Bed & Brea
in France 2008

The AA carries out inspection and classification for its best-selling Bed & Breakfast and Hotel Guides to Britain and Ireland. By joining forces with Gîtes de France we aim to bring you the same reliable, high quality information for France.

You will find an easy-to-use layout, clear gradings, a useful description of the B&B and its facilities and lots of colour photographs. We hope this guide will be invaluable every time you plan a visit to France.

Gîtes de France aims to promote country holidays and breaks by developing quality accommodation. The Gîtes de France logo guarantees that all the accommodation in this guide complies with a national charter and meets specific standards of comfort.

The Gîtes de France grading goes from 1 up to 4 and for this guide we have selected over 4,000 of those with a grade of 3 or 4 to ensure the highest quality and a wide choice. You can rest assured that your host's first priority is to make sure you enjoy your stay.

Produced by AA Publishing 7th edition March 2008
© Automobile Association Developments Limited 2008. Automobile
Association Develpoments Limited retains the copyright in the current
edition and in all subsequent editions, reprints and amendments to
editions. Directory information supplied by and reproduced with the
permission of the Fédération Nationale des Gîtes de France.

Please contact:
Advertisement sales: advertisingsales@theAA.com
Editorial team: lifestyleguides@theAA.com

Picture credit: Front Cover Image: Chateau St. Germain de Livet,
AA World Travel Library/Pete Bennett
Back Cover Image: Village of Sacy, AA World Travel Library/Roger Moss
Typeset by Keenes, Andover, England
Printed and bound by Printer Trento Srl, Italy
A CIP catalogue record for this book is available from the British Library

Published by AA Publishing, a trading name of Automobile Association
Developments Limited, whose registered office is: Fanum House, Basing
View, Basingstoke, Hampshire, RG21 4EA
Registered number 1878835

ISBN 13: 978 0 7495 5571 9
A03287

Maps reproduced with the permission of AD.com,
Charenton-le-Pont, France
© Fédération Nationale des Gîtes de France

BOUCHES-DU-RHÔNE

Provence-Alpes-Côte-d'Azur

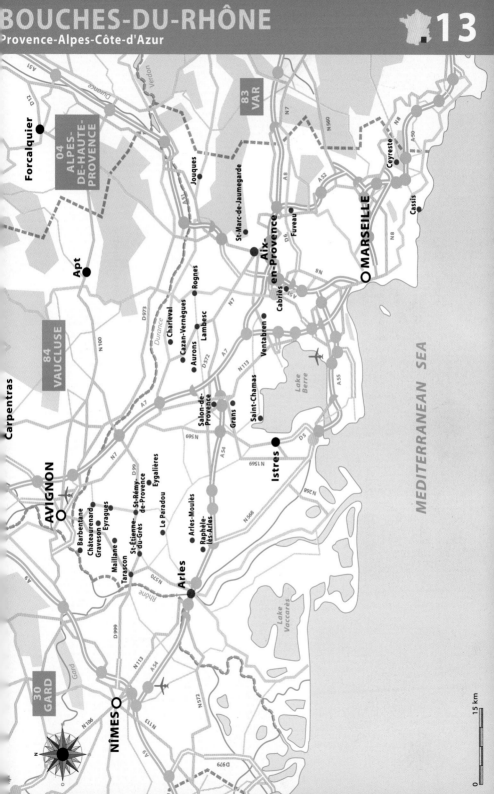

ITALY

Tunnel
de Fréjus

Villar-d'Arêne

Névache

La Salle-
les-Alpes

St-Chaffrey

Briançon

N91

N94

Arvieux

St-Crépin

Risoul

Champcella

Durance

St-Clément-sur-Durance

Barcelonnette

D900

Ubaye

D900

Baratier

**04
ALPES-
DE-HAUTE-PROVENCE**

St-Jean-St-Nicolas

St-Léger-les-Mélèzes

Prunières

Bénévent-et-Charbillac

Buissard

Chabottes

Saint-Jacques-en-Valgaudémar

N85

N94

Lake
Serre-Ponçon

Durance

Gap-Romette

GAP

Romanche

**38
ISÈRE**

Drac

Le Noyer

Poligny

N85

A51

N85

A51

Barcillonnette

N75

Aspres-sur-Buëch

D994

La Piarre

Sigottier

Laragne-
Montéglin

D993

D994

St-André-de-Rosans

N75

Rosans

N91

N85

N75

A51

D993

**26
DRÔME**

Die

D93

D93

D94

Aigues

Ouvèze

Var

Tinée

N
E
S
O

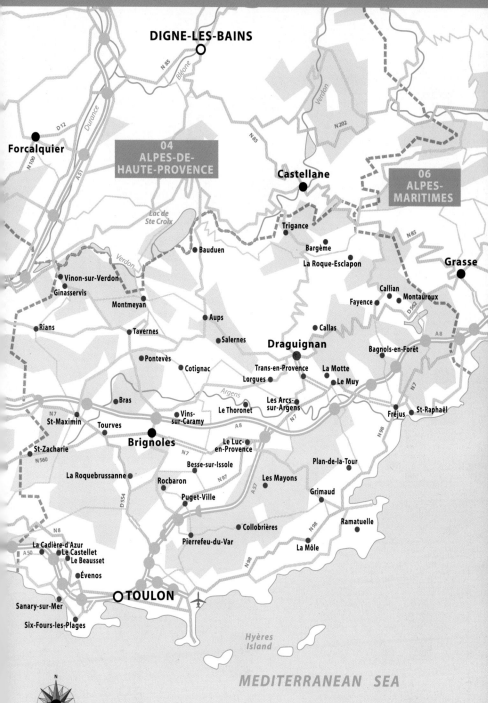

DIGNE-LES-BAINS

N 85

Bléone

Durance

D 12

N 100

A 51

Forcalquier

04
ALPES-DE-
HAUTE-PROVENCE

Castellane

N 85

N 202

Verdon

06
ALPES-
MARITIMES

N 85

Grasse

Lac de
Ste Croix

Trigance

Bargème

La Roque-Esclapon

Bauduen

Verdon

Vinon-sur-Verdon

Ginasservis

Montmeyan

Callian

Fayence

Montauroux

D 562

A 8

Aups

Rians

Tavernes

Salernes

Callas

Draguignan

Bagnols-en-Forêt

Pontevès

Cotignac

Trans-en-Provence

La Motte

Lorgues

Le Muy

N 7

Argens

Bras

Les Arcs-
sur-Argens

Vins-
sur-Caramy

Le Thoronet

A 8

N 7

N 98

Fréjus

St-Raphaël

St-Maximin

Tourves

N 7

Brignoles

Le Luc-
en-Provence

St-Zacharie

N 560

La Roquebrussanne

Besse-sur-Issole

Rocbaron

N 97

A 57

Les Mayons

Plan-de-la-Tour

Grimaud

D 554

Puget-Ville

N 98

Ramatuelle

Collobrières

La Cadière-d'Azur

Le Castellet

Le Beausset

N 8

A 50

Évenos

Pierrefeu-du-Var

La Môle

N 98

Sanary-sur-Mer

TOULON

Six-Fours-les-Plages

Hyères
Island

MEDITERRANEAN SEA

N
O   E
S

0   15 km

VAUCLUSE
Provence-Alpes-Côte-d'Azur

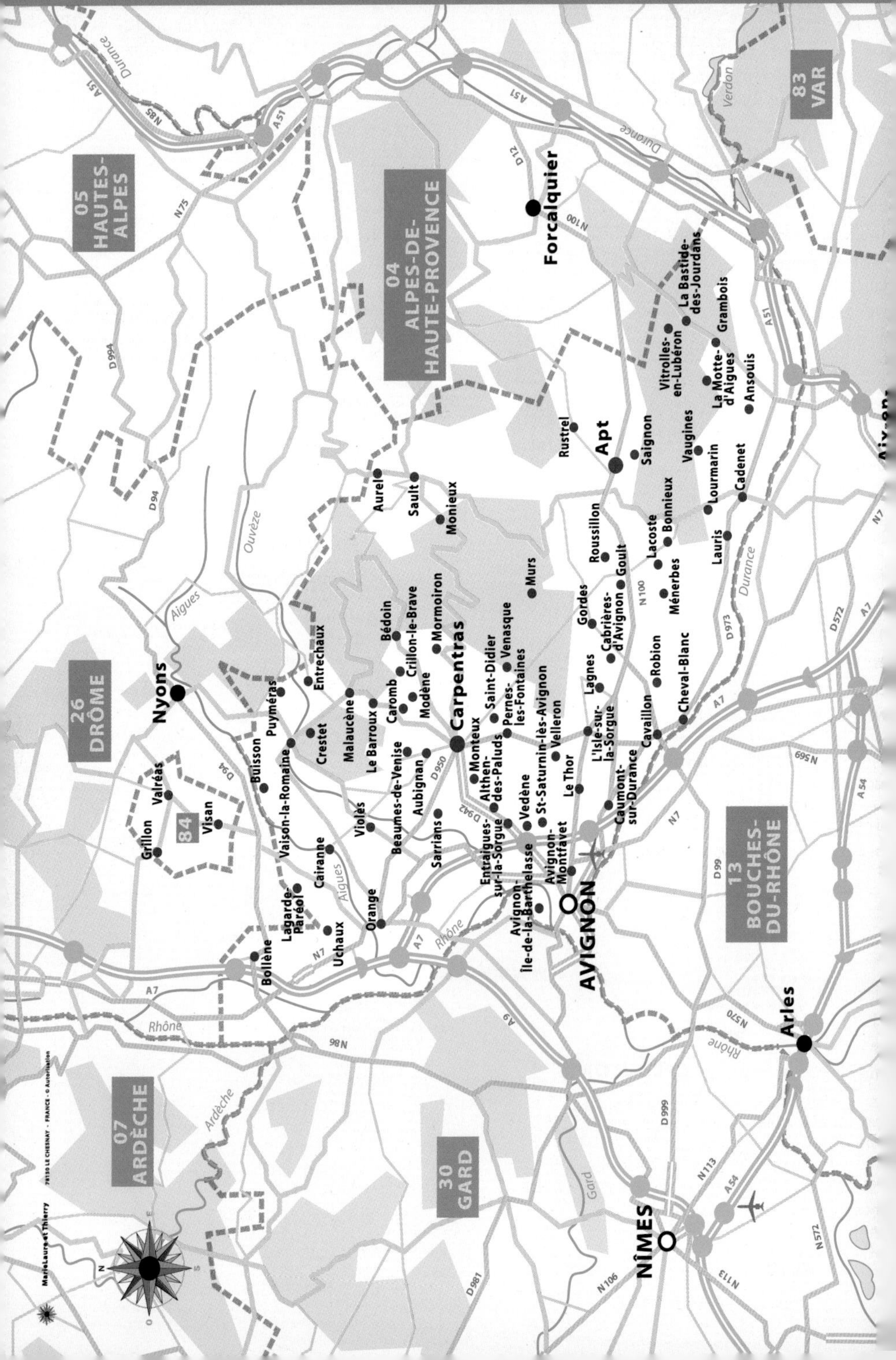

84

83 VAR

05 HAUTES-ALPES

04 ALPES-DE-HAUTE-PROVENCE

26 DRÔME

07 ARDÈCHE

30 GARD

13 BOUCHES-DU-RHÔNE

84

Forcalquier

La Bastide-des-Jourdans
Grambois
Vitrolles-en-Lubéron
La Motte-d'Aigues
Ansouis
Saignon
Vaugines
Lourmarin
Cadenet
Apt
Rustrel
Bonnieux
Ménerbes
Lauris
Roussillon
Lacoste
Goult
Murs
Gordes
Cabrières-d'Avignon
Cheval-Blanc
Robion
Cavaillon
Lagnes
L'Isle-sur-la-Sorgue
Aurel
Sault
Monieux
Bédoin
Mormoiron
Crillon-le-Brave
Modène
Carpentras
Saint-Didier
Venasque
Pernes-les-Fontaines
Saint-Saturnin-lès-Avignon
Velleron
Caromb
Le Barroux
Malaucène
Entrechaux
Puyméras
Crestet
Beaumes-de-Venise
Aubignan
Monteux
Althen-des-Paluds
Vedène
Le Thor
Entraigues-sur-la-Sorgue
Avignon-Montfavet
Violès
Sarrians
Avignon-Ile-de-la-Barthelasse
AVIGNON
Vaison-la-Romaine
Cairanne
Sablet
Orange
Uchaux
Bollène
Lagarde-Paréol
Buisson
Visan
Valréas
Grillon
Nyons

NÎMES
Arles

Durance
Verdon
Ouvèze
Aigues
Rhône
Ardèche
Gard

N85 · A51 · N75 · D994 · D94 · D538 · D976 · D950 · D942 · N7 · A7 · A9 · A54 · N100 · D973 · D212 · N570 · N113 · D999 · D981 · D99

Marie-Laure et Thierry
79100 LE CHESNAY - FRANCE - © Autorisation

RHÔNE-ALPES

AIN

BELIGNEUX

▦ ◉ La Dépendance

Béatrice BREVET

155, Chemin de la Grange, 01360 BELIGNEUX

☎ 06 76 79 68 03

email: ladependance@wanadoo.fr

web: www.ladependance.fr

An historic 19th-century farm in the heart of the village which has been completely renovated. Guests have the use of two lounges and independent access to the first floor bedrooms with their private bathrooms. There is one double, one twin and a double with a single bed. A cot is available.

Prices s €60-€65; d €60-€65; t fr €85; extra person fr €20; dinner fr €24 **On Site** ⚓ Restaurant ⚑ Private ↿ **Nearby** ⚳ 15km ⚗ 3km ⚘ 3km ⚑ 1km ⚵ 1km **Notes** No pets English spoken

BELLEY

▦ *Le Saint Jean*

Martine BARBOT

92, Rue Saint Jean, 01300 BELLEY

☎ 04 79 81 55 27

email: martinebarbot@yahoo.fr

web: www.ausaintjean.com

The five elegantly decorated bedrooms here are in a converted outbuilding. All the rooms are doubles, one with an extra bed, and each has a private bath or shower room and WC. Cots available if needed. Sitting room for guests, and the garden has plenty of furniture. In a quiet location, close to various destinations.

Prices not confirmed for 2008 **Nearby** ⚓ 4km ⚳ 30km ⚗ 2km ⚘ 25km ⚑ 0.5km ⚵ 16km **Notes** No pets

BOHAS

▦ ◉ Le Château

Pierre DUBOURGET

01250 BOHAS

☎ 04 74 51 86 11

email: p.dubourget01@orange.fr

A stone residence in the heart of Revermont, situated in the park of a château. It offers five rooms with private facilities: two rooms for three and three for two people. There is a large living room, lounge with library, terrace, courtyard with garden furniture, parking and table d'hôte meals by reservation. In a quiet location, close to various destinations.

Prices s fr €33; d fr €40; t fr €50; extra person fr €9; dinner fr €15 **Nearby** ⚓ 7km ⚳ 13km ⚗ 5km ↿ 15km Restaurant 2km ⚘ 3km ⚑ 3km ⚵ 15km **Notes** No pets

BRESSOLLES

▦ ◉ Le Clos du Paillot

Alain AVRILLON

01360 BRESSOLLES

☎ 04 78 06 53 10 & 06 09 73 49 41

email: a.avrillon@free.fr

web: www.leclosdupaillot.com

This house is in the heart of a village, 30 kilometres from Lyon. There are three first floor double rooms, all with TV, internet access, private bath/shower room and WC. An extra bed is available. Lounge with wood-burner; garden with terrace and furniture. Meals are available, by arrangement, except Wednesday evenings.

Prices s €60-€65; d €60-€65; extra person fr €20; dinner fr €20 **On Site** Restaurant Private tennis court **Nearby** ⚓ 2km ⚳ 30km ⚗ 2km ↿ 25km ⚘ 10km ⚑ 2km ⚵ 3km **Notes** No pets English spoken Open February to December.

CHAVANNES-SUR-REYSSOUZE

▦ ◉ Les Darbonnets

Charles et Dominique CACLIN

01190 CHAVANNES-SUR-REYSSOUZE

☎ 03 85 36 48 75 ▤ 03 85 30 98 93

email: darbonnets@wanadoo.fr

web: www.darbonnets.fr

In extensive grounds surrounded by farmland, this large house has three bedrooms - a double room, a twin-bedded room and a room for three with a double bed and a single; all have private shower room and WC. Outside is a terrace, barbecue and croquet. Bikes can be borrowed; honey and home-made jams available.

Prices s fr €50; d fr €60; t fr €75; extra person fr €15; dinner €15-€22 **On Site** ⚑ **Nearby** ⚓ 5km ⚳ 15km ⚗ 1.5km Restaurant 5km ⚑ 5km ⚵ 25km **Notes** No pets English spoken

DOMPIERRE-SUR-VEYLE

▦ ◉ Le Mas Bouchy

Kajsa SMITH

01240 DOMPIERRE-SUR-VEYLE

☎ 04 74 30 39 85 & 06 76 63 09 01 ▤ 04 74 30 39 86

email: kajsa@mas-bouchy.com

web: www.mas-bouchy.com

There are views across the private park and lake from this manor house. The five rooms are on three floors, all with private bathrooms, some with fireplaces or balconies. The twin on the ground floor, three suites on the first floor and one suite on the second floor offer a variety of accommodation.

Prices s fr €52; d fr €65; t fr €80; extra person fr €15; dinner fr €20 **On Site** Private tennis court **Nearby** ⚓ 15km ⚳ 8km ⚗ 10km ↿ 10km Restaurant 4km ⚑ 8km ⚵ 18km **Notes** No pets English spoken Open February to November.

GIRON

▦ ⚬ **Le Bellevue**

Martine et Pierre BOUVARD
01130 GIRON
☎ 04 50 59 89 42
email: bellevue.giron@wanadoo.fr
web: www.lebellevuegiron.com

This large non-smoking house in the heart of a village in the Parc Naturel Régional du Haut Jura has three beautifully decorated rooms with separate access (one double with massage shower and a double and twin with spa baths). There is a large library, lounge/diner with TV, and large terrace to enjoy summer meals and beautiful views of the sheltered flower garden. Sauna available. Table d'hôte evening meals can be reserved.

Prices s fr €57; d fr €65; t fr €91; extra person €11-€22; dinner fr €22 **Nearby** ♨ 6km ⌁ 25km ℘ 4.5km ⤏ 20km Restaurant 8km ⚓ 17km ⛵ 0.5km ⊞ 9km ⋈ 20km **Notes** No pets English spoken

LAGNIEU

▦ **Le Jardin d'Alice**

Jocelyne et J-Pierre MAULET
1, Place de la Liberté, 01150 LAGNIEU
☎ 04 74 35 86 62 & 06 81 94 97 36
email: jeanpierre.maulet@wanadoo.fr
web: www.lejardindalice.eu

This is a 19th-century house with three bedrooms, all on the second floor. Two of the rooms are doubles; the other is a family room for four, with a double bed and two singles. Each room has air-conditioning, internet connection, and a private bath or shower and WC. Guest living room; outside is a terrace and garden with trees.

Prices s fr €47; d fr €52; t fr €67 **On Site** ⚘ **Nearby** ♨ 15km ⌁ 30km ℘ 2km Restaurant 0.1km ⚓ 35km ⊞ 0.2km ⋈ 5km **Notes** No pets English spoken

MESSIMY-SUR-SAONE

▦ ⚬ **Pigeonnier du val de Saone**

M et C GUTIERREZ
Chemin Prenois, 01480 MESSIMY-SUR-SAONE
☎ 04 74 67 97 73
email: m.guti@wanadoo.fr

Close to the Saône, this charming 19th-century house offers three rooms with private facilities and access: a double, a twin and a room with a king-size and single bed. Large courtyard with garden furniture, garden and parking. Walks along the river. Near to Dombes and Beaujolais and 35km from Lyon.

Prices s fr €45; d fr €50; t fr €62; dinner fr €18 **On Site** ⚘ **Nearby** ♨ 1km ⌁ 10km ℘ 2km ⤏ 10km Restaurant 4km ⛵ 1km ⊞ 0.7km ⋈ 12km **Notes** Pets admitted English spoken

MIJOUX

▦ ⚬ **Le Boulu**

B et C GROSFILLEY
01410 MIJOUX
☎ 04 50 41 31 47

A historic farmhouse renovated by the owner on the edge of the Valserine at the foot of the Jura's snowy peaks, between the ski resorts of Mijoux-La Faucille and Lélex-Crozet. The en suite rooms include two rooms with either double or twin beds, two with a double and twin beds, one with a double and a single bed. There is a lounge with fireplace and ample breakfasts on offer.

Prices d fr €60; t fr €82; extra person fr €16; dinner fr €19 **On Site** ℘ **Nearby** ♨ 24km ⌁ 6km Restaurant 4km ⚓ 4km ⚘ 4km ⊞ 4km ⋈ 30km **Notes** No pets English spoken Open Christmas, Easter & July to August.

MIRIBEL

▦ ⚬ **La Villa du Rhône**

Christine et Jean CABARDI
58 Chemin de la Lune, 01700 MIRIBEL
☎ 04 78 55 54 16
email: contact@lavilladurhone.com
web: www.lavilladurhone.com

A spacious contemporary house on the side of a hill, with lovely views over the Rhône plain. Rooms available include a grade 2 double room in the house and two double grade 3 rooms in a stone annexe, each with private facilities and possible extra bed. There is a swimming pool and terrace, lounge with fireplace, books, and TV. Minibar and internet access in each room. Table d'hôte meals available. Leisure activities at Miribel Jonage (1km).

Prices s €85-€105; d €90-€110; extra person fr €15; dinner fr €30 **On Site** Private ⤏ **Nearby** ♨ 2.3km ⌁ 4.9km ℘ 1.1km ⚘ 4km ⊞ 1km ⋈ 1.2km **Notes** Pets admitted English spoken

MONTCET

♦♦♦ ⫶◯⫶ Les Vignes

J-L et E GAYET

01310 MONTCET

☎ 04 74 24 23 13 ▤ 04 74 24 23 13

email: gayet-esperanto@wanadoo.fr

web: http://perso.wanadoo.fr/chambresdhoteslesvignes/
source/table.html

An old restored Bressan farm in peaceful parkland with a fishing
lake, private swimming pool and games field. The four comfortable
non-smoking rooms (en suite) have either double or twin beds and
are housed next to the owners' house. There is a lounge, television
room, video, library, courtyard, parking, table tennis and volleyball.
Reservations can be made for healthy table d'hôte meals with free
meals for children under four.

Prices s fr €43.60; d fr €57.20; t fr €71.80; extra person fr €13; dinner fr
€21 **On Site** 🏊 Private 🎣 **Nearby** ⛷ 12km ⚓ 12km Restaurant 1km
♨ 12km 🏛 1.5km ⋙ 12km **Notes** No pets English spoken

NEUVILLE-SUR-AIN

♦♦♦ Bosseron

Annie et Claude RIVOIRE

325, Rte de Geneve, 01160 NEUVILLE-SUR-AIN

☎ 04 74 37 77 06 ▤ 04 74 37 77 06

email: arivoire@free.fr

web: http://arivoire.free.fr

Set in two hectares on the banks of the River Ain, this characterful
house offers four well decorated en suite rooms (two twin and two
doubles). Two large lounges with fireplaces, piano, television, library,
fishing, swimming, table tennis, billiards, and weights are all available
and generous breakfasts are served looking out over the river. Nearby
are the GR59, Tour du Revermont, tennis courts, local crafts and a
restaurant.

Prices s fr €55; d fr €64 **On Site** 🏊 🎣 **Nearby** ⛷ 7km ⚓ 15km
Restaurant 0.3km ⛵ 23km ⚲ 0.2km 🏛 0.3km ⋙ 6km **Notes** No pets
English spoken Open April to October.

PEYZIEUX-SUR-SAONE

♦♦♦ 🌱 Chez Marie

Joël et Marie-Josée CROZIER

Les Maisons Neuves, 01140 PEYZIEUX-SUR-SAONE

☎ 04 74 04 03 42 & 06 82 29 80 11

web: http://chezmarie01.ifrance.com

On a quiet dairy farm, in an extension of the proprietor's home, there
are three spacious and personalised rooms each with private facilities:
a double with single, a double and a two-roomed family suite with
double and two single beds. Large living room with kitchen corner
and lounge, terrace with furniture, grounds. Animals accepted by prior
arrangement. Restaurants 2km; 10 minutes to Beaujolais wine-making.

Prices s fr €35; d fr €45; t €52-€55; extra person fr €22 **Nearby** ⛷ 6km
⚓ 20km ⛵ 1km Restaurant 2km ♨ 15km 🏛 3km ⋙ 10km **Notes** Pets
admitted

PONT-DE-VAUX

♦♦♦ *Chambre d'hôtes*

Michel BOUVARD

11, Grand Faubourg, 01190 PONT-DE-VAUX

☎ 03 85 30 33 16

email: michelbouvard2@wanadoo.fr

Three doubles and a twin room with independent access in an
outbuilding near the owners' home on a former farm, each with
private facilities. Large living room with lounge corner and kitchenette
for guests. Terrace with garden furniture, parking, enclosed courtyard,
table tennis, bikes for hire. Route de la Bresse, Maconnais, Truchère
natural reserve 12km. River port of Pont de Vaux nearby.

Prices not confirmed for 2008 **Nearby** ⛷ 1km ⚓ 7km ⛵ 0.5km
🏛 0.2km ⋙ 20km **Notes** Pets admitted

SANDRANS

♦♦♦ ⫶◯⫶ *Le Petit Bessay*

Sylvie DURAND

01400 SANDRANS

☎ 04 74 55 45 82 ▤ 04 74 55 45 82

email: lepetitbessay@wanadoo.fr

web: http://perso.orange.fr/hubert.bouvier/

An old farmhouse, quietly situated and full of character. There
are three bedrooms. On the ground floor, with private access,
is a two-roomed family suite for four (double bed and singles);
upstairs are two doubles. All have TV and private shower room/WC.
Guests' lounge; garden with beautiful countryside views. Meals by
arrangement, including vegetarian dishes, except Sundays and public
holidays. Bikes available. Closed three weeks in winter.

Prices not confirmed for 2008 **Nearby** ⛷ 0.3km ⚓ 12km ⛵ 3km
🏛 3km ⋙ 10km **Notes** No pets

SERVAS

♦♦♦ ⫶◯⫶ Le Nid à Bibi

Elsie BIBUS

Lalleyriat, 01960 SERVAS

☎ 04 74 21 11 47 ▤ 04 74 21 02 83

email: lenidabibi@wanadoo.fr

web: http://lenidabibi.com

This peaceful, beautifully restored farmhouse has five rooms,
including en suite rooms for two to three people and one with
a spa bath. On site facilities include a library and dining room
(where brunch breakfasts are served), landscaped garden, parking,
tennis courts, indoor heated swimming pool with wave machine,
sauna, weights, table tennis, bicycles. Nearby there is a river, golf
and water-skiing. Reduced rates for extended stays.

Prices s €85-€115; d €100-€130; t fr €155; extra person fr €30;
dinner €25-€30 **On Site** 🎣 Private 🎾 Private tennis court
Nearby ⛷ 15km ⚓ 12km ⛵ 3km Restaurant 3km 🏛 3km ⋙ 7km
Notes Pets admitted English spoken CC

ST-ANDRE-D'HUIRIAT

⧫⧫⧫ ⦿⦿ Château de Bourdonnel

P BRAC DE LA PERRIERE

01290 ST-ANDRE-D'HUIRIAT

☎ 04 74 50 03 40 📄 04 74 50 22 29

Five rooms on the first floor of this château in wooded parkland. There are two grade 3 rooms for two or three people, one grade 2 twin room and a children's room, each en suite. In the summer there is also one with four single beds and one with two single beds. A cot is available. Facilities include a communal lounge and dining room, parking, a courtyard and enclosed grounds.

Prices s fr €44; d fr €54; extra person fr €16; dinner €19–€30
Nearby ⚓ 4km ♨ 15km ⚓ 5km Restaurant 5km 🏛 6km 🚗 20km
Notes Pets admitted English spoken

ST-BERNARD

⧫⧫⧫ ⦿⦿ Le Clos du Chêne

Cheryl et Michel PATAY

370, Chemin du Carré, 01600 ST-BERNARD

☎ 04 74 00 45 39 📄 04 74 08 03 51

email: leclosduchene@orange.fr

Just 30 kilometres from Lyon in wooded grounds beside the Saône, this house has five very comfortable, air-conditioned rooms, one with disabled access. Three are doubles; there is also a twin-bedded room and a two-roomed family suite for four. Each room has a living area, a terrace or balcony and a private bath or shower room. Swimming pool, sauna and boules pitch.

Prices s €112–€190; d €112–€190; extra person fr €20; dinner fr €30 **On Site** ♨ Private **Nearby** ⚓ 8km ♨ 5km ⚓ 0.1km Restaurant 0.8km 🏛 0.5km 🚗 4km **Notes** No pets English spoken
see advert under LYON

ST-JEAN-DE-NIOST

⧫⧫⧫ Le Relais de Saint Jean

Jacqueline HENEUY

57, Rue de la Véquière, 01800 ST-JEAN-DE-NIOST

☎ 04 74 61 88 67

email: le-relais-de-saint-jean@wanadoo.fr
web: http://relaisdestjean.free.fr

A house standing in the centre of a village on the edge of the Dombes region. On the ground floor is a double room with its own entrance; upstairs is another double with a balcony, and a room with two double beds and a dressing room. All rooms have private facilities. Lounge with open fire and books; wooded, flower garden; kitchen for guests' use.

Prices s fr €50; d fr €60; t fr €80; extra person fr €15 **Nearby** ⚓ 3km ♨ 20km ⚓ 0.5km Restaurant 0.1km 🏛 0.1km 🚗 3km **Notes** No pets English spoken

ST-JEAN-SUR-REYSSOUZE

⧫⧫⧫ Mons

Danielle et Daniel GUILLOT

01560 ST-JEAN-SUR-REYSSOUZE

☎ 04 74 52 61 09

email: 2daniel@orange.fr
web: http://perso.orange.fr/2daniel.guillot

The three guest rooms at this property are all on the ground floor, in an annexe to the owners' home. Two are triple rooms (double bed and a single in each), and a split level double room has possible space for one or two extra beds. All have private shower room and WC. Guests have access to a kitchenette.

Prices s fr €43; d fr €50; t fr €60; extra person fr €10 **Nearby** ⚓ 14km ♨ 25km ⚓ 3km ⚓ 10km Restaurant 0.5km ⚓ 10km 🏛 12km 🚗 25km **Notes** No pets

⧫⧫⧫ *Montéfanty*

G et J CLEMENT

01560 ST-JEAN-SUR-REYSSOUZE

☎ 04 74 30 88 43 📄 04 74 30 88 43

email: guy.clement1@libertysurf.fr
web: http://chezguyetjacqueline.chez.tiscali.fr

An old farmhouse built in the local style, which has been renovated to provide three guest rooms, all non-smoking. Two are triples (double bed and single in each); the other is a double with separate sitting area. All have private facilities. Guests' entrance and living room. In the garden is a swimming pool, and plenty of garden furniture.

Prices not confirmed for 2008 **On Site** Private ⚓ **Nearby** ⚓ 8km ♨ 25km ⚓ 6km 🏛 6km 🚗 25km **Notes** No pets English spoken

ST-NIZIER-LE-BOUCHOUX

⧫⧫⧫ ⦿⦿ La Closerie

François BONGARD

Jassans, 01560 ST-NIZIER-LE-BOUCHOUX

☎ 04 74 52 96 67 📄 04 74 52 96 67

email: francois.bongard@wanadoo.fr
web: www.lacloserie.net

Non-smoking accommodation on the level in this extension to the main house. There is separate access to the four en suite rooms and evening meals can be reserved. The farm contains farm artefacts, a local style chimney and Beaujolais and Mâconnais vineyards.

Prices s fr €48; d fr €54; t fr €76; extra person fr €22; dinner fr €18 **Nearby** ⚓ 17km ♨ 30km ⚓ 2km ⚓ 1.5km Restaurant 6km ⚓ 6km ⚓ 15km 🏛 1.5km 🚗 30km **Notes** No pets

ST-RAMBERT-EN-BUGEY

⧫⧫⧫ ⦿⦿ Albarande Chambres d'hôtes

Lucie et Patrick POGGIALI

Grangeneuve, 01230 ST-RAMBERT-EN-BUGEY

☎ 06 33 30 53 77 & 06 13 57 13 15 📄 04 74 37 40 02

email: patrick.poggiali@orange.fr

A 19th-century house in grounds of one hectare, with four spacious air-conditioned rooms in an annexe to the owners' home. The rooms all have double beds, two of them king-sized, and each has a private bath or shower room and WC. Generous breakfasts served in the living room overlooking the grounds; other meals available if pre-booked.

Prices s €80-€110; d €80-€110; dinner fr €25   **On Site** ☂
Nearby ⚓ 5km ♪ 0.2km ☙ 25km ⌂ 1km ⋈ 1km   **Notes** No pets

SULIGNAT

⋈ ⁄◯⁄ *L'Oreiller de la Belle Aurore*

Valérie GALLIC
Le mont, 01400 SULIGNAT
☎ 04 74 55 71 65 & 06 22 16 54 63   ▤ 04 74 55 68 65

This restored 18th-century farmhouse offers three quiet and comfortable guest rooms. There is a double-bedded room; a two-roomed suite with double bed, a small double bed and a single; and another two-roomed suite with four single beds. All rooms have private facilities. Baby's cot, lounge with games, books and piano. Large grounds with children's games and sheltered outdoor area. Meals by arrangement.

Prices not confirmed for 2008   **Nearby** ⚓ 4km ☡ 15km ♪ 4km ⌂ 2km ⋈ 7km   **Notes** No pets English spoken Open March to December.

VERJON

⋈ La Verjonnière

Christian BUATOIS
01270 VERJON
☎ 04 74 51 56 37 & 06 65 25 54 97   ▤ 04 74 51 56 37

Monique and Christian, both keen antique dealers, will be delighted to welcome you to their restored farmhouse, built in the style typical of the area. There are three elegantly decorated guest bedrooms, all on the first floor: two doubles, each with a private shower room/WC; and a family room for three with private WC and bathroom.

Prices s fr €60; d €72-€75; t fr €95   **Nearby** ⚓ 0.5km ☡ 19.5km ♪ 0.4km ⚲ 5km Restaurant 1km ☙ 12km ⌂ 4km ⋈ 20km
Notes No pets Open April to October.

VESCOURS

⋈ ❧ Ferme de Montailbord

André et Chantal PONT
1560 VESCOURS
☎ 04 74 30 76 73   ▤ 04 74 30 76 73

A charming, listed, 15th-century farmhouse on the borders of Bresse and Bourgogne. It has been entirely renovated whilst keeping its historic, local, architectural features. The three en suite, non-smoking rooms on the first floor are furnished with high quality antiques.

Prices s fr €50; d fr €65; t fr €80   **On Site** ♪ ☂   **Nearby** ⚓ 17km ☙ 25km ⚲ 10km Restaurant 5km ☙ 5km ⌂ 5km ⋈ 18km
Notes No pets English spoken Open January to November.

VILLEMOTIER

⋈ ⁄◯⁄ La Recouvrance

Olivier AUDEBERT
Montfollet, 01270 VILLEMOTIER
☎ 04 74 42 01 18
email: la-recouvrance@wanadoo.fr
web: www.la-recouvrance.fr

A typical restored farmhouse set in a botanical garden containing more than 300 varieties of maple and magnolia, swimming pool, veranda and koi carp pond. The accommodation consists of two en suite double rooms (one is grade 2) and one room with three single beds with separate access and cot available. There is a large lounge with satellite TV and fireplace, generous breakfasts on offer and a restaurant nearby. Reduced rates for extended stays out of season.

Prices s €35-€40; d €48-€52; t €63-€67; extra person fr €17
On Site Private ⚲   **Nearby** ⚓ 15km ☡ 17km ♪ 0.5km Restaurant 4km ☙ 6km ☂ 5km ⌂ 3km ⋈ 20km   **Notes** No pets English spoken

⋈ ⁄◯⁄ Le Moulin du Fay

Thierry et Christelle PERRIN
01270 VILLEMOTIER
☎ 04 74 42 01 48 & 06 80 33 84 42
email: thierry.s.perrin@wanadoo.fr
web: www.moulin-du-fay.com

This old watermill, in its green rustic setting, has three spacious and comfortable guest bedrooms, all on the first floor. There is a large family room with a double bed and two singles, and two rooms for three. They all have en suite bath or shower rooms, and a cot is available.

Prices s €45-€50; d €55-€60; t €65-€70; extra person fr €10; dinner fr €18   **On Site** Restaurant ☂   **Nearby** ⚓ 3km ♪ 0.5km ⚲ 5km ☙ 5km ⌂ 5km ⋈ 20km   **Notes** No pets English spoken

VILLEREVERSURE

⋈ ⁄◯⁄ *L'Agnoblens*

A et E GUILLERMIN
01250 VILLEREVERSURE
☎ 04 74 30 60 50 & 06 78 07 27 98

A working farm in the heart of Revermont. The six en suite rooms include four double rooms, one room with double and single bed and one room with double and two singles. There is a large lounge with a television and library, a peaceful, shaded flower garden for meals, private parking, petanque, and table tennis. The table d'hôte evening meals are available by reservation. Freshly cooked bread and galettes are available to taste and buy.

Prices not confirmed for 2008   **On Site** ♪ Private ⚲   **Nearby** ⚓ 6km ☡ 15km ⌂ 1km ⋈ 2km   **Notes** Pets admitted

VILLES

▦ |◎| Chambre d'hôtes Vert Pré

Myriam et Daniel HENRIOUX

6, Rue de la Promenade, 01200 VILLES

☎ 04 50 59 97 29 & 06 73 06 12 02 📄 04 50 59 97 29

email: mhenrioux@free.fr

web: http://mhenrioux.free.fr

Set in a large park in the Retord with beautiful views and a field of horses, three en suite rooms are available (two double and one twin) in the owners' large house. One room has a TV and a cot is available. The guest lounge has satellite TV and library. Also available are a telephone, boules and table tennis with 'Carnotzet' during the evenings.

Prices s €50-€55; d €60-€65; t fr €80; extra person fr €20; dinner fr €18
Nearby ⛷ 6km ⌘ 28km ⚲ 8km ⚓ 6km Restaurant 0.2km ⚑ 20km
⚓ 6km Spa 50km ⚐ 5km ⚑ 2km ⚒ 4km **Notes** No pets

VIRIAT

▦ |◎| *Moulin de Champagne*

Anne-Marie FAMY

01440 VIRIAT

☎ 04 74 25 16 04 & 06 30 91 36 82

email: moulin-champagne@club-internet.fr

On the site of an historic, renovated mill, en suite rooms are in an outbuilding with separate access. Two rooms have one double and one single, one room has three singles and one has a double bed and a single on a mezzanine. There is also a day room and seating areas with a fireplace, grounds and terrace with garden furniture for guests' use. Table d'hôte meals are available.

Prices not confirmed for 2008 **Nearby** ⌘ 5km ⚲ 2km ⚑ 2km ⚒ 5km
Notes No pets English spoken

ARDÈCHE

ALBA-LA-ROMAINE

▦ Le Jeu du Mail

M et M-F ARLAUD

07400 ALBA-LA-ROMAINE

☎ 04 75 52 41 59 📄 04 75 52 41 59

email: lejeudumail@free.fr

web: http://lejeudumail.free.fr/

This 19th-century former silkworm house has retained the simplicity of the local architecture. There are three en suite rooms, and two suites (each sleeping four); two lounges with fireplace, a tree-lined garden and private pool. Enjoy the etchings exhibition, local wines and walks.

Prices d €58-€90; extra person fr €20 **On Site** Private ⚓
Nearby ⛷ 5km ⌘ 20km ⚲ 20km Restaurant 0.2km ⚓ 0.2km ⚐ 10km
⚑ 0.1km ⚒ 16km **Notes** No pets English spoken

ALBOUSSIERE

▦ |◎| Domaine de l'Abeale

V LEGRAND

Quartier de Peygros, 07440 ALBOUSSIERE

☎ 04 75 84 58 10 & 06 80 54 97 75 📄 04 75 25 75 03

email: contactabeale@yahoo.fr

web: www.abeale.com

Not far from the Rhône Valley - four guest rooms, all different, in a building which dates from the 1830s. The rooms sleep from two to four guests, and each one has a private bathroom and WC. The dining room has a lounge area with an open fire. Above-ground swimming pool, and lake. Large room with vaulted ceiling available for meetings.

Prices s fr €53; d fr €63; t fr €78; extra person fr €15; dinner fr €19.50
On Site ⚲ Spa Private ⚓ **Nearby** ⛷ 4km ⌘ 25km Restaurant 3km
⚓ 3km ⚐ 10km ⚑ 4km ⚒ 25km **Notes** No pets English spoken

ARCENS

▦ |◎| L'Ayga

Celine LEYNAUD

Mayas, 07310 ARCENS

☎ 04 75 30 80 73 & 06 12 16 60 98 📄 04 75 30 80 73

email: ayga07@aol.com

web: www.ayga.net

This 17th-century farm is delightfully situated in the heart of the mountains of the Ardèche. With its beautiful green surroundings, it is a haven of peace and tranquillity. It offers four guest bedrooms, sleeping up to four people, all of them with en suite shower rooms and WCs. Delicious traditional meals available.

Prices s fr €45; d fr €45; t fr €60; extra person fr €15; dinner fr €16
Nearby ⚲ 2.8km ⚓ 15km ⚑ 2.8km **Notes** No pets

ARDOIX

▦ |◎| ♿ Beauvoir

H et J-M SEITIER

07290 ARDOIX

☎ 04 75 34 48 82 & 06 83 11 05 39

email: jmseitier@wanadoo.fr

web: http://ardeche.chambres.ifrance.com

Take time to unwind in the peace of green Ardèche at this restored barn in the heart of the St Joseph vineyard. This detached house is an idyllic place for holidays with families and friends. There are three spacious ground-floor rooms with their own entrance, one of which i accessible to the less mobile.

Prices s fr €40; d fr €50; t fr €68; extra person fr €18; dinner fr €18
Nearby ⛷ 5km ⚲ 2km ⚓ 2km Restaurant 5km ⚓ 3km ⚑ 3km
⚒ 7km **Notes** No pets English spoken

BEAULIEU

ⅢⅢ Ⅰ◎Ⅰ Les Pitchounnettes

Pierre LECONTE
place de l'Eglise, 07460 BEAULIEU
☎ 04 75 39 36 23 & 06 87 57 03 92
email: pierre.leconte12@wanadoo.fr
web: www.lespitchounnettes.com

This stone built house, right in the centre of the village, was originally the café. Now it offers three guest rooms, a double, a twin, and one with a double bed and a single. They all have en suite facilities. The rooms have antique furnishings and each is decorated according to a theme.

Prices s fr €45; d fr €55; t fr €65; extra person fr €15; dinner fr €18
Nearby ⛵2km ♂4km ⚲7km ⚓0.5km ⊞0.5km　**Notes** No pets

BEAUMONT

ⅢⅢ Ⅰ◎Ⅰ La Petite Cour Verte

Henri ROUVIERE
La Roche, 07110 BEAUMONT
☎ 04 75 39 58 88 🗎 04 75 39 43 00
email: henri.rouviere@wanadoo.fr
web: www.lapetitecourverte.com

A warm welcome is assured at this superb 16th-century country house, peacefully set overlooking a valley of chestnut trees. En suite bedrooms are charming and comfortable. The large lounge with fireplace opens onto a terrace and garden; there is a heated and covered swimming pool and sauna (charged). Generous table d'hôte meals feature regional dishes and local produce.

Prices s €75-€80; d €75-€80; extra person fr €30; dinner fr €22
On Site Private ⚲　**Nearby** ⛵8km ♂3km ⚓15km ⊞15km
Notes No pets Open April to 15 November.

BERRIAS-CASTELJAU

ⅢⅢ ❦ L'Ensolleiade

Jean NEGRE
Casteljau, 07460 BERRIAS-CASTELJAU
☎ 04 75 39 01 14 🗎 04 75 39 01 14
email: contact@ensolleiade.com
web: www.ensolleiade.com

On a rural holding beside the Gorges du Chassezac and the Bois de Paiolive, between the Gorges of the Ardèche and Cévennes. Five spacious rooms in a charming building adjacent to the owner's house: all are en suite rooms and sleep two to four. Facilities include an enclosed garden, television lounge, kitchen, swimming pool, barbecue, boules, children's games, table tennis, parking. High season tariff from 8 July to 25 August.

Prices d €44-€50; extra person fr €12　**On Site** Private ⚲
Nearby ⛵3km ♂0.8km Restaurant 0.8km ⚘1km ⊞3km
Notes No pets Open 7 April to September.

ⅢⅢ Ⅰ◎Ⅰ La Bastide de Bleu Provence

Cyril HARDOUB
place de l'Eglise, 07460 BERRIAS-CASTELJAU
☎ 04 75 39 58 02
email: labastidebleuprovence@wanadoo.fr
web: www.bastidebleuprovence.com

In the heart of a delightful village of stone-built houses, this 15th-century building has three comfortable, individually decorated rooms. All have double beds, private shower room and WC. Rivers pass close by, and there is good access to way-marked footpaths. Extensive grounds with swimming pools; wide range of outdoor activities available locally. Pets charged for.

Prices s fr €70; d €70-€98; extra person fr €25; dinner fr €25
On Site Private ⚲　**Nearby** ⛵5km ♂2km Restaurant 0.1km ⚓5km
⚘3km ⊞0.5km ⋙70km　**Notes** Pets admitted English spoken

ⅢⅢ Ⅰ◎Ⅰ ♿ La Farigoule

Marc et Michèle AUDIBERT
rte de Casteljau, 07460 BERRIAS-CASTELJAU
☎ 04 75 39 82 72 & 06 89 94 12 83 🗎 04 75 39 82 72
email: info@la-farigoule.info
web: www.la-farigoule.info

On the edge of a little village, typical of the southern Ardèche, close to woods and the Chassenac Gorges. The bedrooms are spacious, and sleep from two to four people. Each has a private shower room and WC, and a fridge. Separate guests' entrance. Heated pool, boules, table tennis, large wooded garden with private parking. Meals by arrangement.

Prices s fr €62; d fr €65; t fr €85; extra person fr €20; dinner fr €23
On Site ⚘ Private ⚲　**Nearby** ⛵4km ♂2km Restaurant 0.6km
⚓5km Spa 40km ⊞0.5km　**Notes** Pets admitted English spoken

BESSAS

ⅢⅢ Ⅰ◎Ⅰ Le Château de Bessas

B et P BONNEFIN
07150 BESSAS
☎ 04 75 38 64 34 & 06 11 50 39 60 🗎 04 75 38 60 90
email: bb.ct@wanadoo.fr
web: www.chateau-de-bessas.com

In a renovated part of the Château de Bessas, close to the Pont d'Arc and the Cèze Valley, four beautiful en suite guest rooms each sleep two or four people. There is a lounge, large sunny terrace, table tennis and swimming pool with hydro-massage jets. Reduced rates available for extended stays and for children.

Prices s €47-€62; d €51-€67; t €67-€83; extra person €8-€16; dinner fr €20　**On Site** Private ⚲　**Nearby** ⛵2km ♂3km Restaurant 3km
⚓4km Spa 4km ⊞4km ⋙15km　**Notes** No pets English spoken
Open March to 15 December. CC

BOFFRES

₩₩ ⦿ **Domaine de Lavenant**

B et R DEMELIN

07440 BOFFRES

☎ 04 75 58 21 82 📄 04 75 58 31 11

email: robert.demelin@wanadoo.fr

web: www.demelin.com

This house is situated in the mountains with lovely views of the countryside, the Rhône Valley and the Alps. In a calm setting by the forest, the house provides three personalised rooms with private bathrooms and table d'hôte meals by reservation, with home-made jams. Guests can walk and mountain bike from the house. Nearby Vernoux has shops, a lake and swimming pool.

Prices s fr €62; d fr €73; t fr €97; extra person fr €22; dinner fr €27 **Nearby** ⛳ 0.8km ∕ 1km ⚞ 10km Restaurant 3km ⌁ 10km ⚑ 10km 🏛 10km ⚓ 30km **Notes** No pets Open 15 April to 15 November.

₩₩ ⦿ ⟐ **Domaine de Reiller**

Sandrine BROTTES

07440 BOFFRES

☎ 04 75 58 15 14 & 06 75 36 86 21

email: domaine.reiller@wanadoo.fr

web: www.reiller.com

A 19th-century property in traditional style, surrounded by chestnut woods and meadows, which has been totally restored to provide three beautiful bedrooms, sleeping from two to four guests. Each has a shower room and WC. Guests' lounge with bar, books and TV; kitchen. Wonderful countryside views. Heated swimming pool, tennis, jacuzzi and sauna.

Prices s fr €30; d fr €60; t fr €72; extra person fr €12; dinner fr €19 **On Site** ∕ Restaurant ⚑ Private ⚞ Private tennis court **Nearby** ⛳ 8km 🏛 2km ⚓ 30km **Notes** Pets admitted English spoken

BOUCIEU-LE-ROI

₩₩ **Hameau du Robert**

G et M DURAND DELLENBACH

07270 BOUCIEU-LE-ROI

☎ 04 75 06 23 66

email: contact@gites-boucieu.com

web: www.gites-boucieu.com

On the slopes of the Doux Valley, close to the village of Boucieu-le-Roi, this 16th-century property has five guest bedrooms in an old

silk-worm house. Each can sleep up to three guests, and they all have en suite facilities. Take your breakfast on the terrace, enjoying the magnificent views, or indoors, in front of the beautiful fireplace dating from the time of the revolution.

Prices d fr €45; t fr €58 **Nearby** ⛳ 12km ∕ 5km ⚞ 20km Restaurant 3km ⌁ 5km ⚑ 12km 🏛 5km ⚓ 22km **Notes** No pets English spoken

BURZET

₩₩ ⦿ **La Clede**

Daniel GUBERNATI

Laligier, 07450 BURZET

☎ 04 75 94 58 04 📄 04 75 94 58 04

email: gubernati.daniel@orange.fr

web: www.laclede-ardeche.com

Overlooking the little village of Burzet, famous for its trout and its mushrooms, this impressive house has four comfortable and cosy rooms, some with a terrace or a balcony. Enjoy traditional French cuisine with the evening meals which are served in the large stone-built arched dining room, with its traditional fireplace. Peaceful, relaxing garden with a babbling spring and birdsong. Quad biking available.

Prices s €55–€75; d €60–€80; extra person fr €20; dinner fr €25 **Nearby** ⛳ 10km ∕ 0.5km ⚞ 15km Restaurant 10km ⌁ 0.5km Spa 10km 🏛 0.5km **Notes** No pets English spoken

CHALENCON

₩₩ ⦿ **Porte de Besse**

P et S CHOLAT

07240 CHALENCON

☎ 04 75 58 15 18

email: ph.cholat@free.fr

web: www.portedebesse.free.fr

This house is part of the original 13th-century fortified village of Chalencon. There is a grade 2 room sleeping two (with separate washing facilities), and two grade 3 three rooms sleeping two to four. A lovely lounge is available for guests' use. Breakfast and dinner (must be booked) are served in a restored medieval dining room using local and home-grown produce.

Prices s fr €46; d fr €49; t fr €62; extra person fr €13; dinner fr €20 **Nearby** ⛳ 4km ∕ 9km ⚞ 9km Restaurant 0.1km ⌁ 1km ⚑ 9km 🏛 0.1km ⚓ 45km **Notes** No pets Open April to November.

CHAMPAGNE

₩₩ **Domaine de Laprette**

Christian CHARDON

07340 CHAMPAGNE

☎ 04 75 34 12 89

web: www.domaine-de-laprette.com

This 17th-century mansion has four very beautiful guest rooms, sleeping from two to four people, all with en suite showers and WCs. There is a small guests' lounge, and a vast dining room. The house has a beautiful central staircase, large rooms and old furniture - all adding to the period atmosphere. Large east-facing courtyard, parking. Restaurant close by.

Prices s €40-€43; d €55-€58; t €70-€73; extra person fr €15
Nearby ♥ 10km ♨ 5km ♣ 15km ♦ 10km Restaurant 1.5km ♨ 5km Spa 12km ⓘ 5km ♒ 15km **Notes** No pets English spoken Open April to 15 October.

CHASSIERS

♥ ♥ i◯i *La Ferme d'Antan*

Jean Remy VALETTE
Chalabreges, 07110 CHASSIERS
☎ 04 75 88 37 79 📄 04 75 88 37 79
email: jean-remy.valette@laposte.net
web: www.lafermedantan.com

A renovated 18th-century working farm offering five en suite guest rooms accommodating two to four guests each. Breakfast is served on the terrace with a view over the Tanargue. Dinner by reservation, or kitchen at guests' disposal. There is a pony for children, billiards and many nearby attractions. Reduced rates for extended stays and groups.

Prices not confirmed for 2008 **Nearby** ♥ 10km ♣ 1km ♦ 20km ♨ 5km ⓘ 5km **Notes** No pets English spoken

CHAUZON

♥ ♥ ♿ **Les Clapas**

C et C CAPELLE
07120 CHAUZON
☎ 04 75 39 79 67
email: infos@lesclapas.com
web: http://lesclapas.com

A welcoming 18th-century farmhouse in a small village with five en suite guest rooms. There is one two-roomed suite sleeping four with disabled access; one suite for four on two floors; two double rooms and one room sleeping three. Closed Xmas and last week of October.

Prices s €38-€42; d €48-€52; t €64-€68; extra person fr €16
On Site Private ♦ **Nearby** ♥ 9km ♣ 0.8km Restaurant 0.1km ♨ 4km Spa 35km ♔ 4km ⓘ 0.1km **Notes** Pets admitted English spoken

CROS-DE-GEORAND

♥ i◯i ♿ **Brin d'Air**

P J TOCHEPRAX
Beauregard, 07510 CROS-DE-GEORAND
☎ 04 75 38 93 62 & 06 27 83 18 50 📄 04 75 38 93 08
email: brindair@wanadoo.fr
web: www.brindair.com

This delightfully located old farm house offers five comfortable and tastefully decorated bedrooms, each with a double bed and a single. They all have en suite WCs and power showers. Enjoy some home-made jam with your breakfast; evening meals using local produce are available by arrangement. Good area for walking and riding.

Prices s fr €50; d fr €50; t fr €70; dinner fr €20 **Nearby** ♥ 5km ♣ 2km Restaurant 2km ♨ 2km ♔ 8km ⓘ 2km **Notes** Pets admitted

DESAIGNES

♥ i◯i **Château du Vergier**

A et L JUPIN
07570 DESAIGNES
☎ 06 86 26 53 29 📄 04 75 06 65 96
email: chateauvergier@aol.com
web: www.lechateauduvergier.com

In a countryside setting, this château dates from the 14th century and features charming old furniture and modern comforts. Each room has a private bathroom and is accessed by a spiral staircase in the 15th century tower; three are spacious family rooms for up to four people. There are large lounges with fireplaces, a dining room for table d'hôte meals, library, billiards, swimming pool with solarium, 26 hectare park, gym room. Equestrian centre 100mtrs.

Prices s fr €84; d fr €107; t fr €130; extra person fr €15; dinner fr €23 **On Site** ♥ Private ♦ **Nearby** ♣ 0.5km ♨ 2km ⓘ 2km **Notes** No pets English spoken

♥ i◯i **Les Rosières**

Liliane VEYRIER
07570 DESAIGNES
☎ 04 75 06 66 90 & 06 11 27 96 15 📄 04 75 06 66 90
web: http://lesrosieres.free.fr

Five minutes from Lamastre, in a small open valley, this house with its relaxing atmosphere has three bedrooms. Two have private shower rooms and WCs; the other has a bathroom with spa bath. There is a swimming pool, and the protected local environment is yours to discover, on foot or mountain bike. Meals available by arrangement, using local produce.

Prices not confirmed for 2008 **On Site** Private ♦ **Nearby** ♥ 3km ♣ 4km ♨ 4km ⓘ 4km **Notes** No pets

ECLASSAN

♥ i◯i *Le Grand Chaleat*

T et D FILIBERTO
07370 ECLASSAN
☎ 04 75 34 35 14
email: filiberto.danielle@wanadoo.fr
web: www.ardeche-grandchaleat.com

An old mill building beside a river in beautiful countryside with woods close by. Five rooms for two or three people each have a private shower room and WC. The house has a large open fireplace, and lots of exposed beams and stonework. Meals are available if pre-booked.

Prices not confirmed for 2008 **On Site** ♣ **Nearby** ♥ 2km ♦ 15km ♨ 5km ⓘ 5km ♒ 20km **Notes** No pets English spoken

EMPURANY

⚞⚟ Le Crouzat

H et D VAN GEERSDAELE
07270 EMPURANY
☎ 04 75 06 56 03 ▤ 04 75 06 58 93
email: d.vangeersdaele@libertysurf.fr
web: http://site.voila.fr/crouzat

In a protected green site, this chambre d'hôtes offers three rooms with private facilities: a double with single bed and two rooms for two people. There is a large living room and dining room with wonderful views. The terrace has a fenced swimming pool and the atmosphere is pleasant and refined. Your hostess will be happy to share her passion for painting and watercolours.

Prices s fr €55; d €60-€70; t fr €80; extra person fr €9   **On Site** ✲ Private ⚲   **Nearby** ⚓ 10km ⚲ 1km Restaurant 1.5km ⚓ 10km 🏛 2km **Notes** No pets English spoken Open Easter to 1 November.

FAUGERES

⚞⚟ ⚟ La Bastide d'Aguyane

M-C et P GONTIER
Le Sabatier, 07230 FAUGERES
☎ 04 75 36 42 31 ▤ 04 75 36 42 31
email: contact@bastide-aguyane.com
web: www.bastide-aguyane.com

A lovely 17th-century stone house in a lovely, sunny setting, overlooking magnificent countryside with a terrace leading down to the valley. It offers two rooms for two people, a triple and a room for four, each with private facilities. Generous table d'hôte meals include regional cuisine, featuring home-grown produce.

Prices s €45-€50; d €49-€56; extra person fr €16; dinner fr €20 **On Site** Private ⚲   **Nearby** ⚓ 0.5km ⚲ 0.5km Restaurant 10km ⚓ 5km ✲ 10km 🏛 2km **Notes** No pets English spoken

GLUIRAS

⚞⚟ ⚟ ⚙ Château de Mours

Pieter DE GROOT
07190 GLUIRAS
☎ 04 75 66 62 32
email: chateaudemours@wanadoo.fr
web: www.chateaudemours.com

An 18th-century house set in a large botanical garden 15 minutes from the valley of l'Eyrieux. The house has a relaxing atmosphere and is artistically decorated with traditional furniture. There is a library, television, separate sitting room and the three en suite rooms are for two or three guests. Dinner is available if booked.

Prices s fr €55; d fr €55; t fr €73; extra person fr €19; dinner fr €21 **On Site** ✲   **Nearby** ⚓ 15km ⚲ 10km ⚲ 17km Restaurant 10km ⚓ 10km 🏛 5km ⚙ 50km **Notes** Pets admitted English spoken Open April to 15 November.

GRAS

⚞⚟ ⚟ Chez Bacchus

Marie Christine PILA
St Vincent, 07700 GRAS
☎ 04 75 04 18 69 ▤ 04 75 04 00 98
email: pila.mariechristine@neuf.fr
web: www.chezbacchus.com

In an area known for its vineyards and fields of lavender, this house has three bedrooms for two to four guests. All have private shower room and WC, two have a private terrace and one has a vaulted ceiling. Meals are available by arrangement. The Gorges de l'Ardèche are 13 kilometres away, and the Rhône Valley about 20 kilometres.

Prices s fr €48; d fr €52; t fr €64; extra person fr €12; dinner fr €22 **Nearby** ⚓ 3km ⚲ 30km ⚲ 13km ⚲ 3km Restaurant 5km ⚓ 3km ✲ 5km 🏛 5km ⚙ 30km **Notes** No pets English spoken

⚞⚟ ⚟ Ferme le Micalin

Patrick MEYCELLE
07700 GRAS
☎ 04 75 04 20 85 & 06 07 62 36 42
email: patrickmeycelle@orange.fr
web: www.lemicalin.com

A beautifully restored farmhouse in a valley bordered by oak trees and fields of lavender. Three superb ground floor bedrooms: two vaulted doubles with a fully fitted private bathroom; one double with bathroom with traditional bathtub and Italian shower, private WC. Each bedroom has access to the grand terrace which catches the morning sun. Lovely dining room with monumental fireplace.

Prices d fr €80; dinner fr €22   **Nearby** ⚓ 8km ⚲ 10km Restaurant 3km ⚓ 4km ✲ 15km 🏛 3km ⚙ 20km **Notes** No pets English spoken Open April to October.

⚞⚟ ⚘ ⚟ Mas de Marquet

M GRANIER-CHAUTARD
07700 GRAS
☎ 04 75 04 39 56

Seven kilometres from St Remèze and St Montan and near the Gorges de l'Ardèche, this farm comes complete with chickens, rabbits, sheep and cows. It offers a choice of three double rooms, one suite for five people, and one similar sized room for four people, all en suite. There is a communal room with piano, library, central heating and covered terrace. Evening meals must be booked; otherwise cooking facilities are available.

Prices s fr €35; d fr €50; t fr €65; extra person fr €15; dinner fr €18 **Nearby** ⚓ 2km ⚲ 13km ⚲ 20km Restaurant 7km 🏛 7km ⚙ 28km **Notes** No pets English spoken

GROSPIERRES

🍴 La Flor Azul

Diny VAN LAARHOVEN

La Ribiere, 07120 GROSPIERRES

☎ 04 75 93 97 24 & 06 77 39 63 77

email: laflor.azul@wanadoo.fr

web: www.laflorazul.com

Four of the five bedrooms of this property have been created in the lower part of the owners' 16th-century Ardéchois farmhouse, and have direct access onto the courtyard. The fifth is in the main part of the house, and can sleep up to four people. All rooms are elegant and tastefully furnished, and each has its own shower and WC.

Prices s fr €50; d fr €55; t fr €70; extra person fr €15 **Nearby** ☘ 5km ⚓ 1km Restaurant 0.5km ⚓ 5km 🎾 0.2km 🏛 0.2km **Notes** Pets admitted English spoken

🍴 🌱 Les Monteils

Pierre TEYSSIER

07120 GROSPIERRES

☎ 04 75 93 67 44 & 04 75 93 94 67

web: www.lesmonteils.fr

Four vaulted en suite guest rooms with separate access in an 18th-century farmhouse, 7km from the Gorges of the Ardèche and Vallon Pont d'Arc. Pleasant open grounds with garden furniture, deckchairs and barbecue. Small kitchen for guests to use, television lounge, washing machine, lavish breakfasts with home-made preserves, restaurant 300mtrs.

Prices s fr €42; d fr €48; t fr €60; extra person fr €12 **Nearby** ☘ 2km ⚓ 40km ⚓ 0.3km ⚓ 20km Restaurant 0.3km ⚓ 0.5km Spa 40km 🏛 1km ⚓ 40km **Notes** Pets admitted Open 16 February to 10 November.

🍴 Mas Calou

N ABSIL

Quartier de l'Eglise, 07120 GROSPIERRES

☎ 04 75 39 67 43 & 06 08 61 21 70

email: mascalou@free.fr

web: www.mascalou.com

An attractive 19th-century building in a large garden with five bedrooms, each sleeping from two to four people. All the rooms have private bath or shower room and WC. The spacious living area has an open fire and kitchenette, and a barbecue is available in the enclosed grounds. Canoeing and kayaking available 7km.

Prices s fr €45; d fr €55; t fr €65; extra person fr €15 **Nearby** ☘ 2km ⚓ 0.7km Restaurant 1km ⚓ 0.2km 🎾 1km 🏛 1km **Notes** Pets admitted English spoken Open March to December.

JAUJAC

🍴 🌱 🍽 La Ferme du Monteil

Catherine BRUN

07380 JAUJAC

☎ 04 75 93 28 56 📠 04 75 93 28 56

email: contact@la-ferme-du-monteil.com

web: www.la-ferme-du-monteil.com

This non-smoking restored stone farmhouse is set in the Regional Natural Park of the Monts d'Ardèche. There are four en suite rooms (two of them suitable for families) sleeping two to four. Facilities include central heating, games room, lounge, terrace and flower meadow and dinner includes produce from the garden, farm and local area.

Prices s fr €45; d fr €51; t fr €66; extra person fr €15; dinner fr €20 **Nearby** ☘ 10km ⚓ 4km ⚓ 7km Restaurant 4km ⚓ 4km 🏛 3.5km **Notes** No pets English spoken Open April to October.

🍴 🌱 Maison d'Hôtes des Roudils

Marie et Gil FLORENCE

07380 JAUJAC

☎ 04 75 93 21 11 📠 04 75 93 21 11

email: le-rucher-des-roudils@wanadoo.fr

web: www.lesroudils.com

This restored farmhouse owned by beekeepers is a haven of peace overlooking a large valley of the Hautes Cévennes. There are three en suite guest rooms: one room sleeps three; one suite sleeps five; and one sleeps two.

Prices d fr €60; t fr €78; extra person fr €18 **Nearby** ☘ 10km ⚓ 4km ⚓ 15km Restaurant 4km ⚓ 4km 🏛 4km ⚓ 12km **Notes** No pets English spoken Open April to 15 November.

JOANNAS

🍴 🌱 🍽 La Maurelle

Muriel et Laurent MALJEAN

07110 JOANNAS

☎ 04 75 88 37 85

email: lamaurelle07@aol.com

web: www.lamaurelle07.com

This large 17th-century house, built in the local style, is situated in the heart of the Monts d'Ardèche regional park, amongst springs, chestnut trees and vines. It has three double rooms, each one with private shower/WC. Your hosts will be delighted to serve evening meals, on request, making the best of local produce and their own inspiration.

Prices s fr €40; d fr €54; t fr €74; extra person fr €15; dinner fr €18 **Nearby** ☘ 10km ⚓ 1.5km Restaurant 1.5km ⚓ 5km 🏛 1km **Notes** No pets English spoken Open April to November.

LA SOUCHE

▦ ⦿ *La Chataîgneraie*

Solange et Gerard LOVERA
Quartier de l'Eglise, 07380 LA SOUCHE
☎ 04 75 37 92 53 ▤ 04 75 37 92 53
email: chambrelasouche@tele2.fr
web: http://lachataigneraie.free.fr

This old house is situated in the heart of the Monts d'Ardèche regional park, just at the top of the village. There are five bedrooms, doubles and triples, all with their own WC and shower room. Dining room, with lounge area.

Prices not confirmed for 2008 **Nearby** ⚱ 13km ⌀ 0.5km ⤳ 16km
⚲ 0.5km 🏛 0.5km **Notes** No pets

LABASTIDE-DE-VIRAC

▦ ⦿ Le Mas Rêvé

G et M-R GOOSSENS
07150 LABASTIDE-DE-VIRAC
☎ 04 75 38 69 13
email: info@lemasreve.com
web: www.lemasreve.com

A 17th-century mas provençale which owes its charm in part to its location beside the cliffs in the Nature Reserve of the Gorges de l'Ardèche. There are four en suite rooms of great comfort, each with separate access and sitting area, a terrace with garden furniture, vaulted lounge and library. Meals are enhanced by use of local produce.

Prices s fr €90-€120; d €90-€120; extra person fr €30; dinner fr €32
On Site ⌀ Private ⤳ **Nearby** ⚱ 5km ⌀ 30km Restaurant 3km
⚲ 5km Spa 45km ⚘ 10km 🏛 3km ⛵ 50km **Notes** No pets
English spoken Open 15 April to 15 October.

LAMASTRE

▦ ⦿ Florette Belle

Chantal et Patrick BANCEL
Valoan, 07270 LAMASTRE
☎ 04 75 06 32 95
email: philip.coutisson@tiscali.fr
web: www.florette-belle.com

Five bedrooms in a hamlet of stone-built houses three kilometres from Lamastre. The rooms sleep from two to four people, and each has a private shower room and WC. Grounds shaded by pine trees, with terraces and swimming pool. Generous breakfasts with home-made and local produce; other meals by arrangement.

Prices s fr €40; d fr €50; t fr €56; extra person fr €9; dinner fr €18
On Site Private ⤳ **Nearby** ⚱ 5km ⚑ 15km ⌀ 1km Restaurant 3km
⚲ 4km Spa 40km 🏛 4km ⛵ 40km **Notes** Pets admitted English spoken

LANAS

▦ ⦿ *Chambre d'hôtes*

P et C VANDENBUSSCHE-SIMONINI
07200 LANAS
☎ 04 75 37 76 39 & 06 32 51 87 06 ▤ 04 75 37 76 39
email: la.borie.de.lanas@wanadoo.fr

On the edge of the village of Lanas, close to the Ardèche region, this 18th-century house, with its welcoming Mediterranean atmosphere, offers three guest bedrooms, one of them a family suite for four. All the rooms have private facilities. Meals are available by arrangement.

Prices not confirmed for 2008 **Nearby** ⚱ 8km ⌀ 0.1km ⤳ 12km
⚲ 2km 🏛 2km **Notes** No pets English spoken Open June to September.

LARGENTIERE

▦ ✾ ⦿ Mas de la Madeleine

Gerard GUILLEMIN
07110 LARGENTIERE
☎ 04 75 39 23 18 ▤ 04 75 39 23 18
email: masdelamadeleine@aol.com
web: www.masdelamadeleine.com

Peacefully situated overlooking the medieval village of Largentière, surrounded by greenery, this beautiful old house has been lovingly restored by its owners. Each of the three spacious and prettily decorated bedrooms - two doubles and a family room - has a private balcony and en suite facilities. Beautiful terrace and gardens, where you can enjoy your breakfast when the weather is good.

Prices d fr €70; t fr €95; extra person fr €25; dinner fr €28
On Site Restaurant **Nearby** ⚱ 6km ⌀ 5km ⚲ 2km 🏛 5km ⛵ 1km
Notes No pets Open April to October.

LEMPS

▦ ⦿ Château Chavagnac

Diana et Aubyn HOWARD
07610 LEMPS
☎ 04 75 08 33 08
email: chateauchavagnac@wanadoo.fr
web: www.chateauchavagnac.com

You will find this Directoire château on the wine route on an agricultural holding of 15 hectares. Two very comfortable en suite rooms are available furnished in 19th-century style; cot and spare beds available. Large dining room and similarly large lounge with library opening out over the terrace. Massage available. Several restaurants in nearby Tournon and L'Hermitage.

Prices s €60-€70; d €70-€85; t €85-€100; extra person €15-€20; dinner fr €28 **On Site** ⚘ Private ⤳ **Nearby** ⚱ 5km ⚑ 15km
⌀ 4km Restaurant 1km ⚲ 8km 🏛 5km ⛵ 15km **Notes** No pets
English spoken

▥ ⅼ◯⒤ Château de Lemps

Nicole DU TREMOLET
07610 LEMPS
☎ 04 75 06 80 08
email: nicole.dutremolet@free.fr
web: www.chateaudelemps.com

In a quiet and relaxing spot at the heart of Lemps village, near the valley of the Rhône and the wine route, this old building offers two en suite family rooms for two to four people and one room for two or three. Dinner (family fare) must be booked and is served in the dining room in medieval style with the proprietor's family.

Prices s €50; d €50; t €62-€70; extra person fr €15; dinner fr €18
Nearby ⅼ 10km ℘ 10km ⅼ 7km ⅼ 7km ⅼ 4km **Notes** No pets
English spoken Open April to September.

▥ Mas de la Garrigue

Marie-Antoinette THEBAULT
Chemin de la Transhumance, 07140 LES VANS
☎ 04 75 88 52 02 ⅼ 04 75 88 52 02
email: thebaultma@wanadoo.fr
web: www.masdelagarrigue.com

Set in acres of olive trees, mulberries and fruit trees near the Bois de Païolive, this old silk house has five lovely en suite rooms which all sleep two (one with extra child's bed in a corner). There is central heating, a television lounge and a swimming pool. Four person gîte also available.

Prices d €65-€73; t €97-€107 **On Site** Private ⅼ **Nearby** ⅼ 5km
ⅼ 50km ℘ 4km Restaurant 2.5km ⅼ 2.5km ⅼ 2.5km **Notes** No pets
English spoken Open 15 February to 15 November.

LES ASSIONS

▥ La Bergerie

Christiane CHARMOT
Le Bosc, 07140 LES ASSIONS
☎ 04 75 94 90 20 & 06 83 00 14 02
email: labergeriecharm@aol.com
web: http://labergeriedecharme.free.fr

These rooms are in a pretty hamlet, in a stone building adjacent to the owner's house. The three double rooms all have en suite showers and WCs. Breakfast is served in the garden or on the enclosed terrace. There is a lounge area next to the bedrooms for guests' exclusive use; also a guests' kitchen near the garden.

Prices s fr €40; d fr €45; t fr €57; extra person fr €12 **Nearby** ⅼ 6km
ⅼ 40km ℘ 2km ⅼ 20km Restaurant 2km ⅼ 4km Spa 30km ⅼ 4km
ⅼ 2km ⅼ 40km **Notes** Pets admitted English spoken

LES VANS

▥ Les Figuiers

Annie RICHARD
Place de l'Eglise, 07140 LES VANS
☎ 04 75 37 32 56
email: annie.richard@tiscali.fr

Quietly situated in a character village in the south of the Ardèche, this large, 18th-century stone-built house has three guest rooms, with their own independent access; two doubles, and a two-roomed family suite for four, all with private facilities. Large lounge with kitchenette, TV and open fireplace. Delicious breakfasts with home-made jams served on the terrace. Swimming pool.

Prices s fr €50; d fr €50; t fr €65; extra person fr €15 **On Site** Private ⅼ
Nearby ⅼ 5km ℘ 1km Restaurant 1km ⅼ 4km ⅼ 2km ⅼ 2km
Notes Pets admitted Open April to 15 December.

▥ ⅼ◯⒤ La Maison Bleue

Marithe et Serge DER LOUGHIAN
Hameau de Ladreyt, 07000 LYAS
☎ 04 75 64 22 44

This house is in a sunny spot on the edge of a pine forest. It has two rooms for two or four people, each with private shower and WC, and a further grade 2 double room with private, but not en suite, facilities. Lounge area with TV, games and books. Terrace, use of owner's pool (limited hours). Meals by arrangement.

Prices s €45-€50; d €55-€60; t €80-€85; extra person fr €25; dinner fr €20 **On Site** Private ⅼ **Nearby** ⅼ 15km ℘ 6km ⅼ 7km ⅼ 7km
ⅼ 40km **Notes** Pets admitted English spoken

MALBOSC

▥ ⅼ◯⒤ La Pauze

Marie Louise DE ROO
07140 MALBOSC
☎ 04 75 36 00 47 ⅼ 04 75 36 00 47
email: lapauze@wanadoo.fr
web: www.lapauze.com

This isolated 18th-century house, built in the local style, is surrounded by chestnut and oak trees, with owls, boars, deer and the open sky for company. It has three rooms, with oriental décor, each one with private facilities. The generous breakfasts are served on the big south-facing terrace, overlooking the valleys of the Cévennes, or in the impressive inner courtyard.

Prices s fr €70; d fr €80; extra person fr €30; dinner fr €30
On Site Private ⅼ **Nearby** ⅼ 3km ℘ 1km ⅼ 6km ⅼ 7km ⅼ 7km
ⅼ 40km **Notes** No pets English spoken

MARCOLS-LES-EAUX

ⅢⅢ ⅣⅢ Domaine de Salomony

Joke RISSON
07190 MARCOLS-LES-EAUX
☎ 04 75 65 61 65 ▤ 04 75 65 61 65
email: joke.risson@wanadoo.fr
web: http://perso.wanadoo.fr/salomony

An 18th-century stone building situated in the wilds of the Parc Naturel des Monts d'Ardèche on the bank of the river, ideal for walks, biking and fishing. Two en suite rooms sleeping two or three, one grade 2 double room and possible room for two children (cot available). Living room, television, interior courtyard, terrace, games, sun loungers, boules. Dinner includes home grown vegetables and herbs and home-made preserves.

Prices s fr €46; d fr €55; t fr €75; extra person fr €20; dinner fr €20 **On Site** ⌖ **Nearby** ⚲ 30km Restaurant 10km ⚓ 0.5km ⚑ 0.5km **Notes** No pets English spoken

MARS

ⅢⅢ La Souche

Jacques MARY
Gourgouras, 07320 MARS
☎ 04 75 30 23 13

A superb traditional farmhouse, completely restored to its original condition, with four en suite guest rooms. Large games room, lounge with open fire and television corner. 9km from St Agrève and 15km from Cheylard.

Prices s fr €48; d fr €55; t fr €78; extra person fr €13 **On Site** ☙ **Nearby** ⚓ 10km ⚒ 5km ⌖ 6km Restaurant 3km ⚑ 9km ⚕ 50km **Notes** Pets admitted English spoken

MERCUER

ⅢⅢ ⅣⅢ Mas de Mazan

Alain et Michele CROZE
07200 MERCUER
☎ 04 75 35 41 88 ▤ 04 75 35 41 88
email: masdemazan@wanadoo.fr
web: www.masdemazan.com

Perfect for ramblers, set between the plateau and south Ardèche, five minutes from Aubenas and Vals les Bains, five en suite guest rooms are offered sleeping two to four. Guests may use the dining room and small kitchen, swimming pool and fishing is 5km. Breakfast, with home-made jams and pastries, may be taken in the shade of the mulberries.

Prices s €48-€50; d €48-€50; t €58-€60; extra person €10 **On Site** Private ⚲ **Nearby** ⚓ 5km ⌖ 5km ⚓ 3km Spa 5km ⚑ 3km ⚕ 40km **Notes** No pets Open 15 March to 15 November.

PAILHARES

ⅢⅢ ⅣⅢ ⅣⅢ Le Petit Marchand

Jacques ANDRY
Cole de Marchand, 07410 PAILHARES
☎ 04 75 06 06 80 ▤ 04 75 06 13 46
email: jacques.andry@wanadoo.fr
web: http://perso.wanadoo.fr/petit.marchand

Enjoying amazing views between the Safari-Parc de Peaugres and Tournon, this old restored farmhouse has four beautiful en suite rooms (one of them grade 2), each with sitting area and fridge. Dinner is based on local produce, regional recipes and specialities of Alsace. Plenty of activities nearby. Reduced rates for half board and children.

Prices s fr €45; d fr €50; t fr €67; extra person fr €17; dinner fr €20 **Nearby** ⚓ 8km ⌖ 2km ⚲ 8km Restaurant 5km ⚓ 5km ⚑ 5km **Notes** Pets admitted English spoken

PEAUGRES

ⅢⅢ ⅢⅢ *La Palisse*

Anne et Gerard MOREL
07340 PEAUGRES
☎ 04 75 67 08 37 & 06 03 34 97 19 ▤ 04 75 67 08 37
email: inforesa@lapalisse-peaugres.com
web: www.lapalisse-peaugres.com

This beautiful modern house, 15 kilometres from the Rhône Valley, is close to the Peaugres Safari Park and has views towards the Alps. There are three bright guest bedrooms, each decorated according to a theme, and each with en suite facilities and direct access to the terrace. A wonderful breakfast is served in the conservatory, which enjoys panoramic views.

Prices not confirmed for 2008 **Nearby** ⚓ 10km ⚲ 10km ⚓ 2km ⚑ 2km ⚕ 20km **Notes** No pets English spoken Open May to October.

PLANZOLLES

ⅢⅢ La Civade

Bruno LE BRIS
07230 PLANZOLLES
☎ 04 75 36 59 72
email: la.civade@wanadoo.fr
web: www.guideweb.com/ardeche/gite/la-civade/

This former silkworm house stands in the heart of a chestnut grove, with the sound of cicadas in the background. There are two beautiful double rooms and a triple, all with private bath or shower room and WC. Guests' kitchen available. There is a swimming pool, and an equipped games area for children.

Prices s fr €40; d fr €45; t fr €55 **On Site** Private ⚲ **Nearby** ⚓ 15km ⚒ 20km ⌖ 15km Restaurant 10km ⚓ 5km ☙ 8km ⚑ 6km ⚕ 35km **Notes** No pets English spoken

PONT-DE-LABEAUME

♯♯♯ ⚄ La Maison de Paul et Cloé

Carole et Christophe POIZAT
Niegles, Le Goux, 07380 PONT-DE-LABEAUME
☎ 04 75 37 31 62 & 06 89 44 26 04 ▤ 04 75 94 14 78
email: maisondepaulcloe@wanadoo.fr
web: www.maisondepaulcloe.com

A house with lots of character, close to a medieval hamlet with a Romanesque church dating back to the 11th century. There is a suite with a double bed, two singles and lounge area; a split-level room with a double bed and a single; and an attic room for up to four people. All have private bath or shower room and WC. Lounge, patio and swimming pool.

Prices s €63-€68; d €63-€68; t €77-€82; extra person €15-€20; dinner fr €22 **On Site** Private ⚄ **Nearby** ⚓ 5km ⚐ 2km ⚓ 2km ⚄ 2km **Notes** No pets English spoken

POURCHERES

♯♯♯ ⚄ La Hameau de la Sourcière

A et M GOETZ
07000 POURCHERES
☎ 04 75 66 81 99 ▤ 04 75 66 81 99
email: marcelle.goetz@wanadoo.fr

Four guest rooms with separate access opening on to the garden, in an old Ardéchois house surrounded by greenery. Dinner (communal or separate) uses produce from the garden and can be vegetarian. The village is situated on the slopes of an old volcano, with lovely walks. Explore astrology, tarot, botany or complementary medicine.

Prices s €39-€44; d €50-€58; t €60-€71; extra person fr €14; dinner fr €20 **On Site** Private ⚄ **Nearby** ⚓ 10km ⚄ 10km **Notes** Pets admitted English spoken Open Easter to 1 November.

PRADES

♯♯♯ La Grange

B et B FERMENT
Chemin de Chanarelles, 07380 PRADES
☎ 04 75 94 18 10 ▤ 04 75 94 18 10
email: contact@lagrange-prades.com
web: www.lagrange-prades.com

A peaceful, typical Ardèche barn, restored to provide three beautiful and comfortable guest rooms - two doubles and one room for two/three, each with private facilities. There is a sitting room with library and lovely vaulted dining room, courtyard, large open area and lawn in the shade of oak trees. Huge breakfasts include home-made preserves, organic foods and local produce. Bedrooms are non-smoking.

Prices d €60-€65; extra person fr €16 **Nearby** ⚓ 12km ⚐ 2km ⚓ 6km Restaurant 2km ⚄ 2km Spa 6km ⚄ 6km ⚄ 2km ⚄ 50km **Notes** No pets

PRADONS

♯♯♯ ⚄ Les Ranchins

Francis RANCHIN
07120 PRADONS
☎ 04 75 93 98 33 & 06 07 10 07 79 ▤ 04 75 93 98 33
email: ranchins@aol.com
web: www.lesranchins.fr

Five en suite guest rooms (three doubles and two rooms sleeping three) in an entirely restored farmhouse, on a vineyard 5km from Ruoms. Living room for guests' use only; central heating; swimming pool; garage; a seven person gîte nearby. Breakfast served on the veranda or on the terrace, and wine is for sale.

Prices s €40-€45; d €50-€55; t €65-€70; extra person fr €15 **On Site** Private ⚄ **Nearby** ⚓ 7km ⚄ 10km ⚄ 0.5km Restaurant 2km ⚄ 5km ⚄ 5km ⚄ 2km ⚄ 50km **Notes** Pets admitted English spoken CC

ROCHESSAUVE

♯♯♯♯ ⚄ Château de Rochessauve

Yannick VIALLE
07210 ROCHESSAUVE
☎ 04 75 65 07 06
email: yannick.vialle@chateau-de-rochessauve.com
web: www.chateau-de-rochessauve.com

This beautiful and charming house is perched on a rocky peak at the heart of the Coiron Massif and has superb views of the valley. There are three peaceful rooms, one of them a suite, which have a sophisticated atmosphere. Swimming pool. Meals available, offering seasonal menus using local produce.

Prices d €100-€110; t fr €125; extra person fr €20; dinner fr €35 **On Site** Private ⚄ **Nearby** ⚓ 6km ⚄ 30km ⚐ 2km Restaurant 5km ⚄ 3km ⚄ 6km ⚄ 30km **Notes** Pets admitted English spoken Open mid March to December.

ROSIERES

♯♯♯ ⚄ L'Oustalou

Philippe ALCALDE
Augnac, 07260 ROSIERES
☎ 04 75 39 57 05
email: loustalou@wanadoo.fr
web: www.loustalou-ardeche.com

CONTINUED

ROSIERES CONTINUED

This beautiful house, three kilometres south of Rosières, has retained its soul and its history after undergoing a major restoration. It has four welcoming bedrooms, each with a private bath or shower room and WC. Cosy lounge with open fireplace and a large dining room which overlooks the grounds. Swimming pool. Meals available, using local produce.

Prices s €52-€60; d €52-€60; t €71-€79; extra person fr €21; dinner fr €19 **On Site** Private ⸯ **Nearby** ⚓ 5km ⌀ 3km ⌇ 3km ⌘ 3km 🏛 3km ⚓ 50km **Notes** No pets English spoken

RUOMS

🏵 **Le Mas St-Michel**

Y et M-C STOLDVISER
07120 RUOMS
☎ 04 75 39 73 33
email: info@le-mas-saint-michel.com
web: www.le-mas-saint-michel.com

A lovely traditional stone mas situated amid vines, at the convergence of four rivers and five minutes from the centre of Ruoms. There are four rooms for two to three people with private bathrooms, a dining room, pretty lounge and terrace next to the swimming pool, shaded by a mulberry tree. Ideally situated for the shops and tourist activities in Ruoms and Vallon Pont d'Arc.

Prices s fr €40; d €52-€56; t fr €70; extra person fr €14
On Site Private ⸯ **Nearby** ⚓ 5km ⌀ 2km Restaurant 1km ⌇ 1km Spa 50km 🏛 2km ⚓ 50km **Notes** No pets

🏵 🍽 **Villa Hugon**

Romain COUTURIER
73 Rue des Brasseries, 07120 RUOMS
☎ 04 75 36 75 72
email: contact@villahugon.com
web: www.villahugon.com

You can immerse yourself in the delights of the Belle Epoque when you visit this villa, which was built by the brewer Hugon in 1900. It has four splendid guest rooms - two suites, a family room and a bedroom - and a Mediterranean garden with swimming pool and jacuzzi. Meals are available by arrangement, and the house offers easy access to Ruoms and Labeaume.

Prices s fr €79; d €89-€135; extra person fr €20; dinner fr €35
On Site ⌀ ⌘ Private ⸯ **Nearby** ⚓ 1km ⌇ 1km 🏛 1km
Notes No pets English spoken Open Easter to September. CC

SALAVAS

🏵 🍽 **Domaine de la Sauvagine**

Florian SAUVAGE
Lalauze, 07150 SALAVAS
☎ 04 75 88 90 94 & 06 74 45 37 37
email: info@domainedelasauvagine.com
web: www.domainedelasauvagine.com

In a green setting, between pine forests and the gorges of the Ardèche, but just two minutes from the centre of Vallon Pont d'Arc,

this house has four bedrooms. They each sleep two or three people, and all have en suite WCs/shower rooms. The hosts offer a very warm welcome, and will be delighted to prepare evening meals, by arrangement.

Prices s €49-€55; d €55-€65; t fr €85; extra person fr €20; dinner fr €25 **On Site** Private ⸯ **Nearby** ⚓ 4km ⌀ 0.8km ⌇ 2km 🏛 1km
Notes No pets English spoken Open 15 March to 1 November.

ST-ALBAN-AURIOLLES

🏵 **Domaine de Champtressac**

Dominique MAZOYER
07120 ST-ALBAN-AURIOLLES
☎ 04 75 93 66 24 & 06 78 30 37 64
email: mazoyerdominique@hotmail.com
web: www.champtressac-ardeche.com

In a unique setting in the heart of the southern Ardèche, this superb 16th-century house has been sensitively restored with local stone, respecting the charm of its unique architecture. It offers four bedrooms and a suite for up to four people, all with private facilities. Breakfast is served in the courtyard overlooking the park, or in the beamed dining room.

Prices s €80-€120; d €80-€120; t €120-€150 **On Site** Private ⸯ
Nearby ⚓ 0.8km ⌀ 2km 🏛 3km **Notes** No pets English spoken Open April to 15 October. CC

🏵 🍽 **Mas St Alban**

Philippe DELATTRE
Quartier Robert, 07120 ST-ALBAN-AURIOLLES
☎ 04 75 89 17 01 📠 04 75 89 17 01
email: christel-philippe@mas-stalban.com
web: www.mas-stalban.com

Situated above St Alban Auriolles, amongst the vines, this place offers all the peace and calm of the countryside of Provence, while still being close to the main tourist sites of the lower Ardèche. There are four bedrooms, doubles and triples, all with private facilities. Enjoy your breakfast on the covered terrace with its superb views.

Prices d €55-€92; t €70-€110; extra person fr €15; dinner fr €20
On Site Private ⸯ **Nearby** ⚓ 1.8km ⌀ 3km Restaurant 3km ⌇ 7km
Spa 30km ⌘ 6km 🏛 3km **Notes** Pets admitted

🏵 🍽 **Mas de Chantressac**

Chantal et Patrick ALTARE
07120 ST-ALBAN-AURIOLLES
☎ 04 75 39 79 05 & 06 07 30 95 67 📠 04 75 39 79 05
email: patrick.altare@wanadoo.fr
web: www.masdechantressac.com

In open countryside at the heart of southern Ardèche, this traditional country house in an oak wood is completely restored. Three en suite carefully appointed rooms for two to four people, swimming pool and special rates for groups. Breakfasts served in the lounge or outside on the stone terraces. Dinner available (except July and August) - booking required.

Prices s €52-€69; d €56-€85; dinner fr €23 **On Site** Private ⸯ
Nearby ⚓ 0.8km ⌀ 2km Restaurant 2km ⌇ 3km ⌘ 2km 🏛 2km
Notes No pets

⁘ Villa St-Patrice

G et M TOURRE
07120 ST-ALBAN-AURIOLLES
☎ 04 75 39 37 78 & 06 73 50 50 92
email: contact@villastpatrice.com
web: www.villastpatrice.com

This Florentine-style house in set in quiet parkland in the middle of a Provençal village. Three double en suite rooms and one suite for two or four people, with lounge. Breakfast is on the terrace opposite the vineyard and Samson's Rock; the living room is shared with the owner. Parking, garden furniture and sunbeds available in the shady grounds.

Prices d €85-€130; extra person fr €15 **On Site** Private ⚡
Nearby ⚓ 0.5km ⚲ 1km Restaurant 0.5km ⚱ 7km ⚑ 7km
⚐ 0.5km **Notes** No pets English spoken CC

ST-ANDEOL-DE-FOURCHADES

⁘ ⦿ La Calmeraie

Sebastien LIABEUF
Longeagnie, 07310 ST-ANDEOL-DE-FOURCHADES
☎ 04 75 29 19 38

A traditional 17th-century farmhouse restored to its original condition 3km from the Lac du St Martial on 100 hectares of open land. Five refined guest rooms with private facilities (one has a bathroom). Lounge with television and open fire; meals (local cuisine) are served under the lime tree. Leisure facilities include painting classes, rambling, cross country skiing and mushroom picking in season.

Prices s €45-€50; d €45-€50; t fr €60; extra person fr €15; dinner fr €16
On Site ⚲ **Nearby** ⚓ 15km ⚑ 35km Restaurant 3km ⚱ 3km ⚑ 18km
⚐ 3km ⚒ 50km **Notes** Pets admitted English spoken

ST-ANDRE-DE-CRUZIERES

⁘ ⚘ ⦿ Les Mûriers

Elisabeth DUMAS
Pierregras, 07460 ST-ANDRE-DE-CRUZIERES
☎ 04 75 39 02 02 ▤ 04 75 39 02 02
email: lesmuriersdumas@aol.com
web: www.ardeche.com/tourism/les-muriers

A Provençal house between the Ardèche and the Gard with four comfortable en suite guest rooms for two or three (spare beds available). Communal living room, television, corner kitchen for guests' use, heating, barbecue. Breakfast may be taken on the shady terrace; restaurants in 4km.

Prices s fr €37; d fr €44; t fr €57; extra person fr €13; dinner fr €17
Nearby ⚓ 10km ⚲ 20km ⚡ 10km Restaurant 4km ⚱ 10km ⚑ 15km
⚐ 0.8km ⚒ 27km **Notes** Pets admitted

ST-CHRISTOL

⁘ ⦿ ⚿ Le Moulinage de St Christol

B et D JOUANNIGOT
Les Echarlives, 07160 ST-CHRISTOL
☎ 04 75 29 00 34 ▤ 04 75 29 96 39
email: lemoulinage@free.fr
web: www.lemoulinage.fr.st

Restored old mill among the mountains and woods 12km from Cheylard, offering a choice of four en suite rooms each sleeping two and a rural gîte sleeping five. You have the use of the lounge or music room and meals are served either outside in the courtyard or in the dining room. Mountain bikes available.

Prices s fr €40; d fr €48; t fr €60; dinner fr €16 **On Site** ⚲ ⚑
Nearby ⚑ 40km ⚡ 12km Restaurant 12km ⚱ 12km ⚐ 12km
Notes No pets English spoken

ST-CIRGUES-DE-PRADES

⁘ ⦿ Domaine de la Graveyre

G ESPANET DALMOLIN
07380 ST-CIRGUES-DE-PRADES
☎ 04 75 93 26 64 & 06 88 17 14 82 ▤ 04 75 93 26 64
email: lagraveyre07@orange.fr
web: www.lagraveyre.com

A 15th-century farmhouse, standing amongst chestnut trees, in the green surroundings of the Ardèche. Three very comfortable bedrooms; outside are extensive grounds with outstanding views over the Cévennes. Guests can enjoy breakfast indoors, or outside on a covered or open terrace. Other meals are available by arrangement.

Prices d fr €62; t fr €75; dinner fr €25 **Nearby** ⚓ 10km ⚡ 5km ⚡
Restaurant 1km ⚱ 1.5km ⚑ 10km ⚐ 1.5km **Notes** No pets

ST-FORTUNAT

⁘ ⦿ Mondon Le Haut

Francois COTTE
Mondon, 07360 ST-FORTUNAT
☎ 04 75 65 30 37
email: mondonlehaut@laposte.net
web: http://mondonlehaut.free.fr

Situated to the south of the Eyrieux Valley, in a very pretty valley bordered with oak trees and orchards, this house has three air-conditioned bedrooms. There are two doubles, one an attic room, each with private WC/shower room. There is another grade 2 room for three, with its own private shower room/WC which is not en suite.

Prices d €42-€44; dinner fr €15 **On Site** ⚑ Private ⚡
Nearby ⚓ 12km ⚑ 20km ⚡ 1km Restaurant 2km ⚱ 0.8km ⚐ 1km
⚒ 10km **Notes** No pets

ST-GENEST-DE-BEAUZON

♦♦♦ Mas du Vieux Chêne

Corinne et Jacquy LEROY
Le Suel, 07230 ST-GENEST-DE-BEAUZON
☎ 04 75 88 53 79 📄 04 75 88 53 79
email: lemasduvieuxchene@tiscali.fr
web: www.vieuxcheneardeche.com

Close to Joyeuse des Vans, this 18th-century stone house provides three rooms decorated in provençal colours and with private facilities: a double, a family room with a double and twin and a family suite with a double and single. There is a communal dining room, terrace, enclosed courtyard, shady lawn with children's games and swimming pool.

Prices d €49-€60; t €64-€75; extra person fr €19   **On Site** Private ⚓
Nearby ⛱ 7km 🏊 5km Restaurant 5km 🚣 3km ⛵ 7km 🏠 5km
🚴 30km   **Notes** No pets   English spoken

ST-GERMAIN

♦♦♦ 🐾 Chambre d'hôtes

Nicole RICHARD
07170 ST-GERMAIN
☎ 04 75 37 77 14 & 06 85 15 37 45 📄 04 75 37 77 14
email: charles.richard2@wanadoo.fr
web: www.chez-nicole-et-charles.chambres-hotes-ardeche.fr

In a small village, full of character, typical of the lower Ardèche region - three bedrooms, for two or three guests, all with private shower room and WC. The rooms are in a building separate from the owners' home, with a pretty, enclosed courtyard full of flowers. Lounge, use of kitchen. Private parking. Air-conditioning in all rooms.

Prices s fr €35; d fr €43; t fr €52; extra person fr €12   **Nearby** ⛱ 7km
🏊 3km ⚓ 10km Restaurant 3km 🚣 3km 🏠 0.2km   **Notes** No pets

ST-JEAN-DE-MUZOLS

♦♦♦ 🍽 Villa Chaumont

Marie Michele CHAUMONT
Route de St Felichen, 07300 ST-JEAN-DE-MUZOLS
☎ 04 75 08 48 04
email: mmchaumont@yahoo.fr
web: www.chaumont-chambredhote.org

Among the vineyards on the heights of Tournon, this house offers a double room, a triple and a family suite for up to five people. All have television, private shower room and WC. Living area and sun terrace, and meals served by arrangement. Good area for walking and mountain-biking; river bathing possible close by.

Prices s fr €48; d €50-€55; t €78-€82; extra person fr €18; dinner fr €20
On Site ⛵ **Nearby** ⛱ 1km 🏊 3km ⚓ 3km Restaurant 2km 🚣 3.5km
🏠 3km 🚴 10km   **Notes** No pets   English spoken   Open 2 February to November.

ST-JEAN-LE-CENTENIER

♦♦♦ L'Ecurie de Margot

Brigitte et Patrice BOYER
Les Rochers, 07580 ST-JEAN-LE-CENTENIER
☎ 04 75 36 73 72 & 06 77 27 05 22
email: lecuriedemargot@hotmail.fr
web: www.lecuriedemargot.com

An old farmhouse nestling at the foot of the cliffs with open views towards Mont Ventoux and the Cévennes. In the converted stable named after grandfather's favourite mare, there are three comfortable, stylishly-decorated double rooms, all with private shower room and WC. Peace and quiet in a wonderful setting with a flower-filled garden, ideal for lazing in the sun.

Prices s fr €37; d fr €47   **Nearby** 🏊 2km ⚓ 10km Restaurant 3km
🚣 10km 🏠 3km   **Notes** No pets   Open Easter to 1 November.

ST-JUST-D'ARDECHE

♦♦♦ 🍽 La Melinas

VANDENBERGHE-DE PERMENTIER
07700 ST-JUST-D'ARDECHE
☎ 04 75 04 61 36
email: la-melinas@wanadoo.fr
web: www.la-melinas.com

Old stones and hearths recall the age of the Knights Templar. Three en suite guest rooms available - two suites for two to four people and one family room for four. Swimming pool with swimming pool, terrace with outdoor furniture, garden, children's play area, large lounge with traditional fireplace. Meals (by reservation) are taken on the terrace or in the kitchen.

Prices s fr €55; d €65-€95; t fr €120; extra person fr €25; dinner fr €30
On Site Private ⚓ **Nearby** ⛱ 2km 🏊 1km 🚣 0.3km 🏠 2km 🚴 10km
Notes Pets admitted   English spoken

ST-LAGER-BRESSAC

♦♦♦♦ 🍽 Château de Fontblachère

Bernard LIAUDOIS
07210 ST-LAGER-BRESSAC
☎ 04 75 65 15 02 & 06 07 62 74 23
📄 04 75 65 18 56
email: chateau@fontblachere.com
web: www.chateau-fontblachere.com

10km off the A7, the 18th-century château stands on the hills overlooking the valley of the Rhône. Choose from three en suite rooms sleeping two or three and a suite for four (cot available). There is a swimming pool and tennis court in the large shaded park, vaulted dining room, terrace with garden furniture. Nearby horse riding centre, golf, marina, flying club. Small dogs welcome.

Prices s €100-€130; d €100-€130; extra person fr €20; dinner fr
€30   **On Site** Spa Privae ⚓ Private tennis court   **Nearby** ⛱ 3km
⛳ 30km 🏊 14km ⛵ 20km 🏠 6km 🚴 20km   **Notes** English spoken
Open April to October and weekends.   CC

₩ ⊙ Le Moulinage

Thibaud QUERE

Quartier Champesteve, 07210 ST-LAGER-BRESSAC

☎ 04 75 65 13 96 📄 04 75 65 13 96

email: info@gite-chambre-ardeche.com

web: www.gite-chambre-ardeche.com

This restored mill building situated midway between Privas and Montelimar, has four spacious and comfortable bedrooms sleeping two to four people. Each room has a private shower and WC, and there is a cot available. Lounge/library, lawn and terrace. There is also a swimming pool, and there is a restaurant five minutes away.

Prices s €65-€95; d €65-€95; t €85-€115; extra person fr €20; dinner fr €25 **On Site** 🛪 Private ↖ **Nearby** ⛷ 2km ⚓ 18km ⚓ 20km Restaurant 3km ⚓ 0.5km Spa 45km ⛳ 5km ⚓ 18km **Notes** No pets English spoken

---

ST-MARTIN-DE-VALAMAS

₩ ⊙ La Croix la Pierre

Dominique RIOU

07310 ST-MARTIN-DE-VALAMAS

☎ 04 75 30 29 25

email: riou-lebon@orange.fr

This is a stone-built house in the Parc Naturel Régional des Monts d'Ardèche, between the Rhône and the source of the River Loire. There are two double rooms, a twin-bedded room and two triples, all with private bathroom and WC. Meals available by arrangement, and the host is a 'chocolatier', which for some guests puts the icing on the cake!

Prices d €50-€70; extra person fr €20; dinner fr €20 **Nearby** ⛷ 20km ⚓ 20km ⚓ 0.5km ↖ 8km Restaurant 0.8km ⚓ 2km ⛳ 10km ⛳ 0.8km **Notes** No pets

---

ST-MONTAN

₩ ⊙ La Pacha

Isabelle MILLION

Route de Viviers, 07220 ST-MONTAN

☎ 04 75 52 57 41 📄 04 75 52 57 41

email: lapacha.lemoure@wanadoo.fr

Restored 18th-century Ardéchois farmhouse with panoramic outlook, near a medieval village and the Gorges de l'Ardèche. Four pretty rooms each with private terrace and garden furniture. Communal living room with open fire, small lounge, games, pétanque, swimming pool. Breakfast served under the arbour during summer; restaurant 3km.

Prices s fr €57; d fr €63; extra person fr €16; dinner fr €23 **On Site** Private ↖ **Nearby** ⛷ 10km ⚓ 25km ⛳ 6km Restaurant 3km ⚓ 3km ⛳ 25km ⛳ 3km ⚓ 17km **Notes** No pets English spoken Open 5 January to 15 December.

ST-PIERREVILLE

₩ *Moulinage Chabriol*

Kim et Gerben BOOGAARD

07190 ST-PIERREVILLE

☎ 04 75 66 62 08 📄 04 75 66 65 99

email: chabriol@infonie.fr

web: www.chabriol.com

This 18th-century silk-spinning mill on the river bank has been remarkably well restored, and has six quality en suite rooms with exposed stones, vaulted ceilings, antique furniture and modern materials. Large lounge with open fire, swimming and fishing on site and displays of silk-making. Good restaurants nearby.

Prices not confirmed for 2008 **On Site** ⛳ Private ↖ **Nearby** ⛷ 25km ⚓ 4km ⛳ 4km **Notes** No pets English spoken

---

ST-REMEZE

₩ ⊙ La Martinade

Sylvette et Gerard MIALON

07700 ST-REMEZE

☎ 04 75 98 89 42

email: sylvetlm@aol.com

web: www.chambres-hotes-la-martinade.fr

This old farmhouse has been in the family for over a century and offers a choice of four en suite rooms for two people (with spare beds available). Ardéchois and regional cuisine is served (dinner reservations may be necessary). No pets allowed in rooms.

Prices s €48-€50; d €50-€55; t €70-€75; extra person fr €20; dinner fr €20 **On Site** Private ↖ **Nearby** ⛷ 6km ⚓ 40km ⛳ 9km Restaurant 2km ⚓ 2km ⛳ 2km ⚓ 20km **Notes** No pets English spoken

---

ST-SAUVEUR-DE-CRUZIERES

₩ ⊙ Mas des Molières

Richard REUTHER

07460 ST-SAUVEUR-DE-CRUZIERES

☎ 04 75 39 08 75 📄 04 75 39 08 75

email: reservation@masdesmolieres.com

web: www.masdesmolieres.com

A typical 16th-century mas among vines and olive trees in the Cruzières, with indoor swimming pool in the courtyard and terraces enjoying a superb view. There are four guest rooms, a vaulted dining room, lounge with television, billiard table, sofas, shaded boules pitch and meals based on seasonal produce. Reduction for stays over three nights (except July and August).

Prices s €56-€66; d €60-€70; extra person fr €19; dinner fr €21 **On Site** Private ↖ **Nearby** ⛷ 4km ⛳ 2.5km Restaurant 7km ⚓ 2km ⛳ 1km ⚓ 30km **Notes** No pets English spoken Open 15 February to 1 November.

ST-THOME

⁂ La Bastide Bernard

Francoise et J-Pierre BERNARD
Chasser, 07220 ST-THOME
☎ 04 75 96 39 72 & 06 83 34 60 54
email: bastide@bastidebernard.com
web: www.bastidebernard.com

A very comfortable modern house beautifully situated among the vineyards, looking towards the medieval village of St-Thomé. The bedrooms - two doubles, a twin-bedded room and a triple - have direct access to a sun terrace which leads to the swimming pool. Each room has an en suite shower room and WC. Three night minimum stay during high season.

Prices s €49-€70; d fr €80; t fr €95; extra person fr €15
On Site Private ⚲ **Nearby** ⚓ 1km ⚴ 15km ⌀ 1km Restaurant 4km ⚲ 1km ⚑ 4km ⚐ 4km ⚒ 15km **Notes** No pets English spoken

⁂ ⏚ Le Moulinage

Laurent JULIENNE
Les Carmes, 07220 ST-THOME
☎ 06 09 48 80 14 📄 04 75 52 60 62
email: famille.julienne@wanadoo.fr
web: www.le-moulinage.com

This totally restored property is situated beside a river in the heart of the Helvie Vineyard, between St Thomé and Alba la Romaine - which is famous as an archaeological site. It has three delightfully furnished and decorated bedrooms, all for two or three people, and each with a spacious en suite bathroom. Sauna and massage available.

Prices s fr €120; d fr €120; t fr €145; extra person fr €25; dinner fr €30 **On Site** Private ⚲ **Nearby** ⚓ 4km ⚴ 15km ⌀ 0.1km Restaurant 5km ⚲ 4km Spa 40km ⚑ 8km ⚐ 5km ⚒ 18km **Notes** No pets English spoken

THUEYTS

⁂ Mas Casta Nea

Guy et Christianne BURATTI
Les Higoux, 07330 THUEYTS
☎ 04 75 36 62 02 📄 04 75 36 62 02
email: ch.buratti@club-internet.fr
web: www.casta-nea.com

Three very comfortable rooms in this 14th-century fortified farmhouse. The rooms can sleep from two to four people; they all have private bath or shower room and WC, and one has its own sitting area. Living room with huge granite fireplace, and kitchenette with fridge and microwave. Bathing in the Ardèche is possible, just five minutes away.

Prices d €55-€70; t €70-€85; extra person fr €15 **Nearby** ⚓ 1.5km ⌀ 1.5km ⚲ 5km ⚲ 1km Spa 5km ⚑ 7km **Notes** Pets admitted English spoken

UZER

⁂ ⏚ Château d'Uzer

Eric et Muriels CHEVALIER
07110 UZER
☎ 04 75 36 89 21 📄 04 75 36 02 59
email: chateau-uzer@wanadoo.fr
web: www.chateau-uzer.com

This very pretty château, with its 12th-century keep, has been restored to combine old and contemporary features. Set in a large park with a swimming pool, it offers three lovely rooms of character including a family room, each with private facilities and views over the park. Guests can sample regional cuisine in the table d'hôte meals. Ideally located on the Aubenas-Alès road and within 30km of plenty of sporting and cultural activities.

Prices s €70-€110; d €80-€120; extra person fr €28; dinner fr €32 **On Site** ⌀ Private ⚲ **Nearby** ⚓ 6km Restaurant 5km ⚲ 6km ⚑ 5km ⚐ 0.6km ⚒ 12km **Notes** No pets English spoken

VALS-LES-BAINS

⁂ ⏚ Château Clement

SARL LE CHATEAU
La Chataigneraie, 07600 VALS-LES-BAINS
☎ 04 75 87 40 13 & 06 72 75 03 36
email: contact@chateauclement.com
web: www.chateauclement.com

This château was built at the end of the 19th century by Auguste Clément, who developed the spa at Vals les Eaux. In this superb setting, there are five very special guest rooms, each decorated in an individual style. Guests also have use of two lounges, a library and a dining room. The splendid breakfasts include home made patisseries and organic produce.

Prices d €120-€210; t €170-€240; extra person fr €30; dinner fr €50 **On Site** Private ⚲ **Nearby** ⚓ 5km ⚴ 45km ⌀ 0.8km Restaurant 0.5km ⚲ 0.8km Spa 0.5km ⚐ 0.5km ⚒ 45km **Notes** Pets admitted English spoken CC

VERNON

⁂ ⏚ Mas de la Cigale

Catherine GOHIER
EURL les Cigales, 07260 VERNON
☎ 04 75 39 68 69 & 06 80 05 89 75
📄 04 75 39 68 69
email: la.cigalle@wanadoo.fr
web: www.lemasdelacigale.com

This sandstone house on the vine terraces of the Ardèche Cévennes has five spacious and refined guest rooms, all en suite. There is a dining room and vaulted sitting room and a swimming pool shared with two rural gîtes.

Prices s fr €75; d fr €80; extra person fr €22; dinner fr €29 **On Site** Private ⚲ **Nearby** ⚓ 10km ⌀ 3km Restaurant 6km ⚲ 7km ⚑ 6km ⚐ 5km **Notes** No pets CC

VERNOUX

♦♦♦ ⃘ Roiseland

Roland ESPOSITO-MASCHIO
10 Rue Boissy D'Anglas, 07240 VERNOUX
☎ 04 75 58 19 32 & 06 14 64 94 77

Beautiful 19th-century family mansion with private park offering five non-smoking, en suite guest rooms: one suite with double and two singles, two doubles, one twin room and one sleeping three. Sitting room for guests with open fire and television, swimming pool, stair-lift, exhibition of engravings, and of Ardéchois painters in July. Possibility of letting entire house. Meals available by reservation.

Prices s fr €47; d fr €54; t fr €70; dinner fr €17　**On Site** Private ⤙
Nearby ⚑ 3km ⚲ 15km ⚘ 0.6km Restaurant 0.1km ⚐ 0.6km
Spa 30km ⚑ 30km　**Notes** No pets Open April to November.

VILLENEUVE-DE-BERG

♦♦♦ ⃘ Chambre d'hôtes de Laudun

Nicole LOYRION
07170 VILLENEUVE-DE-BERG
☎ 04 75 94 83 03 & 04 75 94 75 63　▤ 04 75 94 75 63
email: loyrion@wanadoo.fr
web: www.laudun.com

This old agricultural holding, 1km from the village between the Plateau of Coiron and the Vallée d'Ardèche, has six comfortable guest rooms. The local auberge is only 100mtrs away and offers generous and respectable fare using local ingredients. Shady park with children's playground and relaxing area; themed holidays available.

Prices not confirmed for 2008　**Nearby** ⚑ 3km ⚘ 10km ⤙ 10km
⚐ 1km ⛪ 1km ⚑ 25km　**Notes** Pets admitted English spoken

♦♦♦ ⃘ Domaine de La Manse

V et M GANDOLFO
Le Petit Tournon, 07170 VILLENEUVE-DE-BERG
☎ 04 75 94 74 39 & 06 15 46 88 64
email: contact@lamanse.com
web: www.lamanse.com

This restored 19th-century silkworm house is situated on the tourist route through the valley of the Ibie, 22km from Vallon Pont d'Arc and from Grotte Chauvet. There are five beautiful and comfortable en suite rooms, an enormous vaulted room for breakfast or relaxation, a terrace, park, swimming pool (free until midday) and parking.

Prices s fr €50; d fr €63; t fr €79; extra person fr €20; dinner fr €25
On Site Private ⤙　**Nearby** ⚑ 8km ⚲ 30km ⚘ 15km Restaurant 0.1km
⚐ 2km Spa 22km ⛪ 2km ⛪ 1km ⚑ 30km　**Notes** No pets English spoken

VIVIERS

♦♦♦ ⃘ ♿ *Les Chênes de l'Escoutay*

Sylvie et Patrick MORTAIN
Couijanet, 07220 VIVIERS
☎ 04 75 49 28 81 & 06 87 98 45 05
email: patrick.mortain@wanadoo.fr
web: www.les-chenes-de-lescoutay.com

This superb property, in wooded surroundings not far from Montelimar, overlooks the Rhône Valley. It has five double rooms, each with private facilities, a small lounge area and direct access to its own small garden. Extensive grounds, swimming pool and sauna; meals available by arrangement.

Prices not confirmed for 2008　**On Site** Private ⤙　**Nearby** ⚑ 15km
⚘ 2km ⚐ 2.5km ⛪ 2.5km　**Notes** No pets English spoken CC

DRÔME

ALBON

♦♦♦ ⃘ Le Pré Aux Ânes

Jacques et Nadine TONDUT
Les Barris, 26140 ALBON
☎ 04 75 03 11 73
email: pre.aux.anes@wanadoo.fr
web: www.lepreauxanes.com

On the edge of the green, tranquil region of the Drôme hills. En suite rooms include two bedrooms for two and two for three. There are donkeys, parking and golf nearby; evening meals include regional specialities.

Prices s fr €44; d fr €50; t fr €62; extra person fr €12; dinner fr €16
On Site Private ⤙　**Nearby** ⚑ 15km ⚲ 3km ⚘ 3km Restaurant 2km
⚐ 4km ⛱ 4km ⛪ 1km ⚑ 5km　**Notes** Pets admitted English spoken

ALLAN

♦♦♦ ⃘ Le Mas de la Combe

Lydie BERNARD
Chemin la Combe, 26780 ALLAN
☎ 04 75 46 66 69 & 06 82 38 49 97
email: ld.bernard@wanadoo.fr
web: www.masdelacombe.com

This property, near the ruins of an old village, has a view over the mountains of the Ardèche and good access to footpaths. It has two air-conditioned rooms with en suite bathrooms and WCs, and a further bedroom, also with private facilities, which has direct access to the garden. The house stands in extensive grounds.

Prices s fr €60; d fr €70; t fr €85; extra person fr €15; dinner fr
€23　**On Site** ⛱ Private ⤙　**Nearby** ⚑ 2km ⚲ 26km ⚘ 10km
Restaurant 1.5km ⚐ 1.5km Spa 1.5km ⛪ 1.5km ⚑ 12km
Notes No pets English spoken

ALLEX

▦ La Petite Aiguebonne

Elisabeth MONSARRAT
26400 ALLEX
☎ 04 75 62 60 68 & 06 10 11 19 32
email: contact@petite-aiguebonne.com
web: http://petite-aiguebonne.com

This delightful country property has beautiful views over the surrounding countryside. It has five charming and spacious bedrooms, and a swimming pool and spa bath to help you relax. There is a garden perfumed with rose blossom, and the attentive welcome provided by the hosts will help to make your stay enjoyable and memorable. Parking.

Prices s €85-€120; d €85-€120; extra person fr €20 **On Site** Spa ☀ Private ↖ **Nearby** ⚓ 5km ♨ 7km ⚐ 2km Restaurant 7km ⚘ 2km ⚑ 2km ⚒ 20km **Notes** No pets

BARRET-DE-LIOURE

▦ ⊙ *Mona Lisa*

M SCHMITT et J-M WOLF
26570 BARRET DE LIOURE
☎ 04 75 28 10 38 & 06 60 88 42 42 ▤ 04 75 28 10 38
email: muchang@tiscali.fr
web: www.gite-monalisa.com

The peaceful mountain location of this property, looking towards Mont Ventoux, will make you feel welcome and help you to appreciate the beautiful Toulourenc Valley. This former goat farm has three guest rooms, all with private bath/shower room and WC.

Prices not confirmed for 2008 **On Site** ☀ **Nearby** ⚓ 20km ↖ 7km ⚘ 7km **Notes** No pets English spoken

BEAUMONT-LES-VALENCE

▦ ⊙ La Magnanerie

Olivier et Violette BELLON
26760 BEAUMONT LES VALENCE
☎ 04 75 59 70 80 ▤ 04 75 59 70 80

This 18th-century property is on a working farm. The guest accommodation is in a former silkworm house which has been totally renovated. There are two family bedrooms for four, one room for three, and a double - all with private facilities. Breakfast is served in the converted henhouse, using produce from the farm. Meals are available, by arrangement.

Prices s fr €37; d fr €47; t fr €61; extra person fr €16; dinner fr €17 **On Site** ☀ **Nearby** ⚓ 12km ♨ 4km ↖ 3km Restaurant 4km ⚑ 3.5km ⚒ 12km **Notes** No pets

BOULC

▦ Le Moulin de Ravel

Jutta et Gérard LECOCQ
26410 BOULC
☎ 04 75 21 24 62 ▤ 04 75 21 24 62
email: moulinderavel@orange.fr
web: www.moulin-de-ravel.com

This 17th-century mill, which has been fully restored and enjoys a spacious site, has a one-kilometre frontage to the River Boulc. It has four rooms, all with their individual styles, and all with private bath or shower rooms and WCs. It has a large guests' lounge, as well as a guests' kitchen. The breakfasts are delicious!

Prices s fr €65; d fr €75; extra person fr €15 **On Site** ⚐ ☀ Private ↖ **Nearby** ⚓ 5km ⚘ 6km ⚑ 6km ⚒ 20km **Notes** No pets English spoken Open Easter to 1 November.

BOURDEAUX

▦ ✿ ⊙ Les Junchas

Claudio & Joëlle SAMMARCO
26460 BOURDEAUX
☎ 04 75 53 38 11 & 06 17 31 57 98 ▤ 04 75 53 38 11
email: lesjunchas@wanadoo.fr
web: www.lesjunchas.com

Between Provence and Vecors, with a magnificent view over the Roubion Valley, five double en suite rooms are offered (one on the ground floor). Evening meals are served in a large, light dining room or on the terrace and there is a sitting room for cooler evenings. Camping spot nearby.

Prices s fr €41; d fr €52; t fr €66; extra person fr €15; dinner fr €21 **Nearby** ⚓ 4km ⚐ 2km ↖ 2km Restaurant 2km ⚘ 2km ⚑ 2km ⚒ 25km **Notes** Pets admitted English spoken Open 16 March to 14 November. CC

CHALANCON

▦ ⊙ Les Bayles

Frédéric FRANCOIS
26470 CHALANCON
☎ 04 75 27 24 38 & 06 87 33 43 76
email: lesbayles@wanadoo.fr
web: www.lesbayles.com

At the top of the Oule Valley, nestled under the Eyriot Mountains, this typical farmhouse is situated in a small hamlet. There are three en suite bedrooms on the ground floor and a triple bedroom with a mezzanine, a double bedroom, a bedroom for three and a bedroom for two with twin beds in an independent wing of the farmhouse. Meals use farm meat and organic vegetables, and truffle weekends run from November-January.

Prices s fr €40; d fr €50; t fr €60; extra person fr €11; dinner fr €20 **Nearby** ⚓ 3.5km ⚐ 8km ↖ 5km Restaurant 3.5km ⚘ 3.5km ☀ 3.5km ⚑ 3.5km ⚒ 30km **Notes** No pets English spoken

CHANOS-CURSON

∰ & Ferme des Denis

J-P & J SAUVAJON
26600 CHANOS CURSON
☎ 04 75 07 34 11 & 06 07 27 35 89
email: ferme.des.denis@wanadoo.fr
web: www.lesdenis.com

A warm welcome awaits guests to this renovated 15th-century farmhouse, in the vineyards of Crozes Hermitage. There are four en suite rooms, three for two or three people, a large lounge with kitchen area, swimming pool, games room and home-made preserves and bread.

Prices s fr €42; d fr €53; t fr €73; extra person fr €20 **On Site** ☂
Private ⚲ **Nearby** ⛷2km ≋2km ﹏5km **Notes** No pets English spoken

∰ La Farella

Rose-Marie ROIGE
Les Champs Ratiers, 26600 CHANOS CURSON
☎ 04 75 07 35 44 ▤ 04 75 07 39 90
email: accueil@lafarella.com
web: www.lafarella.com

3km from the A7, in the heart of the orchards and vineyards, this old house has lots of character. Rooms are en suite; one of the bedrooms is furnished and decorated in an antique style. There are two separate courtyards and a swimming pool.

Prices s €45-€49; d €56-€60; t €72-€76; extra person fr €16
On Site Private ⚲ **Nearby** ⛷3km Restaurant 4.5km ≋3km ☂10km
▣8km ﹏8km **Notes** Pets admitted

CHAROLS

∰ ⋈ & Les Griottes

W LAU
26450 CHAROLS
☎ 04 75 90 41 68 & 06 25 51 31 14 ▤ 04 75 90 41 68
email: cetrelau@yahoo.fr
web: www.lesgriottes.com

A beautiful old farmhouse, fully restored and in a quiet rural setting with woods close by. The place has a family atmosphere, and the rooms have their own lounge area and terrace. There are plenty of birds and animals around the place: donkeys, goats, white peacocks, pigeons, chickens, geese, dogs and cats! Meals are available by arrangement.

Prices d €55-€60; extra person fr €16; dinner fr €18 **On Site** ✎
Nearby ⛷3km ≋10km ⚲2km ﹋2km ☂5km ▣2km ﹏18km
Notes No pets English spoken

CHARPEY

∰ ⋈ ⋈ Les Marais-St-Didier

Jean-P et Christiane IMBERT
St-Didier-de-Charpey, 26300 CHARPEY
☎ 04 75 47 03 50 & & 06 27 32 23 65
email: imbert.jean-pierre@wanadoo.fr
web: http://perso.orange.fr/les-marais

This shady farm lies in the middle of the countryside between Valence and Romans, at the foot of the Vercors Mountain, and on beautiful walking and driving routes. There are three bedrooms for two people on the ground floor, a private bathroom, lounge and sitting room area, library, TV, parking and play area. Reductions for children.

Prices s €35-€40; d €45-€50; t €59-€68; extra person €14-€18; dinner fr €16 **Nearby** ⛷3km ﹋3km ☂10km Restaurant 3km ≋10km ☂7km
▣3km ﹏10km **Notes** No pets

CHATEAUDOUBLE

∰ ⋈ Les Péris

Madeleine CABANES
Rte de Combovin, 26120 CHATEAUDOUBLE
☎ 04 75 59 80 51 ▤ 04 75 59 48 78

A large, traditional house in the countryside, set in a small hamlet at the foot of the Massif du Vercors. Three triple en suite bedrooms, dining room, communal sitting rooms, open fireplace, TV, play area. Farm produce and evening meals available.

Prices s fr €39; d fr €50; t fr €70; extra person fr €20; dinner fr €17
Nearby ⛷3km ☂10km ✎0.1km ⚲5km Restaurant 25km ≋5km
Spa 5km ☂0.2km ▣5km ﹏15km **Notes** Pets admitted English spoken

CHATEAUNEUF-SUR-ISERE

∰ Les Communaux

Gérard et Sylvie COMBET
26300 CHATEAUNEUF SUR ISERE
☎ 04 75 84 58 88 ▤ 04 75 84 71 89
email: info@naturedeaux.com
web: www.naturedeaux.com

Five en suite bedrooms: one twin with disabled access; one with four-poster bed; three with mezzanines for three/four people (one double bed and twin beds). Kitchen available for longer stays and jacuzzi available, charge made.

Prices s fr €45; d fr €54; t fr €70; extra person fr €16 **On Site** ⚽ ☂
Nearby ⛷7km ⚲1km ✎0.5km ▣2.5km ﹏6km **Notes** No pets
English spoken CC

CHATUZANGE-LE-GOUBET

††† ΙΟΙ *Chambre d'hôtes*

Florence LAFOREST

26300 CHATUZANGE LE GOUBET

☎ 04 75 05 57 72 & 06 75 04 62 48

email: florence@drome-sweet-home.com

web: www.drome-sweet-home.com

Quietly situated in a small hamlet, this house, with its panoramic views, offers three spacious guest rooms for up to three people, all of them with private shower room and WC. Terrace and shady garden, spa pool, family-style meals available some evenings.

Prices not confirmed for 2008 **On Site** ☼ **Nearby** ☁ 4km ↴ 5km ♨ 8km 🏛 10km ⋙ 10km **Notes** No pets English spoken

††† ΙΟΙ *L'Ecole Buissonnière*

Sylvie SCHUSTER

1 route d'Alixan, 26300 CHATUZANGE LE GOUBET

☎ 04 75 47 32 14

email: ecolebuissonniere26@free.fr

web: www.ecolebuissonniere26.net

At the foot of Vercors and 10 minutes from Romans, this charming building offers five rooms, including a family suite for five, each personalised and with private facilities. Lounge with TV and books, private courtyard, garden, parking. Regional cuisine and home-made jams can be enjoyed in the dining room. Numerous activities nearby, including golf in 10km.

Prices not confirmed for 2008 **Nearby** ☁ 7km ↴ 5km ♨ 1km ♣ 5km ⋙ 10km **Notes** No pets English spoken

CLEON-D'ANDRAN

††† *Le Mas de l'Ancelle*

Pascal & Dany LARRATTE

Chemin Serre Fournier, 26450 CLEON D'ANDRAN

☎ 04 75 90 43 58 ▤ 04 75 90 35 48

email: dany.larratte@orange.fr

web: www.mas-ancelle.com

In provincial Drôme, in open countryside with superb views of the mountains, the Mas de l'Ancelle offers guests a calm and relaxing stay. There are four lovely rooms with private facilities, a lounge, billiards room, swimming pool and parking.

Prices s fr €66; d fr €66; t fr €86; extra person fr €20 **On Site** ☼ Private ↴ **Nearby** ☁ 8km ✐ 10km Restaurant 2km ♨ 2km 🏛 2km ⋙ 20km **Notes** No pets English spoken Open February to November.

COLONZELLE

††† *Le Moulin de l'Aulière*

Marie BERAUD

26230 COLONZELLE

☎ 04 75 91 10 49 ▤ 04 75 91 10 49

A 19th-century building set in a park on the banks of the Aulière. Five en suite bedrooms are available: two rooms for two and three people,

two doubles (one with a terrace) and one triple. There is a kitchen area, lounge, fireplace, TV and parking space.

Prices s fr €50; d fr €60; t fr €85; extra person fr €20 **On Site** ☼ **Nearby** ☁ 4km ↧ 12km ↴ 4km Restaurant 2km ♨ 1km Spa 7km 🏛 2km ⋙ 30km **Notes** Pets admitted English spoken Open 16 December to 14 November. CC

COMPS

††† *Le Château*

Marilou TERROT

26220 COMPS

☎ 04 75 46 30 00 ▤ 04 75 46 30 00

A magnificent setting - a 12th-century château with an adjoining wing close to a farm. The location is beautiful and the atmosphere quiet. There are three bedrooms, for one or two people, each with private shower room and WC. Private parking.

Prices not confirmed for 2008 **Nearby** ☁ 0.5km ↴ 6km ♨ 0.2km 🏛 6km **Notes** No pets Open Easter to 1 November.

DIVAJEU

††† ♥ ΙΟΙ *A la Ferme de Ranchy*

Roselyne LOMBARD

Quartier Ranchy, 26400 DIVAJEU

☎ 04 75 25 29 74 & 06 81 41 99 84 ▤ 04 75 76 71 42

email: vacances.lombard@tiscali.fr

web: http://vacances.lombard.free.fr

Close to the Valence-Montélimar road stands the 17th-century family farm of Ranchy, where we offer a choice of four rooms - two family rooms each sleeping four with private facilities, and two double rooms with shared facilities. Farm produce is the basis of our meals. Also available, two rural gîtes. Child's meal (under 10): €7.50.

Prices not confirmed for 2008 **On Site** ☼ Private ↴ **Nearby** ☁ 7km ♨ 5km 🏛 5km ⋙ 5km **Notes** No pets

ETOILE-SUR-RHONE

††† *La Mare*

Famille CHAIX

Rte de Montmeyran, Quartier la Mare,

26800 ETOILE SUR RHONE

☎ 04 75 59 33 79 ▤ 04 75 59 05 20

email: la.mare@free.fr

web: http://la.mare.free.fr/

Situated in a lovely rural setting, near to the Rhône Valley, with large grounds around the farm and shady parkland. Four (grade 3) bedrooms with separate access and two (grade 2) bedrooms with private bath/shower-rooms and a communal wc shared between two bedrooms. Sitting room with TV and fireplace.

Prices not confirmed for 2008 **On Site** ☼ **Nearby** ☁ 6km ↴ 5km ♨ 3km 🏛 4km ⋙ 15km **Notes** No pets

⦀ Le Vieux Chêne

Jacques FARIN
26800 ETOILE SUR RHONE
☎ 04 75 60 79 97 & 06 15 99 90 77   🖹 04 75 60 79 65
email: contact@levieuxchene.net
web: www.levieuxchene.net

Near the wild waters of the Rhône, which one can imagine as having been just as beautiful since pre-historic times, you will enjoy the peace and serenity of this authentic 17th-century house, built with pebbles from the river. It has three splendid and very comfortable period bedrooms. Nearby you can explore the 1000-year-old village.

Prices s fr €61; d fr €89; t fr €117; extra person fr €28   **On Site** ⛳
Nearby ⛵ 5km ⤓ 20km ✎ 5km ⟓ 15km Restaurant 2km ⛵ 6km
Spa 6km 🏛 4km ⚕ 12km   **Notes** No pets English spoken

EURRE

⦀ ⦁ *A Cote d'Eurre*

M-H GUIROY et N ASTIER
26400 EURRE
☎ 04 75 25 79 90   🖹 04 75 25 79 90
email: chlomani@free.fr
web: www.acotedeurre.com

Something unusual - the buildings of an old silkworm farm in the Drôme Valley, which have been restored and converted to provide three bedrooms, dining room, and a living room used for art exhibitions which change with the seasons. There is a guests' kitchen, parking, and meals are available by arrangement.

Prices not confirmed for 2008   **On Site** ⛳ Private ⟓   **Nearby** ⛵ 4km
⛵ 1km 🏛 3km ⚕ 3km   **Notes** No pets English spoken

EYGALAYES

⦀ ⦁ *La Forge Sainte-Marie*

N et I DERBEZ-MUSE
26560 EYGALAYES
☎ 04 75 28 42 77   🖹 04 75 28 42 77
email: isabelle.muse@wanadoo.fr
web: www.guideprovence.com/
chambres_hotes/forge-ste-marie/

This chambre d'hôtes can accommodate up to 11 guests in its four comfortable rooms, which are on two levels in a building attached to the owners' home, amongst the lavender and the lime trees. It has its own relaxation room, complete with wave bath and sauna.

Prices not confirmed for 2008   **On Site** ⛳ **Nearby** ⛵ 12km ⟓ 7km
⛵ 3km 🏛 8km ⚕ 35km   **Notes** Pets admitted English spoken

FERRASSIERES

⦀ ⦁ ♿ Château la Gabelle

Marguerite BLANC
26570 FERRASSIERES
☎ 06 85 20 80 31 & 04 75 28 80 54   🖹 04 75 28 85 56
email: chateaulagabelle@free.fr
web: www.chateau-la-gabelle.com

This 12th-century building is set on the outskirts of Lubéron and the Haute-Provence Alps, amid prairies and fields of lavender. The bedrooms are comfortable with private bathrooms. In the tower, the lounge and sitting room (with a fireplace) are the ideal setting for meals prepared with farm produce.

Prices s €65-€90; d €65-€90; t €106-€125; extra person fr €33; dinner fr €24   **Nearby** ⛵ 8km ⟓ 8km Restaurant 8km ⛵ 8km ⛳ 8km 🏛 8km
Notes No pets English spoken CC

GRANE

⦀ ♥ ⦁ *Domaine Distaise*

Corinne CHAMBRON
26400 GRANE
☎ 04 75 61 78 58 & 06 80 91 94 28   🖹 04 75 61 41 80
email: earl.dounis@wanadoo.fr
web: http://perso.wanadoo.fr/domaine-distaise/

A chambre d'hôtes on a working farm, in a restored wing of the owners' home. A peaceful setting amongst apricot trees. There is a day room for guests, with books and billiards, where breakfast and other meals (using home-grown produce) are served. Swimming pool, pétanque and table tennis.

Prices not confirmed for 2008   **On Site** ⛳ Private ⟓   **Nearby** ⛵ 0.3km
⛵ 4km 🏛 1km ⚕ 4km   **Notes** No pets English spoken

GRIGNAN

⦀ ⦁ La Maison du Moulin

Philippe & Bénédicte APPELS
Petit Cordy, 26230 GRIGNAN
☎ 04 75 46 56 94 & 06 23 26 23 60
email: info@maisondumoulin.com
web: www.maisondumoulin.com

In the heart of Drôme Provençale, this mill house amidst the lavender, vines and truffle fields is a delightful place to stay. It has five bedrooms, each with a southern feel and its own terrace or garden, where you will hear the sound of water from the river. Interesting meals are served, prepared with local ingredients. Courses in cooking and truffle-hunting.

Prices s €90-€145; d €110-€160; t €140-€190; dinner fr €30
On Site ✎ Restaurant ⛳ Private ⟓   **Nearby** ⛵ 3km ⛵ 3km
🏛 3km ⚕ 25km   **Notes** No pets English spoken

HOSTUN

☳ ⚆ *Les Bruyères*

Serge et Annie NATTIER

26730 HOSTUN

☎ 04 75 48 81 94 & 06 62 81 49 75 ▤ 04 75 48 93 50

email: karine.nattier@wanadoo.fr

web: www.les-bruyeres.net

This large welcoming house is surrounded by a shady park, in two hectares of grounds. En suite rooms include two bedrooms for two, one bedroom for three and one family suite for four. There is a dining room, communal sitting room, private parking, children's meals and golf at 20km.

Prices not confirmed for 2008 **On Site** Private ⚲ **Nearby** ⚑ 1km
⚒ 1km ⚐ 1km ⚒ 10km **Notes** No pets English spoken

LA BATIE-ROLLAND

☳ ⚆ **Le Fabras**

Ghislaine BRECHIGNAC

Quartier St Andéol, 26160 LA BATIE-ROLLAND

☎ 04 75 53 88 20 ▤ 04 75 53 88 20

email: contact@hebergement-fabras.com

web: www.hebergement-fabras.com

This large property is full of character. It has the spaciousness of a real country house, combined with comfort and a warm family atmosphere. It is in a shady and peaceful location, near to vineyards and villages. It has three very comfortable guest rooms, each one with private bath or shower room and WC.

Prices s fr €55; d fr €60; t fr €77; extra person fr €17; dinner fr €20
Nearby ⚑ 2km ⚒ 4km ⚲ 5km Restaurant 5km ⚒ 2km ⚘ 3km ⚐ 2km
⚒ 8km **Notes** No pets English spoken

LA BAUME-D'HOSTUN

☳ ⚆ **Chambre d'hôtes**

Véronique et Daniel CLOP

Grange Vieille, 26730 LA BAUME-D'HOSTUN

☎ 04 75 47 80 72 & 06 19 50 52 42

email: clop@grangevieille.eu

web: www.grangevieille.eu

A large flint-built house standing in its own peaceful grounds between Drôme and Vercours. There are two double rooms, a twin-bedded room and a family room, all upstairs and each with a private bath or shower room and WC. Outside is a fitness area and jacuzzi, and the house is in good walking and cycling country. Meals by arrangement.

Prices s €45-€50; d €55-€65; t fr €75; extra person fr €20; dinner fr €20 **On Site** Restaurant ⚘ **Nearby** ⚑ 4km ⚒ 15km ⚲ 3km ⚲ 12km
⚒ 3km ⚐ 0.7km ⚒ 4km **Notes** No pets English spoken CC

LA BEGUDE-DE-MAZENC

☳ ⚆ **La Piverdière**

Agnès AUMONT

Route de St-Gervais, 26160 LA BEGUDE-DE-MAZENC

☎ 04 75 46 26 42 & 06 89 85 75 27

email: lapiverdiere@wanadoo.fr

web: http://perso.wanadoo.fr/lapiverdiere.aumont/

Situated among the lavender fields 1km from the village of Bégude. A large house furnished with antiques, spacious rooms (one on the ground floor), terraces and gardens, swimming pool with unsurpassed view over the old village. In the evening, by arrangement, guests can dine with the hosts. Out of season catering for hikers and mountain bikers - bikes may be hired and cycling circuit nearby.

Prices s fr €65; d fr €65; t fr €85; extra person fr €20; dinner fr €20
On Site ⚘ Private ⚲ **Nearby** ⚑ 0.6km ⚒ 0.8km ⚐ 1km ⚒ 15km
Notes No pets English spoken Open March to December.

LA GARDE-ADHEMAR

☳ ❦ ⚆ *Ferme des Rosières*

René & Michèle GIRARD

Quartier la Peyssade, 26700 LA GARDE-ADHEMAR

☎ 04 75 04 72 81 ▤ 04 75 04 72 81

email: girard.rosieres@wanadoo.fr

web: www.guideweb.com/provence/bb/rosieres/

At the heart of the Drôme Provençale, among the vines and lavender bushes, you are promised a warm welcome by your hosts who are farmers with a special interest in draught horses. There are two grade 2 and 3 family rooms, and one grade 3 double-bedded room. Meals by arrangement, including poultry from the farm, and home-grown vegetables.

Prices not confirmed for 2008 **On Site** ⚘ **Nearby** ⚑ 1km ⚲ 3km
⚒ 3km ⚐ 3km ⚒ 7km **Notes** No pets

LA GARDE-ADHEMAR

☳ ❦ ⚆ **Gîte du Val des Nymphes**

C et I ANDRUEJOL

26700 LA GARDE-ADHEMAR

☎ 04 75 04 44 54

web: www.valdesnymphes.com

In a quiet orchard setting, on a 30-hectare estate, among the perfume of truffles and apricots, this stone-built 17th-century house has three guest rooms. They are all on the ground floor, with en suite bath or shower rooms. There is a lounge with TV; parking space. Meals, prepared in the traditional Provençal style, are available by reservation.

Prices s €39-€50; d €48-€65; t fr €80; extra person fr €15; dinner fr €18
On Site ⚲ ⚘ Private ⚲ **Nearby** ⚑ 6km ⚒ 3km Restaurant 1.5km
⚒ 0.8km ⚐ 1.5km ⚒ 8km **Notes** Pets admitted English spoken

₩₩ ⚭ & **Mas Bella Cortis**

Alexandre & Anne BUFFARD
Route du Val des Nymphes,
26700 LA GARDE-ADHEMAR
☎ 04 75 04 04 15 & 06 12 04 86 80
email: contact@masenprovence.com
web: www.masenprovence.com

This restored 18th-century house is a restful place, with the warm
shades of its walls, its leather armchairs, and its seven hectares
of grounds criss-crossed by footpaths. It has five delightful and
peaceful bedrooms, and a heated sea-water swimming pool.
Meals by arrangement, with old-fashioned traditional dishes.

Prices d €85-€120; t €120-€160; dinner fr €30   **On Site** Private ⚲
Nearby ⚓ 6km ♨ 2km Restaurant 2km ⚲ 2km ⚜ 5km ⚑ 2km
⚒ 5km   **Notes** No pets English spoken CC

LA REPARA-AURIPLES

₩₩ ⚭ *Les Lombards*

Andrew & Jacqueline BAYLOR
26400 LA REPARA-AURIPLES
☎ 04 75 25 08 76 & 06 84 46 27 05   ⎙ 04 75 25 08 76
email: andrew.baylor@wanadoo.fr
web: www.cote-roche.com

Thirty kilometres from Montelimar and Valence, this Provençal style
house is an ideal base for exploring the Drôme region. It is not far
from a riding centre, and it has three very comfortable guest rooms.
The views are wonderful, the setting rustic, and the welcome warm
and friendly. Meals can be arranged.

Prices not confirmed for 2008   **On Site** ⚲   **Nearby** ⚓ 1.5km ⚲ 8km
⚑ 3km ⚒ 10km   **Notes** No pets English spoken

LA ROCHE-DE-GLUN

₩₩ ⚭ **Le Tinal de l'Hermitage**

Géraldine CLOT
Les Hauts Saviaux, 26600 LA ROCHE-DE-GLUN
☎ 04 75 08 98 12 & 06 87 11 96 38   ⎙ 04 75 08 98 12
email: letinal@aliceadsl.fr
web: www.chambreshotes-letinal.com

This ancient farmhouse has been lovingly restored by its owners,
using natural materials. It is quietly situated amongst orchards and the
Crozes Hermitage vineyards. There are four guest rooms, all of them
decorated to original themes. Sitting around the farmhouse table,
or outside beneath the pines in the summer, the hosts are keen to
share with guests their interests in pottery, woodwork and property
renovation.

Prices s fr €45; d fr €52; t fr €69; extra person fr €17; dinner fr
€18   **On Site** ⚲   **Nearby** ⚓ 7km ⚲ 4km ⚲ 4km ⚑ 4km ⚒ 5km
Notes No pets English spoken

LA ROCHE-SUR-GRANE

₩₩ ⚭ *La Magerie*

Roger et Pierrette BOHLER
26400 LA ROCHE-SUR-GRANE
☎ 04 75 62 71 77   ⎙ 04 75 62 71 77
email: la.magerie@wanadoo.fr
web: www.lamagerie.com

This restored farmhouse is in the middle of the countryside, with a
beautiful view over the old village, the wooded hills and the Vercors
Mountains. There are five en suite bedrooms, communal lounge and
dining room where evening meals are served, parking, play area and
garden. Mediterranean TGV route nearby. Discounts for long stays and
for children.

Prices not confirmed for 2008   **On Site** ⚲ Private ⚲   **Nearby** ⚓ 8km
⚲ 6km ⚑ 7km ⚒ 12km   **Notes** Pets admitted

LE POET-LAVAL

₩₩ ⚘ ⚭ **Le Mas des Alibeaux**

Jean-François EHRET
Route de Mollans, 26160 LE POET-LAVAL
☎ 04 75 46 35 59 & 06 12 64 12 90   ⎙ 04 75 46 35 59
email: j-f.ehret@wanadoo.fr
web: http://masdesalibeaux.com

A delightful location on the edge of a forest, with hills and a river close
by. The property is a farmhouse, built in the local style with small
buildings around a courtyard. There are two double rooms and two
family rooms for three or four, all with private shower and WC. Meals
available by arrangement.

Prices s fr €55; d fr €68; t fr €85; extra person fr €17; dinner fr €23
Nearby ⚓ 1km ♨ 20km ⚲ 0.3km ⚲ 4km Restaurant 0.8km ⚲ 4km
⚲ 5km ⚑ 1km ⚒ 24km   **Notes** No pets English spoken CC

LEONCEL

₩₩ ⚭ *La Vercorelle*

Catherine MACKOWIAK
26190 LEONCEL
☎ 04 75 44 42 85   ⎙ 04 75 44 10 48
email: la-vercorelle@wanadoo.fr
web: www.la-vercorelle.com

On a green road, perched at the side of the valley and opposite a
12th-century Cistercian abbey, this is an ideal place for walking and
resting. It has five individual and comfortable rooms, all with private
facilities. The garden is an excellent place to spend time relaxing, and
the welcoming host will be pleased to serve meals, by reservation.

Prices not confirmed for 2008   **Nearby** ⚓ 18km ⚲ 18km ⚲ 18km
⚲ 4km ⚑ 18km ⚒ 35km   **Notes** Pets admitted English spoken

MALATAVERNE

▦ ⊧◎⊧ *Mas Fa Sua*

Nathalie CATALAN
Chemin des Brebis, 26780 MALATAVERNE
☎ 04 75 90 77 47
email: catalanath@aol.com
web: www.hebergement-malataverne.com

Among the oak trees and lavender bushes of the Drôme Provençale, this restored farmhouse offers three guest rooms. There is a double with private terrace and bathroom/WC, and two family rooms for up to five people, one of them a grade 2 room, which have independent access to a large private terrace. Meals by arrangement; theme weekends - bread baking, truffles, etc.

Prices not confirmed for 2008 **On Site** ⁂ Private ⊀ **Nearby** ⌘ 10km ⊰ 4km ⊟ 3km ⋙ 12km **Notes** No pets English spoken

MARIGNAC-EN-DIOIS

▦ ⊧◎⊧ *La Ferme de l'hermite*

Jacki et Renée SEGOND
26150 MARIGNAC EN DIOIS
☎ 04 75 22 08 51 ▤ 04 75 22 08 51
email: jacki.segond@free.fr
web: http://lafermedelhermite.com

The proprietors of this lovely farmhouse extend a warm welcome at this calm, country location at the foot of the Vercors Massif. There are two double bedrooms, one triple, private bathrooms and lounge; meals include home-grown produce.

Prices not confirmed for 2008 **On Site** ⁂ **Nearby** ⌘ 8km ⊀ 8km ⊰ 7km ⊟ 7km ⋙ 7km **Notes** Pets admitted Open Easter to 1 November.

MIRABEL-ET-BLACONS

▦ **Les Vignes Rouges**

Frédéric TANCHON
Quartier Bellevue, 26400 MIRABEL ET BLACONS
☎ 06 21 19 69 31
email: lesvignes.rouges@laposte.net
web: www.lesvignesrouges.com

An attractive 1930s property right in the heart of the Drôme Valley which offers three bedrooms - two doubles, and a family room for up to three plus a child in a cot. Each room has a private bath or shower room and WC. This is a restful spot, and an ideal base for exploring the area.

Prices s fr €55; d fr €60; t fr €65; extra person fr €10 **Nearby** ⌘ 3km ✐ 1km ⊀ 4km Restaurant 0.1km ⊰ 2km ⁂ 0.1km ⊟ 0.2km ⋙ 2km **Notes** No pets English spoken CC

MIRMANDE

▦ *La Maison de Marinette*

Tieno & Marinette GORIOU
26270 MIRMANDE
☎ 04 75 63 01 15 ▤ 04 75 63 14 06
email: tienogoriou@aol.com
web: www.maisondemarinette.com

Near to one of the most beautiful villages in France, this house has a balcony overlooking the Rhône Valley, with panoramic views over the Vivarais Mountains. The large, comfortable house, near to a sculpture workshop, has three en suite bedrooms for two people with private terraces. Communal sitting room, kitchen and parking area.

Prices not confirmed for 2008 **On Site** ⁂ Private ⊀ **Nearby** ⌘ 20km ⊰ 4km ⁂ 0.5km ⋙ 15km **Notes** No pets Open 15 February to December.

▦ *Le Petit Logis*

Maryse BRUN
La Colline, 26270 MIRMANDE
☎ 04 75 63 02 92 ▤ 04 75 63 02 92
email: lepetitlogis@com02.com
web: www.lepetitlogis.com02.com

Three en suite bedrooms in a house set in the middle of a green and tranquil park with a view over the medieval village. Small kitchen, swimming pool, parking, play area. Dining room and lounge shared with the owners.

Prices not confirmed for 2008 **On Site** ⁂ Private ⊀ **Nearby** ⊰ 4km ⊟ 2km ⋙ 20km **Notes** Pets admitted Open 2 March to November.

MOLLANS-SUR-OUVEZE

▦ *Les Fouzarailles*

Valérie et Marc GRENON
Belle Combe, 26170 MOLLANS SUR OUVEZE
☎ 04 75 28 79 05 & 06 63 42 02 54 ▤ 04 75 28 79 05

With impressive views, this provençale farm nestles between woods and vineyards in the Toulourenc Valley at the foot of Mount Ventoux. Rooms are en suite (three bedrooms for two, one for three). Facilities include table tennis, boules pitch, play area, terrace, private parking, barbecue and fridge; and there are sports and bathing in the Toulourenc, 300mtrs.

Prices not confirmed for 2008 **On Site** ⁂ Private ⊀ **Nearby** ⌘ 4km ⊰ 1km ⊟ 2.5km ⋙ 50km **Notes** Pets admitted English spoken Open Easter to 1 November.

MONTBRISON-SUR-LEZ

▦ ❦ *Roussoullie*

R et M-N BARJAVEL
26770 MONTBRISON SUR LEZ
☎ 04 75 53 54 04 ▤ 04 75 53 54 04
email: barjavel@club-internet.fr
web: www.domainebarjavel.com

The provençale home of winegrowers set in the vineyards of Côtes du Rhône. There are two rural, semi-detached gîtes and three guest bedrooms with private entrances (one en suite double and two bedrooms for two/three people with bathroom). Guests may use the kitchen area and lounge.

Prices not confirmed for 2008 **On Site** ☺ Private ⚲ **Nearby** ⛷7km ♨6km 🎣7km ⚑7km **Notes** Pets admitted

MONTELIMAR

⁜ Domaine de Paissy

P et D BENOIT ROSSI
176 route de Sauzet, 26200 MONTELIMAR
☎ 04 75 46 04 08 📄 04 75 46 04 08
email: montelimar@domainedepaissy.com
web: www.domainedepaissy.com

In the Drôme provençal, a stone's throw from Montélimar, in over 1 hectare of park with specimen trees and a swimming pool, Pierrette and Didier are proud of their magnificent 15th-century home. Impressive decoration, embroidered hangings, old china and silverware in four bedrooms and dining room. Quiet, rest, conviviality and good cuisine will ensure that you enjoy this little paradise. From October to March the fourth night is discounted.

Prices s €60-€80; d €65-€100; extra person fr €20 **On Site** Private ⚲ **Nearby** ⛷5km ♠8km ✎1km Restaurant 2km ♨5km ☺5km 🎣2km ⚑3km **Notes** No pets English spoken

PIEGROS-LA-CLASTRE

⁜ ⅋ *Le Mas Ste Marie*

Daniel GOBANCE
Hameau les Bernards, 26400 PIEGROS LA CLASTRE
☎ 04 75 40 30 42 & 06 14 40 36 58
email: daniel.gobance@wanadoo.fr
web: www.mas-sainte-marie.com

This chambre d'hôtes, an old silk-worm house tucked away below the Forest of Saou, has superb views towards the Balcons de la Drôme. The oldest parts of it date back to the 16th century. There are five bedrooms, one of them a suite, all with private facilities, and it can accommodate up to 12 guests. Lounge with open fire and books. Meals by arrangement.

Prices not confirmed for 2008 **On Site** ☺ **Nearby** ⛷3km ⚲8km ♨8km **Notes** Pets admitted English spoken

PONET-ET-SAINT-AUBAN

⁜ ⅋ La Source

Francis et Françoise DURIEZ
26150 PONET ET SAINT AUBAN
☎ 04 75 22 02 98 & 06 85 16 90 05
email: duriez-francoise@wanadoo.fr
web: www.fermedelasource.com

At the lower end of the Parc Naturel Régional du Vercors, this 19th-century property overlooks a valley planted with pine trees, vines and lavender. There are four rooms: two doubles and two triples (three beds in each), all with private shower and WC. The rooms have their

own entrances and are all individually decorated. Covered terrace, meals by arrangement.

Prices s €50; d €55; t fr €70; extra person fr €15; dinner fr €18 **On Site** ☺ **Nearby** ⛷3km ⚲7km 🎣7km ⚑7km **Notes** No pets English spoken Open 16 January to 14 November.

PONT-DE-BARRET

⁜ ⅋ ⚷ Le Mas Eva

Madeleine et Marc TISSERAND
Les Perrins Sud, 26160 PONT DE BARRET
☎ 04 75 90 78 35 & 06 81 33 37 96 📄 04 75 90 78 35
email: mas_eva2004@yahoo.fr
web: www.mas-eva.qsdf.org

In the countryside not far from Montélimar, this restored old house has magnificent views across the Rhône Valley. There are five spacious and beautifully decorated rooms, all with private facilities. Generous breakfasts are served in the dining room or out on the terrace, in the shade of the 200-year-old oak tree.

Prices d €77-€100; t €97-€120; extra person fr €20; dinner fr €20 **On Site** ♠ ☺ Private ⚲ **Nearby** ⛷3km ✎3km Restaurant 3km ♨3km 🎣3km ⚑25km **Notes** Pets admitted

PONTAIX

⁜ ⅋ Le Moulin de Pontaix

Noël CHEVILLON
26150 PONTAIX
☎ 04 75 21 20 31 & 06 85 66 45 50 📄 04 75 21 21 86
email: nchevillon@wanadoo.fr
web: http://moulindepontaix.tibone.com

A magnificently restored old mill in a medieval village surrounded by vines and lavender bushes. The rooms are spacious, with private terraces where you can relax with the sound of the river in the background. There is a big lounge with a billiard table, and meals are available by reservation.

Prices s fr €56.50; d fr €63; t fr €91.50; extra person fr €10; dinner fr €20 **On Site** ✎ **Nearby** ⛷3km ♠30km ⚲8km Restaurant 0.3km ♨8km ☺10km 🎣5km ⚑8km **Notes** No pets English spoken Open April to 1 November. CC

RHÔNE-ALPES

ROCHEFORT-SAMSON

ⅲ ⓘ○ⅼ *La Balad'ane*

Thierry et Jocelyne BONNET
Le Peu, 26300 ROCHEFORT SAMSON
☎ 04 75 47 40 11 & 06 50 25 97 04
email: jocelyne.bonnet@cegetel.net
web: http://la-baladane.chez.tiscali.fr

This 19th-century farmhouse is peacefully situated in the heart of the countryside, surrounded by sunflowers. The bedrooms have been carefully restored, taking care to combine their traditional feel with a good level of comfort. Meals are available, using local produce. The hosts' donkeys can be used for exploring the countryside.

Prices not confirmed for 2008 **On Site** ⚘ Private ⚡ **Nearby** ⚡ 5km ⚓ 2km 🏛 2km 🚶 20km **Notes** No pets

ROCHEGUDE

ⅲ **Le Portail**

Pierre et Odette BRETON
Ancienne route d'Orange, 26790 ROCHEGUDE
☎ 04 75 98 22 16 & 06 89 35 29 45 🖷 04 75 98 22 16
email: breton.pierre@free.fr
web: http://breton.pierre.free.fr

These guest rooms are in a separate building on the owners' property, in a sheltered location close to a village amongst vineyards and wooded hills. There are three double rooms and a triple, all with private facilities. Lounge; use of kitchen on request. There is a pleasant garden with enclosed parking and a swimming pool.

Prices s fr €40; d fr €50; t fr €65; extra person fr €12 **On Site** Private ⚡ **Nearby** ⚡ 12km ⚓ 🚶 17km **Notes** No pets

SAUZET

ⅲ ⓘ○ⅼ **Le Sagnac**

Jean et Françoise FAUGIER
26740 SAUZET
☎ 04 75 46 71 78 & 06 22 65 70 44 🖷 04 75 46 71 78
web: www.le-sagnac.com

A beautiful, traditional farmhouse, in the countryside on the edges of provençale Drôme. There are three bedrooms for two/three people with private bathrooms and private access. 11km from the A7 on the D105.

Prices s fr €40; d fr €50; t fr €60; dinner fr €15 **Nearby** ⚡ 10km ⚡ 10km Restaurant 2km ⚓ 2km ⚘ 4km 🏛 2km 🚶 10km **Notes** Pets admitted Open 15 February to 30 October.

ST-ANDEOL-EN-QUINT

ⅲ ⓘ○ⅼ *La Lune En Bouche*

J.C et F MENGONI BRONCHART
Hameau de Ribière, 26150 ST-ANDEOL-EN-QUINT
☎ 04 75 21 26 34 🖷 04 75 21 29 40
email: laluneenbouche@valleedequint.com
web: www.valleedequint.com

In a beautiful location on the south side of the Vercors natural park, this house has been restored using natural and environment-friendly materials. The five guest rooms are in converted farm buildings. They all have a private bath or shower room and WC; solar power is used to heat the water and the buildings. Guests' lounge. Meals by arrangement; organic breakfasts available.

Prices not confirmed for 2008 **Nearby** ⚡ 5km ⚡ 12km ⚓ 10km ⚘ 6km 🏛 12km 🚶 12km **Notes** No pets English spoken

ST-AUBAN-SUR-OUVEZE

ⅲ 🌱 ⓘ○ⅼ *La Galane*

J-Y et B ROCHAS-DENUZIERE
26170 ST-AUBAN-SUR-OUVEZE
☎ 04 75 28 62 37 🖷 04 75 28 63 88
email: galane@free.fr
web: www.provence.guideweb.com/chambres_hotes/galane/

In provençale Drôme, this stone farmhouse set in fields of lavender has a view over the village and the valley. Three en suite bedrooms for two people, one bedroom suite for four people, dining room, TV, sitting room on a mezzanine, laundry. No meals on Wednesday and Sunday evenings.

Prices not confirmed for 2008 **On Site** ⚘ **Nearby** ⚡ 15km ⚡ 14km ⚓ 15km 🏛 15km **Notes** No pets English spoken Open Easter to 1 November.

ST-CHRISTOPHE-ET-LE-LARIS

ⅲ ⓘ○ⅼ *La Bouretière*

I et N DENIS ROSTAND
26350 ST-CHRISTOPHE-ET-LE-LARIS
☎ 04 75 45 75 38 🖷 04 75 45 75 38
email: labouretiere@aol.com
web: www.labouretiere.net

This traditional stone-built farmhouse offers a superb view across to the cliffs of Vercors. It is a peaceful place to linger, and one where you will be welcome to explore the delights of a working farm, with its chickens, sheep and rabbits. The tastefully decorated bedrooms are in an annexe. There is a guests' lounge, with kitchen area and open fireplace.

Prices not confirmed for 2008 **On Site** ⚘ **Nearby** ⚡ 10km ⚡ 5km ⚓ 5km 🏛 5km 🚶 35km **Notes** Pets admitted English spoken

ST-JEAN-EN-ROYANS

⫴ **Ferme de Fontepaisse**

Michèle CHABERT

26190 ST-JEAN-EN-ROYANS

☎ 04 75 48 60 65

email: michele.chabert@wanadoo.fr

web: www.fontepaisse.com

An 18th-century farmhouse in a tree-lined setting with two triple bedrooms and two en suite double bedrooms. There is a dining room, sitting room, central heating and cot on request.

Prices s fr €40; d fr €50; t fr €65; extra person fr €15 **On Site** Private ⌇ **Nearby** ⌇ 4.5km ⌇ 5km ⌇ 2.5km ⌇ 1.5km ⌇ 0.9km ⌇ 35km **Notes** No pets

⫴ ○ *Les Tourelons*

Corinne CRAYTON

37 Av de la Fôret de Lente, 26190 ST-JEAN-EN-ROYANS

☎ 04 75 48 63 96

email: corinne@estapade.com

web: www.estapade.com

This restored 18th-century farmhouse in the heart of Royans country, at the foot of the Massif du Vercors and on the Route des Cols, offers three en suite bedrooms for two/three people. Large dining room, private sitting room and parking.

Prices not confirmed for 2008 **On Site** Private ⌇ **Nearby** ⌇ 1km ⌇ 0.5km ⌇ 1km ⌇ 1km ⌇ 15km **Notes** Pets admitted

ST-JULIEN-EN-QUINT

⫴ ○ *Le Moulin du Rivet*

Leni WELENS

26150 ST-JULIEN-EN-QUINT

☎ 04 75 21 20 43 ▤ 04 75 21 20 43

email: contact@moulindurivet.com

web: www.moulindurivet.com

Charming old restored mill in the south of the Parc Naturel Régional du Vercors on the banks of the river with a superb view of the Ambel Mountains and the Quint Valley. Evening meals feature original and inspired recipes using local produce. Very comfortable rooms are en suite and there are reductions for children.

Prices not confirmed for 2008 **On Site** ⌇ **Nearby** ⌇ 10km ⌇ 14km ⌇ 14km ⌇ 13km ⌇ 13km **Notes** No pets English spoken

ST-MARTIN-EN-VERCORS

⫴ ○ **La Ferme du Château**

Christiane PITAVAL

26420 ST-MARTIN-EN-VERCORS

☎ 04 75 48 50 47 & 06 87 81 05 99

email: christiane.pitaval@wanadoo.fr

web: www.alafermeduchateau.com

A restored farmhouse in the Parc Naturel Régional du Vercors with five cosy bedrooms. Three are doubles, one has twin beds and there is a room for three with a double bed and a single. All have private bath or shower room and WC. There is a living room, garden furniture outside, and garage parking.

Prices s fr €52; d fr €72; t fr €92; dinner fr €22 **On Site** ⌇ Restaurant **Nearby** ⌇ 9km ⌇ 9km ⌇ 9km ⌇ 0.5km ⌇ 0.5km ⌇ 0.5km **Notes** Pets admitted CC

SUZE-LA-ROUSSE

⫴ ○ **La Poupaille**

Pierre FOSSOYEUX

St Turquois, 26790 SUZE LA ROUSSE

☎ 04 75 04 83 99 ▤ 04 75 04 83 99

A large provençale house, surrounded by vineyards and the woods of Tricastin. Five double bedrooms with private bathrooms. Facilities include dining room, sitting room with open fireplace, private parking and garden.

Prices s fr €40; d fr €50; t fr €69; extra person fr €19; dinner fr €20 **On Site** Private ⌇ **Nearby** ⌇ 5km ⌇ 9km ⌇ 2km Restaurant 2km ⌇ 2km ⌇ 10km ⌇ 3km ⌇ 15km **Notes** Pets admitted English spoken

⫴ ○ **Les Aiguières**

Brigitte JACQUEMOND

Rue de la Fontaine d'Argent,

26790 SUZE LA ROUSSE

☎ 04 75 98 40 80

email: brigitte@les-aiguieres.com

web: www.les-aiguieres.com

Here you are in a relaxing setting in the heart of the village, in an enclosed garden with an open view of the medieval château. The three welcoming bedrooms, with their warm Provençal colours, promise a restful stay. Meals are available: they can be served on the terrace or indoors, and they make full use of local specialities.

Prices s fr €72; d fr €82; t fr €113; extra person fr €35; dinner fr €25 **On Site** Private ⌇ **Nearby** ⌇ 5km ⌇ 15km Restaurant 0.1km ⌇ 0.5km ⌇ 0.2km ⌇ 0.1km ⌇ 15km **Notes** No pets English spoken

TAULIGNAN

⁂ ○ *La Rialhe*

Aline MARQUIS
Place de la République, 26770 TAULIGNAN
☎ 04 75 53 51 79 & 06 66 34 88 49
email: info@la-rialhe.com
web: www.la-rialhe.com

In the heart of Taulignan village, this old mill has been entirely restored with five spacious, relaxing bedrooms with private bathrooms. On the ground floor, there is a small gîte for four people.

Prices not confirmed for 2008 **Nearby** ☒ 7km ⚲ 7km ☻ 1km ☏ 1km ⌂ 0.3km ⋙ 30km **Notes** No pets English spoken

TULETTE

⁂ ○ ♿ *La Ramade*

A MARTINET DUMARQUEZ
Chemin de Visan Nord, 26790 TULETTE
☎ 04 75 98 31 12 ▤ 04 75 98 31 12
email: laramade.a@wanadoo.fr
web: www.guideweb.com/provence/bb/laramade/

'La Ramade' is a provençale house in a tranquil spot amid vineyards. There are three large bedrooms for two or three people with private bathrooms, a dining room, sitting room, electric heating, private parking, shady terrace and swimming pool.

Prices s fr €60; d fr €70; t fr €90; dinner fr €23 **On Site** Private ⚲
Nearby ☒ 2km ⚲ 50km Restaurant 3km ☻ 2km ☏ 1km ⌂ 1.7km
⋙ 20km **Notes** No pets

VALAURIE

⁂ ○ ♿ *Le Val Léron*

François et M-Claire PROTHON
Rte de St-Paul 3 Châteaux, 26230 VALAURIE
☎ 04 75 98 52 52 ▤ 04 75 98 52 52
email: mcf.prothon@laposte.net
web: www.levalleron.com

Set on a sheep farm which produces organic cheese and truffles, this provençale Drôme home is an old, renovated boarding house offering one en suite bedroom for two and two en suite bedrooms for four with kitchen area. Facilities include private entrances, sitting room, TV, reading room, piano, swimming pool and garden furniture.

Prices s €40-€45; d €53-€60; t fr €68; extra person fr €16; dinner fr €21
On Site Private ⚲ **Nearby** ☒ 5km ⚲ 0.5km Restaurant 1km ☻ 3km
☏ 2km ⋙ 20km **Notes** Pets admitted English spoken Open February to November.

ABONDANCE

⁂ ○ **Champfleury**

Nadine AVOCAT-MAULAZ
Richebourg, 74360 ABONDANCE
☎ 04 50 73 03 00
email: champsfleury@wanadoo.fr

High up in the Abondance Valley, this old chalet has been renovated in the traditional Savoie style. Four en suite guest rooms are furnished with double beds, some with extra singles. There is a sitting room with TV, home-cooked local specialities. Downhill skiing in the valley and other Ports du Solely resorts, skating, swimming and watersports also nearby. Reduced rate for children. Single supplement.

Prices s fr €45; d fr €50; t fr €75; extra person fr €10; dinner fr €15
Nearby ☒ 3km ⚲ 30km ⚑ 0.3km ⚲ 8km Restaurant 1km ☻ 3km
☻ 3km Spa 30km ☏ 1km ☏ 3km ⋙ 30km **Notes** Pets admitted

ALLINGES

⁂ ○ *A La Pince Allinges*

L et D RAMELET
247c, Route du Crêt Baron, 74200 ALLINGES
☎ 04 50 71 89 67 ▤ 04 50 81 56 45
email: ramelet.louis@cegetel.net
web: www.alapinceallinges.com

A stylish modern house, minutes from Lake Geneva and the spa town of Thonon. Three double rooms (one with a cot) and two family rooms each with two double beds all have private facilities. There is a swimming pool right in front of the house and a garden with wonderful views. Meals available by arrangement.

Prices not confirmed for 2008 **On Site** Private ⚲ **Nearby** ☒ 2km
⚑ 1km ☻ 15km ☻ 3km Spa 4km ☏ 2km ⋙ 4km **Notes** No pets
English spoken

BLUFFY

⁂ **Chalet Adagio**

Marie-José et Roland TILLIER
Le Bosson, Route du Bosson, 74290 BLUFFY
☎ 04 50 02 89 85 ▤ 04 50 02 89 85
email: chadagio@orange.fr

Standing at the foot of the Dents de Lanfon and overlooking the Lake of Annecy and the Menton-St-Bernard château, these three en suite guest rooms, grouped around the garden, all have superb views. A warm welcome is extended; there is a large living room with kitchen area and shady terrace. Restaurants, beaches, golf, skiing nearby.

Prices s fr €41; d fr €52 **Nearby** ☒ 3km ⚲ 3km ⚑ 2.5km ⚲ 10km
Restaurant 1km ☻ 10km ☻ 3km Spa 40km ☏ 3km ☏ 2km ⋙ 11km
Notes No pets English spoken

CHAMONIX-MONT-BLANC

ⅲ *La Girandole*

Pierre et Georgette GAZAGNES
46, Chemin de la Persévérance,
74400 CHAMONIX MONT BLANC
☎ 04 50 53 37 58 🖺 04 50 55 81 77
email: la-girandole@wanadoo.fr
web: www.lagirandole.free.fr/

Standing on a sunny slope at the edge of a forest and facing the Mont Blanc range, this beautiful chalet has three comfortable guest rooms: two double and one with twin beds, all en suite..Guests may use the peaceful garden and breakfast in large dining room with panoramic view and fireplace. Parking available.

Prices not confirmed for 2008 **Nearby** ⚓ 1.8km 🏊 1.8km ↖ 1.6km
⛵ 0.5km 🗺 1.6km Spa 20km 🏛 1.3km 🚶 1.8km **Notes** No pets
English spoken Open January to 15 May & 15 June to 15 October.

CHATILLON-SUR-CLUSES

ⅲ ⅧⅢ La Ferme de Béatrix

Brigitte DECAUDIN
Chef-Lieu, 74300 CHATILLON-SUR-CLUSES
☎ 04 50 89 43 97 & 06 74 93 53 40 🖺 04 50 89 44 04

At the crossroads between the great Haute-Savoie, Grand-Massif, Portes du Soleil and Praz de Lys-Sommand ski ranges, this former farm offers three double en suite guest rooms, decorated like forest cabins. Large living room with fireplace and pool table, walled orchard, spacious grounds with beautiful views over the Aravis. Dinner by reservation.

Prices s fr €40; d fr €50; t fr €65; extra person fr €10; dinner fr €20
Nearby ⚓ 6km 🏊 20km 🏊 3km ↖ 5km Restaurant 0.5km ⛵ 9km
🗺 3km Spa 32km 🎣 12km 🏛 0.3km 🚶 5km **Notes** No pets

CHAVANOD

ⅲ L'Epicurien

V et F BAUMONT-KOHLI
150 route de Chez Grillet, 74650 CHAVANOD
☎ 04 50 69 23 40 🖺 04 50 69 23 40
email: gitelepicurien@wanadoo.fr
web: www.gitelepicurien.com

Just 15 minutes from Annecy, in a peaceful country setting, this restored 19th-century house has five bedrooms, each sleeping two to four people. All of the rooms have a private bath or shower room and WC. Lounge with piano; library and games room. Garden with woodland walks.

Prices s fr €55; d fr €63; t fr €78; extra person fr €15 **On Site** 🏊
Nearby ⚓ 4km 🏊 10km ↖ 4km ⛵ 20km 🗺 4km Spa 37km 🏛 1.5km
🚶 7km **Notes** No pets

CORDON

ⅲ Lou Stalet de Jovet

Michèle FONTAINE
Chemin de Jovet, 74700 CORDON
☎ 04 50 90 12 08
email: lou-stalet@wanadoo.fr
web: www.lou-stalet.fr/

A traditional Savoyard chalet offering two double rooms and three triples, all with private facilities. Breakfast is served in a large living room with a panoramic view of Mont Blanc. Kitchenette available, TV if required. Everything supplied for babies under two; non-smoking.

Prices s €70-€85; d €78-€93; t €94-€109; extra person fr €20
On Site 🏊 **Nearby** ⚓ 1.5km 🏊 10km ↖ 5km Restaurant 0.3km
⛵ 1.5km 🗺 1.5km Spa 10km 🏛 0.2km 🚶 4km **Notes** No pets English spoken

CUSY

ⅲ ⅧⅢ Les Jardins du Nant

Philippe MEYRIEUX
La Tropaz, 600 Chemin du Pranant, 74540 CUSY
☎ 04 50 52 52 53 & 06 08 07 45 36 🖺 04 50 52 52 53
email: philippe.meyrieux@wanadoo.fr
web: www.lesjardinsdunant.com

In their organic market garden on the edge of the Bauges Massif, your hosts have created two comfortable family units in this ancient house. There is also a small (grade 2) chalet for three people, with private bath/shower room and WC. Breakfast, using produce from the garden, is served in the dining room or on the south-facing terrace.

Prices s €32-€48; d €42-€58; extra person €19-€29; dinner fr €16.50
Nearby ⚓ 15km 🏊 1km ↖ 15km ⛵ 20km 🗺 15km Spa 15km 🏛 1km
🚶 12km **Notes** Pets admitted English spoken

DINGY-SAINT-CLAIR

ⅲ ⅧⅢ *St Brides*

Raymond SMITH
Provenat, 74230 DINGY-SAINT-CLAIR
☎ 04 50 66 55 44 & 06 16 02 23 49
email: st.brides@laposte.net
web: www.st-brides.net

The Scottish host promises a typically warm welcome in this newly-built, bright and spacious chalet. There are five double rooms, each decorated to the theme of a different country, and each with a private bath or shower and WC. Varied breakfast menus; other meals by arrangement. Lounge with stereo and video, sauna. Terrace, garden bordered by a stream.

Prices not confirmed for 2008 **Nearby** ⚓ 7km 🏊 1.5km ↖ 8km
⛵ 20km 🗺 8km Spa 40km 🏛 8km 🚶 12km **Notes** No pets English spoken

DOMANCY

⋕⋕ ⏣ Mont-Blanc Paradis

Cathy RAMON
446, Route des Lacs, 74700 DOMANCY
☎ 04 50 58 11 70 & 06 88 40 27 02
email: ramon.cathy@wanadoo.fr
web: http://montblanc.paradise.free.fr

Right in the heart of the Mont Blanc region and close to the Passy lakes, this chalet, with lots of flowers, has three comfortable and individually decorated double bedrooms. All of the rooms have a private bath or shower room and WC. Breakfast and, by arrangement, other meals, can be served indoors or out on the terrace. Large garden, bordered by a river.

Prices s fr €60; d fr €72; dinner fr €23　**On Site** 🏌　**Nearby** ⛷ 2km
🏊 10km　🕏 3km　Restaurant 0.5km　🛶 7km　🚴 2km　Spa 3km　🛎 2km
🏛 2km　🚲 3km　**Notes** No pets　English spoken

DRAILLANT

⋕⋕⋕⋕ ⏣ La Ferme du Château de Maugny

D GALOPIN et S ROUSSEL-GALL
74550 DRAILLANT
☎ 04 50 26 46 68 & 06 81 73 58 47
email: infos@lafermeduchateau.com
web: www.lafermeduchateau.com

At the foot of the Col des Moises, dating from the 18th-century, this farm has two rooms, one double and family room that sleeps four. All rooms have access to the swimming pool and are non-smoking.

Prices d fr €85; extra person fr €25; dinner fr €25　**On Site** Private 🕏
Nearby ⛷ 4km　🏊 10km　🏌 3km　Restaurant 6km　🛶 12km　🚴 2km
Spa 8km　🏛 3km　🚲 6km　**Notes** Pets admitted　English spoken

EXCENEVEX

⋕⋕ ⏣ *Le Chemin des Fées - Chevilly*

Louis MEGEVAND
74140 EXCENEVEX
☎ 04 50 72 89 57 & 06 19 56 14 65
email: le_chemin_des_fees@yahoo.fr

A 19th-century property in a delightful green setting five minutes from a lake-side sandy beach. It offers two double rooms, a twin-bedded room and a suite for up to four, all with private bath or shower room and WC. Outside there is a garden and terrace with open views towards the Alps, and the medieval village of Yvoire is nearby.

Prices not confirmed for 2008　**Nearby** ⛷ 0.1km　🏌 1km　🕏 12km
🛶 30km　🚴 2km　Spa 12km　🏛 2km　🚲 12km　**Notes** No pets

GRAND-BORNAND

⋕⋕ ⏣ La Ferme de Vanille

D et A DUFAURE DE LAJARTE
Les Frasses, 74450 GRAND-BORNAND
☎ 04 50 09 08 32　🖹 04 50 09 08 32
email: delajarte@wanadoo.fr
web: www.lafermedevanille.com

At the heart of the Aravis Mountain range, this 18th-century former farmhouse is set in an old village with traditional mountain architecture, ideal for skiing (ski bus 50 metres). There are three comfortable rooms for two or three with private bathrooms. Discover regional delicacies at the table d'hôte, relax in the two lounges with fireplace and meet the donkeys, Vanille and Noisette, in the garden.

Prices s fr €53; d fr €69; dinner fr €20　**Nearby** ⛷ 4km　🏊 5km　🏌 1km
🕏 4km　Restaurant 2km　🛶 2km　🚴 2km　Spa 4km　🛎 4km　🏛 2km
🚲 23km　**Notes** No pets　English spoken

HERY-SUR-ALBY

⋕⋕ ⏣ *Le Galatan*

Philippe et Christele DURAND
2085 Route de Liaudy, 74450 HERY-SUR-ALBY
☎ 04 50 68 25 50 & 06 82 05 19 66
email: info@gite-galatan.com
web: www.gite-galatan.com

Close to Annecy and Aix-les-Bains, Christele and Philippe have restored this old farmhouse to provide a welcoming ambience in three rooms for two or four people, each with shower/WC. Breakfast and table d'hôte meals include Savoyard specialities. Everything for babies supplied; no charge for children under two.

Prices not confirmed for 2008　**Nearby** ⛷ 15km　🏌 3km　🕏 8km
🚴 20km　🚴 3km　Spa 20km　🏛 3km　🚲 8km　**Notes** No pets　English spoken　Open April to 1 November.

LA CHAPELLE-D'ABONDANCE

⋕⋕ ⏣ Le Chat Féroce

Lisa PERRY
La Voraz, 74360 LA CHAPELLE D'ABONDANCE
☎ 04 50 73 58 08　🖹 04 50 73 58 08
email: lisa.perry@wanadoo.fr
web: www.alfinealice.co.uk

An ideal place to stay for sporting activities or a complete rest. Two double rooms, a triple (three single beds) and a room for four (all single beds), each with private bath or shower/WC. Living rooms, open fire, copious breakfasts and meals with an English accent.

Prices s fr €55; d fr €80; t fr €100; extra person fr €20; dinner fr €25 **Nearby** ♿ 1.2km ♨ 25km 🏌 1.2km ➶ 5km Restaurant 1km ♣ 1.2km ♨ 1.2km Spa 33km 🏛 1.2km ⛵ 33km **Notes** No pets English spoken

LA VERNAZ

⁂ 🍴 La Grange aux Oies

Alexandre CHACHAY

74200 LA VERNAZ

☎ 04 50 72 14 23 & 06 17 58 80 76 📠 04 50 72 14 23

email: contact@lagrangeauxoies.fr

web: www.lagrangeauxoies.com

A former farmhouse with four attractively decorated split-level rooms sleeping from two to four people, all with private shower room and WC. Breakfasts are generous and the host, who is a keen cook, is delighted to serve other meals if pre-booked. An excellent location, not far from the Gorges du Pont du Diable and Lake Geneva.

Prices s €30-€35; d €60-€70; extra person €30-€35; dinner fr €20 **Nearby** ♿ 10km ♨ 25km 🏌 3km ➶ 15km Restaurant 4km ♣ 15km ♨ 8km Spa 15km ⛳ 8km 🏛 8km ⛵ 15km **Notes** Pets admitted

LES CONTAMINES-MONTJOIE

⁂ La Ferme de Bon-Papa

Cathy et Joël ROUX-GUERIN

35, Impasse de la Bérangère,

74170 LES CONTAMINES-MONTJOIE

☎ 04 50 90 33 28

email: joelrouxlesconta@tele2.fr

web: www.gites-de-france-haute-savoie.com/
albums_photos/7485601.htm

A restored 17th-century farmhouse within easy reach of Mont Blanc. It has three double rooms and two family rooms for up to four people, each with a private shower and WC. The host is a mountain guide who can give guests a lot of useful information about the area. Non-smoking property.

Prices d fr €65; t fr €85; extra person fr €15 **Nearby** ➶ 1.5km ♨ 15km 🏌 0.2km ➶ 8km Restaurant 0.2km ♣ 1km ♨ 1.5km Spa 13km ⛵ 13km **Notes** No pets English spoken

LES GETS

⁂ 🍴 Chalet L'Envala

Thérèse GOSSET

Route des Platons, 74260 LES GETS

☎ 04 50 75 89 15 & 06 20 04 11 08

email: chalet.lenvala@libertysurf.fr

web: www.lenvala.com

With spectacular panoramic alpine views of the peaks right across to Switzerland, this charming wooden chalet stands on a sunny slope above the village, between Leman and Mont-Blanc. The rooms are

warmly decorated and furnished completely in wood. Sitting room with open fire, flower-filled terrace. Home-made dinner includes numerous local specialities.

Prices not confirmed for 2008 **Nearby** ♿ 2km 🏌 1.5km ➶ 1.5km ♣ 1.5km ♨ 1.5km Spa 35km 🏛 1.5km ⛵ 25km **Notes** No pets English spoken

LES HOUCHES

⁂ 🍴 La Ferme d'en Haut

Marie-Joëlle TURC

152, Route des Aillouds, 74310 LES HOUCHES

☎ 04 50 54 74 87 & 06 62 02 17 14

email: mijoturc@wanadoo.fr

web: www.lafermedenhaut.fr

A peaceful haven for Mont Blanc hill-walkers and mountaineers, this is a charming 19th-century wooden chalet with a snug living room with fireplace and gourmet dining. Sunny terrace, ski runs and paths on the doorstep. Four en suite guest rooms: two double and two with two doubles. Close to Chamonix.

Prices not confirmed for 2008 **Nearby** 🏌 1.5km ➶ 6km ♣ 0.1km ♨ 1.5km Spa 15km 🏛 2km ⛵ 3km **Notes** No pets English spoken

LES OLLIERES

⁂ Chez Joly

Madeleine MERCIER

74370 LES OLLIERES

☎ 04 50 60 89 08

email: madeleinemercier@aol.com

In a rural location not far from Annecy, this beautifully restored old property provides a quiet non-smoking environment for its visitors. There are three bedrooms, accommodating from two to four guests, all with private bath/shower and WC. Lounge with books; music room with piano; pretty garden, outdoor children's games.

Prices s fr €50; d fr €75; t fr €95 **Nearby** ♿ 10km 🏌 3km ➶ 10km ♣ 20km ♨ 5km Spa 50km 🏛 3km ⛵ 10km **Notes** No pets English spoken

LULLY

⁂ Le Pré d'Emma

Agnès CHARMOT

Les Parrets, 74890 LULLY

☎ 04 50 31 75 18 & 04 50 36 34 41

web: http://lepredemma.chez-alice.fr

This chalet stands between Lake Lemoin and the Col de Cou, in the middle of a village. There are four en suite guest rooms, all double, with entrances off their own private terraces. Use of large pleasant wooden living room with TV, library and games, kitchen area, and flowery garden.

Prices s €45-€50; d €60-€55; t €70-€75; extra person fr €15 **Nearby** ♿ 6km ♨ 18km 🏌 0.1km ➶ 11km Restaurant 8km ♣ 13km ♨ 2km Spa 11km 🏛 0.2km ⛵ 11km **Notes** No pets

MAXILLY-SUR-LEMAN

▥ ⭗ *Les Vernes*

Pascal VOISIN
51, Route du Très Clos, 74500 MAXILLY-SUR-LEMAN
☎ 04 50 26 50 02 & 06 82 29 13 57
email: les.vernes@wanadoo.fr

This restored early 20th-century property, in its wooded grounds near to Lake Geneva, has four guest rooms, each for two to four people and with en suite bath or shower room and WC. Use of kitchen. Delicious breakfasts are served in the dining room or in the garden, and other meals are available by arrangement.

Prices not confirmed for 2008 **Nearby** ⚲ 3km 🏌 1km ⚐ 5km ⚓ 6km 🏊 2km Spa 3km 🏛 2km ⛟ 5km **Notes** No pets

MEGEVE

▥ Les Oyats

J-Claude et Cl. Marie TISSOT
745, Route de Lady, Chalet les Oyats, 74120 MEGEVE
☎ 04 50 21 11 56
email: lesoyats3@wanadoo.fr
web: www.lesoyats.fr

This old farmhouse, near Mont Blanc, has been lovingly restored by its owners to transform it into comfortable holiday accommodation. There are four bedrooms for three or four people, with private terraces and en suite bathrooms, plus a further en suite double room in the owners' house. Large lounge and kitchen area for guest use. Walking and hang-gliding available locally.

Prices s fr €74; d fr €84; t fr €112 **On Site** ⚐ **Nearby** ⚲ 2km ⚓ 6km 🏌 2km ⚐ 2km Restaurant 0.8km 🏊 2km Spa 15km ⚑ 0.5km 🏛 1.5km ⛟ 15km **Notes** No pets Open December to September.

MIEUSSY

▥ ⭗ La Maison des Soeurs

Marie-Lise MAERTCHIK
74440 MIEUSSY
☎ 04 50 43 15 74 & 06 08 37 87 81
🖹 04 50 43 15 74
email: mlm@mieussy.net
web: www.mieussy.net

The welcome from the hosts at this property will give you the impression that you are visiting friends you have known all your life. The three spacious non-smoking bedrooms, one of them a suite, are elegant, yet cosy and comfortable. All have en suite facilities. Lounge with TV; meals by arrangement.

Prices s fr €62; d €75-€95; t fr €113; extra person fr €18; dinner fr €22 **Nearby** ⚲ 12km 🏌 15km ⚐ 1km ⚐ 8km Restaurant 0.1km ⚓ 10km 🏊 1.2km ⚑ 10km 🏛 0.2km 🏛 18km **Notes** No pets English spoken

MORZINE

▥ ⭗ Le Chalet des Ardoisiers

Guy VERNET
757, Route des Udrezants, 74110 MORZINE
☎ 04 50 79 00 08 & 06 87 69 01 25
email: chaletdesardoisiers@free.fr
web: http://chaletdesardoisiers.free.fr

Situated in the heart of Morzine, the chalet has been renovated using wood and stone. Four cosy bedrooms for two to four people, two of which are suites and all have private facilities. Large living area with open hearth, where breakfast and evening meals are served using local produce. Parking available.

Prices s €84; d €84-€94; t €104-€114; extra person €20; dinner fr €23 **On Site** ⚐ ⚑ **Nearby** ⚲ 1km ⚐ 1km Restaurant 0.7km ⚓ 1km 🏊 1km Spa 35km 🏛 0.7km 🏛 35km **Notes** No pets English spoken Open December to 10 May & 8 June to September.

ORCIER

▥ ⭗ *La Basse*

Catherine MARTINERIE
120, Chemin des Sources, 74550 ORCIER
☎ 04 50 26 67 02 & 06 03 92 15 48
email: catherine.martinerie@wanadoo.fr
web: www.alabasse.com

A family atmosphere at this country cottage that offers 3 bedrooms (1 family suite); all with private facilities.

Prices not confirmed for 2008 **Nearby** ⚲ 10km ⚐ 4km ⚐ 12km ⚓ 2.5km 🏊 3km Spa 12km 🏛 5km 🏛 12km **Notes** Pets admitted

PLATEAU D'ASSY / PASSY

▥ ⭗ *Gîte La Chouette*

Edwin WILHELM
99, Rue d'Anterne, 74480 PLATEAU D'ASSY / PASSY
☎ 04 50 91 39 79 & 06 11 68 95 52 🖹 04 50 91 54 81
email: info@gitelachouette.com
web: www.gitelachouette.com

This house, with its panoramic view of Mont Blanc, has been totally renovated by its Dutch owners. It has five comfortable bedrooms, all with en suite facilities, and each sleeping from two to four guests. Large lounge area, open fire, terrace. Meals available by arrangement.

Prices s fr €40; d fr €59; t fr €88; extra person fr €29.50; dinner fr €24.50 **Nearby** ⚲ 6km 🏌 20km ⚐ 6km ⚐ 10km Restaurant 0.5km ⚓ 6km 🏊 1km Spa 10km ⚑ 1km 🏛 0.5km 🏛 10km **Notes** Pets admitted English spoken Open 21 December to October. CC

PRAZ DE LYS - TANINGES

⋕⋕⋕ 🍽 *Chalet Le Serac*

A-B BEC

Praz-de-Lys, 74440 TANINGES

☎ 04 50 89 90 32 & 06 86 84 65 49

email: leserac.bec@wanadoo.fr

This chalet, with its panoramic view towards Mont Blanc, offers an ideal location for your winter sports holiday. It is warmly decorated, and has four cosy rooms sleeping two to four people. All the rooms have en suite facilities. Big lounge with an open fire; home-made bread for breakfast; other meals available by arrangement.

Prices not confirmed for 2008 **Nearby** ⚐ 0.5km 🏊 5km ⚡ 0.5km
⚑ 0.1km ⛳ 0.5km Spa 50km 🎏 0.5km ⛷ 24km **Notes** No pets
English spoken

SALES

⋕⋕⋕ 🍽 La Salière

Eric et Chrystelle BENOIT

74150 SALES

☎ 04 50 63 19 22 & 06 19 20 52 39 📄 04 50 63 19 22

email: chrystelle@la-saliere.com

web: www.la-saliere.com

This restored farmhouse has five spacious, charming and comfortable en suite guest. Cot available. Shared sitting room with TV and kitchen area, pleasant garden. Fishing, cycling, riding, skiing, rambling and watersports nearby.

Prices s €57-€75; d €67-€85; t €86-€104; extra person fr €19; dinner fr €26 **On Site** Private ⚡ **Nearby** ⚐ 0.3km ⛳ 15km ⚡ 0.5km Restaurant 2km ⚑ 25km ⛳ 2km Spa 20km 🎏 1km ⛷ 1.5km **Notes** No pets English spoken

SAMOENS

⋕⋕⋕ 🍽 *Chambre d'hôtes*

Gwenaëlle BOTTAGISI

De Plampraz, 74340 SAMOENS

☎ 04 50 34 95 98 📄 04 50 34 95 98

email: gwenaelle.bottagisi@wanadoo.fr

web: www.plampraz.com

Overhanging the Samoëns Valley and opposite the summits of the Haut-Giffre, near Col de Joux-Plane, this farmhouse has three rooms for two to three people with refined décor and private facilities. Family table d'hôte meals available with traditional Savoyard cuisine. Small

lounge with TV, grounds, balconies. Station and historic village nearby. Leisure activities and ski resort at Grand Massif (5km).

Prices not confirmed for 2008 **Nearby** ⚐ 4km ⚡ 0.1km ⛳ 1.7km
⚑ 3km ⛳ 1.7km Spa 50km 🎏 1.7km ⛷ 18km **Notes** No pets English spoken

SERVOZ

⋕⋕⋕ *L'Alpe*

Josiane et Hervé ANSELME

Le Bouchet, Chemin du Rucher, 74310 SERVOZ

☎ 04 50 47 22 66 📄 04 50 91 40 66

email: lalpe@caramail.com

web: www.chez.com/lalpe/

This guest house, in a friendly, untouched village with traditional wooden buildings, is set among tranquil mountains. It has six grade 3 rooms, two of which are family rooms, sleeping up to five people. Use of kitchen, sitting room and large garden. The owner, a ski instructor and mountain guide, offers advice and can arrange activities. Reduced rates for extended stays and for children.

Prices not confirmed for 2008 **Nearby** ⚐ 8km ⚡ 0.1km ⛳ 10km
⚑ 5km ⛳ 0.1km Spa 6km 🎏 0.1km ⛷ 0.8km **Notes** No pets English spoken Open 15 December to 15 May & 15 June to September. CC

SEVRIER

⋕⋕⋕ Maison d'hôtes Nicoline

Eric et Marylin REY

1780, Ancienne Route d'Annecy, 74320 SEVRIER

☎ 04 50 51 11 98 & 06 09 44 81 65

email: info@nicoline.fr

web: www.nicoline.fr

La Villa Nicoline enjoys panoramic views over the lake, and has direct access to the beach. Four bedrooms are available, two doubles and two rooms for three people, all en suite.

Prices s €55-€65; d €65-€75; t fr €85; extra person fr €15
Nearby ⚐ 1.5km ⛳ 20km ⚡ 0.5km ⛳ 1km Restaurant 1km ⚑ 15km ⛳ 1.5km Spa 40km 🎏 1km ⛷ 2km **Notes** No pets English spoken

SEYNOD/VIEUGY

⋕⋕⋕ La Ferme de Vergloz

Nicole et Philippe MARTEL

46, Route de Vergloz, 74600 SEYNOD/VIEUGY

☎ 04 50 46 71 98 📄 04 50 46 71 98

email: fermedevergloz@free.fr

web: www.fermedevergloz.fr

Overlooking the town of Annecy and facing the Semnoz Massif, the Ferme de Vergloz is a collection of buildings typical of the Avant-Pays. Four charming en suite guest rooms have mezzanine and sleep two to four people. Breakfast, which is served beside the fireplace in the dining room, features produce from the farm. The relaxing lounge has panoramic views. Restaurants 2km. Reduced rates for children.

Prices s €40-€42; d €54-€60; t €73-€75; extra person fr €15
Nearby ⚐ 3km ⚡ 4km ⛳ 4km Restaurant 4km ⚑ 17km ⛳ 4km Spa 35km 🎏 2km ⛷ 6km **Notes** No pets Open 16 December to 14 November.

ST-EUSTACHE

♯♯♯ ○ Les Pralets

Colette SAPPEY

Puget, 74410 SAINT-EUSTACHE

☎ 04 50 32 02 93 📄 04 50 32 08 64

email: colette.sappey@wanadoo.fr

web: www.les-pralets.com

This property overlooking Lake Annecy has three bedrooms in a building adjacent to the owners' home. The rooms, some of them split-level, sleep from two to four people, and each room has a private bath/shower and WC. Extra beds available. Large lounge and library. Garden with terrace and lake views. Evening meals, with local specialities, by arrangement.

Prices s fr €40; d €51-€55; t €64-€68; extra person fr €12; dinner fr €17 **Nearby** ⚓ 11km ⚓ 1km ⚓ 14km ⚓ 18km ⚓ 7km Spa 35km 🏛 6.5km ⚓ 16km **Notes** No pets English spoken CC

ST-FELIX

♯♯♯♯ ○ Domaine des Bruyères

Monique BOURRAT

359 route de Mercy, 74540 SAINT-FELIX

☎ 04 50 60 96 53 & 06 07 88 19 45 📄 04 50 60 94 65

email: info@les-bruyeres.fr

web: www.les-bruyeres.fr

Situated close to Annecy and Aix-les-Bains, this renovated residence, set in a hectare of grounds, offers four suites. All have independent access and are en suite.

Prices d fr €90; t fr €115; extra person fr €25; dinner fr €20 **On Site** Private tennis court **Nearby** ⚓ 5km ⚓ 10km ⚓ 1km ⚓ 1km Restaurant 0.1km ⚓ 20km Spa 17km ⚓ 1km 🏛 0.5km ⚓ 5km **Notes** No pets English spoken CC

ST-GERVAIS-LES-BAINS

♯♯♯ ○ La Maison du Vernay

Caroline RUEDA

164, Route de la Mollaz, 74170 SAINT-GERVAIS-LES-BAINS

☎ 04 50 47 07 55 & 06 09 43 93 21 📄 04 50 47 07 55

email: lamaisonduvernay@hotmail.com

web: www.lamaisonduvernay.com

At the foot of Mont Blanc, and close to the cable cars, this former hotel has been fully refurbished to provide five cosy and comfortable

rooms. After a day's walking or skiing, you can relax by the fire before enjoying a good Savoyard dinner. There is also a garden with terrace, and the thermal baths are not far away.

Prices not confirmed for 2008 **Nearby** ⚓ 5km ⚓ 0.7km ⚓ 0.7km ⚓ 0.8km ⚓ 0.7km Spa 5km 🏛 0.1km ⚓ 5km **Notes** No pets English spoken

ST-JEAN-DE-SIXT

♯♯♯ La Passerelle

Marie-Claude MISSILLIER

74450 SAINT-JEAN-DE-SIXT

☎ 04 50 02 24 33

email: info@gites-chaletlapasserelle.com

web: www.gites-chaletlapasserelle.com

In the village between La Clusaz and Grand-Bornand, this pretty chalet stands next to the owners' farmhouse. It houses four cosy en suite guest rooms, each with double bed and extra single, TV and private terrace. Folding bed and cot available. There is a large guests' living room, and breakfast can be enjoyed on a large terrace with views of the Aravis Mountains.

Prices s fr €42; d €58-€60; t fr €90 **Nearby** ⚓ 3km ⚓ 20km ⚓ 8km ⚓ 1.5km Restaurant 0.2km ⚓ 1.5km ⚓ 0.1km Spa 50km ⚓ 3km ⚓ 30km **Notes** Pets admitted

TANINGES

♯♯♯ La Grange

Nicole et M-Jeanne BASTARD

Avonnex, 74440 TANINGES

☎ 04 50 34 31 36

Situated between the Grand Massif and Portes du Soleil, this former farmhouse enjoys spectacular views facing the Aravis, Buet and Marcelly Mountains and is ideal for skiing. The three double en suite guest rooms, housed in a converted barn, are split-level and spacious but cosy. Breakfast is served in a large dining room, with sitting/reading area.

Prices s fr €46; d fr €56; t fr €71; extra person fr €10 **Nearby** ⚓ 7km ⚓ 10km ⚓ 1.5km ⚓ 10km Restaurant 1km ⚓ 7km ⚓ 2km Spa 40km 🏛 1.5km ⚓ 13km **Notes** No pets

THOLLON

♯♯♯ ○ Au Balcon du Léman

Ghislaine GALLAND

Chez les Vesins, 74500 THOLLON-LES-MEMISES

☎ 04 50 70 23 53 & 06 10 97 12 07

email: gallandgy@tiscali.fr

Not far from Lake Geneva, this old village farmhouse makes an excellent base for exploring this beautiful region, very close to the Swiss border. There are three individually decorated bedrooms, each for two people, and all with private facilities. Meals are available by arrangement, offering dishes from various regions of France, and from other countries.

Prices not confirmed for 2008 **Nearby** ⚓ 11km ⚓ 11km ⚓ 11km ⚓ 2km ⚓ 0.5km Spa 11km ⚓ 1km ⚓ 12km **Notes** Pets admitted English spoken

THONES

⚑ Chalet les Lupins

Patricia et Rémi TALEB

Glapigny - la Closette, 74230 THONES

☎ 04 50 63 19 96 & 06 03 15 24 55　🖹 04 50 63 19 19

email: chaletleslupins@orange.com

web: http://perso.orange.fr/leslupins

This chalet stands high up in the heart of the Aravis range, facing La Tournette. It offers three guest rooms, all en suite with double and extra single. Use of sitting room, TV, washing facilities, terrace with panoramic views. Friendly dinners around large farmhouse table, regional specialities. No smoking. Reduced rates for children.

Prices s fr €50; d fr €60; t fr €80; extra person fr €20　**Nearby** ⚘6km ✎5km ↖15km ⚓15km ◡5km Spa 45km ⌂5km ⚶30km
Notes No pets　English spoken

⚑ ⌾ Le Clos Zénon

Michel et Joëlle COLLE

Le Pessey-Route de Bellossier, 74230 THONES

☎ 04 50 02 10 86　🖹 04 50 02 10 86

web: www.thones-chalet-gite.com

In a calm setting between Annecy Lake and the Arakis resorts, and overlooking the mountains, this attractive chalet offers five non-smoking rooms for two to four people with mountain décor and private facilities. Lounge with fireplace, swimming pool, pretty terrace, enclosed garden, garage, horses for hire. The hosts, former restaurateurs, offer traditional regional table d'hôte cuisine. Reductions from two nights and for children.

Prices s fr €50; d €62-€82; t fr €112; extra person fr €30; dinner €28-€35　**On Site** ⌘ Private ↖　**Nearby** ⚘1.5km ✈8km ✎1km Restaurant 1.5km ⚓11km ◡2km Spa 45km ⌂1.5km ⚶20km
Notes No pets　English spoken　Open April to 20 December.

⚑ Pré Varens la Cour

S JOSSERAND-DOUSSOT

Route de la Clusaz, 74230 THONES

☎ 04 50 32 95 76 & 06 70 43 19 57　🖹 04 50 32 95 76

email: s.doussot@wanadoo.fr

web: www.gites-aravis.com

Standing on the riverbank in a pretty garden, this guest house has five rooms: two grade 3 rooms with double bed, sofa and kitchen area; and two doubles and a family room with double and twin beds (grade 2). All have shower rooms and shared wc. Communal room with TV, games, barbecue, table tennis. Reduced rate for children.

Prices s €34-€40; d €40-€46; t €53-€58; extra person fr €9
Nearby ⚘1.5km ✎0.5km ↖1.5km Restaurant 1.5km ⚓10km ◡1.5km Spa 50km ⌂1.5km ⚶20km　**Notes** No pets　English spoken

VALLORCINE

⚑ ⌾ La Fontaine

A DE PLAEN-MEYS

Le Couteray, 74660 VALLORCINE

☎ 04 50 54 64 19

email: adp@lafontaine-vallorcine.com

web: www.lafontaine-vallorcine.com

Close to the Chamonix Valley, in a hamlet which is the starting point for many walks, your hosts are lovingly restoring this old country house. It has a warm atmosphere, a panoramic view, and three cosy bedrooms for two to four people. There is a lounge, and a beautiful terrace which is a quiet place to relax. Meals by arrangement.

Prices d €80-€90; t fr €120; dinner fr €22　**On Site** Restaurant ✿
Nearby ⚘14km ✎0.5km ↖10km ⚓1km ◡2km Spa 30km ⌂2km
⚶0.6km　**Notes** No pets　English spoken　Open January to September.

VAULX

⚑ ⌾ La Ferme sur les Bois

Marie-Christine SKINAZY

Le Biolley, 74150 VAULX

☎ 04 50 60 54 50

email: annecy.attelage@wanadoo.fr

web: www.annecy-attelage.fr

This 19th-century Savoie farmhouse stands in beautiful untouched countryside. It has four cosy en suite guest rooms; three with double and extra single bed and a family room with double and twin beds with its own entrance. Cot available. Use of library, grounds and terrace, parking. Dinner available. Reduced rates for children.

Prices s fr €45; d fr €56; extra person fr €25; dinner fr €23
Nearby ⚘2km ✎5km ↖14km ◡3km Spa 40km ⌂3km ⚶14km
Notes No pets　English spoken

VIUZ-LA-CHIESAZ

⚑ ⌾ Lô Praz Condus

Véronique MOREL

775, route de Lacrevaz, 74540 VIUZ-LA-CHIESAZ

☎ 04 50 77 57 58 & 06 74 95 17 36

email: vemorel@infonie.fr

web: www.chambres-hotes-annecy.com

Situated in a family farm, typical of the region, are four bedrooms sleeping between two to five people. Each room has its own shower and WC. Evening meal is available by reservation Friday, Saturday and Sunday.

Prices s fr €50; d €55-€65; t €75-€85; extra person fr €10; dinner €18
Nearby ⚘7km ↕20km ✎12km ↖9km Restaurant 2km ⚓12km
◡3km Spa 25km ⌂7km ⚶12km　**Notes** No pets　English spoken

ISÈRE

ANNOISIN-CHATELANS

⁂ ⁑ La Maison de la Noisette

Marie-N et Thierry JANIN
La Prairie, 38460 ANNOISIN CHATELANS
☎ 04 74 83 86 09 📄 04 74 83 11 53
email: janin@maison-noisette.com
web: www.maison-noisette.com

Near the medieval city of Crémieu, the caves at la Balme and the Larina archaeological site, and set in a quiet rural location in a lovely enclosed wooded garden. Four delightful en suite bedrooms, lavish family dinners, a large veranda, exposed beams and an open fire. Hiking, mountain biking, horse-riding, ornamental lakes nearby.

Prices s fr €42; d fr €53; t fr €68; extra person fr €15; dinner fr €17 **On Site** Private ⚲ **Nearby** ⛷ 5km ⚓ 20km ⚐ 10km Restaurant 2km ⚲ 10km ⚑ 5km ⚑ 5km ⚑ 20km **Notes** Pets admitted English spoken CC

AUTRANS

⁂ ⁑ Belle Combe

Laurence et Roland CAILLET
Les Gaillards, 38880 AUTRANS
☎ 04 76 94 79 84 📄 04 76 94 79 84
email: belle-combe@tiscali.fr

Choose between five individually decorated en suite guest rooms at this old restored farmhouse. Dining/sitting room with open fire in the old stable, lovely garden and meals under the arbour. Enjoy home-made preserves at breakfast and a friendly atmosphere and local produce at dinner, or take a cookery lesson with the proprietor, a cook by profession.

Prices s fr €52; d fr €65; t fr €85; extra person fr €20; dinner fr €20 **On Site** Spa **Nearby** ⛷ 2km ⚓ 15km ⚐ 0.5km ⚲ 2km Restaurant 0.6km ⚑ 1km ⚑ 0.3km ⚑ 0.5km ⚑ 40km **Notes** No pets English spoken CC

BALBINS

⁂ ⚹ *Les Granges d'Eglantine*

Christian ABEL
345 Chemin du Revollet, Le Revolet, 38260 BALBINS
☎ 04 74 20 56 87 📄 04 76 58 08 99
email: contact@grangesdeglantine.com

This is an ideal place to rest and recharge your batteries! These converted barns overlook the plain of Bièvre and the neighbouring hills. There are six bedrooms sleeping from two to six people, all with individual décor and en suite bathrooms. Breakfasts served by the fire in the lounge, on the patio, or beside the heated swimming pool. Parking.

Prices not confirmed for 2008 **On Site** Private ⚲ **Nearby** ⚐ 3km ⚑ 50km ⚑ 3km ⚑ 20km **Notes** No pets English spoken CC

BESSINS

⁂ Le Maroubra

Jocelyne et Jean M. TOUCHER
Au Mercier, 38160 BESSINS
☎ 04 76 64 11 62 📄 04 76 64 11 62
email: lemaroubra@free.fr
web: http://lemaroubra.free.fr

Old pebble-fronted farmhouse in the traditional architectural style of the Antonin countryside, set in a beautiful estate with swimming pool and large shady garden, sun loungers and garden furniture. In an annexe to the main house are four en suite rooms for two, three or four people. Dining room and sitting room with open fire. Near to tourist sites.

Prices s fr €34; d fr €44; t fr €56; extra person fr €13 **On Site** Private ⚲ **Nearby** ⛷ 10km ⚐ 10km Restaurant 5km ⚲ 10km ⚑ 6km ⚑ 10km ⚑ 10km **Notes** No pets English spoken

BOURG-D'OISANS

⁂ ⁑ Les Petites Sources

Pauline DURDAN
Le Vert, 38520 BOURG D'OISANS
☎ 04 76 80 13 92 📄 04 76 80 13 92
email: durdan@club-internet.fr
web: www.petitessources.free.fr

A warm and comfortable barn conversion in a mountain setting. The balconied first floor offers a range of rooms, and there are two rooms for three on the second floor. The host is a mountain guide and will offer advice or organise cross-country skiing trips for groups in winter.

Prices s €35-€38; d €50-€58; t €70-€78; extra person fr €20; dinner fr €18 **On Site** ⚐ **Nearby** ⚲ 2km ⚑ 15km ⚑ 2km ⚑ 2km **Notes** Pets admitted English spoken Open 15 December to September.

BOURGOIN-JALLIEU

❄ ✿ |◎| Champfort

Monique et Robert DURAND
41 chemin de Champfort, Charbonnières,
38300 BOURGOIN JALLIEU
☎ 04 74 43 35 82 ▤ 04 74 43 35 82
email: monique.durand2@wanadoo.fr
web: http://perso.wanadoo.fr/champfort

A farmhouse situated on a cereal farm on the Champfort Plateau, bordering the valley. Five rooms are available in the owners' house which has a family atmosphere. Meals include farm produce and are served in a vast dining room with fireplace and TV, whilst lovely breakfasts with pastries and home-made jams are taken on the terrace in summer. Guests can relax in the shade of the chestnut tree or wander on the nearby way-marked paths.

Prices s fr €40; d fr €51; t fr €63; extra person fr €11; dinner fr €20
Nearby ⚐ 5km ⚑ 2km ⓘ2km � 6km **Notes** No pets

BOUVESSE-QUIRIEU

❄ |◎| La Reine des Prés

Hoai-linh et Laurent LEFEBURE
Enieu, 38390 BOUVESSE QUIRIEU
☎ 06 67 33 91 79
email: lareinedespres@laposte.net
web: www.lareinedespres.com

A 19th-century maison bourgeoise with charming flower garden opposite the Cliffs of Bugey. Four rooms for two or three people and a two-roomed suite for five, all en suite. Lounge with open fire, library, video recorder, television and large cosy dining room. Near the Blue Valley, Morestel, Crémieu, Walibi theme park.

Prices s fr €52-€62; d fr €58-€70; t fr €80-€100; extra person fr €10; dinner fr €25 **On Site** ✿ Private ⚑ **Nearby** ⚐ 1km Restaurant 2km ⓘ2km ⋈25km **Notes** No pets English spoken

CHAPAREILLAN

❄ Les Tilleuls

M et D OMNES GUITTON
Av de Grenoble, 38530 CHAPAREILLAN
☎ 04 76 45 24 89
email: contact@tilleuls38.com
web: www.tilleuls38.com

A large house near vineyards and ski stations, decorated in patchwork with three lovely, fully equipped, en suite rooms. Tasty breakfasts with patisserie and home made jams. There is a music room, billiard room and large dayroom. The garden has flowers, trees and an aviary. Secure parking.

Prices s fr €39-€45; d fr €48-€57; t fr €71 **Nearby** ⚐ 3km ⚑ 5km ✦ 15km ⓘ0.4km ⋈ 5km **Notes** No pets English spoken

CHARNECLES

❄ *Ferme du Bois Vert*

Jean-Louis et Eugénie ROSSET
38140 CHARNECLES
☎ 04 76 65 26 46 ▤ 04 76 65 28 68
email: fermeboisvert@infonie.fr

Old farm buildings entirely renovated, near the home of the proprietors. Three lovely en suite bedrooms sleeping two, dining room and sitting room with open fire. Breakfast is taken in the dining room or on the terrace under the shade of the lime tree. Enjoy the farm produce - fruits, juices and home-made preserves.

Prices not confirmed for 2008 **Nearby** ⚐ 3km ⚑ 3km ⓘ0.5km ⋈ 3km **Notes** No pets English spoken CC

CHASSE-SUR-RHONE

❄ |◎| Domaine de Gorneton

Jacqueline et Jean FLEITOU
712 Chemin de Violans, 38670 CHASSE SUR RHONE
☎ 04 72 24 19 15 ▤ 04 78 07 93 62
email: gorneton@wanadoo.fr
web: www.gorneton.com

Close to Lyon, Vienne, the Parc Régional du Pilat and the Côtes Rôties vineyard, this 17th-century fortified house has gardens, a lake, fountains and enclosed courtyard. En suite accommodation includes one apartment sleeping four; two double rooms and a suite for two people. Generous family fare served at the dinner table. Swimming pool and tennis.

Prices s fr €100; d €100-€160; extra person fr €30; dinner fr €40 **On Site** ⚐ ♨ Restaurant ✿ Private ⚑ Private tennis court **Nearby** ⚐ 2km ⓘ1.5km ⋈ 2.5km **Notes** No pets English spoken *see advert on page 820*

CHICHILIANNE

❄ |◎| Ruthières

Jean-Luc SAUZE
38930 CHICHILIANNE
☎ 04 76 34 45 98 & 04 76 34 42 20 ▤ 04 76 34 45 98
email: fsauze@gmail.com
web: www.fermederuthieres.com

Traditional farmer's house in a small hamlet. Four guest rooms and two gîtes in an adjoining building. The en suite rooms are large, with English country furniture and a lounge area, and accommodate two to four people. Breakfast and dinner, by reservation, are served in the old vaulted sheep building, where local painters exhibit their watercolours. Large fireplace; board games; bookshelves; small terrace.

Prices s fr €38; d fr €47; t fr €60; extra person fr €15; dinner fr €15 **Nearby** ♨ 2.5km ⚐ 0.2km ⚑ 4km Restaurant 2km ✦ 25km ⓘ7km ⋈ 3km **Notes** Pets admitted

Domaine de Gorneton

Prop: J et J Fleitou

712 Chemin de Violans
38670 Chasse sur Rhone
Tel: 04 72 24 19 15 Fax: 04 78 07 93 62

*at the intersection of A7/A46/A47 towards St
Etienne exit Chasse to 'Centre Commercial' under
railway bridge, then left and right towards
Trembas, 2 km on right. Forest area.*

3 en-suite (bth/shr) (1 fmly), full central heating,
open and covered parking available. Outdoor
swimming pool, tennis, fishing, boule, table tennis
all in a 5 hectares park. English & Spanish spoken.
Travellers cheques accepted.

CHIRENS

ⅲ ⎸Ⓞ⎹ La Maison de Joanny

B et C MICOUD TERREAUD

1490 Route de la Guilletière, 38850 CHIRENS

☎ 04 76 91 04 67 & 06 70 06 23 34

email: c.b.mt@wanadoo.fr

web: www.maison-de-joanny.com

A converted barn, adjacent to the owners' home, about half an hour
from Grenoble and Chambéry. There are four spacious rooms, two
doubles and two triples, all with internet access, private shower and
WC. A full range of baby equipment is available. Grounds with pond,
parking space and stunning views. Meals available if pre-booked.

Prices s fr €55; d fr €70; t fr €85; extra person fr €15; dinner fr €23
Nearby ♿ 5km ♨ 20km ⚑ 4km ⚘ 8km Restaurant 5km ⚓ 35km
🏊 3km ♟ 5km ♟ 2km ⚓ 8km **Notes** No pets English spoken CC

COLOMBE

ⅲ ⎸Ⓞ⎹ La Ferme du Futeau

Brigitte et J-Pierre BILLON

1345 Montée du Futeau, 38690 COLOMBE

☎ 04 76 55 92 45 & 06 87 23 15 25 ▤ 04 76 06 51 44

email: billon-jp.b@wanadoo.fr

web: www.lafermedufuteau.com

Take your meals - prepared with local produce - either in the bright
dining room or under the shade of the lime tree in this sheltered

environment. Three charming rooms on the first floor of the house,
each with a private shower or bath room and WC.

Prices s fr €40; d fr €60; t fr €75; extra person fr €15; dinner fr €20
Nearby ⚑ 8km ⚘ 10km ⚓ 45km ♟ 3km ⚓ 4km **Notes** No pets CC

CORBELIN

ⅲ ♥ ⎸Ⓞ⎹ La Bardelière

N et M MARTIN CORDIER

38630 CORBELIN

☎ 04 74 88 96 70 & 06 82 11 21 56 ▤ 04 74 88 96 70

email: bardeliere@akeonet.com

web: http://la-bardeliere.com

This converted barn, two kilometres from the N75, stands close to
the owners' house on a working farm. There are three pretty first
floor bedrooms, all for two or three people. Each room has en
suite facilities, and a small balcony. Breakfasts (and other meals by
arrangement) are served by the fire or in the garden. Farm produce
for sale.

Prices s fr €41; d fr €52; t fr €67; extra person fr €18; dinner fr €21
On Site Restaurant **Nearby** ♿ 5km ⚑ 5km ♟ 2km ⚓ 12km
Notes Pets admitted

ⅲ ⎸Ⓞ⎹ La Paumanelle

Corinne et Rémi CHAVANON

Route du Saint-Martin, 38630 CORBELIN

☎ 04 74 83 77 72 ▤ 04 74 83 00 37

email: lapaumanelle@lapaumanelle.com

web: www.lapaumanelle.com

This tastefully converted old barn has a panoramic view of the Alps. It
has three spacious ground floor rooms, with French windows opening
to the swimming pool. Each room sleeps two or three people, and
has a private shower room and WC. Meals are served in a convivial
atmosphere, around the table in an old weaving shop.

Prices s fr €45; d fr €55; t fr €70; extra person fr €15; dinner fr €19
On Site Private ⚘ **Nearby** ♿ 4km ⚑ 2km ⚑ 8km Restaurant 4km
🏊 2km ♞ 5km ♟ 2km ⚓ 10km **Notes** No pets English spoken

GRESSE-EN-VERCORS

ⅲ ⎸Ⓞ⎹ La Chicholière

Janick et Gérard MOUTTET

L'Eglise, 38650 GRESSE EN VERCORS

☎ 04 76 34 33 70 ▤ 04 76 34 33 70

In the heart of the old village, a restored farmhouse with a small
mountain shelter and view of the Little Dolomites. Five en suite rooms
for two, three or four guests, dining room with open fire and reading
corner. Sample home-made bread and preserves and the vegetables
from the garden.

Prices s fr €40; d fr €50; t fr €66; extra person fr €16; dinner fr €20
On Site ⚑ Restaurant **Nearby** ⚘ 1km ⚓ 1km ♞ 1.5km ⚓ 13km
Notes No pets CC

⊞ |◎| La Grange aux Loups

Annie MANCHE

La Bâtie, 38650 GRESSE EN VERCORS

☎ 04 76 34 11 08 ▤ 04 76 34 11 08

email: la-grangeauxloups@wanadoo.fr

Completely renovated 18th-century farmhouse at the foot of Mont Aiguille, containing three pretty en suite guest rooms for two or three people in an annexe on the house. Huge living room with an old restored bread oven, library on the flora and fauna of Vercors and tempting tea room.

Prices s fr €38; d fr €49; t fr €61; extra person fr €12; dinner fr €20
On Site ⚘ ⌖ ╱ **Nearby** ⌁ 5km Restaurant 5km ⚓ 8km ⌓ 5km
⚑ 5km ▣ 5km ⋙ 15km **Notes** No pets English spoken Open February to October. CC

HERBEYS

⊞ |◎| La Grange

Anne-Marie TRAMARD

Le Noyaret, Chemin de la Magnanerie, 38320 HERBEYS

☎ 06 71 20 60 42 & 04 76 73 67 95 ▤ 04 76 68 03 79

email: claude.tramard@wanadoo.fr

web: www.lagrange-herbeys.fr

A house with lots of character, standing at the top of the village in extensive grounds with trees, flowers, and mountain views. There are two double rooms, and a suite consisting of a twin-bedded room and a children's room with two stowaway beds. Terrace, swimming pool, secure parking, meals by arrangement.

Prices s €50-€60; d €60-€70; extra person fr €21; dinner fr €20
On Site Private ⌁ **Nearby** ⚓ 20km ▣ 2km ⋙ 6km **Notes** No pets Open May to September.

LA FERRIERE

⊞ |◎| Auberge Nemoz

Francoise et Bertrand JOLAIS

Hameau La Martinette, 38580 LA FERRIERE

☎ 04 76 45 03 10 ▤ 04 76 45 03 10

email: aubergenemoz@wanadoo.fr

web: www.auberge.nemoz.com

This authentic chalet standing on the edge of the forest, is a good place to be at any time of the year. It has five beautiful and distinctive bedrooms, each with independent access and en suite bathrooms. Breakfasts and other meals are served in the country inn, on the ground floor, with its mountain atmosphere!

Prices s €58-€73; d €72-€86; extra person fr €26; dinner fr €26
On Site ⚘ ╱ **Nearby** Restaurant 2km ⚓ 5km ⌓ 3km ⚑ 17km
▣ 17km ⋙ 50km **Notes** No pets English spoken Open December to 20 March & 25 March to October. CC

LA MOTTE-D'AVEILLANS

⊞ Les Signaraux

Catherine MARTINASSO

38770 LA MOTTE-D'AVEILLANS

☎ 04 76 30 79 71 & 06 81 60 70 80 ▤ 04 76 30 66 01

email: b.martinasso@wanadoo.fr

web: www.gite-chambre-signaraux.fr

A peaceful place, with one guest room in the owners' home and two more in a separate building. The rooms combine modern comforts with the traditional style of décor you might expect to find in this mountain region. Horses graze in the meadows, and there is plenty of scope for walking and mountain biking in the forest.

Prices s fr €41; d fr €51; t fr €55; extra person fr €15 **Nearby** ⚘ 7km
⌁ 30km ╱ 5km ⌓ 5km Restaurant 6km ⚓ 32km ⌓ 5km Spa 20km
⚑ 5km ▣ 5km ⋙ 40km **Notes** No pets English spoken

LAVAL

⊞ Le Tresminet

Severine et Jean RAFFIN

Vaugelas, 38190 LAVAL

☎ 04 76 71 30 35 & 06 75 05 72 99 ▤ 04 76 71 30 35

A house in a small hamlet, with views towards the mountain peaks of the Massif de Belledonne. There are two double rooms on the ground floor, and two more, each with a split-level layout, on the first floor. All have private shower room and WC.

Prices s fr €47; d €57-€67; t fr €82; extra person fr €15 **On Site** ╱
Nearby ⌁ 11km Restaurant 3km ⚓ 12km ⚑ 11km ▣ 4km ⋙ 11km
Notes No pets English spoken CC

LE GUA

⊞ |◎| Le Jonier

Isabelle GOUDIN

Route de Miribel, St Barthélémy, 38450 LE GUA

☎ 04 76 13 43 99 & 06 71 56 06 99 ▤ 04 76 13 43 99

email: lejonier@wanadoo.fr

web: www.lejonier.com

This house is in the Parc Naturel du Vercors, about 20 minutes from Grenoble. Four upstairs bedrooms each sleep two or three people, all with private bath or shower room and WC. Baby equipment is available. Wonderful views from the garden, which has a stream running through it. Good area for walking and mountain-biking. Meals by arrangement.

Prices s fr €46; d fr €53; t fr €68; extra person fr €15; dinner fr €18
On Site Restaurant **Nearby** ⚘ 5km ╱ 4km ⚓ 7km ⌓ 8km
⋙ 8km **Notes** No pets English spoken CC

LE PERCY

▦ ⦿ Les Volets Bleus

Cathy et Thierry FUMAT
Hameau des Blancs, 38930 LE PERCY
☎ 04 76 34 43 07 & 06 07 75 77 05
email: info@lesvoletsbleus-isere.com
web: www.lesvoletsbleus-isere.com

A restored 18th-century farmhouse on the tracks of Giono in the Alps with a hint of Provence in the air. Three en suite bedrooms with very individual décor and separate access. Dinner is taken in the large vaulted dining room which opens on to the garden and includes regional dishes from Trieves, the Midi or further afield, all prepared with local produce. Reduced rates after the second day.

Prices s fr €45; d fr €54; t fr €66; extra person fr €15; dinner fr €20 **Nearby** ⛷ 5km ⚲ 2km ⚓ 12km Restaurant 1.5km ⚑ 20km ⚑ 10km ⚑ 4.5km ⚐ 4.5km **Notes** No pets English spoken Open Easter to October.

LE SAPPEY-EN-CHARTREUSE

▦ ⦿ Gîte du Chant de l'Eau

Colette et Bruno CHARLES
Mollard Giroud, 38700 LE SAPPEY-EN-CHARTREUSE
☎ 04 76 88 83 16 & 04 76 88 88 17   ⧉ 04 76 88 83 16
email: gite-chant-de-leau@wanadoo.fr
web: http://gitechantdeleau.free.fr

An old barn of character on the edge of the village facing the forest, adjoining the house of the owners. There are five en suite rooms for two, three or four guests and a large cosy living room with open fire. Friendly proprietors introduce guests to the flora and fauna here in the Parc Naturel Régional de Chartreuse.

Prices s fr €41; d fr €50; t fr €62; extra person fr €12; dinner fr €20 **Nearby** ⚲ 0.5km Restaurant 0.1km ⚑ 0.2km ⚑ 0.2km ⚑ 0.5km ⚐ 12km **Notes** No pets English spoken

LE TOUVET

▦ ⦿ La Ferme de Jeanne

Jocelyne et Jean Paul JACQUIER
104 rue de la Charrière, 38660 LE TOUVET
☎ 04 76 97 38 13   ⧉ 04 76 97 38 13
email: ferme.de.jeanne@wanadoo.fr
web: www.fermedejeanne.fr

There are five beautiful guest rooms, including two family suites for up to four people, in this 18th-century farmhouse. All of the rooms have private bathrooms and WCs. Meals are available by arrangement, with traditional regional dishes. Garden with garden furniture; enclosed parking.

Prices s €49-€57; d €63-€75; t fr €100; extra person fr €15; dinner fr €25 **Nearby** ⛷ 2km ⚲ 2km ⚓ 3km Restaurant 0.5km ⚑ 7km ⚑ 1km ⚑ 0.2km ⚐ 3km **Notes** No pets English spoken

LES COTES-DE-CORPS

▦ ❦ ⦿ ♿ Au Fil des Saisons

D et D OLLIER FLAMBARD
Le Cros, 38970 LES COTES-DE-CORPS
☎ 04 76 30 07 01 & 06 72 21 33 68   ⧉ 04 76 30 07 01
email: aufildessaisons@aol.com
web: www.chambresdhotes-afs.com

A working farm producing honey, organic ewes' milk cheese, and bread. There are five beautiful bedrooms, doubles and twin-bedded, all with private shower room and WC. Breakfast and other meals can be enjoyed in the dining room by the fire, or outside on the terrace where the wonderful view matches the food. Closed one week Xmas.

Prices s fr €41; d fr €50; extra person fr €17; dinner fr €17 **On Site** ⚑ **Nearby** ⚲ 1km ⚓ 5km Restaurant 2km ⚑ 20km ⚑ 2km ⚑ 2km ⚐ 35km **Notes** No pets

MARCOLLIN

▦ ⦿ Le Clos des Collières

Pascale et Christophe BARGE
717 Route de Viriville, 38270 MARCOLLIN
☎ 04 74 56 74 38   ⧉ 04 74 79 17 55
email: leclosdescollieres@orange.fr
web: http://clos.des.collieres.free.fr/

This old flint farmhouse has four first-floor bedrooms, all with themed decorations relating to a region of the world. Extensive grounds with trees and flowers; swimming pool. Meals, including both regional and traditional specialities are available, by arrangement.

Prices s fr €40; d fr €50; t fr €65; extra person fr €10; dinner fr €18 **On Site** Private ⚓ **Nearby** ⛷ 4km ⚲ 5km ⚑ 5km ⚐ 30km **Notes** No pets English spoken

MAUBEC

▦ Château de Césarges

C et P DELAIR -POPINEAU
38300 MAUBEC
☎ 04 37 03 08 22   ⧉ 04 37 03 08 22
email: contact@chateau-cesarges.com
web: www.chateau-cesarges.com

In the middle of parkland, the charming Château de Césarges offers three lovely en suite bedrooms for two or three people looking over the park. Breakfast is served in the dining room by the open fire, or outside in the shade of the 400-year-old lime tree. Drawing room with piano; many restaurants and inns nearby.

Prices s fr €60; d fr €70; t fr €88; extra person fr €18 **Nearby** ⚑ 3km ⚑ 10km ⚲ 8km ⚓ 6km Restaurant 3km ⚑ 3km ⚑ 6km ⚐ 6km **Notes** No pets English spoken Open April to November.

MEYLAN

ⅷ Le Mas du Bruchet

A-M et M FERGUSON

Chemin du Bruchet, 38240 MEYLAN

☎ 04 76 90 18 30 & 06 31 18 58 46 ▤ 04 76 41 92 36

email: amferguson38@aol.com

Just 15 minutes from Grenoble, this place is a calm oasis on a wine-growing estate. Four attractive rooms, all with internet access and modern comforts, have been created in a converted barn. Two of the rooms are split-level, and all have wonderful Alpine views. Breakfasts are served in the bright lounge, with its enormous bay window. Wine tastings available.

Prices s €55-€60; d €60-€65; t fr €88; extra person fr €18
Nearby ⛷ 10km ↣ 1km Restaurant 1km ⚓ 32km 🏛 1km ⛰ 15km
Notes No pets English spoken CC

MOIRANS

ⅷ ⅺ La Pastorale

Bruna et Marcel MUZET

1235 Rue Louis Dellorenzi, 38430 MOIRANS

☎ 04 76 35 33 19 & 06 07 16 17 70 ▤ 04 76 35 33 19

email: lapastorale-38@wanadoo.fr

This is a converted former sheepfold, close to the owners' house and with easy access to two regional parks. It has four first floor bedrooms, one with external access and a little balcony. All have en suite bathrooms. Large lounge. Very generous breakfasts!

Prices s fr €42; d fr €55; extra person fr €17; dinner fr €20
Nearby 🎣 1km ↣ 2km 🏛 2km ⛰ 4km **Notes** No pets English spoken

MORESTEL

ⅷ Chambre d'hôtes de Franciscaines

Odile CHOLAT

205 rue Ravier, 38510 MORESTEL

☎ 04 74 80 56 82 ▤ 04 74 80 04 28

email: franciscainesmorestel@wanadoo.fr

In the historic centre of Morestel, this ancient building is today occupied by the Franciscan sisters. Their four bright and comfortable rooms offer an exceptional place to stay, with a wonderful feeling of serenity. There are two doubles, a triple, and a room for four, all with private facilities. Breakfasts include home-made and local produce. Guests' lounge/library; parking.

Prices s fr €42; d fr €52; t fr €68; extra person fr €16 **Nearby** ⛷ 5km ⛴ 15km 🎣 5km ↣ 0.5km Restaurant 0.2km ⚓ 0.5km 🏛 0.3km ⛰ 17km
Notes Pets admitted English spoken

NANTES-EN-RATIER

ⅷ ⅺ La Voute de Séraphin

Fabienne et Marcel BARD

Serbouvet, 38350 NANTES EN RATIER

☎ 04 76 81 21 46 ▤ 04 76 81 21 46

email: marcel-et-fabienne.bard@wanadoo.fr

web: http://lavoute38.free.fr

A restored family farmhouse, set back from the road near a working farm offering three sunny en suite rooms for two/three. Small sitting area and enormous vaulted dining room in which you can try the dishes of the region - murçon, squash pie, prune tart. Near the Route Napoléon, the Lacs de Laffrey and Notre Dame de la Salette.

Prices s fr €45; d fr €50; t fr €65; extra person fr €15; dinner fr €18
On Site Restaurant **Nearby** 🎣 8km ↣ 3km ⚓ 22km 🚣 3km 🏛 3km ⛰ 36km **Notes** No pets English spoken

PONT-EVEQUE

ⅷⅷ ⅺ Au Manoir des Forges

Danielle et Michel PLAS

22 rue Francisque Cartallier, 38780 PONT EVEQUE

☎ 04 74 16 05 68 & 06 71 87 33 97

email: manoirdesforges@wanadoo.fr

web: www.manoirdesforges.com

A 19th-century building beautifully restored and decorated surrounded by ancient trees in the heart of a World Heritage site. The five large rooms are light and airy with views of the park. Tennis and lake; evening meals can be booked.

Prices s €70-€99; d €90-€113; extra person fr €30; dinner fr €28
On Site Private tennis court **Nearby** ⛷ 5km ⚡ 20km 🎣 0.5km ↣ 5km Restaurant 0.5km 🏛 0.3km ⛰ 4km **Notes** Pets admitted English spoken CC

PRESLES

ⅷ ⅺ Les Fauries

Carmen WINTZENRIETH

38680 PRESLES

☎ 04 76 36 10 50 ▤ 04 76 36 10 50

Quiet old farmhouse with exposed stonework and panoramic views over the Plateau de Vercors. Four en suite bright and comfortable rooms for two/three people looking onto the countryside. Enjoy breakfast in the shade of the lime tree and a family dinner, with natural and varied ingredients. On the edge of the Forest of the Coulmes, Parc Régional Naturel du Vercors and 70km of pistes.

Prices s fr €33; d fr €46; t fr €60; extra person fr €14; dinner fr €17
Nearby 🎣 10km ↣ 18km ⚓ 35km 🎿 11km 🏛 11km ⛰ 18km
Notes No pets Open October to 12 November & 27 January to September.

REVENTIN-VAUGRIS

⬛⬛⬛ ⓘ◎ & Un Soir en Provence

Gabrielleet Christian MALIGOT
238 rue des Ecoles, 38121 REVENTIN-VAUGRIS
☎ 04 37 02 07 81 & 06 10 99 13 90 📄 04 74 78 21 29
email: gmaligot@wanadoo.fr
web: http://unsoirenprovence.com

This tastefully renovated Provençal farmhouse has five spacious guest bedrooms, all with shower or bathroom and private WC. Breakfast and evening meals are served in the dining room by the fireplace, in the garden or by the pool depending on the season. Archaeological sites, Vienne jazz festival and vineyards nearby.

Prices s €70-€90; d €90-€120; t fr €140; extra person fr €20; dinner fr €30 **On Site** Private ↘ **Nearby** ⛷ 10km ⚞ 20km ⌖ 20km Restaurant 0.2km 🏊 1km 🏡 4km ⛰ 8km **Notes** No pets English spoken CC

SICCIEU

⬛⬛⬛ ⓘ◎ Soleil et Cacao

Nadine DE BLOCK
Hameau St Julien, St Julien, 38460 SICCIEU
☎ 04 74 83 68 01 & 06 32 15 65 50 📄 04 74 90 75 65
email: nadine@soleiletcacao.fr
web: www.soleiletcacao.fr

This old farmhouse, stone-built with exposed beams, has been completely restored. It has five spacious and elegantly decorated bedrooms, two of them family rooms for four, all with private shower rooms/WCs. Breakfasts, and other meals by arrangement, can be served in the cosy lounge or outside on the terrace, with its view of the Château de St-Julien.

Prices s fr €43; d fr €53; t fr €68; extra person fr €15; dinner fr €19 **Nearby** ⚞ 10km ⌖ 1.5km ↘ 10km Restaurant 3.5km 🏊 4km 🎿 4km 🏡 4km ⛰ 20km **Notes** No pets English spoken

ST-ANTOINE-L'ABBAYE

⬛⬛⬛ ⓘ◎ Chambre d'hôtes

Catherine BRUAS
Rue Corsière, 38160 ST-ANTOINE-L'ABBAYE
☎ 04 76 36 41 53 📄 04 76 36 41 53
email: catherine@bruas.org

A charming house in the middle of the medieval village of St Antoine, featuring a large lounge with a stove and hearth. There are three

double rooms, a room for three and a large room for four people; each has private washroom and WC. Local artisans and the St Marcellin cheese museum are some of the attractions nearby.

Prices s fr €37; d fr €43; t fr €59; extra person fr €16; dinner fr €16 **Nearby** ⌖ 2km ↘ 10km Restaurant 0.2km 🏊 0.2km 🏡 10km ⛰ 10km **Notes** No pets English spoken

⬛⬛⬛ ⓘ◎ Les Voureys

M.Thérèse et Henri PHILIBERT
38160 ST-ANTOINE-L'ABBAYE
☎ 04 76 36 41 65
email: voureyhote@aol.com
web: http://chambrehote.site.voila.fr

This small farmhouse, typical of the Pays Antonin, has three lovely en suite country-style bedrooms with every modern comfort. Lavish and varied breakfasts are served in the enormous cosy kitchen. Lounge for guests; shady grounds with garden furniture. Nearby railway garden at Chatte and cheese museum at St Marcellin.

Prices s fr €37; d fr €43; t fr €59; extra person fr €16; dinner fr €17 **Nearby** ⌖ 1km ↘ 5km Restaurant 2km ⚞ 30km 🏊 2km 🎿 4km 🏡 2.5km ⛰ 10km **Notes** Pets admitted

ST-APPOLINARD

⬛⬛⬛ ⓘ◎ La Combe de Mouze

Monique et Henri PAIN
38160 ST-APPOLINARD
☎ 04 76 64 10 52

Farmhouse with four cheerful double en suite rooms with views over the slopes of the Pays Antonin and the mountains of Vercors. There is also an annexed en suite four-person duplex, with lounge, open fire and kitchenette, perfect for a family holiday. Dine on farm produce outside or in the huge country-style dining room in front of the fire. Warm atmosphere, terrace and shady flower garden.

Prices s fr €38; d fr €44; extra person fr €20; dinner fr €16 **Nearby** ⌖ 8km ↘ 10km ⚞ 20km 🏡 9km ⛰ 10km **Notes** Pets admitted Open 15 January to 15 December.

ST-AREY

⬛⬛⬛ ⓘ◎ Le Pellenfrey

Framboise et J-Pierre ANALORO
38350 ST-AREY
☎ 04 76 81 17 01 & 06 83 75 17 95 📄 04 76 81 17 01
email: lepellenfrey@online.fr
web: www.lepellenfrey.online.fr

In the heart of the hamlet of Pellenfrey, attractively furnished rooms available in this house include three rooms for two people and a triple, each with private facilities. There is a relaxing space with access to a library and a lounge with fireplace and TV. Cakes and home-made jams are served outside in summer and guests can enjoy the tranquillity, or for the more active there is the Monteynard Lake and walks.

Prices s fr €46; d €50-€65; t fr €70; extra person fr €20; dinner fr €20 **Nearby** ⌖ 2km ↘ 0.5km ⚞ 30km 🏡 7km ⛰ 46km **Notes** No pets Open December to October. CC

ST-BAUDILLE-DE-LA-TOUR

♯♯♯ ⏣ Les Basses Portes

M et V GIROUD DUCAROY

Torjonas, 38118 ST-BAUDILLE-DE-LA-TOUR

☎ 04 74 95 18 23

email: mirvinc@wanadoo.fr

web: www.basses-portes.com

Full of character and restored with care, this house is set in a rural and relaxing spot and has three cheerful en suite rooms with individual décor (one twin, one double and one sleeping three). Sitting room with open fire; enormous living room/kitchen with exposed beams. Flowery and shaded grounds. Close by: Crémieu, archaeological sites, caves at La Balme, mountain biking, caravan routes, climbing.

Prices s fr €42; d €53-€55; t fr €68; extra person €14-€15; dinner fr €19 **On Site** Private ⚲ **Nearby** ⛷ 15km ⚓ 20km ⌖ 10km Restaurant 5km ⚄ 15km ⛬ 10km **Notes** Pets admitted English spoken Open 15 January to 15 November. CC

ST-BONNET-DE-CHAVAGNE

♯♯♯ ⏣ La Boisiere

J-Jacques et Lisbeth FRENKEL

Les Daruds, 38840 ST-BONNET-DE-CHAVAGNE

☎ 04 76 36 40 13

email: laboisiere@free.fr

web: http://laboisiere.free.fr

A contemporary wooden house in a pastoral setting with three carefully decorated rooms. Each room has a shower and toilet and private balcony. Meals are served in a large, airy room or on the terrace and consist of fresh baked bread, cakes and home produce.

Prices s fr €53; d fr €59; extra person fr €14; dinner fr €22 **On Site** ⛷ ⌖ Private ⚲ **Nearby** ⚄ 10km ⛬ 6km ⋈ 8km **Notes** No pets English spoken

♯♯♯ ⛭ Le Mas du Vernay

Isabelle et Pascal GENEREUX

Les Terras, 38840 ST-BONNET-DE-CHAVAGNE

☎ 04 76 38 07 87 & 06 76 21 06 13 🗎 04 76 38 07 87

email: contact@masduvernay.com

web: http://masduvernay.com

Peacefully situated at the foot of the Vercors Massif, this fully restored flint-built farmhouse has five beautiful bedrooms, sleeping from two

to four people, all with private showers/WCs. There is a lounge with exposed beams, and a guests' kitchenette. In the summer, you can enjoy your breakfast outside in the shade of the lime tree.

Prices s fr €50; d €60-€64; t fr €75; extra person fr €15 **On Site** Private ⚲ **Nearby** ⚓ 8km ⚓ 30km ⌖ 4km Restaurant 5km ⚄ 40km ⛬ 6km ⛬ 5km ⋈ 12km **Notes** No pets English spoken

ST-CHRISTOPHE-EN-OISANS

♯♯♯ ⏣ Le Champ de Pin

Christiane AMEVET

La Bérarde, 38520 ST-CHRISTOPHE-EN-OISANS

☎ 04 76 79 24 20 🗎 04 76 79 54 09

email: champdepin@free.fr

web: www.lechampdepin.com

Home to the great mountain guide families of Oisans, this huge chalet enjoys a remarkable alpine location. Four lovely en suite rooms with separate access, terrace, holiday gîte adjacent (accommodates 16). Meals served in the Auberge, a room reserved for guests. Parc des Ecrins nearby.

Prices d fr €53; dinner fr €18 **On Site** ⌖ Restaurant **Nearby** ⚲ 10km ⛬ 8km ⛬ 25km ⋈ 75km **Notes** Pets admitted English spoken Open 15 May to 15 September. CC

ST-HILAIRE-DE-BRENS

♯♯♯ ⏣ Le Saint Hilaire

Andrée et Maurice COUPARD

38460 ST-HILAIRE-DE-BRENS

☎ 04 74 92 81 75 🗎 04 74 92 81 91

email: andree.coupard@wanadoo.fr

web: www.le-st-hilaire.com

Charming house in the middle of the village with small country grocery/café. A warm and attentive welcome is assured from your hosts who offer five lovely en suite rooms with separate access for two/three. Have breakfast in the sun in the enclosed garden, with swimming pool, play table tennis or visit local tourist sites.

Prices s fr €41; d fr €51; extra person fr €15; dinner fr €17 **On Site** Private ⚲ **Nearby** ⌖ 4km ⛬ 5km ⋈ 15km **Notes** No pets Open October to August. CC

ST-JUST-CHALEYSSIN

♦♦♦ La Tuilière

Valérie et Pascal DUCHENE
38540 ST-JUST-CHALEYSSIN
☎ 04 78 96 32 82 & 06 19 88 95 08 📄 04 72 70 31 68
email: ch.hotes.latuiliere@orange.fr
web: www.latuiliere.fr

This 17th-century former tile works, lovingly restored by its owners and in a green rural setting near to Vienne, offers three superb double bedrooms adjacent to the owners' house, all with en suite facilities. Beautiful dining room with open fireplace, and a lounge on the first floor. Large terrace with open view across the countryside. Restaurants close by.

Prices s fr €54; d fr €67; t fr €87; extra person fr €20   **Nearby** ✈ 3km ↘ 5km 🏠 2km ⚓ 10km   **Notes** No pets English spoken

ST-LATTIER

♦♦♦ ❦ ⦿ ⅇ Montena des Collines

Geneviève et Patrick EFFANTIN
38840 ST-LATTIER
☎ 04 76 64 52 59 📄 04 76 64 34 27
email: effantin@montena-des-collines.com
web: www.montena-des-collines.com

A beautiful house in the depths of the countryside between Vercors and Drôme, with large gardens, leisure area and swimming pool. Three bright, comfortable en suite rooms, two rooms for two/three, and one two-roomed suite sleeping five. Sitting room, dining room, sheltered terrace for summer evening parties. Families and small groups welcome. The farm produces cereals, asparagus and nuts and also has animals.

Prices s fr €37; d €47-€52; t €63-€67; extra person fr €16; dinner fr €17 **On Site** Private ✈   **Nearby** ↘ 35km 🏠 3km ⚓ 15km   **Notes** Pets admitted English spoken Open September to June.

ST-MARTIN-DE-LA-CLUZE

♦♦♦♦ ⦿ Château de Paquier

Hélène et Jacques ROSSI
38650 ST-MARTIN-DE-LA-CLUZE
☎ 04 76 72 77 33 📄 04 76 72 77 33
email: hrossi@club-internet.fr
web: http://chateau.de.paquier.free.fr

Charming 16th-century castle with five beautiful guest bedrooms each with private bathroom. Dine with your hosts in the huge dining room on home produced bread, vegetables and fruit from the garden and relax in the shady park. Ponies and games for children, parking. Lac de Monteynard, small tourist train, hiking.

Prices s fr €56; d €66-€80; extra person fr €20; dinner fr €25 **Nearby** ⚐ 10km ⛷ 20km ✈ 8km ✈ 10km Restaurant 3km ⚓ 20km ⊙ 10km ✈ 10km 🏠 1km ⚓ 10km   **Notes** No pets English spoken CC

ST-MICHEL-LES-PORTES

♦♦♦ ⦿ Le Goutarou

J et A BOUVIER GUIHARD
Les Granges de Thoranne, 38650 ST-MICHEL-LES-PORTES
☎ 04 76 34 08 28 📄 04 76 34 13 16
email: aubergedugoutarou@yahoo.fr
web: www.mont-goutaroux.com

This country auberge, an 18th-century restored farm between Trièves and Vercors, has six en suite rooms sleeping three or four, with mezzanine and exposed beams. Breakfast and dinner including classic dishes are taken at the large table in an old vaulted room. Sitting room with open fire, flower-bedecked garden and terrace, parking, laundry. Babies welcome. Reduced rates for stays over two nights. Packed lunches available.

Prices s fr €46; d fr €58; t fr €78; extra person fr €20; dinner fr €20 **Nearby** ✈ 6km Restaurant 6km ⚓ 12km 🏠 6km ⚓ 6km   **Notes** Pets admitted English spoken Open 15 February to 15 December. CC

ST-ONDRAS

♦♦♦♦ ⦿ Le Pas de l'Ane

Josiane et Philippe ROBERGE
145 chemin de la Brocardière, 38490 ST-ONDRAS
☎ 04 76 32 01 78 📄 04 76 32 01 78
email: jroberge@wanadoo.fr
web: www.lepasdelane.com

A beautiful house close to the Château of Virieu with four beautiful bedrooms, all with en suite facilities. Each has a double bed and a living area with a sofa bed. Outside, trees provide shady places for sitting and the only background noise is the sound of a stream and birdsong. Meals are available (pre-booking needed) with local and vegetarian dishes.

Prices s fr €58; d fr €69; t fr €94; extra person fr €25; dinner fr €25 **Nearby** ⚐ 3km ⛷ 9km ⚐ 7km ✈ 4km Restaurant 2km ⚓ 40km ⊙ 1km 🏠 3km ⚓ 3km   **Notes** No pets English spoken CC

ST-PRIM

♦♦♦ ⦿ La Margotine

Lucie BOIDIN
Ch. de Pré Margot, 38370 ST-PRIM
☎ 04 74 56 44 27 📄 04 74 56 44 27
email: lamargotine@wanadoo.fr
web: www.chambredhotelamargotine.com

This very large modern house, in its rural setting, overlooks vineyards and the lake of Roches de Condrieu with its marina. It has six bedrooms, for two or three people, all with TV, air conditioning, private showers and WCs. Large conservatory, with open fire, where breakfasts are served, and other meals by arrangement. Billiards and board games. Enclosed parking.

Prices s fr €45; d fr €50; t fr €65; extra person fr €15; dinner fr €19 **Nearby** ⚐ 0.3km Restaurant 0.2km ⚓ 27km 🏠 1.2km ⚓ 1.2km **Notes** No pets

ST-VERAND

♯♯♯ *Le Clos de Foncemanen*

Martine et André SEVAZ

Les Rollands, 38160 ST-VERAND

☎ 04 76 38 19 94 & 06 60 05 25 83　📄 04 76 38 44 02

email: sevaz@wanadoo.fr

web: http://monsite.wanadoo.fr/foncemanen

A traditional old cob farm in large grounds, on the edge of the forest, that has been completely renovated. There are three rooms that sleep up to three with their own facilities. Guests have the use of a large dining room, mezzanine lounge, sheltered terrace, garden, orchard, paddock with horses.

Prices not confirmed for 2008　**On Site** Private ⌇　**Nearby** 🏌 2km
🏊40km ⛴5km ➤ 2km　**Notes** No pets　English spoken

VAUJANY

♯♯♯ ⭐ **Chalet La Maitreya**

A et P STEENHUIS HAMELYNCK

Le Perrier, 38114 VAUJANY

☎ 04 76 79 11 80 & 06 21 24 57 97　📄 04 76 79 11 80

email: lamaitreya@wanadoo.fr

web: www.lamaitreya.com

This chalet is owned by a talented couple: Anne is a pianist and singer; Pascal is a ski instructor. They have five twin-bedded rooms, four of them with balconies, and all with private shower rooms and WCs. There is a vast lounge with an open fireplace, a sauna, terraces with an open view. Meals are available, by arrangement.

Prices s fr €46; d fr €66; t fr €86; extra person fr €22; dinner fr €24
Nearby 🏌 4km ⛷ 1.5km 🏊 1km 🏛2.5km ➤ 50km　**Notes** Pets admitted　English spoken　Open 15 December to 15 April & 15 May to 15 September.　CC

♯♯♯ ⭐ ⭐ **Solneige**

Jan et Mirjam DEKKER

Pourchery, 38114 VAUJANY

☎ 04 76 79 88 18　📄 04 76 79 58 74

email: solneige@wanadoo.fr

web: www.solneige.com

This tastefully restored old farmhouse near the charming village of Vaujany is an ideal base for ski holidays or summer holidays in the Alps. Five charming en suite rooms for two or three guests, with balcony and outstanding views over the Vallée d'Eau d'Olle (two rooms are in a separate maisonette). Dinner and breakfasts are taken in the comfortable vaulted living room, or in the garden. Two six person gîtes available.

Prices s fr €55; d €69-€70; t fr €90; dinner fr €28　**On Site** Spa
Nearby ⛷10km ⛷40km 🏌 2.5km ⛷ 2.5km　Restaurant 2.5km
⛷2.5km 🏊4km 🎿8km 🏛2.5km ➤ 50km　**Notes** Pets admitted
English spoken　Open 16 December to 16 April & 20 May to 20 September.
CC

VERNIOZ

♯♯♯ **Bois Marquis**

Chantal FRECHET

105 Impasse du Bois Marquis, 38150 VERNIOZ

☎ 04 74 84 49 40

En suite guest rooms in a house adjoining the owners': one double, one room for two and a large room sleeping three. Living room with kitchenette, views of the countryside and shaded grounds with garden furniture.

Prices s fr €35; d fr €42; t fr €53; extra person fr €10　**Nearby** ⛷10km
🏌 3km ⛷ 15km　Restaurant 3km ⛷ 3km 🏛3km ➤ 15km
Notes No pets

VERTRIEU

♯♯♯ ⭐ *Le Relais du Bac*

Marie Dominique DEBAIL

38390 VERTRIEU

☎ 04 74 90 68 06　📄 04 74 90 68 06

email: relaisdubac@club-internet.fr

web: www.relaisdubac.com

This beautiful 18th-century house, just 40 kilometres from Lyon, is situated beside the Rhône, in a small village typical of the Isle Crémieu area. It has four magnificent rooms, which have been lovingly decorated and all have en suite bathrooms. Meals are available, by arrangement, served in the large dining room or the extensive wooded grounds.

Prices not confirmed for 2008　**On Site** 🏌 Private ⌇
Nearby ⛷42km 🏛4km ➤ 10km　**Notes** No pets　English spoken　CC

VIENNE

♯♯♯ **La Reclusière**

Monique et Philippe ROCHE

93 Montée Bon Accueil, 38200 VIENNE

☎ 04 74 85 04 76 & 06 08 16 82 30

email: info@lareclusiere.com

web: www.lareclusiere.com

A magnificent Vienne house built at the end of the 19th century with three first and second floor guest rooms, each with bathroom or shower room and private WC. Views over the gardens and terraces. Ideal for visiting Vienne or Lyon. Vienne has an old theatre, Roman temple and holds a jazz festival.

Prices s €120-€150; d €120-€150; t €120-€150　**Nearby** ⛷5km
🏌 0.5km ⛷ 2km　Restaurant 3km ⛷ 5km 🏛1km ➤ 3km
Notes No pets　English spoken

VILLARD-BONNOT

▦ ◎ Domaine du Berlioz

M-Thérèse et Robert ESSA
Rue du Berlioz, 38190 VILLARD BONNOT
☎ 04 76 71 40 00 📄 04 76 71 40 00
email: domaineduberlioz@wanadoo.fr
web: http://perso.wanadoo.fr/domaineduberlioz

A 12th-century manor set in country surroundings, just a quarter of an hour from Grenoble at the foot of the Belledonne chain. Choose from two beautiful en suite double rooms or one suite sleeping four. Dining room with vast fireplace, television lounge, video, library. Generous dinners, with specialities cooked in the bread oven.

Prices s fr €80; d fr €100; t fr €130; extra person fr €30; dinner fr €35 **On Site** ⚏ Private tennis court **Nearby** ⌀ 2km ⚲ 5km Restaurant 1km �‖ 10km ⬚ 2km ⋙ 2km **Notes** Pets admitted English spoken Open March to 1 November. CC

VILLARD-DE-LANS

▦ ◎ ⚹ La Croix du Liorin

Nicole BERTRAND
Bois Barbu, 38250 VILLARD DE LANS
☎ 04 76 95 82 67 📄 04 76 95 85 75
email: ch-hotes-bertrand@wanadoo.fr

At an altitude of 1235mtrs, the view of the mountains to the east and Vercors is exceptional. Look down onto the village of Corrençon. Cosy inside, there are three bedrooms to choose from. All are small and delightful, and have French windows opening at ground level. All have shower and wc. Share meals with the owners in a friendly atmosphere and relax in front of the big wood fire. Golf at Corrençon.

Prices s fr €43; d fr €46; dinner fr €15 **Nearby** ⚏ 3km ⚲ 3km ⌀ 2km ⚲ 5km Restaurant 1km ⚲ 3km ⬚ 2km ⚲ 2km ⬚ 5km ⋙ 35km **Notes** Pets admitted

▦ ◎ La Framboisine

Lionel et Brigitte MADARY
Bois Barbu, 38250 VILLARD DE LANS
☎ 04 76 95 14 33
email: la.framboisine@wanadoo.fr
web: www.villarddelans.com

A large, pretty, welcoming and contemporary house offering four triple rooms, including two at ground level, each with private

facilities. There is a large lounge with a balcony looking out over the forest. Traditional, regional cuisine is served in a lively, family setting. In summer, guests can play golf or tennis, or ride horses. In winter there is a wide range of activities available including alpine skiing.

Prices s fr €50; d fr €54; t fr €79; extra person fr €25; dinner fr €18 **Nearby** ⚏ 6km ⚲ 7km ⌀ 2km ⚲ 4km Restaurant 0.2km ⚲ 7km ⚲ 3km ⚲ 5km ⬚ 5km ⋙ 35km **Notes** No pets CC

▦ La Jasse

Michel IMBAUD
222 rue du Lycée Polonais, 38250 VILLARD DE LANS
☎ 04 76 95 91 63
email: imbaud.lajasse@wanadoo.fr
web: www.imbaud-lajasse.com

A modern house in the Parc du Vercors in the middle of a lively resort. Cosy rustic interior with three comfortable rooms: one duplex for three people; and two double rooms. Terrace, garden, parking and menus which change regularly.

Prices s fr €43; d fr €52; t fr €67 **Nearby** ⌀ 0.5km ⚲ 0.4km ⚲ 3km ⬚ 0.1km ⋙ 30km **Notes** No pets English spoken

▦ ◎ Le Val Sainte Marie

Dominique et Agnès BON
Bois Barbu, 38250 VILLARD DE LANS
☎ 04 76 95 92 80 📄 04 76 95 92 80
email: levalsaintemarie@orange.fr
web: http://levalsaintemarie.villard-de-lans.fr

In the heart of the Vercors, this traditional farmhouse has three comfortable en suite bedrooms and a friendly table with regional fare in a warm atmosphere. With garden, terrace, stove room, library.

Prices s fr €45; d fr €52; t fr €70; extra person fr €16; dinner fr €18 **On Site** Restaurant ⚹ **Nearby** ⚏ 5km ⚲ 4km ⌀ 1km ⚲ 4km ⚲ 7km ⚲ 3km ⬚ 4km ⋙ 35km **Notes** No pets English spoken

▦ ◎ Les 4 Vents

Jean-Paul UZEL
Bois Barbu, 38250 VILLARD DE LANS
☎ 04 76 95 10 68 📄 04 76 95 10 68

A Vercors farmhouse in a peaceful location, offering five en suite bedrooms, dining room with open fire and sitting room. Tuck into family food prepared using produce from the garden and local area. Breakfast features home-made preserves and Vercors honey. The nearby village provides plenty to do. Garage. Reduced rates available.

Prices d fr €50; extra person fr €15; dinner fr €16 **On Site** ⚹ Restaurant ⚹ **Nearby** ⌀ 3km ⚲ 3km ⚲ 7km ⬚ 6km ⋙ 30km **Notes** No pets English spoken CC

VILLEMOIRIEU

ⅲ 🍴 La Bicyclette Fleurie

Richard et Nathalie KOZIK
Moirieu, 38460 VILLEMOIRIEU
☎ 04 74 90 06 55
email: la-bicyclette-fleurie@club.fr

Just a couple of kilometres from the medieval city of Crémieu, this 19th-century vineyard building has four bedrooms, with their décor inspired by the owners' cycle trips around Europe and further afield. Vast lounge, opening on to the garden with its trees, flowers and children's games. Baby equipment available.

Prices s €60-€68; d €68-€78; t €83-€93; extra person fr €15; dinner fr €22 **Nearby** 🖉 3km ⚘ 18km 🗓 2.5km � 15km **Notes** No pets English spoken

VOREPPE

ⅢⅢ Château Saint-Vincent

Sylvia et Bruno LAFFOND
Chemin Saint Vincent, 38340 VOREPPE
☎ 04 76 50 67 87 📄 04 76 50 88 03
email: chateau.stvincent@wanadoo.fr
web: http://perso.wanadoo.fr/chateau.stvincent

This 16th-century castle combines charm and modernity and has a friendly atmosphere. The five bedrooms have period windows opening onto the park with its stately trees. Tasty breakfast's are served either on the terrace or beside the monumental fireplace at the family dining table. Perfect for exploring the town of Grenoble, with its blend of high-tech, art and history.

Prices s €95-€120; d €115-€155; extra person fr €42 **On Site** 🎾 Private ⚘ **Nearby** ⚘ 3km ⚘ 10km 🖉 4km Restaurant 5km ⚓ 29km 🗓 2km � 4km **Notes** No pets Open 3 January to July and September to 22 December. CC

LOIRE

AMBIERLE

ⅲ 🐓 La Ferme aux Abeilles

Yvette et Maurice PACAUD
Les Alliers, 42820 AMBIERLE
☎ 04 77 65 61 80 & 06 08 07 49 48 📄 04 77 65 61 80
web: http://perso.wanadoo.fr/lafermeauxabeilles/

In open countryside on the Côte Roannaise, this farmhouse has been totally restored and offers four rooms with en suite facilities. There is a guest lounge and a mezzanine for TV, games and reading. The proprietors will gladly share their passion for beekeeping and agriculture, and results of their efforts are on display at breakfast.

Prices d €42-€54; t fr €54 **Nearby** ⚘ 2km ⚘ 10km 🖉 5km ⚘ 10km Restaurant 2km 🗓 2km � 18km **Notes** Pets admitted

CHALAIN-LE-COMTAL

ⅲ 🐓 🍴 Chambre d'hôtes

Régine et J-François COTTIN
Beauplan, 42600 CHALAIN LE COMTAL
☎ 04 77 76 12 58 & 06 08 99 46 88

This restored farmhouse has four bedrooms, a double, a twin, and two triples, all with en suite bathrooms. Extra bed and cot available. Lounge and large terrace, half of which is enclosed and ideal for meals or resting in the shade! Breakfast and other meals make great use of produce from the farm, prepared using your hosts' own recipes.

Prices s fr €36; d fr €46; t fr €62; dinner fr €15 **Nearby** ⚘ 0.6km 🖉 6km ⚘ 10km ⚓ 0.5km ⚘ 10km 🗓 0.5km � 6km **Notes** No pets

CHAMBLES

ⅲ 🐓 🍴 La Grange aux Hirondelles

Christine et Pascal JOUSSERAND
Meyrieux, 42170 CHAMBLES
☎ 04 77 52 95 12 & 06 62 02 77 69
email: jousserand-pascal@wanadoo.fr
web: www.la-grange-aux-hirondelles.com

A barn conversion with five guest bedrooms. There are two doubles, a twin-bedded room, and two rooms for four, one with four single beds, the other with a double bed and two singles. All have private facilities. Enclosed grounds with a beautiful view; meals by arrangement.

Prices s fr €37; d fr €47-€49; t fr €65; extra person fr €15; dinner fr €16 **On Site** ⚘ Restaurant **Nearby** ⚘ 20km 🖉 5km ⚘ 12km ⚓ 5km 🗓 8km � 10km **Notes** No pets English spoken

COMMELLE-VERNAY

ⅢⅢ 🍴 Château de Bachelard

Daniéla et Hervé NOIRARD
42120 COMMELLE VERNAY
☎ 04 77 71 93 67 📄 04 77 78 10 20
email: dhnoirard@chateaubachelard.com
web: www.chateaubachelard.com

In parkland near a 6 hectare lake stands the 17th-century Château de Bachelard. Three double rooms and one suite with a double bed and four singles, each with private facilities and lounge area. Huge reception rooms; lounge with open fire; dining room looking over the swimming pool serving family cuisine with produce from the kitchen garden. Fishing; mallard shooting.

Prices s fr €92; d fr €98; t fr €118; extra person fr €20; dinner fr €23 **On Site** 🖉 🎾 Private ⚘ **Nearby** ⚘ 3km ⚘ 3km Restaurant 1km ⚓ 3km 🗓 2km � 1km **Notes** Pets admitted English spoken

EPERCIEUX-ST-PAUL

⦚⦚⦚ ⦿⦿ Les Barges

Pascale et Hervé GARDON

42110 EPERCIEUX SAINT PAUL

☎ 04 77 26 54 40

email: gardonpascale@wanadoo.fr

web: http://perso.orange.fr/la-vesne

Old restored farmhouse with four en suite guest rooms: one double room, two twin rooms and a room sleeping three. Private lounge, TV room and kitchen available for guest use. Grounds with lawn, boules, garden furniture under the shade of the lime tree, Loire (1km). At dinner enjoy regional recipes and family cuisine using home grown vegetables and preserves.

Prices s fr €34; d fr €41; t fr €53; extra person fr €12; dinner fr €15 **On Site** Restaurant ⚘ **Nearby** ⛵ 5km ⚓ 15km 🖉 1km ⚘ 5km ⚘ 5km 🏛 4km ⚕ 4km **Notes** No pets ⚬

FEURS

⦚⦚⦚ ⦿⦿ La Bussinière

Eliane et Daniel PERRIN

Route de Lyon, 42110 FEURS

☎ 04 77 27 06 36 & 06 88 32 37 15 📠 04 77 27 06 36

email: la-bussiniere@wanadoo.fr

web: www.labussiniere.com

Guests to this old restored farmhouse can choose between three double en suite guest rooms in an adjacent building. Breakfast and dinner served in the living room with sitting area, open fire.

Prices not confirmed for 2008 **On Site** ⚘ **Nearby** 🖉 4km ⚘ 4km ⚘ 4km 🏛 3km ⚕ 3km **Notes** Pets admitted

FOURNEAUX

⦚⦚⦚⦚ *Château de l'Aubépin*

Laure DE CHOISEUL

42470 FOURNEAUX

☎ 06 19 74 20 19 📠 04 77 62 48 40

email: lauredechoiseul@yahoo.fr

A 17th-century castle with impressive Italianate décor overlooking a garden designed by Le Nôtre. Three en suite rooms, guard room with monumental fireplace. The swimming pool is for guest use; also a private lake for fishing.

Prices not confirmed for 2008 **On Site** 🖉 Private ⚘ **Nearby** ⛵ 11km ⚘ 🏛 3km ⚕ 11km **Notes** No pets English spoken Open May to September.

GREZIEUX-LE-FROMENTAL

⦚⦚⦚ 🐓 ⦿⦿ Le Thevenon

Françoise et J-Marc FARJON

42600 GREZIEUX LE FROMENTAL

☎ 04 77 76 12 93

email: ffarjon@free.fr

web: www.chambre-hote-thevenon.info

Four guest rooms in a building adjacent to the proprietors' home. Two twin rooms and two doubles all en suite; folding bed also available. Sitting area; dining room (with TV); fully equipped kitchen with washing machine. Large grounds with outdoor furniture; tennis court; table tennis; volleyball; pétanque. Dinner (by reservation).

Prices s fr €33; d fr €41; extra person fr €14; dinner fr €15 **Nearby** ⛵ 4km ⚓ 5km 🖉 5km ⚘ 7km Restaurant 5km ⚘ 5km ⚘ 7km 🏛 5km ⚕ 5km **Notes** Pets admitted English spoken

LA GRESLE

⦚⦚⦚ ⦿⦿ Le Châlet

J-Bernard CHAPON

Les 4 Croix, 42460 LA GRESLE

☎ 04 74 64 47 27 & 06 08 56 60 88 📠 04 74 64 33 74

email: chaponjb@aol.com

In 2.5 hectare grounds, two double and two twin guest rooms with good views over the surrounding countryside, all with private washing facilities and wc. Gentle strolls in the parklands are perfect after gastronomic meals served on the terrace in the shade of century old cedars. Close to Beaujolais, Burgundy and the Auvergne.

Prices s fr €70; d fr €70; dinner fr €20 **Nearby** ⛵ 10km 🖉 2km ⚘ 5km ⚘ 0.3km ⚘ 5km 🏛 4km ⚕ 22km **Notes** Pets admitted English spoken

LA TERRASSE-SUR-DORLAY

⦚⦚⦚ ⦿⦿ Le Moulin Payre

Myriam et Pierre MARQUET

42740 LA TERRASSE-SUR-DORLAY

☎ 04 77 20 91 46

In the Parc Naturel du Pilat, this old family mansion has five en suite guest rooms, a shady park with swimming pool, private lake and river bank. Sitting room and meals by arrangement. Conveniently located between Lyon and St-Etienne, in the open countryside.

Prices s fr €40; d fr €63; extra person fr €13; dinner fr €20 **On Site** Private ⚘ **Nearby** ⛵ 3km ⚓ 25km 🖉 0.1km Restaurant 3km ⚘ 3km ⚘ 8km 🏛 3km ⚕ 6km **Notes** No pets Open 15 March to 15 October.

MAROLS

♯♯♯ ⊚ L'Ecusson

Josiane FRACHEY

42560 MAROLS

☎ 04 77 76 70 38 & 04 77 32 64 40

A building of character in the village centre, offering four individually styled en suite bedrooms: twin room; room sleeping four; twin with double beds; room sleeping three. Kitchen area; lounge; TV. Closed grounds with interior courtyard; garden furniture; parking. Close to Forez, Auvergne and Velay (on the Circuit des Babets). Evening meal (by reservation).

Prices s fr €37; d fr €49; t fr €65; extra person fr €16; dinner fr €17 **On Site** ⚓ **Nearby** ⚡ 5km ⚓ 15km ⚓ 19km Restaurant 4km ⚓ 4km ⚓ 9km ⚓ 0.2km ⚓ 19km **Notes** Pets admitted Open May to November.

♯♯♯ ⚐ L'Olme

A et P-M DUGAS-SAUSSE

42560 MAROLS

☎ 04 77 76 54 25 ▤ 04 77 76 58 66

email: pmdugas@wanadoo.fr

web: http://perso.wanadoo.fr/grange-au-pre/

Anaïs and Pierre-Marie will welcome you to their former farmhouse where a calm and restful stay is assured. The four bedrooms are equipped with private facilities and two have king-size beds. There is a large guest lounge with a hearth and library. Home-made bread and preserves are served at breakfast, and guests can make use of the south-facing terrace.

Prices s €38-€51; d €44-€57; t fr €72; extra person fr €15 **Nearby** ⚡ 3.5km ⚓ 20km ⚓ 4km ⚓ 9km ⚓ 0.3km ⚓ 20km **Notes** No pets English spoken Open Easter to 1 November & school holidays.

MONTAGNY

♯♯♯ ⊚ La Vache sur le Toit

Denise et Pascal CAUWE

42840 MONTAGNY

☎ 04 77 66 13 61

email: parcelly@free.fr

web: http://parcelly.free.fr

In the heart of the quiet countryside, this property offers five rooms in the owners' house and restored annexe. There are three rooms with en suite bathrooms: two doubles and a single, also two grade 1 rooms (a twin and a triple) with shared facilities. Lounge/library, garden. Meals prepared using local and home-made produce. Horse and trap rides.

Prices s €26-€46; d €32-€49; t €45-€64; dinner fr €15 **Nearby** ⚡ 9km ⚓ 22km ⚓ 8km Restaurant 3km ⚓ 6km ⚓ 15km ⚓ 3km ⚓ 10km **Notes** No pets English spoken

MONTBRISON

♯♯♯ ✿ ⊚ Le Bruchet

Hélène et Bernard COTTIER

42600 MONTBRISON

☎ 04 77 76 98 55 & 06 75 50 70 29 ▤ 04 77 76 98 55

A farmhouse now totally restored, two kilometres from the beautiful village of Montbrison. Five bedrooms all with private bath/shower room and WC; each also has a private terrace. Guests' lounge, with kitchenette. The host, who is a farmer, will delight in telling you all about the region to enable you to make the most of your stay.

Prices s fr €35; d fr €43; extra person fr €15; dinner fr €15 **On Site** ⚓ **Nearby** ⚡ 2km ⚓ 4km ⚓ 2km Restaurant 3km ⚓ 2km ⚓ 2km ⚓ 2km **Notes** No pets English spoken

MONTVERDUN

♯♯♯ Domaine de la Loge

D et J THIOLLIER

42130 MONTVERDUN

☎ 04 77 97 56 96 ▤ 04 77 97 56 96

email: jd.thiollier@libertysurf.fr

web: http://domainedelaloge.free.fr

This restored farmhouse has four bedrooms sleeping from two to four people, each one individual in style and with a private bathroom. There is a lounge with a guests' kitchen area, complete with bread oven, and a garden with garden room. The owners are ceramic artists, and they have restored this house with immense attention to every detail.

Prices d €50-€55; t €70-€80 **On Site** ⚓ **Nearby** ⚡ 3.5km ⚓ 0.8km ⚓ 9km Restaurant 3km ⚓ 9km ⚓ 3.5km ⚓ 9km **Notes** No pets English spoken

NEAUX

♯♯♯ La Ferme du Toine

Jean-Pierre PELTIER

42470 NEAUX

☎ 04 77 62 70 83 & 06 80 26 95 08 ▤ 04 77 62 72 18

email: contact@fermedutoine.com

web: www.fermedutoine.com

An 18th-century farmhouse close to a river with four individually decorated bedrooms, three in an annexe and one in the main house. The annexe rooms are all doubles with en suite facilities; there is also a guests' sitting room. The accommodation in the main house comprises four single beds in two linked rooms, with access to bathroom and WC via the landing.

Prices d €50-€70; t fr €65; extra person fr €15 **On Site** ⚓ Private ⚓ **Nearby** ⚡ 8km ⚓ 15km Restaurant 0.6km ⚓ 3km ⚓ 3km ⚓ 13km **Notes** No pets English spoken Open June to September.

NOAILLY

⚓ 🍽 Château de la Motte

Anny et Alain FROUMAJOU
42640 NOAILLY
☎ 04 77 66 64 60 🖷 04 77 66 68 10
email: chateaudelamotte@wanadoo.fr
web: http://chateaudelamotte.net/accueil.php

This peacefully situated château has six bedrooms - four doubles, a twin, and a room for four - each with an open fireplace, TV, garden view and an en suite bathroom. Non-smoking rooms are available. There is a lounge/library, and meals are served, using local produce. Enclosed grounds with lake and forest; car parking.

Prices s €65-€97; d €74-€105; t fr €121; extra person fr €18; dinner fr €24 **On Site** ℘ 🎾 Private 🎣 **Nearby** ⛷ 4km 🏊 4km 🏛 1km ⚓ 12km **Notes** Pets admitted English spoken CC

⚓ 🍽 La Gourmandière

Annie et Jacquis GAUNE
42640 NOAILLY
☎ 04 77 66 61 20 & 06 08 74 06 01 🖷 04 77 66 61 82
email: aj.gaune@wanadoo.fr

Guests receive a warm welcome at this 19th-century former farmhouse, offering four bedrooms (two doubles and two twins) with en suite facilities. Two of the rooms can be used as a family suite. A large terrace with a barbecue is at guests' disposal, as is the 2,000 metre-square landscaped garden. Table d'hôte meals are served, by prior arrangement to guarantee quality.

Prices s fr €37; d fr €46; t fr €58; extra person fr €12; dinner fr €16 **On Site** ℘ **Nearby** ⛷ 2km 🎣 12km Restaurant 0.5km 🏊 4km 🏛 0.1km ⚓ 12km **Notes** No pets

PANISSIERES

⚓ 🦃 🍽 La Ferme des Puits

Marc BAVOZAT
42360 PANISSIERES
☎ 04 77 28 83 19

A beautiful 16th-century farmhouse in the Monts du Lyonnais with three very comfortable family rooms with period furniture and private facilities. One has three single beds and is a grade 2 room; one has a double bed and a single; and the third has a double bed and three singles. Beautiful views; good walking and mountain-biking country.

Prices s fr €35; d fr €52; t fr €78; extra person fr €26; dinner fr €15 **On Site** ⛷ Restaurant 🎾 **Nearby** 🏊 30km ℘ 2km 🎣 12km 🏊 12km 🏛 1km ⚓ 12km **Notes** Pets admitted English spoken

⚓ 🍽 La Ferme des Roses

Michel BARTHELEMY
Le Clair, 42360 PANISSIERES
☎ 04 77 28 63 63 🖷 04 77 28 63 63
email: jednostka.arabians@free.fr
web: http://lafermedesroses.free.fr

A large restored farmhouse, peacefully situated in the Monts du Lyonnais. In a building adjacent to the owners' home are five bedrooms: two split-level rooms for four (double beds and singles), a twin-bedded room and two rooms with two double beds. All have private facilities. Lounge with open fire, swimming pool, meals by arrangement. Horses are bred on the farm.

Prices s fr €42; d €52-€57; t fr €73; extra person fr €14; dinner fr €16 **On Site** Restaurant Private 🎣 **Nearby** ⛷ 2km ℘ 1.7km 🏊 2km 🎾 10km 🏛 2km ⚓ 12km **Notes** No pets English spoken

RENAISON

⚓ La Ferme d'Irene

Christine DE BATS
Platelin, 42370 RENAISON
☎ 04 77 64 29 12 & 04 77 62 14 79 🖷 04 77 62 14 79
email: contact@platelin.com
web: www.platelin.com

A quiet, south-facing spot with a double and a family room with separate access in the owner's farmhouse each with a shower, WC and television. There is a lounge with satellite television and cooking facilities. In a small, detached house is a two room suite with a double and twin beds, lounge with kitchen corner, divan bed, television and terrace.

Prices s €65-€80; d €70-€85; t €85-€105; extra person €15-€20 **On Site** ℘ 🎾 Private 🎣 **Nearby** ⛷ 8km 🎿 15km Restaurant 0.8km 🏊 1km 🏛 1km ⚓ 12km **Notes** Pets admitted English spoken

SOUTERNON

⚓ 🍽 Le Grapiaud

Alain et Sabine MIRIMANOFF
42260 SOUTERNON
☎ 04 77 65 25 76 & 06 09 45 07 05 🖷 04 77 65 25 76
email: legrapiaud@wanadoo.fr
web: www.legrapiaud.com

An old property, totally restored, in grounds of 12 hectares with exceptional views across a valley. There is a suite for four (double bed and singles); and two double rooms. All have private bathroom/WC, but those for the double rooms are not en suite. Some antique furnishings; meals by arrangement. Swimming pool, and an attractive kitchen garden.

Prices d fr €65; t €80-€120; dinner fr €23   **On Site** Private � **Nearby** ⛷ 3km ♨ 17km ⚓ 0.5km Restaurant 1.5km ⚓ 1.5km ⛳ 9km 🏯 9km � 20km   **Notes** No pets English spoken Open March to November.

ST-JEAN-ST-MAURICE

⫶⫶⫶ 🍽 L'Echauguette

Michèle ALEX

Rue Guy de la Mure, 42155 ST-JEAN-ST-MAURICE

☎ 04 77 63 15 89

email: contact@echauguette-alex.com

web: www.echauguette-alex.com

Four en suite guest rooms of character: one double and one twin; one with three single beds; and a double in a separate maisonette. Lounge, terrace with outdoor furniture. Rooms overlook the village or Loire.

Prices s €57-€67; d €67-€77; t fr €87; extra person fr €20; dinner fr €27   **Nearby** ⛷ 5km ♨ 7km ⚓ 2km ⚓ 14km Restaurant 15km ⚓ 1km 🏯 0.3km � 15km   **Notes** No pets English spoken

ST-JODARD

⫶⫶⫶ 🌱 ♿ Daguet

Claudie et Philippe DUREL

42590 ST-JODARD

☎ 04 77 63 45 34 & 06 82 14 59 67   📄 04 77 63 45 34

email: durel.philippe@wanadoo.fr

A south-facing stone-built property which was restored and converted, to provide three bedrooms, each individually and tastefully decorated. There are two downstairs rooms, a double and a twin, each with a private terrace; upstairs is a room with three single beds. All have private bath/shower room and WC. Lounge, sun room, use of kitchen.

Prices s fr €34; d fr €39; t fr €50; extra person fr €10   **Nearby** ⛷ 15km ♨ 15km ⚓ 2km ⚓ 0.5km Restaurant 1km ⚓ 1.5km 🏯 0.5km � 0.5km **Notes** No pets

ST-JULIEN-MOLIN-MOLETTE

⫶⫶⫶ Castel-Gueret

Daniel COULAUD

Drevard, 42220 ST-JULIEN-MOLIN-MOLETTE

☎ 04 77 51 56 04

email: contact@domaine-castelgueret.com

web: www.domaine-castelgueret.com

Five comfortable en suite rooms in a fine 19th-century castle in the heart of the Parc Naturel du Pilat, between the Loire, the Ardèche and the Isère. Two double rooms; one twin room; two suites each with a double and two single beds. Also a gîte for four to six people. Sitting areas; billiard room; kitchen; park with private swimming pool. St-Joseph and Côtes-Rôties vineyards close.

Prices s fr €60; d €75-€84; t fr €125; extra person fr €23   **On Site** ⛳

Private ⚓   **Nearby** ⛷ 1km ♨ 7km ⚓ 0.2km Restaurant 0.1km ⚓ 0.2km 🏯 0.4km � 30km   **Notes** Pets admitted English spoken

⫶⫶⫶ 🍽 La Rivoire

Denise THIOLLIERE

42220 ST-JULIEN-MOLIN-MOLETTE

☎ 04 77 39 65 44   📄 04 77 39 67 86

email: info@larivoire.net

web: www.larivoire.net

In the Parc Naturel du Pilat, a comfortable 18th-century home with wonderful views and five en suite rooms (two doubles, two twins and one room sleeping four, ideal for a family). Beautiful living rooms. Breakfast and dinner (served on the terrace in season) is based on fruit and vegetables from the garden and other regional produce.

Prices s fr €52; d fr €62; extra person fr €16; dinner fr €19 **On Site** Restaurant   **Nearby** ⛷ 10km ⚓ 0.5km ⚓ 5km ⚓ 5km 🏯 3km � 20km   **Notes** No pets English spoken

ST-MARCEL-D'URFE

⫶⫶⫶ 🍽 Il fût un Temps...

Julien PERBET

Les Gouttes, 42430 ST-MARCEL-D'URFE

☎ 04 77 62 52 19 & 06 03 55 86 13   📄 04 77 62 53 88

email: contact@ilfutuntemps.com

web: www.ilfutuntemps.com

Five guest rooms in an old stone farmhouse in the depths of the country. One double room; two singles; and two large rooms each with double bed and sofa bed, all en suite. Dining room and sitting room with open fire. Story-telling evenings round the fire on occasions.

Prices s fr €51-€69; d €61-€79; t fr €93; extra person fr €15; dinner fr €24 **On Site** ⛳   **Nearby** ⛷ 3km ♨ 20km ⚓ 3km ⚓ 7km Restaurant 3km ⚓ 3km 🏯 3km � 25km   **Notes** No pets English spoken

ST-MARCELLIN-EN-FOREZ

⫶⫶⫶ Chambre d'hôtes

Roland MALCLES

40 Rte de St-Bonnet-le-Château,

42680 ST-MARCELLIN-EN-FOREZ

☎ 04 77 52 89 63 & 06 03 00 23 67   📄 04 77 52 89 63

email: roland.malcles@wanadoo.fr

Five en suite rooms include one two-roomed suite with double and three single beds; two rooms sleeping three; and two double rooms. Dining room, fully equipped kitchen, lounge (with two folding beds available), video and hi-fi system. Enclosed parkland, parking, garden furniture, games. Weekend breaks (booking required).

Prices s fr €34; d fr €45; t €60-€62; extra person fr €17   **On Site** ⛷ Private ⚓   **Nearby** ⚓ 4km � 4km   **Notes** No pets English spoken

ST-MARTIN-LESTRA

ⵌ ⵔⵏⵓ ⴹ Les Blés d'Or

Christine et Denis PERALTA
Bouchala, 42110 ST-MARTIN-LESTRA
☎ 04 77 28 58 76 & 06 80 88 66 64 ▤ 04 77 28 58 76
email: contact@blesdor.com
web: www.blesdor.com

Your hosts fell in love with this old farm, and they will welcome you like friends to their four comfortable and peaceful bedrooms - all with en suite bathrooms. Three rooms have balconies, and they all face west - so you will see some beautiful sunsets! Guests' lounge. Meals available: local produce and hosts' own recipes. Good walking country; bike storage.

Prices s fr €39; d fr €48; t fr €63; extra person fr €15; dinner fr €15 **Nearby** ⛵ 8km ⵔ 5km ⵔ 15km Restaurant 5km ⵀ 5km ⵔ 10km ⵔ 5km ⵔ 15km **Notes** No pets English spoken

ST-MEDARD-EN-FOREZ

ⵌ Chambre d'hôtes La Vallée des Moulins

Cédric DUILLON
Fonfarlan, 42330 ST-MEDARD-EN-FOREZ
☎ 04 77 94 13 09
email: cedric.duillon@wanadoo.fr

A haven of tranquillity situated in open countryside. The four ground floor bedrooms, each with en suite facilities and kitchens, have individual access to the expansive landscaped grounds. There is a huge terrace, with views over the countryside, where breakfasts that utilise home-made preserves and local produce are served. Guests can fish or hike from the gîte.

Prices s fr €32; d fr €42; t fr €50 **Nearby** ⛵ 7km ⵔ 20km ⵔ 0.1km ⵔ 7km Restaurant 1km ⵀ 1.5km ⵔ 0.1km ⵔ 1km ⵔ 7km **Notes** Pets admitted English spoken

ⵌ ⵔⵏⵓ La Ferrière

Jean et Michèle GOUILLON
Place de l'Eglise, 42330 ST-MEDARD-EN-FOREZ
☎ 04 77 94 04 44
email: info@chambresdhotesloire.com
web: www.chambresdhotesloire.com

A restored 18th-century home in the middle of a charming village offering five en suite guest rooms: four double rooms (two with spare bed if required) plus one twin room. Large living room with table; sitting room with TV. Dinner (by reservation).

Prices s fr €36; d fr €47; extra person fr €15; dinner fr €18 **On Site** ⵔ **Nearby** ⛵ 6km ⵔ 1km ⵔ 6km Restaurant 6km ⵀ 6km ⵔ 10km **Notes** Pets admitted English spoken CC

ST-MICHEL-SUR-RHONE

ⵌ ⵔⵏⵓ L'Ollagnière

Georges et Claudette BONNET
42410 ST-MICHEL-SUR-RHONE
☎ 04 74 59 51 01 & 04 74 56 80 74

In the Parc du Pilat, between Lyon and Valence, three guest rooms in an old house near the proprietors' home (two grade 2 rooms - a double and one with three single beds sharing a wc, one grade 3 room with two single beds and child's bed if required). Kitchen, dining room and TV lounge. Breakfast and dinner available. Terrace and summer kitchen. Garden furniture. Wine-tasting nearby.

Prices s fr €32; d fr €42; t fr €52; extra person fr €12; dinner fr €16 **Nearby** ⵔ 2km ⵔ 4km Restaurant 1km ⵀ 7km ⵔ 6km ⵔ 3km ⵔ 4km **Notes** Pets admitted

ST-PIERRE-LA-NOAILLE

ⵌ Domaine Château de Marchangy

Marie-Colette GRANDEAU
42190 ST-PIERRE-LA-NOAILLE
☎ 04 77 69 96 76 ▤ 04 77 60 70 37
email: contact@marchangy.com
web: www.marchangy.com

Three guest rooms in an 18th-century house in a quiet spot with panoramic views; one double room and two suites, one with two double beds and one with a double and two singles. All are en suite with TV and telephones. Lounge with open fire and mini-bar. 2.5 hectare park with garden furniture, swimming pool, bikes. Generous breakfast. Brunch (extra charge). Many walking trails.

Prices s €77-€99; d €85-€110; extra person €18-€27 **On Site** ⵔ Private ⵔ **Nearby** ⵔ 14km ⵔ 12km ⵔ 4km Restaurant 3km ⵀ 4.5km ⵔ 4km ⵔ 15km **Notes** Pets admitted English spoken

ST-PRIEST-LA-ROCHE

ⵌ ⵙ ⵔⵏⵓ Prévieux

A et O ROCHE-MERCIER
42590 ST-PRIEST-LA-ROCHE
☎ 04 77 64 92 12 ▤ 04 77 64 92 12

Plentiful breakfasts using farm produce are on offer in this old house with superb mountain views and peaceful garden. There are three rooms, a double, a grade 2 room with double bed, and a grade 3 double with single bed; each has a fully equipped, private bathroom. Guests also have use of a lounge, library, fireplace and terrace.

Prices s fr €28; d €32-€38; extra person fr €11; dinner fr €13 **On Site** ⵔ **Nearby** ⛵ 7km ⵔ 12km ⵔ 6km ⵔ 10km Restaurant 5km ⵀ 1km ⵔ 5km ⵔ 10km **Notes** Pets admitted English spoken

ST-ROMAIN-LE-PUY

⏸ & Sous le Pic

Dominique PEROL

20 rue Jean Moulin, La Pérolière,

42610 ST-ROMAIN-LE-PUY

☎ 04 77 76 97 10 & 06 64 13 85 49 📄 04 77 76 97 10

email: laperoliere@wanadoo.fr

web: www.laperoliere.com

Situated at the foot of Prieuré, this old restored farmhouse offers a double room, two twins and a twin with extra bed available (one accessible to the less mobile), plus a suite with lounge, TV and coffee-making facilities. Each has refined décor, furnishings and private facilities. Living room with lounge corner and library, telephone, parking. Breakfasts are served on the terrace in the grounds in summer, and include home-made jam and cakes. Farm inns 500mtrs, thermal spa nearby.

Prices s €47-€62; d €55-€70; extra person fr €15 **On Site** 🎣 🌳 **Nearby** ⛷ 7km 🛶 0.5km ⚓ 7km Restaurant 0.8km ⛳ 0.8km 🏛 0.8km ⏸ 1km **Notes** No pets English spoken Open March to December.

ST-ROMAIN-LES-ATHEUX

⏸ & Domaine de Bonnefond

Joëlle FRANC-CAIRE

Centre Equestre, 42660 ST-ROMAIN-LES-ATHEUX

☎ 04 77 39 04 06 & 06 98 44 55 67

email: jcaire42@aol.com

This restored stone-built farmhouse has three bedrooms: a triple, and two rooms for four, with a mezzanine. They all have en suite bathrooms. There is a lounge with open fireplace and a small kitchen area. This is an ideal location for walking, riding, mountain-biking and cross-country skiing. Possible horse accommodation. Country restaurant 2 kilometres away. Open all year by reservation.

Prices s fr €43; d €48-€60; t fr €68-€73; extra person fr €13 **On Site** ⛷ 🌳 Private ⚓ **Nearby** 🛶 12km ⚓ 4km Restaurant 2km ⛳ 10km 🏛 4km ⏸ 7km **Notes** No pets English spoken

ST-VICTOR-SUR-LOIRE

⏸ & Chambre d'hôtes

Martine et René JOSEPH

Boulain, 42230 ST-VICTOR-SUR-LOIRE

☎ 06 75 07 45 37 & 04 77 90 36 90

email: leplateaudeladanse@yahoo.fr

On a listed protected site, this 18th-century house has four bedrooms: a double room, two twin-bedded rooms, and a room for four with a double bed and two singles. Three share a terrace; the fourth is an attic room. All have private facilities and wonderful views. Lounge with open fire, kitchen. Non-smoking property. Garden, swimming pool, games area, pétanque.

Prices s fr €47; d fr €52; t fr €65; extra person fr €15 **On Site** Private ⚓ **Nearby** ⛷ 10km 🛶 10km ⚓ 5km Restaurant 2km ⛳ 2.5km 🏛 3.5km ⏸ 7km **Notes** No pets English spoken

⏸ Chambre d'hôtes

Colette GRIMAND

Pracoin, 42230 ST-VICTOR-SUR-LOIRE

☎ 04 77 90 37 95

email: colettegrimand@club-internet.fr

web: www.chambre-hotes-loire.com

At the gateway to the Gorges of the Loire, three comfortable en suite rooms in an old renovated barn. Guests may use the sitting room and lounge, and enclosed park with swimming pool. Breakfast is served in the barn building or by the side of the pool, and dinner may be enjoyed in the nearby restaurants and auberges.

Prices s fr €36; d fr €45; t fr €60; extra person fr €13 **On Site** Private ⚓ **Nearby** ⛷ 3km 🛶 5km ⚓ 5km Restaurant 4km ⛳ 3km Spa 20km ⛳ 10km 🏛 1km ⏸ 6km **Notes** No pets English spoken

STE-FOY-ST-SULPICE

⏸ 🌱 🍴 Ferme Neuve

Yvette et Clément BROSSAT

42110 STE-FOY-ST-SULPICE

☎ 04 77 27 81 37 📄 04 77 27 81 37

A 19th-century farmhouse now restored. There is a double room, and two two-room suites for four (one with two double beds, the other with a double and two singles). All have private facilities; each room has individual decorations and high-quality furnishings. Day room for guests' use; breakfasts and other meals include home-grown and home-made produce.

Prices s fr €35; d fr €50; t fr €60; extra person fr €10; dinner fr €14 **Nearby** ⛷ 1.5km ⚓ 0.3km ⚓ 8km Restaurant 10km ⛳ 3km 🎣 22km 🏛 10km ⏸ 9km **Notes** No pets

⏸ 🐓 🍴 St-Sulpice

Lucette et René CLAIR

42110 STE-FOY-ST-SULPICE

☎ 04 77 27 81 08 & 06 78 78 78 70

web: http://stsulpice.ifrance.com

Three en suite guest rooms upstairs in a wing of the family house with independent access. One double room and two singles. Spare bed if required. Living room with kitchen available to guests. At dinner enjoy real family cooking with farm and regional produce. Terrace, shady parkland. 5km from the Bastide d'Urfé and Pommiers en Forez.

Prices s fr €32; d fr €42; extra person fr €12; dinner €13-€14 **Nearby** ⛷ 8km ⚓ 9km ⚓ 12km Restaurant 6km ⛳ 4km 🎣 10km 🏛 4km ⏸ 9km **Notes** Pets admitted

USSON-EN-FOREZ

♦♦♦ ΙΟΙ Myrtille

Pascale TISSEUR

Jouanzecq, 42550 USSON EN FOREZ

☎ 04 77 50 90 83

email: tisseur.pasale@aliceadsl.fr

web: http://chambre.myrtille.chez-alice.fr

In open country on the edge of the Auvergne, 20 kilometres from the spectacular Bouriannes lava flow, this restored farmhouse has five bedrooms, all with en suite bathrooms. The rooms sleep two, three or four people (the quad room has a mezzanine). Each room has its own particular style. Breakfast and other meals use produce from the farm. Garage parking.

Prices d €45-€48; t €60-€63; extra person fr €15; dinner fr €15
Nearby ⛷ 5km 🎣 2km 🎿 5km Restaurant 3km 🏊 3km 🎾 5km
🏛 3km 🚶 45km **Notes** No pets English spoken

VENDRANGES

♦♦♦ 🐓 ΙΟΙ *Ferme de Montissut*

Jean et Suzanne DELOIRE

42590 VENDRANGES

☎ 04 77 64 90 96

email: jeanetsuzanne@wanadoo.fr

web: http://montissut.free.fr

Three guests rooms available in this cattle rearing farm: one grade 3 en suite room overlooking the lake with one double and two singles, one en suite grade 3 twin room and a grade 2 double room. Extra bed available. Reading room, lounge, TV, library, open fire. Shady terrace, play area, table tennis, garage. Camping, fishing on the lake. Near to Château de la Roche and Gorges of the Loire.

Prices not confirmed for 2008 **On Site** 🎣 **Nearby** ⛷ 6km 🎿 10km
🏊 1km 🏛 8km 🚶 15km **Notes** No pets English spoken Open March to December.

VERRIERES-EN-FOREZ

♦♦♦ 🐓 ΙΟΙ Le Soleillant

Camille RIVAL

42600 VERRIERES EN FOREZ

☎ 04 77 76 22 73

email: camille.rival@wanadoo.fr

web: www.le-soleillant.com

A working farm in the hills on the edge of the Auvergne. There are three double bedrooms, one with a lounge area, balcony, and

wonderful views. Each has a private shower room and WC. Lounge with old-fashioned furniture, kitchen, washing machine. Generous breakfasts, other meals (including produce from the farm) available by arrangement. Garden with furniture.

Prices s €31-€35; d €40-€45; dinner €13-€17 **On Site** 🎣 🎾
Nearby ⛷ 10km 🎣 10km 🎿 10km Restaurant 1km 🏊 10km Spa 20km
🏛 1km 🚶 13km **Notes** No pets English spoken

VILLEMONTAIS

♦♦♦ 🐦 Domaine de Fontenay

Simon et Isabelle HAWKINS

42155 VILLEMONTAIS

☎ 04 77 63 12 22 & 06 81 03 30 33 📠 04 77 63 15 95

email: hawkins@tele2.fr

web: www.domainedufontenay.com

This renovated house faces due south with a terrace overlooking the vineyards. It has four rooms full of character, one of them a duplex suite, which can sleep two, three or four people. Cot available. One is a non-smoking room, and they all have en suite bathrooms. There is a large guests' lounge with kitchen area.

Prices s fr €55; d fr €65; t fr €75 **On Site** 🎾 **Nearby** ⛷ 5km
🎿 10km 🏊 0.5km 🏛 2km 🚶 10km **Notes** No pets English spoken CC

RHÔNE

AMPUIS

♦♦♦ ΙΟΙ *Entre Eau et Vin*

C et J RIVOIRE

69420 AMPUIS

☎ 04 74 56 20 82

A wine-growing village on the banks of the Rhône, ideal for a holiday or stopover. The hosts are happy to help their guests discover the area and nature, and offer three very comfortable guest rooms: a double, a room with two doubles and a room with four singles each with private facilities. Healthy and generous table d'hôte meals and a friendly environment. Garage and shady walks by the river.

Prices not confirmed for 2008 **On Site** 🎣 **Nearby** ⛷ 13km 🎣 30km
🎿 5km 🏊 2.5km 🎾 4km 🏛 0.5km 🚶 8km **Notes** No pets

♦♦♦ La Gerine

Nine et Bernard THOMAS

2 Côte de la Gerine-Verenay, 69420 AMPUIS

☎ 04 74 56 03 46 & 06 85 06 06 56

email: contact@lagerine.com

web: www.lagerine.com

Standing amongst vineyards, this house perched high on a hillside gives a magnificent view of the Rhône. It has four spacious and comfortable rooms - two for three people and two for four. They all have mezzanines and private shower rooms/WCs. Generous breakfasts are served in the big lounge with its open fire, or in the garden. Swimming pool.

Prices s fr €55; d fr €70; t fr €90; extra person fr €20 **On Site** 🎾
Private 🎿 **Nearby** ⛷ 7km 🎣 10km 🎣 0.1km Restaurant 2.5km
🏊 0.3km 🏛 0.1km 🚶 5km **Notes** No pets English spoken

⌗ *La Maison aux Geraniums*

Gilles et Marie-Alice BARGE
8 Boulevard des Allées, 69420 AMPUIS
☎ 04 74 56 13 90 & 06 81 22 71 54 📄 04 74 56 10 98
email: barge.gilles@wanadoo.fr
web: www.domainebarge.com

A vineyard property on the edge of the Côte-Rôtie region. There are three bedrooms: a twin-bedded room, a triple (double bed and a single) and a grade 2 double. All have private shower room and WC. Use of lounge (shared with hosts), enclosed gardens with vineyard views, wine-tasting possible. Garage parking.

Prices not confirmed for 2008 **On Site** Private ↖ **Notes** Pets admitted English spoken CC

⌗ *Villa Montplaisir*

Marcel GAGNOR
9 Ch de la Vialliere-Verenay, 69420 AMPUIS
☎ 04 74 56 16 43

Set in large grounds with a terrace, this new house above the Rhône, easily reached from the nearest autoroute exit, has three double en suite rooms with independent access. Central heating, television, telephone, living room, cooking area. Explore the Parc du Pilat and the Côtes Rôties vineyard.

Prices not confirmed for 2008 **Nearby** ⛳5km ⚓10km ⚓1km ↖2km ⚓0.2km ⚓5km ⚓1km ⚓5km **Notes** Pets admitted

BAGNOLS

⌗ ✾ *Domaine des Vignes d'Hôtes*

J-P et H GRILLET
Saint-Aigues, 69620 BAGNOLS
☎ 04 74 71 62 98 & 06 63 86 44 26 📄 04 74 71 62 98
email: info@jpgrillet.com
web: www.jpgrillet.com

This distinctive house overlooks the vineyard and the Lyonnais Mountains in the heart of Beaujolais. There is one double room, one twin room and one room with double bed and bunks, all en suite, and a huge day room with open fire, sitting room, fully-equipped kitchen, central heating, parking, lawn and garden furniture. Visit the wine cellar or the Castle of Bagnols.

Prices not confirmed for 2008 **On Site** ⚓ **Nearby** ⛳5km ⚓10km ⚓10km ↖15km ⚓ ⚓1km ⚓15km **Notes** Pets admitted

BEAUJEU

⌗ ⚙ ♿ **Chantemerle en Morne**

Marie et Philippe LAPRUN
Rte de St Joseph-Juliénas, 69430 BEAUJEU
☎ 04 74 04 89 26
email: laprunbeaujeu@aol.com
web: www.chantemerle-en-morne.com

A property right at the heart of the Beaujolais region. On the first floor is a grade 2 twin-bedded room; and a split-level family room with a

double bed, three singles, and a child's bed. A twin-bedded ground floor room has access for disabled guests. All have private bath or shower room and WC. Lounge, courtyard and garden, terrace. Meals by arrangement. Closed Xmas & New Year.

Prices s fr €37; d fr €45; extra person fr €12; dinner fr €15
Nearby ⛳6km ⚓30km ⚓5km ↖12km ⚓3km ⚓2km ⚓1km ⚓12km **Notes** Pets admitted English spoken

BELLEVILLE-SUR-SAONE

⌗ ⚙ **Le Clos Beaujolais**

Aline et Jacques BRUNAND
Les Poutoux, 69220 BELLEVILLE-SUR-SAONE
☎ 04 74 66 54 73 & 06 78 78 38 06 📄 04 74 66 47 86
email: le.clos.beaujolais@wanadoo.fr
web: www.closbeaujolais.com

This 16th-century house stands in extensive grounds. It has four peaceful rooms, each decorated according to a theme: one twin, one double, one family room for four, and one room with a double bed and a bed settee. All have private bath/shower room and WC. Swimming pool, French-style garden. Meals available, by arrangement.

Prices s €60-€80; d €65-€85; t €80-€95; extra person fr €15; dinner fr €22 **On Site** Private ↖ **Nearby** ⛳4km ⚓20km ⚓4km Restaurant 2km ⚓3km ⚓10km ⚓2km ⚓2km **Notes** No pets English spoken CC

BLACE

⌗ ✾ ⚙ **Domaine de la Maison Germain**

M-P et P BOSSAN
Route de Salles - D20, 69460 BLACE
☎ 04 74 67 56 36 📄 04 74 60 55 23
email: patrick.bossan@wanadoo.fr
web: www.bossan.tk

On their estate in mid-Beaujolais, this old restored house, home to winegrowers, has three en suite guest rooms of character: two double rooms and one family room with two single beds and bunk. Spare bed or cot available. Lounge with television, games, reading material. Breakfast served with the family in the dining room or out in the garden. Six camping pitches.

Prices s fr €40; d fr €50; t fr €65; extra person fr €15; dinner fr €17
Nearby ⛳10km ⚓8km ⚓3km ⚓8km **Notes** No pets English spoken CC

BOURG-DE-THIZY

⚑ |○| **La Ferme Fleurie**

Colette DESPORTE

Les Epercelys, 69240 BOURG-DE-THIZY

☎ 04 74 64 09 00 & 06 65 43 14 44

email: desporte.colette@wanadoo.fr

This peaceful country house has four bedrooms. Three are in a restored pigeon loft: a double, a triple, and a room for four, all with en suite bathrooms and a view over the valleys. In the house there is a suite for up to five people, with an en suite shower room and a kitchen corner. Terrace, meals by arrangement.

Prices s fr €35; d fr €40; t fr €55; extra person fr €15; dinner fr €15
Nearby ⚓ 8km ⚲ 20km ⚡ 2km ⚐ 3km Restaurant 2km ⚘ 3km
⚑ 8km ⚑ 2km ⚑ 10km **Notes** Pets admitted English spoken

BRIGNAIS

⚑ |○| **Au Domaine de Cheron**

S et J-P VEYRARD

33 Route de Soucieu, 69530 BRIGNAIS

☎ 04 72 31 06 62 & 06 11 86 62 80

email: cheron@cegetel.net

web: www.cheron.info

En suite guest rooms in adjacent farm buildings set in a quiet, green area (three double rooms, one twin, one single, one for three and one for four). Two spare child's beds. Courtyard with outdoor furniture, wooded parkland, parking. Reduced rates for long stays.

Prices s €38-€45; d €55-€65; extra person fr €20; dinner fr €20
Nearby ⚓ 6km ⚡ 6km ⚐ 1.5km ⚘ 1.5km ⚑ 1.5km ⚑ 15km
Notes No pets English spoken CC

BULLY

⚑ |○| *Le Chene Patouillard*

I et M BIRON

69210 BULLY

☎ 04 74 26 89 50 & 06 10 98 04 16

email: chenepatouillard@free.fr

web: http://gite-de-france-au-chene-patouillard.com

A restored farmhouse in a peaceful spot with fine open views. There are five individually decorated rooms: two doubles, two triples (double bed and a single in each) and a room for four (two double beds). All have private facilities. Separate guests' entrance and a large day room. Outside is a terrace and a swimming pool. Meals by arrangement.

Prices not confirmed for 2008 **On Site** Private ⚐ **Nearby** ⚲ 1.5km
⚲ 15km ⚘ 3km ⚑ 5km ⚑ 2.5km ⚑ 3km **Notes** No pets English spoken

---

CERCIE-EN-BEAUJOLAIS

⚑ ☙ **Domaine de Saint-Ennemond**

M et C BEREZIAT

Lieu-dit Saint Ennemond, 69220 CERCIE-EN-BEAUJOLAIS

☎ 04 74 69 67 17 ▤ 04 74 69 67 29

email: christian.bereziat@wanadoo.fr

web: www.domainebereziat.fr

A vineyard property in the hamlet of Saint-Ennemond offering three comfortable en suite guest rooms with separate access (one twin, two rooms with double and single bed - cot available). Communal living room with open fire. Near RN6, and autoroute A6 exit Belleville S/Saone.

Prices s fr €54; d fr €60; t fr €76; extra person fr €16 **On Site** ⚡
Nearby ⚓ 4km ⚲ 10km ⚐ 4km Restaurant 3km ⚘ 2km ⚑ 8km
⚑ 2km ⚑ 5km **Notes** No pets English spoken CC

CHAMBOST-LONGESSAIGNE

⚑ |○| **Château de Chambost**

V et V DE LESCURE

Route de Panissière, RD 101,

69770 CHAMBOST-LONGESSAIGNE

☎ 04 74 26 37 49 ▤ 04 74 70 63 26

email: infos@chateaudechambost.com

web: www.chateaudechambost.com

This working farm 600 metres up in the Monts du Lyonnais has five guest bedrooms, all with private facilities. There are two double-bedded rooms, two with twin beds, and a two-roomed suite for three. Meals using local produce are available by arrangement, served in the 16th-century dining room with its arched roof.

Prices s €50-€90; d €60-€90; t fr €100; extra person fr €20; dinner fr €15
Nearby ⚓ 6km ⚲ 45km ⚡ 6km ⚐ 12km ⚘ 0.3km ⚑ 6km ⚑ 0.3km
⚑ 15km **Notes** No pets English spoken

CHARENTAY

⚑ ☙ **Les Combes**

Christine et Denis DUTRAIVE

La Tour de la Belle-Mère, 69220 CHARENTAY

☎ 04 74 66 82 21 ▤ 04 74 66 82 21

email: denis.dutraive@wanadoo.fr

web: www.dutraive.com

Five en suite guest rooms in a separate building on a wine estate (three double rooms and two rooms sleeping three). Large guest lounge, huge lounge/library, swimming pool, great open park with the Tour de la Belle-Mère and Beaujolais wine cellars.

Prices s €54-€73; d €60-€80; t fr €93; extra person fr €17
On Site Private ⚐ **Nearby** ⚓ 1km ⚲ 20km ⚡ 10km Restaurant 3km
⚘ 4km ⚑ 5km ⚑ 5km ⚑ 5km **Notes** No pets English spoken Open
3 January to 15 December. CC

CHARLY

♦♦♦♦ *La Maison Curiale*

Michelle et J-Paul AUCLAIR

2 place de l'Église, 69390 CHARLY

☎ 04 72 30 13 13 & 06 19 50 88 65

📄 04 72 30 13 13

This former vicarage dates from the Middle Ages and enjoys a tranquil setting just 12km from Lyon. The very comfortable rooms are arranged in a wing with private facilities and access, and include two twin rooms and a double. Outside, guests can relax in the vast enclosed grounds. Parking available.

Prices not confirmed for 2008 **Nearby** ⚓ 5km 🏌 5km ⬆ 5km 🏊 2km 🏛 1km ⛳ 5km **Notes** No pets

CHIROUBLES

♦♦♦ 🐾 Domaine de la Grosse Pierre

V et A PASSOT

69115 CHIROUBLES

☎ 04 74 69 12 17 & 06 07 47 35 55 📄 04 74 69 13 52

email: apassot@wanadoo.fr

web: www.chiroubles-passot.com

Winegrowers offering five en suite guest rooms with separate access in this Beaujolais house of character (two twins and three doubles). Cot and child's bed available. Large living room with open fire and sitting room. Central heating; swimming pool; terrace; large shady courtyard; garage. Sampling and sale of estate wines.

Prices s fr €50; d fr €60; t fr €70; extra person fr €15 **On Site** Private ⬆ **Nearby** ⚓ 10km 🏌 20km ⬆ 10km Restaurant 3km 🏊 2km ⛳ 8km 🏛 2km ⛳ 10km **Notes** No pets English spoken Open February to November. CC

♦♦♦ 🍽 La Tour

M-F et J-P BERNARD

Le Pont, 69115 CHIROUBLES

☎ 04 74 04 20 26 & 06 10 28 21 43

email: mfjp.bernard@free.fr

web: http://mfjp.bernard.free.fr.

A house in the Beaujolais region with lots of character and four bedrooms. On the first floor is a double room; on the second floor is a triple (double bed and single), a room for four (double bed and twins), and a twin-bedded room. All have private facilities and elegant decor. Large lounge, with piano and billiards. Meals available by arrangement.

Prices s fr €70; d fr €80; t fr €100; extra person fr €10; dinner fr €25 **On Site** Private ⬆ **Nearby** ⚓ 10km 🏌 20km ⬆ 12km Restaurant 5km 🏊 10km Spa 40km ⛳ 7km 🏛 5km ⛳ 10km **Notes** No pets English spoken

La Villa Toscana is set in the heart of the Beaujolais vineyards. 4 lovely guest rooms are available, each individually themed: the Ocean, the East, the countryside and the mountains. Expect a warm welcome from the proprietors Fabienne and Pascal, who offer table d'hôtes on request. Relax in the swimming pool or explore the magnificent region which is sure to win you over!

Fabienne and Pascal Chanudet
La Villa Toscana   Le Bret   69640 COGNY   France
Tel: 04 74 67 35 18
Email: pascal.chanudet@wanadoo.fr

COGNY

♦♦♦ 🍽 La Villa Toscana

Fabienne et Pascal CHANUDET

Le Bret, 69640 COGNY

☎ 04 74 67 35 18 & 06 99 88 79 13

email: pascal.chanudet@wanadoo.fr

web: www.domaine-les-tilleuls.fr.st

This characterful and welcoming house is in a small hamlet in the Beaujolais region. There are four guest rooms. An extra bed is available, and all rooms have en suite shower rooms/WCs. Guests' lounge, shady grounds, swimming pool. Meals by arrangement.

Prices s €55-€79; d €61-€85; t fr €90; dinner fr €23 **On Site** ⛳ Private ⬆ **Nearby** ⚓ 4km 🏌 15km Restaurant 5km 🏊 2km ⛳ 10km 🏛 2km ⛳ 10km **Notes** No pets English spoken

see advert on this page

COURZIEU

▦ Les Gouttes

M BONNEPART

69690 COURZIEU

☎ 04 74 70 80 74

email: gites.bonnepart@club-internet.fr

web: http://gites.bonnepart.free.fr

Five en suite guest rooms in a block of buildings attached to the proprietors' house: three doubles and three rooms each with three single beds. Spare adult and child's beds are available. Guests have the use of a lounge, cooking area and sitting area with television. Terrace, grounds, garden furniture, barbecue.

Prices s fr €35; d fr €45; t fr €60; extra person fr €15 **Nearby** ⛷ 12km ⚓ 20km ✎ 2km ➴ 10km Restaurant 3km ⌚ 3km ⌂ 3km ⛵ 10km **Notes** Pets admitted English spoken Open March to December.

DENICE

▦ ◉ Domaine de Pouilly-le-Chatel

S et B CHEVALIER

69640 DENICE

☎ 04 74 67 41 01 & 06 70 36 55 77

email: bruno.chevalier@pouillylechatel.com

web: www.pouillylechatel.com

In the heart of the Beaujolais region, this beautiful house has two double bedrooms, both with en suite bathrooms. They are decorated in warm colours, and one opens on to a terrace, the other on to an internal courtyard. There is a swimming pool. Your hosts are wine growers, and will be happy to arrange tastings. Meals available, by arrangement.

Prices d €90-€95; dinner fr €30 **On Site** Private ➴ **Nearby** ⛷ 2km ⚓ 15km Restaurant 2km ⌚ 3km ⌂ 3km ⛵ 4km **Notes** Pets admitted English spoken

▦ ☙ ◉ Le Calme

J-Jacques et Mireille DULAC

Aux Bruyères, 69640 DENICE

☎ 04 74 67 34 00 & 06 80 43 07 11 ▤ 04 74 67 34 00

email: jj.dulac@wanadoo.fr

web: www.gites-dulac.com

A character property in the heart of the Beaujolais region with four bedrooms. There are three double rooms, one with private terrace and one with lounge/kitchenette area. There is also a further grade 2 double. All rooms have a private bath or shower room and WC, but those for the grade 2 room are not en suite. Lounge area, upstairs sitting room; swimming pool, wooded grounds.

Prices d €49-€67; extra person fr €16; dinner fr €23 **On Site** Private ➴ **Nearby** ⛷ 1km ⚓ 10km ✎ 6km Restaurant 1km ⌚ 1km ⛵ 4km ⌂ 1km ⛵ 5km **Notes** Pets admitted English spoken

EMERINGES

▦ Domaine de Monsepeys

J-L CANARD et E CONESA

Les Benons, 69840 EMERINGES

☎ 04 74 04 45 11 & 06 70 63 12 86 ▤ 04 74 04 45 19

email: ec.jlc@wanadoo.fr

web: http://perso.wanadoo.fr/domaine.de.monsepeys/

This 18th-century wine-grower's house has five guest rooms, with their own access onto a large flowery terrace, which has garden furniture and views over the Beaujolais region. Downstairs are two bedrooms, a double with a bed-settee, and a twin-bedded room. Upstairs are two doubles and a two-roomed family suite with double bed and bed-settee. All rooms have private facilities. Cot available, kitchenette, wooded grounds.

Prices s fr €46; d fr €52; t fr €64; extra person fr €12 **Nearby** ⛷ 10km ⚓ 25km ✎ 2km ➴ 20km Restaurant 0.5km ⌚ 4km ⛵ 10km ⌂ 2km ⛵ 15km **Notes** No pets English spoken

FLEURIE

▦ Château de la Chapelle des Bois

O SALUS et A MORATEUR

69820 FLEURIE

☎ 04 74 04 10 29 & 06 75 19 58 33

▤ 04 74 69 85 29

email: chapelle.des.bois@wanadoo.fr

web: www.chateaudelachapelledesbois.com

A few steps away from the little Beaujolais village of Fleurie, your hosts Agnès and Olivier look forward to introducing you to their charming mansion and its five superb en suite rooms for one or two people; all have TV and telephone. Living rooms, library, large country park, swimming pool.

Prices s €80-€115; d €95-€130; t fr €185; extra person fr €40 **On Site** Private ➴ **Nearby** ⛷ 15km ⚓ 20km ✎ 7km Restaurant 8km ⌚ 1km ⛵ 15km ⌂ 0.8km ⛵ 5km **Notes** Pets admitted English spoken Open March to December.

▦ Clos des Garands

M-P et J YVES

69820 FLEURIE

☎ 04 74 69 80 01 & 06 12 52 61 73

▤ 04 74 69 82 05

email: mariepauleyves@wanadoo.fr

web: www.closdesgarands.fr

This 18th-century house has a superb view across the Beaujolais region. It has four bedrooms, a ground floor double, with a possible extra bed, and upstairs, three luxury rooms for two or three people. Cot available. All rooms have private facilities. Breakfast served in the lounge, with open fireplace, or on the terrace overlooking the park. Wine tasting can be arranged.

Prices d €84-€104; extra person fr €17 **Nearby** ✎ 6km ➴ 12km ⌂ 1km ⛵ 15km **Notes** No pets English spoken CC

RHÔNE-ALPES

⁙ **Domaine des Marrans**

L et J-J MELINAND

69820 FLEURIE

☎ 04 74 04 13 21 & 06 30 26 98 67 ▤ 04 74 69 82 45

email: domainedesmarrans@wanadoo.fr

web: www.domainedesmarrans.com

This establishment in the heart of the Beaujolais region has four guest rooms, all with private facilities, in two separate parts of the owners' house. There are two double and two twin-bedded rooms, all upstairs, with possible extra bed. Each of the two guest areas has a lounge and kitchenette. Outside are two courtyards, and a children's play area.

Prices s fr €47; d fr €53; extra person fr €15 **Nearby** ⚓25km ✐8km ➘ 8km Restaurant 2km ⬭1km ⛾2km ⓑ2km ⋙4km **Notes** No pets English spoken CC

GLEIZE

⁙ **A L'Orée des Vignes**

M JACQUET

990 Route des Bruyères, 69400 GLEIZE

☎ 04 74 62 91 74 & 06 79 25 28 74

email: contact@aloreedesvignes.com

web: www.aloreedesvignes.com

A 19th-century house on the edge of the Beaujolais region, close to Villefranche. There are three first floor double rooms, one a suite with a lounge area. One is a grade 2 room. All have private facilities, but those for the grade 2 room are not en suite. Extra bed available. Landscaped garden with terrace and garden furniture.

Prices s €60-€70; d €65-€75 **Nearby** ⚓2km ⬭5km ✐5km ➘5km Restaurant 3km ⬭5km Spa 25km ⛾3km ⓑ3km ⋙4km **Notes** Pets admitted English spoken Open April to October.

GRANDRIS

⁙ ⓘⓞⓘ **Le Domaine des Mollières**

N PASQUIER et F FIORDA

Le Bruley, 69870 GRANDRIS

☎ 04 74 60 13 59

email: domainedesmollieres@orange.fr

web: www.ledomainedesmollieres.org

A restored former farmhouse on the edge of a forest with five guest bedrooms. Two are doubles, two are triples (single beds) and there is a room for four (all single beds). Each room has a private shower and WC. Breakfast and (by arrangement) other meals can be served in the house or out on the terrace.

Prices s €40-€50; d €50-€60; t fr €80; extra person fr €20; dinner fr €20 **Nearby** ⚓15km ⬭30km ✐10km ➘5km ⓑ5km ⋙10km **Notes** Pets admitted English spoken

GREZIEU-LA-VARENNE

⁙ *Les Attignies*

Aline et Christian ROBINO

11 Les Attignies, 69290 GREZIEU-LA-VARENNE

☎ 04 78 57 99 54 & 06 74 89 22 72 ▤ 04 78 57 99 54

email: robino.ac@wanadoo.fr

web: www.lesattignies.com

A mid-19th-century restored farmhouse, offering four guest bedrooms on the first and second floors. Two doubles with private bathrooms/ WC. One double and one twin, both with en suite shower room/WC. Extra sofa beds in each room. Ground floor guest living room with small kitchen area. TV lounge, VHS/DVD/broadband, library. Covered terrace, secure courtyard with parking, wooded grounds, swimming pool.

Prices not confirmed for 2008 **On Site** Private ➘ **Nearby** ⚓4km ⬭5km ✐2.5km ➘1km ⛾4km ⓑ0.6km ⋙5km **Notes** No pets English spoken

JULLIE

⁙ **Domaine la Chapelle de Vatre**

Dominique CAPART

Le Bourbon, 69840 JULLIE

☎ 04 74 04 43 57 & 06 85 70 22 00 ▤ 04 74 04 40 27

email: vatre@wanadoo.fr

web: www.vatre.com

On the heights of Jullié overlooking the vineyards, this 17th-century home incorporates a wine business, a gîte, and the owners' accommodation. Three guest rooms of character include an en suite twin room with its own entrance and private terrace, and two twins with private sitting rooms, one en suite. Heated swimming pool. Sampling and sale of estate wines.

Prices s €60-€80; d €70-€95; t fr €115; extra person fr €20 **On Site** Private ➘ **Nearby** ⚓15km ⬭15km ✐2km Restaurant 1.4km ⬭10km ⛾15km ⓑ4km ⋙15km **Notes** No pets English spoken CC

LANCIE

|O| & **Les Pasquiers**

L et J GANDILHON-ADELE

69220 LANCIE

☎ 04 74 69 86 33 🖹 04 74 69 86 57

email: welcome@lespasquiers.com

web: www.lespasquiers.com/

In the middle of Beaujolais, a huge 19th-century house in a park with swimming pool and tennis court. One double room has disabled access, and there is one double and two twin rooms, all en suite. Living room with open fire and central heating. High quality cuisine with market produce and selected wine.

Prices s fr €80; d fr €80; t fr €100; extra person fr €20; dinner fr €30
On Site 🏊 Private 🎾 Private tennis court **Nearby** ⛷ 5km ⚓ 10km
🌳 5km Restaurant 2km ⚒ 7km **Notes** Pets admitted English spoken

LANTIGNIE

Château des Vergers

Natalie et Pierre BASSOULS

69430 LANTIGNIE

☎ 04 74 04 85 63 & 06 98 84 67 78 🖹 04 74 03 83 50

email: chateaudesvergers@wanadoo.fr

web: www.chateaudesvergers.com

This château, renowned for its wines, has a delightful classical façade, extensive landscaped grounds and four beautifully restored bedrooms, all with en suite showers/WCs. There is one twin-bedded room, one double, and two rooms for three, one with a cot. Possible supplementary room. Guests' lounge and vast period kitchen, swimming pool and tennis court. Wine tasting and sales.

Prices s fr €75; d fr €90; t fr €100; extra person fr €10
On Site Private 🎾 Private tennis court **Nearby** ⛷ 5km ⚓ 50km
🌳 10km 🏊 5km 🚲 2km ⚒ 10km **Notes** Pets admitted English spoken CC

Domaine des Quarante Ecus

B et M-C NESME

Les Vergers, 69430 LANTIGNIE

☎ 04 74 04 85 80 🖹 04 74 69 27 79

email: bnesme@wanadoo.fr

A wine-growing estate in the heart of Beaujolais offering five en suite guest rooms in a house of character with an outstanding view. Three double rooms, one room with a double bed and sofa bed and one twin room. Vast shaded garden with private swimming pool; heating; parking; wine tasting and estate wine sales.

Prices not confirmed for 2008 **On Site** Private 🎾 **Nearby** ⛷ 2km
⚓ 25km 🏊 1km 🎾 15km 🚲 1km ⚒ 15km **Notes** No pets English spoken

|O| *Le Tracot*

Jacqueline MOREL

69430 LANTIGNIE

☎ 04 74 69 25 50 🖹 04 74 69 25 50

Three guest rooms, separate from the house, include two grade 3 en suite rooms (one double and one twin) and one grade 2 twin room with separate bathroom. Beautiful views over the vineyards, enclosed courtyard and wine sampling and museum. Dinner by reservation.

Prices not confirmed for 2008 **Nearby** 🌳 8km 🎾 15km 🏊 1km
🎾 3km 🚲 3km ⚒ 12km **Notes** No pets

LE PERREON

|O| **Les Volets Bleus**

Fabienne DUGNY

69460 LE PERREON

☎ 04 74 03 27 65 🖹 04 74 02 84 23

email: fabienne.dugny@free.fr

web: www.lesvoletsbleus.org

A 19th-century town house in the heart of Beaujolais, near the famous village of Clochemerle, with six tastefully decorated en suite guest rooms (three rooms for two/three people, and three suites for four or five, all non smoking). Large lounge; telephone; central heating; small enclosed garden; garage. Meals by reservation in a relaxed, friendly atmosphere.

Prices s fr €40; d fr €50; t fr €60; extra person fr €15; dinner fr €18
On Site Restaurant **Nearby** ⛷ 10km ⚓ 25km 🌳 0.2km 🎾 15km
🏊 0.5km 🚲 0.1km ⚒ 15km **Notes** No pets English spoken

LES ARDILLATS

|O| **La Verrière**

C et G GESSE-LAMY

69430 LES ARDILLATS

☎ 04 74 04 71 46

email: christine.gesse@wanadoo.fr

web: www.alaverriere.com

This house has been in the same family for over a hundred years. Each of its five rooms can be arranged with a double bed or twin beds; one of them has an additional single bed, and another also has a double bed-settee. All the rooms have private facilities. Lounge with open fire; meals by arrangement; swimming pool.

Prices s fr €50; d fr €65; t fr €80; extra person fr €15; dinner fr €22
On Site Private 🎾 **Nearby** ⛷ 12km ⚓ 25km 🌳 2km Restaurant 5km
🏊 5km 🚲 12km 🎾 5km ⚒ 25km **Notes** Pets admitted English spoken

LES HAIES

⫙ ⦿ **Hermitane**

G et G COMBA-DURANTON
Croix-Régis, 69420 LES HAIES
☎ 04 74 87 82 10 & 06 71 86 08 51 📄 04 74 87 84 76
email: hermitane@yahoo.fr

This property has four bedrooms. On the garden level, with separate access, is a double room with kitchenette; upstairs is a twin-bedded room; a room for four with twin beds and double bed; and a further grade 2 double. All rooms have a private shower room and WC, but those for the grade 2 room are not en suite. Lounge, terrace, garden furniture; meals by arrangement.

Prices s €40-€46; d €44-€50; t fr €64; extra person fr €14; dinner fr €18 **On Site** 🍴 **Nearby** ⛷ 0.1km ♨ 25km 🚴 2.5km ⛵ 9km Restaurant 6km 🛶 9km 🏛 9km 🚠 10km **Notes** No pets English spoken

LES HALLES

⫙ ⦿ **Manoir de Tourville**

Isabelle et François GOUBIER
69610 LES HALLES
☎ 04 74 26 66 57 & 06 09 84 37 09 📄 04 74 26 66 57
email: tourville@manoirdetourville.com
web: www.manoirdetourville.com

In the heart of the Lyonnais mountains, this refined 16th-century manor is surrounded by a charming park and is a friendly place to stay close to Lyon and St Etienne. It offers a double room, a twin, two rooms with a double and single bed, and a suite with a double and single room and a lounge in the tower, each with private facilities. Dinners with home-grown produce by reservation in the large dining room, and candlelit dinners possible in the tower. Horses for hire.

Prices s €65-€120; d €65-€120; t €75-€105; dinner fr €24 **Nearby** ⛷ 3km ♨ 40km 🚴 3km Restaurant 1km 🛶 1km ⛵ 5km 🏛 1km 🚠 20km **Notes** Pets admitted English spoken CC

Le Clos du Chêne
25 km north of Lyons, 5 km from Villefranche sur Saône
Only 30 km from the Eurexpo exhibition halls
370 chemin du Carre   01600 Saint Bernard

Le Clos du Chêne is situated on the Saône River, in a large, enclosed park, with private car parking. Guests have access to library, a large living room with fireplace, outdoor terrasses, swimming pool, sauna, and ping pong and also have use of bicycles. Rooms are air conditioned and have river views, either from balconies or terrasses. All rooms have private bath and toilet facilities. Dinner can be made available by reservation.

Contact : Cheryl and Michel Patay Tel. 00.33.4.74.00.45.39
leclosduchene@orange.fr website : www.leclosduchene.com

LIMAS

▓▓▓ Le Clos de la Barre

Monique et Alain JOFFARD
14 Rue de La Barre, 69400 LIMAS
☎ 04 74 65 97 85 & 06 77 81 50 97
🖩 04 74 09 13 28
email: ajoffard@wanadoo.fr
web: www.leclosdelabarre.com

A superb property in the heart of the village of Limas in Beaujolais, with six charming guest rooms situated in magnificently restored stone outbuildings: two doubles and four double suites with TV and small kitchen corner, all with private facilities. Breakfast served in the owner's home or in the enclosed park, with ancient trees. Ideal location for relaxation.

Prices s €85-€145; d €85-€145; extra person fr €15 **Nearby** ⚓ 3km ⚓ 5km ⚐ 5km ↘ 2km Restaurant 0.2km ⚓ 0.5km Spa 30km ⚑ 0.2km ᾄᾄ 2km **Notes** Pets admitted English spoken Open May to 30 August. CC

LYON

Le Clos du Chêne   see advert on page 843

MARCY-SUR-ANSE

▓▓▓ La Maison Dorée de Martine

Martine LAURENT
184, Route de Frontenas, 69480 MARCY-SUR-ANSE
☎ 04 37 55 08 01 & 06 79 07 38 59
email: lamaisondoree2@wanadoo.fr
web: http://lamaisondoree.ifrance.com

This house, in the heart of the Beaujolais region, has one large room with a double bed and two singles; a double room with a further single bed; and a grade 2 double room. All rooms have private facilities, but those for the grade 2 room are not en suite. Breakfast served in the dining room or on the terrace; possible use of kitchen.

Prices not confirmed for 2008 **Nearby** ⚓ 4km ↘ 10km ⚓ 1km ⚑ 3km ᾄᾄ 10km **Notes** No pets English spoken

MONSOLS

▓▓▓ ⦿ Gîte des Humberts

Jeannine TRIBOLET
69860 MONSOLS
☎ 04 74 04 74 03 & 06 78 53 16 86 🖩 04 74 04 57 80
email: gitedeshumberts@wanadoo.fr
web: http://perso.wanadoo.fr/gitedeshumberts/

This characterful stone-built country house, standing in the middle of the countryside, has been fully restored. It has three guest bedrooms, two doubles and a twin, all with private shower rooms/WCs. There is a large lounge with a small guests' kitchen area. Solar heating. Terrace with garden room for guests' use, open grounds. Parking.

Prices not confirmed for 2008 **Nearby** ⚓ 1km ⚐ 10km ↘ 18km ⚓ 2km ⚓ 12km ⚑ 2km ᾄᾄ 25km **Notes** No pets English spoken

MONTROMANT/YZERON

▓▓▓ ♥ Ferme du Thiollet

C et M RADIX
69610 MONTROMANT/YZERON
☎ 04 78 81 00 93 & 06 16 49 91 46 🖩 04 78 81 00 93
email: mc.radix@wanadoo.fr
web: http://ferme.thiollet.free.fr

Amid the Monts du Lyonnais, this restored family farmhouse offers en suite guest rooms with separate access: one double; one triple and two rooms sleeping four. Guests may use the kitchen and sitting room with open fire; breakfast is served in the dining room and there are local restaurants for dinner.

Prices not confirmed for 2008 **Nearby** ⚓ 15km ⚓ 25km ⚐ 1.5km ↘ 10km ⚓ 1.5km ⚓ 15km ⚑ 1.5km ᾄᾄ 18km **Notes** Pets admitted

QUINCIE-EN-BEAUJOLAIS

▓▓▓ ⦿ Domaine Gouillon La Petite Grange

Danielle GOUILLON
69430 QUINCIE-EN-BEAUJOLAIS
☎ 04 74 04 30 41 & 06 11 16 63 50 🖩 04 74 69 00 67
email: contact@domainegouillon.fr
web: www.domainegouillon.fr

A wine-growing property in the heart of the Beaujolais region. The three bedrooms are in a separate building: a double room and two triples, one with three single beds, the other with a double bed and a single. Each has a private shower room and WC. Guests' lounge, use of kitchen. Terrace with table football and children's slide. Meals by arrangement.

Prices s fr €65; d fr €65; t fr €80; extra person fr €15; dinner fr €25 **Nearby** ⚓ 5km ⚓ 12km ↘ 5km Restaurant 0.5km ⚓ 0.5km ⚓ 3km ⚑ 0.5km ᾄᾄ 6km **Notes** Pets admitted CC

▓▓▓ ⦿ Domaine de Romarand

Annie et Jean BERTHELOT
69430 QUINCIE-EN-BEAUJOLAIS
☎ 04 74 04 34 49 🖩 04 74 04 35 92
email: berthelot.romarand.orange.fr
web: www.beaujeu.com/hote_berthelot.html

Three en suite guest rooms with separate access (one twin and two doubles with two spare beds) set in the midst of Beaujolais vines. Large

communal room for guests, sitting area with open fire. Central heating; parking in closed courtyard. Swimming pool with pleasant garden. Wine tasting on the premises; dinner by reservation. Closed Xmas.

Prices s fr €50; d €60-€62; extra person fr €15; dinner fr €23
On Site Private ⊹ **Nearby** ⚓ 10km ⚱ 15km 🏊 15km Restaurant 3km 🍴 3km 🍷 5km 🏛 3km ⛟ 12km **Notes** Pets admitted English spoken CC

▦ 🐾 🍽 Huire

J et G LAGNEAU
69430 QUINCIE-EN-BEAUJOLAIS
☎ 04 74 69 20 70 🖺 04 74 04 89 44
email: jealagneau@wanadoo.fr
web: www.domainelagneau.com

Winegrowers farm this peaceful corner of Beaujolais from their stone house set between pines and vines. Magnificent views can be enjoyed from the four en suite guest rooms with separate access (one two-roomed suite with four single beds; two twin rooms; one double room). Central heating; lounge; television; open grounds with garden furniture. Meals by reservation.

Prices s €50; d €60-€65; t €92-€97; extra person €20; dinner fr €23
Nearby ⚓ 7km ⚱ 35km 🏊 5km ⊹ 12km 🍴 4km 🍷 2.5km 🏛 2.5km ⛟ 12km **Notes** No pets English spoken CC

▦ 🍽 Les Potins du Four

Sylvie et J-Philippe AUGER
La Roche, 69430 QUINCIE-EN-BEAUJOLAIS
☎ 04 74 04 38 82 & 06 75 95 77 00
email: lespotins@wanadoo.fr
web: http://perso.wanadoo.fr/lespotinsdufour

This house is in the heart of the Beaujolais region, with vineyards bordering the garden. A separate guests' entrance leads to four rooms: a double, and three further doubles which also have double sofa beds, making good family accommodation. Each room has en suite facilities and a living area; outside is a terrace and swimming pool. Meals by arrangement.

Prices s fr €53; d €58-€63; t fr €80; extra person fr €17; dinner fr €22
On Site Private ⊹ **Nearby** ⚓ 15km Restaurant 0.2km 🍴 1km 🍷 3km 🏛 0.5km ⛟ 10km **Notes** Pets admitted English spoken

SOUCIEU-EN-JARREST

▦ 🍽 *Carpe Diem*

Joëlle et Patrick CHARTIER
5 Montée du Perron, 69510 SOUCIEU-EN-JARREST
☎ 04 78 05 10 30 & 06 89 92 06 50
email: a-carpediem@wanadoo.fr
web: http://perso.wanadoo.fr/a.carpediem

In a leafy setting in the heart of Soucieu-en-Jarrest, just 20 minutes from Lyon, guests can choose between a double room in the owners' home with possible extra bed, or a double and room for four in an adjoining building. All have private facilities. Breakfast is served in the proprietor's living room or in the garden by the pool.

Prices not confirmed for 2008 **On Site** Private ⊹ **Nearby** ⚓ 5km ⚱ 20km 🏊 20km 🍴 1km 🍷 5km 🏛 0.3km ⛟ 5km **Notes** No pets English spoken CC

ST-ANDRE-LA-COTE

▦ 🐾 🍽 *Le Petit Bois des Terres*

Anne et Marc GUYOT
69440 ST-ANDRE-LA-COTE
☎ 04 78 81 61 16 & 06 73 94 56 80 🖺 04 78 81 61 16
email: chambredhote@lahautsurlamontagne.com
web: www.la-hautsurlamontagne.com

High up in the Monts du Lyonnais, this property has a ground floor double room with its own entrance, and two further family rooms for up to four in a separate building. All have private shower room and WC. The grounds are extensive, with wonderful views. Generous breakfasts; other meals and picnics by arrangement.

Prices not confirmed for 2008 **On Site** ⊹ **Nearby** ⚓ 11km ⊹ 11km 🍴 0.5km 🍷 5km 🏛 5km ⛟ 20km **Notes** Pets admitted English spoken

ST-IGNY-DE-VERS

▦ 🍽 *La Musardière*

Geneviève DIOT
La Fabrique, 69790 ST-IGNY-DE-VERS
☎ 04 74 03 68 25
email: gene.diot@orange.fr

This restored stone house, standing in a quiet spot in the middle of the countryside, has three guest bedrooms, one with an additional small en suite bedroom. The beds can be flexibly arranged, to provide doubles, twins, or rooms for three, all with private facilities. There are extensive shady grounds, with a river nearby. Meals by arrangement, with vegetarian option.

Prices not confirmed for 2008 **Nearby** ⚓ 4km 🏊 5km ⊹ 13km 🍴 3km 🍷 25km 🏛 3km ⛟ 15km **Notes** Pets admitted

ST-JEAN-LA-BUSSIERE

▦ 🍽 *La Clef des Champs*

B THIOLLIER-VILLAVERDE
La Fedolliere, 69550 ST-JEAN-LA-BUSSIERE
☎ 04 74 89 52 18 & 06 87 53 16 94 🖺 04 74 89 52 18
email: brigitte.villaverde@wanadoo.fr

Specially built accommodation at the heart of Beaujolais with one double room with disabled access; one room with double bed and bunks; one room with twin bed and bunks; one double room; and one single room, all en suite. Living room/lounge for guests. Television, terrace, garden furniture, parking. Meals by reservation.

Prices not confirmed for 2008 **Nearby** ⚓ 1km 🏊 1km ⊹ 3km 🍴 3km 🏛 3km ⛟ 5km **Notes** No pets

ST-JEAN-LA-BUSSIERE *CONTINUED*

▦ ⒪ La Mamouniere

F et Y MOUNIER

La Mazille, 69550 ST-JEAN-LA-BUSSIERE

☎ 04 74 89 52 04 & 06 84 11 59 99

email: moufry@wanadoo.fr

A restored stone-built farmhouse with four bedrooms in a separate wing. Three of the rooms are triples; the fourth is a family room for four with a double bed and bunks. Large day room for guests' use, with a kitchenette. Inner courtyard with parking space. Saturday meals available by arrangement. Lake 800 metres away, with recreational opportunities.

Prices s €32-€35; d €45-€48; t €60-€63; extra person fr €15; dinner fr €20 **Nearby** ⚓ 0.8km ♨ 30km ⌁ 0.2km ⤳ 3km Restaurant 0.8km ♒ 1.5km ♣ 1km ⛪ 3km ⅏ 5km **Notes** Pets admitted English spoken

ST-JULIEN-SOUS-MONTMELAS

▦ ✿ Château du Jonchy

C et T DES GARETS

Le Jonchy, 69640 ST-JULIEN-SOUS-MONTMELAS

☎ 04 74 67 53 36 ▤ 04 74 67 58 93

email: caroledesgarets@wanadoo.fr

web: www.chateaudujonchy.com

At this property the three guest rooms are in a separate building close to the owners' house. There is a double room with space for two extra beds; a room with a double bed and a single; and a double/twin room with linking beds. The first two rooms also have a fridge and microwave. Small shady sitting-out area. Breakfast in owners' house or garden.

Prices s €60-€70; d €65-€75; t €80-€90; extra person fr €15 **On Site** Private ⤳ Private tennis court **Nearby** ⚓ 3km ♨ 25km ⌁ 1.5km Restaurant 4km ♣ 20km ⛪ 1.5km ⅏ 10km **Notes** No pets English spoken

ST-LAURENT-D'OINGT

▦ Chambre d'hôtes

R et N GUILLARD

69620 ST-LAURENT-D'OINGT

☎ 04 74 71 27 95 & 06 71 39 01 88

email: roger.guillard@numericable.com

A warm welcome can be expected at this golden stone house offering three rooms: one grade 3 en suite room with double bed plus spare bed; one grade 2 room with double bed and two singles with separate bathroom; and one en suite grade 3 room with separate access sleeping three. Communal room; kitchen available. Courtyard, lawn with children's games, parking. Cellar on site, with sampling and wine sales.

Prices s fr €41; d fr €46; t fr €58; extra person fr €15 **Nearby** ⚓ 6km ♨ 20km ⌁ 5km ⤳ 15km Restaurant 0.5km ♒ 4km ⛪ 5km ⅏ 5km **Notes** No pets English spoken

ST-LAURENT-DE-CHAMOUSSET

▦▦ ⒪ Château de la Charmeraie

Brigitte TREGOUET

Domaine de la Batie,

69930 ST-LAURENT-DE-CHAMOUSSET

☎ 04 74 70 50 70 & 06 62 22 56 40

▤ 04 74 26 59 55

email: contact@chateaudelacharmeraie.com

web: www.chateaudelacharmeraie.com

An impressive house in an exceptional location in the Monts du Lyonnais. There are three double rooms, a twin-bedded room and a family room for four (double bed and two singles). All are air-conditioned with private bathroom and WC. Evening meals are available (pre-booking needed) and there is a conservatory, terrace and swimming pool.

Prices s €70-€150; d €70-€150; extra person fr €30; dinner fr €33 **On Site** ⌁ Private ⤳ **Nearby** ⚓ 2km ♨ 25km Restaurant 8km ♒ 0.2km Spa 30km ⛪ 1km ⅏ 35km **Notes** No pets English spoken CC

ST-VERAND

▦ ⒪ Fondvielle

Catherine et Joël MORAND

Taponas, 69620 ST-VERAND

☎ 04 74 71 62 64 & 06 03 47 64 63

email: fondvielle@wanadoo.fr

web: http://fondvielle.free.fr

Three of the four bedrooms here are in an extension to the owners' house. There is a double room, a twin-bedded room, and a family room with three single beds and its own terrace. In a separate building is a triple room (double bed and a single). All have private facilities. Lounge in owners' house. Large enclosed wooded grounds, garden furniture, boules. Meals by arrangement.

Prices s fr €50; d fr €62; t fr €73; extra person fr €15; dinner fr €19 **Nearby** ⚓ 7km ♨ 20km ⌁ 5km ⤳ 12km ♒ 2km ♣ 12km ⛪ 1.5km ⅏ 15km **Notes** No pets English spoken

THEIZE

▦ ⑩ Le Clos des Pierres Dorées

Christine LACK

Le Boitier, 69620 THEIZE

☎ 04 74 71 26 38 & 06 19 29 40 97

email: leclosdespierresdorees@wanadoo.fr

web: http://perso.wanadoo.fr/closdespierresdorees/

Right in the heart of the Beaujolais vineyards, this is a stone-built property in walled grounds with a swimming pool. The two double rooms and one twin-bedded room, all with private shower room and WC, are in a wing of the owners' house. Guests' sitting room; meals available by arrangement (except Sundays).

Prices d €105-€145; dinner fr €30 **On Site** Private ⚄ **Nearby** ⚄ 10km ⚄ 12km **Notes** No pets English spoken Open March to January.

VAUX-EN-BEAUJOLAIS

▦ ⑩ Les Picorettes

J et F BLETTNER

Montrichard, 69460 VAUX-EN-BEAUJOLAIS

☎ 04 74 02 14 07 📄 04 74 02 14 21

email: francis.blettner@picorettes.com

web: www.picorettes.com

In a beautiful spot in the heart of wine country near Vaux-en-Beaujolais, this welcoming guest house has four rooms with separate access: one room sleeping three with bath and jacuzzi and separate wc; one two-roomed en suite family suite with double bed and two singles; and two double en suite rooms. Meals (by reservation) are served under the arbour; swimming pool; parking.

Prices s €59-€89; d €65-€100; t €100-€115; extra person fr €15; dinner fr €25 **On Site** Private ⚄ **Nearby** ⚄ 10km ⚄ 20km ⚄ 0.2km Restaurant 1.4km ⚄ 2km ⚄ 25km ⚄ 2km ⚄ 12km **Notes** No pets English spoken CC

VERNAY

▦ ⑩ Hameau d'Amignié

Sylvie PERRET

69430 VERNAY

☎ 04 74 69 23 06 & 06 62 52 30 50

email: symax@wanadoo.fr

web: www.hameauamignie.com

This chambre d'hôtes consists of three buildings, one of which houses the guest accommodation. There is a double-bedded room, a twin-bedded room and a family room for four with a double bed and bunks. All have private bath or shower room and WC. Full range of baby equipment available. Landscaped gardens; meals by arrangement.

Prices s fr €70; d fr €75; t fr €90; extra person fr €15; dinner fr €25 **On Site** Spa ⚄ **Nearby** ⚄ 5km ⚄ 25km ⚄ 5km ⚄ 25km Restaurant 7km ⚄ 5km ⚄ 5km ⚄ 20km **Notes** No pets English spoken CC

VILLIE-MORGON

▦ La Maison du Raisin

Jean-Paul BALDECK

278 Rue Pasteur, 69910 VILLIE-MORGON

☎ 04 74 04 24 64 & 06 25 41 00 53 📄 04 74 04 24 20

email: a2jpb@wanadoo.fr

web: www.lamaisonduraisin.com

An old wine-grower's house, peacefully situated in a delightful village in the Beaujolais region. There are three double bedrooms, each with a private bathroom and WC, all decorated in a warm and attractive style. Dining room with kitchenette; enclosed courtyard with pergola.

Prices s fr €75; d fr €80; t fr €120 **Nearby** ⚄ 10km ⚄ 15km ⚄ 4km ⚄ 0.5km Restaurant 0.5km ⚄ 0.5km Spa 3km ⚄ 4km ⚄ 0.5km ⚄ 8km **Notes** No pets English spoken

▦ Le Clachet

Agnes et Jean FOILLARD

69910 VILLIE-MORGON

☎ 04 74 04 24 97 & 06 76 48 48 71 📄 04 74 69 12 71

email: jean.foillard@wanadoo.fr

web: www.leclachet.com

Close to Belleville exit on autoroute, three twin rooms and one double bedroom are spacious with large beds and all are en suite. There is an enormous day room with fireplace, an airy lounge and library for the use of guests.

Prices d €80-€90; extra person fr €16 **Nearby** ⚄ 11km ⚄ 25km ⚄ 3km ⚄ 4km Restaurant 4km ⚄ 0.6km ⚄ 3km ⚄ 0.7km ⚄ 7km **Notes** No pets Open April to 20 December.

YZERON

▦ ⑩ La Maison du Parc

Pascale et J-Yves SCHENCK

2 Grande Rue, 69510 YZERON

☎ 04 78 81 09 21 & 06 68 38 22 33

email: lamaisonduparc@free.fr

web: http://la-maison-du-parc.com

This 19th-century house stands in the heart of the village of Yzeron, 29 kilometres from Lyon. It has four pleasant double rooms, all on the first and second floors and with private shower rooms/WCs. Lounge with books available; dining room opens on to a terrace and shady grounds with a swimming pool. Enclosed parking, meals by arrangement.

Prices s €41-€48; d €48-€55; extra person €10; dinner fr €18 **On Site** Private ⚄ **Nearby** ⚄ 15km ⚄ 1km Restaurant 0.5km ⚄ 1km ⚄ 0.5km ⚄ 25km **Notes** Pets admitted English spoken

RHÔNE-ALPES

SAVOIE

AILLON-LE-JEUNE

♦♦♦ ⊙ Gite de Vieux Four

Robert BAULAT
73340 AILLON-LE-JEUNE
☎ 04 79 54 61 47 & 06 16 54 12 17
web: http://giteduvieuxfour.free.fr

A typical Bauges house, now renovated, looking down onto the village. Three double rooms, one with cot, and one single room, all en suite. Living room, central heating, grounds with garden furniture. Traditional breakfast is served in the dining room. Specialities include gratin, diots, crozets, tartiflette, pizza and organic bread. Walks along forest tracks and skiing at Aillon-le-Jeune. Reduced meal prices for children.

Prices s fr €40; d fr €46; t fr €60; extra person fr €14; dinner fr €15 **Nearby** ⚓ 3km ♟ 0.2km ⇲ 4km Restaurant 2km ⚑ 3km ♨ 3km ❦ 2km ⌂ 1km ⋙ 24km **Notes** No pets English spoken

♦♦♦ ⊙ La Grangerie

V et P CONCEILLON
Les Ginets, 73340 AILLON-LE-JEUNE
☎ 04 79 54 64 71
email: grangerie@libertysurf.fr
web: www.lagrangerie.com

A traditional restored farmhouse with superb views over the valley and Aillon-le-Jeune. Four en suite guest rooms in the mansard roof, each with a double and single bed and one with a balcony. Central heating. Enjoy home-made preserves, a variety of organic bread and specialities including tarte à la tome, fondue savoyarde, and civet. Nearby national park and skiing at Aillon-le-Jeune and le Margériaz. Reduced meal prices for children.

Prices not confirmed for 2008 **Nearby** ⚓ 2km ♟ 2km ⇲ 2km ⚑ 0.5km ♨ 2km ⌂ 1.5km ⋙ 26km **Notes** Pets admitted English spoken

AIME

♦♦♦ ⊙ Ancienne Ecole de Montvilliers

Marie et Yves BONNEAUD
73210 AIME
☎ 04 79 09 75 43 ▤ 04 79 55 32 29
email: yves@gite-de-montvilliers.com
web: www.gite-de-montvilliers.com

Renovated former farmhouse and 19th-century school, situated in a hamlet by an orchard and enjoying views over the mountains and valley of Isère. Rooms include a double, two twins, and three triples, all with private facilities. Grounds, heating, breakfast made to order with regional and seasonal specialities, free transport to activities. Skiing at Montalbert (linked to La Plagne), climbing 10km, hang-gliding 5km, white water 6km.

Prices s €45-€54; d €54-€63; t €66-€76; extra person €13; dinner fr €18 **On Site** Restaurant ❦ **Nearby** ♟ 6km ⇲ 19km ⚑ 4km ♨ 4km ⌂ 1km ⋙ 7km **Notes** Pets admitted English spoken CC

ALBERTVILLE

♦♦♦ Chambre d'hôtes

Kathia et David EXCOFFON
7 Chemin des Galibouds, 73200 ALBERTVILLE
☎ 04 79 31 38 75 & 06 21 09 14 39 ▤ 04 79 31 38 75
email: Kathia.excoffon@free.fr
web: http://leschambresdepauline.free.fr

An attractively restored 1920s house, in a residential area. There are three bedrooms on the ground floor: two doubles and a family suite for four, with a double bed and two singles. Each room has air conditioning, TV, private shower room and WC. Large lounge, leading onto an open terrace. Good choice of food for breakfast.

Prices not confirmed for 2008 **Nearby** ⚓ 5km ♟ 0.5km ⇲ 5km ⚑ 24km ♨ 1km ⌂ 0.5km ⋙ 1km **Notes** Pets admitted

ARECHES-BEAUFORT

♦♦♦ ⊙ Chalet de Bernoline

Luc GOLFIER
La Pierre, 73270 ARECHES-BEAUFORT
☎ 04 79 38 05 56 & 06 19 86 80 77 ▤ 04 79 38 05 56
email: chaletdebernoline@tiscali.fr
web: www.chaletdebernoline.com

This modern chalet is at the foot of a hill, with a view due south towards the mountains. It has four beautifully decorated bedrooms, two doubles and two triples, all with en suite shower rooms and WCs. Central heating. There is a large lounge with an open fireplace. Breakfast includes home-made jams and bread; other meals are available by arrangement.

Prices not confirmed for 2008 **Nearby** ⚓ 7km ♟ 1km ⇲ 2km ⚑ 7km ♨ 2km ⌂ 2km ⋙ 20km **Notes** No pets English spoken

AUSSOIS

♦♦♦ ⊙ La Roche du Croue

Claire TANTOLIN
3 Rue de L'Eglise, 73500 AUSSOIS
☎ 04 79 20 31 07 & 06 70 11 44 59 ▤ 04 79 20 48 28
email: info@larocheducroue.com
web: www.larocheducroue.com

Near the Parc National de la Vanoise, five guest rooms available (one double room; two with three single beds; one with a double and a twin; and one with a double bed and bunks) all en suite and four with balconies. Lounge area with open fire and TV. Washing machine, drier, terrace, central heating. Specialities include crozets, tartiflette, raclette, home-made yoghurt, jams, and various desserts.

Prices not confirmed for 2008 **Nearby** ⚓ 0.5km ♟ 7km ⇲ 7km ⚑ 0.3km ♨ 0.5km ⌂ 0.1km ⋙ 7km **Notes** No pets English spoken CC

AVRIEUX

⚌ *Chambre d'hôtes*

Nathalie et Bruno MUNARI
352 Rue St Thomas, 73500 AVRIEUX
☎ 04 79 20 37 09 📄 04 79 20 37 09
email: lagrange.nat@free.fr
web: www.la-norma.com/lagrange-avrieux/index.html

This 19th-century barn conversion stands in the centre of the village. It has four bedrooms, with an independent entrance. On the ground floor is a double room; on the first floor are two more doubles; on the second floor is a two-roomed suite with twin beds, double beds and a balcony. All rooms have a private shower and WC. Varied breakfasts; kitchenette available.

Prices not confirmed for 2008 **Nearby** ⚌ 8km 🏊 0.1km ⛷ 5km
⚌ 4km ⚌ 4km 🏛 5km ⚌ 5km **Notes** Pets admitted English spoken CC

BONNEVAL-SUR-ARC

⚌ La Rosa

Olga CAVATORE
Vieux Village, 73480 BONNEVAL-SUR-ARC
☎ 04 79 05 95 66 📄 04 79 05 95 66
email: la.rosa-chambresdhote@wanadoo.fr
web: www.la-rosa.info

A traditional style stone-built house, with a beautiful flower-filled garden and terrace. All the rooms are upstairs: a double and a triple with balconies; and two split-level rooms, one with a double bed and the other with a double bed and two singles. All have private shower room and WC. Guests' sitting room. Breakfasts include home-made jams and pastries.

Prices s €50-€58; d €60-€68; t €80-€85; extra person fr €15
Nearby ⚌ 18km 🏊 0.2km ⛷ 17km Restaurant 1km ⚌ 0.3km ⚌ 0.5km
Spa 18km 🏌 0.5km 🏛 0.1km ⚌ 45km **Notes** No pets English spoken

BRAMANS

⚌ 🍴 Chalet Lavis Trafford

F et F DE GROLEE
Le Planay, 73500 BRAMANS
☎ 04 79 05 06 83 📄 04 79 05 08 82
email: info@chalet-lavis-trafford.com
web: www.chalet-lavis-trafford.com/

This wood and stone chalet is situated in the Ambin Valley, surrounded by larch trees and ideal for walking and skiing (16km). The five guest rooms comprise two twins, two doubles and a triple. Two rooms share a wc; the rest have private facilities and balconies. Breakfasts feature home-made jams, honey and regional specialities. The chalet cannot be reached by car in winter and access is by shuttle and snow shoes.

Prices s €64-€88; d €64-€88; dinner fr €22 **On Site** 🏊
Nearby ⚌ 9km ⛷ 18km Restaurant 7km ⚌ 9km Spa 18km 🏌 18km
🏛 7km ⚌ 18km **Notes** No pets English spoken Open December to March & May to October.

CHAMBERY

⚌ *La Ferme du Petit Bonheur*

Chantal et Eric SOULARD
538 Chemin de Jean Jacques, 73000 CHAMBERY
☎ 04 79 85 26 17 & 06 10 28 84 13 📄 04 79 85 26 17
email: info@fermedupetitbonheur.fr
web: www.fermedupetitbonheur.fr

An old renovated Savoyard farmhouse on a hill dominating the town, opposite Nivolet and close to the valley of Charmettes. Three rooms with refined décor in an old grange: a double, a twin and a room with a double and single, each with heating and private facilities. Large living room with Norwegian stove, children's games, big garden with terrace. Breakfasts with home-made jam and Savoie cheeses. Skiing nearby at Le Granier.

Prices s fr €75; d fr €85; t fr €105 **Nearby** ⚌ 3km 🎣 15km 🏊 4km
⛷ 3km Restaurant 1km ⚌ 17km ⚌ 3km Spa 10km 🏌 4km 🏛 1.5km
⚌ 3km **Notes** No pets English spoken

CORBEL

⚌ *Les Terrasses du Frou*

Janine FERTIER
73160 CORBEL
☎ 04 79 65 73 89 📄 04 79 44 39 80
email: contact@terrasses-du-frou.com
web: www.terrasses-du-frou.com

This renovated former presbytery has great views. The three ground-floor rooms with sloping ceilings have a separate entrance. Two doubles, a single with washbasin and shower; WC in each bedroom. Traditional terracotta décor and panelling. Electric heating, wood-burning stove, fireplace, dining area, outside space, shaded terrace with garden chairs. Breakfast in the lounge or on the terrace, homemade jam and local honey.

Prices not confirmed for 2008 **Nearby** ⚌ 12km 🏊 1km ⛷ 16km
⚌ 6km ⚌ 10km 🏛 16km ⚌ 23km **Notes** No pets CC

CREST-VOLAND

⚌ 🍴 Chalet les Campanules

Jackie CHEVRETON
Chemin de la Grange, 73590 CREST-VOLAND
☎ 04 79 31 81 43 & 06 74 84 59 05
email: chanteline@wanadoo.fr
web: www.lescampanules.com

With splendid views over the alpine range of Aravis, this cosy house is in the heart of a ski resort and offers a double room, a twin with balcony and a suite with a double, twin and balcony, each with private facilities. Living room with fireplace, heating, grounds. Generous breakfasts served in the dining room or on the balcony, with home-made jams, cakes and breads. Specialities available. Restaurant nearby.

Prices s fr €66; d fr €66; t fr €89; extra person fr €20; dinner fr
€21 **On Site** ⚌ **Nearby** ⚌ 3km 🎣 13km 🏊 10km ⛷ 14km
Restaurant 0.1km Spa 13km 🏛 0.1km ⚌ 25km **Notes** No pets English spoken

FEISSONS-SUR-SALINS

♯♯♯ ⧉ *Chalet de la Yodine*

Philippe BRANGER
73350 FEISSONS-SUR-SALINS
☎ 04 79 24 24 34 & 06 72 09 91 48
email: info@chaletdelayodine.com
web: www.chaletdelayodine.com

A large restored house in the middle of the village, facing south. There are five bedrooms, all upstairs, sleeping from two to five people. All have en suite facilities, and four have balconies. The rooms are individually decorated and there is a living room with a log-burner. Breakfasts include home-made jams and pastries; other meals available by arrangement.

Prices not confirmed for 2008   **Nearby** ♿ 18km ✐ 10km ➹ 9km ⚓ 10km ⛰ 10km Spa 10km ⛪ 10km ⫘ 11km **Notes** No pets English spoken CC

FLUMET

♯♯♯ ⧉ *Les Glieres*

M et P OUVRIER MONTI
73590 FLUMET
☎ 04 79 31 38 84 & 06 87 34 01 32 ▤ 04 79 31 38 84
email: contact@chalet-marie.com
web: www.chalet-marie.com

A totally restored chalet in a small hamlet. There are four bedrooms, all upstairs: two doubles and two two-roomed suites for four, all with private shower and WC. There is a tastefully-decorated living room, and outside is a terrace with garden furniture. Breakfasts include home-made jams and pastries. Garage for motor-bikes.

Prices not confirmed for 2008   **On Site** ✐   **Nearby** ♿ 8km ➹ 14km ⚓ 5km ⛰ 4km ⛪ 4km ⫘ 27km **Notes** Pets admitted English spoken

JONGIEUX

♯♯♯ *Jongieux le Haut*

A et P JACQUIN
73170 JONGIEUX
☎ 04 79 44 00 29 & 04 79 44 02 35 ▤ 04 79 44 03 05

This guest house is at the entrance to the village on a plateau overlooking the Rhône Valley with views over the Charvaz mountain and vineyards. One double room with a terrace, one room with a double and single bed with balcony; a second room sleeping three, all en suite. Superb day room, use of kitchen, central heating, grounds. Restaurant, climbing, canoeing and sailing nearby.

Prices not confirmed for 2008   **Nearby** ♿ 7km ✐ 4km ➹ 25km ⛰ 7km Spa 24km ⛪ 0.5km ⫘ 19km **Notes** No pets

LA BIOLLE

♯♯♯ *La Villette*

Gilbert et Jeanette GOURY
Sous la Colline, 73410 LA BIOLLE
☎ 04 79 54 76 79 ▤ 04 79 54 70 70
email: souslacolline@wanadoo.fr

Typical Albanais house, situated by a wood. Four en suite guest rooms: one double and three rooms sleeping three, one with sitting area and balcony. Kitchen area, courtyard, garden furniture, children's games. Breakfast served in the dining room or on the terrace with preserves, yoghurt, honey and cheese. Skiing, climbing, restaurant nearby. Reduced rates by agreement.

Prices not confirmed for 2008   **Nearby** ♿ 5km ✐ 5km ➹ 11km ⚓ 27km ⛰ 5km Spa 11km ⛪ 2.5km ⫘ 5km **Notes** No pets

LA BRIDOIRE

♯♯♯ ⧉ **Au Petit Prince**

P et B DELATTRE
Chef-Lieu, 73520 LA BRIDOIRE
☎ 04 76 07 25 60 & 06 03 80 88 29
email: contact@aupetitprince.net
web: www.aupetitprince.net

Right in the middle of the village, this is a cosy comfortable place with three large rooms. There is a double, a triple (double bed plus single) and a suite with a double bed, single bed and cot. All have private facilities. Sitting room with TV, DVD player and music system; garden with parking space. Breakfasts include home-made jams, bread and pastries.

Prices s fr €55; d €60-€70; t fr €80; extra person fr €20; dinner €25 **On Site** ✐   **Nearby** ♿ 0.2km ⛰ 30km ➹ 14km Restaurant 2km ⚓ 30km ⛰ 3km Spa 31km ⫘ 2km **Notes** No pets English spoken

LA COTE-D'AIME

♯♯♯ ⧉ **Le Paradou**

D et M-P CHUZEUL
73210 LA COTE-D'AIME
☎ 04 79 55 67 79 ▤ 04 79 55 67 79
email: chaletleparadou@orange.fr
web: www.chaletleparadou.com

Wooden chalet with lovely views over the mountains offering five en suite guest rooms: three double rooms and two twins. Lounge with open fire, games, electric heating, terrace, grounds, garden furniture. Specialities include gigot, raclette cooked over a wood fire, ham, home-made pastries and jams. Skiing and rafting nearby. Reduced children's rates.

Prices s €60-€70; d fr €70; t €80-€90; dinner fr €20 **On Site** Spa **Nearby** ♿ 15km ⛰ 25km ✐ 5km ➹ 18km Restaurant 1km ⚓ 5km ⛰ 7km ⛪ 5km ⫘ 4km **Notes** No pets English spoken

₩ ⓘ⊙ı **Les Carlines**

M et A FOESSEL

Pre Berard, 73210 LA COTE-D'AIME

☎ 04 79 55 52 07 & 06 14 17 75 17 📄 09 55 27 52 07

email: carlines@free.fr

web: http://carlines.free.fr

This modern house in a small hamlet has pleasing views over the valley of the Isère. It has five bedrooms, all on the first floor. There are three triples with single beds, a room with four single beds, and a twin-bedded room. All have a private shower and WC. Lounge with open fire and TV. Breakfast buffet includes savoury dishes. Garden furniture.

Prices s €28-€31; d €56-€62; t €84-€93; dinner fr €17 **Nearby** ☂ 15km ⌇ 5km ⌲ 18km ⌗ 5km ⌓ 7km ⌼ 5km ⌗ 5km **Notes** No pets

LA NORMA-VILLARODIN-BOURGET

₩₩ ⓘ⊙ı **Che Catrine**

Catherine et Christian FINAS

88 Rue St Antoine,

73500 LA NORMA-VILLARODIN-BOURGET

☎ 04 79 20 49 32 & 06 62 11 49 32

📄 04 79 20 48 67

email: info@che-catrine.com

web: www.che-catrine.com

A 16th-century house with lots of character. There are two double-bedded rooms, a twin-bedded room and two suites for four or five people. All have internet access, private bath or shower room and WC. Meals are available by arrangement, with vegetables from the garden and home-made bread. Sauna and jacuzzi on site; the hosts are ski instructors.

Prices s €59-€79; d €79-€105; t fr €134; extra person fr €15; dinner fr €30 **On Site** Spa **Nearby** ☂ 2km ⌇ 2km ⌲ 2.5km Restaurant 0.2km ⌗ 2.5km ⌓ 0.8km ⌼ 3km ⌗ 3km **Notes** Pets admitted English spoken

LA ROCHETTE

₩₩ **Les Oiseaux**

Isabelle AUTONES

800 Route d'Arvillard, 73110 LA ROCHETTE

☎ 04 79 65 27 69 & 06 75 22 08 37 📄 04 79 36 92 95

email: lesoiseaux.autones@wanadoo.fr

web: http://lesoiseaux.site.voila.fr/

This 100-year old house stands in vast wooded grounds. It has three bedrooms. On the ground floor are two rooms, a double and a single; upstairs is a two-roomed suite with a double bed, twin beds and a child's bed. All of the rooms have a private shower room and WC. Lounge with board games; breakfast includes home-made items; possibility of brunch. Garden furniture.

Prices not confirmed for 2008 **Nearby** ☂ 5km ⌇ 1km ⌲ 1km ⌗ 21km ⌓ 0.6km Spa 11km ⌼ 0.6km ⌗ 11km **Notes** Pets admitted CC

LE CHATELARD

₩₩ ⓘ⊙ı *Chambre d'hôtes*

Francine et Roger LE BRIS

Av Denis Therme, 73630 LE CHATELARD

☎ 04 79 52 02 74 & 06 09 06 28 15 📄 04 79 54 61 60

email: roger.lebris@wanadoo.fr

web: http://lebris.site.voila.fr

A 1960s house, in a village, on a hillside. There are three ground floor rooms, two doubles and a twin. All have private bath or shower and WC. The large dining room has an open fire and a lounge area. The excellent breakfasts offer much variety, including regional specialities. Fridge and microwave; pretty garden with terrace and flowers.

Prices not confirmed for 2008 **Nearby** ☂ 8km ⌲ 2km ⌗ 15km ⌗ 14km ⌓ 0.5km ⌗ 21km **Notes** No pets English spoken CC

LE NOYER

₩₩ ✿ **L'Herbier de la Clappe**

Philippe DURAND

73340 LE NOYER

☎ 04 79 63 49 94 & 06 86 82 51 53 📄 04 79 63 49 94

email: lherbierdelaclappe@wanadoo.fr

web: www.lherbierdelaclappe.com

A beautiful modern house, in a rural setting on the edge of a village, with four bedrooms. On the ground floor is a double; upstairs there is a twin-bedded room, a double, and a triple. All have private shower and WC, and the upstairs rooms have balconies. Terrace with views, varied breakfasts, use of kitchen. Three-day courses: learning about herbs.

Prices s fr €43; d fr €48; t fr €60 **Nearby** ☂ 4km ⌲ 2km ⌗ 21km ⌗ 10km ⌓ 6km Spa 31km ⌗ 6km ⌗ 25km **Notes** No pets

LE VIVIERS-DU-LAC

₩₩ **Chambre d'hôtes**

B MONTAGNOLE

516 Chemin de Boissy, 73420 LE VIVIERS-DU-LAC

☎ 04 79 35 31 26 📄 04 79 35 31 26

Modern house on a hill with a fine view of the cliffs on the Plateau du Revard. Three en suite guest rooms: one twin, one double and one room with single and double bed. Electric heating; cooking facilities available; grounds with garden furniture. Quiet living room. Restaurants, golf and skiing (Le Revard) nearby.

Prices s €30-€35; d €40-€45 **Nearby** ☂ 3km ⌇ 2km ⌗ 3km ⌗ 5km Restaurant 1km ⌗ 22km ⌓ 3km Spa 3km ⌗ 2km ⌗ 5km **Notes** No pets

LEPIN-LE-LAC

⚜⚜⚜ ⏏ La Bageatière

Valerie AMBAL

73610 LEPIN-LE-LAC

☎ 04 79 65 95 61 & 06 88 84 62 83

email: contact@labageatiere.com

web: www.labageatiere.com

A former vineyard property at the foot of Mont Granier, which has been restored to provide three en suite guest rooms, sleeping from two to four people. The rooms have attractive, country-style decorations. A terrace leads to extensive grounds with garden furniture and a barbecue. Generous breakfasts, with home-made items.

Prices s €60-€85; d €68-€90; t €105-€115; extra person €25-€30; dinner fr €24 **Nearby** ⛷ 2km ♨ 25km ⚓ 0.8km ✈ 13km Restaurant 3km ⛵ 33km ♨ 1.5km Spa 25km ♿ 2.5km ⚓ 1km **Notes** No pets English spoken

⚜⚜⚜ ⏏ La Clairière du Moulin

Anita DUNCAN

Hameau du Puits, 73610 LEPIN-LE-LAC

☎ 04 79 36 30 05 📠 04 79 36 30 05

web: www.laclairieredumoulin.com

This former farmhouse is peacefully situated on a hillside overlooking the lake of Aiguebelette. It has five pleasantly decorated guest rooms all with single beds for three or four people, and en suite shower rooms and WCs. Lounge with TV, video, hi-fi and books; open fire. Meals available.

Prices s €70-€90; d €70-€90; extra person fr €18; dinner fr €23 **Nearby** ⛷ 4km ♨ 1.5km ✈ 13km Restaurant 1km ⛵ 33km ♨ 4km ⛺ 1km ⚓ 1km **Notes** No pets English spoken Open January to October. CC

⚜⚜⚜ ⏏ Le Rossignolet

Patricia DUFRESNE

73610 LEPIN-LE-LAC

☎ 04 79 36 09 62 & 06 30 10 68 92 📠 04 79 36 09 62

email: patricia.dufresne@wanadoo.fr

web: http://grangedurossignolet.monsite.wanadoo.fr

This renovated farmhouse is in a hamlet overlooking the lake of Aiguebelette. It has three guest rooms, with exposed beams: two doubles and a room for four, all with en suite shower rooms and WCs. Lounge area with books and tourist leaflets. Central heating. Breakfast served indoors or on the terrace. Other meals by arrangement: local cuisine.

Prices s fr €47; d fr €55; t fr €77; extra person fr €13; dinner fr €18 **On Site** Restaurant **Nearby** ⛷ 3km ♨ 1.5km ✈ 13km ♨ 2km ⚓ 1km ⚓ 2.5km **Notes** No pets English spoken

LES MARCHES

⚜⚜⚜ ⏏ Le Clos de la Tourne

Francoise GAILLARD

Lachat, 73800 LES MARCHES

☎ 04 79 28 05 34 📠 04 79 28 08 49

email: closdelatourne@wanadoo.fr

web: www.closdelatourne.com

This house is set in a vineyard at the foot of Mount Granier and provides three light mansard double rooms with exposed beams and rustic decor, each with private facilities. Guests have use of a lounge area, terrace and large grounds with garden furniture and barbecue. Enjoy splendid views and breakfasts with home-made cakes and yoghurt. Restaurant on site. Skiing, ice-skating and paragliding nearby.

Prices s fr €45; d fr €48; t fr €60; dinner fr €18 **Nearby** ⛷ 8km ♨ 3km ✈ 8km ♨ 15km ♨ 5km Spa 7km ♿ 2km ⚓ 10km **Notes** Pets admitted English spoken CC

MERIBEL-LES-ALLUES

⚜⚜⚜ ⏏ *Chalet Raphael*

Bridget DALEY

Le Raffort, 73550 MERIBEL-LES-ALLUES

☎ 04 79 00 45 69 📠 04 79 00 45 69

email: lesalpesbd@hotmail.com

web: www.lesalpes.co.uk

This renovated old house, with views over the mountain and the valley of Doron, offers six cosy en suite guest rooms in the mansard storey (two double rooms, three twin rooms (one with balcony) and one room sleeping four). Jacuzzi, electric heating, sitting room with open fire, terrace, small garden. House specialities include quail stuffed with chestnuts and chestnut mousse gâteau.

Prices not confirmed for 2008 **Nearby** ⛷ 3km ♨ 0.2km ✈ 3km ♨ 0.2km ♨ 3km Spa 11km ⚓ 1km ⚓ 14km **Notes** Pets admitted English spoken CC

QUEIGE

⚜⚜⚜ ⏏ La Grange aux Loups

P et C CHANTEPERDRIX

Le Villaret, 73720 QUEIGE

☎ 04 79 38 08 32 📠 04 79 38 08 41

email: clotilde.chanteperdrix@freesbee.fr

web: www.grangeauxloups.com

In a clearing in the woods, with views over the mountains of Beaufortain, this house offers six en suite guest rooms: two double rooms and two twin rooms with balconies, one room sleeping three (with balcony) and one room sleeping four. Electric heating, open fire, terrace, grounds. Buffet breakfast features home-made patisserie and preserves. Nearby activities include skiing at Arêches and walking. Reduced rates for children's meals.

Prices s €42-€44; d €50-€52; t €60-€62; extra person €10; dinner fr €16.50 **Nearby** ⛷ 15km ♨ 1.5km ✈ 12km ⛵ 18km ♨ 2km ♨ 4km ⚓ 10km **Notes** Pets admitted English spoken Open 23 December to mid October.

SEEZ

⌗ ⍾ La Ferme D'Angele

Valerie GRAZIANO
Le Noyeray, 73700 SEEZ
☎ 04 79 41 05 71 & 06 07 67 43 20 📄 04 79 41 05 71
email: contact@ferme-angele.com
web: www.ferme-angele.com

Restored farmhouse with a superb mountain-style interior. There
are five bedrooms: a double, three triples, and a room for four. Two
of the triples have a double bed, the other has all singles; the quad
room has a double bed and two singles. All have private facilities;
some have balconies. Lounge, TV, terrace, sauna. Varied breakfast
menu.

Prices s fr €50; d fr €85; t fr €120; dinner fr €25 **Nearby** ⛷ 4km
⌕ 4km ⬈ 7km ⚵ 4km ⌔ 4km 🏛 4km ⋙ 7km **Notes** Pets admitted
English spoken CC

ST-ALBAN-DE-MONTBEL

⌗ La Chesneraie

Jeanne-Marie TEPPAZ
73610 ST-ALBAN-DE-MONTBEL
☎ 04 79 36 04 33 📄 04 79 36 77 31
email: lachesneraie@wanadoo.fr
web: www.lachesneraie.com

This 1910 stone-built house overlooks the lake of Aiguebelette. It
has four spacious and elegant bedrooms, for two or three people,
each with a lounge area, desk, TV, en suite shower and WC.
Varied and delicious breakfasts served indoors, or on the terrace
with panoramic view of the lake. Access to the lake with private
beach: three boats available.

Prices s €90-€100; d €105-€120; t €125-€140 **On Site** ⌕
Nearby ⛷ 5km ↧ 20km ⬈ 10km Restaurant 2km ⚵ 1km
Spa 19km 🏛 0.5km ⋙ 8km **Notes** Pets admitted Open December
to October.

ST-CHRISTOPHE-LA-GROTTE

⌗⌗ ⍾ Ferme Bonne de la Grotte

Astrid AMAYENC
73360 ST-CHRISTOPHE-LA-GROTTE
☎ 04 79 36 59 05 📄 04 79 36 59 31
email: info@ferme-bonne.com
web: www.gites-savoie.com

This 13th-century house has six bedrooms. On the first floor are
four, doubles or twins, all with canopied beds and en suite
bathrooms; on the ground floor there is a room for three and a
room for four, with private facilities, but not en suite. Lounge with
stone fireplace, satellite TV, grounds. Generous and varied
breakfasts, other meals available. Craft boutique.

Prices s fr €62; d €71-€89; t fr €98; dinner fr €27 **Nearby** ⛷ 10km
↧ 20km ⌕ 0.3km ⬈ 4km Restaurant 3km ⚵ 19km ⚵ 4km
Spa 28km ⚘ 3km 🏛 3km ⋙ 22km **Notes** No pets English
spoken CC

ST-NICOLAS-LA-CHAPELLE

⌗ Chalet Pel'Vuoz

C DUMAX VORZET
Route de Chaussice, 73590 ST-NICOLAS-LA-CHAPELLE
☎ 04 79 31 64 37 & 06 78 03 13 31 📄 04 79 31 64 37
email: chaletpelvuoz@wanadoo.fr
web: www.gite-prop.com/73/262601/

A charming property of old wood featuring woven fabrics and
polished furniture. Wooden stairs lead to three double guest rooms
with TV, private facilities and balconies as well as a living room with
fireplace overlooking the countryside. There is a sauna, reading room
and baby room. Large breakfasts are served in the dining room, or on
the terrace in summer overlooking Mont Blanc. Skiing and ice-skating
nearby.

Prices s fr €45; d fr €58 **Nearby** ⛷ 3km ⌕ 2.5km ⬈ 13km ⚵ 3km
⚵ 3km 🏛 3km ⋙ 23km **Notes** No pets CC

ST-PIERRE-D'ALBIGNY

♦♦♦♦ ⏀ **Château des Allues**

S VANDEVILLE
73250 ST-PIERRE-D'ALBIGNY
☎ 04 79 71 48 96 & 06 75 38 61 56
email: info@chateaudesallues.com
web: www.chateaudesallues.com

This feudal manor house, surrounded by three hectares of wooded grounds, has an elegant yet friendly atmosphere. There are three ground floor bedrooms, two doubles and a twin, each decorated to a theme. All of the rooms have a private bath or shower room and WC. Lounge with TV and internet; buffet breakfast; panoramic views.

Prices s €90-€120; d €100-€140; t fr €150; extra person fr €20; dinner fr €40 **Nearby** ⛷ 12km ♨ 20km ♪ 2km ⚲ 10km Restaurant 8km ⚞ 34km ⚘ 2km Spa 10km ⛪ 0.8km ⛷ 1km **Notes** Pets admitted English spoken Open December to October.

TERMIGNON

♦♦♦ **Chambre d'hôtes**

Martine ROSAZ
3 Rue du Scheuil, 73500 TERMIGNON
☎ 04 79 20 53 34 & 06 88 97 72 49 ▤ 04 79 20 53 34
email: martine.rosaz@wanadoo.fr
web: www.locationtermignon.fr

A converted barn in the middle of the village, with good views all around. There is a double room, a twin-bedded room and a family suite for four with a kitchenette. All the rooms have private bath or shower room and WC, and there is a living room with TV. Varied breakfast menus, with many home-made items.

Prices s fr €45; d fr €50; t fr €76 **Nearby** ⛷ 2km ♪ 0.1km ⚲ 7km ⚞ 0.4km ⚘ 0.5km ⛪ 0.1km ⛷ 18km **Notes** No pets English spoken Open 15 December to 10 October.

VAL-D'ISERE

♦♦♦ ⏀ *Le Franchet - Chalet Colinn*

Elisabeth CHABERT
Route de Val d'Isere, 73320 VAL-D'ISERE
☎ 04 79 06 26 99 & 06 60 23 33 28 ▤ 04 79 06 21 83
email: contact@chaletcolinn.com
web: www.chaletcolinn.com

A restored 1840s farmhouse in a small hamlet - a quiet spot with wonderful views all around. There are four very comfortable rooms with twin beds which can be linked to make doubles, and a fifth room with three single beds. All have internet access, private shower room and WC, and there is a sauna on site.

Prices not confirmed for 2008 **Nearby** ⛷ 6km ♪ 1km ⚲ 6km ⚞ 3.5km ⚘ 5km ⛪ 5km ⛷ 29km **Notes** No pets English spoken CC

YENNE

♦♦♦ ⏀ *L'Orée du Bois*

C et R BORGEY
Le Haut Somont, 73170 YENNE
☎ 04 79 36 72 04 & 06 17 23 06 75 ▤ 04 79 36 72 04
email: raymond.borgey@freesbee.fr
web: www.l-oree-du-bois.net

A modern house, standing in a small hamlet, with pleasant views over the surrounding countryside. There are four bedrooms. On the first floor are two doubles and a single; on the second floor is a triple room, with three single beds. All have private facilities. There is a mezzanine lounge area. Varied breakfast menus; other meals using local dishes by arrangement.

Prices not confirmed for 2008 **On Site** Private ⚲ **Nearby** ⛷ 17km ♪ 2km ⚞ 39km ⚘ 4km Spa 19km ⛪ 4km ⛷ 20km **Notes** No pets CC

● Chalons-sur-Saône

○ LONS-LE-SAUNIER

● Louhans

**71
SAÔNE-ET-LOIRE**

**39
JURA**

● Vescours

● St-Nizier-
le-Bouchoux

● Chavannes-
sur-Reyssouze

● Pont-
de-Vaux

● St-Jean-
sur-Reyssouze

● Verjon

● Villemotier

● Saint-Claude

● Mijoux

● Gex

MÂCON ○

● Viriat

● Montcet

**BOURG-
EN-BRESSE** ○

● Villereversure

● Bohas-Meyriat-Rignat

● Nantua

● Giron

● St-André-
d'Huiriat

● Sulignat

● Peyzieux-
sur-Saône

● Dompierre-
sur-Veyle

**St-Julien-
en-Genevois** ●

● Servas

● Neuville-sur-Ain

● Villes

**74
HAUTE-
SAVOIE**

● Messimy-
sur-Saône

● Sandrans

● St-Rambert-en-Bugey

● St-Bernard

● Lagnieu

● Béligneux

● Bressolles

● Miribel

● St-Jean-
de-Niost

● Bellay

○ **LYON**

**69
RHÔNE**

**38
ISÈRE**

● La Tour-du-Pin

○ **CHAMBÉRY**

N

0   15 km

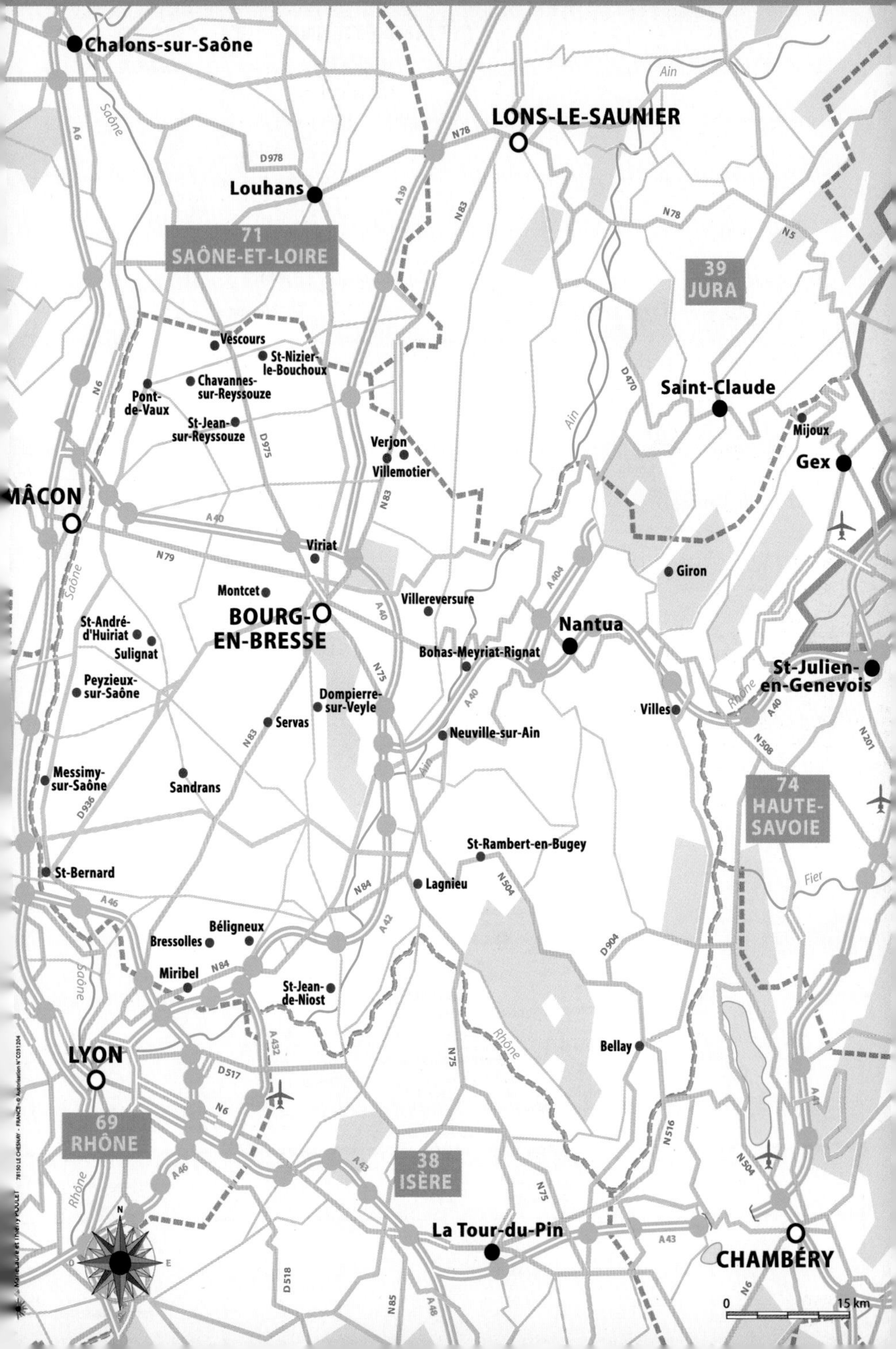

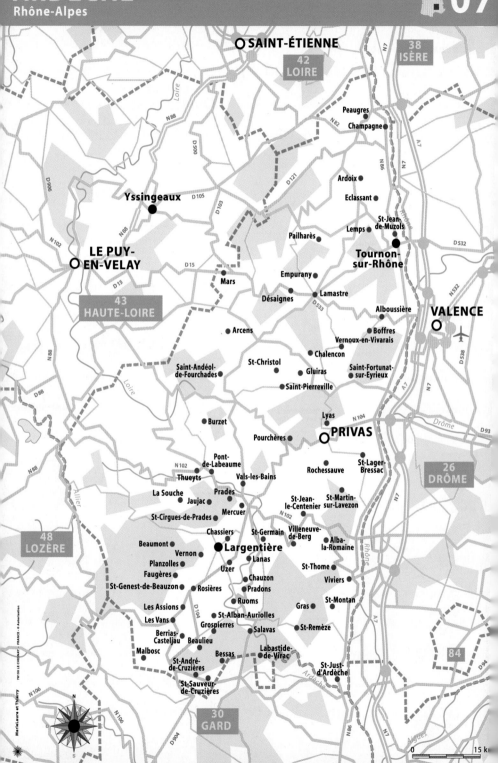

SAINT-ÉTIENNE

38
ISÈRE

42
LOIRE

Peaugres

Champagne

Ardoix

Eclassant

St-Jean-
de-Muzols

Lemps

Yssingeaux

Pailharès

Tournon-
sur-Rhône

LE PUY-
EN-VELAY

Mars

Empurany

Lamastre

Désaignes

Alboussière

VALENCE

43
HAUTE-LOIRE

Arcens

Boffres

Vernoux-en-Vivarais

Chalencon

St-Christol

Gluiras

Saint-Fortunat-
sur-Eyrieux

Saint-Andéol-
de-Fourchades

Saint-Pierreville

Burzet

Lyas

Pourchères

PRIVAS

Pont-
de-Labeaume

Rochessauve

St-Lager-
Bressac

Thueyts

Vals-les-Bains

26
DRÔME

La Souche

Prades

St-Jean-
le-Centenier

St-Martin-
sur-Lavezon

Jaujac

St-Cirgues-de-Prades

Mercuer

Chassiers

St-Germain

Villeneuve-
de-Berg

Alba-
la-Romaine

48
LOZÈRE

Beaumont

Vernon

Largentière

Lanas

Planzolles

Uzer

St-Thome

Faugères

Chauzon

Viviers

St-Genest-de-Beauzon

Rosières

Pradons

St-Montan

Les Assions

Ruoms

Gras

Les Vans

St-Alban-Auriolles

St-Remèze

Berrias-
Casteljau

Grospierres

Salavas

Beaulieu

Malbosc

Bessas

Labastide-
de-Virac

84

St-André-
de-Cruzières

St-Just-
d'Ardèche

St-Sauveur-
de-Cruzières

30
GARD

0   15 k

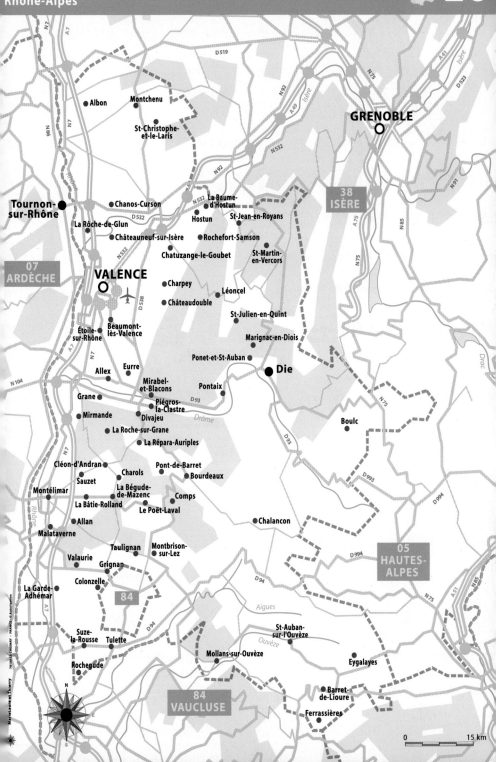

DRÔME
Rhône-Alpes

26

Albon
Montchenu
St-Christophe-et-le-Laris
GRENOBLE

38 ISÈRE

Chanos-Curson
La Baume-d'Hostun
Tournon-sur-Rhône
Hostun
St-Jean-en-Royans
La Rôche-de-Glun
Châteauneuf-sur-Isère
Rochefort-Samson

07 ARDÈCHE

Chatuzange-le-Goubet
St-Martin-en-Vercors
VALENCE
Charpey
Léoncel
Châteaudouble
St-Julien-en-Quint
Étoile-sur-Rhône
Beaumont-lès-Valence
Marignac-en-Diois
Ponet-et-St-Auban
Die
Allex
Eurre
Mirabel-et-Blacons
Pontaix
Grane
Piégros-la-Clastre
Mirmande
Divajeu
Boulc
La Roche-sur-Grane
La Répara-Auriples
Cléon-d'Andran
Pont-de-Barret
Charols
Bourdeaux
Sauzet
La Bégude-de-Mazenc
Montélimar
Comps
La Bâtie-Rolland
Le Poët-Laval
Allan
Chalancon
Malataverne
Taulignan
Montbrison-sur-Lez
05 HAUTES-ALPES
Valaurie
Grignan
Colonzelle
La Garde-Adhémar
84
Suze-la-Rousse
Tulette
St-Auban-sur-l'Ouvèze
Rochegude
Mollans-sur-Ouvèze
Eygalayes
84 VAUCLUSE
Barret-de-Lioure
Ferrassières

0   15 km

SWITZERLAND

N78

N5

39
JURA

D470

Saint-Claude

Lake Geneva

Gex

01
AIN

Thonon-
les-Bains

Maxilly-Léman   N5

Thollon

Excenevex

Allinges

La Chapelle-
d'Abondance

Orcier

N5   N203

Draillant

La Vernaz

Abondance

Lully

Geneva

N205

Ésery-Reignier

Morzine

Les Gets

Mieussy

Saint-Julien-
en-Genevois

N201

Rhône

A40

A41

Bonneville

Taninges

Châtillon-
sur-Cluses

Samoëns

N508

A90

N205

Vallorcine

Plateau-d'Assy

Les Ollières

N203

Le Grand-Bornand

Servoz

Chamonix-Mont-Blanc

Saint-Jean-de-Sixt

Cordon

Vaulx

Dingny-St-Clair

Domancy

ANNECY

St-Gervais-les-Bains

Chavanod

Seynod-Vieugy

Thônes

Tunnel
du Mont-Blanc

Sales

Fier

Bluffy

Les Houches

Sévrier

Megève

N212

St-Félix

Viuz-
la-Chiésaz

St-Eustache

Héry-sur-Alby

Les Contamines-
Montjoie

Cusy

N508

ITALY

N516

Albertville

73
SAVOIE

N504

A43

N90

N90

N90

N6

CHAMBÉRY

A43

Isère

N515

N   NE

O   E

Arc

N6

S

75118 LE CHIGNY • FRANCE • Reproduction
Marie-Laure et Thierry

0   15 km

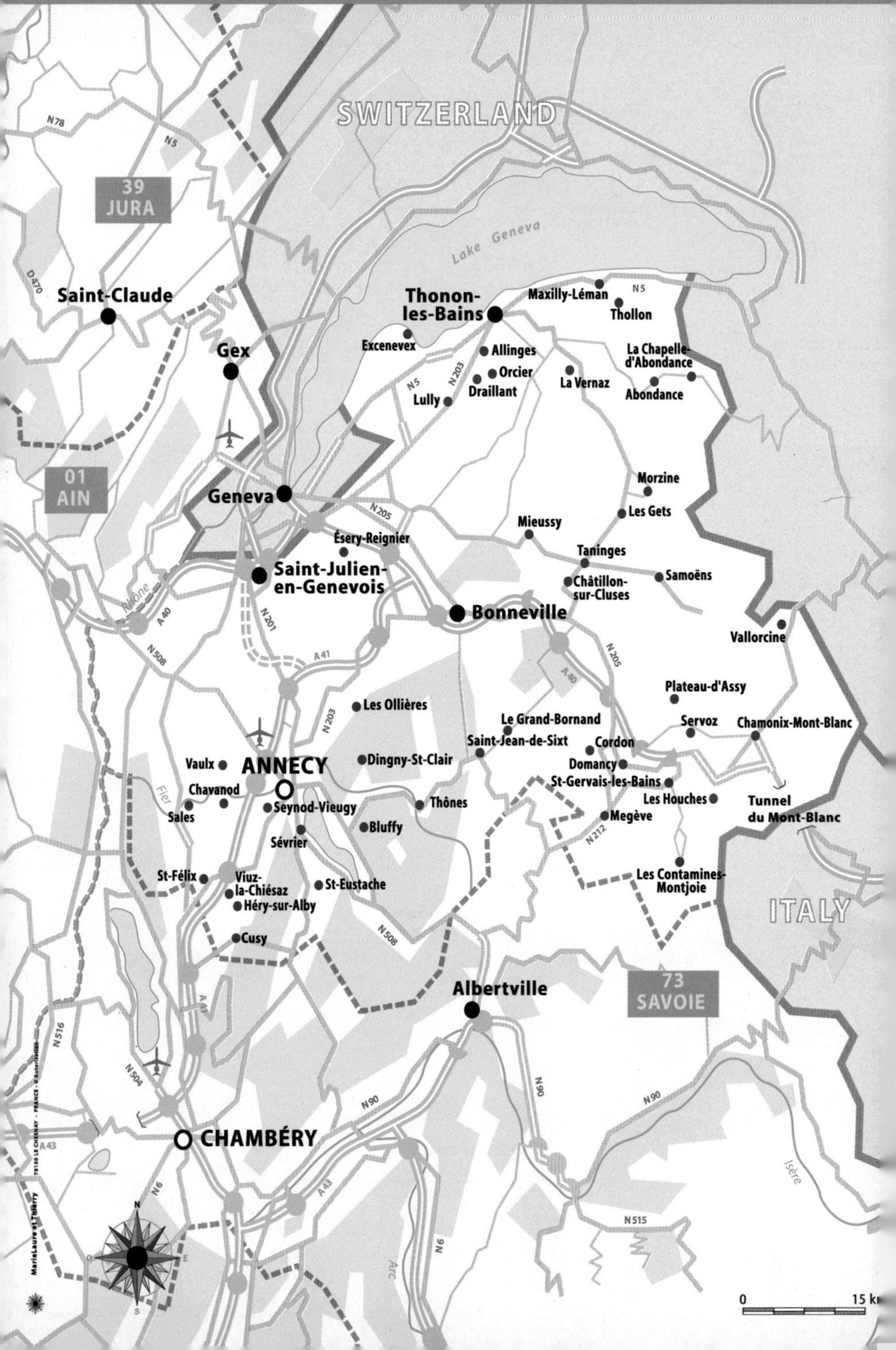

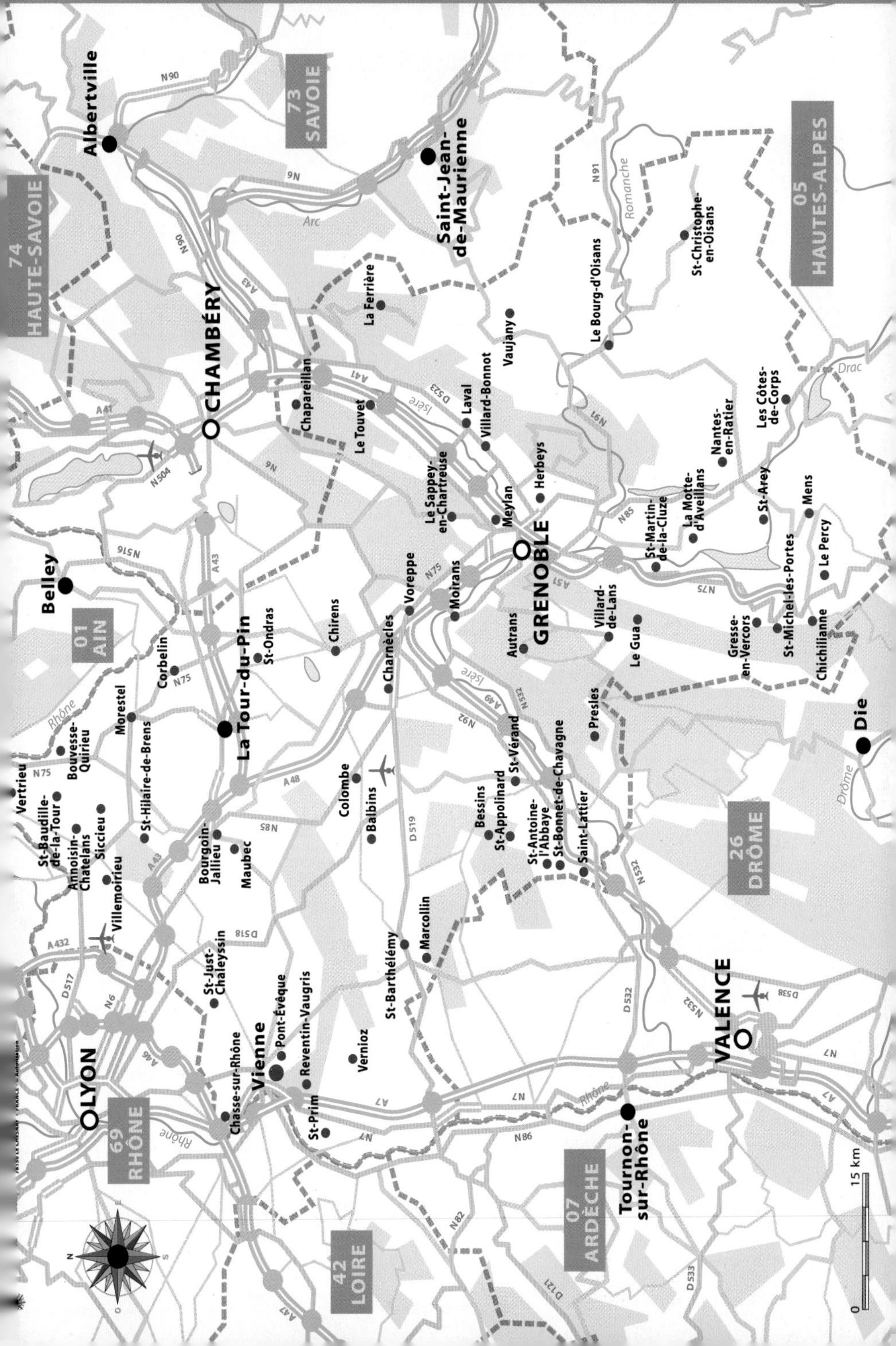

HAUTE-SAVOIE 74

01 AIN

69 RHÔNE

OLYON

42 LOIRE

07 ARDÈCHE

26 DRÔME

05 HAUTES-ALPES

73 SAVOIE

N90

Albertville

9N

Arc

Saint-Jean-de-Maurienne

9N

N91

St-Christophe-en-Oisans

Romanche

Le Bourg-d'Oisans

Drac

CHAMBÉRY

A43

A41

A41

N504

N6

La Ferrière

Chapareillan

Le Touvet

D523

Isère

Laval

Villard-Bonnot

Vaujany

Les Côtes-de-Corps

Nantes-en-Ratier

Le Sappey-en-Chartreuse

Herbeys

Meylan

La Motte-d'Aveillans

St-Arey

Mens

Le Percy

N85

GRENOBLE

Voreppe

Moirans

Villard-de-Lans

St-Martin-de-la-Cluze

St-Michel-les-Portes

Chichilianne

Gresse-en-Vercors

Le Gua

Autrans

Belley

Belley

N516

A43

A48

A41

Corbelin

St-Ondras

Chirens

Charnècles

N75

La Tour-du-Pin

Isère

A49

N92

Presles

St-Vérand

Bessins

St-Appolinard

St-Antoine-l'Abbaye

St-Bonnet-de-Chavagne

Saint-Lattier

Die

Drôme

Die

Rhône

Vertrieu

Bouvesse-Quirieu

Morestel

St-Hilaire-de-Brens

St-Baudille-de-la-Tour

Annoisin-Chatelans

Siccieu

Villemoirieu

Maubec

Bourgoin-Jallieu

Colombe

Balbins

D519

Marcollin

St-Barthélémy

A46

A432

D517

N6

St-Just-Chaleyssin

Chasse-sur-Rhône

Pont-Évêque

Vienne

Reventin-Vaugris

St-Prim

Vernioz

D532

N532

N7

A7

Rhône

VALENCE

N86

D538

Tournon-sur-Rhône

N86

N82

D121

D533

15 km

0

N

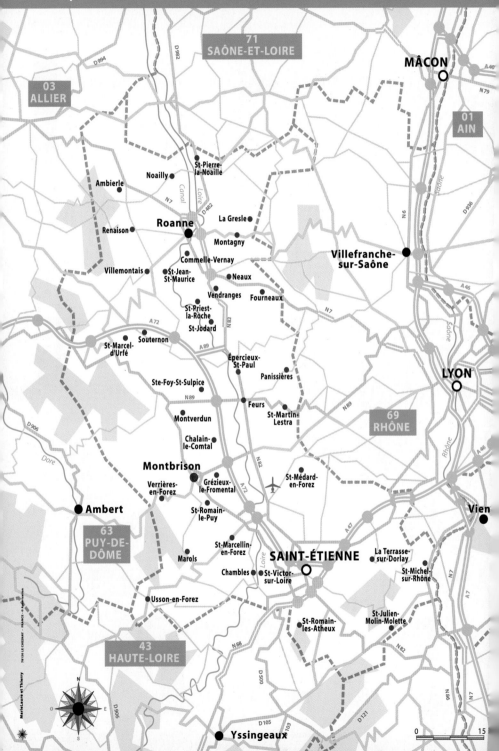

03
ALLIER

71
SAÔNE-ET-LOIRE

01
AIN

MÂCON

St-Pierre-
la-Noaille

Noailly

Ambierle

La Gresle

Roanne

Renaison

Montagny

Villefranche-
sur-Saône

Commelle-Vernay

Villemontais

St-Jean-
St-Maurice

Neaux

Vendranges

Fourneaux

LYON

St-Priest-
la-Roche

St-Jodard

St-Marcel-
d'Urfé

Souternon

Épercieux-
St-Paul

Ste-Foy-St-Sulpice

Panissières

Feurs

69
RHÔNE

St-Martin-
Lestra

Montverdun

Chalain-
le-Comtal

Montbrison

St-Médard-
en-Forez

Verrières-
en-Forez

Grézieux-
le-Fromental

Ambert

St-Romain-
le-Puy

Vien

63
PUY-DE-
DÔME

St-Marcellin-
en-Forez

Marols

SAINT-ÉTIENNE

La Terrasse-
sur-Dorlay

Chambles

St-Victor-
sur-Loire

St-Michel-
sur-Rhône

Usson-en-Forez

St-Julien-
Molin-Molette

St-Romain-
les-Atheux

43
HAUTE-LOIRE

N
O   E
S

0   15

Yssingeaux

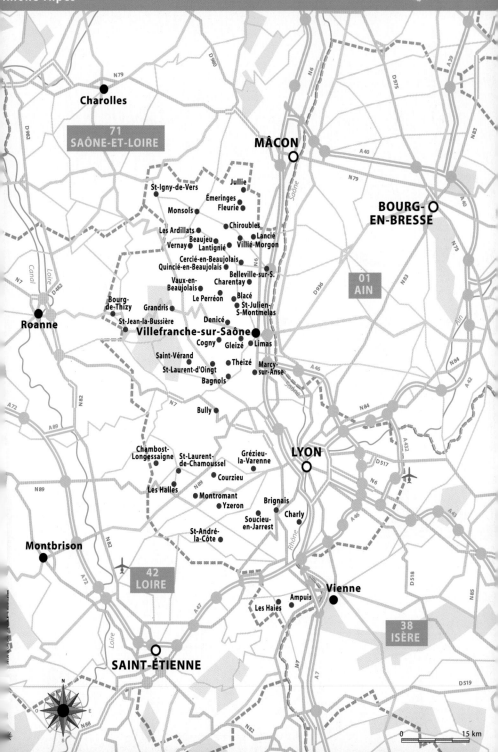

Charolles

71
SAÔNE-ET-LOIRE

MÂCON

**BOURG-
EN-BRESSE**

St-Igny-de-Vers

Jullie

Émeringes

Monsols
Fleurie

Chiroubles

Les Ardillats
Lancié

Beaujeu
Villié-Morgon

Vernay
Lantignié

Cercié-en-Beaujolais

Quincié-en-Beaujolais

Belleville-sur-S.

Vaux-en-
Beaujolais
Charentay

Bourg-
de-Thizy
Le Perréon
Blacé

Grandris
St-Julien-
S-Montmelas

St-Jean-la-Bussière
Denicé

Villefranche-sur-Saône

**01
AIN**

Roanne

Cogny
Gleizé
Limas

Saint-Vérand

St-Laurent-d'Oingt
Theizé
Marcy-
sur-Anse

Bagnols

Bully

Chambost-
Longessaigne
St-Laurent-
de-Chamoussel
Grézieu-
la-Varenne

LYON

Courzieu

Les Halles
Montromant
Yzeron

Brignais

Soucieu-
en-Jarrest
Charly

St-André-
la-Côte

Montbrison

**42
LOIRE**

Vienne

Ampuis

Les Haies

**38
ISÈRE**

SAINT-ÉTIENNE

0   15 km

ITALY

Tunnel du Grand-Saint-Bernard

Tunnel du Mont-Blanc

Bonneval-sur-Arc

Val-d'Isère

Séez

Arc

N6

Isère

Bramans

Aussois

Avrieux

Termignon

La Norma-Villarodin-Bourget

Tunnel de Fréjus

Arêches-Beaufort

Feissons-sur-Salins

Crest-Voland

La Côte-d'Aime

Aime

N90

N515

Méribel-les-Allues

Queige

Flumet

St-Nicolas-la-Chapelle

Albertville

N90

Saint-Jean-de-Maurienne

9N

A40

N212

Arc

N91

N508

Le Châtelard

Le Noyer

Aillon-le-Jeune

St-Pierre-d'Albigny

St-Alban-de-Montbel

La Rochette

A45

N90

74 HAUTE-SAVOIE

ANNECY

N203

Fier

Le Viviers-du-Lac

Chambéry-le-Vieux

A41

Les Marches

38 ISÈRE

Isère

D523

CHAMBÉRY

N504

La Biolle

Jongieux

Yenne

Lépin-le-Lac

St-Christophe-la-Grotte

Corbel

9N

N6

Rhône

N516

N516

A43

La Bridoire

N504

Ruisseau

N75

GRENOBLE

Belley

01 AIN

Marie-Laure et Thierry — 24198 LE CHESNAY - FRANCE - © autorisation

N
E
S
O

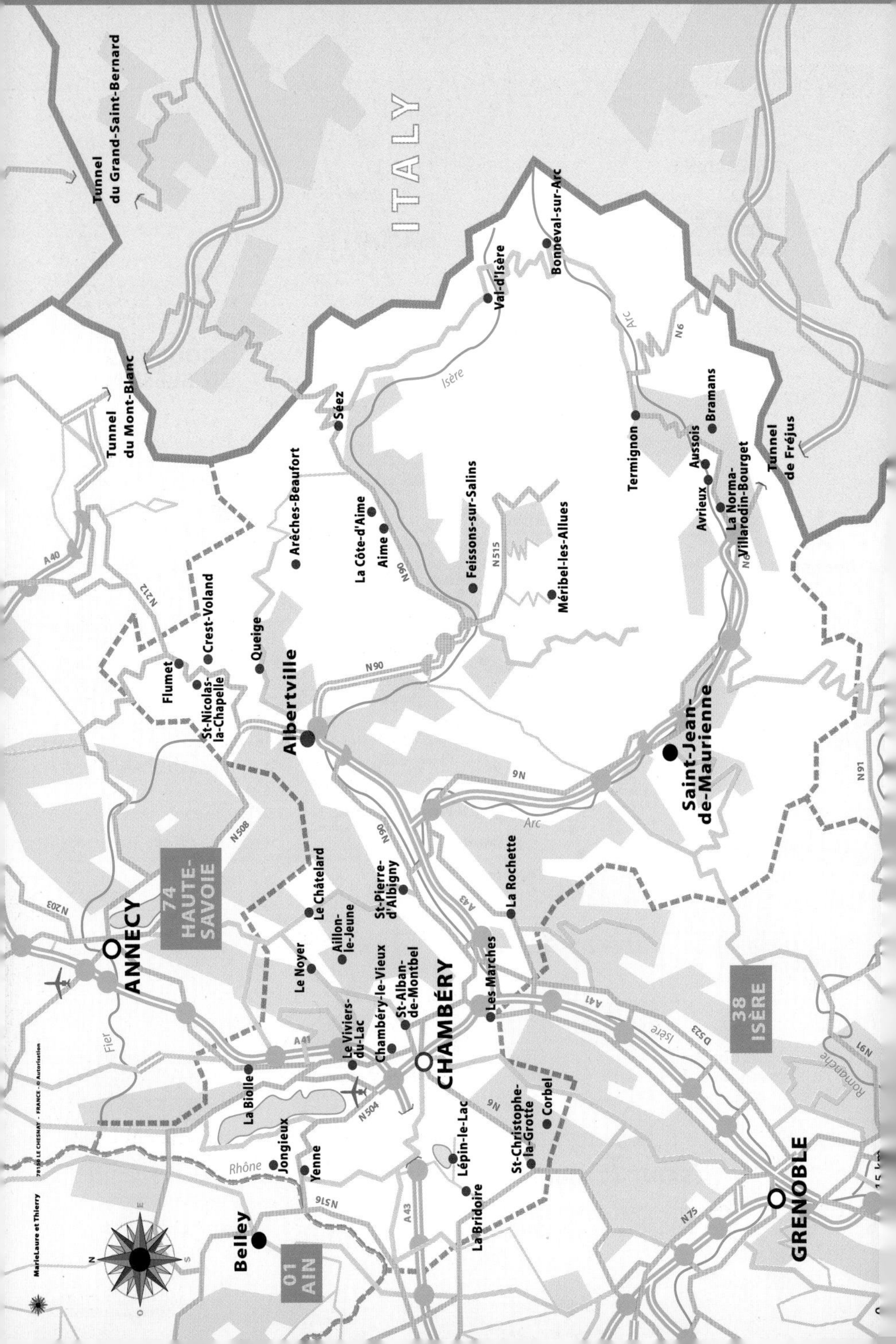

CORSICA

CORSE-DU-SUD

BARBAGGIO

ⅲ ⅰⓄⅰ **Pezzo Brietta**

J-Louis FRATANI

20253 BARBAGGIO

☎ 04 95 37 28 64 & 06 24 33 18 32

email: fratani@libertysurf.fr

web: www.castellu-piattu.fr.st

Set in a vineyard in the countryside, five rooms are offered in a stone outbuilding near the owners' house: four doubles and a room with a double and single bed, each with private facilities and independent access. All the rooms open onto a patio with big swimming pool, six hectares of grounds with trees, and views over the vineyard and the mountain of Sant Angelo. Cot and changing table available. Reductions off-season.

Prices d fr €88; t fr €112; dinner fr €23 **On Site** Sea 🖉 Restaurant 🏊 Private ᛘ **Nearby** ⛷ 5km 🏊 5km Spa 20km 🏛 5km 🚶 20km **Notes** No pets

BONIFACIO

ⅲ ⅰⓄⅰ **Cavallo Morto**

Alain BRUNELLI

20169 BONIFACIO

☎ 04 95 73 05 41 & 06 09 36 35 50 🖹 04 95 73 05 41

email: info@cavallomorto.com

web: www.cavallomorto.com

This 17th-century house is situated out in the country, on an olive farm. On the first floor there is a double bedroom and a single; on the second floor is a large double bedroom. There is a lounge/dining room on the ground floor, with separate access. All rooms have private bath or shower room and WC.

Prices s fr €90; d €120-€150; extra person fr €30; dinner fr €50 **Nearby** ⛷ 1km ᛘ 4km Sea 3km Restaurant 2km 🏊 3km 🏛 3km **Notes** No pets English spoken Open April to October.

CERVIONE

ⅲ *Prunete*

Anne-Marie DOUMENS

Casa Corsa - Acqua Nera, 20221 CERVIONE

☎ 04 95 38 01 40 & 06 25 89 89 32 🖹 04 95 33 39 27

web: www.casa-corsa.net

Three guest rooms of real character in the owner's house. On the ground floor, with private access, a family suite (two double beds) with private bath/wc. On the first floor are two en suite double rooms (one with small terrace). Shared lounge, dining room with television and open fire and communal terrace and picnic area. Folding child's bed and cot available, and two more double rooms in an annexe. Two covered terraces and garden.

Prices not confirmed for 2008 **Nearby** ⛷ 5km ᛞ 45km 🏊 4km 🏛 4km 🚶 40km **Notes** No pets

CORTE

ⅲ 🌱 *Casa Guelfucci*

Antoine GUELFUCCI

Pont de l'Orta, 20250 CORTE

☎ 04 95 61 06 41 & 06 81 87 83 20 🖹 04 95 61 06 41

On the edge of town, close to the owners' farmhouse restaurant, this non-smoking property has four bedrooms and a suite. The bedrooms are all air-conditioned doubles; the suite has a double-bedded room and a lounge with a bed-settee. All rooms have private facilities. Cot available; use of washing machine and dryer. Lounge with internet access, TV, home cinema and stereo.

Prices not confirmed for 2008 **Nearby** ⛷ 2km 🏊 1km 🏛 0.8km 🚶 2km **Notes** No pets English spoken CC

FAVALELLO-DI-BOZIO

ⅲ ⅰⓄⅰ **A Casa Aperta**

Isabelle RIBATTO

Plaine de Féo, 20212 FAVALELLO DI BOZIO

☎ 06 80 58 31 50 & 04 95 61 09 21 🖹 04 95 61 09 21

email: acasaaperta@aol.com

web: www.a-casa-aperta.com

This is a modern three-storey house, out in the country, and it has five bedrooms. There are three doubles, and two with a double bed and a single. All rooms have private bath or shower room and WC. Dining room, lounge with TV. Covered terrace, garden furniture. Meals available Monday, Tuesday, Thursday and Friday.

Prices s fr €54; d fr €60; t fr €66; extra person fr €12; dinner fr €20 **Nearby** ⛷ 3km ᛞ 🏊 9km 🏛 9km 🚶 9km **Notes** Pets admitted Open April to October.

LEVIE

ⅲ ⅰⓄⅰ ⅙ **Aravina**

Jean Yves MORGON

Pianu di Livia, 20170 LEVIE

☎ 04 95 72 21 63 & 06 33 87 04 14 🖹 04 95 72 21 63

email: jeanyves.morgon@wanadoo.fr

A large house in the countryside, built of granite. There are two twin-bedded rooms, and a double room which has possible space for extra beds. All three have private bath or shower room and WC. The living room has an open fireplace and piano; outside are seven hectares of grounds with dramatic views. The Propriano/Porto Vecchio coast-to-coast path passes close by.

Prices s fr €70; d fr €80; t fr €95; extra person fr €15; dinner fr €25 **Nearby** ⛷ 0.5km Sea 28km 🖉 3km Restaurant 0.8km 🏊 6km Spa 15km 🏊 10km 🏛 5km **Notes** Pets admitted English spoken

CORSICA

MONTEGROSSO

ⅲ ⅰⅇⅰ Villa Opvntia

Eléna BONANNO
Route de Montemaggiore, 20214 MONTEGROSSO
☎ 04 95 65 40 76 ▤ 04 95 65 40 76
email: VillaOpvntia@aol.com
web: www.calvi-gite.com

The owners of this countryside villa offer two double rooms and a room with a double and single bed, each with private facilities and personalised decor. Lounge, living room with fireplace, library and TV. Large enclosed grounds with trees and a swimming pool, and views over the sea and Calvi. Parking, airport and port 7km. Table d'hôte meals by reservation.

Prices s €80-€120; d €80-€120; t fr €120; dinner fr €30
On Site Private 🐾 **Nearby** ⛷ 7km ⚓ 7km 🏛 7km ⚑ 7km
Notes No pets English spoken

MONTICELLO

ⅲ Tré Castelli

Christiane BANDINI
Lieu dit Tre Castelli, Route de Reginu,
20220 MONTICELLO
☎ 04 95 60 24 27

On the edge of the village, this house has six air-conditioned guest rooms, with independent access. All of the rooms are doubles, and each has a private terrace. All rooms have private bath or shower room and WC. Breakfast is served on the terrace.

Prices s fr €60; d fr €70; t fr €95 **Nearby** ⛷ 1.5km ⚓ 3km Sea 4km 🏊 3km 🐾 1.5km Restaurant 1.5km ⚓ 1.5km ⛳ 4.5km 🏛 1.5km ⚑ 5km
Notes No pets Open March to October. CC

NESSA

ⅲ 🌿 Chambre d'hôtes

Jean-Marc PINAUD NOBILI
20225 NESSA
☎ 04 95 61 71 01 & 04 95 47 11 89 ▤ 04 95 61 73 07
email: jean-marc.pinaud2b@orange.fr

There are six high-quality rooms available in this country property: four doubles, one of which has a private 30-metre terrace, and two triples. All rooms have shower and WC. Breakfast is served either in the house or on the terrace, where panoramic views can be enjoyed.

Prices s fr €60; d fr €60; t fr €80 **Nearby** ⛷ 7km ⚓ 8km Sea 17km Restaurant 1km ⚓ 4km ⛳ 17km 🏛 1km ⚑ 5km **Notes** No pets English spoken Open April to October.

NONZA

ⅲ *Casa Maria*

Marie-Ange BURINI
20217 NONZA
☎ 04 95 37 80 95 & 06 76 05 40 13 ▤ 04 95 37 80 95
email: casamaria@wanadoo.fr
web: www.casamaria-corse.com

Near the tower, in the heart of the village of Nonza, tastefully decorated rooms are offered in a very well restored small mansion. There are three twin rooms, a double, and a family room with a double and two singles, each with private facilities and air-conditioning. Communal lounge.

Prices not confirmed for 2008 **Nearby** ⚓ 2.5km **Notes** No pets English spoken Open April to October.

OLETTA

ⅲ Les Chênes Verts

Brésilie JOUCK
Chemin de Piedalbuccio, 20217 OLETTA-ST FLORENT
☎ 04 95 39 02 28

All the rooms in this country property are on the ground floor, with independent access. There are two doubles and a twin-bedded room; a cot is available, and also a child's bed. Each room has a private shower room and WC. There is a big shady terrace, lawn, wooded garden with garden furniture, and a boules pitch. On-site parking. Reductions for longer stays.

Prices d fr €80; extra person fr €30 **Nearby** ⚓ 5km Restaurant 1km 🏊 4km ⛳ 6km 🏛 1km ⚑ 15km **Notes** No pets English spoken

OLMETA-DI-TUDA

ⅲ ⅰⅇⅰ *Casa di L'Amanduli*

Dany SAULI
20232 OLMETA DI TUDA - ST FLORENT
☎ 04 95 37 28 87 ▤ 04 95 37 28 87
email: contact@casacorse.com
web: www.casacorse.com

This chambre d'hôtes is out in the country, at the end of a 300 metre unmade road. In a building next to the owners' house, it has four double bedrooms, each with TV, shower room/WC, small terrace and garden furniture. Possible extra bed. Large enclosed terrace with seasonal kitchen. Meals by arrangement; possibility also of packed lunches.

Prices not confirmed for 2008 **On Site** Private 🐾 **Nearby** ⚓ 4km 🏊 5km 🏛 2km ⚑ 16km **Notes** No pets English spoken

ORTIPORIO

⊮⊮⊮ U Vecchju Mulinu

Colette ROUTA

Hameau de Fornoli, 20290 ORTIPORIO

☎ 04 95 28 91 87

email: colette.routa@wanadoo.fr

web: http://monsite.orange.fr/vecchju-mulinu

Surrounded by forest, this property has three thoughtfully planned bedrooms, all of them doubles (one with a king-size bed). Each has a private shower room and WC. Lounge with TV, video recorder and DVD player. There is an old mill in the enclosed wooded grounds, which are bordered by a river.

Prices s fr €62; d fr €72 **On Site** Private � **Nearby** Restaurant 4km ⊞15km ⊯7km **Notes** No pets English spoken

PIEDIGRIGGIO

⊮⊮⊮ ⊱ ⊙⊱ A Ghjuvellina

Simon AGOSTINI

20218 PIEDIGRIGGIO

☎ 04 95 47 68 75 ▤ 04 95 47 68 77

Overlooking the village 350 metres away, this smallholder's house offers five en suite double rooms. Sitting room with TV shared with hosts, large dining room. Enclosed garden, communal terrace with garden furniture, parking

Prices s fr €55; d fr €60; t fr €84; extra person fr €20; dinner fr €23 **Nearby** ⊱5km ⊘7km Restaurant 3km ⊴4km Spa 4km ⊞4km ⊯4km **Notes** No pets Open April to October.

PIETROSELLA

⊮⊮⊮ Villa Ghiatone

Stéphane OTTAVY

Allée du Maquis, Lieu dit Ghiatone, 20166 PIETROSELLA

☎ 04 95 25 53 71 & & 06 14 30 09 76 ▤ 04 95 25 53 71

email: contact@villaghiatone.com

web: www.villaghiatone.com

Facing the sea, on the ground floor of the owners' house, this chambre d'hôtes has two large double rooms and a two-roomed family suite for up to five. All have private shower room/WC, air conditioning, TV and DVD player. Lounge shared with hosts. Enclosed garden, terrace with garden furniture and children's games; shady lawns, parking.

Prices d fr €90; t fr €120; extra person fr €30 **Nearby** ⊱7km Sea 0.5km ⊘0.5km Restaurant 2km ⊴0.5km Spa 5km ⊞1km ⊯25km **Notes** No pets English spoken

PORTO-VECCHIO

⊮⊮⊮ *Palombaggia*

Marta SCHNEIDER

Domaine U Scaleghiu, 20137 PORTO VECCHIO

☎ 04 95 70 03 05 & 06 21 05 68 19 ▤ 04 95 70 03 05

email: Marta2a@aol.com

web: www.marta-hote.com

Facing the Bay of Palombaggia, surrounded by oak trees, this property has three bedrooms in a building close to the owners' home. There is a double room, a room with three singles, and a two-roomed family suite for up to five. Each room has a private terrace with garden furniture, shower room/WC, and a side room with a fridge and coffee-making facilities.

Prices not confirmed for 2008 **Nearby** ⊱2km ⊸13km ⊴2km ⊞2km **Notes** No pets

⊮⊮⊮ Uspitaghju

Nadine GIORGIONE

20137 PORTO VECCHIO

☎ 04 95 26 77 53 & 06 12 51 01 25

email: nadetdom@wanadoo.fr

In the Parc Naturel Régional Corse, this is a stone-built house with three ground floor guest rooms. All have double beds, with possible space for an extra bed or cot, and each room has a private bathroom and WC. Living room with TV and open fire. The garden has trees, flowers, terrace and a decking area ideal for sunbathing.

Prices s €60-€70; d €70-€80; t fr €95 **Nearby** ⊱5km ⊱35km Sea 19km ⊘2km ⊸ Restaurant 0.1km ⊴19km ⊞19km **Notes** No pets English spoken

SAMPOLO

⊮⊮⊮ ⊙⊱ Giovicacce

Julia KUHLING

20134 SAMPOLO

☎ 04 95 24 39 81

email: giovicacce@wanadoo.fr

web: http://perso.orange.fr/corsicaparadiso

This stone-built house has three bedrooms: a double, a twin-bedded room, and a triple with double bed and a single. An extra bed is available. Each room has a private shower room and WC. Lounge with open fire, shared with hosts. Enclosed grounds with garden furniture and a panoramic view towards the mountains. Good for walking: access to several footpaths.

Prices s fr €50; d fr €55; t fr €70; extra person fr €15; dinner fr €22 **Nearby** ⊞6km **Notes** No pets English spoken Open May to October.

CORSICA

SAN-MARTINO-DI-LOTA

⦀ Chambre d'hôtes

Bertrand CAGNINACCI

Château Cagninacci, 20200 SAN MARTINO DI LOTA

☎ 06 78 29 03 94 ▤ 06 76 43 01 44

web: www.chateaucagninacci.com

Three double rooms and one twin in a 17th-century Capucin monastery. Each has a private bathroom and wc. Sitting room just for guests and a dining room with open fireplace. Distinctive furnishings. Extensive park with summer houses. Three restaurants in village.

Prices d fr €110; t fr €127 **Nearby** ⚓ 10km ♨ 8km ☖ 8km ⛰ 11km **Notes** No pets English spoken Open 15 May to September.

SISCO

⦀ ⟨◎⟩ *U San Martinu*

Alain MONEGLIA

Marine de Sisco, 20233 SISCO

☎ 04 95 35 25 78 & 06 24 59 96 70

email: usanmartinu2b@wanadoo.fr

This rural property offers four beautifully decorated air-conditioned double rooms, all in the owners' house and close to three gîtes. Each room has a shower room/WC, TV, terrace and teak garden furniture. Lounge shared with owners, small reading room.

Prices not confirmed for 2008 **Nearby** ⚓ 1km ♨ 2km ☖ 1km ⛰ 14km **Notes** No pets Open March to October. CC

SOLLACARO

⦀ Cigala-Filitosa

Anita TARDIF

Cigala, 20140 SOLLACARO

☎ 06 62 43 13 69 & 04 95 74 29 48

Just three minutes from the prehistoric site at Filitosa is this bed and breakfast. Three rooms (one double and two twins) on the ground floor, with separate access and en suite shower and wc. Sitting area with open fire used by guests and owners. Breakfast on the terrace overlooking enclosed grounds of 1 hectare. Summer kitchen, barbecue and stunning views. Cot and high chair available.

Prices s fr €50; d fr €70; extra person fr €30 **Nearby** ⚓ 7km ⟋ 15km Restaurant 3km ♨ 15km Spa 15km ☖ 5km **Notes** No pets

VICO

⦀ ⟨◎⟩ Chambre d'hôtes

Santa CARLOTTI

Route du Stade, Col de Saint Antoine, 20160 VICO

☎ 04 95 26 71 28 & 06 87 20 25 31

Three rooms in the owners' house, up above the village, with sea views. On the ground floor is a double room with private access; upstairs are two more doubles, each with a little terrace. All three rooms have private shower room/WC, and TV. Two have sea views; the other has a mountain view. Extra bed available. Meals by arrangement.

Prices s fr €50; d fr €60; t fr €78; dinner fr €25 **Nearby** ⚓ 8km ♨ 0.1km Spa 15km ☖ 1.5km **Notes** No pets

VIX

⦀ Taglio Di Sacramento

Annonciade PRIEUR

Villa le Cédre Bleu, 20240 VIX-VENTISERI

☎ 04·95 57 43 83 & 06 24 29 58 84 ▤ 04 95 57 43 83

email: annonciade.prieur@wanadoo.fr

web: www.taglio-di-sacramento.com

A separate building to the side of the owners' home houses these three spacious guest rooms. Two of the rooms have double beds; the third has a double and a single. They all have en suite facilities, and there is a shared lounge and kitchenette. Terraced flower-filled garden with garden furniture and swimming pool. Property is air-conditioned.

Prices d €70-€95; t €100-€140; extra person fr €35 **On Site** ♨ Private ⟋ **Nearby** ⚓ 4km ⟋ 50km Sea 2km Restaurant 0.6km ♨ 2km Spa 15km ☖ 4km **Notes** No pets

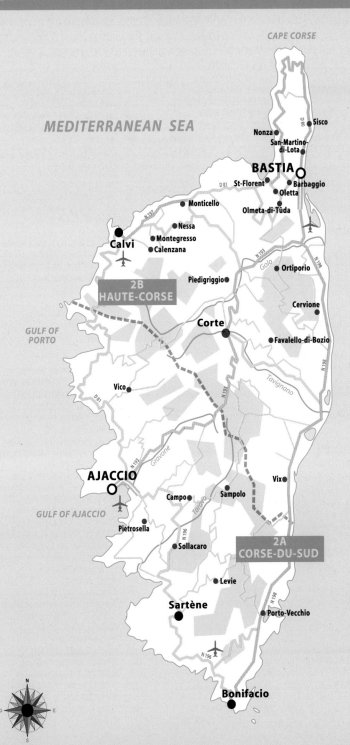

CAPE CORSE

MEDITERRANEAN SEA

Sisco

Nonza
San-Martino-
di-Lota

BASTIA

St-Florent
Barbaggio
Oletta
Olmeta-di-Tûda

Monticello

Nessa
Montegresso
Calenzana

Calvi

Ortiporio

2B
HAUTE-CORSE

Piedigriggio

Cervione

GULF OF
PORTO

Corte

Favalello-di-Bozio

Vico

Tavignano

Golo

Gravone

AJACCIO

Vix

GULF OF AJACCIO

Campo
Sampolo

Pietrosella

2A
CORSE-DU-SUD

Sollacaro

Levie

Sartène

Porto-Vecchio

Bonifacio

N 197
D 81
D 80
D 81
N 193
N 198
N 198
N 193
N 196
N 196

N
O — E
S

0   12 km

Marie-Laure et Thierry   78150 LE CHESNAY - FRANCE © Auréfusion

INDEX OF LOCATIONS

Locations are arranged alphabetically in this index. Chambres d'hôtes are listed in the guide under the nearest town or village, which may be several kilometres away. The location name is followed by the département name and number (in brackets). The page number(s) for each location is shown last. Places beginning 'La', 'Le' and 'Les' appear under 'L'.

INDEX

T

The Automobile Association would like to thank the following photographers, companies and picture libraries for their assistance in the preparation of this book.

Abbreviations for the picture credits are as follows: (t) top; (b) bottom; (l) left; (r) right; (AA) AA World Travel Library.

1(b) AA/Roger Moss; 2(l) AA/Rob Moore; 3(bl) AA/Pete Bennett; 3(br) Tony Oliver; 8(t) AA/Roger Moss; 10(br) AA/Rob Moore; 12(b) AA/Paul Kenward; 17(br) AA/Roger Moss; 194 AA/Alex Kouprianoff.

Every effort has been made to trace the copyright holders, and we apologise in advance for any accidental errors. We would be happy to apply the corrections in the following edition of this publication.

Contents

How to use the Guide

1 Town or village name. This is the nearest town or village to the chambre d'hôtes and corresponds with the location shown on the maps in the guide.

2 Gîtes de France grading (see page 8 for details).

3 A ❤ symbol may appear here if the chambre d'hôtes is on a farm.

4 Table d'hôtes evening meals (see page 10) or a restaurant are available where this ⦿ symbol appears.

5 Places with this ♿ symbol have been assessed by a French disability organisation (l'APF). For precise details of accessibility please contact the host (proprietor) direct.

6 Name of the chambre d'hôtes. Many houses do not have a name so these appear as 'Chambre d'hôtes'. Where the name appears in *italics* the price information has not been confirmed by the establishment for 2008.

7 Contact details for the establishment. The names of the hosts, the address, telephone, fax and e-mail appear where applicable. Website addresses are shown where supplied by the owners. Web addresses vary in France and may start with www. or http:// Some addresses will also be linked to the Gîtes de France website **www.gites-de-france.fr**. The AA cannot be held responsible for the content of these websites or the accuracy of the addresses. Some establishments give their local Gîtes de France Office as their contact address.

8 Optional photograph supplied by establishment.

9 A description of the setting and facilities.

10 Prices appear in Euros (€):
s - one person
d - two people
t - three people
(See page 11 for more details)

11 Further details of facilities at the chambre d'hôtes, and within the immediate vicinity.

---

1 PLATEAU D'ASSY / PASSY

2 ⦿ **Gîte La Chouette** ————— **6**

7 Edwin WILHELM
99, Rue d'Anterne, 74480 PLATEAU D'ASSY / PASSY
☎ 04 50 91 39 79 & 06 11 68 95 52 📠 04 50 91 54 81
email: info@gitelachouette.com
web: www.gitelachouette.com

9 This house, with its panoramic view of Mont Blanc, has been totally renovated by its Dutch owners. It has five comfortable bedrooms, all with en suite facilities, and sleeping from two to four guests. Large lounge area, open fire, terrace. Meals available by arrangement.

10 **Prices** s fr €40; d fr €59; t fr €88; extra person fr €29.50; dinner fr €24.50 **11** **Nearby** ⚓ 6km ⛷ 20km ✐ 6km ↖ 10km Restaurant 0.5km ⚓ 6km **12** ☂ 1km Spa 10km ⛳ 1km 🎣 0.5km ⛤ 10km **Notes** Pets admitted English spoken Open 21 December to October. CC

12 Additional information, e.g. whether pets are admitted, credit cards (CC) accepted, English spoken, etc. Most places are open all year. If not, the opening dates are shown (you are advised to check when booking).

Where in France?

Regions To find the general area of France that you would like to visit, you can use the Key Map on pages 6-7 to identify a French region (e.g Brittany), these are shown in capitals. If you are happy to browse through the whole Region then turn to the Index of Regions (page 18) to find the relevant page number in the guide. Regions are listed in alphabetical order through the guide.

Départements Each Region is made up of départements, and to narrow down your search for a place to stay use the Key Map (page 18) to identify these départements (e.g Finistere within Brittany). Each département has a number as well as a name (e.g Finistere 29). There are map sections at the end of each Region in this guide; each département has its own map page.

Towns and villages If you already know a particular town or village where you plan to stay, you can look through the index at the back of the guide. Many chambres d'hotes (B&Bs) are rurally located so they are listed under the nearest town or village. If there are no chambre d'hotes listed under the town or village you have chosen, you can look at the relevant département map to see if there's somewhere to stay close by. The red dots on these maps indicate the locations of chambre d'hotes in this guide.

Maps Each Region in this guide has a map section, and each département has its own map, which appear in alphabetical order within that region. These maps are intended solely to help you find your way around the guide and should not be used as road maps. We recommend the AA's range of French Atlases at different scales for navigating your way around the country; and there's also a range of 16 AA Touring Maps of France (scale: 1:180,000).

Which chambre d'hôtes?

For general information about staying in a chambre d'hôte and details of the Gîtes de France grading system, turn to page 8-10. The sample entry opposite shows how the information appears in the guide and what the symbols and abbreviations mean.

Directions and Signs

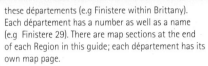

The AA Route Planner for Europe is ideal for obtaining the most convenient route to the location of your chosen chambre d'hote. Go to **www.theaa.com** and follow the links through Travel and The Route Planner, then just enter the name of your port of entry into France and the chambre d'hôtes' location. Every Gîtes de France chambre d'hôtes displays the Gîtes de France sign with the chambres d'hôtes panel.

Places selected for this guide may also display a window sticker identifying them as recommended in this AA guide.

Key to Symbols & Abbreviations

⚲	Bicycle Hire	**CC**	Credit Cards
⛷	Downhill Skiing	**fr**	from
♿	Establishment assessed by French disability organisation (l'APF)	**ha**	hectares
		km	kilometres
		mtrs/m	metres
⚲	Fishing	**s**	price for one person
⛳	Golf	**d**	price for two persons
🐴	Horseriding	**t**	price for three persons
♥	On farm		
▦	Railway Station		
⚓	Swimming Pool		
IOI	Table d'hôtes available		
⚓	Tennis		

GENERAL MAP AND KEY

KEY

Revelles ●   Town or village providing bed & breakfast accommodation

AMIENS ○   Prefecture

Abbeville ●   Sub-Prefecture

━━━━━━   Motorway

◐ ◑ ●   Interchange

◒ ◓   Half interchange

━━━━━━   Dual carriageway

┅┅┅┅┅   Main trunk road

┅┅┅┅┅   Major trunk road

━━━━━━   Road

━ ━ ━ ━   Department boundary

━━━━━━   Border

▬▬▬▬▬   Foreign country

〜〜〜   River

⬭   Lake

▬▬▬▬   Forest or wood

✈   Airport or aerodrome

MarieLaure et Thierry POULET TRESO LE CHESNAY - FRANCE - © Autorisation N°00321204

GREAT BRITAIN
PLYMOUTH
SOUTHAMPTON
CHERBOURG
ROSCOFF
SAINT-LÔ
BREST
50
SAINT-BRIEUC
SAINT-MALO
29
22
QUIMPER
BRITTANY
35
RENNES
56
LORIENT
VANNES
PAYS D.
44
LA LOIR
SAINT-NAZAIRE
ANG
NANTES
LA ROCHE-
SUR-YON
ATLANTIC
OCEAN
85
LA ROCHELLE
N(
17
BORDEAUX
AQUITAI
40
MONT-
DE-MARSAN
BAYONNE
BILBAO
PAU
64
TA
SPAIN

0   110 km

THE ENGLISH CHANNEL

BELGIUM

GERMANY

LUXEMBOURG

DOVER
FOLKESTONE
PORTSMOUTH
ANTWERPEN ●
DÜSSELDORF ●
DUNKERQUE
CALAIS
BOULOGNE
62
NORD-PAS-DE-CALAIS
LILLE ●
BRUSSELS ●
AACHEN ●
COLOGNE ●
BONN ●
LIEGE ●

ARRAS ●
59
AMIENS ●
80
DIEPPE ●
76
HAVRE ●
ROUEN ●
BEAUVAIS ●
PICARDY
02
LAON ●
CHARLEVILLE-MÉZIÈRES ●
LUXEMBOURG ●
FRANKFURT ●

CAEN ●
27
ÉVREUX ●
95
78
VERSAILLES
PARIS ○
60
ÎLE-DE-FRANCE
08
55
57
METZ ●
STUTTGART ●

NORMANDY
ÉVREUX ●
CHARTRES ●
28
ÉVRY
91
MELUN ●
77
51
CHÂLONS-EN-CHAMPAGNE ●
CHAMPAGNE-ARDENNE
BAR-LE-DUC ●
54
NANCY ●
ALSACE-LORRAINE
STRASBOURG ●
67

ALENÇON ●
61
72
LE MANS ●
45
89
TROYES ●
10
52
CHAUMONT ●
88
ÉPINAL ●
COLMAR ●
68

LE MANS ●
41
ORLÉANS ●
AUXERRE ●
70
90
BELFORT ●

TOURS ●
37
CENTRAL FRANCE
BLOIS ●
36
CHÂTEAUROUX ●
18
BOURGES ●
58
NEVERS ●
21
BURGUNDY
DIJON ●
VESOUL ●
25
BESANÇON ●
FRANCHE-COMTÉ
ZÜRICH ●
BERN ●

POITIERS ●
86
MOULINS ●
03
71
MÂCON ●
39
LONS-LE-SAUNIER
SWITZERLAND

POITOU-CHARENTES
87
GUÉRET ●
23
CLERMONT-FERRAND ●
BOURG-EN-BRESSE
69
01
GENÈVE ●
74
ANNECY ●

ANGOULÊME ●
16
LIMOGES ●
LIMOUSIN
63
42
LYON ●
SAINT-ÉTIENNE ●
38
CHAMBÉRY ●
RHÔNE-ALPES
73
MILAN ●

PÉRIGUEUX ●
24
TULLE ●
19
AUVERGNE
15
AURILLAC ●
43
LE PUY-EN-VELAY ●
VALENCE ●
GRENOBLE ●
TURIN ●
ITALY

47
CAHORS ●
46
07
MENDE ●
48
PRIVAS ●
05
GAP ●
GENOA ●

AGEN ●
82
MONTAUBAN ●
RODEZ ●
12
26
04
DIGNE-LES-BAINS ●
06
NICE ●
BASTIA ●
CALVI ●
2B

AUCH ●
2
TOULOUSE ●
ALBI ●
81
LANGUEDOC-ROUSSILLON
30
NÎMES ●
84
AVIGNON ●
PROVENCE-ALPES-CÔTE D'AZUR
CORSICA

MIDI-PYRÉNÉES
31
CARCASSONNE ●
11
34
MONTPELLIER ●
13
MARSEILLE ●
83
TOULON ●
AJACCIO ●
2A

09
FOIX ●
PERPIGNAN ●
66
MEDITERRANEAN SEA
BONIFACIO ●

Staying in a Chambre d'Hôtes

The French 'chambre d'hôtes' literally means 'bedroom of the hosts', where you are welcomed as a guest in someone's home. We use the term 'chambre d'hôtes' throughout this guide and refer to the owners as hosts. All the places in this guide are privately-owned, family homes run by hosts who will welcome you as part of the family and be pleased to help you get to know their local area.

Although the chambre d'hôtes philosophy is similar to that of bed and breakfast in the UK, family homes in France may offer different facilities and services to those you might expect in your own home. Chambres d'hôtes come in all shapes and sizes, from rural farmhouses and village inns, to beautiful manor houses and impressive châteaux with acres of garden or parkland. You might find yourself staying with a farmer and his family or in some cases with a viscount and viscountess. We give you the names of your hosts in this guide so that you can start to get to know them from the moment you first make contact, and we offer some useful tips on French culture and etiquette on page 17.

Change in regulations for accommodation

From December 2007 the French Government are making some changes to requirements for different types of accommodation. Chambres d'hotes will have to have five bedrooms or fewer, accommodating a maximum of 15 guests.

The data for this guide was collected in summer 2007, before these new regulations came into force. You may therefore find that some establishments will have reconfigured their rooms and may be offering a slightly different set up to that quoted, or that they may no longer be calling themselves a chambre d'hotes – please do check before you book that the establishment you have chosen is suitable for your requirements.

Gîtes de France Grading

All the chambres d'hôtes in this book are inspected, assessed and given a grade by Gîtes de France. The grading is the épis or 'ear of corn' which appears as

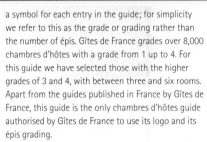

a symbol for each entry in the guide; for simplicity we refer to this as the grade or grading rather than the number of épis. Gîtes de France grades over 8,000 chambres d'hôtes with a grade from 1 up to 4. For this guide we have selected those with the higher grades of 3 and 4, with between three and six rooms. Apart from the guides published in France by Gîtes de France, this guide is the only chambres d'hôtes guide authorised by Gîtes de France to use its logo and its épis grading.

The Gîtes de France grading varies according to the style of architecture and the setting, the level of comfort and the services provided, and is shown to give you a general indication of the different standards of the chambres d'hôtes. At grade 3 you can expect 'a high level of comfort', while at grade 4 you can expect to enjoy 'exceptional levels of comfort, in residences of character in outstanding settings'. Whatever the grade, your hosts' priority is to make sure you enjoy your stay.

Rooms

Chambre d'hôtes rooms in this guide all have fully fitted private bathrooms, however these may not always be en suite. They will have a bath or shower, washbasin and WC. French bathrooms may be as full of character as the house. Do not expect them to be fantastically modern; sometimes French showers don't have shower curtains. Rooms are cleaned daily (for long stays, bedlinen is changed at least once a week and towels etc. twice a week).

Children's facilities

Some owners may provide an extra bed for children in your room, others offer family rooms or suites with connecting rooms. Additional children's facilities may be mentioned in the guide description. Check with the owners when you book that your requirements can be met.

Room prices

Room prices shown are per night, and may vary depending on the number of people sharing the room. Room prices always include breakfast. Please bear in mind that prices are liable to change during the currency of this guide. Some chambres d'hôtes offer

discounts for longer stays or for children, so it is worth asking when booking. Tourist tax (taxe de séjour) is collected locally in France. Tourist tax is charged per person per day.

Prices in the guide are given in euros. Francs are no longer legal tender, but franc notes can be exchanged at the Treasury or the Bank of France until 2012.

Meals
Breakfast

Breakfast is always included in the price shown. This gives you the chance to try local specialities according to your hosts' individual style, which may include home-made bread, jams, home-baked pastries, local cheese and dairy products and local charcuterie (cold meats).

Table d'hôtes evening meals

'Table d'hôtes' means sharing your host's table, for an evening meal. This is usually en famille so you may be joined by members of the hosts' family and other guests. Approximately one third of the chambres d'hôtes in this guide offer an evening meal shown by this symbol ⏞◯⏞. There may be particular days when table d'hôtes meals are not available so do ask to avoid disappointment. Table d'hôtes meals are only offered to resident guests. Some chambres d'hôtes may have a restaurant; this will be indicated in the guide entry.

Meal arrangements

If you wish to have meals with your hosts during your stay you will need to let them know in advance. It is best to ask when you make your booking, especially if you want dinner on the night you arrive. Table d'hôtes can be a flexible arrangement; you can opt for one meal only or full-board. If you have not booked in advance you may be able to make arrangements with your hosts a day in advance or each morning of your stay. Meal times will vary from around 7-9pm; if you wish to eat at a particular time discuss this with your host at the start of your stay, particularly if you have children with you.

continued

Staying in a Chambre d'Hôtes continued

Meal prices

Dinner prices given in the guide are an indication of the cost of the whole meal, starter, main course, cheese and/or dessert, coffee and beverage. Children's meal rates may be available, check when booking. Some chambres d'hôtes may offer special rates for full board.

Alternative meal arrangements

If dinner is not available at your chambre d'hôtes your hosts will be able to advise you of the best local restaurants or inns, where you can enjoy traditional or regional French cooking. Entries mention if there is a restaurant nearby. Local restaurants generally close one day a week, and may not take orders after 9pm.

Payment

Check which payment methods are acceptable when booking. Most chambres d'hôtes will expect payment in cash, some may accept travellers cheques or credit cards but these methods may incur additional charges.

Arrival times

If you are going to be later arriving than you anticipated, please do telephone to let your hosts know, otherwise they may let your room to someone else. Most chambres d'hôtes expect guests to arrive from 4pm onwards. If you have to cancel your booking, let the owners know immediately.

Taking pets

Information on whether pets are permitted or not appears in the entry under NOTES. Please note that if pets are accepted there may be a charge. If you are taking your dog or cat, make sure you let the owners know when booking. Plans to take a pet must be carefully considered and made well in advance. The pet must pass a blood test at least six calendar months before travelling, and stringent import/export regulations apply. For full details of pet passports, microchipping and documentation required, refer to the Pet Travel Scheme (PETS): Hotline 0870 241 1710 (08.30-17.00 Monday to Friday):
Email: pets.helpline@dfra.gsi.gov.uk
Website: www.defra.gov.uk/animalh/quarantine/pets/

Smoking

From February 2008 smoking is banned in public places. Those found in breach of the ban will be fined - 75 euros for individuals and 150 euros for the premises where the offence occured.

Complaints

Most common problems arise from a simple misunderstanding so we strongly urge you to take up any issues with your host at the time, in the spirit of entente cordiale. Of course we are anxious to hear about serious problems which may arise and these will also be forwarded to Gîtes de France for their assessment. If you wish to contact the AA about a complaint arising from using this guide, please write to the Editor, Bed & Breakfast in France, AA Hotel Services, Fanum House, Basing View, Basingstoke, Hampshire, RG21 4EA.

The AA will not in any circumstances act as representative or negotiator or undertake to obtain compensation or enter into further correspondence or deal with the matter in any other way whatsoever. The AA will not guarantee to take any specific action.

CAMPIGNÔN-DE-CURB

Avoid the hassle of breaking down in Europe

It's the last thing you want on your holiday. Fortunately, our European Breakdown Cover brings you all the protection you'd expect, from only £11.88* for AA members. Accessed through a 24 hour English-speaking hotline. So at least you know, you won't be campignôn-de-curb.

The AA gives you 24-hour English speaking telephone assistance, arranging and helping towards the cost of:

- Vehicle recovery back to the UK
- Roadside assistance and emergency repair
- Alternative travel and accommodation

0800 316 9969
theAA.com

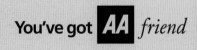
You've got **AA** *friend*

How to Book a Chambre d'hôtes

It is always best to make your reservations in advance. Many of the places in this guide are in popular areas and are quite small, so they may get booked up quickly. Details of public and school holidays are provided on page 16.

Contacting your hosts for information and to make a booking (see also sample letters) '

Each entry in the guide gives you the name of your hosts and the location of the chambre d'hôtes. The address, telephone, fax and e-mail given will usually be for your hosts; however, in some cases Gîtes de France regional offices run a reservation service (SR) and this number may appear instead.

Many hosts speak English and this is indicated in the entry under NOTES. If you prefer to contact your hosts by telephone, remember that France is an hour ahead of the UK.

You can also book any of the chambres d'hôtes on the internet through **www.gites-de-france.com**.

Confirming your booking

In many cases you will be asked for written confirmation and/or a deposit. An agreement may also be drawn up (usual for longer stays); a copy will be sent out to you to complete and return. Do check the details carefully to ensure that you have the correct dates and the types of rooms and beds that you require in particular. You should also have the agreed price and information on payment methods. It is a good idea to make a note of any special requirements on the written confirmation or in your booking letter to avoid any confusion.

You might like to ask a number of questions before you make your booking. Here is a checklist to help you:

- Have they got availability for the dates you require?
- Have they got the right combination of rooms/beds for your party?
- Have you asked about special rates for children/meals?
- Do you want to book any evening meals?
- Do you understand the prices and what is included?
- Have you explained any special requirements e.g. vegetarian food?
- Have you asked about any activities you are interested in e.g. golf, horse-riding?

Sample Letters

Establishment address in full with postcode and country

Your address in full with postcode and country

Date

Dear M/Mme X

I am writing to ask you to send me your brochure, or further information about your chambre d'hôtes, which I found in the AA/Gîtes de France Bed & Breakfast in France Guide. I look forward to hearing from you. Thank you for your help.

Yours sincerely

Your name

Establishment address in full with postcode and country

Your address in full with postcode and country

Date

Monsieur/Madame

Je vous serais reconnaissant de me faire parvenir votre brochure ou des renseignements sur votre chambre d'hôtes, que j'ai vu dans le guide AA/Gîtes de France Bed & Breakfast in France.

J'attends vos renseignements et vous remercie par avance.

Je vous prie d'agréer, Monsieur/Madame, l'expression de mes sentiments distingués.

Your name

Establishment address in full with postcode and countrycountry

Your address in full with postcode and

Date

Monsieur/Madame

Je vous remercie pour votre brochure. Je voudrais réserver ... chambre(s) pour (une personne/deux personnes) avec salle de bain/salle d'eau et WC privés, du (date) jusqu'au (date). Nous sommes ..., ... adulte(s), et ... enfant(s) de ... ans/moins de ... ans. Nous voudrions un lit d'enfant dans la chambre des parents. Est-ce que vous avez des chambres disponibles pour ces nuits?

Je voudrais aussi réserver une table d'hôtes pour ... adulte(s)et ... enfant(s) le soir du (date). Est-ce qu'il y a la possibilité d'un tarif réduit pour les enfants ou pour un séjour prolongé? Est-ce que vous acceptez les cartes de crédit/ les chèques de voyage?

Nous partirons de (place); je vous serais reconnaissant de me communiquer les directions.

En attendant vos renseignements, je vous prie d'agréer, Monsieur/Madame, l'expression de mes sentiments distingués.

Your name

Establishment address in full with postcode and country country

Your address in full with postcode and

Date

Dear M/Mme X

Thank you for sending me your brochure. I would like to reserve ... (single/double) room(s) with private bath/shower and WC, for the nights of (dates). We are a party of ..., comprising ... adults and ... child(ren) aged .../ under ... years. We would like a cot in the parents' room. Do you have any rooms available at that time?

I would also like to book table d'hôtes for (number of adults/children) on (date). Do you offer any discounts for children and/or longer stays? Will I be able to pay by credit card/travellers' cheque?

We will be travelling from (place), please can you send me directions. I look forward to hearing from you.

Yours sincerely

Your name

Travelling in France

Motoring

Documentation You should carry your full valid national driving licence (including the paper part if you have a photo card) or International Driving Permit (IDP), the vehicle registration document, certificate of motor insurance and a letter of authorisation from the owner if the vehicle is not registered in your name. Your vehicle should display the approved standard design International Distinguishing Sign (IDS), for example 'GB' for UK residents. Cycle racks should not obscure your number plate or IDS.

Rules of the road Drive on the right and overtake on the left. Traffic coming from the right has priority (priorité à droite), unless signs say otherwise. The priorité rule no longer applies at roundabouts, which means you give way to cars already on the roundabout. The minimum age to drive in France is 18, and no one is allowed to drive on a provisional licence.

Lights Right-hand drive cars need headlamp beam converters (available as kits) to divert the beam away from drivers of oncoming left-hand drive vehicles. Motorists must carry a warning triangle and are advised to carry a set of replacement bulbs, as it is illegal to drive with faulty lights.

Speed limits In built-up areas 50 kph (31 mph); outside built-up areas 90 kph (55 mph), or 80 kph (49 mph) in wet conditions; dual carriageways with a central reservation 110 kph (69 mph) or 100 kph (62 mph) in wet conditions; motorways 130 kph (80 mph) or 110 kph (69 mph) in wet conditions. Minimum speed on the Paris Périphérique is 80 kph (49 mph); on other urban motorways 110 kph (69 mph). In fog the speed limit on all roads is 50 kph (31 mph). Drivers who have held a licence for less than two years must always observe the reduced speed limits.

Seatbelts must be worn by the driver and the front and back-seat passengers.

Drink Maximum permissible alcohol levels are very low (0.05 per cent) and random breath tests are frequent. It is wiser not to drink at all if you will be driving.

Motorways France has more than 8,000 km of motorways (autoroutes), indicated on maps as A followed by a number. Most of these are toll roads. Prices per km vary and you can pay by cash or credit card at the exit booth (péage). Autoroutes in France are usually much quieter than motorways in Britain, and have resting areas (aire de repos) every 20km or so.

Alternative routes Country roads offer a more picturesque, if slower, alternative to the autoroute. Although routes nationales (indicated by the letter N before the road number) are generally very good, they can become congested in places. Look for roads signed itinéraire bis to avoid trouble spots. The Bison Futé map shows these routes; copies are available from the French Tourist Office. You can also plan your route on the AA website www.theAA.com.

Car hire You will need your driver's licence and preferably an IDP. You may be asked to show your passport.

Eurotunnel run a 24-hour drive-on train service through the Channel Tunnel, from Folkestone to Calais, UK telephone 08705 353535 or see www.eurotunnel.com.

Fuel Petrol stations in France no longer sell leaded petrol, which has been replaced with a substitute unleaded petrol that can be used in vehicles that normally use leaded fuel. Unleaded (sans plomb) may be found as 98 or 95 octane, 'super plus' or 'premium'. Diesel is generally known as gas oil/gazole.

Motoring essentials AA shops at Dover and Eurotunnel sell European Breakdown Insurance, and a wide range of maps, atlases and guides. Motoring abroad essentials such as beam converters and warning triangles can also be purchased here and international driving permits can be obtained. AA shops give a 5% discount off all merchandise to AA members.
    Visability vests are likely to become compulsory throughout the EU. It is recommended that you carry one for each passenger.

AA telephone numbers

European Breakdown Cover
Telephone 0800 444500
Maps, Atlases & Guides
Telephone 01256 491524
Travel Insurance
Telephone 0800 316 2456

AA shops

Travelcentre, Eastern Docks Terminal, Dover
Telephone 01304 208122
Eurotunnel passenger terminal, Folkestone
(access only on day of travel with ticket)
Telephone 0800 072 4372

Motoring websites

www.theAA.com
(route planning, motoring advice, traffic information,
insurance and much more)
www.autoroutes.fr
(information on motorways in France - road works,
tolls, etc.)
www.sytadin.tm.fr
(traffic reports around Paris)
www.franceguide.com
(information on motoring in France)

Train travel

There is an extensive rail network in France. It is
advisable to book popular routes (e.g. Paris-Lyon)
well in advance. You can travel direct from London
Waterloo or Ashford, Kent, to Paris or Lille on the
Eurostar passenger service. Eurostar also offers direct
services to Disneyland Paris and the French Alps. Many
other destinations can be reached by taking the
high-speed TGV from Paris or Lille. For further
information and bookings contact Rail Europe on
08705 371 371. (www.raileurope.co.uk)
    When booking accommodation check that it is
accessible by train if this is your main method of
transport.

Train websites

www.eurostar.co.uk
www.eurotunnel.com
www.raileurope.co.uk

Ferry travel

Ferries operate regularly between France and Britain,
for foot passengers as well as cars. Services are subject
to seasonal variations; check with your travel agent
in advance.

Ferry websites

www.brittanyferries.com
(Brittany Ferries)
www.condorferries.com
(Condor Ferries)
www.norfolkline-ferries.co.uk
(Norfolk Line)
www.poferries.com
(P&O Ferries)
www.seafrance.com
(SeaFrance)
www.speedferries.com
(Speed Ferries)
www.transmancheferries.com
(Transmanche Ferries)

Air travel

The international airports for Paris are Roissy-Charles
de Gaulle and Orly Sud and the national airline,
Air France, has a very extensive domestic network
operating out of both. Other airports used for direct
scheduled flights include Bordeaux, Lyon, Marseille,
Nantes, Nice, Strasbourg and Toulouse.

Airline websites

www.airfrance.co.uk
(Air France)
www.ba.com
(British Airways)
www.flybmi.com
(British Midland)
www.easyjet.com
(easyJet)
www.ryanair.com
(Ryanair)

Student and youth travel

If you are under 26, you can apply for one of a variety
of reasonably priced cards which give discounts
on travel, accommodation and meals. You will
need identification and a photo for all of them. The
International Student Card (ISIC) also entitles you
to cheaper museum entry and beds in university
residences. Contact your local students' union, student
travel office, or the ISIC website (www.isiccard.com)
for an application form. Proof of full-time student
status is required. ISIC also issue International Youth
Travel Cards, (IYTC) to anyone under the age of 26.
A free booklet, Youth Tourism, is available from the
French Tourist Office (www.franceguide.com).

Useful Information

School holidays 2008-2009

France is split into three distinct regions for the dates of when classes break up. The aim is to stagger holiday times so that the roads and public services are not overloaded.

ZONE A: Caen, Clermont- Ferreand, Grenoble, Lyon, Montpellier, Nancy-Metz, Nantes, Rennes, Toulouse

ZONE B: Aix-Marseille, Amiens, Besançon, Dijon, Lille, Limoges, Nice, Orléans-Tours, Poitiers, Reims, Rouen, Strasbourg

ZONE C: Bordeaux, Créteil, Paris, Versailles

Public holidays 2008

New Year's Day	1 January
Easter	23-26 March
Labour Day/Ascension Day	1 May
Victory Day WWII	8 May
Whit Monday	12 May
Bastille Day	14 July
Assumption Day	15 August
All Saints' Day	1 November
Remembrance Day	11 November
Christmas Day	25 December

	Zone A	Zone B	Zone C
Winter	16 Feb-3 Mar	9-25 Feb	23 Feb-10 Mar
Spring	12-18 Apr	5-21 Apr	19 Apr-5 May
Summer	3 Jul-2 Sep	3 Jul-2 Sep	3 Jul-2 Sep
Autumn	27 Oct-8 Nov	27 Oct-8 Nov	27 Oct-8 Nov
Christmas	22 Dec-7 Jan	22 Dec-7 Jan	22 Dec-7 Jan

British consulate

18 bis, rue d'Anjou, 75008, Paris
Tel (1) 44 51 31 00, Fax (1) 44 51 31 27
Open Mon-Fri 9.30am-12.30pm, 2.30-5pm
There are also consulates in Bordeaux, Lille, Lyon and Marseilles.

Emergency Numbers

Fire	18
Police	17
Ambulance (SAMU)	15
Operator	13
Directory Enquiries	12
European Emergency number (use for any emergency service from a mobile phone)	112

Telephones

French telephone numbers are 10 digits (9 from the UK as you drop the initial 0).

To dial France from the UK
Dial 0033 (international access code), then the number minus the first 0.

To call the UK from France
Dial 0044 (international access code) then the UK number minus the first 0.

To call the US and Canada from France
Dial 001 (international access code), then the number.
 Payphones are plentiful, and usually take phone cards (télécartes), which you can buy in newsagents (tabacs) and post offices. Some payphones in cities will take credit cards.

Shopping and business hours

Banks: 9am-noon, 2-4pm weekdays, and closed either Saturday or Monday. Banks close early the day before a public holiday.

Post Offices: 8am-noon, 2-7pm weekdays, 8am-noon Saturdays.

Food shops/supermarkets: 7am-noon, 2-6.30 or 7.30pm

Other shops: 9 or 10am-noon, 2-6.30 or 7.30pm. Many shops close all or half-day Monday. Some food shops (bakers in particular) may open Sunday morning. Shops everywhere usually close for lunch between 12 and 2pm, sometimes longer. Restaurants generally serve food only between 12-2 at lunchtime. Hypermarkets are often open until 9 or 10pm Monday to Saturday (many close on Monday morning). Tourist offices can give you local times.

Tourist information

There are 5,000 local Offices de Tourisme and Syndicats d'Initiative. They can give advice on accommodation, transport, restaurants and entertainment.

Time Changes

From the end of March to the end of October French times change from GMT+1 to GMT+2 (GMT-Greenwich Mean Time)

Credit cards

Make sure you take your bank's 24-hour credit card contact number with you. Cash can be withdrawn from many cash dispensing machines using your UK pin number, check that the machine displays the appropriate symbol. British cards do not usually work in 24-hour petrol machines.

Medical treatment and health insurance

If you regularly take certain medicines, do make sure that you have a sufficient supply for your stay before travelling. If for health reasons you carry drugs or appliances (such as a hypodermic syringe), a letter from your doctor explaining the condition and treatment required may save you from any difficulties in entering France. Before travelling, make sure you are covered by insurance for emergency medical and dental treatment as a minimum. Before taking out extra insurance check whether your homeowner or medical insurance covers travel abroad. Many European countries have reciprocal agreements for medical treatments which require EU citizens to obtain a European Health Insurance Card (which has replaced the E111 form) before travel. You should not rely exclusively on this, however, and personal travel insurance is advisable.

Etiquette and cultural differences

Although your hosts will want you to feel welcome during your stay, you should never forget that you are guests in their home. It is polite to notify them if you're going to arrive earlier or later than arranged, and always ask first before bringing your pet with you. Even if your French is limited to a few textbook phrases, do make the effort to use what you know;

your hosts will appreciate your efforts, even if it is just a friendly bonjour or au revoir as you enter or leave the premises. If your French is good enough to hold a conversation, do remember that you should never use the familiar tu over the more formal vous, unless invited to do so.

When entering a shop, it is courteous to greet the assistant with bonjour, monsieur/ madame/ mademoiselle. Generally, a woman in her twenties or older is addressed as madame, while a younger woman is addressed as mademoiselle. Use these forms of address to attract the attention of a waiter in a restaurant.

Table etiquette is important to the French but a little common sense should be all you need to get by. It is usual to order wine or mineral water to drink with a meal, rather than a fizzy drink or coffee. A basket of bread will come with your meal, whether you order it or not. In a restaurant, service is usually included (look out for the words service compris on the menu or bill) but people generally leave a euro or two on the table as they leave. You will probably need to prompt the waiter to bring your bill; dining out is rarely a hurried affair and most waiters will take the cue from you as to when you're ready to leave. Never ask for a doggy bag, no matter how delicious your dessert.

Index to Regions

ALSACE-LORRAINE

BAS-RHIN

BETSCHDORF

♦♦♦ Chambre d'hôtes

Christian KRUMEICH

23, rue des Potiers, 67660 BETSCHDORF

☎ 03 88 54 40 56 🖹 03 88 54 40 56

Three bedrooms available in the home of a potter. All are grade 3 and have twin beds, one has a kitchen and TV. There is a lounge, a garden with outdoor furniture and a covered parking area. Pottery courses can be arranged.

Prices s €38-€40; d €48-€53; extra person fr €14 **Nearby** ⛳ 10km
🌊 1km ⛲ 0.5km ⚓ 30km ⛴ 0.5km 🏛 0.1km ➹ 10km **Notes** No pets English spoken

BOERSCH

♦♦♦ Bienvenue Willkommen

Alain TAUBERT

3, route de Rosheim, 67530 BOERSCH

☎ 03 88 95 93 06 🖹 03 88 95 99 98

email: alisnata@bienvenue-willkommen.com

web: www.bienvenue-willkommen.com

Situated on the edge of a wine growing town near Obernai, en suite rooms are offered in a house adjoining the owners' residence. There are two triple rooms and a twin room with a double and a single bed. Breakfast is served in the dining room. There is also a lounge area with books, magazines and games available to guests. The panoramic garden has outdoor furniture and parking facilities. Reductions for longer stays.

Prices s fr €50; d fr €60; t fr €70 **On Site** ⚓ ⛴ ⚓ **Nearby** ➹ 3km Restaurant 3km ⚓ 15km ⛲ 3km 🍽 3km 🏛 0.1km ➹ 3km **Notes** No pets English spoken

BREITENBACH

♦♦♦ 🍽 La Cerisaie

Robert HAAS

31, rue des Tilleuls, 67220 BREITENBACH

☎ 03 88 57 05 07 🖹 03 90 56 29 19

email: astrid@la-cerisaie.net

web: www.la-cerisaie.net

Five rooms for two to four people here, two with mezzanine, one with a Jacuzzi, and a ground-floor room suitable for disabled guests in the owners' house on the edge of a quiet village. Breakfast served in the owners' dining room, or on the terrace in summer. Living room with TV and fridge; meals by arrangement. Parking.

Prices s fr €60; d fr €66; t fr €87; dinner fr €18 **Nearby** ⚓ 3km ➹ 3km ⚓ 6km ⛲ 3km 🏛 3km ➹ 10km **Notes** No pets English spoken

CLEEBOURG

♦♦♦ 🍽 Chambre d'hôtes

Anne KLEIN

59, rue Principale, 67160 CLEEBOURG

☎ 03 88 94 50 95 & 06 21 35 07 91 🖹 03 88 94 50 95

email: annejp.klein@laposte.net

web: www.chez.com/cleebourg

Situated in the centre of a small wine-growing village, this house has one family room with a double and a single bed, one double room and one twin room, all en suite. A camp bed is also available. Breakfast is served in a traditionally decorated room and meals based on Alsace specialities are available. There is an enclosed courtyard, garden with furniture, barbecue and parking facilities.

Prices s fr €39; d fr €44; extra person fr €21; dinner fr €14
Nearby ⚓ 6km ⛲ 30km ➹ 10km ➹ 4km Restaurant 0.2km ⚓ 10km 🏛 7km ➹ 10km **Notes** No pets

DAMBACH-LA-VILLE

♦♦♦ Chambre d'hôtes

Michel NARTZ

12, place du Marché, 67650 DAMBACH LA VILLE

☎ 03 88 92 41 11 🖹 03 88 92 63 01

email: nartz.michel@wanadoo.fr

A 17th-century vineyard property complete with wine-tasting cellar, situated in the town centre. There are three double rooms, one with a lounge area, one twin room and one single room, all en suite. Breakfast is served in a small tavern, with traditional food during the summer. Reduced rates available for extended stays.

Prices s fr €40; d €46-€50; extra person fr €10 **Nearby** ⚓ 15km
➹ 2km ➹ 8km Restaurant 1km ⚓ 1km 🍽 8km 🏛 0.1km ➹ 1km **Notes** No pets English spoken Open April to 22 December. CC

DIEBOLSHEIM

☷ Chambre d'hôtes

Pierrette KIENY
12, rue Abbé Wendling, 67230 DIEBOLSHEIM
☎ 03 88 74 84 85
email: pierrette@kieny.com
web: www.ambiance-jardin.com

In a barn on this ancient farm with exposed beams are four rooms, three for two people in twin or double beds, and another sleeping four in single beds. Three of the rooms have balconies, and all have bath or shower/WC. A 'garden' theme runs through the entire establishment, with breakfast served in a greenery-filled room. Wi-fi available. The English garden has furniture; enclosed parking.

Prices d €75-€85; extra person fr €15 **On Site** ℰ Private ♨ Restaurant ℘ **Nearby** ⚲ 10km ♨ 20km ⚹ 15km ⋈ 10km **Notes** No pets English spoken

DIEFFENBACH-AU-VAL

☷ ✿ Les Trois Pierres

Albert GEIGER
2, route de Neuve Eglise, 67220 DIEFFENBACH AU VAL
☎ 03 88 85 69 02 ⬛ 03 88 85 62 03
email: geiger@les3pierres.com
web: www.les3pierres.com

Guest rooms adjoining the owners' house on the edge of a quiet village. There are three double en suite rooms with satellite TV and a cot is available. Breakfast is served in a private guest room, which also has a lounge area and fireplace. Garden area with furniture and covered parking. Reduced price for stays over three nights. No smoking in bedrooms.

Prices not confirmed for 2008 **Nearby** ℰ 2km ⚹ 4km ⋐ 25km ♨ 4km ⬚ 4km ⋈ 10km **Notes** No pets

EICHHOFFEN

☷ ⅙ Les Feuilles d'Or

Francis KUSS
50-52 rue du Vignoble, 67140 EICHHOFFEN
☎ 03 88 08 49 80 ⬛ 03 88 08 49 80
email: kuss.francis@libertysurf.fr
web: www.lesfeuillesdor.fr.st

Five rooms are offered in a house adjacent to the proprietors', situated in the heart of a vineyard with lovely views. There is a triple room, two doubles and two rooms for four, each with TV, telephone and private facilities. Breakfast is served in the dining room, and there is a relaxing room with kitchen area, garden with terrace, furniture and barbecue. Private pond 1km. Parking available.

Prices s fr €65; d fr €75; t fr €100; extra person fr €25 **On Site** ℘ **Nearby** ⚲ 3km ℰ 1km ⚹ 10km Restaurant 0.6km ⋐ 14km ♨ 2km ⬚ 0.5km ⋈ 1km **Notes** No pets English spoken

GERSTHEIM

☷ ⅋ Chambre d'hôtes

Danièle ALBERTUS
53 rue du Rhin, 67150 GERSTHEIM
☎ 03 88 98 37 20
email: famille.albertus@wanadoo.fr
web: www.giterural-albertus.com

In a village setting, this property has four guest bedrooms, all on the first floor of a converted outbuilding adjacent to the owners' house. Three of the rooms are doubles; the fourth is a two-roomed family suite for four. All have a private shower room/WC and a TV. Cot available. Enclosed courtyard with parking; table tennis; meals by arrangement.

Prices s fr €45; d fr €50; t fr €70; extra person fr €15; dinner fr €18 **On Site** ℰ Restaurant **Nearby** ⚲ 3km ♨ 12km ⚹ 7km ℘ 9km ⋈ 7km **Notes** No pets English spoken

GOUGENHEIM

☷ Chambre d'hôtes

M.-Claude et Alain LEBAS
1, rue de la Montée, 67270 GOUGENHEIM
☎ 03 88 70 59 72 & 06 81 39 57 99
email: mclebas@hotmail.com
web: www.aux-quatre-saisons.com

This restored 18th-century farmhouse is conveniently situated not far from Strasbourg. On the first floor are two double rooms, one with an additional sofa bed; on the second floor is a triple room (double bed plus a single) with a kitchenette, microwave, and its own terrace with garden furniture. All rooms have private facilities. Space outside with table tennis, parking. No smoking.

Prices s fr €60; d fr €70; t fr €90; extra person fr €15 **On Site** ℘ **Nearby** ⚲ 10km ♨ 25km ℰ 8km ⚹ 8km Restaurant 5km ♨ 5km ⬚ 5km ⋈ 8km **Notes** No pets English spoken Open 4 January to 19 December

HEILIGENSTEIN

⊞ Chambre d'hôtes

Charles BOCH
6, rue Principale, 67140 HEILIGENSTEIN
☎ 03 88 08 41 26 🖹 03 88 08 58 25
email: charles.boch@wanadoo.fr
web: www.boch-vins-alsace-chambresdhotes.com
A pretty wine maker's house, situated in a vineyard. There are three en suite double rooms, one with a balcony. Extra bed available. Excellent breakfasts are served in a private dining room. Pot luck meals available. There is a garden area with furniture, table tennis and parking.
Prices not confirmed for 2008 **Nearby** ⚓ 10km ⚐ 10km ⚑ 20km ⚒ 2km 🚶 2km **Notes** No pets

HOERDT

⊞ Le Landhome

René et Dorothée STOLL
23, route de la Wantzenau, 67720 HOERDT
☎ 03 88 51 72 29 & 06 08 25 01 51 🖹 03 90 29 00 79
email: stoll.rene@wanadoo.fr
web: http://perso.wanadoo.fr/landhome
Five guest rooms available; three double rooms, one room sleeping four, and one twin. Each is en suite with telephone and one room has a kitchen. Facilities for guests include a dining room and lounge with cable TV.
Prices s fr €44; d fr €52; t fr €62; extra person fr €10 **On Site** Restaurant ⚑ **Nearby** ⚓ 10km ⚐ 3km ⚑ 1km ⚑ 10km ⚒ 1km 🚶 1km **Notes** No pets English spoken CC

HUNSPACH

⊞ Maison Ungerer

3, route de Hoffen, 67250 HUNSPACH
☎ 03 88 80 59 39 🖹 03 88 80 41 46
email: maison-ungerer@wanadoo.fr
web: www.maison-ungerer.com
This renovated farm building offers three twin rooms, each with bathroom facilities, a kitchen and a lounge area. Accommodation can be provided for two additional people. Breakfast is served in the dining room and there is a garden with barbecue, table tennis and garden furniture. Bike hire is available and there are reductions for extended stays.
Prices s fr €30; d fr €47; t fr €71 **On Site** ⚑ **Nearby** ⚓ 12km ⚒ 20km ⚐ 5km ⚑ 10km Restaurant 0.5km ⚒ 0.2km 🏠 0.3km 🚶 1km **Notes** No pets English spoken CC

ITTERSWILLER

⊞ Chambre d'hôtes

Raymond KIEFFER
10, rue Viehweg, Rotland, 67140 ITTERSWILLER
☎ 03 88 85 51 12 🖹 03 88 85 58 18
web: http://perso.wanadoo.fr/coteauxdurotland
These three rooms are on the first floor of the owners' home, in the heart of the vineyard. All of the rooms are twin-bedded, and each has a TV, a private shower room and WC. One of the rooms has a terrace, and one a balcony. Breakfast is served in the hosts' dining room, or on the terrace. Garden furniture, games room, parking.
Prices d €65-€95; t fr €95; extra person fr €15 **On Site** ⚐ Restaurant ⚑ **Nearby** ⚑ 15km ⚒ 1km 🏠 1km 🚶 2km **Notes** No pets English spoken

KURTZENHOUSE

⊞ ⓘ Chambre d'hôtes

Bernard et Agnès SUSAN
50, rue principale, 67240 KURTZENHOUSE
☎ 03 88 72 15 37
email: abza67@wanadoo.fr
web: http://perso.wanadoo.fr/famillesusan/menu/index.htm
A half-timbered village house with three bedrooms. Two of them are doubles, with a private lounge containing a double bed-settee. The third room, with its own entrance, is also a double, with a small lounge area. All rooms have a private shower room and WC. Breakfast served in guests' breakfast room; other meals available by arrangement. Garden furniture, barbecue and swing.
Prices s fr €54; d fr €59; t fr €84; extra person fr €25; dinner fr €23 **On Site** Restaurant ⚑ **Nearby** ⚓ 5km ⚒ 15km ⚐ 2km ⚑ 5km ⚑ 18km ⚒ 0.1km Spa 30km 🏠 0.1km 🚶 0.5km **Notes** No pets English spoken

LUPSTEIN

⊞ Chambre d'hôtes

Francine HUBER - VANDELOISE
40, rue principale, 67490 LUPSTEIN
☎ 03 88 91 49 96 & 06 26 83 59 13 🖹 03 88 91 49 96
email: francine.huber@wanadoo.fr
This half-timbered house has two first-floor guest bedrooms, each with its own private entrance. Each room has a double bed, an additional folding bed, and a private bathroom. The house is situated in the village; it has an enclosed courtyard and private parking.
Prices s fr €37; d fr €48; extra person fr €26 **On Site** ⚐ **Nearby** ⚓ 25km ⚒ 30km ⚑ 10km Restaurant 2.5km ⚒ 10km ⚑ 10km 🏠 2km 🚶 2.5km **Notes** No pets

NEUBOIS

⚜ ⓞ L'Altenberg

Richarde MOSSER

4, rue de l'altenberg, 67220 NEUBOIS

☎ 03 88 85 60 56

email: richarde.mosser@wanadoo.fr

web: www.chambres-de-l-altenberg.net

A typical Alsace house adjoining the owners' residence in quiet surroundings. There are two triple rooms, one twin and a room with a double and a single bed, all en suite with TV. Breakfast is served in the dining room and meals are available, with Alsace specialities. There is a kitchen, veranda, TV, garden furniture, swing and parking. Reductions for extended stays.

Prices s fr €50; d fr €54; t fr €66; extra person fr €12; dinner fr €20
On Site 🏊 **Nearby** ⛵ 2km 🚴 20km ⤳ 6km Restaurant 2km 🛥 15km
🏇 6km 🐎 6km 🚶 12km **Notes** Pets admitted English spoken

ORSCHWILLER

⚜ Rose des Vignes

Régine et Gilbert EHRHARDT

6a, route du Vin, 67600 ORSCHWILLER

☎ 03 88 92 82 29 📠 03 88 92 82 29

email: rose.des.vignes@wanadoo.fr

web: http://perso.wanadoo.fr/rosedesvignes

This flower adorned house is set at the foot of Haut Koenisgsbourg on the wine route. Rooms include a double, a room with a double bed, single, fridge and balcony and a suite with a double room, twin room and kitchenette; each has private facilities and lounge area. Breakfast is served in a room reserved for guests or on the terrace. Shady green grounds with furniture and parking. Gite on site. Reductions from the third night.

Prices d €48-€52; t fr €65; extra person fr €10 **Nearby** ⛵ 5km 🏊 5km
⤳ 6km Restaurant 0.5km 🏇 6km 🚲 2km 🚶 6km **Notes** No pets
English spoken

RIMSDORF

⚜ Au Fenil

Raymond et Annie FORTHOFFER

5, rue Principale, 67260 RIMSDORF

☎ 03 88 00 26 14 📠 03 88 00 26 14

email: aufenil@orange.fr

web: www.aufenil.fr

On the edge of a village, this property has six bedrooms, all in the owners' house. There are five doubles, one grade 1, two grade 2, and three grade 3, including a two-room family suite for four, all with private facilities and one with a private kitchen. Satellite TV and wireless internet access. Garden furniture, barbecue, table-tennis and swing. Meals by arrangement.

Prices s €36-€40; d €45-€50; t €70-€75 **Nearby** ⛵ 3km 🏊 9km
⤳ 7km Restaurant 3km 🏇 4km 🚲 3km 🚶 4km **Notes** Pets admitted

SCHERWILLER

⚜ ⓞ Chambre d'hôtes

Simone SAVA

29, route des Romains, 67750 SCHERWILLER

☎ 03 88 92 84 74 📠 03 88 92 84 74

email: 4saisons.sava@wanadoo.fr

web: www.les-4-saisons.fr

Guest rooms on the first and second floor of the owners' house, situated on the edge of a vineyard. There are two en suite double rooms with TV and video, a relaxing veranda with a jacuzzi, large garden with furniture, indoor pool open June-September, and table tennis. Meals by arrangement.

Prices not confirmed for 2008 **Nearby** ⤳ 🏊 5km 🚶 3km
Notes No pets English spoken

SCHILLERSDORF

⚜ ⓞ ♿ Chambre d'hôtes

Karine VOGEL

27, rue Pasteur Schroeder, 67340 SCHILLERSDORF

☎ 03 88 89 42 80

email: karine@freidbarry.com

web: www.freidbarry.com

This property offers six guest bedrooms in converted farm buildings. On the ground floor are two doubles, one suitable for disabled guests; upstairs are two more doubles, a triple with its own terrace, and a family room for four. All have private bath or shower room. Views across the meadows, where deer can often be seen. Enclosed courtyard with garden furniture. Parking; meals available.

Prices s fr €53; d €58-€69; t fr €84; extra person fr €15; dinner fr €21
Nearby ⛵ 10km 🚴 22km 🏊 20km ⤳ 4km Restaurant 0.7km 🏇 4km
🐎 15km 🏛 4km 🚶 4km **Notes** Pets admitted English spoken CC

HAUT-RHIN

AMMERSCHWIHR

⚜ Chambre d'hôtes

A et O THOMANN-DESMAREST

2, rue des Ponts en Pierre, 68770 AMMERSCHWIHR

☎ 03 89 47 32 83 📠 03 89 47 32 83

email: andre.thomann@laposte.net

web: www.courfranche.com

Formerly a wine-producing farm, this 16th-century house is peacefully situated in a village near a forest. It has one room with a double bed, bunk beds, and a cot, one with a double bed and a child's bed and a third with a double bed, cot and TV, all en suite. There is a guests' sitting room, parking, and a courtyard. Reduced rates for extended stays.

Prices s €35-€45; d €42-€55; t €50-€62; extra person fr €12
Nearby ⛵ 12km 🚴 1km 🏊 12km ⤳ 4km Restaurant 0.5km 🛥 15km
🏇 0.5km 🐎 8km 🏛 0.5km 🚶 8km **Notes** Pets admitted Open 15 April
to 15 November.

⚑ Maison Turquoise

Guy THOMAS

41, Grand rue, 68770 AMMERSCHWIHR

☎ 03 89 78 23 90 🖃 03 89 47 18 90

email: info@maisonthomas.fr

web: www.maisonthomas.fr

There are three bedrooms in this former wine-grower's house. On the ground floor is a double room, and a room with a single bed and bunks; on the second floor is a further double. Each has a kitchenette, lounge area with TV, and a private bath or shower room. Home-made jam and rolls for breakfast; garden with barbecue and garden furniture for guest use.

Prices s fr €42; d €44-€48; t €54-€58; extra person fr €8
Nearby ♨ 4km ♪ 1km ♣ 1km ♥ 3km Restaurant 0.5km ♣ 15km
♨ 1km ♚ 1km 🏠 0.1km ᴍ 8km **Notes** Pets admitted

BEBLENHEIM

⚑ Chambre d'hôtes

Christine COLAIANNI

41, rue de Hoen, 68980 BEBLENHEIM

☎ 03 89 47 82 52 🖃 03 89 47 98 29

email: colaianni1@voila.fr

Peacefully situated with fine views of a vineyard; the proprietors of this house offer one double en suite room and one with double bed and single bed with separate bathroom. A fold-up bed is also available. Breakfast may be taken in the dining room or on the veranda; further facilities include central heating, air conditioning, fridge, courtyard, private parking and garage.

Prices s fr €41; d fr €46; extra person fr €10 **Nearby** ♨ 15km ♪ 5km
♥ 5km Restaurant 0.5km ♣ 20km ♨ 1km ♚ 5km 🏠 0.5km ᴍ 10km
Notes No pets English spoken

CHAVANNES SUR L'ETANG

⚑ 🍴 ♿ Chambre d'hôtes

M BILGER & C COURBAT

32, rue d'Alsace, 68210 CHAVANNES SUR L'ETANG

☎ 03 84 23 48 19 🖃 03 84 23 48 19

email: relais9068@aol.com

web: www.relais9068.com

This property is right on the edge of Alsace - to the extent that guests can choose whether to sleep in Alsace or the Franche-Comté! There are four ground floor bedrooms, two in a separate building with kitchenette and lounge area, and two with direct access to the swimming pool and garden. Each has a private shower room, TV and music system.

Prices s fr €47; d fr €56; t fr €71; extra person fr €15; dinner fr €20
On Site Private ♥ ♨ ♣ Restaurant ♚ **Nearby** ♪ 10km ♣ 35km ♨
🏠 0.2km ᴍ 2km **Notes** No pets English spoken

EGUISHEIM

⚑ Chambre d'hôtes

Monique FREUDENREICH

4, Cour Unterlinden, 68420 EGUISHEIM

☎ 03 89 23 16 44 🖃 03 89 23 16 44

email: maisonhotes@aol.com

An 18th-century house situated in the heart of the village offering three rooms, each with TV and en suite facilities, a double bed and the possibility of adding one or two single beds. Living room with kitchenette and fridge; central heating. Parking in private courtyard.

Prices not confirmed for 2008 **On Site** ♚ **Nearby** ♨ 6km ♪ 10km
♣ 10km ♣ 20km ♨ ᴍ 5km **Notes** Pets admitted English spoken

⚑ Chambre d'hôtes

Christiane GASCHY

3, rue des Fleurs, 68420 EGUISHEIM

☎ 03 89 23 69 09 🖃 03 89 23 69 09

email: christiane.gaschy@laposte.net

This house is peacefully situated close to the edge of the village. There is one twin-bedded room, one double room, and one double room with adjoining single room, all en suite with TV and fridge on landing. Breakfast is served on the veranda, with a view of three châteaux. Parking in enclosed courtyard and air conditioning in summer.

Prices s fr €36; d fr €42; t fr €52 **Nearby** ♨ 3km ♪ 20km ♣ 5km
♥ 5km Restaurant 0.1km ♨ 0.2km 🏠 0.1km ᴍ 3km **Notes** No pets

⚑ Chambre d'hôtes

Jean-Pierre BOMBENGER

8, rue du Bassin, 68420 EGUISHEIM

☎ 03 89 23 13 12 🖃 03 89 23 13 12

email: jpbombenger@free.fr

This modern house is close to the centre of the village. Two double en suite rooms and one room with one double and one single bed, with shared wc and shower room. There is a lounge, and a dining room in which breakfast is served, a garden, courtyard, barbecue, terrace and swing.

Prices s fr €37; d fr €43; t fr €55; extra person fr €13 **Nearby** ♨ 5km
♪ 25km ♣ 5km Restaurant 0.5km ♣ 15km ♨ 1km ♚ 0.5km 🏠 0.4km
ᴍ 1km **Notes** No pets English spoken

⚑ Chambre d'hôtes

Marthe HERTZ

3, rue du Riesling, 68420 EGUISHEIM

☎ 03 89 23 67 74 🖃 03 89 23 67 74

This charming house is situated in the heart of the village and offers three double rooms, one twin room and one triple room. Guests may take breakfast in the living room, on a beautiful veranda with garden views, or in fine weather, on the terrace.

Prices s fr €50; d €60-€70; t fr €80 **Nearby** ♨ 4km ♪ 15km ♣ 20km
♥ 5km Restaurant 0.4km ♨ 10km 🏠 0.5km ᴍ 6km **Notes** No pets
English spoken Open March to December.

GUEBERSCHWIHR

⑪ Chambre d'hôtes

Gilberte SCHNEIDER

42 rue du Nord, 68420 GUEBERSCHWIHR

☎ 03 89 49 25 79   ▤ 03 89 49 25 79

web: http:\\fschneider.skyblog.com

The three very comfortable double rooms offered at this wine-making estate each have en suite facilities and kitchenette. Enjoy panoramic views over the vineyard and the forest from the large courtyard and terraces with seating. Private parking and reductions for extended stays.

Prices s fr €51; d fr €55; extra person fr €25   **Nearby** ⚓ 7km ⚓ 4km ⚓ 7km ⚓ 10km ⚓ 5km ⚓ 3km   **Notes** Pets admitted

⑪ Chambre d'hôtes

Christiane SCHERB

1, route de Rouffach, 68420 GUEBERSCHWIHR

☎ 03 89 49 33 70 & 03 89 49 21 05   ▤ 03 89 49 33 70

On a wine-making estate, these comfortable rooms are en suite and comprise one twin room, two double rooms and two rooms each with one double and one single bed. Facilities include microwave, fridge and garden. Breakfast is served on the veranda with views over the vineyard and the plain of Alsace.

Prices s fr €37; d fr €55; t fr €67; extra person fr €15   **On Site** ⚓ **Nearby** ⚓ 4km ⚓ 4km ⚓ 4km ⚓ 4km   **Notes** No pets

HOLTZWIHR

⑪ Chambre d'hôtes

Liliane MEYER

3, rue des Américains, 68320 HOLTZWIHR

☎ 03 89 47 42 11

email: liliane.meyer@orange.fr

This terraced house has a garden area and three two-person rooms, one three-person room, and one four-person room; all en suite with kitchenette and TV. Child's bed available. Access for less mobile guests to all rooms, with assistance. Guests' sitting room, shady terraces and barbecue, games area, lawn, central heating and private parking. The forest is within 600mtrs. Restaurant in village.

Prices d fr €48; t fr €60; extra person fr €10   **Nearby** ⚓ 5km ⚓ 8km ⚓ 2km ⚓ 5km Restaurant 5km ⚓ 15km ⚓ 4km ⚓ 5km ⚓ 5km ⚓ 5km   **Notes** Pets admitted English spoken

HUNAWIHR

⑪ Le Clos Seiler

Frédérique SEILER

3, rue du Nord, 68150 HUNAWIHR

☎ 03 89 73 70 19   ▤ 03 89 73 70 19

email: gites-seiler@wanadoo.fr

web: www.le-clos-seiler.com

This former wine-maker's house, in the heart of the village, offers five very comfortable en suite rooms. Three rooms have a private kitchenette, one has a sofa bed and there is one two-person room and one room for two people and one child. The grounds are enclosed and private, with garden furniture, barbecue, and courtyard.

Prices d €43-€55; extra person fr €16   **Nearby** ⚓ 12km ⚓ 9km ⚓ 2km ⚓ 2km Restaurant 0.8km ⚓ 7km ⚓ 2km ⚓ 0.3km ⚓ 7km   **Notes** Pets admitted English spoken Open December to February and April to October.

HUSSEREN-LES-CHATEAUX

⑪ *Chambre d'hôtes*

Gilles SCHNEIDER

10, rue du Hagueneck, 68420 HUSSEREN-LES-CHATEAUX

☎ 03 89 86 45 04

email: couette-cafe@wanadoo.fr

web: www.couette-cafe.net

There are four guest rooms on the ground floor of this modern house in the peaceful area at the foot of the three châteaux at Eguisheim. A double and a twin each have en suite facilities; the other two rooms, both doubles, share a shower room and WC. One room has a kitchenette and fridge. Plentiful breakfasts.

Prices not confirmed for 2008   **On Site** ⚓ **Nearby** ⚓ 10km ⚓ 25km ⚓ 5km ⚓ 2km ⚓ 7km   **Notes** No pets English spoken

HUSSEREN-WESSERLING

⑪ Chambre d'hôtes

Yvonne HERRGOTT

4, rue de la gare, 68470 HUSSEREN-WESSERLING

☎ 03 89 38 79 69

web: www.aux-4-couronnes.com

Surrounded by flowers, this beautiful property has four guest rooms accessed by a separate entrance. There is a room with double and single beds and a twin (en suite with a kitchen area), an adjoining room has two single beds and two further en suite twins have a living/kitchen area. Buffet-style breakfast; central heating; garden furniture and heated covered swimming pool (March to October).

Prices d €55-€60; extra person fr €20   **On Site** ⚓ Private ⚓ **Nearby** ⚓ 1km ⚓ 15km ⚓ 1km ⚓ 14km ⚓ 1km ⚓ 2km **Notes** No pets

ALSACE-LORRAINE

KATZENTHAL

⫶⫶ Chambre d'hôtes

Christian AMREIN
128, rue des trois épis, 68230 KATZENTHAL
☎ 03 89 27 48 85 & 06 76 54 17 13 ▤ 03 89 27 35 18
email: sarl.amrein@wanadoo.fr
web: www.gites-amrein.com

This centrally heated house is peacefully situated at the heart of the vineyard, close to the forest. It has two rooms each with one double and one single bed, and one room with three single beds. All rooms have TV, and are en suite. Courtyard; self-catering gîte also available.
Prices not confirmed for 2008 **On Site** 🏊 **Nearby** ⛷ 8km ♨ 3km 🛶 20km 🚲 5km ⭐ 6km **Notes** Pets admitted English spoken

KAYSERSBERG

⫶⫶ Chambre d'hôtes

Daniel et M.Thérèse PICAVET
104, route de Lapoutroie, 68240 KAYSERSBERG
☎ 03 89 47 15 14
email: picavet@les-cedres.org
web: www.les-cedres.org

At the edge of the town, this mansion borders a large park near the forest. The rooms - three grade 2 and two grade 3 - include two double rooms sharing a bathroom and one double, one large twin and two twin doubles sleeping four (with sitting room), all en suite with TV.
Prices s €40-€52; d €45-€68; t €82-€92; extra person fr €10 **Nearby** ⛷ 10km ♨ 5km ✿ 1km ↘ 0.5km Restaurant 0.2km 🛶 15km 🚲 1km 🎣 10km ⭐ 12km **Notes** No pets English spoken Open 15 March to 6 January.

⫶⫶ 🍽 *Les Chambres de la Weiss*

Cécile MERCIER
64A, rue de la Flieh, 68240 KAYSERSBERG
☎ 03 89 78 14 57
email: cecmercier@yahoo.fr
web: www.leschambresdelaweiss.com

Guests at this property, in the heart of Kaysersberg, can enjoy views across the vineyards. On the ground floor are two double rooms, with a terrace and garden furniture; upstairs are two bigger rooms, each for three or four people. All have private baths or showers. Outdoor area with waterside terrace and private parking. Weekend meals, by arrangement.
Prices not confirmed for 2008 **On Site** ✿ **Nearby** ⛷ 10km ♨ 3km 🛶 12km 🎣 10km **Notes** No pets English spoken

KEMBS

⫶⫶ Au Relais de la Poste aux Chevaux

Gilbert WIDMER
45, rue du Maréchal Foch, 68680 KEMBS
☎ 03 89 48 33 98
email: widmerfamily@online.fr
web: http://widmerfamily.online.fr

This guesthouse was once a staging post. There are three very comfortable rooms, each with one double and two single beds and en suite shower and WC. Facilities include Jacuzzi, terrace, closed courtyard parking, large garden. Cot available; bikes for hire; no smoking.
Prices s fr €64; d €70-€78; t fr €100; extra person fr €22 **On Site** ✿ **Nearby** ⛷ 2km ♨ 8km ✿ 0.2km ↘ 4km Restaurant 0.2km 🛶 2km 🎣 0.4km ⭐ 6km **Notes** No pets English spoken

LABAROCHE

₩ La Montagne Verte

Christiane SCHIELE
60, Basse Baroche, 68910 LABAROCHE
☎ 03 89 49 87 12 & 06 85 13 52 28
email: info@montagneverte.com
web: www.montagneverte.com

A warm welcome awaits at this renovated farm and garden set amongst trees. A separate entrance leads to six centrally-heated en suite guest rooms, with the hosts' living and dining room available for relaxation and TV. Breakfasts are generous; table tennis, BBQ, loungers available. Many footpaths in the vicinity, accompanied night walks, caves to visit.

Prices s fr €41; d fr €47; t fr €54; extra person fr €10 **On Site**
Nearby ⚓ 14km ⚑ 2km ⚐ 10km ⚒ 10km Restaurant 4km ⚓ 15km ⚒ 6km ⚑ 4km ⚒ 14km **Notes** No pets English spoken

LAPOUTROIE

₩ ⓘ Chambre d'hôtes

Daniel GARNIER
207, le Brezouard, 68650 LAPOUTROIE
☎ 03 89 47 23 80 ▤ 03 89 47 23 80
email: auberge-du-brezouard@wanadoo.fr
web: www.ferme-aubergedubrezouard.fr

A property with five beautiful rooms situated up in the mountains, including a double room on the ground floor with disabled access. The other rooms are on the second floor: Violet and Marguerite have a double bed and a bed-settee; Poppy has a double bed, a single and bunk beds. All rooms have a private bath or shower room and WC. Meals by arrangement.

Prices s fr €43; d fr €51-€80; extra person fr €20 **Nearby** ⚓ 6km ⚑ 17km ⚐ 3km ⚒ 15km Restaurant 3km ⚒ 6km ⚒ 7km ⚒ 3km ⚒ 30km **Notes** No pets Open 15 February to 20 December.

LAUTENBACH

₩ Chambre d'hôtes

M. RINGLER/PEYRELON
44, rue principale, 68610 LAUTENBACH
☎ 03 89 76 39 21 & 06 60 89 15 83
email: lauten@free.fr
web: http://lauten.free.fr

This establishment, in the Ballon des Vosges park, provides an ideal location for exploring Alsace and the mountains. There are three bedrooms, for two to four people, each with a TV socket, and two of them with a small kitchen area. They all have a private bathroom and WC. Conservatory, garden, garden furniture, possible use of sauna.

Prices s €36-€37; d €40-€41; t €50-€51; extra person fr €10 **On Site** ⚐ Spa **Nearby** ⚓ 3km ⚑ 12km Restaurant 0.1km ⚓ 15km ⚒ 0.1km ⚒ 5km ⚒ 0.1km ⚒ 25km **Notes** Pets admitted English spoken

LINTHAL

₩ ⓘ Chambre d'hôtes

Yves/Claudie BOEHM/GREVET
139, Hilsenfirst, 68610 LINTHAL
☎ 03 89 74 05 23
email: boehm.yves@wanadoo.fr
web: www.chambres-linthal.com

Located in the Ballon des Vosges Park, one room is available to guests in the owner's house, whilst a separate building houses a further two guest rooms. There is a kitchenette area, a bathroom and heating, as well as a garden complete with furniture and a vegetable patch.

Prices s fr €36; d fr €42; t fr €50; extra person fr €12; dinner fr €18
On Site ⚐ **Nearby** ⚓ 15km ⚑ 15km ⚐ 5km ⚒ 10km Restaurant 2km ⚓ 12km ⚒ 3km ⚒ 1.5km ⚒ 30km **Notes** Pets admitted English spoken

MAGSTATT-LE-BAS

₩ ⓘ Chambre d'hôtes

Sandrine KIEFFER
4 rue de l'Eglise, Belys, 68510 MAGSTATT-LE-BAS
☎ 03 89 81 68 22
email: sandrine.kieffer@wanadoo.fr
web: www.belys.info

A peaceful Alsace village provides the setting for this 19th-century farmhouse. There is a family room for four with two double beds (one on a mezzanine) and a kitchenette; and also two double rooms, one with an additional folding bed. Enclosed courtyard with a covered sitting-out area and small garden; parking space.

Prices d €50-€55; t fr €65; extra person fr €15; dinner fr €17
Nearby ⚓ 5km ⚑ 15km ⚐ 10km ⚒ 10km Restaurant 5km ⚓ 30km ⚒ 3km ⚒ 5km ⚒ 5km **Notes** Pets admitted English spoken

MERTZEN

₩ ⓘ Chambre d'hôtes

Marie-Hélène et Léon BILGER
11, rue de Strueth, 68210 MERTZEN
☎ 03 89 25 02 08 & 06 77 80 76 84
email: lesondinesdusundgau@yahoo.fr
web: www.lesondinesdusundgau.fr

This property beside the River Largue offers three guest bedrooms, all on the first floor - two doubles, and a triple with three single beds. All have private bath or shower room. Meals by arrangement, with local specialities and vegetarian options. Cycle path close by.

Prices s fr €35; d €45-€50; t fr €65; extra person fr €15; dinner fr €16
On Site ⚐ Restaurant **Nearby** ⚓ 12km ⚑ 12km ⚒ 6km ⚒ 4km ⚒ 8km ⚒ 8km **Notes** Pets admitted English spoken

MITTELWIHR

♯♯♯ Domaine du Bouxhof

François EDEL
68630 MITTELWIHR
☎ 03 89 47 93 67 📄 03 89 86 02 41

The home of a wine-grower, this centrally heated house in the heart of the vineyard is listed as a historic monument. One twin-bedded room (child bed available), one double room and one twin room are available, all with en suite facilities, hairdryer and TV. There is a fridge, garden furniture and parking.

Prices d fr €57; t fr €70   **On Site** Restaurant   **Nearby** ⛳ 4km ♨ 5km
🎿 5km ⛵ 18km ⛷ 2km 🏌 5km 🏠 1km 🚶 12km   **Notes** No pets
English spoken   Open 15 February to December.

MUNWILLER

♯♯♯ 🍽 Chambre d'hôtes

Yvonne REYMANN
17, rue principale, 68250 MUNWILLER
☎ 03 89 49 68 66 & 03 89 78 50 76
email: yvonne.reymann@club-internet.fr
web: http://perso.club-internet.fr/yvonne.reymann/

Peacefully situated in a village near the Route des Vins, this house offers four comfortable en suite rooms in a farm outbuilding. A room with double and single beds and one with three singles share a kitchen area and sitting room and there is a twin room, all with TV and fridge. Kitchenette, washing machine and dryer, heating, courtyard, garden furniture. Breakfast is served on the terrace. Reduced rates for extended stays.

Prices not confirmed for 2008   **Nearby** ⛳ 5km ♨ 5km ℘ 5km ⛵ 25km
⛷ 5km 🏠 2km 🚶 5km   **Notes** No pets

MURBACH

♯♯♯♯ 🍽 Le Schaeferhof

Sylvie & Robert ROTHENFLUG
6, rue de Guebwiller, 68530 MURBACH
☎ 03 89 74 98 98 📄 03 89 74 98 99
email: chambredhotes@schaeferhof.fr
web: www.schaeferhof.fr

The name of this establishment means 'Shepherd's Court' and each spring there are still lambs to be seen. Situated in a quiet area close to Murbach Abbey, there are four rooms each with a flat screen TV, Wi-fi access and mini-bar. The living room has a fire; there's a garden and spa with sauna. Regional cooking.

Prices s fr €110; d fr €130; t €160-€170; extra person fr €30;
dinner fr €40   **On Site** 🏌   **Nearby** ⛳ 8km ♨ 15km ℘ 1km
🎿 8km Restaurant 0.1km ⛷ 12km ⛷ 7km 🏠 3km 🚶 20km
Notes No pets English spoken

ORBEY

♯♯♯ Chèvremont

Céline GUIDAT
68370 ORBEY
☎ 03 89 71 23 51 📄 03 89 86 51 30
email: chevremont2@wanadoo.fr
web: http://perso.wanadoo.fr/chevremont/

This farmhouse-inn, typical of the Val d'Orbey area, has three beautiful grade 3 first floor bedrooms, all with private bathrooms/ WCs. There are also four family rooms, which do not have en suite facilities. Farmhouse breakfasts, and other local dishes served. Half-board possible; farm produce for sale. Good area for walking.

Prices not confirmed for 2008   **On Site** ℘   **Nearby** ⛳ 0.5km ♨ 15km
⛵ 5km ⛷ 0.1km 🏌 5km 🏠 0.5km 🚶 25km   **Notes** Pets admitted

♯♯♯ Schoultzbach

Sylvie CONREAU
68370 ORBEY
☎ 03 89 71 33 68 & 06 80 32 41 96
email: conreau.sylvie@wanadoo.fr
web: http://perso.wanadoo.fr/ferme.du.schoultzbach/

An old farmhouse, typical of the Val d'Orbey, offering three pretty rooms in a former hayloft. Breakfasts made with farm produce served outside in summer. Fridge and microwave, baby equipment and children's games, courtyard parking, swimming pool. 5km from the ski resort and on numerous walking routes.

Prices s fr €42; d fr €47; t fr €58   **On Site** ℘   **Nearby** ⛳ 1km
♨ 15km 🎿 15km Restaurant 0.3km ⛵ 5km ⛷ 5km 🏌 5km 🚶 25km
Notes No pets English spoken CC

RIXHEIM

♯♯♯♯ ♿ La Grange à Elise

Yves REYMANN
66, Grand rue, 68170 RIXHEIM
☎ 03 89 54 20 71 📄 03 89 54 20 71
email: contact@grange-elise.com
web: www.grange-elise.com

A barn conversion with private gardens, set well back from the main road. There are five bedrooms, sleeping from two to four people, all with private bath or shower room. There is a large indoor living area where guests can relax, with exposed beams, piano and a wood-burning stove. Enclosed courtyard with private parking; non-smoking rooms available.

Prices s fr €72; d fr €94; extra person fr €26   **On Site** ℘
Nearby ⛳ 2km ♨ 10km 🎿 2km Restaurant 0.2km ⛵ 30km
⛷ 1km 🏌 5km ♨ 5km 🚶 2km   **Notes** No pets English spoken
CC

ALSACE-LORRAINE

▓▓▓ Le Clos du Murier

Rosa VOLPATTI

42, Grand rue, 68170 RIXHEIM

☎ 03 89 54 14 81 📄 03 89 64 47 08

email: rosa.volpatti@orange.fr

This attractive, restored 16th-century house with enclosed garden is centrally located. There are two twin-bedded rooms with living area and two double rooms, one with living area. All rooms have private bathroom, kitchenette, TV and central heating. Shared washing machine and dryer. Private parking in an enclosed courtyard; table tennis; bicycles available.

Prices s fr €66; d fr €66; t fr €104; extra person fr €20 **On Site** ♪
♥ **Nearby** ⚐ 2km ♪ 10km ↖ 1km Restaurant 0.3km ⌓ 2km
Spa 25km ♨ 1km **Notes** No pets CC

RORSCHWIHR

▓▓▓ Chambre d'hôtes

M et V FAHRER-ACKERMANN

10 route du Vin, 68590 RORSCHWIHR

☎ 03 89 73 83 69 & 03 89 73 74 48

A traditional Alsace house, dating back to 1709, right in the middle of the village. There are four bedrooms, all with private facilities, and two with a balcony. Fridge for guests' use; courtyard with private parking and garden furniture. On the wine route, close to vineyards. Wine-tasting possible.

Prices not confirmed for 2008 **On Site** ♪ **Nearby** ⚐ 15km ♪ 15km
⌓ 2km ♥ 2km ⚐ 1.3km ♨ 5km **Notes** No pets

▓▓▓ Chambre d'hôtes

Yves ACKERMANN

22 bis, route du Vin, 68590 RORSCHWIHR

☎ 03 89 73 63 87 📄 03 89 73 38 16

email: andre.ackerman@hotmail.fr

This house, conveniently situated on the Route des Vins, has three beautiful upstairs rooms. There is a room for three with its own kitchenette and balcony, and two doubles, one of which also has a balcony. Small terrace; wine tasting can be arranged. Guests' kitchen with fridge and dishwasher; dining room with TV.

Prices s fr €35; d fr €45; t fr €60 **On Site** ♪ Restaurant
Nearby ♪ 15km ↖ 4km ⌓ 2km ♥ 2km ⚐ 1km ♨ 8km
Notes No pets English spoken Open March to December. CC

▓▓▓ Chambre d'hôtes

Fernande MESCHBERGER

1, rue de la Forêt, 68750 RORSCHWIHR

☎ 03 89 73 77 32 📄 03 89 73 77 32

This modern house with veranda and garden is peacefully situated, with a view of the Château of Haut-Koenigsbourg. The four double rooms each have private shower and wc and separate guest entrance. Central heating, fridge, additional bed if required. The enclosed veranda and garden furniture are available for guests to use. Small dogs allowed.

Prices s fr €35; d fr €45; t fr €50 **On Site** ♪ ♥ **Nearby** ⚐ 20km
♪ 15km ↖ 4km Restaurant 2km ⌓ 30km ⚐ 1.5km ♨ 10km
Notes Pets admitted Open 15 March to 20 December.

SEWEN

▓▓▓ ⦿| La Villa du Lac

Yvette RIOUAL

68290 SEWEN

☎ 03 89 82 98 38 📄 03 89 82 98 38

email: villadulac.sewen@tv-com.net

web: www.villa-du-lac-alsace.com

At the foot of the Ballon d'Alsace, opposite Lake Sewen, the Villa du Lac provides guest rooms with private facilities. There are four double rooms and and 2 triple rooms with either views of the lake or the forest. Guests can relax in front of the fire or on the terrace.

Prices s fr €45; d €48-€58; t €65-€70; dinner fr €22 **On Site** ♪
Restaurant **Nearby** ⚐ 5km ♪ 5km ↖ 10km ⌓ 10km ♥ 10km ♨ 10km
⚐ 4km **Notes** No pets

SIGOLSHEIM

▓▓▓ Chambre d'hôtes

Eliane & Marcel ZON

9, rue du Raisin, 68240 SIGOLSHEIM

☎ 03 89 47 13 09

email: marcelzon@yahoo.fr

In a traditional village, right in the heart of the vineyard. There are three double bedrooms, all on the first floor and all with private shower room/WC. Each has a TV. Outdoor area with private parking and a terrace where a good breakfast is served in summer.

Prices not confirmed for 2008 **On Site** ♪ **Nearby** ⚐ 2km ♪ 3km
⌓ 20km ♥ 3km ⚐ 3km ♨ 10km **Notes** No pets

SOULTZEREN

▓▓▓ ❤ ⦿| Chambre d'hôtes

Daniel ROESS

4, Oberer Geisberg, 68140 SOULTZEREN

☎ 03 89 77 02 09 📄 03 89 77 13 72

email: chantal.roess@laposte.net

This chambre d'hôtes is located at a ferme-auberge - a farmhouse restaurant. It has two doubles, and two doubles with an additional single bed; and a room on the ground floor suitable for disabled guests. All of the rooms have a private bath or shower room and WC. Car park; farm produce for sale.

Prices s €42-€47; d €47-€52; t €62-€67; extra person fr €18; dinner fr
€20 **On Site** ♥ **Nearby** ⚐ 4km ♪ 25km ↖ 12km ⌓ 12km ⚐ 4km
♨ 9km **Notes** Pets admitted English spoken

✦✦✦ ⊙ Le Londenbach

Luc GOERTZ

14, chemin du Londenbach, 68140 SOULTZEREN

☎ 03 89 77 00 59

email: luc.goertz@wanadoo.fr

web: www.londenbach.com

A big house, standing on its own above Soultzeren. There are two guest rooms on the ground floor, a double and a family room; on the first floor is another family room; on the second floor are two double rooms. All have private facilities. Meals by arrangement, with local dishes; packed meals also available. Cookery courses. Good area for walking.

Prices d fr €54; t fr €75; extra person fr €21; dinner fr €18 **On Site** ✦ **Nearby** ↧ 25km ℘ 2km ↘ 8km Restaurant 2.5km ⚓ 5km ⌂ 8km Spa 8km 🛝 2km ⋙ 8km **Notes** No pets English spoken

---

ST-HIPPOLYTE

✦✦✦ Chambre d'hôtes

François BLEGER

63 route du Vin, 68590 SAINT HIPPOLYTE

☎ 03 89 73 04 36 & 03 89 73 06 07 📄 03 89 73 06 07

email: domaine.bleger@wanadoo.fr

On the first floor of this wine grower's property are three guest rooms. One has a double bed, TV and shower room; the second has two double beds, TV and shower room; and the third has a double bed and a single bed, also with TV and shower room. A courtyard offers private parking. Wine tasting.

Prices s €46; d fr €52; t fr €63; extra person €11-€27 **On Site** ✦ **Nearby** ⚓ 15km ↧ 20km ℘ 1km ↘ 7km Restaurant 0.1km ⚓ 30km ⌂ ⋙ 7km **Notes** No pets English spoken Open Easter to December.

✦✦✦ *Domaine du Windmuehl*

Claude BLEGER

92, route du Vin, 68590 SAINT-HIPPOLYTE

☎ 03 89 73 00 21 📄 03 89 73 04 22

email: vins.bleger.claude@wanadoo.fr

web: www.vins-bleger.com

On the Route des Vins, right on the edge of the vineyard and with a view of the château of Haut-Koenigsbourg. There are five double bedrooms, all on the first floor with private showers and WCs. Cot and folding bed available. Private parking. The owner is a wine-grower, and tastings are possible.

Prices not confirmed for 2008 **On Site** ℘ **Nearby** ↧ 18km ⚓ 30km ⌂ ⋙ 8km **Notes** No pets

---

STE-MARIE-AUX-MINES

✦✦✦ ✿ ⊙ Ferme La Fonderie

Gabriel DEMOULIN

17, rue Untergrombach,

68160 SAINTE-MARIE-AUX-MINES

☎ 03 89 58 59 51 & 06 83 99 97 29 📄 03 89 58 59 51

email: ferme.lafonderie@wanadoo.fr

web: www.fermelafonderie.com

This restored property, which includes two self-catering gîtes, has a peaceful situation on the borders of the forest and close to the river. There are two en suite double rooms and one room with a double and a single bed, with separate shower room and wc. Heating; communal living room with TV and kitchen for preparing breakfast; TV; courtyard, parking, garden furniture; sampling of local products.

Prices s fr €35; d €45-€50; t €60-€70; extra person fr €20; dinner €15-€20 **On Site** ℘ **Nearby** ⚓ 3km ↧ 5km ↘ 1km Restaurant 1km ⚓ 12km ⌂ 0.5km Spa 35km ⋙ 22km **Notes** No pets

---

THANNENKIRCH

✦✦✦ Chambre d'hôtes

René DUMOULIN

15, rue Sainte-Anne, 68590 THANNENKIRCH

☎ 03 89 73 12 07

Close to the forest in a calm, fresh setting, this house offers four two-person rooms, all en suite with bath or shower and telephone. There is a terrace, garden meadow, private parking and sitting room with TV.

Prices d €43-€45 **On Site** ✦ **Nearby** ⚓ 5km ↧ 10km ℘ 10km Restaurant 5km ⚓ 20km ⌂ 10km 🛝 6km ⋙ 17km **Notes** No pets Open June to 1 November.

MEURTHE-ET-MOSELLE

BELLEAU

✦✦✦ ⊙ Château de Morey

Johann KARST

19, rue Saint Pierre, 54610 BELLEAU

☎ 03 83 31 50 98

email: chateaudemorey@wanadoo.fr

web: www.chateaudemorey.com

This renovated 16th-century château is beautifully situated with views across the valley. It offers five spacious rooms including a family suite, each with one double bed and one single if required. Living area with TV and video, private bathroom. Games room, library, private parking, stables, mountain bikes. The private swimming pool is in a park bordering a forest.

Prices s fr €65; d €65-€75; extra person fr €25; dinner €20-€25 **On Site** ✦ Private ↘ **Nearby** ⚓ 1.5km ℘ 5km Restaurant 5km Water sports 5km ⌂ 8km 🛝 5km ⋙ 15km **Notes** No pets CC

BIONVILLE

ⅲ |◎| *Ferme du Petit Bonheur*

Dieudonné & Michelle HOBLINGRE

21, Les Noires Colas, 54540 BIONVILLE

☎ 03 29 41 12 17 & 06 85 36 08 16 📄 03 29 41 12 17

email: chambre@vosgespetitbonheur.fr

web: www.vosgespetitbonheur.fr

Six high-quality bedrooms in an establishment that lies within a beautiful hamlet. On the first floor there is a room with a single bed and a fold-away double bed and a room with a double bed. There are three double rooms and family room for three people on the third floor. All bedrooms have private facilities. Guests can make use of a lounge and dining room and there is a furnished terrace.

Prices not confirmed for 2008 **On Site** ⚲ **Nearby** ⛵ 15km ⌁ 15km Water sports 6km ⌕ 1km 🏛 1km ⋙ 17km **Notes** Pets admitted English spoken

CHARENCY-VEZIN

ⅲ |◎| Chambre d'hôtes

Viviane & Miro JAKIRCEVIC

1 Grand Rue, 54260 CHARENCY-VEZIN

☎ 03 82 26 66 26 📄 03 82 26 66 26

email: chambreshotes@wanadoo.fr

web: http://perso.wanadoo.fr/chambreshotes54/

At the edge of Luxembourg and Belgium, this restored period house dating from 1804 has three guest rooms, of which two have an adjoining sitting area. Fitted kitchen, dining room, recreation room on the veranda. Terrace, garden, and enclosed parking area. Child's bed available on request.

Prices s fr €36; d fr €46; t fr €64; extra person fr €18; dinner fr €17 **On Site** ⚲ ⚘ **Nearby** ⛵ 5km ⌁ 5km Restaurant 5km Water sports 5km ⌕ 5km ⋙ 10km **Notes** No pets English spoken

CRANTENOY

ⅲ |◎| Chambre d'hôtes

J-M et M-J TROUP

67, rue de Chirmont, 54740 CRANTENOY

☎ 03 83 52 43 32 & 06 81 07 83 36 📄 03 83 52 43 32

email: troupm@aol.com

This is a 16th-century farmhouse, built in the local style, with three guest rooms. There are two twin-bedded rooms, and a two-roomed suite with a double bed, two singles and a folding bed. All have private bath/shower facilities. Terrace, and garden with children's games. Meals by arrangement, made with the family's own produce; guided walks and doll-making courses can be arranged.

Prices s fr €36; d fr €47; t fr €58; extra person fr €13; dinner fr €18 **Nearby** ⛵ 1km ⌁ 30km ⚲ 4km ⌁ 30km Restaurant 3km Water sports 20km ⌕ 8km Spa 47km ⚘ 6km 🏛 6km ⋙ 9km **Notes** No pets

DOMMARTIN-SOUS-AMANCE

ⅲ ❦ ♿ *Ferme de Montheu*

Hubert GRANDDIDIER

54770 DOMMARTIN-SOUS-AMANCE

☎ 03 83 31 17 37 & 06 89 09 97 20 📄 03 83 31 17 37

email: hgrandidier@wanadoo.fr

In picturesque open countryside in relaxing, delightful surroundings with many valleys, this restored farmhouse has four spacious en suite rooms, tastefully decorated and furnished with antiques. Child's bed and additional single bed available. Lounge, library, TV, fridge, microwave. Guests can visit the farm and sample regional products.

Prices s €36-€38; d €47-€49; t €58-€60 **Nearby** ⛵ 2km ⌁ 5km ⚲ 6km ⌁ 6km Restaurant 1km Water sports 20km ⌕ 7km 🏛 5km ⋙ 8km **Notes** Pets admitted English spoken

HATRIZE

ⅲ La Tremloisière

Micheline ARIZZI

Route de Briey, 54800 HATRIZE

☎ 03 82 33 14 30 📄 03 82 20 15 55

email: arizziroger@minitel.net

A family smallholding of two hectares situated outside the village. The house is furnished and decorated with care, with four en suite rooms, a huge sitting room with terrace, lawn, and garden with trees. Numerous restaurants within 5km. Close to the Regional Nature Park of Lorraine and Metz.

Prices s fr €41; d fr €51; t fr €61 **Nearby** ⛵ 5km ⌁ 20km ⚲ 5km ⌁ 5km Restaurant 5km Water sports 20km ⌕ 5km Spa 33km 🏛 5km ⋙ 5km **Notes** No pets English spoken

JAULNY

ⅲ |◎| Château de Jaulny

Anna & Hugues COLLIGNON-DRION

4, rue du Château, 54470 JAULNY

☎ 03 83 81 93 04

email: jaulnychateau@free.fr

web: www.jaulny-chateau.com

The keep of an 11th-century château - according to some historians the last residence of Joan of Arc - is the setting for this chambre d'hôtes. There are three double rooms, one with its own lounge area and one with an open fire, and all with private shower/WC, TV and DVD player. Lounge with books; microwave and fridge. Wooded grounds.

Prices s €50-€70; d €55-€75; dinner fr €30 **On Site** ⚲ ⚘ **Nearby** ⛵ 12km ⌁ 12km ⌁ 22km Restaurant 25km Water sports 12km ⌕ 4km 🏛 4km ⋙ 12km **Notes** No pets English spoken

LANEUVELOTTE

♯♯♯ Les Volets Bleus

Noëlle & Alain DIAQUIN
10, Grande Rue, 54280 LANEUVELOTTE
☎ 03 83 20 41 65 & 06 81 33 81 31
email: adiaquin@yahoo.fr
web: http://voletsbleuslorraine.free.fr

This distinctive 17th-century farmhouse stands at the centre of a small village. There are two triple bedrooms, one with a double bed and a single, the other with three singles; in addition there is a two-roomed suite for four (double bed plus twins). All have private bath/shower room, and the suite has its own lounge. Award-winning garden; good walking area.

Prices s fr €50; d fr €60; t fr €80; extra person fr €25 **On Site** Private ↘
Nearby ☆ 1km ⚓ 5km ✐ 15km Restaurant 1km Water sports 8km
⚑ 3km ⛪ 2km ⋈ 7km **Notes** No pets English spoken

LEMAINVILLE

♯♯♯ Chambre d'hôtes

Ulrike & Gérard FLEURY
22, Grande rue, 54740 LEMAINVILLE
☎ 03 83 25 54 51
email: chambres-fleury@laposte.net

This old house, built in the traditional local style, has three first floor guest bedrooms, all with private bathrooms and WCs. There is a twin-bedded room, and two triples, each with a double bed and a single. Cot available; lounge with open fire, video and books; terrace.

Prices not confirmed for 2008 **On Site** ✐ **Nearby** ☆ 2km ↘ 10km
Water sports 6km ⚑ 2km ⛪ 3km ⋈ 5km **Notes** Pets admitted English spoken

MAIZIERES

♯♯♯ Chambre d'hôtes

Laurent COTEL
69, rue Carnot, 54550 MAIZIERES
☎ 03 83 52 75 57 ▤ 03 83 52 75 57

Three en suite guest rooms available in an attractive house, furnished in country style in a peaceful setting. Facilities include a sitting room for guests and a secluded garden.

Prices s fr €35; d fr €45; t fr €55; extra person fr €10 **Nearby** ☆ 10km
⚓ 15km ✐ 5km ↘ 5km Restaurant 3km Water sports 40km ⚑ 5km
⋈ 6km **Notes** Pets admitted

MANONCOURT-SUR-SEILLE

♯♯♯ Les Chambres d'Ylang

Virginie KUNTZ-ROUSSEL
10, rue du Château, 54610 MANONCOURT-SUR-SEILLE
☎ 03 83 86 50 50 & 06 11 48 28 81 ▤ 03 83 86 51 27
email: info@chateau-de-manoncourt.com
web: www.chateau-de-manoncourt.com

The former stables and outbuildings of a listed 17th-century château make an attractive setting for these three guest bedrooms. Two of the rooms are on the ground floor, each with a lounge area; the third is upstairs. The rooms are air-conditioned, and all three have private bath/shower room. They overlook a Japanese style garden and extensive enclosed grounds.

Prices not confirmed for 2008 **On Site** ☆ ✐ **Nearby** ↘ 12km
Water sports 12km ⚑ 6km ⋈ 12km **Notes** No pets English spoken
CC

SAXON-SION

♯♯♯ Les Hauts de Sion

Nicolas & Catherine DUCHATEL
3, impasse Georges Berger, 54330 SAXON-SION
☎ 03 83 25 10 52 & 06 80 20 02 04 ▤ 03 83 25 17 36
email: duchecat@club-internet.fr

Not far from the Vosges mountains, this elegant property enjoys panoramic views from its hilltop site. There is a two-roomed suite for four with two double beds; a double room, and one additional bedroom. Good walking country, with signposted footpaths; guided horse-riding and hot-air balloon trips available. Prepared tray meals can be arranged.

Prices s €35-€45; d €40-€60; extra person fr €15 **On Site** Restaurant
❀ **Nearby** ☆ 2km ✐ 10km ↘ 18km Water sports 10km ⚑ 6km
Spa 35km ⛪ 6km ⋈ 1.5km **Notes** No pets

STE-GENEVIEVE

♯♯♯ ⦿⦿ Ferme Sainte Geneviève

Marc & Véronique GIGLEUX
4, route de Bézaumont, 54700 SAINTE-GENEVIEVE
☎ 03 83 82 25 55 ▤ 03 83 82 25 55
email: marc.gigleux@wanadoo.fr

An 18th-century Lorraine farmhouse, peacefully situated overlooking the Moselle Valley with three spacious rooms, and a large garden with views. Lounge, TV, telephone, regional cuisine using local produce. Tennis and boules in the village. Nearby museum and abbey.

Prices s fr €40; d fr €45; t fr €60; extra person fr €15; dinner fr €17
Nearby ☆ 7km ⚓ 15km ✐ 3km ↘ 7km Restaurant 7km Water
sports 7km ⚑ 7km ⛪ 7km ⋈ 7km **Notes** Pets admitted English spoken

VIRECOURT

♯♯♯ Les Marguerites

Manuela & François BEYEL

14, rue de la République, 54290 VIRECOURT

☎ 03 83 72 54 20 & 06 10 99 87 59 ▤ 03 83 72 54 20

Three spacious en suite rooms in a renovated country house at the gateway to the Vosges Mountains, each with TV and separate entrance. Lounge with tourist information, dining room, courtyard garden with furniture, games area, table tennis and bicycles. Skiing and restaurants one hour away. Walking routes can be suggested, following marked paths.

Prices s €30-€40; d €40-€50; t €55-€65   **On Site** ♂   **Nearby** ⚓ 15km ↖ 20km Water sports 20km ⚲ 1km ㎞ 1km   **Notes** No pets

MEUSE

ANCEMONT

♯♯♯ ⑩ Château de Labessière

René EICHENAUER

55320 ANCEMONT

☎ 03 29 85 70 21 ▤ 03 29 87 61 60

email: rene.eichenauer@wanadoo.fr

web: www.labessiere.com

An 18th-century château with a Louis XV sitting room is the splendid setting for this chambre d'hôtes. There are five stylishly furnished bedrooms including two which sleep three guests, and a two-roomed suite for two adults and up to four children. They all have private shower rooms and WCs. Shady grounds with swimming pool. Top quality meals available, by arrangement.

Prices d €150-€160   **On Site** Private ↖   **Nearby** ⚓ 2km ⚑ 30km ♂ 1km ⚲ 10km ♛ 12km ㊙ 5km ㎞ 12km   **Notes** No pets English spoken

CHARNY-SUR-MEUSE

♯♯♯ Les Charmilles

Valérie GODARD

12 rue de la Gare, 55100 CHARNY-SUR-MEUSE

☎ 03 29 86 93 49 ▤ 03 29 84 65 30

email: valerie@les-charmilles.com

web: www.les-charmilles.com

In an attractive village not far from Verdun, this property has three non-smoking bedrooms: a twin-bedded room downstairs, and two doubles upstairs. They all have private shower rooms and WCs. TV available. Guests' lounge with books and board games; enclosed garden with terrace, furniture and private parking. Evening meals available, by arrangement.

Prices s fr €45; d fr €55; extra person fr €12; dinner fr €23   **On Site** ♂ **Nearby** ⚓ 8km ⚑ 8km Restaurant 3km ⚲ 1km ㊙ 8km ㎞ 7km **Notes** No pets English spoken

FUTEAU

♯♯♯ � Le Four au Bois

Michel CLO

Hameau de Bellefontaine, 55120 FUTEAU

☎ 03 29 88 22 08

email: michel-clo@wanadoo.fr

web: www.lefouraubois.com

Peace and comfort are guaranteed in this small hamlet tucked away in the forest of Argonne. There are four bedrooms, one of them a ground floor suite with disabled access. The other three rooms are upstairs: a double, a twin, and a room with three singles plus an occasional bed.

Prices s fr €40; d fr €50; extra person fr €15   **On Site** ♂ **Nearby** ⚓ 3km ⚑ 40km ↖ 15km Restaurant 1km ⚲ 10km ㊙ 1km ㎞ 5km   **Notes** No pets English spoken CC

PAREID

♯♯♯ ⑩ Au Coin des Jardins

Delphine SORAIN

13 bis Grande Rue, 55160 PAREID

☎ 06 83 13 88 50 & 03 29 83 97 76 ▤ 03 29 83 97 76

email: aucoindesjardins@wanadoo.fr

web: www.aucoindesjardins.com

This property is in a peaceful and pleasant village. There are five guest bedrooms: two doubles; two more doubles, each with an additional single bed; and a room with a double bed and two singles. All of the bedrooms have private shower rooms and WCs. Large lounge with TV and open fire; meals by arrangement.

Prices s €36-€41; d €44-€49; t €53-€58; extra person €7-€9; dinner €18-€22   **Nearby** ⚓ 7km ⚑ 20km ♂ 7km ↖ 20km Restaurant 7km ⚲ 7km ♛ 20km ㊙ 7km ㎞ 20km   **Notes** No pets English spoken

REVIGNY-SUR-ORNAIN

✷✷✷ ⓖ La Maison Forte

Caroline CHEURLIN
6, place Henriot du Coudray,
55800 REVIGNY-SUR-ORNAIN
☎ 06 63 46 03 26 & 03 29 70 78 94
email: caroline_cheurlin@hotmail.com
web: http://la-maison-forte.monsite.orange.fr

This property was once a fortified house, with a tower and high walls all around. The tower has gone, and now there are four guest bedrooms including a suite. Each has a TV and private bathroom; two have a split-level layout. Three are doubles; one has twin beds with a living room. Guests' lounge; breakfast can be enjoyed on the terrace.
Prices s €65-€80; d fr €65; t fr €110 **Nearby** ⛷ 6km ⌁ 15km 🏊 20km ⚄ 5km Restaurant 1km ⏃ 1km ⚁ 0.5km ⋈ 1km **Notes** Pets admitted English spoken

ST-AUBIN-SUR-AIRE

✷✷✷ ⓘⓞⓘ Le Domaine de Hellebore

Elisabeth POTHIER
28 rue Basse, 55500 ST-AUBIN-SUR-AIRE
☎ 03 29 77 06 61 ▤ 03 29 77 06 61
email: domaine.hellebore@wanadoo.fr
web: http://perso.wanadoo.fr/domaine.hellebore
This country house, full of character, has three guest rooms. On the ground floor is a room with two double beds; upstairs there is a double-bedded room, and a room with a double bed, a single and a cot. All of the rooms have private showers and WCs. Lounge with open fire, and billiard room. Terrace with garden furniture. Meals by arrangement.
Prices s fr €38; d fr €48; t fr €62; dinner fr €21 **Nearby** ⛷ 10km 🏊 10km ⚄ 11km Restaurant 11km ⏃ 11km ⚁ 25km ⚁ 11km ⋈ 13km **Notes** Pets admitted CC

ST-MAURICE-LES-GUSSAINVILLE

✷✷✷ ⓘⓞⓘ La Ferme des Vales

Ghislaine VALENTIN
55400 GUSSAINVILLE
☎ 03 29 87 12 91 ▤ 03 29 87 18 59
email: lafermedesvales@voila.fr
web: http://perso.wanadoo.fr/lafermedesvales
This former farmhouse has four double rooms on the first floor each with private facilities. Living room with open fire, TV and library for guests. Park; garden furniture; climbing frame for children. Table tennis. Table d'hotes by reservation.
Prices s fr €38; d fr €50; extra person fr €12; dinner fr €20
On Site Private ⚄ **Nearby** ⛷ 5km ⌁ 35km 🏊 2km Restaurant 4km ⚁ 20km ⚁ 4km ⋈ 4km **Notes** No pets English spoken

THILLOMBOIS

✷✷✷ ⓘⓞⓘ Le Clos du Pausa

Lise TANCHON
Rue du Château, 55260 THILLOMBOIS
☎ 03 29 75 07 85 ▤ 03 29 75 00 72
email: leclosdupausa@wanadoo.fr
web: http://perso.wanadoo.fr/leclosdupausa
Large character house offering three en suite rooms with park views: two spacious rooms sleep two or three and have a mini-bar, and there's one very comfortable suite, tastefully decorated, with TV and telephone. Coffee and tea-making facilities; lounge with satellite TV; shaded garden with furniture; bicycles; barbecues. Meals available on request. Fly-fishing nearby. Supplement payable for pets.
Prices s fr €50; d €70-€90; t fr €85; extra person fr €14; dinner fr €27
On Site 🏊 **Nearby** ⛷ 25km ⌁ 25km ⚄ 14km Restaurant 10km ⚁ 25km ⚁ 15km ⋈ 12km **Notes** Pets admitted English spoken Open February to October.

WATRONVILLE

✷✷✷ ⓘⓞⓘ La Métairie du Manoir

M-Josée et Christian WURTZ
3 rue Principale, 55160 WATRONVILLE
☎ 06 85 51 15 25
email: wurtz@lametairiedesvergers.com
web: www.lametairiedesvergers.com
Among orchards, in a small village, this property has three individually decorated guest bedrooms, all on the first floor. There are two doubles, one with an additional single bed and one with a folding bed; plus a twin-bedded room. They all have private shower rooms and WCs. Lounge with open fire, books and TV. Meals by arrangement.
Prices s fr €45; d fr €50; t fr €65; extra person fr €10; dinner fr €25
Nearby ⛷ 6km ⌁ 26km 🏊 3km ⚄ 15km ⚁ 6km ⚁ 3km ⋈ 15km **Notes** No pets English spoken Open Easter to 1 November.

WISEPPE

ⅲ ᵢ◯ᵢ Chambre d'hôtes

Joël JODIN

6 rue Montorgueil, 55700 WISEPPE

☎ 03 29 80 81 43 & 06 70 97 01 18

email: jeanpaul.veret@wanadoo.fr

web: http://jodin.joel.monsite.wanadoo.fr

An old farm, dating back to the middle of the 19th century, is the setting for this chambre d'hôtes. There are five rooms, one double on the ground floor, and four doubles upstairs. They all have private bathrooms and WCs. Lounge with open fire; terrace with garden furniture; landscaped gardens. Meals by arrangement.

Prices s fr €55; d fr €61; extra person fr €8; dinner €18–€26 **On Site** ℘ **Nearby** ⌁12km ⚲ 40km Restaurant 7km ⬳3km ⚘7km ⌂7km ⋘40km **Notes** Pets admitted English spoken Open April to 1 November.

WOINVILLE

ⅲ Le Domaine de Pomone

Nicole GERARD

1, ruelle de Haldat du Lys, 55300 WOINVILLE

☎ 06 14 93 55 92 & 03 29 90 01 47

email: ledomainedepomone@wanadoo.fr

web: www.ledomainedepomone.com

Ancient trees and a standing stone add to the attractions of this late 18th-century house in the heart of the Parc Naturel Régional de Lorraine, close to the Lac de Madine. There are three double bedrooms, each with a settee and a private bath or shower room. Guests' dining room and lounge area; books, and garden with furniture.

Prices s €45–€55; d €55–€65; t fr €75; extra person fr €20 **Nearby** ⚘7km ⌁7km ℘7km ⚲10km Restaurant 5km ⬳7km ⚘7km ⌂10km ⋘20km **Notes** No pets English spoken

MOSELLE

ANCY-SUR-MOSELLE

ⅲ Chambre d'hôtes

Paul-Marie et Sylvia THOMAS

2 rue des Quarrés, Haumalet, 57130 ANCY-SUR-MOSELLE

☎ 03 87 30 91 54 & 06 07 21 71 64 ▤ 03 87 30 91 54

email: haumalet@wanadoo.fr

web: http://haumalet.monsite.orange.fr

In the heart of the Lorraine Parc Naturel, this house has a peaceful setting. There are three bedrooms, with a separate guests' entrance: a double with canopied bed; another double with space for an occasional bed for two; and a twin-bedded room, also with space for an additional double. Cot available. All rooms have private showers/WCs. First floor lounge with books and baby's bottle warmer.

Prices s fr €45; d €60–€65; t fr €75; extra person fr €15 **Nearby** ⚘3km ⌁10km ℘1km ⚲2km Restaurant 0.5km ⬳3km ⌂2km ⋘1km **Notes** No pets English spoken Open 21 March to December.

BERIG-VINTRANGE

ⅲ ᵢ◯ᵢ ⅊ Vintrange

Daniel DUVOID

37 place de l'Eglise, 57660 BERIG-VINTRANGE

☎ 03 87 01 73 72

email: daniel.duvoid@wanadoo.fr

web: www.la-dame-blanche.com

This property in eastern Lorraine dates back to the early 18th century, and was once a small farmhouse. Today guests can enjoy the view across the meadow, sloping gently down towards the pond, and the open countryside beyond. Three suites offer complete rest and relaxation, each with a separate entrance, living room and private facilities. Cot and child's bed available; private parking.

Prices s €55–€65; d €60–€70; t €80–€90; extra person fr €20; dinner €22–€30 **On Site** ℘ Private ⚲ Spa **Nearby** ⚘5km ⌁15km Restaurant 5km ⬳5km ⌂5km ⋘5km **Notes** Pets admitted English spoken

BERTHELMING

ⅲ Chambre d'hôtes

Alice et Jean-Claude PEIFFER

47 rue Principale, 57930 BERTHELMING

☎ 03 87 97 82 76

email: jeanclaude.peiffer@free.fr

web: www.val-de-sarre.com

On the edge of Sarre, three en suite double rooms, one with an additional single bed. Two child's' beds available. Kitchenette; lounge; sitting room; TV; video; hi-fi. Garden with furniture and barbecue, access to park, children's play area, bicycles and parking. Reductions for extended stays.

Prices s fr €35; d fr €45; t fr €55 **On Site** ℘ ⚘ **Nearby** ⚘20km ⌁12km ⚲12km Restaurant 0.3km ⬳1km Spa 9km ⌂0.5km ⋘0.5km **Notes** No pets

CUVRY

ⅲ Ferme de la Haute Rive

J-F et B MORHAIN

57420 CUVRY

☎ 03 87 52 50 08

email: mbm21@wanadoo.fr

Three rooms (two rooms and one suite) in a detached house: four single beds and two doubles with separate shower rooms and wcs. Facilities include lounge, dining room, fireplace, reading area, TV, courtyard, enclosed garden, parking. Restaurant in the next village and many tourist attractions in this area.

Prices s fr €45; d fr €55; t fr €65 **On Site** ⚘ **Nearby** ⚘5km ⌁3km ℘10km ⚲4km Restaurant 3km ⬳2km ⌂4km ⋘10km **Notes** No pets English spoken Open 15 March to 15 November.

KOENIGSMACKER

ⅲ ♿ Chambre d'hôtes

J et M-B KEICHINGER
Moulin de Méwinckel, 57970 KOENIGSMACKER
☎ 03 82 55 03 28

This ancient mill has been in the owners' family since the 19th
century. It is set deep in the countryside, where the sound of
running streams seems to keep tune with the seasons. The four
guest rooms and a suite are in a former stable which has been
totally restored; one room is suitable for people of reduced
mobility. Singles, couples and families are all welcome; covered
parking.

Prices s €47-€60; d €55-€70; t fr €68 **Nearby** ✿ 6km ⌚ 18km
♟ 4km ↖ 9km Restaurant 2km ⌚ Spa 15km ☒ 2km ⋈ 12km
Notes No pets CC

LANDONVILLERS

ⅲ ◉ Le Moulin

Clodette WEBER
57530 LANDONVILLERS
☎ 03 87 64 24 81 📄 03 87 64 24 81
email: weber.c2@wanadoo.fr
web: www.studio-synchro.fr/weber

This late 19th-century property has three bedrooms in an old mill,
one of them a split-level suite, and a further room in the owners'
home which can sleep up to four people. The style of them all is a
charming mix of ancient and modern. Ornithologists will delight in
watching the herons, wrens, kingfishers and chaffinches, but there's
also fishing, mountain-biking and walking to enjoy.

Prices not confirmed for 2008 **On Site** ♟ **Nearby** ⌚ 18km ↖ ☒ 4km
⋈ 20km **Notes** No pets English spoken

MAIZIERES LES VIC

ⅲ ◉ Port Sainte Marie

Jean-Yves et Daniele BRETON
57810 MAIZIERES LES VIC
☎ 06 25 92 43 81
email: breton.daniele@wanadoo.fr
web: www.gites57.com

An ancient auberge, fully modernised, situated between the Lindre
and the Vosges, just a few metres from the banks of the canal that
runs from the Marne to the Rhine. The property has four guest
bedrooms, two doubles and two triples, each with a double bed and
a single. All have private bathroom/WC. Meals using local ingredients
are available by arrangement. Children under five free, reduced rate
for three or more nights.

Prices s fr €30; d fr €43; t fr €50; extra person fr €10; dinner fr €17
Nearby ✿ 15km ⌚ 24km ♟ 0km ↖ 20km Restaurant 3km ⌚ 10km
Spa 17km ☒ 3.5km ⋈ 10km **Notes** No pets English spoken

NIDERVILLER

ⅲ *Chambre d'hôtes*

Jean-Marie BURKEL
2 rue de la Faïencerie, 57565 NIDERVILLER
☎ 06 73 72 62 90

Guests to this restored 18th-century house can enjoy lovely walks in
the region north of the Vosges Mountains. Accommodation comprises
three double guest rooms and one triple room; child's bed available.
Lounge, kitchenette, terrace, barbecue. Barge rental available on the
Marne-Rhine canal.

Prices not confirmed for 2008 **Nearby** ⌚ 5km ♟ 1km ↖ 5km ⌚ 1km
⋈ 5km **Notes** No pets

ⅲ Chambre d'hôtes

Marcel et Marinette FETTER
11 rue des Vosges, 57565 NIDERVILLER
☎ 03 87 23 79 96 & 06 22 65 33 14
email: fettermarcel@hotmail.com
web: www.gites57.com

This establishment offers two double rooms and two single rooms,
on the ground floor or first floor. All of the rooms have their own
shower, wc and TV. Parking is available, and a garage is provided for
cycles and motorbikes.

Prices s fr €32; d fr €40; t fr €50 **On Site** ♟ **Nearby** ⌚ 5km ↖ 5km
Restaurant 1km ⌚ ⋈ 5km **Notes** No pets

PELTRE

ⅲ La Cour Basse

Sylvie et Lucien LAURENT
3, rue de Metz, 57245 PELTRE
☎ 03 87 74 16 36 & 06 79 27 28 85 📄 03 87 74 16 36
email: lucien.laurent066@orange.fr

Between fields and forests not far from Metz, this welcoming
farmstead has one double room, and a two-roomed family suite for
four, with a double bed and two singles. Each room has a private
bathroom and WC. Outside there is a terrace and parking space.

Prices s fr €38; d fr €48; extra person fr €16 **Nearby** ✿ 1km ⌚ 5km
♟ 3km ↖ 5km Restaurant 0.5km ⌚ 0.5km ☁ 5km ☒ 0.8km ⋈ 0.4km
Notes No pets English spoken

RHODES

⚏ ❦ Ferme du Domaine les Bachats

Jean-Bernard CORSYN
57810 RHODES
☎ 03 87 03 92 03 & 06 81 71 93 27 📄 03 87 03 56 66
email: jb.corsyn@wanadoo.fr
web: www.domainelesbachats.com

This farmhouse, not far from the Vosges mountains, is ideal for walkers and dates back to the 19th century. Still a working farm (sheep and cereal) it has three two-roomed family suites, all with private facilities and one with direct access to the garden. Mountain biking and horse riding can be arranged, also farm visits. Price reductions available for longer stays.

Prices s €45-€55; d €50-€60; t €60-€70; extra person fr €10
On Site ⚘ ☙ ❧ **Nearby** ⚓ 20km ⚔ Restaurant 2km ⊞ 1km
⚏ 20km **Notes** Pets admitted English spoken Open 5 January to 15 December.

SARREGUEMINES

⚏ Chambre d'hôtes

Loekie et Hubert JAGER
51, rue de Deux-Ponts,
57200 SARREGUEMINES-NEUNKIRCH
☎ 03 87 95 14 54 📄 03 87 95 14 54
email: loekie.jager@wanadoo.fr

In the heart of the village of Neunkirch, this restored traditional-style house has four guest bedrooms. On the first floor is a double room; on the second floor is a suite for two people, with its own lounge; and two more double-bedded rooms. Each of the rooms has a private shower room and WC.

Prices s fr €41; d fr €55; t fr €75; extra person fr €15 **Nearby** ⚓ 0.2km ⚓ 5km ⚘ 1km ⚔ 1km Restaurant 0.3km ⊜ 1km ❦ 3km ⊞ 0.5km ⚏ 3km **Notes** No pets English spoken

SOLGNE

⚏ ⊙ Chambre d'hôtes

Jean BRUNET
16 rue Alsace Lorraine, 57420 SOLGNE
☎ 03 87 57 72 60
email: jean-brunet@wanadoo.fr

This house has four first floor guest bedrooms - a double, one with twin beds, and two with double beds plus a single. Each room has an en suite bath or shower room and WC. High speed internet access; lounge with books; garden and terrace.

Prices s fr €35; d fr €46; t fr €55; dinner fr €17 **On Site** ⚓ **Nearby** ⚓ 15km ⚘ 25km ⊜ 5km ⚏ 5km **Notes** Pets admitted

ST-AVOLD-DOURD'HAL

⚏ Domaine du Moulin

Marie-Paule MULLER
13 rue de la Vallée, 57500 ST-AVOLD-DOURD'HAL
☎ 03 87 92 55 15 & 06 08 53 71 21
email: domaine.du.moulin@free.fr
web: www.gitesdefrance.fr.st

There are buildings on this rural site which go back to the 13th century, but the five guest bedrooms are in an annexe, built using old materials. On the ground floor is a twin-bedded room, and a double; upstairs are two more doubles and a twin-bedded room. Baby equipment available; lounge. Garden furniture, boules.

Prices s fr €60; d fr €70 **On Site** Spa **Nearby** ⚓ 2km ⚓ 12km ⚔ 2km Restaurant 2km ⊜ 2km ⊞ 2km ⚏ 4km **Notes** No pets English spoken CC

ST-HUBERT

⚏⚏ Ferme de Godchure

Annette FLAHAUT
57640 ST-HUBERT
☎ 03 87 77 03 96 & 03 87 77 98 10
email: godchure@wanadoo.fr
web: www.lafermedegodchure.fr

Once the abbey farm for Villiers de Bettnach, this property is a haven of peace and quiet, set in the valley of the Canner in the heart of the forest. In their restoration work Annette and Dominique have 'planted happiness' and reap the rewards - the satisfaction of their guests. Four rooms, one of which has a jacuzzi; another sleeps three people. A spa and sauna are also available for guests' use.

Prices d €70-€90; t fr €100; extra person €10-€20
Nearby ⚓ 15km ⚓ 20km ⚘ 15km ⚔ 20km ⊜ 3km ❦ 18km ⊞ 3km ⚏ 20km **Notes** No pets English spoken

VOSGES

ANOULD

⚏ ⊙ *Domaine des Iris*

M-Claude et J-Yves CONREAUX
563, rue du Val de Meurthe, 88650 ANOULD
☎ 03 29 57 01 09 📄 03 29 57 01 09
email: marie-claude-des-iris@wanadoo.fr
web: www.domainedesiris.com

A spacious home surrounded by 2 hectare grounds with a fishing lake and river. Five en suite guest rooms (four with balcony) include two doubles, two rooms with double bed and single and one with double and two singles. Facilities include cot, central heating, lounge, fireplace, TV, garden swing, boules and a dining room in which to sample regional and garden produce.

Prices not confirmed for 2008 **On Site** ⚘ **Nearby** ⚓ 4km ⚔ 12km ❦ 13km ⊜ 0.5km ⊞ 0.5km ⚏ 10km **Notes** No pets

DARNIEULLES

♯♯♯ Le Moulin

Anne-Marie COSSIN-HIGEL

170, Impasse du Moulin, Le Moulin de Vaudrillot, 88390 DARNIEULLES

☎ 03 29 34 04 23   🖹 03 29 38 36 45

You will receive a warm welcome to this old mill which sits in large grounds set back from the village. An annexe has three doubles with en suite shower rooms, with another room for four children upstairs. A small suite in the hosts' house sleeps 2-3 and a child, with bathroom. Sitting room with kitchenette, dining room shared with hosts.

Prices s fr €40; d fr €50; extra person fr €15   **On Site** ℰ
Nearby ⛷ 1km ♨ 6km ⇌ 5km Restaurant 2km ⌣ 1km Spa 20km
🎾 6km ⛪ 1km ⋘ 7km   **Notes** No pets

ELOYES

♯♯♯ 🍽 Chambre d'hôtes

Christine PIERRE

5, Chemin du Gueuty, 88510 ELOYES

☎ 03 29 32 32 19

Sympathetic renovation has preserved the character and cachet of this ancient Vosgienne farmhouse overlooking the Moselle Valley. There are two double rooms on the first floor with shower/WC, plus a room for four with bathroom; all rooms have TV and central heating. On the ground floor is a large sitting room with open fire and TV. Large terrace with flowers and courtyard; table tennis.

Prices s fr €33; d fr €40; t fr €52; extra person fr €12; dinner fr €15
Nearby ⛷ 10km ♨ 15km ℰ 0.7km ⇌ 12km Restaurant 0.7km ⌣ 36km
⌣ 12km Spa 25km 🎾 12km ⛪ 0.7km ⋘ 15km   **Notes** No pets

GERARDMER

♯♯♯ 🍽 ⚥ Chalet l'Epinette

Famille POIROT-SCHERRER

70, Chemin de la Trinité, 88400 GERARDMER

☎ 03 29 63 40 06   🖹 03 29 63 40 06

email: info@chalet-epinette.com

web: www.chalet-epinette.com

Chalet close to the forest, with 6 guest rooms. Ground floor : one room with a double bed, one room with a canopy bed (double), one double room with disabled access. Dining room, fireplace. First floor: one room with a canopy bed (double), two rooms for 3 people. Shower or bathroom, WC, TV, video, terrace or balcony in each room. Sauna, steam room, billiards. Large grounds.

Prices s fr €53; d fr €62-€67; t fr €85; extra person fr €18; dinner fr €22
Nearby ⛷ 2km ♨ 2km ⇌ 0.5km Restaurant 0.5km ⌣ 3km ⌣ 2km
Spa 40km 🎾 2km ⛪ 1km ⋘ 2km   **Notes** No pets English spoken
Open 9 December to 17 November.

LA BRESSE

♯♯♯ 🍽 Villa Eugene

Claudine EYNIUS

13, route du Chajoux, 88250 LA BRESSE

☎ 03 29 25 68 76 & 06 86 60 56 94

email: villaeugene@wanadoo.fr

web: www.villaeugene.fr

In the Parc Naturel des Ballons des Vosges, this impressive property has three beautifully furnished guest rooms, all upstairs. One is a double; the others have twin beds. All have private bathroom and WC. Guests can enjoy their breakfast in a vast dining room, where the ceiling has some wonderful plaster mouldings.

Prices s fr €49; d fr €59; extra person fr €15; dinner fr €19   **On Site** ℰ
Nearby ⛷ 5km ♨ 45km ⇌ 1.5km Restaurant 1km ⌣ 6km ⌣ 1.5km
Spa 40km ⛪ 1.3km ⋘ 27km   **Notes** No pets English spoken

LA CHAPELLE-AUX-BOIS

♯♯♯ 🍽 *Chambre d'hôtes*

Marie-Claire CHASSARD

9, Les Grands Près, 88240 LA CHAPELLE-AUX-BOIS

☎ 03 29 36 31 00   🖹 03 29 36 31 00

Three comfortable guest rooms in a tastefully restored mansion including one double room, one room with three single beds and one family room with one double and bunk beds. Dining room and sitting room with TV; veranda and washing machine available. Spacious grounds include fishing and self-catering gîtes and are close to thermal spa of Bains-les-Bains.

Prices not confirmed for 2008   **On Site** ℰ   **Nearby** ⛷ 4km ⇌ 25km
⌣ 3km Spa 3km ⛪ 3km ⋘ 3km   **Notes** Pets admitted

LE VAL D'AJOL

♯♯♯ 🍽 La Villa Fleurie

Rosine NOT

38, Grande Rue, 88340 LE VAL D'AJOL

☎ 03 29 30 58 96 & 06 74 28 18 92

email: rosine.not@wanadoo.fr

A beautiful, light and airy early 20th-century house set in a delightful garden, with charmingly decorated rooms. Ground floor dining room, lounge and reading room , and veranda. The two double bedrooms are on the first and second floors and share a kitchen. Both have shower rooms and toilet, one has a TV.

Prices s fr €35; d fr €46; extra person fr €17; dinner fr €16   **On Site** ⛷
ℰ   **Nearby** ⇌ 0.5km Restaurant 0.2km ⌣ 45km ⌣ 0.5km Spa 9km
🎾 0.5km ⛪ 0.5km ⋘ 14km   **Notes** No pets English spoken

REMIREMONT

⚑ Ferme du Grand Bienfaisy

Sylvie et Patrick KIEFFER

1, Route du Fiscal, 88200 REMIREMONT

☎ 03 29 23 28 20 & 06 85 59 59 76 📄 03 29 23 28 20

email: patrick.kieffer10@wanadoo.fr

web: www.legrandbienfaisy.fr

Outside the town of Remiremont at the edge of a wood, this restored former farmhouse offers five guest rooms: on the first floor one room with a double and a single bed, a twin room with a sofa bed, a room with three single beds and a double room. All have shower/WC. There is also a family suite with two rooms, a double and a triple, plus a bathroom and WC. There is a large living room, sitting room, and kitchenette for the guests. TV, fireplace. Washing machine and tumble dryer available.

Prices s fr €32; d €46-€48; t €60-€62; extra person fr €15
Nearby ⚓ 0.3km ♨ 25km 🖉 1km ⤳ 0.3km Restaurant 2km ♣ 30km
♒ 0.3km Spa 11km 🏠 1.5km ⚌ 2km **Notes** No pets English spoken

SAULCY-SUR-MEURTHE

⚑ Le Bout du Chemin

Jean-Claude BOURG

6, rue d'Hadremont, 88580 SAULCY-SUR-MEURTHE

☎ 03 29 50 90 13 & 06 07 84 76 49 📄 03 29 50 90 53

email: bourg.jean-claude@wanadoo.fr

Close to St Dié, this large, renovated house offers five bedrooms. Two double rooms have a private entrance. In addition, there are two single rooms and a double. WC, shower, TV point and private terrace for each bedroom. Large living room with sitting room, TV and fireplace, shared with the owners.

Prices s fr €43; d fr €48; t fr €58; extra person fr €10 **Nearby** ⚓ 3km
♨ 5km 🖉 5km ⤳ 3km Restaurant 0.6km ♣ 25km ♒ 4km 🏠 2km
⚌ 3km **Notes** Pets admitted English spoken

SAULXURES-LES-BULGNEVILLE

⚑ ⦿ Le Château de Bulgneville

Danièle SENGEL

6, rue du Château,

88140 SAULXURES-LES-BULGNEVILLE

☎ 03 29 09 21 73

email: sengel.daniele@wanadoo.fr

web: www.chateaudesaulxures.fr.st

A magnificent 17th-century residence surrounded by a huge parkland garden featuring a majestic lime tree. Four vast guest rooms, named after plants, have oak flooring and period fireplaces, with refined furnishings and elegant decor. The gourmet meals and breakfast are served in the dining room or on the shaded terrace. The library and garden provide total peace and relaxation.

Prices s fr €70; d fr €90; dinner fr €40 **On Site** ♔
Nearby ⚓ 7km ♨ 12km 🖉 1km ⤳ 7km Restaurant 2km ♒ 2km
Spa 5km 🏠 2km ⚌ 7km **Notes** No pets English spoken **Open** February to November. CC

XERTIGNY

⚑ ⦿ ♿ La Charmante

Edith et Joël LACHAUX

563, Route du Coney, Rasey, 88220 XERTIGNY

☎ 03 29 30 18 26

Well-appointed rooms in a restored farmhouse 20 minutes from Epinal. On the ground floor, with independent access, is a double room with disabled access; upstairs are two more rooms, each with a double bed and a single. All have private facilities and TVs. Grounds, with a barbecue. A small shallow lake is close by. Meals by arrangement.

Prices s fr €46; d fr €50; t fr €68; extra person fr €18; dinner fr €20
Nearby ⚓ 3km ♨ 20km 🖉 3km ⤳ 8km Restaurant 10km ♣ 46km
♒ 8km Spa 10km 🏠 8km ⚌ 20km **Notes** No pets

GERMANY

Sarregemines

57 MOSELLE

Wissembourg

Cleebourg

Hunspach

Kutzenhausen

Betschdorf

Rimsdorf

Schillersdorf

Hagueneau

Sarrebourg

Saverne

Lupstein

Hoerdt

Gougenheim

STRASBOURG

Molsheim

Boersch

Heiligenstein

Eichhoffen

Breitenbach

Itterswiller

Gerstheim

88 VOSGES

Dieffenbach-au-Val

Dambach-la-Ville

Saint-Dié

Neubois

Scherwiller

Diebolsheim

Sélestat

Orschwiller

GERMANY

Ribeauvillé

COLMAR

68 HAUT-RHIN

0   15 km

67 BAS-RHIN

88 VOSGES

70 HAUTE-SAÔNE

90 TERRITOIRE DE BELFORT

25 DOUBS

Saint-Dié

Sélestat

Ste-Marie-aux-Mines

Thannenkirch

St-Hippolyte

Rorschwihr

Ribeauvillé

Beblenheim

Hunawihr

Mittelwihr

Kaysersberg

Lapoutroie

Sigolsheim

Ammerschwihr

Holtzwihr

Orbey

Katzenthal

Labaroche

COLMAR

Soultzeren

Eguisheim

Husseren-les-Châteaux

Gueberschwihr

Linthal

Munwiller

Lautenbach

Murbach

Guebwiller

Husseren-Wesserling

Thann

Sewen

Mulhouse

Rixheim

Kembs

Magstatt-le-Bas

Chavannes-sur-l'Étang

Altkirch

Mertzen

BELFORT

Montbéliard

GERMANY

SWITZERLAND

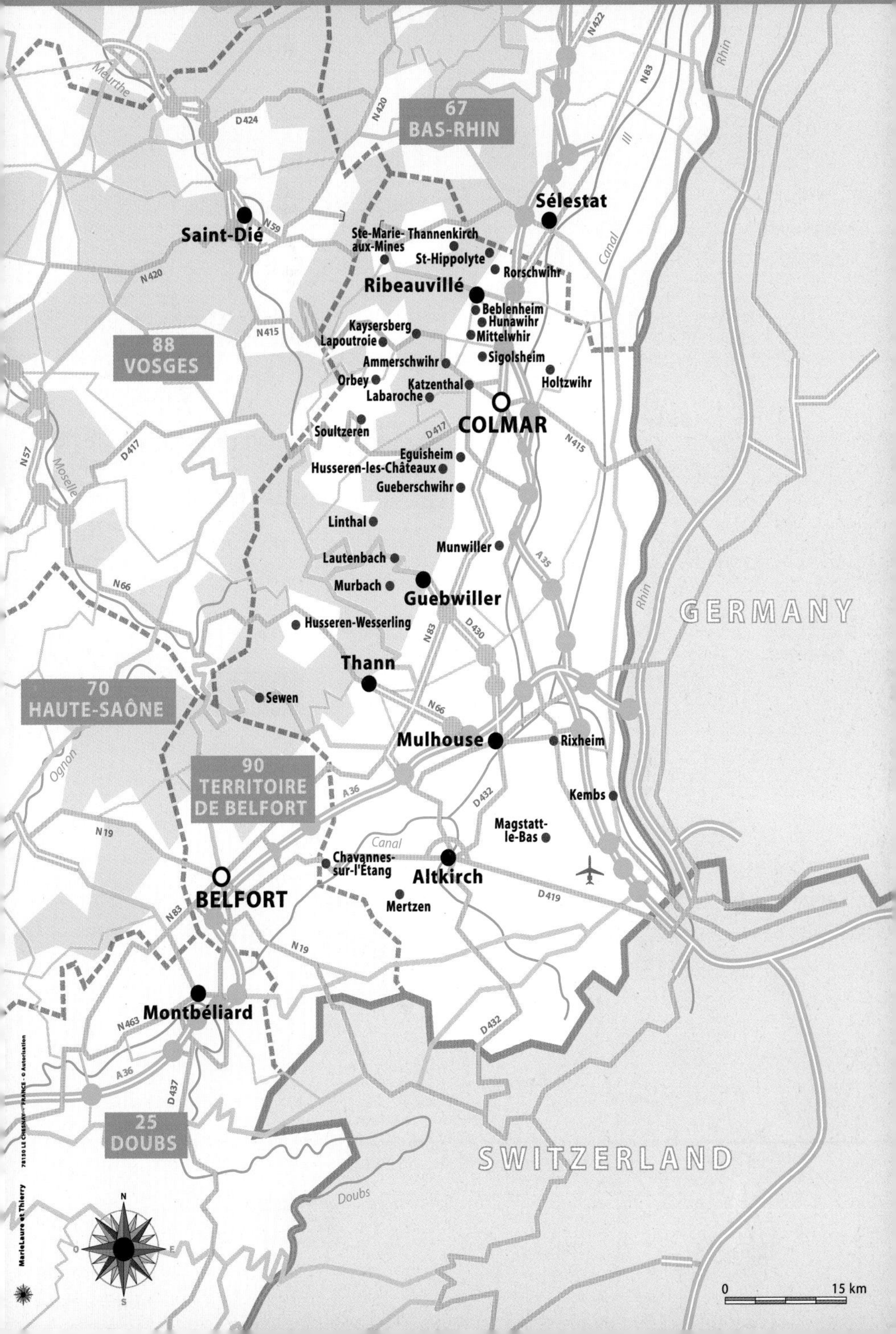

MarieLaure et Thierry   781101 Le Cosseur - FRANCE - © Autorisation

Meurthe

Rhin

Canal III

Moselle

Ognon

Canal

Doubs

N 422

N 83

N 59

N 420

D 424

N 420

N 415

N 57

D 417

N 415

D 417

A 35

N 83

D 430

N 66

N 66

A 36

N 19

N 19

A 36

N 463

D 437

D 432

D 432

D 419

N 83

0   15 km

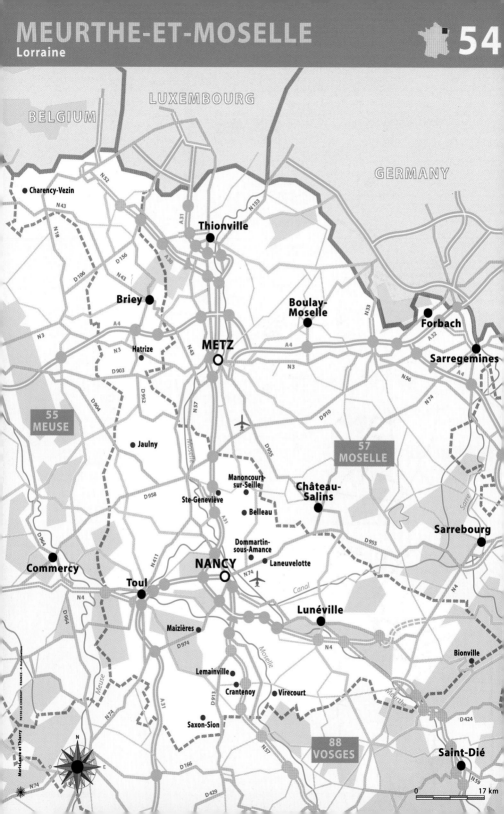

LUXEMBOURG

BELGIUM

GERMANY

N 52

● Charency-Vezin

N 43

N 18

D 156

D 106

N 43

Thionville

N 153

N 31

A 30

Briey ●

A 4

Hatrize ●

METZ ○

N 3

D 903

Boulay-Moselle ●

N 33

Forbach

A 32

Sarregemines

N 3

N 43

D 952

A 4

N 3

N 56

N 74

D 904

55 MEUSE

D 958

Jaulny ●

N 57

Moselle

Ste-Geneviève ●

A 31

Manoncourt-sur-Seille ●

Belleau ●

D 955

Château-Salins ●

57 MOSELLE

Sarre

Sarrebourg ●

Commercy ●

N 411

D 964

NANCY ○

Dommartin-sous-Amance ●

Laneuvelotte ●

N 74

Canal

D 955

N 4

Toul ●

N 4

Maizières ●

D 974

Lunéville ●

N 4

Bionville

Lemainville ●

Crantenoy ●

Virecourt ●

Moselle

D 913

A 31

Saxon-Sion ●

N 74

88 VOSGES

N 57

Meurthe

D 424

Saint-Dié ●

N 39

D 166

D 429

N 74

N

O   E

S

0   17 km

BELGIUM

LUXEMBOURG

D 964

D 977

D 981

08 ARDENNES

Wiseppe

D 947

N 43

N 52

A 31

Meuse

D 905

N 18

D 156

A 30

D 946

● Vouziers

D 964

D 106

N 43

A 4

Briey

D 962

Charney-sur-Meuse

St-Maurice-les-Gussainville

Aisne

N 3

Verdun

Watronville

Pareid

N 3

D 903

D 952

N 57

Meuse

Sainte-Menehould

N 3

A 4

Ancemont

D 964

Meuse

D 904

Futeau

Thillombois

Moselle

D 994

Woinville

N 35

D 958

51 MARNE

Revigny-sur-Ornain

D 994

54 MEURTHE-ET-MOSELLE

BAR-LE-DUC ○

D 964

N 411

N 135

Commercy

Toul

Saint-Aubin-sur-Aire

N 4

N 4

Canal de la Marne

D 964

Saint-Dizier

Meuse

Marne

D 974

52 HAUTE-MARNE

D 384

D 60

N 74

A 31

N

O E

S

0   15 km

MOSELLE
Lorraine

57

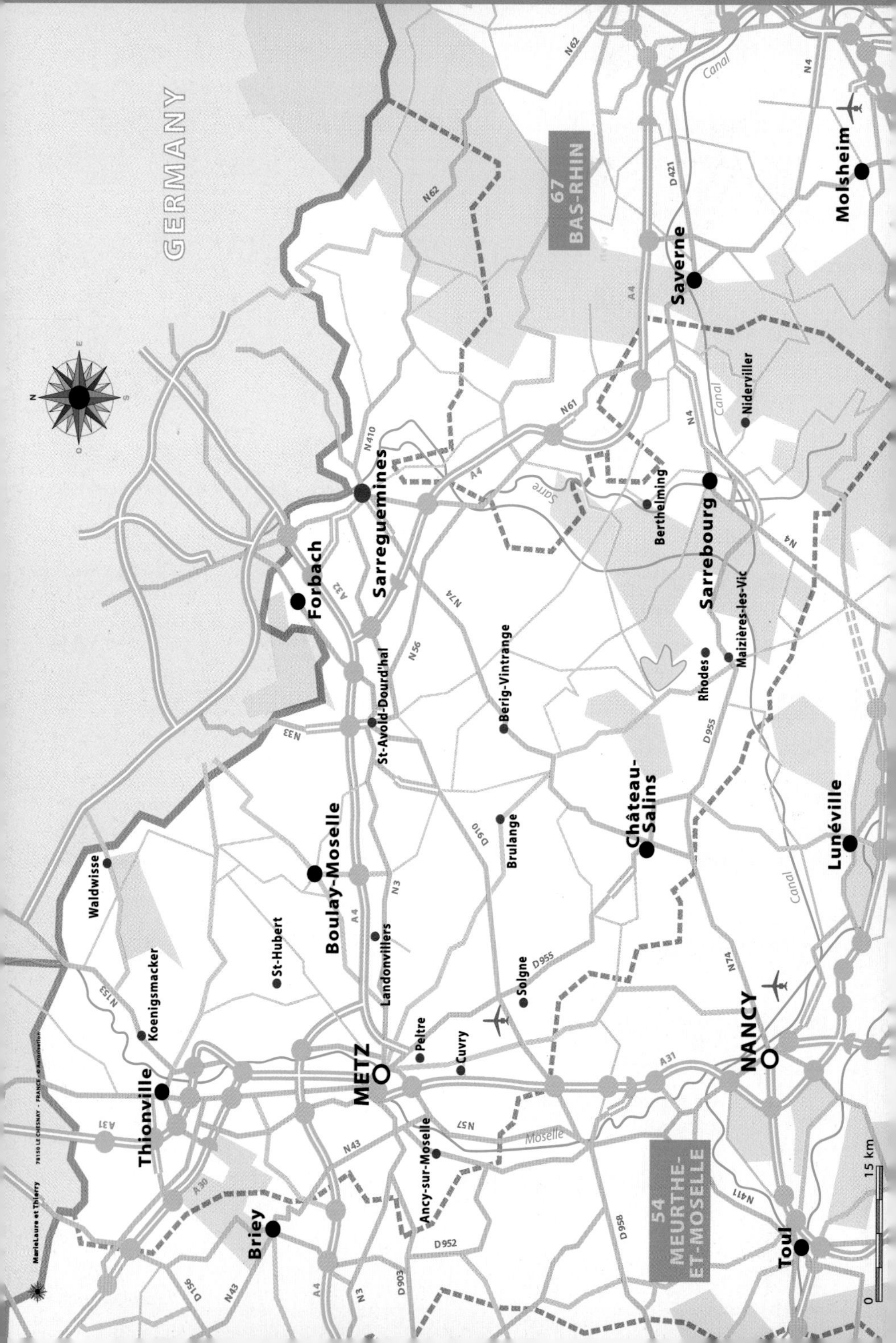
GERMANY
67 BAS-RHIN
54 MEURTHE-ET-MOSELLE
Molsheim
Saverne
Niderviller
Sarrebourg
Berthelming
Sarreguemines
Forbach
St-Avold-Dourd'hal
Berig-Vintrange
Maizières-les-Vic
Rhodes
Château-Salins
Brulange
Lunéville
Boulay-Moselle
Waldwisse
St-Hubert
Landonvillers
Koenigsmacker
Thionville
Solgne
Peltre
Cuvry
METZ
NANCY
Ancy-sur-Moselle
Briey
Toul
Canal
Sarre
Moselle
N62
N4
D421
A4
N61
N410
A32
N74
N56
N33
D910
N3
D955
D955
N74
A31
N153
A31
N57
N43
A30
N411
D958
D952
D903
D156
N43
A4
N3
0
15 km
MarieLaure et Thierry 78150 LE CHESNAY - FRANCE - © Autorisation

67 BAS-RHIN

68 HAUT-RHIN

Guebwiller

Thann

54 MEURTHE-ET-MOSELLE

Saint-Dié

Saulcy-sur-Meurthe

Anould

Gérardmer

La Bresse

90

Éloyes

Moselle

Remiremont

Le Val-d'Ajol

Lunéville

ÉPINAL

Xertigny

La Chapelle-aux-Bois

Damieulles

HAUTE-SAÔNE 70

NANCY

Sâone

Canal

Toul

Saulxures-lès-Bulgnéville

Neufchâteau

55 MEUSE

Meuse

52 HAUTE-MARNE

Meuse

15 km

N E O S

AQUITAINE

DORDOGNE

ARCHIGNAC

⚜ *Pouch*

Francine et Serge BOURGEADE
24590 ARCHIGNAC
☎ 05 53 28 85 02 & SR : 05 53 35 50 01
🖹 05 53 28 90 93
email: sla24@wanadoo.fr
web: www.resinfrance.com/perigord/

Situated in the Périgord Nord region close to Montignac, Sarlat and the Vézère Valley, this stone house is typical of the region. There is a twin and double room with a single bed that can be converted into a double (on a mezzanine level), each with private facilities and TV. Terrace, shady park, ideally situated for rambling. Goose and duck patés are available from the house and there is a restaurant nearby.

Prices not confirmed for 2008   **On Site** Private ⚲   **Nearby** ⛳ 3km ♨ 25km ⚓ 3km ⛵ 8km 🏛 6km ⚑ 16km   **Notes** Pets admitted   Open April to 15 November.

AUDRIX

⚜ **Mas Jeandemai**

Betty et Olivier PREAUX
24260 AUDRIX
☎ 05 53 04 26 96 & SR : 05 53 35 50 01
🖹 05 53 07 67 96
email: preotel@jeandemai.com
web: www.jeandemai.com

This 15th and 17th-century Périgord house lies in 20 hectares of land and dominates Le Bugue area bordered by the Vézère and Dordogne Valleys, in the heart of the Périgord Nord. There are two double rooms and two with double and single bed, each with private (extra bed and cot on request). Drawing room with TV; friendly and tranquil atmosphere; restaurants nearby.

Prices s fr €55; d fr €65   **On Site** 🖉 ♨ Private ⚲   **Nearby** ⛳ 3km ♨ 14km ⛵ 3km 🏛 4km ⚑ 4km   **Notes** No pets English spoken Open 7 April to 3 November. CC

BEAUSSAC

⚜ **Chez Robert**

K et J-M CHAPELL-WELFFENS
24340 BEAUSSAC
☎ 05 53 56 56 51 & SR : 05 53 35 50 01
🖹 05 53 56 56 59
email: jean.m-chapelle@wanadoo.fr
web: www.resinfrance.com/perigord/

This property is ideally situated in a quiet and peaceful area which offers plenty of places to explore. There are two double rooms, and a twin-bedded room. An extra bed may be available for additional guests, and also a baby's cot. All rooms have a private shower room and WC.

Prices s fr €40; d fr €50; extra person fr €15   **On Site** ⛄ **Nearby** 🖉 1km ⚓ 5km ⛵ 5km 🏛 0.5km ⚑ 40km   **Notes** Pets admitted English spoken

CHAMPAGNAC-DE-BELAIR

⚜ **Château de la Borie Saulnier**

Claude et Michel DUSEAU
Saulnier, 24530 CHAMPAGNAC-DE-BELAIR
☎ 05 53 54 22 99 & SR : 05 53 35 50 01
🖹 05 53 08 53 78
email: chateau-de-la-borie-saulnier@wanadoo.fr
web: http://perso.wanadoo.fr/chateaudelaboriesaulnier

This old property, peacefully situated in a wooded area, offers spacious accommodation with antique furnishings. There are four double bedrooms, and one room sleeping three; a cot and an extra bed are also available. All rooms have private facilities. The caring owners give a warm welcome. There is a restaurant close by and many châteaux to visit. Pets allowed on request only. Reservations only November to mid April.

Prices d €73-€79; t €95-€101; extra person €10-€22   **On Site** Private ⚲ **Nearby** ⛳ 6km ♨ 23km 🖉 0.8km Restaurant 3km ⛵ 0.8km ⚽ 3km 🏛 0.8km ⚑ 33km   **Notes** Pets admitted English spoken

CHANTERAC

⧼⧼⧼ *Chaniveau*

Françoise et Claude BRALET

24190 CHANTERAC

☎ 05 53 82 38 25 & SR : 05 53 35 50 01

▤ 05 53 35 50 41

email: contact@chaniveau.com

web: www.resinfrance.com/perigord/

A restored 17th-century farmhouse, situated in a forest clearing is the setting for this chambres d'hôtes. There is a double room and a twin-bedded room; also a family suite of two rooms - a double, and a twin. All rooms have private bath or shower room and WC. Cot available. Enjoy your breakfast outdoors, in the shady garden.

Prices not confirmed for 2008　**Nearby** ⚓ 10km ⚲ 25km ✐ 1km ⚞ 12km ⚐ 4km ⚑ 2.5km ⚒ 11km　**Notes** No pets　Open 15 March to 15 October.

CHERVAL

⧼⧼⧼ **Les Pouyades**

Thérèse et Jean-Marie TRUFFAUX

24320 CHERVAL

☎ 05 53 91 02 96 & SR : 05 53 35 50 01

▤ 05 53 91 02 96

email: sla24@wanadoo.fr

web: www.resinfrance.com/perigord/

This late 19th-century mansion is set in spacious shady grounds on the edge of Le Périgord Vert, in an area known for its Romanesque churches. There are two twin bedrooms and one double, all with their own facilities. An extra bed is available. A generous breakfast is provided, and there is a restaurant nearby.

Prices s fr €75; d €80-€90; extra person fr €20　**Nearby** ⚓ 5km ⚲ 25km ✐ 10km ⚞ 5km Restaurant 5km ⚑ 2km ⚐ 5km ⚒ 40km **Notes** No pets　English spoken

LA CHAPELLE-FAUCHER

⧼⧼⧼ ⊺◎⊺ **Tierchâteau**

Joëlle et Claude BORLOZ

24530 LA CHAPELLE-FAUCHER

☎ 05 53 55 31 90 & SR : 05 53 35 50 01

▤ 05 53 35 50 41

email: claude.borloz@wanadoo.fr

web: www.resinfrance.com/perigord/

In a calm and relaxing spot in the open countryside, near the tourist sites of Périgord Vert. Three rooms with a double and single bed, each with private facilities and possible cot are available in a warm and friendly atmosphere. Lounge with TV, library, and games; garden with furniture. Freshly grown produce served at table d'hôte meals.

Prices s fr €32; d fr €42; t fr €52　**Nearby** ⚓ 12km ⚲ 30km ✐ 4km ⚞ 10km ⚑ 4km ⚐ 10km ⚒ 13km　**Notes** Pets admitted

LA GONTERIE-BOULOUNEIX

⧼⧼⧼ ⊺◎⊺ **Le Coudert**

C et C-B MAGRIN

24310 LA GONTERIE-BOULOUNEIX

☎ 05 53 05 75 30 & SR : 05 53 35 50 01

▤ 05 53 35 50 41

web: www.resinfrance.com/perigord/

A warm welcome, calm and relaxation are assured at this pretty country farmhouse in the heart of the Périgord Vert region. There are three double bedrooms, each with private facilities. An extra bed is also available on request. Canoeing available nearby.

Prices s fr €42; d fr €47; extra person fr €10; dinner fr €17 **Nearby** ⚓ 9km ⚲ 30km ✐ 7km ⚞ 7km Restaurant 6km ⚑ 7km ⚞ 7km ⚐ 7km ⚒ 30km　**Notes** No pets　Open February to December.

LISLE

⧼⧼⧼ ⊺◎⊺ **La Picandine**

Armelle et Olivier LACOURT

24350 LISLE

☎ 05 53 03 41 93 & SR : 05 53 35 50 01

▤ 05 53 03 28 43

email: picandine@aol.com

web: www.picandine.com

This 17th-century farmhouse in a peaceful countryside location has a family atmosphere and provides two double bedrooms, a triple, a room with single bed and double on a mezzanine floor and a suite of two bedrooms (one double and one twin), all with private facilities. Extra single bed and child's bed on request. Sitting room with TV, library, board games, billiard table, terrace and laundry. Evening meals by prior arrangement.

Prices s fr €41; d fr €51; t fr €67; extra person fr €14; dinner fr €21 **On Site** Private ⚞　**Nearby** ⚓ 12km ⚲ 12km ✐ 5km Restaurant 5km ⚑ 5km ⚞ 20km ⚐ 5km ⚒ 20km　**Notes** No pets　English spoken Open 15 February to 15 November.

MENESPLET

⧼⧼⧼ ⊺◎⊺ ⚷ *Les Loges*

M-D et C BERTHIER

24700 MENESPLET

☎ 05 53 81 84 39 & SR : 05 53 35 50 01

▤ 05 53 81 62 74

email: campgite.ber@perigord.tm.fr

web: www.resinfrance.com/perigord/

This house is set in seven hectares of parkland with stables and a stream. There is a twin bedroom and two triples with disabled access and private facilities. An extra bed can be provided. Library, board games, TV available, lovely garden with furniture and activities for children: volleyball, boules, swings, sandpit, table football and table tennis. Wine route 8 km; forest 3 km.

Prices not confirmed for 2008　**Nearby** ⚓ 7km ✐ 3km ⚞ 7km ⚑ 3km ⚐ 7km ⚒ 7km　**Notes** No pets

AQUITAINE

MONTFERRAND-DU-PERIGORD

₩₩ |O| Chambre d'hôtes

J et J-M BELGARRIC

Boulègue, 24440 MONTFERRAND-DU-PERIGORD

☎ 05 53 63 26 42 & SR : 05 53 35 50 01

🖹 05 53 63 26 42

email: jeanmarc.belgarric@aliceadsl.fr

This typical welcoming Périgord house lies in the Couze Valley, at the heart of the Bastide region. There are five double rooms, one with twin beds; child's bed on request. Sitting room with library and TV, terrace area with garden furniture, regional cooking with vegetables from the garden. Near the GR36 walking route and footpaths.

Prices s fr €40; d fr €44; extra person fr €16 **Nearby** ☝ 8km
♨ 20km ✍ 5km ➹ 12km Restaurant 1km ☒ 5km ☖ 5km ₩ 8km
Notes No pets Open March to November.

NAUSSANNES

₩₩ Le Chant des Oiseaux

Brigitte et Christian LE GROS

Le Bourg, 24440 NAUSSANNES

☎ 05 53 27 35 09 & SR : 05 53 35 50 01

🖹 05 53 35 50 41

email: legros.brigitte@wanadoo.fr

web: www.le-chant-des-oiseaux.com

This renovated 15th-century farmhouse, set in a shady landscaped garden, offers peaceful accommodation close to the Route des Vins. There are two double-bedded rooms, and a family suite of two double-bedded rooms, all with their own facilities (extra bed available on request). The welcoming owners provide a wonderful breakfast, with home-made jams and pastries. There is a restaurant close by. Pets only accepted on request.

Prices s fr €64; d fr €64; t fr €98 **On Site** Private ➹ **Nearby** ☝ 5km
♨ 5km ✍ 10km Restaurant 1km ☒ 3km ✾ 10km ☖ 4km ₩ 25km
Notes Pets admitted English spoken Open 3 January to 20 December.

PAULIN

₩₩ |O| ₺ Lou Cantou

Catherine et Michel STEVAUX

Le Pech, 24590 PAULIN

☎ 05 53 30 39 27 & SR : 05 53 35 50 01

🖹 05 53 30 39 27

email: loucantou1@tele2.fr

web: www.resinfrance.com/perigord/dp000620

This old, restored blacksmith's forge in the heart of Périgord Nord, near to Quercy, is an ideal starting point for visiting the tourist sites of the Dordogne. There are two double bedrooms and two twins, each with a shower room and wc. Extra bed on request and evening meals by reservation.

Prices s fr €48; d fr €52; t fr €70; extra person fr €18; dinner fr €20
Nearby ☝ 15km ♨ 15km ✍ 10km ➹ 5km Restaurant 1km ☒ 10km
✾ 20km ☖ 5km ₩ 20km **Notes** Pets admitted English spoken

PROISSANS

₩₩ ✿ |O| Chez Michel

Jeanine et Jacques FUMAT

24200 PROISSANS

☎ 05 53 59 11 79 & SR : 05 53 35 50 01

🖹 05 53 35 50 41

email: jacques.fumat@club-internet.fr

web: www.resinfrance.com/perigord/

This country house, in the heart of Black Perigord, is near to a farm that produces tobacco, cereal crops and raises poultry. There are three double rooms, including one twin room, and two rooms for three people; each with shower room and wc. Three bedrooms are in the annexe. There is a lounge, and a peaceful atmosphere is guaranteed. Near the châteaux of the Dordogne and many tourist sites.

Prices s fr €45; d fr €50; t fr €64 **Nearby** ☝ 10km ♨ 10km ✍ 1km
Restaurant 2km ☒ 2km ☖ 7km ₩ 25km **Notes** No pets Open April to October.

₩₩ ✿ Les Anglards

Isabelle et Thierry VILATTE

24200 PROISSANS

☎ 05 53 29 47 36 & SR : 05 53 35 50 01

🖹 05 53 59 36 72

email: isabelle.vilatte@wanadoo.fr

web: www.resinfrance.com/perigord/

In the heart of the Périgord Noir, this old barn has been restored using the local stone. There is a double and three rooms with a double and single bed, each with a shower room and wc. Cot on request. Sitting room with TV, library and open fireplace, terrace with garden furniture. Private ponds available for fishing. Tobacco, corn, asparagus and walnuts are grown on site. Restaurant and farm inn nearby.

Prices s fr €45; d fr €45; t fr €55 **On Site** ✍ Private ➹
Nearby ☝ 4km ♨ 5km ☒ 1km ☖ 5km ₩ 5km **Notes** No pets

ST-ANDRE-D'ALLAS

₩₩ Les Filolies

Adrienne et Patrick LANCAUCHEZ

24200 ST-ANDRE-D'ALLAS

☎ 05 53 30 31 84 & SR : 05 53 35 50 01

🖹 05 53 30 31 84

email: lesfilolies@hotmail.com

web: www.lesfilolies.com

This old renovated post office lies at the heart of the Périgord Nord within a two-hectare park, bordered by woods and fields, and close to Sarlat and the Dordogne Valley. There are two double bedrooms and two triples, each with private facilities (cot available). Large, varied breakfasts of local produce. Garden with furniture. Rambling, cycling. Restaurant and farm inn nearby.

Prices s fr €47; d fr €51; t fr €64 **On Site** ✾ Private ➹ **Nearby** ☝ 10km
♨ 10km ✍ 10km Restaurant 5km ☒ 3km ☖ 2km ₩ 7km **Notes** No pets
English spoken Open 12 February to 10 November.

ST-PARDOUX-LA-RIVIERE

⦂⦂⦂ ⦿ Fompeyrinière

Jeanine et Jacques VANDAMME

Lapeyronnie, 24470 ST-PARDOUX-LA-RIVIERE

☎ 05 53 60 53 30 & SR : 05 53 35 50 01

▤ 05 53 60 53 30

This old restored farmhouse lies in a charming hamlet, with a wonderful view over lush countryside and a relaxing atmosphere. There are three double rooms and a twin, each shower room and wc. Sitting room with TV, library, board games, terrace and leafy garden. Walks in the high forests or in the Dronne Valley, châteaux nearby and bathing in the pond. Evening meals on request.

Prices s fr €38; d fr €44; dinner fr €18 **Nearby** ♿ 10km ♨ 45km ⟋ 2km ⤳ 10km Restaurant 1.2km ⩊ 10km ⚑ 20km ⌕ 1.2km ⛟ 20km **Notes** No pets

ST-REMY-SUR-LIDOIRE

⦂⦂⦂ *La Mouthe*

Marie-Ange CAIGNARD

24700 ST-REMY-SUR-LIDOIRE

☎ 06 71 52 73 42 & SR : 05 53 35 50 01

email: lamoutheperigord@wanadoo.fr

web: www.resinfrance.com/perigord/

Situated between Bergerac and St-âmilion on 20 hectares of land with vineyards, forests, a pond for fishing, and footpaths. There are two comfortable double bedrooms and one twin, each with private access from the terrace, shower room, wc and individual décor. A cot can be provided on request. Library; board games; telephone; restaurant, farm inn and stables nearby.

Prices not confirmed for 2008 **On Site** ⟋ Private ⤳ **Nearby** ♿ 4km ♨ 25km ⩊ 3km ⌕ 4km ⛟ 11km **Notes** Pets admitted English spoken

VAUNAC

⦂⦂⦂ ❧ Les Guézoux

Béatrice et Pierre FOUQUET

24800 VAUNAC

☎ 05 53 62 06 39 & SR : 05 53 35 50 01

▤ 05 53 62 88 74

email: escargot.perigord@wanadoo.fr

web: www.escargotduperigord.com

This stone farmhouse lies in a lovely, peaceful, wooded area. Guests receive a warm welcome and can learn about snail breeding and tasting. Two double bedrooms and one with a double bed and single bed area with private facilities (cot provided on request). Large breakfasts feature local produce and home-made jams. There is a shady terrace area and a restaurant nearby.

Prices s fr €40.50; d fr €46; t €57-€59.50 **On Site** Private ⤳ **Nearby** ♿ 7km ♨ 25km ⟋ 5km Restaurant 2km ⩊ 3km ⚑ 7km ⌕ 6km ⛟ 6km **Notes** Pets admitted English spoken CC

GIRONDE

AILLAS

⦂⦂⦂ ⦿ Janoutic

Jean Pierre DOEBELE

2, Le Tach, 33124 AILLAS

☎ 05 56 65 32 58 & 06 07 57 74 42 ▤ 05 56 65 33 55

email: jpdoebel@club-internet.fr

web: www.chambresdhotesjanoutic.com

A pretty 19th-century red brick house, typical of the area. It is situated in a hamlet, in its own landscaped grounds, complete with a terrace. On the ground floor is a double bedroom with a bathroom and WC; on the first floor are a further two double rooms, and a shower room with WC.

Prices s fr €45; d fr €55; extra person fr €17; dinner fr €20 **Nearby** ♿ 5km ♨ 25km ⟋ 5km ⤳ 13km Restaurant 8km ⩊ 2km ⌕ 2km ⛟ 13km **Notes** Pets admitted

ANDERNOS

⦂⦂⦂ *Chambre d'hôtes*

Françoise SORET BEDEXAGAR

84, Av J. Marcel Despagne, 33510 ANDERNOS

☎ 05 56 82 56 73 & 06 74 94 54 21 ▤ 05 56 82 56 73

email: soret-francoise@free.fr

This old 19th-century grange, near the owners' house, is typical of this area, and lies near the Arcachon basin. There are two two-person rooms and two triples with shower room and wc. Breakfast room on the veranda (high chair available), large, enclosed garden, terrace and parking.

Prices not confirmed for 2008 **Nearby** ♿ 1.5km ♨ 6km Sea 7km ⟋ 1km ⤳ 1km Restaurant 1km ⩊ 0.8km ⌕ 0.8km ⛟ 10km **Notes** Pets admitted English spoken

⦂⦂⦂ Les Albatros

Jacques MALFERE

10, boulevard de Verdun, 33510 ANDERNOS

☎ 05 56 82 04 46

email: jmalfere@club-internet.fr

web: www.lesalbatros.com

This mid 20th-century house is located very near the Arcachon beaches, in an enclosed country garden surrounded by beautiful countryside and local architecture. There are two themed double bedrooms and a family room for two to four people, each with private facilities. Lounge/dining room, TV, garden furniture, barbecue and summer cooking area with terrace.

Prices s fr €58; d €67-€74; t fr €80 **Nearby** ♿ 2km ♨ 5km Sea 0.1km ⟋ 0.2km ⤳ 0.3km Restaurant 0.5km ⩊ 2km ⌕ 0.6km ⛟ 20km **Notes** No pets English spoken Open February to October.

ARBIS

⌗⌗⌗ Château le Vert

Claude et Martine IMHOFF

Route d'Escoussans, 33760 ARBIS

☎ 05 56 23 91 49 ▤ 05 56 23 91 49

This 19th-century château, in the heart of the Entre-Deux-Mers region, is attached to 13th- and 16th-century buildings and is surrounded by vines and meadows. There is a large twin room, two rooms with two bunk beds and a double suite in a separate wing with lounge; all with private facilities and TV. Swimming pool. Breakfast include home-made jam and farmhouse bread.

Prices d €85-€100 **On Site** Private ⊀ **Nearby** ⛵ 15km ⚓ 20km ⚓ 3km Restaurant 5km ⚓ 2km ⚑ 15km ⚓ 4km ⋙ 10km **Notes** No pets

ARES

⌗⌗⌗ Hameau des Mimosas

Josette et Edmond URTIZVEREA

2, allées des Arbousiers, 33740 ARES

☎ 05 56 82 43 68 & 06 83 35 67 15 ▤ 05 56 82 43 68

This modern house is in a hamlet, close to Cap Ferrat and beaches. There is a spacious double room with private shower/WC and garden access. The second room (Grade 2) is smaller, with its own shower and handbasin in the room, but the WC not en suite. Use of fridge. Peaceful setting, enclosed garden. Sailing school and cycle track nearby.

Prices s €45-€50; d €48-€55; extra person fr €17 **Nearby** ⛵ 4km ⚓ 8kmSea 0.5km ⚑ 0.5km ⊀ 4km Restaurant 1.5km ⚓ 1.5km ⚑ 1.5km ⋙ 26km **Notes** No pets

BALIZAC

⌗⌗⌗ ◎ Les Bordes

Laurent et Marie CHAMBON

1, les Bordes, 33730 BALIZAC

☎ 05 56 25 88 45 & 06 64 13 71 16

email: info@lesbordes.net

web: www.lesbordes.net

This house is right in the heart of the forest in the Parc Naturel des Landes de Gascogne. The four bedrooms comprise three doubles and a twin. The lounge/dining area is available for guests' use, and outside are extensive wooded grounds. Bikes available.

Prices s fr €45; d fr €50; dinner fr €15 **On Site** ⚑ **Nearby** ⛵ 2km ⚓ 20km ⊀ 6km Restaurant 6km ⚓ 2km ⚑ 6km ⋙ 20km **Notes** No pets English spoken

BARSAC

⌗⌗⌗ Chambre d'hôtes

Valérie CASASOLA

8, Campéros, 33720 BARSAC

☎ 05 56 27 15 47 & 06 87 53 71 45 ▤ 05 56 27 11 06

email: valerie.casasola@orange.fr

web: www.lesvignesdecamperos.com

An 18th-century mansion, on a wine-growing property in the Sauternes and Barsac region. There is a large landscaped garden with a swimming pool and beautiful vineyard views. There are two double rooms (one at Grade 2) and a twin-bedded room. All rooms have private facilities. A cot and high chair available. Guests' lounge, dining room and use of kitchen.

Prices s fr €57; d fr €62; t fr €77; extra person fr €15 **On Site** ⚑ Private ⊀ **Nearby** ⛵ 9km ⚓ 9km ⚑ 3km Restaurant 4km ⚓ 2km ⚑ 2km ⋙ 0.8km **Notes** No pets English spoken Open 10 March to November.

BEYCHAC-ET-CAILLAU

⌗⌗⌗ Domaine de Teynac

Valérie DUBOIS

22, Teynac, 33750 BEYCHAC ET CAILLAU

☎ 05 56 72 92 46

email: h-dubois2@wanadoo.fr

web: www.golf-teynac.com

An ideal spot for wine-drinking golfers - this 17th-century property is on an 18-hole golf course in the heart of the Bordeaux vineyards. There is a ground-floor room for three; upstairs is a double room, and a triple. Extra bed available. All rooms have a private bath or shower and WC. Gardens with attractive views.

Prices s fr €55; d fr €65; t fr €80; extra person fr €15 **On Site** ⚑ **Nearby** ⛵ 5km ⚑ 8km ⊀ 10km Restaurant 0.1km ⚓ 2km ⚑ 10km ⚑ 1.5km ⋙ 15km **Notes** No pets English spoken

AQUITAINE

BLAYE

ⅲ **Villa Prémayac**

Léa GOLIAS

13, rue Prémayac, 33390 BLAYE

☎ 06 07 79 64 05 & 05 57 42 27 39 📄 05 57 42 69 09

This 18th-century property is situated in the city of Blayé, near to the Citadel at Vauban and the Gironde estuary. There are four double bedrooms and one twin each with bathroom, wc and TV. There is also a lounge and tea room. Roman garden and enclosed zen garden. Parking nearby.

Prices d fr €90; extra person fr €10 **On Site** ℰ **Nearby** ⚘ 10km ♨ 35km ↗ 1km Restaurant 0.1km ♒ 1km ⌂ 0.1km ⊯ 20km **Notes** Pets admitted English spoken CC

BOSSUGAN

ⅲ ⦿ **Domaine de Barrouil**

Annie EHRSAM

33350 BOSSUGAN

☎ 05 57 40 59 12 📄 05 57 40 59 12

email: info@barrouil.com

web: www.barrouil.com

This 19th-century gentleman's house is in the heart of a vineyard, with well-tended garden and lovely valley views. The ground floor has the dining and sitting rooms, and one guest bedroom that sleeps three. Upstairs there is a double room plus a suite of two rooms with four single beds. All have shower and wc. Meals by arrangement.

Prices s €45-€70; d €50-€85; t €90-€100; extra person fr €20; dinner fr €25 **Nearby** ⚘ 9km ♨ 35km ℰ 4km ↗ 9km Restaurant 1km ♒ 4km ⌂ 3km ⊯ 9km **Notes** No pets English spoken

BOURG-SUR-GIRONDE

ⅲ ♿ **Le Petit Brésil**

Gérard GUERIN

26, le Pain de Sucre, 33710 BOURG SUR GIRONDE

☎ 05 57 68 23 42 & 06 70 34 24 45 📄 05 57 68 23 42

email: guerin.gite@free.fr

web: http://guerin.gite.free.fr/

There are five rooms in this renovated stone house among the vines of Côtes de Bourg on the Gironde estuary; there are lovely valley views from the terrace. On the ground floor is a double with bathroom/WC; upstairs are other doubles with shower and WC. Living room, library and parking.

Prices s €35-€45; d €40-€50; extra person €15 **On Site** ℰ **Nearby** ⚘ 10km ♨ 35km ↗ 2km Restaurant 2km ♒ 2km ⌚ 15km ⌂ 2km ⊯ 15km **Notes** No pets

CAMIRAN

ⅲ ⦿ **La Camiranaise**

Christelle GUY-GRAND

29, Les Faures, 33190 CAMIRAN

☎ 05 56 71 11 26 📄 05 56 71 15 38

email: lacamiranaise@wanadoo.fr

web: http://lacamiranaise.free.fr

A swimming pool is available in the enclosed grounds of this 19th-century barn conversion, which is situated in a small hamlet. There are two twin-bedded rooms on the ground floor, with private bathroom and WC; upstairs are a further three rooms. Meals are available by arrangement.

Prices d €65-€70; t €80-€85; extra person fr €10; dinner fr €20 **On Site** Private ↗ **Nearby** ⚘ 1km ♨ 20km ℰ 1km Restaurant 6km ♒ 1km ⌚ 6km ⌂ 6km ⊯ 6km **Notes** No pets English spoken

CAPIAN

ⅲ ⦿ **Château Grand Branet**

Blanche MAINVIELLE

859, Branet Sud, 33550 CAPIAN

☎ 05 56 72 17 30 & 06 89 42 97 34 📄 05 56 72 36 59

email: d.mainvielle@free.fr

web: http://chateauaugrandbranet.free.fr

This renovated 17th-century château lies in a large, peaceful, wooded park. There are five bedrooms with private facilities, two with communal terraces. Cot provided on request. There is a sitting room, TV, dining room and gallery area. Table tennis. Evening meals on reservation. Wine tasting. Kitchenette available.

Prices s fr €51; d fr €65; t fr €83; extra person fr €18; dinner fr €20 **Nearby** ⚘ 15km ♨ 30km ℰ 8km ↗ 7km Restaurant 9km ♒ 2km ⌚ 10km ⌂ 4km ⊯ 10km **Notes** Pets admitted English spoken

CASTELNAU-DE-MEDOC

₩₩ **Domaine de Carrat**

Laurence PERY

Route de Ste Hélène, 33480 CASTELNAU DE MEDOC

☎ 05 56 58 24 80 📄 05 56 58 24 80

This house has lots of character and is surrounded by woods and meadows with streams. It is a lovely, calm place to relax. There are three rooms including a twin and small suite with a twin and small bedroom for children, all with private facilities. A lounge, TV and kitchen for guest use. Closed Christmas.

Prices s fr €49; d €56-€62; t fr €82 **Nearby** ⛷ 5km ⚓ 10km Sea 25km ⚓ 25km ⚓ 25km Restaurant 5km ⚓ 1.5km Spa 10km ₩ 5km **Notes** Pets admitted English spoken

---

CASTILLON-LA-BATAILLE

₩₩ ♿ **Robin**

Pierrette MINTET

33350 CASTILLON LA BATAILLE

☎ 05 57 40 20 55 📄 05 57 40 20 55

email: pierrette.mintet@libertysurf.fr

This old restored house is situated on one of many wine-growing estates stretching over the valleys of the Dordogne and la Lidoire and is typical of the Gironde region. There are two doubles and a twin bedroom, each with private facilities, a dining/lounge room and hall area. Garden, terrace and veranda.

Prices s fr €45; d fr €50; t fr €63; extra person fr €15 **On Site** Private ⚓ **Nearby** ⛷ 2.5km ⚓ 2km ⚓ 2.5km Restaurant 2km ⚓ 2.5km Spa 10km ⛺ 2.5km ₩ 2.5km **Notes** No pets English spoken

---

CASTRES-SUR-GIRONDE

₩₩ **Le Moulin de Pommarede**

Béatrice DE BOUSSIERS

35, route de Pommarede, 33640 CASTRES-SUR-GIRONDE

☎ 05 56 67 31 28 & 06 67 22 66 08 📄 05 56 67 67 69

email: deboussiers@wanadoo.fr

web: www.pommarede.com

A 13th-century mill on the border of the Gât Mort, entirely restored, on a wine estate, with courtyard, terrace and grounds, and in the area around the Graves vineyards. There is a ground-floor living room and a twin guest bedroom with shower; upstairs are two rooms each for 2/3 people, with shower or bathroom. TV, fridge and microwave. Dogs are accepted by prior arrangement.

Prices s fr €67; d fr €67; t fr €84; extra person fr €17 **On Site** ⚓ **Nearby** ⛷ 2km ⚓ 20km Sea 40km ⚓ 17km Restaurant 1km ⚓ 1km ⛺ 1km ₩ 1.5km **Notes** Pets admitted English spoken

CEZAC

₩₩ ⦿ *Château la Hateau la Baronnerie*

M. BATARD

Sci la Baronnerie, 1, la Baronnerie, 33620 CEZAC

☎ 05 57 68 12 22 & 06 60 02 64 28 📄 05 57 68 12 10

email: la.baronnerie@wanadoo.fr

web: www.labaronnerie.net

Right in the heart of a vineyard, this restored 19th-century manor house has three bedrooms, each with internet access and en suite facilities. There is a large lounge area for guests, and meals are available by arrangement (except weekends). Swimming pool with pool house and shower; attractive walks possible through the vineyards.

Prices not confirmed for 2008 **On Site** Private ⚓ **Nearby** ⛷ 5km ⚓ 25km ⚓ 6km Restaurant 2.5km ⚓ 2.5km ⛺ 2.5km ₩ 3.5km **Notes** No pets English spoken

---

COUTRAS

₩₩ ♥ **Château Le Baudou**

Philippe et M.Christ HEFTRE

Le Baudou, 33230 COUTRAS

☎ 05 57 49 16 33 & 06 11 14 73 72 📄 05 57 49 16 33

email: le.baudou@wanadoo.fr

web: www.chateaulebaudou.com

This restored 18th-century home is situated in four hectares of parkland, woods, meadows and orchards. There is a double room and a room with double and single bed, both with private facilities and access. Lounge/dining room with fireplace, board games, library and table tennis. Terrace and parking.

Prices d €65-€105; extra person fr €20 **Nearby** ⛷ 3km ⚓ 20km ⚓ 0.5km ⚓ 1.3km Restaurant 1.3km ⚓ 1.3km ⛽ 16km ⛺ 1.3km ₩ 1.5km **Notes** No pets English spoken

---

EYNESSE

₩₩ ⦿ *Aux Trois Fontaines*

Catherine COLARDELLE

27, La Beysse, 33220 EYNESSE

☎ 05 57 41 02 28 & 06 80 35 12 32 📄 05 57 41 02 28

email: colardel@club-internet.fr

web: www.auxtroisfontaines.com

This 19th-century house in the Dordogne Valley has views over the vineyards and is set in large grounds with enclosed courtyard, terrace and garden furniture. Rooms, in an annexe, include a triple with kitchen area, three double rooms (one Grade 2) and a room for 2-4 people, all with private facilities. Sitting room with TV, billiard room, fireplace and dining room. Evening meals on request. Pets admitted under certain conditions.

Prices not confirmed for 2008 **On Site** Private ⚓ **Nearby** ⛷ 3km ⚓ 15km ⚓ 1km Restaurant 8km ⚓ 7km ⛺ 7km ₩ 7km **Notes** Pets admitted English spoken

ⅲⅲ ⅼ◎ⅼ **Le Grand Renom**

Francine SERAS

Manoir Le Grand Renom, 33220 EYNESSE

☎ 05 57 41 02 10 & 06 11 56 34 72

email: augrandrenom@tele2.fr

web: www.augrandrenom.com

This 19th-century manor house lies amongst the vines in a shady park. There is a sitting room, dining room and three double bedrooms and a triple, each with shower room or bathroom and wc.

Prices d €52-€55; t fr €72; extra person fr €20; dinner fr €20
Nearby ⚡ 6km ⅃ 15km ⌔ 2km ⚲ 6km Restaurant 7km ⚘ 6km
⚑ 7km 🏠 2km ⋙ 7km **Notes** No pets

FARGUES-DE-LANGON

ⅲⅲ ⅼ◎ⅼ **Les Acanthes**

Claude et Maryse GENVRIN

16, rte de Mounic, 33210 FARGUES DE LANGON

☎ 05 56 63 05 33

email: claude.genvrin@wanadoo.fr

web: www.gite-prop.com/33/33201

A 19th-century manor house in a hamlet in the Sauternes wine-growing region, close to the edge of the Landes forest. There are three bedrooms, a double and two twins, with a private upstairs terrace area. On the ground floor is a lounge, a music room with piano, and a kitchen area for guest use. Meals by arrangement; swimming pool.

Prices d €70-€75; t €90-€95; extra person fr €20; dinner fr €25 **On Site** ⚑ Private ⚲ **Nearby** ⚡ 1km ⅃ 4km ⌔ 5km Restaurant 3km ⚘ 1km 🏠 3km ⋙ 3km **Notes** No pets English spoken

GAJAC-DE-BAZAS

ⅲⅲ *Cabirol*

Xavier DIONIS DU SEJOUR

33430 GAJAC DE BAZAS

☎ 05 56 25 15 29 & 06 12 75 23 95 📄 05 56 25 15 29

email: dominique.dionis@free.fr

In the heart of the countryside, this restored 18th-century house is typical of the region. There are four two-person bedrooms, each with private facilities and a sitting room/dining room/library leading out onto a terrace. Large country garden, parking. Games room, billiard table and table tennis. Special rates for groups and stays over four nights.

Prices not confirmed for 2008 **On Site** Private ⚲ **Nearby** ⚡ 4km ⅃ 20km ⌔ 1km Restaurant 4km ⚘ 4km 🏠 4km ⋙ 15km **Notes** No pets English spoken

GANS

ⅲⅲ ⅼ◎ⅼ *Domaine du Bouchon*

Thierry DE LA PRADE

Catalot, 33430 GANS

☎ 05 56 65 11 97

email: domaine-du-bouchon@cario.fr

This 19th-century mansion stands in its own grounds above the village. On the ground floor it has a lounge, a dining room, and two double bedrooms. There are two more double rooms upstairs. All of the rooms have private showers and WCs. Grounds, garden with a terrace. Meals available with 48 hours notice.

Prices not confirmed for 2008 **On Site** Private ⚲ **Nearby** ⚡ 0.5km ⅃ 17km ⌔ 2km Restaurant 5km ⚘ 5km 🏠 5km ⋙ 17km **Notes** Pets admitted

ILLATS

ⅲⅲ ⅼ◎ⅼ **La Milleva**

Sabine BOLZAN

10, Barrouil Ouest, 33720 ILLATS

☎ 05 56 27 00 63 & 06 17 95 27 11 📄 05 56 27 00 63

email: lamilleva@wanadoo.fr

web: www.lamilleva.com

Peacefully situated in a quiet hamlet in the Sauternes, this pretty 19th-century house, built in the local style, has extensive grounds and a swimming pool. There are four spacious double rooms, two on the ground floor and two upstairs, all with en suite facilities. Extra single beds are available. Meals available by arrangement.

Prices s fr €60; d fr €66; extra person fr €23; dinner fr €35 **On Site** Private ⚲ **Nearby** ⚡ 7km ⅃ 15km ⌔ 6km Restaurant 4km ⚘ 5km ⚑ 10km 🏠 4km ⋙ 4km **Notes** No pets English spoken

ⅲⅲ ⅼ◎ⅼ **La Vignereine**

Claude et Michèle BRAY

1, Le Mouréou, 33720 ILLATS

☎ 05 56 27 14 33 & 06 07 47 98 41 📄 05 56 27 14 33

email: la.vignereine@wanadoo.fr

web: www.lavignereine.com

An old wine-makers house, situated in the vineyards of Graves and Sauternais between Cérons and Barsac. It offers a double with cot, two rooms with a double and single, and one with a double and two singles, each with private facilities. Dining room and lounge corner. Table d'hôte meals by reservation.

Prices s fr €45; d fr €57; t fr €72; extra person fr €15; dinner €15-€22 **On Site** ⚑ Private ⚲ **Nearby** ⚡ 16km ⅃ 16km ⌔ 5km Restaurant 4km ⚘ 3km 🏠 4km ⋙ 3km **Notes** Pets admitted English spoken

AQUITAINE

LA RIVIERE

▦ Château la Rivière

James GREGOIRE
SNC Armonia, 33126 LA RIVIERE
☎ 05 57 55 56 51 & 05 57 55 56 56
📄 05 57 55 56 54
email: reception@chateau-de-la-riviere.com
web: www.chateau-de-la-riviere.com

Standing on the site of a defensive camp established by
Charlemagne, this château was built in the 16th century and
restored in the 19th. It is now a wine estate, with 60 hectares of
vineyards and three vast cellars holding 900 barrels of wine. It
has five bedrooms, all with private facilities. Swimming pool and
tennis court in extensive grounds.

Prices s €130-€170; d €150-€190; extra person fr €20
On Site Private ⚓ ⚒ **Nearby** ⚓ 5km ⚒ 24km ⚐ 2km
Restaurant 1km ⚒ ⛫ 4km ⚑ 8km **Notes** No pets English spoken
CC

LISTRAC-MEDOC

▦ ⚘ Château Cap Léon Veyrin

Maryse MEYRE
33480 LISTRAC MEDOC
☎ 05 56 58 07 28 📄 05 56 58 07 50
email: capleonveyrin@aol.com
web: www.vignoble-meyer.com

This refined house has been renovated and lies within vineyards (cru
Bourgeois du Médoc). There are five bedrooms each sleeping two
people with private facilities, a large lounge, dining room with fireplace
and TV. Washing machine, barbecue and telephone. Visit the owners'
wine cellar and taste the wines. There is a forest and river nearby.

Prices s fr €39; d fr €44; t fr €55 **Nearby** ⚓ 5km ⚒ 20km Sea 30km
⚐ 3km ⚓ 10km Restaurant 3km ⚒ 2km ⛫ 10km ⛫ 3km ⚑ 5km
Notes No pets English spoken

MIOS

▦ Les Tilleuls

M. LAGOUEYTE-COUGET
17 bis, rue des Ecoles, 33380 MIOS
☎ 05 56 26 67 85 & 06 14 39 22 54 📄 05 56 26 49 35
email: gitemios@club-internet.fr
web: www.gitemios.free.fr

Situated in a village, in the heart of the Landes de Gascogne Regional
Park and near the Arcachon Basin. Rooms are in the old outbuildings
of this manor house, built in the local Arcachon style and dating back
to the early 1900s. There is a suite with a double bedroom and a twin,
and two double rooms, all with private facilities. TV, video and library.
Large, tree-lined garden and parking area.

Prices s €49-€52; d €52-€58; t fr €73; extra person fr €15
Nearby ⚓ 1km ⚒ 15km Sea 20km ⚐ 0.5km ⚓ 11km Restaurant 0.5km
⚒ 0.3km ⛫ 0.5km ⚑ 4km **Notes** No pets
Open May to 1 November.

MOULIS

▦ 🍴 Domaine Quittignan Brillette

Pascale MERCEUR
Av de la Gironde, Le Bourg Ouest, 33480 MOULIS
☎ 06 63 09 77 31 & 05 57 88 70 48 📄 05 57 88 70 48
email: contact.quittignanbrillette@wanadoo.fr
web: www.quittignanbrillette.com

This late 18th-century house is on the edge of a small town. In an
annexe to the owners' home, it has three bedrooms including a suite.
All have private facilities, and there is a guests' lounge. Outside are
enclosed gardens, covered parking and a swimming pool. A peaceful
spot, with easy access to many interesting places to visit.

Prices d fr €80; extra person fr €15; dinner fr €25 **On Site** Private ⚓
Nearby ⚓ 10km ⚒ 5km Sea 40km ⚐ 10km Restaurant 0.1km ⚒ 5km
⛫ 0.1km ⛫ 0.8km ⚑ 5km **Notes** No pets English spoken

NEAC

▦ Château Belles Graves

Xavier PITON
33500 NEAC
☎ 05 57 51 09 61 & 06 80 32 02 78 📄 05 57 51 01 41
email: x.piton@belles-graves.com
web: www.belles-graves.com

This very beautiful 18th-century former monastery is situated on the
slopes of the Barbane Valley. A terrace in the French-style garden
overlooks the renowned Pomerol vineyard, where wine tastings are
available. There is one ground-floor double bedroom; upstairs are a
twin bedroom, and another double. All rooms have private bath or
shower room, and WC. Library, and maze in the grounds.

Prices s €78-€93; d €85-€100; t fr €105 **On Site** ⚐ ⛫
Nearby ⚓ 5km ⚒ 15km ⚓ 3km Restaurant 3km ⚒ 2km ⛫ 3km
⚑ 5km **Notes** No pets English spoken CC

PAUILLAC

▦ Lou Bercail

Dany HAUSELMANN
26, Grande Rue, St Lambert, 33250 PAUILLAC
☎ 05 57 75 28 04 & 06 82 01 22 97
email: loubercail@wanadoo.fr
web: www.lou-bercail.com

This stone-built 19th-century house is in a small hamlet at the heart of
the Médoc wine-growing region. It has three upstairs bedrooms which
can sleep from two to four people, and a further (Grade 2) twin-
bedded room. All have private bath/shower room and WC. Enclosed
gardens with picnic tables and BBQ available, along with parking
space. Wi-fi available.

Prices s €58-€65; d €60-€68; extra person fr €15 **On Site** Private ⚓
Nearby ⚓ 7km ⚒ 31km Sea 25km ⚐ 2km Restaurant 1.2km ⚒ 2km
⛫ 1.5km ⛫ 1.5km ⚑ 4km **Notes** No pets English spoken

PESSAC-SUR-DORDOGNE

⦀ 🌱 🍽 ♿ Château de Carbonneau

J/W FRANC DE FERRIERE

33890 PESSAC SUR DORDOGNE

☎ 05 57 47 46 46 🖷 05 57 47 42 26

email: carbonneau@wanadoo.fr

web: www.chateau-carbonneau.com

Situated on a winegrowers' estate, this 19th-century château has an amazing conservatory and is surrounded by parkland and vineyards. There are five double rooms, all with private facilities. Lounge, dining room and parking.

Prices s €75-€85; d €85-€95; extra person fr €15; dinner fr €22 **On Site** Private ↖ **Nearby** ⛵ 5km ♨ 20km ♬ 3km Restaurant 2km ♨ 2km ♣ 2km ⓕ 2km ⋈ 12km **Notes** No pets English spoken Open March to November CC

PUJOLS-SUR-DORDOGNE

⦀ 🍽 Les Gues Rivières

Margotte et Olivier BERNARD

5, place du Général de Gaulle,

33350 PUJOLS SUR DORDOGNE

☎ 05 57 40 74 73 & 06 70 52 32 07 🖷 05 57 40 73 26

email: margotte.olivier@wanadoo.fr

web: http://perso.wanadoo.fr/margotte.olivier/

A pretty 19th-century Gironde house in the heart of a village near L'Entre-Deux-Mers and Côtes de Castillon. Enclosed landscaped garden with covered terrace, lounge and dining room available to guests. Rooms with private facilities include a king size room, a large room with a king size (converts to twins) and two singles and a suite with a king size and two singles.

Prices d fr €65; t fr €85; extra person fr €20; dinner fr €23 **On Site** ♨ ♣ **Nearby** ⛵ 4km ♨ 15km ♬ 4km ↖ 6km Restaurant 0.1km ♨ ⓕ 0.1km ⋈ 6km **Notes** No pets English spoken

RIONS

⦀ Château Salins

Marie-Claude GAY

33410 RIONS

☎ 05 56 62 92 09 🖷 05 56 76 90 75

email: chateausalins@wanadoo.fr

web: http://chateausalins.monsite.wanadoo.fr

A wine-growing property on the edge of a medieval village on the right bank of the Garonne, this 17th-century house offers a twin-bedded room, and two doubles - all with private shower room/WC and internet access. Billiard room. Wooded grounds with ancient trees and enclosed parking.

Prices d fr €57; extra person fr €18 **On Site** Private ↖ **Nearby** ⛵ 12km ♨ 15km ♬ 0.2km Restaurant 0.1km ♨ 0.2km Spa 50km ⓕ 0.3km ⋈ 5km **Notes** No pets English spoken Open April to November.

⦀ Château du Broustaret

M. BRUNET

33410 RIONS

☎ 05 56 62 96 97 🖷 05 56 76 93 73

email: broustaret@libertysurf.fr

web: www.broustaret.net

A beautiful country house in its own grounds, with lots of character and views over the vineyards and woods. There are five bedrooms, doubles and triples, all with private bath or shower rooms and WCs. There is a day room for guests, with kitchenette, high chair and ironing board.

Prices s €50-€55; d €50-€55; t €60-€65; extra person fr €10 **On Site** ♬ **Nearby** ♨ 20km ↖ 5km Restaurant 5km ♨ 5km ⓕ 5km ⋈ 8km **Notes** No pets Open Easter to 1 November.

SADIRAC-CREON

⦀ ♿ Le Prieuré de Mouquet

Pierre MARCHIVE

6, chemin de Mouquet, 33670 SADIRAC-CREON

☎ 05 56 23 26 57 & 06 22 56 48 48 🖷 05 56 23 26 57

email: p.marchive@wanadoo.fr

web: www.prieure-de-mouquet.com

This former 16th-century priory, with its internal courtyard and covered terrace, is situated in the heart of the Entre-Deux-Mers region. It has a suite for up to four people, with a double bed and a bed-settee; another suite for four with two double beds; and two double rooms. All of the rooms have private facilities. Wooded grounds, swimming pool.

Prices d €60-€74; t €75-€89; extra person fr €15 **On Site** Private ↖ **Nearby** ⛵ 0.1km ♨ 10km ♬ 10km Restaurant 0.5km ♨ 5km ♣ 0.5km ⓕ 1km ⋈ 30km **Notes** No pets English spoken

SALIGNAC

⦀ *Chambre d'hôtes*

Francis FORT

7, Laubertrie, 33240 SALIGNAC

☎ 05 57 43 48 00 & 06 07 21 66 67 🖷 05 57 43 67 19

email: laubertrie@wanadoo.fr

In a hamlet, situated between vines and woodland, this 19th-century house has a large semi-enclosed garden, with a lake and a covered terrace. On the ground floor is a double bedroom, with dressing-room; upstairs is another double room and a room for three people (one double and one single bed). All rooms have private facilities. Music room, library/TV room, billiard room.

Prices not confirmed for 2008 **On Site** Private ↖ **Nearby** ⛵ 5km ♨ 30km Sea 15km ♬ 4km Restaurant 6km ♨ 3km ⓕ 2km ⋈ 8km **Notes** No pets English spoken

ST-BRICE

▦ ⋈ **La Maison Chevalier**

Elisabeth et Alain FREDOU

11 bourg sud, 33540 SAINT BRICE

☎ 05 56 71 65 22

email: maison.chevalier@wanadoo.fr

web: www.caruso33.net

This beautiful house, with a terrace and garden, is situated in the countryside on a winegrower's estate. There is a lovely view over the coast, lakes and woods and fishing nearby. The three large, light rooms sleep two to three people, each with private facilities. Dining room, small kitchen with an annexe room for meals. Reduction for longer stays.

Prices s fr €35; d fr €45; extra person fr €17; dinner fr €17 **On Site** ⌂
Nearby ⛵ 15km ↧ 35km ⌕ 7km ⤢ 4km Restaurant 1.5km ⌂ ⛳ 5km
⌂ 0.2km ⋈ 18km **Notes** No pets English spoken

ST-CAPRAIS-DE-BORDEAUX

▦ ⋈ **Château Sogeant**

Florence et Jacques BOREL

30, route de Cenac-BP7,

33880 ST CAPRAIS DE BORDEAUX

☎ 05 56 20 71 20 ▤ 05 56 20 01 10

email: contact@chateausogeant.com

web: www.chateausogeant.com

Built on the ruins of a medieval château, this property stands in 15 hectares of grounds in the Entre-Deux-Mers wine-growing region. A beautiful stone staircase leads from the entrance hall to three upstairs bedrooms and two suites, all with telephone, private bath/shower room and WC. Outside guests can enjoy the French-style gardens. Meals by reservation only.

Prices s fr €120; d €140-€180; t fr €200; extra person fr €20; dinner
fr €45 **On Site** Private ⤢ **Nearby** ⛵ 5km ↧ 15km Restaurant 5km
⌂ 0.7km ⌂ 0.7km ⋈ 15km **Notes** No pets English spoken

ST-CIERS-DE-CANESSE

▦ *Château Rousselle*

Vincent LEMAITRE

33710 ST CIERS DE CANESSE

☎ 05 57 42 16 62 ▤ 05 57 42 19 51

email: chateau@chateaurousselle.com

web: www.chateaurousselle.com

In the heart of the Côtes de Bourg and Côtes de Blaye vineyards, the guest rooms at this property are in the annexe of a 19th-century château. There is a spacious double room, a twin-bedded room, and a split-level room for four, with a double bed and two singles. All the rooms have private bathrooms and WCs.

Prices not confirmed for 2008 **Nearby** ⛵ 15km ↧ 35km ⌕ 2km
Restaurant 4km ⌂ 1.5km ⌂ 4km ⋈ 20km **Notes** Pets admitted English
spoken CC

▦ **Château les Tours de Seguy**

J François et M Agnès BRETON

2, le Seguy, 33710 ST CIERS DE CANESSE

☎ 05 57 64 99 57 & 06 72 70 59 32

email: chateau-les-tours-seguy@wanadoo.fr

web: www.chateau-les-tours-seguy.com

This property consists of a 19th-century château and an adjacent 18th-century mansion. There are three double rooms (two on the ground floor) and a large room for three, with a double bed and a single. All rooms have a private bath or shower room and WC. Baby equipment available. Breakfast served in the dining room, which opens onto the garden.

Prices s €50-€55; d €54-€59; t fr €75; extra person fr €15
Nearby ⛵ 15km ↧ 35km ⌕ 12km ⤢ 9km Restaurant 5km ⌂ 6km
⌂ 5km ⋈ 21km **Notes** No pets English spoken CC

ST-EMILION

▦ **Château Meylet**

Marie France FAVARD

La Gomerie, 33330 ST EMILION

☎ 05 57 24 68 85 ▤ 05 57 24 77 35

email: chateau.meylet@free.fr

web: http://chateau.meylet.free.fr

This renovated 18th-century Gironde house is on a winegrower's estate in the St-Emilion wine region. Two double rooms (extra bed possible) and two triples (one is on a mezzanine level). Rooms have private facilities and antique furnishings; there is a private entrance, day room, sitting room, TV, small kitchen, garden, shady terrace and parking. Stays over three nights include use of bicycles, a washing machine, tumble dryer and ironing room. 8% reduction over 7 nights.

Prices s €46-€58; d €52-€58; t €68-€72; extra person fr €10 **On Site** ⛳
Nearby ⛵ 15km ↧ 10km ⌕ 15km ⤢ 6km Restaurant 1.5km ⌂ 6km
⌂ 1.5km ⋈ 3km **Notes** Pets admitted English spoken

▦ **Château Millaud Montlabert**

Claude BRIEUX

33330 ST EMILION

☎ 05 57 24 71 85 ▤ 05 57 24 62 78

email: claude.brieux@wanadoo.fr

A typical Gironde 18th-century family home offering three two-person attic rooms, a triple with a TV and cot and another large room for two people, all with private facilities. Dining room with lounge area and fireplace, sitting room/library with TV, kitchen and dining room. Situated on a winegrower's estate, near Saint-Emilion and Pomerol. Wine tasting.

Prices s fr €48; d €55-€60; t fr €75; extra person fr €25
Nearby ⛵ 3.5km ↧ 30km ⌕ 3.5km ⤢ 1.5km Restaurant 0.5km ⌂ 3km
Spa 0.5km ⌂ 3.5km ⋈ 3.5km **Notes** No pets English spoken Open
March to December.

ST-GERMAIN-DE-LA-RIVIERE

⋕⋕⋕ Château de l'Escarderie

Bénédicte CLAVERIE

2, rue Goffre, 33240 ST GERMAIN DE LA RIVIERE

☎ 05 57 84 46 28 ▤ 05 57 84 46 28

email: lescarderie@free.fr

web: http://lescarderie.free.fr

A small château, in the middle of the Fronsadais coastline, with walking routes and woody parkland surrounding. The four bedrooms have private bathrooms and include three rooms for two, one with balcony and private terrace, and a room suitable for three to four people (twin beds). Dining room and lounge leading onto a lovely terrace area.

Prices s fr €60; d fr €70; t fr €90   **On Site** ☂ **Nearby** ⛵ 8km ⛷45km ⚘ 3km ⚓ 3km Restaurant 0.5km ◔ 3km ▣ 3km ♨ 10km **Notes** No pets English spoken

ST-MARIENS

⋕⋕⋕ Château de Gourdet

Yvonne et Daniel CHARTIER

33620 ST MARIENS

☎ 05 57 58 05 37 & 06 14 42 50 10 ▤ 05 57 58 05 37

email: chateau.gourdet@free.fr

This beautiful 18th-century home lies on the Blaye coast, on a small vineyard. There are three en suite bedrooms for two to three people, a dining room and lounge. Beds for small children available. Horses are reared on this property and there are many walking routes from the house. This is a lovely, calm spot with a beautiful view across vineyards and forests.

Prices s fr €45; d fr €50; extra person fr €15   **Nearby** ⛵ 3km ⛷15km ⚘ 4km ⚓ 16km Restaurant 5km ◔ 4km ▣ 5km ▣ 3km ♨ 1.5km **Notes** No pets

ST-MARTIN-DE-LERM

⋕⋕⋕ ⃔◯⃕ La Lézardière

Marie Hélène MATTEI

33540 ST MARTIN DE LERM

☎ 05 56 71 30 12

email: lalezardiere@free.fr

web: http://lalezardiere.free.fr

These restored old stables at a 17th-century smallholding offer four bedrooms for 2-3 people with private facilities. There is a sitting room, dining room, library, fireplace, cot and high chair. Table tennis, terrace, large garden and parking. Stables opposite the fortified windmills of Loubens and Bagas, halfway between St-Emilion and Sauternes. Children's meals available.

Prices s fr €50; d fr €65; t fr €80; extra person fr €10; dinner fr €20 **On Site** ⚘ Private ⚓ **Nearby** ⛵ 1km ⛷18km Restaurant 6km ◔ 6km ▣ 6km ♨ 6km **Notes** Pets admitted English spoken

ST-MICHEL-DE-FRONSAC

⋕⋕⋕ Closerie Saint Michel

Marie-Christine AGUERRE

1 Larriveau, 33126 ST MICHEL DE FRONSAC

☎ 05 57 24 95 81 ▤ 05 57 24 95 30

email: contact@laclosseriedefronsac.com

web: www.laclosseriedefronsac.com

This old 17th-century house is situated on a small wine-producing property, on which guests may taste and purchase wines. The two 2/3 person bedrooms are attached to the proprietor's house with independent access and private facilities. There is a dining room with lounge, kitchen area and open fireplace, a terrace, parking and garden. Bordeaux is 30 minutes away.

Prices s fr €87; d fr €97-€117; extra person fr €30   **Nearby** ⛵ 2km ⛷10km ⚓ 5km Restaurant 1km ◔ 1.5km ▣ 5km ▣ 1km ♨ 6km **Notes** No pets English spoken CC

ST-PHILIPPE-D'AIGUILLE

⋕⋕⋕ Chambre d'hôtes

Christine LECOMTE

2, le Sac, 33350 ST PHILIPPE D'AIGUILLE

☎ 08 72 43 25 15 & 06 27 76 12 61 ▤ 05 57 40 62 30

email: christine.lecomte1@free.fr

web: www.lapetitegirondine.fr

A beautiful 18th-century house, close to the site of the Battle of Castillon which marked the end of the 100 Years War. There are two double rooms on the ground floor, while upstairs there is another double, and a suite with two double beds. All have private facilities, and there is a guests' lounge. Garden, patio, swimming pool. Good walking country.

Prices d €55-€90; t fr €106; extra person fr €16   **On Site** Private ⚓ **Nearby** ⛵ 3km ⛷25km ⚘ 20km Restaurant 10km ◔ 1km Spa 10km ▣ 7km ▣ 7km ♨ 7km **Notes** Pets admitted English spoken

ST-SEURIN-DE-CADOURNE

⋕⋕⋕ ⃔◯⃕ Real

Violaine LAPEYRERE

6, Rue Clément Lemaignan,

33180 ST SEURIN DE CADOURNE

☎ 05 56 59 31 04 ▤ 05 56 59 31 04

email: real-en-medoc@wanadoo.fr

web: http://perso.wanadoo.fr/real-en-medoc

Six generations in the care of the same family have given this house, built in 1800, a very special quality. There are two double bedrooms, one on the first floor and one on the second with a balcony and wonderful views over the vineyard. Both rooms are delightfully arranged and decorated, with private bath/shower and WC. Landscaped gardens with a swimming pool.

Prices s fr €55; d fr €64; t fr €80; extra person fr €15; dinner fr €23 **On Site** ▣ Private ⚓ **Nearby** ⛵ 20km ⛷40km Sea 30km ⚘ 3km Restaurant 12km ◔ 0.5km ▣ 0.3km ♨ 12km **Notes** No pets English spoken CC

ST-SEVE

▦ ◉ Domaine de la Charmaie

France CHAVEROU

33190 ST SEVE

☎ 05 56 61 10 72 ▤ 05 56 61 10 72

email: lacharmaie@hotmail.com

web: http://monsite.wanadoo.fr/domainedelacharmaie

A 12th-century manor house with two two-person bedrooms and a twin room, each with private facilities. There is also a sitting room with fireplace, dining room, TV, billiard room and library. Set in a three-hectare park with walking, horse riding and cycling routes.

Prices d €70-€105; dinner fr €28 **On Site** Private ↖
Nearby ☀4km ♨18km ♠4km Restaurant 4km ☺4km ⌂4km
⋙4km **Notes** No pets English spoken

ST-YZANS-DE-MEDOC

▦ ♥ Château la Hourqueyre

Corinne BATAILLEY

42, rue de la Hourqueyre, 33340 ST YZANS DE MEDOC

☎ 05 56 09 05 10 & 06 72 88 68 14

email: corinbat@wanadoo.fr

An old 19th-century house on a vineyard, between Fleuve and the sea. Accommodation comprises a double room, a twin and a king-size each with private facilities, and guests have use of the lounge, dining room and enclosed garden with garage. Reductions for stays longer than one night.

Prices s €46-€48; d €51-€53; extra person €15-€18 **Nearby** ☀10km
Sea 25km ♠2km ↖10km Restaurant 4km ☺4km ⌂1km ⋙10km
Notes Pets admitted English spoken

▦ ◉ Le Moulin

Michèle POGNOT

5, route de Queyzans, 33340 ST YZANS DE MEDOC

☎ 05 56 09 02 80 ▤ 05 56 09 02 80

email: contact@medoc-hote.com

web: www.medoc-hote.com

Dating from the 18th-century and totally renovated, this former miller's house has a tower and is set in a park at the heart of a Médoc vineyard, on a small wine-producing property. Four pretty king-size rooms with private facilities, a lounge/dining room and large terrace available to guests. Cot available.

Prices s fr €52; d fr €60; t fr €78; extra person fr €18; dinner fr €23
Nearby ☀10km ♨30km Sea 25km ♠2km ↖12km Restaurant 2km
☺2km ♥12km ⌂0.2km ⋙12km **Notes** No pets English spoken

STE-FOY-LA-LONGUE

▦ *Ferme de Mouline*

Daniel CARMAGNAT

Mme Lesley FLOOD, 33490 STE FOY LA LONGUE

☎ 05 56 76 44 25 ▤ 05 56 76 44 25

email: a2zagency@tiscali.fr

web: www.a2z-agency.com

Overlooking an expanse of vineyards, this farmhouse has been totally restored to offer four guest bedrooms. All are upstairs, with private bath or shower room, and each is decorated according to a theme. A kitchenette is available for guests' use. The medieval village of St-Macaire and the walled town of Sauveterre de Guyenne are both close by.

Prices not confirmed for 2008 **Nearby** ☀2km ♨9km ♠5km ↖7km
Restaurant 7km ☺2km ⌂7km ⋙7km **Notes** Pets admitted English spoken

VENDAYS-MONTALIVET

▦ La Cadichonne

Max BAHOUGNE

182, Le Dehes, 33930 VENDAYS MONTALIVET

☎ 05 56 41 70 54 ▤ 05 56 41 79 57

email: max.bahougne@libertysurf.fr

web: http://lacadichonne.chez.alice.fr

This beautiful 18th-century Médocaine-style house is situated in a large country garden in the heart of the countryside, in a forest area. There are three double bedrooms, shower room, wc and dining room.

Prices s €56-€62; d €62-€70; extra person fr €30 **On Site** Private ↖
Nearby ☀6km Sea 10km ♠10km Restaurant 2km ☺2km ♣2km
⌂2km ⋙12km **Notes** No pets English spoken Open May to October.

VERTHEUIL

▦ ◉ Château le Souley

Jean-Pierre CHIAMA

33180 VERTHEUIL

☎ 05 56 41 98 76 & 06 87 76 40 87

email: jpchiama@club-internet.fr

web: http://perso.club-internet.fr/jpchiama

This 19th-century house has been restored but retains its country atmosphere. Situated in large grounds, in a Médoc vineyard, there is a terrace with garden furniture and climbing vines. Three double rooms, a suite with one double and a twin room, all with private facilities. Dining room, sitting room/library, TV and fireplace. Evening meals by reservation.

Prices s €51-€55; d €58-€65; t €74-€83; extra person fr €16; dinner fr €22 **Nearby** ☀3km ♨25km Sea 30km ♠2km ↖10km
Restaurant 5km ☺10km ♣10km ⌂0.5km ⋙10km **Notes** No pets English spoken

VILLENAVE-DE-RIONS

ⵜ ⵦ **Les Batarelles**

Danielle et André TANDONNET

103, Deyma, 33550 VILLENAVE DE RIONS

☎ 05 56 72 16 08 & 06 08 28 42 54 🖹 05 56 72 16 08

email: tandonnet.danielle@wanadoo.fr

web: http://lesbatarelles.free.fr

An historic, restored house in the heart of the Entre-Deux-Mers and Cadillac vineyards with lounge/dining room, enclosed garden and terrace. There is a Grade 2 double room with shower and toilet. On the first floor is a twin room with shower, bath and toilet and a Grade 2 double with shower and toilet. Brunch is available on request and a kitchen is available for guests use.

Prices d €50-€60; extra person fr €20; dinner fr €30   **On Site** Private ⵗ
Nearby ⵜ 10km ⵌ 13km ⵦ 3km Restaurant 3km ⵗ 1km Spa 8km
ⵦ 5km ⵦ 4km ⵦ 6km   **Notes** Pets admitted

LANDES

ANGRESSE

ⵜ **Ty Boni**

Bernard et Bab BONIFACE

1831 route de Capbreton, 40150 ANGRESSE

☎ 05 58 43 98 75

email: info@ty-boni.com

web: www.ty-boni.com

Lovely shady garden with outdoor furniture and barbecue, rolling down towards a pond and swimming pool. Three pretty bedrooms with private bathrooms, (two of which have further rooms for two people attached). Kitchen, washing machine. 20 minutes from Biarritz and five from the beaches. Special rates off season and for extended stays.

Prices d fr €80; extra person fr €25   **On Site** ⵦ Private ⵗ
Nearby ⵜ 4km ⵌ 3km Sea 4km Restaurant 4km ⵗ 1.8km
Watersports 4km ⵦ 3km ⵦ 1.8km ⵦ 8km   **Notes** No pets English spoken

---

BELUS

ⵜ ⵦ **Maison Bel Air**

Alain et Françoise PARANT

Route de Cagnotte, 40300 BELUS

☎ 05 58 73 24 17 & 06 15 41 63 84 🖹 05 58 73 03 26

email: marie-francoise.parant@wanadoo.fr

web: www.maison-belair.com

In the highest village in the Landes, in an area renowned for its gastronomy and tourist attractions, this restored 18th-century mansion has three spacious bedrooms. It also offers a family suite sleeping four. All rooms have private bath or shower rooms with WC.

Prices s fr €45; d fr €50; t fr €65; extra person fr €15; dinner fr €18
On Site ⵦ   **Nearby** ⵜ 10km ⵌ 20km Sea 20km ⵦ 6km ⵗ 6km
Restaurant 3km ⵗ 6km Spa 15km ⵦ 2km ⵦ 6km   **Notes** No pets

BETBEZER-D'ARMAGNAC

ⵜ ⵦ **Domaine de Paguy**

Albert DARZACQ

40240 BETBEZER D'ARMAGNAC

☎ 05 58 44 81 57 & 06 86 92 03 82 🖹 05 58 44 68 09

email: domaine-de-paguy@wanadoo.fr

The four rooms in this peaceful 16th-century property sleep up to three and have private shower rooms. The property has superb views over the vineyards and an open-air swimming pool. Also on site are a farm hotel, gîtes and the opportunity to purchase regional specialities.

Prices s €55-€63; d €58-€68; t €79-€85   **On Site** ⵦ Private ⵗ
Nearby ⵜ 15km ⵌ 25km ⵗ 5km ⵦ 4km ⵦ 32km   **Notes** No pets

CAMPET-ET-LAMOLERE

ⵜ ⵦ **Lamolère**

Béatrice DE MONREDON

SERVICE RESERVATION ACCUEIL LANDES

☎ 05 58 06 04 98 & 06 60 38 71 64 🖹 05 58 06 04 98

email: lamolere@wanadoo.fr

web: www.lamolere.net

This beautiful house has lots of character, and lies in the middle of 12 hectares of parkland, bordered by a river. There are four pretty bedrooms, one a two-bedroom suite, all with private facilities. Evening meals by reservation all year, except July and August.

Prices d €45-€60; extra person fr €15; dinner fr €20   **Nearby** ⵜ 1km
ⵌ 12km ⵦ 1km ⵗ 5km ⵗ 1km ⵦ 4km ⵦ 4km   **Notes** No pets
English spoken

CASTETS

ⵜ **Le Gahoun**

Nicole et Jacky AUBERT

2270 route de Cabillon, 40260 CASTETS

☎ 05 58 91 51 35 & 06 75 20 29 94 🖹 05 58 91 65 42

email: mathieu.aubert@wanadoo.fr

web: monsite.wanadoo.fr/legahoun/

This property stands in a vast clearing at the end of a forest road. It has four bedrooms and a suite, all attractively decorated, and can sleep up to ten guests. There is a kitchenette for guests' use; outside is a swimming pool. Beautiful peaceful surroundings.

Prices d fr €60; t fr €75; extra person fr €15   **On Site** Private ⵗ
Nearby ⵜ 5km ⵌ 19km Sea 18km ⵦ 5km Restaurant 2km ⵗ 3km
ⵦ 2km ⵦ 20km   **Notes** No pets English spoken

CREON-D'ARMAGNAC

⊞ ⊚ Le Poutic

Henri SUBRA

SERVICE RESERVATION ACCUEIL LANDES

☎ 05 58 44 66 97 & 06 66 44 92 19

email: lepoutic@wanadoo.fr

web: www.lepoutic.com

A charming farmhouse, totally restored, with a stone frontage and original timbers. It has three bright, spacious rooms, which have been furnished and decorated with an eye for detail and comfort. This property, in the heart of Armagnac, encourages relaxation.

Prices s fr €50; d €55-€62; t fr €70; extra person fr €14; dinner fr €20 **Nearby** ⚓ 8km ⚓ 19km ⚓ 2km ⚓ 5km Restaurant 5km ⚓ 5km Spa 5km ⚓ 1km ⚓ 25km **Notes** No pets English spoken CC

GAMARDE-LES-BAINS

⊞ ⊚ La Gamardaise

Romuald MILLOT

SERVICE RESERVATION ACCUEIL LANDES

☎ 05 58 98 62 79 ▤ 05 58 98 62 79

email: romualdmillot@aol.com

web: www.chambreslandes.com

This beautifully restored old property - a converted sheepfold - stands amongst fields of maize. There are three bedrooms, all decorated to individual themes, and non-smoking rooms are available. Outside, guests can enjoy the garden with its terrace and swimming pool along with a sauna and gym. Parking place.

Prices d fr €45; t fr €58; dinner fr €17 **On Site** ⚓ Private ⚓ **Nearby** ⚓ 4km ⚓ 40km Sea 40km ⚓ 4km ⚓ 4km ⚓ 4km ⚓ 17km **Notes** No pets English spoken

HERM

⊞ ⊚ Au Logis des Becs Fins

Jean Marc et Josée CATHERINEAU

370 route de Tachette, 40990 HERM

☎ 05 58 91 77 06 & 06 23 96 30 56 ▤ 05 58 91 77 06

email: becfin40@orange.fr

Deep in the countryside, yet close to the forest and beaches, this property offers beautifully decorated guest accommodation. There are two double bedrooms, a family room and a suite, all with private bath or shower room and WC. A large dining room with a beautiful fireplace is where meals can be served, by prior arrangement.

Prices d €50; t €62-€70; extra person fr €15; dinner fr €18 **Nearby** ⚓ 10km ⚓ 27km Sea 23km ⚓ 10km ⚓ 12km ⚓ 3km ⚓ 12km ⚓ 3km ⚓ 14km **Notes** Pets admitted English spoken

LESPERON

⊞ Chambre d'hôtes des Bruyères

Gilles et Nicole GONON

162, Allée des Bruyères, 40260 LESPERON

☎ 05 58 89 65 54 ▤ 05 58 89 65 54

email: gilles.gonon@tiscali.fr

There are three bedrooms with private bathrooms in this home, situated in a lovely, tranquil setting on the edge of a pine wood, 800 metres from the village and just two minutes from the beach. Breakfasts are served at a large communal table.

Prices d fr €52; extra person fr €25 **On Site** ⚓ **Nearby** ⚓ 15km ⚓ 25km Sea 20km ⚓ 15km Restaurant 0.8km ⚓ 10km ⚓ 0.8km ⚓ 15km **Notes** No pets

LINXE

⊞ La Palombiere

Nicole BOURGEOIS

89 route de Retgeyre, 40260 LINXE

☎ 06 77 81 59 64 ▤ 01 53 01 46 78

email: nd.bourgeois@free.fr

web: http://nd.bourgeois.free.fr

Just ten minutes from the sea, this beautiful 19th-century house has exposed beams and other interesting architectural features. There are three spacious upstairs bedrooms, all with private bath/shower room. A kitchenette is available, and there is Wi-fi internet access. Cot available.

Prices s €40-€60; d €55-€65; extra person €15-€20 **Nearby** ⚓ 10km ⚓ 15km Sea 11km ⚓ 10km ⚓ 27km Restaurant 0.3km ⚓ 1km ⚓ 0.3km ⚓ 0.3km ⚓ 27km **Notes** No pets English spoken

LUGLON

ⵀⵀⵀ ⵀⵀ Les Engoulevents

Jean-Guy RODRIGUEZ
SERVICE RESERVATION ACCUEIL LANDES
☎ 05 58 07 56 86
email: les.engoulevents@wanadoo.fr
web: http://perso.orange.fr/engoulevents

This old manor house has a timeless charm - a wonderful place to relax.It has been tastefully restored and stands in a hectare of grounds, surrounded by meadows where there are horses. There are five double bedrooms, all upstairs and four with private shower and WC, and one with a bath and WC plus a private garden. A cot is available.

Prices s fr €45; d €50-€70; t fr €90; extra person fr €15; dinner fr €20 **On Site** ⚑ **Nearby** ⚑ 35km Sea 45km ⚐ 15km ⟋ 8km ⟑ 1km
🏠 8km ⵀⵀ 30km **Notes** No pets

MAGESCQ

ⵀⵀⵀ *Le Cassouat*

Marlène DESBIEYS
314, Route d'Herm, 40140 MAGESCQ
☎ 05 58 47 71 55

This pleasant modern house, situated amongst oak trees, has four bedrooms. Possible use of a kitchenette. On site there is a lake with pedalos, and a stream where fishing is possible. Permanent water-colour exhibition in the house; reduced rate for stays of longer that two nights.

Prices not confirmed for 2008 **On Site** ⚐ **Nearby** ⚑ 15km ⚐ 15km
Sea 18km ⟋ 15km ⟑ 1.5km 🏠 1.5km ⵀⵀ 15km **Notes** Pets admitted
English spoken

MAYLIS

ⵀⵀⵀ ⵝ Saint Germain

Odile et Bernard RECURT
SERVICE RESERVATION ACCUEIL LANDES
☎ 05 58 97 72 89 📠 05 58 97 95 21
email: maylis@hotes-landes.com
web: www.hotes-landes.com

Guests can expect a warm welcome when visiting this beautiful, 17th-century family farm. Five bedrooms (for two to three people) with old fireplaces and private bathrooms. Cot available. Kitchen and fridge. Garden furniture outside.

Prices s fr €40; d fr €45; t fr €58; dinner fr €20 **Nearby** ⚑ 10km
⟋ 25km ⚐ 1km ⟑ 10km Restaurant 5km ⟑ 10km 🎣 10km 🏠 6km
ⵀⵀ 35km **Notes** No pets English spoken

MIMIZAN

ⵀⵀⵀ Simjan

Marie PLANTIER
SERVICE RESERVATION ACCUEIL LANDES
☎ 06 81 60 46 76 & 05 58 09 33 29 📠 05 58 09 01 47
email: simjan@club-internet.fr
web: www.simjan.com

This large art deco house, in the small forestry town of Mimizan, five kilometres from wide sandy beaches, is where Jean Cocteau found his inspiration. The house has two suites and two bedrooms, all with private facilities, and a library/TV room, all with Louis XV and XVI style decorations. Cot available on request.

Prices d €85-€100; t fr €100 **Nearby** ⚑ 5km ⟑ 3km Sea 5km ⚐ 3km
⟋ 0.1km Restaurant 0.2km ⟑ 4km 🎣 0.1km 🏠 0.2km ⵀⵀ 2.5km
Notes No pets Open 15 April to October

MORCENX-BOURG

ⵀⵀⵀ ⵀⵀ Château d'Agès

Christiane STEVENS KINTZ
40110 MORCENX BOURG
☎ 05 58 08 16 25 & 06 63 14 75 35
email: mail@chateaudages.com
web: www.chateaudages.com

A château dating back to the days of Napoleon III, standing in two hectares of grounds, bordered by a stream. There are four spacious guest rooms, one a family suite for four with two bedrooms and lounge. All have private facilities. Cot available. Meals by arrangement using organic products. Kennels available for dogs, also stabling for horses. Owners are bee-keepers.

Prices s €45-€55; d €60-€80; t fr €95; extra person fr €15; dinner fr €22
Nearby ⚑ 1km Sea 35km ⚐ 0.2km ⟑ 2km ⟑ 2km 🏠 2km ⵀⵀ 2km
Notes Pets admitted English spoken

ORTHEVIELLE

ⵀⵀⵀ ⵀⵀ Basta

Valérie TUR
SERVICE RESERVATION ACCUEIL LANDES
☎ 05 58 73 15 01 & 06 79 64 79 66 📠 05 58 73 15 01
email: basta.t@club-internet.fr
web: www.gite-basta.com

A beautiful 18th-century dwelling, calmly set in one hectare of grounds. The four spacious and comfortable rooms have private facilities. Table d'hôte meals are served, either on the terrace or the veranda. A warm and restful stay is assured, and cycling and table tennis are provided, with other sporting activities available nearby.

Prices s fr €49; d fr €53; extra person fr €13; dinner fr €20
On Site Private ⟑ **Nearby** ⚑ 10km ⟋ 25km Sea 28km ⚐ 7km
Restaurant 3km ⟑ 4km 🏠 3km ⵀⵀ 7km **Notes** No pets English spoken

OUSSE-SUZAN

♨♨♨ ⊙ Domaine d'Agès

Elisabeth HAYE

SERVICE RESERVATION ACCUEIL LANDES

☎ 05 58 51 82 28 📄 05 58 51 82 29

email: giteslandes@hotmail.fr

web: www.hotes-landes.fr

This old property lies in the heart of the Landaise forest, surrounded by horses, a swimming pool and old trees. There are three double bedrooms, each with bathrooms, two of which make up a suite. Large breakfasts and reserved evening meals are served in a pretty dining room. Cot available.

Prices s €56-€70; d €65-€77; extra person fr €20; dinner fr €22 **On Site** ♨ Private ⚲ **Nearby** ⚓ 10km ⚲ 20km Sea 45km ⚲ 10km ⚲ 2km 📷 5km ⚲⚲ 5km **Notes** Pets admitted English spoken

SABRES

♨♨♨ Le Plaisy

Gwenaëlle BACON

40630 SABRES

☎ 05 58 07 50 29 📄 05 58 07 50 29

Set in a lovely five-hectare park, peace is guaranteed at this manor house. There are three bedrooms, each with private facilities, a sitting room with TV, heating and swimming pool. Barbecue area, garden furniture. Breakfasts can be taken in the owners' dining room or on the terrace. Tennis and mountain biking nearby.

Prices d fr €50; t fr €63 **On Site** ⚲ Private ⚲ **Nearby** ⚓ 8km ⚲ 40km Sea 45km ⚲ 3km 📷 3km ⚲⚲ 18km **Notes** No pets English spoken Open May to October.

♨♨♨ Le Plaisy

Stéphane BACON

SERVICE RESERVATION ACCUEIL LANDES

☎ 05 58 07 56 92 & 06 86 08 40 87 📄 05 58 07 50 29

email: stephane.bacon@wanadoo.fr

Near to the eco-museum of Marquèze, in the heart of the Landes forest, this property enjoys a beautiful parkland setting with pond and private fishing. It has a swimming pool with a shelter, and a barbecue. It is a delightful house, simply and tastefully furnished offering three bedrooms, all with private facilities.

Prices d fr €50; extra person fr €13 **On Site** ⚲ Private ⚲ **Nearby** ⚓ 8km ⚲ 35km Sea 45km ⚲ 3km 📷 3km ⚲⚲ 20km **Notes** No pets

♨♨♨ ⊙ Les Arbousiers

Monique LABRI

Le Gaille, 40630 SABRES

☎ 05 58 07 52 52 & 06 81 13 28 09

email: lesarbousiers@aol.com

web: www.chambres-landes.com

A traditional building on a one hectare plot at the heart of the forest. There are five bedrooms with private facilities and showers, plus individual lounges and dining rooms. Calm and comfort are assured, as is a friendly, family atmosphere. Table d'hôte meals, served in the evenings by arrangement, are taken at one table with the proprietors.

Prices s fr €42; d fr €52; extra person fr €20; dinner fr €20 **On Site** Private ⚲ **Nearby** ⚓ 11km Sea 40km ⚲ 40km Restaurant 9km ⚲ 7km ⚲ 9km 📷 9km ⚲⚲ 15km **Notes** Pets admitted English spoken

SARBAZAN

♨♨♨ ⊙ Chambre d'hôtes

Stephanie BERGES

SERVICE RESERVATION ACCUEIL LANDES

☎ 05 58 45 75 92

email: berges.stephanie@wanadoo.fr

web: http://site.voila.fr/pratdessus

Calm and tranquillity are the watchwords in this estate surrounded by pine forests and fields. Each of the four rooms has either a private bath or shower room; between them they sleep up to eleven people. Guests can relax in the sauna, and evening meals can be booked.

Prices s fr €50; d fr €55; extra person fr €15; dinner fr €19 **On Site** Restaurant ♨ Private ⚲ **Nearby** ⚓ 5km ⚲ 1km ⚲ 1km ⚲⚲ 30km **Notes** Pets admitted English spoken Open 31 Mar-29 Oct

SAUBUSSE

♨♨♨ Bezincam

Claude DOURLET

Rte de l'Adour, 40180 SAUBUSSE LES BAINS

☎ 05 58 57 70 27 📄 05 58 57 70 27

email: dourlet.bezincam@tiscali.fr

A 19th-century dwelling, in a large quiet park with mature woodland on the edges of the Adour. Guests are offered a warm and personal welcome, and there are three two-person bedrooms with spacious, private bathrooms.

Prices s fr €60; d fr €70; t fr €90; extra person fr €20 **On Site** ⚲ ♨ **Nearby** ⚓ 5km ⚲ 18km Sea 18km ⚲ 1km Restaurant 0.6km ⚲ 1km 📷 1km ⚲⚲ 15km **Notes** No pets English spoken

SEIGNOSSE

ⵌ A l'Orée de la Forêt

Pascal FROESCH
40510 SEIGNOSSE
☎ 05 58 49 81 31 🖹 05 58 49 81 31
email: info@loreedelaforet.com
web: www.loreedelaforet.com

Calm and relaxation are guaranteed in this house, set in a pine forest. There are five bedrooms for two, three or four people (two are in a suite), each with private bathroom and access. Summer kitchen and garden available to guests. Special rates except July and August.

Prices s €54-€77; d €63-€87; extra person €20-€25 **On Site** 🏊 Private ⚲ **Nearby** ⛷ 3km ♨ 3km Sea 4km Restaurant 1km 🛒 1km ⛳ 4km 🎣 1km ⛵ 10km **Notes** No pets English spoken Open mid March-mid November.

ⵌ 🍴 L'Accalmie

Maria et Claude GIRARD
SERVICE RESERVATION ACCUEIL LANDES
☎ 05 58 49 84 10 & 06 72 24 82 43 🖹 05 58 49 84 10
email: accalmie40@wanadoo.fr
web: http://accalmie40.site.voila.fr

This modern house, adjacent to the forest and in its own grounds will guarantee a relaxing time. It has three very comfortable bedrooms, all beautifully arranged and with their private entrance. Each has its own shower room and WC, with direct access to the swimming pool and garden. Meals available by arrangement.

Prices not confirmed for 2008 **On Site** Private ⚲ **Nearby** ⛷ 5km ♨ 3km Sea 6km ⛳ 4km Restaurant 3km 🛒 4km ⛵ 3km 🎣 1.5km ⛵ 30km **Notes** No pets

SORE

ⵌ 🍴 ♿ La Bergerie de Pinot

Danièle DAMBON
SERVICE RESERVATION ACCUEIL LANDES
☎ 05 58 07 67 05 & 06 85 14 96 49
email: danielle.dambon@wanadoo.fr
web: www.chambres-pinot.com

This 19th-century farm has four charming double bedrooms in a sympathetically converted sheepfold. All rooms have private bath/shower room and WC. Meals can be served, by arrangement.

Prices s €48-€51; d €53-€56; dinner fr €20 **Nearby** ⛷ 18km ♨ 1km ⚲ 2km Restaurant 8km 🛒 2km 🎣 2km **Notes** Pets admitted

ⵌ 🍴 Le Moulin de Sore

Nathalie MELEY
SERVICE RESERVATION ACCUEIL LANDES
☎ 05 58 07 68 26 🖹 05 58 07 63 68
email: lemoulindesore@wanadoo.fr
web: www.lemoulindesore.fr

An interesting property - an old mill which has been restored in a contemporary style in keeping with the natural surroundings. Five guest bedrooms, four of which are upstairs: two doubles with single beds, each with shower room/WC; and three doubles, each with bath and WC. They have themed decoration based on the owner's travels. A cot is available, and meals can be provided by arrangement.

Prices s €46-€54; d €51-€59; extra person fr €16; dinner fr €18 **On Site** 🏊 Restaurant **Nearby** ⛷ 10km ♨ 40km Sea 45km ⚲ 1km 🛒 1km 🎣 0.8km ⛵ 35km **Notes** No pets English spoken

ST-GEIN

ⵌ 🍴 ♿ La Méniguère

Dominique MAJOURAU-POUYSUS
SERVICE RESERVATION ACCUEIL LANDES
☎ 05 58 03 27 55 & 06 12 52 88 73 🖹 05 58 03 27 55
email: lameniguere@orange.fr
web: www.lameniguere.com

Once a farm, this establishment situated by a stretch of water was restored around a former wine-store. It offers three rooms, one with disabled access, each no smoking with private facilities and separate access. Fridge available, cot on demand, parking. Table d'hôte meals by reservation. No animals allowed.

Prices s fr €65; d fr €70; t fr €85; dinner fr €30 **On Site** 🏊 Private ⚲ **Nearby** ⛷ 5km ♨ 30km Restaurant 1.3km 🛒 8km ⛳ 25km 🎣 1km ⛵ 19km **Notes** No pets English spoken

ST-JUSTIN

ⵌ 🍴 Pinchaou

Dominique et Jean DUBRANA
SERVICE RESERVATION ACCUEIL LANDES
☎ 05 58 44 68 96 & 06 62 35 06 39 🖹 05 58 44 68 96
email: jeandubrana@wanadoo.fr
web: www.gite-prop.com/40/50101

This farmhouse dates back to 1800, and is built in a style typical of the region. It stands in 22 hectares of meadows and woods. The four bedrooms, one of them a suite, all have private facilities. There is a spacious day room with lounge area and an open fire. Outside is a boules pitch, table-tennis and table football.

Prices s €42-€45; d €48-€50; t €63-€70; extra person fr €15; dinner fr €17 **Nearby** ⛷ 10km ♨ 30km ⚲ 5km ⛵ 20km 🛒 4km 🎣 8km ⛵ 32km **Notes** No pets

ST-MAURICE-SUR-L'ADOUR

ⅲ ⅰ⊙ⅰ **Trouilh**

Nadine VINIANE-SAVARY
SERVICE RESERVATION ACCUEIL LANDES
☎ 05 58 71 08 68
email: trouilh@tiscali.fr
web: www.trouilh.fr.fm

In a tree-lined rural setting, this restored characterful farmhouse offers three personalised and tastefully decorated rooms, including a suite for four people, each with private facilities and separate access. Table d'hôte meals by reservation. Cot and parking available.

Prices d €45-€50; t fr €65; extra person fr €15; dinner fr €20
On Site Sea **Nearby** ⚽ 4km ⚓ 10km ⚑ 3km ⚑ 4km Restaurant 4km ⚑ 4km Spa 10km ⚑ 4km ⚑ 10km **Notes** Pets admitted

TARNOS

ⅲ **Chambre d'hôtes**

André et Hélène LADEUIX
26, Rue Salvador Allendé, 40220 TARNOS
☎ 05 59 64 13 95 ⓘ 05 59 64 13 95
email: heleneladeuix@hotmail.com
web: www.enaquitaine.com

This large, tastefully furnished Basque house has a swimming pool and is surrounded by a quiet wood. Of the five bedrooms, four are in an annexe and have private bathroom and wc. Also a communal guest room, washing machine, mountain biking, swimming, table tennis and barbecues.

Prices d fr €75 **On Site** Private ⚑ **Nearby** ⚽ 5km ⚓ 10km Sea 5km ⚑ 5km Restaurant 3km ⚑ 0.5km Spa 10km ⚑ 3km ⚑ 0.3km ⚑ 3km
Notes No pets

ⅲ ⅰ⊙ⅰ **Ferme de Honzac**

Gilles HOURQUEBIE
SERVICE RESERVATION ACCUEIL LANDES
☎ 05 59 55 29 23 & 06 60 78 21 19 ⓘ 05 59 55 79 52
email: ferme-de-honzac@wanadoo.fr
web: http://perso.wanadoo.fr/fermedehonzac/

This former farmhouse has been fully restored and offers five double bedrooms. Non-smoking rooms available. The rooms have hairdryers, tea and coffee making facilities, and independent access. Cot and high chair available. Library, garden furniture, garage and washing machine. Meals available by reservation only.

Prices d €50-€63; extra person fr €16; dinner fr €21 **Nearby** ⚽ 8km ⚓ 8km Sea 9km ⚑ 2km ⚑ 5km Restaurant 3km ⚑ 5km Spa 14km ⚑ 3km ⚑ 7km **Notes** No pets English spoken Open February to 5 November. CC

TOSSE

ⅲ **Le Bosquet**

J.Pierre et Monique ARNAUDIN
rue du Hazan, 40230 TOSSE
☎ 05 58 43 03 40 ⓘ 05 58 43 04 68
email: jpm.arnaudin@wanadoo.fr
web: www.lebosquet-landes.com

This beautiful contemporary house is situated on the outskirts of the village 8km from the beach. Set in nearly 5 hectares of wooded land, the property has three pretty, double rooms, each with a private terrace, shower room and wc. There is garden furniture, table tennis, parking and footpaths in the village.

Prices s fr €40; d fr €48; extra person fr €15 **Nearby** ⚽ 3km ⚓ 5km Sea 8km ⚑ 3km ⚑ 10km Restaurant 0.1km ⚑ 0.1km ⚑ 0.1km ⚑ 4km **Notes** No pets

ASTAFFORT

ⅲ **La Fougère**

Michel ESTEBAN
Barbonvielle, 47220 ASTAFFORT
☎ 05 53 66 39 34 ⓘ 05 53 77 53 45
email: m.esteban@astaffort.com
web: www.astaffort.com/lafougere

On the St-Jacques-de-Compostella way in the Pays de Brulois, this renovated farmhouse offers two double rooms and two rooms with a double and single bed, each with private facilities and air-conditioning. Lounge with fireplace, books and games, large breakfasts with home-made jams. Tree-lined garden with swimming pool. 5km from Astaffort and 14km from Lectoure with thermal spa.

Prices s fr €55; d fr €55; extra person fr €20 **On Site** Private ⚑ Restaurant ⚑ **Nearby** ⚽ 3km ⚑ 3km ⚑ 5km ⚑ 20km **Notes** No pets English spoken Open May to October

AURADOU

ⅲ ⅰ⊙ⅰ **Le Roc**

Rémi et Françoise COMMANDRE
Le Jardin de la Paresse, 47140 AURADOU
☎ 06 88 27 97 93
email: remietfrancoise@aol.com
web: http://francoisetremi.free.fr

Expect a warm and friendly welcome at this 18th-century home. There is a room with a double bed and a single bed and en suite bathroom; two interconnecting rooms, (a double and a single) and a private bathroom; and two suites, both with a double room and a twin room with an extra bed available if required, and private facilities. South-western cooking and local wines.

Prices s €48-€56; d €53-€65; t €75-€86; extra person fr €15; dinner fr €23 **On Site** Private ⚑ **Nearby** ⚽ 5km ⚓ 10km ⚑ 5km Restaurant 6km ⚑ 4km Spa 25km ⚑ 6km ⚑ 4km **Notes** Pets admitted

BALEYSSAGUES

ⅠⅠⅠ ⅠOⅠ **Mounica**

Jocelyne PAZZAGLIA
Domaine du Pech, 47120 BALEYSSAGUES
☎ 05 53 83 33 52 & 06 81 39 46 55　📄 05 53 84 52 81
email: jocelyne.pazzaglia@wanadoo.fr
web: www.domaine-du-pech.com

House of character set in 1500 hectares of superb grounds and gardens. The comfortable rooms have been renovated exposing beams and flagstones and include two double rooms and one with a double and single bed, all with shower and wc. Also a separate family suite for four with a large lounge, bathroom and private terrace. Small private lounge. Mountain bikes, tennis, golf, horseriding all available nearby.

Prices s fr €48; d fr €53; t fr €77; extra person fr €21; dinner €16-€19 **On Site** Private ↘ **Nearby** ⚓ 3km ♨ 15km ✐ 1km Restaurant 3km ⊴ 3km Spa 40km ♞ 3km ⓢ 3km ⋙ 24km **Notes** No pets English spoken

BOUGLON

ⅠⅠⅠⅠ ⅠOⅠ **Le Mas de Campech**

Richard ANDREA
47250 BOUGLON
☎ 05 53 64 14 55
email: lemasdecampech@hotmail.fr
web: www.lemasdecampech.fr

At the top of the little commune of Bouglon, this restored 18th-century house is open all year. It has four charming grade 4 bedrooms with private facilities: two large family rooms, a double and a twin. Guest dining room and lounge with fireplace. TV, books, telephone. Evening meals, open terrace and garden room.

Prices s €85-€90; d €90-€95; t €105-€115; extra person fr €20; dinner fr €27 **On Site** Private ↘ **Nearby** ⚓ 8km ♨ 8km ✐ 1km Restaurant 8km ⊴ 8km Spa 8km ⓢ 0.8km ⋙ 15km **Notes** No pets

CASTELCULIER

ⅠⅠⅠ ⅠOⅠ **La Sevelotte**

Claudine et Jean DUPHIL
47240 CASTELCULIER
☎ 06 83 44 87 55
email: chateausevelotte@yahoo.fr
web: www.chateausevelotte-bnb.com

This 18th-century property has two double bedrooms, and a Grade 2 twin-bedded room. All of the rooms are upstairs; they are all well-appointed, and they all have private shower rooms and WCs; those for the Grade 2 room are not en suite. Large lounge with TV, small lounge with books; extensive grounds with garden furniture, swimming pool.

Prices s €45-€60; d €60-€70; dinner fr €23 **On Site** Private ↘ **Nearby** ⚓ 3km ♨ 7km ✐ 0.5km Restaurant 5km ⊴ 5km ⓢ 5km ⋙ 11km **Notes** No pets English spoken

CLAIRAC

ⅠⅠⅠ ♥ ⅠOⅠ **Caussinat**

Aimé et Gisèle MASSIAS
47320 CLAIRAC
☎ 05 53 84 22 11　📄 05 53 84 22 11

Accommodation comprises one double and one twin room rated Grade 3 with washbasins, sharing bathroom and wc and a twin and two double rooms rated Grade 1 with en suite facilities. Table tennis.

Prices s €38-€47; d €42-€51; t fr €69; extra person fr €18; dinner fr €18 **On Site** ♞ Private ↘ **Nearby** ⚓ 20km ♨ 15km ✐ 2km Restaurant 2km ⊴ 2km ⓢ 2km ⋙ 7km **Notes** No pets Open 15 April to 15 October. CC

COURBIAC

ⅠⅠⅠ ♥ ⅠOⅠ **Château de Rodie**

Paul HECQUET
47370 COURBIAC
☎ 05 53 40 89 24　📄 05 53 40 89 25
email: chateau.rodie@wanadoo.fr
web: www.chateauderodie.com

A 13th to 16th-century fortified castle restored to a warm family home, with vast living rooms and five beautiful bedrooms furnished with antiques: three double rooms; a suite in the round tower and a double room with living room and access to the watchtowers in the square tower. In an area full of sites of historic, natural and sporting interest, including a bird sanctuary and a rare breed of sheep.

Prices d €75-€106; t fr €88; extra person fr €18; dinner fr €15 **On Site** Private ↘ **Nearby** ⚓ 15km ♨ 30km ✐ 20km Restaurant 5km ⊴ 1km ♞ 5km ⓢ 5km ⋙ 40km **Notes** Pets admitted English spoken CC

DONDAS

⊪ ｜◎｜ **Gourraud**

Jean et Myriam MARTY
47470 DONDAS
☎ 05 53 95 43 11 📄 05 53 95 46 79
email: myriam@gite-marty.com
web: www.hotes-marty.com

In Pays de Serres, this peaceful 16th-century fortress has a large double room with cot, a room with a double and single bed and a suite with a large double and two twin beds, in a delightful alcove. All accommodation is en suite.

Prices s fr €70; d fr €90; t fr €110; extra person fr €20; dinner fr €40
On Site Restaurant 🌳 Private 🔾   **Nearby** ⛵ 8km ⌕ 15km 🎣 2km
🏛 8km ⋒ 20km   **Notes** Pets admitted   English spoken   CC

DOUDRAC

⊪ **Keur du Monde**

Jacques BODIN
Boulègue, 47210 DOUDRAC
☎ 05 53 71 74 08
email: keurdumonde47@aol.com
web: http://keurdumonde.monsite.orange.fr

An old farmhouse surrounded by meadows, this property has four guest bedrooms, all on the first floor. Two of the rooms are doubles; one has twin beds, and the fourth is a family suite for four, with a double bed and two singles. All have private facilities. Lounge, dining room with open fire, terrace, pétanque pitch, mountain bikes.

Prices s fr €42; d fr €47; t fr €57; extra person fr €5   **On Site** 🌳
Nearby ⛵ 5km ⌕ 20km 🎣 5km 🎣 5km 🏛 5km ⋒ 30km
Notes No pets   CC

DOUZAINS

⊪ 🐓 ｜◎｜ **Le Capy**

Thérèse JACQUOT
47330 DOUZAINS
☎ 05 53 36 83 68 📄 05 53 36 83 68
email: lecapy@yahoo.fr

Situated on the edge of the Périgord, in it own grounds with plenty of trees and flowers, this 18th-century mansion offers two double bedrooms, with private facilities. There is another room (grade 2) for up to four people which has its own bathroom, plus a private WC which is not directly accessed from the room. Barbecue, evening meals by arrangement.

Prices s €31-€34; d €36-€39; t €45-€48; extra person fr €10; dinner fr €14   **Nearby** ⛵ 3km ⌕ 18km 🎣 6km 🔾 4km Restaurant 4km 🎣 4km
🏛 4km ⋒ 28km   **Notes** Pets admitted   Open April to October.

DURAS

⊪ ｜◎｜ & **Botte**

Michel CHAUGIER
47120 DURAS
☎ 05 53 83 81 27 📄 05 53 83 81 27
email: michel.chaugier@wanadoo.fr
web: http://michel.chaugier.monsite.wanadoo.fr

Situated between the Dordogne and the vineyards of Bordelais, Duras is known for its castle, wines and prunes. This old restored house offers three rooms, one double, one with double and single bed, and one with three single beds. There is one bathroom and two shower rooms, stair-lift, library, veranda, garden with furniture and outdoor games. Gastronomic dinners on request, children's menu and picnic hampers.

Prices s fr €33; d fr €45; t fr €54; extra person fr €12; dinner fr €16
Nearby ⛵ 4km ⌕ 27km 🎣 0.6km 🔾 10km Restaurant 2km 🎣 4km
🌳 4km 🏛 4km ⋒ 25km   **Notes** No pets   English spoken   Open April to 1 November.

ENGAYRAC

⊪ **Le Rhodier**

Hélène et Olivier AILLET
Engayrac, 47470 BEAUVILLE
☎ 05 53 95 40 48 📄 05 53 95 40 48
email: o.aillet@wanadoo.fr
web: www.lerhodier.com

You will find three charming and comfortable rooms for two to four people, each with bathroom and WC, in this 18th-century squire's house in the heart of the Guyenne. Fenced pool with pool-house and kitchenette.

Prices s fr €50; d fr €65; extra person fr €20   **On Site** Restaurant
Private 🔾   **Nearby** ⛵ 3km ⌕ 25km 🎣 3km 🎣 3km 🏛 3km ⋒ 30km
Notes No pets   English spoken

GAVAUDUN

⁞⁞⁞ ⁞◎⁞ Domaine de Majoulassie

Guy FEVRY

47150 GAVAUDUN

☎ 05 53 40 34 64 📃 05 53 40 34 64

email: domaine.majoulassie@wanadoo.fr

web: www.villereal-tourisme.com/majoulassie

On the borders of a fishing lake, 1km from the village, this restored 17th-century windmill is situated in five hectares, with a pool. There is a family suite and four rooms on the first floor, each with private facilities and balcony. TV room with fireplace, terrace, park, boules, mountain biking and rock climbing nearby. Dinner available on request; picnics on site. Hunting dogs kept on the estate.

Prices s €40-€45; d €50-€60; t €68-€75; extra person fr €16; dinner fr €25 **On Site** 🏊 ⚐ Private ⚐ **Nearby** ⚓ 10km ⚓ 30km Restaurant 1km 🚲 5km 🏛 5km ⚓ 10km **Notes** Pets admitted English spoken

GRANGES-SUR-LOT

⁞⁞⁞ ⁞◎⁞ Chambre d'hôtes

Thierry JARDONNET

8, place Papon Lagrave, 47260 GRANGES-SUR-LOT

☎ 05 53 88 28 99 📃 05 53 88 01 90

email: thierry.jardonnet@wanadoo.fr

This is a big house, full of character, in a beautiful rural setting just a few minutes from Villeneuve-sur-Lot. There are two double bedrooms, each with private bathroom. A cot and high chair are available on request. Outside you will find a lot of greenery, some ancient fruit trees, roses and a vast kitchen garden.

Prices s fr €50; d fr €70; t fr €85; dinner fr €21 **Nearby** ⚓ 15km ⚓ 10km ⚓ 0.1km ⚓ 3km Restaurant 0.8km 🚲 0.5km 🏛 7km ⚓ 14km **Notes** No pets

LA SAUVETAT-SUR-LEDE

⁞⁞⁞ 🐓 ⁞◎⁞ Château Saint-Sulpice

Frédéric et June FILLIETTE

47150 LA SAUVETAT-SUR-LEDE

☎ 06 84 79 03 89

email: chateausaintsulpice@wanadoo.fr

web: www.chateausaintsulpice.com

In a calm valley of Lède, this 16th-century château is set on a mature, tree-lined park and offers a family atmosphere. It offers spacious and light rooms, full of character with old, period furniture, including a family suite for four, two rooms for two and two further family suites, each with private facilities. Table d'hôte meals are available by reservation and there are reductions for children. The proprietors raise horses for sport and produce foie gras.

Prices s fr €52; d €64-€78; dinner fr €25 **On Site** Private ⚐ **Nearby** ⚓ 6km ⚓ 5km ⚓ 6km Restaurant 3km 🚲 3km 🍷 6km 🏛 7km ⚓ 35km **Notes** No pets English spoken

LANNES

⁞⁞⁞ ⁞◎⁞ Château Brichot

P MAURER et I LAGARDE

47170 LANNES

☎ 05 53 65 47 82

email: chateaubrichot@free.fr

web: www.chateaubrichot.com

One of the oldest wine-growing châteaux in the region, this 18th-century residence is in the hills of Gascogne in Marmagnac. Very comfortable rooms are authentically furnished and include Médicis (double), Margot (king-size) and Fleurette (a suite with a double and single room), each with private facilities and TV on demand. Lounge with library, fireplace, billiards and dining rooms. Shady park with copse of rare trees. Guests may taste and buy Armagnac.

Prices d €130-€150; t fr €175; extra person fr €25; dinner fr €40 **On Site** Restaurant 🍷 Private ⚐ **Nearby** ⚓ 3km ⚓ 25km ⚓ 2km 🚲 6km 🏛 6km ⚓ 40km **Notes** No pets English spoken Open Easter to October.

LUSIGNAN-PETIT

⁞⁞⁞ Dantounet

P PALHORIES & A MARCHAIS

47360 LUSIGNAN-PETIT

☎ 05 53 66 63 98

email: palhomarc@wanadoo.fr

An 18th-century property standing among 12 hectares of woods, meadows and orchards. It has been faithfully restored by its owners, who will make you feel very welcome. The spacious bedrooms are all furnished with old family furniture. All of the rooms are doubles, and they all have private bathrooms and WCs. Extensive wooded grounds with swimming pool.

Prices s fr €65; d fr €75 **On Site** Private ⚐ **Nearby** ⚓ 16km ⚓ 10km ⚓ 3km 🚲 3km 🏛 4km ⚓ 10km **Notes** No pets CC

MADAILLAN

⁞⁞⁞ Chambre d'hôtes

Lina BERNINI

47360 MADAILLAN

☎ 05 53 87 55 66

Peaceful, undulating countryside provides the setting for this old property. It has three guest rooms, all of them upstairs. Two of them have double beds (one a small double), and the third has twin beds. Each room has a private bath or shower room and WC. Guests can enjoy their breakfast in the dining room, or outside on the enclosed terrace.

Prices s fr €45; d fr €55 **Nearby** ⚓ 6km ⚓ 22km ⚓ 9km ⚓ 6km Restaurant 8km 🚲 8km 🏛 5km ⚓ 15km **Notes** Pets admitted

AQUITAINE

MONCAUT

⋇ Manoir de Pouzergues

Christiane DOUBESKY
47310 MONCAUT
☎ 05 53 97 53 97 ▤ 05 53 97 15 25

This late 18th-century manor house in a peaceful setting, 10km from the airport, offers two double rooms with terraces, one suite with double and twin beds and another double room in the attic. All rooms have telephone, bathroom and kitchenette. There is a library, lounge with TV, conservatory and heated pool. Boat trips on the Baise Canal, walks in three hectares of park with old and rare trees. Local drinks tasting.

Prices s fr €65; d fr €72; t fr €106; extra person fr €34
On Site Private ⚲ **Nearby** ⛵ 6km ⚐ 15km ⚑ 10km Restaurant 5km
⚓ 4km ⛻ 4km ⋔ 12km **Notes** No pets Open 10 January to
23 December. CC

MONTAGNAC-SUR-AUVIGNON

⋇ ⧈ Laloubin

Marie-France AGUILERA
47600 MONTAGNAC-SUR-AUVIGNON
☎ 05 53 97 33 97
email: laloubin@wanadoo.fr
web: http://laloubin.monsite.orange.fr

18th-century house set in three shady hectares with spring and stream, close to a countryside village, in the hills of Albret. It has two rooms for two and a triple, each with private facilities. Lounge, library, TV, board games, dining room, covered terrace, garden furniture, barbecue, table tennis. Dinner by reservation, picnics possible for rambles. 16km from Agen with rambling and mountain bike trails; 12km from Nearc with its château and tourist attractions.

Prices s fr €42; d fr €52; extra person fr €15; dinner fr €22
Nearby ⛷ 12km ⚐ 20km ⚲ 12km Restaurant 12km ⚓ 12km Spa 30km
⛳ 20km ⛻ 0.3km ⋔ 15km **Notes** No pets English spoken

MONTAYRAL

⋇ ⧈ La Ferme de Myriam

Les Trembles, Av de Cézérac, 47500 MONTAYRAL
☎ 05 53 70 49 83 & 06 74 14 21 59
email: lafermedemyriam@lafermedemyriam.com
web: www.lafermedemyriam.com

This 19th-century farmhouse is in the heart of the Lot valley. There are two bedrooms, one a double and one a family room, with access via an external staircase. Both have private bath/shower room and WC. On the ground floor is a large lounge/dining room with open fire. Meals are available by arrangement, with regional dishes and garden produce.

Prices s fr €50; d fr €60; t fr €110; extra person fr €15; dinner fr €22
On Site Private ⚲ **Nearby** ⛷ 2km ⚐ 20km ⚑ 0.5km Restaurant 1.5km
⚓ 1.5km ⛳ 2km ⛻ 0.3km ⋔ 3km **Notes** Pets admitted English
spoken CC

NERAC

⋇ ⧈ Le Cauze

Isabelle POPE
Domaine du Cauze, 47600 NERAC
☎ 06 70 89 09 20
email: cauze.pope@wanadoo.fr
web: www.domaineducauze.com

In a peaceful setting of wooded parkland with commanding views, this ancient restored farmhouse has four double rooms each with shower and wc. Pool, large terrace with a summer house, large living room with billiards, satellite TV, piano, boules, table tennis and parking. Walks and places of interest nearby. Meals available on request.

Prices s fr €46; d fr €53; t fr €69; dinner fr €24 **On Site** Private ⚲
Nearby ⛷ 5km ⚐ 10km ⚑ 10km Restaurant 2km ⚓ 2km ⛻ 2km
⋔ 25km **Notes** No pets English spoken CC

⋇ ⧈ Ferme de Pehillo

Henry PICQUET
47600 NERAC
☎ 05 53 97 11 96 & 001 908 684 48 78
email: henrypicquet@aol.com
web: www.pehillo.info

This house has a peaceful setting in the heart of Gascony, in 17 hectares of grounds with plenty of trees and flowers. It has been sensitively restored, with exposed beams and stonework. There are three bedrooms: one with twin beds, and a further two twin-bedded rooms which make up a family suite for four. All have private bathroom and WC.

Prices s fr €40-€50; d fr €50-€60; t fr €70-€80; dinner fr €17 **On Site** ⛳
Private ⚲ **Nearby** ⚐ 10km ⚑ 4km Restaurant 3km ⚓ 4km ⛻ 3km
⋔ 33km **Notes** No pets English spoken

PRAYSSAS

⋇ Domaine du Roubillou

Françoise BOIDIN
Vignoble de Rebel, 47360 PRAYSSAS
☎ 05 53 47 14 30 ▤ 05 53 66 88 29
email: domaineduroubillou@clubinternet.fr
web: www.domaineduroubillou.com

Not far from Agen, this ancient property has four hectares of enclosed grounds, complete with a heated swimming pool. There are three air-conditioned bedrooms, all upstairs and all with private facilities. Two are doubles, one with a private terrace, and the third is a family room for three. Dining room, lounge and billiard room.

Prices s fr €75; d fr €85; t fr €95 **On Site** Private ⚲
Nearby ⛷ 2km ⚐ 5km ⚑ 0.3km Restaurant 2km ⚓ 2km ⛻ 2km
⋔ 7km **Notes** No pets English spoken Open Easter to November.
CC

SAMAZAN

ⅲ ⅰⓄⅰ Château de Cantet

Jean-Bernard DE LA RAITRIE

47250 SAMAZAN

☎ 05 53 20 60 60 & 06 09 86 68 77

email: jbdelaraitrie@wanadoo.fr

18th-century manor with a big park offering one suite of two rooms with separate shower and wc, one room with bathroom, wc and dressing room and a double with shower and wc. Activities include table tennis, croquet, badminton, French billiards and horse boxes available. Meals provided on request.

Prices s €55-€60; d €60-€75; t €85-€100; extra person fr €25; dinner fr €25 On Site ⚡ Private Nearby ⚓ 6km ⚓ 12km ⚓ 2km Restaurant 6km ⚓ 10km ⚓ 2km ⚓ 12km Notes No pets English spoken

ST-LEGER

ⅲ ⅰⓄⅰ Château de Grenier

Chantal BRETON-LE-GRELLE

47160 ST-LEGER

☎ 05 53 79 59 06 ᐧ 05 53 79 59 06

email: info@chateaudegrenier.com

web: www.chateaudegrenier.com

Full of character, this 18th-century residence is on the borders of the Pays d'Albret and Pays de Serres, set in a shady park. It offers three double rooms, a twin and a suite with two rooms for two, each with private facilities. Dinner (by reservation) and breakfast are served in the dining room overlooking the terrace. Lounge with fireplace, parking and painting classes. Route of bastides and châteaux, river walks and vineyards nearby.

Prices s fr €75; d fr €90; extra person fr €25; dinner fr €30 On Site ⚡ ⚓ Nearby ⚓ 8km ⚓ 20km ⚓ 3km Restaurant 4km ⚓ 3km ⚓ 3km ⚓ 3km Notes No pets English spoken

VIANNE

ⅲ La Maison Remparts de Jourdain

Luce et Roger BERNARD

47230 VIANNE

☎ 05 53 65 16 57

email: roger.bernard16@wanadoo.fr

Five en suite double rooms located in the south-western ramparts of a 13th-century renovated country house. Breakfast is served in rooms or out on the terrace. There are restaurants in the village and parking nearby. Living room with TV, games room and secret walled garden with a terrace.

Prices s fr €45; d fr €50; t fr €70; extra person fr €15 On Site ⚡ Nearby ⚓ 10km ⚓ 5km ⚓ 8km Restaurant 0.5km ⚓ 8km Spa 25km ⚓ 0.3km ⚓ 0.2km ⚓ 25km Notes Pets admitted

VILLEREAL

ⅲ ⅰⓄⅰ ⚬ Château du Rayet

Anne VAN HULLEBUS

47210 LE RAYET-VILLEREAL

☎ 05 53 36 76 63 ᐧ 05 53 36 76 63

email: chateaudurayet@wanadoo.fr

web: www.chateaudurayet.com

This is an 18th-century manor house with extensive grounds. The large bedrooms have been restored in traditional style, but with modern comforts. There are two doubles, and three family rooms for three. All have television, private bathroom and WC. Grounds with woods, fishpond and swimming pool. Meals are available two or three days a week. Conference room available.

Prices s fr €89; d fr €98; t fr €158; extra person fr €29; dinner fr €29 On Site ⚡ ⚓ Private Nearby ⚓ 8km ⚓ 15km Restaurant 3km ⚓ 3km ⚓ 3km ⚓ 25km Notes No pets English spoken

PYRÉNÉES-ATLANTIQUES

AAST

ⅲ Maison Rémy

Yves TUGAYE

64460 AAST

☎ 05 62 32 55 04 & 06 86 64 35 05

web: www.gites64.com/chez-remy

The three rooms here are tastefully decorated with exposed beams, open out onto the pool and with views of the Pyrenees. The dining room has an open fire and you will be warmly welcomed with a friendly drink.

Prices s fr €38; d fr €48; t fr €58 On Site Private Nearby ⚓ 12km ⚓ 18km ⚓ 3km Restaurant 5km ⚓ 40km ⚓ 5km Spa 40km ⚓ 18km ⚓ 5km ⚓ 17km Notes No pets

ACCOUS

ⅲ Maison L'Arrayade

J-F LESIRE

64490 ACCOUS

☎ 05 59 34 53 65 & 06 70 71 89 45 ᐧ 05 59 34 53 65

email: jean-francois.lesire@tele2.fr

web: http://chambresdhotes-larrayade.com

Large Bearnese house with sheltered garden in a peaceful village in the Aspe Valley region. The house has a kitchenette, television room, laundry, garden furniture and barbecue. There are also restaurants nearby and numerous activities in the village, including mountain biking, paragliding and walking.

Prices s fr €35; d fr €45 Nearby ⚓ 3km ⚓ 1km ⚓ 25km Restaurant 0.5km ⚓ 25km ⚓ 25km ⚓ 3km ⚓ 0.5km ⚓ 25km Notes Pets admitted English spoken

ARRIEN

⍾ La Picharotte

Alain FOUCART

1 chemin de la Picharotte, 64420 ARRIEN

☎ 05 59 04 19 75 & 06 30 54 02 02

email: alain@picharotte.fr

web: www.picharotte.fr

There are four guest rooms, for up to three people, in this family home which dates from the 19th century. You can enjoy superb views of the Pyrénèes from the terrace or beside the swimming pool. Alain, the host, is a wonderful raconteur, and will delight in telling you stories of the area or offering advice for excursions.

Prices s fr €50; d fr €55; t fr €75 **On Site** ⍦ Private ⚲ **Nearby** ⚵ 3km ⚶ 10km ⚯ 5km Restaurant 5km ⚱ 3km ⚸ 5km ⚹ 18km **Notes** No pets English spoken Open April to November.

ARZACQ

⍾ ⍥ ⚿ Chambre d'hôtes

Suzanne LANGLOIS

chemin de Saubole, 64410 ARZACQ

☎ 05 59 04 55 16 ⚏ 05 59 04 55 16

Three bedrooms, two doubles and a single, all with disabled access, are offered in this 18th-century house. Each room has an en suite shower room/WC, and a private terrace. The house has exposed beams and a lot of character. Outside, guests will find a pleasant courtyard with garden furniture and barbecue. Meals are available, by arrangement.

Prices s fr €28; d fr €35; dinner fr €13 **Nearby** ⚵ 30km ⚶ 30km ⚯ 2km ⚲ 2km Restaurant 2km ⚱ 2km ⚸ 2km ⚹ 35km **Notes** No pets English spoken

ASCAIN

⍾ Galardia

Tina VACQUIE

Col de St Ignace, 64310 ASCAIN

☎ 05 59 54 28 37

Located at the neck of Saint Ignace at the foot of La Rhune, guests will find peace and fresh air on the beaches and walks. Three rooms are available in this pretty Basque house, with living room and terrace.

Prices s fr €40; d fr €49; t fr €63; extra person fr €15 **Nearby** ⚵ 5km ⚶ 9km Sea 9km ⚲ 3km ⚱ 3km ⚸ 3km ⚹ 10km **Notes** No pets

⍾ ⚘ Haranederrea

J-L GRACY

64310 ASCAIN

☎ 05 59 54 00 23 ⚏ 05 59 54 00 23

This authentic Basque farmhouse is surrounded by meadows and woods, and has a lounge, library, ping-pong, private walled garden, terrace with flowers, and parking. There are four rooms with bathroom facilities. Spain 10km.

Prices s fr €44; d fr €54; t fr €65 **Nearby** ⚵ 3km ⚶ 5km Sea 5km ⚲ 1km Restaurant 2km ⚱ 1km ⚸ 0.5km ⚹ 5km **Notes** No pets Open January to November.

⍾ ⚘ Maison Arrayoa

A-M IBARBURU

64310 ASCAIN

☎ 05 59 54 06 18

A farmhouse near the charming village of Ascain, the coast and the Spanish border. Bedrooms provided include one twin and two double rooms with private facilities. Living room, TV room with fireplace, and car shelter. Home produced lamb and duck.

Prices s fr €42; d fr €55 **Nearby** ⚵ 6km ⚶ 6km Sea 6km ⚲ 0.6km Restaurant 0.6km ⚱ 0.6km Spa 6km ⚸ 0.6km ⚹ 6km **Notes** Pets admitted English spoken

ASCARAT

⍾ Maison Idioinia

Pierre GUERACAGUE

64220 ASCARAT

☎ 05 59 37 03 12 & 06 80 44 45 26

web: http://gueracague.pierre.neuf.fr

Close to St Jean Pied de Port, this authentic farmhouse dates back several generations and has a warm atmosphere. A relaxing stay here can include visiting nearby places of interests, walking and wine-tasting sessions.

Prices d fr €48 **Nearby** ⚵ 2km ⚶ 45km ⚯ 10km ⚲ 3km Restaurant 5km ⚱ 2km Spa 45km ⚸ 2km ⚸ 2km ⚹ 2.5km **Notes** No pets

ASTE-BEON

⍾ Lo Saunei

Marite DESSEIN

Village d'Aste, 64260 ASTE-BEON

☎ 05 59 82 63 32

web: www.losaunei.com

This wooden house in a peaceful little village in the Ossau Valley offers four comfortable rooms, all with private facilities, each one decorated in the colours of the seasons. There is a separate guests' entrance, kitchenette, garden furniture and private parking. Outside are wonderful views of the surrounding mountains.

Prices s fr €46; d fr €51; extra person fr €20 **Nearby** ⚵ 10km ⚶ 40km ⚯ 0.5km ⚲ 4km Restaurant 2km ⚴ 16km ⚱ 4km ⚸ 4km ⚹ 40km **Notes** No pets

BIDACHE

♨ **Maison Gelous**

Catherine CANDERATZ

1970, chemin de Gelous, 64520 BIDACHE

☎ 05 59 56 00 06 & 06 83 65 75 75

email: gelous@wanadoo.fr

web: www.chambresdhotesdupaysbasque.com

Surrounded by fields and forests, this restored farmhouse is full of character, and offers five spacious and cheerful first-floor bedrooms, all with private facilities. Rest and relaxation are guaranteed. Breakfast is served in the kitchen or on the terrace, from where guests can enjoy wonderful views of the countryside.

Prices s fr €45; d fr €55; t fr €72; extra person fr €18   **Nearby** ⚓ 6km ⛷ 22km Sea 35km ◢ 1km ⟲ 4km Restaurant 5km ◔ 4km ⊠ 5km ⛵ 9km   **Notes** No pets   English spoken

---

BIDARRAY

♨ ◉ **Gastanchoanea**

Marie HARAN

64780 BIDARRAY

☎ 05 59 37 70 37

email: haranmarie@orange.fr

web: www.bastanondo.com

An imposing 19th-century Basque farmhouse in a quiet corner surrounded by mountains, on the banks of a river. Home cooking, a reading corner, and a pretty garden are all on offer, along with four rooms for two to three people. In the village there is rafting, canoeing, mountain biking and rambling. Meals by arrangement.

Prices s fr €41; d fr €46; t fr €53; dinner fr €15   **Nearby** ⚓ 5km ⛷ 25km Sea 40km ◢ 0.1km ⟲ 18km Restaurant 0.5km ◔ 17km ⚑ 1km ⊠ 1km ⛵ 0.5km   **Notes** No pets   Open February to 15 November.

BILHERES-D'OSSAU

♨ ⚲ **L'Arrajou**

Veronique CAMBIER

Quartier de l'Eglise, 64260 BILHERES-D'OSSAU

☎ 05 59 82 62 38 & 06 81 41 31 46

email: contact@larrajou.com

web: www.larrajou.com

In a mountain village overlooking the Ossau Valley, this property enjoys a magical location. Whether you look from the bay windows, balconies or the terraces, the mountains are there - offering relaxation or exercise, as you wish! There is an open fire in the circular lounge. Four prettily decorated rooms comprise a triple with three beds, a triple with double and single bed, and two doubles. All are equipped with TV and en suite shower/WC; one of the bedrooms has disabled access.

Prices s fr €54; d fr €59; extra person fr €17   **Nearby** ⚓ 5km ◢ 3km ⟲ 8km Restaurant 3km ◔ 23km ⊠ 10km Spa 15km ⚑ 2.5km ⛵ 30km   **Notes** No pets   English spoken

BORCE

♨ ◉ ⚲ *Chambre d'hôtes*

Celine FLORES

Quartier Biella, 64490 BORCE

☎ 05 59 34 87 75 & 06 79 26 58 43

email: coustet.flores@planetis.com

web: http://celine.flores.chez-alice.fr/

This sympathetically restored grange retains the local building style with its slate roof and use of stone and wood. Five guest bedrooms include one with disabled access, all have connecting private facilities. Panoramic views of the mountains can be enjoyed from the south-facing terrace. Enjoy regional cooking with your host.

Prices not confirmed for 2008   **Nearby** ⚓ 8km ⟲ 35km ◔ 15km ◔ 1km ⚑ 1km ⛵ 35km   **Notes** No pets

---

BOSDARROS

♨♨ ◉ **Maison-Trille**

Christiane BORDES

chemin de Labau, 64290 BOSDARROS

☎ 05 59 21 79 51 & 06 83 78 40 67

🖹 05 59 21 57 54

email: christiane.bordes@libertysurf.fr

web: www.gites64.com/maison-trille

A beautiful 18th-century Bearnese house with inside courtyard and spectacular porch. Peaceful location and interesting architecture. Rooms have their own entrance and are decorated to a high standard. Excellent breakfast, and dinner by arrangement.

Prices s fr €60; d fr €70; dinner €25-€35   **Nearby** ⚓ 10km ⛷ 10km ◢ 0.5km ⟲ 10km Restaurant 0.3km ◔ 40km ⊠ 5km ⚑ 8km ⛵ 3km ⛵ 10km   **Notes** No pets   English spoken

---

BUZY

♨ **La Maison de Lucie**

Lucie AUGAREILS

4 rue Bonnehon, 64260 BUZY

☎ 05 59 21 02 53 & 06 89 54 97 49

email: lucieaugareils@free.fr

web: www.lamaisondelucie.net

Situated in a pretty mountain village, this restored barn bears witness to the past. On the first floor, amongst impressive ancient stones and beams, are three pretty rooms and a comfortable lounge. The light woodwork, and the bright colours of the walls provide a pleasing contrast. The owner serves breakfast in front of the fire, or in the flower garden.

Prices s fr €43; d fr €52; extra person €17-€20   **Nearby** ⚓ 10km ⛷ 25km ◢ 2km ⟲ 5km Restaurant 0.1km ◔ 30km ⊠ 0.5km Spa 5km ⚑ 6km ⛵ 0.1km ⛵ 1km   **Notes** No pets   English spoken

⊮ |◯| **Maïnade**

Rolande AUGAREILS

6 place Cazenave, 64260 BUZY

☎ 05 59 21 01 01 & 06 75 23 59 25

email: rolandeaugareils@free.fr

There are five double guest bedrooms at this property, which is a working farm in a village in the Ossau region. It is perfectly located for lots of mountain walks. Meals, available by arrangement, use farm and local produce.

Prices s €43–€50; d €52–€60; extra person fr €18; dinner €18–€20
Nearby ⛷ 15km ♨ 10km ✐ 1km ↖ 5km Restaurant 5km ⛵ 35km
⌕ 0.5km ⋙ 1km **Notes** No pets

CAMBO-LES-BAINS

⊮ **Maison Garatia**

Liliane CAUDROY

rue de l'Ecole, 64250 CAMBO-LES-BAINS

☎ 05 59 29 28 64

email: cajalima@msn.com

web: www.gites64.com/garatia

This house is situated in the centre of an area which is typical of lower Cambo. It has three beautiful bedrooms, all with private facilities. The welcoming owners serve a generous and varied breakfast in the dining room or in the garden. In the evening, you can relax in the lounge choosing from the wide selection of books.

Prices s fr €56; d fr €62 **Nearby** ⛷ 10km ♨ 10km Sea 20km ✐ 10km
↖ 1.5km Restaurant 0.1km ⌕ 1.5km Spa 20km ⬚ 1km ⋙ 0.5km
Notes No pets

CASTEIDE-CANDAU

⊮ |◯| **Domaine de Compostelle**

Michelle DRUCBERT

Maison Lacrouts, 64370 CASTEIDE-CANDAU

☎ 05 59 81 43 48   🖹 05 59 81 43 48

email: m.drucbert@free.fr

web: http://gite.compostelle.free.fr

This tastefully restored house is in a peaceful rural setting just a very short distance from the interesting village of Morlanne. The family bedrooms are in an annexe, all for four people, and have been planned with children in mind. Outside is a swimming pool and a pétanque pitch. Meals are available, by arrangement.

Prices s fr €47; d fr €55; t fr €64; extra person fr €5; dinner fr €16
On Site Restaurant Private ↖ **Nearby** ⛷ 3km ♨ 29km ⌕ 7km
Spa 30km ⬚ 7km ⋙ 25km **Notes** No pets

COARRAZE

⊮ |◯| *Chambre d'hôtes*

Marie-Noelle PEE

3 cote du Bois de Benejacq, Beth Soureilh, 64800 COARRAZE

☎ 05 59 53 70 75 & 06 07 66 90 11   🖹 05 59 53 70 75

email: beth.soureilh-chambredhote@wanadoo.fr

This is a magnificent modern house, with wide bay windows looking towards the Pyrenees. The non-smoking bedrooms are carefully and elegantly decorated, with themes drawn from Marie-Noëlle's travels around the world. Breakfast and, by arrangement, evening meals, all with organic produce, are served in the bright dining room or out on the south-facing terrace.

Prices not confirmed for 2008 **Nearby** ⛷ 7km ♨ 20km ↖ 15km
⌕ 2km ⬚ 2km ⋙ 3km **Notes** No pets English spoken

COSLEDAA

⊮ |◯| **La Noyeraie**

Eugene LAUTECAZE

64160 COSLEDAA

☎ 05 59 68 02 90   🖹 05 59 68 02 90

This newly built villa is at the entrance to the village and has a lounge with TV, a garden and furniture, a shaded terrace, central heating and games. There are two bedrooms on the ground floor and two more upstairs with private bathrooms. Guests can walk and fish in the restful surroundings of the Bearnese countryside.

Prices d fr €40; t fr €50; extra person fr €15; dinner fr €25
Nearby ⛷ 15km ♨ 25km ↖ 15km Restaurant 1km ⛵ 45km ⌕ 5km
⬚ 15km ⋙ 25km **Notes** Pets admitted

ESPELETTE

⊮ **Irazabala**

Marikita TOFFOLO

Quartier Laharketa, 64250 ESPELETTE

☎ 05 59 93 93 02 & 06 07 14 93 61   🖹 05 59 93 80 18

email: irazabala@wanadoo.fr

web: www.irazabala.com

This house has a lot of character, and it has been carefully furnished in a warm style. It has four bedrooms, and can sleep up to a total of ten guests. The owners keep a breed of Basque ponies, which graze amongst the trees in the meadows surrounding the property. Pony-trekking with a qualified guide can be arranged.

Prices s fr €54; d €65–€68; extra person fr €19 **Nearby** ⛷ 10km
♨ 4km Sea 20km ✐ 0.5km ↖ 3km Restaurant 1.5km ⌕ 3km ⬚ 1.5km
⋙ 18km **Notes** No pets English spoken

AQUITAINE

ESTIALESCQ

Maison Naba

Jeanne PERICOU

8 Chemin Carrere, 64290 ESTIALESCQ

☎ 05 59 39 99 11 ▤ 05 59 36 14 92

email: maisonnaba@aol.com

web: www.maison-naba-bearn.com

Beautiful restored 18th-century Bearnese farmhouse with four rooms and separate entrance. In a peaceful rural setting, a shady park with flowers surrounds the property. Near the valleys of Aspe and Osseau, and the Soule in the Pays-Basque.

Prices s fr €35; d fr €48; extra person fr €15 **On Site** ✿
Nearby ☘ 0.5km ♨ 25km ⚓ 6km ✈ 6km Restaurant 6km ⛵ 50km
⛳ 0.5km ⛲ 6km ⇝ 6km **Notes** Pets admitted English spoken

FAGET-D'OLORON

▯◎▮ Maison Millage

Beatrice ALBRECHT

Le Faget, 64400 OLORON SAINTE MARIE

☎ 05 59 36 10 22 & 06 32 36 89 32

email: beatrice.albrecht@wanadoo.fr

web: http://site.voila.fr/beatrice-albrecht

Three rooms are available with three double beds, a single and private facilities, in a grange adjoining the 16th-century stone house of the proprietors. 7km from Oloron, it has a lovely aspect with picture windows overlooking the terrace and Pyrénées range. The decor is contemporary and there is a living room and lounge area with TV.

Prices s fr €40; d fr €46; t fr €61; dinner fr €18 **Nearby** ☘ 3km
♨ 25km ⚓ 7km ✈ 6km Restaurant 7km ⛵ 3km ⛲ 7km ⇝ 7km
Notes Pets admitted English spoken

GUICHE

▯◎▮ Maison Huntagnères

Jean-Marie LAPLACE

64520 GUICHE

☎ 05 59 56 87 48 & 06 80 70 64 90 ▤ 05 59 56 87 48

email: contact@hount.com

web: www.hount.com

This 17th-century farmhouse offers a room with its own entrance on the ground floor. The house is surrounded by lovely countryside and a pretty river flows nearby. Home cooking available.

Prices s fr €46; d fr €50; t fr €63; extra person fr €13; dinner fr €16
Nearby ☘ 2.4km ♨ 35km Sea 35km ✈ 4.5km Restaurant 5km ⛵ 1km
Spa 20km ⛲ 1km ⇝ 12km **Notes** No pets English spoken

HASPARREN

Maison Haitz Ondo

Sandrine BRUNET

27 Chemin d'Olasogaraia, 64240 HASPARREN

☎ 05 59 29 62 88 & 06 81 93 55 87 ▤ 05 59 29 62 88

email: haitzondo@orange.fr

web: www.gites64.com/haitzondo

This house is built in the modern Basque style. It has spacious guest accommodation: two bedrooms, one suite with a balcony leading off, and a guests' lounge with unrestricted views over the mountains and the village. Enjoy its peaceful setting, in its own grounds with many shady terraces, or let the owner help you to plan a route to explore the area.

Prices d €54-€75; t €69-€90; extra person fr €15 **Nearby** ☘ 3km
♨ 30km Sea 30km ⚓ 5km ✈ 1km Restaurant 1km ⛵ 1km Spa 10km
⛲ 0.5km ⇝ 10km **Notes** No pets English spoken

IRISSARRY

❧ ▯◎▮ & Chambre d'hôtes

Pierre ETCHEBEHERE

Herriesta, 64780 IRISSARRY

☎ 05 59 37 67 22

If you seek a relaxing holiday, this 16th-century farmhouse is ideal. There are three rooms on the ground floor with their own entrance and chances to learn about agriculture and animal husbandry. The village is crossed by the Chemins of St Jacques de Compostelle. Dinner is available three nights a week from September to June.

Prices s fr €35; d fr €42; extra person fr €15; dinner fr €15 **On Site** ✿
Nearby ☘ 20km ♨ 35km Sea 48km ⚓ 0.1km ✈ 18km Restaurant 7km
⛵ 0.5km ⛲ 0.8km ⇝ 18km **Notes** Pets admitted English spoken

ISESTE

Chambre d'hôtes

Jean ASNAR

4 Av Georges Messier, 64260 ISESTE

☎ 05 59 05 71 51 & 06 30 16 87 47 ▤ 05 59 05 71 51

email: jean-lili.asnar@tele2.fr

web: http://gite.ossau.free.fr

Three double rooms on the ground floor of a large old manor house in the valley of Osseau. The friendly hosts offer an ample breakfast. An ideal location for those who want to relax under the trees.

Prices s fr €40; d fr €45; t fr €62 **Nearby** ☘ 2km ♨ 25km ⚓ 0.5km
✈ 2km Restaurant 0.2km ⛵ 20km ⛵ 0.3km ⛲ 0.3km ⇝ 2km
Notes No pets English spoken

ISPOURE

⁂ Ferme Etxeberria

M. MOURGUY

64220 ISPOURE

☎ 05 59 37 06 23 ▤ 05 59 37 06 23

email: domainemourguy@hotmail.com

Open views across a working vineyard provide a wonderful setting for this property. There are four bedrooms, with an independent entrance for guests. Outside on the terrace, guests can enjoy their breakfast and the view at the same time.

Prices d fr €48; extra person fr €15   **Nearby** ⚓ 10km ⚓ 40km
⚓ 0.8km Restaurant 0.1km ⚓ 0.8km ⚓ 0.8km ⚓ 0.8km
Notes No pets English spoken

ISSOR

⁂ ⎮◎⎮ La Ferme aux Sangliers

Francoise CAZAURANG

Micalet, 64570 ISSOR

☎ 05 59 34 43 96 & 06 08 45 66 97 ▤ 05 59 34 43 96

email: delhaybernard@wanadoo.fr

Three upstairs rooms in a Bearnese converted grange, on a farm, with two lounges, TV, open fire, two terraces with furniture and fantastic panoramic views of the surrounding mountains. Plenty of outdoor and mountain leisure activities are available.

Prices s fr €47; d fr €57; t fr €74; extra person fr €18; dinner fr €17
Nearby ⚓ 11km ⚓ 10km ⚓ 10km Restaurant 5km ⚓ 27km ⚓ 10km
⚓ 6km ⚓ 5km ⚓ 14km **Notes** No pets

ISTURITZ

⁂ ⎮◎⎮ Urruti Zaharria

Andre FILLAUDEAU

64240 ISTURITZ

☎ 05 59 29 45 98

email: urruti.zaharia@wanadoo.fr

web: www.urruti-zaharria.fr

Expect a warm welcome at this spacious, fully restored 11th-century house. The bedrooms and suite are beautifully decorated. Oak beams, living room, library and games room, fireplace and terrace. Tasty regional dishes offered, using local produce.

Prices s fr €47; d €59-€76; t €72-€99; dinner fr €21   **Nearby** ⚓ 10km
⚓ 30km Sea 45km ⚓ 0.1km ⚓ 10km Restaurant 2km ⚓ 10km
Spa 35km ⚓ 10km ⚓ 35km **Notes** No pets

ITXASSOU

⁂ Gure Gostuan

Xantal ITHURRY-BORGEAIS

64250 ITXASSOU

☎ 05 59 29 89 20 & 06 75 07 20 25

The property stands in beautiful grounds, in a village well known for its cherry trees and warm, friendly atmosphere. The three bedrooms have en suite facilities. Guests have an independent entrance, and their own lounge and dining room.

Prices s fr €50; d fr €55; extra person fr €17   **Nearby** ⚓ 4km ⚓ 15km
Sea 25km ⚓ 0.5km ⚓ 3km Restaurant 0.1km ⚓ 1km ⚓ 5km ⚓ 0.5km
⚓ 0.7km **Notes** No pets English spoken

⁂ Soubeleta

M-Francoise REGERAT

64250 ITXASSOU

☎ 05 59 29 22 34 & 06 23 19 70 24

In this charming village, this little 17th-century castle is surrounded by greenery and cherry trees. Five rooms with breathtaking views over the mountains, a kitchenette, living rooms, antiques and open fire.

Prices s fr €45; d €52-€60; extra person fr €15   **Nearby** ⚓ 10km
⚓ 10km Sea 25km ⚓ 0.5km ⚓ 3km Restaurant 0.5km ⚓ 1km Spa 4km
⚓ 4km ⚓ 1km ⚓ 4km **Notes** No pets English spoken

⁂ Zakataka-Enia

Denis THOMAS

chemin Apesteguia, 64250 ITXASSOU

☎ 05 59 93 46 88 & 06 23 68 55 57

email: zakataka@neuf.fr

web: www.chambresdhotes-zakataka.com

Surrounded by a big garden and 20 minutes from the sea, this 19th-century house has four second-floor bedrooms, all with private facilities. Also available are billiards and a Jacuzzi. While you are in this village - which is famous for its cherries - you can choose between rafting on the River Nive, taking your first glider flight, or simply going for a very long walk.

Prices s fr €50; d fr €55; extra person fr €15   **Nearby** ⚓ 20km ⚓ 10km
Sea 20km ⚓ 0.1km ⚓ 3km ⚓ 1km Spa 3km ⚓ 3km ⚓ 1.5km ⚓ 2km
Notes No pets English spoken

LA BASTIDE-CLAIRENCE

⫘ ⑩ *Argizagita*

Marie BUCK

Maison Argizagita/Bidau, Quartier Pessarou,
64240 LA-BASTIDE-CLAIRENCE

☎ 05 59 70 15 59 & 06 77 33 07 78

email: buck@argizagita.com

web: www.argizagita.com

This authentic 15th-century Basque farmhouse is on the edge of a listed village. Three spacious bedrooms, including one with a small adjoining lounge, are found in the converted hayloft. Evening meals with your hosts are available three times a week and at other times by arrangement. Garden and terraces, good walking country.

Prices not confirmed for 2008 **Nearby** ⛷ 10km ⚓ 28km Sea 28km ⚐ 5km ≋ 5km 🚲 5km 🚄 28km **Notes** No pets English spoken Open May to October.

⫘ **Le Clos Gaxen**

Nathalie ZELLER

64240 LA-BASTIDE-CLAIRENCE

☎ 05 59 29 16 44 & 06 19 62 56 17 📄 05 59 29 16 44

email: gaxen@wanadoo.fr

web: www.leclosgaxen.com

A warm welcome awaits guests to this 18th-century Basque house set in a tranquil little valley very close to a 14th-century listed village. Three rooms are available.

Prices s €60-€65; d €63-€70 **On Site** ⚐ Private ⚓ **Nearby** ⛷ 8km ⚓ 25km Sea 25km Restaurant 2km ≋ 3km ⚑ 2km 🏛 2km 🚄 20km **Notes** Pets admitted English spoken

⫘ ⑩ **Maison Marchand**

Gilbert FOIX

rue Notre Dame, 64240 LA-BASTIDE-CLAIRENCE

☎ 05 59 29 18 27 & 06 19 21 21 24

email: valerie.et.gilbert.foix@wanadoo.fr

web: http://perso.wanadoo.fr/maison.marchand

A 16th-century house in a listed village integrating the Basque and Gascon cultures, with five rooms all differently decorated (two of which are mezzanine). The friendly hosts offer good food and plenty of advice on how to discover the Pays-Basque and its culture. Evening meals two nights a week.

Prices s €50-€55; d €55-€70; t fr €70; extra person fr €15; dinner fr €25 **Nearby** ⛷ 6km ⚓ 20km Sea 30km ⚐ 10km ⚑ 0.5km Restaurant 0.5km ≋ 0.5km 🚄 27km **Notes** Pets admitted English spoken Open 16 March to 14 November.

⫘ ⑩ ♿ **Maison Maxana**

Ana BERDOULAT

rue Notre Dame, 64240 LA-BASTIDE-CLAIRENCE

☎ 05 59 70 10 10 & 06 32 42 65 99

email: ab@maison-maxana.com

web: www.maison-maxana.com

Situated in one of the most beautiful villages in France, this 17th-century property promises a quiet and peaceful stay in elegant and welcoming surroundings not far from the coast. It can accommodate up to ten guests in its five bedrooms, all with private bath or shower room and WC.

Prices d fr €110; dinner fr €35 **On Site** Private ⚑ **Nearby** ⛷ 6km ⚓ 25km Sea 30km ⚐ 2km Restaurant 0.2km ≋ 0.5km Spa 20km 🚄 20km **Notes** No pets English spoken

⫘ ⑩ **Maison la Croisade**

Sylvianne DARRITCHON

64240 LA BASTIDE CLAIRENCE

☎ 05 59 29 68 22 & 06 74 28 29 65 📄 05 59 29 62 99

email: lacroisade@aol.com

web: www.la-croisade.com

An old coaching inn of St Jacques de Compostelle, this 17th-century building offers breakfast in its magnificent garden. The four guest rooms are upstairs. Guests can enjoy the peace and charm of this family home with its antique furniture, old flagstones, and vast fireplace. Meals on request with traditional Basque cuisine.

Prices s fr €57; d fr €60; t fr €75; extra person fr €15; dinner fr €23 **Nearby** ⛷ 8km ⚓ 25km Sea 25km ⚑ 3.5km Restaurant 2km ≋ 3.5km 🏛 3.5km 🚄 36km **Notes** Pets admitted English spoken

LACARRY

⫘ **Chambre d'hôte Etché**

Louise ETCHEGOYHEN

64470 LACARRY

☎ 05 59 28 55 14 📄 05 59 28 75 55

email: etchep@aol.com

web: www.etche.online.fr

This house, which enjoys a pastoral setting, offers three bright and spacious rooms and a warm welcome from its owner. It provides a good base for exploring la Soule, an unspoilt region of upland pastures, caves, the gorges of Holzarte and Kakuetta, and the wild cattle-rearing areas of the Ahusquy plateaux.

Prices s fr €35; d fr €45; t fr €60; extra person fr €15 **Nearby** ⛷ 12km ⚑ 13km ⚓ 30km ≋ 13km 🏛 7km **Notes** No pets

LANNE-EN-BARETOUS

⧟ ⍾ Château de Porthos

Michele CLUZANT-LAHER

Le Bourg, 64570 LANNE-EN-BARETOUS

☎ 06 07 96 53 47 & 06 08 90 88 40

email: chateaudeporthos@hotmail.fr

web: www.gites64.com/chateaudeporthos

This early 17th-century château is in the village of Lanne. The building is full of character, with mullioned windows and four beautifully decorated and spaciously comfortable bedrooms - all with en suite shower/WC, TV and telephone. The grounds extend to one hectare, and there is an open terrace which catches the morning sun. Parking is close by; meals are available by arrangement, or there is a restaurant in the village.

Prices s fr €58; d fr €68; extra person fr €15; dinner fr €20 **Nearby** ⛷ 0.5km ♣ 40km 🏊 3km ➹ 0.2km Restaurant 0.3km ⚓ 30km ≋ 0.5km ▣ 0.2km ⋙ 17km **Notes** No pets English spoken

⧟ ⍾ Maison Rachou

Evelyne MASERO

64570 LANNE-EN-BARETOUS

☎ 05 59 34 10 30 ▤ 05 59 34 10 30

web: www.gites64.com/maison-rachou

This converted barn, overlooking the village, has five bedrooms and can sleep up to a total of twelve guests. One of the rooms has disabled access. Breakfast (and other meals by arrangement) can be enjoyed indoors, or out beside the swimming pool.

Prices s fr €46; d fr €48; extra person fr €15; dinner fr €18 **On Site** Private ➹ **Nearby** ⛷ 0.5km ♣ 40km 🏊 8km Restaurant 1km ⚓ 30km ≋ 4km ▣ 1.5km ⋙ 17km **Notes** No pets English spoken

LARCEVEAU

⧟ ⍦ ⍾ ♿ Maison Arantzeta

Michele AMPO

Quartier Cibits, 64120 LARCEVEAU

☎ 05 59 37 37 26 & 06 81 17 92 54

email: ampochristophe@aol.com

web: http://arantzeta.fr

This quiet little village provides an ideal base for exploring the heartland of the Basque country. The house, which has beautiful views, dates back to the 18th century and has three spacious bedrooms, all with private bath or shower room and WC. There is a large lounge for guests' use, and meals using farm produce are served two evenings a week.

Prices s fr €45; d fr €50; t fr €65; extra person fr €15; dinner fr €15 **Nearby** ⛷ 15km ♣ 35km 🏊 15km ➹ 15km Restaurant 1.5km ⚓ 3km ☘ 15km ▣ 1.5km ⋙ 15km **Notes** No pets English spoken Open May to 30 October.

⧟ ⍾ Maison Oyhanartia

Chantal ISAAC-JACQUEMIN

rte de Bunus, 64120 LARCEVEAU

☎ 05 59 37 88 16 & 06 80 85 61 73

email: contact@oyhanartia.com

web: www.oyhanartia.com

A Navarrian farmhouse, surrounded by prairies and bordered by woods and rivers. The house is in a beautiful, peaceful setting in the Basse Navarre. Guests can enjoy evening meals using farm produce, served at their hosts' table. The cosy library has an open fire and is the ideal place to relax.

Prices s €55-€60; d €60-€65; t €75-€80; extra person fr €15; dinner €15-€25 **On Site** ➹ **Nearby** ⛷ 15km ♣ 35km ➹ 15km ≋ 15km Spa 35km ▣ 2km ⋙ 15km **Notes** No pets English spoken

LARRAU

⧟ Chambre d'hôtes

Marcel ACCOCEBERRY

Etxandi, 64560 LARRAU

☎ 05 59 28 60 35

17th-century renovated property with three converted rooms, in the heart of a pretty village at the foot of the Orhi peak and the forest of Iraty. Living room with fireplace and TV, heating, garden and terrace. Several walks and hikes round the gorges of Holzarte and Kakueta.

Prices d fr €46; t fr €54; extra person fr €14 **On Site** 🏊 **Nearby** ⛷ 20km ➹ 17km Restaurant 0.1km ⚓ 30km ≋ 12km ☘ 12km ▣ 0.1km ⋙ 45km **Notes** No pets

LASSEUBE

⧟ Ferme Dague

J-P MAUMUS

Chem Croix de Dagué, 64290 LASSEUBE

☎ 05 59 04 27 11 & 06 24 34 33 92 ▤ 05 59 04 27 11

email: famille.maumus@wanadoo.fr

web: www.ferme-dague.com

Four rooms and a suite are available in the outbuildings of this lovely 18th-century Bearnese farm with its traditional square courtyard. The farm is on ten hectares of land with exceptional views of the Pyrénées and is a suitable stop for riders and horses.

Prices s €42-€62; d €51-€62; t fr €82 **Nearby** ⛷ 10km ♣ 10km 🏊 1km ➹ 6km Restaurant 0.9km ⚓ 45km ≋ 1km ▣ 1km ⋙ 18km **Notes** No pets English spoken Open Easter to November.

ⵍⵍ **Maison Priats**

Annie LABORDE

Quartier Rey, 64290 LASSEUBE

☎ 05 59 04 24 65   🖷 05 59 04 24 65

email: labordese@wanadoo.fr

web: www.maisonpriats.com

This renovated traditional Béarnais farmhouse, surrounded by woods and meadows, offers peaceful and comfortable accommodation in a charming location. It has a beautiful outlook towards the Pyrénées. There are two bedrooms, and a suite, which open onto the swimming pool.

Prices s fr €40; d €55-€70; t fr €85; extra person fr €15
On Site Private ⵗ **Nearby** ⴻ 8km ⴵ 10km ⵁ 2km Restaurant 2km ⵂ 45km ⵃ 10km Spa 35km ⵄ 20km ⵅ 2km ⵆ 20km **Notes** No pets Open Easter to 1 November.

ⵍⵍ ⵏⵎ *Maison Rancesamy*

Isabelle BROWNE

Quartier Rey, 64290 LASSEUBE

☎ 05 59 04 26 37 & 06 13 55 54 02   🖷 05 59 04 26 37

email: missbrowne@wanadoo.fr

web: www.missbrowne.com

This beautiful Bearnese farm from the 18th century has an inside courtyard and pool. Through a separate entrance there are five rooms with splendid views over the Pyrenees. Guests can relax under the shade of the walnut tree or in the blossoming bower of the garden.

Prices not confirmed for 2008 **On Site** Private ⵗ **Nearby** ⴻ 8km ⴵ 10km ⵂ 45km ⵃ 1.5km ⵅ 1.5km ⵆ 12km **Notes** No pets English spoken

---

LAY-LAMIDOU

ⵍⵍ ⵤ ⵏⵎ **La Grange de Georges**

Georges LABERDESQUE

17 rue de la Hount, 64190 LAY-LAMIDOU

☎ 05 59 66 50 45 & 06 82 79 65 03   🖷 05 59 66 50 45

email: lagrangedegeorges@wanadoo.fr

web: www.lagrangedegeorges.fr/

A newly restored barn at the heart of a small village in the valley of Gave d'Oloron. Guests can enjoy the friendly family atmosphere and meals making use of home-grown produce. Cycling, ping-pong, piano, games and large terrace.

Prices s fr €34; d fr €42; t fr €52; extra person fr €10; dinner fr €15
Nearby ⴻ 5km ⴵ 25km ⵁ 2km ⵗ 5km Restaurant 5km ⵃ 5km ⵅ 5km ⵆ 25km **Notes** Pets admitted

LECUMBERRY

ⵍⵍ ⵏⵎ **Chambre d'hôtes**

J-P JACQUES

Ur-Aldea, 64220 LECUMBERRY

☎ 05 59 37 24 18

email: gredesvents@wanadoo.fr

Old restored property edged by a river at the foot of the forest of Iraty. Enjoy home-cooked south-western specialities, and if you have time fly over the Basse Navarre in a hot air balloon.

Prices d fr €56; extra person fr €14; dinner fr €24 **Nearby** ⴻ 20km ⴵ 50km ⵁ 3km ⵗ 7km Restaurant 0.1km ⵃ 7km ⵅ 7km ⵆ 7km **Notes** No pets English spoken

---

LIVRON

ⵍⵍ **La Maison de l'Ousse**

M. VIDAL-GIRAUD

14 Rue de la Mairie, chemin Pecastaing, 64530 LIVRON

☎ 05 59 53 71 15 & 06 71 72 46 60

email: anne@chambres64.com

web: www.chambres64.com

This big house, built in the local style, stands in a small village on the River Ousse. It has two bedrooms on the ground floor and one upstairs, all with private facilities. A lavish breakfast is served in the vast kitchen, which has a view over the orchard. Extensive grounds running down to the river.

Prices s fr €42; d fr €48; t fr €56; extra person fr €10 **Nearby** ⴻ 6km ⴵ 15km ⵁ 12km ⵗ 5km Restaurant 5km ⵃ 5km ⵅ 5km ⵆ 15km **Notes** No pets English spoken

---

LOUHOSSOA

ⵍⵍ ⵏⵎ **Domaine de Silencenia**

Philippe MALLOR

64250 LOUHOSSOA

☎ 05 59 93 35 60 & 06 13 23 76 02   🖷 05 59 93 35 60

email: domaine.de.silencenia@wanadoo.fr

web: www.domaine-silencenia.com

Dating from 1881, this charming mansion is surrounded by three hectares of parkland with a small lake at the foot of the Basque mountains. The bedrooms, with their four poster beds, are exceptionally comfortable. The table is fit for the gourmand and Philippe is a wine connoisseur.

Prices s fr €70; d fr €85; extra person fr €15; dinner fr €30
On Site Private ⵗ **Nearby** ⴻ 6km ⴵ 10km Sea 25km ⵁ 10km Restaurant 0.8km ⵃ 3km Spa 7km ⵅ 3km ⵆ 8km **Notes** No pets English spoken Open April to 30 October.

AQUITAINE

MONEIN

ⅲ ⅴ ⅰ◎ⅰ Maison Canterou

Marie-Jose NOUSTY
Quartier Laquidée, 64360 MONEIN
☎ 05 59 21 41 38 & 06 32 38 80 98
email: nousty.mariejosee@wanadoo.fr
web: www.gites64.com/maison-canterou

A friendly welcome awaits guests to this lovely Bearnese farm with enclosed courtyard along the wine routes of Jurancon. There are five bedrooms that are both comfortable and peaceful. Vineyards to explore and meals served out on the terrace (except on Saturdays).

Prices s €44-€54; d €54-€64; t €69-€79; extra person fr €15; dinner fr €20 **On Site** Private **Nearby** ⅎ 13km ⅉ12km ⌖ 1km Restaurant 3km ⅊ 6km ⅇ 6km ⅈ6km ⅉ 25km **Notes** Pets admitted English spoken

MONSEGUR

ⅲ ⅰ◎ⅰ Maison Cap Blanc

Francine MAUMY
64460 MONSEGUR
☎ 05 59 81 54 52 & 06 07 65 61 84
email: maumy.francine@wanadoo.fr

Monségur is near the Madiran and Gers vineyards, twenty minutes from the venue of the Marciac Jazz Festival. The rooms are in a separate house and guests may use the lounge with library, TV, shaded garden with pool and private terrace.

Prices s fr €60; d €65-€70; t €85-€90; extra person fr €20; dinner fr €30 **On Site** Private **Nearby** ⅎ 1km ⅉ20km Restaurant 7km ⅊0.5km ⅈ1km ⅉ 20km **Notes** No pets English spoken

PAGOLLE

ⅲ ⅰ◎ⅰ Elixondoa

Michel WALTHER
64120 PAGOLLE
☎ 05 59 65 65 34 & 06 16 95 17 35
email: jean.walther@wanadoo.fr
web: www.elixondoa.com

At the entrance of a small village surrounded by hills; these four rooms include a suite for five. Enjoy bread and home-made jams for breakfast, and good home-cooking around the big table for dinner. Basque region, crossing paths of St Jacques, walks and mountain biking.

Prices s fr €48; d fr €50; t €65-€68; extra person €15-€18; dinner fr €22 **On Site** Private **Nearby** ⅎ 10km ⅉ40km ⌖ 10km Restaurant 5km ⅊ 15km Spa 40km ⅇ 25km ⅈ12km ⅉ 40km **Notes** Pets admitted English spoken

PAU

ⅲ ⅴ ⅰ◎ⅰ La Ferme du Hameau de Pau

Vincent ROUSSET-SEGER
73 Av Copernic, 64000 PAU
☎ 05 59 84 36 85
email: la-ferme-du-hameau-de-pau@wanadoo.fr
web: http://perso.wanadoo.fr/lafermeduhameaudepau

This renovated farmhouse is close to an old town, just 40km from the Pyrénées. The farm grows red fruits and has sheep and poultry. There is a lounge with kitchen area for guests, separate access, parking, a shady garden with furniture and table tennis. Table d'hôte meals (by reservation) feature farm produce and home-made jams are available to buy. Discover weaving in the owner's studio.

Prices s fr €40; d fr €50; t fr €65; extra person fr €15; dinner fr €14 **Nearby** ⅎ 0.1km ⅉ5km ⌖ 6km ⌖ 0.3km Restaurant 1km ⅊ 2km Spa 2km ⅇ 5km ⅈ1km ⅉ 6km **Notes** No pets English spoken

POEY-D'OLORON

ⅲ ⅴ ⅰ◎ⅰ ⅇ Domaine Pédelaborde

Thierry CIVIT
64400 POEY D'OLORON
☎ 05 59 39 59 93 ⅰ 05 59 39 59 93
email: civit.earl@wanadoo.fr
web: http://perso.wanadoo.fr/civit

Outbuildings of a 19th-century mansion house, offering two ground floor and two upstairs rooms set in a green, tranquil park. Swimming pool, and meals prepared with home-grown farm produce.

Prices s fr €33; d €47-€50; t fr €59; extra person fr €10; dinner fr €18 **On Site** Private **Nearby** ⅎ 4km ⅉ25km ⅊ 5km ⅈ10km ⅉ 10km **Notes** Pets admitted

PONTIACQ-VIELLEPINTE

ⅲ ⅰ◎ⅰ Chambre d'hôtes

Nicole VIGNOLO
rte de Montaner, 64460 PONTIACQ-VIELLEPINTE
☎ 05 59 81 91 45 & 06 62 45 94 88
email: nicole.vignolo@wanadoo.fr
web: www.gites64.com/vignolo

Five rooms in a lovely Bearnese home near Lourdes and the Hautes Pyrénées, with views onto a park. Enjoy meals made with farm produce at the dining table and a friendly atmosphere.

Prices s fr €35; d fr €45; t fr €59; dinner fr €17 **Nearby** ⅎ 4km ⅉ25km ⌖ 10km Restaurant 3km ⅊ 5km Spa 25km ⅈ10km ⅉ 25km **Notes** Pets admitted

SALIES-DE-BEARN

⊞ ⦿ La Closerie du Guilhat

M-C POTIRON

Quartier du Guilhat, 64270 SALIES-DE-BEARN

☎ 05 59 38 08 80 ▤ 05 59 38 08 80

email: guilhat@club-internet.fr

In a green oasis, this old and serene Bearnese mansion has a park, golf, fishing, nursery and casino nearby. Around the table, guests can enjoy good regional cuisine, by reservation.

Prices s fr €45; d €54-€59; t fr €67; extra person fr €14; dinner fr €22 **On Site** ⛳ **Nearby** ⚓ 5km ⚐ 3km ⌁ 5km ⚘ 3km Restaurant 4km ⌇ 3km Spa 3km ⌂ 4km ⋙ 30km **Notes** No pets English spoken

⊞ ⦿ Maison Léchémia

Helene CAMOUGRAND

Quartier du Bois, 64270 SALIES-DE-BEARN

☎ 05 59 38 08 55 ▤ 05 59 38 08 55

web: www.gites64.com/maison-lechemia

This 16th-century family house is on the woody hillsides of the salt city and sleeps eight. Discover the flavours of rural cooking over a wood fire, in either the converted grange near the old press or under the chestnut trees.

Prices s fr €40; d €53-€55; t fr €65; extra person fr €13; dinner fr €23 **Nearby** ⚓ 3km ⚐ 3km ⌁ 2km Restaurant 3km ⚘ 2km Spa 3km ⌂ 3km ⋙ 8km **Notes** Pets admitted English spoken

SARE

⊞ Aretxola

Trini DEVOUCOUX

rte des Grottes, 64310 SARE

☎ 05 59 54 28 33 & 06 12 48 82 93 ▤ 05 59 54 28 33

email: info@aretxola.com

web: www.aretxola.com

The owners of this chambre d'hôtes are horse lovers and they will be delighted to welcome you to Aretxola, their stone-built house, which stands in its own grounds with an uninterrupted view of the nearby Spanish peaks. There are three cosy and comfortable rooms, one a family room.

Prices s fr €60-€80; d €60-€80; t fr €100; extra person fr €20 **Nearby** ⚓ 5km ⚐ 18km Sea 18km ⚘ 3km Restaurant 3km ⚘ 3km Spa 18km ⌂ 1.5km ⋙ 18km **Notes** No pets English spoken

⊞ La Halte du Temps

Jeanine HARISMENDY

Xoko-Maitea, Chemin Olanda, 64310 SARE

☎ 05 59 47 53 22

At the end of the lane in a beautiful green setting, this property provides an ideal base from which to explore the Basque country - and the Spanish border is not so very far away. Breakfast is served in the family dining room, on the terrace, or beneath the 300-year-old oak trees in the garden. The owners are gardeners and bee-keepers,

and almost everything served here is home-made. Three en suite double rooms, one with bath/WC and two with shower/WC.

Prices d €60-€80; extra person fr €20 **Nearby** ⚓ 2.5km ⚐ 15km Sea 15km ⚘ 0.2km ⚘ 2.5km Restaurant 0.5km ⚘ 2.5km ⌂ 2.5km ⋙ 15km **Notes** No pets English spoken Open April to 1 October.

⊞ ⦿ Maison Ttakoinenborda

Alain ARRIETA

64310 SARE

☎ 05 59 47 51 42 & 06 67 73 76 45

email: alain-et-mary.arrieta@wanadoo.fr

web: http://ttakoinenborda.ifrance.com

Character 17th-century house by the river in a rural setting, offering four rooms. Meals are available on certain nights of the week and include fresh farm produce and daily home-baked bread.

Prices s fr €45; d fr €50; t fr €65; dinner fr €16 **Nearby** ⚓ 4.5km ⚐ 17km Sea 17km ⚘ 4km Restaurant 1km ⚘ 4km ⌂ 1.5km ⋙ 17km **Notes** No pets English spoken Open March to November.

⊞ Uhartea

Michel ECHEVESTE

Quartier Elbarun, 64310 SARE

☎ 05 59 54 25 30 & 06 20 44 54 97

email: echeveste.mikel@wanadoo.fr

web: www.uhartea.com

There are five bedrooms in this authentic 15th-century Basque farmhouse, as well as a living room, lounge and kitchenette. At the foot of Louis XIV's fort and the mountain of the Rhune, guests can take walks, go fishing, or have a round of golf.

Prices s fr €57; d fr €60; t fr €75 **Nearby** ⚓ 3km ⚐ 12km Sea 12km ⚘ 12km ⚘ 2km Restaurant 2km ⚘ 2km Spa 12km ⌂ 2km ⋙ 12km **Notes** No pets

SAUGUIS

ⵜ Maison Biscayburu

Pantxo ETCHEBEHERE

64470 SAUGUIS

☎ 05 59 28 73 19 & 06 10 55 14 04

email: informations@chambres-hotes-pays-basque.com

web: www.chambres-hotes-pays-basque.com

A typically renovated farmhouse with exposed beams and stonework, in the village of Sauguis, nestling in the Soule Valley. A warm atmosphere prevails and there are mountain views. Your hosts are former bakers, and offer guests excellent home-made breakfasts.

Prices s €45-€50; d €50-€55; t €62-€65; extra person fr €12
On Site Private ⚡ **Nearby** ⛷ 3km 🏊 0.5km Restaurant 3km ⛵ 8km
🚣 8km 🚲 3km **Notes** No pets English spoken

SEVIGNACQ-MEYRACQ

ⵜ Les Bains de Secours

Anne-Marie PAROIX

64260 SEVIGNACQ-MEYRACQ

☎ 05 59 05 89 70 & 06 86 79 84 47

email: bdsref@club-internet.fr

web: www.sejour-en-pyrenees.com

A 19th-century spa house with a beautiful green setting, in the middle of the countryside. There are five double rooms, all with private facilities. The decor has been carefully chosen, and the house has a happy atmosphere - especially around the fire in the lounge. Chalybeate baths on site; relaxation classes, therapeutic massage available.

Prices s fr €45; d fr €56; t €66-€74 **On Site** Spa **Nearby** ⛷ 3km
🏊 20km ⛵ 4km ⚡ 5km Restaurant 0.1km ⛷ 35km 🏊 5km ⛵ 6km
🚣 3km 🚲 8km **Notes** No pets English spoken

ⵜ ⅠⓄⅠ *Maison Lagrave*

Yves GRUGEON

Hauteur de Marere, 64260 SEVIGNACQ-MEYRACQ

☎ 05 59 05 55 94 & 06 73 39 24 33

email: maisonlagrave@free.fr

web: www.maisonlagrave.com

This farmhouse, with views towards the Pyrenees, has been totally restored by its owners. The guest rooms are in converted outbuildings; all five are upstairs, and two have their own entrance. All have private bath/shower room and WC. There is a large, pleasant day room; outside is a garden with fruit trees, children's games area and a swimming pool.

Prices not confirmed for 2008 **On Site** Private ⚡ **Nearby** ⛷ 8km
🏊 20km ⛵ 35km ⚡ 5km 🚣 8km 🚲 23km **Notes** Pets admitted English spoken

ST-ESTEBEN

ⵜ Jaureguia

Annie DURRUTY

64640 SAINT-ESTEBEN

☎ 05 59 29 65 34 & 06 84 25 06 47

13th-century stately home, now a dairy farm, with four large rooms (three double, one three-quarter and two single beds). There is also a lounge, TV, fireplace, and garden with furniture. A hilly region at the heart of the Pays-Basque, half way between the sea and the mountains, with plenty of walking.

Prices s fr €35; d fr €40; t fr €51; extra person fr €10 **Nearby** ⛷ 30km
🏊 40km Sea 40km ⚡ 8km ⚡ 10km Restaurant 0.5km 🏊 10km
Spa 20km 🚣 10km 🚲 35km **Notes** Pets admitted

ST-ETIENNE-DE-BAIGORRY

ⵜ ⅠⓄⅠ Maison Idiartekoborda

Sandrine BIBES

Idiartekoborda, Route de Belexi,

64430 SAINT-ETIENNE-DE-BAIGORRY

☎ 05 59 37 46 29

email: idiartekoborda@wanadoo.fr

web: www.gites64.com/idiartekoborda

This 17th-century Basque farmhouse, with its wonderful views of the changing mountain colours, has been restored to provide five spacious bedrooms with exposed beams and stonework. Breakfasts include home-made jams and pastries, and other meals are available by arrangement, except July and August. The hosts will be delighted to help you plan walks and mountain-bike rides.

Prices s fr €50; d fr €54; t fr €74; extra person fr €15; dinner fr €20
Nearby ⛷ 10km 🏊 37km ⚡ 2km Restaurant 2.5km 🏊 2km Spa 15km
🚣 2km 🚲 12km **Notes** No pets English spoken

ST-JEAN-PIED-DE-PORT

ⵜ *Maison Donamaría*

Sylvia MENDIZABAL

1 Chemin d'Olhonce, 64220 SAINT-JEAN-PIED-DE-PORT

☎ 05 59 37 02 32 & 06 26 11 54 50

email: donamaria2002@wanadoo.fr

web: http://perso.wanadoo.fr/maisondonamaria

Beside the river, and two minutes' walk from the old town, this is a characterful house where wood and stone are in harmony. There are three comfortable rooms, one a family room, each with its own style. The garden has views of the waterfall and the Roman bridge, and the fireside provides evening comfort.

Prices not confirmed for 2008 **Nearby** ⛷ 3km 🏊 45km ⚡ 1km 🏊 1km
🚣 1km 🚲 2km **Notes** Pets admitted English spoken

ST-PALAIS

⋕⋕⋕ 🍴 Maison d'Arthezenéa

Francois BARTHABURU

42 rue du Palais de Justice, 64120 SAINT-PALAIS

☎ 05 59 65 85 96 & 06 15 85 68 64 📄 05 59 65 85 96

email: francois.barthaburu@wanadoo.fr

web: www.gites64.com/maison-darthezenea

This family home has bright and spacious rooms with antique furnishings. There are four guest bedrooms, all with private bath or shower room and WC. Outside is an attractive garden, with lots of flowers. Meals are available by arrangement using local and home-produced ingredients, and your host will be delighted to tell you all about the Pays-Basque region.

Prices s €63-€68; d €68-€73; extra person fr €22; dinner fr €25 **On Site** 🌳 **Nearby** ✿ 0.5km ♨ 30km ⌛ 0.1km ⚓ 0.5km Restaurant 0.2km ☁ 0.5km Spa 30km ⓘ 0.5km 🚐 40km **Notes** No pets English spoken Open April to December.

ST-PEE-SUR-NIVELLE

⋕⋕⋕ ⌖ Bidachuna

Isabelle ORMAZABAL

RD 3, 64310 SAINT-PEE-SUR-NIVELLE

☎ 05 59 54 56 22 📄 05 59 54 55 07

email: isabelle@bidachuna.com

web: www.bidachuna.com

A charming home at the edge of a protected forest. Facing the Pyrénées, this 19th-century walled farm is set in quiet surroundings.

Prices s fr €105; d fr €115 **Nearby** ✿ 6km ♨ 4km Sea 15km ⚓ 15km Restaurant 6km ☁ 6km ⓘ 6km 🚐 15km **Notes** No pets English spoken Open Easter to 1 November.

⋕⋕⋕ 🍴 Ehaltzekoborda

Marc VERDIER et Soisick JUPAS

64310 SAINT-PEE-SUR-NIVELLE

☎ 05 59 85 94 29 & 06 60 19 93 85

web: www.ehaltzekoborda.fr.st

This old Basque property has five guest bedrooms, all on the ground floor with independent access and all with private bath/shower room and WC. There is a lounge for guests, and outside is a swimming pool with pool house and space for parking. The views are beautiful, and the site is in an environmental conservation area.

Prices s fr €63; d fr €68; t fr €85; extra person fr €17; dinner fr €24 **On Site** Private ⚓ **Nearby** ✿ 2km ♨ 3km Sea 14km ⚓ 2km Restaurant 0.5km ☁ 0.2km Spa 14km 🌳 14km ⓘ 2km 🚐 14km **Notes** Pets admitted English spoken

⋕⋕⋕ Ferme-Uxondoa

PhilippePOULET

Quartier Elbarron, 64310 SAINT-PEE-SUR-NIVELLE

☎ 05 59 54 46 27 & 06 85 87 84 75

email: poulet.uxondoa@wanadoo.fr

web: www.chambres-d-hotes-uxondoa.com

Three spacious rooms upstairs and two suites for three with terraces are on offer at this renovated country farmhouse. Complete with stone, beams, baked earth and white-washing it offers warmth and modern comforts in natural settings and six hectares of land at the edge of the Nivelle. Only ten minutes from the ocean.

Prices s €56-€70; d €60-€75; t fr €85 **On Site** ⚓ **Nearby** ✿ 2km ♨ 9km Sea 9km ⚓ 3.5km Restaurant 1.5km ☁ 2km 🌳 2km ⓘ 1km 🚐 9km **Notes** No pets

⋕⋕⋕ 🍴 Larrun Bixta

Yvette COLAS

Chemin Isabelenea, 64310 SAINT-PEE-SUR-NIVELLE

☎ 05 59 54 17 66 & 06 19 31 37 00

email: colasclaude@neuf.fr

web: www.gites64.com/larrun-bixta

This typical Basque house, close to the sea and the mountains, offers five spacious rooms. A generous breakfast is served in the dining room or on the terrace opposite the Rhune, in front of the swimming pool, which you can enjoy at your leisure. Dinner with your hosts offers varied traditional dishes. Pétanque.

Prices s fr €55; d fr €60; extra person fr €10; dinner fr €20 **On Site** Private ⚓ **Nearby** ✿ 1km ♨ 9km Sea 12km ⚓ 6km Restaurant 1km ☁ 2km 🌳 1km ⓘ 1km 🚐 12km **Notes** No pets English spoken

STE-ENGRACE

⋕⋕⋕ 🍴 Maison Elichalt

Ambroise BURGUBURU

Prebenda, 64560 SAINTE-ENGRACE

☎ 05 59 28 61 63 & 06 83 69 70 54 📄 05 59 28 75 54

email: a.burguburu@wanadoo.fr

web: www.gites-burguburu.com

Four rooms with shower and one with bathroom at this typical Basque house with stunning views over the Ehujarre gorges. At the foot of the mountain, this charming village has an exceptional 11th-century Norman church. Ample dining table and private parking.

Prices s fr €37; d fr €43; dinner fr €15 **Nearby** ✿ 18km ⚓ 33km Restaurant 10km ☁ 11km ☁ 10km ⓘ 18km **Notes** No pets English spoken

SUHESCUN

▦ ⦿ *Gordagia*

Maite SARAGUETA

64780 SUHESCUN

☎ 05 59 37 60 93

Guests have use of their own entrance, kitchenette and living room, TV, central heating, sheltered garden and terrace. Two rooms with double and twin beds, and another with two double beds. Meals on request except on Sundays. Numerous trails nearby.

Prices not confirmed for 2008 **Nearby** ⛷ 5km ⚓ 11km ⚓ 11km ⚑ 5km ⚒ 11km **Notes** No pets

URCUIT

▦ ⦿ Chambres d'Hotes L'Ardanavy

J-P BERGEMAYOU

Maison la Tourterelle, chemin des Tourterelles, 64990 URCUIT

☎ 05 59 42 95 66 & 06 24 29 23 39 ▤ 05 59 42 95 66

This beautifully peaceful property has been extensively restored to offer four spacious guest rooms, all on the ground floor with private bath or shower room and WC. Meals are available by arrangement, prepared with local produce. Garden with terrace, swimming pool and parking space.

Prices s €80-€90; d fr €100; t fr €130; dinner fr €30 **On Site** ⚓ Restaurant ⚑ Private ⚓ **Nearby** ⛷ 10km ⚓ 15km Sea 17km ⚓ 2km ⚑ 0.3km ⚒ 11km **Notes** No pets English spoken

▦ ⦿ Relais Linague

Marie BLEAU

64990 URCUIT

☎ 05 59 42 97 97 ▤ 05 59 42 97 97

email: linague@wanadoo.fr

web: www.relaislinague.com

Four rooms in a beautiful blue-timbered Basque house with restored furniture and fabrics a few minutes from the Basque hills. An ideal spot for riders and horse lovers. There are magnificent views of the surroundings from the terrace where breakfast is served. Full meals on request three nights a week out of season.

Prices s fr €50; d €52-€60; extra person fr €18; dinner €15-€18 **On Site** ⚑ **Nearby** ⛷ 10km ⚓ 15km Sea 15km ⚑ 3km ⚓ 10km Restaurant 3km ⚓ 0.5km Spa 15km ⚑ 3km ⚒ 10km **Notes** No pets

URRUGNE

▦ ❦ Manttu-Baïta

J-P IRAZOQUI

Quartier Olhette, 64122 URRUGNE

☎ 05 59 54 46 72 & 06 20 43 49 25

email: manttu@wanadoo.fr

web: www.gites64.com/manttu

This 18th-century Basque farmhouse is situated at the foot of the Rhune mountain. It has three double rooms, and one with twin beds,

all with private bath/shower room and WC. Guests' kitchenette. The pretty garden has lots of flowers, and is decorated with antique farm implements and machines. Breakfasts include home-made pastries and local specialities. Good walking country.

Prices d fr €65; extra person fr €20 **Nearby** ⛷ 12km ⚓ 8km Sea 8km ⚑ 0.1km ⚓ 4km Restaurant 0.5km ⚓ 4km Spa 12km ⚑ 4km ⚒ 12km **Notes** No pets

USTARITZ-ARRAUNTZ

▦ Bereterraenea

Nicole SINDERA

Quartier Arrauntz, 64480 USTARITZ

☎ 05 59 93 05 13 & 06 81 26 91 82 ▤ 05 59 93 27 70

email: bereter.nicole@wanadoo.fr

web: http://perso.wanadoo.fr/bereterraenea/

Only ten minutes from the sea, Bereterraenea offers ground floor and upstairs rooms with their own entrance. This is a 17th-century coaching inn overlooking forests and rivers.

Prices s fr €51; d €51-€63; extra person fr €17 **Nearby** ⛷ 5km ⚓ 2km Sea 10km ⚑ 0.3km ⚓ 4km Restaurant 3km ⚓ 4km ⚑ 10km ⚑ 4km ⚒ 7km **Notes** No pets English spoken

VIALER

▦ Le Bidou

Andre FOURCADE

Ch de l'Eglise, 64330 VIALER

☎ 05 59 04 07 58 ▤ 05 59 04 07 58

email: fourcade.andre@wanadoo.fr

web: www.lebidou.fr

This 18th-century Béarnaise house provides guests with the opportunity to discover the joys of French country living. There is a picnic area, a terrace with fine views, a shaded park and a boules court, plus four bedrooms.

Prices s fr €35; d fr €45; t fr €65; extra person fr €15 **Nearby** ⛷ 2km ⚓ 10km ⚑ 10km ⚓ 3km Restaurant 2km ⚓ 15km ⚑ 10km ⚒ 36km **Notes** No pets

VILLEFRANQUE

▦ Chambre d'hôtes

J-B LASCARAY

Chemin D137, 64990 VILLEFRANQUE

☎ 05 59 44 94 52 & 06 29 82 71 04

web: www.gites64.com/lascaray

This property has three upstairs bedrooms, all decorated with great charm and originality. There is an exceptional view towards the Pyrenees, and an unusual portrait gallery of members of the family. The delicious breakfasts include home-made pastries and are served on the terrace in summer.

Prices s fr €50; d €55-€60; extra person fr €20 **Nearby** ⛷ 5km ⚓ 10km Sea 10km ⚓ 5km Restaurant 1km ⚓ 3km ⚑ 1km ⚒ 5km **Notes** No pets

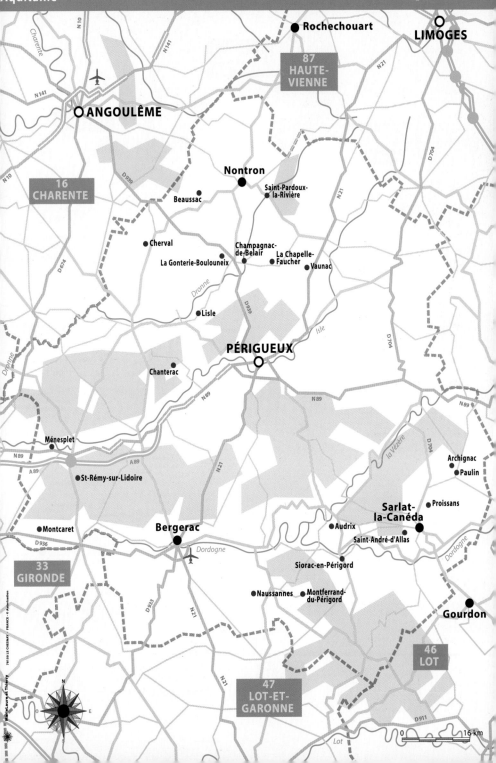

Rochechouart

LIMOGES

**87
HAUTE-
VIENNE**

ANGOULÊME

**16
CHARENTE**

Nontron

Saint-Pardoux-
la-Rivière

Beaussac

Cherval

Champagnac-
de-Belair

La Chapelle-
Faucher

La Gonterie-Boulouneix

Vaunac

Dronne

Lisle

D 939

Isle

PÉRIGUEUX

Chanterac

N 89

N 89

N 89

la Vézère

Ménesplet

St-Rémy-sur-Lidoire

A 89

Archignac

Paulin

Proissans

**Sarlat-
la-Canéda**

Montcaret

Bergerac

Audrix

Saint-André-d'Allas

D 936

Dordogne

Dordogne

**33
GIRONDE**

Siorac-en-Périgord

Naussannes

Montferrand-
du-Périgord

Gourdon

**46
LOT**

**47
LOT-ET-
GARONNE**

N

O   E

S

D 911

0   16-km

Lot

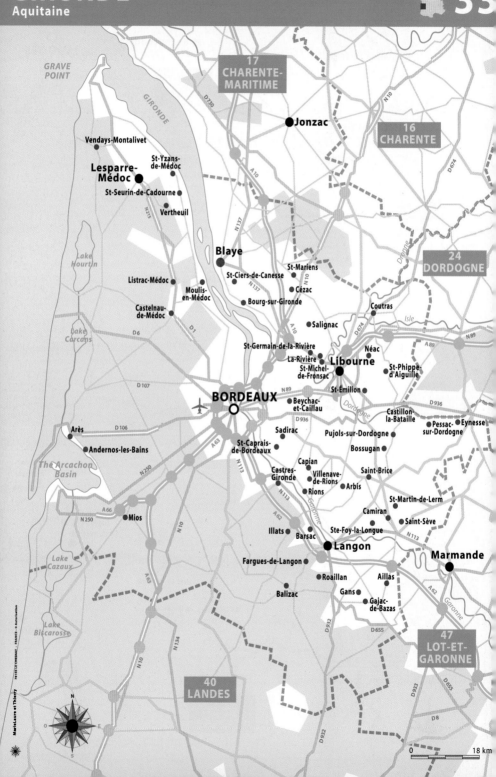

GRAVE POINT

GIRONDE

17 CHARENTE-MARITIME

16 CHARENTE

● Jonzac

Vendays-Montalivet

St-Yzans-de-Médoc

Lesparre-Médoc ●

St-Seurin-de-Cadourne

Vertheuil

Lake Hourtin

Listrac-Médoc

Moulis-en-Médoc

Castelnau-de-Médoc

● Blaye

St-Mariens

St-Ciers-de-Canesse

Cézac

Bourg-sur-Gironde

24 DORDOGNE

Coutras

Salignac

Isle

St-Germain-de-la-Rivière

La-Rivière

St-Michel-de-Fronsac

Néac

Libourne ●

St-Phippe-d'Aiguille

Lake Carcans

D 6

D 1

St-Émilion

BORDEAUX

Beychac-et-Caillau

Dordogne

Castillon-la-Bataille

D 936

Pessac-sur-Dordogne

Eynesse

Arès

D 106

Sadirac

Pujols-sur-Dordogne

Bossugan

Andernos-les-Bains

St-Caprais-de-Bordeaux

The Arcachon Basin

Capian

Saint-Brice

Castres-Gironde

Villenave-de-Rions

Arbís

Rions

St-Martin-de-Lerm

Mios

Illats

Camiran

Saint-Sève

Ste-Foy-la-Longue

Barsac

Langon ●

● **Marmande**

Fargues-de-Langon

Lake Cazaux

Roaillan

Aillas

Balizac

Gans

Gajac-de-Bazas

Lake Biscarosse

47 LOT-ET-GARONNE

40 LANDES

0   18 km

N
O   E
S

Marie-Laure et Thierry   PATRICE/ORMINAC — FRANCE — © Annoisation

Marmande

47 LOT-ET-GARONNE

33 GIRONDE

32 GERS

A 62

D 655

D 8

D 933

D 933

D 655

D 932

D 932

D 931

N 124

Douze

Midour

Adour

D 935

D 934

N 134

Créon-d'Armagnac

Betbezer-d'Armagnac

Sarbazan

St-Justin

St-Gein

St-Maurice-sur-Adour

N 124

D 933

D 933

D 932

Midouze

Campet-et-Lamolère

MONT-DE-MARSAN

N 134

Sore

Sabres

Morcenx-Bourg

Ousse-Suzan

N 134

N 134

N 10

A 63

N 10

Maylis

Adour

D 924

Gamarde-les-Bains

N 124

Dax

D 947

N 117

Mimizan

Lesperon

Castets

Herm

Linxe

Magescq

Lake Cazaux

Lake Biscarrosse

ATLANTIC OCEAN

Tosse

Seignosse

Angresse

A 63

N 10

Adour

Bélus

Orthevielle

Saubusse

Tarnos

N
O
E
S

0   15 km

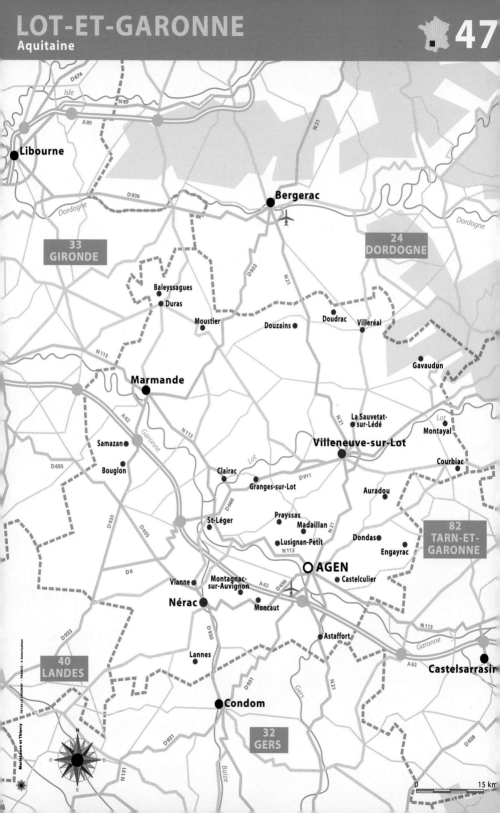

LOT-ET-GARONNE
Aquitaine

47

33 GIRONDE

24 DORDOGNE

82 TARN-ET-GARONNE

40 LANDES

32 GERS

Libourne

Bergerac

Baleyssagues
Duras
Moustier
Douzains
Doudrac
Villeréal

Gavaudun

Marmande

La Sauvetat-sur-Lédé
Montayal

Samazan
Bouglon

Villeneuve-sur-Lot

Courbiac

Clairac
Granges-sur-Lot

Auradou

St-Léger
Prayssas
Madaillan
Dondas
Engayrac

Lusignan-Petit

Vianne
Montagnac-sur-Auvignon
AGEN
Castelculier

Nérac
Moncaut

Astaffort

Lannes
Castelsarrasin

Condom

Isle
Dordogne
Dordogne
Garonne
Lot
Lot
Garonne
Gers
Baïze

D674
N89
A89
D936
D933
N21
N113
A62
D655
D666
D933
D655
D8
D930
D931
D933
D931
N131
D911
N21
N113
A62
D656
N113
D928

N
O E
S

0   15 km

Marie-Laure et Thierry
79150 LE RETAIL - FRANCE - © Autorisation

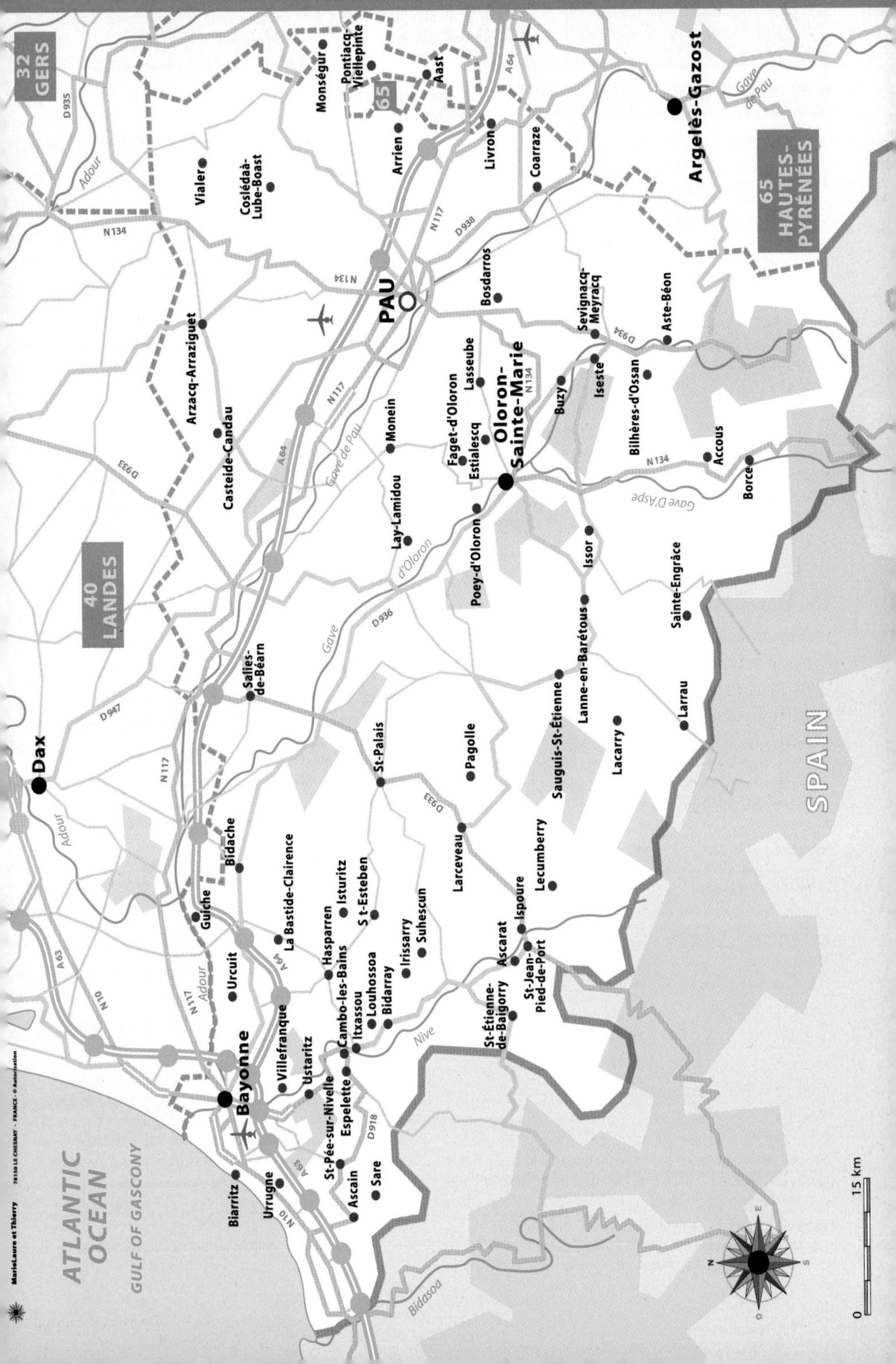

32 GERS

65

HAUTES-PYRÉNÉES

40 LANDES

SPAIN

ATLANTIC OCEAN

GULF OF GASCONY

Adour

D 935

D 933

N 134

Gave de Pau

Gave de Pau

Gave d'Oloron

Gave d'Oloron

Gave

Gave d'Aspe

Adour

Nive

Bidasoa

N 117

N 134

D 938

D 934

D 936

D 947

D 933

A 64

A 63

A 64

N 10

N 117

D 918

PAU

Oloron-Sainte-Marie

Bayonne

Dax

Argelès-Gazost

Monségur
Pontiacq-Vieillepinte
Aast
Arrien
Livron
Coarraze
Vialer
Coslédaà-Lube-Boast
Bosdarros
Sevignacq-Meyracq
Aste-Béon
Arzacq-Arraziguet
Lasseube
Buzy
Iseste
Bilhères-d'Ossan
Accous
Casteide-Candau
Faget-d'Oloron
Estialescq
Borce
Monein
Lay-Lamidou
Poey-d'Oloron
Issor
Sainte-Engrâce
Salies-de-Béarn
Lanne-en-Barétous
Larrau
St-Palais
Pagolle
Sauguis-St-Étienne
Lacarry
Lacarry
Bidache
Larceveau
Guiche
Urcuit
La Bastide-Clairence
Isturitz
St-Esteben
Lecumberry
Hasparren
Ispoure
Villefranque
Cambo-les-Bains
Itxassou
Louhossoa
Irissarry
Suhescun
Ascarat
St-Jean-Pied-de-Port
Ustaritz
Espelette
Bidarray
St-Étienne-de-Baïgorry
Biarritz
St-Pée-sur-Nivelle
Urrugne
Ascain
Sare

15 km

0

N
E
S
O

AUVERGNE

ALLIER

AGONGES

♯♯♯ ⏁◯⏁ Les Fours

Ettie et Koofs HAZENBERG
03210 AGONGES
☎ 04 70 43 98 40 & 06 70 34 81 03
email: info@lesfours.com
web: www.lesfours.com

18th-century residence of some note gives a choice of three rooms (with separate access), and the use of a salon and living room. Enclosed garden with terrace, barbecue and garden furniture. The Forest of Bagnolet is on the doorstep. Extra persons can be accommodated. English, German and Dutch are spoken.

Prices s fr €40; d fr €45; t fr €55; extra person fr €10; dinner fr €17 **Nearby** ↓18km ℘4km ⤳10km Restaurant 5km ⤳8km ⛳16km ⌂2km ⤳16km **Notes** Pets admitted English spoken Open April to October.

AUDES

♯♯♯ ❦ ⏁◯⏁ *Roueron*

Jacques & Véronique SION
Domaine de Roueron, 03190 AUDES
☎ 04 70 06 00 59 ▤ 04 70 06 16 81
email: jv.sion@wanadoo.fr

Beautifully restored Bourbonnais stables providing a double room with three single beds, a triple room, a twin, a room with twin beds and a child's bed, and one with double bed and cot, each with private facilities. Breakfast room, lounge and fireplace. Discount for stays over three days.

Prices not confirmed for 2008 **On Site** ℘ **Nearby** ⤳7km ↓6km ⤳15km ⤳3km ⛳18km ⌂3km ⤳10km **Notes** Pets admitted Open 15 March to 15 November.

AUTRY-ISSARDS

♯♯♯ ⏁◯⏁ Chambre d'hôtes

Jean Claude ROUX
Le Bourg, 03210 AUTRY ISSARDS
☎ 04 70 43 66 80 & 04 70 43 66 73 ▤ 04 70 43 66 73
email: chez-lgars-roux@wanadoo.fr

This house is close to the church, in a small village with an abundance of flowers. It has a double room on the ground floor, while upstairs there is a triple (double bed and single), a split-level room for four (double bed and twins), and a family room for five (double bed plus singles). All have private facilities; cot available. Good walking country.

Prices s fr €35; d fr €45; t fr €55; extra person fr €10; dinner fr €18 **On Site** ⛳ **Nearby** ⤳10km ↓25km ℘0.2km ⤳8km Restaurant 5km ⤳ ⤳20km **Notes** Pets admitted English spoken CC

BELLERIVE-SUR-ALLIER

♯♯♯ ⏁◯⏁ Les Marm'hôtes Chemin de Preux

Jean Francois RANDANNE
03700 BELLERIVE SUR ALLIER
☎ 04 70 32 05 78 & 06 82 09 90 70
email: les.marm.hotes@segetel.net
web: http://monsite.wanadoo.fr/visualisation

A large, modern house, close to the forest, with three first floor bedrooms. All are non-smoking, with private facilities. Breakfast area in the big, American-style kitchen; lounge available. Outside are attractive grounds with a terrace, table tennis, pétanque pitch, and above-ground swimming pool.

Prices s €41-€49; d €52-€57; t fr €68; extra person fr €10; dinner fr €16 **On Site** Private ⤳ **Nearby** ⤳4km ↓1km ℘4km Restaurant 1km ⤳1km ⛳4km ⌂1km ⤳4km **Notes** No pets English spoken Open February to 15 December.

BIZENEUILLE

♯♯♯ ⏁◯⏁ *Château de Bagnard*

Emmanuel DE MONTAIGNAC
03170 BIZENEUILLE
☎ 06 09 18 50 79 & 04 70 07 85 40 ▤ 04 70 07 85 40
email: e.de-montaignac@wanadoo.fr

A 19th-century château with five bedrooms, all decorated and furnished in keeping with their period, comprising four doubles and a twin. All are upstairs and equipped with private facilities. Extensive grounds with swimming pool. Quad bikes, cycles and horses are available for hire. Meals by arrangement.

Prices not confirmed for 2008 **On Site** ⤳ ℘ ⛳ Private ⤳ **Nearby** ↓15km ⤳8km ⤳8km ⤳15km **Notes** No pets English spoken Open March to November.

BRAIZE

♯♯♯ Grange Florie Jean

F et J-C LENAY CESSIECQ
Ferme de Beauregard, 03360 BRAIZE
☎ 04 70 06 15 09 & 06 71 40 45 01 ▤ 04 70 06 15 09
email: jean-florie@wanadoo.fr
web: www.grangefloriejean.net

This barn conversion, just across from the owners' house on a working farm, has a large entrance hall and lounge. The three bedrooms, all with private bath/shower room and WC, one with a split-level layout, are upstairs. Outside is a courtyard, grassed area, and a swimming pool.

Prices d €65-€75; t €72-€82; extra person fr €7 **On Site** Private ⤳ **Nearby** ⤳10km ↓25km ℘1km Restaurant 4km ⤳2km Spa 25km ⛳2km ⌂2km ⤳14km **Notes** Pets admitted English spoken

BUXIERES-LES-MINES

⫴ ıⓄı **Renière**

Geneviève BREGEOT
03440 BUXIERES LES MINES
☎ 04 70 66 00 13 📄 04 70 66 00 13

A working farm next to a private forest with enclosed garden and shaded park, grazing for horses, fishing and picnic areas. Double room and twin, and in a separate building, refurbished in local stone and wood, there is a double and room with a double and single bed. All have private facilities. Shared lounge with fireplace, dining room, washing machine. Table d'hôte meals on reservation. Walking trails nearby.

Prices s fr €36; d fr €43; t fr €53; extra person fr €10; dinner fr €15
On Site ⌇ **Nearby** ⛷ 12km ⏚ 30km ⤳ 11km ⌇ 3.5km ⌇ 5.5km
⌂ 3.5km ⛫ 30km **Notes** No pets

CHARROUX

⫴⫴ ıⓄı **La Grange du Belvedere**

Colleen SHARPE
03140 CHARROUX
☎ 04 70 56 80 02 📄 04 70 56 80 02
email: lagrangedubelvedere@wanadoo.fr
web: www.lagrangedubelvedere.com

Right at the centre of a medieval village, classified as one of the most beautiful in France, this is a restored farmhouse with three bedrooms. Two are doubles; the other has a double and a single bed, and all have private bath or shower rooms and WCs. Elegant decorations, with some antique furniture. Lounge available for guests; garden with terrace and garden furniture.

Prices s fr €65; d fr €80; t fr €95; dinner fr €30 **On Site** ⌇
Nearby ⛷ 4km ⏚ 20km ⌇ 4km ⤳ 12km Restaurant 0.1km
⌇ 6km Spa 25km ⌂ 0.1km ⛫ 10km **Notes** No pets English spoken

⫴ ıⓄı **Le Relais de l'Orient**

Susette THYS
Grande Rue, 03140 CHARROUX
☎ 04 70 56 89 93
email: relais-orient@charroux.com
web: www.relais-orient.charroux.com

In the heart of a listed medieval village, this distinctive house, with internal courtyard and pigeon loft, stands in quiet private grounds, with many fruit trees. It has one suite of two double rooms with power shower/WC, and two rooms for three people, both with private facilities. Library, swimming pool, working farmyard. Meals available by request.

Prices s fr €40; d €48-€60; t €63-€73; extra person fr €15; dinner
fr €24 **On Site** ⌇ Private ⤳ **Nearby** ⛷ 4km ⏚ 20km ⌇ 4km
Restaurant 0.1km ⌇ 6km ⌂ 0.1km ⛫ 8km **Notes** Pets admitted
English spoken

⫴⫴ **La Maison du Prince de Condé**

Jon SPEER
8 Place d'Armes, 03140 CHARROUX
☎ 04 70 56 81 36 & 06 88 71 10 59
📄 04 70 56 81 36
email: jspeer@club-internet.fr
web: www.maison-conde.com

The house of the Prince de Condé, an old to 13th to 18th-century hunting lodge, in a medieval cité classed as one of France's beautiful villages. It offers five doubles, with a duplex in one of the fortified towers. Each has private facilities, three with spa baths. TV available. Library, lounge with fireplace, dining room in the 13th-century cellar. Enclosed wooded garden. Non-smoking house. Two restaurants in the village.

Prices s fr €50; d €58-€82; t €86; extra person fr €15
On Site Restaurant **Nearby** ⛷ 6km ⏚ 20km ⌇ 4km ⌇ 6km
⌇ 20km ⌂ 10km ⛫ 6km **Notes** No pets English spoken CC

CHATEAU-SUR-ALLIER

⫴⫴ ıⓄı **Château de Saint Augustin**

Jehan DE L'ALLIER
Les Amis de Saint Augustin,
03320 CHATEAU SUR ALLIER
☎ 04 70 66 42 01
email: chateau-saint-augustin@wanadoo.fr
web: www.chateau-saint-augustin.fr

A listed château, the oldest parts of which date back to the 16th century, with four guest bedrooms, all on the first floor, each decorated and furnished in a period style. The rooms are all doubles with private bath/shower room and WC, and one has a canopied bed. Lounge and billiard room available for guest use. The entire site is non-smoking.

Prices d €130-€180; extra person €25-€45; dinner fr €60
Nearby ⛷ 15km ⏚ 30km ⌇ 2km ⤳ 6km Restaurant 6km ⌇ 6km
⌂ 6km ⛫ 12km **Notes** No pets English spoken

AUVERGNE

CHOUVIGNY

⊞ ⦿ La Chouvignotte

Gisèle et J Claude DURIAUX
03450 CHOUVIGNY
☎ 04 70 90 91 91 & 06 77 19 37 66 📄 04 70 90 91 91
email: contact@chouvignotte.com
web: www.chouvignotte.com

Tucked away among the gorges of the Sioule, a favourite river for anglers, this stone-built house offers three first floor guest bedrooms. There are two rooms with double beds, each with two additional singles on a mezzanine, and a further bedroom with three singles. Each room has private shower/WC. There is another triple in a small separate building. Terrace facing river; meals by arrangement.

Prices s €40-€45; d €45-€50; t fr €60; extra person fr €12; dinner fr €18 **On Site** ⚓ **Nearby** ⚓ 10km ⚓ 25km ⚓ 20km Restaurant 0.6km ⚓ 10km ⚓ 20km ⚓ 9km ⚓ 25km **Notes** Pets admitted Open April to 15 November.

COULANDON

⊞ ⦿ La Grande Poterie

Jean Claude POMPON
9 rue de la Grande Poterie, 03000 COULANDON
☎ 04 70 44 30 39 & 06 68 22 20 73
📄 04 70 44 30 39
email: jcpompon@lagrandepoterie.com
web: www.lagrandepoterie.com

An old restored barn next to the owner's house, which has been beautifully decorated with both antique and modern furniture. There are two doubles, a twin and a room with a double and single bed, each with a private shower and wc. Cot available. Facilities include a lounge, dining room, terrace, trail bikes and swimming pool. Table d'hôte meals available if booked in advance. Forest and walking trails nearby.

Prices s fr €55; d fr €66; t fr €77; extra person fr €17; dinner fr €25 **On Site** ⚓ Private ⚓ **Nearby** ⚓ 2km ⚓ 10km ⚓ 1.5km Restaurant 2km ⚓ 4km Spa 20km ⚓ 4km ⚓ 9km **Notes** No pets Open 16 March to October.

COULEUVRE

⊞ ⚓ Le Champ du Taillis

H et R KILKENS BEKENKAMP
03320 COULEUVRE
☎ 04 70 66 68 42 📄 04 70 66 68 42
email: henron@wanadoo.fr

Four spacious bedrooms have been created in this converted barn, close by the owners' home. On the ground floor is a double room and a twin-bedded room, with the same again upstairs. All four have private shower room and WC, and additional beds are available. Guest living room, terrace, meals by arrangement.

Prices s fr €40; d fr €50; t fr €65 **Nearby** ⚓ 10km ⚓ 20km ⚓ 1km ⚓ 2km Restaurant 5km ⚓ 4km ⚓ 7km ⚓ 1km ⚓ 45km **Notes** Pets admitted English spoken

COUZON

⊞ ⚘ ⦿ Manoir de la Beaume

Mme BIEWER-BARRITAUD
La Beaume, 03160 COUZON
☎ 04 70 66 22 74 📄 04 70 66 22 74
email: labeaume@wanadoo.fr
web: http://perso.orange.fr/maisondelabeaume

On the Allier horse-riding trail, this small 17th-century manor house is on an equestrian farm. There is a room with a queen bed and single bed, a twin and two doubles (one with double couch), all with private facilities. Cot available. There is a lounge, dining room and open fire, walks, riding lessons, pony trekking and pony club.

Prices s €37-€52; d €50-€62; t €64-€70; dinner fr €18 **Nearby** ⚓ 22km ⚓ 25km ⚓ 1km ⚓ 12km Restaurant 5km ⚓ 12km Spa 18km ⚓ 22km ⚓ 12km ⚓ 22km **Notes** Pets admitted English spoken

DEUX-CHAISES

⊞ ⦿ Château de Longeville

Geneviève & Rodolphe MARCHAND
Longeville, 03240 DEUX CHAISES
☎ 04 70 47 32 91
email: châteaudelongeville@hotmail.com
web: www.chateaudelongeville.com

This 19th-century château has four guest bedrooms, with striking decorations and stylish furnishings. There are two double rooms, a triple (double bed and a single), and a two-room family suite for four, with a double bed and twins. Each has a private bathroom and WC. Lounge, dining room, billiard table, and extensive grounds.

Prices s fr €60; d fr €75; t fr €90; extra person €15-€20; dinner fr €28 **On Site** ⚓ **Nearby** ⛷ 20km 🚣 30km Restaurant 7km 🏊 1km ✤ 15km 🚲 4km ⚘ 40km **Notes** Pets admitted English spoken

DIOU

♨ ⁙○⁙ ⚒ **Le Cloitre**

Catherine et Gilles FONTENIAUD
89 Grande rue, 03290 DIOU
☎ 04 70 34 60 89 & 06 87 46 07 61 📄 04 70 34 60 89
email: fonteniaud.c@wanadoo.fr
web: www.lecloitre.fr

In a village close to the Loire, this property stands in walled gardens with a swimming pool. There is one double room, three triples (double bed and a single in each) and a two-roomed suite. An additional bed and a cot are available. Guests have use of a kitchen, and outside there is garden furniture and a barbecue. Footpaths nearby.

Prices s fr €50; d fr €60; t fr €75; extra person fr €15; dinner fr €25 **On Site** ⚓ ✤ Private ⚲ **Nearby** ⛷ 15km 🚣 30km Restaurant 5km 🏊 0.2km 🏛 0.2km ⚘ 5km **Notes** Pets admitted English spoken

DOYET

♨ **Bord**

Chantal & Jacques CHATEAU
03170 DOYET
☎ 04 70 07 74 83 & 06 80 33 17 26 📄 04 70 07 74 83
email: gitesdebord@wanadoo.fr
web: www.pour-les-vacances.com

This restored former barn, standing in its own wooded grounds among many flowers, offers four rooms. In the barn are one double room and one single; in a converted farm building are two twin-bedded rooms. These two rooms also share a small lounge. All four rooms have private facilities. Meals by arrangement. Large external room with bread oven, swimming pool.

Prices s fr €43; d fr €58; extra person fr €20; dinner fr €23 **On Site** Private ⚲ **Nearby** ⛷ 15km 🚣 12km ⚓ 1.5km Restaurant 0.4km 🏊 3km Spa 12km ✤ 15km 🏛 3km ⚘ 12km **Notes** Pets admitted English spoken

EBREUIL

♨ ⁙○⁙ **Chavagnat**

Christian BOUTONNET
03450 EBREUIL
☎ 04 70 90 73 56 📄 04 70 90 73 56
email: cboutonnet03@aol.com
web: www.chavagnat.fr

A fully restored old farmhouse in a hamlet overlooking the countryside. One room with a double and single bed, a room with a double and twin beds, one with two doubles and a large room with a double bed and two double sofa beds, each with private facilities. There is a lounge, sitting room, library, terrace and garden furniture. Also a holiday cottage to let.

Prices s fr €38; d fr €45; t fr €53; extra person fr €12; dinner fr €17 **On Site** Restaurant **Nearby** ⛷ 2km ⚓ 2km 🏊 2km ✤ 2km 🏛 3km ⚘ 12km **Notes** No pets English spoken

ESPINASSE-VOZELLE

♨ ⁙○⁙ **Aux Jardin des Thévenets**

Lynn CHAULIEU
03110 ESPINASSE VOZELLE
☎ 04 70 56 57 04 & 06 81 14 39 11
email: jardins-des-thevenets@wanadoo.fr
web: www.jardins-des-thevenets.com

Just 8 kilometres from Vichy, surrounded by nine hectares of woods and medicinal plants, this house dating from the 17th and 19th centuries offers five guest bedrooms, all with private facilities. Lounge and dining room shared with hosts; garden furniture; indoor swimming pool available.

Prices s €63-€73; d €70-€80; extra person fr €20; dinner fr €28 **On Site** ✤ Private ⚲ **Nearby** ⛷ 6km 🚣 3km ⚓ 8km Restaurant 3km 🏊 8km Spa 8km 🏛 2km ⚘ 8km **Notes** No pets English spoken

FLEURIEL

₩ǁ ꜰⓄꜰ **Le Corgenay**

Manuela et Louis STERCKX
Le Bourg, 03140 FLEURIEL
☎ 04 70 56 94 12 ▤ 04 70 56 90 88
web: www.valdesioule.fr

A completely restored 1820s house on a working farm with superb views over the Bourbonnais and Puy mountains. There is a twin room, two doubles and two rooms with king-sized beds, all with private facilities. Shared lounge, dining room, library, jacuzzi, terrace, veranda and garden furniture. Table d'hôte meals must be booked in advance.

Prices s fr €58; d €60-€88; extra person fr €15; dinner fr €20
On Site Private ⭠ **Nearby** ⛄ 20km ♨ 15km ♂ 8km ⌔ 8km ♥ 12km ☖ 8km ⋈ 30km **Notes** No pets English spoken Open Easter to 1 November.

FRANCHESSE

₩ǁ ꜰⓄꜰ **Les Communs Bouquetraud**

Christian AMMANN
03160 FRANCHESSE
☎ 04 70 66 25 27 ▤ 04 70 66 23 86
email: gite.bouquetraud@wanadoo.fr
web: http://perso.wanadoo.fr/gite.bouquetraud/

This large restored house stands in 2 hectares of wooded parkland with ponds, in the grounds of an old castle. One double room in a wing of the castle with separate entrance, plus three rooms upstairs in the main house. Lounge reserved for guests, library, games including table football, table tennis, billiards. Pets accepted by prior arrangement. Visit the volcanoes at Auvergne (1hr 30min).

Prices s fr €40; d fr €45; t fr €55; extra person fr €10; dinner fr €16
On Site ♂ ♥ **Nearby** ⛄ 6km ♨ 23km ⭠ Restaurant 7km ⌔ 10km Spa 7km ☖ 3km ⋈ 25km **Notes** Pets admitted English spoken

GANNAT

₩ǁ Ꝡ ꜰⓄꜰ ♿ **Domaine de Rouzat**

Martine et Christian MATHINIER
Route de St Priest l'Andelot, 03800 GANNAT
☎ 04 70 90 20 04 & 06 74 58 23 54 ▤ 04 70 90 20 04
web: http://membres.lycos.fr/domainederouzat/

In a former sheepfold backing on to the owners' house, the four guest bedrooms have been built from old materials to retain the character of the building. On the ground floor are a double and a triple; upstairs are two more rooms, each with a double bed and a single. All have private facilities. Cot available. Shady grounds, wonderful views.

Prices s fr €44; d fr €49; t fr €62; extra person fr €12; dinner fr €17
Nearby ⛄ 3.5km ♨ 15km ♂ 5km ⭠ 3km Restaurant 3km ⌔ 3km ♥ 3km ☖ 3km ⋈ 3km **Notes** Pets admitted English spoken

₩ǁ ꜰⓄꜰ **Domaine des Chambons**

Marie Laure SOCCOL
03800 GANNAT
☎ 04 70 90 27 39 & 06 62 59 11 08 ▤ 04 70 90 27 39

This interesting house, standing in its walled garden, dates from the 18th century. There are three guest bedrooms: a double, a twin and a triple, each with private WC/shower room. Outside there is a terrace and garden room offering panoramic views over the mountains of the Auvergne.

Prices not confirmed for 2008 **On Site** Private ⭠ **Nearby** ⛄ 1km ♨ 20km ♂ 3km ⌔ 3km ♥ 3km ☖ 3km ⋈ 3km **Notes** Pets admitted Open April to October.

GOUISE

₩ǁ ꜰⓄꜰ **Les Rubis**

Marie et Yves LEBRUN
03340 GOUISE
☎ 04 70 43 12 70
email: lesrubis.gouise@wanadoo.fr
web: http://pro.wanadoo.fr/lesrubis

In the converted outbuildings of this 19th-century property are four bedrooms. A twin-bedded ground floor room is suitable for guests with limited mobility. There is a further twin-bedded room, one with a double bed plus a single, and a fourth with double bed and bunks. All have private WC/shower. Cot available; garden and garden room. Meals by arrangement in school holidays; guests' kitchenette.

Prices s fr €38; d fr €45; t fr €50; extra person fr €10; dinner fr €15
Nearby ⛄ 3km ♨ 12km ♂ 8km ⭠ 18km Restaurant 6km ⌔ 6km Spa 20km ♥ 20km ☖ 6km ⋈ 20km **Notes** No pets Open April to 29 October.

HURIEL

₩ǁ ꜰⓄꜰ **Les Malvaux**

Nathalie et Pascal NICOLAS
03380 HURIEL
☎ 04 70 06 44 09 & 06 21 56 39 10
email: lesmalvaux@aliceadsl.fr
web: http://lesmalvaux.free.fr

In a hamlet near the village of La Chapelaude, in a barn conversion next to the family home; there are three rooms for two, three or four people, each with a private shower and wc. Cot available. Large lounge with open fire, library and kitchenette, large lawned courtyard, garden furniture, barbecue, parking and stabling for horses.

Prices s fr €35; d fr €45; t fr €59; extra person fr €14; dinner fr €17
Nearby ⛄ 4km ♨ 18km ♂ 7km ⭠ 10km Restaurant 1km ⌔ 1.5km Spa 20km ♥ 7km ☖ 1.5km ⋈ 10km **Notes** Pets admitted English spoken

ISLE-ET-BARDAIS

▥ ⦿ **La Tour de Bouis**

Marie Aude DEVRED

03360 ISLE ET BARDAIS

☎ 04 70 66 60 13 & 06 33 23 25 03 📄 04 70 66 60 17

email: latourdebouis@wanadoo.fr

Situated in the Tronçais forest, this restored barn close to the owners' house offers three ground floor rooms - two doubles, and one with three single beds. Extra bed and cot available. All rooms have private bath or shower room and WC. Large lounge with open fire, small kitchen area for guests' use, meals available by arrangement.

Prices s fr €39; d fr €50; t fr €61; dinner fr €18 **Nearby** ⛷ 15km ⚓ 35km ⚐ 3.5km ⚑ 25km Restaurant 4km ⚓ 3.5km ⚑ 7km ⚑ 7km ⚑ 26km **Notes** Pets admitted English spoken

LA FERTE-HAUTERIVE

▥▥ ⦿ **Demeure d'Hauterive**

Jérome LEFEBVRE

03340 LA FERTE HAUTERIVE

☎ 04 70 43 04 85 📄 04 70 43 04 85

email: j.lefebvre@demeure-hauterive.com

web: www.demeure-hauterive.com

A big house, typical of the Sologne Bourbonnais, in a large enclosed park. It has a double room, two rooms with a double and a single bed and a two-room suite with four single beds and extra bed available. There is a dining room, lounge, billiard room, terrace, garage, summerhouse and ornamental ponds. Pets accepted by prior arrangement; kennels available.

Prices s fr €65; d fr €80; t fr €105; dinner €20-€25 **On Site** ⚑ Private ⚑ **Nearby** ⛷ 20km ⚓ 12km ⚐ 0.5km Restaurant 0.5km ⚓ 0.2km ⚑ 2km ⚑ 20km **Notes** Pets admitted English spoken CC

LE MAYET-DE-MONTAGNE

▥ ⦿ **De Chez Breuil**

Noelle Dominique MOUSSIERE

03250 LE MAYET DE MONTAGNE

☎ 04 70 59 75 03

web: www.chezbreuil.com

Situated on a working cattle farm in a mountain village, this property has three bedrooms in a building adjoining the owners' home. There is a double, a room with a double and a single, and a room with a double and two singles. Each room has its own shower/WC. Extra bed available. Courtyard with lawn, garden furniture.

Prices s fr €34; d fr €44; t fr €54; extra person fr €10; dinner fr €15 **Nearby** ⛷ 3km ⚓ 20km ⚐ 3km ⚑ 2.5km Restaurant 2.5km ⚓ 2.5km Spa 25km ⚑ 20km ⚑ 2.5km ⚑ 20km **Notes** No pets

▥ ⦿ **Le Couturon**

Mireille Christian MONAT

La Cartonnée, 03250 LE MAYET DE MONTAGNE

☎ 04 70 56 45 14 & 06 64 85 06 29

email: mireille.monat@wanadoo.fr

web: www.le-couturon.com

In the heart of the leafy Bourbonnaise mountains, this former farmhouse is near a stretch of water and offers a room with a double and twin beds, two double rooms, a twin and a room with a single and double bed, each with private facilities. There is a lounge with fireplace and TV, living room, terrace with garden furniture, portico and enclosed green space. Non smoking house; baby equipment available. Walks nearby. Vichy 30km.

Prices s fr €35; d fr €43; t fr €55; extra person fr €17; dinner fr €17 **Nearby** ⛷ 3km ⚓ 30km ⚐ 0.5km ⚑ 4km Restaurant 4km ⚓ 1km Spa 30km ⚑ 20km ⚑ 4km ⚑ 30km **Notes** No pets

LE PIN

▥ ⚘ ⦿ **La Noux**

Michele et Alain DECERLE

03130 LE PIN

☎ 04 70 55 62 62 📄 04 70 55 65 51

A working farm with rooms in the owner's house including a room with three single beds, two twin rooms and a double room, each with bathroom and wc. The owner's lounge with fireplace is for guests' use and meals are based on farm produce. There is a lake on site.

Prices s fr €40; d fr €50; t fr €62; extra person fr €12; dinner fr €16 **On Site** ⚐ ⚑ **Nearby** ⛷ 2km ⚓ 15km ⚑ 15km Restaurant 6km ⚓ 10km ⚑ 3km ⚑ 15km **Notes** Pets admitted English spoken

LE THEIL

▥ ⦿ ♿ **Château du Max**

Dominique PESSAR MAZET

03240 LE THEIL

☎ 04 70 42 35 23 📄 04 70 42 34 90

email: chateaudumax@club-internet.fr

web: www.chateaudumax.com

Guest rooms in a separate wing of this 13th-15th century château, surrounded by a moat. One suite of two rooms with two double four-poster beds, a room with two single four-poster beds, and a double room in the château tower. All have private facilities; additional beds available. The lounge and dining room are shared with the owners. Guests may walk in the grounds and woods, and fish in the moat.

Prices s fr €60; d €70-€80; t €80-€90; extra person fr €10; dinner fr €25 **On Site** ⚐ ⚑ **Nearby** ⛷ 10km ⚓ 15km ⚑ 15km Restaurant 10km ⚓ 5km ⚑ 4km ⚑ 35km **Notes** Pets admitted English spoken

LE VERNET

₩₩₩ Moulin St Jean

Jean Philippe LALOY
Rte de Ferrières, 03300 CUSSET
☎ 04 70 96 05 51 & 06 07 63 68 10 📠 04 70 96 05 51
email: florence.laloy@club-internet.fr
web: www.moulinsaintjean.com

In a beautiful riverside location, not far from Vichy, this 18th-century mill, still in working order, has five bedrooms - three doubles, a twin-bedded room, and a family room for four. All have private facilities. Cot available; TV for hire. Lounge with books, billiards. Extensive grounds with terrace, garden furniture, children's games and swimming pool.

Prices s fr €50; d fr €60; t fr €72; extra person fr €12   **On Site** 🏌 ♨ Private ⟋   **Nearby** ⛵ 5km ♨ 8km Restaurant 1.5km ♨ 2km 🏛 2km ₩ 5km   **Notes** No pets English spoken

LOUCHY-MONTFAND

₩₩₩ i◎i Le Courtiau

C J AYRAULT DUBOIS
5 rue du Courtiau, 03500 LOUCHY MONTFAND
☎ 04 70 45 91 03 📠 04 70 45 91 03
email: ayrault.christian@wanadoo.fr

A former vineyard property, with three first floor bedrooms - two with independent access. All of the rooms are doubles, and each has a private shower room and WC. Possible occasional use of an additional twin-bedded room. Lounge, covered terrace, enclosed grounds. Non-smoking rooms available; meals by arrangement.

Prices s fr €42; d fr €47; extra person fr €16; dinner fr €18   **Nearby** ⛵ 15km ♨ 3km ⟋ 1km ⟋ 3km Restaurant 3km ♨ 3km ♨ 3km 🏛 3km ₩ 25km   **Notes** No pets English spoken Open April to 30 October.

LOUROUX-DE-BEAUNE

₩₩₩ L'étang du Champfournier

E JALLET et L FAUDEMER
Les Roumeaux, 03600 LOUROUX DE BEAUNE
☎ 04 70 64 95 04 & 06 84 48 88 37

In the heart of a large wooded area with a private pond, this old farm guesthouse has a twin room and three double, each with a private shower and wc. Other facilities include a lounge, sitting room, large terrace, parking and garden furniture. Trail bikes are available for local trips and table d'hôte meals are served at weekends.

Prices s fr €45; d fr €55   **Nearby** ⛵ 5km ♨ 30km ⟋ 16km ⟋ 18km Restaurant 5km ♨ 8km ♨ 18km 🏛 8km ₩ 18km   **Notes** No pets English spoken Open March to November.

LOUROUX-DE-BOUBLE

₩₩₩ Le Bourg

Ennio TURCY
03330 LOUROUX DE BOUBLE
☎ 04 70 90 48 04 📠 04 70 90 48 04

Close to the Colettes forest, and in the heart of the village, this property offers three first floor guest rooms: two doubles, and one with two large singles and a child's bed. All rooms have private facilities; there is also a first floor lounge/library. The garden has an enclosed area and a terrace. Garage available.

Prices s fr €38; d fr €42; t fr €54   **Nearby** ⛵ 17km ♨ 30km ⟋ 2km ⟋ 22km Restaurant 0.8km ♨ 17km ₩ 0.5km   **Notes** No pets English spoken

LURCY-LEVIS

₩₩₩ i◎i La Platrière

Jackie et Andrew DIAPER
03320 LURCY LEVIS
☎ 04 70 67 94 26 & 06 85 50 67 07 📠 04 70 67 94 26
email: info@laplatriere.co.uk
web: www.laplatriere.co.uk

An old farmhouse which has been totally restored to provide five guest rooms, all upstairs. There is one bedroom for four (all single beds), three twin-bedded rooms, and a single room, all with en suite facilities. Outside guests can enjoy the wooded grounds, with swimming pool and a boules pitch.

Prices s fr €45; d €60-€75; t fr €75; dinner fr €30   **On Site** ♨ Private ⟋   **Nearby** ⛵ 6km ♨ 28km ⟋ 5km Restaurant 4km ♨ 4km ♨ 7km ₩ 40km   **Notes** No pets English spoken

₩₩₩ ♿ La Porte

Guy et Catherine DE TURCKHEIM
03320 LURCY LEVIS
☎ 04 70 67 87 28
email: turckheim-et-compagnie@wanadoo.fr
web: www.laporteallier.fr

This farm has four bedrooms, sleeping from two to four people, each with a private bath or shower room and WC. One of the rooms has disabled access; two of them are on the first floor. Guests' lounge, with kitchenette available. Large garden with terrace and furniture; games area for children; small pond.

Prices s fr €35; d fr €45; t fr €58; extra person fr €13   **On Site** ♨   **Nearby** ⛵ 10km ♨ 28km ⟋ 2km ⟋ 15km Restaurant 2km ♨ 2km Spa 20km 🏛 2km ₩ 40km   **Notes** No pets English spoken

LUSIGNY

♯♯♯ ❦ ⓘⓞⓘ Ferme de Treveze

Evelyne JOLY
Treveze, 03230 LUSIGNY
☎ 04 70 42 44 87
email: s.joly@03.sideral.fr
web: http://perso.orange.fr/treveze

This Sologne farmhouse, surrounded by meadows, lakes and woods, has three guest rooms. There are two attic rooms - one with a double bed plus a single, and the other with a double, a single and a cot. There is a further twin-bedded room downstairs. All rooms have private facilities. Garden with garden furniture and children's games. Stabling available.

Prices s fr €35; d fr €44; t fr €56; extra person fr €12; dinner fr €15 **Nearby** ⚓ 12km ⚡ 15km ⚲ 7km ➚ 12km Restaurant 7km ◡ 7km ⚑ 10km ⚐ 7km ⚒ 8km **Notes** No pets English spoken

MARIOL

♯♯♯ ⓘⓞⓘ Les Breuils

Catherine ARNAUD
8 route de St Yorre, 03270 MARIOL
☎ 04 70 41 00 03 ▤ 04 70 41 00 12
email: canayma@wanadoo.fr

Guest rooms available in a completely renovated house of much character: two twins, a double and a room with a double and single bed. Each has private facilities; extra beds and cot available. There is a washing machine, large shady garden with furniture, parking and barbecue and the owner's lounge and dining room is open to guests. Pets accepted if booked. Discounts out of season after the fourth night and for groups.

Prices s fr €42; d fr €48; t fr €59; extra person fr €11; dinner fr €17 **On Site** ⚲ ⚑ **Nearby** ⚓ 5km ⚡ 15km ➚ 5km Restaurant 4km ◡ 5km Spa 15km ⚒ 2km ⚐ 15km **Notes** Pets admitted English spoken

MEAULNE

♯♯♯♯ ⓘⓞⓘ Manoir du Mortier

Catherine GRENINGER
Le Mortier, 03360 MEAULNE
☎ 06 62 21 08 82 & 04 70 06 99 87
email: manoirdumortier@yahoo.fr
web: www.manoirdumortier.com

On the edge of the Tronçais forest, this 18th-century manor house offers three guest bedrooms. There are two intercommunicating doubles, and a two-roomed suite, also with two double beds. All have en suite bathrooms. There is a guests' lounge with books to read. Horse riding is possible in the forest.

Prices s fr €115; d €115-€160; t fr €150; extra person fr €25; dinner fr €25 **On Site** ⚓ Restaurant Private ➚ **Nearby** ⚡ 12km ⚲ 6km ⚑ 6km ⚐ 26km ⚒ 7km ⚐ 30km **Notes** No pets English spoken Open April to December. CC

MONTEIGNET L'ANDELOT

♯♯♯ La Marivole

Annick SUPPLISSON
Le Bourg, 03800 MONTEIGNET L'ANDELOT
☎ 04 70 90 58 53 ▤ 04 70 90 58 53
email: annick.supplisson@wanadoo.fr

Four rooms in this lovely house near Andelot: two twins, a double and a room with a double and single bed - all with private facilities. The owners share the lounge and dining room with guests and there are large, shady grounds, a terrace and garden furniture, table tennis, and bikes for guests to use.

Prices s €35-€42; d €42-€48; t €54-€60; extra person fr €12 **On Site** ⚑ **Nearby** ⚓ 5km ⚡ 7km ⚲ 5km ➚ 8km Restaurant 2km ◡ 8km ⚒ 2km ⚐ 6km **Notes** Pets admitted English spoken

MONTILLY

♯♯♯ Manoir des Hérards

Pierrette et Rémi BLOCH
Les Hérards, 03000 MONTILLY
☎ 04 70 46 51 26 & 06 89 26 71 71 ▤ 04 70 76 51 26

A 17th-century manor house belonging to a painter offering non-smoking rooms with independent access through a 15th-century tower and each with private bath and wc - two double rooms and one with a double and single bed. Shared lounge and dining room. Table tennis, fishing and garden furniture for use on the terrace and in the grounds. Table d'hôte meals by reservation. Painting and drawing lessons available.

Prices s fr €49; d fr €56; t fr €73; extra person fr €17 **Nearby** ⚓ 12km ⚡ 12km ⚲ 0.2km ➚ 8km Restaurant 8km ◡ 1km ⚐ 8km ⚒ 8km ⚐ 8km **Notes** No pets English spoken Open May to September.

NEUILLY-LE-REAL

♯♯♯ ⓘⓞⓘ Domaine des Chatards

Grazia VARRONE
Les Chatards, 03340 NEUILLY LE REAL
☎ 04 70 43 28 05 & 06 08 30 61 06
email: leschatards@orange.fr
web: www.masoe-des-chatards.com

Enclosed grounds of 150 acres, criss-crossed by streams and with four ponds, make a very attractive setting for this property. There are four twin-bedded rooms downstairs, with a separate guest entrance; a fifth is upstairs. All have private bath or shower room and WC. Garden with terrace and furniture; swimming pool. Bikes and quad bikes available for hire. Meals available if reserved.

Prices s fr €59; d fr €79; extra person fr €10; dinner fr €34 **On Site** ⚲ ⚐ Private ➚ **Nearby** ⚓ 3km ⚡ 3km Restaurant 3km ◡ 3km ⚒ 3km ⚐ 15km **Notes** Pets admitted English spoken CC

NEURE

♨ ✿ ⍟ ♿ **Le Grand Brimerand**

Albert LATOUR

03320 NEURE

☎ 04 70 66 41 19 & 06 07 89 07 65 ▤ 04 70 66 43 21

email: albert.latour@free.fr

web: www.brimerand.com

This large farmhouse stands surrounded by woods and meadows on a mixed cereal and dairy farm. On the first floor are two rooms - a double, plus another with double bed, single bed and a cot. Both have en suite facilities. A further grade 2 family suite offers two small doubles, with private shower room/WC reached via the landing. Extensive grounds with swimming pool.

Prices s €50-€65; d €55-€65; t €65-€70; extra person fr €10; dinner €15-€25 **On Site** Private ⍩ **Nearby** ⛷ 7km ⌓ 2km ⌇ 2km ⍟ 16km ⌂ 2km ⍭ 20km **Notes** Pets admitted English spoken

NOYANT D'ALLIER

♨ ✿ ⍟ **Les Jobineaux**

Caroline J.Dominique CARRELET

03210 NOYANT D'ALLIER

☎ 04 70 47 29 71

email: jean-dominique.carrelet@wanadoo.fr

Five rooms with beautiful views, on a dairy farm in the Bourbonnais countryside near Souvigny. Each room has a shower and wc and four are grade 3, one is grade 2. Large, shared lounge with open fire, table tennis, table football, trail bikes and guests can take part in the milking. Horse riders welcome.

Prices s fr €32; d fr €42; t fr €56; dinner fr €14 **On Site** ⌓ **Nearby** ⛷ 18km ⌇ 25km ⍩ 13km Restaurant 3km ⍟ 3km ⌇ 10km ⌂ 2.5km ⍭ 21km **Notes** Pets admitted English spoken

PARAY-LE-FRESIL

♨ ⍟ **Le Château**

Esmeralda DE TRACY

03230 PARAY LE FRESIL

☎ 04 70 43 68 02 & 04 70 43 42 36 ▤ 04 70 43 42 36

web: www.chateaudeparay.com

Two double rooms and a twin room offered in a château of local brick, each with bath, wc and television. Cots available. The day room

and lounge are shared with the owners and there is table tennis on site as well as large grounds, a swimming pool, stabling and hunting. Table d'hôte meals must be booked in advance.

Prices s fr €70; d fr €85; t fr €92; extra person fr €7; dinner fr €30 **On Site** Private ⍩ **Nearby** ⛷ 5km ⌇ 25km ⍩ 3km Restaurant 7km ⍟ 7km ⌂ 0.5km ⍭ 25km **Notes** Pets admitted English spoken

PARAY-SOUS-BRIAILLES

♨ ⍟ **Les Caissons**

Michèle et Gérard MAUSSAN

Route de Marcenat, 03500 PARAY SOUS BRIAILLES

☎ 04 70 45 03 00 & 06 33 27 96 99

email: maussan.michele@wanadoo.fr

Right in the countryside, three annexe rooms on a traditional farm include two doubles and a room with a double, two singles and a cot. Each room has a private bath and wc. There is also a lounge, library and kitchenette, a large green open area, garden furniture, barbecue and car port. An equestrian property, bicycles for hire. Table d'hôte meals can be booked. Special rates for family groups. Go-karts 4 km.

Prices s fr €43; d fr €47-€49; t fr €55; extra person fr €10; dinner fr €18 **On Site** ⌇ **Nearby** ⛷ 12km ⌇ 5km ⍩ 2km Restaurant 10km ⍟ 3km ⌂ 6km ⍭ 17km **Notes** Pets admitted English spoken

POUZY-MESANGY

♨ ✿ **Le Plaix**

Claire RAUCAZ

03320 LURCY LEVIS

☎ 04 70 66 24 06 ▤ 04 70 66 25 82

email: leplaix@yahoo.fr

This 16th-century manor house is on a farm near forests and rivers and offers five rooms for two to three people with private facilities and entrance through tower stairs. A kitchenette is available and table d'hôte meals may be reserved. Facilities in the summer include pétanque, table tennis, barbecue and trails for walkers and cyclists.

Prices s fr €42; d fr €46; t fr €60 **On Site** ⍩ **Nearby** ⛷ 10km ⌇ 30km ⍩ 15km Restaurant 4km ⍟ 5km ⍟ 7km ⌂ 4km ⍭ 35km **Notes** Pets admitted English spoken Open 15 March to 15 November.

SAULCET

▦ Château de Piroy

Cécile DEL CHEVALERIE
03500 SAULCET
☎ 04 70 47 51 28 & 06 75 67 28 95
📄 04 70 47 51 28

A vineyard provides the setting for this 19th-century château with its five guest rooms. On the first floor are three doubles and a twin, all with refrigerators and en suite bathrooms, two of them with spa baths. On the second floor is a two-room family suite for four (single beds) with shower room. Lounge with TV, billiard table; garden furniture.

Prices s fr €65; d €70-€95; extra person fr €25　**On Site** Restaurant ❦ Private ↘ **Nearby** ⚓ 28km ♨ 7km ♪ 3km ⛵ 3km 🏠 3km
⛰ 14km　**Notes** No pets English spoken Open July to August.

▦ ⊙ La Fontaine

Barbara & Serge SCHWOPE
03500 SAULCET
☎ 04 70 47 57 73　📄 04 70 47 57 73
email: serge.schwope@wanadoo.fr

This property offers three rooms in a wine grower's converted barn. On the ground floor is a double room; upstairs is a further double room and a room for three. All rooms have private shower room and WC. Extra bed on request. Use of owners' lounge; outside is a garden room and a barbecue. Meals by arrangement.

Prices s fr €40; d €50-€61; t fr €67; extra person €12-€15; dinner fr €18
Nearby ⚓ 28km ♨ 7km ♪ 3km ↘ 3km Restaurant 0.5km ⛵ 3km
Spa 28km ⛵ 28km 🏠 3km ⛰ 28km　**Notes** No pets

ST-AUBIN-LE-MONIAL

▦ ✿ ⊙ La Gare

Anne Marie et Louis MERCIER
03160 SAINT AUBIN LE MONIAL
☎ 04 70 67 00 20

Four rooms in a Bourbonnais house: a double room, a triple room with alcove, a suite of two rooms with two double beds and a single with room for an extra bed, and one room with a double and single bed. All have private facilities and guests have sole use of a lounge and dining room. Washing machine, telephone, garage, shaded green area and forest. Table d'hôte meals available if reserved.

Prices s fr €35; d fr €45; t fr €62; extra person fr €15; dinner fr €15
Nearby ⚓ 3km ♨ 40km ♪ 2km ↘ 7km Restaurant 7km ⛵ 2km
Spa 8km ⛵ 15km 🏠 3km ⛰ 29km　**Notes** Pets admitted

ST-BONNET-DE-ROCHEFORT

▦ ⊙ La Ferme de Rochefort

Sabine et Philippe BONNAL
4 Chemin des Vignes,
03800 SAINT BONNET DE ROCHEFORT
☎ 04 70 58 57 26 & 06 71 08 46 19
email: lafermederochefort@wanadoo.fr
web: http://chez.tiscali.fr/ferme-de-rochefort

Five guest rooms with a double and single bed on a farm near the Gorges de la Sioule; two have a private entrance and all have private shower and wc. In the owner's lounge, sitting room and library are available to guests. Table d'hôte meals must be booked. The grounds offer a swimming pool, garden furniture and barbecue. Horse riders welcome.

Prices s fr €39; d fr €43; t fr €56; extra person fr €13; dinner fr €17
On Site Private ↘ **Nearby** ⚓ 4km ♨ 30km ♪ 0.5km Restaurant 4km
⛵ 4km Spa 25km ⛵ 4km 🏠 4km ⛰ 10km　**Notes** Pets admitted
English spoken Open April to December.

ST-BONNET-TRONCAIS

▦ La Beaume

Laurence et Jehan DE POMYERS
03360 SAINT BONNET TRONCAIS
☎ 04 70 06 83 76
email: jehan.de_pomyers@orange.fr

An old smithy in the Forêt de Tronçais offering two twin rooms and a suite of two rooms with a double and single bed in the main house, and a double and twin room in a nearby outbuilding; all have private facilities. The lounge is shared with the owners and there are guided walks in the forest and table d'hôte meals by reservation. Discounts for stays of two nights (5%), three or four nights (10%), and five nights or more (15%).

Prices s fr €35; d fr €46; t fr €55　**Nearby** ⚓ 10km ♨ 20km ♪ 0.5km
↘ 30km Restaurant 3km ⛵ 0.5km Spa 30km ⛵ 0.5km 🏠 0.5km
⛰ 20km　**Notes** No pets English spoken

ST-DESIRE

▦ ♥ ⦿ ⅙ Domaine du Petit Lage

Francis LEROY
03370 SAINT DESIRE
☎ 04 70 07 10 03
email: gitedelage@wanadoo.fr

A renovated 18th-century grange, opposite the home of the cereal farming proprietors. It has a double room, a twin, a room with a double and single, and a room with disabled access with a double and two singles, all with private facilities and access to the garden. Extra bed available on demand. Lounge with fireplace, garden with furniture and walking routes on site. Wi-fi available in rooms. Table d'hôte meals by reservation.

Prices s fr €37; d fr €48; t fr €64; extra person fr €16; dinner fr €16 **Nearby** ⛷ 14km ♨ 15km ⚘ 4km ⤳ 26km Restaurant 3km ⚓ 3km ❀ 4km 🎣 3km ⋙ 28km **Notes** Pets admitted English spoken

ST-DIDIER-EN-DONJON

▦ ⦿ Les Dibois

Mirjam et Yves LAGARDETTE
03130 SAINT DIDIER EN DONJON
☎ 04 70 55 63 58 & 06 79 95 52 57 📄 04 70 55 63 58
email: lagardette.y@orange.fr

Three bedrooms in a converted sheepfold close to the owners' home. One of the rooms is a double; another has twin beds, and the third has a double bed and a single. Each has a private bathroom/WC, and two of the rooms have a private terrace. Guests lounge; swimming pool; fishing available. Good walking country. Meals by arrangement.

Prices s fr €40; d fr €55; t fr €50; extra person fr €10; dinner fr €15 **On Site** ⚘ ❀ Private ⤳ **Nearby** ⛷ 30km ♨ 20km Restaurant 6km ⚓ 5km 🎣 6km ⋙ 25km **Notes** No pets English spoken

ST-GERAND-LE-PUY

▦ ⦿ Demeure des Payratons

Christiane POULET
03150 SAINT GERAND LE PUY
☎ 04 70 99 82 44 📄 04 70 99 82 44

An 18th-century house with a wide range of antique furniture and shaded grounds. The rooms consist of three doubles (one in Louis XV), a triple and a suite of two rooms with a double and two single beds, each with private facilities. Shared lounge and dining room and TV available.

Prices s €54-€64; d €69-€98; t fr €89; extra person fr €20; dinner fr €24 **Nearby** ⛷ 12km ♨ 20km ⚘ 8km ⤳ 8km Restaurant 1.5km ⚓ 1km Spa 22km ❀ 10km 🎣 1km ⋙ 12km **Notes** No pets English spoken CC

ST-GERMAIN-DE-SALLES

▦ ⦿ *Chambre d'hôtes*

Elisabeth et Bart GIELENS
1 Allée des Gandins, 03140 SAINT GERMAIN DE SALLES
☎ 04 70 56 80 75 📄 04 70 56 80 75
email: lesgandins@wanadoo.fr
web: www.domainelesgandins.com

Three rooms in a typical Bourbonnais mansion, set in an enclosed, wooded park on the banks of the River Sioule. Two doubles and a triple room, all with their own entrance and shower room and wc. Lounge reserved for guests and three self-catering cottages and camping for ten tents on site.

Prices not confirmed for 2008 **On Site** ⚘ **Nearby** ⛷ 5km ♨ 12km ⤳ 10km ⚓ 6km ❀ 10km 🎣 10km ⋙ 10km **Notes** No pets English spoken

ST-LEON

▦ ⦿ *Château de Montpeyroux*

F et E FIZZAROTTI
Montpeyroux, 03220 SAINT LEON
☎ 04 70 42 18 34 & 06 08 78 32 47
email: emmanuel.fizzarotti@cario.fr

There are three first-floor bedrooms in this 18th-century château, which stands in two hectares of grounds. All the rooms have double beds, and private bath/shower room and WC. There is a guest lounge and an outdoor swimming pool. Views across the meadows, where the owners keep sheep and horses.

Prices s fr €70; d fr €75; extra person fr €25; dinner fr €30 **On Site** ⛷ ❀ Private ⤳ **Nearby** ♨ 30km ⚘ 5km Restaurant 10km 🎣 3km ⋙ 30km **Notes** No pets English spoken

AUVERGNE

ST-PRIEST-EN-MURAT

♯♯♯ Chambre d'hôtes

Jacques ROSIER

Place de l'Eglise, 03390 SAINT PRIEST EN MURAT

☎ 04 70 02 97 41

email: lesrosiers_sp@yahoo.fr

A large house, full of character, situated in a village. There are three bedrooms: on the ground floor a triple (double bed plus a single), with bathroom and WC; on the first floor a double with shower/WC, and another triple (double bed plus single) with shower/WC and its own sitting room; there is also a guest lounge on the ground floor.

Prices s €32-€44; d €48-€54; t €55-€64 **Nearby** ♨ 26km ♣ 30km ♬ 5km ⚘ 21km Restaurant 0.5km ⚐ 7km ⚑ 26km ⚐ 7km ⚑ 30km
Notes No pets English spoken Open May to October.

♯♯♯ ⚏ La Charvière

Robert ENGELS

03390 SAINT PRIEST EN MURAT

☎ 04 70 07 38 24 📄 04 70 02 91 27

email: robert.engels@wanadoo.fr

web: www.lacharviere.nl

A Dutch family welcome you to their restored farmhouse, which has a double room, a room with a double and single bed, and a room with two double beds, all with private facilities. The lounge with open fire is shared and there is a terrace. Self-catering cottages and camping on site.

Prices s fr €30; d fr €48; t fr €58; extra person fr €10; dinner fr €16
On Site Private ⚘ **Nearby** ♨ 25km ♬ 30km ⚘ 5km Restaurant 4km ⚐ 5km ⚑ 35km ⚐ 7km ⚑ 30km **Notes** Pets admitted English spoken
Open March to 24 October.

ST-REMY-EN-ROLLAT

♯♯♯ ⚏ Château de Gerbe

Xavier SIWA

03110 SAINT REMY EN ROLLAT

☎ 04 70 41 96 03 & 06 24 98 07 16 📄 04 70 41 96 03

email: eurlsaintmarc@aol.com

web: www.chateau-de-gerbe.com

Just 300 metres from the River Allier, this 16th- and 19th-century château offers five bedrooms. There are three doubles; one two-roomed family suite with two double beds plus a single; and one room with two four-foot beds. All rooms have private facilities. Lounge, terrace, garden furniture, billiards and table tennis. Stabling possible. Meals by arrangement.

Prices s fr €58; d €67-€95; t fr €82; extra person fr €15; dinner €20-€25
On Site ⚘ Private ⚘ **Nearby** ♨ 7km ♬ 9km Restaurant 2km ⚐ 9km ⚑ 9km ⚐ 3km ⚑ 7km **Notes** No pets English spoken Open March to 30 October.

THIONNE

♯♯♯ ⚏ ⚐ La Maison du Lac - Les Clayeux

Ghislaine NAUROY

03220 THIONNE

☎ 04 70 34 74 23 & 06 16 38 77 46 📄 04 70 34 74 23

email: nauroyghislaine@yahoo.fr

Set in a clearing, an extension of the proprietor's character property offers two double bedrooms with separate access and small terraces with canopies. An old house in the garden has two more rooms with a double and single bed; all with private facilities. Bikes for loan and fishing in private pond. Le Pal theme park nearby.

Prices s fr €35; d fr €45; t fr €55; extra person fr €12; dinner fr €18
On Site ⚘ ⚘ **Nearby** ♨ 8km ♬ 17km ⚘ 13km Restaurant 15km ⚐ 7km ⚑ 4km ⚑ 23km **Notes** Pets admitted English spoken

TRONGET

♯♯♯ ⚏ Château de la Sauvatte

P BELOT et D ALTHERR

03240 TRONGET

☎ 04 70 47 15 28 & 06 60 29 71 88 📄 04 70 47 15 28

email: dorothea.altherr@gmx.ch

web: www.sauvatte.eu

Five hectares of grounds surround this 19th-century château, in the heart of the Bourbon region. There are three guest suites, each consisting of two rooms. The first has four single beds; the second has two doubles and a single; the third has five single beds. All have en suite bath/shower rooms and WCs. Lounge and dining room shared with the hosts.

Prices s €47-€55; d €57-€65; t fr €80; extra person fr €20; dinner €10-€15 **Nearby** ♨ 20km ♬ 17km ⚘ 4km ⚘ 17km Restaurant 4km ⚐ 4km Spa 20km ⚑ 25km ⚐ 4km ⚑ 30km **Notes** Pets admitted English spoken

♯♯♯ ⚏ La Roche

Michèle et Olivier BAES

03240 TRONGET

☎ 04 70 47 16 43

email: baes.o@wanadoo.fr

web: www.fermedelaroche.com

Three double rooms in a Bourbonnais farm surrounded by fields and woods; one with a child's bed and another with extra single bed (all with private facilities). The dining room is shared with the owners and meals are made with farm produce.

Prices s fr €33; d fr €40; t fr €53; extra person fr €13; dinner fr €15
Nearby ♨ 20km ♬ 40km ⚘ 4km ⚘ 20km Restaurant 4km ⚐ 4km Spa 45km ⚑ 25km ⚐ 4km ⚑ 30km **Notes** No pets English spoken

AUVERGNE

VALIGNAT

ⅢⅢ ⏀ Château de L'Ormet

Patricia et Pierre LAEDERICH
RD183, 03330 VALIGNAT
☎ 04 70 58 57 23 ▤ 04 70 58 57 19
email: lormet@wanadoo.fr
web: www.chateaudelormet.com

Set in wooded grounds facing the Puy-de-Dôme and the Montagne Bourbonnais, this unique non-smoking house is a good starting point for walks. It has two rooms with a double and single bed and a twin room, all with private bath and wc. The owner will be delighted to show you his three miniature railways, of different gauges, that circle the garden and grounds. Meals available by reservations, Friday and Saturday only.

Prices s €64-€75; d €72-€83; dinner fr €25 **On Site** Private ⚲ **Nearby** ⛷ 6km ⚓ 25km ⚐ 6km Restaurant 5km ⚑ 6km ✤ 6km ⚑ 6km ⋙ 6km **Notes** No pets English spoken Open 29 March to 16 November.

VERNEUIL-EN-BOURBONNAIS

ⅢⅢ ⏀ Place de la Fontaine

Rachel & Christopher LEONARD
03500 VERNEUIL EN BOURBONNAIS
☎ 04 70 45 55 96 & 06 12 50 59 11
email: placedelafontaine.verneuil@wanadoo.fr
web: www.placedelafontaine.com

Right in the heart of the village, this house has four bedrooms, all on the first floor. There is a double room, a twin bedded room, and two rooms for three, each with a double bed and a single. Each room has a private bathroom/WC, and two have a private terrace. Cot available. Lounge, terrace, garden furniture. Meals by arrangement.

Prices s €50-€75; d €60-€85; t fr €100; extra person fr €15; dinner fr €25 **On Site** Restaurant ✤ **Nearby** ⛷ 5km ⚓ 8km ⚐ 2km ⚲ 5km ⚑ 5km ⋙ 20km **Notes** No pets English spoken

YGRANDE

ⅢⅢ ☙ Les Ferrons

Agnès et Henri VREL
03160 YGRANDE
☎ 04 70 66 31 67 ▤ 04 70 66 32 64

A 19th-century house set in large grounds, offering two double rooms (one in an annexe), a room with a double and single bed and a suite of two rooms with a double and two single beds, all with private shower and wc. Guests have sole use of a lounge, television and library. Washing machine and cot available. Meals may be provided. Stable and field for horses on site; close to the Allier equestrian rides.

Prices s fr €35; d fr €48; t fr €70; extra person fr €15 **Nearby** ⛷ 4km ⚓ 45km ⚐ 4km ⚲ 10km Restaurant 2km ⚑ 2.5km Spa 10km ✤ 12km ⚑ 2.5km ⋙ 32km **Notes** No pets

ALBEPIERRE-BREDONS

ⅢⅢ ⏀ Auzolles-Bas

Martine NAIRABEZE
15300 ALBEPIERRE BREDONS
☎ 04 71 20 00 80 & 06 86 91 96 93
email: martine.nairabeze@wanadoo.fr
web: http://cantal.gite.free.fr

The owner of this house offers two double rooms, a twin and a room with a double and single bed, all with private bathrooms. Heating, lounge, terrace, garden with trees. Shops in Murat, Plom du Cantal, Super Lioran, Garabit. Table d'hôte meals are available by reservation.

Prices s fr €37; d €44-€46; t fr €59; dinner fr €15 **On Site** ⚐ **Nearby** ⛷ 5km ⚓ 10km Restaurant 3km ⚑ 5km ⚲ 3km Spa 10km ⚑ 3.5km ⋙ 3.5km **Notes** No pets

ANGLARDS-DE-SALERS

ⅢⅢ ☙ ⏀ Les Sorbiers

Géraldine RIBES
15380 ANGLARDS DE SALERS
☎ 04 71 40 02 87

Six rooms in a house near the owners' home: two rooms with double and single bed, a twin room and three doubles with private shower and wcs. The dining room and lounge with library and fireplace are for guests' use and there is an enclosed garden with furniture. The ground floor serves as a ferme auberge at weekends. Discounts for children.

Prices s fr €42; d fr €48; t €52-€60; dinner fr €17 **Nearby** ⛷ 20km ⚓ 10km ⚐ 1km ⚲ 8km Restaurant 10km ⚲ ✤ 6km ⚑ 0.2km ⋙ 8km **Notes** No pets

ARPAJON-SUR-CERE

𝗜𝗢𝗜 Le Cambon

Jacqueline et Angelo LENA

15130 ARPAJON-SUR-CERE

☎ 04 71 63 52 49 & 06 76 76 01 40 ▤ 04 71 63 52 49

email: lena.jacqueline@wanadoo.fr

web: www.jacqueline.lena.fr

This property has a calm and restful location, close to Aurillac. There are three second-floor rooms: the pink room (double), the blue room (twin with private lounge and possible extra bed), and the twin-bedded yellow room (grade 2). All rooms have private facilities and TV socket, central heating. TV lounge, garden room, courtyard and enclosed garden area. Meals by arrangement.

Prices s fr €37; d €45-€48; dinner fr €20 **On Site** 🏊 **Nearby** ⛷ 2km
⛰ 6km Restaurant 2km 🚴 40km 🏊 2km Spa 2km 🏛 3km 🚶 3km
Notes No pets

BADAILHAC

𝓎 ♿ Calmejane

Jean-François TROUPEL

15800 BADAILHAC

☎ 04 71 62 47 54 ▤ 04 71 62 47 54

Overlooking a remarkable valley panorama, three rooms with a double and single bed and private facilities are offered in a building separate from the owner's house. There is electric heating, a communal lounge, a terrace with furniture, a courtyard and table d'hôte meals. Vic sur Cère is 10km away, or tour the Monts du Cantal.

Prices s fr €35; d fr €42; t fr €52 **Nearby** ⛷ 8km ⛰ 8km 🏊 0.2km
Restaurant 8km 🏊 7km 🎣 0.2km 🏊 8km 🚶 8km **Notes** No pets
English spoken

𝓎 𝗜𝗢𝗜 La Calsade

Jean MORZIERE

15800 BADAILHAC

☎ 04 71 47 40 54

email: morzieres@9online.fr

In a small hamlet near Badailhac, a farming couple welcome you to their restored house with two double and a family room containing a double and a single bed, all with heating, private shower rooms and wcs, and a TV point. The lounge, shared with the owners, has a fireplace and TV; there is a terrace and courtyard.

Prices s fr €42; d fr €45; t fr €54; dinner fr €12 **Nearby** ⛷ 10km
⛰ 15km 🏊 3km Restaurant 12km 🏊 30km 🏊 12km Spa 20km 🏛 12km
🚶 12km **Notes** No pets

BEAULIEU

𝓎 Chambre d'hôtes

SARL EYZAT

Le Bourg, 15270 BEAULIEU

☎ 06 83 61 72 03

email: fermegitebeaulieu@orange.fr

web: www.fermegitebeaulieu.com

Enjoying views over the lakes, Monts du Cantal and the Château de Val, the five rooms include two doubles, and two twins and a triple with mezzanines that can accommodate an extra bed. Facilities include private shower rooms and wcs, dining room, sitting room with TV and heater, fridge, table tennis, enclosed garden with furniture and barbecue. Out of season discounts are available.

Prices s €36-€45; d €36-€45; t €45-€50 **Nearby** ⛷ 10km ⛰ 15km
🏊 0.8km Restaurant 0.1km 🏊 4km Spa 45km 🏛 4km 🚶 10km
Notes Pets admitted English spoken Open April to 15 November.

CHALIERS

𝗜𝗢𝗜 Champ Grand Sud

Michel SIQUIER

La Besse, 15320 CHALIERS

☎ 04 71 23 48 80 & 06 80 05 37 85 ▤ 04 71 23 48 80

A small farm on the fringes of Cantal, Lozère and Haute Loire, with many walking routes nearby. The accommodation offers five double rooms (two with extra single) in a barn, with independent access, private facilities and mezzanine. Extra beds available. The communal lounge has a TV and an open fire - where food is prepared. Heating, courtyard, garden and terrace. Near the GR4, the Vallée de la Truyère, Aubrac, Monts du Cantal and Saint Flour.

Prices s fr €40; d €48-€57; t fr €62; dinner €16 **On Site** 🏊
Nearby ⛷ 10km Restaurant 4km 🏊 30km 🏊 10km 🏛 10km 🚶 20km
Notes Pets admitted English spoken

CONDAT

𝓎 Les Sorbiers

Véronique PHELUT

Le Veysset, 15190 CONDAT

☎ 04 71 78 62 96

email: veronique.phelut@libertysurf.fr

web: www.les-sorbiers.net

Two double rooms and two family rooms with their own entrances, shower rooms and wcs are available, together with a dining room, heating, and gardens, in which the host grows strawberries, raspberries and blueberries. Kitchen available in season and table d'hôte meals are offered in April, May, September and October. Close to Condat, the Lastioules Dam and the Lac de la Crégut.

Prices s fr €40; d fr €46; t fr €60 **Nearby** ⛷ 1km 🏊 3km
Restaurant 3km 🏊 3km 🏛 3km 🚶 40km **Notes** No pets

FAVEROLLES

♯♯♯ *Chambre d'hôtes*

Nelly COMBES

Le Bourg, 15320 FAVEROLLES

☎ 04 71 23 45 90 & 06 83 70 57 44

The proprietors of this house offer two double rooms, a double with a single, a triple and a family room with a double and two singles, all with private facilities. Lounge, corner kitchen, heating and courtyard. Nearby attractions include shops at Faverolles, a restaurant in the village, dam at Grandval, caves at Truyere, park with bisons at Margeride, château at Chassan. Chaudes-Aigues 25km. St Flour 20km.

Prices not confirmed for 2008 **On Site** ⚓ **Nearby** ⌀ 5km ⚓ 40km ⚓ 0.5km ⚓ 20km **Notes** Pets admitted

FRIDEFONT

♯♯♯ ♥ ⃝ **Le Bourg**

Marinette GUILBOT

15110 FRIDEFONT

☎ 04 71 23 51 72 & 06 86 15 81 26 📄 04 71 23 51 72

email: mguilbot@terre-net.fr

web: www.ferme-guilbot.fr

This is a working cattle and dairy farm. The setting is green and peaceful, and the welcome warm and cheery. The house has three double bedrooms, one on the ground floor and two upstairs with their own access. All have private shower/WC. Guest lounge, attractive gardens with furniture and views.

Prices s fr €32; d fr €39; dinner fr €13 **Nearby** ⚓ 30km ⌀ 3km ⚓ 13km ⚓ 13km ⚓ 30km **Notes** No pets English spoken

GIOU-DE-MAMOU

♯♯♯ ♥ ⃝ **Barathe**

Pierre et Isabelle BRETON

15130 GIOU-DE-MAMOU

☎ 04 71 64 61 72

email: barathe@wanadoo.fr

web: http://barathe.monsite.wanadoo.fr

This charming Auvergne manor house, with many original features, enjoys a peaceful location, overlooking beautiful countryside where cow bells ring. On the second floor are three double rooms and a triple; on the first floor is another double. All rooms have private showers and WC. Central heating. Two of the rooms are rated at grade 2. Shared lounge, meals available.

Prices s fr €48; d fr €48; dinner fr €13 **On Site** ⌀ **Nearby** ⚓ 5km ⚓ 10km Restaurant 7km ⚓ 30km Spa 7km ⚓ 8km ⚓ 8km **Notes** No pets

JALEYRAC

♯♯♯ ♥ ⃝ **La Salterie**

Alain CHAVAROCHE

15200 JALEYRAC

☎ 04 71 69 72 55

email: chavaroche.alain@wanadoo.fr

web: www.lasalterie.com

Three rooms in a building adjoining the owner's house: two rooms with a double and single bed on a mezzanine and a twin. All have private facilities, heating and an extra bed is available. Guests have access to a communal lounge, fridge, microwave, and grounds with garden furniture. Out of season discounts. Climbing or micro-lighting nearby, or visit Salers, Puy Mary, Le Falgoux and Monts du Sancy.

Prices s fr €30; d fr €40; t fr €49; dinner fr €11 **Nearby** ⚓ 10km ⚓ 7km ⌀ 2km Restaurant 7km ⚓ 7km ⚓ 7km ⚓ 7km **Notes** No pets English spoken Open April to November.

JOURSAC

♯♯♯ ⃝ *Recoules*

Alain NICOLLEAU

15170 JOURSAC

☎ 04 71 20 59 12 📄 04 71 20 59 12

email: barajade@wanadoo.fr

web: www.chambres-hotes-cantal.com

This typical farmhouse is south of Cézallier with views of the Massif Cantalien. It has a room with queen size bed, two triple rooms with room for an extra bed, a room with a double and single bed and a double room, all with private facilities and access. Shared dining room with an alcove and lounge. Library, garden, and regional cooking.

Prices not confirmed for 2008 **Nearby** ⚓ 15km ⌀ 5km ⚓ 10km ⚓ 7km ⚓ 7km **Notes** Pets admitted

LA CHAPELLE-D'ALAGNON

♯♯♯ ⃝ *Gaspard*

Denis et Joëlle MEDARD

15300 LA CHAPELLE-D'ALAGNON

☎ 04 71 20 01 91

email: denis.medard@wanadoo.fr

This old farmhouse is set in a hamlet on the fringes of Alagnon, in the heart of Cantal, and has pretty views from the three double rooms and a twin. Rooms have private showers, wcs and heating, and guests have use of a dining room, lounge, telephone and table d'hôte meals. Nearby attractions include the Grandval Dam, the Maison de la Faune, the Monts du Cantal and mountain biking.

Prices not confirmed for 2008 **On Site** ⌀ **Nearby** ⚓ 7km ⚓ 12km ⚓ 4km ⚓ 4km ⚓ 4km **Notes** Pets admitted

LADINHAC

₩ ❤ ⏺ ⚬ Ferme la Valette

Gilberte ESCARPIT

15120 LADINHAC

☎ 04 71 47 80 33 & 06 75 34 48 46 📄 04 71 47 80 16

email: info@ferme-la-valette.com

web: www.ferme-la-valette.com

This countryside farm offers self-catering cottages, camping, farmhouse produce and regional cooking, as well as six guest rooms. They include a double room, three triples and a twin in an annexe (grade 3) and a double room in the house (grade 2); all have private facilities and TV socket. Washing machine, fridge, gas cooker, private terrace with furniture, garden and field, games area and pond.

Prices s fr €39; d €46-€49; dinner fr €14 **On Site** 🏊 **Nearby** ⛷ 5km ♨ 20km Restaurant 0.1km 🚲 2km 🎿 30km 🏠 2km 🚶 22km

Notes Pets admitted

LE FALGOUX

₩ ⏺ La Michie

Guy SUPERSAC

15380 LE FALGOUX

☎ 04 71 69 54 36

email: Guyll.supersac@wanadoo.fr

web: http://perso.wanadoo.fr/guy.supersac

Rooms in this large, impressive house include three doubles and two family suites in the attic (one with double and single room and the other with two twin rooms), all with private facilities. Lounge shared with the owner, open fire, heating, table d'hôte meals and use of the grounds. Nearby: shops in Falgoux, Vallée du Mars, the Cirque du Falgoux, Puy Mary, Salers and the GR400.

Prices s €50-€58; d €50-€58; t fr €66; dinner fr €18 **On Site** ♨ **Nearby** ⛷ 25km Restaurant 0.3km 🚲 0.4km 🏠 0.4km 🚶 28km

Notes No pets Open May-September

LE MONTEIL

₩ ⏺ Le Miniou

Marie et Bernard SOYEZ

Bélière, 15240 LE MONTEIL

☎ 04 71 40 69 10 & 06 08 71 21 73 📄 04 71 40 69 10

email: msoyez@nordnet.fr

This converted barn in unfenced grounds is deep in the countryside. A separate guest entrance leads to the upstairs rooms: a two-roomed family suite (double bed in one, large single bed in the other); a double with shower/WC and a double with bath/WC. Guest living room, library, billiard table, internet access; outside there is a large terrace with garden furniture. Meals by arrangement; mountain bikes available.

Prices d fr €50; dinner fr €16 **On Site** 🎿 **Nearby** ⛷ 3km ♨ 25km ♨ 4km Restaurant 10km 🚲 10km 🏠 10km 🚶 30km **Notes** No pets

LE VIGEAN

₩ ❤ ⏺ Lasbordes

Daniel et Chantal CHAMBON

15200 LE VIGEAN

☎ 04 71 40 01 59

email: chantal.et.daniel.chambon@wanadoo.fr

Between Mauriac and Anglards de Salers, this farm provides two double rooms, two twins and a room with a double and single bed, all with private facilities; additional bed available. Table d'hôte meals are served in a communal room with fireplace and seating area, and there is heating, a TV, terrace, and shady park. Discounts for children under 10. Micro-lights, Mauriac, Salers and Monts du Cantal nearby.

Prices s fr €41; d fr €45; t fr €57; extra person fr €12; dinner fr €14 **Nearby** ⛷ 10km 🚲 5km ♨ 5km Restaurant 5km 🚲 5km 🎿 5km 🏠 5km **Notes** No pets English spoken Open Apr-Nov

LEYNHAC

₩ ❤ Martory

J-Marie & Jeanine CAUMON

15600 LEYNHAC

☎ 04 71 49 10 47 📄 04 71 49 14 61

email: jean-marie.caumon@wanadoo.fr

A renovated 19th-century barn on a cattle farm, offering three double rooms and three rooms with double and single bed. Three have kitchenette and all have their own entrance, terrace, shower rooms and wcs. Shared dining room and lounge, courtyard, garden, games room, bicycle hire, rides in a pony and cart, swimming pool. Out of season discounts available. Near Conques, Figeac, Rocamadour, Rodez, Laguiole, and Salers.

Prices s €30-€38; d €41-€46; t €50-€55 **On Site** Private ⚬ 🎿 **Nearby** ⛷ 3km 🚲 40km ♨ 1km Restaurant 3km 🚲 3km 🏠 10km 🚶 10km **Notes** Pets admitted English spoken

LORCIERES

₩ ⏺ *Chambre d'hôtes*

Clément et Odette COUTAREL

Le Bourg, 15320 LORCIERES

☎ 04 71 23 49 79 & 06 86 72 04 33 📄 04 71 78 17 39

email: clement.coutarel@wanadoo.fr

web: http://monsite.wanadoo.fr/chez_odette_clement

A family home with a double room, a twin and a room with double and single bed, each with their own shower room and wc. The communal lounge has an alcove and table d'hôte meals offer a range of local specialities such as truffade and aligot. The hosts can advise guests on best local walks and places to visit.

Prices not confirmed for 2008 **On Site** ♨ **Nearby** ⛷ 5km 🚲 9km 🏠 9km 🚶 20km **Notes** No pets

AUVERGNE

MAURS

⦀ ❤ 🍴 La Drulhe

Annie et Michel SEYROLLES

15600 MAURS

☎ 04 71 49 07 33   📄 04 71 49 07 33

A renovated house on a cattle farm providing rooms in an annexe with a lounge and terrace: two double rooms and two rooms with double and single beds, each with private facilities and baby facilities available. Heating, courtyard and garden. Shops, lakes of Figeac and Tolerme and the Vallée du Lot nearby.

Prices s fr €38; d fr €42; t fr €56; dinner fr €15   **Nearby** ⛷ 10km ⚓25km 🏌 1km Restaurant 5km 🏊 5km Spa 20km 🎣 5km 🚶 5km
Notes Pets admitted

ORADOUR

⦀ 🍴 La Roseraie

Brigitte DUSSUELLE

Le Bourg, 15260 ORADOUR

☎ 04 71 23 92 43   📄 04 71 23 94 55

email: dominique.dussuelle@wanadoo.fr

web: http://perso.wanadoo.fr/gite.laroseraie

A 19th-century house in wooded parkland providing a double room, a twin and room with a queen size bed, all with private facilities and heating. Shared dining room and lounge with fireplace; washing machine and cot available. Table d'hôte meals by reservation. Shops in Pierrefort, Chaudes Aigues, Gorges de la Truyère, Plomb du Cantal and the Viaduc de Garabit nearby.

Prices s fr €38; d fr €47; dinner fr €16   **Nearby** ⛷ 15km 🏌17km 🏌 3km Restaurant 9km 🏊 28km 🏊 9km Spa 25km 🎣9km 🚶25km
Notes No pets English spoken Open March-14 November.

⦀ 🍴 Lieuriac

G WEIL et C GIRAUD

15260 ORADOUR

☎ 04 71 23 39 78

email: sandine.hotes@club-internet.fr

web: www.sardine.cantal.fr.free

Rooms with panoramic views include a grade 2 double (sharing a wc) and a double, twin and room with double and single bed, all with mezzanines and private facilities. Rooms have separate entrances; additional bed available. Guest lounge with fireplace and kitchenette

looking over the courtyard, orchard with seating, heating and washing machine. Hot springs, Neuvéglise, Chaudes Aigues, the Gorges de la Truyère and Pierrefort. Closed Christmas.

Prices s fr €37; d fr €42; t fr €51; dinner fr €11   **Nearby** ⛷ 12km 🏌15km 🏌 12km Restaurant 9km 🏊 11km Spa 17km 🎣11km 🚶22km
Notes No pets English spoken

PAULHAC

⦀ 🍴 ♿ La Sagnette

SARL VAYSSADE-RIGAL

15430 PAULHAC

☎ 04 71 73 34 98 & 04 71 73 30 02

email: marie-pierre.vayssade@wanadoo.fr

web: http://monsite.wanadoo.fr/aubergedelasagnette

There are four ground floor bedrooms at this property, in an annexe to the owners' home. There is one double room; two split-level rooms, each with a double bed plus twins; and a room with disabled access which has two double beds, one of them on a mezzanine. All have private shower/WC. Farmhouse restaurant on site.

Prices s fr €35; d €45-€55; t fr €57; dinner fr €13   **On Site** 🏌
Nearby ⛷ 1km Restaurant 3km 🏊 3km 🏊 12km 🎣 13km 🎣7km 🚶 13km   **Notes** Pets admitted English spoken

PLEAUX

⦀ 🍴 Les Ombrages

David et Carol JACKSON

Rue d'Empeyssine, 15700 PLEAUX

☎ 04 71 40 47 66 & 06 81 65 82 78   📄 04 71 40 47 66

email: info@les-ombrages-cantal.com

web: www.les-ombrages-cantal.com

There are four first floor bedrooms at this property. Two of the rooms are doubles; one is a triple, with a double bed and a single; and the fourth is a grade 2 twin-bedded room. All have private bath/shower room and WC, but those for the twin-bedded room are not en suite. Guest lounge; extensive wooded grounds; meals by arrangement.

Prices s €60-€70; d €60-€70; extra person fr €25; dinner fr €25
On Site ⛷ **Nearby** 🏌 2km 🏊0.5km 🚶20km   **Notes** No pets
English spoken

ROFFIAC

⦀ Chambre d'hôtes

Jean-Louis & Josette BROUARD

Le Bourg, 15100 ROFFIAC

☎ 04 71 60 45 75

Two double rooms and a twin with private access, facilities and heating, located in the owners' house. The lounge is reserved for guests and there is a terrace, garden and farmhouse hotel 300m away. Visit the Viaduc de Garabit, Château d'Alleuze, Château du Saillant and Chaudes Aigues.

Prices s fr €43; d fr €48   **On Site** 🏌 **Nearby** ⛷ 3km
Restaurant 0.1km 🏊30km 🏊 3km 🎣3km 🚶 3km   **Notes** No pets

RUYNES-EN-MARGERIDE

♦♦♦ ♿ L'Oustar de Tougnini

Luc et Ghislaine BONY

Trailus, 15320 RUYNES EN MARGERIDE

☎ 04 71 23 46 42

Four first-floor bedrooms in the semi-detached end of the owners' home, with its own guest entrance: two double rooms called 'Jeanne' and 'Marie'; a twin-bedded room called 'Albertine'; and a triple called 'Berthe' (double and single beds); all have shower room and WC. Extra beds available for children. Dining and sitting rooms, kitchenette, terrace.

Prices s fr €41; d fr €45; extra person fr €16 **Nearby** ⛷ 3km ✗ 2km Restaurant 3km ♨ 18km ✦ 3km ▨ 3km ⚓ 18km **Notes** No pets

SALERS

♦♦♦ 🍽 La Jourdanie

Barbara GANDILHON

15140 SALERS

☎ 04 71 40 77 99 & 06 30 35 33 92 📠 04 71 40 77 99

email: b.gandilhon@wanadoo.fr

In a medieval city classed as one of the most beautiful in France, rooms with private facilities are offered in an 18th-century residence. 'Poppy' is a twin and 'Lys Martagon', 'Gentian' and 'Blue Thistle' are doubles. There is a communal living room and lounge with fireplace, heating, TV and telephone. Garden with flowers and trees and table tennis. Guests can enjoy the authentic taste of regional specialities made with local produce.

Prices not confirmed for 2008 **Nearby** ⛷ 10km ✗ 6km ♨ 0.8km ⚓ 20km **Notes** No pets

♦♦♦ La Maison de Barrouze

Yves LESAGE

Av de Barrouze, 15140 SALERS

☎ 04 71 40 78 08 & 06 87 86 38 34

email: lamaisondebarrouze@orange.fr

web: http://monsite.wanadoo.fr/location.salers.bray

Right in the heart of the medieval part of the town, this 19th-century house has three double bedrooms, one with a relaxing area and all with private shower and WC. Extensively renovated, the house retains a lot of character. There is a day room for guests, with an open fire. Walking guides and snow shoes available.

Prices s €52-€60; d €46.50-€57.50; extra person fr €15.75 **Nearby** ⛷ 5km ⚘ 45km ✗ 3km Restaurant 0.1km ♨ 0.5km ▨ 0.1km ⚓ 7km **Notes** No pets English spoken

♦♦♦ 🐓 Le Jardin du Haut Mouriol

J-Pierre et Eliane VANTAL

Route du Puy Mary, 15140 SALERS

☎ 04 71 40 74 02 📠 04 71 40 74 02

email: eliane.vantal@wanadoo.fr

Four rooms with their own entrance in the owner's house: two doubles, a twin and a room with a double and single bed, all with private facilities. Dayroom and lounge with TV, seating in the garden, children's games and parking. Crafts, museums, exhibitions, walks on GR400, Puy Mary nearby.

Prices s €40-€44; d €45-€50; t fr €60 **Nearby** ⛷ 8km ⚘ 20km ✗ 5km Restaurant 1km ♨ 0.2km Spa 40km ▨ 0.8km ⚓ 18km **Notes** Pets admitted English spoken

SIRAN

♦♦♦ 🐓 La Sablière

M-P SARRAUSTE DE MENTHIERE

15150 SIRAN

☎ 04 71 46 08 00

There are three bedrooms at this property, all in the owners' home. On the ground floor is a double room, and a family suite, with a double bed and a single. Upstairs is another double room. All have private bath/shower room and WC. There is a guests' lounge. Grounds not enclosed.

Prices s fr €30; d fr €43; t fr €62 **Nearby** ⛷ 10km ✗ 2.5km Restaurant 3km ♨ 2.5km ✦ 2.5km ▨ 2.5km ⚓ 2.5km **Notes** Pets admitted

ST BONNET-DE-CONDAT

♦♦♦ Régheat

Stéphanie GASTON

15190 ST BONNET-DE-CONDAT

☎ 04 71 78 43 86 📠 04 71 78 43 86

email: stgaston@wanadoo.fr

web: http://chardousse.monsite.wanadoo.fr

This restored Auvergne farm offers four first floor rooms: two doubles, one twin, and one for three people. All rooms have private showers and WC. Lounge shared with the owners; meals available. Own grounds, gas central heating.

Prices s €40-€55; d €45-€55; t fr €60 **On Site** Restaurant ✦ **Nearby** ⛷ 15km ✗ 3km ⚘ 30km ♨ 12km ▨ 1km ⚓ 30km **Notes** No pets English spoken

ST BONNET-DE-SALERS

Le Pont Tougouze

Jérome et Delphine QUINTARD
Tougouze, 15140 ST BONNET-DE-SALERS
☎ 04 71 40 76 55 & 06 87 51 56 28
email: lemoulindupont@yahoo.fr
web: www.le-moulin-du-pont.com

This property has five rooms. On the first floor are two doubles and a twin; on the ground floor are two doubles. All have private showers and WCs. Shared lounge with open fire; central heating. Landscaped gardens with terrace and pond.

Prices s fr €45; d fr €48; dinner fr €18 **On Site** ✍ **Nearby** ✪ 15km ⚓ 15km Restaurant 3km ⚓ 3km Spa 43km ⌂ 2.2km ✈ 17km **Notes** No pets English spoken

ST-ETIENNE-DE-CARLAT

Lou Ferradou

Jacky BALLEUX
Caizac, 15130 ST-ETIENNE-DE-CARLAT
☎ 04 71 62 42 37 & 06 65 25 49 79 ▤ 04 71 62 42 37
email: balleux@louferradou.com
web: www.louferradou.com

This traditional, stone Auvergne house offers a warm welcome and rooms in a renovated annexe: two rooms with a double and two single beds, two double rooms and a twin. All have private facilities. Dining room with fireplace and seating, lounge and table tennis. Visit the local châteaux, Monts du Cantal, Vallée de la Cère or Aurillac.

Prices s €45-€55; d €45-€55; dinner fr €15 **On Site** ✍ **Nearby** ✪ 10km ⚓ 5km Restaurant 5km ⚓ 40km ⚓ 10km Spa 15km ⌂ 12km ✈ 15km **Notes** No pets

ST-MARTIN-CANTALES

Sept-Fons

Jean-Louis & Denise CHANUT
15140 ST-MARTIN-CANTALES
☎ 04 71 69 40 58
email: chambres-sept-fons@wanadoo.fr

A lovely property in the heart of the country offering two Grade 3 double rooms (one with possible extra beds) and a Grade 2 twin room, all with private facilities and heating. Shared dining room, lounge and garden with seating. Nearby attractions: Martin Valmeroux, Salers, the Château d'Anjony and Lac d'Enchanet.

Prices s €34-€39; d €39-€44 **Nearby** ✪ 10km ⚓ 40km ✍ 2km Restaurant 8km ⚓ 10km Spa 34km ⌂ 2km ✈ 34km **Notes** No pets Open May to October.

ST-MARY-LE-PLAIN

Nozerolles

Bernard et Maryse CHALIER
15500 ST-MARY-LE-PLAIN
☎ 04 71 23 05 80 ▤ 04 71 23 05 80

Large traditional family house with private facilities and heating, including a room with a double and single bed, and two doubles (one with small lounge with a double sofa-bed). Shared living room with open fire, courtyard, open garden and meals with regional products. St Flour 18km.

Prices s fr €34; d fr €42; t fr €55; dinner fr €12 **Nearby** ✪ 18km ✍ 2.5km Restaurant 7km ⚓ 13km ⚓ 26km ⌂ 13km ✈ 18km **Notes** Pets admitted

ST-PONCY

Chausse

Lucien et Marie BONNAFOUX
15500 ST-PONCY
☎ 04 71 73 10 04

A double and a twin room available in the owners house with lounge area, and a further double room in an annex building, all with private facilities. Heating, lounge with fireplace, relaxation room, enclosed gardens for guests' use. Shops in nearby Chapelle Laurent, Massiac 12km, St Flour 20km.

Prices s fr €34; d fr €48 **Nearby** ✪ 20km ✍ 1km Restaurant 2km ⚓ 12km ⌂ 3km ✈ 12km **Notes** Pets admitted

ST-PROJET-DE-SALERS

Chambre d'hôtes

Thérèse CHAMBON
Le Bourg, 15140 ST-PROJET-DE-SALERS
☎ 04 71 69 23 01

A family welcome in the heart of the Parc des Volcans; this house has two double rooms and a room with double and single beds, all with private entrances and facilities. Guests' sitting room with kitchenette and a lounge with open fire shared with the owners. Facilities include heating, a terrace, courtyard, and garden. Out of season discounts available. Visit the Vallée de la Bertrande and Monts du Cantal.

Prices s fr €32; d fr €43; t fr €50 **On Site** ✍ **Nearby** ✪ 10km ⚓ 15km ✈ 30km **Notes** No pets

THIEZAC

⁂ ⦿ La Maison de Muret

Marie-Claude LABORIE

15800 THIEZAC

☎ 04 71 47 51 23 📄 04 71 47 51 23

email: m-claude.laborie@wanadoo.fr

web: www.maisondemuret.com

This charming and welcoming house offers spacious accommodation. On the first floor are a double room, a twin and a room which can sleep four people. On the second floor is another double. All rooms have private facilities. There is a shared lounge, and the dining room has an open fire. Central heating. Garden with pond. Meals available.

Prices s fr €39; d fr €48; extra person fr €15; dinner fr €15
Nearby 🖉 1km Restaurant 3.5km 🛶 16km 🏊 3km 🎣 3km 🚶 3km
Notes No pets

VEBRET

⁂ 🐓 ⦿ Verchalles

Guy et Simone GALVAING

15240 VEBRET

☎ 04 71 40 21 58 & 06 87 08 28 29

email: guy-galvaing@wanadoo.fr

web: http://perso.wanadoo.fr/guy.galvaing

Guest rooms including two Grade 2 rooms (a double, and one with a double and single bed) and four Grade 3 rooms in an annexe (a double and three with a double and single bed). All have private facilities. Shared lounge with TV, library, fireplace, heating, washing machine, terrace, grounds with garden furniture, swimming pool. Children's toys, table tennis, trail bike hire, camping on the farm. Supplement payable for pets, discounts available for children and out of season.

Prices s fr €45; d fr €50; t fr €61; extra person fr €12; dinner €12–€20
On Site Private 🎣 **Nearby** 🛶 10km 🛷 25km 🖉 1km Restaurant 3km
🏊 5km 🎣 3km 🚶 5km **Notes** Pets admitted English spoken

VIC-SUR-CERE

⁂ 🐓 ⦿ La Prade

Auguste et Noëlle DELRIEU

15800 VIC-SUR-CERE

☎ 04 71 47 51 64

A 14th-century farmhouse offering a double room, a room with a double and single bed and a suite with two double rooms (Grade 3) and a Grade 2 double room, all with private facilities. There is heating, telephone, TV, open fire, library, garden, play area. Family cooking offering regional dishes and home-made jams for breakfast. Discounts for children. Close to Aurillac, numerous waterfalls, and the health resort and spa of Vic Sur Cère.

Prices s fr €39; d fr €44; dinner fr €13 **Nearby** 🛶 0.5km 🖉 0.2km
Restaurant 1km 🛷 17km 🏊 0.5km 🎣 0.5km 🚶 0.5km **Notes** No pets

HAUTE-LOIRE

ALLEGRE

⁂ ⦿ L'Ancienne Baronnie

Stéphanie et Fabien CHARREYRE

5 place du Marchédial, 43270 ALLEGRE

☎ 04 71 00 22 44

email: stephanie-charreyre@club-internet.fr

This typical 15th-century building, with elegant antique furniture, is situated between the gorges of the Loire and the stunning countryside of the Allier region. There are two double bedrooms and three bedrooms with a lounge (one with open fireplace and balcony), all with private bathrooms. Small lounge area with TV and large dining room with an open fireplace.

Prices s €40–€54; d €45–€54; t fr €54; dinner fr €18 **Nearby** 🛷 3km
🛶 25km 🏊 5km 🎣 12km Restaurant 0.1km 🏊 0.2km 🎣 0.2km 🚶 25km
Notes No pets English spoken Open March to 15 October

ALLY

⁂ 🐓 ⦿ Chambre d'hôtes

Marie et Paul MASSEBOEUF

43380 ALLY

☎ 04 71 76 78 34

Near the Allier gorges, in peaceful windmill country between Velay and the volcanic Puy area, this house is on a farm. The hosts provide a warm welcome and meals using produce straight from the farm and garden. All bedrooms have private bathrooms and there is a communal eating area with open fireplace, library, lounge and covered terrace.

Prices s fr €35; d fr €40; t fr €46; extra person fr €10; dinner fr €15
Nearby 🛷 13km 🖉 10km 🎣 15km Restaurant 0.1km 🏊 22km 🎣 15km
🛷 20km 🚶 20km **Notes** Pets admitted

BAINS

⁂ 🐓 ⦿ Chambre d'hôtes

Patricia et Daniel RAVEYRE

Route du Puy, 43370 BAINS

☎ 04 71 57 51 79 & 06 83 59 93 47

email: patricia.raveyre@wanadoo.fr

In a village, at the heart of the volcanic region, a warm welcome awaits at this characterful renovated home. All of the bedrooms have a bathroom, wc and TV. Outside there is a garden and parking. Fresh farm produce is offered and the young owners are happy to help guests discover this beautiful region. Near the Saint-Jacques-de-Compostelle pilgrimage route.

Prices s fr €28; d fr €36; t fr €45; extra person fr €9; dinner fr €12
On Site 🎣 **Nearby** 🛷 5km 🖉 15km 🎣 5km Restaurant 3km 🏊
🚶 12km **Notes** Pets admitted English spoken

BAINS CONTINUED

▥ ⦿ Fay

C DE RANCOURT-DE-GROSSOUVRE
43370 BAINS
☎ 04 71 57 55 19   ▤ 04 71 57 55 19
email: c.derancourt@nta43.com

In the volcanic Velay region, known for its remarkable volcanic craters, lakes and picturesque villages, this carefully preserved country house is full of character and situated in a lovely village. All bedrooms are en suite and non-smoking with antique furniture, and there is a lounge and open fireplace. Traditional cooking is available and outside there are horse boxes, a park, and garage. Pick up can be arranged on request; discounts for off-peak holidays.

Prices s fr €33; d fr €40; t fr €42; dinner fr €20   **On Site** ⌖
Nearby ⛷ 15km ⚓ 10km ⚲ 15km Restaurant 15km ⌁ 15km Spa 15km
⌂ 3km ⋈ 15km   **Notes** No pets English spoken

▥ ❦ Jalasset

Monique et Marcel PELISSE
43370 BAINS
☎ 04 71 57 52 72 & 04 71 57 58 22

This restored farmhouse is deep in the countryside, in a small, peaceful hamlet in the volcanic Velay region near Livradois-Foez. There are two double bedrooms, a room for three and one for four: all with shower rooms and wc. The lounge has a TV, library and open fireplace. Outside, there is a garden, parking, and play area. Meals can be ordered and are made from farm produce.

Prices s fr €30; d fr €36; t fr €45; extra person fr €9   **Nearby** ⚲ 10km
⚲ 6km ⌁ 1km Restaurant 1km ⌂ 1km ⋈ 12km   **Notes** Pets admitted

▥ ⦿ Montbonnet

Xavier DE GROSSOUVRE
43370 BAINS
☎ 06 84 62 77 25

This is a 17th-century farmhouse with lots of character. It can sleep up to 11 guests in its three bedrooms, all with private facilities, which are in a building separate from the owners' house. There is a lounge with a big open fireplace, and a separate dining room. Mountain bikes available for hire.

Prices s fr €35; d fr €42; t fr €49; extra person fr €7; dinner fr €25
On Site ⌖ Private ⚲   **Nearby** ⛷ 15km ⚲ 10km Restaurant 0.3km
⌁ 15km ⌂ 3km ⋈ 15km   **Notes** No pets English spoken Open March to November.

BAS-EN-BASSET

▥ ⦿ Le Cendron

Nathalie et Yvan VEROT
43210 BAS-EN-BASSET
☎ 04 71 66 94 21 & 06 10 60 48 49
email: verot.nathalie@wanadoo.fr
web: http://ch-dhotesducendron.monsite.wanadoo.fr

This lovingly restored old house, tucked away among the meadows

just 100 metres from the Loire, has four bedrooms, each decorated in an individual style and all with en suite facilities. Meals are available by arrangement, and there is a covered swimming pool. Riverside walks, fishing, and lots of farm animals to interest the children.

Prices s fr €45; d fr €55; extra person fr €15; dinner fr €16
On Site Private ⚲   **Nearby** ⛷ 10km ⚲ 0.1km Restaurant 10km
⌁ 5km ⌂ 5km ⋈ 10km   **Notes** Pets admitted English spoken

BEAULIEU

▥ ❦ ⦿ Les Varennes

Jacqueline JOUBERT-MATHIEU
Les Rouzeyroux, 43800 BEAULIEU
☎ 04 71 08 18 02 & 06 30 91 56 94   ▤ 04 71 08 18 02
email: jacqueline.joubert-mathieu@wanadoo.fr
web: www.chambres-hotes-varennes.com

An old farmhouse dating from 1900, in a beautiful green setting not far from the gorges of the Loire. There are four very comfortable guest rooms, one a family room, and all with private bath/shower room and WC. Large lounge with books. Meals are available, by arrangement.

Prices d €59-€66; t €76-€80; extra person fr €18; dinner fr €22
Nearby ⛷ 1km ⚲ 1km ⚲ 2km Restaurant 3km ⌁ 1km ⌂ 3km
⋈ 9km   **Notes** Pets admitted English spoken

BEAUNE-SUR-ARZON

▥ ⦿ ♿ Le Clos St-François

Karine CHOUVET
43500 BEAUNE-SUR-ARZON
☎ 04 71 01 23 95
web: www.leclosstfrancois.com

Four fully equipped rooms in an historic 18th-century convent set in the heart of the small village of Forez. There are two rooms with two double beds, one room with a double and a single and a family room with a double and two singles. There is a large lounge, enclosed courtyard and garden plus a garage.

Prices s fr €50; d €55-€65; t €80-€85; extra person fr €15; dinner fr €18
Nearby ⛷ 14km ⚓ 30km ⚲ 2km ⚲ 10km Restaurant 2km ⌁ 2km
⌂ 5km ⋈ 40km   **Notes** Pets admitted English spoken Open March to November.

BLESLE

♦♦♦ ⭐⬤ Bousselargues

Gisèle et Michel LUBIN
43450 BLESLE
☎ 04 71 76 27 38 📠 04 71 76 27 38
web: perso.orange.fr/themyghaal/bousselargues

This tiny typical Cezallier village, near Blesle, is classed as one of the most beautiful in France. A restored winegrower's house provides two bedrooms for three people and one grade 2 room for four. There is also a lounge with open fireplace, a dining room, terraces and parking.

Prices s fr €35; d fr €40; extra person fr €13; dinner fr €13 **On Site** ✐ **Nearby** ⛴ 4km ⭢ 8km Restaurant 6km ⛵ 4km 🏛 4km 🚲 8km **Notes** No pets English spoken

BOURNONCLE-ST-PIERRE

♦♦♦ ⭐ ⭕ Bard

Christiane & Bernard CHAZELLE
43360 BOURNONCLE-SAINT-PIERRE
☎ 04 71 76 01 12 📠 04 71 76 01 12
email: c.chazelle1@tiscali.fr

This modern house has en suite bedrooms, a communal lounge room with open fireplace and TV, terrace, garden and parking. Farm produce available. The owners speak some English. Nearby Briode is known for the magnificent Roman basilica of Auvergne, the salmon museum and the old quarters; also worth exploring are the picturesque gorges of Allier and Allagnon.

Prices s fr €32; d fr €48; t fr €62; extra person fr €15 **Nearby** ⛴ 4km ✐ 7km ⭢ 7km Restaurant 7km ⛵ 7km 🏛 4km 🚲 4km **Notes** Pets admitted Open 15 March to September.

♦♦♦ ⭐⬤ L'Oustal

Marie-Hélène CLAVILIER
43360 BOURNONCLE-SAINT-PIERRE
☎ 04 71 76 99 83
email: hélène.clavilier@laposte.net

This is an interesting property - an old school building right in the middle of the village. There are two double bedrooms, and a family room for four, with a double bed and two singles. All rooms are upstairs and equipped with en suite bathroom and WC.

Prices s fr €35; d fr €45; t fr €55; extra person fr €15; dinner fr €15 **On Site** Restaurant ⛲ **Nearby** ⛴ 12km ✐ 5km ⭢ 4km ⛵ 12km 🏛 5km 🚲 5km **Notes** Pets admitted Open November to September.

CHANTEUGES

♦♦♦ ⭐ ⭕ La Grande Maison

Marloes DER KINDEREN
43300 CHANTEUGES
☎ 04 71 74 01 91 & 06 20 38 67 77
email: info@la-grande-maison.com
web: www.la-grande-maison.com

This beautifully renovated 15th-century house lies at the foot of the Roman abbey and has lots of character. There are a number of spacious rooms available, each with private bathroom and antique furniture. Lounge room with open fireplace; garden and terrace outside with a wonderful view over the village and Allier region. Creative art workshops available for individuals or groups. The gorges of Allier are nearby and evening meals are available on request.

Prices s €35-€110; d €65-€110; dinner €12-€25 **Nearby** ⛴ 12km ✐ 0.5km ⭢ 5km Restaurant 0.1km ⛵ 5km 🏛 0.1km 🚲 5km **Notes** No pets English spoken Open April to 15 November.

CHASPUZAC

♦♦♦ ⭕ La Maison Vieille

Robert PILLAY
43320 CHASPUZAC
☎ 04 71 08 68 50
email: robert.pillay@wanadoo.fr

This restored 17th-century farmhouse has lots of character and lies in a village at the heart of the volcanic region of Puy-en-Velay. There are two double rooms, one for three and two for four, each with private bathrooms. Lounge with beautiful old, open fireplace, dining/kitchen room and enclosed courtyard. The owner offers tasty meals and can help guests plan rambling in the surrounding area. Aerial sports 1km.

Prices s fr €32; d fr €40; t fr €48; extra person fr €8; dinner fr €15 **On Site** Restaurant **Nearby** ⛴ 5km ✐ 3km ⭢ 10km ⛵ 2km 🏛 2km 🚲 13km **Notes** Pets admitted English spoken Open 15 March to 15 October.

CRAPONNE-SUR-ARZON

♦♦♦ Doulioux

Marie-Claude ROUYER
La Crapounette, 43500 CRAPONNE-SUR-ARZON
☎ 04 71 03 20 32 📠 04 71 03 20 32
email: marieclaude.rouyer@wanadoo.fr
web: www.crapounette.com

This beautiful restored, stone farmhouse is situated in the Livradois Forez Park, well known for its music festivals, lava flow formations and numerous walking routes. There are three bedrooms with private bathrooms and a big lounge with fireplace, television area, library and board games. There is also a garden with children's play area.

Prices not confirmed for 2008 **Nearby** ⛴ 16km ✐ 3km ⭢ 3km ⛵ 3km 🏛 3km 🚲 20km **Notes** No pets English spoken

FAY-SUR-LIGNON

⅏ ❦ ⅋ La Maison des Chevres

T et B BOUTARIN et DESAGE
Abries, 43430 FAY-SUR-LIGNON
☎ 04 71 59 56 66 📄 04 71 56 31 89
email: maison-des-chevres@wanadoo.fr
web: http://perso.wanadoo.fr/maison-des-chevres/

A restored stone house situated on a goat farm, offering bedrooms
with private bathroom. There is a dining room, lounge, library and
terrace. The hosts offer a warm welcome and will be happy to help
guests explore this region. Evening meals and farm produce are
available on request.

Prices s fr €40; d fr €50; t fr €65; extra person fr €15; dinner fr €18
Nearby ☂ 1km ⚓ 15km ⚲ 0.2km ⚘ 15km Restaurant 5km ⚲ 15km
⚑ 15km 🏛 5km ⅏ 35km **Notes** No pets English spoken

GREZES

⅏ ❦ ⅋ Bugeac

Martine et Paul CUBIZOLLE
43170 GREZES
☎ 04 71 74 45 30 📄 04 71 74 45 30

Accommodation is available on this small dairy farm, in the heart of
Gevaudan. There are two double beds and seven single beds; four
in a separate room; each room with private facilities. Lounge, dining
room and charming garden. This old farm is typical of the region
with its mix of austere granite and warm wood. Bread, salamis, meat,
vegetables, cheeses, jams, honey are all served as house specialities.

Prices d fr €46; extra person fr €15; dinner fr €15 **On Site** ⚲
Nearby ☂ 10km ⚘ 10km Restaurant 10km ⚲ 10km 🏛 10km ⅏ 25km
Notes No pets English spoken Open Easter to 1 November.

JULLIANGES

⅏⅏ Domaine de la Valette

Michèle MEJEAN
43500 JULLIANGES
☎ 04 71 03 23 35 & 04 75 01 04 15
email: mmejean@wanadoo.fr
web: http://pro.wanadoo.fr/domaine.valette/

A 19th-century manor house, built of granite, and standing in
extensive grounds with plenty of trees and flowers. It has five
bedrooms, two of them suites, and all with private bath/shower
room and WC. Large lounge with open fire and books; kitchen
available for guests' use. Prepared food available on site.

Prices s fr €57; d €70-€95; extra person fr €20 **On Site** ⚲
Nearby ⚘ 12km ⚲ 6km ⅏ 35km **Notes** No pets English spoken
Open mid June to mid September.

LA CHAISE-DIEU

⅏⅏ ⅋ La Jacquerolle

Jacqueline CHAILLY
rue Marchedial, 43160 LA CHAISE-DIEU
☎ 04 71 00 07 52
email: lajacquerolle@hotmail.com
web: www.jacquerolle.com

In the Livradois Forez Park, near the famous Chaise-Dieu Abbey, this
house has been entirely renovated and is full of character. There
are five non-smoking bedrooms with private facilities, a lounge with
open fireplace, dining room, piano and terrace. Picnics, main meals
and large breakfasts of local produce can be prepared on request.
Prestigious music festival held at the abbey nearby. 7th night is free
except July and August.

Prices s fr €52; d €57-€60; t fr €77; extra person fr €17; dinner fr €24
Nearby ☂ 1km ⚲ 1km ⚘ 15km Restaurant 0.1km ⚲ 1km ⚑ 1km
🏛 0.1km ⅏ 40km **Notes** Pets admitted English spoken

LAFARRE

⊞ ❦ ⅘ Ferme Souchon

Dominique et Romano SILVESTRI

Ferme-Auberge Illa Fara, Souchon, 43490 LAFARRE

☎ 04 71 57 14 38

In peaceful surroundings near the Loire, on a secluded family-run goat farm with meals on offer in the farm/hotel. Of the five rooms, one has disabled access. All the rooms have private bathrooms and separate toilets. The lounge contains books and games.

Prices d fr €45; t fr €55; extra person fr €10; dinner €16–€22
On Site ✐ ❦ **Nearby** 🏛10km 🚣25km **Notes** Pets admitted
Open February to December CC

⊞ ⧉ La Longerine

Catherine CARON-LABRIOT

La Théoule, 43490 LAFARRE

☎ 04 71 57 39 01

email: cath@lalongerine.eu

web: www.lalongerine.eu

This old farmhouse has been totally restored. It has four guest bedrooms, all on the ground floor and all with private bath/shower room and WC. Large lounge with open fire. Outside are open grounds with garden furniture and barbecue; on-site parking and beautiful views.

Prices s fr €48; d fr €48; dinner fr €15 **On Site** Restaurant
Nearby ⛷4km ✐0.5km ⚓11km ⛵25km 🏛4km 🚣40km
Notes No pets English spoken Open April to October.

LAPTE

⊞ ❦ ⧉ Les Brus de Verne

Josette et Auguste MOUNIER

43200 LAPTE

☎ 04 71 59 38 30 📄 04 71 59 38 30

In a peaceful village setting, this restored old farmhouse is linked to the owners' house and has five comfortable bedrooms with private bathrooms (one with a mezzanine). There is also large communal room with fireplace and small kitchen, and a courtyard and terrace. This forest region is ideal for rambling and is near many tourist routes.

Prices not confirmed for 2008 **Nearby** ⛷10km ✐5km ⚓10km
⚓4km 🏛3km 🚣25km **Notes** No pets English spoken

LAVAUDIEU

⊞ ⅘ La Buissonnière

Andrée et Michel ISABEL

43100 LAVAUDIEU

☎ 04 71 76 49 02 & 06 30 95 48 27

email: andree.isabel@wanadoo.fr

This is a former wine-grower's house on the edge of the fortified village of Lavaudieu, which is one of the most beautiful villages in France. There is one ground floor room with disabled access, and three on the first floor. All rooms have private facilities. There is a garden with an enclosed area, terraces and garden furniture.

Prices s fr €46; d fr €50; extra person fr €15 **On Site** ✐
Nearby ⛷5km ⚓9km Restaurant 0.1km ⚓9km ⚓9km 🏛5km
🚣9km **Notes** No pets Open Easter to 15 November.

⊞ La Maison d'à Côté

Marie ROBERT

43100 LAVAUDIEU

☎ 04 71 76 45 04

email: lamaisondacote@wanadoo.fr

This restored house, linked to the owners' house, has a number of twin/double bedrooms with private bathrooms. In addition, there is a dining room with lounge area and panoramic views. Two restaurants on site. The peaceful old fortified village is next to the clear waters of the Sénouire and surrounded by meadows and wooded hillsides, and has a Benedictine abbey, museum, cloisters and stained-glass windows.

Prices s fr €48; d fr €52 **On Site** ✐ **Nearby** ⛷5km ⚓9km
Restaurant 0.1km ⚓9km ⚓9km 🏛9km 🚣9km **Notes** No pets Open
Easter to 1 October

⊞ Le Colombier

Pascal COLTRI

route de Fontannes, 43100 LAVAUDIEU

☎ 04 71 76 09 86 & 06 82 74 67 13 📄 04 73 35 99 24

email: colombier.chambredhote@wanadoo.fr

web: www.lecolombier-lavaudieu.com

This modern house stands on a hillside overlooking Lavaudieu, one of France's most beautiful villages, and the Senouire Valley. Three double rooms with private balconies are in the owners home; there is a fourth in a separate building, a converted pigeon house. All have private facilities. Enclosed grounds with swimming pool and parking.

Prices s fr €60; d fr €65; t fr €95 **On Site** Private ⚓ **Nearby** ⛷4km
✐1km Restaurant 0.1km ⚓7km 🏛5km 🚣7km **Notes** No pets
English spoken Open May to 15 October. CC

LE BOUCHET-ST-NICOLAS

▦ ⦿ **Chambre d'hôtes**

Andrée et Augustin REYNAUD

43510 LE BOUCHET-SAINT-NICOLAS

☎ 04 71 57 31 91   🖹 04 71 57 31 91

A restored house in the village, near the Lac du Bouchet, containing three bedrooms, one with a mezzanine and en suite facilities. There is a guest lounge and dining room and a balcony. The area is the home of the Puy lentil.

Prices s fr €32; d fr €40; t fr €48; extra person fr €8; dinner fr €14
Nearby ⛷ 12km ⛷ 6km ℘ 1.5km ⊀ 12km Restaurant 0.1km ⌕ 6km
🚢 20km **Notes** Pets admitted Open Easter to 1 November.

▦ ❦ **Chambre d'hôtes**

Colette et Pierre VILLESECHE

43510 LE BOUCHET-SAINT-NICOLAS

☎ 04 71 57 35 34   🖹 04 71 57 30 93

This is a newly built house on the edge of the village. There are two rooms for four, with a mezzanine, and one room for three, all of them spacious, with private facilities and direct access to a terrace. The village is between the valleys of the Allier and the upper Loire. Meals available at the farmhouse restaurant on site.

Prices s fr €35; d fr €39; t fr €49; extra person fr €10; dinner fr €14
On Site Restaurant **Nearby** ⛷ 12km ⛷ 20km ℘ 1.5km ⊀ 12km
⌕ 4km ⌘ 4km 🏛 4km 🚢 20km **Notes** Pets admitted Open
15 February to 15 December. CC

LEOTOING

▦ ⦿ **A La Buissonnière**

Claudine CORMERAIS

1, rue de l'Ecole, 43410 LEOTOING

☎ 04 71 76 31 41

email: reservation@alabuissonniere.com

web: www.alabuissonniere.com

This is a restored country house on the edge of town. It enjoys an exceptional medieval site, overlooking the valley of the Alagnon and with a beautiful view of the Massif Cézallier. It has four rooms with private facilities, one of them with a mezzanine, and one family room for four. Conservatory, library, and garden with furniture. Parking close by. Meals by reservation, but only on certain days.

Prices d €70-€90; extra person fr €20; dinner fr €17 **On Site** Private ⊀
Nearby ⛷ 8km ℘ 1km Restaurant 1km ⌕ 12km Spa 30km ⌘ 12km
🏛 6km 🚢 6km **Notes** Pets admitted English spoken Open 15 April to
December.

▦ ⦿ **Le Moulin du Bateau**

Claude et Catherine QUANTIN

43410 LEOTOING

☎ 04 71 76 57 07

email: lemoulindubateau@wanadoo.fr

An old mill, restored with much loving care, provides a special setting for this chambre d'hôtes. There are four attractively decorated

bedrooms, two doubles and two rooms for four (double bed plus two singles), all on the second floor and all with en suite bathroom and WC. Breakfast in the hosts' large dining room. Outside are flowery terraces which go right down to the river.

Prices s fr €50; d fr €55; t fr €73; extra person fr €18; dinner fr €20
On Site ℘ **Nearby** ⛷ 10km ⊀ 10km Restaurant 0.4km ⌕ 6km
🏛 6km 🚢 10km **Notes** Pets admitted

LES ESTABLES

▦ ⦿ **Francillon**

Marie-Josée DURAND

43150 LES ESTABLES

☎ 04 71 08 39 56

This is a restored former farmhouse on the edge of the village. It enjoys a beautiful view of the Massif du Mézenc. It has three bedrooms on the first floor, all with private facilities. There is a large shared lounge area, with a fireplace, and two further lounges. It has a garden with terraces and garden furniture.

Prices d fr €55; t fr €60; extra person fr €10; dinner fr €18
Nearby ⛷ 15km ℘ 0.8km ⊀ 5km ⌔ 0.4km ⌕ 0.5km 🏛 0.8km
🚢 36km **Notes** No pets English spoken

▦ ⦿ **La Maison du Rocher Tourte**

Karine et Bruno TOMOZYK-HERRY

Chamard, 43150 LES ESTABLES

☎ 04 71 08 30 53   🖹 04 71 08 30 53

email: lamaisondurochertourte@orange.fr

This typical stone country house has a magnificent view over Mézenc and the Cévennes. All the guest rooms have private bathrooms and there is a lounge with kitchen area and dining room. With a large garden, the house is ideally situated for rambling, tennis and cross-country skiing.

Prices s fr €44; d fr €44; t fr €54; extra person fr €10; dinner fr €16
On Site ⌘ **Nearby** ⛷ 10km ⛷ 30km ℘ 3km Restaurant 3km ⌔ 3km
⌕ 3km 🏛 3km 🚢 35km **Notes** No pets English spoken

▦ ⦿ ♿ **La Vacheresse**

Catherine LAURENT

La Bartette, 43150 LES ESTABLES

☎ 04 71 08 31 70

email: labartette.chambresdhotes@club-internet.fr

web: www.labartette.fr

This beautiful stone-built house dating from 1875 has been totally restored. It has four bedrooms, one with a split-level arrangement, and can sleep up to 12 guests. All the rooms have a private bath or shower room and WC. Dining room with open fire, and lounge with books. A stream borders the property.

Prices s fr €35; d fr €50; t fr €66; extra person fr €16; dinner fr €16
On Site ℘ **Nearby** ⛷ 15km ⛷ 35km ⊀ 11km Restaurant 4km ⌔ 4km
⌕ 4km ⌘ 4km 🏛 4km 🚢 32km **Notes** No pets

LISSAC

♨ ❦ ⊙ ⊹ Freycenet

Nicole et Alain SIGAUD
Route de Darsac, 43350 LISSAC
☎ 04 71 57 02 97

A modern house with four bedrooms, one with access for disabled guests. The rooms sleep from two to four people, and all have en suite facilities. Lounge with open fire; meals by arrangement. Guests who know their lentils will be delighted to know that the authentic green 'Lentilles du Puy' are cultivated right here!

Prices s fr €28; d fr €36; t fr €44; extra person fr €8; dinner fr €12
Nearby ⚓ 8km ⌁ 18km ⚘ 3km ⚲ 7km Restaurant 5km ⛵ 0.5km
⚑ 7km ⌂ 7km ⩊ 1km **Notes** Pets admitted English spoken

LORLANGES

♨ ❦ ⊙ Lachaud

Suzanne et J-Claude BOUDON
43360 LORLANGES
☎ 04 71 76 03 03 ⊟ 04 71 76 03 03

In a hamlet in the Allier/Margeride region, this renovated farm contains two grade 3 bedrooms with private bathrooms and three bedrooms with mezzanine levels. There is a lounge and drawing room with fireplace, a garden, terrace, children's play area and parking in an enclosed courtyard. Fishing is possible in the private lake and camping is also available on the farm.

Prices s fr €45; d fr €45; t fr €60; extra person fr €15; dinner fr €14
Nearby ⚓ 12km ⚘ 9km ⚲ 9km Restaurant 4km ⛵ 9km ⌂ 9km
⩊ 9km **Notes** Pets admitted

MALVALETTE

♨ ❦ ⊙ Chambres d'hôtes de Malvalette

Dany et Jean-Marc BUFARD
43210 MALVALETTE
☎ 04 71 66 77 30 & 06 81 66 48 44
email: dany.bufard@free.fr

This new house is situated on a goat farm in a small village on the edge of the Auvergne region. Each bedroom has a private bathroom and there are private entrances to three bedrooms (with a mezzanine) for four people and two rooms for two. Outside there is a covered terrace and enclosed courtyard. There are tourist attractions nearby including a good bird watching site and it is an ideal location for rambling or horse riding. Meals by reservation.

Prices s fr €32; d fr €42; t fr €50; extra person fr €10; dinner fr €16
Nearby ⚓ 4km ⚘ 3km ⚲ 8km Restaurant 8km ⛵ 8km ⌂ 8km
⩊ 8km **Notes** Pets admitted English spoken

MONLET

♨ ⊙ La Maison du Lac

Joëlle LE JEAN
Lac de Malaguet, 43270 MONLET
☎ 04 71 00 21 48
email: lacdemalaguet@wanadoo.fr
web: www.lac-de-malaguet.com

This stylish modern property has been created by the conversion of a former ribbon factory in a delightful spot, right beside Lac Malaguet. There are five bedrooms, doubles and twins, three on the ground floor and two upstairs. All have en suite bath or shower room and WC. Outside, guests will find garden furniture and reclining chairs, and fly fishing is available.

Prices s €40-€45; d €55-€60; extra person €15; dinner €22
On Site ⚘ **Nearby** ⚓ 2km ⚲ 15km Restaurant 5km ⛵ 5km ⌂ 5km
⩊ 30km **Notes** No pets English spoken Open March to November. CC

MOUDEYRES

♨ ⊙ ⊹ Le Moulinou

Lucia et Bertrand GABORIAUD
43150 MOUDEYRES
☎ 04 71 08 30 52
email: lucia.gaboriaud@wanadoo.fr
web: http://lemoulinou.free.fr

This welcoming 18th-century Mézenc farm property has a warm family atmosphere and is situated on a volcanic plateau with peaceful pastures. It has five bedrooms with lots of character and private facilities. There is also a drawing room, lounge with huge fireplace, terrace, jacuzzi, enclosed courtyard and parking. Warm yourself in front of the fire after a day's skiing, and enjoy the wild flowers in warmer months..

Prices s fr €45; d fr €53; t fr €65; extra person fr €12; dinner fr €18
On Site ⚘ **Nearby** ⚓ 10km ⌁ 10km ⚲ 10km Restaurant 2km ⚓ 8km
⛵ 5km Spa 0.1km ⌂ 5km ⩊ 25km **Notes** No pets English spoken
Open January to mid November.

POLIGNAC

♨ ⊙ La Gourmantine

Lydie et Freddy SAIMOUR
Chemin de Ridet, 43000 POLIGNAC
☎ 04 71 05 94 29 ⊟ 04 71 05 94 29
email: contact@gourmantine.fr
web: www.gourmantine.fr

This beautifully restored 18th-century stone farmhouse lies in woodland in a delightful village, at the foot of a 10th-century feudal fortress. There is a non-smoking family room for four with two bedrooms and a private bathroom, plus a lounge, dining room with fireplace and piano. Outside, there is an enclosed garden and terrace with a beautiful view over the Cévennes massif and Mézenc. Freshly baked bread and organic wine are served. Closed Christmas.

Prices s €45-€53; d €50-€58; t €68-€73; extra person €15; dinner €20
On Site Restaurant **Nearby** ⚓ 5km ⌁ 5km ⚘ 3km ⚲ 5km ⚓ 30km
⛵ 5km ⌂ 0.1km ⩊ 5km **Notes** Pets admitted English spoken

AUVERGNE

QUEYRIERES

▒▒▒ ⵁⵁⵁ La Bòria delh Chastèl

Catherine CHALOT-LEVRAT
Le Bourg, 43260 QUEYRIERES
☎ 04 71 57 70 81 & 06 25 67 06 54
email: contact@laboria-queyrieres.com
web: http://perso.wanadoo.fr/laboria/

This is a restored farmhouse with a wonderful view, situated in a beautiful village in the Meygal area. It has four rooms, two of them with mezzanines, and all with private bath or shower room and WC. Lounge with open fire, TV, books and games. Small museum of local traditions. Covered parking.

Prices s fr €40; d fr €50; t fr €67; extra person fr €13; dinner fr €16
Nearby ⚓ 8km ⤳ 15km ⤢ 8km ⚘ 20km ⤵ 8km ⑁ 8km ⤛ 20km
Notes No pets English spoken

RETOURNAC

▒▒▒ ⵁ ⵁⵁⵁ ⵁ Les Revers

Béatrice et J-Pierre CHEVALIER
43130 RETOURNAC
☎ 04 71 59 42 81 ⵁ 04 71 59 42 81
email: jean-pierrechevalier589@orange.fr
web: www.lesrevers.fr.st

This restored farm lies in countryside with picturesque valleys and some of the oldest Loire châteaux and remarkable Roman churches. There are four bedrooms (two have a mezzanine), each with bathroom and wc. There is a large lounge room with open fireplace, TV, library and large garden. Farm produce is also available on the farm. Horse riding can be organised. Pets admitted except dogs.

Prices s fr €33; d fr €45; t fr €57; extra person fr €12; dinner fr €16
On Site ⚓ ⵁ **Nearby** ⤳ 1km ⤢ 4km Restaurant 4km ⚘ 5km
⑁ 6km ⤛ 5km **Notes** English spoken Open April to September.

ROSIERES

▒▒▒ ⵁ ⵁⵁⵁ La Colombière

Pierre VEROT
Chiriac, 43800 ROSIERES
☎ 06 87 06 53 39 ⵁ 04 71 57 91 08
email: pierre.verot@wanadoo.fr
web: www.lacolombiere-auvergne.fr

This is a working farm, not far from the Loire Valley. The three guest rooms are in a building adjacent to the owners' home. Each one has themed decorations, and they all have en suite facilities. Large day room with kitchenette, enclosed courtyard with garden furniture and barbecue. Meals are available by arrangement.

Prices s fr €30; d fr €43; t fr €50; extra person fr €12; dinner fr €13
Nearby ⚓ 5km ⤢ 1km ⤳ 5km Restaurant 10km ⚘ 0.5km ⑁ 0.5km
⤛ 12km **Notes** Pets admitted English spoken

SANSSAC-L'EGLISE

▒▒▒ ⵁ Chambre d'hôtes

Florence et Patrick LIABEUF
43320 SANSSAC-L'EGLISE
☎ 04 71 08 64 15 & 06 33 11 45 50
email: alounna@orange.fr

In the middle of the countryside, in the heart of a small quiet village, this old restored farmhouse has bedrooms with private bathrooms. The dining room/lounge has a fireplace and TV and there is an enclosed courtyard and terrace. Nearby: Puy lentil growing area, amazing volcanic craters, lovely villages and the châteaux of Saint-Vidal and Rochelambert.

Prices s fr €32; d fr €42; t fr €50; extra person fr €8 **Nearby** ⚓ 1km
⤵ 5km ⤢ 10km ⤳ 8km ⚘ 5km ⵁ 10km ⑁ 5km ⤛ 10km **Notes** Pets admitted

SAUGUES

▒▒▒ ⵁⵁⵁ Le Rouve

Jean-Pierre & Hélène BLANC
43170 SAUGUES
☎ 04 71 77 64 15 ⵁ 04 71 77 83 84

This house, with lovely countryside views of the 'wild nut' country, is set in two hectares of land on the outskirts of a village. There are bedrooms with private bathrooms and independent entrances, a communal room and terrace with a large open courtyard and parking. Evening meals can be provided. Saugues, the small, lively town on the Saint-Jacques-de-Compostelle route, is nearby.

Prices d fr €43; dinner fr €17 **Nearby** ⚓ 4km ⤢ 0.3km ⤳ 4km
Restaurant 4km ⚘ 4km ⑁ 4km ⤛ 20km **Notes** Pets admitted Open
April to 1 November.

▒▒▒ ⵁ ⵁⵁⵁ Les Gabales

Pierre GAUTHIER
route du Puy, 43170 SAUGUES
☎ 04 71 77 86 92
email: contact@lesgabales.com
web: www.lesgabales.com

This 1930s manor house is on the route from Saint-Jacques de Compostelle and has non-smoking rooms with private facilities including two suites (four people in each), each with a different style. Lounge with library, dining room, terrace and parkland with walking routes. Half board tariff and special rates for children available. This is granite countryside, a fitting home for the Beast of Gévaudan (a local legend).

Prices d fr €50; t fr €60; extra person fr €17; dinner fr €17 **On Site** ⤢
Nearby ⚓ 1km ⤳ 0.8km Restaurant 0.1km ⚘ 0.8km ⵁ 1km ⤛ 20km
Notes No pets English spoken

SENEUJOLS

🌼 ◯ Chambre d'hôtes

Bernard et Colette BOYER
Route de St Christophe, 43510 SENEUJOLS
☎ 04 71 03 19 69 📄 04 71 03 19 69
email: colettebernardboyer@tiscali.fr

In the heart of the volcanic region, this stone renovated farmhouse is in a small, peaceful village near the Bouchet Forest and lake. The bedrooms all have private bathrooms and a separate house there is a kitchenette, communal lounge, library, kitchen area, courtyard, terrace with garden furniture and children's games. Communal meals are served in the owners' dining room; picnics on request. Horses are welcome and walkers can be picked up.

Prices s fr €30; d fr €42; t fr €50; extra person fr €6; dinner fr €14
Nearby 🏌 15km ♨ 8km 🎣 8km ⚡ 15km Restaurant 3km ♨ 🅿 5km
🚴 15km **Notes** Pets admitted Open April-15 November.

ST-BEAUZIRE

🌼 🐓 Les Chaumasses

Hélène et Dominique CHAZELLE
43100 SAINT-BEAUZIRE
☎ 04 71 76 81 00 📄 04 71 76 81 00
email: dominique.chazelle@wanadoo.fr
web: www.chaumasses.com

This property has comfortable bedrooms with private bathrooms, lovely patios and wonderful views. Guests may use the lounge and garden. The house is near Broude, with its wonderful Roman basilica, and the superb gorges of Allier with its river and wild salmon.

Prices s fr €40; d fr €45; t fr €55; extra person fr €5 **Nearby** 🏌 9km
🎣 8km ⚡ 8km Restaurant 0.3km ♨ 0.4km ⛳ 8km 🅿 8km 🚴 8km
Notes No pets English spoken

ST-CHRISTOPHE-SUR-DOLAIZON

🌼 🐓 ◯ ♿ Le Champ de l'Oustau

Virginie et Hervé CHAMARD
Eycenac, 43370 SAINT-CHRISTOPHE-SUR-DOLAIZON
☎ 04 71 01 51 55 & 06 26 17 72 24
email: fami.chamard@wanadoo.fr

A restored farm building at the entrance to the village, with five guest bedrooms. All of the rooms, a mixture of doubles and triples, have private bath or shower room and WC. Some have a split-level layout. Enclosed grounds with garden furniture and parking space. Farm produce is for sale, and meals are available by arrangement.

Prices s fr €30; d fr €40; t fr €50; extra person fr €10; dinner fr €15
Nearby 🏌 10km ♨ 10km 🎣 3km ⚡ 5km Restaurant 5km ♨ 5km
🅿 3km 🚴 5km **Notes** Pets admitted English spoken

ST-CIRGUES

🌼 ◯ Chez les Bougnats

Jean-Louis DUCRETTET
Le Bourg, 43380 SAINT-CIRGUES
☎ 04 71 77 44 69 & 06 60 17 83 72
email: chezlesbougnats@wanadoo.fr
web: http://chezlesbougnats.monsite.wanadoo.fr

This restored house is right in the heart of a village in the Allier Gorges area. There are four bedrooms, all upstairs, each with a private bath or shower room and WC. Cold meals available in the evening by arrangement, and packed lunches can be provided for days out. Good walking area; watersports close by.

Prices s fr €33; d fr €45; t fr €59; extra person fr €14; dinner fr €15
On Site ♨ **Nearby** ⚡ 2km ⚡ 13km ♨ 0.8km 🅿 0.8km 🚴 13km
Notes No pets

ST-DIDIER-D'ALLIER

🌼 ◯ La Grangette

Jacqueline MONTAGNE
43580 SAINT-DIDIER-D'ALLIER
☎ 04 71 57 24 41
email: avoine-montagne@wanadoo.fr

This isolated renovated farm lies amongst the magnificent Allier gorges, in a village perched on the edge of one. Two of the bedrooms have a mezzanine level and all have a private bathroom. Living room, library and dining room with kitchen area, courtyard. Salmon and white-water country with canyoning, rafting and mountain biking available.

Prices s fr €32; d fr €38; t fr €48; extra person fr €10; dinner fr €14
Nearby ♨ 26km ♨ 10km Restaurant 5km ♨ 6km ⛳ 6km 🅿 6km
🚴 15km **Notes** Pets admitted English spoken Open April to October.

ST-DIDIER-EN-VELAY

⌘ ⚲ Au Delà des Bois

Laura et Guy FRANC
Montcoudiol, 43140 SAINT-DIDIER-EN-VELAY
☎ 04 71 61 08 09
email: audeladesbois43@wanadoo.fr
web: http://membres.lycos.fr/laurafranc/

A typical 17th-century farm in a small hamlet surrounded by forest. Three individual guest rooms with private facilities. Large communal lounge with an open fire. Terrace and children's play area. Many activities on offer nearby.

Prices s fr €34; d fr €44; t fr €54; extra person fr €10; dinner fr €16
Nearby ⚓ 1km ℘ 2km ⚲ 3km Restaurant 3km ⚲ 3km ⚲ 8km
⚲ 3km ⚲ 20km **Notes** Pets admitted English spoken

⌘ ⚲ Les Chenelettes

Bernard ROUSSET
43140 SAINT-DIDIER-EN-VELAY
☎ 04 71 61 11 67 & 06 30 90 32 99
email: info@chenelettes.com
web: www.chenelettes.com

Four well equipped rooms in old farm buildings next to the owner's home. This peaceful hamlet has lovely countryside views. There is a large guest living room. All the rooms have private bathrooms and offer a double, two rooms with a double and a single bed and a family room with two double beds. Wi-fi available.

Prices s fr €34; d fr €44; t fr €54; extra person fr €10; dinner fr €16
On Site ⚲ **Nearby** ⚓ 2km ℘ 2km ⚲ 1.5km Restaurant 1.5km
⚲ 12km ⚲ 1.5km ⚲ 2km ⚲ 10km **Notes** No pets English spoken

ST-FRONT

⌘ ⚲ La Vidalle d'Eyglet

C.-Paule et François LELOUSTRE
43550 SAINT-FRONT
☎ 04 71 59 55 58 📠 04 71 59 55 58
email: vidalle@free.fr
web: www.vidalle.fr

A 16th-century building in an exceptionally delightful pastoral setting. There are five guest rooms, full of character, all with private facilities. Reading rooms and an art room available; art exhibition in the house. Art courses from May to October. Facilities for horse riders. Meals available by arrangement, except July and August, with authentic local produce.

Prices s €75-€85; d €75-€95; extra person fr €25; dinner fr €25
Nearby ⚓ 6km ⚲ 25km ℘ 1km ⚲ 12km Restaurant 5km ⚲ 6km
⚲ 12km ⚲ 5km ⚲ 5km ⚲ 27km **Notes** No pets English spoken

⌘ ⚲ Les Bastides du Mézenc

Erik DEN HAESE
43550 SAINT-FRONT
☎ 04 71 59 51 57 📠 04 71 59 51 57
email: lesbastidesfrance@wanadoo.fr
web: www.lesbastidesfrance.com

At the top of Lauzes, with views over the volcanoes and the high plateaux of Velay, this old country house has been restored in the local style. There are bedrooms for two people and two suites with private bathroom, a sitting room with open fireplace, dining room, library, piano and billiards table. Large garden and terrace. Dog driving (the owner is a professional dog trainer) and horse riding can be arranged.

Prices s fr €47; d fr €63; dinner fr €26 **Nearby** ⚓ 6km ⚲ 20km
℘ 15km ⚲ 30km Restaurant 5km ⚲ 10km ⚲ 6km ⚲ 10km ⚲ 30km
Notes Pets admitted English spoken CC

ST-GENEYS-PRES-ST-PAULIEN

⌘ Bel Air

Annick et Serge CHABRIER
43350 ST-GENEYS-PRES-SAINT-PAULIEN
☎ 04 71 00 45 56
email: belairvert@aol.com
web: www.bienvenue-a-la-campagne-haute-loire.com/belair

This old restored farmhouse is in a lovely position in the village. Each bedroom has a private bathroom and there is also a lounge with TV and library, and large garden with furniture. Located in the volcanic Velay/Livradois-Forez area, there are several walking routes nearby.

Prices s fr €35; d fr €39; t fr €49; extra person fr €9.50 **Nearby** ⚓ 3km
⚲ 15km ℘ 1km ⚲ 3km Restaurant 1km ⚲ 3km Spa 20km ⚲ 3km
⚲ 15km **Notes** Pets admitted Open March to 1 November.

ST-JEURES

⌘ ⚲ Le Fougal

Martine FAURE
43200 SAINT-JEURES
☎ 04 71 59 66 64 📠 04 71 59 66 64
email: lefougal@yahoo.fr
web: www.chambres-dhotes-lefougal.com

A house on the edge of the village with a large lounge, courtyard, games room and parking. Four large, well-equipped rooms, all have private bathrooms. On the first floor are two twin rooms and a family room with a double bed and two singles on a mezzanine. In an annexe is a further room with three single beds.

Prices s fr €40; d fr €44; t fr €56; extra person fr €13; dinner fr €16
On Site ⚲ **Nearby** ⚓ 10km ℘ 1km ⚲ 10km Restaurant 2km
⚲ 30km ⚲ ⚲ 0.1km ⚲ 20km **Notes** No pets English spoken

ST-JULIEN-D'ANCE

¦¦¦ ⑩ Chambre d'hôtes

Françoise et Pascal SAIVET
Le Roure, 43500 SAINT-JULIEN-D'ANCE
☎ 04 71 03 24 02 & 06 68 18 63 63
email: lechantdelance@wanadoo.fr
web: www.le-chant-de-lance.fr

An old farmhouse, built in the local style, agreeably restored to provide very comfortable accommodation in an environmentally protected area in the Livradois-Forez park. There are five bedrooms, three doubles and two triples, all with private shower and WC. Lounge with open fire; enclosed wooded grounds; meals available by arrangement.

Prices s fr €46; d fr €51; t fr €61; extra person fr €11; dinner fr €20
On Site ♿　**Nearby** ⚓ 5km ⌁ 40km ⚲ 5km 🛒 5km 🐎 5km 🎣 3km
🚶 10km　**Notes** No pets　English spoken　Open mid April to mid November.

ST-JULIEN-MOLHESABATE

¦¦¦ La Maison d'En Haut

Roland SIGRIST
Malatray, 43220 SAINT-JULIEN-MOLHESABATE
☎ 04 71 61 96 20 📄 04 71 61 96 20
email: roland.sigrist@nornet.fr
web: www.maison-den-haut.com

A beautiful spacious home which has been renovated in keeping with the local style. It has three non-smoking double rooms, tastefully decorated and furnished. Each has private bath/shower room and WC. There is a small guests' lounge with direct access to the beautiful flowery garden which overlooks the valley. Good area for walking or mountain-biking.

Prices s €75-€85; d €75-€85　**On Site** ♿　Private 🏊
Nearby ⚓ 10km ⌁ 20km ⚲ 10km Restaurant 6km 🎣 6km
🚶 45km　**Notes** No pets　English spoken

ST-PAL-DE-SENOUIRE

¦¦¦ ⑩ La Grange

Lieke ZUIDEMA
43270 SAINT-PAL-DE-SENOUIRE
☎ 04 71 00 09 07
email: liekezuidema@hotmail.com
web: www.zuidenwind.net

La Grange is a 19th-century manor house, in a secluded spot right in the heart of the Livradois-Forez park. Here three individually-decorated twin-bedded rooms all have en suite shower room and WC. Breakfasts and evening meals (by arrangement) are served in the large living room downstairs. A bright and cheery place, with superb views.

Prices s fr €35; d fr €40; dinner fr €15　**Nearby** ⚓ 8km ⚲ 15km
Restaurant 7km 🛒 7km 🎣 6km 🚶 45km　**Notes** Pets admitted　English spoken

ST-PAL-EN-CHALENCON

¦¦¦ 🐓 Chambre d'hôtes

Christine et Pascal COCHARD
Le Villard, 43500 SAINT-PAL-EN-CHALENCON
☎ 04 71 61 38 50

This is a restored farm building, standing in a village. It has four big double bedrooms, all on the first floor. They all have private showers and WCs. On the ground floor is a day room with lounge area and kitchenette. There is an enclosed courtyard with garden furniture, and a farmhouse restaurant is on site.

Prices s fr €29; d fr €36; t fr €45　**Nearby** ⚓ 15km ♿ 3km ⚲ 3km
Restaurant 3km 🚲 20km 🛒 3km 🎣 3km 🚶 15km　**Notes** No pets　CC

¦¦¦ ⑩ Chambre d'hôtes

Corinne SOLA
Boisset-Bas, 43500 SAINT-PAL-EN-CHALENCON
☎ 04 71 75 29 35
email: laboissette@orange.fr

Beautifully restored farm on the edge of the village with three double rooms in an annexe to the main house. There is on site parking, a courtyard, and enclosed garden with furniture. The annexe also contains a kitchen and large lounge. Each bedroom has a private bathroom.

Prices s fr €37; d fr €45; extra person fr €10; dinner fr €18　**On Site** 🚲
🐎　**Nearby** ⚓ 17km ⌁ 40km ♿ 1km ⚲ 2km Restaurant 1km 🛒 3km
🎣 3km 🚶 28km　**Notes** Pets admitted　English spoken

ST-PAULIEN

⊞ ♥ ℣ L'Orée du Viaye

Nathalie LASSON

Chassagnoles, 43350 SAINT-PAULIEN

☎ 04 71 00 56 39

email: auroreboreal22@hotmail.com

Near the picturesque town of Puy en Velay, the owners of this renovated farm offer rooms for two rooms for two people and two for three with private facilities. Living room, lounge corner, grounds, parking. No smoking.

Prices s fr €34; d fr €42; t fr €51; extra person fr €9; dinner fr €16
On Site ⚓ **Nearby** ⌁20km ℐ3km ⅄ 3km Restaurant 3km ⌁ 3km
🏠3km ᴍ 10km **Notes** No pets English spoken

ST-PIERRE-EYNAC

⊞ ♥ ℣ ♿ Montoing

Germaine et Michel JULIEN

43260 SAINT-PIERRE-EYNAC

☎ 04 71 03 00 39 & 06 81 29 89 28 🗎 04 71 03 00 39

This old restored farm is near Puy-en-Velay in a volcanic area with a rich Roman heritage evident in the churches and museums. The bedrooms each have a private bathroom and one has a mezzanine area for nine people. There is also a lounge, TV, sitting room, library, large, enclosed garden, terrace and parking.

Prices s fr €28; d fr €40; t fr €50; extra person fr €12; dinner fr €14
On Site ᵉ **Nearby** ⚓ 5km ℐ5km ⅄ 10km ⌁6km 🏠3km ᴍ12km
Notes No pets

ST-VICTOR-MALESCOURS

⊞ ℣ Le Grand Fayard

Zahra et Michel FUCHS

La Tourette, 43140 SAINT-VICTOR-MALESCOURS

☎ 04 77 39 92 98 🗎 04 77 39 93 16

email: michel.fuchs.43@wanadoo.fr

web: www.chambredhotesympa.com

An 18th-century farm in the heart of the countryside, near Jonzeiux in the Loire; ideal for active people and families. There are five quiet and comfortable bedrooms, each with a private bathroom, a dining room with open fireplace and pond with ducks and fish. There are a number of routes and signposted walks from the house.

Prices s fr €33; d fr €42; t fr €54; dinner fr €17 **On Site** ⚓ Spa ᵉ
Nearby ⌁40km ℐ1km ⅄ 10km Restaurant 4km ⌁4km 🏠4km
ᴍ 25km **Notes** Pets admitted English spoken

ST-VINCENT

⊞ ℣ La Buissonnière

P MONCHIET et N VAN DURME

Chalignac, 43800 SAINT-VINCENT

☎ 04 71 08 54 41

email: buiss@free.fr

web: www.buissonniere-auvergne.com

This beautiful and charming dwelling is magnificently situated in large grounds in the Loire gorges, surrounded by volcanic cones. There are five bedrooms (each with private bathroom), a music room with piano and library, landscaped garden and parking. Home-grown produce and meals can be provided. Numerous walks nearby.

Prices s €47-€50; d €53-€60; extra person fr €18; dinner fr €18
Nearby ⚓ 20km ⌁30km ℐ0.5km ⅄ 4km Restaurant 1.5km ⌁5km
Spa 4km ᵉ 4km 🏠4km ᴍ 5km **Notes** Pets admitted English spoken

⊞ ℣ Les Pierres Bleues

Annie et Jean-Pierre LORRAIN

Ceneuil, 43800 SAINT-VINCENT

☎ 04 71 08 58 67 & 06 87 79 04 81

email: jp.lorrain@orange.fr

web: www.mes-vacances-en-auvergne.com

In a quiet, pleasant village setting, this renovated former farmhouse has three upstairs guest bedrooms, one of them a split-level family room for four (double bed and two singles), with en suite shower/WC; the other two rooms are a twin with shower/WC and a double with bathroom/WC. Living room on the ground floor with books and games. Enclosed courtyard and part-covered terrace with loungers and hammocks.

Prices s €50-€55; d €55-€60; t fr €70; extra person fr €15; dinner €10-
€18 **Nearby** ⚓7km ⌁25km ℐ2km ⅄ 4km Restaurant 3km ⌁7km
ᵉ 4km 🏠4km ᴍ 4km **Notes** No pets English spoken Open April to
November.

TENCE

☷ ❦ ⒪ **Les Grillons**

Elyane et Gérard DEYGAS
La Pomme, 43190 TENCE
☎ 04 71 59 89 33

This beautifully restored house is situated in large grounds in the countryside, with a terrace, parking area and golf-putting course. There are bedrooms with private bathrooms, a lounge with an open fireplace and a drawing room with TV. The hosts are young farmers and offer guests a warm welcome. Meals are available on request.

Prices s fr €32; d fr €43; t fr €60; dinner fr €16 **Nearby** ⚡ 3km ⛳ 3km
🏹 3km ⚓ 3km 🏛 3km ⛵ 17km **Notes** Pets admitted

☷ ♿ **Salettes**

Dominique BOURGEOIS
1, rue du Pré Long, 43190 TENCE
☎ 04 71 56 35 80
email: thomas.bourgeois@freesbee.fr
web: www.lesprairies.com

This bourgeois house is set in a shady, enclosed one hectare park, and the proprietors offer a warm welcome. There are five personalised spacious guest rooms in a wing: a family room for four and four double rooms, each with private facilities and lovely old furniture. There is a large living room with fireplace and books, and children's games. Parking available. Close to the tourist resort of Chambon Sur Lignon.

Prices s fr €63; d fr €71; extra person fr €20 **On Site** Private ⚓
❦ **Nearby** ⚡ 0.8km ⛳ 0.5km 🏹 0.3km ⛵ 50km **Notes** Pets admitted English spoken Open 16 April to October.

THORAS

☷ ❦ ⒪ **Chazelles**

Bernard PASCAL
43170 THORAS
☎ 04 71 74 42 47 📠 04 71 74 42 47

Right in the heart of a small granite-built village in the Margeride this old, restored farmhouse has lovely views. One room on the ground floor and two on the first floor each with well-fitted, private bathrooms. Meals use local farm produce wherever possible and local delicacies are on sale.

Prices s fr €39; d fr €53; t fr €65; extra person fr €12; dinner fr €14
Nearby ⛳ 1km 🏹 13km Restaurant 4km ⚓ 13km 🏛 4km ⛵ 25km
Notes English spoken No pets Open mid March to mid November.

VERNASSAL

☷ ❦ ⒪ **Domaine de Tarra**

Magali et Robert VAUCANSON
Darsac, 43270 VERNASSAL
☎ 04 71 57 00 92 & 06 77 42 19 36
email: domainedetarra@club-internet.fr
web: www.domaine-de-tarra.com

This restored 18th-century farmhouse is built from volcanic stone, close to the owners' home. All the bedrooms have a private bathroom. Communal lounge with an open fireplace, library, terrace, courtyard, large tree-lined and enclosed garden with furniture and swimming pool, plus parking. Picnics and evening meals provided on request. Nearby: 10-hole mini golf, Puy lentil growing area, volcanic craters, châteaux, footpaths and bike trails.

Prices s fr €45-€55; d fr €50-€60; extra person fr €15; dinner fr €20
On Site ⚡ Private 🏹 **Nearby** ⛳ 1km Restaurant 4km ⚓ 0.3km
❦ 5km 🏛 6km ⛵ 0.5km **Notes** Pets admitted English spoken Open May to September.

VIEILLE-BRIOUDE

☷ ⒪ ♿ **L'Ermitage Saint-Vincent**

Frédérique TOURETTE
place de l'Eglise, 43100 VIEILLE-BRIOUDE
☎ 04 71 50 96 47 & 06 09 15 38 40
web: www.ermitage-saintvincent.fr

This old presbytery has been converted to provide five very attractive guest rooms, each of which sleeps three, either in three single beds or in a double bed plus a single; all have en suite shower room and WC. There is an upstairs conservatory with reclining chairs; outside is a terrace and large garden with fine views. Fishing available, also mushroom gathering in season. Meals by arrangement.

Prices s fr €45; d fr €50; extra person fr €19; dinner fr €20 **On Site** ⛳
Nearby ❦ 5km 🏹 3km Restaurant 0.3km ⚓ 0.5km ❦ 4km 🏛 0.1km
⛵ 4km **Notes** No pets English spoken Open March to November.

☷ ❦ ⒪ **La Coustade**

Anne-Marie et Gérard CHANTEL
Chemin du Stade, 43100 VIEILLE-BRIOUDE
☎ 04 71 50 25 21 📠 04 71 50 20 45
email: anne-marie.chantel@laposte.net

This newly built house in the Haut-Allier/Margeride region, has five bedrooms with bathrooms, one of which is suitable for disabled guests. Sitting room with open fireplace and TV, terrace area, veranda, large garden with play area. The young farm owners offer a warm welcome and are happy to help guests appreciate all this region has to offer.

Prices s fr €35; d fr €45; t fr €55; dinner fr €15 **Nearby** ⚡ 7km
⛳ 0.5km 🏹 3km Restaurant 1km ⚓ 1km ❦ 3km 🏛 3km ⛵ 3km
Notes Pets admitted Open mid April to mid October.

VIEILLE-BRIOUDE CONTINUED

ⅢⅢ ♿ Le Panorama

Verena MEDBOUHI

Coste-Cirgues, 43100 VIEILLE-BRIOUDE

☎ 04 71 50 94 35 & 06 62 14 94 35　📄 04 71 50 92 45

email: chambresdhotes@9online.fr

A spacious modern villa with a panoramic view over the Allier Valley. There are three guest rooms on the ground floor, all with bathrooms and private entrances plus a lounge, kitchen, large covered terrace and garden. Ideal location for walking, bathing and white-water sports as well as exploring the local tourist sites.

Prices s fr €43; d fr €49; extra person €10–€17　**On Site** ⚑
Nearby ⛷ 5km ⚓ 0.5km ⏴ Restaurant 0.3km ⚓ 5km ⚓ 0.4km
⚓ 4km　**Notes** No pets English spoken

YSSINGEAUX

ⅢⅢ ⏵⦶ Le Chambonnet

Régine PHALIPPON

43200 YSSINGEAUX

☎ 04 71 56 06 92 & 06 88 33 92 69

A quiet hamlet is the setting for this old farmhouse. It has four bedrooms: two doubles, a twin and a triple. All have private shower/WC, but the WC for one of the doubles is not en suite, and this room is rated at grade 2. Baby equipment available. Lounge with billiards; leisure room in adjacent barn. Enclosed grounds, garden furniture, barbecue.

Prices d fr €45; t fr €55; extra person fr €15; dinner fr €15　**On Site** ⚓
Nearby ⛷ 6km Restaurant 4km ⚓ 8km ⚓ 2km ⚓ 10km　**Notes** Pets admitted

---

PUY-DE-DÔME

ARLANC

ⅢⅢ ⏵⦶ Ma Cachette

Johan BERNARD

10 rue du Onze Novembre, 63220 ARLANC

☎ 04 73 95 04 88

email: cachette@club-internet.fr

web: www.ma-cachette.com

Four rooms available in the owners' house: a twin room and three doubles, each with private facilities. Dining room, lounge with fireplace, enclosed garden and garage.

Prices s €50–€55; d €55–€60; dinner fr €25　**Nearby** ⛷ 10km ⚓ 3km
⏴ 16km Restaurant 0.3km ⚓ 3km ⚑ 15km ⚓ 0.3km　**Notes** No pets English spoken CC

AURIERES

ⅢⅢ ♥ ⏵⦶ Chambre d'hôtes

Christiane RANDANNE

63210 AURIERES

☎ 04 73 65 67 55　📄 04 73 65 67 55

web: www.ferme-randanne.com

This house offers a room with a double and single bed and terrace and two doubles, each with private shower and wc. Sitting room, lounge and garden. Nearby watersports and fishing, the Romanesque church of Orcival, the Col de Guéry, the lac de Guéry, and the Chaîne de Guéry.

Prices s fr €35; d fr €45; t fr €60; dinner fr €15　**Nearby** ⏴ 20km
⚓ 27km ⚓ 13km ⚓ 26km　**Notes** No pets English spoken

AYDAT

ⅢⅢ Grange de Phialeix

Michèle et Daniel FRANCIONE

Route de Fohet, 63970 AYDAT

☎ 04 73 78 33 10　📄 04 73 78 33 10

email: daniel.francione@orange.fr

web: www.lagrangedephialeix.fr.st

In the heart of the Parc Régional des Volcans d'Auvergne, near to the Puy de Dôme. This property has three rooms, all on the first floor: one twin bedded room, and two for three people. They all have private facilities. On the ground floor is a lounge with an open fire; outside is an unfenced garden with a terrace.

Prices s fr €36; d fr €45; t fr €60　**Nearby** ⛷ 10km ♨ 20km ⚓ 1km
⏴ 25km Restaurant 3km ⚓ 25km ⚓ 3km Spa 15km ⚑ 3km ⚓ 1km
⚓ 25km　**Notes** No pets English spoken Open Easter to 1 November.

ⅢⅢ ⏵⦶ Le Moulassat

Françoise & J-Pierre GOLLIARD

rue Yvon Chauveix, 63970 AYDAT

☎ 04 73 79 30 44

email: jpfgolliard@wanadoo.fr

web: www.moulassat.fr

Four rooms in the owners' house, consisting of two double rooms, a twin and a room with a double and single bed. All rooms have private facilities. A lounge and sitting room with open fire and bread oven, TV and snow lodge are available. Hiking trails and fishing nearby.

Prices s fr €35; d fr €41; t fr €55; dinner fr €15　**Nearby** ⛷ 12km
♨ 20km ⚓ 2km ⏴ 18km Restaurant 0.2km ⚓ 36km ⚓ 0.1km
Spa 12km ⚑ 2km ⚓ 0.1km ⚓ 20km　**Notes** No pets English spoken

₩₩ ⚶ Ponteix

Véronique et Didier VERBRUGGHE
63970 AYDAT
☎ 04 73 79 33 70

Two of the guest rooms at this establishment are located in an annexe separate from the main house. They comprise a double room at ground floor level and a double room on the first floor with a balcony. On the ground floor of the main house there are two double rooms. All the rooms have private facilities. There is a shared lounge and dining room, a courtyard and garden and table football.

Prices s fr €34; d fr €39; dinner fr €15　**Nearby** ⚑ 10km ⚑ 15km
⚑ 3km ⚑ 20km Restaurant 2km ⚑ 38km ⚑ 2km ⚑ 3km ⚑ 2km
⚑ 20km　**Notes** No pets　English spoken

BAGNOLS

₩₩ ⚶ & Domaine de Bos

Kees et Ans VAN DE GOOR
63810 BAGNOLS
☎ 04 73 22 27 83
email: domainedebos@wanadoo.fr
web: http://monsite.orange.fr/domainedebos

This property has four double rooms and one room sleeping six (three double beds). All rooms have private shower and WC. A sitting room with a stove is shared with the owners. Unfenced garden. Full board available. Horse riding, mountain biking and hiking (guided night hikes in the summer) are all possible nearby.

Prices s fr €33; d fr €45; t fr €62; dinner fr €17　**Nearby** ⚑ 5km
⚑ 30km ⚑ 7km ⚑ 1km Restaurant 1km ⚑ 15km ⚑ 7km Spa 25km
⚑ 10km ⚑ 1km ⚑ 25km　**Notes** Pets admitted　English spoken

BEAUREGARD-VENDON

₩₩ Chaptes

Elisabeth BEAUJEARD
63460 BEAUREGARD-VENDON
☎ 04 73 63 35 62

On the first floor of a characterful 18th-century house, accommodation here comprises three double rooms, each with private facilities. The house is furnished with antique pieces. There is a dining room with a fireplace, a covered terrace with table tennis and a landscaped garden.

Prices s €65-€70; d €70-€75; extra person fr €25　**Nearby** ⚑ 6km
⚑ 25km ⚑ 10km ⚑ 7km Restaurant 6km ⚑ 6km ⚑ 2km ⚑ 9km
Notes No pets　English spoken

La Randonnée

John, Estelle and their two little ones welcome you in their comfortable attic rooms, where everything is there to assure you of a most relaxing stay. Enjoy a good breakfast before discovering this beautiful area and come back to the smells of a home cooked meal served in our bright dining room overlooking the medieval village of Besse.

Rue de la Croix de la Combe
63610 Besse et St Anastaise
Tel: 04 73 79 56 30　Fax: 04 73 78 51 10
Mob: 06 29 49 43 27
www.mes-vacances-a-besse.com

BESSE-ET-SAINT-ANASTAISE

₩₩ ⚶ La Randonnée

John et Estelle SYKES
Rue de la Croix de Combe,
63610 BESSE ET SAINT-ANASTAISE
☎ 04 73 79 56 30 & 06 20 93 81 83　⚑ 04 73 78 51 10
email: jesykes@orange.fr
web: www.mes-vacances-a-besse.com

There are five first floor double bedrooms in this big house, which has an independent guests' entrance. Each room has a private shower room and WC, and there is a lounge which is shared with the hosts. There are two gîtes on the same site. Outside there is a terrace; the grounds are not enclosed.

Prices s €41-€51; d €48-€58; extra person fr €15; dinner fr €16
On Site ⚑ ⚑　**Nearby** ⚑ 6km Restaurant 0.5km ⚑ 7km ⚑ 1km
⚑ 6km ⚑ 0.5km ⚑ 30km　**Notes** No pets　English spoken　CC

see advert on this page

BOURG-LASTIC

⫿⫿ Artiges

Chantal et Denis DUGAT-BONY
63760 BOURG-LASTIC
☎ 04 73 21 87 39
email: chantaldugatbony@orange.fr
web: www.artiges-chambresdhotes.com

Accommodation is in an old restored family house comprising two rooms with a double and single bed and a double room, each with private bathroom and wc. Guests can use the lounge and kitchenette, courtyard, garden, barbecue, boules pitch and table tennis table. Restaurants 2km and fishing at Chavanon (5km).

Prices s fr €35; d fr €44; t fr €56; extra person fr €12 **On Site** ⛵ **Nearby** ⬇30km ⛳5km ⭢26km Restaurant 2km ⛵33km ⊖2km ⒶΖ2km 🚴20km **Notes** No pets English spoken Open 10 January to 20 December.

BROMONT-LAMOTHE

⫿⫿ ❦ ◉ Le Pre du Roc

Christine et Vincent GUILLOT
Haute Roche, 63230 BROMONT-LAMOTHE
☎ 04 73 88 7122 & 06 76 61 22 65 📠 04 73 88 74 22
email: contact@lepreduroc.com
web: www.lepreduroc.com

A spacious old farm building which has been converted to provide ground-floor living room and WC as well as bedrooms upstairs: on the first floor, two triples each with double bed and a single; on the second floor is a family suite (double room plus twin room), and another triple with double bed and single; all have en suite shower room and WC. Outside there is a terrace for guests' use, also parking space. Meals available by arrangement. Closed Christmas.

Prices s fr €40; d fr €48; t fr €65; dinner fr €17 **Nearby** ⬇25km ⬇25km ⛳2km ⭢20km Restaurant 3km ⊖3km Spa 30km Ⓐ3km 🚴3km **Notes** No pets

CEILLOUX

⫿⫿⫿ Domaine de Gaudon

Alain & Monique BOZZO
le Château, 63520 CEILLOUX
☎ 04 73 70 76 25
email: domainedegaudon@wanadoo.fr
web: www.domainedegaudon.fr

A parkland setting, with trees and a lake, adds to the attractions of this 19th-century house. It has five bedrooms - three doubles and a twin on the first floor, and a room with a double and a single bed on the second floor. All of the rooms have a phone, private bath or shower room and WC. Lounge and dining room with open fires. Pets admitted by arrangement.

Prices s fr €80; d fr €98; t fr €110; extra person fr €20 **On Site** ⛳ **Nearby** ⬇0.5km ⬇40km ⭢10km Restaurant 2km ⊖1km ⭐3km Ⓐ5km 🚴40km **Notes** Pets admitted

CHAMBON-SUR-LAC

⫿⫿ Le Pavillon Bleu

C et S GONNET-LE CONTELLEC
63790 CHAMBON SUR LAC
☎ 04 73 88 89 52
email: pavillonbleuchrisyl@orange.fr
web: http://perso.orange.fr/pavillonbleuchrisyl

This lakeside house has three first-floor bedrooms: two doubles (one with a balcony), and a grade 2 triple (double bed plus a single), also with a balcony. All have private facilities, but those for the grade 2 room are not en suite. Garden with parking, and garaging for motor bikes and cycles.

Prices d fr €60; extra person fr €15 **On Site** ⛳ **Nearby** ⛵2km ⭢9km Restaurant 0.2km ⛵21km ⊖2km ⭐0.8km Ⓐ0.5km 🚴32km **Notes** No pets English spoken

CHARBONNIERES-LES-VARENNES

⫿⫿ ◉ La Vedrine

Fabienne et Alexis GARCIN
63410 CHARBONNIERES-LES-VARENNES
☎ 04 73 33 82 85

Four guest rooms in the owners' house: two rooms with a double and single bed and two double rooms, all with private shower and wc. Guests may use a sitting room, terrace, and adjacent garden. Reduced weekly rates available (except in July, August and school holidays). Table d'hôte meals provided at weekends during school holidays.

Prices not confirmed for 2008 **Nearby** ⛳16.5km ⭢13.5km Ⓐ3km 🚴8.5km **Notes** No pets English spoken Open March to 15 November.

CISTERNES-LA-FORET

⫿⫿ ◉ La Picote

Maryse et Alain BRUNET
Les Imbauds, 63740 CISTERNES-LA-FORET
☎ 04 73 87 89 34 & 06 83 53 15 83 📠 04 73 87 83 92
web: http://lapicote.free.fr

There are five bedrooms at this property, in an annexe to the owners' home: three doubles, a triple (double bed plus a single) and a two-roomed family suite for four with a double bed and two singles. Each has a private bath/shower room and WC. Outside there is a terrace and parking space. Meals available by arrangement, fishing close by.

Prices s fr €40; d fr €50; extra person fr €10; dinner fr €17 **Nearby** ⛵12km ⬇25km ⛳1km ⭢15km Restaurant 6km ⊖11km ⭐15km Ⓐ10km 🚴15km **Notes** No pets English spoken CC

AUVERGNE

CLEMENSAT

★ ❦ ⏣ Chambre d'hôtes

André et Chantal TRUCHOT

63320 CLEMENSAT

☎ 04 73 71 10 82 ▤ 04 73 71 10 82

email: lavoute@wanadoo.fr

Accommodation is offered on a working farm, comprising two double rooms, a room with a double and single bed and one with a double and two singles. All have private facilities. Dining room with fireplace, covered terrace, courtyard, garden and parking. Meals can be provided by reservation. Bathing, sailing, windsurfing, canoes, kayaks, and fishing available at Lac de Chambon (21km).

Prices s fr €36; d fr €45; t fr €62; dinner fr €17   **On Site** ⛷
Nearby ⌁40km ⌇2km ⚲2km Restaurant 5km ⚄29km ⚊2km
⚇12km ⛪5km ⋈12km   **Notes** No pets English spoken

COMBRONDE

★ Chambre d'hôtes

Lise et André CHEVALIER

105, rue Etienne Clémentel, 63460 COMBRONDE

☎ 04 73 97 16 20 ▤ 04 73 97 16 20

Two doubles, a room with a double and single bed, and a twin room, all with private facilities, offered in the owners' house. Dining room, lounge with open fire, courtyard, terrace, barbecue, garden and parking. Restaurants in Combronde.

Prices s fr €42; d fr €49; t fr €64; extra person fr €15   **On Site** ⚲
Nearby ⛷3km ⌁9km ⌇2km ⚲7km Restaurant 2km ⛪0.2km
⋈9km   **Notes** No pets Open mid February to mid November.

DAVAYAT

★★★ *Chambre d'hôtes*

Nicole et Stephan HONNORAT

25 rue de l'Eglise, 63200 DAVAYAT

☎ 04 73 63 58 20 & 06 63 90 73 67

email: honnorat.la.treille@wanadoo.fr

web: http://honnorat.la.treille.free.fr

A 19th-century outbuilding of the proprietor's bourgeois house offering three double rooms (one with cot) and a family room with four single beds, all with private facilities. There is a dining room with fireplace and lounge, landscaped park with trees, and restaurants in nearby Châtel-Guyon.

Prices not confirmed for 2008   **Nearby** ⚲7km ⛪6km ⋈7km
Notes No pets English spoken

DORE-L'EGLISE

★ ⏣ Domaine de Sault

Sylvie ROUSSEL

Le Sault, 63220 DORE-L'EGLISE

☎ 04 73 95 08 21 & 06 83 33 59 14

email: lesault@wanadoo.fr

web: www.domaine-de-sault.skyblog.com

This property, on the edge of the Auvergne and close to Velay, has something of a time-warp feel about it. It is a 19th-century farmhouse, in a forest clearing with fine views. There are two double rooms and a twin-bedded room, each with en suite shower room and WC. Living room and kitchen for guests' use.

Prices s fr €50; d fr €55; dinner fr €15   **Nearby** ⛷10km ⌁0.5km
⚲3km Restaurant 1km ⚄30km ⚇10km ⛪3km ⋈36km   **Notes** Pets
admitted English spoken

★ ⏣ Domaine la Reveille

Anne et Jef NELISSEN

La Reveille, 63220 DORE-L'EGLISE

☎ 04 73 95 09 94

email: jef.nelissen@wanadoo.fr

web: www.la-reveille.com

Right in the heart of the Parc Régional Naturel du Livradois Forez, this property dates from the 14th century, adapted and tastefully modernised over the years. There are three grade 3 rooms (two doubles and a triple), and two grade 2 doubles, each with shower room and WC. Enclosed garden and grounds with swimming pool, pond and parking; meals by arrangement.

Prices d €55-€60; dinner €18.50-€20   **On Site** ⚇ Private ⚲
Nearby ⛷9km ⚲3km Restaurant 0.1km ⚊3km ⛪3km ⋈30km
Notes No pets English spoken

FLAT

★ ⏣ Coquelitcots

Nathalie et Frédéric BIDON

Le Bourg, 63500 FLAT

☎ 04 73 71 50 49 ▤ 04 73 71 50 49

email: reservation@coqueLITcots.com

web: www.coqueLITcots.com

Three first floor bedrooms in the hosts' house. One single and two twin rooms, each with shower room and WC. Shared dining room, lounge and veranda. Private parking with carport, secure internal courtyard, unfenced grounds. Discount depending on length of stay. Evening meals by arrangement; child meal discount. Pétanque, table-tennis, walking routes.

Prices s fr €45; d fr €58; t fr €78; dinner fr €19   **Nearby** ⛷8km ⌁5km
⚲5km Restaurant 4km ⚄40km ⚊5km Spa 30km ⚇5km ⛪5km
⋈5km   **Notes** Pets admitted

GIAT

⛊ ‖○‖ ⌖ *Chambre d'hôtes*

Gérard et Catherine DALE
rue de la Clinique, 63620 GIAT
☎ 04 73 21 60 02 🗒 04 73 21 60 02
email: catherine.gdale@wanadoo.fr
web: http://monsite.wanadoo.fr/lvpgdale

A 19th-century house offering two double rooms (one with disabled access), a twin and a room with a double and single, each with private bathroom. Communal facilities include a dining room-lounge with library and fireplace, parking, garage, enclosed garden with terrace. Table d'hôte meals available by reservation using home-grown vegetables. Reductions of 10% from the third night except in school holidays, and for children.

Prices not confirmed for 2008   **Nearby** ⌖ 5km ⌖ 45km
Notes No pets English spoken CC

⛊ ❦ *Rozery*

Joëlle BRIQUET-DESBAUX
63620 GIAT
☎ 04 73 21 60 08 🗒 04 73 21 60 08
email: briquet-desbaux.joelle@wanadoo.fr

Three bedrooms in the owners' house on a working farm: two double rooms and a room with a double and single bed with private facilities. Dining room, lounge, courtyard, and adjoining garden. Restaurants nearby.

Prices not confirmed for 2008   **Nearby** ⌖ 5km ⌖ 30km   **Notes** Pets admitted English spoken

JOZE

⛊ La Serita

Isabelle & Jacques FLORENCON
1, route de Vichy, 63350 JOZE
☎ 04 73 70 28 63 & 06 63 80 82 61
email: florencon@wanadoo.fr
web: www.laserita.net

A converted 19th-century stable block in extensive grounds with lots of trees and flowers. There are three double rooms with private shower and WC, all on the first floor. A kitchenette is available for guest use. Enclosed grounds with swimming pool, tennis and parking space.

Prices d fr €110   **On Site** ⌖ Private ⌖   **Nearby** ⌖ 4km ⌖ 7km
⌖ 5km Restaurant 1km ⌖ 0.5km ⌖ 18.5km   **Notes** No pets English spoken

LA BOURBOULE

⛊ ‖○‖ La Lauzeraie

Martine et J.Claude GOIGOUX
577 Les Suchères, 63150 LA BOURBOULE
☎ 04 73 81 15 70 & 06 78 14 37 74
email: goigoux.martine@wanadoo.fr
web: www.lalauzeraie.net

In a peaceful spot, overlooking the spa town of La Bourboule, this property has three guest bedrooms, two doubles and a twin, all on the first floor and each with en suite bath or shower room and WC. There are two lounges with open fires, a home cinema, terraces and a swimming pool. Enclosed wooded grounds; meals by arrangement; internet access.

Prices s €75-€100; d €105-€125; dinner fr €25   **On Site** ⌖ Private ⌖
Nearby ⌖ 0.1km ⌖ 7km Restaurant 0.5km ⌖ 11km ⌖ 0.5km Spa 0.5km
⌖ 7km   **Notes** No pets Open mid March to mid October

LE MONT-DORE

⛊ La Closerie de Manou

Françoise LARCHER
Le Genestou BP 30, 63240 LE MONT-DORE
☎ 04 73 65 26 81 & 06 08 54 50 16
email: lacloseriedemanou@club-internet.fr
web: www.lacloseriedemanou.com

An 18th-century house providing two grade 3 double rooms, a grade 4 room with a double and single bed and two grade 3 attic rooms, one triple and the other double. All have private shower and wc. Marked paths for walkers, river and inn nearby.

Prices s €55-€65; d €80-€85; t fr €105; extra person fr €20   **On Site** ⌖
Nearby ⌖ 3km ⌖ 2km ⌖ 3km Restaurant 20km ⌖ 4.5km ⌖ 3km
Spa 3km ⌖ 3km ⌖ 2km   **Notes** No pets English spoken Open mid April to mid October.

⛊ ‖○‖ Le Mirabeau

Marie et Christian LEGOUT
13 rue Sidoine Apollinaire, 63240 LE MONT-DORE
☎ 04 73 65 25 82
email: lemirabeau@wanadoo.fr
web: www.lemirabeau.fr

This house has three rooms for three and two rooms for two, all en suite in the owners' house. Guests have use of a sitting room, library and courtyard and table d'hôte meals can be reserved. Mont Dore, a ski resort and spa, is in the Parc des Volcans, which is great walking country.

Prices s €56-€67; d €60-€75; t €87-€95; dinner fr €20   **Nearby** ⌖ 1km
⌖ 3km ⌖ 15km ⌖ 5km Restaurant 0.1km ⌖ 5km ⌖ 0.5km ⌖ 0.1km
⌖ 0.5km   **Notes** No pets English spoken

LES MARTRES-DE-VEYRE

⍦ La Tour Richelieu

Gerd et Jean STARACE

15 rue St-Martial, 63730 LES MARTRES-DE-VEYRE

☎ 04 73 39 29 49 ⧗ 04 73 39 91 97

email: gerd.starace@club-internet.fr

web: www.tour-richelieu.com

Rooms available in a wing of the proprietors' house including a double, a room with a double and single bed and a room with a mezzanine floor, double and two single beds. All have private facilities. Dining room with open fire, lounge with library, courtyard and balcony. Special rates for four people. Canoeing, walking and fishing nearby.

Prices s fr €40; d fr €48; t fr €61; extra person fr €19 **Nearby** ⌀ 0.5km ↖ 5km Restaurant 0.2km ☙ 35km ⛺ 0.5km **Notes** No pets English spoken

LOUBEYRAT

⍦ ⛷ Beaulieu

Nicole et Guy GARDARIN

63410 LOUBEYRAT

☎ 04 73 86 66 60 ⧗ 04 73 86 66 60

Three rooms available in the attic of the proprietors' home: a twin, a double and a double with child's bed, each with private facilities. Dining room with fireplace, kitchen corner, lounge, open garden. Breakfasts with organic produce and table d'hôte meals by reservation. Tariff reductions after three nights except in July and August. Nearby: Château de Chazeron, Châtel-Guyon with thermal spa, Volvic, Gour de Tazenat and the Sioule caves.

Prices s fr €39; d €46-€52; extra person fr €21 **Nearby** ⌀ 3km ♨ 12km ⌀ 15km ↖ 5km Restaurant 2km ⛺ 5km ♧ 5km ⛺ 5km ⛄ 12km **Notes** No pets Open 15 April to 15 November.

MANZAT

⍦ Chambre d'hôtes

Martine BERNA

Voie Romaine, Les Oulanières, 63410 MANZAT

☎ 06 75 87 17 35 & 04 73 86 96 55 ⧗ 04 73 86 99 76

email: berna.hotes@wanadoo.fr

web: http://oulanieres.monsite.wanadoo.fr

This beautiful house, in a wooded parkland setting, has three guest rooms on the second floor. There is one twin room, one double, and one family room for four. All rooms have private bath or shower room and WC. Ground floor: veranda and terrace.

Prices s €35-€40; d €44-€48; extra person fr €15 **Nearby** ⛺ 12km ♨ 18km ⌀ 4km ↖ 11km Restaurant 0.5km ⛺ 1km ♧ 14km ⛺ 0.5km ⛄ 18km **Notes** No pets English spoken

⍦ Les Cheix

M-Thérèse & Manuel PEREIRA

63410 MANZAT

☎ 04 73 86 57 74 ⧗ 04 73 86 57 74

web: http://maisondefour.free.fr

Three bedrooms in a building opposite the owners' house: a double and two rooms with a double and single bed, all with private facilities. There is a sitting room with open fire, a terrace and garden. Restaurant 1km. The Fades Besserbe offers bathing, sailing, sailboarding, motor boating, canoeing and fishing.

Prices not confirmed for 2008 **Nearby** ⌀ 5km ↖ 10km ⛺ 50km ⛺ 1km ⛄ 20km **Notes** No pets

MAREUGHEOL

⍦ ⍉ Les Etoiles

Catherine MILLOT

Longchamps, 63340 MAREUGHEOL

☎ 04 73 71 40 04 ⧗ 04 73 71 40 04

email: millot.catherine@wanadoo.fr

web: http://catherinelesetoiles.monsite.orange.fr

This house offers a double room, a twin, a room with three singles and one with four singles with private facilities. Dining room with open fire, lounge with TV and fireplace, terrace, courtyard and garden. Meals can be booked in advance. Children under 2 free. Fort de Mareugheol and the Château de Villeneuve-Lembron nearby.

Prices s fr €52; d fr €74; extra person fr €17; dinner €19 **Nearby** ⛺ 15km ⌀ 10km ↖ 9km Restaurant 3km ⛺ 30km ⛺ 10km ⛺ 10km ⛄ 10km **Notes** No pets English spoken

MIREFLEURS

⍦ ⛦ Domaine de Pomeix

Jeannine et Jean DURIF

8, rue de Pomeix, 63730 MIREFLEURS

☎ 04 73 39 90 79 & 06 81 38 63 13 ⧗ 04 73 39 90 79

email: jeannine.durif@wanadoo.fr

web: www.pomeix-mirefleurs.com

This property has four guest bedrooms in a building facing the owners' home. There are two double rooms on the ground floor; upstairs is another double room and a family suite for four. Each has a private bath or shower room and WC. Lounge with open fire; outdoors are enclosed grounds and a terrace with covered parking.

Prices s fr €47; d fr €55; t fr €70; extra person fr €15 **On Site** ⛺ ⌀ Restaurant **Nearby** ↖ 5km ⛺ 3km ⛄ 3km **Notes** Pets admitted English spoken Open March to October.

AUVERGNE

MONTCEL

▦ ⏻ ⚹ Le Peyroux

Marie-Elise SOLITO
63460 MONTCEL
☎ 04 73 97 36 24 ▤ 04 73 97 36 24
email: lepeyrouxauvergne@free.fr
web: http://lepeyrouxauvergne.ifrance.com

Standing in enclosed grounds, this property has three guest rooms: a twin-bedded room on the ground floor, and a double and a triple upstairs. All have private bath or shower room and WC, with cot available. Fitness room on site, and terrace for guest use.

Prices s €39-€40; d €46-€49; t fr €62; dinner fr €20 **On Site** ⚘
Nearby ⛷ 3km ♨ 40km ♬ 2km ⇥ 14km Restaurant 5km ⚓ 10km
▣ 3km ᴟ 14km **Notes** No pets English spoken Open Easter to 1 November.

▦ Les Chanteaux

Annie DELISLE
63460 MONTCEL
☎ 04 73 33 03 09 & 06 10 89 18 63
email: annie.delisle@wanadoo.fr
web: www.leschanteaux.com

A property with three first-floor bedrooms, doubles and twins, one with a child's bed and all with bath or shower room and WC. There is a conservatory, and outside are the enclosed grounds with terrace and swimming pool. Accommodation by reservation only in winter.

Prices s fr €50; d fr €60; extra person fr €15 **On Site** Private ⚓ ⚘
Private ⇥ **Nearby** ⛷ 10km ♨ 15km ♬ 1.5km Restaurant 2.5km
Spa 15km ▣ 3.5km ᴟ 15km **Notes** No pets

MONTPEYROUX

▦ Chambre d'hôtes

Edith et Claude GRENOT
Les Pradets, 63114 MONTPEYROUX
☎ 04 73 96 63 40 ▤ 04 73 96 63 40
email: claude.grenot@wanadoo.fr

Rooms here include a grade 4 twin room, a grade 4 room with a double and single bed and grade 3 room with mezzanine, double and single bed and terrace, in a detached pavilion. All have private facilities. Dining room, lounge with fireplace and piano, and enclosed shady garden.

Prices s fr €68; d fr €72; extra person fr €20 **Nearby** ⛷ 6km
♨ 30km ♬ 3km ⇥ 6km Restaurant 0.3km ⚓ 39km ⚓ 0.3km
Spa 18km ▣ 2km ᴟ 3km **Notes** Pets admitted

▦ ✿ ⏻ Chambre d'hôtes

Dominique DELHERME
Rue des Granges, La Vigneronne, 63114 MONTPEYROUX
☎ 04 73 96 66 71 ▤ 04 73 96 66 71
web: http://perso.wanadoo.fr/delherme.lavigneronne/

Four rooms available in the home of the proprietors, situated in one of the most beautiful villages in France. There are two double rooms, a triple and a room with a double and single bed, all with private facilities. Dining room, lounge, terrace and enclosed garden with parking. Nearby Issoire is a centre of Roman art (14km).

Prices not confirmed for 2008 **Nearby** ⇥ 8km ▣ 2km ᴟ 2km
Notes Pets admitted Open February to November.

▦ Le Cantou

Hermann & Jacqueline VOLK
Place de la Croix du Bras, 63114 MONTPEYROUX
☎ 04 73 96 92 26 ▤ 04 73 96 92 26

The guest rooms here are all on the first floor of the owners' house. There is a double-bedded room, and two rooms with linked twin beds, one of which has an extra single bed. All rooms have a private shower and WC. Lounge with books; guests also have use of a former stable with vaulted roof as a lounge area. Tennis court.

Prices s €39-€49; d €46-€58; t fr €69 **Nearby** ⛷ 5km ♨ 20km
♬ 3km ⇥ 10km Restaurant 0.4km ⚓ 39km ⚓ 10km ▣ 3km ᴟ 3km
Notes Pets admitted English spoken

▦ Les Chambres Boissiere

Joëlle BOISSIERE
Rue de la Poterne, 63114 MONTPEYROUX
☎ 04 73 96 69 42 & 06 08 51 81 82 ▤ 04 73 96 95 39
email: jules.boissiere@wanadoo.fr
web: www.chambres-boissiere.com

This property offers five guest bedrooms in an annexe to the owners' home. Four of the rooms are doubles; the fifth has twin beds. All have private bath or shower room and WC. Four of the rooms have a private terrace; the room which does not have a terrace has a jacuzzi. On-site restaurant, mountain bikes for hire.

Prices s €51-€55; d €56-€60 **Nearby** 🏊 1km 🎣 10km
Restaurant 0.2km 🚲 39km ⛷ 0.5km 🐎 3km 🚶 18km **Notes** Pets admitted English spoken

---

MUROL

🏠 La Forge de Gabriel

Monique PETIT-GOYON

Chemin de la Pardaniche, 63790 MUROL

☎ 04 73 88 60 73 & 06 08 99 14 52 📄 04 73 88 60 73

email: info@laforgedegabriel.com

web: www.laforgedegabriel.com

Dating back to the early 19th century, this house has a double room on the ground floor, and two more doubles upstairs, each with a television and private bath or shower room; a cot is available. Outside are enclosed grounds with a terrace and views of the Château de Murol.

Prices d €75-€110 **Nearby** 🏊 1km ⛷ 40km 🎣 1km 🎣 4km
Restaurant 0.2km 🚲 18km ⛷ 5km 🐎 1km 🐎 0.5km 🚶 40km
Notes No pets English spoken Open April to September.

NEBOUZAT

🏠 🍴 ♿ Les Granges

Jocelyne GAUTHIER

Recoleine, 63210 NEBOUZAT

☎ 04 73 87 10 34 & 06 89 93 99 54 📄 04 73 87 10 34

email: gauthier.jocelyne@free.fr

web: http://lesgranges2.free.fr

Guest rooms here include a family suite in a building adjoining the owners' house, with two rooms with a double and two single beds, a triple room and a room with double and single bed. All have private facilities and there is a sitting room, terrace and garden. Table d'hôte meals available by reservation and there is an inn at Recoleine.

Prices s fr €34; d €44-€48; t €59-€63; extra person fr €15; dinner fr €16
Nearby 🏊 10km ⛷ 15km 🎣 10km 🎣 18km Restaurant 0.2km 🚲 30km
⛷ 20km 🐎 10km 🐎 2km 🚶 22km **Notes** No pets English spoken
Open April to 15 November.

OLBY

🏠 ♥ L'Abri du Berger

Paul BONY

Bravant, 63210 OLBY

☎ 04 73 87 12 28 📄 04 73 87 19 00

Five rooms are available in a former farm building close to the owners' house. There are four rooms with a double and single bed (two with mezzanine) and a triple, all with private facilities. A kitchen is available for guests and there is a sitting room with fireplace, a courtyard, an open garden and parking. Reduced rates are available outside July and August and children under two years are free.

Prices s fr €35; d fr €40; t fr €54 **Nearby** 🏊 5km ⛷ 7km 🎣 2km
🎣 18km Restaurant 2km 🚲 31km ⛷ 3km Spa 20km 🐎 5km 🐎 2km
🚶 20km **Notes** No pets Open 16 February to 14 November.

OLLIERGUES

🏠 🍴 Chambre d'hôtes

Annie-Paule CHALET

19 rue Jean de Lattre de, Tassigny, 63880 OLLIERGUES

☎ 04 73 95 52 10 📄 04 73 95 52 10

email: chaletannie@aol.com

Three family suites in the proprietor's house, each with two rooms with one double and one single bed, private bathroom and wc and a library. There is a sitting room with a library, a terrace, garden and garages.

Prices s fr €37; d fr €48; t fr €65; extra person fr €17; dinner fr €15
On Site 🎣 **Nearby** 🏊 20km 🎣 10km Restaurant 0.1km 🚲 30km
⛷ 4km 🐎 0.1km 🚶 26km **Notes** Pets admitted English spoken

ORCINES

🏠 Domaine de Ternant

Catherine PIOLLET

63870 ORCINES

☎ 04 73 62 11 20 📄 04 73 62 29 96

email: domaine.ternant@free.fr

web: http://domaine.ternant.free.fr

Set in the Auvergne Volcanic Regional Park, near the Puy-de-Dôme site, this 19th-century family home has a family suite of a double and a twin; a family suite of two rooms with four single beds, two double rooms, and one twin. All rooms have private bathrooms. Guests share a lounge, billiard room and dining room with the owner and there is a ten hectare wooded park and tennis court. Golf, paragliding and restaurant nearby. 10% reduction after the third night or for the rental of all the rooms.

Prices s €70-€82; d €78-€90; t fr €115; extra person fr €23
On Site Private 🐎 **Nearby** 🏊 6km ⛷ 6km 🎣 15km 🎣 10km
Restaurant 3km 🚲 45km Spa 10km 🐎 8km 🐎 3km 🚶 15km
Notes No pets English spoken Open mid March to mid November.

PESCHADOIRES

₩₩ ¡O¡ Chambre d'hôtes

Gilles BOLLET

Chemin des Torrents, 63920 PESCHADOIRES

☎ 04 73 51 37 78 📃 04 73 51 61 79

email: info@les-torrents.com

web: www.les-torrents.com

This chambre d'hôtes offers three guest rooms, all in the owners' house. On the ground floor is a room with three single beds; upstairs there is a double room, and a room with a double bed and a single. They all have a private bath or shower room and WC. Lounge with wood-burning stove, kitchenette, terrace.

Prices s fr €40; d €47-€49; t €62-€65; extra person fr €15; dinner fr €16 **On Site** ⚓ ⛲ Private ⚓ **Nearby** ⚓ 35km 🏌 0.6km ⚓ 35km ⚓ 5km 🏛 0.7km 🚶 1km **Notes** Pets admitted English spoken

PRONDINES

₩₩ *Vedeux*

Danielle et André MONNERON

Au Belhetre, 63470 PRONDINES

☎ 04 73 87 84 55 📃 04 73 87 84 55

This house on a dairy farm offers a double room, a room with three single beds, and a room with a double and a single bed. All have private facilities. Day room with kitchen area, terrace, open garden, barbecue and enclosed parking. Reductions offered out of season and for longer stays. Restaurants 1km.

Prices not confirmed for 2008 **Nearby** 🏌 5km ⚓ 30km ⚓ 42km 🏛 8km 🚶 45km **Notes** No pets English spoken

RENTIERES

₩₩ 🌱 ¡O¡ Le Chausse-Haut

Marie-Jo et Philippe BOYER

63420 RENTIERES

☎ 04 73 71 84 28 📃 04 73 71 84 28

email: pmj.boyer@wanadoo.fr

web: http://monsite.wanadoo.fr/mariejo.lesaubepines/

This property has one room for three people on the ground floor; one double room on the first floor, together with another room (grade 3) for three people. All rooms have a private bath or shower room and WC. Table tennis, and lounge/dining room with two open fires. Reservations required mid November to mid March.

Prices s fr €33; d fr €43; t fr €58; extra person fr €15; dinner fr €15 **Nearby** ⚓ 8km 🏌 0.5km ⚓ 15km Restaurant 2km ⚓ 35km ⚓ 2km ⛲ 25km 🏛 2km 🚶 20km **Notes** Pets admitted English spoken

ROCHEFORT-MONTAGNE

₩₩ La Nichée

François MONTEL

Bomparent, Route d'Ourceyre,

63210 ROCHEFORT-MONTAGNE

☎ 04 73 65 88 53 & 06 24 23 02 43 📃 04 73 65 88 53

email: info@lanichee.com

web: www.lanichee.com

Three guest bedrooms on the second floor of this house. Two have twin beds with shower room and WC. One family suite made up of two rooms, one double and one single, bathroom and WC. Shared dining room with bread oven, lounge. Baby equipment available. Cycle hire, pets by arrangement.

Prices s €42-€50; d €50-€57; t fr €71; extra person fr €12 **Nearby** ⚓ 3km 🏌 1km ⚓ 35km Restaurant 2km ⚓ 19km ⚓ 1km Spa 15km ⛲ 15km 🏛 1.5km 🚶 13km **Notes** Pets admitted English spoken Open 10 February to 5 November.

ROYAT

₩₩₩ Château de Charade

Marc et M-Christine GABA

Charade, 63130 ROYAT

☎ 04 73 35 91 67 📃 04 73 29 92 09

email: gaba@chateau-de-charade.com

web: www.chateau-de-charade.com

A château offering two double rooms, a suite consisting of two rooms (each with three single beds) and another suite of two rooms (one with a double and single bed, the other with a double). All rooms have private facilities. Dining room, billiard room and library, large garden, boules and parking. 5% reduction for stays of more than two nights.

Prices s €72-€80; d €78-€86; t fr €110; extra person fr €25 **On Site** ⚓ ⚓ Restaurant **Nearby** ⚓ 5km ⚓ 40km ⛲ 3km 🏛 4km 🚶 6km **Notes** No pets English spoken Open end March to October.

SAURIER

₩₩ 🌱 ¡O¡ Rozier

Joël RODDE

63320 SAURIER

☎ 04 73 71 22 00 📃 04 73 71 24 06

email: joel.rodde@wanadoo.fr

web: www.lesrosiers.fr

A farmhouse with rooms housed in the attic: two double rooms, two twins, a room with a double and single bed and a room with a double and two single beds, all with private facilities and two connecting. Sitting room with fireplace and TV, terrace, courtyard, garden and parking. Walking, mountain biking, cross-country skiing with instruction.

Prices s fr €38; d fr €46; extra person fr €18; dinner fr €15 **On Site** ⛲ **Nearby** ⚓ 12km 🏌 2km ⚓ 12km ⚓ 22km ⚓ 10km 🏛 2km 🚶 20km **Notes** No pets English spoken

SAUXILLANGES

♯♯♯ La Haute Limandie

Patricia et J-Claude ANGLARET
63490 SAUXILLANGES
☎ 04 73 96 84 95

Three rooms in the owners' house: a double with cot, a twin and a room with a double and single bed; all with private shower and wc. Guests have use of a day room with TV, a courtyard and open garden.

Prices s €28-€31; d €38-€40; t fr €52　**Nearby** ⚘ 3km　Restaurant 3km ⛷ 3km ♨ 15km　**Notes** No pets　Open mid March to mid October.

SINGLES

♯♯♯ ⍟ L'Estive

Christophe,Coralie DEBORD
Plagnes, 63690 SINGLES
☎ 04 73 21 12 22 & 06 61 43 60 68
email: christophedebord@aol.com
web: www.chambresdhotes-estive.com

This house has three guest bedrooms: on the ground floor a double with en suite shower room, and a triple (double bed plus a single) with en suite bathroom; and upstairs a family room with double bed and two singles, with shower room. Baby equipment available. Open grounds, with terrace and parking space. Good base for walks in the Monts de Sancy.

Prices s fr €37; d fr €50; t fr €65; extra person fr €15; dinner fr €15 **Nearby** ⚘ 3km ⚘ 18km　Restaurant 6km ⚓ 23km　Spa 17km ⛷ 9km ♨ 18km　**Notes** Pets admitted　English spoken

ST-BONNET-PRES-ORCIVAL

♯♯♯ ⍟ *Vareilles*

Michelle et Thierry GAIDIER
63210 ST-BONNET-PRES-ORCIVAL
☎ 04 73 65 87 91
email: thierry.gaidier@cegetel.net
web: www.vareilles-nature.com

Three bedrooms in a building adjacent to the proprietors' house: two en suite doubles and a family room with a double and two single beds, bathroom and wc. Dining room with fireplace, microwave and refrigerator, lounge, terrace, garden and parking. Table d'hôte meals. Reduced rates for more than three nights and out of season. Donkey available to carry children or baggage on walking trips.

Prices not confirmed for 2008　**Nearby** ⚘ 3km ⚘ 25km ⚓ 27km ⛷ 3km ♨ 25km　**Notes** Pets admitted　English spoken

ST-DIER-D'AUVERGNE

♯♯♯ Les Martinanches

Arnaud DE CADIER DE VEAUCE
Château des Martinanches, 63520 ST-DIER D'AUVERGNE
☎ 04 73 70 81 98
email: info@chateau-des-martinanches.com
web: www.chateau-des-martinanches.com

This château, the earliest parts of which date back to the 11th century, is open to the public. There are two double rooms on the first floor, and a room for three on the ground floor, all with private bath or shower room and WC. There are enclosed grounds with drainage streams running through.

Prices s fr €80; d fr €120-€150; extra person fr €30　**On Site** ⚘ ⚘ **Nearby** ⛷ 5km ⚘ 19km　Restaurant 5km ♨ 5km　Spa 2km ⛷ 5km ♨ 19km　**Notes** No pets　English spoken　Open Easter to 1 November.

ST-GEORGES-DE-MONS

♯♯♯ ⍟ Le Tilleul

Eliane CHAUMONT
Genestouze, 63780 ST-GEORGES-DE-MONS
☎ 04 73 86 77 23
email: eliane.chaumont@tiscali.fr
web: http://chambredhote63.com

This converted barn houses five first floor guest rooms, three with double beds and two with twin beds. All of the rooms have a private shower room and WC. There is a lounge and kitchen area on the ground floor, and two sitting areas on a mezzanine level. Terrace and parking; meals by arrangement.

Prices s fr €40; d fr €45; dinner fr €15　**On Site** ⚘ Restaurant **Nearby** ⚘ 5km ⛷ 4km ♨ 6km　**Notes** Pets admitted　Open February to November.

ST-GERMAIN-LEMBRON

♯♯♯ ⍟ La Maison de Marie-Camille

Fabien MAROTTE
4, rue de la Porte Vieille, 63340 ST-GERMAIN LEMBRON
☎ 04 73 96 45 73
email: la-maison-de-mariecamille@wanadoo.fr
web: www.la-maison-de-mariecamille.com

This property stands right in the village. It has five bedrooms, each sleeping two or three people and having private shower and WC. Baby equipment is available. Billiard room; enclosed grounds; meals served by arrangement. A good base for exploring the Allier Gorges, and the Romanesque church at Issoire is close by.

Prices s €51-€62; d €64-€84; extra person fr €22; dinner fr €24 **On Site** ⚘ Restaurant　**Nearby** ⛷ 5km ⚘ 11km ⚓ 45km ♨ 11km **Notes** No pets　English spoken

AUVERGNE

ST-GERVAIS-D'AUVERGNE

₩₩ Montarlet

Elyane et Jean-René PELLETIER
63390 ST-GERVAIS-D'AUVERGNE
☎ 04 73 85 87 10 📃 04 73 85 87 10
email: contact@montarlet-chambresdhotes.com
web: www.montarlet-chambresdhotes.com

A building adjoining the owners' house with two double rooms and an attic room with a double and two single beds. All have private shower and wc. Lounge with fireplace, dining room, garden and private parking. St Gervais d'Auvergne is nearby, with restaurants and lake with sail-boarding and fishing. Mountain bikes available for loan.

Prices s fr €40; d fr €53; t fr €66; extra person fr €20   **Nearby** ⚓ 10km
⛴ 30km 🏊 2km ⤴ 2km Restaurant 3km 🦢 2km 🎿 2km 🏛 3km 🚴 2km
Notes Pets admitted English spoken Open March to December.

ST-GERVAZY

₩₩ 🐾 🍽 *Chambre d'hôtes*

Patrick TROUILLER
Auberge du Moncelet, 63340 ST-GERVAZY
☎ 04 73 96 44 51 📃 04 73 96 55 85
email: patrick.trouiller@wanadoo.fr
web: http://aubergedumontcelet.free.fr

Set on a farm, four twin bedrooms with private facilities are situated in an annexe to the owners' house on a farm. There is a sitting room/ kitchenette reserved for guests and private parking. Meals can be taken at the inn. Special rates for children.

Prices not confirmed for 2008   **On Site** 🏊   **Nearby** ⤴ 5km 🦢 50km
🏛 5km 🚴 15km   **Notes** No pets

ST-IGNAT

₩₩ Les Trèfles

Nicole et Jacques RODRIGUEZ
2 impasse de la Forge, 63720 ST-IGNAT
☎ 04 73 33 22 32 & 06 78 55 53 33 📃 04 73 33 22 32
email: rodriguezlestrefles@orange.fr

This 19th-century house is attached to the owner's home and provides three double rooms and two rooms with a double and single bed, each with their own shower and wc. Guests have use of a reception room, sitting room, and games room with books. Trail bikes, terrace and garage available.

Prices s fr €48; d €54-€59; t fr €79; extra person fr €20   **On Site** 🎿
Nearby ⚓ 12km ⛴ 13km 🏊 4km ⤴ 13km Restaurant 4km 🦢 5km
🏛 4km 🚴 13km   **Notes** No pets CC

ST-NECTAIRE

₩₩ Chambre d'hôtes

Audrey et David CELLIER
Villa du Pont Romain, 63710 ST-NECTAIRE
☎ 04 73 88 41 62 & 06 88 45 38 25
email: cellier.david@free.fr
web: http://lavilladupontromain.free.fr

Not far from Lake Chambon, this house has three guest rooms: two doubles and a triple, each with private shower room and WC. Baby equipment available. Billiard table; enclosed grounds with parking space. Swimming possible at Lake Chambon.

Prices s fr €35; d fr €47; extra person fr €15   **On Site** 🏊
Nearby ⚓ 15km ⤴ 1.5km Restaurant 0.5km 🦢 25km 🦢 2km 🎿 8km
🏛 1.8km 🚴 23km   **Notes** No pets English spoken

₩₩ Les Fleurs

René et Simone MAEDER
Saillant, 63710 ST-NECTAIRE
☎ 04 73 88 54 83 & 06 82 22 40 89 📃 04 73 88 51 95
email: rene.monette.maeder@wanadoo.fr

An old farm building close to the owners' home, restored to provide three first-floor bedrooms. There are two double rooms, one with a small private dining area, and a room for three. All have private bath or shower room and WC. Enclosed garden with space for parking.

Prices s fr €45; d fr €50; t fr €65   **Nearby** ⛴ 30km 🏊 0.2km ⤴ 1km
Restaurant 0.8km 🦢 24km Spa 1km 🎿 15km 🏛 1km 🚴 25km
Notes No pets English spoken

ST-PIERRE-LE-CHASTEL

₩₩ 🍽 *Bonnabaud*

Martine et Joël PARROT
Les Genêts Fleuris, 63230 ST-PIERRE-LE-CHASTEL
☎ 04 73 88 75 81 📃 04 73 88 97 47
web: http://perso.wanadoo.fr/genets-fleuris

Three rooms in a former farmhouse, all with a double and single bed and their own shower and wc. Sitting room, terrace and garden. Meals can be reserved and children's meals are available. Reduced rates outside school holidays. Nearby are the Puy-de-Dôme (paragliding available), the Parc de Volcans, the Châine des Puys and the Valley of the Sioule. Activities include hiking, fishing and mountain biking.

Prices not confirmed for 2008   **Nearby** 🏊 1km ⤴ 28km 🦢 30km
🏛 5km 🚴 4km   **Notes** Pets admitted

ST-PIERRE-ROCHE

♦♦♦ ⦿ **Champlaurent**

Florence CARTIGNY
63210 ST-PIERRE-ROCHE
☎ 04 73 65 92 98
email: cartignyflor@orange.fr

In a small, calm hamlet, this traditional stone-built house offers three guest rooms. One has a double and two single beds, the second has two singles and the third has a double bed. All have private facilities. There is a dining room with a fireplace, a garden and a terrace. Dinners feature fruit and vegetables grown in the proprietors' garden, but are not available on Sundays in July and August.

Prices s €39-€41; d €42-€49; extra person €14-€18; dinner fr €15 **Nearby** ⛳ 5km ♨ 18km ✎ 0.1km ⟿ 18km Restaurant 4km 🏊 5km Spa 20km ⚑ 18km 🏛 4km ⛵ 15km **Notes** No pets English spoken Open April to mid November.

ST-PRIEST-BRAMEFANT

♦♦♦ ⦿ **La Fermette**

Michèle et Francis ROCHE
Domaine du Casson, 63310 ST-PRIEST-BRAMEFANT
☎ 04 70 59 08 56 & 06 62 77 82 35 📄 04 70 59 08 56
email: la-fermette@club-internet.fr
web: http://perso.club-internet.fr/rembertmichele/
lafermette

Accommodation in an old farmhouse, an annexe of the owner's house. Ground floor twin with private terrace, bathroom/WC. First floor double with shower room/WC; double with bathroom/WC, double with balcony, shower room/WC (access via a steep staircase). Shared sitting room, lounge area with fireplace. Evening meal, children's meal reduction. Pets by arrangement. Terrace, private parking, open outside space.

Prices s €40-€45; d €45-€50; dinner fr €13 **On Site** Restaurant ⚑ **Nearby** ✎ 2km ⟿ 5km 🏛 3km ⛵ 12km **Notes** Pets admitted English spoken

ST-PRIEST-DES-CHAMPS

♦♦♦ ⦿ **Montpied**

Dominique DELLISSE
63640 ST- PRIEST-DES-CHAMPS
☎ 04 73 52 59 32 📄 04 73 52 59 32
email: dominique.dellisse@wanadoo.fr
web: www.chambres-hotes-noisetiere.com

Guest rooms are divided between the proprietor's house and an annexe opposite with its own entrance. In the main house there is a double with shower/WC and a room with a double and a single, bathroom/WC. In the annexe there is a lounge and family accommodation of one double and one twin with bathroom/WC. Shared lounge with wood-burning stove, dining room. Open space and terraces.

Prices s fr €38; d fr €46; t €60-€70; extra person fr €16; dinner fr €16 **Nearby** ⛳ 12km ✎ 3km ⟿ 3km Restaurant 3km 🏛 3km ⛵ 10km **Notes** No pets English spoken

ST-REMY-DE-CHARGNAT

♦♦♦♦ **Château de Pasredon**

Henriette et Henri MARCHAND
63500 ST-REMY-DE-CHARGNAT
☎ 04 73 71 00 67 📄 04 73 71 08 72

A château with two hectare of grounds, offering a twin room with sitting room, two doubles and a twin with dressing rooms and a double room, all with private facilities. Dining room, lounge, private tennis court and garage parking. Situated between Parc de Volcans and Parc du Livradois-Forez.

Prices s €60-€80; d €70-€90 **Nearby** ⛳ 15km ✎ 8km ⟿ 8km Restaurant 2km 🏊 8km 🏛 6km ⛵ 8km **Notes** No pets English spoken Open mid April to mid October.

ST-SATURNIN

♦♦♦♦ **La Maison des Archers**

Catherine et Charles BOUSQUET
Rue de la Boucherie, Centre Historique,
63450 ST-SATURNIN
☎ 04 73 39 31 42 📄 04 73 39 31 42
email: lamaisondesarchers@wanadoo.fr
web: www.lamaisondesarchers.com

This house, the former home of Queen Margot's riding master, has three guest bedrooms, all on the first floor. There are two double rooms and a twin-bedded room, each with a private bath or shower room and WC. There is a lounge with fireplace, and a terrace.

Prices s fr €50; d fr €60; t fr €68 **Nearby** ⛳ 10km ♨ 10km ✎ 0.1km ⟿ 15km Restaurant 0.2km ⚓ 31km 🏊 0.1km Spa 15km 🏛 0.1km ⛵ 21km **Notes** No pets English spoken

ST-SAUVES-D'AUVERGNE

⌗⌗⌗ ⍟ ⴜ **Domaine de Goulandre**

Daniel et Christiane PERRAULT
63950 ST-SAUVES-D'AUVERGNE
☎ 04 73 22 01 93 🖺 04 73 22 01 93
email: goulandre@wanadoo.fr
web: http://gite.goulandre.free.fr

This house has five guest bedrooms - a mixture of doubles and twin-bedded rooms - all with private bath or shower room and WC. On the ground floor is a lounge with wood-burner and books to read; outside are open grounds with a terrace and space to park cars. Meals available by arrangement.

Prices s fr €42; d fr €46; dinner fr €17 **On Site** ⚲ ⌀ Restaurant **Nearby** ⌕15km ⌕12km ⌕ ⌕10km ⌕3km ⌕5km **Notes** No pets English spoken

ST-SYLVESTRE-PRAGOULIN

⌗⌗⌗ **La Poivrière**

J-F et G RIBOULET-RATTERO
5 rue du Château, 63310 ST-SYLVESTRE-PRAGOULIN
☎ 04 70 59 01 11 🖺 04 70 59 01 11

Two ground-floor rooms in a renovated farm building opposite the owners' house; both rooms are doubles, one with shower/WC and the other with bath/WC. Dining room with open fire and bread oven; enclosed garden, parking.

Prices s €41-€44; d €44-€48; extra person fr €14 **On Site** ⌀ **Nearby** ⚲15km ⌕9km ⌕3km Restaurant 3km ⌕3km Spa 9km ⌕3km ⌕9km **Notes** Pets admitted Open March to October.

ST-VICTOR-LA-RIVIERE

⌗⌗⌗ ⍟ **La Cambuziere**

Christelle & Patrick JALLET
Bessolles, 63790 ST-VICTOR-LA-RIVIERE
☎ 04 73 88 87 99 🖺 04 73 88 87 99
email: cambuziere@aol.com
web: www.lacambuziere.com

This house, built in the distinctive local style, has four guest rooms - three doubles on the ground floor, and upstairs, with dormer windows, a room with a double bed and a single. They all have a private bath or shower room and WC. Lounge with open fire; garden, terrace and parking. Meals by arrangement.

Prices s fr €40; d €51-€58; extra person fr €18; dinner fr €16 **Nearby** ⚲7km ⌕3km ⌕8km Restaurant 0.5km ⚲12km ⌕2km Spa 7km ⌕3km ⌕2km ⌕28km **Notes** No pets

ST-VICTOR-MONTVIANEIX

⌗⌗⌗ ⍟ **Chambre d'hôtes**

J-P, P FORCE-MOULIER
Domaine Montvianeix, 63550 ST-VICTOR-MONTVIANEIX
☎ 04 73 94 02 95 🖺 04 73 94 02 95
email: domaine@montvianeix.com
web: www.montvianeix.com

Open grounds extending to 14 hectares surround this property, which has five upstairs bedrooms. The rooms are all doubles, each with a private bath or shower room. There are two lounges - one on the ground floor with an open fire, and one on the first floor with a stove and books to read. Terrace, and space for parking.

Prices s fr €70; d fr €80; extra person fr €15; dinner fr €28 **Nearby** ⚲9km ⌕35km ⌀ 8km ⌕ 5km Restaurant 2km ⌕5km ⌕7km ⌕15km **Notes** No pets English spoken

⌗⌗⌗ ⍦ ⍟ *Dassaud*

Michel GIRARD
63550 ST-VICTOR-MONTVIANEIX
☎ 04 73 94 38 10 🖺 04 73 94 38 10
email: gitegirdassaud@tiscali.fr
web: http://gite.girard.free.fr

This former farm building, adjacent to the owner's house, has a triple room, a room with double and single and two double rooms, all with private shower and wc. Garden and private parking. Rates vary according to season; reductions for children under 12. Nearby: Thiers, the Vallée de Rouets and the Creux de l'Enfer contemporary arts centre.

Prices not confirmed for 2008 **On Site** ⌀ **Nearby** ⌕15km ⌕15km ⌕23km **Notes** No pets Open March to October.

STE CHRISTINE

⌗⌗⌗ ⍟ **Le Tilleul**

Nicole et Laurent BIANCHERI
Les Abouranges, 63390 STE CHRISTINE
☎ 04 73 85 87 60
email: laurent.biancheri@wanadoo.fr
web: http://perso.wanadoo.fr/lesabouranges

Three guest bedrooms in a former farm building typical of the region. One room with double and single beds, shower room, WC; one double with bathroom, WC; one double with shower room and WC. Shared dining room with fireplace, lounge, terrace, enclosed exterior. Open all year (winter by reservation). Evening meal by reservation. Walking and cycle hire.

Prices s fr €40; d fr €46; extra person fr €16; dinner fr €18 **Nearby** ⚲8km ⌕20km ⌀ 0.5km ⌕ 12km Restaurant 4km ⌕4km ⌕4km ⌕4km **Notes** Pets admitted English spoken

TAUVES

ᚎ ᘯ ⵔ Les Escladines

Sylvie FEREYROLLES
63690 TAUVES
☎ 04 73 21 13 02 & 04 73 21 10 53
email: sylvie.fereyrolles@free.fr
web: http://escladines.chez-alice.fr

Guest rooms in a former farmhouse opposite the owner's home include a double, a single and a triple, all with private facilities. Sitting room with fireplace, games room and garden. Table d'hôte meals can be booked in advance and a children's menu is available. The Mont-Dores and lakes are nearby.

Prices s fr €40; d €48-€52; t €60-€65; dinner fr €17 **Nearby** ⚓ 1km ⵗ 20km ⵢ 1km ⵟ 15km Restaurant 2.5km ⵣ 26km ⵞ 2.5km Spa 15km ⵥ 2.5km ⵦ 2.5km ⵧ 15km **Notes** No pets English spoken Open February to November.

TEILHEDE

ᚎ ⵔ Château des Raynauds

Nathalie SIMON
63460 TEILHEDE
☎ 04 73 64 30 12 & 06 82 24 28 37
email: info@chateau-raynauds.com
web: www.chateau-raynauds.com

Dating from the 16th-century, this hunting lodge offers four double rooms with private facilities. There is a dining room, lounge, enclosed garden, mountain bikes and car port. Dinner available by reservation.

Prices d fr €81; dinner fr €29 **Nearby** ⚓ 8km ⵗ 14km ⵢ 8km ⵟ 7km Restaurant 3km ⵞ 7km ⵥ 7km ⵦ 5km ⵧ 14km **Notes** No pets English spoken CC

ᚎ La Grange

Renée et Guy EDIEU
Les Plaines, 63460 TEILHEDE
☎ 04 73 63 39 00 ⵕ 04 73 63 39 31
email: lagrange.deteilhede@wanadoo.fr
web: http://perso.wanadoo.fr/la-grange-de-teilhede

This converted barn, with its sweeping view over the plain, has three guest bedrooms, all on the first floor. There are two rooms for three, with a double bed and a single, and a double-bedded room. All of the rooms have a private shower room and WC. Lounge, terrace, parking.

Prices s fr €40; d fr €48; t fr €66; extra person fr €16 **Nearby** ⚓ 7km ⵗ 9km ⵢ 10km ⵟ 8km Restaurant 8km ⵞ 8km ⵦ 4km ⵧ 8km **Notes** No pets

TOURS-SUR-MEYMONT

ᚎ ᘯ Ferme de Pied Froid

P et G MAJEUNE-MALLET
63590 TOURS-SUR-MEYMONT
☎ 04 73 70 71 20 & 06 89 75 83 47 ⵕ 04 73 70 71 20
email: philmajeune@orange.fr

A former farm building adjacent to the owner's house offering a twin room, a double room and a room with a double and two single beds, all en suite. Guests have use of a sitting room with fireplace and a garden with table tennis. Table d'hôte meals can be booked. Rates reduced from the fourth night. Fishing and walking available locally.

Prices s fr €33; d €41-€43; t fr €51; extra person fr €16 **Nearby** ⚓ 6km ⵢ 5km ⵟ 5km Restaurant 5km ⵣ 40km ⵞ 2km ⵥ 1km ⵧ 30km **Notes** No pets English spoken

VARENNES-SUR-USSON

ᚎ Les Baudarts

Hélène VERDIER-BRIOUDES
63500 VARENNES-SUR-USSON
☎ 04 73 89 05 51 ⵕ 04 73 89 05 51

Accommodation is in three rooms in the owners' house and includes a family room with four single beds and two twin rooms (one with lounge), all with private facilities. Guests have the use of a lounge, dining room with fireplace and library, garden and parking. Attractions in the area include Usson, the Château of Queen Margot; Le Vernet-la-Varenne, the Château de Parentignat; and Sauxillanges.

Prices d €72-€85; extra person fr €20 **On Site** Private ⵟ **Nearby** ⚓ 5km ⵗ 40km Restaurant 2km ⵞ 4km ⵥ 4km ⵦ 2km ⵧ 6km **Notes** No pets English spoken Open 1 May to 1 October.

VENSAT

ᚎ ⵔ Château de Lafont

Marie-Anne VERDIER
2, rue de la Côte Rousse, 63260 VENSAT
☎ 04 73 64 21 24
email: info@chateaudelafont.com
web: www.chateaudelafont.com

The oldest parts of this château date from the end of the 16th century. It has three bedrooms, all on the first floor: two doubles, and a family room for four. All rooms have a private bath or shower room and WC. Lounge with open fire, terrace, sauna. Wooded grounds with lake, tennis court and swimming pool. Stabling is possible.

Prices s €90-€105; d €95-€110; t fr €150; extra person fr €15; dinner fr €25 **On Site** Private ⵟ **Nearby** ⚓ 4km ⵗ 15km ⵢ 16km Restaurant 5km Spa 25km ⵦ 3km ⵧ 5km **Notes** No pets English spoken

VERNEUGHEOL

⏐⏐⏐ ✿ ⍥ Le Glufareix

Christiane & Bernard THOMAS
63470 VERNEUGHEOL
☎ 04 73 22 11 40 📄 04 73 22 11 40

Four bedrooms in the owners' house: a family suite with two doubles and a single bed, two with a double and single and a double room, all with private facilities. Lounge, dining room, courtyard, terrace and parking. Table d'hôte meals can be reserved. The nearby observatory of Verneugheol offers lectures on astronomy.

Prices s fr €38; d €44-€46; t fr €59; extra person fr €15; dinner fr €16 **Nearby** ⛷ 20km ⚓ 40km ✎ 5km Restaurant 1km ⛵ 45km ◈ 9km ◉ 9km ⛪ 3km ✈ 9km **Notes** Pets admitted English spoken

VERNINES

⏐⏐⏐ ✿ *Bessat*

Roger MORANGE
63210 VERNINES
☎ 04 73 65 68 03
email: hélene.morange@voila.fr

An old farm building adjoining the proprietor's home in open grounds, offering a double room, a twin and a family suite composed of two rooms with a double and single bed. Each has a private bathroom. Living room available. Reductions off-season and depending on length of stay. Animals accepted for a charge. Restaurant 2km.

Prices not confirmed for 2008 **Nearby** ◈ 22km ⛵ 23km ⛪ 2km ✈ 29km **Notes** Pets admitted English spoken

VEYRE-MONTON

⏐⏐⏐ ⍥ Au Fond de la Cour

C et N KALSRON-LEGOUEIX
1 Av de l'Occitanie, 63960 VEYRE-MONTON
☎ 04 73 69 76 64 & 06 07 30 95 43
📄 04 73 69 65 32
email: contact@aufonddelacour.com
web: www.aufonddelacour.com

These rooms are in an annexe to the owners' manor house, which dates from 1850. They are all on the first floor: two doubles, and a two-roomed family suite with a double bed and twin beds. Each room has air-conditioning, power showers and WCs. Lounge with open fire, and sitting room on mezzanine level. Terrace, internal courtyard. A gym, sauna and Jacuzzi are also available for guests use.

Prices s fr €90; d fr €120; t fr €160; extra person fr €20; dinner fr €30 **On Site** ✎ Spa **Nearby** ⛵ 3km ⚓ 20km ◈ Restaurant 5km ⛵ 36km ⛪ 15km ⛪ 0.1km ✈ 15km **Notes** Pets admitted English spoken

VILLOSANGES

⏐⏐⏐ ⍥ La Ferme de l'Etang

Christiane QUEYRIAUX
La Verrerie, 63380 VILLOSANGES
☎ 04 73 79 71 61

Six rooms in the owner's house attached to a country cottage which has its own private lake for fishing. There is a twin room, three doubles and two rooms with a double and a single bed, all with private facilities. Lounge with a mezzanine floor and TV, dining room with fireplace, terrace, garden and parking. Table d'hôte meals if booked in advance.

Prices s fr €38; d fr €48; t fr €63; dinner fr €17 **On Site** ⛪ **Nearby** ⛵ 15km ✎ 0.1km ◈ 15km Restaurant 7km ◉ 3km ⛪ 3km ✈ 15km **Notes** No pets Open March to January.

VOLLORE-VILLE

⏐⏐⏐ ⍥ *Le Troulier*

Arlette et Bernard MOIGNOUX
Le Temps de Vivre, 63120 VOLLORE-VILLE
☎ 04 73 53 71 98
email: troulier@libertysurf.fr
web: www.letroulier.com

Two double rooms and a triple with private facilities, provided at this farmhouse. Guests have the use of a sitting room with fireplace and library, a large flower garden and a table tennis table. Table d'hôte meals can be provided using the garden's vegetables. In July concerts of classical music are held at Vollore-Ville. Fishing and walking nearby.

Prices not confirmed for 2008 **Nearby** ✎ 5km ◈ 12km ⛵ 35km ⛪ 4km ✈ 15km **Notes** Pets admitted English spoken

SAÔNE-ET-LOIRE
71

42
LOIRE

58
NIÈVRE

18
CHER

23
CREUSE

63
PUY-DE-DÔME

Roanne

Loire
Canal

Le Pin

St-Didier-en-Donjon

St-Léon

Thionne

Le Mayet-
de-Montagne

Mariol

Vichy

Le Vernet

Bellerive-
sur-Allier

Espinasse-
Vozelle

Montoldre
St-Rémy-
en-Rollat

Monteignet-
sur-l'Andelot

Gannat

Charroux

St-Bonnet-
de-Rochefort

Riom

Paray-le-Frésil

Lusigny

Neuilly-le-Réal

Gouise

St-Gérand-le-Puy

Paray-sous-Briailles

La Ferté-Hauterive

MOULINS

Châtel-
de-Neuvre

Verneuil-
en-Bourbonnais

Saulcet

St-Germain-
de-Salles

Chouvigny

Ébreuil

Valignat

Louroux-de-
Bouble

Montilly

Coulandon

Noyant-d'Allier

Deux-Chaises

Le Theil

Louchy-Montfand

Fleuriel

Couzon

Agonges

Autry-
Issards

St-Aubin-le-Monial

Tronget

St-Priest-en-Murat

Château-
sur-Allier

Neure

Pouzy-Mésangy

Franchesse

Couleuvre

Lurcy-
Lévis

Isle-et-Bardais

Ygrande

Buxières-les-Mines

Bizeneuille

Doyet

St-Bonnet-Tronçais

Braize

Meaulne

Montluçon

Louroux-de-Beaune

Audes

Saint-Désiré

Huriel

Saint-Amand-
Montrond

Cher

15 km

0

Loire
Canal

Allier

Sioule

N81
D994
D978
D982
D994
N79
D979
D973
D973
N2079
N79
N7
N7
D60
D951
N144
D943
N145
A71
A71
N371
N144
N9
N7
N209
D6
6N
D46
D46
N145
A719
A719
D2009N
D907
D906
D906 b
A72
A72
A72
A71
N7

Canal

NE
SW

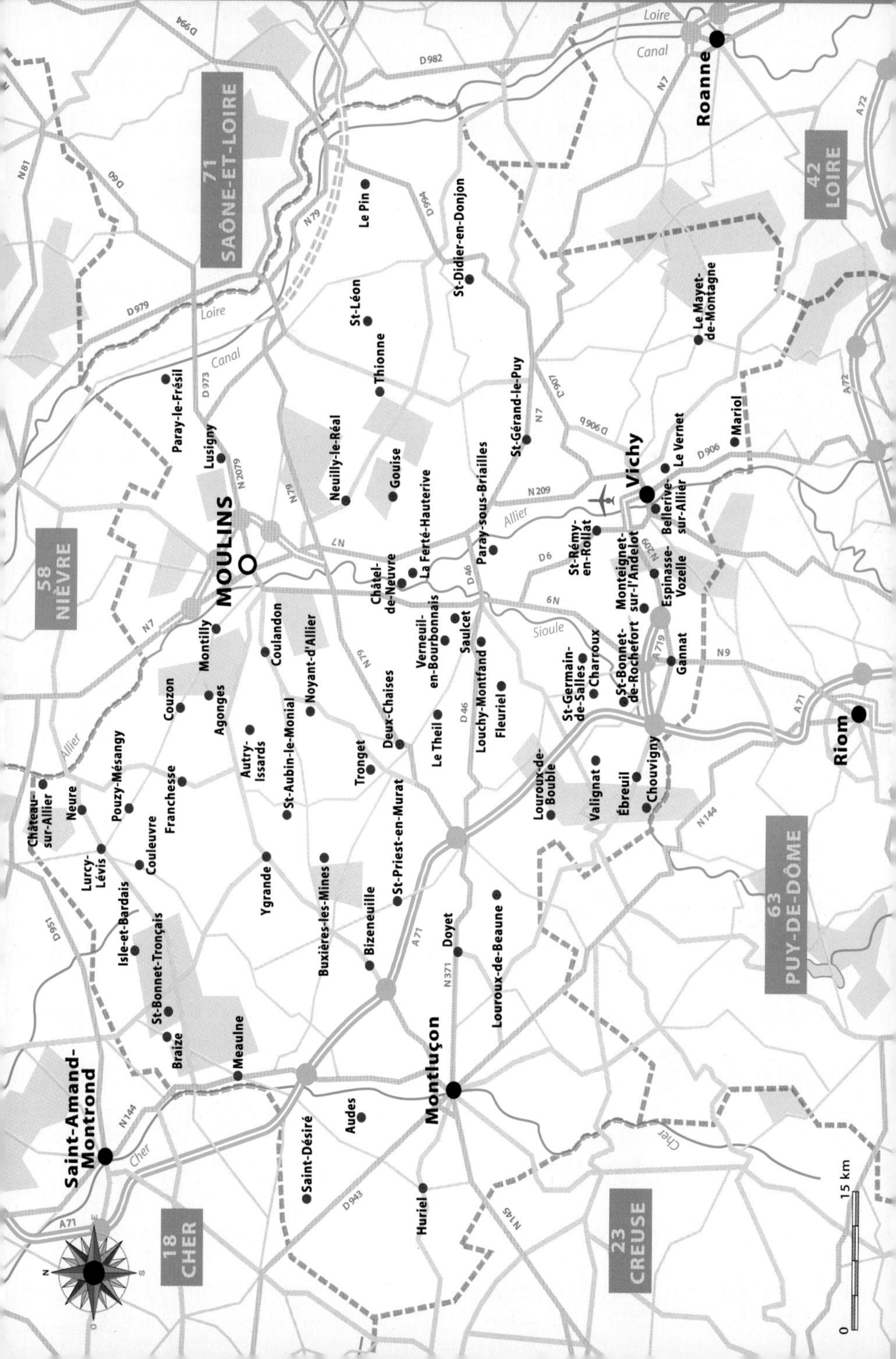

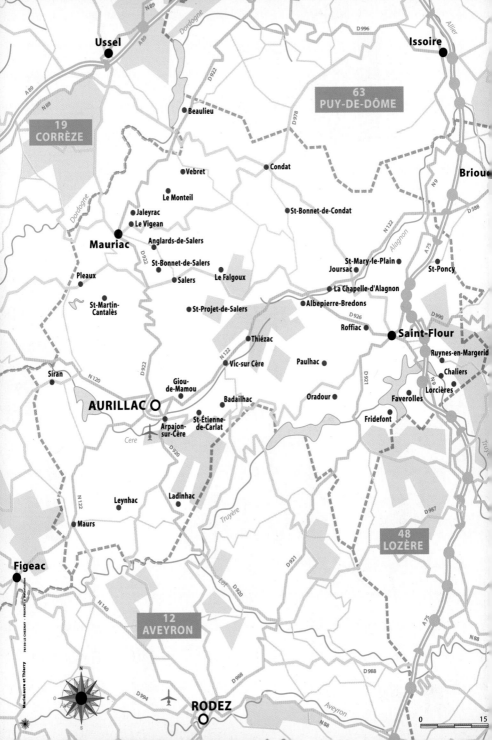

CANTAL
Auvergne

15

Ussel

Issoire

63
PUY-DE-DÔME

Beaulieu

Brioude

19
CORRÈZE

Vebret

Condat

Le Monteil

St-Bonnet-de-Condat

Jaleyrac
Le Vigean

Mauriac

Anglards-de-Salers

St-Mary-le-Plain
Joursac

St-Poncy

Pleaux

St-Bonnet-de-Salers

Salers

Le Falgoux

La Chapelle-d'Alagnon

St-Martin-
Cantalès

St-Projet-de-Salers

Albepierre-Bredons

Roffiac

Saint-Flour

Siran

Thiézac

Vic-sur-Cère

Paulhac

Ruynes-en-Margeride

Chaliers

Lorcières

AURILLAC

Giou-
de-Mamou

Badailhac

Oradour

Faverolles

Arpajon-
sur-Cère

St-Étienne-
de-Carlat

Fridefont

Leynhac

Ladinhac

48
LOZÈRE

Maurs

Figeac

12
AVEYRON

RODEZ

0   15

Cère
Dordogne
Truyère
Alagnon
Allier

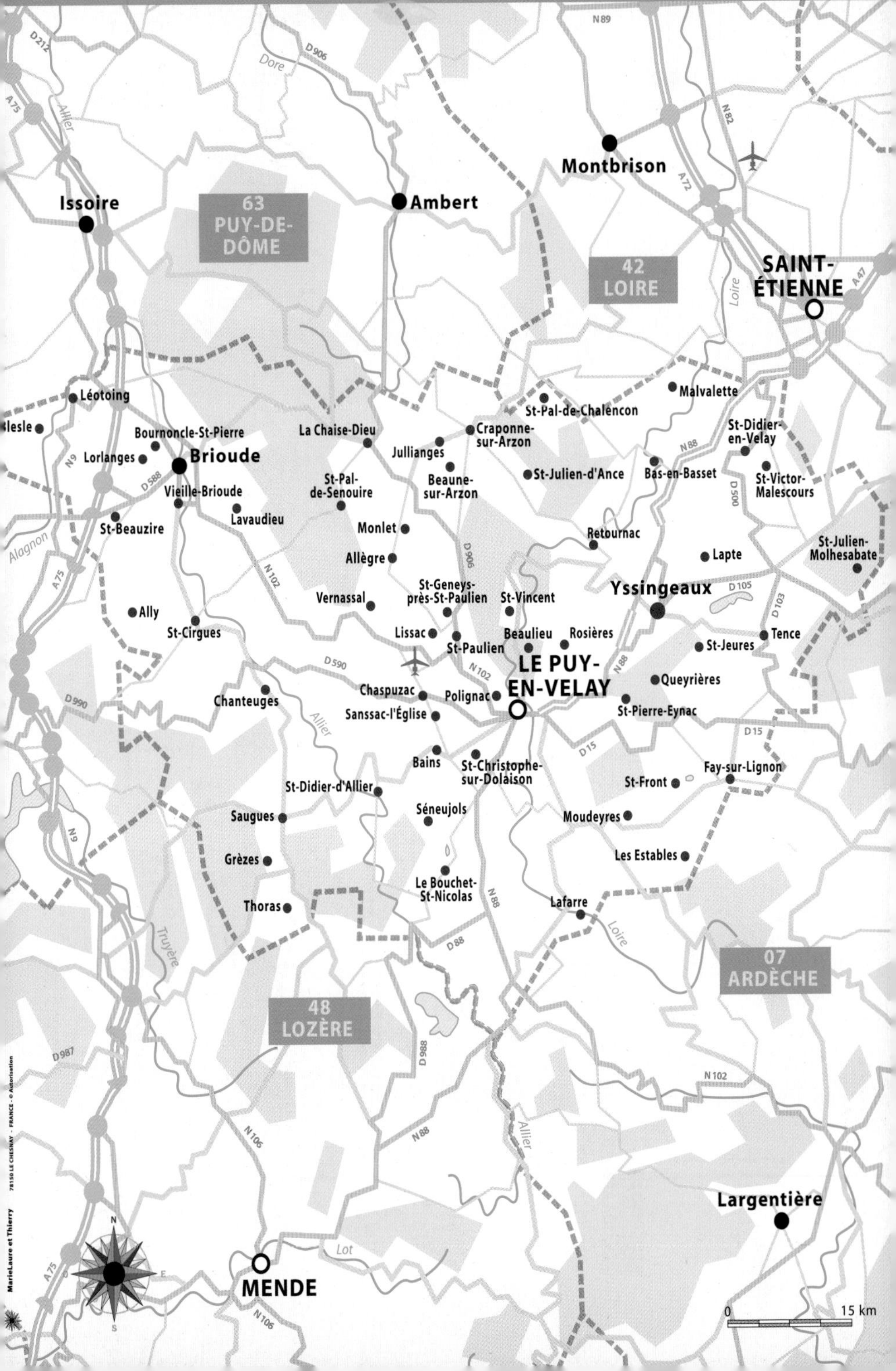

D 212
D 906
Dore
N 89
N 82

Issoire

63
PUY-DE-DÔME

Ambert

Montbrison

42
LOIRE

Loire

A 72

SAINT-ÉTIENNE

A 47

Léotoing
Bournoncle-St-Pierre
Lorlanges
Brioude
Vieille-Brioude
St-Beauzire
Lavaudieu
Ally
St-Cirgues

La Chaise-Dieu
St-Pal-de-Senouire
Monlet
Allègre
Vernassal

Jullianges
Beaune-sur-Arzon

St-Pal-de-Chalençon
Craponne-sur-Arzon
St-Julien-d'Ance

Malvalette
St-Didier-en-Velay
St-Victor-Malescours

Bas-en-Basset

Retournac
Lapte

St-Julien-Molhesabate

St-Geneys-près-St-Paulien
St-Vincent
Yssingeaux

D 105

Lissac
Beaulieu
Rosières
St-Paulien
Chaspuzac
LE PUY-EN-VELAY
Polignac
Sanssac-l'Église

St-Jeures
Tence

Queyrières
St-Pierre-Eynac

D 15

Chanteuges

Bains
St-Christophe-sur-Dolaison

St-Front
Fay-sur-Lignon

St-Didier-d'Allier
Séneujols
Moudeyres

Sauges
Les Estables

Grèzes
Le Bouchet-St-Nicolas
Lafarre

Thoras

07
ARDÈCHE

48
LOZÈRE

Largentière

MENDE

Lot

0   15 km

Loire
Canal
Roanne

Montbrison

N7

A89

A72

N89

42
LOIRE

Ambert

Dore-l'Église

Arlanc

03
ALLIER

Thiers

Vollore-Ville

Olliergues

D906

Tours-sur-Meymont

Celloux

43
HAUTE-LOIRE

St-Victor-Montvianeix

St-Priest-Bramefant

Peschadoires

St-Didier-d'Auvergne

Sauxillanges

Varennes-sur-Usson

St-Rémy-de-Chargnat

Brioude

Vichy

St-Sylvestre-Pragoulin

D906

N209

Allier

D6

N9

Sioule

A719

A71

Beauregard-Vendon

St-Ignat

Joze

Mirefleurs

Les Martres-de-Veyre

Veyre-Monton

Montpeyroux

Flat

Issoire

Mareugheol

St-Germain-Lembron

St-Gervazy

Rentières

Vensat

Montcel

Combronde

Teilhède

Davayat

RIOM

N9

CLERMONT-FERRAND

St-Saturnin

Aydat

St-Nectaire

Murol

Clémensat

Saurier

Besse-et-St-Anastaise

Manzat

Loubeyrat

Charbonnières-les-Varennes

Royat

Orcines

Nébouzat

Aurières

Vernines

Bagnols

Ste-Christine

N144

Saint-Gervais-d'Auvergne

St-Priest-des-Champs

St-Georges-de-Mons

Villossanges

Bromont-Lamothe

Saint-Pierre-le-Chastel

Olby

Prondines

Saint-Pierre-Roche

Saint-Bonnet-près-Orcival

Rochefort-Montagne

La Bourboule

Le Mont-Dore

Chambon-sur-Lac

Saint-Victor-la-Rivière

15
CANTAL

Cher

Cisternes-la-Forêt

D941

Giat

Verneugheol

Bourg-Lastic

St-Sauves-d'Auvergne

Tauves

Singles

Dordogne

D922

23
CREUSE

15 km

MarieLaure et Thierry

0

BRITTANY

CÔTES-D'ARMOR

BOURSEUL

⦀ 🌿 🍴 Saint-Maleu

Eric TRANCHANT

22130 BOURSEUL

☎ 02 96 83 01 34   📄 02 96 83 01 34

email: eric-tranchant@wanadoo.fr

web: www.gitesdarmor.com/saintmaleu

On a farm close to the Côte d'Emeraude, a stone-built house in a rural setting. There are six bedrooms, all upstairs except one, and four of which are en suite: three doubles and a triple; another double shares a shower room and WC with another triple. Baby equipment is available. Meals by arrangement; fishponds in the grounds.

Prices s fr €38; d fr €40; t fr €50; dinner fr €17 **Nearby** ⛷ 5km 🏊 3km Sea 15km ⛳ 0.5km 🚴 12km Restaurant 1.5km Water sports 15km 🏊 1km Spa 26km 🏛 1km 🚶 6km **Notes** Pets admitted

CALORGUEN

⦀ *Tréliger*

Josette LOQUEN

Chambres d'Hôtes Les Glycines, Tréliger,

22100 CALORGUEN

☎ 02 96 88 00 08 & 06 11 50 20 02

email: jc.treliger@wanadoo.fr

web: http://treliger.free.fr

An old farmhouse situated 600 metres from the River Rance and four kilometres from the town of Dinan. It has three bedrooms. On the ground floor is a double; upstairs is another double and a two-roomed family suite for four. All of the rooms have private facilities, but they are not all en suite. Garden furniture and barbecue.

Prices not confirmed for 2008 **Nearby** ⛷ 5km 🏊 30km Sea 25km 🚴 4km Water sports 5km 🏊 1.5km 🏛 1.5km 🚶 6km **Notes** No pets English spoken

CREHEN

⦀ 🍴 La Belle Noë

Chantal BIGOT

22130 CREHEN

☎ 02 96 84 08 47 & 06 89 94 69 18

email: belle.noe@wanadoo.fr

web: www.crehen.com

This 18th-century house is near the owner's property, in wooded grounds with a rose garden, close to St-Jacut de la Mer and St Cast le Guildo. It has a double room with private patio, a room with a double and single bed, and one with a double and two single beds, all en suite. Lounge, cycling, badminton, table tennis, parking. Meals can be arranged. Special rates for groups of four.

Prices s €50-€80; d €60-€90; t €80-€110; extra person fr €20; dinner fr €27 **Nearby** ⛷ 2km 🏊 8km Sea 4km ⛳ 3km 🚴 8km Restaurant 2km Water sports 6km 🏊 1km Spa 17km 🏛 1km 🚶 4km **Notes** Pets admitted English spoken

⦀ Villa Belle-vue

Albert EVEN

10 rue du Port, Port du Guildo, 22130 CREHEN

☎ 02 96 41 08 21   📄 02 96 41 08 21

email: even-nicole@wanadoo.fr

web: www.gitesdarmor.com/villabellevue

This large centrally heated house has sea views and a large garden. There are four double and two twin rooms, all en suite, a guests' lounge, parking, garage, balcony and terrace. Breakfast is served in the dining room and on the veranda. Restaurant nearby. Local attractions: Créhen, Port du Guildo, ruins of the Château du Guildo, Pleudihen, St Cast and St Malo.

Prices s fr €48; d fr €52; t fr €70 **Nearby** ⛷ 6km 🏊 6km Sea 0.2km ⛳ 6km 🚴 6km Restaurant 0.1km Water sports 1.5km 🏊 2km Spa 25km 🏛 0.2km 🚶 25km **Notes** No pets

ERQUY

⦀ *Le Dréneuf*

Roselyne GORIN

Le Dreneuf, 22430 ERQUY

☎ 02 96 72 10 07 & 06 19 71 86 72   📄 02 96 72 10 07

email: gorin.bernard@wanadoo.fr

web: www.gitesdarmor.com/lahazaie

An annexe of a small farm providing two double en suite rooms and a family suite of two rooms with a double and two single beds. Cooking facilities are available. The beaches and cliffs of Cap d'Erquy and Cap Fréhel, Mont St Michel and La Côte de Granit Rose are nearby, as is the GR34 path.

Prices not confirmed for 2008 **Nearby** ⛷ 10km 🏊 3.5km Sea 1km ⛳ 3.5km 🚴 8km Water sports 1km 🏊 4km 🏛 2km 🚶 18km **Notes** No pets

ETABLES-SUR-MER

♨ ❧ ⓘ La Ville Jacob

Florence LE CORVAISIER

Chemin de la roulerie, 22680 ETABLES-SUR-MER

☎ 02 96 73 32 68 & 06 08 57 28 18

email: gite-etables@wanadoo.fr

web: http://lagarenne.canalblog.com

Welcoming farm offering three en suite double rooms and a well-equipped kitchen. Breakfast is served in the dining room and there is a garden with terrace, barbecue, children's room and bikes for guests use. Walking and cycling trails nearby.

Prices s fr €30; d fr €40; extra person fr €12; dinner fr €16
Nearby ☘ 1km ♨ 2km Sea 2km ⚓ 1km ⚲ 1.5km Restaurant 2km Water sports 2km ⚑ 2km ⓘ 1.5km ⚐ 15km **Notes** No pets English spoken CC

FREHEL

♨ Ker Léon

Isabelle BARRANDON

La Porte Morin, Plévenon, 22240 FREHEL

☎ 02 96 41 55 75 & 06 60 08 15 23

email: kerleon@wanadoo.fr

web: www.kerleon.com

This house, stone-built and dating from the late 19th century, has an open south-facing garden with a sculpture workshop. There are five upstairs bedrooms, some with double beds, some with twins. They all have private facilities; some of them have sea views and some of them overlook the garden.

Prices s fr €50; d fr €60-€70 **Nearby** ☘ 4km ♨ 8km Sea 1km ⚓ 3km ⚲ 12km Restaurant 0.3km Water sports 1km ⚑ 4km Spa 40km ⓘ 3km ⚐ 20km **Notes** No pets English spoken

GOMENE

♨ ⓘ La Hersonnière d'en Haut

Gérard LE MEAUX

22230 GOMENE

☎ 02 96 28 48 67

email: gerard.lemeaux@wanadoo.fr

web: www.gitesdarmor.com/la-hersonniere

This 19th-century house is at the heart of Brittany and has a twin room, two double rooms, a suite with a double and single bed, and a two-room family suite, all with private bathrooms. Breakfast and evening meals include local dishes and garden vegetables. There is a sitting room with views over the lake, where guests can fish, a garden and conservatory.

Prices s €50-€55; d €55-€60; t fr €84; extra person fr €24; dinner fr €22 **Nearby** ☘ 5km ⚓ 0.1km ⚲ 5km Restaurant 3km ⚑ 5km ⓘ 5km ⚐ 20km **Notes** No pets English spoken Open 3 January to 24 December.

HENGOAT

♨ ♿ Le Rumain

J.François DUYCK

22450 HENGOAT

☎ 02 96 91 30 92 & 06 83 49 18 39

🖺 02 96 91 30 92

email: jf.duyck@libertysurf.fr

web: www.lerumain.com

Rooms available on the site of a 16th-century manor house, set in grassland and woods. There is a grade 3 studio with disabled access and a double room, single room and small kitchen, a grade 3 double room and two grade 4 rooms with a double and single bed; all have private facilities. Living room with fireplace, library, washing machine, kitchen, barbecue, stables, bikes for hire. Special prices out of season.

Prices s €34-€42; d €44-€52; t €63-€67 **On Site** ⚑
Nearby ☘ 5km ♨ 15km Sea 15km ⚓ 5km ⚲ 10km Restaurant 8km Water sports 15km ⚑ 10km ⓘ 5km ⚐ 20km **Notes** No pets English spoken CC

KERBORS

♨ ⓘ Manoir de Troezel Vras

J.Marie & Françoise MAYNIER

22610 KERBORS

☎ 02 96 22 89 68 🖺 02 96 22 90 56

email: troezel.vras@free.fr

web: http://troezel.vras.free.fr

Five rooms in a 17th-century renovated manor house set in two hectares: a three-room family unit, three double rooms and a three person family room, all with private bathrooms. Extra beds available. Sitting room, library, garden with furniture and terrace. Home-made jams, yoghurt and children's meals served.

Prices s fr €65; d fr €74; t fr €105; extra person fr €21; dinner fr €21 **Nearby** ☘ 7km ♨ 19km Sea 3km ⚓ 3km ⚲ 10km Restaurant 2km Water sports 3km ⚑ 7km ⚑ 5km ⓘ 2km ⚐ 15km **Notes** No pets English spoken Open April to October.

♨ Troëzel Bian

J.Claude & Annick BOUCHER

22610 KERBORS

☎ 02 96 22 98 63

email: jclaudeboucher@aol.com

web: www.troezelbian.com

An 18th-century manor in the heart of wild countryside. A granite staircase leads to large guest rooms including Art Déco (double and single bed), Bourgogne (king-size and single), Bretagne and Bord de Mer (twins), each with private facilities. Dining room and lounge with fireplace, kitchenette, bikes, table-tennis, interior courtyard with garden furniture. Surrounding tourist sites include the Côte du Granit Rose, Bréhat, Paimpol, Château de la Roche and Jagu.

Prices s €45-€50; d €51-€56; t fr €72 **On Site** ⚑
Nearby ☘ 10km ♨ 29km Sea 3km ⚓ 3km ⚲ 8km Restaurant 1km Water sports 16km ⚑ 3km ⓘ 1km ⚐ 15km **Notes** No pets

LA ROCHE-DERRIEN

♦♦♦ ৬ Quillevez Vraz

Georges BEAUVERGER
22450 POMMERIT-JAUDY
☎ 02 96 91 52 81 & 06 23 50 75 80

Between the Côte de Granit Rose and the Ile de Bréhat, on land
that was once part of a working farm, this property has three triple
bedrooms (double bed plus single) all with en suite bathroom and
WC. The room on the ground floor is suitable for disabled guests; the
other two are upstairs. A very agreeable spot, with plenty of flowers
and a restful atmosphere; covered parking.

Prices s fr €38; d fr €43; t fr €53 **Nearby** ♣ 0.3km ♨ 10km Sea 15km
♬ 1km ↖ 5km Water sports 15km ⊜ 2km ☖ 1.5km ⋈ 20km
Notes No pets Open Easter to October.

LANNION

♦♦♦♦ Manoir du Launay

Florence & Ivan CHARPENTIER
Servel, 22300 LANNION
☎ 02 96 47 21 24 & 06 87 61 91 13
email: manoirdulaunay@wanadoo.fr
web: www.manoirdulaunay.com

This beautiful residence has been entirely renovated by Florence
and Ivan, and combines the authentic pink granite with modern
comfort. Five light and spacious rooms, decorated tastefully, are
all doubles with bathroom and WC. Generous breakfasts feature
home-made and regional products. Games room with billiards.
Country garden with furniture, table tennis. Five minutes from
town centre.

Prices s €75–€105; d €80–€110; t fr €150; extra person fr €22
Nearby ♣ 7km ♨ 7km Sea 6km ♬ 5km ↖ 10km Restaurant 3km
Water sports 7km ⊜ 10km ☖ 3km ⋈ 4km **Notes** No pets English
spoken

LE FAOUET

♦♦♦ *Le Rohiou*

Germaine LE DIUZET
22290 LE FAOUET
☎ 02 96 52 34 99 & 06 61 78 26 47
email: c.lediuzet@infonie.fr

A farmhouse offering four en suite rooms with bathrooms: two rooms
with a double and single bed, a family suite with two grade 2 rooms
(one double and two single beds) and a double room. Sitting room
with kitchen, courtyard, and garden.

Prices not confirmed for 2008 **Nearby** ♣ 2km ♨ 20km Sea 14km
♬ 0.3km ↖ 15km Water sports 6km ⊜ 6km ☖ 0.2km ⋈ 17km
Notes No pets English spoken

LEZARDRIEUX

♦♦♦ Chambre d'hôtes

Marie Yvette GUILLOU
5 rue de Kervoas, 22740 LEZARDRIEUX
☎ 02 96 20 14 53 📠 02 96 20 14 53

This renovated former stable is on the Sauvage peninsula and
provides four en suite rooms (one with a double and single bed). The
owners' house has a further two grade 1 twin rooms with communal
bathroom and wc. Large breakfasts, sitting room, TV, garden, terrace,
barbecue, picnic area and bowls. The GR34 footpath is close by.

Prices s fr €42; d €44–€46; t fr €66; extra person fr €16 **Nearby** ♣ 3km
♨ 20km Sea 3km ♬ 3km ↖ 8km Restaurant 0.5km ⊜ 3km Spa 4km
☖ 3km ⋈ 3km **Notes** No pets English spoken

♦♦♦ ৬ Croas Hent

Michel et M.line CARRIOU
22740 LEZARDRIEUX
☎ 02 96 22 21 82 📠 02 96 22 21 82
email: michel.carriou@wanadoo.fr
web: www.gites-du-croas-hent.com

Set on a vegetable farm, this family accommodation is in a private
annexe and includes a double bed and twin beds, with private
facilities, as well as a well-equipped kitchen area and veranda. Another
annexe has four rooms; two with disabled access and a double and
twin room on the first floor, both en suite. Communal veranda and
kitchen, garden. Nearby: Paimpol, Bréhat and beaches.

Prices s €42–€45; d €50–€55; t fr €75; extra person fr €16
Nearby ♣ 4km ♨ 15km Sea 1km ♬ 1km ↖ 7km Restaurant 1km
⊜ 2km Spa 30km ☖ 2km ⋈ 7km **Notes** Pets admitted English spoken

♦♦♦ *Lan Caradec*

Edith et Toshihiko WAKE
Lan Caradec route des Perdrix, 22740 LEZARDRIEUX
☎ 02 96 20 10 25
email: edith.wake@tiscali.fr
web: www.lan-caradec.com

Extensive accommodation in this quiet bourgeois-style house: four
units, all with balcony and bath/WC, include two two-room family
suites and can sleep up to fifteen people. Direct access to sea, views
over port.

Prices not confirmed for 2008 **Nearby** ♣ 8km ♨ 10km Sea 0.2km
♬ 0.2km ↖ 6km Water sports 0.2km ⊜ 2km ☖ 1km ⋈ 6km
Notes No pets English spoken

LOUANNEC

♨ ⌕ **Goas Ar Lan**

Nicole MICHEL
22700 LOUANNEC
☎ 02 96 49 08 54 & 06 13 60 75 94
email: goas-ar-lan@wanadoo.fr
web: www.goasarlan.com

In the heart of the Côte du Granit Rose, this old restored house is set in five hectares and offers four rooms for two people (Hortensia, Camélia, Céanothe and Agapanthe) and Rhododendron with a double and single, each with private facilities. Parking, tranquil garden with maples, rose bushes and conifers, furniture, barbecue.

Prices s fr €55; d fr €55; t fr €80 **Nearby** ⚓ 5km ⚘ 5km Sea 2km ⚑ 2km ⚒ 5km Restaurant 2km Water sports 2km ⚓ 2km ☕ 2km ⛺ 2km ⚑ 5km **Notes** No pets English spoken

♨ ⦿ **Le Colombier de Coat Gourhant**

Erwan FAJOLLES
22700 LOUANNEC
☎ 02 96 23 29 30
email: le-colombier-coat-gourhant@wanadoo.fr

In a private wing of this renovated farm there are four en suite attic rooms, including two double rooms, a room with a small double bed and a twin room. Communal sitting room, large aquarium, conservatory and parking. Breakfast is served at individual tables and picnics are possible in the grounds. The resort of Perros Guirac is nearby.

Prices s fr €45; d fr €50; extra person fr €15; dinner €15-€30
Nearby ⚓ 6km ⚘ 10km Sea 2.5km ⚑ 2.5km ⚒ 8km Restaurant 2.5km Water sports 2.5km ⚓ 3km Spa 6km ⛺ 2km ⚑ 10km **Notes** No pets English spoken

MINIHY-TREGUIER

♨ **Le Penquer**

Françoise LE MEE
22220 MINIHY-TREGUIER
☎ 02 96 91 57 03 ▤ 02 96 91 58 58
email: gildas.lemee@wanadoo.fr
web: http://membres.lycos.fr/lepenquer

Guest rooms have independent access in the annexe: a family suite on the ground floor comprises a double and a twin, shower and WC; upstairs is a twin and a double, both with shower and WC. Within the hosts' stone-built house on the ground floor is another family room with a double and twin beds, bathroom and WC. Breakfast served in large dining room. Library, kitchenette (evenings only), and TV/DVD room. Garden/furniture.

Prices not confirmed for 2008 **Nearby** ⚓ 2km ⚘ 25km Sea 11km ⚒ 4km Water sports 11km ⚓ 4km ⛺ 3km ⚑ 20km **Notes** No pets

MONCONTOUR

♨ ⦿ **À la Garde Ducale**

Christiane LE RAY
10 place de Penthièvre, 22510 MONCONTOUR
☎ 02 96 73 52 18 ▤ 02 96 73 52 18
email: alagardeducal@orange.fr
web: www.gitesdarmor.com/a-la-garde-ducale

This 16th-century house offers four en suite bedrooms: two rooms with a double and two single beds, a room with a double and single bed and a double room. Sitting room, dining room, kitchen, yard, terrace, garden furniture and barbecue. Meals are served on demand.

Prices s fr €45; d fr €50; t fr €75; dinner fr €20 **Nearby** ⚓ 5km ⚘ 25km Sea 20km ⚒ 0.8km Restaurant 0.1km Water sports 20km ⚓ 0.5km ⛺ 0.1km ⚑ 17km **Notes** No pets CC

PAIMPOL

♨ **Gardenn Zant Vignoc**

Françoise BOUCHARD
Lanvignec, 22500 PAIMPOL
☎ 02 96 20 72 21
email: gites.bouchard@free.fr
web: http://gites.bouchard.free.fr

Just 900 metres from the centre of Paimpol, this traditional house nevertheless enjoys a quiet location. There are two ground floor rooms: a double, and (in an annexe) a room with a double bed and a single. Upstairs is a further double room. All rooms have private bath or shower rooms and WCs. Traditional breakfasts served, with local specialities.

Prices not confirmed for 2008 **Nearby** ⚓ 0.2km ⚘ 10km Sea 1km ⚑ 1km ⚒ 0.2km Water sports 1km ⚓ 0.2km ⛺ 0.8km ⚑ 1km **Notes** No pets English spoken

♨♨ **Pondervann**

Katerine CHABOUD
Chemin de Pont Erwann, 22500 PAIMPOL
☎ 02 96 22 09 89 & 06 14 59 56 96
▤ 02 96 22 09 89
email: jpkchaboud@wanadoo.fr
web: www.pondervann.com

A large typical 17th-century residence, authentically Bretonne and set in a two hectare park with pond and woods. Rooms have private facilities and include Hortensia (double), Tilleul (twin) and Abricot (double with views over the estuary) with English style décor, and a room with a king-size and a single bed. Lounge with fireplace, games and TV. Garden furniture, bikes. Situated by the Trieux estuary and near the landing stage for Bréhat. Picnic by the sea and sail with your host.

Prices s €65-€80; d €75-€90; t €90-€105 **On Site** ⚑ ⚒ **Nearby** ⚓ 3km ⚘ 8km Sea 8km ⚒ 3km Restaurant 2km Water sports 2km ⚓ 3km ⛺ 3km ⚑ 3km **Notes** No pets English spoken Open February to 15 December.

⚡ Villa Keralinec

Gabriel PELLAN

7 av de Chateaubriand, 22500 PAIMPOL

☎ 02 96 22 06 98

email: gabriel.pellan@wanadoo.fr

web: http://perso.wanadoo.fr/keralinec

Built by an Admiral at the end of the 19th-century, this house offers a calm, relaxing stay and is ideal for discovering the Côte du Goëlo and the Côte du Granit Rose. Four spacious rooms include a room with a king-size and double bed, a triple and two double rooms (one with a lounge, one with a kitchen corner), each with private facilities. Enclosed grounds, garden with furniture and barbecue, and parking.

Prices s €39-€42; d €46-€49; t fr €69; extra person fr €20
Nearby ⚓ 8km ⬇ 25km Sea 0.2km ⚐ 4km ⚲ 1km Restaurant 0.2km
⬡ 1km Spa 35km ⬚ 0.2km ⩗ 0.1km **Notes** No pets English spoken

---

PENVENAN

⚡ La Marine

Gérard & Monique MENOU

6 rue de la Poste, 22710 PENVENAN

☎ 02 96 92 82 89 📠 02 96 92 82 89

email: gerard.menou22@laposte.net

A 19th-century residence close to walking trail GR 34. It offers two double rooms and two rooms with a double and single bed, each with private facilities. Living room with fireplace, small lounge and garden with furniture and barbecue.

Prices not confirmed for 2008 **Nearby** ⚓ 3km ⬇ 16km Sea 3km
⚐ 3km ⚲ 6km Water sports 3km ⬡ 0.1km ⬚ 0.1km ⩗ 18km
Notes No pets English spoken

⚡ Leur Min

Bernard & Maryvonne GUYOMAR

Leur Min No 19, 22710 PENVENAN

☎ 02 96 92 67 10 & 06 85 23 88 39

email: bernard.guyomar@wanadoo.fr

A large peaceful garden full of flowers surrounds the house. There are four guest rooms, three doubles and a twin, all of them upstairs. All have private facilities, but for two of the rooms, which are Grade 2, the WC is accessed via the landing. Garden with barbecue and garden furniture.

Prices not confirmed for 2008 **Nearby** ⚓ 4km ⬇ 20km Sea 1.5km
⚐ 1.5km ⚲ 7km Water sports 3km ⬡ 1km ⬚ 0.5km ⩗ 15km
Notes No pets

PERROS-GUIREC

⚡ *Chambre d'hôtes*

J.Noël & Gaby LE SOUDEER

16 rue de Feuten Léo, 22700 PERROS-GUIREC

☎ 02 96 91 28 74

Gaby and J-Noël's home lies between the port and the woods, a light, modern house with four guest rooms, all with shower and WC. On the ground floor, two doubles with sea views; on the first floor another two double rooms. Breakfast in dining room or on terrace. Living room with open fire, TV; conservatory, BBQ. 1.5 kilometres from Trestraou beach. Reductions in low season.

Prices not confirmed for 2008 **Nearby** ⚓ 10km ⬇ 10km Sea 0.2km
⚐ 0.2km ⚲ 10km Water sports 1km ⬡ 2km ⬚ 0.2km ⩗ 10km
Notes No pets English spoken

PLELO

⚡ 🐓 🍽 Le Char à Bancs

Famille LAMOUR

Moulin de la ville Geffroy, 22170 PLELO

☎ 02 96 74 13 63 📠 02 96 74 13 03

email: charabanc@wanadoo.fr

web: www.aucharabanc.com

Four rooms are available in this house, which is also a local museum. All rooms have wc and washbasin and one has a bath. Guest sitting room and meals available at the farm inn (500mtrs). Shetland pony rides for children accompanied by their parents, fishing and pedalos can be hired on the River Leff.

Prices s €59-€85; d €65-€90; t €90-€104; extra person fr €15;
dinner €15-€25 **On Site** ⚐ **Nearby** ⚓ 15km ⬇ 10km Sea 13km
⚲ 5km Restaurant 2km Water sports 13km ⬡ 5km ⬚ 2km ⩗ 2km
Notes No pets English spoken

PLEUDIHEN-SUR-RANCE

⚡ L'Hôpital

Xavier & Typhaine TARDIF

Les Kériaden's, 22690 PLEUDIHEN-SUR-RANCE

☎ 02 96 83 29 49

email: leskeriadens@hotmail.com

web: www.leskeriadens.com

A fully restored 18th-century house with a large garden and four guest bedrooms. On the first floor are two rooms for three (each with a double bed plus a single); on the second floor are two attic rooms, both doubles. All have private facilities. Barbecue, garden furniture, children's games. Good access to footpaths. Breakfasts include local specialities.

Prices s €48; d €48; t €65; extra person €15 **Nearby** ⚓ 5km ⬇ 14km
Sea 14km ⚐ 4km ⚲ 2km Water sports 6km ⬡ 2km ⬚ 1.7km ⩗ 12km
Notes Pets admitted English spoken

BRITTANY

PLEUDIHEN-SUR-RANCE *CONTINUED*

⁜⁜ La Maison de la Vallée

Françoise CHENU
Le Val Hervelin, 22690 PLEUDIHEN-SUR-RANCE
☎ 02 96 83 35 61 📄 02 96 83 38 43
email: chenu.francoise@hotmail.com
web: www.maisondelavallee.fr

A magnificent house in Mont-St-Michel Bay with lovely views. There are four bedrooms with private bathrooms (one of which is on the first floor). A family rooms is available on the second floor. Two living rooms with open fires are available, and breakfast is served on a veranda overlooking the water. TV in some rooms.

Prices d €72-€78; t €95-€115; extra person fr €15 **Nearby** ☝ 5km ⚓ 7km Sea 15km 🏌 6km ⤳ 9km Restaurant 3km Water sports 15km 🏊 3km 🎣 12km 🏛 3km ⩜ 9km **Notes** No pets

⁜⁜ *Le Val Hervelin*

Sylvie BRIGNON
22690 PLEUDIHEN-SUR-RANCE
☎ 02 96 88 20 99 & 06 18 43 96 86
email: hervelines@hotmail.com
web: www.leshervelines.com

Themed rooms are available at this charming establishment: La Campagnarde (triple en suite), la Bretonne (en suite double) and La Romantique is ideal for couples. Sitting room, garden; forest and Malouine coast nearby.

Prices not confirmed for 2008 **On Site** Private ⤳ **Nearby** ☝ 5km ⚓ 7km Sea 15km 🏌 1km Water sports 3km 🏊 3km 🏛 3km ⩜ 12km **Notes** Pets admitted English spoken

PLEUMEUR-GAUTIER

⁜⁜ Chambre d'hôtes

Loïc & Chantal RAOULT
6 rue de Pleubian, 22740 PLEUMEUR-GAUTIER
☎ 02 96 20 14 11
web: http://chambres-compadre.francevasion.net

An old longhouse, restored and converted to provide four guest bedrooms: two doubles on the ground floor and two triples upstairs (double bed and a single in each). All have private facilities. Not far from the Côte de Granit Rose, the Ile de Bréhat and the Sillon du Talbert, a remarkable seaside area with a 15-kilometre network of footpaths.

Prices s fr €40; d fr €45; extra person fr €15 **Nearby** ☝ 4km ⚓ 22km Sea 4km 🏌 4km ⤳ 6km Restaurant 4km Water sports 4km 🏊 6km Spa 30km 🏛 0.2km ⩜ 10km **Notes** No pets

PLEVEN

⁜ ⍥ La Rompardais

Michelle BLANCHARD
22130 PLEVEN
☎ 02 96 84 43 08 📄 02 96 84 41 86

A renovated 19th-century cottage with a double room, a room with a double and single bed (both en suite) and upstairs a double and a single room. Breakfast is served in the living room or on the veranda. Activities include mountain biking and fishing; farm d'Antan at Plédéliac and medieval castle nearby.

Prices s fr €37; d fr €44; t fr €54; extra person fr €10; dinner fr €18 **Nearby** ☝ 10km ⚓ 20km Sea 20km 🏌 1km ⤳ 17km Restaurant 5km Water sports 20km 🏊 1km 🏛 1km ⩜ 17km **Notes** Pets admitted English spoken

PLOEZAL

⁜⁜ Ferme de Kerléo

Roselyne & J. Louis HERVE
22260 PLOEZAL
☎ 02 96 95 65 78 & 06 31 27 16 33 📄 02 96 95 14 63
email: kerleo.herve@wanadoo.fr
web: www.kerleo.com

Four rooms here include two grade 3 en suite rooms (one with a double and single bed; the other a double) and two grade 1 double rooms sharing a bathroom. All rooms have private entry. Sitting room and garden. Gîte on the site. The Côte du Granit Rose, 15th-century castle of la Roche Jagu and steam train from Pontrieux to Paimpol nearby.

Prices s €34-€40; d €39-€46; extra person fr €14 **Nearby** ☝ 5km ⚓ 15km Sea 10km 🏌 5km ⤳ 15km Restaurant 3km Water sports 3km 🏊 3km Spa 20km 🏛 3km ⩜ 3km **Notes** No pets English spoken

PLOUBAZLANEC

⁜⁜ La Maison des Iles

Yveline LE ROUX
29, Route de la Vieille Côte, 22620 PLOUBAZLANEC
☎ 02 96 55 87 01 & 06 84 39 53 94
📄 02 96 55 87 01

This house with its lovely sea views out to the islands is the ideal spot for a reviving holiday. On the first floor are the 'Bretonne' with two double beds and shower/WC, and the 'Exotique', a double with bathroom and WC; on the second floor are two more doubles, the 'Marine Bleue' and the 'Marine Rouge', both with shower/WC. Shared living room, enclosed garden, private parking, conservatory and BBQ.

Prices s fr €66; d fr €72; t fr €94; extra person fr €22 **On Site** Sea Water sports **Nearby** ☝ 7km ⤳ 7km 🏊 2.5km 🏛 2.5km ⩜ 7km **Notes** Pets admitted English spoken CC

PLOUER-SUR-RANCE

♦♦♦ La Renardais - Le Repos

Jean & Suzanne ROBINSON
22490 PLOUER-SUR-RANCE
☎ 02 96 86 89 81 📠 02 96 86 99 22
email: suzanne.robinson@wanadoo.fr
web: http://perso.orange.fr/suzanne.robinson.bnb/

A warm welcome awaits at this elegant country house which offers two rooms with a double and single bed, a double and a twin room, all en suite. Extra bed available. Sitting room with open fireplace and breakfast in the flower garden. Nearby sites include Mont-St-Michel, Cap Fréhel, Dinard, and St Malo.

Prices s fr €80; d fr €80; t fr €100; extra person fr €20 **Nearby** ♿ 1km ♨ 15km Sea 15km 🏌 1km ⚓ 8km Water sports 8km 🚣 1km 🏠 1km 🚲 8km **Notes** No pets English spoken CC

PLOUEZEC

♦♦ *Hent Straou Glève*

M.Thérése PATRY
7 Hent Straou Glève, 22470 PLOUEZEC
☎ 02 96 55 44 20 & 06 24 88 36 18
email: contact@izel-vor.com
web: http://izel-vor.com

A peaceful spot, on the bay of Paimpol, with views towards the Ile de Bréhat. In a building adjacent to the owners' home there are three bedrooms: a double, a twin-bedded room, and a triple (three single beds), all with private bathroom and WC. Big garden, with garden furniture, terrace and parking space.

Prices not confirmed for 2008 **Nearby** ♿ 10km ♨ 8km Sea 3km 🏌 3km ⚓ 6km Water sports 3km 🚣 6km 🏠 1km 🚲 6km **Notes** No pets

PLOUGRESCANT

♦♦♦ Chambre d'hôtes

M.Claude JANVIER
15 rue du Castel Meur, 22820 PLOUGRESCANT
☎ 02 96 92 52 67 & 06 71 07 32 32 📠 02 96 92 52 67

A Breton house with three en suite rooms including a double with views of the sea, a double with extra bed and a twin, both with library. There is a fridge for guests, a sitting room, patio and parking. The airport is at Lannion.

Prices s fr €40; d €46-€52; t fr €62 **Nearby** ♿ 8km ♨ 25km Sea 1km 🏌 1km ⚓ 7km Restaurant 1km Water sports 1km 🚣 1km Spa 22km 🏠 1km 🚲 20km **Notes** No pets English spoken

♦♦♦ Le Tourot

Gilles LE BOURDONNEC
22820 PLOUGRESCANT
☎ 02 96 92 50 20 & 06 87 52 64 62
web: www.gitesdarmor.com/letourot/

This renovated cottage offers four very spacious en suite double rooms (one with private access) in an annexe. Large sitting room, dining room and kitchen. The farm enjoys a fine sea view and has a dovecote. Trips available on sailing boats and in kayaks; good walking country.

Prices s fr €36; d fr €43 **Nearby** ♿ 9km ♨ 22km Sea 0.2km 🏌 0.3km ⚓ 7km Restaurant 1.5km Water sports 0.2km 🚣 2km 🚲 7km 🏠 2km 🚲 23km **Notes** No pets English spoken

PLOUGUIEL

♦♦♦ 🍴 Kerlilou

Pascaline & Patrick CORTOPASSI
3 Calvary, 22220 PLOUGUIEL
☎ 02 96 92 24 06 & 06 17 84 31 08
email: kerlilou@free.fr
web: www.kerlilou.fr

This restored property has three bedrooms - a double-bedded room, one with twin beds, and one with two doubles. All of the rooms have private bath or shower rooms, and there is a cot available. Guests have use of a lounge, and outside there is garden furniture.

Prices s fr €50; d fr €60; t fr €75; dinner fr €20 **Nearby** ♿ 5km ♨ 25km Sea 5km 🏌 1km ⚓ 2km Restaurant 2km Water sports 5km 🚣 2km Spa 15km 🏠 0.5km 🚲 14km **Notes** No pets English spoken

♦♦♦ *La Roche Jaune*

Elisabeth CORBEL
Kéraret, 22220 PLOUGUIEL
☎ 02 96 92 57 65 📠 02 96 92 00 83
email: yves.corbel2@wanadoo.fr
web: www.ifrance.com/keraret

Elisabeth and Yves offer the comfort of their old farmhouse, which has, on the first floor, three double rooms and a triple, all en suite with shower and WC. On the second floor is a family suite of two rooms, shower and WC. Large living room, fully-equipped kitchen (fridge, microwave, dishwasher, gas cooker), reception room with library, laundry room. Special rates for weekends or stays of more than four nights. Small oyster port of la Roche Jaune nearby.

Prices not confirmed for 2008 **Nearby** ♿ 5km ♨ 30km Sea 4km 🏌 0.5km ⚓ 7km Water sports 4km 🚣 4km 🏠 2km 🚲 20km **Notes** Pets admitted CC

PLOUHA

☷ ও *Rungagal*

M.Andrée ROSE

Les Gîtes du Goëlo, 22580 PLOUHA

☎ 02 96 22 40 20 & 06 30 62 29 57 ▤ 02 96 20 23 46

email: contact@lesgitesdugoelo.com

web: www.lesgitesdugoelo.com

A comfortable stone-built property two kilometres from the sea. The three guest bedrooms and one family suite, all with separate entrance and TV, are in an annexe to the main building. On the ground floor, a double with a child's bed and a room with two double beds; upstairs another room with two doubles, and a family unit with kitchenette which can sleep four. All rooms have en suite bath or shower room and WC. Gourmet breakfasts. Wooded grounds with barbecue, meadows with ponies.

Prices not confirmed for 2008 **Nearby** ⇵ 0.8km ⌁ 8km Sea 2km ℘ 2km ⋏ 10km Water sports 5km ⌁ 2.5km 🏛 2km ₩ 25km **Notes** No pets English spoken CC

PLOULEC'H

☷ ⬚ **Chambre d'hôtes**

Nadia BEECKMANN

20 Rte de Kerhervrec, 22300 PLOULEC'H

☎ 02 96 46 42 33 & 06 78 69 55 67

email: nadia.beeckmann@wanadoo.fr

web: http://perso.wanadoo.fr/nadia.loc.vacances/

Quietly situated at the end of a no-through road, this renovated farm house offers three bedrooms, a double and two twins. They all have private shower rooms/WCs. There is a lounge with books to read, and a garden with furniture and a barbecue. Use of washing machine is possible.

Prices s €45-€48; d €48-€53; t fr €60; dinner fr €20 **Nearby** ⇵ 10km ⌁ 11km Sea 5km ⋏ 13km Restaurant 1km Water sports 7km ⌁ 4km Spa 8km 🏛 1km ₩ 2.5km **Notes** No pets English spoken

PLUMIEUX

☷ ❦ ⬚ **Le Breil Sablé**

A-Marie & Dominique GUILLAUME

22210 PLUMIEUX

☎ 02 96 26 77 16 & 06 68 77 15 73 ▤ 02 96 26 66 13

email: anne-marie@gitedubreil.com

web: www.gitedubreil.com

An annexe to this farmhouse offers three rooms, a double, a single and a triple room (one double bed and one single), two en suite and one with bathroom. Dining room, sitting room/kitchen with dining area, courtyard, garden, garden furniture and barbecue. Reduced rates for children. Walking on the banks of the Lié, 15th and 16th-century churches and the forests of Brocéliande, Loudéac, and Lanouée are nearby.

Prices s €33-€35; d €42-€44; t €56-€58; extra person €16-€18; dinner fr €18 **On Site** Private ⋏ **Nearby** ⇵ 15km ⌁ 5km ℘ 5km Restaurant 5km Water sports 40km ⌁ 5km ❦ 15km 🏛 5km ₩ 15km **Notes** No pets

PLURIEN

☷ ❦ **Guitrel**

Colette MORIN

22240 PLURIEN

☎ 02 96 72 35 37

email: guitrel@wanadoo.fr

web: www.guitrel.com

A completely renovated house with flower garden, south facing terrace and five guest rooms, all with private shower and wc. A family unit on the ground floor sleeps four, and has disabled access. Upstairs are two double rooms and two twin rooms. Breakfast is served in a rustic room. Close to the sea, between the cliffs at Cap Fréhel and the beaches at les Sables d'Or Les Pins.

Prices s fr €40; d fr €45; t fr €55 **Nearby** ⇵ 2.5km ⌁ 1.5km Sea 1.5km ℘ 2km ⋏ 15km Restaurant 1.5km Water sports 1.5km ⌁ 0.6km Spa 30km 🏛 0.6km ₩ 20km **Notes** No pets

& *Les Sables*

M.Christine MEHOUAS-HOUZE
16/18 chemin de la Nonne, 22240 PLURIEN
☎ 02 96 72 11 12 & 06 08 94 26 26 📱 02 96 72 11 12
email: mcmehouas@netcourrier.com
web: www.les-sables-erquy.com

Marie-Christine welcomes you to the four comfortable, en suite rooms in the annexe of her home. One double room has a single bed, an independent entrance and a view of the sea. There are three more double rooms: two with king size beds and one with an extra single. In the house there is a two-room family suite and en suite facilities.

Prices not confirmed for 2008 **Nearby** ⛳ 0.8km ♨ 1km Sea 0.8km
♦ 2km 🏕 15km Water sports 0.8km 🌲 1km 🏛 0.8km ⚓ 20km
Notes No pets

POMMERIT-LE-VICOMTE

🍴 *Manoir Le Cosquer*

A SINCLAIR et M LECCACORVI
22200 POMMERIT-LE-VICOMTE
☎ 02 96 21 74 12 & 06 99 38 43 04
email: lecosquer@tiscali.fr
web: www.lecosquer.com

These three bright rooms are on the first floor of a wing of a restored manor house. There are two double rooms, and a twin-bedded room, all with private facilities. There is a well-equipped fitness room, badminton, table tennis, table football, darts, croquet, an above-ground swimming pool, walking and fishing. Meals available by arrangement.

Prices s fr €57; d €75-€95; t fr €110; extra person fr €15; dinner fr €27 **On Site** 💧 Private 🏕 **Nearby** ⛳ 5km ♨ 12km Sea 15km Restaurant 3km Water sports 15km 🌲 0.3km 🏛 0.3km ⚓ 10km
Notes No pets English spoken

PONTRIEUX

🍴 *Les Korrigannes*

Frédérique FORNER
10 Rue des Fontaines, 22260 PONTRIEUX
☎ 02 96 95 12 46 & 06 08 01 17 82
email: korrigannesgaby@wanadoo.fr
web: http://monsite.orange.fr/korrigannes

A typical bourgeois house owned by artists and restored using old and natural materials. Five rooms, all with shower room and WC; one room has an en suite reception room. Studio, exhibition gallery and tea room are on site. Conservatory, library, lounge with open fire and hi-fi. Walled garden, stream, wash-house. Ideal departure point for excursions by foot, on horseback, by boat or kayak.

Prices s €62-€87; d €72-€97; extra person fr €18; dinner fr €25
On Site Water sports **Nearby** ⛳ 4km ♨ 15km Sea 15km ♦ 0.1km
🏕 15km Restaurant 0.1km 🌲 0.1km 🏵 0.1km 🏛 0.1km ⚓ 0.5km
Notes No pets English spoken Open 15 March to 8 January.

PORDIC

💚 & **Chambres d'hôtes**

Henriette TREHEN
St Halory, 22590 PORDIC
☎ 02 96 79 41 11 & 06 88 28 29 15 📱 02 96 79 41 11

A renovated cottage beside the owner's home on a dairy farm. There is a double room, a twin room and a family unit with two rooms sleeping four people, all with private bathrooms. Sitting room, dining room, small kitchen, terrace, lawn, garden furniture, yard and barbecue. Activities include trail walking, mountain bike circuits, a velodrome (1km), beaches, the sailing school (2km) and canoeing.

Prices s fr €38; d fr €42; t fr €62; extra person fr €15 **Nearby** ⛳ 5km
♨ 6km Sea 2.5km ♦ 2.5km 🏕 6km Restaurant 1km Water sports 2.5km
🌲 1km 🏵 4km 🏛 1km ⚓ 7km **Notes** No pets English spoken

Manoir de la Ville Evêque

Isabelle & J-Yves LE FEVRE
Keryos, 56 rue de la Ville Evêque, 22590 PORDIC
☎ 02 96 79 17 32 & 06 87 71 76 38
email: keryos@wanadoo.fr
web: www.keryos.com

Isabelle and J-Yves offer four rooms furnished with antiques in their manor house by the sea. On the first floor with bathroom and WC are 'Neptune', a twin, and 'Egypt', a grade 4 suite (extra bed available). On the second floor with shower and WC are 'Licorne', and 'Phoenix', both doubles. Reading room, conservatory. Extensive grounds with direct private access to the sea. English, Italian, Spanish spoken.

Prices s €65-€95; d €70-€100; extra person fr €20 **Nearby** ⛳ 5km
♨ 10km Sea 0.5km ♦ 0.5km 🏕 3km Restaurant 2km Water sports 2km
🌲 2km 🏛 2km ⚓ 10km **Notes** No pets English spoken Open 15 March to 15 November.

QUEVERT

🍴 **Argenteil - la Borgnais**

Stéphane LESAGE
22100 QUEVERT
☎ 02 96 85 46 59
email: argenteil@free.fr
web: http://argenteil.free.fr

On the outskirts of Dinan, this unusual country property has three family units (Retro, Anglais and Safari) each for four people with marble bathrooms, a double and two single beds. Guests may prepare their own meals, or enjoy home-cooked meals in the Art Deco dining room. The tree-lined grounds run alongside the River Argenteil and have a swimming pool, games, fishing and walking. Washing machine and internet access. Reduced rates for children.

Prices s €45-€65; d €48-€68; t €62-€82; dinner fr €20
On Site Private 🏕 **Nearby** ⛳ 0.8km ♨ 20km Sea 17km
Restaurant 3km Water sports 3km 🌲 1km Spa 20km 🏛 3km ⚓ 3km
Notes Pets admitted English spoken

BRITTANY

147

QUINTIN

▦ La Pommeraie

M-Pierre LE LOUET

Le Foeil, 22800 QUINTIN

☎ 02 96 74 80 09 📄 02 96 74 80 09

This property is not far from Quintin, which often describes itself as 'a little city of character'. There are three bedrooms: a double on the ground floor, and another upstairs, where there is also a two-roomed family suite for three. Each room has a private bath or shower room and WC. Garden with furniture.

Prices d fr €40; t fr €55 **Nearby** ♿ 10km ♨ 20km Sea 25km 🏌 3km ⚓ 3km Restaurant 3km Water sports 25km ♨ 3km Spa 30km 🏛 3km ⚒ 3km **Notes** No pets

▦▦ ◉ Le Clos du Prince

M. Madeleine GUILMOTO

10 rue des Crois Jarrots, 22800 QUINTIN

☎ 02 96 74 93 03 📄 02 96 74 93 03

email: info@leclosduprince.com

web: www.leclosduprince.com

An 18th-century house with antique furniture, exquisite decorations and four guest bedrooms - three doubles and a suite for four. All have private bath or shower room and WC. Grounds with mature trees, including a superb redwood. Meals are available outside the main tourist season.

Prices s fr €60; d €75-€85; t fr €98; extra person fr €23; dinner fr €20 **Nearby** ♿ 8km ♨ 25km Sea 15km 🏌 0.5km ⚓ 0.3km Restaurant 0.2km Water sports 15km ♨ 0.1km 🏛 0.3km ⚒ 15km **Notes** No pets

SQUIFFIEC

▦ ◉ Manoir de Kercadic

Karen & Stéphen GEIPEL

22200 SQUIFFIEC

☎ 02 96 43 26 69 📄 02 96 43 26 69

email: s.geipel@wanadoo.fr

web: www.kercadic.com

This old 19th-century farmhouse is in a peaceful spot not far from Trieux. It has five spacious bedrooms, four of them split-level, all with independent access and private bath or shower rooms. A cot is available. There is a lounge area with table tennis, table football, books and a bar.

Prices s €30-€42; d €56-€84; t €74-€110; extra person €18; dinner fr €22 **Nearby** ♿ 16km ♨ 13km Sea 25km 🏌 0.5km ⚓ 11km Water sports 25km ♨ 7km Spa 25km 🎿 11km 🏛 7km ⚒ 10km **Notes** Pets admitted English spoken Open 15 March to 15 November. CC

ST-ALBAN

▦ 🌥 Malido

Huguette LE GRAND

22400 ST-ALBAN

☎ 02 96 32 94 74 📄 02 96 32 92 67

email: legrand.malido@wanadoo.fr

web: www.malido.com

This accommodation is in an annexe of the owner's farmhouse and comprises five grade 3 rooms and a grade 2 room, four with private access. There are two double rooms, two triples and a family unit with two rooms, one with balcony. Sitting room with open fireplace, well-equipped kitchen and baby-sitting service. Play area and leisure park, sandy beaches and a walking trail nearby.

Prices s fr €37; d €37-€55; t €55-€61; extra person €18-€17 **Nearby** ♿ 4km ♨ 4km Sea 4km 🏌 10km ⚓ 4km Restaurant 2km Water sports 4km ♨ 4km Spa 20km 🏛 2km ⚒ 10km **Notes** No pets English spoken

ST-CARADEC

▦ 🌥 ◉ Goizel

Loïc LE MAITRE

22600 ST-CARADEC

☎ 02 96 25 05 30 & 06 20 15 68 12 📄 02 96 25 05 30

email: loic.le-maitre@wanadoo.fr

Set on the edge of La Rigole de l'Hilvern, this pretty cottage on a farm has two double rooms, a twin room and a triple room with a double and a single bed, all with private facilities. Meals using local produce are served in a family environment. In summer, guests can ride in a carriage to the market at Loudéac farm.

Prices s €35; d €40; t €54; dinner fr €20 **Nearby** ♿ 9km ♨ 10km Sea 40km 🏌 1.5km ⚓ 9km Restaurant 45km Water sports 10km ♨ 1.5km Spa 9km 🏛 1.5km ⚒ 9km **Notes** No pets English spoken

ST-DONAN

▦ 🌥 ◉ ♿ La Ville Suzanne

Michel CORBEL

Le Cheval et le Paysan, 22800 ST-DONAN

☎ 02 96 73 95 03 & 06 70 48 16 14 📄 02 96 73 86 41

email: corbelm@wanadoo.fr

web: www.vacancesenbretagne.com

A renovated farm cottage, offering two double en suite guest rooms on the first floor, with cooking alcove. In an outbuilding with independent access, a two unit bedroom with kitchen corner, and an en suite double room on the ground floor, sitting room with open fireplace, and a twin room with bathroom upstairs. Small communal kitchen, garden, barbecue and meals with local produce. Horses may be stabled here.

Prices s fr €40; d €40-€49; t fr €66; extra person fr €15; dinner fr €23
Nearby ⚓ 10km ♨ 25km Sea 12km ♪ 2km ⚘ 10km Water sports 2km
🛒 3km 🏛 3km ⛵ 10km **Notes** No pets CC

ST-LORMEL

††† ⭕ La Pastourelle

Evelyne LEDE
22130 ST-LORMEL

☎ 02 96 84 03 77 & 06 87 57 78 92 📄 02 96 84 03 77
email: la-pastourelle-stlormel@wanadoo.fr
web: www.gitesdarmor.com/la-pastourelle

A lovely cottage with outdoor sitting area, lawn and games. It offers
five double rooms and a family unit with two rooms and bathroom. The
cottage is well presented with fine porcelain and beautiful
furniture, and with stone walls in the sitting and dining rooms. Only a
few kilometres from the beaches of the emerald coast with Cap
Fréhel, Fort-La-Latte, St Malo, and Dinan.

Prices s fr €45; d fr €47; t fr €62; dinner fr €18 **Nearby** ⚓ 10km
♨ 10km Sea 10km ♪ 1km ⚘ 10km Restaurant 3km Water sports 10km
🛒 2km Spa 25km 🏛 1.5km ⛵ 4km **Notes** No pets English spoken
Open Easter to 15 November.

ST-POTAN

††† *Ferme de Bonne Vie*

Denise RENOUARD
22550 ST-POTAN

☎ 02 96 41 02 91 & 06 83 16 99 45
email: ferme.bonne.vie@wanadoo.fr

By the sea and with much charm, this family property has a double
room, and two rooms with a double and single bed. Breakfast is
served with produce from the dairy farm and picnics in the large
garden and organised walks can be arranged. Meals are served on
Monday, Wednesday, Friday or Saturday.

Prices not confirmed for 2008 **Nearby** ⚓ 4km ♨ 4km Sea 4km ♪ 3km
⚘ 4km Water sports 4km 🛒 4km 🏛 4km ⛵ 25km **Notes** No pets

††† 🌱 ⭕ Les Bérouelleucs

Henri & Danielle BINET
22550 ST-POTAN

☎ 02 96 83 72 92 & 06 87 57 46 93

Danielle and Henri will welcome you to their simple Breton-style
house. Upstairs is a double with bathroom and WC; a double with
shower room and WC; and a two-room suite with two double beds,
shower and WC.Living room and salon with open fire. Meals using
farm produce by arrangement (not Sundays or public holidays),
served on the veranda. Courtyard, lawn, children's games.

Prices s €34-€35; d €40-€42; t €58-€60; extra person €18-€20;
dinner fr €16 **Nearby** ⚓ 6km ♨ 10km Sea 10km ♪ 10km ⚘ 10km
Restaurant 1.5km Water sports 10km 🛒 10km Spa 35km 🏛 1.5km
⛵ 20km **Notes** No pets

ST-SAMSON-SUR-RANCE

††† Le Petit Châtelier

Pierrette PAPAIL
22100 ST-SAMSON-SUR-RANCE

☎ 02 96 39 47 89 & 06 66 10 86 62
email: pierrette@lepetitchatelier.com
web: http://lepetitchatelier.com

The guest accommodation here is in a separate wing of a restored
farmhouse. There are four bedrooms, all upstairs: a double, another
double with an additional folding bed, and two split-level family rooms
for four, each with a double bed and two singles. All have private
facilities. Wooded grounds with garden furniture and children's games.

Prices s €45-€50; d €50-€65; t €80-€85 **Nearby** ⚓ 5km ♨ 10km
Sea 20km ♪ 1km ⚘ 8km Restaurant 1km Water sports 4km 🛒 4km
Spa 25km 🏛 1.5km ⛵ 7km **Notes** No pets English spoken

TONQUEDEC

†††† Le Queffiou

Alain & Chantal REGRAIN
Route du Château, 22140 TONQUEDEC

☎ 02 96 35 84 50 & 06 68 09 89 97
📄 02 96 35 84 50
web: http://lequeffiou.free.fr

A large early 20th-century bourgeois house built from the
local granite. The five very comfortable first-floor rooms offer
combinations of grade 3 or grade 4 doubles and twins, two
with bathroom/WC and three with shower/WC. Living room and
conservatory; large grounds and parking. River fishing (trout,
salmon) and walks nearby.

Prices s fr €88; d fr €88; t fr €123 **Nearby** ⚓ 1km ♨ 16km
Sea 18km ♪ 0.8km ⚘ 10km Restaurant 7km Water sports 18km
🛒 2km 🏛 0.5km ⛵ 10km **Notes** No pets

TREGUIER

††† Tara

Guy & Malou ARHANT
31 rue Ernest Renan, 22220 TREGUIER

☎ 02 96 92 15 28
web: www.paysdetreguier.com/tara.htm

This 16th-century house is in the capital of Trégor and has five en
suite rooms: four doubles can have an additional bed, and the triple
has disabled access. Breakfast is at the communal table in the period
dining room and there is a small kitchen, dining area and parking in
the garden.

Prices s fr €48; d fr €58; t fr €75; extra person fr €17 **Nearby** ⚓ 2km
♨ 20km Sea 1km ⚘ 1km Restaurant 0.3km Water sports 4km 🛒 1km
Spa 17km 🏛 0.1km ⛵ 18km **Notes** No pets English spoken Open
November to September. CC

TRELEVERN

₩ La Ferme de l'Etang

Christian LEROY

Le Launay, 22660 TRELEVERN

☎ 02 96 91 70 44   📄 02 96 91 79 96

A 19th-century cottage on a large property with a pond. There are three rooms with a double and single bed, and a twin room, all en suite. Babies are welcome. Breakfast may be served in the dining room or garden and there is garden furniture and table tennis. Visit the Côte de Granit Rose, the reserve of the seven islands and Bréhat on the GR34.

Prices s fr €40; d fr €55; t fr €70; extra person fr €15 **Nearby** ☘ 14km ⚓ 20km Sea 3.5km ✐ 3.5km ↘ 14km Restaurant 6.5km Water sports 3.5km 🏊 3km Spa 6km 🏛 3km 🚣 8km **Notes** No pets Open Easter to October.

TREMEREUC

₩ *La Ville Patouard*

Gérard DELEPINE

25 la Ville Patouard, 22490 TREMEREUC

☎ 02 96 27 88 29

email: delepinegerard@caramail.com

web: http://gwenael.delepine.free.fr

Three rooms are available in this detached property with a shady garden: oneo double and two (grade 1) triples with a double and single bed, all with private bathroom. Guests have use of the kitchen, sitting room, barbecue and parking. Local activities include volleyball, football, basketball, golf, horse riding, mountain biking and walking. Countryside and sea nearby with the Vallée du Frémur and de la Rance taking you to Dinan.

Prices not confirmed for 2008 **Nearby** ☘ 2km ⚓ 0.5km Sea 8km ✐ 2km ↘ 7km Water sports 8km 🏊 0.1km 🏛 1km 🚣 13km **Notes** No pets English spoken

TRESSAINT-LANVALLAY

₩ 🐾 🍽 La Ville Ameline

Huguette/Yvon LEMARCHAND

22100 TRESSAINT-LANVALLAY

☎ 02 96 39 33 69 & 06 22 63 48 33

email: lemarchand.huguette@free.fr

web: www.lavilleameline.com

A farm near the magnificent Vallée de la Ronce and close to the emerald coast and the town of Dinan. Accommodation is in three family units with two rooms for four people each, and one additional double room, all with private bathrooms. There is a dining room, large park with trees, a vast lawn, garden furniture, play area and bowls.

Prices s fr €40; d €45-€48; t €60-€63; extra person fr €11; dinner fr €19 **Nearby** ☘ 6km ⚓ 15km Sea 25km ✐ 2km ↘ 3km Restaurant 2km Water sports 25km 🏊 2km Spa 25km 🏛 2km 🚣 4km **Notes** No pets

TREVE

₩ 🍽 ♿ Le Bois d'en Haut

Paulette DONNIO

22600 TREVE

☎ 02 96 25 44 53 & 06 64 47 02 25   📄 02 96 25 44 53

email: paulette.donnio@caramail.com

This renovated house on a horse-breeding farm has four rooms with a small kitchen and separate entrance; all with private facilities and sitting room. Two are double rooms (one grade 2) and the other two are doubles with a mezzanine so can sleep three. Set in grounds of one hectare, the garden offers a barbecue, sitting area and games.

Prices s fr €35; d €42-€46; t €55-€60; extra person fr €15; dinner fr €15 **Nearby** ☘ 4km ⚓ 20km Sea 35km ✐ 4km ↘ 4km Restaurant 2km Water sports 20km 🏊 4km 🎾 4km 🏛 2km 🚣 0.5km **Notes** No pets English spoken

UZEL

₩ 🐾 🍽 Bizoin

M.Annick CADORET

22460 UZEL

☎ 02 96 28 81 24 & 06 21 35 69 30   📄 02 96 26 28 42

email: bizoin22@aol.com

The accommodation on this charming farm is in two grade 2 rooms (double room; room with double and single bed) and two grade 3 rooms (double room; room with double and single bed), all en suite. Dining room, kitchen, courtyard, terrace and garden furniture. Evening meals are served. Pony club 7km. Local sites: Lac du Bosméléac and Quintin.

Prices s €35-€38; d €36-€40; t €48-€52; dinner fr €15 **Nearby** ☘ 12km ⚓ 40km Sea 30km ✐ 0.1km ↘ 15km Restaurant 5km Water sports 12km 🏊 3km 🎾 12km 🏛 3km 🚣 3km **Notes** Pets admitted English spoken

YFFINIAC

₩ *Chambre d'hôtes*

Régine BERTHO

13, Le Val Josselin, 22120 YFFINIAC

☎ 02 96 72 62 63

email: regine.bertho@wanadoo.fr

web: www.le-val-josselin.c.la

This property, with all its flowers, is between the sea and the country. All the bedrooms are upstairs, and all have private facilities. There is a room for four (double plus twins) with a lounge area; a two-roomed family suite with two doubles and a single; a double room. Generous and varied breakfasts; barbecue, places for picnics.

Prices not confirmed for 2008 **Nearby** ☘ 1km ⚓ 6km Sea 1.5km ✐ 1km ↘ 6km Water sports 6km 🏊 1km 🏛 0.5km 🚣 7km **Notes** No pets English spoken

♯♯♯ Domaine du Grenier

M.Reine LOQUIN
route de Plédran, 22120 YFFINIAC
☎ 02 96 72 64 55 & 06 62 16 84 71
email: accueil@domainedugrenier.fr
web: www.domainedugrenier.fr

A large house on a farm offering a family unit, double room and a room for three people with cooking area; all have private facilities. Sitting room, dining room, barbecue and garden with children's play area and bikes. The house is half way between Cap Fréhel and la Côte de Granit Rose.

Prices d €41-€44 **Nearby** ♿ 0.2km ⚓ 10km Sea 8km 🎣 3.5km
⤢ 8km Water sports 10km ⚓ 3.5km 🏛 3km ⛪ 8km **Notes** No pets

♯♯♯ *La Fontaine Ménard*

François & Josiane PENNORS
22120 YFFINIAC
☎ 02 96 72 66 68 & 06 31 62 67 31 📠 02 96 72 66 63
email: fpennors@infonie.fr
web: www.gitesdarmor.com/la-fontaine-menard/

An annexe of an old restored stone manor offering accommodation including a large room with a double and two single beds, a room with a double and single and two doubles, all with private facilities. Kitchen, sitting room, washing machine, terrace with barbecue and courtyard. Special rate for four people. Animals are welcome by prior arrangement. Walking trails 2km, hippodrome 800mtrs, and ice rink 4km.

Prices not confirmed for 2008 **Nearby** ♿ 0.8km ⚓ 8km Sea 6km
🎣 1km ⤢ 6km Water sports 6km ⚓ 6km 🏛 3km ⛪ 8km
Notes English spoken

♯♯♯ ☙ *Les Villes Hervé*

Elisabeth JOUAN
22120 YFFINIAC
☎ 02 96 72 50 31 📠 02 96 72 50 31

Between Cap Fréhel and Perros Guirec, in an ideal walking area, there are two grade 3 rooms (a double and twin) with private bathroom and a grade 2 twin room with hand basin, bath and separate wc. Breakfast includes farm produce and there is a large garden with terrace, furniture and barbecue. Fishing on the river only 500m from the farm.

Prices not confirmed for 2008 **Nearby** ♿ 0.5km ⚓ 10km Sea 8km
🎣 0.5km ⤢ 8km Water sports 15km ⚓ 2km 🏛 2km ⛪ 5km
Notes No pets

FINISTÉRE

ARGOL

♯♯♯ *La Ferme Hizou*

Nicole BLONDEAU
Trovéoc, 29560 ARGOL
☎ 02 98 27 74 49
email: accueil.blondeau@tiscali.fr
web: www.la-ferme-hizou.fr.fm/

This restored house, not far from the sea, successfully combines ancient and modern. There are three guest rooms: a ground floor double, with dressing room and space for an extra bed, and a double room and a family suite upstairs. All rooms have private bath or shower room and WC. Mezzanine with sitting area. Generous breakfasts, garden with furniture.

Prices not confirmed for 2008 **Nearby** ♿ 9km ⚓ 30km Sea 0.9km
🎣 0.9km ⤢ 12km Water sports 8km ⚓ 5km ⛪ 12km 🏛 3km ⛪ 12km
Notes No pets English spoken Open April to 15 November

ARZANO

♯♯♯♯ Nivinen

Catherine SEZNEC
29300 ARZANO
☎ 02 98 71 77 09 & 06 08 88 14 55
email: seznecdedecat@aol.com
web: www.nivinen.com

In south Finistère, on the edge of Morbihan, this is a longhouse adjacent to the owners' home, with five very comfortable bedrooms. Two are doubles, two are twins, and there is a room for three (double bed and a single). En suite facilities (bath or shower) to all the rooms, which also have TV and individual entrance. Swimming pool.

Prices s fr €60; d fr €75; extra person fr €20 **On Site** Private ⤢
Nearby ♿ 2.5km ⚓ 15km Sea 18km 🎣 1km Restaurant 6km
Water sports 18km ⚓ 2.5km ⛪ 9km 🏛 0.7km ⛪ 10km
Notes No pets English spoken

BANNALEC

♯♯♯ ☙ *Sainte-Anne*

Nicole & Jean René CHRISTIEN
29380 BANNALEC
☎ 02 98 39 53 44 & 06 85 20 56 25 📠 02 98 39 53 44
email: jr.christien@wanadoo.fr
web: http://perso.wanadoo.fr/christien/

Charming, tranquil house at the gateway to Cornouaille, close to Pont-Aven, Quimperlé, Quimper and Concarneau. A family farm in relaxing, verdant countryside, offering a double room, a twin and a room with a double and single bed, all comfortable with private facilities. Lounge with fireplace and TV, washing machine, high chair, kitchen available on request. Garden with furniture. Country walking footpaths nearby.

Prices not confirmed for 2008 **Nearby** ⚓ 30km Sea 22km 🎣 5km
⤢ 15km Water sports 22km ⚓ 1km ⛪ 3km 🏛 2.5km ⛪ 15km
Notes No pets English spoken

BRITTANY

BRASPARTS

⚐ ⊙ *Domaine de Rugornou Vras*

Romy CHAUSSY

29190 BRASPARTS

☎ 02 98 81 46 27 & 06 82 91 37 36 ▤ 02 98 81 47 14

email: romy.chaussy@wanadoo.fr

Between mountains and sea, in a verdant setting overlooking the town of Brasparts, this stone longbarn has four pretty bedrooms: three doubles and a twin, each with independent access, shower room and wc. Fireplace, TV, lounge, gazebo, garden with furniture and terrace. Evening meals available by reservation. Walking footpaths from the house; close to the Parc Naturel Régional d'Armorique.

Prices not confirmed for 2008 **Nearby** ⛳ 0.5km ⚓ 40km Sea 35km
⚐ 2km ⚲ 15km Water sports 15km ⚘ 2km ⚑ 0.5km ⚒ 2km ⚕ 15km
Notes No pets English spoken

BRIGNOGAN-PLAGE

⚐ ⊙ **La Terre du Pont**

Odile BERTHOULE

29890 BRIGNOGAN-PLAGE

☎ 02 98 83 58 49 & 06 32 26 85 56

email: accueil@terredupont.com

web: www.terredupont.com

An 18th-century thatched cottage with four rooms, an en suite double on the ground floor and en suite twin and double upstairs (one also has a shower). There is also a room with a double and a single bed. Both the large dining room, where you can reserve dinner, and the lounge, have fireplaces. No smoking. Reduced prices out of season.

Prices s €55-€85; d €65-€95; extra person fr €25; dinner fr €25 **On Site** Private ⚲ **Nearby** ⛳ 5km ⚓ 5km Sea 0.1km
⚐ 0.1km Water sports 0.5km ⚘ 3km ⚑ 1km ⚒ 1.5km ⚕ 20km
Notes No pets English spoken Open 15 March to 15 November.

CAST

⚐ ⊙ *Kernir*

Madeleine & Pierre PHILIPPE

29150 CAST

☎ 02 98 73 54 31 & 06 70 18 70 19 ▤ 02 98 73 61 07

email: contact@kernir.com

web: www.kernir.com

Near the bay of Douarnenez and Locronan, this comfortable, tastefully restored longbarn is on a livestock farm. There is a twin room in the main house, and an annexe houses two twin rooms and two doubles with a single bed on a mezzanine level, each with private facilities. Typical Breton reception room and fireplace, TV in the two sitting rooms, garden with terrace area and evening meals served by reservation.

Prices not confirmed for 2008 **Nearby** ⛳ 5km ⚓ 35km Sea 7km
⚐ 7km ⚲ 9km Water sports 7km ⚘ 3km ⚑ 3km ⚕ 9km
Notes No pets English spoken

CLEDER

⚐ **Manoir de Kerliviry**

Christine PONTHIEUX

29233 CLEDER

☎ 02 98 61 99 37 & 06 23 50 27 08 ▤ 02 98 61 99 37

email: kerliviry@wanadoo.fr

web: www.kerliviry.com

In the two hectares of park of this renovated 18th-century manor, donkeys and goats graze peacefully by the lake. On the ground floor is a family room for four with bathroom and wc; separate entry. Upstairs are two double rooms with bath and wc. Spare bed and cot available. Lavish Breton style breakfasts are served in a dining room with open fire. Garden, games equipment, barbecue, parking. Close to the sea, with several castles within the parish boundary.

Prices d €60-€80; extra person €18-€26 **Nearby** ⛳ 4km ⚓ 25km
Sea 4km ⚐ 0.5km ⚲ 17km Water sports 4km ⚘ 3km ⚑ 3km ⚒ 3km
⚕ 20km **Notes** No pets English spoken

CLOHARS-CARNOET

⚐ ♥ **Au Vieux Moulin**

Thierry et Anne LYMES

Kerguilan, 29360 CLOHARS CARNOET

☎ 02 98 39 92 61 & 06 25 04 60 14

email: auvieuxmoulin@free.fr

web: http://auvieuxmoulin.free.fr

Between the sea and the forest, Anne and Thierry invite you to their farm, renovated with traditional materials, offering three en suite independent rooms. On the ground floor is a room for three, suitable for persons with mobility difficulties; upstairs are a double and a twin. Spare bed available. Walking in pastures and forests or coastal paths and beaches, or just … relax.

Prices d fr €52; t fr €67; extra person fr €15 **Nearby** ⛳ 2km ⚓ 15km
Sea 1.5km ⚐ 1.5km ⚲ 10km Restaurant 1km Water sports 2km
⚘ 1.5km ⚑ 2km ⚒ 2km ⚕ 12km **Notes** No pets English spoken
Open March to November and school holidays.

⚐ ⊙ *Kergastel*

Dominique PHILIBOT

29360 CLOHARS CARNOET

☎ 02 98 71 48 99 & 06 75 71 25 72 ▤ 02 98 71 62 87

email: dominique.philibot@free.fr

South facing, in grounds of 2.5 hectares, this restored property has three bedrooms. Two are in the owners' house - a double room, and a twin-bedded room. The third is a two-roomed suite, in a small separate building: a twin-bedded room downstairs and a double upstairs. All have private facilities. Baby equipment available. Lounge with wood-fired stove, TV, children's games. Garden with terrace and furniture.

Prices not confirmed for 2008 **Nearby** ⛳ 8km ⚓ 8km Sea 4km
⚐ 4km ⚲ 10km Water sports 4km ⚘ 4km ⚑ 4km ⚒ 4km ⚕ 10km
Notes No pets

₩Ⅲ iOi **Kergreven**

Dominique LE STUNFF
29360 CLOHARS CARNOET
☎ 02 98 71 64 06 & 06 18 16 89 34
email: dominique.le-stunff@wanadoo.fr
web: http://chambresdhotes-kergreven.net/

A smallholding in a wooded valley not far from the sea, with four bedrooms. All are upstairs: two doubles, a twin-bedded room, and a room for three (double bed and a single). Each has a private shower and WC. There is a lounge, and meals are available by arrangement.

Prices d fr €51; t fr €66; extra person fr €15; dinner fr €20
Nearby ⚓ 1km ♨ 15km Sea 3km ♟ 3km ⚘ 12km Water sports 3km
♨ 5km ♜ 3km ⌂ 2km ⋙ 12km **Notes** Pets admitted English spoken

---

COMBRIT-SAINTE-MARINE

₩Ⅲ *Le Stang*

Betty & Michel FOLCHER
Les fermes de Betty, 29120 COMBRIT
☎ 02 98 51 99 14
email: b-m.folcher@wanadoo.fr

In the heart of the countryside, on the edge of the forest - this old farmhouse has been transformed to offer quality accommodation in its four themed bedrooms, each with private outdoor space. There are two doubles and a twin-bedded room on the ground floor; upstairs is a family room for five. All have private facilities. Garden with terraces and furniture, bike hire.

Prices not confirmed for 2008 **On Site** ♜ **Nearby** ⚓ 2km ♨ 10km
Sea 3km ♟ 3km ⚘ 5km Water sports 3km ♨ 5km ⌂ 0.3km ⋙ 20km
Notes No pets

CONCARNEAU

₩Ⅲ iOi *La Boissière-L'Orée de l'Océan*

Joëlle & Michel LE BRIGAND
Croastalhouroum, 29900 CONCARNEAU
☎ 02 98 97 12 47 & 06 61 24 32 79 📄 02 98 97 12 47
email: joelleetmichel.le-brigand@wanadoo.fr
web: www.gites-finistere.com/gites/laboissiere/

Close to Concarneau, this beautifully converted longhouse was built in 1881. It has three spacious bedrooms: a double on the ground floor, fully accessible for disabled guests, and a double and a triple upstairs. All have private shower room and WC. Meals are available by arrangement, also packed lunches for days out.

Prices not confirmed for 2008 **Nearby** ⚓ 5km ♨ 6km Sea 6km
♟ 6km ⚘ 8km Water sports 6km ♨ 8km ♜ 6km ⌂ 4km ⋙ 10km
Notes No pets

DINEAULT

₩Ⅲ **Rolzac'h**

André & Anne-Marie L'HARIDON
29150 DINEAULT
☎ 02 98 86 22 09 📄 02 98 86 22 09
email: evolakarem@orange.fr

Rooms available in a flower-filled, restful spot on a small restored farm in the Aulne Valley. They include 'Anais' (double), 'Elise' (double) and 'Iris' has a double bed and private lounge room with fridge. Cot on request. Use of kitchen, private gardens with furniture and barbecue area.

Prices s fr €44; d fr €48 **Nearby** ⚓ 3km ♨ 30km Sea 12km ♟ 3km
⚘ 3km Restaurant 3km Water sports 12km ♨ 3km ♜ 3km ⌂ 3km
⋙ 2km **Notes** No pets English spoken

DOUARNENEZ

₩Ⅲ **Manoir de Kervent**

Marie-Paule LEFLOCH
29100 DOUARNENEZ
☎ 02 98 92 04 90 📄 02 98 92 04 90
email: mariepaule.lefloch@free.fr
web: www.gites-finistere.com/gites/kervent/
50460/indexgb.php

This manor house is near the Douarnenez exit and lies in countryside in a flower-filled park on an arable farm. Two double rooms (one with extra single), and a family room with a double and twin beds are offered, all with shower room, wc and cot on request. Breakfast of Breton specialities are served in the light and spacious dining room. Table tennis, croquet and many footpaths on the property; guidebooks on the region can be provided.

Prices s fr €40; d €48-€50; t €60-€68 **Nearby** ⚓ 3km ♨ 30km
Sea 2km ♟ 2km ⚘ 3km Restaurant 2km Water sports 3km ♨ 3km
Spa 3km ♜ 2km ⌂ 2km ⋙ 25km **Notes** No pets

ELLIANT

₩Ⅲ **Chambre d'hôtes**

Monique LE BERRE
Quélennec, 29370 ELLIANT
☎ 02 98 59 10 43 & 06 72 78 28 49

Ten minutes from Quimper, in the heart of the countryside, this welcoming 1945 family home offers four individual double bedrooms (one with extra single), all with private facilities. Lounge/sitting room with TV, kitchen. Horses and riders welcome. The house is ideally located for long walks and the countryside has a wonderful historic and natural heritage: Chapel of Kerdévot 5 km, the site of Stangala, megaliths and old manors are all close by. Price reductions out of season.

Prices s fr €40; d €43-€45; extra person €15-€20 **On Site** ♟
Nearby ⚓ 0.1km ♨ 22km Sea 22km ⚘ 8km Restaurant 10km Water sports 13km ♨ 8km ♜ 10km ⌂ 9km ⋙ 10km **Notes** No pets English spoken

ELLIANT *CONTINUED*

⚜ *Les Camélias*

Catherine & Marcel TERRIER
Cosquéric, 29370 ELLIANT
☎ 02 29 20 10 57 & 06 78 85 90 53
email: mar-cath.terrier@laposte.net
web: www.chambres-camelias.com/

In the countryside, but not far from Quimper and Concarneau, this property offers comfort and a peaceful location. In a separate building are four rooms: a double and a single downstairs, and two doubles upstairs. There is another double on the first floor of the owners' house, with private access. All rooms have private shower room and WC. Garden furniture, barbecue, baby-sitting.

Prices not confirmed for 2008 **Nearby** ⚘ 2km ⚘ 15km Sea 15km
⚘ 0.5km ⚘ 1km Water sports 15km ⚘ 1km ⚘ 7km ⚘ 2km ⚘ 7km
Notes Pets admitted English spoken

ERGUE-GABERIC

⚜ Trolan

Alain & Odile JOURDREN
29500 ERGUE-GABERIC
☎ 02 98 59 62 83
web: www.gite-breton.com/

Three bedrooms at this property, in an extension to the owners' home. All the rooms are doubles, one downstairs and two upstairs, with private facilities; extra single beds are available, also baby equipment. Separate guests' entrance, and lounge with stove. Use of kitchen; organic breakfasts. Enclosed garden, with terrace, barbecue and garden furniture. Footpaths close by.

Prices s fr €38; d fr €44; extra person fr €15 **Nearby** ⚘ 9km ⚘ 18km
Sea 18km ⚘ 3km ⚘ 9km Water sports 12km ⚘ 5km ⚘ 12km ⚘ 5km
⚘ 12km **Notes** No pets English spoken

GOUESNAC'H

⚜ Chambre d'hôtes

Alfred LE SCOUR
11 Hent Kerjoly, 29950 GOUESNAC'H
☎ 02 98 54 63 12 & 06 83 14 77 42

A newly built house, quietly situated in the countryside, with four guest rooms. On the ground floor are three double rooms, with independent access. Upstairs is a twin-bedded room, with space for an additional folding bed. All the rooms have private shower room and WC. Lounge with open fire. Garden enclosed by banks and bushes. Terrace with garden furniture.

Prices s fr €45; d fr €50; t fr €75; extra person fr €20 **Nearby** ⚘ 6km
⚘ 5km Sea 8km ⚘ 2km ⚘ 8km Restaurant 2km Water sports 8km
⚘ 8km ⚘ 8km ⚘ 2km ⚘ 10km **Notes** No pets

GUIPAVAS

⚜ La Châtaigneraie

Michelle & Gaëlle MORVAN
Kéraveloc, 29490 GUIPAVAS
☎ 02 98 41 52 68
email: la-chataigneraie@wanadoo.fr
web: http://perso.orange.fr/la-chataigneraie

A spacious house offering two double rooms (extra bed possible), and a suite of a double and twin room, all with private facilities and TV. Large mezzanine area in the library, billiard room, use of kitchen and garage, and terrace with panoramic views over the botanical garden and boat harbour in Rade de Brest. Wooded park with games, garden furniture and barbecue and heated swimming pool and solarium available in high season. Close to Vallon de Stangalac'h (footpaths), Moulin Blanc beach, Brest and Océanopolis.

Prices s €42-€45; d €50-€55; t fr €75; extra person fr €15
On Site Private ⚘ **Nearby** ⚘ 10km ⚘ 10km Sea 2km ⚘ 2km Water
sports 2km ⚘ 4km ⚘ 5km ⚘ 3km ⚘ 4km **Notes** No pets English
spoken

ILE-DE-BATZ

⚜ Ty Va Zadou

Marie Pierre PRIGENT
Bourg, 29253 ILE DE BATZ
☎ 02 98 61 76 91

Your hosts will help you discover traditional Breton life in their ancestral home with antique furniture, next to a farm in a market town and opposite the sea. They offer two double rooms, a twin and a family room with double bed and twin beds, all with private facilities. Dining room, sitting room with fireplace and TV, small garden with furniture. The port of Roscoff is close by; from there you can cross to Ile-de-Batz in only 15 minutes.

Prices s fr €40; d fr €60; t fr €70; extra person fr €10 **Nearby** ⚘ 1.5km
⚘ 20km Sea 0.2km ⚘ 0.2km Restaurant 0.2km Water sports 0.4km
⚘ 15km Spa 15km ⚘ 0.3km ⚘ 15km **Notes** No pets Open February
to 15 November.

KERLAZ

⚜ *Chambre d'hôtes*

Michel & Cathy KERVOALEN
29100 KERLAZ
☎ 02 98 92 85 49 📠 02 98 92 85 49
email: kervoalen@free.fr

Close to the sea, discover the charms of the countryside at this dairy farm with beautiful views of Douarnenez bay, the fishing port, the Locronan mountains and Ménez Hom. There are two double rooms, a twin and a family room with a double bed and twin beds, all with private shower rooms and wcs. Independent access, sitting room, billiard room, table tennis, garden furniture, barbecue. Horses welcome. Reduced rates out of season.

Prices not confirmed for 2008 **Nearby** ⚘ 5km ⚘ 25km Sea 0.8km
⚘ 3km ⚘ 2.5km Water sports 5km ⚘ 2km ⚘ 3km ⚘ 2km ⚘ 20km
Notes No pets

₩₩ Lanevry

René & Josy GUEGUEN - GONIDEC
29100 KERLAZ
☎ 02 98 92 14 87 & 06 75 79 63 63
email: info@lanevry.com
web: www.lanevry.com

Between Douarnenez fishing port and the small town of Locronan, this restored farmhouse is set in a prize-winning flower garden in a lovely area. Relax in 'La ville d'Y's' (double with sea views), 'Tristan' (twin), or 'Korrigan', 'Gradlon' and 'Iseult' (doubles). Each has a private bathroom. Large breakfasts feature regional specialities. Use of kitchen out of season, lounge with TV, garden furniture. Four grade 3 gites also available.

Prices d €50-€55 **On Site** Spa **Nearby** ⛉ 5km ⌇ 20km Sea 0.8km ♬ 1km ⤳ 2km Restaurant 3km Water sports 5km ⌇ 2km ⚹ 3km ⌑ 2km ₩ 20km **Notes** Pets admitted English spoken

KERNILIS

₩₩ Chambre d'hôtes

Jo UGUEN
1 Route de Kerbrat, 29260 KERNILIS
☎ 02 98 25 54 02 ▤ 02 98 25 54 02

A dairy farm, near the Aber Wrac'h Valley, offering independent access to three guest bedrooms: a double, a twin and a triple, each with private facilities. Extra bed on request. Sitting room and TV, kitchen, garden with furniture and bikes. Plouguerneau is 7km away and Brest is 23km.

Prices s fr €33; d fr €40; t fr €55 **On Site** ⚹ **Nearby** ⛉ 10km ⌇ 25km Sea 7km ♬ 0.8km ⤳ 8km Restaurant 8km Water sports 7km ⚹ 0.4km ⌑ 0.4km ₩ 22km **Notes** Pets admitted

LAMPAUL-GUIMILIAU

₩₩ Chambre d'hôtes

Odile & Jean Marc PUCHOIS
26, Kerverez, 29400 LAMPAUL GUIMILIAU
☎ 02 98 68 62 02 & 06 67 03 23 26 ▤ 02 98 68 62 02
email: odileetjm.puchois@wanadoo.fr
web: http://perso.orange.fr/ojmpuchois/

This property is in the heart of the Pays des Enclos Paroissiaux ideal for discovering the north Finistère region. There are two double rooms and a twin, with shower rooms, wc and TV and one has a lounge area. Fridge and cot available. Garden with furniture, barbecue, enclosed parking, four bikes available. The GR380 is nearby and guidebooks and various detailed maps are provided.

Prices s fr €32; d €42-€43 **On Site** ⚹ **Nearby** ⛉ 5km Sea 20km ♬ 2km ⤳ 5km Restaurant 1.5km Water sports 15km ⚹ 2km ⌑ 2km ₩ 5km **Notes** Pets admitted English spoken

LANDREVARZEC

₩₩ ♿ Chambre d'hôtes de Penn ar Yeun

Guy & Anne-Marie BOTHOREL
Penn ar Yeun, 29510 LANDREVARZEC
☎ 02 98 57 36 64 & 06 85 95 93 24
email: guy.botherel@wanadoo.fr
web: http://perso.orange.fr/guy.bothorel

This is a good base for exploring the southern part of Finistère. The guest accommodation is part of a group of buildings dating from the 17th century. One bedroom on the ground floor has disabled access; two further rooms upstairs are a double and a triple (double bed plus single). All have en suite shower and WC. Kitchenette, lounge and terrace; bikes for hire. Guests can be collected from station or airport.

Prices d fr €50; extra person fr €15 **On Site** ⚹ **Nearby** ⛉ 10km ⌇ 18km Sea 20km ♬ 0.5km ⤳ 10km Restaurant 0.8km Water sports 20km ⚹ 3km ⌑ 2.5km ₩ 10km **Notes** Pets admitted English spoken

₩₩ ᴏɪ Ti Braz

H et M-L HANEL-COURTIN
Kervéguen, 29510 LANDREVARZEC
☎ 02 29 40 13 93 & 06 32 70 14 55
email: tibraz@cegetel.net
web: www.tibraz.perso.cegetel.net

A traditional, restored Breton style house situated in a small hamlet. There are three upstairs bedrooms: a double with a canopied bed, a twin-bedded room, and a family room for four. All have private shower room and WC. Lounge with TV and internet access, garden; meals by arrangement, also packed lunches.

Prices d €50-€53; t €65-€68; extra person €15; dinner fr €20 **Nearby** ⛉ 12km ⌇ 30km Sea 18km ♬ 2km ⤳ 14km Restaurant 4km Water sports 18km ⚹ 5km Spa 25km ⚹ 14km ⌑ 2km ₩ 18km **Notes** No pets English spoken

LANHOUARNEAU

ⅲ Kergollay

Marie France QUEGUINEUR

29430 LANHOUARNEAU

☎ 02 98 61 47 35 & 06 12 64 76 24 📄 02 98 61 82 81

A warm welcome awaits at this vegetable-growing farm, in a calm and flower-filled setting. It has two double rooms and a twin, each with private facilities, plus a TV, terrace and garden with furniture. Walking routes on site. Crêperie, restaurant, beach and Roscoff ferry nearby.

Prices s fr €40; d fr €45; extra person fr €15 **On Site** 🌐
Nearby ⚓ 8km ⚴ 30km Sea 8km 🏸 8km Restaurant 10km Water sports 8km 🛶 0.8km 🏛 0.8km 🚍 17km **Notes** No pets English spoken

LANILDUT

ⅲ Chambre d'hôtes

M-F GOURMELON

13, route de Mézancou, 29840 LANILDUT

☎ 02 98 04 43 02

email: mfgourm@hotmail.com

web: http://leclosdildut.free.fr

The former residence of the harbour-master, this 17th-century granite house now offers two double rooms and a further double in an outbuilding. Each with old furniture, a fireplace and private facilities. Breakfasts are served in the Breton dining room with fireplace, TV and phone. Garden with furniture, barbecue and terrace available to guests.

Prices d fr €53; extra person fr €20 **Nearby** ⚓ 3km ⚴ 5km Sea 0.5km
🌐 0.5km 🏸 20km Water sports 0.5km 🛶 5km 🎣 2km 🏛 0.5km
🚍 22km **Notes** No pets Open March to 15 November.

ⅲ ♿ Le Nid d'Iroise

Dominique et Anne LE TARNEC

4, hent Kergaradec, 29840 LANILDUT

☎ 02 98 04 38 41

email: lenidiroise@hebergement-nature-bretagne.com

web: www.hebergement-nature-bretagne.com

Set in a small, tranquil village which runs the length of the Aber Ildut, this beautiful stone house overlooks the countryside and sea and has rooms decorated in a nautical theme: two doubles, a twin and a four-poster room, all with private facilities. Lounge with open fireplace, private sitting room with TV and library. Huge, enclosed garden with furniture. Baby equipment available. Footpaths and a small stream nearby. Boat trips to the Ile d'Ouessant from the port in July and August.

Prices d €55-€65; extra person fr €20 **On Site** Spa 🎣
Nearby ⚓ 6km ⚴ 8km Sea 3km 🌐 3km 🏸 20km Restaurant 2km Water sports 3km 🛶 2km 🏛 2km 🚍 23km **Notes** No pets English spoken

LE JUCH

ⅲ *Le Carbon*

Anne-Marie YOUINOU

29100 LE JUCH

☎ 02 98 92 21 08 & 06 33 73 63 41

email: yves.youinou@wanadoo.fr

A warm welcome awaits in this old farmhouse, with its large flower courtyard, surrounded by gardens. There is a room with a double and a single bed, a double and a family room with two doubles and a single, each with private facilities. Cot on request. TV, garden with furniture, and large, home-made breakfasts served in a beautiful Breton room. Restaurant, beach and coastal footpaths 3km.

Prices not confirmed for 2008 **Nearby** ⚓ 6km ⚴ 25km Sea 3km
🌐 3km 🏸 4km Water sports 5km 🛶 4km 🏛 4km 🚍 25km
Notes No pets English spoken

LOC-BREVALAIRE

ⅲ 🍴 Pencreach

René & Germaine BOZEC

29260 LOC BREVALAIRE

☎ 02 98 25 50 99 & 06 76 61 48 58

email: bozec.rene@wanadoo.fr

web: www.gites-finistere.com/gites/pencreach

A sunny, calm, welcoming and non-smoking family home with two doubles and a twin, all with private shower rooms. There is a large garden where fresh produce for the dinner table is grown, a veranda where breakfast is served and a lounge for guests. The menus are simple but generous and there are lots of local walks to discover.

Prices d fr €42; dinner fr €12 **Nearby** ⚓ 15km Sea 9km 🌐 0.5km
🏸 6km Water sports 12km 🛶 0.2km 🎣 7km 🏛 6km 🚍 18km
Notes No pets

LOC-EGUINER-ST-THEGONNEC

ⅲ 🍴 *Ty Dreux*

Benoît MARTIN

29410 LOC EGUINER SAINT THEGONNEC

☎ 02 98 78 08 21 📄 02 98 78 01 69

email: ty-dreux@club-internet.fr

web: http://tydreux.com

In open countryside lies the dairy farm of Ty Dreux. In the new farmhouse (where three generations live) there are three guest bedrooms. A ground floor room has a canopied four poster, shower and wc. Upstairs there are a room for three and a double room, each with private facilities. Living room with open fire.

Prices not confirmed for 2008 **Nearby** ⚓ 5km ⚴ 25km Sea 18km
🌐 0.3km 🏸 5km Water sports 5km 🛶 6km 🏛 4km 🚍 12km
Notes No pets English spoken Open Mid March to September

♨ ✿ ⁛ *Ty Dreux*

Annie MARTIN

29410 LOC EGUINER SAINT THEGONNEC

☎ 02 98 78 08 21 📄 02 98 78 01 69

email: ty-dreux@club-internet.fr

web: http://tydreux.com

A peaceful old weaver's farm in the heart of the countryside with an exhibition of Breton costumes. The four rooms, all with shower rooms, are on the first and second floors. There are two doubles, one single and one with a double and a single bed. Dinners of local produce are offered at the weekend and during school holidays.

Prices not confirmed for 2008 **Nearby** ⌂ 8km ⚓ 20km Sea 18km ⚲ 5km ⟲ 5km Water sports 5km ♨ 6km ⚐ 4km ⌂ 4km ⋘ 18km **Notes** No pets

---

LOCRONAN

♨ **Rodou Glaz**

Famille JAIN-CAMUS

29180 LOCRONAN

☎ 02 98 73 52 41 & 06 99 22 91 60

email: contact@rodou-glaz.com

web: www.rodou-glaz.com

In the Pointe du Raz, close to charming Locronan with its arts activities and shops; guests are warmly welcomed in this large restored home, surrounded by a lovely flower garden. It has three double rooms, a twin and a family room with a double and twin beds, all with TV and private bathrooms. Large breakfasts are served in the airy lounge or on the veranda. Walks in the forest or on the fine sandy beaches of Douarnenez Bay (5 minutes away).

Prices s fr €42; d fr €47; t fr €63; extra person fr €16 **Nearby** ⌂ 10km Sea 5km ⚲ 10km ⟲ 10km Restaurant 1.5km Water sports 10km ♨ 5km ⚐ 10km ⌂ 1.5km ⋘ 15km **Notes** No pets English spoken Open Easter to September.

LOCUNOLE

♨ **Sterwen**

Cécile NICOLAS

Le Pouldu, 29310 LOCUNOLE

☎ 02 98 71 31 63 & 06 03 51 25 37

email: ster.wen@free.fr

Not far from Quimper, in the part of Brittany known as le Cornouaille, this 18th-century house has four comfortable bedrooms - three with twin beds, and the fourth with a double bed and a single. All have private WC and shower. A rural spot, and a good base for exploring inland Brittany as well as the coast.

Prices s fr €47; d fr €52; extra person fr €12 **Nearby** ⌂ 5km Sea 20km ⚲ 3km ⟲ 3km Water sports 20km ♨ 5km ⚐ 5km ⋘ 8km **Notes** No pets English spoken

---

LOGONNA-DAOULAS

♨ ⁛ **Gouelet Ker**

Gwenaël MARCHAND

29460 LOGONNA DAOULAS

☎ 02 98 20 69 42

email: info@gouelet-ker.com

web: http://gouelet-ker.com

Between the sea and the river, this is a 100-year old restored house. It has four guest rooms: a double on the ground floor, a double and a twin on the first floor, and a double on the second floor - all with private facilities. Some have a sea view, some a garden view.

Prices d fr €48; t fr €63; extra person fr €15; dinner fr €17 **Nearby** ⌂ 8km ⚓ 15km Sea 0.5km ⚲ 0.5km ⟲ 18km Water sports 1.5km ♨ 1.5km ⚐ 18km ⌂ 1.5km ⋘ 20km **Notes** No pets English spoken Open April to October.

MAHALON

♨ ✿ **Kérantum**

Anne OLIER

29790 MAHALON

☎ 02 98 74 51 93 & 02 98 74 58 04

email: gitesetchambres.kerantum@wanadoo.fr

web: www.gites-finistere.com/gites/kerantum

On the outskirts of Cap Sizun, on the Pointe du Raz road, this old farmhouse is ideally situated for the Douarnenez and Audierne bays. There are large, comfortable bedrooms with private facilities and entrances: a twin, a double with queen-size bed and a double with a single bed as well. Relax in the sitting room, or courtyard, and lawn with garden furniture. Parking, barbecue, table tennis and use of kitchen possible.

Prices s fr €38; d fr €45; t €55-€60; extra person fr €10 **On Site** ⚲ **Nearby** ⌂ 1.5km ⚓ 32km Sea 9km ⟲ 10km Water sports 10km ♨ 5km ⚐ 10km ⌂ 3km ⋘ 25km **Notes** No pets English spoken

BRITTANY

NEVEZ

♦♦♦ Kerambris

Yveline GOURLAOUEN

Port Manech, 29920 NEVEZ

☎ 02 98 06 83 82

email: gites-kerambris@orange.com

web: www.gites-finistere.com/gites/kerambris

Yveline lives in an old weaving village near Pont-Aven. The 16th-century stone farmhouse is in a very quiet and relaxing location. One ground floor double room; upstairs one double and two twin rooms, all with shower and wc. Veranda with view over garden and orchard. Coastal footpath. Picturesque port and beach at Port Manech 1km.

Prices d fr €45 **Nearby** ☂ 3km ⌁ 25km Sea 0.3km ✐ 1km ↘ 18km Restaurant 0.5km Water sports 1km ☯ 0.5km ♥ 5km 🏠 5km ✹ 25km **Notes** No pets

♦♦♦ Le Chêne

Béatrice LE TORREC

Kérado, 29920 NEVEZ

☎ 02 98 06 85 89

email: keradohote@yahoo.fr

This converted farm building is in the land of the standing stones, and not far from Pont-Aven - well-known for its Gauguin connections and artistic heritage. It is a converted longhouse with four comfortable first-floor bedrooms, two with balconies: two doubles, a small double and a twin; all have en suite shower room/WC. Use of washing machine, Wi-fi access, and lounge with an enormous open fireplace where guests can pass the winter evenings.

Prices not confirmed for 2008 **Nearby** ☂ 3km ⌁ 30km Sea 2.5km ✐ 2km ↘ 10km Water sports 4km ☯ 4km ♥ 1km 🏠 0.5km ✹ 20km **Notes** No pets English spoken

PENMARC'H

♦♦♦ ⃝ Chambre d'hôtes

H et D GOMPERTZ-VOLANT

241 rue de Feunteunigou, 29760 PENMARC'H

☎ 06 18 04 56 40 & 02 98 58 56 07 ▤ 02 98 58 56 07

Very close to la Pointe de la Torche, famous for its windsurfing, this property has three guest rooms in a complex of small thatched cottages. There is a two storey family suite for up to five, a double room, and a twin-bedded room, all with private facilities. Baby equipment available, also baby-sitting by arrangement. Washing machine; packed lunches available in summer.

Prices s fr €40; d fr €48; t fr €60; extra person €12-€15; dinner fr €17 **Nearby** ☂ 1km ⌁ 18km Sea 2km ✐ 1.5km ↘ 9km Restaurant 1km Water sports 1.5km ☯ 2km Spa 15km ♥ 9km 🏠 1km ✹ 24km **Notes** No pets

PEUMERIT

♦♦♦ Lespurit-Coat

Georges L'HELGOUALC'H

29710 PEUMERIT

☎ 02 98 82 92 27 & 06 60 88 43 76 ▤ 02 98 82 92 27

web: http://lespurit.coat.free.fr

In the Bigouden countryside, this restored farm offers welcoming bedrooms in a longbarn annexe: three double rooms, a single and a twin, each with private facilities. Breakfast is served in a communal room with fireplace. There is a terrace, garden with furniture and barbecue.

Prices s fr €41; d fr €53; t fr €66 **Nearby** ☂ 6km ⌁ 22km Sea 4km ✐ 2km ↘ 12km Restaurant 3km Water sports 15km ☯ 1km Spa 25km ♥ 3km 🏠 1km ✹ 18km **Notes** No pets English spoken

PLOGASTEL-ST-GERMAIN

♦♦♦ Kerguernou

Jean Marie LE HENAFF

29710 PLOGASTEL SAINT GERMAIN

☎ 02 98 54 56 30 ▤ 02 98 54 57 00

Rooms offered in an old renovated longbarn, in a lovely calm setting on a dairy farm, near the family house. There are four double bedrooms and a twin, all with private facilities, plus a lounge with fireplace, kitchen, garden, barbecue and play area.

Prices s fr €35; d fr €43; t fr €53 **Nearby** ☂ 6km ⌁ 23km Sea 10km ✐ 0.2km ↘ 18km Restaurant 5km Water sports 17km ☯ 5km ♥ 10km 🏠 5km ✹ 18km **Notes** No pets

PLOGOFF

▦ ◉ **An Tiez Bihan**

Jean Paul GANNE
Kerhuret, 29770 PLOGOFF
☎ 02 98 70 34 85
web: www.fumoir-delapointeduraz.com

In a coastal village, 2km from the Pointe du Raz, an old comfortable
farmhouse has independent entrances to five bedrooms: three
doubles, a double with twin beds on a mezzanine, and a double with
single mezzanine bed and lounge, each with private facilities. Cot
on request. Lounge with fireplace, courtyard, garden with furniture
and play area. Evening meals on request, featuring farm products or
local produce (smoked salmon, fish paté, langoustines, rabbit paté).
Diving 1km.

Prices d fr €43; extra person fr €12; dinner fr €20 **Nearby** ⚓ 1km
♨ 15km Sea 0.5km ⚓ 1km ⚓ 10km Restaurant 0.5km Water
sports 10km ⓐ 2.5km **Notes** Pets admitted

▦ *Chambre d'hôtes*

René & Marie Yvonne LE CORRE
29 Rue des Hirondelles, Lescoff, 29770 PLOGOFF
☎ 02 98 70 38 24
email: lecorre.marieyvonne@wanadoo.fr
web: http://perso.orange.fr/chambre-pointeduraz

One kilometre from the famous Pointe du Raz, just off the main road,
this old, renovated farmhouse has three bedrooms with independent
access: a twin and two doubles, each with shower room and wc.
Lounge with TV and telephone, enclosed garden with furniture,
terrace, and parking.

Prices not confirmed for 2008 **Nearby** ⚓ 3km Sea 0.5km ⚓ 1km
⚓ 28km Water sports 1km ⚓ 3km ⚓ 3km ⓐ 2km **Notes** Pets
admitted English spoken

▦ ◉ *Kerguidy-Izella*

Annick & Jean Noël LE BARS
Ferme de Kerguidy-Izella, 29770 PLOGOFF
☎ 02 98 70 35 60
email: jean-noel.le-bars@wanadoo.fr
web: www.fermelebars.com/

Five kilometres from the Pointe du Raz, this farmhouse is set in
a valley with an enclosed garden with furniture and a terrace. All
bedrooms have en suite shower and wc. On the ground floor, there
is a double room, and a room with two double beds and disabled
access. Upstairs, a double room and two rooms which can have twin
or king-size beds, and a room with a double and a single bed. Cot on
request. Lounge with library, TV and games. Evening meals on request
(except Saturdays, Sundays and holidays), based on farm produce.
Reduced prices out of season.

Prices not confirmed for 2008 **Nearby** ⚓ 1km ♨ 15km Sea 1km
⚓ 2km ⚓ 28km Water sports 12km ⚓ 1km ⚓ 1km ⓐ 1km
Notes No pets

PLOGONNEC

▦ *Le Croezou*

Marie Louise KERMOAL
29180 PLOGONNEC
☎ 02 98 51 80 89 🗎 02 98 51 80 89
email: marielouise.kermoal@wanadoo.fr
web: www.gites-finistere.com/gites/kermoal

There are three en suite rooms at this property, which is near
the dramatic Pointe du Raz, the 'Land's End' of France. There is a
double room, a twin-bedded room and a room for three - all very
comfortable, and each with its own decorative theme. Breakfasts are
in keeping with the superb dining room where they are served. Large
garden; kitchen.

Prices not confirmed for 2008 **Nearby** ⚓ 5km Sea 10km ⚓ 2km
⚓ 13km Water sports 10km ⚓ 2.5km ⚓ 10km **Notes** No pets

▦ *Leurbiriou*

Jacqueline DELLIERE
29180 PLOGONNEC
☎ 02 98 91 76 79

A comfortable, traditional Breton home with three first floor rooms,
two doubles and one twin, all with en suite shower rooms. The
lounge, with fireplace, television and telephone, overlooks the
enclosed, flower-filled garden with terrace and portico. The house is
hung with paintings created by your host.

Prices s fr €40; d €47-€50; extra person fr €13 **Nearby** ⚓ 3km ♨ 20km
Sea 8km ⚓ 8km ⚓ 8km Restaurant 2km Water sports 8km ⚓ 2km
⚓ 2km ⓐ 2km ⚓ 10km **Notes** No pets Open Easter to November.

PLOMODIERN

▦ ♿ **Sainte Marie du Ménez-Hom**

Michelle JACQ
29550 PLOMODIERN
☎ 02 98 81 54 41 & 06 08 63 68 99 🗎 02 98 81 59 20
email: michellejacq@hotmail.com
web: http://gitesjacq.free.fr

A dairy farm at the foot of the Menez Hom (330mtrs), by Presqu'île
de Crozon and the Pointe du Raz. The longbarn houses two gîtes and
four guest rooms: a double and twin with disabled access, a double
with a single bed on a mezzanine and two rooms with a double, and
twin beds on a mezzanine. Each has a shower and wc. Sitting room
for guests, kitchen may be used in the evenings, heating, terrace and
garden furniture. Crêperie 100mtrs.

Prices d €48-€55; t fr €65; extra person fr €15 **Nearby** ♨ 32km
Sea 5km ⚓ 1km ⚓ 11km Restaurant 0.1km Water sports 5km ⚓ 3km
⚓ 10km ⓐ 3km ⚓ 11km **Notes** No pets English spoken Open March
to November.

PLONEOUR-LANVERN

⊞ Chambre d'hôtes Kerc'Hoat

Nathalie LE GOFF
Kerc'Hoat, 29720 PLONEOUR LANVERN
☎ 02 98 82 62 18
web: www.gites-finistere.com/gites/kerchoat

This old farmhouse is peacefully situated amongst the trees. There are three guest rooms - two doubles and a twin - in an extension to the main house, also a lounge area. In a separate converted barn are a further double-bedded room, and a room with single beds which could sleep a family. All rooms have private facilities. Baby-sitting available.

Prices s fr €35; d fr €45; extra person fr €12 **Nearby** ⛳ 10km ⚓ 20km Sea 10km ♞ 1km ✈ 8km Restaurant 8km Water sports 12km ♨ 8km ⚑ 8km ⛨ 8km ⋙ 15km **Notes** No pets

⊞ ⦿ Kergaviny

Marcelle TIRILLY
29720 PLONEOUR LANVERN
☎ 02 98 82 64 49 & 02 98 87 61 97 🖨 02 98 82 63 75
email: gitestirilly@orange.fr

This chambres d'hôtes has three rooms in a traditional Breton style house adjacent to the owners' home. All the bedrooms are doubles, with private bath or shower rooms, and there is a cot available. Breakfasts are generous, with home-made local specialities, and evening meals are available by arrangement. Lounge with books and TV, lawn with garden furniture.

Prices s fr €35; d fr €42; extra person fr €20; dinner fr €16 **Nearby** ⛳ 6km ⚓ 20km Sea 8km ♞ 1km ✈ 12km Restaurant 5km Water sports 12km ♨ 5km Spa 18km ⚑ 5km ⛨ 2.5km ⋙ 18km **Notes** No pets

PLOUEGAT-MOYSAN

⊞ *Pen an Néac'h*

Familles THOMAS et SCARELLA
Le Puits de Jeanne, 29650 PLOUEGAT MOYSAN
☎ 02 98 79 20 15 🖨 02 98 79 22 73
email: contact@lepuitsdejeanne.com
web: http://gites.penaneach.com/

This beautiful comfortable 1950s house has rustic style furniture and lies in a large park with magnificent views over undulating countryside. There are two family rooms with twin beds and a double, and two twin rooms, all with private facilities. Fireplace, TV, telephone, washing machine, baby equipment and garden with furniture. Terrace, lounge room, gazebo and garage. Baby sitting, cooking and bike hire can be arranged. Farm inn on site.

Prices not confirmed for 2008 **Nearby** ⛳ 6km ⚓ 20km Sea 12km ♞ 0.5km ✈ 15km Water sports 15km ♨ 6km ⚑ 6km ⛨ 0.5km ⋙ 15km **Notes** Pets admitted

PLOUENAN

⊞ Lopreden

Allain & Sylvie CAZUC
29420 PLOUENAN
☎ 02 98 69 50 62 & 06 60 07 50 62 🖨 02 98 69 50 02
email: allain.cazuc@wanadoo.fr
web: www.dormiralopreden.com

This farm is typical of the region and has three large bedrooms in an old longbarn built of local stone: two doubles and a twin, each with shower room and wc. A lovely, relaxing setting with a flower garden, children's play area and footpaths from the house, leading to the forest (1km). Use of kitchen on request.

Prices s fr €35; d fr €45; extra person fr €13 **Nearby** ⛳ 3km ⚓ 10km Sea 8km ♞ 8km ✈ 8km Restaurant 8km Water sports 8km ♨ 3km Spa 20km ⚑ 8km ⛨ 3km ⋙ 15km **Notes** Pets admitted English spoken

PLOUESCAT

⊞ ⦿ Penkéar

C et F SCHOCK-LE JEUNE
29430 PLOUESCAT
☎ 02 98 69 63 64 & 06 88 12 94 34
email: lejeune.ferland@free.fr
web: www.gites-plouescat.com

A market garden, just a kilometre outside town, is the setting for these three guest rooms. One is on the ground floor, the others upstairs, and each has a shower/WC, its own entrance and a TV. Meals are available by arrangement, except weekends and public holidays. Well placed for beaches and country walks, and Roscoff is just 15 kilometres away.

Prices d €45-€60; extra person fr €15; dinner fr €18 **Nearby** ⛳ 6km ⚓ 20km Sea 2.5km ♞ 2.5km ✈ 15km Restaurant 0.8km Water sports 2.5km ♨ 1km Spa 18km ⚑ 1km ⛨ 1km ⋙ 32km **Notes** No pets English spoken

PLOUGAR

⊞ ✿ Keramis

Jean Vincent & Yvonne LOUSSAUT
29440 PLOUGAR
☎ 02 98 68 56 21 & 02 98 68 54 26 🖨 02 98 68 56 31
email: jv.loussaut@wanadoo.fr
web: http://perso.orange.fr/keramis/

Between the sea and the Pays des Enclos Paroissiaux (parochial enclosures); there are three bedrooms in this modern house: a double (extra bed on request), and two triples (double bed and a single), all with private facilities. Lovely garden, parking and barbecue. Breakfasts served in the lounge/sitting room with open fireplace. TV and games provided. Nearby: restaurant, crêperie, stretch of water, the Château de Kerjean.

Prices s fr €40; d fr €43; extra person fr €15 **Nearby** ⛳ 12km Sea 13km ♞ 5km ✈ 12km Water sports 13km ♨ 5km ⚑ 12km ⛨ 5km ⋙ 12km **Notes** No pets

PLOUGASNOU

⌂ ⓘ◯ *Le Clos Saint Sauveur*

Claire & Luc TOURNIER

8 rue Jean Jaurès, 29630 PLOUGASNOU

☎ 02 98 67 34 94 📄 02 98 67 34 94

email: cltournier@aol.com

Five non-smoking rooms, ten minutes walk from the beach in an old school building. There are two doubles, a twin-bedded room, and two triple rooms (double bed plus a single). Each room has a private shower/WC. Large games room with table tennis and table football. Outside is a big lawn with two boules pitches. Meals available by arrangement.

Prices not confirmed for 2008 **Nearby** ⚓ 3km ⚲ 20km Sea 1km ⚐ 0.8km ⚹ 18km Water sports 2km ⚘ 0.2km ⚑ 0.5km ⚑ 0.3km ⚑ 14km **Notes** No pets English spoken

⌂ **Merdy Bras**

Chantal & Gilbert FILY

Route de Pontplaincoat, 29630 PLOUGASNOU

☎ 02 98 67 34 12

web: www.chambredhote-fily.com

A restored longbarn near the sea, between the pink granite coast and Roscoff. There are three guest rooms with independent entrances: a family room with double bed on a mezzanine and twin beds, a double and a twin, all with shower room and wc. Extra bed on request. Large lounge with TV, kitchen and tree and flower filled garden with furniture. Coastal footpaths 3km.

Prices s fr €38; d fr €42; t fr €51; extra person fr €10 **Nearby** ⚓ 3km ⚲ 20km Sea 3km ⚘ 2km ⚹ 18km Restaurant 2km Water sports 4km ⚑ 1km ⚑ 2km ⚑ 20km **Notes** No pets

PLOUGASTEL-DAOULAS

⌂ *Ker-Bili*

Paul GUILLEMETTE

55 Chemin de Coat Pehen,

29470 PLOUGASTEL DAOULAS

☎ 02 98 37 80 65 📄 02 98 37 80 65

email: ker-bili@wanadoo.fr

In a protected site, right on the edge of the water, this architect-designed house stands in enclosed grounds full of trees and flowers. There are three non-smoking double-bedded first floor guest rooms, with their own bath or shower room and WC - although for one room the facilities are not en suite. Possible child's bed, use of kitchen. Garden furniture.

Prices not confirmed for 2008 **On Site** Sea ⚘ Water sports **Nearby** ⚓ 4.5km ⚲ 12km ⚹ 15km ⚘ 2.5km ⚑ 4km ⚑ 1.2km ⚑ 15km **Notes** No pets

PLOUGONVELIN

⌂ **Kéryel**

Monique & Marcel SALIOU

29217 PLOUGONVELIN

☎ 02 98 48 33 35 & 06 62 06 33 35

email: saliou.monique@wanadoo.fr

web: www.keryel.fr.st

Guest rooms in an annexe of the main house include a double, a twin and two family suites with double and twin beds, all with private facilities. Garden with furniture and terrace area and camping possible in the farm grounds. Baby sitting service. Plougonvelin, Finistère point, the Trez Hir, Pointe Saint Mathier, Bertheaume Fort and Le Conquet (fishing port) are all nearby. Coastal footpath 10km.

Prices s €40-€65; d €48-€65; t fr €68; extra person fr €10 **Nearby** ⚓ 0.5km ⚲ 15km Sea 1.5km ⚘ 1.5km ⚹ 3km Water sports 3km ⚘ 2km ⚑ 4km ⚑ 1.5km ⚑ 20km **Notes** No pets

PLOUIDER

⌂ ❦ *Kermabon*

Thérèse CORBE

29260 PLOUIDER

☎ 02 98 25 40 28

email: therese.corbe@wanadoo.fr

There are four guest rooms with views of the sea in this country location: a double in the owner's home, and three in a renovated farmhouse nearby include a twin and two doubles, one with mezzanine. Each has a private bathroom. Kitchen and communal sitting room with fireplace. Beautiful walks along the seashore, land yachting, bird sanctuary, restaurants and shops nearby. Airport 30km.

Prices not confirmed for 2008 **Nearby** ⚓ 4km ⚲ 25km Sea 2km ⚘ 2km ⚹ 5km Water sports 4km ⚘ 2km ⚑ 3km ⚑ 3km ⚑ 20km **Notes** Pets admitted English spoken

⌂ ⓘ◯ *Kersehen*

Claudine ROUE

Kersehen, 29260 PLOUIDER

☎ 02 98 25 40 41 & 06 81 04 10 87

email: claudine.roue@wanadoo.fr

The owners welcome you to their farmhouse, in which they offer three double bedrooms, each with private facilities. Cot available on request. Lounge, TV, library, large garden with furniture, children's swing and bikes. Meals (including children's) available by reservation. Land yachting nearby.

Prices not confirmed for 2008 **Nearby** ⚓ 3km Sea 2.5km ⚘ 3km ⚹ 5km Water sports 5km ⚑ 1.5km ⚑ 20km **Notes** Pets admitted English spoken

BRITTANY

PLOUIGNEAU

₩ ﾼ⃞ ₺ **Luzivilly**

Herveline LE FER
29610 PLOUIGNEAU
☎ 02 98 79 22 80 ▤ 02 98 79 22 80
web: http://bm-web.phpnet.org/lefer/

This restored building offers four guest bedrooms at ground level, with a south facing garden. Two double rooms, one room for three, one family room with a double plus twin beds on a mezzanine, all with shower or bath and wc. Enjoy a country style breakfast (crêpes, home-made preserves, hams). Near a river, private lake, the sea, and the Parc d'Armorique. Meals by arrangement. Barbecue, covered gallery, table tennis, football pitch.

Prices s €36-€48; d €42-€52; t fr €63; extra person fr €16; dinner fr €22 **Nearby** ♥ 4km ♨ 18km Sea 15km ⚐ 1km ↖ 4km Restaurant 4km Water sports 15km ☲ 4km ☂ 4km 🏛 4km ⚒ 16km **Notes** No pets Open 2 March to 14 November.

PLOURIN-LES-MORLAIX

₩ ❦ **Chambre d'hôtes**

Patrick HELARY
Lestrezec, 29600 PLOURIN LES MORLAIX
☎ 02 98 72 53 55 & 06 09 61 44 54
▤ 02 98 72 53 55
email: phelary@yahoo.fr
web: http://perso.wanadoo.fr/tourisme.bretagne

This dairy farm is at the foot of the Arée Mountains and has charmingly decorated rooms including two doubles and a twin, with private facilities. A family welcome awaits guests to the simple granite Breton house, with large bay windows looking onto the country garden. Large lounge, sitting room with fireplace, kitchen. Reduced rates October to April (on reservation).

Prices d €60-€65; t fr €80; extra person fr €20 **On Site** ☂ **Nearby** ♥ 10km ♨ 20km Sea 10km ⚐ 1km ↖ 8km Restaurant 8km Water sports 20km ☲ 4km Spa 45km 🏛 4km ⚒ 10km **Notes** No pets English spoken

PLOUVIEN

₩ **Croas Eugan**

Maurice & Denise LE JEUNE
29860 PLOUVIEN
☎ 02 98 40 96 46 & 06 77 13 82 30
email: le.jeune.maurice@wanadoo.fr

A property in North Finistère, at the centre of the Abers region and the 'Côte des légendes'. There is independent access to the two double bedrooms (one grade 2 bedroom with wc on the landing) and a twin room with bathroom, sitting room and TV. Use of kitchen, fireplace, TV, heating and dining room.

Prices not confirmed for 2008 **On Site** ☂ **Nearby** ♥ 6km ♨ 10km Sea 10km ⚐ 5km ↖ 10km Water sports 10km ☲ 2km 🏛 1.5km ⚒ 18km **Notes** No pets

PLOUZANE

₩ **Lannevel Vras**

Irène & Pierre GOURVENNEC
29280 PLOUZANE
☎ 02 98 05 94 60

A lovely family house, quiet and welcoming, with a view over the countryside and the port of Brest. Three double guest rooms in the owner's house, with two gîtes nearby. One of the rooms has a sitting area. Spare bed available. Large living room/lounge with open fire and television. Garden with terrace, barbecue; covered gallery.

Prices s €40-€45; d €45-€50; t fr €65 **Nearby** ♥ 4km ♨ 5km Sea 3km ⚐ 4km ↖ 6km Water sports 10km ☲ 2km ☂ 5km 🏛 1km ⚒ 7km **Notes** No pets

₩ ❦ ﾼ⃞ ₺ *Lézavarn*

Christiane PHILIPOT
29280 PLOUZANE
☎ 02 98 48 41 28 & 06 63 46 02 98 ▤ 02 98 48 93 29
email: christiane.philipot@wanadoo.fr
web: www.gites-finistere.com/gites/lezavarn

A pig and dairy farm close to Brest, offering four bedrooms with independent access in an annex: three doubles, one with disabled access, and a twin, plus a grade 2 family room in the owners' house with a double and twin beds. All have TV, telephone and private facilities. Extra bed possible. Kitchen, washing machine, gazebo with table tennis, table football and billiards, play area, farm visits. Evening meals possible except on Sundays, free for children under four.

Prices not confirmed for 2008 **Nearby** ♥ 5km ♨ 10km Sea 8km ↖ 12km Water sports 3km ☲ 3km ☂ 10km 🏛 3km ⚒ 15km **Notes** Pets admitted

PLOVAN

₩ ﾼ⃞ *Corn Goarem*

Olivier ROUSSET
29720 PLOVAN
☎ 06 62 76 86 45
email: o.rousset@ch-cornouaille.fr

Just a stone's throw from the sea yet situated in the countryside in the heart of the Pays Bigouden, this house dates from 1924 and has been fully renovated in a traditional style. After a continental breakfast guests can walk along the coastal path around the Bay of Audierne or explore both the coast and countryside between Penmarc'h and the Pointe du Raz by bicycle or car. Meals available; no smoking.

Prices not confirmed for 2008 **Nearby** ♥ 8km ♨ 25km Sea 1km ⚐ 1km ↖ 15km Water sports 20km ☲ 5km ☂ 3km 🏛 0.5km ⚒ 30km **Notes** No pets English spoken

PLOZEVET

⫴ *Kérongard Divisquin*

Claudine TREPOS
29710 PLOZEVET
☎ 02 98 54 31 09 & 06 27 53 33 91
email: claudine.trepos@wanadoo.fr
web: http://monsite.wanadoo.fr/trepos/

In Audierne Bay, this home is in a small, peaceful village 30km from the Pointe du Raz, the Pointe de Penmarc'h and Bénodet, Quimper and Locronan. There are two double rooms and a twin with independent access and private facilities. TV, fridge, garden furniture and boules pitch. Generous breakfasts of home-made crêpes and Breton gateaux. Beach, footpaths and restaurant nearby. Varying rates depending on length of stay.

Prices not confirmed for 2008　**Nearby** ⚓ 8km ♨ 25km Sea 1km
⚐ 1km ⤔ 15km Water sports 10km ⚉ 4km ⚑ 4km ⚒ 4km ⚏ 25km
Notes No pets

⫴ ◉ **Lesneut**

Evelyne BOURDIC
29710 PLOZEVET
☎ 02 98 54 34 33
email: le-vent-solaire@wanadoo.fr
web: www.bretagne-vacance.com

This 18th-century farm is 2km from the sea on the Pointe du Raz road. The longbarn has three comfortable non-smoking bedrooms, and a second building has a family suite for four people, all with private facilities. Large lounge and sitting room with chimney, library and TV, washing machine, tumble dryer, fridge. Evening meals featuring seafood and garden produce are served in the garden with sea views, furniture and picnic area in the orchard.

Prices s €50; d €55; t fr €70; extra person fr €15; dinner €20-€22
Nearby ⚓ 7km ♨ 30km Sea 2km ⚐ 2km ⤔ 17km Restaurant 4km
Water sports 2km ⚉ 5km Spa 17km ⚑ 2km ⚒ 2km ⚏ 25km
Notes No pets English spoken

PONT-AVEN

⫴ **Kermentec**

Véronique LAROUR
29930 PONT AVEN
☎ 02 98 06 07 60 & 06 89 43 04 52
email: hanoi.michel@free.fr
web: http://hanoi.michel.free.fr/1.htm

High up in Pont Aven, close to the 'city of painters' and the 'Bois d'Amour', guests can expect a warm welcome at this pretty stone house. It has a twin room and two doubles with private facilities, a large lounge with corner seating area, kitchen and extra beds on request. Breakfasts can be enjoyed outside or next to the fireplace. Tranquil countryside with lovely walks near the beaches. Quimper, Locronan, Concarneau and many activities nearby.

Prices d €43-€45; extra person fr €14　**Nearby** ⚓ 0.5km ♨ 25km
Sea 5km ⚐ 0.5km ⤔ 15km Water sports 7km ⚉ 0.5km ⚑ 15km
⚒ 0.3km ⚏ 18km　**Notes** No pets

⫴ *Kérévennou*

Nadine EVEN
29930 PONT AVEN
☎ 02 98 06 03 19 ▤ 02 98 09 11 25
email: chambres-kerevennou@wanadoo.fr
web: http://perso.wanadoo.fr/chambres-kerevennou/

Just ten minutes from the sea, this property is situated in an area famous for its artists. There are three guest rooms on the second floor of the family home, at the entrance to a working farm. Two of the rooms have double beds, and the other has twin beds. They all have a private shower and WC. Separate guests' entrance; meals by arrangement.

Prices not confirmed for 2008　**Nearby** ⚓ 6km ♨ 25km Sea 8km
⚐ 0.4km ⤔ 14km Water sports 10km ⚉ 3km ⚑ 5km ⚒ 3km ⚏ 14km
Notes No pets

PONT-CROIX

⫴ **La Glycinière**

Alain et Corinne SIRHENRY
Rue de la Métairie, 29790 PONT CROIX
☎ 02 98 70 58 50 ▤ 02 98 70 58 50
email: la glyciniere@free.fr
web: http://laglyciniere.free.fr/

Not far from la Pointe du Raz, this chambre d'hôtes is in a wonderful location. There are four guest rooms, all on the first floor of the owners' house: two doubles, a twin and a triple, all with private shower room and WC. Baby equipment available. Lounge; attractively laid-out garden with furniture; fishing equipment available. Picnics on request.

Prices s fr €42; d €45-€48; t €55-€58; extra person fr €14　**On Site** ⚓
⚐ ⚑ Private ⤔　**Nearby** ♨ 30km Sea 5km Water sports 5km ⚉
⚏ 30km　**Notes** Pets admitted English spoken

POULLAN-SUR-MER

⫴⫴ **Manoir de Kerdanet**

Sid & Monique NEDJAR
29100 POULLAN SUR MER
☎ 02 98 74 59 03 ▤ 02 98 74 59 03
email: manoir.kerdanet@wanadoo.fr
web: www.manoirkerdanet.com

This beautiful 15th-century manor house nestles in the hollow of a verdant valley near Douarnenez, in a three hectare park with large pond. Stone stairs lead up to a period bedroom with a fireplace and a four-poster bed and there are two double rooms and a bedroom/sitting room suite with a double and twin beds; all are no smoking with private facilities and have king-size beds. In the sitting room there is a carved stone fireplace, where shields of the former lords of the manor are displayed.

Prices d €98-€128; extra person €32　**Nearby** ⚓ 4km ♨ 30km
Sea 4km ⚐ 10km ⤔ 5km Restaurant 2km Water sports 5km
⚉ 5km Spa 5km ⚑ 5km ⚒ 2km ⚏ 30km　**Notes** No pets English
spoken　Open May to 1 November.

POULLAOUEN

⚜ ⎮◎⎮ *Goasvennou*

Ghislaine DEGRYSE-BRIAND

Les Tilleuls, 29246 POULLAOUEN

☎ 02 98 93 57 63

email: degemer-mad@goasvennou-les-tilleuls.com

This beautiful property is less than thirty minutes from the sea and near to Huelgoat, 'the forest of 1001 legends', in a green, tranquil setting with small pond and large flower garden with furniture and terrace. Guests are warmly welcomed and can enjoy farm life, walks, mountain biking and 4x4 driving. There are four double bedrooms, each with shower room and wc. Cot and baby equipment available. Outdoor play area for the children. Picnic baskets on request.

Prices not confirmed for 2008 **On Site** ⌘ **Nearby** ⌘ 3km ⌘ 6km Sea 30km ⌖ 1km ⌁ 5km Water sports 40km ⌂ 4km ⌂ 4km ⌬ 10km
Notes No pets English spoken

QUEMENEVEN

⚜ *Nanclic*

P et M JEZEQUEL-SQUIVIDAN

29180 QUEMENEVEN

☎ 02 98 73 51 86 ⌸ 02 98 73 51 86

email: P.Dulieu.Jezequel@wanadoo.fr

In the heart of the Cournouaille countryside, close to Locronan and Plonévez Porzay, this dairy farm has two double rooms, a twin, and a room with a single and double bedroom, each with shower room and wc. Lounge with fireplace and TV. Baby equipment available. Garden with furniture, terrace, barbecue and gazebo. Evening meals on reservation, except July and August.

Prices not confirmed for 2008 **Nearby** ⌘ 2km ⌘ 16km Sea 6km ⌖ 6km ⌁ 12km Water sports 12km ⌂ 2km ⌂ 2km ⌬ 8km
Notes No pets English spoken

QUIMPER

⚜ Le Logis du Stang

Annie HERVE

Stang Youenn, 29000 QUIMPER

☎ 06 81 55 73 83 & 02 98 52 00 55

email: logis-du-stang@wanadoo.fr

web: www.logis-du-stang.com

Ten minutes from the old town of Quimper, in the countryside, this 19th-century manor house at Ergué-Armel is on the cider route. It has a twin room, and two family rooms in a nearby longbarn having two double beds looking onto private terraces, and two single beds on a mezzanine level, TV and telephone. All have private facilities. Large garden with high stone walls.

Prices s fr €49; d €65-€82; extra person fr €20 **Nearby** ⌘ 9km ⌘ 12km Sea 12km ⌖ 5km ⌁ 5km Restaurant 2km Water sports 5km ⌂ 5km Spa 15km ⌂ 5km ⌂ 2km ⌬ 5km
Notes No pets English spoken CC

QUIMPERLE

⚜ ⎮◎⎮ *Domaine de Kervail*

F et J-Y DELATOUCHE-HERVE

29300 QUIMPERLE

☎ 02 98 35 06 47

email: francoise@domaine-de-kervail.com

web: http://domaine.kervail.free.fr/

A restored and converted longhouse, full of character, is the setting fo these four comfortable rooms. Three of the rooms are doubles; the other has twin beds. Two are on the ground floor, one with its own terrace and garden furniture. All have TV and private bath or shower room; extra beds available. Generous breakfasts.

Prices not confirmed for 2008 **Nearby** ⌘ 0.5km ⌘ 20km Sea 14km ⌖ 1km ⌁ 1km Water sports 15km ⌂ 0.5km ⌂ 14km ⌂ 0.5km ⌬ 1km
Notes No pets

ROSNOEN

⚜ ❦ ⌇ *Le Seillou*

Familles TROADEC et LE PAPE

29590 ROSNOEN

☎ 02 98 81 92 21 ⌸ 02 98 81 07 14

email: fermeaubergeduseillou@wanadoo.fr

web: www.gites-finistere.com/gites/seillou

A typical Breton family farm offering six bedrooms above the farm an in an annexe: four doubles, a twin and a double with a single bed; each has private facilities and lounge area. Garden with furniture, par and play area; meals of farm produce and home-made crêpes served on reservation. Set back from the D791, on the Presqu'île de Crozon crossroads and 300mtrs from the Rade de Brest.

Prices not confirmed for 2008 **Nearby** ⌘ 10km ⌘ 25km Sea 0.3km ⌖ 0.3km ⌁ 20km Water sports 18km ⌂ 5km ⌂ 3km ⌂ 6km ⌬ 15km
Notes No pets English spoken CC

ROSPORDEN

⚜ Kérantou

Monique BERNARD

29140 ROSPORDEN

☎ 02 98 59 27 79

email: monique.bernard7@wanadoo.fr

web: http://perso.wanadoo.fr/kerantou/

Guest rooms available in old farm buildings, close to the owners' home, 2km from Rosporden and 15km from Concarneau and Pont-Aven. Discover Breton traditions with the hosts and choose between three double rooms, two twins and a family room with a double bed and two singles, each with private facilities. Kitchen, sitting room, garden with furniture, barbecue, covered area, games, walks nearby. Baby sitting service. Fishing 2km.

Prices s fr €38; d fr €44; extra person fr €16 **Nearby** ⌘ 10km ⌘ 18km Sea 15km ⌖ 2km ⌁ 3km Restaurant 2km Water sports 15km ⌂ 3km ⌂ 3km ⌂ 2km ⌬ 3km **Notes** Pets admitted English spoken

⍟ Manoir de Coat Canton

Diana SIMON

Grand bois, 29140 ROSPORDEN

☎ 02 98 66 31 24

In a rural setting, this 13th-17th century manor house warmly welcomes guests. Two double rooms and a family room with a double and twin beds are available in a renovated longbarn, all comfortable with shower room and wc. Baby-sitting can be arranged. TV, telephone, washing machine, garden with furniture. Visits to the private museum and horse riding lessons on site. Close to the beach, Concarneau port, Quimper and Pont Aven.

Prices s fr €45; d fr €45; t fr €65   **Nearby** ⚑ 10km ⚓ 10km Sea 13km ⚓ 1km ⚓ 1km Water sports 13km ⚓ 1km ⚓ 0.5km ⚓ 0.5km ⚓ 1km
Notes No pets   English spoken

SANTEC

⍟ Chambre d'hôtes

Marie Pierre RIVOALLON

83 route du Dossen, 29250 SANTEC

☎ 02 98 29 70 65

email: mariepierre.rivoallon@wanadoo.fr

web: http://perso.wanadoo.fr/mariepierre.rivoallon/

Expect a warm welcome at this typically Breton home, in a green, tranquil setting. There is a family suite of two bedrooms (a double and twin), and three twin rooms, all with private facilities. Cot available. Flower garden with furniture, terrace, barbecue and parking. A large beach is only 1.5 km away, where you can enjoy land yachting, sea kayaking and surfing. Forest walks, creperie and several restaurants nearby. Roscoff 6km.

Prices not confirmed for 2008   **Nearby** ⚑ 15km ⚓ 15km Sea 1.5km ⚓ 1.5km ⚓ 2.5km Water sports 1.5km ⚓ 5km ⚓ 5km ⚓ 3km ⚓ 3km
Notes No pets   English spoken

SCAER

⍟ Kerloaï

Gabrielle & Hervé PENN

29390 SCAER

☎ 02 98 59 42 60 & 06 65 47 06 99

email: ti.penn@wanadoo.fr

web: www.gites-finistere.com/gites/kerloai

Situated between Armor (the sea region) and Argoat (the wood region), this property has four doubles and a twin room, all with private facilities. Enjoy calm evenings in the lovely garden and large breakfasts in the lounge, around the fireplace. Breton is spoken. Visit Pont Aven, Concarneau, Quimper and discover inner Brittany.

Prices s fr €40; d fr €50; extra person fr €20   **Nearby** ⚑ 15km ⚓ 15km Sea 20km ⚓ 4km ⚓ 4km Restaurant 4km Water sports 20km ⚓ 4km ⚓ 4km ⚓ 4km ⚓ 10km   **Notes** Pets admitted   English spoken

SCRIGNAC

⍟ Le Cloître

Lionel COTONNEC

29640 SCRIGNAC

☎ 02 98 78 23 17

This old renovated farmhouse is situated near to the cattle and dairy farm of the owners. There are three double guest rooms with shower room and wc. Enjoy the family atmosphere and tranquillity around the stretch of water and flower garden outside, and walking, fishing and nature discovery in the woods around the farm. Baby sitting by arrangement and telephone available.

Prices s fr €38; d fr €42; extra person fr €10   **Nearby** ⚑ 15km ⚓ 7km Sea 30km ⚓ 1km ⚓ 15km Restaurant 8km Water sports 15km ⚓ 7km ⚓ 15km ⚓ 7km ⚓ 15km   **Notes** Pets admitted   English spoken

SIBIRIL

⍟ Chambre d'hôtes

M-Claude et Michel DIMEY

29250 SIBIRIL

☎ 02 98 29 95 12 & 06 61 53 57 16

email: marieclaude.dimey@wanadoo.fr

These three rooms are on the first floor of the owners' home. There are three double rooms, all with private bath or shower room and WC. The lounge has an open fire and TV. Outdoors, there is a garden with terrace and garden furniture, and covered parking.

Prices d fr €50   **Nearby** ⚑ 7km ⚓ 12km Sea 3km ⚓ 1km ⚓ 9km Restaurant 3km Water sports 3km ⚓ 3km ⚓ 9km ⚓ 3km ⚓ 20km
Notes Pets admitted   English spoken

SPEZET

⍟ ◯ Manoir de Toullaeron

Nicole LASSAIGNE

29540 SPEZET

☎ 02 98 93 97 58

email: toullaeron@wanadoo.fr

Surrounded by flowers and greenery, this manor house has four guest bedrooms, all on the second floor. Two doubles and a twin-bedded room all have en suite facilities; there is also a grade 2 family suite for four, with private but not en suite bathroom/WC. Extra beds and baby-sitting can be arranged. Generous breakfasts, other meals by arrangement. Good walking area.

Prices not confirmed for 2008   **Nearby** ⚑ 5km ⚓ 12km Sea 45km ⚓ 6km ⚓ 4km Water sports 45km ⚓ 4km ⚓ 4km ⚓ 12km
Notes No pets

ST-JEAN-DU-DOIGT

ⅷ ⅳ⊙ *Ty Fumi*

Lionel et Yumi FACCENDA
9, Lot. de Pen Ar C'Hra, 29630 SAINT JEAN DU DOIGT
☎ 02 98 67 37 41 & 02 81 10 61 00
email: tyfumi@wanadoo.fr
web: http://www.tyfumi.fr

A friendly welcome is assured in this modern house overlooking the beach. There are three themed bedrooms, all on the ground floor: a twin-bedded room, a double, and a split-level family room with double bed and futons for a further four people. All have private facilities, TV and independent access. Baby equipment available. Garden with furniture; terrace with sea views.

Prices not confirmed for 2008 **Nearby** ⚓ 5km 🏊 25km Sea 1.4km
🌲 1.4km ⅈ 18km Water sports 6km 🚣 3.4km 🐎 3.5km 🏛 0.6km
🚴 20km **Notes** Pets admitted English spoken Open February to December

ST-MARTIN-DES-CHAMPS

ⅷ **Keréliza**

Marie-Noëlle ABIVEN
29600 SAINT-MARTIN-DES-CHAMPS
☎ 02 98 88 27 18

A charming renovated 19th-century manor house with five lovely bedrooms, all with private facilities: two twins, two doubles and a room with a double bed and single bed. Situated on a farm, with a large flower garden, parking is provided. There is also a sitting room with TV, kitchen, table tennis, billiards and baby equipment.

Prices s fr €32; d fr €45; t fr €55; extra person fr €10 **Nearby** ⚓ 10km
🏊 14km Sea 3km 🐎 3km ⅈ 2km Restaurant 0.5km Water sports 10km
🚣 2km 🐎 3km 🏛 2km 🚴 3km **Notes** Pets admitted English spoken

ST-THEGONNEC

ⅷ ⅳ⊙ *Ar Presbital Koz*

Christine PRIGENT
18, rue Lividic, 29410 SAINT THEGONNEC
☎ 02 98 79 45 62 📄 02 98 79 48 47
email: ar.presbital.koz@free.fr

In the Enclos Paroissiaux and Arrée mountains, this house was the Presbyterian church of Saint Thégonnec for two centuries. There are six spacious, comfortable bedrooms with private facilities: three doubles, two twins and a room with a double and single bed. The owners are happy to advise on the region. Bike hire, parking and meals using local specialities and regional produce available on reservation. Crêperie, restaurants and shops within 300mtrs. Discount after two nights.

Prices not confirmed for 2008 **On Site** 🐎 **Nearby** ⚓ 10km 🏊 12km
Sea 14km 🌲 1km ⅈ 6km Water sports 20km 🚣 🏛 0.5km 🚴 12km
Notes No pets English spoken

ST-THONAN

ⅷ 🌿 *Veuleury*

Marie Jo EDERN
29800 SAINT THONAN
☎ 02 98 20 26 99 & 06 85 75 18 72 📄 02 98 20 27 13
email: marie-jo.edern@wanadoo.fr

Three rooms available in this large, modern house: a family room with a double bed, twin beds, and a sitting area; a double room; a room with twin beds and a single. All have separate access, shower room, wc, heating and telephone. Sitting room, kitchen, terrace, garden with furniture, two gîtes available. Footpath and Chapelle St-Herbot 200m; visits to pig farm. Reduced rates between September and June, and after a week. Sports teams welcome.

Prices not confirmed for 2008 **Nearby** ⚓ 6km 🏊 9km Sea 15km
🌲 6km 🐎 6km Water sports 20km 🚣 2.5km 🏛 2.5km 🚴 5km
Notes No pets

ST-YVI

ⅷ **Kervren**

Odile LE GALL
29140 SAINT-YVI
☎ 02 98 94 70 34 & 06 08 06 54 93 📄 02 98 94 81 19
email: o.legall@wanadoo.fr

Near to Quimper, Concarneau, Bénodet and Pont-Aven, a longbarn on a 19th-century farm, 2.5km from town has six guest bedrooms: four doubles and two twins with shower room and wc. Sitting room with fireplace, kitchen, large breakfasts, lovely parkland with panoramic views. Shops, tennis court, swimming pool and river (for fishing) five minutes away; beach and golf course fifteen minutes.

Prices s fr €40; d fr €47 **Nearby** ⚓ 5km 🏊 10km Sea 10km 🌲 8km
🐎 5km Restaurant 8km Water sports 20km 🚣 5km Spa 20km 🏛 2km
🚴 10km **Notes** No pets Open March to December.

TOURC'H

ⅷ ⅳ⊙ *Ti ar Vourc'hized*

Rémy & Odette LE BOURHIS
Le Bourg, 29140 TOURC'H
☎ 02 98 59 15 42 📄 02 98 59 01 41
email: ti-ar-vourchized@wanadoo.fr

A large house in open countryside, between Concarneau and the Trévarez Château and opposite the 16th-century church. There are two double rooms and two twins, each with a TV and private facilities. Large dining room, sitting room and enclosed garden with terrace. Evening meals available, made from farm produce (duck pâté and poultry). Farm 2 km; shops close by.

Prices not confirmed for 2008 **Nearby** ⚓ 6km 🏊 30km Sea 20km
🌲 1km 🐎 7km Water sports 20km 🚣 7km 🚴 7km **Notes** No pets
Open 15 June to 15 September.

BRITTANY

TREOGAT

⑪⑪⑪ Kéramoine ·

Hélène & Michel FAOU
29720 TREOGAT

☎ 02 98 87 63 98 & 06 31 29 15 69   🖹 02 98 87 63 98

web: www.gites-finistere.com/gites/keramoine/

This house is 500 metres from the sea, and 15 kilometres from sandy beaches. It has three bedrooms, all on the first floor. A double room and a room for three both have en suite shower room/WC. There is also a grade 2 family room for five with private but not en suite facilities. Fridge available; garden with furniture and barbecue.

Prices s fr €40; d fr €45; t fr €60   **Nearby** 🚲 7km 🎣 15km Sea 0.5km ⚓ 0.5km 🏹 15km Water sports 10km 🏊 7km 🎾 7km 🏛 3km ♨ 30km
Notes No pets

ILLE-ET-VILAINE

ANTRAIN-SUR-COUESNON

⑪⑪⑪ ⍩⃝ Chambre d'hôtes

Claire LAGOUTTE-PERRIN
2, rue de Couesnon, 35560 ANTRAIN-SUR-COUESNON

☎ 02 99 98 43 76 & 06 70 25 08 66

email: claire.perrin5@wanadoo.fr

web: www.lamaisondeclaire.fr

This stone-built 18th-century house stands in the centre of the village. It has an enclosed courtyard with trees and garden furniture, and the interior of the house has much exposed woodwork and mouldings. It has one double room and two triples, all with private, but not en suite, facilities. Lounge area with TV; excellent breakfasts; other meals available by arrangement.

Prices not confirmed for 2008   **Nearby** 🎣 30km 🏹 25km 🏊 2km
Notes No pets

BAGUER-MORVAN

⑪⑪⑪ Les Sageais

Maurice et Yvonne PAPAIL
Baguer Morvan, 35120 DOL-DE-BRETAGNE

☎ 02 99 80 90 45

This restored stone house lies in wooded, green countryside and has two family suites, each containing two bedrooms, and a double room with private bathroom. Kitchen, lounge/dining room with fireplace and library on a mezzanine level available for guests' use. Outside, there are landscaped grounds with garden furniture, parking and children's games. Highlights include a warm welcome and generous breakfasts.

Prices s fr €38; d €40-€45; t €70; extra person fr €15   **Nearby** 🚲 2km 🎣 2km Sea 15km ⚓ 5km 🏹 5km Restaurant 1.5km 🏊 3km Spa 25km 🏛 1km ♨ 5km   **Notes** No pets

⑪⑪⑪ 🐓 ⍩⃝ Manoir de Launay Blot

B et G MABILE
35120 DOL-DE-BRETAGNE

☎ 02 99 48 07 48 & 06 09 21 60 26   🖹 02 99 80 94 47

email: launayblot@wanadoo.fr

web: www.launayblot .com

A 17th-century house built in the local style, not far from St-Malo. There are five very attractive rooms, two doubles, a triple, a family room for four, and a suite for four, all with en suite bathrooms. Garden with a pond and parking space; bike hire; meals by arrangement (not Sundays).

Prices not confirmed for 2008   **On Site** 🎣 ⚓   **Nearby** Sea 12km 🏹 6km 🏛 2km ♨ 6km   **Notes** Pets admitted English spoken

BAGUER-PICAN

⑪⑪⑪ Le Grand Villouët

Valérie et Jerome NIORT
35120 BAGUER-PICAN

☎ 02 99 80 94 29 & 06 23 36 12 95

email: valerie.niort@club-internet.fr

web: www.jardin-coramille.com

This 17th-century country house, with its English-style garden, is decorated and furnished in a natural style, with wood, whitewash, sea-grass and linen. It has three bedrooms. Upstairs are two triples (double beds plus singles), with an extra bed and cot available. The third room is a double, in a separate building in the garden. All the rooms have private facilities.

Prices not confirmed for 2008   **Nearby** 🎣 5km Sea 7km 🏹 2km 🏊 2km 🏛 2km ♨ 2km   **Notes** No pets English spoken

BAINS-SUR-OUST

⑪⑪⑪ Chambre d'hôtes

Marie ROBERT
23 rue de la Fosse Piquet, 35600 BAINS-SUR-OUST

☎ 02 99 91 60 10 & 06 98 83 39 32

In a small, rural village, known for the Ile au Pies, this modern house lies amongst large flowery, country grounds. There are three bedrooms for two people, each with a bathroom, a lounge/sitting room for guests and a terrace with garden furniture. A farm inn is 1.5km away and the beaches and sea of the Atlantic coast are an hour away.

Prices not confirmed for 2008   **Nearby** 🎣 15km Sea 35km ⚓ 3km 🏹 6km 🏊 1km ♨ 5km   **Notes** No pets English spoken

BETTON

�Ⅰ ❧ Bas Cheneze

Odile et Roger BESNIER

35830 BETTON

☎ 02 99 55 82 92 & 06 32 76 58 88 📄 02 99 55 31 44

email: roger.besnier.cheneze@orange.fr

A pretty farmhouse in lovely verdant countryside with terraces, garden furniture, a play area, volleyball pitch, animal park, private pond with fishing and walks. There is a family suite (double bed, three singles and kitchen) with a very spacious mezzanine level opening onto terraces, another family suite (two rooms with a double, cot and twin beds), two double rooms and a twin, all with private facilities. Lounge, sitting room with fireplace, kitchen with fridge and generous breakfasts available.

Prices s fr €32; d €38-€40; t €49-€51; extra person €11-€15
On Site ♈ **Nearby** ⚓ 4km ⚐ 10km ↘ 10km Restaurant 3km ⚓ 3km
Spa 10km ⚐ 3km ⚑ 2.5km **Notes** No pets

BRAIN-SUR-VILAINE

ⅢⅢ ⅠⅪ La Grand'Maison

Cathy et François BERTIN

La Grand'Maison Grande rue,

35660 BRAIN-SUR-VILAINE

☎ 06 22 52 58 30 & 02 99 70 25 81

email: bertinfrancois@wanadoo.fr

web: www.la-grand-maison.com

A beautiful 17th-century residence, entirely renovated and offering three double rooms and a four-person suite; all have private facilities and views over the grounds and La Vilaine. Regional specialities are served at breakfast and dinner (by reservation). Guests can explore the extensive walled and landscaped grounds.

Prices s fr €50; d fr €60; t fr €75; extra person fr €15; dinner fr €20 **Nearby** ⚓ 8km ⚐ 40km ♈ 0.1km ↘ 10km Restaurant 4km
⚓ 4km ⚑ 18km ⚐ 3km ⚑ 3km **Notes** Pets admitted English spoken Open February to November.

BREAL-SOUS-MONTFORT

ⅢⅢ ⅠⅪ ⅙ *Le Grenier d'Ernestine*

Julie NOGIER

Les Basses Barres, 35310 BREAL-SOUS-MONTFORT

☎ 02 99 60 34 03 & 06 81 11 17 33

email: contact@grenier-ernestine.com

web: www.grenier-ernestine.com

There are five rooms at this property, a 16th/17th-century country house. There is a ground floor triple room with disabled access, two further triple rooms, and two split-level family suites for four. All have en suite facilities. Cot available. Garden with terrace and parking space; table tennis and bike hire. Meals by arrangement.

Prices not confirmed for 2008 **Nearby** ⚐ 15km ♈ 5km ↘ 10km
⚓ 3km ⚐ 3km ⚑ 10km **Notes** Pets admitted CC

CANCALE

ⅢⅢ *Chambre d'hôtes*

Eric et Martine LOCHET

66, rue des Français Libres, 35260 CANCALE

☎ 02 99 89 63 32 & 06 81 13 99 44

email: contact@metairie-du-vauhariot.com

web: www.metairie-du-vauhariot.com

This 16th-century agricultural house is just five minutes on foot from the renowned oyster port of Cancale. It has four bedrooms, all with en suite shower room and two with sea views. There is a landscaped garden, with garden furniture and on-site parking. Beautiful breakfasts served in the dining room or out on the terrace. The hosts' fridge, microwave and living room with TV and open fire are all at guests' disposal.

Prices not confirmed for 2008 **Nearby** ⚐ 15km Sea 0.3km ♈ 1km
↘ 10km ⚓ 1km ⚐ 1km ⚑ 6km **Notes** No pets

ⅢⅢ *Chambre d'hôtes*

Sophie VERDON

No 68, av Général de Gaulle, 35260 CANCALE

☎ 06 50 39 61 53

email: sophie@chambre-cancale.com

An attractive modern house with three guest rooms, each decorated to an individual theme. Two of the rooms are doubles; the third has twin beds, and they all have TV and private bath or shower room. Extra beds available. Fitness room and sauna. Quiet enclosed garden with boules pitch, lots of flowers and a swimming pool. Parking on site.

Prices not confirmed for 2008 **On Site** Private ↘ **Nearby** ⚐ 15km
Sea 1km ♈ 1km ⚓ 0.5km ⚐ 1km ⚑ 15km **Notes** No pets

ⅢⅢ ⅠⅪ La Maison de la Marine

Christian POUSSET

23 rue de la Marine, 35260 CANCALE

☎ 02 99 89 88 53 📄 02 99 89 83 27

email: info@maisondelamarine.com

web: www.maisondelamarine.com

This property, now a luxurious and welcoming chambre d'hôtes, was originally an office building. It has two double rooms and three suites for four guests, with décor inspired by English bathing scenes from the beginning of the last century. All have private bath or shower room, TV and internet access. Lounge with books, open fire and piano; meals by arrangement.

Prices s fr €90; d €110-€140; t fr €155; extra person fr €15; dinner fr €26 **Nearby** ⚓ 5km ⚐ 15km Sea 0.3km ♈ 0.3km ↘ 0.3km
Restaurant 0.5km ⚓ 1km Spa 15km ⚑ 1km ⚐ 0.2km ⚑ 15km
Notes Pets admitted English spoken CC

⚑ ⍥ **Les Bulots**

Aline et ses enfants GALLAND

9, rue Roger Vercel, 35260 CANCALE

☎ 02 99 89 89 86 & 06 84 92 27 75 ▤ 02 99 89 89 86

email: lesbulots@free.fr

web: http://lesbulots.free.fr

This is a modern house, five minutes from the town centre and ten minutes from the coast. It has three bedrooms, all with private facilities and themed decorations relating to the sea. On the ground floor is a double room, also a room for four with its own entrance. Upstairs is another double. Lounge; generous breakfasts; enclosed garden with terrace and garden furniture.

Prices s €42-€47; d €47-€52; t €52-€57; extra person fr €10; dinner fr €20 **Nearby** ⤓0.5km Sea 1km ⌗1km ⤸15km Restaurant 0.5km ⌁0.5km Spa 15km ⌖0.5km ⌂1km ⇻10km **Notes** Pets admitted

---

CHAUVIGNE

⚑ **La Haunaie**

Aimée et Jean COUDRAY

35490 CHAUVIGNE

☎ 02 99 97 77 19 ▤ 02 99 95 02 09

This old, renovated house offers a warm welcome and is set in the countryside. There are two double rooms and a triple with private bathrooms, a sitting room with TV and a shady garden with furniture, large flowery courtyard and children's play area.

Prices s fr €25; d fr €35; t fr €47; extra person fr €12 **Nearby** ⤓10km ⌗4km ⤸15km ⌁20km ⌂4km ⇻40km **Notes** Pets admitted

---

CHERRUEIX

⚑ **L'Hamelinais**

Marie-Madeleine GLEMOT

Hamelinais, 35120 CHERRUEIX

☎ 02 99 48 95 26 & 06 17 47 53 49 ▤ 02 99 48 89 23

This old, restored house is situated in a small park with flowers and shade, between Mont Saint Michel and St Malo, and has warm personalised rooms. There are two double rooms, a triple and two rooms for four with a mezzanine, each with private bathroom. Lounge/ sitting room with old, granite open fireplace, terrace and parking.

Prices d fr €46; t fr €61; extra person fr €15 **Nearby** ⛵10km ⤓7km Sea 4km ⌗4km ⤸4km Restaurant 4km ⌁4km ⌖4km ⌂4km ⇻4km **Notes** No pets

---

⚑ **La Croix Gailliot**

Jean-Michel TAILLEBOIS

35120 CHERRUEIX

☎ 02 99 48 90 44

email: jmtaillebois@club-internet.fr

web: http://taillebois.club.fr

This 19th-century stone-built house stands between Mont-St-Malo and St-Malo. There are three double rooms and two triples, all with private bath or shower room and WC. Guest lounge, use of kitchen. Attractively laid out gardens with garden furniture and parking space.

Prices s €36-€40; d €42-€46; t €53-€57; extra person €10 **Nearby** ⤓15km Sea 2km ⌁2km ⤸7km Restaurant 2km ⌁2km Spa 25km ⌖5km ⌂2km ⇻7km **Notes** No pets English spoken

⚑ **La Pichardière**

Au manoir de la Pichardière

35120 CHERRUEIX

☎ 02 99 48 83 82

This old house lies on the coast near to Saint-Anne Chapel. It has a room with a double bed and four singles, one with two double beds, and two double rooms, all with private facilities. There is a lounge, sitting room with TV and fireplace, and large terrace area.

Prices s fr €35; d fr €45; t fr €60; extra person €15 **Nearby** ⤓18km Sea 0.1km ⤸15km Restaurant 2km ⌁3km Spa 40km ⌂2.5km ⇻10km **Notes** No pets

⚑ & **Le Lac**

Jeanne GUITTON

124, rue du Han, 35120 CHERRUEIX

☎ 02 99 48 93 77

email: guitton.julien@wanadoo.fr

web: http://perso.wanadoo.fr/le.lac

Half-way between Mont St-Michel and St-Malo, this 19th-century house has four bedrooms. On the ground floor is a double room with disabled access and space for an extra bed; upstairs are three more doubles. All of the rooms have private facilities and two of them have sea views. Footpath access to the shore. Generous breakfasts, lounge with books, garden with terrace and furniture.

Prices not confirmed for 2008 **On Site** Sea **Nearby** ⤓18km ⤸7km ⌁2km ⌂1km ⇻7km **Notes** No pets English spoken

---

COESMES

⚑ ⍥ **Manoir du Plessix**

Geneviève ANJOT

35134 COESMES

☎ 02 99 47 77 33 ▤ 02 99 47 79 74

email: j.j.anjot@wanadoo.fr

web: www.manoirduplessix.com

Your host will entrance you with the history of her house, part of which dates back to 1186, situated in a small hamlet. There are two suites for two to four people, each with private facilities; additional beds available. Breakfast and evening meals feature home produce; large garden with furniture.

Prices s fr €46; d fr €55; t fr €70; extra person fr €15; dinner fr €20 **Nearby** ⛵5km ⤓30km ⌗1km ⤸20km Restaurant 4km ⌂4km ⇻4km **Notes** No pets CC

BRITTANY

DINARD

⑪ ⑩ **Le Clos d'Enhaut**

Maïté et Alain BERNARD

42 rue de la Ville es Meniers, 35800 DINARD

☎ 02 99 46 27 82 & 06 73 37 90 75

email: leclosdenhaut@orange.fr

This is a 19th-century longhouse, close to the sea and mid-way between Mont-St-Michel and Cap Fréhel. There is a double room on the ground floor; upstairs is another double, and a family suite for four (double bed plus singles). All have individually themed decorations and en suite facilities; extra beds are available. Meals by arrangement, with local specialities.

Prices s fr €57; d fr €62; extra person fr €15; dinner fr €25
Nearby ⛵ 1km ⚓ 5km Sea 1.2km ✎ 5km ➷ 1.5km ⛰ 1km Spa 1.5km
⛳ 1.5km ⛴ 0.8km ⋙ 8km **Notes** No pets English spoken

DOL-DE-BRETAGNE

⑪ ⑩ *Chambre d'hôtes*

Catherine COSTARD-SOULABAILLE

La Begaudière, Mont-Dol, 35120 DOL-DE-BRETAGNE

☎ 02 99 48 20 04 ▤ 02 99 48 20 04

email: bonds@club-internet.fr

web: www.begaudiere.com

On the edge of a river, this house of character has two double bedrooms, a triple and two four-person split-level bedrooms, all with private facilities. Lounge with fireplace, garden and terrace overlooking tree-lined parkland.

Prices not confirmed for 2008 **Nearby** ⚓ 10km Sea 8km ➷ 1.5km
⛰ 1km ⛴ 1km ⋙ 1.5km **Notes** Pets admitted English spoken

⑪ *Haute Lande*

Riekus et Ineke RENTING

35120 DOL-DE-BRETAGNE

☎ 02 99 48 07 02 ▤ 02 99 48 07 02

email: renting@wanadoo.fr

web: www.lahautelande.fr

There are two double bedrooms and a triple, each with private bathroom, in this old 17th-century manor house with a garden and lawn. There is also a lounge/sitting room and terrace with garden furniture. The house is situated on a farm, near to numerous towns and tourist sites such as Dol, Dinan, Saint Malo, Mont Saint-Michel, Combourg.

Prices not confirmed for 2008 **Nearby** ⚓ 3km ➷ 3km ⛰ 3km ⛴ 3km
⋙ 3km **Notes** No pets English spoken

⑪ *L'Aunay Begasse*

Alain RONCIER

35120 DOL-DE-BRETAGNE

☎ 02 99 48 16 93 ▤ 02 99 48 16 93

There is a double and two triple rooms in this stone, country house, each with a bathroom. Set in a lovely flower garden with a friendly atmosphere. Large breakfasts, sitting room and TV. Fishing can be enjoyed 1km away.

Prices not confirmed for 2008 **Nearby** ⚓ 7km Sea 8km ➷ 1km
⛰ 0.5km ⛴ 1km ⋙ 1km **Notes** No pets

⑪ ⑩ **La Loubatais**

Annick DAUMER

35120 DOL-DE-BRETAGNE

☎ 02 99 48 19 27

web: www.laloubatais.com

A peaceful and relaxing place to go back to, after your day spent on the beach or exploring this area. It has a double room, a room for three (double bed and single) and a room for four (double bed and two singles), all with private facilities. Meals are available by arrangement in the winter period (mid-October to mid-April).

Prices s fr €35; d fr €42-€44; extra person €12-€15; dinner fr €18
Nearby ⛵ 8km ⚓ 10km Sea 10km ➷ 3km Restaurant 3km ⛰ 3km
Spa 25km ⛴ 3km ⋙ 3km **Notes** Pets admitted

EPINIAC

⑪ **Cadran**

Régine SANGUY

Vallée de Cadran, 35120 EPINIAC

☎ 02 99 80 03 55

This modern house is tucked in a peaceful green valley, close to the bay of Mont St-Michel. It has a double room on the ground floor, with another double and a very spacious triple upstairs. All the rooms have private facilities. Lounge, flower garden; good centre for touring.

Prices d €41-€47; t €56-€62 **Nearby** ⛵ 4km ⚓ 4km Sea 25km
✎ 1km ➷ 7km Restaurant 6km ⛰ 1km Spa 25km ⛴ 1.5km ⋙ 6km
Notes No pets

ESSE

⑪ ⑩ ♿ **L'Arthurais**

Françoise et Marcel MARTIN

35150 ESSE

☎ 02 99 47 06 17 & 06 08 26 47 99

A restored farmhouse, peaceful and welcoming, surrounded by greenery. It has four guest rooms, one with disabled access. Two are doubles; the other two are triples, and they all have private shower rooms/WCs. Lounge and dining room with open fire; breakfasts are generous, and can be served outdoors in the summer. There is a pond in the grounds.

Prices s fr €41; d fr €51; t fr €69; extra person fr €18; dinner fr €20
Nearby ⚓ 35km ➷ 14km ⛰ 1km ⋙ 4km **Notes** No pets

⊪ *La Roche aux Fées*

Béatrice ROZE

35150 ESSE

☎ 02 99 47 73 84 & 06 07 06 04 22 🖹 02 99 47 79 25

email: relais-des-fees@wanadoo.fr

web: www.roche-aux-fees.com

Four bedrooms available in the owner's house: three rooms for two and one for four, each with a bathroom. Generous home-made breakfasts and the house is attached to an inn, where you can enjoy local produce. Outside, there is a terrace with garden furniture and close by, the largest dolmen in Brittany (the Roche aux Fées), with its summer spectacles.

Prices not confirmed for 2008   **Nearby** ℰ 5km ↖ 15km ♨ 3km 🖾 3km 🚌 3km   **Notes** Pets admitted English spoken CC

GAHARD

⊪ **La Rogerie**

André et Angèle HOUDUSSE

Le Bourg, 35490 GAHARD

☎ 02 99 39 50 17 & 06 88 15 85 79

There are three bedrooms available in this stone house: two triples and a room for two, all with private facilities. Extra bed on request. There is a lounge/sitting room with fireplace, kitchen and grounds with garden furniture. Fishing can be enjoyed nearby and there is a pony club on site.

Prices s fr €30; d €38-€40; t €49-€51; extra person fr €13   **On Site** ♨ **Nearby** ♨ 30km ℰ 6km ↖ 10km Restaurant 0.2km ♨ 0.1km 🚌 12km **Notes** No pets

⊪ ⊙ **Les Viviers**

V et A DUGUEPEROUX

35490 GAHARD

☎ 02 99 39 50 19 & 02 99 45 75 61

email: les.viviers@laposte.net

This house is full of character and attached to a dairy farm, in a verdant setting between Rennes and Mont-St-Michel. There are two rooms for two and two triples, each with private bathroom. Extra bed possible. There is a lounge/drawing room with TV for guests, evening meals available on request and a garden with child's play area and terrace. Fishing 6km away and hiking possible from the property.

Prices not confirmed for 2008   **Nearby** ♨ 30km Sea 40km ↖ 10km ♨ 1km 🖾 1km 🚌 12km   **Notes** Pets admitted

---

GUICHEN

⊪⊪ **Château de Bagatz**

Daniel et Christiane DIOT

35580 GUICHEN

☎ 02 99 57 09 88 & 06 22 15 40 91

🖹 02 99 57 02 48

email: chateaudebagatz@aol.com

web: www.chateaudebagatz.com

In an enchanting and romantic setting, this pretty 15th-century property lies in sixty-five hectares of parkland and woods including a pond. Rooms include two double rooms (one with lounge in a tower), a triple and a suite for four people, each with spacious bathrooms. There is a lounge and games room with books, TV and table tennis, and a terrace with garden furniture where guests can enjoy generous breakfasts. On site there are walking paths, an equestrian centre and nearby attractions include Rennes and the Brocéliande Forest.

Prices s €65-€70; d €80-€90; t €100-€110; extra person fr €20   **On Site** ♘ **Nearby** ♨ 0.1km ♨ 6km ℰ 0.1km ↖ 10km Restaurant 2km ♨ 3km 🖾 2km 🚌 20km   **Notes** No pets English spoken

---

GUIPRY

⊪ **La Bouetelaie**

C RENAUD et P LEROY

35480 GUIPRY

☎ 02 99 34 76 12 & 06 18 01 45 87

email: gitecorbinieres@free.fr

web: http://gitecorbinieres.free.fr

This old longhouse is in a tranquil wooded spot, with much to offer anglers and walkers. There are three bright bedrooms, all upstairs, and all with en suite facilities. One room is a double, another has twin beds, and the third is a family room. Lounge with books, and a corner where guests can make hot drinks; varied breakfast menu.

Prices not confirmed for 2008   **Nearby** ↖ 3km ♨ 3km 🖾 2.5km 🚌 3km   **Notes** No pets English spoken Open February to 21 December.

HIREL

⊪ **Chambre d'hôtes**

Marlène et Michel HARDOUIN

10 rue du Domaine, 35120 HIREL

☎ 02 99 48 95 61 & 06 83 57 96 34

email: hardouinm@wanadoo.fr

This rural house is near Mont Saint-Michel bay and has four rooms for two and one for four guests, all with private bathrooms. Extra beds may be available on request. There is a lounge area, reading area, sitting room with TV, garden and parking.

Prices not confirmed for 2008   **Nearby** ♨ 15km Sea 0.8km ↖ 15km ♨ 0.1km 🖾 0.2km 🚌 8km   **Notes** Pets admitted

HIREL *CONTINUED*

⊞ *Le Clos des Chaumières*

Yvelyne et Patrick DESHOUX

24 la ville es Fleurs, 35120 HIREL

☎ 02 99 80 86 29

email: matthieu.deshoux@wanadoo.fr

web: http://monsite.wanadoo.fr/leclosdeschaumieres

Near to Mont St Michel, this establishment offers a family room for four people and two double rooms, all with private facilities. The house features a lounge, an open fire, a garden and large terraces. Generous breakfasts are served.

Prices not confirmed for 2008 **Nearby** ⌀15km Sea 2km ⌀10km ⌁6km ⌁1.5km ⌁2km ⋙6km **Notes** No pets English spoken

IFFENDIC

⊞ ⎰⎱ *Le Château du Pin*

Catherine et Luc RUAN

35750 IFFENDIC-PRES-MONTFORT

☎ 06 80 22 45 26

email: luc.ruan@wanadoo.fr

web: www.chateaudupin-bretagne.com

This welcoming 19th-century château is surrounded by a park and offers two suites for four people and a double room, each with private facilities and decorated with a literary theme: Victor Hugo, George Sand and Marcel Proust. A lounge featuring an exhibition of art and photography can be reserved, and watercolour lessons are available. Breakfasts with home-made cakes and delicious dinners are served in the dining room, and there is a lounge with books and fireplace.

Prices not confirmed for 2008 **Nearby** ⌀20km ⌁3km ⌁3km ⌁3km ⋙3km **Notes** No pets English spoken CC

LA BOUEXIERE

⊞ *La Ferme Gourmande*

Marie-Thérèse FEUGUEUR

35340 LA BOUEXIERE

☎ 02 99 04 43 90

email: lefermegourmande@wanadoo.fr

web: http://ferme.gourmande.free.fr

These two rooms are in a magnificent stone-built village inn, in green surroundings with lots of trees and a wonderful view. One room is a double with its own lounge and convertible bed; the other is also a double, with a cot. Both rooms have private showers and WCs. Lounge with books and TV. Grounds with terrace and garden furniture. Meals available.

Prices not confirmed for 2008 **Nearby** ⌀21km ⌁7km ⌁2km ⌁0.5km ⋙8km **Notes** No pets

LAILLE

⊞ *La Renouette*

Laurence et Jacques RENOU

35890 LAILLE

☎ 02 23 61 49 12 & 06 64 99 71 27 ▤ 02 99 67 65 91

email: renoujacques@wanadoo.fr

There are two ground floor rooms at this property: a double, and a two-roomed family suite for four. Upstairs there is a further double room, and a triple. All have private facilities. This is a traditional longhouse, in the countryside ten minutes from Rennes. Four hectares of grounds, with a lake where fishing is available.

Prices not confirmed for 2008 **On Site** ⌀ **Nearby** ⌁10km ⌁5km ⌁3km ⋙5km **Notes** No pets

LANDEAN

⊞ ⎰⎱ *La Haute Bourdière*

Thérèse LASSERRE

35133 LANDEAN

☎ 02 99 97 21 52 ▤ 02 99 97 33 09

email: haute-bourdiere@wanadoo.fr

web: www.haute-bourdiere.com

Ample accommodation in this typical Breton house, with three doubles and a room for three or four, all with shower/WC, and another family room for four with bath/WC. Plentiful home-cooked breakfasts.

Prices not confirmed for 2008 **Nearby** Sea 35km ⌁15km ⌁5km ⌁5km **Notes** Pets admitted CC

LA RICHARDAIS

⊞ *Le Berceul*

Annie et René DUAULT

24 rue de la Theaudais, 35780 LA RICHARDAIS

☎ 02 23 17 06 00 & 06 63 29 86 21 ▤ 02 23 17 06 01

email: berceul@wanadoo.fr

web: www.berceul.com

Back in the 18th century, this property was the home of a ship-owner. Today it has three very attractive and individually decorated guest bedrooms: a double room, a twin-bedded room, and a two-roomed suite. Each has its own entrance, private bath/shower room and WC. Dinard is five minutes away, and the River Rance is just 800 metres from the house.

Prices d €66-€81; extra person fr €16 **Nearby** ⌀3km ⌀6km Sea 2km ⌀0.8km ⌁4km Restaurant 1km ⌁0.8km Spa 5km ⌁5km ⌁0.5km ⋙10km **Notes** No pets English spoken

BRITTANY

LE GRAND-FOUGERAY

⚞ **Manoir des Hautes Joussardais**

M-Claude MARZELIERE

35390 LE GRAND-FOUGERAY

☎ 02 99 08 42 59

A restored 17th-century manor house, now used as an equestrian property. It has three double bedrooms, each individually decorated, and all with private bath or shower room and WC. Cots are available. There is a pleasant lounge with open fire and TV; breakfasts are generous, and can be served outdoors in the summer.

Prices s fr €45; d fr €55; t fr €65; extra person fr €15   **Nearby** ⌖ 1km ⚞ 15km Restaurant 0.6km ⚌ 1km ⌂ 0.5km ⋙ 12km   **Notes** No pets

LE TRONCHET

⚞ ⚟ **Le Baillage**

Catherine SCALART

35540 LE TRONCHET

☎ 02 99 58 17 98 & 06 19 56 28 47

email: info@lebaillage.com

web: www.lebaillage.com

A beautiful home, full of character and charm, with three large and beautifully decorated double rooms with TV, bathrooms and private wcs. There is also a sitting room, lounge with open fireplace and terrace with garden furniture. You can enjoy golf in Le Tronchet or the forest in Mesnil.

Prices s fr €65; d €75–€80; extra person fr €20; dinner fr €27   **Nearby** ⌖ 3.5km ⚞ 0.5km Sea 20km ⚐ 0.2km ⚞ 7km Restaurant 1km Spa 20km ⚑ 10km ⌂ 0.1km ⋙ 8km **Notes** No pets English spoken

LOHEAC

⚞ **Chambre d'hôtes**

Maïté POUSSIN

34 rue de la Poste, 35550 LOHEAC

☎ 06 80 63 38 95 ▤ 02 99 34 08 93

email: loheac.loisirs@wanadoo.fr

web: www.loheac-colibri.com

This guesthouse has been entirely renovated, and decorated with an aviation theme. On the ground floor is a triple room with shower and WC, suitable for the disabled. On the first floor are a double with bathroom and two triples, each with shower and WC. TV, lounge, billiards; cot available; terrace, garden. Car museum nearby.

Prices s fr €50; d fr €50   **Nearby** ⌖ 5km ⚞ 10km ⚐ 5km ⚞ 5km Restaurant 0.5km ⚌ 0.5km ⋙ 30km   **Notes** Pets admitted

MARCILLE-RAOUL

⚞ ⚘ ⚟ *Chambre d'hôtes*

Annick et Louis RAULT

Le Petit Plessis, 35560 MARCILLE-RAOUL

☎ 06 61 47 28 29

email: rault.annick@tiscali.fr

web: http://petit.plessix.chez.tiscali.fr

This house offers a four-person bedroom and a communicating room with a double and twin beds, a room with a double bed and sofa bed for two and two doubles, all with private facilities. Lounge/sitting room, kitchen, lawn with garden furniture and barbecue. Evening meals by reservation, apart from Saturdays and Sundays. Visit the farm or go fishing 3km away. Restaurant 1km.

Prices not confirmed for 2008   **Nearby** ⚞ 18km Sea 30km ⚞ 9km ⌂ 1km ⋙ 10km   **Notes** Pets admitted

MINIAC-MORVAN

⚞ ⚟ **Estival**

Tina et Malcolm KINZETT

La Ville Blanche, 35540 MINIAC-MORVAN

☎ 02 96 83 33 30 & 06 70 11 48 40 ▤ 02 96 88 26 56

email: estival@tiscali.fr

web: www.estivalbrittany.com

A stone house on the banks of the river, with a large flower garden and grounds, terrace and garden furniture. There is a family suite of two bedrooms (a double and twin) and four double bedrooms with private bathrooms. Breakfasts and meals are served in the dining room or on the summer terrace and include home-made and local produce.

Prices s €44–€52; d €50–€58; t €66–€73; extra person fr €16; dinner fr €20   **Nearby** ⚞ 5km ⚞ 8km Sea 15km ⚞ 10km Restaurant 2km ⚌ 3km Spa 22km ⌂ 3km ⋙ 4km   **Notes** No pets English spoken Open March to 15 November.

⚞ **La Chalandière**

Marcel et Marie PITON

35540 MINIAC-MORVAN

☎ 02 99 58 00 91

This is the annexe of an old manor house, peacefully situated in the countryside. It has three bedrooms, a double and two triples, all upstairs and all with private bath or shower room and WC. There is a guests' lounge close to the bedrooms, and breakfasts are served in the superb dining room. Garden furniture and swings.

Prices s fr €48; d fr €52; t fr €65; extra person fr €12   **On Site** ⚐ **Nearby** ⚞ 6km ⚞ 5km Sea 12km ⚞ 12km Restaurant 5km ⚌ 8km Spa 15km ⌂ 5km ⋙ 3km   **Notes** No pets

BRITTANY

MINIAC-MORVAN CONTINUED

∰ ⏀ La Maison Neuve

Nicole BARBOT

35540 MINIAC-MORVAN

☎ 06 85 01 21 73 & 02 99 58 05 38 📄 02 99 58 05 38

email: fbarbot@wanadoo.fr

web: www.la-maison-neuve.com

Two triple rooms on the ground floor, and two doubles and a triple upstairs, all with bath and WC; extra beds can be arranged. Massive grounds, an ideal mix of countryside and seaside.

Prices s €65-€68; d €72-€75; t €87-€92; extra person €15-€17; dinner fr €28 **Nearby** ⌕6km Sea 14km ⌔6km ⤳12km ⌕2km ⌕2km ⌕1km **Notes** No pets English spoken CC

MONT-DOL

∰ ⏀ Au Château de Mont-Dol

Yannick GOULVESTRE

1, rue de la Mairie, 35120 MONT-DOL

☎ 02 99 80 74 24 & 06 24 31 87 49

email: yannick.goulvestre@wanadoo.fr

web: www.chateaumontdol.com

An attractive house dating from the early 19th century, with five guest bedrooms. There is a triple room with terrace and private garden, two double rooms, a suite and a family room. All have private bathroom and WC. Lounge with books, games and an open fire. Yannick, your host, is a very experienced cook who prepares delicious meals from local produce.

Prices s fr €65; d fr €70; t fr €80; extra person fr €15; dinner fr €30 **Nearby** ⌕11km Sea 5km ⤳2km ⌕2km ⌕2km **Notes** No pets English spoken

∰ La Roche

François-Xavier et Joëlle LAIR

35120 MONT-DOL

☎ 06 82 75 78 36

A stone-built house situated at the foot of Mont Dol and not far from the bay of Mont-St-Michel. It has three bedrooms, all with private bath or shower room and WC. There is a lounge, and games for children. Possible use of kitchen, off-road parking.

Prices s fr €37; d €42-€45; t fr €54 **Nearby** ⌕4km ⌕10km Sea 5km ⤳3km Restaurant 3km ⌕4km Spa 25km ⌕1km ⌕4km **Notes** No pets

NOYAL-SUR-VILAINE

∰ ❤ Le Val Froment

Michel et Edith LEHUGER

35530 NOYAL-SUR-VILAINE

☎ 02 99 00 66 29 & 06 88 01 05 85

email: edith.lehuger@wanadoo.fr

There are two double bedrooms and a triple with private facilities available in this restored property, in a lovely, green setting. Extra bed or cot available on request. Lounge/sitting room with a fireplace and kitchen area; terrace with garden furniture. Learn about their farming life and enjoy farm produce at breakfast.

Prices not confirmed for 2008 **Nearby** ⌕5km ⤳6km ⌕1km ⌕0.5km ⌕1km **Notes** No pets English spoken

ORGERES

∰ Bouharée

Elisabeth BILLAND

35230 ORGERES

☎ 02 99 57 73 23 & 06 32 29 14 19

email: elisabeth-billand@hotmail.fr

web: www.elisabeth-billand.com

Just a few minutes from Rennes, but in a quiet and attractive setting among plenty of greenery. This property has three double rooms, all with private bath or shower room and WC. An extra bed is available, and there is a separate guests' entrance. The lounge has an open fire, and the breakfasts are bountiful. Closed at Christmas.

Prices s fr €39; d fr €49; extra person fr €15 **Nearby** ⌕10km ⤳7km ⌕1km ⌕1km ⌕15km **Notes** No pets English spoken

PAIMPONT

∰ La Corne de Cerf

Annie et Robert MORVAN

Le Cannée, 35380 PAIMPONT

☎ 02 99 07 84 19 📄 02 99 07 84 19

There are prettily decorated bedrooms in this house of character, situated in the Brocéliande forest: two triples, a room for four and a double with private bathroom. There is a lounge with fireplace, sitting room for guests, library, park with garden furniture and terrace attached to the house. Forest with a number of footpaths and hiking routes nearby.

Prices s fr €47; d fr €55; t fr €71; extra person fr €16 **Nearby** ⌕27km ⌔2km ⤳7km Restaurant 1km ⌕2km ⌕2km ⌕2km ⌕45km **Notes** No pets Open February to December.

PIRE-SUR-SEICHE

∰ ♿ Les Epinays

René COLLEU

35150 PIRE-SUR-SEICHE

☎ 02 99 00 01 16 & 06 12 02 38 22

email: lesepinays@wanadoo.fr

There are three comfortable double rooms and a triple with private facilities in this charming restored 18th-century longère, set in flower adorned grounds in a small valley. There is a large sitting room with fireplace, a room with disabled access and evening meals available on request.

Prices not confirmed for 2008 **Nearby** ⌕12km ⤳10km ⌕6km ⌕12km **Notes** No pets English spoken

PLECHATEL

☷ *Tillac*

Valérie BETAIL

35470 PLECHATEL

☎ 02 23 50 21 33 & 06 85 57 42 69

email: vbetail@wanadoo.fr

web: http://tillac.monsite.orange.fr

This character property has three bedrooms, two doubles and a triple, all with en suite facilities. It is a tastefully restored old farmhouse, on the edge of a forest, in a good area for walks. Outside is a big garden, with a terrace for sitting out. Breakfasts include home-made jams and pastries.

Prices not confirmed for 2008　**Nearby** ⚓ 17km 🎣 2km ⚡ 8km ⚘ 8km ⚑ 2km ⚓ 2km　**Notes** No pets　English spoken

PLEINE-FOUGERES

☷ ❧ *La Costardière*

Gérard et Isabelle HERVE

35610 PLEINE-FOUGERES

☎ 02 99 48 55 92

email: lacostardiere@aol.com

web: www.la-costardiere.com

This 16th-century manor house lies on a working farm and has a two-person room, a triple and a room for four, all with private facilities; two with fireplace. Sitting room available; parkland with animals and kids' games, fields, woods, a stretch of water for fishing and boating and river around the property.

Prices not confirmed for 2008　**Nearby** ⚓ 15km ⚡ 0.2km ⚡ 11km ⚘ 2km　**Notes** No pets　English spoken

PLELAN-LE-GRAND

☷ Hôtel Jouet

Patrice et Edwige LEFEBVRE

35380 PLELAN-LE-GRAND

☎ 02 99 06 98 66

web: www.hotel-jouet-broceliande.com

This renovated Breton longhouse has three double rooms with shower/WC, and a suite for up to five people with bathroom and WC. Plenty of stone and beams, old furniture and paintings, and generous breakfasts.

Prices s fr €40; d fr €46; t fr €56; extra person fr €10　**Nearby** ⚓ 20km ⚡ 20km Sea 45km ⚡ 5km Restaurant 3km ⚘ 5km Spa 30km ⚑ 2.5km ⚓ 30km　**Notes** No pets　English spoken

PLEUGUENEUC

☷ ◎ *Les Bruyères*

Françoise KOPP

35720 PLEUGUENEUC

☎ 02 99 69 47 75　🖹 02 99 69 47 75

Three charming rooms with private facilities (two doubles and a twin) are provided in this 17th-century property, which offers a warm welcome in a tranquil and pretty setting. Facilities include a lounge with fireplace and satellite TV, table d'hôte meals by reservation and bikes are also available. Close to Dinan, Combourg, St Malo and Mont St Michel.

Prices not confirmed for 2008　**Nearby** ⚓ 10km Sea 25km ⚡ 10km ⚘ 4km　**Notes** Pets admitted　English spoken

☷ Lézard Tranquille

Julie de LORGERIL

35720 PLEUGUENEUC

☎ 02 99 69 40 36 & 06 03 96 12 38

This magnificent property is situated in the grounds of the 17th-century Bourbansais château. There are five bedrooms, each with private bathrooms and wc, a TV and lounge/sitting room with fireplace, table tennis and bikes available. Direct access to the château, its parkland and zoo.

Prices s fr €40; d fr €45; t fr €55　**Nearby** ⚔ 20km ⚓ 10km Sea 25km ⚡ 10km Restaurant 2km ⚘ 0.5km Spa 30km ⚓ 10km　**Notes** Pets admitted　English spoken

PLEURTUIT

☷ La Métairie

Nathalie GARREC MERVIN

La Mettrie Labbé, 35730 PLEURTUIT

☎ 02 99 16 02 94　🖹 02 99 46 54 37

email: nathalie@chambrelametairie.com

web: www.chambrelametairie.com

This pretty renovated property is set near to Dinan and just 6km from the sea and provides a family atmosphere in a rustic setting. It offers four guest rooms: a double, two triples and a room for four with private facilities and TV. Parking is available.

Prices d €45-€56; t €56-€65; extra person fr €13　**Nearby** ⚔ 5km ⚓ 6km Sea 5km ⚡ 2km ⚡ 6km Restaurant 5km ⚘ 5km Spa 0.6km ⚑ 3km ⚓ 15km　**Notes** No pets　English spoken

REDON

☷ La Maison Jaune

Sylvie et Patrice HULBERT

31 rue de Vannes, 35600 REDON

☎ 02 99 72 22 30 & 06 66 50 95 81　🖹 02 99 72 22 30

email: chambredhote.redon@wanadoo.fr

web: http://lamaisonjaune.monsite.wanadoo.fr

Close to the centre of the fascinating historic town of Redon, this 1930s property has three bedrooms. Two are doubles, and there is

CONTINUED

REDON CONTINUED

a family room for four. All have en suite shower rooms, and a cot is available. The town, with its canals, pleasure port, swimming pool and multiplex cinema is on the doorstep.

Prices s fr €50; d fr €55; extra person fr €20   **On Site** 🏊
Nearby ⛷ 7km ♨ 15km Sea 40km ⚓ 1km 🏊 3km 🎣 3km 🏛 0.5km
🚶 1km   **Notes** No pets English spoken

ROZ-LANDRIEUX

☰ ⟨○⟩ *Les Champs de Roz*

Marie-Odile MAINSARD
8, Grande Rue, 35120 ROZ-LANDRIEUX
☎ 02 99 48 25 19 🖹 02 99 48 25 19
email: marieodile.mainsard@wanadoo.fr
web: http://monsite.wanadoo.fr/leschamps.deroz/

This stone-built house has five guest bedrooms. On the ground floor is a double room with a child's bed on a mezzanine; on the first floor is a family room for up to five; on the second floor are two doubles and a room for three. All of the rooms have private bath or shower room and WC.

Prices not confirmed for 2008   **Nearby** ♨ 4km Sea 10km ⚓ 5km
🏊 1.5km   **Notes** No pets

☰ *Manoir de la Mettrie*

Claude JOURDAN
35120 ROZ-LANDRIEUX
☎ 02 99 48 29 21 🖹 02 99 48 29 21
email: manoirmettrie@wanadoo.fr
web: www.manoir-de-la-mettrie.com

Three double bedrooms and two bedrooms for three/four people, each with bathroom, in this magnificent 13th and 16th-century manor house. Lounge, reading room and sitting room with TV. Garden with furniture and children's play area.

Prices not confirmed for 2008   **Nearby** ♨ 4km ⚓ 4km 🏊 0.5km 🏛 3km
🚶 3km   **Notes** No pets

ROZ-SUR-COUESNON

☰ ⟨○⟩ *Chambre d'hôtes*

Marie-Jo MANCHERON
2 rue des Mondrins, Fleur de Sel,
35610 ROZ-SUR-COUESNON
☎ 02 99 80 20 60 & 06 30 90 96 09
email: mjtmancheron@wanadoo.fr
web: http://membres.lycos.fr/mjtmancheron/

This is a beautiful 18th-century house in wooded grounds three kilometres from the sea and six kilometres from Mont-St-Michel. It has four comfortable, spacious rooms: two doubles, and two family rooms for four. All have private bath/shower room and WC. Lounge with TV, use of kitchenette. Breakfasts include home-made crêpes and jam, and other meals are available except during July and August.

Prices not confirmed for 2008   **Nearby** ♨ 20km Sea 3km ⚓ 12km
🏊 0.8km 🏛 0.8km 🚶 12km   **Notes** No pets

☰ *La Bergerie*

Jacky PIEL
La Poultière, 35610 ROZ-SUR-COUESNON
☎ 02 99 80 29 68 🖹 02 99 80 29 68
web: www.la-bergerie-mont-saint-michel.com

A large 17th and 18th-century granite property with five bedrooms for between two and four people, each with private bathroom. There is a lounge/sitting room and kitchen area for guests, a lawn and parking. The house is situated in Mont Saint-Michel bay, between Cancale and Mont-Saint-Michel.

Prices not confirmed for 2008   **Nearby** ♨ 13km ⚓ 18km 🏊 9km
🏛 0.2km 🚶 8km   **Notes** Pets admitted English spoken

☰ ♿ *La Roselière*

Bernard et Odile MOUBECHE
35610 ROZ-SUR-COUESNON
☎ 02 99 80 22 05 🖹 02 99 80 22 05
web: www.la-roseliere.com

This 16th-century home produces foie gras paté and has three triple bedrooms (one with disabled access) and two four-people rooms, all with private bathrooms. There is a lounge with TV, courtyard and garden, and food can be provided on request. The house is on the tourist route, near Pontorson, Saint Malo, the coast and the river.

Prices s fr €41; d fr €45; t fr €50   **Nearby** ♨ 15km ⚓ 20km 🏊 1km
🏛 1km 🚶 15km   **Notes** Pets admitted Open April to September. CC

☰ *Les Cotterets*

Nadine et Christian BESNARD
35610 ROZ-SUR-COUESNON
☎ 06 80 62 24 75
email: lescotterets@wanadoo.fr
web: www.lescotterets.com

A farmhouse just 15 minutes from Mont St-Michel where local produce and homemade ice cream are on offer. The spacious rooms all have private shower rooms with toilet. There are two doubles and a large family room for four with bathroom on the landing. Also for guest use are a kitchenette with fridge and garden furniture.

Prices not confirmed for 2008   **Nearby** Sea 3km ⚓ 18km 🏛 2km
🚶 8km   **Notes** No pets

SIXT-SUR-AFF

☰ ⟨○⟩ *Manoir de Pommery*

Pascal et Frédérique MORRIER
35550 SIXT-SUR-AFF
☎ 02 99 70 07 40 & 06 68 55 51 26
email: infos@manoir-pommery.com
web: www.manoir-pommery.com

The three attractive rooms available in this pretty 16th-century building feature fireplaces and old flagstones, as well as private facilities. They include two doubles and a twin room, with a cot available on request. There is a dining room and lounge opening onto the park, which has trees, flowers and garden furniture. This tranquil setting is less than an hour from the beach and guests can expect a warm welcome. Closed 1 to 15 July.

Prices not confirmed for 2008   **Nearby** ♨40km Sea 45km ✎2.5km ➚8km ♨8km 🏚2.5km ⋙15km   **Notes** No pets   English spoken

⸬⸬ **Manoir de Tregaray**

Annie BARRETEAU

Le Village de Tregaret, 35550 SIXT-SUR-AFF

☎ 02 99 70 08 32 & 06 80 16 09 08

📠 02 99 70 06 99

email: manoirdetregaray@orange.fr

web: www.manoir-de-tregaray.com

A 16th-century manor house, now an equestrian establishment, splendidly set in 20 hectares of wooded parkland and meadows. There are four guest suites, each with a private lounge, bathroom, WC, television and complimentary mini-bar. Indoor swimming pool, conservatory, billiard room, tennis court.

Prices s €310-€460; d €310-€460   **On Site** Private ➚ Private tennis court   **Nearby** ♨2km ✎0.8km Restaurant 1km Spa 15km ♘1km 🏚1km ⋙15km   **Notes** No pets   English spoken   CC

ST-BENOIT-DES-ONDES

⸬⸬ ⓰ **La Grande Mare**

M-N et F FOULON

46, Bord de Mer, 35114 ST-BENOIT-DES-ONDES

☎ 06 89 18 86 32

email: lagrandemare@aol.com

Facing the bay of Mont-St-Michel (which is itself only 20 minutes away) this old fisherman's house, just 100 metres from the sea, has five very comfortable bedrooms. All the rooms sleep three people; each is decorated in an individual style, and they all have private shower rooms/WCs. Heated swimming pool (south-facing) available from May to September. Lounge and terrace.

Prices not confirmed for 2008   **On Site** Private ➚   **Nearby** ♨15km Sea 0.1km ✎0.1km ♨1.5km ⋙10km   **Notes** No pets   English spoken

ST-BRIAC-SUR-MER

⸬⸬ **Le Clos-du-Pont-Martin**

Daniel COUPLIERE

35800 ST-BRIAC-SUR-MER

☎ 02 99 88 38 07 & 06 68 37 62 65

email: info@briac.com

web: www.briac.com

Furnished with antiques and tastefully decorated, this house has three double rooms (two can be used for four people), with TVs, mini-bars and private facilities. One has a terrace; another has a lounge area. There is also a lounge with fireplace; garage and parking. The house is situated in an enclosed, tree and flower lined park with canopied area, garden furniture and a barbecue.

Prices not confirmed for 2008   **Nearby** ♨3km Sea 2km ➚3km ♨1km 🏚2km ⋙12km   **Notes** No pets   English spoken

ST-BRIEUC-DES-IFFS

⸬⸬ *L'Hormondais*

Michel et Cécile ADGNOT

35630 ST-BRIEUC-DES-IFFS

☎ 02 99 45 82 79   📠 02 99 45 82 79

email: michel.adgnot@wanadoo.fr

web: http://perso.wanadoo.fr/hormondais

Half-way between Rennes and St-Malo, this restored house is in a beautiful setting. It has one double bedroom on the ground floor; upstairs there is a triple room (double bed and a single), and a family room for up to four (double bed and two singles). Each room has a private shower room and WC. Generous breakfasts; garden furniture.

Prices not confirmed for 2008   **Nearby** ♨30km Sea 40km ➚15km ♨4km 🏚3km ⋙15km   **Notes** No pets   English spoken

ST-BROLADRE

⸬⸬ *Petit Angle*

P et M-M LAUNAY

35120 ST-BROLADRE

☎ 02 99 80 26 24   📠 02 99 80 26 24

This pretty countryside stone house provides four guest rooms: two doubles, a twin and a room with a double and single bed, with extra beds possible. Facilities include a pretty living room with TV where generous breakfasts can be enjoyed, and grounds with a terrace and garden furniture. Nearby guests can sand-yacht and fish in Mont St Michel Bay.

Prices not confirmed for 2008   **On Site** Sea   **Nearby** ♨15km ✎2km ➚10km ♨1km 🏚1km ⋙9km   **Notes** No pets

ST-COULOMB

⸬⸬ *La Guimorais*

Brigitte et Alain SORRE

3, impasse du Moulin de la Mer, 35350 ST-COULOMB

☎ 02 99 89 07 03 & 06 87 47 45 50

email: brigitte.sorre@wanadoo.fr

Close to the beach at Guimorais and with good access to footpaths, this stone-built house has two double rooms and two triples. All have en suite facilities, and an extra bed is available. Lounge with TV; pleasant enclosed garden; breakfast can be served on the terrace.

Prices not confirmed for 2008   **Nearby** Sea 0.1km ✎0.3km ➚10km ♨2.5km 🏚2.5km ⋙8km   **Notes** No pets   English spoken

⁺⁺⁺ *Le Hindre*

Catherine ROBIN

35350 ST-COULOMB

☎ 06 63 48 23 30

email: chambre@lehindre.com

web: www.lehindre.com

There are four double bedrooms and one for four people, each with private bathroom, in this old renovated house. Sitting room/lounge with open fireplace, kitchen area and large garden.

Prices not confirmed for 2008 **Nearby** ♨ 15km Sea 2.5km ⚓ 8km
🏊 1.5km 🏛 1.5km ⚓⚓ 8km **Notes** No pets English spoken

⁺⁺⁺ **Les Landes**

Jeanine HIREL

35350 ST-COULOMB

☎ 02 99 89 01 27

An 18th-century farmhouse situated close to the sea on the Côte d'Eméraude. On the first floor it has two double bedrooms, also a two-roomed family suite for up to five guests (double bed and three singles). All the rooms have a private bath/shower and WC. Lounge, garden with furniture. Good footpath access.

Prices s fr €40; d €45-€46; t fr €58 **Nearby** ♨ 25km ⚓ 10km
🏊 2.5km 🏛 3km ⚓⚓ 10km **Notes** No pets

⁺⁺⁺ *La Lande Grêle*

Jacques HESRY

35430 ST-JOUAN-DES-GUERETS

☎ 02 99 82 46 94 & 06 63 37 46 94

email: hesryjacques@wanadoo.fr

web: www.lalandegrele.fr.tc

Not far from St-Malo and Cancale, and close to the River Rance, this longhouse is in a delightful spot. There are two double rooms, and a two-roomed family suite for five, all with en suite bath/shower room. Landscaped garden with garden furniture and lots of flowers. Generous breakfasts with home-made specialities; lounge area, parking space.

Prices not confirmed for 2008 **Nearby** ♨ 15km Sea 2km ⚓ 6km
🏊 2km 🏛 2.5km ⚓⚓ 7km **Notes** No pets

⁺⁺⁺ *La Ruaudais*

Louisette et Francis PES

35800 ST-LUNAIRE

☎ 02 99 46 31 92 & 06 72 73 30 35

This house built in 1856, and surrounded by a lawned garden, offers three double rooms, plus a triple and one for four, both with private facilities. Terrace with chairs and BBQ, a conservatory and living room with TV. Home-made jams are included in the generous breakfasts.

Prices not confirmed for 2008 **Nearby** ♨ 3km Sea 3km ⚓ 3km 🏊 3km
Notes No pets

⁺⁺⁺ *Goeletterie Quelmer*

Raymonde TREVILLY

35400 ST-MALO

☎ 02 99 81 92 64 🗎 02 99 82 27 01

email: raymonde.trevilly@wanadoo.fr

web: www.la-goeletterie..fr

There are four double bedrooms and a room for four/five people in this house with lots of character, on the banks of the Rance. Each room has a private bathroom and two have a lovely view. The property is situated in a peaceful and relaxing area and has a sitting room with open fireplace, TV and play area. Port 4km and there are several footpaths on site.

Prices not confirmed for 2008 **Nearby** ⚓ 4km 🏊 4km 🏛 2km ⚓⚓ 5km
Notes No pets

⁺⁺⁺ **La Petite Hulotais**

J, M et L BANGE

15, rue G. Onfroy, 35400 ST-MALO

☎ 02 99 88 91 69 & 06 08 67 46 23 🗎 02 99 88 91 69

email: jacques.bange@wanadoo.fr

web: www.lapetitehulotais.com.fr

This 17th-century house is in a quiet and very attractive part of St-Malo, not far from the walled town and the sea. It has two double rooms, a triple, and a two-roomed family suite for four, all with en suite bathrooms, TVs, DVDs and internet access. Generous breakfasts, with a strong regional flavour.

Prices s fr €50; d €62-€82; t €87-€99; extra person €15-€17
Nearby ⛳ 10km ♨ 10km Sea 2km 🏖 2km ⚓ 2km Restaurant 2km
🏊 2km Spa 2km 🎣 2km 🏛 0.3km ⚓⚓ 2km **Notes** No pets English spoken Open February to December. CC

⁺⁺⁺ **La Petite Ville Mallet**

Joëlle COQUIL

Le Gué, 35400 ST-MALO

☎ 02 99 81 75 62 🗎 02 99 81 75 62

email: lapetitevillemallet@orange.fr

web: www.lapetitevillemallet.com

A warm welcome awaits at this Breton home situated in wooded parkland. There is a double room, a triple and a family suite (a twin room, double room and extra single bed), all with private bathrooms.

Lounge area with a library and terrace with garden furniture, where generous home-made breakfasts are served.

Prices s fr €65; d fr €70 **Nearby** ♨ 3km ⚓ 10km Sea 2km ⌇ 3km Restaurant 2km ⏆ 3km ⏱ 3km ⏒ 1km ⛵ 5km **Notes** Pets admitted English spoken

⚑⚑⚑⚑ Malouinière du Mont-Fleury

Bob HABY

2, rue du Mont Fleury, 35400 ST-MALO

☎ 02 23 52 28 85 & 06 80 25 61 75

email: bob.haby@wanadoo.fr

web: www.lemontfleury.com

This property, built in the typical local style, dates from the early 18th century. It has two double rooms, and two large split-level rooms, one for five people and one for six, each with a double bed plus singles. All the themed bedrooms private showers and WCs. Lounge with TV and open fire; generous breakfasts; terrace and wooded grounds.

Prices s fr €65; d €75-€105; t €108-€128; extra person fr €23 **Nearby** ♨ 3km ⚓ 12km Sea 1.5km ⌇ 1.5km Restaurant 1km ⏆ 1.5km Spa 1.5km ⏒ 1km ⛵ 1.5km **Notes** Pets admitted English spoken CC

see advert on this page

ST-MELOIR-DES-ONDES

⚑⚑⚑ La Ferme du Point du Jour

Famille BUNOUF

Le Buot, 35350 ST-MELOIR-DES-ONDES

☎ 06 30 03 93 40

email: ferme.pointdujour@wanadoo.fr

web: www.gites-point-du-jour.fr

On the bay of Mont-St-Michel, this property has four bedrooms: a double, two triples, and a two-roomed family suite for four. All have private bath or shower room and WC. Lounge. Outdoors is a swimming pool, children's games area and garden furniture.

Prices s fr €36; d €46-€52; t €56-€62; extra person fr €10 **On Site** ⏆ Private ⌇ **Nearby** ♨ 1km ⚓ 16km Sea 0.3km ⌁ 0.3km Restaurant 0.3km ⏆ 2km Spa 15km ⏒ 2.5km ⛵ 4km **Notes** Pets admitted English spoken

⚑⚑⚑ ♿ *Langavan*

Loïc COLLIN

35350 ST-MELOIR-DES-ONDES

☎ 02 99 89 22 92

email: sopcollin@wanadoo.fr

web: http://membres.lycos.fr/langavan35

This renovated 18th-century barn has a terrace with views of the sea and the Mont Saint-Michel bay. There are two double rooms and three for four people (one with disabled access). Each has a private

CONTINUED

179

BRITTANY

ST-MELOIR-DES-ONDES CONTINUED

bathroom. There is also a dining room, terrace with sea views and garden with lawn. Special rates for groups.

Prices not confirmed for 2008 **Nearby** ↓ 25km ↗ 12km ≈ 5km
🏠 5km ⛴ 12km **Notes** Pets admitted English spoken Open April to September.

⌗ *Le Grand Pré*

J-Louis et M-Paule MAZIER
35350 ST-MELOIR-DES-ONDES
☎ 06 61 89 32 34
email: mazier.marie.paule@wanadoo.fr
web: http://le-grand-pre.chez.tiscali.fr

Three double rooms and a triple are available on this vegetable farm, in Mont St Michel Bay. Guests also have use of a living room, lounge, TV, kitchenette with possibility to make evening meals and parking.

Prices not confirmed for 2008 **Nearby** ↓ 16km ↗ 10km ≈ 2km
🏠 2.5km ⛴ 2.5km **Notes** No pets

⌗ *Le Petit Porcon*

E FRABOULET
35350 ST-MELOIR-DES-ONDES
☎ 06 88 09 47 46
email: edithfraboulet@wanadoo.fr
web: www.lepetitporcon.com

This renovated farmhouse enjoys a calm setting just five minutes from the beach at Porcon and coastal walking routes. Rooms available include a family room with a double and three single beds, three triple rooms and a double with possible child's bed; each has private facilities. There is a large living room with fireplace for breakfast, a lounge with TV, garden furniture and parking.

Prices not confirmed for 2008 **Nearby** ↓ 15km Sea 0.5km ⚓ 0.5km
↗ 10km ≈ 3km 🏠 3km ⛴ 3km **Notes** No pets

⌗ 🌱 *Le Pont Prin*

Marie-Jo BOUTIER
35350 ST-MELOIR-DES-ONDES
☎ 06 07 75 56 76
email: gites-du-pont-prin@wanadoo.fr
web: www.gites-du-pont-prin.com

This individual house, in a peaceful area near the Emerald Coast, is surrounded by a tree-lined garden and has two double bedrooms and a family suite of two separate bedrooms (for four people), all with private bathrooms and separate access. Lounge/sitting room, kitchen, lawn with garden furniture and play area for children.

Prices not confirmed for 2008 **Nearby** ↓ 10km Sea 5km ⚓ 5km
↗ 4km ≈ 2km 🏠 2km ⛴ 4km **Notes** No pets English spoken

⌗ *Le Tertre Nande*

Madeleine LOCHET
35350 ST-MELOIR-DES-ONDES
☎ 02 99 89 10 86

Near the Mont Saint-Michel bay, between St-Malo and Cancale, this 16th-century farmhouse has parkland with donkeys. There is a triple room and two doubles, all with private facilities and one with kitchen area. Sitting room with open fireplace, guests' lounge/sitting room, terrace area and south-facing garden.

Prices not confirmed for 2008 **Nearby** ↓ 15km Sea 0.5km ↗ 6km
≈ 1km 🏠 2.5km ⛴ 2.5km **Notes** No pets

⌗ *Les Chesnais*

Monique et Michel RENAULT
35350 ST-MELOIR-DES-ONDES
☎ 06 63 29 43 16
email: leschesnais@aol.com
web: www.leschesnais.com

Close to the sea yet in the quiet of the countryside, this welcoming renovated longhouse has a double and a family room on the ground floor, and upstairs two further family suites each for up to four people; all have private facilities. Living room with TV and kitchenette.

Prices not confirmed for 2008 **Nearby** ↓ 10km Sea 6km ↗ 4km
≈ 2km 🏠 2km ⛴ 4km **Notes** No pets

ST-OUEN-LA-ROUERIE

⌗ 🍽 *Le Guiborel*

Christelle RIOUAT
35460 ST-OUEN-LA-ROUERIE
☎ 02 99 98 25 33 & 06 22 16 38 86
email: caclan@club-internet.fr
web: www.lesmarchesdumont.com

An 18th-century farmhouse, restored and with plenty of flowers all around. There are four very comfortable bedrooms, with independent access. On the ground floor are two doubles; upstairs are two split-level rooms for four. They all have private bath or shower room and WC. Cot and high chair available. Garden furniture, and private parking.

Prices d fr €40; t fr €50; extra person fr €10; dinner fr €16
Nearby ⚡ 5km Sea 25km ⚓ 5km ↗ 20km Restaurant 6km ≈ 5km
🏠 4km ⛴ 44km **Notes** No pets Open mid January to mid December.

ST-PERAN

⌗ *Chambre d'hôtes*

Marie-Claire RENAULT
Chemin des Demoiselles, 35380 ST-PERAN
☎ 02 99 06 98 67 & 06 24 60 09 22
email: saintperan@lechampdesoiseaux.eu
web: www.lechampdesoiseaux.eu

In a green setting at the edge of the forest of Brocéliande and close to the interesting little village of St-Péran, this property has three bedrooms. All are doubles with en suite facilities, and an extra bed is available. Breakfasts and other meals (served by arrangement) use local produce where possible. Large garden with plenty of trees.

Prices not confirmed for 2008   **Nearby** ⚑ 5km ⤢ 7km ⚓ 5km
Notes No pets

TEILLAY

🍴 🍽 **Domaine du Prieuré**

Brigitte GAULTIER
35620 TEILLAY
☎ 02 99 47 30 67
email: patrick.gaultier@resteco.fr
web: www.domaine-du-prieure-35.com

There are four individually decorated rooms at this property - three doubles and a triple, all with en suite facilities. Cot and extra beds available. The house, which has a good-sized garden with trees and flowers, is in a village with lots of character. Breakfasts and other meals are prepared using the best traditions of local cuisine.

Prices s fr €45; d fr €52; t fr €72; extra person fr €20; dinner €25-€31
Nearby ⛷ 8km ⬇ 40km ⤢ 10km Restaurant 15km ⚓ 10km Spa 40km
⋙ 20km   **Notes** No pets English spoken

TRANS-LA-FORET

🍴 🍽 **Le Clos St Michel**

Nathalie et Yvan PAPAIL
5 rue de St-Malo, 35610 TRANS-LA-FORET
☎ 02 99 48 59 66 & 06 79 41 16 92
email: yvanpapail@orange.fr

This restored property stands in its own enclosed grounds close to the forest. It has two double rooms and a triple, all with individual decorations and private facilities. There is a lounge with an open fire, where the hosts serve generous breakfasts. Meals by arrangement, but not in July and August.

Prices s fr €37; d fr €44; t fr €59; extra person fr €13; dinner fr €18
Nearby ⛷ 5km ⬇ 15km Sea 18km ⤢ 2km ⤢ 12km Restaurant 8km
⚓ 9km ☖ 2km ⋙ 13km   **Notes** No pets English spoken

TRESBOEUF

🍴 🍽 **Lunel**

Hervé et Chantal DANAIRE
35320 TRESBOEUF
☎ 06 10 38 34 44 & 02 99 44 64 85   🖨 02 99 44 64 85

In undulating wooded countryside about half an hour from Rennes, this house has two double and two triple bedrooms, all with private bath or shower room and WC. Kitchenette for guests' use; traditional style breakfasts. Good access to local footpaths.

Prices s fr €40; d fr €50; t fr €65; extra person fr €15; dinner fr €16
Nearby ⛷ 15km ⬇ 30km ⤢ 3km ⤢ 12km Restaurant 10km ⚓ 3km
☖ 2km ⋙ 12km   **Notes** Pets admitted

VEZIN-LE-COQUET

🍴 *La Touche Thebault*

M-A et P LOUAPRE
35132 VEZIN-LE-COQUET
☎ 02 99 60 19 74 & 06 03 51 04 43
email: mannicklouapre@aol.com

Five minutes from Rennes, this family farm offers a warm atmosphere in the beautifully decorated, renovated house. It provides a room for two, one for four, a family room with a mezzanine level, sleeping five, and a family suite of two bedrooms for five people and a possible extra bed. Each has a private bathroom and kitchen area with fridge and washing machine. Lounge/sitting room. Garden with children's play area. Reductions after the fourth night.

Prices not confirmed for 2008   **Nearby** ⬇ 8km ⤢ 3km ⚓ 3km ☖ 3km
⋙ 8km   **Notes** Pets admitted

🍴 **Le Rouvray**

Catherine et Michel THOUANEL
35132 VEZIN-LE-COQUET
☎ 06 30 94 32 33 & 02 99 64 56 38
email: catherine.thouanel@wanadoo.fr

There are two triple bedrooms and three doubles (one with disabled access) in this renovated Brittany house near Rennes, in the heart of Brittany. Each has a private bathroom and there is a sitting room/lounge with TV and a lovely garden with flowers and furniture. A 10% reduction is available after the fourth night.

Prices s fr €32; d fr €38; extra person fr €15   **Nearby** ⬇ 2km ⤢ 4km
⚓ 4km ☖ 0.8km ⋙ 5km   **Notes** No pets English spoken

MORBIHAN

AMBON

☷ Le Listy d'en Bas

Jean & Patricia COELIS
56190 AMBON
☎ 02 97 41 04 33 & 06 92 64 68 73
email: patriciacoelis@wanadoo.fr
web: www.itea.fr/G56/pages/56173.html

A warm welcome awaits at this renovated long-house, 1.5km from Ambon and 10km from hiking trail 34. There are four en suite double rooms, a dining room and lounge reserved for guests, a garden with furniture/barbecue, and fishing available in the private lake. Kitchen facilities are provided at an extra cost.

Prices s €40-€45; d €45-€50; extra person fr €15 **Nearby** ☘ 7km ♨ 20km Sea 3km ♙ 3km ᛏ 25km Restaurant 3km Water sports 3km ◗ 1.5km ♣ 6km ⌂ 1.5km ᴍ 25km **Notes** No pets English spoken Open May to September.

AUGAN

☷ La Ville Ruaud

Gilles DE SAINT JEAN
56800 AUGAN
☎ 02 97 93 44 40 & 06 07 38 78 96 📠 02 97 93 44 40
email: gwen@cap-broceliande.com
web: www.cap-broceliande.com

An attractive old building at the edge of the Forêt de Brocéliande, with four bedrooms. There is a double room on the first floor of the owners' house; in a separate building are two doubles, and a two-room suite for up to four guests. All the rooms have private bath/shower room and WC. Cot available. Billiards, garden with furniture, barbecue, table tennis table.

Prices s fr €40; d fr €58; t fr €76; extra person fr €18 **On Site** Private ᛏ **Nearby** ☘ 5km ♨ 7km ♙ 2km Restaurant 3.5km Water sports 7km ◗ 6km ♣ 6km ⌂ 6km **Notes** No pets English spoken CC

BELZ

☷ ⍟ Keryargon

Françoise LEBLOIS
SARL Leblois, Keryargon - Route des Pins, 56550 BELZ
☎ 06 08 21 31 47 📠 02 97 55 94 25
email: keryargon@free.fr

In a village of holiday cottages and chambres d'hôtes, this property has two double rooms on the ground floor, and upstairs a further double plus a triple. All have private bath or shower room, and each has independent access. Child's bed available (up to age five). Shared facilities include a garden with swing, swimming pool and sauna (supplement payable).

Prices d €69-€82; t €63-€93; extra person fr €8; dinner fr €24 **On Site** Restaurant Private ᛏ **Nearby** ☘ 4km ♨ 4km Sea 5km ♙ 5km Water sports 5km ◗ 2km ⌂ 2km ᴍ 10km **Notes** No pets English spoken Open 31 March to 11 November.

☷ Les Ferme de Kercadoret

Jean-François ROLLAND
Kercadoret, Route de Ninezur, 56550 BELZ
☎ 02 97 55 44 01 & 06 77 98 37 49
email: rolland.jeanfrancois@wanadoo.fr

Only 50 metres from the Ria d'Etel and 5km from hiking trails 34 and 341, this secluded traditional house has four en suite rooms: two triples and two doubles. Guests may use the lounge with TV and garden with furniture, barbecue, table tennis and boules. Extra facilities include use of a kitchen and washing machine for a charge.

Prices s fr €36; d fr €45; t fr €65; extra person fr €15 **Nearby** ☘ 5km ♨ 5km Sea 3km ♙ 0.5km ᛏ 12km Restaurant 0.7km Water sports 5km ◗ 1km Spa 10km ♣ 1km ⌂ 0.7km ᴍ 10km **Notes** No pets English spoken

BERNE

⛤ ⓘⓞⓘ **Marta**

Isabelle HELLO

56240 BERNE

☎ 02 97 34 28 58 🖹 02 97 34 28 58

web: http://pagesperso.aol.fr/Martamorbihan/marta.htm

In a rural setting 30 minutes from the coast, this house provides two triple rooms and four first floor doubles, all en suite. Hairdryer, cot and kitchen with washing machine, microwave, refrigerator and freezer are available. Lounge with TV, parking, garden with furniture, swing, table tennis and heated private pool. Fishing and forest walks nearby. Reductions apply except in the summer months.

Prices s fr €40; d fr €46; t fr €60; extra person fr €10; dinner fr €15
On Site Private ⚲ **Nearby** ⚑ 9km ⚑ 20km Sea 30km ⚐ 2km
Restaurant 10km Water sports 10km ⚑ 5km ⚑ 5km ⚑ 25km
Notes No pets English spoken

BRANDERION

⛤ **L'Hermine**

Mouche ZETUNIAN

Route d'Hennebont, 56700 BRANDERION

☎ 02 97 32 96 17

email: lhermine.mouche@wanadoo.fr

Situated one kilometre from Brandérion and surrounded by five acres of woodland, this charming house has three double en suite guest rooms. Guests are welcome to relax in the lounge and garden. Hiking trail 34E is within 10 kilometres.

Prices s fr €50; d fr €50; extra person fr €10 **Nearby** ⚑ 3km ⚑ 12km
Sea 12km ⚐ 1km ⚲ 15km Water sports 5km ⚑ 1km ⚑ 1km ⚑ 5km
Notes No pets English spoken Open June to August and Easter holidays.

CARNAC

⛤ **Ker Kristal**

Jurgen et Jocelyne HEILIGTAG

Kerguearec no 12, 56340 CARNAC

☎ 02 97 56 73 57 & 06 84 91 43 36 🖹 02 97 56 73 57

email: kerkristal@yahoo.fr

web: www.kerkristal.com

Ker Kristal lies in extensive grounds near to the Carnac standing stones. There is a twin room, a room for three and a family room for up to four people. All rooms have en suite washroom or bathroom. A cot is available on request. Breakfast is served in the spacious guest lounge, which has an open fire.

Prices d €48-€62; extra person €10-€20 **On Site** ⚑ **Nearby** ⚑ 2km
⚑ 6km Sea 5.5km ⚐ 3km ⚲ 6km Restaurant 2km Water sports 6km
⚑ 2km ⚑ 4.5km ⚑ 7km **Notes** Pets admitted English spoken

⛤ **L'Alcyone**

Marie-France ALLAIN-BALSAN

Impasse de Beaumer, 56340 CARNAC

☎ 02 97 52 78 11

Set in secluded, enclosed gardens within a kilometre of hiking trail 341 and only 500 metres from the sea. This house has five double en suite rooms with telephone and optional TV, a lounge with TV and terrace with garden furniture. Local recreational facilities include thalassotherapy at Carnac-Plage and a casino. Reduced rates apply out of season. Pets accepted by prior arrangement.

Prices d fr €62; extra person fr €20 **On Site** ⚑ **Nearby** ⚑ 1km
⚑ 5km Sea 0.5km ⚐ 0.5km ⚲ 1km Restaurant 2km Water sports 0.5km
⚑ 0.3km Spa 1km ⚑ 0.5km ⚑ 8km **Notes** Pets admitted English spoken

⛤ **Le Lac**

Evelyne AUDIC

56340 CARNAC

☎ 02 97 55 78 75 & 06 99 64 39 34

web: www.lamaisondelaria.com

Situated on the banks of the River Crach, with fine views of the Sound, this house provides en suite double bedrooms and also rooms suitable for families. Facilities include a comfortable lounge with TV, garden, terrace with furniture, microwave and fridge available for guests' use. Hiking trail nearby.

Prices s fr €45; d €47-€50; t €56-€59; extra person fr €13
Nearby ⚑ 2km ⚑ 10km Sea 3km ⚐ 0.1km ⚲ 6km Restaurant 3km
Water sports 3km ⚑ 3km ⚑ 3km ⚑ 3km ⚑ 12km **Notes** No pets
Open 15 February to 1 October and All Saints holiday.

⛤ **Ty-Me-Mamm**

Anne-Sophie DANIEL

Quelvezin, 56340 CARNAC

☎ 02 97 52 45 87

email: tymemam@wanadoo.fr

web: www.gites-de-france-morbihan.com/tymemam

Idyllically situated in the Carnac countryside, this house offers three double rooms and a triple, all en suite; one suitable for disabled guests. Lounge with open fireplace and large garden with furniture available. Breakfast is served in a room reserved for guests, which also has a TV. Hiking and cycling in the vicinity.

Prices s fr €37; d fr €50; t fr €60; extra person fr €13 **Nearby** ⚑ 1.5km
⚑ 3km Sea 5km ⚐ 0.5km ⚲ 6km Restaurant 3km Water sports 7km
⚑ 3km Spa 6km ⚑ 5km ⚑ 2km ⚑ 3km **Notes** Pets admitted English spoken

CLEGUEREC

▶ Ferme de Lintever

Claire & Nicolas RAFLE

56480 CLEGUEREC

☎ 02 97 38 03 95 & 06 71 66 27 44 📄 02 97 38 03 95

email: fermedelintever@wanadoo.fr

web: www.gites-de-france-morbihan.com/lintever

A big country house with its own orchard, this property has four guest rooms. There is a double on the ground floor; upstairs there is another double, and two family rooms. There is a separate guests' entrance, and all of the rooms have en suite facilities. Large lounge, kitchenette; garden with furniture and picnic area; and an unusual extra - home-made cider!

Prices s fr €38; d fr €44; t fr €60; extra person fr €16 **Nearby** ☝ 6km
♨ 20km ♠ 1km ↖ 7km Restaurant 4km Water sports 12km 🏊 4km
Spa 25km 🏛 4km 🚶 8km **Notes** No pets English spoken

CRACH

Coët-Kerzuc

Michel & Andrée ELHIAR

Kerzuc, 56950 CRACH

☎ 02 97 55 03 41 & 06 78 33 12 72

A charming house with three double guest rooms: two en suite and one grade 2 room with separate bathroom/wc. The dining room, lounge, terrace and a large garden with furniture are at guests' disposal.

Prices s fr €38; d fr €42; extra person fr €18 **Nearby** ☝ 7km ♨ 10km
Sea 5km ♠ 2km ↖ 6km Water sports 5km 🏊 2km 🏛 1km 🚶 8km
Notes No pets

Kergoët

Hélène KERVADEC

56950 CRACH

☎ 02 97 55 06 91

This attractive detached house has five en suite guest rooms with a separate entrance: three doubles and two triples. Kitchen facilities are available at a cost and there is a lounge with TV and garden with furniture.

Prices s fr €29; d fr €38; t fr €47 **Nearby** ☝ 7km ♨ 10km Sea 7km
♠ 0.5km ↖ 7km Restaurant 5km Water sports 7km 🏊 3km 🎾 7km
🏛 3km 🚶 8km **Notes** Pets admitted English spoken

Keruzerh-Brigitte

Nelly FRAVALO

56950 CRACH (SUR LA D 768)

☎ 02 97 56 47 62 & 06 88 51 06 33

This sunny house provides a triple room with its own entrance off the terrace, and three double rooms with TV, all en suite. Kitchen, lounge, library, terrace with garden furniture, garden with barbecue and private parking.

Prices s fr €30; d fr €38; t fr €46 **Nearby** ☝ 8km ♨ 8km Sea 10km
♠ 10km ↖ 3km Restaurant 0.8km Water sports 10km 🏊 6km Spa 8km
🏛 1.5km 🚶 3km **Notes** Pets admitted

ELVEN

Kergonan

Nadine FRENKEL

56250 ELVEN

☎ 02 97 53 37 59 & 06 80 23 57 05 📄 02 97 53 37 59

email: frenkelkergonan@aol.com

web: www.kergonan.fr

A wing of a rural 18th-century house offering three double rooms with separate access and a family room sleeping up to four people, all en suite. Facilities include dining room with TV, fridge, table tennis table, garden furniture and woodland walks.

Prices s fr €48; d fr €52; extra person fr €18 **Nearby** ☝ 14km ♨ 30km
Sea 20km ♠ 0.5km ↖ 14km Restaurant 2km Water sports 20km 🏊 2km
Spa 30km 🎾 14km 🏛 2km 🚶 14km **Notes** No pets English spoken
Open April to November.

Kerniquel

Michel LE VANNIER

Ty Nehué, 56250 ELVEN

☎ 06 77 84 22 63 & 02 97 53 34 36 📄 02 97 53 34 36

email: michel.le-vannier@wanadoo.fr

This detached house five kilometres from Elven offers on the first floor a family suite for two to four people, with separate bathroom and WC, with another double room with shower and WC. On the ground floor is a double with en suite bathroom, TV and direct access to the terrace. Garden with picnic table and BBQ.

Prices s fr €40; d fr €40; t fr €50; extra person fr €10 **Nearby** ☝ 8km
♨ 24km Sea 25km ♠ 1km ↖ 20km Water sports 25km 🏊 5km 🏛 5km
🚶 20km **Notes** No pets

Ty Néhué - Camarec

Chantal & Michel GUILLOT

56250 ELVEN

☎ 02 97 53 36 99 & 06 14 98 51 63

email: michel-chantal.guillot@wanadoo.fr

web: www.gites-de-france-morbihan.com/ty-nehue

Pleasant enclosed wooded grounds surround this property. It has three bedrooms, all doubles. One is downstairs; the other two (one with a small lounge area) are upstairs. Each room has its own entrance, and a private bath or shower room and WC. The knowledgeable hosts will be delighted to advise you about places to visit. Internet access.

Prices d fr €53; extra person fr €20 **Nearby** ☝ 8km ♨ 24km Sea 20km
♠ 1km ↖ 20km Restaurant 5km Water sports 20km 🏊 5km 🏛 5km
🚶 15km **Notes** No pets

GESTEL

♯♯♯ ⑩ Domaine de Kerguestenen

Gilles GUEGUEN

56530 GESTEL

☎ 02 97 05 15 03 & 06 61 83 28 55

email: ng.gueg@wanadoo.fr

This modern property has three ground floor rooms. There are two doubles, each with independent access and en suite facilities, and a two-roomed suite suitable for a single family, where the two rooms share a shower room and WC. There is an indoor swimming pool, and meals are available by arrangement.

Prices d €70-€74; t fr €74; extra person fr €25; dinner fr €20   **On Site** ⬍ Private ⭦   **Nearby** ⚓0.5km Sea 10km ⌀ 3km Restaurant 2.5km Water sports 10km ☾ 2km ⚑ 2.5km ⓢ 1km ⋙ 12km   **Notes** Pets admitted English spoken Open April to 4 November.

GUEHENNO

♯♯♯ ⚬ Les Chimères

R et F BLANCHARD-LUCAS

3 Rue Saint-Pierre, 56420 GUEHENNO

☎ 02 97 42 30 14 & 06 67 17 94 92 ▤ 02 97 42 30 14

email: leschimeres56@wanadoo.fr

web: www.leschimeres.com

A charming house in Guéhenno, a Breton heritage site. En suite guest rooms are reached via a separate entrance and include a twin room with disabled access, two split-level rooms sleeping three with traditional Breton box beds; and a split-level family room. Cot and other baby equipment available. Shared use of a kitchen and washing machine for small charge. The garden has a picnic area, play area and parking.

Prices s fr €36; d fr €46; extra person fr €16   **Nearby** ⚓ 15km ⚐ 18km Sea 25km ⭦ 18km ⭦ 5km Water sports 18km ☾ 0.5km ⚑ 18km ⓢ 0.5km ⋙ 25km   **Notes** Pets admitted English spoken CC

GUERN

♯♯♯ ⑩ ⚬ Kersalous

Annie PENNARUN

S.C.I Kersalou, 56310 GUERN

☎ 02 97 27 71 77 & 06 17 52 58 53

email: kersalou@orange.fr

web: www.gites-de-france-morbihan.com/kersalous/

There are five large rooms containing a mix of double and single beds, all with en suite showers/WCs, in this 17th-century property within the boundaries of the chapel of Quelven, where free concerts take place during July and August. There's a heavy accent on horses here, with seven boxes available for visiting equestrians, and long bridlepaths for riding, biking or walking nearby. Evening meals by reservation.

Prices s fr €40; d fr €50; extra person fr €15; dinner fr €20   **On Site** ⚘ **Nearby** ⚓ 3km ⚐ 5km ⌀ 0.5km ⭦ 10km Restaurant 0.3km Water sports 10km ☾ 2km ⓢ 2km   **Notes** Pets admitted English spoken

GUIDEL

♯♯♯ Chambre d'hôte à Coatroual

Christine HAMONIC

Coatroual, 56520 GUIDEL

☎ 02 97 02 94 41 & 06 73 50 53 48

email: f.hamonic@wanadoo.fr

web: www.coatroual.fr.st

Christine will be pleased to welcome you to her quiet village house not far from the River Laita. It has which has two, ground floor double rooms, and another two doubles upstairs all with en suite shower/WC. Guests are welcome to use the lounge with TV, and the kitchen. Beaches are nearby.

Prices s fr €36; d fr €48; extra person fr €12   **Nearby** ⚓ 4km ⚐ 10km Sea 8km ⌀ 0.5km ⭦ 10km Restaurant 5km Water sports 8km ☾ 5km ⓢ 5km ⋙ 15km   **Notes** No pets English spoken

♯♯♯ ⚬ Ty Horses

Robert HAMON

Le Rouho - Route de Locmaria, 56520 GUIDEL

☎ 02 97 65 97 37

Accommodation available in two houses, situated in parkland at Guidel. An annexe with its own entrance contains four en suite guest rooms for three people; two ground floor and two 1st floor rooms. Garden with outdoor furniture, kitchenette available for a charge and breakfast is served on the veranda. Baby equipement; paddock for horses.

Prices s fr €45; d fr €55; t fr €70; extra person fr €18   **Nearby** ⚓ 4km ⚐ 8km Sea 5km ⌀ 1km ⭦ 8km Restaurant 4km Water sports 5km ☾ 4km ⚑ 5km ⓢ 4km ⋙ 15km   **Notes** Pets admitted English spoken

JOSSELIN

♦♦♦ La Butte Saint-Laurent

Jean GUYOT
56120 JOSSELIN
☎ 02 97 22 22 09 & 06 14 44 74 63
email: chez.guyot@wanadoo.fr
web: www.chambres-bretagne.com

This house is 500 metres from the town, in shady grounds providing walks and a play area, and enjoys panoramic views of the Oust Valley and the Château de Josselin. Accommodation comprises an en suite triple room, an en suite double and two Grade 2 double rooms with separate facilities.

Prices s €47-€50; d €52-€55; t fr €70; extra person fr €15
Nearby ♿ 5km ♨ 12km Sea 45km ✿ 0.5km ↘ 10km Water sports 8km
♨ 1km ⌂ 0.5km ⋈ 45km **Notes** No pets English spoken Open July to 15 September.

KERNASCLEDEN

♦♦♦ ⓘ Ti Er Mad

Béatrice LENZ
Kerihuel, 56540 KERNASCLEDEN
☎ 02 97 28 20 75 & 06 32 29 90 80 ▤ 02 97 28 20 75
email: beatrice@tiermad.com

This large, renovated longhouse near the Scorff Valley offers four double rooms, all have private shower and WC. There is a large day room, just for guest use, with eating area, books to read, games area for children and a great countryside views. Use of washing machine (chargeable). Large garden with barbecue; good walking country; local fishing available.

Prices s fr €37; d fr €47; extra person fr €15; dinner fr €15
Nearby ♿ 7km ♨ 20km Sea 35km ✿ 2km ↘ 10km Restaurant 0.5km
Water sports 10km ♨ 10km ⌂ 2km ⋈ 30km **Notes** Pets admitted English spoken

LA CROIX-HELLEAN/JOSSELIN

♦♦♦ Les Hortensias

M et H NICOLAS
La Ville Robert, 56120 LA CROIX-HELLEAN
☎ 02 97 75 64 37 & 06 81 90 05 75 ▤ 02 97 75 64 37
email: nicolasmo@wanadoo.fr
web: www.geocities.com/h_m_nicolas/

In part of a lovingly restored barn conversion, accommodation comprises a double room, which is accessed directly from the terrace, and a triple room, both are en suite with kitchen areas. The garden with outdoor furniture, barbecue, table tennis table and lounge/veranda with TV are available for guests' use. Hiking trail 37 is only 2km away.

Prices s fr €36; d fr €45; t fr €59; extra person fr €15 **Nearby** ♿ 1km
♨ 11km Sea 45km ✿ 3km ↘ 8km Restaurant 2km Water sports 11km
♨ 3km ⌂ 3km ⋈ 40km **Notes** Pets admitted English spoken

LANDEVANT

♦♦♦ ⓘ ♿ Talvern

Patrick et Christine GILLOT
56690 LANDEVANT
☎ 02 97 56 99 80 & 06 16 18 08 75
email: talvern@chambre-morbihan.com
web: www.chambre-morbihan.com

In this old farmhouse which belonged to the Château of Lannouan, your host Patrick, once a head chef in Paris, and Christine offer delicious regional cooking. Double with en suite shower on the ground floor (semi-private access), and upstairs two doubles and a family suite, each with en suite shower. On the second floor there is a family room for four, with en suite bathroom.

Prices s fr €60; d fr €60; dinner fr €20 **Nearby** ♿ 10km ♨ 10km
Sea 4km ✿ 1km ↘ 10km Restaurant 1km Water sports 20km ♨ 1km
♔ 10km ⌂ 1km ⋈ 1km **Notes** No pets English spoken

LARMOR-BADEN

♦♦♦♦ ⓘ *La Saline*

Martine et Michel RIO-LE GAL
17 la Saline, 56870 LARMOR-BADEN
☎ 02 97 56 24 06 & 06 82 01 82 72
email: lasalinelarmor@yahoo.fr

Just a stone's throw from the Golfe du Morbihan, close to a protected environmental area, this peaceful and comfortable house has four guest rooms. On the ground floor is a double and a triple (double bed plus single); upstairs is another triple, and a family suite for four. All have private facilities. Guest lounge; garden with sunny terrace where breakfast may be served.

Prices not confirmed for 2008 **Nearby** ♿ 2km ♨ 3km Sea 0.7km
✿ 0.7km ↘ 10km Water sports 0.7km ♨ 1.5km ⌂ 1.5km ⋈ 10km
Notes No pets English spoken

LARMOR-PLAGE

♦♦♦ Villa des Camélias

Paulette ALLANO
9, Rue des Roseaux, 56260 LARMOR-PLAGE
☎ 02 97 65 50 67 ▤ 02 97 65 50 67

Situated on the coast road, this large house provides a single and five double guest rooms, either en suite or grade 2 with private facilities. Lounge with TV, garden, terrace, free use of the kitchen from June to September and parking. Hiking trail 34 is 5km.

Prices s €45-€47; d €47-€50 **Nearby** ♿ 1km ♨ 5km Sea 0.3km
✿ 0.3km ↘ 3km Restaurant 0.3km Water sports 0.3km ♨ 0.5km
♔ 0.5km ⌂ 0.5km ⋈ 3km **Notes** No pets English spoken

LE COURS

🍴 Le Moulin du Pont de Molac

Christian RESTOIN

Kermelin, 56230 LE COURS

☎ 02 97 67 52 40 & 06 18 92 50 79 📠 02 97 67 52 40

email: moulinmolac@club-internet.fr

web: www.moulinmolac.fr.st

Expect a warm welcome at this 18th-century mill, on the banks of the River Arz. There are three double rooms and a triple, all en suite and the owner's long house provides an en suite double bedroom with a separate entrance. Breakfast is served in the mill and there is a garden extending to the river.

Prices s €45-€50; d €50-€60; t fr €75; extra person fr €15 **On Site** 🔗 **Nearby** ♨ 5km ♿ 25km Sea 30km ➴ 12km Restaurant 4km Water ports 15km ♨ 1km ⛳ 12km 🏛 4km ⛵ 12km **Notes** No pets

---

LE CROISTY

🍴 🍽 Ty Houarn

Mark PULFORD

Cornhospital, 56540 LE CROISTY

☎ 02 97 28 29 34 & 06 70 32 20 26

email: ty.houarn@yahoo.fr

This house is in green countryside, in the heart of Brittany. On the first floor are two bedrooms for three people; on the second are two doubles. All have private facilities. The hosts, Alison and Mark, both experienced and enthusiastic former chefs, are pleased to prepare pre-arranged evening meals or packed lunches for guests.

Prices s fr €38; d fr €47; t fr €58; dinner fr €17 **Nearby** ♨ 7km ♿ 30km Sea 35km 🔗 3km ➴ 10km Restaurant 1km Water sports 3km ♨ 1km Spa 45km 🏛 2km ⛵ 30km **Notes** No pets English spoken Open February to November.

LOCMARIAQUER

🍴 🍽 An Degemeriad

Jacques et Bettina MADEC

Allée Er Vechelec, 56740 LOCMARIAQUER

☎ 02 97 57 36 74 & 06 86 43 46 85

email: bettina.madec-lec@laposte.net

web: www.an-degemeriad.fr

This house is in a peaceful setting, just five minutes walk from the town and the beach. It has three bedrooms: a double and a twin-bedded room upstairs, and another double downstairs. Each has a private shower room and WC. Day room with billiards and books, garden with garden furniture. Meals available, by arrangement, on Tuesdays and Saturdays.

Prices s fr €45; d fr €50; t fr €66; extra person fr €10; dinner fr €21 **Nearby** ♨ 13km ♿ 15km Sea 0.5km 🔗 0.5km ➴ 13km Restaurant 0.5km Water sports 1km ♨ 0.5km ⛳ 0.5km 🏛 0.5km ⛵ 15km **Notes** No pets English spoken Open February to 1 November.

🍴 Chambre d'hôtes

Michelle et Jean COUDRAY

2 Impasse de la Ruche, 56740 LOCMARIAQUER

☎ 02 97 57 33 16 & 06 81 91 76 82 📠 02 97 57 33 16

email: j.coudray@wanadoo.fr

Only five minutes from the port, accommodation here includes two grade 2 rooms (a room for four and a double) and an annexe houses three grade 3 rooms (two doubles and a triple), all with private facilities. A lounge overlooking the garden is reserved for guests. Fridge and microwave available.

Prices d €47-€51; extra person fr €16 **Nearby** ♨ 12km ♿ 15km Sea 0.5km 🔗 0.5km ➴ 12km Restaurant 0.4km Water sports 0.4km ♨ 0.4km ⛳ 0.3km ⛵ 12km **Notes** No pets English spoken Open mid March to mid November.

🍴 La Troque Toupie

Catherine LE ROUZIC

Kerouarch, 56740 LOCMARIAQUER

☎ 02 97 57 45 02 & 06 63 58 45 02

email: chambredhotetroque@wanadoo.fr

This country house, typical of the region, has views over the Gulf of Morbihan. On the ground floor it has two double rooms, and two rooms for three; upstairs is a further room for three. All rooms have private facilities. There is a large sitting room with a fireplace and breakfast is served in the living room; the garden leads directly onto the coastal path.

Prices s fr €63; d fr €69; t fr €88; extra person fr €21 **On Site** Sea 🔗 **Nearby** ♨ 6km ♿ 15km ➴ 10km Restaurant 0.4km Water sports 3km ♨ 2.5km ⛳ 2.5km 🏛 2.5km ⛵ 12km **Notes** No pets English spoken Open 15 March to 15 November.

LOCOAL-MENDON

🍴 Kerohan

Jean-François LE NY

56550 LOCOAL-MENDON

☎ 02 97 24 65 08

Located in its own grounds on an old farm, this charming house provides a family room sleeping up to five people, with separate shower-room/WC and two en suite double rooms. Facilities include a living room, lounge with fireplace, TV and video, fridge, and use of barbecue and garden furniture. Small pets are accepted.

Prices s fr €35; d fr €45; extra person fr €15 **Nearby** ♨ 12km ♿ 6km Sea 6km 🔗 6km ➴ 12km Restaurant 5km Water sports 12km ♨ 3km 🏛 3km ⛵ 8km **Notes** Open April to September.

🍴 🌱 🍽 Kervihern

Gabriel & M.-Thérèse MAHO

56550 LOCOAL-MENDON

☎ 02 97 24 64 09 📠 02 97 24 64 09

email: gabriel.maho@orange.fr

web: www.gites-de-france-morbihan.com/kervihern

This 17th-century house, situated on farmland close to the Ria d'Etal, has four double rooms (one on the ground floor) and a triple, all en

CONTINUED

BRITTANY

LOCOAL-MENDON CONTINUED

suite. A separate en suite family room is also available in a renovated barn, providing four beds (single or dual king). Dinner by prior arrangement, except in high season. Facilities include a guests' TV lounge, a washing machine, garden furniture and table tennis.

Prices d fr €45; t fr €60; extra person fr €15; dinner fr €16
Nearby ♿ 4km ⚓ 5km Sea 5km ⚲ 5km ⚹ 10km Restaurant 5km
Water sports 12km ⚲ 2km ⚽ 0.1km 🏛 2km ⚒ 10km **Notes** No pets English spoken

⚑ ⚐ Manescouarn

Jean & Edith NICOLAS
56550 LOCOAL-MENDON
☎ 02 97 24 65 18

A renovated farm complex adjoining the owner's house, offering four double rooms and a family room sleeping two to five people, all en suite. Dining room, lounge with open fireplace and TV reserved for guests, who may also use the garden with furniture. Delightful meals are cooked by the hosts, Edith and Jean.

Prices d fr €45; extra person fr €16; dinner fr €17 **Nearby** ♿ 7km
⚓ 2km Sea 7km ⚲ 7km ⚹ 11km Restaurant 8km Water sports 7km
⚲ 3km ⚽ 8km 🏛 3km ⚒ 11km **Notes** Pets admitted

MALANSAC (ROCHEFORT EN TERRE)

⚑ Manoir de St Fiacre

Roger & Denise GOAPPER
56220 MALANSAC
☎ 02 97 43 43 90 & 06 18 06 05 25 📠 02 97 43 43 40
email: denise.goapper@orange.fr

Accommodation provided in a wing of a 17th-century manor house, surrounded by landscaped wooded parkland: a double, one family room, and three triples (two in an annexe with separate access), all en suite. Living room/TV and garden with furniture.

Prices s €65-€80; d €65-€80; t fr €100; extra person fr €20
Nearby ♿ 10km ⚓ 5km Sea 25km ⚲ 0.5km ⚹ 25km Restaurant 1.5km
Water sports 0.5km ⚲ 0.5km 🏛 1.5km ⚒ 12km **Notes** No pets English spoken

MENEAC

⚑ Manoir de Bellouan

Emilienne BELLAMY
56490 MENEAC
☎ 02 97 93 35 57 & 06 19 16 09 30 📠 02 97 93 35 57
web: www.itea.fr/G56/pages/56192.html

A 17th-century manor house set in five acres of natural woodland, offering traditionally furnished en suite rooms comprising three doubles and a triple. Living room, lounge and independent kitchen facilities are available at a charge.

Prices d €50-€70; extra person fr €15 **Nearby** ♿ 20km ⚓ 25km
⚲ 1km ⚹ 6km Restaurant 1km Water sports 20km ⚲ 2km 🏛 1.2km
Notes Pets admitted English spoken Open Easter to 1 November.

MOHON

⚑ ⚐ La Charbonnière

Marylène FOUR
Bodegat, 56490 MOHON
☎ 02 97 93 96 80 & 06 65 00 62 65 📠 02 97 93 97 41
email: charbonniere2@orange.fr
web: http://perso.wanadoo.fr/charbonniere

This house of character is situated only 500 metres from the Bronze Age town of Mohon and close to the Lanouée Forest, close to hiking trail 37. It provides four en suite double rooms, a living room with open fireplace, and a large garden with furniture. Pony-trekking is available.

Prices d €44; t €62; extra person €18; dinner fr €18 **On Site** ♿ ⚲
Restaurant **Nearby** ⚲ 17km ⚹ 15km Water sports 17km 🏛 1.5km
Notes Pets admitted English spoken

NEULLIAC

⚑ La Bretonnière

Adèle MILOUX
Bel-Air, 56300 NEULLIAC/PONTIVY
☎ 02 97 39 62 48 & 06 86 65 86 04 📠 02 97 39 62 48
email: miloux.bretonniere@wanadoo.fr
web: www.gites-de-france-morbihan.com/bretonniere

This detached house offers an en suite, double room (one grade 3), a grade 2 double with separate bathroom/WC and a grade 3 triple en suite room. Facilities include a lounge with open fireplace, a 3 hectare enclosed garden and boules. Hiking trail 37 is only 3km away. Booking essential.

Prices d fr €45; t fr €60; extra person fr €15 **Nearby** ♿ 2km ⚓ 3km
⚲ 1.5km ⚹ 3km Restaurant 3km Water sports 10km ⚲ 3km ⚽ 3km
🏛 3km **Notes** No pets English spoken

NIVILLAC

⚑ Au Fil de l'Eau

Michel et Maryse ARNOU
Port de Folleux, 56130 NIVILLAC
☎ 02 99 90 96 61 & 06 23 12 96 48
email: michel.arnou@wanadoo.fr
web: www.gites-de-france-morbihan.com/folleux

Set in landscaped gardens on the banks of the River Vilaine, this old stone house provides en suite accommodation in two double rooms and a triple on the ground floor. Veranda, garden furniture, loungers and BBQ. River trips in the owners' boat can be arranged and the nearby restaurant provides a free ferry service. Dinner by prior arrangement. Not recommended for children as there are cliffs close by.

Prices s fr €43; d fr €48; t fr €60 **Nearby** ♿ 5km ⚓ 15km Sea 25km
⚲ 0.1km ⚹ 5km Water sports 0.1km ⚲ 5km 🏛 5km ⚒ 25km
Notes Pets admitted English spoken Open Easter to 1 November.

⌗⌗⌗ La Genetière

Fabienne LAPTEFF
Port Folleux, 56130 NIVILLAC
☎ 02 99 90 88 04 & 02 97 41 46 90
🖹 02 97 41 46 90
email: lagenetiere56@wanadoo.fr
web: www.lagenetiere.fr.st

La Genetière towers over Folleux, a beautiful sailing and fishing
port which has inspired poems and songs. Guests can enjoy
panoramic views over the River Vilaine and choose between
five double, en suite rooms (3 rooms are Grade 4), which have
either a river or garden view. A comfortable and revitalising stay is
assured. 5 minutes from la Roche Bernard and 20 from Redon.

Prices s €57-€60; d €63-€67; extra person fr €18 **Nearby** ♨ 6km
♨ 15km Sea 25km ⚓ 0.1km ↴ 5km Water sports 0.1km ⚐ 5km
🏛 5km ⛟ 25km **Notes** Pets admitted English spoken

⌗⌗ ✲ ⦿ Le Moulin du Couëdic

Joseph CHESNIN
Saint-Cry, 56130 NIVILLAC
☎ 02 99 90 62 47 & 06 76 57 68 44 🖹 02 99 90 62 47
email: moulin-couedic@wanadoo.fr

Accommodation available on a farm; two double rooms and two
triple, all with private entrances and en suite. Lounge with open
fireplace, TV and video. Garden furniture and boules. Dinner is
available as an extra, except Sundays. Rates vary for length of stay.

Prices s fr €38-€40; d €40-€44; extra person fr €16; dinner fr €16
Nearby ♨ 12km ♨ 15km Sea 30km ⚓ 2km ↴ 9km Water sports 12km
⚐ 7.5km 🏛 8km ⛟ 22km **Notes** No pets

NOYAL-MUZILLAC

⌗⌗ Maisonneuve

Yves BONNAL
Route de Berric, 56190 NOYAL-MUZILLAC
☎ 02 97 67 02 66 & 06 08 06 58 01
email: yves.bonnal@free.fr

This longhouse has the twin attractions of the sea and the countryside.
It has three bedrooms: on the ground floor of the owners' home, with
its own entrance, is a double room with TV; in an adjoining building is
another double room, and a two-roomed suite for up to four people,
suitable for family accommodation. All rooms have private facilities.

Prices d fr €50; extra person fr €17 **Nearby** ♨ 15km ♨ 25km
Sea 15km ⚓ 3km ↴ 12km Restaurant 3km Water sports 15km ⚐ 2km
Spa 20km ⚑ 15km 🏛 12km ⛟ 15km **Notes** Pets admitted English
spoken

PLOEMEL

⌗⌗⌗ Kerimel

Nicolas MALHERBE
56400 PLOEMEL
☎ 02 97 56 83 53 & 06 83 40 68 56
email: chaumieres.kerimel@wanadoo.fr
web: http://kerimel.free.fr

Among a group of 17th-century cottages in a peaceful village, this
property has four upstairs bedrooms. Two are twin-bedded rooms;
two are triples (three single beds). All have en suite shower room and
WC, hair-dryer and kettle. Baby equipment available. Living room for
guest use; garden with chairs.

Prices d fr €70; t fr €90; extra person fr €20 **Nearby** ♨ 3km ♨ 2km
Sea 7km ↴ 7km ⚓ 7km Restaurant 2km Water sports 8km ⚐ 1km
⚑ 4km 🏛 1km ⛟ 6km **Notes** No pets English spoken

PLOEMEUR

⌗⌗⌗ Chapelle Sainte Anne

Christiane LE LORREC-BELLEC
3 bis rue de St Deron, 56270 PLOEMEUR
☎ 02 97 86 10 25 & 06 72 70 76 48
email: chris.lelorrec@laposte.net
web: www.gites-de-france-morbihan.com/deron

Only 4km from the beaches and close to the aquatic leisure centre,
Océanis, this is also an ideal area for walking. The main house
has a triple room, whilst the annexe provides two doubles, all en
suite. Books, TV, garden with furniture and barbecue. There is a 5%
reduction on bookings of five days and over. Closed November

Prices s fr €42; d fr €52; t fr €68 **On Site** Restaurant ⚑
Nearby ♨ 3km ♨ 7km Sea 4.5km ⚓ 4km ↴ 0.7km Water sports 8km
⚐ 1km 🏛 0.2km ⛟ 7km **Notes** No pets

PLOUGOUMELEN

⌗⌗⌗ *Lohenven*

Joëlle SCRIZZI
56400 PLOUGOUMELEN
☎ 02 97 57 82 94 & 06 64 61 30 31
email: scrizzi@wanadoo.fr
web: http://perso.wanadoo.fr/almanto.scrizzi

Midway between Vannes and Auray, and five minutes from Morbihan
Golf Course, this establishment offers three double rooms (one on
the ground floor). Beautiful views from the house over the wooded
grounds. Generous breakfasts are served in the dining room, and
guests have use of a small kitchen.

Prices not confirmed for 2008 **Nearby** ♨ 6km ♨ 6km Sea 10km
⚓ 10km ↴ 3km Water sports 10km ⚐ 4km 🏛 1.5km ⛟ 6km
Notes No pets English spoken

PLOUHARNEL

⁂ Kercroc

Serge ROUSSEAU

56340 PLOUHARNEL

☎ 06 72 11 73 04

email: rousseau.odile56@wanadoo.fr

web: http://mongite.free.fr

A house in a quiet village cul-de-sac close to Plouharnel, offering two en suite doubles (one on the ground floor)and a family room sleeping up to five people with separate bathroom/wc. Dining room, lounge area with open fireplace and TV, terrace and enclosed garden. Baby equipment available.

Prices s fr €39; d fr €48; t fr €57; extra person fr €13   **On Site** ☞   **Nearby** ⚓ 5km ♨ 10km Sea 0.2km 🌊 0.2km ⌁ 4km Restaurant 0.5km Water sports 2km ⊇ 3km 🏠 1km ⋈ 3km   **Notes** No pets   English spoken   Open February to December.

⁂ Kerfourchelle

Louis et Anne-Marie LE TOUZO

14 Rue Kerfourchelle, 56340 PLOUHARNEL

☎ 02 97 52 34 38 & 06 70 43 96 35

A comfortable, detached house offering a double room, a room for three and a room suitable for up to five people. All rooms have en suite facilities. There is a lounge with a TV and a microwave, and there is a large garden.

Prices d fr €46; t fr €60; extra person fr €18   **Nearby** ⚓ 5km ♨ 7km Sea 0.5km 🌊 2.5km ⌁ 3km Water sports 2.5km ⊇ 3km 🏠 0.8km ⋈ 0.5km   **Notes** No pets   English spoken

⁂ Kerzivienne

Anne-Marie LE BARON

56340 PLOUHARNEL

☎ 02 97 52 31 44 & 06 78 54 72 47

web: www.gites-de-france-morbihan.com/kermarquer/

This house is situated between Carnac and Quiberon and provides two grade 3 en suite double rooms with sea views, and a grade 2 triple room with a separate shower-room/wc. TV lounge, garden with furniture, barbecue and table tennis. Hiking trails 34 and 341 are within 1.5km.

Prices s fr €40; d €44-€47; t €59-€62; extra person fr €15   **Nearby** ⚓ 4km ♨ 8km Sea 2km 🌊 7km ⌁ 4km Restaurant 0.8km Water sports 3km ⊇ 2km Spa 4km ☞ 3.5km 🏠 0.8km ⋈ 0.2km   **Notes** No pets   English spoken   Open March to November.

PLOUHINEC

⁂ ⦿ Kerzine

Sylvie LE PENNEC

56680 PLOUHINEC

☎ 02 97 85 86 29 & 06 79 07 93 08

web: www.chambres-bretagne-sud.com

In a village not far from the sea, this house has four guest bedrooms. There are two doubles on the ground floor, and two triples upstairs,

all with en suite shower room and WC. Baby equipment available; use of kitchen. Garden with furniture; good access to footpaths.

Prices s fr €42; d fr €48; extra person fr €14; dinner fr €19   **Nearby** ⚓ 10km ♨ 12km Sea 1.5km 🌊 1.5km ⌁ 20km Restaurant 1km Water sports 1.5km ⊇ 1km ☞ 5km 🏠 1km ⋈ 20km   **Notes** No pets English spoken

PLUMELIN

⁂ Gostrevel

Bernard et Dominique CAPPY

56500 PLUMELIN

☎ 02 97 44 20 92 & 06 70 43 97 54

email: bernard.cappy@yahoo.fr

This pleasant house, situated 4km from Plumelin and 7km from Locminé, provides a family room sleeping up to four people, triple (both en suite) and a grade 2 double room with separate shower-room/wc. Situated in the heart of the Morbihan region, Locminé is the ideal base from which to explore the many tourist, leisure and cultural sites nearby. Hiking trail 341 is 16km away.

Prices s fr €40; d fr €48; t fr €65; extra person fr €17   **Nearby** ♨ 25km Sea 45km 🌊 12km ⌁ 7km Restaurant 6km Water sports 35km ⊇ 6km 🏠 6km ⋈ 35km   **Notes** No pets English spoken

PLUMERGAT

⁂ ⦿ Le Clos de Kerhouil

Catherine COZIGOU

56400 MERIADEC (SAINTE-ANNE D'AURAY)

☎ 02 97 57 79 19 & 06 11 97 15 12

email: clos-de-kerhouil@cegetel.net

A few kilometres from Carnac and the Golfe du Morbihan, this modern property stands in spacious enclosed grounds. There are two double rooms: one on the ground floor with air-conditioning, and another upstairs. Both have en suite facilities. Also upstairs is a grade two-roomed suite with shared facilities, suitable for a single family.

Prices s €46-€61; d €50-€65; t fr €91; extra person fr €20; dinner fr €30   **Nearby** ⚓ 4km ♨ 10km Sea 15km 🌊 10km ⌁ 10km Restaurant 1.5km Water sports 15km ⊇ 2km ☞ 1.5km 🏠 2km ⋈ 10km   **Notes** No pets

PLUNERET

⁂ ♿ Tréguévir

Josiane NAVEOS

4 Impasse de Tréguévir, 56400 PLUNERET

☎ 02 97 24 40 90 & 06 63 85 31 80

email: famille.naveos@wanadoo.fr

In the centre of a village not far from Auray, this property has three bedrooms in a building adjacent to the owners' home. On the ground floor is a double room; upstairs is another double, and a triple. All the rooms have a private bath or shower room and WC. Baby equipment available; kitchenette. Pleasant views of the orchard, where guests can relax.

Prices s fr €45; d fr €53; extra person fr €15   **Nearby** ⚓ 5km ♨ 6km Sea 15km 🌊 3km ⌁ 3km Restaurant 1km Water sports 15km ⊇ 1.5km ☞ 2km 🏠 1.5km ⋈ 3km   **Notes** No pets English spoken

PLUVIGNER

⏸ ⏸ Chaumière de Kerréo

Gérard & Nelly GREVES
56330 PLUVIGNER
☎ 02 97 50 90 48 🖹 02 97 50 90 69
web: www.gites-de-france-morbihan.com/kerreo

This 17th-century cottage, in a peaceful rural location with landscaped gardens, has five double, en suite guest rooms. Comfortable and traditional furnishings throughout. The highlight of a visit is undoubtedly the meals, prepared by a former cookery teacher. Baby equipment available.

Prices s fr €45; d €57-€63; extra person fr €15; dinner fr €22
Nearby ⛰ 6km ⚓ 15km Sea 20km ✦ 5km ⚘ 7km Restaurant 6km Water sports 25km ♨ 7km 🏛 7km ⚕ 16km **Notes** No pets English spoken Open April to 15 November.

⏸ ⏸ Kerdavid Duchentil

Marie-Claire COLLET
56330 PLUVIGNER
☎ 02 97 56 00 59 & 06 08 57 05 00
web: www.gites-de-france-morbihan.com/kerdavid

This traditional long house enjoys a rural location in large, shaded grounds. There are four double bedrooms and a family room, each en suite with private entrance. A kitchen, lounge, living room, TV, garden with furniture and BBQ are at guests' disposal. Numerous historic sites, the Gulf of Morbihan, beaches and forests are all within easy reach.

Prices s fr €38; d fr €45 **On Site** ✦ **Nearby** ⛰ 3km ⚓ 13km Sea 25km ⚘ 13km Restaurant 5km Water sports 18km ♨ 13km ✦ 5km ⚕ 15km **Notes** Pets admitted

⏸ Melin Keraudran

Fernand et Marie MADEROU
56330 PLUVIGNER
☎ 02 97 24 90 73 & 06 07 18 59 51
email: fernandmaderou@club-internet.fr
web: www.gites-de-france-morbihan.com/melin

Full of character, this cottage is situated in a two hectare park with private pond which is available for fishing. An outbuilding houses a king-size room and two rooms for two, each en suite. Lounge with TV, guests' living room with fireplace, garden furniture and barbecue.

Prices d fr €70; t fr €90 **On Site** ✦ **Nearby** ⛰ 5km ⚓ 13km Sea 25km ⚘ 10km Restaurant 5km Water sports 18km ♨ 5km ✦ 6km 🏛 5km ⚕ 15km **Notes** No pets English spoken Open April to September.

QUEVEN

⏸ Le Mané

Marie-Louise KERMABON
Route de Kerdual, 56530 QUEVEN
☎ 02 97 84 83 20
web: www.gites-de-france-morbihan.com/lemane/

This two-acre setting is close to Lorient and within easy reach of beaches, Val Quéven golf course and Pont-Scorff zoo. There is a family suite with a double room and room sleeping two children with separate bathroom/wc, a grade 2 double room with separate shower-room/wc and a further en suite double. TV lounge, terrace with garden furniture and parking. Hiking trails 34E and 38E are 1km away.

Prices s fr €43; d €46-€50; t fr €66; extra person fr €15 **Nearby** ⛰ 3km ⚓ 3km Sea 6km ✦ 3km ⚘ 6km Restaurant 3km Water sports 3km ♨ 3.5km Spa 30km 🏛 0.5km ⚕ 2km **Notes** No pets English spoken

⏸ ⏸ Manoir de Kerlebert

Guirec et Sophie DEWAVRIN
Rue de Kerlebert, 56530 QUEVEN
☎ 02 97 80 22 37 🖹 02 97 80 20 83
email: manoirkerlebert@wanadoo.fr
web: www.gites-de-france-morbihan.com/manoir-kerlebert

This 17th-century manor, close to the town centre, sits in extensive grounds featuring many old trees. There are three first-floor rooms, two doubles and a triple; two with en suite bath and WC, and one with shower and WC. Use of small kitchen at an additional charge; evening meals and picnic baskets by prior arrangement.

Prices s fr €45; d fr €55; t fr €80; extra person fr €25; dinner fr €20
Nearby ⛰ 0.1km ⚓ 2km Sea 10km ✦ 10km ⚘ 10km Water sports 10km ♨ 0.5km 🏛 0.5km ⚕ 6km **Notes** No pets English spoken

⏸ ⏸ Saint-Nicodème

Marcel et Françoise LAURENT
56530 QUEVEN
☎ 02 97 05 17 48 & 06 19 94 11 33
email: marcel.laurent405@orange.fr
web: http://alt64.gotdns.com/closstnicodeme

In a small village not far from the Lorient, this house has three double bedrooms; one is on the ground floor, and they all have private shower room and WC. The large attractive garden makes an ideal place for guests to relax.

Prices s fr €40; d fr €47; extra person fr €15; dinner fr €20
Nearby ⛰ 1.5km ⚓ 2km Sea 6km ✦ 5km ⚘ 4km Restaurant 0.6km Water sports 6km ♨ 2km Spa 25km ✦ 5km 🏛 2km ⚕ 4km **Notes** No pets English spoken Open March to 20 November.

RIANTEC

♦♦♦ Kervassal

Maya WATINE
56670 RIANTEC
☎ 02 97 33 58 66 📄 02 97 33 58 66
email: gonzague.watine@wanadoo.fr
web: www.tymaya.com

Not far from the beach, in a quiet little village, this 17th-century
cottage has three spacious bedrooms. There are two large double
rooms that can sleep up to three people; all have private shower
room and WC. Tea-making equipment and a hair-dryer in each room;
guests' lounge on the ground floor. Attractive flower garden with
garden furniture.

Prices d fr €64; extra person fr €20 **Nearby** ⚓ 1.5km ⚓ 18km
Sea 1.5km ⚓ 1km ⚓ 1km Restaurant 1km Water sports 1.5km ⚓ 1km
Spa 30km ⚓ 1km ⚓ 1km ⚓ 12km **Notes** No pets English spoken
Open April to October.

RUFFIAC

♦♦♦ Ferme de Rangera

Gilbert COUEDELO
56140 RUFFIAC
☎ 02 97 93 72 18 📄 02 97 93 72 18

This property, adjacent to a gîte, has three rooms, all with private
shower rooms and WCs. There is a double room on the ground
floor, and two triple rooms upstairs. Lounge area with TV;
microwave. In the owners' house are two more rooms: a double and
a triple, again with private facilities. Garden, garden furniture, boules,
barbecue.

Prices s fr €37; d fr €43; t fr €56; extra person fr €16 **Nearby** ⚓ 25km
⚓ 20km Sea 45km ⚓ 3km ⚓ 18km Restaurant 1km Water sports 18km
⚓ 2km ⚓ 8km ⚓ 1.5km ⚓ 30km **Notes** No pets Open 15 April to
15 November.

ST-AIGNAN

♦♦♦ Croix Even

Micheline HENRIO
56480 SAINT-AIGNAN
☎ 02 97 27 51 56 & 06 86 31 62 06

Not far from the Canal de Nantes, in its own grounds, this house has
three bedrooms. On the ground floor is a double room, and a room
for three; upstairs is another double, with its own balcony overlooking
the garden; all have private shower room/WC. Baby equipment, guests'
lounge, use of kitchen. Shady enclosed grounds, with garden furniture.

Prices s fr €35; d fr €45; t fr €55; extra person fr €15 **Nearby** ⚓ 10km
⚓ 25km ⚓ 10km ⚓ 20km Restaurant 2km Water sports 10km ⚓ 4km
⚓ 4km **Notes** Pets admitted English spoken

ST-GRAVE

♦♦♦ Vaugrenard

Silvaine LE DOUARON
56220 SAINT-GRAVE
☎ 02 97 43 44 20 & 06 30 15 33 68
email: silvaine.le-douaron@wanadoo.fr
web: http://perso.orange.fr/levaugrenard/

There is a choice of two double rooms on the ground floor and two
three-person rooms on the first floor at this renovated farmhouse;
all have en suite facilities. The house lies on a four-hectare property
where guests can meet the owners' goats, horses and sheep. A lounge
and a small kitchen are available, and guests can also enjoy the
garden with its BBQ and boules.

Prices s fr €40; d fr €48; t fr €62; extra person fr €15 **Nearby** ⚓ 3km
⚓ 7km Sea 30km ⚓ 0.1km ⚓ 17km Restaurant 3km Water sports 5km
⚓ 3km ⚓ 10km ⚓ 6km ⚓ 17km **Notes** Pets admitted English spoken
Open mid March to mid January.

ST-JACUT-LES-PINS

♦♦♦ Le Pilori

Josie MORICE
La Lardrie, 56220 SAINT-JACUT-LES-PINS
☎ 02 99 91 20 14 & 06 85 92 48 77 📄 02 99 91 20 14
email: josiemorice@free.fr

On the edge of the forest, on a footpath between a windmill and
a watermill, this house has a wonderful, peaceful location. On the
ground floor are two linked rooms, which can be taken together (to
sleep up to five) or separately. Upstairs are two more double rooms;
all rooms have en suite facilities. Baby equipment available. Lounge
with open fire, music and books.

Prices s fr €47; d fr €55; t fr €80; extra person fr €20 **Nearby** ⚓ 5km
⚓ 9km Sea 38km ⚓ 0.5km ⚓ 13km Restaurant 2km Water sports 5km
⚓ 2km ⚓ 2km ⚓ 13km **Notes** No pets English spoken Open May to
15 September.

ST-PHILIBERT

▦ **Kernivilit**

Christine GOUZER

17 Route de Quéhan, 56470 SAINT-PHILIBERT

☎ 02 97 55 17 78 & 06 78 35 09 34   📄 02 97 30 04 11

email: fgouzer@club-internet.fr

web: www.residence-mer.com

This oyster farm affords panoramic views of the River Crach and offers three en suite guest rooms with a separate entrance: a double room, a triple with kitchenette and a family room with kitchenette accommodating up to four people. A lounge area, garden with terrace and furniture are at guests' disposal.

Prices s €60-€80; d €65-€80; extra person fr €20 **Nearby** ⚓ 5km ⚓ 7km Sea 0.1km ✎ 0.1km ↖ 5km Restaurant 0.5km Water sports 0.1km ⚓ 0.1km Spa 6km ☘ 2km 🏛 3km ⋔ 9km **Notes** No pets English spoken

SULNIAC

▦ ○| *Le Grand Clos*

Christian et Joan BOUTELOUP

La Hellaye, 56250 SULNIAC

☎ 02 97 53 10 97 & 06 03 17 88 84

email: jbouteloup@wanadoo.fr

web: www.gites-de-france-morbihan.com/bouteloup

This house lies in a large garden between Questembert and Sulniac and offers guests a choice of three en suite rooms: two rooms for two and a room for three. Guests can play boules, table tennis and darts; table d'hôte meals by prior arrangement. Situated near the beaches at Damgan and d'Ambon, and ideal for exploring nearby character towns.

Prices not confirmed for 2008 **Nearby** ⚓ 4km ⚓ 20km Sea 18km ✎ 0.5km ↖ 4km Water sports 20km ⚓ 4km 🏛 4km ⋔ 4km **Notes** Pets admitted English spoken

▦ ○| **Quiban**

V et G LE JALLE-FOUCHER

56250 SULNIAC

☎ 02 97 53 29 05

email: gilles.lejalle@wanadoo.fr

web: www.gites-de-france-morbihan.com/quiban

This house is full of character and stands in wooded grounds. It has three double rooms on the ground floor and one double upstairs (awaiting classification), all of them with en suite bath or shower rooms and WCs. Baby equipment available. Enclosed gardens with garden furniture; breakfast served in the lounge, or, in good weather, on the veranda. Meals by arrangement.

Prices s fr €45; d fr €50; extra person fr €18; dinner fr €20 **Nearby** ⚓ 2km ⚓ 25km Sea 20km ✎ 5km ↖ 2km Restaurant 1.5km Water sports 20km ⚓ 2km 🏛 2km ⋔ 14km **Notes** No pets English spoken

SURZUR

▦ **Kerguezec**

Patrick GAUTHIER

56450 SURZUR

☎ 02 97 42 09 33 & 06 63 22 79 68

email: pa.gauthier@wanadoo.fr

web: www.kerguezec.com

A 17th-century manor house with five bedrooms, all upstairs. There are four double rooms with en suite shower and WC, plus a split-level, two-room unit for four guests, suitable for a single family. Meals by prior arrangement. A wonderful spot where guests can discover what country life is all about.

Prices d €65-€75; extra person fr €20 **Nearby** ⚓ 3km ⚓ 18km Sea 6km ✎ 6km ↖ 10km Restaurant 3km Water sports 9km ⚓ 2km Spa 20km ☘ 10km 🏛 1.5km ⋔ 10km **Notes** No pets English spoken

▦ **Le Petit Kerbocen**

Claude GAUGENDAU

56450 SURZUR

☎ 02 97 42 00 75   📄 02 97 42 00 75

web: www.itea.fr/G56/pages/5657.html

A restored annexe of a house on a working farm, providing four double rooms and two triples, all en suite. Facilities include a TV lounge, baby equipment, children's games and free use of the kitchen. Child's bed on request. Hiking trail 34 is 6km away.

Prices s fr €41; d fr €46; t fr €60; extra person fr €14 **Nearby** ⚓ 4km ⚓ 15km Sea 6km ✎ 6km ↖ 13km Water sports 8km ⚓ 1km 🏛 1km ⋔ 16km **Notes** Pets admitted

THEIX

⊪ *Le Bézit*

G et J LE BOURSICAULT

10 Allée Ty Er Beleg, 56450 THEIX

☎ 02 97 43 13 75

This 17th-century farmhouse is near the Gulf of Morbihan and close to hiking trail 34. There are two grade 2 doubles with a separate entrance and two grade 3 doubles in the mansion house, all en suite. Lounges, TV, shared kitchen facilities and garden with furniture.

Prices not confirmed for 2008 **Nearby** ⛳ 15km ♨ 14km Sea 12km 🏊 2km ⚓ 8km Water sports 12km 🍴 2km 🏛 2km ⛺ 8km **Notes** No pets English spoken

⊪ **Le Petit Clérigo**

Guy LE GRUYERE

56450 THEIX

☎ 02 97 43 03 66 & 06 32 07 80 10

This detached house is situated on a farm and offers three en suite double guest rooms with a private entrance, and a garden with furniture. Hiking trail 34 is within 14 km.

Prices s fr €35; d fr €40 **Nearby** ⛳ 20km ♨ 20km Sea 4km 🏊 4km ⚓ 10km Restaurant 0.8km Water sports 12km 🍴 1km Spa 30km 🏛 1km ⛺ 10km **Notes** No pets Open March to November.

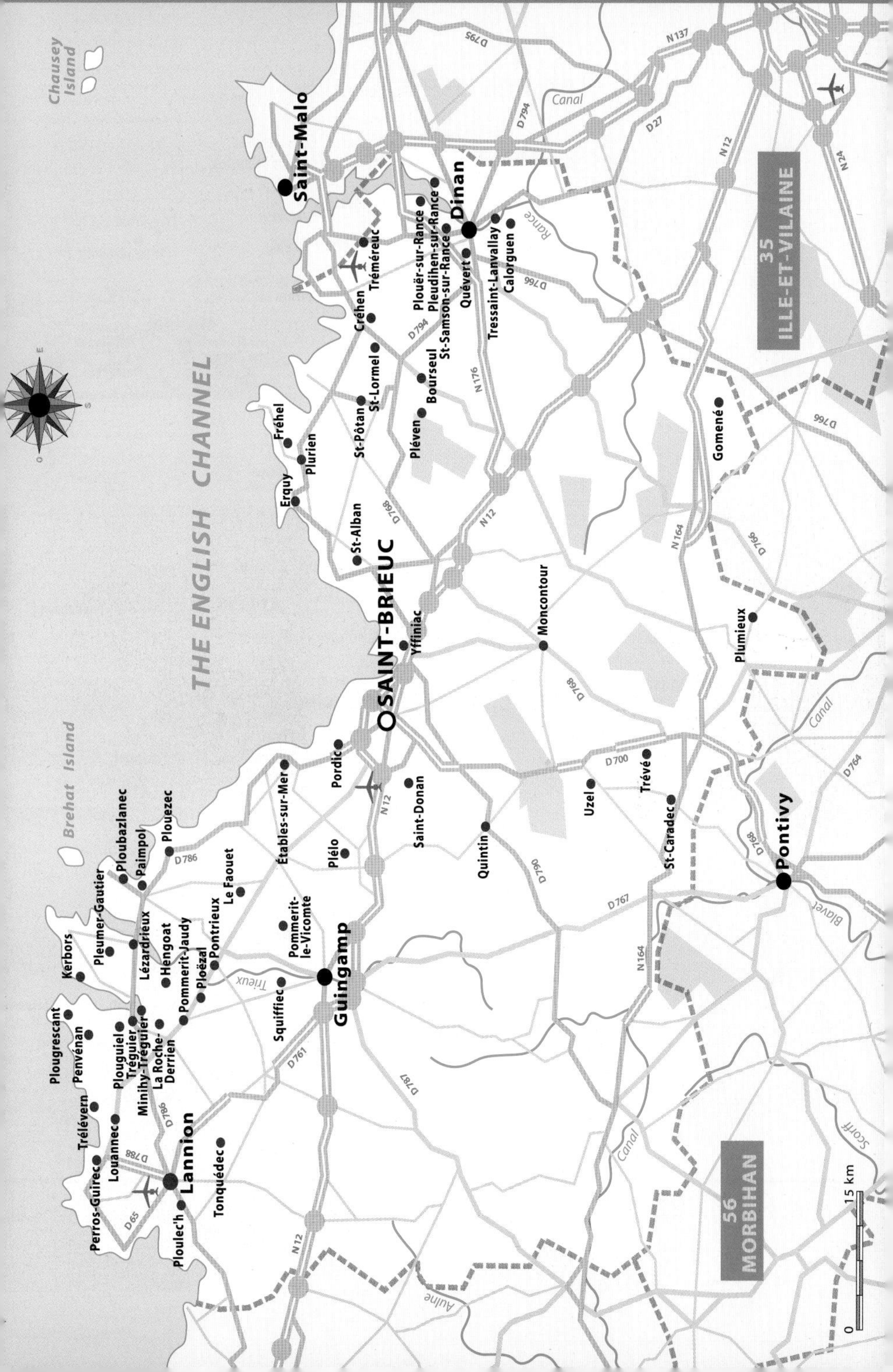

THE ENGLISH CHANNEL
Chausey Island
Brehat Island
Saint-Malo
Dinan
Plouër-sur-Rance
Pleudihen-sur-Rance
St-Samson-sur-Rance
Quévert
Tressaint-Lanvallay
Calorguen
Trémereuc
Créhen
St-Lormel
Bourseul
Pléven
St-Pôtan
Fréhel
Plurien
Erquy
St-Alban
OSAINT-BRIEUC
Yffiniac
Moncontour
Gomené
Plumieux
Pordic
Saint-Donan
Étables-sur-Mer
Plélo
Quintin
Uzel
Trévé
St-Caradec
Pontivy
Plouezec
Paimpol
Ploubazlanec
Pleumer-Gautier
Lézardrieux
Le Faouet
Pontrieux
Hengoat
Pommerit-Jaudy
Ploëzal
Pommerit-le-Vicomte
Guingamp
Squiffiec
Kerbors
Plougrescant
Penvénan
Plouguiel
Tréguier
Minihy-Tréguier
La Roche-Derrien
Trélévern
Louannec
Perros-Guirec
Lannion
Ploulec'h
Tonquédec
35 ILLE-ET-VILAINE
56 MORBIHAN
Canal
Rance
Trieux
Blavet
Aulne
Scorff
D795
N137
D794
D27
N12
N24
D766
N176
D768
N164
D700
D764
D790
D767
D786
D761
D787
D788
D65
0
15 km

FINISTÈRE
Brittany

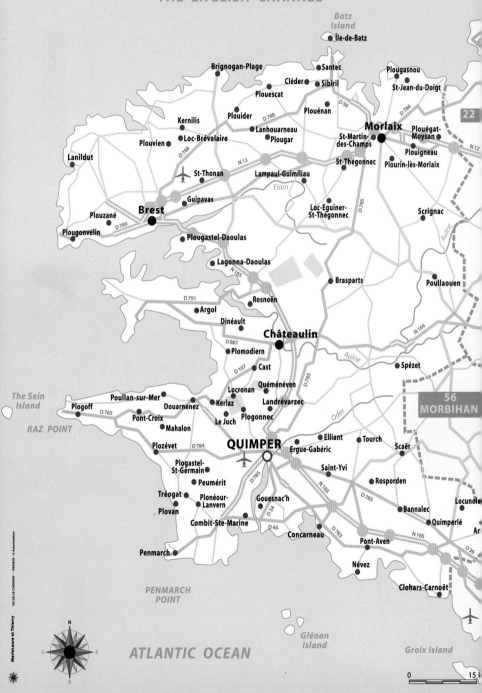

THE ENGLISH CHANNEL

Batz Island
●Île-de-Batz

Brignogan-Plage●
●Santec
Cléder● ●Sibiril
Plouescat●
Plouénan●
Plouider●
Kernilis●
Lanhouarneau●
●Loc-Brévalaire ●Plougar
Plouvien●
Lanildut●
St-Thonan●
N12

Plougasnou●
St-Jean-du-Doigt●
D786

Morlaix
Plouégat-Moysan●
St-Martin-des-Champs●
Plouigneau●
St-Thégonnec● Plourin-lès-Morlaix●
Lampaul-Guimiliau●
22
N12

Elorn

Brest●
Guipavas●
Plouzané●
Plougonvelin●
D789
Plougastel-Daoulas●

Loc-Eguiner-St-Thégonnec●
D785

Scrignac●

Aulne

Lagonna-Daoulas●
N165

Brasparts●
Poullaouen●

D791
Rosnoën●
Argol●
Dinéault●
D887
Châteaulin●
Plomodiern●
D107 Cast●
Quéménéven●
Locronan●
Landrévarzec●

Aulne

N164

Spézet●

D785

The Sein Island
Plogoff● D765
RAZ POINT

Poullan-sur-Mer●
Douarnenez● Kerlaz●
Pont-Croix●
Mahalon●
Plozévet● D784
Le Juch● Plogonnec●

QUIMPER ◉
Plogastel-St-Germain●
Peumérit●
Tréogat● Plonéour-Lanvern●
Plovan●
Combit-Ste-Marine●
Penmarch●

Odet
MORBIHAN 56

Elliant● Tourch●
Ergue-Gabéric● Scaër●
Saint-Yvi●
N165 Rosporden●
D765
Locunolé
Gouesnac'h● Bannalec●
D34 Quimperlé● Ar
D44 N165 D26
Concarneau● Pont-Aven●
D783
Névez●
Clohars-Carnoët●

PENMARCH POINT

Glénan Island
Groix Island

MarieLaure et Thierry

ATLANTIC OCEAN

0   15

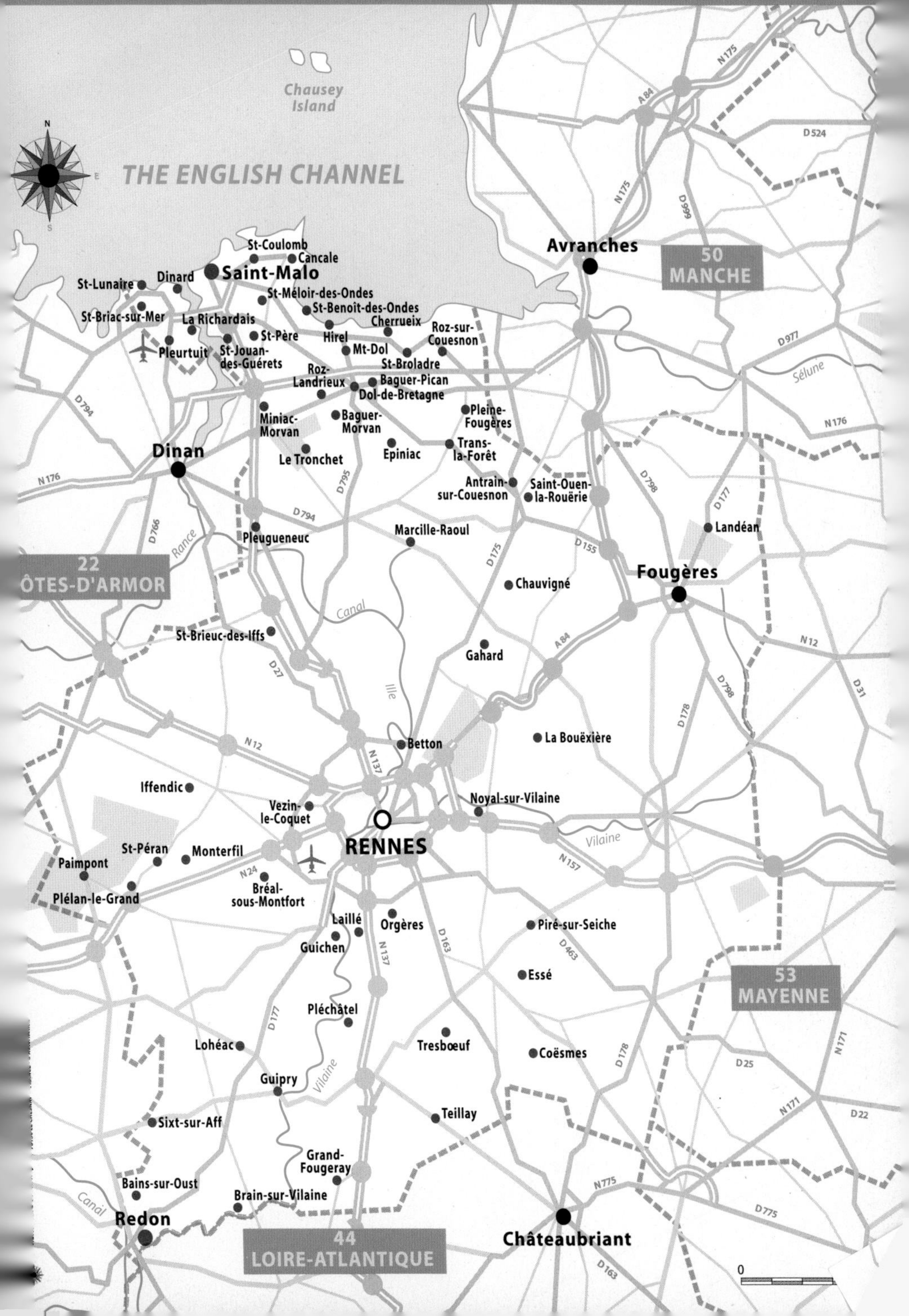

Chausey
Island

THE ENGLISH CHANNEL

N

50
MANCHE

Avranches

St-Coulomb
Cancale
Dinard
Saint-Malo
St-Lunaire
St-Méloir-des-Ondes
St-Briac-sur-Mer
St-Benoit-des-Ondes
La Richardais
Cherrueix
Roz-sur-
Couesnon
St-Père
Hirel
Pleurtuit
St-Jouan-
Mt-Dol
St-Broladre
des-Guérets
Roz-
Landrieux
Baguer-Pican
Dol-de-Bretagne
Miniac-
Baguer-
Pleine-
Morvan
Morvan
Fougères
Dinan
Le Tronchet
Epiniac
Trans-
la-Forêt
N 176
Antrain-
Saint-Ouen-
sur-Couesnon
la-Rouërie
Pleugueneuc
Marcille-Raoul
Landéan

**22
ÔTES-D'ARMOR**

St-Brieuc-des-Iffs
Chauvigné
Fougères

Gahard

N 12
Betton
La Bouëxière

Iffendic
Noyal-sur-Vilaine
Vezin-
le-Coquet
St-Péran
Monterfil
RENNES
Vilaine
Paimpont
Bréal-
Plélan-le-Grand
sous-Montfort
Laillé
Orgères
Pîré-sur-Seiche
Guichen
Essé

**53
MAYENNE**

Pléchâtel
Lohéac
Tresbœuf
Coësmes
Guipry
Teillay
Sixt-sur-Aff
Grand-
Fougeray
Bains-sur-Oust
Brain-sur-Vilaine
Redon

**44
LOIRE-ATLANTIQUE**

Châteaubriant

0

MORBIHAN
Brittany

56

35 ILLE-ET-VILAINE
22 CÔTES-D'ARMOR
29 FINISTÈRE
44 LOIRE-ATLANTIQUE
Redon
Augan
Ruffiac
St-Gravé
St-Jacut-les-Pins
Ploërmel
Malansac-Rochefort-en-Terre
Nivillac
Ménéac
Mohon
La Croix-Helléan
Josselin
Guéhenno
Le Cours
Noyal-Muzillac
Sulniac
Ambon
Elven
Theix
Noyalo
Surzur
VANNES
Pontivy
Neulliac
Plumelin
Plumergat
Plougoumelen
Larmor-Baden
Locmariaquer
Pluvigner
Pluneret
St-Aignan
Cléguérec
Guern
Baud
Crach
Saint-Philibert
Landévant
Locoal-Mendon
Carnac
Plouharnel
Brandérion
Belz
Inzinzac-Lochrist
Kernascléden
Le Croisty
Berné
Plouhinec
Quéven
Gestel
Lorient
Larmor-Plage-près-Lorient
Guidel
Ploëmeur
Groix Island
ATLANTIC OCEAN
QUIBERON PENINSULA
Belleisle-en-Mer
Canal
Vilaine
Rance
Blavet
Scorff
N24
N12
N164
N165
N166
D766
D775
D773
D774
D780
D700
D764
D767
D768
D781
D26
D765
MarieLaure et Thierry 78150 LE CHESNAY - FRANCE - © Autorisation

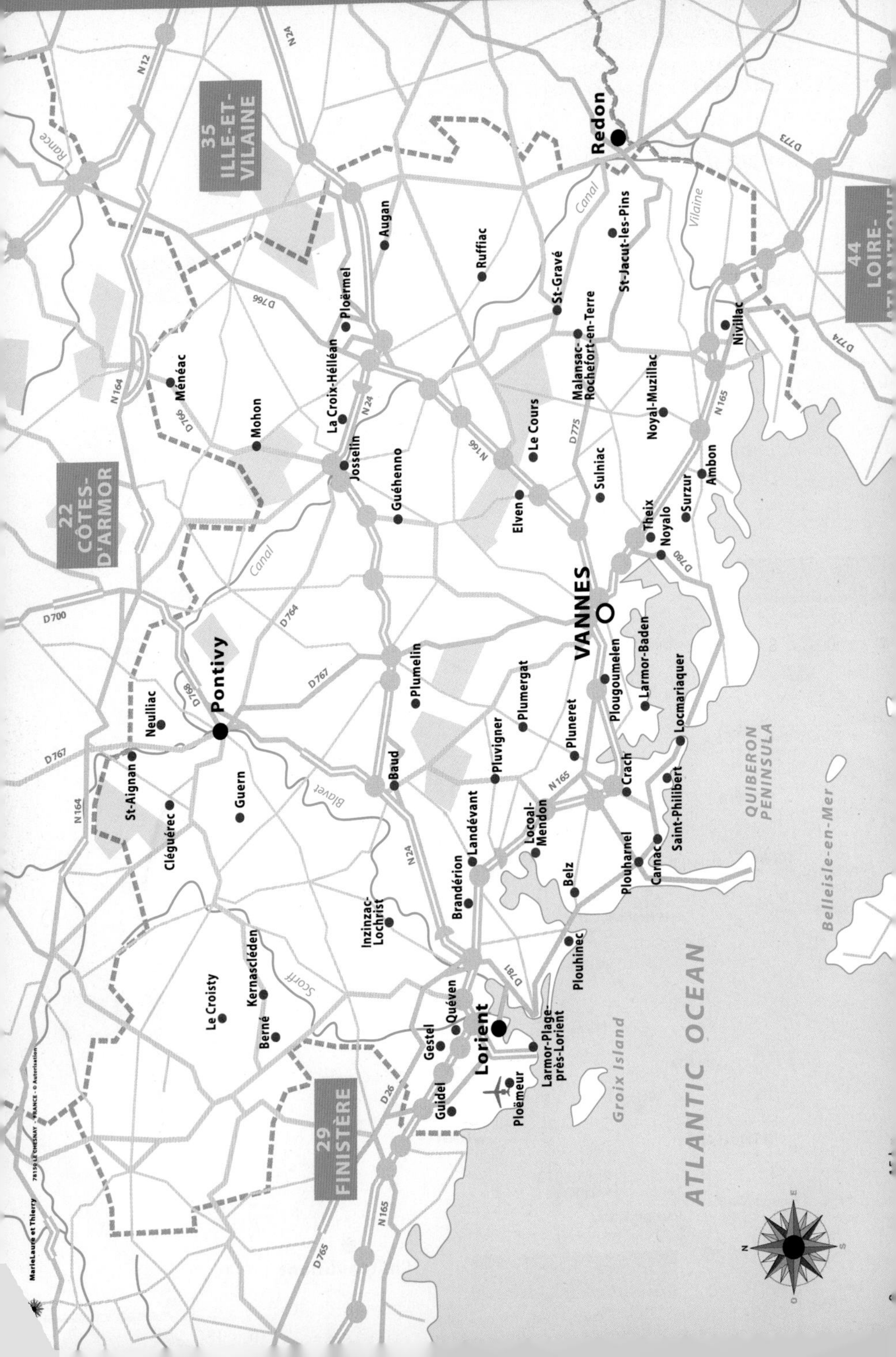

BURGUNDY

CÔTE-D'OR

AIGNAY-LE-DUC

▓▓ 🍽 Chambre d'hôtes

Claude BONNEFOY
rue Sous les Vieilles Halles, 21510 AIGNAY-LE-DUC
☎ 03 80 93 90 07
email: claude.o.bonnefoy@wanadoo.fr
web: www.maisonlademoiselle.com

This 18th-century mansion has fine views of the village with its 13th-century church. The three double bedrooms and one triple room have a private entrance and are en suite (cot available). Central heating, wi-fi available, a lounge with TV and library. Evening meals available on request, served in the living room. Garden with barn.

Prices s fr €30; d fr €40; t fr €50; dinner fr €17 **On Site** Restaurant **Nearby** ⛳ 15km 🚴 15km 🏖 1km 🎣 34km 🚣 34km **Notes** Pets admitted

---

AISY-SOUS-THIL

▓▓ Les Forges

D et F GIROUDEAU
21390 AISY-SOUS-THIL
☎ 03 80 64 53 86 & 06 77 51 42 27
email: dangiroudeau@aol.com

Situated on an old farm in the heart of the countryside, four en suite bedrooms sleep up to three people. Guests are welcome to use the kitchen and the living room with open fireplace. Safe storage is provided for bicycles and motorcycles, and parking is available for cars.

Prices s fr €40; d fr €45; t fr €50; extra person fr €10 **Nearby** ⛳ 13km 🚴 5km 🏖 0.1km 🎣 11km Restaurant 1km 🏊 1km 🛒 2km 🚣 30km **Notes** No pets English spoken

ARGILLY

▓▓ Maison de Soi

Edith PIAT
rue de l'Eglise, 21700 ARGILLY
☎ 03 80 62 59 83 📠 03 80 62 59 55
email: piat.vincent@wanadoo.fr

In the outbuildings of the old rectory are three guest rooms decorated in local craft style and each with its own entrance. They all sleep either two or three people, with private shower rooms, toilets and central heating. There is also a lounge, sitting room, library, enclosed courtyard and garden.

Prices s fr €47; d fr €55; t fr €60 **On Site** 🎾 Private 🎣 **Nearby** ⛳ 10km 🚴 15km 🏖 7km Restaurant 8km 🏊 0.5km 🛒 8km 🚣 8km **Notes** No pets English spoken

---

ATHEE (COTE D'OR)

▓▓ 🍽 Chambre d'hôtes

Gilbert MILLIERE
17 rue Serpentiere, 21130 ATHEE
☎ 03 80 37 36 33 📠 03 80 37 36 33
email: gc-milliere@ifrance.com
web: www.gc-milliere.ifrance.com

Enjoying a peaceful, rural location with views of the 3.5 hectare garden or a courtyard planted with trees, this old farmhouse offers three en suite guest rooms (one grade 2), all with private entrances. Facilities include central heating, a living room, lounge, open fireplace, games, shady terraces, floral displays, garages and table d'hôte meals on request.

Prices s fr €41; d fr €44; t €54-€61; dinner fr €20 **Nearby** ⛳ 12km 🚴 20km 🏖 2km 🎣 3km Restaurant 5km 🏊 6km 🛒 0.5km 🚣 4km **Notes** Pets admitted

ATHEE (COTE D'OR) CONTINUED

▦ ⃝ *Les Laurentides*

Michelle ROYER-COTTIN
27 rue du Centre, 21130 ATHEE
☎ 03 80 31 00 25 🖹 03 80 31 00 25
email: michrobroyer@wanadoo.fr

Four bedrooms form part of an old farm dating back to the 19th-century: a grade 2 room sleeps up to three people, and there are two grade 3 doubles and a grade 3 triple, all en suite. Heating, living room, lounge with TV, fully equipped kitchen, parking and garden. Table d'hôte meals may be booked at weekends and public holidays, and there is a restaurant within 2km.

Prices not confirmed for 2008 **Nearby** ⛷ 4km ⌁30km ⌀1km ⚡4km
⌇4km 🛏4km ⋘4km **Notes** Pets admitted

AUXEY-DURESSES

▦▦ Château de Melin

Hèléne et Arnaud DERATS
Hameau de Melin, 21190 AUXEY-DURESSES
☎ 03 80 21 21 19 🖹 03 80 21 21 72
email: derats@chateaudemelin.com
web: http://chateaumelin.free.fr

This 16th-century château lies in the heart of a Beaune vineyard, and guests are welcome to taste and buy wines from the estate. The en suite accommodation comprises one double room and two adjoining rooms, one double and the other twin-bedded. Heating, lounge, terrace, parking and five acres of land with a small lake. Restaurant within 2km.

Prices s €80–€85; d €85–€100; t fr €115 **Nearby** ⛷ 4km ⌁13km
⌀10km ⚡9km ⌇2km 🛏4km ⋘12km **Notes** Pets admitted
English spoken

BAUBIGNY (ORCHES)

▦▦ Rocault

F & B ROCAULT
Orches, 21340 BAUBIGNY
☎ 03 80 21 78 72 🖹 03 80 21 85 95
email: francois.blandine.rocault@wanadoo.fr
web: www.bourgogne-rocault.com

This winegrowers' house is situated at the foot of some cliffs on a vineyard overlooking the hamlet. There are five en suite guest rooms, three doubles and two rooms sleeping three. Facilities include heating, a living room, garden and parking. Wine-tasting tours of the vineyard are available for guests.

Prices s fr €48; d fr €59; t fr €74; extra person fr €12 **Nearby** ⛷ 0.5km
⌁15km ⌀10km ⚡15km Restaurant 3km ⌇3km ⚑15km 🛏8km
⋘15km **Notes** No pets English spoken CC

BEAUNE

▦ ⃝ Chambre d'hôtes

Elisabeth SEROUART
Chemin du Dessus de Bressandes, La Montagne,
21200 BEAUNE
☎ 03 80 22 93 50
email: denis.serouart@wanadoo.fr
web: www.maisonbressandes.com

This large, welcoming house has a unique view of the vineyard and the town of Beaune. The en suite accommodation comprises one suite and two other guest rooms, all tastefully furnished. Heating, TV, lounge and library. Spacious grounds with parking and swimming pool surrounded by garden. Table d'hôte meals available on request; within 500 metres.

Prices s €65–€80; d €65–€80; t €100; dinner fr €25 **On Site** Private ⚡
Nearby ⛷ 5km ⌁5km ⌀8km Restaurant 2km ⌇3km ⚑2km 🛏2km
⋘3km **Notes** No pets Open March to November.

▦▦ La Terre d'Or

Christine MARTIN
Rue Izembart 21200 BEAUNE
☎ 03 80 25 90 90 & 06 85 08 61 49
email: jlmartin@laterredor.com
web: www.laterredor.com

Only two minutes from Beaune and in an idyllic position amidst trees and birds overlooking the vineyard; Les Tilleuls (the larger of two buildings) is a contemporary, welcoming house with five en suite guest rooms. Huge lounge, kitchenette, books, TV and heating. Parking and garage available; swimming pool and 13th-century gardens. Cooking lessons are available and wine tasting in the cellar.

Prices s €165–€210; d €180–€225; t fr €210 **On Site** Private ⚡
Nearby ⛷ 6km ⌁6km ⌀8km ⌇2km 🛏2km ⋘4km
Notes No pets English spoken CC

see advert on opposite page

BELLENOT-SOUS-POUILLY

▦▦ ⃝ Chambre d'hôtes

Martine DENIS
21320 BELLENOT-SOUS-POUILLY
☎ 03 80 90 71 82
email: mrdenis@club-internet.fr
web: www.ifrance.com/chambres-hotes-bellenot/

Two double en suite guest rooms housed in this traditional property adjoining the owners' home and a further room sleeping up to four people in a small 18th-century house, with shower-room/wc and a kitchenette. Facilities include a kitchenette, lounge, heating, TV, books, garden with parking. Table d'hôte meals provided on request.

Prices s fr €35; d fr €45; t fr €57; dinner fr €17 **On Site** ⚑
Nearby ⛷ 10km ⌁3km ⌀2km ⚡12km ⌇2km 🛏2km ⋘45km
Notes No pets

BESSEY-LES-CITEAUX

⁂ ⦿ Château de Bessey-Les-Citeaux

P et F AUBERT
24 rue de la rivière, 21110 BESSEY-LES-CITEAUX
☎ 03 80 29 73 27 📄 03 80 29 61 91
email: aubertphil@infonie.fr
web: www.chateau.bessey.free.fr

Set in 5 hectares of wooded parkland, an 18th-century castle offers spacious rooms: four doubles and a family room for four people, all with private bathroom. Lounge and salon restored in period style, with open fireplace and beautiful tapestries. Television. Meals by reservation. Patchwork courses: fixed price weekends.

Prices d fr €85; t fr €100; extra person fr €15; dinner fr €30 **On Site** 🏊 Private ⤹ **Nearby** ⛷ 2km ⤓ 20km Restaurant 3km 🏊 0.2km 🌳 7km 🏛 1.5km 🚣 20km **Notes** Pets admitted English spoken CC

BLIGNY-LES-BEAUNE

⁂ ⦿ Curtil

Bruno et Fabienne GUILLEMIN
rue de la Cardine, 21200 BLIGNY-LES-BEAUNE
☎ 03 80 22 38 89 & 06 22 75 79 72
📄 03 80 24 79 37
email: bruno@bed-and-breakfast-beaune.com
web: www.bed-and-breakfast-beaune.com

Gardens and two hectares of vineyards surround this 18th-century house. All with a cosy ambience, the five bedrooms comprise four doubles and triples and one is a suite sleeping up to five people; all have private bathroom and WC. Meals are available by arrangement, and outside is a swimming pool with views across the vineyards. Restaurant a stroll away.

Prices s fr €80; d €120-€160; t €145-€175; extra person fr €25; dinner fr €25 **On Site** 🏊 Private ⤹ **Nearby** ⛷ 4km ⤓ 5km 🌳 2km Restaurant 1.5km 🏊 0.3km 🏛 3km 🚣 3km **Notes** Pets admitted English spoken Open February to November. CC

La Terre d'Or

A unique setting with unforgettable surroundings. A charming chambre d'hôtes in the heart of BEAUNE, surrounded by trees and nature, within close proximity to BEAUNE. With the help of the proprietors, discover the culture of the region of Burgundy, its villages, cuisine, restaurants, the wines of Burgundy and the art of wine tasting, within 500 metres. Day trips available on reservation (walking, biking or diving).

La Montagne - Rue Izembart 21200 BEAUNE
Tel: +33 (0)3 80 25 90 90
E Mail: jlmartin@laterredor.com
Web: www.laterredor.com

BOUSSENOIS

⁂ ⦿ La Chamade - Chambres et Table d'Hôtes

Sylvie MAUBLANC
30 Grande rue, 21260 BOUSSENOIS
☎ 03 80 75 56 21 & 06 82 70 50 57
email: sylpat.gaia@wanadoo.fr
web: www.lachamade.fr

This former vineyard property between Dijon and Langres has four bright and comfortable bedrooms comprising two doubles, a twin and a triple (double bed plus single); two rooms can be linked to provide family accommodation. All have private shower and WC. Use of fridge and microwave; good quality, generous meals are available by arrangement. 10% reduction for stays over four nights.

Prices s €34; d €45-€50; t €56; extra person €11; dinner fr €19 **On Site** 🌳 **Nearby** ⛷ 10km ⤓ 25km 🌳 5km ⤹ 5km Restaurant 5km 🏊 5km 🏛 5km 🚣 17km **Notes** Pets admitted English spoken

BOUZE-LES-BEAUNE

♦♦♦ ♿ La Cadolle

Corinne PAWLOWSKI

Grande rue, 21200 BOUZE-LES-BEAUNE

☎ 03 80 26 08 99 & 06 09 07 07 16 ▤ 03 80 26 08 99

email: lacadolle@free.fr

web: www.lacadolle.com

In the Hautes Côtes de Beaune, this old house has been restored to provide three bright guest bedrooms, all with private showers and WCs. Lounge, and enclosed garden with private parking. According to season, breakfast is served in the old stable block or in the garden.

Prices s fr €45; d fr €55; t fr €60 **Nearby** ♿ 5km ⌁ 10km
♦ 5km ⌁ 7km Restaurant 0.1km ⌁ 8km ⌁ 8km ⌁ 5km ⌁ 8km
Notes No pets Open February to November.

CHAMBOEUF

♦♦♦ ◯◯ Chambre d'hôtes

C et D MONCEAU

23 rue du Sus-Amont, 21220 CHAMBOEUF

☎ 03 80 51 84 65 & 06 20 51 75 32 ▤ 03 80 49 77 24

email: les.sarguenotes@hotmail.com

Situated on the edge of a wood in an elevated position, this beautiful house has panoramic views of Mont Vergy. There are five double en suite bedrooms opening out on to a terrace and large garden. Living room, lounge, TV, heating and kitchen area.

Prices s fr €55; d fr €61; t fr €78; dinner fr €15 **On Site** Private ⌁
Nearby ♿ 10km ⌁ 28km ♦ 14km ⌁ 6km ⌁ 6km ⌁ 14km
Notes No pets

CHAMPDOTRE

♦♦♦ ◯◯ Le Poulain Ranch

Carole SCHMITT

4 rue de l'Abreuvaille, 21130 CHAMPDOTRE

☎ 03 80 39 46 65 & 06 64 62 29 79

email: poulainranch@akeonet.com

web: http://poulainranch.monsite.orange.fr

In the heart of the Val de Saône, this old farmhouse has three guest bedrooms for two or three people. Each has a private shower and WC, and there is an independent guests' entrance. Lounge with books; terrace and garden; secure parking. Possibility of stabling. Meals are available by arrangement.

Prices s €40; d €48-€50; t €60-€65; extra person €10-€15; dinner fr €22 **Nearby** ♿ 5km ⌁ 28km ♦ 5km ⌁ 8km ⌁ 8km ⌁ 5km ⌁ 6km
Notes No pets English spoken

CHATEAUNEUF-EN-AUXOIS

♦♦♦ *Chambre d'hôtes*

Annie BAGATELLE

rue des Moutons, 21320 CHATEAUNEUF-EN-AUXOIS

☎ 03 80 49 21 00 ▤ 03 80 49 21 49

email: jean-michel.bagatelle@wanadoo.fr

This former shepherd's cottage is situated in the heart of a medieval village renowned for its 12th-15th century château and its quaint houses. It offers four en suite rooms, each accommodating up to four guests, with mezzanine. A living room, garden and parking are available and the village has a choice of restaurants. The Burgundy Canal and public footpaths are nearby.

Prices not confirmed for 2008 **Nearby** ♿ 5km ⌁ 12km ♦ 1.5km
⌁ 5km ⌁ 10km **Notes** No pets English spoken

CHEVANNES

♦♦♦ ◯◯ *Chambre d'hôtes*

Gerard et Martine FRICOT

4 place de la Margelle, 21220 CHEVANNES

☎ 03 80 61 42 12

email: la.hulottiere.chevannes@wanadoo.fr

web: http://lahulottiere-chambredhotes.ifrance.com

In the middle of a vineyard, in a restful and lush location, this lovely Burgundy country house has three double rooms. Each has shower and wc. Large living room with open fireplace and exposed beams. Central heating. Parking. Terrace with fine view. Meals by arrangement

Prices not confirmed for 2008 **Nearby** ♿ 4km ⌁ 20km ♦ 3km
⌁ 10km ⌁ 4km ⌁ 4km ⌁ 10km **Notes** No pets

CHOREY-LES-BEAUNE

♯♯♯ L'Escale des Grands Crus

Henri DESCHAMPS
15 rue d'Aloxe Corton, 21200 CHOREY-LES-BEAUNE
☎ 03 80 24 08 13 📄 03 80 24 08 01
email: henri.deschamps@wanadoo.fr
web: www.lescaledesgrandscrus.com

These six guest en suite rooms are right in the heart of the vineyards
and comprise five double rooms and a room sleeping three. A lounge
with TV, central heating, garden and garage are available. The
bedrooms are non-smoking.

Prices s fr €44; d fr €50; t fr €50 **Nearby** ⚓ 3km ♨ 6km
🏊 8km ✈ 3km Restaurant 3km ☂ 3km ♟ 3km 🏛 1.5km ₩ 3km
Notes No pets English spoken Open March to November.

♯♯♯♯ *Le Château*

Francois GERMAIN
21200 CHOREY-LES-BEAUNE
☎ 03 80 22 06 05 📄 03 80 24 03 93
email: chateau-de-chorey@wanadoo.fr
web: www.chateau-de-chorey-les-beaune.fr

The six guest rooms boast a fine setting in a 13th-17th-century
château owned by a family of winegrowers. There are two double
rooms, three rooms accommodating three and a suite for four
people, all en suite with telephone. Living room, lounge and
terrace; restaurant nearby. Sample and purchase the estate's
wines.

Prices not confirmed for 2008 **Nearby** ⚓ 3km ♨ 6km ✿ 2km
✈ 3km ☂ 3km ♟ 3km ₩ 3km **Notes** Pets admitted English
spoken Open Easter to November. CC

CLAMEREY (PONT-ROYAL)

♯♯♯ ⦿ Maison du Canal

Pont Royal, 21390 CLAMEREY
☎ 03 80 64 62 65
email: gdf.lamaisonducanal@wanadoo.fr

Located beside an attractive port on the Burgundy Canal, this
beautifully restored house offers six en suite bedrooms, each for two
or three people. There is a living room with a typically Burgundian
fireplace and TV, heating and a stone terrace with garden furniture
affording a panoramic view of wooded valleys. Parking and small pets
permitted.

Prices s fr €43; d €49-€53; t fr €59; dinner fr €21 **Nearby** ⚓ 0.2km
♨ 5km ✿ 0.2km ✈ 9km ☂ 12km ♟ 9km 🏛 9km ₩ 25km
Notes Pets admitted English spoken

COLOMBIER

♯♯♯ ⦿ Chambre d'hôtes

Yvette BROCARD
21360 COLOMBIER
☎ 03 80 33 03 41 & 06 12 57 23 16 📄 03 80 33 03 41

Three double rooms and two triples (en suite) are situated in a
quiet little village in a stone house separate from the owner's home.
Heating, living room with open fireplace, lounge and kitchen area
available. Outside there is a parking area, meadow and stables. Inn
9km.

Prices s fr €36; d fr €46; t fr €60; dinner fr €20 **Nearby** ⚓ 10km
♨ 30km ✿ 2km ✈ 25km Restaurant 2km ☂ 7km Spa 25km 🏛 9km
₩ 25km **Notes** No pets

COMBLANCHIEN

⑪ ○○ Le Clos des Chenevieres

L GOUSSOT et A CHOPIN
Rue de Pleurey, 21700 COMBLANCHIEN
☎ 03 80 62 74 94 & 06 09 11 06 77
email: chops3@wanadoo.fr

In the heart of the Côte de Nuits wine region, this old vineyard property is in a quiet, green setting. Three double rooms have been sympathetically restored using old materials, each with private shower room and WC, and direct access onto the terrace. Meals offer the best of local cuisine; also wine-tasting. Open views across the vineyard. Enclosed courtyard, parking.

Prices s €54-€58; d €59-€63; t fr €73; dinner fr €24 **Nearby** ☼ 5km ♨ 10km ✎ 4km ⌖ 5km ☲ 5km ⊕ 5km ⋙ 5km **Notes** No pets English spoken Open March to November.

CORBERON

⑪ ○○ Chambre d'hôtes

Hèléne ARDAENS
2 route de Beaune, 21250 CORBERON
☎ 03 80 26 65 59 ▤ 03 80 26 56 24
email: lamarellecotedor@aol.com
web: http://lamarellecotedor.com

A village house with six differently themed bedrooms and a heated swimming pool. Evening meals can be ordered in advance. Guests have use of a lounge, courtyard, terrace, garage and parking. Two of the rooms adjoin and they all have private bath or shower rooms with toilet and air-conditioning.

Prices s fr €50; d fr €75; t fr €100; dinner fr €25 **On Site** Private ⌖ **Nearby** ☼ 3km ♨ 9km ✎ 0.5km Restaurant 6km ☲ 5km ❀ 12km ⊕ 1km ⋙ 13km **Notes** Pets admitted English spoken

CORPEAU

⑪ ⅕ Domaine de la Perrière

Monique CHENU
3 rue de Braux, 21190 CORPEAU
☎ 03 80 21 38 24 ▤ 03 80 21 95 93

On a wine-growing property, three guest rooms in a restored outbuilding. Each room is decorated in a different style, and has private shower room or bathroom and wc. The guests' living room has television and a cooking area. Terrace, courtyard and garden. Sample wines from our cellars.

Prices s fr €50; d fr €58; t fr €72 **Nearby** ☼ 10km ♨ 12km ✎ 3km ⌖ 3km Restaurant 0.1km ☲ 3km ❀ 2km ⊕ 0.5km ⋙ 3km **Notes** No pets English spoken

CRUGEY

⑪ *Le Pre Vert*

Roland et Catherine CARTAUT
rue de l'Odeu, 21360 CRUGEY
☎ 03 80 33 09 80 & 06 83 08 82 27
email: rc.leprevert@wanadoo.fr

A very well restored building, near the valley of l'Ouche, with good views. One double room, two triples, and one separate room sleeping five with private terrace. Private shower room or bathroom with wc. Living room with open fire, television and kitchenette. Enclosed courtyard. Restaurants in the village. Riding, walking and mountain-biking trails.

Prices not confirmed for 2008 **Nearby** ☼ 5km ♨ 25km ✎ 0.2km ⌖ 23km ☲ 0.2km ⊕ 8km ⋙ 25km **Notes** No pets Open April to November.

CURTIL-VERGY

⑪ ○○ Domaine de Pellerey

Sarah BARDET
21220 CURTIL-VERGY
☎ 03 80 61 46 46 ▤ 03 80 61 49 57
email: domaine.de.pellerey@wanadoo.fr
web: www.domainedepellerey.com

Guests receive a warm welcome in this elegant family home tucked away amongst the vineyards seven kilometres from Nuits-Saint-Georges. There are three double bedrooms, two of which are grade 3. All the rooms have a private bath or shower room and WC. Lounge with books, and magnificent grounds with a stream and ancient trees.

Prices d €70-€80; extra person €20-€30; dinner fr €40 **On Site** ✎ **Nearby** ☼ 1km ♨ 20km ⌖ 8km Restaurant 1km ☲ 1km ⊕ 1km ⋙ 8km **Notes** No pets English spoken

▦ ⦾ **Pellerey**

Brigitte PUVIS DE CHAVANNES
Le Val de Vergy, 21220 CURTIL-VERGY
☎ 03 80 61 41 62 ▤ 03 80 61 41 62
email: puvis-de-chavannes@wanadoo.fr
web: www.valdevergy.com

This winegrowers' house dates from the 18th century and boasts a magnificent wine cellar. Three en suite guest rooms enjoy an elevated position right in the heart of the Hautes-Côtes vineyard and include two triple rooms and a double. Living room with exposed beams and open fireplace, heating, meadow and garden with terrace. Table d'hôte meals once a week on request.

Prices s €50-€60; d €56-€66; t €70-€95; dinner €25-€35 **On Site** ⌀
Nearby ⊄ 2km ⌁ 20km Restaurant 0.6km ⊇ 1km ▣ 2km ⋙ 8km
Notes No pets Open March to December.

▦ *Une clé dans le Pré*

Nathalie TERRAND
rue de Montceau, 21360 CUSSY-LA-COLONNE
☎ 03 80 20 26 75 ▤ 03 80 20 26 75
email: cledanslepre@neuf.fr
web: http://cledanslepre.neuf.fr

This accommodation is in a group of farm buildings in a quiet village close to the Ouche Valley. Four pretty rooms, all very comfortable, comprise three doubles and a two-roomed family suite, all with private facilities. Outside there is a terrace and courtyard, with children's games. Parking on site.

Prices not confirmed for 2008 **Nearby** ⊄ 15km ⌁ 25km ⌀ 15km
⤳ 20km ⊇ 10km ▣ 10km ⋙ 22km **Notes** No pets English spoken

ECHALOT

▦ ⦾ **Les Chambres de Rita**

Rita BONNEFOY
Bas du Village, 21510 ECHALOT
☎ 03 80 93 86 84
web: www.leschambresderita.com

Two grade 3 guest rooms accommodating three people and one grade 2 double room, all en suite, are available in this charming house. Facilities include heating, a living room, lounge with TV, garden with terrace and parking area. Meals can be provided on request.

Prices s fr €30; d fr €40; t fr €50; dinner fr €17 **Nearby** ⊄ 6km ⌁ 6km
⌀ 5km Restaurant 10km ⥉ 6km ▣ 10km ⋙ 30km **Notes** Pets admitted

EPERNAY-SOUS-GEVREY

▦ **Les Tilleuls**

Neil et Pam AITKEN
2 place des Tilleuls, 21220 EPERNAY-SOUS-GEVREY
☎ 03 80 36 61 76 ▤ 03 80 36 64 68
email: bacchus.neil@wanadoo.fr
web: http://perso.orange.fr/athomeinburgundy

Five en suite guest rooms are located on the first floor of this old restored inn: two double rooms, one room sleeping three and two rooms sleeping up to four people. The property has heating, a lounge, books, a garden and parking facilities.

Prices s fr €50; d fr €70; t fr €90; extra person fr €20 **Nearby** ⊄ 4km
⌁ 6km ⌀ 2km ⤳ 5km Restaurant 5km ⊇ 5km ▣ 4km ⋙ 8km
Notes No pets English spoken

FIXIN

▦▦ *Chambre d'hôtes*

Domaine Philippe Naddef
30 Route des Grands Crus, 21220 FIXIN
☎ 03 80 51 45 99 ▤ 03 80 58 83 62
email: domaine.phil.naddef@wanadoo.fr
web: www.bourgogne-naddef.com

This 16th/17th-century house in the heart of a village on the Grands Crus route has three double rooms, each with a private shower room. The large lounge has a beautiful fireplace and a small library. Central heating, secure parking, courtyard and garden. 300mtrs from a restaurant and close to wine cellars and the motorway.

Prices not confirmed for 2008 **Nearby** ⊄ 12km ⌁ 25km ⌀ 1km
⤳ 7km ⊇ 0.5km ▣ 5km ⋙ 11km **Notes** No pets English spoken
CC

FLAGEY-ECHEZEAUX

▦▦ *Petit Paris*

Nathalie BUFFEY
6 rue du Petit Paris, Pont Chevalier-Gilly,
21640 FLAGEY-ECHEZEAUX
☎ 03 80 62 84 09 ▤ 03 80 62 83 88
email: petitparis.bourgogne@free.fr
web: www.petitparis.bourgogne.free.fr

The guest rooms are located in the annexe of a 17th-century house, on the banks of the River Vouge surrounded by parkland. There are four en suite rooms centred around a large engraving and painting studio. Extra beds are available for children or teenagers. Living room, lounge, books, garden, river and fishpond.

Prices s fr €85; d fr €85; extra person fr €20 **Nearby** ⊄ 4km
⌁ 15km ⌀ 5km ⤳ 0.8km Restaurant 0.3km ⊇ 0.8km Spa 2km
▣ 0.1km ⋙ 4.5km **Notes** No pets English spoken

FLAMMERANS

♯♯♯♯ ◎ Le Château

Guy BARRIER
rue de Remily, 21130 FLAMMERANS
☎ 03 80 27 05 70 📄 03 80 31 12 12
email: info@chateaudeflammerans.com
web: www.chateaudeflammerans.com

Luxury in an 18th-century castle in 4 hectares of parkland; five rooms including suites with superb bathrooms and open fires. King and queen size beds. Television and telephone. Guests' salon. Hearty breakfasts. Fine evening meals (with specialities or themed) by reservation. Billiards. Heated pool. Orangery with terrace.

Prices s €83-€170; d €88-€175; t €180-€200; extra person fr €25; dinner fr €45 **On Site** Private ⚲ **Nearby** ⛷ 12km ♨ 14km ℘ 3km Restaurant 5km ♨ 7km Spa 30km 🏛 7km ⛵ 7km **Notes** No pets English spoken CC

FRANCHEVILLE

♯♯♯♯ Chambre d'hôtes

Pierre et Denise DROUOT
3, rue de la Folie, 21440 FRANCHEVILLE
☎ 03 80 35 01 93 📄 03 80 35 07 27
email: denise-pierre.drouot@numeo.fr

Situated in a quiet, wooded area, this large, old house offers three en suite guest rooms, heating, a living room, kitchen, lounge with open fireplace and TV, parking and a garden with a play area. There is a choice of restaurants nearby, and hiking trails 2 and 7. Reductions for bookings over three nights.

Prices s fr €35; d fr €45; t fr €50 **Nearby** ⛷ 7km ♨ 35km ℘ 15km ⛷ 18km Restaurant 0.5km ♨ 0.2km 🏛 9km ⛵ 20km **Notes** No pets

GEVREY-CHAMBERTIN

♯♯♯♯ Chambre d'hôtes

Genevieve SYLVAIN
14 rue de l'Eglise, 21220 GEVREY-CHAMBERTIN
☎ 03 80 51 86 39 📄 03 80 51 86 39
email: sylvain.pierre5@wanadoo.fr
web: www.mrocz.com/gevrey/

Three en suite guest rooms in a large, plush house situated close to vineyards in the centre of the village. There is also a dining room and very pleasant, small garden. The village offers a choice of restaurants and hiking trail 7 is in the vicinity. Some English is spoken.

Prices s €45-€50; d €55-€60 **On Site** ⚲ **Nearby** ⛷ 11km ♨ 15km ℘ 2km ⛷ 5km Restaurant 0.2km ♨ 1.5km 🏛 0.5km ⛵ 3km **Notes** No pets English spoken

GEVROLLES

♯♯♯♯ Chambre d'hôtes

Jacques PELLISER
7 Petite rue, 21520 MONTIGNY-SUR-AUBE
☎ 03 80 93 56 15 📄 03 80 93 56 15
email: jacques.pelliser@wanadoo.fr

This old house has been restored to offer three guest bedrooms, all doubles. One room is rated at grade 3 and has a private shower room and WC; the others are rated at grade 1 with shared shower room and WC. Separate guests' entrance; lounge and courtyard; meals by arrangement.

Prices not confirmed for 2008 **Nearby** ℘ 12km ⛷ 32km 🏛 4km ⛵ 35km **Notes** No pets Open May to February.

GILLY-LES-CITEAUX

♯♯♯♯ La Closerie de Gilly

Sandrine et André LANAUD
16 Av Bouchard, 21640 GILLY-LES-CITEAUX
☎ 03 80 62 87 74 & 06 60 73 10 11
📄 03 80 62 87 74
email: contact@closerie-gilly.com
web: www.closerie-gilly.com

This historic 18th-century residence is located in a pretty village on the wine-growing slopes. The five spacious and comfortable en suite guest rooms are all decorated and furnished in an elegant, individual style and overlook a garden with 100-year-old trees. Living room, lounge, TV, heating, parking, play area and mountain bike rental. Local attractions include the vineyard at Vougeot and Cîteaux Abbey (15km).

Prices d €70-€85; t €90-€105 **On Site** Restaurant ☕ Private ⚲ **Nearby** ⛷ 3km ♨ 20km ℘ 0.2km ♨ 1km 🏛 1km ⛵ 5km **Notes** No pets English spoken CC

LA ROCHE-EN-BRENIL

♯♯♯♯ ◎ Clef des Champs

Michelle et René LEGRAND
Chenesaint le Bas, 21530 LA ROCHE-EN-BRENIL
☎ 03 80 64 79 06 & 06 65 38 73 75
email: courrier@clefdeschamps-bourgogne.com
web: www.clefdeschamps-bourgogne.com

In the Parc Regional du Morvan is this typical local farm, beautifully redecorated, with private pool, parking, garden and lounge. There are five fully equipped rooms all with their own bathrooms: two doubles, a triple and two family rooms that sleep four. Cot and children's meals available.

Prices d fr €55; t fr €70; dinner fr €25 **On Site** Restaurant Private ⚲ **Nearby** ♨ 15km ℘ 3km 🏛 3km ⛵ 3km **Notes** No pets English spoken Open March to November.

LADOIX-SERRIGNY

₩₩ Les Demoiselles de Ladoix

Maryse PIANETTI

47-49 Route de Beaune, 21550 LADOIX-SERRIGNY

☎ 03 80 20 70 44 & 03 80 20 71 80

🖹 03 80 20 70 44

email: info@lesdemoiselles.com

web: www.lesdemoiselles.com

Right amongst the Côtes de Beaune vineyards, this 1889 house has three ground floor double bedrooms (one twin-bedded), each with beautiful bathroom/WC and complete with antique floor tiles. Breakfast is served on the veranda, overlooking the beautiful green garden and swimming pool. Wi-fi available. Local wine and other produce available; restaurant in the village.

Prices d fr €95; extra person fr €15   **On Site** Restaurant Private ⚲ **Nearby** ⚓ 4km ⚑ 16km ⚐ 6km ⚑ 6km ⚑ 0.1km ⚑ 10km **Notes** Pets admitted English spoken CC

LAMARCHE-SUR-SAONE

₩₩ ⃝ Chambre d'hôtes

Martine CLEMENT

15 rue du Pont, 21760 LAMARCHE-SUR-SAONE

☎ 03 80 47 17 04

email: chambres.clement@free.fr

web: www.chambresclement.supersite.fr

In the heart of the Burgundy countryside and on the banks of the River Saône, this charming old house provides four en suite guest rooms. Facilities include a colourful courtyard and garden situated in sunny, enclosed grounds, heating, table football, a variety of games and a private swimming pool. Restaurants are located nearby.

Prices d €55-€65; extra person fr €15; dinner fr €26   **On Site** ⚲ Private ⚲ **Nearby** ⚓ 10km ⚑ 30km Restaurant 1km ⚐ 1km ⚑ 5km ⚑ 0.3km ⚑ 15km **Notes** No pets

---

LAPERRIERE-SUR-SAONE

₩₩ ⃝ Chambre d'hôtes

Sylvie et Frédéric RICHARD

12 rue des Varennes, 21170 LAPERRIERE-SUR-SAONE

☎ 03 80 39 15 65 & 06 82 36 00 49

email: ticoltanbert@wanadoo.fr

web: http://perso.orange.fr/ticoltanbert/

Sylvie and Frédéric welcome you to their chambre d'hotes just five minutes from Saint-Jean de Losne (France's principal river port). Four rooms are available, one of which is on the ground floor. Each has a shower and WC. There's a living room with an open fire, a games room, terrace, courtyard and garden. Small pets welcome. Children under two free (bring own child's bed).

Prices not confirmed for 2008   **Nearby** ⚓ 15km ⚑ 25km ⚲ 0.5km ⚲ 15km ⚑ 8km ⚑ 10km **Notes** English spoken

LEVERNOIS

₩₩ Couettes et Capucines

Blandine D'ARDHUY

3 Grande rue, 21200 LEVERNOIS

☎ 03 80 22 29 42 & 06 83 12 98 68

email: couettescapucines@free.fr

web: http://couettescapucines.free.fr

A peaceful house in the heart of the village with courtyard and small garden. There is a typical Burgundian annexe offering two communicating rooms, for two adults/two children. In the main house are two further family rooms and kitchenette. All have their own shower rooms. There is also a lounge and central heating.

Prices s €51-€57; d €51-€57; t fr €68   **On Site** ⚑ ⚲ **Nearby** ⚓ 5km ⚲ 5km ⚐ ⚑ 5km ⚑ 5km **Notes** Pets admitted English spoken

---

LONGECOURT-EN-PLAINE

₩₩ *Chambre d'hôtes*

Arielle MERLE

22 rue du Murot, 21110 LONGECOURT-EN-PLAINE

☎ 03 80 39 73 68

email: arielle.manu@free.fr

En suite accommodation is provided in three rooms in a detached house reserved for guests within a few kilometres of vineyards and Citeaux Abbey. The private entrance opens into a large living room with a lounge area and there is a kitchen, garden, parking and full range of shops in the village. The Canal de Bourgogne runs through the village, where fishing and cycling are popular activities.

Prices not confirmed for 2008   **On Site** ⚲ **Nearby** ⚓ 6km ⚑ 12km ⚲ 6km **Notes** No pets

---

MAGNY-LES-VILLERS

₩₩ ⃝ Chambre d'hôtes

Jocelyne GAUGEY

La Maison des Abeilles, route de Pernand,

21700 MAGNY-LES-VILLERS

☎ 03 80 62 95 42

email: joel.gaugey@wanadoo.fr

web: http://perso.orange.fr/maison-des-abeilles/

A large Burgundian house in a peaceful, wine producing village. Six rooms (three are grade 2), each with private facilities and entrance. There are three doubles, one large room that sleeps four with sitting area and fridge, and two further rooms that sleep up to four. Also for guest use is a large lounge with kitchenette.

Prices s fr €55; d fr €55; t fr €70; dinner fr €24   **Nearby** ⚓ 1km ⚑ 9km ⚲ 7km ⚲ 8km ⚐ 0.2km ⚑ 1km ⚑ 9km **Notes** No pets English spoken

MAREY-LES-FUSSEY

₩₩ *Chambre d'hôtes*

Sarah LOCK

Grande Rue, 21700 MAREY-LES-FUSSEY

☎ 03 80 62 90 64 📄 03 80 62 90 64

email: sarah.lock@wanadoo.fr

web: www.chambres-marey-les-fussey.com

Situated in a small wine-growing village between Nuits-St-Georges and Beaune. Three bedrooms (one double and two sleeping three) in an old vineyard house. Each with shower and wc. Separate access. Large living room with open fire. Central heating. Courtyard and large garden opening out onto the vineyard. Restaurant 1km.

Prices not confirmed for 2008　**Nearby** ⚓ 2km ♨ 15km ✈ 15km ✦ 11km ♨ 4km ⓕ 3km ₩ 12km　**Notes** No pets　English spoken

MESSANGES

₩₩ **Chambre d'hôtes**

Marie-Louise RUCH

23A Grande rue, 21220 MESSANGES

☎ 03 80 61 41 29

email: j.ruch@wanadoo.fr

web: http://monsite.orange.fr/gite.ruch

In a fully renovated old house with central heating, terrace, lawn and parking is a double room with private shower room and toilet. With its own entrance is a small flat with two communicating double rooms, lounge, kitchen, dining room and private bathrooms.

Prices s €50; d €55; t €75　**Nearby** ⚓ 2km ♨ 20km ✈ 2km ✦ 7km ♨ 7km ⓕ 2km ₩ 7km　**Notes** No pets　Open March to 20 December.

₩₩ ⓘⓞⓘ **Chambre d'hôtes**

Y et J-L HUGUENIN-VUILLEMIN

2 Grande rue, 21220 MESSANGES

☎ 03 80 61 48 93

email: mesanges21@free.fr

web: www.les-mesanges.com

An old wine-maker's house is the setting for this B&B, in the heart of a village in the Hautes-Côtes de Nuits. Three charming rooms have shower or bath and private WC; one shower room is in a separate vaulted cellar. One room has a kitchenette and living space with sofabed, and all rooms have independent access. Meals by reservation, free for under-6s. Central heating.

Prices s €50-€75; d €60-€80; t €90-€100; extra person fr €10; dinner fr €25　**Nearby** ⚓ 2km ♨ 25km ✈ 9km ✦ 7km Restaurant 2km ♨ 5km ✦ 20km ⓕ 2km ₩ 7km　**Notes** No pets　English spoken　Open March to November.

MESSIGNY-ET-VANTOUX

₩₩ *Chambre d'hôtes*

Annette DESCHAMPS

20 rue de la Maladiere, 21380 MESSIGNY-ET-VANTOUX

☎ 03 80 35 48 54 & 06 21 66 25 94

email: deschamps.annette@wanadoo.fr

This newly constructed house offers five guest rooms, four en suite and one with separate shower-room/wc. The house has heating, a living room, lounge, kitchen, parking and landscaped gardens with mature trees. Horse-riding facilities and the Jouvence woods are nearby.

Prices not confirmed for 2008　**Nearby** ⚓ 0.5km ♨ 3km ✈ 8km ♨ 0.5km ⓕ 0.3km ₩ 10km　**Notes** Pets admitted　English spoken

MEULSON

₩₩ ⓘⓞⓘ **Le Clos Lucotte**

Simonne DESTEPHANIS

rue Haute, 21510 MEULSON

☎ 03 80 93 85 81 📄 03 80 93 85 81

A charming 17th-century property adjoining the owner's house, offering two double rooms with a lounge area and a twin, all en suite with optional TV. Heating, dining room, lounge, garden and private swimming pool. Table d'hôte meals available on request. 10% reduction on bookings over one week. Pets permitted, except in rooms.

Prices s fr €39; d fr €48; t fr €63; dinner fr €20　**On Site** Private ✦ **Nearby** ⚓ 20km ♨ 18km ✈ 2km Restaurant 5km ♨ 4km ⓕ 5km ₩ 40km　**Notes** Pets admitted　English spoken

MEURSAULT

₩₩ **Chambre d'hôtes**

Brigitte LANOE

29 rue de Mazeray, 21190 MEURSAULT

☎ 03 80 21 68 81

email: lanoe-brigitte@tele2.fr

web: www.maison-du-charmes.com

Close to the famous Meursault vineyards, this house has three bedrooms for up to four people, all with private shower room and WC. One room has its own independent access. Guest lounge, kitchenette, and garden with courtyard. Parking space; restaurant in the village. Beaune is just seven kilometres away.

Prices s fr €50; d fr €55; t fr €65　**Nearby** ⚓ 4km ♨ 7km ✈ 0.3km ✦ 10km ♨ 0.5km ⓕ 0.2km ₩ 4km　**Notes** No pets　Open 21 January to 22 December.

⊞⊞ *Les Écureuils*

Pascal MOLINOT
20 rue Pierre Joigneaux, 21190 MEURSAULT
☎ 03 80 21 27 82 & 06 78 02 82 81 📄 03 80 21 27 82
email: info@lesecureuils-meursault.com
web: www.lesecureuils-meursault.com

In the famous, white wine producing village of Mersault this old wine-growers house with lounge, courtyard and parking, offers three rooms for 2-3 people each with private shower room and electric heating. A fourth room is now available and all rooms are non-smoking. Prices decrease after the fourth night. There are local restaurants and the motorway nearby.

Prices not confirmed for 2008 **Nearby** ⛵ 10km ⚓ 10km ⚓ 5km
⚓ 7km ⚓ 1km ⚓ 0.2km ⚓ 8km **Notes** No pets

MONTCEAU-ECHARNANT

⊞⊞ ✿ ⃝ *Chambre d'hôtes*

Elisabeth et Bernard LAGRANGE
Ferme du Pigeonnier, 21360 MONTCEAU-ECHARNANT
☎ 03 80 20 23 23 📄 03 80 20 23 23
email: bernard.lagrange@free.fr
web: www.ferme-du-pigeonnier.fr

On a Charollais cattle farm, this attractive house offers three en suite guest rooms with a private entrance: a double, a triple and two adjoining rooms (one double and two single beds) with their own lounge. Heating, living room, lounge and garden with parking. Table d'hôte meals need to be booked on Sundays. A reduction of 10% on bookings over four nights. Supplement for pets.

Prices not confirmed for 2008 **Nearby** ⛵ 10km ⚓ 20km ⚓ 6km
⚓ 20km ⚓ 3km ⚓ 6km ⚓ 20km **Notes** Pets admitted CC

MOREY-SAINT-DENIS

⊞⊞ *Caveau Saint-Nicolas*

Francoise BEAUMONT-PALISSES
13 rue Haute, 21220 MOREY-SAINT-DENIS
☎ 03 80 58 51 83 & 06 10 31 03 96 📄 03 80 58 56 48
email: contact@le-saint-nicolas.com
web: www.le-saint-nicolas.com

This property has housed generations of winegrowers and provides three en suite bedrooms, a living room, heating, lounge area with TV and kitchenette. There is also a studio with separate entrance, providing a double and two single beds, shower-room/wc and kitchen. Terrace, park, wine tasting and purchasing possible. Restaurant in the village.

Prices not confirmed for 2008 **Nearby** ⛵ 0.5km ⚓ 14km ⚓ 2km
⚓ 2km ⚓ 2km ⚓ 7km **Notes** Pets admitted

MUSSY-LA-FOSSE

⊞⊞ ⃝ **Le Clos Mussy**

Andre ARMAND
rue du Château, 21150 MUSSY-LA-FOSSE
☎ 03 80 96 97 87 & 06 80 12 26 62 📄 03 80 96 97 87
email: closmussy@yahoo.fr
web: www.closmussy.fr

This house, parts of which date back to the 13th and 16th centuries, has three spacious bedrooms in a very desirable setting: two twin-bedded rooms and a double, all with private shower and WC. Living room with open fire; outside is a garden and orchard, with a sheltered sitting-out area.

Prices s €55-€70; d €65-€80; extra person fr €15; dinner fr €30
Nearby ⛵ 15km ⚓ 3km ⚓ 3km ⚓ 20km Restaurant 2km ⚓ 2km
⚓ 3km ⚓ 3km ⚓ 20km **Notes** No pets English spoken

NOIRON-SUR-BEZE

⊞⊞ ♿ *Chambre d'hôtes*

Bernard et Bernadette SUBLET
ACCUEIL ET VACANCES EN COTE-D'OR
☎ 03 80 36 79 18

Three en suite guest rooms for two or three people are provided in this newly built house, which has views of the river. Facilities include a kitchen area, lounge, books, heating, garden and parking. There is a reduction of 10% on reservations over four nights.

Prices not confirmed for 2008 **Nearby** ⛵ 10km ⚓ 25km ⚓ 20km
⚓ 5km ⚓ 5km ⚓ 5km ⚓ 28km **Notes** Pets admitted

PLOMBIERES-LES-DIJON

⊞⊞ ⃝ **Chambre d'hôtes**

C et J-C TOURTET
rue du Moulin, 21370 PLOMBIERES-LES-DIJON
☎ 03 80 45 00 61 📄 03 80 43 29 73
email: chateau-de-plombieres@wanadoo.fr
web: www.chateau-de-plombieres.com

Colette and J-Claude extend a warm welcome to their superbly decorated château. The six large rooms all have private bath or shower facilities. Enjoy the Bourgogne wines served with the dishes prepared by your hostess. Relax in the lounge, dining room, garden and courtyard. Parking. Some English and German spoken.

Prices s fr €58; d fr €60; t fr €95; dinner fr €32 **On Site** ⚓
Restaurant ⚓ **Nearby** ⛵ 1km ⚓ 4km ⚓ 0.1km ⚓ 0.5km ⚓ 3km
Notes No pets English spoken CC

POMMARD

▥ Clos du Colombier

Marie-Christine POTHIER

1 route d'Ivry, 21630 POMMARD

☎ 03 80 22 00 27 & 06 09 15 13 88

email: mc.pothier@wanadoo.fr

web: http://perso.orange.fr/closducolombier/
index.htm

Set in a village famous for its wine, this house has been in the same family since 1835. Totally renovated, it still retains its charm and authenticity. Comfortable bedrooms are set around a library/living room, all have private bathrooms and separate WCs. The breakfast room opens onto a beautiful flower garden.

Prices s €90-€95; d €90-€110; t fr €125   **On Site** ❦ Private ⚲ **Nearby** ⛷ 7km ♨ 7km ⚓ 7km ⛴ 0.5km ⚑ 4km   **Notes** No pets English spoken CC

▥ Les Nuits de Saint-Jean

E et T VIOLOT-GUILLEMARD

9 rue Sainte-Marguerite, 21630 POMMARD

☎ 03 80 22 49 98 📄 03 80 22 94 40

email: violot.pommard@cegetel.net

web: www.violot-guillemard.fr

In the heart of a vineyard, this old renovated house provides five rooms including four rooms for two people and a suite for four, each with private or shared facilities and heating. Guests have the use of a lounge and living room with fireplace and TV, a kitchen area, a large courtyard and small garden and parking. English is spoken and there is a restaurant nearby.

Prices s €64; d €69; t fr €89; extra person fr €20   **On Site** ⚲ Private ⚲ **Nearby** ⛷ 4km ♨ 6km ⚓ 2km Restaurant 0.5km ⚓ 0.5km ⚑ 4km ⛴ 0.5km ⚑ 5km   **Notes** No pets English spoken

PONTAILLER-SUR-SAONE

▥ ⦿ Les Clematites

Daniel et Christiane PITEY

65 rue du 8 Mai 1945, 21270 PONTAILLER-SUR-SAONE

☎ 03 80 36 11 01

email: dankiki@wanadoo.fr

web: www.maison-des-clematites.net

A 17th-century house with garden combining English and exotic styles of landscaping. There are two large en suite guest rooms, each with sitting room. Lounge with TV, CDs and library. Mountain bike hire and painting/stained glass courses available. Regional dishes are provided on request and are served in the dining room or on the veranda.

Prices s €58-€65; d €58-€65; t €72-€86; dinner €15-€21 **Nearby** ⛷ 6km ♨ 20km ⚓ 0.1km ⚲ 13km ⚓ 0.3km ⚑ 16km **Notes** No pets English spoken

PULIGNY-MONTRACHET

▥ Chambre d'hôtes

Anne-Sophie et Pierre RAVAUT

La Cle des Vignes, 14 rue de Poiseul,
21190 PULIGNY-MONTRACHET

☎ 03 80 22 65 49 & 06 75 09 00 27

email: la-cle-des-vignes@wanadoo.fr

In the centre of a village, facing the vineyards, this elegantly decorated property has four bedrooms sleeping from two to four people. All have private shower or bathroom and WC. Direct access to the terrace and garden. The guest accommodation is in a building separate from the owners' home. Large breakfast room, with use of kitchenette.

Prices s fr €55; d fr €60; t fr €75   **Nearby** ⛷ 12km ♨ 20km ⚓ 8km ⚲ 4km ⚓ 0.2km ❦ 10km ⛴ 0.1km ⚑ 6km   **Notes** No pets English spoken

▥ Chambre d'hôtes

Maria ADAO

17 rue Drouhin, 21190 PULIGNY-MONTRACHET

☎ 03 80 21 97 46 📄 03 80 21 97 46

email: adaomaria@free.fr

A house in the Burgundy style, amongst vines, in a very peaceful environment. Four guest rooms with shower or bathroom and wc. Sitting room with cooking area, salon with television. Courtyard. Wi-fi available.

Prices s fr €40; d €49-€59; extra person fr €10   **On Site** ❦ **Nearby** ⛷ 15km ♨ 10km ⚓ 7km ⚲ 4km ⚓ 8km ⛴ 0.1km ⚑ 4km **Notes** No pets

SALIVES (LARCON)

ⅢⅢ ❦ ⅠⓄⅠ Larcon

Simone RAMAGET
21580 SALIVES
☎ 03 80 75 60 92

The five en suite guest rooms, each accommodating two or three people, are situated on a farm. Facilities include a living room, TV, books, heating, a garden with play area and parking. Table d'hôte meals using farm produce are available.

Prices s fr €30; d fr €45; t fr €65; dinner fr €17   **On Site** ⅃
Nearby ⅏ 5km ⅌ 10km ⅂ 20km Restaurant 5km ⅌ 5km ⅌ 15km
⅏ 30km   **Notes** No pets

SANTENAY-EN-BOURGOGNE

ⅢⅢ *Chambre d'hôtes*

Francoise MONIOT-NIE
44 Grande rue, 21590 SANTENAY-EN-BOURGOGNE
☎ 03 80 20 60 52 & 06 77 49 80 19   📄 03 80 20 60 52
email: bourgognemoniot@wanadoo.fr
web: www.premiumorange.com/bourgognemoniot

Four guest rooms are located in a charming farmhouse on a vineyard. There are two double and two triple rooms, all en suite with TV. Extra beds can be supplied. Heating and living room provided for guests. Hiking trail 7 is close by and the village offers a choice of restaurants.

Prices not confirmed for 2008   **Nearby** ⅏ 1km ⅃ 15km ⅌ 1km ⅂ 1km
⅌ 1km ⅌ 0.1km ⅏ 5km   **Notes** Pets admitted

SAUSSY

ⅢⅢ ❦ ⅠⓄⅠ Chambre d'hôtes

Nicolas et Christelle SIMONET
rue de la Mare, 21380 SAUSSY
☎ 03 80 35 46 29 & 06 65 56 64 31   📄 03 80 35 46 29
email: laclefdesbois@yahoo.fr
web: www.laclefdesbois.fr

This is a sensitively restored farm building in a quiet little village amongst the woods. There are five double rooms, one on the ground floor, with views over the fields and forest. Each room has a private shower and WC. Lounge with books and open fire. Courtyard and garden with a covered terrace. Meals available by arrangement.

Prices s fr €45; d fr €50; t fr €60; dinner fr €20   **On Site** Private ⅂
Nearby ⅏ 1km ⅃ 8km ⅌ 0.2km ⅌ 20km ⅌ 9km ⅏ 2km
Notes No pets English spoken

SEURRE

ⅢⅢ Chambre d'hôtes

Christine VERNAY
15 quai du Midi, 21250 SEURRE
☎ 03 80 20 46 32 & 06 87 84 47 35
email: givernay@wanadoo.fr
web: http://perso.orange.fr/au-bord-de-saone/accueil.html

Situated on the banks of the River Saône in a pleasant little town, this 18th-century house offers four en suite guest rooms. Facilities include a guest lounge with TV, heating, a courtyard and parking. A special offer of four nights for the price of three applies. There is a restaurant within 50 metres.

Prices s fr €41; d fr €46   **On Site** ⅌   **Nearby** ⅏ 15km ⅃ 18km
⅂ 0.5km Restaurant 0.5km ⅌ 1km Spa 35km ⅌ 0.5km ⅏ 0.5km
Notes No pets English spoken

ST-BERNARD

ⅢⅢ ⅠⓄⅠ *Chambre d'hôtes*

Jeanne ESMONIN
ACCUEIL ET VACANCES EN COTE-D'OR
☎ 03 80 62 81 60 & 06 20 52 69 19
email: les-rolanges@wanadoo.fr

A quiet detached building near the owner's property offers three double en suite bedrooms with direct access to the garden via a terrace with furniture, and an en suite twin room in the main house. Parking, restaurant within three kilometres. Cîteaux Abbey, Vouget vineyard and the Nuits-Saint-Georges wine slope nearby.

Prices not confirmed for 2008   **Nearby** ⅏ 18km ⅃ 23km ⅌ 3km
⅂ 5km ⅌ 5km ⅌ 7km ⅏ 7km   **Notes** No pets

ST-NICOLAS-LES-CITEAUX

ⅢⅢ ⅠⓄⅠ L'Oree du Bois

Daniel et Brigitte NAUDIN
rue du Pasquier Haut,
21700 SAINT-NICOLAS-LES-CITEAUX
☎ 03 80 61 19 34   📄 03 80 61 19 34
email: danaudin@wanadoo.fr
web: www.l-oree-du-bois.fr

Close to the forest of Cîteaux and its famous abbey, this property has two comfortable rooms, individually and tastefully decorated and equipped with television and telephone; each has a private shower room and WC. Facing the park is a double, plus a room for four (double bed and two singles) with garden views. Garden with plenty of flowers and shady spots for sitting, complete with swimming pool.

Prices s fr €58; d €68-€71; t €88-€91; dinner fr €27   **On Site** Private ⅂
Nearby ⅏ 13km ⅃ 20km ⅌ 2km Restaurant 9km ⅌ 0.5km ⅌ 9km
⅌ 9km ⅏ 9km   **Notes** Pets admitted English spoken

ST-ROMAIN

⚜ Chambre d'hôtes

Véeronique MOIROUD-MONNOT
rue de la Perriere, 21190 SAINT-ROMAIN
☎ 03 80 21 68 08 & 06 20 39 08 58
email: accueil@domainecorgette.com
web: www.domainecorgette.com

With wine cellar and terrace with view over the cliffs this house is named in local dialect after its small courtyard. There are five charming rooms, one en suite, all with own bath or shower room and toilet. There is private access, use of a lounge and reading room and central heating.

Prices d €70-€100; t €115-€130 **Nearby** ⛷ 5km ♨ 12km
🎣 5km ⚲ 12km Restaurant 0.1km ⚓ 5km 🏛 6km ⚑ 12km
Notes No pets English spoken

STE-MARIE LA BLANCHE

⚜ Chambre d'hôtes

Nicole MOKOTOWITCH
20 rue de la Poste, 21200 SAINTE-MARIE-LA-BLANCHE
☎ 03 80 26 61 14 & 06 75 51 22 14 📄 03 80 26 61 14

A charming house set in the village centre overlooking a pond. There are three bedrooms upstairs - two cosy rooms with showers and WCs and one bedroom (Grade 2) with WC that shares a bathroom on the ground floor. There's a lounge, a garden with covered terrace, and parking on site.

Prices s fr €55; d fr €65; t fr €80 **Nearby** ⛷ 2km ♨ 3km 🎣 4km
⚲ 6km 🏛 6km ⚑ 6km **Notes** No pets

VANDENESSE-EN-AUXOIS

⚜ ⅼ◯ⅼ Chambre d'hôtes

Sami et Catherine YAZIGI
Peniche Lady A, Port du Canal - Cidex 45,
21320 VANDENESSE-EN-AUXOIS
☎ 03 80 49 26 96
email: ladyabarge@yahoo.fr
web: www.peniche-lady-a.com

Three very comfortable cabins on a barge, moored on the Burgundy Canal, just below the medieval town of Châteauneuf-en-Auxois. The cabins can be arranged with double beds or twins, and they all have private shower rooms and WCs. Day room, lounge with TV and books, sundeck with summer flowers. Meals are available by arrangement.

Prices s fr €60; d fr €65; dinner fr €25 **On Site** 🎣 Restaurant ♨
Nearby ⛷ 5km ♨ 10km ⚲ 7km 🏛 40km **Notes** No pets English spoken CC

⚜ Domaine de Serrigny

Marie-Pascale CHAILLOT
Le Village, 21320 VANDENESSE-EN-AUXOIS
☎ 03 80 49 28 13 & 06 86 50 08 35
📄 03 80 49 28 13
email: chaillot.mp@wanadoo.fr
web: www.domaine-de-serrigny.com

A beautiful 18th-century house, with splendid views over the medieval town of Châteauneuf-en-Auxois. There are three spacious guest rooms, each with a double bed and a single. All the rooms have a private bath and shower room, plus a lounge area. Sitting room with open fire, exposed beams, and books. Grounds with trees and roses, swimming pool and tennis court.

Prices s €87-€112; d €87-€112; t €104-€129; extra person fr €17
On Site Private ⚲ Private tennis court **Nearby** ⛷ 7km ♨ 12km
🎣 2km ⚓ ♨ 0.1km 🏛 7km ⚑ 40km **Notes** Pets admitted English spoken

VILLARS-FONTAINE

⚜ Château le Pre aux Dames

Anne-Marie et Bernard HUDELOT
21700 VILLARS-FONTAINE
☎ 03 80 62 31 94 📄 03 80 61 02 31
email: bernard.hudelot@wanadoo.fr
web: www.lepreauxdames.com

Your hosts here are wine growers, and they can provide wine-tasting courses for guests. Their 18th-century family home, surrounded by parkland, has five beautiful and spacious bedrooms, four doubles and a single. All have private bath/shower room and WC, and some period furnishings. This is a non-smoking property.

Prices d €90-€150 **Nearby** ⛷ 2km ♨ 15km 🎣 8km ⚲ 5km
Restaurant 0.1km ⚓ 5km 🏛 4km ⚑ 4km **Notes** No pets English spoken CC

VILLEFERRY

⚜ ⅼ◯ⅼ Le Verger sous les Vignes

John SPENCER MERSKY
21350 VILLEFERRY
☎ 03 80 49 60 04 📄 03 80 49 60 04
email: info@bourgogne-en-douce.com
web: http://Bourgogne-en-Douce.com

In a secluded position amidst the Auxois hills, with a beautiful view of the undulating countryside, this old winegrowers' house is by an orchard. There are two rooms with private terrace and garden and a split-level apartment with kitchen area and private garden, all en suite with private entrance. Table d'hôte meals are available on request.

Prices s €56-€59; d €62-€80; extra person fr €15; dinner fr €22
On Site Spa ♨ **Nearby** ⛷ 10km ♨ 10km 🎣 1km ⚲ 0.5km
Restaurant 6km ⚓ 3km 🏛 3km ⚑ 8km **Notes** Pets admitted English spoken

NIÈVRE

BAZOCHES

♯♯♯ ❧ |O| Domaine de Rousseau

Nadine et Philippe PERRIER
58190 BAZOCHES
☎ 03 86 22 16 30 📄 03 86 22 11 81
email: fermeauberge.bazoches@wanadoo.fr
web: www.auberge-bazoches.com

This detached 18th-century mansion overlooks the Château de Bazochesis and is close to the Parc du Morvan and Clamecy, Vezelay and Avallon. There are three double rooms and two triples, each with heating and private bathroom facilities. An extra bed is available. Table d'hôte except for Wednesday and Sunday evenings. Beautiful views over surrounding countryside.

Prices s fr €42; d fr €42; t fr €57; extra person fr €20; dinner fr €17 **Nearby** ⛷ 8km ♣ 6km ⚓ 20km Restaurant 11km ♨ 8km ☘ 11km 🏠 8km ⚓ 20km **Notes** No pets

♯♯♯ Ferme d'Ecosse

Chantal PERRIER
58190 BAZOCHES
☎ 03 86 22 14 57 📄 03 86 22 14 57
email: fermedecosse@wanadoo.fr
web: http://perso.wanadoo.fr/fermedecosse

This centrally heated house occupies an agricultural setting at the foot of the Château de Bazoches in Morvan. There are two double rooms and a triple with private facilities, a living room, kitchen area and garden. Visit the farm and its Charolais cattle. Signposted walking routes offer superb views over surrounding countryside. Farmhouse inn 800mtrs.

Prices s fr €37; d fr €42; t fr €54 **Nearby** ⛷ 5km ♣ 5km ⚓ 22km Restaurant 1km ♨ 10km ☘ 10km 🏠 1km ⚓ 25km **Notes** No pets English spoken

BEAUMONT-LA-FERRIERE

♯♯♯♯ *Sauvages*

M GONDRAND
58700 BEAUMONT LA FERRIERE
☎ 03 86 38 12 17 📄 03 86 38 12 17

This beautiful 17th-century château, registered in France's inventory of historic monuments, offers two spacious rooms of 33 sq metres in the tower, both with en suite bathrooms. Another slightly smaller room with shower, WC and kitchenette in a tower separate from the castle is ideal for longer stays - the perfect wedding present! Salon/library, dining room, magnificent park.

Prices not confirmed for 2008 **Nearby** ⛷ 8km ♣ 4km ⚓ 18km ♨ 18km ☘ 10km ⚓ 18km **Notes** No pets English spoken Open Easter to 1 November.

BLISMES

♯♯♯ |O| Château de Poussignol

Margreet UNINGE
58120 BLISMES
☎ 03 86 84 98 02 📄 03 86 84 98 03
email: poussignol@wanadoo.fr
web: www.chateau-poussignol.com

This 19th-century château stands in extensive grounds in the Morvan Regional Park. The setting is a peaceful one, and there are five guest rooms. Four are doubles; the fifth has two double beds, and its own lounge and kitchen area. All have private bathrooms/WCs. Children's games and play area, tennis court, stabling.

Prices s €45-€60; d €60-€80; t fr €95; extra person fr €15; dinner fr €25 **On Site** Private tennis court **Nearby** ⛷ 12km ♣ 5km ⚓ 12km ☘ 12km 🏠 12km ⚓ 20km **Notes** Pets admitted English spoken CC

CERCY-LA-TOUR

♯♯♯ |O| Chambre d'hôtes

M et L BOUMA-VERBAARSCHOT
2 Rue des Grandes Brunettes, 58250 CERCY-LA-TOUR
☎ 03 86 50 54 66 & 06 77 37 79 77
email: l.bouma@wanadoo.fr
web: www.maisonlesdeux.com

A pretty house with a garden and terrace. There's a sitting room with open fire; two twin rooms and a room for four with private facilities. Table d'hote available on reservation. The owners organise themed outings including wine tasting at a nearby vineyard. Close to a National Park. English, Dutch and German spoken.

Prices s €38-€40; d €53-€58; t fr €78; dinner fr €15 **Nearby** ⛷ 5km ♣ 2km ⚓ 2km Restaurant 1km ♨ 2.5km ☘ 12km 🏠 0.5km ⚓ 0.2km **Notes** Pets admitted English spoken

CHALLUY

♯♯♯ |O| Le Pavillon

Nicolas et Stephanie GODDET
4 Rue du Pavillon, 58000 CHALLUY
☎ 03 86 90 30 39 & 06 09 24 19 93 📄 03 86 90 30 39
email: contact@le-pavillon.eu
web: www.le-pavillon.eu

This 19th-century manor house with a twin-bedded room and two doubles is near the town of Nevers. The style of decoration is elegant, and each room has a private bath or shower room and WC. Guest living room and dining room. The house is 50 metres from a canal, and a cycle route passes close by.

Prices s €50-€60; d €60-€70; extra person fr €20; dinner fr €25 **On Site** ☘ **Nearby** ⛷ 8km ♣ 0.1km ⚓ 4km Restaurant 1km ♨ 3km 🏠 1km ⚓ 5km **Notes** Pets admitted English spoken

CHAMPALLEMENT

ⅢⅢ **Château De Champallement**

Donatienne VAN CAILLIE
58420 CHAMPALLEMENT
☎ 03 86 29 02 18 📄 03 86 29 02 18
email: manoirchampallement@yahoo.fr
web: www.manoir-champallement.com

A 10th-century château, with three bedrooms and a family suite.
On the ground floor is a guest lounge with a grand piano;
upstairs are two twin-bedded rooms, a double room and a family
suite for four. All have private bath/shower room and WC, but
those for the family room are not en suite. Wooded grounds with
fine views. Pets admitted by reservation only.

Prices d €55-€90 **On Site** ❀ **Nearby** ⅙ 5km ↗ 45km ✎ 1km
↖ 30km Restaurant 15km ⌂ 6km Spa 40km ⓔ 6km ⋙ 44km
Notes Pets admitted English spoken

CHAMPLEMY

ⅢⅢ ⚘ **Chambre d'hôtes**

Marie-Noelle MONANGE
Le Bourg, 58210 CHAMPLEMY
☎ 03 86 60 15 08
web: www.champlemy.com

Right in the centre of a village not far from the attractive little towns
of Vézelay and la Charité-sur-Loire, this house has a double bedroom
and two rooms for four. All the rooms have private shower room and
WC, and there is a living room for guests. Garden with parking space,
and possible accommodation for horses.

Prices s fr €32; d €44-€48; t €60-€64; dinner fr €15 **On Site** Restaurant
Nearby ⅙ 14km ↗ 30km ✎ 3km ↖ 15km ⋙ 30km **Notes** Pets
admitted English spoken

CHATILLON-EN-BAZOIS

ⅢⅢ ⚘ **Le Couvent**

Ginette LAPORTE
1 Rue de Vauclaix, 58110 CHATILLON-EN-BAZOIS
☎ 03 86 84 07 43 & 06 19 07 86 47 📄 03 86 84 07 43
email: ginette.laporte@wanadoo.fr
web: www.lecouventenbazois.com

This former convent is situated in the centre of the town, on a loop of
the Nivernais Canal. It has three upstairs double bedrooms, one with

its own kitchenette. All of them have private shower room and WC.
There is an enclosed interior courtyard and the beautiful ground floor
reception room is available for guests' use.

Prices s fr €54; d €58-€62; t fr €72; extra person fr €14; dinner fr €25
On Site ✎ **Nearby** ⌂ ⋙ 40km **Notes** No pets

CHATIN

ⅢⅢ ⚘ **Champs De La Croix**

Rita MEEMS
58120 CHATIN
☎ 03 86 85 03 34
email: info@champsdelacroix.nl
web: www.champsdelacroix.nl

This house is in the Morvan regional park, and close to several lakes
which offer opportunities for fishing and water sports. There are also
plenty of possibilities for walking and cycling. Upstairs are three twin-
bedded rooms, and also a split-level room which can sleep four (two
double beds). All have private shower room and WC.

Prices not confirmed for 2008 **On Site** ✎ **Nearby** ↖ 7km ⌂ 7km
ⓔ 7km ⋙ 35km **Notes** Pets admitted English spoken Open March to
December.

CHAULGNES

ⅢⅢ ⚘ **Le Margat**

Cheryl TRINQUARD
Beaumonde, 58400 CHAULGNES
☎ 03 86 37 86 16 & 06 15 74 85 48
📄 03 86 37 86 16
email: cheryl.jj.trinquard@wanadoo.fr
web: www.gites-de-france-nievre.com/beaumonde/

Your Australian hostess Cheryl can offer three double rooms, a
twin, and a room with two double beds in her well-renovated
house, each with en suite bath, WC and TV. Central heating.
Exercise room, swimming pool and terrace with garden furniture.
Large grounds with lake and footpaths. Reductions on stays of
more than three nights.

Prices s fr €60; d €65-€80; t fr €95; extra person fr €15; dinner fr
€24 **On Site** ✎ ❀ Private ↖ **Nearby** ⌂ 4km Restaurant 4km
⌂ 5km ⓔ 3km ⋙ 5km **Notes** No pets English spoken Open
February to November.

CHAUMARD

ⅢⅢ ⚘ **Le Chateau**

Charles VAISSETTE
58120 CHAUMARD
☎ 03 86 78 03 33 📄 03 86 78 04 94
email: chateauchaumard@minitel.net

This property is in the Morvan regional park, with its many lakes and
woods. There are six bedrooms, four doubles and two singles. A
family atmosphere in a peaceful setting, with meals available certain
evenings. Accommodation for horses.

Prices d fr €49; t fr €54; extra person fr €10; dinner fr €24 **On Site** ❀
Nearby ⌂ 10km ✎ 0.2km Restaurant 0.2km ⓔ 0.3km ⋙ 60km
Notes Pets admitted Open 10 March to 30 December.

CORVOL-D'EMBERNARD

▦ ⭐ **Le Colombier**

Robert COLLET

58210 CORVOL-D'EMBERNARD

☎ 03 86 29 79 60 📠 03 86 29 79 33

email: contact@lecolombierdecorvol.com

web: www.lecolombierdecorvol.com

Le Colombier is an old farmhouse built in 1812, where all five bedrooms, en suite with bath and WC, open on to a terrace overlooking the swimming pool. Refined rooms in idyllic location; electric heating. Elaborate high-quality evening meals. Badminton, exercise course in grounds; village with old washhouse and manor near by.

Prices s fr €97; d €97-€107; t €115-€125; extra person fr €20; dinner fr €43 **On Site** Private ↖ **Nearby** ⛵ 6km ⚓ 40km ⚑ 6km Restaurant 8km 🏊 6km 🏛 6km 🚍 30km **Notes** No pets English spoken CC

COSNE-SUR-LOIRE (SAINT-PERE)

▦ ⭐ **L'Oree des Vignes**

Marie Noelle KANDIN

21 Croquant, 58200 SAINT-PERE

☎ 03 86 28 12 50 📠 03 86 28 12 50

email: loreedesvignes@wanadoo.fr

web: www.loreedesvignes.com

A small restored farmhouse, offering five charming and individually furnished rooms, each with private shower/wc in spacious wooded grounds. Sitting room with fireplace and piano, bread oven, games room, and terrace with garden furniture. Parking; meals by reservation. Farm produce, wine, mountain bike rental and hiking are all nearby. Available for birthdays, family reunions, and foie gras trips; seventh night free.

Prices s fr €47; d fr €58; t fr €70; extra person fr €25; dinner fr €25 **Nearby** ⛵ 2km ⚓ 4km ↖ 2km Restaurant 2km 🏊 2km 🍽 2km 🏛 2km 🚍 2km **Notes** No pets English spoken

DOMPIERRE-SUR-HERY

▦ ⭐ **La Belle Grange**

Doreen et John BROADBENT

Reugny, 58420 DOMPIERRE-SUR-HERY

☎ 03 86 29 68 04

email: brumboo2@aol.com

web: www.tasteofburgundy.com

In a quiet and restful spot 30 minutes from Vézelay, this is a beautiful barn conversion, with three guest bedrooms. Two of the rooms are doubles, and the third has twin beds. All have private facilities. There is a dining room and lounge for guests to use.

Prices s fr €50; d fr €60; dinner fr €25 **On Site** Private ↖ **Nearby** ⛵ 1km ⚓ 4km Restaurant 10km 🏊 3km 🏛 6km 🚍 6km **Notes** No pets English spoken

DONZY

▦ ⭐ **Jardins de Belle Rive**

Laura et Billy JUSTE

Bagnaux, 58220 DONZY

☎ 03 86 39 42 18 📠 03 86 39 49 15

email: jardinsdebellerive@free.fr

web: http://jardinsdebellerive.free.fr

This detached house is situated in a pleasant wooded region and provides four comfortable guest rooms, each with private bathroom and wc and heating. There is a guests' sitting room, with pretty views of the garden and countryside and a swimming pool. A first-class restaurant is situated in river valley.

Prices s fr €52; d fr €55; t fr €70; extra person fr €15; dinner fr €20 **On Site** Private ↖ **Nearby** ⛵ 17km ⚓ 23km ⚑ 0.3km Restaurant 1.5km 🏊 1.5km 🍽 1.5km 🏛 1.5km 🚍 17km **Notes** No pets English spoken

EMPURY

▦ ⭐ ♿ **La Brosse**

Karin RYDSTROM-COLOMB

58140 EMPURY

☎ 03 86 22 34 90

email: labrosse.morvan@wanadoo.fr

web: www.labrosse-morvan.com

This old farmhouse has fine views towards the Morvan hills. It has four spacious bedrooms: a twin-bedded ground floor room with access for disabled guests, plus another twin-bedded room, a double and a triple upstairs. All of the rooms have private bath or shower room and WC. Guests have their own entrance, and use of a large lounge. Meals available by arrangement. Swedish spoken.

Prices s fr €42; d fr €48; t fr €60; dinner fr €19 **Nearby** ⛵ 3km ⚑ 1km Restaurant 5km 🏊 6km 🍽 15km 🏛 6km 🚍 25km **Notes** No pets English spoken

FACHIN

▦ ⭐ **Le Chatelet**

Claudine JUBERT

Moulin des Morvans, 58430 FACHIN

☎ 03 86 85 00 46

email: moulindesmorvans@wanadoo.fr

web: www.chambres-hotes-morvan.com

An 18th-century mill beside the River Yonne, in a beautiful green setting on an estate of five hectares. Three rooms have a rustic feel about them: a twin-bedded room on the ground floor, with a double and another twin upstairs. Here you are not far from Château-Chinon, and Bibracte is the famous site of an ancient settlement - a fascinating visit.

Prices s fr €55; d fr €60; dinner fr €22 **On Site** ⚑ **Nearby** ⛵ 8km ⚓ 30km ↖ 8km Restaurant 5km 🏊 5km 🍽 8km 🏛 5km 🚍 30km **Notes** No pets English spoken

BURGUNDY

GACOGNE

⅏ ⅩⅠ L'Huis Pillavoine

Eveline VECTEN
Hameau de Rhuère, 58140 GACOGNE
☎ 03 86 22 78 45 ▤ 03 86 22 78 45
email: lhuis-pillavoine@wanadoo.fr
web: www.lhuis-pillavoine-morvan.com

Rooms in an old farmhouse close to the hamlet of Rhuère, in quiet countryside with superb views. Upstairs are a double, and a triple with cot, both with shower and WC; on the ground floor is a family suite of two rooms with a double and twin beds and en suite bathroom and WC. Play area for children; horse-riding nearby.

Prices s fr €39; d fr €45; t €56-€66; dinner fr €18 **Nearby** ☝ 3km ℓ 8km ⚲ 25km Restaurant 5km ⚲ 8km ⚲ 8km ⚲ 8km ⚲ 18km
Notes No pets English spoken

GERMENAY

⅏ ⅩⅠ Cray

Marie-Christine OLIVIER
La Chaume, 58800 GERMENAY
☎ 03 86 29 04 93 & 06 85 66 24 54 ▤ 03 86 29 04 93
email: lachaume-cray@wanadoo.fr
web: www.lachaume-cray.com

Once this was a small farm surrounded by pastures. Now it has three air-conditioned guest rooms, one a mezzanine, one with bathroom and two with shower and WC. There is a large lounge, and meals are available by arrangement. Close to a canal, and several lakes which offer a range of leisure opportunities; also a good base for walking and cycling. Occasional embroidery courses.

Prices s fr €45; d fr €60; t fr €65; dinner fr €16 **Nearby** ☝ 8km ℓ 10km ⚲ 20km ⚲ 10km ⚲ 20km **Notes** Pets admitted English spoken

GIMOUILLE

⅏⅏ Château du Marais

Bernadette et Thierry GRAILLOT
58470 GIMOUILLE
☎ 03 86 21 04 10 & 06 22 65 19 22
▤ 03 86 21 04 10
email: le.marais@online.fr
web: http://le.marais.online.fr

In a beautiful château, built in the 14th century, this establishment offers three pleasant guest rooms, each of which has private facilities. The château is near the medieval village of Apremont and the Formula 1 circuit. Bicycles and table tennis are among the facilities on offer to guests.

Prices s fr €80; d fr €80-€90; t €100-€110 **On Site** ℓ ⚲
Nearby ☝ 8km ⚲ 6km ⚲ 2km ⚲ 4km ⚲ 7km **Notes** No pets English spoken Open April to 1 November.

LA CHARITE-SUR-LOIRE

⅏ Chambre d'hôtes

Christine TARDIF
9 Rue du Point, 58400 LA CHARITE-SUR-LOIRE
☎ 03 86 70 11 25 & 06 03 79 42 53
email: logisdupont@wanadoo.fr

Just a few steps from the abbey, this 16th-century building is steeped in history. It has four bedrooms, all with carefully preserved original features. Two of the rooms are doubles; one has twin beds; the fourth has a double bed and a single. All have private shower and WC.

Prices not confirmed for 2008 **On Site** ℓ **Nearby** ☝ 15km ⚲ 0.5km ⚲ 0.5km ⚲ 0.5km **Notes** Pets admitted English spoken

LA FERMETE

⅏ ⅩⅠ Château de Prye

Magdalena DU BOURG DE BOZAS
58160 LA FERMETE
☎ 03 86 58 42 64 ▤ 03 86 58 47 64
email: info@chateaudeprye.com
web: www.chateaudeprye.com

This château was built between the 17th and 19th centuries and is situated in a walled estate of some 160 hectares, with stables and a river - a haven of peace and greenery. It has two suites and two rooms, all with private facilities. Billiards, table tennis, piano, TV and video are available, together with fishing in the grounds. Weddings and conferences can be arranged.

Prices s €90-€125; d €90-€125; dinner fr €35 **On Site** ℓ
Nearby ☝ 5km ⚲ 15km ⚲ 5km Restaurant 4km ⚲ 5km ⚲ 5km ⚲ 5km **Notes** No pets English spoken Open 15 April to 15 October. CC

LORMES

⅏ ⅩⅠ ⅙ Gîte de Chevigny

M PIERSON et J-L MENET
58140 LORMES
☎ 03 86 22 57 40

Five rooms to sleep seven people, each with private facilities. Rooms are all on the same level, so ideal for anyone with mobility problems. The rooms all have private access. There's a large terrace with panoramic views of the Morvan. Table d'hotes with home-grown produce. Trout fishing. Near to the Morvan Lakes, Château de Bazoches and several museums.

Prices s fr €40; d fr €45; t fr €60; dinner fr €21 **Nearby** ☝ 7km ℓ 1km ⚲ 35km Restaurant 4km ⚲ 4km Spa 40km ⚲ 15km ⚲ 4.5km ⚲ 35km **Notes** Pets admitted English spoken

BURGUNDY

MAGNY-COURS

♦♦♦ ⦿ **Nioux**

Sylvie BESSON

58470 MAGNY-COURS

☎ 03 86 58 17 94 & 06 99 43 34 61 🖹 03 86 58 17 94

This former 18th-century hunting lodge on a Charolais estate has four guest rooms: two double rooms, a twin and a family room sleeping five, with kitchen and living area in an annexe. Rooms have private facilities and heating and there is fitness equipment, a lounge with library and playing cards, table tennis, and games room.

Prices s fr €37; d fr €47; dinner fr €23 **Nearby** ⛷ 15km ⚓ 5km 🎣 2km Restaurant 3km 🏊 10km ♞ 15km 🎿 5km ⛰ 6km **Notes** No pets

MARIGNY-L'EGLISE

♦♦♦ ⦿ **Le Pré Marigny**

et P CAPY-CHAMBRIS

58140 MARIGNY-L'EGLISE

☎ 03 86 22 60 23

In the Parc Naturel du Morvan, this property has four guest rooms, three doubles and a triple, all on the first floor and all with private bathrooms and WCs. Lounge, garden and meadow available for guests' use. Meals available by arrangement, gastronomic menus possible.

Prices not confirmed for 2008 **Nearby** ⛷ 20km 🎣 3km ⚓ 20km ⛰ 8km ♞ 20km **Notes** No pets English spoken

METZ-LE-COMTE

♦♦♦♦ **Chambre d'hôtes**

Walter et Chantal MEYER

Route de Vezelay, Les Frenes, 58190 METZ-LE-COMTE

☎ 03 86 29 87 63 🖹 03 86 29 87 63

This 17th-century building oozes character, sitting as it does beside the route of St Jacques de Compostelle on the crossroads between Vézelay, Clamecy, Tannay and Corbigny. One double room with en suite shower and WC, and two triples - both with mezzanine and en suite bathroom and WC. Lounge, library, games, TV, open fire; central heating. Nivernais canal 2 kilometres.

Prices s fr €54; d €65-€85; t €88-€100; extra person fr €16 **Nearby** 🎣 2km ⚓ 15km Restaurant 3km 🏊 3km ♞ 15km 🎿 5km ⛰ 15km **Notes** No pets English spoken Open April to October.

MONT-ET-MARRE

♦♦♦♦ **Manoir du Chagnot**

A PETERSE et M FERNANDEZ

58110 MONT-ET-MARRE

☎ 03 86 84 06 75 🖹 03 86 84 09 63

email: info@manoirduchagnot.fr

web: www.manoirduchagnot.fr

One suite, two double rooms and a single room, all with private shower/bathroom and WC en suite. One room has a private lounge. Guests have use of an elegant and spacious lounge and dining room on the ground floor. Adjacent to the dining room is a small kitchen with facilities for making coffee, tea and sandwiches, and a fridge with soft drinks, beer and wine. A two hectare walled garden is also available to guests. There are plenty of restaurants in the area.

Prices s €60-€110; d €75-€110; extra person fr €20 **On Site** Private ⚓ **Nearby** ⛷ 5km 🎣 2km Restaurant 1km 🏊 4km ♞ 2km 🎿 2km ⛰ 45km **Notes** No pets English spoken Open 15 March to 15 November. CC

MONTIGNY-SUR-CANNE

♦♦♦♦ ⦿ **Château le Bailly**

Pedro ARRIOLA

58340 MONTIGNY-SUR-CANNE

☎ 03 86 50 06 50 🖹 03 86 50 06 50

email: chateau-le-bailly@wanadoo.fr

web: www.chateau-le-bailly.com

In this romantic renaissance-style château guests can expect to find peace and relaxation. The six rooms (one of them a suite) are spacious and bright, with elegant decorations. They all have private bathrooms and WCs. Lounge, reading room, billiard room, gym and tennis court. Parkland setting with mature trees.

Prices s €110-€125; d €130-€145; dinner €30-€45 **On Site** Private tennis court **Nearby** ⛷ 5km 🎣 1.5km ⚓ 4km Restaurant 12km Spa 10km ♞ 8km ⛰ 8km **Notes** No pets English spoken CC

MONTSAUCHE-LES-SETTONS

♦♦♦ ⦿ **La Vieille Diligence**

Michel MACE

Lac des Settons Rive Droite,

58230 MONTSAUCHE-LES-SETTONS

☎ 03 86 84 55 22

email: info@lvd-fr.com

web: www.morvan.com.fr/diligence

Five bedrooms in a charming old hostel near the Lac des Settons. The rooms sleep between two and four people and have private shower and wc. There is a shared lounge that has a fire and offers views over the lake. Numerous activities are available nearby, and guests can make use of a sauna. Table d'hôte dinners are served on request.

Prices not confirmed for 2008 **On Site** 🎣 **Nearby** ⛷ 10km 🏊 1km ♞ 5km ⛰ 25km **Notes** Pets admitted Open March to November except 2nd week in June.

MOULINS-ENGILBERT

⊪⊪ *La Grande Sauve*

Dominique et Marc DERANGERE

Route de Limanton, 58290 MOULINS-ENGILBERT

☎ 03 86 84 36 40

email: derangeredom@club-internet.fr

web: www.gites-de-france-nievre.com/grandesauve

Charming bedrooms with individual décor in a house furnished with antiques and surrounded by a one-and-a-half hectare park. There is a double room and two rooms with a double and a single bed. Each room has a private bathroom and wc. Horses can be stabled here, by arrangement. Guests can play boules, badminton and table football on-site, and there are many attractions nearby.

Prices not confirmed for 2008 **On Site** ♒ **Nearby** ⟍ 2km ⌁ 2km ⌂ 2km ⋙ 20km **Notes** No pets English spoken Open March to November.

NARCY

⊪⊪ La Cuvellerie

Francoise PERDRIZET-MADEGARD

Rue de L'Enfer, 58400 NARCY

☎ 03 86 69 16 34 & 01 42 08 68 65

email: francoise.perdrizet@free.fr

web: www.gites-de-france-nievre.com/la-cuvellerie/

This is an 18th-century manor house standing in its own grounds and bordered by a stream. It has two family suites, each with a double bed and twins, plus a double-bedded room. All three rooms have private bathrooms and WCs. Breakfast can be enjoyed in the lounge, on the terrace, or in the garden. Meadows available for horses.

Prices s €55-€60; d €60-€65; t fr €75; extra person fr €10 **On Site** ♒ **Nearby** ⟍ 18km ⌁ 23km ♒ 0.1km ⟍ 9km Restaurant 6km ⌁ 18km ⌂ 9km ⋙ 9km **Notes** Pets admitted English spoken

NEUFFONTAINES

⊪⊪ ⟆○⟇ Le Pigeonnier

J-P et C LAMARQUE

Le Bourg, 58190 NEUFFONTAINES

☎ 03 86 24 89 21 ⧉ 03 86 24 89 21

email: pigeonnierbourguignon@voila.fr

web: http://lepigeonnier.site.voila.fr

A welcoming 17th-century house full of character, in a country village. There are four bedrooms and a suite, all with private bath or shower room and WC. Meals are available, by arrangement, with tasty and varied home-made dishes. Good area for walking and horse riding.

Prices s €59-€64; d €66-€70; extra person fr €25; dinner fr €26 **On Site** ♒ Restaurant **Nearby** ⟍ 15km ⟍ 20km ⌁ 15km ⌂ 15km ⋙ 20km **Notes** No pets English spoken

OUROUER

⊪⊪ Château de Nyon

Catherine HENRY

58130 OUROUER

☎ 03 86 58 61 12

web: www.gites-de-france-nievre.com/chateau-de-nyon

This handsome non-smoking house is surrounded by a country park and has three double guest rooms, tastefully decorated, with private bathrooms and wcs and a dining room and lounge. There are numerous walks in the forest of Amognes and Nevers, city of art and history, is nearby. Reduced rates for stays over three nights.

Prices s fr €45; d fr €60 **Nearby** ⟍ 4km ⌁ 30km ♒ 9km ⟍ 9km Restaurant 6km ⌁ 6km ⟍ 15km ⌂ 9km ⋙ 15km **Notes** Pets admitted

POUILLY-SUR-LOIRE

⊪⊪ ⟆○⟇ La Pouillyzotte

Anne-Marie ROMMEL

Charenton, 58150 POUILLY-SUR-LOIRE

☎ 03 86 39 17 98 & 06 80 05 37 23 ⧉ 03 86 39 17 98

email: pouillyzotte@wanadoo.fr

web: http://pouillyzotte.free.fr

This property is in the heart of the Pouilly and Sancerre wine-growing region, in wooded parkland among lots of flowers. There are four guest rooms, each one with an independent entrance, and one with disabled access. All the rooms have a private bath or shower room and WC. Meals are available by arrangement, except Wednesdays and Sundays.

Prices d €49-€54; t €55-€60; dinner fr €20 **On Site** ♒ Private ⟍ **Nearby** ⟍ 8km ⌁ 12km ♒ 0.6km Restaurant 2km ⌁ 4km ⌂ 2km ⋙ 3km **Notes** No pets English spoken

RAVEAU

⏟ ✿ 🍽 Le Bois-Dieu

D et J MELLET-MANDARD
58400 RAVEAU
☎ 03 86 69 60 02 📠 03 86 70 23 91
email: leboisdieu@orange.fr
web: www.leboisdieu.com

This family house is close to a farm bordering the forest of Bertranges, on the pilgrim road of St Jacques de Compostelle. It offers four double non-smoking rooms with private bath/wc, lounge, library, and sitting room. Table d'hôte meals can be booked (except for Sunday evenings), and include farm produce and local wine. Numerous historic sites and monuments are nearby, as well as the vineyards of Pouilly/Loire and Sancerre.

Prices s fr €48; d fr €58; dinner fr €25 **On Site** 𝒫 **Nearby** ⛷ 2km
⛷ 30km ⚲ 6km ♨ 2km ☂ 8km ⛪ 6km ⋈ 6km **Notes** No pets
English spoken Open April to 15 November.

SAUVIGNY-LES-BOIS

⏟⏟⏟ Château de Marigny

Christine BELZ-HENSOLDT
58160 SAUVIGNY-LES-BOIS
☎ 03 86 90 98 49 📠 03 86 90 98 45
email: belz.marigny@wanadoo.fr
web: http://perso.wanadoo.fr/marigny/

A pretty Napoleon III-era château with wonderful views over the Loire Valley. There are three very comfortable guest rooms with private facilities. The château is furnished with antiques and surrounded by a landscaped park. Nearby facilities for equestrians are good, and there are opportunities to fish and play tennis. Pets admitted by reservation.

Prices s €90-€95; d €100-€110 **On Site** ⛷ **Nearby** ⚲ 10km
𝒫 1km ⚲ 1km Restaurant 2km ♨ 1km ⛪ 0.8km ⋈ 8km
Notes Pets admitted English spoken

SEMELAY

⏟⏟⏟ ✿ 🍽 Domaine de la Chaume

Pierre et Valérie D'ETE
58360 SEMELAY
☎ 03 86 30 91 23 📠 03 86 30 91 23
email: dete.pierre59360@orange.fr
web: http://perso.wanadoo.fr/pierre.dete/

Set in open country with superb views, this house is close to walks, hiking routes, sites of historical interest like Mont-Beuvray, caves (Beaune) and an organic farm. There are three double rooms (one with kitchen) and a four-person room with mezzanine floor, all with private facilities. Stabling for horses, shelter for bikes and cars, children's games, table tennis and cycles available. Equestrian centre within 12km.

Prices s fr €41; d fr €45; dinner fr €17 **On Site** ♨ **Nearby** ⛷ 12km
𝒫 2km ⚲ 10km Restaurant 3km ♨ 10km ⛪ 3km ⋈ 12km
Notes No pets English spoken

ST-AMAND-EN-PUISAYE

₩ **La Berjatterie**

René MANNEHEUT

58310 SAINT-AMAND-EN-PUISAYE

☎ 03 86 39 67 14   🖨 03 86 39 65 97

email: manneheut@aol.com

web: http://gites-de-france-nievre.com/la-berjatterie

Close to the pottery region of St-Amand, this house is set peacefully among flowers and trees. The proprietors offer two double rooms, two twins and a triple room, each with private bathroom and wc. Large sitting room, games room with library, TV, parking, extensive grounds. Restaurants within 3 km, and several museums and châteaux and are close by, including the Château of St-Fargeau, with its son et lumière.

Prices s fr €43; d fr €53; t fr €68   **Nearby** ♿ 6km ♨ 35km ⚓ 0.5km ⛷ 19km Restaurant 3km ♒ 3km 🏛 3km 🚉 17km   **Notes** No pets CC

ST-ELOI

₩ 🍽 **Domaine de Trangy**

Guy et Chantal DE VALMONT

8 Route de Trangy, 58000 SAINT-ELOI

☎ 03 86 37 11 27 & 06 08 57 15 77   🖨 03 86 37 18 75

email: chambreshotestrangy@free.fr

web: http://chambreshotestrangy.free.fr

A late 18th-century house with two double and two twin rooms available, each with private shower and wc; child bed available. Living room, library, swimming pool, table tennis, badminton, pony club. Meals can be ordered. The house is set in open countryside, with forested land within 2km.

Prices s fr €45; d fr €53; t fr €72; dinner fr €23   **On Site** ♿ ⛷ Private ⛷   **Nearby** ♨ 15km Restaurant 3km ♒ 4km 🎾 4km 🏛 4km 🚉 6km   **Notes** No pets English spoken

---

ST-GRATIEN-SAVIGNY

₩ 🍽 **La Marquise**

Huguette et Noël PERREAU

58340 SAINT-GRATIEN-SAVIGNY

☎ 03 86 50 01 02 & 06 16 53 11 85   🖨 03 86 50 07 14

email: hcollot@aol.com

web: http://perso.wanadoo.fr/la-marquise

This pretty mansion house has two furnished suites, each with two double and two twin rooms, with private bathroom and wc. There is a large room with kitchenette and living/sitting area, heating, TV, telephone, parking, heated swimming pool in summer and garden. Loose-boxes for horses available. Children under 6 years free.

Prices s fr €40; d fr €55; t fr €84; dinner fr €25   **On Site** 🎾 Private ⛷   **Nearby** ♿ 10km ⚓ 1km Restaurant 3km ♒ 1km Spa 10km 🏛 4km 🚉 5km   **Notes** Pets admitted English spoken

---

ST-HILAIRE-EN-MORVAN

₩ *La Ferme des Archers*

Edith et Jacques CAUMONT

Courcelles, 58120 SAINT-HILAIRE-EN-MORVAN

☎ 03 86 85 08 90   🖨 03 86 85 08 90

This typical Morvan farmhouse has been restored to provide four comfortable guest rooms, one with disabled access, and all with superb views and private facilities. Breakfast room reserved for guests, animal park of 20 hectares, traditional farm animals, archery and table tennis available. Close by are the lakes of the Morvan, the museum and archaeological excavations at Glux-en-Glenne, and a costume museum at Château-Chinon. Non-smoking.

Prices not confirmed for 2008   **Nearby** ♿ 8km ⚓ 10km ⛷ 7km ♒ 16km 🏛 8km   **Notes** No pets English spoken Open Easter to September.

ST-HONORE-LES-BAINS

₩ 🍽 **La Rouveyre**

Karen HENGENS

27 Av Eugene Collin, 58360 SAINT-HONORE-LES-BAINS

☎ 03 86 30 61 44

email: info@larouveyre.nl

web: www.larouveyre.com

Beautiful grounds of about a hectare surround this 19th-century manor house. The four spacious bedrooms are all upstairs: two double rooms, a twin-bedded room, and a triple (three single beds). All have private bathroom and WC. Close to the Morvan nature park with its lakes, and not far from Bibracte, the place where Vercingétorix was elected in 52 BC!

Prices s €40; d €55; t €60; dinner €15-€17.50   **On Site** Spa   **Nearby** ♿ 1km ♨ 45km ⚓ 2km ⛷ 0.2km ♒ 0.5km 🏛 0.2km 🚉 17km   **Notes** Pets admitted English spoken

---

ST-JEAN-AUX-AMOGNES

₩ 🍽 **Château de Sury**

Hubert DE FAVERGES

58270 SAINT-JEAN-AUX-AMOGNES

☎ 03 86 58 60 51   🖨 03 86 68 90 28

email: sury58@wanadoo.fr

web: www.chateau-de-sury.com

two double rooms and a twin with private facilities are available in this 17th-century château, peacefully situated a few kilometres from Nevers in the region of Amognes. Nearby attractions include the Formula One circuit at Magny-Cours, the vineyards of Pouilly, Sancerre, and Côteaux du Giennois, and the Nivernais Canal. Mountain bikes can be hired.

Prices s fr €50; d fr €70; dinner fr €30　**On Site** ❦ Private ↖
Nearby ⚓ 2km 🏊 0.5km Restaurant 2km ⛳ 6km 🚲 6km 🚶 15km
Notes Pets admitted English spoken CC

ST-LOUP

🏠 🍴 **Chauffour**

Elvire DUCHET

Saint-Loup, 58200 COSNE-SUR-LOIRE

☎ 03 86 26 20 22

Your hostess Elvire will welcome you warmly to this small 19th-century farmhouse, with its old brick and exposed beams. All three guest rooms are on the first floor, and comprise two doubles and a triple with mezzanine; each has shower and WC. Electric heating. Living room with open fire, library, games. Exterior chimney for BBQ grills. Evening meals by arrangement. Sancerre and Pouilly vineyards nearby.

Prices s fr €45; d fr €54; t fr €68; dinner fr €23　**Nearby** ⚓ 10km
↖ 25km ⛳ 12km ↖ 12km 🏊 12km 🏛 12km 🚶 12km　**Notes** No pets
Open April to 1 November.

ST-MARTIN-DU-PUY

🏠 🍴 **Montcreçon**

S et E WILHELM-FISCHER

58140 SAINT-MARTIN-DU-PUY

☎ 03 86 22 63 58　📃 03 86 22 63 58

email: wilfis@wanadoo.fr

web: www.4saisons-en-morvan.com

Three peaceful rooms with independent entry, surrounded by countryside with views over woods and groves. One large double room and two twin-bedded rooms each have en suite bath and WC. Shared living and dining rooms; kitchenette. Evening meals by reservation. Horses and riders welcome; also ideal for walkers and mountain bikers.

Prices s €40-€50; d €45-€55; t €60-€70; extra person fr €15; dinner fr
€17　**On Site** Restaurant ❦　**Nearby** ⚓ 20km ⛳ 3km 🏊 7km 🏛 2km
🚶 20km　**Notes** No pets English spoken

TANNAY

🏠 🍴 ♿ **L'Abricotier**

Anny et Michel GERVAIS

Cuzy le Bourg, 58190 FLEZ-CUZY

☎ 03 86 29 37 13 & 06 27 95 42 02

email: gervais.anny@wanadoo.fr

web: http://perso.wanadoo.fr/giteabricotier

The hosts' interests here include nature, the countryside, and motor bikes! Their home, which is close to the River Yonne and the Nivernais Canal, has five guest bedrooms. There is a double room with disabled

access on the ground floor; upstairs are three doubles and a family room for five. Each room has a bathroom/WC and a television.

Prices not confirmed for 2008　**Nearby** ⚓ 30km ⛳ 0.2km ↖ 17km
🏊 2km 🏛 2km 🚶 0.5km　**Notes** Pets admitted English spoken

TRACY-SUR-LOIRE

🏠 **La Charbonnière**

Florence et Franck LANTHIEZ

58150 TRACY-SUR-LOIRE

☎ 03 86 26 13 58 & 06 33 42 98 42

email: ff.lanthiez@wanadoo.fr

web: http://monsite.wanadoo.fr/charbonniere

At the heart of a Pouillyssois vineyard, 8km from Sancerre and Chavignol, this renovated family farmhouse offers two rooms with two double beds and a twin room, each with private facilities. Lounge, dining room, calm atmosphere and exceptional views. Nearby activities include golf, swimming, tennis, visits to the caves and goats' cheese making.

Prices s fr €45; d fr €50; t fr €65; extra person fr €15　**On Site** ❦
Nearby ⚓ 5km ↖ 3km ⛳ 0.5km ↖ 3km Restaurant 3km 🏊 3km
🏛 4km 🚶 3km　**Notes** No pets English spoken

VAUCLAIX

🏠 🍴 **Domaine de Chaumes**

Maryse et Pierre DUMOULIN

58140 VAUCLAIX

☎ 03 86 22 75 37

email: pierre.dumoulin5@wanadoo.fr

web: www.domainedeschaumes.fr

An organic farming enterprise, with a river, providing two double rooms and three rooms sleeping two to three, each with private facilities. Horse riding, canoeing, and boating are available. Rates reduced by 10% for two nights or more; fifth night free.

Prices s fr €40; d fr €45; t fr €50; dinner fr €20　**On Site** ⚓ ⛳
Nearby 🏊 7km 🏛 7km 🚶 30km　**Notes** Pets admitted

VILLE-LANGY

🏠 *La Hersandière*

Claudine et René HERSANT

La Chapelle, 58270 VILLE-LANGY

☎ 03 86 60 21 07 & 06 16 67 50 11

Three rooms in a modern house, each room has two single beds and private facilities. Guests have independent access to the rooms. There is a lounge and a kitchenette, as well as a garden. Shops and restaurants are 5km away.

Prices not confirmed for 2008　**Nearby** ⚓ 15km ⛳ 5km ↖ 15km
🏊 15km 🏛 5km 🚶 15km　**Notes** No pets

SAÔNE-ET-LOIRE

ALLERIOT

▦ ⊙ Chambre d'hôtes

Claudine et Alain FRANCK
Rue de L'Etang Bonnot, 71380 ALLERIOT
☎ 03 85 47 58 58
email: franck-71380@libertysurf.fr
web: www.nos-sens-a-table.com/chambres.htm

This 18th-century farm is set on the banks of the Saône and has three guest rooms for four and two people, with private facilities. Sitting room for guests and huge enclosed wooded grounds. Gourmet discovery weekends can be booked in advance.

Prices s fr €42; d fr €50; t fr €63; extra person fr €15; dinner fr €22 **Nearby** ⚓ 2km ♨ 10km ♬ 0.1km ⌇ 12km Restaurant 0.1km ⛳ 10km
🎿 10km 🏛 6km ⚕ 12km **Notes** No pets English spoken Open 20 March to 20 September & 8 October to November.

AMANZE

▦ ⊙ Chambre d'hôtes des Collines

Philippe et M-Christ PAPERIN
Gaec des Collines, 71800 AMANZE
☎ 03 85 70 66 34 📠 03 85 70 63 81
email: philippe.paperin@wanadoo.fr
web: www.fermeaubergedescollines.com

There are four spacious rooms on offer in this very old farm building in the heart of Brionnais. One double room, one triple and two rooms for four, one with mezzanine with individual bathrooms. Communal lounge, enclosed grounds, children's games. Local cycle discovery route and Roman churches nearby.

Prices s fr €39; d fr €52; t fr €67; extra person fr €15; dinner fr €19 **Nearby** ♬ 3km ⌇ 10km Restaurant 10km ⛳ 5km 🎿 10km 🏛 10km ⚕ 10km **Notes** No pets English spoken Open 15 March to November.

AUTUN

▦ Maison Sainte-Barbe

Jérôme et Marie-Luce LEQUIME
7 Place Sainte-Barbe, 71400 AUTUN
☎ 03 85 86 24 77 📠 03 85 86 19 28
email: maison.sainte.barbe.autun@wanadoo.fr
web: www.maisonsaintebarbe.fr.st

At the heart of old Autun and beside St-Lazare Cathedral, three double rooms set out on the first floor of a 15th-18th century building. Rooms have private facilities. There is a breakfast room with a fire and there is a garden. Restaurants and amenities are nearby.

Prices s fr €58; d fr €64; t fr €79 **Nearby** ⚓ 2km ♨ 2km ♬ 2km ⌇ 2km Restaurant 0.1km 🎿 1km ⛳ 1km 🏛 0.3km ⚕ 2km **Notes** Pets admitted English spoken

▦ ⊙ Moulin Renaudiots

Peter SORENSEN & Jan WIJMA
Chemin du Vieux Moulin, 71400 AUTUN
☎ 03 85 86 97 10 & 06 16 97 47 80
email: contact@moulinrenaudiots.com
web: www.moulinrenaudiots.com

Close to Autun, this is a renovated 17th-century mill with modern interior decorations. There are four bedrooms, all doubles with private shower room/WC. Two are on the ground floor with their own lounge; the other two are upstairs and very large. One has its own lounge. There is a large day room with lounge area for guests' use. Private parking.

Prices d €92-€118; extra person fr €25; dinner €32-€36 **On Site** Private ⌇ **Nearby** ⚓ 3km ♨ 2km ♬ 2km Restaurant 2km 🎿 2km 🏛 2km ⚕ 4km **Notes** Pets admitted English spoken Open April to 15 November.

AZE

▦ Chambre d'hôtes

Laurent GALLIMBERTI
Le Bourg, 71260 AZE
☎ 03 85 33 44 20
email: laurent.gallimberti@wanadoo.fr
web: www.chambreshotesaze.com

A village house in the Mâcon wine-growing area, a few kilometres from Cluny. There are four bedrooms, sleeping from two to four people, with independent garden access and vineyard views. All have private shower room/WC and television, and one has provision for a baby. Guests' breakfast room, terrace and enclosed grounds.

Prices s fr €40; d fr €51; t €62-€74; extra person fr €13 **On Site** Private ⌇ **Nearby** ⚓ 1km ♨ 10km ♬ 1km Restaurant 0.3km 🎿 1km ⛳ 14km 🏛 0.3km ⚕ 20km **Notes** No pets English spoken

ⅢⅢ En Rizerolles

Roger BARRY

71260 AZE

☎ 03 85 33 33 26 ▤ 03 85 33 40 13

email: r.barry.aze@infonie.fr

Five en suite comfortable rooms in a pretty and typical house halfway between Cluny and Mâcon. Communal room with lounge reserved for guests, heating, balcony, courtyard, terrace and enclosed garden. Golf 10km, caves 250mtrs. Restaurants around the corner.

Prices s fr €38; d fr €48; t fr €65; extra person fr €17 **Nearby** ⚓ 0.8km ⛷ 10km ♨ 0.5km ⚲ 0.5km Restaurant 0.2km ⚑ 0.2km Spa 17km ⚑ 12km ⊞ 0.5km ⋔ 17km **Notes** Pets admitted Open 15 March to 5 November.

BAUDRIERES

ⅢⅢ La Chaumière

Arlette VACHET

Route de Saint Etienne, 71370 BAUDRIERES

☎ 03 85 47 32 18 & 06 07 49 53 46

email: arlette.vachet@wanadoo.fr

web: www.lachaumierebaudrieres.com

Three beautifully decorated, romantic bedrooms with double beds, antique furniture and private facilities in a house of character, each with TV. Garden and parking on site. Breakfast is served on the terrace and features home-made jams.

Prices s fr €65; d €65-€85; extra person fr €20 **On Site** ⚑ Private ⚲ **Nearby** ⚓ 7km ⚑ 17km ⚑ 1km Restaurant 1km ⚑ 0.5km ⊞ 0.1km ⋔ 17km **Notes** No pets English spoken Open 15 April to 15 October.

BISSEY-SOUS-CRUCHAUD

ⅢⅢ La Combe

Jean et Marie-Anne COGNARD

71390 BISSEY-SOUS-CRUCHAUD

☎ 03 85 92 15 40 & 06 83 48 42 77 ▤ 03 85 92 19 54

email: macognard@free.fr

web: www.champs-de-bey.com

A wine-producing enterprise of the Côte Chalonnaise, 3km from Buxy Four, providing four comfortable double rooms with private facilities. Breakfast room and lounge exclusively for visitors. Swimming pool. Footpaths and vineyards all around.

Prices not confirmed for 2008 **On Site** Private ⚲ **Nearby** ⚓ 8km ⚑ 9km ⚑ 3km ⊞ 3km ⋔ 15km **Notes** No pets English spoken

BOURGVILAIN

ⅢⅢ ⚑ Les Arbillons

C et S DUBOIS-FAVRE

Le Moulin des Arbillons, 71520 BOURGVILAIN

☎ 03 85 50 82 83 ▤ 03 85 50 86 32

email: moulin@arbillon.fr

web: www.club-internet.fr/perso/arbillon

Outbuildings of an 18th-century mill near Cluny offer five rooms with shower or bath and wc, one of which is accessible for disabled guests. Lounge with fireplace and TV, and breakfasts are served in the orangery. Regional wines and crafts are sold in the cellar. Internet access possible at hosts' house. Restaurant 300mtrs.

Prices not confirmed for 2008 **On Site** ⚑ **Nearby** ⚓ 8km ⚑ 8km ⚑ 8km ⊞ 0.5km ⋔ 25km **Notes** No pets Open April to 15 November.

BOYER

ⅢⅢ La Maison des Coeur

Monique et Michel JOLY

Pingeon, 71700 BOYER

☎ 03 85 51 78 14 & 06 77 66 35 32 ▤ 03 85 51 78 14

There are three comfortable guest rooms for two/four people, in a pretty house on the outskirts of Tournus. The rooms have been decorated and furnished with care, each with its own bathroom and WC. Living and breakfast rooms. Shady terrace and huge tree-filled garden. No smoking. Restaurants, swimming pool, tennis, shops nearby.

Prices s €70; d fr €70; t €85-€90; extra person fr €20 **Nearby** ⚓ 10km ⚑ 20km ⚑ 0.1km ⚑ 2km Restaurant 3km ⚑ 2km ⊞ 2km ⋔ 2km **Notes** No pets English spoken

BRANDON

ⅢⅢ La Grange de la Ferdière

Véronique SAINZ

71520 BRANDON

☎ 03 85 50 40 09

email: lagrange@laferdiere.com

web: www.laferdiere.com

Just a few kilometres from Cluny, this 18th-century barn has three spacious first floor bedrooms, each with a private bath or shower room and WC. On the ground floor is a large lounge area, with kitchenette. Enclosed courtyard and extensive shady grounds.

Prices s fr €47; d fr €55; t fr €69 **Nearby** ⚓ 7km ⚑ 30km ⚑ 0.5km ⚑ 8km Restaurant 2km ⚑ 5km Spa 30km ⚑ 7km ⊞ 5km ⋔ 15km **Notes** No pets English spoken Open April to 1 November.

BRAY

♦♦♦ ⫷◎⫸ & Toury

Marie-Antoinette CHOPELIN
71250 BRAY
☎ 03 85 50 08 64 & 06 82 12 75 10
email: machopelin@wanadoo.fr
web: www.tantine.eu

In a quiet hamlet a few kilometres from Taizé, this property has three bedrooms for two to four people. One of the rooms is on the ground floor, with disabled access; each room has a private shower room and WC. There is a large lounge area which opens onto extensive grounds. Enclosed courtyard; parking.

Prices s fr €38; d fr €45; t fr €64; dinner fr €18 **Nearby** ⛷ 16km
🏊 2km ⚓ 10km ♨ 10km ⊞ 10km ⚏ 30km **Notes** No pets Open 15 March to 15 November.

BRESSE-SUR-GROSNE

♦♦♦ La Griolette

Micheline WELTER
71460 BRESSE-SUR-GROSNE
☎ 03 85 92 62 88 ▤ 03 85 92 63 47
email: la-griolette@club-internet.fr
web: www.france-bonjour.com/la-griolette/

In the centre of the village, this house has two quiet and comfortable suites, which can each sleep up to five people. Each has its own bathroom with shower, bath and WC. Breakfast served in the garden in summer. Very attractive large enclosed garden, with shady spots for sitting. There is a swimming pool, and parking space on site. Internet access possible.

Prices s fr €53; d fr €61; t fr €74; extra person fr €13 **On Site** Private ⚓
Nearby ⛷ 6km 🏊 2km ♨ 0.2km ⊞ 8km ⚏ 14km **Notes** Pets admitted English spoken

Le Château

Benoit et Isabelle DE MURARD
71460 BRESSE-SUR-GROSNE
☎ 03 85 92 51 36 ▤ 03 85 92 51 36
email: benoit.de-murard@orange.fr
web: www.chateau-de-bresse-sur-grosne.com

This château, standing in its 20-hectare park, dates back to the 14th century. In one of its towers it has three double bedrooms, and each room has a private bath or shower room and WC. Breakfast is served in the château's dining room. There is an orchard, and the vineyard begins at the edge of the park.

Prices s €55-€70; d €60-€75; extra person fr €25 **On Site** 🏊
Nearby ⛷ 6km 🏌 40km ⚓ 14km Restaurant 2km ♨ 0.5km ⊞ 8km
⚏ 17km **Notes** Pets admitted English spoken

CHARBONNIERES

♦♦♦ ⫷◎⫸ La Renaudière

Pierre et Martine MARSAL
Les Renauds, 71260 CHARBONNIERES
☎ 03 85 23 01 07 ▤ 03 85 23 01 07
email: info@larenaudiere.com
web: www.larenaudiere.com

A beautifully restored 18th-century building located on a vineyard, this establishment offers five comfortable bedrooms, carefully laid out on the first floor. Each has private facilities. There is a breakfast lounge and a terrace, as well as landscaped grounds. Dinner is served by arrangement. Reductions in room rate are offered to guests staying longer than three nights at certain times of the year. Open alternate weeks July and August.

Prices s fr €60; d €70-€75; extra person fr €15; dinner fr €23
On Site Private ⚓ **Nearby** ⛷ 3km 🏌 2km 🏊 0.5km Restaurant 5km
♨ 1km ⊞ 5km ⚏ 8km **Notes** No pets English spoken

CHASSEY-LE-CAMP

♦♦♦ La Vierge Romaine

Corinne LE VOT-GRONDAHL
Valotte, 71150 CHASSEY-LE-CAMP
☎ 03 85 87 26 92 ▤ 03 85 87 26 92
email: bienvenue@laviergeromaine.com
web: www.laviergeromaine.com

On the edge of a vineyard, near to Santenay, this old house has three delightful and comfortable rooms, one of them with a terrace. There

BURGUNDY

is a separate guests' entrance, and all of the rooms have private bath or shower rooms and WCs. Kitchen available to guests. There is an enclosed courtyard, and direct access to public footpaths.

Prices s €70-€95; d €75-€100; extra person fr €25 **Nearby** ⛷ 2km
♨ 20km ♬ 2km ⚓ 1.5km Restaurant 2km ⚘ 1.5km ⚐ 2km ⋈ 4km
Notes Pets admitted English spoken

CHATEL-MORON

▦ ⦿ *L'Abergement*

Marie et Dominique LEBEAU
71510 CHATEL MORON
☎ 03 85 96 96 98 & 06 22 61 13 88
email: mariedomlebeau@orange.fr
web: www.labergement.com

This small village house has been beautifully restored, and has three pretty double bedrooms, all on the first floor, and all with private facilities. In addition to providing a warm welcome, Marie, the hostess, is also a Cordon Bleu cook. Breakfast and dinner can be served on indoor or on the terrace. Lounge with books.

Prices s fr €38; d fr €46; extra person fr €15; dinner fr €19
Nearby ⛷ 6km ♬ 3km ⚓ 6km ⚘ 10km ⚐ 10km ⋈ 20km
Notes No pets English spoken

CHATENAY

▦ ⦿ *Lavaux*

Paulette GELIN
71800 CHATENAY
☎ 03 85 28 08 48 ▤ 03 85 26 80 66
email: ferme-auberge-lavaux@wanadoo.fr

Five guest rooms in a farmhouse full of character, each with access to an outside gallery and with private facilities. Set in grounds with a pond, and fishing available. Farm produce 500mtrs. Fresh honey in the village.

Prices not confirmed for 2008 **On Site** ♬ **Nearby** ⛷ 12km ⚓ 8km
⚘ 8km ⚐ 4km ⋈ 8km **Notes** No pets English spoken Open Easter to 11 November.

CHENOVES

▦ *La Boutière*

S.A.R.L COLLIN
71390 CHENOVES
☎ 03 85 44 03 76 ▤ 03 85 44 07 44
email: laboutiere@wanadoo.fr
web: www.laboutiere.com

Tucked away in ancient parkland, among the vines, this late 17th-century house has six bedrooms. There is a double room, two triples, and a family room for four. There are also two grade 2 double rooms. Each room has a private bath or shower room and WC, but for the grade 2 rooms the WCs are not en suite. Dining room, guests' lounge.

Prices s €37-€58; d €42-€65; t fr €80; extra person fr €20
Nearby ⛷ 15km ♬ 3km ⚓ 15km ⚘ 5km ⚐ 3km ⋈ 20km
Notes Pets admitted English spoken Open 15 January to 15 November.

CHEVAGNY-LES-CHEVRIERES

▦ *Chambre d'hôtes*

Marie-Thérèse MARIN
Le Bourg, 71960 CHEVAGNY-LES-CHEVRIERES
☎ 03 85 34 78 60 ▤ 03 85 20 10 99
email: marie-therese.marin@wanadoo.fr

Three rooms for two or four people with private facilities in a 17th-century agricultural house in the heart of the Mâconnais, on the wine and Roman church trail. Panoramic view over Solutré, Vergisson. Courtyard, garden, wine-tasting and wine sales. Restaurant 100mtrs. Internet access possible.

Prices not confirmed for 2008 **Nearby** ⛷ 1km ♬ 5km ⚓ 5km ⚘ 5km
⚐ 0.1km ⋈ 5km **Notes** No pets

CLUNY

▦ *Chambre d'hôtes*

Philippe et Hélène BEAULIEU
18 Av Charles de Gaulle, 71250 CLUNY
☎ 03 85 59 19 46 ▤ 03 85 59 19 46
email: contact@lamaisondesgardes.com
web: www.lamaisondesgardes.com

Three pretty rooms in an 18th-century building of character at the heart of the village. On the ground floor there is a suite for three people with a private bathroom and wc. On the first floor there is a double room and a twin room; both have private facilities. There is a shared breakfast lounge with a fire. Local amenities are nearby. Internet access possible.

Prices s fr €52; d fr €60; t fr €75; extra person fr €15 **Nearby** ⛷ 1km
♬ 0.1km ⚓ 0.8km Restaurant 0.3km ⚘ 0.8km ⚑ 1km ⚐ 0.1km
⋈ 20km **Notes** No pets English spoken

CRECHES-SUR-SAONE

▦ *Les Tournesols*

M et P ROUVEYROL-LAFOND
1147 Route de Drace, 71680 CRECHES-SUR-SAONE
☎ 03 85 36 50 22 ▤ 03 85 36 50 22
web: www.rouveyrol.com

This is an old house, built in the local style, with five bedrooms. On the ground floor are three doubles, two of them small studio rooms with a kitchenette. On the second floor are two more doubles, both non-smoking and air-conditioned, each with a lounge area. All rooms have private facilities. Enclosed courtyard with covered parking; swimming pool (heated in summer months).

Prices not confirmed for 2008 **On Site** Private ⚓ **Nearby** ⛷ 5km
♬ 2km ⚘ 1km ⚐ 1km ⋈ 1km **Notes** Pets admitted

DEMIGNY

₩₩ *Le Meix des Hospices*

Francoise THIERY

Rue Basse, 71150 DEMIGNY

☎ 03 85 49 98 49

email: lemeix@wanadoo.fr

web: http://perso.orange.fr/demigny-chambres-hotes/

In an old farmhouse once belonging to the Hospices de Beaune there are three large rooms for two to four people with showers and WCs, a large living room full of character, and kitchenette. Well-tended estate with pétanque and BBQ. Restaurant 4km and vineyard nearby. Internet access possible.

Prices not confirmed for 2008 **Nearby** 🌳 0.5km ➷ 7km 🏊 0.2km 🏛 0.2km 🚶 7km **Notes** No pets English spoken

DENNEVY

₩₩ 🍴 Le Petit Dennevy

Esther COSTE

18 route de Chagny, 71510 DENNEVY

☎ 03 85 45 48 96 & 06 76 30 34 30

email: lepetitdennevy@yahoo.fr

web: www.lepetitdennevy.fr

This establishment, on the edge of the village, was once a wine-grower's house. Now it has five guest rooms, two doubles, two twins and a triple, all with their own shower room and WC. Baby equipment available. Large lounge with TV, a garden and courtyard. Meals by arrangement; good area for walking, cycling and fishing.

Prices s fr €45; d fr €50; t fr €65; extra person fr €15; dinner fr €20 **On Site** ⚜ **Nearby** ⚓ 10km 🌳 0.5km ➷ 12km 🏊 12km 🏛 2km 🚶 12km **Notes** Pets admitted English spoken Open 9 January to 22 December.

ECUELLES

₩₩ L' Arbramante

Gabrièle ECHTELER

9 Route de la Foret, Molaise, 71350 ECUELLES

☎ 03 85 91 90 35

email: gabi.echteler@wanadoo.fr

web: www.arbramante.fr.ms

In the peaceful countryside of the Saône valley, 17km from Beaune, this pretty house has three bedrooms for two or three people. All rooms have a private bath or shower room and WC. There are three rivers close by, and the house is close to the forest. Good walking area.

Prices s €38-€45; d €44-€51; t fr €60; extra person fr €10 **Nearby** ⚓ 20km 🌳 2km ➷ 6km 🏊 6km 🏛 6km 🚶 10km **Notes** No pets English spoken

FARGES-LES-CHALON

₩₩ *Les Barongères*

Jacques et Chantal DION

3 Rue du Boubouhard, 71150 FARGES LES CHALON

☎ 03 85 41 90 47 & 06 61 17 90 47 📄 03 85 48 24 05

email: lesbarongeres@fr.st

web: http://lesbarongeres.com

A warm welcome awaits in the heart of the Chalonnais vineyards, where Chantal and Jacques offer three guest rooms. Each room can accommodate two to four people, have a private entrance, and has en suite shower and WC. Living room, salon and kitchenette for guest use. Forest, footpaths and restaurants within 3kms.

Prices not confirmed for 2008 **On Site** Private ➷ **Nearby** ⚓ 3km 🌳 7km 🏊 5km 🏛 5km 🚶 5km **Notes** No pets English spoken

FLEY

₩₩ Chambre d'hôtes

Francoise et André DAVID

Le Bourg, 71390 FLEY

☎ 03 85 49 21 85 & 06 07 09 54 81 📄 03 85 49 21 85

email: anddavid@club-internet.fr

web: http://larandonneeafley.free.fr

Three charming, comfortable rooms (one a suite for three people) in a house in a Chalonnais village. Each room has separate access and private facilities. Day room and sitting room exclusively for visitors, tended enclosed courtyard, gallery. Internet access possible. Reduced rates for stays of 3 nights.

Prices s fr €45; d fr €55 **Nearby** ⚓ 20km 🌳 3km ➷ 6km 🏊 6km 🏛 3km 🚶 20km **Notes** No pets English spoken Open 15 March to 20 September.

FUISSE

₩₩₩ Bergerie-Fuissé

Monique RUSCH

71960 FUISSE

☎ 03 85 35 64 38

email: bergerie.rusch@wanadoo.fr

web: www.bergerie-fuisse.com

In the heart of the Mâcon wine-growing area, this superb 17th-century house has tremendous character. There are five bedrooms, three of them two-roomed suites; all have private bath or shower room, and one has a sauna. An internal courtyard has a BBQ and a covered terrace. Shady grounds; enclosed parking.

Prices s €80-€145; d €80-€145; t fr €180; extra person fr €30 **Nearby** ⚓ 2km ⛷ 8km 🌳 4km ➷ 6km Restaurant 0.8km 🏊 6km 🏛 5km 🚶 3km **Notes** Pets admitted English spoken Open 8 April to 8 October.

HURIGNY

⊞⊞⊞ Château des Poccards

Catherine et Ivan FIZAINE
120 Route des Poccards, 71870 HURIGNY
☎ 03 85 32 08 27   📄 03 85 32 08 19
email: chateau.des.poccards@wanadoo.fr
web: www.chateau-des-poccards.com

Guests are warmly welcomed to this renovated, early 19th-century château, which is surrounded by a three-hectare park. There are six spacious and comfortable bedrooms of different styles, with private bathrooms and wc. Breakfast is taken either inside or on the terrace looking out over the grounds. Large lounge; swimming pool. Restaurants 7kms.

Prices s €75-€125; d €100-€140; extra person fr €20
On Site Private ⚲ **Nearby** ⛷ 5km ⚓ 7km ℘ 7km Restaurant 7km ⚓ 0.5km Spa 7km 🏠 0.5km ⋙ 7km **Notes** No pets English spoken Open 15 March to 20 December.

IGE

⊞⊞ ⍥ Château des Pommiers

Steve et Vivienne TAYLOR
71960 IGE
☎ 03 85 33 41 46   📄 03 85 33 35 18
email: burgundyxp@wanadoo.fr
web: www.burgundyxp.com

In the heart of the Mâcon wine-growing area, five spacious guest rooms have been created in this old 18th-century wine-grower's house. Each room sleeps two or three people, and has a private bath or shower room and WC. Lounge with TV, and a breakfast room opening onto the garden. Terrace, and an unenclosed wooded garden.

Prices d €80-€90; extra person fr €20; dinner €27.50-€29.50
On Site Private ⚲ **Nearby** ⛷ 12km ⚓ 6km ℘ 5km Restaurant 1km ⚓ 2km ⚽ 12km 🏠 1km ⋙ 15km **Notes** No pets English spoken Open March to October.

IGUERANDE

⊞⊞ ⍥ Les Montées

Denise et Maurice MARTIN
Outre-Loire, 71340 IGUERANDE
☎ 03 85 84 09 69   📄 03 85 84 09 69
email: mart1dmonty@gmail.com
web: http://lesmonty.free.fr

Four vast rooms with private facilities in an old farmhouse deep in the Brionnais, a few kilometres from the banks of the Loire. Peace and quiet guaranteed: rustic décor, living room with sitting area. Enclosed shady grounds, mountain bike circuit. Possible stabling for horses. Meals if booked.

Prices s fr €46; d fr €52; t fr €68; dinner fr €25 **Nearby** ⛷ 8km ⚓ 13km ℘ 1km ⚲ 10km Restaurant 2.5km ⚓ 2.5km ⚽ 6km 🏠 2.5km ⋙ 20km **Notes** No pets English spoken

LA BOULAYE

⊞⊞ ⍥ Le Bois du Caveau

Christian TORRIONE
71320 LA BOULAYE
☎ 03 85 79 58 43 & 06 07 22 89 64   📄 03 85 79 58 43
email: torrione.christian@wanadoo.fr
web: www.le-moulin-renove.com

This 19th-century mill on the edge of the Morvan region has been totally restored to provide three spacious double rooms, all with private bathrooms and WCs. The guests' lounge has lots of space and plenty of character, plus TV and books. Internet access possible. Sauna; mountain bikes available. Meals by arrangement. There is a Buddhist temple just one kilometre away.

Prices s fr €85; d fr €85; t fr €100; dinner €20-€30 **On Site** ⚽ **Nearby** ⛷ 5km ⚓ 30km ℘ 0.5km ⚲ Restaurant 0.5km ⚓ 5km 🏠 5km ⋙ 20km **Notes** Pets admitted English spoken

LA CHAPELLE-SOUS-BRANCION

⊞⊞ ⍦ Château de Nobles

B et F DE CHERISEY
71700 LA CHAPELLE-SOUS-BRANCION
☎ 03 85 51 00 55
email: cheriseyb@free.fr

Three characterful en suite rooms, one with mezzanine, for three to five people in a wing of this 15th-century castle. Breakfast in the castle's great hall; wooded park.

Prices d fr €79; t fr €101; extra person fr €22 **Nearby** ⛷ 7km ℘ 1km ⚲ 15km ⚓ 7km 🏠 10km ⋙ 15km **Notes** Pets admitted English spoken Open April to October.

BURGUNDY

LA COMELLE

⁂ *Maison de Bourgogne*

Bernard et Virginie JOOS
Bieux, 71990 LA COMELLE
☎ 03 85 82 56 09 📠 03 85 82 56 09
email: maisondebourgogne@wanadoo.fr

This property is on the edge of the Morvan region, in the countryside close to Bibracte. There are two double bedrooms, one of which also has a cot, plus a room for three. All the rooms have a private bath or shower room and WC, and there is a separate guests' entrance. Large lounge, and an outdoor area.

Prices not confirmed for 2008 **Nearby** ☂ 8km ✎ 3km ⚲ 8km ⚐ 8km 🏠 8km ⚑ 8km **Notes** No pets Open 23 April to September.

LA GRANDE-VERRIERE

⁂ Les Dues

Paul et Jeannette CARE
71990 LA GRANDE VERRIERE
☎ 03 85 82 50 32

Three very comfortable rooms (one for families) in an old renovated barn in a hamlet in the Parc du Morvan. Each room has shower and wc and there is a breakfast room, living room and terrace and quiet grounds.

Prices s fr €37; d fr €43 **Nearby** ☂ 1.5km ✎ 1.5km ⚲ 15km ⚐ 15km 🏠 3km ⚑ 15km **Notes** Pets admitted

LA GUICHE

⁂ Le Rompoix

Nadine SACCHETI
L'Hermitage, 71220 LA GUICHE
☎ 03 85 24 68 55 📠 03 85 24 68 55
email: contact@hermitagelaguiche.com
web: www.hermitagelaguiche.com

Three double rooms in a large, quiet stone house by a wooded park, each with private facilities and one with extra child's bed. Dining room, television for hire. Horses can be accommodated in stables or on grass.

Prices s fr €60; d fr €68; t fr €90 **Nearby** ☂ 20km ⚲ 30km ✎ 4km ⚲ 0.5km Restaurant 4km ⚐ 0.5km 🏠 0.5km ⚑ 25km **Notes** Pets admitted English spoken

LA LOYERE

⁂ Domaine Sainte-Marie

M-Henriette et Marc LELEDY
71530 LA LOYERE
☎ 03 85 45 79 25 📠 03 85 45 71 60
web: www.domaine-saintemarie.com

Four comfortable rooms in a pretty, totally restored property, all with independent access. Each room has private facilities. There is a breakfast room and a lounge with a kitchenette for guests' use. Restaurants 1.5kms

Prices s fr €50; d fr €56; t fr €80 **On Site** ✿ **Nearby** ☂ 5km ⚲ 10km ✎ 1km ⚲ Restaurant 1.3km ⚐ 12km 🏠 6km ⚑ 8km **Notes** No pets

LA ROCHE-VINEUSE

⁂ Somméré

Eliane HEINEN
71960 LA-ROCHE-VINEUSE
☎ 03 85 37 80 68 📠 03 85 37 80 68

A noteworthy house giving a fine view over the rocks of Solutré and Vergisson. There are two double rooms and a room for two to four people, all with bath or shower and wc. Lounge, courtyard, grounds and parking. On the Lamartinien Circuit.

Prices s fr €40; d fr €50 **Nearby** ☂ 2km ✎ 2km ⚲ 8km Restaurant 3km ⚐ 2km 🏠 2km ⚑ 5km **Notes** No pets English spoken

LA VINEUSE

⁂ ⦿ ⚙ A la Maîtresse

Ghislaine DE CHALENDAR
Le Bourg, 71250 LA VINEUSE
☎ 03 85 59 60 98 📠 03 85 59 65 26
email: info@alamaitresse.fr
web: www.alamaitresse.fr

Five comfortable rooms (one accessible to guests with disabilities), each with private facilities and TV. Set in exceptional enclosed ground with swimming pool. Breakfast room and kitchen for guests. Meals available Saturday, Sunday and Monday.

Prices d €85-€105; t fr €125; extra person fr €20; dinner fr €28 **On Site** Private ⚲ **Nearby** ☂ 2km ⚲ 25km ✎ 5km Restaurant 8km ⚲ 7km 🏠 7km ⚑ 25km **Notes** No pets English spoken Open February to December. CC

LAIZY

⁂ ⚘ ⦿ Ferme de la Chassagne

Francoise GORLIER
71190 LAIZY
☎ 03 85 82 39 47 📠 03 85 82 39 47
email: francoise.gorlier@wanadoo.fr

Four comfortable double rooms with private facilities, in a noteworthy farmhouse set in managed grounds with a terrace. There is a breakfast room and sitting room with television. Meals with farm produce by reservation, except Sunday evening.

BURGUNDY

Prices s €37-€46; d fr €45; t fr €58; dinner fr €18　**Nearby** ⚓ 5km
⛷ 12km ⚲ 4km ↖ 12km　Restaurant 6km　⚓ 4km ▣ 7km ⋙ 7km
Notes No pets　English spoken　Open 15 February to 15 November.

LE BREUIL

⦀ ⦿ Domaine de Montvaltin

Maurice DELORME

71670 LE BREUIL

☎ 03 85 55 87 12 & 06 88 57 21 86　▤ 03 85 55 54 72

email: domainedemontvaltin@hotmail.com

web: www.domainedemontvaltin.com

This former farmhouse, deep in the countryside, has five guest
bedrooms, all with private shower room, WC and broadband internet
access. Three of them also have a private terrace. Breakfast can be
enjoyed indoors or on the veranda. Landscaped grounds with boules
and covered swimming pool. Meals by arrangement.

Prices s €65-€85; d €70-€90; extra person fr €15; dinner €15-€25
On Site ⚲ Private ↖ Private tennis court　**Nearby** ⚓ 0.2km ⚐ 3km
Restaurant 3km ▣ 1km ⋙ 5km　**Notes** No pets　English spoken　Open
March to January.　CC

LE ROUSSET

⦀ ⦿ Le Grand Fussy

Dominique BRUN

71220 LE ROUSSET

☎ 03 85 24 60 26　▤ 03 85 24 60 26

email: la-fontaine-du-grand-fussy@wanadoo.fr

A few kilometres from Cluny, this large and beautiful 18th-century
house is surrounded by a extensive garden. Guests may choose
between five comfortable en suite rooms, all carefully appointed.
Salon, small kitchen, library, terrace, swimming pool and breakfast
room.

Prices s fr €59; d €65-€75; t €78-€88; extra person fr €19; dinner fr €18
On Site Private ↖　**Nearby** ⚓ 8km ⚲ 20km ⚐ 2km　Restaurant 6km
⚓ 6km ▣ 6km ⋙ 20km　**Notes** Pets admitted　English spoken

LEYNES

⦀ *Chambre d'hôtes*

Annie-Cl. et Vincent SANGOUARD

Le Bourg, Le Clos des Monnets, 71570 LEYNES

☎ 03 85 35 13 26　▤ 03 85 35 13 38

email: vincent.sangouard@wanadoo.fr

At the heart of the village and in the Beaujolais wine-growing region,
this old house has four warm and simple rooms, including a family
suite for five, in an annexe near the main house. Each room has
private bath or shower facilities and wc. There is a lounge and a
kitchen for guests, who can also make use of the large terrace and a
nearby restaurant.

Prices not confirmed for 2008　**Nearby** ⚓ 7km ⚐ 1km ↖ 15km
⚓ 0.5km ▣ 0.1km ⋙ 12km　**Notes** Pets admitted

⦀ *Prieuré du Bois de Leynes*

Nadine et Bruno JEANDEAU

71570 LEYNES

☎ 03 85 35 11 56 & 06 62 37 11 56　▤ 03 85 35 15 15

email: bruno.jeandeau@wanadoo.fr

web: http://prieure.suivezlagrappe.com/bleuet.php

At the heart of the Beaujolais wine region, guests are warmly
welcomed to this vineyard. There are four bedrooms for two or three
people in a restored outbuilding, including one room at ground-floor
level; all have private washrooms and wc. There is a guest lounge and
a kitchen area, as well as a garden and courtyard. Restaurants 2km.

Prices not confirmed for 2008　**Nearby** ⚓ 6km ⚐ 2km ↖ 15km
⚓ 2km ▣ 2km ⋙ 12km　**Notes** Pets admitted

MALAY

⦀ ⦿ Le Clos Morelle

Martine MORELLE

Le Bourg, 71460 MALAY

☎ 03 85 50 77 47 & 06 07 66 01 89　▤ 03 85 50 77 47

email: martine.m@leclosmorelle.com

web: www.leclosmorelle.com

There are four bedrooms in this pretty house, right in the centre
of a small village. One is in the owners' house; the other three are
in a separate building. All have private bath/shower room and WC.
Breakfast can be enjoyed in the house or in the garden, and there
is a guests' kitchenette. Above-ground swimming pool; meals by
arrangement; reduced rates for over 4 nights.

Prices s €43-€47; d €52-€55; t €63-€67; extra person fr €12; dinner fr
€22　**On Site** ⚲ Private ↖　**Nearby** ⚲ 42km ⚐ 2km　Restaurant 2km
⚓ 7km ▣ 2.5km ⋙ 43km　**Notes** No pets　English spoken　CC

MANCEY

▦ *Dulphey*

Francoise LAMBOROT-DEREPAS
71240 MANCEY
☎ 03 85 51 10 22
email: francoise.lamborot@wanadoo.fr
web: www.chezderepas.com

Four quiet rooms in a house with a wooded park; all have private facilities. There is a lounge, and guests have use of a microwave oven. Horse-riding, fishing, swimming and tennis are all on offer in the locality and there is a restaurant just a stone's throw away.

Prices not confirmed for 2008 **Nearby** ⚓ 3km ✦ 1.5km ⚲ 5km ⚘ 5km ⋔ 5km **Notes** Pets admitted English spoken

MARCIGNY

▦ Chambre d'hôte de Charme de la Tour du Moulin

A MARAZANNOFF et B FOURNIER
11 Rue la Tour du Moulin, 71110 MARCIGNY
☎ 03 85 25 04 54
web: www.chambresdecharme-marcigny.com

The hosts at this 19th-century property are a decorator and an antique dealer - so the three comfortable bedrooms are very carefully maintained. Each room has a private bath or shower room and WC. Guests' lounge, and a shady sitting-out area.

Prices d fr €95; t fr €110 **Nearby** ⚓ 10km ⚘ 5km ✦ 1km ⋔ 0.3km Restaurant 0.2km ⚘ 0.2km ❦ 0.2km ❒ 0.2km ⋔ 21km **Notes** No pets Open April to 1 November.

▦ La Musardiere

Jean-Pierre RICOL
50 Rue de la Tour, 71110 MARCIGNY
☎ 03 85 25 38 54 & 06 08 26 92 14
email: pierreaxel.ricol@wanadoo.fr
web: www.lamusardiere.net

On the Roman church trail, at the entrance to the village, a 19th-century house of character offers three guest rooms, one with cooking facilities. All have bathroom and wc. Quiet is guaranteed in the lush well-managed parkland. Private swimming pool and parking with car shelter.

Prices s €40-€50; d €55-€70; extra person fr €15 **On Site** Private ⋔ **Nearby** ⚓ 8km ⚘ 8km ✦ 2km Restaurant 0.6km ⚘ 0.7km ❒ 0.3km ⋔ 30km **Notes** Pets admitted English spoken

▦ ⓘⓞⓘ Les Recollets

Michelle et Yves COTTIN
4 Place du Champ de Foire, 71110 MARCIGNY
☎ 03 85 25 05 16 🖹 03 85 25 05 16
email: contact@lesrecollets.com
web: www.lesrecollets.com

Five guest rooms (each with bathroom and wc) in a house of some character. Lounge, sitting room, television, library, games room. Garden with shaded terrace. Meals if booked.

Prices s fr €59; d €72-€78; t fr €92; extra person fr €20; dinner fr €22 **On Site** Private ⋔ **Nearby** ⚓ 3km ⚘ 9km ✦ 2km Restaurant 0.2km ⚘ 0.5km ❒ 0.5km ⋔ 30km **Notes** Pets admitted English spoken

MAZILLE

▦ ⓘⓞⓘ Le Domaine du Vernay

Laurence et Christian NICOLOT
Routede Charolles, 71250 MAZILLE
☎ 03 85 50 85 51
email: contact@domaineduvernay.com
web: www.domaineduvernay.com

This former wine-growing property eight minutes from Cluny has five vast bedrooms. They include two twin-bedded rooms, a triple, and a room for four, all upstairs and all with en suite facilities. There is a kitchenette for guest use, and outside is an enclosed garden and courtyard.

Prices d €55-€65; extra person fr €15; dinner fr €24 **Nearby** ⚓ 1.5km ⚘ 20km ✦ 1km ⋔ 7km Restaurant 0.3km ⚘ 0.5km ❒ 1km ⋔ 12km **Notes** Pets admitted English spoken CC

MELLECEY

⦀ Le Clos Saint-Martin

Kate et Stephan MURRAY-SYKES
Route de la Vallee, 71640 MELLECEY
☎ 03 85 45 25 93 📄 03 85 45 25 93
email: stephan.murraysykes@freesbee.fr

Amongst the vineyards of the Côte Chalonnaise, this beautiful property
is surrounded by an enclosed wooded park. It has six extremely
comfortable rooms for two to four people, all equipped with private
bath or shower. Television, heated private swimming pool. Non-
smoking establishment. Restaurant 300mtrs.

Prices s €70-€130; d €90-€150; t €140-€170; extra person €20-€30
On Site Private ⚲ **Nearby** ⛵ 2km ⚓ 10km ✈ 0.1km Restaurant 0.3km
🚲 1km 🎿 4km 🏛 0.3km ⛰ 10km **Notes** No pets English spoken
Open Easter to 1 November. 2 November to Easter by reservation only. CC

MENETREUIL

⦀ 🍴 Le Devu

Herve et Francine BEUDET
71470 MENETREUIL
☎ 03 85 74 28 13
email: ledevu@wanadoo.fr
web: http://ledevu.free.fr

This is a farmhouse, full of character, built in the 18th century and
subsequently restored. The guest accommodation is in a separate
building: a suite for up to five people, a small suite for three, and a
double room. All have private facilities, and the building is decorated
with many theatrical souvenirs belonging to the owner. Enclosed
grounds; meals by arrangement.

Prices not confirmed for 2008 **Nearby** ✈ 1km ⚲ 9km 🚲 🏛 3km
⛰ 9km **Notes** Pets admitted English spoken

MONT-ST-VINCENT

⦀ ♿ La Croix de Mission

Madeleine GONNOT
71300 MONT-SAINT-VINCENT
☎ 03 85 79 87 69 📄 03 85 79 87 69

This substantial home is at the village entrance and has splendid views
from the terrace and gardens. There is a living room with television,
four rooms for two or three people, all with private facilities and a twin
room suitable for disabled guests.

Prices not confirmed for 2008 **Nearby** ⛵ 10km ✈ 4km ⚲ 10km
🚲 5km 🏛 0.3km ⛰ 10km **Notes** No pets Open 15 March to 15
November.

MONTBELLET

⦀ 🍴 Moulin de Buffière

Martine LESCOUET
71260 MONTBELLET
☎ 03 85 27 99 01 & 06 81 40 35 61
email: marc.lescouet@wanadoo.fr
web: www.moulindebuffiere.com

This 17th-century mill has two family suites on the second floor, and
a further suite in a separate small house with lounge, kitchenette,
mezzanine bedroom and a covered terrace. All of the rooms have
a private bath or shower and WC. Guests' kitchen; swimming pool.
Meals are available by arrangement.

Prices s €50-€55; d €60-€65; t fr €80; extra person fr €20; dinner €17-
€25 **On Site** ✈ Private ⚲ **Nearby** ⛵ 8km ⚓ 6km Restaurant 1.2km
🚲 1km 🎿 10km 🏛 7km ⛰ 11km **Notes** Pets admitted English spoken

MOROGES

⦀ 🍴 L'Orangerie

N. LIEROW & D. EADES
Vingelles, 71390 MOROGES
☎ 03 85 47 91 94 📄 03 85 47 98 49
email: info@orangerie-moroges.com
web: www.orangerie-moroges.com

In a huge country house between vineyards and meadows, choose
between five elegant rooms, each with private facilities. Beautiful day
room, enclosed shady park. Telephone in each room. Meals can be
booked.

Prices s €67-€92; d €72-€102; t fr €122; extra person fr €20; dinner
€25-€40 **On Site** Private ⚲ **Nearby** ⛵ 3km ⚓ 15km ✈ 5km
Restaurant 5km 🚲 2km 🏛 5km ⛰ 15km **Notes** No pets English
spoken Open March to November.

⦀ 🍴 Moulin Brûlé

Francoise PAUPE
71390 MOROGES
☎ 03 85 47 90 40 & 06 03 78 33 83 📄 03 85 47 97 10
email: moulin.brule@wanadoo.fr
web: www.moulinbrule.com

In a Chalonnais vineyard, this enormous house is surrounded by
a wooded park. There are four rooms with refined decor for two
or three people located in the old mill, each with shower, wc and
television points. Breakfast room and salon. Meals can be booked.
Restaurant 2km.

Prices not confirmed for 2008 **On Site** ✈ **Nearby** ⛵ 10km ✈ 10km
🚲 2km 🏛 5km ⛰ 12km **Notes** No pets English spoken

BURGUNDY

POISSON

⦀ ⦿ Château de Martigny

Edith DOR

71600 POISSON

☎ 03 85 81 53 81 📄 03 85 81 59 40

email: chateau-martigny@wanadoo.fr

web: http://chateau-martigny.chez.alice.fr

Four bedrooms in a restored 18th-century castle set in a shaded park. Two double rooms and two triples, and the possibility of a children's room, all with bathroom and wc. Lounge and sitting room with television, garage and farm produce. Performances and theatre at the castle.

Prices s €85-€115; d €90-€120; t €95-€130; extra person €12-€12; dinner fr €40 **On Site** Private ⚲ **Nearby** ⚑ 4km ⌂ 2km Restaurant 1.5km ⌘ 3km ⌂ 12km ⋙ 12km **Notes** Pets admitted English spoken Open April to 1 November.

⦀ *Sermaize*

Maguy et Paul MATHIEU

71600 POISSON

☎ 03 85 81 06 10 📄 03 85 81 06 10

email: mp.mathieu@laposte.net

A 14th-century Charollais hunting lodge offering a family room (five beds), two double rooms and two triple rooms, each with shower room and wc. Living room, library, parkland, courtyard, garage. Restaurant 4km.

Prices not confirmed for 2008 **Nearby** ⚑ 4km ⌂ 0.2km ⚲ 12km ⌘ 4km ⌂ 4km ⋙ 11km **Notes** Pets admitted English spoken Open 15 March to 11 November.

PRUZILLY

⦀ Le Raisin Bleu

Catherine et Christian SIGOT

71570 PRUZILLY

☎ 03 85 35 10 17 📄 03 85 35 10 17

email: leraisinbleu@free.fr

web: http://leraisinbleu.free.fr

In Beaujolais, this establishment offers pretty rooms with independent access, looking out over the Juliénas Vineyard. All bedrooms have private washroom and wc. There is a covered terrace, a landscaped garden and a swimming pool.

Prices s fr €45; d fr €52; t fr €68; extra person fr €16 **On Site** Private ⚲ **Nearby** ⚑ 15km ⌂ 25km ⌂ 4km Restaurant 3km ⌘ 0.3km ⚘ 15km ⌂ 4km ⋙ 10km **Notes** No pets English spoken

SAGY

⦀ Chez Sophie

Sophie MAILLOT

Le Bourg, 71580 SAGY

☎ 03 85 74 05 90 📄 03 85 74 08 35

Five guest rooms are available in this modern house in a quiet village. On the ground floor, a room with shower and WC; on the first floor, four more rooms, all with en suite bathrooms and one with its own sitting room and baby bed. Host's living room has open fire. Enclosed garden. Most facilities within half a kilometre.

Prices s fr €50; d fr €60; t fr €70; dinner fr €25 **On Site** ⌂ ⚘ **Nearby** ⚑ 8km ⌂ 25km ⚲ 8km Restaurant 0.2km ⌘ 0.5km ⌂ 0.5km ⋙ 7km **Notes** Pets admitted

SALORNAY-SUR-GUYE

⦀ Les Epaux

C et A DE BUZONNIERE

14 rue du Château, 71250 SALORNAY-SUR-GUYE

☎ 03 85 59 48 77

email: lesepaux@free.fr

web: http://lesepaux.free.fr

This old 15th-century property houses three large bedrooms, each for two guests. Two extra beds are available. Each room has a private bath and WC. Enclosed wooded grounds, with a terrace.

Prices s €58-€60; d €65-€67; t €87-€90; extra person fr €23 **Nearby** ⚑ 10km ⌂ 20km ⌂ 0.2km ⚲ 12km Restaurant 0.5km ⌘ 0.2km ⚘ 8km ⌂ 0.1km ⋙ 25km **Notes** Pets admitted English spoken

SENNECE-LES-MACON

⦀ Le Clos Barault

Roger JULLIN

425 rue Vremontoise, 71000 SENNECE LES MACON

☎ 03 85 36 00 12 📄 03 85 36 00 12

A house with lots of character in an attractive rural setting. There are two double rooms with an adjacent lounge, and a separate two-roomed suite for up to four people. All three rooms have a private bath or shower room and WC. Breakfast is served in the rustic dining room, which is used exclusively by guests. Enclosed garden with covered parking.

Prices s fr €40; d fr €50; t fr €75; extra person fr €15 **Nearby** ⚑ 5km ⌂ 3km ⌂ 2km ⚲ 5km Restaurant 0.5km ⌘ 5km ⌂ 2km ⋙ 6km **Notes** No pets

SENOZAN

ⅲ ⅰ◯ⅰ **Chambre d'hôtes**

Susan BADIN
Le Bourg, 71260 SENOZAN
☎ 03 85 36 00 96
email: clos.de.leglise@wanadoo.fr
web: www.ch-hote-badin.com

Five guest rooms three doubles, one triple and one family room sleeping up to five people with private bathroom and wc, in an old restored house. Garden and private parking.

Prices s fr €45; d fr €58; t fr €75; extra person fr €18; dinner fr €25
Nearby ⌁ 4km ⌁ 2km ⌁ 8km Restaurant 3km ⌁ 0.5km ⌁ 8km
⌁ 10km **Notes** No pets English spoken

SIVIGNON

ⅲ **L'Ecousserie du Bas**

Jean-Claude GEOFFROY
71220 SIVIGNON
☎ 03 85 59 66 66

Half an hour from the major tourist and cultural sites of south Burgundy, this family mansion is set in the calm and relaxation of the emerald setting of the Monts du Charolais. Guests can enjoy fishing and the flower garden. Restaurant nearby.

Prices s €38-€44; d fr €50; t fr €66 **On Site** ⌁ Private ⌁
Nearby ⌁ 15km ⌁ 35km Restaurant 3km ⌁ 8km ⌁ 8km ⌁ 20km
Notes No pets English spoken

SOMMANT

ⅲ ⅰ◯ⅰ ⌁ **Château de Vareilles**

C et R VAN DE BAAREN
71540 SOMMANT
☎ 03 85 82 67 22   ▤ 03 85 82 69 00
email: info@chateaudevareilles.com
web: www.chateaudevareilles.com

Six huge, comfortable double rooms (one adapted for disabled guests) each have private bathroom and wc and possible extra beds. This early 19th-century house offers panoramic views, a lounge, dining room, library and video room, salon with television and open fire. 7 hectares park with terrace and swimming pool.

Prices s fr €79; d €98-€112; t €133-€147; extra person fr €35; dinner €25-€30 **On Site** ⌁ Private ⌁ **Nearby** ⌁ 0.5km ⌁ 2km Restaurant 15km ⌁ 4km ⌁ 10km ⌁ 15km **Notes** No pets English spoken CC

ST-AMOUR-BELLEVUE

ⅲ **Le Paradis de Marie**

Marie et Stephane LEFAUCHEUX
71570 ST-AMOUR-BELLEVUE
☎ 03 85 36 51 90
email: contact@leparadisdemarie.com
web: www.leparadisdemarie.com

This house is in a quiet spot, on the borders of the Beaujolais and Mâcon wine-growing areas. There are four big bedrooms: a double, a triple, and one for four people, all with private bath or shower rooms and WCs. Kitchen and lounge area. Billiards, hammocks and a garden with a large shady enclosed area.

Prices s fr €80; d fr €80; t fr €100; extra person fr €20 **On Site** ⌁
Nearby ⌁ 4km ⌁ 12km ⌁ 0.5km ⌁ 12km Restaurant 0.2km ⌁ 0.5km
⌁ 4km ⌁ 8km **Notes** No pets English spoken Open 15 January to 15 December.

ST-AUBIN-SUR-LOIRE

||| |◯| **Château des Lambeys**

Famille BUSSIERRE

Les Lambeys, 71140 ST-AUBIN-SUR-LOIRE

☎ 03 85 53 92 76 📄 03 85 53 98 28

email: leslambeys@wanadoo.fr

Five guest rooms in an 18th-century house on the banks of the Loire. Each double room has a large bed, bathroom and wc. Dining room and billiard room reserved for guests. Huge shady park. Thermal health spa (Damona at Bourbon-Lancy) 5km.

Prices s fr €55; d €70-€110; t fr €110; extra person fr €15; dinner €25-€30 **Nearby** ⚓ 6km ⚓ 7km ⬚ 0.5km ⚓ Restaurant 6km ⬚ 6km Spa 7km ⬚ 6km ⬚ 3km ⬚ 35km **Notes** Pets admitted English spoken Open April to December.

ST-BOIL

||| **Chaumois**

Sylvie et Pascal MANEVEAU

71390 ST-BOIL

☎ 03 85 44 07 96 & 06 76 75 56 90

email: sylvie.maneveau@orange.fr

web: www.chaumois.com

This restored house is in a village situated in the Côte Chalonnaise wine-growing area. Four large and comfortable rooms all have private bathroom and WC; two are doubles, and two triples each have a double bed and a single. Living area with a kitchenette, and enclosed courtyard outside.

Prices s fr €37; d fr €48 **On Site** ⬚ **Nearby** ⚓ 0.5km ⬚ 1km ⚓ 12km ⬚ 4km ⬚ 4km ⬚ 20km **Notes** Pets admitted English spoken

ST-DESERT

||| **Maison Romaine**

Patrick NEYRAT

29 Av de Bourgogne, 71390 ST-DESERT

☎ 03 85 47 91 81 & 06 08 47 85 58 📄 03 85 47 91 81

email: maisonromaine@wanadoo.fr

web: www.maison-romaine.com

At the heart of the village lies this beautiful 18th-century winegrower's house, surrounded by a huge landscaped garden. There are three comfortable bedrooms for two to three people. Rooms are equipped with private washroom or bathroom and wc. A dining room and lounge are available to guests.

Prices d €70-€95; extra person fr €20 **On Site** Private ⚓ **Nearby** ⚓ 0.5km ⬚ 12km ⬚ 15km Restaurant 0.1km ⬚ 0.1km Spa 15km ⬚ 4km ⬚ 0.1km ⬚ 15km **Notes** Pets admitted English spoken

ST-DIDIER-SUR-ARROUX

||| *Moulin de Bousson*

J DE VALK et T NIJZINK

71190 ST-DIDIER-SUR-ARROUX

☎ 03 85 82 35 07 📄 03 85 82 25 41

email: moulin.bousson@wanadoo.fr

web: www.bousson.fr

This beautifully restored old mill on the edge of a lake, with its wonderful mountain views, can accommodate up to eight guests in its three rooms. Each room has a private shower room and WC, and a cot is available. Lounge, large kitchen for guests' use. Wooded grounds.

Prices not confirmed for 2008 **On Site** ⬚ **Nearby** ⬚ 3km ⚓ 11km ⬚ 8km ⬚ 2km ⬚ 8km **Notes** Pets admitted English spoken

ST-FORGEOT

||| |◯| **Château de Millery**

Gérard PERRETTE

71400 ST-FORGEOT

☎ 03 85 52 18 51 📄 03 85 52 81 27

email: chateau_de_millery@hotmail.fr

Beautiful wooded parkland surrounds this 19th-century house. There are five comfortable bedrooms: four which can be arranged as doubles or twins, and a family room for four. All have private facilities, and baby equipment is available. Breakfast room and guests' lounge. Enclosed grounds with terrace; meals by arrangement.

Prices s fr €50; d €55-€70; t fr €70; extra person fr €20; dinner fr €20 **Nearby** ⚓ 1.5km ⬚ 4km ⬚ 0.5km ⚓ 4km Restaurant 2.5km ⬚ 4km ⬚ 4km ⬚ 4km ⬚ 4km **Notes** Pets admitted English spoken Open April to 1 November.

ST-GENGOUX-LE-NATIONAL

||| |◯| **Chambre d'hôtes**

M-Claude & J-Luc REUMAUX

7 rue de la Tuilerie, 71460 ST-GENGOUX-LE-NATIONAL

☎ 03 85 92 55 76

email: reumauxjl@aol.com

web: www.tilleuls71.com

In the heart of a medieval town, this house with its grounds full of ancient trees has three guest bedrooms, one of which is a two-roomed suite. Each room has a private bath or shower room and WC. Lounge with books, enclosed grounds, vineyard.

Prices s fr €40; d fr €48; t fr €58; extra person fr €10; dinner fr €17 **Nearby** ⬚ 5km ⚓ 18km ⬚ 0.8km **Notes** Pets admitted

ST-GERVAIS-EN-VALLIERE

Champseuil

Martine LYSSY

1 rue du Bief, 71350 ST-GERVAIS-EN-VALLIERE

☎ 03 85 91 80 08 & 06 71 00 54 08   📄 03 85 91 80 08

email: martine.lyssy-chambres-dhotes@wanadoo.fr

A village house situated a few kilometres from Beaune and Verdon. The three rooms offered are both quiet and comfortable, with bath and wc. Breakfast room for guests' use, courtyard and enclosed garden. Meals may be booked.

Prices not confirmed for 2008   **Nearby** ⌀ 0.3km ⤳ 12km 🏊 12km 🏛 4km 🚴 14km   **Notes** No pets English spoken Open February to November.

ST-LOUP-DE-VARENNES

Chambre d'hôtes

Pascale Yvette ROMERO

36, rue de Varennes, 71240 ST-LOUP-DE-VARENNES

☎ 03 85 44 27 46 & 06 63 15 82 45

email: chambres.claires@wanadoo.fr

Four double rooms in a restored 17th-century house. All rooms have private washrooms and wc. There is a lounge and a garden.

Prices not confirmed for 2008   **Nearby** ⌀ 4km ⤳ 6km 🏊 0.5km 🏛 3km 🚴 9km   **Notes** Pets admitted Open 15 March to 15 November.

ST-MAURICE-DE-SATONNAY

Moulin de Bugy

Sandra et Bernard ELOY

71260 ST-MAURICE-DE-SATONNAY

☎ 03 85 33 42 38   📄 03 85 33 42 38

email: moulin.de.bugy@wanadoo.fr

web: http://moulindebugy.com

This mill house is situated on the wine route, an equal distance from Mâcon, Tournus and Cluny. It has been sensitively restored, and retains all the charm of old houses in this area. There are five comfortable and bright bedrooms, all upstairs. Breakfast room with fireplace, lounge with books. Outside are enclosed grounds with a swimming pool. Meals by arrangement.

Prices d €65-€80; extra person fr €15; dinner fr €24   **On Site** ⌀ Private ⤳   **Nearby** ⛷ 2km 🏊 2km 🚴 13km   **Notes** No pets English spoken

ST-MAURICE-LES-CHATEAUNEUF

La Violetterie

Madeleine CHARTIER

71740 ST-MAURICE-LES-CHATEAUNEUF

☎ 03 85 26 26 60   📄 03 85 26 26 60

email: madeleinechartier@yahoo.fr

This traditional Brionnais home offers double rooms with shower and wc. Extra bed possible. Dining room and lounge with open fire, TV

and books, shady garden and courtyard. On the Roman Church Trail. Antique shops and restaurant in the village.

Prices s €42-€45; d fr €55; t fr €68; extra person fr €12; dinner fr €18   **On Site** ⛷   **Nearby** ⌀ 20km ⤳ 1km ⤳ 7km Restaurant 0.2km 🏊 0.3km 🏛 10km 🏛 0.5km 🚴 7km   **Notes** No pets English spoken Open Easter to 11 November.

ST-PIERRE-LE-VIEUX

Château des Colettes

Corinne et Jacques LORON

71520 ST-PIERRE-LE-VIEUX

☎ 03 85 50 40 96   📄 03 85 50 40 96

email: jcloron@yahoo.fr

17th-century manor house on the borders of Mâconnais and Beaujolais. There are rooms for two or three people with shower room and wc, and a guests' lounge with open fire, television and library. Enclosed garden. Baby equipment. Meals with themed menus available.

Prices not confirmed for 2008   **On Site** Private ⤳   **Nearby** ⌀ 0.8km 🏊 7km 🏛 7km 🚴 27km   **Notes** Pets admitted English spoken Open 15 March to 23 December.

ST-PRIX

L'Eau Vive

Catherine DENIS

71990 ST-PRIX

☎ 03 85 82 59 34

email: redenis@club-internet.fr

web: www.leauvive.over-blog.com

In the Parc du Morvan, near to Mont Beuvray, four comfortable guest rooms, each with bathroom and wc and a salon with open fire. Private pond, walking trails, mountain biking. Archaeological site of Bibracte 6km. Walking trails. High quality evening meals.

Prices s fr €39; d fr €47; t fr €58; dinner fr €20   **On Site** Restaurant **Nearby** ⌀ 0.1km 🏛 4km 🚴 15km   **Notes** No pets English spoken Open 22 March to 15 June & July to 3 November.

ST-SERNIN-DU-PLAIN

La Providence

Thierry et M-Claire VIGOUREUX

Mazenay, 71510 ST-SERNIN-DU-PLAIN

☎ 03 85 49 62 37   📄 03 85 49 62 37

email: mazenay@orange.fr

web: http://mazenay.free.fr

On the Beaune to Cluny wine route, this old restored house contains three comfortable rooms with private facilities and entrances. One room sleeps four (one double bed and two singles). Sitting room with television, kitchen available for use. Courtyard and enclosed wooded grounds. Bathing 7km. Meals must be booked.

Prices s fr €40; d fr €53; t fr €67; extra person fr €12   **Nearby** ⛷ 12km 🏊 25km ⌀ 5km ⤳ 7km Restaurant 2km 🏊 3km 🏛 3km 🚴 15km   **Notes** Pets admitted English spoken

ST-SYMPHORIEN-DE-MARMAGNE

✦ ⏽❍⏽ La Maison Bleue

Verena MATHYS

71710 SAINT-SYMPHORIEN-DE-MARMAGNE

☎ 03 85 78 22 97 ▤ 03 85 78 22 06

email: vmathys@wanadoo.fr

web: www.maison-bleue.net

This house has four spacious and well-decorated bedrooms. There are two double rooms, each with a lounge with fireplace; a family suite with a double bed and four bunks; and a double room. Each room has a private bath or shower room and WC. Large terrace and shady grounds; meals by arrangement. Closed November.

Prices s €38-€47; d €50-€63; t fr €63; dinner fr €18 **On Site** ⚘
Nearby ⚓ 20km ⚴ 16km ⚗ 20km ⚘ 16km Restaurant 1km ⚘ 0.3km
Spa 50km ⚑ 0.5km ⚒ 0.5km **Notes** Pets admitted English spoken

ST-USUGE

✦ ✿ ⏽❍⏽ *La Chaviere*

Claudette et Charles JAEGGI

Charangeroux, 71500 ST-USUGE

☎ 03 85 72 18 13 ▤ 03 85 72 18 13

The owners of this restored property are farmers, producing goats' cheese and the famous Bresse chickens. There is a two-roomed suite with two double beds, and a double-bedded room, both with private bath/shower room and WC. Large conservatory, a garden with lots of flowers, and a pond-side barbecue. Meals can be arranged.

Prices not confirmed for 2008 **On Site** ⚘ **Nearby** ⚓ 10km ⚘ 10km
⚘ 6km ⚑ 2km ⚒ 10km **Notes** No pets English spoken

✦ ⏽❍⏽ La Ferme des Fourneaux

Fabienne THEBERT

Les Chyses, 71500 ST-USUGE

☎ 03 85 72 18 12 & 06 89 33 30 51 ▤ 03 85 72 17 08

email: fc.thebert@fermedesfourneaux.com

web: www.fermedesfourneaux.com

In a typical Bressane house, guest rooms laid out in style include a room for three, one for four and two double rooms, each with private facilities. Rustic breakfast room and sitting room with TV. Courtyard, shady enclosed park. Evening meals may be booked.

Prices d €45-€70; t €81-€89; extra person fr €20; dinner fr €25
Nearby ⚓ 2km ⚴ 30km ⚗ 0.5km ⚘ Restaurant 1km ⚘ 1km
Spa 30km ⚑ 1km ⚒ 5km **Notes** No pets

ST-YTHAIRE

✦ ⏽❍⏽ Domaine de Morlay

Corinne LIEVRE

71460 ST-YTHAIRE

☎ 03 85 92 67 95 & 06 89 79 87 35

email: domaine@morlay.fr

web: www.morlay.fr

On the site of an age-old vineyard overlooking Cormatin, this property offers five beautiful rooms with their own entrance. The rooms sleep from two to four people, all have private bath or shower room/WC, and a cot is available. Enclosed grounds with delightful views of the hills and villages around. Horse riding and cycling possible; meals by arrangement.

Prices s fr €48; d €58-€68; t €73-€78; extra person fr €12; dinner fr €18
On Site ⚓ **Nearby** ⚘ 2km ⚴ 18km Restaurant 5km ⚘ 6km ⚑ 5km
⚒ 30km **Notes** Pets admitted

TINTRY

✦ ⏽❍⏽ Lusigny

Jean-Pierre BERTRAND

71490 TINTRY

☎ 03 85 82 98 98 & 06 72 17 59 93

email: lalison2@wanadoo.fr

Between Beaune and Autun, near the vineyards of Couchois. Three charming and spacious guest rooms, one with covered terrace, each with shower room and wc. Lounge area, gym, well-tended garden. Meals must be booked.

Prices s fr €34; d €38-€46; t fr €56; dinner fr €16 **Nearby** ⚓ 10km
⚘ 23km ⚘ 10km ⚑ 3km ⚒ 23km **Notes** No pets English spoken

TOURNUS

✦ Marie-Clementine

Francoise DOURNEAU

1 quai de Saone, 71700 TOURNUS

☎ 03 85 51 04 43 ▤ 03 85 51 04 43

email: francoise.dourneau@wanadoo.fr

web: http://perso.wanadoo.fr/marie.clementine.chambres.hotes/

Three rooms in a house of character on the banks of the Saône. Breakfast room with lounge area, library, television and enormous enclosed shady garden. The bedrooms sleep two or three, and have private shower and wc. Booking required out of season.

Prices s fr €60; d fr €75; t fr €95; extra person fr €15 **On Site** ⚗
Nearby ⚓ 6km ⚴ 10km ⚘ 1km Restaurant 0.1km ⚘ 1km ⚑ 0.1km
⚒ 1km **Notes** No pets English spoken Open Easter to 1 November.

UCHIZY

⁂ Domaine de l'Arfentière

Annick SALLET

oute de Chardonnay, 71700 UCHIZY

☎ 03 85 40 50 46 & 06 89 93 02 75 📄 03 85 40 58 05

our rooms in a distinctive house, peacefully located on a wine
growing estate. The rooms sleep between two and four guests and
include a bath or shower and wc. Cooking area for guests' use, living
oom, courtyard, games, parking. Wine-tasting on the premises.

Prices s fr €38; d fr €50; t fr €65; extra person fr €15 **Nearby** � 15km
15km ♪ 2km ⅃ 10km Restaurant 5km ⌕ 10km ⌖ 10km ⌗ 0.5km
🚗 2km **Notes** No pets English spoken

VARENNES-SAINT-SAUVEUR

⁂ ⁑ La Petite Grange

Cathy et Gilles KOBLET

71480 VARENNES-SAINT-SAUVEUR

☎ 03 85 74 63 92 & 06 71 06 00 46

email: petitegrange@yahoo.fr

Right in the countryside, close to the Jura Mountains, this farmhouse
is typical of the region. It has been sympathetically restored, and has
three rooms, doubles and twins, all with private bath or shower room/
WC. Swimming pool, and on-site parking. Footpaths and fishing are
close by; meals are available by arrangement.

Prices s fr €45; d fr €59; t fr €70; extra person fr €10; dinner €25
On Site Private ⌕ **Nearby** ♪ 1km ⌕ 4km ⌗ 4km 🚗 18km
Notes No pets English spoken Open June to September.

VARENNES-SOUS-DUN

⁂ ⁑ ⁑ La Saigne

Alain et Michele DESMURS

71800 VARENNES SOUS DUN

☎ 03 85 28 12 79 & 06 84 67 14 81 📄 03 85 28 12 79

email: michele-alain.desmurs@orange.fr

web: http://perso.orange.fr/michele.desmurs

Between meadows and forest, on a traditional Charolais Brionnais
agricultural estate, this property is separate from the owner's home
and provides three rooms (one a suite for four people) with private
facilities. Kitchen area, heating and meals by reservation.

Prices s fr €39; d fr €49; t fr €64; extra person fr €15; dinner fr €21
On Site ♪ **Nearby** ⌖ 10km ⌕ 4km Restaurant 4km ⌕ 4km ⌖ 4km
⌗ 4km 🚗 4km **Notes** No pets English spoken

VENDENESSE-LES-CHAROLLES

⁂ ⁑ ⁑ La Dougade

Jean et Anne MALACHER

71120 VENDENESSE LES CHAROLLES

☎ 03 85 24 70 22 📄 03 85 24 70 22

email: jean.malacher@wanadoo.fr

web: www.sud-bourgogne.francevasion.net

In a calm and verdant setting on a restored farm, this establishment
offers four rooms with independent access, two of which are at
ground-floor level. Each room has private facilities. Panoramic views
can be enjoyed from the property. There is a lounge with a fire.
Breakfasts are served on a veranda looking out over the garden.

Prices s fr €45; d fr €52; t fr €65; extra person fr €13 **Nearby** � 10km
♪ 30km ⌖ 3km ⌕ 7km ⌕ 4km ⌗ 4km 🚗 24km **Notes** No pets
English spoken

VEROSVRES

⁂ ⁑ ⁑ Le Rocher

Roger et Ginette CARETTE

71220 VEROSVRES

☎ 03 85 24 80 53 & 06 83 55 68 16

Three guest rooms in a new house situated in the birthplace of
Ste-Marguerite Marie Alacoque. There are two rooms sleeping two or
three people and a suite of two rooms sleeping four or five, all with
panoramic views, separate access and showers and wcs. Living room
with fireplace and television, terrace, courtyard, enclosed grounds.
Restaurants nearby.

Prices s fr €42; d €48-€54; t €63-€64; extra person fr €13
Nearby ⌖ 0.8km ⌕ 5km Restaurant 4km ⌗ 0.2km 🚗 30km
Notes Pets admitted

VINZELLES

⁂ ⁑ ⁑ ⅃ Les Galopières

Pierre-Yves SPAY

71680 VINZELLES

☎ 03 85 32 90 32 & 06 20 52 65 83 📄 03 85 35 67 65

email: cavedechaintre@wanadoo.fr

web: www.cavedechaintre.com

In the heart of the Pouilly-Fuissé vineyards, host Pierre-Yves, a grower
and wine buff, has prepared four huge and comfortable rooms with
en suite bathrooms. Two doubles and a family room for four, and
one room suitable for the disabled. Breakfast room, small lounge
with open fire; sauna and Jacuzzi. Terrace and garden. Restaurant
800 metres.

Prices not confirmed for 2008 **On Site** Private ⌕ **Nearby** � 2km
⌖ 5km ⌕ 2km ⌗ 5km 🚗 3km **Notes** Pets admitted CC

VIRE

♦♦♦ ⟨◎⟩ **Poiseuil**

Jean-Christophe ROBINET

71260 VIRE

☎ 03 85 33 11 15 & 06 60 88 85 11 📠 03 85 27 98 37

email: info@poiseuil.com

web: www.poiseuil.com

This beautiful house, dating from the 18th and 19th centuries, stands in extensive grounds. It has five guest rooms, each with a private shower room and WC. There is a kitchen available for guests' use; TV on request. Lounge and breakfast room, board games, terrace.

Prices s fr €60; d €65-€100; t €80-€115; extra person fr €15; dinner fr €25 **On Site** ※ Private **Nearby** ⛵ 3km ⚓ 2.5km 🏌 3km Restaurant 1.5km 🛥 3km Spa 14km 🏛 3km 🚶 14km **Notes** Pets admitted English spoken

---

VITRY-EN-CHAROLLAIS

♦♦♦ *Les Terres de Pouilly*

Cécile et Bernard MICHELET

71600 VITRY-EN-CHAROLLAIS

☎ 03 85 81 33 96 📠 03 85 81 33 96

A peacefully situated restored farmhouse. There are two double rooms, and a family suite for four with a lounge area and a convertible bed-settee. They all have private shower room and WC. Enjoy breakfast indoors or out on the terrace. The attractively laid-out garden offers shady sitting space.

Prices not confirmed for 2008 **Nearby** ⛵ 6km 🏌 1km 🔫 6km 🛥 3km 🏛 6km 🚶 6km **Notes** No pets Open Easter to 1 November.

YONNE

ANCY-LE-FRANC

♦♦♦ *Le Moulin*

M-P et J Louis GUIENNOT

Chemin de Halage, 89160 ANCY LE FRANC

☎ 03 86 75 02 65

email: info@moulin-ancy.com

web: www.moulin-ancy.com

Situated by the palace of Ancy le Franc, on an island of two hectares, this 17th-century windmill is on the Bourgogne canal. It offers four bedrooms, one of which has a private roof terrace, for two to four people. There is a park with horses, patios by the canal, an art gallery and a stained glass window workshop. Fishing and regional wines are available.

Prices not confirmed for 2008 **On Site** 🏌 **Nearby** ⛵ 11km 🏌 12km 🔫 17km 🛥 1km 🏛 1km 🚶 8km **Notes** No pets English spoken Open April to October.

APPOIGNY

♦♦♦ ⟨◎⟩ **Le Puits d'Athie**

B FEVRE et P SIAD

1, rue de l'abreuvoir, 89380 APPOIGNY

☎ 03 86 53 10 59 & 06 08 71 82 97 📠 03 86 53 10 59

email: bnbpuitsdathie@wanadoo.fr

Former outbuildings of the château Régennes in a pretty 18th-century Burgundian estate: a charming and comfortable stop-off. It offers two suites and a room with own facilities, American billiards, parking and a shady garden with flowers.

Prices s €69-€160; d €69-€160; t €102-€138; dinner fr €45 **Nearby** ⛵ 7km 🏌 30km 🔫 3km 🛥 10km 🏛 2km 🚶 10km **Notes** Pets admitted English spoken

---

AUXERRE-VAUX

♦♦♦ ♿ **Chambre d'hôtes**

André et Catherine DONAT

Domaine Bon-Boire, 19, rue de Vallan,

89290 AUXERRE-VAUX

☎ 03 86 53 89 99

email: ca@dessusbonboire.com

web: www.dessusbonboire.com

In a peaceful village four kilometres south of Auxerre, this vineyard property offers five bedrooms, all with independent entrance; one on the ground floor is suitable for handicapped access. They comprise two twin-bedded rooms with shower/WC; two triples (double bed and single), one with bathroom and one with shower/WC; and a family room for up to five people with private bathroom. A kitchen and barbecue are available for guest use. The vineyard is given over to organic wine production; the wines are available for guests to enjoy, and also cherries in season.

Prices s fr €46; d fr €56; t fr €70 **On Site** ※ **Nearby** ⛵ 3km 🏌 35km 🔫 0.3km 🔫 3km Restaurant 0.5km 🛥 0.6km Spa 4.5km 🏛 3km 🚶 4km **Notes** No pets English spoken Open March to December. CC

CHAMPIGNELLES

♦♦♦ ⟨◎⟩ **La Ferme des Perriaux**

Noël et Marie France GILET

89350 CHAMPIGNELLES

☎ 03 86 45 17 91 📠 03 86 45 17 99

email: contact@lafermedesperriaux.com

web: www.lafermedesperriaux.com

A 16th-century house surrounded by greenery and flowers, on an agricultural operation. It provides three guest rooms on the first floor, each with private facilities. One room has a cooking area and can accommodate four persons.

Prices s fr €51; d €55-€65; t fr €80; extra person fr €17; dinner fr €25 **On Site** Restaurant **Nearby** ⛵ 3km 🏌 30km 🔫 3km 🔫 12km 🛥 3.5km 🏛 3km 🚶 45km **Notes** No pets Open March to 11 November.

CHARNY

⛲ ❤ 🍽 Ferme du Gué de Plénoise

Daniel et Dominique ACKERMANN

89120 CHARNY

☎ 03 86 63 63 53 📠 03 86 63 63 53

email: mail.ack@wanadoo.fr

Four guestrooms with private facilities, on a working cattle farm on the edge of a river in the countryside. There is a lounge, bookcase and television. Set meals are available by reservation and are free for babies. Toboggan and indoor games available; walking paths nearby. Guests can discover the art of milking on site. There is a weekly bus to Paris-Charny. Swimming available July and August only.

Prices s fr €36; d fr €49; t fr €64; extra person fr €15; dinner fr €18 **On Site** 🎣 **Nearby** ⛷ 5km ⌀ 30km ⚓ 5km Restaurant 5km ⌁ 5km 🏊 5km ➴ 35km **Notes** No pets

CHATEL-CENSOIR

⛲⛲ 🍽 Chambre d'hôtes

Michel et Michelle SAMSON

4, rue du Moulin, 89660 CHATEL CENSOIR

☎ 03 86 81 05 37

email: maison.st.francois@voila.fr

web: http://demeurestfrancois.free.fr

In a delightful village close to the Yonne and the Canal du Nivernais, this beautiful 17th-century house has three double rooms full of character, all upstairs and all with private shower room and WC. Non-smoking throughout; meals by arrangement.

Prices s fr €75; d fr €80; extra person fr €15; dinner fr €28 **On Site** 🎣 Restaurant 🖘 **Nearby** ⛷ 5km ⚓ 15km ⌁ 🏊 0.5km **Notes** No pets English spoken

CHEVANNES

⛲ ♿ Château de Ribourdin

Claude et M.Claude BRODARD

89240 CHEVANNES

☎ 03 86 41 23 16 📠 03 86 41 23 16

email: chateau.de.ribourdin@wanadoo.fr

web: www.chateauderibourdin.com

Five bedrooms arranged in the outbuildings of a 16th-century castle in the country, 300mtrs from a village. Each bedroom has a private bathroom and one has disabled access. A lounge, flower garden, swimming pool and parking are available to guests. Shops and a restaurant are nearby and mountain bikes can be hired. Permit required for fishing.

Prices s fr €55; d €70-€80; t €85-€95; extra person fr €15 **On Site** 🏊 Private ⚓ **Nearby** ⛷ 3km ⌀ 30km 🎣 7km Restaurant 0.5km ⌁ 1km 🏊 0.5km ➴ 7km **Notes** No pets English spoken

COLLAN

⛲ La Marmotte

Gilles et Elisabeth LECOLLE

2, Rue de l'école, 89700 COLLAN

☎ 03 86 55 26 44 & 06 89 45 42 82

email: lamarmotte.glecolle@wanadoo.fr

web: www.bonadresse.com/bourgogne/collan.htm

Three bedrooms in an old renovated house in the heart of the village, 6km from Chablis. There is a twin and two double bedrooms on the first floor, each with its own bathroom. Parking and garden for guests' use, marked footpaths in the surrounding area. Supplement for children aged 3-10.

Prices s fr €40; d fr €45; extra person fr €17 **Nearby** ⛷ 8km ⌀ 20km 🎣 6km ⚓ 10km ⌁ 🏕 6km ➴ 10km **Notes** No pets English spoken

COULANGES-LA-VINEUSE

⛲ *Chambre d'hôtes*

Jean Pierre et Odile MALTOFF

20, rue d'Aguesseau, 89580 COULANGES LA VINEUSE

☎ 03 86 42 32 48 📠 03 86 42 24 92

email: domainej-p.maltoff@wanadoo.fr

Right in the village, this house has four rooms for two to four people, all with private bath/shower room and WC. Breakfast is served in the old fermenting room - a vast place with stonework and exposed beams. Outside is a terrace and courtyard with lots of flowers. Vineyard visits and wine-tasting available; accommodation for riders and their horses.

Prices not confirmed for 2008 **Nearby** ⛷ 10km 🎣 3km ⚓ 15km ⌁ ➴ 3km **Notes** Pets admitted English spoken CC

DISSANGIS

⛲ 🍽 Domaine de Rochefort

89440 DISSANGIS

☎ 03 86 33 80 52

email: info.rochefort@laposte.net

web: www.domaine-de-rochefort.com

In the middle of the countryside, on the edge of Morvan, this old farmhouse has four bedrooms, all on the first floor. There are four doubles, and a suite for four people which has not yet been graded. All have private bathrooms and WCs. On the ground floor is the breakfast room, and a lounge, with books. Terrace, mountain bikes, swimming pool.

Prices d fr €58; t fr €70; dinner fr €26 **On Site** 🎣 🏊 Private ⚓ **Nearby** ⛷ 12km ⌀ 30km Restaurant 3km ⌁ 3km 🏕 3km ➴ 17km **Notes** No pets

ESCOLIVES-STE-CAMILLE

✱✱✱ �🍴 *Chambre d'hôtes*

Régine BORGNAT

1, Rue de l'Eglise, 89290 ESCOLIVES STE CAMILLE

☎ 03 86 53 35 28   📄 03 86 53 65 00

email: regine@domaineborgnat.com

On a wine-growing estate, this beautiful fortified house stands above 700 square metres of cellars. On the first floor are five bedrooms, sleeping from two to five people, all with private bath or shower rooms and WCs. Separate guests' entrance. Lounge with books. Garden with furniture and table tennis. Cellar visits and wine tasting; meals by arrangement.

Prices not confirmed for 2008   **On Site** Private ↘   **Nearby** ⚓4km
⚓30km ✏2km ♨2km 🏛3km ➳3km   **Notes** Pets admitted   English spoken CC

✱✱✱ *La Cour Barrée*

Raymond TRIPOT

12bis, rte de Vaux, 4, rue du canal,
89290 ESCOLIVES STE CAMILLE

☎ 03 86 53 35 98 & 06 87 12 56 92   📄 03 86 53 35 98

email: rtrip@wanadoo.fr

web: http://perso.wanadoo.fr/raymond.tripot/

A five-bedroom guest house on a farm set in a pretty park. Each bedroom has bathroom facilities and independent access; one is suitable for a family of four. There is a lounge, TV room, kitchen, books, fireplace, swimming pool, parking, boules pitch, garden, barbecue and table tennis.

Prices not confirmed for 2008   **On Site** ✏ Private ↘   **Nearby** ⚓20km
⚓25km ♨1km 🏛1km ➳1km   **Notes** No pets

FONTAINES

✱✱✱ �🍴 *La Bruère*

Guy et Chantal JORRY

89130 FONTAINES

☎ 03 86 74 30 83

Three guest rooms on the first floor of a working cattle-breeding farm, set in the heart of the countryside. There is a lounge with a fireplace, a garden and parking.

Prices d fr €43; dinner fr €16   **Nearby** ⚓8km ♨20km ✏3km ↘8km Restaurant 8km ♨8km ✝15km 🏛8km ➳32km   **Notes** No pets

FONTENAILLES

✱✱✱✱ �🍴 **Relais Fontenailles**

Pierre ROVET

20, rue de l'église, 89560 FONTENAILLES

☎ 03 86 41 57 14 & 06 60 41 59 63

email: pierre@relaisfontenailles.com

web: www.relaisfontenailles.com

Five double rooms in fully restored old farm buildings overlooking the undulating countryside, on the edge of an historic village. All the rooms have private facilities and guests have use of a lounge with fireplace, library and private swimming pool. Evening meals can be reserved.

Prices d fr €75; dinner fr €28   **On Site** Private ↘   **Nearby** ⚓5km
♨40km ✏15km Restaurant 5km ♨5km ✝20km 🏛5km ➳20km
Notes No pets   English spoken   Open Easter to 15 October.

FONTENAY-PRES-VEZELAY

✱✱✱ �🍴 **Soeuvres**

Bruno et Marie DEMOINET

Les Chenevieres-48, Grande Rue,
89450 FONTENAY PRES VEZELAY

☎ 03 86 32 37 80 & 06 71 71 98 35   📄 03 86 32 37 80

email: bruno.demoinet@wanadoo.fr

web: www.chenevieres-soeuvres.com

A characterful house in a park extending to several acres, with an ancient mill and waterfall. Four first-floor en suite rooms. Living room with open fire. Swimming pool (unsupervised) shared with hosts and another let property. Table tennis, bar football; walks in the woods.

Prices s €52-€69; d €58-€75; t €80-€92; extra person fr €17; dinner fr €20   **On Site** Private ↘   **Nearby** ⚓5km ✏10km ♨5km 🏛6km ➳18km   **Notes** No pets   English spoken

GERMIGNY

✱✱✱ �🍴 **La Clef des Champs**

Yvon et Evelyne PEYRONNON

44 Grande Rue, Vieux Champs, 89600 GERMIGNY

☎ 03 86 35 34 26

This barn conversion is in a peaceful little hamlet. There are five guest bedrooms, each for two or three people, and all on the first floor. All have private bath or shower room and WC. There is a large day room for guests, complete with an open fire, and outside are enclosed grounds. Meals are available by arrangement.

Prices s fr €38; d €48-€50; extra person fr €15; dinner fr €17
Nearby ⚓5km ♨25km ✏1km ↘5km Restaurant 5km ♨5km
✝30km 🏛1km ➳5km   **Notes** Pets admitted   English spoken

GIGNY

♦♦♦ La Grande Vèvre

Aldo et Agnès MAGNO-BATIS
Route de Nicey, 89160 GIGNY
☎ 03 80 81 41 88 & 06 80 41 14 46　▤ 03 80 81 41 88
email: la-grande-vesvre@wanadoo.fr

At the crossroads of three departments, this ancient farm is close to forest and waterways. There are three spacious, comfortable bedrooms, each with private facilities. Open air concerts, theatre and exhibitions. English and Italian spoken.

Prices s fr €60; d fr €70; t fr €90; extra person fr €20　**Nearby** ⚓ 8km ⚐ 18km ⚐ 0.1km ⚑ 25km Restaurant 5km ⚒ 18km ⚓ 20km ⚐ 4km ⚒ 30km　**Notes** No pets　English spoken

GY-L'EVEQUE

♦♦♦ Chambre d'hôtes

Martial et Chantal MOYER
2, Rue de la Fontaine, 89580 GY L'EVEQUE
☎ 03 86 41 61 64　▤ 03 86 41 74 17
email: chantal.moyer@orange.fr
web: www.gite-prop.com/89/2052

Five guest rooms on the first floor of an old restored building on a working farm, each with its own bathroom facilities. There is a lounge with fireplace and set meals are available at weekends by reservation. The house is located in a village well-known for the Marmot cherry and during May and June, guests are invited to taste and pick the cherries.

Prices s fr €42; d €50-€55; t fr €60; extra person fr €20　**On Site** Private tennis court　**Nearby** ⚓ 5km ⚐ 25km ⚐ 9km ⚑ 9km Restaurant 5km ⚓ 9km ⚐ 0.1km ⚒ 9km　**Notes** No pets　English spoken　Open February to November.

JOUX-LA-VILLE

♦♦♦ ♿ Le Clos du Merry

Maryse et Jean Paul GUEUNIOT
4 rue Crété, 89440 JOUX LA VILLE
☎ 03 86 33 65 54
email: closmerry@free.fr

Guest rooms arranged in an old farm barn include three double rooms (one with disabled access), and two rooms for families of four or five people. There is independent access to the rooms, a garden with patio, picnic area, boules pitch and various games. Guided walks are available during high season, for groups of ten to fifteen people. Reservations required October to Easter.

Prices s fr €35; d fr €45; t fr €55　**Nearby** ⚐ 10km ⚑ 16km ⚐ 16km ⚒ 16km　**Notes** No pets

LAIN

♦♦♦ ⦿ ♿ Art'Monie

Jacques et Arlette ELZIERE
6 rue du Bourgelet, 89560 LAIN
☎ 03 86 45 20 39　▤ 03 86 45 21 76
email: arlette@artmonie.net
web: www.artmonie.net

This old Burgundian farm has five rooms sleeping two to four people with private bathrooms. One bedroom has disabled access. There is a guest lounge and set meals can be provided on Thursdays, Fridays and Saturdays by reservation. Table tennis, games area and picnic area; walking, fishing, horse riding and bathing nearby. Animals welcome by arrangement.

Prices not confirmed for 2008　**Nearby** ⚓ 12km ⚐ 10km ⚑ 18km ⚒ 4km ⚒ 30km　**Notes** Pets admitted　English spoken　Open February to 11 November.

LEZINNES

♦♦♦ Chambre d'hôtes

Jean et Madeleine PIEDALLU
5 Route d'Argentenay, 89160 LEZINNES
☎ 03 86 75 68 23

A new house of regional character with three bedrooms with private facilities, a lounge reserved for guests, an enclosed courtyard with parking and a garden shaded by trees. Shops, a restaurant, tennis and a train station are available in the village. The castles of Tanlay and Ancy le Franc are nearby.

Prices not confirmed for 2008　**On Site** ⚐　**Nearby** ⚒ 8km ⚑ 10km ⚒ 10km　**Notes** No pets

LINDRY

♦♦♦ ⦿ La Bichonnière

S et J DE WELLENSTEIN
37/39, Rue de Charbuy, Les Houches, 89240 LINDRY
☎ 03 86 47 19 85 & 03 86 47 11 47
▤ 03 86 47 19 85
email: labichonniere@free.fr
web: www.la-bichonniere.com

Hidden from the road, this early 19th-century farm has been carefully restored. It offers five tranquil non-smoking rooms for two to three people; two can be combined for a family of four, and all have either bathroom or shower/WC. Facilities include internet access, microwave, kettle and fridge, and a cot is available.

Prices s fr €66; d fr €72; t fr €86; dinner fr €20　**On Site** Restaurant　**Nearby** ⚒ 2km ⚑ 15km ⚐ 3km ⚑ ⚒ 12km ⚐ 2km ⚒ 15km　**Notes** No pets　English spoken

LINDRY *CONTINUED*

⁂ 🕿 *La Vederine*

Eliane et Gérard BONFANTI

Cidex 500-No28, Chazelles, 89240 LINDRY

☎ 03 86 47 10 86 & 06 82 92 02 95 📄 03 86 47 10 86

This old renovated farm is situated in a small, very quiet hamlet in over 8 hectares of land with a garden, boules pitch, patio and parking. There are five rooms, one with disabled access, all with private bathrooms. Lounge with fireplace, books and kitchen area.

Prices not confirmed for 2008 **Nearby** ⛵ 4km ⚓ 15km 🏊 5km ↘ 3km ⚓ 3km 🏢 3km ⋈ 16km **Notes** Pets admitted

⁂ À la Métairie

Brigitte MARTINIGOL

16, Hameau de La Métairie, 89240 LINDRY

☎ 03 86 98 20 56 📄 03 86 98 20 56

email: alametairie@wanadoo.fr

web: www.alametairie.com

A warm welcome and comfortable rooms await at this 18th-century traditional longhouse. Two first-floor doubles have independent access; a separate small building houses a double on two levels, with bread oven. All rooms have private facilities. Shared salon, living room, games, library. Kitchenette, fridge, BBQ, table tennis. Reductions for longer stays; pets by arrangement. No smoking.

Prices s €55-€65; d €65-€75; extra person fr €25 **On Site** Private ↘ **Nearby** ⛵ 2km ⚓ 10km 🏊 5km Restaurant 7km ⚓ 3km 🏊 10km 🏢 8km ⋈ 12km **Notes** Pets admitted English spoken

LIXY

⁂ 🍽 *Chambre d'hôtes*

Alain et Catherine BALOURDET

16, Place de la Liberté, 89140 LIXY

☎ 03 86 66 11 39 & 06 86 65 53 87 📄 03 86 66 11 39

email: clos-melusine@wanadoo.fr

web: www.clos-melusine.com

An old Burgundian farm in the centre of a village with three guest rooms arranged in a separate barn, built on a 12th-century crypt. Each room has its own bathroom facilities and there is a lounge with books about the surrounding region and a garden. Set meals are accompanied by Yonne wines.

Prices not confirmed for 2008 **On Site** ⚓ **Nearby** ⛵ 4km 🏊 10km ↘ 15km ⚓ 4km 🏢 2km ⋈ 10km **Notes** No pets

MASSANGIS

⁂ 🍽 Carpe Diem

Anselme CABON

53, Grande Rue, 89440 MASSANGIS

☎ 03 86 33 89 32

email: carpediem.ser@infonie.fr

web: www.acarpediem.com

There are three converted bedrooms in this 19th-century farmhouse, all en suite and two of which have mezzanines. Sitting room with open fire, farmyard, enclosed grounds. Private parking.

Prices s €54-€60; d €57-€65; extra person fr €15; dinner fr €27 **On Site** 🏊 **Nearby** ⛵ 15km ⚓ 30km ↘ 22km Restaurant 4km ⚓ 4km 🏢 4km ⋈ 22km **Notes** No pets English spoken

MERRY-LA-VALLEE

⁂ Chambre d'hôtes

Marc et Catherine LECOIN

2, Route d'Arthe, Hameau de Maurepas,

89110 MERRY LA VALLEE

☎ 03 86 44 19 04

email: marc.lecoin@neuf.fr

web: www.hameaudemaurepas.com

Set in the countryside, this old farmhouse has three spacious and elegant bedrooms, full of character. There are two rooms which can sleep from two to four people, plus a double room. There is a separate guests' entrance, and all the rooms have a private bath or shower and WC. Breakfasts, including organic produce, are served on the terrace in the summer.

Prices s fr €55; d fr €60; t fr €80 **Nearby** ⛵ 2km ⚓ 16km 🏊 2km ↘ 4km Restaurant 4km ⚓ 4km 🏢 4km ⋈ 20km **Notes** No pets English spoken

MERRY-SEC

⁂ 🍽 Demeure de Forterre

Luc et Dominique POSTIC

9, Rue du Château, 89560 MERRY SEC

☎ 03 86 41 61 94 📄 03 86 41 67 66

email: luc.postic@wanadoo.fr

web: www.demeure-de-forterre.com

An old fortified house dating back to the 16th century, in beautiful green surroundings. There are four guest bedrooms, three on the ground floor and one upstairs. All the rooms have private facilities. Gourmet meals are available by arrangement.

Prices s fr €72; d €76-€80; t fr €110; extra person fr €30; dinner fr €40 **On Site** Private ↘ **Nearby** ⛵ 2km 🏊 15km Restaurant 9km ⚓ 15km 🏊 17km 🏢 17km ⋈ 17km **Notes** No pets English spoken

MEZILLES

⚑ *Le Moulin Grenon*

ris Théodora VAN ROYEN
9130 MEZILLES
☎ 03 86 45 49 92
email: iris@vanroyen.fr
web: www.moulingrenon.fr

n old mill, surrounded by water, attractively situated and now
estored. There are four guest rooms, three doubles and a single, all
with private bath or shower room and WC. Lounge with open fire;
breakfast can be served outside on the terrace.

rices not confirmed for 2008 **On Site** ℘ **Nearby** ☘ 5km ⚓ 30km
⚑ 10km ⚲ 2km ⚑ 10km ⚑ 33km **Notes** No pets English spoken

MOLAY

⚑ ⊙ & **Le Calounier**

ascal et Corinne COLLIN
, Rue de la Fontaine, Arton, 89310 MOLAY
☎ 03 86 82 67 81 ⊟ 03 86 82 67 81
email: info@lecalounier.fr
web: www.lecalounier.fr

his charming house, full of character, is situated in the quiet
ountryside. There are four bedrooms with private bathroom facilities,
f which two are double bedrooms for families of up to five people
nd one has disabled access. There is a lounge and rooms with
ooks and games, a large garden and meals are available and feature
egional dishes.

rices s fr €56; d fr €61; t fr €79; dinner €17–€24 **On Site** ℘
earby ☘ 6km ⚲ 19km ⚲ 3km ⚑ 8km ⚑ 19km **Notes** No pets
nglish spoken

NEUVY-SAUTOUR

⚑ ⊙ *Le Grange de Boulay*

ascal et Christiane GRON
9570 NEUVY SAUTOUR
☎ 03 86 56 43 52 ⊟ 03 86 56 43 52
email: christiane-laurent@wanadoo.fr

etween Auxerre and Troyes, this old renovated house in a hamlet
as a tree-filled garden and river frontage. Five en suite rooms (one
n the ground floor) can accommodate from one to four people.
ving room, dining room, library; French billiards. Two swimming
ools (unsupervised) shared with hosts. Meals by arrangement;
rivate parking.

rices not confirmed for 2008 **On Site** Private ⚲ **Nearby** ☘ 4km
⚓ 30km ⚲ 2km ⚑ 2km ⚑ 9km **Notes** Pets admitted English spoken

NOYERS-SUR-SEREIN

⚑ **Château d'Archambault**

Claude MARIE
Cours, 89310 NOYERS SUR SEREIN
☎ 03 86 82 67 55 ⊟ 03 86 82 67 87
email: chateau-archambault@wanadoo.fr
web: www.chateau-archambault.com

Five guest rooms in a 19th-century mansion house, set in a
wooded park, each with private facilities. Two of the rooms are
doubles, suitable for a family. There is a lounge with fireplace.
The 12th-century village of Noyers-sur-Serein is nearby.

Prices d €70–€90; extra person €25–€30 **On Site** ℘
Nearby ⚑ 1.5km ⚑ 24km **Notes** No pets English spoken
Open 15 March to November. CC

⚑ ⊙ & **Le Clos Malo**

Marie Noëlle MALOSZEK
22 Rue de la République, 89310 NOYERS SUR SEREIN
☎ 03 86 75 97 36 ⊟ 03 86 82 65 13
email: le-clos-malo@noyers-sur-serein.fr
web: www.noyers-sur-serein.fr

In the 13th century this building was a hospital. It stands right in
the village centre, facing the old wash-house. There are four quiet
bedrooms, one of them a two-roomed suite. All are on the ground
floor, and they all have private bath/shower room and WC. Three
rooms open onto an enclosed garden. Private parking; meals by
arrangement.

Prices s fr €63; d fr €65; extra person €10–€15; dinner €20–€25
On Site Restaurant ♨ **Nearby** ☘ 10km ⚓ 20km ℘ 0.1km ⚲ 20km
⚲ 10km ⚑ 20km **Notes** Pets admitted English spoken

OUANNE

⚑ *Duenne*

Michel et Blandine JOZON
2, Duenne, 89560 OUANNE
☎ 03 86 47 66 23 ⊟ 03 86 47 64 89
email: blamijozon@aol.com
web: www.chambres-hotes-ouanne.com

A house dating from the 18th century situated on a working mixed
farm, in a quiet hamlet amongst rolling green fields. Three guest
bedrooms, all en suite, one of which is family-sized. Sitting room for
guests; walks around the property. Restaurant 7km.

Prices not confirmed for 2008 **Nearby** ☘ 7km ⚲ 15km ⚲ 3km ⚑ 3km
⚑ 25km **Notes** No pets

POILLY-SUR-SEREIN

₩₩ iOi **Le Moulin**

Robert et Yvette GILLES
1, Rue des Fossés, 89310 POILLY SUR SEREIN
☎ 03 86 75 92 46
email: info@lemoulindepoilly.com
web: www.lemoulindepoilly.com

A vast 19th-century mill, on the edge of a village. There are five
bedrooms, all with private bath or shower room and WC. The setting
is quiet and peaceful, in spacious grounds with a lot of greenery.
There is a lounge with books; parking is on-site, and there is a long-
distance footpath close by.

Prices s fr €50; d €65-€69; t €75-€80; extra person fr €15; dinner fr €26
On Site ⟋ ⟡ **Nearby** ⚓ 3km ⚐ 15km ⚘ 10km Restaurant 3km ⚲
⚑ 0.4km ⋙ 9km **Notes** No pets English spoken Open February to 14
December.

SANTIGNY

₩₩ **Domaine d'Ecuseaux**

Olivier et Valérie LE ROY
17 Grande Rue, 89420 SANTIGNY
☎ 03 86 32 00 93 & 06 80 84 63 20
email: info@domaine-ecuseaux.com
web: www.domaine-ecuseaux.com

This restored 19th-century manor house is in the heart of the village.
Two double rooms and a family room for up to five, all with private
bath/shower room and WC, enjoy views across the grounds. Lounge
with open fire and table football. An outside portico provides a
sheltered spot for children to play.

Prices s €60-€90; d €60-€90; t fr €105 **Nearby** ⚓ 20km ⚐ 60km
⟋ 8km ⚘ 22km Restaurant 7km ⚲ 20km ⚑ 10km ⋙ 20km
Notes No pets English spoken

SAUVIGNY-LE-BEUREAL

₩₩ iOi *La Forlonge*

Famille NOIROT
5 Rue de la Vallée de Beauvoir,
89420 SAUVIGNY LE BEUREAL
☎ 03 86 32 58 80 ⧉ 03 86 32 58 80

An authentic Burgundian farm set in a village offers five rooms in the
attic, all with private bathrooms and heating. There is a restored room

with an open fireplace, a garden, billiards, table tennis and fishing in a
private lake. Footpaths in the surrounding area.

Prices not confirmed for 2008 **On Site** ⟋ **Nearby** ⚓ 5km ⚘ 5km
⚲ 2km ⚑ 2km ⋙ 17km **Notes** No pets

ST-MARTIN-DES-CHAMPS

₩₩ iOi **Les Salzards**

William VAN BOCKEL
L'ancienne Poterie, 89170 SAINT MARTIN DES CHAMPS
☎ 03 86 74 18 10
email: lessalzards@wanadoo.fr
web: www.lessalzards.com

An old pottery, with four bedrooms sleeping from two to four people.
All of the rooms have a private bath or shower room and WC. The
setting is very attractive, amongst orchards and meadows. Lounge and
swimming pool. Meals are available, by arrangement.

Prices s €39-€49; d fr €63; t fr €79; dinner fr €19 **On Site** Private ⚘
Nearby ⚓ 6km ⚐ 30km ⟋ 6km Restaurant 5km ⚲ 5km ⚡ 5km
⚑ 5km ⋙ 35km **Notes** Pets admitted English spoken

ST-SAUVEUR-EN-PUISAYE

₩₩ *Les Sapins*

Fabrice BRANGEON-BONNARD
89520 SAINT SAUVEUR EN PUISAYE
☎ 03 86 45 50 32 & 06 74 20 20 34
email: lessapins-chambresdhotes@wanadoo.fr
web: www.domaine-des-sapins.com

This 19th-century house of immense character stands in its own
grounds of three hectares surrounded by countryside. It offers three
twin-bedded rooms, all with private bathroom and WC. Lounge with
TV; swimming pool in the grounds. Plenty of woodland, and good
walking country.

Prices not confirmed for 2008 **On Site** Private ⚘ **Nearby** ⚓ 4km
⟋ 3km ⚲ 2km ⚑ 2km ⋙ 35km **Notes** No pets English spoken Open
Easter to 1 November.

STE-MAGNANCE

⚜⚜⚜ 🍴 **Chambre d'hôtes**

E et J-C BRIEN-ROQUES
Domaine des Roches, 6 Rue Chaume Lacarre,
89420 SAINTE MAGNANCE
☎ 03 86 33 14 87
email: domainedesroches225@orange.fr
web: www.domainedesroches89.com

This totally restored longhouse close to the Morvan regional park has three bedrooms: a double, a triple (double bed and a single), and a room with four single beds. All have private bathroom and WC. Living room with open fire, and garden with parking space. Meals are available by arrangement.

Prices s €55-€65; d €60-€70; t €75-€85; dinner fr €25
On Site Restaurant **Nearby** ⛷ 4km ⚲ 25km 🏌 10km 🏛 3km
🚶 13km **Notes** No pets English spoken

TANNERRE-EN-PUISAYE

⚜⚜ 🍴 **Moulin de la Forge**

René et Chantal GAGNOT
89350 TANNERRE EN PUISAYE
☎ 03 86 45 40 25
email: renegagnot@aol.com

A 14th-century mill set in four hectares of wooded grounds with a lake and swimming pool. There are five bedrooms, one with disabled access, and all with private facilities. There is a kitchen area, a lounge with fireplace and a covered barbecue for guests' use. Fishing available on site.

Prices s fr €54; d fr €54; t fr €69 **On Site** ⛷ ⚲ Private 🏌
Nearby ⚲ 25km 🏊 1km 🏛 7km 🚶 40km **Notes** Pets admitted

THIZY

⚜⚜ 🍴 **L'Esperluette**

Marie Josée BRUN
10 Rue Edme Marie Cadoux, 89420 THIZY
☎ 03 86 32 04 59 📠 03 86 32 04 59
email: info@lesperluette.com
web: www.lesperluette.com

The former house of the sculptor Edme Marie Cadoux situated on the edge of a picturesque village. There are three bedrooms for two or three people, with bathroom facilities. Lounge with a piano and books, large garden and shaded park. Set meals are available by reservation. Animals welcome by arrangement.

Prices s €40-€48; d €50-€58; t fr €68; dinner fr €26 **Nearby** ⛷ 18km
🏊 30km 🏌 4.5km 🏌 15km 🏊 4.5km 🏛 4.5km 🚶 15km **Notes** English spoken

VALLERY

⚜⚜⚜ 🍴 ♿ **La Margottière**

Didier et Colette DELIGAND
89150 VALLERY
☎ 03 86 97 57 97 📠 03 86 97 53 80
email: contact@lamargottiere.com
web: www.lamargottiere.com

Six guest rooms arranged in a detached Burgundian residence, on the working farm of the 17th-century castle of Conde. The bedrooms have separate bathroom facilities, a telephone and TV and one room has disabled access. Lounge with a 17th-century fireplace, enclosed courtyard, children's games, table tennis and table football. Set meals available on reservation.

Prices s fr €70; d fr €70; t fr €85; extra person fr €15; dinner fr €30
On Site 🎯 **Nearby** ⛷ 2km 🏌 4km 🏌 1km 🏌 20km Restaurant 0.8km
🏊 5km 🏛 0.5km 🚶 14km **Notes** No pets English spoken

VAUDEURS

⚜⚜⚜ 🍴 *Les Brissots*

Frédéric et Nathalie BANCE
6 Les Brissots, 89320 VAUDEURS
☎ 03 86 96 44 80
email: ide8921@yahoo.fr
web: http://chdhotesyonne.ifrance.com

On the tourist 'route of the cider presses' in peaceful countryside, Frédéric and Nathalie will welcome you to their old farm. Three guest rooms all offer en suite facilities. Living room. In the nearby hamlet is a cider museum and a major hiking route.

Prices not confirmed for 2008 **Nearby** ⛷ 5km 🏌 24km 🏌 24km
🏊 2km 🏛 5km 🚶 24km **Notes** No pets English spoken

VENOY

⚜⚜⚜⚜ **Domaine Ste-Anne**

Alain et Béatrice MAGNE
Soleines le Haut, 89290 VENOY
☎ 03 86 94 10 16 📠 03 86 40 26 58
email: info@domainesainteanne.com
web: www.domainesainteanne.com

This property has three south-facing upstairs bedrooms: a double, a twin-bedded room, and a room for three (double bed and a single), all with private bath/shower room and WC. This is an impressive 18th-century house, standing in an isolated spot surrounded by trees. Separate guest entrance, and a living room with open fire and television.

Prices d €65-€74; t fr €88 **On Site** 🏌 **Nearby** ⛷ 10km 🏌 15km
🏌 8km Restaurant 0.8km 🏊 1.5km 🏌 7km 🏛 7km 🚶 7km
Notes No pets English spoken Open April to October.

VEZELAY

₩ Chambre d'hôtes

B et S VAN DEN BOSSCHE
Le Porc Epic, 80 Rue St Pierre, 89450 VEZELAY
☎ 03 86 33 32 16
email: sylvie@le-porc-epic.com

Near the Basilique, this is a beautiful building built over a 12th century pilgrims' room, which is still visible. A ground floor studio displays the work of sculptors Monsieur and Madame Van den Bossche. There are four no-smoking guest rooms with private facilities, one of which is grade 2. Breakfast is served in a conservatory.

Prices s €70-€90; d €75-€95 **Nearby** ₺ 3km ✐ 3km ⚓ 12km Restaurant 0.5km ☕ Spa 50km ₩ 10km **Notes** No pets

VEZINNES

₩ ⦿ Chambre d'hôtes St-Nicolas

Philippe & Gwenaelle PACAULT
1 Place de L'Eglise, 89700 VEZINNES
☎ 03 86 55 56 14 & 06 18 17 92 52 📄 03 86 55 58 98
email: ligne-g@wanadoo.fr
web: www.chambres-st-nicolas.com

This property offers two split-level rooms for four, each with a double bed and two singles, a private shower room and a WC. They make an ideal holiday base for families. Courtyard and garden reserved for guest use. Theme weekends arranged in winter.

Prices s fr €60; d fr €65; t fr €85; dinner fr €20 **On Site** ✐ **Nearby** ₺ 15km ⚓ 10km ⚓ 5km Restaurant 3km ☕ 5km ✎ 5km ☖ 5km ₩ 5km **Notes** No pets English spoken CC

VILLIERS-LOUIS

₩ ⦿ Le Ménestrel

Pierre et Georgette COUTANT
5 Rue de L'Église, 89320 VILLIERS LOUIS
☎ 03 86 88 24 98 & 06 08 61 96 72
email: coutant.pierre.georgette@wanadoo.fr

A village house with three bedrooms. There is a double room on the ground floor; upstairs are two more rooms which can each sleep up to four people. All of the rooms have private facilities. There is a lounge with books, and top quality meals are available, with home-made bread and pastries. Garage.

Prices s fr €39; d fr €47; t fr €63; extra person fr €16; dinner fr €25 **Nearby** ₺ 9km ⚓ 12km ⚓ 5km ⚓ 12km Restaurant 8km ☕ Spa 50km ☖ 10km ₩ 12km **Notes** No pets

VILLIERS-SUR-THOLON

₩ ⦿ Chambre d'hôtes

Alain et Myriam DESESSARTS
2A Chemin du Champ Guibert,
89110 VILLIERS SUR THOLON
☎ 03 86 63 83 63 & 03 86 63 83 84 📄 03 86 63 83 84
email: alain.desessarts@wanadoo.fr

This is a modern house in a quiet and peaceful spot with a large garden. The village is charming, on the edge of the Puisaye region. The four bedrooms comprise two doubles, a twin-bedded room, and a family room for four (double bed and twins). Separate entrance for guests. Good area for walking.

Prices s €45-€60; d €50-€60; t fr €70; extra person fr €16; dinner fr €22 **Nearby** ₺ 11km ⚓ 5km ⚓ 4km ⚓ 2km ☕ 2km ☖ 2km ₩ 12kr **Notes** No pets

10
AUBE

CHAUMONT

D417

52
HAUTE-
MARNE

Gevrolles

Meuse

Marne

N19

A5

A31

Langres

89
YONNE

Seine

Aube

D965

D980

D905

N71

D67

Meulson

Aignay-le-Duc

Salives

Échalot

D996

Boussenois

N4

A31

Montbard

D980

Mussy-la-Fosse

Saussy

Noiron-
sur-Bèze

Villeferry

Francheville

Messigny-
et-Vantoux

A6

Seine

D70

Aisy-
sous-Thil

Clamerey
(Pont-Royal)

Plombières-lès-Dijon

N71

A38

DIJON

Pontailler-sur-Saône

A39

Lamarche-
sur-Saône

N6

Bellenot-
sous-Pouilly

Fixin

N74

Canal

N5

Flammerans

Athée

Chamboeuf

Vandenesse-en-Auxois

Châteauneuf-en-Auxois

Morey-St-Denis

Longecourt-
en-Plaine

Champdôtre

Crugey

Curtil-Vergy

Flagey-Echézeaux

Bessey-lès-Citeaux

Messanges

Colombier

Chevannes

Villars-
Fontaine

Épernay-sous-Gevrey

St-Bernard

St-Nicolas-les-Citeaux

Comblanchien

Marey-lès-Fussey

Ladoix-Serrigny

Argilly

Saône

Dole

N6

A36

Chorey-
lès-Beaune

Villy-
le-Moutier

N73

Montceau-
Écharnant

Bouze-
lès-Beaune

Cussy-la-Colonne

Beaune

St-Romain

Pommard

D973

Seurre

D980

Baubigny

Auxey-Duresses

Bligny-lès-Beaune

N81

Santenay-
en-Bourgogne

Meursault

Puligny-
Montrachet

71
SAÔNE-
ET-LOIRE

Doubs

N73

D973

D978

N

S

0   15 km

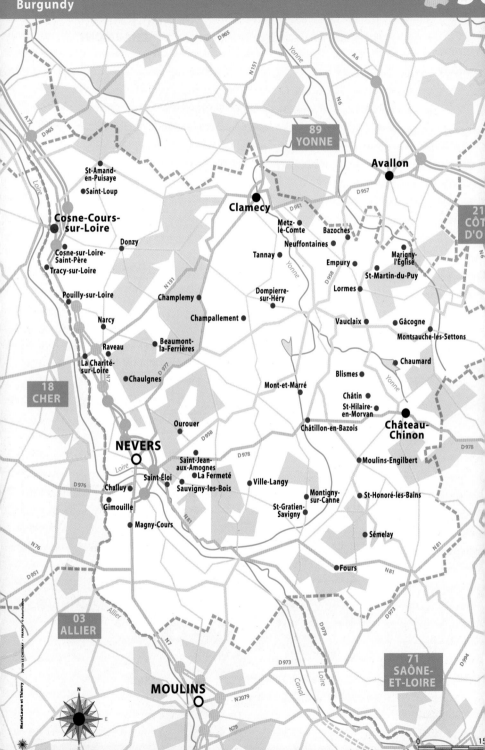

NIÈVRE

89 YONNE

21 CÔTE D'O

18 CHER

03 ALLIER

71 SAÔNE-ET-LOIRE

Avallon

St-Amand-en-Puisaye
●Saint-Loup

Clamecy

Cosne-Cours-sur-Loire

Metz-le-Comte
Bazoches
Donzy
Neuffontaines
Cosne-sur-Loire-Saint-Père
Tannay
Empury
Marigny-l'Eglise
Tracy-sur-Loire
St-Martin-du-Puy

Pouilly-sur-Loire
Champlemy
Dompierre-sur-Héry
Lormes

Narcy
Champallement
Vauclaix
Gâcogne

Raveau
Beaumont-la-Ferrières
Montsauche-les-Settons

La Charité-sur-Loire
Chaumard

Chaulgnes
Blismes
Mont-et-Marré
Châtin
St-Hilaire-en-Morvan

Ourouer
Château-Chinon

Châtillon-en-Bazois

NEVERS
Moulins-Engilbert

Saint-Jean-aux-Amognes
La Fermeté
Saint-Éloi
Ville-Langy
Challuy
Sauvigny-les-Bois
Montigny-sur-Canne
St-Honoré-les-Bains

Gimouille
St-Gratien-Savigny

Magny-Cours
Sémelay

Fours

MOULINS

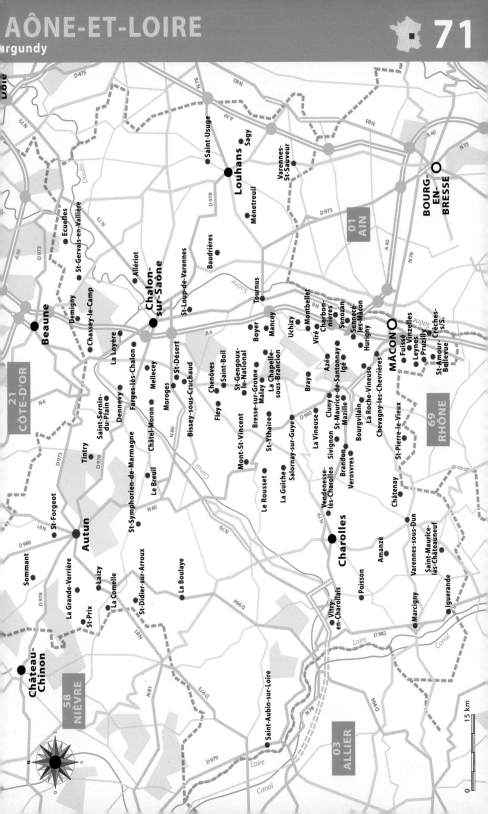

YONNE
Burgundy

89

Nogent-sur-Seine

10 AUBE

TROYES

Lixy

Vallery

Villiers-Louis

Sens

Vaudeurs

Neuvy-Sautour

Germigny

45 LOIRET

Charny

Villiers-sur-Tholon

Appoigny

Vézinnes

Collan

Merry-la-Vallée

Venoy

Lézinnes

Lindry

AUXERRE

Poilly-sur-Serein

Ancy-le-Fra

Champignelles

Chevannes

Escolives-Ste-Camille

Môlay

Tannerre-en-Puisaye

Gy-l'Évêque

Mézilles

Fontaines

Coulanges-la-Vineuse

Noyers-sur-Serein

Ouanne

St-Martin-des-Champs

St-Sauveur-en-Puisaye

Merry-Sec

Massangis

Dissangis

Lain

Joux-la-Ville

Thizy

Santigny

Châtel-Censoir

Fontenailles

Avallon

Sauvigny-le-Beuréal

Vézelay

Ste-Magnance

Clamecy

Fontenay-près-Vezelay

21 CÔTE D'O

Cosne-Cours-sur-Loire

58 NIÈVRE

N
O E
S

0 15

CENTRAL FRANCE

CHER

ALLOGNY

▦ *Domaine de L'Orée de Sologne*

Sylvie et Joël BARDON
Le Rabillon, 18110 ALLOGNY
☎ 02 48 64 08 19 ▤ 02 48 64 00 53
email: l.oree.de.sologne@wanadoo.fr
web: http://perso.orange.fr/l.oree.de.sologne/

Anyone who appreciates nature will love this large house, with its 2-hectare fishing lake and woods, to say nothing of the warm welcome. One double room and three rooms sleeping two to four, with kitchenette and dining area; all are en suite. Guests' sitting room with open fire, TV, swimming pool, jacuzzi, billiards, table tennis. Covered terrace. Hiking trails. 10% discount for over three days. Wi-fi access.

Prices not confirmed for 2008 **On Site** ⚓ Private ⤳ **Nearby** ⤳ 3km Water sports 25km 🚣 3km 🏛 3km 🚴 25km **Notes** No pets English spoken

ARCAY

▦ Château de Belair

Roger et Claudette MAGINIAU
18340 ARCAY
☎ 02 48 25 36 72

Four double bedrooms and two triple rooms in a 19th-century château surrounded by an extensive wooded park; one has an additional room for two children and one has a sitting room with open fire. Each has shower, wc and television. Lounge and salon.

Prices d fr €49; extra person fr €17 **On Site** Private ⤳ **Nearby** ⚓ 12km ⚓ 15km ⚓ 5km Restaurant 3km Water sports 14km 🚣 0.8km Spa 20km 🏛 5km 🚴 20km **Notes** Pets admitted English spoken

ARDENAIS

▦ iOi *La Folie*

Annick JACQUET
18170 ARDENAIS
☎ 02 48 96 17 59
email: la.folie@wanadoo.fr
web: http://perso.wanadoo.fr/cher.berry.la.folie

An 18th-century farmhouse set in a hectare of woods, with a double room and a suite with a double and two singles, all with separate entry and facilities. Lounge/dining room with TV and open fireplace, reading room with documents about the region and tourist information. Your hostess can recommend routes around the region. Nearby: naval base at Sidiailles, river banks, forest, hiking.

Prices not confirmed for 2008 **Nearby** ⚓ 12km ⚓ 4km ⤳ 15km Water sports 20km 🚣 4km 🏛 8km 🚴 13km **Notes** No pets English spoken

AUGY-SUR-AUBOIS

▦ ❦ iOi **Ferme Auberge des Pirodelles**

Sandrine GUIENOT
Les Pirodelles, 18600 AUGY-SUR-AUBOIS
☎ 02 48 74 51 26 ▤ 02 48 74 51 26
email: pirodelles@wanadoo.fr
web: http://monsite.wanadoo.fr/pirodelles

On the first floor of this farm-auberge are three rooms, all with en suite shower and WC. The rooms, accessed by a private entrance, can each sleep three people, and you are welcome to share the hosts' living room and TV. Here, deep in the countryside, you can relax and watch the day-to-day running of this mixed farm.

Prices s fr €40; d €45-€60; t fr €65; extra person fr €15; dinner fr €18 **On Site** Restaurant **Nearby** ⚓ 14km ⚓ 6km ⤳ 12km Water sports 6km 🏛 5km 🚴 30km **Notes** No pets English spoken CC

BELLEVILLE-SUR-LOIRE

▦ **Chambre d'hôtes**

Gery et Christine DE JENLIS
20, route de Beaulieu, 18240 BELLEVILLE-SUR-LOIRE
☎ 02 48 72 49 60 & 06 11 61 41 57
email: g.de.jenlis@wanadoo.fr
web: www.lecrotpansard.com

At the edge of Loiret and the Nièvre, these old, renovated stables, set across from the owners' home, house four double guest rooms, all with shower room and wc. TV lounge, dining room and kitchenette for guests' use. Fine wooded grounds with water garden and the canal alongside the Loire.

Prices s fr €40; d fr €43; extra person fr €12 **On Site** ⚓ ⚓ **Nearby** ⚓ 20km ⤳ 0.5km 🚣 🚴 15km **Notes** No pets English spoken

BERRY-BOUY

▦ ❦ *L'Ermitage*

Géraud DE LA FARGE
18500 BERRY-BOUY
☎ 02 48 26 87 46 ▤ 02 48 26 03 28
email: domaine-ermitage@wanadoo.fr

A stunning family mansion set on a mixed and cattle farm just west of Bourges. There are three double rooms, a room for three and one for four, all with private facilities and TV. Two are in a wing of the house, and three in an adjacent mill. Lounge for guests, park with old trees and parking. Restaurants 3km. Closed Christmas and New Year.

Prices not confirmed for 2008 **On Site** ⚓ **Nearby** ⚓ 5km ⤳ 5km Water sports 8km 🚣 5km **Notes** No pets English spoken

BLET

▦ *Chassy*

F et M DE VILDER ET HULSHOF

18350 BLET

email: dom.dechassy@wanadoo.fr

web: www.chassy.org

Accommodation is offered in this charming 18th-century house and 14th-century pigeon-house, in a quiet and secluded spot. There are three double rooms each with separate access, shower or bathroom and wc. Living room/lounge with open fireplace; extensive grounds with furniture; bikes and cot available.

Prices not confirmed for 2008   **On Site** Private ↖   **Nearby** ♿ 20km ℘ 15km Water sports 30km ♨ 7km 🏛 3km ⛵ 40km   **Notes** No pets English spoken Open April to October.

BRINON-SUR-SAULDRE

▦ |◎| **Château des Bouffards**

C et C FORTIN DE GUILLEBON

18410 BRINON-SUR-SAULDRE

☎ 02 48 58 59 88 & 06 07 21 36 64

▤ 02 48 58 32 11

email: bouffards@wanadoo.fr

web: http://perso.wanadoo.fr/bouffards/

A 19th-century hunting lodge in 2.5-hectare park, peacefully situated ten kilometres from Lamotte-Breuvon. It offers a family suite for four, a double-bedded room, a twin and a triple; all rooms have private bath or shower room and WC. Lounge, dining room and billiard room, mountain bikes all available. Heated swimming pool.

Prices s fr €60; d fr €115; t fr €115; extra person fr €20; dinner fr €25   **On Site** Private ↖   **Nearby** ♿ 7km ℘ 0.5km Water sports 25km 🏛 10km ⛵ 5km   **Notes** Pets admitted English spoken

CHARENTON-LAUGERE

▦▦ **La Serre**

Claude et Claude MOREAU

route de Dun, 18210 CHARENTON-LAUGERE

☎ 02 48 60 75 82 & 06 14 90 23 56

▤ 02 48 60 75 82

Three double rooms with shower and wc in a 100-year-old house, harmoniously combining art deco and contemporary furnishings. Park and garden with outdoor furniture. Two living rooms and a dining room for guests. Learn about topiary and French gardens.

Prices s fr €60; d fr €75-€90; extra person fr €20   **On Site** ℘   **Nearby** ♿ 4km ♨ 20km ↖ 15km Restaurant 15km Water sports 6km ♨ 3km 🏛 3km ⛵ 15km   **Notes** No pets English spoken Open April to September.

CIVRAY

▦ & **La Maison de Philomène**

Martine et Jacques BLIN

4 impasse du Parc, Le Grand Entrevins, 18290 CIVRAY

☎ 02 48 26 25 63 & 06 64 71 89 41   ▤ 02 48 26 25 31

email: maisondephilomene@wanadoo.fr

web: http://perso.orange.fr/maisondephilomene/

Between Bourges and Issoudun, this renovated farmhouse offers a warm welcome and a hearty breakfast. Accommodation consists of three double rooms and one triple, all individually decorated, with bath or shower and WC. Being on the ground floor, they are suitable for the disabled. A large living room has a lovely view to open countryside.

Prices s fr €45; d fr €50; t fr €70; extra person fr €20   **On Site** Private ↖   **Nearby** ♿ 10km ℘ 3km ♨ 7km 🏛 7km ⛵ 7km   **Notes** No pets English spoken

CLEMONT

▦ |◎| **Chambre d'hôtes**

Roland et M-José DAUDE

Domaine des Givrys, 18410 CLEMONT

☎ 02 48 58 80 74   ▤ 02 48 58 80 74

email: givrys@wanadoo.fr

web: www.domainedesgivrys.com

Rooms for two people, with private facilities, in a charming farmhouse in the midst of forests and lakes. Living room/lounge with TV. Kennels for dogs and stables for three horses. Many tourist sites nearby, plus tennis, horse riding, golf, fishing and the wine trail.

Prices s fr €57; d fr €65; extra person fr €26; dinner fr €30   **On Site** ℘   **Nearby** ♿ 5km ♨ 10km ↖ 10km Restaurant 5km Water sports 10km ♨ 2km 🏛 4km ⛵ 34km   **Notes** No pets English spoken

Domaine de la Dijonnière

Jeanine et Claude AUCHER
18410 CLEMONT
☎ 02 48 58 65 50 📠 02 48 58 65 95
email: ladijonniere@orange.fr

This restored sheepfold, facing the owner's home, is on a hunting estate that enjoys a peaceful setting. It offers six double bedrooms, all with private bath or shower room and WC. Guests' lounge. Guests can explore the extensive grounds, with their woods, lakes and rivers. Kennels available.

Prices not confirmed for 2008 **On Site** 🏊 Private 🎣 **Nearby** ⛷ 7km Water sports 15km 🏊 7km 🏛 7km ♨ 25km **Notes** No pets English spoken Open March to January.

COUST

⫘ ⦿ La Madenrie

Henri et Madeleine VOLCOVICI
Le Haut de Changy, 18210 COUST
☎ 02 48 63 52 84 & 06 14 61 18 62
email: lamadenrie@tiscali.fr

Guests will be welcomed with a glass of wine at La Madenrie, a 19th-century farmhouse with en suite rooms sleeping 2-5 people. Lounge with TV, table tennis and lovely flower garden. Nearby sites: Château d'Ainlay le Vieil, Abbaye de Noirlac, Jardin du Prieuré d'Orsan and the Forest of Tronçais. Special rates for five people.

Prices s fr €40; d fr €52; t fr €70; extra person fr €20; dinner fr €25 **Nearby** ⛷ 4km 🥾 11km 🏊 2km Restaurant 9km Water sports 8km 🏊 2km Spa 11km ♨ 9km 🏛 11km ♨ 10km **Notes** Pets admitted English spoken Open April to 15 November.

CREZANCY-EN-SANCERRE

⫘ La Maison de Margot

Karine et Hubert CHARLON
Reigny, 18300 CREZANCY-EN-SANCERRE
☎ 02 48 79 05 43
email: contact@chambres-margot.com
web: http://chambres-margot.com

Set in the heart of the Sancerre vineyards, in a village famous for its wine production. Three double rooms and one room for two or four are available in this renovated barn, each with private shower room and WC; ground floor rooms available. Lounge area for guests, terrace with garden furniture. Private parking; walking and cycle routes. Restaurants 7km.

Prices d €48-€60; t €62-€72; extra person fr €12 **Nearby** 🏊 9km 🎣 9km Water sports 14km 🏊 9km 🏛 9km ♨ 20km **Notes** Pets admitted English spoken

ENNORDRES

⫘ ⦿ Les Châtelains

Marylène et Daniel GENEVIEVE
18380 ENNORDRES
☎ 02 48 58 40 37 & 06 07 29 67 98
email: contact@leschatelains.com
web: www.leschatelains.com

This 19th-century property, built in a style typical of the area, offers two suites, each with a double and a twin-bedded room, a private terrace and a lounge area. There are also two further double-bedded rooms, and a triple. All rooms have private bath or shower room and WC. There is a large guests' lounge/dining room in a separate building. Certain pets accepted by prior arrangement.

Prices d €75-€105; t €95-€125; extra person fr €20; dinner fr €28 **On Site** 🏊 Private 🎣 **Nearby** ⛷ 10km Restaurant 3.5km Water sports 20km 🏊 6km ♨ 12km 🏛 8km ♨ 25km **Notes** Pets admitted English spoken CC

FOECY

⫘ ⦿ Au Petit Prieuré

Pierre DALTON
7 rue de l'Eglise, 18500 FOECY
☎ 02 48 51 01 76
email: info@philosophes.com
web: www.philosophes.com

In the heart of Berry, this small priory, built in 1760, is now a musician's house, and has an enchanting atmosphere and gardens, with the possibility of musical performances. There are three double bedrooms, all with shower and wc; one has a private sitting room and another has access to a living room and kitchen area. Parking. Courses in watercolour painting and music.

Prices s €57-€67; d €59-€69; extra person €16-€21; dinner €35 **On Site** Private tennis court **Nearby** ⛷ 2km 🎣 0.5km 🏊 6km Restaurant 4km Water sports 25km 🏛 0.2km ♨ 0.2km **Notes** No pets English spoken Open 4 February to 22 December.

GRON

▦ ❦ Les Chapelles

Stéphanie MEFFERT
18800 GRON
☎ 02 48 68 51 49   📄 02 48 68 51 13
email: spmeffert@wanadoo.fr
web: www.chambredhote-leschapelles.eu

Between Sancerre and Bourges, three en suite double rooms with independent access adjoining the main house. Wooded and flower-filled grounds with garden furniture, guests' living room/lounge with TV and parking available. Lavish breakfasts served. Restaurant 5kms.

Prices s fr €35; d fr €47; extra person fr €12   **On Site** ℘
Nearby ⚲ 13km Restaurant 5km ⊰ 4km ⌂ 0.4km ⋙ 13km
Notes Pets admitted English spoken

HENRICHEMONT

▦ ❦ Le Lac aux Fées

J-Claude et M-Odile MORIN
18250 HENRICHEMONT
☎ 02 48 26 71 23
email: morin.earl@worldonline.fr
web: www.lelacauxfees.chez.tiscali.fr

This charming restored farmhouse - The Lake of the Fairies - has guest rooms with independent access in an extension to the main house. One room for three and one for two to four, a double and triple, all with private facilities and TV, plus a small sitting room and kitchen, and lounge area for guests. Wooded grounds, terrace, garden furniture. Restaurants close by. Reduction in tariff over four days.

Prices not confirmed for 2008   **On Site** ℘   **Nearby** ⚲ 10km ⚲ 12km ⊰ ⋙ 30km   **Notes** No pets English spoken CC

HERRY

▦ Domaine des Butteaux

Jean-Christophe GRAILLOT
18140 HERRY
☎ 06 87 04 73 68 & 02 48 79 56 11   📄 02 48 79 51 03
email: domainedesbutteaux@wanadoo.fr
web: www.domainedesbutteaux.com

At the gateway to two notable wine areas, your host, an artist and framemaker, has given guest rooms names of the perfumes they contain. A 19th-century family mansion on the banks of the Loire, it contains a double room and two rooms for three, each with shower, wc and independent access. Cots available. Living room/lounge for guests. Extensive wooded grounds with swimming pool. Garage, parking. Restaurants 2km.

Prices not confirmed for 2008   **On Site** Private ⚲   **Nearby** ⚲ 10km ℘ 1km ⊰ 2km ⌂ 5km ⋙ 15km   **Notes** No pets English spoken

JARS

▦ ❦ La Brissauderie

Madeleine JAY
18260 JARS
☎ 02 48 58 74 94   📄 02 48 58 74 94
email: madeleine.jay@wanadoo.fr
web: www.labrissauderie.com

Calm reigns at this mid-Sancerrois house, set in 10 hectares of woods. The comfortable rooms have painted furniture and murals and include a double room ('The Tulips') and two two-roomed suites ('The Bees' and 'The Sunflowers') for three to six people, all with private facilities. Day room, lounge with TV for guests, parking. Substantial breakfast with fresh goats' cheese from Chavignol. Restaurant 4km.

Prices not confirmed for 2008   **Nearby** ⚲ 10km ℘ 4km ⚲ 12km Water sports 4km ⊰ 2km ⌂ 4km ⋙ 22km   **Notes** No pets Open 15 February to 15 December.

LAZENAY

▦ ⌾ La Maison Bleue

Jacky LANGELEZ
7 Les Cocuas, 18120 LAZENAY
☎ 02 48 26 38 42 & 06 85 42 56 80

Two double rooms and a triple, each with shower or bath and WC, as well as a living room with open fire and TV, are at your disposition at this renovated 19th-century farmhouse. This is an ideal place to relax, in the garden or swimming pool. Homely and flavoursome cooking. Enclosed parking.

Prices d €59-€80; t fr €100; dinner fr €20   **On Site** Private ⚲ **Nearby** ⚲ 10km ⚲ 15km ℘ 2km Restaurant 5km Water sports 24km ⊰ 5km ⌂ 6km ⋙ 15km   **Notes** No pets English spoken

LE CHATELET

▦ ⌾ Estiveaux

Odette de FAVERGES
18170 LE CHATELET
☎ 02 48 56 22 64
email: odefaverges@yahoo.fr

In the heart of Berry, south of the Route Jacques Coeur, this striking house is in the middle of a large shady park with a lake for fishing, and offers peace, comfort and a warm welcome. It has three double rooms with canopy beds, shower and wc, a dining room with wood fire, books, games and fitness room and living rooms. Parking. Meals by prior arrangement.

Prices s fr €75; d €87-€97; dinner €25-€31   **On Site** ℘ **Nearby** ⚲ 36km ⚲ 30km ⚲ 25km Restaurant 2km Water sports 19km ⊰ 2km Spa 30km ⌂ 2km ⋙ 25km   **Notes** No pets Open 2 January to 30 December.

LIGNIERES

⊞ ⏍ **L'Ange Blanc**

Odile et Alain OLAIZOLA
18160 LIGNIERES
☎ 06 14 64 76 47 & 02 48 60 27 70
web: http://langeblanc.lignieres.free.fr

A barn conversion combining wood, stone and steel located near the town centre. There are three rooms - two doubles and family room for up to four, all upstairs and all with private bath or shower room. Cots available, and extensive grounds with terraces and a swimming pool. Horse paddocks available.

Prices d €45-€52; dinner fr €20 **On Site** ✧ Private ⇗
Nearby ⛄ 8km ⚓ 1.5km Restaurant 0.8km ⬙ 0.2km ⌂ 0.8km ⛶ 17km
Notes No pets

LUNERY

⊞ *La Vergne*

Francis et M-Hélène JACQUIER
18400 LUNERY
☎ 02 48 68 01 07
email: la-vergne@wanadoo.fr
web: www.alavergne.com

A 17th-century family home, overlooking the Valley of Cher, offering comfort, quiet and charm in five guest rooms housed in the old outbuildings. Each accommodates two to four guests, all with private shower and TV. Library, living/dining room for guests. Terrace, garden, outdoor furniture. Restaurant nearby.

Prices not confirmed for 2008 **Nearby** ⛄ 10km ⚓ 10km ⇗ 25km
Water sports 10km ⬙ 2km ⌂ 2km ⛶ 25km **Notes** Pets admitted
English spoken

MARCAIS

⊞ ⏍ **Le Moulin du Pont**

B REGNAULT DE LA MOTHE
18170 MARCAIS
☎ 02 48 96 44 43 & 06 15 05 43 06
email: bertrand.regnault546@orange.fr

A 19th-century house on the site of an old watermill, in beautiful grounds with lawns and flowers. There is a twin-bedded room, a double, and a family suite for four, all with private shower room and WC. A quiet and peaceful place, with a very friendly welcome. Meals by reservation.

Prices s fr €47; d fr €52; dinner fr €20 **On Site** ⚓ **Nearby** ⛄ 7km
⚐ 20km ⇗ 15km Restaurant 10km ⬙ 1km ⌂ 6km ⛶ 15km
Notes No pets English spoken Open March to December.

MARSEILLES-LES-AUBIGNY

⊞ ⏍ **Chambre d'hôtes/Croisières**

Carlo CIACCHELLA
Bateau Alphonsia Maria, Rue du Port - BP5,
18320 MARSEILLES-LES-AUBIGNY
☎ 02 48 76 14 41 & 06 21 38 01 60
email: alphonsia@tele2.fr
web: www.peniche-alphonsia.com

Why not be tempted by something a little different, and book a stay aboard this 33-metre, renovated Dutch barge? It offers two double cabins, each with shower room and WC. The 80 square metre bridge makes a wonderful terrace for breakfasts and dinners; there's even a small swimming pool.

Prices s €68; d €78; dinner fr €30 **On Site** ⚓ Restaurant Water sports
Private ⇗ **Nearby** ⛄ 6km ⬙ ⛶ 12km **Notes** No pets English spoken

⊞ **Château Vert**

Marie-Christine de CHAMPS
18320 MARSEILLES-LES-AUBIGNY
☎ 02 48 76 04 91 🖷 02 48 76 09 60
email: marie-christine.dechamps@voila.fr
web: www.chambredhote-chateauvert.com

This 19th-century château sits in its vast estate of woods and fields, where the owners raise cattle and breed horses. There is independent access to a first-floor double room, and a three-person suite of two rooms; both have en suite shower and WC. The spacious accommodation is tastefully furnished and features fine porcelain painted by your hostess. Horses welcome.

Prices s €47-€50; d €52-€55; extra person €22-€25 **Nearby** ⛄ 7km
⚓ 1km ⇗ 11km Restaurant 2km Water sports 20km ⬙ 1km ✧ 12km
⌂ 1km ⛶ 11km **Notes** No pets English spoken

MEHUN-SUR-YEVRE

⅏ 🍽 Les Aubuees

Françoise DENIS

51, route de Montcorneau, 18500 MEHUN-SUR-YEVRE

☎ 02 48 57 08 24

email: les.aubuees@wanadoo.fr

web: www.lesaubuees.free.fr

A 19th-century manor house in nearly three hectares of enclosed grounds, with a swimming pool. Three rooms are all on the ground floor: two triples, one with a terrace, and a twin-bedded room. All have private bathroom and WC. Cot and high chair available; terrace with garden furniture. Mountain bikes; meals by arrangement. Closed Christmas and New Year.

Prices s fr €68; d fr €78; t fr €98; extra person fr €20; dinner €20-€35 **On Site** ❧ Private ➤ **Nearby** ☞ 15km ⚓ 10km ⚑ 0.5km Restaurant 1.5km ≋ 1.5km 🏠 1km 🚉 1.5km **Notes** Pets admitted

⅏ *Les Buissons*

Jeanne COMPAGNIE-GUIDOT

107, Av Jean Chatelet, 18500 MEHUN-SUR-YEVRE

☎ 02 48 57 31 22

email: les-buissons-gite-mehun@wanadoo.fr

Set above the Valley of the Yèvre, this accommodation is comfortable and decorated in the style of the Berry region. Two double rooms and a triple with shower and wc and separate access in outbuildings of a 19th-century farm. Living/dining room for guests, reading room and TV. Porcelain and art displays, garden with furniture and parking. Forest and vineyards nearby. Cot available. Restaurants in town.

Prices not confirmed for 2008 **On Site** ⚑ **Nearby** ☞ 4km ➤ Water sports 6km ≋ **Notes** No pets English spoken Open 15 March to 15 November.

MENETREOL-SUR-SAULDRE

⅏ 🍽 *Manoir de Bellevue*

Monique et Jean-Pierre TRIPAUL

Route de Souesmes, 18700 MENETREOL SUR SAULDRE

☎ 02 48 58 29 65

email: contact@manoirdebellevue.com

web: www.manoirdebellevue.com

This is a beautiful place from which to explore la Sologne: a 19th-century manor house in four hectares of enclosed wooded grounds, with a heated swimming pool. There are five rooms, all upstairs: four doubles, and one with twin beds. Guests are welcome to explore the manor house, which is situated between Aubigny and Salbris.

Prices not confirmed for 2008 **On Site** Private ➤ **Nearby** ☞ 20km ⚑ 0.2km ≋ 0.3km 🏠 9km 🚉 20km **Notes** Pets admitted English spoken

MONTIGNY

⅏ ❧ 🍽 Domaine de la Reculée

Elisabeth GRESSIN

18250 MONTIGNY

☎ 02 48 69 59 18 🖨 02 48 69 52 51

email: e.gressin@wanadoo.fr

web: www.domainedelareculee.fr

Five double guest rooms with separate access on a farm, all with private facilities. Dine and relax in the living room with its open fire, TV and antique furniture, opening on to the garden where on fine days the proprietor serves breakfast. Meals except Sundays; restaurant nearby. 10% reduction for over three nights.

Prices s fr €48; d fr €56; extra person fr €22; dinner fr €24 **On Site** Private ➤ **Nearby** ⚑ 10km ≋ 10km **Notes** Pets admitted English spoken Open April to 15 November.

MONTLOUIS

⅏ ❧ 🍽 *Domaine de Bourdoiseau*

Isabelle HUE-RIBAUDEAU

18160 MONTLOUIS

☎ 02 48 60 06 44 🖨 02 48 60 06 44

email: bourdoiseau@wanadoo.fr

This beautiful 16th-century house is on a cereal and cattle breeding farm. There are three bedrooms - a ground floor double, and two first-floor rooms sleeping from two to four people; all have private shower and WC. Large dining room with lounge area, and a separate small lounge with TV. Garden furniture, outdoor games. Meals available by arrangement.

Prices not confirmed for 2008 **On Site** ⚑ **Nearby** ☞ 7km ➤ 20km Water sports 12km ≋ 7km 🏠 7km 🚉 20km **Notes** Pets admitted English spoken

⅏ 🍽 Les Varennes

Anne et Michel LUMET

Domaine des Varennes, 18160 MONTLOUIS

☎ 02 48 60 11 86 🖨 02 48 60 45 92

email: lumet.varennes@wanadoo.fr

web: www.domaine-de-varennes.com

This 18th-century manor house is set in mature woodland and has 5 comfortable rooms available for guests. Three double rooms with bath and WC, 2 rooms for 4 people (1 double and 2 single beds) with bath, shower and WC. Sheltered terrace, landscaped gardens, French billiards, table football, large heated pool. Possibility of ordering filled picnic basket. Tables d'hotes available on reservation.

Prices d €70-€100; extra person fr €20; dinner fr €25 **On Site** ⚓ Private ➤ **Nearby** ☞ 5km ⚑ 5km Restaurant 5km Water sports 12km ≋ 7km Spa 45km 🏠 7km 🚉 5km **Notes** No pets English spoken Open April to December.

NANCAY

▦ ⦿ **Les Crocus**

Arlette GUERU

7 rue du Grand Meaulnes, 18330 NANCAY

☎ 02 48 51 88 28

email: lescrocus@cario.fr

web: www.lescrocus.com

Arlette is an artist who loves to share her enthusiasm for music, philosophy and gastronomy. Five rooms are available including family suites and two with independent access; all have en suite shower and WC. Dining room, living room, library and art gallery are at guests' disposal, as well as flower-filled gardens where exotic meals can be served.

Prices s fr €55; d fr €55; extra person fr €15; dinner fr €25
On Site Private ⤻ **Nearby** ⛷ 10km ⚓ 3km ⚐ 3km Restaurant 0.3km Water sports 14km ◔ 0.8km 🏛 0.2km ⋈ 15km **Notes** Pets admitted

NEUVY-LE-BARROIS

▦ *Les Grandes Molles*

B et G DEPREZ-PERRIN

18600 NEUVY-LE-BARROIS

☎ 02 48 80 07 65 & 06 07 04 15 55 📄 02 48 76 21 14

email: brigitte-perrin@wanadoo.fr

web: www.labouinaude.com

A Berry house offering a relaxing stay in the countryside. It has two double rooms and one triple room, all with WC, bath or shower, and independent access. Shared lounge, terrace, park with trees and ponds. Restaurants nearby. Also nearby: Bec d'Allier with its bird reserve, Aprement with flower-filled park, Tronçais forest. 17km from the Nevers-Magny-Cours racing circuit.

Prices not confirmed for 2008 **On Site** Private ⤻ **Nearby** ⛷ 3km ⚐ 4km Water sports 30km ◔ 6km 🏛 1km ⋈ 15km **Notes** No pets English spoken

ORVAL

▦ ⦿ **La Trolière**

Marie-Claude DUSSERT

18200 ORVAL

☎ 02 48 96 47 45

Four double rooms, all with bath or shower and WC, in a home of character with a shady park close to a river and forest. Two rooms are air conditioned. Living room and lounge for guests, parking. The hostess will serve meals based on seasonal produce, by prior arrangement. Parking.

Prices s fr €43-€63; d fr €48-€68; t fr €59; extra person fr €11; dinner fr €22 **On Site** ⚐ **Nearby** ⛷ 6km ⚓ 25km ⤻ 3km Restaurant 3km Water sports 15km ◔ 2km Spa 50km ⋈ 3km **Notes** No pets English spoken

PARASSY

▦ ⦿ *La Montagne*

J DAGALLIER et I AUZOLLE

18220 PARASSY

☎ 02 48 64 23 25 & 06 71 89 34 93

email: isabelle@archicool.net

web: www.lamontagnedeparassy.com

On the edge of the forest and surrounded by vines, this property has three double rooms, either on the first floor of the hosts' house, or in a separate building. Each room has a private bathroom or power shower and WC, plus separate access. Lounge with books; outside lawned area for guests.

Prices not confirmed for 2008 **Nearby** ⛷ 12km ⚐ 1.2km ⤻ 4km ◔ 2km 🏛 4km ⋈ 25km **Notes** Pets admitted

PLAIMPIED-GIVAUDINS

▦ ⦿ **Les Glycines**

Régis et Martine VANDAMME

1 rue de l'Abbaye, 18340 PLAIMPIED-GIVAUDINS

☎ 02 48 25 64 28

email: glycines.plaimpied@wanadoo.fr

web: http://monsite.wanadoo.fr/lesglycinesplaimpied

Rooms on the first floor of a large 19th-century building opposite the 12th-century Roman abbot's house in a quiet little village. Expect a warm welcome and choose between a room for four, one for three, and a double, all with shower and wc. Living room/lounge for guests, parking, closed courtyard, garden furniture. Restaurant, Bourges cathedral, nuits lumière and the châteaux on the Jacques Coeur trail are all nearby.

Prices d €34-€38; extra person fr €13; dinner fr €15 **On Site** ⚐ **Nearby** ⛷ 10km ⚓ 8km ⤻ 10km Restaurant 0.3km Water sports 10km ◔ ⋈ 10km **Notes** No pets English spoken

RIANS

▦ ✿ ⦿ **La Chaume**

Yves et Odile PROFFIT

18220 RIANS

☎ 02 48 64 41 58 📄 02 48 64 29 71

email: contact@domaine-la-chaume.com

web: www.domaine-la-chaume.com

On the way to the Sancerrois, in a quiet spot, a warm welcome awaits guests. There are two double rooms, two for three and a room for four, all with separate access and facilities. Cot available. Guests' living room/lounge with TV, kitchen available. Meals by prior arrangement, except Sunday.

Prices s fr €40; d fr €50; extra person fr €21; dinner fr €20 **On Site** ⚘ **Nearby** ⛷ 25km ⚓ 30km ⚐ 5km ⤻ 4km Restaurant 4km Water sports 20km ◔ 4km 🏛 4km ⋈ 20km **Notes** Pets admitted English spoken

RIANS   *CONTINUED*

▦ *Le Gué*

Sandra et Etienne LOISEAU

18220 RIANS

☎ 02 48 64 21 21 & 06 88 30 12 87

email: loiseau.etienne@wanadoo.fr

Quietly situated between Bourges and Sancerre, next to a river and just 7km from the vineyards at Menetou. There are three bedrooms, one double and two twin rooms, all with private shower room and WC, plus a private terrace. Wi-fi access, microwave and a cot are all available to guests. 10% reduction over 3 nights.

Prices not confirmed for 2008 **On Site** ℰ **Nearby** ⛷ 8km ⚲ 2.5km ⚓ 1km ⚑ 2.5km ⚒ 2.5km **Notes** No pets English spoken

SANCERRE

▦ **Les Logis du Grillon**

Pascal et Nadia CHARPENTIER

3-5 rue du Chantre, 18300 SANCERRE

☎ 06 14 42 16 33

email: reservation@chambres-hotes-sancerre.com

web: www.chambres-hotes-sancerre.com

Enjoy peace and quiet in this large restored house dating from the 15th and 16th centuries, right in the historic city. The beautiful rooms sleep either two to three, or four to six people. Lavish breakfasts. Wine-sampling, gastronomy, hiking and more.

Prices d fr €70; extra person fr €30 **Nearby** ⛷ 5km ⚲ 2km ℰ 2km ⚓ 2km Water sports 2km ⚑ 2km ⚕ 2km ⚒ 11km **Notes** No pets English spoken

SIDIAILLES

▦ **Chezelles**

Jocelyne et Jacques DEFORGE

18270 SIDIAILLES

☎ 02 48 56 78 73 ▤ 02 48 56 78 73

email: jdeforge@orange.fr

web: www.logisdechezelles.com

A converted stable block in wooded grounds, at the point where the Auvergne meets the Limousin. There are four big bedrooms, two doubles and two triples, all with private bath or shower room and WC.

A cot is available. There is a ground-floor lounge, and upstairs is a large day room with books and games. Generous breakfasts. Garden furniture, boules pitch.

Prices s fr €35; d fr €40; t fr €55; extra person fr €15 **On Site** ℰ **Nearby** ⛷ 18km ⚲ 25km ⚓ 29km ⚑ 5km Spa 40km ⚕ 5km ⚒ 25km **Notes** No pets

▦ ❏❘ *La Fosse-Ronde*

G GARIH et U CARLI

18270 SIDIAILLES

☎ 02 48 56 61 25 ▤ 02 48 56 61 25

email: carligarih@wanadoo.fr

On the Route Jacques Coeur, between the Roman Oppidum of Chateaumeillant and the medieval town of Culan with its restaurants and castle forts. Three double rooms in a renovated house, each with bath and shower. Living room/lounge, TV, open fires, large grassed grounds, terrace, outdoor furniture, farm animals, parking. Animals welcome in kennels. Meals if booked.

Prices not confirmed for 2008 **Nearby** ⛷ 7km ℰ 5km ⚓ 28km Water sports 5km ⚑ 2.5km ⚕ 2.5km ⚒ 28km **Notes** Pets admitted English spoken

ST-BAUDEL

▦ ❧ *Parassay*

C CARTERON et F DUCLUZEAUD

18160 ST-BAUDEL

☎ 02 48 60 14 18 & 06 21 12 58 31

email: christophe-carteron164@orange.fr

Guests will find comfort, quiet and hospitality here, in an old building on an isolated farm. There are four double rooms with shower/wc, grounds with pond, furniture and children's games. Lounge/dining room with TV and open fire. Several châteaux, restaurants and leisure area nearby. 7th night free.

Prices not confirmed for 2008 **On Site** ℰ **Nearby** ⛷ 10km ⚓ 24km Water sports 7km ⚑ 7km ⚕ 2km ⚒ 9km **Notes** No pets English spoken

ST-ELOY-DE-GY

▦ *La Grande Mouline*

Jean et Chantal MALOT

Bourgneuf, 18110 ST-ELOY-DE-GY

☎ 02 48 25 40 44 ▤ 02 48 25 40 44

email: jean-m4@wanadoo.fr

Very old house with a genuine welcome in the quiet of the countryside. Enjoy a summer stroll in the forest and the warmth of an open fire in winter. The rooms are in a main house and large outbuilding; there are three rooms for four guests, each with mezzanine and small lounge, a triple and an apartment for three plus two, all with private facilities. Sitting room/library, dining room, games, TV, terrace and garden furniture.

Prices not confirmed for 2008 **Nearby** ⛷ 11km ℰ 1km ⚓ 11km Water sports 13km ⚑ 11km **Notes** No pets English spoken

ST-GEORGES-SUR-LA-PREE

⫸ Chambre d'hôtes

Jacqueline et Daniel LEFEVRE
10, chemin des Menoux,
18100 ST-GEORGES-SUR-LA-PREE
☎ 02 48 52 00 51 & 06 32 03 89 47

A renovated 17th-century farmhouse on the way to the Sologne, with three double rooms with private facilities. There is a dining/living room with open fire and extensive grounds with furniture, parking, courtyard, and terrace.

Prices s fr €35; d fr €40; t fr €50; extra person fr €10   **Nearby** ⚑ 15km ⚓ 15km ♪ 3km ⚘ 15km ♨ 1.5km 🏛 15km ⚕ 15km   **Notes** No pets

ST-GERMAIN-DU-PUY

⫸ ❦ Jacquelin

Irène et Jean-Paul JOLLY
18390 ST-GERMAIN-DU-PUY
☎ 02 48 30 84 97
email: chambresjolly@wanadoo.fr
web: http://monsite.wanadoo.fr/jollychambres

At the gateway to Bourges, guests can enjoy the peace of the country in this beautiful farmhouse and its rural setting. Five double rooms with private facilities and access, TVs and lounge areas in a 15th-century main house and outbuildings. Kitchen, wooded park and garden furniture. Wi-fi access.

Prices s €50-€60; d €60-€70; extra person fr €20   **Nearby** ⚑ 7km ♪ 3km ⚓ 7km ⚘ 1km Restaurant 1km Water sports 7km ♨ 1km Spa 7km 🏛 1km ⚕ 7km   **Notes** Pets admitted English spoken CC

ST-SATUR

⫸ Chambre d'hôtes

N et J AUDIBERT-AMAGAT
La Chancelière, 5 rue Amagat, 18300 ST-SATUR
☎ 02 48 54 01 67
email: jaudibert@wanadoo.fr
web: www.la-chanceliere.com

At the foot of Sancerre, this 18th-century chancellory was the residence of the administrator of the adjacent abbey. The luxurious en suite rooms (all upstairs) comprise three doubles and a suite for three. Television and video available. South facing terrace with magnificent view over the vineyards and hills of Sancerre. Continental breakfast served on the terrace or in the dining room. Private, secure parking.

Prices not confirmed for 2008   **Nearby** ⚑ 10km ♪ 2km ⚓ 2km Water sports 2km ♨ 2km ⚕ 10km   **Notes** No pets English spoken CC

SURY-EN-VAUX

⫸ ◉ *Tréprot*

Patricia LAMACQ
18300 SURY-EN-VAUX
☎ 02 48 79 35 38 & 06 07 87 35 36
email: patricia.lamacq897@orange.fr

A comfortable old farmhouse standing among the vineyards seven kilometres from Sancerre. There are four bedrooms, for three or four people, all with bathroom or shower/WC. Three are upstairs in the main house; the fourth is on the ground floor of a separate building. Attractive wooded grounds. Meals by arrangement; home-made pastries for breakfast.

Prices not confirmed for 2008   **Nearby** ⚑ 7km ♪ 1.5km ⚓ 7km Water sports 7km ♨ 7km 🏛 2km ⚕ 12km   **Notes** Pets admitted English spoken

THENIOUX

⫸ Le Petit-Nançay

J et M BARDIOT-JOBLEAU
5 route de Genouilly, 18100 THENIOUX
☎ 02 48 52 01 58   🖶 02 48 52 01 58
email: bardiot-jobleau@orange.fr
web: www.le-petit-nancay.com

Five rooms for two to five people in 15th-century farm buildings, each with separate access and shower and wc. Communal living room, two sitting rooms, library and cooking area at guests' disposal. Indoor and outdoor kitchen with barbecue, swimming pool. Restaurant nearby.

Prices s fr €40; d fr €45; t fr €60; extra person fr €15   **On Site** ♪ Private ⚓   **Nearby** ⚑ 7km ♪ 10km Restaurant 0.5km Water sports 2km ♨ 0.5km 🏛 1.5km ⚕ 9km   **Notes** No pets English spoken

VIGNOUX-SOUS-LES-AIX

⫸ ◉ *La Petite Noué*

J-François et Danielle GILBERT
18110 VIGNOUX-SOUS-LES-AIX
☎ 02 48 64 56 55
email: jfgilbert1@hotmail.com
web: http://perso.orange.fr/lapetitenoue

Guests can expect a hospitable and comfortable stay at this beautiful restored 19th-century farmhouse, near the châteaux on the Route Jacques Coeur. There are rooms for two or three people, each with shower and wc, a living room/lounge with open fire and TV and large wooded grounds with ornamental lake and terrace with garden furniture.

Prices not confirmed for 2008   **Nearby** ⚑ 12km ♪ 3km ⚓ 12km Water sports 12km ♨ 12km 🏛 1km ⚕ 12km   **Notes** Pets admitted

VIGNOUX-SUR-BARANGEON

⫴ Villemenard

Jacques GREAU
18500 VIGNOUX-SUR-BARANGEON
☎ 02 48 51 53 40 ▤ 02 48 51 58 77
web: www.villemenard.com

A charming property in a peaceful setting at the gateway to the
Sologne. The large 19th-century bourgeois house is built on an
ancient site and offers six rooms (three doubles, two for three guests
and one for four). Dining room, wooded park, river, ponds (fishing
and boating), garden furniture. Many restaurants nearby.

Prices s fr €50; d fr €55; extra person fr €16 **On Site** ⟋ Spa Private ⤚
Nearby ⛷ 2km ♨ 10km Restaurant 4km Water sports 25km ⌕ 5km
⊞ 8km ✈ 10km **Notes** No pets English spoken

VOUZERON

⫴ *La Petite Ferme*

Catherine et Pascal COUQUET
3, route du Feuillage, 18330 VOUZERON
☎ 06 74 23 09 33
email: la-petite-ferme-du-feuillage@wanadoo.fr
web: http://la-petite-ferme-monsite-wanadoo.fr

This 18th-century house has extensive grounds with woods, lake,
and an enclosed park area with trees, flowers, swimming pool and
children's games. There are two ground floor rooms and one upstairs,
all for up to three people and all with private bath or shower room
and WC. Large lounge for guests' use, with books and piano.

Prices not confirmed for 2008 **On Site** ⟋ Private ⤚ **Nearby** ⛷ 0.1km
⌕ 3km ⊞ 3km ✈ 9km **Notes** Pets admitted English spoken

EURE-ET-LOIR

BAILLEAU-L'EVEQUE

⫴ ⦿ *Levesville*

Bruno et Nathalie VASSEUR
Av du Château, 28300 BAILLEAU-L'EVEQUE
☎ 02 37 22 97 02 ▤ 02 37 22 97 02

Large farmhouse situated in a peaceful area. There are two adjoining
twin rooms and two double rooms with space for an extra bed, all
with private facilities and non-smoking. Guests' living room, garage
and garden.

Prices not confirmed for 2008 **Nearby** ⛷ 5km ⟋ 3km ⤚ 8km
Restaurant 2km ⌕ 8km ⊞ 3km ✈ 10km **Notes** No pets English
spoken

BLEURY

⫴ Bonville

Sandrine et Bruno ROY
17 Rue du Four à Chaux, 28700 BLEURY
☎ 02 37 31 82 94
email: roybruno9@yahoo.fr
web: www.gitedebleury.com

Between Paris and Chartres, in its own wooded grounds, this house
has three guest rooms, each decorated to a theme. There are two
double rooms, and a large family suite, all with private bath or shower
room and WC.

Prices s fr €49; d fr €63; extra person fr €21 **On Site** ⟋ ⌁
Nearby ⛷ 5km ⤚ 10km Restaurant 3km ⌕ 10km ⊞ 3km ✈ 10km
Notes Pets admitted

COURBEHAYE

⫴ ⦙ Moronville

Florence et Yves HURBAULT
2 Moronville, 28140 COURBEHAYE
☎ 02 37 99 70 03 ▤ 02 37 99 83 39
email: hurbault.yves@wanadoo.fr
web: www.gitedemoronville.com.fr

This fortified farmhouse has two second floor bedrooms, with their
own entrance via the 16th-century square tower. There is a twin-
bedded room, with a possible linked single room; also a double room
Cot available, small kitchenette. Downstairs is a two-roomed family
suite for up to five. All rooms have private bath or shower room and
WC. Garden.

Prices s fr €38; d fr €48; extra person fr €20 **On Site** ⌁
Nearby ⛷ 25km ⟋ 5km ⤚ 5km Restaurant 10km ⌕ 9km ⊞ 5km
✈ 15km **Notes** No pets English spoken

COURVILLE-SUR-EURE

⫴ ⦿ ♿ Domaine du Tronchay

Ezilda et Jean-Louis LAPLASSE
28190 COURVILLE-SUR-EURE
☎ 06 27 74 27 32 & 02 37 33 37 46
email: lejardindesgourmandise@wanadoo.fr
web: www.domainedutronchay.fr

Between Chartres and Nogent-le-Rotrou, a beautiful farm bursting
with flowers. On the ground floor is a spacious suite with a double

bedroom and a lounge with open fire. Upstairs is another double room, and a two-room family suite. All the rooms have private shower and WC. Generous breakfasts include cold meats, pastries and home-made jam.

Prices s fr €70; d fr €90; dinner fr €15   **Nearby** ⚓ 3km ⛷ 18km ⬝ 1km ⟋ 1km Restaurant 1km ⯊ 1km ☆ 20km ⬚ 0.3km ⋙ 0.4km
Notes No pets   English spoken

DANGEAU

⬝⬝⬝ La Chesnaye

Monique AYMARD

2 La Chesnaye, 28160 DANGEAU

☎ 02 37 96 72 09   ▤ 02 37 96 72 09

email: aymardmonique@aol.com

web: http://lachesnayedangeau.free.fr

This restored farmhouse with its attractively laid-out gardens makes an ideal location for a stopover or a longer stay. Peace and quiet guaranteed. There are three spacious rooms with TVs, two are family suites, one of which has a split-level layout. All rooms have private facilities, and there is a kitchenette available. Garden with children's games and reclining chairs.

Prices s fr €40; d fr €50-€60; extra person €15-€20   **On Site** ☆
Nearby ⚓ 8km ⟋ 2km ⬝ 8km Restaurant 2km ⯊ 2km ⬚ 2km
⋙ 8km   **Notes** Pets admitted   English spoken

GOMMERVILLE

⬝⬝⬝ *Arnouville*

Claire et Pascal GARROS

28310 GOMMERVILLE

☎ 02 37 99 53 49 & 06 08 41 41 00

email: bassecour@wanadoo.fr

web: www.bassecour.fr

This working farm has three family suites in a building separate from the owners' home. Each suite sleeps up to four people, and is decorated according to a theme. One has a split-level layout, and another includes a kitchenette. Baby equipment is available, also mountain bikes. Artists occasionally in residence.

Prices not confirmed for 2008   **On Site** ☆   **Nearby** ⚓ 15km ⬝ 5km Restaurant 5km ⯊ 5km ⬚ 5km ⋙ 4km   **Notes** No pets

LA LOUPE

⬝⬝⬝ *La Muloterie*

M. et Mme FERRE

28240 LA LOUPE

☎ 02 37 81 03 66

email: christiane.ferre@wanadoo.fr

A very restful environment with three well equipped rooms in an old farm. There are two double rooms on the ground floor, and on the first floor a room with a double bed and a large single. Each room has a private shower and toilet.

Prices not confirmed for 2008   **Nearby** ⚓ 3km ⟋ 1km ⬝ 1km Restaurant 1km ⯊ 1km ☆ 1km ⬚ 1km ⋙ 1km   **Notes** No pets

MIERMAIGNE

⬝⬝⬝ Les Bois

Marie-Christine HAMEON

28420 MIERMAIGNE

☎ 06 15 37 73 16

An interesting house on the edge of the woods in the middle of the Parc Natural Regional du Perch. There is a restful lounge with library and fireplace. The three, tastefully furnished, well equipped, double rooms each have a shower room and toilet.

Prices s €39-€44; d €47-€52; t fr €64; extra person fr €14
Nearby ⚓ 15km ⛷ 6km ⟋ 3km ⬝ 7km Restaurant 5km ⯊ 3km
☆ 12km ⬚ 7km ⋙ 12km   **Notes** No pets   English spoken   Open March to October.

MONTIGNY-SUR-AVRE

⬝⬝⬝ 🐓 Ferme équestre de Montigny

Aude de la BOURDONNAYE

250 Route du Petit Sault, 28270 MONTIGNY-SUR-AVRE

☎ 06 88 04 71 78   ▤ 02 37 48 26 67

email: fermemontigny@club-internet.fr

web: www.montignysuravre.com

Three ground-floor rooms in the main house of this busy equestrian farm; all have their own bathrooms and WCs. The farm is ideally situated to discover Normandy and the Perche nature park. Horse and pony rides throughout the valley and forest. Baby cot and equipment by request. Lawns with garden furniture and BBQ. Reductions for three nights or more.

Prices s fr €30; d fr €40   **On Site** ⚓   **Nearby** ⟋ 1km ⬝ 8km Restaurant 8km ⯊ 8km ☆ 1km ⬚ 8km ⋙ 8km   **Notes** No pets   English spoken

NOGENT-LE-PHAYE

⬝⬝⬝ Chambre d'hôtes

André LEBOUCQ

1 Rue de la Boissière, 28630 NOGENT-LE-PHAYE

☎ 06 09 39 54 60

This contemporary house, nestled in a peaceful grassy enclosure full of flowers close to Chartres, has five guest rooms: two twins and three

CONTINUED

NOGENT-LE-PHAYE CONTINUED

doubles, one with extra single and all with TV and private facilities. Dining room and living room available to guests.

Prices s fr €49; d €59-€64; t fr €89　**Nearby** ⚓3km ⚓14km ⚑7km ⚓7km　Restaurant 0.8km ⚘ ⚒8km　**Notes** No pets

---

OINVILLE-SOUS-AUNEAU

⋕⋕⋕ **Chambre d'hôtes**

Caroline LETHUILLIER

2 rue des Prunus, Cherville,

28700 OINVILLE-SOUS-AUNEAU

☎ 02 37 31 72 80 & 06 22 05 91 02　📠 02 37 31 38 56

email: info@cherville.com

web: www.cherville.com

Breakfast is served in the welcoming ambience of a converted barn at this 19th-century farm on 'the wheat route'. Four rooms, each thematically decorated and with en suite bath or shower and WC, are a mix of doubles, twins and triples; two of the rooms are interconnected. One room on the ground floor has independent access. Kitchenette.

Prices s €47-€53; d €56-€60; t €69-€73; extra person fr €14　**Nearby** ⚓5km ⚓20km ⚑2km ⚓5km Restaurant 18km ⚘5km 🏠3km ⚒5km　**Notes** No pets English spoken

---

OINVILLE-ST-LIPHARD

⋕⋕⋕ 🍽 **Chambre d'hôtes**

Annette MAILLAUX

3 Rue du Moulin, 28310 OINVILLE-ST-LIPHARD

☎ 02 37 90 28 76

email: bnb28@orange.fr

web: http://bnb28.monsite.orange.fr

Between Paris and Orléans, this house offers non-smoking rooms with their own entrance, TV and private shower room: the 'yellow' room (double), 'blue' room (double with single) and 'green' room (two adjoining rooms, one double with single and a twin). Cot available. Grounds with trees and parking; restaurants nearby. Discounts for stays over three nights. Evening meals by reservation.

Prices s fr €40; d fr €50; t fr €70; extra person fr €20; dinner fr €25　**On Site** 🌳　**Nearby** ⚓4km Restaurant 4km ⚘4km 🏠4km ⚒4km　**Notes** No pets English spoken

---

SANCHEVILLE

⋕⋕⋕ 🍂 🍽 **Baigneaux**

Claire et J-Marc VANNEAU

10 Baigneaux, 28800 SANCHEVILLE

☎ 02 37 44 02 26　📠 02 37 44 02 26

email: VANNEAUJ@aol.com

web: www.baigneaux.com

This farmhouse has three guest rooms in the attic, reached by an outside staircase. Two of the rooms have double beds; the third has twin beds. All of the rooms have private bath or shower rooms and WCs. Guests' lounge available.

Prices not confirmed for 2008　**Nearby** ⚓15km ⚑3km ⚓12km Restaurant 3km ⚘1km 🏠3km ⚒12km　**Notes** No pets English spoken

---

ST-AUBIN-DES-BOIS

⋕⋕⋕ **Chazay**

Yveline et J-Marie GUINARD

38 Rue Jean Moulin, 28300 ST-AUBIN-DES-BOIS

☎ 02 37 32 80 53

email: jmguinard@aol.com

web: www.erablais.com

In the grounds of a 19th-century farm on the edge of the forest, this converted stable has three spacious non-smoking bedrooms, with their own separate access. All of the rooms - two doubles and a twin - have private bathrooms and WCs. Baby equipment is available, and there is a guests' lounge area and kitchen. Closed 23 December to January.

Prices s fr €35; d fr €47; extra person fr €12　**On Site** 🌳　**Nearby** ⚓15km ⚑6km Restaurant 3km ⚘2km 🏠3km ⚒5km　**Notes** No pets English spoken

---

ST-ELIPH

⋕⋕⋕ 🍂 **L'Auberdière**

Jean-Pierre BOUDET

28240 ST-ELIPH

☎ 02 37 81 10 46

Three double bedrooms (one with extra single) on a farm in the Perche region, each with shower and sharing a wc. Corner living room with TV, ideal for reading and reception with telephone. Outdoor furniture and barbecue.

Prices not confirmed for 2008　**Nearby** ⚓10km ⚑0.6km ⚓2km Restaurant 1km ⚘0.6km 🌳2km 🏠2km ⚒2km　**Notes** No pets

---

ST-LAURENT-LA-GATINE

⋕⋕⋕ **Chambre d'hôtes**

Bernadette et Francis JAMES

Clos Saint-Laurent, 6 Rue de l'Eglise,

28210 ST-LAURENT-LA-GATINE

☎ 02 37 38 24 02

email: james@clos-saint-laurent.com

web: www.clos-saint-laurent.com

This 19th-century house in a peaceful location offers three half-timbered bedrooms: a twin and two doubles, one with child's bed and all with private shower and wc. The ground floor has a living room with open fire, with a furnished patio. Golf course 15km. Closed Christmas and New Year.

Prices s fr €65; d €70-€88; extra person fr €20　**Nearby** ⚓6km ⚓15km ⚑7km ⚓6km Restaurant 6km ⚘4km Spa 6km 🏠6km ⚒8km　**Notes** No pets English spoken

ST-LUBIN-DE-CRAVANT

⚜ Chambre d'hôtes

Claudine et Dany CHUTAUX
Le Domiane des Peupliers, 1 Place de la Mairie,
28270 ST LUBIN DE CRAVANT
☎ 06 99 25 32 42 & 02 37 48 36 21
email: dany.chutaux@wanadoo.fr

This is a peaceful spot, at the edge of the attractive Perche region.
The 19th-century house, which is beside a river, has three very
pleasant rooms, all tastefully decorated, and all with private bath
or shower room and WC. Excellent breakfasts with home-made
ingredients.

Prices d €70-€90; extra person fr €30 **On Site** ☺
Nearby ☖ 10km ⌗ 15km ♪ 15km ↗ 15km Restaurant 3km
📷 3km ⋒ 15km **Notes** No pets English spoken Open May to
October.

ST-LUPERCE

⚜ ❧ La Ferme de Mousseau

Marie-Laure PERRIN
28190 ST-LUPERCE
☎ 02 37 26 85 01
email: gillesperrin2@wanadoo.fr
web: www.lafermedemousseau.com

In a calm and peaceful environment between Beauce and Perche,
near the River Eure, three guest rooms are available in an outbuilding
above an old stable on a farm. There are two double rooms 'Bouton
d'Or' (also contains single bed) and 'Myosotis' and a twin room
Tournesol.' Each has a private bathroom and wc.

Prices s €45-€50; d €55; t €75; extra person €20 **On Site** ♪
Nearby ☖ 9km ↗ 9km Restaurant 6km 📷 2km 📷 2km ⋒ 9km
Notes No pets English spoken Open March to 15 November.

ST-MAIXME-HAUTERIVE

⚜ ❧ ⍟ La Rondellière

Catherine et J-Paul LANGLOIS
11 Rue de la Mairie, 28170 ST-MAIXME-HAUTERIVE
☎ 02 37 51 68 26 📠 02 37 51 08 53
email: jeanpaul.langlois@wanadoo.fr
web: www.ferme-rondelliere.com

The owners welcome guests to their farm in a small village which has
two twin rooms and two doubles (one with a sofa bed), all with private
facilities. Extra beds and cot available. Wi-fi available in bedrooms.
Facilities include a reception with living room, open fire and TV, a
kitchen for family gatherings and tennis court and bikes, whilst archery
and golf are nearby. Evening meals may be booked in advance.

Prices s fr €33; d fr €42; extra person fr €10; dinner fr €15 **On Site** ☺
Nearby ☖ 2km ⌗ 2km ↗ 5km Restaurant 5km 📷 0.1km 📷 5km
⋒ 20km **Notes** No pets English spoken

VER-LES-CHARTRES

⚜ La Varenne

Cécile et Guillaume PICAULT
20 Rue de Tachainville, 28630 VER-LES-CHARTRES
☎ 02 37 26 45 32 & 06 14 53 34 80
email: lavarenne28@free.fr
web: http://lavarenne28.free.fr

A detached and peaceful pavilion in the Eure Valley provides two
double rooms and two adjoining rooms with a double, single and
possible second single bed; all with private facilities. Kitchenette
available. Large garden, parking and covered pool heated between
April and October.

Prices s €45-€50; d €50-€60; t €60-€75; extra person fr €15
On Site Private ↗ **Nearby** ☖ 2km ⌗ 20km ♪ 3km Restaurant 3km
📷 2km 📷 3km ⋒ 7km **Notes** No pets English spoken

AZAY-LE-FERRON

⚜ Domaine de la Botterie

Andree LEGROS
24 rue Louis Cassas, 36290 AZAY-LE-FERRON
☎ 02 54 39 23 77 & 06 81 16 14 74
email: j.a.legros@wanadoo.fr
web: www.domainedelabotterie.com.fr

Guests will receive a warm welcome at this restored longhouse with
its three romantic bedrooms. There is a triple room (double bed plus
a single) on the ground floor with independent access; upstairs are
two doubles, one with an extra folding bed; all the bedrooms have a
private shower room and WC. Landscaped gardens with terrace and
garden furniture.

Prices s fr €55; d fr €60; extra person fr €20 **On Site** ♪ ☺
Nearby ☖ 20km ⌗ 40km ↗ 15km Restaurant 0.5km Water sports 20km
📷 1km 📷 1km ⋒ 50km **Notes** No pets English spoken

BOUGES-LE-CHATEAU

⬥⬥⬥ Petit Château de Ste Colombe

M-A DAQUEMBRONNE
36110 BOUGES-LE-CHATEAU
☎ 02 54 35 88 33 🖷 02 54 35 15 21
email: saintecolombe@wanadoo.fr
web: http://stecolombe.com

A small 15th-century château with three guest rooms. On the ground floor is a double with TV and private entrance; upstairs is another double, and a suite for two to four people; all have private shower room and WC. Conservatory, where breakfast is served. Guests' kitchenette in a separate building. Swimming pool, barbecue, garden furniture.

Prices s €45-€80; d €45-€80 **On Site** Private ↖ **Nearby** ⚓ 3km
⚓ 29km Water sports 28km ⚓ 6km ⚓ 6km ⚓ 29km **Notes** No pets
English spoken

CEAULMONT-LES-GRANGES

⬥⬥⬥ Chambre d'hôtes

Marc-Yves HEMBERT
8 rue Saint-Vincent, Villarnoux,
36200 CEAULMONT-LES-GRANGES
☎ 02 54 47 75 56 🖷 02 54 47 75 56
email: marc.hembert@wanadoo.fr
web: www.villarnoux.free.fr

A tranquil artist's house in the charming village of Villarnoux. Breakfasts are served in the gallery whilst the rooms are in a separate building. On the first floor are two double rooms and a triple, each with its own shower room and toilet. On the ground floor are a lounge area, kitchen, terrace and enclosed garden.

Prices s fr €45; d fr €50; t fr €58 **Nearby** ⚓ 10km ⚓ 20km 🔎 1km
↖ 5km Restaurant 2km Water sports 5km ⚓ 2km ⚓ 2km ⚓ 5km
Notes No pets English spoken

CHATILLON-SUR-INDRE

⬥⬥⬥⬥ ⬤ La Poignardière

Maryse LHEUREUX
36700 CHATILLON-SUR-INDRE
☎ 02 54 38 78 14 & 06 11 97 37 21
🖷 02 54 38 95 34
email: maryse_lheureux@yahoo.fr
web: http://lapoignardiere.fr

Parkland with many species of trees, some of them very ancient, surrounds the house. There are five first-floor bedrooms, four doubles with king-size beds plus a twin-bedded room; all have private bath or shower room and WC. Swimming pool and tennis court.

Prices s fr €85; d fr €90; extra person fr €15; dinner fr €25
On Site 🔎 ⚓ Private ↖ Private tennis court **Nearby** ⚓ 5km
⚓ 15km Restaurant 15km ⚓ 4km **Notes** No pets English spoken
Open May to November.

CHEZELLES

⬥⬥⬥ ⬤ Chambre d'hôtes du Priouzé

M et G BABLIN
4 rue du Priouzé, 36500 CHEZELLES
☎ 02 54 36 66 28 🖷 02 54 36 66 28

A lovely 18th-century house in a shaded park by a river near the Brenne natural park. There are three guest rooms with two large double beds and two smaller doubles, with bathrooms, TV and telephone. Dining room, living room with open fire (TV, games, books, hi-fi), kitchen for longer stays. Patio, garden furniture, barbecue, table tennis, outdoor games, and picnic area.

Prices s fr €50; d fr €60; extra person fr €20; dinner fr €22
Nearby ⚓ 15km ⚓ 6km 🔎 15km ↖ 15km Restaurant 6km ⚓ 0.3km
⚓ 6km ⚓ 15km **Notes** No pets

CLERE-DU-BOIS

⬥⬥⬥⬥ ⬤ Les Effes

Christian MEUNIER
36700 CLERE-DU-BOIS
☎ 02 54 38 72 43 & 06 76 75 06 05
🖷 02 54 38 86 06
web: gen.meunier@orange.fr

Bedrooms available at the heart of a vast 17th-century manor surrounded by a wooded park: two doubles with en suite, one with king-size bed, an en suite twin room and one suite with sofa bed. Large lounge. Château d'Azay-le-Ferron 9kms. Also nearby is the Parc de la Haute Touche at Obterre where visitors can see many animals.

Prices s fr €70; d fr €80; extra person fr €40 **Nearby** ⚓ 10km
⚓ 25km ↖ 10km Restaurant 4km ⚓ 8km Spa 25km ⚓ 10km
⚓ 10km ⚓ 50km **Notes** Pets admitted English spoken

CLUIS

⬥⬥⬥⬥ Chambre d'hôtes

D et T VAN DEN OEVER
route d'Orsennes, 36340 CLUIS
☎ 02 54 31 22 52 & 06 33 35 43 56
🖷 02 54 31 22 52
email: info@lacigognedelahaye.com
web: www.lacigognedelahaye.com

This 18th-century house is in a small town in the area where George Sand was well known. On the ground floor is a suite for two people, and on the first floor are two double rooms, all with private bath or shower room and WC. There is a garden with trees and flowers, and an enclosed courtyard with parking space. Lounge with open fire and books to read.

Prices s fr €60-€80; d fr €75-€95; extra person fr €25 **Nearby** ⚓ 3km
⚓ 20km ↖ 20km Restaurant 0.1km Water sports 20km ⚓ 1km
Spa 0.1km ⚓ 0.1km ⚓ 25km **Notes** No pets English spoken

COINGS

⁑ ⃝ *Domaine de Villecourte*

Claudine DAGUET-RAULT

Route de la Champenoise, Moulin de Notz-Villecourte,
6130 COINGS

☎ 02 54 22 12 56   📄 02 54 22 12 56

mail: claudine.daguet2@wanadoo.fr

Lovers of wild life will be delighted to see the hares, pheasant
and deer on this cereal farm. There are two double bedrooms
with excellent shower rooms/WCs, TVs, internet connections and
kitchenettes. Lounge with billiards, terrace. There are two further
ground floor double rooms in a separate building, with their own
showers and kitchen area. Wooded grounds, stream and lake.

Prices not confirmed for 2008   **Nearby** ♿ 15km ⛷ 17km ➴ 8km
⚓ 15km 🏠 7km ⛵ 10km   **Notes** No pets   English spoken

⁑ ⃝ *Le Château*

Dominique COTILLON

6130 COINGS

☎ 02 54 07 02 48   📄 02 54 07 02 48

mail: coings.lechateau@free.fr

Guests are assured of a relaxing stay at this 19th-century residence
flanked by a 15th-century tower (containing a lounge conversion) and
situated in nine hectares of parkland. There are two double rooms, a
single and a twin, all with private bathroom or WC. There is a 24-hour
restaurant five minutes away and a kitchenette for guests' use.

Prices not confirmed for 2008   **Nearby** ♿ 10km ⛷ 15km ➴ 8km Water
sports 30km 🏊 8km 🏠 7km ⛵ 8km   **Notes** No pets   English spoken

DUN-LE-POELIER

⁑⁑ ⃝ *Le Gué Rabot*

Michel DESGROLARD

36210 DUN-LE-POELIER

☎ 02 54 40 68 26 & 06 14 57 18 51

email: michel.desgrolard@wanadoo.fr

web: www.leguerabot.fr

A paradise for those who truly love nature, and surrounded by
woods and lakes, this establishment offers accommodation in
three rooms, one with a private terrace and one a family suite. In
summer there is a terrace and in winter guests can sit by an open
fire in the lounge. Heated covered swimming pool; picnics made
by prior arrangement.

Prices s fr €80; d €90-€100; extra person fr €30; dinner fr €20
On Site 🏊 Private ➴ Private tennis court   **Nearby** ♿ 3km ⛷ 50km
🎣 10km 🏠 10km ⛵ 25km   **Notes** Pets admitted   English spoken

FLERE-LA-RIVIERE

⁑⁑ ⃝ *Le Moulin du Bourg*

Danielle AUMERCIER

36700 FLERE-LA-RIVIERE

☎ 02 54 39 34 41

email: lemoulindeflere@wanadoo.fr

An old mill beside the river provides the setting for this chambres
d'hôtes. There are three bedrooms - a double on the ground floor,
and a triple (double bed plus a single) and a two-roomed family suite
for four upstairs; all have private shower room and WC. The mill's
former gear room is now the dining room. Barbecue, garden furniture,
table tennis, fishing.

Prices s fr €42; d fr €50; t fr €70; extra person fr €15; dinner fr €23
Nearby ♿ 2km ⛷ 30km ➴ 5km Water sports 30km 🏊 5km 🏠 0.1km
Notes Pets admitted   English spoken   Open May to 15 October.

GARGILESSE-DAMPIERRE

⁑⁑ *Le Haut Verger*

S et F DE BUEGER

36190 GARGILESSE

☎ 02 54 47 76 95   📄 02 54 47 76 95

email: francis.gargilesse@wanadoo.fr

A tranquil, picturesque oasis near the artist village of Gargilesse,
with three spacious grade 2 and 3 rooms. Double with en suite
shower room and toilet. Double with adjacent bathroom and WC.
The third room contains a double bed, divan for two, fireplace and
adjacent bathroom. There is a terrace, private parking and two further,
accessible, small gîtes.

Prices not confirmed for 2008   **Nearby** ♿ 13km ⛷ 35km ➴ 13km
Water sports 5km 🏊 13km 🏠 5km ⛵ 13km   **Notes** Pets admitted
English spoken   Open January to 20 December.

CENTRAL FRANCE

INGRANDES

⚜ Château d'Ingrandes

Jacqueline DROUART
place de l'Eglise, 36300 INGRANDES
☎ 02 54 37 46 01 & 06 19 41 29 37
📠 02 54 28 64 55
email: jdrouart@aol.com
web: http://perso.wanadoo.fr/chambres

Renovated 11th-15th century château beside a river, which is open to the public. There is a double room, a large attic room for five people (one double bed and three singles), one room in the castle keep with a canopied bed, and a suite of a double room and twin room, all with private facilities. Dining room with fireplace, large living room/library, TV and telephone. Outdoor furniture, BBQ and parking. Restaurant 50mtrs

Prices s fr €55; d fr €60-€80; t fr €75-€85; extra person fr €10
On Site 🏊 Private 🎣 **Nearby** ⚓ 15km ⚡ 10km Water sports 9km 🏛 0.1km 🚲 50km **Notes** Pets admitted English spoken Open 16 June to September (April to 15 June by reservation).

LE POINCONNET

⚜ Les Divers

A et L DROUIN
Allee Paul Rue, 36330 LE POINCONNET
☎ 02 54 35 40 23 📠 02 54 35 40 23

An 18th-century house in a 15-hectare park, with two suites for two to five people with living room, bathroom and adjoining WCs; and a double room with private shower. Living room and TV room. Outdoor furniture, 9-hole golf course (clubs provided), and stables in the grounds. Opportunity for shooting weekends. National forest nearby.

Prices s fr €50; d fr €50; t fr €65; extra person fr €15 **Nearby** ⚓ 3km ⚡ 15km 🎿 6km Restaurant 0.5km Water sports 8km 🏊 0.5km Spa 40km 🏛 0.5km 🚲 8km **Notes** No pets English spoken

LINGE

⚜ 🍽 Champ Rocher

Karel SAERENS
36220 LINGE
☎ 02 54 37 92 40 📠 02 54 37 92 40
email: info@champ-rocher.com
web: www.champ-rocher.com

Extensive wooded grounds with seven lakes provide a wonderful setting for this property. On the first floor are three double rooms, two with king-size beds; on the second floor is a two-roomed family suite for four. Each room has a lounge area, a private bath or shower room and WC. Lounge with open fire.

Prices s fr €60; d fr €65; t fr €90; extra person fr €25; dinner fr €25
On Site 🎣 🚲 **Nearby** ⚓ 5km ⚡ 17km Restaurant 5km Water sports 18km 🏊 30km 🏛 15km 🚲 47km **Notes** Pets admitted English spoken

MAUVIERES

⚜ 🍽 ⚐ Les Petites Ages

Martial Duval
36370 MAUVIERES
☎ 02 54 37 97 32 & 06 20 53 89 02
email: lespetitesages@aol.com
web: http://lespetitesages.free.fr

Deep in the countryside, this restored farmhouse offers real peace and quiet. There are six bedrooms (five doubles and a triple), all on the ground floor and all with private bathrooms/WCs. One is suitable for disabled guests. Lounge, use of kitchen, terrace with barbecue. Meals by arrangement. Horse riding available; hire of owners' boats to explore the River Anglin is possible.

Prices s fr €45; d fr €48; t fr €62; dinner fr €16 **On Site** 🚲
Nearby ⚓ 0.1km ⚡ 10km 🎣 1km Restaurant 4km Water sports 5km 🏊 5km 🏛 3km 🚲 38km **Notes** Pets admitted English spoken

MERS-SUR-INDRE

⚜ Le Lac

Francoise GATESOUPE
36230 MERS-SUR-INDRE
☎ 02 54 36 29 49

Situated in a detached house next to the owner's home in a forest with 30-hectare wooded park which is great for long walks and off-road cycling. Five double rooms with private facilities are offered. Large communal dining room with a fireplace, living room and small kitchen. Outdoor furniture, parking and picnic table. Free fishing in the lake.

Prices s fr €28; d fr €38; t fr €48; extra person fr €10 **Nearby** ⚓ 7km ⚡ 20km 🎿 6km Restaurant 5km 🏊 5km Spa 20km 🏛 5km 🚲 20km **Notes** No pets

MONTIPOURET

♯♯♯ ♚ ⸎ **Maison Voilà**

Ingrid PLUYLAAR

La Brande, 36230 MONTIPOURET

☎ 02 54 31 17 91 & 06 24 76 57 61

email: maisonvoila@yahoo.com

web: www.maisonvoila.com

Martin and Ingrid would like you to experience the total peace and quiet of their three refined guest rooms, each on split-level and having shower and WC. Downstairs is a double sofabed, while upstairs are twin beds. Each duplex has a furnished terrace. Tennis, heated swimming pool, jacuzzi. Conservatory for reading; barn with games.

Prices s €50-€60; d €70-€80; t fr €120; dinner fr €25
On Site Private ⚡ Private tennis court **Nearby** ⚓ 20km ⛷ 15km
⚑ 10km Restaurant 10km Water sports 20km Spa 15km ⛽ 5km
⋘ 20km **Notes** No pets English spoken

NEUVY-SAINT-SEPULCRE

♯♯♯ ♚ **Etrechet**

M et J-L MARSAIS

36230 NEUVY-SAINT-SEPULCRE

☎ 02 54 30 89 89 & 06 87 51 19 14 📄 02 54 30 89 89

email: madeleine.marsais@wanadoo.fr

web: www.gitesmarsais.fr

An old farmhouse with a warm, peaceful atmosphere and offering three guest bedrooms. Two of the rooms are doubles; the third is a two-roomed family suite for four; all have private shower room/WC, TV and internet access. There is a lounge with TV and open fire, kitchenette, and meals can be arranged on an occasional basis. Garden with trees; swimming pool mid June to mid September.

Prices not confirmed for 2008 **On Site** Private ⚡ **Nearby** ⚓ 4km
⛷ 30km Water sports 29km ⛽ 2km ⛽ 2km ⋘ 29km **Notes** No pets
English spoken CC

NOHANT-VIC

♯♯♯ ♚ **Ripoton**

Martine COLOMB

36400 NOHANT-VIC

☎ 02 54 31 06 10

email: colomb.martine@wanadoo.fr

web: http://perso.wanadoo.fr/ripoton

In George Sand's village, in the heart of the Vallée Noire, this old restored family farmhouse is next to the River Indre. There are four double guest rooms (one is Grade 2), each with a shower room and wc and one with an extra single bed. Large communal room with a fireplace, books, tourist and walking information. Outdoor furniture and covered parking.

Prices not confirmed for 2008 **Nearby** ⛷ 18km ⚡ 9km ⛱ 7km ⛽ 8km
⋘ 30km **Notes** Pets admitted English spoken Open March to October.

PARNAC

♯♯♯ **La Villonniere**

C et S HILL

36170 PARNAC

☎ 02 54 24 89 05 & 06 89 11 77 96 📄 02 54 24 89 05

email: la-villonniere@wanadoo.fr

This small restored farmhouse is in a quiet little hamlet, not far from Lac Chambon. There are three guest bedrooms, two doubles and a triple (double bed plus single), all with private bath or shower room and WC. There is a lounge/dining area with TV, books and games, and a courtyard with parking space. Enclosed wooded grounds with barbecue, garden furniture and plenty of flowers.

Prices s fr €40; d fr €45; t fr €60; extra person fr €15 **Nearby** ⚓ 10km
⛷ 25km ⚡ 12km Water sports 10km ⛱ 5km ⛽ 5km ⋘ 12km
Notes Pets admitted English spoken

POULIGNY-NOTRE-DAME

♯♯♯ **Le Gachet**

Monique DELACHATRE

36160 POULIGNY-NOTRE-DAME

☎ 02 54 30 20 52 & 02 54 30 11 12

email: m.delachatre@free.fr

web: http://le-gachet.com

Restored in a style typical of the region, this farm offers rooms in rustic, warm surroundings. There are two double rooms (one with lounge) with independent entrances, a room with double bed and single, kitchen and living room and a room for three. All have private facilities. Large living/dining room/bar, TV lounge, outdoor furniture and parking. Special rate for a week's stay. Golf and spa treatments 500mtrs.

Prices not confirmed for 2008 **Nearby** ⚓ 15km ⛷ 0.5km ⚡ 10km
Water sports 30km ⛱ 0.5km ⛽ 0.5km ⋘ 45km **Notes** Pets admitted

REUILLY

↻ *Les Bouchauds*

M et M MULLER

36260 REUILLY

☎ 02 54 49 25 17 & 06 24 91 38 49 📄 02 54 49 25 17

Martine and Michel welcome you to their typical 18th-century Berry longhouse, which has been entirely restored. Three rooms have been harmoniously decorated, all having shower room and WC. Breakfast is served in a vast dining room where fodder racks and mangers can still be seen. Garden furniture; parking. Walks, vineyards, clay pigeon shooting and fishing nearby.

Prices not confirmed for 2008   **Nearby** ♿ 15km ♨ 15km ↖ 15km Water sports 15km ♒ 1.5km ⚓ 2km ⛵ 15km   **Notes** No pets

ROSNAY

↻ **Domaine de la Crapaudine**

Thierry DANYAUD

13 rue Saint-Andre, 36300 ROSNAY

☎ 02 54 37 77 12

email: thierry.danyaud@voila.fr

web: www.lacrapaudine.fr.st

In the heart of the Brenne, and just a step away from several paths and lakes. The 17th- and 18th-century, red sandstone residence offers a ground-floor double room with park views, and upstairs a triple and a room for four people; all have en suite shower and WC. Traditional meals (by arrangement) feature seasonal produce from the orchard and vegetable garden. Terrace, garden furniture, parking.

Prices s fr €55; d fr €60; t fr €75; extra person fr €15; dinner fr €28   **Nearby** ♿ 9km ♨ 15km ♬ 0.9km ↖ 15km Restaurant 0.1km Water sports 15km ♒ 0.8km ⚡ 0.1km ⚓ 0.1km ⛵ 45km **Notes** No pets   English spoken

SARZAY

Château de Sarzay

Richard HURBAIN

36230 SARZAY

☎ 02 54 31 32 25 📄 02 54 31 32 25

email: sarzay@wanadoo.fr

Four guest rooms in a 14th-century château open to the public (guided visits available). There is a double room and three rooms with two doubles and two singles with private facilities, plus a large living room with fireplace, piano, kitchen, comfy corner with TV and video. Large interior court (with various displays), meeting hall for weddings and family celebrations.

Prices s fr €46; d fr €50; t fr €65; extra person fr €15   **Nearby** ♿ 10km ♨ 15km ↖ 7km Water sports 40km ♒ 7km ⚓ 7km ⛵ 7km   **Notes** Pets admitted

↻ **Montgarni**

Michel LABAURIE

36230 SARZAY

☎ 02 54 31 31 05 & 06 30 78 73 96 📄 02 54 31 30 10

email: contact@sarzay-hotes.com

web: www.sarzay-hotes.com

A 19th-century mansion, surrounded by greenery and some magnificent trees. There are three rooms on the first floor, two doubles and a twin; on the second floor is another double and a family room for four; all have private bath/shower room and WC. Above-ground swimming pool. Meals are available by arrangement, and there is a farmhouse restaurant close by.

Prices s fr €38; d fr €44; t fr €70; extra person fr €13; dinner fr €18   **On Site** Private ↖   **Nearby** ♿ 12km ♨ 23km Water sports 40km ♒ 7k ⚓ 7km ⛵ 36km   **Notes** No pets   English spoken   CC

SAULNAY

La Marchandière

A et J RENONCET

36290 SAULNAY

☎ 02 54 38 42 94

email: alain-renoncet@wanadoo.fr

A working farm is the peaceful setting for this chambre d'hôtes. On the ground floor are two double rooms, one of them a Grade 2 room Upstairs is a separately-accessed family room with a double bed and three singles. All rooms have private shower rooms and WCs. A converted barn provides a games room with kitchen area. Terrace and garden furniture.

Prices not confirmed for 2008   **Nearby** ♿ 2km ♨ 22km ↖ 16km Wate sports 30km ♒ 9km ⚓ 9km ⛵ 45km   **Notes** No pets

ST-BENOIT-DU-SAULT

La Chatille

Michel BAILLY

36170 SAINT-BENOIT-DU-SAULT

☎ 02 54 47 50 12 & 06 81 36 49 50 📄 02 54 47 50 12

Nestling in a village by a river, this house looks onto the medieval town with its 11th-century church, 15th and 18th-century priories and fortified gate. Ideal for nature lovers, it is set in extensive enclosed shady grounds with picnic tables, archery and fishing on site. The waterfalls at Rocs-Martes and dolmens at Gorces and Passebonneau are nearby. Rooms include a double and two rooms with two double each with private facilities, and a large lounge with TV.

Prices s fr €50; d fr €54; extra person fr €16   **On Site** ♬ **Nearby** ♿ 5km ♨ 50km ↖ 20km Restaurant 0.5km Water sports 20km ♒ 2km Spa 50km ⚓ 1km ⛵ 20km   **Notes** No pets

⑪ Le Portail

Marie-France BOYER-BARRAL
8 rue Emile Surun, 36170 SAINT-BENOIT-DU-SAULT
☎ 02 54 47 57 20 🗎 02 54 47 57 20

full of character, a 14th-15th century house which acts as a fortified
gateway to the city. There is a double room, a room with a double
bed and two singles, and a room with small double bed and single
bed. The latter rooms have TV and lounge area, and all have private
facilities. Kitchen, small terrace, artist's studio and parking.
Prices s €45-€55; d €50-€60; extra person €12-€18 **Nearby** ⛷ 7km
28km 🏊 8km ⚓ 18km Restaurant 0.2km Water sports 20km ⛳ 1km
🏇 0.5km 🚲 0.1km ✈ 18km **Notes** No pets English spoken Open
February to December.

THENAY

⑪ *Chambre d'hôtes*

Martine BERTHELIN
3 rue du Gue de l'Ille, La Ribere, 36800 THENAY
☎ 02 54 47 02 73 & 06 24 86 42 03
email: la.ribere@gmail.com
web: www.la-ribere.eu

former farmhouse dating back to the 19th century in the Brenne
regional park. On the first floor are a double room and a triple, with
another double on the second floor. Additional beds are possible.
There is a separate guests' entrance, and each room has a shower
room and WC. Garden furniture, table tennis. Hiking trails nearby.
Prices not confirmed for 2008 **Nearby** ⛷ 8km ♨ 30km ⚓ 8km Water
sports 27km ⛳ 2km 🚲 3km ✈ 8km **Notes** Pets admitted English
spoken Open Easter to 1 November.

TOURNON-SAINT-MARTIN

⑪ Chambre d'hôtes

C et A SIMONNET
4 bis, route de la Blanc,
36220 TOURNON-SAINT-MARTIN
☎ 02 54 28 77 34 & 06 86 75 25 97 🗎 02 54 28 77 34

urrounded by a landscaped garden together with a swimming pool
and outdoor furniture, this property is in Mille Etangs country, near
Creuse. There are three double guest rooms each with a bathroom,
WC and private patio. Open all year by reservation only.
Prices s fr €60; d fr €65; t fr €78; extra person fr €18 **On Site** Private ⚓
Nearby ⛷ 8km ♨ 12km 🏊 0.2km Restaurant 0.2km Water sports 0.2km
⛳ 0.2km Spa 12km 🚲 0.2km ✈ 35km **Notes** No pets

AMBOISE

⑪ Le Manoir de la Maison Blanche

Annick DELECHENEAU
18 rue de l'Epinetterie, 37400 AMBOISE
☎ 02 47 23 16 14 & 06 88 89 33 66
email: annick.delecheneau@wanadoo.fr
web: www.lamaisonblanche-fr.com

This beautiful manor house dates from the late 17th century. Just five
minutes from the Château of Amboise, it stands in three hectares of
grounds. There are four spacious bedrooms, all with independent
access, private bath or shower room, TV and Wi-fi. Kitchen available
for guests. Reduced price after 3 nights.
Prices s fr €80; d fr €90; t fr €100; extra person fr €20 **Nearby** ⛷ 10km
♨ 15km 🏊 2km ⚓ 0.8km Restaurant 1.5km ⛳ 5km ⚑ 1.5km 🚲 1km
✈ 2km **Notes** No pets English spoken

AZAY-LE-RIDEAU

⑪ Chambre d'hôtes

Alain et Cathy SARRAZIN
9 Chemin des Caves, 37190 AZAY-LE-RIDEAU
☎ 02 47 45 31 25
email: sarrazin.alaincathy@wanadoo.fr
web: www.troglododo.com

Guest accommodation here faces due south along the Indre Valley
and consists of three independent rooms. Two are in troglodyte caves
and the third is a loft conversion and has a king-size bed. Each has
private bathroom facilities and a kitchenette. An extra bed and a cot
are available.
Prices s €47-€56; d €56-€68; t €76-€88; extra person €20
Nearby ⛷ 15km ♨ 12km 🏊 0.2km ⚓ 0.5km ⛳ 0.5km 🚲 1km ✈ 3km
Notes Pets admitted English spoken

AZAY-LE-RIDEAU *CONTINUED*

♨ & La Petite Loge

Christine BANTAS

15 route de Tours, 37190 AZAY-LE-RIDEAU

☎ 02 47 45 26 05 & 06 81 61 94 07

email: lapetiteloge@free.fr

Five guest rooms with separate access in a small old farmhouse in wooded grounds of one hectare, near the centre of Azay-le-Rideau. There is a room with two doubles, a twin and three doubles, all with shower and wc. Kitchen area available for use. Parking, garden furniture, BBQ.

Prices s fr €42; d €45-€55; t fr €75; extra person fr €10 **Nearby** ♘ 8km ♒ 14km ✎ 1km ⇗ 1km ⌇ 1km ❦ 2km ⌂ 1.5km ⋙ 1.5km
Notes No pets English spoken Open April to October.

AZAY-SUR-CHER

♨ Domaine du Coteau

Comtesse DE LARREA

37270 AZAY-SUR-CHER

☎ 02 47 50 47 47 📄 02 47 50 49 60

email: 3g@wanadoo.fr

web: www.domaine-du-coteau.com

Six rooms in the clock house of a romantic 19th-century property, in a 12 hectare wildlife park, on the edge of River Cher. There are four twin rooms (can be doubles), a double and a one flat with sitting room, cooking area, a double room and triple room. All have private facilities and TV. Living room with piano for guests' use. Swimming pool. Hot-air ballooning.

Prices s €77-€93; d fr €98; t fr €152; extra person fr €30 **On Site** ♘
Spa Private ⇗ **Nearby** ♒ 15km Restaurant 4km ⌇ 5km ⌂ 2km
⋙ 17km **Notes** No pets English spoken CC

see advert on opposite page

♨ ⍥ Le Clos des Augers

Danny et Philippe HELLIO

37270 AZAY-SUR-CHER

☎ 02 47 50 49 49 📄 02 47 50 49 51

email: closdesaugers@wanadoo.fr

web: www.closdesaugers.fr

A farm with donkeys, goats, sheep and geese wandering around the two hectares of meadows and a lake. There is a double room and two split-level family suites, each for 2/6 people and with private access; all rooms have shower and TV. Meals by arrangement are served in the hosts' dining room, or in the garden in summer.

Prices not confirmed for 2008 **Nearby** ♘ 1km ✎ 3km ⇗ 3km ⌇ 3km ⌂ 3km ⋙ 15km **Notes** No pets English spoken

AZAY-SUR-INDRE

♨ ⍥ La Bihourderie

Francis et Naomi BERTHONNEAU

37310 AZAY-SUR-INDRE

☎ 02 47 92 58 58

email: labihourderie@hotmail.com

web: www.labihourderie.com

This house is typical of Lochois and is a first-prize winner for 'gîtes in bloom'. There is a twin room, a double and two triples, each with private facilities. Cot available. Living room for guests with kitchen, TV and video. Garden with table tennis and pétanque.

Prices s fr €50; d €55-€65; t fr €70; extra person fr €15; dinner fr €20
Nearby ♘ 10km ♒ 15km ✎ 2.5km ⇗ 10km Restaurant 6km ⌇ 6km ⌂ 5km ⋙ 10km **Notes** No pets English spoken CC

♨ Moulin de la Follaine

Danie LIGNELET

37310 AZAY-SUR-INDRE

☎ 02 47 92 57 91 📄 02 47 92 57 91

email: moulindelafollaine@wanadoo.fr

web: www.moulindefollaine.com

Between the Val de Loire and south Touraine, this ancient hunting estate of the Marquis de La Fayette offers rooms in a working mill. Guests can enjoy the tranquillity of the two-hectare park with fishing, visit the nearby châteaux or relax in the living room with an open fire. There is a double room, a suite with three singles and a suite with a double bed, medium bed and single, with bathroom, wc and TV.

Prices d €65-€75; t fr €95; extra person fr €20 **On Site** ✎
Nearby ♘ 6km ♒ 20km ⇗ 10km Restaurant 3km ⌇ 3km ❦ 8km ⌂ 3km ⋙ 10km **Notes** No pets English spoken

ALLAN-MIRE

⊮⊮⊮ Château du Grand Bouchet

Dominique DEVANT

37510 BALLAN-MIRE

☎ 02 47 67 79 08 📄 02 47 67 79 08

email: chateau@grandbouchet.fr

web: www.grandbouchet.fr

This non-smoking property is in the converted outbuildings of the former farm of the Château du Grand Launay. There are three rooms - a double, a twin and a triple, all with old furniture and elegant décor. All have a private bath or shower room and WC. Dining room with open fire, large lounge with TV; garden with furniture.

Prices s fr €105; d fr €105; t fr €130; extra person fr €25

On Site Private ⁊ **Nearby** ⬥2km ⌇2km ⌀1km Restaurant 3km ⌇1km ⌇2km ⬚2km ⋙7km **Notes** No pets English spoken Open Easter to 15 November. CC

⊮⊮ ⛬ Le Château des Templiers

yrille AUBRY-LEBORGNE

7 rue de la Commanderie, 37510 BALLAN-MIRE

☎ 02 47 53 94 56 & 06 25 79 81 95 📄 02 47 53 94 57

mail: contact@chateaudestempliers.com

web: www.chateaudestempliers-touraine.com

he 12th-century Château des Templiers has five very comfortable edrooms in a former stable block. There are three doubles, a twin-edded room, and a room for three (single beds). All have en suite ath or shower room and WC. The six hectares of grounds provide lenty of space for walking, and the Loire cycle circuit passes about)0 metres away.

rices s €85-€95; d €95-€105; t fr €125; extra person fr €20

n Site Private ⁊ **Nearby** ⬥0.5km ⌇1km ⌀0.5km Restaurant 1km ⋅1km ⌇7km ⬚1km ⋙10km **Notes** No pets English spoken CC

EAUMONT-LA-RONCE

⊮⊮ ❦ La Louisière

Michel CAMPION

7360 BEAUMONT-LA-RONCE

☎ 02 47 24 42 24

 working farm on the edge of town is the setting for these three hambres d'hôtes. There is a twin-bedded room; a room for three ith a double bed and a single; and a room for five with a double ed and three singles; all rooms have private facilities. Cot available. ounge with open fire and TV; kitchenette. Children's games. estaurant 300mtrs.

rices s fr €42; d fr €48; t fr €63; extra person fr €15 **Nearby** ⬥15km ⌇11km ⌀0.5km ⁊20km ⌇1km ⬚0.1km ⋙8km **Notes** Pets dmitted English spoken

Château du Coteau

The Domaine du Coteau is a haven of tranquillity half way between Tours and Chenonceau surrounded by 9 hectares of magnificent woodland and a flower filled park. This elegant establishment was visited by Chopin. The bedrooms as well as the bathrooms have been superbly decorated with an emphasis on comfort.There is a large lounge with piano and a dining room with a romantic feel. The animal park houses goats, geese, a pony, deer and pigs. The heated swimming pool will aid your relaxation.

CLAUDIE TASSI Comtesse de Larrea
37270 AZAY-SUR-CHER
Tel : 02 47-50-47-47   Fax : 02 47-50-49-60
Email: 3g@wanadoo.fr
www.domaine-du-coteau.com

BENAIS

⊮⊮⊮ La Sourderie

Noëlle MAGNE

37140 BENAIS

☎ 02 47 97 09 17

email: info@sourderie.com

web: www.sourderie.com

This lovely 18th and 19th-century house is set in three hectares of tranquil grounds, amid woods and vines. It provides three spacious rooms with private facilities and access: one with a king-size bed and lounge (can be twin), a room with a double, mezzanine and lounge with sofa bed for two and a further king-size room.

Prices s €50-€68; d €60-€79; t fr €105; extra person fr €18

Nearby ⬥20km ⌇25km ⌀3km ⁊15km ⌇2km ⋙7.5km **Notes** No pets English spoken

⊮⊮⊮ Le Grand Moulin

Claire BOHADAS

37140 BENAIS

☎ 02 47 97 38 76 & 06 81 27 30 70

email: michel.cottereau@cario.fr

web: www.le-grand-moulin.com

This 17th-century mill is set on the meandering River Changeon. It offers three guest rooms on the first floor, reached by a private door. A double room has its own shower room, and both the triple rooms have an en suite bathroom. Cot available. Reception room with TV,

CONTINUED

CENTRAL FRANCE

BENAIS CONTINUED

and kitchenette. Vast grounds and 800 metres of river bank. Enclosed car park.

Prices s fr €54.60; d fr €60; t fr €75; extra person fr €15   **On Site** ℴ
Nearby ⚓ 9km ⚓ 22km ⚓ 6km ⚓ 5km ⚓ 5km ⚓ 3km ⚓ 5km
Notes No pets Open 11 July to 9 June.

BERTHENAY

⦙⦙⦙ |◎| La Grange aux Moines

Janine MILLET

37510 BERTHENAY

☎ 02 47 50 06 91 & 06 07 99 71 65   🖹 02 47 50 06 91

email: jaber.millet@wanadoo.fr

web: http://grangeauxmoines.free.fr

Five rooms in a restored 17th-century farmhouse in a hamlet on the banks of the Loire: there are two rooms with a double bed and two singles, two double rooms and a twin room. (Two rooms are Grade 2). All have separate access, shower and wc; one is on the ground floor. Shady grounds, garage, swimming pool.

Prices s fr €55; d €64-€69; t €89-€110; dinner fr €25   **On Site** Private ⚓
Nearby ⚓ 6km ⚓ 8km ℴ 4km Restaurant 2km ⚓ 6km ⚓ 7km ⚓ 6km
⚓ 6km   **Notes** No pets Open 16 March to 10 November.

BOSSEE

⦙⦙⦙ |◎| Au Clos de Beaulieu

Thaddée TILLIEUX

37240 BOSSEE

☎ 02 47 92 29 47 & 06 86 84 04 51   🖹 02 47 92 29 47

email: auclosdebeaulieu@wanadoo.fr

web: www.auclosdebeaulieu.com

Not far from the Loire châteaux, this pretty stone-built house makes a peaceful place for a holiday. There are two double rooms and a room for four (double bed plus twins), all with private bath or shower room and WC. There are three hectares of grounds with a swimming pool, fishing pond, boules pitch, fitness room, children's games, and more.

Prices d €85-€95; t €105-€115; extra person fr €20; dinner fr €35
On Site ℴ ⚓ Private ⚓   **Nearby** ⚓ 15km ⚓ 25km Restaurant 12km
⚓ 10km ⚓ 2km ⚓ 35km   **Notes** No pets English spoken

BOURGUEIL

⦙⦙⦙ |◎| Le Moulin de Touvois

Myriam MARCHAND

37140 BOURGUEIL

☎ 02 47 97 87 70   🖹 02 47 97 87 70

email: info@moulindetouvois.com

web: www.moulindetouvois.com

This 18th-century mill is 5km from Bourgueil and near to walking trails. It houses four double rooms (can be twin) and a twin, all with private facilities. Guests may use the swimming pool, set in a large lawn reached by a wooden bridge over a stream. Meals available by reservation.

Prices s fr €54; d fr €60; t fr €75; extra person fr €15; dinner fr €20
On Site ⚓ ℴ ⚓ Private ⚓   **Nearby** ⚓ 15km Restaurant 4km ⚓ 4km
⚓ 4km ⚓ 6km   **Notes** No pets English spoken Open April to October.

BRAYE-SUR-MAULNE

⦙⦙⦙ |◎| Domaine de la Bergerie

Colette DEFOND

37330 BRAYE-SUR-MAULNE

☎ 02 47 24 90 88   🖹 02 47 24 90 88

email: clairedefond@gmx.net

web: www.domaine-bergerie.fr

A haven of quiet in a lovely setting, this château is on a romantic estate dating from 1850 and set in 12 hectares of parkland with huge ornamental lake and 200-year-old trees. The rooms have air conditioning, large double beds, bathrooms and WCs and a suite offers an additional two single beds. Private lounge for guests. Meals, using estate produce, may be booked.

Prices d fr €80; extra person fr €25; dinner fr €30   **On Site** ℴ
Nearby ⚓ 4km ⚓ 8km ⚓ 12km ⚓ 2.5km ⚓ 3km ⚓ 12km
Notes Pets admitted English spoken

BREHEMONT

⦙⦙⦙ Chambre d'hôtes

Josiane YVERNAULT

16 Av du 11 novembre, 37130 BREHEMONT

☎ 02 47 96 42 53 & 06 76 28 45 80

email: josjean.yvernault@free.fr

This former presbytery makes an ideal base for exploring the UNESCO world heritage site of the Loire Valley. There are four bedrooms: two can be doubles or twins, a further double (with river view), and a room for four (all single beds). All have private bath or shower room/WC. Interesting breakfast menus, good riverside walks and boat trips on the Loire.

Prices d €45-€57; t fr €73; extra person fr €5   **On Site** ℴ Private ⚓
Nearby ⚓ 1km Restaurant 0.5km ⚓ 0.5km ⚓ 0.5km ⚓ 0.2km ⚓ 6km
Notes No pets English spoken Open Easter to October.

⦙⦙⦙ |◎| *Les Devants de Rupuanne*

Marie-Claude HENRY

10 les Devants de Rupuanne, 37130 BREHEMONT

☎ 02 47 95 49 36 & 06 60 47 60 61

email: rupuanne@wanadoo.fr

web: http://rupuanne.monsite.wanadoo.fr

A stone-built house in enclosed wooded grounds, with four bedrooms. There is an air-conditioned, split-level room for four; a double room; and two more doubles on the second floor which can be let as a family suite. A cot is available, and all rooms have a private bath or shower room and WC. Lounge, garden furniture, table tennis, BBQ. Meals by prior arrangement.

Prices not confirmed for 2008   **Nearby** ⚓ 8km ⚓ 25km ℴ 0.4km
⚓ 8km ⚓ 8km ⚓ 3.5km ⚓ 7km   **Notes** No pets English spoken

CANDES-ST-MARTIN

⦀ *Les Sarments*

Marylène LHERBETTE

5 rue Trochet, 37500 CANDES-SAINT-MARTIN

☎ 02 47 95 93 40 🗋 02 47 95 93 40

email: sarments@wanadoo.fr

web: http://lessarments.free.fr

ate 19th-century farmhouse high in the village of Candes, with
anoramic views of the confluence of the Vienne and the Loire.
 provides a double room; one sleeping four (double bed and
wo singles) and a suite (two double beds and one single). TV if
equested. Large garden with terrace and views over Montsoreau and
he vineyards.

Prices not confirmed for 2008　**Nearby** ⚓ 10km ⚲ 7km ✐ 1km ⟋ 8km
▸ 1km 🎦 0.5km ⋒ 12km　**Notes** No pets　English spoken

CHAMBOURG-SUR-INDRE

⦀ ⦶ *La Tuilerie de l'Isle Auger*

Martine et Olivier MICHAULT

7310 CHAMBOURG-SUR-INDRE

☎ 02 47 91 51 56 & 06 18 07 09 53

email: michaultco@wanadoo.fr

web: http://perso.wanadoo.fr/latuilerie.michault

his property, with its three elegant bedrooms, is on a wooded site
eside the River Indre, close to the medieval city of Loches. The
edrooms each have a double bed and a single; one is on the ground
oor with its own entrance; all have private shower and WC. Baby
quipment available; meals by arrangement (except Wednesday
venings). Many walks lead from the property.

Prices not confirmed for 2008　**On Site** ✐　**Nearby** ⚓ 2km ⚲ 18km
5km ⋒ 5km 🎦 5km ⋒ 5km　**Notes** Pets admitted

⦀ ⦶ Le Petit Marray

aymonde et Nicolas GACHADOIT

0 route de Marray, 37310 CHAMBOURG-SUR-INDRE

☎ 02 47 92 50 67 🗋 02 76 34 11 11

email: nature@petit-marray.fr

web: http://petit.marray.free.fr

he farmhouse dates from 1830 and offers four large rooms with
eparate access: a two-roomed suite (one double bed, two singles),
 double room, a room with a double and two singles with disabled
ccess and a suite with lounge, pull-out bed and double bed with
ower and wc. Rooms have private facilities and TV; three have
icrowave and fridges. Books, games, large garden. Meals by
eservation.

Prices s fr €54; d fr €62; t fr €75; extra person fr €13; dinner fr €20
Nearby ⚓ 4km ⚲ 15km ✐ 2km ⟋ 4km Restaurant 2km ⋓ 2km
4km ⋒ 4km　**Notes** Pets admitted　English spoken

CHANCAY

⦀ Chambre d'hôtes

Claire LEHOREAU

19 rue du Château de Vaux, 37210 CHANCAY

☎ 06 82 48 33 83 & 02 47 52 98 63

email: lehoreau@infonie.fr

web: http://vallee-de-vaux.com

This 18th-century residence is set in a small valley which produces
Vouvray wine. The three rooms available have separate access and
facilities, and include a double room with fireplace, a suite with king-
size bed, single, kitchenette, TV and fireplace, and another suite in a
loft accessed by a covered terrace, with a lounge, kitchenette, TV and
two double beds. Laundry facilities are available.

Prices s fr €55; d fr €65; t fr €80; extra person fr €15　**Nearby** ⚓ 11km
⚲ 4km ✐ 2km ⟋ 7km ⋓ 2km 🎦 4km ⋒ 15km　**Notes** Pets admitted
English spoken

⦀⦀ Le Moulin de Bacchus

Didier et Françoise SURIN

37210 CHANCAY

☎ 02 47 52 27 90 & 06 17 61 04 77

email: didier-surin@wanadoo.fr

web: www.moulin-de-bacchus.com

In the heart of Vouvrillon, this extensive 17th-19th century mill
is on a four-hectare estate with a river, between Chançay and
Vernou. It offers a suite with a double and two single beds, a
double room, a twin and two air-conditioned rooms sleeping
four in a double and two singles. All are non-smoking with
private facilities. Reading/sitting room with TV, a covered heated
swimming pool, solarium, sunbeds, summer kitchen, BBQ and
table tennis.

Prices s €62-€71; d €69-€78; t fr €98; extra person fr €20
On Site ✐ Private ⟋　**Nearby** ⚓ 15km ⚲ 30km Restaurant 7km
⋓ 3km ✐ 15km 🎦 3km ⋒ 12km　**Notes** No pets　English spoken

CHARENTILLY

▥▥ La Roche Buard

Patricia et Gilles LAMOUREUX
37390 CHARENTILLY
☎ 02 47 56 62 71
email: patricia@rochebuard.com
web: www.rochebuard.com

This converted 19th-century barn nestles at the bottom of a valley in a lovely wooded garden with stream running through. The striking interior houses a double and a triple, each with private shower and WC; an additional suite accessed by an outside staircase can sleep five, also with shower and WC. Reductions for longer stays.

Prices s fr €48; d €55-€70; t €75-€85; extra person fr €15; dinner fr €20 **On Site** ⚲ **Nearby** ⛵ 7km ♨ 2km ⚓ 10km Restaurant 1km ♨ 2km 🏠 2km ⋈ 6km **Notes** No pets English spoken

See advertisement under TOURS

CHARNIZAY

▥▥ ♥ ⦶ ⚿ *Les Bénestières*

Martine et Henri ROBERT
37290 CHARNIZAY
☎ 02 47 94 56 78 🗎 02 47 94 41 70
email: henri-martine.robert@wanadoo.fr

A working farm producing cereals and beef, near the Valleys of the Creuse and Brenne. There is a double room with disabled access, a room for four, and two for three, all with shower and wc. Kitchen area, lounge, garden with lawn. Visit the farm and the nearby archaeological sites, or walk in the forests. Meals by reservation (except Tuesdays). Reductions for stays of two days or more; half board available.

Prices not confirmed for 2008 **Nearby** ⛵ 12km ♨ 16km ⚓ 5km ⚓ 5km ♨ 5km 🏠 5km ⋈ 30km

CHAVEIGNES

▥▥▥ La Varenne

DRU-SAUER
37120 CHAVEIGNES
☎ 02 47 58 26 31 🗎 02 47 58 27 47
web: www.la-varenne.com

This lovely house has a unique architectural style and is set on an estate dedicated to the production of walnuts and honey, in countryside 4km from Richelieu. Very large and quiet, the three guest rooms have bath and wc, and either a double bed or two singles. Cosy sitting room with piano and open fireplace; generous breakfasts. Heated swimming pool, table tennis, 5 hectares of woods, footpaths, bikes and mopeds for hire.

Prices s €78-€103; d €85-€110; extra person fr €26 **On Site** ⚲ Private ⚓ **Nearby** ⛵ 15km ♨ 30km ⚓ 4km Restaurant 4km ♨ 3km 🏠 4km ⋈ 28km **Notes** No pets English spoken

CHENONCEAUX

▥▥ Clos Mony

Betty LE CLAINCHE
6 rue des Bleuets, 37150 CHENONCEAUX
☎ 02 47 23 82 68 🗎 02 47 23 82 68
email: clos.mony@wanadoo.fr
web: www.france-bonjour.com/clos-mony/

Three rooms in a late 19th-century house in a quiet area in the centre of Chenonceaux, just 500mtrs from the entrance to its famous château. There are two double rooms and one twin, each with shower and wc, all on the upper floor. There are two further bedrooms (both Grade 2) located in a neighbouring house. Large, secure garden with lovely ornamental pond.

Prices s €46-€49; d €52-€54; t €72-€76; extra person €20-€22 **Nearby** ⛵ 9km ♨ 20km ⚓ 1km ⚓ 6km Restaurant 0.1km ♨ 0.5km ⚓ 0.1km 🏠 0.1km ⋈ 0.4km **Notes** No pets English spoken

▥▥ *La Baiserie*

Claude GUYOMARD
37150 CHENONCEAUX
☎ 02 47 23 90 26
email: info@labaiserie.com
web: www.labaiserie.com

A restored 15th-century farmhouse in a quiet environment, near the château and village. There is a double room and separate access, and two rooms for three, all with private facilities, TVs and fridges; as well as a dining/sitting room with TV reserved for guests. One hectare par with farm animals, terrace, parking, garden furniture. Enclosed car pa with remote control access.

Prices not confirmed for 2008 **Nearby** ⚓ 1km ⚓ 6km ♨ 0.6km 🏠 0.6km ⋈ 0.5km **Notes** No pets

CHISSEAUX

⋕ ⏅ *Chambre d'hôtes*

Mireille ANSAR

rue du Perpassé, 37150 CHISSEAUX

☎ 02 47 23 81 20

email: lestilleulsduperpasse@wanadoo.fr

Accommodation on a 19th-century vineyard, in the village, comprising a double, a twin, a triple and a family room sleeping five, all with separate facilities. The owners serve dinner (booking required) in the basement dining room or on the terrace with pleasant garden and organic kitchen garden.

Prices not confirmed for 2008 **Nearby** ⌁ 15km ⍛ 0.5km ⚮ 10km ⚮ 0.5km ⌂ 2km � 2km **Notes** No pets English spoken

⋕ **Les Clos des Lys**

André BESSOU

6 rue du Perpassé, 37150 CHISSEAUX

☎ 02 47 23 83 54 & 06 80 58 10 92

email: info@leclosdeslys.com

web: www.leclosdeslys.com

One and a half kilometres from the town, this property has one bedroom and two suites. In the main house is a ground floor twin-bedded room with its own terrace, and a first floor suite for four. There is another suite, also with a terrace, in a separate building. Barbecue, kitchenette with microwave, heated pool.

Prices s fr €60; d fr €75; t fr €68; extra person fr €22 **On Site** Private ⚮ **Nearby** ⌁ 5km ⍛ 15km ⚮ 1km Restaurant 1km ⌁ 0.5km ⌂ 2km � 1.5km **Notes** No pets English spoken

CINAIS

⋕ ⏅ **Le Noisillet**

Annie-P et Christian BARTHEL

chemin du Noisillet, 37500 CINAIS

☎ 02 47 95 97 28 & 06 07 64 43 42

email: contact@noisillet.com

web: www.noisillet.com

This chambre d'hotes is a former farm dating from the 17th century, and nestles in a small valley where cave-dwellers once settled. Four luxurious and spacious suites are available for guests, each with shower room (one has a bath) and private WC. One room for four people with mezzanine; two triple rooms and one double. The dining area has an open fire and a library for guests. Table d'hotes by reservation. Shared facilities include fridge, and a swimming pool. 300mtrs from equestrian centre.

Prices s fr €65; d fr €79; t fr €93; extra person fr €8; dinner fr €29 **On Site** ⌁ Private ⚮ **Nearby** ⍛ 15km ⚮ 2km Restaurant 8km ⌁ 6km ⌂ 6km � 7km **Notes** No pets English spoken

⋕ ⏅ **Les Jards**

Marie-Anne LEBLEU

37500 CINAIS

☎ 02 47 95 88 48 & 06 17 46 74 34

On the road out of Chinon, this house has two bedrooms and one suite. There is a family room with a double bed and bunks, a triple room (double bed plus a single), and a two roomed suite for five, with a double bed and three singles. All have shower room and WC; cots available. Large enclosed garden with swimming pool.

Prices s fr €46; d fr €51; t fr €63; dinner fr €16 **On Site** Private ⚮ **Nearby** ⌁ 2km ⍛ 15km ⚮ 2km Restaurant 2km ⌁ 7km Spa 0.1km ⌂ 7km � 8km **Notes** Pets admitted English spoken

CINQ-MARS-LA-PILE

⋕ **La Meulière**

M. MANIER

Rue du Breuil, 37130 CINQ-MARS-LA-PILE

☎ 02 47 96 53 63 & 06 03 53 76 59

email: cgmanier-lameuliere@wanadoo.fr

web: http://lameuliere.free.fr

Three rooms in a bourgeois house near the station. Two double rooms and a family room with two double beds, all with private facilities. Television lounge available.

Prices s fr €40-€44; d fr €46-€54; t fr €62-€66; extra person fr €12 **On Site** ⌁ **Nearby** ⍛ 8km ⚮ 1km ⚮ 4km Restaurant 0.5km ⌁ 0.5km ⌂ 0.5km � 0.5km **Notes** No pets English spoken

CIVRAY-DE-TOURAINE

⋕ ⏅ **La Marmittière**

Marie BOBLET

22 vallée de Mesvres, 37150 CIVRAY-DE-TOURAINE

☎ 02 47 23 51 04 & 06 88 83 82 48

email: marmittiere@libertysurf.fr

web: http://marmittiere.chez-alice.fr/chambres.htm

An early 20th-century building beside a 17th-century mansion housing two double rooms and a suite with a double and two single beds, kitchen, dining area, sitting room and TV; all have private facilities. Partly wooded 3 hectare park with donkeys, chickens and a gîte, table tennis and meals prepared using organic produce available by reservation. 10% reduction on stays of more than three nights.

Prices s fr €50; d fr €58; t fr €80; extra person fr €16; dinner fr €24 **Nearby** ⌁ 10km ⍛ 3km ⚮ 3km Restaurant 2km ⌁ 2km ⚮ 2km ⌂ 1.2km � 2.5km **Notes** No pets English spoken Open 6 March to 15 November.

CRISSAY-SUR-MANSE

Les Vallées

Louis GUERIN
37220 CRISSAY-SUR-MANSE
☎ 02 47 97 07 81 📄 02 47 97 07 81
email: louisguerin.chambres-dhotes@wanadoo.fr

On a south-facing hillside, overlooking the Manse Valley and the listed village of Crissay, this property has three rooms in an annexe. On the ground floor is a double room; upstairs is a room for four (double bed plus a sofabed). Also upstairs is a large grade 2 room for five. All have private facilities. Courtyard and covered parking.

Prices not confirmed for 2008 **Nearby** ⚓ 10km 🏊 2km ↖ 7km 🏛 4km 🏰 4km ⛵ 10km **Notes** Pets admitted English spoken

---

EPEIGNE-LES-BOIS

La Boissière

Geneviève et Daniel MALASSINET
9 rte des Vignes, 37150 EPEIGNE-LES-BOIS
☎ 02 47 23 83 46 & 06 64 66 16 84
email: la-boissiere@tele2.fr

A restored long-house dating from 1850, surrounded by famous châteaux such as Chenonceau and Amboise, and no less attractive sites like Loches and Montrésor. Three ground floor rooms with independent access comprise a twin-bedded room with shower/WC, and another twin and a double both with en suite bathroom. Cot available; meals can be arranged.

Prices s €35-€39; d €44-€49; dinner fr €17 **Nearby** ⚓ 2km 🏊 25km 🏰 3km ↖ 10km ⛵ 5km 🏛 3km ⛵ 7km **Notes** No pets English spoken

Les Doumées

Vasco & Martine COSTA
La Lézardière, 2 route d'Echédan,
37150 EPEIGNE-LES-BOIS
☎ 02 47 23 84 21 & 06 71 52 81 60
email: quima@wanadoo.fr

In a hamlet not far from Chenonceaux and Montrichard, this is a traditional style house with three first-floor bedrooms, a double and two triples, all with private bath or shower room/WC. Lounge with open fire, shady enclosed garden; meals available by arrangement.

Prices s fr €48; d fr €56; t fr €68; extra person fr €16; dinner fr €24 **Nearby** ⚓ 0.5km 🏊 25km 🏰 2.5km ↖ 10km Restaurant 5km ⛵ 5km 🏛 2.5km ⛵ 10km **Notes** Pets admitted English spoken

ESVRES-SUR-INDRE

Domaine de la Guillotière

Anne DIGNAM
37320 ESVRES-SUR-INDRE
☎ 02 47 34 80 53
email: dignam@wanadoo.fr
web: www.frenchguesthouse.com

Set in a magnificent six-hectare park in Indre, the Irish owners of this restored 18th-century château extend a warm welcome. They offer four rooms with private facilities: two with king-size beds, a twin and a room with a double and single bed in an annexe. Lounge with TV, swimming pool, fishing and walks in the park. Animals accepted by prior agreement.

Prices s fr €85; d fr €90; t fr €120; extra person fr €15 **On Site** 🏰 Private ↖ **Nearby** ⚓ 4km 🏊 20km Restaurant 3km ⛵ 2.5km Spa 20km ⛵ 5km 🏛 2.5km ⛵ 2.5km **Notes** Pets admitted English spoken

La Lubinerie

Elizabeth AUBERT
3 rue des Ecoles, 37320 ESVRES-SUR-INDRE
☎ 02 47 26 40 87 & 06 13 30 59 66
email: lalubinerie@orange.fr
web: www.lalubinerie.com

In the middle of a village, yet only 20 minutes from Tours, Azay-le-Rideau, Amboise and Loches, this property is in an ideal location. There are two double rooms, one on the ground floor, and a first-floor suite for four with a double bed and a single. All rooms have private bath or shower room and WC, also working fireplaces. Landscaped gardens.

Prices s fr €65; d fr €70; t fr €90; extra person fr €15; dinner fr €25 **Nearby** ⚓ 4km 🏊 10km 🏰 0.2km ↖ 0.2km Restaurant 0.2km ⛵ 0.2km ⛵ 4km 🏛 0.2km ⛵ 0.5km **Notes** No pets English spoken

---

FAYE-LA-VINEUSE

La Tour Ménagée

Serge BENARD
3 rue de la Corderie, 37120 FAYE-LA-VINEUSE
☎ 02 47 95 68 94 📄 02 47 95 63 81
email: reservations@la-tour-menagee.com
web: www.la-tour-menagee.com

A medieval village provides a peaceful location for this old farmhouse property with its little 12th-century tower and three delightful guest rooms, doubles and twins, all with private bathrooms and WCs. The hosts are passionate about literature, and like to share their vast library with guests. Internal courtyard, and wooded garden with a covered terrace.

Prices s €65-€75; d €70-€120; extra person fr €15; dinner fr €26 **Nearby** ⚓ 7km 🏊 20km 🏰 7km ↖ 7km Restaurant 7km ⛵ 7km 🏛 7km ⛵ 25km **Notes** No pets English spoken

FONDETTES

⌗ Le Grenadier

Martine BUTTERWORTH

rue des Patys, 37230 FONDETTES

☎ 02 47 42 08 32

email: martine@legrenadier.net

web: www.legrenadier.net

This 1750s stone-built residence, typical of the area around Tours, has wonderful views overlooking the village and its church. Three guest rooms in a converted annexe comprise a double, a triple and a room for four people, all with bath or shower and WC. Reductions for longer stays, except July/August. Cot available.

Prices s fr €60; d fr €70; t fr €90; extra person fr €20 **Nearby** ⌕ 4km 15km ⚲ 1.5km ⬈ 4km Restaurant 2km ⬙ 1km ⬗ 7km
Notes No pets English spoken

FRANCUEIL

⌗ ⍥ La Haute Traversière

M et Mme CHAMBON

rue Léopold Deschamps, 37150 FRANCUEIL

☎ 02 47 23 87 59

email: lahautetraversiere@wanadoo.fr

web: http://lahautetraversiere.com

Situated by the river in the village, La Haute Traversière is a large former farm, comprising a collection of rural 19th-century buildings. Rooms have private facilities and include two suites with a king-size and two single beds (one with kitchen corner) and a king-size room. Garden, orchards, large landscaped courtyard for relaxation. Table d'hôte meals by reservation. Close to Cher and the château of Chenonceau.

Prices s €43-€55; d €49-€60; t €68-€75; extra person fr €15; dinner fr €22 **Nearby** ⌕ 20km ⚲ 20km ⚲ 5km ⬈ 7km ⬙ 7km ⬗ 0.2km ⬗ 2km **Notes** No pets

⌗ ⍥ Le Moulin

Jean-Claude JOYEZ

8 rue du Moulin Neuf, 37150 FRANCUEIL

☎ 02 47 23 93 44

email: moulinfrancueil@aol.com

web: www.moulinfrancueil.com

Five rooms in a 19th-century mill, each with private bathroom and WC, set in parkland with rivers, waterfall, pond and ducks. There is a large lounge, winter garden, heated swimming pool, parking, outdoor furniture and breakfast served by the water. Midday picnic hamper and wine tasting available. 15% reduction from October to March inclusive.

Prices s €102-€122; d €110-€130; t €126-€150; extra person fr €16; dinner fr €25 **On Site** ⚲ Private ⬈ **Nearby** ⌕ 20km ⚲ 20km Restaurant 4km ⬙ 6km ⬗ 0.5km ⬗ 8km **Notes** No pets English spoken CC

HOMMES

⌗⌗ ⍥ Domaine du Château de Hommes

Albine HARDY

Relais du Vieux Château, 37340 HOMMES

☎ 02 47 24 95 13 ▤ 02 47 24 68 67

email: levieuxchateaudehommes@wanadoo.fr

web: http://le-vieux-chateau-de-hommes.com

A 15th-century tithe barn with five double or twin rooms, one with disabled access, and each with private facilities. Large living room for use of guests, with open fire, TV and telephone, park, courtyard and swimming pool. Meals can be booked.

Prices d €107-€117; t fr €127; extra person fr €25; dinner fr €30
On Site ⚲ Private ⬈ **Nearby** ⌕ 2.5km ⚲ 7km Restaurant 5km ⬙ 4km ⬗ 3km ⬗ 14km **Notes** No pets English spoken CC

HUISMES

⌗ ⍥ L'Ermitage

Marie-Chantal DE VERNEUIL

37420 HUISMES

☎ 02 47 95 52 40 ▤ 02 47 95 58 71

There are three guest bedrooms at this 17th-century manor house on a watercress farm. One is a double, the second has twin beds (which can be joined), and the third is a grade 2 room for six, with two double beds and two singles. All have private bathroom. Lounge with TV, garden with furniture; meals by arrangement.

Prices s €32-€47; d €35-€50; t fr €40; extra person fr €7; dinner fr €12 **Nearby** ⌕ 4km ⚲ 25km ⚲ 4km ⬈ 5km Restaurant 3km ⬙ 1km ⬗ 3km ⬗ 1km **Notes** No pets English spoken

LA CELLE-ST-AVANT

▓▓▓ Le Grignon

Claude CHUIT

3 allée du Grignon, 37160 LA CELLE-SAINT-AVANT

☎ 02 47 65 13 61 & 06 86 50 61 92

email: nicoleclaudechuit@wanadoo.fr

web: www.chambredugrignon.com

Located between Celle-Saint-Avant and Descartes (the birthplace of the philosopher), this small restored farmhouse is in a hamlet and offers two double rooms and a suite with double, two singles and child's bed. Private facilities; extra children's beds available. Living room with TV and open fireplace, lawned garden and parking. Golf 35 minutes.

Prices s €37-€40; d €47-€50; t €57-€60; extra person fr €10
Nearby ⛷ 7km ⚓ 30km 🏊 5km ⚲ 6km Restaurant 6km 🍴 6km
Spa 30km 🏛 6km ⚑ 12km **Notes** No pets Open February to December.

LA CROIX-EN-TOURAINE

▓▓▓ Chambre d'hôtes

Daniel COCHIN

103 rue d'Amboise, 37150 LA CROIX-EN-TOURAINE

☎ 02 47 57 94 55

On the outskirts of the old village, on a hill overlooking the Cher Valley, this establishment enjoys magnificent views. Four rooms, two twins and two doubles, each have private shower/WC. The stone fireplace in the living room is the work of the stonemason owner. Kitchenette, cot and high chair available. Large lawned garden. Discount on three nights or more.

Prices s fr €40; d fr €45; extra person fr €15 **Nearby** ⛷ 12km ⚲ 0.3km
⚲ 2km 🍴 2km 🏛 0.5km ⚑ 1km **Notes** No pets

LANGEAIS

▓▓▓ Chambre d'hôtes

Martine SANTENS

27 rue Anne de Bretagne, 37130 LANGEAIS

☎ 02 47 96 08 52 & 06 80 74 91 11

email: d.santens@laposte.net

This 19th-century squire's house in the heart of Langeais only 100 metres from the château has three comfortable rooms on the first floor, each with en suite bath or shower. Two to four people can be accommodated in each room, all of which are stylishly furnished.

A terrace looks out over the landscaped enclosed garden. Private parking.

Prices not confirmed for 2008 **Nearby** ⛷ 2km ⚓ 18km ⚲ 0.2km
⚲ 0.8km 🍴 1km ⚑ 0.5km **Notes** No pets English spoken

▓▓▓ iOi La Brosse

Laurence GARANTIE

37130 LANGEAIS

☎ 02 47 96 37 86 & 06 22 29 74 31

email: les-chambres-des-charmes@wanadoo.fr

web: http://perso.wanadoo.fr/les-charmes

A few minutes from the banks of the Loire and the château at Langeais, this house has three double bedrooms, all with private shower/WC. The owners are keen gardeners, and the house is on the edge of the woods, so visitors here are close to nature. Use of kitchen weekend meals by arrangement. Accommodation for horses, in stable or meadow.

Prices s fr €41; d fr €49; extra person fr €10; dinner fr €16
Nearby ⛷ 7km ⚓ 15km ⚲ 7km ⚲ 7km 🍴 6km 🏛 7km ⚑ 7km
Notes Pets admitted

LARCAY

▓▓▓ Manoir de Clairbois

Huguette ZEILER

37270 LARCAY

☎ 02 47 50 59 75 📠 02 47 50 59 76

email: info@manoirdeclairbois.com

web: www.manoirdeclairbois.com

One of the most gracious buildings in the area, this 19th-century manor house is elegantly decorated, set in large, tree filled grounds. On the first floor - a large suite with a double bed and convertible bed for two, bath, shower and WC; two double rooms with own bathroom and WC. There is a guest lounge and private pool.

Prices d €115-€140; extra person fr €25 **On Site** Private ⚲
Nearby ⛷ 5km ⚲ 0.1km Restaurant 0.1km 🍴 1km ⚲ 3km
🏛 0.5km ⚑ 7km **Notes** Pets admitted English spoken CC

LERNE

⦀ La Grande Cheminée

Suzanne BLANCHARD

37500 LERNE

☎ 02 47 95 94 46 & 06 73 05 82 74 📄 02 47 95 94 46

A 17th-century poultry farm on the borders of Poitou, Touraine and Anjou, providing three rooms with separate access, shower and wc: twin, a double and a suite with double and two single beds. Extra beds and baby equipment available. Small sitting room, kitchen area and large shady garden for guests to enjoy, as well as farm produce and wine.

Prices s €40-€43; d €45-€47; t fr €65; extra person fr €16
Nearby ⚓ 2km ⚘ 4km 🎣 6km ⚲ 15km Restaurant 7km ⛳ 1km
🚲 12km 🏛 7km ⛵ 12km **Notes** Pets admitted

LIGNIERES-DE-TOURAINE

⦀ Chambre d'hôtes

Jean-Pierre DUVEAU-CHARDON

22 la Croix des Durets, 37130 LIGNIERES-DE-TOURAINE

☎ 02 47 96 85 04

email: jp-b.duveau@terre-net.fr

web: http://duveauchardon.free.fr

Your hosts offer four en suite guest rooms on this fruit farm (apples and pears) in the heart of the Loire Valley. A suite in the old bakehouse has living room, kitchenette and can sleep four. A triple on the ground floor has its own entrance. Upstairs is a family room for four, and a triple. Antique furnishings, fridge, use of kitchen, shaded garden.

Prices s fr €47; d fr €50; t fr €62; extra person fr €10 **Nearby** ⚓ 6km
⚲ 17km 🎣 0.5km ⚲ 7km ⛳ 3km 🏛 7km ⛵ 7km **Notes** Pets admitted

---

LIGRE

⦀ ⦶ Au Prince Grenouille

Anne-Isabelle GEAIX

Le Manoir de Beauvais, 37500 LIGRE

☎ 02 47 93 49 97 📄 02 47 98 08 29

email: info@auprincegrenouille.fr

web: www.auprincegrenouille.fr

A 17th-century house listed as an historic monument, standing in its own walled grounds. There are four bedrooms, a double, two triples, and a room for four. All have private bath or shower room and WC, cots are available, and two of the rooms are Grade 4. Lounge with piano; swimming pool, table tennis, accommodation for horses. Meals by arrangement.

Prices s €75-€95; d €90-€120; t €115-€145; extra person fr €25; dinner fr €28 **On Site** 🎣 Private ⚲ **Nearby** ⚓ 3km ⚘ 10km Restaurant 7km ⛳ 2km 🎾 7km 🏛 7km ⛵ 7km **Notes** Pets admitted English spoken

---

LUSSAULT-SUR-LOIRE

⦀ Château de Pintray

Marius RAULT-COUTURIER

37400 AMBOISE

☎ 02 47 23 22 84 📄 02 47 57 64 27

email: marius.rault@wanadoo.fr

web: www.chateau-de-pintray.com

This 17th and 19th-century château is set on a six hectare wine-growing estate of Mountlouis. It provides three double rooms (one with sofa-bed), and two singles and a king-size bed, each with private facilities and charmingly decorated and furnished. Guests have use of a lounge with fireplace, TV and billiards.

Prices s fr €97; d fr €105; t fr €131; extra person fr €26
Nearby ⚓ 7km ⚘ 30km 🎣 2km ⚲ 6km Restaurant 3km ⛳ 6km
Spa 7km 🎾 7km ⛳ 3km ⛵ 7km **Notes** Pets admitted English spoken CC

LUZILLE

⦀ ⦶ La Rabottière

André et Annie SIMKHOVITCH

37150 LUZILLE

☎ 02 47 30 28 66

email: larabottiere@wanadoo.fr

Half-way between Chenonceaux and Loches in a rural location, this beautiful 18th-century property has three bedrooms on the first floor of the owners' home. There is a double room, and two triples - one with a double bed and a single, the other with three single beds. All have bathroom or shower room with WC. Meals available by arrangement.

Prices s fr €48; d fr €55; t fr €70; dinner fr €20 **Nearby** 🎣 4km
⚲ 10km ⛳ 3km 🏛 10km ⛵ 12km **Notes** Pets admitted

MANTHELAN

⦀ ⦶ Le Vieux Tilleul

Laurence VAN HAVERE

8 rue Nationale, 37240 MANTHELAN

☎ 02 47 92 24 32 & 06 76 37 09 79

email: le-vieux-tilleul@wanadoo.fr

web: www.le-vieux-tilleul.net

This large elegant house dates from 1820. It stands in the centre of a small town, but the garden offers peace and quiet. There are three bedrooms - two of them suites - all with single beds which can be linked to form doubles. All rooms have private showers and WCs. Garden with a huge lime tree and garden furniture. Meals by arrangement.

Prices s fr €60; d €65-€85; t fr €105; dinner fr €22 **Nearby** ⚓ 5km
⚘ 23km 🎣 0.5km ⚲ 15km Restaurant 15km ⛳ 0.5km 🎾 15km
⛵ 25km **Notes** No pets English spoken

MONTHODON

♦♦♦ ⏥ La Maréchalerie

Patricia et Danny NIEDBALSKI
Hameau Le Sentier, 37110 MONTHODON
☎ 02 47 29 61 66
email: info@lamarechalerie.fr
web: www.lamarechalerie.fr

This 19th-century half-timbered blacksmith's house, separate from the owners', is perched above a pretty valley, in a green and quiet spot. Near the Loire and Amboise with its châteaux; there are six rooms sleeping two up to five people with shower and wc. Sitting/dining room for guests in the old forge, with open fireplace. Country garden of one hectare, with terraces, furniture and leisure area. Stream, donkeys and children's games.

Prices s fr €36; d fr €40; t fr €49; extra person fr €9; dinner fr €15
Nearby ⚓ 12km ⚓ 20km ⚓ 2km ⚓ 9km Restaurant 3km ⚓ 9km
⚓ 4km ⚓ 9km **Notes** No pets English spoken

MONTRESOR

♦♦♦ Le Moulin

Alain et Sophie WILLEMS
37460 MONTRESOR
☎ 02 47 92 68 20 ⏚ 02 47 92 74 65
email: alain.willems@wanadoo.fr

Four rooms in a 19th-century mill built on the Indre, in a hectare of grounds with private swimming pool. There is a double room, a room with a double and two single beds, a twin and a room with four singles, all with private facilities. Large lounge/sitting room with abundant character and views of the millstream. Several restaurants nearby.

Prices s €57-€60; d €60-€65; extra person fr €16 **On Site** Private ⚓
Nearby ⚓ 20km ⚓ 17km ⚓ 3km ⚓ 0.5km ⚓ 0.3km **Notes** No pets English spoken

MONTS

♦♦♦ Château de la Roche

Diane DE CHAMBURE
37260 MONTS
☎ 02 47 26 70 08

In an outstanding location on the banks of the Indre, this 19th-century château is set in parkland and forest, near Tours and Azay-le-Rideau. Two doubles and one twin room, each with private facilities, TV and telephone; child's bed available (supplementary charge).

Prices d fr €130 **Nearby** ⚓ 3km ⚓ 3km ⚓ 3km ⚓ 12km
Notes No pets English spoken

♦♦♦ ⏥ La Tourainière, Les Gasniers

P et S MESNARD-GRATZL
37260 MONTS
☎ 02 47 34 99 68 ⏚ 02 47 26 60 66
email: la.tourainiere@wanadoo.fr
web: www.la-tourainiere.com

Set in a large, placid landscaped garden with a swimming pool, this characterful house dating from 1850 offers a vast suite and two bedrooms. One of the bedrooms has independent access. There is a communal guest lounge/dining room with French windows opening onto the pool. 10% discount is offered to guests staying more than three nights.

Prices s fr €64; d fr €72; t fr €87; dinner fr €25 **On Site** ⚓ Private ⚓
Nearby ⚓ 5km ⚓ 6km ⚓ 3km Restaurant 2.5km ⚓ 2.5km Spa 5km
⚓ 3km ⚓ 5km **Notes** No pets English spoken

MOSNES

♦♦♦ Chambre d'hôtes

Jean-Marc CHARPIN
La Lice, 67 rue Nationale, 37530 MOSNES
☎ 02 47 57 38 26 & 06 78 78 41 37
email: la-lice2@wanadoo.fr
web: http://perso.wanadoo.fr/la-lice

An aristocratic house of the late 19th century in a village by the Loire. The decoration of the house reflects the owners' passion for medieval chivalry. Three bedrooms - two on the first and one on the second floor - each with a private WC and washroom or bathroom. Garden terrace with furniture.

Prices s €41-€43; d €48-€50; t €61-€63; extra person fr €13
Nearby ⚓ 6km ⚓ 9km ⚓ 0.7km ⚓ 9km ⚓ 9km ⚓ 0.1km ⚓ 9km
Notes No pets

♦♦♦ Le Buisson

Marie-France BAQUET
37530 MOSNES
☎ 02 47 57 31 09 ⏚ 02 47 57 61 43
email: lebuisson@tiscali.fr
web: http://lebuisson.chez.tiscali.fr

This farmhouse is in an elevated position close to the Loire, between Blois and Tours, and is an ideal base for exploring the Touraine. It offers a double room and two triples, each with private facilities. There is a lounge/sitting room with open fire and TV, kitchen, terrace, parking, organic kitchen garden, lakes and farmyard on site.

Prices s fr €38; d €45-€55; t fr €63; extra person fr €12 **On Site** ⚓
Nearby ⚓ 3km ⚓ 2.5km ⚓ 2.5km Restaurant 2km ⚓ 2km ⚓ 2.5km
⚓ 12km **Notes** No pets

NAZELLES-NEGRON

ⵌ **Château de Nazelles**

Véronique FRUCTUS

16 rue Tue la Soif, 37530 NAZELLES-NEGRON

☎ 02 47 30 53 79 ▤ 02 47 30 53 79

email: info@chateau-nazelles.com

web: www.chateau-nazelles.com

Three guest rooms in an authentic 16th-century home which is a classified historic monument, constructed by Thomas Bohier (builder of the Château de Chenonceau). The house looks over the Loire Valley to the south and the Château d'Amboise and has grounds with terraces, cave dwellings and a swimming pool. There is a double room in a house and a double and twin in the château, all with private facilities and a large lounge. Closed Christmas and New Year.

Prices d €100-€130; extra person fr €25 **On Site** Private ⵛ **Nearby** ⵛ 1.5km ⵛ 9km ⵛ 0.5km Restaurant 3km ⵛ 1.5km ⵛ 0.2km ⵘ 2km **Notes** No pets English spoken

NEUIL (SACHE)

ⵌ ⵅ **Les Hautes Mougonnières**

Soline MESTIVIER

37190 NEUIL

☎ 02 47 26 87 71

email: jp.mestivier@voila.fr

web: http://perso.wanadoo.fr/jp.mestivier

A working farm that produces foie gras and strawberries and raises poultry offers five guest rooms, each with private shower and wc: a suite for four; two rooms for three (one of which has separate access and a cooking area); a double room; a single room. Lounge area with books, living room with antique furniture, cooking facilities. Parking, garden, awning, veranda. Regional produce for sale.

Prices s fr €46; d fr €46; t €62-€80; extra person fr €17; dinner fr €24 **Nearby** ⵛ 15km ⵛ 5km ⵛ 10km ⵛ 2km ⵛ 2km ⵘ 10km **Notes** No pets English spoken CC

NOIZAY

ⵌ ⵅ **Le Moulin Tresneau**

Antoine GUEGNAUD

563 route de Vernou, 37210 NOIZAY

☎ 02 47 52 17 21

email: resa@le-moulin-tresneau.com

web: www.le-moulin-tresneau.com

Set amongst the vineyards of Vouvray in château country, this 19th-century mill has five large guest bedrooms on the first floor. All rooms sleep two to four people, with shower or bath en suite. The wooded parkland garden has a kilometre of the Cisse river bank which feeds into the Loire. Function room and swimming pool.

Prices d €60-€70; t €75-€85; dinner fr €23 **On Site** ⵛ Restaurant Private ⵛ **Nearby** ⵛ 5km ⵛ 3km ⵛ 6km ⵛ 0.5km ⵘ 1km **Notes** No pets English spoken

PERNAY

ⵌ **L'Hérissaudière**

Claudine DETILLEUX

37230 PERNAY

☎ 02 47 55 95 28 & 06 03 22 34 45

▤ 02 47 55 97 45

email: lherissaudiere@aol.com

web: www.herissaudiere.com

A pretty renovated former coaching inn nestling in a seven hectare park. The five rooms available have a warm and refined atmosphere and include a suite with a king-size and single bed, a suite with a king size and two singles, a suite with four singles, a double room and a twin, each with private facilities and antique furniture. There is a library, wood fire, flowered terraces, tennis courts, heated swimming pool and table-tennis. Wi-fi and summer kitchen available. Golf and pony club nearby.

Prices s €130-€150; d €140-€160; t €165-€175; extra person fr €20 **On Site** ⵛ Private ⵛ Private tennis court **Nearby** ⵛ 3km ⵛ 12km ⵛ 5km Restaurant 3km ⵛ 3km ⵘ 15km **Notes** No pets English spoken

RAZINES

ⵌ ⵅ *La Prunelière*

M. MENANTEAU-BERTON

37120 RAZINES

☎ 02 47 95 67 38

email: la.pruneliere@infonie.fr

web: www.la-pruneliere.com

A restored farmhouse in a style typical of the area dating back to the 16th century. There are three first floor rooms: a double, a twin-bedded room, and a two-roomed family suite for four with baby's cot, fridge and microwave. All have TV and private facilities. Lounge, complete with an old wine-press; piano, boules pitch, landscaped garden with terraces.

Prices not confirmed for 2008 **Nearby** ⵛ 5km ⵛ 4km ⵛ 4km ⵛ 8km ⵘ 20km **Notes** No pets

RESTIGNE

ⵌ ⵙ ⵅ *Chambre d'hôtes*

Annette GALBRUN

15 rue Croix des Pierres, 37140 RESTIGNE

☎ 02 47 97 33 49 ▤ 02 47 97 46 56

email: annette.galbrun@wanadoo.fr

web: http://perso.wanadoo.fr/croix.des.pierres

Three rooms in a Tourangel house on a wine estate, each with separate access, shower and wc: a double room, a single and a room sleeping four. Kitchen, parking, garden and meals by reservation. Enjoy farm activities, learn the game of Boule de Fort and try some wine in a picturesque cellar (Vin de Bourgueil from the estate). Restaurant 1km.

Prices not confirmed for 2008 **Nearby** ⵛ 20km ⵛ 3km ⵛ 8km ⵛ 4km ⵛ 0.5km ⵘ 3km **Notes** No pets

RICHELIEU

▥ Chambre d'hôtes

Michèle COUVRAT-DESVERGNES
6 rue Henri Proust, 37120 RICHELIEU
☎ 02 47 58 29 40 ▤ 02 47 58 29 40
email: lamaisondemichele@yahoo.com
web: www.lamaisondemichele.com

A beautiful bourgeois home dating from the early 19th century and situated in a group of 17th-century buildings in Richelieu, opening onto a quiet enclosed park. There are two twin rooms and two doubles, all with private bathroom and wc; a large living room with open fire, telephone and TV. Indoor parking and garage. Animals accepted under certain conditions.

Prices s fr €80; d fr €100; t fr €120; extra person fr €20 **Nearby** ⚐ 7km ↧ 20km ⚐ 1km ⚐ 0.5km Restaurant 0.2km ⚐ 0.5km Spa 50km ⚐ 6km ⚐ 0.1km ⚐ 50km **Notes** Pets admitted English spoken Open 15 April to September.

▥ Chambre d'hôtes

Marie-Josephe LEPLATRE
1 rue Jarry, 37120 RICHELIEU
☎ 02 47 58 10 42

Four stylish guest rooms for two or three people in a house of character in the middle of Richelieu, all with private facilities and quality furniture. Winter garden exclusively for guests and French gardens. Restaurants, pony-trekking and 'swing-golf' nearby.

Prices s €48-€50; d fr €66; t fr €80; extra person fr €9 **On Site** ⚐ **Nearby** ⚐ 0.5km ⚐ 0.5km ⚐ 0.5km ⚐ 0.5km ⚐ 0.5km **Notes** No pets Open February to December.

RIVARENNES

▥ ▯▯ La Buronnière

Marie-Anne KUHN
2 route des Sicots, 37190 RIVARENNES
☎ 02 47 95 47 61 & 06 84 07 31 36
email: la-buronniere@wanadoo.fr
web: www.laburonniere.com

A former wine-growing property, in the heart of châteaux country, is the location for this chambres d'hôtes. It has four individually-themed rooms: a double, two twin-bedded rooms, and a split-level suite for four, with a double bed and two singles. All have private bath or shower room and WC. Lounge, use of washing machine, meals by arrangement.

Prices s fr €45; d fr €52; t €62-€70; extra person fr €10; dinner fr €19 **On Site** ⚐ **Nearby** ⚐ 2km ↧ 18km ⚐ 2km ⚐ 10km Restaurant 1km ⚐ 5km ⚐ 0.2km ⚐ 1km **Notes** No pets English spoken

RIVIERE

▥ ▯▯ Chambre d'hôtes

Jeanne MALEZY
Domaine du Héron, 9 rue des Pêcheurs,
37500 RIVIERE
☎ 02 47 93 10 32 & 06 85 84 25 15
email: hote@domaineheron.com
web: www.domaineheron.com

Overlooking the Vienne with direct riverside access, this 19th-century house has wonderful views over this tributary to the river Loire. There are two double rooms, and a suite for four (double bed plus singles), all with en suite facilities. The internal courtyard backs onto the village church. Garden and terrace; parking space. Wine tasting on site (the owner is a wine-grower).

Prices s fr €58; d €70-€80; t €90-€100; extra person fr €10; dinner fr €25 **On Site** ⚐ **Nearby** ⚐ 10km ↧ 15km ⚐ 5km Restaurant 4km ⚐ 5km ⚐ 5km ⚐ 5km **Notes** No pets Open March to November.

SAVIGNE-SUR-LATHAN

⌗ ○| & Chambre d'hôtes

Jean-Marie RONGIER

3 Faubourg de la Rue, 37340 SAVIGNE-SUR-LATHAN

☎ 02 47 24 04 44 ▤ 02 47 24 15 69

email: info@efgh.fr

web: www.efgh.fr

Back in the 18th century, this house was a cottage hospital. The village is famous for its many streams and is in good walking country, with a bird sanctuary nearby. It has five bedrooms: three doubles, a triple, and a room for four (double bed plus singles). All have private facilities. Meals by arrangement; courtyard and garden.

Prices s €45; d €45-€60; t fr €76; extra person fr €17; dinner fr €22
On Site Restaurant **Nearby** ⛷ 5km ⚓ 4km ✐ 3km ↖ ⌁ ⋙ 17km
Notes No pets English spoken

SAVIGNY-EN-VERON

⌗ Cheviré

Marie-Françoise CHAUVELIN

11 rue Basse, 37420 SAVIGNY-EN-VERON

☎ 02 47 58 42 49 ▤ 02 47 58 42 49

email: chauvelin.michel@wanadoo.fr

web: www.ch-hotes-chevire.fr

This 19th-century barn, attached to the owners' beautiful home, is in a wine-growing village in the Regional Natural Park and offers non-smoking accommodation. There are two double rooms (one with two extra folding beds) and a triple, all with private facilities. Cot available. Large living room with kitchen area, courtyard, garden, meadow with picnic area and garage.

Prices s €30-€37; d €40-€48; t €57-€60; extra person fr €12
Nearby ⛷ 8km ⚓ 15km ✐ 2km ↖ 4km Restaurant 1km ⌁ 1km
⚓ 4km ⋙ 8km **Notes** No pets English spoken Open 16 January to 14 December.

SEMBLANCAY

⌗ La Ferme du Grand Launay

Laurence PERREAU

37360 SEMBLANCAY

☎ 02 47 40 97 42 & 06 16 33 38 18

email: contact@legrandlaunay.com

web: http://legrandlaunay.com

In a converted outbuilding of what was once the farm of the château of Grand Launay are three bedrooms, all on the ground floor. There is a twin-bedded room, a double, and a room for four (double bed plus singles). All have private bath or shower room and WC. Garden with furniture; table tennis table. Good area for walking and cycling. Entirely non-smoking.

Prices s fr €60; d fr €70; t fr €85; extra person fr €10 **On Site** ✐
Nearby ⛷ 3km ⚓ 4km ✐ 18km ↖ 15km Restaurant 1km
⌁ 1.5km ⚓ 1.5km ⋙ 15km **Notes** No pets English spoken

SEPMES

⌗ ♥ ○| La Ferme des Berthiers

Anne-Marie VERGNAUD

37800 SEPMES

☎ 02 47 65 50 61 ▤ 02 47 65 50 61

email: lesberthiers@libertysurf.fr

Six rooms in a 19th-century family mansion on a Tourangel farm: two triple rooms, a double and a suite with a single and medium bed; and a twin and room for four in a separate building. All rooms have private facilities; cot and children's beds available. Living room, sitting room, courtyard, shady garden.

Prices s fr €44; d fr €53; t fr €64; extra person fr €10; dinner fr €24
On Site ♞ **Nearby** ✐ 3km ↖ 7km ⌁ 0.5km Spa 30km ⚓ 0.5km
⋙ 7km **Notes** No pets English spoken

SEUILLY

⌗ ○| Manoir de l'Abbaye

Franck COVIN

2 route de l'Abbaye, 37500 SEUILLY

☎ 02 47 95 81 02 & 06 75 21 33 94

email: manoir-abbaye.seuilly@wanadoo.fr

web: http://manoir.abbaye.free.fr

This property is a charming 15th-century manor house which overlooks the village of Seuilly. It has four first-floor bedrooms: a double-bedded room, a room with three single beds, a suite with two double beds, and a suite with a double bed and two singles. All rooms have private bath or shower room/WC, and there is a swimming pool.

Prices s fr €75; d €80-€110; t €95-€120; extra person fr €20; dinner
fr €26 **On Site** Private ↖ **Nearby** ⛷ 5km ⚓ 10km ✐ 4km
⌁ 4km ⚓ 6km ⋙ 7km **Notes** Pets admitted English spoken

SOUVIGNE

⌗ Le Clos de Launay

Pierre et Colette BESNIER

37330 SOUVIGNE

☎ 02 47 24 58 91 ▤ 02 47 24 58 91

email: besnier.pierre@wanadoo.fr

web: www.loisirscampagne.com

This large house stands in the middle of the countryside, overlooking a large lake. It has six first-floor bedrooms: three doubles; a twin-bedded room; a room for three, with double bed and a single; and a suite for four with a double bed and two singles. All rooms have private facilities. Cot and high chair; extensive grounds; fishing available.

Prices s fr €53; d €58-€60; t fr €74; extra person fr €16 **On Site** ✐
Nearby ⚓ 10km ↖ 18km ⌁ 2km ⚓ 2km ⋙ 25km **Notes** No pets
English spoken

ST-BAULD

⛉ ⍟ Le Moulin du Coudray

Sylvie PERIA

37310 SAINT-BAULD

☎ 02 47 92 82 64 & 06 67 20 02 17 📄 02 47 92 82 64

email: sylvie.peria@free.fr

web: www.lemoulinducoudray.fr.st

Three rooms in a restored 16th-century mill, situated on 3 hectares of parkland with a large pond (fishing possible). All rooms have luxury bathrooms and sleep two, either in double beds or twins. Day room reserved for guests and sitting room with open fire. Shaded paved terrace overlooking the park. Gym available. Dinners by reservation except Wednesday.

Prices s fr €49; d €60-€65; t fr €80; extra person fr €15; dinner fr €23 **On Site** 🎣 **Nearby** ⛳ 3km ⌀ 5km 🏛 10km ⚓ 15km **Notes** Pets admitted English spoken

ST-BRANCHS

⛉ ⍟ ⚐ Le Logis de la Paqueraie

Monique BINET

37320 SAINT-BRANCHS / CORMERY

☎ 02 47 26 31 51

email: monique.binet@wanadoo.fr

web: http://perso.wanadoo.fr/lapaqueraie/

A very beautiful restored house overlooking a lawn with a one hectare park with parking, garage and swimming pool. Two double rooms and two twins, all with private facilities and a lounge with open fireplace.

Prices s fr €80; d fr €85; extra person fr €20; dinner fr €28 **On Site** 🎣 Private ⚓ **Nearby** ⛳ 3km ⌀ 12km 🏊 2km Restaurant 3km ⌀ 3.5km 🏛 3.5km ⚓ 3km **Notes** Pets admitted English spoken

ST-EPAIN

⛉ ⍟ La Maison Rouge

Josseline ROSSI

37800 SAINT-EPAIN

☎ 02 47 65 89 55 & 06 12 44 59 09

email: chambredhote@aol.com

web: www.lachambredhote.com

At the centre of a complex of old farm buildings, overlooking the Manse Valley, this late 17th-century property has three enormous guest bedrooms, two on the ground floor and one upstairs. Each room has a double bed and two single folding beds; the upstairs room has independent access by an external staircase. All have private shower rooms/WCs.

Prices s €50-€55; d €50-€55; t €62-€67; extra person fr €12; dinner fr €23 **Nearby** ⛳ 1km ⌀ 20km 🏊 7km ⚓ 10km Restaurant 2km ⌀ 2.5km 🏛 2.5km ⚓ 6km **Notes** Pets admitted English spoken

ST-JEAN-ST-GERMAIN

⛉ Chambre d'hôtes

Nicole TAUZI

La Palombière, 2 impasse de la Garenne,

37600 SAINT JEAN SAINT GERMAIN

☎ 02 47 94 80 24 & 06 98 43 92 36

email: marcel.tauzi@wanadoo.fr

web: www.gites-lapalombiere.com

Right in the middle of this charming village not far from Loches and several other châteaux, this one-time farmhouse has three beautiful bedrooms. There is a double room, a twin-bedded room and a triple (double bed and a single). All have private shower room and WC. The house has been sensitively and extensively restored; rooms and garden are non-smoking. Enclosed garden.

Prices d fr €68; extra person fr €20 **On Site** 🎣 **Nearby** ⛳ 3km ⌀ 10km 🏊 2km ⚓ 9km ⌀ 3km Spa 50km 🏛 6km ⚓ 8km **Notes** No pets

⚜ ⋔◎⋔ La Maison Neuve

Clarisse et Stéphane GODEFROY
37600 SAINT JEAN SAINT GERMAIN
☎ 02 47 91 97 23 & 06 87 61 20 30 📄 02 47 91 97 23
email: contact@domainedelamaisonneuve.com
web: www.domainedelamaisonneuve.com

Big, bright rooms combining brick, stone and wood make this quite a stunning building. Overlooking the Indre Valley and close to the ancient town of Loches, it is a converted farmhouse with two double rooms and two triples (double beds plus singles). All have private bath or shower room and WC. Baby equipment available; internet access.

Prices s fr €63; d fr €70; t fr €88; extra person fr €18; dinner fr €28 **Nearby** ⚓ 4km ⚲ 3km ✐ 0.5km ➤ 5km Restaurant 1km ⌂ 3km 🏠 2.5km ⋙ 6km **Notes** No pets English spoken

---

⚜ST-MARTIN-LE-BEAU

⚜ Domaine Aurore de Beaufort

MOYER
23 rue des Caves, 37270 SAINT-MARTIN-LE-BEAU
☎ 02 47 50 61 51 📄 02 47 50 27 56
email: aurore.de.beaufort@wanadoo.fr

In the heart of Montlouis wine country, this 19th-century wine estate has five rooms with separate access, shower, wc and TV: a double; two sleeping five in single beds (three on mezzanine); a double with extra convertible double; a twin. Large lounge with telephone, books and fireplace and kitchenette. Garden with furniture and parking. Wine sampling and restaurant nearby.

Prices s fr €40-€45; d fr €48-€58; t fr €75; extra person fr €10 **Nearby** ⚓ 4km ⚲ 30km ✐ 2km ➤ 8km ⌂ 2km ✪ 8km 🏠 2km ⋙ 2km **Notes** Pets admitted English spoken

---

⚜ST-QUENTIN-SUR-INDROIS

⚜ La Bertinière

Françoise DUBOIS
Route de Chenonceaux,
37310 SAINT-QUENTIN-SUR-INDROIS
☎ 02 47 92 57 89
email: labertiniere@infonie.fr
web: www.labertiniere.fr.st

A suite and two bedrooms with independent entrances housed in a character 17th-18th century building that stands in seven square kilometres of wooded parkland surrounded by open countryside. The suite comprises a double room with en suite and a library-lounge with a double sofa-bed and a stereo system. The two triple bedrooms each have private washroom and WC.

Prices s fr €50-€57; d fr €60-€70; t fr €71-€81; extra person fr €15 **On Site** Private ➤ **Nearby** ⚓ 8km ⚲ 15km ✐ 3km Restaurant 10km ⌂ 5km ✪ 10km 🏠 10km ⋙ 10km **Notes** No pets English spoken Open April to October.

⚜ ⋔◎⋔ La Sauvagère

Marie-Thérèse BURIET
37310 SAINT-QUENTIN-SUR-INDROIS
☎ 02 47 92 29 96
email: contact@sauvagere.com
web: www.sauvagere.com

This 16th-century farmhouse is situated in a relaxing, tranquil setting in open countryside. It provides a double room, a twin and a suite with a large double and two single beds, each with private bathrooms. Guests also have use of a lounge with TV. Fishing at Indrois (4km) and Loches, Amboise and Chenonceaux are about 15 minutes away.

Prices s fr €47; d €52-€59; t fr €60; extra person fr €10; dinner fr €20 **Nearby** ⚓ 8km ⚲ 15km ✐ 4km ➤ 5km ⌂ 5km ✪ 10km 🏠 5km ⋙ 10km **Notes** No pets English spoken

---

TAUXIGNY

⚜ *Chambre d'hôtes*

Ludovic et Valérie MERIAUX
La Maison des Sources, 2 ruelle des Sources,
37310 TAUXIGNY
☎ 02 47 92 13 91 & 06 60 62 12 74
email: valerie.meriaux@aliceadsl.fr

Half way between Tours and Loches, this 17th-century bourgeois house has lots of character and offers three en suite rooms (a triple, a twin and a room for four) opening onto a courtyard with a spring; two have separate entrances. Kitchen area for guests. Raised garden with outdoor furniture.

Prices not confirmed for 2008 **Nearby** ⚓ 2km ⚲ 20km ✐ 0.2km ➤ 6km ⌂ 0.3km ⋙ 18km **Notes** No pets English spoken

---

THENEUIL

⚜ ⋔◎⋔ Les Bournais

Philippe MARTINEZ
37220 THENEUIL
☎ 02 47 95 29 61
email: les.bournais@orange.fr
web: www.lesbournais.net

There are three large guest rooms in this renovated farm which dates back to the 15th century. Accessed independently, each room has a large double bed, a single bed, a small sitting area and private shower/WC. Horse-riding and horse-drawn carriage rides. Artists' workshop. Evening meals. English and Spanish spoken.

Prices s fr €60; d fr €65; t fr €77; extra person fr €12; dinner fr €20 **Nearby** ⚓ 4km ⚲ 22km ✐ 2km ➤ 2km Restaurant 2km ⌂ 2km ✪ 2km 🏠 2km ⋙ 15km **Notes** No pets English spoken

TOURS

Nestled in a valley bordered by streams and ponds, Roche Buard is an 18th-century restored barn. Three rooms with private bathroom on the first floor. Right in the middle of the Chateaux of the Loire, Roche Buard is only 20 minutes from Tours and 10 minutes from Tours Loire Valley airport. Quiet and peace guaranteed in this piece of heaven.

Patricia et Gilles Lamoureux
La Roche Buard
F 37390 CHARENTILLY
Tel: 00 33 2 47 56 62 71
www.rochebuard.com

TRUYES

ⅢⅢ Ⅰ○Ⅰ Manoir de Chaix

Francis FILLON
37320 TRUYES
☎ 02 47 43 42 73
email: manoirdechaix@aol.com
web: www.manoir-de-chaix.com

A 16th-century manor 3km from the village of Truyes with six bedrooms: three double rooms, a triple and two rooms for two, three or four people; all roomy, quiet and with private facilities. Lounge for use of guests. Private swimming pool. Meals can be booked.

Prices s fr €47; d €60-€65; t €78-€85; extra person fr €13; dinner fr €21
On Site Private ⌇ **Nearby** ⚓ 8km ⚓ 15km ⚐ 3km ⚐ 3km ⚑ 3km
⚑ 20km **Notes** Pets admitted English spoken

VALLERES

ⅢⅢ Le Clos de la Baubinière

Caroline et Alain ALSEMBACH
15 la Bobinière, 37190 VALLERES
☎ 02 47 45 91 33 & 06 14 14 87 74
email: labaubiniere@aol.com

Well-placed for Langeais, Villandry and Azay-le-Rideau, this house has three guest rooms, two doubles and a twin-bedded room, all with private shower and WC. Alain, the host, collects vintage cars; Caroline prepares rather special breakfasts. Garden with lawn and space to park.

Prices s €45-€52; d €51-€58; extra person fr €15 **Nearby** ⚓ 9km
⚓ 5km ⚓ 4km ⚓ 4km Restaurant 1km ⚓ 4km ⚐ 4km ⚑ 2.5km
⚑ 4km **Notes** No pets English spoken

VERNOU-SUR-BRENNE

ⅢⅢ Ferme des Landes

Geneviève BELLANGER
Vallée de Cousse, 37210 VERNOU-SUR-BRENNE
☎ 02 47 52 10 93 ▤ 02 47 52 08 88

This 15th-century farmhouse has six rooms with antique furniture and private bathrooms and wcs, comprising three doubles, two twin rooms and a room for four.

Prices s fr €48; d €60-€63; t fr €67; extra person fr €10 **Nearby** ⚐ 7km
⚓ 7km ⚓ 7km ⚑ 3km ⚑ 15km **Notes** Pets admitted

ⅢⅢ Ⅰ○Ⅰ Le Moulin des Landes

Claude et Juliette BRUNEAU
10 rue Aristide Briand, 37210 VERNOU-SUR-BRENNE
☎ 02 47 52 08 21 & 06 13 03 02 24 ▤ 02 47 52 08 21
email: info@moulindeslandes.com
web: www.moulindeslandes.com

In the heart of the Vouvray vineyard, and close to many of the most important Loire châteaux, this 15th-century mill has five bedrooms. A cot is available; meals by arrangement. Use of owners' swimming pool.

Prices d €70-€100; t fr €85; extra person fr €25; dinner fr €30
On Site Private ⌇ **Nearby** ⚓ 10km ⚓ 2km ⚐ 1km ⚑ 0.1km ⚑ 0.3km
⚑ 12km **Notes** No pets English spoken

VOUVRAY

⌗⌗⌗ La Rochelière

Anneli TULKKI
6 rue Victor Hérault, 37210 VOUVRAY
☎ 02 47 52 61 47 📄 02 47 40 04 29
email: info@la-rocheliere.com
web: www.la-rocheliere.com

A classic 18th-century, south-facing town house next to the church with a stunning staircase in the main courtyard. Every room is non-smoking with private shower room and toilet. Two are doubles, one contains a double and a single bed, and one has three singles. There is a lounge and guests can use the owner's pool.

Prices s €60-€70; d €65-€80; t €95-€100; extra person €15-€20 **On Site** Private ↖ **Nearby** ⚓ 12km ♨ 2km ♪ 1km Restaurant 0.5km ⚘ 0.5km ⋙ 8km **Notes** No pets English spoken

⌗⌗⌗ ◎ *Le Manoir du Grand Echeneau*

Noël TERRY
Rue du Petit Côteau, 37210 VOUVRAY
☎ 02 47 52 75 43 📄 02 47 52 70 45
email: mail@chateaux4u.com
web: www.chateaux4u.com

An elegant south-facing Louis XV manor house among the Vouvray vineyards offers five luxury guest rooms with large double beds and bathrooms. Booked meals are served in the magnificent panelled dining room full of sculptures. Drawing room, library and satellite TV. Rose terraces. Troglodytic 16th-century chapel. Tennis 100 metres.

Prices not confirmed for 2008 **On Site** Private ↖ **Nearby** ⚓ 6km ♨ 15km ♪ 1km ⚘ 0.1km ⊞ 0.3km ⋙ 8km **Notes** No pets English spoken

LOIR-ET-CHER

AZE

⌗⌗⌗ ◎ Ferme de Crislaine

Christian & Annie GUELLIER
Crislaine, 41100 AZE
☎ 02 54 72 14 09 📄 02 54 72 18 03
email: annie.guellier@free.fr
web: www.crislaine.com

This dairy farm provides a suite for four, a family room, and a twin room, all with independent access, private facilities, possible extra bed and nursery facilities. Mezzanine with TV, opening onto communal room with cooking area. In the orchard there is a swimming pool, pétanque, outdoor furniture, farming activities (dairy and organic farming). Meals available if booked, except Sundays. Arrangements can be made to collect from train station.

Prices s €42-€44; d €45-€48; t €56-€58; extra person fr €10; dinner fr €18.50 **On Site** Private ↖ **Nearby** ⚓ 3km ♨ 12km ♪ 2.5km Restaurant 5km ⚘ 2.5km ⚘ 0.1km ⊞ 2.5km ⋙ 5km **Notes** Pets admitted English spoken

⌗⌗⌗ ♥ ◎ La Ferme de Gorgeat

Michel & Nadège BOULAI
Gorgeat, 41100 AZE
☎ 02 54 72 04 16 📄 02 54 72 04 94
email: michel.boulai@wanadoo.fr
web: http://perso.wanadoo.fr/gorgeat

This organic farm with pigs, chickens and cereals is located on the edge of the forest, and offers organic produce for sale. There are four double rooms and two family rooms, all with shower and wc (one with balneotherapy bath). Living room with cooking area for guests; meals available if booked. Animals by prior arrangement. Near the station (owner can organise lifts).

Prices s fr €45; d €42-€52; t fr €62; extra person fr €10; dinner fr €19 **On Site** ♪ Private ↖ **Nearby** ⚓ 1.5km ♨ 22km Restaurant 6km Water sports 4km ⚘ 1.5km ⚘ 6km ⊞ 2km ⋙ 3km **Notes** Pets admitted English spoken

BOURRE

⚜ Domaine de la Salle du Roc

Patricia BOUSSARD

69 Route de Vierzon, Manoir de la Salle, 41400 BOURRE

☎ 02 54 32 73 54 🖷 02 54 32 47 09

email: boussard.patricia@wanadoo.fr

web: http://manoirdelasalleduroc.monsite.wanadoo.fr

In the heart of the Cher Valley, four rooms in an 18th-century manor house include three double rooms, and a triple; all have private facilities. Large landscaped garden.

Prices s €60-€100; d €70-€110; t fr €130; extra person fr €28 **On Site** 🏊 **Nearby** ⛵ 10km ⛷ 20km ⚓ 5km Restaurant 1km Water sports 10km 🏊 5km Spa 25km 🎾 5km 🏛 1km 🚶 5km **Notes** No pets English spoken CC

⚜ Le Clos du Veret

Anne et Aimé JOSSEAU

9 Route des Vallées, 41400 BOURRE

☎ 02 54 32 75 51

email: contact@lestabourelles-leveret.com

web: www.lestabourelles-leveret.com

This 18th-century house is on the wine route, four kilometres from Montrichard, 20 kilometres from Chenonceaux, Chaumont and the Beauval Zoo. There are three bedrooms, two doubles and a room for four, all with private shower and WC. Wine-tasting and vineyard visits can be arranged.

Prices s fr €50; d fr €55; t fr €70; extra person fr €15 **Nearby** ⛵ 7km ⛷ 25km ⚓ 1km Restaurant 0.8km Water sports 4km 🏊 4km 🎾 4km 🏛 0.5km 🚶 5km **Notes** No pets English spoken

CANDE-SUR-BEUVRON

⚜ Le Court au Jay

C et L MARSEAULT

41120 CANDE-SUR-BEUVRON

☎ 02 54 44 03 13 🖷 02 54 44 03 13

email: letcl.marseault@wanadoo.fr

web: www.lacourtaujay.org

Situated in a farmhouse, one room for three (double and single bed), a double room and a twin, all with private facilities, heating and possible extra bed for each room. Dried flower workshop.

Prices s fr €42; d fr €45; t fr €60; extra person €10-€15 **On Site** 🎾 **Nearby** ⛵ 10km ⛷ 10km ⚓ 1km ⚓ 40km Restaurant 0.8km Water sports 16km 🏊 1km 🏛 1km 🚶 8km **Notes** No pets Open March to October.

CHAUMONT-SUR-LOIRE

⚜ Les Hauts de Chaumont

Dany GOMBART

2 Rue des Argillons, 41150 CHAUMONT SUR LOIRE

☎ 02 54 33 91 45

email: leshautsdechaumont@free.fr

web: www.france-bonjour.com/hauts-de-chaumont/

Close to the Château de Chaumont/Loire and the International Garden Festival, this property offers two double rooms and a twin with private facilities. Also available is a living room with breakfast tables, kitchenette, television, open fire, board games, swimming pool terraces, table tennis, cycle hire and parking. Special price for one or two people out of season (November to March) and after 3 nights.

Prices s €53-€60; d €53-€60; t €70-€73; extra person fr €15 **On Site** 🎾 Private ⚓ **Nearby** ⛵ 1km ⛷ 3km ⚓ 1km Restaurant 0.2km Water sports 15km 🏊 0.2km 🏛 0.5km 🚶 3km **Notes** No pets English spoken

CHAUMONT-SUR-THARONNE

⚜ La Gentil'Hommière

Jean Pierre GENTIL

5 Rue des Pres, 41600 CHAUMONT SUR THARONNE

☎ 02 54 96 60 22

email: gentilhommieres@wanadoo.fr

web: www.lagentilhommiere.com

A house with lots of character in a rural setting less than two kilometres from CenterParcs. There are two double rooms on the ground floor and a triple upstairs, with room for an extra bed. All three rooms have private shower and WC. Cot available. Enclosed grounds, garden furniture and lots of flowers. Fridge and microwave available. Secure parking.

Prices s fr €45; d fr €55; t fr €70; extra person fr €15 **On Site** ⚓ 🎾 **Nearby** ⛵ 9km ⛷ 14km ⚓ 10km Restaurant 5km 🏊 0.4km 🏛 0.5km 🚶 10km **Notes** Pets admitted

⚜ Le Petit Clos

Thierry LE MOING et René BARIL

6 Rue de la Folie, 41600 CHAUMONT SUR THARONNE

☎ 02 54 88 28 17 & 06 86 18 47 59

email: petitclos6@aol.com

web: www.lepetitclos.com

An old, brick-built, wisteria-clad house surrounded by a lovely garden with amusing gazebo from which to enjoy fine days. On offer are 2 doubles, 1 triple, 1 twin, and a family room for four. All have en suite shower and WC. Rooms are all named after châteaux on the Loire. Meals can be booked in advance, and pets are accepted with prior notice.

Prices s €55-€60; d €55-€60; extra person fr €15 **Nearby** ⭑ 18km ⬧ 15km 🏊 0.2km ⬥ 7km Restaurant 0.1km 🏊 0.2km ⛵ 9km **Notes** Pets admitted English spoken

CHEVERNY

⏐⏐⏐ ❍⏐ Ferme des Saules

Didier MERLIN
41700 CHEVERNY
☎ 02 54 79 26 95 📄 02 54 79 97 54
email: merlin.cheverny@wanadoo.fr
web: http://chambresdhotes.fr/lessaules

Close to the Château of Cheverny, in an area of forest and open countryside, guests can choose between two bedrooms for four and a double room and a double, each with private facilities (child's bed available). Swimming pool. Dinner (by reservation) on Friday, Saturday and Monday, with local produce prepared by the owner (a chef). Restaurants 1.6km. English and Dutch spoken.

Prices d €65-€75; t €89-€99; dinner fr €25 **On Site** Private ⬥ **Nearby** ⭑ 3km ⬧ 1.5km 🏊 5km Restaurant 1.6km Water sports 10km 🏊 5km 🏛 3km 🏛 2km ⛵ 18km **Notes** No pets English spoken

⏐⏐⏐ ❍⏐ La Levraudière

Sonia MAURICE
Route de Contres, 41700 CHEVERNY
☎ 02 54 79 81 99 📄 02 54 79 81 99
email: lalevraudiere@aol.com
web: http://lalevraudiere.free.fr

The five guest rooms here can accommodate a total of fourteen people. The heart of this 19th-century farmhouse has been restored with the greatest comfort of guests in mind. The house is surrounded by acres of meadows, and sits opposite the 18-hole golf course of the Château of Cheverny. Meals by arrangement.

Prices s fr €43; d fr €53; t fr €69; extra person fr €16; dinner fr €22 **Nearby** ⭑ 2km ⬧ 2km 🏊 5km Restaurant 1km Water sports 15km 🏊 0.5km 🏛 1.5km ⛵ 16km **Notes** No pets English spoken

CHITENAY

⏐⏐⏐⏐ Le Clos Bigot

Roland & Colette BRAVO MERET
41120 CHITENAY
☎ 02 54 44 21 28
email: clos.bigot@wanadoo.fr
web: www.gites-cheverny.com

In a peaceful location by the Châteaux of the Loire, 6km from Cheverny, a 17th-century property of considerable character. The 16th-century pigeon loft houses a double room, a suite for two or four people, and a flat for two to four. Garden with furniture and lavish breakfasts; many restaurants nearby. The owner, a lover of architecture, can advise guests on visits to châteaux in the area.

Prices s €50-€68; d €59-€90; t €90-€112; extra person fr €22 **On Site** 🏊 **Nearby** ⭑ 1km ⬧ 5km 🏊 5km ⬥ 5km Restaurant 1km Water sports 15km 🏊 1km 🏛 2km ⛵ 1km **Notes** Pets admitted English spoken

CHOUE

⏐⏐⏐ Grange de Choue

Christiane BASSET
Le Moulin Neuf, 41170 CHOUE
☎ 02 54 80 88 53 📄 02 54 80 88 53
email: cricri.basset@orange.fr
web: http://monsite.orange.fr/grange-de-choue

This beautiful old barn, with its six hectares of grounds, has an exceptional location by the river. The town is 600 metres away, and Paris just 42 minutes by high speed train. There are two bedrooms on the ground floor and one upstairs, all with private shower/WC. There is a large lounge/TV/games room, and a large garden with flowers.

Prices s €42-€47; d €47-€53; extra person fr €15 **On Site** 🏊 **Nearby** ⭑ 2km ⬥ 2km Restaurant 0.8km 🏊 2km 🏊 3km 🏛 0.9km ⛵ 25km **Notes** Pets admitted English spoken

CONTRES

⏐⏐⏐⏐ La Rabouillère

Martine THIMONNIER
Chemin de Macron, 41700 CONTRES
☎ 02 54 79 05 14 📄 02 54 79 59 39
email: rabouillere@wanadoo.fr
web: www.larabouillere.com

In Châteaux country, near Cheverny, this typical house is situated within a park. On offer are four rooms for two and one triple room, along with a suite in an annexe for four people with living room and open fire. All have private facilities. Sitting room and communal kitchen shared between two rooms. Restaurant 3km.

Prices s fr €50; d €65-€110; t €110-€140 **On Site** 🏊 **Nearby** ⭑ 0.5km ⬧ 6km 🏊 10km ⬥ 3km Restaurant 3km Water sports 20km 🏊 3km 🏛 3km ⛵ 25km **Notes** No pets English spoken CC

CORMERAY

⚏ ⫟ ᕚ Les Chambres Vertes

Sophie GELINIER
Le Clos de la Chartrie, 41120 CORMERAY
☎ 02 54 20 24 95 🖹 02 54 20 24 95
email: sophie@chambresvertes.net
web: www.chambresvertes.net

Between Chambord, Amboise and Chenonceau, these restored old farm buildings are set in a large peaceful garden. They offer three single rooms and two doubles, two of which can form a family suite, each with private facilities. Enormous living room, terrace and conservatory. Parking, swings and children's games in the grounds. Meals with organic produce may be booked.

Prices s fr €40; d €55-€60; extra person fr €18; dinner fr €23
On Site ⚘ **Nearby** ⛵ 0.5km ⚲ 5km 🏇 2km 🏊 4km 🖂 5km ᕱ 15km
Notes No pets English spoken Open March to November. CC

COULOMMIERS-LA-TOUR

⚏ ⫟ Chambre d'hôtes

Patricia BLUET
15 Rue Vendomoise, 41100 COULOMMIERS-LA-TOUR
☎ 02 54 77 00 33
email: patriciabluet@wanadoo.fr

Restored tower house near Vendome offering a twin room, a double, and a family room with a double and three single beds, each with private facilities. Guests may use the dining room, lounge with TV, baby facilities, indoor and outdoor games, table tennis, children's pedal go-karts and garden furniture.

Prices s fr €36; d fr €46; t fr €62; extra person fr €16; dinner fr €18
Nearby ⛵ 6km ⚲ 10km 🏌 0.1km 🏇 6km Water sports 6km 🏊 0.7km
🖂 6km ᕱ 8km **Notes** No pets English spoken

COUR-CHEVERNY

⚏ Le Béguinage

Brice & Patricia DELOISON
41700 COUR-CHEVERNY
☎ 02 54 79 29 92 🖹 02 54 79 94 59
email: le.beguinage@wanadoo.fr
web: www.lebeguinage.fr

Close to the Château de Cheverny, in a house of character in a country park, offering hot air ballooning from the grounds and fishing

in the river at the foot of the garden. It has four rooms for two, a triple room and a family room for four, all with private facilities. Parking available. Restaurant five minutes on foot.

Prices s €50-€75; d €52-€80; t €80-€85; extra person €5-€20
On Site 🏌 ⚘ **Nearby** ⛵ 3km ⚲ 3km 🏇 4km Restaurant 5km Water sports 15km 🏊 1km 🖂 5km ᕱ 15km **Notes** No pets English spoken Open February to December. CC

COUR-SUR-LOIRE

⚏ ⫟ ᕚ Château de la Rue

Véronique DE CAIX DE REMBURES
Fleury, 41500 COUR-SUR-LOIRE
☎ 02 54 46 82 47 🖹 02 54 46 88 17
email: chateau-de-la-rue@wanadoo.fr
web: www.chateaudelarue.com

A magnificent and fully restored 18th-century residence at the historic heart of the Loire Valley. The opulent house is surrounded by five hectares of landscaped grounds that contain a swimming pool. Delicious home-made preserves, made with fruit from the orchard, are served at breakfast. There are four charming rooms, with views over the grounds and en suite bathrooms. A guest lounge is available.

Prices s €80-€112; d €92-€158; t €130-€168; extra person fr €30; dinner €35-€49 **On Site** ⚘ Private 🏇 **Nearby** ⛵ 3km ⚲ 15km 🏌 0.6km Restaurant 1.5km Water sports 5km 🏊 0.5km 🖂 1km ᕱ 5km **Notes** No pets English spoken

CROUY-SUR-COSSON

⚏ ⫟ Le Moulin de Crouy

Nathalie HARRAULT
3 Route de la Cordellerie, 41220 CROUY-SUR-COSSON
☎ 02 54 87 56 19 🖹 02 54 87 56 19
email: lemoulindecrouy@wanadoo.fr
web: www.lemoulindecrouy.com

In a quiet spot 90 minutes from Paris, rooms in this mill have been personally designed by the owners, who are interior decorators. They include four double rooms and a family suite with one double bed, four singles and a sofa bed, all with private facilities. Very large living room with fireplace and TV, opening onto a terrace. The 14 hectare park has a tennis court. Meals may be booked.

Prices s fr €63; d fr €68; extra person fr €15; dinner fr €25 **On Site** 🏌 Private 🏇 Private tennis court **Nearby** ⛵ 4km ⚲ 10km Restaurant 4km Water sports 12km 🏊 1km ᕱ 15km **Notes** No pets English spoken CC

⚏ ⫟ Les Renardières

Joël & Nathalie SAINSON
41220 CROUY-SUR-COSSON
☎ 02 54 87 02 68 & 02 54 44 51 20
email: sainsonjoel@free.fr

In the Sologne, this ancient farm just one kilometre from town offers a suite comprising a double and a twin with bathroom and WC; two additional large guest rooms both sleep three, with a double bed and a single, and their own bathrooms. Breakfasts feature the honey from the estate, home-made jams and gingerbread. In the grounds there are walks in the woods and a huge lake.

Prices s fr €55; d fr €55; t fr €70; extra person fr €15　**Nearby** ☾ 4km ☖ 15km ✿ 2km ➴ 8km Restaurant 4km ⌣ 2km ⛫ 1km ⋘ 15km **Notes** No pets　English spoken

DANZÉ

⊞ La Borde

Michel KAMETTE

41160 DANZÉ

☎ 02 54 80 68 42　📄 02 54 80 63 68

email: michel.kamette@orange.fr

web: www.la-borde.com

This house of much character is situated between Danzé and la Ville aux Clercs, on a wooded estate of 10 hectares. Five very comfortable rooms each have a private shower and wc, and an extra bed if required. Television lounge for guests and garden with furniture. Price reduction over two nights.

Prices s €37-€54; d €50-€65; t fr €84; extra person fr €15　**On Site** ✿ ✾ Private ➴　**Nearby** ☾ 6km ☖ 20km Restaurant 2km Water sports 15km ⌣ 2km ⛫ 2km ⋘ 10km **Notes** Pets admitted　English spoken

FAVEROLLES-SUR-CHER

⊞ ▯❍▮ Domaine de la Chapelle

Rebecca SACKER

1 Route de Maugères, 41400 FAVEROLLES-SUR-CHER

☎ 02 54 32 58 48

email: domaine-de-la-chapelle@wanadoo.fr

web: www.domaine-de-la-chapelle.net

A beautiful situation - close to the Touraine vineyards, two kilometres from Montrichard, and in peaceful wooded grounds. There are two

double rooms, and a family suite for up to five. All have private bath or shower room and WC. Baby equipment, bikes for hire, garden with furniture and picnic area.

Prices d fr €55; t fr €67; extra person fr €12; dinner fr €20　**Nearby** ☾ 9km ☖ 20km ✿ 3km ➴ 2km Restaurant 3km Water sports 2km ⌣ 2km ✾ 3km ⛫ 2km ⋘ 4km **Notes** Pets admitted　English spoken

⊞ ▯❍▮ La Bigottière

B et R POLLET DAL SANTO

8 Route de la Bigotterie, 41400 FAVEROLLES-SUR-CHER

☎ 02 54 32 86 80　📄 02 54 32 90 62

email: roselyne@la-bigottiere.com

web: www.la-bigottiere.com

Five rooms, including a family suite of two rooms, in a restored, genuine 19th-century wine growing farm. Guests have use of a television room and kitchen equipped with oven, microwave and fridge. Baby equipment and children's games available. Pétanque ground and table tennis. Evening meals can be booked.

Prices s €44-€52; d €52-€57; t €65-€71; extra person fr €14; dinner fr €20　**On Site** ✾ Private ➴　**Nearby** ☾ 5km ☖ 8km ✿ 2km Restaurant 2km Water sports 2km ⌣ 3km ⛫ 2km ⋘ 4km **Notes** Pets admitted　English spoken

⊞ ▯❍▮ La Clémencerie

Maryse PERCHAT

27 Rue de la Clémencerie, 41400 FAVEROLLES-SUR-CHER

☎ 02 54 32 95 15

email: laclemencerie@wanadoo.fr

web: http://laclemencerie.com

On the wine route and in the heart of the châteaux country, La Clémencerie has a spacious suite for five, three double rooms and a twin-bedded room. All have private bath or shower and WC. Guests' lounge, games room, kitchenette and boules pitch. Garden with orchard and picnic area; good footpath access.

Prices s €55-€60; d €60; t €66-€71; extra person fr €15; dinner fr €20 **Nearby** ☾ 15km ☖ 25km ➴ 1.5km Restaurant 1km ⛫ 1km ⋘ 1km **Notes** No pets

FEINGS

⊞ Le Petit Bois Martin

Régis & Denise PAPINEAU

Favras, 41120 FEINGS

☎ 02 54 20 27 31

web: www.web-de-loire.com/C/41H1105.htm

Set in the Loire Valley, with its museums, châteaux and abbeys, close to Blois, this 18th-century house of character is in a shady park with cultural events in summer (classical music concerts, historical re-enactments, son et lumières). It has one suite for four, a suite for three, and one room for two, all with TV and private facilities, plus a games room and kitchen area. Enjoy lavish breakfasts with home-made preserves. Reduced prices for more than three nights.

Prices s fr €40; d €48-€60; t €60-€70; extra person fr €12　**On Site** ✿ **Nearby** ☾ 5km ☖ 8km ⛫ 5km ⋘ 18km **Notes** No pets　English spoken　Open March to 15 November.

FEINGS CONTINUED

〰 Les Roseaux

Jean & Gisèle LIONDOR

Favras, 41120 FEINGS

☎ 02 54 20 27 70

These rooms are on an old wine estate on the Châteaux of the Loire route, 20km from Blois in a wooded park with pond. There is a room for four, a triple room and a room for two. All have TVs and private facilities. Breakfast served in the family dining room. Separate kitchen with fireplace and individual fridges for guests.

Prices s fr €50; d fr €55; t fr €65 **On Site** 🌳 🎾 **Nearby** ⛵ 4km ⚓ 6km 🏊 3km 🚲 3km 🚶 18km **Notes** No pets Open Easter to October.

FONTAINES-EN-SOLOGNE

〰 Le Bois Fontaines

Bernard & Liliane MOUREN

591 Route d'Arian, 41250 FONTAINES-EN-SOLOGNE

☎ 02 54 46 44 98

email: liliane.mouren@orange.fr

web: www.leboisfontaines.com

A 17th-century longhouse in a peaceful spot between Cheverny and Chambord. There is a double room, a twin-bedded room, and a split-level room with a double bed and two singles. Each has a private shower room and WC; an extra bed is available, also a baby's cot. Lounge with open fire, use of kitchen.

Prices s €55-€60; d €60-€65; t fr €80; extra person fr €15 **Nearby** ⛵ 8km ⚓ 7km 🎾 2km Water sports 20km 🏊 2km 🎾 2km 🏛 2km 🚶 15km **Notes** No pets English spoken

FRETEVAL

〰 Château de Rocheux

L et M GUERRE GENTON

41160 FRETEVAL

☎ 02 54 23 29 74 📠 02 54 23 29 74

email: chateauderocheux@orange.fr

web: www.chateauderocheux.com

Three rooms, each with en suite bathroom, are available at this beautiful 18th-century château, which is surrounded by an 18-hectare park. There is a guest lounge where television and games are

provided, and a breakfast room that also contains a kitchenette for guests' use in the evenings. A lake with a beach (supervised in summer) is six kilometres away.

Prices s fr €50; d fr €57; t fr €69; extra person fr €15 **On Site** 🌳 **Nearby** ⛵ 12km ⚓ 4km 🎾 7km Restaurant 4km Water sports 6km 🏊 7km 🏛 4km 🚶 4km **Notes** No pets English spoken

GIEVRES

〰 La Pierre

Isabelle VATIN

41130 GIEVRES

☎ 02 54 98 66 93 & 06 63 74 49 89

email: vat-isa@club-internet.fr

web: www.lechampdupre.com

Just off the Tours/Vierzon road on a cereal farm; rooms here have separate access and include three rooms with a double and two single beds and private facilities. Extra bed possible. Sitting room, lounge with fireplace and kitchen area reserved for guests. Pond, covered parking, garden furniture and children's games. Animals accepted with prior notice. Closed holidays in February and Christmas.

Prices s fr €35; d fr €45; t fr €55; extra person fr €10 **On Site** 🌳 **Nearby** ⛵ 8km ⚓ 40km 🎾 3km Restaurant 2km Water sports 5km 🏊 3km 🎾 6km 🏛 5km 🚶 3km **Notes** Pets admitted

LA FERTE-SAINT-CYR

〰 ♿ Althaea

Alexandre LAVADO

4 Route de Ligny, 41220 LA FERTE-SAINT-CYR

☎ 02 54 87 90 05

email: althaeachambres@aol.com

web: http://membres.lycos.fr/althaea/

This five hectare property has two ponds and is set on the edge of a forest, near to Chambord. Four rooms are available: a double, a double with a single bed, a double with two singles and a room for six with three double beds, all with private facilities. Guests have use of a TV, barbecue and garden furniture.

Prices s fr €48; d fr €55; t fr €70; extra person fr €17 **On Site** ⛵ 🌳 🎾 Private 🎾 **Nearby** Water sports 15km 🏊 0.5km 🚶 15km **Notes** Pets admitted

LANGON

〰 Nocfond

Thierry COUTON PROD'HOMME

41320 LANGON

☎ 02 54 98 16 21

email: prodhomme.dominique@wanadoo.fr

An old restored farmhouse in a large flower-filled and shady park in the open Sologne countryside. Rooms include 'Bagatelle' (twin) and three doubles: 'Berthe St James', 'La Varende' and 'Les Guernazelles', all with private facilities. Parking. Dogs accepted.

Prices s fr €46; d fr €50; extra person fr €15 **Nearby** ⛵ 4km ⚓ 20km 🎾 3km 🏊 10km 🏛 6km 🚶 17km **Notes** Pets admitted English spoken

AVARDIN

ⅢⅢ Saint Eloy

ue & Harry PORTER
v des Reclusages, 41800 LAVARDIN
☎ 02 54 72 65 38
mail: susanporter@wanadoo.fr
web: www.loire-lavardin-accom.com

19th-century house perched on a hillside close to the River Loir,
one of the most beautiful villages of France. There are three two-
oomed suites for four, each with a double bed and two singles; a
iple room with a double bed and a single; and a twin-bedded room.
ll five rooms have private facilities, and some enjoy wonderful views.

Prices s €42-€50; d €52-€60; t €62-€70; extra person fr €10
On Site ✎ Private ⚲ **Nearby** ⚡ 10km Restaurant 0.8km ⚓ 1km
◻ 0.5km ⋙ 20km **Notes** No pets English spoken

ES MONTILS

ⅢⅢⅢ Château de Frileuse

Nicolas MARTIN DE BARRY
41120 LES MONTILS
☎ 02 54 44 19 59 🖷 02 54 44 98 33
email: frileuse@chateau-de-frileuse.com
web: www.chateau-de-frileuse.com

This château dates from the 12th to 18th centuries and stands in
its own large private grounds. There are three double rooms, one
with a linked single room. They are all decorated in an antique
style, and they all have private bathrooms. Apartment for five also
available. Guests' lounge, with a terrace overlooking the gardens.
Owner makes perfumes; workshop visits possible.

Prices s fr €110; d €120-€140; t fr €160; extra person fr €20
On Site ❀ **Nearby** ⚡ 1km ⚓ 8km ✎ 1km Restaurant 2km Water
sports 4km ⚓ 0.5km ⋙ 7km **Notes** No pets English spoken
Open Easter to 1 November.

AREUIL-SUR-CHER

ⅢⅢ ⅠⅭⅠ Les Aulnaies

hantal BODIC
Rue des Aulnaies, 41110 MAREUIL-SUR-CHER
☎ 02 54 75 43 89 & 06 08 92 28 21
mail: lesaulnaies@aol.com
web: www.lesaulnaies.com

ld sheep farm among the vineyards and forest offering three double
ooms and two sleeping four with bathroom and wc. Television with
uropean channels, swimming pool, pond in three hectare park,
shing, cycles, volleyball court available. Beauval Zoo 2km. Closed
hristmas to 1 January.

rices s fr €60; d €75-€95; t fr €105; extra person fr €18; dinner fr €27
n Site Private ⚲ **Nearby** ⚡ 5km ⚓ 25km ✎ 4km Restaurant 4km
Vater sports 6km ⚓ 5km ◻ 4km ⋙ 6km **Notes** No pets English
poken

ⅢⅢ Les Mariniers

Viviane & Patrick VINCENT
119 Rue de la République, 41110 MAREUIL-SUR-CHER
☎ 02 54 71 56 53 & 06 67 53 67 17
email: viviane.vincent@wanadoo.fr
web: www.lesmariniers.com

A large 19th-century house in the midst of the vineyards and châteaux
of the Loire region and just three kilometres from the Zoo at Beauval.
There are three comfortable double bedrooms, all with private
bath/shower room and WC. Lounge with television, and enclosed
landscaped gardens of one hectare.

Prices s €48-€50; d €56-€65; extra person fr €15 **On Site** ✎
Nearby ⚡ 3km ⚓ 3km Water sports 3km ⚓ ◻ 3km ⋙ 5km
Notes Pets admitted

MAZANGE

ⅢⅢⅢ Moulin d'Echoiseau

Madeleine LAUTMAN
Le Gue du Loir, 41100 MAZANGE
☎ 02 54 72 19 34 🖷 02 54 72 19 34
email: moulin-echoiseau@wanadoo.fr
web: www.moulin-echoiseau.fr

This charming old mill, once the summer residence of Alfred de
Musset, would be an ideal place to stay for naturalists. The quiet
and sprawling grounds have ponds, water courses and a waterfall.
The renovated building offers a family suite, and a charming attic
room with twin beds and a view over the grounds is decorated
and furnished in the Mozart style, each with bathroom and WC.
All European languages spoken. Free for children under 5.

Prices d €60-€80; extra person fr €15 **On Site** ✎ Private ⚲
Nearby ⚡ 3km ⚓ 30km Restaurant 2.5km Water sports 3km
⚓ 7km ◻ 1.5km ⋙ 5km **Notes** Pets admitted English spoken

MER

♦♦♦ Le Clos

Joëlle MORMICHE

9 Rue Jean et Guy Dutems, 41500 MER

☎ 02 54 81 17 36 📄 02 54 81 70 19

email: mormiche@wanadoo.fr

web: www.chambres-gites-chambord.com

Two triple rooms, two doubles (one with possible spare bed) and a two-roomed suite with four single beds are available here, with lots of character and private facilities. Guests have a kitchenette, sitting room, billiards and garden with enclosed parking at their disposal. Display and sale of paintings. Leisure area. Two country gîtes nearby.

Prices s €49-€52; d €58-€65; t €73-€80; extra person fr €15
On Site 🏊 🌳 **Nearby** ⛵ 0.5km 🚴 12km ⟋ Water sports 0.5km
🏕 0.5km 🚶 0.5km **Notes** No pets English spoken Open February to December. CC

MEUSNES

♦♦♦ Chambre d'hôtes

Patrick & Dominique LEGRAS

210 Rue Jean Jaures, 41130 MEUSNES

☎ 02 54 32 59 66 & 06 16 03 83 14

email: plegras5@hotmail.com

web: www.chez.com/closeriedemeusnes/

A charming and tranquil girls' school dating from the end of the 18th-century, converted to offer four bedrooms opening onto a walled garden: a double suite with day bed, a room with double and single beds and two double rooms (with possible extra double bed). All have private facilities and guests can enjoy the swimming pool, garden furniture and picnic in the park.

Prices s €50-€65; d €56-€75; t €78-€87; extra person €9-€20
On Site Private ⟋ **Nearby** ⛵ 12km 🚴 30km ⟋ 0.5km Water sports 12km 🏕 0.5km 🏛 0.2km 🚶 6km **Notes** Pets admitted English spoken

MONDOUBLEAU

♦♦♦ 🍴 Carrefour de l'Ormeau

I PEYRON et A GAUBERT

7 Carrefour de l'Ormeau, 41170 MONDOUBLEAU

☎ 02 54 80 93 76 📄 02 54 80 93 76

email: peyron.isa@wanadoo.fr

web: www.carrefour-de-lormeau.com

Your hosts in this large 17th-century house are a talented cook and a furniture designer. Perfectly situated to explore the region or relax in the calm, enclosed garden. The four spacious rooms sleep up to six - one is en suite. Evening meals can be reserved between April and September. Ideal for training courses.

Prices s fr €41; d €45-€50; t fr €64; extra person fr €16; dinner fr €23
On Site Restaurant 🌳 **Nearby** ⛵ 5km 🚴 40km ⟋ 0.3km ⟋ 0.5km
🏕 0.5km 🏛 20km 🚶 26km **Notes** Pets admitted English spoken

MONT-PRES-CHAMBORD

♦♦♦ La Giraudière

Eliane & Jean Luc PION

256 Rue de la Giraudière,

41250 MONT-PRES-CHAMBORD

☎ 02 54 70 84 83 & 06 86 80 33 05

In the heart of Loire châteaux country, set in a large, flower-filled garden with above ground pool. Breakfast is served in the family's room. The three en suite guest rooms are on the first floor - two doubles and a twin.

Prices s fr €45; d €50-€55 **On Site** Private ⟋ **Nearby** ⛵ 6km
🚴 12km ⟋ 2km Restaurant 0.8km Water sports 15km 🏊 1km 🌳 8km
🏛 1km 🚶 15km **Notes** Pets admitted English spoken Open Easter to 1 November.

MONTEAUX

♦♦♦ Les Cedres

Michelle LECOMTE

20 Rue du Colonel Rol-Tanguy, 41150 MONTEAUX

☎ 02 54 70 20 09

email: michel.lecomte2@freesbee.fr

web: www.chambres-les-cedres.com

Near the village centre, on the Vineyard Trail, two double rooms with separate access and a suite for two to four people with two double beds (one with canopy) and kitchenette. All have private facilities; extra bed and baby equipment available. Enclosed garden, parking.

Prices s €45-€55; d €50-€60; t €60-€70; extra person fr €10 **On Site** ⟋
Nearby ⛵ 10km 🚴 8km ⟋ 2km ⟋ 10km Restaurant 1km 🏊 5km
🚶 2km **Notes** Pets admitted

MONTLIVAULT

♦♦♦ Les Salamandres

Jean Claude PARZY

1 Rue de Saint Dye, 41350 MONTLIVAULT

☎ 02 54 20 69 55 📄 02 54 20 69 55

email: mail@salamandres.fr

web: http://salamandres.fr

An ancient wine-growing farm between Loire and Chambord, at the gateway to the Sologne, offering three double rooms, a triple and a suite with a double and two single beds, all with private facilities.

arking, garden and traditional meals with the owners - booking
equired. Cycling, tennis and rambling nearby.

rices s fr €46.50; d €49.50-€58.50; t fr €68.50; extra person fr
15   **On Site** 🎾 Private 🏇   **Nearby** ⚓ 2km ♨ 12km ⛵ 1km
estaurant 0.2km Water sports 4km 🛶 0.5km 🏛 0.3km ⛪ 12km
lotes No pets English spoken

MONTRICHARD

ⅲ ⅰⓞⅰ Maison Carre

ierre & Evelyne FILIOZAT
0 Rue de Tours, 41400 MONTRICHARD
☎ 06 70 71 43 15 & 02 54 32 60 24
mail: filiozat.pierre@wanadoo.fr
veb: http://monsite.wanadoo.fr/maison.carre

hree spacious guest rooms have been created in the outbuildings of
his early 19th-century family house. Each room has a double bed, a
ouble sofabed, TV, shower, basin and WC. The vast gardens have a
rivate lake, and a beach area on the River Cher with canoes and
edalos. Private parking. Shops 500 metres.

rices s fr €55; d fr €60; t fr €75; extra person fr €15; dinner fr €20
Nearby ⚓ 10km ♨ 20km ⛵ 0.2km 🏇 0.5km Restaurant 0.5km Water
ports 1km 🛶 1km 🏛 0.3km 🏛 0.5km ⛪ 0.2km   **Notes** No pets
nglish spoken

NOYERS-SUR-CHER

ⅲ La Noisetière

rançoise & Raoul COUETTE
9 Rue du Port, 41140 NOYERS-SUR-CHER
☎ 02 54 75 06 25
mail: noisetiere.hotes@wanadoo.fr
veb: www.noisetiere.com

property well-placed for visits to the châteaux and wine cellars of
his region, overlooking the Canal du Berry and close to the River
her. The three bedrooms have individually themed decorations, and
ach has a private shower room and WC. Guests' lounge area on
nezzanine floor. Fishing close by; Beauval zoo 5km.

rices s fr €50; d €55-€65; extra person fr €15   **On Site** ⛵
Nearby ⚓ 1km ♨ 15km 🏇 3km Restaurant 0.5km Water sports 2km
🛶 0.5km 🎾 3km 🏛 3km ⛪ 1.5km   **Notes** Pets admitted

PONTLEVOY

ⅲⅲⅲ *Chambre d'hôtes*

Robert INGRAM
9 Rue de la Cure, 41400 PONTLEVOY
☎ 02 54 32 01 29 📄 02 54 32 02 93
email: la-cure@wanadoo.fr
web: www.la-cure.com

In the heart of Pontlevoy, near the Abbey and amidst the
châteaux of the Loire Valley, this 17th-century house offers
five individually decorated guest bedrooms. Patio and peaceful
internal garden area. Full breakfast, internet, private garage. Cots
on request.

Prices not confirmed for 2008   **On Site** ⚓   **Nearby** ♨ 20km
⛵ 7km Water sports 7km 🛶 ⛪ 7km   **Notes** No pets English
spoken

ⅲ ⅰⓞⅰ La Ferme d'O

Alain DELMAS
10 Rue de Paradis, 41400 PONTLEVOY
☎ 02 54 32 58 07 📄 02 54 32 58 07
email: contact@ferme-do.com
web: www.ferme-do.com

Right in the heart of the châteaux country, this 1860s farmhouse has
been beautifully and sensitively restored. There are five bedrooms,
all triples (double bed and a single in each), and all with private
shower room and WC. There is a large living room; meals, and
relaxation massage, are available by arrangement. Vineyard visits can
be arranged.

Prices s €65-€85; d €65-€85; t €75-€95; extra person fr €15; dinner fr
€25   **On Site** Private tennis court   **Nearby** ⚓ 2km ♨ 15km ⛵ 7km
🏇 7km Restaurant 0.5km Water sports 7km ⛪ 7km   **Notes** No pets
English spoken

ROCE

ⅲ La Touche

Jean Louis NOUVELLON
41100 ROCE
☎ 02 54 77 19 52 📄 02 54 77 06 45
email: jl_nouvellon@yahoo.fr
web: http://gite.latouche.free.fr/.

Five kilometres east of Vendôme, in a green and relaxing spot. One
twin room, two rooms sleeping three with sitting area and a family
room on two levels for four to five people, with small kitchen. All have
separate facilities. Volleyball, archery, table tennis and mountain bikes.

Prices s fr €40; d fr €50; t fr €65; extra person fr €15   **On Site** ⛵ 🎾
Private 🏇   **Nearby** ⚓ 8km Restaurant 6km Water sports 14km 🛶 6km
🏛 6km ⛪ 7km   **Notes** Pets admitted English spoken Open 15 June to
August.

SAMBIN

▦ Le Pré Karvain

Karine & Sylvain CARLO

5 Rue de la Croix, 41120 SAMBIN

☎ 02 54 20 17 25 & 06 65 15 80 40 ▤ 02 54 20 17 25

email: karine.sylvain@wanadoo.fr

web: www.leprekarvain.org

A restored farmhouse dating back to the early 19th century. On the ground floor is a twin-bedded room with its own entrance; upstairs is a double, and a two-roomed family suite with two double beds, two singles and a baby's cot. All have private shower room and WC. Guests' kitchen, billiard table, terrace with garden furniture, landscaped grounds.

Prices s fr €40; d fr €50; t fr €65; extra person fr €15 **On Site** ❦ **Nearby** ⚲ 6km ⚑ 12km ℘ 10km ⚞ 20km ⌕ 0.5km ⋙ 20km **Notes** Pets admitted English spoken

SANTENAY

▦ Herceux

Bernard THOMAS

La Ferme d'Herceux, 41190 SANTENAY

☎ 02 54 46 12 10 ▤ 02 54 46 18 17

email: lafermedherceux@wanadoo.fr

web: http://lafermedherceux.monsite.wanadoo.fr

Ten minutes from the Amboise exit on the A10 motorway, and close to Blois, this ancient renovated farm is a haven of quiet. A family suite has two rooms which could sleep six, a bathroom and WC; a double has en suite shower and WC, and a twin has bathroom and WC. Games room; garden furniture and veranda. Reduced rates for three or more nights.

Prices s fr €49; d fr €59-€79; t fr €99 **On Site** ❦ Private ⚞ **Nearby** ⚲ 5km ⚑ 5km ℘ 10km Restaurant 9km ⌕ 10km ⚑ 10km ⋙ 10km **Notes** No pets

▦ ✿ Le Bas Beau Pays

Jean & Monique DEUTINE

41190 SANTENAY

☎ 02 54 46 12 33 & 06 72 71 18 96 ▤ 02 54 46 12 33

email: j.deutine@wanadoo.fr

web: www.ferme-beau-pays.com

Four guest rooms on an agricultural estate in the Loire Valley, near the châteaux. There is a room with a double bed and single, a room for four, a twin room and a double. Each has shower, wc and separate entry. Central heating, shady garden.

Prices s fr €36; d fr €45; t fr €62; extra person fr €17 **Nearby** ⚲ 20km ⚑ 20km ℘ 10km ⚞ Water sports 20km ⌕ 4km ⚑ 4km ⋙ 14km **Notes** No pets

SARGE-SUR-BRAYE

▦ La Vougrerie

Claude & Martine ROUSSEAU

41170 SARGE-SUR-BRAYE

☎ 02 54 72 78 24 ▤ 02 54 72 75 96

email: rousseaumcjk@wanadoo.fr

web: http://vougrerie.free.fr

A farmhouse in open country four kilometres out of town, with panoramic views over the Percheron countryside. It has three rooms with private facilities, a sitting room for guests, kitchen, swimming pool, ten-speed bikes and mountain bikes available. Silk-painting lessons. Animals accepted with prior notice.

Prices s fr €35; d fr €43; t fr €53; extra person fr €12 **On Site** ❦ Private ⚞ **Nearby** ⚲ 4km ⚑ 25km ℘ 4km Restaurant 3km Water sports 20km ⌕ 4km ⚑ 3km ⋙ 20km **Notes** Pets admitted English spoken

▦ Les Ganeries

Josiane JEULIN

41170 SARGE-SUR-BRAYE

☎ 02 54 72 78 44 ▤ 02 54 72 78 44

email: lesganeries@free.fr

web: http://lesganeries.free.fr

A country retreat with: Poppy, a double room with small lounge and en suite shower; Cornflower has a four poster and a single, small lounge, spa bath; Foxglove is a double with spa bath; Iris is a family suite with three singles and a double bed, spa bath and child bath. Lounge and fireplace, kitchenette, above ground pool and games.

Prices s fr €35; d fr €45; t fr €55; extra person fr €10 **On Site** ❦ Private ⚞ **Nearby** ⚲ 2km ⚑ 30km ℘ 2km Restaurant 8km Water sports 20km ⌕ 2km ⚑ 5km ⋙ 20km **Notes** No pets English spoken

SELLES-SAINT-DENIS

▦ Les Atelleries

Caroline QUINTIN

41300 SELLES-SAINT-DENIS

☎ 02 54 96 13 84 ▤ 02 54 96 13 78

email: caroline.quintin@wanadoo.fr

web: www.lesatelleries.com

At the heart of Sologne in 65 hectare grounds, this farmhouse has guest rooms available in the outbuildings. A double room and room with a double and single bed are in a bakery, restored along with its ovens, and in a half-timbered building there is a triple room. All have private facilities. Kitchen and lounge reserved for guests.

Prices d fr €50; t fr €60; extra person fr €10 **Nearby** ⚲ 20km ⚑ 40km ℘ 5km ⚞ 15km Restaurant 5km Water sports 13km ⌕ 5km ⚑ 10km ⚑ 5km ⋙ 15km **Notes** Pets admitted English spoken Open April to December.

SERIS

⚞ ❤ ⟨◎⟩ **Chambre d'hôtes**

ean Yves & Annie PESCHARD
0 Chemin de Paris, 41500 SERIS
☎ 02 54 81 07 83 ▤ 02 54 81 39 88
email: jypeschard@wanadoo.fr
web: http://fermepeschard.free.fr

n the Loire Valley with its famous châteaux, this working farm
ffers rooms in its 19th-century farmhouse: three doubles (one with
onvertible double bed), a twin with two extra beds, and a room with
ouble bed, single bed, spare bed and cot. All have private facilities.
iving room for guests in old cellar, covered garden area with outdoor
ames, bikes available for hire and possible guided tours. Preserve
haking on site.

Prices s €45-€48; d €49-€52; t fr €70; extra person €13-€15;
inner €18-€19 **On Site** ❀ **Nearby** ⚲ 8km ⚳ 15km ✍ 7km
⚓ 7km Restaurant 4km Water sports 15km ⌚ 5km ⛫ 5km ⋙ 7km
Notes English spoken CC

SEUR

⚞ **La Valinière**

ean Pierre D'ELIA
0 Route de Cellettes, 41120 SEUR
☎ 02 54 44 03 85
email: la.valiniere@laposte.net
web: http://lavaliniere.free.fr

n unusual property in the heart of the châteaux country with three
etro-style bedrooms, all with private bathroom and WC. The hosts,
ho have more than 20 years experience, pride themselves on the
uality and variety of the breakfasts they serve. Kitchenette for guest
se.

Prices s €42-€52; d €50-€64; t €67-€77; extra person €10-€12
On Site ✍ ❀ **Nearby** ⚲ 10km ⚳ 10km ✈ 10km Restaurant 3km
Water sports 10km ⌚ 3km ⛫ 3km ⋙ 10km **Notes** No pets English spoken

---

ST-AIGNAN-SUR-CHER

⚞ **Chambre d'hôtes Sousmont**

Geneviève BESSON
66 Rue Maurice Berteaux, Sousmont,
41110 ST-AIGNAN-SUR-CHER
☎ 02 54 75 24 35 ▤ 02 54 75 24 35

A town house near the châteaux of the Loire, with charming guest
rooms: a stylish two-roomed suite with two double beds, a twin room,
a room for four opening onto the garden and a room with double
bed and large single. All have private facilities.

Prices d fr €60; extra person fr €18 **On Site** ✍ Water sports
Nearby ⚲ 3km ⚳ 25km ✈ 0.5km Restaurant 0.1km ⛫ 0.5km
⋙ 2km **Notes** No pets

⚞ **Le Clos Dassault**

Francine CHALONS
41110 ST-AIGNAN-SUR-CHER
☎ 02 54 75 59 43 & 06 75 71 86 30 ▤ 02 54 75 59 43
email: chabodo@orange.fr
web: http://le-clos-dassault.site.voila.fr

This is an exceptional house, in extensive grounds overlooking the
River Cher. Three spacious ground floor bedrooms, two doubles and a
triple, all with private bath or shower room and WC, open onto a
terrace overlooking the river, and there is a large impressive courtyard.

Prices s €50-€75; d €75; t fr €95; extra person fr €20 **On Site** ✍
Nearby ⚲ 2km ✈ 0.5km Restaurant 1km Water sports 1km ⌚ 1.5km
❀ 1km ⛫ 1km ⋙ 2.5km **Notes** Pets admitted English spoken Open
Easter to November.

ST-CLAUDE-DE-DIRAY

▐▐▐ Le Relais de Nozieux

Lysiane & Alain GILLMETT

2 Rue de Nozieux, 41350 ST-CLAUDE-DE-DIRAY

☎ 02 54 20 63 50 ▤ 02 54 20 63 50

email: a.gillmett@wanadoo.fr

web: http://lerelaisdenozieux.free.fr

This is an old coaching inn dating from the 16th and 17th centuries, less than a kilometre from the River Loire and facing the château of Ménard on the opposite bank. There are three double bedrooms, all with private shower room/WC; also a sauna, multi-gym, billiards and table-tennis.

Prices s fr €55; d fr €60; extra person fr €16   **On Site** ☜
Nearby ⛷ 2.5km ♨ 12km ♪ 0.9km ⸲ 4km Restaurant 1.5km Water sports 4km ⤓ 4km ⟐ 1.5km ⋙ 9km   **Notes** No pets   English spoken

ST-DENIS-SUR-LOIRE

▐▐▐ ⅙ Harmonies

M CHAURIN et M-A CHESNEAU

46 Rue du Château d'eau, Villeneuve,

41000 ST-DENIS-SUR-LOIRE

☎ 02 54 74 16 45 & 06 81 31 42 06 ▤ 02 54 78 40 23

email: chaurin.marc@wanadoo.fr

web: http://monsite.wanadoo.fr/chambresharmonies

Three rooms have been created here from an attic and a room which once housed the wine press. There is a family room with a double bed and three singles; a room with a double bed and a convertible, and a double room with access for disabled guests. All have private facilities. Use of kitchen, terrace with garden furniture.

Prices s €43-€50; d €55-€60; t fr €80   **Nearby** ⛷ 6km ♨ 20km ♪ 1km ⸲ 6km Restaurant 1km Water sports 6km ⤓ 1km ☜ 4km ⟐ 1km ⋙ 6km   **Notes** No pets   English spoken

▐▐▐ ⦿⦿ La Villa Médicis

Muriel CABIN-SAINT-MARCEL

Mace, 41000 ST-DENIS-SUR-LOIRE

☎ 02 54 74 46 38 ▤ 02 54 78 20 27

email: medicis.bienvenue@wanadoo.fr

An 18th/19th-century house in parkland on the banks of the Loire, 3km from Blois. It has a double room, two rooms sleeping four and three sleeping two, each with private facilities. Guests have use of

the sitting room and library. Meals may be booked. Special rates for groups of four.

Prices s €58-€88; d €68-€98; t €78-€118; dinner fr €32
On Site Restaurant   **Nearby** ⛷ 2km ♨ 15km ♪ 0.5km ⸲ 5km Water sports 0.5km ⤓ 0.3km ⟐ 1km ⋙ 5km   **Notes** No pets   English spoken

ST-DYE-SUR-LOIRE

▐▐▐ L'Échappée Belle

Francis BONNEFOY

120 Rue Nationale, 41500 ST-DYE-SUR-LOIRE

☎ 02 54 81 60 01

email: fbonnefoy@libertysurf.fr

web: http://perso.libertysurf.fr/fbonnefoy

Francis and Béatrice open their 19th-century artists' house to guests and will be pleased to assist in their cultural and culinary exploits. The house is set in a romantic garden, very close to the Loire, and just four kilometres from the river-port and château of Chambord. There are three characterful bedrooms with en suite facilities.

Prices s fr €65; d fr €70; t fr €100   **On Site** ♪   **Nearby** ⸲ 3km ♨ 10km ⸲ 8km Restaurant 0.5km Water sports 8km ⤓ 14km Spa 14km ⋙ 8km   **Notes** No pets   English spoken   Open April to September.

ST-GEORGES-SUR-CHER

▐▐▐ ⅙ La Prieuré de la Chaise

Daniele DURET-THERIZOLS

8 Rue du Prieuré, 41400 ST-GEORGES-SUR-CHER

☎ 02 54 32 59 77 ▤ 02 54 32 69 49

email: prieuredelachaise@yahoo.fr

web: www.prieuredelachaise.com

Near the châteaux of the Loire, the 14th-century Priory de la Chaise is set on a peaceful wine estate, with 12th-century chapel. There are two double rooms and a two-roomed apartment with two double beds and a two-person pull-out bed, each with private facilities.

Prices d €60-€120; t €100-€120   **On Site** ☜ Private ⸲
Nearby ⛷ 2km ♨ 30km ♪ 2km Restaurant 2km ⸲ 2km ⟐ 2km ⋙ 5km   **Notes** No pets   English spoken

ST-JULIEN-DE-CHEDON

▐▐▐ Le Clos du Haut Villiers

Marc & Corinne BLANCQUAERT

2 Allée de Villiers, 41400 ST-JULIEN-DE-CHEDON

☎ 02 54 32 19 38

email: mc.blancquaert@wanadoo.fr

web: www.leclosduhautvilliers.com

Standing above the valley of the Cher looking towards the medieval keep of Montrichard, this 18th-century building has tremendous character. There are three double bedrooms, all with private bath/shower room and WC. Baby equipment is available. Breakfast is served in the vaults which have been transformed into a retro bar and family room. Landscaped gardens and table tennis.

Prices s €55-€60; d €60-€65; extra person fr €17   **Nearby** ⛷ 6km ♨ 27km ♪ 2km ⸲ 2.5km Restaurant 2.5km Water sports 2.5km ⤓ 0.7km ⟐ 2.2km ⋙ 5km   **Notes** No pets   English spoken

ST-VIATRE

⊯ Villepalay

Jean Yves & Danièle NAVUCET

Route de Nouan le Fuzelier, 41210 ST-VIATRE

☎ 02 54 88 22 35

email: navucet@wanadoo.fr

Enclosed grounds with a fishing lake provide an attractive setting for this restored longhouse, which offers two double rooms and a family room for four (all single beds), all with en suite facilities and television. There is a big day room with an open fireplace, and a dining room where organic breakfasts are served. Massage available by reservation.

Prices s €53-€65; d €58-€70; t fr €78; extra person fr €20 **On Site** 🏊 🎣 **Nearby** ⛵ 10km ⚓ 15km ➹ 10km Restaurant 2km 🏊 10km Spa 30km 🏠 2km ✈ 10km **Notes** No pets English spoken Open April to February.

SUEVRES

⊯ Moulin de Choiseaux

Marie Françoise SEGUIN

8 Rue des Choiseaux, 41500 SUEVRES

☎ 02 54 87 85 01 📄 02 54 87 86 44

email: choiseaux@wanadoo.fr

web: www.choiseaux.com

Guests will love the quietness and the wildlife at this 18th-century water mill in the Loire Valley, between Chambord and Blois. The hosts can advise guests on visits and walks and offer four lovely bedrooms (a double, a single, and two sleeping three) with bath and wc, and a family suite (double and two singles). Enormous country garden with swimming pool. Restaurant 1km.

Prices s fr €65; d €58-€85; t fr €91; extra person fr €16 **On Site** 🎣 Private ➹ **Nearby** ⛵ 5km ⚓ 15km Restaurant 1km Water sports 5km 🏊 1km 🏠 1km ✈ 5km **Notes** No pets English spoken CC

THEILLAY

⊯ ⟨○⟩ Château la Frégeolière

Antoin HOEZEN

41300 THEILLAY

☎ 02 54 83 19 70 📄 02 54 83 19 70

email: lafregeoliere@wanadoo.fr

web: www.freewebs.com/fregeolierefrance

This property, on the southern edge of the Sologne region with good access from main routes, stands in four hectares of grounds close to the village. There are five well-appointed double rooms, each with a lounge area and private shower/WC. Meals are available by arrangement.

Prices s fr €50; d fr €60; t fr €75; extra person fr €15; dinner fr €20 **On Site** 🎣 **Nearby** ⚓ 2km ⚓ 15km 🏊 2km **Notes** Pets admitted English spoken

THENAY

⊯ ⟨○⟩ La Serrerie

Guylaine MOREAU

12 Chemin de la Fagoterie, 41400 THENAY

☎ 02 54 71 08 04

email: guylaine@chambresnature.net

web: www.chambresnature.net/

This restored 19th-century farmhouse lies between the two majestic rivers, the Loire and the Cher. There are three spacious rooms, of which one is a family room of 50 sq metres. All have private entrance and en suite facilities. A huge living room, kitchen, salon, library with open fire and garden furniture are at guests' disposal. Extra bed/cot available. Pets by arrangement.

Prices s €45-€60; d €50-€65; t €65-€75; extra person fr €12; dinner fr €20 **On Site** 🏊 **Nearby** ⛵ 3km ⚓ 20km 🎣 3km ➹ 12km Restaurant 5km 🏊 3km 🏠 3km ✈ 12km **Notes** Pets admitted English spoken

THOURY

⊯ ⟨○⟩ ♿ La Ferme de la Maugerie

Gérard LANGE

8 Route de la Maugerie, 41220 THOURY

☎ 02 54 87 05 07 📄 02 54 87 05 06

email: lamaugerie@aol.com

web: www.la-maugerie.com

Right out in the countryside, a renovated old barn with five comfortable en suite rooms. One of the rooms is specifically adapted for those with mobility problems. The large bay windows of the dining room look out over the view, the terrace and the private pool. Evening meals are available. Pony riding and stabling, and children's games on site.

Prices s fr €50; d fr €55; t fr €69; extra person fr €83; dinner fr €20 **On Site** ⛵ Private ➹ **Nearby** ⚓ 25km 🎣 2km Restaurant 12km Water sports 25km 🏊 2km 🏌 0.1km 🏠 1km ✈ 12km **Notes** Pets admitted English spoken CC

⊯ La Grange aux Herbes

C et D VERMET-GOBY

4 Rue du Pavillon, 41220 THOURY

☎ 02 54 87 55 79

email: lagrangeauxherbes@caramail.com

web: www.lagrangeauxherbes.fr

Just 300mtrs from the entrance to the Park of Chambord and near the Sologne, with its forests, hiking and riding. This old farmhouse is in a shady park with pond and has three double rooms and two triples, plus a family room (double bed and two singles), all with private facilities. Cot available. Kitchen and television lounge with open fire for guests' use. Parking available. Fee payable for bigger dogs.

Prices s fr €40; d €50-€60; t €65-€75; extra person fr €15 **On Site** 🎣 **Nearby** ⚓ 8km ⚓ 10km Restaurant 6km Water sports 10km 🏊 3km 🏌 0.3km 🏠 1km ✈ 10km **Notes** Pets admitted English spoken Open March to 15 December.

TROO

♯♯♯ Côté Sud

Dominique JEHL-CALEGARI

7 rue Haute, Côté Sud, 41800 TROO

☎ 02 54 72 61 38 & 06 13 38 43 43

email: cotesud@troo.com

web: www.troo.com/cotesud.html

In the heart of this troglodyte village, a character 17th-century residence has a warm and relaxed atmosphere, and its own troglodyte salon and bar. The diverse rooms are themed: the Greek, the Tourangelle and the Indi are all double rooms equipped with own bath or shower and WC. There's even a half-troglodyte room with kitchenette, shower and WC. Generous breakfasts served in the family dining room.

Prices s fr €50; d €52-€60; extra person fr €15   **On Site** 🏊
Nearby ⚓ 10km 🏌 0.5km ⛷ 6km Restaurant 0.5km 🎣 0.1km 🚴 5km
🚣 25km   **Notes** No pets English spoken Open 21 January to 19 December.

VENDOME

♯♯♯ 🍽 La Bretonnerie

Yves & Claudine SALAÜN

32 Route du Bois la Barbe, 41100 VENDOME

☎ 02 54 77 46 22

email: salaun-claudine@wanadoo.fr

web: www.la-bretonnerie.com

Near Vendome, three guest rooms in a 2 hectare wooded park: a room with a double and single bed, a two-roomed suite with a double bed, bunks and a cot and a double room, all with private facilities, heating and TV. Lounge, garden furniture and barbecue, baby equipment. Meals by reservation. Animals accepted with prior notice.

Prices s fr €34; d fr €45; t fr €56; extra person fr €11; dinner fr €18
On Site 🏊 **Nearby** ⚓ 3km ⛷ 7km 🏌 1km ⛷ 1.5km Restaurant 1.5km
Water sports 2km 🎣 1.5km 🚴 1.5km 🚣 2.5km   **Notes** Pets admitted

VERNOU-EN-SOLOGNE

♯♯♯ Grand Pas

Daniel VILLAIN

Route de Chambord, 41230 VERNOU-EN-SOLOGNE

☎ 02 54 98 27 84 📄 02 54 98 27 84

web: www.grand-pas.fr

Total rural peace and quiet in the heart of the Sologne region. This property stands in 23 hectares of grounds with a lake. There are three double bedrooms with king-size beds. Each has a private bathroom and WC.

Prices s fr €65; d fr €75   **On Site** 🏌 **Nearby** ⚓ 5km ⛷ 20km
🎣 10km 🚴 2km 🚣 18km   **Notes** No pets

VILLEBAROU

♯♯♯ ♿ Francillon

Jacques & Agnès MASQUILIER

8 Rte de la Chaussee St Victor, Le Retour - Francillon, 41000 VILLEBAROU

☎ 02 54 78 40 24 📄 02 54 56 12 36

email: contact@leretour.fr

web: www.leretour.fr

Four guest rooms with private facilities in a distinctive house - three doubles with separate entrances (one with disabled access) and a large suite with mezzanine and two double beds. Fully equipped large kitchen/dining area, communal TV. Flower filled courtyard with parking, table tennis, shaded park.

Prices s €43-€60; d €48-€68; t €58-€81; extra person fr €14   **On Site** 🏊
Nearby ⚓ 5km ⛷ 10km 🏌 5km Restaurant 1km Water sports 10km
🎣 1km 🚴 1km 🚣 5km   **Notes** Pets admitted English spoken

VILLERBON

♯♯♯ Villejambon

Elisabeth LESOURD

3 Route des Greves, Villejambon - Cidex 8520, 41000 VILLERBON

☎ 02 54 46 83 16 📄 02 54 46 83 16

On an old farm near Blois, a restored wine store provides two double rooms and one twin, each with shower and wc. Guests' lounge and living room with local style furniture, games and kitchen for guests. The garden is available for leisure and picnicking by arrangement. Animals if pre-booked.

Prices s fr €43; d fr €47; extra person fr €15   **Nearby** ⚓ 10km ⛷ 10km
🏌 5km ⛷ 10km Restaurant 8km 🎣 2km 🏊 10km 🚴 8km 🚣 10km
Notes Pets admitted English spoken Open April to November.

VILLIERS-SUR-LOIR

▥ Chambre d'hôtes

Hans & Adèle TIMMERS
/6 Av du 11 Novembre, 41100 VILLIERS-SUR-LOIR
☎ 02 54 72 72 49
email: hansadele41@aol.com
web: http://home.wanadoo.nl/a.huybrechts/index.htm

Close to Vendôme, in the village centre, this old house has three ground-floor family rooms with en suite facilities - one room with our single beds, and two with a single and a double. Electric heating. Hosts happy to taxi guests to and from the railway station (TGV), 3 kilometres away. Large enclosed garden.

Prices s fr €37; d fr €44; t fr €54; extra person fr €10   **Nearby** ⚓ 5km 20km ⚲ 0.5km ➹ 7km Restaurant 0.2km Water sports 0.5km ⛵ 1km ⛳ 0.5km ⛲ 0.1km ⚑ 3km   **Notes** Pets admitted English spoken

VINEUIL

▥ Le Clos Fleuri

Christian & Yvette FAUVINET
Rue de Greffier, 41350 VINEUIL
☎ 02 54 42 74 90 & 06 89 38 83 43
email: christian.fauvinet@wanadoo.fr
web: www.chambredhoteschambord.com

Between Blois and Chambord and less than two hours from Paris, this restored farmhouse stands in enclosed grounds with a forest and river close by. There are three double rooms, two of which have a living area; all have private facilities. Fridge, microwave and kettle are available. Picnic area and heated swimming pool; bikes available.

Prices s fr €58; d fr €65; t fr €82; extra person fr €16   **On Site** ⛲ Private ➹ **Nearby** ⚓ 3km ⚲ 10km ⛳ 0.5km Restaurant 5km ⛵ 5km ⛳ 4km ⚑ 6km   **Notes** Pets admitted English spoken

VOUZON

▥ ♿ Château le Corvier

Geneviève DE HENNIN
41600 VOUZON
☎ 02 54 83 04 93
email: chateaulecorvier@hotmail.com
web: www.chateaulecorvier.com

There are five guest rooms here in a Louis XIII-style château in the Sologne, as well as 100 acres of wooded grounds and a lake to wander around. A ground-floor double room has an access suitable for people with reduced mobility. On the first floor are three double rooms and a family suite, all with bath or shower and WC. Extra bed available. Heated swimming pool.

Prices s €73-€112; d €82-€112; t €100-€130; extra person fr €18 **On Site** ⛲ Private ➹ **Nearby** ⚓ 8km ⚲ 10km ⛳ 3km Restaurant 3km ⛳ 8km ⚑ 8km   **Notes** Pets admitted English spoken

YVOY-LE-MARRON

▥ ▥◯▥ ♿ Château Mont Suzey

Dominique DOUVIN
41600 YVOY-LE-MARRON
☎ 02 38 24 06 79
email: dom@douvin.fr
web: www.chateau-mont-suzey.com

Five well-equipped rooms in this Anglo-Norman style château. Secluded amongst wooded walks, with a lake full of fish and a swimming pool. The individually decorated rooms, one a suite, all have independent bathrooms and toilets. There is a guest television lounge and kitchenette. Bookable evening meals from a Vietnamese and local menu. Pets welcome if booked in advance.

Prices s €60-€90; d €70-€100; extra person fr €15; dinner fr €15 **On Site** ⛳ ⛲ Private ➹ **Nearby** ⚓ 13km ⚲ 13km Restaurant 3km Water sports 40km ⛳ 3km ⚑ 12km   **Notes** Pets admitted English spoken Open Easter to 1 November. CC

LOIRET

AILLANT-SUR-MILLERON

⚑ ⍥ Les Beaupieds

Jacques MAILLOT

39 Les Beaupieds, 45230 AILLANT-SUR-MILLERON

☎ 02 38 97 41 10

email: jacques.maillot45@wanadoo.fr

web: http://perso.wanadoo.fr/jacques.maillot45/

A peaceful, rural property on the edge of the Burgundy region with three guest bedrooms. All are doubles, and the Indian Ocean provides the theme for the decoration. Each room has a private bath or shower room and WC. There is a large lounge and billiard room, and meals can be arranged.

Prices s €80-€100; d €80-€100; dinner fr €35 **Nearby** ↨ 35km ⌖ 5km ↴ 30km 🏠 8km ⋈ 15km **Notes** No pets English spoken

BRAY-EN-VAL

⚑ Les Saules

Monique et Jacques BEZIN

18 Rue des Jardins du Coulouis, 45460 BRAY-EN-VAL

☎ 02 38 29 08 90 & 06 72 47 07 73

Between Loire and the Forest of Orléans, this old restored property offers three elegant guest rooms with private bath or shower rooms, including two doubles and a large room with a double and two single beds. Cot or extra single bed available. Lounge and billiard room, terraces with garden furniture, walks in the wooded and landscaped park (3 hectares) crossed by a river. Picnics possible, heating, car park.

Prices s €42-€52; d €49-€59; t €70-€75; extra person fr €16 **Nearby** ↨ 1km ↴ 12km ⌖ 0.3km ↴ 8km 🏠 0.3km ⋈ 35km **Notes** Pets admitted English spoken

BRETEAU

⚑ ❦ ⍥ ♿ La Chenauderie

Brigitte ROBILLIART

45250 BRETEAU

☎ 02 38 31 97 88 🖹 02 38 29 69 38

email: la-chendaurie@wanadoo.fr

web: www.giteschambresettablesdhotes-loiret.com

On a working farm, this converted barn offers five spacious guest rooms, close to the Puisaye lakes (fishing). There is a room equipped for disabled guests, a room with a double and two single beds, plus three bedrooms with four singles and two double beds; each with private facilities. Large dining room and lounge, garden furniture. Table d'hôte meals available on reservation.

Prices s fr €38; d fr €48; t fr €58; extra person fr €10; dinner fr €19 **On Site** ⌖ **Nearby** ↨ 5km ↴ 3km Restaurant 3km 🌊 4km 🎾 15km 🏠 3km ⋈ 25km **Notes** Pets admitted English spoken CC

BRIARE

⚑ La Thiau

Bénédicte FRANCOIS-DUCLUZEAU

45250 BRIARE

☎ 02 38 38 20 92 & 06 62 43 20 92 🖹 02 38 38 06 20

email: lathiau@club-internet.fr

web: http://lathiau.club.fr

Between Gien and Briare, this 18th-century, Mansart-style house is set in a three-hectare landscaped park by the Loire. There are three rooms with double and single beds and a room with kitchen, double bed, single bed (extra single bed available) and fireplace. All have private facilities. Lounge with TV, books and games, washing machine, tennis, table tennis, children's play area. Two mountain bikes for hire. Pets accepted for a charge. 10% reduction after three nights.

Prices s fr €49; d €53-€61; t €69-€81; extra person fr €16 **On Site** ⌖ 🎾 Private tennis court **Nearby** ↨ 6km ↴ 25km ↴ 4km Restaurant 4km 🏠 4km ⋈ 4km **Notes** Pets admitted English spoken

CERDON

⚑ Les Vieux Guays

Sandrine et Alvaro MARTINEZ

45620 CERDON-DU-LOIRET

☎ 02 38 36 03 76 & 06 80 16 53 76

🖹 02 38 36 03 76

email: alydrine@aol.com

web: www.lesvieuxguays.com

This peacefully situated old property is full of character, and it stands in the middle of a forest in front of a pond. It has three large guest bedrooms, in a wing of the house which has been completely re-modelled in the style of the area. Big lounge, with books and video. Swimming pool, fishing and tennis.

Prices s fr €60; d fr €75 **On Site** ⌖ Private ↴ Private tennis court **Nearby** ↨ 6km ↴ 12km Restaurant 3km 🎾 12km 🏠 3km ⋈ 25km **Notes** Pets admitted English spoken

CHAILLY-EN-GATINAIS

⚑ Ferme de Grand Chesnoy

Benoit CHEVALIER

45260 CHAILLY-EN-GATINAIS

☎ 02 38 96 27 67 & 06 72 14 68 78 🖹 02 38 96 27 67

email: bclechesnoy@yahoo.fr

This house is set in wooded grounds bordering the Orléans canal (fishing possible), and is linked to the forest by footpaths. There are two double rooms and a twin with views, and a suite with a double bed and lounge with a single bed; all have private facilities. Lounge/dining room, billiards room.

Prices s fr €60; d fr €65; t fr €80; extra person fr €15 **Nearby** ↨ 6km ↴ 25km ⌖ 0.2km ↴ 7km Restaurant 5km 🌊 🏠 6km ⋈ 20km **Notes** No pets English spoken

CHATEAURENARD

ⅲ Le Clos Saint Nicolas

Maria CESPEDES

50 Rue Paul Doumer, 45220 CHATEAURENARD

☎ 02 38 95 25 79 📄 02 38 95 25 79

email: xavier.cespedes@gmail.com

web: www.clos-saint-nicolas.fr

This is a large and beautiful 18th-century house in spacious grounds, ideal for a restful stay. A ground-floor double room has shower and WC. Upstairs are two more rooms, one containing one small double bed, the other with two small double beds, and both with shower/WC. All three rooms have broadband access, and the hosts' living room can be used.

Prices s fr €40; d fr €60; extra person fr €15 On Site 🏊
Nearby ⛳ 2km ♨ 20km ♪ 0.1km ⚲ 14km Restaurant 0.1km ⚓ 17km
♠ 0.1km ⚶ 17km Notes No pets English spoken

CHATILLON-SUR-LOIRE

ⅲ ♿ Les Brûlis

Robert et Micheline EDMET

45360 CHATILLON-SUR-LOIRE

☎ 02 38 31 42 33

email: robert.edmet@orange.fr

Three guest rooms are offered at this renovated rural property, peacefully set close to the banks of the Loire, Gien and the Sancerrois. There is a twin room and two doubles with private facilities, a lounge/dining room, kitchenette, TV and telephone. Garden furniture and use of owners' swimming pool.

Prices s fr €40; d fr €50; t fr €68 On Site 🏊 Private ⚲
Nearby ⛳ 15km ♨ 40km Restaurant 4km ⚓ 4km ⚑ 5km 🏠 5km
⚶ 10km Notes Pets admitted

CHECY

ⅲ Les Courtils

Brigitte et Jacques MONTHEL

Rue de l'Ave, 45430 CHECY

☎ 02 38 91 32 02 & 06 88 26 22 14 📄 02 38 91 14 90

email: infos@les-courtils.com

web: www.les-courtils.com

An ancient restored barn, standing on the church square of a small village, is the setting for this chambres d'hôtes. It has four bedrooms, including one on the ground floor, each sleeping two or three people. All rooms have private bathrooms and WCs. Lounge with open fire, terrace and enclosed garden with views of the canal and the Loire.

Prices s fr €45; d fr €53; t fr €70 On Site ♪ Nearby ⛳ 5km ♨ 6km
♪ 1km Restaurant 0.1km ⚓ 🏠 0.1km ⚶ 12km Notes No pets English
spoken

CHEVILLON-SUR-HUILLARD

ⅲ *Chambre d'hôtes*

Frédéric et Brigitte TOSTAIN

218 Route de Saint-Maurice,

45700 CHEVILLON-SUR-HUILLARD

☎ 02 38 97 97 93

email: les-deux-chenes@gmail.com

web: www.les-deux-chenes.com

This converted barn, close to the owners' house, has three attractive bedrooms. There are two doubles on the ground floor, and a room for four (double bed and two singles) upstairs. All rooms have private showers and WCs; those downstairs also have TVs. Garden furniture, table tennis. Grounds with lake.

Prices not confirmed for 2008 Nearby ⛳ 1.8km ♨ 8km ♪ 0.5km
⚲ 8km 🏠 8km ⚶ 10km Notes No pets

COURTENAY

ⅲ Chambre d'hôtes

Laurette BEAUFILS

36 Rue Nationale, 45320 COURTENAY

☎ 02 38 97 33 40

web: http://lechateaudecourtenay.chez.tiscali.fr/

Three upstairs rooms in this restored 18th-century château, which was itself built on the site of a medieval building: a twin-bedded room, a double room, and a room for four with twin beds and a sofabed. All have private bathroom and WC. Garden with garden furniture.

Prices s fr €50; d €60-€70; extra person fr €20 Nearby ⛳ 10km
♨ 10km ♪ 2km ⚲ 0.5km Restaurant 10km ⚶ 25km Notes No pets

FEROLLES

ⅲ Chambre d'hôtes

Susan DE SMET

8 Route du Martroi, La Bretêche, 45150 FEROLLES

☎ 02 38 59 79 53

Newly built house in a very tranquil village offering a twin room and two doubles (extra double bed can be installed) with private shower room and wc. Large, enclosed, tree-lined garden.

Prices s fr €36; d fr €46; t fr €56; extra person fr €12 Nearby ⛳ 5km
♨ 6km ♪ 10km ⚲ 10km Restaurant 3km ⚑ 3km 🏠 3km ⚶ 20km
Notes No pets English spoken

GERMIGNY-DES-PRES

ⅲ 🍴 Chambre d'hôtes

Marie et Laurent KOPP

28 Route de Châteauneuf, 45110 GERMIGNY-DES-PRES

☎ 02 38 58 21 15

email: koppm@wanadoo.fr

web: www.kopp.fr

In a small Ligérien village, famous for its Carolingian Oratory, five very peaceful bedrooms for 2-4 people, with single and/or double beds

CONTINUED

GERMIGNY-DES-PRES *CONTINUED*

opening onto a large landscaped garden. Extra beds available; all have private facilities. Guests may use the barbecue, garden furniture, children's games, equipped kitchen and lounge with books, games and TV. Local artists' exhibition and parking on site. Table d'hôte meals by reservation from October to March.

Prices s fr €39; d fr €50; t fr €60; dinner fr €20 **On Site** ℰ
Nearby ⛳ 4km ↟ 15km ⚓ 4km Restaurant 4km ⚲ 4km ⌂ 4km
⚞ 30km **Notes** No pets English spoken

GIEN

Domaine des Grands Chênes

Gérard PONTILLON
Le Chétif Puits, 45500 GIEN
☎ 02 38 05 08 42 & 06 75 08 85 69
email: gpontillon@grandschenes.net
web: www.grandschenes.net

Your hosts Michelle and Gérard will welcome you to their 19th-century hunting lodge on the Jacques Coeur route, with its 3-hectare garden and ancient trees. The three bedrooms have their own bathrooms and WCs; one of the bedrooms is part of a family suite with entrance hall and living room. TV, hi-fi, games, library, microwave in main house.

Prices s fr €53–€75; d €58–€80; t fr €95 **On Site** ⚲ **Nearby** ⛳ 10km
↟ 25km ℰ 5km ⚓ 5km Restaurant 5km ⚲ 5km ⌂ 4km ⚞ 4km
Notes No pets English spoken

GUILLY

Domaine de la Croix Tibi

B et O VAN DEN BROEK
45600 GUILLY
☎ 02 38 58 17 71 & 06 76 39 56 24

This property has five rooms in the converted outbuildings of a manor house facing the basilica of Saint-Benoît-sur-Loire, in a loop of the River Loire. All the rooms are upstairs: two doubles, two twin-bedded rooms, and a family room for four. All have shower room and WC.

Prices s fr €50; d fr €60; t fr €85 **Nearby** ⛳ 2km ↟ 3km ℰ 0.3km
⚓ 7km Restaurant 6km ⚲ 6km ⌂ 6km ⚞ 35km **Notes** No pets
English spoken

LA BUSSIERE

La Chesnaye

M et M MARTIN-DENIS
45230 LA BUSSIERE
☎ 02 38 35 99 39

Five spacious rooms are available at the little Château de la Chesnaye, a 19th-century building. There are two double rooms, two double suites, and a grade 2 family suite with double bed, single bed and cot/child bed. All have private facilities.

Prices d €53–€61; extra person fr €23 **On Site** Private ⚓
Nearby ⛳ 10km ↟ 15km ℰ 0.8km Restaurant 10km ⚲ 0.1km ⌂ 0.8km
⚞ 10km **Notes** Pets admitted English spoken

Le Petit Boucherot

92300 LA BUSSIERE
☎ 01 47 48 19 55   ⎙ 01 47 48 19 56
email: concretiser@wanadoo.fr

7km from Gien, in a tranquil setting, this old renovated residence is surrounded by two hectares of private gardens. It has four single or double rooms with refined decor and lovely private bathrooms. Warm lounge with fireplace and TV. Breakfast is served in the dining room or on the pergola by the swimming pool or small pond.

Prices s fr €100; d fr €120 **On Site** Private ⚓ **Nearby** ⛳ 15km
↟ 12km Restaurant 8km ⚲ 3km ⚞ 7km **Notes** No pets English spoken

LAILLY-EN-VAL

⊙ Domaine de Montizeau

Jacqueline ABEILLE
Monçay, 45740 LAILLY-EN-VAL
☎ 02 38 45 34 74
email: ja.montizeau@wanadoo.fr
web: www.domaine-montizeau.com

Four elegant rooms, each with its own entrance, in a converted stable block on an old hunting estate. On the ground floor are a double room and a twin-bedded room; upstairs is another double, and a suite with double bed plus a bed-settee in the lounge. All have private facilities and high-speed internet access. Kitchenette; meals by arrangement.

Prices s fr €70; d €70–€95; t fr €115; extra person fr €20; dinner fr €28 **Nearby** ⛳ 7km ↟ 5km ℰ 3km ⚓ 8km Restaurant 8km
⚲ 3km Spa 15km ⌂ 8km ⚞ 8km **Notes** No pets English spoken

LIGNY-LE-RIBAULT

Chambre d'hôtes

Sylvie BARDINE
351 Rue du Gal Leclerc, 45240 LIGNY-LE-RIBAULT
☎ 02 38 45 44 37 & 06 07 26 16 55

A big house on the edge of the village in the heart of the Sologne region, with three upstairs guest bedrooms. Two are doubles; the thi is a two-roomed family suite for four. All have private bathroom and WC. Lounge for guests' use, billiard table and secure parking.

Prices s fr €50; d fr €56; t fr €76; extra person fr €15; dinner fr €22
Nearby ⛳ 3km ↟ 13km ℰ 1km ⚓ 13km Restaurant 2km Spa 13km
⚞ 13km **Notes** Pets admitted English spoken

⚏ ⏣ Communs de Bon Hôtel

Marcel FICHELLE

Chemin de Saint-Laurent, 45240 LIGNY-LE-RIBAULT

☎ 02 38 45 66 90 & 06 11 22 85 26 📠 02 38 45 66 90

email: ccbonhotel@wanadoo.fr

web: www.communsdebonhotel.fr

In the forest of Sologne, two kilometres from a village, this property has two suites and two triple rooms. One of the triples has three single beds, the other a double bed and a single. Each of the suites has a double bed and two singles; one also has a cot. All have private facilities. Extensive wooded grounds, garden furniture.

Prices s €47-€52; d €55-€60; t €70-€75; extra person fr €15; dinner fr €24 **Nearby** ⚓ 6km ⛷ 15km 🏊 3km ⚲ 15km Restaurant 2km 🅿 2km ⚶ 15km **Notes** No pets English spoken

MALESHERBES

⚏ ⏣ La Lilandière

D et P LAGRUE-DIEUDONNE

Chemin de la Messe, Hameau de Trézan, 45330 MALESHERBES

☎ 02 38 34 84 51 & 08 71 50 02 20

email: la-lilandiere@wanadoo.fr

web: www.lalilandiere.com

La Lilandière is in a hamlet on the edge of the forest of Fontainebleau, about an hour from Paris. There are three beautiful rooms, each sleeping three people, in old farm buildings dating back to 1702. All the rooms have private shower room and WC. Extensive grounds with an enclosed garden and terrace. Meals available by arrangement.

Prices s fr €56; d fr €60; t fr €82; dinner fr €25 **On Site** 🏊 ⚲ **Nearby** ⚓ 0.5km ⛷ 4km ⚲ 2km Restaurant 2km 🅿 1.5km ⚶ 1km **Notes** Pets admitted English spoken

MENESTREAU-EN-VILLETTE

⚏ La Ferme des Foucault

Rosemary BEAU

45240 MENESTREAU-EN-VILLETTE

☎ 02 38 76 94 41 📠 02 38 76 94 41

email: rbeau@wanadoo.fr

web: www.ferme-des-foucault.com

Very comfortable accommodation in the heart of the Sologne forest, in a beautiful and peaceful setting. There is a suite with two double beds, lounge and fireplace, TV and independent access and two very large double bedrooms (extra bed possible), one of which has a private terrace, with TV. Rooms have private facilities. Large, verdant grounds with garden furniture; many walks nearby. Swimming pool available.

Prices s €65-€75; d €75-€85; extra person fr €20 **On Site** Private 🏊 **Nearby** ⚓ 5km ⛷ 8km 🏊 6km Restaurant 6km ⚲ 10km 🅿 6km ⚶ 15km **Notes** English spoken

MEUNG-SUR-LOIRE

⚏ Hameau de la Nivelle

Raymonde BECHU

30 Rue de la Bâtissière, 45130 MEUNG-SUR-LOIRE

☎ 02 38 44 34 38 📠 02 38 44 34 38

email: raymonde.bechu@orange.fr

In a very peaceful hamlet, this house is surrounded by a tree and flower-lined garden. There is a double room, a twin room with private facilities, and a double room with an adjoining children's room (twin beds), sharing a bathroom and wc. TV aerial in each room. Large terrace, garden with furniture, bicycle hire. Discounted tariff after two nights.

Prices s €37-€40; d €47-€50; extra person fr €15 **On Site** ⚲ **Nearby** ⚓ 3km ⛷ 10km 🏊 0.3km ⚲ 3km Restaurant 2km ⚒ 3km 🅿 3km ⚶ 3km **Notes** No pets English spoken

⚏ ♿ La Bonnerie

Chantal et Philippe MAHE

135 Route de Clan, 45130 MEUNG-SUR-LOIRE

☎ 02 38 44 28 26

email: philippe@labonnerie.com

web: www.labonnerie.com

Mid-way between Orléans and Beaugency, La Bonnerie has three ground floor bedrooms, one of which is suitable for people of reduced mobility. The rooms, all doubles, are in an annexe built in wooded surroundings close to the owner's home. Each room has a large shower room with a separate WC. Depending on the time of the year, breakfast is served in the garden or in the dining room of the hosts' home.

Prices s fr €43; d fr €52; extra person fr €14 **Nearby** ⚓ 3km ⛷ 15km 🏊 0.5km ⚲ 3.5km Restaurant 3.5km ⚒ 3.5km ⚲ 0.1km 🅿 3.5km ⚶ 3km **Notes** No pets English spoken

MONTLIARD

⁙ ⏐◎⏐ Château de Montliard

Annick et François GALIZIA
5 Route de Nesploy, 45340 MONTLIARD
☎ 02 38 33 71 40 📄 02 38 33 86 41
email: a.galizia@infonie.fr
web: www.chateau-de-montliard.com

Surrounded by moats and a peaceful 14-hectare park, at the edge of the Forest of Orléans and 100km from Paris, this charming château has belonged to the same family since 1384. The four very comfortable and spacious guest rooms have stacks of character, elegant décor and private facilities, plus baby equipment if required. Park, bicycles, table tennis, games, TV, stables and kennels. Pets are not permitted in the bedrooms. Close to several châteaux.

Prices s €56-€80; d €66-€89; extra person fr €15; dinner €23-€32 **Nearby** ⅄ 5km ⅃ 25km ✎ 5km ⤳ 5km Restaurant 5km ☕ 5km 🏛 2km ⇟ 25km **Notes** Pets admitted English spoken

NANCRAY-SUR-RIMARDE

⁙ ⏐◎⏐ Ancienne Poterie

Michelle et J.Claude PEROT
36 Rue Jules César, 45340 NANCRAY SUR RIMARDE
☎ 02 38 32 25 27
email: l-ancienne-poterie45@wanadoo.fr
web: http://monsite.orange.fr/lanciennepoterie/

This property is in a quiet village on the edge of the forest of Orléans. There are three bedrooms: a twin-bedded room downstairs, and a double and a triple upstairs - all with private shower room and WC. There is a garden behind the house, and meals are available by arrangement. Kitchenette for guests' use.

Prices s fr €40; d fr €46; t fr €56; dinner fr €18 **Nearby** ⅄ 10km ⅃ 40km ✎ 3km ⤳ 6km Restaurant 0.1km 🌊 3km ☕ 15km 🏛 3km ⇟ 40km **Notes** No pets English spoken

NEVOY

⁙ Sainte-Barbe

Annie LE LAY
45500 NEVOY
☎ 02 38 67 59 53 & 06 73 93 10 50 📄 02 38 67 28 96
email: s.barbe@hotmail.fr
web: www.sainte-barbe.net

Overlooking the garden, this 19th-century rural property has lots of character and offers two double rooms (extra single bed possible in one) and a single with private facilities and separate entrances. There is a reception room and a lounge with TV. Tennis courts on site.

Prices s €40-€50; d €65; t fr €80 **On Site** ✎ ☕ Private ⤳ Private tennis court **Nearby** ⅄ 10km ⅃ 25km Restaurant 5km 🏛 5km ⇟ 5km **Notes** No pets English spoken Open 7 January to 19 December.

PUISEAUX

⁙ ⏐◎⏐ La Maison Rose

Véronique FOURNIER
34,36 Rue des Viviers, 45390 PUISEAUX
☎ 02 38 34 33 61 & 06 63 69 96 38
email: lamaisonrose45@neuf.fr

One hour from Paris, and a similar distance from the Loire Valley, this property has four bedrooms, in a pink house next to the owners' home. There are three double rooms, one on the ground floor and two upstairs. Also upstairs is a family room for four with a double bed and two singles. All rooms have private showers and WCs. Meals by arrangement.

Prices s fr €42; d fr €49; t fr €68; extra person fr €15; dinner fr €20 **On Site** ☕ **Nearby** ⅄ 3km ⅃ 8km ✎ 3km ⤳ 12km Restaurant 0.3km 🌊 0.3km 🏛 0.3km ⇟ 12km **Notes** No pets English spoken

CENTRAL FRANCE

ST-BENOIT-SUR-LOIRE

ⅲ ❤ iOi ᱐ **La Borde**

Dominique & Mireille BOUIN
Chemin de la Borde, 45730 SAINT-BENOÎT-SUR-LOIRE
☎ 02 38 35 70 53 & 06 76 05 69 72 📄 02 38 35 10 06
email: Mireille-Dominique.BOUIN@wanadoo.fr
web: www.fermedelaborde.com

Mireille and Dominique invite you to their chambre d'hôte, located on a cereal farm between Sully-sur-Loire and Saint-Benoît. There are three twin rooms, a triple, a suite for four, and further twin room for disabled guests in a separate house in the garden. All have private facilities. Reception room and equipped kitchen available. Pleasant tree-lined garden with vegetable patch and garden furniture.

Prices s €48-€53; d €53-€58; t €75-€89; dinner fr €20 **Nearby** ⚑ 6km 12km ⌖ 2km ⟋ 7km Restaurant 2km ⌂ 2km ⚘ 0.1km ⓔ 2km ⋇ 25km **Notes** Pets admitted English spoken CC

TAVERS

ⅲ iOi **Le Clos de Pont-Pierre**

Patricia et Pierre FOURNIER
115 Rue des Eaux Bleues, 45190 TAVERS
☎ 02 38 44 56 85 & 06 07 17 93 26
email: closdepontpierre@wanadoo.fr
web: www.clos-de-pontpierre.com

Peacefully set in the Loire Valley, this renovated 18th-century farm offers pleasant guest rooms with independent access and views over the park. Two bedrooms on the ground floor and two on the first floor, all with private shower and wc. Lounge with antique furnishings, shady, flower-filled park, swimming pool, table tennis, parking, garden furniture. Meals on reservation (except Sunday) prepared by the owner, a professional chef.

Prices s €51-€61; d €61-€76; t fr €92; extra person fr €16; dinner fr €23 **On Site** Private ⟋ **Nearby** ⚑ 10km ⌖ 10km ⟋ 2km Restaurant 0.2km ⌂ 1km ⓔ 0.1km ⋇ 2km **Notes** No pets English spoken

VIENNE-EN-VAL

ⅲ **La Bâte**

Aurore et Frédérick LECONTE
45510 VIENNE-EN-VAL
☎ 02 38 58 89 24 & 06 74 52 11 82
email: aurore.leconte@cegetel.net
web: http://gitedelabate.free.fr

Close to Sully and Châteauneuf , and 50km from Chambord, this traditional local home offers two ground floor rooms, both doubles with a shower room. On the first floor is a family room with one double and two single beds, bathroom, shower room, toilet and its own entrance. There is a lounge-diner with microwave, fridge and sink for guest use. Horse boxes available.

Prices s fr €50; d fr €60; t fr €85; extra person fr €25 **Nearby** ⚑ 6km ⌖ 10km ⟋ 20km Restaurant 1km ⓔ 1km ⋇ 25km **Notes** No pets English spoken

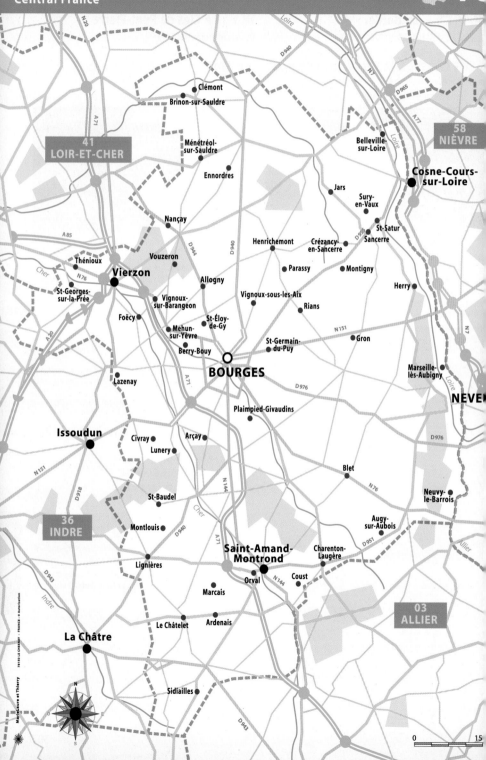

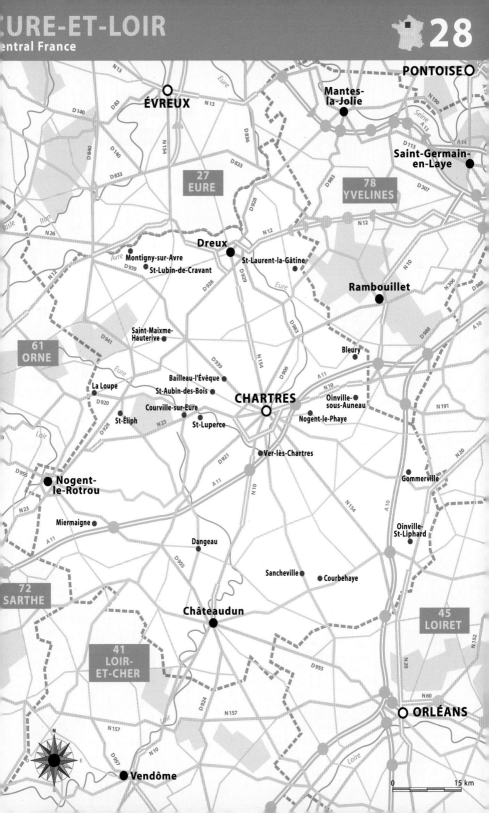

A 11

Sarthe

D 304

N 138

A 28

N 23

N 157

N 10

Loir

D 957

Vendôme

D 924

La Flèche

Loir

D 306

N 10

D 957

Monthodon

D 766

A 28

Braye-sur-Maulne

D 766

Beaumont-la-Ronce

BLOIS

Souvigné

D 959

Semblançay

A 10

N 152

Loire

D 764

Savigné-sur-Lathan

Charentilly

Chançay

Nazelles-
Négron

D 138

Pernay

Vernou-
sur-Brenne

Mosnes

Hommes

Fondettes

Noizay

Amboise

Vouvray

Lussault-sur-L.

A 85

Berthenay

TOURS

Larçay

St-Martin-
le-Beau

Civray-
de-Touraine

N 76

Langeais

Cinq-Mars-
la-Pile

Ballan-
Miré

Azay-
sur-Cher

La Croix-
en-Touraine

Chisseaux

Cher

Lignières-
de-Touraine

N 143

Chenonceaux

Benais

Vallères

A 85

Monts

Restigné

Bréhémont

D 751

Francueil

Bourgueil

Rivarennes

Azay-
le-Rideau

Esvres-sur-Indre

Épeigné-les-Bois

Saumur

Savigny-en-Véron

D 75

Truyes

Indre

Huismes

St-Branchs

Tauxigny

Luzillé

Candes-
St-Martin

St-Quentin-
sur-Indrois

Lerné

Chinon

Neuil

Saint-Bauld

Azay-
sur-Indre

Chambourg-sur-Indre

Montrésor

Cinais

Rivière

St-Epain

Manthelan

Seuilly

Vienne

A 10

N 10

Loches

N 147

Theneuil

Bossée

St-Jean-
St-Germain

D 147

Chaveignes

Sepmes

Richelieu

La Celle-St-Avant

Razines

Faye-
la-Vineuse

Charnizay

N 143

Creuse

D 975

N 147

Châtellerault

A 10

Vienne

N
O   E
S

N 149

Vienne

0   15 km

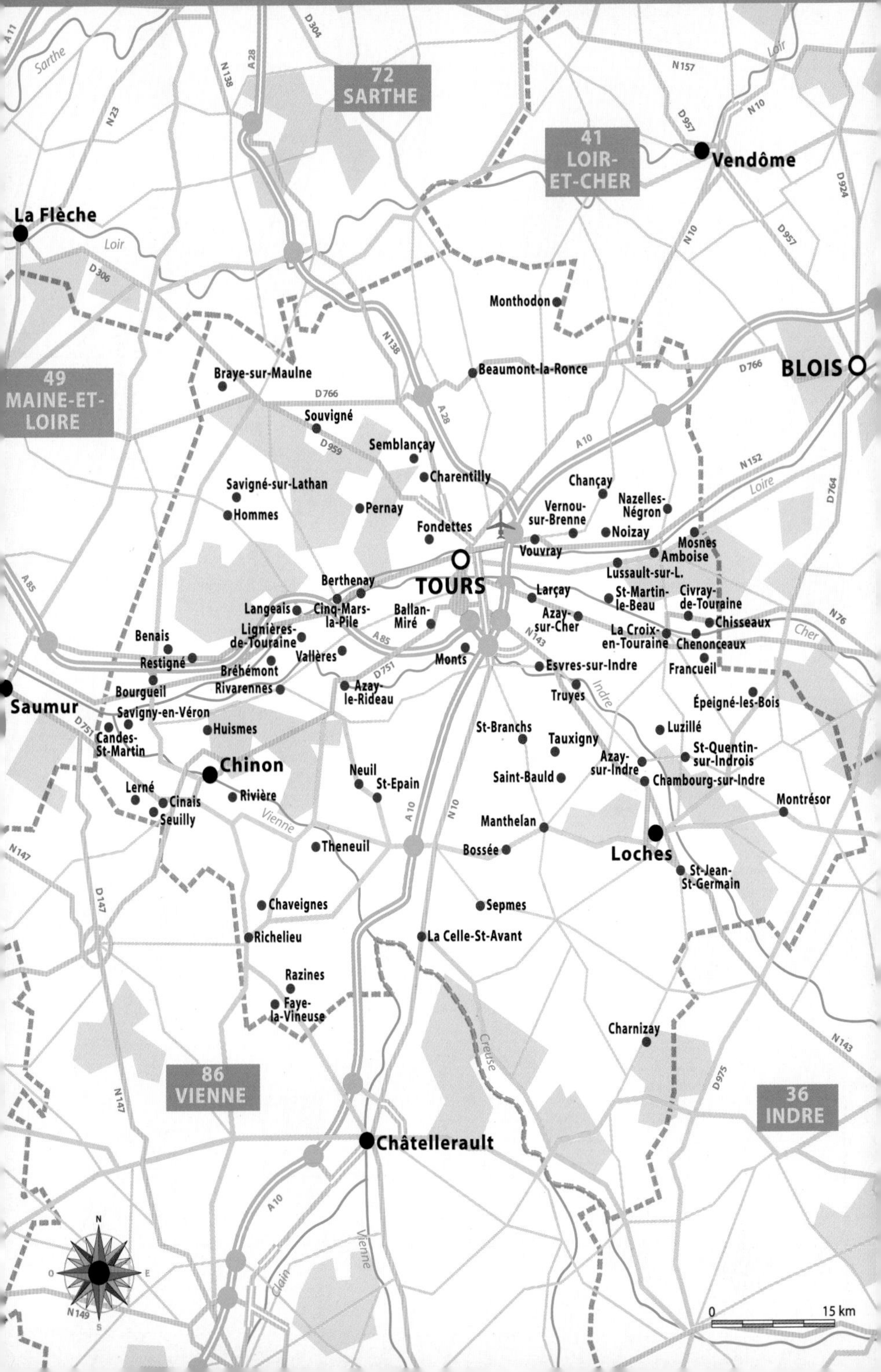

LOIR-ET-CHER
Central France

41

ORLÉANS
45 LOIRET
28 EURE-ET-LOIR
18 CHER
36 INDRE
37 INDRE-ET-LOIRE
72 SARTHE
Châteaudun
Vendôme
BLOIS
Romorantin-Lanthenay
Vierzon
TOURS
Vouzon
Yvoy-le-Marron
Chaumont-sur-Tharonne
St-Viâtre
Selles-St-Denis
Theillay
Langon
Gièvres
Vernou-en-Sologne
La Ferté-Saint-Cyr
Crouy-sur-Cosson
St-Dyé-sur-Loire
Thoury
Fontaines-en-Sologne
Mer
Suèvres
Montlivault
St-Claude-de-Diray
Mont-près-Chambord
Cour-Cheverny
Cheverny
Contres
Seris
Villerbon
Cour-sur-Loire
St-Denis-sur-Loire
Vineuil
Chitenay
Cormeray
Feings
Noyers-sur-Cher
Meusnes
Seur
Villebarou
Les Montils
Thenay
Bourré
Sambin
Chaumont-sur-Loire
Pontlevoy
Montrichard
Candé-sur-Beuvron
Monteaux
Santenay
St-Julien-de-Chédon
Mareuil-sur-Cher
St-Aignan-sur-Cher
Faverolles-sur-Cher
St-Georges-sur-Cher
Fréteval
Rocé
Coulommiers-la-Tour
Danzé
Azé
Mazangé
Villiers-sur-Loir
Lavardin
Troo
Choue
Mondoubleau
Sargé-sur-Braye
Loire
Loir
Cher
Indre
N60
N152
N20
A71
D944
N76
A85
D951
D955
D765
A10
N157
D924
D957
N10
D764
D766
N143
N138
D959
D751
N
S
E
O
MarieLaure et Thierry 78150 LE CHESNAY - FRANCE - © Autorisation

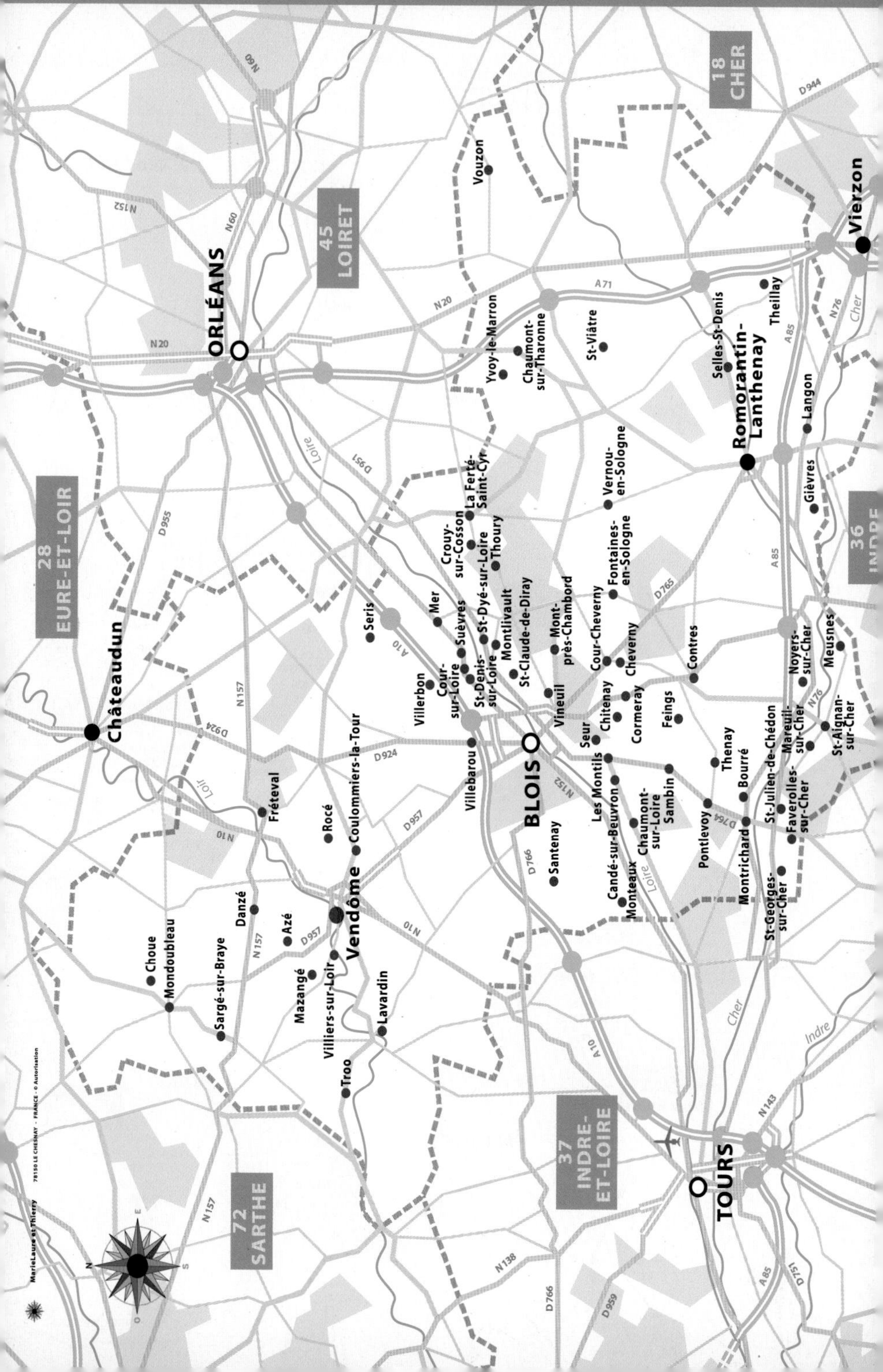

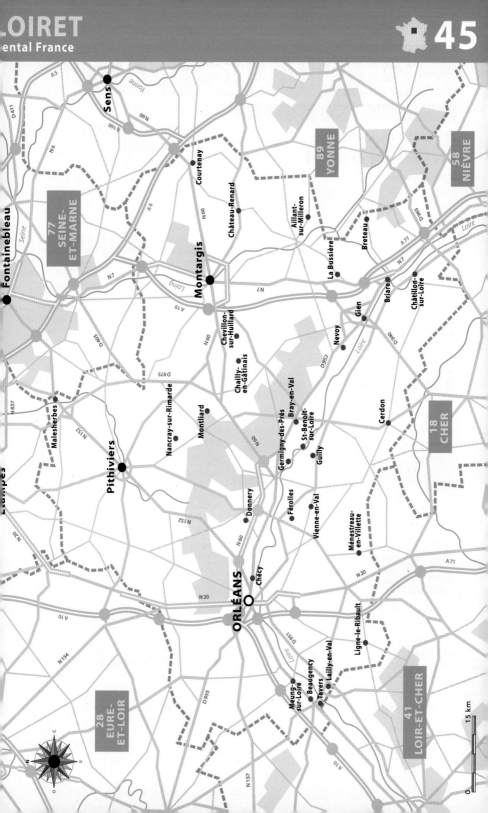

CHAMPAGNE-ARDENNE

ARDENNES

AUBIGNY-LES-POTHEES

♦♦♦ ⦿ Domaine de la Faneraie

Marie-Hélène & José LAGARD
Grand'Rue, 08150 AUBIGNY-LES-POTHEES
☎ 03 24 32 32 87 & 06 70 24 63 98 🗎 03 24 32 32 87
email: marielagard@wanadoo.fr
web: www.gitardennes.com/fr/chambres/9951.html

A stone-built house in a rural setting, with a stream close by. The five bedrooms are all upstairs: three doubles, and two family rooms for four. All the rooms have private bath or shower room and WC. A cot is available. Downstairs there is a lounge with TV; outside are extensive grounds. Meals by arrangement.

Prices s fr €38; d fr €45; t fr €55; extra person fr €10; dinner fr €17
On Site 🏊 **Nearby** ⛷ 20km ⚲ 20km ⚲ 20km Restaurant 25km
⚲ 10km 🏛 3km ⚲ 25km **Notes** Pets admitted

BRIENNE-SUR-AISNE

♦♦♦ Chambre d'hôtes

Jacqueline, J.Pierre LERICHE
13 route de Poilcourt Sydney, 08190 BRIENNE-SUR-AISNE
☎ 03 24 72 94 25 & 06 24 02 69 85 🗎 03 24 72 94 25
web: www.gitardennes.com/fr/chambres/9905.html

In the calm and relaxed atmosphere of this working farm, four en suite rooms of character with TVs accommodating seven. Centrally heated, there are also cooking facilities for snacks and a living room downstairs. Leisure activities include games room with table tennis and a private museum nearby.

Prices s fr €30; d fr €42; t fr €55; extra person fr €15 **Nearby** ⛷ 5km
⚲ 4km 🏊 1km ⚲ 18km 🏛 2km ⚲ 10km **Notes** No pets

CHATEL-CHEHERY

♦♦♦♦ ⦿ Château de Chatel

Jacques & Simone HUET
08250 CHATEL-CHEHERY
☎ 03 24 30 78 54 & 06 25 35 70 05
🗎 03 24 30 25 51
email: jacques.huet9@wanadoo.fr
web: http://perso.wanadoo.fr/chateaudechatel/

Three bedrooms are available in this exceptional and picturesquely located 18th-century château. Doubles and single rooms are en suite and sleep seven in total. Table d'hôte meals are by reservation only and there are snack making facilities in one of the rooms. There is a heated swimming pool (May to September) and fishing.

Prices s fr €65; d fr €85; t fr €115; extra person fr €30; dinner fr €24
On Site 🏊 🎾 Private ⚲ Private tennis court **Nearby** ⛷ 15km
⚲ 65km 🏛 10km ⚲ 25km **Notes** No pets English spoken CC

FLOING

♦♦♦ La Maison de l'Etang

Jacqueline & J.F. LAMBERTY
Chemin des Hautes, 08200 FLOING
☎ 06 86 44 87 64 & 06 81 55 74 42 🗎 03 24 29 48 25
email: jflamberty@free.fr
web: www.lamaisondeletang.com

This ancient building is set in its own parkland full of trees and flowers with a private lake. Four charming rooms, one of which has an annexe making it suitable for four people, all have TV, en suite shower and WC. The dining and living rooms and a kitchenette are at the disposal of guests. Cot, laundry, fishing and mountain bikes all available (no charge).

Prices s fr €35; d fr €45; t fr €75; extra person fr €15 **On Site** 🏊 🎾
Nearby ⛷ 5km ⚲ 20km ⚲ 3km Restaurant 3km ⚲ 3km 🏛 0.8km
⚲ 3km **Notes** No pets English spoken

FUMAY

♦♦♦ Chambre d'hôtes

Liliane LORENT
3 rue du Docteur Bourgeois, 08170 FUMAY
☎ 03 24 41 29 66 & 06 89 52 22 97
email: f08170@aol.com
web: www.gitardennes.com/fr/chambres/9942.html

Three en suite rooms are available in this lovely 18th-century house bordering the Meuse: a double room with an en suite shower room and wc; and two double rooms with en suite bathroom and wc. Extra folding bed possible. There is a guest lounge and sitting room with TV and central heating.

Prices s fr €45; d fr €50; extra person fr €18   **On Site** 🌳
Nearby ⚑ 15km ⚓ 40km ⚒ 0.5km   Restaurant 0.2km 🏊 0.5km
⛵ 0.2km 🏛 0.2km ⋙ 2km   **Notes** No pets

GIVET

🏵🏵🏵 🍽 Orchidee Rose

Pierre & Quân GLIN

41 rue de Tivoli, 08600 GIVET

☎ 03 24 57 27 88 & 06 65 35 43 80   📄 03 24 57 27 88

email: lane@orchideerose.com

web: www.orchideerose.com

This modern house, with views over the River Meuse and the town
of Givet, has four guest rooms. On the first floor with separate access
is a lounge, kitchenette, and three double bedrooms. On the ground
floor are two linked bedrooms, a double and a twin; all have en suite
facilities. Cot and folding bed; meals available June-September.

Prices s fr €43; d fr €48; d fr €63; extra person fr €15; dinner fr €20
Nearby ⚑ 2km ⚓ 25km 🎣 0.5km ⚒ 2km   Restaurant 0.7km 🏊 0.5km
⛵ 3km 🏛 0.7km ⋙ 2km   **Notes** No pets   English spoken

JANDUN

🏵🏵🏵 🍽 Chambre d'hôtes

Jocelyne et Joël BOURNONVILLE

11 rue de Milaville, 08430 JANDUN

☎ 03 24 52 86 05 & 06 08 98 97 71   📄 03 24 52 86 05

email: bournonville.jocelyne@wanadoo.fr

web: www.gitardennes.com/fr/chambres/9953.html

This 17th-century house stands in the centre of the village. It has three
bedrooms: a double, a triple, and a split-level family suite for up to four
people with its own independent access. All rooms have TVs and private
facilities; the suite also has a fridge and washing machine. Cot available;
conservatory lounge area; extensive grounds with private parking.

Prices s fr €35; d €42-€45; t €54-€55; extra person fr €12; dinner fr €16
Nearby ⚑ 1km ⚓ 15km 🎣 11km ⚒ 16km 🏊 6km ⛵ 1km ⋙ 16km
Notes No pets   English spoken

LALOBBE

🏵🏵🏵 🍽 La Besace

Danièle & Claude CARPENTIER

08460 LALOBBE

☎ 03 24 52 81 94

web: www.gitardennes.com/fr/chambres/9940.html

Escape to this charming house in the middle of a forest which offers
four en suite listed bedrooms (two grade 2 double rooms, one double
grade 3, and a grade 3 double suite includes a single). There is a
large, beautiful garden and plenty of pastimes. A drinks inclusive table
d'hôte menu is on offer by reservation.

Prices s €32-€35; d €42-€45; t fr €55; extra person fr €10; dinner €20-
€30   **Nearby** ⚑ 5km ⚓ 25km 🎣 5km   Restaurant 5km 🏊 5km ⛵ 5km
🏛 5km ⋙ 25km   **Notes** No pets   English spoken

ROCROI

🏵🏵🏵 🍽 *Chambre d'hôtes*

Françoise DUMONCEAU

5 rue d'Hersigny, 08230 ROCROI

☎ 03 24 53 86 37   📄 03 24 53 86 37

email: levdum@tiscali.fr

web: www.gitardennes.com/fr/chambres/9938.html

On the Franco-Belgian border, this is a great stop-off point for pilgrims
of St-Jacques de Compostelle. There are grade 2 and 3 doubles and
a twin room with a possible extra single and double bed, all non
smoking with TV and most sharing bathroom facilities. Washing
machine; terrace; sitting room; table d'hôte meals by reservation only,
drinks inclusive. 50% discount for children under twelve.

Prices not confirmed for 2008   **Nearby** ⚑ 7km 🎣 8km ⚒ 🏊 8km
⋙ 12km   **Notes** No pets

VIEL-ST-REMY

🏵🏵🏵 Chambre d'hôtes

Thérèse & René TURQUIN

Margy, 08270 VIEL-ST-REMY

☎ 03 24 38 56 37   📄 03 24 38 56 37

email: rturquin@voila.fr

web: www.gitardennes.com/fr/chambres/9930.html

Three bedrooms created in an old farm. A rural location with an
orchard and a lake for free fishing. On the first floor, with a separate
entrance is a double room and two rooms both sleeping three
(double bed and one single). All rooms come with showers and wcs
and are decorated with the personal touch of the proprietor. There is
a sitting room, and the partially covered terrace has a wonderful view.

Prices s fr €32; d fr €40; t fr €52; extra person fr €13   **On Site** 🌳
Nearby ⚑ 7km ⚓ 22km ⚒ 15km   Restaurant 10km 🏊 6km ⛵ 15km
🏛 15km ⋙ 15km   **Notes** No pets

AUBE

BAROVILLE

Le Vieux Pressoir

S.A.R.L. URBAIN FRERES
Cote Sandray, 10200 BAROVILLE
☎ 03 25 27 00 36 📠 03 25 27 78 80
email: champagne.urbain@wanadoo.fr
web: http://levieuxpressoir.barsuraube.net

This is an old wine-growing property which has been totally restored. It is on the Champagne tourist route. There are four bedrooms - three doubles and a family room for four; all have private facilities. There is a day room, and guests have use of a kitchenette.

Prices d fr €50; extra person fr €10 **Nearby** 25km 3km 6km Restaurant 6km Water sports 25km 6km 6km 6km **Notes** No pets English spoken CC

BOUILLY

Les Sargaillons

Jean-Paul et Michèle BENOIT
27 rue de Bois, 10320 BOUILLY
☎ 03 25 40 25 35 📠 03 25 40 25 35
email: chambred'hotebouilly10@yahoo.fr

Close to the RN77 and Auxerre, 30 minutes from the lakes and on the edge of the Othe forest, Michèle and Jean-Paul will welcome you to their timber-framed farmhouse with its flowered courtyard, shaded gardens and children's games. Two double rooms, both with en suite bathroom and WC, one with twin beds as well. Copious breakfasts feature home-made jams and pastries. Evening meals by reservation.

Prices s €38-€44; d €44-€50; extra person fr €15; dinner fr €19 **Nearby** 8km 20km 25km 13km Restaurant 8km Spa 15km 15km **Notes** Pets admitted

BOUY-LUXEMBOURG

Les Epis d'Or

S.A.R.L. BOUVRON
10220 BOUY-LUXEMBOURG
☎ 03 25 46 31 67 📠 03 25 46 31 67
email: earl.bouvron@wanadoo.fr
web: http://perso.wanadoo.fr/lesepisdor/

This welcoming working family farm offers four en suite bedrooms in a separate renovated building: two bedrooms with a double and a single bed and two double bedrooms, one of which also contains bunk beds. Extra bed possible. Kitchen and large lounge. Visit the 15th/16th century church nearby.

Prices not confirmed for 2008 **Nearby** 18km 11km 20km Water sports 24km 3km 8km 20km **Notes** Pets admitted

BREVONNES

La Bergeotte

Gilles ANTOINE
6 rue de Dienville, 10220 BREVONNES
☎ 03 25 46 31 44

This quiet house in a big shaded garden is located amongst the large lakes of the Forest of Orient. There are three en suite bedrooms: two doubles and one bedroom with a double and a single bed. Extra beds can be provided. A small kitchen and a barbecue are available for guest use. Children's games are also available. Table d'hôte meals on reservation.

Prices s fr €30; d fr €41; t fr €50; extra person fr €9; dinner fr €17 **Nearby** 12km 14km 5km 30km Restaurant 0.3km Water sports 10km 10km 13km 30km **Notes** No pets

COURTERON

Ferme de la Gloire Dieu

10250 COURTERON
☎ 03 25 38 20 67 📠 03 25 38 22 78

Situated in part of a large 16th-century fortified farm on the Champagne route. There are three en suite bedrooms with exposed stone and pastel drawings: one twin and two doubles. There is a flower-filled garden and nearby ramblers' route.

Prices s fr €40; d fr €45; t fr €60; extra person fr €15; dinner fr €18 **Nearby** 30km 30km 20km Restaurant 3km Water sports 30km 15km 6km 3km 50km **Notes** Pets admitted Open February to December.

EAUX-PUISEAUX

La Ferme des Hauts Frênes

Marie Paule LAMBERT
6 Voie de Puiseaux, 10130 EAUX-PUISEAUX
☎ 03 25 42 15 04 📠 03 25 42 02 95
email: les.hauts.frenes@wanadoo.fr
web: www.les-hauts-frenes.com

This welcoming farm offers three fully equipped en suite bedrooms with TV: one double, one twin and one bedroom with a double, bunk bed and a single bed. Children's games are available. Mountain bike hire is available on site. Cider museum in the village.

Prices s fr €32; d fr €43; t fr €54; extra person fr €11 **On Site** **Nearby** 5km 20km 5km 20km Restaurant 0.5km Water sports 30km 5km 1km 35km **Notes** No pets English spoken

ESSOYES

ⅢⅢ **Chambre d'hôtes**

Maite RUFFIN

14 rue de l'Extra, 10360 ESSOYES

☎ 03 25 29 01 93

email: marie-therese.ruffin@wanadoo.fr

web: www.le-relais-st-georges.com

A good starting point for walks and opposite Renoir's house and studio right in the heart of the village. The generous breakfasts are served outside in fine weather in the shaded garden. There is a family room, a double and a twin, each with private shower room. The large day room has a fireplace and seating area.

Prices s fr €55; d fr €65; t fr €75; extra person fr €25 **On Site** ✍ ❧ **Nearby** ⛷ 10km ⚓ 30km ↖ 30km Restaurant 0.1km Water sports 35km ⌕ 0.2km 🏠 0.1km ⋙ 50km **Notes** No pets English spoken

---

ESTISSAC

ⅢⅢ Ⅰⓞ & **Domaine du Moulin d'Eguebaude**

Alexandre & Sandrine MESLEY

36 Rue Pierre Brossolette, 10190 ESTISSAC

☎ 03 25 40 42 18 📄 03 25 40 40 92

email: eguebaude@aol.com

This house was designed by a French architect renowned for his woodwork, Jean-Louis Valentin. Three spacious and original ground-floor rooms (no smoking), one of which is suitable for the disabled, look out on the banks of the Vanne River. Excellent breakfasts featuring local produce are served in the restored mill. Satellite TV, jacuzzi, boutique, kitchenette, riverside terrace.

Prices s €43-€51; d €50-€72; extra person fr €20; dinner fr €22 **On Site** ✍ **Nearby** ⛷ 9km ⚓ 30km ↖ 23km Restaurant 1km Water sports 50km ⌕ 2km 🏠 1km ⋙ 25km **Notes** No pets English spoken

ⅢⅢ Ⅰⓞ **Le Domaine du Voirloup**

Jacqueline HULO

3 place Betty Die, 7B rue Costel Laurent, 10190 ESTISSAC

☎ 03 25 43 14 27 & 06 83 16 36 32

email: resavrlp@free.fr

web: www.vrlp.com

Three rooms in a 1900s mansion each with telephone, video and internet access. In summer the generous breakfasts are served under the arbour and home-cooked evening meals, which must be booked in advance, consist of regional specialities. Walk in the large, shady grounds with a river or in the nearby Othe Forest.

Prices s fr €60; d fr €60; t fr €80; extra person fr €10; dinner fr €25 **On Site** ❧ **Nearby** ⛷ 15km ✍ 0.5km ↖ 3km Restaurant 0.3km 🏠 0.3km ⋙ 20km **Notes** No pets English spoken

ⅢⅢ **Les Fontaines du Betrot**

Isabelle KARKOWSKI

23 rue Jean Hector, 10190 ESTISSAC

☎ 03 25 40 67 01 & 06 19 80 97 59

Just an hour and a half from Paris, this property stands in pleasant grounds with a stream and a small pond. There are four spacious bedrooms, all with TV, private bath/shower room and WC (three have a spa bath). Extra beds are available. Two covered swimming pools which are heated from May to October; children's games. Meals by arrangement.

Prices s fr €39; d €48-€50; t €57-€60; extra person €7.50-€15; dinner fr €17 **On Site** Private ↖ ✍ **Nearby** ⛷ 3km ⚓ 30km Restaurant 0.3km Water sports 35km ⌕ 1km 🏠 0.4km ⋙ 25km **Notes** Pets admitted English spoken

GYE-SUR-SEINE

⊞⊞⊞ La Jouette

Claude OLIVIER

6 Grande Rue, 10250 GYE-SUR-SEINE

☎ 03 25 38 40 23

email: cljolivier@wanadoo.fr

web: www.gite-prop.com/10/860

This house stands on a pretty village square, in the heart of the Champagne region. It has three double bedrooms. All have private facilities. There is a sitting room with open fire, a garden room and delightful pergola. Breakfasts are generous and varied. Visits to Champagne wine cellars can be arranged.

Prices s €30-€47; d €35-€52 **On Site** 🖉 **Nearby** ⛷ 8km ⚓ 28km ⛵ 35km Restaurant 0.2km Water sports 30km 🏊 0.5km ⛳ 28km **Notes** Pets admitted English spoken Open 30 March to November.

JEUGNY

⊞⊞⊞ Ⅰ○Ⅰ La Louviere

Jean CHALONS

22 rue de Villeneuve, 10320 JEUGNY

☎ 03 25 40 21 93

email: jean.chalons@worldonline.fr

web: www.la-louviere.fr

Guests to this old wooden farmhouse have a choice of two single bedrooms, one triple bedroom and one bedroom with one double and one single bed, all sharing bathroom facilities. There is also a communal room and parking and dinner available, with an aperitif and wine included. Countryside rich with mushrooms and game is ideal for long walks and cycle rides; also nearby are Troyes, the Champagne route and the Forest of Orient.

Prices s €34; d fr €42; t fr €50; dinner fr €20 **Nearby** ⛷ 20km ⚓ 14km ⚓ 35km ⛵ 25km Restaurant 10km Water sports 35km 🏊 25km Spa 25km ⛳ 4km ⛳ 25km **Notes** No pets

LA MOTTE-TILLY

⊞⊞⊞ *Les Bienvenues*

Robert RONDEAU

12 rue de Chêne, 10400 LA MOTTE-TILLY

☎ 03 25 39 83 85 ▤ 03 25 39 75 22

This separate house in a farm courtyard is situated in the Seine Valley, close to the castle of Motte Tilly. One twin bedroom, suitable for the less mobile guest, and four double bedrooms each have bathroom facilities and a TV point. A kitchen is available for guests and plentiful breakfasts include pastries and home-made jams.

Prices not confirmed for 2008 **On Site** ⚓ Water sports **Nearby** ⚓ 4km ⚓ 4km ⛳ 4km **Notes** No pets

LA VILLENEUVE-AU-CHENE

⊞⊞⊞ Ⅰ○Ⅰ La Renouillere

Edwige PREVOT

3 rue aux Chèvres, 10140 LA VILLENEUVE-AU-CHENE

☎ 03 25 81 64 05 ▤ 03 25 81 64 05

email: la-renouillere@wanadoo.fr

web: http://perso.orange.fr/la-renouillere/

Five individually decorated rooms in an interesting 19th-century house set in the peaceful Parc de la Forêt d'Orient. On the first floor are a twin room, and double room with sitting area. On the second are three doubles, one with a sitting area. There is a communal lounge on each floor. The hearty breakfasts and bookable evening meals use local produce.

Prices s fr €35; d €44-€52; extra person fr €15; dinner fr €22 **On Site** ⚓ **Nearby** ⚓ 1km ⚓ 5km ⚓ 4km ⛵ 25km Restaurant 4km Water sports 20km 🏊 6km ⛳ 6km ⛳ 6km **Notes** No pets English spoken

LAUBRESSEL

⊞⊞⊞ ❦ Au Colombage Champenois

Joelle JEANNE

33 rue du Haut, 10270 LAUBRESSEL

☎ 03 25 80 27 37 ▤ 03 25 80 80 67

email: aux.colombages.champenois@wanadoo.fr

web: www.pnrfo.org/partenaires/lescolombages/fr/

Set in wooded, flower-filled grounds on the tourist route of the Parc Naturel de la Forêt d'Orient. The six en suite bedrooms are in an old barn and pigeonry (one double; two triples; one with four single beds; two with two double beds) and two have a kitchen area. Washing facilities, a garden, barbecue and parking are available. Plentiful breakfasts include home-made yoghurt, pastries and jams.

Prices s fr €32; d fr €45; t fr €52; extra person fr €8 **Nearby** ⛷ 15km ⚓ 8km ⚓ 8km ⛵ Restaurant 3km Water sports 8km 🏊 7km ⛳ 4km ⛳ 12km **Notes** No pets

LESMONT

⫟⫟⫟ ⍥ **Domaine des Lacs**

Francois BRADIER

10500 LESMONT

☎ 03 25 92 00 70 ▤ 03 25 92 00 70

email: mail@domainedeslacs.com

web: www.domainedeslacs.com

Five comfortable rooms, a mix of doubles and triples, all with TV, en suite bathrooms and WCs, feature in this old hunting lodge, next to woods and the River Aube. Guests can relax in the salon after a swim in the pool or a game of tennis, or roam further afield on foot or a hired mountain bike. Aerodrome 3 kilometres, golf 17 kilometres.

Prices s fr €50; d fr €60; t fr €75; extra person fr €15; dinner fr €20 **On Site** 🎣 🎾 **Nearby** ⚓ 10km ⤳ Restaurant 0.2km Water sports 10km 🏠 0.2km ⋙ 30km **Notes** No pets English spoken

LEVIGNY

⫟⫟⫟ ⍥ 🦽 **Le Tryon**

Henriette et Hubert DESPEYROUX

8 rue du Chateau, 10200 LEVIGNY

☎ 03 25 92 78 95 ▤ 03 25 92 78 95

This renovated house has two rooms with a double and single bed, a twin room and a double, all with private facilities and separate access. Terrace with views of the countryside. Meals can be taken with the family by reservation; the proprietor lives nearby in a champagne vineyard.

Prices s fr €40; d fr €48; t fr €60; extra person fr €10; dinner fr €20 **Nearby** ⚓ 20km 🏊 30km 🏌 20km ⤳ 10km Restaurant 10km Water sports 15km 🏊 10km 🎾 15km 🏠 10km ⋙ 10km **Notes** No pets

LONGCHAMP-SUR-AUJON

⫟⫟⫟ **Les Tremieres**

Gilberte BRESSON

Hameau d'Outre Aube, 10310 LONGCHAMP-SUR-AUJON

☎ 03 25 27 80 17 ▤ 03 25 27 87 69

email: gilberte.bresson@wanadoo.fr

Guests to this traditional house at the foot of the Abbey of Clairvaux, in the Aube Valley, may choose between two triple bedrooms and one double with bathroom facilities and sharing a communal wc. There is a reception room with fireplace, veranda, garage and garden. Breakfast includes farm milk and home-made breads and jams. Visits to the Abbey are available every Saturday afternoon.

Prices d fr €42; t fr €58 **On Site** Water sports **Nearby** ⚓ 18km 🏊 25km 🏌 0.2km ⤳ 14km Restaurant 0.2km 🎾 14km 🏠 2km ⋙ 14km **Notes** No pets English spoken Open May to 30 October.

LUSIGNY-SUR-BARSE

⫟⫟⫟⫟ ⍥ **La Florestine**

Pascal GIRARDEL

29 rue Georges Clemenceau,

10270 LUSIGNY-SUR-BARSE

☎ 03 25 41 22 78

email: contact@laflorestine.fr

web: www.laflorestine.com

This late 19th-century property is in the centre of an historic village, only 15 kilometres from Troyes. It has been renovated to provide three high standard en suite rooms: a twin-bedded room with bathroom, and two doubles with shower/WC. Telephone, TV, internet access. Lakeside beaches close by. No children accepted.

Prices s fr €85; d fr €90; dinner fr €30 **On Site** Restaurant 🎾 **Nearby** ⚓ 4km 🏊 11km 🏌 0.5km ⤳ Water sports 4km 🎾 0.2km 🏠 0.3km ⋙ 17km **Notes** No pets English spoken

MARAYE-EN-OTHE

⫟⫟⫟ 🐓 ⍥ 🦽 **Les Furets**

Patricia PERIN

16 route de Vaucorbat, Champsicourt (D23),

10160 MARAYE-EN-OTHE

☎ 03 25 76 72 51 ▤ 03 25 80 58 13

email: jean-patricia.perin@wanadoo.fr

web: www.lesfurets.fr.st

Five individually themed rooms on a farm. On the ground floor is a twin-bedded room with disabled access; upstairs is another twin-bedded room, two doubles and a family room for four. All have private facilities. There is a lounge area and terrace. Meals are available, made with local produce.

Prices s fr €40-€50; d fr €50-€60; extra person fr €15; dinner fr €20 **Nearby** ⚓ 10km 🏌 15km ⤳ 18km Water sports 50km 🎾 5km 🏠 10km ⋙ 25km **Notes** No pets English spoken

MEURVILLE

⫟⫟⫟ 🦽 **L'Haubette**

route de Spoy, 10200 MEURVILLE

☎ 03 25 27 40 56 & 06 87 33 11 80 ▤ 03 25 27 01 69

email: champagne-perron-beauvineau@wanadoo.fr

web: www.gite-prop.com/10/863

Three rooms available, situated in the outbuildings of a wine-producing farm. There is a twin room with disabled access, and two rooms with a double and single bed, all with private facilities. Lounge with relaxing corner and large breakfasts include home-made pastries. Visits to the farm possible.

Prices s fr €38; d fr €46; t fr €54; extra person fr €8 **Nearby** ⚓ 20km 🏊 30km 🏌 10km ⤳ 10km Restaurant 3km Water sports 20km 🎾 10km 🎾 0.1km 🏠 10km ⋙ 10km **Notes** Pets admitted CC

CHAMPAGNE-ARDENNE

MOUSSEY

ⅢⅢ Domaine de la Creuse

Patrick LE BORGNE
10800 MOUSSEY
☎ 03 25 41 74 01 & 06 80 63 33 10
📄 03 25 73 13 87
email: contact@domainedelacreuse.com
web: www.domainedelacreuse.com

Very careful attention has been paid to restoring this charming, peaceful, 18th-century, timber-framed, traditional house. The three comfortable and beautifully decorated rooms are on level access and breakfasts can be served in the large well-tended garden full of trees and flowers. Closed Xmas to New Year.

Prices s €95-€110; d €100-€115; extra person fr €30
Nearby ⚓ 5km ⚑ 15km ⚑ 5km ⚑ 10km Restaurant 2km Water sports 15km ⚑ 5km ⚑ 10km ⚑ 2km ⚑ 15km **Notes** No pets English spoken

POUGY

ⅢⅢ Château de Pougy

Antoine MORLET
Grande Rue, 10240 POUGY
☎ 03 25 37 09 41
email: antoine.morlet@wanadoo.fr

This superb 18th-century property is situated in a park full of old trees and lakes, offering fishing opportunities. There are three double bedrooms, with the possibility of an extra bed, one double bedroom and one bedroom with one double and two single beds, all en suite. There is a small relaxing lounge with tourist information.

Prices s fr €35; d fr €40; t fr €44; extra person fr €48 **Nearby** ⚓ 15km ⚑ 15km ⚑ 2km ⚑ 30km Restaurant 5km Water sports 15km ⚑ 5km ⚑ 15km ⚑ 0.1km ⚑ 30km **Notes** Pets admitted English spoken

ST-GERMAIN

ⅢⅢ Les Beauchots

Marie MEEKEL
412 route de Lepine, 10120 ST-GERMAIN
☎ 03 25 79 51 92 📄 03 25 79 51 92
email: paul.meekel@wanadoo.fr
web: www.lesbeauchets.fr

This charming house with flower-filled park and an orangery is situated 6km from the centre of Troyes. It offers five guest rooms, all double or twin and non smoking.

Prices s fr €60; d €65-€95; extra person fr €20 **On Site** ⚓ Water sports ⚑ **Nearby** ⚑ 20km ⚑ 5km ⚑ 3.5km Restaurant 1km ⚑ 1km ⚑ 0.4km ⚑ 5.5km **Notes** No pets English spoken Open 10 January to December.

VILLEHARDOUIN

ⅢⅢ |○| La Ferme de Croit

T et J P MEURVIL
5 rue Gauliere, 10220 VILLEHARDOUIN
☎ 03 25 46 40 28 📄 03 25 46 32 39
email: jp.meurville.dethune@wanadoo.fr
web: www.pem.net/meurville/

A warm welcome can be expected at this farm, set in a small village by the Natural Park of the Forêt d'Orient and full of the charms of Aube rural life. There are five rooms offering accommodation for two to four people, as well as a kitchen, dining room, library and indoor and outdoor games. Animals are admitted if pre-booked, and table d'hôte meals are available by reservation.

Prices s €25-€32; d €39-€49; t €46-€55; extra person fr €10; dinner fr €18 **Nearby** ⚓ 10km ⚑ 7km ⚑ 25km Water sports 10km ⚑ 5km ⚑ 4km **Notes** Pets admitted Open 16 January to 14 December.

VIVIERS-SUR-ARTAUT

ⅢⅢ ⚘ |○| ⚐ *La Combernée*

Francine CORNET
4 Grande Rue, 10110 VIVIERS-SUR-ARTAUT
☎ 03 25 38 41 49 & 06 83 37 47 24 📄 03 25 38 41 49
email: lacombernee@wanadoo.fr
web: http://perso.wanadoo.fr/combernee.cornet/

Look out over the vineyard surrounding the owner's house from one of the three rooms with private showers and toilets. Meals use farm grown produce. Get a feel for local life on grape-picking days, or hire a donkey, or visit experimental vineyards.

Prices not confirmed for 2008 **Nearby** ⚓ 10km ⚑ 3km ⚑ 30km Water sports 30km ⚑ 3km ⚑ 3km ⚑ 50km **Notes** No pets

VULAINES

ⅢⅢ Le Saule Fleuri

Fandard SCHMITE
7 rue de l'Ancienne Gare, 10160 VULAINES
☎ 03 25 40 80 99 📄 03 25 40 80 99
email: fandardschmite@wanadoo.fr

A four bedroom 19th-century house full of character. The rooms are bright and have been carefully decorated, all rooms are en suite and non-smoking. Guests will enjoy the quiet, flower-filled garden and terrace. Plentiful, varied breakfasts are served, including pastries and home-made jams and there is a restaurant nearby.

Prices s fr €45; d fr €55; extra person fr €15 **On Site** Restaurant ⚑ **Nearby** ⚓ 8km ⚑ 5km ⚑ 8km Water sports 50km ⚑ 3km ⚑ 3km ⚑ 28km **Notes** No pets

HAUTE-MARNE

BAY-SUR-AUBE

▦ ⦿ *La Maison Jaune*

Marian JANSEN-GERRETSEN
rue Principale, 52160 BAY-SUR-AUBE
☎ 03 25 84 99 42 ▤ 03 25 87 57 65
email: jwjansen@club-internet.fr

Next to the River Aube, La Maison Jaune is a beautiful four-bedroom house set in large grounds, with authentic paintings and antique furniture. Breakfast and table d'hôte meals use local produce. Picnics are popular and a hamper can be arranged. TV, games and books, private parking and courtyard. Fishing and swimming in the river.

Prices not confirmed for 2008   **On Site** 🎣   **Nearby** ⛷ 4km
⭢ 12km Water sports 25km ▣ 4km ⋔ 35km **Notes** No pets
English spoken

CHALINDREY

▦ ⦿ **Gîte des Archots**

erge et Véronique FRANCOIS
2600 CHALINDREY
☎ 03 25 88 93 64 ▤ 03 25 88 93 64

et in five hectares bordered by an old Roman road, and at the edge
f a large, wild forest, this house has five en suite bedrooms: two
ooms sleep five, two are double/twins, and the fifth sleeps four.
ames room, children's play area, selection of books and living room.
able d'hôte meals by reservation.

rices s fr €33; d fr €45; t fr €57; extra person fr €12; dinner fr €15
earby ⛷ 3km ⋣ 30km 🎣 5km ⭢ 10km Restaurant 3km Water
orts 10km ≋ 3km ▣ 3km ⋔ 3km **Notes** Pets admitted English
poken

CHAMOUILLEY

▦ **Chambre d'hôtes**

iliane et Antoine MARSAL
Route d'Eurville, 52410 CHAMOUILLEY
☎ 03 25 55 02 26 & 06 74 19 22 09
mail: liliane.bereche@wanadoo.fr

his is a four-bedroom house with plenty of character. Two rooms
re double/twins, and two each sleep three; all have private facilities.
V, courtyard, parking, billiards room and cooking facilities. Separate
uest entrance.

rices s fr €40; d fr €45; t fr €50; extra person fr €15 **Nearby** ⛷ 8km
° 1km ⭢ 8km Restaurant 1km Water sports 12km ⁓ 8km ▣ 1km
⋔ 8km **Notes** Pets admitted English spoken

▦ ⦿ **Le Moulin**

Sylvie et Regis FORET
52410 CHAMOUILLEY
☎ 03 25 55 81 93 & 06 12 30 23 87
▤ 03 25 55 81 93
email: lemoulinchamouilley@wanadoo.fr

This is a house with plenty of character, and it stands in two hectares of grounds beside the Marne River. There is a separate guests' entrance to the five bedrooms, all of which have their own shower rooms and WCs. Lounge with TV and books; use of the kitchen.

Prices s fr €49; d €56-€60; t fr €70; extra person fr €15; dinner fr
€29   **On Site** 🎣 Restaurant ⁓ Private ⭢ **Nearby** ⛷ 8km ⋣ 8km
Water sports 12km ≋ 2km ⋔ 7km **Notes** Pets admitted English
spoken

DOULEVANT-LE-CHATEAU

▦ ⦿ **Joie de Vivre**

Wanda GEUSENS
13 Rue Haute, 52110 DOULEVANT-LE-CHATEAU
☎ 03 25 05 74 81 & 06 23 58 81 43
▤ 03 25 05 74 81
email: joie-de-vivre@club-internet.fr
web: http://joie-de-vivre.monsite.wanadoo.fr

A large and ancient house, surrounded by lots of greenery. There are five double bedrooms, all with private shower and WC. Extra beds available. There is a big lounge with books, an orangery and a heated swimming pool. Mountain bikes available; children's games. Meals, including vegetarian dishes, available on request; also packed lunches. Enclosed parking.

Prices s €55-€90; d €60-€95; t €80-€110; dinner fr €18
On Site 🎣 Private ⭢ **Nearby** ⛷ 10km Water sports 20km
⋔ 20km **Notes** No pets English spoken

DROYES

⊞ *La Maison de Marie*

Sylvie GRAVIER

11 rue de la Motte, 52220 DROYES

☎ 03 25 04 62 30

email: lamaison.marie@wanadoo.fr

An attractive half-timbered house with three rooms, two of them making a family suite for up to five people (two double beds and a single), with shower room/WC. The other room is a double with bathroom. There is an enclosed garden, and not far away is the largest reservoir in Europe, the Lac du Der.

Prices not confirmed for 2008 **Nearby** ⚘ 15km ⚲ 9km ⚹ 25km Water sports 9km ⌂ 7km ⋘ 25km **Notes** Pets admitted English spoken Open 15 January to 15 December

⊞ Les Coccinelles

Sandrine et P-Jean CHARUEL

8 Rue Papillon, 52220 DROYES

☎ 03 25 94 60 38 ▤ 03 25 04 22 81

email: sandrine.charuel@wanadoo.fr

The welcome at this old farmhouse has a warm, family feel about it. The building was renovated in 2005, and its three bedrooms all have private shower room and WC. There is a lounge with a supply of books, a kitchenette, an enclosed courtyard and garage.

Prices s fr €40; d fr €50; t fr €65; extra person fr €10 **Nearby** ⚘ 12km ⚲ 7km ⚹ 30km Restaurant 7km Water sports 7km ⌁ 1km ⚶ 7km ⌂ 7km ⋘ 30km **Notes** No pets

FLAGEY

⊞ ❦ ⎐ La Ferme du Soleil de Langres

Sylvie JAPIOT

52250 FLAGEY

☎ 03 25 84 45 23

email: sylvie.japiot@wanadoo.fr

web: www.fermedusoleildelangres.com

A family house, renovated by its owners, with four bedrooms sleeping twelve comfortably. Three kilometres from a small village and an old farm; it also boasts a prize-winning garden. The amenities offered are private facilities, lounge, sitting room, TV, books, electric heating and a garage. Mountain bikes hire nearby.

Prices s fr €48; d fr €55; t fr €73; dinner fr €16 **On Site** ⚶ **Nearby** ⚘ 10km ⌁ 30km ⚲ 5km ⚹ 12km Restaurant 5km Water sports 5km ⌁ 2km ⌂ 5km ⋘ 14km **Notes** No pets

LONGEVILLE-SUR-LA-LAINES

⊞ ⎐ Domaine de Boulancourt

P et C VIEL-CAZA

52220 LONGEVILLE-SUR-LA-LAINES

☎ 03 25 04 60 18 ▤ 03 25 04 60 18

email: dom.boulancourt@wanadoo.fr

This house sits in quiet parkland with a pond and river and offers five double/twin bedrooms with showers and wcs. One bedroom has an adjoining suite for two children. Nearby for visits: churches, a wildlife museum and an old railway line. Table d'hôte meals by reservation.

Prices s €60-€70; d €65-€75; extra person fr €18; dinner fr €25 **On Site** ⚲ **Nearby** ⚘ 8km ⚹ 40km Restaurant 10km Water sports 15km ⌁ 2km ⚶ 15km ⌂ 10km ⋘ 35km **Notes** No pets English spoken Open March to 10 December.

LOUVEMONT

⊞ Le Relais du Blaiseron

Jean Jacques & Corine Kesler

6 rue du Four, 52130 LOUVEMONT

☎ 03 25 04 02 74 & 06 84 97 93 31

email: corinne.ney@wanadoo.fr

web: www.chambre-hotes-louvemont.com

A big house, full of character, dating from the end of the 19th century. At one time it was a staging post for the horses which hauled the barges along the neighbouring canal. Today it has five double bedrooms, all with private shower and WC. Guests' lounge, use of kitchen, beautiful gardens. Attractive village setting. Mountain bikes, tennis, stabling.

Prices s fr €60; d fr €70; extra person fr €15 **Nearby** ⚘ 0.3km ⚲ 0.2km ⚹ 12km Restaurant 10km Water sports 8km ⌁ 0.2km ⚶ 10km ⌂ 6km ⋘ 12km **Notes** No pets English spoken

LOUVIERES

✦ ⋈ Au Pré l'Eau d'Anirol

Annie SASTRE
Rue Pacotte, 52800 LOUVIERES
☎ 03 25 32 16 49
email: prelot.anirol@wanadoo.fr
web: http://perso.orange.fr/au-pre-leau-danirol

Pré l'Eau d'Anirol is in an area with plenty of outdoor activities including mountain biking, horse riding and donkey walks, along with woodland to explore. This house offers one bedroom and two-room suites, with private facilities. Also a living room, sitting room, TV and books. Table d'hôte meals are offered along with regional cuisine by reservation. Parking available.

Prices s fr €40; d fr €50; t fr €63; extra person fr €13; dinner fr €18 **Nearby** ⇄ 7km ↨ 25km ✎ 1km ↖ 15km Restaurant 17km Water sports 15km ⌂ 7km ⋙ 17km **Notes** Pets admitted

MANDRES-LA-COTE

✦ ⋈ Relais de la Côte

Christiane et Robert LESPRIT
Rue de Normandie, 52800 MANDRES-LA-COTE
☎ 03 25 01 94 03 ▤ 03 25 01 94 03

This old renovated farm offers accommodation for eleven. There are two double/twin rooms, one room sleeping four, and the two room suite sleeps five; all are en suite with TVs. Other amenities include books, living room and playground. Parking available.

Prices s fr €28; d fr €38; extra person fr €15; dinner fr €14 **Nearby** ⇄ 4km ↨ 22km ✎ 25km ↖ 4km Restaurant 4km Water sports 25km ≋ 1km ⌂ 1km ⋙ 18km **Notes** No pets

PRANGEY

✦ L'Orangerie

Monique et Patrick TRINQUESSE
52190 PRANGEY
☎ 03 25 87 54 85 & 06 74 88 47 05
email: lorangerie0787@orange.fr

The owners welcome guests to this charming three-bedroom property set in peaceful countryside next to a château. Each bedroom has a private bathroom and wc. There are two doubles and one twin room. Guests' sitting room. Covered parking. Reservations necessary out of season.

Prices s fr €50; d fr €60-€65; extra person fr €20 **Nearby** ⇄ 20km ↨ 30km ✎ 8km ↖ 2km Water sports 2km ≋ 2km ⌂ 2km ⋙ 15km **Notes** No pets English spoken

PRESSIGNY

✦✦ ⋈ Maison Massin-Perrette

Evelyne et Michel POOPE
24 rue Augustin Massin, 52500 PRESSIGNY
☎ 03 25 88 80 50 ▤ 03 25 88 80 49
email: e.m.poope@wanadoo.fr
web: www.massin-perrette.com

A modern house of original design, built from red cedar, in the heart of the pine forest. Golfing holidays can be arranged, and the bedrooms are named after golf courses. St. Andrews and Sperone are double rooms; Augusta has a double bed and a single. All have private shower and WC, air conditioning, and DVD player. Swimming pool, jacuzzi, table tennis and boules.

Prices s fr €45; d €50-€65; t €65-€80; extra person fr €15; dinner fr €16 **On Site** ✎ **Nearby** ⇄ 15km ↖ 15km Water sports 30km ⋙ 25km **Notes** No pets English spoken

SAVIGNY

✦ ⋈ La Renaissance

C et W VAN ROOY-KADMAER
34 rue du Festival, 52500 SAVIGNY
☎ 03 25 88 69 17 & 06 77 47 20 66
email: renaissance@libertysurf.fr

This house has a lot of character. It has four individually decorated bedrooms, each with private shower room and WC, enjoying views over the village or towards some attractive woodland. There is a warm and comfortable lounge with TV, and the whole place has a pleasant, typically Flemish, feel about it.

Prices s fr €45; d €58-€83; extra person fr €15; dinner fr €24 **On Site** ✎ **Nearby** ⇄ 20km ↨ 3km ↖ 3km Restaurant 12km Water sports 22km ≋ 12km ⌂ 12km ⋙ 18km **Notes** No pets English spoken

THONNANCE-LES-JOINVILLE

✦✦ ❧ ⋈ Le Moulin aux Ecrevisses

J.Pierre GEERAERT
Route de Nancy, 52300 THONNANCE-LES-JOINVILLE
☎ 03 25 94 13 76 & 06 07 82 90 91 ▤ 03 25 94 02 52
email: jean.geeraert@wanadoo.fr
web: http://pro.wanadoo.fr/lemoulin/index.htm

This mill bordering a forest offers four en suite rooms. Centrally heated throughout there is also a lounge, sitting room, TV, fireplace

CONTINUED

THONNANCE-LES-JOINVILLE *CONTINUED*

and games room, plus a selection of books and videos. A free visit to a crayfish breeding farm is offered, as well as private fishing facilities.

Prices s fr €40; d €50-€65; t fr €60; extra person fr €15; dinner €23-€32 **Nearby** ℓ 1km ⚓ 30km Restaurant 1km Water sports 30km ⬛ 3km ⫶ 3km **Notes** No pets English spoken

VECQUEVILLE

⫿ ⦿ & Ferme de Sossa

Maria et Thierry PAQUET
52300 VECQUEVILLE
☎ 03 25 94 32 18 & 06 87 61 21 81 📄 03 25 94 32 18
email: tpaquet@wanadoo.fr
web: www.sossa.fr

A charming, sunny family farmhouse in a village at the heart of the Champagne, with a vast flowery garden overlooking a valley and fish-filled river. It provides three rooms with private facilities and access, a living room with fireplace and TV, library, parking, cot and nine horse boxes. Walks and canoeing in the nearby river.

Prices s fr €47; d fr €50; t fr €65; extra person fr €15; dinner fr €20 **Nearby** ⛷ 14km ⚲ 20km ℓ 2.5km ⚓ 30km Restaurant 2.5km Water sports 25km ⚄ 2.5km ⚘ 2.5km ⬛ 2.5km ⫶ 2.5km **Notes** No pets English spoken

VILLEGUSIEN-LE-LAC

⫿ ⦿ & Les Lilas

Geneviève/Dominique ROBIN
21 rue de l'Eglise, 52190 VILLEGUSIEN LE LAC
☎ 03 25 87 38 33 & 03 25 84 49 53
email: leslilas52@wanadoo.fr

This property has three bedrooms, each for three people, all with private shower rooms and WCs. One has full provision for disabled guests. There is a cot available. The rooms have TV sockets and private safe deposit boxes. Lounge, with kitchenette and microwave.

Prices s fr €40; d fr €50; t fr €65; dinner fr €15 **On Site** ℓ Water sports **Nearby** ⛷ 8km ⚲ 20km ⚓ 14km Restaurant 4km ⚄ 4km Spa 25km ⬛ 2km ⫶ 16km **Notes** No pets

VILLIERS-SUR-SUIZE

⫿ ⚘ ⦿ Domaine du Bas Bois

Roselyne et Eric GRUOT
52210 VILLIERS-SUR-SUIZE
☎ 03 25 31 11 80 & 06 80 30 16 11 📄 03 25 31 11 80
email: fermebasbois@wanadoo.fr

For stargazers, this renovated farmhouse is situated close to a private observatory and with starlit walks in the local countryside. The house has two rooms sleeping three and one double/twin, all en suite. Extra beds available. Centrally heated. Lounge, garage parking and garden furniture.

Prices s fr €43; d fr €52; t fr €63; dinner fr €19 **On Site** ⛷ ℓ **Nearby** ⚲ 15km ⚓ 17km Restaurant 2km Water sports 25km ⚘ 17km ⬛ 0.1km ⫶ 17km **Notes** No pets English spoken

MARNE

AVIZE

⫿ Le Vieux Cèdre

Imogen/Didier PIERSON-WHITAKER
14 route d'Oger, 51190 AVIZE
☎ 03 26 57 77 04 📄 03 26 57 97 97
email: champagnepiersonwhitaker@club-internet.fr

A typical family home, built around 1840, includes amongst its many attractions three en suite guest bedrooms (one double, one twin, and a grade 2 double). In the heart of the Côte des Blancs region there are plenty of wine related activities to pursue. Closed two weeks in August & Xmas.

Prices d fr €60; extra person fr €13 **Nearby** ⚲ 30km ⚓ 10km ⚄ 10km ⚘ 10km ⬛ 0.1km ⫶ 10km **Notes** No pets English spoken

BANNAY

⫿ ⦿ Chambre d'hôtes

J.Pierre/Muguette CURFS
51270 BANNAY
☎ 03 26 52 80 49 📄 03 26 59 47 78
email: mjpcurfs@aliceadsl.fr

In a rustic setting this charming house offers comfort and relaxation. There are three en suite bedrooms: a double and two triples. In a separate building there is accommodation for a further four people, featuring a kitchenette. Sample the local farm produce at table d'hôte meals.

Prices s €47-€59; d €51-€63; t €68-€80; extra person €17-€29; dinner €29-€35 **Nearby** ⛷ 30km ⚲ 4km ⚓ 15km ⚄ 10km ⬛ 3km ⫶ 30km **Notes** No pets English spoken

BASLIEUX-SOUS-CHATILLON

⫿ Chambre d'hôtes

Hervé et Thérèse ROUILLERE
5 rue du Vieux Moulin,
51700 BASLIEUX-SOUS-CHATILLON
☎ 03 26 58 15 26 & 06 79 43 30 45 📄 03 26 58 15 26
email: champagne.rouillere@wanadoo.fr

Well-placed in a small village 15 kilometres from Epernay, 20 kilometres from Reims, and one hour from Disneyland Paris, this house has two double rooms and a twin-bedded room, each with private bath or shower room and WC. Breakfast is served in the dining room, where a big bay window looks out onto the lawn. Living room, mini-bar, enclosed parking.

Prices not confirmed for 2008 **On Site** ℓ **Nearby** ⚲ 7km ⚲ 15km ⚓ 15km ⚄ 7km ⬛ 7km ⫶ 18km **Notes** No pets English spoken

BAYE

⚑ Ambiances

Isabelle LENOIR-COLLIN

9 Grande rue, 51270 BAYE

☎ 03 26 52 13 01 & 06 84 34 65 88

email: i.lenoir@libertysurf.fr

house with a lot of character, extensively restored, in a wine-growing village with a long history. There are three rooms: a double with two single beds, a double with additional sofabed, and a triple; all have themed decoration and private bath/shower room. A cot is available, and children's games. The garden and courtyard are pleasant places to relax. Enclosed parking available.

Prices s fr €44; d fr €52; t fr €67; extra person fr €15   **Nearby** ⛷ 12km ☇ 30km ⌖ 3km ⚓ 15km Water sports 25km ⚓ 15km Spa 25km ☇ 25km ⛟ 25km   **Notes** Pets admitted English spoken Open 3 January to 31 July & 16 August to 23 December.

BELVAL-SOUS-CHATILLON

⚑ Hameau du Paradis

Daniel GRAFTIEAUX

51480 BELVAL-SOUS-CHATILLON

☎ 03 26 58 13 15

email: daniel.graftieaux@wanadoo.fr

web: http://hameau.des.paradis.free.fr

Perfectly situated between forests and vineyards, this charming renovated farmhouse sleeps six, in three en suite double rooms. Table d'hôte meals are available by reservation except Tuesdays.

Prices s fr €45; d fr €55; extra person fr €15   **Nearby** ⛷ 15km ⚓ 15km ☇ 10km ⌖ 15km Restaurant 8km Water sports 20km ⚓ 10km ⚓ 15km ☇ 7km ⛟ 15km   **Notes** No pets English spoken

BOURSAULT

⚑ Les Impériales

Françoise/Dominique CUCHET

rue de l'Ascension, 51480 BOURSAULT

☎ 03 26 58 63 71 & 06 87 83 53 19   📠 03 26 57 87 94

email: fdcuchet@aol.com

web: www.les-imperiales.com

Set in vineyards by forest on the hillside of the Marne Valley, this old house offers five rooms with private showers and wcs. There is lounge with park view, sitting room with TV, terrace and garden

furniture, separate guest entry, and numerous walks and sites to explore locally.

Prices s fr €45; d fr €51; extra person fr €17   **Nearby** ⛷ 8km ⚓ 15km ⌖ 2km ⌖ 10km Restaurant 3km ⚓ 3km ☇ 0.1km ⛟ 8km   **Notes** No pets CC

BOUZY

⚑ ♿ Les Barbotines

Marie Thérèse BONNAIRE

1 place A. Tritant, 51150 BOUZY

☎ 03 26 51 70 70 & 03 26 57 07 31

📠 03 26 58 26 36

email: contact@lesbarbotines.com

web: www.lesbarbotines.com

On the tourist route through Champagne, in the heart of the village of Bouzy, you can sleep in the home of a 19th-century master winemaker. Five guest bedrooms are decorated with refinement in the colours of the seasons, all with en suite facilities. A ground-floor room is suitable for the disabled. Two dining rooms, reading room, terrace with inner courtyard.

Prices s fr €70; d fr €90; t.fr €106; extra person fr €25   **On Site** 🎾 **Nearby** ⛷ 10km ⚓ 20km ⌖ 6km ⌖ 16km Restaurant 2km ⚓ ⛟ 17km   **Notes** No pets English spoken Open 2 February to 1 August and 12 August to 14 December. CC

BROUILLET

⚑ ♥ La Brouilletière

Rémi et Marie ARISTON

4-8 Grande Rue, 51170 BROUILLET

☎ 03 26 97 43 46   📠 03 26 97 49 34

email: contact@champagne-aristonfils.com

web: www.champagne-aristonfils.com

This delightful 18th-century house in the Vallee de l'Ardre is a perfect stopover on the Champagne tourist trail. There are three en suite doubles with TV in each room. Visit cellars and try out some of the wines, or just stroll through the countryside.

Prices d €50-€55   **On Site** ⌖ **Nearby** ⛷ 11km ⚓ 10km ⌖ 25km Water sports 25km ⚓ 10km ☇ 11km ⛟ 25km   **Notes** No pets English spoken

BROUILLET *CONTINUED*

▓▓ ◉ Les Délices de Marie

Marie-France/David TYROU

3 Grande Rue, 51170 BROUILLET

☎ 03 26 08 40 46 & 06 87 83 17 48

email: lesdelicesdemarie@free.fr

web: www.lesdelicesdemarie.com

Right at the heart of the most attractive part of the Marne region, the Ardre Valley, this 18th-century property has been extensively and sensitively restored. There are three double bedrooms, all with private shower rooms/WCs and direct access to the garden, where there are lots of fruit trees. Delicious, generous meals are available by reservation. Closed one week in February, two weeks in July & Xmas.

Prices s fr €45; d fr €50; dinner €23-€38 **Nearby** ⚓ 15km ⚓ 25km ⚓ 15km ⚓ 30km Water sports 25km ⚓ 10km ⚓ 12km ⚓ 25km **Notes** No pets English spoken

BRUGNY-VAUDANCOURT

▓▓▓ Le Logis des Elfes

Rachelle DEMIERE

15 rue de Breux, 51530 BRUGNY VAUDANCOURT

☎ 03 26 56 48 65

email: contact@lelogisdeselfes.com

web: www.lelogisdeselfes.com

There are panoramic views of the vineyard from this property, close enough to the wooded slopes south of Epernay to enjoy the sounds and the smells of the forest. There are three elegantly decorated rooms, a double and two twins, all with private bathroom and WC. Extra beds available. Jacuzzi, steam room and games room.

Prices s fr €70; d €100-€140; extra person fr €40 **Nearby** ⚓ 7km ⚓ 30km ⚓ 20km ⚓ 7km Restaurant 5km ⚓ 7km ⚓ 3km ⚓ 5km ⚓ 7km **Notes** No pets English spoken

see advert on opposite page

CONDE-SUR-MARNE

▓▓ ◉ Chambre d'hôtes

Bruno BARRAULT

7 rue Albert Barré, 51150 CONDE-SUR-MARNE

☎ 03 26 67 95 49 & 03 26 66 90 61 📄 03 26 66 82 97

email: barrault.home@wanadoo.fr

A stylishly decorated converted farmhouse situated in a town in the heart of the Champagne vineyard tourist trail. Three en suite bedrooms, a twin and two doubles, sleep six in comfort. There is also a kitchen, dining room, sitting room with TV, veranda and lawn all reserved for the guests' use. Activities including mountain biking. Table d'hôte meals served by reservation.

Prices s fr €32; d fr €45; extra person fr €15; dinner fr €20 **On Site** 🖊 **Nearby** ⚓ 10km ⚓ 20km 🖭 4km ⚓ 20km **Notes** No pets

CONGY

▓▓ ◉ Chambre d'hôtes

André/Marie-Thérèse TRUFFAUT

20 rue St Rémy, 51270 CONGY

☎ 03 26 59 31 23 📄 03 26 59 60 07

Come and explore Champagne from this charming family-run house of great charm and character. Accommodation provided includes three double and two twin rooms, all with en suite facilities. There is also a lounge, sitting room and a lawn to enjoy, along with local food and wine to sample. Closed during holidays.

Prices s fr €43; d fr €54; t fr €69; extra person fr €15; dinner fr €34 **Nearby** ⚓ 15km 🖊 9km ⚓ 20km Restaurant 10km ⚓ 20km ⚓ 4km ⚓ 25km **Notes** No pets

CRAMANT

▓▓ Chambre d'hôtes Champagne

Carole et Eric ISSELEE

350 rue des Grappes d'Or, 51530 CRAMANT

☎ 03 26 57 54 96 & 06 86 41 73 74 📄 03 26 53 91 76

email: champagneissele.e@wanadoo.fr

web: www.champagne-eric-isselee.com

In this village, right in the heart of the Champagne wine-growing area, peace and quiet are almost guaranteed. The property has three bedrooms, two doubles and a triple, all with private shower and WC. A cot is available. Panoramic views; wine-cellar visits and Champagne sales. Closed during holidays.

rices d fr €45; t fr €60; extra person fr €15 **On Site** ☁
earby ⚓ 5km ⚲ 15km ⚹ 6km Restaurant 7km ◷ 2km ⌂ 0.3km
8km **Notes** No pets CC

RUGNY

▦ ⃝ La Maison Bleue

Gilles DE BOHAN
46 rue Haute, 51170 CRUGNY
☎ 03 26 50 84 63 🖹 03 26 97 43 92
email: maisonbleue@aol.com
web: www.la-maison-bleue.com

La Maison Bleue offers an exceptional setting as you follow the
Champagne route, just over an hour from Paris. There are four
spacious rooms, two suitable for families, and all with double
beds and private bathrooms. Large gardens have a stream and
lake; a heated pool, sauna and Jacuzzi, with terrace, loungers and
a play area make for an unforgettable stay. Meals by reservation.

Prices s €50-€85; d €91-€106; t €134-€150; dinner fr €26
On Site ⚲ ☁ **Nearby** ⚓ 10km ⚲ 10km ⚹ Restaurant 8km
◷ 1km ⌂ 0.5km ▦ 8km **Notes** Pets admitted English spoken
Open February to 22 December. CC

GERMAINE

▦ *La Clairière*

régoire & Karine VERDONK
1160 GERMAINE
☎ 03 26 58 16 46 & 06 72 81 43 18 🖹 03 26 52 84 08
mail: gverdonk@orange.fr

en kilometres from Epernay, this wonderful converted barn has five
double rooms, all with private bath or shower room and WC. Extra
eds are available, also baby equipment. Guests have their own
ntrance, lounge and dining room. Local produce for sale includes
oney and snails. Good area for mountain biking and walking.

rices not confirmed for 2008 **Nearby** ⚓ 10km ⚲ 25km ⚹ 15km
⚹ 15km Water sports 15km ◷ 15km ⌂ 3km ▦ 1km **Notes** No pets
nglish spoken

GIFFAUMONT-CHAMPAUBERT

▦ Chambre d'hôtes

nnie NOAILLES
5 rue du Lac, 51290 GIFFAUMONT
☎ 03 26 72 64 16

lose to a lake known as a gathering point for migrating birds, this
ouse in the village centre offers every comfort, with three rooms
omprising a double, a twin and a triple; all have private facilities.
he grounds are enclosed and private, with a terrace and loungers.
ou can jet-ski or take to the water at the watersports centre only 100
netres away.

rices s fr €40; d fr €50; t fr €65 **On Site** ⚲ ⚲ Water sports
earby ⚓ 9km ⚹ 25km ◷ 9km ▦ 25km **Notes** No pets English
poken

HERMONVILLE

▦ ♿ Les Grattières

Christelle LEGER
Route de Bouvancourt, 51220 HERMONVILLE
☎ 03 26 02 10 60 & 06 22 69 49 52 🖹 03 26 02 10 60
email: pascal.coutie@tele2.fr
web: www.domainedesgrattieres.com

A quiet relaxing spot, 15 kilometres from Reims, 90 minutes from Paris
and on the Champagne tourist route. There are three comfortable
rooms here - two doubles and a twin-bedded room, all with private
bath or shower room and WC.

Prices d fr €55; t fr €75; extra person fr €15 **Nearby** ⚓ 2km ⚲ 18km
⚲ 12km ⚹ 2km Restaurant 9km Water sports 25km ◷ 10km ⚹ 15km
⌂ 15km ▦ 16km **Notes** No pets English spoken

JOISELLE

❦ *Chambre d'hôtes*

Guy/Yvana DEGOIS
Rue de la Fontenelle, Hameau Champagnemay,
51310 JOISELLE
☎ 03 26 81 52 13   📄 03 26 81 52 13

This is a dairy farm in a peaceful village with lots of flowers. In a purpose-built annexe, two ground floor double bedrooms each have a private shower room and WC. Cot available. Furnishings are rustic in style; living room with TV and a kitchenette for guest use. Garden furniture, barbecue; footpaths close by.

Prices not confirmed for 2008   **Nearby** ⛷ 4km 🏊 40km 🎣 1km ⛳ 16km 🏌 6km 🛒 6km 🚶 3km   **Notes** No pets

JUVIGNY

Château de Juvigny

Brigitte CAUBERE
51150 JUVIGNY
☎ 06 78 99 69 40   📄 03 26 64 86 24
email: brigitte.caubere@wanadoo.fr
web: www.chateaudejuvigny.com

A wing of this 17th-century château on the Champagne route offers three charming rooms and a two-room suite, all with private entrance and en suite facilities. A ground-floor room has a four-poster bed. Breakfast is served in the old château kitchens. The château has its private park and fishing lake. Winter stays by arrangement.

Prices s fr €40; d €90-€130; extra person fr €30   **On Site** ⛳ **Nearby** ⛷ 5km 🏊 28km 🎣 9km 🚶 12km   **Notes** No pets English spoken

LA BERTONNERIE

La Bertonnerie

Christian et Odile LE BEUF
51360 LA BERTONNERIE EN CHAMPAGNE
☎ 03 26 49 10 02   📄 03 26 49 17 13

This characterful old house benefits from a beautiful garden. There is a double room, a family room for three, and two double rooms with a communicating door. Extra beds can be arranged. The rooms have independent access. Guests can make use of the lounge, with its TV, books and games or play table tennis in the garden.

Prices s fr €47; d fr €56; t €79-€87; extra person fr €19 **Nearby** ⛷ 20km 🏊 15km 🎣 8km Restaurant 0.6km 🏊 12km 🛒 2km 🚶 12km   **Notes** No pets English spoken

LAVANNES

Les Célestines

Jean/Anne-Laure GARNOTEL
Rue des Ladres, 51110 LAVANNES
☎ 03 26 49 05 11   📄 03 26 97 03 28
email: contact@lescelestines.com
web: www.lescelestines.com

The calm setting and ancient buildings of this old farm offer four tastefully decorated guest rooms, each with shower room and WC. Extra children's beds available, use of kitchenette, and shared sitting room. There are enclosed gardens with lawns, furnished terrace and play area. Covered parking and Champagne for sale on the premises

Prices s €40-€45; d €47-€50; extra person fr €12   **Nearby** ⛷ 10km 🏊 15km 🎣 12km Restaurant 5km 🏊 0.5km 🎿 10km 🛒 4km 🚶 12km **Notes** No pets English spoken

LE MESNIL-SUR-OGER

Chambre d'hôtes

Jany MICHAUDET-BARADON
58 Grande rue, 51190 LE MESNIL-SUR-OGER
☎ 03 26 57 19 70   📄 03 26 57 15 01
email: info@champagne-baradon-michaudet.com
web: www.champagne-baradon-michaudet.com

Two of the three spacious rooms in a separate building at this Champagne estate house have their own saunas, and all have fridge and TV, indicating the luxury that awaits you. Breakfast is served in a dining room with open fire; then you can enjoy the panoramic views while tasting and buying the product of the vineyard.

Prices s €54-€62; d €59-€69; extra person fr €16   **On Site** 🎿 **Nearby** ⛷ 12km 🏊 30km ⛳ 0.5km 🎣 5km Restaurant 0.1km 🏊 🛒 0.1km 🚶 12km   **Notes** Pets admitted English spoken

LES CHARMONTOIS

♯♯ ⁝◯⁞ ⅋ **Chambre d'hôtes**

Bernard/Nicole PATIZEL
5 rue St Bernard, 51330 LES CHARMONTOIS
☎ 03 26 60 39 53　📄 03 26 60 39 53
email: nicole.patizel@wanadoo.fr
web: www.chez.com/patizel

In a rural setting this renovated farmhouse provides accommodation for seven: two doubles and a room sleeping three, all with en suite facilities. The guests also have the use of a sitting room, garden, lounge and a piano. Closed Xmas & New Year.

Prices s fr €32; d €38-€42; extra person fr €12; dinner fr €16
On Site 🏊　**Nearby** ⛷ 8km 🏊 20km Restaurant 9km ⛵ 9km ⛳ 9km
🚴 5km 🚶 20km　**Notes** Pets admitted

LES GRANDES-LOGES

♯♯ ⅋ **Chambre d'hôtes**

Martine et Etienne JANSON
50 rue Principale, 51400 LES GRANDES LOGES
☎ 03 26 67 32 38　📄 03 26 67 32 38
email: em.janson@orange.fr

An old family house on a farm, sleeping seven in three en suite rooms, one of which has wheelchair access. During the day guests may use the courtyard, swing and garden furniture. In the evening, why not relax by the fire and play games? There are also kitchen facilities and covered parking, as well as tennis and table tennis in the town nearby.

Prices s fr €31; d fr €42; t fr €52　**Nearby** ⛷ 15km 🏊 25km ⛵ 6km
⛳ 13km 🚴 🏠 11km 🚶 18km　**Notes** No pets

♯♯ ❦ ⅋ **Ferme de la Fauvette**

Michel LEFEVRE
1 rue de l'Eglise, 51400 LES GRANDES LOGES
☎ 03 26 67 33 05　📄 03 26 67 33 05
email: gite.martine@free.fr
web: http://gite.martine.free.fr

Overlooked by vineyards, this farm has three guest bedrooms. On the ground floor and accessible for disabled guests is a twin-bedded room. Upstairs are a double and a triple (double bed and a single). They all have private bath or shower room and WC. Use of kitchen; outside is a garden and terrace with furniture.

Prices s fr €35; d fr €45; t fr €55　**Nearby** ⛷ 8km 🏊 30km ⛵ 5km
⛳ 15km Restaurant 3km ⛵ 0.1km 🏠 13km 🚶 13km　**Notes** No pets

MANCY

♯♯ ⅋ **L'Atelier des Artistes**

S et A BRITES-GIRARDIN
19 rue du Bas, 51530 MANCY
☎ 03 26 59 70 78 & 06 11 63 06 41　📄 03 26 59 70 78
email: info@latelierdesartistes.com
web: www.latelierdesartistes.com

The owners of this property are wine-growers, and enthuse guests with their way of life. Accommodation is in the semi-detached house adjacent to the owners' home. A twin-bedded room on the ground floor has disabled access; upstairs there is a double room, and two communicating rooms for up to four people (double bed in one room, two singles in the other). All have private shower room and WC. Outside the terrace faces south-east. Closed during holidays.

Prices s fr €49; d fr €58; extra person fr €13　**Nearby** ⛷ 4km 🏊 20km
⛵ 7km ⛳ 7km Restaurant 7km ⛵ 6km ⛳ 7km 🏠 5km 🚶 7km
Notes No pets English spoken CC

MAREUIL-SUR-AY

♯♯ ⁝◯⁞ **Chambre d'hôtes**

Guy CHARBAUT
12 rue du Pont, 51160 MAREUIL-SUR-AY
☎ 03 26 52 60 59　📄 03 26 51 91 49
email: champagne.guy.charbaut@wanadoo.fr
web: www.champagne-guy-charbaut.com

Chambre d'hôtes, 12 rue du Pont

An ideal place for those who enjoy good French food and wine. Seven kilometres from Epernay and owned by Champagne producers, this old house has six distinctive rooms, each en suite with independent access. A sitting room with minibar, and large enclosed garden are at the visitors' disposal. Special table d'hôte meals are served in an old Champagne cellar. Small pets are welcome. Closed Xmas & New Year.

Prices s fr €62; d fr €70; t fr €107; dinner fr €45　**On Site** ⛵
Nearby ⛷ 1km 🏊 30km ⛵ 7km Restaurant 1.2km ⛵ 0.5km 🏠 0.1km
🚶 7km　**Notes** Pets admitted English spoken CC

MAREUIL-SUR-AY *CONTINUED*

▦ Chambre d'hôtes

Yves/Martine GIRAUD
11 rue Sadi Carnot, La Marotière,
51160 MAREUIL-SUR-AY
☎ 03 26 52 11 00 & 03 26 52 03 13
▤ 03 26 52 95 30
email: lamarotiere@wanadoo.fr
web: www.lamarotiere.com

An 18th-century winegrower's home, this comfortable house has activities and amenities to suit almost every taste. There are three en suite bedrooms, two doubles, and a duplex grade 3 double with extra sofa bed. Kitchen facilities are provided along with a dining room. Table d'hôte meals are available by reservation, except on Sunday.

Prices s €62-€70; d €70-€82; t €80-€97 **On Site** ⚓ ⚐ Restaurant **Nearby** ⚓ 30km ⚓ 6km Water sports 0.5km ⚓ 0.5km ⚐ 6km ⚓ 0.1km ⚓ 3km **Notes** No pets English spoken Open March to January. CC

MARGERIE-HANCOURT

▦ ⏣ Le Clos de Margerie

Maurice/Claudine BRASSART
4 rue des Clos, 51290 MARGERIE HANCOURT
☎ 03 26 41 02 14 & 06 07 44 34 75

On the site of an old farm in the centre of a village, this property has three spacious bedrooms, two doubles and a triple. All the rooms have independent access, and their own shower rooms/WCs. Cot available. Lounge with books; peace and quiet guaranteed. Champagne meals by arrangement; bikes available.

Prices s fr €29; d fr €39; t fr €52; extra person fr €11; dinner €15-€23 **Nearby** ⚓ 10km ⚐ 1km ⚓ 20km Restaurant 1km Water sports 18km ⚓ 5km ⚓ 6km ⚓ 20km **Notes** No pets

MATOUGUES

▦ ⏣ ⏣ Chambre d'hôtes

Jacques/Nicole SONGY
Chemin St Pierre, La Grosse Haie, 51510 MATOUGUES
☎ 03 26 70 97 12 ▤ 03 26 70 12 42
email: songy.chambre@wanadoo.fr

An extremely comfortable house surrounded by lush countryside close to Champagne vineyards and with a relaxed atmosphere. A must for those who enjoy their food and wine, this house offers gourmet meals, raclette and fondue evenings (except Sundays). There are three en suite rooms, a grade two double, and two grade three rooms sleeping 2-4. Mountain biking and walking available.

Prices s fr €36; d fr €48; t fr €53; dinner €19-€28 **On Site** ⚐ **Nearby** ⚓ 12km ⚓ 18km ⚓ 10km Restaurant 9km Water sports 45km ⚓ 0.1km ⚓ 5km ⚓ 10km **Notes** No pets

see advert on opposite page

MOUSSY

▦ ⏣ ♿ La Loge

Nicole/Claude RICHARD
La Loge Turbanne, 51530 MOUSSY
☎ 03 26 59 73 62 & 06 07 47 64 63 ▤ 03 26 51 05 20
email: champagnemarcelrichard@wanadoo.fr
web: www.alaloge.com

A wine-producing and agricultural farm in the verdant hills south of Epernay. Rooms are in a separate farm building with garden, terrace and parking and include a twin with disabled access, a room with a double and two single beds, a room with a double and single and a double with cot. Each has private facilities and two have mezzanines with extra beds available. Kitchen, lounge with fireplace, books, TV and games, baby equipment. Hire of entire house possible.

Prices s €46-€56; d €51-€61; t €76-€91; extra person fr €20 **Nearby** ⚓ 15km ⚓ 30km ⚐ 5km ⚓ Restaurant 5km ⚓ 3km ⚐ 5km ⚓ 2km ⚓ 6km **Notes** Pets admitted English spoken CC

MUTIGNY

▦ Manoir de Montflambert

G etS LHEUREUX-PLEKHOFF
51160 MUTIGNY
☎ 03 26 52 33 21 ▤ 03 26 59 71 08
email: contact@manoirdemontflambert.fr
web: www.manoirdemontflambert.fr

In the heart of the Champagne region, this 17th-century former hunting lodge has six bedrooms, all with private showers/WCs. The grounds are vast and full of wildlife, with magnificent views and a romantic lake. Peace and quiet are assured. Breakfast is served in the panelled dining room, with its enormous fireplace.

Prices s €95-€100; d €95-€105; t €130-€155 **On Site** ⚐ **Nearby** ⚓ 3km ⚓ 25km ⚓ 7km Restaurant 3km ⚓ 2km ⚐ 7km ⚓ 2km ⚓ 2km **Notes** No pets English spoken CC

NUISEMENT-SUR-COOLE

ⅲ ❦ Chambre d'hôtes

Patrick/Régine PICARD
rue du Moulin, 51240 NUISEMENT SUR COOLE
☎ 03 26 67 62 14 & 08 77 96 66 92 📄 03 26 67 79 45
Email: pat.picard@wanadoo.fr
Web: http://chambres.site.voila.fr

This establishment is located in a small village in the Coole Valley. There are two double rooms with independent access, and there are two double rooms in the main house that have an interconnecting door. A cot can be provided free of charge. Each room has private facilities. The furnished terrace provides guests with a calm spot to relax.

Prices s fr €32; d fr €42　**Nearby** ⛱ 5km ⚓ 20km ⊀ 10km Restaurant 10km Water sports 50km ♞ 10km ⌂ 10km ⚒ 10km　**Notes** No pets

OGER

ⅲ Chambre d'hôtes

Brigitte DREMONT-LEROY
rue du Fort, 51190 OGER
☎ 03 26 57 94 78 📄 03 26 59 17 41
Email: brigitte.dremont@orange.fr

This typical Champagne house offers a suite of two rooms and two other guest rooms, each with private bathrooms and WCs and two with private access. Guests have use of microwave and fridge. The dining room is furnished with curiosities from the Champagne region, and there is a lounge, TV and games such as bar-football and table-tennis. Champagne for sale. The nearby village of Oger is famed for its ancient washhouses and weather vanes.

Prices s fr €44; d €48-€51; t fr €64　**Nearby** ⛱ 5km ⚸ 2km ⊀ 7km Restaurant 3km ⚓ 2km ♞ 12km ⌂ 1.5km ⚒ 12km　**Notes** No pets Open February to December.

PASSY-GRIGNY

₩ La Ferme du Temple

Philippe/Didier HINCELIN

51700 PASSY-GRIGNY

☎ 03 26 52 91 02 📄 03 26 59 36 59

email: scai-le-temple@wanadoo.fr

web: www.fermedutemple.fr

A peaceful, rural spot, but only 15 minutes from Reims, 20 minutes from Epernay and an hour from Paris. There are four bedrooms: a double, a twin, a triple, and a family room for four. Generous breakfasts. Footpaths pass near the farm.

Prices s fr €48; d fr €50; t fr €65 **Nearby** ⛳ 10km ⚓ 2km ⚶ 10km
Notes No pets English spoken

see advert on page 331

RILLY-LA-MONTAGNE

₩ *Au Cherubin*

Didier JEANGOUT

3 rue Gervais, 51500 RILLY LA MONTAGNE

☎ 03 26 03 41 90 & 06 10 02 80 58 📄 03 26 03 49 39

email: aucherubin@aol.com

web: www.jeangout-didier.com

In the home of a wine grower, three en suite bedrooms have room to sleep eight people (two triple rooms and a double). Kitchen and barbecue facilities are available as well as a guest room. This house is close to all local amenities and restaurants and is free for children under three.

Prices not confirmed for 2008 **Nearby** ⚓ 20km ⚶ 12km ⚓
Notes No pets

ROSNAY

₩ ⦿ Chambre d'hôtes

Annette/Philippe MEUNIER

14 Grande rue, 51390 ROSNAY

☎ 03 26 03 46 46

email: annette.meunier@wanadoo.fr

web: http://perso.orange.fr/rosnayhotes/

This completely renovated small farm sits within its walls in a charming flower-filled village. Three finely decorated double rooms each have their own theme (Oriental, Egyptian and Champagne), while a twin-bedded room has a Roman accent. All have their own shower rooms and WCs. A large sitting room for guests leads out on to a furnished terrace and lawn. Meals by reservation.

Prices s fr €49; d fr €59; dinner €26-€30 **Nearby** ⛳ 6km ⚓ 2km
⛳ 10km ⚶ 12km Restaurant 9km Water sports 20km ⚓ 2km ⚶ 9km
⛳ 2km ⚶ 2km **Notes** No pets English spoken

SACY

₩ Maison Damien Buffet

Véronique/Henry DAMIEN

1 rue de Chatillon, 51500 SACY

☎ 03 26 49 23 62 & 06 08 93 66 87 📄 03 26 49 78 47

email: champagne.damienh@caramail.com

web: www.maison-damien-buffet.com

Surrounded by hills, this village house stands between Reims and Epernay, on the Champagne tourist route. The owners are farmers and wine-growers, who have put much thought and effort into the planning and decoration of this accommodation. There are two double rooms and a family room for five people, all with private facilities. Champagne is made on site and tasting is included in price. Good area for walking.

Prices s fr €58; d fr €65; t fr €85; extra person €10-€20 **Nearby** ⛳ 4km
⚓ 6km ⛳ 12km ⚶ 6km Restaurant 5km ⚓ 1km ⚶ 6km ⛳ 6km
⚶ 10km **Notes** No pets

SARRY

₩ ⦿ ⦿ ⦿ La Janenquelle

Christine/Hervé MAILLET

rue Basse, 51520 SARRY

☎ 03 26 21 44 88 & 06 87 21 33 47 📄 03 26 68 39 12

email: lajanenquelle@free.fr

This property, adjacent to a farm, combines a country setting with easy access to the town. There are four upstairs rooms - one with twin beds; two triples; and a family suite with a double bed and two singles. Downstairs is another triple, with disabled access. All rooms have private facilities. Cot available. Games room, garden furniture, meals by arrangement (Mondays to Fridays).

Prices s fr €33; d fr €42; t fr €52; extra person fr €17; dinner fr €18
On Site ⛳ **Nearby** ⛳ 5km ⚓ 20km ⚶ 5km Restaurant 0.2km ⚓
⛳ 5km ⛳ 0.2km ⚶ 12km **Notes** No pets English spoken CC

SELLES

₩ ⦿ Chambre d'hôtes

Hélène GUERIN

10 Grande Rue, 51490 SELLES

☎ 03 26 48 70 60

This small manor house in the heart of the village is only fifteen minutes from Reims and 2 kilometres from the nearest restaurant. It offers two rooms, each with bath- or shower-room and WC. The welcome is warm and the breakfast copious. Calm surroundings, garden, garage.

Prices s fr €32; d fr €40; t fr €57; extra person fr €15 **Nearby** ⚓ 5km ⚓ 20km ⚡ 5km Restaurant 4km 🚣 2km 🏠 1km ⚕ 20km **Notes** Pets admitted

ST-ETIENNE-AU-TEMPLE

♯♯ ⵔⵔ **Chambre d'hôtes**

Nadine HAMANT
Chemin de la Jorne, 51460 ST-ETIENNE-AU-TEMPLE
☎ 03 26 66 32 02 & 06 26 58 19 30
email: hamant.nadine@wanadoo.fr

Surrounded by the plains and vineyards of Champagne, this B&B has independent access for guests. The accommodation comprises two double rooms and a twin, each with private shower and WC. The hosts' living rooms offer peace and quiet, or TV and games. Cot and/or additional bed can be arranged. Evening meals by reservation. Closed Xmas & New Year.

Prices s fr €32; d fr €43; t fr €51; dinner fr €18 **Nearby** ⚓ 10km ⚓ 9km ⚡ 10km ⟋ 9km Restaurant 9km 🚣 10km 🏠 9km ⚕ 10km **Notes** Pets admitted

ST-GERMAIN-LA-VILLE

♯♯ ♥ ⵔⵔ **Les Perrières**

Nicole/Denis LESAINT
7 rue de Chalons, 51240 ST-GERMAIN-LA-VILLE
☎ 03 26 67 51 13 & 06 70 35 40 32 🖹 03 26 68 49 37
email: denis.lesaint@wanadoo.fr
web: http://perso.wanadoo.fr/lesperrieres

A welcoming guest house in the Champagne region, providing a twin and two double rooms with private showers and wc's along with guest sitting room, TV and kitchenette. Snacks available without prior reservation.

Prices s fr €29; d fr €40; t fr €49; dinner fr €16 **On Site** ⚡ ⵔ **Nearby** ⚓ 5km ⚓ 20km ⟋ 10km Restaurant 2km Water sports 10km 🚣 4km 🏠 0.1km ⚕ 14km **Notes** No pets English spoken

ST-MARTIN-D'ABLOIS

♯♯♯ **Chambre d'hôtes**

Christian DAMBRON
7, route de Vauciennes, Montbayen,
51530 SAINT-MARTIN-D'ABLOIS
☎ 03 26 59 95 16 & 06 81 85 74 23
email: christine.dambron@wanadoo.fr
web: www.francanada.com/marne

This vintner's house is well situated, with fabulous views, between a forest and the vineyards. The house offers three en suite double rooms and a triple with an attached children's bedroom. There is also a kitchenette, sitting room with TV and stereo, garden and parking. Wine tasting nearby; special rates for children and off season.

Prices s fr €41; d fr €50; t fr €66; extra person fr €16 **Nearby** ⚓ 6km ⚓ 20km ⚡ 10km ⟋ 10km 🚣 1km 🏠 1km ⚕ 12km **Notes** Pets admitted English spoken

STE-EUPHRAISE-ET-CLAIRIZET

♯♯♯ ⵔⵔ ♿ **Chambre d'hôtes**

Jacky DELONG
24 rue des Tilleuls, 51390 STE-EUPHRAISE-ET-CLAIRIZET
☎ 03 26 49 20 86 & 06 79 53 61 22 🖹 03 26 49 24 90
email: guydelongch@wanadoo.fr
web: www.domainedelong.com

This wine-growing family home has four en suite bedrooms (three doubles and a twin). Guests have the use of a large reception room for breakfasts as well as courtyard and garden furniture. A selection of local excursions and the lovely countryside are sure to please. Closed Xmas.

Prices s fr €48; d fr €58; extra person fr €27; dinner fr €28 **On Site** ⚡ **Nearby** ⚓ 5km ⚡ 6km ⟋ 12km Restaurant 3km 🏠 2km ⚕ 15km **Notes** No pets CC

TOULON-LA-MONTAGNE

♯♯♯♯ ⵔⵔ **Les Corettes**

Jean Marie SALMON
Chemin du Pati, 51130 TOULON LA MONTAGNE
☎ 03 26 59 06 92 & 06 76 74 16 28
🖹 03 26 59 06 92

Nicole and Jean-Marie will welcome you to their beautifully decorated five-bedroomed accommodation, only 3 kilometres from Marais de St-Gond and 12 kilometres from the famous white grape vineyards. Four of the rooms have their own bathroom and WC, the fifth offers a shower-room and WC. A delicious evening meal may feature duckling or fish or nut tart. Terrace, French billiards, bicycles.

Prices s fr €52; d fr €60; extra person fr €25; dinner fr €38 **On Site** Restaurant ⚡ **Nearby** ⚓ 30km ⚓ 35km ⟋ 15km ⟋ 15km 🚣 12km 🏠 3km ⚕ 25km **Notes** Pets admitted Open 2 March to 29 November.

VAL-DE-VESLE

♿ Chambre d'hôtes

Joy et Laurent LAPIE
1 rue Jeanne d'Arc, 51360 VAL DE VESLE
☎ 03 26 03 92 88 ▤ 03 26 02 76 16
email: joyhello@free.fr

A fine family home at the foot of a Champagne vineyard providing five charmingly decorated rooms, en suite with separate access. Guests have use of a dining room, kitchen and sitting room with TV. Many local sights, including a 12th-century church and visits to cellars and vineyards, are on the doorstep.

Prices s fr €41; d fr €51; t fr €65 **On Site** ⚓ **Nearby** ⚓ 15km ⚓25km ⚓ 18km Restaurant 3km ⚓18km ⚓5km ⚓7km ⚓2km **Notes** Pets admitted English spoken

VERTUS

Chambre d'hôtes

Serge JUMEL
31 Av de Bammental, 51130 VERTUS
☎ 03 26 52 02 80 & 06 81 97 23 18 ▤ 03 26 52 06 58
email: serge.jumel@wanadoo.fr

A wine-making couple welcome guests to this peaceful, lush area at the heart of the Champagne vineyards. Separate access to three tastefully decorated en suite double rooms plus one twin room. Additional bed and cot possible. Lounge, TV, fireplace. Terrace with garden furniture. Indoor parking. Restaurants and shops close by.

Prices s fr €38; d fr €48; extra person fr €16 **On Site** Restaurant **Nearby** ⚓20km ⚓40km ⚓2km ⚓0.5km ⚓1km ⚓1km ⚓20km **Notes** No pets English spoken Open March to December.

⚫ La Madeleine

René/Huguette CHARAGEAT
51130 VERTUS
☎ 03 26 52 11 29 & 06 85 20 57 92 ▤ 03 26 59 22 09
email: charageat.la.madeleine@wanadoo.fr

In a peaceful setting close to the forest in the Champagne vineyards, this welcoming farmer's home offers two double rooms with mezzanine and balcony and a further room for three people, all en suite. Lounge, TV and phone, additional bed and cots available. Climbing and sports ground 800mtrs, tourist and walking routes, vineyard visits. Table d'hôte meals by reservation (except Sunday).

Prices s fr €40; d fr €49; t fr €62; extra person fr €13; dinner €22-€30 **Nearby** ⚓2km ⚓2km Restaurant 2km ⚓2km ⚓18km ⚓2km ⚓18km **Notes** Pets admitted English spoken

VERZY

Chambre d'hôtes

Pierre/Véronique BARBIER
1 rue de Louvois, 51380 VERZY
☎ 03 26 97 90 29 & 06 11 23 23 38
email: letihlia.barbier@orange.fr
web: www.letihlia.com

In the heart of the regional Montagne de Reims parklands, in a flower bedecked village, you will receive a warm welcome at this working vineyard. A double and two triple rooms, each with en suite, ensure a quiet, relaxing stay. Large terrace and independent access. Cot available. Enclosed parking. Restaurants and shops in village, wine museum 1 kilometre away. Closed Xmas & New Year.

Prices s fr €45; d €55-€60; t fr €70 **On Site** Restaurant **Nearby** ⚓20km ⚓25km ⚓20km ⚓20km **Notes** No pets English spoken CC

VILLENEUVE-RENNEVILLE

⚫ Château de Renneville

Marie-Thérèse COLLARD
51130 VILLENEUVE RENNEVILLE
☎ 03 26 52 12 91 ▤ 03 26 51 10 49

At the heart of the Côte des Blancs vineyard, on a wine growing estate, three en suite double guest rooms (one grade 4) in a peaceful setting. Gastronomic meals by reservation, six people minimum. No charge for children under two; reduced rates after three nights. Jacques Collard Champagne sold on site: visit the cellars and wine press.

Prices s fr €56; d €68-€70; t fr €80; dinner fr €38 **On Site** ⚓ **Nearby** ⚓4km ⚓4km ⚓4km ⚓4km ⚓20km **Notes** No pets

WARMERIVILLE

Val des Bois

Nicole/Christian LACROIX-LEDUC
6 bis rue du 8 Mai 1945, 51110 WARMERIVILLE
☎ 03 26 40 90 81 ▤ 03 26 91 02 07

Close to the Ardennes and the vineyards of Champagne, this comfortably furnished old station building has three bedrooms. There are two linked doubles, with private but not en suite shower room and WC, plus a triple room with en suite facilities. Breakfasts are served in the old waiting room, or outdoors, with home-made jams and gingerbread. Garden furniture; enclosed parking.

Prices s fr €45; d fr €58; t fr €75 **On Site** ⚓ **Nearby** ⚓0.3km ⚓18km ⚓20km Restaurant 0.3km Water sports 40km ⚓0.3km ⚓0.3km ⚓17km **Notes** No pets English spoken

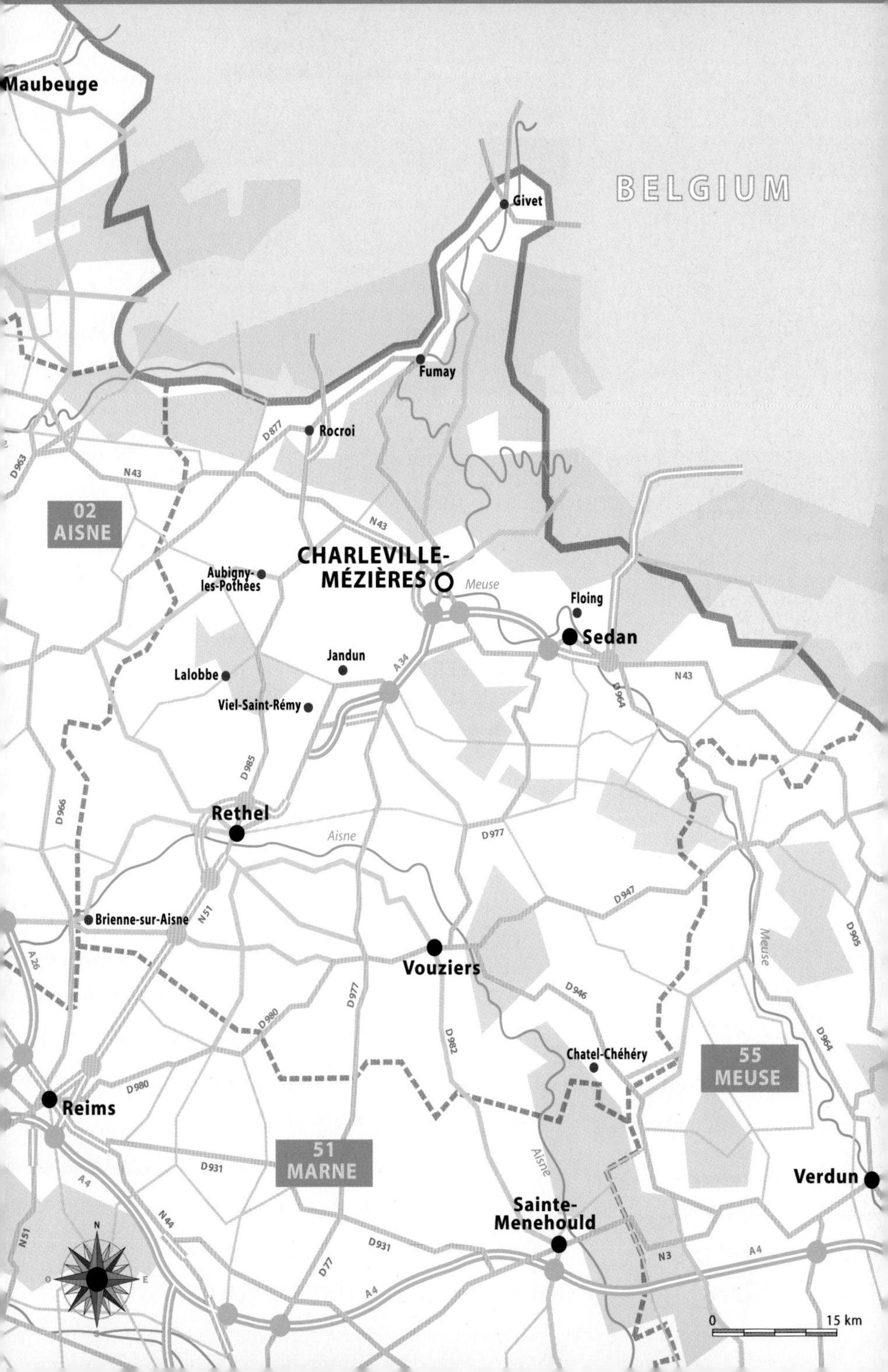

BELGIUM

Maubeuge

Givet

Fumay

D 877

Rocroi

D 963

N 43

02
AISNE

N 43

CHARLEVILLE-
MÉZIÈRES

Meuse

Aubigny-
les-Pothées

Floing

Sedan

Jandun

D 34

N 43

Lalobbe

D 964

Viel-Saint-Rémy

D 985

Rethel

Aisne

D 977

D 966

D 947

Meuse

D 905

Brienne-sur-Aisne

N 51

A 26

Vouziers

D 977

D 980

D 946

D 902

D 964

Chatel-Chéhéry

55
MEUSE

Reims

D 980

A 4

51
MARNE

D 931

Verdun

N 51

N

N 44

D 77

D 931

Sainte-
Menehould

Aisne

N 3

A 4

O   E

S

0   15 km

Map Labels

CHÂLONS-EN-CHAMPAGNE

51 MARNE

D 951
D 933
D 933
D 5
N 77
A 26
N 4
N 44

Vitry-le-François

N 4

D 951

D 373

D 951

Aube

D 441

Seine

N 19

N 77

A 26

Nogent-sur-Seine

La Motte-Tilly

Pougy

Lesmont

D 400

Villehardouin

Aube

Bouy-Luxembourg

D 960

Brévonnes

TROYES

Laubressel

Lévigny

A 5

Estissac

Saint-Germain

Seine

Lusigny-sur-Barse

Villeneuve-au-Chêne

Bar-sur-Aub

Vulaines

N 60

N 19

Baroville

Meurville

Maraye-en-Othe

Bouilly

A 5

Moussey

N 71

A 5

Longch sur-A

N 77

Eaux-Puiseaux

Jeugny

Viviers-sur-Artaut

D 905

Gye-sur-Seine

Essoyes

Courteron

N 71

D 943

89 YONNE

Armançon

Seine

D 905

D 965

21 CÔTE-D'OR

N 77

AUXERRE

D 965

A 6

Yonne

0   15

Marie-Laure et Thierry
74195 LE CHESNAY – FRANCE – © Reproduction

51 MARNE

BAR-LE-DUC

Commercy

Toul

N4

N411

N135

N4

Saint-Dizier

Chamouilley

55 MEUSE

Canal de la Marne

D964

D974

Louvemont

Marne

Droyes

D384

Vecqueville

Thonnance-lès-Joinville

D60

Meuse

N74

Longeville-sur-la-Laines

Doulevant-le-Château

D60

Neufchâteau

88 VOSGES

A31

D166

10 AUBE

N67

N74

D74

Bar-sur-Aube

N19

Meuse

A31

D429

CHAUMONT

D417

Mandres-la-Côte

Saône

Louvières

Marne

D65

A5

N19

Villiers-sur-Suize

Aube

Langres

Bay-sur-Aube

Chalindrey

21 CÔTE-D'OR

Flagey

Pressigny

N19

Prangey

N4

Villegusien-le-Lac

Savigny

70 HAUTE-SAÔNE

A31

Prauthoy

Saône

Seine

D396

D67

D70

Saône

N

O   E

S

0   15 km

MARNE
Champagne-Ardenne

LAON

02
AISNE

N44

N2

D966

D965

Rethel

08
ARDENNES

D977

Vouziers

D946

Aisne

N51

Warmerville

Hermonville

Lavannes

Selles

Reims

D980

Crugny

Rosnay

St-Euphraise-
et-Clairizet

La Bertonnerie

D931

Brouillet

N31

N44

Sacy

Val-de-Vesle

Belval-
sous-
Châtillon

Rilly-
la-Montagne

Verzy

D931

Germaine

N44

D980

Passy-
Grigny

Baslieux-
sous-
Châtillon

Mutigny

Bouzy

Les Grandes-Loges

D77

Sainte-
Menehould

Épernay

Mareuil-
sur-Ay

Condé-sur-Marne

A4

Marne

Boursault

N3

Moussy

Juvigny

St-Etienne-au-Temple

N3

Château-
Thierry

St-Martin-d'Ablois

Cramant

Matougues

CHÂLONS-
EN-CHAMPAGNE

D994

Les Charmontois

Brugny-Vaudancourt

Avize

D951

Oger

D1

Mancy

Le Mesnil-sur-Oger

Vertus

Villeneuve-
Renneville-Chevigny

Sarry

St-Germain-la-Ville

N44

D933

Bannay

D933

D5

N77

Nuisement-
sur-Coole

Baye

Congy

Toulon-
la Montagne

N4

Vitry
le-François

N4

Joiselle

D951

Saint-Diz

N4

D373

Margerie-
Hancourt

Giffaumont-
Champaubert

D394

52
HAUTE-
MARNE

Aube

D441

Seine

N19

Nogent-
sur-Seine

N77

A26

10
AUBE

D400

D60

A5

TROYES

D960

Aube

N

Bar-sur-Aube

A5

Seine

N19

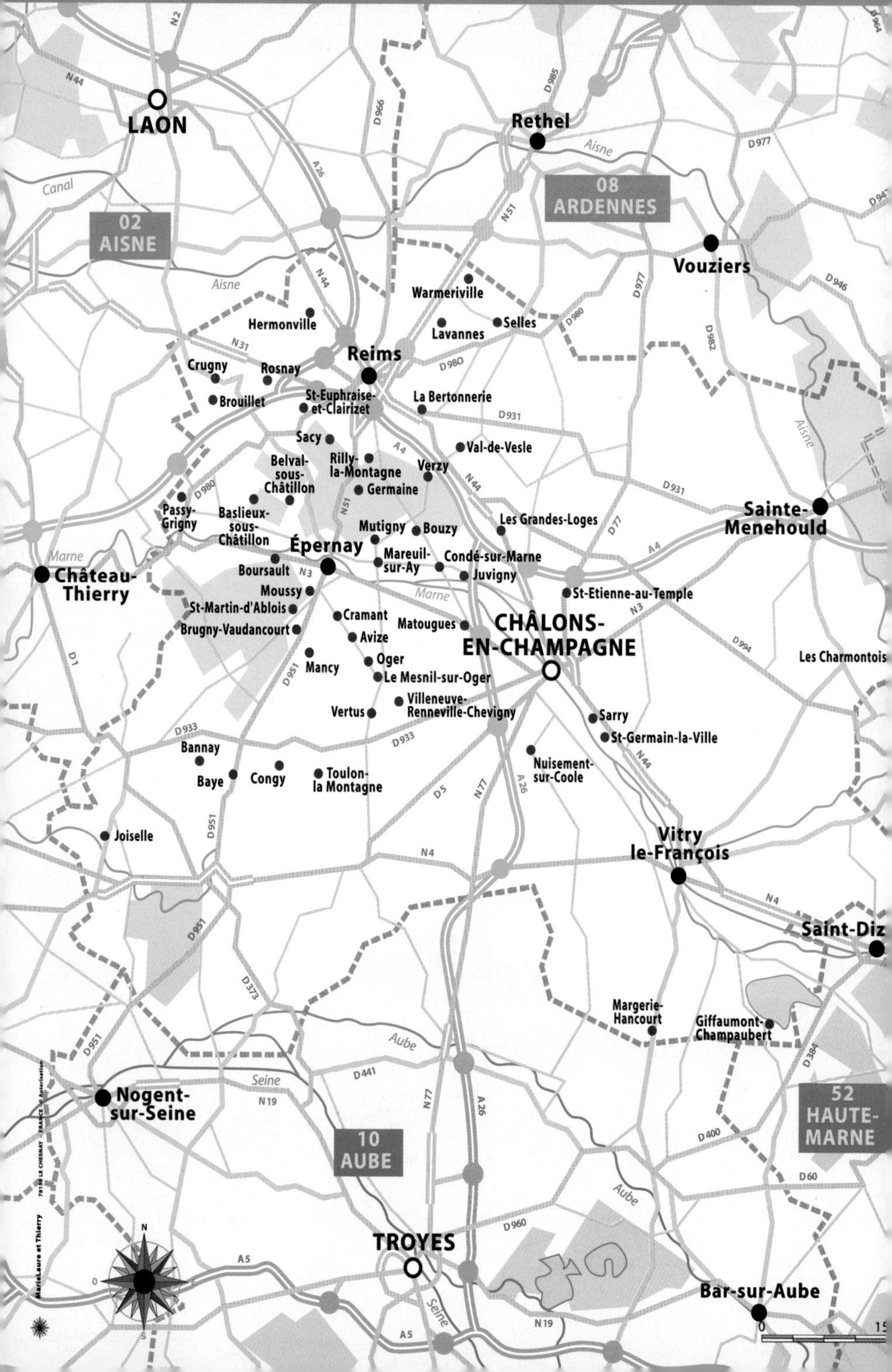

FRANCHE-COMTÉ

DOUBS

ARC-SOUS-CICON

⋔ ⦿ *Le Ferme d'Arc*

Marie-Claude POURCELOT

rue des frères Vuillemin, 25520 ARC-SOUS-CICON

☎ 03 81 69 90 76   🖹 03 81 69 90 76

web: http://perso.wanadoo.fr/lafermedarc/

his house, on a working farm, has three guest bedrooms, sleeping
rom two to four people and named after the seasons of the year. On
he ground floor is a room with a kitchen range; upstairs is a lounge
with TV and books. Baby equipment available; shady garden with
arden furniture. Possible farm visits.

rices not confirmed for 2008   **On Site** ⚅   **Nearby** ⛷ 17km   ⚲ 12km
⟨ 15km   ⚘ 3km   ⚴   ⋔⋔ 20km   **Notes** No pets

AUBONNE

⋔ ✿ ⦿ **La Ferme du Château**

 et I LOMBARDOTV CHOGNARD

 rue du Château, 25520 AUBONNE

☎ 03 81 69 90 56

web: www.gites-de-france-doubs.fr

lose to the Loue and Lison valleys, this 18th-century residence offers
hree en suite guest rooms each sleeping four with a double and sofa
r bunk beds. There is a lounge with TV, a library, a huge park within
he grounds with garden furniture and table tennis and a smallholding.
Meals (except Mondays) feature produce from the farm.

rices s fr €40; d fr €45; t fr €55; extra person fr €10; dinner fr €14
Nearby ⛷ 23km   ⚲ 20km   ⟨ 15km   Restaurant 8km   ⚘ 35km   ⚴ 5km
⚲ 20km   🖫 6km   ⋔⋔ 15km   **Notes** No pets   English spoken   Open
ebruary to 10 November.

BAUME-LES-DAMES

⋔ ✿ **Saint-Ligier**

atrice et Véronique RAMEL

Direction A36, 25110 BAUME-LES-DAMES

☎ 03 81 84 09 13   🖹 03 81 84 09 13

mail: vero.ramel@wanadoo.fr

web: www.gites-de-france-doubs.fr

he four guest bedrooms here are above the farmhouse restaurant
which the owners run. All the rooms sleep three guests and they all
ave private shower room/WC. There is space for an extra folding bed
n each room. Small lounge area on the first floor; living room with
itchenette on the second floor.

rices s €41-€45; d €47-€51; t €67-€71; extra person fr €20
Nearby ⛷ 15km   ⚲ 2km   ⟨ 30km   ⚴ 2km   ⚘ 2km   🖫 2km   ⋔⋔ 2km
Notes No pets   English spoken   Open 31 January to 20 December.   CC

BRETONVILLERS

⋔⋔⋔ *La Joux*

Patrick DORGET

25380 BRETONVILLERS

☎ 03 81 44 35 78

web: www.gites-de-france-doubs.fr

This old farm building is typical of the Haut-Doubs region and is
entered via a covered bridge. It offers four en suite rooms: the 'Mont
du Frêne' room has four single beds; 'Prés du Fol' is a double room;
'Pierre Perthuis' has three single beds and the fourth room, 'La
Racine', is a twin-bedded room. Communal lounge with books and TV,
garden furniture within the grounds. Walking trails from the property,
and rock climbing is 5km. Restaurant in the village.

Prices not confirmed for 2008   **On Site** ⚅   **Nearby** ⛷ 20km   ⚲ 5km
⟨ 20km   ⚲ 20km   ⚴ 6km   🖫 4km   ⋔⋔ 30km   **Notes** No pets   English
spoken

BUFFARD

⋔⋔ ♿ **Le Détour**

Sandrine et Joël ROY

27, rue de Besançon, 25440 BUFFARD

☎ 03 81 57 50 77   🖹 03 81 57 50 77

email: ledetour@chambres-hote.com

web: www.chambres-hote.com

A small 17th-century château in wooded grounds, with six guest
bedrooms in the converted outbuildings. On the ground floor is a
double room with access suitable for disabled guests, a room for four
(double bed and two singles), a living room and dining room. Upstairs
are three double rooms and a triple (double bed and a single). The
rooms all have private shower and WC. Terrace, enclosed parking.

Prices not confirmed for 2008   **On Site** ⚲   **Nearby** ⛷ 14km   ⟨ 14km
⚴ 30km   ⚴   🖫 5km   ⋔⋔ 7km   **Notes** Pets admitted   English spoken   CC

CHARQUEMONT

⋔⋔⋔ **Le Bois de la Biche**

Sylvie MARCELPOIX

Chalet Les Grillons, 25140 CHARQUEMONT

☎ 03 81 44 07 01

Rooms at this house include two accessed by a private exterior
staircase: the double Grillon ('cricket') 1 and Grillon 2 (a grade 3
room) has a double and single bed. Two further rooms are in a
neighbouring wing opening onto the terrace: Grillon 3 with three
single beds, telephone and TV and Grillon 4 (grade 3) is a twin
room. Rooms have private facilities, extra bed on request. Dining
room, library, terrace.

Prices s fr €40; d fr €48; t fr €68; extra person fr €20   **On Site** ⚅
Nearby ⛷ 12km   ⚲ 25km   ⟨ 12km   Restaurant 0.1km   ⚴ 2km
⚴ 12km   🖫 6km   ⋔⋔ 25km   **Notes** No pets

CLERVAL

✦✦✦ Chambre d'hôtes

Robert et Colette CORNEILLE

31 bis, Av Gaston Renaud, 25340 CLERVAL

☎ 03 81 97 84 31 & 06 88 55 33 99

web: www.gites-de-france-doubs.fr

This guest accommodation is on the first floor of the owners' home: a room with double bed, and a two-roomed family suite for four (double bed and two singles). Both have private bathroom and WC. On a mezzanine floor there is a living area for guest use. Outside are large grounds and a courtyard, all enclosed, with garden furniture.

Prices s fr €37; d fr €47; t fr €67 **On Site** 🐴 **Nearby** ⚲ 8km
⚓15km ⌁ 30km Restaurant 1.5km ⚒ 15km Spa 0.6km ⋒ 0.1km
Notes No pets

CROSEY-LE-PETIT

✦✦✦ ❦ ⎧◎⎫ ⚲ *La Montnoirotte*

Joëlle et Alain BOUCHON

Relais Equestre Montnoirotte, Route de Vellevans, 25340 CROSEY-LE-PETIT

☎ 03 81 86 83 98 📄 03 81 86 82 53

email: bouchona@wanadoo.fr

web: www.fermeequestredelamontnoirotte.com

This typical Franche-Comté farm is peacefully set in a secluded location on the Lomont range. There is a twin room, two double rooms, one with a child's bed if required, and one with bunk-beds and a room with two sets of bunk-beds and two single beds; all with private facilities. Dining room, covered terrace, kitchenette, lounge area with books, TV and video, washing machine, tumble dryer, TV, swimming pool, garden furniture and barbecue. The owners breed horses, and riding is available.

Prices not confirmed for 2008 **On Site** ⚲ 🐴 Private ⌁
Nearby 🏌 7km ⚒ 10km 🏠 10km ⋒ 16km **Notes** Pets admitted

DANNEMARIE-SUR-CRETE

✦✦✦ Domaine des Chaumes

R GRANDPERRIN et A RABOLIN

27 rue des Chanets, 25410 DANNEMARIE-SUR-CRETE

☎ 03 81 58 69 68

web: www.gites-de-france-doubs.fr

Four tastefully decorated and furnished rooms in a cottage: three double rooms and a twin, each with private facilities and TV. Lounge with unusual natural rock décor, dining room, terrace, parking, large wooded park. Special tariffs available.

Prices s fr €45; d fr €58 **Nearby** ⚲ 4km 🏌 6km ⌁ 12km
Restaurant 1km ⚒ 3km 🏠 7km ⋒ 7km **Notes** No pets CC

DOMMARTIN

✦✦✦ ⎧◎⎫ Chambre d'hôtes

Josette PETITE

2 Grande rue, 25300 DOMMARTIN

☎ 03 81 39 21 67 & 06 84 91 72 46

email: le.champi@wanadoo.fr

web: www.gites-de-france-doubs.fr

These three beautiful rooms are in the owners' home. There is a double room, a triple, and a room for four. Beds can be made up as doubles or singles, as required. Each room has a private shower room and WC. Enclosed storage for skis and bikes. Garden. Closed second week in September.

Prices s fr €45; d fr €58; t fr €67; extra person fr €16; dinner €16-€24
On Site 🏌 **Nearby** ⚲ 3km ⚓ 10km ⌁ 5km Restaurant 1km ⚒ 12km
⚒ 5km 🏠 1km ⋒ 6km **Notes** Pets admitted English spoken

GENEUILLE

✦✦✦ ⎧◎⎫ ⚲ *Chambre d'hôtes*

A BITARD et P SCHMITT

18 Rue de l'Abreuvoir, 25870 GENEUILLE

☎ 03 81 55 68 99

email: info@lelavoirdesreves.com

web: http://lelavoirdesreves.com

Vast grounds with lots of greenery provide the setting for these five rooms, in a separate building close to the owners' home. On the ground floor are two doubles (one with disabled access) and a triple; on the first floor, with access by an outside staircase, are another double and a triple. All have private facilities. Meals by arrangement.

Prices not confirmed for 2008 **On Site** 🏌 **Nearby** ⚲ 7km 🏌 0.5km
⌁ 10km ⚒ 7km 🏠 5km ⋒ 10km **Notes** Pets admitted English spoken

---

LARNOD

✦✦✦ *Chez Lou*

Christelle et Mikaël DEMENGE

20 route de la Maltournée, 25720 LARNOD

☎ 03 81 57 37 15

email: chezlou@neuf.fr

web: www.chambreshotes-chezlou.com/francais/

This 18th-century house has three guest bedrooms: two doubles, one of them with a child's bed, and a family suite with a double bed, twin beds and a cot. All rooms have a private shower room and WC. Extra beds available, also baby equipment. Lounge, pleasant garden. Meals and wine-tasting by arrangement.

Prices not confirmed for 2008 **On Site** Private ⌁ **Nearby** ⚲ 10km
🏌 6km 🏠 2km ⋒ 6km **Notes** No pets English spoken

LAVANS-VUILLAFANS

♥ *Chambre d'hôtes*

Famille BOURDIER

Ferme du Rondeau, 25580 LAVANS-VUILLAFANS

☎ 03 81 59 25 84 & 03 81 59 26 64 ▤ 03 81 59 29 31

email: lerondeau@terre-net.fr

web: www.lfrance.com/fermerondeau/

This farm-inn offers comfortable rooms in the main building (two doubles, a triple and a room with double and three single beds) and a room for four in a separate chalet close by with lounge area. Rooms have private facilities. Guests can sit out on the terrace and enjoy meals and breakfasts of a high standard, with farm produce for sale. Longer stays possible.

Prices not confirmed for 2008 **Nearby** ⚓ 10km ♪ 12km ↖ 10km ⚡ 2km ♨ 9km ⋙ 9km **Notes** Pets admitted English spoken Open January to November.

LES ECORCES

Bois Jeunet

Paul et Marie-Thérèse PERROT

25140 LES ECORCES

☎ 03 81 68 63 18 ▤ 03 81 68 63 18

web: www.gites-de-france-doubs.fr

In a delightful rural setting, this typical Haut-Doubs house offers three guest rooms next to three other holiday homes: a single with balcony, a double and a room with double and twin beds, all with private facilities (cot on request). Laundry room, library; set in large park with terrace, swimming pool, table tennis, garden furniture and parking. Table d'hôte meals available by reservation; restaurants 2km. Pets are admitted at a charge. Reductions for children and stays over one night.

Prices not confirmed for 2008 **On Site** ♨ Private ↖ **Nearby** ⚓ 8km ♪ 5km ⚡ 2km ♨ 2km ⚑ 2km ⋙ 25km **Notes** Pets admitted English spoken

LODS

Chambre d'hôtes

Janine BRULET

4 chemin des Forges, Au fil de l'eau, 25930 LODS

☎ 03 81 60 92 21 & & 06 89 32 15 83

email: aufildelo.brulet@wanadoo.fr

web: www.amiesenfranchecomte.com/pro_jan.htm

A beautiful 18th-century house beside the river, with an enclosed garden. There are four split-level bedrooms, all with private bath or shower room and WC. Two of the rooms are doubles; the third is a triple, and the fourth is a family room with a double bed and singles. Baby equipment is available. Good area for walking and other outdoor activities.

Prices not confirmed for 2008 **On Site** ♪ **Nearby** ⚓ 20km ↖ 19km ⚡ 20km ♨ ⋙ 19km **Notes** No pets English spoken

LOMBARD

Chambre d'hôtes

Jean-Luc et Andrée CARRIERE

16 Grande rue, 25440 LOMBARD

☎ 03 81 63 67 95 & 06 87 48 88 40

email: carrierejl@aol.com

web: www.chambres-hotes-lombard.com

This very attractive 'maison bourgeoise' offers three spacious double guest rooms, two with additional child's bed, and each with private facilities (cot available). Guests have use of a lounge with books, TV and internet. There is a tree-lined garden with furniture and parking.

Prices s fr €40; d fr €50; extra person fr €15 **Nearby** ⚓ 30km ♪ 0.5km ↖ 22km Restaurant 4km ♨ 4km Spa 20km ⚑ 4km ⚡ 4km ⋙ 4.5km **Notes** Pets admitted English spoken

MALPAS

◎ *Chambre d'hôtes*

Carmen et Patrick DAVID

109 route des Grangettes, 25160 MALPAS

☎ 03 81 69 68 69 ▤ 03 81 69 64 09

email: attelages.2lacs@wanadoo.fr

web: http://wanadoo.fr/attelages.2lacs/

There are four guest bedrooms at this equestrian establishment, standing in the forest. On the first floor, but with level access, are two doubles, each with a convertible single bed. On the second floor is a family suite for five, and a twin-bedded room. All rooms have private bath or shower room and WC. On the ground floor are a lounge, kitchenette, and additional toilets and showers.

Prices not confirmed for 2008 **On Site** ⚑ **Nearby** ⚓ 12km ♪ 4km ↖ 14km ⚡ 12km ♨ 14km ⚑ 4km ⋙ 14km **Notes** Pets admitted English spoken

MEREY-SOUS-MONTROND

Les Granges du Liège

Guy LAUT

25660 MEREY-SOUS-MONTROND

☎ 03 81 81 88 22 ▤ 03 81 81 88 23

email: les.granges.du.liege@wanadoo.fr

web: www.besac.com/lesgrangesduliege/chambres.htm

This large rural site offers three rooms in the owners' house, and three in an annexe. The rooms accommodate two, three or four people, and they all have private showers and WCs. One of the annexe rooms has a kitchenette. In the extensive grounds is a swimming pool and part of the garden is arranged as an "outdoor room".

Prices not confirmed for 2008 **On Site** ⚑ Private ↖ **Nearby** ⚓ 6km ♪ 12km ♨ 3km ⚑ 5km ⋙ 10km **Notes** No pets English spoken CC

MONTBENOIT

♯♯♯♯ ⏁⦶⏁ Les Essarts

Catherine et Mimi ROLAND

25650 MONTBENOIT

☎ 03 81 38 12 84

email: lesessarts@wanadoo.fr

web: www.maisondhoteslesessarts.com

Right in the heart of the countryside, this is an old farmhouse which has been superbly restored. It has five bedrooms: two doubles, a twin, a triple and a two-room family suite for four (two double beds). Children's beds and baby equipment are available, and all rooms have private facilities. Guests' lounge area. Meals by arrangement.

Prices s fr €73; d fr €78; extra person fr €27 **Nearby** ⛷ 15km ⛳ 3km ⏁ 10km Restaurant 4km ⌕ 6km ⌕ 6km 🕍 6km ᴍ 12km **Notes** No pets English spoken

NANS-SOUS-SAINTE-ANNE

♯♯♯ Chambre d'hôtes

Béatrice et Brendan MURPHY

29 Grande Rue, 25330 NANS-SOUS-SAINTE-ANNE

☎ 03 81 86 65 87

email: reservations@residencedevaux.com

web: www.residencedevaux.com

A very pretty house dating from the 19th century, which stands in 50 hectares of grounds. There are three bedrooms, all with double beds, and private bath or shower room and WC. Two of the rooms open onto small balconies. Guest lounge on the ground floor; outside is a large terrace with garden furniture.

Prices s €65-€85; d €65-€85 **On Site** ⛳ ❀ **Nearby** ⛷ 7km ⌁ 40km ⏁ 13km Restaurant 1km ⌕ 45km ⌕ 11km Spa 14km 🕍 11km ᴍ 23km **Notes** No pets English spoken

♯♯♯♯ Chambre d'hôtes

David et Cynthia PRICE

6 rue du Château, 25330 NANS-SOUS-SAINTE-ANNE

☎ 03 81 86 54 72 🖷 03 81 86 43 29

email: dlcprice25@aol.com

web: www.frenchcountryretreat.com

An 18th-century house, formerly connected with the château, which has been superbly restored. It stands in 17 hectares of enclosed grounds. There are four double bedrooms, all with private bath or shower room - in one case the shower room is not en suite. Lounge with books, dining room; outside there is garden furniture.

Prices s €90-€100; d €90-€100 **On Site** ⛳ ❀ **Nearby** ⛷ 7km ⏁ 13km Restaurant 3km ⌕ 45km ⌕ 11km Spa 14km 🕍 0.1km ᴍ 25km **Notes** No pets English spoken Open May to October.

ORNANS

♯♯♯ ⏁⦶⏁ Le Jardin de Gustav

Marylène RIGOULOT

28 rue Edouard Bastide, 25290 ORNANS

☎ 03 81 62 21 47 🖷 03 81 62 21 47

web: www.lejardindegustav.fr

This 19th-century house has three tastefully-furnished guest rooms. They are all doubles, two of them with an additional single bed. All rooms have a private bath or shower room and WC. Lounge and sitting room shared with hosts; meals by arrangement. Large enclosed garden with access to river; bikes available.

Prices s €60-€78; d €60-€78; t fr €90; extra person fr €12; dinner fr €25 **On Site** ⛳ **Nearby** ⛷ 10km ⌁ 20km ⏁ Restaurant 0.2km Water sports 0.5km ⌕ 1km ❀ 0.5km 🕍 0.5km ᴍ 25km **Notes** Pets admitted English spoken

OUGNEY-LA-ROCHE

♯♯♯ ⏁⦶⏁ Auberge Chez Soi

D et N Vercammen-Van Wezer

Rue du Rechandet, 25640 OUGNEY-LA-ROCHE

☎ 03 81 55 57 05

email: info@chez-soi-france.com

web: www.chez-soi-france.com

These three rooms are in a beautiful stone-built house on the edge of the Doubs. All of the rooms have twin beds, and one of them has a little lounge area. They all have private shower rooms and WCs. Rustic-style dining room, garden with garden furniture. Small boat available; meals by arrangement.

Prices s fr €56; d fr €64; t fr €92; dinner fr €23 **On Site** ⛳ ❀ **Nearby** ⛷ 7km ⏁ 22km Restaurant 1.5km ⌕ 8km 🕍 8km ᴍ 9km **Notes** Pets admitted English spoken

RAHON

▦ ⍥ Chambre d'hôtes

Noël et Marie-Paule BRAND
25430 RAHON
☎ 03 81 86 80 46
web: www.gites-de-france-doubs.fr

Close to a long-distance footpath, this property has five bedrooms in a building adjacent to the owners' home, all with independent access. On the first floor are four doubles, with a shared living area with fridge and microwave; on the second floor is a family room for five. All have private facilities, and baby equipment is available. Bike hire; meals by arrangement.

Prices s fr €28; d fr €38; t fr €50; extra person fr €12; dinner fr €12 **Nearby** ⛸ 11km ⚓ 25km ᔍ 15km ᔎ 30km Restaurant 0.5km ᔏ 3.5km ❀ 2km 🏠 1km 🐾 10km **Notes** No pets English spoken

RANG

▦ ⍥ Les Charmettes

Catherine et Laurent DERVAUX
10 Grande Rue, 25250 RANG
☎ 03 81 92 84 19 & 06 07 90 50 01
email: laurent.dervaux@cegetel.net
web: www.chambre-hote-lescharmettes.com

This former coaching inn is in the middle of the village on the N83 road. There are four bedrooms, all on the second floor: a double room, a room with a double futon, a room for four (twin beds and a sofa bed), and a triple (double bed plus a single). All have private facilities and internet connection, baby equipment is also available.

Prices s fr €55; d fr €60; extra person fr €15; dinner fr €20 **On Site** ᔍ Private ᔎ **Nearby** ⛸ 20km ⚓ 15km Restaurant 4km ᔏ 4km ❀ 15km 🏠 4km 🐾 4km **Notes** Pets admitted English spoken

VALONNE

▦ ❧ ⍥ *Chambre d'hôtes*

Maryline et Stéphane PONCOT
1 rue des Carrières, 25190 VALONNE
☎ 03 81 93 35 09 & 06 75 05 69 41
email: stephane.poncot@wanadoo.fr
web: www.chambres-hotes-ferme.com

There are five attractive rooms in this building adjacent to the owners' home. On the ground floor are two family rooms for four; upstairs are two doubles and a twin-bedded room. There are guests' lounge areas on both floors; downstairs there is also a kitchenette. All rooms have private shower room and WC. Baby equipment; meals by arrangement.

Prices not confirmed for 2008 **Nearby** ⛸ 15km ᔍ 10km ᔎ 30km ᔏ 30km ᔐ 10km 🐾 15km **Notes** No pets

VAUDRIVILLERS

▦ ⍥ ♿ Chez Mizette

Marie-Josephe PHILIPPE
3 rue de l'église, 25360 VAUDRIVILLERS
☎ 03 81 60 45 70 🗎 03 81 60 45 70
email: mizette@orange.fr
web: www.mizette.com

Situated in open grounds in a little village on the Lomont plateau, this house offers four double guest rooms, each with private shower and wc. A child's bed can be added. There is a guest lounge with colour TV, books and kitchenette. Special tariffs available, breakfast included.

Prices s fr €35; d fr €45; t fr €61; extra person fr €17; dinner fr €17 **Nearby** ⛸ 12km ⚓ 15km ᔍ 8km ᔎ 15km Restaurant 4km ᔏ 45km ᔐ 12km ❀ 15km 🏠 3km 🐾 15km **Notes** No pets English spoken

VERCEL

▦ ⍥ Chambre d'hôtes

Martine et Patrice HAÜY
18 Voie de la Grâce de Dieu, 25530 VERCEL
☎ 03 81 58 38 83 & 06 81 64 41 44
email: hauy.martine@wanadoo.fr
web: www.aux-couleurs-des-saisons.com

This property has three bedrooms, all in the owners' house. On the ground floor is a double room and a twin-bedded room; upstairs is a triple room (three single beds). All the rooms have private shower room and WC, and an extra bed is available. Guests' lounge with kitchenette. Garden, and terrace with furniture. Meals by arrangement.

Prices s fr €45; d fr €50; extra person fr €15; dinner €19-€22 **Nearby** ⛸ 1.5km ⚓ 5km ᔎ 8km Restaurant 5km ᔏ 11km ᔐ 1km 🐾 8km **Notes** No pets

HAUTE-SAÔNE

ARGILLIERES

▦ ⍥ Les Clochettes d'Argillieres

Jean-François CHARLOT
70600 ARGILLIERES
☎ 03 84 31 34 06 🗎 03 84 31 34 06
email: borie-yvette@wanadoo.fr
web: www.gites-de-france70.com

A restored farmhouse on the edge of the village and close to walking tours. There are three double bedrooms, all on the first floor, all with private facilities. There is a lounge area on a mezzanine, an internal courtyard and the dining room is in an old barn. The hosts keep goats and make goats' cheese. Boules court.

Prices s fr €40; d fr €50; dinner fr €20 **On Site** ❀ **Nearby** ⛸ 6km ⚓ 40km ᔍ 10km ᔎ 15km Restaurant 10km ᔏ 0.2km 🏠 10km 🐾 25km **Notes** Pets admitted English spoken

CHAMPAGNEY

⁕ ⁺◯⁺ Le Clos Fleuri

Brigitte et André TAQUARD

3, rue sous les Chênes, 70290 CHAMPAGNEY

☎ 06 66 59 58 71

email: contact@clos-fleuri.net

web: www.clos-fleuri.net

Situated in a quiet corner of a small town, this property has a warm country feel about it. There are four double bedrooms, one with an additional single bed, all of them upstairs. All of the rooms have private bath or shower rooms and WCs. Wooded surroundings in the Ballons des Vosges Regional Park, not far from Belfort.

Prices s fr €37; d fr €47; t fr €57; extra person fr €15; dinner fr €17
On Site ⌖ **Nearby** ⛷ 4km ⚓ 30km ⟲ 15km Restaurant 2km ⚲ 15km
⋙ 2km **Notes** Pets admitted

COLOMBOTTE

⁕ ⁺◯⁺ Chambre et Tables d'hôtes la Tourelle

T et M VAN VOOREN / MULLER

Rue Haute, 70240 COLOMBOTTE

☎ 03 84 78 77 60

email: info@colombotte.nl

web: www.colombotte.nl

A restored country house on the edge of the village. On the first floor is a double room and a room for four (double bed and singles); on the second floor is another double, and a triple (double bed and single). In a separate building is a two-roomed suite with two double beds. All rooms have private facilities.

Prices s fr €67; d €38-€69; t fr €79; extra person fr €15; dinner fr €19.50 **On Site** ⚑ **Nearby** ⛷ 10km ⚓ 10km ⚑ 1km ⟲ 12km Restaurant 10km ⚲ 5km Spa 19km ⚑ 4km ⋙ 12km **Notes** Pets admitted English spoken Open April to October.

CULT

⁕⁕ ⁺◯⁺ *Les Egrignes*

Fabienne LEGO-DEIBER

Château de Cult, rte d'Hugier, 70150 CULT

☎ 03 84 31 92 06 & 06 84 20 64 91

email: lesegrignes@wanadoo.fr

web: www.les-egrignes.com

A warm welcome awaits guests to this beautiful country mansion built in 1854. Peaceful surroundings, elegant decor and excellent cuisine are offered, together with two double suites and the one twin room, all with private facilities. Pastries, home-made jams and cereals are served for breakfast, whilst terrines, magret de canard aux griottines and croustillant d'escargots are served at table d'hôte meals. Lounge, board games, table tennis, large grounds and bicycles.

Prices not confirmed for 2008 **Nearby** ⛷ 20km ⚓ 25km ⚑ 5km ⟲ 20km ⚑ 4km ⋙ 25km **Notes** No pets English spoken

DAMPIERRE-SUR-SALON

⁕ ⁺◯⁺ Chambre d'hôtes la Tour des Moines

Odette et Bernard MONNEY

7, rue de Fouvent, La Tour des Moines, 70180 DAMPIERRE-SUR-SALON

☎ 03 84 67 16 37 & 06 30 47 86 64

email: stephanie.monney@wanadoo.fr

web: www.latourdesmoines.com

This 18th-century house is in a quiet corner of the town. It is an old property, with some wonderful architectural features, which has been sensitively restored in a rural style. It has two double rooms and a triple, with private, but not in all cases en suite, facilities. Kitchen, extensive grounds with plenty of shade.

Prices s fr €40; d fr €48; t fr €60; dinner fr €20 **On Site** ⚑ **Nearby** ⛷ 2km ⚑ 0.2km ⟲ 15km Restaurant 0.2km ⚲ 0.2km ⚑ 0.2km ⋙ 35km **Notes** Pets admitted

ESMOULINS

⁕⁕⁕ Au Hêtre Pourpre

Marie-Claude VEZZOLI

4, rue de la Tenise, Au Hêtre Pourpre, 70100 ESMOULINS

☎ 03 84 67 45 16 & 06 74 37 33 39 🗎 03 84 64 89 44

email: au-hetre-pourpre@wanadoo.fr

web: www.auhetrepourpre.com

In a quiet village, an 18th-century house in magnificent wooded grounds with a stream running through. There are three bedrooms, tastefully and individually decorated, each with private facilities and its own lounge area. Baby equipment is available. Breakfasts offer lots of choice; other meals are available by arrangement.

Prices s fr €47; d fr €50; t fr €70; extra person fr €20; dinner fr €20
On Site 🏊 **Nearby** ⛷ 6km ♨ 40km 🎣 6km Restaurant 6km 🛒 6km
🚲 6km 🚶 4km **Notes** No pets

FRAHIER

▦ ❦ 🍴 Les Gros Chênes

Elisabeth et Philippe PEROZ
70400 FRAHIER
☎ 03 84 27 31 41
email: e.peroz@wanadoo.fr
web: www.amiesenfranchecomte.com/pro_eli.htm

This house is situated in undulating countryside at the foot of the
Ballon d'Alsace and the Ballon de Servance. One wing with a separate
entrance is reserved for guests and has two double rooms, one twin
and one room with four single beds, each with shower and wc. Guests
can use the furnished terrace, attractive grounds and veranda. 15%
discount for bookings over 4 days. Children under 5 free. Mini-golf 12
km. Chapelle de Notre Dame du Haut, designed by Le Corbusier, in
Ronchamp 12 km.

Prices s fr €37; d fr €45; t fr €58; extra person fr €14; dinner €14-€18
On Site 🏊 **Nearby** ⛷ 5km ♨ 35km 🎣 10km Restaurant 0.5km
Spa 39km 🚲 1km 🚶 10km **Notes** Pets admitted English spoken

MAGNY-JOBERT

▦ 🍴 Vue du Lavoir

Thiébaud COMTE
3, rue du Lavoir, De la Chapelle des Cornottes,
70200 MAGNY-JOBERT
☎ 03 84 63 15 81
web: http://site.voila.fr/cornottes

This old farmhouse in a village at the foot of the Vosges has been
restored in a rural style - complete with a working bread oven. The
bedrooms are on the first floor: a twin-bedded room, a triple (three
single beds), and a split-level family suite for up to five people. All
rooms have private showers and WCs.

Prices s fr €30; d fr €43; t fr €60; extra person fr €10; dinner fr €19
On Site 🏊 **Nearby** ⛷ 4km ♨ 33km 🎣 10km Restaurant 6km 🛒 8km
Spa 29km 🚲 8km 🚶 8km **Notes** Pets admitted English spoken

MELISEY

▦ ❦ 🍴 ♿ La Ferme des Guidons

Daniel et Elisabeth GAVOILLE
70270 MELISEY
☎ 03 84 63 20 43 & 06 82 12 27 16
email: courrier@ferme-des-guidons.fr
web: www.ferme-des-guidons.fr

On the ground floor of this modern house are three double rooms,
one with disabled access; upstairs is a family room for four, with
a double bed and two singles. All have private showers and WCs.
Spacious well-equipped kitchen; mezzanine reading area. Big games
room and terrace; extensive grounds. Meals by arrangement.

Prices s fr €40; d fr €50; extra person fr €15; dinner fr €18 **On Site** 🏊
Private 🎣 **Nearby** ⛷ 4km ♨ 20km Restaurant 4km 🛒 4km Spa 20km
🚲 3km 🚶 13km **Notes** Pets admitted

PALANTE

▦ Champ Lallemant

Denis DANEK
4, rue du Champ Lallemand, 70200 PALANTE
☎ 03 84 63 03 48 📄 03 84 63 03 48
email: ste.genevieve@pele2.fr

In a beautiful green setting on the edge of the village, this old house
has been extensively restored. It has two double guest bedrooms, and
a two-roomed family suite for four with a double bed and two singles.
All of the rooms have private showers and WCs. Lounge/dining area;
extensive grounds.

Prices s fr €26; d fr €45; t fr €55; extra person fr €15 **Nearby** ⛷ 4km
♨ 31km 🏊 8km 🎣 7km 🛶 30km Spa 28km 🚲 7km 🚶 7km
Notes Pets admitted

PUSY-EPENOUX

▦ 🍴 Château d'Epenoux

E HOLZ et S HUBBUCH
5, rue Ruffier d'Epenoux, 70000 PUSY-EPENOUX
☎ 03 84 75 19 60 📄 03 84 76 45 05
email: chateau.epenoux@orange.fr
web: www.chateau-epenoux.com

This château has five guest bedrooms, all on the first floor. There
are four double rooms, and a twin-bedded suite with its own
living area adjacent. All five rooms have private bath or shower
room and WC. On the ground floor is a lounge and dining room,
and meals are available by arrangement.

Prices s €85-€100; d €90-€100; extra person fr €25; dinner fr €24
Nearby ⛷ 12km ♨ 25km 🏊 5km 🎣 5km Spa 20km 🚲 5km
🚶 5km **Notes** No pets English spoken CC

RUPT-SUR-SAONE

▦ ♿ Chambre d'hôtes

Colette et Jean-Paul DULAC
5, chemin du Petit Breuil, 70360 RUPT-SUR-SAONE
☎ 03 84 92 72 77
email: dorlotines@yahoo.fr
web: www.dorlotines.com

On the edge of a pretty village in the heart of the Saône Valley, this
beautifully restored property is in a peaceful location. There are two
double bedrooms, and a family room with a double bed and singles.
All have private bath/shower rooms and WCs. Lounge/dining room on
the ground floor.

Prices s fr €42; d fr €50; extra person fr €16 **Nearby** ⛷ 6km ♨ 9km
🏊 5km 🎣 6km Restaurant 6km 🚲 6km 🚶 24km **Notes** No pets

TERNUAY

††† ‖◎‖ Hameau de Melay

Maurizio DELLA FIORENTINA
Melay, 70270 TERNUAY
☎ 03 84 20 48 46 📄 03 84 20 48 46
email: josiedemelay@club-internet.fr
web: www.gites-de-france70.com

A farmhouse, in a style typical of the southern Vosges, which has been nicely restored. On the first floor is a double room, and a split-level room for four (double bed and singles). On the second floor is a triple room (double plus single) and a room for four (double and singles). All have private facilities. Lounge area on a mezzanine floor.

Prices s fr €46; d fr €51; t fr €68; extra person fr €17; dinner fr €18
Nearby ⚓ 7km ⚲ 20km ⚑ 10km ➴ 18km Restaurant 3km ⛵ 29km ⌇ 7km Spa 18km ⌂ 7km ⋈ 18km **Notes** Pets admitted English spoken

VOLON

††† ‖◎‖ ⚬ Chambre d'hôtes

C et J-L KLUMPP - BAUMANN
2, Grande rue, 70180 VOLON
☎ 03 84 31 37 53 📄 01 58 16 43 72
email: contact@les-3-pierres.com
web: www.les-3-pierres.com

This farmhouse, which has been fully restored and modernised, is a good place to come and recharge your batteries. On the ground floor is a double room, and a twin-bedded room with disabled access. Upstairs are two more doubles, and a triple (double bed and single). All have private facilities. Fitness room, sauna, lounge, and bright dining room. Table tennis, bikes available.

Prices s fr €57; d fr €65; t fr €83; extra person fr €18; dinner fr €20
On Site Private ➴ **Nearby** ⚓ 11km ⚲ 20km ⚑ 9km Restaurant 4km ⌇ 2km ⌂ 9km ⋈ 25km **Notes** No pets English spoken

VY-LES-LURE

††† *Chambre d'hôtes*

Emmanuel GEORGES
23 grande rue, 70200 VY-LES-LURE
☎ 03 84 63 93 43
email: leparc-egeorges@wanadoo.fr
web: www.hotesduparc.com

A tastefully restored manor house in the Ognon Valley, with a remarkable central staircase leading up from the hall to the guest rooms. For garden lovers a visit here is a must, as it is listed in the Racine guide to the 750 most beautiful gardens in France - particularly for its peonies and varieties of old rose. Two rooms on the first floor are a double and a small double; on the second floor are a triple (double bed and a single) and a twin-bedded room. All rooms have private facilities.

Prices not confirmed for 2008 **Nearby** ⚓ 6km ⚲ 21km ⚑ 1km ➴ 6km ⛵ 30km Spa 25km ⌂ 6km ⋈ 6km **Notes** No pets English spoken CC

JURA

ARLAY

††† ‖◎‖ Le Jardin de Misette

M Claude et Christian PETIT
Rue Honoré Chapuis, 39140 ARLAY
☎ 03 84 85 15 72
email: cmc.petit@aliceadsl.fr
web: http://misette.blog.lemonde.fr/misette

This old winegrower's house is set beside a river in an historic village with a rich cultural heritage. The pretty flower garden offers plenty of shade, and is a tranquil place in which to relax. One of the bedrooms is located in a little house in the garden. Guests have use of a music room, a reading room with library of books and an open fireplace.

Prices d fr €50; t fr €67; extra person fr €17; dinner fr €24 **On Site** ⚑ Restaurant ⚘ **Nearby** ⚓ 10km Water sports 30km ⌇ ⋈ 10km **Notes** Pets admitted English spoken

BARESIA-SUR-L'AIN

††† *Le Verger de Pommiers*

Cheryl et Nick BEARE
37 Rue de la Chapelle, 39130 BARESIA SUR L'AIN
☎ 03 84 25 80 08
email: baresia39@tiscali.fr

A renovated farmhouse in a small village, ideal for fishing, walking and mountain biking. Two bedrooms, a double and a twin, both with television and en suite bathroom. Living room with open fire, shaded garden, terrace and pool. Meals with Jura wines can be booked.

Prices not confirmed for 2008 **Nearby** ⚓ 5km ⚑ 2km ⛵ 29km Water sports 2km ⌇ 5km ⌂ 5km ⋈ 25km **Notes** No pets English spoken Open April to October.

BAUME LES MESSIEURS

††† La Grange a Nicolas

Felicette DEBONIS
Rue Saint Jean, 39210 BAUME LES MESSIEURS
☎ 03 84 85 20 39
email: contact@lagrangeanicolas.com
web: www.lagrangeanicolas.com

This 18th-century grange is in wonderful gardens bordered by a gently flowing river. It is full of character with beams, stone walls and features such as a working bread oven. It has been carefully and authentically restored, and all five of its bedrooms have individually themed decorations. They all sleep two people and each has its own bathroom and WC.

Prices s €75-€100; d €85-€110; extra person fr €25 **On Site** ⚑ ⚘ **Nearby** ⚓ 12km ➴ 15km Restaurant 0.2km Water sports 20km ⌇ 11km ⌂ 7km ⋈ 15km **Notes** No pets English spoken

BERSAILLIN

▓ 🍽 ♿ Ferme du Château de Bersaillin

Marie GONTCHAROFF
Rue de la Poste, 39800 BERSAILLIN
☎ 03 84 25 91 31 📠 03 84 25 93 62
email: contact@ferme-du-chateau.fr
web: www.ferme-du-chateau.fr

A magnificent classified 'monument historique' with a large range of accommodation for up to twenty people, which includes suites for up to six people and a twin-bedded room with handicapped access. Three suites have en suite shower/WC and three have en suite bathroom. The site also functions as a cultural centre running courses in the arts, exhibitions, theatrical performances, festivities and conferences.

Prices s fr €65; d fr €82; extra person fr €35; dinner fr €25 **Nearby** 5km 20km 2km 10km Restaurant 10km Water sports 40km 10km Spa 20km 10km 5km 20km **Notes** Pets admitted English spoken

▓ 🍽 Le Risoux

Mirella PAGNIER
6 rue de la Poste, 39800 BERSAILLIN
☎ 03 84 25 90 52 📠 03 84 25 90 52
email: mirella.pagnier@wanadoo.fr
web: http://monsite.wanadoo.fr/lerisoux

Three bedrooms have been created in this beautifully restored farmhouse, just a few yards from the château. The rooms sleep from two to four people, they all have private facilities, and one of them has its own private entrance into the garden. Meals featuring local dishes are available by arrangement.

Prices s fr €48; d €58-€62; t €77-€80; extra person €19-€22; dinner fr €24 **Nearby** 5km 5km Restaurant 4km Water sports 40km 8km Spa 20km 6km 22km **Notes** Pets admitted English spoken

BONLIEU

▓ 🐾 ♿ Chambre d'hôtes

Christine/Dominique GRILLET
12 Rue de la Maison Blanche, 39130 BONLIEU
☎ 03 84 25 59 12
email: dominique.grillet@wanadoo.fr

Set in the heart of the lake region, at the gateway to the Haut-Jura, this early 19th-century farm has been completely renovated to provide four comfortable guest rooms with private bathrooms. There is a delightful garden, a large terrace and a courtyard with garden furniture.

Prices d fr €38; t fr €46; extra person fr €8 **On Site** 🍽 **Nearby** 1km 3km Restaurant 4km 30km Water sports 2km 5km 10km 10km **Notes** No pets English spoken

CERNANS

▓ 🍽 ♿ La Grange Combaret

Florence et Denis MOREL
23 Rue de Salins, 39110 CERNANS
☎ 03 84 73 52 90
email: info@grange-combaret.com
web: www.grange-combaret.com

Not far from the spa town of Salins-les-Bains, this immense house has been completely renovated to offer four individually decorated bedrooms, each with either a terrace or a balcony. Rooms sleep two to four people, with several king-size beds; all the rooms have TV and telephone and all have en suite shower room/WC except the triple room, which has an en suite bathroom. The hosts are happy to involve guests in their eco-friendly agricultural business.

Prices s fr €48; d fr €61; t fr €16; dinner fr €22 **Nearby** 5km 5km 5km Restaurant 5km 30km Water sports 30km 5km 5km 15km **Notes** No pets English spoken

CERNON

▓ 🍽 Le Chalet de Fanny

Françoise et André LAMARCHE
Viremont, 39240 CERNON
☎ 03 84 35 75 17
email: lechaletdefanny@wanadoo.fr
web: www.lechaletdefanny.fr

Set in a region with a rich natural heritage, this peaceful, comfortable property offers wonderful views of the surrounding countryside. The guest rooms are situated in a chalet, each with their own bathroom. Meals feature produce from the garden. Numerous lakes and forests nearby.

Prices s fr €50; d fr €52; t fr €68; extra person fr €16; dinner fr €18 **On Site** 🍽 **Nearby** 12km 2km Restaurant 3km Water sports 5km 15km 30km **Notes** No pets English spoken Open April to October.

CHARCHILLA

▓ 🍽 Le Clos d'Estelle

Christine/J. Pierre THEVENET, 1, La Marcantine, 39260 CHARCHILLA
☎ 03 84 42 01 29 📠 03 84 42 01 29
email: leclosdestelle@wanadoo.fr
web: www.leclosdestelle.com

This magnificent country house provides a warm atmosphere in a calm and peaceful setting. It has three rooms for two or three people, and one suite for up to five. The restored rooms, all with private facilities, have their individual character. The dining room has a bread oven, and there is a lounge with books to read. Evening meals by arrangement.

Prices s €62-€120; d €62-€120; t €80-€120; dinner fr €19 **Nearby** 3km 20km 1km Restaurant 3km 25km Water sports 1km 3km 3km 3km 40km **Notes** No pets English spoken

CHAREZIER

♥♥♥ ⧉ & Chambre d'hôtes

Guy et Jacqueline DEVENAT
17 rue du Vieux Lavoir, 39130 CHAREZIER
☎ 03 84 48 35 79

Set in the lake region, this property offers three rooms with private bathrooms in a little house in the garden and one further room in the proprietor's house. Guests have use of a lounge, TV room and terrace. The surrounding area has wide pastures, forests, lakes and waterfalls.

Prices s fr €35; d fr €40; t fr €45; extra person fr €8; dinner fr €11
Nearby ⛷5km 🚴1km ⛵30km Water sports 5km 🏊5km 🏬5km
🚶20km **Notes** Pets admitted

CHATEAU-CHALON

♥♥♥ ⧉ Chambre d'hôtes

Agnès et Gérard VIDAL
Rue de la roche, 39210 CHATEAU-CHALON
☎ 03 84 44 98 56
email: relaisdesabbesses@wanadoo.fr
web: www.chambres-hotes-jura.com

An old house in the heart of one of France's most beautiful villages. Sit on the terrace and admire the unobstructed view across the valley, or relax in the library/lounge. The four rooms will sleep either 2 or 3 and their private facilities are meticulously maintained.

Prices d €65-€70; extra person fr €15; dinner fr €24 **On Site** Restaurant
🎿 **Nearby** ⛷8km 🏊5km 🎿15km Water sports 25km 🏊15km
🏬5km 🚶5km **Notes** No pets Open February to November.

CHATELAY

♥♥♥♥ Les Chambres d'Aude

Aude et Patrick BADONNEL
5 rue de la Gare, 39380 CHATELAY
☎ 03 84 37 70 09 & 06 78 30 20 90
email: audedagnet@leschambresdaude.com
web: www.leschambresdaude.com

In Pasteur's birth town, on the edge of the Forest of Chaux, four comfortable and elegant rooms in the owner's home. There are three doubles and a two room family suite, each with television and lovely bathroom. Take breakfast in the lovely dining room overlooking the park. Guests have use of a lounge, library, games, kitchen and bicycles.

Prices s fr €55; d fr €60; t fr €75; extra person fr €15
Nearby ⛷15km 🏊22km 🏊5km Restaurant 6km Water sports 2km 🏊4km 🏬5km 🚶9km **Notes** No pets English spoken

CHATENOIS

♥♥♥ & A La Thuilerie des Fontaines

Françoise/Michel MEUNIER
LOISIRS ACCUEIL JURA
☎ 03 84 70 51 79 📠 03 84 70 57 79
email: michel.meunier2@wanadoo.fr
web: http://perso.wanadoo.fr/hotes-michel.meunier/michel.htm

On the borders of Franche-Comté and Burgundy, between the Serre Massif and the Chaux forest, and close to the lower Doubs Valley. This mid-18th century residence offers four guest rooms with private facilities and guests have use of a reading room and library. There is a heated swimming pool and garden furniture in the shady park adjacent.

Prices s fr €50; d fr €50; t fr €65; extra person fr €15
On Site Restaurant 🎿 **Nearby** ⛷2km 🏊15km 🏊2km Water sports 2km 🏊 Spa 25km 🏬2km 🚶6km **Notes** No pets English spoken

CHILLY-SUR-SALINS

♥♥♥ 🌿 ⧉ Au Petit Bonheur

M Claude et Roger CLERC
39110 CHILLY SUR SALINS
☎ 03 84 73 12 93 & 06 80 23 13 85 📠 03 84 73 12 21
email: marieclaude.clerc@wanadoo.fr
web: www.ptitbonheur.net

This very pretty renovated farmhouse is surrounded by magnificent flowers and offers rooms for two, three or four people with private facilities and lovely views. Table d'hôte meals, including home-made jams and farm produce, are available between October and April.

Prices s fr €40; d fr €45; t fr €60; extra person fr €15; dinner fr €15
Nearby ⛷3km 🏊25km 🎿6km Restaurant 13km 🏊40km 🏊1km Spa 6km 🏬6km 🚶25km **Notes** No pets Open October to April

COLLONDON

♥♥♥ La Belle Verte

Florence LEGRAND
370 rue du Manoir, 39130 COLLONDON
☎ 03 84 25 71 61
email: labellevertejura@wanadoo.fr

At the heart of the lake region, this former farm contains two- or three-person bedrooms with private facilities. There is a large wooded park, a barbecue and garden furniture, and games for children.

Prices s fr €40; d fr €45; t fr €50; extra person fr €5 **On Site** 🎿
Nearby ⛷3km 🏊2km Restaurant 2km Water sports 5km 🏊2km 🏬2km 🚶25km **Notes** No pets English spoken

OMMENAILLES

⏸ ⏸ La Ferme de la Rechassière

ristine et Denis CONTE
e des Forges, 39140 COMMENAILLES
☎ 03 84 44 18 77 & 08 77 53 76 89
mail: conte.denis2@wanadoo.fr

estored farmhouse with four bedrooms which can sleep from two
four people. Each has a lounge area, a private bath or shower
m, and independent access. There is a lounge with open fire for
sts' use. Meals are available, by arrangement, and there is outdoor
ommodation for horses.

ces s fr €36; d €46-€48; extra person fr €20; dinner fr €18
Site 🖉 Restaurant Nearby ⛷ 6km ⛷ 5km Water sports 50km
.8km 🖪 7km 🚿 20km

OURBOUZON

⏸ 🍽 ⏸ Escargot Comtois

riel et David BLANCHARD
ISIRS ACCUEIL JURA
03 84 24 15 29
ail: info@escargot-comtois.com
b: www.escargot-comtois.com

he heart of Revermont and in the centre of the old village, rooms
two to three people have been carefully decorated in this ancient
se of character and exposed stone walls. Large living room,
ace, and enclosed garden with stream running through. Snails are
ned here and served as a speciality. Internet access.

ces s fr €41; d fr €49; t €59-€68; extra person fr €10; dinner €20-€23
Site 🖉 Nearby ⛷ 2km ⛷ 3km ≭ 3km Restaurant 3km Water
ts 25km ⅏ 3km Spa 3km 🎾 3km 🖪 3km 🚿 3km Notes No pets
ish spoken Open January to October.

⏸ Les Volets Verts

gine HUGUET
ISIRS ACCUEIL JURA
03 84 43 25 95 & 06 89 35 32 65
ail: huguet.regine@wanadoo.fr

rbouzon is a village with plenty of water: seven springs, two wash-
ses and a waterfall! The chambre d'hôtes has three bedrooms
double, a twin-bedded room, and a room for three (double bed
a single). All have private shower and WC, but those for the twin-
ded room are not en suite. Large living room, garden with terrace
orchard.

es s €38-€40; d €42-€48; t fr €58; extra person fr €15; dinner fr €10
Site 🖉 Nearby ⛷ 4km Water sports 30km ⅏ 2km 🎾 3km 🖪 3km
km Notes No pets

CRENANS

⏸ 🍽 La Compagnie des Anes

Françoise BESSIERES
Hameau de Couloubre, 39260 CRENANS
☎ 03 84 42 68 83 & 06 83 29 55 33
email: bessieres.francoise@wanadoo.fr
web: www.lacompaigniedesanes.fr

In the heart of the Regional Natural Park of Haut-Jura, and close to the
Vouglans lake, this property has four rooms for two people, all with
private facilities. There is originality in the decoration and layout of the
accommodation, and meals in the traditional style of the region are
served in a cheerful atmosphere. Numerous excursions possible.

Prices d €46-€48; extra person fr €18; dinner fr €18 Nearby ⛷ 0.9km
🖉 3km ≭ 20km Restaurant 4km ⅏ 25km Water sports 5km ⅏ 4km
🎾 15km 🖪 4km 🚿 20km Notes No pets English spoken Open
February to November.

ECLEUX

⏸ 🍽 ⛇ Che'val d'Amour

Dominique PREVITALI
LOISIRS ACCUEIL JURA
☎ 03 84 37 66 16
email: domprevi@aol.com
web: http://cheval.damour.free.fr

There are three bedrooms at this former farmhouse, which stands
on the edge of a forest and close to a lake. The rooms sleep from
three to six people, and all have private shower room and WC. A
terrace accessible from the bedrooms has garden furniture. Meals are
available by arrangement; pony and trap rides may be arranged.

Prices s fr €38; d fr €45; t fr €56; extra person fr €11; dinner fr €20
On Site ⛷ 🖉 Nearby ⛷ 20km ≭ 4km Restaurant 1km Water
sports 2km ⅏ 4km 🎾 4km 🖪 3km 🚿 5km Notes Pets admitted English
spoken

FONCINE-LE-HAUT

⏸ 🍽 Les Biches et Les Genévriers

Bernadette et Daniel PRETET
56 Le Bayard, 39460 FONCINE LE HAUT
☎ 06 80 35 03 49 🖹 03 84 51 94 56
email: pretet.bernadette@wanadoo.fr
web: www.lebayard.com

These chambres d'hôtes are in two chalets on Mont Bayard, with
a superb view towards the Jura Mountains. The rooms and suites,
for up to five people, all have private bathrooms/WCs, and coffee
making facilities. One room has a small kitchenette. Guests'
lounge with books and video. Painting and botany courses; fitness
suite, jacuzzi. Meals by arrangement.

Prices s €75-€115; d €77-€120; t €90-€145; extra person fr €25;
dinner fr €26 On Site 🖉 🎾 Nearby ⛷ 3km Restaurant 3km
≭ 3km Water sports 18km ⅏ 2km 🖪 3km 🚿 18km
Notes No pets English spoken

GERUGE

♥ ♿ La Grange Rouge

M BARAUX

39570 GERUGE

☎ 03 84 47 00 44 📄 03 84 47 34 15

web: www.la-grange-rouge.com

This ferme-auberge has lots of character and is situated in beautiful surroundings. Each bedroom has its own bathroom, and there is a living room with TV. The large garden has several shady terraces.

Prices s fr €34; d fr €46; extra person fr €12; dinner fr €15 **On Site** ⚓ ◆ **Nearby** ⛷ 6km Water sports 20km ⊃ 9km Spa 9km 🏛 4km ⛵ 12km **Notes** Pets admitted English spoken Open 3 January to 17 December.

GEVRY

◎ La Bonardiere

D et J-G CHAUVEAU/PILLOUD

3 rue du puits, 39100 GEVRY

☎ 03 84 71 05 93 & 06 89 33 06 17 📄 03 84 71 08 08

email: gabriel.pilloud@wanadoo.fr

web: www.labonardiere.fr

There are five rooms at this property, which is in a small village a few minutes from Dole. Two of the rooms are doubles (one with disabled access), one is a triple, and there are two family suites for up to five. All have private facilities (power showers). Garden, games room for children; meals (available by arrangement) include local specialities.

Prices s fr €42; d fr €48; t €57-€74; extra person fr €15; dinner fr €19 **On Site** Water sports **Nearby** ◆ 1km ⚓ 6km ⊃ 7km 🏛 7km ⛵ 8km **Notes** Pets admitted

LAJOUX

◎ La Trace

Nathalie et Jean-Luc NEUSEL

Le Manon, 39310 LAJOUX

☎ 03 84 41 25 70 & 06 85 70 64 15

email: info@latracejura.com

web: www.latracejura.com

In the hamlet of Manon, well-placed for footpaths and cross-country skiing, this old farmhouse has five bedrooms, sleeping up to five people. All rooms have private facilities; there is a lounge with books, and a beautiful large dining room with an old-fashioned stove. Meals are available by arrangement, and the owner is a ski and mountain bike enthusiast.

Prices s fr €58; d fr €58; t fr €78; extra person fr €20; dinner fr €18 **Nearby** ⛷ 10km ⛷ 5km ◆ 5km Restaurant 1km ⚓ 5km Water sports 5km ⊃ 5km 🏛 7km ⛵ 20km **Notes** No pets English spoken

LAVANS-LES-ST-CLAUDE

♿ La Boutonnière

Jeanne et Alain GROJEAN

23 Ter Rue de la Cueille,

39170 LAVANS LES SAINT CLAUDE

☎ 03 84 42 24 96 & 06 83 53 32 18

email: boutonniere@wanadoo.fr

web: http://boutonniere.monsite.wanadoo.fr

This property is a converted and restored small button factory. Ther are two bedrooms for up to three guests, both with private bath/ shower room and WC. A third room is available, a Grade 1 double, which does not have en suite facilities. Terrace and small garden. A good location for walks in the summer and cross-country skiing in the winter.

Prices s fr €45; d fr €50; extra person fr €18; dinner fr €16 **Nearby** ⛷ 8km ◆ 4km Restaurant 3km ⚓ 25km Water sports 13km ⊃ 2km ⚓ 3km ⛵ 9km **Notes** No pets English spoken

LE FRASNOIS

Chambre d'hôtes

Christian MONNERET

Hameau La Fromagerie, 39130 LE FRASNOIS

☎ 03 84 25 50 60 📄 03 84 25 50 38

email: vedier@wanadoo.fr

web: www.eolienne.net

This large chalet is situated in the middle of a small valley, in the heart of the lakes. The four guest rooms sleep between three and f people and have private shower room and wc, a seating area and access to a private terrace. Two rooms also have a mezzanine level There is a large lounge and inn 100mtrs away. Botanical garden an exhibition on site.

Prices s fr €40; d €50-€56; t €65-€71; extra person fr €12 **Nearby** ⛷ 0.5km ◆ 0.5km ⚓ 20km Water sports 12km ⊃ 2km 🏛 3 ⛵ 10km **Notes** No pets English spoken

◎ ♿ Chambre d'hôtes

Laurence et Philippe COLOMBATO

66 route des Lacs, 39130 LE FRASNOIS

☎ 03 84 25 51 32 📄 03 84 25 51 32

email: pcolomba@wanadoo.fr

web: www.5lacs.fr

This old renovated farm, in the heart of the lakes, offers five rooms with private bathrooms, one of which is suitable for disabled guest: There is a mezzanine lounge with TV, books and fire; guests can al sit out on the terrace or in the garden. Baby facilities available. No smoking.

Prices s fr €47; d fr €54; t fr €70; extra person fr €16; dinner fr €17 **On Site** ⚓ Restaurant **Nearby** ⛷ 25km ◆ 0.5km ⚓ 20km Water sports 12km ⊃ ⛵ 6km **Notes** No pets English spoken

ES PLANCHES-EN-MONTAGNE

▮ ¡○¡ Montliboz

dier PREVOT
chemin de la Montagne Ronde,
150 LES PLANCHES EN MONTAGNE
☎ 03 84 51 53 98 ▤ 03 84 51 59 48
mail: didiermicheleprevot@wanadoo.fr

a very restful countryside location, this huge old Jura farmhouse has
en completely renovated to provide charming, tasteful guest rooms.
gional cuisine is served at table d'hôte meals every evening except
day. The river and Gorges de la Langouette are close by.

ces not confirmed for 2008 **On Site** ⚲ **Nearby** ⛷ 6km ⚓ 10km
ter sports 12km ⛳ 4km ⛪ 3km ⋙ 3km **Notes** No pets Open
December to 15 January & February to 15 September.

ARIGNY

▮ ¡○¡ ⛨ Les Sittelles

nès et Christian HENZLER
Rue des Voituriers, 39130 MARIGNY
☎ 03 84 25 71 32
mail: sittelles.marigny@wanadoo.fr
eb: www.sittelles-marigny.fr

old house in a peaceful spot just a very short distance from Lake
 alain. There are five bedrooms, sleeping from two to five people,
with private shower room and WC. Garden with terrace. Meals are
ilable by arrangement, except on Sundays.

ces s fr €40; d fr €48; t fr €56; extra person fr €10; dinner fr €17
Site Restaurant ⚲ **Nearby** ⛷ 3km ⚲ 0.5km Water sports 0.5km
km ⛪ 5km ⋙ 15km **Notes** Pets admitted English spoken

ONTFLEUR

▮ Plume et Notes

rie-Ella et Frédéric LOUVET
320 MONTFLEUR
☎ 03 84 44 37 42 & 06 60 18 62 16
mail: louvet.frederic@wanadoo.fr
eb: www.plumenotes.com

ormer village grocer's shop makes an unusual setting for these
mbres d'hôtes. Four pleasant rooms, doubles and twins, are all
ned after writers or musicians; two can be linked for family use and
have private facilities. Guests can enjoy breakfast on the terrace,
home-made jams and conserves. Garage space for motorbikes.

ces s fr €43; d €49-€52; t €59-€62 **Nearby** ⛷ 5km ⚲ 0.5km
aurant 0.5km Water sports 15km ⛳ 7km ⛪ 7km ⋙ 25km
es Pets admitted

MONTIGNY-LES-ARSURES

▮▮▮▮ Château de Chavanes

I et F DE CHAVANES
Rue De Saint Laurent,
39600 MONTIGNY LES ARSURES
☎ 03 84 37 47 95 & 06 83 23 26 89
▤ 03 84 37 47 95
email: chambres-hotes@chateau-de-chavanes.com
web: www.chateau-de-chavanes.com/chambres-hotes

A picturesque village amongst the vineyards, with some beautiful
houses built of red stone. The château, which has been owned
by the same family since the 16th century, has five bedrooms,
one of them a family suite, with king-size beds and private bath/
shower room. Visits to wine cellars with tastings can be arranged;
meals served by arrangement.

Prices d €105-€125; extra person fr €15; dinner €20-€30
On Site ⚲ **Nearby** ⛷ 1km ⛳ 35km ⚲ 10km ⌖ 2km Water
sports 20km ⛳ 2km ⛪ 2km ⋙ 6km **Notes** No pets English
spoken

PLAINOISEAU

▮▮▮ La Fontaine aux Loups

Jocelyne et Régis DUFERT
39210 PLAINOISEAU
☎ 03 84 25 35 59 & 06 79 64 79 29
email: la.fontaine.aux.loups@orange.fr

In this beautiful stone-built house which has been extensively restored
there are three guest rooms. They all sleep two people, and all have
a private bath or shower room and WC. A lounge and kitchen are
available for the use of guests. Outside, the flowery garden and the
terrace are ideal places to have breakfast.

Prices s fr €45; d fr €48; t fr €65; extra person fr €15 **Nearby** ⛷ 12km
⛳ 15km ⚲ 9km ⌖ 3km Restaurant 5km Water sports 30km ⛳ 10km
Spa 3km ⛪ 4km ⋙ 4km **Notes** No pets

PONT-D'HERY

▮▮▮ Le Moulin Chantepierre

Chantal et Pierre GODIN
Moutaine, 39110 PONT D'HERY
☎ 03 84 73 29 90 & 06 07 32 17 87 ▤ 03 84 37 97 06
email: chante-pierre@tele2.fr
web: www.chantepierre.com

A peaceful haven just minutes from the spa of Salins-les-Bain. There
are three individually decorated rooms in this old mill each with
its own bathroom facilities. Guests have sole use of a lounge with
fireplace and television. Enjoy the sound of the river from the terrace
with its garden furniture.

Prices s fr €55; d fr €60; extra person fr €15 **On Site** ⚲
Nearby ⛷ 8km ⛳ 40km ⌖ 4km Restaurant 0.2km ⛳ 2km Spa 4km
⚲ 10km ⛪ 4km ⋙ 13km **Notes** No pets English spoken Open
February to November.

PRESILLY

▒ ⁱ◎ı La Baratte

Régine et Jean-François CHALET
39270 PRESILLY
☎ 03 84 35 55 18 ▤ 03 84 25 43 49
email: labaratte@free.fr
web: www.labaratte.fr

Présilly is a small village on a plateau, close to the Vouglans lake and home to a 11th-13th century castle. This old village farmhouse has been completely renovated to provide 4 guest rooms with private bathrooms and TV. There is a large lounge with open fireplace and regional dishes at the table d'hôte, the price of which includes wine.

Prices not confirmed for 2008 **Nearby** ⛷ 4km ⌀ 4km Water sports 8km ⌀ 4km ⌀ 4km ⌀ 15km **Notes** No pets

PUPILLIN

▒ ⁱ◎ı La Part des Anges

Stéphanie et Olivier ISTACE
Rue des Chenevières, 39600 PUPILLIN
☎ 08 71 03 23 34 & 03 84 37 47 35
email: alapartdesanges@free.fr
web: www.alapartdesanges.com

In the heart of the Arbois vineyard, this 18th-century house has four individually-decorated rooms, sleeping from two to four people. All the rooms have a private bath or shower room and WC, and there is a lounge and a magnificent garden for guests' use. Superb food and wine are served, and everything about this place will make your stay unforgettable.

Prices s fr €46; d fr €52; t fr €64; extra person fr €12; dinner €18-€20 **On Site** ⌀ **Nearby** ⛷ 10km ⌀ 35km ⌀ 2km ⌀ 3km Restaurant 3km Water sports 22km ⌀ 2km ⌀ 3km ⌀ 3km **Notes** No pets Open February to mid November.

RAHON

▒ ⁱ◎ı Le Temps des Moisson

Agnès et Jean-Michel MOISSON
LOISIRS ACCUEIL JURA
☎ 03 84 81 86 99
email: j2m@letempsdesmoisson.com
web: www.letempsdesmoisson.com

Between Dole and Chaussin, and close to three different rivers - this old farmhouse has five spacious rooms, for two to five people. Two rooms are on the ground floor, and three are upstairs; all have a shower room and WC. Meals featuring local specialities are served by candle light and with your hosts wearing medieval costume!

Prices s fr €40; d fr €48; t fr €63; extra person fr €15; dinner fr €20 **On Site** ⌀ **Nearby** ⛷ 0.8km ⌀ 0.2km ⌀ 15km Restaurant 5km Water sports 15km ⌀ 0.8km Spa 15km ⌀ 5km ⌀ 15km **Notes** No pets English spoken

SAMPANS

▒ Au Champs du Bois

Colette LAGE
Route de Dole, 39100 SAMPANS
☎ 03 84 82 25 10 ▤ 03 84 82 25 10
email: champdubois@ifrance.com
web: www.champsdubois.ifrance.com

This pretty manor house dates from the beginning of the last centur and is situated 4km from Dole, Pasteur's birthplace. The three stylish bedrooms each have private facilities and there is a large, enclosed wooded park with parking for boats and trailers. Guests may use the library and TV lounge.

Prices s fr €38; d fr €48; t fr €60; extra person fr €15 **On Site** ⌀ **Nearby** ⛷ 5km ⌀ 8km ⌀ 4km Restaurant 1.8km Water sports 4km ⌀ 4km ⌀ 4km ⌀ 4km **Notes** Pets admitted English spoken

SOUVANS

▒ ⁱ◎ı *Chambre d'hôtes*

C et N IULIANELLA/GOUX
LOISIRS ACCUEIL JURA
☎ 03 84 80 00 35 & 06 23 37 66 84 ▤ 03 84 80 00 35
email: la.maison.bleue.@wanadoo.fr
web: http://monsite.wanadoo.fr/_la_maison_bleue_/

Each of the three rooms has a private balcony in this beautifully restored old house. There are two doubles with own bathrooms and family room with bathroom on the landing. Guests have use of sittir area and terrace. Evening meals can be booked. You are a stone's throw from Pasteur's birthplace.

Prices not confirmed for 2008 **Nearby** ⛷ 10km ⌀ 2km Water sports 2km ⌀ 4km ⌀ 14km **Notes** Pets admitted English spoken

ST-AMOUR

▒ L'Achapt

Rita et Hans NAEGELI
6 Av de Lyon, 39160 SAINT AMOUR
☎ 03 84 48 75 70 ▤ 03 84 48 70 50

This beautiful, late 18th-century residence dominates the town of Saint-Amour. The park is planted with old trees, while a large, beaut rotunda borders the pool and opens onto a flower-filled garden. Th five double rooms have private bathrooms, and there is a reading room, TV and sauna.

Prices s fr €59; d fr €75 **Nearby** ⌀ 1km Water sports 9km ⌀ **Notes** No pets English spoken Open April to 15 October.

T-MAUR

❀ ⦿ Chambre d'hôtes

érard et Marie VIVENOT
chemin de la gare, 39570 SAINT-MAUR
☎ 03 84 44 23 34 & 06 78 10 15 91
mail: mg.vivenot@wanadoo.fr
eb: www.aubier.monsite.orange.fr

is big house on the edge of the village has four bedrooms, each for
ree or four people, and all with private shower room and WC. There
a large lounge area, a kitchen for guests, and outside a garden
d courtyard with garden furniture. The house is close to lakes and
neyards, and the mountain views are wonderful.

ices s fr €38; d fr €45; t fr €52; extra person fr €13; dinner fr
7 **On Site** ❀ ❀ **Nearby** ⦿ 10km Water sports 10km ⦿ 10km
a 10km ⦿ 10km ⥲ 10km **Notes** Pets admitted English spoken

T-PIERRE

❀ Chez les Hypolites

olette et Jean-Pierre LEYDER
Grande Rue, 39150 SAINT-PIERRE
03 84 60 83 44 & 06 80 95 17 73
mail: colette.leyder@wanadoo.fr
eb: www.chezleshypolites.free.fr

the heart of the Haut Jura Parc Naturel, this farmhouse has three
uble rooms, each with a TV and private facilities. Use of kitchen,
vate parking, courtyard with garden furniture and wonderful view of
Jura Mountains. Good starting point for walking and cross-country
ing; close to lakes and waterfalls.

ices d fr €47; t fr €57; extra person fr €10 **Nearby** ⦿ 10km ⦿ 20km
3km ⥲ 5km ⦿ 20km Water sports 20km ⦿ 2.5km ⦿ 2.5km
2.5km **Notes** No pets

OULOUSE-LE-CHATEAU

❀ Chambre d'hôtes

anine et Jean BERNARD
e de l'Eglise, 39230 TOULOUSE LE CHATEAU
03 84 85 54 78
mail: jean.jeaninebernard@orange.fr

minating the village with a lovely view, this old renovated house
ers rooms for two with private facilities. Guests have use of a large
ng room with billiards, table-football, lounge, library, terrace and
den with furniture. Supplement for stays of one night only.

ces s fr €45; d fr €50; extra person fr €15 **On Site** ❀
arby ⦿ 5km ⦿ 20km ⦿ 2km ⥲ 20km Restaurant 2km Water
rts 15km ⦿ 20km ⦿ 2km ⥲ 1km **Notes** No pets

VERTAMBOZ

❀❀❀ Chambre d'hôtes

M.Claude et Serge DEVENAT
495 Rue des Fontaines, 39130 VERTAMBOZ
☎ 03 84 44 77 36
web: www.les-4-lacs.com

In the heart of the Pays des Lacs, in a very pretty little village, this large
restored house has three upstairs bedrooms sleeping from two to four
people; all have private bath or shower room and WC. One room has
an independent entrance and a kitchenette. Streams and waterfalls
flow through the grounds outside.

Prices s fr €34; d €38-€52; extra person fr €10 **Nearby** ⦿ 6km ⦿ 30km
⦿ 0.3km Restaurant 5km ⦿ 30km Water sports 10km ⦿ 7km ⦿ 7km
⥲ 25km **Notes** Pets admitted English spoken

VILLERS-ROBERT

❀❀❀ ⦿ Le Moulin

Jacqueline MONAMY
39120 VILLERS ROBERT
☎ 03 84 71 52 39
web: www.lemoulindemamere.com

This old restored mill offers bedrooms with private bathrooms. Guests
may use the dining room and lounge with open fireplace. The tree-
lined park borders the river, and private fishing is possible within the
grounds.

Prices s fr €55; d €65-€70; t fr €86; extra person fr €16; dinner fr €22
On Site ⦿ **Nearby** ⦿ 5km ⥲ Restaurant 8km Water sports 15km
⦿ 15km ⦿ 1km ⥲ 15km **Notes** Pets admitted English spoken

VOITEUR

❀❀❀ Chambre d'hôtes

Colette MONACI
5 Route de Menetru, 39210 VOITEUR
☎ 03 84 85 28 43
email: jean-marie.monaci@wanadoo.fr

This modern house nestles in a verdant riverside setting at the heart of
the Jura vineyards. Bedrooms have their own bathrooms, and guests
are welcome to use the lounge or sit out on the terrace or in the
garden. There is a private pool and bicycles can be borrowed. Table
d'hôte meals served by prior arrangement.

Prices s fr €50; d fr €57 **On Site** ⦿ ❀ **Nearby** ⦿ 10km ⦿ 15km
⥲ 10km Restaurant 1km Water sports 20km ⦿ 10km ⦿ 0.5km ⥲ 2km
Notes No pets English spoken

VOITEUR *CONTINUED*

▦ *Château Saint-Martin*

Brigitte et Mickaël KELLER

39210 VOITEUR

☎ 03 84 44 91 87 🖹 03 84 44 91 87

email: kellerbr@wanadoo.fr

Most of this huge, beautiful house dates back to the 14th century, although it was extended in the 17th and 18th centuries. There are five guest rooms with three double and three single beds. The large park contains a kitchen garden, small vineyard, large terraces and old trees. Closed Xmas & New Year.

Prices not confirmed for 2008 **On Site** ✎ **Nearby** ⛷15km Water sports 10km ⌇10km ⋙10km **Notes** Pets admitted English spoken

---

▬ TERRITOIRE-DE-BELFORT

BOUROGNE

▦ ǀOǀ **Côté Grange**

M-C et J BONIN

16 rue Bernardot, 90140 BOUROGNE

☎ 03 84 27 74 52 🖹 03 84 27 74 52

email: jacques.bonin@wanadoo.fr

web: www.cote-grange.fr

Guests are promised a warm welcome at this peaceful old farmhouse, which has five very comfortable bedrooms. There is a sauna, lounge with television, a terrace and garden. Mountain bikes are available, and from June to September boat trips can be arranged. Meals are available, by arrangement.

Prices s €42-€52; d €52-€62; t fr €82; extra person fr €20; dinner fr €22 **On Site** ❦ Private ⤳ **Nearby** ⛷4km ⌇30km ✎1km Restaurant 0.5km ⌇1km ⌂0.5km ⋙15km **Notes** No pets English spoken CC

ETUEFFONT

▦ ǀOǀ ♿ **Chambre d'hôtes**

Daniel ELBERT

10, rue de la Chapelle, 90170 ETUEFFONT

☎ 03 84 54 68 63

email: champsbayex@orange.fr

web: http://perso.wanadoo.fr/chambres-tourisme/

A warm, welcoming atmosphere is assured at this property which has three very comfortable guest rooms. Two are in the owners' house, one on the ground floor and one upstairs, and there is a suite for four people in an adjacent building. Each room has a fridge and a kettle. Attractive garden.

Prices s €51-€54; d €58-€69; t €70-€86; dinner fr €25 **On Site** ✎ ❦ **Nearby** ⛷11km ⌇4km ⤳ Restaurant 4km ⌇ ⋙15km **Notes** Pets admitted English spoken

---

LARIVIERE

▦ ǀOǀ *Le Village*

Maryse et Alain LIGIER

4 rue du Margrabant, 90150 LARIVIERE

☎ 03 84 23 80 46 🖹 03 84 23 80 46

email: ligier.Alain@wanadoo.fr

web: www.hote-montebello.com

This restored house is built in the traditional Alsace style, and it stands in the centre of the village. There are three very comfortable bedrooms: two rooms for three on the second floor, and a grade 4 room for three on the first floor. All the rooms have private bath or shower rooms and WCs. There is an attractive terraced garden, and a swimming pool.

Prices not confirmed for 2008 **On Site** ❦ Private ⤳ **Nearby** ⛷5km ⌇10km ⌇2km ⌂2km ⋙15km **Notes** No pets English spoken

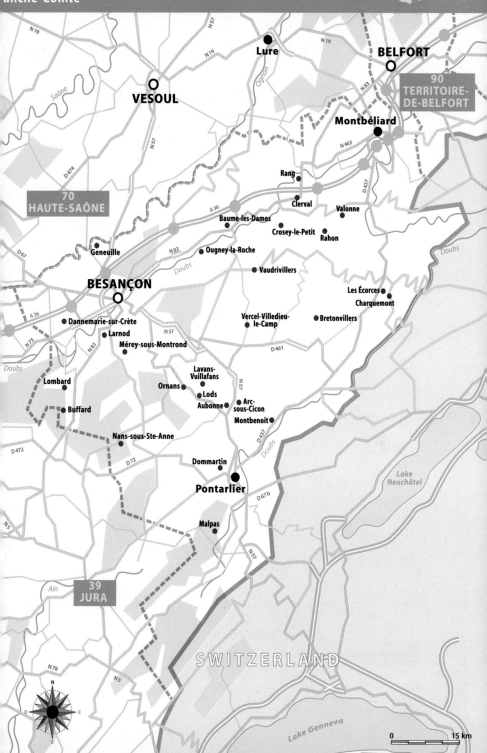

LURE

BELFORT

**90
TERRITOIRE-
DE-BELFORT**

VESOUL

Montbéliard

Rang

**70
HAUTE-SAÔNE**

Clerval

Valonne

Baume-les-Dames

Crosey-le-Petit

Rahon

Geneuille

Ougney-la-Roche

Vaudrivillers

BESANÇON

Les Écorces

Charquemont

Vercel-Villedieu-
le-Camp

Bretonvillers

Dannemarie-sur-Crète

Larnod

Mérey-sous-Montrond

Lombard

Lavans-
Vuillafans

Ornans

Lods

Buffard

Aubonne

Arc-
sous-Cicon

Montbenoit

Nans-sous-Ste-Anne

Dommartin

Pontarlier

Malpas

**39
JURA**

*Lake
Neuchâtel*

SWITZERLAND

Ain

N

O   E

S

Lake Genneva

0   15 km

HAUTE-SAÔNE
Franche-Comté

70

N 74

D 166

D 429

D 74

D 166

ÉPINAL

A 31

D 429

D 3

88
VOSGES

D 164

N 57

D 417

Meuse

Saône

Canal

D 26

Moselle

N 66

52
HAUTE-
MARNE

D 64

N 57

Ternuay-Melay-
et-St-Hilaire

Mélisey

Ognon

Champagney

N 19

N 19

Lure

Palante

Argillières

Rupt-
sur-Saône

Colombotte

N 19

Magny-Jobert

Frahie

Volon

Vy-lès-Lure

VESOUL

D 67

D 70

Saône

Dampierre-
sur-Salon

N 57

Montbélia

N 463

D 474

A 36

D 70

Esmoulins

N 83

Doubs

25
DOUBS

D 67

Cult

BESANÇON

N 57

39
JURA

A 36

N 73

D 461

N 83

N 57

Doubs

N

E

S

0   1

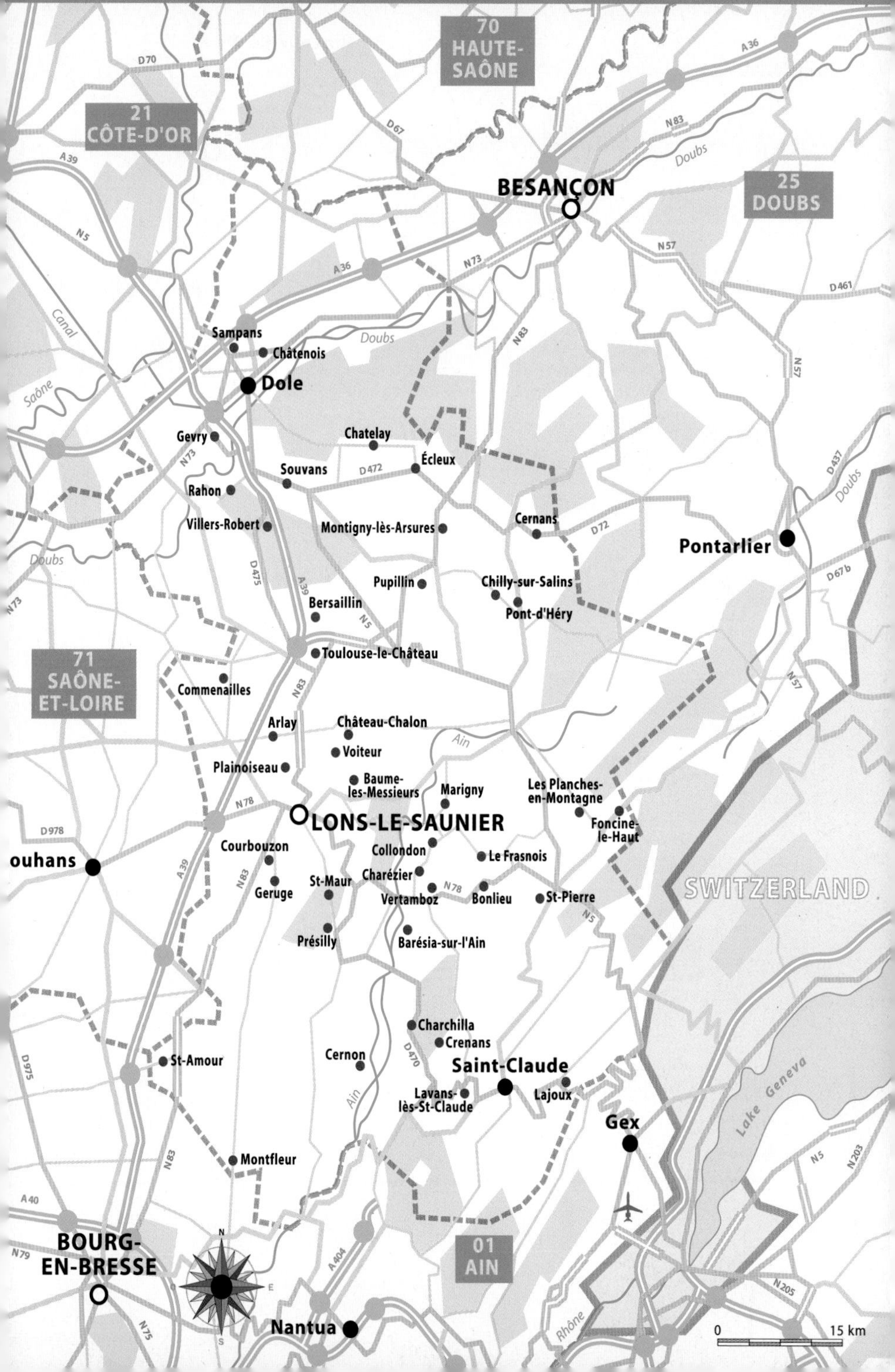

70
HAUTE-
SAÔNE
21
CÔTE-D'OR
25
DOUBS
71
SAÔNE-
ET-LOIRE
01
AIN
SWITZERLAND
BESANÇON
Sampans
Châtenois
Dole
Gevry
Chatelay
Écleux
Souvans
Rahon
Villers-Robert
Montigny-lès-Arsures
Cernans
Pontarlier
Pupillin
Chilly-sur-Salins
Pont-d'Héry
Bersaillin
Toulouse-le-Château
Commenailles
Arlay
Château-Chalon
Voiteur
Plainoiseau
Baume-
les-Messieurs
Marigny
Les Planches-
en-Montagne
Foncine-
le-Haut
LONS-LE-SAUNIER
Courbouzon
Collondon
Le Frasnois
ouhans
Geruge
St-Maur
Charézier
Vertamboz
Bonlieu
St-Pierre
Présilly
Barésia-sur-l'Ain
Charchilla
Crenans
Cernon
Saint-Claude
St-Amour
Lavans-
lès-St-Claude
Lajoux
Gex
Lake Geneva
Montfleur
BOURG-
EN-BRESSE
Nantua
Rhône
Doubs
Saône
Canal
Ain
A39
A36
A40
A404
N5
N73
N83
N57
N78
N79
N75
N203
N205
D70
D67
D461
D472
D475
D437
D72
D67b
D978
D975
D470
N
E
S
0
15 km

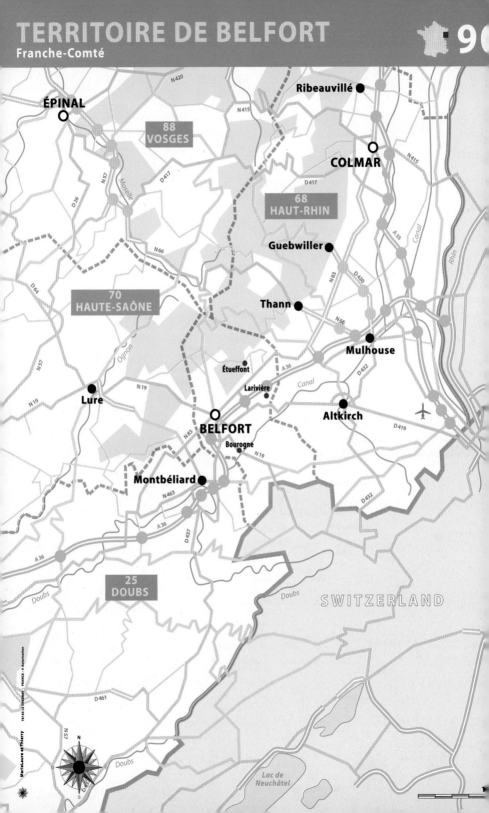

ILE-DE-FRANCE

ESSONNE

D'HUISON-LONGUEVILLE

ⅢⅢ Chambre d'hôtes

Françoise & J-Pierre DAVOINE
26 rue de Cerny, 91590 D'HUISON-LONGUEVILLE
☎ 01 64 57 73 31 & 06 82 70 78 01
email: closdusequoia91@neuf.fr
web: www.closdusequoia.com

In the centre of a small village, this restored property has four pretty guest rooms, three doubles and a twin, all with private shower room and WC. The garden, with all its flowers and greenery, is a quiet relaxing spot, and guests can enjoy their breakfast, complete with home-made jam, on the terrace or in the dining room.

Prices s fr €50; d fr €60 **Nearby** ⚓ 2km ⚘ 5km ⚐ 5km ⚑ 10km Restaurant 5km ⚒ 5km 🏛 4km ⛵ 4km **Notes** No pets

FONTAINE-LA-RIVIERE

ⅢⅢ ⚅ La Grange aux Grains

Daniel & Yvonne GATINEAU
rue des Vignes, 91690 FONTAINE-LA-RIVIERE
☎ 01 64 95 67 22 & 06 22 32 52 67 📠 01 64 95 67 22

This house stands in the centre of the village. On the ground floor is a large living room where breakfast is served, and a bedroom suitable for disabled guests with three single beds. Upstairs are three double rooms; all have private facilities. Go-karting, fly-fishing and walking are all near by; Chartres, Orléans, Versailles and Paris are within 60 kilometres. Pets admitted by reservation. Closed last fifteen days of January.

Prices s fr €45; d fr €50; t fr €65 **Nearby** ⚓ 2km ⚘ 20km ⚐ 4km ⚑ 7km Restaurant 2km ⚒ 7km 🏛 3km ⛵ 10km **Notes** Pets admitted Open February to 16 January.

GUIGNEVILLE-SUR-ESSONNE

ⅢⅢ La Ferme de Clercy

Patricia DESROUSSEAUX
0 rue de Clercy, 91590 GUIGNEVILLE-SUR-ESSONNE
☎ 01 64 57 61 84 📠 01 64 57 61 84
email: contact@lafermedeclercy.fr
web: www.lafermedeclercy.fr

A fully restored 18th-century riverside farmhouse in the Gâtinais National Park. Ground floor dining room with fireplace, generous breakfasts. Two hectares of grounds with lake and river. Kayaks may be hired and fishing by permit. Two doubles, one triple, one family room (double and twin). Annexe with suite for four people and dining room. All have private facilities. Wi-fi available.

Prices s €49-€54; d €64-€69; t €81-€84; extra person fr €15 **On Site** ⚐ **Nearby** ⚓ 5km ⚘ 5km ⚑ 12km Restaurant 2km ⚒ 2km 🏛 2km ⛵ 3km **Notes** No pets English spoken

MAUCHAMPS

ⅢⅢ Chambre d'hôtes

J-Jacques & Françoise RICHER
12, rue des Templiers, La Manounière,
91730 MAUCHAMPS
☎ 01 60 82 77 10 & 06 74 05 20 35
email: lamanouniere@tiscali.fr
web: www.chambres-manouniere.com

Françoise and Jean-Jacques and their typical Hurepoix farmhouse offer a warm welcome in the heart of this village of 275 people. With independent access, four first-floor comfortable rooms, three doubles and a twin, each have en suite shower and WC. Downstairs, a living room with TV, and a dining room where generous breakfasts are served. Courtyard, parking. Reductions for longer stays.

Prices s fr €42; d fr €52 **On Site** ⚓ **Nearby** ⚑ 10km ⚐ 5km ⚑ 8km Restaurant 1km ⚒ 4km 🏛 4km ⛵ 4km **Notes** No pets

MOIGNY-SUR-ECOLE

ⅢⅢ ⅠⅪ Campagnie des Clos

Frédéric LENOIR
9 rue du Souvenir, 91490 MOIGNY-SUR-ECOLE
☎ 01 64 98 47 84 & 06 76 95 56 87
email: lenoirf1@aol.com
web: www.compagnie-des-clos.com

Situated in a pretty village, this character property offers two double rooms and a suite with two single beds (extra beds possible). Each room has TV and private facilities. Breakfast room with kitchenette, huge lounge, landscaped garden with furniture. Table d'hôte meals served by prior arrangement. GR11 path, restaurant and Forest of Fontainebleau nearby. Limited parking.

Prices s fr €35; d fr €63; t fr €76; extra person fr €13; dinner fr €18 **On Site** Private ⚑ **Nearby** ⚘ 0.5km ⚐ 7km ⚑ 1km Restaurant 3km ⚒ 3km 🏛 3km ⛵ 9km **Notes** Pets admitted

NAINVILLE-LES-ROCHES

♯♯♯♯ & Le Clos des Fontaines

Geneviève SOTON

3 rue de l'Eglise, 91750 NAINVILLE-LES-ROCHES

☎ 01 64 98 40 56 & 06 61 92 04 00

email: soton@closdesfontaines.com

web: www.closdesfontaines.com

There are five elegantly decorated bedrooms at this property, all of them large and one with disabled access. The rooms are in a separate building from the owners' home, and each has satellite TV. Sauna, tennis, trampoline, fitness equipment and boules are also available. There are open views over the wooded grounds, and the forest is close by.

Prices s €70-€80; d €85-€105; extra person fr €25   **On Site** ⚴
Private tennis court   **Nearby** ⚑ 3km ⚴ 4km ⚓ 10km ⚓
Restaurant 2km 🏠 3km ⛵ 8km   **Notes** No pets   English spoken   CC

SACLAS

♯♯♯♯ Ferme des Prés de la Cure

André et Françoise SOUCHARD

17 rue Jean Moulin, 91690 SACLAS

☎ 01 60 80 92 28

This beautiful 15th-century farm with lots of character, situated in a village, welcomes guests in three double rooms with private facilities, access and TV point. Extra single bed on request. A huge breakfast is served in the living room, and guests have access to the terrace and garden. The farm is close to a landscaped garden with a stretch of water and the GR111 walking path.

Prices s fr €40; d fr €48; extra person fr €11   **On Site** ⚴
Nearby ⚑ 5km ⚴ 25km ⚓ 0.1km ⚓ 6km Restaurant 0.1km ⚓ 0.1km
🏠 0.1km ⛵ 8km   **Notes** No pets

VERT-LE-PETIT

♯♯♯♯ & Chambre d'hôtes

Bruno & Monique MERCIER

36 rue du Général Leclerc, 91710 VERT-LE-PETIT

☎ 01 64 93 24 39 📄 01 64 93 24 39

email: merciermo@wanadoo.fr

Your hosts welcome you to the five guest rooms in their restored barn, in the heart of the village. There are four double rooms and a twin, each with private shower and wc, TV, and separate access. Breakfast is served in the guests' dining room or on the terrace. Reduced tariffs for longer stays. Fishing is available in the lake nearby.

Prices s fr €45; d €55-€60; extra person fr €16; dinner fr €18
Nearby ⚑ 1km ⚴ 5km ⚓ 0.5km ⚓ 5km Restaurant 0.5km ⚓ 0.5km
⚴ 5km 🏠 0.5km ⛵ 3km   **Notes** No pets   English spoken

ACHERES-LA-FORET

♯♯♯ ◎ La Courtiliere

Cidalia et François LE BAIL

16 rue du Closeau, Meun, 77760 ACHERES LA FORET

☎ 01 64 69 88 41 & 06 70 98 87 21

email: reservations@lacourtiliere.com

web: www.lacourtiliere.com

A tastefully restored country house, in an attractive garden with flowers and trees. The three bedrooms - two doubles and a twin - are in a separate building, all with private bath or shower room and WC. Extra bed available. There is a lounge/dining room with kitchenette. Shady terrace, table tennis, loan of bikes. Meals by arrangement, prepared with local produce.

Prices s fr €50; d fr €55; extra person fr €25; dinner €15-€25
Nearby ⚑ 1km ⚴ 12km ⚓ 10km ⚓ 12km Restaurant 3km ⚓ 12km
🏠 3km ⚓ 12km   **Notes** No pets   English spoken

AMILLIS

♯♯♯ ✿ ◎ Chambre d'hôtes

Delphine et Olivier ROUSSEAU

No1 Fontenelle, 77120 AMILLIS

☎ 01 64 75 41 25 & 06 16 51 55 50 📄 01 64 75 41 25

email: rousseauolivier@free.fr

web: www.fermedefontenelle.com

Tastefully restored, this farmhouse is the centre of a working farm. Three split-level family bedrooms, all upstairs, each have a double bed and two singles. Each has its own private shower room and WC, and a cot is available. There is a games room, with billiards and table football, and fishing can be arranged. Brunch can be served by arrangement.

Prices s fr €55; d fr €65; extra person fr €20; dinner fr €25   **On Site** ⚓
Nearby ⚑ 10km ⚴ 20km ⚓ 8km Restaurant 8km ⚓ 1km 🏠 8km
⛵ 8km   **Notes** No pets   English spoken

BOISSISE-LA-BERTRAND

♯♯♯ Domaine de l'Orangerie du quai de Seine

J-Pierre et Bénédicte PIERRAIN

1570 Quai de Seine, 77350 BOISSISE LA BERTRAND

☎ 01 64 37 09 99

email: contact@domaine-orangerie.com

web: www.domaine-orangerie.com

A former orangery and outbuildings from the 19th century on the banks of the Seine, set in four hectares of beautiful grounds. Bedrooms and breakfast room are upstairs. Double with shower room/WC; family suite with a double room and twin room, shower room/WC. Further family suite with one separate entrance, a double room and a twin room, shower room/WC. Terrace and flower garden.

Prices s fr €62; d fr €68; extra person fr €26   **On Site** ⚓
Nearby ⚑ 2km ⚴ 4km ⚓ 3km Restaurant 2km ⚓ 2km ⚓ 4km 🏠 2km
⛵ 2km   **Notes** No pets   English spoken

BOURRON-MARLOTTE

▦ Château de Bourron

Estrella & Guy DE CORDON
14 bis rue du Maréchal Foch,
77780 BOURRON MARLOTTE
☎ 01 64 78 39 39 ▤ 01 64 78 35 35
email: bourron@bourron.fr
web: www.bourron.fr

A wonderful 17th-century château which stands in 40 hectares of grounds, seven kilometres from Fontainebleau and 70 kilometres from Paris. There are four double rooms, two on the first floor and two on the second. All are non-smoking, with private bathroom and WC, king-size bed, telephone, internet access and hi-fi. Antique furniture, 18th-century library - and a very warm welcome!

Prices d €160-€300; extra person fr €20 **On Site** ✎ Restaurant Private tennis court **Nearby** ⛳ 7km ⚓ 7km ⚒ 7km ⛴0.1km
⚓ 0.6km **Notes** No pets English spoken

BREAU

▦ ⚲ Ferme Relais du Couvent

Nicole et Jacques LEGRAND
77720 BREAU
☎ 01 64 38 75 15 ▤ 01 64 38 75 75
email: ferme.couvent@wanadoo.fr
web: www.lafermeducouvent.com

A very pretty restored farm with six hectares of land; this property offers lots of activities including tennis, mountain biking and hot-air ballooning. There is a double room, one with a double and two single, and one with a double and single bed, all en suite. Phone, breakfast room and baby-sitting service available.

Prices s fr €50; d fr €60; extra person fr €30 **Nearby** ⛳ 3km ⚓ 5km
✎ 2km ⚒ 7km Restaurant 3km ⛴ 1km ⚓ 7km **Notes** Pets admitted English spoken

BUTHIERS

▦ La Perrichonniere

Alain ROBERT
5 rue Grande, Herbeauvilliers, 77760 BUTHIERS
☎ 01 64 24 14 46 & 06 20 65 01 97
email: mediagreen@wanadoo.fr

A tastefully decorated beautiful property with large landscaped garden, set in a pretty village near Fontainebleau and Malesherbes. Ground floor large dining room, upstairs family suite (one double room and one twin), own bathroom and WC. Upstairs in an annexe is a family suite with one double room and one twin, shower room and WC. Breakfast is served in a pretty winter garden or on the terrace.

Prices s fr €80; d €80-€85; extra person fr €50 **Nearby** ⛳ 8km ⚓ 2km
⚒ 5km ⛴5km ⚓ 5km **Notes** No pets English spoken

CESSOY-EN-MONTOIS

▦ Le Clos Thibaud de Champagne

Martine LECOINTRE
1 rue du Souci, Le Petit Cessoy,
77520 CESSOY-EN-MONTOIS
☎ 01 60 67 32 10
email: closthibaud-de-champagne@orange.fr
web: www.closthibaud.com

This house enjoys a rural setting, not far from the medieval city of Provins and 35 minutes from Disneyland. There are three comfortable bedrooms: Vanilla and Lavender each have a double bed and a single; Cinnamon is a two-roomed family suite for five. All rooms have en suite facilities. Lounge with billiard table; function room for hire; terrace and landscaped garden.

Prices s €55-€62; d €61-€68; extra person fr €26 **Nearby** ⛳ 0.1km
⚓ 15km ✎ 0.2km ⚒ 15km Restaurant 1km ⚓ 3km ⛴ 4km ⚓ 12km
Notes No pets English spoken

CHARTRETTES

▦ Château de Rouillon

Peggy MORIZE-THEVENIN
41 Av Charles de Gaulle, 77590 CHARTRETTES
☎ 01 60 69 64 40 & 06 12 52 79 91
▤ 01 60 69 64 55
email: chateau.de.rouillon@club-internet.fr
web: www.chateauderouillon.net

A magnificent 17th-century property, situated in two hectares of lovely parkland on the banks of the Seine. The grounds include a French garden and terrace; there is a lounge, dining room, book and a video library. Rooms include three double rooms (one a suite with views over the Seine and the park, and a lounge area), a single and another suite with a double and twin room. All rooms have a bathroom and wc.

Prices s fr €75; d €82-€104; extra person fr €28 **On Site** ✎ ⚲
Nearby ⛳ 2km ⚓ 2km ⚒ 5km Restaurant 1km ⚓ 2km ⛴1km
⚓ 3km **Notes** No pets English spoken

ILE-DE-FRANCE

CHATEAUBLEAU

⋕⋕ Les Castelblotines

Catherine DALMARD

27 rue Prosper Desplats, 77370 CHATEAUBLEAU

☎ 01 64 01 65 12 📄 01 64 01 66 30

web: www.provins.net

Just 15 kilometres from the ancient town of Provins, and only 75 kilometres from Paris, this property has three attractive and tastefully arranged bedrooms - a twin-bedded room on the ground floor, an upstairs room with a double bed and a sofa bed, plus a family room. Outside is a garden and terrace; brunch can be served by arrangement.

Prices s fr €50; d fr €56; extra person €15-€20 **Nearby** ⛳ 15km
♨ 15km 🏊 15km 🕯 9km Restaurant 3km ⌛ 9km Spa 9km 🏩 3km
🎣 9km **Notes** No pets English spoken

CHATRES

⋕⋕ ⦿ Le Portail Bleu

Dominique et Pierre LAURENT

2 route de Fontenay, 77610 CHATRES

☎ 01 64 25 84 94 📄 01 64 25 84 94

email: leportailbleu@voila.fr

web: www.leportailbleu.com

This welcoming, renovated old farm offers two bedrooms with lots of character: a comfortable double and a family room with a double bed and three singles, both with private facilities. There is an enclosed country garden, table tennis, excellent walks nearby and picnic baskets prepared on request. Baby-sitting service available. Wi-fi available.

Prices s fr €50; d fr €60; extra person fr €21; dinner fr €21
Nearby ⛳ 5km 🏊 25km ♨ 1km 🕯 3km Restaurant 5km ⌛ 0.3km
🏩 3km 🎣 7km **Notes** No pets English spoken

CHAUMES-EN-BRIE

⋕⋕ ♥ ♿ Ferme de Forest

Marie-Joseph VANDEWEGHE

77390 CHAUMES EN BRIE

☎ 01 64 06 27 35 & 06 14 74 11 21 📄 01 64 06 25 33

email: vandeweghe@wanadoo.fr

web: http://perso.wanadoo.fr/ferme-forest/

This lovely old farm in the heart of quiet Brie countryside offers four spacious ground-floor bedrooms comprising three doubles and a triple, all with en suite bathroom and WC. Convivial welcome, with breakfast served in a large rustic dining room. Function rooms also available. Bikes, table tennis; footpaths close by.

Prices s fr €50; d fr €55; extra person fr €15 **Nearby** ⛳ 8km 🏊 20km
♨ 2km 🕯 Restaurant 2km ⌛ 2km Spa 20km 🏩 2km 🎣 5km
Notes No pets English spoken

see advert on opposite page

CHOISY-EN-BRIE

⋕⋕ ⦿ La Marvalière

Catherine et Jean MORRIOT

10 rue Bulot, Champbonnois, 77320 CHOISY EN BRIE

☎ 01 64 04 46 80 & 06 15 09 15 86

email: cjmorriot@aol.com

web: www.marvaliere.com

Situated 35 minutes from Disneyland Paris, between Coulommiers and La Ferté-Gaucher, this large house, typical of the Brie region, has been tastefully renovated, and has a large flower garden and terrace. Ideal for peace and relaxation, four bedrooms (for 2 to 4 people) and a family room with cot, each have private bathrooms. The lounge/drawing room has a large fireplace, books and television.

Prices s fr €53; d fr €60; extra person fr €25; dinner fr €20 **On Site** ⛲
Nearby ⛳ 5km 🏊 10km ♨ 3km 🕯 Restaurant 5km ⌛ 3km 🏩 5km
🎣 15km **Notes** No pets English spoken

COURPALAY

⊞ ⓘ◎ La Cle des Songes

Clément et Christine SAADIA

7 cour Durand, Le Grand Bréau, 77540 COURPALAY

☎ 01 64 42 95 12 & 06 84 23 78 74 📄 01 64 42 95 12

email: saadia.clement@wanadoo.fr

web: www.lacledessonges.com

This property is conveniently placed for Disneyland Paris, which is only 25 kilometres away. Four guest rooms comprise two with double beds, a twin-bedded room, and (in a separate building) a family room for four. All have private bath or shower room and WC. Baby equipment is available. Breakfast served inside or out on the terrace; brunch available by arrangement.

Prices s fr €47; d fr €62–€78; extra person fr €20; dinner €25–€30
On Site ♚ **Nearby** ⚓ 3km ♨ 8km ✗ 4km ↖ 1km Restaurant 1km
🖼 1km ♨ 7km � 10km **Notes** No pets English spoken

CRECY-LA-CHAPELLE

⊞ La Herissonière

F et S BORDESSOULE-BESSELIEVRE

4 rue du Barrois, 77580 CRECY LA CHAPELLE

☎ 01 64 63 00 72

email: laherissoniere@free.fr

In the heart of the village, bordered by a branch of the Morin River, a warm, friendly atmosphere can be found in these five comfortable, tastefully decorated en suite bedrooms. Four have a double and single bed, and one is a double; all have TVs. Charming garden with large terrace and floral pergola, lounge and dining room where a set menu can be served on request.

Prices s fr €50; d fr €54; extra person fr €18 **On Site** ✗
Nearby ⚓ 5km ♨ 4km Restaurant 10km ♨ 0.4km 🏠 0.1km � 0.8km
Notes Pets admitted English spoken

CRISENOY

⊞ Chambre d'hôtes

Josette et Alain VALERY

5 rue de l'Eglise, 77390 CRISENOY

☎ 01 64 38 83 20 📄 01 64 38 83 20

This very beautiful house is set within a village and offers well maintained en suite rooms: three double bedrooms with a cot and independent access to a fourth double bedroom, overlooking the enclosed garden with terrace. Warm atmosphere and friendly welcome, breakfast room and rustic lounge with open fire and cooking area.

Prices s fr €45; d fr €53; extra person fr €20 **On Site** ♚
Nearby ⚓ 10km ♨ 18km ✗ 10km Restaurant 0.5km ♨ 1km 🏠 6km
� 12km **Notes** Pets admitted English spoken

Ferme de Forest

77390 Chaumes en Brie
Tel: 01 64 06 27 35
Web: vandeweghe@wanadoo.fr

Marie-joseph welcomes you to her farm, in the heart of Brie. The bedrooms are spacious, comfortable, entirely renovated with resembling "les chambres de charme" Les rooms have been rated 3 épi by Gites de France. You can visit the region's chateaux, various historic sites and Disneyland Paris. Alternatively explore the region by rambling or biking on the GR1 path.
40 mins from Paris. Take the A4 from La Porte de Bercy towards Reims. Take the exit signed Melun/Nancy onto the N4. After 8 kms take the 2nd intersection on the left follow signs for N36 Chaumes en Brie then Forest

CROUY-SUR-OURCQ

⊞ Chambre d'hôtes

Marie-Thérèse FROGNEUX

1 Place du Marché, 77840 CROUY SUR OURCQ

☎ 01 64 35 67 41 & 01 64 35 61 38

email: mt.frogneux@free.fr

Crouy-sur-Ourcq is a pleasant village in the valley of the same name. This B&B in a renovated house in the village centre has plentiful accommodation on the first and second floors, which includes a family suite sleeping five, three doubles and a twin, all with shower and WC. Dining room on ground floor; huge terrace. Champagne cellars near by.

Prices s fr €40; d fr €48; extra person fr €18 **Nearby** ⚓ 1km ♨ 25km
✗ 10km Restaurant 0.1km ♨ 0.5km 🏠 0.5km � 1km **Notes** No pets
English spoken

ECHOUBOULAINS

⊞ ❦ Ferme de la Recette

Famille DUFOUR

Echou, 77830 ECHOUBOULAINS

☎ 01 64 31 81 09 📄 01 64 31 89 42

email: info@fermedelarecette.com

web: www.fermedelarecette.com

This large farm has stacks of charm and tasteful décor. There are three double bedrooms, each with a shower and wc, and a breakfast room.

CONTINUED

ECHOUBOULAINS CONTINUED

This is an ideal spot for rambling and mountain biking. Self-catering gîtes available.

Prices s fr €46; d fr €55; extra person fr €16 **On Site** 🖉 Restaurant **Nearby** ⛳ 10km ⚓ 15km ⤳ 20km ⛵ 2.5km 🏇 20km 🏛 2.5km 🚶 10km **Notes** No pets English spoken CC

EGREVILLE

🍴 🎱 La Borde

Catherine -J-Pierre LATSCHA

10 Route de Villebéon, 77620 EGREVILLE

☎ 01 64 29 58 58 & 06 64 10 36 48

email: info@loisirsengatinais.com

web: www.les2noyers.com

This is a beautiful old house, in landscaped grounds one and a half kilometres from the local village. It has a double room, a room for four (double bed plus singles), and two family suites for four. All have private facilities, and the whole place is beautifully decorated. There are terraces outside, where guests can enjoy breakfast in summer.

Prices s fr €60; d fr €70; extra person fr €30; dinner fr €25 **On Site** 🍷 **Nearby** ⛳ 1km ⚓ 15km 🖉 10km ⤳ Restaurant 1.5km ⛵ 1.5km 🏛 1km 🚶 12km **Notes** No pets English spoken

EVRY-GREGY

🍴 Le Prieuré de Vernelle

Suzanne et Eric TEXIER

77166 EVRY GREGY

☎ 01 60 62 71 47 & 01 60 62 78 96

📠 01 60 62 78 96

email: contact@vernelle.fr

web: www.vernelle.fr

An old Bénédictine priory dating back to the 12th century, standing in five hectares of grounds with a river passing through. The guest rooms are upstairs, in the oldest part of the house: a double room, and a room with two double beds, both with private facilities. Breakfasts are served in the lounge, leading off the cloisters. A delightful property in an exceptional location.

Prices s fr €100; d €120-€155; t fr €145; extra person fr €25 **On Site** ⛳ **Nearby** ⚓ 8km 🖉 0.5km Restaurant 3km ⛵ 2km 🏛 3km 🚶 12km **Notes** No pets English spoken

FAVIERES

🍴 Le Relais du Petit Paris

G et M MEUNIER-FENNAS

2 rue du Marronnier, 77220 FAVIERES

☎ 06 74 83 47 70 & 01 64 07 29 33

email: lerelaisdupetitparis@wanadoo.fr

web: http://perso.wanadoo.fr/lerelaisdupetitparis/

In a charming village, but with easy access to Disneyland and Paris, this old inn has been fully restored. On the first floor are two double rooms; on the second floor are two triples, each with a double bed and a single. Cot available. All rooms have a private bathroom and WC, and are cheerfully decorated. Enclosed grounds, covered parking.

Prices not confirmed for 2008 **Nearby** ⛳ 3km ⚓ 7km 🖉 0.2km Restaurant 0.2km ⛵ 3km 🏛 3km 🚶 3km **Notes** No pets English spoken

GOUVERNES

🍴 Au Victor Hugo

Monique et Daniel VERNET

27 rue Victor Hugo, 77400 GOUVERNES

☎ 01 60 31 03 85 & 06 84 58 89 32 📠 01 64 02 87 81

email: chambres-gouvernes@wanadoo.fr

web: www.chambres-gouvernes.com

A typical Briard restored farmhouse in a village 28 kilometres from Paris and 15 kilometres from Disneyland. On the first floor is a two-roomed family suite for four, with a double bed and two singles, and its own bathroom/WC. Another family room with its own entrance has a similar arrangement of beds and en suite facilities. Cot available. Garden with terrace and parking.

Prices not confirmed for 2008 **Nearby** ⛳ 0.5km ⚓ 1km 🖉 2km Restaurant 1km ⛵ 0.5km 🏛 2km 🚶 2km **Notes** Pets admitted English spoken

GRISY-SUR-SEINE

🍴 🐓 🎱 Ferme de Toussacq

Dominique et J.Louis COLAS

Grisy-sur-Seine, 77480 VILLENAUXE-LA-PETITE

☎ 01 64 01 82 90 📠 01 64 01 82 90

email: toussacq@wanadoo.fr

web: http://hameau-de-toussacq.com

A farm by the River Seine, with five bedrooms in a converted outbuilding, two on the ground floor and three upstairs. All have private shower or bathroom and WC, and TVs are available. Dining room with kitchenette, lounge, garden with garden furniture. Meals by arrangement (not Sundays or Tuesday evenings), including vegetarian options using organic produce from the garden.

Prices s fr €42; d fr €50; extra person fr €19; dinner fr €15 **Nearby** ⛳ 10km ⚓ 35km 🖉 0.1km ⤳ 15km Restaurant 6km ⛵ 3km 🏛 6km 🚶 18km **Notes** Pets admitted English spoken

JUILLY

🍴 🐓 La Ferme de l'Abbaye

Franck CORVISIER

1 place de l'Oratoire, 77230 JUILLY

☎ 01 64 36 14 04 & 06 07 41 57 19 📠 01 60 44 40 89

email: garros.traiteur@wanadoo.fr

web: www.fermedelabbaye.fr

A complex of farm buildings 41 kilometres from Paris and 25 kilometres from Disneyland. There are five attractively decorated bedrooms: two doubles with shower/WC and a family room for four (double bed and two singles) with bathroom/WC; and in an annexe, a large ground floor double with bathroom and WC, and upstairs a double with shower room/WC. Tennis court, also meeting rooms where catering can be provided for functions.

Prices not confirmed for 2008　**Nearby** ✿ 0.2km ⚓ 25km ✐ 6km Restaurant 3km ▣ 0.2km ᚽ 3km　**Notes** No pets　English spoken

LA CHAPELLE-LA-REINE

⁇ ⏐◯⏐ **Le Clos du Tertre**

S DAGNICOURT et V SIMON

6 Chemin des Vallées, 77760 LA CHAPELLE LA REINE

☎ 01 64 24 37 80 & 06 20 14 70 17

email: leclosdutertre@wanadoo.fr

web: www.bonadresse.com/ile-de-france/
la-chapelle-la-reine.htm

In a village bordering the Forest of Fontainebleau, this ancient house has been renovated with taste. On the first floor, two doubles and a twin each have their own shower and WC. Downstairs is a reception room with kitchenette. Breakfast served on the terrace in summer. Large lawned gardens, parking in courtyard. Meals by reservation. Walks and rock climbing nearby.

Prices s fr €50; d fr €55; extra person fr €20; dinner fr €22 **Nearby** ✿ 3km ⚓ 14km ✐ 7km ⤢ 12km Restaurant 0.3km ⤲ 5km Spa 3km ♟ 12km ▣ 0.5km ᚽ 14km　**Notes** No pets　English spoken

LA CHAPELLE-RABLAIS

⁇⁇ **Château des Moyeux**

Brigitte GALAZOMMATIS

77370 LA CHAPELLE RABLAIS

☎ 01 64 08 49 51　▤ 01 64 08 42 74

email: n.g@alphacomgroup.com

web: www.chateau-des-moyeux.com

Rebuilt in the 18th century and situated in a large, 30-hectare park, this château offers three double rooms, each with a bathroom and wc and cot available. There is a lounge with large fireplace, a small music room, dining room, library with fireplace and an orangery housing a swimming pool. Breakfast available; restaurants nearby. Explore the chapel crypt or the beautiful park. Discounts for week-long bookings or long weekends.

Prices s €80-€110; d €100-€130; extra person fr €30　**On Site** ♟ Private ⤢　**Nearby** ✿ 5km ⚓ 3km Restaurant 3km ⤲ 7km ▣ 5km ᚽ 5km　**Notes** No pets　English spoken

LE CHATELET-EN-BRIE

⁇ ❦ **La Fauconnière**

Christophe DUMORTIER

RN 105, 77820 LE CHATELET-EN-BRIE

☎ 01 60 69 40 45 & 06 70 63 76 49　▤ 01 60 69 40 45

email: lafauconniere77@wanadoo.fr

A very pretty, well maintained farm with a cosy feel. There are three double rooms and a twin, each with shower and WC. Breakfast room on the ground floor.

Prices s fr €42; d fr €48　**Nearby** ✿ 2km ⚓ 7km ✐ 1km ⤢ 8km Restaurant 3km ⤲ 3km ▣ 3km ᚽ 7km　**Notes** No pets

LES ORMES-SUR-VOULZIE

⁇ ❦ ⏐◯⏐ **Chambre d'hôtes**

Pierre et Sylvie LASSEAUX

9 rue de la Rivière, 77134 LES ORMES SUR VOULZIE

☎ 01 64 01 79 38 & 06 33 46 74 31

email: piersyl2@wanadoo.fr

A lovely farmhouse with large garden offering guest bedrooms in an annexe with separate entrance. Breakfast room with tea-making area, breakfast in the garden in summer. Ground floor room with a double and a single bed, shower room/WC. Upstairs bedroom with a double and single, separate shower room and WC. One triple with shower room/WC. Evening meal by arrangement using the farm's produce.

Prices not confirmed for 2008　**Nearby** ✿ 5km ⚓ 25km ✐ 6km Restaurant 6km ⤲ 6km ▣ 6km ᚽ 6km　**Notes** No pets

LIZINES

⁇ ❦ **Chambre d'hôtes**

Christine et J-C DORMION

2 rue des Glycines, 77650 LIZINES

☎ 01 60 67 32 56　▤ 01 60 67 32 56

This pretty house is situated opposite the owners' farm and offers a warm welcome and family atmosphere. There are five bedrooms for two to three people, each with bathroom and wc. TV on request, children's games, flower-filled garden with furniture, kitchen area and barn converted into a summer room with open fireplace, barbecue and bar area. Meals with farm produce can be provided Monday to Wednesday. Guests can be met at the station.

Prices s fr €40; d fr €47; extra person fr €15　**Nearby** ✿ 12km ⚓ 12km ✐ 15km ⤢ 13km Restaurant 7km ⤲ 4km ♟ 12km ▣ 7km ᚽ 7km **Notes** No pets　English spoken

⁇ ❦ ⏐◯⏐ **Chambre d'hôtes**

Annick et Jean-Marie DORMION

24 rue du Perré, 77650 LIZINES

☎ 01 60 67 32 47　▤ 01 60 67 32 47

email: ajmdormion@wanadoo.fr

Adjacent to a pretty 18th-century church, this welcoming farm has a friendly, family atmosphere. There are two doubles (one with separate access) and a room with a double and single bed, all with private facilities. Breakfast room, kitchen, TV and small garden available. Table d'hôte meals with the farm's own produce are served each evening (except Fridays) by prior arrangement. Animals admitted at owners' discretion. Reduced rates, depending on length of stay.

Prices s fr €40; d fr €47; extra person fr €15; dinner fr €14 **Nearby** ✿ 12km ⚓ 12km ✐ 15km ⤢ 12km Restaurant 4km ⤲ 4km ▣ 4km ᚽ 7km　**Notes** English spoken

ILE-DE-FRANCE

NOISY-SUR-ECOLE

⊞⊞ **Les Nuelles**

Josette et Christian SANDER
109 Rue Grande, 77123 NOISY SUR ECOLE
☎ 01 60 71 80 57 & 06 08 97 17 36 📄 01 60 71 80 57
email: christian.sander@free.fr

A property in the village of Noisy, only five kilometres from Milly-la-Forêt. There are two double rooms and a twin-bedded room, all with private bath or shower room and WC. The breakfast room has a corner where hot drinks can be made. Outside are large enclosed grounds, and many leisure possibilities close by include rock climbing, walking and riding.

Prices s fr €55; d fr €60; extra person fr €20 **On Site** ♚
Nearby ⚓ 2km ⚲ 12km ⚲ 10km ⚲ 5km Restaurant 3km ⚲ 2km
⚏ 5km ⚲ 10km **Notes** No pets English spoken

POMMEUSE

⊞⊞ ⏐◯⏐ **Le Moulin de Pommeuse**

Annie et Jacky THOMAS
32 Av du General Huerne, 77515 POMMEUSE
☎ 01 64 75 29 45 📄 01 64 75 29 45
email: infos@le-moulin-de-pommeuse.com
web: www.le-moulin-de-pommeuse.com

A warm welcome awaits at this 14th-century water-mill, in a typical Brie village in a valley. Convenient for many cultural and leisure activities, the mill is set in a three-hectare park beside the river with easily accessible island. Vast rooms include a large dining room with open fireplace and five characterful rooms, of which two are family rooms; all with private facilities and views over the river or park. Outdoor activities include table tennis, fishing, mountain biking and rambling.

Prices s fr €52; d fr €62; extra person fr €25; dinner €25-€30
On Site ⚲ **Nearby** ⚓ 1km ⚲ 4km Restaurant 2km ⚲ 2km ⚏ 2km
⚲ 2km **Notes** No pets English spoken

PREAUX

⊞⊞ **Les Tremieres**

Cécile et Patrice GREGOIRE
23 rue des Prés, 77710 PREAUX
☎ 01 64 31 41 51 & 06 85 02 47 75 📄 01 64 31 49 19
email: lestremiere@voila.fr
web: www.lestremieres.fr

A group of farm buildings 30 kilometres from Fontainebleau with three very attractive guest rooms, all upstairs: a double room, a triple (double bed plus a single), and a room for four (double bed plus two singles); each has a private shower room and WC. Guests can enjoy breakfast around the fire in winter or out in the garden amongst the flowers in the summer; brunch and other meals by arrangement. Bikes and kitchen available for guests use.

Prices s fr €50; d fr €60; extra person fr €22 **On Site** ♚
Nearby ⚓ 3km ⚲ 12km ⚲ 3km ⚲ 6km Restaurant 5km ⚲ 5km
⚏ 3km ⚲ 15km **Notes** No pets English spoken

PROVINS

⊞⊞⊞ **Demeure des Vieux Bains**

Véronique et Nicolas DESSERY
7 rue du Moulin de la Ruelle, 77160 PROVINS
☎ 06 74 64 54 00 📄 01 60 52 07 32
web: www.demeure-des-vieux-bains.com

This beautiful 12th-century house is a luxuriously-appointed listed building in the medieval city of Provins. It has a double-bedded room; a large two-roomed suite with two double beds; and in an annexe, a three-roomed suite for five people. All of the rooms have private facilities, some with power showers and spa baths. Lounge, billiard room, patio.

Prices s €100-€140; d €100-€250 **Nearby** ⚓ 2km ⚲ 25km
⚲ 10km ⚲ 0.3km Restaurant 0.1km ⚲ 0.2km ⚏ 0.1km ⚲ 0.8km
Notes No pets English spoken CC

♯♯♯ ☙ Ferme du Chatel

Annie et Claude LEBEL
5 rue de la Chapelle St Jean,
77160 PROVINS-VILLE HAUTE
☎ 01 64 00 10 73 📄 01 64 00 10 99
email: fermeduchatel@wanadoo.fr
web: www.provins.net

This farm is located near the ramparts of a listed medieval town,
which offers lots of activities during the summer. There is a double
room, two triples and two rooms for four, each with private facilities.
Small seminar room for 12-15 people and a breakfast room with
kitchen area and grill. Baby sitting and picnics can be arranged. Horses
welcome.

Prices d €64-€66; extra person fr €20 **Nearby** ☝ 4km ⚓ 24km
⚐ 10km ⚲ 0.5km Restaurant 0.2km ⚑ 1km 🏠 1km ﹏ 1km
Notes No pets English spoken

SIVRY-COURTRY

♯♯♯ ⧉ Château de Courtry

D et P BRUNN-SERVOUZE
Hameau de Courtry, 77115 SIVRY COURTRY
☎ 01 60 69 36 01 & 06 62 79 78 20 📄 01 60 69 36 01
email: brunndagga@tiscali.fr
web: www.chateaudecourtry.com

Stay at this impressive 16th to 17th-century château with two hectares
of grounds. The breakfast room and lounge are on the ground floor of
the right wing. On the second floor a vast family room has a double,
sofa bed and single on a mezzanine, bathroom and WC. A further
double and sofa bed with bathroom and WC, and a further double
with bathtub and washbasin. Private WCs on the landing. Evening
meal by arrangement. Cycle hire. Terrace, garden furniture. Friendly
service and warm welcome.

Prices s fr €58; d fr €68; extra person fr €25; dinner €28-€38
On Site ⚲ **Nearby** ☝ 10km ⚓ 10km ⚐ 7km ⚲ Restaurant 2km
⚑ 2km 🏠 2km ﹏ 7km **Notes** Pets admitted English spoken

SOUPPES-SUR-LOING

♯♯♯ ⧉ Au Domaine des Roses

Pascal GUITTONNEAU
6 rue du Marais Brule, Champs sur les Bois,
77460 SOUPPES SUR LOING
☎ 01 60 55 09 81 & 06 07 04 71 46
email: kat9@tiscali.fr

Set in four hectares of enclosed grounds, near Souppes-sur-Loing, this
B&B has five comfortable and personalised rooms: two with a double
and single bed and three doubles, each with private facilities. Dining
room and lounge with fireplace, TV and French billiards. Child's bed,
high chair, games, brunch and picnic baskets available. Stables on site
with horse boxes and horse hire; numerous walks and tourist sites
nearby.

Prices s €50-€55; d €55-€60; extra person fr €10; dinner fr €20
Nearby ☝ 2km ⚓ 10km ⚐ 2km ⚲ 8km Restaurant 2km ⚑ ⚲ 2km
🏠 2km ﹏ 2km **Notes** Pets admitted

SOURDUN

♯♯♯ ⧉ La Loutiniere

Valérie PLANCKAERT
13 rue Creuse, 77171 SOURDUN
☎ 01 60 58 06 33

A village house only four kilometres from the medieval town of
Provins. Four air-conditioned bedrooms sleep from two to four
people, all with private shower room and WC. Cot and high chair
available. Breakfast room and lounge with open fire; brunch available.
Livestock on site includes donkeys and chickens.

Prices s fr €46; d fr €56; t fr €94; extra person fr €20; dinner fr €15
Nearby ☝ 4km ⚐ 5km ⚲ 4km Restaurant 4km ⚑ 0.1km 🏠 4km
﹏ 4km **Notes** No pets

ST-AUGUSTIN

♯♯♯ ⧉ Château la Roseraie du Poncet

Marie-France LAGIER
1b, rue de la Cascade, 77515 SAINT AUGUSTIN
☎ 01 64 03 93 18 📄 01 64 03 93 18
email: lagierptitcoinparadis@wanadoo.fr

This château stands in ten hectares of grounds where lakes, waterfalls
and horses create a wonderful ambience. It has a family suite for up
to five, with two double beds and a single, and a double room. Each

CONTINUED

ST-AUGUSTIN *CONTINUED*

has a private bathroom and WC. Accommodation available for horses as well as their riders; meals and packed lunches by arrangement.

Prices s fr €62; d fr €68; extra person fr €26; dinner €25-€35
On Site 🏊 🎾 **Nearby** ⚓ 2km ⛳ 10km ✈ 6km Restaurant 1.5km ⛵ 1km 🚲 1km 🚠 2km **Notes** No pets English spoken Open March to October.

ST-DENIS-LES-REBAIS

⚜ 🍴 Brie-Champagne

Anne BODIN
22 Chantareine, 77510 SAINT DENIS LES REBAIS
☎ 01 64 65 46 45 & 06 23 44 78 11 🖹 01 64 65 46 45
email: contact@chambres-brie-champagne.com
web: www.chambres-brie-champagne.com

In a hamlet 12 kilometres from Coulommiers, this 18th-century house has been beautifully restored. On the ground floor is a double room; on the first floor is a three-roomed suite for six people; in the attic is a two-roomed suite for four. All of these beautifully-appointed rooms have a private bath or shower room and WC. Lounge, terrace, vast garden with trees and flowers.

Prices s fr €55; d fr €65; t fr €95; extra person fr €30; dinner fr €23
Nearby ⚓ 2km ⛳ 20km ⛳ 5km ✈ 5km Restaurant 2km ⛵ 2km
🏇 12km 🚲 2km 🚠 12km **Notes** No pets English spoken

ST-GERMAIN-SUR-MORIN

⚜ La Rose des Vents

Véronique et Bernard RICHEFEU
8 Sente des Jardins, Montguillon,
77860 SAINT GERMAIN SUR MORIN
☎ 01 64 63 50 13 & 06 19 45 34 68 🖹 08 70 27 65 43
email: larose.desvents@free.fr
web: www.rosedesvents.net

Peacefully situated on a hillside, but only seven kilometres from Disneyland, this property has four individually-decorated rooms, looking out onto a large wooded garden. On the ground floor are two double rooms; upstairs a twin-bedded room and a family room for four. All rooms have a private bath or shower room and WC; extra beds and cot available.

Prices s fr €50; d fr €58; extra person fr €20 **Nearby** ⚓ 1km ⛳ 2km ⛳ 1km ✈ 15km Restaurant 1km ⛵ 1km Spa 1km 🚲 1km 🚠 7km **Notes** No pets English spoken

⚜ Les Hauts de Montguillon

Chantal LEGENDRE
22 rue de St Quentin, Montguillon,
77860 ST GERMAIN SUR MORIN
☎ 01 60 04 45 53
email: chantal.legendre@wanadoo.fr
web: www.les-hauts-de-montguillon.com

Enjoy peace and quiet at this tastefully restored local style home set in large grounds. Only 7km from Disneyland with easy access to the RER station at Chessy. Separate entrance. Lounge with games area (bridge table, board games). Terrace, garden furniture. Three guest bedrooms with private facilities: one ground floor double; two first floor doubles each with singles on a mezzanine. Lovely walking area, warm welcome assured.

Prices s fr €55; d fr €70; extra person fr €20 **Nearby** ⚓ 2km ⛳ 5km ⛳ 2km ✈ 5km Restaurant 2km ⛵ 1.5km 🚲 1.5km 🚠 2km **Notes** Pets admitted English spoken

ST-LOUP-DE-NAUD

⚜ Ferme de la Haute Maison

Jean DHENIN
77650 SAINT LOUP DE NAUD
☎ 01 64 08 62 56 & 06 07 46 60 19 🖹 01 64 08 60 20
email: jean.dhenin@wanadoo.fr

This property is in a remarkable situation, on the site of an old monastery overlooking the village of St-Loup-de-Naud and its Roman church. It has three elegant and comfortable double rooms, and two family suites for four in a separate building. All of these beautifully-appointed rooms have a private bath or shower room and WC. Generous breakfasts, swimming pool.

Prices s fr €65; d fr €72; extra person fr €28 **On Site** Private ✈ **Nearby** ⚓ 4km ⛳ 15km ⛳ 10km Restaurant 2km ⛵ 7km 🚲 4km 🚠 4km **Notes** No pets English spoken

ST-OUEN-EN-BRIE

⚜ 🍴 Le Logis Brie-Art

Rosine et Alain GOHET
41 rue de la Mairie, 77720 SAINT OUEN EN BRIE
☎ 01 64 08 46 38 & 06 83 28 21 47 🖹 01 64 08 46 38
email: alain.gohet@wanadoo.fr
web: www.chambres.com.fr/brie-art

Located in the countryside near Nangus, the medieval city of Provins, tourist sites and 40km from Disneyland Paris. There is a double with

cot, private access and fireplace, another double and a room with a
double and single bed, each with private facilities. Table d'hôte meals
(by reservation) feature home-grown produce. The proprietors, a
painter and photographer of art, are happy to share their passion for
their work.

Prices s fr €48; d fr €57; extra person fr €25; dinner fr €28
Nearby ⛵ 0.1km ⚓ 3km ⚑ 3km Restaurant 3km ⚓ 3km 🏠 3km
⚑ 6km **Notes** Pets admitted

ST-REMY-DE-LA-VANNE

⚑ 🍴 Les Puits du Lettrée

C et F GENESTE-POULUSSEN
6 Hameau de Lettrée, 77320 SAINT REMY DE LA VANNE
☎ 01 64 04 58 72 & 06 07 09 55 41
email: info@lespuits.com
web: www.lespuits.com

This beautifully restored house with large wooded grounds is in a
quiet hamlet. It has three double rooms and a triple, all tastefully
decorated. Each has private bath or shower room. Ground floor small
reception room and large lounge with fireplace. Summer dining area
on the terrace.

Prices s fr €80; d fr €90; extra person fr €30; dinner fr €30
Nearby ⛵ 3km ⚓ 25km ⚑ 2.5km Restaurant 2km ⚓ 1km 🏠 2.5km
⚑ 17km **Notes** No pets English spoken

STE-COLOMBE

⚑ La Villa L'Orchidée

Fanjanirina FOURTIER
60 bis Av de la Libération, 77650 SAINTE COLOMBE
☎ 06 86 78 98 24 📠 01 60 67 23 48
email: villaorchidée@orange.fr

Close to the medieval town of Provins, this modern house is in the
pretty village of Sainte Colombe. Extensive accommodation comprises
two doubles with shower and WC on the ground floor, a double with
bathroom on the first floor; with independent access are an upstairs
double, and a ground-floor family room for four, both with shower
and WC. Hospitable hosts serve breakfast by the fire in winter, on the
terrace in summer.

Prices not confirmed for 2008 **Nearby** ⛵ 3km ⚓ 30km ⚑ 10km
Restaurant 2km ⚓ 3km 🏠 0.5km ⚑ 0.8km **Notes** No pets English
spoken

THOMERY

⚑ Les Cours de la Seine

Isabelle BADER
149 Av Gl de Ségur, 77810 THOMERY
☎ 01 64 70 80 52 📠 01 60 96 40 62
email: isabelle.bader@libertysurf.fr
web: www.bonadresse.com

This 18th-century house with its beautiful interior garden and paved
courtyard is in a village which stands in the heart of the forest. It is
a charming and peaceful location. It has three large, individually-
decorated bedrooms, each for two or three people. All rooms have

a private bath or shower room and WC. Gardens close to the River
Seine. Language courses.

Prices not confirmed for 2008 **On Site** ⚑ **Nearby** ⛵ 5km ⚓ 8km
Restaurant 1km ⚓ 2km 🏠 2km ⚑ 2km **Notes** No pets English spoken

TRILBARDOU

⚑ Chambre d'hôtes

Evelyne et Patrick CANTIN
2 rue de l'Eglise, 77450 TRILBARDOU
☎ 01 60 61 08 75 & 06 11 23 87 23 📠 01 60 61 08 75
email: cantin.evelyne@voila.fr

Adjoining the church in this quiet and pretty village, behind a walled
garden, this solid 19th-century house offers a first-floor family suite
(one double, one twin) with bathroom and WC, and a balcony for
total relaxation. In the old housekeeper's cottage, with independent
access, are a triple and a room for four, both with private facilities.
Warm welcome guaranteed.

Prices s fr €50; d fr €58; extra person fr €20 **On Site** ⚑
Nearby ⛵ 4km ⚓ 8km ⚓ 5km Restaurant 6km ⚓ 0.5km 🏠 1km
⚑ 1km **Notes** No pets English spoken

VERDELOT

⚑ Ferme Saint Georges

Carole et Marc GENDRE
77510 VERDELOT
☎ 01 64 04 91 99 📠 01 64 04 95 92
email: contact@fermesaintgeorges.com
web: www.fermesaintgeorges.com

Five kilometres from the village, this restored farm sits in an agreeable
and quiet spot. Two doubles and a family suite (a double and a twin),
all with shower and WC, are found on the first floor. On the ground
floor are a large dining room, open fire and kitchenette. Meals by
reservation. Terrace and garden; horses on site.

Prices s fr €50; d fr €55; extra person fr €20 **Nearby** ⛵ 4km ⚓ 30km
⚑ 5km Restaurant 5km ⚓ 5km 🏠 5km ⚑ 12km **Notes** No pets
English spoken

VILLEMER

⚑ Le Gallois

Ghislaine et Dominique BON
1 rue du Pimard, 77250 VILLEMER
☎ 01 64 24 97 61 & 06 72 71 49 82
email: legallois.ch@wanadoo.fr
web: www.legallois.net

A tiny hamlet found one kilometre from the village, in the heart of
quiet countryside. An old renovated house with 5-acre garden offers
plentiful accommodation with independent access: two doubles, two
triples and a family room for four with double bed and two singles; all
rooms have shower and WC. Breakfast room on first floor. Reductions
for stays of several nights.

Prices s fr €50; d €60–€75; extra person fr €25; dinner fr €25
On Site ⚑ **Nearby** ⛵ 0.5km ⚓ 7km ⚑ 3km ⚓ Restaurant 3km
⚓ 0.8km 🏠 1km ⚑ 10km **Notes** No pets English spoken

VILLENEUVE-LE-COMTE

ⵌ Chambre d'hôtes

Eliane et René TEISSEDRE
55 Boulevard de l'Est, 77174 VILLENEUVE LE COMTE
☎ 01 60 43 28 27 📄 01 60 43 10 42
email: contact@chambres-erteissedre.com
web: www.chambres-erteissedre.com

This welcoming house with garden and terrace is set in the grounds of the owners' property. There is a lounge/dining room, a breakfast room, a double bedroom and four bedrooms suitable for four people, each with twin beds on a mezzanine. Rooms have private facilities and heating.

Prices s fr €48; d fr €57; extra person fr €22 **Nearby** ⵎ 10km ⵎ 10km ⵌ 12km Restaurant 0.1km ⵎ 0.1km ⵌ 0.2km ⵎ 4km **Notes** Pets admitted

---

VILLIERS-SAINT-GEORGES

ⵌ ⵜ ⵜ Chambres d'hôtes de Villiers St Georges

Brigitte et Emmanuel MORISSEAU
40 rue de Nogent, 77560 VILLIERS ST GEORGES
☎ 01 64 01 95 85 & 06 72 01 33 93 📄 01 64 01 25 88
email: emmanuel.morisseau@wanadoo.fr
web: http://perso.wanadoo.fr/emmanuel.morisseau

Just 14 kilometres from the medieval town of Provins, this property has three guest rooms in a converted farm building separate from the owners' home. Upstairs is a twin-bedded room and a double. On the ground floor is another twin-bedded room, with access suitable for disabled guests. All have private shower room and WC. Generous breakfasts; use of kitchen. Garden and orchard.

Prices s fr €43; d fr €49; extra person fr €20 **Nearby** ⵌ 18km ⵎ 40km ⵎ 4km Restaurant 3km ⵎ ⵌ 0.5km ⵎ 14km **Notes** No pets English spoken

VILLIERS-SOUS-GREZ

ⵌ ⵌ⌾ La Cerisaie

Christiane et André CHASTEL
10 rue de Larchant, 77760 VILLIERS SOUS GREZ
☎ 01 64 24 23 71 & 06 66 22 65 92 📄 01 64 24 23 71
email: andre.chastel@free.fr

A tastefully renovated detached house in a charming village on the edge of the forest, where André will share his passion for photography with you. On the first floor are a twin, a double, and a family suite with a single and a double room, all with own bathroom and WC. Meals by arrangement feature local products. Large living room, courtyard, terrace, garden.

Prices s fr €65; d fr €70; extra person fr €28; dinner fr €25 **Nearby** ⵌ 4km ⵎ 12km ⵌ 2km ⵌ 4km Restaurant 4km ⵌ 0.5km ⵌ 10km ⵌ 4km ⵌ 12km **Notes** No pets English spoken

---

VILLIERS-SUR-MORIN

ⵌ Castel-Morin

Catherine et Jacques SALEMBIER
23 rue du Bas de Villiers, 77580 VILLIERS SUR MORIN
☎ 01 64 63 72 14 & 06 60 41 22 69 📄 01 60 04 48 35
email: castelmorin@gmail.com

This village, which has inspired many artists, is in a forest 45 kilometres from Paris and close to Disneyland. The beautifully decorated 19th-century house has two double rooms, and a family suite for four with a double bed and two singles. Each has a private bath or shower room and WC. One hectare of grounds, bordered by a river.

Prices d €65-€80; extra person fr €20 **Nearby** ⵌ 2km ⵎ 5km ⵌ 0.5km ⵌ 5km Restaurant 0.6km ⵌ 3km ⵌ 0.5km ⵌ 0.6km **Notes** No pets English spoken

VAL-D'OISE

BREANCON

ⵌ Chambre d'hôtes

Doris BOURGEOIS
Le Château des Gourmets, 2, rue de l'Eglise,
95640 BREANCON
☎ 01 34 66 60 12
email: manoir.breancon@club.fr

Large airy bedrooms set in calm surroundings in an agricultural area of the Parc Naturel Régional du Vexin. One room with two double beds and bathroom with bathtub; one room with a double and a single, shower room, one room with two doubles and shower room. Cot free.

Prices s €70-€85; d €80-€90; t fr €110 **Nearby** ⵌ 5km ⵎ 4km ⵌ 10km ⵌ 10km Restaurant 3km ⵌ 3km ⵌ 2km ⵌ 12km **Notes** No pets English spoken

CHAUMONTEL

▦ Beauvilliers

Doris MANDY
oute de Baillon, 95270 CHAUMONTEL
☎ 01 30 29 99 61 & 06 81 25 28 46
email: doris@beauvilliers.com
web: www.beauvilliers.com

A former hunting lodge in a forest clearing in the Parc Naturel Régional d'Oise offering three beautiful double guest bedrooms, one of which has an additional folding bed; all have private shower room and WC. Several golf courses are close by, and Charles de Gaulle airport at Roissy is 25 kilometres away.

Prices s €60-€70; d €63-€75; extra person fr €15 **Nearby** ⛳ 1km ⊖ 5km ₶ 10km ⌖ 10km Restaurant 2km ♨ 2km ⊕ 10km ⑤ 2km ⌂ 4km **Notes** No pets English spoken

CHERENCE

▦ Le St-Denis

Andrée PERNELLE
rue des Cabarets, 95510 CHERENCE
☎ 01 34 78 15 02

This rural character house is peacefully set in a delightful, flower-filled garden in the heart of the village, on the border of the Parc Régional du Vexin Français. The five bedrooms each have private facilities and there is a dining room, open fireplace, TV, lounge, heating, terrace, garden furniture, and parking. Local attractions include the Château and Valley of the Seine, gliding, hot-air ballooning, the Route des Crêtes, the gardens at Giverny.

Prices not confirmed for 2008 **On Site** ⛳ **Nearby** ⊖ 4km ₶ 2km ⌖ 15km ♨ 4km ⌂ 16km **Notes** No pets English spoken

GENICOURT

▦ Chambre d'hôtes

Annette ROLLAND
Hameau de Gérocourt, 6 Rue Saint Mellon,
95600 GENICOURT
☎ 01 34 42 72 38 & 06 12 14 06 63 📄 01 34 42 70 91
email: annette.rolland@gmail.com
web: www.fermedegerocourt.free.fr

This property is on a large cereal farm. There are three spacious first floor rooms: two with twin beds, and a third with a double bed plus a single. All are bright and airy, with private bath or shower room and WC. Large living room with an open fire. There are grounds of about one hectare, with parking space.

Prices not confirmed for 2008 **Nearby** ⛳ 4km ⊖ 6km ₶ 5km Water sports 10km ♨ 6km ⊕ 2km ⌂ 3km **Notes** No pets

JAGNY-SOUS-BOIS

▦ ⦿ La Gentilhommière

Bernard et Marie RAYNAUD
42 rue Jeanest, 95850 JAGNY-SOUS-BOIS
☎ 01 34 71 85 08 & 06 03 64 52 31
email: gentilhommiere@neuf.fr
web: www.lagentilhommieredejagny.com

This large 19th-century house stands in its own quiet wooded grounds in the smart village of Jagny. The ground floor reception room is where breakfast is served. On the first floor is a huge triple room; on the second floor are a double room, a twin room, and a small salon. All have shower/WC facilities. A cot is available. The accommodation is smartly decorated, and the house has a warm pleasant feel.

Prices s €51-€66; d €66-€78; t fr €95; dinner fr €25 **Nearby** ⛳ 5km ⊖ 3km ₶ 10km ⌖ 5km Restaurant 4km ♨ 0.5km Spa 15km ⑤ 3km ⌂ 5km **Notes** No pets English spoken

PARMAIN

▦ Chambre d'hôtes

Laurent DELALEU
131 rue du Maréchal Foch, 95620 PARMAIN
☎ 01 34 73 02 92 📄 01 34 08 80 76
email: chambresdhotes.parmain@wanadoo.fr

This large working farm has an enclosed courtyard complete with tennis court. There are three large double bedrooms and a room with two singles and a double; all with private bathroom and wc. Kitchen and breakfast room, TV room in the vaulted cellar, indoor parking and terrace with garden furniture. Ideally located for guests without their own transport, there is lots to see and do in the immediate vicinity.

Prices not confirmed for 2008 **Nearby** ⛳ 2km ⊖ 2km ₶ 0.5km ⌖ 1km ⑤ 0.5km ⌂ 0.5km **Notes** No pets English spoken

PRESLES

▦ Chambre d'hôtes

Hervé et Blandine CLEMENT
12, ruelle Tortue, 95590 PRESLES
☎ 01 30 34 31 72 & 06 86 38 23 04
email: blandine.clement1@free.fr
web: www.gites-val-doise.com

This is a large restored 19th-century house, about half a kilometre outside the village. The accommodation comprises two units with independent access sleeping up to six people. Each unit has a mezzanine with small double bed and additional single, plus a double bed below with shower room/WC and kitchenette. Cot available. Landscaped grounds with orchard, parking space, terrace and games area.

Prices not confirmed for 2008 **Nearby** ⛳ 4km ⊖ 1km ₶ 0.5km ⌖ 4km ⑤ 0.5km ⌂ 0.2km **Notes** No pets English spoken

YVELINES

GARANCIERES

🎖️ 🐦 *La Ferme du Château*

M LAVENANT

5 route de Boissy, Hameau de Breuil - D42,
78890 GARANCIERES

☎ 01 34 86 53 94

This former farmhouse, dating from the 17th century, is in a pleasant setting about 30 kilometres from Versailles. Three attractively-decorated double bedrooms each have a private bath or shower room and WC, television and internet access. Large garden with furniture; two bikes available. Non-smoking property.

Prices not confirmed for 2008 **Nearby** ⚓ 5km ⚓ 4km ⚓ 5km Restaurant 3km ⚓ 3km ⚓ 3km ⚓ 4km **Notes** No pets English spoken

LA BOISSIERE-ECOLE

🎖️ ⚿ La Gâtine

M et M CHANZY-OLIVIE

15 route de Faverolles, 78125 LA BOISSIERE ECOLE

☎ 01 34 94 32 79

email: marion@lagatine.fr

web: www.lagatine.com

In a peaceful spot on the edge of the forest of Rambouillet, this property has six elegant and very comfortable bedrooms. On the ground floor are three doubles; upstairs is a triple room (double bed and a single) and two linked rooms - one with a double bed, one with twin beds. All rooms have private bathrooms and WCs. Cot, leisure area, large garden.

Prices d fr €75; t fr €95; extra person fr €20 **Nearby** ⚓ 2km ⚓ 17km ⚓ 15km ⚓ 15km Restaurant 10km ⚓ 4km ⚓ 15km ⚓ 3km ⚓ 15km **Notes** No pets English spoken

MOISSON

🎖️ 🍽️ **Chambre d'hôtes**

Brigitte LEVI

4, allée du Jamborée, 78840 MOISSON

☎ 01 34 79 37 20 🖨 01 34 79 37 58

email: blc.blevi@orange.fr

A 16th-century priory in a flower-filled garden in a village on a loop in the Seine. On the first floor are a double bedroom with private shower room, wc and sauna bath, and a second en suite room with small double bed. On the second floor is an en suite double room. Further bedrooms are available in an annexe. Video room, heated swimming pool (May to October), barbecue. Generous breakfasts and sometime brunch. Vintage car rides can be arranged.

Prices s fr €57; d fr €69; dinner fr €24 **On Site** 🏊 Private ⚓ **Nearby** ⚓ 1km ⚓ 1km ⚓ 0.5km Restaurant 0.1km ⚓ 1km ⚓ 0.1km ⚓ 7km **Notes** No pets English spoken

NEAUPHLE-LE-CHATEAU

🎖️ **Le Clos Saint Nicolas**

Marie-France DROUELLE

33, rue Saint Nicolas, 78640 NEAUPHLE-LE-CHATEAU

☎ 01 34 89 76 10 🖨 01 34 89 76 10

email: mariefrance.drouelle@wanadoo.fr

web: www.clos-saint-nicolas.com

Set in the middle of a park in the village of Neauphle-le-Château, this Napoleonic residence offers three very comfortable first-floor guest rooms with independent access from the winter garden. There are two double rooms and one twin, each with private bathroom facilities. Guests have use of period lounge. Pets admitted by reservation.

Prices s fr €90; d fr €90; extra person fr €21 **On Site** 🏊 **Nearby** ⚓ 3km ⚓ 5km ⚓ 3km Restaurant 0.1km ⚓ 1km ⚓ 0.2km ⚓ 3km **Notes** Pets admitted English spoken CC

ILE-DE-FRANCE

ORGEVAL

ⅲ La Thuilerie

Isabelle RENARD-DELAHAYE

321, rue de la Chapelle, 78630 ORGEVAL

☎ 01 39 75 40 23 & 06 80 62 25 04 📄 01 39 75 40 23

email: contact@lathuilerie.com

web: www.lathuilerie.com

This 19th-century house has a lot of character. It stands in its own enclosed gardens, in the heart of the village. There are two first floor bedrooms - a double, and one which can be a double or a twin. On the second floor is another double. All have private facilities and Wi-fi connection. A child's bed is available. Generous and varied breakfasts.

Prices s fr €90; d fr €90   **Nearby** ⚓ 2km ♫ 2km ✐ 1km ↖ 6km Restaurant 0.3km ⊕ 0.2km ❀ 10km 🏛 0.3km ⋙ 5km   **Notes** No pets English spoken   Open March to December.

PARAY-DOUAVILLE

ⅲ ❤ ♿ Lenainville

Philippe et Isabelle COUTEAU

4 rue de la Plaine, 78660 PARAY-DOUAVILLE

☎ 01 30 59 01 96 & 06 19 85 43 70 📄 01 30 59 01 96

email: icout@wanadoo.fr

web: www.vallee-aux-pages.com

Set in a quiet hamlet, this farmhouse offers comfortable, carefully decorated bedrooms. Ground floor room with a double and single, private shower/WC. Living room with fireplace. Upstairs double with own shower/WC and twin with bathroom and WC. Large open garden, conservatory. Baby equipment available. Breakfast can be taken on the terrace. Discount after two nights.

Prices s fr €60; d fr €65; extra person fr €15   **Nearby** ⚓ 8km ⊙ 25km ✐ 8km ↖ 8km Restaurant 8km ⊕ 8km 🏛 3km ⋙ 5km **Notes** No pets English spoken

SOINDRES

ⅲ ❤ Chambre d'hôtes

M-Claudine et Didier RAUX

20 bis rue Henri Duverdin, 78200 SOINDRES

☎ 01 34 76 57 44 & 06 78 79 51 48 📄 01 34 76 57 83

email: mc.rauxleduff@wanadoo.fr

web: http://perso.wanadoo.fr/fermedesvallees

This farm stands in the heart of a village and offers three beautiful bedrooms, with their own entrance. On the ground floor is a double room; upstairs is a single room, and a further double. Cot and extra bed available. All of the rooms have a TV, private bath or shower room and WC. Private terrace, enclosed grounds, garden furniture, parking. Closed last two weeks of August.

Prices s fr €50; d fr €57; extra person fr €19   **On Site** ❀ **Nearby** ⚓ 5km ♫ 5km ✐ 4km Restaurant 2km 🏛 2km ⋙ 5km **Notes** No pets English spoken   Open September to 14 August.

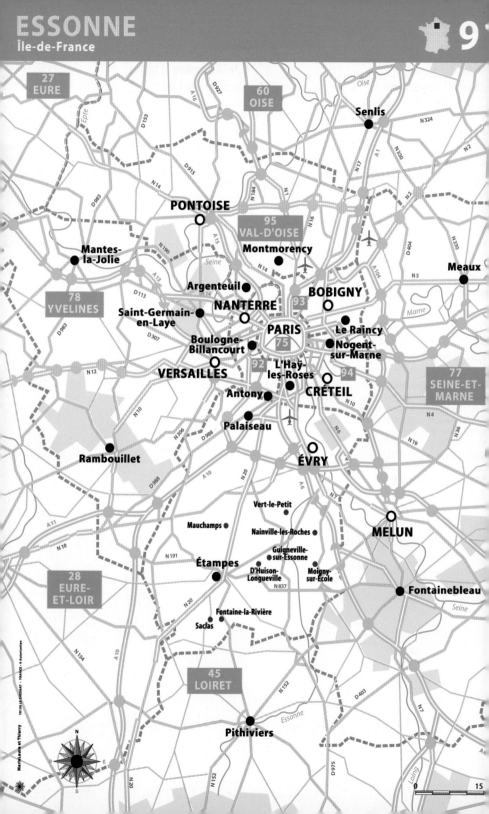

EINE-ET-MARNE
e-de-France

77

60 OISE

02 AISNE

95 AL-D'OISE

Senlis

Crouy-sur-Ourcq

Château-Thierry

Marne

Juilly

ontmorency

Meaux

BOBIGNY

93

Trilbardou

ANTERRE

PARIS

75

Le Raincy

Nogent-sur-Marne

Marne

St-Germain-sur-Morin

Gouvernes

Crécy-la-Chapelle

Villiers-sur-Morin

Pommeuse

Verdelot

St-Denis-lès-Rebais

51 MARNE

L'Haÿ-les-Roses

94

CRÉTEIL

Villeneuve-le-Comte

Favières

St-Augustin

St-Rémy-la-Vanne

Antony

aiseau

Choisy-en-Brie

Châtres

Amillis

ÉVRY

Evry-Grégy

Chaumes-en-Brie

Courpalay

Villiers-St-Georgès

Crisenoy

Châteaubleau

Provins

Bréau

St-Ouen-en-Brie

St-Loup-de-Naud

MELUN

Sivry-Courtry

Sourdun

Boissise-la-Bertrand

Lizines

Ste-Colombe

Nogent-sur-Seine

La Chapelle-Rablais

Chartrettes

Le Châtelet-en-Brie

Cessoy-en-Montois

Échouboulains

Les Ormes-sur-Voulzie

91 ESSONNE

Thomery

Seine

10 AUBE

Grisy-sur-Seine

Achères-la-Forêt

Fontainebleau

Bourron-Marlotte

Noisy-sur-École

Villiers-sous-Grez

La Chapelle-la-Reine

Villemer

Buthiers

Préaux

ithiviers

Souppes-sur-Loing

Egreville

Sens

45 LOIRET

89 YONNE

0   15 km

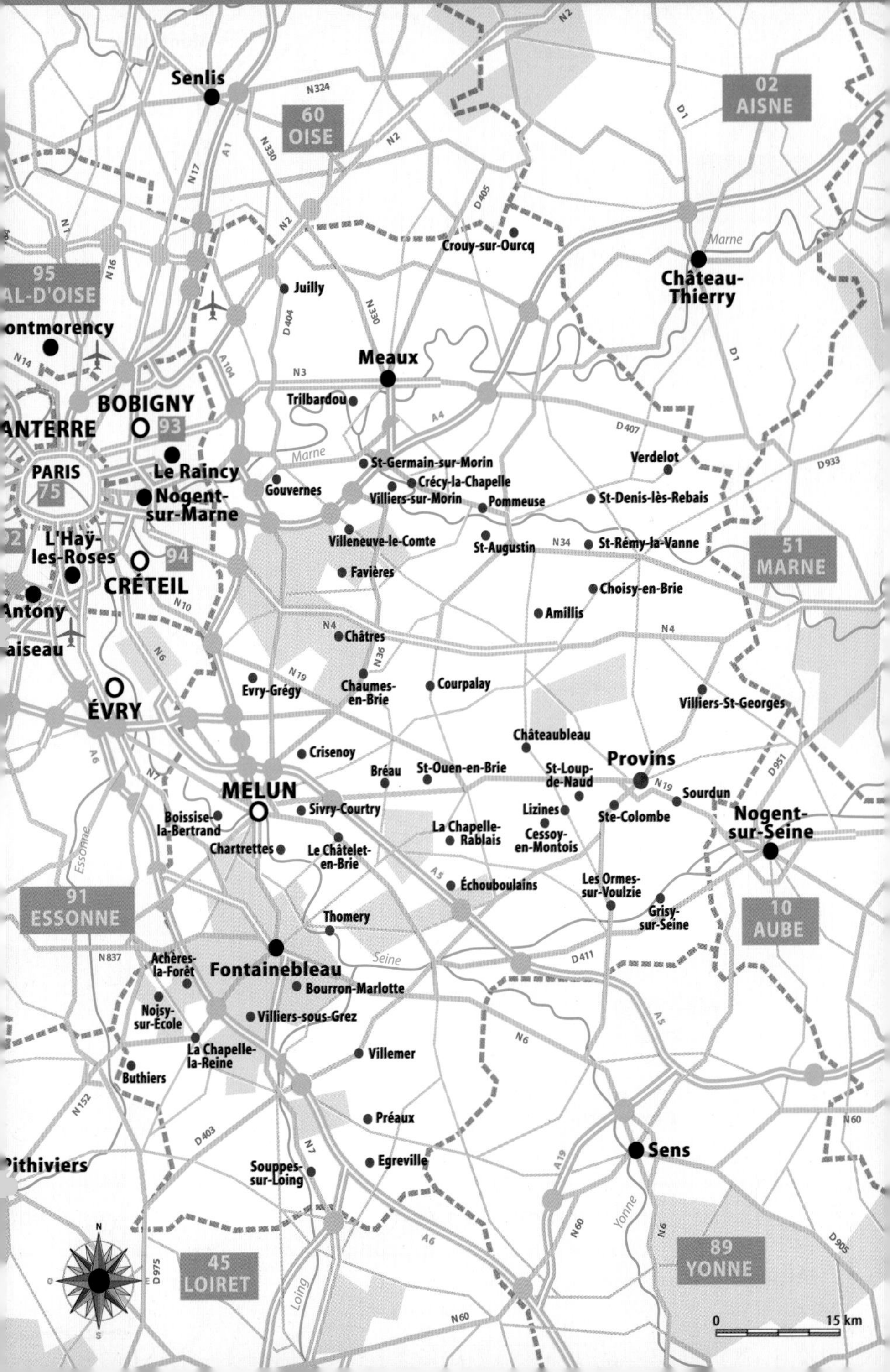

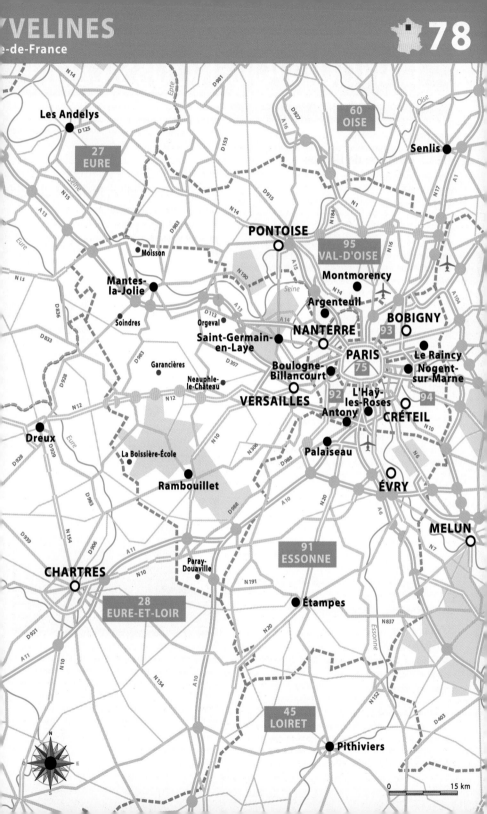

LANGUEDOC-ROUSSILLON

AUDE

ALBIERES

⚓ ॏ◯ⱡ **Domaine de Boutou**

Christian LAFARGUE

11330 ALBIERES

☎ 04 68 70 04 05

In the heart of Cathar country, five first-floor, double rooms with private facilities are available in this house, close to a small Corbières village. The centrally heated house has a lounge, large terrace, well-kept garden. Close to hiking trails and the castles of Arques, Termes and Peyrepertuse. Information about the surrounding area is available.

Prices s fr €48; d fr €50; t fr €70; extra person fr €20; dinner fr €20 **Nearby** ⚓7km ✿4km ⭢35km Restaurant 15km ♨7km ⓑ10km ⋙32km **Notes** No pets Open March to November.

ALZONNE

⚓ ॏ◯ⱡ **Villa les Cèdres**

Pascale CHARPENTIER

2 Rue des Ecoles, 11170 ALZONNE

☎ 04 68 76 93 43 & 06 25 98 03 28

email: maud.charpentier2@wanadoo.fr

web: www.villalescedres.com

Just 15 kilometres from Carcassonne, this 19th-century mansion has a beautiful village location, close to interesting places to visit. It has three first floor bedrooms (one grade 2, two grade 3), all with private facilities. Breakfast can be served in the garden; other meals available by arrangement. The owner, who is an artist, will be delighted to introduce you to the delights of the Cathar country.

Prices s €55-€60; d €58-€68; t fr €78; dinner fr €22 **On Site** ✿ Private ⭢ **Nearby** ⚓5km ⭢12km ✿1km Restaurant 0.3km ♨0.5km Spa 15km ⋙15km **Notes** No pets English spoken

See advert under CARCASSONNE

ANTUGNAC

⚓ **Domaine de Mournac**

J.Claude et Arlette BEZIAU

11190 ANTUGNAC

☎ 04 68 74 21 10 & 06 03 90 63 06 🖷 04 68 74 21 10

email: contact@mournac.com

web: www.mournac.com

Old oaks and walnut trees surround this former coaching inn. There are four bedrooms (three doubles and a family suite for four), all with en suite facilities. The building has been extensively renovated; outside are terraces, a swimming pool, and stunning views towards the Pyrenees. An unforgettable place in a special location. Barbecue available. Reductions for longer stays.

Prices s €85-€100; d €90-€100; t fr €130; extra person fr €30 **On Site** Private ⭢ **Nearby** ⚓15km ⭢40km ✿3km Restaurant 4km Freshwater sports 5km ♨3km ✿4km ⓑ4km ⋙7km **Notes** No pets English spoken CC

AZILLE

⚓ **Chambre d'hôtes Pierre et Claudine**

Pierre et Claudine TENENBAUM

5 Av du Minervois, 11700 AZILLE

☎ 04 68 91 56 90

email: pierreetclaudine@tele2.fr

web: www.pierreetclaudine.com

In the centre of a Minervois, this house has a private garden with furniture and offers four en suite guest rooms: a triple with sitting room and three doubles, one with private terrace and another with sitting room and fireplace. Central heating, communal room and lounge. Nearby attractions include the footpaths, walks along the Canal du Midi, and Lake Jouarres with bathing.

Prices d €57-€59; extra person fr €17 **Nearby** ⚓8km ⭢30km Sea 48km ✿4km ⭢ Restaurant 0.1km ♨ ✿3km ⓑ0.1km ⋙30km **Notes** Pets admitted English spoken CC

⚓ ॏ◯ⱡ **Les Cordeliers**

Herve et Christine LEON

22 Allee Pol Lapeyre, 11700 AZILLE

☎ 04 68 91 31 72

email: cordeliersducomtal@wanadoo.fr

web: http://lescordeliers.c.la

With an ideal location between Béziers and Carcassonne this house is an excellent base for exploring the many attractions of the area. It has four bedrooms: three doubles and a family room for four, all with private facilities. The enclosed interior garden is an ideal spot for breakfast; other meals available at weekends by arrangement.

Prices s fr €60; d fr €65; extra person fr €15; dinner fr €25 **On Site** Restaurant ✿ **Nearby** ⚓3km Sea 48km ✿2km ⭢2km ♨ ⓑ10km ⋙10km **Notes** Pets admitted English spoken

BAGES

⫟⫟⫟ ⚑ Les Palombières d'Estarac

M PENFEYREF et S AEBY

Prat De Cest, 11100 BAGES

☎ 04 68 42 45 56 & 06 76 82 77 82

📄 04 68 42 45 56

email: estarac@wanadoo.fr

web: www.palombieres-estarac.com

This magnificent and charming property is set in 3 hectares of richly wooded parkland, and enjoys the peace of an outstanding area at the heart of a National Reserve. Relax in the reading room, music room, lounge with open fire and TV. The comfortable rooms include the Océane with a dressing room, the Soleilad du Olivine with balcony and a suite with sitting room, balcony and extra bed if required. Each has private facilities.

Prices s €58-€120; d €68-€130; t fr €143; extra person fr €13; dinner fr €25 **Nearby** ⌁ 6km Sea 18km ✎ 3km ⚲ 6km Restaurant 3km ⚘ 6km ⛪ 5km ⚒ 10km **Notes** No pets English spoken Open February to 14 December. CC

BIZANET

⫟⫟⫟ *Domaine St Jean*

Didier DELBOURG

1200 BIZANET

☎ 04 68 45 17 31 & 06 03 25 31 24 📄 04 68 45 17 31

email: didierdelbourgbizanet@yahoo.fr

Deep in the Cathar region, this house is in a winemaking area in the heart of Corbières and offers four guest rooms with private facilities in an independent building, including one family room with mezzanine and a triple room with terrace. Lounge and dining room; breakfast can be taken on the terrace where guests can enjoy the gardens.

Prices not confirmed for 2008 **Nearby** ⚓ 15km Sea 25km ✎ 12km ⚲ 3km ⛪ 3km ⚒ 12km **Notes** No pets CC

⫟⫟⫟ *Domaine de la Barthe St-Pierre*

Jean MALRIC

1200 BIZANET

☎ 04 68 45 17 27 & 04 68 45 10 66

Not far from the village, in the vineyards of Frontfroide with its Cistercian abbey, this beautiful family house has a shady garden full of flowers. The proprietors are winegrowers and provide three lovely upstairs bedrooms, each with shower and wc, and are happy to share their large lounge and sitting room with its open fire. Guests are encouraged to visit the local church and cemetery with tombs of the local seigneurs.

Prices not confirmed for 2008 **Nearby** ⚓ 15km Sea 25km ✎ 12km ⛪ 1km ⚒ 12km **Notes** No pets CC

⫟⫟⫟ *La Margelide*

Blaise et Halima ANDREO

27 Rue De La Gare, 11200 BIZANET

☎ 04 68 48 39 68 & 06 63 62 32 03

email: reservation@lamargelide.com

This village property is in Corbières, close to the Abbey of Fontfroide and many of the Cathar Castles. It offers four upstairs bedrooms: two are doubles, one has three single beds, and one has a double bed and a single. All have private facilities, and are heated by solar energy. The rooms are beautifully arranged, and outside are attractive gardens.

Prices not confirmed for 2008 **Nearby** ⚓ 12km Sea 22km ✎ 9km ⚒ 12km **Notes** Pets admitted CC

BOUTENAC

⫟⫟⫟ ⚑ Domaine du Griffon

Brigitte et Patrick DELVAULX

8 Route De Ferrals, 11200 BOUTENAC

☎ 04 68 27 07 29 & 06 25 15 92 66 📄 04 68 27 07 29

email: domaine-du-griffon@wanadoo.fr

web: www.domaine-du-griffon.fr

In a village below the Château of Boutenac, the centre of the Corbières wine region, the hosts have created five rooms on the first floor of a 19th-century wine-grower's house. Each characterful room - all with private facilities - recalls the history of the Cathar country, and makes you want to explore this historic area. Meals can be served in the garden.

Prices s fr €78; d fr €78; extra person fr €20; dinner fr €25 **On Site** ⚘ **Nearby** ⚓ 35km Sea 30km ✎ 6km ⚲ 7km Restaurant 7km ⛪ 0.3km ⚑ 0.2km ⚒ 2km **Notes** No pets English spoken

CABRESPINE

⫟⫟⫟ ⚑ Chambre d'hôtes

Marie Elisabeth THOMAS

rue Pierre Duhem, L'Olivette, 11160 CABRESPINE

☎ 04 68 26 19 25

email: olivette.cabrespine@wanadoo.fr

web: http//perso.wanadoo.fr/olivette.cabrespine

A family home in the heart of the village, with a terraced garden full of flowers, with all their many perfumes and colours. There are two double rooms and a grade 2 family room, all with private bath or shower rooms and WCs. Walkers will appreciate the easy access to footpaths. Meals are available, by arrangement.

Prices s fr €45; d fr €50; t fr €60; extra person fr €10; dinner fr €18 **Nearby** ⚓ 5km ✎ 0.5km Restaurant 5km ⛪ 5km ⚑ 5km ⚒ 30km **Notes** No pets Open March to January. CC

CARCASSONNE

Villa Les Cèdres
Chambres d'hôtes de Charme
En Pays Carcassonnais
AUDE
2, rue des écoles
11170 Alzonne

10 minutes from the famous medieval city of Carcassonne, Villa les Cèdres offers charming guestrooms in a lovely 19th-century manor surrounded by greenery in the middle of a little village. Local attractions include Châteaux de Lastours, Saissac and Canal du Midi. Pascale and Alain invite you to share their knowledge of their region and to enjoy meals created using local produce.
Parking facilities available.

Tel: 00 33 (0)4 68 76 93 43
maud.charpentier2@wanadoo.fr
www.villalescedres.com

CASCASTEL

▦▦▦▦ Domaine Grand Guilhem

Severine et Gilles CONTREPOIS
11360 CASCASTEL
☎ 04 68 45 86 67 & 06 88 79 26 98
🖷 04 68 45 29 58
email: gguilhem@aol.com
web: www.grandguilhem.com

This pretty 14th-century winemaker's house, built from local stone and with wooded grounds, has four very comfortable rooms, each with lounge and private facilities. There is a dining room with fireplace and piano, lounge, heating, car park, swimming pool. Breakfast can be taken in the garden with panoramic views of the château and surrounding vineyards.

Prices s fr €78; d fr €85; t fr €102; extra person fr €20   **On Site** 🌊 Private ⭧   **Nearby** ⛷ 7km ♨ 30km Sea 25km Restaurant 0.2km ⤸ 2km ⛳ 0.3km ⋈ 30km   **Notes** No pets English spoken

CASTELNAU-D'AUDE

▦▦▦ Clos Cavailles

Maite CHINCHOLLE-WULVERYCK
2 av du Paradis, 11700 CASTELNAU D'AUDE
☎ 04 68 49 06 62 & 06 80 32 66 96
email: contact@closcavailles.com
web: www.closcavailles.com

A village between Corbières and Minervois, just two kilometres from the Canal du Midi, is the location for this beautiful house. It has four double bedrooms, all with private facilities. There is an enclosed garden, a terrace with garden furniture, and on-site parking. Reductions out of season.

Prices s fr €55; d fr €65; extra person fr €15   **Nearby** ⛷ 10km Sea 45km ♨ 1km ⤸ 10km Restaurant 2km ⤸ 0.2km ⛳ 10km 🏛 0.1km ⋈ 11km   **Notes** No pets English spoken Open Easter to October. CC

CAUX-ET-SAUZENS

▦▦▦ Domaine des Castelles

Isabelle PUAUD
11170 CAUX ET SAUZENS
☎ 04 68 72 03 60 🖷 04 68 72 03 60

This pretty house was once home to winemakers and now offers three very large guest rooms: the 'Sunflower Room', the 'Pink Laurel Room' and the 'Palm-tree' suite, all for five people with private facilities and views of the park. In summer, breakfast is served on the terrace. No smoking.

Prices s €60-€65; d €65-€70; t fr €90; extra person fr €20 **Nearby** ⛷ 7km ♨ 7km ♨ 2km ⤸ 5km Restaurant 1km ⤸ 5km ⛳ 5km 🏛 1km ⋈ 7km   **Notes** No pets English spoken

CONQUES-SUR-ORBIEL

▦▦▦ ⭕ La Maison Pujol

Veronique PHI
17 Rue Frederic Mistral, 11600 CONQUES SUR ORBIEL
☎ 04 68 26 98 18
email: info@lamaisonpujol.com
web: http://lamaisonpujol.com

In the Cathar country, not far from Carcassonne, the Canal du Midi, and the vineyards of Cabardès and Minervois, this bright and cheerful house with its warm atmosphere, striking décor and modern paintings has four non-smoking bedrooms. One of the rooms is a suite for four, and all of them have private facilities. Meals and picnic lunches available by arrangement.

Prices s fr €70; d fr €80; dinner fr €25   **Nearby** ⛷ 10km ♨ 10km Restaurant 0.4km ⤸ 1km ⛳ 10km 🏛 8km ⋈ 8km   **Notes** No pets English spoken

CUCUGNAN

⑪ *L'Ecurie de Cucugnan*

oel et Lydie GAUCH

0 rue A.Mir, 11350 CUCUGNAN

☎ 04 68 33 37 42 & 06 76 86 38 52 🗐 04 68 33 37 42

mail: ecurie.cucugnan@orange.fr

his is the village of Alphonse Daudet's famous fictional character, the uré de Cucugnan. The property has five very comfortable double edrooms, all with air-conditioning, private bathroom and WC. arge lounge with open fire. Outside, guests will find a garden and errace with wonderful views across the countryside and vineyards of orbières.

rices not confirmed for 2008 **Nearby** ⚓ 1km Sea 50km ⚑ 3km
⦁ 8km 🏠 4km 🚶 45km **Notes** No pets English spoken

DOUZENS

⑪ ⓘ **Chambre d'hôtes**

atricia DENIAUX

Domaine Du Parc, 3 Rue Du Barri, 11700 DOUZENS

☎ 06 77 88 48 53 & 04 68 24 88 78

mail: domaineduparc@free.fr

web: http://domaineleparc.free.fr

etween Narbonne and Carcassonne, just three kilometres from ne Canal du Midi, this air-conditioned house has some beautifully estored guest rooms. They sleep from two to four people, they are right with plenty of space, and they all have views over the grounds. ll the rooms have private showers and WCs. Swimming pool, terrace, oules, garden with ancient trees.

rices d €67–€82; extra person fr €15; dinner fr €21   **On Site** Private ⚓ **earby** ⚓ 10km Sea 35km ⚑ 0.5km ⛲ 0.5km 🚶 10km **Notes** Pets dmitted English spoken CC

DURBAN-CORBIERES

⑪ *Le Clos des Rosalines*

elle GALINIER

v des Corbieres, 11360 DURBAN-CORBIERES

☎ 04 68 45 84 60 & 06 83 07 38 45 🗐 04 68 45 86 44

mail: contact@chambreshotes-rosalines.com

web: www.chambreshotes-rosalines.com

 the heart of Corbières, on the route of the Châteaux Cathares, this elcoming home is full of charm and offers four characterful rooms or two to three people, equipped with private facilities. Guests can ke breakfast on the patio.

rices not confirmed for 2008 **Nearby** Sea 25km ⚑ 1km ⛲ 1km
⦁ 25km **Notes** No pets English spoken CC

ESPERAZA

⑪⑪ **La Maison du Chapelier**

Andrew RICHARDSON

7 Rue Elie Sermet, 11260 ESPERAZA

☎ 04 68 74 22 49

email: andy@esperaza.net

web: www.esperaza.net

Not far from the famous village of Rennes-le-Château, this property has five guest bedrooms. One room is on the ground floor, and four are upstairs. All have private bath/shower rooms and WCs, but those for one of the first-floor rooms are not en suite. Lounge, extensive grounds with plenty of shade.

Prices s €60; d €75; t €95; extra person €20 **Nearby** ⚓ 6km ⚑ 1km
↖ ⛲ 1km Spa 5km 🍽 1km **Notes** No pets English spoken CC

FABREZAN

⑪⑪ ⓘ *La Maison de Leonie*

Hubert et Elisabeth DE GIACOMI

GITES DE FRANCE SERVICES AUDE

☎ 04 68 27 68 52 & 06 33 05 75 76

email: degiacomi.hubert@wanadoo.fr

web: http://perso.orange.fr/lamaisondeleonie/

A 19th-century stone-built property in Corbières, close to the abbeys of Lagrasse and Fontfroide and convenient for visiting several of the Cathar sites. Three air-conditioned rooms comprise a double, a twin and a triple, all with bath or shower room and WC. Outside are olive trees and vineyards. Meals are available by arrangement.

Prices not confirmed for 2008 **Nearby** ⚓ 10km Sea 40km ⚑ 4km
⛲ 4km 🏠 10km 🚶 10km **Notes** No pets CC

FANJEAUX

⑪⑪ **Relais St Dominique**

Norbert et Nadine MICOULEAU

11170 FANJEAUX

☎ 04 68 24 68 17 🗐 04 68 24 68 18

email: norbert.micouleau@wanadoo.fr

web: www.lerelaisdesaintdominique.com

At the foot of the medieval village of Fanjeaux, half-way between Carcassonne and Mirepoix, this is an ideal base for exploring a fascinating area. There are six bedrooms, each sleeping from two to four people, all with private bathrooms and WCs. Attractive grounds with swimming pool.

Prices s fr €53; d fr €70; t fr €91; extra person fr €15 **On Site** Private ⚓ **Nearby** Restaurant 2km ⛲ 2km 🏠 0.2km 🚶 5km **Notes** No pets English spoken CC

FERRALS-LES-CORBIERES

⊞ Le Logis de Dame Salimonde

Christine et Pierre LAFITTE

18 Rue Des Nobles, 11200 FERRALS-LES-CORBIERES

☎ 04 68 43 57 35 & 06 70 48 70 04

email: contact@logisdamesalimonde.com

web: www.logisdamesalimonde.com

The home of winegrowers, this property is located at the crossing of the Frontfroide Abbey and the Cathars Castle roads, at the heart of Corbières wine country. Two rooms have private shower/wc; the family suite has a bathroom. On the Mediterranean patio, you can sample the wines of Corbières and local produce. Parking nearby; garage available.

Prices s fr €40; d fr €50 **On Site** ⌂ Restaurant ⌘ **Nearby** ⌘ 7km Sea 45km ⌁ 7km ⌂ ⌘ 7km **Notes** No pets

FLEURY-D'AUDE

⊞ Domaine la Tour la Pagèze

Miguel et Claudine MODESTIN

Route des Cabanes, 11560 FLEURY D' AUDE

☎ 04 68 33 85 06 📄 04 68 33 72 82

web: www.domaine-lapageze.com

Three rooms in a working vineyard property between the Aude estuary and the sea. An unforgettable location in the beautiful setting of a natural park. Wine-tasting of the estate's produce available. Rooms for two to four people are on the first floor, with en suite bathrooms. Large living room with terrace overlooking the sea. There are plenty of small local restaurants.

Prices d €60-€70; t fr €80; extra person fr €5 **Nearby** ⌘ 4km ⌁ 25km Sea 3km ⌁ 3km ⌁ 4km Restaurant 4km ⌂ 4km ⌂ 4km ⌂ 18km **Notes** No pets English spoken CC

GINCLA

⊞ Chambre d'hôtes

Jean-Charles BRUCHET

2 route de Boucheville, 11140 GINCLA

☎ 04 68 20 50 92 & 06 75 17 92 23 📄 04 68 20 50 92

email: j.charles.bruchet@wanadoo.fr

web: www.multimania.com/bruchet

Magnificent forests with plenty of footpaths surround this beautiful village house, between the Aude and the eastern Pyrenees. There are five bedrooms (two of them grade 2), sleeping from two to four people, all with private facilities. The owner is a cabinet maker who has made most of the furniture. River close by, with trout fishing.

Prices not confirmed for 2008 **On Site** ⌁ **Nearby** ⌘ 8km ⌂ 7km ⌂ 14km ⌂ 25km **Notes** Pets admitted English spoken Open April to September.

HOMPS

⊞ |◯| Le Jardin d'Homps

Nina BOURDON

21 Grande Rue, 11200 HOMPS

☎ 04 68 91 39 50 & 06 11 29 12 71

📄 04 68 91 41 50

email: ljdh@wanadoo.fr

web: www.jardinhomps.com

This mansion, located in its own wooded grounds in the heart of a village on the Canal du Midi, has five beautiful rooms, all with their own bath or shower room and WC. Lounges available for guest use; garden with terraces, tennis courts, swimming pool, enclosed parking, meals available.

Prices s €75-€95; d €84-€105; extra person fr €30; dinner fr €30 **On Site** Restaurant ⌘ Private ⌁ Private tennis court **Nearby** ⌘ 3km Sea 20km ⌁ 2km ⌂ 0.1km ⌂ 8km **Notes** No pets English spoken CC

⊞ |◯| Relais des Chevaliers de Malte

Pascale HAYT

3 Av du Languedoc, 11200 HOMPS

☎ 04 68 49 90 94

email: pascale.rey5@wanadoo.fr

web: http://perso.wanadoo.fr/relaischevaliers/

In a village on the Canal du Midi, between Carcassonne and Narbonne, this beautiful and historic house has five bedrooms, all with private facilities. Four are on the first floor, with a family suite for four on the second floor. The house has a splendid stone circular staircase and outside is a courtyard where breakfast and (by arrangement) other meals can be served.

Prices d fr €85; extra person fr €20; dinner fr €18 **Nearby** ⌘ 3km ⌂ 30km Sea 35km ⌁ 1km Restaurant 0.1km ⌂ Spa 30km ⌂ 8km **Notes** No pets Open April to October (open in winter for groups). CC

LABASTIDE-ESPARBAIRENQUE

⊞ |◯| Chambre d'hôtes

Dominique et Pascale COIGNET

Coumo Jama, 11380 LABASTIDE ESPARBAIRENQUE

☎ 04 68 26 35 44 📄 04 68 26 35 44

email: coumojama@wanadoo.fr

In the heart of the Montagne Noire, surrounded by meadows and chestnut trees, this converted sheepfold has wonderful views across the valley. There are three guest rooms, two with a split level arrangement involving wooden steps which are not suitable for children aged under seven. All the rooms have private bath or shower and WC. Meals by arrangement.

Prices not confirmed for 2008 **Nearby** ⌘ 4km ⌁ 1km ⌂ 3km ⌂ 5km ⌂ 28km **Notes** No pets CC

LABECEDE-LAURAGAIS

▦ ❦ ⵔ◯⵩ *Domaine de Villemagne*

CEA LAFOUCADE

ina GACQUIERE, 11400 LABECEDE LAURAGAIS

☎ 04 68 60 44 89 & 06 12 76 59 56 ▤ 04 68 60 44 89

mail: jean.gacquiere@wanadoo.fr

This house has a wonderful setting with panoramic views of the Pyrenees from its south-facing terrace. The three bedrooms, each sleeping two or three guests, all have private shower rooms and WCs. There is a guests' kitchen and lounge. Good access to footpaths and the Lac de St-Ferreol.

Prices not confirmed for 2008 **On Site** ⵔ **Nearby** ℰ 15km ♨ 3km ⵏ 15km ⵏ 15km **Notes** Pets admitted English spoken CC

LANET

▦ ⵔ◯⵩ *La Maison du Pont de l'Orbieu*

Jean-Marie LIVET

1330 LANET

☎ 04 68 70 09 34

In the heart of the Corbières, this house - formerly a basket-maker's - overlooks the Orbieu River. It is surrounded by oak forests and limestone gorges. There are four guest rooms, all with private facilities. The hosts have a great love of this area, and hope to pass some of that on to their guests. Lounge with open fire, meals available.

Prices not confirmed for 2008 **On Site** ℰ **Nearby** ⵔ 15km ♨ 7km ⵏ 7km **Notes** No pets

LAURE-MINERVOIS

▦ ❦ ⵔ◯⵩ & *Domaine du Siestou*

vie BRUNEL

1800 LAURE MINERVOIS

☎ 04 68 78 30 81

mail: domainedusiestou@wanadoo.fr

web: www.lesiestou.com

This smallholding property has four non-smoking upstairs bedrooms, three doubles and a triple. Downstairs there is a family room for five, with its own entrance. Large dining room with lounge area; garden with shade from pine trees. Wine-tasting; meals by arrangement, except Wednesdays and Sundays.

Prices s fr €55; d fr €70; extra person fr €20; dinner fr €20 **On Site** ⵩ rivate ⵏ **Nearby** ♨ 18km ℰ 4km Restaurant 3km ♨ 3km ⵏ 4km ⵏ 18km **Notes** Pets admitted English spoken CC

LEUCATE

▦ *Les Maisons de Pierre*

ierre VIGIER

GITES DE FRANCE SERVICES AUDE

☎ 04 68 40 98 55 ▤ 04 68 40 98 55

mail: lesmaisonsdepierre@laposte.net

Three distinctive guest rooms in a family house on the main street of a winemaking village: a family suite and two double rooms with private facilities. Dining room, lounge with fireplace and television, courtyard garden, car park and patio. Walks and bike riding are possible around the lakes and cliffs of the area. Visit the oyster-farms, the local windsurfing centre and the Leucate cellar where you can sample the wines. Wi-fi available.

Prices s fr €50; d fr €50; t fr €81; extra person fr €15 **On Site** ⵩ **Nearby** ⵔ 3km ♨ 30km Sea 2km ℰ 3km ⵏ 1km Restaurant 0.1km ♨ 0.8km Spa 15km ⵩ 0.1km ⵏ 4km **Notes** No pets English spoken

LIMOUX

▦ ⵔ◯⵩ *Domaine de la Moneze Basse*

M et Mme DEVRIES

11300 LIMOUX

☎ 04 68 74 29 63 & 06 26 46 08 75

email: devries.martine@wanadoo.fr

web: http://lamonezebasse.monsite.wanadoo.fr

Close to Limoux, this stone built house is on the slopes where the grapes for the Blanquette de Limoux sparkling wine are grown. There are five bedrooms, each for two or three people, and all with en suite facilities. A large lounge opens onto a south-facing terrace, with garden furniture and plenty of shade.

Prices not confirmed for 2008 **Nearby** ⵔ 4km ℰ 1km ♨ 2.5km ⵩ 2.5km ⵏ 2.5km **Notes** No pets

MAILHAC

▦ *Le Coq du Nord*

Iain et Patricia SINCLAIR

27 Chemin Des Fonts, 11120 MAILHAC

☎ 04 68 44 07 75 & 06 31 22 56 69 ▤ 04 68 44 07 75

email: info@lecoqdunord.com

web: www.lecoqdunord.com

In the village of Mailhac, amongst the Minervois vineyards and olive groves, this beautiful house stands in its own extensive grounds. The five bedrooms all have telephones, private shower rooms and WCs. Breakfasts can be served outdoors, in the conservatory or in the dining room. The Scottish hosts will be happy to tell you all about the area.

Prices d fr €75; extra person fr €15 **On Site** Private ⵏ **Nearby** ⵔ 5km Sea 30km ℰ 5km ♨ 2km ⵏ 15km **Notes** No pets English spoken CC

MAS-SAINTES-PUELLES

▦ ⦿ Peniche Kapadokya

Nathalie AUGUSTE
Ecluse de la Mediterranee, 11400 MAS SAINTES PUELLES
☎ 04 68 23 46 71 & 06 86 95 71 36
email: kapadoky@wanadoo.fr
web: www.enpeniche.com

These three chambres d'hôtes are on board a canal boat, moored at a lock near Castelnaudary on the Canal du Midi. All of the rooms have private showers and WCs, and a large lounge gives access to two sun terraces from which you can appreciate the peaceful beauty of the location. The towpath can be explored on foot or by mountain bike. Meals by arrangement.

Prices s fr €70; d fr €70; dinner fr €25   **On Site** ⌁ ☀   **Nearby** ⌚ 8km Restaurant 2km ⚘ 6km ⌂ 2km ⋙ 10km   **Notes** No pets English spoken

MONTREAL

▦ Domaine de Caraman

William VAN DEN AKKER
11290 MONTREAL
☎ 04 68 76 31 33
email: info@domainecaraman.com
web: www.domainecaraman.com

This is a beautifully rural spot with wonderful views, three kilometres from the village and 20 kilometres from Carcassonne. There are four double rooms, all on the first floor with private shower room and WC. A large living area with an open fireplace leads onto a south-facing terrace. Way-marked mountain bike circuits close by.

Prices not confirmed for 2008   **Nearby** ⌚ 10km ⌁ 3km ⚘ 3km ⌂ 3km ⋙ 7km   **Notes** No pets English spoken

MOUSSOULENS

▦ La Rougeanne

Monique et Paul Andre GLORIEUX
11170 MOUSSOULENS
☎ 04 68 24 46 30 & 06 61 94 69 99
email: info@larougeanne.com
web: www.larougeanne.com

Between the Canal du Midi and the Montagnes Noire, just 13 kilometres from Carcassonne, this beautiful country house stands in its own wooded grounds. It has four fine bedrooms: two split-level rooms for up to five people, and two others which have access to a terrace with views of the Pyrenees. Children's books; internet connections in bedrooms.

Prices s €70-€80; d €75-€85; t €90-€100; extra person fr €15   **On Site** ⌁   **Nearby** ⌚ 8km ⚘ 1km ⋙ 13km   **Notes** No pets English spoken CC

MOUX

▦ ❦ ⦿ Relais de l'Alaric

Francoise DUFOUR
4 Chemin Des Clauzes, 11700 MOUX
☎ 04 68 43 97 68 & 06 62 48 63 53   ▤ 04 68 43 97 70
email: relaisdalaric@wanadoo.fr

This family house, on the edge of a village, has five first-floor bedrooms, all with private bath or shower rooms and WCs. Lounge with open fire, books and TV. Painting, sculpture, basketwork and aeroplane flights can be arranged, as well as wine-tasting and an introduction to geo-biology.

Prices not confirmed for 2008   **Nearby** ⌚ 8km Sea 42km ⌁ 5km ⚘ 12km ⌂ 1km ⋙ 12km   **Notes** Pets admitted English spoken Open 16 April to December. CC

NARBONNE

▦ Château de Joncquières

11100 NARBONNE
☎ 04 68 42 70 01 & 06 30 74 10 98
email: visagesetvins@vvo.fr
web: www.chateaudejonquieres.com

Close to Narbonne, and on the edge of the Parc Naturel de la Narbonnaise, this house has four beautiful double bedrooms, all air-conditioned and with en suite bathrooms, WCs and televisions. There is a sauna; wine-tasting can be arranged, and there is good access to footpaths.

Prices s fr €83; d fr €96; extra person fr €12   **On Site** Private ⚲ Private tennis court   **Nearby** ⌚ 8km Sea 20km ⌁ 10km ⌂ 1km ⋙ 4km   **Notes** Pets admitted English spoken CC

▦ ⦿ ♿ Domaine de Gleizes

Guy MARTEIL
11100 NARBONNE
☎ 04 68 32 94 48 & 06 72 70 38 85
email: domainedegleizes@wanadoo.fr
web: www.domaine-de-gleizes.com

Not far from the beaches, Narbonne and the Parc Naturel, this property has three ground floor double bedrooms, all with private facilities, in the converted outbuildings of a wine-growing property. A large internal courtyard has ancient plane trees and parking space; footpaths lead past lakes and pink flamingoes to the village of Bages, and also to the centre of Narbonne.

Prices d fr €65; t fr €80; dinner fr €28   **On Site** ☀   **Nearby** ⌚ 3km ⚲ 3km Sea 15km ⌁ 2km Restaurant 3km ⚘ 4km ⌂ 3km ⋙ 5km   **Notes** Pets admitted English spoken CC

🍴 *Domaine de Grand Beaupré*

athy et Laurent GRAND

e d'Armissan, 11100 NARBONNE

☎ 04 68 65 85 57 & 06 23 42 26 23

mail: cathy.cabes@wanadoo.fr

ose to the beautiful town of Narbonne, in the heart of a wine-
owing area and only 15 kilometres from the beach, this property has
ur upstairs bedrooms for two or three people. Each has a private
throom (with spa bath) or shower room, and a WC. Large sitting
om for guests, and a lounge which opens onto a terrace. Baby
uipment available. Wine tasting.

ices not confirmed for 2008　**Nearby** ⚽4km Sea 12km 🏊1km
4km 🏛1km ᵚ4km　**Notes** No pets CC

EYRIAC-DE-MER

🍴 ⦿ **La Milhauque**

erard et Florence BARBOUTEAU

440 PEYRIAC-DE-MER

☎ 04 68 41 69 76 & 06 17 61 03 85 📠04 68 41 69 76

mail: barbouteau@wanadoo.fr

the heart of the Narbonne Natural Park, this property has three
drooms, one in the owners' home and two in a separate building.
e rooms sleep from two to four people, and they all have en
ite facilities. Breakfast and other meals can be served outdoors,
erlooking vineyards and the lakes which supply fresh fish for the
ble.

ices s fr €50; d €53-€70; extra person fr €10; dinner fr €20
Site ⚘　**Nearby** ⚽12km ⛳8km Sea 18km 🏊5km ↖8km
staurant 3km ⛲8km 🏛3km ᵚ15km　**Notes** No pets

ORTEL-DES-CORBIERES

🍴 **Le Relais de Tamaroque**

igitte & Jean-Luc COULTEAUX

2 Av des Corbieres, 11490 PORTEL-DES-CORBIERES

☎ 06 73 91 20 13

mail: contact@relaisdetamaroque.com

eb: www.relaisdetamaroque.com

is former coaching inn is situated in the main road of a wine-
owing village and enjoys panoramic views over the river and
rbières from the garden. Five rooms are on offer including three
oms sleeping four or five. There is a large room for watching films,
ncing or playing games, a terrace and garage. Terra Vinéa, with its
es and olive trees, and the Notre Dame des Ourbiels church are
arby.

ices s €55-€70; d €65-€75; t €85-€90; extra person fr €18
Site 🏊　**Nearby** ⚽1km Sea 10km ⛲1km ᵚ20km
tes No pets English spoken

🍴 **Les Campets**

Myriam PASTERNAK

11490 PORTEL-DES-CORBIERES

☎ 04 68 48 89 79 & 06 62 73 54 38 📠04 68 48 89 79

email: lapierrechaude@yahoo.fr

web: www.lapierrechaude.com

In the middle of wine country, in the hollow of Corbières and close to
the sea, this house is a blend of northern and southern Mediterranean
in its unique decorative style, with a Moorish patio and a mosaic
based on a design by Gaudi. The guest rooms are spacious and very
comfortable with refined décor. Guests can relax on the wide, sunny
terrace, in the scent of the surrounding pine forest.

Prices d €78-€85; extra person fr €25　**Nearby** ⚽3km Sea 15km
🏊0.5km Restaurant 2km ⛲2km 🏛3km ᵚ18km　**Notes** No pets
English spoken Open March to December.

POUZOLS-MINERVOIS

🍴 ⦿ **Domaine de Creva-Tinas**

Anne CHARDONNET-TORRES

1 Chemin de Sainte Valiere, 11120 POUZOLS MINERVOIS

☎ 04 68 46 38 69 📠04 68 46 38 71

email: anne.chardonnet-torres@wanadoo.fr

web: www.pouzols-minervois.com/creva-tinas

Four charming en suite double rooms are offered in this centrally
heated family house. There is a lounge and library, and breakfast can
be taken in the garden. Owned by winemakers, the house is close to
footpaths and bike-trails and is only 300mtrs from the pretty village
of Pouzols.

Prices s fr €46; d fr €52; extra person fr €15; dinner fr €19
Nearby ⚽6km ⛳20km Sea 35km 🏊6km ↖2km Restaurant 3km ⛲
🏊4km 🏛4km ᵚ15km　**Notes** Pets admitted English spoken CC

PUICHERIC

🍴 ⦿ ♿ **Domaine des Fontanelles**

Irene TALIEU

11700 PUICHERIC

☎ 04 68 43 72 11 📠04 68 43 72 11

email: les.fontanelles@wanadoo.fr

Near a village and on the banks of the Canal du Midi, this chambre
d'hôtes has an ideal setting for exploring nature, flowers, fauna and a
pond on foot or by bike. One room is available in the owners' house
and two are situated in an annexe; each has private facilities. There is
a large veranda and a garden where breakfasts are served, and table
d'hôte meals are available by reservation including regional cuisine
and the house wines.

Prices s fr €40; d fr €47; t fr €62; extra person fr €17; dinner fr €20
On Site 🏊 ⚘　**Nearby** ⚽5km ⛳5km ↖ Restaurant 1km ⛲1km
🏛1km ᵚ22km　**Notes** Pets admitted CC

PUIVERT

✦✦✦ ⓘ◎ La Cocagniere

Mme GUERIN

3 Place du Pijol, Hameau de Campsylvestre,
11230 PUIVERT

☎ 04 68 20 81 90

email: lacocagniere@wanadoo.fr

web: www.lacocagniere.com

A truly rural spot in a hamlet between the Cathar castles of Puivert
and Montségur. Four bedrooms are available: a double, a twin-
bedded room, a triple (double bed and a single), and one with four
single beds. All have private facilities. Meals available by arrangement
featuring organic produce. Shady garden; plenty of footpaths in the
area.

Prices s €43-€53; d €48-€58; extra person fr €15; dinner fr €18
On Site ♟ **Nearby** ⚓ 3km 🖋 3km ⤳ 11km Restaurant 11km ⚓ 6km
🏠 6km 🚤 12km **Notes** No pets English spoken CC

ROQUETAILLADE

✦✦✦ ⓘ◎ Maison de Léoncie

Eric BLONDEL

18 Grand Rue, 11300 ROQUETAILLADE

☎ 04 68 31 58 54

email: blondel.eric@free.fr

web: www.leoncie.com

Set in the heart of a village whose inhabitants cut stone and vines
with equal skill, this house has four double or triple rooms, all en
suite. Heating, dining room, lounge area with bread oven, fireplace
and library with specialist works and documents about the Cathar
region. The village and its 11th-century château overlook the vineyards
and there are many spectacular views. Evening meal available by
reservation.

Prices s fr €40; d €50-€55; extra person fr €15; dinner fr €20
Nearby ⚓ 15km ⚓ 40km 🖋 10km ⤳ 10km Restaurant 10km ⚓ 10km
♟ 10km 🏠 10km 🚤 10km **Notes** No pets English spoken

SAISSAC

✦✦✦ ⓘ◎ *Le Lampy Neuf*

Claude BOUDET

11310 SAISSAC

☎ 04 68 24 46 07   📄 04 68 24 44 81

Close to the Canal du Midi, in the heart of the Lampy arboretum, this
19th-century house offers four en suite guest rooms, one of which is a
double. Lounge, library and breakfast, and evening meals served in the
large dining room. Lake nearby and fable-themed evenings available.

Prices not confirmed for 2008 **On Site** 🖋 **Nearby** ⚓ 5km ⚓ 5km
🏠 5km 🚤 25km **Notes** Pets admitted English spoken

✦✦✦ ⓘ◎ *Les Balcons du Cabardes*

C et C MORINI-RAVAGE

24 av Georges Clemenceau, 11310 SAISSAC

☎ 04 68 24 98 11 & 06 60 39 04 47

email: christel.morini@wanadoo.fr

web: www.lesbalconsducabardes.com

This property, in a village close to Carcassonne and the Canal du Mid
has tremendous character and a wonderful view of the Pyrenees and
the Aude Valley. Five bedrooms comprise two doubles, two twins,
and a triple, all with private bath or shower room and WC. Enclosed
wooded grounds, with walking close by. Good spot for exploring the
Cathar country.

Prices not confirmed for 2008 **Nearby** ⚓ 5km 🖋 5km ⚓ 1km
🚤 25km **Notes** No pets CC

SALLELES-D'AUDE

✦✦✦ ⓘ◎ Domaine de Truilhas

Carole LINOSSIER

11590 SALLELES-D'AUDE

☎ 04 68 46 09 55

email: domaine-de-truilhas@club-internet.fr

web: www.truilhas.com

French-style gardens surround this house, on a wine-growing proper
close to the Canal du Midi and the Cathar country. There are three
first floor bedrooms, two doubles and a family room for five, all with
private facilities. Games room; meals available by arrangement.

Prices d €58-€70; extra person fr €10; dinner fr €18 **Nearby** ⚓ 3km
⚓ 8km Sea 25km 🖋 0.3km ⤳ 4km Restaurant 2km ⚓ 3km ♟ 3km
🏠 3km 🚤 12km **Notes** Pets admitted English spoken CC

✦✦✦ ⓘ◎ Les Volets Bleus

Isobel EVANS

43 Quai D, Alsace, 11590 SALLELES-D'AUDE

☎ 04 68 46 83 03 & 0844 2325841

email: izevans@wanadoo.fr

web: www.salleles.net

A large 19th-century house in the heart of the village, 15 minutes fro
Narbonne and half an hour from the sea. There is a large hall on the
first floor, and five bedrooms: three doubles (two at grade 2) and tw
twins. All have private bath or shower room and WC. Meals available
by arrangement. Canal close by.

LANGUEDOC-ROUSSILLON

ices d €60-€70; extra person fr €15; dinner fr €25 **On Site** ⌀
staurant ⌁ **Nearby** ⚐ 2km Sea 25km ⚑ 0.2km ⚒ 12km
otes Pets admitted English spoken CC

ALSIGNE

⚘ ⌁ **Domaine de Combestremières**

ARL COMBESTREMIERE
600 SALSIGNE
☎ 04 68 77 06 97 & 06 18 97 74 08 ▤ 04 68 77 56 39
nail: lafage.andre@wanadoo.fr

ur double rooms and one triple, all with private facilities, are
ailable in this family house, part of a farming property. The
agnificent restored farmhouse is surrounded by woods, near to
e Cathar fortress of Lastours and many hiking trails running along
e Cabardès. Evening meals include the farm's own produce, and
e served in the attractive dining room with fireplace. Picnics can be
ovided and mountain bikes are available for hire.

ices not confirmed for 2008 **Nearby** ⚐ 10km ⚑ 6km ⚑ 12km
4km ⚒ 25km **Notes** Pets admitted Open April to August.

GEAN

⌁ **Chambre d'hôtes**

édéric et Dorothée LECLERCQ
Rue De La Liberte, 11130 SIGEAN
☎ 04 68 48 62 75 & 06 65 16 62 75
nail: d-f-leclercq@neptune.fr

the village of Sigean, just steps from the sea and the preserved
tural areas of coastal Corbières, this old vineyard house has been
stored with care and displays the owner's own paintings. The three
vely rooms sleep two to four people, and there is also a garden,
tio where meals are served.

ices s €40-€46; d €50-€56; extra person fr €15; dinner fr €24
earby ⚐ 5km Sea 6km ⚑ 3km ⚑ 0.2km ⚒ 5km **Notes** No pets
glish spoken Open March to November.

OULATGE

⌁ **La Giraudasse**

et K SOMOZA TIBERGHIEN
330 SOULATGE
☎ 04 68 45 00 16 ▤ 04 68 45 05 40
nail: info@giraudasse.com
eb: www.giraudasse.com

7th-century family mansion providing five large non-smoking
oms with private facilities. Set halfway between the Cathar
ongholds of Quéribus and Peyrepertuse and the Galamus gorge,
ests can enjoy breakfast in the large garden with fruit trees or relax
the fire in the lounge with its reading corner. Try the cassoulet,
obit and lamb on offer at dinner.

ices s fr €55; d fr €65; t fr €75; dinner fr €25 **Nearby** ⚐ 20km
1km Restaurant 0.1km ⚑ 8km ⚑ 8km ⚒ 50km **Notes** No pets
glish spoken Open 2 March to 29 November.

ST-HILAIRE

▥▥▥ **Chambre d'hôtes**

P HOYOS et J THEVENOT
3 Av De Limoux, 11250 ST-HILAIRE
☎ 04 68 69 41 21 ▤ 04 68 69 69 02
email: auxdeuxcolonnes@aol.com
web: http://auxdeuxcolonnes.com

This guest house is situated in the heart of one of the world's oldest
vineyards and has five guest rooms with private facilities. Breakfast can
be taken in the dining room or in the small garden with patio. Visit the
village's two abbeys and swim in the Lauquet River.

Prices not confirmed for 2008 **Nearby** ⚐ 7km ⚑ 1km ⚑ 15km
Notes No pets CC

ST-MARTIN-LALANDE

▥▥▥ ⚘ ⌁ **La Capelle**

Jacques SABATTE
11400 ST-MARTIN-LALANDE
☎ 04 68 94 91 90 & 06 65 41 82 57
email: lacapelle1@aol.com
web: http://la-capelle.site.voila.fr

This property, set amongst green countryside, is on a farm, and 50
metres from the owners' home. It has three grade 3 rooms, each
with shower room, toilet, small lounge and kitchen. Electric heating,
payphone on site. The Canal du Midi and Castelnaudary - renowned
for its cassoulet - are close by. Panoramic view towards the Pyrenees.

Prices d fr €60; t fr €75; extra person fr €16; dinner fr €23
Nearby ⚐ 10km ⚑ 2km ⚑ 2km ⚑ 2km ⚒ 6km **Notes** No pets

ST-MARTIN-LE-VIEIL

▥▥▥ ⌁ **Villelongue Côté Jardins**

Claude ANTOINE
11170 ST-MARTIN-LE-VIEIL
☎ 04 68 76 09 03
email: avillelongue@free.fr
web: http://avillelongue.free.fr

In a building which was once part of an old abbey, surrounded by
impressive grounds with rare and ancient trees, this chambre d'hôtes
has two spacious and comfortable first-floor bedrooms. There is a
separate guests' entrance, and the rooms have private facilities. Meals
are available by arrangement, in the low season.

Prices s fr €45; d fr €58; extra person fr €15; dinner fr €20
Nearby ⚐ 15km ⚑ 5km ⚑ 5km ⚑ 5km ⚒ 12km **Notes** Pets
admitted English spoken CC

TALAIRAN

▓ Chambre d'hôtes

Paule CHERTIER

Place de la Republique, 11220 TALAIRAN

☎ 04 68 44 09 92 & 06 76 86 97 88 ▤ 04 68 44 09 92

email: p-chertier@wanadoo.fr

This house of character stands in a village on the Cathar Castles Route, ideal for circular walking routes and for visits to the local cellars for some wine-sampling. It provides four rooms for two to three people, all large and tastefully furnished. There is a large terrace solarium for guests, as well as a reception room and sitting room, and breakfast is served on the terrace. Garage available.

Prices s fr €55; d €55-€65; t fr €83; extra person fr €18 **Nearby** ⚓ 8km Sea 40km ✦ 10km ↰ 20km ♨ ♣ 20km ⋙ 20km **Notes** No pets English spoken

TRAUSSE-MINERVOIS

▓ Sous l'Olivier

M SAN FRANCISCO et F FREU

33 rue de la Montagne Noire,

11160 TRAUSSE MINERVOIS

☎ 04 68 78 32 11

email: souslolivier@club-internet.fr

This old vineyard house, in the heart of the Minervois region, is full of lots of interesting antique items. It has three first-floor bedrooms, all with private bath or shower rooms and WCs. The whole property is non-smoking. Baby equipment is available. The dining room leads out onto a pretty stone terrace.

Prices s fr €55; d fr €65; extra person fr €15 **On Site** ♣
Nearby ⚓ 4km ↕ 5km ✦ 3km ↰ 4km Restaurant 2km ♨ 3km
🏛 0.3km ⋙ 25km **Notes** No pets

VILLARDONNEL

▓ ❦ ⭗ Abbaye de Capservy

Denise MEILHAC

11600 VILLARDONNEL

☎ 04 68 26 61 40 ▤ 04 68 26 66 90

email: daniel.meilhac@wanadoo.fr

Dating from the 11th century, this former abbey is set in stunning rural surroundings and has three distinctive guest rooms; two en suite rooms for five with mezzanines and a double room with private bathroom. There is a dining room with fireplace, a reading room, garden with furniture, small lake and swimming pool. Local delicacies at dinner (available by reservation, except Sunday and Tuesday).

Prices s fr €65; d fr €70; extra person fr €15; dinner fr €25 **On Site** ✦
Private ↰ **Nearby** ⚓ 6km Restaurant 3km ♨ 5km 🏛 2km ⋙ 17km
Notes Pets admitted English spoken Open 16 February to 14 November.

▓ ❦ ⭗ *Domaine de la Calm*

Eric et Pilar MARTIN

11600 VILLARDONNEL

☎ 04 68 26 52 13 ▤ 04 68 26 58 30

email: lacalm@free.fr

Set on the Carcassonne plain, in Cathar country, this sheep farm offers a choice of four attractive guest rooms with private facilities. Evening meals available by reservation, featuring the farm's own produce and served in the dining room with traditional fireplace made of local stone. Breakfast featuring home-made jam is served on the terrace. Archery sessions possible.

Prices not confirmed for 2008 **Nearby** ⚓ 5km ✦ 5km ♨ 5km 🏛 4km
⋙ 25km **Notes** No pets

VILLENEUVE-MINERVOIS

▓ ⭗ Le Clos du Moulin

Frederique et Jacques BUFFIERE

34 route de L'Aven, 11160 VILLENEUVE MINERVOIS

☎ 04 68 26 37 16

email: info@closdumoulin.net

web: www.closdumoulin.net

Vines and olive trees surround this 1930s house, which stands amongst cedar trees in its own grounds. There are three air-conditioned rooms, sleeping from two to four people, all with private shower room and WC. Bikes available; themed weekends can be arranged. Meals can be served by reservation. Good area for walking.

Prices s €61-€68; d €61-€68; extra person fr €17; dinner fr €25
On Site ✦ ♣ **Nearby** ⚓ 0.3km ↕ 15km ↰ 5km Restaurant 0.2km
♨ 0.2km ⋙ 15km **Notes** No pets English spoken CC

VILLESEQUE-DES-CORBIERES

▓ ♿ Château du Haut Gléon

Léon Nicolas DUHAMEL

11360 VILLESEQUE DES CORBIERES

☎ 04 68 48 85 95 ▤ 04 68 48 46 20

email: contact@hautgleon.com

web: www.hautgleon.com

Six charming guest rooms are available at this winemaking château, set in a Corbières valley 25km from the Mediterranean coast. Guest rooms are situated in the former shepherd's quarters or those of the grape-pickers and include two rooms with separate bathroom and four en suite rooms. Dining room with lounge area and fireplace, courtyard, car park and shady grounds.

Prices d fr €70; extra person fr €8 **Nearby** ⚓ 7km Sea 25km
✦ 2km ↰ 0.2km Restaurant 3km ♨ 5km ♣ 20km 🏛 5km ⋙ 20km
Notes Pets admitted English spoken CC

GARD

AIGUES-VIVES

♯ *Chambre d'hôtes*

M-Odile et J-Pierre STAJANO
Lou Felibre, 30670 AIGUES-VIVES
☎ 04 66 35 30 00 & 06 81 95 08 51
email: contact@lou-felibre.fr
web: www.lou.felibre.com

Near the village centre, this 19th-century country house stands on its
own in a wooded park, between Nîmes and Montpellier. Three rooms
decorated in the colours of the south open off a wide corridor with a
large living room reserved for guests. Every room has a shower, wash
basin and wc. The living room has games, books and music. Sunny
enclosed swimming pool. Secure parking within the grounds. Near the
beaches and ports.

Prices not confirmed for 2008 **On Site** Private ₹ **Nearby** ₺ 13km
Sea 25km ⌀ 13km ⌁ 0.5km ⌂ 0.2km ⋈ 3km **Notes** Pets admitted
English spoken

ALES

♯ **Chambre d'hôtes**

P et D DELAPORTE
Mas de Rochebelle, 44 Chemin Sainte-Marie, 30100 ALES
☎ 04 66 30 57 03
email: masderoche@masderochebelle.fr
web: www.masderochebelle.fr

This pretty residence is set in a wooded park of one hectare, with
swimming pool and parking, and is ideal for mountain biking, walks,
horse-riding and fishing. It offers two suites for two to five people in
the main house and a separate building provides seven single beds
and three doubles with a kitchen. There is a lounge with TV and
another with fireplace, library, board games and terraces.

Prices s fr €50; d €60-€80; t fr €120; extra person fr €30
On Site Private ₹ **Nearby** ₺ 0.5km ⌀ 0.5km Restaurant 0.5km
⌁ 1km Spa 10km ⌂ 0.5km ⋈ 2km **Notes** Pets admitted English
spoken

ANDUZE

♯ ❦ **Le Cornadel**

Carine ANFOSSO
30140 ANDUZE
☎ 04 66 61 79 44 & 06 08 24 15 18 ▤ 04 66 61 80 46
email: anfosso@cornadel.fr
web: www.cornadel.fr

Old restored farm with one large room for two or three guests, two
rooms for two guests, and two suites for two or four people. Each
room has a fridge, TV, video recorder and air conditioning. Dining
room with fireplace. Local specialities include ceps, truffles, pork, trout
and aioli de morue.

Prices s €79-€95; d €99-€119; t €119-€135 **On Site** ₺ Private ₹
Nearby Sea 40km ⌀ 3km ⌁ 1km ⌂ 2km ⋈ 15km **Notes** Pets
admitted CC

♯♯♯ **Mas Paulet**

Chantal VIGNOLLE
3550 Chemin du Mas Paulet, 30140 ANDUZE
☎ 04 66 83 57 03 & 06 15 12 51 79
email: regisvignolle@aol.com
web: www.mas-paulet.com

A three storey 19th-century house, one of a group of buildings on a
50-hectare wine-growing estate. The four bedrooms all have private
bathroom, WC, television and open views to the south across the
estate. Lounge, dining room, large conservatory and terrace.

Prices s €65-€70; d €75-€80; t fr €85 **On Site** Private ₹
Nearby ₺ 4km ⌀ 6km ⌁ 0.5km Restaurant 3km ⌁ 3.5km ❦ 3km
⌂ 3km ⋈ 12km **Notes** No pets English spoken CC

ARGILLIERS

♯♯♯ **La Bastide de Boisset**

G et P DE CORNEILLAN
Le Village, 30210 ARGILLIERS
☎ 06 88 09 11 96 & 04 66 22 91 13 ▤ 04 66 22 91 13
email: phdecorneillan@yahoo.fr
web: www.bastidedeboisset.com

Beautiful restored old stone house with antique furniture and
comfortable décor assuring peace and quiet. Bedrooms comprise a
twin and two suites with private facilities, and a double with shower
and separate wc. Library with fireplace, swimming pool, terrace,
parking and garden.

Prices d €70-€85; t fr €99; extra person fr €20 **On Site** Spa Private ₹
Nearby ₺ 3km ⌀ 5km ⌁ 4km Restaurant 0.3km ⌁ 3km ⌂ 3km
⋈ 30km **Notes** Pets admitted English spoken Open 6 January to 19
December.

ARPHY

♯♯♯ **La Baumelle**

Anne et Patrick GRENOUILLET
30120 ARPHY
☎ 04 67 81 12 69 ▤ 04 67 81 12 69
email: labaumelle@tele2.fr
web: www.cevennes-hebergement30.com

This chambre d'hôtes is a stone building amongst chestnut trees,
separate from the owners' home. The three guest rooms, all with
private facilities, have their own garden which is bordered by a stream.

CONTINUED

ARPHY *CONTINUED*

Swimming pool, wonderful open views, and the house is in good walking country.

Prices s €47-€55; d €52-€60; t €69-€89; extra person fr €8
On Site Private ⚲ **Nearby** ♿ 4km 🏊 3km Restaurant 3km ⛵ 2km
🎿 7km 🏛 3km **Notes** Pets admitted English spoken

AUBORD

⅏ 🍴 **La Bergerie**

Fabienne CORBALAN
17 Chemin des Mas, 30620 AUBORD
☎ 04 66 71 67 58 & 06 11 27 85 30
email: info@bergerie-de-faby.com
web: www.bergerie-de-faby.com

In a magical location in wooded grounds on the edge of the Camargue, this former sheepfold offers three guest bedrooms, with themed decorations. Each room has a double bed and a single; there is a cot available, and an extra bed. All rooms have private bathroom and WC. A lounge is available for guests. Theme evenings; picnics for when you explore the region.

Prices s €50-€60; d €59-€69; t fr €74; extra person €10-€15; dinner €17-€26 **On Site** Spa 🎿 **Nearby** ♿ 3km ⛵ 8km Sea 30km 🏊 8km ⚲ 9km Restaurant 2km ⛵ 0.5km 🏛 0.3km 🚶 10km **Notes** Pets admitted English spoken CC

AUBUSSARGUES

⅏⅏ 🍴 **Mas Conil**

Beat SCHURMANN
Chemin de Collorgues, 30190 AUBUSSARGUES
☎ 04 66 63 97 00 & 06 85 77 77 16
📄 04 66 63 97 01
email: hotes@masconil.com
web: www.masconil.com

Spacious comfortable rooms, each with their individual style of decoration and all with large bathrooms are a feature of this renovated 19th-century property close to Uzès. The dining room has a vaulted ceiling and a beautiful fireplace. Extensive grounds with a large shady terrace and swimming pool. Carefully prepared meals, by arrangement.

Prices s fr €85; d fr €100; t €130-€150; dinner fr €28
On Site Private ⚲ **Nearby** ♿ 5km 🏊 10km 🏛 8km 🚶 30km
Notes Pets admitted English spoken CC

BARJAC

⅏⅏ **La Domaine de la Sérénité**

Catherine L'HELGOUALCH
Place de la Mairie, 30430 BARJAC
☎ 04 66 24 54 63 & 06 76 84 85 48
email: catherine@la-serenite.fr
web: www.la-serenite.fr

A beautiful 18th-century house in the village square, with a superb view of the Cévennes. One suite (one double, one single bed) with large sitting room, a double room and a family suite with two bedrooms (one double, one twin). The rooms are vast and comfortable with antique furniture and fittings (the owner is an antique dealer) and all have private facilities. Wooded garden with enormous terrace for breakfast plus a relaxing, sitting room and library. No smoking.

Prices s €80-€135; d €80-€135 **Nearby** ♿ 3km ⛵ 30km
🏊 6km ⚲ 7km Restaurant 0.1km ⛵ 0.5km 🏛 0.1km 🚶 30km
Notes No pets English spoken Open Easter to 30 October.

BELLEGARDE

ⅲ *Péniche Farniente*

Laurent MICHEL
Port de Plaisance, 30127 BELLEGARDE
☎ 04 66 01 45 52 & 06 10 69 59 81
email: penichefarniente@free.fr
web: http://penichefarniente.free.fr

A canal boat with three air-conditioned cabins, moored on the Rhône-sète canal, close to the Camargue region. The cabins each have private power shower and WC; there is a lounge area shared by all the guests, and outside is a shady terrace with lots of flowers and a view of the port.

Prices not confirmed for 2008   **On Site** ⌀   **Nearby** ⌘ 0.3km
Sea 45km ⤢ 15km ⌘ 1km ⌂ 1km ⋈ 15km   **Notes** No pets   English spoken

---

BELVEZET

ⅲ ⅼⵔ *Chambre d'hôtes*

Carine DE ROBIANO
Le Mas de Paiolive, Le Village, 30580 BELVEZET
☎ 04 66 57 50 79 & 06 03 52 34 91   ▤ 04 66 59 69 72
email: contact@lemasdepaiolive.com
web: www.lemasdepaiolive.com

This is a restored 17th-century farmhouse in a quiet village. For guests, he has a double room, a triple with three single beds, and a suite for four or five people. All have private facilities, and a cot is available. There is a garden with a terrace and swimming pool, and meals can be served by arrangement.

Prices not confirmed for 2008   **On Site** Private ⤢   **Nearby** ⌘ 10km
⌂ 10km ⌂ 10km ⋈ 35km   **Notes** No pets

BEZ-ET-ESPARON

ⅲ ⅼⵔ **Château Massal**

Françoise DU LUC
30120 BEZ-ET-ESPARON
☎ 04 67 81 07 60 & 06 14 35 45 04   ▤ 04 67 81 07 60
email: francoiseduluc@aol.com
web: www.cevennes-massal.com

A 19th-century castle, in an exceptional setting of oak and chestnut forests with views over the Arre Valley. Three double rooms, each with separate facilities and entrance. Guests can dine and relax in the wooded and flower-filled garden and large lounge. Meals can be booked in advance. Nearby, visit the forests of l'Aigoual, the Causses, the Cirques de Navacelle and caves.

Prices s fr €64; d €68-€88; dinner fr €28   **Nearby** ⌘ 1km ⌀ 0.3km
⤢ 7km Restaurant 5km ⌘ 1km ⌓ 7km ⌂ 5km   **Notes** No pets   English spoken   Open April to 1 November.

CALVISSON

ⅲ ⅼⵔ *Chambre d'hôtes*

R et C BURCKEL DE TELL
Pays de Nîmes, Grande Rue 48, 30420 CALVISSON
☎ 04 66 01 23 91   ▤ 04 66 01 42 19
email: burckedetell@hotmail.fr
web: www.bed-and-art.com

Near the village, this restored 16th-century property provides three bedrooms overlooking an enclosed patio, with individual bathrooms and wcs. Sitting room with fireplace, terraces and parking. There are guided tours of Arles, Nîmes, Montpellier and Avignon. Painting exhibition on the premises.

Prices not confirmed for 2008   **Nearby** ⌘ 5km   Sea 20km ⌀ 8km ⤢ ⌘ 8km   **Notes** Pets admitted   English spoken   Open February to October.

CAMPESTRE-ET-LUC

ⅲ ⅼⵔ *Le Luc*

Jean-Michel MOHA
Domaine du Luc, Au Pays des Templiers,
30770 CAMPESTRE-ET-LUC
☎ 04 67 82 01 01   ▤ 04 67 82 01 01
email: domaineduluc@free.fr

A warm welcome and relaxed ambience await at this 1850s home - perfect for recharging your batteries. It offers six rooms with private facilities, and a garden with terrace and parking. Meals using regional produce may be enjoyed at the inn. La Couvertoirade, Lac du Salagou, Cirque de Mourèze, Grottes de Labeil and de Clamouse are nearby.

Prices not confirmed for 2008   **On Site** Private ⤢   **Nearby** ⌘ 3km ⌀ 15km ⌂ 15km ⋈ 30km   **Notes** Pets admitted   English spoken

---

CASTILLON-DU-GARD

ⅲ **Chambres d'hôte Vic**

Michel VIC
3 Chemin du Mas de Raffin, 30210 CASTILLON-DU-GARD
☎ 04 66 37 13 28   ▤ 04 66 37 62 55
email: viccastillon4@aol.com
web: www.chambresdhotes-vic.com

In the heart of the vineyards and open countryside, this restored old house guarantees rest and relaxation. There are two vaulted rooms and a beamed room for two to three people, one room with a kitchen bar sleeping two to four, and another room for two or three; all with private facilities. TV, courtyard and parking. The cellar specialises in Côtes du Rhône (red and rosé). Close to the Pont du Gard and Uzès.

Prices s fr €59; d €72-€92; t fr €112   **Nearby** ⌘ 4km ⌁ 14km ⌀ 4km ⤢ Restaurant 0.4km ⌘ 2km ⌂ 0.4km ⋈ 24km   **Notes** Pets admitted   English spoken

CASTILLON-DU-GARD CONTINUED

⟨O⟩ ⟨⟩ L'Estel

Philippe CHAMAND

La Bastide des Pins, Chemin du Bosquet,
30210 CASTILLON-DU-GARD

☎ 04 66 22 74 30 & 06 80 42 64 23

▤ 04 66 57 23 87

email: contact@bastide-des-pins.com

web: www.bastide-des-pins.com

A beautiful pine wood shelters this property, which offers double and triple rooms, and split-level rooms for four. All have TVs, air-conditioning, adjoining bathrooms and WCs, and garden views. Disabled access to some rooms. Cots, high-chairs, etc. Air-conditioned dining room. Table tennis, swimming pool, tennis, canoes. Enclosed parking, locked at night. Meals available.

Prices not confirmed for 2008 **On Site** Private ⟨ **Nearby** ⟨ 4km ⟨ 0.1km ⟨ 1km ⟨ 2km ⟨ 22km **Notes** Pets admitted English spoken CC

CHAMBORIGAUD

⟨⟩ ⟨O⟩ Le Mas du Seigneur

Serge et Yvonne HORNUNG

Altayrac, 30530 CHAMBORIGAUD

☎ 06 64 33 06 58

email: horsy.bike@wanadoo.fr

web: www.mas-du-seigneur.com

This 16th-century Cévennes house is set amid 15 hectares of pines and mature chestnuts. There are five renovated and carefully decorated double en suite rooms, with separate access. Extra bed available. Library, swimming pool, bowling alley, parking. Enjoy walking, flower and fruit-picking, and swimming. Half board minimum stay of one week.

Prices not confirmed for 2008 **On Site** Private ⟨ **Nearby** ⟨ 10km ⟨ 1km ⟨ 4km ⟨ 4km ⟨ 5km **Notes** No pets English spoken CC

COLOGNAC

⟨O⟩ Domaine de la Clédette

I TYMRUK et B DUPRE

Le Grand Bois, 30460 COLOGNAC

☎ 04 66 85 46 93

email: lacledette@wanadoo.fr

web: www.domaine-de-la-cledette.com

In the heart of the Cevennes, this house is in a quiet, secluded area. Three tastefully decorated rooms, two doubles and one twin/triple room, each with WC and bathroom. Living room, dining room and kitchen available. Garden and parkland. Table d'hotes on request. Plenty to do within an hour's drive - museums, craft workshops, festivals, markets and lovely scenery.

Prices not confirmed for 2008 **Nearby** ⟨ 6km ⟨ 1km ⟨ 5km ⟨ 3km ⟨ 3km ⟨ 40km **Notes** No pets English spoken

CORCONNE

Crémal

Heidi et Renzo SARTORI

Chemin de Mailhac, 30260 CORCONNE

☎ 04 66 77 76 06 ▤ 04 66 77 76 06

email: r.sartori@libertysurf.fr

Situated on a hill surrounded by vines, oaks, olive trees and the perfume of lavender, thyme and rosemary; five rooms available each with private facilities and magnificent views. French window, games, washer-dryer, parking. Breakfasts served in the garden with swimming pool. Relax and explore nearby Montpellier, Nîmes, Cevennes and the sea.

Prices not confirmed for 2008 **On Site** Private ⟨ **Nearby** ⟨ 3km ⟨ 30km Sea 40km ⟨ 6km ⟨ 6km ⟨ 6km ⟨ 33km **Notes** No pets English spoken

COURRY

⟨O⟩ Croix-Parens

Anne et François BOUCHE

La Picholine, 30500 ST-AMBROIX

☎ 04 66 24 13 30 ▤ 04 66 24 09 63

email: picholine@wanadoo.fr

web: www.lapicholine.net

Guests can be sure of quiet, comfort and a warm welcome at this old restored house, with its 100-year-old vaults and antique furnishings. Three guest rooms with private facilities, a dining room, two sitting rooms with TV, terrace, garden, pool and parking. Evening meals are available if pre-booked. Tennis, mountain-biking, walking, table tennis, boules nearby. Visit the Cévennes National Park, the Bambouseraie, the Ardèche Gorges. Pets permitted for a charge.

Prices not confirmed for 2008 **On Site** Private ⟨ **Nearby** ⟨ 6km ⟨ 7km ⟨ 0.3km ⟨ 0.3km ⟨ 7km **Notes** Pets admitted English spoken CC

CROS

⟨O⟩ Le Bouzigaud

Paul et Anne MOREAU

Mas du Bouzigaud, 30170 CROS

☎ 06 89 62 29 79

email: paul.moreau1@wanadoo.fr

web: www.bouzigaud.com

This house, which dates back to the 16th and 19th centuries, stands on the edge of the little village of Cros. It has a double room on the ground floor, and two triples upstairs. A child's bed is available, and each room has a private shower and WC. Garden with terrace and swimming pool. Meals by arrangement include local dishes and garden vegetables.

Prices s fr €55; d fr €60; t fr €75; extra person fr €15; dinner fr €25 **On Site** Private ⟨ **Nearby** ⟨ 8km ⟨ 0.2km Restaurant 4km ⟨ 5km ⟨ 4km ⟨ 50km **Notes** No pets English spoken

DURFORT

⁞⁞⁞ ⅼⓄⅼ *La Bruguière*

Pascale NUSSWITZ

Route de Canaules, 30170 DURFORT

☎ 04 66 80 40 45 & 08 26 35 97 82

email: pascale@labruguiere.com.fr

web: www.labruguiere.com.fr

This property has an exceptional setting between the Garrigue and the Cévennes. Guest accommodation consists of three bedrooms with private bathroom, terrace and lounge. A cot is available. There is also a gîte which can sleep up to eight people. Swimming pool, quality meals available, theme weekends organised - olives, truffles, wine and laundry service.

Prices not confirmed for 2008   **On Site** Private ↖   **Nearby** ☝ 7km
Sea 45km ℘ 7km ⌣ 7km 🏠 8km ⋙ 30km   **Notes** No pets   English spoken   CC

GAGNIERES

⁞⁞⁞ ⅼⓄⅼ *Chambre d'hôtes*

Patrick JARRE

Quartier de la Poste, 30160 GAGNIERES

☎ 06 86 71 77 50

email: pjarre@mageos.com

web: http://cevennes-gard.com

A big house in a village, close to where the Gard region meets the Ardèche. There are four upstairs rooms: three triples (two of them air-conditioned), and a two-roomed suite for four. All have private bath/shower room and WC. Use of kitchen; meals available by arrangement. Terrace and gardens.

Prices not confirmed for 2008   **Nearby** ☝ 6km ℘ 1km ↖ 1km ⌣ 1km
🏠 0.5km ⋙ 5km   **Notes** Pets admitted

GALLICIAN

⁞⁞⁞ ⅬＯⅼ ⅼⓄⅼ ⅼ *Montcalm*

Jo WAELDELE

Route d'Aigues Mortes, Montcalm Mas Apolline,
30600 GALLICIAN

☎ 04 66 73 52 20   📄 04 66 73 52 20

email: masapolline@camargue.fr

web: www.masapolline.camargue.fr

A house in the heart of the Camargue region, between the vineyards and the sea. It has three bedrooms, each with individual decoration, private bathroom and WC. Shady grounds of about one hectare. A perfect location for visiting such places as Arles, Nîmes and Aigues-Mortes.

Prices not confirmed for 2008   **Nearby** ☝ 4km Sea 20km ℘ 3km
⌣ 25km 🏠 11km ⋙ 12km   **Notes** No pets

ISSIRAC

⁞⁞⁞ ⅼⓄⅼ *Chambre d'hôtes*

Pascale CHAVE

Chez Dame Tartine, Rue de la Fontaine, 30760 ISSIRAC

☎ 04 66 82 17 06 & 06 08 41 02 24

email: dame.tartine@9online.fr

web: www.chambres-hotes-dame-tartine.com

Set in a landscape of lavender and cherries, in this pretty and quiet village of Issirac with its typical bell tower overlooking the Gorges de l'Ardèche and the Cèze Valley. This charming stone-built house offers three guest rooms with shower, wc and balcony. The large garden has a lovely view, and footpaths and mountain bike tracks lead into beautiful countryside.

Prices not confirmed for 2008   **Nearby** ☝ 10km ℘ 6km ↖ 2km
⌣ 6km   **Notes** Pets admitted   English spoken

LA BRUGUIERE

⁞⁞⁞ ⅼⓄⅼ **Le Mas des Santolines**

Marie-Claude PARMENTIER

Le Village, 30580 LA BRUGUIERE

☎ 04 66 72 85 04 & 04 66 72 91 62

📄 04 66 72 87 38

email: mas-santolines@wanadoo.fr

web: www.mas-santolines.com

Early 19th-century house with four rooms and a suite, all of which are very comfortable and prettily decorated. The lounge, kitchen and dining room are large, light and welcoming and there is a huge garden with Mediterranean plants and swimming pool. Dogs are allowed. Hearty buffet breakfast served on the terrace. Transport to the station or airport can be arranged. Close to the Camargue and the Mediterranean.

Prices s fr €87; d fr €95; t fr €120; extra person fr €15; dinner fr €28
On Site Private ↖   **Nearby** ☝ 5km ⌛ 10km Sea 45km ℘ 10km
⌣ 2km 🏠 3km ⋙ 25km   **Notes** Pets admitted   English spoken   CC

LASALLE

⫟⫟⫟ Domaine de Soulages

Guillaume GOURGAS
Saint-Louis-de-Soulages, 30460 LASALLE
☎ 04 66 85 41 83 & 06 11 08 04 51
email: ggourgas@free.fr

Situated on a 38-hectare estate this property is a haven of peace and solitude, with beautiful views. The estate was extensively altered when magnificent granite-walled terraces and dams were built. The guest rooms and a suite are large and pleasant, each with bath and wc, and furniture and ornaments are in period style.

Prices s fr €80; d fr €88; t fr €128; extra person fr €30
On Site Private ⚲ **Nearby** ⚡ 2km ⚑ 30km Sea 50km ✎ 10km
Restaurant 5km ⚓ 2km ⌂ 1.5km **Notes** No pets

LAUDUN

⫟⫟⫟ ⚲ Villa Thébaïde

Supy et André DULAS
250, rue Albert Camus, 30290 LAUDUN
☎ 04 66 79 23 82 & 06 08 65 84 94 ▤ 04 66 33 05 48
email: villathebaide@wanadoo.fr
web: www.villathebaide.com

This house is in enclosed grounds, five minutes from the centre of a village, in the Côtes du Rhône wine-growing region. Five ground floor guest bedrooms all have private shower room and WC, and direct access to the garden. Accommodation comprises a king-size double, another double, two twin-bedded rooms, and a family suite for up to five people. The landscaped garden has shady sitting areas, a swimming pool with pool house and a Jacuzzi.

Prices s fr €70; d fr €70; extra person fr €15 **On Site** Private ⚲
Nearby ⚡ 5km ⚑ 27km ✎ 10km ⚓ 2km ⌂ 1km ⛬ 25km
Notes No pets English spoken

see advert on opposite page

LAVAL-PRADEL

⫟⫟⫟⫟ ⟨◎⟩ Le Mas de la Cadenede

Maxime TURC
Le Mas de Dieu, 30110 LAVAL-PRADEL
☎ 04 66 30 78 14
email: masdelacadenede@free.fr
web: www.masdelacadenede.free.fr

A place for gentle living, organised to make your stay in the Cevennes memorable. On the ground floor, rooms with bath shower and wc, TV, hairdryer and private terrace. Billiard room, games room, library and swimming pools. Midday and evening meals can be arranged. Private parking.

Prices s fr €60; d fr €70; t fr €85; extra person fr €15; dinner fr €20
On Site Private ⚲ **Nearby** ⚡ 8km ⚑ 10km ✎ 10km
Restaurant 8km ⚓ 3km ⌂ 3km ⛬ 8km **Notes** Pets admitted
English spoken CC

LE CAILAR

⫟⫟⫟ Mas St Maurice

Jean-Claude TROUGNAC
Route de Codognan, 30740 LE CAILAR
☎ 04 66 73 35 86 & 06 16 25 92 34
email: jc.trougnac@free.fr
web: www.mas-saint-maurce.camargue.fr

This is a typical mas in the Camargue wine-growing region where guests can discover the horse and bull traditions of the area. Two ground floor rooms with washbasin, shower and private WC. Terrace and garden. Fridge. Two first floor rooms, one with en suite bathroom and a child's room; the other with en suite shower and separate WC. Garage for motorcycles may be available. Reductions after the second night.

Prices s fr €55; d fr €60; t fr €75; extra person fr €15 **Nearby** ⚡ 0.5km
Sea 20km ✎ 1km ⚲ 5km ⚓ 10km ⌂ 2km ⛬ 5km **Notes** Pets
admitted English spoken

LEDENON

⫟⫟⫟ Chambre d'hôtes

F LEMEAUX et C LEPAN
3, Impasse du Porche, La Maison de l'Olivier,
30210 LEDENON
☎ 06 62 80 66 27
email: lamaisondelolivier@wanadoo.fr
web: http://lamaisondelolivier.free.fr

The main part of a 17th-century mill with a small flowery garden on one side and a quiet cul-de-sac on the other. It provides three rooms and a suite, each with private facilities, TV. Solarium available and large dining room for breakfast. Between Avignon and Nîmes, 5km from Pont du Gard. Reductions in tariff according to the season and special rates for stays of a week.

Prices s €60-€100; d €60-€100; t €75-€100; extra person fr €15
Nearby ⚡ 8km ⚑ 20km Sea 45km ✎ 3km ⚲ 5km Restaurant 0.3km
⚓ 5km Spa 15km ⌂ 0.1km ⛬ 15km **Notes** No pets English spoken

LES MAGES

⫟⫟⫟ *Les Rois Mages*

L DEBEAUX et S NOUGIER
Le Village, 30960 LES MAGES
☎ 04 66 24 75 74 ▤ 04 66 24 75 74
email: ldebeaux@wanadoo.fr
web: http://lesroismages.monsite.orange.fr

A stone-built house, once a coaching inn, which dates back to the early 18th century. It has two double rooms, and a room for four (double bed plus singles). All are individually decorated and air-conditioned, with private bath or shower room and WC. Home-made jams and cakes for breakfast, served on the terrace.

Prices not confirmed for 2008 **Nearby** ⚡ 5km ✎ 5km ⚲ 2km ⚓ 1km
Notes No pets English spoken

LUSSAN

ⅢⅢ Ⅰ◎Ⅰ Les Buis de Lussan

Thierry VIEILLOT
Rue de la Ritournelle, 30580 LUSSAN
☎ 04 66 72 88 93 & 06 79 72 53 27
email: buisdelussan@free.fr
web: http://buisdelussan.free.fr

In the heart of the medieval village of Lussan, this restored house with its true southern French atmosphere offers four guest rooms. There are three doubles and a twin, with a separate entrance, and each with private shower and WC. Central heating and lounge for guests' use. Enjoy the Mediterranean garden, complete with jacuzzi pool and a panoramic view!

Prices s fr €70; d €74-€76; dinner fr €30 **On Site** Private ↘
Nearby ⚓5km ⚓17km ⚓1km Restaurant 0.2km ⚓1km ⚓9km
⚓0.2km ⚓30km **Notes** No pets English spoken

ⅢⅢ ❤ Mas des Garrigues

Christian DOLLFUS
La Lèque, 30580 LUSSAN
☎ 04 66 72 91 18 ▤ 04 66 72 97 91
web: www.masdesgarrigues.com

A beautiful house in a picturesque hamlet is the setting for this chambre d'hôtes. There are four comfortable and tastefully decorated rooms, all with private bath and WC. Central heating. Large lounge with open fire, billiard table, swimming pool. River la Cèze close by, walking and horse riding: loose boxes and paddocks available.

Prices s fr €54; d fr €62; t fr €72 **On Site** ⚓ Private ↘ Private tennis court **Nearby** ⚓12km Restaurant 0.1km ⚓15km ⚓4km ⚓40km
Notes No pets English spoken Open February to December. CC

MEYNES

ⅢⅢ Ⅰ◎Ⅰ *Le Mas du Micocoulier*

Jacques THIEULIN
Quartier du Théron, 30840 MEYNES
☎ 06 10 48 32 98
email: micocoulier@free.fr
web: www.guideprovence.com/bb/micocoulier/

This mas is situated in a calm countryside setting of two hectares of orchards, and your hosts are keen to share with you the charms of the region including cultural activities, walks and historic sites. There are two guest rooms with private facilities, a communal living room, terrace and garden, and table d'hôte meals are available in the evenings by reservation.

Prices not confirmed for 2008 **On Site** Private ↘ **Nearby** ⚓1km
Sea 25km ⚓4km ⚓3km ⚓2km ⚓25km **Notes** No pets

Villa Thébaïde

This chambre d'hotes is situated in the heart of the Cotes du Rhone vineyards near to Avignon, Pont du Gard, The Ardeche Gorges and a 40 min drive from Nîmes and Avignon airport. You can expect a warm welcome at this haven of tranquillity and comfort. Guests can take pleasure in the landscaped garden with swimming pool. Enjoy a hearty breakfast in the garden or dining room including homemade jams and seasonal local fruits.

André & Supy DULAS
250 Rue Albert Camus, 30290 LAUDUN
Tél : +33 (0)4 66 79 23 82
Fax : +33 (0)4 66 33 05 48
Portable : +33 (0)6 08 65 84 94
Email : villathebaide@wanadoo.fr
www.villathebaide.com

MOLIERES-SUR-CEZE

ⅢⅢ Ⅰ◎Ⅰ Chambre d'hotes

René et Joëlle ARNAUX
Les Brousses, 30410 MOLIERES-SUR-CEZE
☎ 04 66 24 27 69
▤ 04 66 24 27 69
email: joelle.arnaux2@tele2.fr

All of the guest suites at this property consist of two rooms - a lounge with a fridge, and a bedroom with bathroom and WC. There is a guests' lounge area, and meals are available by arrangement.

Prices s fr €39; d fr €48; t fr €57; dinner fr €13 **Nearby** ⚓10km
⚓15km ⚓4km ↘ Restaurant 5km ⚓8km ⚓4km ⚓4km
Notes Pets admitted English spoken

ⅢⅢ Ⅰ◎Ⅰ Les Brousses

Denise COLLADO
30410 MOLIERES-SUR-CEZE
☎ 04 66 24 63 35 & 06 12 21 81 43
▤ 04 66 24 25 62
email: collado.michel2@wanadoo.fr
web: http://lachouettequidd.com

This is an ideal location for a peaceful holiday in a beautiful verdant setting. There are three rooms, all with private bathroom and WC. One is self-contained on the ground floor, the other two are on the

CONTINUED

MOLIERES-SUR-CEZE *CONTINUED*

first floor. There is a large garden and a terrace with views over the Cévennes. Public footpaths close by.

Prices s fr €57; d fr €62; t fr €82; extra person fr €15; dinner fr €30
On Site Private **Nearby** 10km 30km 4km
Restaurant 10km Spa 15km 4km 4km **Notes** Pets admitted

MONOBLET

Le Mas de l'Aubret

Robert COYNEL
La Pause, 30170 MONOBLET
☎ 04 66 85 42 19 & 06 23 20 06 15
email: nr.coynel@laubret.com
web: www.laubret.com

Between Anduze and St-Hippolyte-du-Fort, Monoblet is a typical Cevennes village, nestling between vineyards and chestnut forests. In a lovely green setting close to the village, this large house comprises six bedrooms for two or three people, each with a bathroom and WC. Cot available. There's also a terrace, large sitting room with open fire, library and kitchenette.

Prices s fr €35; d fr €45; t fr €55; extra person fr €15 **Nearby** 10km 12km 7km 7km 0.2km 50km **Notes** Pets admitted English spoken

MONTAREN-SAINT-MEDIERS

Chambre d'hôtes

Thérèse STENGEL-DELBOS
Cruviers Larnac, Route de St Ambroix,
30700 MONTAREN-SAINT-MEDIERS
☎ 04 66 22 10 89
email: contact@mas-cruviers.com
web: www.mas-cruviers.com

Four en suite rooms in a house of real character set in open countryside, where a restful stay is assured. Evening meals using farm produce are available by prior arrangement, and feature preserves, duck, chicken, fruit and asparagus. Heating, swimming pool and terrace with views over Uzès.

Prices s fr €50; d fr €60; t fr €70; dinner fr €20 **On Site** Private **Nearby** 5km 5km 5km Restaurant 5km 5km 5km 5km 30km **Notes** Pets admitted

MUS

La Ringole

Muriel ST-PIERRE
121, Impasse du Muscat, 30121 MUS
☎ 04 66 35 37 42 & 06 03 64 42 41
email: contact@la-ringole.com
web: www.la-ringole.com

A very welcoming place, not far from the Cévennes and the sea, conveniently located for many interesting visits. There are three double bedrooms, all with king-size beds, their own bathrooms and WCs, and a lounge area. Use of fridge. Attractive gardens with swimming pool.

Prices not confirmed for 2008 **On Site** Private **Nearby** 25km Sea 25km 20km 2km 2km 2km **Notes** No pets Open 15 March to 1 October.

NAVACELLES

Les Hauts de Séguissous

Mireille et Gérard CARRIERE
Hameau de Cal, 30580 NAVACELLES
☎ 04 66 24 87 45 & 06 81 15 52 59
email: mireille.carriere@wanadoo.fr
web: www.leshautsdeseguissous.com

This house stands on a rocky outcrop in the Valley of the Cèze, in a hamlet 500mtrs from the Thermales des Fumades, and is ideal for walking. Two rooms for four people and three twin rooms, all en suite. Hairdryer, balcony, kitchen and day room with open fireplace where meals may be prepared.

Prices not confirmed for 2008 **Nearby** 1km 5km 5km 5km 4km 14km **Notes** No pets English spoken

NIMES

La Magne

Josyane PIERSON
296D, Impasse des Troënes, 30900 NIMES
☎ 06 12 58 43 57
email: josyane.pierson@club-internet.fr
web: www.chambres-la-magne.com

A beautiful stone-built house just ten minutes from the centre of Nîmes. There are three bedrooms, individually decorated, with private shower and WC, television and fridge. Outside are extensive grounds with a large shady terrace, barbecue and swimming pool.

Prices s €72-€80; d €80-€90; t fr €110; extra person fr €25
On Site Private **Nearby** 0.5km 2km Sea 45km 10km Restaurant 0.6km 0.5km Spa 0.8km 3km 1km 3km **Notes** No pets English spoken CC

ⅲ ℺ **Le Garric**

Laurence MARTIN
31 Chemin d'Engance, 30000 NIMES
☎ 04 66 26 84 77 📄 04 66 26 84 77
web: http://chambreslegarric.free.fr

This modern house is surrounded by dry-stone walls in the heart of a protected scrubland area. In this magnificent landscape, peace and quiet are guaranteed and there are five double rooms with separate bathroom and wc, and a terrace or balcony. TV, telephone, shaded park, boules, table tennis, billiards. Breakfast and evening meals are taken in a communal room beside the pool. Reductions for longer stays.

Prices s fr €93; d €100-€107; t fr €140; extra person fr €23; dinner fr €30 **On Site** Spa Private ↝ **Nearby** ⚓ 5km ⚓ 8km Sea 45km ⌔ 15km Restaurant 5km ⚒ 3km ℘ 5km ⚏ 3km ⚉ 5km **Notes** No pets English spoken

POMPIGNAN

ⅲ ℺ *Chambre d'hôtes*

Carole FALLET
Hameau de Tourres, 30170 POMPIGNAN
☎ 04 66 77 76 57
email: auberge.tourres@laposte.net
web: www.aubergedetourres.com

The guest rooms here are in a building adjacent to the old family house. Two of the rooms are downstairs, one of them with disabled access; the other two are upstairs. Each room has a shower and WC. There is a lounge; an adjacent inn serves meals which offer traditional dishes from the Mediterranean and the Cévennes.

Prices not confirmed for 2008 **Nearby** ⚓ 12km Sea 50km ⌔ 8km ↝ 9km ⚒ 4km ⚏ 4km ⚉ 40km **Notes** No pets

PONT-SAINT-ESPRIT

ⅲ ℺ *Domaine du Pont d'Ardèche*

Ghislaine DE VERDUZAN
30130 PONT-SAINT-ESPRIT
☎ 04 66 39 29 80 📄 04 66 39 51 80
email: pontdardèche@aol.com
web: www.pont-dardeche.com

This is an old country house beside the Ardèche, with its own private beach. There are five guest bedrooms, all on the first floor, and each with a private bath or shower room and WC. The grounds, which extend to one and a half hectares, contain a variety of fruit trees. Meals are available by arrangement.

Prices not confirmed for 2008 **On Site** ⌔ Private ↝ **Nearby** ⚓ 3km ⚒ 3km ⚏ 3km ⚉ 7km **Notes** Pets admitted English spoken

POULX

ⅲ ⚿ *Les Cigales*

Régis BOUVART
241 Rue des Amandiers, 30320 POULX
☎ 06 70 62 84 00
email: contact@lescigales.net
web: www.lescigales.net

This is a modern house, in extensive enclosed grounds in a quiet and peaceful setting. It has five spacious guest rooms - three on the ground floor and two on the first, all opening on to a terrace leading to the garden and swimming pool. They all have TVs, private bathrooms and WCs. Lounge, enclosed parking, swimming pool.

Prices not confirmed for 2008 **On Site** Private ↝ **Nearby** ⚓ 3km Sea 40km ⚒ 3km ⚏ 1km ⚉ 10km **Notes** Pets admitted

REMOULINS

ⅲ **Bize de la Tour**

Pierre DUCRUET
2, Place du Portail, 30210 REMOULINS
☎ 04 66 22 39 33 & 06 64 96 19 54
📄 04 66 63 97 25
email: 2.dupartet@wanadoo.fr
web: www.bizedelatour.com

A big house, with a 12th-century tower, in the historic part of the village. There are three rooms with themed decoration, all with private facilities, TV, internet access , and high-quality fittings. There are two lounges (one for smokers) and all the furnishings and decorations throughout the house are in keeping with the style and period of the property.

Prices s fr €75; d fr €75; extra person fr €15 **On Site** ⌔ **Nearby** ⚓ 8km ⚓ 8km Sea 50km ↝ 5km Restaurant 0.1km ⚒ 0.3km ℘ 0.1km ⚏ 0.1km ⚉ 20km **Notes** No pets English spoken CC

REMOULINS CONTINUED

♦♦♦♦ La Terre des Lauriers

Gérard et Marianick LANGLOIS
Av du Pont du Gard, 30210 REMOULINS
☎ 04 66 37 19 45 & 06 30 10 69 28
email: langlois@laterredeslauriers.com
web: www.laterredeslauriers.com

A big country house 900 metres from the Pont du Gard, with five spacious double rooms. All the rooms have king-size beds, private bath or shower room and WC, television and air-conditioning. Terrace with views over the grounds; swimming pool and table tennis. Good access to forest and riverside walks.

Prices s fr €89; d fr €99; t fr €124; extra person €25 **On Site** ♦
♦ Private ♦ **Nearby** ♦ 8km ♦ 8km Sea 50km Restaurant 0.5km
♦ 1km ♦ 1km ♦ 20km **Notes** No pets English spoken

REVENS

♦♦♦♦ ♦♦ St Pierre de Revens

Hubert et Madeleine MACQ
30750 REVENS
☎ 05 65 62 27 99
email: madeleine.macq@wanadoo.fr
web: http://hermitage.st.pierre.site.voila.fr

The wild beauty of the Dourbie Valley, between Saint-Véran and Cantobre, provides the setting for this property, a restored priory dating back to Roman times. There are five guest rooms, all with a private bathroom and WC, and one with a kitchenette. Furnishings are antique and rustic in style. Four of the rooms have canopied beds. Evening meals available out of season, by arrangement.

Prices s fr €74; d fr €79; extra person fr €15; dinner fr €25
On Site ♦ **Nearby** ♦ 14km Restaurant 5km ♦ 10km ♦ 10km
♦ 20km **Notes** No pets

ROCHEFORT-DU-GARD

♦♦♦♦ Chambre d'hôtes

Anne et Gilbert PASQUER
Chemin de Bellevue, L'Oustau,
30650 ROCHEFORT-DU-GARD
☎ 06 86 70 97 65
email: gilbertpasquer@voila.fr
web: http://loustau_bellevue.site.voila.fr

This modern house is between Avignon and the Pont du Gard, on a quiet hillside with views of Mont Ventoux. It has three rooms: Glycines and Tournesol are doubles with private bathrooms; Griotte (twin) and Eglantine (double) share a shower room and are ideal for a family or two couples. Private entrances and terraces; breakfasts served on the terrace in the summer.

Prices s fr €60; d fr €65; extra person fr €15 **Nearby** ♦ 2.5km ♦ 15km
♦ 9km ♦ 7km ♦ 2km ♦ 10km **Notes** No pets English spoken

SAUVE

♦♦♦♦ ♦ Chambre d'hôtes

Stephane MEILHAC
La Pousaranque, 30610 SAUVE
☎ 06 81 95 09 90
email: aubergelapousaranque@free.fr
web: www.aubergelapousaranque.com

A 19th-century farmhouse of architectural interest, offering four nicely decorated and themed rooms for two to four people, each with private facilities. There are carved ceilings in the lounges and superb mosaics on the ground. Breakfasts feature home-made jams and guests can relax in the swimming pool and park.

Prices not confirmed for 2008 **On Site** ♦ Private ♦
Nearby ♦ 1km ♦ 2km ♦ 2km ♦ 35km **Notes** Pets admitted English spoken

♦♦♦♦ La Renaudière

Annie RENAULT
Perdiguier-Bas, 30610 SAUVE
☎ 06 03 22 46 14
email: la-renaudiere@wanadoo.fr
web: www.larenaudiere.com.fr

Country house on enormous plot of land, among vines, on the banks of the Crieulon. Enjoy peace and relaxation by the pool or in the shade of the trees, with rambling, walking routes and mountain biking nearby. Guest rooms with private facilities, terrace, swimming pool and parking. Breakfast in the dining room.

Prices not confirmed for 2008 **On Site** Private ♦ **Nearby** ♦ 3km
♦ 5km **Notes** No pets

♦♦♦♦ La Traversière

Katy ROMIEU
5 Grand Rue, 30610 SAUVE
☎ 04 66 77 15 40 & 06 67 35 51 43
email: romieu.jerome@wanadoo.fr

This is a 19th-century house at the heart of a medieval village. The spacious rooms have been fully restored in the style of their time. There is a double room (possible extra bed) and a triple, both with private facilities. There is a further double room with its own lounge and shower/WC. Dining room and terrace for guests.

Prices d €60-€75; t €75-€90; extra person fr €15 **Nearby** ♦ 2km
Sea 40km ♦ 7km Restaurant 0.1km ♦ 10km ♦ 0.1km ♦ 30km
Notes No pets English spoken

SERVIERS-ET-LA-BAUME

♨ ❧ *Mas d'Alzas*

Nicolas FOURNIER
30700 SERVIERS-ET-LA-BAUME
☎ 06 81 73 81 82
email: masdalzas1@wanadoo.fr
web: www.masdalzas.com

This is an old farmhouse in the countryside, close to the Pont du Gard and the historic town of Uzès. It has five very comfortable bedrooms; outside there is a terrace and swimming pool. The owners also run a farmhouse restaurant which is on the same site.

Prices not confirmed for 2008 **On Site** Private ⚲ **Nearby** ⚑ 6km ⚲ 2km ⚲ 6km ⚑ 6km ⚑ 40km **Notes** Pets admitted English spoken

SOMMIERES

♨ ♿ **Mas Font Claire**

Colette LABBE
8 Av Emile Jamais, 30250 SOMMIERES
☎ 04 66 77 78 69 📄 04 66 77 78 69
email: masfontclaire@free.fr
web: http://masfontclaire.free.fr

Situated in a peaceful medieval village between the sea and the Cévennes, there are two double rooms and a room for four (one double, two singles), all with private facilities. Terrace, garden, pool and restaurant serving regional cuisine on site. Tennis courts in the village.

Prices s fr €68; d fr €80; extra person fr €20 **On Site** ⚲ Private ⚲ **Nearby** ⚑ 0.5km Sea 24km ⚲ 0.5km Restaurant 0.1km ⚲ 0.2km ⚲ 0.2km ⚑ 30km **Notes** No pets English spoken

ST-ANASTASIE

♨ **Le Mazet / Hameau de Russan**

Guy et Dominique GARRIGUE
Domaine du Mazet, 30190 ST-ANASTASIE
☎ 04 66 63 19 59 & 06 03 20 04 38
email: ggarrigue1@aol.com
web: http://ggarrigue.free.fr

There are three guest rooms in this former silk-worm house, on a farm half way between Nîmes and Uzès, near the Pont du Gard. A lounge and a small guests' kitchen are available. Satellite TV, swimming pool. Breakfast (with home-made jams and fresh fruit in season) is served on the terrace, or in the former sheepfold with its arched ceiling.

Prices s fr €55; d fr €75; t fr €80 **On Site** Private ⚲ **Nearby** ⚑ 1km Sea 40km ⚲ 1km ⚲ 6km ⚲ 3km ⚑ 12km **Notes** Pets admitted English spoken

ST-CHRISTOL-LES-ALES

♨ 🍽 **Boujac**

Clotilde SALLIERES
Boujac Les Micocouliers, 128 Chemin des Brusques,
30380 ST-CHRISTOL-LES-ALES
☎ 04 66 60 71 94 & 06 83 83 21 10
email: lesmicocouliers@wanadoo.fr
web: www.maslesmicocouliers.fr

This is a large restored Provençal house in the heart of the country, where quiet and relaxation are a certainty. Four rooms and a family suite, with private facilities, are offered, and a separate country cottage with its own entrance. Heating, large day room with open fire. Provençal cuisine, using seasonal produce. Horse-riding nearby. Reductions for children under seven.

Prices s €45-€60; d €55-€80; t €75-€90; dinner €12-€20 **On Site** Private ⚲ **Nearby** ⚑ 2km ⚲ 9km ⚲ 2.5km ⚑ 5km **Notes** Pets admitted

ST-GILLES

♨ *Chambre d'hôtes*

Claude DUPLISSY
Mas Plisset, Route de Nîmes, 30800 ST-GILLES
☎ 04 66 87 18 91 📄 04 66 87 18 91
email: claude.duplissy@free.fr

Five large, authentically renovated rooms for two or four people, each with WC and bathroom. Air conditioning, satellite TV, private garage,

CONTINUED

LANGUEDOC-ROUSSILLON

ST-GILLES CONTINUED

pretty garden. Private outdoor pool and sauna, Turkish bath and jacuzzi. The estate's rice fields can be visited.

Prices not confirmed for 2008 **On Site** Private ⚡ **Nearby** ⚓ 5km ⚓ 8km Sea 35km ✎ 4km ☟ 3km ⛺ 2km ⋙ 17km **Notes** No pets English spoken

▦ ⚲ La Fosse

Christine ABECASSIS
Domaine de la Fosse, 30800 ST-GILLES
☎ 04 66 87 05 05 & 06 17 69 47 58
▤ 04 66 87 40 90
email: christine.abecassis@domaine-de-la-fosse.com
web: www.domaine-de-la-fosse.com

Situated close to the Petit Rhône, this property has five large and beautifully restored rooms, all with private bathrooms and WC. Satellite TV and air conditioning. Attractive garden, private garage. Outdoor and indoor swimming pools, sauna, steam room, fitness room. Possible visits to nearby rice farm. The welcoming hosts will be delighted to provide meals on request.

Prices s €120-€130; d €135-€145; t €150-€160; extra person fr €15; dinner fr €28 **On Site** Private ⚡ **Nearby** ⚓ 4km ☟ 12km Sea 20km ✎ 2km Restaurant 6km ☟ 7km Spa 20km ⛺ 7km ⋙ 20km **Notes** No pets English spoken CC

see advert on page 399

ST-JEAN-DE-VALERISCLE

▦ ⚲ Mas Fraissinet

Ghislaine ROS
Rue des Granges, 30960 ST-JEAN-DE-VALERISCLE
☎ 04 66 83 13 18
email: info@mas-fraissinet.com
web: www.mas-fraissinet.com

On the outskirts of a small medieval village, rooms are available in an annexe of the owners' mas, surrounded by mature cedars and overlooking the valley. Three large, comfortable rooms and two suites with private facilities and TV. Cot available, heating, terrace for guests, keep fit room with jacuzzi, table tennis, mountain bikes, parking.

Prices s fr €110; d fr €120; t fr €150; extra person fr €30; dinner fr €30 **On Site** ✎ ⚲ **Nearby** ⚓ 0.5km Restaurant 0.5km ☟ 1.5km ⋙ 15km **Notes** No pets English spoken

ST-JEAN-DU-GARD

▦ ⚲ Les Fromentières

Gladys CHAGNOLLEAU
Les Plaines, 30270 ST-JEAN-DU-GARD
☎ 04 66 85 10 25 ▤ 04 66 85 10 25
email: gladys.chagnolleau@wanadoo.fr
web: http://perso.wanadoo.fr/chambres-lesFromentieres

A 16th-century farmhouse in the woods, with a double room and two split-level rooms for four (double bed and two singles in each). All the rooms are upstairs with private shower and WC, and a guests'

terrace. Downstairs is a living room, kitchen with a fridge, and access to the garden.

Prices not confirmed for 2008 **Nearby** ⚓ 5km ✎ 1.5km ⚡ 2.5km ☟ 2.5km ⛺ 2.5km ⋙ 25km **Notes** No pets English spoken

ST-JULIEN-DE-LA-NEF

▦ ⚲ ⚲ Château d'Isis

M. ROUDIER et Mme VILLARD
Rive Droite de l'Hérault, 30440 ST-JULIEN-DE-LA-NEF
☎ 04 67 73 56 22 ▤ 04 67 73 56 22
email: castelisis@free.fr
web: www.chateau-isis.com

A peaceful 14th-century castle in grounds with streams, waterfalls, woods and meadows. Three guest room with private facilities: the twin Pink Room with a French-style ceiling and ancient floor; the double Blue Room overlooking the park; the Green Room for four in two four-posters; plus another twin room with two towers. Lounge with open fire. Local cuisine: spit-roast leg of lamb, game birds, crayfish, foie gras.

Prices s fr €40; d €55-€75; t €75-€91; extra person fr €20; dinner fr €23 **On Site** ⚲ **Nearby** ⚓ 3km ✎ 0.5km ⚡ 0.5km ☟ 5km ⛺ 6km ⋙ 70km **Notes** Pets admitted English spoken Open April to December. CC

ST-LAURENT-D'AIGOUZE

▦ ⚲ Mas de la Montille

M. PANIER WIDAD
Rte des Stes Maries de la Mer,
30220 ST-LAURENT-D'AIGOUZE
☎ 04 66 35 59 43 & 06 18 92 63 37
email: masdelamontille@free.fr

This chambre d'hôtes is situated on a poultry and vegetable farm, in the wild countryside of the Camargue. There are three spacious, air-conditioned guest bedrooms, all with large double beds and good quality furniture. The rooms are decorated in an oriental style, and each has a large bathroom/WC. There is a jacuzzi and swimming pool.

Prices s fr €80; d fr €120; extra person fr €15; dinner €25-€30 **On Site** Spa Private ⚡ **Nearby** ⚓ 3km ☟ 17km Sea 10km ✎ 2km Restaurant 3km ☟ 4km ⛺ 4km ⋙ 3km **Notes** No pets English spoken Open February to December.

ST-LAURENT-LES-ARBRES

∰ ΙΟΙ Après la Sieste

Chloé MINET

358, rue Alexis Martin, 30126 ST-LAURENT-LES-ARBRES

☎ 04 66 50 33 94 & 06 61 84 58 40

email: info@apreslasieste.com

web: www.apreslasieste.com

This is a delightful property, fifteen minutes from Avignon and well-placed for visiting many tourist sites in the region. Three double bedrooms, one with bathroom, two with shower/WC; and two double suites, one with bathroom, the other with shower/WC, and both with salon and terrace. Outside is a garden and swimming pool heated in season.

Prices s €76-€102; d €90-€120; t €105-€135; extra person fr €15; dinner fr €29 **On Site** 🎾 Private 🔨 **Nearby** ⛷ 1km ᚐ 20km 🏊 5km Restaurant 0.1km 🏊 0.2km 🛒 0.2km 🚉 15km **Notes** No pets English spoken

ST-MAMERT

∰ ΙΟΙ La Mazade

Eliette COUSTON

2 Rue de la Mazade, 30730 ST-MAMERT

☎ 04 66 81 17 56 📄 04 66 81 17 56

email: couston.eliette@yahoo.fr

web: www.bbfrance.com/couston.html

Nineteenth-century building now restored, offering two double rooms, and one with double and twin beds, all en suite and overlooking the courtyard and garden. Heating.

Prices s fr €45; d €60-€65; extra person fr €20; dinner fr €25 **Nearby** ⛷ 6km ᚐ 10km Sea 40km 🏊 15km 🔨 11km Restaurant 14km 🏊 14km 🍴 14km 🛒 0.1km 🚉 14km **Notes** No pets

ST-MICHEL-D'EUZET

∰ Le Nid des Hirondelles

Isabelle et Patrice RIGAUD

Place Jean Jaurès, 30200 ST-MICHEL-D'EUZET

☎ 04 66 82 16 25 📄 04 66 82 16 25

email: rigaud-patrice@orange.fr

In a forest clearing between Cèze and Ardèche, this 18th-century vineyard property has three stylish bedrooms: a double room with canopied bed; a suite with a canopied bed and a single; and a suite with twin beds and a folding double. All have private shower and WC. Only 15 minutes walk from the famous Sautadet waterfalls.

Prices d €55-€70 **On Site** Spa **Nearby** ⛷ 1km ᚐ 40km 🏊 1km 🔨 8km Restaurant 0.1km 🏊 6km 🛒 7km 🚉 40km **Notes** No pets English spoken Open April to September.

ST-PAULET-DE-CAISSON

∰ Le Mas Canet

Bernard PELLOUX

Mas Canet, 30130 ST-PAULET-DE-CAISSON

☎ 04 66 39 25 96

email: pelloux.bernard@wanadoo.fr

web: www.mascanet.com

At the gateway to Provence and the Languedoc, in a lovely national forest, this beautiful farmhouse of exposed stone was built by monks in the 16th century. There are six double rooms with large beds and TV points - TV hire possible. Swimming pool shared with owners. Close to Chartreuse-de-Valbonne and Pont-Saint-Esprit, with its Saturday market.

Prices d fr €77 **On Site** Private 🔨 **Nearby** ⛷ 8km ᚐ 40km 🏊 9km 🏊 3km Spa 40km 🍴 7km 🛒 4km 🚉 10km **Notes** No pets

ST-QUENTIN-LA-POTERIE

∰ Les Pins de Jols

Michèle DELCOR

30700 ST-QUENTIN-LA-POTERIE

☎ 06 16 28 92 88

email: lespinsdejol@orange.fr

web: http://lespinsdejol.free.fr

Four rooms for two or three guests, each with private shower and wc; and two rooms with kitchenette, in a charming house. Quiet, comfort and good company, surrounded by parkland with pines and a pool, minutes from Uzès and the Pont du Gard, and 45 minutes from the Cévennes and the gorges of the Ardèche.

Prices s fr €60; d €65-€70; t fr €85; extra person fr €15 **On Site** Private 🔨 **Nearby** ⛷ 2km ᚐ 6km 🏊 15km Restaurant 2km 🏊 2km 🍴 2km 🛒 2km 🚉 30km **Notes** No pets English spoken Open February to 2 January.

LANGUEDOC-ROUSSILLON

ST-SEBASTIEN-D'AIGREFEUILLE

⊞⊞ ⲓ◯⌷ Le Mas des Sources

Sandra NABZDYJAK

Anduze, 30140 ST-SEBASTIEN-D'AIGREFEUILLE

☎ 04 66 60 56 30

email: lemasdessources@wanadoo.fr

web: www.mas-des-sources.fr

At the foot of the Cévennes, in a 17th-century silkworm house, five spacious rooms are offered with bath, wc, and TV. Large living room, kitchen, laundry. Breakfast and other meals served on the terrace or on the patio. The 8-hectare park setting gives room for relaxation and picnics. Reduced tariff for children. Meals by arrangement.

Prices s fr €70; d fr €82; t fr €98; extra person fr €16; dinner fr €28 **Nearby** ⛷ 5km ⛰ 6km ✎ 2km ⚓ 5km Restaurant 1.5km ⛵ 4km ⌂ 4km ⋈ 10km **Notes** Pets admitted English spoken

THOIRAS

⊞⊞⊞ ⲽ Massies

Paul et Danièle GUYOT

30140 THOIRAS

☎ 04 66 85 11 66

web: http://membres.lycos.fr/chguyot/

Not far from Gardon, in a small hamlet typical of the Cévennes, this house has four guest rooms. There is a double room, a triple (double bed plus a single), a room for four and a room for five (both with double beds plus singles). All have private facilities. Kitchenette, terrace and garden.

Prices s fr €42; d fr €50; t fr €58 **Nearby** ⛷ 4km ✎ 0.8km ⚓ 4km Restaurant 4km ⛵ 4km ⌂ 4km ⋈ 20km **Notes** Pets admitted Open April to November.

UCHAUD

⊞⊞⊞⊞ Les Aliziers

Louisette ROTA-LONJON

19 Rue Jean Moulin, 30620 UCHAUD

☎ 06 03 80 16 86 ▤ 04 66 71 54 77

email: rotalonjon@aol.com

web: www.les-aliziers.camargue.fr

This 19th-century village house, cool in the summer and warm in the winter, stands in lawned grounds amongst 100-year-old trees. There are three bedrooms, with parkland views. Two of them have double beds; the third has a double and a single. All rooms have a private shower room and WC. Lounge with fireplace and books; swimming pool, barbecue and table tennis.

Prices s fr €80; d fr €93; extra person fr €20 **On Site** ⛲ Private ⚓ **Nearby** ⛷ 10km ⛰ 10km Sea 20km ✎ 5km Restaurant 0.2km ⛵ 1km ⌂ 0.2km ⋈ 15km **Notes** No pets Open Easter to 1 November.

VALLABREGUES

⊞⊞⊞ ⲽ ⲓ◯⌷ Le Mas de Donat

André et Martine MARIN

8, Route de Mézoargues, 30300 VALLABREGUES

☎ 04 66 59 43 10

email: lemasdedonat@wanadoo.fr

web: www.lemasdedonat.com

This peacefully situated house is on a fruit farm. There are three double ground floor guest rooms, all with private shower and WC. A cot and an extra bed are available on request. Guest lounge with TV; terrace and garden. Breakfast includes fruit from the farm, and home-made bread and charcuterie. Award-winning evening meals are available, by arrangement.

Prices s €45-€60; d €48-€62; t €69-€86; extra person €18-€25; dinner €18-€25 **On Site** Private ⚓ **Nearby** ⛷ 7km Restaurant 0.3km ⛵ 0.5km ⌂ 0.5km ⋈ 7km **Notes** No pets

⊞⊞⊞⊞ Mas de l'Ilon

Corinne et Jean Noël SABATIER

Chemin de l'Ilon, 30300 VALLABREGUES

☎ 04 66 59 53 41 & 06 32 67 96 68

email: jnsabati@club-internet.fr

web: www.masdelilon-provence.com

This Provençal house, surrounded by orchards, is in the old village of Vannier. It has air-conditioned rooms, each with TV, shower and WC. Guest lounge with open fire, private terrace. Swimming pool, enclosed parking. Traditional markets, local festivals and bullfighting are all available in the area.

Prices d €65-€95; extra person fr €20 **On Site** Private ⚓ **Nearby** ⛷ 10km ⛰ 10km Sea 50km ✎ 5km Restaurant 6km ⛵ 0.8km ⛲ 10km ⌂ 0.2km ⋈ 6km **Notes** No pets

VALLERAUGUE

⊞⊞⊞ ⲓ◯⌷ ⚿ La Coconnière

Lydie et Yannick CARLE

Rue Neuve, 30570 VALLERAUGUE

☎ 04 67 82 00 13 ▤ 04 67 82 07 86

email: lacoconniere@tiscali.fr

web: http://lacoconniere.chez.tiscali.fr

Five bedrooms in a village house with mountain views. All the rooms have private bath or shower room and WC; there is a lounge, a game room, a covered terrace and a boules pitch. The house is in enclosed wooded grounds, close to a river. Meals are available by arrangement

Prices not confirmed for 2008 **Nearby** ⛷ 20km ✎ 0.1km ⛵ 0.5km ⌂ 0.1km **Notes** No pets English spoken

▦ ⏣ *Mas de Cougnet*

Sabine et François SERRA
Route de l'Aigoual, 30570 VALLERAUGUE
☎ 06 81 56 36 15
email: masducougnet@aliceadsl.fr
web: www.masdecougnet.com

This house stands in eight hectares of parkland, which has streams running through. A separate guests' entrance leads to the four bedrooms: all are upstairs, and all have a private shower room and WC. There is a lounge with TV and games, and an attractive garden. A bus service passes close by.

Prices not confirmed for 2008   **Nearby** ⚓ 20km ✎ 0.1km ⌘ 0.7km ⚑ 1km   **Notes** No pets

▦ Domaine de Beauregard

Grâce DIAS DAS ALMAS
RN 572, 30600 VAUVERT
☎ 04 66 51 62 90 & 06 08 66 84 82 📄 04 66 88 12 26
email: domainebeauregard@wanadoo.fr
web: www.domainebeauregard.com

A big house, in a quiet spot, with three bedrooms. There are two double rooms, one of them with views across the garden and direct access to the terrace; the third room is a suite for four guests, with a double bed and two singles. All have private bath or shower room and WC. Lounge with TV; swimming pool.

Prices s fr €65; d fr €85   **On Site** Private ⚲   **Nearby** ⚓ 0.8km ⚑ 15km Sea 20km ✎ 1km Restaurant 0.8km ⌘ 6km ⚑ 10km ⚑ 3km ⚑ 8km   **Notes** No pets   English spoken

▦ ⏣ ⚿ La Fénière

Nathalie et Michel CHIOUSSE
Le Clau de la Garde, Route de Bagnols, 30200 VENEJAN
☎ 06 88 48 90 89

This 19th-century property in the heart of the vineyards was originally a lavender distillery. The en suite guest accommodation is all on the ground floor, where there is also a living room with access to the garden and grounds. Small kitchen garden, and farmyard animals. Meals available by arrangement.

Prices s fr €55; d fr €60; t fr €80; extra person fr €30; dinner fr €16   **On Site** Restaurant ⚲ Private ⚲   **Nearby** ⚓ 0.1km ✎ 3km ⌘ 1km ⚑ 1.5km ⚑ 30km   **Notes** No pets   English spoken

▦ ⏣ *La Bégude de Vers-Pont-du-Gard*

Pierre-Jean et Martine TURION
Le Mas de mon Père, 30210 REMOULINS
☎ 04 66 37 16 25 & 06 86 90 44 84
email: contact@masdemonpere.com
web: www.masdemonpere.com

Four upstairs guest rooms in an old family house, 1km from the Pont du Gard. Each room has a mezzanine, shower room and wc. Sitting room with open fireplace and TV; patio; painting exhibition. F1 circuit, monuments and historic sites nearby.

Prices not confirmed for 2008   **On Site** ✎   **Nearby** ⚓ 4km Sea 50km ⚲ 13km ⌘ 1km ⚑ 3km ⚑ 25km   **Notes** Pets admitted   Open Easter to October.

▦ ⏣ *Chambre d'hôtes*

Dany LEGRELE
Rue Basse, La Maison du Farfadet, 30360 VEZENOBRES
☎ 06 79 54 21 94
email: dany@lamaisondufarfadet.com
web: www.lamaisondufarfadet.com

A medieval village between Anduze and Uzès is the setting for this chambre d'hôtes. The three bedrooms are all doubles; one is a suite with a lounge and TV, and one has its own terrace. All have private shower room and WC. Kitchen and swimming pool. The breakfasts are generous; other meals can be served by arrangement.

Prices not confirmed for 2008   **On Site** Private ⚲   **Nearby** ⚓ 1km ✎ 2km ⌘ 2km ⚑ 10km   **Notes** Pets admitted   English spoken

▦ Les Ecuries des Chartreux

Pascale LETELLIER
66, Rue de la République,
30400 VILLENEUVE-LES-AVIGNON
☎ 04 90 25 79 93
email: pascale.letellier@wanadoo.fr
web: www.ecuries-des-chartreux.com

This property is situated close to Avignon, in the heart of a historic village. There are three rooms - a double, a twin and a room for four - in a detached restored house, all with private bathrooms and WCs. Part of the grounds is reserved for guests.

Prices s €72-€107; d €82-€122; t €100-€121   **Nearby** ⚓ 2km ⚑ 3km ⚲ 0.4km Restaurant 0.1km ⌘ 0.4km ⚑ 0.8km ⚑ 3km   **Notes** No pets   English spoken

VILLENEUVE-LES-AVIGNON   CONTINUED

⫲ Les Jardins de la Livrée

Irène et Jean-Paul GRANGEON
4 Bis Rue Camp de Bataille,
30400 VILLENEUVE-LES-AVIGNON
☎ 04 90 26 05 05
email: la-livree@numericable.fr
web: www.la-livree.com

In the old centre of historic Villeneuve-les-Avignon, (papal city and art centre), this house has an enormous, peaceful garden. Four rooms, each with shower and wc, terrace, pool and parking. Enjoy regional cuisine at the dinner table. Good base for exploring Provence and Languedoc.

Prices s €50-€80; d €60-€90; t €80-€95; dinner €21-€25
On Site Private ⤳ **Nearby** ⛷ 3km ⌖ 1km Restaurant 0.1km ⌁ 0.5km
⋙ 3km **Notes** No pets English spoken

HÉRAULT

BESSAN

⫲ Chambre d'hôtes

Lucien PAUL
30, Av De La Victoire, 34550 BESSAN
☎ 04 67 77 40 07 & 06 63 66 61 23 🖺 04 67 77 40 07

Four rooms in a family mansion in a village near the main road. One three-bedded room, two rooms (for two and three) and a suite for four, each with private facilities and heating. Day room exclusively for visitors, TV, fridge/freezer, use of washing machine, table tennis, 3 hectare enclosed garden, parking.

Prices s fr €45; d fr €50; t fr €80 **Nearby** ⛷ 10km ⌁ 6km Sea 10km
⌖ 1km ⤳ 6km Restaurant 0.5km ⌁ ⋙ 6km **Notes** No pets

BRIGNAC

⫲ La Missare

Jean-Francois MARTIN
9, Route De Clermont, 34800 BRIGNAC
☎ 04 67 96 07 67
email: la.missare@free.fr
web: http://la.missare.free.fr

Nestling in a verdant setting, vast rooms available on a wine-making estate dating from the 19th century. There is a room with a double

and single bed, a twin room and two double rooms with private facilities and heating. Communal living room with antique furniture and fireplace, washer-drier, garden with furniture, terrace, swimming pool and garage. Wi-fi available.

Prices s fr €70; d fr €70; t fr €86 **On Site** Private ⤳ **Nearby** ⛷ 3km
Sea 35km ⌖ 6km Restaurant 3km ⌁ 3km Spa 30km ⌖ 3km ⌂ 3km
⋙ 35km **Notes** No pets English spoken

BRISSAC

⫲ ⍥ Les Rameaux

Patricia et Alan LOPEZ
188 rue du Lirou, Coupiac, 34190 BRISSAC
☎ 04 67 71 45 02
email: contact@lesrameaux.com

This 19th-century house is in a small hamlet to the south of the Cévennes and close to the Hérault gorges. Three bedrooms, a double and two triples, are all upstairs; each has private bath or shower room and WC. A cot is available, also meals by arrangement. Terrace with garden furniture; footpaths close by.

Prices not confirmed for 2008 **Nearby** ⛷ 3km ⌖ 3km ⤳ 10km
⌁ 5km ⌂ 4km ⋙ 45km **Notes** No pets

⫲ ⍥ Mas de Coulet

Alain et Celine WEISS
Sarl le Mas de Coulet, 34190 BRISSAC
☎ 04 67 83 72 43 & 06 18 47 80 01 🖺 04 67 83 72 43
email: masdecoulet@yahoo.fr
web: www.masdecoulet.com

A non-smoking property to the south of the Cévennes and not far from Montpellier. The guest accommodation is in a restored and converted farm building. The five rooms are all doubles, with television, internet connection, private shower/WC, and access to a patio and swimming pool. Four holiday cottages and an 'auberge' are on the same site.

Prices s €50-€60; d €65-€75; dinner €22-€32 **On Site** Restaurant
Private ⤳ **Nearby** ⛷ 7km ⌁ 10km Sea 50km ⌖ 4km ⌁ 10km
Spa 50km ⌂ 4km ⋙ 40km **Notes** No pets English spoken Open
October to 14 September. CC

CABRIERES

⫲ ⛭ Le Cadran Solaire

Margareta AVERMAETE
Route Des Crozes, 34800 CABRIERES
☎ 04 67 88 19 44 🖺 04 67 88 19 44
email: info@le-cadran-solaire.fr
web: www.le-cadran-solaire.fr

In the heart of the Hérault, surrounded by oak trees and with an open view across the hills, this modern house on the edge of the village offers five rooms for two to four people, all with en suite showers and WCs. Lounge complete with books, central heating. Wooded garden with terrace, private parking. This is a non-smoking house. Reduction for more than one night.

Prices s fr €44; d fr €56; t fr €68; extra person fr €12 **Nearby** ⛷ 5km
⌁ 20km Sea 35km ⌖ 12km ⤳ 4km ⌁ Spa 35km ⌖ 8km ⋙ 40km
Notes Pets admitted English spoken

CAPESTANG

⏶ ⏵⃝ Le Murier Platane

Anne WAUTERS

Bis Rue Voltaire, 34310 CAPESTANG

☎ 04 67 93 78 45

email: lemurierplatane@orange.fr

web: http://perso.orange.fr/lemurierplatane

This is a vine-grower's house in the old village and close to the Canal du Midi. There is one twin-bedded room and one double, also two rooms with mezzanine, which accommodate three or four people. All rooms have private facilities. Lounge with books, use of washing machine. Electric heating. Small courtyard and flower-filled garden. Enclosed swimming pool, meals by arrangement.

Prices s fr €48; d fr €62; t fr €76; dinner €20　**On Site** Restaurant Private ⏌　**Nearby** ⏛ 30km Sea 23km 🏌 0.3km ⛵ 0.3km Spa 40km ♨ 0.3km 🚲 15km　**Notes** No pets English spoken CC

CAUSSE-DE-LA-SELLE

⏶ ⏵⃝ Les Hauts d'Issensac

Fabienne COULET

Route De Ganges, 34380 CAUSSE-DE-LA-SELLE

☎ 04 67 73 37 09 & 06 11 55 55 91

email: hauts.issensac@free.fr

web: www.hauts-issensac.com

In the upper Hérault Valley, between St-Guilhem-le-Désert and Ganges, your hosts will be delighted to welcome you to this centuries old house. There is a family room for four on the ground floor; upstairs there are two doubles and a twin. All have private facilities. Central heating, lounge, terrace and games room. Meals by arrangement - local wine and food specialities.

Prices s €45-€53; d €54-€58; t fr €72; extra person fr €14; dinner fr €19　**On Site** 🏌　**Nearby** ⏛ 12km Sea 45km ⏌ 13km Restaurant 5km ♨ 5km 🚲 13km 🚣 40km　**Notes** No pets English spoken Open March – November.

CAZOULS-D'HERAULT

⏶⏶ Villa Saint Germain

Richard GUY

13 route de la Grange, 34120 CAZOULS-D'HERAULT

☎ 04 67 25 28 06

email: aetrguy@tiscali.fr

web: www.villa-saint-germain.com

This is a beautiful 19th-century house, on the edge of a village in the heart of the Hérault Valley. There are three bedrooms: a twin-bedded room, a triple (double bed and a single), and a two-roomed suite for four (double bed and two singles). All have private facilities. Outside are extensive grounds and a swimming pool.

Prices s fr €65; d fr €75; t €95-€105; extra person fr €15　**On Site** 🏊 Private ⏌　**Nearby** ⏛ 6km ⏛ 20km Sea 25km 🏌 1km Restaurant 0.5km ⛵ 4km Spa 20km 🚲 6km 🚣 28km　**Notes** No pets English spoken

CAZOULS-LES-BEZIERS

⏶ ⏵⃝ La Noria

Famille RAMOS

Domaine De La Plaine, 34370 CAZOULS-LES-BEZIERS

☎ 04 67 93 58 27 & 06 76 50 96 73

email: la.noria@wanadoo.fr

web: http://perso.orange.fr/la.noria/lanoria.htm

Authentic 19th-century Languedoc house on an established wine estate, 7km from the Canal du Midi. One suite for four people, two rooms for three, and a double, each with private facilities. TV points, lounge, sitting room, heating, telephone. Outside, enjoy the terrace, garden furniture, barbecue, play area, pergola, bowling alley, summer kitchen with fridge. Laundry, parking and garage.

Prices s fr €39; d fr €45; t fr €55; dinner fr €15　**On Site** Restaurant 🏊　**Nearby** ⏛ 8km Sea 24km 🏌 4km ⏌ 8km ⛵ 5km 🚲 1.2km 🚣 8km　**Notes** Pets admitted English spoken

CRUZY

⏶ ⏵⃝ Le Clos Mazerolles

Henriette et Jean LOPEZ

17 Rue Du Camp Du Pal, 34310 CRUZY

☎ 04 67 89 77 27 & 06 89 15 42 42　▤ 04 67 38 00 12

email: closmazerolles@free.fr

web: http://closmazerolles.free.fr

In the heart of the Saint-Chinian vineyards, five kilometres from the Canal du Midi, this village property has four bedrooms: two doubles, a triple (double bed and a single) and a family room for four (two double beds). They all have private facilities, and a cot is available on request. The garden has a terrace with furniture.

Prices s fr €50; d fr €60; t fr €75; extra person fr €15; dinner fr €20　**Nearby** ⏛ 5km ⏛ 30km Sea 30km 🏌 5km ⏌ 5km Restaurant 1km 🏊 12km 🚣 20km　**Notes** No pets English spoken

FABREGUES

⏶ ⏵⃝ La Bastide Ghislaine

Alain DARCOURT

114, rue des Troenes, 34690 FABREGUES

☎ 04 67 85 27 54 & 06 80 87 24 06　▤ 04 67 27 55 05

email: maisondhotes@labastideghislaine.com

web: www.labastidedeghislaine.com

A newly built country house on the edge of a village. On the ground floor is a double room; upstairs is a family suite for five (two double beds and a single), and a family suite for four (two double beds). All rooms have private facilities, and the two suites also have air-conditioning. Two swimming pools, one indoors. Meals by arrangement.

Prices s fr €100; d fr €110; t fr €145; extra person fr €35; dinner fr €30　**On Site** Private ⏌　**Nearby** ⏛ 2km ⏛ 15km Sea 10km 🏌 0.1km Restaurant 1km 🏊 0.2km Spa 20km 🚲 1km 🚣 12km　**Notes** No pets English spoken

LANGUEDOC-ROUSSILLON

GARRIGUES

⦀ ⦿ **Château Roumanières**

Amélie GRAVEGEAL

34160 GARRIGUES

☎ 04 67 86 49 70 & 06 79 77 14 06

email: gravegeal.amelie@wanadoo.fr

web: www.chateauroumanieres.fr

This château, standing in its vineyard in the middle of the village, has
five guest bedrooms. There are three double rooms, a suite for three
people, and a split-level family room for four. All rooms have a private
bath or shower room and WC. The 14th-century dining room has a
vaulted roof. Conservatory, roof solarium, courtyard with flowers and
garden furniture. Meals by arrangement.

Prices s €75-€85; d €80-€90; t €100-€110; extra person fr €20; dinner
fr €35   **Nearby** ⛷7km ♨20km Sea 38km ✐ 7km Restaurant 4km ♨
Spa 38km ⚜20km 🏠7km ⋙25km   **Notes** No pets English spoken

GIGNAC

⦀ ☙ ⦿ **Domaine de Pélican**

B et I THILLAYE DE BOULLAY

34150 GIGNAC

☎ 04 67 57 68 92 📄 04 67 91 24 37

email: domaine-de-pelican@wanadoo.fr

A large Languedoc house overlooking the valley, surrounded by
vines and the typical garrigue (scrubland). There are three rooms
for four with mezzanine and sitting area and a double room, all with
private facilities. Heating, washing machine, balcony. Parking in open
courtyard.

Prices s €55-€60; d €60-€70; t fr €81; dinner fr €23   **On Site** Restaurant
Private ⚘   **Nearby** ⛷10km ♨20km Sea 40km ✐ 4km ♨3km
Spa 30km ⚜15km 🏠3km ⋙25km   **Notes** No pets English spoken

⦀ ☙ ⦿ **Mas Cambounet**

Fabienne PERRET

34150 GIGNAC

☎ 04 67 57 55 03 📄 04 67 57 55 03

email: perret.cambounet@wanadoo.fr

In a truly rural setting, this is a magnificently restored wine-growing
and olive-growing property. It has a room for three and a family room
for four, both with TV, private facilities and use of fridge. In an annexe
are two further rooms, a twin and a double, with private showers/
WCs. Central heating and guests' lounge, garden. Meals available.

Prices s fr €64; d fr €80; t fr €100; dinner fr €24   **On Site** Restaurant
Private ⚘   **Nearby** ⛷8km ♨20km Sea 40km ✐ 10km ♨8km
Spa 30km ⚜8km 🏠3km ⋙25km   **Notes** No pets English spoken
Open April to October. CC

GRABELS

⦀ ♿ **Le Mazet**

Philippe et Suzanne ROBARDET

253, Chemin Du Mas De Matour, 34790 GRABELS

☎ 04 67 03 36 57

email: lemazet253@aol.com

web: www.lemazetdegrabels.info

Just 4km from Montpellier, this typical Languedoc house offers three
rooms: La Provençale (double) and l'Exotique (twin or double) each
with mezzanine and extra single bed, and La Méditerranéenne for
two guests with TV lounge. Rooms have private facilities. Swimming
pool, shaded parking. Breakfast served in rooms. Nearby restaurants.
Reductions for children under three. Dogs permitted for a charge.

Prices s fr €45; d fr €55; t fr €70   **On Site** ⚜ Private ⚘
Nearby ⛷4km ♨5km Sea 16km ✐ 0.5km Restaurant 1km ♨0.3km
🏠1km ⋙8km   **Notes** Pets admitted English spoken

JONQUIERES

⦀ **Château de Jonquières**

F et I DE CABISSOLE

34725 JONQUIERES

☎ 04 67 96 62 58 & 06 03 23 57 71 📄 04 67 88 61 92

email: contact@chateau-jonquieres.com

A vineyard property in an exceptional setting in the heart of the villag
It has four second floor rooms with beautiful views over the grounds.
There are three double rooms and a twin-bedded room, all with
private bath or shower room and WC. Lounge, dining room, terrace
with garden furniture.

Prices d €85-€90; extra person €20   **On Site** ⚜   **Nearby** ⛷10km
Sea 40km ✐ 8km ⚘   Restaurant 2.5km ♨ 🏠4km ⋙40km
Notes No pets English spoken Open April to 10 November.

LA LIVINIERE

⦀ ⦿ **Le Domaine de la Pinsonniere**

Stephanie HARMAND

12 route de Notre Dame, 34210 LA LIVINIERE

☎ 04 68 65 10 38 & 06 79 67 15 82

email: contact@lapinsonniere.fr

Not far from the Canal du Midi in a wine-growing village, this
19th-century house has five spacious bedrooms: a double, two twin-
bedded rooms and two triples; one twinned room has a bathroom,

the others all have a shower and WC. Two of the rooms have access to a sun terrace. Wooded grounds with swimming pool and parking space. Meals available by arrangement.

Prices s €50-€55; d €60-€65; t fr €80; dinner fr €20　**On Site** Private ⚲
Nearby ⚑ 7km　Sea 40km ♬ 6km ♨ 0.2km 🏠 0.2km ⛟ 30km
Notes No pets　English spoken

LA TOUR-SUR-ORB

⊞ ⧈ ♿ **Montbarri**

Roland BEC

34260 LA TOUR-SUR-ORB

☎ 04 67 95 09 97 　🗎 04 67 95 09 97

email: roland.bec@gmail.com

This property, bordered by a river, lies between the sea and the mountains, with a panoramic view over the hills. The bedrooms are modern, but with traditional charm. There are five of them, doubles and twins, all with private bath or shower room and WC. Solar heating. Garden with terrace. Meals by arrangement. Guided walks and horse riding.

Prices s fr €55; d fr €60; dinner fr €20　**On Site** ⚑ ♬ Restaurant
Nearby Sea 45km ⚲ 6km ♨ 4km 🏠 6km ⛟ 6km　**Notes** Pets admitted　English spoken

MARSEILLAN

⊞ **Domaine de la Mandoune**

Francoise COT

34340 MARSEILLAN

☎ 04 67 77 21 14 　🗎 04 67 77 29 00

email: mandoune@libertysurf.fr

web: www.mandoune.com

This property on a wine-growing estate has views across the Thau lake. It offers three double rooms and a twin on the ground floor, and a family room (double bed and two singles) on the first floor. Extra bed available. All rooms have private shower and WC. Electric heating. Lounge, garden with terrace.

Prices s fr €70; d fr €82　**Nearby** ⚑ 5km　Sea 10km ♬ 0.5km ⚲ 10km Restaurant 4km ♨ 5km ☂ 10km 🏠 4km ⛟ 12km　**Notes** No pets Open February to December.　CC

MARSILLARGUES

⊞ ⧈ **Au Soleil**

Catherine MAUREL

9, rue Pierre Brossolette, 34590 MARSILLARGUES

☎ 04 67 83 90 00 & 06 89 54 26 69

email: catherine.maurel@ausoleil.info

web: www.ausoleil.info

A big 18th-century house in the centre of a village on the edge of the Camargue. There are three double rooms, two with additional folding single beds, and all with private bath or shower room and WC. Lounge, dining room, and patio. Possible garage space for car. Meals available by arrangement.

Prices s fr €58; d fr €63; dinner fr €20　**On Site** Restaurant ☂
Nearby ⚑ 3km　Sea 17km ♬ 0.5km ⚲ 4km ♨ 🏠 0.2km ⛟ 2km
Notes No pets　English spoken　CC

⊞ **Relais Saint-Georges**

Veronique BERMANNE

5 bis R.Jean Jacques Rousseau, 34590 MARSILLARGUES

☎ 04 67 83 53 53 & 06 07 74 32 12 　🗎 04 67 83 53 53

email: patantiq@wanadoo.fr

This is an old vineyard property with five bedrooms, four on the ground floor and one upstairs. Four are doubles, and one is a triple with a double bed and a single; all of them have en suite facilities. There are two hectares of grounds, with a terrace and parking space.

Prices s fr €65; d fr €70; t fr €85; extra person fr €15　**Nearby** ⚑ 7km ⚑ 15km　Sea 15km ♬ 0.5km ⚲ 8km　Restaurant 0.5km　Spa 15km 🏠 0.5km ⛟ 25km　**Notes** No pets　English spoken

MAUREILHAN

ᛗ ᛁᎾᛁ Les Arbousiers

B et J FABRE-BARTHEZ
34370 MAUREILHAN
☎ 04 67 90 52 49 & 06 74 68 03 14 📄 04 67 90 50 50
email: ch.d.hotes.les.arbousiers@wanadoo.fr
web: www.gites-de-france34.com/les-arbousiers

A wine-grower offers six rooms in the centre of a village, five
kilometres from the Canal du Midi. Four air-conditioned rooms for
two or three guests and two for two or four, all with private facilities.
Guests' living room, reading room, TV, telephone, fireplace. Garden,
games area, shady terrace, enclosed parking.

Prices s €38-€49; d €46-€55; t €60-€67; extra person €14-€15;
dinner fr €20 **Nearby** ☂ 1km ⚓ 10km Sea 20km ✐ 4km ⚹ 9km
Restaurant 3km ⚓ 0.2km 🏛 0.1km ⚌ 9km **Notes** Pets admitted
English spoken

MURVIEL-LES-MONTPELLIER

ᛗ *Le Devois du Moulin*

J-C TESCH et J ROGER
Route de Bel Air, 34570 MURVIEL-LES-MONTPELLIER
☎ 04 67 07 28 42 📄 04 67 07 28 43
email: jengski.tesch@wanadoo.fr

This is a modern house a few kilometres northwest of Montpellier.
There are four bedrooms, three doubles and a family room for four,
all with private bath or shower room and WC. Outside are open
grounds with a terrace, swimming pool and ponds. Parking on site
and good access to footpaths.

Prices not confirmed for 2008 **On Site** Private ⚹ **Nearby** ☂ 8km
Sea 15km ✐ 25km ⚓ 2km 🏛 6km ⚌ 15km **Notes** No pets English
spoken

NOTRE-DAME-DE-LONDRES

ᛗ Le Pous

Elisabeth NOUALHAC
34380 NOTRE-DAME-DE-LONDRES
☎ 04 67 55 01 36 & 06 11 74 21 41

A beautiful 18th-century house in extensive grounds surrounded by
woods and scrubland. Six double rooms with private shower or bath
and wc. Heating, lounge, telephone.

Prices s €48-€50; d €52-€60 **Nearby** ☂ 2km Sea 40km ✐ 12km
⚹ 30km Restaurant 2km ⚓ 2km Spa 30km 🏛 9km ⚌ 30km
Notes No pets English spoken

OLONZAC

ᛗ Maison d'Hôtes

Henri MIGAUD
3, Av d'Homps, 34210 OLONZAC
☎ 04 68 91 17 70 & 06 80 47 46 78
email: levoyageurimmobile@wanadoo.fr
web: www.webzinemaker.com/voyageur/

This old posting inn, in the centre of the village and close to a park,
has five second floor rooms, all created using old materials. There are
two double rooms, two triples, and a family room for four. All rooms
have private bath or shower room and WC. Lounge with books,
kitchen available, garden.

Prices s fr €60; d fr €65; t fr €80; extra person fr €15 **Nearby** ☂ 10km
⚓ 35km Sea 45km ✐ 2km ⚹ 15km ⚓ 0.4km Spa 35km ✐ 4km
🏛 0.3km ⚌ 15km **Notes** No pets English spoken

POUSSAN

ᛗ ᛙ Chambre d'hôtes

Mireille et Pierre BARBE
65, Bis Rue Des Horts, 34560 POUSSAN
☎ 04 67 78 29 39 & 06 60 74 71 97
email: bbe2000@aol.com

At the foot of La Moure hill and the Massif de la Gardiole, this new
building offers five rooms: three twin rooms and two doubles with
private facilities. Geothermal heating and air conditioning, lounge/
sitting room, mezzanine library, fireplace. Enclosed grounds, garden
furniture, parking and table tennis. Reduced tariff for stays over a
week.

Prices s €55-€65; d fr €65; t fr €80 **On Site** Restaurant
Nearby ☂ 1km Sea 12km ✐ 5km ⚹ 12km ⚓ 1km ⚌ 8km
Notes No pets English spoken

POUZOLLES

ᛗ ᛁᎾᛁ Biens au Soleil

Paul HARREN
10, Boulevard Aristide Briand, 34480 POUZOLLES
☎ 04 67 24 84 27 📄 04 67 24 84 27
email: biens.au.soleil@wanadoo.fr
web: www.biensausoleil.fr

In the centre of a village in a wine-growing area, this 19th-century
house offers four guest bedrooms. They are all on the first floor: thre

win-bedded rooms, and a two-roomed family suite with four single
eds. All the rooms have private bath or shower room and WC.
ounge, garden with furniture, laundry facilities, meals by
rrangement.

Prices s fr €49; d fr €66; t fr €83; extra person fr €17; dinner fr €25
Nearby ⚓ 8km ⚓ 12km Sea 31km ✎ 7km ✈ Restaurant 3km ⚓ 1km
✈ 0.5km ⚓ 18km **Notes** No pets English spoken Open 15 March to
November.

⊪ ⦿ Domaine l'Eskillou

Brigitte GELLY
4, rue de la Distillerie, 34480 POUZOLLES
☎ 04 67 24 60 50 ▤ 04 67 24 60 50
email: brigitte.gelly@wanadoo.fr

Wine-growers offer five rooms for two to four people in a house
djacent to their home, all with air conditioning and private facilities.
iving room/sitting room, heating, open fire, TV, telephone, fridge.
wimming pool, parking, garden, shady terrace. Evening meal with
ine included. Motorbikes, swings, board games and table tennis in
ames room. Reductions after 7 nights in low season.

Prices s fr €63; d fr €70; t fr €90; extra person fr €20; dinner fr €20
On Site Private ✈ **Nearby** ⚓ 8km Sea 31km ✎ 10km ⚓ ⚓ 6km
Notes Pets admitted English spoken Open April to November. CC

QUARANTE

⊪ ⦿ Chambre d'hôtes

Helge WOLFF
4, Grande Rue, 34310 QUARANTE
☎ 04 67 89 34 72 ▤ 04 67 89 30 64
email: wolffhelge@hotmail.com

ocated between the sea and the mountains, this countryside location
ideal for rambling. The 19th-century family mansion is 4km from
ne Canal du Midi in a 3.5 hectare, shady park. Four large rooms each
eep 3-4 people and have a private bathroom and wc. Sitting room
ith TV and open fire, parking, swimming pool, pétanque, cycling.
Meals available if booked. Restaurants nearby.

Prices not confirmed for 2008 **On Site** Private ✈ **Nearby** ⚓ 4km
ea 35km ✎ 4km ⚓ ⚓ 25km **Notes** Pets admitted English spoken

OUBES

⊪ Les Terrasses du Peret

ierre SOULAIROL
53 Chemin de Peret, 34700 SOUBES
☎ 04 67 44 22 63 ▤ 04 67 44 22 63
email: lesterrassesduperet@yahoo.fr

he three bedrooms here are in a modern building adjacent to the
wners' home and looking down towards a picturesque village. They
e on different levels, all of them triples (double bed plus a single in
ach) with private bathroom and WC. Living room and conservatory,
nd outside are open grounds with garden and parking space.

Prices s fr €50; d fr €65; t fr €80 **Nearby** ⚓ 5km ✎ 2km ✈ 5km
⚓ 5km **Notes** No pets English spoken

ST-ANDRE-DE-BUEGES

⊪ ⦿ Bombequiols

A-M BOUEC-DANN
Route De Brissac, 34190 SAINT-ANDRE-DE-BUEGES
☎ 04 67 73 72 67 & 06 83 54 44 60 ▤ 04 67 73 72 67
email: bombequiols@wanadoo.fr
web: http://masdebombequiols.free.fr

Medieval country house, in a peaceful, preserved spot among the hills.
Dine on local produce and wine under the arches of the terrace or in
front of the fire. Two rooms, one duplex and three suites (with open
fires), each with their own access, set around the closed courtyard
with private baths and wcs. Swimming pool, 50 hectare park, lake.
Explore St-Guilhem-le-Désert, La Couvertoirade, the Roman churches,
Grottes des Demoiselles, the Bambouseraie.

Prices d €90-€125; t €150; dinner fr €30 **On Site** ✎ Private ✈
Nearby ⚓ 8km Restaurant 5km ⚓ 5km ✈ 9km ⚓ 5km ⚓ 42km
Notes No pets

⊪ ⦿ Mas de Luzière

Arnaud DELRUE
34190 SAINT-ANDRE-DE-BUEGES
☎ 04 67 73 34 97 ▤ 04 67 73 34 97
email: arnaud@luziere.com

In the heart of the Buegus Valley and the foot of the Seanne
mountains, this 19th-century mansion is surrounded by ten hectares
of field and woodland. There are three rooms available, all with private
facilities. Lounge with open hearth, car parking, garden furniture and
swimming pool.

Prices s fr €60; d fr €60; t fr €70; extra person fr €10; dinner fr €24
On Site Private ✈ **Nearby** ⚓ 20km ✎ 5km Restaurant 5km ⚓ 5km
⚓ 15km ⚓ 50km **Notes** No pets English spoken Open Easter to 1
November. CC

ST-NAZAIRE-DE-LADAREZ

⊪ ⦿ Chambre d'hôtes

J et S CATANZANO-FARRUGIA
rue Francaise, Les Semailles,
34490 SAINT-NAZAIRE-DE-LADAREZ
☎ 04 67 89 56 28

In the centre of the village, known for its quarry of crimson marble,
this 19th-century wine-making house is surrounded by some of the
oldest vineyards in France. On the ground-floor is a lounge with
open hearth and on the second floor, two double rooms with private
facilities. Meals available on request.

Prices s €43-€46; d €46-€50; t fr €96; dinner fr €25 **Nearby** Sea 45km
✎ 9km ✈ 18km ⚓ 9km ⚓ 9km ⚓ 25km **Notes** No pets

VIAS

ⵌ Domaine de la Gardie

Sandrine DUPLAN
34450 VIAS
☎ 04 67 21 79 22   📄 04 67 21 79 22
email: eduplan@wanadoo.fr

Ideally located in a shady pine-forest on a verdant wine-growing estate, less than 3km from the beaches. There are five rooms at street level for two and three people with terraces and private facilities. Lounge/living room, heating, fireplace, TV, telephone, parking, garden with furniture and children's games, table tennis, basketball and volleyball.

Prices s €54-€59; d €54-€59; t fr €67   **Nearby** ⚓ 3km Sea 3km ⚐ 3km ⟋ 4km ⌕ 1km 🏠 1km ⵜ 4km   **Notes** No pets English spoken Open April to 6 November. CC

VIC-LA-GARDIOLE

ⵌ ⬥ Mas de Jacquet

Nathalie SOLIVE
23 Bld Des Aresquiers, 34110 VIC LA GARDIOLE
☎ 04 67 78 43 03
email: masdejacquet@wanadoo.fr
web: www.masdejacquet.com

Two kilometres from the beach, this old wine-growing property in the village centre has six spacious bedrooms. On the ground floor is a twin-bedded room, and a two-room family suite with a double bed and two singles. Upstairs are three doubles, and another family suite similar to the one downstairs. All rooms have private bath/shower room and WC. Lounge, terrace, garden furniture.

Prices s fr €60; d fr €60; t fr €95   **Nearby** ⚓ 1km Sea 2km ⚐ 1km ⟋ 5km ⌕ 0.5km ⚑ 0.2km 🏠 9km ⵜ 9km   **Notes** No pets Open March to October.

LOZÈRE

BADAROUX

ⵌ ⵙ Lou Rastel

Monique CHAPERON
48000 BADAROUX
☎ 04 66 47 70 04

Guests receive a warm welcome here and the hosts are eager to help and to share their passion for the Lozère lifestyle. The house has a large wooded and lawned garden, plus a terrace and courtyard. The table d'hôte dinners are notable. There are three double rooms; two extra beds can be arranged for families.

Prices s fr €47; d €50-€52; extra person fr €17; dinner fr €17
On Site ⚐   **Nearby** ⚓ 3km ⚒ 25km ⟋ 5km Restaurant 5km ⌕ Spa 10km ⚑ 5km 🏠 6km ⵜ 6km   **Notes** No pets English spoken

BARJAC

ⵌ ⵙ ⬥ Domaine de Recoulettes

Patrick et Nicole DIEUDONNE
48000 BARJAC
☎ 06 85 57 81 39
email: recoulettes@wanadoo.fr
web: www.domainederecoulettes.com

A beautiful old house which has been restored to offer comfortable accommodation for nine guests. There are four upstairs double room one with an additional single bed; all have TV, private bathroom and WC. Downstairs there is a large lounge, bar and dining room; outside is a garden with terrace and garden furniture. Meals by arrangement.

Prices s fr €48; d fr €54; t fr €70; extra person fr €16; dinner fr €15
On Site ⚐ ⚒   **Nearby** ⚓ 5km ⟋ 5km Restaurant 14km ⌕ 5km ⵜ 14km   **Notes** Pets admitted English spoken

BARRE-DES-CEVENNES

ⵌ ⵎ ⵙ Le Mazeldan

Claude BOISSIER
48400 BARRE-DES-CEVENNES
☎ 04 66 45 07 18
email: chambresdhotes.boissier@wanadoo.fr

Situated in a small village at an altitude of 700 metres, with a magnificent view over the Cévennes, a warm welcome awaits at this sheep and cattle rearing farm with its traditional farmhouse. En suite rooms, sitting-dining room with open fire and TV, patio and parking.

Prices d €42-€44; t €53-€55   **Nearby** ⚓ 7km ⟋ 19km ⌕ 5km 🏠 5kr
Notes No pets

CHANAC

ⵌ Le Jas

J-Pierre et Sylvie DURAND
L'Oustal del jas, 48230 CHANAC
☎ 04 66 48 22 93
email: sylvie.japy@orange.fr
web: http://cardoule.com/durand/

This farm is situated between the Gorges du Tarn and the Vallee du Lot, and offers three en suite guest rooms with space for eight guests in the proprietors' home. Conservatory, TV corner, washing

machine, kitchen, baby equipment, BBQ and parking. Walking trips.
advanced booking is essential; reductions for children and for stays
ver 7 nights.

rices s fr €42; d €47-€54; t fr €61; extra person fr €12 **On Site** ❦
Nearby ☘ 5km ⚓ 20km ✎ 6km ↖ 5km Restaurant 5km ⚓ 5km
16km ⛵ 7km **Notes** No pets

FONTANS

♨ ⬭ Les Sapins Verts

lexandre CRUEIZE
hazeirollettes, 48700 FONTANS
☎ 04 66 48 30 23 📄 04 66 48 30 23
mail: alexandre.crueize@wanadoo.fr
veb: www.lessapinsverts.com

n old house offering five en suite, centrally heated rooms for two
r three people. Traditional family cooking includes local specialities
cluding game, truffles etc. Lots of activities in the area: walking, bison
ark 12 km, wolf park 20 km, Lac de Naussac 40 km.

rices s fr €40; d fr €52; t fr €73; extra person fr €21; dinner €12-€24
earby ☘ 10km ↖ 18km ⚓ 7km 🏇 4km ⛵ 15km **Notes** No pets
nglish spoken Open April to mid October.

GATUZIERES

♨ Chambre d'hôtes

uriel TRESCARTE
150 GATUZIERES
☎ 04 66 45 64 10 & 06 74 58 28 85
mail: tresjlm@aol.com
eb: www.causses-cevennes.com/gatuzieres

commodation at this peaceful, mosaic-tiled gite is located in a
ouse neighbouring the proprietors'. Two bedrooms have a double
d two single beds, and the third has a double bed; all have private
ashrooms and wc.

ices s fr €42; d fr €48; t fr €59; extra person fr €9 **Nearby** ☘ 6km
6km ⚓ 6km 🏇 6km ⛵ 46km **Notes** No pets English spoken Open
arch to November.

RANDRIEU

♨ 🐦 Bellelande

oi ASTRUC
600 GRANDRIEU
☎ 04 66 46 30 53 📄 04 66 46 30 53

is guest house offers two grade 2 rooms and two grade 3 rooms
with private wc and private or shared bath or shower room.
mmunal sitting room with TV, dining room with open fire, patio,
nservatory and parking. Reservation essential and children up to
ee are free. Meals are served using local specialities.

ices s fr €23; d fr €46; t fr €69 **On Site** ✎ **Nearby** ☘ 5km ⚓ 20km
24km ⚓ 6km 🏇 6km ⛵ 24km **Notes** No pets Open 16 April to
November.

LA CANOURGUE

♨ ⬭ & La Vialette

Jean et Anne-Marie FAGES
48500 LA CANOURGUE
☎ 04 66 32 83 00
email: contact@gite-sauveterre.com
web: www.gite-sauveterre.com

A warm welcome awaits in this 15th-century Caussenarde farmhouse,
which provides six rooms, all with en suite facilities and TV.

Prices d fr €52; t fr €66; dinner fr €16 **On Site** ❦ **Nearby** ☘ 10km
⚓ 8km ↖ 0.1km Restaurant 10km ⚓ 10km 🏇 10km ⛵ 13km
Notes Pets admitted

LA TIEULE

♨ ⬭ Les Ecuries de Sauveterre

Sylviane RIVOIRE
48500 LA TIEULE
☎ 04 66 48 82 83 & 06 77 40 28 80 📄 04 66 48 89 23
email: ecuries-sauveterre@wanadoo.fr
web: www.ecuriesdesauveterre.com

A former monastery, well placed near Millau and the Gorges du
Tarn. Five bedrooms sleep from two to six people, each having
private bathroom and WC. Meals are available by arrangement, with
traditional local dishes. Outside is a garden with terrace and swimming
pool. Horses, bikes and motorbikes can all be accommodated.

Prices s fr €52; d fr €58; t fr €78; extra person fr €20; dinner fr €18
On Site ✎ ⚓ Private ↖ **Nearby** ☘ 5km ⚓ 7km ⚓ 7km 🏇 12km
⛵ 50km **Notes** Pets admitted English spoken Open 15 March to
11 November.

LANGOGNE

♨ Villa Les Roches

Christine COOPER
48300 LANGOGNE
☎ 04 66 46 69 53 & 06 33 58 08 91
email: info@villa-les-roches.com
web: www.villa-les-roches.com

In a wonderful setting perched up above a rocky outcrop, this house
overlooks the green valley of the River Langouyrou. Three beautifully
decorated rooms at terrace level all have private bathroom (one of the
rooms is not en suite); on the first floor are two twin-bedded rooms
CONTINUED

LANGOGNE CONTINUED

(can be made into doubles), one with bathroom, the other with shower room and WC. Outside are peaceful wooded grounds, with a river and spectacular wild countryside beyond.

Prices s €40-€47; d €48-€55; extra person fr €15 **On Site** 🖉
Nearby 🏇 3km ⚓ 0.5km 🎣 1km Restaurant 1km 🏊 1km 🎾 1km
🏛 1km 🚶 1.5km **Notes** No pets English spoken Open April to 1 November.

LE COLLET-DE-DEZE

🏳 🌱 🍽 Chambre d'hôtes

Bernard et Josiane LEROUX
Lou Rey, 48160 LE COLLET-DE-DEZE
☎ 04 66 45 58 58 & 06 08 33 09 32 📄 04 66 45 58 59
email: lourey.gfa@wanadoo.fr
web: http://lou-rey.com

On the edge of the Parc National des Cévennes, this fortified 13th-century farmhouse has three quiet and comfortable guest bedrooms: two are triples and the third is a two-roomed suite for four with two double beds; each room has a shower and WC. Outside, guests will find a terrace, chestnut trees, and a great view of the Cévennes. The owners keep goats, donkeys and horses.

Prices s fr €40; d fr €58; t fr €85; dinner €12-€16 **On Site** 🚴
Nearby ⚓ 10km 🖉 4km 🎣 10km Restaurant 5km 🏊 4km 🚶 14km
Notes Pets admitted

🏳 🍽 Mas Lou Prat

Marlène et Pascal TOURNEUX
La Dévèze, 48160 LE COLLET-DE-DEZE
☎ 04 66 45 46 47
email: louprat@wanadoo.fr
web: http://chambre-hotes-cevennes.fr

This house is on the edge of the Parc National des Cévennes, and offers four guest bedrooms. All of them have private shower room and WC, but for one of the rooms (which is grade 2) the WC, although private, is not en suite. Meals are available by arrangement. Many outdoor activities near by include walking, rock-climbing and canoeing.

Prices s €36-€40; d €58-€60; t fr €85; extra person fr €25; dinner €14
Nearby 🚴 4km 🖉 3km 🎣 12km Restaurant 0.5km 🏊 4km 🎾 10km
🏛 4km 🚶 30km **Notes** Pets admitted English spoken Open April to December.

LE POMPIDOU

🏳 🌱 🍽 Chambre d'hôtes

Jean-Marie CAUSSE
Le Village, 48110 LE POMPIDOU
☎ 04 66 60 31 82 & 06 98 28 80 96
email: j.m.causse@libertysurf.fr
web: www.chambres-hotes-cevennes.com

Situated at the junction of two valleys in an area rich in history and spectacular scenery; this is a well appointed house, in a small village on the edge of the Cévennes. It offers four en suite rooms for two to three people, a sitting room with fridge and a terrace with conservatory and garden with parking.

Prices s fr €41; d fr €48; t fr €66; extra person fr €11; dinner fr €16 **On Site** Restaurant **Nearby** 🚴 12km 🖉 5km 🏊 🎾 8km
Notes No pets Open 8 January to 20 December.

LE PONT-DE-MONTVERT

🏳 🍽 Finiels

J GALZIN et M PANTEL
Maison Victoire, 48220 LE PONT-DE-MONTVERT
☎ 04 66 45 84 36
email: jacqueline.galzin@free.fr
web: www.gites-mont-lozere.com

This restored house offers five comfortable en suite rooms and is set in the heart of the Cévennes National Park and on Stevenson's trail (GR 70) in a peaceful village on the slopes of the Mont Lozère. Meals using home-made and local produce are served in front of the 16th-century fireplace. Forest walks.

Prices s fr €58; d fr €58 **On Site** 🖉 Restaurant **Nearby** 🚴 25km
🎣 15km 🎾 10km 🏛 6km 🚶 35km **Notes** Pets admitted English spoken

🏳 🌱 🍽 Le Merlet

Catherine et Philippe GALZIN
48220 LE PONT-DE-MONTVERT
☎ 04 66 45 82 92 📄 04 66 45 80 78
email: lemerlet@wanadoo.fr
web: www.lemerlet.com

This 16th-century farmhouse in the Cévennes National Park offers six double en suite rooms. Meals using local specialities are served. Mapped local walking routes are available.

Prices s fr €51; d fr €102; dinner fr €20 **Nearby** 🖉 0.5km 🎣 0.5km
Restaurant 5km 🏊 6km Spa 30km 🎾 29km 🏛 8km 🚶 25km
Notes No pets English spoken CC

LE ROZIER

⊯ La Pause

rancis ESPINASSE

.oute de Capluc, 48150 LE ROZIER

☎ 05 65 62 63 06 ▤ 05 65 61 03 87

mail: gite.la.pause@wanadoo.fr

 veb: www.chambres-hotes-gorgesdutarn.com

his property is near the Gorges du Tarn and La Jonte, on the edge f the village. There are six en suite guest rooms in the home of the roprietor: four double rooms, one room sleeping three and one om sleeping four. There is a patio with conservatory, pool and walks arting from the house.

rices s fr €38; d fr €45; t fr €60; extra person fr €18　**On Site** ℘
Private ⟍　**Nearby** ⛷ 5km Restaurant 0.3km ⌇ 0.8km ⋙ 20km
otes Pets admitted English spoken

1ARCHASTEL

⊯ ⍥ Chambre d'hôtes

eanine BOYER

3260 MARCHASTEL

☎ 04 66 32 53 79

ve en suite rooms with separate access are available in an old family anor house. This charming home is situated in the heart of Aubrac a pretty and peaceful village. There is a dining room with small tchen and washing machine. Meals feature local specialities.

rices s €40-€42; d €47-€49; t €63-€65; dinner €16-€50
earby ⛷ 5km ⟍ 20km ⌇ 5km ⓶ 5km ⋙ 20km **Notes** Pets mitted Open 30 March to 5 November.

1AS-SAINT-CHELY

⊯ ⛤ Les Aires de la Carline

aussignac, 48210 MAS SAINT CHELY

☎ 04 66 48 54 79

nail: lesairesdelacarline@wanadoo.fr

eb: www.hote-causse-mejean.com

stone building in the traditional style, standing in its own wooded ounds in a hamlet of about 20 people seven kilometres from the orges du Tarn. There are four very comfortable bedrooms, all with vate bath or shower room and WC, as well as TV, telephone, ernet access, hairdryer and minibar. On-site parking.

ices s fr €55; d fr €55; t fr €65　**Nearby** ⛷ 15km ↧ 30km ⟍ 15km 7km ⓶ 7km **Notes** No pets English spoken Open 15 April to 15 tober.

NAUSSAC

⊯ Les Genêts d'Or

Michèle BANDON

48300 NAUSSAC

☎ 04 66 69 17 47

web: www.lozere.online.com/lesgenetsdor

Beautifully decorated, this newly renovated house is situated between Langogne and Lake Naussac in the village of Pomeyrols. It has three double rooms, a triple and a four bedded-room, all en suite. Kitchen, sitting room with open fire and TV, telephone, conservatory and parking.

Prices s fr €45; d fr €45; t fr €58; extra person fr €13　**Nearby** ⛷ 8km ↧ 4km ℘ 2km ⟍ 5km Restaurant 5km ⌇ 5km ⓶ 5km ⓶ 5km ⋙ 5km
Notes Pets admitted English spoken Open Easter to 1 November.

RIEUTORT-DE-RANDON

⊯ ⛤ ⍥ ⛭ La Ferme de Saltel

Edith et Benoît NOETINGER

48700 RIEUTORT-DE-RANDON

☎ 04 66 47 38 51 ▤ 04 66 47 38 11

email: fermedesaltel@wanadoo.fr

web: www.lozere.com

To the south of the Margeride, in one of the strongholds of the war-time resistance groups and not far from the Charpal Lake, this property has three beautiful bedrooms including a double and a twin-bedded room. All have en suite facilities, and one is fully accessible for disabled guests. There is on-site parking.

Prices s fr €48-€60; d fr €53-€65; t fr €75-€90; extra person €25-€40; dinner €27-€36　**On Site** ℘ Restaurant ⓶　**Nearby** ⛷ 4km ⟍ 10km ⌇ 2km ⓶ 2km ⋙ 15km **Notes** Pets admitted English spoken Open 15 March to 15 November.　CC

ST-ANDRE-DE-CAPCEZE

⊯ ⍥ Au Portaou

P THOLET et H-D RÖCHER

Valcrouzès, 48800 ST-ANDRE-DE-CAPCEZE

☎ 04 66 46 20 10 ▤ 04 66 46 20 10

email: au-portaou@wanadoo.fr

web: www.cevennes-mont-lozere.com

The hamlet of Valcrouzès is right on the edge of the Cévennes, near Villefort. The house is built of granite, in the traditional style of the region, with an internal courtyard, vine-covered arbours and terraces. Four bedrooms comprise three doubles and one room for three, all with private bath or shower room and WC. Meals available by arrangement.

Prices s fr €34; d fr €48; t fr €58; extra person fr €10; dinner fr €18
Nearby ⛷ 6km ↧ 12km ℘ 6km ⟍ 4km Restaurant 1.5km ⌇ 7km
Spa 40km ⓶ 6km ⓶ 6km ⋙ 6km **Notes** No pets English spoken Open February to 15 November & Xmas to New Years Day.

ST-ANDRE-DE-LANCIZE

❦ ⭗ Le Valès

Séverine KIEFFER

48240 ST-ANDRE-DE-LANCIZE

☎ 04 66 45 93 20 ▤ 04 66 45 93 20

email: anesvales@wanadoo.fr

web: www.gite-cevennes.fr

This property is in a small peaceful hamlet and has a triple room (one double and one single bed) and two family rooms (one double and two mezzanine single beds), all en suite. There is a garden, a conservatory and terrace; donkey and pony trips nearby. Local farm products for sale.

Prices s fr €45; d fr €50; extra person €22-€40 **Nearby** ⛷ 10km 🏊 4km 🎣 20km 🚴 15km 🎾 15km 🏛 12km 🚶 45km **Notes** No pets English spoken

ST-FREZAL-DE-VENTALON

⭗ Le Viala

Katrien VANDENBROUCKE

48240 ST-FREZAL-DE-VENTALON

☎ 04 66 45 54 08

email: leviala@gmail.com

web: www.leviala.com

A 16th-century house built in the local style, in the heart of the Parc National des Cévennes. Four bedrooms, each with independent access, comprise three doubles and a triple with three single beds; all have private shower and WC. Before meals an aperitif is offered, around the fire in winter and beneath the grapevines in summer. Attractive garden, and good walking country beyond.

Prices s €48; d €58; extra person €15; dinner fr €23 **Nearby** 🏛 11km 🚶 45km **Notes** No pets English spoken

ST-GERMAIN-DE-CALBERTE

⭗ La Fare

Julien BONNAL

Mas Lou Abeilhs La Fare,

48370 ST-GERMAIN-DE-CALBERTE

☎ 04 66 45 94 91 & 06 60 86 85 49

email: bonnal.julien@wanadoo.fr

web: www.causses-cevennes.com/mas-abeilhs/

This property has four rooms, all of them with private terraces overlooking a wild valley. Each room has a private shower and WC. The location of the house provides a panoramic view across the valleys of the Cévennes. Central heating; good mobile phone signal for Itinéris and Bouygtel!

Prices s fr €48; d fr €48; dinner fr €18 **Nearby** ⛷ 5km 🏊 2km 🎣 5km Restaurant 5km 🚴 5km 🏛 6km 🚶 50km **Notes** Pets admitted English spoken Open April to 30 October.

⭗ Lou Pradel

Pol et Maria HOSTENS

48370 ST-GERMAIN-DE-CALBERTE

☎ 04 66 45 92 46 ▤ 04 66 45 92 46

email: lou.pradel@wanadoo.fr

web: www.loupradel.com

At the heart of the Cévennes overlooking the valleys, this property ha three comfortable en suite guest rooms, a sitting room with open fire and a library. Mountain bike hire, donkey enclosure. Meals are serve on request on Wednesday and Saturday. Bar is 1km.

Prices s fr €50; d fr €62; t fr €76; extra person fr €17; dinner fr €26 **On Site** Restaurant **Nearby** ⛷ 5km 🎣 12km 🚴 12km 🎾 30km 🏛 8km 🚶 20km **Notes** No pets English spoken Open March to 11 November.

❦ ⭗ Vernet

Sabine et Gérard LAMY

48370 ST-GERMAIN-DE-CALBERTE

☎ 04 66 45 91 94

email: gerardsabine.lamy@wanadoo.fr

web: www.vernet-cevennes.com

Six en suite guests rooms offered, together with a sitting room with open fire and heating, a library and a terrace. Guests have the chanc to see the donkeys and the sheep, and at the right time of year colle raspberries with the farmer. Meals are prepared with garden and farr produce.

Prices s fr €40; d fr €50; t fr €66; extra person fr €16; dinner fr €17.50 **Nearby** ⛷ 10km 🏊 10km Restaurant 10km 🚴 10km 🏛 10km 🚶 40kr **Notes** Pets admitted English spoken Open 15 March to 15 November.

ST-MARTIN-DE-LANSUSCLE

⭗ Château de Cauvel

Hubert et A-Sylvie PFISTER

48110 ST-MARTIN-DE-LANSUSCLE

☎ 04 66 45 92 75 ▤ 04 66 45 94 76

email: lecauvel@lecauvel.com

web: www.lecauvel.com

Guests can enjoy peace and beautiful surroundings at this family home. There is a large library, an open fire, comfortable rooms. Interesting cuisine includes freshly baked bread and jam.

Prices s fr €60; d fr €65; dinner fr €20 **On Site** 🎾 **Nearby** ⛷ 9km 🏊 4km 🎣 12km Restaurant 9km 🏛 9km 🚶 55km **Notes** No pets English spoken

T-PIERRE-DES-TRIPIERS

▦ ❚◎❚ La Volpilière

anielle et Michel GAL
e Choucas, 48150 ST-PIERRE-DES-TRIPIERS
☎ 04 66 45 64 28
eb: http://cardoule.com/lechoucas/

ith splendid views, this house is set on le Causse-Méjean, above the
orges du Tarn. Three charming en suite rooms sleeping two to four
eople are offered. There is a large sitting room with open fire and TV,
rrace and walking routes nearby. Some English spoken.

ices s fr €48; d fr €53; extra person fr €13; dinner fr €16
earby ⛷ 15km ⌧ 40km ⚲ 8km ⌤ 17km Restaurant 4km ⌇ 17km
17km 🏛 8km ⋙ 38km **Notes** No pets Open May to September.

T-PRIVAT-DE-VALLONGUE

▦▦ *La Baume*

Richard THEME
48240 ST-PRIVAT-DE-VALLONGUE
☎ 04 66 45 58 89 📄 04 66 45 48 84
email: contact@labaume-cevennes.com
web: www.labaume-cevennes.com

A warm welcome awaits at this traditional 17th-century Cévenole
building. Rooms include 'Magnanerie' (en suite double), the
'Bruyère Suite' (en suite double with two singles, and sitting
room), 'La Clède' (double with sitting room and private patio)
and 'Tilleul' (double with single sofa bed, sitting room and
bathroom). Dining room, two sitting rooms, billiard room,
parking, conservatory, telephone, terrace, and guided walks from
La Baume.

Prices not confirmed for 2008 **Nearby** ⚲ 0.3km ⌇ 0.1km 🏛 1km
⋙ 40km **Notes** Pets admitted English spoken Open Easter to
December.

T-ROME-DE-DOLAN

▦ Combelasais

erre CALMELS
500 ST-ROME-DE-DOLAN
04 66 48 80 08
nail: yvonnepierre.calmels@club-internet.fr
eb: http://saint-rome-de-dolan.com/combelasais.htm

s stone built farmhouse is four kilometres from the Gorges du
n. It has an open view to the south. It has a room for four people
uble bed and two singles) with en suite shower and WC; it also
s a double room and a twin with private showers and a shared WC.
rden terrace.

ces s €30-€35; d €40-€45; t fr €60; extra person fr €15
arby ⛷ 6km ⌧ 20km ⚲ 10km ⌤ 40km Restaurant 2km ⌇ 2km
0km 🏛 2km ⋙ 10km **Notes** Pets admitted

STE-COLOMBE-DE-PEYRE

▦▦ Chaudoudoux

Annie et Georges PAUC
48130 STE-COLOMBE-DE-PEYRE
☎ 04 66 42 93 39
email: chaudoudoux@tiscali.fr

This small traditional farm offers four en suite rooms, heating, an open
fire, garden and garage. Pick-up from the station if required. Walking,
mountain biking and cross-country skiing available; Déroc waterfall
20km. Half board discount after 4 nights.

Prices s fr €40; d fr €50; extra person fr €15 **Nearby** ⛷ 20km ⌧ 30km
⚲ 0.3km ⌤ 18km ⌇ 20km ⌖ 20km 🏛 10km ⋙ 10km **Notes** No pets

TERMES

▦▦ ❚◎❚ La Narce

Alain CHALVET
48310 TERMES
☎ 04 66 31 64 12 📄 04 66 31 64 12
email: lanarce@orange.fr

The old, traditionally restored farmhouse of La Narce guarantees
peace and quiet. Access is by a private road and the farm is situated
in three hectares of parkland between Aubrac and Margeride just
500mtrs from the village. Accommodation is in twin rooms with
private facilities. There is a large dining room and kitchen with stove.
Meals available by arrangement.

Prices s fr €40; d fr €47; dinner fr €15 **On Site** ⛷ ⚲
Nearby ⌧ 25km ⌤ 10km Restaurant 0.4km ⌇ 5km Spa 18km ⌖ 10km
🏛 5km ⋙ 10km **Notes** No pets English spoken

VILLEFORT

▦▦ ❧ ❚◎❚ *Mas de l'Affenadou*

Nelly MANIFACIER
11 Rue des Amandiers, 48000 MENDE
☎ 04 66 49 27 42 & 04 66 46 97 23
email: manifacier.nelly@free.fr
web: www.gite-lozere.com

This 16th-century farmhouse on the GR68 path is a former mule
trail inn. On the edge of the Cévennes national park and close to
the Ardèche, it has a wonderful view towards Mont Lozère. It has
four rooms, two doubles and two triples, each with private shower
and WC. Meals available, many using ducks from the farm. Excellent
fishing area.

Prices not confirmed for 2008 **Nearby** ⛷ 1km ⌧ 3km ⌤ 1km ⌇ 1km
🏛 1km ⋙ 1km **Notes** No pets English spoken Open April to 15
November.

LANGUEDOC-ROUSSILLON

PYRÉNÉES-ORIENTALES

ARBOUSSOLS

⚜ Les Fenêtres du Soleil

F et C CHOLLOT-DEVILLE
rue de la Fontaine, 66320 ARBOUSSOLS
☎ 04 68 05 56 25 & 06 11 08 60 41 📄 04 68 05 56 25
email: lesfenetresdusoleil@wanadoo.fr
web: www.lesfenetresdusoleil.com

There are four spacious and elegant bedrooms, two of them family rooms, in this restored house in the pretty village of Arboussols. The house has an exceptional view over the Pic du Canigou and the valley below. The hosts will make you very welcome, either in front of the fire or out on the sunny terrace.

Prices s €53-€63; d €63-€73; t fr €90; extra person fr €17   **On Site** 🍽
Nearby ☘4km ♨2.7km ♟4km ♝45km ⚓0.1km Spa 20km 🏛4km
♨4km **Notes** No pets English spoken CC

BAGES

⚜ 🍴 Mas de la Prade

Claudette GILJEAN
66670 BAGES
☎ 04 68 37 58 19 📄 04 68 37 58 19
email: masdelaprade@aol.com

An 18th-century restored farm building is the setting for three large and delightful bedrooms, all of them doubles. The house is on the edge of a village, surrounded by meadows. The breakfasts are generous, and other meals, showing off the delights of the local cuisine, are available by arrangement.

Prices s fr €65; d fr €75; dinner fr €25   **On Site** 🍽 **Nearby** ☘0.5km
Sea 15km ♟2km Restaurant 5km ⚓2km Spa 25km 🏛2km ♨10km
Notes No pets English spoken Open April to September.

BROUILLA

⚜ L'Ancienne Gare

Joaquina CASENOBAS
Le Millery, 66620 BROUILLA
☎ 04 68 89 88 21 📄 04 68 89 88 21
email: ancienne-gare@wanadoo.fr

There are five spacious guest rooms in this restored former railway station. There is a wooded garden, with "outdoor room" style spaces. The location is quiet, and slightly outside the village. The hosts will be delighted to tell you about the places to visit in the area.

Prices not confirmed for 2008   **Nearby** ☘3km Sea 10km ♟5km
Spa 8km ♨7.5km **Notes** No pets English spoken

CABESTANY

⚜ ⅙ Domaine du Mas Boluix

Jean-Louis CEILLES
Chemin Du Pou De Les Coulobres,
66100 PERPIGNAN
☎ 04 68 08 17 70 📄 04 68 08 17 71
web: www.domaine-de-boluix.com

Situated in a 30 hectare vineyard in Cabestany, ten minutes from the beaches of Canet, this renovated 18th-century mas offers five charming rooms and a family suite with refined décor, air-conditioning and satellite TV. Tours of the vineyard possible with the owner.

Prices s fr €83; d fr €91; t fr €130   **On Site** Restaurant 🍽
Nearby ☘4km ♨4km Sea 8km ♟3km ♝3km ⚓3km
Spa 30km 🏛1km ♨3km **Notes** No pets

CAMELAS

⚜ 🍴 Mas Bellecroze

Charles-André HARREAU-RELAVE
66300 CAMELAS
☎ 04 68 53 67 11 📄 04 68 53 67 11
email: masbellecroze@tiscali.fr
web: www.masbellecroze.com

This big Mediterranean house has three bedrooms and a suite, and can accommodate up to eight guests. A travel theme runs through the decoration of the rooms. There is a spacious lounge with an open fir and books to read. The surrounding forest, and the terraces around the swimming pool, provide space for rest and relaxation. Meals by arrangement.

Prices s €80-€90; d €80-€90; t fr €105; dinner fr €24
On Site Private ♝ **Nearby** ☘5km Sea 35km ♟10km Restaurant 5k
Spa 35km 🏛7km ♨20km **Notes** No pets English spoken

⚜ 🍴 Mas del Roc

André ARCIS
66300 CAMELAS
☎ 04 68 53 05 43 & 06 61 49 10 12 📄 04 68 53 05 43
email: ch.arcis@wanadoo.fr

Panoramic views over Roussillon and the Mediterranean come free with these five large rooms! The host is passionate about cooking ar Catalan meals (by reservation) are served by the pool.

Prices d €85-€100; t fr €100; dinner fr €24   **On Site** Private ♝
Nearby ☘10km Sea 35km ♟10km Spa 35km 🏛7km ♨13km
Notes No pets English spoken

CASTELNOU

♯♯♯ ⏺ **La Figuera**

Nicole et Michel DESPREZ

3 Carrer De La Fount D'Avall, 66300 CASTELNOU

☎ 04 68 53 18 42

email: lafiguera@wanadoo.fr

web: www.la-figuera.com

This property has four charming guest rooms, in a house of character in one of the most beautiful villages in France. The rooms are comfortably arranged and beautifully decorated. In summer, breakfast is served on the terrace in the shade of the fig trees. A peaceful spot in an enclosed garden full of flowers.

Prices d €70-€80; dinner fr €25   **On Site** Restaurant ♜
Nearby ⛵ 5km ⚓ 20km Sea 25km 🎣 25km ⌇ 5km ⛵ 5km Spa 20km
🏛 5km ᴘᴘ 20km   **Notes** No pets

CERET

♯♯♯ ⚮ **Mas Terra Rosa**

Simone JOSSE-ROUX

Las Bourgueres, 66400 CERET

☎ 04 68 87 34 00 & 06 09 06 76 63

This quiet wooded property has three guest rooms. In fine weather breakfast is served on the sunny terrace with a splendid view over the Canigou Massif. Secure parking available. Many routes for walking directly from the farmhouse.

Prices s fr €50; d fr €55; t fr €65   **On Site** Restaurant ♜
Nearby ⛵ 10km Sea 30km 🎣 2km ⌇ ⛵ Spa 10km 🏛 3km ᴘᴘ 3km
Notes No pets English spoken

FONT-ROMEU-ODEILLO-VIA

♯♯♯ **Les Roches**

Rita SIDLER

112 Av Marechal Joffre, 66120 FONT ROMEU

☎ 04 68 30 31 84 🖷 04 68 30 31 84

email: lesroches66@yahoo.fr

This is a modern house, with a delightful view of the mountains. There are four very individual guest rooms, each with its own subtle style and antique furnishings. There is a TV in each room. Storage for skis and bikes; possible parking space in the garden.

Prices s fr €55; d fr €65   **On Site** ⚓   **Nearby** ⛵ 3km 🎣 3km ⌇ 2km
Restaurant 0.1km ⛵ 1km Spa 8km 🏛 0.1km ᴘᴘ 2km   **Notes** No pets
English spoken CC

ILLE-SUR-TET

♯♯♯ ⏺ **Le Magnolia**

Hélène ROSIER

8 Rue Pierre Fouche, 66130 ILLE SUR TET

☎ 04 68 84 14 84 & 06 12 93 22 92

email: lemagnolia66@yahoo.fr

A 19th-century house in the middle of the village, with three guest bedrooms. All of the rooms have private shower and WC; some of the furnishings are antiques, and the style of decoration is elegant. Outside is a terrace with a day room; guests have use of the garden. Meals are available, including Catalan specialities prepared with local ingredients.

Prices not confirmed for 2008   **Nearby** ⛵ 10km Sea 37km 🎣 6km
ᴘᴘ 1km   **Notes** No pets English spoken

♯♯♯ ⏺ **Les Buis**

Patricia QUERRIEN

37 Rue Carnot, 66130 ILLE SUR TET

☎ 04 68 84 27 67 & 06 09 76 73 77

🖷 04 68 56 93 50

email: mquerrien@wanadoo.fr

web: www.lesbuis.com

There are four large guest rooms, each with stylish decorations, in this substantial village house. There is a big lounge with an open fire and a selection of books. Breakfast is served in the garden, on tables under the trees. This is a good base for visiting Conflent, an area rich in tourist sites which are too good to miss.

Prices s €70-€85; d €65-€90; t fr €110; extra person fr €20; dinner fr €27   **On Site** Restaurant Private ⌇   **Nearby** ⛵ 10km Sea 37km
🎣 10km ⛵ Spa 30km 🏛 0.1km ᴘᴘ 0.3km   **Notes** No pets English
spoken Open April to September.

LA BASTIDE

♯♯♯ ⏺ **Domaine des Aspres**

Delphine LASNES

Mas Can Pere Courreu, 66110 LA BASTIDE

☎ 04 68 39 42 28

email: delphine.lasnes@orange.fr

web: www.domainedesaspres.fr

This place enjoys a truly rural location, on the slopes of the Tech Valley (or Vallespir), overlooking Roussillon and the Mediterranean. There are four double bedrooms, attractively furnished and decorated, all with private bath or shower room and WC. Meals available by arrangement.

Prices s €45-€75; d €55-€85; t fr €100; dinner fr €20   **Nearby** ⛵ 1km
⚓ 32km 🎣 2km Restaurant 12km Spa 28km 🏛 12km ᴘᴘ 28km
Notes No pets English spoken

LANGUEDOC-ROUSSILLON

LE TECH

ⅢⅢ ꜰⓄꜰ Sanglier Lodge

Jan TEEDE

6 Route Royale, 66230 LE TECH

☎ 04 68 39 62 51 & 06 12 06 24 76 📄 04 68 39 62 51

email: jteede@wanadoo.fr

web: www.sanglierlodge.com

This large characterful house in the village is quite unusual - part of it was the former village bakery. The garden is on three levels with a swimming pool and view of the surrounding area. Four guest bedrooms include one family room. Municipal parking 50mtrs.

Prices s €35-€45; d fr €68; dinner fr €25 **On Site** ⌀ Restaurant Private ⋏ **Nearby** ⛷ 4km ⓛ 20km Sea 45km ⬥ 40km ⓢ Spa 12km **Notes** Pets admitted English spoken

LOS MASOS

ⅢⅢ ꜰⓄꜰ Mas de l'Estruc

Christiane WARGNIER

9 Traverse de Prades, 66500 LOS MASOS

☎ 06 20 45 91 34 📄 04 68 05 37 19

email: mas-de-lestruc@wanadoo.fr

This property is a working farm (the owners keep ostriches) between the sea and the mountains. Three individually decorated bedrooms, two of them family rooms, each have a living area and a private bath or shower room and WC. Meals are available by arrangement.

Prices s €70-€75; d €75-€80; t fr €90; dinner fr €20 **On Site** Restaurant **Nearby** ⛷ 2km ⓛ 6km Sea 50km ⌀ 2km ⋏ 2km ⬥ 50km ⓢ 0.9km Spa 10km 🎾 2km 🏛 1.5km ⋙ 1.5km **Notes** Pets admitted English spoken

MOSSET

ⅢⅢ ꜰ⸕ꜰ La Forge

Judith CARMONA

Mas Lluganas, 66500 MOSSET

☎ 04 68 05 00 37 📄 04 68 05 04 08

email: maslluganas@orange.fr

This former Catalan smithy has been renovated to offer three guest rooms and one suite, all with private access. There is a dining room with open fireplace, a flower garden with furniture and a barbecue. A trout river flows past the 2-hectare property. Meals can be taken in a nearby inn.

Prices s fr €39; d fr €50 **On Site** ⌀ **Nearby** Restaurant 3km Spa 5km 🎾 12km 🏛 1km ⋙ 13km **Notes** No pets English spoken CC

PERPIGNAN

ⅢⅢ Les Jardins St-Jacques

Jérôme VAN LEEUWEN

1066 Chemin De La Glaciere, 66000 PERPIGNAN

☎ 04 68 51 10 41 & 06 27 85 32 54

email: info@jardins-st-jacques.com

web: www.jardins-st-jacques.com

This prettily restored 18th-century house is set in a shady park with flower gardens and courtyard. It has a swimming pool and private parking, satellite TV and air-conditioning in the bedrooms. Four bedrooms and one suite are comfortably furnished and beautifully decorated.

Prices s €65-€75; d €75-€85; t fr €125 **On Site** Private ⋏ **Nearby** ⛷ 1km ⓛ 10km Sea 8km ⌀ 8km Restaurant 0.2km ⓢ 5km Spa 20km 🏛 2km ⋙ 4km **Notes** No pets English spoken

PORT-VENDRES

ⅢⅢ *Domaine de Valcros*

Louis NIVET

Paulilles, 66660 PORT-VENDRES

☎ 04 68 82 04 27 & 06 85 87 14 23

email: valcros@wanadoo.fr

This renovated vineyard house is on a listed environmental site. It offers three bedrooms in an annexe. There is a guests' lounge, and wine is sold on site. From the house it is possible to walk to the rocky coast and towards the Albères Massif. The house is close to a road which can become busy in the summer.

Prices not confirmed for 2008 **Nearby** ⛷ 15km Sea 0.3km ⌀ 0.3km Spa 29km 🏛 2km ⋙ 2km **Notes** Pets admitted

PRADES

⚏⚏ ⓘ⚑ **Castell Rose**

Evelyne WALDVOGEL

Chemin De La Litera, 66500 PRADES

☎ 04 68 96 07 57 & 06 32 68 72 26

🖹 04 68 96 07 57

email: castell.rose@wanadoo.fr

web: www.castellrose-prades.com

Well-placed half-way between the sea and the mountains, this big house stands in its own grounds, surrounded by ancient trees. There are five bedrooms, and the stylish furniture and meticulous decorations give the place a feeling of quality. Swimming pool and tennis courts in the grounds.

Prices s €69-€89; d €79-€105; extra person fr €15; dinner fr €25 **On Site** Private ⚐ Private tennis court **Nearby** ⚓ 5km Sea 45km
⚑ 1km Restaurant 1km ⚘ 40km Spa 5km ⚑ 1km ⚑ 1km ⚒ 1km
Notes No pets English spoken

SERRALONGUE

⚏⚏ ⓘ⚑ **Case Guillamo**

E et P BRACCKEVELDT

66230 SERRALONGUE

☎ 04 68 39 60 50　🖹 04 68 39 60 50

web: www.caseguillamo.com

A farm tucked away in a forest that promises peace and quiet, natural surroundings and good food. Accommodation consists of two rooms and a family suite with a shady terrace and parking. Fishing and walking. The farm is reached by a 1.8 kilometre rough track.

Prices d fr €80; t fr €100; dinner fr €25 **On Site** ⚑ Private ⚐
Nearby ⚓ 4km ⚑ 18km Restaurant 18km ⚘ 50km ⚑ 4km Spa 25km
⚑ 4km **Notes** No pets

ST-ANDRE

⚏⚏ **Les Vignes**

Jeanne et Pierre LACREU

40 rue des Alberes, 66690 SAINT ANDRE

☎ 04 68 89 18 13 & 06 09 84 71 89

email: pierre.lacreu@wanadoo.fr

web: http://sebastien.lacreu.neuf.fr

This is a newly built village house, with five air-conditioned rooms, one of them a family room. Each room has a TV, and a small kitchen is available for guests' use. The hosts will be delighted to share with you their love of Catalan folklore, and can also arrange visits to the cellar of the local wine co-operative.

Prices s fr €57; d fr €60; t fr €68 **Nearby** ⚓ 6km ⚑ 6km Sea 6km
⚑ 6km ⚐ 4km Restaurant 0.1km Spa 15km ⚑ 4km **Notes** No pets

ST-HIPPOLYTE

⚏⚏ **Casa Clara**

Claudine CREPAIN

21 Rue Des Commercants,

66510 SAINT HIPPOLYTE

☎ 04 68 28 48 14

email: casa-clara@orange.fr

web: www.casa-clara.com

There are three double bedrooms here, in a house which stands in the heart of the village. They have been decorated with care and originality, each to a theme, and they each have private shower room and WC. Outside in the Mediterranean courtyard guests can cool down in the Jacuzzi, or laze in the shade.

Prices s fr €55; d fr €68; extra person fr €20 **On Site** ⚝ Private tennis court **Nearby** ⚓ 2km Sea 10km ⚑ 10km ⚑ 15km **Notes** Pets admitted English spoken

ST-LAURENT-DE-CERDANS

⚏⚏ **Damia Noell**

Mario LOPES

4 rue de la Sort, 66260 SAINT LAURENT DE CERDANS

☎ 04 68 85 32 24 & 06 19 25 38 03

A large house right in the centre of the village, with three spacious, bright and comfortable double rooms, all with private shower and WC. A beautiful central staircase gives access to the lounge and dining room, as well as to the bedrooms. Outside, the terrace which overlooks the village makes an ideal spot for guests to relax.

Prices s fr €45; d €60-€70 **On Site** Restaurant ⚝ **Nearby** ⚓ 1km
⚑ 6km ⚑ 1km ⚐ ⚑ **Notes** No pets English spoken

TAURINYA

⚏⚏ ⓘ⚑ *Las Astrillas*

Bernard LOUPIEN

12 Carrer D'Aval, 66500 TAURINYA

☎ 04 68 96 17 01　🖹 04 68 96 17 01

email: lasastrillas@yahoo.fr

web: www.gite-prop.com/66/220401

Five guest rooms and a family suite offered in a renovated farmhouse, full of character, at the foot of the Canigou. Guests share the dining room with open fireplace with the owner, but the sitting room is

CONTINUED

TAURINYA *CONTINUED*

reserved for guests. Flower garden with outdoor furniture and small museum on site.

Prices not confirmed for 2008 **On Site** ℘ **Nearby** ⛵4km Sea 50km ⚓30km Spa 10km ⛫1km ⋈5km **Notes** No pets English spoken Open March to November.

TAUTAVEL

⅋ 🍽 Le Cellier de l'Henriette

Sophie FONT

route d'Estagel, 66820 TAUTAVEL

☎ 04 68 86 44 89 & 06 76 94 53 59

email: sabg1@wanadoo.fr

web: www.cellier-henriette.fr

On the edge of the village, this stone-built barn has been converted to provide four comfortable bedrooms, two doubles, a twin-bedded room, and a triple with double bed and a single. All have private facilities. The conversion and decoration have been tastefully done, and the place has a warm feel about it. A good base for exploring the Cathar castles.

Prices s fr €60; d €60-€65; t fr €80; dinner fr €20 **On Site** Restaurant ⛲ **Nearby** ⛵4km Sea 30km ℘0.5km ⚓ ⛵ ⛫0.5km ⋈20km **Notes** No pets English spoken

TRESSERRE

⅋ *La Majucecave*

Valérie BESSOU

Hameau De Nidoleres, 66300 TRESSERRE

☎ 04 68 83 92 57 📄 04 68 83 92 57

email: lamajucecave@tiscali.fr

An old wine store provides the setting for this chambre d'hôtes. There are five bedrooms, one of them a suite, all with private facilities and individually and tastefully decorated. For relaxation, there is a beautifully arranged upstairs lounge area, and a peaceful spot beside the swimming pool. Use of kitchen.

Prices not confirmed for 2008 **On Site** Private ⚓ **Nearby** ⛵15km Sea 20km ℘3km Spa 3km ⛫2km ⋈20km **Notes** No pets English spoken Open March to October.

VILLEFRANCHE-DE-CONFLENT

⅋ 🍽 Casa Penalolen

Mireille PENA

3 Domaine Sainte Eulalie,

66500 VILLEFRANCHE DE CONFLENT

☎ 04 68 96 52 35

email: mireille.pena@wanadoo.fr

A house in the Pyrénées Orientales, just a few minutes from the historic town of Villefranche-de-Conflent. Three individually decorated guest rooms, one of them a family suite, all have private shower room and WC. The River Têt passes close by the property (fishing available), and there is a swimming pool in the garden.

Prices s fr €55; d fr €70; extra person fr €18; dinner fr €20 **On Site** ⛲ Private ⚓ **Nearby** ⛵6km ⚓15km Restaurant 3km ⛵50km ⚓5km Spa 6km ⛫0.5km ⋈1.5km **Notes** No pets English spoken

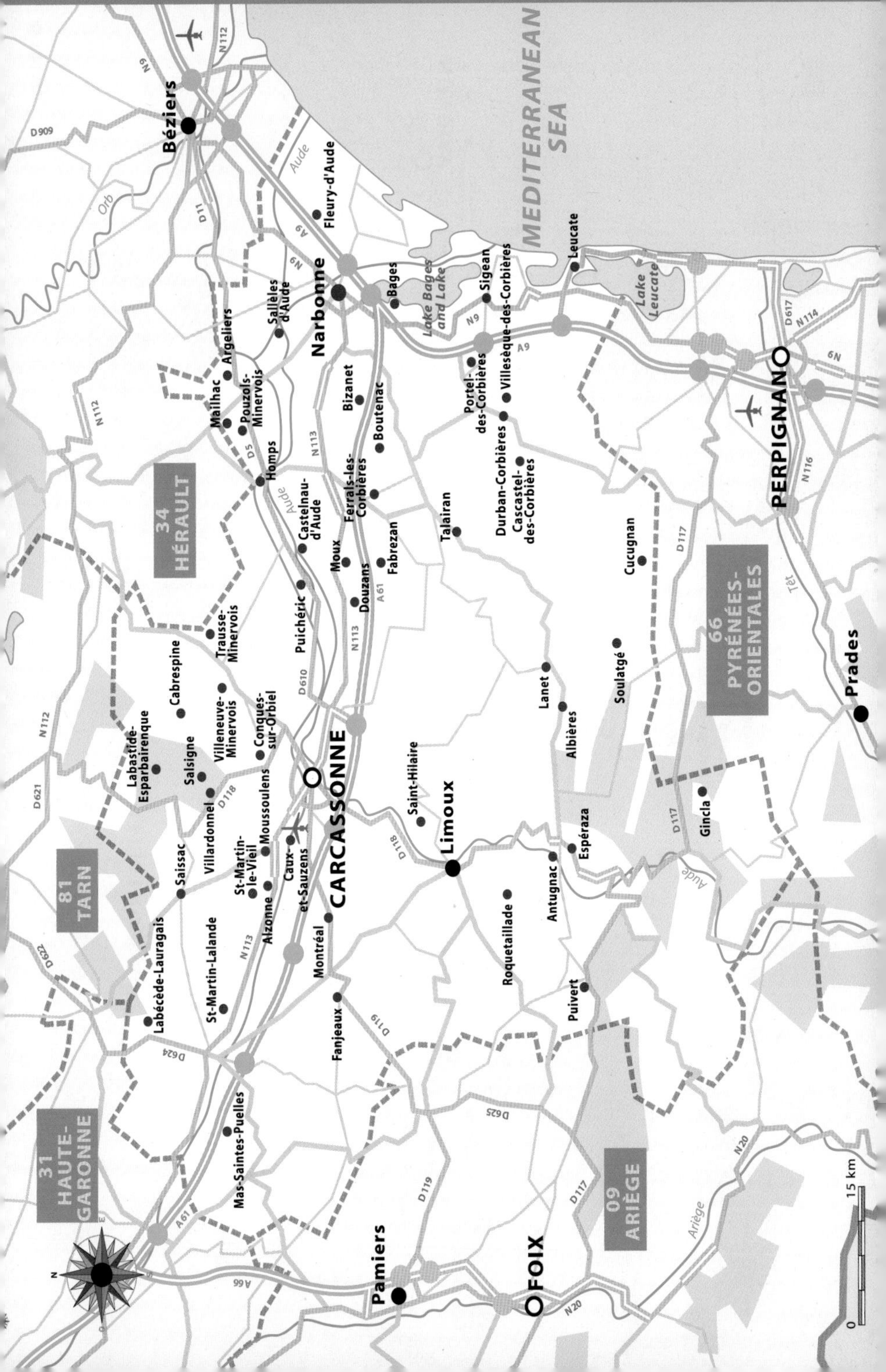

MEDITERRANEAN SEA
Béziers
Narbonne
CARCASSONNE
PERPIGNAN
Limoux
Pamiers
FOIX
Prades
34 HÉRAULT
81 TARN
31 HAUTE-GARONNE
09 ARIÈGE
66 PYRÉNÉES-ORIENTALES
Fleury-d'Aude
Sallèles d'Aude
Argeliers
Mailhac
Pouzols-Minervois
Homps
Bages
Lake Bages and Lake
Sigean
Leucate
Lake Leucate
Villesèque-des-Corbières
Portel-des-Corbières
Durban-Corbières
Cascastel-des-Corbières
Bizanet
Boutenac
Ferrals-les-Corbières
Castelnau-d'Aude
Talairan
Moux
Fabrezan
Douzans
Cucugnan
Puichéric
Trausse-Minervois
Cabrespine
Villeneuve-Minervois
Conques-sur-Orbiel
Labastide-Esparbairenque
Salsigne
Villardonnel
Moussoulens
St-Martin-le-Vieil
Saissac
Caux-et-Sauzens
Alzonne
Labécède-Lauragais
St-Martin-Lalande
Montréal
Fanjeaux
Mas-Saintes-Puelles
Saint-Hilaire
Lanet
Albières
Soulatgé
Gincla
Espéraza
Antugnac
Roquetaillade
Puivert
Orb
Aude
Têt
Ariège
A9
A61
A66
N9
N20
N112
N113
N114
N116
D5
D11
D117
D118
D119
D610
D617
D621
D622
D624
D625
D909
15 km
0

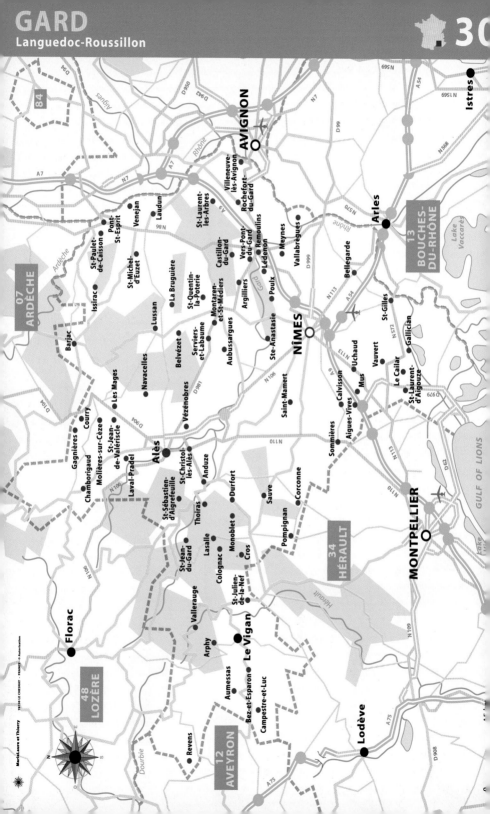

GARD
Languedoc-Roussillon

30

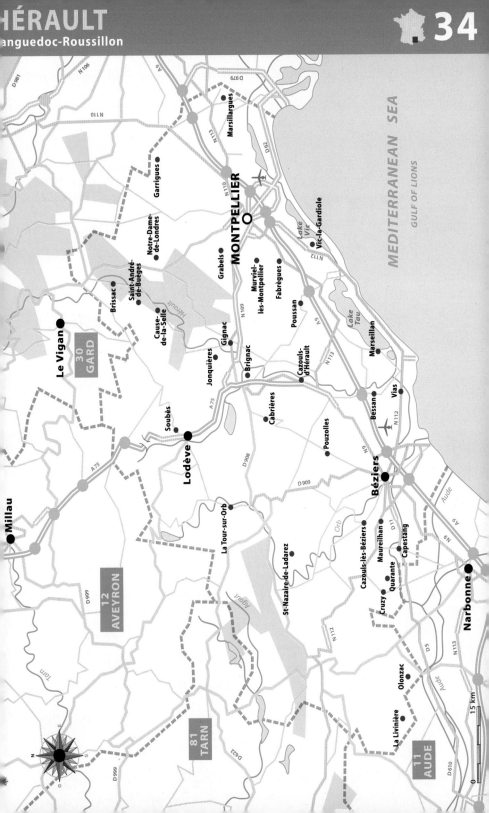

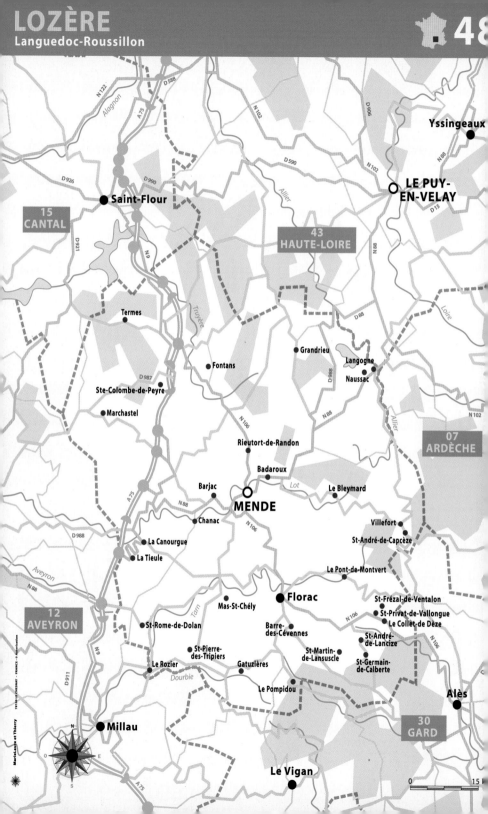

LOZÈRE
Languedoc-Roussillon

48

Yssingeaux

LE PUY-EN-VELAY

15 CANTAL

Saint-Flour

43 HAUTE-LOIRE

Termes

Grandrieu

Fontans

Langogne

Naussac

Ste-Colombe-de-Peyre

Marchastel

07 ARDÈCHE

Rieutort-de-Randon

Badaroux

Barjac

Le Bleymard

MENDE

Chanac

Villefort

St-André-de-Capcèze

La Canourgue

La Tieule

Le Pont-de-Montvert

12 AVEYRON

St-Frézal-de-Ventalon

Mas-St-Chély

Florac

St-Privat-de-Vallongue

St-Rome-de-Dolan

Le Collet-de-Dèze

Barre-des-Cévennes

St-André-de-Lancize

St-Pierre-des-Tripiers

St-Martin-de-Lansuscle

St-Germain-de-Calberte

Le Rozier

Gatuzières

St-Martin-de-Lansuscle

Le Pompidou

Alès

Millau

30 GARD

Le Vigan

0   15

Mariet Jean et Thierry - 78190 LE CHESNAY - FRANCE - © réservé la reproduction

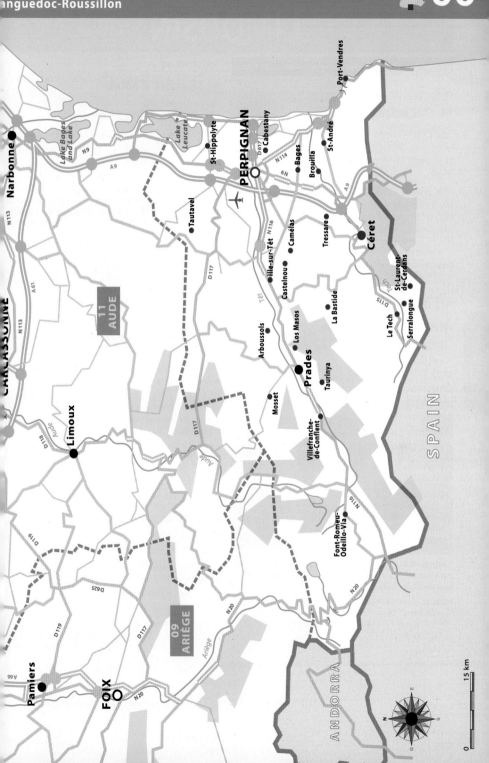

LIMOUSIN

CORRÈZE

AIX

⏣ ⏹ *Chalons d'Aix*

Nathalie FAGEOLLE
La Navade, 19200 AIX
☎ 05 55 94 31 17
email: n.fageolle@free.fr
web: http://n.fageolle.free.fr

This Limousin cattle farm is in a peaceful and verdant setting and offers home cooking with farm produce including pork, beef, cep mushrooms, and bilberries. The three bedrooms are in the owners' house and have private facilities and a shared sitting room. Meals provided out of season by reservation only.

Prices not confirmed for 2008   **On Site** ✍   **Nearby** ⛵ 6km ⌀ 35km ↖ 15km ≋ 4km 🏛 4km ⋙ 4km   **Notes** No pets

ALTILLAC

⏣ ⏹ **La Majorie Basse**

Christine GILLIERON
19120 ALTILLAC
☎ 05 55 91 28 70   ▤ 05 55 91 28 70
email: lamajorie@wanadoo.fr
web: http://monsite.wanadoo.fr/marjorie

A large house in enchanting surroundings near the Dordogne offering four bedrooms (one a suite for four people), an equipped kitchen, a living room and a terrace.

Prices s €37-€42; d €44-€53; t fr €63; extra person fr €10; dinner fr €17   **On Site** ✍ Private ↖   **Nearby** ⛵ 15km ⌀ 10km Restaurant 1km ≋ 1km 🏛 1km ⋙ 5km   **Notes** No pets English spoken

ARGENTAT

⏣ **Chambre d'hôtes**

Montserrat PARLANT
4 Route du Chastang, 19400 ARGENTAT
☎ 05 55 28 87 14   ▤ 05 55 28 83 31
email: monsep@aol.com
web: www.parlant.com.fr

On the way into the pretty village of Argentat this idyllic haven of peace in 5,000m² of park is the spot for a warm and friendly break. Three rooms with ground-level access, one with a king-size bed and hydro-massage shower. Television and fridge in each room. Library. Parking in the grounds. For those who like fishing, the waters of the Dordogne and the Maronne are waiting.

Prices s fr €40; d €49-€54; t fr €60; extra person fr €10   **On Site** ✍ Private ↖   **Nearby** ⛵ 2km ≋ 1km ⋙ 40km   **Notes** No pets English spoken

⏣ **Chambre d'hôtes**

Alice DENOT
38 Rue Bombal, La Croix Verte, 19400 ARGENTAT
☎ 05 55 91 19 36
email: richarddenot@aol.com
web: www.lacroixverte-argentat.com

This house on a hill 800 metres from Argentat offers three bedrooms, one of them a family room for four and all with en suite bathroom and WC. The terrace with a wonderful view is a great place to have breakfast; there is also a living and dining room for guest use.

Prices s €37; d €47-€50; t fr €58; extra person fr €10   **On Site** ✍ **Nearby** ⛵ 12km ⌀ 20km ✍ 1km ↖ 1km ≋ 1km 🏛 0.5km ⋙ 30km **Notes** No pets English spoken

BEAULIEU-SUR-DORDOGNE

⏣ *Chambre d'hôtes*

J-C et C HENRIET
11 Rue de la Gendarmerie,
19120 BEAULIEU-SUR-DORDOGNE
☎ 05 55 91 24 97   ▤ 05 55 91 51 27
email: lamaison19@wanadoo.fr
web: http://lamaison19.chez-alice.fr

Situated a stone's throw away from the Dordogne in the heart of Beaulieu, this house offers four bedrooms that look out either onto an interior patio full of flowers or the garden with its swimming pool. Each one is unusually decorated with Indian, 1930s, bridal or bird themes. Guests also have the use of a large room with fireplace. Special rates for groups.

Prices not confirmed for 2008   **On Site** ✍ Private ↖   **Nearby** ⛵ 8km ⌀ 17km ≋ 🏛 0.2km ⋙ 7km   **Notes** No pets Open April to September.

LIMOUSIN

BEYNAT

♨ ⑩ *Chambre d'hôtes*

Françoise DEMARTY
Place de la Mairie, 19190 BEYNAT
☎ 05 55 85 50 57 📄 05 55 85 51 03
email: lejardindagathe@wanadoo.fr

In the heart of the Limousin, on the borders of Périgord, Quercy and the Auvergne, this old property has three first floor guest bedrooms, all with antique furnishings. There is a large lounge with books, games and a piano. Generous breakfasts, complete with home-made jam; other meals by arrangement, with local dishes.

Prices not confirmed for 2008 **On Site** Private ⚡ **Nearby** ⚓ 10km ⚡ 10km ⚡ 4km ⚘ 4km ⚘ 20km **Notes** No pets English spoken Open 5 January to December.

BILHAC

♨ ♥ ⑩ **La Ferme du Masvidal**

Marielle et P & M SIMBILLE
19120 BILHAC
☎ 05 55 91 53 14 & 06 70 24 91 53 📄 05 55 91 08 74
email: lafermedumasvidal@laposte.net
web: www.masvidal.fr

Overlooking the Dordogne Valley, this establishment is within easy reach of many tourist areas such as Curemonte, Collonge-la-Rouge and Turenne. Three bedrooms, one with loggia, each have a shower, WC and heating. There is a lounge with television, reading material and access to a shady park with garden furniture. A riding school is only 500mtrs away.

Prices s €40-€43; d €40-€43; t €48-€51; extra person fr €8; dinner fr €11 **On Site** Restaurant **Nearby** ⚓ 0.5km ⚡ 10km ⚡ 3km ⚡ 3km ⚘ 10km ⚘ 3km ⚘ 10km **Notes** Pets admitted English spoken

BORT-LES-ORGUES

♨ **Chambre d'hôtes**

C BOURDOUX
1 Boulevard de la Nation, place de l'Eglise,
19110 BORT-LES-ORGUES
☎ 05 55 96 00 58 📄 05 55 96 00 58

Set in a small village on the banks of the Dordogne bordering the Cantal; there are two en suite bedrooms, one with a view of Les Orgues rock formations and garden, the other overlooking the church of Bort. Very spacious lounge with large windows, garden furniture and a barbecue. Micro-light lessons can be arranged, or you can go walking, mountain-biking, or fishing in the dam and river three kilometres away.

Prices s fr €31; d fr €40; t fr €50 **Nearby** ⚓ 5km ⚡ 20km ⚡ 3km ⚘ 1km ⚘ 1km **Notes** Pets admitted

♨ ⑩ **Chambre d'hôtes**

J BRETAGNOLLE et E BRANDELY
Route d'Ussel, 19110 BORT-LES-ORGUES
☎ 05 55 96 84 55
web: http://chambresbortoises.free.fr

This barn conversion offers exceptional views across the Bort-les-Orgues dam and the Monts du Cantal. There are four bedrooms, all with private bathrooms and WCs. Lounge with books, TV and an open fire. Fishing and water skiing.

Prices s fr €36; d fr €46; t fr €56; dinner fr €15 **On Site** ⚡ **Nearby** ⚓ 10km ⚡ 20km ⚡ 1km Restaurant 0.5km ⚘ 1km ⚘ 7km ⚘ 1km ⚘ 1km **Notes** Pets admitted English spoken

BRIGNAC-LA-PLAINE

♨ ⑩ ⚕ **La Maison de la Plaine**

E CAPELLE et M-F DAUTRAIT
1, Route du Rouvet, 19310 BRIGNAC-LA-PLAINE
☎ 05 55 85 25 75 & 06 14 11 94 59
email: capelle.f@wanadoo.fr
web: www.lamaisondelaplaine.com

Two generations pursue their respective hobbies here, one couple enjoys cooking and the other likes to restore old cars and show you around the local area. Relax and enjoy some of their traditional and creative cooking, or take a walk in the lovely grounds.

Prices d fr €60; extra person fr €20; dinner fr €20 **On Site** ⚘ **Nearby** ⚓ 1km ⚡ 12km ⚡ 10km ⚡ 10km Restaurant 10km ⚘ 1km ⚘ 0.3km ⚘ 15km **Notes** No pets English spoken

BRIVEZAC

♨ ⑩ **La Grèze**

Anne FRANCE
19120 BRIVEZAC
☎ 05 55 91 08 68 📄 05 55 91 08 68
email: anne-odile-france@wanadoo.fr
web: www.chateaudelagreze.com

Surrounded by ancient trees in the Dordogne Valley, this 18th-century château offers peace and quiet in a wonderful setting. Five airy, spacious and individually decorated bedrooms combine the charm of the past with modern comforts. Cooking uses the best of local produce. Closed Xmas.

Prices s €67-€98; d €73-€104; extra person fr €25; dinner fr €25 **On Site** ⚓ Private ⚡ **Nearby** ⚡ 25km ⚡ 0.5km Restaurant 4km ⚘ 4km ⚘ 4km ⚘ 10km **Notes** No pets English spoken

CHAMBOULIVE

✦ ⍟ **Orliac de Virolle**

M DALLAIRE & P LOPEZ

Orliac de Virolle Chamboulive, 19450 CHAMBOULIVE

☎ 05 55 21 40 73

email: arbreafruits@free.fr

web: http://arbreafruits.free.fr

Deep in the country, five kilometres from the village, this sympathetically restored farmhouse has five bedrooms, furnished with a pleasing blend of styles. All have private facilities. Breakfasts, and dinners which reflect a fusion of the Mediterranean and French Canadian origins of the hosts, are served at individual tables inside or out on the terrace.

Prices s €70-€80; d €75-€85; t fr €100; dinner €28-€32
Nearby ✪ 5km ♨ 25km ⚲ 5km ↖ Restaurant 4km ♒ 5km
♞ 10km ◍ 5km ⋙ 20km **Notes** No pets English spoken

CLERGOUX

✦ ⍟ **Leix**

Sylvie SOUDANT

19320 CLERGOUX

☎ 05 55 27 75 49 ▤ 05 55 27 75 49

email: asoudant@wanadoo.fr

web: www.ferme-de-leix.com

This peaceful farmhouse with character offers four bedrooms joined to the owners' house, each with its own separate entrance, shower room and wc. Evening meals using farm produce are served. Horse riding and harnessing on the premises. Near a lake and three kilometres from a village. Special rates for groups.

Prices s fr €34; d fr €45; t fr €56; extra person fr €10; dinner fr €17
On Site ⚲ **Nearby** ✪ 5km ↖ 10km Restaurant 3km ♒ 8km ♞ 3km
◍ 3km ⋙ 21km **Notes** No pets English spoken Open March to 14 November.

COLLONGES-LA-ROUGE

✦ ⍟ **Maison d'hôtes Jeanne**

Brigitte et Pascal MONTEIL

Le Bourg, 19500 COLLONGES-LA-ROUGE

☎ 05 55 25 42 31 & 06 86 70 63 53

▤ 05 55 25 47 80

email: info@jeannemaisondhotes.com

web: www.jeannemaisondhotes.com

A beautiful Collonges-la-Rouge house with 15th-century tower, set on an ancient estate in one of the most beautiful villages in France. It offers five tastefully decorated and comfortable rooms, and has a quiet and charming country garden. In the evenings, guests may join the hosts for meals in a friendly atmosphere.

Prices s fr €90; d fr €90; extra person fr €10; dinner fr €32
Nearby ✪ 6km ♨ 20km ⚲ 20km ↖ 2km Restaurant 0.2km
♒ 2km Spa 25km ◍ 2km ⋙ 25km **Notes** No pets English spoken CC

✦ **Peyrelimouze**

Jean François VITTOZ

19500 COLLONGES-LA-ROUGE

☎ 05 55 84 07 17 & 06 77 07 00 26

Not far from Collonges-la-Rouge, one of the most beautiful villages o' France, this property has three comfortable bedrooms, one of them a suite for four. All have a private bath or shower room and WC, and one has disabled access. Beautiful gardens with views across the valle and towards Quercy.

Prices s €42-€47; d €54-€67; t €85-€87 **Nearby** ✪ 5km ♨ 20km
⚲ 10km ↖ 4km Restaurant 2km ♒ 4km ♞ 4km ◍ 4km ⋙ 15km
Notes Pets admitted English spoken Open April to 30 October.

COMBRESSOL

⚞ ❦ ⵔ **Les Chaussades**

Marcelle MIGNON

19250 COMBRESSOL

☎ 06 81 41 92 02

mail: marcelle.mignon@orange.fr

stone house typical of the Plateau de Millevaches offering two
edrooms with private showers and one bedroom with a bathroom.
tuated near Meymac, a centre of contemporary art. Riders are
elcome; this is a good area for hiking.

rices d fr €40; t fr €52; extra person fr €10; dinner fr €16
earby ⚑ 5km ⚲ 15km ⚘ 1km ⚹ 5km Restaurant 3km ⚾ 3km
ɔa 15km ☒ 1.5km ⚲ 6km **Notes** No pets

CORNIL

⚞ ⵔ **La Lupronne**

M P et L LESIEUR

Le Mons, 19150 CORNIL

☎ 05 55 27 26 47

email: lalupronne@free.fr

web: http://lalupronne.free.fr

Built by one of Napoleon's admirals in the 18th century, this
family house has views of 17th- and 18th-century buildings,
formal gardens and countryside. Dining room with 12th-century
fireplace. Bread and meals (by arrangement) baked in the
traditional bread oven. Picnic baskets on request. Courses and
weekend cinema. 5% discount after 2nd night.

Prices s €55-€67; d €55-€67; t €77-€78; extra person fr €10; dinner
€19-€21 **Nearby** ⚑ 6km ⚲ 6km ⚘ 2km ⚹ 5km Restaurant 4km
⚾ 0.4km ☒ 2km ⚲ 2km **Notes** No pets English spoken

CORREZE

⚞ ⵔ **Chambre d'hôtes**

GOVAERTS et A PEETERS

v de la Gare, Le Parc des Quatre Saisons,

9800 CORREZE

☎ 05 55 21 44 59

mail: annick.peter@wanadoo.fr

eb: www.leparc.info

is old mansion and barn are surrounded by a magnificent garden
ɔrdered by trees. The setting is both soothing and inspiring. The five
ɔmfortable rooms, decorated in a warm style with an artistic feel, all
ve en suite showers and WCs. Swimming pool and sauna. Meals by
rangement; vegetarian dishes on request.

ices s €53-€73; d €60-€85; extra person €15-€20; dinner fr €25
1 Site ⚘ Private ⚹ Private tennis court **Nearby** ⚑ 8km ⚲ 35km
4km **Notes** No pets English spoken

La Queyrie

⚞ ⵔ **La Queyrie**

Nadia PESCHEL

19800 CORREZE

☎ 05 55 21 34 16 ▤ 05 55 21 34 16

email: bernard.peschel@wanadoo.fr

web: http://monsite.wanadoo.fr/la.topiane.fr

In a peaceful green setting, in grounds of one hectare, this property
has an exceptional view over the delightful medieval village of Corrèze.
Your hosts will offer you a warm welcome to their magnificent
chambre d'hôtes with its comfortable bedrooms.

Prices s €40-€50; d €47-€59; extra person fr €13; dinner fr €18
Nearby ⚑ 8km ⚘ 1km ⚹ 1km ⚾ 1km ☒ 1km ⚲ 4km
Notes No pets English spoken Open Easter to October.

CUREMONTE

⚞ ❦ ⵔ **Chambre d'hôtes**

Fernande RAYNAL

Le Bourg, 19500 CUREMONTE

☎ 05 55 25 35 01

Accommodation offered in the heart of a medieval city in one of the
most beautiful areas of France. Guests can choose between three very
comfortable rustic-style rooms in a former barn; each with its own
shower room. Calves and ducks are reared on this farm. Reservations
necessary.

Prices s fr €40; d fr €58; t fr €75; dinner fr €19 **Nearby** ⚑ 7km
⚲ 20km ⚘ 12km ⚹ 12km Restaurant 0.1km ⚾ 10km ⚽ 12km ☒ 12km
⚲ 35km **Notes** Pets admitted Open 15 March to November. CC

FORGES

⚞ ⵔ **La Souvigne**

Ian et Jacquie HOARE

1, Impasse La Fontaine, 19380 FORGES

☎ 05 55 28 63 99 ▤ 05 55 28 65 62

email: info@souvigne.com

web: www.souvigne.com

Discover this restored period residence with three bedrooms with
private facilities. Living room available for guests' use. Heating, library,
parking. Evening meal by reservation.

Prices s €33-€36; d €36-€39; extra person fr €12; dinner fr €18
On Site ⚘ Restaurant **Nearby** ⚑ 11km ⚲ 15km ⚹ 11km ⚾ 11km ⚽ 11km
☒ 11km ⚲ 16km **Notes** No pets English spoken

LAFAGE-SUR-SOMBRE

⚞ ⵔ **Vergne**

Guy et Yolande LEJAY

19320 LAFAGE-SUR-SOMBRE

☎ 05 55 27 83 51

email: lejayguy@aol.com

web: www.lagrangeaucoq-correze.com

This old barn, dating from 1798, houses five charmingly decorated
guest rooms, all with private showers and WCs. It is situated in the

CONTINUED

LAFAGE-SUR-SOMBRE CONTINUED

heart of the forest, surrounded by footpaths which provide pleasant walks in the area. Meals by arrangement: your host prepares regional specialities and makes delicious pâtisseries.

Prices s fr €35; d fr €42; t fr €55; dinner fr €15   **Nearby** ⚓ 15km
🏊 2km ⚑ 15km 🍴 7km 🏛 5km ⛵ 15km   **Notes** Pets admitted
English spoken

LISSAC-SUR-COUZE

⁂ Château de Lissac

Catherine MEYJONADE
Le Bourg, 19600 LISSAC-SUR-COUZE
☎ 05 55 85 14 19 & 06 75 24 06 31
email: chateaudelissac@wanadoo.fr
web: www.chateaudelissac.com

This château dates back to the 12th century with 15th- and 18th-century additions. It is in the heart of Corrèze near the Brive basin. Three characterful rooms offer comfortable and spacious accommodation. The grounds have exceptional views over lake Causse. Near to Sarlat, Rocamadour and Collonges-la-Rouge.

Prices d €110-€220   **On Site** Restaurant 🎯   **Nearby** ⚓ 6km
🏊 6km ⚑ 0.3km ⚑ 0.3km 🍴 6km ⛵ 10km   **Notes** No pets
English spoken   Open April to November.

MARCILLAC-LA-CROISILLE

⁂ *La Teyssonnière*

Jean-Claude CLEMENT
19320 MARCILLAC-LA-CROISILLE
☎ 05 55 27 58 99 & 06 73 36 96 79
email: lamaisonpresdulac@free.fr
web: www.lamaisonpresdulac.com

Discover the 'house near the lake' in a hamlet set in wonderful Corrèzian scenery in the Dordogne Valley, where rest and tranquillity are guaranteed. Only 600 metres from the lake, this friendly residence has an inglenook fireplace and four comfortable, elegantly decorated bedrooms, each with its own bathroom. There are four restaurants offering regional specialities two kilometres away. Special rates for groups.

Prices not confirmed for 2008   **On Site** ⚑   **Nearby** ⚓ 6km ⚑ 8km
🍴 2km 🏛 2km ⛵ 19km   **Notes** No pets

MEYSSAC

⁂ Chambre d'hôtes

Jean-Luc LEBAS
La Dame Blanche, 19500 MEYSSAC
☎ 05 55 84 05 96 & 06 83 30 53 99

A red sandstone property which features a 17th-century tower. Situated in the old village of Meyssac, near Turenne and Curemonte, the accommodation consists of four spacious bedrooms.

Prices s fr €40; d fr €50; t fr €60; extra person fr €10   **Nearby** ⚓ 5km
🍴 15km ⚑ 10km ⚑ 0.1km Restaurant 0.1km 🍴 0.4km Spa 20km
⛵ 20km   **Notes** No pets English spoken

MILLEVACHES

⁂ Le Magimel

Maryline DESASSIS
19290 MILLEVACHES
☎ 05 55 95 61 24 🖷 05 55 95 17 27

This detached property with upstairs bedrooms is peacefully situated in the heart of the Plateau de Millevaches. A reception room plus an exterior terrace with garden furniture is available. Two kilometres from a village, with fishing and pleasant woodland walks.

Prices s fr €40; d fr €45   **On Site** ⚑ Private ⚑   **Nearby** ⚓ 15km
🍴 10km Restaurant 1km 🏛 11km ⛵ 15km   **Notes** No pets   Open July to August.

MONCEAUX-SUR-DORDOGNE

⁂ Saulières

Marie-José LAFOND
19400 MONCEAUX-SUR-DORDOGNE
☎ 05 55 28 09 22 🖷 05 55 28 09 22
email: mariejo.lafond@free.fr
web: www.chambredhotes-saulieres.com

This cattle rearing and walnut farm is set in the heart of the Dordogne Valley. The individually decorated bedrooms are situated in an extension of the contemporary house, each with shower and private wc. An equipped kitchen, lounge with fireplace, dining room and terrace are at the guests' disposal. There is a picnic area on the riverbank.

Prices s fr €30; d fr €45; t fr €55   **On Site** ⚑ Private ⚑
Nearby ⚓ 6km 🍴 20km Restaurant 3km ⚑ 3km 🏛 7km ⛵ 40km
Notes Pets admitted English spoken

NAVES

⁂ Ⓐ *Gourdinot*

B et J-M PERROT
19460 NAVES
☎ 05 55 27 08 93
email: brunhild.perrot@wanadoo.fr
web: www.hotes-naves-correze.com

At this charming, typical Corrèze house guests can relax and sample the local gastronomy, or try bread-making lessons with the proprietor. There are three tastefully refined bedrooms, one with a large canopied bed and comfortable lounge, one with a double bed verlooking a loggia, the third with two single beds. Living room, brary, TV and large kitchen with an open fireplace, where evening meals are taken.

rices not confirmed for 2008 **Nearby** ⚓ 3km ⚓ 25km ⚓ 2km ⚓ 3km ⚓ 7km ⚓ 5km ⚓ 12km **Notes** No pets English spoken

⚓ ⏾ *Vimbelle*

DA SILVA & E THOUVENEL

9460 NAVES

☎ 05 55 29 31 42

mail: helenedasi@free.fr

veb: www.larosabelle.fr.cx

estling in verdant countryside by the lovely trout-stocked Vimbelle ver; this house was once a dance hall. After a walk in the nearby rest, guests can relax and enjoy excellent meals at the table d'hôte y reservation).

rices not confirmed for 2008 **On Site** ⚓ **Nearby** ⚓ 3km ⚓ 25km ⚓ 3km ⚓ 4km ⚓ 9km **Notes** Pets admitted English spoken

IESPOULS

⚓ ⏾ ⏾ **Aux Sabots du Causse**

oi et Marie-France LALLE

elveyre, 19600 NESPOULS

☎ 05 55 85 84 47

mail: aux-sabots-du-causse@orange.fr

xpect a warm welcome and calm environment at this restored old sidence. Cosy nights are guaranteed in the four tastefully decorated edrooms, each with their own shower rooms and wc.

rices s fr €30; d €35-€40; t €40-€50; dinner €15-€25 **Nearby** ⚓ 10km ⚓ 10km ⚓ 6km ⚓ 15km Restaurant 5km ⚓ 5km ⚓ 6km ⚓ 2km ⚓ 15km **Notes** No pets Open April to September.

⚓ ⏾ **Le Clos de Combes**

atricia et J.Marie MERCIER

9600 NESPOULS

☎ 05 55 85 82 19

is property is in a peaceful village on the edge of the Lot and the ordogne. It is a beautiful barn conversion, with five guest rooms, one them a family room, and two with kitchenettes. Meals, including elicious local specialities, are available by arrangement.

ices s fr €35; d €45-€50; t €56-€61; extra person fr €11; dinner fr €17 **earby** ⚓ 15km ⚓ 15km ⚓ 8km ⚓ 15km Restaurant 5km ⚓ 15km 0.4km ⚓ 15km **Notes** No pets English spoken

NEUVIC

⚓ ⏾ ⏾ **Ferme de Bêchefave**

J CHASTAING

19160 NEUVIC

☎ 05 55 95 97 60

email: bechefave@orange.fr

web: http://bechefave.free.fr

In the upper Corrèze, in an area renowned for mushrooms, this establishment is just a stone's throw from a lake with an enchanting view of the Puy-de-Dome and Cantal Mountains. An ideal place to discover the region and gastronomic cooking. There are three guest rooms, plus lounge with fireplace, TV and heating.

Prices s fr €38; dinner fr €17 **Nearby** ⚓ 2km ⚓ 2km ⚓ 2km ⚓ 2km Restaurant 1km ⚓ 1km ⚓ 1km ⚓ 1km ⚓ 20km **Notes** Pets admitted

NEUVILLE

⚓ ⏾ **La Closeraie du Sirieix**

Philippe GIRODROUX

19380 NEUVILLE

☎ 05 55 28 64 29 & 06 87 73 25 09

🖷 05 55 28 55 70

email: contact@closerie-de-sirieix.com

web: www.closeraie-de-sirieix.com

Restored 18th-century farmhouse and buildings in grounds of nearly two hectares, with views across the hills of the Auvergne. There is a bread oven in working order, and a huge barn fashioned in the shape of an upturned ship's hull. Upstairs in the farmhouse are a double room and a suite, and on the ground floor of the grange is an independent apartment. All are equipped with double beds and private bathrooms. Large living rooms, a swimming pool in the grounds, and the property is in good walking country.

Prices d €88-€118; extra person fr €15; dinner fr €23 **On Site** Private ⚓ **Nearby** ⚓ 15km ⚓ 15km ⚓ 8km Restaurant 2km ⚓ 6km ⚓ 20km **Notes** No pets English spoken Open 5 January to 30 March.

NOAILHAC

⚓ ⏾ *La Diligence*

J-C et M VIGUIER

Le Peyratel, 19500 NOAILHAC

☎ 05 55 25 47 50 & 06 70 53 36 16

email: ladiligencenoailhac@free.fr

web: www.la-diligence-noailhac.fr

This very pleasant property dates back to the 19th century, and has panoramic views over the village and the surrounding countryside. There are two doubles, and a room for four guests which has a separate sitting area. Evening meals make full use of local specialities.

Prices not confirmed for 2008 **Nearby** ⚓ 15km ⚓ 20km ⚓ 4km ⚓ 5km ⚓ 5km ⚓ 6km ⚓ 15km **Notes** No pets English spoken

NOAILLES

ⅢⅢ ⅠⓄⅠ Les Dependances du Château

Sylvie GAY

Place du 11 Novembre, 19600 NOAILLES

☎ 05 55 85 85 11

email: j.gay2@tiscali.fr

This magnificent residence once belonged to the Counts of Noailles. Four rooms sleep two to five people and a cot is available. Situated at the junction of the Corrèze, Lot and Dordogne, the house has a private swimming pool (14mtrs x 8mtrs), tennis court and billiard room. Evening meal by arrangement.

Prices s fr €70; d fr €70; t €60-€90; dinner fr €20
On Site Private ⚷ Private tennis court **Nearby** ⚓ 8km ⚘ 8km
⚘ 5km Restaurant 7km ⚑ 0.1km ⚓ 7km **Notes** Pets admitted English spoken

OBJAT

ⅢⅢ Chambre d'hôtes

Henri GUIONY

10 Av Georges Clémenceau, 19130 OBJAT

☎ 05 55 25 00 17 & 06 82 31 86 03

email: guiony@free.fr

A warm welcome awaits guests to this fine mansard-style family home, dating from the early 1900s. This renovated property offers a choice of three spacious bedrooms; one double room can accommodate a couple plus three children. There is a large living room. Close to Limousin, the Auvergne, the Quercy and Perigord and the prehistoric sites of the Dordogne and Vézère Valleys.

Prices s fr €41; d fr €48; t fr €58; extra person fr €13 **On Site** Private tennis court **Nearby** ⚓ 10km ⚘ 15km ⚘ 0.5km **Notes** No pets

ⅢⅢ *Stahlhana*

Béatrice et Eric-Marie DOUCET

14 Av Raymond Poincaré, 19130 OBJAT

☎ 06 84 82 40 91

email: familledoucet@stahlhana.com

web: www.objat.com

A beautiful restored 19th-century home, Stahlhana is half way between the stud farm of Pampadour and Brive la Gaillard, on the edge of Périgord and Haut-Quercy. Stahlhana offers the choice of a room or two suites, whose charm reflects the attentive welcome of Béatrice and Eric-Marie. Guests have use of the library and private lounge.

Prices not confirmed for 2008 **On Site** Private ⚷
Nearby ⚓ 10km ⚘ 15km ⚘ 1km ⚑ 0.8km ⚓ 1km
Notes No pets English spoken

PALAZINGES

ⅢⅢ ⅠⓄⅠ Chambre d'hôtes

Dominique et Nicole CURE

Le Bourg, 19190 PALAZINGES

☎ 05 55 84 63 44

An exceptional view and five spacious guest bedrooms are offered at this restored barn full of old-world charm, each equipped with showe and wc. Dinner is served for residents. Close to Tulle and Brive.

Prices s fr €40; d fr €45; t fr €60; extra person fr €15; dinner fr €17
Nearby ⚓ 4km ⚘ 4km ⚘ 4km ⚷ 18km Restaurant 4km ⚘ 18km ⚑ 4km
⚓ 8km **Notes** Pets admitted English spoken Open April to 1 November.

SARRAN

ⅢⅢ ⅠⓄⅠ *Chambre d'hôtes*

Anne Marie BARSACQ

Le Bourg, 19800 SARRAN

☎ 05 55 21 31 54 & 06 03 82 40 36 ▤ 05 55 21 37 59

A 19th-century barn, beautifully restored. There are four bedrooms, all with private bath or shower rooms and WCs. Lounge with television, open fire and books. In the winter months, from November to Februar three-day foie gras courses are arranged, on a full board basis.

Prices not confirmed for 2008 **Nearby** ⚓ 10km ⚘ 2km ⚷ 8km ⚘ ⚑ 8km ⚓ 8km **Notes** No pets English spoken

SARROUX

ⅢⅢ ⚘ ⅠⓄⅠ Puy de Bort

Roger VENNAT

19110 SARROUX

☎ 05 55 96 05 10

An organic beef and dairy farm with four guest rooms with private w and shower rooms. There is a living room and sampling of the farm produce. Views of the Orgues rock formations, Puy Mary and le Sanc

Prices s fr €30; d fr €50; t fr €60; extra person fr €10; dinner fr €15
Nearby ⚓ 12km ⚘ 30km ⚘ 5km ⚷ 5km Restaurant 5km ⚘ 5km
Spa 30km ⚑ 5km ⚓ 5km **Notes** Pets admitted English spoken

SEGONZAC

ⅢⅢ Lauregie

Jacques DERRIEN-PAYOT

19310 SEGONZAC

☎ 05 55 84 17 39 & 06 30 56 30 18

email: payot-derrien@tiscali.fr

web: www.prelaminon.com

This traditional barn has been converted to provide three very comfortable guest bedrooms, sleeping from two to four people. Here, at the crossroads of Périgord and the Limousin, you can enjoy a refreshing break in a unique area, with lots of places to visit and things to do.

Prices s fr €40-€50; d €52-€60; t €67-€80; dinner fr €18
Nearby ⚓ 3km ⚘ 50km ⚘ 1km ⚷ Restaurant 5km ⚘ 3km
⚑ 6km ⚓ 30km **Notes** Pets admitted English spoken Open April to September.

ST-BAZILE-DE-MEYSSAC

⚜⚜⚜ La Brunie

Pierre et Jacqueline APPERT
19500 ST-BAZILE-DE-MEYSSAC
☎ 05 55 84 23 07
email: appierre@wanadoo.fr
web: www.manoirlabrunie.com

A magnificent 18th-century manor house with three beautiful bedrooms. The decorations are elegant, and there is a delightful atmosphere about the place. Two of the bedrooms can be linked to make a family suite. A small lounge is available for guests' use, for reading or relaxation.

Prices d €80–€100; extra person fr €30 **On Site** ⚙
Nearby ⚑ 5km ⚓ 30km ⚐ 1km ⚬ 5km Restaurant 2km ⚒ 6km
⚑ 2km ⚖ 25km **Notes** No pets English spoken

ST-BONNET-ELVERT

⚜⚜⚜ 🍴 Bétaillole

Martine MOULARD
19380 ST-BONNET-ELVERT
☎ 05 55 28 44 16
email: mamoulard@wanadoo.fr

This is an old farmhouse, built in the local style, with the fine views so typical of the Limousin region. The setting is quiet, close to the valley of the Dordogne. It has six beautifully spacious bedrooms, and there is access for guests with limited mobility.

Prices not confirmed for 2008 **Nearby** ⚑ 12km ⚬ 5km ⚐ 12km
⚒ 12km ⚖ 7km ⚖ 25km **Notes** Pets admitted English spoken

ST-BONNET-L'ENFANTIER

⚜⚜⚜ 🦢 🍴 La Borde

Nadine BUGE
19410 ST-BONNET-L'ENFANTIER
☎ 05 55 73 72 44 ▤ 05 55 73 72 44

In a green and peaceful setting, five kilometres from the A20, this geese-rearing farm is surrounded by walnut groves. There are five bedrooms, each with full bathroom facilities. At the dining table you will discover a traditional cuisine in a warm and friendly family atmosphere. Kitchen, board games and outdoor games on the premises. Foie gras weekends in winter.

Prices not confirmed for 2008 **Nearby** ⚑ 20km ⚬ 20km ⚐ 10km
⚬ 10km ⚒ 3km ⚖ 1km ⚖ 15km **Notes** No pets Open April to August.

ST-CERNIN-DE-LARCHE

⚜⚜⚜ 🍴 Le Moulin Vieux de la Roche

Michel ANDRIEUX
19600 ST-CERNIN-DE-LARCHE
☎ 05 55 85 40 92 ▤ 05 55 85 34 66

Six bedrooms are available at this 13th-century cistercian mill. Each room has a TV, private facilities and access and has been comfortably and tastefully decorated. Large fireplaces and old earthenware tiles accentuate the charm of the property and copious breakfasts are served in the large dining room. The property overlooks the picturesque village of Laroche and the cliffs of the Cirque de la Doux.

Prices not confirmed for 2008 **Nearby** ⚑ 5km ⚓ 5km ⚐ 0.6km
⚬ 0.6km ⚒ 3km ⚖ 1km ⚖ 3km **Notes** No pets English spoken
Open 15 March to 15 November.

ST-CHAMANT

⚜⚜⚜ 🍴 🦽 Chambre d'hôtes

Madeleine et Germain COUTAL
Le Bourg, 19380 ST-CHAMANT
☎ 05 55 28 05 46 ▤ 05 55 28 84 03

This large house is situated in a very quiet part of the village. There are six bedrooms with private shower and wc, one of which has access for disabled guests and two have private living rooms. A communal lounge with TV is available, as are evening meals upon demand.

Prices s fr €37; d fr €42; t fr €62; dinner fr €16 **Nearby** ⚑ 6km ⚓ 25km
⚐ 6km ⚬ 6km Restaurant 0.2km ⚒ 4km ⚖ 24km **Notes** No pets

ST-CLEMENT

⚜⚜⚜ 🍴 Serendipity

Timothy HAINSWORTH
Le Mayne, 19700 ST-CLEMENT
☎ 05 55 27 08 37
email: hainsworthlisa@wanadoo.fr
web: www.holidaycorreze.co.uk

This big house, full of character, is not far from the town yet it is in a quiet location. It has three bedrooms, all with their own showers and WCs, and one with a jacuzzi. It has big grounds, with a terrace and a swimming pool. Meals are available, by arrangement.

Prices s fr €60; d fr €70–€95; extra person fr €15; dinner fr €20
On Site ⚙ Private ⚬ **Nearby** ⚑ 3km ⚓ 20km ⚐ 1km
Restaurant 6km ⚒ 1km ⚖ 1km ⚖ 10km **Notes** No pets English spoken

ST-EXUPERY-LES-ROCHES

₩ *Chambre d'hôtes*

Jean-Paul SONNIER

2 Rue des Haras, 19200 ST-EXUPERY-LES-ROCHES

☎ 06 87 65 30 95

email: jpson@wanadoo.fr

In this former barn there are five spacious guest rooms, all with independent access. They have TV sockets, en suite showers and WCs. Spacious lounge with open fireplace; well-equipped guest kitchen available. Pompon and Pomponette, two little donkeys, are available for rides.

Prices not confirmed for 2008 **Nearby** ⚓ 8km ♨ 30km ✐ 0.5km
↖ 8km ♨ 0.1km ⛩ 7km ⋘ 8km **Notes** Pets admitted

ST-GERMAIN-LES-VERGNES

₩ ◯ La Clauzade

Carmen LINFORD

Domaine la Clauzade, 19330 ST-GERMAIN-LES-VERGNES

☎ 05 55 27 92 97 ▤ 05 55 27 92 97

email: c.linford@tiscali.fr

web: www.domainedelaclauzade.com

This 17th-century stone-built property, adjacent to the owners' home, has four bedrooms - two on the ground floor and two upstairs. There are three doubles, one with a cot, and a family room for three or four. All have private facilities, and there is a guests' lounge with kitchenette. Garden with pond; hosts can suggest leisure activities or arrange theme holidays.

Prices s €50-€55; d €60-€65; t €70-€75; extra person €10; dinner fr €22
On Site ✐ ⚘ **Nearby** ⚓ 10km ♨ 15km ↖ 5km Restaurant 10km
♨ 5km ⛩ 5km ⋘ 15km **Notes** No pets English spoken

ST-JULIEN-PRES-BORT

₩ ◯ La Garenne à Nuzejoux

Eric MESNIL

19110 ST-JULIEN-PRES-BORT

☎ 05 55 94 83 83 ▤ 05 55 94 83 83

In the heart of the Artense, this period residence is set in wooded parkland and has a completely renovated interior, comprising four tasteful bedrooms equipped with shower, private wc, veranda and dining area. Guests also have use of a TV, games and swimming pool. Fishing; gastronomic delights.

Prices s fr €41; d fr €51; t fr €62; extra person fr €13; dinner €18-€21
On Site Private ↖ **Nearby** ⚓ 3km ♨ 20km ✐ 5km Restaurant 2km
♨ 8km Spa 40km ⛩ 8km ⋘ 20km **Notes** No pets

TROCHE

₩ ◯ La Petite Brunie

J et M CROUZILLAC

19230 TROCHE

☎ 05 55 73 34 17 ▤ 05 55 73 57 25

email: martine.crouzillac@netcourrier.com

web: www.isasite.net/la-petite-brunie

In the heart of the Limousin, and close to the Périgord, this totally renovated detached building on a cattle and apple farm has five comfortable guest rooms. Each room has en suite shower and WC, electric heating, fireplace and lounge area. There is a lake on the farm. Your hosts are pleased to provide meals, by arrangement.

Prices not confirmed for 2008 **On Site** ✐ **Nearby** ⚓ 5km ↖ 3km
♨ 2km ⛩ 3km ⋘ 3km **Notes** Pets admitted Open 15 March to 15 November.

TUDEILS

₩₩ *Château de la Salvanie*

Edmond POUJADE

19120 TUDEILS

☎ 05 55 91 53 43

In this peaceful, charming period château, there are three guest rooms and one suite with wc, washbasin and shower. There is also a living room, TV, fireplace, lounge, microwave, fridge and terrace at guests' disposal.

Prices s fr €45; d €55-€60; t €65-€70; extra person fr €10
Nearby ⚓ 15km ♨ 20km ✐ 8km ↖ 8km Restaurant 8km ♨ 8km
⛩ 8km ⋘ 15km **Notes** No pets English spoken Open April to 15 October.

TURENNE

₩ *Au Bontemps*

Jean-Pierre SOUSTRE

19500 TURENNE

☎ 05 55 85 97 72

email: jean-pierre.soustre@wanadoo.fr

Discover an old, peaceful, isolated farm in one of the most beautiful villages of France, on the edge of Quercy. Accommodation consists of six rooms with private shower rooms in a barn restoration, plus living room, TV and library. Breakfast served in the owners' dining room. Special rates for groups.

Prices not confirmed for 2008 **Nearby** ⚓ 13km ♨ 15km ✐ 5km
↖ 10km ♨ 8km ⛩ 3km ⋘ 15km **Notes** No pets

₩ ◯ La Croix de Belonie

C COUVRAT-DESVERGNES

19500 TURENNE

☎ 06 10 61 46 92

email: bruno.couvrat-desvergnes@cegetel.net

A restored former bell founder's residence just 400 metres from the historic town of Turenne, listed as one of the most beautiful in France.

On a hill surrounded by meadows, the refined residence has antique furniture, tasteful décor and flower arrangements. Panoramic views, large garden, swimming pool, TV lounge, and local reading material.

Prices s fr €55; d fr €62; t fr €72; extra person fr €22; dinner fr €20
On Site Private ⚡ **Nearby** ⚓ 10km ⚓ 10km ⚓ 2km ⚓ 5km ⚓ 0.5km
⚓ 17km **Notes** No pets English spoken

⊞ ⏀ Le Clos Marnis

Denis SOURZAT
Le Bourg, 19500 TURENNE
☎ 05 55 22 05 28
email: keny.sourzat@wanadoo.fr

A beautiful group of buildings built by monks in 1711 in one of the most beautiful villages in France, this property has six bedrooms - two in the owners' home and four in a separate wing. Those in the main building reflect the charm of their period, with vaulted ceilings and canopied beds; the other rooms are elegant and tastefully decorated. Meals by arrangement.

Prices d €57-€78; t fr €69; extra person fr €12; dinner fr €22
Nearby ⚓ 10km ⚓ 15km ⚓ 0.1km Restaurant 0.1km ⚓ 6km ⚓ 0.2km
⚓ 0.1km ⚓ 15km **Notes** Pets admitted

VARETZ

⊞ ⏀ ⚲ Les Cailloux

Francis BROCHETON
19240 VARETZ
☎ 05 55 85 09 37 & 06 11 09 64 20
email: coloniale@free.fr
web: http://coloniale.free.fr

This is a beautiful air-conditioned villa, nine kilometres from Brive and five kilometres from the A89 and A20 motorways. It has five bedrooms, some of them extremely spacious, all with TV and internet connections. Meals are available, and can be served indoors or out on the terrace.

Prices s €45-€75; d €55-€80; extra person fr €20; dinner fr €19.50-€24.50 **On Site** Restaurant Private ⚡ **Nearby** ⚓ 9km ⚓ 9km
⚓ 3km ⚓ 2km ⚓ 10km ⚓ 2km ⚓ 2km **Notes** Pets admitted
English spoken CC

VITRAC-SUR-MONTANE

⊞ ⏀ Domaine du Mons

Raphaëlle de SEILHAC
19800 VITRAC-SUR-MONTANE
☎ 05 55 27 60 87 & 06 62 85 70 76
email: raphaelledeseilhac@yahoo.fr
web: www.vacances-en-correze.com

This property, which dates from 1620 and feels full of history, has four spacious and comfortable rooms. It provides an ideal starting point for exploring the area and discovering its historic buildings, slate quarries, interesting villages and natural environment. Guest lounge with TV, books, board games and piano. Meals available (using local produce) by arrangement.

Prices s fr €50; d fr €55; extra person fr €15; dinner fr €19
Nearby ⚓ 15km ⚓ 40km ⚓ 1km ⚓ 13km Restaurant 3km ⚓ 3km
⚓ 2km ⚓ 20km **Notes** No pets English spoken

VOUTEZAC

⊞ ⏀ Sajueix

Jean-Charles RELIER
Sajueix 14, 19130 VOUTEZAC
☎ 05 55 25 80 70 ▤ 05 55 25 80 70
email: gentilhommierecorreze@wanadoo.fr

'La Gentilhommière' is a charming home situated in a small village in the heart of the Vézère and Loyre Valley. There are three upstairs rooms, one with a suite. This is the ideal place to laze around and enjoy good food. Near Pompadour and Objat. Canoes and kayaks 5km.

Prices not confirmed for 2008 **Nearby** ⚓ 15km ⚓ 27km ⚓ 1.5km
⚓ 7km ⚓ 7km ⚓ 2km ⚓ 7km **Notes** Pets admitted Open July to September.

CREUSE

BANIZE

⊞ ⏀ Meyzoux

Maryse GUY
23120 BANIZE
☎ 05 55 66 07 17

Four guest rooms have been created in an old manor house situated in parkland in the middle of the countryside. There is a room for four, a single and two doubles, all with private facilities, TV and heating. Living room with a dining area, TV and library. Cross-country skiing 18km away.

Prices s fr €30; d fr €46; dinner fr €16 **Nearby** ⚓ 3km ⚓ 40km
⚓ 20km ⚓ 12km Restaurant 2.5km ⚓ 5km ⚓ 4km ⚓ 14km
Notes No pets Open April to September.

BUSSIERE-DUNOISE

⊞ Les Couperies

Paule et Roger BOUERY
13, Les Couperies Basses, 23320 BUSSIERE-DUNOISE
☎ 06 81 57 04 93
email: bouery@wanadoo.fr

You might believe you were in a magic place in this lovely, quiet village in the middle of the Pays des Trois Lacs with its remarkable sites. Three rooms of great comfort (private facilities, fridge, television) restored with refinement and authenticity in small stone farmhouses. Two double rooms, and one room for three with a single bed and an electric double bed. Private shady parking.

Prices not confirmed for 2008 **Nearby** ⚓ 6km ⚓ 4km ⚓ 13km
⚓ 4km ⚓ 4km ⚓ 13km **Notes** Pets admitted English spoken

BUSSIERE-ST-GEORGES

♯♯♯ ʘ *Couchardon*

Edith GUILBERT

23600 BUSSIERE-ST-GEORGES

☎ 06 89 86 28 36

email: edith.guilbert@wanadoo.fr

On the edge of two tree-lined lakes, four extremely comfortable double guest rooms with private facilities in a converted farm building dating from the last century. Friendly welcome, a lounge-dining room with TV and library. Restaurants 5km.

Prices not confirmed for 2008　**On Site** ⚓ Private ⚓　**Nearby** ⚓ 15km ⚓ 15km ⚓ 10km ⚓ 5km　**Notes** Pets admitted　English spoken

CHAMBON-STE-CROIX

♯♯♯ ʘ *Chambre d'hôtes*

Antoine et Martine PICARD

2 Rue de la Mairie, 23220 CHAMBON-STE-CROIX

☎ 05 55 89 24 80　🖹 05 55 89 24 80

This old property dates from the last century, and is located near the homes of the Crozant impressionists. There are two double rooms with child's beds and one room for four; each has a TV and private shower room. Guests can use the living room, gardens and terrace with furniture. Central heating. Restaurants 6km. Special rates for groups and children.

Prices not confirmed for 2008　**On Site** ⚓　**Nearby** ⚓ 20km ⚓ 12km ⚓ 12km　**Notes** Pets admitted

CHAMPSANGLARD

♯♯♯♯ **La Villa des Cagnes**

Corinne LEROY

23220 CHAMPSANGLARD

☎ 05 55 51 98 95

email: lescagne@wanadoo.fr

web: www.lavilladescagnes.com

Situated at the heart of the "Pays des Trois Lacs", in its own landscaped grounds, this early 20th-century former hunting lodge has a wonderful view over the surrounding countryside. The welcoming hosts offer four very comfortable guest rooms, each with TV and private bathroom/WC. Wooded grounds, heated swimming pool. Enclosed parking.

Prices s fr €85; d fr €90　**On Site** Private ⚓　**Nearby** ⚓ 5km ⚓ 20km ⚓ 2km Restaurant 3km ⚓ 5km ⚓ 5km ⚓ 15km **Notes** No pets　English spoken

FRESSELINES

♯♯♯ ʘ **Confolent**

D DEMACHY-DANTIN

23450 FRESSELINES

☎ 06 70 97 14 65

email: demachydantin.daniele@neuf.fr

This fine Creuse house dates from the 17th and 18th centuries, and is located on the site immortalised by Claude Monet, where the two Creuse rivers meet. There are two double rooms and one single with private facilities and heating. Guests have use of a living room, lounge with TV and library, and car park. Restaurant 10km.

Prices s fr €66; d €72-€78; dinner fr €24　**Nearby** ⚓ 10km ⚓ 30km ⚓ 0.3km ⚓ 0.5km ⚓ 10km ⚓ 30km **Notes** Pets admitted　English spoken

GENTIOUX-PIGEROLLES

♯♯♯ ʘ *Pallier la Commanderie*

V et J-M LECHEVALLIER

La Commanderie, 23340 GENTIOUX-PIGEROLLES

☎ 05 55 67 91 73

email: info@pallier23.com

web: www.pallier23.com

Originally a fortified house, this property dates back to the 18th century. It has five bedrooms: on the ground floor are two doubles; on the first floor are two more doubles, and on the second floor is a family room with three singles and a cot. All have private facilities. Landscaped grounds, with ponds.

Prices not confirmed for 2008　**On Site** ⚓　**Nearby** ⚓ 10km ⚓ 10km ⚓ 27km ⚓ 9km ⚓ 4km　**Notes** Pets admitted　English spoken

LA CELLE-DUNOISE

♯♯♯ ʘ **Joie de Vivre**

Carolyn et Michael PLOWS

9 L'âge, 23800 LA CELLE-DUNOISE

☎ 05 55 89 92 24

email: joiedevivre-creuse@wanadoo.fr

web: www.joiedevivre-creuse.com

In the heart of the Pays des Trois Lacs, this traditional-style house has three spacious non-smoking double rooms, each decorated in an individual style. They all have private facilities, but those for one of the upstairs rooms are not en suite. Possible children's room (twin beds) on the second floor. First floor lounge area.

Prices s €44-€49; d €56-€70; t €74-€88; dinner fr €22 **On Site** Private ⚓　Private tennis court　**Nearby** ⚓ 4km ⚓ 25km ⚓ 1km Restaurant 4km ⚓ 4km ⚓ 4km ⚓ 15km **Notes** No pets　English spoken

LA CHAPELLE-ST-MARTIAL

⚜⚜ Chambre d'hôtes

Alain COUTURIER
Le Bourg, 23250 LA CHAPELLE ST-MARTIAL
☎ 05 55 64 54 12

This detached house has stacks of character and has three double bedrooms, one with a view of the garden and swimming pool, and all with TV, private shower and wc. There is a living room, heating, terrace with garden furniture, and a restaurant 6km away.

Prices s €38-€55; d €45-€60　**On Site** Private ⚓ **Nearby** ⚑ 6km
⚑ 18km ⚑ 4km Restaurant 6km ⚑ 4km ⚑ 11km ⚑ 7km ⚑ 23km
Notes No pets English spoken

MERINCHAL

⚜ Le Montaurat

Didier et Odile LABAS
23420 MERINCHAL
☎ 05 55 67 25 99 & 06 83 05 11 88

Accommodation available in a detached stone house: an en suite triple, a double and another triple, each with separate bathrooms and wc. There is a living room, lounge with TV and local reading material, kitchen, heating, grounds, car park. Restaurant 3km.

Prices s fr €34; d €42-€52; t fr €58　**Nearby** ⚑ 10km ⚑ 45km
⚑ 4km ⚓ 30km Restaurant 3km ⚑ 4km Spa 40km ⚑ 4km ⚑ 3km
Notes Pets admitted

MOUTIER-MALCARD

⚜ ⦿ Chambre d'hôtes

Corrie et Ronald DE HOOG
5 Route du Geay, 23220 MOUTIER-MALCARD
☎ 05 55 80 66 08 & 06 83 23 95 69 ▤ 05 55 80 66 11
email: corrieron@wanadoo.fr
web: www.veilouqueri.com

The hosts of this delightful property, which stands in wooded grounds, are delighted to welcome tourists to their five guest rooms. There are four double rooms and a room for three, all of them on the first floor. Lounge with books, games and TV. Attractively laid out garden.

Prices s €38-€45; d €47-€55; t €61-€70; extra person fr €12; dinner €19　**Nearby** ⚑ 15km ⚑ 12km ⚑ 3km ⚓ 10km Restaurant 7km ⚑ 7km ⚑ 15km ⚑ 0.5km ⚑ 30km　**Notes** Pets admitted English spoken

PARSAC

⚜ ⦿ La Maison Bleue

G PASCAL et J-P REGNAULT
Montignat, 23140 PARSAC
☎ 05 55 81 88 80 & 06 10 26 87 19
▤ 05 55 81 86 69
email: lamaisonbleue2002@yahoo.fr
web: www.la-maison-bleue-en-creuse.com

A pretty farmhouse, attractively restored, in a small hamlet. It has three spacious and comfortable bedrooms. On the ground floor is a double, and upstairs is a family room for four with a double bed and singles. A further two-room family suite has a double bedroom, plus a single bed in the lounge. All rooms have private facilities.

Prices s fr €50; d fr €70-€75; t fr €85; dinner fr €25　**On Site** ⚑
⚑ **Nearby** ⚑ 25km ⚑ 10km ⚓ 25km Restaurant 10km ⚑ 10km
⚑ 5km ⚑ 25km　**Notes** Pets admitted English spoken

PIONNAT

⚜ ⦿ Las Brouas - Au Beau Rivage

Janice et Peter HILL
23140 PIONNAT
☎ 05 55 62 40 27 ▤ 05 55 62 40 81
email: enquiries@aubeaurivage.com
web: www.aubeaurivage.com

Beneath the Eiffel viaduct which crosses the Creuse, this is an attractive, beautifully decorated house which has five non-smoking guest bedrooms. Four are doubles, and the fifth has twin beds. Two of the rooms also have a child's bed, and they all have private shower room/WC. There is a lounge with TV and board games, and outside is a terrace.

Prices s fr €38; d fr €48; t fr €58; dinner fr €17　**On Site** ⚑ Restaurant
Nearby ⚑ 10km ⚑ 20km ⚓ 16km ⚑ 5km ⚑ 7km ⚑ 0.5km
Notes Pets admitted English spoken CC

ROCHES

⊞ ⏁⏁ **La Vergnolle**

Nelly et Philippe BOURET

23270 ROCHES

☎ 05 55 80 81 97 & 06 63 42 23 14 ▤ 05 55 80 88 12

email: bouret.philippe@wanadoo.fr

web: www.lavergnolle.com

This pleasant residence offers four delightful bedrooms: two double rooms, a twin and one triple, all with TV. Guests may use the living room with TV and reading material, the gardens, car park and children's play area. There is a swimming pool, lakes and several farm animals on the premises. Fishing rods are available at no extra charge. Child's menu; children under four free. Prices vary according to season.

Prices s fr €44; d fr €52; t fr €62; dinner fr €21 **On Site** ⌒ Private ⌁ **Nearby** ⛄ 12km ♨ 25km ♒ 5km ⌂ 5km ⋈ 22km **Notes** Pets admitted English spoken

SAGNAT

⊞ ⅋ **La Roche - La Grange**

Maria et Thierry FAITY

23800 SAGNAT

☎ 05 55 89 10 50 & 06 76 08 42 59

email: lagrange23@voila.fr

web: http://lagrange-en-creuse.monsite.orange.fr

An attractive old building in a peaceful rural setting. There are three non-smoking guest bedrooms. One is on the ground floor, and they all have private bath or shower room and WC. There is a separate guests' entrance. Fishing is available on-site, and many other activities are available close by.

Prices s fr €50; d fr €55 **On Site** ⌒ **Nearby** ⛄ 10km ⌁ 15km Restaurant 5km ♒ 5km ♒ 5km ⌂ 4km ⋈ 15km **Notes** Pets admitted English spoken

SOUBREBOST

⊞ ⏁⏁ *Le Masmontard*

Bernard HAYEZ

23250 SOUBREBOST

☎ 05 55 64 59 27

email: hayezbernard@wanadoo.fr

In Martin Naduad country, this early 20th-century house is in a magical setting and offers two double rooms and a room with a double and single bed. Living room, lounge with books, children's games and parking. Extra bed possible.

Prices not confirmed for 2008 **Nearby** ⛄ 6km ♨ 10km ⌒ 3km ♒ 10km **Notes** No pets

ST-AVIT-DE-TARDES

⊞ ⏁⏁ **Le Moulin de Teiteix**

Y BRUN et L DAUPHIN

23200 ST-AVIT-DE-TARDES

☎ 05 55 67 34 18 & 06 76 18 47 56

email: lemoulindeteiteix@yahoo.fr

web: http://perso.wanadoo.fr/moulin-de-teiteix

Close to Aubusson and right beside the Tardes, a top class trout river, this house has four bedrooms. On the ground floor is a family room for four; upstairs are two double rooms, with another double in a separate building. All have en suite bath/shower room and WC. Attractive grounds with terrace and parking space. Meals available by arrangement.

Prices s fr €55; d fr €75; t fr €95; dinner fr €22 **On Site** ⌒ **Nearby** ⛄ 17km ♨ 35km ⌁ 15km Restaurant 5km ♒ 15km ⌂ 15km ⋈ 15km **Notes** No pets English spoken

ST-BARD

⊞ ⏁⏁ **Château de Chazelpaud**

Patrick et Madeleine ALBRIGHT

23260 ST-BARD

☎ 05 55 67 33 03 & 06 83 12 58 61 ▤ 05 55 67 30 25

email: albrightpatrick@aol.com

web: http://membres.lycos.fr/chazelpaud/

This neo-renaissance château, set in a 100-year-old park, offers a period dining room and a Louis XVI lounge with TV. There is a double three triples and a suite for four people with private facilities. Heating, car park, covered heated swimming pool, gym and children's games.

Prices s fr €70; d €70-€115; t €85-€130; dinner fr €25 **On Site** Private ⌁ **Nearby** ⛄ 8km ♨ 40km ⌒ 0.5km Restaurant 5km ♒ 8km Spa 30km ⌂ 8km ⋈ 20km **Notes** Pets admitted English spoken Open April to October.

ST-DIZIER-LEYRENNE

⊞ *Le Masbeau*

Jean-Pierre et Nicole PELEGE

23400 ST-DIZIER-LEYRENNE

☎ 05 55 64 40 11 ▤ 05 55 54 95 84

email: bourganeuf.immobilier@wanadoo.fr

A converted outbuilding dating from the early 1900s has three bedrooms of character: three doubles, two with two child's beds and all with private facilities. There is a living room with TV, heating, a games room and use of a kitchen. Outside are landscaped grounds, a swimming pool, a garage and a car park. Restaurant 4km.

Prices not confirmed for 2008 **On Site** Private ⌁ **Nearby** ⌒ 2km ♒ 2km ⌂ 2km **Notes** No pets English spoken Open March to November.

ST-ETIENNE-DE-FURSAC

Chambre d'hôtes

Dominique et Josette BASSE
44, Paulhac, 23290 ST-ETIENNE-DE-FURSAC
☎ 05 55 63 36 02
email: info@delacure.com
web: www.delacure.com

This 18th-century restored vicarage is near the Knights Templar command post and is set in a park with views of the Monts d'Ambazac. Accommodation comprises four non-smoking bedrooms: a twin, and three doubles with private facilities; extra bed and TV on request. There are lounge areas, library and TV. Gardens with terrace, furniture, children's games and car park.

Prices s €58-€67; d €64-€72; dinner fr €22   **Nearby** ☆ 10km
♨ 20km ♪ 3km ⚓ 6km Restaurant 3.5km ⚓ 4km ⛵ 14km
Notes No pets

ST-HILAIRE-LA-PLAINE

Le Grand Villard

Trudy et Mark WAIN
23150 ST-HILAIRE-LA-PLAINE
☎ 05 55 81 30 39 & 06 72 08 20 41   📧 05 55 81 19 61
email: mark.wain@wanadoo.fr
web: www.hiddenfrance.co.uk

This is a quiet little village, and Le Grand Villard is a beautiful old farmhouse set in its own grounds. It offers three attractive, tastefully decorated bedrooms: two doubles and a family room for four, all with en suite facilities. Meals are available by arrangement. There is a garden with terrace, and much to see and do in the area.

Prices s fr €38; d fr €48; t fr €58; dinner fr €18   **Nearby** ☆ 17km
♨ 30km ♪ 8km ⚓ 16km ⚓ 5km 🏠 5km ⛵ 16km   **Notes** Pets admitted English spoken

ST-HILAIRE-LE-CHATEAU

La Chassagne

M-Christine FANTON
23250 ST-HILAIRE-LE-CHATEAU
☎ 05 55 64 55 75 & 06 14 61 08 16
email: m.fanton@tiscali.fr
web: www.chateau-lachassagne.com

A magnificent 15th and 17th-century château overlooking the Thaurian Valley, with a shady park of five hectares bordered by a trout river. There are four bedrooms (three double beds and two singles) and one suite in the guard house (one double and one single). All rooms have private facilities. There is also a living room with TV lounge area and heating. Excellent restaurants nearby.

Prices s €90-€100; d €95-€120; t €110-€120; dinner fr €30
On Site ♪   **Nearby** ☆ 3km ♨ 14km ⚓ 24km ⚓ 11km 🏠 3km
⛵ 30km   **Notes** Pets admitted English spoken

ST-PARDOUX-LE-NEUF

Les Vergnes

Sylvie et Patrick DUMONTANT
23200 ST-PARDOUX-LE-NEUF
☎ 05 55 66 23 74   📧 05 55 67 74 16

Six bedrooms are available in this beautiful 18th-century farmhouse with private lake: five with double beds and two singles plus an en suite room with two single beds. Each room has its own shower and wc, one has a spa bath. There is a living room with open fireplace, lounge, TV and library, heating and an adjoining park and terrace.

Prices s €48-€66; d €57-€79; t fr €88; dinner €16-€28   **On Site** ♪
Private ⚓   **Nearby** ☆ 15km ♨ 30km Restaurant 6km ⚓ 6km
Notes Pets admitted English spoken Open April to October.

ST-PARDOUX-LES-CARDS

Le Mont Gapier

Ghislaine et Dominique JUHEL
23150 ST-PARDOUX-LES-CARDS
☎ 05 55 62 35 16   📧 05 55 62 35 16

16th-century house of character built on the former site of the Château of Villemonteix, in the Limousin cattle-raising area. There is a living room with lounge area, TV, library, and fireplace, a garden and children's games. Rooms include three doubles, a single with child's bed and one suite with a double bed, each with private facilities. There are two double-bedded rooms and shower room on the second floor. Restaurants 3km. Special rates for groups. Animals accepted except in bedrooms.

Prices s €48-€50; d €58-€60; t fr €77; dinner fr €20   **On Site** ♪
Nearby ☆ 23km ♨ 11km ⚓ 4km Restaurant 4km ⚓ 1.5km Spa 45km
🏠 3km   **Notes** English spoken

ST-SILVAIN-BELLEGARDE

Les Trois Ponts

I et G VAN IPENBURG
23190 ST-SILVAIN-BELLEGARDE
☎ 05 55 67 12 14   📧 05 55 67 12 14
email: info@lestroisponts.nl
web: www.lestroisponts.nl

A riverside setting, surrounded by greenery, makes this 18th-century mill a very attractive place. It has five comfortable rooms, all with private facilities. There are two twin-bedded rooms, two with three singles, and a family room with five singles. Lounge with TV, books and board games; guests' kitchenette. Games area - volleyball, boules, etc. Meals available.

Prices s fr €50; d fr €75; t fr €105; dinner fr €25   **On Site** ♪
♨ Private ⚓   **Nearby** ☆ 7km ♨ 25km Restaurant 12km ⚓ 3km
🏠 12km ⛵ 14km   **Notes** Pets admitted English spoken CC

LIMOUSIN

ST-YRIEIX-LA-MONTAGNE

††† |Ol Gibouleaux

Richard et Danièle DARDUIN

23460 ST-YRIEIX-LA-MONTAGNE

☎ 05 55 66 03 27 ▤ 05 55 66 05 82

This individual house dates from 1863 and offers two double rooms with a child's bed, and one room for four, each with shower and wc. There is a living room/lounge with TV, heating, landscaped grounds and a car park.

Prices s fr €40; d fr €50; t fr €65; dinner fr €16   **On Site** ☙
Nearby ⚓ 6km ⚓ 30km ♣ 8km ⚓ 20km Restaurant 4km ⚓ 6km
🏠 6km   **Notes** Pets admitted English spoken Open January to November.

VALLIERE

†††† *La Lombrière*

Frédérique et Yannick CROUTEIX

23120 VALLIERE

☎ 05 55 66 94 41

A warm welcome is promised in this 100-year-old farmhouse, on a working farm. It has four bedrooms: a double and a triple on the first floor, and the same again upstairs. All rooms have private bath or shower room and WC. Lounge with kitchen, and sitting room with TV and books. Outside play area; two mountain bikes available.

Prices not confirmed for 2008   **On Site** ♣   **Nearby** ⚓ 3km
⚓ 15km ⚓   **Notes** Pets admitted English spoken

††† |Ol Le Masvaudier

Yvette DESMICHEL

23120 VALLIERE

☎ 05 55 66 03 18

A small farmhouse with a family atmosphere. There are three bedrooms: a double, and two triples (each with a double bed plus a single) which also have televisions. All have private bath or shower room and WC. Lounge, landscaped grounds, boules pitch. Meals available, by arrangement.

Prices s fr €30; d fr €37; t fr €42; dinner fr €12   **Nearby** ⚓ 9km ♣ 1km
⚓ 12km Restaurant 12km ⚓ 3km 🏠 3km ⚓ 12km   **Notes** Pets admitted English spoken

VIDAILLAT

†††† |Ol Chez Jallot

Denise DANIEL & Doug IBBS

23250 VIDAILLAT

☎ 05 55 64 50 77

email: info@chezjallot.com

web: www.chezjallot.com

In the heart of the Creuse department, and 15 minutes from the Lac de Vassivière, this 19th-century house was featured in Channel 4's Grand Design Abroad and known as 'The Creuse House'. It offers five beautiful en suite bedrooms; four are doubles; the fifth is a two-roomed suite for four (two sets of twin beds). A cot and an additional single bed are available. Meals are available by arrangement, and the house is non-smoking.

Prices s fr €60; d fr €75-€115; t fr €95; dinner fr €30
On Site Restaurant ☙   **Nearby** ⚓ 10km ⚓ 15km ♣ 2km ⚓ 30km
⚓ 20km   **Notes** Pets admitted English spoken

HAUTE-VIENNE

ARNAC-LA-POSTE

††† |Ol Chambre d'hôtes

Jeanine et William KERR

Rond Point du Marronnier, 87160 ARNAC-LA-POSTE

☎ 05 55 76 87 26

This restored house with its shady garden looks on to the small village square with its chestnut tree, near to the fortified church. There are three rooms, on the first and second floors, all with private bath/ shower rooms and WCs and electric convector heaters. Guests' lounge with open fire, TV and books.

Prices d fr €46; t fr €56; dinner fr €17   **Nearby** ♣ 10km ⚓ 10km
Restaurant 7km ⚓ 0.3km 🏠 0.1km ⚓ 10km   **Notes** No pets English spoken Open 26 May to 16 September.

BEAUMONT-DU-LAC

†††† *Chambre d'hôtes*

Lorrell BYRNE

Le Bourg, 87120 BEAUMONT-DU-LAC

☎ 05 55 69 63 98 ▤ 05 55 69 63 98

email: lorrell.byrne@wanadoo.fr

web: www.lescavaliers.bravehost.com

This is an attractive stone-built house, with English hosts, in a village on the road to the Lac de Vassivière. It has five bedrooms, sleeping from two to five guests, each with a private bath or shower room and WC. Some of the rooms are on the ground floor.

Prices not confirmed for 2008   **Nearby** ♣ 4km ⚓ 6km ⚓ 4km 🏠 4km
⚓ 6km   **Notes** Pets admitted English spoken

BELLAC

▦ Chambre d'hôtes

ean-Paul et Odile FONTANEL
Rue du Docteur Vetelay, 87300 BELLAC
☎ 05 55 68 11 86 📄 05 55 68 78 96
mail: bellac@free.fr
eb: http://bellac.free.fr

hese rooms are in a 17th-century house full of character, in the heart
the old part of Bellac. There are three rooms, which can sleep up
five people, on the first and second floors. They all have private
athrooms and WCs. Lounge, private parking, courtyard and compact
ounds with lawn.

rices s fr €40; d €40-€50; t fr €50; extra person fr €10 **Nearby** ⛷ 4km
15km ⚲ 1km ⚘ 1km Restaurant 1km ⚓ 1km ⋔ 0.5km
otes No pets English spoken

▦ ⑩ *Chambre d'hôtes*

tephen ARMSTRONG-JAMES
Place de la République, 87300 BELLAC
☎ 05 55 68 47 61 & 06 77 60 81 68
mail: steve@maisonbellachonne.com
eb: www.maisonbellachonne.com

is is a house full of character, dating back to the 17th century, in the
d part of Bellac which overlooks the valley of the Vincou. It has four
drooms, all on the second floor, each sleeping from two to four
ests. All have private bath or shower room and WC. Dining room
th lounge area on the first floor.

ices not confirmed for 2008 **On Site** Restaurant **Nearby** ⛷ 2km
0.2km ⚓ 0.5km ⋔ 0.5km **Notes** Pets admitted English spoken

ERSAC-SUR-RIVALIER

▦ ⑩ *Domaine du Noyer*

an et Anna MASDOUMIER
370 BERSAC-SUR-RIVALIER
05 55 71 52 91 📄 05 55 71 51 48
mail: noyer.prats@free.fr
eb: http://noyer-prats.com

ur bedrooms are available in this 16th-century stately residence, in
e heart of a property of 20 hectares, with gym, swimming pool and
ycles. There are four double rooms (three double beds and two
gle beds) with showers and private wc, and a living room, lounge,
place, library and games room. In addition, there are loose boxes
horses and training areas. Lake for fishing on the estate.

ices not confirmed for 2008 **On Site** ⚲ Private ⚘
arby Restaurant 6km ⚓ 3km ▦ 2km ⋔ 6km **Notes** Pets admitted
glish spoken

BESSINES-SUR-GARTEMPE

▦ ⑩ Chambre d'hôtes

Ana Mery et Gérard VAN HOOFT
Av du 11 Novembre, 87250 BESSINES-SUR-GARTEMPE
☎ 05 55 76 78 42
email: chateau_constant@yahoo.com
web: www.chateau-constant.com

Wooded grounds are the setting for this grand late 19th-century
house. Five very comfortable first floor bedrooms sleep two to four,
with private facilities. The lounge has a large entrance opening onto
the terrace and grounds. Loggia and library. Evening meals can be
enjoyed while hearing about your hosts' travels.

Prices s fr €65; d fr €75; t fr €85; extra person fr €10; dinner fr
€20 **On Site** ⚘ **Nearby** ⛷ 9km Restaurant 1km ⚓ 1km ⋔ 15km
Notes Pets admitted English spoken

▦ ❦ ⑩ Morterolles-sur-Semme

Jean-Marie et Andrée TESSIER
Chez Doussaud, 87250 BESSINES-SUR-GARTEMPE
☎ 05 55 76 06 94 📄 05 55 76 58 35

This cattle farm is situated in a small hamlet and the proprietors offer
guided tours of the farm and home-made rabbit and chicken rillettes.
Three very large, cheerful bedrooms opening onto a terrace and
garden have been built in an annexe separate from the house. Each
is en suite and accommodates two to four people. Lounge for guests;
meals available on demand, except Sunday evenings.

Prices s fr €30; d fr €40; t fr €50; extra person fr €10; dinner fr €15
Nearby ⛷ 5km ⚲ 35km ⚘ 15km ⚘ 12km Restaurant 5km ⚓ 5km
▦ 5km ⋔ 15km **Notes** No pets English spoken

BLANZAC

▦ ❦ ⑩ Rouffignac

Catherine KUBIAK-LE QUERE
87300 BLANZAC
☎ 05 55 68 02 14 📄 05 55 68 86 89
email: catkubiak@hotmail.com
web: www.visitorama.com/87/rouffignac.html

This farm is close to the mountains of Blond, Bellac and Mortemart,
and the centre of la Mémoire d'Oradour-sur-Glane. There are five
very comfortable en suite bedrooms (two split level) for four and five
people. There is a mezzanine over a huge living room with modern
décor, and a games room with billiard table, TV lounge and piano.
Meals are generous and feature farm produce.

Prices s €40-€48; d €48-€59; t fr €59; extra person fr €9; dinner fr €17
On Site ⚘ **Nearby** ⛷ 8km Restaurant 4km ⚓ 4km ▦ 4km ⋔ 4km
Notes No pets English spoken CC

BLOND

♦♦♦ ◉ *Thoveyrat*

Myriam et Pierre MORICE
87300 BLOND
☎ 05 55 68 86 86 ▤ 05 55 68 86 86
email: chambrehote@freesurf.fr
web: www.visitorama.com/87/chambre-d-hote/
thoveyrat.html

This is a big house, full of character, near to the Blond hills. It has four comfortable guest rooms for up to four people, all with private shower room/WC. Lounge with open fire. Meals available: in season, the host serves lamb, and organic pork from the farm. Delicious vegetarian meals are also available on request.

Prices not confirmed for 2008   **Nearby** ♯ 7km ✐ 1km ✈ 3km Restaurant 3km ⌣ 3km ⛉ 3km ⋙ 3km   **Notes** No pets English spoken

---

BOISSEUIL

♦♦♦ *Domaine de Moulinard*

Brigitte ZIEGLER
87220 BOISSEUIL
☎ 05 55 06 91 22 ▤ 05 55 06 98 28
email: ph.ziegler@laposte.net
web: http://membres.lycos.fr/moulinard

This 18th-century mansion, on a sheep farm and tree cultivation business near Moulinard and Limoges, has been restored to provide five bedrooms. They are all light and spacious with antique furniture, private bathrooms, and views of the quiet, shady garden surrounding the house. There are restaurants 2km away and at 6km, a challenging 18-hole golf course.

Prices not confirmed for 2008   **Nearby** ♯ 13km ✐ 6km ✈ 9km Restaurant 2km ⌣ 2km ⛉ 2km ⋙ 7km   **Notes** No pets English spoken Open April to October.

BONNAC-LA-COTE

♦♦♦ **Château de Saint-Antoine**

Nathalie et Olivier RAIMBAULT
22 Av de Maison Rouge, 87270 BONNAC-LA-COTE
☎ 05 55 36 61 71 & 06 15 76 28 83 ▤ 05 55 36 61 72
email: gite@chateau-de-st-antoine.com
web: www.chateau-de-st-antoine.com

Close to Limoges, this château was built in the 18th and 19th centuries, on the site of an old coaching inn on the road to Paris. It now has five guest bedrooms, including a family suite in one of the towers. All of the rooms have private bath or shower rooms and WCs. Lounge and kitchen available for guests.

Prices s €60-€110; d €73-€120; t €95-€135; extra person fr €12; dinner fr €15   **Nearby** ♯ 3km ⌁ 15km ✐ 2.5km ✈ 15km Restaurant 1km ⌣ 3km ⛉ 2km ⋙ 10km   **Notes** Pets admitted English spoken

CHAMPAGNAC-LA-RIVIERE

♦♦♦♦ ◉ **Château de Brie**

Pierre DU MANOIR DE JUAYE
87150 CHAMPAGNAC-LA-RIVIERE
☎ 05 55 78 17 52 ▤ 05 55 78 14 02
email: chateaudebrie@wanadoo.fr
web: www.chateaux-france.com/brie

15th-century château set in three hectares of parkland with swimming pool and tennis court. There are four character bedrooms with private bathroom and wc. Guests can use the lounge, dining room and library. Fishing, forest walks and cycling on the property.

Prices d fr €110; dinner fr €40   **On Site** ✐ Private ✈ Private tennis court   **Nearby** ♯ 11km Restaurant 5km ⛲ 1km ⛉ 5km ⋙ 13km   **Notes** Pets admitted English spoken Open April to 1 November.

CHAMPSAC

♦♦♦ ◉ *Moulin de Cros*

Trudi et Patrick DEMPSEY
87230 CHAMPSAC
☎ 05 55 78 16 54
email: patrick.dempsey@lionheartholidays.com
web: www.lionheartholidays.com/b_b

Situated in the Parc Naturel Régional Périgord-Limousin, this property has three beautiful bedrooms. Two are doubles (one with a king-size bed); the third has twin beds and all three have en suite bath/shower room and WC. Superb living room, and a garden with covered terrace and swimming pool. Meals are available by arrangement.

Prices not confirmed for 2008   **Nearby** ✐ 0.5km ✈ Restaurant 7km ⛉ 7km ⋙ 7km   **Notes** No pets

---

CHATEAU-CHERVIX

♦♦♦ ❧ ◉ **La Chapelle**

Patrick et Mayder LESPAGNOL
87380 CHATEAU-CHERVIX
☎ 05 55 00 86 67 ▤ 05 55 00 70 78
email: lespagno@club-internet.fr
web: http://gite.lachapelle.free.fr

This small traditional house on an organic goat farm offers four bedrooms, each with individual shower and wc. Other amenities include a living room with reading material, a kitchen area and a garden, games corner, grounds and car park. Meals (by reservation, July-August only); and there is a forest on the property and a river 3km away.

Prices s fr €36; d fr €44; t fr €49; extra person fr €8; dinner fr €10 **Nearby** ♯ 6km ✐ 6km Restaurant 4km ⌣ 4km ⛉ 4km **Notes** No pets English spoken

HATEAUNEUF-LA-FORET

₩ ⵔ◯⵰ La Croix du Reh

eter et Galina FENTON

'130 CHATEAUNEUF-LA-FORET

05 55 69 75 37

mail: lacroixdureh3@aol.com

eb: www.lacroixdureh.com

is impressive house stands in its own grounds, with plenty of
eenery and flowers. There is a double bedroom downstairs, with
ur more rooms upstairs - two of which can be linked to form a suite.
have en suite facilities. Comfortable lounge with an open fire, and
grand dining room where evening meals can be served.

ices s €50-€55; d €65-€70; t €70-€75; extra person fr €5; dinner fr
9 **Nearby** ⚘ 8km ✍ 1km ⤢ 10km Restaurant 0.5km ♨ 🏠 0.3km
10km **Notes** Pets admitted English spoken

HATEAUPONSAC

₩ ⵔ◯⵰ *Domaine des Baux*

arie-Claire POTHIER

'290 CHATEAUPONSAC

05 55 68 80 46

mail: marieclairepothier@wanadoo.fr

eb: www.domaine-des-baux.com

a hamlet 6km from the Lac de Saint-Pardoux, this house has lovely
ounds. Three ground floor bedrooms with shower room and private
C, dining room, reading area and mezzanine. Meals are served in
large sympathetically restored dining room by the fire or on the
race.

ices not confirmed for 2008 **Nearby** ⚘ 2km ✍ 6km ⤢ 6km
staurant 4km ♨ 6km 🏠 4km **Notes** Pets admitted Open April to 30
tober.

IEUX

₩ ⵔ◯⵰ Les Volets Bleus

thy et Tony FRENCH

10 rte d'Oradour-sur-Glane, 87520 CIEUX

05 55 03 26 97 📠 05 55 03 26 97

mail: voletsbleuscieux@aol.com

s house looks onto a garden of flowers and trees, bordered
a stream, and is located near Lake Cieux (43 hectares, bathing
ssible) in a village at the foot of the Monts. There are three carefully
corated en suite bedrooms, a dining room, lounge with fireplace,
ary and TV reserved for guests. Meals (by reservation), including a
getarian menu. No smoking. Discover the legendary standing stones
arby and numerous footpaths, horse and bike trails.

ces s fr €43; d fr €48; dinner fr €19 **Nearby** ⚘ 6km ⚓ 17km
0.1km Restaurant 0.8km ♨ 1km ⛳ 10km 🏠 0.8km 🚣 12km
tes No pets English spoken Open 15 May to 15 September.

COMPREIGNAC

₩₩₩ ⵔ◯⵰ *Chambre d'hôtes*

Béatrice et Gilbert SALLET

6-7 Place du 11 Novembre, 87140 COMPREIGNAC

☎ 05 55 71 23 51

email: gilbert.sallet@wanadoo.fr

A house of character with fine granite terraces, situated in the town
of Compreignac, near the old fortified church. There are three guest
rooms, sleeping two to four people, with private facilities. The Lake
of Saint-Pardoux (330 hectare) offers all the joys of bathing, fishing
and sailing.

Prices not confirmed for 2008 **Nearby** ⚘ 12km ✍ 3km
Restaurant 13km ♨ 3km 🚣 13km **Notes** No pets

COUSSAC-BONNEVAL

₩₩₩ *Las Gouttas*

Nicole et Marcel PENAUD

87500 COUSSAC-BONNEVAL

☎ 05 55 75 24 25 📠 05 55 75 24 25

This house is situated amongst the meadows of a small sheep farm,
close to the rivers Corrèze and Dordogne. It has two double rooms
and a family suite for up to four. All rooms have private bath or
shower room and WC. Use of kitchen.

Prices not confirmed for 2008 **Nearby** ⚘ 14km ✍ 3km ⤢ 14km
Restaurant 3km ♨ 3km 🏠 3km 🚣 14km **Notes** No pets Open April
to November.

₩₩₩ ⵔ◯⵰ Le Moulin de Marsaguet

Renaud et Valérie GIZARDIN

87500 COUSSAC-BONNEVAL

☎ 05 55 75 28 29 📠 05 55 75 28 29

email: gizardin.renaud@akeonet.com

web: www.tourismorama.moulindemarsaguet.com

Three en suite bedrooms for two or three can be found in this old
mill, on the banks of a fine 13-hectare lake. A large ironmonger's
house, where guests may sample farm produce (foie gras, conserves,
duck fillet), and vegetables from the garden. Special foie gras
weekends.

Prices s fr €41; d fr €46; extra person fr €11; dinner fr €20 **On Site** ✍
Nearby ⚘ 14km ⚓ 40km ⤢ 14km Restaurant 3km ♨ 3km 🏠 3km
🚣 12km **Notes** No pets English spoken Open April to September.

CUSSAC

₩₩₩ ⵔ◯⵰ Chambre d'hotes

Josette et René COLOMBIER

La Mazaurie, 87150 CUSSAC

☎ 05 55 70 97 30 & 06 74 42 54 14

This is a quietly situated restored farmhouse in a small hamlet in the
Parc Naturel Régional. There are three bedrooms, all upstairs. Two of
the rooms have private facilities, and the third, a suite for four or five
guests, has its own bathroom and WC on the landing. Baby

CONTINUED

443

LIMOUSIN

CUSSAC CONTINUED

equipment available. Lounge with books and games; table tennis. Meals by arrangement. Accommodation by reservation only out of season.

Prices s fr €39; d fr €45; t fr €56; extra person fr €16; dinner fr €17
Nearby ⚓ 6km ♨ 42km ✎ 4km ↖ 11km Restaurant 3km ♨ 3km
♣ 6km 🏠 3km ⛵ 20km **Notes** No pets English spoken

DOURNAZAC

⚓ ❦ ⊚ *Le Mas du Loup*

Laurence et Philippe CHAPLAIN
87230 DOURNAZAC
☎ 05 55 78 11 59 & 06 60 42 89 98
email: lemasduloup@wanadoo.fr
web: www.masduloup.monsite.wanadoo.fr

Situated in the Parc Naturel Régional, this old fortified farmhouse dates from the 17th century. At the entrance to the property is an unusual porch/pigeon-loft. It has three rooms for two or three people, and a suite for four, all with private bath or shower room and WC. Lounge with fireplace; grounds with panoramic views. Swimming pool. Meals by arrangement.

Prices not confirmed for 2008 **On Site** Private ↖ **Nearby** ⚓ 7km
✎ 10km Restaurant 10km ♨ 3km 🏠 3km ⛵ 10km **Notes** Pets admitted English spoken Open 2 March to October.

EYMOUTIERS

⚓ ❦ ⊚ *La Tour d'Ayen*

Maryline et Romain HUBERT
Le Bourg, 87120 EYMOUTIERS
☎ 05 55 69 76 05
email: Tourdayen@aol.com
web: www.tourdayen.com

This is a restored Renaissance house in the heart of Eymoutiers, formerly a centre of the tannery industry. On the first floor there are two rooms for three people and a duplex family suite for four, with lounge and kitchenette. All rooms have private facilities. Breakfast, with home-made jams, is served in a pretty flowery courtyard. Meals by arrangement.

Prices s fr €42; d fr €56; t fr €66; extra person fr €10; dinner fr €18
Nearby ⚓ 20km ♨ 30km ✎ 1km ↖ 1km Restaurant 0.5km ♨ 1km
🏠 0.5km ⛵ 1km **Notes** No pets English spoken

⚓ ⊚ *Peyrassou*

David et Susan SMALL
87120 EYMOUTIERS
☎ 05 55 69 68 12
email: peyrassou@tele2.fr
web: www.stepintofrance.com

This isolated house stands between forest and pastures, in the hills of Eymoutiers. There are two double rooms and a suite for four, all on the second floor and all with private bath or shower rooms and WCs. Excellent walks are available in the hills of the Limousin; English owners.

Prices not confirmed for 2008 **On Site** Private ↖ **Nearby** ✎ 2km Restaurant 5km 🏠 5km ⛵ 5km **Notes** No pets English spoken

FEYTIAT

⚓ Chambre d'hôtes

Danielle et Bernard BRULAT
Le Vieux Crezin, 87220 FEYTIAT
☎ 05 55 06 34 41 🖶 05 55 48 37 16

A spacious barn conversion in a small, peaceful hamlet five minutes from Limoges town centre. It offers three en suite mezzanine bedrooms above a living room with billiard table.

Prices s fr €50; d €60-€67; t €75-€82; extra person fr €15
Nearby ⚓ 7km ♨ 4km ✎ 0.8km ↖ Restaurant 0.2km ♨ 2km ♣ 1km
🏠 0.8km ⛵ 6km **Notes** Pets admitted

⚓ ⊚ Chambre d'hôtes

Mady et Gérard CHASTAGNER
Allée du Puy Marot, 87220 FEYTIAT
☎ 05 55 48 33 97 🖶 05 55 30 31 86
email: gerardchastagner@wanadoo.fr

A peaceful 16th-century priory situated overlooking the Valoine Valle There are three en suite bedrooms, one a family suite and one a luxury bedroom, which look onto the park surrounding the house, a enjoy panoramic views of the valley. Proprietors are passionate abou porcelain, and the property is just 10 minutes from Limoges, the capital of kiln arts with its porcelain and enamel museums.

Prices s fr €58; d fr €68; t fr €100; dinner fr €28 **On Site** ♣
Nearby ⚓ 4km ✎ 7km ↖ 5km Restaurant 5km ♨ 1km 🏠 1km
⛵ 5km **Notes** No pets English spoken

FLAVIGNAC

⚓ Les Mingoux

T et M-F VIVIANT-MOREL
87230 FLAVIGNAC
☎ 05 55 36 08 62 & 05 55 36 93 47
email: th.viviant@wanadoo.fr
web: www.vivacesflavignac.com

On the site of an old mill, this house has three attic rooms, looking out onto a garden terrace. The rooms are all doubles, with private facilities; an extra bed is available. The owners - a nurserywoman an

landscape architect - take great pleasure in sharing with their guests
e beauty of this wonderful place in the Périgord-Limousin natural
ark.

ices s fr €38; d fr €43; t fr €51 **On Site** 🏊 **Nearby** ⚓ 11km
6km Restaurant 4km 🚲 4km 🐎 4km 🐎 18km **Notes** Pets admitted

---

ROMENTAL

ⅢⅠ ⊙Ⅰ *Le Moulin du Goutay*

athalie EMERY
7250 FROMENTAL
☎ 05 55 76 14 59
nail: le-moulin-du-goutay@wanadoo.fr
eb: www.moulindugoutay.fr

is restored mill in a picturesque location is ideal for exploring the
nbazac Hills, on foot or on horseback. On the first floor are two
mfortable rooms, one with a small kitchenette. They have private
owers and shared WC. There are also two large family rooms, each
th private shower/WC. Library; central heating, washing machine.
eals by arrangement.

ices not confirmed for 2008 **On Site** ⚓ 🏊 **Nearby** ⚓ 9km
staurant 10km 🏠 10km 🐎 11km **Notes** Pets admitted

ⅢⅢ ⊙Ⅰ **Château Montautre**

Norma RIVA-SCHIPPER
87250 FROMENTAL
☎ 05 55 76 69 81 & 06 72 30 22 20
email: montautre@aol.com
web: www.montautre.com

This restored 15th-century manor house, with its square keep
towering over the woods and meadows, has four distinctive guest
rooms, all with private facilities. Lounge with books; meals by
arrangement. The hosts run courses in dance, yoga and cooking
(booking necessary).

Prices s fr €65; d fr €80; t fr €95; dinner fr €25 **On Site** 🏊
Private ⚓ **Nearby** ⚓ 6km Restaurant 10km 🚲 7km 🏠 4km
🐎 10km **Notes** No pets English spoken Open April to December.

ⅼLE

Ⅱ **Château de la Chabroulie**

:nédicte DE LA SELLE
'170 ISLE
05 55 36 13 15 & 06 77 04 87 09
nail: dls@chateau-chabroulie.com
eb: www.chateau-chabroulie.com

is château is set in grounds of 70 hectares, 6km from Limoges, and
ers the warmth and quality of an old family home. Four bedrooms
h private bathrooms and wc have been built for guests, plus a
inge, library area and fireplace. Explore the property by bicycle.

ces s fr €65; d fr €70; t fr €85 **On Site** Private ⚓ **Nearby** ⚓ 6km
1km Restaurant 6km 🚲 2km 🏠 1.5km 🐎 7km **Notes** No pets
:lish spoken

JANAILHAC

ⅢⅢ ⊙Ⅰ *Chambre d'hôtes*

Isabelle et Bernard VARNOUX
Le Bourg, 87800 JANAILHAC
☎ 05 55 00 40 18 & 06 83 25 35 90
email: contact@lepreauchene.com
web: www.lepreauchene.com

The guest rooms in this originally decorated house open onto a
courtyard with old wells, patio garden and covered, heated swimming
pool. The rooms sleep up to five, each with a shower room and toilet.
On the ground floor is a lounge, and your artist hostess serves meals
using her home-grown produce.

Prices not confirmed for 2008 **On Site** Private ⚓ **Nearby** 🏊 10km
Restaurant 7km 🚲 7km 🏠 7km 🐎 7km **Notes** No pets English spoken

---

JOUAC

ⅢⅢ ⊙Ⅰ **L'Ancien Chais**

Marina PRICE
Le Bourg, 87890 JOUAC
☎ 05 55 60 49 41
email: bandb.jouac@hotmail.com

The three bedrooms at this property are in a house adjacent to the
hosts' home, in a little village overlooking the Benaize River. One of
the bedrooms is on the ground floor; the others are upstairs and all
have private shower room and WC. There is a lounge area for guests.
Outside is a covered terrace and private parking.

Prices s fr €45; d fr €50; t fr €60; dinner fr €20 **On Site** 🏊
Nearby Restaurant 6km 🚲 5km 🏠 8km 🐎 20km **Notes** Pets admitted
English spoken

LA CHAPELLE-MONTBRANDEIX

ⅢⅢ ⊙Ⅰ *Lartimache*

Evelyne et Bernard GUERIN
87440 LA CHAPELLE-MONTBRANDEIX
☎ 05 55 78 75 65 📄 05 55 78 75 65
web: www.visitorama.com/ppi/87/lartimache.htm

15th-century renovated farm building with a family atmosphere, in
a verdant setting with two private lakes in the Périgord-Limousin
Regional Park. There are four bedrooms with exposed beams, and a
family suite for four to six people, all with private facilities. Large room
with fireplace, terrace, washing machine, kitchen area, table tennis
and board games. Bicycle hire; fishing lessons; walkers and horses
welcomed.

Prices not confirmed for 2008 **On Site** 🏊 **Nearby** ⚓ 5km ⚓ 15km
Restaurant 5km 🚲 5km 🏠 9km 🐎 20km **Notes** No pets English
spoken

LE VIGEN

⚜ Boissac

Agnès et Robert NICOT

87110 LE VIGEN

☎ 05 55 00 54 76   🖹 05 55 00 56 91

email: nicot2@wanadoo.fr

In a hamlet near Limoges, this property offers three first floor rooms in one of the oldest barns in the village, adjacent to the owners' home. All rooms have private bathrooms. The lounge, with open fireplace, opens on to a pleasant flower garden where you can enjoy your breakfast in the summer. Mushroom gathering in the autumn.

Prices s fr €36; d fr €42; t fr €50; extra person fr €8   **Nearby** ⚲ 10km ⚲ 10km ⚲ 4km ⚲ 15km Restaurant 5km ⚲ 4km Spa 10km ⚲ 6km ⚲ 8km   **Notes** No pets English spoken Open 20 March to 15 November.

MAGNAC-BOURG

⚜ ⏚ Le Bos Grenier

M et P GAULTIER-DUBOIS

87380 MAGNAC-BOURG

☎ 05 55 00 77 84 & 06 81 89 42 91

email: martine.gaultier-dubois@wanadoo.fr

web: http://ch.d.hotes.sittelle.monsite.wanadoo.fr

Not far from Magnac-Bourg, this modern house opens directly onto the meadows. There are three guest bedrooms, all with private facilities and direct access to the garden. Delicious home-made meals are available, made from local produce. After dinner, you may like to enjoy a game of pétanque with your hosts.

Prices not confirmed for 2008   **Nearby** ⚲ 8km ⚲ 6km Restaurant 1km ⚲ 0.5km ⚲ 0.5km   **Notes** No pets English spoken

MASLEON

⚜ ⏚ & Chambre d'hôtes

F et M CHARBONNIAUD

Le Bourg, 87130 MASLEON

☎ 05 55 57 00 63   🖹 05 55 57 00 63

email: marylene.charbonniaud@wanadoo.fr

Guest accommodation offered in the home of Limousin cattle breeders, in a village near the lakes at Bujalef and Châteauneuf-la-Forêt, which are ideal for swimming. There are four rooms with private facilities, two living rooms with fireplace, TV and reading matter, and a

kitchen with fridge and washing machine. Outside there is a terrace, garden furniture, pétanque and table tennis.

Prices s fr €38; d €40-€50; t fr €60; extra person fr €15; dinner fr €20   **Nearby** ⚲ 10km ⚲ 20km ⚲ 3km ⚲ 10km Restaurant 7km ⚲ 8km ⚲ 10km ⚲ 0.1km ⚲ 7km   **Notes** No pets

MORTEMART

⚜ ⏚ Chambre d'hôtes

Raymond THOMAS

2 Place des Carmes, 87330 MORTEMART

☎ 05 55 60 20 23   🖹 05 55 60 20 23

email: raymond.thomas5@wanadoo.fr

web: www.carmes87.com

A 14th-century Carmelite convent in Mortemart, classed as one of the most beautiful villages in France. The beautiful, enclosed garden is very restful and meals are served in the dining room by your host, an ex-chef. There are three large rooms on the first floor - one is a family room for four with shower room and toilet.

Prices s fr €50; d fr €50; t €60-€70; extra person fr €10; dinner fr €18   **Nearby** ⚲ 5km ⚲ 2km ⚲ 10km Restaurant 4km ⚲ 5km ⚲ 4km ⚲ 13km   **Notes** Pets admitted English spoken

PAGEAS

⚜ Domaine de la Ribière

SARL DOMAINE DE LA RIBIERE

87230 PAGEAS

☎ 05 55 78 44 35   🖹 05 55 78 56 71

email: mbonn1950@aol.com

web: www.domainedelaribiere.com

Grounds of 47 hectares surround this property, in the Parc Régional Périgord-Limousin. The building is a barn conversion, and it has six first floor bedrooms, each with a private shower room and WC, and fridge. There is a lounge and kitchenette. Outside there are two ponds, a swimming pool, sauna, and a boules pitch. Packed lunches available by arrangement.

Prices not confirmed for 2008   **On Site** ⚲ Private ⚲   **Nearby** ⚲ 10km Restaurant 6km ⚲ 2km ⚲ 6km ⚲ 16km   **Notes** Pets admitted English spoken

⚜ Le Mazaubert

B et E KELLNER-DESSEIN

87230 PAGEAS

☎ 05 55 78 75 03 & 06 89 36 07 87

email: etienne.kellner@wanadoo.fr

This is an impressive barn conversion in the Parc Naturel Régional Périgord-Limousin. There are three first floor bedrooms, each for two or three people, and all with private bath or shower room. The grounds extend to more than four hectares, and plenty of walks are possible in the area. Fishing is available nearby (purchase of permit necessary).

Prices not confirmed for 2008   **Nearby** ⚲ 0.5km ⚲ 3km Restaurant 6km ⚲ 3km ⚲ 3km ⚲ 6km   **Notes** No pets

LIMOUSIN

PANAZOL

ⅠⅠⅠⅠ **Domanine de Forest**

Jane BRUNTON
87350 PANAZOL
☎ 05 55 31 33 68 📄 05 55 31 85 08
email: domainedeforest@wanadoo.fr
web: www.domainedeforest.com

Your hosts are golf enthusiasts, and their restored 18th-century manor house borders an excellent golf course near Limoges (preferential green fees for guests). They have five luxurious rooms, two of them family suites, all with private facilities and TV. The lounge and the billiard room have an open view over the Vienne Valley. Swimming pool, fitness suite, tennis.

Prices s fr €95; d fr €105; extra person fr €25 **On Site** ✐ Private ↴ Private tennis court **Nearby** ✿ 2km ↲ 0.5km Restaurant 2km ✾ 2km 🏠 2km 🚲 5km **Notes** No pets English spoken

PENSOL

Ⅰ ❦ ⅠⅠ *Le Moulin*

Catherine BERTHELOT
7440 PENSOL
☎ 05 55 78 21 31 📄 05 55 78 21 31
mail: moulin.de.pensol@wanadoo.fr
web: www.ferme-auberge-pensol.com

This former mill situated in the Parc Naturel Régional has three first floor guest rooms for two to four people, all with private shower rooms/WCs. On the ground floor is a small lounge, where meals from the adjacent farmhouse restaurant are served, using such things as poultry, rabbits and fruits from the farm to delight your taste buds.

Prices not confirmed for 2008 **On Site** ✐ **Nearby** ✿ 10km ↴ 15km Restaurant 15km ✾ 5km 🏠 15km 🚲 16km **Notes** No pets English spoken Open February to 15 December.

PEYRAT-LE-CHATEAU

ⅠⅠⅠ ❦ ⅠⅠ **Villards**

Bernard BLONDEL
Ferme Equestre de Villards, 87470 PEYRAT-LE-CHATEAU
☎ 06 85 52 81 80 & 05 55 69 21 36
email: fermequestrevillards@wanadoo.fr
web: www.fermequestrevillards.com

This beautiful stone house stands amongst the forests and meadows of Millevaches, which your hosts will invite you to explore on foot, horseback or mountain bike. It has one ground floor room and four upstairs, for two to four people, all with private bath/shower room and WC. Lounge with open fireplace, TV, books and snooker table. Bike hire.

Prices s fr €40; d fr €46; t fr €54; extra person fr €9; dinner fr €17 **On Site** ✿ ✾ **Nearby** ✿ 2km ↴ 12km Restaurant 2km ✾ 2km 🏠 2km 🚲 12km **Notes** No pets English spoken

PIERRE-BUFFIERE

ⅠⅠⅠ ⅠⅠ **Chambre d'hôtes**

Philippe FRUGIER
53 Av de la République, 87260 PIERRE-BUFFIERE
☎ 05 55 00 91 00
email: lebriancais@hotmail.fr

This 19th-century property, in a picturesque little town one kilometre from the A20 and 17 kilometres from Limoges, has four large guest bedrooms. The rooms can sleep from two to four people, and they all have private showers and WCs. Lounge with open fire, enclosed garden.

Prices s fr €50; d fr €55; t fr €60; extra person fr €5; dinner fr €20 **Nearby** ✿ 5km ↲ 1km ↴ 15km Restaurant 1km ✾ 1km 🚲 1km **Notes** Pets admitted English spoken

REMPNAT

ⅠⅠⅠⅠ ⅠⅠ **Château de la Villeneuve**

Jean-Claude AEN
87120 REMPNAT
☎ 05 55 69 99 28 📄 05 55 69 99 26
email: jean-claude.aen@wanadoo.fr
web: www.jalcary.com

Classes in silk painting and painting miniatures are available at this 19th-century manor house, in the foothills of the Plateau de Millevaches. The three en suite bedrooms, one of which is a suite, look onto the river or extensive park surrounding the house. Lounge with fireplace, dining room, snooker table, indoor heated swimming pool. Private fishing (killing of fish prohibited) on the Vienne, and tasty meals.

Prices d fr €75; t fr €90; extra person fr €15; dinner fr €37 **On Site** ✐ Private ↴ **Nearby** ✿ 8km Restaurant 5km ✾ 4km 🏠 4km 🚲 15km **Notes** No pets English spoken

RILHAC-RANCON

₩ *Chambre d'hôtes*

Valérie et Denis MALABOU

Route des Bardys-Les-Thermes, 87570 RILHAC-RANCON

☎ 06 82 93 37 64

email: denis.malabou@orange.fr

This contemporary house is on the edge of Limoges, but in its own grounds with oak trees, terrace and swimming pool. It has five bedrooms, each for two or three people, all on the first floor with private bath or shower room and WC. The style is modern; breakfast is served in a bistro-style mezzanine area with juke-box and electric billiards.

Prices not confirmed for 2008 **On Site** Private ↖ **Nearby** ☝ 11km ℘ 0.4km Restaurant 2km ⌇ 1.5km ⓐ 1.5km ⋈ 10km **Notes** No pets English spoken Open June to September.

ROCHECHOUART

₩ ⓘ **La Roseraie**

Mary et Ralph VELTHOEK

12 Rue Porte Beraud, 87600 ROCHECHOUART

☎ 05 55 03 60 08 ▤ 05 55 03 12 85

email: info@laroseraiefrance.com

web: www.laroseraiefrance.com

Old renovated house in a city of character, on a little street which climbs to the castle. The three large guest rooms are sympathetically decorated, each with a sitting area, shower and wc. Enclosed rose garden. Rochechouart is built on the site of a 200-million-year-old meteor impact.

Prices s fr €40; d fr €55; t fr €65; extra person fr €10; dinner fr €19 **Nearby** ☝ 11km ⌇ 15km ℘ 1km ↖ 14km Restaurant 1km ⌇ 1km ❦ 15km ⓐ 0.1km ⋈ 7km **Notes** Pets admitted English spoken

ST-AUVENT

₩ ⓘ *Coufiegeas*

Geoffroy et Païvi TILLEUL

87310 ST-AUVENT

☎ 05 55 48 16 12 ▤ 05 55 48 16 12

email: gt87@wanadoo.fr

web: www.domainedecoufiegeas.com

Set on a hill overlooking the Gorre, between Rochechouart and Saint-Junien, this charming farm has been renovated by a welcoming

Franco-Finnish couple and is set in calm, green countryside. Four en suite bedrooms and meals with farm produce, such as rillette, patés, ham and local dishes.

Prices not confirmed for 2008 **Nearby** ☝ 11km ℘ 10km Restaurant 7km ⌇ 1km ⓐ 7km ⋈ 7km **Notes** No pets English spoke

ST-BRICE-SUR-VIENNE

₩ ⓘ **La Musardière**

M ET M DUHAMEL OLDROYD

2 route de St Victurnien, 87200 ST-BRICE-SUR-VIENNE

☎ 05 55 03 34 07

email: monique.michael@yahoo.fr

web: www.lamusardiere.eu

A large contemporary house on a hill looking over the Vienne Valley, offering five rooms for two or four people. Living room with fire and lounge corner and books on a mezzanine. Terrace leading onto a tre lined garden. Nearby: Centre de la Mémoire d'Oradour-sur-Glace an Espace Météorite de Rochechouart.

Prices s fr €46; d fr €51; t fr €61; dinner fr €17 **Nearby** ☝ 3km ⌇ 10km ℘ 3km Restaurant 7km ⓐ 3km ⋈ 2km **Notes** No pets English spoken Open Easter to September.

ST-HILAIRE-BONNEVAL

₩ ⓘ *La Forge*

D et A BATAILLER

87260 ST-HILAIRE-BONNEVAL

☎ 05 55 00 68 57

email: contact@jardin-de-la-forge.com

web: www.jardin-de-la-forge.com

A converted old forge with three bedrooms with private showers an wc, and adjoining blacksmith's house with one guest room. All the rooms look out onto a flowery, green park and there is a large loung with fireplace. Set in a small village typical of the Briance Valley. Mea available by reservation.

Prices not confirmed for 2008 **Nearby** ☝ 3km ℘ 2km ↖ 16km Restaurant 5km ⌇ ⓐ 5km ⋈ 4km **Notes** Pets admitted English spok

ST-JUNIEN-LES-COMBES

⊞ ⊙ Château de Sannat

C et J de SAINTE-CROIX
87300 ST-JUNIEN-LES-COMBES
☎ 05 55 68 13 52 🖹 05 55 60 85 51
email: chateausannat@wanadoo.fr
web: www.chateausannat.com

Discover this 18th-century château built on an ancient stronghold with panoramic views of the Blond Mountains. Accommodation consists of four spacious double rooms, with private shower or bathroom, one of which is grade 3. There is also a large lounge with TV, and dining room and the property is set in a huge wooded park of 500 hectares, with a French-style hanging garden, tennis court and swimming pool (May to October).

Prices s fr €120; d fr €120; extra person fr €20; dinner fr €40
On Site ⅃ 🖉 Private ⅄ Private tennis court **Nearby** ⅍ 3km Restaurant 9km 🖺 7km ⋙ 7km **Notes** Pets admitted English spoken Open May to November.

ST-LAURENT-SUR-GORRE

⊞ ⊙ Charlet

Agnès TRAGETT
87310 ST-LAURENT-SUR-GORRE
☎ 05 55 00 09 72 🖹 05 55 00 09 72
email: charlet@tragett.net
web: www.tragett.net/charlet

A secluded house, set on a 50 hectare estate. Gardens beyond the terrace lead to a wood with several fishing lakes. There are 3 double rooms with private bathrooms on the first floor (children's beds are available by arrangement). Lounge with fire place and dining room; billiards and table tennis available. The Tragett family have created this oasis of calm and organise courses in dance, pottery painting and cookery.

Prices s fr €35; d fr €45; t €55-€60; extra person fr €10; dinner fr €16
On Site 🖉 **Nearby** ⅍ 10km ⅃ 20km ⅄ 13km Restaurant 4km ⅊ 5km Spa 13km 🐾 13km 🖺 5km ⋙ 13km **Notes** No pets English spoken

⊞ ⊙ Les Bellunies

Babette et Daniel VILLEMIN
87310 ST-LAURENT-SUR-GORRE
☎ 05 55 48 16 63 🖹 05 55 48 16 63
email: bellunies@free.fr
web: http://bellunies.free.fr

Wooded grounds surround this house, which has three guest bedrooms. The rooms sleep from two to four guests, and all have private bath or shower room and WC. Lounge and billiard room open into the garden where there is a barbecue. Breakfast includes home-made jams and pastries, and other meals are available by arrangement, including some local specialities.

Prices not confirmed for 2008 **On Site** 🖉 **Nearby** ⅄ 12km Restaurant 2km ⅊ 3km 🖺 2km ⋙ 18km **Notes** No pets English spoken

ST-LEGER-LA-MONTAGNE

⊞ ⊙ Lasgorceix

Anne et Pascal BRUNEAU
87340 ST-LEGER-LA-MONTAGNE
☎ 05 55 39 89 38
email: lasgorceix@hotmail.com
web: http://lasgorceix.wifeo.com

Three charming and comfortable en suite bedrooms sleeping two to four people have been installed in this fine, wooden house in the heart of the Ambazac Mountains. This is ideal for restful holidays, with healthy, family cooking (vegetarian meals available). Painting exhibition on the premises. Close to horse riding centres, tennis courts, wild-mushroom picking and walks. Reduced rates for extended stays.

Prices s fr €30; d fr €40; t fr €50; extra person fr €10; dinner fr €15
Nearby ⅍ 12km ⅃ 30km 🖉 6km ⅄ 30km Restaurant 7km ⅊ 30km Spa 30km 🐾 30km 🖺 7km ⋙ 7km **Notes** Pets admitted English spoken

ST-LEONARD-DE-NOBLAT

⊞ *Chambre d'hôtes*

Françoise BIGAS
20 Rue Jean Jaures, 87400 ST-LEONARD-DE-NOBLAT
☎ 05 55 56 19 47 🖹 05 55 56 19 47

Two grade 1 rooms with shared shower and wc and three bedrooms with private facilities in an adjoining house, in the remarkable medieval village of St-Léonard-de-Noblat. There is a lounge, dining room, kitchen area for longer stays, washing machine, and garden full of flowers. The proprietor's hobbies include enamel work and dried flower arranging and a special welcome is reserved for cyclists: champion cyclist Raymond Poulidor hails from this area.

Prices not confirmed for 2008 **Nearby** ⅍ 11km 🖉 2km ⅄ 0.5km Restaurant 0.5km ⅊ 0.5km ⋙ 1km **Notes** No pets

ST-PARDOUX

⊞ ⊙ Château de Vauguenige

Alain et Marick CLAUDE
87250 ST-PARDOUX
☎ 05 55 76 58 55 🖹 05 55 76 57 11
email: vauguenige@wanadoo.fr
web: www.vauguenige.com

The proprietors of this 19th-century château (a yoga teacher, Gestalt practitioner and dietician and a PE teacher and lifeguard) offer themed holidays. These could be based on swimming, fitness, relaxation or health, taking advantage of the heated covered swimming pool, sauna, jacuzzi and equestrian centre on the premises. There are five large bedrooms with private facilities, and lounges with TV, library, and piano.

Prices s €58-€60; d €65-€85; t €90-€98; dinner fr €23 **On Site** ⅍ 🖉 🐾 Private ⅄ **Nearby** Restaurant 3km ⅊ 3km 🖺 3km ⋙ 35km **Notes** No pets English spoken Open April to 15 November.

ST-PARDOUX CONTINUED

♨ ⚇ **Villarcoin**

Jane et Yvan REYNOLDS
87250 ST-PARDOUX
☎ 05 55 76 51 81 📄 05 55 76 51 81
email: janeandivan@wanadoo.fr
web: www.mrmcgregors.co.uk

An old, granite-built house in a hamlet near the lake of St-Pardoux.
The three beamed bedrooms are on the first floor decorated in
country-style. Your hosts offer you candle-lit dinners and summer
breakfasts served under the flowered arbour in their English garden.

Prices s fr €33; d fr €50; t fr €68; dinner fr €20 **On Site** ♨
Nearby ⚓ 2km ⌗ 2km ⚲ Restaurant 5km ⚲ 2km 🏛 2km ♨ 20km
Notes No pets English spoken

ST-SYLVESTRE-GRANDMONT

♨ ⚇ *Les Chênes*

Edith et Lorenzo RAPPELLI
87240 ST-SYLVESTRE-GRANDMONT
☎ 05 55 71 33 12
email: les.chenes@wanadoo.fr
web: www.leschenes-st-sylvestre.com

In the heart of the Ambazac Hills, this quiet, beautiful house is
surrounded by forests and lakes. The hosts give a warm welcome
to their three smart and comfortable rooms, all sleeping two to four
people and with private bathrooms and WCs. Meals available: healthy
home cooking, vegetarian dishes on request. Art exhibition. Walks,
mushroom gathering, tennis, riding all available.

Prices not confirmed for 2008 **Nearby** ⚓ 8km ⌗ 8km Restaurant 8km
⚲ 8km 🏛 8km ♨ 8km **Notes** No pets English spoken Open June to
1 September.

ST-SYMPHORIEN-SUR-COUZE

♨ ⚇ **Chasseneuil**

J et K RICHARDSON
87140 ST-SYMPHORIEN-SUR-COUZE
☎ 05 55 53 59 01 & 06 33 63 22 80
email: keith.richardson@wanadoo.fr

A small cattle farm in a hamlet near the Lac de St Pardoux, with rooms
on the first floor of an enormous renovated barn. Five bedrooms
sleep two to six people with rustic décor and private facilities. Ground
floor large lounge with dining area, TV and fireplace. Local forest
walks. Local produce used in cooking.

Prices s fr €35; d fr €45; t fr €60; extra person fr €15; dinner fr €20
Nearby ⚓ 2km ⌗ 1km Restaurant 10km ⚲ 4km 🏛 10km ♨ 11km
Notes Pets admitted English spoken

ST-VICTURNIEN

♨ *La Chapelle Blanche*

A-M et M LALOYAUX
87420 ST-VICTURNIEN
☎ 05 55 03 58 20
email: am.laloyaux@orange.fr

This farm, typical of the region, produces Baronnet lamb and provides
a family room with a double and two single beds, and two double
rooms, all en suite. There is also a large enclosed courtyard and table
tennis. Various pretty walks can be enjoyed through the farm lanes.

Prices not confirmed for 2008 **Nearby** ⌗ 2km ⚲ 4km 🏛 3km
♨ 13km **Notes** No pets Open 15 April to September.

ST-VITTE-SUR-BRIANCE

♨ ⚇ **Lapeyrousse**

Marie-Christine DELORT
Manin, 87380 ST-VITTE-SUR-BRIANCE
☎ 05 55 71 83 23 & 05 55 71 70 60
email: Marie-Christine.Delort@wanadoo.fr

This cattle farm, in the birthplace of the Limousin breed, also breeds
draught horses and ornamental fowls. It has four guest rooms in an
annexe to the owners' house, all with en suite bath/shower rooms.
Central heating, lounge, TV, garage. Meals by arrangement. Microlight
club close by.

Prices s fr €32; d fr €37; t fr €47; extra person fr €5; dinner fr €13
Nearby ⚓ 5km ⚱ 40km ⌗ 6km Restaurant 5km ⚲ 6km 🏛 5km
♨ 5km **Notes** Pets admitted English spoken

LIMOUSIN

STE-ANNE-ST-PRIEST

‖‖ ﾏﾔ Les Bruges

an et Richard ROGERS
87120 STE-ANNE-ST-PRIEST
☎ 05 55 69 42 39
email: info@chezlachouette.com
web: www.chezlachouette.com

A former grange near the family home, in the countryside with lovely walks on the doorstep. It has four rooms for two to four people each with private facilities and a kitchenette. The hosts only speak English. Vassevière Lake of 1000 hectares, le Plateau de Millevaches, Saint-Léonard-de-Noblat and Eymoutiers to explore in the vicinity.

Prices s fr €48; d fr €55; t fr €68; extra person fr €10; dinner fr €25 **Nearby** ✍ 9km ✈ 8km Restaurant 8km ⛳ 9km 🏛 8km 🚶 8km **Notes** No pets English spoken

VERNEUIL-MOUSTIERS

‖‖ ﾏﾔ Domaine du Fan

Suzanne NOZARI
87360 VERNEUIL-MOUSTIERS
☎ 05 55 68 25 30 📠 05 55 60 14 56
email: contact@domainedufan.com
web: www.domainedufan.com

A fine avenue of oak trees leads to this 18th-century manor house situated in an idyllic spot, in 60 hectares in the Brenne National Park. It offers accommodation of five bedrooms for two to four people with private shower and wc, a living room, reading room and video room.

Prices s €49-€60; d €60-€75; t €70-€90; extra person fr €12; dinner €15-€19 **On Site** ✍ ☺ Private ✈ Private tennis court **Nearby** ✍ 7km Restaurant 5km 🏛 4km 🚶 16km **Notes** Pets admitted English spoken CC

VERNEUIL-SUR-VIENNE

‖‖ L'Oustalet

S et E BARELAUD-TKACZUK
2, Rue de Tranchepie, 87430 VERNEUIL-SUR-VIENNE
☎ 05 55 00 17 35
email: tkaczuk@wanadoo.fr

This converted old farmhouse is located in a hamlet, five minutes from the western exit from Limoges. In this large, modern house you can choose from one ground floor room for four, with bath and wc, and two upstairs rooms, each sleeping three, with private facilities.

Prices s €55-€65; d €65-€75; t €75-€85; extra person fr €10 **Nearby** ✍ 5km ✈ 10km ✍ 7km ✈ 11km Restaurant 5km ⛳ 3km Spa 10km 🏛 4km 🚶 13km **Notes** No pets English spoken

VEYRAC

‖‖ Grand Moulin

Guy et Gisèle DORIDANT
87520 VEYRAC
☎ 06 63 79 30 28
email: gisele.doridant@wanadoo.fr

This converted old Limousin barn is situated near the home of the owners' and provides three spacious bedrooms with private facilities. There is also a dining room, mezzanine lounge, and beautiful swimming pool. Closed on Tuesday evenings. Close to the porcelain and enamel museums.

Prices not confirmed for 2008 **Nearby** ✍ 10km ✍ 6km ✈ 16km Restaurant 16km ⛳ 1km 🏛 1km 🚶 16km **Notes** No pets English spoken Open Easter to 1 November.

LIMOUSIN

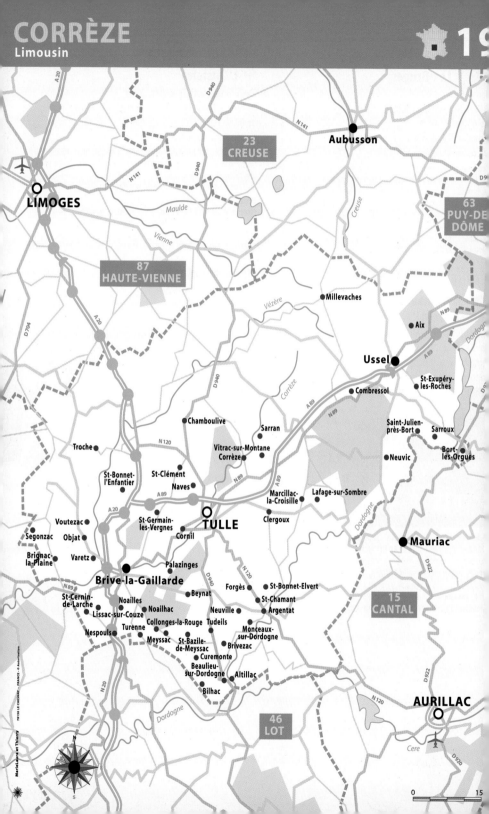

CORRÈZE
Limousin

19

23 CREUSE

Aubusson

LIMOGES

63 PUY-DE-DÔME

87 HAUTE-VIENNE

Maulde

Vienne

Vézère

Millevaches

Aix

Ussel

St-Exupéry-les-Roches

Combressol

Corrèze

Chamboulive

Sarran

Saint-Julien-près-Bort

Sarroux

Troche

Vitrac-sur-Montane
Corrèze

Bort-les-Orgues

Neuvic

St-Bonnet-l'Enfantier

St-Clément

Naves

Marcillac-la-Croisille

Lafage-sur-Sombre

Voutezac

St-Germain-les-Vergnes

TULLE

Clergoux

Dordogne

Segonzac

Objat

Cornil

Mauriac

Brignac-la-Plaine

Varetz

Palazinges

Brive-la-Gaillarde

Beynat

Forgès

St-Bonnet-Elvert

St-Chamant

15 CANTAL

St-Cernin-de-Larche

Noailles

Noailhac

Neuville

Argentat

Lissac-sur-Couze

Collonges-la-Rouge

Tudeils

Monceaux-sur-Dordogne

Nespouls

Turenne

Meyssac

St-Bazile-de-Meyssac

Brivezac

Curemonte

AURILLAC

Beaulieu-sur-Dordogne

Altillac

Bilhac

46 LOT

Dordogne

Cere

0   15

REUSE
mousin
23

Saint-Amand-Montrond
Cher
N144
18 CHER
D943
Indre
N151
Creuse
D927
La Châtre
36 INDRE
A71
D943
Montluçon
Moutier-Malcard
Bussière-St-Georges
Fresselines
D951
D940
A20
Chambon-Ste-Croix
Sagnat
La Celle-Dunoise
Bussière-Dunoise
Champsanglard
Roches
N145
N145
N145
Parsac
GUÉRET
Pionnat
St-Étienne-de-Fursac
St-Hilaire-la-Plaine
Creuse
Gartempe
D942
St-Pardoux-les-Cards
Cher
La Chapelle-St-Martial
St-Martial-le-Mont
St-Dizier-Leyrenne
A20
D940
St-Hilaire-le-Château
Soubrebost
Vidaillat
St-Silvain-Bellegarde
Aubusson
N141
St-Bard
Vallière
St-Pardoux-le-Neuf
Mérinchal
St-Avit-de-Tardes
LIMOGES
N141
D940
St-Yriex-la-Montagne
Banize
D941
63 PUY-DE-DÔME
Maulde
Creuse
Gentioux-Pigerolles
Vienne
87 HAUTE-VIENNE
N89
Vézère
19 CORRÈZE
Dordogne
A89
Ussel
D922
D940
Corrèze
A89
N89
0
15 km
N
O
E
S

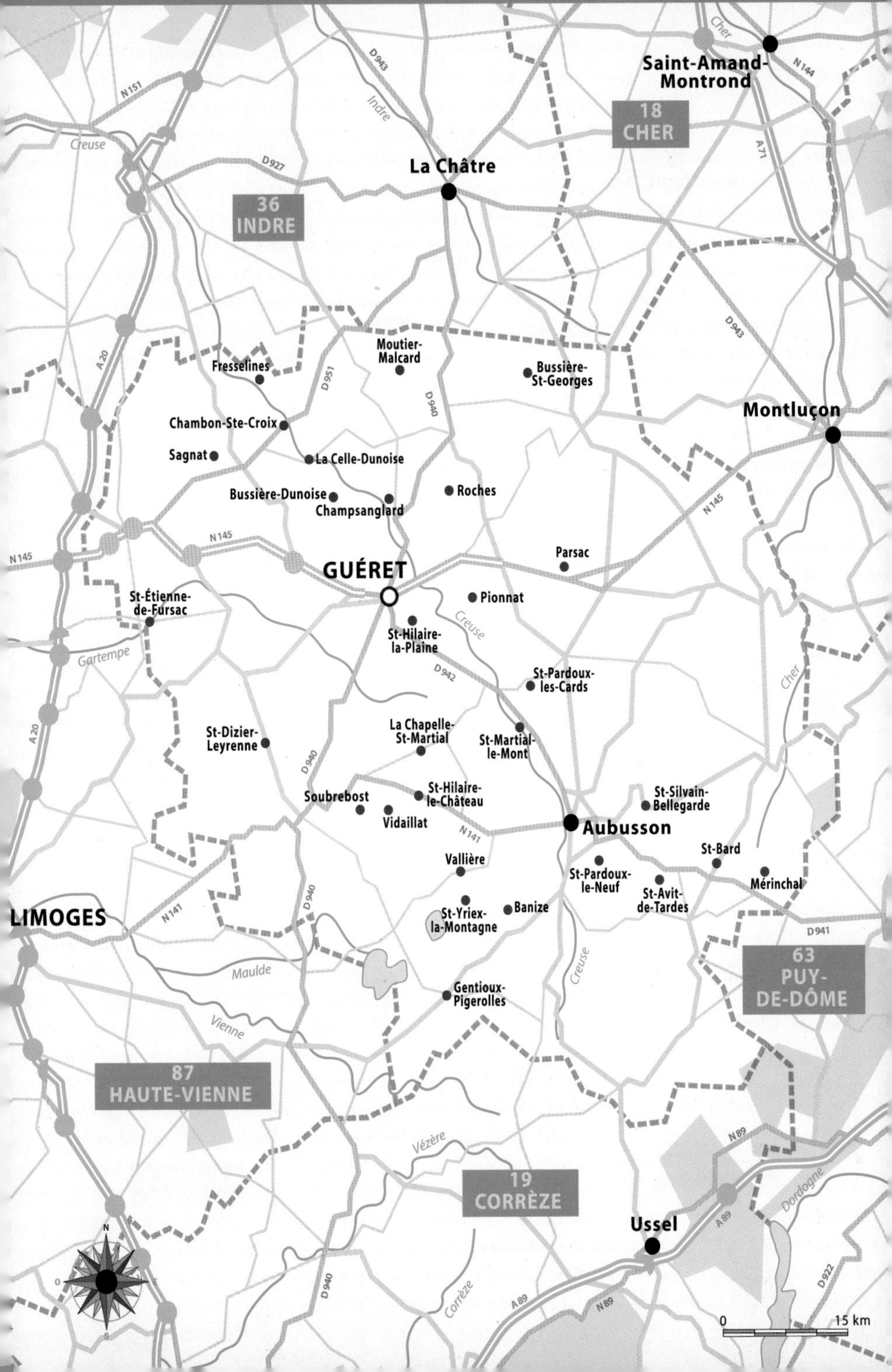

La Châ▮

N 147

Montmorillon

Jouac

Verneuil-Moustiers

N 147

Arnac-
la-Poste

GUÉRET

D 951

N 145

Creuse

N 145

D 942

Fromental

Gartempe

Blanzac

Châteauponsac

D 951

Bellac

Bessines-
sur-Gartempe

St-Junien-
les-Combes

St-Pardoux

Bersac-
sur-Rivalier

Vienne

Mortemart

Blond

St-Symphorien-
sur-Couze

St-Léger-
la-Montagne

D 940

Confolens

N 147

Compreignac

St-Sylvestre-
Grandmont

Cieux

Bonnac-
la-Côte

D 951

D 940

N 141

Vienne

Veyrac

Rilhac-
Rancon

St-Victurnien

Panazol

St-Léonard-
de-Noblat

N 141

Rochechouart

Verneuil-
sur-Vienne

Isle

LIMOGES

Maulde

Peyrat-
le-Château

St-Auvent

Feytiat

Vienne

St-Laurent-sur-Gorre

Boisseuil

Masléon

Beaumont-du-Lac

N 21

Cussac

Champsac

Flavignac

Le Vigen

St-Hilaire-Bonneval

Éymoutiers

Champagnac-
la-Rivière

Pageas

Pierre-
Buffière

Châteauneuf-
la-Forêt

Ste-Anne-
St-Priest

Rempnat

La Chapelle-
Montbrandeix

Pensol

Dournazac

Janailhac

Magnac-
Bourg

St-Vitte-sur-Briance

Château-Chervix

D 704

Nontron

Coussac-
Bonneval

N 21

A 20

D 940

Corrèze

N 120

A 89

A 89

0   15

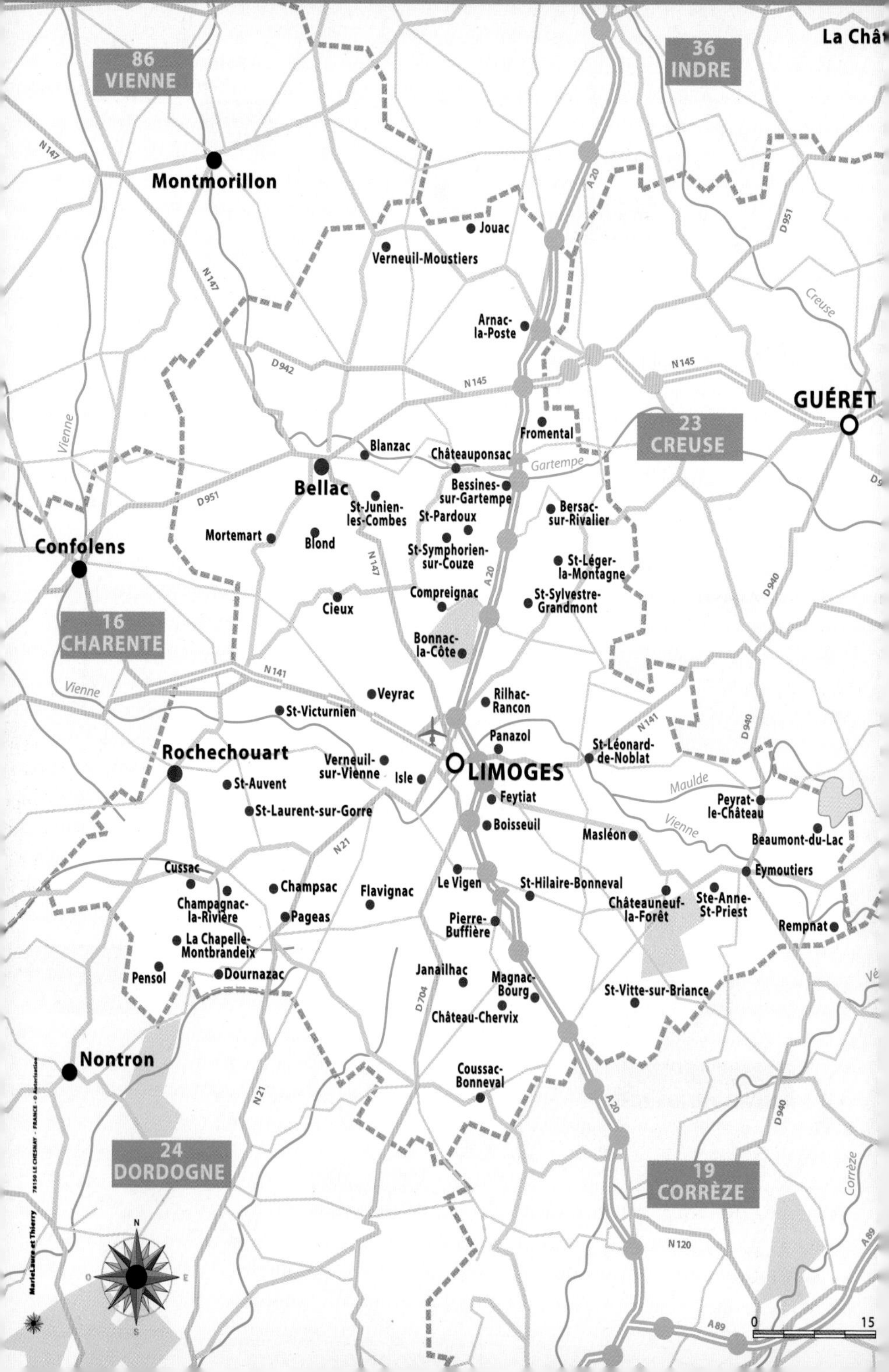

MIDI-PYRÉNÉES

ARIÈGE

BÉNAC

⁂ ⓘ Château de Bénac

erge et Sylvie DOUMENC
9000 BENAC
☎ 05 61 02 65 20

17th-century château situated in the Barguillère valley offering three ouble guest rooms and three rooms with a double and single bed. Il have a bathroom/wc and heating. There is a guests' living room ith TV, open fireplace, books and children's games.

rices d fr €60; t fr €75; dinner fr €20   **On Site** ❦ **Nearby** ⚓ 3km
20km ⚐ 1km ↘ 2km ᠍ 2km ᠍ 2km ⬩ 8km   **Notes** Pets admitted

FOUGAX-ET-BARRINEUF

⁂ *Oh! Les Beaux Jours*

et M BIREBENT
oute de Montségur, 09300 FOUGAX-ET-BARRINEUF
☎ 05 61 01 64 42 & 06 75 46 58 27
mail: oh.lesbeauxjours@free.fr
eb: http://oh.lesbeauxjours.free.fr

he owners of this property, in a quiet spot with a river close by, are eeders of Angora goats. The guest rooms are in a converted farm uilding. On the ground floor is a bedroom with disabled access; upstairs e two split-level double rooms; a twin-bedded room; and a family om for four; all have private facilities. Lounge and kitchenette available.

rices not confirmed for 2008   **On Site** ⚐ **Nearby** ⚓ 15km ↘ 15km
20km ᠍ 6km ᠍ 1km   **Notes** No pets

LERAN

⁂ ⓘ Bon Repos

arie-Anne DE BRUYNE
9600 LERAN
☎ 05 61 01 27 83   ᠍ 05 61 01 27 83

ree en suite guest rooms on a working dairy/breeding farm. Dining om, lounge with open fireplace and piano. Facilities include

swimming pool, table tennis, picnic area and shady garden. Mountain biking or micro-lighting available. Local tourist attractions include go-karting, textile museum, museum of agricultural machinery, Montségur, Mirepoix, Camon, Foix and Puivert. All-inclusive price for two people available.

Prices s €45-€50; d fr €50; t fr €65; dinner fr €20   **On Site**
Nearby ⚓ 1.5km ⚐ 3km Restaurant 1.5km ⚓ 25km ᠍ 1.5km ᠍ 3km
⬩ 35km   **Notes** No pets Please contact for opening dates

⁂ ⓘ Chambre d'hôtes

John et Lee-Anne FURNESS
1 Impasse du Temple, 09600 LERAN
☎ 05 61 01 50 02 & 06 88 19 49 22
email: john.furness@wanadoo.fr
web: www.chezfurness.com

This 18th-century house has been restored by an Australian couple and sits by a small stream. There is a lounge and living room with access to a courtyard, where breakfast and evening meals are served. En suite rooms include three double rooms, a room with a double and single bed, and a suite of two rooms (one double, one twin). Guests are invited to sample regional specialities and Australian cuisine.

Prices s €53-€58; d €65-€70; t €83-€88; extra person fr €18; dinner fr €22   **On Site** Restaurant ❦ Private ↘ **Nearby** ⚓ 0.5km ⚐ 2km
᠍ 0.5km ⬩ 46km   **Notes** No pets English spoken CC

455

LUDIÈS

⅋⅋⅋⅋ ⅋⊙⅋ Le Château

L BOGULINSKI FINES
09100 LUDIES
☎ 05 61 69 67 45 🖹 05 61 69 67 45
email: maud.bogulinski@wanadoo.fr

The Château de Ludies has recently been completely rebuilt using authentic materials. Three double rooms, two twins (one with single in an alcove) and a family suite are available. Table d'hôte meals using local produce, TV lounge, library, painting studio, games room with billiard table, garden with swimming pool, terrace and gazebo are provided.

Prices s €60-€70; d €70-€85; t €96-€105; extra person fr €20; dinner fr €24 **On Site** ⅋ **Nearby** ⅋ 4km ⅋ 40km ⅋ 2km Restaurant 4km ⅋ 6km ⅋ 6km **Notes** Pets admitted English spoken

MONTAUT

⅋⅋⅋⅋ ⅋⊙⅋ Domaine du Pégulier

Jacques MAES
09700 MONTAUT
☎ 05 61 68 30 65 🖹 05 61 68 30 65
email: pegulier@wanadoo.fr
web: www.pegulier.com

This 18th-century building (a registered building of character), has terrific natural scenery and serenity. The five guest rooms have lovely décor and include two suites for three with lounge, a family suite with three bedrooms and a sitting area and two double rooms, each with private facilities. Enjoy badminton, table tennis, boules and swimming in the heated pool.

Prices s €65-€70; t €70-€85; extra person fr €20; dinner fr €24 **On Site** ⅋ Private ⅋ **Nearby** ⅋ 3km ⅋ 35km Restaurant 5km ⅋ 3km Spa 35km ⅋ 3km ⅋ 5km **Notes** No pets English spoken

⅋⅋⅋ ⅋⊙⅋ La Vernoune

Marie-Joëlle JAUMOT
09700 MONTAUT
☎ 05 61 69 23 12 & 06 60 20 73 62
email: vernoune@club.fr
web: www.vernoune.com

A 19th-century farmhouse in four hectares of grounds with a view towards the Pyrénées. There are three double-bedded rooms, one a two-roomed suite, and a family room for up to four. All have en suite facilities. There is a guest living room on the first floor, and downstairs the dining room opens onto the rear terrace, with a meadow beyond. Jacuzzi available for guest use. Pets by reservation.

Prices s €55-€57; d €60-€63; extra person fr €18; dinner fr €22 **Nearby** ⅋ 4km ⅋ 3km ⅋ 7km Restaurant 6km ⅋ 7km ⅋ 7km ⅋ 3km ⅋ 5km **Notes** Pets admitted English spoken

RABAT-LES-TROIS-SEIGNEURS

⅋⅋⅋ ⅋⊙⅋ Les Forges d'Enfalits

Eric et Nathalie PELLERIN
09400 RABAT-LES-TROIS-SEIGNEURS
☎ 05 61 03 83 45 & 06 73 05 88 34
email: enfalits@tiscali.fr
web: www.forgesdenfalits.com

This stone built house, beside the river and on the site of the old Rabat forge, has five guest rooms. Three are doubles and two are family rooms, all with private bath or shower room and WC. Large guest lounge and billiard room, games room. In the grounds are woods, lakes, waterfalls. Tennis, table tennis, badminton and volleyball available.

Prices s fr €48; d fr €54; t fr €70; dinner fr €20 **On Site** Spa Private tennis court **Nearby** ⅋ 10km ⅋ 38km ⅋ 5km ⅋ 5km Restaurant 0.5k ⅋ 5km ⅋ 5km ⅋ 5km **Notes** No pets English spoken

RIEUCROS

⅋⅋⅋ ⅋⊙⅋ Le Domaine de Marlas

Eric & Joelle CHETIONI
09500 RIEUCROS
☎ 05 61 69 29 88 & 06 73 57 18 24
email: contact@domainedemarlas.com
web: www.domainedemarlas.com

This old farmstead incorporates a rural gîte, and five guest rooms in the owner's home: four doubles and a family room for three, each with private facilities. Guests have the use of the garden and private swimming pool, a dining room with open fire and relaxing room with communal TV. The 13 hectare estate is traversed by a river.

Prices s €55-€58; d €65-€68; t €83-€88; extra person fr €18; dinner fr €20 **On Site** ⅋ ⅋ Private ⅋ **Nearby** ⅋ 12km ⅋ 30km Restaurant 3km ⅋ 2km Spa 30km ⅋ 7km ⅋ 12km **Notes** No pets English spoken CC

SAVERDUN

⅋⅋⅋ ⅋⊙⅋ *Domaine de Roudeille*

J et B JANSSENS
09700 SAVERDUN
☎ 05 61 60 58 62 🖹 05 61 60 78 03
email: jeanette.janssens@wanadoo.fr
web: www.roudeille.com

Standing in its own grounds of one hectare, 40 kilometres from Toulouse, this property has five double bedrooms, all with en suite facilities. On the ground floor is a large communal room with billiard table, games, TV, fireplace and looking out onto the terrace

nd swimming pool. Jeanette is a former cookery teacher, happy to
rovide meals if pre-booked and meet guests at the airport.

rices not confirmed for 2008 **On Site** Private ⚲ **Nearby** ⚓ 6km
3km 🏠 3km **Notes** Pets admitted

T-AMADOU

ⅲ ⅰ◎ⅰ **Sabaranis**

rançois CARPENTIER
9100 SAINT-AMADOU
☎ 05 61 69 34 46 & 06 11 65 56 17 📄 05 61 69 34 46
mail: francois.carpentier14@wanadoo.fr
veb: www.sabaranis.fr

farmhouse dating from 1790, in a peaceful spot on a 34-hectare
rm, complete with a fitness trail for guests to use. A separate
ntrance leads to five bedrooms, doubles and triples, all with private
ath or shower room and WC. Living room with a wood-burner stove;
ardens. Accommodation for horses is possible.

rices s fr €50; d fr €55; extra person fr €15; dinner fr €20
earby ⚓ 4km ⚑ 30km ⚑ 3km ⚲ 7km Restaurant 7km 🎣 7km
3km 🚶 7km **Notes** No pets English spoken

T-PAUL-DE-JARRAT

ⅲ **Hélianthe 09**

ène et Georges MONTAGNE
1 Av de Foix, 09000 SAINT-PAUL-DE-JARRAT
☎ 05 61 03 69 78
mail: helianthe09@free.fr
eb: http://helianthe09.free.fr

is delightful, detached house is surrounded by forests and fields
d has two double rooms and a twin, all en suite (two grade 3 and
e other grade 2). Cot available on request. Lounge with TV and
chenette. Local activities include hang-gliding and water-skiing.

ices s fr €43; d fr €48 **On Site** ⚑ **Nearby** ⚓ 9km ⚑ 15km ⚲ 4km
staurant 2km ⚓ 47km Water sports 4km 🎣 0.1km Spa 35km 🎿 4km
0.1km 🚶 6km **Notes** No pets English spoken

TE-FOI

ⅲ ⅰ◎ⅰ **Domaine La Trille**

orence GAILLARD
omaine de la Trille, 09500 SAINTE-FOI
 05 61 67 89 82 & 06 71 21 21 33 📄 05 61 67 78 08
nail: info@domainedelatrille.com
eb: http://domainedelatrille.com

South-facing farmhouse in the heart of the country, with the working
m behind it. There are three double bedrooms, all with en suite
ilities. The sitting room has an open fireplace, TV and DVD player.
tside is a garden with shady sitting places, garden furniture,
ldren's swing. Accommodation available for horses and their riders.

ices s fr €50; d fr €50; t fr €60; extra person fr €10; dinner fr €12
 Site ⚑ **Nearby** ⚓ 10km ⚑ 40km ⚲ 3km Restaurant 3km
 45km 🎿 3km 🏠 3km 🚶 20km **Notes** Pets admitted English
ken

TARASCON-SUR-ARIÈGE

ⅲ ⅰ◎ⅰ *Domaine Fournié*

Pierre MARIE
09400 TARASCON-SUR-ARIEGE
☎ 05 61 05 54 52 📄 05 61 02 73 63
email: contact@domaine-fournie.com
web: www.domaine-fournie.com

A variety of rooms to suit all needs are offered in this large 17th-
century mansion, surrounded by parkland and conservation woodland.
There are three double rooms, a room with a king-sized bed and two
singles, another with a double and two single beds, all en suite. Table
d'hôte meals, half board bookings for two and prices for four people
available on request. Indoor swimming pool.

Prices not confirmed for 2008 **On Site** Private ⚲ **Nearby** ⚓ 36km
🎣 1km Spa 5km 🏠 1km 🚶 1km **Notes** No pets English spoken

AVEYRON

ALPUECH

ⅲ ⅰ◎ⅰ ♿ *La Violette*

Benoît IZARD
Air Aubrac, 12210 ALPUECH
☎ 05 65 44 33 64 & 05 65 68 52 36
email: airaubrac@wanadoo.fr
web: www.airaubrac.fr

A house surrounded by fields, with five guest bedrooms: four double-
bedded rooms and a family room, all with private bath or shower
room and WC. Lounge with open fire; outside, guests can enjoy the
garden with its terrace and boules pitch. For a different perspective on
things, hot air balloon trips are available close by.

Prices not confirmed for 2008 **On Site** ⚑ **Nearby** ⚓ 8km ⚲ 20km
⚓ 15km 🎣 8km 🏠 3km **Notes** No pets English spoken Open 7 April
to 2 October, 27 October to 4 November & 29 December to 2 January.

BOUILLAC

ⅲ ⅰ◎ⅰ **Nissols**

Camille AUFFRET
12300 LES ALBRES BOUILLAC
☎ 05 65 80 41 03
email: camille.auffret@orange.fr
web: http://perso.orange.fr/camille.auffret

A small hamlet deep in the countryside and overlooking the Lot
valley is the setting for this chambre d'hôtes. There are three double
rooms, all on the first floor, all with private shower room and WC. Vast
lounge, opening to a wonderful panoramic view. Large grounds, with
terrace and garden furniture. Meals available by arrangement, except
Thursday evenings.

Prices s fr €40; d fr €52; extra person fr €15; dinner fr €18
Nearby ⚓ 8km ⚑ 10km ⚲ 10km Restaurant 0.5km 🎣 13km 🏠 5km
🚶 15km **Notes** Pets admitted English spoken Open March to October.

BOURNAZEL

♨ ♥ La Borde

Pilar et Roland MATHAT
12390 BOURNAZEL
☎ 05 65 64 41 09

Expect a warm welcome at this old sheep farm, with two guest rooms in an annexe for two or three guests, two family rooms with mezzanine for two to four, with independent entrances, shower and wc. Communal living room with open fire and TV, grounds, summer kitchen, barbecue, table tennis, spare bed and cot available. Camping on farm. Farm-auberge 300mtrs.

Prices s fr €30; d fr €40; t fr €50; extra person fr €10 **Nearby** ☕ 7km ♨ 35km ♂ 1km ↘ 7km Restaurant 0.3km ☕ 0.2km ☕ 7km ♨ 9km **Notes** No pets Open April to November.

BOZOULS

♨ Les Brunes

Monique PHILIPPONNAT-DAVID
12340 BOZOULS
☎ 05 65 48 50 11 & 06 80 07 95 96
email: lesbrunes@wanadoo.fr
web: www.lesbrunes.com

Situated on le Causse, between Rodez and la Vallée du Lot, this pretty house is in a vast wooded space. The four guest rooms have private facilities and guests can use the communal living room with TV and fireplace and garden with terrace and furniture. Breakfasts are taken in the large stone-flagged kitchen with charming fireplace and bread oven. Restaurants 5 km.

Prices s €74-€117; d €81-€124; extra person fr €20 **Nearby** ☕ 5km ♨ 19km ♂ 5km ↘ 14km Restaurant 5km ☕ 5km ☕ 14km ☕ 5km ♨ 17km **Notes** No pets English spoken

CALMELS ET LE VIALA

♨ ○ Sermet

Suzanne et Philippe SCHMAL
12400 CALMELS ET LE VIALA
☎ 05 65 99 16 48 📄 05 65 99 16 48
email: domaine.sermet@free.fr
web: www.sermet.fr

The four elegantly decorated double bedrooms in this property occupy a separate wing of the owners' recently restored home. The setting is rural, on a goat farm. One room is on the ground floor; the other two are upstairs. All have private shower rooms/WCs; a cot and non-smoking rooms are available. Large terrace with garden furniture. Meals by arrangement.

Prices not confirmed for 2008 **Nearby** ☕ 6km ♂ 0.1km ↘ 12km ☕ 12km ☕ 15km ♨ 40km **Notes** No pets English spoken Open February to 1 November & Xmas.

COMPEYRE

♨ ♥ ○ Quiers

Véronique LOMBARD
12520 COMPEYRE
☎ 05 65 59 85 10
email: quiers@wanadoo.fr
web: www.quiers.net

Six rooms in an annexe on a farm in the remote Causse foothills: five doubles and a room for five, all with private bath or shower/wc. Extra beds possible; garden room. No meals Sunday evening or Monday, other times by reservation.

Prices s fr €45; d fr €54; t fr €68; dinner fr €17 **Nearby** ☕ 15km ♂ 5km ↘ 12km Restaurant 7km ☕ 5km ☕ 7km ♨ 13km **Notes** Pets admitted Open April to 1 November.

CORNUS

♨ ○ Sorgues

Patrick et Yvonne GIANSILY
12540 CORNUS
☎ 05 65 97 50 21
web: www.chateaudesorgues.fr

An ancient château, in the heart of the Parc Naturel Régional, close to the source of the river Sorgues. The four bedrooms - two doubles and two family rooms - are all upstairs, with private shower room and WC. Extra beds and a cot are available. Outside are attractive grounds with trees and a shady terrace.

Prices not confirmed for 2008 **On Site** ♂ **Nearby** ☕ 20km ↘ 20km ☕ 10km ☕ 7km ♨ 40km **Notes** No pets

COUPIAC

♨ ○ Lapaloup

Monique et Donald VERHOEFF
12550 COUPIAC
☎ 05 65 99 71 49
email: info@lapaloup.com
web: www.lapaloup.com

There are panoramic views across meadows and forests from this house, with its three first floor bedrooms. Two are doubles and the third is a room for four; all have private shower room and WC. Lounge with open fire; garden with terrace, barbecue and garden furniture. Swimming pool. Good area for walking, riding, or mountain biking.

Prices not confirmed for 2008 **On Site** Private ↘ **Nearby** ♂ 12km ☕ 5km ☕ 5km ♨ 45km **Notes** Pets admitted English spoken

ENTRAYGUES-SUR-TRUYERE

ⅲⅼ ⅼ◯ⅼ **Le Clos St-Georges**

Catherine RETHORE
9 Coteau de St Georges,
12140 ENTRAYGUES-SUR-TRUYERE
☎ 05 65 48 68 22 & 06 70 44 78 52
email: catherine.rethore@hotmail.fr

This beautiful old mansion is on the edge of the town of Entraygues, which is on two rivers - the Lot and the Truyère. It has four first floor bedrooms - three doubles, and a family room for three adults with an additional bed for a child (up to age four). All rooms have private shower rooms/WCs. Lounge with TV and garden furniture.

Prices s fr €47; d fr €57; t fr €72; extra person fr €15; dinner fr €18 **On Site** 🖉 **Nearby** ⅎ 3km ⅎ 32km ⅎ 0.5km Restaurant 0.5km ⅎ 34km ⅎ 0.5km Spa 45km ⅲ 45km **Notes** No pets English spoken Open 2 January to 20 December.

ESTAING

ⅲ ❤ ⅼ◯ⅼ **Cervel**

André et Madeleine ALAZARD
Route de Vinnac, 12190 ESTAING
☎ 05 65 44 09 89 🖻 05 65 44 09 89

This farmhouse is in a small hamlet in the Lot Valley, at the foot of the Aubrac, and has traditional furniture, and views over the shady courtyard and flowery terrace with furniture. Two double rooms and two triples are available with shower, wc and TV. Spare beds available. Panelled salon for use of guests, with open fire, piano, bookshelves, TV.

Prices s fr €42; d fr €51; extra person fr €18; dinner fr €17 **Nearby** ⅎ 7km ⅎ 20km 🖉 1.5km ⅎ 5km Restaurant 5km ⅎ 30km ⅎ 5km ⅎ 4km ⅲ 30km **Notes** No pets Open April to 15 November.

GISSAC

ⅲ ⅼ◯ⅼ **St-Etienne**

Anne-Marie et Gilbert BOSC
12360 GISSAC
☎ 05 65 99 59 27

This countryside family mansion opens onto a paved courtyard, surrounded by old vaulted buildings. The rooms have stone paving slabs and white-washed walls and include two double rooms and two rooms for two to four people, each with shower and wc. Lounge with open fire, living room, courtyard, garden with furniture. Reduced rates for longer stays and half board. The hosts can help visitors discover south Aveyron and the Parc des Grands Causses.

Prices s fr €42; d fr €52; t fr €67; dinner fr €20 **Nearby** ⅎ 10km ⅎ 10km ⅎ 23km Restaurant 6km ⅎ 10km ⅎ 23km 🖻 10km ⅲ 25km **Notes** No pets English spoken Open February to November.

LA FOUILLADE

ⅲ ⅼ◯ⅼ *Chambre d'hôtes Alisa*

Isabelle et Alain FRANZ
Route de Laudinie, 12270 LA FOUILLADE
☎ 05 65 29 67 78 & 06 14 66 57 48
email: isabelle@aveyron-hotes
web: www.aveyron-hotes.com

This property is in a peaceful village, and the rooms are in a separate building from the owners' house. There are four non-smoking doubles, all with en suite facilities. An extra bed is available if needed. There is a lounge and dining room for guests' use, and outside there is a good-sized garden with a garden room and barbecue.

Prices not confirmed for 2008 **On Site** 🖉 **Nearby** ⅎ 5km ⅎ 5km ⅲ 6km **Notes** No pets English spoken Open March to September.

ⅲ ⅼ◯ⅼ *La Serène*

Catherine et Gérard DREVET
12270 LA FOUILLADE
☎ 05 65 29 67 93 & 06 18 47 05 78
email: laserene@wanadoo.fr
web: http://monsite.wanadoo.fr/laserene

Three non-smoking first floor rooms, in a hamlet amongst the Gorges de l'Aveyron. There is a double room, and two two-roomed family suites, one for three guests, the other for four. All have private bath or shower room and WC. Lounge; garden with furniture, barbecue and swimming pool. Meals by arrangement; creative arts workshops can be provided.

Prices not confirmed for 2008 **On Site** Private ⅎ **Nearby** ⅎ 16km 🖉 2km ⅎ 4km 🖻 4km ⅲ 21km **Notes** No pets English spoken

---

ⅲ ⅼ◯ⅼ **Le Moulin de Martre**

Michelle CELERIEN
12270 LA FOUILLADE
☎ 05 65 29 77 74 & 06 19 23 39 35
email: moulin-de-martre@tiscali.fr
web: www.moulin-de-martre.com

This sympathetically restored property stands in magnificent wooded grounds. There are three double bedrooms, one in the owners' house but with independent access, the other two in a separate building. All have private bath or shower rooms and WCs. Cot available; guests' lounge. Terrace, garden furniture, barbecue, pétanque.

Prices s fr €63; d fr €68; dinner fr €20 **On Site** Private ⅎ **Nearby** ⅎ 15km ⅎ 50km 🖉 0.1km Restaurant 4km ⅎ 3km ⅎ 17km 🖻 3km ⅲ 20km **Notes** No pets English spoken Open April to October.

LACROIX-BARREZ

ⅲ ❦ ⚇ *Vilherols*

Jean LAURENS

12600 LACROIX-BARREZ

☎ 05 65 66 08 24 & 06 07 42 30 15 ▤ 05 65 66 19 98

web: www.gite-vilherols.net

In the house of the proprietors, there is a family room for three people with access to a sitting room with open fire and TV, and an annexe offers three double rooms with TV and one with private terrace. All have private facilities and cooking. Garden with furniture, meadowland, parking, disabled access. A terrific vista over the wild valley of the Truyère. Restaurants and gym nearby.

Prices not confirmed for 2008 **Nearby** ⚞ 10km ⚲ 6km ⚈ 4km ⧉ 8km
Notes No pets

LAGUIOLE

ⅲ ❦ ⓘ◎ **Bouet**

Evelyne et Michel CHAYRIGUES

12210 LAGUIOLE

☎ 05 65 44 33 33 & 06 77 00 53 87

Delightful small château with four spacious guest rooms for three/four people, with separate access, private facilities and TV. Communal lounge with open fire; washing machine; refrigerator; courtyard and herb garden; garden furniture; barbecue. Tariff reductions for groups of four and longer stays.´

Prices s fr €40; d fr €52; dinner fr €18 **Nearby** ⚞ 8km ⚲ 5km
⚊ 1km ⚲ 20km Restaurant 1km ⚌ 6km ⚈ 1km ⧉ 1km ⚏ 56km
Notes No pets Open 15 April to 15 November.

ⅲ ❦ **Ferme de Moulhac**

Claudine et Philippe LONG

12210 LAGUIOLE

☎ 05 65 44 33 25 & 06 07 30 55 77

web: http://perso.wanadoo.fr/moulhac

On a cattle farm on the Aubrac plateau, these guest rooms are in a converted barn adjacent to the family house. Charming decoration mixes traditional and modern materials and there are three double rooms and one sleeping four, all with private facilities. Living room with open fire, cooking area, garden, small lake. Animals accepted by prior booking.

Prices s €55-€90; d €65-€95; extra person fr €18 **On Site** ⚲
Nearby ⚞ 10km ⚲ 6km ⚲ 20km Restaurant 3km ⚌ 8km ⚈ 3km
⚲ 6km ⧉ 3km **Notes** Pets admitted English spoken

LAPANOUSE-DE-CERNON

ⅲ *Chambre d'hôtes*

Jacques PELISSIER

Place de l'Eglise, 12230 LAPANOUSE-DE-CERNON

☎ 05 65 62 72 07 ▤ 05 65 62 72 07

email: jacques.pelissier7@wanadoo.fr

A village house with three bedrooms, one double and two triples, all on the second floor and all with private shower room and WC.

The communal living room has an open fireplace. Outside there is an enclosed courtyard with furniture and barbecue. Excellent walking country, with lots of footpaths.

Prices not confirmed for 2008 **On Site** ⚲ **Nearby** ⚞ 6km ⚲ 9km
⚈ 3km ⧉ 3km ⚏ 25km **Notes** Pets admitted

LAPANOUSE-DE-SEVERAC

ⅲ **Chambre d'hôtes**

Armelle et Henri COSTES

Rue des Rosiers, 12150 LAPANOUSE-DE-SEVERAC

☎ 05 65 71 64 40 ▤ 05 65 71 64 40

email: armellecostes@wanadoo.fr

web: www.chambres-letrefle.com

In a small village with an 11th-century church in the Parc Naturel Régional des Grands Causses Lapanouse, this converted barn offers a double room, a room with mezzanine sleeping four and a duplex for five. Each is non-smoking with cooking facilities, shower and wc. Baby equipment available. Private lounge with open fire and TV. Terrace, small garden, outdoor furniture, barbecue. Restaurant 1km.

Prices s fr €45; d fr €52; t fr €71; extra person fr €19 **Nearby** ⚞ 8km
⚲ 1km ⚲ 3km Restaurant 1km ⚈ 3km ⚲ 3km ⧉ 3km ⚏ 3km
Notes Pets admitted English spoken Open March to November.

MILLAU

ⅲ ❦ **Montels**

Henriette CASSAN

12100 MILLAU

☎ 05 65 60 51 70

web: www.chambrehotes-montels.com

A hillside farm with attractive views of the town of Larzac. There is a family room for four, and two double rooms (one at grade 2). All have TV, private shower room and WC, although those for the grade room are not en suite. Lounge; garden with terrace, garden furniture and barbecue. Good area for walking and hang-gliding.

Prices s fr €45; d fr €50; t fr €60; extra person fr €10 **Nearby** ⚞ 12km
⚲ 7km ⚲ 5km Restaurant 2km ⚈ 5km ⧉ 5km ⚏ 5km
Notes No pets

see advert on opposite page

MONTPEYROUX

⚑ ❤ **Esparou**

Christiane et Christian PEGUES

12210 MONTPEYROUX

☎ 05 65 44 37 74

In the rural heart of the Aubrac, this farm property has three bedrooms in a barn conversion close to the owners' home. There is a double room and two triples, all with private bath or shower room and WC. There is a guests' lounge with TV and kitchenette, and a courtyard with garden furniture and a children's swing. On-site parking.

Prices s fr €40; d fr €51; t fr €61 **Nearby** ⚓ 8km ♨ 5km ↗ 19km Restaurant 7km ♒ 8km Spa 50km ⛪ 9km ⛷ 50km **Notes** Pets admitted English spoken

---

ONET-LE-CHATEAU

⚑ ❤ *Les Cabaniols*

Nadine CONSTANS

EARL Les Acacias, 12850 ONET-LE-CHATEAU

☎ 06 82 08 57 63

email: naconstans@wanadoo.fr

web: www.lescabaniols.com

From strolling on the nearby Causses, hiking towards the Conques, the Lakes of Levezou or Aubrac, to golfing at nearby Fontanges - there is plenty to do here. Three bedrooms (for two, three or four) in a converted barn and a room for two in a separate small building, all with private facilities. Cot available. Kitchen area and lounge with TV and books. Garden with furniture and barbecue.

Prices not confirmed for 2008 **Nearby** ⚓ 10km ♟ 7km ↗ 4km ♒ 2km ⛪ 4km ⛷ 4km **Notes** No pets Open 15 February to 5 December.

PONT-DE-SALARS

⚑ *La Coste*

Michel et Mireille BEDOS

12290 PONT-DE-SALARS

☎ 05 65 46 84 14 & 06 83 46 42 71

email: mbedos@free.fr

web: http://mbedos.free.fr

Two double rooms and a twin in the proprietors' house opposite the gendarmerie, with separate entrance, shower, wc and satellite TV. Communal lounge, lovely garden with furniture, river and sailing. Dinner by reservation except Sundays. Restaurant 500mtrs. Reduction for longer stays out of season; advice on tourist attractions. Pets by reservation only.

Prices not confirmed for 2008 **On Site** ♟ **Nearby** ⚓ 4km ↗ 3km ♒ 20km **Notes** No pets English spoken Open 15 March to 5 November.

MADAME CASSAN HENRIETTE
MONTELS
12100 MILLAU

TEL : 05.65.60.51.70
MOBILE : 06.30.85.63.48
HTTP://WWW.CHAMBREHOTES-MONTELS.COM

Mme Cassan will offer you a very warm welcome at this chambre d'hôtes in Millau. The atmosphere is one of serenity and tranquillity. Expect to feel as if you are amongst friends. An ideal location from which you can discover the local region. There are three characterful bedrooms, a living room and a dining room which opens out onto the terrace. Guests can feel free to use the shady garden at will.

RIGNAC

⚑ **La Garissonnie**

André et Monique PRADEL

12390 RIGNAC

☎ 06 73 86 45 40

email: monique.pradel@wanadoo.fr

web: www.lagarissonnie.com

Near to Rodez, explore the cathedral, visit Belcastel and sample the local wine in the producer's home. Two double rooms and a grade 3 triple, with mezzanine, exposed beams, covered terrace and private facilities. Shady garden with furniture; barbecue and picnicking possible. Two horses available for guests. Animals accepted with prior booking. Restaurants and farm-auberge nearby.

Prices s fr €40; d fr €50; t fr €65; extra person fr €15 **Nearby** ⚓ 15km ♟ 5km ↗ 5km ♒ 5km ⛪ 5km ⛷ 25km **Notes** Pets admitted English spoken Open April to 15 December.

RIVIERE-SUR-TARN

⚑ ⦿ *Boyne*

Julie et Patrick BOULOUIS

Les Gargouilles, 12640 RIVIERE-SUR-TARN

☎ 06 71 73 64 47

email: patrick.boulouis@wanadoo.fr

web: www.millau-chambre-hote.com

Set back from the Gorges du Tarn road, this property has a terrace in front and a little garden behind, squeezed in between the house and

CONTINUED

RIVIERE-SUR-TARN *CONTINUED*

the cliff. There are five bedrooms: three doubles and two rooms for four, all with private showers/WCs. Shared lounge, private swimming pool, terrace and small garden with garden furniture.

Prices not confirmed for 2008   **On Site** 🖋 Private 🔭   **Nearby** ⚓ 3km ⛴ 1km 🏛 3km 🚣 16km   **Notes** No pets   Open March to October.

SALLES-LA-SOURCE

🍴 🍽 Cougousse

Jean et Claudette TORRUBIANO
12330 SALLES-LA-SOURCE
☎ 05 65 71 85 52 & 06 71 72 35 52
email: gites.de.cougousse@wanadoo.fr
web: http://gites.cougousse.free.fr

A ground-floor double room with independent access and shower/WC, also with kitchenette and TV, plus gites in this old convent. Terrace, conservatory, BBQ, stream.

Prices s fr €45; d fr €52; t fr €67; extra person fr €15; dinner fr €20 **On Site** 🖋   **Nearby** ⚓ 10km 🔭 2km ⛴ 2km 🏛 3km 🚣 12km **Notes** Pets admitted   Open April to 15 October.

SANVENSA

🍴 🍽 Monteillet

Pierre et Monique BATESON
12200 SANVENSA
☎ 05 65 29 81 01   📠 05 65 65 89 52

This house has two double rooms with shared terrace and separate access, and a room for two to four in an annexe, with kitchenette and terrace; all have private facilities. Lounge with TV and open fire, open courtyard, garden furniture, barbecue, table tennis. Evening meals except Tuesday, Thursday and Sunday, unless booked.

Prices s fr €40; d fr €46; t fr €58; extra person fr €12; dinner fr €19 **Nearby** ⚓ 8km ⛷ 10km 🖋 5km 🔭 11km Restaurant 8km ⛴ 1km 🚣 11km   **Notes** Pets admitted   English spoken

---

SAUVETERRE-DE-ROUERGUE

🍴 🍽 Jouels

Evelyne et Pascal LABBE
Lou Cambrou, 12800 SAUVETERRE-DE-ROUERGUE
☎ 05 65 72 13 40 & 06 10 86 42 06
email: nina.labbe@wanadoo.fr
web: www.loucambrou.fr

Once this was a convent; now it provides rather more comfortable accommodation for up to eleven guests. There are three double-bedded rooms and a family room for up to five, all on the first floor with private shower room and WC. There is a sitting room, a terrace with garden furniture, and on-site parking. Meals are available by arrangement.

Prices s €44-€52; d €52-€63; t €67-€82; extra person fr €13; dinner fr €17   **On Site** 🖋   **Nearby** ⚓ 4km 🔭 4km Restaurant 4km ⛴ 2km 🏛 4km 🚣 10km   **Notes** No pets

---

SEVERAC-LE-CHATEAU

🍴 🍽 *Le Villaret*

Gérard et Denise BONNIER
Le Rocher de Corbières, 12150 SEVERAC-LE-CHATEAU
☎ 06 81 38 82 24
email: d.bonnier@worldonline.fr
web: www.lerocherdecorbieres.com

A house built in the shape of a letter U, with a large open-ended courtyard in the middle. Two double rooms (one at grade 2), and two family rooms for three to five people all have private facilities. Outside are grounds with wonderful views across the rolling countryside. Meals are available by arrangement.

Prices not confirmed for 2008   **Nearby** ⚓ 6km 🖋 4km 🔭 4km ⛴ 4km 🏛 6km 🚣 6km   **Notes** No pets

---

SONNAC

🍴 🍽 *Chambre d'hôtes*

Claude et Jo RONCIN
L'Oustal, Le Bourg, 12700 SONNAC
☎ 06 77 74 78 42
email: loustalous@free.fr
web: www.loustalous.com

There are three bedrooms at this property, in a very pleasant setting on the edge of a village. All the rooms have double beds, with en suite shower room and WCs. A lounge/dining area is in the conservatory; outside are gardens with trees, lots of flowers, and a swimming pool. Plenty of good walks in the area.

Prices not confirmed for 2008   **On Site** Private 🔭   **Nearby** ⚓ 3km 🖋 3km ⛴ 4km 🏛 4km 🚣 4km   **Notes** Pets admitted   English spoken Open 3 January to 22 December.

🍴 🍽 *La Mélessens*

Valérie et Emmanuel PESSO
12700 SONNAC
☎ 05 65 80 86 59   📠 05 65 80 86 56
email: bienvenue@la-melessens.fr
web: www.la-melessens.fr

A peaceful village setting and a warm welcome await you at this property. There are three non-smoking guest rooms, on the first floor of a separate building from the owners' home. The rooms are all split-level, sleeping up to five people, and all have en suite facilities. Cot available; private lounge with TV and books; garden. Meals by arrangement, including vegetarian.

Prices not confirmed for 2008   **On Site** 🖋 Private 🔭   **Nearby** ⚓ 4km ⛴ 4km 🏛 12km 🚣 12km   **Notes** No pets   English spoken   Open 15 February to 15 December.

ST-GEORGES-DE-LUZENCON

⊞ ⭘ *Luzençon*

Claude PIRO et Bruno VALES
La Saisonneraie, 12100 ST-GEORGES-DE-LUZENCON
☎ 05 65 62 58 86 & 06 84 47 18 72
email: claude.bruno@lasaisonneraie.com
web: www.lasaisonneraie.com

Claude and Bruno welcome their guests as friends in their stone-built house in the heart of the Parc Naturel Régional des Grandes Causses. The views are stunning, and each of the tastefully decorated ground floor rooms has its own character. There is a double, two triples, and a two-roomed family suite for four, all with private facilities. Baby equipment; meals by arrangement.

Prices not confirmed for 2008 **Nearby** ⚓ 2km ⚲ 1.5km ⋒ 12km
Notes No pets Open 15 March to September.

ST-JEAN-ET-ST-PAUL

⊞ *Le Moulin de Gauty*

Jocelyne et Hervé GARCIA
12250 ST JEAN ET ST PAUL
☎ 05 65 97 51 90
email: contact@moulindegauty.com
web: www.moulindegauty.com

Not far from Millau, this place is like an open door to the Parc Naturel Régional. The village is picturesque, with lots of flowers, and close to the Gorges du Tarn. There are three bedrooms, two doubles and a triple, all with private shower room and WC. Guest sitting room with fireplace; kitchenette and garden with furniture.

Prices not confirmed for 2008 **On Site** Private ⚲ **Nearby** ⚓ 14km ⚲ 2km ⚲ 14km ⛫ 7km ⋒ 32km **Notes** No pets English spoken

ST-VICTOR-ET-MELVIEU

⊞ ⭘ *Le Clos des Raspes*

Maryvonne FAUCHET
Melvieu, 12400 ST-VICTOR ET MELVIEU
☎ 05 65 58 18 11
email: mary@leclosdesraspes.com
web: www.leclosdesraspes.com

This welcoming property, in the heart of the floral village of Melvieu, provides a gateway to the Parc Naturel Régional des Grandes Causses. It has three bedrooms in the owners' house, but with independent access. Two are doubles, the other a triple; all have private shower rooms/WCs. Guests' lounge and kitchenette; garden with furniture.

Prices not confirmed for 2008 **Nearby** ⚓ 22km ⚲ 3km ⚲ 3km ⚲ 0.1km ⛫ 0.1km ⋒ 15km **Notes** Pets admitted English spoken

VALADY

⊞ ⭘ **Les Auges**

C et A BUEY-TIDBALL
Place de l'Eglise, 12330 VALADY
☎ 05 65 72 77 54 & & 06 78 64 44 31 📄 05 65 72 77 55
email: lesauges@wanadoo.fr
web: http://perso.wanadoo.fr/lesauges/

Charming old house in the village centre, with many original features. Three double rooms, all with bath and WC, on the first floor with independent access. Shared living room with TV, open fire, garden room, restaurant in village.

Prices s fr €50; d fr €52; t fr €70; extra person fr €18; dinner fr €20 **On Site** ⚲ **Nearby** ⚓ 4km ⚲ 9km ⚲ 6km ⋒ 1km **Notes** Pets admitted English spoken Open Easter to 15 October.

VERRIERES

⊞ ⭘ ♿ *La Villa des Pins*

Cathie et Jean-Claude ARGUEL
12520 VERRIERES
☎ 05 65 58 82 32 📄 05 65 58 82 34
email: villadespins@wanadoo.fr
web: www.villadespins.net

This property stands in a small hamlet, and it has four individually-styled bedrooms in an annexe to the owners' house. Two of the rooms are family rooms, and all four have private bath/shower rooms and WCs. There is a split-level guests' lounge with an open fire, TV and games. Terraced grounds with garden furniture, barbecue, table tennis, boules, swimming pool and summer kitchen.

Prices not confirmed for 2008 **On Site** Private ⚲ **Nearby** ⚓ 6km ⚲ 3km ⚲ 9km ⛫ 17km ⋒ 17km **Notes** Pets admitted English spoken Open 5 April to 12 November.

⊞ ⭘ **Le Sans Souci**

Monique GELY
La Graillerie, 12520 VERRIERES
☎ 05 65 59 83 95

A stone-built house in good walking country with three attractively-decorated bedrooms. The rooms, two doubles and a triple, are all on the first floor, all with private shower and WC. Guests' lounge; enclosed courtyard with barbecue and garden furniture. Meals by arrangement, except Sunday evenings.

Prices d fr €55; t fr €70; extra person fr €20; dinner fr €20 **On Site** ⚲ **Nearby** ⚓ 3km ⚲ 10km Restaurant 3km ⚲ 4km ⚲ 10km ⛫ 4km ⋒ 10km **Notes** Pets admitted Open Easter to 1 November.

VILLEFRANCHE-DE-PANAT

⊪ ⏅ **Mas Bertrand**

Hughette et Jean-Pierre CARTON
12430 VILLEFRANCHE DE PANAT
☎ 05 65 78 93 13 & 06 88 14 05 51
email: mas.bertrand@wanadoo.fr
web: www.mas-bertrand.com

An 18th-century property deep in the countryside overlooking the Tarn valley, not far from two lakes. Four bedrooms, all upstairs: a family room for four, and three rooms for two or three guests. Each room has shower room and WC, and a cot is available. Outside is a courtyard with garden furniture. Hiking. Accommodation for horses. Meals available by arrangement.

Prices s fr €42; d fr €49; extra person fr €13; dinner fr €18
Nearby ⚓ 7km ⚓ 50km ✎ 8km Restaurant 6km ✎ 8km 🏛 8km
🎣 45km **Notes** No pets English spoken

VILLEFRANCHE-DE-ROUERGUE

⊪ ✿ **Le Mas de Comte**

Agnès et Philibert JAYR
Les Pesquiés, 12200 VILLEFRANCHE-DE-ROUERGUE
☎ 05 65 81 16 48 ▤ 05 65 81 16 48
email: masdecomte@wanadoo.fr
web: http://masdecomte.free.fr

Whether you sleep in the Provençal bedroom or the African, you will love the charm and the ambience of the Mas de Comte. Two double rooms and a room for three with private facilities, a kitchenette/living room and lounge with open fire and TV. Spare bed and cot available. Garden with furniture. Reduced rates for extended stays.

Prices s fr €40; d fr €50; t fr €60; extra person fr €10 **Nearby** ⚓ 6km ✎ 1km ✈ 6km Restaurant 6km ✎ 6km 🏛 6km 🎣 6km **Notes** Pets admitted English spoken Open February to December.

GERS

AUBIET

⊪ **La Toulette**

Frédérique LABEDAN
32270 AUBIET
☎ 05 62 65 84 48
email: latoulette@free.fr
web: http://latoulette.free.fr

This totally renovated house, standing in a large garden, has four guest rooms. All the rooms are upstairs - three doubles and a room with a double bed and twin beds. One of the rooms has a balcony, and they all have a private bath or shower room and WC. There is a fishing lake in the grounds.

Prices s fr €47; d fr €52; extra person fr €17 **Nearby** ⚓ 5km ⚓ 18km ✎ 2km ✈ 7km ✎ 2km 🏛 7km 🎣 15km **Notes** Pets admitted English spoken Open 5 January to 20 December.

AUCH

⊪ **Le Castagne**

Véronique SEMEZIES-DUPUY
Route de Toulouse, 32000 AUCH
☎ 06 07 97 40 37
email: lecastagne@wanadoo.fr
web: www.domainelecastagne.com

A restored house at the gates of Auch, with impressive views over the castle and countryside. A room with a double and twin beds, a triple and two with double and single beds are available, all with own shower and wc. There is a lounge with corner kitchen (fridge), living room with fireplace and TV, cot, laundry and heating available. Leisure activities include mini-golf, mountain biking, camping, pool and games room.

Prices s fr €40; d fr €50; t fr €60 **On Site** ✎ Private ✈
Nearby ⚓ 8km ✎ 8km Restaurant 3km ✎ 4km 🏛 4km 🎣 4km
Notes No pets English spoken

AUTERRIVE

⊪ ⏅ *Domaine de Poudos*

Jean-Jacques ASTAU
32550 AUTERRIVE
☎ 05 62 61 00 93 & 06 87 48 97 18
email: poudos@wanadoo.fr
web: http://perso.wanadoo.fr/poudos

This property is in shady, flowery grounds. In the main house is a double room with lounge; in an annexe are a further four rooms sleeping two or three people, and a small kitchenette. All have a private bath/shower room and WC. Lounge with books, TV, central heating. Swimming pool, table tennis. Meals by arrangement (not Tuesdays).

Prices not confirmed for 2008 **On Site** Private ✈ **Nearby** ⚓ 5km ⚓ 12km ✎ 1km ✎ 5km 🏛 5km 🎣 8km **Notes** No pets English spoken

BARCELONNE-DU-GERS

⊪ **La Tuilerie**

Marie-France LUPART
Route de Nogaro, 32720 BARCELONNE-DU-GERS
☎ 06 82 58 65 34
email: marie-france.lupart@wanadoo.fr
web: http://alatuilerie.free.fr

Magnificent views of the Pyrénées are a bonus for guests at this property. It is a big house, with four upstairs bedrooms: three doubles and a room for three (single beds), all with shower room and WC. Living room with internet access, terrace outside.

Prices d €60-€70; t fr €85; extra person fr €15 **Nearby** ⚓ 2km ⚓ 20km ✎ 3km ✈ 4km Restaurant 2km ✎ 4km 🏛 2km 🎣 31km **Notes** No pets English spoken

BEAUMARCHES

⏛ *A Labeyrie*

Marie-Edith SAMSON-LARRIEU
32160 BEAUMARCHES
☎ 05 62 69 49 11 & 06 75 34 00 11
email: marie-edith@alabeyrie.com
web: www.multimania.com/alabeyrie

A warm family welcome is promised at this farmhouse with its three guest bedrooms. Two of the rooms are doubles, one of them with room for two extra single beds; the third is a twin-bedded room with a small lounge area. All rooms have private bath or shower room and WC. Outside, guests can enjoy the wooded grounds and lake.

Prices not confirmed for 2008　**Nearby** ⚓ 7km ⚓ 15km ⚓ 7km ⚓ 7km ⚓ 2km 🏠 7km ⚓ 45km　**Notes** No pets

BERAUT

⏛ ⏛ *Le Hour*

Florence BONNEVILLE
32100 BERAUT
☎ 06 85 63 96 03
email: david.bonneville@libertysurf.fr
web: www.le-hour.com

A house in a peaceful spot on the side of a hill, surrounded by woods and meadows. There are five double rooms, with original and tasteful decorations. Each has a private bath or shower room and WC. Cots and children's beds are available, and there is a lounge and kitchenette.

Prices not confirmed for 2008　**On Site** Private ⚓　**Nearby** ⚓ 6km ⚓ 25km ⚓ 7km ⚓ 6km 🏠 6km ⚓ 46km　**Notes** Pets admitted English spoken

BOUZON-GELLENAVE

⏛ ⏛ *Château du Bascou*

Annie et Xavier DESTRADE
32290 BOUZON-GELLENAVE
☎ 05 62 69 04 12 📄 05 62 69 06 09
email: chateau.du.bascou@free.fr
web: www.chateaudubascou.com

A pretty 19th-century residence on a wine-growing estate, furnished and decorated with taste. It has a room with a canopied double bed and a single, two twin rooms and a double, all with private facilities. Communal rooms include a living room with TV. Table d'hôte meals available except Wednesdays.

Prices s fr €74; d fr €74; t fr €89; extra person fr €15; dinner €20-€28　**On Site** Private ⚓　**Nearby** ⚓ 20km ⚓ 25km ⚓ 6km Restaurant 5km ⚓ 7km 🏠 7km　**Notes** No pets English spoken CC

BRETAGNE-D'ARMAGNAC

⏛ ⏛ ⚓ *Les Sapinettes*

Pascale MIGLIORI
32800 BRETAGNE-D'ARMAGNAC
☎ 06 09 65 22 30
email: pascale.migliori@wanadoo.fr

Peace and quiet and a warm welcome are promised in this beautiful late 19th-century house. There are three ground floor double bedrooms, each with its own entrance, private shower and WC. Meals are available, by arrangement. Reduced accommodation rates for stays of longer than three nights.

Prices s fr €65; d fr €74; extra person fr €20; dinner €18-€35　**On Site** ⚓　**Nearby** ⚓ 1km ⚓ 2km ⚓ 2km ⚓ 2km Restaurant 2km ⚓ 2km 🏠 5km　**Notes** No pets English spoken

CASTELNAU-D'ARBIEU

⏛ ⏛ *La Bordeneuve*

Claudine BRUNEAU-DUQUESNOY
32500 CASTELNAU-D'ARBIEU
☎ 05 62 64 27 66 & 06 98 24 61 36
email: bruneau.claudine@wanadoo.fr
web: www.labordeneuve.com

A restored house looking out over the small valleys of the Gers countryside. There are three ground floor bedrooms, all doubles, each with a private shower room and WC, and direct access to a terrace. Large lounge with open fire and books. Meals are available by arrangement.

Prices s fr €53; d fr €58; extra person fr €20; dinner fr €20　**Nearby** ⚓ 6km ⚓ 15km ⚓ 4km ⚓ 8km Restaurant 8km ⚓ 3km Spa 10km ⚓ 7km 🏠 8km ⚓ 40km　**Notes** No pets English spoken

CASTERA-LECTOUROIS

⏛ ⏛ *La Boulègue*

Jean-Michel BORRELLY
Au Village, 32700 CASTERA-LECTOUROIS
☎ 05 62 68 78 84 & 06 80 67 74 12
email: jean-michel.borrelly@wanadoo.fr
web: www.laboulegue.com

A double and triple room, both with shower and WC, on the first floor of the owners home, with independent access. For guest use are a living room with TV, sauna and covered terrace. Meals available July and August, Tuesday to Thursday, reduced for children; gastronomic options.

Prices s fr €60; d fr €67; t fr €89; extra person fr €22; dinner fr €23　**On Site** Restaurant ⚓ Private ⚓　**Nearby** ⚓ 13km ⚓ 20km ⚓ 2km ⚓ 7km 🏠 7km ⚓ 28km　**Notes** No pets English spoken

MIDI-PYRÉNÉES

CAUSSENS

⚜ *Le Vieux Pressoir*

Laurent MARTIN
Saint-Fort, 32100 CAUSSENS
☎ 06 88 15 22 54
email: auvieuxpressoir@wanadoo.fr
web: http://perso.orange.fr/vieuxpressoir/

Large 17th-century stone building with flower garden containing pool and jacuzzi. The dining room opens out onto a terrace, and there are pleasant views over the hills. A family room, a twin, and two large singles are offered, with bathroom facilities. TV, central heating, communal lounge, washing machine, gastronomic meals and farm produce including foie gras. Reductions for stays over three nights.

Prices not confirmed for 2008 **On Site** Private ⬝ **Nearby** ⬝ 6km ⬝ 28km ⬝ 0.5km ⬝ 8km ⬝ 8km ⬝ 40km **Notes** No pets English spoken CC

COLOGNE

⚜ Les Musardises

M et J-C COURANT
10 place de la Halle, 32430 COLOGNE
☎ 06 86 86 32 58 & 05 62 58 39 81
email: martinecourant@hotmail.com

Not far from Toulouse, this 13th-century house has three large and comfortable bedrooms, each with individually themed decorations. Two of the rooms are doubles, the third a triple (double bed and a single). Each has a private bath or shower room, and two folding beds are available. Downstairs is a living room with internet access, outside is an attractive flower garden.

Prices s fr €60; d fr €75; t fr €95; extra person fr €20 **Nearby** ⬝ 0.5km ⬝ 6km ⬝ 4km ⬝ 14km ⬝ 14km **Notes** Pets admitted English spoken Open 5 January to 19 December.

DURBAN

⚜ ⁄◯⁄ Les Linottes

Laurence GATEAU-BROCHARD
Porteteny, 32260 DURBAN
☎ 05 62 61 04 79
email: contact@leslinottes.com
web: www.leslinottes.com

This old farmhouse has been carefully restored, using traditional and eco-friendly techniques. There are three guest bedrooms - two doubles and a twin - with their own access, in a separate wing of the house. Each room has its own shower room/WC, and a small terrace. Meals are available by arrangement.

Prices s fr €54; d fr €60; extra person fr €20; dinner fr €20 **On Site** ⬝ **Nearby** ⬝ 10km ⬝ 20km ⬝ 3km ⬝ 15km Restaurant 6km ⬝ 15km Spa 50km ⬝ 8km ⬝ 15km **Notes** Pets admitted English spoken

EAUZE

⚜ Hourcazet

Claude LEJEUNNE
32800 EAUZE
☎ 05 62 09 99 53
email: claude.lejeunne@wanadoo.fr
web: http://site.voila.fr/hourcazet

Tucked away among the vines, in its grounds full of trees and flowers, this half-timbered farmhouse offers a calm and pleasant setting for a holiday. There are two double rooms on the ground floor of an annexe, and two more rooms, each with a double bed and a single, upstairs in the owners' house. Lounge, terrace and garden furniture.

Prices s fr €55; d fr €65; extra person fr €20 **Nearby** ⬝ 6km ⬝ 6km ⬝ 3km ⬝ 3km Restaurant 6km ⬝ 6km ⬝ 6km ⬝ 6km ⬝ 50km **Notes** Pets admitted English spoken

⚜ ⬝ ⁄◯⁄ *Mounet*

Bernard et Monique MOLAS
Av de Parleboscq, 32800 EAUZE
☎ 05 62 09 82 85 ⬝ 05 62 09 77 45
email: contact@ferme-de-mounet.com
web: www.ferme-de-mounet.com

Manor house surrounded by parkland with three double rooms, one with extra bed, all with private facilities. Family dining room with TV and fireplace, a den, lounge with TV and library, gastronomic meals. Visit the farm and buy farm produce. Spa 12km away.

Prices not confirmed for 2008 **Nearby** ⬝ 3km ⬝ 3km ⬝ 4km ⬝ 3km ⬝ 3km ⬝ 4km **Notes** No pets English spoken CC

ESTIPOUY

⚜ La Grange aux Arts

Bernard et Pascale DILL
La Bache, 32300 ESTIPOUY
☎ 06 74 06 53 23
email: bern.dil@wanadoo.fr
web: www.lagrangeauxarts.fr

Occasional art exhibitions take place at this house, which is in an attractive garden, three kilometres from Mirande. Three double rooms, all upstairs, one with an extra bed if needed; all have private shower room and WC. There is a large sitting room downstairs, with a kitchenette for guests' use.

Prices d fr €50; extra person fr €16 **On Site** Private ⬝ **Nearby** ⬝ 5km ⬝ 15km ⬝ 4km Restaurant 3km ⬝ 4km ⬝ 3km ⬝ 25km **Notes** No pets English spoken

FLEURANCE

⫶⫶⫶ **En Marsan**

Martine COTTIN
Route de Terraube, 32500 FLEURANCE
☎ 05 62 06 08 20
email: cottinmarsan@wanadoo.fr
web: www.cottin.org

This 19th-century house, quietly situated close to Fleurance, has three guest rooms, located in two detached outbuildings which have been fully refurbished. There is a double room, a family suite for four, and a family room for four, all with private bathrooms/WCs. Games room, billiard room. There are large attractive grounds, with a swimming pool.

Prices s fr €66; d fr €72; extra person fr €25   **On Site** Private ↖
Nearby ⛵ 8km ♨ 20km ♬ 1km ⌘ 1.5km 🏠 1km ⋙ 25km
Notes No pets   English spoken   Open 15 April to 15 October.

GONDRIN

⫶⫶⫶ *Chambre d'hôtes*

Jean-Philippe DROUADAINE
32330 GONDRIN
☎ 05 62 29 10 43
email: drouadaine.genets@wanadoo.fr
web: http://resid.genets.monsite.wanadoo.fr

This was once a railway station, but the last train has long since departed. Upstairs it now has a lounge and three bedrooms: two doubles, and a family room with a double bed and two singles - all with a shower room and WC. Downstairs is a lounge/dining room shared with the hosts. Swimming pool, garden furniture. Four gîtes share the same site.

Prices not confirmed for 2008   **On Site** Private ↖   **Nearby** ⛵ 15km
♨ 13km ♬ 5km ⌘ 1km 🏠 1km   **Notes** No pets   English spoken

IDRAC-RESPAILLES

⫶⫶⫶ *Au Noby*

Alain FILLOS
Les Quatre Saisons, 32300 IDRAC-RESPAILLES
☎ 05 62 66 60 74 & 06 31 17 95 01
email: alain.fillos@wanadoo.fr

A new home overlooking the countryside and lake, near a farm. It has four double en suite rooms, a corner kitchen with fridge, washing machine, heating and lounge and gastronomic meals. Special prices for stays of three days or more.

Prices not confirmed for 2008   **Nearby** ⛵ 6km ♨ 25km ♬ 3km ↖ 3km
⌘ 3km 🏠 3km ⋙ 21km   **Notes** No pets   English spoken

JEGUN

⫶⫶⫶ ⫶◎⫶ **Chambre d'hôtes**

Rolande MENGELLE
32360 JEGUN
☎ 05 62 64 55 03 & 06 84 92 86 54

An old stone house which has been restored without losing any of its character. There are four upstairs bedrooms: a double room, a triple (with double canopied bed), and two family rooms each with a double bed and two singles. A fifth (grade 2) room is downstairs. All have private facilities. Guests' living room, kitchenette, meals available by arrangement.

Prices s fr €45; d fr €53; t fr €60; extra person fr €20; dinner fr €25
Nearby ⛵ 10km ♨ 15km ♬ 5km ↖ 13km Restaurant 4km ⋙ 18km
Notes No pets   Open March to October.

⫶⫶⫶ **L'Houresté**

Louis et M-Josephe CAVERZAN
32360 JEGUN
☎ 05 62 64 51 96

This is a farmhouse, in a very attractive spot, with a lake and possible fishing on-site. There are two double rooms and a family room for four, all upstairs and each with a private shower room and WC. A cot is available, and there is a sitting room with an open fireplace and books to read.

Prices s fr €30; d fr €50; t fr €78; extra person fr €16   **Nearby** ⛵ 10km
♨ 20km ♬ 0.1km ↖ 10km Restaurant 5km ⌘ 3km 🏠 2.5km ⋙ 20km
Notes Pets admitted   Open 22 March to December.

JUILLAC

⫶⫶⫶ ⫶◎⫶ **Au Château**

Yves et Hélène de RESSEGUIER
32230 JUILLAC
☎ 05 62 09 37 93 & 06 15 90 25 31
email: deresseguier@marciac.net
web: www.auchateaujuillac.com

This 18th-century monastery has a large sheltered park with flowers and century old trees and provides two doubles and a twin room in a wing adjoining the owners' home, with a day-room with fireplace and corner kitchenette. Heating, laundry service, cot and child's bed. Gastronomic meals served.

Prices s €48-€58; d €50-€60; t €65-€75; extra person fr €15; dinner fr €20   **Nearby** ⛵ 5km ♨ 10km ♬ 0.3km ↖ 5km ⌘ 5km 🏠 5km
⋙ 40km   **Notes** No pets

L'ISLE-JOURDAIN

Au Pigeonnier de Guerre

Eliane BAJON
32600 L'ISLE-JOURDAIN
☎ 05 62 07 29 17
email: eliane.bajon@free.fr
web: www.chambres-pigeonnier-gers.com

This converted cowshed adjoining the traditional house has views of the valley and provides two doubles, and a room with a double and single, all with private facilities. Groups of up to eight are received. Living room with TV and fireplace, library, terrace and outdoor furniture. Gastronomic meals and special price for stays of three nights or more.

Prices s €47-€67; d €52-€72; t €65-€87; dinner fr €20 **On Site** Spa **Nearby** 7km 4km 0.2km 3km Restaurant 3km 3km 3km 2km 2km **Notes** No pets English spoken Open 11 January to 24 December.

Chambre d'hôtes Haouré

Monique DANGLA
Chemin de Beaupuy, 32600 L'ISLE-JOURDAIN
☎ 05 62 07 06 71
email: haoure@free.fr
web: www.haoure.fr.tc

Close to Toulouse, but in the quiet of the countryside, this old farmhouse has four bedrooms adjacent to the owners' home. There is a double room, a twin, a triple with a mezzanine, and a family suite with a mezzanine and lounge area. All rooms have private shower room/WC, and there is a guests' dining room with kitchenette, available at midday.

Prices s fr €42; d €52-€54; t €64-€68; extra person fr €9; dinner fr €20 **On Site** Private **Nearby** 4km 4km 2.5km Restaurant 3km 2.5km 4km 5km **Notes** Pets admitted English spoken

Le Fiouzaire

M-Claude CHAUVIGNE
Chemin de Ninets, Route de Grenade,
32600 L'ISLE-JOURDAIN
☎ 05 62 07 18 80 & 06 63 37 55 06
email: chauvign@club-internet.fr
web: www.chambres-fiouzaire-gers.com

A farmhouse with a double room with lounge, TV and heating in the owner's house, and two doubles (one with extra single) and two rooms with double and twin beds, kitchenette, mezzanine and TV in an annexe; all have private facilities. Terrace, barbecue, shared lounge, TV, washing machine, dining corner, fireplace and pool. Specialist foie gras produced. Mountain biking, walks and cookery course. Gastronomic meals available. Reductions for stays of four nights or more.

Prices not confirmed for 2008 **On Site** Private **Nearby** 4km 4km 4km 4km 4km 3km **Notes** Pets admitted

LAAS

Marchou

Paul et Odette DUFFAR
32170 LAAS
☎ 05 62 67 57 14

A large building, once a farmhouse, with a garden full of flowers. There are four upstairs bedrooms: a double, a family room for up to four or five (plus cot), and two grade 2 doubles. All have private facilities, but the WCs for the grade 2 rooms are accessed via the landing. Terrace, awning for outdoor eating, meals by arrangement.

Prices s €35-€40; d €40-€50; t €57-€67; extra person fr €17; dinner €17-€26 **Nearby** 3km 4km 3km 10km 0.2km 4km 35km **Notes** Pets admitted

LARTIGUE

Garrigas

Marie-Claire FORGET
32450 LARTIGUE
☎ 05 62 65 42 10 05 62 65 49 25

An annexe opening out onto a large wooded garden, with flowers an garden furniture, overhanging the valley of Arratz. Two doubles and a twin room are offered, each with shower and wc (cot available), and there is a dining room and TV lounge. Hunting, walking and fishing excursions, views of the hillsides of Haut Astarac and farmhouse inn 5km away. Toulouse and Pyrénées an hour away.

Prices s fr €44; d fr €48; t fr €68 **Nearby** 20km 0.5km 18km 6km 6km 17km **Notes** Pets admitted English spoken Open 1 March to 15 November

Moulin de Mazeres

Régine BERTHEAU
32450 LARTIGUE
☎ 05 62 65 98 68 05 62 65 83 50

Four rooms in an old water-mill and lovely buildings among lawns, meadows and trees. One double, a twin and a triple and "The Owl Barn"- a double room with seating area and fireplace. All have privat facilities and heating. Pool and ping-pong available.

Prices s fr €67; d fr €74; t fr €81; dinner fr €25 **On Site** Private **Nearby** 15km 20km 12km 7km 20km **Notes** Pets admitted English spoken

LAUJUZAN

Campané

Sylvain et Chantal HOSY
32110 LAUJUZAN
☎ 05 62 09 18 05 & 06 25 27 90 54
email: hosyc@aol.com
web: www.visitorama.com/32/le-campane.html

A peaceful place with five hectares of grounds, among the Armagna vineyards. The guest accommodation is in an annexe. On the groun floor is a living room leading to a terrace and swimming pool, and one double bedroom. Upstairs are three more rooms: two doubles

nd a triple with three single beds. All have private facilities. Large
arden.

rices not confirmed for 2008　**On Site** Private ⚲　**Nearby** ⚓ 10km
18km ⚐ 3km ♨ 6km 🏠 6km ⚓ 36km　**Notes** No pets　Open 15
nuary to 15 December.

LAURAET

⊞ ⚹ Cap Vert

ierre MORARDET

eillot, 32330 LAURAET

☎ 05 62 29 51 85

web: www.capvert32.com

restored Gascon farmhouse, in a green setting of four hectares.
vo double rooms, a room with two large singles and sofa-bed, and
vo family rooms with double and twin beds, all with private facilities.
ivate living and dining rooms, large reception room in the annexe,
ool and paddling pool for kids. Museum of Armagnac and cathedral
earby.

rices s fr €56; d fr €65; t fr €80; extra person fr €21　**On Site** ♨
ivate ⚲　**Nearby** ⚓ 15km ⚡ 15km ⚐ 6km Restaurant 4km ♨ 0.5km
4km ⚓ 40km　**Notes** No pets　English spoken

⊞ ⊙ Le Fezandier

oland VAN OUDENHOVE

2330 LAURAET

☎ 05 62 29 49 82

is restored 18th-century house is in a beautiful setting, surrounded
lots of flowers and greenery. It has four upstairs triple bedrooms:
ree with double beds plus a single, and one with three single beds.
ey all have private bath/shower rooms and WCs. Accommodation
horses is available.

ices s fr €43; d fr €55; t fr €75; dinner fr €19　**On Site** ♨
earby ⚓ 5km ⚡ 15km ⚐ 5km Restaurant 2km ♨ 12km 🏠 5km
48km　**Notes** Pets admitted　English spoken

E HOUGA

⊞ ⊙ Le Glindon

mes HARDMAN

2460 LE HOUGA

☎ 05 62 08 97 61

mail: leglindon@wanadoo.fr

eb: www.leglindon.com

restored 17th-century half-timbered farmhouse, not far from the
rests of the Landes where the deer roam free. A guest entrance
ds to three double-bedded rooms, all with private bath or shower
om/WC. Guests have plenty to do here - there is a swimming
ol, as well as darts, skittles, pétanque and board games. Patio with
rniture.

ices s fr €60; d fr €60; t fr €75; dinner fr €20　**On Site** Restaurant ♨
vate ⚲　**Nearby** ⚓ 3km ⚡ 20km ⚐ 0.8km ♨ 4km 🏠 5km ⚓ 32km
tes No pets　English spoken　Open March to October.　CC

LOMBEZ

⊞ Le Parc de Pétrarque

Jean-François BECANNE

11, rue Notre Dame, 32220 LOMBEZ

☎ 05 62 62 32 70 & 06 20 51 45 20

email: jfmoi@msn.com

web: www.leparcdepetrarque.new.fr

An 18th-century mansion, just below the cathedral, in five hectares of
private riverside grounds - at one time the bishop's gardens. On the
ground floor is a triple room (double bed and a single); upstairs are
two double rooms (one at grade 2), and a family room with a double
bed and twins. Living room with books.

Prices s €48-€54; d €58-€64; t €78-€84; extra person €20
Nearby ⚓ 2km ⚡ 2km ⚐ 0.1km ⚲ 0.3km Restaurant 0.1km ♨ 0.1km
♨ 2km 🏠 0.1km ⚓ 25km　**Notes** Pets admitted　English spoken　Open
school holidays and weekends May, June and September.

MANCIET

⊞ ⊙ Domaine du Passage

Alain et Nathalie CESI

Mounissot, 32370 MANCIET

☎ 05 62 08 53 71 & 06 11 11 42 29　📄 08 72 16 04 67

email: lusitanien32@free.fr

web: http://ledomainedupassage.ifrance.com

This equestrian property has 70 hectares of grounds, some of them
forested, and a fishing lake. There are five twin-bedded rooms, all
upstairs, each with a private shower room and WC. The rooms are
bright and cheerful, with themed decorations. The living room has a
piano and books to read. Meals are available by arrangement.

Prices s fr €49; d fr €55; extra person fr €20; dinner fr €17　**On Site** ⚐
Nearby ⚓ 18km ⚡ 5km ⚲ 15km Restaurant 4km ♨ 4km ♨ 4km
🏠 4km ⚓ 50km　**Notes** No pets

MAUROUX

⊞ ⊙ *La Ferme des Etoiles*

Bruno MONFLIER

Le Corneillon, 32380 MAUROUX

☎ 05 62 06 09 76　📄 05 62 06 24 99

email: contact@fermedesetoiles.com

web: www.fermedesetoiles.com

Bruno and Betty are your hosts in this Gascon house which has been
carefully restored. One ground floor bedroom sleeping three, with
bathroom and wc; two upstairs rooms for three, with bathroom.
Communal rooms in a gîte with a theme - astronomical observation
platform, dome, planetarium, telescopes, projection room, television,
video. Woods and flower garden with swimming pool.

Prices not confirmed for 2008　**On Site** Private ⚲　**Nearby** ⚓ 15km
⚡ 15km ⚐ 4km ♨ 4km 🏠 4km ⚓ 40km　**Notes** No pets　English
spoken　Open April to 1 November

MIRADOUX

⊪ Maison Lou Casaù

A et B LANUSSE CAZALE

5 place de la halle, 32340 MIRADOUX

☎ 05 62 28 73 58

email: loucasau@wanadoo.fr

web: www.loucasau.fr.vu

A warm welcome awaits at this 18th-century property, in the heart of a small tranquil village. Elegant and spacious rooms include a double, twin and family suite with a double and three single beds, all with quality furniture and décor and private facilities. Dining room, living room, garden and terrace, pool with power jets available.

Prices s fr €65; d fr €75; t fr €97; extra person fr €26 **On Site** 🏊 Private ⚓ **Nearby** ⛷ 13km ♨ 24km ⚓ 3km Restaurant 0.2km ⚓ 0.4km Spa 17km 🏛 0.2km ⚓ 30km **Notes** No pets English spoken Open May to November

MIRANDE

⊪ ⏚ Au Président

Jacques PIQUEMIL

Route d'Auch, 32300 MIRANDE

☎ 06 10 37 28 36

email: jacques.piquemil@wanadoo.fr

web: www.chez.com/aupresident

This large renovated house opens out onto a big flower garden with views of the Pyrénées. It has two double rooms with sofa-bed, each with own access through a small garden and terrace, and a family room with mansard roof, double and twin beds. All have private facilities. There is a games room with billiards, and golf at Pallane or jazz in Marciac during the first two weeks of August. Waterpark 1km.

Prices s €45-€50; d €50-€55; t €70-€75; extra person fr €20 **Nearby** ⛷ 4km ♨ 20km ♟ 1.5km ⚓ 1.5km Restaurant 7km ⚓ 1.5km 🏛 1km ⚓ 25km **Notes** No pets English spoken CC

⊪ ⏗ La Brasserie des Arts

Hervé REYNAUD

5 Bd Centulle III, 32300 MIRANDE

☎ 06 81 02 22 44

email: reservation@brasseriedesarts.fr

web: www.brasseriedesarts.fr

Right in the centre of Mirande, in a building separate from the owners' home, this property has four sensitively decorated bedrooms. Upstairs are two double rooms and a room for four with two double beds; there is a further double room downstairs. All have private facilities. Large, private interior garden.

Prices d €60-€75; dinner fr €20 **On Site** Spa **Nearby** ⛷ 2km ♨ 15km ♟ 0.3km ⚓ 0.3km Restaurant 0.1km ⚓ 0.3km 🏛 0.3km ⚓ 20km **Notes** Pets admitted English spoken

MONFERRAN-PLAVES

⊪ Les Merisiers

Louisette LEBRUN

32260 MONFERRAN-PLAVES

☎ 05 62 66 20 90 & 05 62 61 79 00

email: augustelebrun@wanadoo.fr

At the top of a hill, this small Gascon farmhouse has a twin room and double with fold-up, opening out onto a terrace and another double room, all with private facilities. Cot and bedding available. Lounge with TV, fireplace, library, hi-fi, washing machine, heating, outdoor furniture, terrace with dining area in summer and hunting trips or foie gras courses.

Prices s fr €45; d fr €50; t fr €90 **Nearby** ⛷ 10km ♨ 10km ♟ 10km ⚓ 3km Restaurant 2km ⚓ 10km 🏛 2km ⚓ 15km **Notes** Pets admitted

MONFERRAN-SAVES

⊪ Le Meillon

Anne-Marie LANNES

32490 MONFERRAN-SAVES

☎ 05 62 07 83 34 & 06 78 78 62 02

email: lannes.anne-marie@wanadoo.fr

A farmhouse with large garden and views of the valleys, providing three doubles and one twin room with private facilities. There is a dining and living room, laundry service, pool, jacuzzi and lake fishing.

Prices s fr €50; d fr €70; extra person fr €25 **On Site** Private ⚓ **Nearby** ⛷ 7km ♨ 5km ♟ 7km Restaurant 0.5km ⚓ 7km Spa 30km 🏛 7km ⚓ 3km **Notes** No pets English spoken Open 31 January to 20 December.

MONTESQUIOU

⊪ ⏗ Le Petit Haget

F-L et J-P BRAZZALOTTO

La Ferme des Grisettes, 32320 MONTESQUIOU

☎ 06 16 58 84 40

email: jean-pierre.brazzalotto@wanadoo.fr

Jean-Pierre and France-Laure invite you to take a break on their farm. Five guest rooms in a renovated cowshed. Two ground floor rooms with separate access. Upstairs three rooms each sleep up to four. Large living room with cooking area. Try a visit to the goose farm. Washing machine (payable). Table football. Home made preserves for sale.

Prices s fr €41; d fr €48; extra person fr €15; dinner fr €17 **Nearby** ⛷ 7km ♟ 0.3km ⚓ 10km ⚓ 1km 🏛 3km ⚓ 50km **Notes** Pets admitted Open April to 15 October. CC

MIDI-PYRÉNÉES

▦ |◯| **Maison de la Porte Fortifiée**

Carsten LUTTERBACH
Au Village, 32320 MONTESQUIOU
☎ 05 62 70 97 06
email: maison@porte-fortifiee.eu
web: www.porte-fortifiee.eu

This late 18th-century house adjoins the 13th-century fortified gate in a very quiet road in the picturesque village of Montesquiou, on the route of 'Bastides and Castelnaus.' Rooms available include 'Apricot' and 'Gris-Manet' (with canopied doubles) and 'Green' and 'Blue' (twins), all with private facilities. Lounge with fireplace reserved for guests, opening onto the terrace. Table d'hôte meals available by reservation.

Prices s €60-€90; d €80-€110; dinner €29-€39   **Nearby** ♿ 6km ♨ 20km ♬ 0.4km ↘ 3km Restaurant 3km 🏊 0.5km 🏛 0.5km ⚑ 29km   **Notes** No pets English spoken

---

OLASTRON

▦ |◯| **Lou-Cantou**

ouis et Lise BENEDET
J Village, 32130 POLASTRON
☎ 05 62 62 41 71

renovated house in the heart of the village of Polastron offering he Blue Roses" (twin) and "The Thirties", "Countryside" and "At andma's" (doubles), all with shower and wc. Dining room with en fire, washing machine, meals on request. Farm produce for sale. sits to the preserve factory.

ices s fr €65; d fr €75; extra person fr €20; dinner €20-€40 **1 Site** ♿ **Nearby** ♨ 30km ♬ 5km ↘ 8km Restaurant 8km 🏛 8km 12km   **Notes** Pets admitted   Open February to November.

UYLAUSIC

▦ |◯| *Techeyre*

nnie COT
220 PUYLAUSIC
06 86 84 94 74
nail: cot@fr.fm
eb: www.cot.fr.fm

the borders of Gers, this traditionally renovated farmhouse in scon country offers three comfortable ground floor double rooms h private facilities and access. Large communal living room with meals available. Reductions after the third night and for children. as' market from October to April and museum of foie gras nearby.

ices not confirmed for 2008   **Nearby** ♿ 7km ♨ 28km ♬ 6km ↘ 6km 6km 🏛 6km ⚑ 50km   **Notes** No pets English spoken

---

OQUELAURE

▦ *En Boutan*

an et Jeanne DAUZERE
810 ROQUELAURE
05 62 65 54 66

ree hectares of parkland surround this beautiful property which ers three guest bedrooms. Upstairs are two double rooms with en

suite shower and WC; downstairs is a further (grade 2) double, where the facilities are not en suite. Living room for guests, and a games room with a billiard table. Garden with plenty of furniture.

Prices not confirmed for 2008.   **Nearby** ♿ 1km ♨ 8km. ♬ 1km ↘ 3km 🏊 3km 🏛 8km ⚑ 8km   **Notes** No pets   English spoken   Open May to 30 October.

SAMATAN

▦ ❦ |◯| **Latrillote**

Monique MORVAN
Route de Gimont, 32130 SAMATAN
☎ 05 62 62 31 17

Three guestrooms in a small farmhouse with views of the Pyrénées, 3km from Samatan. Two grade 3 double rooms and a grade 2 double, all with private facilities. Dining room, lounge, heating, covered terrace, camping on the grounds and extra children's room (two singles). Traditional Gascon cuisine. Special price for stay of three nights or more.

Prices s €32-€36; d €37-€47; dinner fr €18   **Nearby** ♿ 3km ♨ 35km ♬ 3km ↘ 3km Restaurant 3km 🏊 3km 🏛 3km ⚑ 15km   **Notes** Pets admitted   Open 7 January to 20 December.

SARRAGACHIES

▦ *La Buscasse*

Fabienne et J-Michel ABADIE
32400 SARRAGACHIES
☎ 05 62 69 76 07
email: fabienne.abadie@laposte.net
web: http://buscasse.free.fr

A beautiful 18th-century house within parkland, with magnificent views of farmland and vineyards. Three pretty en suite rooms include two doubles and a twin, and there is a dining/living room with fireplace, kitchen and washing machine. Pool, bicycles, archery, visits to wine cellars and several monuments and leisure parks nearby.

Prices not confirmed for 2008   **On Site** Private ↘   **Nearby** ♿ 15km ♬ 20km ♬ 5km 🏊 1.5km 🏛 5km ⚑ 40km   **Notes** Pets admitted English spoken

---

SCIEURAC-ET-FLOURES

▦ |◯| **Setzères**

Christine FURNEY
32230 SCIEURAC-ET-FLOURES
☎ 05 62 08 21 45
email: setzeres32@aol.com
web: www.setzeres.com

A warm welcome to this quiet and beautifully situated Gascon house is promised by your host. There are three rooms: a double, a twin and a family room, all with private baths and WCs. Lounge shared with the British owner, TV room. English style garden with panoramic views, swimming pool, croquet and table tennis. Meals by reservation and out of season only.

Prices s fr €80; d fr €110; t fr €150; dinner fr €40   **On Site** Private ↘ **Nearby** ♿ 12km ♨ 8km ♬ 5km Restaurant 5km 🏊 5km Spa 12km 🏛 5km ⚑ 50km   **Notes** No pets English spoken   Open 8 January to 17 December.

MIDI-PYRÉNÉES

SIMORRE

♦♦♦ ℮◉ **La Ferme de Marie Barrailh**

Maryse BARRAILH

Le Peydousset, 32420 SIMORRE

☎ 05 62 65 36 48 ▤ 05 62 59 27 54

email: maryse.barrailh@club-internet.fr

web: www.lafermedemariebarrailh.com

This is a large restored mansion, among the meadows on the heights of Simorre. It has three spacious guest rooms for up to three people, all including two single beds which can be zipped together. All have en suite facilities, and each room has an independent entrance. Swimming pool. Large guests' lounge, with open fire.

Prices s fr €60; d fr €70; t fr €90; extra person fr €20; dinner fr €20
On Site ♣ Private ⚘ **Nearby** ♿ 1km ♨ 16km ♪ 1km Restaurant 1km
♨ 1km Spa 50km ⌂ 1km ⋔ 50km **Notes** No pets English spoken CC

ST-CLAR

♦♦♦ **Chambre d'hôtes**

Nicole et J-François COURNOT

12 Place de la Mairie, 32380 ST-CLAR

☎ 05 62 66 47 31 ▤ 05 62 66 47 70

email: nicole.cournot@wanadoo.fr

web: www.lagarlande.com

Stone mansion house with 13th-century hall and walled garden. Rooms include a double with fold up for child and own entrance, a double with single room attached, and two twins (one for children), all with private facilities. Large lounge and shared kitchen, dining room with fireplace. Meals available on request except Tuesdays and Thursdays.

Prices s fr €49; d €57-€68; t fr €84; extra person fr €14
Nearby ♿ 15km ♨ 10km ♪ 1km ⚘ 10km Restaurant 0.5km ♨ 1km
♣ 12km ⌂ 0km ⋔ 10km **Notes** No pets English spoken Open March to 5 November.

♦♦♦ ℮◉ **Les Deux Puits**

Daniel et Rosalind LEGER

9 Av de Gascogne, 32380 ST-CLAR

☎ 06 74 06 42 52 & 05 62 66 49 04

email: deuxpuits@wanadoo.fr

web: www.deuxpuits-saintclar.com

Two minutes' walk from the picturesque village of St-Clar, a house with a large garden, a warm welcome and five bedrooms. The two ground floor doubles have garden access; upstairs you will find a twin-bedded room, a triple (double bed and a single), and a room for four (double and twins). All have private facilities. Lounge areas; meals by arrangement.

Prices s €45; d €55; t €65; extra person €10; dinner fr €22
On Site Restaurant Private ⚘ **Nearby** ♿ 10km ♨ 13km ♪ 10km
♨ 0.3km Spa 15km ⌂ 0.3km ⋔ 44km **Notes** No pets English spoken Open April to October. CC

ST-LARY

♦♦♦ ℮◉ **Le Cousteau**

Yann MALARET

32360 ST-LARY

☎ 05 62 64 53 50

web: http://aubergelecousteau.chez-alice.fr

Five guestrooms in a Gascon house with rustic furnishings, a living room, terrace, pool and heating. There are four doubles and a room for four with private facilities. At weekends, enjoy Gascon cooking and foie gras.

Prices s fr €45; d fr €50; t fr €68; dinner €20-€30 **On Site** Private ⚘
Nearby ♿ 20km ♨ 15km ♨ 15km ⌂ 6km ⋔ 14km **Notes** No pets English spoken

ST-MARTIN-D'ARMAGNAC

♦♦♦ ℮◉ *Au Peyré*

Francis et Colette LAURENT

Castaignet, 32110 ST-MARTIN-D'ARMAGNAC

☎ 05 62 09 18 64 & 06 08 89 21 45

email: fclaurent@tiscali.fr

This house, on a mixed farming/wine-growing property, has been full restored in traditional style. On the ground floor is a room with two double beds, and disabled access; upstairs are three more rooms for four, one with a double bed and two singles, the others each with two double beds. All have private facilities. Lounge; swimming pool under construction.

Prices not confirmed for 2008 **On Site** Private ⚘ **Nearby** ♿ 20km
♨ 30km ♪ 0.1km ♨ 2km ⌂ 7km ⋔ 25km **Notes** No pets English spoken

ST-MAUR

♦♦♦ **Domaine de Loran**

Jean et Marie NEDELLEC

32300 ST-MAUR

☎ 05 62 66 51 55 ▤ 05 62 66 78 58

A large home in beautiful parkland has two family rooms with double and twin beds and two doubles, each with private facilities. Extra heating and cot available. Living room, games room with billiards and ping-pong, and library.

Prices s fr €40; d €50-€55; t fr €70; extra person fr €15 **Nearby** ♿ 3k
♨ 12km ♪ 0.5km ⚘ 3km Restaurant 1km ♨ 3km ⌂ 3km ⋔ 28km
Notes Pets admitted

⫙ Noailles

Marthe SABATHIER
32300 ST-MAUR
☎ 05 62 67 57 98 ▤ 05 62 67 64 60

Three guest rooms in the owners' house: a double, a twin and a family room with two double beds, all with private facilities. There is a dining room, living room, corner kitchen, shaded walled garden and barbecue. Walks and working farm on site.

Prices s fr €38; d fr €42; t fr €65; extra person fr €18 **Nearby** ⛷ 4km ≈ 5km ♠ 2km ↖ 7km ◷ 1km ⌂ 7km ⋒ 32km **Notes** Pets admitted

---

ST-ORENS

⫙ Au Pichet

Christiane COURTOIS
32120 ST-ORENS
☎ 05 62 06 72 47
email: jacourt@wanadoo.fr
web: www.aupichet.com

A restored former farmhouse surrounded by woods and meadows, complete with a medieval garden and a kitchen garden maze. The welcome is friendly; there are views towards the Pyrénées, and animals at the property include a donkey, Natisse. There are three first floor rooms, a double and two twins, all with private bath or shower room and WC. Pets by arrangement only.

Prices s fr €40; d fr €50; extra person fr €25 **Nearby** ⛷ 6km ⤳ 28km ≈ 5km ↖ 4.5km Restaurant 4km ⌂ 4.5km ⋒ 55km **Notes** Pets admitted English spoken

---

ST-ORENS-POUY-PETIT

⫙ ⲓ◎ι Le Tuco

Marie-France SARHAN
32100 ST-ORENS-POUY-PETIT
☎ 05 62 28 39 50
email: le.tuco@wanadoo.fr
web: http://letuco.free.fr

In the heart of Gers, the land of Armagnac and foie gras, Marie-France and Gerard are happy to welcome you to their 18th-century residence. The stone buildings, which were entirely restored in 2004, are set on a lovely hill with panoramic views of their 12-hectare property. The five luxurious bedrooms, table d'hôte, swimming pool and park are all unforgettable.

Prices not confirmed for 2008 **On Site** Private ↖ **Nearby** ⛷ 10km ⤳ 25km ♠ 0.2km ◷ 6km ⌂ 6km ⋒ 40km **Notes** No pets Open April to 2 November.

ST-PUY

⫙ ⲓ◎ι La Lumiane

Alain et Gisèle EMAN
32310 ST-PUY
☎ 05 62 28 95 95 ▤ 05 62 28 59 67
email: info@lalumiane.com
web: www.lalumiane.com

In the heart of a small village in Gascony, the hosts at this 17th-century house promise a warm welcome. There are four bedrooms, two of them in a separate wing of the house: two doubles, a twin-bedded room with a bed-settee, and a family room with two doubles. They are all very well furnished, and have private bathrooms and WCs. Terrace, swimming pool.

Prices s €41-€57; d €49-€65; extra person fr €15; dinner fr €21 **On Site** Private ↖ **Nearby** ⛷ 5km ⤳ 35km ♠ 2km Restaurant 0.1km ◷ 0.1km ⌂ 10km ⋒ 35km **Notes** No pets English spoken

---

STE-MERE

⫙ ⲓ◎ι Au Chien Pèlerin

Pascale HENNEBOIS
Au village, 32700 STE-MERE
☎ 05 62 68 95 33
email: auchienpelerin@wanadoo.fr
web: http://auchienpelerin.monsite.orange.fr

Ideal for a stopover or a longer stay, this village house sits quietly in the Gascony countryside. There is a triple room (double bed and a single), a twin-bedded room with a single sofa bed, and a double room. All have private bath or shower room, and a cot is available.

Prices s fr €55; d fr €60; t fr €75; dinner fr €18 **Nearby** ⛷ 17km ⤳ 25km ♠ 8km ↖ 10km Restaurant 5km ◷ 0.5km ⌂ 0.5km ⋒ 35km **Notes** Pets admitted English spoken Open April to 12 November, 21-26 December & 28 December to 2 January.

TERMES-D'ARMAGNAC

₩ ❤ ꙰ *Domaine de Labarthe*

C et M LARDENOIS

32400 TERMES-D'ARMAGNAC

☎ 05 62 69 24 97 & 05 62 61 79 00 ▤ 05 62 69 24 97

In the valley of Adour, once part of the Tour de Termes d'Armagnac, this farm has three double rooms, two with extra single beds, with own facilities. There are two seating areas and living and dining rooms. The garden is surrounded by fish ponds, ancient moats and fortresses. Foie gras made on the farm.

Prices not confirmed for 2008 **Nearby** ⛳ 20km ✎ 1.5km ⚐ 7km ≋ 7km ⌂ 7km ⛟ 50km **Notes** No pets

₩ ꙰ Le Pouy

Robert et Cathy ROUCHON

32400 TERMES-D'ARMAGNAC

☎ 05 62 69 27 32

email: Cathy.Rouchon@wanadoo.fr

web: www.lepouy.com

This recently restored property, with wonderful views towards the Pyrénées, has three guest rooms on the first floor of the owners' house. Two of the rooms have double beds, and the other has twin beds. Each room has a private bathroom and WC. Antique furniture and high standard of decoration. Meals by arrangement, with local specialities. Horse box available.

Prices s €70-€80; d €75-€85; t fr €115; dinner €20-€30 **Nearby** ⛳ 20km ♨ 30km ✎ 14km ⚐ 6km Restaurant 6km ≋ 7km ⌂ 7km **Notes** No pets English spoken Open March to December.

TERRAUBE

₩ ꙰ ⚐ Maison Ardure

Michel GHYS

32700 TERRAUBE

☎ 05 62 68 59 56 ▤ 05 62 68 97 61

email: reservations@ardure.fr

web: www.ardure.fr

A restored wing of the owners' house is the location for these four rooms. There is a ground floor double, with independent access, suitable for disabled guests. Upstairs are three rooms: a double, a room with a double bed and a single, and a split level family room with double bed and two singles. All rooms have private facilities. Guests' lounge; wooded grounds.

Prices s €65-€75; d €75-€85; extra person fr €25; dinner fr €25 **On Site** ☂ Private ⚐ **Nearby** ⛳ 18km ♨ 15km ✎ 8km Restaurant 2km ≋ 1km ⌂ 6km ⛟ 30km **Notes** Pets admitted English spoken Open February to November & Xmas. CC

VALENCE-SUR-BAÏSE

₩ ꙰ La Maison des Lys

Keith SWIFT

35 Grande Rue, 32310 VALENCE-SUR-BAÏSE

☎ 05 62 28 92 79 & 06 85 13 07 51 ▤ 05 62 28 96 77

email: info@lamaisondeslys.com

web: www.lamaisondeslys.com

An old merchant's house dating back to 1817, one of three similar houses in this village. There are three spacious first floor rooms: a double room, a twin-bedded room, and a double-bedded suite. All have private bath or shower room and WC. Attractive gardens; summer kitchen. Meals are available by arrangement.

Prices s €55-€85; d €60-€90; dinner fr €25 **Nearby** ⛳ 2km ♨ 26km ✎ 1km ⚐ 8km ≋ 0.5km ⌂ 0.2km ⛟ 35km **Notes** No pets English spoken Open February to November.

VERGOIGNAN

₩ Lahitte

P-J LEEMAN et A VAN DER KROGT

32720 VERGOIGNAN

☎ 05 62 08 47 89

email: info@chateaudelahitte.com

web: www.chateaudelahitte.com

Extensive grounds with views towards the Pyrénées provide a fine setting for this house. There are three twin-bedded rooms, all upstairs. Each has a private bath or shower room and WC. Lounge with books and TV; swimming pool, sauna and fitness room.

Prices s fr €80; d fr €90 **On Site** Private ⚐ **Nearby** ⛳ 2km ♨ 18km ✎ 2km Restaurant 4km ≋ 2km ☗ 4km ⌂ 2km ⛟ 35km **Notes** No pets English spoken

HAUTE-GARONNE

ANTIGNAC

⫲⫲ **Suberbielo**

M CALVET et P JEAN
Av de Montréjeau, 31110 ANTIGNAC
☎ 05 61 94 37 03
email: contact@suberbielo.com
web: www.suberbielo.com

At Suberbielo, Michelle, Philippe and their children will welcome you to their 19th-century home in a quiet village, a stone's throw from Luchon with its thermal springs, walking tracks, spas. On the ground floor is the dining room where regional family cuisine is occasionally served; a communal living room with open fire, library, video recorder, board games; one bedroom with mezzanine sleeping three; and one bedroom sleeping four. Upstairs is a double room and an alcove room with bunks.

Prices s €52; d €60; t €80; extra person €20 **On Site** Private ↖
Nearby ⚲ 1.5km ⬇ 4km ✎ 0.5km Restaurant 3.5km ❅ 4km ⌇ 5km
Spa 5km ⌇ 4km ⬚ 2km ⫴ 3km **Notes** No pets English spoken Open 26 December to 10 October.

AUTERIVE

⫲⫲ ◎ **La Maison de Pierrette**

Patrice BOURDEAU
Rue Michelet, Route de Cintegabelle, 31190 AUTERIVE
☎ 05 61 50 81 31 & 06 08 01 28 98
email: maisondepierrette@cegetel.net
web: http://m.d.p.perso.cegetel.net

Guestrooms in a small suburban tavern, restored by the hosts. Dining room, heating, swimming pool, parking and shaded garden with lovely views of the countryside. The three main rooms have private facilities and can be reached via an external staircase.

Prices s fr €46; d fr €49; t fr €60; extra person fr €10; dinner fr €20
On Site Restaurant Private ↖ **Nearby** ❅ 4km ✎ 15km ⌇ 1.5km
⌇ 1.5km ⬚ 1km ⫴ 1.8km **Notes** No pets English spoken

⫲⫲ **La Manufacture**

Valérie BALANSA
2 Rue des Docteurs Basset, 31190 AUTERIVE
☎ 05 61 50 08 50 & 06 73 01 02 82
email: manufacture@manufacture-royale.net
web: www.manufacture-royale.net

Bedrooms in an 18th century building that once manufactured sheets for royalty. There is a twin room, two doubles, a triple and a room with a double and single bed, all with bathroom facilities (two with TV points). Dining room, another room with a stove and a TV shared with the hosts. Garden, courtyard, park, swimming pool, bikes, porch, table tennis, games and parking are all available.

Prices s €55-€60; d €75-€80; t €95-€105; extra person €20-€25
On Site ✎ ⌇ Private ↖ **Nearby** ⬇ 30km ⌇ 0.5km ⬚ 0.1km
⫴ 0.5km **Notes** No pets English spoken Open April to October.

AUZAS

⫲⫲ *Chambre d'hôtes*

Angeline SCHMITT
31360 AUZAS
☎ 05 61 90 23 61

Situated on a working farm, four bedrooms are available, one with a double bed and two singles and each with private facilities. Large room with fireplace and TV reserved for guests, swimming pool. Visit the farm, take part in breadmaking and buy farm produce.

Prices not confirmed for 2008 **On Site** Private ↖ **Nearby** ⌇ 5km
✎ 1km ⌇ 1km ⬚ 5km ⫴ 10km **Notes** Pets admitted

AVIGNONET-LAURAGAIS

⫲⫲ ◎ **Péniche Isatis**

M MANDRILE et S DAVIDENKO
Port Lauragais, 31290 AVIGNONET-LAURAGAIS
☎ 06 86 40 00 75
email: peniche-isatis@freesurf.fr

This chambre d'hôtes is a barge on the Canal du Midi. It sleeps six guests in three air-conditioned cabins, all of them with private facilities. One has a double bed; the rest are singles. There is a lounge area, bar and dining room. The prices given apply when the boat is moored; for cruise prices, please contact the owners.

Prices s €70-€80; d €70-€80; t €70-€80; dinner fr €25 **On Site** ✎
Nearby ⚲ 20km ↖ 10km Restaurant 3km ⌇ 10km ⌇ 3km ⬚ 2km
⫴ 2km **Notes** Pets admitted English spoken Open March to December.

AYGUESVIVES

⫲⫲ ⬅ **La Pradasse**

Christine ANTOINE
39 Chemin de Toulouse, 31450 AYGUESVIVES
☎ 05 61 81 55 96 & 06 19 21 36 71 ▤ 05 61 81 89 76
email: contact@lapradasse.com
web: www.lapradasse.com

This delightful place, not far from the Canal du Midi, offers a new perspective on wrought-iron and glasswork, thanks to the interests of its owner. It offers five guest rooms, four doubles and a twin, all with a private bath or shower room and WC. There is a vast lounge with an enormous fireplace and an open view over the park and lake.

Prices s fr €68; d fr €88; extra person fr €25 **On Site** ⌇ Private ↖
Nearby ⚲ 5km ✎ 15km ✎ 10km Restaurant 3km ⌇ 1km Spa 20km
⬚ 1km ⫴ 3km **Notes** No pets English spoken

MIDI-PYRÉNÉES

AZAS

♦♦♦ En Tristan

Gérard et Chantal ZABE

31380 AZAS

☎ 05 61 84 94 88 🗎 05 61 84 94 88

email: en.tristan@free.fr

web: http://en.tristan.free.fr

An old restored farm, 2 km from the village in the direction of Garrigues. Large lounge with fireplace and TV, reading room, lounge area for guests and four bedrooms with private facilities (a twin and three triples). Garden, courtyard, barbecue, games area and patio.

Prices s €40-€45; d €45-€50; t €55-€60 **Nearby** ⛷ 5km ⚓ 7km ⚓ 3km ⚓ 5km ⚓ 8km ⚓ 8km **Notes** No pets English spoken

BAGNERES-DE-LUCHON

♦♦♦♦ ⚲ Pavillon Sévigné

Catherine SEITER

2 Av Jacques Barrau, 31110 BAGNERES-DE-LUCHON

☎ 05 61 79 31 50 & 06 79 47 59 49

email: seiter@pavillonsevigne.com

web: www.pavillonsevigne.com

A 19th century manor house offering refined and luxurious accommodation. The five double rooms, named after aristocratic French ladies, all have private bath or power shower/WC. Close to Luchon spa, and hiking, skiing, golf and casino are all close by. Living room opening on to a terrace and park.

Prices s fr €80; d fr €90; t fr €120; extra person fr €30; dinner fr €25 **Nearby** ⛷ 1.5km ⚓ 0.5km ⚓ 0.5km Restaurant 0.5km ⚓ 0.5km ⚓ 0.5km ⚓ 0.5km ⚓ 1km **Notes** No pets English spoken

♦♦♦ ⚲ Villa Florida

Daniel et Nicole ISSANCHOU

21, Cours des Quinconces,

31110 BAGNERES-DE-LUCHON

☎ 05 61 79 77 42 & 06 11 48 56 16

email: contact@villaflorida-luchon.net

web: www.villaflorida-luchon.net

This house has a remarkable location opposite the spa in Luchon, and just a few steps from the town centre shops. There are three bedrooms, all upstairs: a twin-bedded room (the beds can be linked);

a room with a double bed and a single, and a room with a double bed and a cot. All have en suite facilities.

Prices s fr €65; d fr €75; t fr €95; dinner fr €25 **Nearby** ⛷ 2km ⚓ 1.5km ⚓ 1km ⚓ 0.2km Restaurant 0.2km ⚓ 0.5km ⚓ 0.5km ⚓ 0.1km ⚓ 2km **Notes** No pets English spoken Open 10 December to 20 October.

BARBAZAN

♦♦♦ ⚲ Le Beau Site

Johnny et Brigitte MARGERIE

Route de Luscan, 31510 BARBAZAN

☎ 06 20 44 80 72

email: j.margerie@wanadoo.fr

web: www.aubeausite.com

Once a hotel, this place is now a pleasant rural chambre d'hôtes. There are three family rooms for four or five people, and a double room. All have en suite shower room and WC. Open garden with space for parking, and many good walks in the area.

Prices not confirmed for 2008 **Nearby** ⛷ 4km ⚓ 8km ⚓ 1km ⚓ 8km ⚓ 30km ⚓ 1km ⚓ 1.5km ⚓ 8km **Notes** No pets English spoken

BOULOGNE-SUR-GESSE

♦♦♦ ⚲ L'Ampelopse

Anne POVEDA

17, Place de la Mairie, 31350 BOULOGNE-SUR-GESSE

☎ 05 61 95 20 60 & 06 14 90 10 31 🗎 05 61 95 20 60

email: jcapoveda@wanadoo.fr

web: www.ampelopse.com

This beautiful house, on the main square of Boulogne-sur-Gesse, makes an ideal base for exploring this area, with its hilly countryside and rich history. Four very attractive bedrooms, three doubles and a twin-bedded room, all have private bath or shower room and WC. Meals are available by arrangement; attractive garden with furniture. Closed 19 to 27 January and last week of August.

Prices s €41-€51; d €52-€62; t fr €70; extra person fr €10; dinner fr €20 **On Site** ⚓ Restaurant **Nearby** ⛷ 12km ⚓ 18km ⚓ 0.5km ⚓ 0.5km ⚓ 35km **Notes** No pets English spoken

BUZET-SUR-TARN

♦♦♦ La Parro

Claire et Antoine STEFFAN

591, Chemin Parro, 31660 BUZET-SUR-TARN

☎ 05 61 84 06 33 🗎 05 61 84 06 33

email: steffan@laparro.com

This peacefully situated 18th-century farmhouse, surrounded by trees, has three guest bedrooms. There are two doubles, one on the ground floor, and a family room with a double and twin beds. They all have private bath/shower room and WC. Lounge, and small sitting room; table tennis, above-ground swimming pool, parking space.

Prices not confirmed for 2008 **On Site** Private ⚓ **Nearby** ⛷ 6km ⚓ 0.5km ⚓ 1km ⚓ 0.5km ⚓ 3km ⚓ 3km **Notes** No pets

CABANAC-SEGUENVILLE

ⅲ ⅠOⅠ Château de Séguenville

Jean-Paul et Marie LARENG
31480 CABANAC-SEGUENVILLE
☎ 05 62 13 42 67 📄 05 62 13 42 68
email: info@chateau-de-seguenville.com
web: www.chateau-de-seguenville.com

Guestrooms full of character, situated in a tranquil park with hundred-year-old trees, at the heart of the Gascony region. The ground floor is solely for the use of guests and has a TV room, a large room with fireplace, dining room and patio. There is a suite of three non-smoking double bedrooms, all en suite.

Prices s €100-€105; d €120-€125; t €130-€135; dinner fr €25
On Site ❧ Private ↖ **Nearby** ⛷ 12km ♨ 24km ⌀ 5km
Restaurant 1km ⇲ 7km 🛍 12km ⋙ 50km **Notes** No pets English spoken Open 15 January to 15 December.

CASTAGNAC

ⅲ La Plaine

Nicole RIVIERE
Vallee de la Leze, 31310 CASTAGNAC
☎ 05 61 90 21 90
web: www.leguideariege.com/aubergeschambresdhotes/laplaine.htm

Among the hills of Volvestre, this old farmhouse has a panoramic view over villages, fields, woods and lakes. There are three non-smoking rooms for two to four people, with private showers/WCs. Lounge with open fire, kitchen with small eating area.

Prices s fr €39; d fr €46; t fr €60 **On Site** ❧ **Nearby** ⛷ 6km ♨ 25km
⌀ 3km Restaurant 4km ⇲ 3km 🛍 3km ⋙ 16km **Notes** No pets

CASTELNAU-D'ESTRETEFONDS

ⅲ Domaine de Saint-Guilhem

Esméralda et Philippe LADUGUIE
1619 Chemin de St-Guilhem,
31620 CASTELNAU-D'ESTRETEFONDS
☎ 05 61 82 12 09 📄 05 61 82 65 59

Four guestrooms in a wine-maker's residence, situated 2.5km from the village. There are two triple bedrooms (one with cot) and two twins, all non-smoking with independent access, private facilities and a fireplace. There is a lounge with a TV and large wooded area with outdoor swimming pool.

Prices s €44-€50; d €50-€58; t €61-€69; extra person fr €11 **On Site** ❧
Private ↖ **Nearby** ⛷ 7km ♨ 15km ⌀ 12km Restaurant 3km ⇲ 2.5km
🛍 2.5km ⋙ 8km **Notes** No pets English spoken

CAZARIL-TAMBOURES

ⅲ ⅠOⅠ *Aux Jardins de Tambourès*

Luc et Bernadette DRECHSEL
31580 CAZARIL-TAMBOURES
☎ 05 61 94 12 97
email: lucdrechsel@wanadoo.fr
web: www.aujardindetamboures.com

Three double rooms and a triple, all with private shower/WC, have been created in an outbuilding of this impressive 19th-century grange. There is a dining room and huge living room with open fire, shared with your hosts, and a swimming pool is planned. Gourmet breakfasts, and delicious evening meals.

Prices not confirmed for 2008 **Nearby** ⛷ 12km ♨ 12km ⌀ 5km
↖ 12km ⚓ 45km ⥥ 4km 🛍 12km ⋙ 12km **Notes** No pets

CORNEBARRIEU

ⅲ *Pontié*

Gilles et Chantal de FALETANS
51 Route de Bouconne, 31700 CORNEBARRIEU
☎ 05 61 85 20 05 📄 05 61 85 54 09
web: www.chateau-de-pontie.com

In its vast wooded grounds on a working farm not far from Toulouse, this large red brick house has an exceptional location. All of the bedrooms are upstairs - a double and two twins, all with private facilities. Downstairs there are two lounges for guests' use. Swimming pool; walks in the grounds.

Prices not confirmed for 2008 **On Site** ↗ Private ↖ **Nearby** ⛷ 10km
♨ 6km ⇲ 5km 🛍 1km ⋙ 6km **Notes** No pets

FIGAROL

ⅲ ⅠOⅠ Chourbaou

Neil et Jean ADAMSON
31260 FIGAROL
☎ 05 61 98 25 54 📄 05 61 98 25 54
email: info@figarolgites.com
web: www.figarolgites.com

Full of character, this old renovated farm dates from 1878, and has a panoramic view over the Pyrénées. There is a double room, two twins and a family suite, all with bathroom facilities. Dining room with fireplace and TV area, enclosed flowery, shaded garden for picnics, and parking.

Prices s €40-€47; d €45-€55; t fr €60; dinner fr €18 **Nearby** ⛷ 7km
♨ 30km ⌀ 2km ↖ 7km ⚓ 30km ⥥ 4km 🛍 5km ⋙ 10km
Notes No pets English spoken

FRONTIGNAN-DE-COMMINGES

⫴ ΙΟΙ *Relais des Frontignes*

Yann DE BRUYCKER

31510 FRONTIGNAN-DE-COMMINGES

☎ 05 61 79 61 67 & 06 76 51 23 90

email: relaisdesfrontignes@free.fr

web: www.relaisdesfrontignes.com

In the heart of Frontignes in a pretty Pyrenean village, the owners of this house offer a room with a double and two singles, one with four singles, the African and Chinese rooms with double beds and the Polynesian room with double and single. Heating, dining room, lounge and games room. Enjoy walks in the large park and programmes of activities to explore the region.

Prices not confirmed for 2008 **Nearby** ⚑ 10km ⚓ 14km ⚲ 1km ⚹ 6km ⚋ 18km ⚑ 1km 🏠 6km ⚌ 14km **Notes** No pets English spoken

GRENADE

⫴⫴ Cayssel

Doris SCHAUMANN

31330 GRENADE

☎ 05 61 82 72 68 & 06 13 16 55 58

A large 19th-century house set in a marvellous park, providing an ideal location for relaxation and visiting the Midi Toulousain and nearby Toulouse. Rooms are full of character and include Trésor (double and single beds), Sublime (double) and Violette (family room sleeping four), each with private facilities. Dining room with fireplace, lounge with TV opening onto terraces and park with swimming pool.

Prices s fr €58-€62; d €63-€68; t €88-€93; extra person fr €25 **On Site** Private ⚹ **Nearby** ⚑ 5km ⚓ 16km ⚲ 4km ⚑ 4km 🏠 4km ⚌ 7km **Notes** No pets English spoken

JUZET-DE-LUCHON

⫴ ΙΟΙ Le Poujastou

Elodie et Thierry COTTEREAU

Rue du Sabotier, 31110 JUZET-DE-LUCHON

☎ 05 61 94 32 88 & 06 88 30 00 20

email: info@lepoujastou.com

web: http://lepoujastou.com

This renovated former café, near Luchon, provides two single rooms, two triples and a room with four single beds, all with private facilities. Dining room and room with a fireplace on the ground floor, enclosed garden and garage.

Prices s fr €40; d fr €49; t fr €67; extra person fr €22; dinner fr €18 **Nearby** ⚑ 2km ⚓ 3km ⚲ 2km ⚹ 2km ⚋ 2km ⚑ 2km 🏠 2km ⚌ 2km **Notes** No pets English spoken

LATOUR

⫴ ΙΟΙ Primoulas

Marie-Paule BELVISO

31310 LATOUR

☎ 05 61 97 46 87 & 06 84 19 42 64 📄 05 61 90 33 57

email: namaste@primoulas.com

web: www.primoulas.com

A guesthouse offering accommodation in four triple rooms, one with access to the garden, and all with private facilities. Large communal dining room with huge fireplace, TV, video and hi-fi. The garden has beautiful views over the Pyrénées and dance, yoga and pottery classes are available.

Prices s fr €40; d fr €50; t fr €70; dinner fr €20 **On Site** ⚹ Private ⚹ **Nearby** ⚑ 12km ⚓ 50km ⚲ 7km Restaurant 5km ⚑ 6km 🏠 7km ⚌ 20km **Notes** Pets admitted English spoken CC

LAVALETTE

⫴ ΙΟΙ *La Poterie*

J-L THIBAUD et J-P DEPONT

Route de Lavaur, D112, 31590 LAVALETTE

☎ 05 61 84 34 49 📄 05 61 84 99 19

email: lapoterie@free.fr

web: http://lapoterie.free.fr

This former pottery has been completely restored and offers four comfortable guest rooms with access to the garden: two twins, a double and a room with a double and two single beds, all with private facilities. Dining room with fireplace and kitchen.

Prices not confirmed for 2008 **Nearby** ⚑ 2km ⚓ 10km ⚲ 5km ⚹ 5km ⚑ 1km 🏠 5km ⚌ 5km **Notes** No pets English spoken

LES VARENNES

⫴⫴ ΙΟΙ Château des Varennes

Béatrice et Jacques MERICQ

31450 LES VARENNES

☎ 05 61 81 69 24 📄 05 61 81 69 24

email: j.mericq@wanadoo.fr

web: www.chateaudesvarennes.com

Built in the 16th century using pink bricks, the Château des Varennes stands in a park with ancient trees, and gives you a choice of four guest rooms with superb views over the hills. On the ground floor are an immense entrance hall, sitting room, dining room with open fire (shared with the owners), library, billiard room, all for guests to use. Choose from the Bedouin room (ground floor double); the Tower room (double, with child's bed in adjoining room); the Bird room and the Newlyweds room (both doubles). All have private bathrooms. Stroll in the park or float in the pool.

Prices s fr €95-€125; d €105-€140; dinner fr €35 **On Site** Private ⚹ **Nearby** ⚑ 0.2km ⚓ 20km ⚲ 10km Restaurant 2km ⚑ 0.2km Spa 22km ⚌ 22km **Notes** Pets admitted English spoken Open March to October. CC

MOLAS

⁂ ⁍◎⁍ *Les Figuiers*

Annick VALENTIN

31230 MOLAS

☎ 05 61 94 15 46 & 06 83 49 07 12

email: annick@lesfiguiers.net

web: http://lesfiguiers.net

At Les Figuiers you will be received as a friend. The house is on the hillside in the village of Molas with a large garden facing the Pyrénées. There are three big guest rooms: 'Félicia' sleeps three, with private bathroom; 'Cornelia' is a double, with shower; 'Francesca' is a family room for up to five, with a shower. Central heating. Guests' sitting room with television and library. Meals by arrangement. Parking area.

Prices not confirmed for 2008 **Nearby** ⚓ 15km ⚓ 20km ⚐ 5km ⚓ 5km ⚓ 5km ⚓ 5km ⚓ 45km **Notes** No pets English spoken

MONS

⁂ **Domaine de Gilède**

Michel LAFFONT

Route de Drémil, 31280 MONS

☎ 05 61 83 92 32 & 06 11 88 65 74 ▤ 05 61 83 92 32

email: gilede@free.fr

web: http://chambreshotesgilede.free.fr

An 18th-century manor house which makes an agreeable stopover in countryside typical of the area around Toulouse. Downstairs are two day rooms with internet access; one of them leads onto a terrace, with the garden and swimming pool beyond. Upstairs are two double bedrooms and a triple (double bed and a single), all with shower room/WC.

Prices s €45-€55; d €50-€60; t fr €75; extra person fr €20 **On Site** ⚐ Private ⚓ **Nearby** ⚓ 1km ⚓ 5km ⚐ 1km ⚓ 1km ⚓ 1km ⚓ 15km **Notes** No pets English spoken

MONTAUBAN-DE-LUCHON

⁂ ⁍◎⁍ **Papilio**

Hermione OOSTRA

Route de Subercarrère, 31110 MONTAUBAN-DE-LUCHON

☎ 05 61 89 29 82 & 06 99 27 22 65

email: rolfemarni@hotmail.com

web: www.papilio-luchon.com

Not far from Luchon, this pretty house with its blue shutters has three guest rooms, all upstairs. There is a double room, a family room with twin beds (which can be linked) plus bunks, and a room with three single beds. All have en suite bathrooms/WCs. Enclosed garden with games for children.

Prices s fr €44; d fr €54; t fr €68; extra person fr €16; dinner €6-€18 **Nearby** ⚓ 1km ⚓ 1km ⚐ 1km ⚓ 1km Restaurant 1km ⚓ 1km ⚓ 0.5km ⚓ 1km ⚓ 1km ⚓ 1km **Notes** No pets English spoken

MONTBERAUD

⁂ ⁍◎⁍ ♿ **Toubies**

Birgit ALBRECHT

31220 MONTBERAUD

☎ 05 61 98 14 35

An isolated renovated old farm has lovely views over the Pyrénées and offers rooms arranged around a patio area, including two double rooms and a room with a double and two singles, all with private facilities. There is a communal lounge with fireplace, kitchenette, table tennis and games available.

Prices s fr €32; d fr €44; dinner fr €17 **On Site** Private ⚓ **Nearby** ⚓ 6km ⚓ 30km ⚐ 5km Restaurant 5km ⚓ 5km ⚓ 25km ⚓ 5km ⚓ 12km **Notes** Pets admitted English spoken

MONTBRUN-BOCAGE

⁂ ⁍◎⁍ **Pave**

Josette PARINAUD

31310 MONTBRUN-BOCAGE

☎ 05 61 98 11 25

A small-enclosed farm in warm surroundings, providing three double rooms and two triples, each with private facilities. There is a dining room with fireplace, where the evening meals are served around the family table.

Prices s fr €44; d fr €49; t fr €69; dinner fr €20 **Nearby** ⚓ 15km ⚓ 30km ⚐ 1km ⚓ 20km Restaurant 5km ⚓ 5km ⚓ 5km ⚓ 20km **Notes** No pets English spoken

MONTESQUIEU-LAURAGAIS

⁂ **La Maison d'Hôtes de Bigot**

Irène et Joseph PINEL

Bigot, 31450 MONTESQUIEU-LAURAGAIS

☎ 05 61 27 02 83 ▤ 05 61 27 02 83

email: joseph.pinel@libertysurf.fr

web: http://hotebigot.chez-alice.fr

An entirely renovated farm, surrounded by a garden in flowery countryside. There is a double room, a room with double and single bed, plus three rooms with three double beds and two singles, all with separate facilities. Large reception room with kitchen, room with TV and bookcase, lawn, covered patio and car shelter. Patchwork demonstrations.

Prices s €45-€55; d €50-€65; t €70-€80; extra person €15-€20 **On Site** Private ⚓ **Nearby** ⚓ 7km ⚓ 20km ⚐ 0.1km ⚓ 1km ⚓ 6km ⚓ 25km **Notes** No pets English spoken

MONTESQUIEU-VOLVESTRE

▦ ⦿ *La Halte du Temps*

Marie-Andrée GARCIN

72 Rue Mage, 31310 MONTESQUIEU-VOLVESTRE

☎ 05 61 97 56 10 ▤ 05 61 90 49 03

email: lahaltedutemps@free.fr

A 17th century building with access through a charming central courtyard. A Louis XIII staircase leads to the bedrooms, which include three double rooms, a single and triple with private facilities and fireplace for each. Dining room with large fireplace, music room, patio and enclosed garden.

Prices not confirmed for 2008 **On Site** Private ↖ **Nearby** ⚓ 5km ⚓ 15km ⚑ 0.5km ⚒ 0.5km ⚙ 11km **Notes** Pets admitted English spoken

▦ *Testory*

S CASTERAN et G ZIPSTEIN

31310 MONTESQUIEU-VOLVESTRE

☎ 06 98 80 18 98

email: zipstein@wanadoo.fr

The restoration of this old farmhouse, with its magnificent views towards the Pyrénées, has given it a modern, spacious feel. There are four guest rooms: a double, a twin and two triples, all with private bath or shower room and WC. There is a large lounge, with open fire and books. Outside are two terraces and a swimming pool.

Prices not confirmed for 2008 **On Site** Private ↖ **Nearby** ⚓ 7km ⚐ 7km ⚒ 2.5km ⚑ 2.5km ⚙ 10km **Notes** No pets English spoken

RAMONVILLE-SAINT-AGNE

▦ ⦿ **Péniche Soleïado**

M VERGEZ et P PEYRAMAURE

Pont de Mange-Pommes,

31520 RAMONVILLE-SAINT-AGNE

☎ 06 86 27 83 19

email: peniche.soleiado@cegetel.net

Close to Toulouse, this property offers a double room and two nearby cabins with double beds, each with private facilities, heating and air-conditioning (extra single cabin possible). Large communal living room, terrace overlooking the bridge. No animals allowed. Relax on the quay or a cruise depending on the season and discover life on board a barge on the Canal du Midi.

Prices d €80-€90; dinner fr €30 **On Site** ⚐ ⚜ **Nearby** ⚓ 7km ↖ 1km ⚒ 1km ⚑ 1km ⚙ 1.5km **Notes** No pets English spoken

ST-ELIX-LE-CHÂTEAU

▦ **Domaine des Marcoujans**

Stéphane CADIO

Route de Lafitte, 31430 ST-ELIX-LE-CHATEAU

☎ 05 61 87 19 76 ▤ 05 61 87 19 76

email: marcoujans@orange.fr

web: http://domaine-marcoujans.com

This old wine-growing property stands in an historic village, between Toulouse and St-Gaudens. It has four guest rooms: a double, two with two double beds, and one with a double bed plus a large single. All rooms have private bath or shower room and WC. Lounge with books; pleasantly laid-out grounds behind the house. Function room for up to 150 guests can be hired.

Prices not confirmed for 2008 **On Site** Private ↖ **Nearby** ⚓ 8km ⚐ 4km ⚒ 0.5km ⚑ 0.5km ⚙ 8km **Notes** No pets English spoken

ST-FRAJOU

▦ ⦿ **Moulères**

Chantal BUTERY

Route des Crêtes, 31230 ST-FRAJOU

☎ 05 61 94 14 14 ▤ 05 61 94 14 14

email: butery.chantal@wanadoo.fr

On the hillsides of the Commingca, this farm rears heavy horses and produces berries. The garden is set out around a pond. Upstairs two family guest rooms for up to four, and two double rooms, each have private shower and wc. Separate access is possible. On the ground floor, the living room (with open fire and piano) is shared between hosts and guests. Large parking area.

Prices s fr €40; d fr €50; t fr €72; extra person fr €22; dinner fr €16 **On Site** Restaurant **Nearby** ⚓ 15km ⚑ 40km ⚐ 11km ↖ 11km ⚒ 11km Spa 40km ⚑ 11km ⚙ 25km **Notes** No pets English spoken

ST-LEON

▦ **Pagnard**

Anne-Marie LAMOUROUX

31560 ST-LEON

☎ 05 61 81 92 21

A large 18th century renovated house housing a ferme-auberge and five rooms containing four doubles and five single beds, all with private facilities. Dining room with fireplace, small private room with TV and covered swimming pool.

Prices s fr €40; d fr €44; t fr €57 **On Site** ⚐ Private ↖ **Nearby** ⚑ 40km Restaurant 5km ⚒ 5km ⚑ 5km ⚙ 10km **Notes** No pets English spoken

ST-MARCET

▦ ⦿ **Parc de Lacoste**

Patrick et Carine LAVRIL

Route de Boulogne (D5), 31800 ST-MARCET

☎ 05 61 79 32 10

email: parc.lacoste@orange.fr

web: http://perso.wanadoo.fr/parc.lacoste

Perched on a hillside in the middle of a forest, this renovated smallholding property offers a calm and relaxing environment for a

liday. There are four non-smoking guest rooms - two doubles, one
h outside access; a double with a double bed-settee; and a family
te with a double bed and twins. All rooms have private facilities.
rge lounge, covered outdoor terrace.

ices s fr €50; d fr €55; t fr €75; dinner fr €20   **On Site** Private ⚲
earby ⛄ 10km ♨ 20km ✎ 2km Restaurant 10km 🏊 1.5km 🎾 12km
12km 🚶 12km   **Notes** No pets English spoken

see advert on this page

T-PAUL-D'OUEIL

❚ Maison Jeanne

ichèle GUERRE
110 ST-PAUL-D'OUEIL
☎ 05 61 79 81 63
eb: www.maison-jeanne-luchon.com

is exposed stone house welcomes guests into warmly decorated
rroundings. There is a family room with a double and two single
ds and two rooms with a double bed and two singles, each with
vate facilities and TV. Dining room and large enclosed garden.
unch available. Skiing and walking nearby.

ices s fr €64; d fr €74; t fr €103   **On Site** ✎ **Nearby** ⛄ 6km ♨ 6km
6km Restaurant 4km 🏊 6km 🎾 6km 🏛 6km 🚶 6km   **Notes** No pets

---

T-SAUVEUR

❚ La Castellane

an-Christophe FELIPE
Chemin de la Castellane, 31790 ST-SAUVEUR
☎ 05 61 35 50 49 & 06 61 23 47 75 📠 05 61 35 50 49
eb: www.la-castellane.com

old flint and brick farmhouse, with a contemporary feel to the
terior. Accommodation comprises a room with a double bed and a
ngle; a room with three single beds (two can be linked); and a suite
 three (double bed plus a single) with its own loggia. All are non-
noking, with internet access and private facilities. Kitchen available,
rden with barbecue.

ices s €58-€68; d €65-€75; t €88-€98; extra person fr €23   **On Site** 🎾
earby ⛄ 10km ⚲ 7km 🏊 0.2km 🏛 3km   **Notes** No pets CC

ERNET

❚❚❚ Château de Dussède

Modesta TROUCHE
31810 VERNET
☎ 05 61 08 39 30

On the edge of Toulouse, rooms in enchanting surroundings
comprising two doubles (Louis XIII and Louis XVI), a 'Rétro'
double room and a Louis XV suite, each with private facilities.
Dining room, billiards room and patio. Relax in the park, by the
swimming pool, or play tennis on the private court.

Prices s fr €140-€275; d €150-€220; t €320   **On Site** ✎ Private ⚲
Private tennis court   **Nearby** ⛄ 6km ♨ 12km 🏛 2km 🚶 2km
Notes No pets English spoken Open April to September.

VIGOULET-AUZIL

❚❚❚❚ Château d'Arquier

Pierre et M. Renée ESPAGNO
17 Av des Pyrénées, 31320 VIGOULET-AUZIL
☎ 05 61 75 80 76 & 06 21 59 43 94
email: infos@arquier.com
web: www.arquier.com

This property has an exceptional location, standing amongst trees on
the hills overlooking Toulouse. All of the accommodation is on the
ground floor. There are three bedrooms - a double, a twin and a
triple, all with private bath or shower room and WC. The owner is
related to the composer Saint-Saëns, and his influence on the
surroundings is apparent.

Prices s fr €85; d fr €95; t fr €130   **On Site** Private ⚲
Nearby ⛄ 0.5km ♨ 4km ✎ 5km 🏊 0.5km 🏛 4km 🚶 15km
Notes Pets admitted English spoken

481

VILLENOUVELLE

☷ ◎ **Maison Joséphine**

Paul et Gwenaëlle REID

1, Rue des Ecoles, 31290 VILLENOUVELLE

☎ 05 34 66 20 13 📄 05 34 66 20 13

email: paul.reid@wanadoo.fr

web: http://maison.josephine.free.fr

This village house has four guest rooms. On the first floor is a double room with a further single bed in the adjoining library; on the second floor are a double, a twin and a triple. All rooms have private facilities. Downstairs is a lounge, and a dining room and billiard room which overlook the village. Baby equipment available; swimming pool.

Prices s fr €55; d fr €65; t fr €80; dinner fr €20 **On Site** Restaurant ☜ Private ☇ **Nearby** ☇ 10km ☇ 15km ☞ 2km ☇ 0.5km ☇ 5km ☇ 5km **Notes** No pets English spoken

HAUTES-PYRÉNÉES

ARCIZAC-EZ-ANGLES

☷ **Chambre d'hôtes**

Amélie TARBES

65100 ARCIZAC-EZ-ANGLES

☎ 05 62 42 92 63 & 06 81 45 69 30 📄 05 62 42 92 63

Situated in a small village of 150 people, guest rooms available in the owner's house include three doubles and a single with private facilities, possible extra bed. There is an enclosed courtyard with a lawn and parking area. Sailing is available at a lake 5km away.

Prices s fr €30; d fr €40; t fr €50 **Nearby** ☇ 8km ☇ 4km ☇ 4km Restaurant 5km ☇ 20km ☇ 4km Spa 13km ☇ 5km ☇ 4km **Notes** No pets

ARCIZANS-AVANT

☷ **Chambre d'hôtes**

Marie-Thérèse VERMEIL

3 rue du Château, 65400 ARCIZANS-AVANT

☎ 05 62 97 55 96

Dating from 1855, this Bigourdane house lies in a small quiet village and has three bedrooms for one, three and five people, each with private facilities. Kitchen area with TV and terrace with lovely views over the mountains. Restaurants in the village, thermal spa 3km and ski resort (alpine and cross country) 10km. The owner is a mountain guide.

Prices s fr €30; d fr €48; t fr €68; extra person fr €20 **Nearby** ☇ 4km ☇ 15km ☞ 0.5km ☇ 2km Restaurant 0.2km ☇ 10km ☇ 2km Spa 3km ☇ 2km ☇ 2km ☇ 15km **Notes** No pets English spoken

☷ ☙ ◎ **Chambre d'hôtes**

Françoise AGUILLON

49 Camin d'Azun, 65400 ARCIZANS-AVANT

☎ 05 62 97 13 69 & 06 84 57 48 95

This former farmhouse has an exceptional view over the Mont du Ge and Hautacam. It has three double rooms, each with private shower rooms and WCs. Gas central heating, lounge and dining room.

Prices not confirmed for 2008 **Nearby** ☇ 3km ☇ 20km ☇ 3km Spa 3km ☇ 3km ☇ 20km **Notes** No pets

ARIES-ESPÉNAN

☷ ◎ **Moulin d'Aries**

Dorit WEIMER

65230 ARIES-ESPÉNAN

☎ 05 62 39 81 85 📄 05 62 39 81 82

email: Moulindaries@aol.com

web: www.poterie.fr

Although near the D929, the atmosphere is quiet in this renovated 14th century mill, on the borders of the Gers region. There is a double and four twin rooms, two of which can sleep two adults and two children or three adults (using an extra double bed). Each has a shower and wc. There are two lounges, one with a library, satellite TV video, board games and children's games.

Prices s fr €45; d fr €60; t fr €72; dinner fr €20 **Nearby** ☇ 22km ☇ 22km ☇ 1km Restaurant 4km ☇ 1km Spa 30km ☇ 4km ☇ 25km **Notes** Pets admitted English spoken Open 15 May to October.

ARRAS-EN-LAVEDAN

☷ ◎ **Les Gerbes**

Didier THEIL

65400 ARRAS-EN-LAVEDAN

☎ 05 62 97 93 94 & 06 82 76 44 21 📄 05 62 97 93 94

email: lesgerbes@wanadoo.fr

web: www.pyrenees-chambres-hotes.com

A characterful residence with five guest bedrooms - each one with a double bed, and four with an additional single bed. All the rooms have a private bath or shower room and WC. Guests' lounge and dining room. Jacuzzi available. Meals, including local specialities, are served by arrangement, but check availability when booking. Paragliding, ski lessons.

Prices s €55-€60; d €60-€65; t €76-€83; dinner €20-€22 **Nearby** ☇ 3km ☇ 8km ☇ 10km Restaurant 2km ☇ 15km ☇ 1km Spa 10km ☇ 18km **Notes** Pets admitted English spoken

RRENS-MARSOUS

▓ *La Condorinette*

▓ et C FRANQUEVILLE

rue de la Gourgoutière, 65400 ARRENS-MARSOUS

☎ 05 62 92 06 39 & 06 78 90 37 41

mail: co_franqueville@yahoo.fr

web: www.lacondorinette.com

17th-century house right in the heart of the village. There are five
martly-decorated rooms, with internet access charged at cost. Three
e doubles and two are triples (double bed plus a single); two rooms
an be linked for family accommodation and each has an en suite
mower room and WC.

rices not confirmed for 2008 **Nearby** ♨20km ⚹ 1km ⚒20km
⚹ 1km 🏛1km ⚓20km **Notes** No pets English spoken

▓ ⦿ **Maison Sempé**

ichel GUILLET

rue Marque de Dessus, 65400 ARRENS-MARSOUS

☎ 05 62 97 41 75

mail: maisonsempe@orange.com

web: www.gites-de-france-65.com/maisonsempe

ne of the most beautiful houses in the village, this 18th-century
ome offers four guest bedrooms (a family room can be made from
o linked bedrooms), each with private facilities. Lounge and dining
om shared with the owners, fireplace, wood burning stove, library,
, terrace, garden with furniture. Evening meals using regional
pecialities available. Cross-country skiing and mountain biking in the
lley.

rices s fr €40; d fr €52; t fr €70; dinner fr €45 **Nearby** ♨6km
25km ⚹ 1km Restaurant 10km ⚒20km ⚓1km Spa 25km 🏛10km
a 25km **Notes** No pets English spoken

RTIGUES

▓ **Chambre d'hôtes**

olette CAPDEVIELLE

rtigues, 65100 LOURDES

☎ 05 62 42 92 42

mail: colette.capdevielle@wanadoo.fr

web: www.chambres-hotes-lourdes-pyrenees.fr

ituated in a small village, this farmhouse is typical of the Bigourd
gion and has a double room, a suite of a double room with single
ofa bed and twin room, and a room with double bed, double sofa
ed and fireplace. Each has a shower room, separate access and views
the fields. Kitchen area, terrace with garden furniture and barbecue.
tting room shared with the owners.

rices s fr €36; d €42-€45; extra person fr €10 **Nearby** ♨5km ♨5km
5km ⚒20km ⚓5km Spa 15km 🏛5km ⚓5km **Notes** No pets
nglish spoken

ASQUE

▓▓ ⦿ **La Ferme du Buret**

Pierre FAYE

Cami de Buret, 65130 ASQUE

☎ 05 62 39 19 26 📄 05 62 39 16 06

email: info@lafermeduburet.com

web: www.lafermeduburet.com

This is a former farmhouse in an exceptional location. It has two
rooms which can be arranged as doubles or twins, and two triple
rooms. Disabled access to one room. All have air conditioning
and private facilities. Lounge/dining room and kitchen for guests'
use. Library, board games. Terrace, garden. Ski tuition can be
arranged. Meals available, not Wedensday.

Prices s €70-€90; d €80-€100; extra person fr €15; dinner fr €22
Nearby ♨20km ♨15km ⚹ 5km ⚹ 18km Restaurant 10km
⚒40km ⚓18km Spa 12km ⚓20km 🏛20km ⚓45km
Notes No pets English spoken Open February to November.

AULON

▓▓ ⦿ **Maison Gachot**

J-B et M DUBARRY

Quartier du Castéra, 65240 AULON

☎ 05 62 39 29 47 & 06 81 32 36 10

A 14th-century Pyrenean farmhouse, in an exceptional location in the
heart of a mountain village. There are three double rooms, each with
a private bath or shower room and WC. Two extra beds are available.
Guest lounge with stereo system; sauna; attractive gardens.

Prices s fr €75; d fr €80; t fr €100; dinner fr €20 **Nearby** ♨6km
♨30km ⚹ 4km ⚹ 12km Restaurant 0.2km ⚒12km ⚓0.2km
Spa 12km ⚓10km 🏛6km ⚓35km **Notes** No pets

BARTRÈS

▓▓ ❧ **Ferme Laurens**

Daniel et Angela LAURENS

3 route d'Adé, 65100 BARTRÈS

☎ 05 62 42 34 96 📄 05 62 42 34 96

email: ferme.laurens@wanadoo.fr

This working farm is in the heart of a village with lots of character
and close to the great sites of the Pyrénées. The house offers five
guest rooms (three double beds, six singles and two sofa beds), one
of which is accessible to the less mobile. Dining room, sitting room
shared with the owners, with fireplace, TV and library. Courtyard,
enclosed garden with furniture, parking and a restaurant 80mtrs away.

Prices s fr €30; d fr €40; t fr €47 **Nearby** ♨3km ♨3km ⚹ 3km
Restaurant 0.8km ⚒25km ⚓3km Spa 25km 🏛16km ⚓3km
Notes No pets

BAZET

▥ ⁕☺ **Le Clos Martel**

Dominique PIERSON-MARTEL

6 rue du 8 Mai, 65460 BAZET

☎ 05 62 33 42 55 & 06 33 69 14 13

email: dominique.pierson-martel@wanadoo.fr

web: http://leclosmartel.free.fr/

At the heart of the village, this beautiful residence dating back to 1820 offers three bedrooms, two of which are family rooms (three doubles and five singles altogether), with private facilities. Dining room, wooded park, parking, garden room, table-tennis table. Electric heating. Your host may offer to demonstrate his skills in knife-making. Evening meal by arrangement.

Prices s fr €45; d fr €53; t fr €65; extra person fr €12; dinner fr €20 **Nearby** ⚓ 2km ♨ 7km ⚐ 0.5km ↻ 7km Restaurant 3km ⚓ 45km Spa 30km ⛺ 0.5km ⋙ 7km **Notes** No pets English spoken

BEAUCENS

▥ ☺ **Chambre d'hôtes**

Ione et Henri VIELLE

15 route de Vielle, 65400 BEAUCENS

☎ 05 62 97 90 02 ▤ 05 62 97 90 02

email: contact@beryepetit.com

web: www.beryepetit.com

Three guest rooms with lots of character, each with new double and single beds and one with 19th-century furniture and balcony; all have private facilities. Guests have use of a large sitting room with chimney, TV and library, a microwave, fridge, shady terrace, garden, kitchen garden, field and parking. Restaurants nearby. Evening meals between November and April, at weekends or on request.

Prices d €56-€63; extra person €18; dinner fr €20 **Nearby** ⚓ 6km ♨ 15km ⚐ 2km ↻ 5km Restaurant 0.1km ⚓ 15km ⛱ 5km Spa 2km ⛺ 5km ⋙ 15km **Notes** No pets English spoken

▥ ☺ **Las Vignes**

Adrien FORCA

19 rue des Malapets, 65400 BEAUCENS

☎ 05 62 97 28 20 & 06 63 15 80 09

email: maison.lasvignes@free.fr

web: www.maison-lasvignes.com

This house stands high up in the spa town of Beaucens, and has a beautiful mountain view. It has three bedrooms, two doubles and one with three single beds. One of the rooms is on the ground floor, and they all have a private bath or shower room and WC. The host trains birds of prey, and can advise on good locations for bird-watching.

Prices s fr €43; d fr €48; t fr €59; dinner fr €20 **Nearby** ⚓ 10km ♨ 13km ⚐ 3km ↻ 5km Restaurant 1km ⚓ 15km ⛱ 5km Spa 5km ⛺ 5km ⋙ 18km **Notes** No pets English spoken

BETPOUEY

▥ ❤ ☺ **Chambre d'hôtes**

J-L et C LASSALLE

65120 BETPOUEY

☎ 05 62 92 88 50

email: christine.lassalle723@orange.fr

A barn conversion in a mountain village, with four guest bedrooms. There is a room for three (double bed and a single) on the ground floor; upstairs are two double rooms and another triple (three single beds). All have private shower room and WC. Lounge with open fire and TV. Meals by arrangement, in winter months only.

Prices not confirmed for 2008 **Nearby** ♨ 34km ↻ 3km ⚓ 3km ⛱ 3km Spa 3km ⛺ 10km **Notes** No pets English spoken

BOI-SILHEN

▥ ☺ **Les Aillans**

Franck BROUILLET

10 chemin de Silhen Debat, 65400 BOI-SILHEN

☎ 05 62 97 59 22 & 06 87 57 57 39 ▤ 05 62 97 59 22

email: fc.brouillet@orange.fr

web: www.brouilletfranck.com

A renovated barn, near the owners' 15th-century house, in an isolate hamlet in green countryside. Three guest rooms (one is a family roor with two communicating rooms) with private bathrooms. Dining roor and separate sitting room, fireplace, TV, library, video and hi-fi, plus a courtyard, enclosed parkland, garden furniture and garage. The owne will be happy to help you discover the Hautes Pyrénées in his 4 x 4.

Prices not confirmed for 2008 **Nearby** ♨ 12km ↻ 2.5km ⚓ 4km ⛱ 2.5km ⋙ 13km **Notes** No pets English spoken

BORDÈRES-LOURON

▥ ☺ **La Flambée**

H et A-L CHAMARY-BRACHET

Le Village, 65590 BORDÈRES-LOURON

☎ 05 62 99 98 89 ▤ 05 62 99 98 89

email: ch.hote.borderes@wanadoo.fr

web: www.laflambee.fr.tc

A renovated farm, which has a double room and four rooms with a double bed and single bed, each with private bathroom. Communal dining room and sitting room, garden with furniture and lawn. Set in valley offering activities such as skiing, paragliding, walking, mountain biking.

Prices not confirmed for 2008 **Nearby** ♨ 8km ↻ 8km ⚓ 12km ⛱ Spa 8km ⛺ 30km **Notes** Pets admitted

MIDI-PYRÉNÉES

OURG-DE-BIGORRE

⊪ ⊧◌⊩ **La Caminade**

érald MAGNIEN
5130 BOURG-DE-BIGORRE
☎ 05 62 39 08 63
mail: magnienlacaminade@tiscali.fr
web: www.chambres.com.fr/lacaminade

his property has two bright and comfortable ground floor rooms,
nd a spacious first floor room, accessed by its own staircase, with
eams, parquet floor and dressing room. All rooms have private bath/
ower rooms and WCs. Guests' kitchen, washing machine. Terrace,
vimming pool, table tennis, barbecue. Hosts will be delighted to
dvise about visits, etc.

rices s €52-€58; d €57-€62; t €69-€74; extra person fr €16; dinner
1-€20 **On Site** Private ⚲ **Nearby** ⚓ 15km ⚲ 15km ⚲ 0.1km
estaurant 10km ⚲ 33km ⚲ 2.5km Spa 9km ⚐ 7km ⚲ 15km
otes No pets

AMPAN

⊪ *Chambre d'hôtes Lahore*

atherine ABADIE
hemin d'Angoué, 65710 CAMPAN
☎ 05 62 91 77 95 & 06 08 78 18 94 ⎙ 05 62 91 73 60
mail: lahore@wanadoo.fr
web: http://perso.wanadoo.fr/lahore

vo twin rooms and a double with mezzanine are offered in a
novated grange adjacent to the owner's home. Guests have use of a
tchen area and dining room and there is an orchard, kitchen garden
nd a green space with garden furniture and barbecue. Your hosts
'll share the various activities available nearby, including climbing,
ountain biking and racket games.

rices not confirmed for 2008 **Nearby** ⚲ 7km ⚲ 5km ⚲ 18km ⚲ 2km
a 6km ⚐ 5km ⚲ 2km **Notes** No pets English spoken

⊪ ⊧◌⊩ **La Laurence**

ascal HUTEAU
5710 CAMPAN
☎ 05 62 91 84 02
mail: contact@lalaurence-pyrenees.fr
web: www.lalaurence-pyrenees.fr

comfortable chalet with panoramic views over the valley and
ountains, offering independent guest rooms with shower room and
c, lounge area, balcony or terrace. Three of the rooms have a kitchen
ea (one room is grade 2). Dining room shared with the owners,
ting room, library, TV, picnic baskets and heating. Reductions
ssible for groups (out of season).

rices s fr €41; d fr €52.50; t fr €72; dinner fr €19 **On Site** ⚲
estaurant **Nearby** ⚲ 15km ⚲ 15km ⚲ 6km Spa 15km ⚐ 4km
18km **Notes** No pets English spoken

CAMPARAN

⊪⊪ *La Couette de Bieou*

B et M-T MOREILHON
65170 CAMPARAN
☎ 05 62 39 41 10 & 06 70 15 86 40 ⎙ 05 62 39 41 10

At the entrance to a small village, this mountain farm offers rooms in
a house retaining much of its original character, with views over the
Aure valley and surrounding peaks. There is a double, a twin and a
room with a double bed and twins, each with private shower room.
Mezzanine level and communal dining room, courtyard, balcony,
garden furniture, parking, lounge area, TV and fireplace. Ski resorts
and spas nearby.

Prices not confirmed for 2008 **Nearby** ⚲ 35km ⚲ 4km ⚲ 4km ⚲ 4km
Spa 4km ⚐ 35km ⚲ 35km **Notes** No pets

CASTELNAU-MAGNOAC

⊪⊪ *Au Verdier*

Nathalie CARRILLON FONTAN
Route de Lamarque, 65230 CASTELNAU-MAGNOAC
☎ 05 62 39 85 45 & 06 81 49 56 10 ⎙ 05 62 39 85 45
email: Verdier@terre-net.fr
web: www.coteaux-bigorre.com/

There are three beautiful bedrooms (four double beds and one
single) with private bathrooms in this converted grain store. In the
lounge, the large locally-made table has pride of place, where you can
enjoy breakfasts. TV, telephone and library. From the balcony, you can
admire the park, flowerbeds, fishing lake and terrace.

Prices not confirmed for 2008 **Nearby** ⚲ 15km ⚲ 2km Spa 25km
⚐ 2km ⚲ 20km **Notes** No pets

⊪⊪ *Manoir de la Grange*

Bernard VERDIER
65230 CASTELNAU-MAGNOAC
☎ 05 62 99 85 33 & 06 07 29 80 36
⎙ 05 62 99 85 33
email: mandelagrange@wanadoo.fr

This 16th century manor house between Gascony and the
Pyrénées offers three bedrooms with private facilities, one a suite
for three people. Dining room, sitting room, library and small
kitchen reserved for guests. Enclosed parkland, swimming pool,
garden furniture and parking. One hour from the Pic du Midi;
walking, horse riding, tennis and aerial sports are all available on
the doorstep.

Prices not confirmed for 2008 **Nearby** ⚲ 25km ⚲ ⚲ 0.5km
Spa 25km ⚐ 27km **Notes** No pets English spoken

CASTELNAU-RIVIÈRE-BASSE

ⅲ ᠄◯᠄ *Flanerie*

Jean-Louis et Nicole GUYOT

Hameau de Mazères, 65700 CASTELNAU-RIVIÈRE-BASSE

☎ 05 62 31 90 56 & 06 13 08 00 92 ᠁ 05 62 31 90 56

email: flanerie.65@wanadoo.fr

This 18th century Gascony farm rears Pyrénées donkeys and offers two double rooms, two rooms for two people, and a suite for three, all with private facilities and heating (one with fireplace). Sitting and dining room with fireplace, TV, library, enclosed courtyard and garden. Babies free. Evening meals on request.

Prices not confirmed for 2008 **Nearby** ⚓ 20km ⤳ 3km ⊰ 3km ⚲14km **Notes** Pets admitted English spoken

CAUTERETS

ⅲ ᠄◯᠄ **Les Ruisseaux**

Glenn ALDERMAN

Route de Pierrefitte, 65110 CAUTERETS

☎ 05 62 92 28 02 ᠁ 05 62 92 28 02

email: les-ruisseaux@wanadoo.fr

web: http://perso.orange.fr/les-ruisseaux/

This is a large house on a hillside, in extensive wooded grounds with springs and waterfalls. Four bedrooms, all upstairs, have private bath or shower room/WC. All the rooms have double beds; two of them also have an additional single bed, and one has its own salon. Guest sitting room with TV; gardens.

Prices s fr €42; d fr €52; t fr €72; dinner fr €20 **On Site** ⚓ **Nearby** ⚓30km ⌖3km ⤳ 7km ⊰3km ⚑7km ⚲3km ⚭ 18km **Notes** No pets English spoken CC

CHELLE-DEBAT

ⅲ *Villa de Giverny*

Howard WHITLEY

Route de Cabanac, 65350 CHELLE-DEBAT

☎ 05 62 35 15 74 & 06 85 95 16 82

email: craig.whitley@wanadoo.fr

This spacious villa offers four guest rooms, two doubles and two twins. Each room has an en suite shower room and WC. Guests' lounge with TV; central heating. Garden room, extensive landscaped grounds with terrace and barbecue, swimming pool.

Prices not confirmed for 2008 **Nearby** ⚓15km ⤳ ⚑40km ⊰3km Spa 18km ⚲18km ⚭12km **Notes** No pets English spoken

CHÈZE

ⅲ **Le Palouma**

Marie-Hélène THEIL

65120 CHÈZE

☎ 05 62 92 90 90 ᠁ 05 62 92 90 90

email: rene.theil.le.palouma@wanadoo.fr

Next to the owners' home, this house is situated in a small village in the mountains, with a beautiful view over the Luz-Saint-Sauveur valley. There are three bedrooms (two double beds and three singles) with private facilities. Dining room and sitting room with fireplace, TV, library, shared with the owners. Enclosed garden with flowerbeds and children's toys, terrace with garden furniture and parking.

Prices s fr €30; d fr €40; t fr €50 **Nearby** ⚑ 5km ⚓30km ⚑ 3km ⤳ 5km Restaurant 5km ⚑15km ⊰5km Spa 5km ⚑ 5km ⚲5km ⚭5km **Notes** No pets

GALAN

ⅲ ᠄◯᠄ **Maison d'Hôtes Namasté**

Jean FONTAINE

13 rue de la Baïse, 65330 GALAN

☎ 05 62 99 77 81 ᠁ 05 62 99 77 81

email: jean.fontaine65@wanadoo.fr

web: www.namaste-pyrenees.com

On the edge of the village, this is a typical 19th-century farmhouse. There are five rooms, all with independent access and private bath/ shower rooms and WCs. Beds can be singles or doubles, as agreed at time of reservation. Lounge with open fire, books, TV and piano. Enclosed grounds. Meals prepared using local or organic produce; vegetarian meals on request.

Prices s fr €55; d fr €60; t fr €75; dinner fr €25 **Nearby** ⚑ 4km ⚑50km ⊰1km ⊰0.5km ⚭12km **Notes** No pets English spoken

see advert on opposite pag

GUCHAN

ⅲ ᠄◯᠄ **Chez Annie et Loïc**

Loïc et Annie LIBÉ

Le Village, 65170 GUCHAN

☎ 05 62 39 92 68 & 06 09 16 81 36

email: pyrenees@annieloic.net

web: http://annieetloic.free.fr

In the centre of a small quiet village, 800 metres up in the mountains, this restored 18th-century farmhouse has five guest bedrooms, for two or three people. All rooms have a private bath or shower room and WC. There is a large lounge for guests, with books, piano and a children's corner. Shady south-facing garden; delicious meals served, by arrangement.

Prices s fr €59; d fr €64; t fr €82; dinner fr €19 **On Site** ⚑ Restaurant **Nearby** ⚓35km ⤳ 4km ⚑12km ⊰2km Spa 4km ⚑4km ⚲2km ⚭30km **Notes** No pets English spoken

UILLAN

❦ *Chambre d'hôtes*

atrick et Nathalie COUILLOUX
rue Voltaire, 65290 JUILLAN
☎ 05 62 32 01 06 & 06 81 80 28 55 🖹 05 62 32 01 06
mail: contact@loubatistou.com
eb: www.loubatistou.com

ur bedrooms with lots of character in a restored and converted
9th-century barn, in the heart of a village. There are two double
oms, a twin-bedded room, and a triple (double bed and a single).
l have private facilities. Pleasant garden; above-ground swimming
ol and outdoor jacuzzi, private parking.

rices not confirmed for 2008 **Nearby** ♨3km ⚑5km ⚓30km ⚴
a 25km ⌂25km ⋈5km **Notes** No pets English spoken

UNCALAS

❦ **Chambre d'hôtes**

aniel COUMES
1 rue de Castelloubon, 65100 JUNCALAS
☎ 05 62 94 76 26 🖹 05 62 94 76 26

ree bedrooms in the owners' house, with private bathrooms: three
ouble beds and one single. TV, library, lounge room and sitting
om for guests. Outside, there is garden furniture, parking and a
urtyard. In the village, guests can enjoy swimming, golf, horse riding
d fishing.

rices s fr €30; d fr €40; t fr €50 **Nearby** ♦8km ♨7km ✐5km
7km Restaurant 1km ⚓17km ⚴7km Spa 16km ⚘7km ⌂7km
7km **Notes** No pets English spoken Open April to 30 October.

❦ ⚶ *Maison Monseigneur Laurence*

obert ASSOUERE
5100 JUNCALAS
☎ 05 62 42 02 04 🖹 05 62 94 13 91
mail: robert.assouere@wanadoo.fr
eb: www.maisondeleveque.com

onseigneur Laurence, the priest of the Lourdes apparitions, spent
rt of his childhood at this characterful house. It has four rooms
vo double) with private facilities, two also with small sitting room,
eplace and TV. Dining room with lots of character, lounge, TV,
rage, parking, private courtyard, garden furniture and barbecue.
ady park with stream, mountain biking, fishing trips, mountain trips,
ening grills. Sailing 7km.

rices not confirmed for 2008 **Nearby** ♨7km ⚑7km ✐17km ⚴7km
a 15km ⌂15km ⋈6km **Notes** No pets English spoken

Namasté

Namasté is a former 19th Century farm, which has 2
ground floor bedrooms that open out into the garden. One
bedroom sleeps 3 people and the other, a family room,
sleeps 4. On the first floor there are 2 double rooms and 1
family room equipped with private WCs and rated 3 *épi*.
(Double beds 180cm, single beds 90). From summer 2005
a pool will be available.

Table d'hotes available on request, where typical southern
dishes are prepared using organic products where
possible, Vegetarian meals on request. Home-baked
organic bread.

During the summer you are invited by your hosts to attend
evenings out (theatre, concerts etc . . .)

65330 Galan Tel: 05 62 99 77 81
Email: jean@namaste-pyrenees.com
Web: www.namaste-pyrenees.com

LABASTIDE

❦❦ ⚶ *Lauga*

Evelyne DASQUE
Route d'Esparros D26, 65130 LABASTIDE
☎ 05 62 98 80 27 🖹 05 62 98 20 57
email: alain.dasque@worldonline.fr

This old shepherd's house has four bedrooms for two/four people,
with a private bathroom in each. There is a lounge for guests with
fireplace, a sitting room with billiard table and a TV room. Outside,
there is a covered, heated swimming pool, a covered tennis court, a
gym, courtyard, garden and parking.

Prices not confirmed for 2008 **Nearby** ♨12km ⚑ ✐25km ⚴
Spa 10km ⌂10km **Notes** Pets admitted

LABORDE

❦❦ ⚶ *Chambre d'hôtes*

Jean et Gi VIDAL
65130 LABORDE
☎ 05 62 39 07 53 🖹 05 62 39 07 53
email: gijean.vidal@free.fr

Situated in the heart of a valley, with impressive views, this renovated
19th-century house is opposite the church. There are four guest
rooms, each with private facilities, a lounge area, fireplace, library,
games, garden, parking and traditional cooking available. Activity
holidays possible: cooking, drawing, watercolours, pottery.

Prices not confirmed for 2008 **Nearby** ♨20km ⚑10km ✐30km
⚴10km Spa 20km ⌂20km **Notes** No pets

LOUBAJAC

⌘ ❦ ⁺◎ Chambre d'hôtes

Jean-Marc et Nadine VIVES

28 route de Bartres, 65100 LOUBAJAC

☎ 05 62 94 44 17 ▤ 05 62 42 38 58

email: nadine.vives@wanadoo.fr

web: www.anousta.com

In a house typical of the Bigourd region, surrounded by a garden, there are two double bedrooms, one room with a double bed and single bed, and two bedrooms with two double beds, each with private facilities. Private sitting room with TV and library, garden furniture. Special rates for groups of four. Sailing and lake 5km away.

Prices s fr €35; d €40-€45; t €50-€55; dinner fr €15 **Nearby** ⛷ 8km ⛷ 5km ♟ 3km ⚐ 5km Restaurant 5km ⚓ 30km ⚓ 5km Spa 17km ⛺ 17km ⚠ 5km **Notes** No pets English spoken Open February to 15 November. CC

LOUDENVIELLE

⌘ ⁺◎ Chambre d'hôtes

Laurence CAPOT

2 chemin des Noisetiers, 65510 LOUDENVIELLE

☎ 05 62 98 60 54 & 06 20 70 12 40

email: pyreneesplaisirs@free.fr

web: www.noisetiers-pyrenees.com

A traditional house in a mountain village in the heart of the Louron valley offering four double-bedded first floor rooms. They all have a private bath or shower room and WC. There is a guests' lounge with TV and stereo, and a dining room with an open fire.

Prices s fr €56; d €56-€61; t fr €76; dinner fr €16 **On Site** ♟ Restaurant ⚐ **Nearby** ⚓ 40km ⚐ 8km ⚓ 15km ⛺ 0.5km ⚠ 35km **Notes** No pets

---

LUZ-SAINT-SAUVEUR

⌘ ⁺◎ ⚐ Chambre d'hôtes

Christine et Petxu CALDERON

14 route de Villenave, 65120 LUZ-SAINT-SAUVEUR

☎ 05 62 92 90 79 & 06 80 73 20 78

email: christinepetxu@orange.fr

Near Luz-St-Sauveur and 25 minutes from the Pic du Midi, this is a property with five guest rooms. One has twin beds which can be linked, and is suitable for disabled guests; three are double rooms (one with panoramic views); the fifth is a split-level family room for four. All have private bath or shower room. The owners are mountain guides. Dinner by reservation.

Prices s fr €40; d €55-€65; t €65-€70; dinner fr €18 **On Site** ♟ **Nearby** ⛷ 20km ⛷ 30km ⚐ 0.5km Restaurant 0.5km ⚓ 1km ⚓ 1km Spa 3km ⚓ 0.5km ⛺ 0.5km ⚠ 25km **Notes** Pets admitted English spoken Open December to October.

⌘⌘⌘⌘ Le Clos de rue de L'art

Jean-Louis DE LA RONCIÈRE

2 rue de l'Art, 65120 LUZ-SAINT-SAUVEUR

☎ 05 62 92 97 75 & 06 19 15 00 69

email: florence.delaronciere@wanadoo.fr

web: www.luz-hebergements.com

A beautiful 14th-century house in the quiet, historic part of Luz-St-Sauveur. There are three spacious first floor bedrooms, two doubles and a triple (three single beds, one of them a large single). All have private facilities. Guests' lounge with TV; garden with furniture. Fitness centre close by.

Prices s €55-€65; d €60-€75; t €70-€85 **On Site** Spa **Nearby** ⛷ 10km ⛷ 30km ⚐ 0.5km ⚐ 0.3km Restaurant 0.1km ⚓ 10km ⛺ 0.1km ⛺ 0.1km ⚠ 0.3km **Notes** No pets English spoken

---

MAUBOURGUET

⌘⌘⌘ Chambre d'hôtes

Leïla BAKER

203 rue Auguste Gerdessus, 65700 MAUBOURGUET

☎ 05 62 31 90 48 ▤ 05 62 31 90 48

email: isom@maisonbel-air.com

A comfortable, elegantly decorated 200-year old house of character. Three bedrooms include one family room (one king-size double, two doubles and a single), private WC and shower or bathrooms. Guest lounge, terrace, garden. Fluent English and Spanish spoken. Marciac jazz festival 15km. Open all year, gas central heating. Bedrooms have phone and internet access. Restaurant in village.

Prices s €35-€40; d €60-€65; t fr €75; extra person fr €15 **Nearby** ⛷ 5km ⛷ 25km Restaurant 1km ⚓ 1km Spa 50km ⛺ 50km ⚠ 25km **Notes** No pets English spoken

---

⌘⌘⌘ ❦ ⁺◎ *Domaine de la Campagne*

H-P et F NOUVELLON

65700 MAUBOURGUET

☎ 05 62 96 45 71 & 06 81 57 02 23 ▤ 05 62 96 45 71

email: hpnou@wanadoo.fr

Close to Maubourguet, in extensive grounds and with views of the Pyrénées, this property has three bedrooms. On the ground floor is a double room and a twin-bedded room; upstairs is a grade 2 double room. All have private facilities, but those for the grade 2 room are n fully en suite. Swimming pool; meals by arrangement.

Prices not confirmed for 2008 **Nearby** ⛷ 18km ⚐ 2km Spa 50km ⛺ 2km ⚠ 30km **Notes** No pets English spoken

ORINCLES

ⅲ Chambre d'hôtes

Françoise GRIMBERT
Passage du Moulin, 65380 ORINCLES
☎ 05 62 45 40 65 & 06 84 78 86 69 📄 05 62 45 60 50
email: francoise.g12@wanadoo.fr

Near to Lourdes, there is easy access to the valleys of the Pyrénées from this old renovated mill. There are two bedrooms with double and single bed, and a double bedroom with a mezzanine with twin beds. Each has a private bathroom. The sound of the water is calming and peaceful and cycling, fishing and bathing are available. Hiking possible nearby with qualified guides.

Prices s fr €51; d fr €62; t fr €73 **On Site** 🎣 🏖 **Nearby** ⚓ 4km ⚡ 10km ⚘ 10km Restaurant 4km ⛱ 10km 🏠 4km ⚑ 10km **Notes** Pets admitted English spoken Open February to 30 October.

OSSUN

ⅲ La Grange du Suisse

Véronique TORRALVA
7 rue Aristide Briand, 65380 OSSUN
☎ 05 62 32 73 40 & 06 79 32 34 17
email: veronique-lagrange2004@wanadoo.fr
web: www.lagrangedusuisse.skyblog.com

Just 10 kilometres from Lourdes, this property has three double/twin bedded rooms (the twin beds can be linked). One of the rooms is on the ground floor. They all have TVs and private bathrooms, one of them with a spa bath. Guests' dining room with lounge area, garden, swimming pool, table tennis, children's games room.

Prices s fr €60; d fr €70; t fr €85; extra person fr €15 **On Site** Private ⚘ **Nearby** ⚓ 2km ⚡ 10km ⚘ 20km Restaurant 3km ⚘ 30km ⛱ 1km Spa 22km 🏖 10km 🏠 0.3km ⚑ 12km **Notes** No pets English spoken

OUEILLOUX

ⅲ ⚐ Chambre d'hôtes

Alain et Rachel GUIDICI
5 Cami Deth Barboutou, 65190 OUEILLOUX
☎ 05 62 35 07 66 📄 05 62 35 07 66

The only thing you will regret about your stay in this property at the foot of the Pyrénées is having to leave at the end! In the former stable and attic there are three upstairs rooms, each with four single beds, shower and private WC. Guests lounge with enclosed fire, TV. Garden with shady lawn.

Prices not confirmed for 2008 **Nearby** ⚡ 13km ⚘ 7km ⚘ 35km ⛱ 7km Spa 13km 🏠 13km **Notes** No pets

OUZOUS

ⅲ *Chambre d'hôtes*

Pierre NOGUEZ
Chemin de l'Eglise, 65400 OUZOUS
☎ 05 62 97 24 89 & 06 66 09 55 55 📄 05 62 97 29 87
email: p.noguez@wanadoo.fr
web: www.chambres-hotes-pyrenees.com

18th-century farmhouse with lots of character, in a small mountain village in the Argeles valley. It has four bedrooms with two twin beds, four double beds, and two extra beds, each with private bathroom. Lounge, sitting room, library, peaceful flower garden and gazebo with garden furniture and lovely views over the valley. Restaurant typical of the region nearby.

Prices not confirmed for 2008 **Nearby** ⚡ 10km ⚘ 4km ⚘ 10km ⛱ 4km Spa 4km 🏠 4km **Notes** Pets admitted English spoken

PIERREFITTE-NESTALAS

ⅲ ⚐ ⚑ La Ferme Peylat

Noël et Claire DUBARRY
21 rue Parmentier, 65260 PIERREFITTE-NESTALAS
☎ 05 62 92 74 77 📄 05 62 92 74 77

This quiet and restful farmhouse property, at the meeting point of five valleys, offers four guest rooms in a former barn. There are two double rooms, a twin, and a room with two double beds. All have private shower rooms and WCs. Large lounge with open fire.

Prices s fr €31; d fr €40; t fr €50; dinner fr €15 **On Site** Private tennis court **Nearby** ⚓ 10km ⚡ 18km ⚘ 1km ⚘ 5km Restaurant 0.2km ⚘ 11km Spa 5km 🏖 6km 🏠 0.2km ⚑ 17km **Notes** No pets Open February to September.

PINAS

ⅲ Domaine de Jean-Pierre

Marie-Sabine COLOMBIER
20 route de Villeneuve, 65300 PINAS
☎ 05 62 98 15 08 & 06 84 57 15 69 📄 05 62 98 15 08
email: marie@domainedejeanpierre.com
web: http://domainedejeanpierre.com

In a peaceful setting on the Lannemezan plateau, this large house has lots of character and a shady park. There are three beautiful bedrooms with private wcs and bathrooms, pretty interior décor, sitting room, library and piano. Your hostess and her small dog are very welcoming. Restaurant 3km.

Prices s €48; d €53; t €68; extra person €15 **On Site** 🎣 🏖 **Nearby** ⚓ 3km ⚡ 3km ⚘ 5km ⚘ 50km ⛱ 1km 🏠 0.8km ⚑ 5km **Notes** Pets admitted English spoken

SAILHAN

⅏⅏⅏ ⅋○⅋ Le Relais de l'Empereur

Pierre et Fabienne VÉDÈRE

Failhan, St Lary, 65170 SAILHAN

☎ 05 62 40 09 18 & 06 80 05 62 45

🗎 05 62 40 09 18

email: vedere.pierre@wanadoo.fr

web: www.lerelaisdelempereur.com

A beautiful 16th-century house in a small mountain village. There are four bedrooms, each for two to four guests. All have private facilities. Meals available, with local specialities. Lounge and garden. The hosts will be delighted to share their local knowledge and enthusiasm for the area. Rock climbing and skiing are available locally, and a long-distance footpath passes close by.

Prices s fr €70; d €80-€85; extra person fr €15; dinner fr €22 **Nearby** ⛷ 2km ♨ 35km 🏊 2km ⚓ 2km Restaurant 0.5km ⛵ 2km 🎣 2km Spa 2km ⛳ 2km 🏛 2km ♒ 20km **Notes** Pets admitted English spoken Open March to April, June to September & December to January.

SALIGOS

⅏⅏⅏ 🐾 ⅋○⅋ La Munia

Monique LABIT

65120 SALIGOS

☎ 05 62 92 84 74 & 06 70 55 10 72

Small, calm, restful village with a lovely view over the mountains. There are three bedrooms with a mezzanine (three double beds, four single beds), each with private facilities. TV, telephone, library, board games, terrace, garden furniture, barbecues, parking.

Prices s fr €29; d fr €40; t fr €47; dinner fr €12 **On Site** 🏊 **Nearby** ⛷ 10km ♨ 35km 🏊 2km Restaurant 2km ⛵ 10km 🎣 2km Spa 3km ⛳ 2km 🏛 2km ♒ 20km **Notes** No pets

SOMBRUN

⅏⅏⅏ ⅋○⅋ *Château de Sombrun*

Gillian QUIRK

65700 SOMBRUN

☎ 05 62 96 49 43 🗎 05 62 96 01 89

email: gillian@sombrun.com

web: www.sombrun.com

The château of this charming small village offers a suite of two bedrooms (twin and double) and a double and twin room in an outbuilding, all with private facilities. Sitting room, piano, billiard room, library, TV, music room, dining room. Dinner on reservation (except Sunday). On the Maridan wine route, the château is situated within six hectares of parkland with a swimming pool and pond.

Prices not confirmed for 2008 **Nearby** 🏊 0.5km ♒ 30km **Notes** No pets English spoken

ST-LARY-SOULAN

⅏⅏⅏ ⅋○⅋ La Ferme de Soulan

Laurence AMELOT

Village Soulan, 65170 SAINT-LARY-SOULAN

☎ 05 62 98 43 21

email: fermedesoulan@orange.fr

web: http://fermedesoulan.free.fr

This is a quiet and comfortable renovated farmhouse in Soulan, a typical mountain village. It has four rooms, three doubles and one triple, all full of character. The lounge has an open fire, books and a stunning view; outside there is a small garden and terrace. Sauna with steam room. Home-made jams and patisseries. Meals available, traditional cuisine.

Prices s €73-€75; d €85-€88; dinner fr €23 **Nearby** ⛷ 6km ⚓ 30km ♨ 6km 🏊 5km Restaurant 3km ⛵ 3km 🎣 5km Spa 5km ⛳ 6km 🏛 5km ♒ 30km **Notes** No pets English spoken

ST-LAURENT-DE-NESTE

⅏⅏⅏ ⅋○⅋ Chambre d'hôtes

Fabienne GARCIA

4 rue de l'Ancienne Poste,

65150 SAINT-LAURENT-DE-NESTE

☎ 05 62 39 76 01

email: info@souleillane.com

web: www.souleillane.com

In a village at the foot of the Pyrénées, this old manor farm house dates from 1822. There are three spacious and comfortable bedrooms: a room in the owner's house with a double and twin beds and two double rooms in an adjoining annexe, each with private facilities. There is a garden for relaxation and meals, which feature local produce, can be provided on Wednesdays, Fridays, and Sundays by reservation.

Prices s fr €40; d fr €50; t fr €60; extra person fr €10; dinner fr €17 **On Site** ♨ **Nearby** ⚓ 8km 🏊 8km Restaurant 0.5km ⛵ 35km 🎣 0.5km 🏛 0.2km ♒ 8km **Notes** No pets English spoken

ST-PÉ-DE-BIGORRE

⅏⅏⅏ 🐾 ⅋○⅋ Ferme Campseissillou

Marie-Luce ARRAMONDE

Quartier du Mousques, 65270 SAINT-PÉ-DE-BIGORRE

☎ 05 62 41 80 92

email: marie-luce.arramonde@wanadoo.fr

web: www.ferme-campseissillou.com

3km from the centre of the village, in the middle of the mountains and forests, there are three bedrooms with private bathrooms and lovely views. (Three double beds and two single beds.) Lounge with TV and sitting room, terrace, garden furniture and evening meals featuring farm produce available.

Prices d fr €45; extra person fr €10; dinner fr €15 **Nearby** ⛷ 2km ⚓ 15km ♨ 4km 🏊 4km Restaurant 4km 🎣 4km Spa 45km ⛳ 15km 🏛 4km ♒ 15km **Notes** No pets English spoken Open 15 March to 30 October.

⊞ ⃟ **Ferme Versailles**

Cécile AZENS
Route des Grottes de Bétharram,
65270 SAINT-PÉ-DE-BIGORRE
☎ 05 62 41 80 48 & 06 85 79 67 19 ▤ 05 62 41 80 48
web: www.gites-de-france-65.com/Fversaille

Built by the owner's grandparents in 1863, this large Bigourd house
has three comfortable bedrooms, each with private facilities and
heating. TV room, large dining room with antique furniture, parking in
farm courtyard. Evening meals featuring farm produce are available.
Walking, excursions, and local visits are all possible. Half rate for children under 12.

Prices s fr €37; d fr €40; dinner fr €17　**Nearby** ⛳ 6km ↧ 9km
✎ 2km ⋆ 1.5km Restaurant 3km ⚓ 50km ⌿ 1km Spa 40km ⛲ 1.5km
⋈ 1.5km　**Notes** No pets English spoken

VIC-EN-BIGORRE

⊞ ⃟ **Chambre d'hôtes**

Lucienne BROQUA
94 impasse des Bouleaux, 65500 VIC-EN-BIGORRE
☎ 05 62 96 26 29 & 06 87 22 75 54
email: broqua@wanadoo.fr

Rooms here include two doubles and a twin with bunks with kitchen
next to the owner's house, and a double room in the main house, all
with shower and wc. Courtyard, enclosed parkland, garden furniture,
barbecue, parking, sand pit, park with lots of flowers, summer dining
room for guests. Available on site: boules and model aircraft making.
Stretch of water, archery and interesting monuments nearby.

Prices s fr €36; d fr €40; t fr €50; dinner fr €18　**Nearby** ⛳ 5km
↧ 19km ⋆ 1km ⋆ 0.8km Restaurant 1km ⌿ 0.8km Spa 37km ⛲ 1km
⋈ 17km　**Notes** No pets

VIDOUZE

⊞ ⃟ **A Lamic**

Joël et Edith THEN
Quartier Arriagosse, 65700 VIDOUZE
☎ 05 62 96 37 36 ▤ 05 62 96 37 36
email: joelthen@hotmail.fr
web: www.chambredhotealamic.com

In the heart of the Côteaux de Gascogne wine-growing region, a
restored farmhouse dating back to the mid-19th century. On the
ground floor is a twin-bedded room with disabled access; upstairs is
a double room, and a suite for four with two double-bedded rooms. All
have private shower room and WC.

Prices s fr €47; d fr €55; t fr €62; dinner fr €17　**On Site** Private ⋆
Nearby ⛳ 3km ↧ 35km ✎ 10km Restaurant 7km ⌿ 12km ⛲ 35km
⋈ 35km　**Notes** No pets English spoken

VIELLA

⊞ ❤ ⃟ **Eslias**

Marcel et Jocelyne LAPORTE
Hameau Les Cabanes, 65120 VIELLA
☎ 05 62 92 84 58 ▤ 05 62 92 84 58
email: jocelyne.laporte4@wanadoo.fr

This is a quiet spot with beautiful mountain views, 300 metres from
the road leading up to the Tourmalet pass. There is a triple room
(double bed and single) upstairs; downstairs is a double room and
a family room for four, all with private facilities. Living room, large
terrace, and pre-booked meals are available.

Prices s fr €35; d fr €48; t fr €60; dinner fr €15　**Nearby** ⛳ 5km ↧ 2km
✎ 1km ⋆ 2km Restaurant 2km ⚓ 5km ⌿ 2km Spa 3km ✾ 2km
⛲ 2km ⋈ 30km　**Notes** No pets English spoken

VIELLE-AURE

⊞ *Chambre d'hôtes*

Claude FOURCADE-ABBADIE
Rue de l'Église, 65170 VIELLE-AURE
☎ 05 62 39 42 33 ▤ 05 62 39 42 33

In the heart of the Aure valley, at an altitude of 800mtrs, three
peaceful rooms are available in the owners' typical Pyrenean house,
each with shower room and wc. Dining room for breakfast, garden
furniture, parking. Special rate for groups of four. Walking (GR10),
Néouvielle nature reserve, horse riding, ski resorts, mountain biking,
paragliding, canyoning, rafting and climbing all nearby.

Prices not confirmed for 2008　**Nearby** ↧ 40km ⋆ 2km ⚓ 10km ⌿
Spa 2km ⛲ 40km ⋈ 40km　**Notes** No pets

VIGNEC

⊞ *Chambre d'hôtes*

Daniel VERDOT
65170 VIGNEC
☎ 05 62 39 54 53

A twin room and three doubles in the owner's house, each with
private facilities, situated on a farm with small campsite, in a typical
village. Small sitting room and large room with fireplace, tree lined
park. Visit the herds or watch haymaking in the summer.

Prices not confirmed for 2008　**Nearby** ⋆ 2km ⚓ 2km ⌿ 2km
Spa 2km ⛲ 2km ⋈ 25km　**Notes** No pets

LOT

ALBAS

🏠 Le Soleil

Jean François FERRON
Rivière-Haute, 46140 ALBAS
☎ 05 65 30 91 90 & 06 62 17 38 07 📠 05 65 30 91 90
email: le-soleil@wanadoo.fr
web: www.chambredhote-lesoleil.com

This character house offers guest rooms with separate entrances including a double, a room with two doubles and one with a double and twin, each non-smoking with private facilities and TV. Terrace, garden furniture, barbecue, boules pitch, covered swimming pool, wooded park. Washing machine, refrigerator, heating, piano, evening events.

Prices s fr €47; d fr €52; t fr €67 **On Site** Private ⸲ **Nearby** ⸲ 20km
⸲ 0.2km Restaurant 0.2km ⸲ 3km ⸲ 3km ⸲ 3km ⸲ 22km
Notes No pets English spoken

ALVIGNAC

🏠 🍽 Le Bout du Roc

Marie LASCOSTE
46500 ALVIGNAC-LES-EAUX
☎ 05 65 33 70 18 📠 05 65 33 70 18
email: leboutduroc@wanadoo.fr
web: www.leboutduroc.com

This traditional house, set in peaceful open countryside between Rocamadour and Padirac, has rooms with separate access and facilities: 'Safranée' (double); 'Primevère' (twin); 'Cannelle' (double with spare double bed); 'Eté Indien' (double with single). Breakfast, with home-made patisseries, is served on the terrace in summer.

Prices s fr €35; d fr €40; t fr €48; dinner fr €18 **Nearby** ⸲ 10km
⸲ 20km ⸲ 15km Restaurant 3km ⸲ 3km Spa 4km ⸲ 6km ⸲ 3km
⸲ 1.5km **Notes** Pets admitted English spoken

🏠 🍽 Mazeyrac

Elie LASCOSTE
Route de Rocamadour, 46500 ALVIGNAC
☎ 05 65 33 61 16

Rooms in a Quercynois house of 1818 including a double room with spare bed and separate entrance, another double and a room for four,

each with private facilities, heating and fridge available. Meals must be booked in advance.

Prices s fr €35; d fr €40; t fr €48; dinner fr €16 **Nearby** ⸲ 8km
⸲ 25km ⸲ 2km ⸲ 8km Restaurant 2km ⸲ 12km ⸲ 8km ⸲ 2km
⸲ 4km **Notes** Pets admitted Open April to September.

AUJOLS

🏠 🍽 Chambre d'hôtes

Pierre et Françoise LAVILLE
Le Bourg, 46090 AUJOLS
☎ 05 65 21 19 72 📠 05 65 21 19 72
email: laville.pierre@wanadoo.fr
web: http://perso.wanadoo.fr/loustalet-aujols/

This village property, built in a style typical of the region, offers three guest rooms in an annexe to the main house. On the ground floor is a room with a double bed and a single; upstairs are two double rooms, one with additional twin beds on a mezzanine. All rooms have a lounge area and en suite facilities. Cot and child's bed available. Meals available except Wednesday and Sunday.

Prices s fr €44–€51; d fr €48–€55; t fr €65; extra person fr €11; dinner fr €18
On Site ⸲ **Nearby** ⸲ 5km ⸲ 30km ⸲ 10km ⸲ 8km Restaurant 14km
⸲ 8km ⸲ 8km ⸲ 8km **Notes** No pets English spoken Open February to November.

BERGANTY

🏠 🍽 Chambre d'hôtes

Serge et Mireille JARLAN
Lapeyre-Basse, 46090 BERGANTY
☎ 05 65 30 24 38
email: jarlan.mireille@wanadoo.fr
web: http://perso.wanadoo.fr/jarlan/accueil.htm

This is a working farm with three bedrooms, two of them family rooms. The accommodation is in converted outbuildings - an old bakehouse and two barns. The bakehouse has a split-level layout, with a double bed, three singles and a sitting area. One barn room is a double; the other is a room for four. All have private bath or shower room/WC.

Prices d €40–€50; t €55–€60; dinner fr €18 **Nearby** ⸲ 6km ⸲ 40km
⸲ 10km ⸲ 19km Restaurant 6km ⸲ 7km Spa 20km ⸲ 6km ⸲ 6km
⸲ 20km **Notes** No pets English spoken

BOISSIERES

🏠 🍽 Chambre d'hotes Lydia Michel

Lydia WOLTERS VAN DER WEY
Bertouille, 46150 BOISSIERES
☎ 05 65 21 43 29 📠 05 65 21 43 29

This house, built in the local style, has four bedrooms. On the first floor are two doubles and a twin, and a small guests' lounge area. On the second floor, a further double room also has a study corner. All rooms have private bath or shower room and WC, also a minibar. The first floor rooms have independent access. Home-made bread and pastries, meals by arrangement.

Prices s €56-€70; d €61-€75; extra person fr €18; dinner fr €22 **On Site** Private ⚲ **Nearby** ⚐ 12km ⚲ 20km ⚑ 15km Restaurant 3km ⚲ 8km ⚲ 0.8km ⛰ 15km **Notes** No pets English spoken Open 6 January to 10 December.

⊞ La Garrigue

Jean Claude BOUVIER
46150 BOISSIERES
☎ 05 65 30 98 40

In a 17th-century house typical of the region and with a large landscaped garden, guest rooms on offer here comprise two double rooms, a suite with a double and a single bed, and a single room, all with private washroom and WC. There are impressive views over the forest, and a restaurant is nearby.

Prices s fr €33; d fr €43; extra person fr €20 **Nearby** ⚐ 8km ⚑ 8km ⚲ 3km Restaurant 3km ⚲ 3km ⚲ 15km ⚲ 1km ⛰ 15km **Notes** Pets admitted English spoken

BOUSSAC

⊞ ⧈ Domaine des Villedieu

Martine VILLEDIEU
46100 BOUSSAC
☎ 05 65 40 06 63 ⧈ 05 65 40 09 22
email: villedi@aol.com
web: www.villedieu.com

There are four bedrooms at this property, all on the ground floor and with independent access. Three are doubles; the fourth is a suite for four, with a double bed and two singles. All have private bath or shower room and WC. Living room with books. Outside there is garden furniture and a swimming pool.

Prices s €64-€118; d €64-€118; t fr €137; dinner fr €28 **On Site** Restaurant ⚲ Private ⚲ **Nearby** ⚐ 10km ⚑ 2km ⚲ 10km ⚲ 10km ⛰ 10km **Notes** Pets admitted English spoken CC

CAHORS

⊞ ⧈ Saint Henri

Noël MASCHERETTI
46000 CAHORS
☎ 05 65 22 56 47 & 06 81 55 55 36
email: n.mascheretti@wanadoo.fr

The owners' home provides three double beds and four singles, each with TV, heating and private facilities. Private swimming pool.

Prices s fr €38; d fr €42; t fr €50; extra person fr €8; dinner fr €20 **On Site** Private ⚲ **Nearby** ⚐ 5km ⚲ 15km ⚑ 2km Restaurant 2km ⚲ 6km ⚲ 3km ⛰ 5km **Notes** No pets

CALES

⊞ ✿ ⧈ Lac Boutel

Alain VERGNES
46350 CALES
☎ 05 65 37 95 70 ⧈ 05 65 41 90 89

Rooms in an annexe of the owners' house offering four double beds and three singles, each with private shower and wc, heating and terrace. Refrigerator available and extra double bed available. Private swimming pool.

Prices s fr €36; d fr €42; t fr €51; dinner fr €17 **On Site** Private ⚲ **Nearby** ⚐ 1km ⚑ 7km Restaurant 2km ⚲ 7km ⚲ 13km ⚲ 9km ⛰ 12km **Notes** Pets admitted English spoken

CALVIGNAC

⊞ ⧈ ⛇ Chambre d'hôtes Pech Blanc

M-I et W VOGEL
Pech Blanc, 46160 CALVIGNAC
☎ 05 65 21 99 65
email: info@pechblanc.com
web: www.pechblanc.com

This is a barn conversion in the heart of the Parc Naturel Régional des Causses du Quercy, with wonderful views over the valleys and countryside. On the ground floor is a twin-bedded room and a double; upstairs are two more doubles, each with a little sitting area. All rooms have television, and private shower room and WC.

Prices s fr €44; d fr €54; extra person fr €15; dinner fr €19 **Nearby** ⚐ 4km ⚑ 5km ⚲ 4.5km Restaurant 4.5km ⚲ 4.5km ⚲ 4.5km ⚲ 4.5km ⛰ 30km **Notes** No pets English spoken

⊞ ⧈ Les Salamandres

Laurence DECOBERT
Pars, 46160 CALVIGNAC
☎ 05 65 50 19 22
email: contact@chambresdhotes-lot.com
web: www.chambresdhotes-lot.com

An old farmhouse built in the local style and nestling in five acres of wooded grounds. Three bedrooms comprise a family room for four with a double bed and bunks in a ground floor extension to the owners' home; two further rooms are in an annexe, both on the first

CONTINUED

CALVIGNAC *CONTINUED*

floor: a double and a twin-bedded room. All have private shower room and WC; cot available. Canoe hire 0.5km.

Prices s fr €35; d fr €45; t fr €55; extra person fr €10; dinner fr €16 **Nearby** ⚓ 0.8km 🏊 10km ⭢ 8km Restaurant 8km 🚣 3km ⛪ 8km 🚉 8km ⛰ 30km **Notes** Pets admitted English spoken

CARENNAC

▥ L'Oustal Nau les Combes

Colette LEMANT

46110 CARENNAC

☎ 05 65 10 94 09 & 06 88 18 13 43 🗎 05 65 50 27 49

email: lemant@club-internet.fr

web: www.oustalnau-carennac.com

This tastefully decorated property overlooks the Dordogne valley. It has five bedrooms: a double and a single on the ground floor, and two grade 2 doubles (one with an additional folding bed) and a twin-bedded room upstairs. All the rooms have private facilities, but those for the grade 2 rooms are not en suite. Use of kitchen. Garden, games area.

Prices s €80-€90; d €90-€100; t €100-€120 **Nearby** ⚓ 5.5km ⚘ 13km 🏊 0.5km ⭢ 0.2km Restaurant 0.1km 🚣 0.8km ⛪ 0.5km 🚉 0.1km ⛰ 9km **Notes** No pets English spoken CC

CASTELNAU-MONTRATIER

▥ 🍽 Ancienne école de Ganic

Julie CONTINI

46170 CASTELNAU MONTRATIER

☎ 05 65 22 45 70 & 06 88 08 63 58

email: contact@couetteetchocolat.com

web: www.couetteetchocolat.com

This old village school has three bedrooms on a mezzanine level, one with its own entrance. Two are doubles; the other is a triple. Each room includes a small lounge area, and each has its own bath/shower room and WC. Private parking, courtyard and garden. There are plans for a guests' kitchen, games room and a swimming pool.

Prices d €55-€60; extra person fr €18; dinner fr €22 **Nearby** ⚓ 12km ⭢ 5km Restaurant 5km 🚣 5km 🚉 5km ⛰ 25km **Notes** No pets English spoken

▥ 🍽 Lacombe

Michèle LELOUREC

46170 CASTELNAU MONTRATIER

☎ 05 65 21 84 16 & 06 84 77 07 53

email: michele.lelourec@jmail.com

web: www.domaine-lacombe.com

Guest rooms in a typical Quercynois house and its associated buildings: 'Le Figuié' (double); 'Les Chênes' (triple); 'La Source' (two double beds), each with private entrance and facilities, terrace, heating and TV. Garden and private covered swimming pool.

Prices d €63-€84; t €96-€103; extra person fr €20; dinner fr €29 **On Site** Private ⭢ **Nearby** ⚓ 6km 🏊 1km Restaurant 5km 🚣 3km 🚉 5km ⛰ 30km **Notes** Pets admitted English spoken CC

CAZALS

▥ La Caminade

Christian et Joëlle GAU

46250 CAZALS

☎ 05 65 21 66 63 🗎 05 65 21 66 63

email: la.caminade@laposte.net

web: www.lacaminade.com

A former presbytery offering characterful rooms: a single with lounge corner on the ground floor and three double rooms and bathroom facilities upstairs; all are no smoking. Lounge, large terraces, enclosed garden available to guests.

Prices s €95-€115; d €95-€115; extra person fr €20 **Nearby** ⚓ 8km 🏊 0.5km ⭢ 3km Restaurant 0.5km 🚣 0.5km 🚉 0.5km ⛰ 15km **Notes** No pets English spoken

CENEVIERES

▥ Mas de Labat

Héléne LEMAIRE

46330 CENEVIERES

☎ 05 65 24 39 11 & 06 09 60 70 66

email: maslabat@free.fr

web: www.mas-de-labat.com

In the heart of the countryside 15 kilometres from the cliff-edge village of St-Cirq-Lapopie, this modern property has four comfortable, bright rooms. In an annexe are two ground floor rooms, each with private terrace and own garden furniture plus covered barbecue; in the house are two upstairs rooms, each with a sitting area, one a double and the other with twin beds that can be made into a double. All have private shower room/WC. Additional beds available.

Prices s €41-€45; d €49-€53; extra person fr €15 **Nearby** ⚓ 6km 🏊 2km ⭢ 8km Restaurant 6km 🚣 4km ⛪ 6km 🚉 2km ⛰ 35km **Notes** Pets admitted English spoken

COMIAC

▥ 🍽 Chambre d'hôtes

André CAYROL

Proupech, 46190 COMIAC

☎ 05 65 33 85 67

email: andre.cayrol@orange.fr

web: http://monsite.orange.fr/proupech-comiac/

In the midst of the Quercy countryside, a farming family home built in 1821. Four guest rooms comprise a double and a triple on the ground floor, with shower/WC; upstairs are two doubles, also with shower room, and a guest living room. Meals feature fresh farm produce and regional specialities.

Prices s fr €40; d fr €45; extra person fr €10; dinner fr €15 **Nearby** ⚓ 20km 🏊 2km ⭢ 10km Restaurant 7km 🚣 2km ⛪ 20km 🚉 10km ⛰ 8km **Notes** No pets

DURAVEL

▦ ⑩ **Chambre d'hôtes**

Philippe DUCOUM
46700 DURAVEL
☎ 06 73 38 21 46 & 05 65 36 54 27
📄 05 65 36 44 14
email: philippeetisabelle.ducoum@club-internet.fr
web: www.chateau-de-rouffiac.com/

In this château, in a Cahors vineyard, there are four guest rooms. On the ground floor is a twin-bedded room; upstairs are two double rooms and a double room with two further single beds and its own lounge. All have private bath or shower room and WC. Central heating. Room with satellite TV and books to read. Extensive grounds.

Prices not confirmed for 2008　**On Site** Private ⚲　**Nearby** ⚓ 3km 🏊 4km 🚣 3km 🛍 5km 🚵 14km　**Notes** No pets　Open April to October.　CC

ESPAGNAC-SAINTE-EULALIE

▦ ⑩ **Sainte Eulalie**

Isabelle POUTINE
46330 ESPAGNAC SAINTE EULALIE
☎ 05 65 50 26 57
email: lesanonsducele@free.fr
web: http://lesanonsducele.free.fr

A 19th-century building formerly used for drying tobacco makes an unusual setting for these three rooms: a twin-bedded room, a double-bedded room, and a triple room (double bed plus a single). All have private shower and WC, and one room has its own entrance and private terrace.

Prices s fr €43; d €49–€62; t fr €72; dinner fr €17　**On Site** Restaurant ⚲　**Nearby** 🏊 0.1km 🚣 17km 🛍 6km 🚵 17km　**Notes** Pets admitted English spoken

FAYCELLES

▦ ⑩ **La Madeleine**

Marie-José DUBOST
La Boudousquerie, 46100 FAYCELLES
☎ 05 65 34 63 26 & 06 80 33 70 78　📄 05 65 34 63 26
email: dubostgerard@wanadoo.fr
web: www.laboudousquerie.com

This property has four bedrooms, in the hosts' house: three double rooms, two with their own lounge area; and a two-roomed suite, also with a lounge area. All rooms have TV, private shower and WC. Extra beds are available.

Prices s fr €59; d fr €74; t fr €94; dinner fr €28　**On Site** Private ⚲ **Nearby** ⚓ 0.5km 🏊 0.1km 🚣 6km 🛍 6km 🚵 6km　**Notes** No pets English spoken

FIGEAC

▦ **Manoir de Conjat**

Hubert et Agnès EVRARD
46100 FIGEAC
☎ 05 65 34 37 95 & 06 72 72 63 79
email: manoirdeconjat@free.fr

Three kilometres from Figeac, this former manor house overlooks a valley, and there is a swimming pool in the grounds. It offers three bedrooms, two with a separate entrance. A double room has its own kitchenette, and two triple rooms each have a double bed and a single; all have private bath or shower room and WC.

Prices d €70–€90; t €100–€120　**On Site** Private ⚲　**Nearby** ⚓ 3km 🏊 3km Restaurant 1km 🚣 3km 🎾 3km 🛍 3km 🚵 3km　**Notes** No pets English spoken

FONS

▦ **Domaine de la Piale**

Adeline SPINDLER
46100 FONS
☎ 05 65 40 19 52 & 06 87 39 84 73　📄 05 65 40 19 52
email: accueil@domainedelapiale.com
web: www.domainedelapiale.com

This 18th-century property stands in seven hectares of grounds, bordered with vines, chestnut trees, orchards and meadows, overlooking the Dourmelle valley. There are four double rooms, two of them with their own sitting rooms, all with private bath or shower room and WC. Indoor swimming pool.

Prices s €70–€110; d €70–€110; extra person fr €20　**On Site** Private ⚲ **Nearby** ⚓ 10km 🚴 30km 🏊 2km Restaurant 2km 🚣 10km 🎾 10km 🛍 10km 🚵 10km　**Notes** Pets admitted English spoken

FRAYSSINET-LE-GELAT

▦ **Le Clos de la Thèze**

Jean-Pierre MALGOUYAT
46250 FRAYSSINET LE GÉLAT
☎ 05 65 36 65 39
email: closdelatheze@free.fr
web: www.closdelatheze.fr

In the heart of Bouriane, between Quercy and Périgord, these three rooms are in an annexe to the owners' 16th-century house. There are two double rooms and a twin-bedded room; each room has a lounge area, and a private shower room and WC. The guests' rooms have their own entrance, and there is a lounge area with books.

Prices d €52–€75; extra person fr €10; dinner fr €10　**Nearby** ⚓ 4km 🏊 4km ⚲ 6km Restaurant 0.8km 🚣 4km 🎾 14km 🛍 4km 🚵 7km **Notes** No pets

GRAMAT

☷☷☷ ⋈ Domaine du Cloucau

Francine BOUGARET

46500 GRAMAT

☎ 05 65 33 76 18 & 06 30 07 44 98

🖹 05 65 33 76 18

email: lecloucau@wanadoo.fr

web: www.domaineducloucau.com

A huge 18th-century house in the heart of the Causse de Gramat. Non-smoking rooms include 'L'Hortensia' and 'Le Pigeonnier' (doubles) and two suites, 'La Caussanette' (double room and two single beds) and 'La Brocantine' (double with twin beds in adjoining room). Swimming pool with diving board, TV, piano, heating and rambling trails nearby.

Prices d €73–€78; extra person fr €18; dinner fr €24 **On Site** Private ⤻ **Nearby** ⛷ 4km ⌁ 20km ⌖ 4km Restaurant 4km ⌁ 4km ⌰ 4km ⋙ 4km **Notes** Pets admitted Open March to November.

☷☷☷ ⓴ Ferme du Gravier

Lydia et Patrice RAVET

Le Gravier, 46500 GRAMAT

☎ 05 65 33 41 88 & 06 84 48 67 99 🖹 05 65 33 41 88

email: admin@fermedugravier.co.uk

web: www.fermedugravier.co.uk

In a small farmhouse typical of the Causse, there are five rooms with four double beds, three singles and two bunks. Each room has shower, wc and heating; extra beds available. Library and terrace with garden furniture.

Prices s fr €45; d fr €45; t fr €55; extra person fr €12; dinner fr €20 **Nearby** ⛷ 5km ⌖ 1km Restaurant 1km ⌁ 1.5km Spa 8km ⌖ 1km ⌰ 1km ⋙ 0.8km **Notes** No pets English spoken

☷☷☷ ⋈ Montanty

Brigitte DUMAS

46500 GRAMAT

☎ 05 65 33 41 65

email: contact@montanty.com

web: www.montanty.com

A converted barn offering four double guest rooms, each with shower room and wc. Cot and spare bed available. Two more rooms are in the process of construction.

Prices s fr €36; d fr €38; t fr €50; dinner fr €16 **Nearby** ⛷ 3.5km ⌁ 15km ⌖ 10km ⤻ 3.5km Restaurant 3km ⌁ 3.5km Spa 10km ⌖ 3km ⌰ 3.5km ⋙ 3.5km **Notes** No pets English spoken

☷☷☷ ⋈ Moulin de Fresquet

Claude RAMELOT

46500 GRAMAT

☎ 05 65 38 70 60 & 06 08 85 09 21

🖹 05 65 33 60 13

email: info@moulindefresquet.com

web: www.moulindefresquet.com

A house of character and charm in a genuine 17th-century Quercynois water mill. Five guest rooms (four double and one with two double beds) available with private shower and wc; three have direct access to the 3 hectare shady park and private courtyard. Heating, terrace, library, TV lounge/reading room. Fishing on private stretch of water.

Prices s €64–€74; d €64–€97; t fr €125; extra person fr €15; dinner fr €25 **On Site** ⌖ **Nearby** ⛷ 0.8km ⌁ 15km ⤻ 0.8km Restaurant 0.8km ⌁ 0.8km ⋙ 1km **Notes** No pets English spoken Open April to October.

LALBENQUE

☷☷☷ ⋈ Le Vayssade

Pierre et Joëlle BAYSSE

46230 LALBENQUE

☎ 05 65 24 31 51 🖹 05 65 24 31 56

email: jpbaysse@lavayssade.com

web: www.lavayssade.com

This barn conversion has five guest bedrooms. On the ground floor there are two doubles; upstairs are three more doubles, two of them with bed-settees. Each room has a power shower and WC. Terrace, garden and swimming pool with wave machine. Courses in water-colour painting.

Prices d €69–€79; dinner fr €25 **On Site** Private ⤻ **Nearby** ⛷ 10km ⌁ 30km ⌖ 8km Restaurant 0.1km ⌁ ⌖ 6km ⌰ 0.3km ⋙ 16km **Notes** No pets Open December to February & April to September. CC

☷☷☷ ❦ ⋈ Mas de Cérès

Louis et Nicole COUCHOUD

Fournet, 46230 LALBENQUE

☎ 05 65 24 79 20 🖹 05 65 24 79 20

email: Louis.Couchoud@wanadoo.fr

web: http://monsite.wanadoo.fr/chambres_hotes_lot

Three guest rooms split between those in the proprietors' house and those in an outbuilding. One room is a double, the second has two double beds and a corner lounge, and the third has a double bed and a bunk bed; all have washroom and WC. Guests can use the courtyard and grounds, there are also several footpaths in the area.

Prices s fr €47; d €42–€49; t €58–€66; dinner €13–€17 **Nearby** ⛷ 5km ⌁ 25km ⌖ 1km ⤻ 7km Restaurant 7km ⌁ 7km ⌖ 15km ⌰ 7km ⋙ 7km **Notes** No pets English spoken

MIDI-PYRÉNÉES

E BASTIT

♯ ⊠ & **Bel Air**

ncine CHAMBERT

500 LE BASTIT

☎ 05 65 38 77 54 ▤ 05 65 38 85 18

eb: www.domaine-de-bel-air.com

s Quercynois house of character provides two twin rooms, a triple
d three doubles, each with private facilities and heating. Salon, TV,
eshment room, cooking area, shaded terrace, boules area, garden
niture, caving, paths. Near the sites of Rocamadour and Padirac.

es s fr €43; d fr €47; t fr €59; dinner fr €19 **Nearby** ⛷ 8km
0km ⚓ 30km ↖ 10km Restaurant 4km 🚲 8km ⚑ 9km 🚉 8km
)km **Notes** Pets admitted English spoken Open March to November.

E MONTAT

♯ ⊠ **Domaine Les Tuileries**

dré CARRIER

090 LE MONTAT-CAHORS

☎ 05 65 21 04 72 ▤ 05 65 21 04 72

ail: domainelestuileries@yahoo.fr

b: http://perso.orange.fr/domainelestuileries

n from Cahors, three guest rooms include a room for four, one
eping three, and a double room, all non-smoking with shower,
TV and heating. Garden furniture, paddock for horses and winter
fle hunts. On the St Jacques de Compostelle pilgrim route, with
ked walking trails.

es s fr €44; d fr €56; t fr €69; extra person fr €10; dinner fr €17
arby 🚲 15km ⚓ 8km ↖ 8km 🚲 1km 🚉 6km ⚑ 6km
tes No pets English spoken

E VIGAN

♯ **La Pradelle**

n-Claude et Colette HUPIN

vers, 46300 LE VIGAN

☎ 05 65 37 40 87 & 06 08 37 85 36 ▤ 05 65 37 40 87

ail: jc.hupin@wanadoo.fr

b: www.la-pradelle.com

s house was built recently, but in the traditional local style. It has
ee rooms: a twin-bedded room with lounge area, and two double-
ded rooms. An extra bed is available. All rooms have private bath
shower room and WC, and a private terrace.

Prices s fr €55; d fr €60; extra person fr €20 **Nearby** ⛷ 4km ⚓ 4km
↖ 5km 🚲 4km 🚉 4km ⚑ 5km **Notes** No pets English spoken Open
March to October.

♯♯♯ ⊠ **Manoir de la Barrière**

Peter et Marie ROBINSON

46300 LE VIGAN

☎ 05 65 41 40 73 & 06 78 85 92 80 ▤ 05 65 32 56 12

email: perobinson@wanadoo.fr

web: www.manoirlabarriere.com

A beautiful old manor house dating back to the 13th century which
stands on the edge of the village of Le Vigan. In the grounds, which
offer plenty of shade, is a swimming pool and parking. Accommodation
comprises two family rooms for up to four people (double bed plus
two singles) with shower/WC, one with its own entrance; two double
rooms, one a king-size, both with bathroom and salon; and a suite for
two on two levels, with upstairs bedroom and ground floor bathroom,
sitting room and own access. Meals by reservation.

Prices s €50-€75; d €75-€95; extra person fr €25; dinner fr €25
On Site ⚑ Private ↖ **Nearby** ⛷ 2km 🚲 12km ⚓ 0.5km
Restaurant 0.1km 🚲 0.5km 🚉 0.1km ⚑ 5km **Notes** No pets English
spoken

LEBREIL

♯♯♯ ⊠ **Mas Labrugade**

Madeleine BIBARD

46800 LEBREIL

☎ 05 65 31 84 66 & 06 26 25 06 82 ▤ 05 65 31 84 58

email: mas.labrugade@orange.fr

web: www.mas-labrugade.com

In an attractive countryside location among flowers and woods, rooms
with separate access and facilities, offering three double beds, a single,
a spare and a cot. Heating, courtyard, sitting room, library. In summer
relax on the shady terrace with its outdoor furniture; in winter enjoy
the warmth of the open fire.

Prices s fr €33; d fr €46; t fr €60; extra person fr €12; dinner fr €17
On Site ⚓ **Nearby** ⛷ 15km Restaurant 4km 🚲 4km ⚑ 4km 🚉 4km
⚑ 30km **Notes** Pets admitted

LES QUATRE ROUTES

♯♯♯ ⊠ **Chambres et Tables d'Hôtes Saint-Julien**

R EYMAT et J CHABOY

46110 LES QUATRE ROUTES

☎ 05 65 32 11 82

email: josette.chaboy@wanadoo.fr

web: www.cafecouette-st-julien.com

Guest rooms in the proprietors' home, with separate access, include
'Tilleul' (double with TV), 'Tournesol' (with two double beds and TV)
and 'Lavande' (double bed). All have private facilities and heating. The
host offers truffle hunting expeditions.

Prices s €40-€45; d €45-€50; t fr €62; dinner fr €17 **Nearby** ⛷ 15km
🚲 15km ⚓ 6km ↖ 8km Restaurant 1km 🚲 15km ⚑ 10km 🚉 1km
⚑ 1km **Notes** No pets Open April to November.

LISSAC-ET-MOURET

☶ ⏏ L'Oasienne - Claviès

Gérard GAY

46100 LISSAC ET MOURET

☎ 05 65 34 40 98 & 06 84 69 79 03 ▤ 05 65 34 40 98

email: loasienne@hotmail.com

web: www.oasienne.com

This farm has rooms in the owners' house with three double beds, two singles and a child's bed in total, all with private facilities. There is also a gîte and camping sharing two swimming pools and a jacuzzi. Trampoline, mini-golf, refreshment room, table tennis. Restaurant 7km.

Prices s fr €35; d €39-€44; t fr €45; extra person fr €5; dinner fr €17 **On Site** Private ⚲ **Nearby** ⛷ 4km ✿ 3km ⚲ 2km ☚ 7km ⚑ 8km ⚏ 8km **Notes** No pets

LUZECH

☶ Le Peyrou

Nienke MARTINOT

46140 LUZECH

☎ 05 65 30 51 98 ▤ 05 65 30 51 98

email: m.martinot@wanadoo.fr

A former wine-growing estate set amongst vines, offering three rooms in the owner's residence and an outbuilding, each with king-size canopied bed and private facilities. Guests have use of a lounge with kitchen corner and a large park with swimming pool, tennis, children's games and boules.

Prices d €58-€72 **On Site** Private ⚲ Private tennis court **Nearby** ⛷ 10km ✿ 0.2km ⚑ 0.6km ⚏ 16km **Notes** No pets English spoken

MARTEL

☶ ⏏ Baboyard

Marie HUREAU

46600 MARTEL

☎ 05 65 32 59 73 & 06 24 05 14 72

email: leshauts.deloupchat@free.fr

web: www.chambres-hotes-lot.com

Four bedrooms, each with an independent entrance, in a house with attractive views, built in the style typical of the area. All of the rooms are doubles; all have private bath or shower room, and one has space for an extra bed. There are ten hectares of grounds, with woods, meadows and a swimming pool. Meals by reservation.

Prices s fr €42; d fr €64; t fr €77; dinner fr €20 **On Site** Private ⚲ **Nearby** ⛷ 4km ⚓ 20km ✿ 4km Restaurant 4km ☚ 10km ⚑ 4km ⚏ 15km **Notes** No pets English spoken

☶ ⏏ *Domaine de la Vaysse*

Nelly et Maurice CHAVANT

Route de Creysse, 46600 MARTEL

☎ 05 65 32 49 87

email: domaine.vaysse@wanadoo.fr

web: www.domaine-de-la-vaysse.com

This is a barn conversion standing in 19 hectares of grounds not far from the valley of the Dordogne. The five rooms, all upstairs, compr a triple with bathroom, a double with shower/WC, a twin with show room and living area, a room for four (double bed and two singles) with shower, and a twin-bedded room with bathroom and its own exterior access and private terrace.

Prices not confirmed for 2008 **On Site** Private ⚲ **Nearby** ⛷ 4km ⚲ 2km ⚑ 2km ⚏ 5km **Notes** Pets admitted CC

☶ La Cour au Tilleul

Myriam JOUVET

Av du Capitani, 46600 MARTEL

☎ 05 65 37 34 08

email: myriam.jouvet@wanadoo.com

web: www.lacourautilleul.fr

In the little medieval village of Martel, this Lotois house has three charming guest rooms with independent access opening on to the interior courtyard. There is a room with double and single bed, a room with a double and two singles and a double room, each with private facilities and heating. Breakfast served on the terrace in the summer.

Prices s fr €55; d fr €60; extra person fr €15 **Nearby** ⛷ 4km ✿ 4km ⚲ 10km Restaurant 0.2km ⚲ 2km ⚑ 0.1km ⚏ 5km **Notes** Pets admitted

☶ La Croix-Matthieu

Lilianne MACAINE

46600 MARTEL

☎ 05 65 37 41 78 & 06 83 51 14 98

email: croix.matthieu@wanadoo.fr

web: http://perso.wanadoo.fr/croix.matthieu/sommaire.htm

Guest rooms available include a triple room with double and cot in adjoining room and three rooms in an annexe with separate access two triple rooms and a twin. All have private facilities; extra beds possible. Lounge/living room with TV and open fire. Picnicking in th grounds, swimming pool shared with owners and covered terrace with barbecue.

Prices s fr €45; d fr €62; t fr €85; extra person fr €15 **On Site** ☚ Private ⚲ **Nearby** ⛷ 8km ⚓ 14km ✿ 5km Restaurant 1km ⚲ 1km ⚑ 1km ⚏ 8km **Notes** No pets English spoken

₩ La Tuilerie

uy RAYNAL

luges, 46600 MARTEL

☎ 05 65 27 04 47 📄 05 65 27 04 48

mail: guyraynal @aol.com

eb: www.latuilerie.akoonet.com

is delightful 19th-century house has five bedrooms. There are two
n the first floor - a double with lounge area, and a twin. On the
cond floor are two doubles, one with a lounge area, and another
in. Extra bed available. All rooms have private bath or shower room
d WC. Eight acres of grounds, and a billiard table in the orangery.

ices d €59-€90; extra person fr €15 **Nearby** ⚓ 7km ⚲ 18km
0.3km Restaurant 0.5km ⚑ 0.5km ⚐ 0.3km ⚑ 5km ⚑ 4km
otes No pets English spoken

1AUROUX

₩ Le Mas de Laure

an Louis TREBOSSEN

5700 MAUROUX

☎ 05 65 30 67 39 📄 05 65 30 67 39

nail: contact@mas-de-laure.com

eb: www.mas-de-laure.com

an old farmhouse of character, rooms with their own access include
ouché de Soleil' and 'Abri des Vents' (twins), 'Sous Ciel Etoilé'
ouble with two singles on a mezzanine), 'Plain Sud' (triple) and
ise d'Antan') (double). All have shower, wc and heating. Swimming
ol, table tennis, 4 x 4 tracks (except July and August), theme
eekends and lakes and walking trails nearby.

ices s fr €70; d fr €70; t fr €85; extra person fr €15 **On Site** Private ⚲
earby ⚓ 2km ⚲ 20km ⚐ 8km Restaurant 2km ⚑ 0.5km ⚐ 13km
1km ⚑ 13km **Notes** No pets English spoken

1AYRAC

₩ ⚑ Villa Touloumo

Andrée LAVIS DE LAUW

46200 MAYRAC

☎ 05 65 27 12 94 & 06 22 60 72 20

📄 05 65 27 14 27

email: villa-touloumo@wanadoo.fr

web: www.villatouloumo.com

With panoramic views over the Dordogne valley and its cliffs,
his house offers personalised, contemporary rooms with private
acilities: 'Rocamadour' (king-size bed and two singles on a
nezzanine), 'Carennac' (double) and 'Figeac' (twin). Buffet-style
oreakfasts. Pets accepted by reservation only.

Prices s fr €62; d €69-€87; t fr €104; dinner fr €29
On Site Private ⚲ **Nearby** ⚓ 4km ⚲ 8km ⚐ 2km Restaurant 3km
⚑ 2km ⚐ 8km ⚑ 3km ⚑ 8km **Notes** Pets admitted English
spoken

MERCUES

₩ |◯| Le Mas Azemar

Claude PATROLIN

46090 MERCUES

☎ 05 65 30 96 85 📄 05 65 30 53 82

email: masazemar@aol.com

web: www.masazemar.com

A beautiful home in the heart of Cahors wine territory, with a
room with double and single bed, two doubles, a room with two
doubles and a single, a twin and a triple. All have private facilities
and heating. Sitting room available.

Prices s €75-€105; d €75-€105; t fr €122; extra person fr €17;
dinner fr €32 **Nearby** ⚓ 8km ⚲ 30km ⚐ 5km Restaurant 1km
⚑ 5km ⚐ 6km ⚑ 0.3km ⚑ 10km **Notes** No pets English spoken

MIERS

₩ Le Vieux Séchoir

Josiane LAVERGNE

46500 MIERS

☎ 05 65 33 68 33 📄 05 65 33 68 33

email: levieuxsechoir@wanadoo.fr

web: www.levieuxsechoir.com

Rooms in an old restored barn by the owners' house, with five double
beds, a single, two bunks, a spare bed, and a cot. All rooms have
shower and wc. Heating, garden furniture, barbecue. Golf 15km.

Prices s fr €35; d fr €40; t fr €48; extra person fr €8 **Nearby** ⚓ 10km
⚲ 15km ⚐ 8km ⚑ 4km Restaurant 1.5km ⚑ 1.5km ⚑ 1.5km ⚑ 10km
Notes No pets Open April to September.

MILHAC

₩ ⚑ |◯| Château-Vieux

Christian BOUDET

46300 MILHAC

☎ 05 65 41 02 11 & 06 86 74 69 83 📄 05 65 41 02 11

email: chateau_vieux@hotmail.com

web: www.internet46.fr/chateau_vieux.html

One room with disabled access with two double beds, three triple
rooms and a double, all with shower, wc and heating. Table d'hôte on
request and children catered for. Lake 3km.

Prices not confirmed for 2008 **Nearby** ⚓ 2km ⚐ 4km ⚲ 7km ⚑ 1km
⚑ 7km ⚑ 7km **Notes** Pets admitted

₩ |◯| La Relinquière

Marie-Claire POINOT

Le Bourg, 46300 MILHAC

☎ 05 65 32 03 35

email: marie-claire@relinquiere.com

web: www.relinquiere.com

This old farmhouse has three guest rooms. On the ground floor
"Harvest" has a double bed; on the first floor "Wine Harvest" has twin

CONTINUED

MILHAC *CONTINUED*

beds, with space for a third; on the third floor "Sowing" has a double with space for an extra single. All rooms have private shower room and WC. Cot available, lounge shared with hosts.

Prices s fr €52; d fr €58; t fr €74; dinner fr €22 **On Site** Private ⚲ **Nearby** ⚓ 1km ⚓ 10km ⚐ 7km Restaurant 3km ⚓ ⚓ 4km ⚑ 5km ⚐ 7km **Notes** No pets English spoken Open March to 15 November.

MONTBRUN

⚲ La Treille

Emmanuel PRADINES
46160 MONTBRUN
☎ 05 65 40 77 20 & 06 22 49 69 91

This house stands beside the River Lot and has two double rooms, one twin and one sleeping four with independent access, heating, shower and wc. Cots and spare bed available. Private lounge and garden furniture.

Prices s fr €30; d fr €38; t fr €42; extra person fr €10 **Nearby** ⚓ 10km ⚓ 20km ⚐ 0.1km ⚲ 8km Restaurant 8km ⚓ 8km Spa 40km ⚓ 8km ⚑ 8km ⚐ 20km **Notes** No pets

ORNIAC

⚲ Le Couffin

Carmen NEHRKORN
46330 ORNIAC
☎ 05 65 31 33 96

Accommodation here is laid out within the proprietors' house, which occupies a pleasant setting. There are two rooms with two double beds, and a family suite with a double bed and two singles in an adjoining room. All have private facilities. There is a lounge with an open fire and guests can use the garden and terrace.

Prices s €30-€43; d €36-€47; t fr €52; extra person fr €18; dinner fr €15 **Nearby** ⚓ 6km ⚐ 5km ⚲ 15km Restaurant 5km ⚓ 4km ⚑ 5km ⚐ 25km **Notes** Pets admitted English spoken

PADIRAC

⚲ Latreille

Philippe LESCALE
46500 PADIRAC
☎ 05 65 33 67 57 ▤ 05 65 33 67 57

In the proprietors' house, guest rooms include three triples and a double, all with shower and wc. Three spare beds and heating available. Special price for four people.

Prices s fr €32; d fr €39; t fr €45; dinner fr €15 **Nearby** ⚓ 10km ⚐ 8km ⚲ 0.3km Restaurant 1km ⚓ 10km ⚑ 10km ⚐ 9km **Notes** Pets admitted

PARNAC

La Condamine

Georges DELMAS
46140 PARNAC
☎ 05 65 30 73 84 & 05 65 30 98 21 ▤ 05 65 30 98 21
email: lecruduquercy@wanadoo.fr
web: www.domainesdelmas.com

Four double rooms, with views of the Lot river, on the second floor of the proprietor's house, set in the heart of the vineyards, one room has a double sofa bed and would suit a family of four. All rooms have bath or shower room and private WC. Terrace and gardens; tasting and purchase of nuts and wine.

Prices d €60-€90; t fr €90 **On Site** ⚲ **Nearby** ⚓ 4km ⚲ 4km ⚓ 1km ⚑ 4km ⚐ 18km **Notes** No pets English spoken CC

PEYRILLES

Trespécoul

André et Jacqueline CHRISTOPHE
46310 PEYRILLES
☎ 05 65 31 00 91 & 06 80 81 86 15 ▤ 05 65 31 00 91
email: j-et-a-christophe@wanadoo.fr
web: www.trespecoul.com

Two double rooms and one sleeping three, each with private facilities and heating. Extra bed available. Garden furniture, barbecue, cooking area, table tennis. Restaurant 2km.

Prices s fr €34; d €37-€42; t fr €54; extra person fr €5 **On Site** ⚐ **Nearby** ⚓ 15km ⚲ 2km Restaurant 2km ⚓ 2km ⚑ 2km ⚐ 15km **Notes** Pets admitted English spoken Open April to 1 November.

PUY-L'EVEQUE

Maison Rouma

Bill ARNETT
2 rue du Docteur Rouma, 46700 PUY L'EVEQUE
☎ 05 65 36 59 39 ▤ 05 65 36 59 39
email: williamarnett@hotmail.com

Next to the river in Puy-l'Evèque, this house offers two double rooms (The Blue Room and Nicki's Room) and a twin (Henry's Room), all with private facilities. Courtyard, terrace for breakfast, parking and open air swimming pool.

Prices s fr €50; d fr €55; t fr €60 **On Site** ⚐ Private ⚲ **Nearby** ⚓ 8km ⚓ 30km Restaurant 0.2km ⚓ 0.5km ⚓ 5km ⚑ 0.5km ⚐ 33km **Notes** No pets English spoken

RIGNAC

⫸ Les Bourruts

atrick BALAYSSAC

6500 RIGNAC

☎ 05 65 33 69 31

mail: francoise.balayssac@wanadoo.fr

our rooms on the first floor of the owners' home, but with a separate uests' entrance. Two of the rooms are doubles, with space for a hild's bed; the other two are rooms for four, each with a double bed nd two singles. All rooms have private shower and WC. Grounds, th shady picnic spots - table available.

rices d fr €39; t fr €45; extra person fr €10 **Nearby** ☘ 0.6km
22km ⚘ 15km ⚹ 3km Restaurant 3km ♨ 3km ⛪ 3km ⤛ 3km
otes No pets Open April to September.

ROCAMADOUR

⫸ Maison Neuve

dette ARCOUTEL

6500 ROCAMADOUR

☎ 05 65 33 62 69 & 06 75 41 19 97

poms here include two doubles, a room with double bed and two ngles and a room with double and single, all with private facilities d heating. Possible spare single bed.

ices s fr €32; d €37-€44; t fr €52; extra person fr €13
earby ☘ 10km ⚘ 30km ⚹ 10km ⛪ 10km Restaurant 1km ♨ 1km
1km ⤛ 3km **Notes** Pets admitted

AIGNES

⫸ La Mazotière

éronique et Gérard PUISNEY

6500 SAIGNES

☎ 05 65 33 75 31 & 06 71 44 35 21 🖹 05 65 33 75 31

mail: lamazotiere@wanadoo.fr

an annexe to the owners' home with independent access, there are o triple rooms and a double room with disabled access, each with vate facilities. Living room/lounge reserved for guests with TV and eo, terrace and garden.

ices s fr €38; d fr €45; t fr €55; extra person fr €10 **Nearby** ☘ 8km
3km ⚹ 8km ♨ 8km ⛪ 8km ⤛ 8km **Notes** Pets admitted English oken Open May to September.

OUILLAC

⫸ 🍴 ♿ Chambres d'hôtes

orinne et Bernard PETIT

 Roc, Par Souillac, 46200 SOUILLAC

 05 65 37 08 45

mail: artesienne@wanadoo.fr

eb: www.artesienne-le-roc.com

is property is tucked away in a quiet spot in the Dordogne valley. e guest bedrooms are all upstairs in the owners' house, but with a parate entrance. The three rooms comprise a room for four (double

---

bed and two singles), one for three (double bed and single) and a double, each with shower room/WC; the room for four has its own small terrace area.

Prices s fr €43; d fr €49; t fr €64; extra person fr €15; dinner €19
On Site Private ⚹ **Nearby** ☘ 6km ⚘ 15km ⚹ 1km ♨ 3km ⛪ 5km
🏠 5km ⤛ 5km **Notes** Pets admitted English spoken Open Easter to November.

⫸ Le Clos Fleury

Georges FLEURY

149 Route de Sarlat, 46200 SOUILLAC

☎ 05 65 37 68 25 & 06 11 87 07 50 🖹 05 65 37 68 25

web: www.chez.com/pierre233

Three first floor rooms here, in a wing of the owners' house, right beside the Dordogne river. The grounds extend to one hectare, and include a riverside beach. There are two double rooms, one with space for an extra bed, and a two-roomed family suite for four. One double has a bathroom, the other rooms have shower/WC. Large living room in stone with TV and games.

Prices s fr €45; d fr €55; t €70-€80 **On Site** ⚘ ⛪ **Nearby** ☘ 2km
⚹ 2km Restaurant 0.4km ♨ 2km 🏠 0.4km ⤛ 1km **Notes** No pets

⫸ Le Prieuré

Martin et Saskia LANDMAN

Cieurac-Lanzac, 46200 SOUILLAC

☎ 05 65 32 74 61 & 06 74 66 27 66

email: contact@le-prieure.net

web: http://gdf.le-prieure.net/

This former priory still has its chapel and offers a double room with adjoining single room, and three further doubles, one with sofa bed. Each has private facilities and heating.

Prices s €42-€53; d €48-€65; t €75-€85 **On Site** Private ⚹
Nearby ☘ 2.5km ⚘ 1km Restaurant 2km ♨ 2.5km ⛪ 2km 🏠 3km
⤛ 2.5km **Notes** Pets admitted English spoken Open April to 1 October.

ST-CHAMARAND

⫸ 🍴 Les Cèdres de Lescaille

B MAGNIN et C VOCK

46310 SAINT CHAMARAND

☎ 05 65 24 50 02 🖹 05 65 24 50 78

email: info@lescaille.com

web: www.lescaille.com

Four rooms, each with a double and single bed, and a double room are available, each with shower and wc. Spare bed available. Heating, terrace, garden, swimming pool shared with owners. Groups taken out of season.

Prices s fr €50; d €58-€68; t €70-€80; dinner fr €20 **On Site** Private ⚹
Nearby ☘ 7km ⚘ 4km Restaurant 10km ♨ 4km ⛪ 10km 🏠 4km
⤛ 10km **Notes** No pets CC

ST-CIRGUES

⫴ ⵙ Château Lantuéjouls

J-M et R LASSALE
46210 SAINT CIRGUES
☎ 05 65 40 32 93
email: webmaster@lot-chambres-hotes.com
web: www.lot-chambres-hotes.com

This house has a beautiful rural setting, high up, amongst woods, meadows and streams. There are three rooms, all on the first floor of the owners' house. There is one double room, and three family rooms for four, each with a double bed or twins, plus bunks. All rooms have private bath or shower room and WC. Terrace.

Prices s fr €41; d fr €49; t fr €64; extra person fr €18; dinner fr €18
Nearby ⛷ 12km ⌇ 40km ⌖ 15km ⋏ 10km Restaurant 10km ⌁ 10km
⌂ 10km ⋙ 10km **Notes** No pets English spoken

ST-DENIS-LES-MARTEL

⫴ ⵙ Cabrejou

Jean-Paul ANDRIEUX
46600 SAINT DENIS LES MARTEL
☎ 05 65 37 31 89 ▤ 05 65 37 31 89
web: www.ferme-cabrejou.com

On the first floor of a converted barn next to the owner's house are four double rooms, all with bath or shower and WC.

Prices s fr €35; d fr €40; t fr €45; dinner fr €17 **Nearby** ⛷ 5km ⌖ 6km
⋏ 5km Restaurant 1km ⌁ 5km ⌘ 5km ⌂ 3km ⋙ 5km **Notes** No pets

⫴ ⵙ La Ferme de Cabrejou

Roger et Marinette ANDRIEUX
46600 SAINT DENIS LES MARTEL
☎ 05 65 37 31 89 ▤ 05 65 37 31 89
web: www.ferme-cabrejou.com

This property has three rooms, two on the ground floor and another on the first floor, with its own lounge. One is a twin-bedded room; the others can sleep three people. All rooms have private bath or shower room and WC. Central heating. Garden rooms.

Prices s fr €35; d fr €40; t fr €45; dinner fr €17 **Nearby** ⛷ 5km
⌇ 17km ⌖ 5km ⋏ 8km Restaurant 3km ⌁ 7km ⌘ 7km ⌂ 3km
⋙ 7km **Notes** No pets Open Easter to 11 November.

ST-GERY

⫴ Domaine du Porche

Jean-Claude LADOUX
46330 SAINT GERY
☎ 05 65 31 45 94 ▤ 05 65 31 45 94

In a house in the village, with separate access, guest rooms offered include a double and three rooms with a double plus single bed, each with private facilities. Cot available. Summer kitchen, swimming pool, shaded terrace and garden for picnics.

Prices s fr €33; d fr €39; t fr €44 **On Site** Private ⋏ **Nearby** ⛷ 8km
⌇ 20km ⌖ 0.2km Restaurant 20km ⌁ 0.2km Spa 20km ⋙ 20km
Notes No pets English spoken

⫴ ⵙ Le Mas de la Pommeraie

Marc et Danielle MAUDUIT
46330 SAINT GERY
☎ 05 65 31 99 43 & 06 33 65 33 45
email: contact@mas-pommeraie.com
web: www.mas-pommeraie.com

An 18th-century barn is the setting for this chambre d'hôtes. There are four rooms: three doubles, plus a larger double which has a lounge area which could provide space for up to two extra beds. All rooms have private bath or shower room and WC. There is a lounge, terrace and courtyard. Picnics prepared by arrangement. Canoes and kayaks available 3km.

Prices s €49-€52; d €54-€70; extra person fr €20; dinner €19-€29
On Site Private ⋏ **Nearby** ⛷ 6km ⌖ 3km Restaurant 2km ⌁ 3km
⌂ 3km ⋙ 25km **Notes** No pets

ST-MARTIN-LABOUVAL

⫴⫴ ⵙ Le Clos de la Roseraie

Fabrice et Corinne PIEDELEU
Le Bourg, 46330 SAINT MARTIN LABOUVAL
☎ 05 65 21 90 46
email: closdelaroseraie@aol.com
web: www.closdelaroseraie.com

A delightful 19th-century house, tucked away in the Lot valley not far from St-Cirq-Lapopie. The three elegant bedrooms are in a totally restored outbuilding. All are doubles; each has an independent entrance, private shower and WC. An extra bed is available. In the grounds are rose bushes, hydrangeas, shady terraces and a swimming pool.

Prices d €68-€71; extra person fr €18; dinner fr €23
On Site Private ⋏ **Nearby** ⛷ 10km ⌖ 0.5km Restaurant 0.1km
⌁ 0.5km ⌘ 10km ⌂ 1km ⋙ 35km **Notes** Pets admitted English spoken

ST-PANTALEON

⫴ ⵙ Lartigue

Annick DUBOIS
46800 SAINT PANTALEON
☎ 05 65 31 89 29 & 06 87 36 49 72 ▤ 05 65 31 89 29
web: www.domaine-de-lartigue.com/

A ground-floor suite sleeping four, with shower and WC. Non-smoking house. Gastronomic menu available (supplement).

Prices s fr €40; d €50-€60; t fr €75; dinner fr €19 **On Site** ⛷
Nearby ⌇ 10km ⌖ 10km ⋏ 10km Restaurant 1km ⌁ 10km ⌂ 10km
⋙ 15km **Notes** Pets admitted English spoken

ST-SIMON

▦ ⏱ ㅎ **Les Moynes**

Pascale ARETS
46320 ST SIMON
☎ 05 65 40 48 90 🗎 05 65 40 48 90
email: les.moynes@free.fr
web: http://les.moynes.free.fr

...ve rooms on an old restored sheep farm, on a 12 hectare estate in ...e Causses de Quercy Regional Park. There are two double rooms, ...e triple and two sleeping four, all with private shower and wc, and ...e with disabled access. Swimming pool and paddling pool, park, ...rrace, boules, table tennis, piano, billiards, library, TV lounge, hiking ...ails.

Prices s fr €38; d €50-€60; t €56-€65; extra person fr €12; dinner fr €19
On Site Private ⌁ **Nearby** ⛷ 1km ⚓ 25km ⚑ 10km Restaurant 8km
⚓ 8km ⚑ 8km ⚑ 8km **Notes** Pets admitted English spoken Open ...ril to October.

ST-SOZY

▦ ⏱ **Le Mas Rambert**

Françoise TIERCE
46200 ST SOZY
☎ 05 65 37 14 07 & 06 32 07 73 79 🗎 05 65 37 14 07
email: f.tierce@wanadoo.fr
web: http://lemasrambert.free.fr

...e owner's house accommodates three guest rooms including two ...ubles, one with possible two extra single beds in an adjoining ...om, and a room for four. All have private facilities and TV point. The ...operty is on the Causse de Martel, close to numerous interesting ...es. Evening meal not available in July and August.

Prices s fr €48; d fr €56; dinner fr €15 **On Site** Private ⌁
Nearby ⛷ 3km ⚑ 2.5km Restaurant 2km ⚓ 2km ⚓ 10km ⚑ 10km
Notes No pets English spoken

▦ ⏱ **Le Pech Grand**

Charles HINSSEN
46200 ST SOZY
☎ 05 65 32 27 98
email: pechgrand@wanadoo.fr
web: www.pechgrand.com

The guest rooms of this property are housed in an extension to the owners' house, with a separate entrance: a double room, two twin-bedded rooms, a room with three beds, and a room with four single beds. All rooms have private bath or shower room and WC.

Prices s fr €45; d €52-€62; t €67-€77; extra person fr €15; dinner fr €24 **On Site** ♨ **Nearby** ⛷ 7km ⚓ 10km ⚑ 1km ⌁ 0.5km
Restaurant 0.5km ⚓ 0.5km ⚓ 0.5km ⚑ 15km **Notes** English spoken
Open March to 1 November.

THEDIRAC

▦ ⏱ **Manoir de Surgès**

Joëlle DELILLE
46150 THÉDIRAC
☎ 05 6521 22 45 & 06 75 26 79 44
email: manoirdesurges@orange.fr
web: www.manoirdesurges.fr.st

A 17th-century manor set in 36 hectare grounds, offering a double four-poster room, a duplex with double four-poster plus two single beds, and a room with double and single beds. All have bathroom, wc and heating; two spare beds available. TV lounge with open fire, terrace with garden furniture, swimming pool shared with owners.

Prices d €65-€70; t €80-€85; extra person fr €20; dinner fr €22
On Site Private ⌁ **Nearby** ⛷ 8km ⚑ 8km Restaurant 4km
⚓ 2km ⚓ 7km ⚑ 20km **Notes** No pets

TOUR-DE-FAURE

❚❚❚ ◯ **Combe de Redoles**

Philippe DRUOT
46330 TOUR DE FAURE
☎ 05 65 31 21 58 & 06 82 61 43 56
📄 05 65 31 21 58
email: druot@club-internet.fr
web: www.chambre-redoles.com

A typical Quercynois farmhouse on the edge of the forest offering rooms with private facilities and heating. Dining room and lounge for guests, piano, summer kitchen, barbecue, garden furniture, outdoor games. Swimming pool and children's pool.

Prices s fr €45; d €46-€55; t €60-€75; extra person fr €13; dinner fr €17 **On Site** ❧ Private ↰ **Nearby** ♿ 10km ✐ 1km 🏊 1km 🏠 1km ⚒ 35km **Notes** Pets admitted English spoken

❚❚❚ *Maison Redon*

Patrice REDON
La Combe, 46330 TOUR DE FAURE
☎ 05 65 30 24 13 📄 05 65 30 24 13
email: patrice@maisonredon.com
web: www.maisonredon.com

This 19th-century house is in a small village close to St-Cirq-Lapopie. It stands in extensive wooded grounds and offers five bedrooms: three doubles and two triples. One of the triples has a double bed and a single; the other has three single beds. All of the rooms have private bathrooms and WCs.

Prices not confirmed for 2008 **Nearby** ♿ 8km ✐ 1km 🏊 0.5km 🏠 0.4km ⚒ 30km **Notes** No pets English spoken

VERS

❚❚❚ ◯ **Le Clos des Dryades**

Thierry CREPIN
46090 VERS
☎ 05 65 31 44 50 📄 05 65 31 44 50
email: contact@closdesdryades.com
web: www.closdesdryades.com

A large house in two hectares of grounds in a quiet location. A double room is on the ground floor; upstairs are two more doubles, and a room for three with a double bed and a single. All have private bathroom and WC. Guests' sitting room and plenty of garden furniture. Wide choice of meals (must be pre-booked).

Prices d fr €46; t fr €57; extra person fr €15; dinner fr €15 **On Site** ❧ Private ↰ **Nearby** ♿ 2km ✐ 4km Restaurant 4km 🏊 4km 🏠 4km ⚒ 20km **Notes** Pets admitted English spoken

❚❚❚ ◯ **Mas de Balmes**

Philippe HUGONENC
46090 VERS
☎ 05 65 24 77 54
email: hugonenc.philippe@free.fr
web: http://hugonenc.philippe.free.fr/

This property on the edge of the Causses du Quercy offers five bedrooms, two of which can communicate for family use. All the rooms are doubles (one with twin beds) with en suite shower and WC. Dining room, terrace, extensive wooded grounds.

Prices s fr €34; d fr €39; t fr €45; dinner €15-€17 **Nearby** ♿ 4km ✐ 4km ↰ 15km Restaurant 3km 🏊 4km ❧ 3km 🏠 3km ⚒ 15km **Notes** Pets admitted

TARN

ALGANS

❚❚❚ ◯ **Montplaisir en Rose**

Thierry MAZZIA
En Rose, 81470 ALGANS
☎ 05 63 75 02 33 📄 05 63 75 02 33
email: contact@montplaisirenrose.com
web: http://montplaisirenrose.com

This 17th-century gentleman's residence has been attractively restored and is in the heart of the Cocagne countryside with the Pyrénées in the distance. There is a twin room, two doubles plus a single bed and two triples, all with own wc and shower. Dining room with corner sitting area and TV, washing machine, fridge. Large garden with space for games, swimming pool, table tennis, badminton. Meals and baby sitting on request.

Prices s fr €50; d fr €60; t fr €80; dinner fr €18 **On Site** Private ↰ **Nearby** ♿ 6km ⚓ 12km ✐ 10km 🏊 6km 🏠 6km ⚒ 12km **Notes** No pets English spoken Open April to October.

AMBIALET (ST CIRGUE)

❚❚❚ ◯ **Regain**

Michele et Alain AVET
81340 SAINT CIRGUE
☎ 05 63 53 48 72
email: avet.regain@wanadoo.fr
web: http://chambres-hotes-regain.com

This ancient and peaceful stone farmhouse, with its view of the Tarn valley, has four spacious and charming guest rooms. On the ground floor is a double; upstairs is another double with private entrance, a room for four, and a room with twin beds which can be zipped together. All have private facilities. Cot available. Meals by arrangement, using garden produce.

Prices d €50-€56; t fr €72; extra person fr €17; dinner fr €19 **Nearby** ♿ 6km ⚓ 27km ✐ 4km ↰ 21km Restaurant 4km 🏊 5km 🏠 4km ⚒ 27km **Notes** No pets English spoken Open 6 January to 15 December.

BELLEGARDE

⊪ **La Borie Neuve**

Esmeralda FRANCISCO
1430 BELLEGARDE
☎ 05 63 55 33 64 🖹 05 63 55 33 64
email: laborieneuve@aol.com
web: www.laborieneuve.com

A beautiful house with a cheery relaxed atmosphere in a truly rural setting. There are three rooms for two (doubles or twins), one with a kitchenette; a suite for three (double bed and a single); and a suite for four (two double beds). All have private facilities. Use of kitchen; garden with barbecue and garden furniture; swimming pool; table tennis.

Prices s fr €43-€50; d €47-€54; t fr €62; extra person fr €16
On Site Private ⚹ **Nearby** ⚐ 10km ⚑ 15km ⚘ 5km Restaurant 4km
⚓ 0.3km ⌂ 5km ⚏ 12km **Notes** No pets English spoken

CASTANET

⊪ ⦿ **Naussens**

Jean Michel MALBREIL
1150 CASTANET
☎ 05 63 55 22 56

In wine-growing country, a few kilometres from Albi and Cordes, this house has two double rooms (one with two single beds) with separate entrance and terrace. The adjacent converted barn has two more doubles and a room with a double and single bed. All have own shower and wc. Evening meal using local ingredients. Reductions for babies.

Prices s fr €40; d fr €40; t fr €55; extra person fr €15; dinner fr €15
Nearby ⚐ 3km ⚑ 15km ⚘ 6km ⚹ 6km Restaurant 6km ⚓ 6km
⚘ 6km ⚏ 15km **Notes** No pets Open 15 April to 30 October.

CASTELNAU-DE-LEVIS

⊪ ⦿ **Jussens**

Michele et Serge ROOSE
1150 CASTELNAU DE LEVIS
☎ 05 63 45 59 75 & 06 80 67 13 22
🖹 05 63 45 21 83
email: michele.roose@wanadoo.fr
web: www.chambre-hote-tarn.com

Not far from Albi, this quietly situated restored farmhouse has three bedrooms. On the ground floor is a double room, with a small study area. Upstairs is a room with twin beds, and another with a canopied double bed plus a single bed. All of the rooms have a private shower and WC. Garden, library, giant game of draughts.

Prices s €37-€42; d €46-€52; t €56-€62; extra person fr €10; dinner fr €18 **On Site** ⚏ **Nearby** ⚐ 5km ⚑ 10km ⚘ 1km ⚹ 2km ⚓ 8km
⚓ 2km ⚏ 2km **Notes** Pets admitted English spoken Open 15 January to 15 December.

CASTELNAU-DE-MONTMIRAL

⊪ ⦿ **Artichaud**

Jos et Liliane JANSSENS
Castel et Merlarie, 81140 CASTELNAU DE MONTMIRAL
☎ 05 63 57 20 42 🖹 05 63 57 20 72
email: liliane@artichaud.fr
web: www.artichaud.fr

Tucked away amongst the villages and vineyards, this traditional house has three bedrooms. All the guest accommodation is upstairs: two double rooms and a suite for three, with a cot and extra beds available. All have private facilities. Sitting room with open fireplace, garden with pool.

Prices s fr €50; d €55-€72; extra person fr €16; dinner fr €25
On Site Private ⚹ **Nearby** ⚐ 8km ⚘ 1km Restaurant 4km ⚓ 1km
⚓ 4km ⚏ 12km **Notes** No pets English spoken Open February to November.

⊪ ⦿ **La Croix du Sud**

C et G SORDOILLET
Mazars, 81140 CASTELNAU DE MONTMIRAL
☎ 05 63 33 18 46 & 06 80 27 63 20 🖹 05 63 33 18 46
email: catherine@la-croix-du-sud.com
web: www.la-croix-du-sud.com

Three comfortable rooms are available in this renovated house, deep in wine-growing and bastide country. There are two rooms with a double and single bed and a double, all with private facilities. Extra single beds, cot and bedroom TV on request. Living and sitting room, swimming pool, petanque and ping-pong. Gourmet meals or local specialities by arrangement; picnics on request. Reduced rates for longer stays.

Prices s fr €70; d fr €80; extra person fr €16; dinner fr €27
On Site Private ⚹ **Nearby** ⚐ 12km ⚑ 20km ⚘ 3km Restaurant 1km
⚓ 4km ⚘ 1km ⚓ 1km ⚏ 10km **Notes** No pets English spoken

CASTRES

⊪ ⦿ **Le Castelet**

Annette et Alain DUBOIS
St Hippolyte, 81100 CASTRES
☎ 05 63 35 96 27 🖹 05 63 35 90 11
email: contact@lecastelet.fr
web: www.lecastelet.fr

Hidden amongst ancient oak trees, this peaceful 19th-century house provides a warm welcome and comfortable accommodation. Upstairs are two double rooms; a suite with a double bed and a double bed-settee in the adjacent lounge; and a family room with a double bed, two singles, and a cot. All have private facilities. Terrace, swimming pool, meals by reservation.

Prices s €75-€120; d €90-€130; dinner fr €30 **On Site** Private ⚹
Nearby ⚐ 5km ⚑ 5km ⚘ 2km Restaurant 5km ⚓ 5km ⚘ 5km
⚓ 5km ⚏ 5km **Notes** Pets admitted English spoken

CORDES-SUR-CIEL

✦✦✦ Le Kerglas

Famille KERJEAN

La Védillerie, Les Cabannes, 81170 CORDES SUR CIEL

☎ 05 63 56 04 17 & 06 82 83 94 78 📄 05 63 56 04 17

email: le.kerglas@orange.fr

Expect a warm welcome at this family farmstead dating from 1730. Outbuildings have been converted to provide five guest rooms, all with either a king-size bed, one or three singles, and with private facilities and entrance. Rooms have panoramic views over Cordes, or overlook the verdant countryside and garden. Long-distance footpaths nearby.

Prices s €46-€54; d €50-€56; t €69-€75 **Nearby** ⛪ 12km ⬇ 30km 🏊 3km ⭢ 3km ⬇ 3km 🏠 5km ⬆ 6km **Notes** No pets Open 15 June to 15 September.

✦✦✦ �🍽 Les Tuileries

Annie et Christian RONDEL

81170 CORDES

☎ 05 63 56 05 93 📄 05 63 56 05 93

email: christian.rondel@wanadoo.fr

In a quiet and leafy setting near Cordes, this gentleman's residence and working farm has five spacious two, three and four-bed guest rooms, all with own shower and wc. There are shady chestnut trees, wonderful views, and an attractive swimming pool. Evening meals featuring produce from the farm are served by the fireside in winter or outdoors in summer. Garage, play-space, sitting room with TV, ping-pong, additional children's beds available.

Prices s fr €56; d fr €64; t fr €72; extra person fr €8; dinner fr €21 **On Site** 🏊 Private ⭢ **Nearby** ⛪ 12km ⬇ 22km Restaurant 0.8km 🏊 0.8km ⭢ 1km 🏠 0.8km ⬆ 5km **Notes** No pets English spoken Open March to November.

DONNAZAC

✦✦✦✦ �🍽 Les Vents Bleus

Valerie et Filippo GROPALLO

rue de la Caussade, 81170 DONNAZAC

☎ 05 63 56 86 11 📄 05 63 56 86 11

email: lesventsbleus@orange.fr

web: www.lesventsbleus.com

In the Gaillac countryside, this house offers a triple room, a double, a suite with three single beds and a bunk bed and another with a double and single. The spacious rooms have TV, own bath and wc. Fridge, crockery, walled garden, swimming pool, play-space, ping-pong, two gîtes, badminton, four adult bikes. Meals available (Thursday and Sunday in July/August).

Prices d €80-€150; dinner fr €25 **On Site** 🏊 Private ⭢ **Nearby** ⛪ 11km ⬇ 22km 🏊 5km Restaurant 5km ⬇ 5km 🏠 5km ⬆ 7km **Notes** No pets English spoken Open 21 March to October.

DOURGNE

✦✦✦ Les Peyrounels Hauts

Francoise CORCELLE

81110 DOURGNE

☎ 05 63 74 29 87 📄 05 63 74 29 87

email: frcorcelle@hotmail.com

web: www.lespeyrounels.com

This restored farmhouse, at the end of the road and 312 metres above sea level, has three bedrooms. On the ground floor is a triple room; on the mezzanine is a suite for four and on the first floor is a double. All have private facilities. Guests' lounge, and kitchenette with fridge.

Prices s €42-€47; d €53-€59; t €63-€70; extra person fr €10 **On Site** Private ⭢ **Nearby** ⛪ 12km ⬇ 16km 🏊 10km Restaurant 2km ⬇ 7km 🎣 10km 🏠 2km ⬆ 15km **Notes** No pets

ESCOUSSENS

✦✦✦ �🍽 La Blancarie

Marina et Eric ALEXANDRE

81290 ESCOUSSENS

☎ 05 63 50 21 86 & 06 88 88 08 04

web: http://lemouscaillou.free.fr/index.html

This property has a wonderful rural location, with a view of the Montagne Noire and the plain of Castres. There is a double room, a triple (double bed and single), and a family room with four single beds which can be linked to form doubles. All have private facilities. Lounge with TV and coffee corner; fridge and cafetière available. Garden furniture, hammock.

Prices s fr €38; d fr €48; t €58-€68; extra person fr €12; dinner fr €19 **Nearby** ⛪ 10km ⬇ 16km 🏊 6km ⭢ 15km Restaurant 7km ⬇ 1.5km Spa 30km 🏠 8km ⬆ 8km **Notes** No pets Open 15 March to 3 November.

✦✦✦ �🍽 ♿ *Mont St Jean*

Marie-Therese ESCAFRE

81290 ESCOUSSENS

☎ 05 63 73 24 70 & 06 14 40 41 53

At the foot of the Black Mountain, this farmhouse once belonged to the Carthusians and is on the old pilgrim route to Santiago de Compostela. There is a room with a double and single bed, a twin and a double with single and child's bed. All have own facilities; cot available. An additional family room has a double bed, single bed and wash-basin. Living room with TV and open fireplace, covered terrace, garden, barbecue, ping-pong and meals available.

Prices not confirmed for 2008 **Nearby** ⛪ 14km ⬇ 14km 🏊 0.2km ⭢ 14km ⬇ 14km 🏠 7km ⬆ 7km **Notes** Pets admitted English spoken

ESPERAUSSES

♯♯ ◯ La Maison de Jeanne

Florence ARTERO
e Bourg, 81260 ESPERAUSSES
☎ 05 63 73 02 77

350-year-old house in the village centre. It has been completely
restored, exposing the original beams and stonework, and now
provides two doubles and two rooms with a double and single bed,
each with private shower and wc. Communal lounge and living room,
fireplace, TV, billiards, terrace, garden furniture, barbecue. Table d'hôte
meals can be served. Fishing. No charge for babies. Reduced rates for
longer stays.

Prices s fr €37; d fr €42; t fr €52; extra person fr €10; dinner fr €19
On Site ✍ **Nearby** ➟ 10km ⚓ 35km ➟ 11km Restaurant 7km
⚑ 11km Spa 35km 🏛 11km ⋙ 35km **Notes** No pets English spoken
Open March to October.

GAILLAC

♯♯ ✿ *Domaine de Gradille*

Lyne et Denis SOULIE
a Grouillere, 81310 LISLE SUR TARN
☎ 05 63 41 01 57   ▤ 05 63 40 39 10
email: lynesoulie@wanadoo.fr
web: www.domainedegradille.com

Close to Albi and Cordes, this wine-growing property has a quiet and
charmingly rustic setting with panoramic views. There are three double
rooms, two with extra single beds and all with own bathroom, wc and
seating. Guests' sitting room, TV, library, open fireplace. Attractive
terrace, shared swimming pool, shady park and pleasant 15-minute
walk to a lake. Three gites nearby.

Prices not confirmed for 2008 **On Site** Private ➟ **Nearby** ➟ 10km
⚓ 12km ⚐ 0.5km ⛱ 5km 🏛 5km ⋙ 5km **Notes** No pets English
spoken

♯♯ Face à l'Abbatiale

Lucile PINON
Place St Michel, 81600 GAILLAC
☎ 05 63 57 61 48   ▤ 05 63 57 61 48
email: lucile.pinon@wanadoo.fr

Deep in the Gaillac countryside, this 17th-century residence has views
over the Abbey of St-Michel, the River Tarn and the old town. There
are six rooms with a total of five double beds and three singles, all
with TV, bathroom and wc. The house is furnished with antiques and
there is a splendid stone staircase, sitting rooms with TV and prettily
painted courtyard and outbuildings. Breakfast served in the rooms or
on a covered terrace.

Prices s fr €43; d fr €55; t fr €70 **Nearby** ➟ 10km ⚓ 12km ⚐ 0.1km
⛱ 0.4km ⛱ 0.4km ⋙ 1km **Notes** Pets admitted English spoken

♯♯ ◯ *Le Mas de Sudre*

Philippa RICHMOND-BROWN
81600 GAILLAC
☎ 05 63 41 01 32   ▤ 05 63 41 01 32
email: masdesudre@wanadoo.fr

In a tranquil setting among the Gaillac vineyards, this large country
house has hospitable English owners. Of the four bright and spacious
rooms, two (one double, one twin) are in the annexe, and two (one
double, one twin) in the main house, all with private shower and wc.
Shared sitting and living room, TV, telephone and piano. Large garden
with terrace, tennis court, swimming pool, boules, table tennis.

Prices s fr €50; d fr €70; extra person fr €25 **On Site** ⛱ Private ➟
Private tennis court **Nearby** ➟ 7km ⚓ 7km ⚐ 20km Restaurant 4km
🏛 4km ⋙ 4km **Notes** No pets English spoken

GIROUSSENS

♯♯ ✿ Le Pepil

J-Paul et M-Josee RAYNAUD
81500 GIROUSSENS
☎ 05 63 41 62 84   ▤ 05 63 41 62 84
email: jearaynaud@wanadoo.fr
web: www.alpepil.com

A family look forward to welcoming guests to their traditional farm
with four rooms: two doubles, a room with a double and single bed,
and a twin plus bunk bed, all with own shower and wc. Big sitting
room with open fireplace, TV, kitchen, fridge, washing machine,
library. Garden, outside bread oven, barbecue, bikes, ping-pong.

Prices d fr €43; t fr €57; extra person fr €16 **On Site** ⛱ Private ➟
Nearby ➟ 14km ⚓ 10km ⚐ 10km Restaurant 3km ⛱ 4km 🏛 3km
⋙ 6km **Notes** Pets admitted English spoken Open 6 January to 20
October & November to 28 December.

LAMONTELARIE

♯♯ ◯ *La Tranquille*

R CLERC et T MAITE
81260 LAMONTELARIE
☎ 05 63 74 56 54   ▤ 05 63 74 56 54
email: latranquille@wanadoo.fr
web: www.la-tranquille.com

This home is deep in the leafy countryside of the Haute-Languedoc
regional park, just a step from la Ravière lake. Four double rooms and
an additional room with bunk bed, shower and wc. Cots and

CONTINUED

LAMONTELARIE CONTINUED

additional beds available. Living and sitting room with open fireplace, washing machine, terrace and large garden, ping-pong.

Prices not confirmed for 2008 **On Site** ℘ **Nearby** ☂ 12km ⚓ 15km
↖ 12km ⚲ 12km ⚿ 8km ⇩ 50km **Notes** No pets English spoken

LARROQUE

▦ ⃝ La Salette

Robin et Rosie JENNINGS
81140 LARROQUE
☎ 05 63 33 25 59
email: rosie.jennings@wanadoo.fr
web: www.lasalette81.com

A restored farmhouse close to one of the most beautiful villages in France. There are three bedrooms: two doubles, and a family room with a double bed and bunk beds. All have private shower room and WC. Lounge with TV and books; gardens with garden furniture. Evening meals available, by arrangement. Good area for walking, riding and mountain-biking.

Prices s fr €50; d fr €55; t fr €70; extra person fr €15; dinner fr €22
Nearby ☂ 2km ⚓ 40km ℘ 12km ↖ 15km Restaurant 0.5km ⚲ 2km
⚘ 6km ⚿ 3km ⇩ 20km **Notes** No pets English spoken

LAUTREC

▦ *Cadalen*

Alain ROUQUIER
81440 LAUTREC
☎ 05 63 75 30 02 & 06 74 88 02 25
email: cadalen81@aol.com
web: www.cadalen81.com

Situated in the quiet of the Lautrec plain between Castres and Albi, this is a house of some character. Bedrooms (with period furnishings) include three upstairs rooms, sleeping two or three people; all have large shower rooms and wc. Communal sitting and dining rooms. Television can be provided in bedrooms if required. Garden; table tennis; library; games; two fine pigeon lofts. Leisure centre, medieval village, walking trails.

Prices not confirmed for 2008 **Nearby** ☂ 5km ⚓ 15km ℘ 3km ↖ 4km
⚲ 3km ⚿ 3km ⇩ 15km **Notes** No pets

▦ ⃝ La Fontaine de Lautrec

Joel et Dominique TSIN
Domaine du Buguet, 81440 LAUTREC
☎ 05 63 75 53 28 ▤ 05 63 75 53 28
email: contact@fontaine-lautrec.com

A 19th-century house surrounded by ancient trees in grounds of one hectare, with a wonderful view of the medieval village of Lautrec. Three ground floor rooms are in an annexe: two are doubles; the third is a split-level room with a double bed and three singles. All have private facilities and individual terraces. Meals by arrangement.

Prices s fr €55; d €59-€69; t €84; extra person fr €25; dinner fr €25 **Nearby** ☂ 6km ⚓ 15km ℘ 2km ↖ 2km ⚲ 1.5km ⚿ 2km **Notes** No pets English spoken

▦ ⃝ La Terrasse de Lautrec

Dominique DUCOUDRAY
rue de l'Eglise, 81440 LAUTREC
☎ 05 63 75 84 22
email: d.ducoudray@wanadoo.fr
web: www.laterrassedelautrec.com

This beautiful 17th-century house, with its garden designed by Le Nôtre, is in Lautrec, a listed medieval village. It has one double room, and two rooms with twin beds which can be linked. Extra bed available. All of the rooms are on the first floor, and have a private bath or shower room and WC. Lounge, library, swimming pool.

Prices d €70-€100; t €105-€125; extra person fr €25; dinner fr €25 **On Site** Private ↖ **Nearby** ☂ 1.5km ⚓ 16km ℘ 1km Restaurant 0.5km ⚲ 0.5km ⚘ 15km ⚿ 0.3km ⇩ 10km **Notes** No pets English spoken Open April to October.

LE BEZ

▦ ⃝ La Bertrandie

J-Pierre et A-Marie REGALI
Guyor, 81260 LE BEZ
☎ 05 63 74 59 91 & 06 31 68 03 29
email: nanou.regali@orange.fr

Three warm rooms, in the area known as Le Sidobre. There is a double room, and two triples (each with double bed and a single, on also with a baby's cot). All have private shower and WC. Meals and picnic lunches by arrangement. The garden is on the other side of the road, which carries little traffic. Good area for walking.

Prices s fr €38; d €42-€48; extra person fr €12; dinner fr €16 **On Site** ℘ **Nearby** ☂ 4km ⚓ 18km ↖ 7km ⚲ 7km ⚿ 7km ⇩ 14km **Notes** No pets

LEMPAUT

▦ ⃝ La Bousquetarie

Charles SALLIER
81700 LEMPAUT
☎ 05 63 75 51 09 ▤ 05 63 75 51 09
web: www.chateau-bousquetarie.com

This château, facing the Montagne Noire, stands among ancient oak trees. It is a peaceful place, with a warm, welcoming atmosphere. It has a double room, a twin-bedded room, and a suite which can accommodate up to five people. All the rooms have a private bath or shower room and WC. Lounge; washing machine; meals by arrangement.

Prices s fr €50; d fr €75; t fr €97; extra person fr €22; dinner fr €20 **On Site** Private ↖ Private tennis court **Nearby** ☂ 10km ⚓ 20km ℘ 10km Restaurant 7km ⚘ 10km ⚿ 2km ⇩ 30km **Notes** No pets English spoken Open March to November.

LESCURE-D'ALBIGEOIS

⚌ ◎ **Le Pignié**

Philippe DESCHAMPS
1380 LESCURE D'ALBIGEOIS
☎ 05 63 60 44 31 & 06 15 73 06 90
email: lepignie.deschamps@wanadoo.fr
web: http://lepignie.com

Stay in comfort in spacious guest rooms in this house in the open country of the Tarn valley a few kilometres from Albi - peace and rest guaranteed. Four ground floor rooms with shower and wc; one upstairs room with separate access with bathroom; television in bedrooms. Grounds, table tennis, 5 x 10m swimming pool. Evening meals and picnic hampers can be organised.

Prices s €40-€47; d €48-€55; t fr €68; dinner fr €17 **On Site** Private ⊀ **Nearby** ⚐ 3km ⚑ 7km ⚘ 5km ⚑ 5km ⚑ 4km ⚒ 6km **Notes** No pets English spoken

MARSAL

⚌ ◎ **Maison Mambre**

Wim et Veerle VANDEPITTE
1430 MARSAL
☎ 05 63 47 91 27 & 06 73 41 97 59 ▨ 05 63 47 33 55
email: info@maisonmambre.com
web: www.maisonmambre.com

A former convent in the heart of the forest, with views of the Tarn. There are five upstairs bedrooms: three doubles; a room with twin beds which can be linked; and a room with double bed and bunks. All have private facilities. Lounge; games room with billiards, table football. Enclosed grounds with parking and swimming pool. Generous breakfasts with home-baked items.

Prices s fr €70; d fr €72; dinner fr €25 **On Site** ⚘ Private ⊀ **Nearby** ⚐ 10km ⚑ 25km ⚘ 3km Restaurant 6km ⚑ 8km ⚑ 5km ⚒ 10km **Notes** No pets English spoken Open 2 April to 4 November.

MAURENS-SCOPONT

⚌ ❦ ◎ **Combe Ramond**

Marie-Bernadette VIGNAU
1470 MAURENS SCOPONT
☎ 05 63 58 77 60 & 06 61 15 77 60 ▨ 05 63 58 57 27
email: vignau@wanadoo.fr
web: www.comberamond.fr

In the Cocagne countryside, in the Albi/Castres/Toulouse triangle, the owners offer guest rooms beside their organic goat and sheep farm (mohair items for sale). Substantial country house with rooms on the second floor sleeping two or three, all with television and telephone. Most rooms have a bath, one has a shower. Parkland, terrace, swimming pool. Cot (up to two years old) free. Evening meal available Monday/Tuesday. Large lake with fishing. Picnic hampers if desired.

Prices not confirmed for 2008 **On Site** ⚘ Private ⊀ **Nearby** ⚐ 6km ⚑ 5km ⚑ 6km ⚒ 12km **Notes** No pets English spoken Open 2 January to 22 December. CC

NOAILLES

⚌ ◎ *Les Vignes*

Fred et Christine CHALLIS
81170 NOAILLES
☎ 05 63 40 59 22
email: fchallis@photohols.com
web: www.photohols.com

This attractive house is in a village which makes an ideal base for walkers and cyclists. There are four first floor bedrooms, two doubles and two with twin beds. Cot available, and a child's bed. All rooms are non-smoking, and each has a private shower room and WC. Internet access; enclosed grounds, with garden and terrace.

Prices not confirmed for 2008 **Nearby** ⚐ 12km ⚑ 25km ⚘ 1km ⊀ 8km ⚑ 7km ⚑ 15km ⚒ 8km **Notes** No pets English spoken

PARISOT

⚌ ◎ **Le Causse**

Michel et Martine CUENCA
81310 PARISOT ·
☎ 05 63 40 44 07 ▨ 05 63 40 47 04
email: michel.cuenca@dorylee.com
web: www.letreslongcausse.fr

A mansion house dating from the late 18th century, restored in the local style. The 7 hectare of grounds include 1 hectare of woodland. One downstairs and three upstairs rooms, sleeping two or three. Cot and/or spare bed available. Communal dining room; private sitting room with open fire and television. Shaded park with terrace and garden furniture; courtyard; parking under shelter. Local produce features at evening meals, grilled over a wood fire; Périgord specialities and Provençal dishes. Picnic hampers.

Prices s fr €36; d fr €43; t fr €55; extra person fr €12; dinner fr €18 **Nearby** ⚐ 3km ⚑ 22km ⚘ 3km ⊀ 4.5km ⚑ 3km ⚑ 4.5km ⚒ 4.5km **Notes** No pets English spoken Open April to 30 October.

PAULINET

⚌ ◎ *Domaine Equestre les Juliannes*

M-Christine et Nick HUDSWELL
81250 PAULINET
☎ 05 63 55 94 38 ▨ 05 63 55 97 49
email: contact@lesjuliannes.com
web: www.lesjuliannes.com

A family-run 17th-century farm offering two double rooms, a triple and two suites (one sleeps four, the other sleeps six), all with own bathroom and wc. Dining room overlooking shady terrace, sitting room with fireplace, traditional cooking, games room and children's toys. Gîte for ten people, shared swimming pool, stables with horses and ponies. Transport can be arranged from Albi station. Price reductions for longer stays.

Prices not confirmed for 2008 **On Site** ⚘ Private ⊀ **Nearby** ⚑ 40km ⚘ 1km ⚑ 6km ⚒ 6km ⚒ 35km **Notes** No pets English spoken Open 31 March to 11 November.

PAYRIN

♦♦♦ ⏚ *Les Oliviers*

Brigitte FAURY

86 Chemin de Palazy, 81660 PAYRIN

☎ 05 63 98 65 47 & 06 75 77 99 66 🗎 05 63 98 63 24

email: chambres.d.hotes.les.oliviers@wanadoo.fr

At the foot of the Montagne Noire, about 10 kilometres from Castres, this property has three bedrooms in a modern setting. On the ground floor is a double-bedded room suitable for disabled guests, and a family room for four. Upstairs is a double-bedded room with a sofa bed and a small child's bed. All have television, private shower and WC.

Prices not confirmed for 2008 **On Site** Private ⤳ **Nearby** ⛵ 3km ⚓ 2km ⛳ 8km ⛲ 10km ⛪ 1km ⛵ 7km **Notes** No pets English spoken Open 2 January to December.

PUYCALVEL

♦♦♦ ⏚ **Plaisance**

Minerve CAYLA

81440 PUYCALVEL

☎ 05 63 75 94 59

email: minerve.cayla@tiscali.fr

In the Cocagne countryside near the medieval village of Lautrec, this old farmstead stands in 13 hectares of woods and meadows. Overlooking a sheltered terrace, two double rooms and a triple have their own entrance and shower and wc. Additional beds available. Spacious dining room with open fireplace, library and TV. Meals by arrangement, reductions for children, themed evenings. Riders welcome (horses available), and courses in leatherworking. Canoe rental 7km.

Prices s fr €30; d fr €40; t fr €50; extra person fr €10; dinner fr €15 **On Site** ⛵ **Nearby** ⚓ 17km ⛳ 5km ⤳ 7km Restaurant 8km ⛲ 7km ⛪ 7km ⛲ 2km ⛵ 8km **Notes** Pets admitted English spoken

PUYLAURENS

♦♦♦ ⏚ **Les Justices**

Janine MERCIER

81700 PUYLAURENS

☎ 05 63 70 26 61 🗎 05 63 70 31 71

email: sncmis@aol.com

Three first floor rooms, in an attractive house between Toulouse and Castres. All the rooms are doubles, one with a cot in an adjoining room. Each has a private bath or shower room and WC; baby equipment is available. Living room with books and piano; use of kitchenette and washing machine. Indoor jacuzzi, children's games, swimming pool. Meals by arrangement.

Prices s fr €70; d fr €70; t fr €85; dinner fr €20 **On Site** Spa Private ⤳ **Nearby** ⛵ 4km ⚓ 10km ⛳ 20km Restaurant 2km ⛲ 4km ⛪ 2km ⛵ 20km **Notes** No pets Open 15 April to 15 October.

ROUAIROUX

♦♦♦ ⏚ **La Ranquière**

Marc et Christiane LECOUTRE

81240 ROUAIROUX

☎ 05 63 98 87 50 & 06 87 09 86 48

email: ranquiere@aol.com

In the Black Mountain region, surrounded by forests and close to lakes, this large 17th-century farmhouse has four guest rooms, three doubles and a twin, all with private bath or shower room and WC. Extra bed available. Guests' lounge with open fire, south facing garden and terrace with swimming pool. Table tennis and table football.

Prices s €50-€60; d €60-€70; t €85; extra person fr €15; dinner fr €25 **On Site** Private ⤳ **Nearby** ⛵ 4km ⚓ 17km ⛳ 5km ⛲ 4km ⛪ 1km ⛵ 17km **Notes** No pets English spoken Open April to November.

SALVAGNAC

♦♦♦ ⏚ *Domaine de Lagarrigue*

Michele et J-Jacques VEDY

81630 SALVAGNAC

☎ 05 63 33 29 72 🗎 05 63 33 29 72

email: info@chambre-hotes-tarn.com

web: www.chambre-hotes-tarn.com

This 18th century farmhouse, near the village, has attractive rooms including a triple, two doubles, and two rooms with a double and two single beds, all with own shower and wc. Cots and additional beds available. TV, evening meals, picnic lunches can be provided. Shady terrace, extensive garden, swimming pool, ping-pong, boules, play-space.

Prices not confirmed for 2008 **On Site** Private ⤳ **Nearby** ⛵ 6km ⚓ 28km ⛳ 0.5km ⛲ 1km ⛪ 1.5km ⛵ 18km **Notes** No pets English spoken

SENOUILLAC

♦♦♦ ⏚ *La Maison de Vieulac*

Simone VARGAS

3100, Route de Lincarque, 81600 SENOUILLAC

☎ 05 63 57 46 65 & 06 76 16 79 93

email: simonevargas@tele2.fr

web: www.chambres-hotes-albi-tarn.com

This remote and peaceful house amongst the vines has three tastefully decorated rooms: one double, one triple, and one with two double beds, all with private shower/WC. Guests' lounge with open fire and books. Washing machine. Well-tended flowery garden, with garden room. Meals available; also introductory sessions to the wine and food of the south-west (minimum eight people).

Prices not confirmed for 2008 **Nearby** ⛵ 4km ⚓ 8km ⛳ 5km ⤳ 8km ⛲ 8km ⛪ 6km ⛵ 8km **Notes** Pets admitted English spoken Open March to October.

⌗ Le Mas des Cistes

Myriam POIRSON

Cirvals, 81600 SENOUILLAC

☎ 05 63 41 52 64

email: le-mas-des-cistes@wanadoo.fr

web: www.le-mas-des-cistes.fr.st/

This big building of white stone stands in the heart of the ancient Gaillac vineyards. There are three double rooms, all on the ground floor with independent access. All of the rooms have a lounge area, private bath or shower room and WC. Extra bed and cot available. Lounge with books and piano; enclosed garden, swimming pool and table tennis.

Prices s fr €70; d fr €80; extra person fr €20   **On Site** Private ⚡
Nearby ⚽ 0.5km ♨ 10km ⚓ 10km Restaurant 5km ♨ 7km ♨ 7km
♨ 7km ♨ 7km   **Notes** No pets English spoken

SOREZE

⌗ ⦿ Moulin de l'Abbé

Eliane et Roland PINEL

route de Durfort, 81540 SOREZE

☎ 05 63 74 25 57 & 06 19 94 70 69   ▤ 05 63 74 31 79

email: eliane.pinel@wanadoo.fr

An old flour mill in a hectare of wooded grounds, with lots of water all round. There are four upstairs bedrooms, one of them a two-roomed suite for four (two double beds). All have private facilities. Kitchenette, microwave, use of washing machine. Grounds, terrace and private parking. Table tennis. Meals by arrangement - local produce, garden vegetables.

Prices not confirmed for 2008   **On Site** ⚓   **Nearby** ⚡ 3km ♨ 25km
⚡ 4km ♨ 3km ♨ 4km ♨ 25km   **Notes** Pets admitted English spoken

⌗ Moulin du Chapitre

B et V GALY-FAJOU

81540 SOREZE

☎ 05 63 74 18 18

email: moulin.chapitre@wanadoo.fr

web: www.moulinduchapitre.com

A stone's throw from the lake of St Ferréol, this old flour mill is the perfect spot for a break in the country. Two double ground floor rooms have independent access. Upstairs there are two family rooms, each sleeping four. All have shower and wc. Guests' living room with cooking area. Communal sitting room/lounge. Washing machine and fridge for guests. Terrace. Véronique offers courses in creative expression. Also on site - a small gîte, covered walkway, table tennis.

Prices s €35-€42; d €39-€46; t fr €62; extra person fr €13   **On Site** ⚓
Nearby ⚽ 3km ⚡ 3km Restaurant 3km ♨ 3km Spa 5km ♨ 3km
♨ 13km ♨ 20km   **Notes** No pets English spoken

ST-JULIEN-GAULENE

⌗ ⦿ La Bergerie du Bousquet

M VAN RIESEN

81340 ST JULIEN GAULENE

☎ 05 63 56 57 84 & 06 72 65 30 30

email: wulfwilhelm@free.fr

Near the Aveyron and the Tarn valley, this old farmhouse has been completely restored and modernised to provide four spacious guest rooms. Three have double beds, and the fourth room has three singles. A cot is available. Guest living room, with a courtyard and garden furniture outside. Meals are available if pre-booked.

Prices not confirmed for 2008   **Nearby** ⚽ 10km ♨ 21km ⚓ 13km
⚡ 21km ♨ 20km ♨ 5km ♨ 21km   **Notes** No pets English spoken

ST-LIEUX-LES-LAVAUR

⌗ Le Château

Lizette DORVAL

81500 ST LIEUX LES LAVAUR

☎ 05 63 41 60 87   ▤ 05 63 41 61 23

This 19th-century château is in quiet and attractive surroundings in the village of St Lieux in the heart of the Cocagne country. There are five double rooms all with TV, own bath and wc. Cot available. Private sitting room, dining room, ping-pong, billiard room. Large, well-wooded garden with raised round swimming pool. Restaurants and other facilities nearby.

Prices s fr €60; d fr €60; extra person fr €20   **On Site** Private ⚡
Nearby ⚽ 2km ♨ 10km ⚓ 1km Restaurant 0.1km ♨ 1km ♨ 10km
♨ 0.5km ♨ 6km   **Notes** Pets admitted English spoken

STE-GEMME

⌗ ⦿ Le Peyrugal

Danielle FOREST

81190 STE GEMME

☎ 05 63 76 59 86   ▤ 05 63 76 59 86

email: lepeyrugal@wanadoo.fr

web: www.lepeyrugal.com

Away from it all - an 18th-century farmhouse in two hectares of shady grounds. There are three triple rooms (double bed and a single in each one), all with private shower and WC. Each has its own entrance and private terrace. Baby equipment available. Lounge, garden furniture, swimming pool. Meals available by arrangement, also prepared picnics.

Prices not confirmed for 2008   **On Site** Private ⚡   **Nearby** ⚽ 3km
♨ 30km ⚓ 0.5km ♨ 5km ♨ 5km ♨ 5km   **Notes** Pets admitted

VALENCE-D'ALBIGEOIS (PADIES)

L'Amartco

P DUMETZ et S MANESSE
Saint Marcel, 81340 PADIES
☎ 05 63 76 38 47
email: lamartco@wanadoo.fr
web: www.lamartco.com

Close to the Tarn valley, this is a house with much venerable charm. There is a family room (two double beds) on the ground floor, and also a double room. Upstairs is another family room with a double bed and two singles. All have private shower/WC, and the ground floor rooms have independent access.

Prices not confirmed for 2008 **On Site** Private **Nearby** 22km 35km 2km 15km 6km 10km **Notes** No pets English spoken

VAOUR

Seréne

Brigitte et Francis BESSIERES
81140 VAOUR
☎ 05 63 56 39 34 05 63 56 39 34
email: francis.bessieres@freesbee.fr

A stone farmhouse in lovely countryside which once belonged to the Knights Templar. It has a twin room (with disabled access), and two doubles plus a suite with double bed and sitting room with two single beds, all with own facilities. Cot available. Living room and large sitting room with fireplace, shared swimming pool and terrace. Evening meals available. Botanical trail nearby.

Prices not confirmed for 2008 **On Site** Private **Nearby** 8km 35km 12km 10km 15km 12km **Notes** No pets English spoken Open March to 15 November.

VIANE

La Bessière

Myriam BARDY
81530 VIANE
☎ 05 63 37 01 26
email: myriam.bardy@cerfrance.fr
web: www.pageloisirs.com/labessiere

Among green and wooded hills on the edge of the valley, this cattle farm offers a warm welcome and rooms comprising a double, a triple and a room with two double beds, all with private facilities. Washing machine, living room with TV, sitting room with fireplace and meals using farm produce available. Garden with furniture, farm tours, mushroom picking in season. Lovely walks and trout fishing nearby.

Prices s fr €40; d fr €50; t fr €61; extra person fr €12; dinner fr €18 **Nearby** 27km 50km 1km 12km 3km 3km 50km **Notes** Pets admitted English spoken

VIRAC

Lasserre

Klaus VOGDT
81640 VIRAC
☎ 05 63 56 43 17 05 63 56 43 17
email: klaus.vogdt@wanadoo.fr

This calm and quiet country house between Cordes and Albi has two twin-bedded rooms on the first floor. In an annexe, with independent access, are two more twin-bedded rooms. All rooms have a lounge and private shower room/WC. Organic garden, swimming pool. Meals by arrangement.

Prices not confirmed for 2008 **On Site** Private **Nearby** 9km 20km 3km 9km 6km 10km **Notes** No pets English spoken Open 15 April to 14 October.

TARN-ET-GARONNE

ANGEVILLE

Le Cantou

Aline et Jackie BERNARDIN
Les Jauberts, 82210 ANGEVILLE
☎ 05 63 95 36 61
email: contact@le-cantou.com
web: www.le-cantou.com

Stay in your hosts' house with grounds and swimming pool. Enjoy evening meals by arrangement either inside or outdoors. Stay in one of four themed, individually decorated bedrooms: one triple with shower/WC; two doubles with bath/WC, one double with shower/WC Shared lounge and dining room with TV and books. Broadband in one bedroom. Cot free.

Prices s €45-€55; d €60-€65; t €75-€80; extra person €15; dinner fr €22 **On Site** Private **Nearby** 15km Restaurant 6km 2km 8km 9km **Notes** Pets admitted English spoken

AUVILLAR

Le Cap de Pech

Annick et Jacques SARRAUT
82340 AUVILLAR
☎ 05 63 39 62 45 & 06 08 35 18 02
email: annick.sarraut@wanadoo.fr

The bedrooms at this property are delightfully arranged, and there is the bonus of a pleasant guest lounge. There are two double rooms, and a room with a double bed plus another small double. They all have private bath or shower rooms and WCs. Washing machine and cooker; big garden with swimming pool. Walking routes nearby.

Prices s fr €35; d fr €50; t fr €75; extra person fr €25 **On Site** Private ⚓ **Nearby** ⛵4km ⚓1km ♪1km Restaurant 0.4km ⚓0.3km ⚓0.4km ⚓5km **Notes** Pets admitted English spoken

CASTANET

⸫ *Cambayrac*

Daniel et Myriam VIDAL

82160 CASTANET

☎ 05 63 24 02 03 & 06 61 17 36 89

email: dvidal@wanadoo.fr

web: http://cambayrac.net

In tranquil countryside, the slate roof and stone walls of this rustic house are typical of old barns. There are three double rooms and a twin with private facilities. Swimming pool, mountain biking, table tennis on site. The host can guide you on beautiful walks on a number of footpaths.

Prices not confirmed for 2008 **On Site** Private ⚓ **Nearby** ⛵7km ♪6km ⚓6km ⚓9km ⚓11km **Notes** No pets English spoken

CASTELSARRASIN

⸫ **Dantous Sud**

Rosine FUNG

82100 CASTELSARRASIN

☎ 05 63 32 26 95

email: rosinefung@aol.com

web: www.gite-lesdantous.com

Five bedrooms with a private entrance in a pretty house: four with a single bed and double bed and one with twin beds and a double bed. Shower room and wc in each. Enclosed shady garden, games area, boules pitch, garden furniture, TV. Garonne canal 100mtrs. Numerous tourist sites nearby.

Prices s fr €38-€40; d fr €42-€45; t fr €58-€60; extra person fr €15 **On Site** Private ⚓ **Nearby** ⛵11km ♪4km ⚓3km ⚓3km ⚓3km **Notes** No pets English spoken Open January to 16 December.

⸫ **L'Ile**

Christine SEILLIER

82100 CASTELSARRASIN

☎ 05 63 04 49 06 & 06 22 67 46 74

email: seillier.jean-louis@wanadoo.fr

web: www.domainedelile.fr

This converted barn has three first floor guest rooms, with their own entrance. There are two triple rooms, with double bed and a single; and a double room with a bed-settee. All three rooms have TVs, shower rooms and WCs. Guests' kitchen. Equestrian accommodation and equipment.

Prices s fr €40; d fr €45; t fr €55; extra person fr €10 **Nearby** ⛵19km ♪0.2km ⚓1km ⚓1km ⚓1km ⚓1.5km **Notes** Pets admitted

CAZES-MONDENARD

⸫ ⚪ **La Grange**

Claude MAURET

Martissan, 82110 CAZES-MONDENARD

☎ 06 07 96 86 87

email: grange_mauret@yahoo.com

web: www.chambre-grange.com

A family home in which each bedroom evokes a style, country or tradition. The 'Heritage' bedroom has three antique single beds, 'Julie' and 'Melissa' have double and single beds. All have private facilities and there is a guest sitting room, dining room, garden with furniture, sun loungers and swimming pool.

Prices s fr €50; d fr €63; t fr €75; dinner €8-€20 **On Site** ♪ Private ⚓ **Nearby** ⛵15km ♪10km Restaurant 6km ⚓6km ⚓6km ⚓24km **Notes** Pets admitted English spoken CC

CORBARIEU

⸫ **Lautouy**

Pascale SANTOS

892, chemin du Loup, 82370 CORBARIEU

☎ 05 63 31 72 81 & 06 89 14 25 29

email: lautouy@orange.fr

web: http://perso.orange.fr/lautouy

This house sits on top of a hill overlooking the Tarn valley, in enclosed grounds. The immediate surroundings are peaceful, but Montauban is not far away. There are four double rooms, all with private bath or shower room and WC. Sitting room with open fireplace and books.

Prices s €46-€54; d €56-€64; extra person €15 **On Site** Private ⚓ **Nearby** ⛵14km ♪14km ♪2km ⚓10km ⚓2km ⚓7km **Notes** Pets admitted English spoken

ESCATALENS

⸫ ⚪ **Chambre d'hôtes**

Claudine CHOUX

Place de la Mairie, 82700 ESCATALENS

☎ 05 63 68 71 23 📄 05 63 30 25 90

email: claude.choux@wanadoo.fr

web: www.maisondeschevaliers.com

Relax around the swimming pool of this 18th century building or in one of the guest rooms. 'Des Chevaliers' is a suite with a double and single room; 'Les Romantiques' has a double and twin bed; 'Côté Sud' has a double and twin; 'Romeo and Juliette' is a triple. All have private facilities and there is a private sitting room, TV, library, shady garden, children's games room. Kitchen, dining room and sitting room in the cellars.

Prices s fr €60; d fr €75; t fr €110; extra person fr €15; dinner fr €22 **On Site** Private ⚓ **Nearby** ⛵10km ♪20km ♪1.5km Restaurant 4km ⚓0.2km ⚓8km ⚓4km ⚓12km **Notes** Pets admitted English spoken

LAFRANCAISE

⚐ ❍ La Maison du Saula

S et B BONCOMPAIN

82130 LAFRANCAISE

☎ 05 63 65 80 24   🖷 05 63 26 44 35

email: bboncompain@aol.com

web: www.la-maison-du-saula.com

Extensive grounds with Lebanon cedars surround this property, which has three spacious first floor guest bedrooms. There is a double room, a twin-bedded room, and a family room with a double bed plus a small double. All of the rooms have private bath or shower rooms and WCs. Extra bed available.

Prices   d €60-€85; t €80-€100; extra person fr €15; dinner €21-€30
Nearby ⚇ 10km 🏊 0.1km ↘ 3km 🚴 3km 🏪 2km 🚶 20km
Notes Pets admitted   English spoken

⚐ ❍ Le Platane

Christa HORF

Coques Lunel, 82130 LAFRANCAISE

☎ 05 63 65 92 18 & 06 73 30 93 62   🖷 05 63 65 88 18

email: le.platane@wanadoo.fr

web: www.leplatane.fr.tt

This farm has stables, a riding school, pigeon loft, wonderfully restored manor house, parkland with a lake and a swimming pool. It offers two double bedrooms with sitting room area and a further double, each with TV, shower room and wc.

Prices s fr €65; d fr €70; extra person fr €20; dinner fr €25 **On Site** ⚇
🏊 Private ↘ **Nearby** ⚇ 25km Restaurant 2km 🚴 5km 🎾 8km 🏪 5km
🚶 12km **Notes** Pets admitted

⚐ 🌿 ❍ Les Trouilles

J-F et F GUFFROY

82130 LAFRANCAISE

☎ 05 63 65 84 46   🖷 05 63 65 97 14

email: lestrouilles@free.fr

web: http://lestrouilles.free.fr

A very enjoyable stay is assured here. Choose between four bedrooms with independent access (double bed and single bed in each), a double room and one with a double and single bed. All have private facilities and access to swimming pool. Half board available.

Prices not confirmed for 2008 **On Site** Private ↘ **Nearby** ⚇ 19km
🏊 2km 🚴 2km 🏪 2km 🚶 20km **Notes** Pets admitted English spoken
Open 6 February to December.

LAMOTHE-CAPDEVILLE

⚐ La Maison de Manon

Manon PICO

122 chemin Antoine de Cadillac,

82130 LAMOTHE-CAPDEVILLE

☎ 05 63 31 36 29 & 06 16 57 34 90

email: manon.pico@wanadoo.fr

web: www.lamaisondemanon.com

On a clear day, there are distant views of the Pyrénées from this house, peacefully situated in beautiful countryside. There is a double room; a two-roomed family suite for up to five, on two floors; and a split-level room for three. All have private bath or shower room and WC. A cot is available.

Prices s €70-€75; d €70-€75; t fr €95; extra person fr €25
On Site Private ↘ **Nearby** ⚇ 8km 🏊 4km 🏊 2km Restaurant 7km
🚴 2km Spa 4km 🏪 2km 🚶 8km **Notes** No pets English spoken

MAUBEC

⚐ ❍ ♿ Le Jardin d'en Naoua

Michèle ROUX

82500 MAUBEC

☎ 05 63 65 39 61 & 06 87 24 29 93   🖷 05 62 06 95 03

email: gite.naoua@free.fr

web: www.en-naoua.com

At the foot of the fortified village of Maubec, this 13th-century farm has been recently restored. It offers a family suite with disabled access (double and twin room), a grade two twin room, a triple and two double rooms, one with a cot and one with an extra single bed. All have private facilities. Garden, terrace. Evening meals by reservation.

Prices s €43-€47; d €57-€65; t €84-€89; extra person €15-€20; dinner €20-€27 **On Site** Private ↘ **Nearby** ⚇ 6km 🏊 2km 🚴 2km 🏪 2km
🚶 45km **Notes** Pets admitted English spoken

MEAUZAC

⚐ ❍ Manoir des Chanterelles

Nathalie BRARD

82290 MEAUZAC

☎ 05 63 24 60 70 & 06 11 08 96 33

🖷 05 63 21 56 49

email: nathalie@manoirdeschanterelles.com

web: www.manoirdeschanterelles.com

On the first floor of this house is a suite with a double canopied bed and two single beds; a twin-bedded room; and a double-bedded room. On the second floor are two more double rooms. All rooms have internet access, private bath or shower rooms and WCs. Lounge, dining room and games room on the ground floor. Large grounds, swimming pool.

Prices s €60-€120; d €70-€120; t €100-€145; extra person fr €25; dinner fr €25 **On Site** 🎾 Private ↘ Private tennis court
Nearby ⚇ 10km 🏊 15km 🏊 2km Restaurant 5km 🏪 2km 🚶 15km
Notes Pets admitted English spoken

See advertisement under MONTAUBAN

MIDI-PYRÉNÉES

MONTASTRUC

▦ iOi **Chambre d'hôtes**

Renata STILMANT
chemin des Combes, 82130 MONTASTRUC
☎ 05 63 26 47 59　📠 05 63 26 47 59
email: info@lagariere.com
web: www.lagariere.com

A typical 1930s house, beautifully restored with great attention to detail. The guest accommodation is all upstairs: two double rooms and a twin-bedded room, all with private shower room and WC. A cot is available. A galleried area provides guests with space to relax.

Prices s fr €60; d fr €63; extra person fr €15; dinner fr €20
On Site Private ⚲　**Nearby** ⚽ 10km ⚓ 12km ✦ 2km Restaurant 5km
⚲ 5km ♞ 12km ▣ 5km ⋙ 14km　**Notes** No pets

MONTAUBAN

▦ **Le Mas des Anges**

Juan et Sophie KERVYN
1623 rte de Verlhac Tescou, 82000 MONTAUBAN
☎ 05 63 24 27 05 & 06 14 32 93 24
email: info@lemasdesanges.com
web: www.lemasdesanges.com

This property has three ground floor guest rooms, all in an annexe to the main house. There are three doubles, carefully arranged and decorated. One has private power shower and WC; the others have private spa baths and WC. Terrace, table tennis, garden furniture beneath the trees.

Prices s fr €55; d fr €60; t fr €80　**On Site** Private ⚲　**Nearby** ⚽ 6km
✦ 4km ⚲ 4km ▣ 4km ⋙ 4km　**Notes** No pets English spoken

▦ *Ramierou*

Brigitte et Sabrina KAYSER
960 chemin du Ramierou, 82000 MONTAUBAN
☎ 05 63 20 39 86
email: sabrina@leramierou.com
web: www.leramierou.com

In a lovely green space, rooms include a double with private sitting room (TV, fireplace, sofa bed), private terrace with garden furniture, barbecue and leafy garden. In another building there are two bedrooms with private sitting rooms, a double and sofa bed in each. All have private facilities. Communal terrace with garden furniture and kitchen.

Prices not confirmed for 2008　**Nearby** ⚽ 6km ✦ 4km ⚲ 2km ⚲ 2km ▣ 2km ⋙ 4km　**Notes** No pets English spoken

Manoir des Chanterelles

The main house, built in 1881, is set in a pine wood. The manor offers beautifully decorated rooms within a charming, tranquil, luxurious setting which has an emphasis on wellbeing, relaxation, quality and refinement. Open all year.

Games room * Secure parking * Themed weekends

**Bernon Boutounelle
82290 MEAUZAC
France**

Tel: 00 33 (0)5 63 24 60 70
Fax: 00 33 (0)5 63 24 60 71
www.manoirdeschanterelles.com
Nathalie@manoirdeschanterelles.com

MONTPEZAT-DE-QUERCY

▦ iOi **Domaine de Lafon**

Micheline PERRONE
82270 MONTPEZAT-DE-QUERCY
☎ 05 63 02 05 09
email: micheline.perrone@domainedelafon.com
web: www.domainedelafon.com

This beautiful pink 19th-century manor house overlooks the fragrant Quercy countryside. The 'Indienne' and 'Perroquets' rooms have a double and single bed, and the 'Baldaquin' room is a twin. Each has private facilities. Large sitting room with TV and fireplace, guest dining room and lovely paintings. Evening meals on reservation. Painting courses available. Pets accepted on request.

Prices s fr €60; d fr €73; t fr €87; dinner fr €25　**Nearby** ⚽ 8km ✦ 4km ⚓ 4km Restaurant 12km ⚲ 4km ♞ 12km ▣ 4km ⋙ 13km **Notes** Pets admitted English spoken

NEGREPELISSE

✦✦✦ ⍥ Les Brunis

Christine et Serge BARRAS

4965 route de Montricoux, 82800 NEGREPELISSE

☎ 05 63 67 24 08 & 06 10 17 80 08 ▤ 05 63 67 24 08

email: barras.serge@wanadoo.fr

web: www.chambres-aveyron.com

This is a beautiful house, situated at the entrance to the Aveyron Gorges. It offers a family suite comprising a twin bedroom linked to an attic room with bunk-beds; two doubles; and two twins (one with balcony) - each with private facilities and TV. Sitting room with lounge area, swimming. Special rates for groups of four.

Prices s €45-€65; d €55-€65; t €80-€105; extra person fr €14; dinner fr €22 **On Site** ⍤ Private ⚲ **Nearby** ♿ 3km ⚲ 1km Restaurant 3km ⚲ 1km ⌂ 2km ⋒ 12km **Notes** Pets admitted English spoken

PARISOT

✦✦✦ Belvésé

Colette NORGA

82160 PARISOT

☎ 05 63 67 07 58 ▤ 05 63 67 07 58

A beautifully restored building in a lovely country location. There are three double guest rooms, each with a lounge area and private facilities, and a lounge, fireplace and kitchen.

Prices s fr €38; d fr €56 **Nearby** ♿ 15km ⚲ 30km ⚲ 3km ⚲ 15km Restaurant 1.5km ⚲ 3km ⌂ 3km ⋒ 31km **Notes** No pets English spoken

SAVENES

✦✦✦ ⍥ Lou Pitchou Bosc

Raoul et Maryvonne ROUSSEL

Chemin de la Forêt, 82600 SAVENES

☎ 05 63 64 31 75 & 06 63 22 33 05 ▤ 05 63 64 46 75

email: maryvonne.roussel@wanadoo.fr

web: www.lou-pitchou-bosc.com

In the heart of the countryside, but not far from Toulouse, this former farmhouse has three bedrooms. Two are doubles, and the third is a family suite for four, with a double bedroom and a twin-bedded room. Each has a private bathroom and WC. Guests' sitting room, and the whole property has a spacious feel set, inside and out.

Prices s fr €60; d fr €65; extra person fr €15; dinner fr €20 **On Site** ⍤ **Nearby** ♿ 5km ⚲ 20km ⚲ 5km ⚲ 12km Restaurant 3km ⚲ 5km ⌂ 3km ⋒ 6km **Notes** No pets English spoken

ST-ANTONIN-NOBLE-VAL

✦✦✦ ⍦ ⍥ Bes de Quercy

Joseph et Denise COSTES

82140 ST-ANTONIN-NOBLE-VAL

☎ 05 63 31 97 61

Typical stone house with garden, near the owner's home, in a lovely relaxing setting. Bedrooms include a family suite with two double

bedrooms, a room with a double bed and single bed and two double rooms, all with private facilities.

Prices s fr €31; d fr €42; t fr €53; extra person fr €10; dinner fr €15 **Nearby** ♿ 17km ⚲ 9km ⚲ 9km ⚲ 9km ⌂ 8km ⋒ 19km **Notes** Pets admitted

✦✦✦ ⍥ La Résidence

Sabine et Evert WEIJERS

37, rue Droite, 82140 ST-ANTONIN-NOBLE-VAL

☎ 05 63 67 37 56

email: info@laresidence-france.com

web: www.laresidence-france.com

Situated among the Aveyron gorges, in the heart of the medieval village of St-Antonin-Noble-Val, this house has been beautifully restored to give it a totally authentic feel. There are five bedrooms, a mix of doubles and twin-bedded rooms, all with private bathroom and WC (in one case the facilities are not en suite).

Prices s €70-€85; d €70-€85; t fr €85; extra person fr €15; dinner fr €25 **Nearby** ♿ 5km ⚲ 0.2km ⚲ 0.5km ⚲ 0.5km ⚲ 0.5km ⌂ 0.5km ⋒ 20km **Notes** No pets English spoken

ST-NAUPHARY

✦✦✦ Domaine du Roussillon

David et Maylis FRESQUET

82370 ST-NAUPHARY

☎ 05 63 67 85 47 & 06 76 86 21 21 ▤ 05 63 67 85 47

email: contact@domaineroussillon.com

web: www.domaineroussillon.com

This beautiful farm lies in the Roussillon area and has a grade 2 room with a double and single bed, and a grade 3 room with independent access, double bed and bunk-beds; all have private facilities. Lovely, comfortable sitting room with TV, covered terrace with garden furniture. Large wooded grounds and swimming pool. Breakfast served in front of the fireplace (in season).

Prices s €42-€44; d €48-€58; t fr €72 **On Site** ⍤ Private ⚲ **Nearby** ♿ 3km ⚲ 15km ⚲ 1km ⚲ 8km ⌂ 0.5km ⋒ 8km **Notes** No pets English spoken

ST-PORQUIER

✦✦✦ Chambre d'hôtes

Bernard BARTHE

Rue Ste Catherine, 82700 ST-PORQUIER

☎ 05 63 31 85 57

email: bernard-barthe075@orange.fr

web: www.chambres-hotes-leshortensias.com

All of the bedrooms at this property are non-smoking and on the ground floor. There is a double room, a twin-bedded room, and a room with a double bed plus a small double. All rooms have private bath/shower rooms and WCs. Lounge, covered terrace, bikes available, swimming pool. Pets admitted by reservation.

Prices s fr €60; d fr €60; t fr €80; extra person fr €15 **On Site** ⍤ Private ⚲ **Nearby** ♿ 10km ⚲ 8km ⚲ 0.5km Restaurant 0.1km ⚲ 0.5km ⌂ 0.5km ⋒ 7km **Notes** Pets admitted

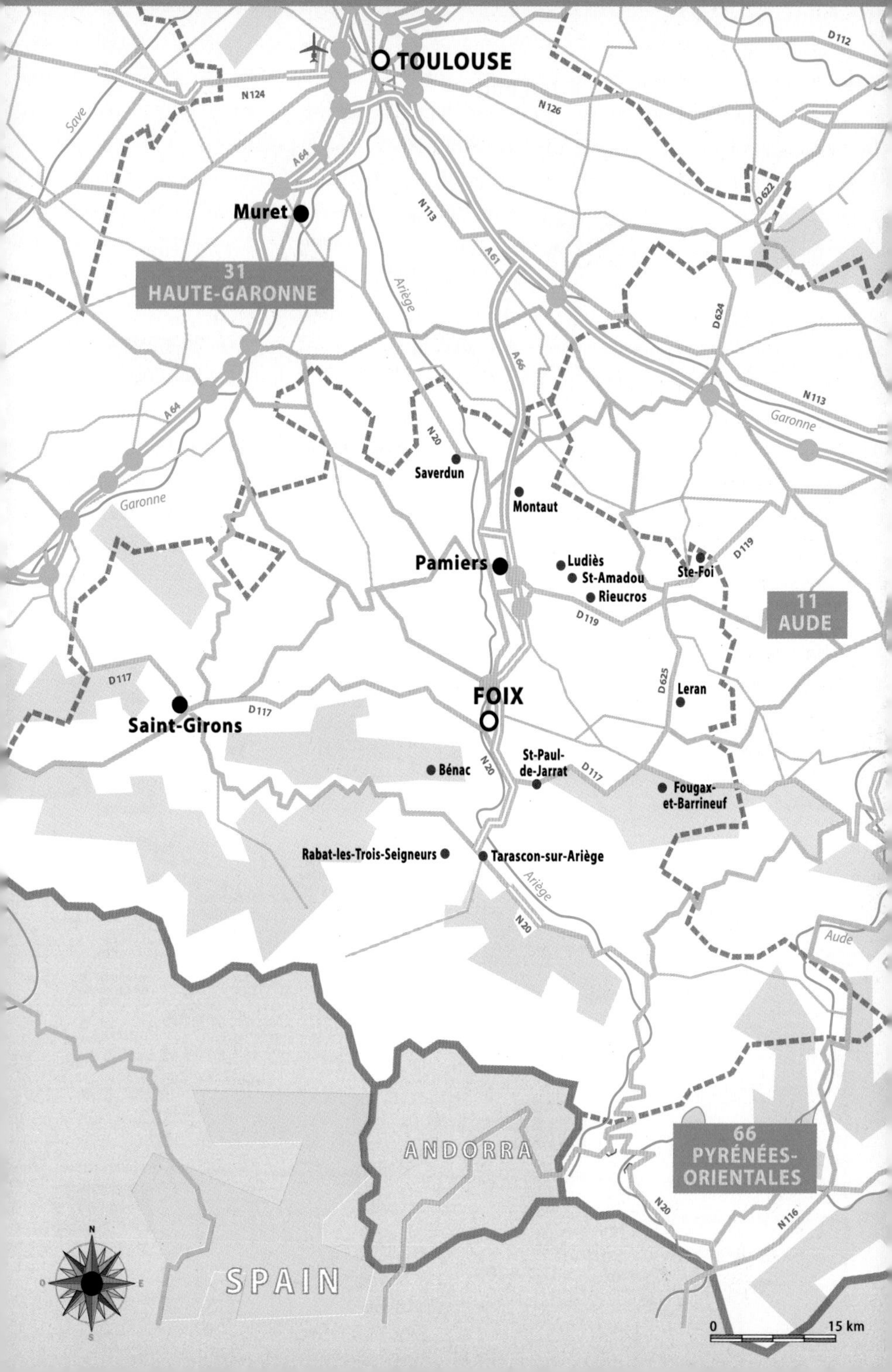

TOULOUSE

Muret

N124

N126

D112

A64

N113

Ariège

A61

31
HAUTE-GARONNE

A66

N20

Saverdun

Garonne

N113

Garonne

D622

D624

D117

Saint-Girons

D117

Pamiers

Montaut

Ludiès
St-Amadou
Rieucros

D119

Ste-Foi

D119

11
AUDE

FOIX

D625

Leran

Bénac

N20

St-Paul-
de-Jarrat

D117

Fougax-
et-Barrineuf

Rabat-les-Trois-Seigneurs

Tarascon-sur-Ariège

Ariège

N20

Aude

ANDORRA

66
PYRÉNÉES-
ORIENTALES

N20

N116

SPAIN

N

O   E

S

0   15 km

N 122

N 120

D 921

N 9

AURILLAC

Cere

D 920

D 987

Truyère

46
LOT

15
CANTAL

N 122

Alpuech

Lacroix-Barrez

Truyère

Entraygues-
sur-Truyère

Figeac

Montpeyroux

Laguiole

48
LOZÈRE

A 75

Bouillac

N 140

D 921

Sonnac

Les Albres

Estaing

D 920

Lot

N 88

Valady

Bozouls

D 922

Bournazel

Salles-la-Source

D 988

D 988

St-Rémy

Rignac

Onet-le-Château

Aveyron

D 994

Aveyron

Lapanouse

Villefranche-
de-Rouergue

RODEZ

N 88

Sévérac-
le-Château

D 911

D 911

Sanvensa

Pont-de-Salars

Rivière-
sur-Tarn

Dourbie

D 922

Sauveterre-
de-Rouergue

Verrières

D 911

La Fouillade

Peyreleau

Viaur

Compeyre

Millau

D 902

Villefranche-
de-Panat

St-Victor
et-Melvieu

D 600

Tarn

St-Georges-
de-Luzençon

N 88

Lapanouse-
de-Cernon

A 75

N 88

Tarn

Calmels-
et-le-Viala

ALBI

Coupiac

D 999

St-Jean-
et-St-Paul

Cornus

81
TARN

D 631

D 999

Gissac

Lodèv

N 112

34
HÉRAULT

N

Agout

D 112

Castres

D 622

Agout

D 622

D 90

0

MarieLaure et Thierry   79155 LE CHESNAY - FRANCE - © Autolmonde

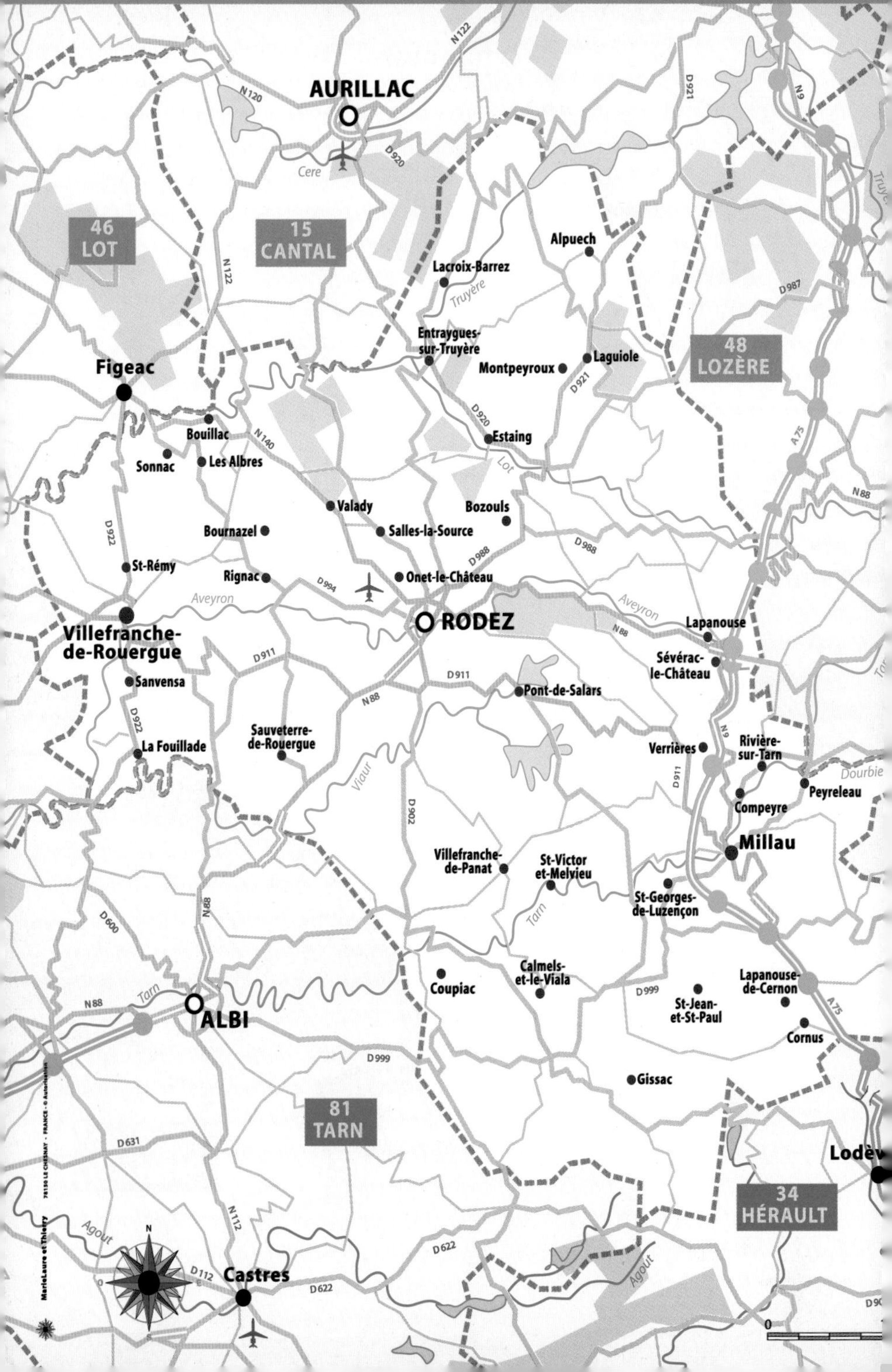

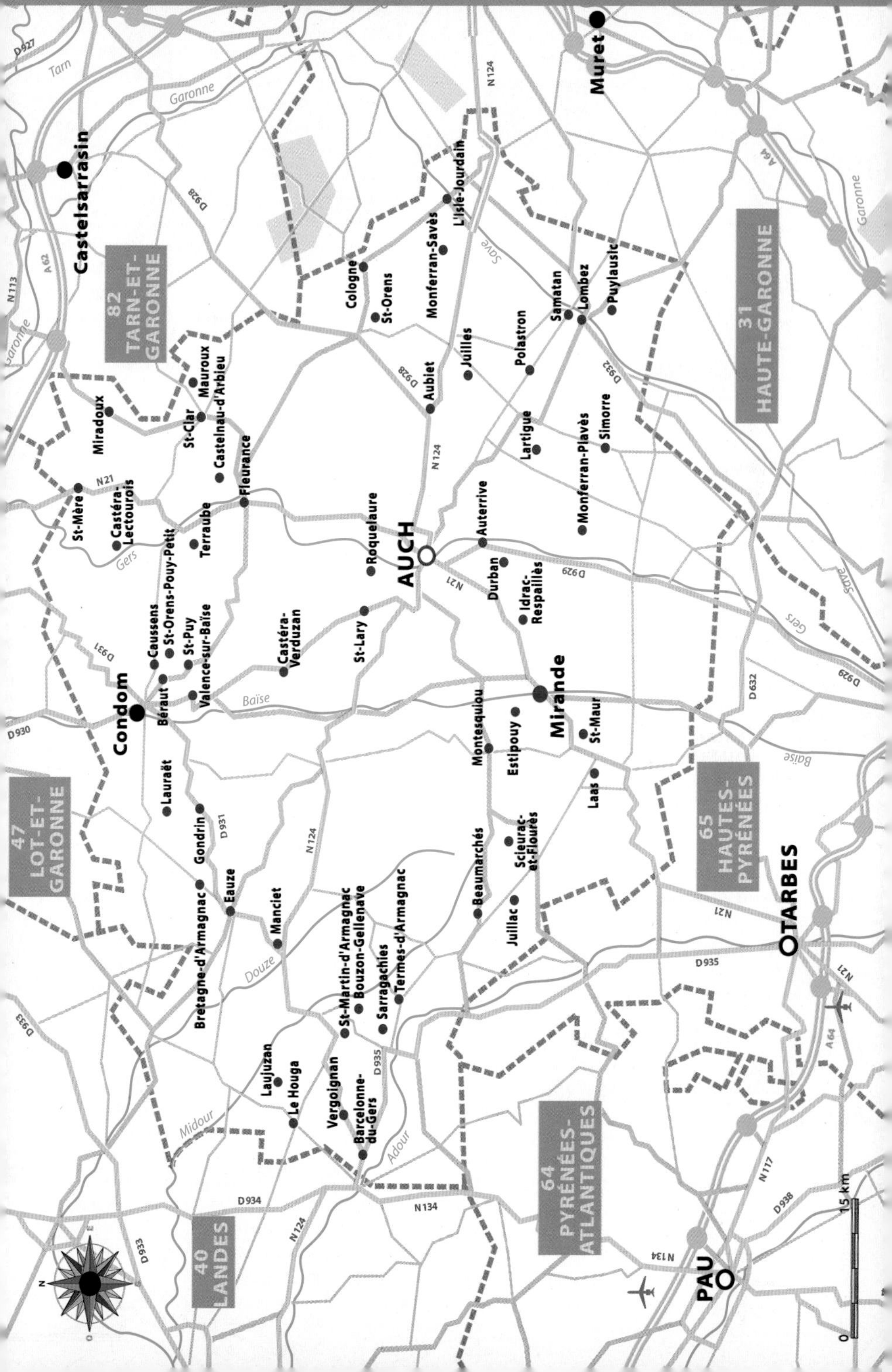

Muret

Castelsarrasin

82 TARN-ET-GARONNE

31 HAUTE-GARONNE

Tarn
Garonne
Garonne

N124

L'Isle-Jourdain
Cologne
St-Orens
Monferran-Savès
Lombez
Samatan
Puylausic
Juilles
Polastron
Aubiet
Lartigue
Monferran-Plavès
Simorre

Miradoux
St-Clar
Mauroux
Castelnau-d'Arbieu
Fleurance
Terraube

St-Mère
Castéra-Lectourois
N21
Gers

Roquelaure
AUCH
N124
Auterive
Durban
Idrac-Respaillès

Ceussens
St-Orens-Pouy-Petit
St-Puy
Valence-sur-Baïse
Castéra-Verduzan
St-Lary

Condom
Béraut
D931
Baïse

47 LOT-ET-GARONNE

Mirande
St-Maur
Montesquiou
Estipouy
Las

Lauraët
Gondrin
Eauze
Manciet
D931
N124
Douze

Bretagne-d'Armagnac
St-Martin-d'Armagnac
Bouzon-Gellenave
Sarragachies
Termes-d'Armagnac
Beaumarchés
Scieurac-et-Flourès
Juillac

Laujuzan
Le Houga
Vergoignan
Barcelonne-du-Gers
Midour
Adour

65 HAUTES-PYRÉNÉES

OTARBES

64 PYRÉNÉES-ATLANTIQUES

40 LANDES

PAU

N124
N134
D934
D933

15 km
0

HAUTE-GARONNE
Midi-Pyrénées

31

82 TARN-ET-GARONNE

81 TARN

32 GERS

AUCH

TOULOUSE

Cabanac-Séguenville

Grenade

Castelnau-d'Estrétefonds

Buzet-sur-Tarn

St-Sauveur

Azas

Cornebarrieu

Lavalette

Mons

Ramonville-Saint-Agne

Muret

Vigoulet-Auzil

Varennes

Vernet

Ayguesvives

Villenouvelle

Montesquieu-Lauragais

St-Léon

Avignonet-Lauragais

Auterive

Molas

Saint-Frajou

Boulogne-sur-Gesse

St-Elix-le-Château

Montesquieu-Volvestre

Castagnac

Latour

11 AUDE

Cazaril-Tamboures

St-Marcet

Auzas

Montberaud

Montbrun-Bocage

Saint-Gaudens

Pamiers

Barbazan

Figarol

09 ARIÈGE

Frontignan-de-Comminges

Saint-Girons

FOIX

St-Paul-d'Ueil

Antignac

Juzet-de-Luchon

Bagnères-de-Luchon

Montauban-de-Luchon

SPAIN

ANDORRA

Marie-Laure et Thierry

78100 LE CHESNAY - FRANCE - © Autoédition

0   1

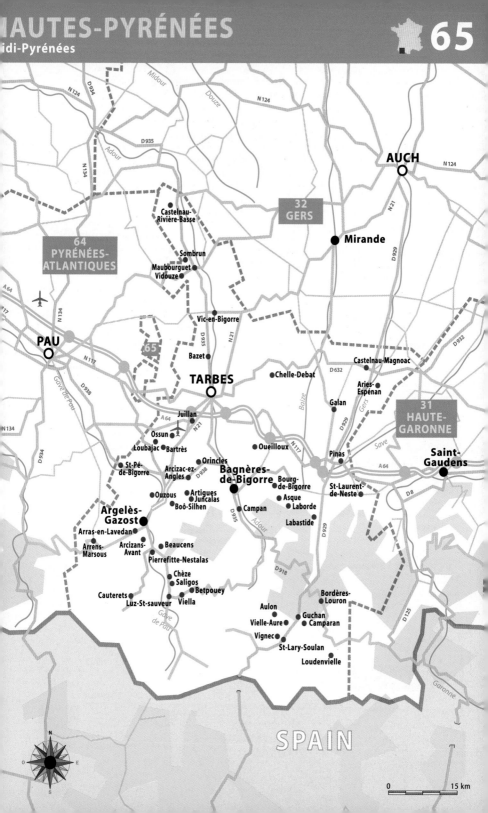

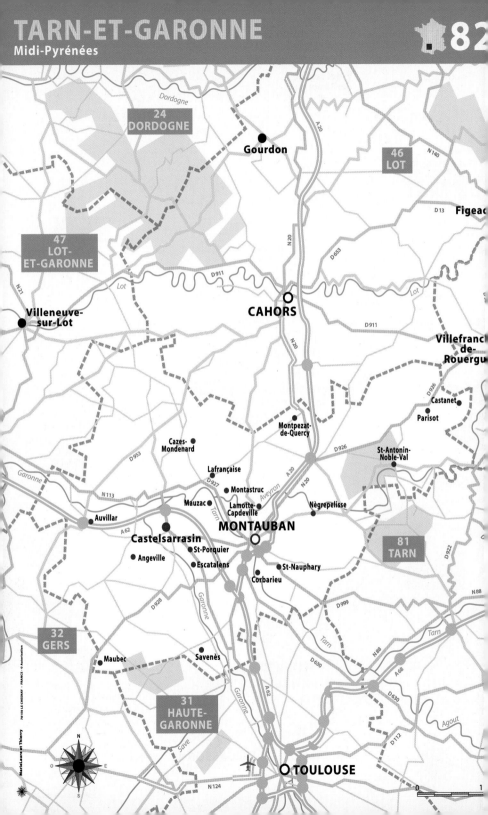
24 DORDOGNE

Dordogne

46 LOT

N 140

D 13   **Figeac**

47 LOT-ET-GARONNE

N 21

Lot

D 911

Villeneuve-sur-Lot

N 20

CAHORS

D 653

D 911   Lot

N 20

Villefranc-de-Rouergu

D 926

Castanet

Parisot

Montpezat-de-Quercy

Cazes-Mondenard

D 953

St-Antonin-Noble-Val

D 926

Lafrançaise

D 927

Montastruc

A 20

N 20

Garonne

N 113

Mauzac

Aveyron

Lamotte-Capdeville

Nègrepelisse

Auvillar

A 62

Tarn

MONTAUBAN

Castelsarrasin

81 TARN

D 922

Angeville

St-Porquier

Escatalens

Corbarieu

St-Nauphary

N 88

Garonne

D 928

D 999

32 GERS

Tarn

Tarn

Maubec

Savenès

D 630

N 88

A 68

D 630

31 HAUTE-GARONNE

Garonne

A 62

D 112

Save

Agout

N

O   E

S

TOULOUSE

N 124

0   1

NORD-PAS-DE-CALAIS

NORD

BAIVES

ⅲ Les Prés de la Fagne

Guy CONSTANT

5 rue Principale, 59132 BAIVES

☎ 03 27 57 02 69 📄 03 27 57 02 69

email: la.fagne@wanadoo.fr

web: www.lespresdelafagne.new.fr

In the area known as Little Switzerland, this 19th-century establishment is renovated in contemporary style but with plenty of traditional exposed timbers. Separate from the owners' dwelling are five charming double en suite rooms. Meals provided, drinks extra. Riding stables, guests' horses welcome.

Prices s €43-€50; d €50-€52; extra person fr €15 **Nearby** ☱ 0.1km 🏊 8km ⚲ 8km 🦆 8km 🎱 8km 🚶 15km **Notes** No pets English spoken

BANTEUX

ⅲ ⚴ Ferme de Bonavis

F DELCAMBRE

59266 BANTEUX

☎ 03 27 78 55 08 📄 03 27 78 55 08

email: contact@bonavis.fr

web: www.bonavis.fr

There are three attractive guest rooms on the first floor of the Bonavis farmstead 2km north of the village: one double with balcony; one triple and one with two double and two single beds, all en suite with TV. Central heating; double glazing; children's toys; table football; boules; parking; garage. Footpaths to Vaucelles Abbey 2km; aerodrome with gliding 9km.

Prices s €42-€48; d €49-€58; t €71-€86 **Nearby** ☱ 2km 🏊 40km ⚲ 2km 🦆 12km Restaurant 0.5km 🎱 13km 🚶 5km 🚶 12km **Notes** No pets English spoken

BEAUCAMPS-LIGNY

ⅲ Chez Julie

C TILMANT-DANJOU

rue de Radinghem, 59134 BEAUCAMPS-LIGNY

☎ 03 20 50 33 82 📄 03 20 50 34 35

email: ctilmant@wanadoo.fr

web: http://perso.orange.fr/chezjulie/indexab.htm

Next to the owners' house, this old farmstead in the village square has three guest rooms with separate access. There is a double room, a triple and a room with a double and two single beds, all en suite with telephone. Cot and TV available. Living and sitting room with wood stove. Terrace, garden, table tennis, parking, garage. Restaurant and shop 50mtrs.

Prices s fr €35; d fr €49; t fr €63 **On Site** Restaurant 🍴 **Nearby** ☱ 5km 🏊 10km ⚲ 5km 🦆 8km 🎱 0.2km 🚶 5km **Notes** No pets English spoken

BEAUDIGNIES

ⅲ *Chambre d'hôtes*

M. TELLIER

3 Rue Haute, 59530 BEAUDIGNIES

☎ 03 27 46 36 18 📄 03 27 25 83 47

email: les.vergers.tellier@wanadoo.fr

web: www.lesvergerstellier.com

This former brewery houses five guest rooms; three are doubles; the other two sleep four people (double bed plus twins). All have private showers and WCs. Lounge with kitchenette. Breakfast includes local foods. Lawn and parking area.

Prices not confirmed for 2008 **Nearby** ☱ 7km 🏊 8km ⚲ 2km 🦆 10km 🎱 2km 🏛 2km 🚶 3km **Notes** No pets

BIERNE

ⅲ ⚴ Chambre d'hôtes

Chantal et Alain VEREECKE

11 route de Watten, 59380 BIERNE

☎ 03 28 68 66 98 📄 03 28 68 68 03

email: ac.vereecke@wanadoo.fr

This mixed farm, 2km from the fortified town of Bergues, has four guest rooms separate from the owners' dwelling. There are two doubles and two twins, all en suite. Breakfast room and kitchenette; sitting area with TV and garden.

Prices s fr €36; d fr €45; t fr €77; extra person fr €20 **Nearby** ☱ 6km 🏊 4km Sea 10km ⚲ 0.1km 🦆 10km Restaurant 0.5km 🎱 1km Spa 1km 🍴 10km 🏛 1km 🚶 0.8km **Notes** No pets English spoken

BOLLEZEELE

ⅲ 🍴 ⚴ Le Pantgat-Hof

F et J-F CHILOUP-GEY

27 rue de Metz, 59470 BOLLEZEELE

☎ 03 28 68 00 87 📄 03 28 68 00 87

email: pantgat.hof@wanadoo.fr

web: http://pantgat.free.fr

This old farmstead is close to the Marais Audomarois Nature Park and offers en suite rooms in a building next to the owners' house. There are three doubles, one triple and a twin-bedded suite. Gardens; woodland; artist's studio; lace-making instruction; weekend guided walking tours; ponies and donkeys. Loose boxes to let. Special weekend rates November to April. Village centre 2km.

Prices s fr €41; d fr €50; t fr €60; dinner fr €22 **On Site** ☱ **Nearby** 🏊 20km Sea 20km ⚲ 5km 🦆 10km Restaurant 1.5km 🎱 11km 🍴 7km 🏛 2km 🚶 10km **Notes** No pets

BOURBOURG

⁂ Le Withof

Camille BATTAIS

Chemin du Château, 59630 BOURBOURG

☎ 03 28 62 32 50 ▤ 03 28 62 38 88

This fortified farmstead with its pony, geese, ducks and chickens dates from the 16th century. Guest rooms in the owners' house include a suite with two double beds, own bath and own wc on the landing, two doubles and two triples, all with own bath and wc. TV. Ground floor sitting and living room with antique furniture. Cot available. Garden with extensive lawn, 3 hectares of grazing, fishing. Closed Xmas and New Year.

Prices s fr €41; d fr €52; t fr €63; extra person fr €11   **On Site** ⌀
Nearby ⛵ 12km ⚓ 20km Sea 10km ⮜ 2km Restaurant 2km ⚲ 4km
⛫ 2.5km ⋙ 4km   **Notes** No pets CC

BOUSBECQUE

⁂ ⦿ La Valandiere

Martine & Frédéric CATRY

37 ch du Blaton, Hameau du Crumesse, 59166 BOUSBECQUE

☎ 03 20 98 83 66 & 06 84 04 13 36

email: info@lavalandiere.com

web: www.lavalandiere.com

An age-old four-square farmhouse forming an enclosed courtyard in the Normandy style. It offers three guest bedrooms, one of them a two-roomed family suite for four, and two more double rooms, all with private bath or shower room and WC. Non-smoking house. Guests' kitchenette, meals by arrangement. Outside are French-style gardens, with a rose-garden and ponds.

Prices s €55-€70; d €70-€85; t fr €95; dinner fr €20
Nearby ⛵ 0.3km ⚓ 10km ⚲ 1km ⮜ 7km ⚲ 0.3km ⛫ 0.5km
⋙ 10km   **Notes** No pets English spoken CC

BOUVINES

⁂ Ferme de la Place

Nadine et François DERVAUX

261 rue du Maréchal Foch, 59830 BOUVINES

☎ 03 20 41 12 13 & 06 78 19 87 22 ▤ 03 20 41 21 47

email: f.dervaux1@free.fr

web: http://f.dervaux1.free.fr/s2

Three bedrooms in a building separate from the hosts' home. On the ground floor are two doubles; upstairs is a triple room (three single beds). The rooms have private facilities, TV and internet access. Living room, kitchenette, lawned area, terrace, barbecue, and enclosed parking. By arrangement, use of heated pool, sauna, tennis court.

Prices s €60; d €75; t €85; extra person fr €15   **Nearby** ⛵ 2km
⚓ 7km ⚲ 5km Restaurant 0.5km ⚲ 0.3km ⛫ 0.1km ⋙ 15km
Notes No pets English spoken

CASSEL

⁂ ♿ *Les Sources*

V et J-B VINCENT-DE POORTER

326 Rue d'Aire, 59670 CASSEL

☎ 03 28 48 26 26 & 06 12 09 53 10 ▤ 03 28 48 26 26

email: valejean@free.fr

web: http://les.sources.cassel.free.fr

In a protected environment on the south side of Mont Cassel, this property has five rooms in the owners' house, but with a separate entrance. On the ground floor are two double rooms, one with disabled access. Upstairs are three rooms, each with a double bed and a single. All rooms have private facilities. The ground floor lounge has a regional artists' exhibition.

Prices not confirmed for 2008   **Nearby** ⛵ 5km ⚓ 20km Sea 30km
⚲ 0.5km ⮜ 10km ⚲ 0.5km ⛫ 0.5km ⋙ 2km   **Notes** No pets English spoken

CREVECOEUR-SUR-ESCAUT

⁂ ⦿ ♿ Ferme de Montécouvez

Géraldine et Franck PUCHE

Hameau de Montecouvez, 59258 CREVECOEUR SUR ESCAUT

☎ 03 27 82 02 01 ▤ 03 27 74 62 04

email: franck.puche@wanadoo.fr

web: www.ferme-montecouvez.com

This property is in a pleasant little hamlet on a working farm. There are four bedrooms: two on the ground floor with access for disabled guests are doubles with en suite shower; upstairs are a double and a triple (double bed plus single), both with bathroom. Lounge, kitchenette, meals by arrangement. Outside is a terrace, lawn and parking space.

Prices s €48-€54; d €55-€65; t fr €70; extra person fr €15; dinner fr €25   **On Site** ⚲   **Nearby** ⛵ 25km ⚓ 30km ⚲ 12km ⮜ 15km Restaurant 7km ⚲ 3km ⛫ 3km ⋙ 15km   **Notes** No pets English spoken

EECKE

⊞ ⦾ *De Kortepoeje*

Francine et Marc LEQUENNE

357, rue des 3 Moulins, 59114 EECKE

☎ 03 28 40 11 56 & 03 20 40 54 10

email: lequenne.marc@wanadoo.fr

This former farmhouse now renovated, enjoys a pleasant country setting. There are three guest rooms, two for three people and one for five. One of the triples has independent access; they all have en suite shower rooms and WCs. Stabling for horses also available. Exhibition of the host's paintings. Walking country, windmills to visit.

Prices not confirmed for 2008 **Nearby** ⚓ 5km ⥮ 35km Sea 40km ⚘ 1km ⌇ 10km ⚬ 5km ⌂ 3km ⇞ 12km **Notes** No pets English spoken

---

ESQUELBECQ

⊞ ☙ ♿ Ferme de Guernonval

P et O VANPEPERSTRAETE

7, rue du Souvenir, 59470 ESQUELBECQ

☎ 03 28 65 61 29 & 06 62 79 63 13 ▤ 03 28 62 98 12

email: opvpp@wanadoo.fr

web: http://site.voila.fr/ferme-guernonval

A mixed working farm is the setting for this chambre d'hôtes, with its five rooms, all with en suite facilities, in an annexe to the owners' home. There are two ground floor rooms with disabled access - a double and a triple; upstairs are two more doubles and another triple. Lounge with TV, use of kitchen. Breakfast in hosts' house.

Prices s fr €38; d fr €45; t fr €56; extra person fr €16 **Nearby** ⚓ 0.5km ⌇ 10km Sea 20km ⚘ 2km ⌇ 5km Restaurant 1km ⚬ 0.5km ⚜ 1km ⌂ 1km ⇞ 0.7km **Notes** No pets English spoken

---

FAUMONT

⊞ Chambre d'hôtes

Renée DEWAS

143 rue du Général de Gaulle, 59310 FAUMONT

☎ 03 20 59 27 74

This old farm has three guest rooms adjacent to a gîte and with separate access: an en suite twin and a double and a triple with own shower and wc on the landing. Ground floor reception room with TV, fridge, microwave and coffee-maker. Breakfast served in main building. Lawn and paved courtyard. Covered parking. Farm shop and restaurants nearby.

Prices s fr €32; d fr €43; t fr €52 **Nearby** ⚓ 1.5km ⌇ 8km ⚘ 1km ⌇ 5km Restaurant 1.5km ⚬ 8km Spa 15km ⌂ 1km ⇞ 8km **Notes** No pets

---

FOURNES-EN-WEPPES

⊞ ☙ ⦾ Ferme de Rosembois

Francine BAJEUX

Hameau du Bas Flandres, 59134 FOURNES EN WEPPES

☎ 03 20 50 25 69 ▤ 03 20 50 60 75

email: famillebajeux@wanadoo.fr

Guests to this mixed farm in a quiet setting 10km from Armentières can choose between three en suite guest rooms, one double, one twin, and one triple. Sitting room with TV and open fireplace. Garden furniture. Restaurant in the village. Leisure centre, tennis courts, gym and golf nearby.

Prices s €34-€36; d €42-€45; t fr €55; extra person fr €10; dinner €16-€18 **Nearby** ⚓ 5km ⌇ 5km ⌇ 10km Restaurant 1.5km ⚬ 5km ⌂ 1.5km ⇞ 8km **Notes** No pets English spoken Open 3 January to 22 December. CC

HALLUIN

⊞ ♿ La Ferme du Nid de Mousse

Marie-Joseph DELESALLE

94 chemin du Billemont, Mont d'Halluin, 59250 HALLUIN

☎ 03 20 37 02 05 ▤ 03 20 03 82 73

email: niddemousse@aol.com

This mixed farm with chickens and horses has three guest rooms above two gîtes separate from the owners' house. There is a triple, a double and a twin with a suite with two single beds. Shared sitting room with TV and living room and library. Breakfast room; parking; terrace and small shared open area with garden furniture.

Prices s fr €29; d fr €36; t fr €40; extra person fr €13 **Nearby** ⚓ 4km ⌇ 10km ⚘ 2km ⌇ 2km Restaurant 1.5km ⚬ 3km ⌂ 2km ⇞ 10km **Notes** No pets English spoken

---

HONDSCHOOTE

⊞ ⦾ ♿ Ons Kot

C et G LOUWYCK-COOLEMAN

1200 Chemin du Clachoire, 59122 HONDSCHOOTE

☎ 03 28 20 76 87 ▤ 03 28 20 75 82

email: info@onskot.com

web: www.onskot.com

Close to the Belgian border, this group of former farm buildings has six guest rooms. On the ground floor is a double, with disabled access, and a triple room (double bed and a single); upstairs are two doubles, a twin-bedded room, and a triple (double bed and a single). All of the rooms have TV and private facilities. Meals by arrangement.

Prices s fr €40; d fr €50; t fr €60; extra person fr €10; dinner fr €20 **Nearby** ⚓ 18km ⌇ 18km Sea 18km ⚘ 5km ⌇ 11km ⚬ 5km ⌂ 5km ⇞ 15km **Notes** No pets English spoken

JENLAIN

⊞⊞⊞ Château d'En Haut

Michel DEMARCQ

59144 JENLAIN

☎ 03 27 49 71 80 & 03 27 07 05 72

▤ 03 27 35 90 17

email: chateaudenhaut@free.fr

web: http://chateaudenhaut.free.fr

Standing in extensive parkland, this 18th-century château has six en suite guest rooms. There are four doubles, another double with a single bed in an adjoining room, and a triple. Sitting room and open fireplace. Garden furniture. Restaurants in the village.

Prices s €48-€58; d €67-€80; t €75-€90; extra person fr €15
Nearby ⛷ 10km ↕ 10km ⚓ 10km ⌁ 10km ◷ 10km 🏛 6km
⋈ 8km **Notes** No pets English spoken

JOLIMETZ

⊞⊞⊞ ⓘⓄⓘ Chambre d'hôtes Jolimessine

M-A GUILLET-MASSON

15 Rue du Pave, BP 36, 59530 JOLIMETZ

☎ 03 27 26 41 81   ▤ 03 27 26 41 81

email: chambres.auberge.jolimessine@wanadoo.fr

In the middle of the village and only 100mtrs from the Mormal Forest, this house has five en suite guest rooms with separate access. There are four doubles and one twin, a sitting and living room and open fireplace. TV available, meals by arrangement. Adjacent to country inn. Large lawn and garden furniture. Spacious courtyard with parking. Bikes for hire.

Prices s fr €45; d fr €50; t fr €70; dinner fr €20   **On Site** Restaurant
❀ **Nearby** ⛷ 5km ↕ 5km ⚓ 3km ⌁ 20km ◷ 20km 🏛 3km ⋈ 3km
Notes Pets admitted English spoken

LA GROISE

⊞⊞⊞ Relais du Toillon

Hélène et Michel DEMARCQ

18 route de Landrecies, 59360 LA GROISE

☎ 03 27 07 05 72 & 03 27 49 71 80

email: relaisdutoillon@easyneuf.fr

web: http://relaisdutoillon.free.fr

Early 19th-century décor and mahogany furniture give this stately property a period feel. Five rooms all have double beds, some of

them canopied, and all with private bath or shower room and WC. The dining and living rooms are in keeping with the style of the place. Extensive grounds have an enclosed area, and garden furniture.

Prices s €51-€56; d €56-€64   **Nearby** ⛷ 10km ↕ 35km ⚓ 6km
⌁ 12km Restaurant 0.9km ◷ 7km ❀ 10km 🏛 4km ⋈ 15km
Notes No pets English spoken CC

LE DOULIEU

⊞⊞⊞ ⓘⓄⓘ Chambre d'hôtes

Elisabeth & J-Marie DECHERF

190 Grand'Rue, 59940 LE DOULIEU

☎ 03 28 49 39 25   ▤ 03 28 40 85 85

email: elisabeth.decherf@ac-lille.fr

Just 12km from Belgium and 25km from Lille, this establishment offers three bedrooms; two rooms are on the first floor of the proprietors' house, and the third is in a separate building. All rooms have private facilities. The first room has a double bed and a single bed, the second has a double bed and the third has a double and two single beds. There is a lounge and garden.

Prices s €38-€45; d €43-€50; t €50-€60; extra person €9-€10; dinner fr €20   **On Site** ❀   **Nearby** ⛷ 0.2km ↕ 15km ⌁ 12km ◷ 8km
Restaurant 5km ◷ 0.2km 🏛 0.2km ⋈ 7km   **Notes** Pets admitted English spoken

LEDERZEELE

⊞⊞⊞ ⓘⓄⓘ La Ferme des Capucines

Dominique et Christian MENTEL

9 route de Watten, 59143 LEDERZEELE

☎ 03 28 62 40 88

email: christian.mentel@wanadoo.fr

This property, once a farm, has four guest bedrooms in a building separate from the owners' home. All the rooms are doubles (two of them king-size), complete with private bath or shower room. On the ground floor is a breakfast room with open fire, a living room and a kitchenette. Meals by arrangement. Outside is a courtyard and terrace with garden furniture.

Prices s €41-€42; d €48-€52; t fr €66; extra person fr €17; dinner fr €22
Nearby ⛷ 5km ↕ 10km Sea 30km ⚓ 10km ⌁ 10km ◷ 10km 🏛 1km
⋈ 10km   **Notes** No pets English spoken CC

LIESSIES

⊞⊞⊞ *La Forge de L'Abbaye*

Christine et Franck PLATEAU

13 rue de la Forge, 59740 LIESSIES

☎ 06 86 88 58 53

email: contact@chateaudelamotte.fr

Once this was a blacksmith's forge attached to the old abbey; now it is a chambre d'hôtes with four comfortable rooms. On the ground floor are a shared living room and kitchenette, and a double room with twin beds. Upstairs are two small doubles, and a triple (double bed and single); all have shower/WC except the triple which has a bathroom. TV, DVD, internet access. Outside is a terrace, and parking space.

Prices not confirmed for 2008   **Nearby** ⛷ 2km ↕ 30km ⚓ 0.5km
⌁ 2km ◷ 1km 🏛 1km ⋈ 12km   **Notes** Pets admitted CC

LOCQUIGNOL

⌘ **La Touraille**

O RENARD-FREMY

2 La Touraille, 59530 LOCQUIGNOL

☎ 03 27 34 20 65 📄 03 27 34 20 65

email: latouraille@laposte.net

web: www.latouraille.com

This residence in the Mormal Forest has four rooms: two doubles, a suite with a single bed and a family room, all en suite. Breakfast room with open fireplace. Leisure corner with TV. Garden and conifer park. Enclosed parking. Bridle paths and equestrian centre. Restaurants 1km.

Prices s fr €40; d €50-€52; t fr €70 **Nearby** ⛷ 6km ⌁ 15km ⌁ 2km ⟶ 8km Restaurant 1km ⌁ 7km Spa 30km ⌁ 20km ⌁ 6km ⌁ 9km
Notes No pets

LOMPRET

⌘ *Ferme Blanche de Lassus*

Olivier DELEVAL

Rue Pasteur, 59840 LOMPRET

☎ 03 20 92 99 12 & 03 20 54 29 82 📄 03 20 57 13 09

email: dadeleval@nordnet.fr

With its own entrance, the accommodation in this 18th-century building consists of three charming rooms. There are two doubles and a twin, all en suite and two with sitting areas. Living room with fireplace and large secluded grassed area. Bikes, table tennis, private lake, garage. Lille Metro stop 1km. Restaurants, leisure centre and transport to Lille nearby.

Prices not confirmed for 2008 **Nearby** ⛷ 5km ⌁ 5km ⌁ 4km ⟶ 4km ⌁ 1km ⌁ 0.5km ⌁ 2km **Notes** Pets admitted English spoken

MAROILLES

⌘ ⍟ **Vert Bocage**

M-France VILBAS

555 Rue des Juifs, 59550 MAROILLES

☎ 03 27 77 74 22 & 06 30 39 46 39 📄 03 27 77 74 91

email: jean_noel.vilbas@wanadoo.fr

This old farmhouse has three non-smoking en suite guest rooms, two with their own entrance: one double with additional room with single bed, one triple and a twin. Sitting room, library, TV, guests' billiard room, parking. Ground floor breakfast room with wood fire, games, table football. Large shared leafy garden with views over the countryside. Restaurants, forest and golf nearby.

Prices s fr €40; d fr €50; t €70-€72; extra person fr €15; dinner fr €20
Nearby ⛷ 5km ⌁ 15km ⌁ 0.5km ⟶ 10km Restaurant 0.5km ⌁ 0.8km ⌁ 35km ⌁ 0.5km ⌁ 10km **Notes** No pets English spoken

MILLAM

⌘ ⍟ ⌀ **La Ferme des Saules**

Cathy et J-Bernard LEDUC

337, rue de l'Eglise, 59143 MILLAM

☎ 03 28 68 05 32

email: la-ferme-des-saules@wanadoo.fr

This property, a former farm building, has two guest rooms in a building adjacent to a gîte. There is a ground floor double room, with disabled access, and a twin-bedded room upstairs. There is also a family room in the owners' house. All rooms have a private bath or shower room and WC. Breakfast is served in the hosts' house. Enclosed garden, parking.

Prices s fr €50; d fr €60; t fr €75; extra person fr €15; dinner fr €25 **Nearby** ⛷ 10km ⌁ 10km Sea 20km ⌁ 2km ⟶ 10km Restaurant 6km ⌁ 0.5km ⌁ 0.5km ⌁ 5km **Notes** No pets English spoken

OSTRICOURT

⌘ *Chambre d'hôtes*

Caroline et J-Claude SABRE

998 rue E. Macquart, 59162 OSTRICOURT

☎ 03 20 87 20 99 & 06 07 16 64 70

📄 03 20 87 20 99

email: jcsabre@wanadoo.fr

This house is full of character. It enjoys a parkland setting, with a lake, bordering a forest. It has four bedrooms: two doubles, a triple with TV, and a suite for three with lounge and TV. All have en suite bathrooms and WCs. Lounge with TV, piano, billiards and books. Indoor tennis, sports room.

Prices not confirmed for 2008 **On Site** ⌁ **Nearby** ⛷ 2km ⌁ 1km ⟶ 6km ⌁ 1km ⌁ 1km ⌁ 3km **Notes** No pets English spoken

PONT-SUR-SAMBRE

⌘ **Aux Berges de Sambre**

Christelle FRECHEIN

117/119 Grand Rue, 59138 PONT SUR SAMBRE

☎ 03 27 39 05 76 📄 03 27 39 17 53

email: sarl.les4c@wanadoo.fr

web: www.auxbergesdesambre.net

These five rooms are on the first floor of a country inn, which is a listed building. They have a separate entrance. There are three doubles and two triples, all with en suite bathrooms and WCs. Wood block flooring and antique furniture. Breakfast served in the heated conservatory.

Prices s fr €55; d fr €60; t fr €65 **Nearby** ⛷ 10km ⌁ 15km ⌁ 0.1km ⟶ 4km ⌁ 5km ⌁ 0.1km ⌁ 4km **Notes** Pets admitted English spoken CC

QUAEDYPRE

⚑ ❦ Chambre d'hôtes

Ghyslaine et Gérard REUMAUX
Ferme du Cheval Noir, 59380 QUAEDYPRE
☎ 03 28 68 68 85 📄 03 28 68 68 85
email: greumaux@free.fr
web: www.reumaux.net

This farm grows traditional local crops (potatoes, flax, raspberries and strawberries) and has four guest rooms with separate access. There is a double, a twin, and two triples. Cot available. Supplement payable for pets. Breakfast room with open fireplace; kitchen; sitting room with TV (satellite and cable). Outdoor furniture in the courtyard and farm produce for sale.

Prices s fr €39; d fr €48; t fr €58   **Nearby** ⚓ 5km ↟ 8km Sea 15km
✎ 5km ⬎ 5km Restaurant 1km 🏊 5km Spa 3km ♔ 4km 🏛 3km
🚣 5km   **Notes** Pets admitted English spoken

RIBECOURT-LA-TOUR

⚑ Le Clos Xavianne

Anne et Xavier LERICHE
20, rue de Marcoing, 59159 RIBECOURT LA TOUR
☎ 03 27 37 52 61 📄 03 27 74 51 17
email: ferme.leriche@free.fr
web: http://ferme.leriche.free.fr

This working farm has three bedrooms. On the ground floor is a double-bedded room; upstairs is another double, and a family room. They all have TVs, private bath/shower rooms and WCs. Lounge with TV; kitchenette. Enclosed courtyard, lawn, flower-filled garden with garden furniture. Exhibition of antique farming implements.

Prices s €53-€65; d €60-€75; t fr €85; extra person fr €22
Nearby ⚓ 0.1km ↟ 40km ✎ 5km ⬎ 10km Restaurant 10km 🏊 0.1km
🏛 3km 🚣 10km   **Notes** No pets

SAINGHIN-EN-MELANTOIS

⚑ ❦ ◎ Chambre d'hôtes

Nelly et Dominique POLLET
832 Rue Pasteur, 59262 SAINGHIN EN MELANTOIS
☎ 03 20 41 29 82 📄 03 20 79 06 99
email: dominique-nelly.pollet@wanadoo.fr
web: http://perso.wanadoo.fr/dpollet

Near Noyelle Wood and the Rivière de la Marque, this 18th-century working farm specialises in cattle breeding and strawberry growing. The four guest rooms, all en suite with TV, have their own entrance and comprise two doubles, a twin and a triple. Kitchenette; breakfast room; lawn, garden furniture. Meals by arrangement. Charge for pets.

Prices s fr €34; d fr €43; t fr €54; extra person fr €12; dinner fr €16
On Site ♔   **Nearby** ⚓ 2km ↟ 6km ✎ 3km ⬎ 5km Restaurant 4km
🏊 2km 🏛 2km 🚣 12km   **Notes** Pets admitted English spoken

SEMERIES-ZOREES

⚑ ◎ Chambre d'hôtes

Nadine & Didier TOUBON
2 rue du Calvaire, 59291 SEMERIES ZOREES
☎ 03 27 59 80 26 & 06 85 97 80 37
email: didier.toubon5@libertysurf.fr
web: www.gite-prop.com/59/4701

All four rooms in this renovated farmhouse are upstairs: three of them are double rooms, and the fourth has three single beds. There is a separate guests' entrance, and all the rooms have TV, phone/internet connection, private shower and WC. Lounge with TV, books and board games; kitchenette. Meals by arrangement. Good walking area, with easy access to footpaths.

Prices s fr €42; d fr €46; t fr €52; extra person fr €10; dinner fr €19
Nearby ⚓ 2km ↟ 2km ✎ 2km ⬎ 7km 🏊 2km 🏛 3km 🚣 3km
Notes No pets CC

ST-HILAIRE-SUR-HELPE

⚑ La Grange de Saint Hilaire

C et L VANCOMPERNOLLE
8 route d'Aulnoye, 59440 SAINT HILAIRE SUR HELPE
☎ 03 27 57 07 15 & 06 85 93 00 44
email: luc.vancompernolle@wanadoo.fr
web: http://grange.saint.hilaire.free.fr

A two-year-old barn conversion, with five splendid bedrooms: a twin bedded room on the ground floor, three doubles, and a family room for three. One of the doubles is a suite with its own sitting room, and all have en suite bath or shower room. Outside are enclosed grounds with garden furniture and parking space.

Prices s €45-€60; d €50-€70; t fr €70   **On Site** ♔
Nearby ⚓ 2km ✎ 0.2km ⬎ Restaurant 5km 🏊 5km 🏛 5km
🚣 5km   **Notes** No pets English spoken

ST-PIERRE-BROUCK

⫩⫩⫩ ⏺ Le Château

Nathalie DUVIVIER-ALBA
287 route de la Bistade,
59630 SAINT-PIERRE-BROUCK
☎ 03 28 27 50 05 🖹 03 28 27 50 05
email: contact@lechateau.net
web: www.lechateau.net

Situated twenty minutes from the coast and near Cap Gris Nez and the Belgian border; charming en suite guest rooms available in a home full of character complete with antique furniture. One twin, two doubles and a suite with canopied double bed and single bed. Sitting room with open fireplace. Terrace and extensive grounds. No smoking establishment.

Prices s €70-€100; d €80-€100; t €100-€120; extra person fr €20; dinner fr €28 **Nearby** ⛴ 15km ⚓ 15km Sea 15km ✒ 1km ⤳ 7km Restaurant 7km ⊋ 7km ⌖ 10km 🖭 7km 🚣 7km **Notes** No pets English spoken

ST-SOUPLET

⫩⫩⫩ Chambre d'hôtes

Dorothée et Jean-Luc MERIAUX
35 rue de la Fabrique, 59360 SAINT SOUPLET
☎ 03 27 77 79 35 & 06 29 91 57 27 🖹 03 27 77 79 42
email: jlmeriaux@wanadoo.fr

Five hectares of grounds, with woods, meadows, river and lake, provide an attractive setting for this 19th-century house with its three guest rooms. On the first floor is a family room, with a double bed and two singles; on the second floor are two doubles. All of the rooms have a private bath or shower room and WC. Guests' lounge with TV.

Prices s fr €45; d fr €50; t fr €70 **Nearby** ⛴ 7km ⚓ 30km ✒ 0.1km ⤳ 7km Restaurant 7km ⌖ 0.5km 🚣 7km **Notes** No pets English spoken

see advert on this page

TETEGHEM

⫩⫩⫩ ⏺ La Demeure du Galgouck

Nelly et Jean-Luc SUING
157 rue des Pierres, 59229 TETEGHEM
☎ 03 28 26 00 35 & 06 07 99 46 61 🖹 03 28 51 19 16
email: jlsuing@aol.com
web: www.legalgouck.com

This property has three bedrooms, all on the first floor of the owners' house. There is a twin-bedded room; a double-bedded room with a cot; and a triple room with a double bed and a single. All of the rooms have en suite facilities. Meals, with local specialities, available by arrangement. Terrace, enclosed lawn, garden.

Prices s fr €42; d fr €48; t fr €63; extra person fr €15; dinner fr €22 **On Site** Restaurant **Nearby** ⛴ 2km ⚓ 3km Sea 7km ✒ 3km ⤳ 7km ⊋ 1km Spa 40km ⌖ 7km 🖭 1km 🚣 5km **Notes** No pets English spoken

Les Etoiles d'Eau

Jean-Luc et Dorothée MERIAUX
35 rue de la Fabrique　　　　59360 Saint Souplet
France

A peaceful country retreat ideal for relaxation. A 5-hectare property with park, wood, river pond, the main house built in the 19th Century has two double rooms as well as a family room which can accommodate 4 people. Each has its own private bathroom and WC. Near to: Matisse Museum and Château Fort du Duc de Guise. No pets.

Email : JLMeriaux@wanadoo.fr
Tel : 00 33 (0)3 27 77 79 35
Mobile : 00 33 (0)6 29 51 59 81

THUMERIES

⫩⫩⫩ Château Beghin

Nathalie et Jamal ELFAIZ
14 rue Joseph Béghin, 59239 THUMERIES
☎ 03 20 86 86 86 & 06 80 58 54 51 🖹 03 20 86 86 86
email: nathalie.elfaiz@wanadoo.fr
web: www.chambre-dhote-chateau-beghin.com

A house with lots character dating back to the late 19th century, standing in three hectares of grounds. There are four bedrooms: three doubles, each with a lounge area, and a family room for four with a double bed and two singles. All have private bath or shower room and WC. Secure parking, possible accommodation for guests' horses.

Prices s fr €45; d fr €50; t fr €62; extra person fr €10 **Nearby** ⛴ 0.3km ⚓ 1km ✒ 1km ⤳ 6km Restaurant 0.5km ⌖ 0.1km 🚣 3km **Notes** Pets admitted English spoken

VERLINGHEM

⫩⫩⫩ Ferme de la Forterie

Françoise et André DUTHOIT
11, chemin noir, 59237 VERLINGHEM
☎ 03 20 51 64 73 🖹 03 20 51 64 73
web: www.gitedefrance.com

This working farm has three first floor bedrooms - a double, a twin and a triple - separate from the owners' house. All the rooms have modem sockets, a lounge area and private bath/shower rooms and

CONTINUED

NORD-PAS-DE-CALAIS

VERLINGHEM *CONTINUED*

WCs. Breakfast room in the hosts' house. Courtyard with furniture, private parking, garden.

Prices s fr €34; d fr €44; t fr €48 **Nearby** ⚓ 1km ♨ 8km ✎ 3km ✈ 1km Restaurant 0.1km ⛵ 2km 🏛 2km ⚒ 6km **Notes** No pets English spoken

VIEUX-CONDE

⍩ Chambre d'hôtes

M.Paule et Albert MATHYS

Mont de Peruwelz, 935 Rue de Calonne, 59690 VIEUX CONDE

☎ 03 27 40 16 13

This working farm has three guest rooms in the owners' house: a double, a twin and a family room, all en suite. Two gîtes and a small child's bed available. Shared terrace; shops nearby. Station 18km, Amaury leisure centre in Bonsecours in Belgium 4km, Parc St-Amand spa 15km.

Prices s fr €31; d fr €39; t fr €46 **Nearby** ⚓ 6km ♨ 4km ✎ 2km ✈ 4km Restaurant 3km ⛵ 2km 🏛 2km ⚒ 18km **Notes** No pets

WALLON-CAPPEL

⍩ *La Ferme des Longs Champs*

Isabelle et Bruno MENTASTI

98, rue des Longs Champs, 59190 WALLON CAPPEL

☎ 03 28 40 09 07 & 06 08 54 53 38 🖺 03 28 40 09 07

email: leslongschamps@aol.com

web: www.fermedeslongschamps.com

The guest rooms at this property are in a building separate from the owners' home, a restored 18th-century farmhouse. Downstairs there is a double room; upstairs are two rooms with a double bed and a single. All rooms have a TV, private bath or shower room and WC. Breakfast is served in the hosts' house. Kitchenette; garden furniture.

Prices not confirmed for 2008 **Nearby** ⚓ 1km ♨ 25km Sea 50km ✎ 4km ✈ 4km ⛵ 4km 🏛 4km ⚒ 4km **Notes** No pets English spoken

WAMBRECHIES

⍩ 🍽 Péniche Fantasia

J-M DEFAUT et G LECOCQ

Port de Plaisance, Quai de l'Ecluse, 59118 WAMBRECHIES

☎ 03 28 52 47 97 & 06 16 44 09 82 🖺 03 28 52 47 97

email: contact@peniche-fantasia.com

web: www.peniche-fantasia.com

A boat moored on the Deûle Canal, with three comfortable, air-conditioned double cabins, all non-smoking. Each has a private shower room and WC. There is a lounge with TV and stereo, and a sun deck with a covered terrace. Parking available; meals by arrangement.

Prices s fr €80; d fr €80; dinner fr €32 **Nearby** ✎ 3km ♨ 3km ✎ 0.5km ✈ 3km Restaurant 1km ⛵ 1km 🏛 0.1km ⚒ 1km **Notes** No pets English spoken

---

ALEMBON

⍩ 🍽 Les Volets Bleus

Veronique BRETON

1A, rue du Cap Gris Nez, 62850 ALEMBON

☎ 03 21 00 13 17 & 06 23 80 84 41

email: d.breton2@libertysurf.fr

web: www.les-volets-bleus.com

This little farmhouse has three double rooms and two twins, all en suite with TV and child's bed by request. There is a sitting room, living room, library, garden, outdoor furniture and parking. Breakfast and other meals (by arrangement) served in the sitting room in front of a wood stove or on the sunny terrace. Lake 3km, forest 3km. Riding stables nearby.

Prices s fr €40; d fr €48; t fr €58; extra person fr €10; dinner fr €25 **Nearby** ⚓ 0.5km ♨ 18km Sea 22km ✎ 3km ✈ 18km Restaurant 8km ⛵ 18km 🏛 3km **Notes** No pets English spoken

ANZIN-ST-AUBIN

⍩ 🍽 Les Volets Bleus

P et P ROUSSEAU

47, rue Briquet Taillandier, 62223 ANZIN-ST-AUBIN

☎ 03 21 23 39 90 & 06 09 12 58 49

email: rousseau_philippe@yahoo.fr

web: www.voletsbleus.com

Opposite Arras golf course, this property has three top quality guest rooms, situated in the owners' house. There is a twin-bedded room and two doubles, one with a double bed-settee. All of the rooms have a private shower room and WC. TV available on request, also internet connection. Baby equipment, excellent breakfasts, other meals by arrangement.

Prices s €55-€72; d €59-€76; extra person fr €15; dinner €21-€37 **On Site** ✎ 🏌 **Nearby** ⚓ 4km ♨ 0.1km ✈ 4km Restaurant 0.1km ⛵ 1km 🏛 4km ⚒ 4km **Notes** No pets English spoken

ARDRES

❦ Le Manoir de Bois en Ardres

Françoise ROGER

1530 rue de Saint-Quentin, 62610 ARDRES

☎ 03 21 85 97 78 & 06 15 03 06 21 📄 03 21 36 48 07

email: roger@aumanoir.com

web: www.aumanoir.com

Guests are warmly welcomed to this restored manor house set in a five hectare park in a quiet countryside setting just twenty minutes from the Channel Tunnel. Guest rooms comprise a triple, a twin, and a suite of two rooms with one double and two single beds. Cot available. Parking; garden, table tennis. Special rates for groups.

Prices s €55-€60; d €65-€70; t €87-€92; extra person fr €22 **On Site** ❀ **Nearby** ⚓ 2km ⚐ 15km Sea 12km ⚐ 2km ⚐ 8km ⚐ 2km ⚐ 2km **Notes** No pets English spoken

AUBIN-ST-VAAST

❦ *Chambre d'hôtes*

Marie RICHAUD

Aubin des Auges, 253, rue des Pâtures,

62140 AUBIN-ST-VAAST

☎ 03 21 86 67 79 & 06 73 39 34 98

email: richaud.marie@wanadoo.fr

A restored farmhouse in the centre of the village, with two bedrooms in the owners' house and one in a separate building. One room has twin beds; the other two have double beds, and all have private bath/shower room and WC. A cot is available, and there is a lounge for guest use.

Prices not confirmed for 2008 **On Site** ⚐ **Nearby** ⚓ 5km ⚐ 20km Sea 40km ⚐ 12km ⚐ 5km ⚐ 5km ⚐ 5km **Notes** No pets

AUCHY-AU-BOIS

❦ ⚑ Chambre d'hôtes

Brigitte DE SAINT-LAURENT

13 rue Neuve, 62190 AUCHY-AU-BOIS

☎ 03 21 25 80 09

email: brigitte.de.saint-laurent@wanadoo.fr

web: http://fermedelavallee.free.fr

In the middle of the village, this brick-built farmhouse has four guest rooms (a double, a twin, and two triples) with their own entrance and one suite with twin beds, all en suite. Guests have use of sitting room, kitchenette, living room, games room, open fireplace, TV, library, parking and garden.

Prices s fr €30; d fr €42; t fr €52; dinner fr €16 **On Site** ❀ **Nearby** ⚓ 12km ⚐ 4km ⚐ 8km ⚐ 7km ⚐ 3km ⚐ 8km **Notes** No pets

AUDEMBERT

❦ Chambre d'hôtes

Robert et Viviane GILSOUL

La Buissonnière, 20 rue de la Mairie, 62250 AUDEMBERT

☎ 03 21 92 85 87 📄 03 21 92 27 14

email: robert.gilsoul@wanadoo.fr

web: http://perso.wanadoo.fr/robert.gilsoul/

The owners of this house offer guests a choice of two double rooms and a twin, each with private bathroom and wc. A child's bed may also be available. Guests can relax with a book in the living room, and enjoy good breakfasts. Set in the middle of the village, guests have use of the garden and parking. Restaurant 4km.

Prices s fr €40; d fr €48; extra person fr €15 **Nearby** ⚓ 4km Sea 4km ⚐ 3km ⚐ 20km Restaurant 4km ⚐ 4km ⚐ 6km **Notes** No pets English spoken

AUDINGHEN

❦ Chambre d'hôtes

Danielle et J-Claude MAERTEN

Ferme des 4 Vents, 62179 AUDINGHEN

☎ 03 21 32 97 64 📄 03 21 83 62 54

email: ferme.des.quatre.vents@wanadoo.fr

web: http://fermedes4vents.fr

This farmhouse has six en suite guest rooms, four with sea views. The accommodation includes a suite with two doubles, a twin, a suite with one double and two singles, a double with sitting room, kitchenette and TV, and a triple with living room, kitchenette, TV and sitting area. Extra double bed available. Living room, sitting room, fully equipped kitchen, garden and parking.

Prices s fr €40; d €50-€55; extra person fr €15 **Nearby** ⚓ 10km ⚐ 12km Sea 1km ⚐ 5km ⚐ 16km ⚐ 5km ⚐ 15km ⚐ 2km ⚐ 15km **Notes** No pets

❦ ⚐ Le Repos des Mouettes

Sylvie DUTERTE

Haringzelle, 62179 AUDINGHEN

☎ 03 21 32 97 20 📄 03 21 32 97 20

email: reposdesmouettes@aol.com

web: www.lesmouettes.free.fr

Set outside the village between Audinghen and Audresselles and only three kilometres from Cap Gris Nez, this detached house is next to a pig farm. There are three double rooms with TV point, kitchenette, and a family room with a double and two twin beds, TV point and kitchenette, all en suite. Garden; parking; adjacent restaurant.

Prices s fr €35; d fr €50; t fr €65 **On Site** Restaurant **Nearby** ⚓ 15km Sea 2km ⚐ 20km ⚐ 10km ⚐ 1km ⚐ 10km **Notes** Pets admitted

AUTINGUES

✦ ⚹ Au Petit Tambour d'Autingues

Agnès de SAINT-JUST

288, rue de Louches, 62610 AUTINGUES

☎ 03 21 36 25 38 & 06 70 03 45 49

email: contact@petit-tambour.com

web: www.petit-tambour.com

Twenty minutes from the beach, in six hectares of wooded parkland, this 18th-century house has five bedrooms, each with a lounge area. There are three double rooms, one twin-bedded room, and a suite with double and twin beds. All of the rooms have a private shower room and WC. Possible extra beds, garden furniture, games room, barbecue. Possible stabling.

Prices s €40-€48; d €55-€58; extra person fr €15 **Nearby** ✿ 6km ↟ 20km Sea 15km ⚲ 1km ⚹ 8km ⚇ 1km ⚐ 1km ⚘ 15km **Notes** No pets English spoken

AZINCOURT

✦ La Gacogne

Patrick et Marie-José FENET

62310 AZINCOURT

☎ 03 21 04 45 61 ▯ 03 21 04 45 61

email: fenetgeoffroy@aol.com

web: www.gacogne.new.fr

This house is full of medieval character and stands on the site of the Battle of Agincourt. It offers four en suite guest rooms with their own entrance. There is a kitchenette and a sitting room with open fireplace, and breakfast is served in the owners' part of the house. Attractive garden, wooded park. Parking.

Prices d fr €54; t fr €65 **Nearby** ✿ 3km ↟ 35km ⚲ 6km ⚹ 30km Restaurant 1km ⚇ 1km ⚘ 3km ⚐ 6km ⚘ 4km **Notes** No pets English spoken

BAINGHEN

✦ ▯⚬ Retour aux Sources

Catherine STEVENART

38, rue Beaurietz, 62850 BAINGHEN

☎ 03 21 83 20 87

email: reserver@retourauxsources.net

web: www.retourauxsources.net

A chalet-type house of character in a village, offering a twin room, a double and a room with two doubles, each with private facilities. Living room and communal lounge, garden, parking.

Prices s fr €42; d fr €46; t fr €55; extra person fr €13; dinner fr €25 **Nearby** ✿ 7km Sea 25km ⚲ 6km ⚹ 25km ⚇ 25km ⚘ 5km ⚐ 5km ⚘ 25km **Notes** No pets

BAZINGHEN

✦ Le Clos des Sarcelles

Claudine DARRAS

63 Chemin du Marais, 62250 BAZINGHEN

☎ 03 21 92 88 00 & 06 87 53 94 07 ▯ 03 21 92 88 00

email: leclosdessarcelles@wanadoo.fr

web: http://perso.wanadoo.fr/leclosdessarcelles

Just outside the village, this establishment offers three guest rooms. It also boasts a wooded garden. There is a double room, a double room with a lounge, and a room with a double and two single beds. Extra beds for children can be arranged. All rooms have private facilities.

Prices s fr €40; d €46-€54; extra person fr €15 **Nearby** ✿ 1km ⚹ 7km Sea 5km ⚲ 1km ⚹ 12km ⚇ 10km **Notes** No pets English spoken

BEUGNY

✦ Chambre d'hôtes

A et F DRUGBERT

15 rue de Bapaume, 62124 BEUGNY

☎ 06 82 04 22 32 ▯ 03 21 58 92 38

email: f.a.drugbert@wanadoo.fr

In a central village location. Four well equipped bedrooms in a former stable block with parking and a garden. Two doubles and a twin with own shower rooms and WCs (grade 3); double with shower room and WC (grade 2). Sitting room, dining room, child's bed available.

Prices d fr €52; extra person fr €15; dinner €15-€20 **On Site** ⚘ **Nearby** ✿ 15km ↟ 20km ⚲ 15km ⚹ 20km ⚇ 5km ⚐ 3km ⚘ 20km **Notes** No pets English spoken

BEUSSENT

✦ Hamot le Ménage

Daniel BARSBY

124 route d'Hucqueliers, 62170 BEUSSENT

☎ 03 21 90 91 92 ▯ 03 21 86 38 24

In the quiet and leafy setting of a 9 hectare park beyond the village, this 19th-century manor house has five en suite double guest rooms, each with a TV and sitting area. Child's bed available. Sitting room; garden; covered parking. Guests are welcome to visit the owner's studio and sculpture gallery. Children under five free.

Prices s fr €85; d fr €90 **On Site** ✿ **Nearby** ↟ 20km Sea 22km ⚲ 3km ⚹ 3km Restaurant 2km ⚇ 20km Spa 20km ⚘ 13km **Notes** Pets admitted English spoken

BLANGY-SUR-TERNOISE

✦ Chambre d'hôtes

Bernard DECLERCQ

3 rue de la Gare, 62770 BLANGY-SUR-TERNOISE

☎ 03 21 47 29 29

This small manor house has four en suite double guest rooms. Additional beds can be provided. Sitting room. Garaging for two cars by arrangement. No charge for children under two.

CONTINUED

Prices d fr €45; extra person fr €20 **Nearby** ☘ 10km Sea 45km
⚓ 5km ⌇ 20km ⛱ 12km ⋒ 12km **Notes** Pets admitted

BONNINGUES-LES-ARDRES

▦ ◎ Le Manoir

Sylvie BREEMERSCH
40 route de Licques, 62890 BONNINGUES-LES-ARDRES
☎ 03 21 82 69 05 🖹 03 21 82 69 05
email: pierre.breemersch@wanadoo.fr
web: www.lemanoirdebonningues.com

This restored manor house dating from the time of Napoleon III
stands in the centre of the village. It has five guest rooms - three
doubles, one triple and one family room; all have en suite bathrooms/
WCs. There is a delightful old lounge, and meals are available by
arrangement. The grounds are wooded, and include a garden room.
Prices s fr €42; d fr €60; t fr €74; extra person fr €14; dinner €25-€40
On Site ⚑ **Nearby** ☘ 15km ⌇ 10km Sea 25km ⚓ 5km ⌇ 7km
Restaurant 7km ⛱ 3km ⌂ 3km ⋒ 7km **Notes** No pets English spoken

BONNINGUES-LES-CALAIS

▦ L'Opalienne

Hubert et Christiane CUGNY
31 chemin du Beauregard,
62340 BONNINGUES-LES-CALAIS
☎ 06 75 84 38 28
email: opalienne@wanadoo.fr
This property is outside the village, and it stands in a large wooded
garden. There are two double rooms, and one triple, with an extra
child's bed available. They all have fridges, TVs and en suite bath
or shower rooms and WCs. Lounge shared with hosts. Garage, and
further parking space.
Prices s fr €45; d fr €60; t fr €75; extra person fr €15; dinner fr €25
Nearby ☘ 13km ⌇ 18km Sea 7km ⚓ 15km ⌇ 13km Restaurant 4km
⛱ 13km ⚑ 9km ⌂ 4km ⋒ 6km **Notes** No pets English spoken

BREXENT-ENOCQ

▦ Ferme du Hodicq

M CLAIDIERE
22, rue d'Haudique, 62170 BREXENT-ENOCQ
☎ 03 21 86 56 80 & 06 74 64 71 95 🖹 03 21 86 56 81
email: claidiere-fermeduhodicq@wanadoo.fr
web: www.fermeduhodicq-picardieweb.com
This equestrian property, situated in a small hamlet, has three guest
rooms. There is one double room, a room with a double bed and
a single, and a suite with a double bed and three singles. All of the
rooms have a TV, private shower room and WC. Garden, parking;
horse and carriage rides.
Prices s fr €51; d €59-€69; t €75-€85; extra person fr €16
Nearby ☘ 7km ⌇ 7km Sea 10km ⚓ 3km ⌇ 5km Restaurant 5km
⛱ 5km ⚑ 7km ⌂ 7km ⋒ 5km **Notes** No pets English spoken

BRIMEUX

▦ ♿ Ferme du Saule

La Famille TRUNNET
20 rue de l'Eglise, 62170 BRIMEUX
☎ 03 21 06 01 28 & 06 08 93 77 91 🖹 03 21 81 40 14
email: fotrunnet@wanadoo.fr
web: http://perso.wanadoo.fr/fermedusaule

Four guest rooms in the centre of the village, comprising one triple in
the owners' house, and two triples and one double on the farm, all en
suite with TV. Extra bed and child's bed available. Garden, courtyard
and enclosed parking. Adjacent restaurant. Beach 18km.
Prices s fr €45; d fr €50; t fr €65 **On Site** ⚓ ⚑ **Nearby** ☘ 18km
Sea 18km ⌇ 6km Restaurant 6km ⛱ ⌂ 0.1km ⋒ 6km **Notes** No pets
English spoken

CAMPAGNE-LES-GUINES

▦ ◎ Le Château de la Garenne

M. TASSART
451, rue du Court Gain, 62340 CAMPAGNE-LES-GUINES
☎ 03 21 34 58 24 & 06 74 00 66 53 🖹 03 21 85 35 32
email: thomas.tassart@wanadoo.fr
web: www.gites62.com/
An 18th-century château on the edge of the village, with three guest
bedrooms in the owners' home. They all have double beds, and each

CONTINUED

CAMPAGNE-LES-GUINES CONTINUED

has an en suite shower room and WC. A cot is available. Lounge for guest use, with internet access.

Prices s fr €60; d fr €65; extra person fr €10; dinner fr €25
Nearby ⛷ 1km ⚓ 20km Sea 17km ⚐ 3km ↘ 17km Restaurant 5km
⚘ 3km ⚑ 5km ⛪ 2km ⋒ 10km **Notes** No pets English spoken CC

ⅲ ꙮ **Le Moulin de Campagne**

Linda AUBRY

1, route de Licques, 62340 CAMPAGNE-LES-GUINES
☎ 03 21 85 92 58
email: lemoulindecampagne@wanadoo.fr
web: http://perso.wanadoo.fr/lemoulindecampagne

Just outside the village, this property has two guest rooms in the owners' home. One room is a double; the other is a family room with a double bed and two singles. Both rooms have en suite facilities and television. The sitting room has a large open fireplace, and evening meals are served, by arrangement, in the conservatory dining room.

Prices s fr €50; d fr €60; extra person €10-€15; dinner €15-€20
Nearby ⛷ 0.3km ⚓ 20km Sea 12km ⚐ 5km ↘ 13km Restaurant 3km
⚘ 2km ⛪ 2km ⋒ 13km **Notes** Pets admitted English spoken

CONCHIL-LE-TEMPLE

ⅲ **Chambre d'hôtes**

Nicole FROISSART

51 rue de la Mairie, 62180 CONCHIL-LE-TEMPLE
☎ 03 21 81 11 02 ▤ 03 21 81 88 32
email: philippe.froissart@wanadoo.fr
web: http://perso.wanadoo.fr/philippe.froissart

This old property of great character has been renovated and contains four en suite guest rooms including a double with cot, a family room with a double and two single beds, and two triples. Child's bed available. Sitting and living room with TV. Garden.

Prices s fr €45; d fr €50; t fr €60; extra person fr €10 **On Site** ⚐
⚘ **Nearby** ⛷ 6km ⚓ 3km Sea 6km ↘ 6km Restaurant 6km ⚘ 6km
⛪ 3km ⋒ 6km **Notes** Pets admitted English spoken

DANNES

ⅲ *Le Moulin*

Christine LECAILLE

40 rue du Centre, 62187 DANNES
☎ 06 62 27 60 33
email: christine.lecaille@free.fr
web: www.au-moulin.com

This property is in the centre of the village, and has three double-bedded guest rooms in the owner's house. All of the rooms have a private shower room and WC. There is a lounge which is shared with the hosts. Garden, parking.

Prices not confirmed for 2008 **On Site** ⛷ **Nearby** Sea 2km ⚐ 2km
↘ 5km ⚘ 5km **Notes** No pets

DELETTES

ⅲ ꙮ **Les Dornes**

Gilles BLONDEL

520 rue des Deux Upen, 62129 DELETTES
☎ 03 21 95 87 09 & 06 88 82 55 96
email: lesdornes@lesdornes.com
web: www.lesdornes.com

Situated in a hamlet, four well equipped bedrooms in the proprietor's house. Ground floor double with extra sofa bed; twin room, each with shower room and own WC. Upstairs: double with optional extra bed, shower room and private WC, double with bathroom and private WC. Lounge, dining room, TV, internet access.

Prices s fr €40; d fr €48; t fr €60; dinner fr €20 **Nearby** ⛷ 10km
⚓ 20km Sea 45km ⚐ 2km ↘ 15km ⚘ 2km ⋒ 15km **Notes** No pets

ECHINGHEN

ⅲ **Chambre d'hôtes**

J BOUSSEMAERE

Rue de l'Eglise, 62360 ECHINGHEN
☎ 03 21 91 14 34 ▤ 03 21 91 06 41
email: jp-boussemaere@wanadoo.fr

In a quiet and attractive setting, this little 18th-century farmhouse in the middle of the village has four en suite guest rooms. There is a double with microwave, fridge and private terrace, a twin, a triple, and a double. Kitchenette; living and sitting room; garden; courtyard; parking; stabling. Reductions for stays of more than two nights. Restaurant 500mtrs.

Prices s fr €38; d €48-€55; t €60-€67; extra person fr €10
Nearby ⛷ 2km ⚓ 10km Sea 5km ⚐ 5km ↘ 5km ⚘ 4km ⋒ 4km
Notes No pets English spoken

ECQUEDECQUES

ⅲ ⅰ◎ⅰ ♿ Chambre d'hôtes

égine CABOCHE

4 rue Principale, 62190 ECQUEDECQUES

☎ 03 21 02 33 19 & 06 85 89 30 69

mail: regine.caboche@wanadoo.fr

web: www.ursuledepaon.com

house with five bedrooms, right in the centre of the village. Four of
he rooms are doubles; the other is a twin-bedded room. All have
rivate shower and WC. There is a lounge with TV, and meals are
vailable by arrangement. Farm produce on sale.

Prices s fr €33; d fr €38; dinner fr €16 **Nearby** ☂ 5km ⚓ 12km ⚐ 5km
⚓ 11km Restaurant 4km ⚲ 14km ⚑ 2km ⚒ 2km **Notes** No pets

ⅲ ⅰ◎ⅰ Chambre d'hôtes

lelen CAUCHY-DEMEY

3, rue Principale, Le Jardin d'Hélant, 62190
CQUEDECQUES

☎ 06 14 82 65 84 ⎙ 03 21 57 40 44

mail: jardin-helant@cegetel.net

web: www.lejardindhelant.com

ght in the centre of the village, this property has five double rooms,
ach one with a private shower room and WC. An extra bed is
vailable if needed. The breakfast room has an open fire, and a sitting
oom and games room with billiards table are available for daytime
elaxation.

rices s fr €40; d fr €45; extra person fr €10; dinner fr €20 **On Site** ⚑
earby ☂ 5km ⚓ 13km ⚐ 2km ⚓ 2km Restaurant 1km ⚲ 13km
1km ⚒ 1km **Notes** No pets CC

FAUQUEMBERGUES

ⅲ ⅰ◎ⅰ La Rêverie

Michèle BLANQUAERT

19 rue Jonnart, 62560 FAUQUEMBERGUES

☎ 03 21 12 12 38 ⎙ 03 21 12 12 38

email: bblareverie@orange.fr

web: www.lareverie.net

A white stone house in the village centre with a garden and parking.
Three bedrooms, one with its own bathroom and WC, two with their
own shower room and one WC. Extra bed available with supplement.
Sitting room, dining room and library.

Prices s fr €50; d fr €60; extra person fr €19; dinner €30 **On Site** ⚑
Nearby ☂ 7km ⚓ 13km Sea 45km ⚐ 5km ⚓ 10km Restaurant 0.5km
⚲ 20km **Notes** Pets admitted English spoken

FILLIEVRES

ⅲ ⅰ◎ⅰ Chambre d'hôtes

Bernadette LEGRAND

16 rue de Saint-Pol, 62770 FILLIEVRES

☎ 03 21 41 13 20 & 06 82 62 30 15

email: contact@moulindefillievres.com

web: www.moulindefillievres.com

An 18th-century mill in the village centre with en suite rooms. There
is a double, a triple, a family room and a suite, each with one double
and two single beds. Child's bed available. Shared sitting and living
room with TV and library, garden and table d'hôte with drinks/apéritif
included. Restaurant, lake, river and forest nearby; mountain bikes and
canoeing available. Children under five free.

Prices s €43-€45; d €50-€54; t €64-€68; extra person fr €14; dinner
fr €21 **On Site** ☂ ⚐ ⚑ **Nearby** Sea 45km ⚲ 12km ⚒ 12km
Notes Pets admitted English spoken

FOSSEUX

ⅲ *Chambre d'hôtes*

Geneviève DELACOURT

3 rue de l'Eglise, 62810 FOSSEUX

☎ 03 21 48 40 13

Close to woodland, this charming house in attractive gardens has
three guest rooms, two doubles and a twin, all en suite. Child's
bed available. Sitting and living room with TV and library. Garage.
Restaurant 5km. No charge for children under five.

Prices not confirmed for 2008 **Nearby** ☂ 7km ⚓ 18km ⚐ 12km
⚓ 17km ⚲ 17km ⚑ 5km ⚒ 17km **Notes** No pets English spoken

GOUY-SOUS-BELLONNE

⋕⋕ ⃝ La Ferme de la Sensée

G et F NICOLAS-MARTIN

5 rue de l'Eglise, 62112 GOUY-SOUS-BELLONNE

☎ 03 21 50 21 68 & 06 60 77 71 31   🖹 03 21 59 55 83

email: contact@fermedelasensee.com

web: www.fermedelasensee.com

This house, which stands in the centre of the village, has three guest rooms. They are all doubles, and they all have private bath or shower room and WC. There is a small kitchen area which is shared between all the guests. Lounge shared with the owners.

Prices s fr €60; d fr €65; extra person fr €15; dinner fr €25   **On Site** ⌂
Nearby ⌀ 5km ⌀ 7km ⌁ 7km Restaurant 4km ⌁ Spa 5km ⌁ 7km
Notes No pets English spoken CC

see advert on opposite page

HAMES-BOUCRES

⋕⋕ *L'Opalienne*

Benoît MOUCHON

2901, route d'Hames, 62340 HAMES-BOUCRES

☎ 03 21 96 43 36 & 06 26 57 28 77   🖹 03 21 85 22 63

email: chateaudubarondesaintpaul@wanadoo.fr

An 18th-century château in five hectares of grounds is the setting for this chambre d'hôtes. There are three bedrooms. On the ground floor is a double with a lounge area; upstairs are two twin-bedded rooms. All of the rooms have a private shower room and WC. Possible extra bed. Guests' lounge, kitchenette.

Prices not confirmed for 2008   **Nearby** ⌀ 3km ⌀ 20km Sea 10km
⌀ 1km ⌁ 10km ⌁ 10km ⌁ 5km   **Notes** No pets

HARDELOT

⋕⋕ *La Claire Eau*

Sylvie DELASSUS

Rond-Point du Centre Equestre, 62152 HARDELOT

☎ 06 22 70 70 08

email: contact@chambres-hardelot.com

web: www.chambres-hardelot.com

This old but newly renovated building has five en suite double guest rooms with their own entrance. Child's bed available and children under five are free. Sitting and living rooms, TV, reading, garden, terrace and parking. Table tennis and restaurant nearby.

Prices not confirmed for 2008   **On Site** ⌀ ⌀ Sea ⌀   **Notes** No pets

HAUTEVILLE

⋕⋕ ⌂ La Solette

J et J-M DEBAISIEUX

10 rue du Moulin, 62810 HAUTEVILLE

☎ 03 21 58 73 58

email: lasolette@yahoo.fr

web: www.lasolette.com

On the edge of the village, this charming house has three en suite double guest rooms with their own entrance. Child's bed available. Breakfast served in family dining room; sitting area with TV and kitchenette. Garden, courtyard, open-air games. On the Six Châteaux walking route. Restaurant 3km. Forest 15km. Children under 6 free.

Prices s fr €35; d fr €50; extra person fr €15   **Nearby** ⌀ 4km
⌀ 10km ⌀ 20km ⌁ 20km Restaurant 3km ⌁ 10km ⌁ 10km ⌁ 3km
Notes No pets English spoken

HERVELINGHEN

⋕⋕ La Leulène

Catherine PETITPREZ

708, rue Principale, 62179 HERVELINGHEN

☎ 03 21 82 47 30

email: laleulene@aol.com

web: http://catherine.petitprez.free.fr

Just five minutes from the Channel Tunnel, this attractive restored farmhouse has three en suite guest rooms: a triple, a double and a room plus suite with four single beds and two bathrooms. Child's bed available. Sitting and living room shared with owners, TV, library, grand piano. Garden, barbecue, outdoor furniture, open fireplace, children's games, parking. Special rates for groups.

Prices s fr €52; d fr €68; t fr €90; extra person fr €15   **Nearby** ⌀ 3km
⌀ 15km Sea 3km ⌁ 15km ⌁ 3km ⌁ 3km   **Notes** No pets

HUCQUELIERS

⚜ *Chambre d'hôtes*

Isabelle BERTIN
9 rue de l'Eglise, 62650 HUCQUELIERS
☎ 03 21 86 37 10 📠 03 21 86 37 18
mail: abertin@club-internet.fr
web: www.clos.info

This 19th-century residence stands in landscaped gardens in the middle of the village and offers six en suite guest rooms with their own entrance. Four are apartments each with twin beds, kitchenette and sitting room, and two are suites (child's bed available). Two sitting rooms with TV, one with open fireplace, plus dining room for exclusive use of guests. Outdoor furniture, barbecue, children's games.

Prices not confirmed for 2008 **On Site** ⚓ **Nearby** ⚓ 25km Sea 25km ⚑ 5km ⚓ 11km ⚓ **Notes** No pets

LA COUTURE

⚜ La Pilaterie

Jean-Michel DISSAUX
129 route d'Estaires, 62136 LA COUTURE
☎ 03 21 26 77 02 & 06 86 44 84 34 📠 03 21 02 71 05
mail: jmicheldissaux@aol.com
web: www.lapilaterie.free.fr

This establishment is outside the village and has three doubles and one twin available, all en suite with TV and their own entrance. Child's bed available. Sitting and living room for exclusive use of guests. Garden and parking. Children under two are free.

Prices s fr €34; d fr €40; extra person fr €10 **On Site** ⚑ **Nearby** ⚓ 5km ⚓ 7km ⚑ 5km ⚓ 10km Restaurant 5km ⚓ 7km ⚑ 5km ⚓ 10km **Notes** No pets CC

LILLERS

⚜⚜ Château de Philiomel

Claire et Frédéric DEVYS
Le Mensecq, 62190 LILLERS
☎ 03 21 61 76 76 & 06 09 10 81 95
email: contact@philiomel.com
web: www.lechateaudephiliomel.com

A 19th-century manor house right in the centre of the village, with four bedrooms. All are double-bedded, one with a folding bed as well, and each room has television and a private bath or shower room/WC. A cot is available if needed. For daytime entertainment there is a games room, and a terrace with garden furniture.

Prices d €75-€115 **On Site** ⚑ **Nearby** ⚓ 5km ⚓ 12km ⚑ 2km ⚓ 2km Restaurant 2km ⚓ 2km ⚑ 2km ⚓ 2km **Notes** No pets English spoken CC

see advert on this page

NORD-PAS-DE-CALAIS

LOCON

♦♦♦ Chambre d'hôtes

Maxime NOULETTE

464 rue du Pont d'Avelette, 62400 LOCON

☎ 03 21 27 41 42 📄 03 21 27 80 71

In the middle of the village, this restored house has six guest rooms: two grade 2 doubles with shared shower, and four grade 3 doubles all en suite with TV. Sitting and living room with TV; kitchen and garage for six vehicles and parking. Children under three free. All year skiing.

Prices s fr €34; d fr €42; extra person fr €13 **Nearby** ⚓ 1km
🏊 8km ⚘ 5km Restaurant 4km ⛵ 15km ♨ 1km 🏠 1km 🚌 5km
Notes No pets English spoken CC

LOISON-SUR-CREQUOISE

♦♦♦ La Commanderie

Marie-Hélène FLAMENT

3 allée des Templiers, 62990 LOISON-SUR-CREQUOISE

☎ 03 21 86 49 87

web: www.lacommanderieloison.com

In the village centre, this building was once a residence of the Knights Templar. The three guest rooms include a twin and a double with kitchenette and veranda, both en suite, a twin and a suite with double bed separated by bathroom. Cot available. Sitting room, games room, library, TV, open wood fire. Garden, outdoor furniture, parking. River and forest nearby.

Prices s €50-€62; d €62-€70 **Nearby** ⚓ 3km ⚘ 20km Sea 25km
🏊 0.1km ⚘ 12km Restaurant 3km ♨ 3km ⚘ 3km 🏠 3km 🚌 3km
Notes No pets English spoken

LONGFOSSE

♦♦♦ Chambre d'hôtes

J-Christophe et Sylvie NOEL

5 rue de Wierre au Bois, La Ferme Louvet,
62240 LONGFOSSE

☎ 03 21 91 65 06 📄 03 21 91 65 06

email: noel.jean-christophe@wanadoo.fr

web: http://chambredhotelelouvet.free.fr

This farmhouse is outside the village, and it offers four guest rooms, all with televisions. One is a suite for four; the other three are all doubles. All have private shower rooms and WCs. Extra bed available. Lounge, garden, parking space and barbecue. Guests are welcome to explore the farm.

Prices not confirmed for 2008 **On Site** ⚓ **Nearby** Sea 15km 🏊 5km
⚘ 5km ♨ 5km 🏠 5km **Notes** No pets

LONGVILLIERS

♦♦♦ La Longue Roye

M DELAPORTE

3 rue de l'Abbaye, 62630 LONGVILLIERS

☎ 03 21 86 70 65 📄 03 21 86 71 32

email: delaporte@la-longue-roye.com

web: www.la-longue-roye.com

Originally built by the Cistercians, this farmstead has been restored and has six en suite guest rooms with their own entrance. There are two twins and four doubles with TV, telephone and sitting room. Additional beds including child's bed available. Shared living room with open fireplace. Outdoor furniture; mountain bikes. Pets welcome (no cats).

Prices s fr €53; d fr €58; extra person fr €17 **Nearby** ⚓ 4km ⚘ 10km
Sea 15km 🏊 5km ⚘ 10km Restaurant 3km ♨ 3km ♣ 10km 🏠 10km
🚌 10km **Notes** Pets admitted English spoken

MARESQUEL

♦♦♦ Château de Ricquebourg

Emmanuelle PRUVOST

62990 MARESQUEL-ECQUEMICOURT

☎ 03 21 90 30 96 📄 03 21 90 30 96

email: emmanuelle.pruvost1@free.fr

web: http://chateaudericquebourg.free.fr/index.htm

Three bedrooms in a small 18th-century château: two doubles, one with a canopied bed, each of which has a private bath or shower room and WC; the third, a Grade 2 room, has a double bed and a single, and private but not en suite facilities. Extra beds available; lounge with open fire; garden with barbecue and garden furniture.

Prices s fr €48; d €55-€65; t fr €66; extra person fr €16 **Nearby** ⚓ 6km
⚘ 28km Sea 24km 🏊 2km ⚘ 14km Restaurant 1km ♨ ♣ 0.5km
🏠 0.5km **Notes** Pets admitted English spoken

MARQUISE

♦♦♦ 🍴 Chambre d'hôtes

Marie-Claude DUTERTRE

40, rue de la République, 62250 MARQUISE

☎ 06 14 82 63 32

email: marie-claude.dutertre@wanadoo.fr

web: www.cap-opale.com

In the centre of a village between Calais and Boulogne, this house ha three en suite guest bedrooms, all of them doubles and one with a small adjoining living room with space for an extra bed. Evening mea are available by arrangement. Outside is an attractive garden; not far away are the beaches at Wimereux and the attractions of Boulogne-sur-Mer.

Prices not confirmed for 2008 **Nearby** ⚓ 7km ⚘ 7km Sea 6km 🏊 6km
⚘ 7km ♨ 7km **Notes** No pets

MONTREUIL-SUR-MER

ⅲ ⅒ **Chambre d'hôtes**

)anièle LOUCHEZ

7 rue Pierre Ledent, 62170 MONTREUIL-SUR-MER

☎ 03 21 81 54 68 & 06 84 01 36 84

mail: louchez.anne@wanadoo.fr

veb: www.larodiere.com

et in the centre of town and full of character, this 18th-century brick
nd stone house has a twin and two doubles, all en suite with sitting
'ea and TV. Guests have use of a sitting room and garden. Canoeing
vailable.

rices s fr €50; d fr €60; t fr €70; extra person fr €15   **On Site** 🌳 🌾
earby ⛵ 10km Sea 15km 🏹 Restaurant 0.1km 🏊 🏪 0.1km 🚃 1km
otes Pets admitted

NEUFCHATEL-HARDELOT

ⅲ ⅒ **Chambre d'hôtes**

laudie MACRET

1 rue du Chemin, D119,

2152 NEUFCHATEL-HARDELOT

☎ 03 21 33 85 23 🖨 03 21 30 84 27

mail: green-field@wanadoo.fr

veb: http://perso.wanadoo.fr/green-field

nis large house in a peaceful setting outside the village and close to
e Hardelot Forest has four twin-bedded guest rooms (non-smoking),
I en suite. Facilities include sitting and living room, TV, central
eating, landscaped garden, terrace, veranda, garden furniture and
arking. Evening meals for eight or more by arrangement except July
nd August.

rices s fr €45; d fr €59; t fr €85; extra person fr €15; dinner €18-€20
n Site Restaurant   **Nearby** ⛵ 3km 🏊 2km Sea 4km 🌾 3km 🏊 2km
0.1km 🚃 12km   **Notes** Pets admitted English spoken Open January
November.

NIELLES-LES-ARDRES

ⅲ ⅒ **Les Hortensias**

M. et Mme CAILLIERET

130 route Départementale 227,

62610 NIELLES-LES-ARDRES

☎ 03 21 82 86 22 🖨 03 21 82 86 22

email: bruno.caillieret@wanadoo.fr

web: http://perso.wanadoo.fr/caillieret

This restored brick farmhouse built around a courtyard has three en
suite guest rooms with separate entrance. There is a double with TV
and kitchenette, a triple with kitchenette and a twin. Cot and additional
child's bed available. Shared sitting and living room with TV. Evening
meal during the week by arrangement including drinks.

Prices s fr €40; d fr €50; t fr €65; extra person fr €15; dinner fr €20
On Site 🌾   **Nearby** ⛵ 6km 🏊 10km Sea 20km 🌾 3km 🏹 8km
Restaurant 1.5km 🏊 3km 🏪 2km 🚃 8km   **Notes** No pets English
spoken

NUNCQ-HAUTECOTE

ⅲ *La Pommeraie*

Eric MORVAN

13 route Nationale, 62270 NUNCQ-HAUTECOTE

☎ 03 21 03 69 85 🖨 03 21 47 28 02

email: eric.morvan01@infonie.fr

web: www.multimania.com/chambredhote

Standing in a tree-filled garden in the village, there are four en suite
guest rooms available in this village establishment: three doubles
and a triple. Child's bed available. Sitting room; fridge; gas cooker;
washing machine and drier; TV; library; garden furniture, barbecue.
Restaurant 3km.

Prices not confirmed for 2008   **Nearby** ⛵ 7km 🌾 8km 🏹 3km 🏊 3km
🚃 10km   **Notes** No pets

CONTINUED

NORD-PAS-DE-CALAIS

PEUPLINGUES

ⅢⅢ ¡◯¡ Chambre d'hôtes

Sylvie GRIGNON

143 rue du Moulin, 62231 PEUPLINGUES

☎ 03 21 85 02 03

email: grignongerard@aol.com

web: www.cote-dopale.com/gite_moulin/index.html

Three separate rooms are available in this restored old house in the village centre. One double and one twin plus one room with a double and a single, all with private shower room, WC and TV. Lounge, dining room with TV and telephone. Evening meals by arrangement.

Prices s fr €45; d fr €55; t fr €69; dinner €12-€25 **Nearby** ☰ 5km ⅃ 20km Sea 4km 🏊 4km ⚓ 10km Restaurant 5km 🛒 0.1km ⅲ 5km **Notes** No pets English spoken

REBERGUES

ⅢⅢ Le Rouge Fort

Sandrine WINTREBERT

1355 route de Licques, 62850 REBERGUES

☎ 03 21 85 57 84 & 06 12 70 87 33

email: sandrine.wintrebert@free.fr

web: http://rougefort.free.fr

An 18th-century château with garden and parking, also grazing available for horses. There are four guest bedrooms sharing a dining room, library and kitchen. One bedroom has a double and single, the other three are doubles, all have their own bathroom and WC. Cot available with supplement.

Prices s €45-€53; d €55-€65; t fr €70; extra person fr €5 **On Site** 🏊 **Nearby** ☰ 3km ⅃ 12km Sea 30km 🏊 2km ⚓ 15km Restaurant 3km 🛒 2km ⅲ 2km **Notes** No pets English spoken

RICHEBOURG

ⅢⅢ Au Temps des Roses

Agnès et Philippe SENECHAL

20 rue Martin Maux, 62136 RICHEBOURG

☎ 03 21 25 09 09 & 06 78 27 98 16

email: philippe.senechal6@free.fr

web: http://autempsdesroses.free.fr

Situated on the outskirts of the village in a renovated former farmhouse with garden and parking. Three separate bedrooms comprising two doubles with own bathrooms and WCs; one room with a double and a single also with own bathroom and WC. Sitting room. Children's bed available with a supplement.

Prices s fr €40; d fr €45; t fr €55; extra person fr €10 **Nearby** ☰ 1km ⅃ 6km ⚓ 25km Restaurant 2km 🛒 1km 🏊 0.1km 🛒 1km ⅲ 14km **Notes** No pets English spoken

ⅢⅢ Chambre d'hôtes

André et Christiane BAVIERE

Ferme les Caperies, 106 rue des Charbonniers, 62136 RICHEBOURG

☎ 03 21 26 07 19 📠 03 21 26 07 19

email: abaviere@orange.fr

A fine old farmstead with four guest rooms in a building adjacent to the owners' residence: a single, a double and two triples, all en suite. Shared ground floor sitting room with TV, kitchen, garden furniture, veranda, BBQ. No charge for children under five. Leisure centre 6km

Prices s fr €29; d fr €39; t fr €49; extra person fr €10 **On Site** 🏊 **Nearby** ☰ 2km ⅃ 5km 🏊 5km ⚓ 18km Restaurant 5km 🛒 1km ⅲ 9km **Notes** No pets English spoken

NORD-PAS-DE-CALAIS

⚜ *La Niche*

érard et Nicole PETIT
1 rue Marsy, 62136 RICHEBOURG
☎ 03 21 65 33 13 📄 03 21 26 14 17
mail: la-niche2@wanadoo.fr

lovely countryside outside the village, this building has four guest
ooms, three doubles and a single (one grade 2), all en suite with own
ntrance, TV and telephone. Extra bed available. Guests have their
vn kitchen, dining area, living room, library and games. Mountain
kes. Shop selling local products. No charge for children under five;
duced rates for longer stays. Forest 10km.

rices not confirmed for 2008   **Nearby** Sea 15km 🏌 3km
otes No pets

ANGATTE

⚜ **Kerloan**

ylvie LEROYE
37, Route Nationale, 62231 SANGATTE
☎ 03 21 82 08 50 & 06 65 66 97 85
mail: admin@kerloan.com
veb: www.kerloan.com

ur doubles and a suite with two double beds, each with private
cilities available in this recently built house in a village. Guests have
se of the living room, library, heating, garden and parking.

rices s €50-€55; d €65-€68; t fr €88; extra person fr €20   **On Site** ⚓
Nearby Sea 0.1km ➔ 6km Restaurant 0.1km ⚓ 0.2km ⛽ 0.3km
6km **Notes** No pets English spoken Open 5 March to 5 January.

T-ETIENNE-AU-MONT

⚜ **La Roseraie**

ylvaine et Pascal DAMEZ
3, rue Eugène Huret, 62360 ST-ETIENNE-AU-MONT
☎ 03 21 10 00 16 & 06 18 96 48 23 📄 03 21 10 00 19
mail: laroseraie@laroseraie.fr
eb: www.laroseraie.fr

is house, built in a style typical of the area, has four guest
drooms. They are all doubles, and each one has an en suite bath or
ower room and WC. Extra beds are available, and there is a guests'
unge on the first floor. Television, table football and piano. Wooded
ounds, enclosed parking.

ices s €40-€45; d €50-€55; extra person fr €15   **Nearby** ⚓ 3km
4km Sea 5km 🏌 3km ➔ 5km Restaurant 1km ⚓ 5km ⛽ 5km
0.5km ⚓ 0.5km **Notes** No pets English spoken

⚜ **Le Plein Air**

Anne-Catherine MARCOTTE
77, rue Madaré, 62360 ST-ETIENNE-AU-MONT
☎ 03 21 10 73 34 & 06 85 31 24 66
email: infos@lepleinair.com
web: www.lepleinair.com

In the village centre, in a hectare of grounds, this 19th-century villa has
four bedrooms. There are two grade 2 rooms - a double and a twin;
also two grade 3 rooms - a double, and a suite for four with double
and twin beds. All of the rooms have a private bath or shower room
and WC. Lounge with TV and books, garden.

Prices d fr €65   **Nearby** ⚓ 4km ⚓ 4km Sea 3km 🏌 3km ➔ 10km
Restaurant 2km ⚓ 5km ⛽ 0.5km ⚓ 2km **Notes** Pets admitted

ST-MARTIN-LEZ-BOULOGNE

⚜ **La Grange Dimière**

Elisabeth NOURY
Rue de la Cluse, 62280 ST-MARTIN-LEZ-BOULOGNE
☎ 03 21 91 12 27
email: mazenoury@aol.com
web: www.lagrangedimiere.com

A former farm building outside the village, offering a double, a
room with double, two singles and mezzanine, and a grade 2 twin
room, each with private facilities. Cot available. Guests' lounge,
communal living room, billiards room, terrace, garden, parking. Can
accommodate six horses in boxes or pastures. Restaurant 1.5km.
Children under 3 free.

Prices s €46-€65; d €60-€65; t €75-€80; extra person fr €15   **On Site** ⚓
Nearby ⚓ 6km ⚓ 8km Sea 4km ➔ 0.5km Restaurant 1.5km ⚓ 1km
⚓ 4km **Notes** No pets English spoken

SURQUES

ⵌ ⎧◯⎫ Manoir de Brugnobois

Ghyslaine LORGNIER
205, rue Manoir de Brugnobois, 62850 SURQUES
☎ 03 21 32 32 54 📄 03 21 32 63 40
email: aubergealaferme@aol.com
web: www.brugnobois.com

The owners of this farmhouse provide four double rooms, each with private facilities and three with TV. Extra bed possible. Living room and lounge with TV reserved for guests. Located in the centre of the village, with parking and restaurant on site.

Prices s €36-€48; d €40-€52; extra person fr €15; dinner €10-€25 **On Site** Restaurant **Nearby** ⌖ 10km ⌇ 15km Sea 20km ⌒ 7km ⌁ 15km ⌇ 25km ⌇ 10km 🖾 4km ⋙ 25km **Notes** No pets CC

TENEUR

ⵌ ⎧◯⎫ Chambre d'hôtes

M-E et J-C VENIEZ-QUENIART
11 rue Marcel Dollet, 62134 TENEUR
☎ 03 21 41 62 34 📄 03 21 41 62 34
email: jean-claude.veniez@wanadoo.fr
web: www.chez.com/chambres

A green and peaceful valley in the Ternois countryside is the setting for this old barn which has been converted into three en suite double guest rooms with sitting areas. Child's bed available. Kitchen for use of guests; garden; barbecue; parking; mountain bikes. Children under five free. On the GR21 long-distance footpath.

Prices s fr €35; d fr €40; t fr €50; dinner fr €16 **On Site** ⌒ **Nearby** ⌖ 10km ⌇ 45km Sea 50km ⌁ 15km Restaurant 5km ⌇ 5km ⌇ 10km 🖾 3km ⋙ 3km **Notes** No pets English spoken

TIGNY-NOYELLE

ⵌ ⎧◯⎫ ⌖ Le Prieuré

Roger DELBECQUE
Impasse de l'Eglise, 62180 TIGNY-NOYELLE
☎ 03 21 86 04 38 📄 03 21 81 39 95
email: r.delbecque@wanadoo.fr
web: www.leprieure-tigny.com

This charming house outside the village has five en suite guest rooms with TV. There is a double, a family room with a double and two

single beds, two twins, and a suite with a double and two single beds. Child's bed available. Sitting room; garden; off-site parking. Meals by arrangement or restaurant 2km. Marquenterre bird sanctuary 20km.

Prices s fr €55; d €70-€98; t €90-€118; extra person fr €20; dinner fr €28 **On Site** ⌒ **Nearby** ⌖ 10km ⌇ 1km Sea 10km ⌁ 10km Restaurant 2km ⌇ 10km ⌇ 10km 🖾 3km ⋙ 8km **Notes** Pets admitted English spoken CC

TUBERSENT

ⵌ Chambre d'hôtes

Marie-Claire DELAPORTE
101, rue de Courteville, 62630 TUBERSENT
☎ 03 21 81 26 48 & 06 66 01 00 47 📄 03 21 81 03 26
email: jodelaporte@wanadoo.fr
web: www.sous-la-roque.fr

On a road leading out of the village, this house has four guest rooms all with TV, including three doubles (one set in a tower) and a triple. There is a breakfast room for guests to use, a garden and parking facilities.

Prices s €50-€55; d fr €56; t fr €80; extra person fr €15 **On Site** ⌒ **Nearby** ⌖ 5km ⌇ 10km Sea 10km ⌁ 5km ⌇ 5km Spa 10km 🖾 5km ⋙ 5km **Notes** No pets

ⵌ Les Coquennes

Anne-Marie et Alain BOITREL
1, impasse des Coquennes, 62630 TUBERSENT
☎ 03 21 86 73 53 📄 03 21 86 09 78
email: lescoquennes@free.fr
web: http://lescoquennes.free.fr

In a country setting outside the village, this house has two guest bedrooms in the owners' home. Both have double bed and private shower and WC. There is a further grade 2 room where the facilities, although private, are not en suite, plus two grade 1 double rooms which share a shower room and WC. Garden with furniture and barbecue.

Prices s fr €40; d fr €48; t fr €75; extra person fr €15 **On Site** ⌇ **Nearby** ⌖ 6km Sea 8km ⌁ 1km ⌁ 5km Restaurant 3km ⌇ 12km 🖾 5km ⋙ 5km **Notes** No pets

VERTON

ⱽ La Mouillère

F ROUCH-HAGNERE

42 Rue de la Gloriette, 62180 VERTON

☎ 03 21 09 59 11 & 06 79 18 03 53 📄 03 21 09 59 35

email: contact@lamouillere.com

web: www.lamouillere.com

Enjoy extensive facilities including an enclosed wooded park, terraces, lake and swimming pool. There are five double rooms with private WC and bathroom (one of these has twin beds and one has a private terrace and entrance). Lounge with satellite TV, internet in every bedroom. Secure outdoor parking.

Prices d fr €65 **On Site** ⚲ Private ⤥ **Nearby** ☼ 4km ↕ 5km Sea 3km Restaurant 1km ⌣ 5km Spa 15km ❀ 4km ⌂ 0.7km ⋇ 3km **Notes** No pets English spoken

ⱽ Villa Marie

Viviane BROCARD

12 rue des Ecoles, 62180 VERTON

☎ 06 20 07 82 34

email: phbrocar@wanadoo.fr

web: http://monsite.wanadoo.fr/villamarie

This detached house stands in a large walled garden and has four en suite guest rooms, three of them in a separate building. There are two doubles and a twin, and a suite of two rooms with a double and two single beds, all with TV. Extra bed and cot available. Shared cooking facilities and parking. Special rates for groups.

Prices s fr €53; d fr €58; t €78-€95; extra person fr €20 **Nearby** ☼ 3km ↕ 13km Sea 5km ⚲ 5km ⤥ 5km ⌣ 5km ⋇ 3km **Notes** Pets admitted

WAIL

ⱽ Ferme de la Wawette

Anielle COURQUIN

1 rue de Wawette, 62770 WAIL

☎ 03 21 41 88 38 📄 03 21 04 54 74

email: anielle.courquin@wanadoo.fr

web: www.lafermedelawawette.fr.fm

Only 30 minutes from the coast, this old farmhouse has been completely renovated and has four ground floor guest rooms with separate entrance. There is a twin, a double, and two triples, all en suite. Two additional single beds available. Guests have use of a sitting and living room with wood fire and there is parking. Restaurant nearby and Croix-en-Ternois motor-racing circuit 20km.

Prices s fr €45; d fr €50 **On Site** ☼ ⚲ **Nearby** ↕ 20km Sea 45km ⤥ 10km Restaurant 2km ⌣ 6km ❀ 7km ⌂ 7km ⋇ 7km **Notes** No pets English spoken

WILLENCOURT

ⱽ Le Clos de la Cascade

Geneviève et Patrice MARLIER

2 rue du Moulin, 62390 WILLENCOURT

☎ 03 21 41 33 89 & 06 77 70 72 47

email: closdelacascade@orange.fr

web: www.closdelacascade.com

On the outskirts of the village, five guest rooms are available in this restored former windmill with large landscaped park and parking. Three double rooms, one double plus optional sofa bed, one twin. All with private shower room and WC. Guest lounge, dining room and library. Telephone available. Child bed and extra single bed possible with supplement.

Prices s €58; d €63-€70; t €86-€93; extra person fr €23 **On Site** ☼ ⚲ **Nearby** ↕ 20km Sea 30km ⤥ 10km Restaurant 2km ⌣ 2km ⌂ 2km ⋇ 20km **Notes** No pets English spoken

WIMILLE

ⱽ Ferme de Tiembrique

Patrick BOUTROY

2 route d'Etiembrique, 62126 WIMILLE

☎ 03 21 87 10 01 📄 03 21 87 10 01

web: www.fermedetiembrique.com

Outside the village, this house has three guest rooms with their own entrance. There are two doubles and a triple with kitchenette, all en suite. Shared sitting room available.

Prices s fr €35; d fr €45; t fr €55 **Nearby** ☼ 5km ↕ 5km Sea 5km ⚲ 6km ⤥ 10km Restaurant 5km ⌣ 5km ❀ 5km ⌂ 5km ⋇ 5km **Notes** No pets English spoken

WIRWIGNES

ⱽ ❦ ❐ Ferme du Blaisel

Hervé NOEL

Rue de la Lombardie, 62240 WIRWIGNES

☎ 03 21 32 91 98 📄 03 21 87 46 12

email: blaisel@wanadoo.fr

web: www.fermeaubergedublaisel.com

This old building in the centre of the village has been renovated and has three ground floor guest rooms with separate entrance and shared kitchenette. There is a double, a triple, and a family room with one double and two single beds, all with TV and en suite. Guests' sitting area, parking and ferme-auberge on site with meals available. Closed Xmas & New Year.

Prices s fr €40; d fr €50; t fr €65; dinner €11-€23 **On Site** Restaurant **Nearby** ☼ 15km Sea 16km ⚲ 6km ⤥ 4km ⌣ 4km ⌂ 5km ⋇ 12km **Notes** No pets English spoken CC

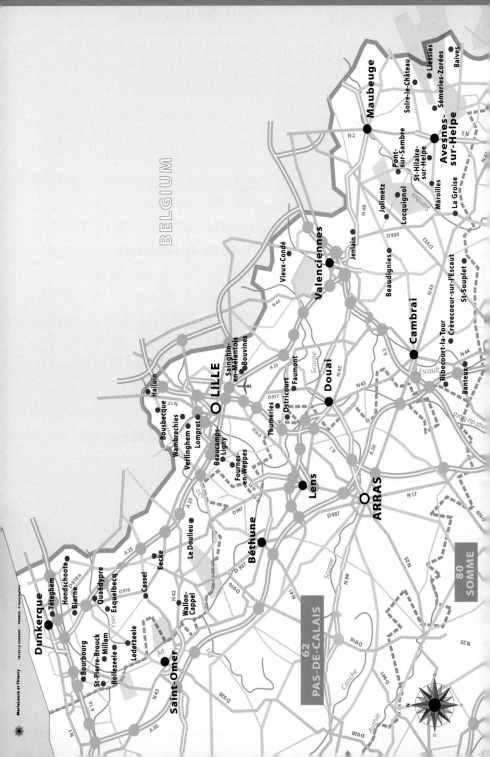

BELGIUM

Maubeuge

Liessies
Solre-le-Château
Sémeries-Zorées
Balves

N2

Pont-sur-Sambre
St-Hilaire-sur-Helpe
Avesnes-sur-Helpe

Jolimetz
Locquignol
Maroilles
La Groise

N49

N2

Valenciennes

Jenlain

Vieux-Condé

Beaudignies

Cambrai

N45

N43

Ribecourt-la-Tour
Crèvecoeur-sur-l'Escaut
St-Souplet

Escaut

N44

Banteux

Douai

N45

A23

Sainghin-en-Mélantois
Bouvines

Scarpe

N43

A2

Halluin

LILLE

Thuméries
Ostricourt
Faumont
D917

Bousbecque
Wambrechies
Verlinghem
Lompret
Beaucamps-Ligny
Fournes-en-Weppes

N17

A26

Lens

ARRAS

N17

Le Doulieu

Béthune

D947

D937

A25

Eecke

Cassel

Wallon-Cappel

N42

Scarpe

N39

80 SOMME

Dunkerque
Téteghem
Hondschoote
Bierne
Quaëdypre
Esquelbecq

Bourbourg
St-Pierre-Brouck
Millam
Bollezeele
Lederzeele

Saint-Omer

A16

N43

Yser
Aa

62 PAS-DE-CALAIS

Canche

D928

Authie

Marie-Laure et Thierry

PAS-DE-CALAIS

Nord-Pas-de-Calais

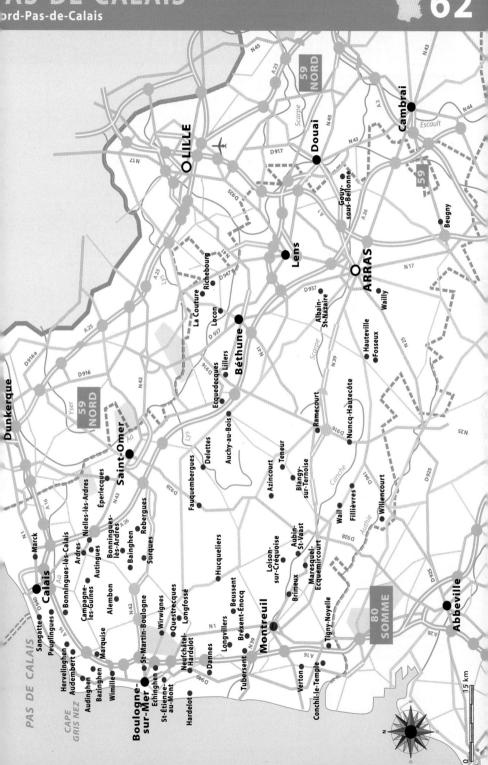

NORMANDY

CALVADOS

AUTHIE

⚑ Chambre d'hôtes

Annick et Raoul LEMOINE

2 rue Henri Brunet, 14280 AUTHIE

☎ 02 31 26 00 35 & 06 64 64 36 14

email: annicketraoul@neuf.fr

This attractive stone house is only 15 minutes from the Côte de Nacre beaches and Caen. It provides spacious, tasteful guest rooms with private showers: two double rooms and one triple; extra beds available. Garden with furniture.

Prices s fr €34; d fr €44; t fr €58; extra person fr €14 **Nearby** ⚽ 2km ⚓ 10km Sea 15km ✎ 12km ➴ 5km Restaurant 2km Water sports 15km ⚑ 🏠 0.1km ➽ 10km **Notes** No pets

---

BANVILLE

⚑ Ferme le Petit Val

Gérard LESAGE

24 rue du Camp Romain, 14480 BANVILLE

☎ 02 31 37 92 18 📄 02 31 37 92 18

Two double or triple rooms with private shower or bathroom are offered in the main part of this property. An independent building also provides two double rooms and a suite consisting of two double rooms, both with private shower. Lounge with TV.

Prices s fr €45; d fr €53–€60; t fr €75–€82; extra person fr €22 **On Site** ⚓ **Nearby** ⚽ 3km ⚓ 10km Sea 3km ✎ 3km ➴ 3km Restaurant 2km Water sports 3km ⚑ 3km 🏠 0.1km ➽ 20km **Notes** No pets English spoken

---

BASLY

⚑ Clos de la Barre

F et A DELABARRE

10 Place de l'Eglise, 14610 BASLY

☎ 02 31 96 38 90 & 06 16 99 36 83 📄 02 31 96 38 90

email: info@calvadosbnb.com

web: www.calvadosbnb.com

A complete restoration has given the rooms of this old inn a beautiful feel, with each of them decorated to a different theme. There are two doubles and three twins, all on the first floor and all with en suite bathrooms/WCs. Breakfast room with lounge area, fireplace and books. Separate guests' entrance.

Prices s €50–€65; d €55–€90; t €80–€110; extra person fr €15 **Nearby** ⚽ 5km ⚓ 9km Sea 5km ✎ 5km ➴ 5km Restaurant 3km Water sports 6km ⚑ 0.5km Spa 8km ➴ 5km ➽ 12km **Notes** No pets English spoken

---

BAVENT

⚑ ⚐ La Rivaudière

J-B et C LAGARDE

1 Rue du Lavoir, 14860 BAVENT

☎ 02 31 78 16 06

email: larivaudiere@lagarde.ws

web: http://larivaudiere.free.fr

Cabourg is only about a quarter of an hour from here. The house has three double bedrooms, each with private shower room and WC; one is on the ground floor with its own entrance. There is a cot, and an extra room could be available for a family with children. Meals by arrangement.

Prices not confirmed for 2008 **Nearby** ⚽ 14km ⚓ 14km Sea 12km ➴ 15km Water sports 12km ⚑ 15km ➽ 15km **Notes** No pets English spoken

---

BAYEUX

⚑ Chambre d'hôtes

Guy et Yvette BELLEE

4 rue Tardif, 14400 BAYEUX

☎ 02 31 21 17 02 & 06 25 32 21 63 📄 02 31 51 70 99

email: yvette.bellee@wanadoo.fr

An 18th-century house just behind the cathedral, well-placed for exploring the historic town centre. On the first floor is a double bedroom; on the second floor are two more rooms which can each sleep two or three guests. All have private showers and WCs, and an extra bed is available. Separate guests' entrance, day room, garden furniture.

Prices not confirmed for 2008 **Nearby** ⚽ 2km ⚓ 8km Sea 10km ✎ 8km ➴ 1km Water sports 10km ⚑ 1km ➽ 0.8km **Notes** No pets

---

⚑ Chambre d'hôtes de Charme

F BOURDON-FOUCHENNERFT

Place Saint Patrice, 12 rue du Marché, 14400 BAYEUX

☎ 06 08 09 62 69

email: contact@hotel-de-sainte-croix.com

web: www.hotel-de-sainte-croix.com

An impressive 18th-century town house, full of character, right in the heart of Bayeux. Three upstairs bedrooms are all triples (double bed and a single in each) with private shower and WC. Outside is a fine walled garden and parking space. An ideal base for exploring the town of Bayeux and the Normandy landing beaches.

Prices s fr €52; d fr €73; t fr €105; extra person fr €20 **On Site** ⚓ **Nearby** ⚽ 1km ⚓ 10km Sea 10km ✎ 4km ➴ 0.5km Restaurant 0.1km Water sports 10km ⚑ 0.5km 🏠 0.5km ➽ 1km **Notes** No pets English spoken

₦₦₦ Les Remparts

François & Christèle LECORNU
4 rue Bourbesneur, 14400 BAYEUX
☎ 02 31 92 50 40 📠 02 72 64 98 32
email: info@lecornu.fr
web: www.lecornu.fr

This beautifully appointed house stands in the centre of Bayeux, overlooking the square where General de Gaulle made his famous speech in June 1944. There are three elegant bedrooms. On the first floor is a room for three, and a family suite for four. On the second floor is another triple. All rooms have private shower rooms/WCs. Terrace with garden furniture.

Prices s fr €53; d €55-€70; t fr €75; extra person €20-€30
Nearby ☂ 2km ☂ 10km Sea 9km 🏊 4km ☂ 1km Restaurant 0.2km
Water sports 9km 🏊 1km ☂ 1km 🏛 0.2km ⛵ 1km **Notes** No pets
English spoken CC

ᵗᵗᵗ Manoir Guérin de la Houssaye

François et Isabelle GAUTHRON

13 Rue Montfiquet, 14400 BAYEUX

☎ 02 31 22 35 68 & 06 23 61 58 45 🖹 02 31 51 89 87

email: info@bandb-bayeux.com

web: www.bandb-bayeux.com

Right in the heart of Bayeux, this beautiful 15th-century house offers a pleasing mix of traditional and modern. There are three air-conditioned double bedrooms, one with an extra bed in an adjoining room. The rooms are stylishly and very comfortably furnished, and each has a private bath or shower room and WC. There is a lounge, and a courtyard with garden furniture.

Prices s fr €50; d fr €65; t fr €95; extra person fr €20 **On Site** ✿ **Nearby** ⚓ 3km ⛵ 1km Sea 10km ↖ 1km Water sports 10km ◒ 1km ᴍ 1.5km **Notes** No pets English spoken

see advert on page 549

ᵗᵗᵗ ᵚ Chambre d'hôtes

J. Luc et Frédérique COSTIL

9 rte de Courseulles, 14440 BENY SUR MER

☎ 02 31 80 08 32 & 06 87 24 18 61

email: frederique.costil@wanadoo.fr

These spacious and beautifully arranged rooms are in a building adjoining the owners' home. On the ground floor is a double room suitable for the less mobile guest; upstairs there are three doubles. All have en suite shower rooms and WCs. Extra bed available. Separate entrance, and a room for guests' use with lounge and kitchen areas. Garden furniture.

Prices not confirmed for 2008 **Nearby** ⚓ 4km ⛵ 15km Sea 4km ⛳ 4km ↖ 15km Water sports 4km ◒ 4km 🏛 4km ᴍ 15km **Notes** Pets admitted

ᵗᵗᵗ ᵗ◯ᵗ Ferme de l'Oudon

Patrick et Dany VESQUE

12 rte d'Ecots, 14170 BERVILLE L'OUDON

☎ 02 31 20 77 96 🖹 02 31 20 67 13

email: contact@fermedeloudon.com

web: www.fermedeloudon.com

This house offers guests a choice of three bedrooms with original decor and private facilities. A triple room is available in the main house in the mansard, and a triple and double room with lounge area are available in an adjacent building, with separate access. Guests can relax on garden furniture and meet the farm animals. Table d'hôte meals are available by reservation.

Prices s fr €75; d fr €95; dinner fr €40 **On Site** ⛳ Spa ✿ **Nearby** ⚓ 2km ⛵ 6km Sea 35km ↖ 3km Restaurant 2km Water sports 40km ◒ 2km 🏛 2km ᴍ 15km **Notes** Pets admitted English spoken CC

ᵗᵗᵗ Le Rivaliere

Audrey POTIER

Le Val Rivier, 14130 BONNEVILLE LA LOUVET

☎ 02 31 65 45 89 & 06 11 36 01 37 🖹 02 31 65 06 79

email: la.rivaliere@wanadoo.fr

web: www.larivaliere.com

Set in a delightful village, this rural house promises peace and relaxation. It has one double room on the ground floor, and a double and a triple upstairs. Each room has an en suite bath or shower room and WC. There is a lounge with armchairs; outside there is a garden room. Easy access to Honfleur, Deauville and Lisieux.

Prices s fr €55; d €60-€68; t fr €85 **Nearby** ⚓ 5km ⛵ 10km Sea 23km ⛳ 12km ↖ 23km Restaurant 4km Water sports 12km ◒ 2km ⛳ 12km 🏛 5km ᴍ 12km **Notes** No pets English spoken

ᵗᵗᵗ ᵚ *Ferme de la Belle Épine*

Vincent et Stéphanie CLOUET

14430 BOURGEAUVILLE

☎ 02 31 65 27 26 & 06 61 17 83 82 🖹 02 31 65 27 26

In the heart of the Auge region, between the seaside resorts of Cabourg and Deauville, this farmhouse offers four spacious rooms housed in a former cider press. The rooms sleep between two and four people and have private facilities. Set in green and peaceful surroundings, with a garden with furniture.

Prices not confirmed for 2008 **On Site** ⚓ **Nearby** ⛵ 8km Sea 8km ⛳ 8km ↖ 1.5km Water sports 8km ◒ 1.5km 🏛 3km ᴍ 10km **Notes** No pets English spoken

ᵗᵗᵗ Le Pressoir de Glatigny

Serge et Yvette DELACOUR

14170 BRETTEVILLE SUR DIVES

☎ 02 31 20 68 93

This farmhouse dates back to the 18th century. Upstairs in the main house is a double bedroom with an adjoining double which together make a suite for four; there is also another room for four. In an adjacent building is a double room with kitchenette. There is a day room, and outside is garden furniture.

Prices s fr €36; d fr €46; t fr €60; extra person fr €15 **Nearby** ⚓ 2.5km ⛵ 30km Sea 35km ⛳ 2.5km ↖ 2.5km Restaurant 2.5km ◒ 2.5km 🏛 2.5km ᴍ 20km **Notes** No pets

BRETTEVILLE-SUR-LAIZE

�� 🍴 Château des Riffets

Alain CANTEL

Les Riffets, 14680 BRETTEVILLE SUR LAIZE

☎ 02 31 23 53 21 📄 02 31 23 75 14

email: chateau.riffets@wanadoo.fr

web: www.chateau-des-riffets.com

This majestic château offers guests the choice of two double or triple rooms and two family suites with private bathrooms. Lounge with TV. Covered swimming pool, heated in season, and 15 hectare wooded park.

Prices s fr €110; d fr €110; t fr €160; dinner fr €45
On Site Private ⚲ **Nearby** ⚐ 4km ⚑ 4km Sea 24km ⚐ 10km
Restaurant 1km Water sports 24km ⚐ 4km Spa 25km ⚑ 4km
⚐ 0.8km ⚐ 20km **Notes** No pets English spoken

BRICQUEVILLE

ⅲ Chambre d'hôtes

Pierre et Mireille DUFOUR

L'Eglise, 14710 BRICQUEVILLE

☎ 02 31 51 74 71 & 06 84 54 36 03 📄 02 31 51 05 32

email: mireille.dufour@relais-du-marais.com

web: www.relais-du-marais.com

Fifteen minutes from the Normandy landing beaches, this beautiful, calm house offers three beautiful bedrooms, with themed decorations. There are two doubles, with private facilities, and another grade 2 double which has its own shower room/WC, which is not en suite. All rooms are on the first floor. Garden furniture.

Prices not confirmed for 2008 **Nearby** ⚐ 5km ⚑ 22km Sea 15km
⚐ 22km Water sports 18km ⚐ 5km ⚐ 5km ⚐ 12km **Notes** No pets
English spoken Open February to 1 November.

CAHAGNES

ⅲ La Foulerie

Irène TALLEC

4240 CAHAGNES

☎ 02 31 77 79 53 & 06 20 51 24 41

email: jean.tallec@wanadoo.fr

web: www.lafoulerie.net

This former cider press has been tastefully restored to provide three guest rooms with refined decor: a room for three, one for two and a large mansard room for five, each with private facilities and access. Guests have use of a comfortable lounge with fireplace and billiards room.

Prices not confirmed for 2008 **Nearby** ⚐ 8km ⚑ 30km Sea 30km
⚐ 1km ⚐ 25km Water sports 30km ⚐ 1km ⚐ 1km ⚐ 30km
Notes No pets English spoken CC

CAHAGNOLLES

ⅲ Ferme du Château

Francis et Nathalie SIMON

14490 CAHAGNOLLES

☎ 02 31 22 75 61

email: francis.simonn@wanadoo.fr

An old stone-built house in the country, well-placed for visiting Bayeux and the landing beaches. On the ground floor is a double room; upstairs are two larger rooms which can sleep up to four people. All have private shower and WC. Use of kitchen. Garden with furniture, and a river passing close by. Hot air balloon trips one kilometre away.

Prices not confirmed for 2008 **On Site** ⚐ **Nearby** ⚐ 1.5km ⚑ 24km
Sea 24km ⚐ 16km Water sports 24km ⚐ 1km ⚐ 9km ⚐ 16km
Notes No pets English spoken

CAMBREMER

ⅲ Les Marronniers

Jean et Chantal DARONDEL

Englesqueville, 14340 CAMBREMER

☎ 02 31 63 08 28 📄 02 31 63 92 54

email: chantal.darondel@wanadoo.fr

web: www.les-marronniers.com

One double room and two rooms sleeping three to four people are available in this 17th-century house. Two further double rooms are housed in the former cider press. Rooms are decorated with a personal touch and have private bathroom facilities and entrances. Kitchen for guests' use in the summer, garden with furniture. Surrounded by a park, with wonderful views of the Dives valley.

Prices not confirmed for 2008 **Nearby** ⚐ 7km Sea 22km ⚐ 17km
Water sports 22km ⚐ 4.5km ⚐ 4.5km ⚐ 17km **Notes** No pets English
spoken

ⅲ Manoir de Cantepie

Arnaud et Christine GHERRAK

14340 CAMBREMER

☎ 02 31 62 87 27 📄 02 31 62 87 27

The well-balanced and distinctive décor of this 17th-century Norman manor forms a large part of its charm. Three double or triple rooms with private bathroom facilities are available.

Prices s fr €55; d fr €70; extra person fr €10 **Nearby** ⚐ 5km ⚑ 15km
Sea 25km ⚐ 11km Restaurant 0.5km Water sports 25km ⚐ 1km
Spa 25km ⚑ 15km ⚐ 1km ⚐ 11km **Notes** No pets English spoken
Open March to 15 November.

CAMBREMER CONTINUED

⁂ Villa les Tilleuls

Danielle KORAITEIM

D50 Le Cadran, 14340 CAMBREMER

☎ 02 31 62 27 42 & 06 60 26 31 95 🖹 02 31 62 27 42

email: danielle.koraiteim@wanadoo.fr

A 19th-century villa well-placed for visiting the seaside towns of the Côte Fleurie - Honfleur, Cabourg, Deauville, as well as the attractive hinterland. The three bedrooms are all doubles, large and tastefully decorated, one with a balcony overlooking the garden. All have private bath or shower room/WC.

Prices d fr €70 **Nearby** ⚓ 6km ⚲ 17km Sea 25km ⮝ 11km Water sports 25km ⚄ 3km 🏛 3km ⇔ 11km **Notes** No pets English spoken Open Easter to 1 November.

CAMPIGNY

⁂ ♿ *Chambre d'hôtes*

Eric et Carole GIBERT

Hameau de Fontenay, 14490 CAMPIGNY

☎ 02 31 21 71 95 & 06 88 45 19 25 🖹 02 31 21 71 95

email: gibert.eric.carole@wanadoo.fr

This farm is a few kilometres from the town of Bayeux and the landing beaches. There are four bedrooms, in a building adjacent to the owners' home. On the ground floor is a double with disabled access; upstairs are a double and a triple. All have en suite shower rooms/ WCs. Extra bed and cot available. Guests' lounge, garden.

Prices not confirmed for 2008 **Nearby** ⚓ 5km ⚲ 18km Sea 20km ⚡ 3km ⮝ 7km Water sports 20km ⚄ 7km 🏛 7km ⇔ 7km **Notes** Pets admitted English spoken

CLECY-LE-VEY

⁂ La Ferme du Manoir

Louise PELLIER

14570 CLECY-LE-VEY

☎ 02 31 69 73 81

A restored Norman manor house which offers a suite consisting of a double and single room and a triple room in the main building, and an additional family room for four people in an annexe with a separate entrance. Guest rooms are comfortable and pleasant with private facilities, and breakfast is served in a rustic setting. Boules available.

Prices s fr €35; d fr €43; t fr €55; extra person fr €16 **Nearby** ⚓ 3km ⚲ 3km Sea 50km ⚡ 2km ⮝ 10km ⚄ 2km 🏛 3km ⇔ 40km **Notes** No pets

⁂ *La Ferme du Vey*

SCS LEBOUCHER-BRISSET

14570 CLECY-LE-VEY

☎ 02 31 69 71 02 🖹 02 31 69 69 33

email: pbrisset@9online.fr

web: www.la-ferme-du-vey.com

Three first floor bedrooms, two with garden views, on a farm not far from Clécy. The rooms are in an annexe to the owners' home. They

are all doubles, an extra bed is available, and they all have private shower room and WC. There is a kitchen for guests' use; outside is garden furniture, and a nice corner for picnics.

Prices not confirmed for 2008 **Nearby** ⚓ 1km ⚲ 3km Sea 50km ⚡ 1km ⮝ 11km ⚄ 1km 🏛 1km ⇔ 25km **Notes** Pets admitted CC

⁂ Le Manoir de Miette

André et Denise LEBOUCHER

14570 CLECY-LE-VEY

☎ 02 31 69 45 80 🖹 02 31 69 69 33

This unique house is surrounded by an attractive garden. The accommodation offered consists of two double or triple rooms with private facilities and a double room housed in an independent cottage with private shower and kitchen. Lounge with TV and garden with furniture. The area has many diverse attractions.

Prices s fr €38; d fr €43; t fr €51 **Nearby** ⚓ 5km ⚲ 3km Sea 50km ⚡ 1km ⮝ 10km Restaurant 0.1km ⚄ 1km 🏛 1km ⇔ 35km **Notes** Pets admitted Open March to December.

COLLEVILLE-SUR-MER

⁂ ♥ ⋈ *Ferme du Clos Tassin*

D et M-T PICQUENARD

14710 COLLEVILLE SUR MER

☎ 02 31 22 41 51 🖹 02 31 22 29 46

email: clostassin@wanadoo.fr

web: www.clostassin.fr.st

In the main building of this working farm, one grade 2 double room and three grade 3 rooms (double, triple and four-person family room) are available. One grade 3 suite with double and connecting twin room is housed in an annexe. All have private facilities. Evening meals are available on reservation. Only five minutes from the sea and the D-Day beaches.

Prices not confirmed for 2008 **Nearby** ⚓ 7km ⚲ 7km Sea 2km ⚡ 2km ⮝ 15km Water sports 2km ⚄ 0.5km 🏛 3km ⇔ 15km **Notes** No pets Open February to December.

⁂ *Ferme du Loucel*

Bernard PETIT

14710 COLLEVILLE SUR MER

☎ 02 31 22 40 95 🖹 02 31 22 40 95

email: fermeduloucel@wanadoo.fr

web: http://perso.wanadoo.fr/fermeduloucel

Near the historic sites and beaches of Débarquement, this residence is typical to the region and provides a triple room and two rooms for two and three people, with private facilities. Guests can relax in the courtyard with lawn and garden furniture.

Prices not confirmed for 2008 **Nearby** ⚓ 6km ⚲ 6km Sea 1km ⮝ 15km Water sports 1km ⚄ 0.5km 🏛 5km ⇔ 16km **Notes** Pets admitted

COLOMBIERES

⌘ ⍥ **Manoir de Thionville**

Michel et Nicole FERNANDO

14710 COLOMBIERES

☎ 02 31 21 35 11 📄 02 31 21 35 11

email: reservation@manoir-thionville.com

web: www.manoir-thionville.com

This large house, on a site which is protected for its environmental interest, offers three elegant guest rooms in a wing which has been beautifully restored. There is a double room, a twin, and a two-roomed suite for three. All have private facilities. There is a guests' lounge with sofas and a billiard table, and garden furniture.

Prices s fr €70; d €80-€130; t fr €160; extra person fr €30; dinner €30 **On Site** ⍩ **Nearby** ⛵ 7km ⚓ 15km Sea 10km ⚲ 4km Restaurant 10km Water sports 12km ⚓ 7km 🏛 7km 🚲 12km **Notes** No pets English spoken Open March to November.

COMMES

⌘ **Chambre d'hôtes**

Michel et Lilou CAIRON

église, 14520 COMMES

☎ 02 31 21 71 08 📄 02 31 21 95 87

Two grade 3 double rooms and one suite with two connecting double rooms are available in this modern house, all with private facilities. Perfect for families and a warm welcome is guaranteed. Pleasant terrace. Close to the D-Day beaches.

Prices s fr €37; d €42; t fr €57 **Nearby** ⛵ 2km ⚓ 3km Sea 2km ⚲ 2km ⚓ 9km Restaurant 1km Water sports 2km ⚓ 2km 🏛 2km 🚲 10km **Notes** No pets

⌘ **Ferme d'Escures**

Charles & Christiane HAELEWYN

14520 COMMES

☎ 02 31 92 52 23 📄 02 31 92 52 23

This traditional Norman house has two double rooms, a family room and a suite sleeping four people, all with private facilities. The comfortable house is close to a pretty fishing town and the D-Day beaches.

Prices s fr €38; d €42-€45; t €57-€60; extra person fr €15 **Nearby** ⛵ 3km ⚓ 1.5km Sea 2km ⚲ 2km ⚓ 7km Restaurant 2km Water sports 2km ⚓ 2km ⍩ 7km 🏛 1.5km 🚲 8km **Notes** No pets English spoken

⌘ ❧ **Le Logis**

Florence et Gilles HAELEWYN

14520 COMMES

☎ 02 31 21 79 56 📄 02 31 21 79 56

email: lelogis.haelewyn@wanadoo.fr

web: http://monsite.wanadoo.fr/le.logis

Near to the fishing town of Port-en-Bessin, this farmhouse offers a triple room, two double rooms and a suite consisting of two connecting double rooms, all with private facilities. An extra bed is available. Comfortable house with lounge and garden with furniture. Close to the D-Day beaches.

Prices not confirmed for 2008 **Nearby** ⛵ 2km ⚓ 2km Sea 2km ⚓ 6km Water sports 2km ⚓ 2km 🏛 2km 🚲 7km **Notes** No pets English spoken

COURSEULLES-SUR-MER

⌘ **Chambre d'hôtes**

Gérard et Marie-Noëlle WILLE

1 rue Arthur Leduc, 14470 COURSEULLES SUR MER

☎ 02 31 37 86 46 & 06 78 26 70 07

email: marie-noelle.wille@wanadoo.fr

web: http://monsite.wanadoo.fr/gmnwille

This very attractive house is in the centre of a seaside resort, just 400 metres from the beach. It offers three triple rooms, one of which is very large, and a double room, all tastefully decorated with private shower facilities. Garden with furniture.

Prices s fr €40; d €48-€50; t fr €63; extra person fr €15 **Nearby** ⛵ 1km ⚓ 20km Sea 0.2km ⚓ 0.5km Water sports 1km ⚓ 0.5km 🚲 17km **Notes** No pets English spoken

⌘ **La Roseraie**

Jacques et Bernadette JORIS

13 rue de Reviers, 14470 COURSEULLES SUR MER

☎ 02 31 37 48 98

email: laroseraie.joris@free.fr

web: http://laroseraie.joris.free.fr/

This comfortable house, set in a colourful garden, has three bright and welcoming double rooms, all on the first floor and with independent access. Each room has an en suite bath or shower room and WC. Cot available. Garden room. Courseulles, with its sandy beach and fish market, is ten minutes' walk away.

Prices s fr €40; d fr €48; t fr €63; extra person fr €15 **Nearby** ⛵ 1km ⚓ 17km Sea 0.5km ⚲ 10km ⚓ 1km Water sports 0.5km ⚓ 0.5km 🏛 0.5km 🚲 20km **Notes** No pets English spoken

COURSON

⌘ ⍥ *La Plaine Postel*

Daniel et Elisabeth GUEZET

14380 COURSON

☎ 02 31 68 83 41 & 06 63 21 09 87 📄 02 31 68 83 41

email: daniel.guezet@wanadoo.fr

web: www.chambresdhotes-guezet.com

This working farm offers one grade 1 double room and one grade 1 room for four people, with communal bathroom. The house also has three grade 3 double rooms with private facilities. Guests can enjoy the calm atmosphere of the Norman countryside and try local specialities. Billiard table, swimming pool.

Prices not confirmed for 2008 **On Site** ⚲ **Nearby** ⛵ 7km ⚓ 17km Sea 40km ⚓ 3km ⚓ 3km 🏛 3km 🚲 15km **Notes** Pets admitted English spoken

CREPON

Manoir de Crépon

Anne-Marie POISSON
Route d'Arromanches, 14480 CREPON
☎ 02 31 22 21 27 📠 02 31 22 88 80
email: manoirdecrepon@wanadoo.fr
web: www.manoirdecrepon.com

Surrounded by a large park planted with trees, this 18th-century manor house offers four guest rooms: two 3-4 person suites and two double rooms, each with private facilities. Lounge and garden with furniture. Bicycles can be borrowed and the D-Day beaches are nearby.

Prices s fr €60; d fr €75; t fr €90; extra person fr €20
Nearby ♿ 5km ⚓ 12km Sea 4km 🎣 12km ✈ 10km Water sports 4km 🚊 4km 🏠 0.1km ᛗ 10km **Notes** Pets admitted English spoken CC

CRESSEVEUILLE

Longueval

J DE LONGCAMP
14430 CRESSEVEUILLE
☎ 02 31 79 22 01
email: philippe.de-longcamp@wanadoo.fr

An attractive manor house offering three large and comfortable guest rooms: a double room in the main building, a triple with TV in an adjoining building with separate entrance and a further double with TV situated in another annexe. All have private facilities. The house has a lounge with TV and garden with furniture and is surrounded by a leafy park.

Prices s €41-€50; d €47-€60; t fr €65; extra person fr €75
Nearby ♿ 5km ⚓ 14km Sea 9km 🎣 0.5km ✈ 1km Water sports 9km 🚊 0.5km 🏠 5km ᛗ 16km **Notes** No pets English spoken

CRICQUEBOEUF

Chambre d'hôtes

B et S HAUCHECORNE
A la Villa des Rosiers, 14113 CRICQUEBOEUF
☎ 02 31 98 25 22 & 06 81 01 11 03
email: villa.rosiers@wanadoo.fr
web: http://monsite.wanadoo.fr/villadesrosiers

Two double rooms and two triple or double rooms are provided at this guest house, each grade 3 with private facilities. A grade 2 double room is also available, with private shower and wc on the landing. Extra single bed available. Situated between Honfleur and Deauville.

Prices not confirmed for 2008 **Nearby** ♿ 2km ⚓ 3km Sea 1km ✈ 7km Water sports 7km 🚊 1km 🏠 1km ᛗ 7km **Notes** No pets English spoken

CROISSANVILLE

Le Presbytère

M. France BEAUVISAGE
14370 CROISSANVILLE
☎ 02 31 23 83 88 & 06 76 71 93 03 📠 02 31 23 83 88
email: marie-france.beauvisage@wanadoo.fr

A beautiful wisteria adorns this peacefully located 18th-century stone built house. It offers three cosy and smart rooms. On the first floor ar two doubles, with a cot; on the ground floor, with a separate entranc there is another double. All have private bath/shower rooms and WC Garden furniture.

Prices not confirmed for 2008 **Nearby** ♿ 5km ⚓ 15km Sea 20km 🎣 3km ✈ 18km Water sports 20km 🚊 6km 🏠 6km ᛗ 6km **Notes** No pets English spoken

EQUEMAUVILLE

La Ferme Chevalier

J-Yves et Françoise GREGOIRE
14600 EQUEMAUVILLE
☎ 02 31 89 18 14
email: lafermechevalier@wanadoo.fr

An 18th-century family house, formerly a horseman's rest, with two double rooms, two triples and a room for five, with mezzanine. All rooms have private facilities and entrances. Garden with furniture ar courtyard with a magnificent 18th-century well.

Prices s fr €40; d fr €50; t fr €60; extra person fr €10 **Nearby** ♿ 3km ⚓ 4km Sea 4km ✈ 4km 🚊 1km 🏠 1km ᛗ 12km **Notes** No pets English spoken

FIRFOL

Bethanie

J.François & Corinne MARIN
Chemin de la Haie aux Prêtres, 14100 FIRFOL
☎ 02 31 61 16 86 & 06 61 66 98 56 📠 02 31 61 16 86
email: clos.bethanie@neuf.fr
web: www.clos.bethanie.free.fr

An old convent building which has been delightfully restored to provide three individually decorated bedrooms, two downstairs, one on the first floor. All the rooms sleep three people, and each has a private shower and WC. A quiet, relaxing place, with garden views from the bright and spacious rooms. Garden furniture.

rices s fr €45; d fr €50; t fr €65; extra person fr €15   **Nearby** 🏌 1km
16km Sea 30km 🎣 7km ⬆ 7km Water sports 20km 🚣 7km
Da 30km ⛵ 7km 🏛 3km ⚓ 7km   **Notes** No pets English spoken

FORMIGNY

🏵 *Ferme du Mouchel*

Odile LENOURICHEL
14710 FORMIGNY
☎ 02 31 22 53 79 & 06 15 37 50 20
email: odile.lenourichel@wanadoo.fr
web: www.ferme-du-mouchel.com

This large dairy farm offers attractively decorated rooms, including
three rooms for two to four people, with private shower facilities and
a suite with two connecting double rooms, housed in an annexe to
the main building. Lounge and garden with furniture. Close to the
D-Day beaches.

Prices not confirmed for 2008   **Nearby** 🏌 5km ⚓ 15km Sea 4km
🎣 4km ⬆ 15km Water sports 4km 🚣 4km 🏛 5km ⚓ 15km
⬆ 15km   **Notes** No pets

🏵 ♿ *Quintefeuille*

Janine DELESALLE
14710 FORMIGNY
☎ 02 31 22 51 73 📠 02 31 22 51 73

Peacefully situated five minutes from the landing beaches, this elegant
15th- and 16th-century house offers three guest rooms, all with
private facilities. Upstairs is a room for four, and a room for three
which links with another triple. In an annexe, on the ground floor, is a
double room, which links to a further double. The annexe rooms have
disabled access. Lounge, table tennis.

Prices s fr €33; d fr €48; t €55-€63; extra person fr €9   **Nearby** 🏌 3km
⚓ 4km Sea 5km 🎣 3km ⬆ 15km Water sports 6km 🚣 3km 🏛 3km
⬆ 15km   **Notes** Pets admitted English spoken Open February to
November.

GEFOSSE-FONTENAY

🏵 *Manoir de l'Hermerel*

Agnès et François LEMARIE
14230 GEFOSSE FONTENAY
☎ 02 31 22 64 12 📠 02 31 22 76 37
email: lemariehermerel@aol.com
web: www.manoir-hermerel.com

Guest rooms in this 15th-century farmhouse retain their traditional
character and are decorated in blue, green or pink. There is a double
room, a suite for four people and an attic room with mezzanine which
sleeps four to five. Private shower facilities for each room; cot and
extra bed available. Independent guest entrance, picnic corner and
garden with furniture. Breakfast is served in front of the impressive
place.

Prices not confirmed for 2008   **Nearby** 🏌 15km ⚓ 30km Sea 1km
🎣 4km ⬆ 20km Water sports 4km 🚣 4km 🏛 4km ⚓ 20km
Notes No pets English spoken Open February to November. CC

🏵 🍽 **Manoir de la Rivière**

Gérard et Isabelle LEHARIVEL
14230 GEFOSSE FONTENAY
☎ 02 31 22 64 45 & 06 81 58 25 21 📠 02 31 22 01 18
email: manoirdelariviere@wanadoo.fr
web: www.chez.com/manoirdelariviere

This fortified farmhouse dates from medieval times and benefits
from spacious, meticulously decorated rooms, with exposed beams
and antique furniture. One double room and two triple rooms, all
with private facilities, are offered. Evening meals are available on
reservation and are served in the vaulted dining room with fireplace
and baker's oven.

Prices s fr €57; d €58-€60; t fr €80; extra person fr €20; dinner fr €23
Nearby 🏌 12km ⚓ 25km Sea 1.5km 🎣 3km ⬆ 20km Water sports 3km
🚣 3km 🏛 3km ⚓ 20km   **Notes** No pets English spoken CC

GENNEVILLE

🏵 **Le Grand Clos de St Martin**

Daniela COIGNARD
Hameau St Martin, 14600 GENNEVILLE
☎ 02 31 87 80 44 & 06 33 95 95 27 📠 02 31 87 80 44
email: legrandclosdesaintmartin@wanadoo.fr
web: www.legrandclosdesaintmartin.com

Inland from Honfleur, tucked away in a small valley, this house has
four attractively decorated bedrooms. Two double rooms are on the
ground floor; upstairs is a suite for four people, with a living room.
All have television and DVD player, and private shower room/WC.
Pleasant garden with furniture, and good local walks.

Prices s fr €70; d €80-€105; t fr €125; extra person fr €20
Nearby 🏌 10km ⚓ 10km Sea 10km 🎣 4km ⬆ 10km Restaurant 5km
🚣 10km Spa 20km ⛵ 10km 🏛 7km ⚓ 15km   **Notes** No pets English
spoken

GONNEVILLE-SUR-MER

🏵 **Ferme des Glycines**

Hugues et Elizabeth EXMELIN
Carrefour Manerbe, 14510 GONNEVILLE SUR MER
☎ 02 31 28 01 15

Surrounded by orchards, this typical Norman farm complex offers
large rooms, decorated with a personal touch. One room for four
people (including a mezzanine for two), one triple and one double
room, all with private wc and shower. Guest rooms benefit from
independent entrances, which open onto the attractive garden with
furniture, trees and flowers.

Prices s fr €43; d fr €51; t fr €65; extra person fr €15   **Nearby** 🏌 4km
⚓ 1km Sea 3km 🎣 3km ⬆ 4km Restaurant 3.5km Water sports 5km
🚣 3km 🏛 3.5km ⚓ 6km   **Notes** No pets Open April to November.

GRANDCAMP-MAISY

♿ Les Piéris

M et L CHAPERON-SCHMIT
14450 GRANDCAMP MAISY
☎ 02 31 92 33 63
email: gites.les-pieris@laposte.net
web: http://lespieris.free.fr

Just two minutes from the sea at Grandcamp-Maisy, this house has four beautifully decorated rooms, two of them with disabled access. They are in an annexe to the owners' house - two downstairs and two upstairs. All of the rooms sleep three people, and they all have private shower rooms/WCs. There is an extra bed available. Garden furniture.

Prices s fr €39; d fr €45; t fr €56; extra person fr €11   **On Site** ☆
Nearby ⚓ 2km ⚁ 23km Sea 2km ♟ 2km ⚐ 25km Water sports 2km
⚂ 2km ⚃ 2km ⚄ 15km   **Notes** Pets admitted English spoken

GRAYE-SUR-MER

Les 4 Saisons

Isabelle et Frederic LEVILLAIN
17, route de Ste Croix, 14470 GRAYE SUR MER
☎ 02 31 37 76 10 & 06 30 10 84 96   📄 02 31 37 76 10
email: 4.saisons@free.fr
web: www.4saisons.biz

This establishment is located in a small, typical village 1km from the sea and the resort of Courseulles-sur-Mer. It has three rooms (one for three and two for two) decorated on the theme of seasons, each with private facilities, separate access and TVs. There is garden furniture, and bikes may be borrowed.

Prices s fr €42; d fr €50; t fr €62; extra person fr €10   **On Site** ☆
Nearby ⚓ 1.5km ⚁ 18km Sea 1km ♟ 10km ⚐ 1.5km Restaurant 2km
Water sports 1km ⚂ 1.5km ⚃ 1.5km ⚄ 20km   **Notes** No pets English spoken

HONFLEUR

Chambre d'hôtes

Janine NINOVE
33 rue Bourdet, 14600 HONFLEUR
☎ 06 07 16 02 02   📄 02 31 89 10 83
email: janine.ninove@wanadoo.fr

In Honfleur, five minutes walk from the Vieux Bassin, this 19th-century house offers four themed rooms. On the first floor a double room; on the second floor two more doubles; on the third floor a suite for four, with a double bed and twins. All rooms have private facilities. You can enjoy your breakfast in the enclosed terraced garden.

Prices s €88-€98; d €96-€166; t €119-€174; extra person €8-€23
Nearby ⚓ 1km ⚁ 10km Sea 1km ♟ 1km ⚐ 1km Water sports 1km
⚂ 1km ⚃ 0.5km ⚄ 16km   **Notes** No pets Open February to November.

Chez Oncle Alphonse

Jérôme et Christel ARNOULD
23 Cours Albert Manuel, 14600 HONFLEUR
☎ 06 30 81 10 15   📄 02 31 89 58 15
email: hotehonfleur@aol.com
web: www.chezonclealphonse.com

In the heart of Honfleur, just a few metres from the Vieux Bassin, this property offers five individually decorated rooms. On the ground floor is a twin-bedded room; on the first floor are a twin and a double; on the second, a double and another double linking through to a twin. All have private bath or shower room and WC. Lounge, garden.

Prices s fr €85; d €95-€120; t €115-€130; extra person fr €20
Nearby ⚓ 3km ⚁ 7km Sea 2km ♟ 1km ⚐ 1km
Water sports 1km ⚂ 0.5km Spa 15km ⚅ 0.1km ⚃ 0.2km ⚄ 15km
Notes No pets English spoken Open February to November.

Le Moulin St-Nicol

Gérard et Joëlle DARDOL
Cote d'Equemauville, 14600 HONFLEUR
☎ 02 31 14 68 37
email: info@moulinsaintnicol.com
web: www.moulinsaintnicol.com

A 19th-century mill in a quiet spot, almost encircled by a river. There are two double bedrooms and a room for four, all with television, private bathroom and WC. Lounge with open fire and books; outside a pleasant garden with garden furniture where guests can relax.

Prices s fr €75; d €90-€125; t fr €140; extra person fr €15
Nearby ⚓ 0.5km ⚁ 6km Sea 1.5km ♟ 1.5km ⚐ 1.5km Water sports 1.5km ⚂ 1.5km ⚃ 1.5km ⚄ 15km   **Notes** No pets English spoken

LA CAMBE

Ferme de Savigny

Régine LE DEVIN
14230 LA CAMBE
☎ 02 31 21 12 33 & 02 31 21 18 75   📄 02 31 21 18 75
email: re.ledevin@libertysurf.fr
web: http://perso.wanadoo.fr/ferme-savigny/

A pretty house, where the tower staircase leads to four cosy, tasteful decorated bedrooms. There are three doubles, and a triple with three single beds. Extra beds are available, and all the rooms have private bathroom and WC. Separate guests' entrance. There is a kitchenette, and a courtyard with garden furniture.

Prices s €36-€41; d €44-€48; t fr €60; extra person fr €8
Nearby ⚓ 6km ⚁ 20km Sea 6km ♟ 6km ⚐ 26km Restaurant 5km
Water sports 6km ⚂ 6km ⚅ 6km ⚃ 6km ⚄ 15km   **Notes** No pets English spoken

LA POMMERAYE

❖ *Ferme de la Couture*

Pascal et Isabelle QUERON
14690 LA POMMERAYE
☎ 02 31 69 02 67 & 06 62 21 74 32 📄 02 31 69 02 67
email: fermedelacouture@tiscali.fr

19th-century farmhouse in the attractive, hilly region known as La
Suisse Normande. In a converted outbuilding are two double rooms,
a triple (all single beds), and a room for four (all singles also). Each
attractively decorated room has a private shower and WC; the quad
room also has a baby's cot and a lounge area. Day room and garden.

Prices not confirmed for 2008 **Nearby** ⚑ 1km ⚘ 7km Sea 47km
🏊 4km ⚓ 12km Water sports 47km ⛳ 6km 🏛 6km 🚉 35km
Notes No pets Open Easter to 1 November.

LE HOME-VARAVILLE

❖ **Manoir de la Marjolaine**

Eric FAYE
Av du Président Coty, 14390 LE HOME VARAVILLE
☎ 06 82 82 78 59 📄 02 31 91 77 10
email: eric.faye@orange.fr
web: http://manoirdelamarjolaine.free.fr

Only 300 metres from the sea and 20km from golf courses, this bourgeois
house is set in a verdant, tree-lined park in a romantic spot. The owner
provides four rooms with TV and private facilities: a suite for three people
with two rooms and a terrace, a triple and two rooms for two people.
There is a games and keep fit room, bike loan and garden furniture.

Prices s €70-€110; d €80-€120; t fr €130 **On Site** ✿
Nearby ⚑ 0.2km ⚘ 0.2km Sea 0.3km 🏊 2km ⚓ 2km Restaurant 0.1km
Water sports 2km ⛳ 2km Spa 20km 🏛 0.8km 🚉 2km **Notes** No pets
English spoken

LE MESNIL-DURAND

❖ **Domaine de la Fromagerie**

Monique QUESNOT
Chemin de la Fromagerie, 14140 LE MESNIL DURAND
☎ 02 31 63 51 50
email: monique.quesnot@tele2.fr
web: http://home.tele2.fr/domainefromagerie

This 18th-century house, with its half-timbered and brick exterior, is in
a style typical of the region. It has three double bedrooms, each with
en suite bath or shower room and WC. There is an extra room which is

suitable for two children. The rooms are spacious, and have such features
as original mouldings, marble fireplaces, etc. Garden and garden room.

Prices s €45-€55; d €50-€60 **Nearby** ⚑ 2km ⚘ 30km Sea 45km
🏊 2km ⚓ 15km Restaurant 7km Water sports 45km ⛳ 7km ✿ 7km
🏛 7km 🚉 16km **Notes** No pets

LE MESNIL-MAUGER

❖ ◉ *Saint Crespin*

William et Ginette GRUCHY
Ferme de la Thillaye, 14270 LE MESNIL MAUGER
☎ 02 31 63 46 26 📄 02 31 63 16 04
email: gruchy-william@wanadoo.fr
web: http://william.gruchy.free.fr

Once a farmhouse, this half-timbered property now has three guest
rooms in converted outbuildings. Two of the rooms are doubles; the
third is a triple, and all have en suite facilities. An ideal spot to recharge
your batteries, but if you are looking for something more energetic, a
swimming pool and exercise equipment is on site. Meals by arrangement.

Prices not confirmed for 2008 **On Site** Private ⚓ **Nearby** ⚑ 4km
Sea 28km Water sports 28km ⛳ 4km 🏛 3km 🚉 6km **Notes** Pets
admitted Open 15 March to 15 November.

LE MESNIL-VILLEMENT

❖ *Les Deux Lumières*

Gareth et Jennifer BRITAIN
Route des Isles Bardel, 14690 LE MESNIL VILLEMENT
☎ 02 31 69 14 93
email: lesdeuxlumieres@wanadoo.fr

This beautiful house in the Suisse Normande, with its comfortable
rooms and lovingly tended garden has a fine view over the Orne
valley. On the first floor is a grade 2 double bedroom with its own,
but not self-contained, shower/WC; there are also two further doubles
with full en suite facilities. Extra bed, lounge, garden furniture.

Prices not confirmed for 2008 **Nearby** ⚑ 4km ⚘ 14km Sea 45km
⚓ 17km ⛳ 4km 🏛 4km 🚉 25km **Notes** No pets English spoken
Open Easter to 1 November.

LE MOLAY-LITTRY

❖ ◉ *Le Prieuré*

Eric et Catherine GUILLOCHIN
Rue Retot, 14330 LE MOLAY LITTRY
☎ 02 31 51 91 97 & 06 17 07 59 95
email: guillochin.eric@wanadoo.fr
web: http://perso.wanadoo.fr/le-prieure

Wooded grounds surround this property, which has three comfortable
and tastefully decorated double bedrooms, all on the first floor. All
of the rooms have private showers/WCs, and one of them has a
possible linking room to provide family accommodation for four. Extra
beds and a cot are available. Meals, based on fine local cuisine, by
arrangement. Garden furniture.

Prices not confirmed for 2008 **Nearby** ⚑ 2km ⚘ 15km Sea 15km
🏊 5km ⚓ 25km Water sports 15km ⛳ 1km 🏛 1km 🚉 15km
Notes Pets admitted English spoken

LE PIN

▦ ᐁ᐀ **Ferme de la Pomme**

Isabelle RICHET

14590 LE PIN

☎ 02 31 61 96 09 & 06 87 17 16 12

email: contact@fermedelapomme.com

web: www.fermedelapomme.com

Built as a farmhouse in the 17th century, this typical Normandy building has been fully restored. On the ground floor is a double room; upstairs is another double with an adjoining room with two single beds, plus a two-roomed suite for four. All have private facilities. Outside is a garden with furniture for sitting out and enjoying the beautiful location.

Prices s €58; d €58; t fr €70; extra person fr €20; dinner fr €22
Nearby ⏛ 4km ♨ 12km Sea 26km ✐ 6km ⚲ 12km Water sports 12km
♨ 2.5km ⚄ 2km ⋈ 12km **Notes** No pets English spoken

LES-AUTHIEUX-SUR-CALONNE

▦ **Les Bélières**

François & Françoise LE ROUX

Route de Blangy le Château,

14130 LES AUTHIEUX SUR CALONNE

☎ 02 31 64 67 28 ᐁ 02 31 64 67 28

email: les-belieres@wanadoo.fr

web: www.lesbelieres.com

Peaceful and comfortable rooms housed in a modern building with an attractive garden. One double room with independent entrance and two double or triple rooms, each connecting with a further double room. All rooms have private facilities.

Prices s fr €55; d fr €58; t €74-€90; extra person fr €16 **Nearby** ⏛ 4km
♨ 6km Sea 18km ✐ 2km ⚲ 18km Water sports 8km ♨ 6km ⚄ 8km
⋈ 8km **Notes** No pets

LINGEVRES

▦ ᐁ ᐁ᐀ **Chambre d'hôtes**

Charles et Marie POLIDOR

14250 LINGEVRES

☎ 02 31 80 91 17 ᐁ 02 31 08 37 78

email: lelandey.p@libertysurf.fr

web: http://lelandey.chez.tiscali.fr/

In the main building of this farmhouse, three double or triple guest rooms are available, all with private shower facilities. An adjoining building provides two further triple rooms with private showers. Table d'hôte meals are available.

Prices not confirmed for 2008 **Nearby** ⏛ 5km Sea 20km ⚲ 12km
♨ 3km ⚄ 3km ⋈ 12km **Notes** No pets

LIVRY

▦ ᐁ᐀ **La Suhardière**

Alain et Françoise PETITON

14240 LIVRY

☎ 02 31 77 51 02 ᐁ 02 31 77 51 02

email: petiton.alain@wanadoo.fr

This restored 17th-century farmhouse offers a triple room and two double or triple rooms with a connecting double room, all with private facilities. Independent entrance, lounge and garden with furniture. The rooms enjoy a restful country setting with fishing available on site.

Prices not confirmed for 2008 **On Site** ✐ **Nearby** ⏛ 1km Sea 20km
⚲ 10km ♨ 1km ⚄ 0.5km ⋈ 23km **Notes** Pets admitted

LONGUES-SUR-MER

▦ ᐁ **Ferme de la Tourelle**

J-M et J LECARPENTIER

Hameau de Fontenailles, 14400 LONGUES SUR MER

☎ 02 31 21 78 47 ᐁ 02 31 21 84 84

email: lecarpentier2@wanadoo.fr

web: www.multimania.com/tourelle

Housed in an annexe to this 17th-century former farmhouse are three rooms with exposed stone walls accommodating three to four people, with private shower facilities and an independent entrance. Lounge with kitchen, fitness room and garden with furniture. Internet access. Close to the sea.

Prices not confirmed for 2008 **Nearby** ⏛ 7km ♨ 7km Sea 1km
✐ 4km ⚲ 7km Water sports 7km ♨ 4km ⚄ 2km ⋈ 7km
Notes Pets admitted

LONGVILLERS

▦ ᐁ᐀ **La Nouvelle France**

Anne-Marie GODEY

14310 LONGVILLERS

☎ 02 31 77 63 36 ᐁ 02 31 77 63 36

email: courrier@la-nouvelle-france.com

web: www.la-nouvelle-france.com

Three double rooms with private shower facilities are available in this former barn, which is built from local stone and forms part of a farm complex. The rooms are decorated in a comfortable rustic style and there is also a large, shady lawn. Calm environment and footpaths for walkers.

Prices not confirmed for 2008 **Nearby** ⏛ 2km ♨ 24km Sea 35km
✐ 4km ⚲ 3km Water sports 35km ♨ 3km ⚄ 4km ⋈ 30km
Notes No pets English spoken

ⅲ *Mathan*

ean et A-Marie DE MATHAN
4310 LONGVILLERS
☎ 02 31 77 10 37 📄 02 31 77 49 13
mail: mathan.normandie@caramail.com

deally situated for stopovers between Normandy and Brittany, this
5th-century manor house offers large, pleasant and distinctive
uest rooms with king size beds. Two suites, both consisting of
vo connecting double rooms, and a double room, all with private
cilities. Lounge with fireplace and private guest entrance.

rices not confirmed for 2008 **Nearby** ⚓ 0.5km ⚓ 35km Sea 35km
5km Water sports 35km ⚓ 4km ⛪ 4km ⛥ 30km **Notes** No pets
nglish spoken Open April to November.

MAGNY-EN-BESSIN

ⅲ ❦ ⅰ◎ⅰ *Ferme de l'Église*

et L LE MONNIER
4400 MAGNY EN BESSIN
☎ 02 31 51 87 41 & 06 03 11 60 06 📄 02 31 51 87 41

his restored farmhouse with its flowery garden offers three
omfortable and tastefully decorated bedrooms, with independent
ccess. There are two triple rooms, and a two-roomed suite for four
eople. They all have en suite shower rooms and WCs. Extra bed and
t available. Garden room. Five minutes from Arromanches, with its
h historical associations.

rices s fr €30; d fr €45; t fr €55; extra person fr €13; dinner fr €16
earby ⚓ 7km ⚓ 12km Sea 5km ⚓ 10km ⚓ 6km Restaurant 2km
ater sports 7km ⚓ 5km ⛤ 6km ⛪ 4km ⛥ 6km **Notes** Pets admitted
nglish spoken

MALTOT

ⅲ *Le Cottage*

cques LARSON
Chemin du Longrais, 14930 MALTOT
02 31 26 96 10 & 06 13 55 68 88 📄 02 31 26 96 10
nail: jack.larson@wanadoo.fr

ar to Caen with its impressive Mémorial museum, this property
ers spacious rooms in a very peaceful setting. On the first floor of
e house there are three rooms, each for up to three people, one
which has a linking room for two. All have private bath or shower
om and WC. Garden furniture.

ices not confirmed for 2008 **Nearby** ⚓ 8km ⚓ 10km Sea 25km
8km ⚓ 6km Water sports 25km ⚓ 6km ⛪ 3km ⛥ 8km
tes No pets

MANDEVILLE-EN-BESSIN

ⅲ ⅰ◎ⅰ *La Beuffrerie*

Jeanne VALEC
14710 MANDEVILLE EN BESSIN
☎ 02 31 21 41 95 & 06 63 12 69 53
email: jeanne.valec@wanadoo.fr
web: www.beuffrerie.com

A good place to recharge your batteries: a 19th-century house in
a small hamlet with nicely decorated rooms looking out over the
garden. On the first floor is a double room, which links to a twin-
bedded room; there are two more doubles in a separate wing of
the house. Big garden, lots of flowers, garden furniture. Meals by
arrangement.

Prices s €35-€40; d €45-€49; t €60-€65; extra person fr €10; dinner
fr €18 **Nearby** ⚓ 3km ⚓ 9km Sea 7km ⚓ 7km ⚓ 12km Water
sports 7km ⚓ 3km ⛪ 3km ⛥ 12km **Notes** Pets admitted English
spoken

MANERBE

ⅲ *La Katounette*

Micheline VALETTE
14340 MANERBE
☎ 02 31 61 14 66 & 06 13 58 99 41

This welcoming half-timbered Norman house is surrounded by
greenery and offers three double rooms, a connecting double room
and a family room, also with connecting double room. All rooms have
TV and private facilities, and are decorated with a personal touch.
Garden with furniture.

Prices s fr €36; d fr €44; t fr €55; extra person fr €12 **Nearby** ⚓ 4km
⚓ 14km Sea 16km ⚓ 3km ⚓ 4km Water sports 16km ⚓ 3km ⛪ 1km
⛥ 6km **Notes** Pets admitted

MANVIEUX

ⅲ *La Bréhollière*

Sandrine PASTRE
14117 MANVIEUX
☎ 02 31 22 19 66 & 06 73 68 71 64 📄 02 31 22 93 48
email: sandrine.pastre@wanadoo.fr
web: www.labreholliere.com

A pretty stone house set in a peaceful environment between
Arromanches and Port en Bessin. Charming guest rooms include two
double or triple rooms and a split-level family room for four people,
all with private shower facilities. Cot available. Independent guest
entrance and garden with furniture.

Prices not confirmed for 2008 **On Site** Private ⚓ **Nearby** ⚓ 6km
⚓ 8km Sea 1.5km Water sports 2km ⚓ 3km ⛪ 3km ⛥ 8km
Notes No pets English spoken

MAROLLES

⁂ Chambre d'hôtes

Lucien et Christiane SIX
Route de Fumichon, 14100 MAROLLES
☎ 02 31 63 64 39 & 06 78 68 64 69
email: lucien.six@wanadoo.fr

This large, traditional half-timbered house offers two double rooms and a triple, all with private shower. Independent entrance and garden with furniture. The dining room benefits from a large fireplace which is lit at breakfast and in the evenings, during the winter months. Discover the rich heritage of the local Norman villages, easily accessible on foot or by bicycle.

Prices s fr €30; d fr €40; t fr €48 **Nearby** ⚓ 0.5km ⚲ 18km Sea 30km ✎ 18km ⚲ 9km Water sports 30km ⚲ 2km ⚐ 2.5km ⚲ 9km **Notes** Pets admitted English spoken

⁂ *La Ferme aux Alpines*

Evelyne PILON
Le Mont Hérault, 14100 MAROLLES
☎ 02 31 61 96 11 ⚟ 02 31 61 96 11

This stone farmhouse offers three very comfortable double rooms, with private facilities. Cot and extra bed available. Inviting and restful lounge for guests and garden with furniture. Extensive opportunities for walking nearby.

Prices not confirmed for 2008 **Nearby** ⚓ 5km ⚲ 27km Sea 35km ⚲ 12km Water sports 35km ⚲ 0.5km ⚐ 4km ⚲ 12km **Notes** No pets English spoken

MONDRAINVILLE

⁂ Manoir de Colleville

Monique GROSS
14210 MONDRAINVILLE
☎ 02 31 80 96 75

This house, built in a style typical of the area, offers three spacious and tastefully decorated rooms, all on the first floor. They are all doubles, and they all have private shower rooms and WCs. There is the possibility of an extra room. Lounge and garden furniture.

Prices s fr €35; d fr €45; t fr €60 **Nearby** ⚓ 6km ⚲ 20km Sea 25km ✎ 1km ⚲ 12km ⚲ 4km Spa 12km ⚐ 1km ⚲ 12km **Notes** No pets

MONTCHAMP

⁂ Le Champ Fleury

Simone LAIMAN
14350 MONTCHAMP
☎ 02 31 68 24 95
email: simonelaiman@wanadoo.fr

Le Champ Fleury is a pretty house built in the local style, standing in a peaceful spot with a south-facing garden. Two upstairs double rooms in the house, and a twin-bedded room in a separate building, are all decorated to individual styles and have private bath or shower room. A cot is available; outside there is garden furniture.

Prices s fr €35; d fr €45 **Nearby** ⚓ 6km ⚲ 12km ✎ 6km ⚲ 12km Water sports 12km ⚲ 6km ⚐ 1.5km ⚲ 12km **Notes** Pets admitted English spoken

MOSLES

⁂ Château d'Argouges

Thibault JEANNE
14400 MOSLES
☎ 02 31 92 52 90 ⚟ 02 31 21 19 99
email: chateauargouges@aol.com
web: www.chateau-argouges.com

Five minutes from Omaha beach and the Port en Bessin golf course, this château has wonderful views over the undulating countryside. On the first floor is a double bedroom, and a suite with two double rooms. On the second floor are two doubles and a triple. All have en suite bathrooms and WCs. Lounge, billiard room, wooded grounds good for walks.

Prices s €90-€135; d €90-€135; t fr €120 **Nearby** ⚓ 5km ⚲ 5km Sea 5km ✎ 0.8km ⚲ 10km Restaurant 5km Water sports 5km ⚲ 5km Spa 30km ⚲ 5km ⚐ 5km ⚲ 10km **Notes** No pets English spoken CC

MOYAUX

⁂ *La Costardière*

Aude LOUVEL
Haras des Auviers, 14590 MOYAUX
☎ 02 31 63 13 50 & 06 74 08 93 36 ⚟ 02 31 63 13 50
email: haras.des.auviers@wanadoo.fr

This property, adjacent to the owners' home, has three designer style rooms, where the use of wood and the décor are very original. All of the rooms are doubles, and one of them has a linking room with child-size twin beds. They all have private bath or shower room and WC. Separate guests' entrance; large garden, garden furniture, horse riding.

Prices not confirmed for 2008 **On Site** ⚓ **Nearby** ⚲ 14km Sea 32km ⚲ 12km Water sports 32km ⚲ 1km ⚐ 1km ⚲ 12km **Notes** No pets

NOYERS-BOCAGE

‼️ ✿ *La Cordière*

Philippe & A-Marie FLAGUAIS

14210 NOYERS BOCAGE

☎ 02 31 77 18 64 & 06 81 17 48 89 📄 02 31 77 18 64

email: anne-marie@fermedelacordiere.com

web: www.fermedelacordiere.com

This equestrian farm offers five south-facing rooms accommodating two, three and five people, all with private shower facilities. Lounge with TV and fireplace, leafy garden with swimming pool. Numerous equestrian activities are available, accompanied and with instructor. Riding school, sandpit and clubhouse with eating area. Inn on site.

Prices not confirmed for 2008 **On Site** ⛄ Private ⌇ **Nearby** ⌇ 15km Sea 25km 🏌 5km Water sports 25km 🌲 1km 🏛 1km � 20km **Notes** Pets admitted English spoken

PARFOURU-SUR-ODON

‼️ *La Garenne Ruaudet*

Remy et Liliane DESQUESNES

14310 PARFOURU SUR ODON

☎ 02 31 77 68 39 & 06 87 34 89 02

email: remi.desquesnes@wanadoo.fr

web: www.leruaudet.net

A magnificent 17th-century manor house, with lots of charm and character. A separate guests' entrance leads to three bedrooms - all doubles, and each with a private bath or shower room and WC. Outside, guests can enjoy the garden, which offers a great deal of variety and interest.

Prices s fr €40; d fr €50; t fr €80 **On Site** ⚘ **Nearby** ⛄ 6km ⌇ 40km Sea 35km ⌇ 4km Restaurant 4km Water sports 35km 🌲 4km 🏛 4km � 25km **Notes** Pets admitted English spoken

PONT-L'EVEQUE

‼️ **Les Vikings**

C ADVIELLE et J ROY

15 Av de la Libération, 14130 PONT L'EVEQUE

☎ 02 31 64 14 44 & 06 81 30 46 94

email: contact@lesvikings.fr

web: www.lesvikings.fr

A beautiful villa with three stylish and very comfortable rooms. They are all on the first floor; one is a double and the other has twin beds. All have private shower and WC. Terrace with garden furniture, and trees in the garden. Not far from the sea at Deauville.

Prices s €59-€69; d €70-€80; t fr €79; extra person €10 **Nearby** ⛄ 0.5km ⌇ 3km Sea 12km 🏌 3km ⌇ 12km Restaurant 1km Water sports 0.5km 🌲 1km Spa 12km ⚘ 12km 🏛 0.8km � 1km **Notes** No pets English spoken

PREAUX-ST-SEBASTIEN

‼️ *La Cour du Houx*

Frédéric et Micheline MONTHUY

14290 PREAUX ST SEBASTIEN

☎ 02 31 32 55 76 & 06 09 95 64 68

email: lacourduhoux@wanadoo.fr

web: http://alacourduhoux.monsite.wanadoo.fr/

In a peaceful setting, this totally restored property has three guest rooms. There is a grade 2 twin-bedded room in the owners' home, with private but not en suite shower room/WC; on the first floor of a separate building is a double room, and a room for four with double and twin beds, both with en suite showers/WCs. Garden furniture.

Prices not confirmed for 2008 **Nearby** Sea 45km 🏌 10km ⌇ 20km 🌲 10km 🏛 10km � 20km **Notes** No pets

PRETREVILLE

‼️ 🍴 *La Sauvagine*

C CAILLOT-FAUQUE

Route de Fervaques, 14140 PRETREVILLE

☎ 02 31 62 80 98

email: la.sauvagine@wanadoo.fr

web: http://sauvagine.normandie.free.fr

This charming house, attractively situated in an area rich in flora and fauna, has five tastefully restored bedrooms. There are four doubles and one room for three, all with private bathrooms and WCs. Two of the rooms have independent access. There is a lounge with TV and an open fireplace. Terrace, garden room. Fishing on site; meals available by arrangement.

Prices not confirmed for 2008 **On Site** 🏌 **Nearby** ⛄ 2km ⌇ 25km Sea 35km ⌇ 9km Water sports 35km 🌲 9km 🏛 9km � 9km **Notes** No pets English spoken

RAPILLY

‼️ **Le Clos Vaucelles**

R et J LETOURNEUR

14690 RAPILLY

☎ 02 31 69 36 47 📄 02 31 69 36 47

This is a modern house with a delightful view and a beautiful flowery garden. It has three double first floor rooms, each with an en suite shower and WC. It has a guests' lounge and a garden room. Possibility of seeing around this dairy farm, which is also close to the GR36 footpath.

Prices s fr €40; d fr €43; t fr €56; extra person fr €10 **Nearby** ⛄ 6km ⌇ 14km Sea 45km ⌇ 17km Restaurant 7km 🌲 6km Spa 40km 🏛 6km � 25km **Notes** No pets

REVIERS

⊞ *La Malposte*

J-Michel et Patricia BLANLOT

15 rue des Moulins, 14470 REVIERS

☎ 02 31 37 51 29   📄 02 31 37 51 29

email: jean-michel.blanlot@wanadoo.fr

web: www.lamalposte.com

This former mill, set on the edge of the sea in a village with authentic architecture, has been fully restored and offers two double rooms and a suite of two double rooms, all with shower facilities and TVs. Lounge and kitchen at guests' disposal. Garden with furniture.

Prices not confirmed for 2008   **On Site** ℘   **Nearby** ⛷ 2.5km ⚓ 15km Sea 2.5km ➔ 2.5km Water sports 2.5km ⌕ 🏛 2.5km ⋙ 18km **Notes** Pets admitted English spoken

⊞ ⋈ *Le Clos St-Bernard*

Michel et Nicole VANDON

36 rue de l'église, 14470 REVIERS

☎ 02 31 37 87 82   📄 02 31 37 87 82

email: leclosbernard@wanadoo.fr

web: www.leclosbernard.com

Tucked away in a little road leading out into the country, this beautiful 18th-century house has three tasteful bedrooms. On the first floor are a double room and a triple; on the second is another double, with its own lounge. Extra bed available. All rooms have private facilities. Guests' lounge with TV opens onto the garden; kitchenette, garden furniture.

Prices not confirmed for 2008   **Nearby** ⛷ 3km ⚓ 15km Sea 3km ℘ 0.3km ➔ 3km Water sports 3km ⌕ 0.3km 🏛 3km ⋙ 15km **Notes** No pets English spoken Open February to 15 December.

ROSEL

⊞ ⋈ ♿ *La Gran'Caye*

B et S LEMANISSIER

11 Chemin du Clos Joli, 14740 ROSEL

☎ 02 31 80 32 99 & 06 87 70 34 17

email: bernard.lemanissier@tiscali.fr

web: www.chambresrosel.com

Just 15 minutes from Caen with its famous Mémorial, this beautiful property has four bedrooms. On the second floor of the hosts' house there are two double rooms, while a separate building provides two more doubles (one with disabled access), each with a linking mezzanine room which can sleep two more people. All rooms have private facilities. Garden furniture.

Prices s €39-€41; d €49-€51; extra person €16-€18; dinner fr €22 **Nearby** ⛷ 3km ⚓ 10km Sea 12km ➔ 8km Water sports 12km ⌕ 4km Spa 15km 🏛 2km ⋙ 8km **Notes** No pets English spoken

RUBERCY

⊞ ⋈ **La Part des Anges**

Michel et Nicole DUVAL

La Poterie, 14710 RUBERCY

☎ 02 31 21 99 60 & 06 82 32 30 43

email: m.n.duval@wanadoo.fr

web: www.la-part-des-anges.fr

A stone-built house not far from Bayeux, with bright and very pleasant rooms. On the ground floor is a double; upstairs is another double which links to an annexe room for two; also a triple, with a linked room suitable for two children (bunk beds). Separate guests' entrance, garden with furniture.

Prices s fr €42; d €52-€62; t fr €78; extra person fr €16; dinner fr €19 **On Site** Restaurant Private ➔   **Nearby** ⛷ 4km ⚓ 12km Sea 12km ℘ 0.3km Water sports 12km ⌕ 4km 🏛 4km ⋙ 15km **Notes** No pets English spoken

SECQUEVILLE-EN-BESSIN

⊞ *Chambre d'hôtes*

Vincent et Annick LE RENARD

14740 SECQUEVILLE EN BESSIN

☎ 02 31 80 39 42

email: famille.lerenard@free.fr

web: http://famille.lerenard.free.fr/fr

This farmhouse offers tastefully restored, restful guest rooms and a warm welcome. The accommodation consists of a double room, a suite with a double and single room, and a further suite with two double rooms. All have private facilities. Garden with furniture available.

Prices not confirmed for 2008   **Nearby** ⛷ 6km ⚓ 20km Sea 15km ➔ 15km Water sports 15km ⌕ 1km 🏛 3.5km ⋙ 15km **Notes** No pets

SOMMERVIEU

⊞ ♥ ⋈ ♿ **Ferme de la Croix de Caugy**

Emmanuel et Sonia BOUET

rue des Sablières, 14400 SOMMERVIEU

☎ 02 31 51 86 32 & 06 14 22 43 31   📄 02 31 51 86 32

email: sonia-manu.bouet@cegetel.net

NORMANDY

This 17th-century farmhouse has five peaceful rooms, each decorated in an individual style. On the ground floor is a double room with disabled access; upstairs are three rooms, doubles and triples, plus a Grade 2 double room which has a linking room for two more people. All rooms have private facilities. Extra bed available. Lounge with TV, kitchen available.

Prices s fr €35; d €40-€45; t €52-€57; extra person fr €12; dinner fr €17 **Nearby** ❤ 2km ⚓ 8km Sea 8km 🏌 8km ⛷ 3km Restaurant 3km Water sports 7km ⛵ 2km Spa 15km 🏛 4km 🚶 5km **Notes** Pets admitted English spoken

ST-AIGNAN-DE-CRAMESNIL

⁂ *Chambre d'hôtes*

E et G DECHAUFOUR

Le Bourg, 14540 ST AIGNAN DE CRAMESNIL

☎ 02 31 23 51 01 📄 02 31 23 13 07

email: edechaufour@cgb-france.fr

web: http://perso.wanadoo.fr/eric-gaetane/accueil.html

This stone building, on a farm and adjacent to the owners' home, has three smart and spacious bedrooms, each with its distinctive style and with frescos on the walls. There is a large bedroom for four, and two double rooms. Each has a private bath or shower room and WC. Courtyard outside.

Prices not confirmed for 2008 **Nearby** ❤ 10km ⚓ 3km Sea 27km 🏌 6km ⛷ 11km Water sports 27km ⛵ 3km 🏛 6km 🚶 12km **Notes** No pets English spoken

ST-CHARLES-DE-PERCY

⁂ Le Château

Jacques DESORMEAU

14350 ST CHARLES DE PERCY

☎ 02 31 66 91 03

email: jacques.desormeau@wanadoo.fr

web: http://perso.wanadoo.fr/chateau-saint-charles

This 18th-century château has architecture reminiscent of Tuscany, and offers two double or triple rooms and a suite of two double rooms. The rooms have exposed floorboards and are equipped with private shower facilities. Inviting and relaxing lounge, garden with furniture and park planted with trees.

Prices s €60-€65; d €70-€80; t fr €70 **On Site** ⛷ **Nearby** ❤ 5km ⚓ 25km Sea 45km ⛷ 14km Restaurant 5km Water sports 50km ⛵ 4km 🏛 14km 🚶 14km **Notes** No pets English spoken Open March to October.

ST-COME-DE-FRESNE

⁂ La Fontaine

et H MARTRAGNY

allée de la Fontaine, 14960 ST COME DE FRESNE

☎ 02 31 22 34 70 & 06 16 82 57 64 📄 02 31 22 34 70

This house overlooks the artificial port of Arromanches, which played such a vital part in the D-day landings. There are three bright double bedrooms, two of which also have a child's bed. All rooms have

private bath or shower room and WC. Cot available. Garden with garden furniture.

Prices s fr €38; d fr €45; t fr €55; extra person fr €10 **Nearby** ❤ 5km ⚓ 12km Sea 0.2km 🏌 0.2km ⛷ 10km Restaurant 1km Water sports 2km ⛵ 2km ⛵ 2km 🏛 2km 🚶 12km **Notes** No pets

ST-DESIR-DE-LISIEUX

⁂ ♿ La Cour St-Thomas

Brigitte BESNEHARD

14100 ST DESIR DE LISIEUX

☎ 02 31 62 87 46 & 06 84 16 08 64 📄 02 31 62 87 46

email: la.cour.st.thomas@wanadoo.fr

web: www.la-cour-saint-thomas.com

Charming accommodation here includes two double rooms and a suite of two double rooms, all with private facilities. Extra beds are available. The kitchen and lounge with TV and fireplace available to guests. Disabled access. Donkey rides offered for children.

Prices d €55-€60 **Nearby** ❤ 15km ⚓ 15km Sea 32km 🏌 1km ⛷ 5km Restaurant 3km Water sports 32km ⛵ 5km ⛵ 5km 🏛 3km 🚶 4km **Notes** No pets Open Easter to 1 November. CC

ST-ETIENNE-LA-THILLAYE

⁂ Le Friche St-Vincent

Guy et Monique BARATTE

14950 ST ETIENNE LA THILLAYE

☎ 02 31 65 22 04 & 06 03 22 29 78 📄 02 31 65 10 16

email: gp.m.baratte@wanadoo.fr

Four double and triple rooms with private shower facilities are available in this comfortable and calm modern house, built in the typical local style. The garden is equally charming and has furniture for guests' use.

Prices s fr €40; d fr €50; t fr €60; extra person fr €10 **Nearby** ❤ 3km ⚓ 4km Sea 8km 🏌 3km ⛷ 8km Restaurant 3km Water sports 3km ⛵ 3km Spa 8km 🏛 3km 🚶 3km **Notes** No pets

ST-GERMAIN-DE-LIVET

⁂ Chambre d'hôtes

Astrid et Gérard MARLET

Route du Château, 14100 ST GERMAIN DE LIVET

☎ 02 31 31 18 24

Set on a hillside, which forms part of a wonderful valley in the Auge area, this house offers two triple rooms and a double, all with private shower facilities. Garden with furniture and château nearby.

Prices s fr €43; d fr €53; t fr €65; extra person fr €14 **Nearby** ❤ 7km ⚓ 25km Sea 35km 🏌 0.5km ⛷ 7km Restaurant 6km ⛵ 7km Spa 30km 🏛 3km 🚶 6km **Notes** No pets

ST-JEAN-LE-BLANC

▦ ⍟ **Les Treize Vieilles**

Pierre et Séverine KELLER

14770 ST JEAN LE BLANC

☎ 02 31 68 80 46 & 06 98 17 71 09

web: www.les13vieilles.com

A complex of old farm buildings dating back to the 18th century, with three spacious, tastefully-decorated en suite double bedrooms. One is on the ground floor; the other two are upstairs, with the possibility of an adjoining room being made available for a child. Living room, and garden with furniture. Meals by arrangement. Accommodation for horses; bungee-jumping close by!

Prices s fr €43; d fr €49; t fr €69; extra person fr €20; dinner fr €21
Nearby ⛳ 17km ⚓ 15km ✐ 2km ⚞ 15km Restaurant 10km ⌕ 3km
⛲ 15km ⌂ 10km ⇷ 22km **Notes** No pets

ST-LAURENT-DU-MONT

▦ *La Vignerie*

Marie-France HUET

14340 ST LAURENT DU MONT

☎ 02 31 63 08 65 ▤ 02 31 63 08 65

email: mfhuet@club-internet.fr

Once used as a cider press, this building is part of a 17th-century complex and houses a double room, family room and three triple rooms, all spacious and with private bathrooms. Communal lounge with fireplace and TV, garden with furniture.

Prices not confirmed for 2008 **Nearby** ⛳ 2km Sea 25km ⚞ 15km
Water sports 25km ⌕ 3km ⌂ 3km ⇷ 15km **Notes** Pets admitted
English spoken

ST-MARTIN-DE-LA-LIEUE

▦ **Vallée Barrée**

J DESHAYES et M LIABEUF

14100 ST MARTIN DE LA LIEUE

☎ 02 31 62 41 28 & 06 75 08 81 07 ▤ 02 31 62 41 28

email: ferme.valleebarre@wanadoo.fr

web: www.chambres-ferme-vallee-barree.com

This old cheese dairy is a delightful mixture of traditional and modern. It stands next to the owners' home, and has three double bedrooms, one on the ground floor and two upstairs. All rooms have a private shower room and WC. The superb garden, with terrace and garden room, has fine views across the valley and towards Lisieux.

Prices s fr €42; d fr €50; t fr €66; extra person fr €16 **Nearby** ⛳ 15km
⚓ 23km Sea 35km ✐ 5km ⚞ 6km Restaurant 2km Water sports 35km
⌕ 6km ⛲ 0.8km ⌂ 2km ⇷ 6km **Notes** No pets English spoken Open
Easter to 1 November.

ST-MARTIN-DES-ENTREES

▦ *Chambre d'hôtes*

P et M LAUMONNIER

9, rue Michel Montaigne, 14400 ST MARTIN DES ENTREES

☎ 02 31 92 76 31 & 06 70 30 08 44

email: pierre.laumonnier@wanadoo.fr

web: http://perso.wanadoo.fr/laumonnier

Close to the D-Day beaches and only five minutes from the historical town of Bayeux, this house offers three triple rooms with private shower facilities and separate access. Additional facilities include a picnic area.

Prices not confirmed for 2008 **Nearby** ⛳ 2km ⚓ 8km Sea 8km ✐ 4km
⚞ 2km Water sports 8km ⌕ 0.5km ⌂ 1km ⇷ 1km **Notes** No pets
English spoken

ST-PIERRE-DU-MONT

▦ **Le Château**

Jean et Marie José BECK

14450 ST PIERRE DU MONT

☎ 02 31 22 63 79 ▤ 02 31 22 63 79

email: chateaustpierre@orange.fr

web: www.chambredhotes-bayeuxarromanchesgrandcamp.com

This 16th-century château has large, warm bedrooms, where the tower has been incorporated into the room - in one case as a superb retro bathroom.

Prices s fr €50; d fr €65; t fr €85; extra person fr €15 **Nearby** ⛳ 11km
⚓ 17km Sea 4km ✐ 4km ⚞ 22km Restaurant 0.2km Water sports 6km
⌕ 4km ⛲ 4km ⌂ 4km ⇷ 0.3km **Notes** No pets

▦ ⍟ **Le Clos Fleuri**

Isabelle WEIDNER

Hameau Lefèvre, 14450 ST PIERRE DU MONT

☎ 02 31 22 96 22 ▤ 02 31 22 96 22

In the main house are two first floor double bedrooms. A separate building offers a bedroom sleeping three guests, all rooms have private shower and wc. A cot is available. Close to the sea, the property has a south facing garden with furniture. Nearby are the historical sites of the landing beaches.

Prices s fr €50; d fr €60; t fr €70; extra person fr €10; dinner fr €23
Nearby ⛳ 15km ⚓ 12km Sea 0.3km ✐ 4km ⚞ 25km Restaurant 4km
Water sports 4km ⌕ 4km ⛲ 4km ⌂ 4km ⇷ 25km **Notes** No pets
English spoken

STE-MARGUERITE-DES-LOGES

▦ **Le Moulin**

Monique LEMESLE

14140 STE MARGUERITE DES LOGES

☎ 02 31 63 13 14 & 02 31 62 70 06

email: moulindecharme@tiscali.fr

web: www.moulindecharme.com

These cosy and tastefully decorated rooms are in a traditional half-timbered Normandy building, in a grassy riverside setting close to the owners' home. On the ground floor is a double room; upstairs is another double and a triple, also an additional room with two beds. All rooms have private facilities. Small kitchen, guests' lounge. Fishing possible locally.

Prices s fr €50; d €55-€65; t fr €70 **Nearby** ⚓ 1km Sea 40km ✎ 4km ⚐ 13km Restaurant 3km Water sports 40km ⚓ 3km 🏠 3km ⚑ 18km **Notes** No pets

SUBLES

⚑⚑⚑⚑ Moulin de Hard

Hélène FICHOT

14400 SUBLES

☎ 02 31 21 37 17 & 06 13 30 53 28

email: contact@moulin-de-hard.com

web: www.moulin-de-hard.com

The landscaped grounds of this beautiful 18th-century mill, with their flowers and streams, make this place exceptional. There are three tastefully decorated double and twin bedrooms, with independent access, on the first and second floors. All have private bath or shower rooms and WCs. Lounge with sofa and fireplace, garden room. Private fishing on site.

Prices s fr €75; d €90-€110; t €115-€135; extra person fr €25 **On Site** ✎ **Nearby** ⚓ 5km ⚐ 12km Sea 13km ⚐ 5km Restaurant 5km Water sports 18km ⚓ 5km ⚑ 5km 🏠 5km ⚑ 5km **Notes** No pets English spoken

TILLY-SUR-SEULLES

⚑⚑⚑ ⊙ Les Tilleuls

Nelly BARATTE

6 Route d'Audrieu, 14250 TILLY SUR SEULLES

☎ 02 31 80 82 10 📄 02 31 80 82 10

Set in a small hamlet in a charming rustic setting, this traditional Norman farmhouse offers two double rooms, one triple room and a family room for four people, all with private bathroom facilities. The kitchen is for guests' use and the hostess offers an excellent range of cuisine and a warm welcome.

Prices s fr €39; d fr €44; t fr €54; extra person fr €8; dinner fr €18 **Nearby** ⚓ 8km ⚐ 20km Sea 20km ✎ 1km ⚐ 12km Restaurant 3km Water sports 20km ⚓ 1km Spa 30km 🏠 1km ⚑ 12km **Notes** No pets

TORTISAMBERT

⚑⚑⚑ Ferme de la Biquetière

M et D FRENEHARD

La Varinière, 14140 TORTISAMBERT

☎ 02 31 62 74 35 📄 02 31 31 57 27

email: clos.la.biquetiere@orange.fr

web: www.ferme-la-biquetiere.com

A goat farm where organic cheese is made. Three double rooms, one of which is in the attic, with an adjoining room for two suitable for family use. All have private bath/shower room, but the facilities for one of the rooms are not en suite. Exceptional views over the lush hillsides of the Pays d'Auge.

Prices s fr €40; d fr €50; t fr €70 **On Site** ✎ **Nearby** ⚓ 7km Sea 48km ✎ 2km ⚐ 15km Restaurant 4km Water sports 48km ⚓ 4km 🏠 4km ⚑ 22km **Notes** No pets English spoken

USSY

⚑⚑⚑ ⊙ *Le Hamel*

Guillaume & Virginie DUCRET

14420 USSY

☎ 02 31 90 32 79

email: guivir@wanadoo.fr

This is a 19th-century house with three individually decorated upstairs bedrooms - two doubles and a room for four, all with private bath or shower room. Guests have their own entrance and living room; outside is a garden with furniture. Not far from Falaise and its château, and well-placed also for exploring the Suisse Normande, with its craggy landscape and wooded hills.

Prices not confirmed for 2008 **Nearby** ⚓ 3km ⚐ 12km Sea 35km ✎ 4km ⚐ 9km Water sports 35km ⚓ 9km 🏠 3km ⚑ 30km **Notes** No pets

VAUCELLES

⚑⚑⚑ Le Relais de l'Aure

Christine et René FATRAS

Hameau Nihault, Bayeaux Vaucelles, 14400 VAUCELLES

☎ 02 31 10 00 45 & 06 72 38 48 82 📄 02 31 10 00 45

email: contact@relaisdelaure.com

web: www.relaisdelaure.com

This pretty 17th-century house is situated a few minutes from the centre of Bayeux. All the bedrooms are bright and spacious: two doubles and a room for four on the first floor; another double with a linking twin on the second floor. Guests have an independent entrance, and all rooms have private facilities. Conservatory and garden with garden room.

Prices s fr €65; d fr €75; t fr €100; extra person fr €25 **Nearby** ⚓ 1km ⚐ 2km Sea 10km ✎ 1.5km Restaurant 0.5km Water sports 10km ⚓ Spa 1km 🏠 1.5km ⚑ 1.5km **Notes** No pets English spoken CC

See advert under BAYEUX

VAUX-SUR-AURE

⚑ Le Hutrel

Jacques et Josiane DANJOU

14400 VAUX SUR AURE

☎ 02 31 92 13 51 & 06 32 38 36 29 📄 02 31 92 13 51

email: jdanjou@tele2.fr

This 18th-century former presbytery is close to Bayeux and the landing beaches. There is one double room on the first floor of the main house; in an adjacent building there is a ground floor room for four, while upstairs there is a double room. All these rooms have private facilities. Also on the first floor is a supplementary twin-bedded room.

Prices s fr €40; d €43-€48; t fr €65; extra person fr €12 **On Site** ☂
🎾 **Nearby** ⚓ 10km Sea 3km 🏌 5km ⚞ 2km Restaurant 3km Water sports 6km ♨ 3km 🎱 1km 🚲 4km **Notes** No pets English spoken

---

VIEUX-FUME

⚑ Le Mesnil d'O

Guy DE CHABANEIX

14270 VIEUX FUME

☎ 02 31 20 01 47 & 06 78 83 69 43 📄 02 31 20 32 87

email: lemesnildo@wanadoo.fr

web: www.lemesnildo.com

This 18th-century château, with its extensive wooded grounds, has four individually decorated guest rooms. On the first floor are two double rooms; and a suite for three people. All of the rooms have a private bathroom and WC. Garden furniture. Convenient for the Abbey of Saint-Pierre-sur-Dives.

Prices s fr €60; d fr €110; t fr €140; extra person fr €30 **Nearby** ⚞ 7km
⚓ 15km Sea 20km 🏌 5km ⚞ 20km Restaurant 5km Water sports 22km
♨ Spa 40km 🎾 20km 🎱 5km 🚲 5km **Notes** No pets English spoken
CC

VOUILLY

⚑ Le Château

James et Marie-José HAMEL

14230 VOUILLY

☎ 02 31 22 08 59 📄 02 31 22 90 58

email: chateau.vouilly@wanadoo.fr

web: www.chateau-vouilly.com

Two double rooms, one triple room and two family suites are available in this 18th-century château, encircled by a moat. There is independent access to the rooms, which all have private bathroom facilities, look over the park, and are spacious and comfortable. Lounge and garden with furniture and picnic area.

Prices s €60-€80; d €70-€90; t fr €110; extra person fr €20
Nearby ☂ 10km ⚓ 28km Sea 10km ⚞ 18km Restaurant 7km Water sports 10km ♨ 7km 🎾 7km 🎱 7km 🚲 10km **Notes** No pets
English spoken Open March to November. CC

ACQUIGNY

⚑ ♿ La Roseraie

Claude et Michèle HEULLANT

Quartier Saint Mauxe, 27400 ACQUIGNY

☎ 02 32 50 20 10 & 08 72 94 78 30 📄 02 32 50 20 10

email: cheullant@wanadoo.fr

web: http://monsite.wanadoo.fr/claude.heullant

Expect a warm welcome in this peaceful home, just a few steps from the gardens of the Château at Acquigny. There are three doubles, a twin, and a single, all with own facilities. Cot available. Kitchenette, open fireplace, living room with billiard table for guests' use. Secure parking.

Prices s €36-€39; d €41-€48; extra person fr €15 **On Site** ☂ 🏌
Restaurant 🎾 **Nearby** ⚓ 8km ⚞ 5km Water sports 0.5km ♨ 0.2km
🎱 1km 🚲 12km **Notes** Pets admitted English spoken

AIZIER

⚑ ◯ Chambre d'hôtes

M.Thérèse et Yves LAURENT

BP 1, Bourneville, 27500 AIZIER

☎ 02 32 57 26 68 📄 02 32 57 42 25

web: www.les-sources-bleues.com

On the 'Route des Chaumières' and overlooking the River Seine, this fine 19th-century brick building is close to the owners thatched house. There are three double rooms and two singles, all with private facilities. Sitting and living room, stair lift and three hectare garden.

Prices not confirmed for 2008 **On Site** 🏌 **Nearby** ☂ 10km ⚓ 15km
Sea 20km ⚞ 15km Water sports 15km ♨ 3km 🎱 5km 🚲 40km
Notes Pets admitted CC

AMECOURT

⚑ ☙ Le Domaine du Pâtis

Jacques et Françoise BODESCOT

1 place du Pâtis, 27140 AMECOURT

☎ 02 32 55 51 51 & 06 89 54 09 01 📄 02 32 55 99 37

email: domainedupatis@free.fr

web: www.domaine-du-patis.com

An 18th-century farmhouse in a forest clearing, with five comfortable bedrooms. There is a two-roomed suite for four (double bed,

ingle bed, and child's bed), and four double rooms. All the guest
accommodation is upstairs, and each of the attractively-decorated
rooms has a private shower room and WC. There are plenty of
interesting towns and villages to visit near by.

Prices s fr €45; d fr €55; t fr €80; extra person fr €25; dinner €12-€15
Nearby ☾ 8km ⌙ 25km ☞ 1km ⚘ 14km Restaurant 8km Water
ports 15km ⚲ 14km ⚐ 5km ⋙ 14km **Notes** No pets English spoken

---

APPEVILLE-ANNEBAULT

⫸ ⦿ **Les Aubépines**

et F CLOSSON MAZE
Aux Chauffourniers, 5 Chemin de la Bergerie,
27290 APPEVILLE ANNEBAULT
☎ 02 32 56 14 25 & 06 72 26 18 59 ▤ 02 32 56 14 25
email: clossonmaze@wanadoo.fr
web: http://perso.wanadoo.fr/lesaubepines/

Completely restored by the proprietors, this 18th-century Norman
farmstead stands in lovely gardens with views over the valley of the
river Risle, which can be explored by canoe or bike. There are two
rooms with double or twin beds and a family suite with two doubles
in separate rooms, all with private facilities and baby equipment.
Dining room with open fireplace. Parking. Montfort Forest nearby.

Prices s fr €55; d fr €60; t fr €80; extra person fr €17; dinner fr €25
Nearby ☾ 15km ⌙ 30km Sea 35km ☞ 15km ⚘ 12km Restaurant 3km
Water sports 13km ⚲ 5km Spa 40km ⚐ 12km ⋙ 40km **Notes** No pets
English spoken Open April to September.

BARNEVILLE-SUR-SEINE

⫸ **Chambre d'hôtes**

rnaud et Françoise BILLY
hemin des côtes, 27310 BARNEVILLE SUR SEINE
☎ 02 32 56 08 87 & 06 24 59 48 08 ▤ 02 32 56 08 87
email: francoise.billy@wanadoo.fr
web: www.chambrebilly.com

This half-timbered house in Norman style is near to the owner's
home and is set within the Regional Nature Park of the Lower
Seine, with unforgettable views over the river from the hang-glider
launching area only 200 metres away. There is a double and two
triples, all with own shower and wc. Reception room and kitchenette
for use of guests.

Prices s fr €35; d fr €46; t fr €54; extra person fr €10 **Nearby** ☾ 5km
⌙ 12km ⚘ 12km Restaurant 1km Water sports 12km ⚲ 1km ⚐ 1km
⋙ 30km **Notes** No pets English spoken

BOSC-BENARD-COMMIN

⫸ **Les Noés**

cques et Evelyne AUVARD
58 Route de Brotonne, 27520 BOSC BENARD COMMIN
☎ 02 32 56 26 24 ▤ 02 32 56 26 24

This charming house is surrounded by apple orchards and grazing
dairy cows. There are two doubles and a triple, all with own facilities.
A corner of the kitchen is for exclusive use of guests.

Prices s fr €32; d fr €42; t fr €51 **Nearby** ☾ 3km ⌙ 20km ☞ 15km
⚘ 12km Restaurant 2km Water sports 25km ⚲ 6km ⚐ 2km ⋙ 30km
Notes No pets

BOURG-BEAUDOUIN

⫸ ✿ **Ferme du Coquetot**

Bénédicte et J.Luc DELAVOYE
46 rue du Coq, 27380 BOURG BEAUDOUIN
☎ 02 32 49 09 91 & 06 16 09 05 00 ▤ 02 32 49 09 91
web: http://fermeducoquetot.free.fr

The proprietors have taken great pride in restoring this farmstead
with its splendid dovecote, which is in a peaceful area near several
châteaux and the RN 14. There are two doubles and a triple room,
all with own facilities and individual décor, a sitting room with open
fireplace and kitchenette for guests' use.

Prices s fr €34; d fr €41; t fr €56; extra person fr €10; dinner fr €16
Nearby ☾ 15km ⌙ 24km ☞ 4km ⚘ 12km Restaurant 4km Water
sports 20km ⚲ 4km Spa 12km ⚐ 4km ⋙ 18km **Notes** No pets
English spoken

BOURGTHEROULDE

⫸ **Château de Boscherville**

Bernadette DU PLOUY
27520 BOURGTHEROULDE
☎ 02 35 87 62 12 & 02 35 87 61 41 ▤ 02 35 87 62 12

An elegantly restored 18th-century château in peaceful parkland, close
to several abbeys and the Lower Seine Regional Nature Park. There
are two doubles, a twin and two triples, all with own facilities. Farm
produce for sale.

Prices s fr €45; d fr €55; t fr €65 **Nearby** ☾ 3km ⌙ 15km ⚘ 12km
Water sports 15km ⚲ 3km ⚐ 3km ⋙ 15km **Notes** Pets admitted
English spoken

BROSVILLE

⫸ ⦿ *Broc Fontaine*

Olivier et Déborah PIVAIN
36 rue Saint Fiacre, 27930 BROSVILLE
☎ 02 32 34 61 78 & 02 32 24 14 72
email: brocfontaine@aol.com

This is a village house in beautiful countryside. There are three
bedrooms - a double and a two-roomed family suite for four in the

CONTINUED

BROSVILLE CONTINUED

main house, and a further family suite in a separate building in the garden. All the rooms have private bath or shower facilities. The garden is exceptional, and leads down to a river.

Prices not confirmed for 2008 **On Site** 🖉 **Nearby** ☆ 1.6km ♨ 16km ⚲ 16km Water sports 20km ♨ 4km ⚌ 6km **Notes** Pets admitted English spoken

CAHAIGNES

♯♯♯♯ Château de Requiecourt

Emmanuelle MILON

5 rue de la Chartreuse, 27420 CAHAIGNES

☎ 02 32 55 37 02 📄 02 32 27 27 28

email: welcome@chateauderequiecourt.com

web: www.chateauderequiecourt.com

This is a 19th-century château, standing in landscaped wooded grounds with a lake. It has five spacious double rooms, each with private bath or shower room and WC. Two of the rooms have terraces, and two are intercommunicating so that they can be used as a suite. Large dining room and conservatory, with view of the grounds and mature woodlands.

Prices s €80-€120; d €85-€125 **On Site** ❄ **Nearby** ☆ 10km ♨ 20km 🖉 10km ⚲ 15km Restaurant 5km Water sports 15km ♨ 5km 🏛 5km ⚌ 15km **Notes** No pets English spoken CC

CAMPIGNY

♯♯♯ Le Clos Mahiet

Régine VAUQUELIN

27500 CAMPIGNY

☎ 02 32 41 13 20

web: http://closmahiet.free.fr

In a peaceful setting, the three guest rooms in this charming half-timbered house include a twin and two doubles, all with own shower and wc. Extra single bed if needed. Sitting room with open fireplace and lovely leafy garden with furniture. Parking. Riders welcome (loose boxes and fodder). Good local walking, riding and mountain biking.

Prices s €41; d €47; extra person €18 **Nearby** ☆ 5km ♨ 37km Sea 30km 🖉 3km ⚲ 5km Restaurant 5km Water sports 8km ♨ 6km Spa 35km 🏛 6km ⚌ 25km **Notes** No pets

CAPELLE-LES-GRANDS

♯♯♯ ⦿ Le Val Perrier

Pierre et Micheline BEAUDRY

27270 CAPELLE LES GRANDS

☎ 02 32 44 76 33 📄 02 32 43 03 15

In the Pays de la Charentonne, Pierre and Micheline welcome guests to their flower-bedecked house in the countryside. Upstairs the green room sleeps three and has independent access, a sitting room and kitchenette. The blue room has a double bed. Both have shower and wc. In the garden, the yellow room sleeps five, with double room, bathroom and kitchenette on the ground floor; and beds for three on a mezzanine. Bike hire. Normandy cuisine is served, with bread baked in a wood-fired oven.

Prices s €33; d €44; t €57; extra person €14; dinner €18 **On Site** ❄ **Nearby** ☆ 3km ♨ 30km 🖉 5km ⚲ 10km Restaurant 5km Water sports 30km ♨ 5km 🏛 5km ⚌ 10km **Notes** Pets admitted English spoken

CAUMONT

♯♯♯ *Maison d'Hôtes de Caumont*

Frédéric et Isabelle PIRON

33 quai de Seine, 27310 CAUMONT

☎ 02 35 68 64 50 📄 08 73 64 78 69

email: piron.caumont@free.fr

web: http://bascaumont.free.fr

This 19th-century house is situated close to the River Seine, and offers guests the unusual sight of big ships apparently moving through the countryside. There are three second floor bedrooms for up to three people, all with private bath or shower room. Plenty of walks are possible.

Prices not confirmed for 2008 **Nearby** ☆ 1km ♨ 8km ⚲ 6km Water sports 8km ♨ 2km 🏛 2km ⚌ 18km **Notes** No pets English spoken

CONCHES-EN-OUCHE

♯♯♯ A L'Orée des Bois

Françoise et Jean CAUVIN

1 chemin de la Mare Sensuelle, Valeuil,

27190 CONCHES EN OUCHE

☎ 02 32 30 49 95 & 06 81 33 64 22

This house is pleasantly situated in a hamlet near to Conches-en-Ouche. It has a double room and a twin (both grade 1) which share bathroom and WC, and a room for three people with private facilities which is grade 3. Cot available. Pleasant lounge with open fireplace, arden with terrace for breakfast in the summer, enclosed courtyard, rest walks.

Prices s €29-€35; d €36-€46; t fr €56; extra person fr €11 **Nearby** ⚓ 3km ⚓ 17km ⚓ 4km ⚓ 2km Restaurant 1km Water ports 40km ⚓ 2km ⚓ 1km ⚓ 1km ⚓ 1km **Notes** No pets English poken

---

CONDE-SUR-RISLE

ⅢⅢ ⅠⓄⅠ ⅋ *Le Nonchaloire*

.Pierre et M.Estelle LOIDON
e Village, 27290 CONDE SUR RISLE
☎ 02 32 56 46 71 & 06 21 02 00 45 ▤ 02 32 56 46 71
mail: jpmeloidon@aol.com

hese 19th-century half-timbered buildings in the Risle valley have een restored to provide accommodation on two floors: on the round floor a double room with access for disabled guests, and a oom for three (double bed and a single) with its own access; upstairs double with its own access, and a two-roomed suite with double nd twin beds. Each room has a private bath or shower room. Dining nd sitting rooms; table tennis, boules. River, lake and forest nearby.

rices not confirmed for 2008 **Nearby** ⚓ 5km ⚓ 40km Sea 40km ⚓ 0.3km ⚓ 10km Water sports 12km ⚓ 0.3km ⚓ 10km ⚓ 25km **lotes** No pets English spoken

---

CONTEVILLE

ⅢⅢ ⅠⓄⅠ *Le Bois des Pierres*

aurence ROUICH
oute d'Honfleur, 27210 CONTEVILLE
☎ 02 32 56 09 71
mail: le-bois-des-pierres@wanadoo.fr
eb: www.leboisdespierres.com

his Norman residence is in a peaceful setting at the gateway Honfleur and has a double room with its own entrance. An utbuilding, also in Norman style, offers two triples and a family room th a double and a single bed, plus a children's corner with two ngle beds. All have private facilities. Breakfast featuring home-made stries and jams is served in the sitting room with open fireplace. rking.

ices not confirmed for 2008 **Nearby** ⚓ 4km ⚓ 30km Sea 20km ⚓ 1km ⚓ 10km Water sports 20km ⚓ 10km ⚓ 30km **Notes** No pets

---

ⅢⅢ **Le Clos Potier**

erre et Odile ANFREY
7210 CONTEVILLE
☎ 02 32 57 60 79 ▤ 02 32 57 60 79

uests are welcomed by the friendly atmosphere of this Norman-style untry home with its antique furniture and, in season, its display of wers. There are four doubles, two in an annexe and all with private cilities. Sitting room with TV, garden, 17th-century cider press. Farm oduce for sale.

ices s fr €55; d fr €60; extra person fr €15 **Nearby** ⚓ 4km ⚓ 30km a 19km ⚓ 3km ⚓ 4km Water sports 10km ⚓ 4km ⚓ 1.5km 13km **Notes** No pets

---

CORNEVILLE-SUR-RISLE

ⅢⅢ **Manoir de Nielles**

Dominique HOCHART
151 Chemin Blanc, Hameau Cardourie,
27500 CORNEVILLE SUR RISLE
☎ 02 32 41 35 02 & 06 09 38 08 64
email: manoirdenielles@wanadoo.fr
web: www.manoirdenielles.free.fr

A warm welcome, spacious rooms, a comfortable house - all you need for a very pleasant stay! On the ground floor is a twin-bedded room; upstairs is a room for four (double bed plus twins), and a double room. A cot is available, and all the rooms have private bathroom and WC. Deer roam in the grounds.

Prices s fr €45; d fr €60; t fr €80; extra person fr €20 **Nearby** ⚓ 10km ⚓ 35km Sea 28km ⚓ 1km ⚓ 6km Water sports 10km ⚓ 6km ⚓ 6km ⚓ 6km **Notes** Pets admitted English spoken

---

EPEGARD

ⅢⅢ ⅋ *La Paysanne*

Maurice et Edith LUCAS
8, rue de l'Eglise, 27110 EPEGARD
☎ 02 32 35 08 95 ▤ 02 32 35 08 95
email: lmauricelucas@club-internet.fr

A spacious and well-restored 17th-century Norman home with a sitting room, kitchen and large wooded garden at guests' disposal. There is a twin and a triple with disabled access, both grade 3, a grade 3 triple and double, and a grade 2 twin. All rooms have own shower and wc.

Prices not confirmed for 2008 **Nearby** ⚓ 0.5km ⚓ 2km ⚓ 20km ⚓ 5km Water sports 30km ⚓ 5km ⚓ 5km ⚓ 30km **Notes** Pets admitted English spoken

---

FATOUVILLE-GRESTAIN

ⅢⅢ ⅠⓄⅠ **La Conterie**

Valérie FRANCOIS-ROZET
Le Bourg, 27210 FATOUVILLE GRESTAIN
☎ 02 32 42 31 25 & 06 14 47 99 80
email: valerie.francois9@wanadoo.fr
web: http://gite.laconterie.free.fr

A few minutes from Honfleur, a large tastefully restored cottage-style property. There is a split-level family suite, with three double-bedded rooms, two of them linked; in an annexe are two more split-level rooms: a double, and a room with two double beds. Each has a lounge area, private bath/shower room and WC. Garden and swimming pool; meals by arrangement.

Prices s €42-€60; d €45-€60; t €80-€85; extra person €20-€30; dinner fr €23 **On Site** Private ⚓ **Nearby** ⚓ 15km ⚓ 15km Sea 8km ⚓ 14km Water sports 14km ⚓ 8km ⚓ 8km ⚓ 20km **Notes** No pets English spoken

FLEURY-LA-FORET

▦ Château de Fleury la Forêt

Pierre et Kristina CAFFIN

27480 FLEURY LA FORET

☎ 02 32 49 63 91 & 06 16 41 64 94 📄 02 32 49 71 67

email: info@chateau-fleury-la-foret.com

web: www.chateau-fleury-la-foret.com

A 17th-century château, with three bedrooms: two doubles, one on the ground floor and one on the first; and a suite for four on the second floor (two rooms - a double and a twin). All have private facilities. Enjoy breakfast in the kitchen, with its collection of copper utensils. Grounds with lime trees; stabling for horses.

Prices s fr €65; d fr €72; t fr €100; extra person fr €15
Nearby ⛷ 5km ⚓ 40km 🎣 3km ⚲ 5km Restaurant 5km Water sports 40km 🏊 5km Spa 25km 🏛 5km 🚶 25km **Notes** No pets English spoken

GAILLON

▦ *Chez Claudine*

Claudine LIONS

2 chemin de Sainte Barbe, 27600 GAILLON

☎ 02 32 52 96 67 & 06 15 07 56 05 📄 02 32 52 96 67

email: c.lions@wanadoo.fr

web: http://claudineagaillon.freesurf.fr

Stop off at Claudine's, at an entrancing spot in the Seine valley, in the park of the remarkable Renaissance Château de Gaillon. Prepare to be enchanted by the comfort and decor of the rooms, and by the welcome from the proprietor. A choice of two independent double rooms in an annexe and one twin room upstairs in the main house, with separate access. Lovely living room with fire, where breakfast is served. Laze on the terrace or in the garden or stroll freely in the parkland on the edge of the forest.

Prices not confirmed for 2008 **Nearby** ⛷ 6km ⚓ 1km 🎣 10km ⚲ 1km Water sports 25km 🏊 0.5km 🏛 0.4km 🚶 4km **Notes** Pets admitted English spoken

GIVERNY

▦ Le Bon Maréchal

Marie Claire BOSCHER

1, rue du Colombier, 27620 GIVERNY

☎ 02 32 51 39 70 📄 02 32 51 39 70

email: aubonmarechal@giverny.fr

web: www.giverny.fr

A former family boarding house in the middle of a village, once frequented by Monet and other artists. It offers a double, a twin with single and a triple with sitting area with satellite TV, in a converted artist's studio. All have private facilities and independent access. Parking available. Breakfast served in sitting room or in the flower-filled garden.

Prices s €55-€65; d €60-€70; t €75-€85; extra person fr €15
On Site 🎣 **Nearby** ⛷ 15km ⚓ 10km ⚲ 4km Water sports 25km 🏊 4km 🚶 4km **Notes** Pets admitted English spoken

▦ Le Clos Fleuri

Claude et Danielle FOUCHE

5 Rue de la Dîme, 27620 GIVERNY

☎ 02 32 21 36 51

email: leclosfleuri27@yahoo.fr

Wander round the large garden or into the famous Impressionist's village of Giverny, or chat to your hosts about their 30 years in Australia. The first floor room can sleep up to three, whilst the two doubles on the ground floor have sitting areas and open onto the terrace. Every room has its own shower room and toilet.

Prices s fr €75; d fr €80; t fr €100; extra person fr €20 **On Site** 🎣 **Nearby** ⛷ 10km ⚓ 15km ⚲ 4km Water sports 25km 🏊 4km 🚶 4km **Notes** No pets English spoken Open April to October.

HONDOUVILLE

▦ ⟮◎⟯ Côté Campagne

J-F et E HOUDAYER

14 Rue du Général de Gaulle, 27400 HONDOUVILLE

☎ 02 32 40 24 98 & 06 83 14 61 52

email: cotecampagne.hotes@orange.fr

web: http://perso.orange.fr/cote.campagne

A pretty village in the Iton valley makes a good setting for this 19th-century house. In an annexe to the owners' home are three individually-decorated bedrooms - a double, a triple and a family suite for four, all with en suite bath or shower room. A cot is available if needed.

Prices s fr €40; d fr €48; t fr €60; extra person fr €12; dinner fr €12 **On Site** Restaurant **Nearby** ♿ 4km ♿ 16km ♿ 1km ♿ Water sports 20km ♿ 1km ♿ 15km ♿ 16km **Notes** No pets English spoken

JUMELLES

ⅲ La Huguenoterie

Jacqueline POITRINEAU
27220 JUMELLES
☎ 02 32 37 50 06 📠 02 32 37 83 36
email: jpoitrineau@hotmail.com
web: www.chez.com/huguenoterie

This old farm building has been converted to house five comfortable guest rooms: a ground floor double and twin and a first floor twin and two triples, all with own shower and wc. Enjoy a gourmet start to the day in the breakfast room.

Prices s fr €41; d fr €52; t fr €70 **Nearby** ♿ 10km ♿ 15km ♿ 10km ♿ 14km Restaurant 4km Water sports 45km ♿ 3km ♿ 4km ♿ 14km **Notes** No pets

LA CROIX-ST-LEUFROY

ⅲ ⅼ◯ⅼ Ferme de la Boissaye

Clotilde et Gérard SENECAL
Hameau de la Boissaye, 27490 LA CROIX ST LEUFROY
☎ 02 32 67 70 85 📠 02 32 67 03 18
email: chambreslaboissiere@wanadoo.fr
web: http://chambres-la-boissiere.com

15th-century manor house providing three doubles and two twins, all with own shower and wc. Lovely sitting room with open fireplace, kitchenette and TV. Games room. Pond with ornamental fowl. Meals by arrangement.

Prices not confirmed for 2008 **Nearby** ♿ 10km ♿ 8km ♿ 3km ♿ 8km Water sports 3km ♿ 3km ♿ 3km ♿ 10km **Notes** No pets

LA HAYE-MALHERBE

ⅲ Château d'Argeronne

Guillemette MARTIN-LAVIGNE
27400 LA HAYE MALHERBE
☎ 06 21 82 36 86 & 02 32 25 11 60 📠 02 32 25 11 58
email: argeronne@wanadoo.fr
web: www.chateau-argeronne.com

This is quite an exceptional place - a fine half-timbered house in an area with lots of forests and beautiful walks all around. It offers four double rooms and a twin-bedded room, all with private bath/shower room and WC. Free internet access; accommodation for horses and their riders.

Prices not confirmed for 2008 **Nearby** ♿ 5km ♿ 15km ♿ 13km Water sports 18km ♿ 2km ♿ 17km **Notes** No pets English spoken

LA LANDE-ST-LEGER

ⅲ La Grange de Saint Léger

Maryvone et Denis ROUSSEL
27210 LA LANDE SAINT LEGER
☎ 02 32 42 28 42 📠 02 32 42 74 99
web: www.grange-saint-leger.com

A vast barn conversion with five bedrooms. Four are upstairs, one with a double bed and a cot, and three triples (double beds plus singles). One of the triples is a split-level room. On the ground floor there is one double room. Each bedroom has a private bath/shower and WC. Guests always appreciate the lounge, with its enormous fireplace.

Prices s fr €45; d fr €50; t fr €62; extra person fr €10 **Nearby** ♿ 4km ♿ 12km Sea 20km ♿ 10km ♿ 23km Water sports 12km ♿ 8km ♿ 8km ♿ 12km **Notes** Pets admitted English spoken

LIEUREY

ⅲ ⅼ◯ⅼ Les Hauts Vents

C et V ANGEVIN CANTAYRE
27560 LIEUREY
☎ 02 32 57 99 27 & 06 19 43 25 21
email: corine.angevin@free.fr
web: http://leshautsvents.free.fr

Protected by banks and hedges, the garden here is like an updated version of the traditional enclosed orchards of the area. An outside staircase leads up to the bedrooms: two doubles, and a family room with a double bed and three singles. All the rooms have private bath/shower and WC. Good area for walking, mountain-biking, or horse-riding.

Prices s fr €47; d fr €57; t fr €70; extra person fr €13; dinner fr €15 **Nearby** ♿ 4km ♿ 25km Sea 30km ♿ 4km ♿ 7km Restaurant 1km Water sports 14km ♿ 1km ♿ 10km ♿ 1km ♿ 18km **Notes** Pets admitted English spoken

LIVET-SUR-AUTHOU

⌗ 🍽 Le Moulin Ponchereux

Yvette et Francis MASCART
Rue de la Vallée, 27800 LIVET SUR AUTHOU
☎ 02 32 45 73 21 & 02 32 43 11 95
email: francis.mascart@free.fr
web: http://francis.mascart.free.fr

Restored with passion by Yvette and Francis, le Moulin Ponchereux is a wonderful place to stop in the Pays de Risle. A real welcome awaits you in this great building. Two ground floor double rooms, and an upstairs room for three, all with private facilities and independent access. Your hosts offer painting classes, both watercolours and in oil.

Prices s fr €52; d fr €58; t fr €73; dinner fr €22 **On Site** 🎣
Nearby ⛵ 5km ♨ 20km Sea 45km ⚲ 15km Restaurant 2km Water sports 5km 🚲 10km 🐎 5km 🏔 5km ⛷ 20km **Notes** No pets English spoken

LORLEAU

⌗ Le Séquoia

Jeanine et Marcel LECOMTE
Hameau Saint Crespin, 9 Rue Bernard Buffet,
27480 LORLEAU
☎ 02 32 48 13 37 📄 02 32 48 13 37
email: info@lesequoia-lecomte.com
web: www.lesequoia-lecomte.com

Three guest rooms have been created here, in two outbuildings. In one, there is a double room downstairs, and a triple (double bed plus a single) upstairs, accessed by an exterior staircase. The other building makes a suite for five, with a double downstairs and a triple (double bed plus single) upstairs. All have private facilities. Big garden, with an ancient redwood.

Prices s fr €40; d €50-€55; t €65-€75; extra person fr €20
Nearby ⛵ 2km ♨ 30km 🎣 2km ⚲ 4km Restaurant 4km Water sports 20km 🚲 4km 🐎 4km 🏔 5km ⛷ 30km **Notes** No pets English spoken

LOUVERSEY

⌗ Le Buisson Margot

Medames BESNARD et JOSSET
19 Route de Beaumont, 27190 LOUVERSEY
☎ 06 89 47 87 73 & 02 32 31 27 96
email: christine.besnard2@wanadoo.fr

Louversey is in a delightful area surrounded by forests and valleys, not far from the attractive little town of Conches-en-Ouche with its half-timbered houses and lively atmosphere. This property right in the village offers a twin-bedded room, a triple, and a split-level family room that can sleep up to five, all with private facilities.

Prices not confirmed for 2008 **Nearby** ⛵ 4km ♨ 20km 🎣 3km ⚲ 3km Water sports 8km 🚲 4km 🏔 3km ⛷ 3km **Notes** No pets English spoken

MAINNEVILLE

⌗ Ferme Sainte Geneviève

J.C et Jeannine MARC
27150 MAINNEVILLE
☎ 02 32 55 51 26 📄 02 32 55 82 27

A farmstead standing in a peaceful setting amid leafy parkland. The five rooms, all with own shower and wc, include two doubles and three triples. Two rooms have access to a kitchenette in an annexe. Parking. Good walking and cycling.

Prices s fr €43; d fr €48; t fr €60 **Nearby** ⛵ 10km ♨ 10km 🎣 6km ⚲ 10km Restaurant 5km Water sports 20km 🚲 10km 🏔 6km ⛷ 15km **Notes** No pets English spoken

MANNEVILLE-SUR-RISLE

⌗ 🍽 Le Clos de la Hudraie

Michèle et Frédéric VINCENT
Le Hudar, 27500 MANNEVILLE SUR RISLE
☎ 06 14 41 92 81
email: frvcent@caramail.com
web: http://closdelahudraie.free.fr

Not far from Pont-Audemer, le Clos de la Hudraie in the Parc des Boucles de la Seine Normande is within striking distance of Honfleur, the Normandy coast and the Route des Abbayes. Departure point for many walking routes. The finely decorated rooms open on to the garden and the countryside. One double room downstairs; one room for three and a twin room upstairs. Preserves such as rhubarb and elder jelly are served at breakfast.

Prices not confirmed for 2008 **Nearby** ⛵ 0.5km ♨ 40km Sea 40km 🎣 4km ⚲ 5km Water sports 7km 🚲 1km 🏔 5km ⛷ 35km **Notes** No pets English spoken Open school holidays and weekends.

MANTHELON

⌗ Le Nuisement

Mélina et Gaël GARNIER
27240 MANTHELON
☎ 02 32 30 96 90 & 06 30 35 37 84 📄 02 32 30 92 44

Guests will receive a warm welcome at this Norman farmstead. The four rooms include a double with whirlpool bath, two doubles with massage shower, and a single in an adjacent room. Spacious living room with open fireplace, kitchen, and sitting and breakfast room. TV if required. Billiard room, fitness room, bikes. Farmhouse foie gras, rillettes and duck confit. Good local walking.

Prices not confirmed for 2008 **Nearby** ⛵ 2km ♨ 20km 🎣 6km ⚲ 8k Water sports 10km 🚲 8km 🏔 6km ⛷ 8km **Notes** No pets English spoken

MARCILLY-LA-CAMPAGNE

⌗ La Mare aux Loups

Suzanne DOUR
Le Moussel, 30 rue de l'Orme,
27320 MARCILLY LA CAMPAGNE
☎ 02 32 60 18 55

Set in a little corner of Normandy and full of character, this large contemporary timbered house is bordered by woods. It has two double rooms and a room with a double and single with private facilities. Breakfasts are served in the large living room with fireplace or on the terrace overlooking the countryside.

Prices s fr €40; d fr €50; t fr €60 **Nearby** ⛷ 6km ⚓ 15km 🏊 8km ⛴ 20km Restaurant 5km 🛝 5km Spa 20km 🏠 1km 🚶 6km **Notes** No pets English spoken

MARTAGNY

⌗ La Rouge Mare

Marie-France LAINE
21 rue de la Chasse, 27150 MARTAGNY
☎ 02 32 55 57 22 📄 02 32 55 14 01

This restored house on a farm is close to the owners' home. There are two triples and a family room with two double beds. Shared shower and wc. Living room, kitchenette, and attractive garden. Close to Lyons-la-Forêt.

Prices s fr €40; d fr €48; t fr €57; extra person fr €13 **Nearby** ⛷ 10km ⚓ 15km 🏊 6km ⛴ 10km Restaurant 6km Water sports 10km 🛝 10km 🏠 3km 🚶 20km **Notes** Pets admitted English spoken

MENILLES

⌗ IOI Les Granges

Chantal et Michel MARCHAND
7 rue Grand Cour, 27120 MENILLES
☎ 02 32 26 45 86 & 06 70 46 87 57 📄 02 32 26 26 45
email: chant.mich.marchand@wanadoo.fr

This pretty little farmhouse, stone-built and timber-framed, is in a delightful village in the Eure valley. The three guest rooms are in an annexe: on the ground floor is a split-level suite for four, and a double-bedded room. Upstairs there is a triple, which has a small linking twin-bedded room, a sauna and a fitness area. All rooms have private facilities. Use of kitchen; garden.

Prices s fr €40; d fr €60; t fr €75; extra person fr €15; dinner fr €20 **On Site** ⚓ **Nearby** ⛷ 5km ⚓ 17km 🏊 0.2km ⛴ 3km Water sports 35km 🛝 1.5km 🏠 3km 🚶 10km **Notes** No pets English spoken

MISEREY

⌗ ❦ IOI La Passée d'Août

DY et V BERTOUT
1 rue du stade, 27930 MISEREY
☎ 02 32 67 06 24 📄 02 32 34 97 95
email: passeedaout@wanadoo.fr
web: http://perso.wanadoo.fr/passee-d-aout

A large family house built of local stone offering four guest rooms in a converted barn. There is a twin, a double, a triple and a family suite with a double and three single beds, all with own shower and wc. Cot available. Sitting room with open fireplace and TV. Meals featuring regional dishes made with farm produce and home-made jams. Attractive garden.

Prices s fr €38; d fr €48; t fr €60; extra person fr €10; dinner €12-€16 **Nearby** ⛷ 5km ⚓ 10km 🏊 8km ⛴ 10km Restaurant 3km 🛝 10km ⚓ 10km 🏠 5km 🚶 10km **Notes** No pets English spoken

NEAUFLES ST MARTIN

⌗ IOI *La Neauflière*

Patrick et Martine MARTY
1 Route de Vernon, 27830 NEAUFLES SAINT MARTIN
☎ 02 32 27 52 26 📄 02 32 27 17 67
email: laneaufliere2@orange.fr

A picturesque place in the Epte valley, bordered by a little river. The rooms are on the first floor: two doubles (can be arranged as twins), and a suite for four (double bed and two singles). All have private facilities. Guests can enjoy a stroll in the garden, or just take things easy. The food is excellent - breakfasts and other meals.

Prices not confirmed for 2008 **On Site** 🏊 **Nearby** ⛷ 3km ⚓ 13km ⛴ 10km 🛝 3km 🏠 3km 🚶 3km **Notes** No pets English spoken

NOTRE-DAME-DE-L'ISLE

⋕⋕⋕ ⊙ *Au Champ du Renard*

N et J-L DESWARTE-DAUCHY

14, rue de Mezières, Pressagny le Val,

27940 NOTRE DAME DE L'ISLE

☎ 02 32 52 64 01

email: auchampdurenard@free.fr

web: http://auchampdurenard.free.fr

An old farmhouse, full of character, built from the local stone, overlooking the River Seine. There are three upstairs rooms, plus a fourth in a converted dovecote. Two of the rooms are doubles; two have twin beds. All the rooms have private shower and WC. Lounge, with books; meals by arrangement (not weekends or public holidays).

Prices not confirmed for 2008   **Nearby** ⛳ 4km ⚓ 10km ⛳ 8km ⟋ 10km Water sports 4km ♨ 4km ▣ 4km ⋔ 10km   **Notes** Pets admitted   English spoken

PONT ST PIERRE

⋕⋕⋕ ⊙ ♿ **Le Cardonnet**

E et E BOQUET THIBERT

27380 PONT ST PIERRE

☎ 02 35 79 88 91   ▤ 02 32 55 97 92

email: emmanuel.eliane@tiscali.fr

web: http://ticketvert.com

Four guest rooms in a separate building, on a farm in quiet and peaceful surroundings on the edge of woodland. There is a triple with disabled access, and three first floor rooms including a family suite with two double beds and four singles, all with own facilities. Spacious sitting room with open fireplace. Stabling for horses available. Close to Rouen, the Seine Valley, Lyons-la-Forêt, and fishing.

Prices s €33-€36; d €41-€46; t €53-€58; extra person fr €12; dinner fr €17   **Nearby** ⛳ 8km ⚓ 25km ⛳ 5km ⟋ 5km Restaurant 5km Water sports 25km ♨ 5km ♟ 25km ▣ 5km ⋔ 25km   **Notes** Pets admitted English spoken

RADEPONT

⋕⋕⋕⋕ **Château de Bonnemare**

A et S VANDECANDELAERE

27380 RADEPONT

☎ 02 32 69 44 33 & 02 32 49 03 73   ▤ 02 32 69 41 07

email: svdc2@wanadoo.fr

web: www.bonnemare.com

A wonderfully impressive place, full of history which your hosts will be delighted to share with you. On the first floor are two luxurious suites with period décor, each consisting of a bedroom, living room and dressing room; downstairs are a further two rooms, a double and a triple, with their own outdoor access. All have private bath/shower room and WC.

Prices s €88-€237; d €96-€245; extra person fr €25   **Nearby** ⛳ 3km ⚓ 15km ⛳ 5km ⟋ 5km Restaurant 5km Water sports 20km ♟ 15km ▣ 3km ⋔ 15km   **Notes** No pets English spoken Open March to December.

REUILLY

⋕⋕⋕ **Clair Matin**

J.Pierre et Amaia TREVISANI

19, rue de l'Eglise, 27930 REUILLY

☎ 02 32 34 71 47   ▤ 02 32 34 97 64

email: bienvenue@clair-matin.com

This delightful manor has a double room plus a family room with twin beds and two single beds on a mezzanine accessed from the courtyard, and a two-room suite with a double and two single beds or the first floor. Lovely garden.

Prices s €45-€55; d €55-€70; t €70-€100; extra person fr €15   **Nearby** ⛳ 5km ⚓ 10km ⛳ 5km ⟋ 10km Water sports 25km ♨ ▣ 5km ⋔ 10km   **Notes** No pets English spoken

ROMILLY-SUR-ANDELLE

⋕⋕⋕ **Les Rives de l'Andelle**

Pascal et Pascale GERARD

11 Chemin du Moulin des Ponts,

27610 ROMILLY SUR ANDELLE

☎ 02 32 48 25 40 & 06 15 66 81 97

email: pascale.gerard12@wanadoo.fr

Not far from the Seine valley with its famous meanders, and in truly beautiful surroundings, this is an excellent spot to recharge your batteries. There are four rooms: two doubles and two triples (double bed and a single in each), all with private shower room and WC. Your hosts will be delighted to advise on the many walks possible from here.

Prices s fr €45; d €50-€55; t fr €65; extra person fr €10; dinner fr €14   **On Site** ⟋   **Nearby** ⛳ 20km ⚓ 20km ⟋ 2km Water sports 20km ♨ 2km ⋔ 20km   **Notes** No pets English spoken

ST-AUBIN-DE-SCELLON

⋕⋕⋕ ⊙ **La Charterie**

Marie Hélène FRANCOIS

27230 ST AUBIN DE SCELLON

☎ 02 32 45 46 52

email: la.charterie@wanadoo.fr

web: http://monsite.orange.fr/la.charterie

An old ribbon factory, now housing four guest bedrooms in the main house. Have a break on the threshold of the Pays d'Auge, where Madame François will be waiting with a warm welcome, and if you wish, she will cook some regional specialities for you. The rooms are upstairs; one double room and three which sleep three. Each has adjacent shower and wc. Living room and dining room on ground floor.

Prices s fr €55; d fr €60; t fr €75; extra person fr €15; dinner fr €23   **Nearby** ⛳ 7km ⚓ 25km Sea 42km ⛳ 15km ⟋ 15km Restaurant 5km Water sports 20km ♨ 4km ▣ 4km ⋔ 15km   **Notes** No pets English spoken

ST-AUBIN-LE-GUICHARD

⊪ **Manoir du Val**

Michel et Mauricette PARENT

27410 ST AUBIN LE GUICHARD

☎ 02 32 44 41 04 & 06 87 15 17 03

A warm welcome is guaranteed at this 16th-century residence with dovecote. The comfortable and spacious rooms include two doubles and a family suite with a double bed and a single bed in a small adjoining room, all with own facilities. Breakfast served in living and dining room with open fireplace. Cider for sale.

Prices s fr €48; d fr €55; t fr €75; extra person fr €20   **Nearby** ⚓ 3km ⚲ 25km ⚐ 9km ⚘ 15km Restaurant 8km Water sports 9km ⚑ 2km Spa 15km 🏠 8km 🚶 15km   **Notes** No pets

ST-CYR-LA-CAMPAGNE

⊪ **Chambre d'hôtes**

Brigitte MAUGER

Mairie Saint Cyr la Campagne,

27370 ST CYR LA CAMPAGNE

☎ 02 35 81 90 98 📠 02 35 81 22 76

Guests are offered rooms in this old brick-built town hall, which has been renovated in contemporary style and is located in the green and leafy valley of the River Oison. Each double room has telephone and own bath and wc. Additional beds available. TV in shared sitting room. Four garages. Several long-distance footpaths.

Prices s fr €32; d fr €37; extra person fr €8   **Nearby** ⚓ 10km ⚲ 15km ⚐ 5km ⚘ 7km Restaurant 2km Water sports 20km ⚑ 0.5km 🏠 1.5km 🚶 8km   **Notes** No pets

ST-DENIS-LE-FERMENT

⊪ *La Levrière*

Sandrine et Pascal GRAVIER

24 rue Guérard, 27140 ST DENIS LE FERMENT

☎ 02 32 27 04 78 & 06 79 43 92 77 📠 02 32 27 04 78

email: pascalgravier@hotmail.com

web: www.normandyrooms.com

A traditional Normandy longhouse dating back to the 18th century. Two converted outbuildings house the three comfortable bedrooms. There is a twin-bedded room, a triple (double bed plus a single), and a room with a double bed and three singles. The house is in the heart of the village, with a river running through the grounds. Good for walking and mountain-biking.

Prices not confirmed for 2008   **Nearby** ⚓ 2km ⚲ 15km ⚐ 0.5km ⚘ 6km Water sports 8km ⚑ 6km 🏠 0.1km 🚶 6km   **Notes** No pets English spoken

ST-GEORGES-DU-VIEVRE

⊪ **La Pommeraie**

Marie et Patrick BELACEL

Route de Giverville, 27450 ST GEORGES DU VIEVRE

☎ 02 32 42 53 92 & 06 77 55 83 21

email: marie.belacel@wanadoo.fr

web: www.lapommeraie27.com

A lovely 19th-century property in Anglo-Norman style, set in peaceful surroundings. There is a double in a completely renovated Norman building, and a double and twin in another building with separate entrance. All have private facilities; cot available. Shared sitting and dining rooms. Stabling and feed for horses. Walking routes close by. Baby-sitting by arrangement.

Prices s fr €45; d fr €52; extra person fr €10   **On Site** ⚓ **Nearby** ⚲ 25km Sea 35km ⚐ 6km ⚘ 0.5km Restaurant 0.1km Water sports 6km ⚑ 0.5km 🌳 0.5km 🏠 0.1km 🚶 20km   **Notes** Pets admitted English spoken

ST-GERMAIN-LA-CAMPAGNE

⊪ *Le Feugrés*

Jean Luc et Denise BREHIN

27230 ST GERMAIN LA CAMPAGNE

☎ 02 32 44 78 10 & 06 71 71 77 13

email: feugres@free.fr

web: http://feugres.free.fr

The hosts here give a warm welcome, and pay attention to the important details. The rooms are bright, with modern comforts. On the ground floor is a double-bedded room; upstairs are two rooms which can be arranged as doubles or twins. Each room has a private shower and WC. Lounge, dining room, use of kitchen.

Prices not confirmed for 2008   **Nearby** ⚓ 6km ⚲ 40km ⚐ 6km ⚘ 15km Water sports 35km ⚑ 3km 🏠 7km 🚶 15km   **Notes** No pets

⊪ *Le Grand Bus*

B et L DE PREAUMONT

27230 ST GERMAIN LA CAMPAGNE

☎ 02 32 44 71 14 📠 02 32 46 45 81

email: chambrepreaumont@libertysurf.fr

web: http://perso.libertysurf.fr/depreaumont

This fine 18th-century residence is set in a lovely wooded park. Rooms include a double and double linked with a twin, a twin and a suite with a double plus two single beds in an adjoining room. All rooms have own facilities. Games room and billiards. Small pets welcome. Bike hire and GR26 footpath nearby.

Prices not confirmed for 2008   **Nearby** ⚓ 3km ⚲ 40km ⚐ 6km ⚘ 16km Water sports 35km ⚑ 1km 🏠 6km 🚶 16km   **Notes** Pets admitted English spoken

ST-OUEN-DES-CHAMPS

₩ ⶮⵔⵇ Les Trois Cornets

Marc et Martine LANGLOIS
27680 SAINT OUEN DES CHAMPS
☎ 02 32 56 83 58 & 06 20 54 49 99 📄 02 32 56 83 58
email: marc.langlois7@wanadoo.fr
web: www.lestroiscornets.com

In the Parc Naturel Régional des Boucles de la Seine, a magnificent
old barn on a grand scale, which has been skilfully converted into a
spacious house. Three double rooms and two rooms for four (double
bed and twin beds in each), all with en suite facilities. Guest lounge,
covered swimming pool. Meals available by arrangement.

Prices s fr €38; d fr €43; t fr €53; extra person fr €10; dinner fr €20
On Site Private ⵟ **Nearby** ⵛ 15km ⵒ 35km Sea 30km ⵔ 7km ⵟ
Water sports 10km ⵓ 7km ⵘ 2km ⵯ 7km **Notes** No pets English
spoken

ST-PIERRE-DE-CORMEILLES

₩ La Grange Saint Pierre

Agnés et Pascal BAUDERE
Le Boulay, 27260 SAINT PIERRE DE CORMEILLES
☎ 02 32 42 23 09 & 06 89 42 32 00
web: www.la-grange-saint-pierre.com

Wonderful views from this house, especially from the terrace which
looks over the Calonne valley. Three triple rooms, each with a double
bed and a single, all have private shower and WC. Lounge and salon
available.

Prices s fr €53; d fr €58; t fr €73 **Nearby** ⵛ 2km ⵒ 15km Sea 23km
ⵔ 15km ⵟ 15km Restaurant 1km Water sports 12km ⵓ 2km Spa 25km
ⵘ 2km ⵯ 15km **Notes** No pets English spoken

ST-PIERRE-DU-VAL

₩ ⶮⵔⵇ Le Pressoir du Mesnil

Bruno et Martine MATYJA
27210 ST PIERRE DU VAL
☎ 02 32 56 12 48 & 06 08 02 44 76 📄 02 32 56 12 48
email: mcroizie@yahoo.fr
web: http://lepressoirdumesnil.com

A few minutes from Honfleur, this half-timbered house's modern
decorations complement its ancient building materials. There are three
double rooms, and a family suite with three double beds. The suite
and one of the double rooms have kitchenettes, and all the rooms
have private bath or shower room and WC. Terrace, with furniture;
meals by arrangement.

Prices s €75-€80; d €80-€85; t €90-€95; extra person fr €10; dinner
fr €30 **On Site** ⵞ **Nearby** ⵛ 5km ⵒ 20km Sea 10km ⵔ 10km
ⵟ 10km Water sports 7km ⵓ 10km Spa 25km ⵘ 4km ⵯ 20km
Notes No pets English spoken

ST-SIMEON

₩ ⶮⵔⵇ ⵛ Le Coquerel

Jean Marc DRUMEL
27560 ST SIMEON
☎ 02 32 56 56 08 📄 02 32 56 56 08
email: moreau-drumel@wanadoo.fr
web: http://perso.wanadoo.fr/chambreshotes

This great half-timbered house is perfect for a charming stop-over,
tucked away in a countryside rich in local legends. One double and
one room for three on the ground floor; one double and two rooms
sleeping four upstairs. All have private facilities. Guests' lounge with
fireplace. The breakfast preserves and bread are home made.

Prices s €46-€51; d €50-€58; t €56-€67; extra person fr €14; dinner
fr €22 **Nearby** ⵛ 4km ⵒ 40km Sea 35km ⵔ 15km ⵟ 10km
Restaurant 0.7km Water sports 15km ⵓ 5km ⵘ 5km ⵯ 25km
Notes Pets admitted English spoken

ST-SYLVESTRE-DE-CORMEILLES

₩ ⶮⵔⵇ La Maison Pommerose

Geneviève VAN HOVE
Le village, 27260 ST SYLVESTRE DE CORMEILLES
☎ 02 32 57 13 05 & 06 83 38 74 69
email: genevieve.vanhove@wanadoo.fr
web: www.pommerose.com

A faithfully restored 17th-century, half-timbered house with superb
views. Generous breakfasts are served in the beautiful dining room
or on the terrace using seasonal produce. The first floor bedrooms
offer a range of accommodation: double, double with single bed
on a mezzanine, family room with double, single and child beds.
Each room has a private shower or bathroom. Pets admitted by
reservation.

Prices s fr €55; d fr €60; t fr €75; extra person fr €15; dinner fr €20
Nearby ⵛ 7km ⵒ 17km Sea 30km ⵔ 2km ⵟ 17km Restaurant 1.5km
Water sports 17km ⵓ 2km Spa 30km ⵞ 1.5km ⵘ 1.5km ⵯ 17km
Notes Pets admitted English spoken

ST-SYMPHORIEN

♯♯♯ ⊙ & La Ferme Saint Nicolas

Corinne MARCHAND

27500 ST SYMPHORIEN

☎ 02 32 56 67 36 & 06 17 50 26 86   📄 02 32 56 67 36

email: corinne.marchand@tiscali.fr

web: www.lafermesaintnicolas.com

Bright and cheerful accommodation in the green countryside. There are four bedrooms in an annexe to the owners' home: a double-bedded room and a twin-bedded room downstairs, and two more doubles upstairs. Each upstairs room has a lounge area, and all rooms have private facilities. Meals are available by arrangement - Madame Marchand is a keen cook.

Prices s €50-€60; d €58-€68; t fr €90; extra person €10-€15; dinner fr €22.50   **On Site** ❦   **Nearby** ⛷ 2km ♨ 17km Sea 20km ♬ 7km ⤳ 9km Restaurant 2km Water sports 12km ♨ 2km Spa 30km ⓔ 2km ⋙ 15km   **Notes** No pets English spoken

STE-OPPORTUNE-LA-MARE

♯♯♯ ⊙ La Vallée

E et J BLONDEL

Quai de la Forge, 27680 STE OPPORTUNE LA MARE

☎ 02 32 42 12 52   📄 02 32 42 12 52

This is a fine half-timbered house with views across the lake. There are three upstairs rooms, two doubles and a triple (double bed and single). All the rooms have private bath or shower room and WC. Downstairs is a lounge with an open fire. Mountain bikes are available.

Prices s fr €35; d fr €44; t fr €55; extra person fr €10; dinner fr €23   **On Site** ❦   **Nearby** ⛷ 7km ♨ 30km Sea 30km ♬ 12km ⤳ 7km Restaurant 2km Water sports 8km ♨ 10km ⓔ 2km ⋙ 10km   **Notes** No pets

VERNEUIL-SUR-AVRE

♯♯♯♯ ⊙ Château de la Puisaye

Diana COSTES

Lieu dit La Puisaye, 27130 VERNEUIL SUR AVRE

☎ 02 32 58 65 35 & 06 85 07 61 24

📄 02 32 58 65 35

email: info@chateaudelapuisaye.com

web: www.chateaudelapuisaye.com

Re-energise yourselves wandering round the beautifully wooded parkland surrounding this charming 19th-century château. Or relax in the large lounge with its piano or make use of the bicycles, table tennis or fishing on offer. There is a range of suites on two floors each with their own bathroom. Ask about the group or long stay discounts.

Prices s €75-€100; d €85-€110; t fr €150; extra person fr €20; dinner €14-€45   **On Site** ♬   **Nearby** ⛷ 1km ♨ 9km ⤳ 3km Water sports 20km ♨ 3km ⓔ 3km ⋙ 3km   **Notes** No pets English spoken CC

MANCHE

ANGOVILLE-AU-PLAIN

♯♯♯ Ferme la Guidonnerie

Maurice LEONARD

50480 ANGOVILLE AU PLAIN

☎ 02 33 42 33 51

This cattle farm, ten kilometres from the landing beaches, has three guest rooms in a building separate from the owners' home. On the first floor there is a double room and a triple; in an extension, with its own entrance, is a split-level room with two double beds. All have private facilities, and there are two kitchen areas. Meals by arrangement.

Prices s fr €33; d fr €38; t fr €43   **Nearby** ⛷ 9km ♨ 15km Sea 9km ♬ 1km ⤳ 5km ♨ 5km ❦ 5km ⓔ 5km ⋙ 6km   **Notes** No pets English spoken

ARDEVON

♯♯♯ Chambre d'hôtes

Juliette HALLAIS

La Rive, 50170 ARDEVON

☎ 02 33 60 80 30 & 06 87 29 64 63

email: juliette.hallais@wanadoo.fr

web: http://juliette.ifrance.com

This is a modern house, surrounded by garden, standing in the countryside close to a small village. A separate guests' entrance leads to the first floor, where there are two double rooms, and a two-room suite with two double beds. All rooms have a private shower room/WC. There is a kitchenette for guests' use. Footpaths pass close by.

Prices s fr €30; d fr €36; t fr €50; extra person fr €10   **Nearby** ⛷ 5km ♨ 15km Sea 40km ♬ 4km Restaurant 0.5km ♨ 10km ❦ 2km ⓔ 2km ⋙ 7km   **Notes** Pets admitted

AUCEY-LA-PLAINE
❦ La Jouvenelle
Pierre et Janine DESCAMPS
14 Rue des Fourchemins, 50170 AUCEY LA PLAINE
☎ 02 33 48 60 01 🖹 02 33 48 60 01
email: la.jouvenelle@wanadoo.fr
web: http://perso.wanadoo.fr/la.jouvenelle

In a small village on the bay of Mont-St-Michel, the owners of this restored stone-built house run a snail farm. All the bedrooms are upstairs: a double, two triples, and a family room for four. All have private shower room/WC. An extra folding bed is available. Large lounge and guests' kitchenette; meals are available by arrangement.

Prices s fr €35; d fr €45; t fr €60; extra person fr €10 **Nearby** ⚓ 10km ℰ 3km Restaurant 5km ⌇ 3km ⋈ 4km **Notes** No pets

BARNEVILLE-CARTERET
La Tourelle
Gérard LEBOURGEOIS
5 rue du Pic Mallet, 50270 BARNEVILLE CARTERET
☎ 02 33 04 90 22 & 06 88 71 97 97

In the little town of Barneville not far from the sea, this 16th-century house has a double room, a triple, and a room for four. In a separate building, looking on to an enclosed courtyard is another double room. All rooms have a private bath or shower room and WC. Separate access for guests; lounge; garage for cycles and motor bikes.

Prices s fr €39; d €44-€47; t fr €60; extra person fr €10 **Nearby** ⚓ 2km ⌇ 2km Sea 2km ℰ 1km ⌇ 2km ⚲ 2km ⋈ 28km **Notes** No pets

BEAUVOIR
❦ Ferme Saint Joseph
Michel et M.Brigitte FAGUAIS
Polder Saint-Joseph, 50170 BEAUVOIR
☎ 02 33 60 09 04 & 06 84 17 10 38 🖹 02 33 48 62 25
email: mbfaguais@wanadoo.fr
web: www.chez.com/fermesaintjoseph

All the bedrooms at this market garden property have views of Mont St-Michel. On the ground floor is a triple room, with a kitchenette; upstairs are two more triples, and a two-roomed suite with a double bed and twins. There is another double room in a separate building. All have private facilities. Large lounge with guests' kitchenette on the first floor.

Prices s fr €40; d fr €50; t fr €60; extra person fr €10 **Nearby** ⚓ 3km ⌇ 20km ℰ 0.5km ⚲ 20km Restaurant 1km ⌇ 7km Spa 45km ⚲ 2km ⌂ 3km ⋈ 7km **Notes** Pets admitted

BENOISTVILLE
La Cuvette
Sylvie et Jean Marie PEZET
5 la Cuvette, 50340 BENOISTVILLE
☎ 02 33 01 02 02 & 06 08 63 68 11 🖹 02 33 01 00 77
email: jm.pezet@wanadoo.fr
web: www.domaine-la-cuvette.com

A property ideally situated for discovering the Anse de Sciotot, with its impressive waves and memorable sunsets, or for walks in the Cotentin valleys. Three rooms, each with double bed, shower room and WC, are on the first floor of an extension to the owners' house with independent access. Kitchenette, living area and salon. Boules pitch.

Prices not confirmed for 2008 **Nearby** ⚓ 1.5km ⌇ 20km ℰ 1km Restaurant 2km ⌇ 2.5km ⋈ 17km **Notes** No pets English spoken

BLAINVILLE-SUR-MER
♿ Village Grouchy
Robert et Jacqueline SEBIRE
11 rue du Vieux Lavoir, 50560 BLAINVILLE-SUR-MER
☎ 02 33 47 20 31 🖹 02 33 47 20 31
email: jr.sebire@free.fr
web: http://jr.sebire.free.fr

This 17th-century stone and granite family home is in an old seaside fishing village. Three first-floor bedrooms for two or three guests and one double all have private WC and shower room. An outbuilding houses a further ground-floor double with private shower room and WC. Lounge, summer kitchen, garden rooms, cycle hire. Barbecue available.

Prices s fr €32; d fr €42; t fr €52 **On Site** ⚲ **Nearby** ⚓ 2km ⌇ 2km ℰ 2km ⚲ 12km Restaurant 1km ⌇ 2km ⌂ 0.5km ⋈ 12km **Notes** No pets

BRICQUEBEC
La Butte
Denise MESNIL
14 rue de Bricqueville, 50260 BRICQUEBEC
☎ 02 33 52 33 13

In the centre of a small town, opposite the château, this farmhouse is 100 metres from a voie verte ("green way" for walkers and cyclists). On the ground floor is a double room; upstairs is a room (grade 2) and annexe for up to four people. Another double room, with kitchenette, is in a small annexe. All rooms have private facilities.

Prices s fr €32; d fr €42; t fr €56; extra person fr €16 **Nearby** ⚓ 15km ⌇ 17km Sea 15km ℰ 1km ⚲ 13km Restaurant 0.1km ⌇ 0.8km ⌂ 0.1km ⋈ 13km **Notes** Pets admitted

CEAUX

⦚ Le Mée Provost

Henri et Agnès DELAUNAY
50220 CEAUX
☎ 02 33 60 49 03

This attractive 18th-century farmstead has five guest rooms: two adjacent doubles and a family room (double) with its own entrance and three rooms with six beds in a separate building. All rooms have own shower and wc. Sitting room and kitchen. Breakfasts feature the arm's produce. Special rates for groups of four.

Prices s fr €38; d fr €43; t fr €60; extra person fr €8 **Nearby** ⛷ 4km ⚓ 6km ✎ 1km ⟲ 6km Restaurant 1.5km ☕ 6km Spa 25km ☂ 3km ⌂ 5km ⚑ 9km **Notes** No pets Open January to November.

COUTANCES

⦚ Manoir de l'Ecoulanderie

Béatrice de PONFILLY
50200 COUTANCES
☎ 02 33 45 05 05
email: contact@l-b-c.com
web: www.l-b-c.com

This lovely 18th-century property with grounds and terrace enjoys panoramic views of the cathedral. Second floor bedrooms comprise a spacious double with optional adjoining room for two. In a garden outbuilding, two further bedrooms (twin or double beds). Private bathrooms and WCs. TV in bedrooms, kitchenette. Gourmet breakfast served in the shade of the magnolia. Non-smoking bedrooms. Closed parking. Indoor swimming pool, heated all year.

Prices s €90-€110; d €110-€130; t fr €155; extra person fr €25 **On Site** ☂ Private ✎ **Nearby** ⛷ 3km ⚓ 9km Sea 9km ✎ 1km Restaurant 1km ☕ 0.3km ⌂ 0.3km ⚑ 3km **Notes** No pets English spoken

FERMANVILLE

⦚ Fort du Cap Lévi

, le Cap Lévi, 50840 FERMANVILLE
☎ 02 33 05 96 07 ▤ 02 33 23 68 69
mail: chambre.fermanville@cg50.fr

fantastic location, which you can really appreciate from the breakfast om, with its uninterrupted panoramic views of the sea. Five marine-emed bedrooms with shower room or bathroom and private WCs.

rices s fr €40; d €60-€65; t fr €85; extra person fr €20 **On Site** ✎ **earby** Sea 0.1km Restaurant 3km ☕ 15km ⌂ 0.2km ⚑ 25km **otes** No pets English spoken CC

FRESVILLE

⦚ Manoir de Vauville

Maryse VIEL
Vauville, 50310 FRESVILLE
☎ 02 33 21 15 77 & 06 99 67 11 57 ▤ 02 33 21 15 77
email: manoirdevauville@wanadoo.fr
web: http://perso.wanadoo.fr/manoirdevauville

A peaceful spot in the Parc Naturel Régional, not far from the landing beaches. There are three bedrooms, doubles and twins, all on the ground floor of a converted farm outbuilding. All have private showers/WCs, and there is a folding bed available. Lounge with kitchenette; garden furniture; baby equipment available.

Prices s fr €35; d fr €45 **Nearby** ⛷ 10km ⚓ 8km ✎ 2km ⟲ 15km Restaurant 7km ☕ 7km ☂ 7km ⌂ 7km ⚑ 15km **Notes** No pets English spoken

GATTEVILLE-LE-PHARE

⦚ Chambre d'hôtes

Daniel et Francette LETERRIER
7 rue Nehean, 50760 GATTEVILLE LE PHARE
☎ 02 33 23 10 19 & 06 80 17 51 94

The peace and quiet offered by this 18th-century stone house surrounded by green countryside are as much appreciated as the attentive welcome by its owners. The rooms, all with shower room/ WC, have independent access and comprise a ground floor double; a large double upstairs on a mezzanine with salon and view to the lighthouse; and a suite for four people with direct access to the terrace and garden, with double bed downstairs and two singles upstairs. Private parking.

Prices s fr €50; d €56-€68; t fr €93; extra person fr €25 **Nearby** ⛷ 6km ⚓ 15km ✎ 1km Restaurant 1km ☕ 0.6km ☂ 1km ⌂ 0.1km ⚑ 25km **Notes** No pets English spoken Open April to 1 November.

⦚ ⦿ Manoir de l'Epine

M-E BOILLETOT
4 Chemin du Brot, Hameau Denneville,
50760 GATTEVILLE-LE-PHARE
☎ 02 33 22 04 55 ▤ 02 33 22 04 55
email: manoirdepine@gmail.com
web: www.manoir-epine.com

An authentic 16th-century manor house - an attractive and peaceful spot in the Saire valley 15 minutes from Cherbourg and just two kilometres from the sea. There are three double bedrooms, one on the first floor and two on the second. All rooms have private shower and WC.

Prices s fr €58; d fr €68; extra person €18 **Nearby** ⛷ 8km ⚓ 15km ⟲ 25km Restaurant 2km ☕ 2km ☂ 2km ⌂ 3km ⚑ 25km **Notes** Pets admitted English spoken Open 2 March to 14 November.

GENETS

⌗⌗ Le Moulin

Louis DANIEL
50530 GENETS
☎ 02 33 70 83 78   📠 02 33 70 83 78

A lovingly restored watermill with waterfall, retaining much charm. Guest rooms are on the second floor with a separate entrance. Three doubles and a twin, private WCs and shower rooms. Guest dining room. Maison de la Baie 300mtrs.

Prices s fr €30; d fr €40   **Nearby** ⚓ 1km Restaurant 0.1km 🏊 0.5km ⋙ 9km   **Notes** No pets English spoken

GRAIGNES

⌗⌗ Domaine du Mémorial

Marcel et Denise DELAUNAY
3 place de la Libération, 50620 GRAIGNES
☎ 02 33 56 80 58   📠 02 33 56 80 58

This restored building within a park is at the heart of an area renowned for horse breeding. First-floor bedrooms comprise two doubles, a grade 2 twin room and a room with annexe which has two doubles. All have private WC and bath or shower. Breakfast is served in a charming dining room. One night free after five nights (except Jul-Aug).

Prices s €38-€43; d €43-€49; t fr €66; extra person fr €20   **On Site** ⛲ **Nearby** ⚓ 5km 🎣 12km ⛳ 2km ⛵ 🏊 12km ⋙ 12km   **Notes** Pets admitted English spoken

HUISNES-SUR-MER

⌗⌗ Bel Horizon

Martine THEBAULT
9 rue du Moulin de la Butte, 50170 HUISNES SUR MER
☎ 02 33 70 94 07 & 06 89 24 27 64   📠 02 33 70 94 07
email: thebault.chambrehote@wanadoo.fr
web: http://thebaultchambrehote.monsite.wanadoo.fr

A big stone house with an unrestricted view of Mont-St-Michel and the bay. A peaceful spot, and an ideal base for exploring all this area has to offer. There are four first floor bedrooms: two doubles, a triple (double bed and a single), and a double with an adjoining double room. All have private facilities. Guests' entrance; kitchenette.

Prices not confirmed for 2008   **Nearby** ⚓ 6km Restaurant 0.2km 🏊 3km ⋙ 7km   **Notes** No pets

⌗⌗ ⚕ Le Moulin de la Butte

Béatrice RABASTE
11 rue du Moulin de la Butte, 50170 HUISNES SUR MER
☎ 02 33 58 52 62 & 06 82 30 49 16   📠 02 33 58 52 62
email: beatrice.rabaste@club-internet.fr
web: www.bedandbreakfastineurope.com/lemoulindelabutte

This large new house has a marvellous hillside location in a charming village, and has guest rooms with views of Mont-St-Michel. The two twin rooms include one with disabled access, and there are three double rooms; all with own shower and wc. Breakfast and sitting room. Summertime carriage rides.

Prices not confirmed for 2008   **Nearby** ⚓ 6km ⛳ 6km Restaurant 0.3km 🏊 3km ⋙ 7km   **Notes** No pets

JUILLEY

⌗⌗ ❧ Ferme du Grand Rouet

Christian et Isabelle FARDIN
50220 JUILLEY
☎ 02 33 60 65 25 & 06 80 42 78 18
email: c.fardin@wanadoo.fr
web: http://perso.wanadoo.fr/christian.fardin

A farm offering four guest rooms including a family room, all with own shower and wc and a separate entrance. Kitchenette for exclusive use of guests. Views of garden and pool. Country inn 3km.

Prices s fr €42; d fr €50; t fr €55; extra person fr €10   **Nearby** ⚓ 6km ⛳ 3km 🎣 15km Restaurant 4km 🏊 3km 🏛 4km ⋙ 15km   **Notes** No pets English spoken

⌗⌗ Les Blotteries

Jean-Malo TIZON
50220 JUILLEY
☎ 02 33 60 84 95
email: bb@les-blotteries.com
web: www.les-blotteries.com

This pretty, 18th-century property is situated where Brittany meets Normandy. There is one guest room in the main house, with a double bed and two singles. In a separate building is a family room for four; in another building is a double-bedded room. All rooms have private facilities. Ample breakfasts are served in the owners' house. Garden furniture.

Prices s fr €50; d €67-€72; t €82-€90; extra person fr €15   **On Site** ⛳ ⛲ **Nearby** ⚓ 5km Restaurant 5km 🏊 6km ⋙ 10km   **Notes** Pets admitted English spoken CC

JUVIGNY-LE-TERTRE

♥ Le Logis de Juvigny

Marylène FILLATRE
50520 JUVIGNY LE TERTRE
☎ 02 33 59 38 20 📄 02 33 59 38 20
email: fillatre.claude@wanadoo.fr
web: http://gitefillatre.free.fr

Enjoy local produce and homemade jam at this manor farm dating back to the 17th century. The first-floor bedroom here has a double and twin beds. In the separate former pigeonnier there is a ground-floor double and upstairs a double and two mezzanine singles. Private WC and shower rooms. Separate entrances. Lounge and kitchen area.

Prices s €31-€35; d €38-€42; t €48-€52; extra person fr €10 **On Site** ✍ **Nearby** ⛵ 12km Restaurant 2km ⚓ 2km ⟁ 25km **Notes** Pets admitted English spoken

LA BESLIERE

Le Manoir

Michel et Marguerite BENSET
0320 LA BESLIERE
☎ 02 33 61 32 23

An old farmhouse, with an adjacent gîte rural, peacefully situated in the green countryside. On the ground floor is a double room with kitchenette; upstairs there are two more doubles and a triple. Folding bed available. All rooms have private showers/WCs, and there is a separate guests' entrance.

Prices s fr €33; d fr €40; t fr €50 **Nearby** ⛵ 6km ⚓ 10km Restaurant 3km ⚓ 4km ⟁ 12km **Notes** No pets

LA CROIX-AVRANCHIN

Mouraine

Evelyne MESLIN
0240 LA CROIX AVRANCHIN
☎ 02 33 48 35 69 📄 02 33 48 35 69
email: bnb1@nooplanet.com
web: www.nooplanet.com

Madame Meslin, the owner of this property, is keen to share her love of nature and of Normandy with her guests. In a beautiful green setting, her restored farmhouse has one (grade 2) double bedroom, and two further doubles with their own separate entrance.

Prices not confirmed for 2008 **Nearby** ⛵ 5km ⚓ 40km ✍ 5km Restaurant 5km ⚓ 5km ⟁ 9km **Notes** No pets English spoken

LA GLACERIE

Source des Oiseaux

Daniel et Cathy AVENEL
Bas de la Loge, 50470 LA GLACERIE
☎ 02 33 22 13 30 & 06 81 80 49 31 📄 02 33 22 24 76
email: avenel.daniel@neuf.fr
web: http://sourcedesoiseaux.neuf.fr

Midway between the impressive views at la Hague and the unusual countryside of the Saire valley, this age-old property once provided

drinking water for the entire Cherbourg community. The restored house is spacious and comfortable, and the wooded grounds still yield inexhaustible spring water. Double room, and a family room with double bed and sofa bed, both with shower room/WC.

Prices s fr €55; d fr €60 **Nearby** ⛵ 5km ⚓ 7km Sea 3km ✍ 3km ✈ 3km Restaurant 3km ⚓ 3km ⚓ 3km ⟁ 1km ⟁ 1.5km **Notes** Pets admitted English spoken

LAMBERVILLE

Le Château

F et E de BRUNVILLE
50160 LAMBERVILLE
☎ 02 33 56 15 70 & 06 80 40 96 02 📄 02 33 56 35 26
email: ef.brunville@wanadoo.fr

Between Mont-St-Michel and the landing beaches, this property has belonged to the same family for generations. The rooms are upstairs in a converted outbuilding: two spacious doubles and a twin-bedded room, all with private bath/shower room and WC, and views across the grounds and lake. Lounge with open fire and guests' kitchen. Fishing, boating, cycling possible.

Prices s fr €45; d fr €55 **On Site** ✍ **Nearby** ⛵ 10km ⚓ 40km Restaurant 8km ⚓ 7km ⚓ 9km ⟁ 9km ⟁ 17km **Notes** No pets

LE MESNIL-AUBERT

Ferme de la Peurie

Antoinette DAVENEL
4 rue du Calvaire, 50510 LE MESNIL AUBERT
☎ 02 33 51 96 31

Rémy and Antoinette welcome you to their restored 17th-century farmhouse in a quiet country location. First-floor bedrooms comprise two doubles and a twin with private WC and shower. In addition a spacious canopied double with mezzanine, hydro-massage shower and WC. Guest lounge. Separate entrance.

Prices s €35-€45; d €40-€50; t fr €70; extra person fr €20 **On Site** ✍ **Nearby** ⛵ 5km ⚓ 12km Restaurant 5km ⚓ 5km ⟁ 10km **Notes** No pets

LE VAL-SAINT-PERE

La Maraîcherie

René DESGRANGES
50300 LE VAL ST PERE
☎ 02 33 58 10 87 & 06 72 67 10 11
web: www.chambre-hotes-maraicherie.c.la

This 18th-century farmhouse stands on the edge of Mont-St-Michel Bay. The three guest rooms in a separate building all have their own shower and wc. Kitchen for exclusive use of guests.

Prices s fr €40; d fr €45; extra person fr €12 **On Site** ⚓ **Nearby** ⛵ 0.5km ⚓ 5km ✍ 0.5km ✈ 5km Restaurant 3km ⚓ 5km ⟁ 5km ⟁ 5km **Notes** No pets

LES PIEUX

▦ La Couerie

Catherine et Roland SAUVAGE

13 la Couerie, 50340 LES PIEUX

☎ 02 33 20 46 06

email: sauvage.roland@wanadoo.fr

web: http://alehautdainville.monsite.wanadoo.fr

Well-presented chambre d'hotes, situated in a typical peaceful Cotentin hamlet. One twin room on the ground floor, two double rooms on the first floor, each with private facilities. Kitchenette, barbecue and garden furniture. Non-smoking. Rates reduce depending on length of stay. Ideal for exploring the local area and enjoying the superb seascapes. 18km from Cherbourg. Land-yachting nearby.

Prices s €37-€45; d €42-€50; extra person fr €15 **Nearby** ⚓ 1km ⚲ 18km Sea 1km ℘ 1km ↖ 2km Restaurant 1km ⌔ 2km Spa 3.5km 🏛 2km ⋈ 18km **Notes** No pets English spoken

LES VEYS

▦ Haras du Vieux Château

Denis et Myriam AVENEL

50500 LES VEYS

☎ 02 33 71 00 38 🗐 02 33 71 63 38

email: contact@haras-vieux-chateau.com

web: www.haras-vieux-chateau.com

A stud farm dating back to the 16th century in an exceptional setting, offering a combination of old-world charm and modern comforts. There are five guest rooms, four doubles and a single, all upstairs, and all with private shower room/WC. There is a separate guests' entrance, and guests have their own lounge.

Prices s fr €65; d fr €80 **On Site** Private ↖ **Nearby** ⚲ 30km ℘ 1km Restaurant 1km ⌔ 5km ℘ 8km 🏛 1km ⋈ 8km **Notes** No pets Open April to 1 November.

LIEUSAINT

▦ Le Haut-Pitois

André et Ghislaine MOUCHEL

50700 LIEUSAINT

☎ 02 33 40 19 92

A home full of regional history with bedrooms in the main house and a separate building. Main house: second floor family room. Separate building first floor: one double, two triples, one room with annexe for four people. Shower room and private WC for each bedroom. Guest kitchen, lounge and fireplace. Breakfast served around one large table in the hosts' lounge.

Prices s fr €36; d fr €43; t fr €54; extra person fr €11 **Nearby** ⚓ 20km ⚲ 16km ℘ 0.3km ↖ 5km Restaurant 5km ⌔ 5km 🏛 5km ⋈ 5km **Notes** No pets

LINGREVILLE

▦ Blanchepré

Christine et Thierry GAUTIER

7 Rue des Chouers, Village Hue, 50660 LINGREVILLE

☎ 02 33 07 91 24 & 06 78 23 06 33

email: thierry.gautier13@wanadoo.fr

web: www.chez.com/blanchepre

This stylish white house stands out in the middle of a country garden. The ground-floor bedroom and annexe overlook the garden and comprise a double and two singles. Upstairs there is a large room with double (160cm) bed and another individually styled double. Private WCs and bathrooms. Kitchen available for guests. Games area. Quiet surroundings, fine sandy beach.

Prices s fr €39; d fr €39; t fr €49; extra person fr €10 **Nearby** ⚓ 3km ⚲ 6km Sea 1.5km ℘ 6km ↖ 15km Restaurant 3km ⌔ 1km ℘ 3km 🏛 1km ⋈ 15km **Notes** No pets English spoken

LONGUEVILLE

▦ Le Manoir de Longueville

Ludovic et Sandrine BOUCHART

50290 LONGUEVILLE

☎ 02 33 50 66 60 & 06 03 48 88 22 🗐 02 33 50 66 60

web: www.chateau-longueville.com

This 18th-century château, with its park and lakes, makes a grand setting for a holiday. On the first floor is a twin-bedded room; a two-roomed suite for two; and a suite for four (two doubles). On the second floor is a three-roomed suite for six (two doubles and twins). All have private facilities, some with power shower or jacuzzi.

Prices s €90-€115; d €120 **Nearby** ⚓ 2km ⚲ 2km Sea 2km ↖ 5km Restaurant 4km ⌔ 2km Spa 5km ⋈ 5km **Notes** Pets admitted Open Easter to 1 November.

MONTCHATON

▦ Le Quesnot

J et G GERMANICUS

3 rue du Mont César, 50660 MONTCHATON

☎ 02 33 45 05 88

With its landscaped garden, this attractive stone house is close to a traditional village, which has a hilltop church with lovely views of the surrounding countryside. There are three double rooms with private facilities, in a separate building with its own sitting and breakfast room. Canoeing 500mtrs.

Prices s fr €40; d fr €45 **Nearby** ⚓ 4km ⚲ 5km Sea 4km ℘ 1km ↖ 5km Restaurant 1km ⌔ 4km ℘ 4km 🏛 0.5km ⋈ 6km **Notes** No pets English spoken

MONTFARVILLE

▓▓▓ Clémasine

Patrick GANCEL

49 rue de la Grandville, 50760 MONTFARVILLE

☎ 02 33 22 08 63 & 06 83 12 25 85

email: patrick.gancel@clemasine.com

web: www.clemasine.com

A pretty 17th-century house which happily combines ancient and modern thanks to its tasteful restoration. It can sleep up to 12 people: two ground floor rooms each have double bed with twin beds on a mezzanine level; upstairs are a further two double rooms; all have private shower room/WC. Huge living room and salon at guests' disposition. Courses in patchwork and painting sometimes arranged. No smoking.

Prices s €55-€65; d €65-€70; t €83-€88; extra person fr €18
Nearby ⚓ 5km ⚴ 20km Sea 1km ⚑ 1km ➴ 30km Restaurant 1km ⚖ 2km ⛪ 2km ⊯ 25km **Notes** No pets English spoken

MONTGARDON

▓▓ ✿ ⦿ Le Mont Scolan

Yves et Nicole SEGUINEAU

50250 MONTGARDON

☎ 02 33 46 11 27 ▤ 02 33 46 11 27

A working farm between the sea and the countryside. Upstairs in the owners' home is a twin-bedded room and a room for three; in an annexe are two double rooms. All have private shower/WC; the rooms in the annexe share a lounge area and kitchenette. Games room with billiards and table football.

Prices s fr €40; d fr €46; t fr €62; extra person fr €16; dinner fr €19
Nearby ⚓ 2km ⚴ 25km ⚑ 5km ➴ 25km Restaurant 2km ⚖ 2km ➴ 15km ⛪ 2km ⊯ 25km **Notes** Pets admitted

NEGREVILLE

▓▓▓▓ Château de Pont Rilly

Jean Jacques ROUCHERAY

50260 NEGREVILLE

☎ 02 33 40 47 50

email: chateau-pont-rilly@wanadoo.fr

web: www.chateau-pont-rilly.com

Guests can have a taste of château life in this superb, meticulously restored 18th century property. There are three elegant and comfortable wood-panelled double rooms, plus a two-roomed suite. Luxurious bathrooms, with Valognes stonework. Set in 15 hectares of grounds with ancient trees, their own system of waterways and a mill.

Prices s fr €150; d fr €150; t fr €150 **On Site** ⚑ **Nearby** ⚓ 6km ⚴ 15km ➴ 5km Restaurant 5km ⚖ 6km ➴ 15km ⛪ 5km ⊯ 5km **Notes** No pets English spoken CC

ORVAL

▓▓▓ Chambre d'hôtes

Catherine SIMON

8 Rue du Pois de Senteur, 50660 ORVAL

☎ 02 33 45 59 29 & 06 88 59 32 45 ▤ 02 33 45 59 29

email: cath1.simon@wanadoo.fr

Bedrooms are in a former farm building. Grade 2 second floor rooms: double with adjoining private shower room and WC; and a room with two doubles, bathroom and private WC on the landing. In an extension with separate entrance, first floor bedrooms: one with a double and single, private shower room and WC; one double with private WC and bathroom. Large guest lounge and kitchen. Garden room, table-tennis, paddling pool and portico.

Prices s €35-€40; d €40-€45; t fr €55; extra person fr €10
Nearby ⚓ 2km ⚴ 9km ⚑ 0.2km ➴ 5km Restaurant 5km ⚖ 0.2km ⊯ 5km **Notes** Pets admitted English spoken Open July to August.

PORTBAIL

▓▓▓ Le Hameau de Gouey

Bernadette VASSELIN

16 Rue Gilles Poërier, 50580 PORTBAIL

☎ 02 33 04 80 27 & 06 67 75 31 52 ▤ 02 33 04 80 27

A beautifully restored stone longhouse, close to the beach and town. Ground-floor bedroom with double and single; first floor two bedrooms for two/three and one double, with adjoining room for three. Each has private shower room and WC. Separate entrances. Spacious well-equipped guest lounge with fireplace. Private terrace and garden. Enclosed courtyard with parking.

Prices s fr €40; d fr €45; t fr €60; extra person fr €10 **Nearby** ⚓ 1km ⚴ 5km Sea 1.5km ⚑ 10km Restaurant 1km ➴ 1km ⛪ 1km ⛪ 1km ⊯ 25km **Notes** No pets

RAUVILLE-LA-PLACE

▓▓▓ La Cour

Monique TARDIF

50390 RAUVILLE LA PLACE

☎ 02 33 41 65 07

email: mt.lacour@wanadoo.fr

web: www.chambres-lacour.com

An old manor house dating back to the 14th century, with Norman ceilings and terracotta floor tiles. On the first floor are two spacious rooms - two double beds or one double plus children's bunks. There are two further double rooms, and a twin-bedded room. All have private facilities, and there is a separate guests' entrance. Guests' lounge.

Prices s €37-€40; d €42-€47; t fr €60; extra person fr €10
Nearby ⚓ 14km ⚴ 20km ⚑ 3km ➴ 3km Restaurant 3km ⚖ 3km ➴ 3km ⛪ 3km ⊯ 14km **Notes** Pets admitted

REGNEVILLE-SUR-MER

⊞ & Le Clos Postel

Robert et Lydie FRIAUX
5 route d'Urville, village d'Urville,
50590 REGNEVILLE SUR MER
☎ 02 33 07 12 38 & 06 14 19 20 19
email: clospostel@hotmail.com
web: www.clospostel.com

This former 17th-century presbytery overlooks the Sienne bay. The interior is beautifully decorated with lovely books, paintings and antiques. First-floor suite of two rooms, one with double and single beds; one duplex at garden level (one double and one single), with kitchenette. The dovecote has two bedrooms (one double). Private shower or bathroom and WC. Guest lounge. Cycle hire.

Prices s fr €75; d €75-€95; t fr €100   **On Site** ⚲   **Nearby** ⚑ 9km ⚓ 9km ✐ 0.1km ⚹ 9km Restaurant 3km ⌇ 9km Spa 22km ⌂ 4km ⋙ 9km   **Notes** No pets English spoken Open February to November.

SERVON

⊞ Chambre d'hôtes

Patrick et Fabienne BAUBIGNY
30 rue du Pont Morin, 50170 SERVON
☎ 02 33 60 34 14 & 06 82 14 55 71
email: fabienne@servon.net
web: www.servon.net

Four bright and spacious guest bedrooms have been created in an old inn adjacent to the owners' home. On the first floor are a triple room and a family room; on the second floor are two doubles. All have private shower rooms/WCs. Extra bed available. Breakfasts served in the lounge, which also has a kitchenette for guests' use.

Prices s fr €32; d €38-€42; t fr €50; extra person fr €9   **On Site** ✐ **Nearby** ⚑ 7km ⚓ 15km ⚹ 15km Restaurant 1km ⌇ 10km ⌂ 10km ⋙ 10km   **Notes** No pets English spoken

ST-AUBIN-DE-TERREGATTE

⊞ ❤ ⫶◯⫶ & Ferme de la Patrais

Jean-Pierre et Hélène CARNET
3 La Patrais, 50240 ST AUBIN DE TERREGATTE
☎ 02 33 48 43 13 ▤ 02 33 48 59 03
email: helene.carnet@laposte.net
web: www.fermedelapatrais.com

Four guest rooms on a farmstead including a double and three family rooms for four (one with disabled access and another with sitting area). All have their own entrance, shower and wc; additional beds available. A separate building has a kitchenette, sitting area and games room for use of guests. Meals by arrangement.

Prices s fr €35; d fr €42; t fr €52; extra person fr €10; dinner fr €18 **Nearby** ⚑ 3km ⚓ 40km ✐ 3km ⚹ 15km Restaurant 2km ⌇ 2km Spa 40km ⚲ 15km ⌂ 5km ⋙ 18km   **Notes** No pets English spoken

ST-CYR-DU-BAILLEUL

⊞ ❤ Chambre d'hôtes

Jean et Antoinette HARDY
Le Bourg, 50720 ST CYR DU BAILLEUL
☎ 02 33 59 43 89 ▤ 02 33 59 39 85

A stone house in the heart of the village. First floor double and separate annexe with two singles and one grade 2 double. Private WC and shower room. In a half-timbered former stable, a further double and in a separate annexe two singles. Private bathrooms and WCs. Guest lounge and kitchen area. Cycle hire, baby equipment, games. Farm visits on request. Climbing 8 km. Pet supplement charged. Discounts available for longer stays and children under 12.

Prices not confirmed for 2008   **Nearby** ⚑ 7km ⚓ 30km ✐ 8km Restaurant 0.1km ⌇ 5km ⋙ 30km   **Notes** Pets admitted

ST-JAMES

⊞ ⫶◯⫶ La Gautraie

Catherine et François TIFFAINE
50240 ST JAMES
☎ 02 33 48 31 86 ▤ 02 33 48 58 17
email: ctiffaine@hotmail.fr
web: http://tiffaine.perso.cegetel.net

A farmhouse, in a pleasant setting, with a real local flavour. All the guest rooms are upstairs: two family rooms for four, one with a kitchenette, and two double rooms. All the bedrooms have a private bath or shower room and WC. Table tennis. Meals are available by arrangement.

Prices s fr €40; d €50-€55; t fr €60; extra person fr €10; dinner €18 **On Site** ⚲   **Nearby** ⚑ 2km ⚓ 40km ✐ 4km ⚹ 20km Restaurant 2km ⌇ 2km ⌂ 1km ⋙ 15km   **Notes** No pets English spoken

ST-MARTIN-DE-VARREVILLE

⊞ Manoir de Juganville

Pascal et Chantal JEAN
39 Les Mézières, 50480 ST MARTIN DE VARREVILLE
☎ 02 33 95 01 97 & 06 31 67 72 01
email: cp-jean@wanadoo.fr
web: www.juganville.com

A 16th-century manor house, with its own quiet grandeur. The hosts give a warm welcome, and can also provide courses in relaxation and stress management. A stone circular staircase leads to the first floor, with its two-roomed suite for four; a triple room; and a double room with canopy bed, all with private facilities. Lounge with books; accommodation for horses.

Prices s €55-€80; d €70-€90; t €85-€105; extra person fr €15 **Nearby** ⚑ 7km ⚓ 7km ✐ 15km ⚹ 20km Restaurant 4km ⌇ 4km ⚲ 10km ⌂ 5km ⋙ 15km   **Notes** No pets English spoken

ST-MICHEL-DES-LOUPS

‖‖ ⓘⓞ⑤ & Ferme de Cheux

Yolaine HALLEGUEN

50740 ST MICHEL DES LOUPS

☎ 02 33 48 14 88 & or 06 73 33 86 51

email: message@fermedecheux.eu

web: www.fermedecheux.eu

A remarkable architectural ensemble from the 18th century, conveniently situated between Mont St Michel and Granville. Separate entrance. Ground floor bedroom with 160cm double and an accessible twin room. First floor double, single and twin rooms, each with sofa and private facilities.

Prices s fr €60; d fr €70; t fr €88; extra person fr €18; dinner fr €20 **Nearby** ⛳ 2km ⚓ 15km Sea 5km ♪ 2km Restaurant 5km ⌇ 5km ⚑ 5km ⓑ 5km ⚐ 10km **Notes** No pets English spoken

STE-MERE-EGLISE

‖‖ Ferme-Manoir La Fière

Yves et Chantal POISSON

12 rte du M des Parachutistes, 50480 STE MERE EGLISE

☎ 02 33 41 31 77 & 06 11 17 29 26

email: poisson.yves2@wanadoo.fr

A traditional Normandy manor house, in the Cotentin peninsula on the site of the 1944 landings. In a separate building from the owners' home is a double room with its own kitchenette, and a split-level triple room (three single beds). In the manor house is a first floor double room, with an inter-communicating single room. All have TV and private facilities.

Prices s fr €32; d fr €42; t fr €57 **On Site** ♪ **Nearby** ⛳ 3km ⚓ 12km ✈ 18km Restaurant 0.3km ⌇ 3km ⚑ 3km ⓑ 3km ⚐ 15km **Notes** Pets admitted English spoken

TAMERVILLE

‖‖ Manoir de Bellauney

C ALLIX DESFAUTEAUX

50700 TAMERVILLE

☎ 02 33 40 10 62 🖩 02 33 40 10 62

email: bellauney@wanadoo.fr

web: www.bellauney.com

This former stately home dating from the 15th and 16th centuries has been sympathetically restored. Overlooking the park, each double

bedroom tells the story of a period of its history. Norman times on the ground floor, Medieval and Louis upstairs. Private WCs and bath or shower rooms. Separate entrance.

Prices s €45-€65; d €55-€75; t fr €100 **Nearby** ⛳ 7km ⚓ 10km ♪ 2km Restaurant 3km ⌇ 3km ⚑ 3km ⚐ 3km **Notes** No pets English spoken Open April to mid October.

TESSY-SUR-VIRE

‖‖ & La Minoterie

Serge et Josy LESAGE

chemin de la Minoterie, Route de Pont Farcy,

50420 TESSY SUR VIRE

☎ 02 33 56 98 55

email: chambres@la-minoterie.com

web: www.la-minoterie.com

The Vire valley is a delightful area, and this house is just a few yards from the towpath. It has three individually-designed rooms which can be arranged as doubles or twins, all on the ground floor and one with disabled access. All have a private bath or shower room and WC. Garden furniture and kitchen for guests use; bikes available nearby.

Prices s fr €50; d fr €55; extra person €10 **Nearby** ⛳ 5km ⚓ 15km ♪ 0.1km ✈ 15km Restaurant 3km ⌇ 0.5km ⚑ 0.2km ⓑ 0.2km ⚐ 15km **Notes** No pets

TOURLAVILLE

‖‖ Manoir Saint-Jean

Honoré et Simone GUERARD

50110 TOURLAVILLE

☎ 02 33 22 00 86

Close to the Ravalet château and not far from the Pointe de Barfleur and the Cap de la Hague, this property has three bedrooms, all upstairs. There is a double, plus a child's bed; a twin-bedded room; and another double room with separate entrance. All the rooms have a private bath or shower room and WC. Easy access to footpaths.

Prices s €51-€55; d €54-€58 **Nearby** ⛳ 3km ⚓ 2km Sea 4km ♪ 4km ✈ 4km Restaurant 3km ⌇ 2.5km ⚑ 6km ⓑ 2.5km ⚐ 6km **Notes** No pets

VALOGNES

✦✦✦ Manoir de Savigny

Eric et Corinne BONNIFET

50700 VALOGNES

☎ 02 33 08 37 75 & 06 72 40 88 04

email: reservation@manoir-de-savigny.com

web: http://manoir-de-savigny.com

This fine house on a dairy farm has three guest rooms furnished in country style and with their own entrance. There is a double with separate room for two, another double, and a family room with a double and two single beds, all with own shower and wc. Superior breakfasts. Laundry room. Restaurants and inn nearby. Granville 20km.

Prices s €55-€95; d €60-€110; t €115-€125; extra person fr €15 **Nearby** ♿ 2km ♨ 15km ♣ 1km Restaurant 2km ♒ 2km ♒♒ 2km **Notes** No pets English spoken

VAUDRIMESNIL

✦✦✦ ♿ La Rochelle

Alain et Olga BERTHOU

12 rte de Coutances, 50490 VAUDRIMESNIL

☎ 02 33 46 74 95

A 17th-century farmhouse, in the heart of the peaceful Manche countryside. On the ground floor is a bedroom for three; upstairs are two more similar rooms, one with a kitchenette. All the rooms have their own showers/WCs. Separate guests' entrance. In the grounds, near to a lake, a pigeon loft dating back to the Middle Ages serves as a games room.

Prices s fr €38; d fr €45; t fr €57 **Nearby** ♿ 5km ♨ 9km Sea 15km ♣ 1km ♣ 12km Restaurant 3km ♒ 3km ♒ 20km ♒ 3km ♒♒ 12km **Notes** No pets

VERGONCEY

✦✦✦✦ Château de Boucéel

R et N de ROQUEFEUIL

50240 VERGONCEY

☎ 02 33 48 34 61 ▤ 02 33 48 16 26

email: chateaudebouceel@wanadoo.fr

web: www.chateaudebouceel.com

This property dates back to the 12th century. The main château, built in 1763, is decorated with ancestral portraits. Ground floor suite for three. First floor: two suites for three, all with private bathrooms and WCs; two double rooms, spacious bathrooms and private WCs. Non-smoking bedrooms. Dining room, library, billiard table. Separate entrance. English style grounds, lakes and chapel. Baby equipment.

Prices s €135-€160; d €140-€165; t €160-€180; extra person fr €20 **Nearby** ♿ 6km ♨ 37km ♣ 13km Restaurant 6km ♒ 6km **Notes** No pets English spoken Open February to December.

VESSEY

✦✦✦ ♥ ⦿ La Butte

Rachel et François TRINCOT

50170 VESSEY

☎ 02 33 60 20 32 ▤ 02 33 58 48 84

This working farm has four guest bedrooms, upstairs in a converted outbuilding close to the owners' home. Three of the rooms are doubles; the other has twin beds. All the rooms have private shower rooms/WCs. Lounge for guests' use, with kitchenette and open fire. Breakfasts and other meals (by arrangement) served in the owners' dining room.

Prices s fr €35; d fr €44; dinner fr €16 **Nearby** ♿ 10km ♨ 25km ♣ 1km Restaurant 10km ♒ 1km ♒ 10km ♒ 3km ♒♒ 10km **Notes** No pets

✦✦✦ ♥ ⦿ La Senellée

Thérèse CHARTOIS

50170 VESSEY

☎ 02 33 60 11 51 ▤ 02 33 60 11 51

email: lasenellee@orange.fr

web: http://chambresvessey.ifrance.com

Five twin bedrooms with private washrooms and WC. One room is at ground-floor level and has its own entrance. There is a lounge and a kitchenette available for guests' use. An extra bed can be provided for a supplement.

Prices s fr €34; d fr €44; t fr €54; extra person fr €10; dinner fr €16 **Nearby** ♨ 30km ♣ 3km ♣ 22km Restaurant 6km ♒ 3km ♒ 6km ♒ 6km ♒♒ 6km **Notes** No pets English spoken

VIDECOSVILLE

✦✦✦ Manoir Saint-Laurent

Annick LEVAILLANT

50630 VIDECOSVILLE

☎ 02 33 54 17 58

A character house close to a former farm. Tasty breakfasts are served in a superb lounge with traditional Norman furnishings and fireplace. One double and one room with double and single on the first floor. Private WC and shower room. Guest lounge.

Prices s fr €35; d €47-€52; t fr €63; extra person fr €12 **Nearby** ♿ 5km ♨ 8km ♣ 10km Restaurant 5km ♒ 8km ♒ 5km ♒ 5km ♒♒ 10km **Notes** Pets admitted

ORNE

ALENCON-SUR-VALFRAMBERT

ⅢⅢ ⅠⓄⅠ Château de Sarceaux

H et J GICQUEL DES TOUCHES
61250 ALENCON SUR VALFRAMBERT
☎ 02 33 28 85 11
email: chateaudesarceaux@yahoo.fr
web: www.chateau-de-sarceaux.com

An 18th-century hunting lodge which has been in the same family
for generations. There are two double rooms and a twin-bedded
room, and two suites which can accommodate up to three guests.
All have private bath or shower room and WC. Lounge, kitchen,
and 12 hectares of grounds with lake.

Prices s €100-€140; d €100-€140; t €140-€185; extra person fr
€20; dinner fr €47 **On Site** ℰ **Nearby** ₫ 3km ⅃7km ⤴ 3km
Restaurant 3km Water sports 25km ⌁2km Spa 45km 🖼2km
⋙3km **Notes** Pets admitted English spoken CC

ⅢⅢ Château des Requêtes

Colette DESNOS
61250 ALENCON SUR VALFRAMBERT
☎ 02 33 27 11 76 & 02 33 29 43 29
web: www.chateau-des-requetes.com

A small château close to Alençon. All the bedrooms are upstairs: a
double, three triples (double beds and singles), and a two-room suite
for four, with two double beds. All rooms have private bath or shower
room and WC. There is a lounge, and outside are attractive grounds.

Prices s €45-€85; d €54-€90; t €63-€135; extra person fr €10
Nearby ₫ 3km ⅃10km ℰ 1km ⤴ 3km Restaurant 0.5km Water
sports 25km ⌁2km Spa 45km ⅌4km 🖼2km ⋙2km **Notes** Pets
admitted English spoken CC

ARGENTAN-SUR-OCCAGNES

ⅢⅢ Le Mesnil

Rémy et Janine LAIGNEL
61200 OCCAGNES
☎ 02 33 67 11 12

A farm in the Haras region which offers a double room with possible
extra single and TV in the owner's house and two double rooms with
extra singles in a separate building with mini kitchenette. All have
private facilities and heating. For trail bike fans there is a circuit nearby.

Prices s €30; d fr €42; t fr €48; extra person fr €5 **Nearby** ₫ 5km
⌁2km ⤴ 5km Water sports 5km ⌁5km Spa 50km 🖼5km ⋙5km
Notes No pets

ARGENTAN-SUR-SARCEAUX

ⅢⅢ Ferme de la Gravelle

Claude et Odile SINEUX
61200 ARGENTAN SUR SARCEAUX
☎ 02 33 67 04 47
email: odilesineux@aol.com

In the Région des Haras, accommodation in this large country house
comprises a double room with kitchenette, open fire and TV and two

further double rooms and a triple, all with private facilities. Living
room with cooking area reserved for guests. Mountain bike circuit
nearby.

Prices s fr €40; d fr €50; t fr €55; extra person fr €5 **On Site** ℰ ⅌
Nearby ₫ 2km ⤴ 2km Restaurant 0.5km Water sports 2km ⌁2km
Spa 40km 🖼2km ⋙2km **Notes** No pets English spoken

AUBRY-EN-EXMES

ⅢⅢ Ⅴ ⅠⓄⅠ La Grande Ferme

Catherine et Philippe PLASSAIS
Sainte Eugénie, 61160 AUBRY EN EXMES
☎ 02 33 36 82 36 & 06 19 65 35 05 📄 02 33 36 99 52
email: ste.eugenie@free.fr

A large house on the edge of a farm with small stream in the grounds.
Guests have sole use of a lounge with television and small kitchen.
Three of the four rooms have private access. On the first floor are a
suite with a double and a single bed, and three double rooms, all with
private shower rooms.

Prices s fr €38; d fr €45; t fr €52; extra person fr €11; dinner fr €17
On Site ⅌ **Nearby** ₫ 0.2km ℰ 10km ⤴ 10km Restaurant 5km
Water sports 6km ⌁4km Spa 40km 🖼5km ⋙10km **Notes** Pets
admitted English spoken

AUBRY-LE-PANTHOU

ⅢⅢ La Pognandière

Paul PONTONE & Chris MOSS
61120 AUBRY LE PANTHOU
☎ 02 33 39 55 02
email: enquiries@bedbreakfastnormandy.com
web: www.bedbreakfastnormandy.com

This property, peacefully situated amongst the valleys of the Pays
d'Auge, has three bedrooms, for two or three people, all on the first
and second floors of the owners' attractive house. Each room has TV
and private facilities. There is another room which could be used for
extra accommodation for a large family group. Lounge, garden with
garden room.

Prices s fr €40; d fr €50; t fr €60; extra person fr €10 **On Site** ⅌
Nearby ₫ 5km ℰ 1km ⤴ 10km Restaurant 5km Water sports 10km
🖼10km ⋙22km **Notes** No pets English spoken

BELLEME

ⅢⅢ ⅠⓄⅠ Château de la Grand Maison

A ISSAHAR-ZADEH

33-37 rue d'Alençon, 61130 BELLEME

☎ 02 33 73 37 25 & 06 86 62 12 77

📄 02 33 73 69 40

email: info@chateaudelagrandmaison.fr

web: www.chateaudelagrandmaison.fr

This restored 18th-century château once belonged to the Marquis de Bellême. An equestrian property, the stables have two boxes and three stalls available for horses plus eight hectares of grazing with forest access (prices on request). Two ground floor lounges, two dining rooms, library. First floor double, second floor two doubles; all with bathroom/WC. One suite with two doubles, bathroom/WC; further suite with double and extra double, bathroom and WC. Car port. Enclosed garden, central heating, large grounds.

Prices s €100-€170; d €120-€190; t fr €240; dinner fr €37
On Site ※ **Nearby** ≛ 0.8km ⌷ 0.8km ♬ 2km ⚲ 0.2km Water sports 20km ≋ 0.2km 🏛 0.3km ⋘ 20km **Notes** No pets English spoken CC

BOECE

ⅢⅢ ⅠⓄⅠ *La Maison Pervenche*

Gilles COLARD

61560 BOECE

☎ 02 33 83 05 16

email: maisonpervenche@hotmail.com

An old farmhouse with all you would expect: blue shutters, roses in the garden, lime trees and willows, antique furniture and exposed beams. In the main house is an attic room for three; in a converted outbuilding is a double room, and three triples. All have private facilities. In the outbuilding there is a guests' lounge and a kitchenette.

Prices not confirmed for 2008 **Nearby** ≛ 10km ♬ 7km ⚲ 7km Water sports 7km ≋ 0.5km Spa 52km 🏛 7km ⋘ 32km **Notes** Pets admitted English spoken

CHAMBOIS

ⅢⅢ *Le Château*

Micheline CLAPEAU

4 Rue des Polonais, 61160 CHAMBOIS

☎ 08 77 03 37 11

email: chambois@wanadoo.fr

web: www.clapeau.com

An Empire-style château at the foot of the Donjon of Chambois, near the famous Haras du Pin close to the Pays d'Auge. This comfortable house offers three double rooms and two triples, each with private facilities and heating.

Prices not confirmed for 2008 **Nearby** ≛ 6km ♬ 0.5km ⚲ 12km Water sports 6km ≋ 0.5km Spa 45km 🏛 7km ⋘ 12km **Notes** No pets English spoken

CONDE-SUR-SARTHE

ⅢⅢ Le Clos des Roses

Simone et Pierre PELLEGRINI

10 rue de la Jardinière, 61250 CONDE SUR SARTHE

☎ 02 33 27 70 68

web: pellegrini.pierre@wanadoo.fr

This renovated house stands at the gateway to the Alpes Mancelles, overlooking the Sarthe. The garden has a collection of roses, a summerhouse, fancy ironwork, and a fountain. There is a room for three with cot if required and two double rooms (one grade 2), all with private facilities and heating. Lounge and veranda available.

Prices s fr €30; d fr €45; t fr €55; extra person fr €12 **On Site** ⚲ **Nearby** ≛ 4km ⌷ 5km ⚲ 1km Restaurant 1km Water sports 24km ≋ Spa 42km 🏛 1km ⋘ 5km **Notes** No pets

COUDEHARD

ⅢⅢ ⅠⓄⅠ Le Champ Massé

John et Jeanette EGGLETON

61160 COUDEHARD

☎ 02 33 35 00 65

email: john.eggleton@wanadoo.fr

web: www.bikenormandy.com

A modern house with fantastic views and a warm welcome to motorcyclists. Facilities include weights room, games, garage and garden; fireplace, TV and piano in the lounge; a ground floor double with bathroom; on the first floor are a room with a double and a single bed, and two rooms with four singles, each with shower room and WC. Meals by arrangement.

Prices s fr €50; d fr €70; t fr €85; dinner fr €20 **Nearby** ≛ 2km ⚲ 15km Restaurant 2km Water sports 6km ≋ 5km Spa 50km 🏛 5km ⋘ 18km **Notes** No pets English spoken

DOMFRONT

ⅢⅢ ⅠⓄⅠ Belle Vallée

V et R HOBSON-COSSEY

61700 DOMFRONT

☎ 02 33 37 05 71

email: info@belle-vallee.net

A peaceful, newly renovated manor house with lovely countryside views, set in a flowered garden. The spacious, beautifully decorated rooms are centrally heated. There is a double with bathroom, a grade 3 double with bathroom and a double with shower and two-person bath. There is a carport and loose boxes.

Prices s €54-€74; d €60-€80; t fr €95; extra person €8-€15; dinner fr €20 **On Site** ※ **Nearby** ≛ 15km ⌷ 15km ♬ 2km ⚲ 20km Restaurant 0.7km Water sports 10km ≋ 2km Spa 18km 🏛 1km ⋘ 20km **Notes** No pets English spoken

ESSAY

Château de Villiers

Franck et Fabienne ROLLO
61500 ESSAY
☎ 06 84 37 89 86 & 02 33 31 16 49
email: info@chateau-normandie.com
web: www.chateau-normandie.com

This building is a château dating from the 16th, 17th and 18th centuries, surrounded by a moat. It has been carefully restored and decorated by its owners, and offers three bedrooms - two doubles and a triple - all with private facilities. The house is electrically heated, and it has a guest lounge and garden. Loose boxes and grazing for horses.

Prices s €60-€110; d €60-€135; t fr €145; dinner fr €35 **On Site** **Nearby** 4km 20km 20km Restaurant 5km Water sports 14km 8km Spa 65km 5km 5km **Notes** No pets English spoken

FAVEROLLES

Le Mont Rôti

Sylviane et Bernard FORTIN
61600 FAVEROLLES
☎ 02 33 37 34 72 & 06 09 85 92 09 02 33 37 34 72

A farmhouse in open country between the bocage and Suisse Normande with charming accommodation situated in the mansard roof. One room for three people; one suite for three; and one double with separate access; all have private facilities and heating. Veranda for guests. Many sites to discover in the neighbourhood.

Prices s fr €30; d fr €38; t fr €48; extra person fr €10; dinner fr €15 **Nearby** 10km 10km 5km 10km Restaurant 4km Water sports 13km 18km Spa 17km 19km 8km **Notes** No pets English spoken

FONTENAI-SUR-ORNE

La Ferme de l'Isle aux Oiseaux

Ghislaine et Alain PICARD
rue du Bourg au Marais, 61200 FONTENAI SUR ORNE
☎ 02 33 67 05 47
email: alain.picard253@orange.fr

An old fortified farmhouse, with an archway leading into an enclosed courtyard. Three upstairs bedrooms have been tastefully restored and are decorated with original paintings. Two of the rooms are doubles, and the third has twin beds; all have private shower and WC. Lounge and conservatory. Art courses can be provided, according to demand.

Prices s €45-€55; d €55-€65; t €80-€90; extra person €20-€35; dinner €12-€35 **Nearby** 4km 30km 0.1km 4km Restaurant 0.8km Water sports 4km 4km Spa 3km 2km 3km **Notes** No pets

GEMAGES

Le Moulin de Gémages

Anna IANNACCONE
61130 GEMAGES
☎ 02 33 25 15 72 02 33 25 18 88
email: annieriv.iann@wanadoo.fr
web: http://moulindegemages.free.fr

Le Moulin de Gémages lies in the hollow of a green valley in the Regional Natural Park of Perche, and has a millrace, lock gates, wheel and river. Old hay lofts at this renovated mill house have been converted to house three rooms, each with double and single bed, private facilities and heating. Garden with river and pond.

Prices s €65-€75; d €75-€85; t €90-€100; dinner fr €30 **On Site** **Nearby** 1km 12km 10km Restaurant 1.2km Water sports 15km 5km Spa 12km 1.2km 15km **Notes** No pets English spoken

HEUGON

Le Pressoir

Robert et Margaret HIND
à La Thibaudière, 61470 HEUGON
☎ 02 33 36 68 99 & 06 26 03 02 96 02 33 36 68 99
email: robert.hind@wanadoo.fr

A restored and converted cider press, with its equipment intact, exposed brickwork and beams, standing in two and a half hectares of land. Upstairs are three double rooms of which two family rooms have three additional single beds on a mezzanine level. All the rooms have a power shower and WC. Lounge with TV and DVD; pétanque, bikes, volley-ball and badminton.

Prices s fr €40; d fr €55; t fr €70; extra person fr €15; dinner fr €16 **On Site** **Nearby** 5km 5km 10km Restaurant 2km Water sports 15km 4km 2km 25km **Notes** Pets admitted English spoken CC

NORMANDY

JUVIGNY-SOUS-ANDAINE

▦ Manoir Ste Cécile

Averill GIBSON

61140 JUVIGNY SOUS ANDAINE

☎ 02 33 38 11 21 📄 02 33 38 11 21

email: reservations@manoirstececile.com

web: www.manoirstececile.com

Not far from the elegant spa town of Bagnoles-de-l'Orne, this house has three second floor guest rooms. All have double beds, with additional beds and sofa beds if needed. Each room has en suite facilities, with a power shower and WC. There is a guest lounge, garden, and possible accommodation for horses. Table tennis.

Prices s fr €50; d fr €60; t fr €80; extra person fr €20 **Nearby** ⛵ 7km ⚓ 7km ♟ 5km ↝ 7km Restaurant 1km Water sports 12km ⌇ 1km Spa 7km 🏛 3km ⋈ 20km **Notes** No pets English spoken CC

LA CHAPELLE-PRES-SEES

▦ ❦ ⏀ Les Tertres

O et J-C BESNIARD

61500 LA CHAPELLE PRES SEES

☎ 02 33 27 74 67 & 06 88 08 94 47 📄 02 33 27 74 67

email: jc.besniard@wanadoo.fr

web: www.fedestertres.com

This farm, near the Forest d'Ecouves, gives visitors the chance to explore the country by horse or pony. There are five double rooms, one with sofa bed, and all with private facilities and heating. Guests' lounge, garden. Cathedral at Sées nearby.

Prices s fr €37; d €42-€45; t fr €52; extra person fr €10; dinner fr €15 **On Site** ⛵ **Nearby** ♟ 5km ↝ 20km Restaurant 4km Water sports 18km ⌇ 5km ⚑ 4km 🏠 4km ⋈ 4km **Notes** Pets admitted English spoken

---

LA FERTE-FRESNEL

▦ ⏀ Le Château

Mr KAMPLIN et Mme BARBIER

61550 LA FERTE FRESNEL

☎ 02 33 24 23 23 📄 02 33 24 50 19

email: chateau.fertefresnel@free.fr

web: http://chateau.fertefresnel.free.fr

This listed 19th-century château is situated among rare plants in a French-style park with a large lake. It has four rooms: two doubles, a

twin, and a room for four (two double beds). Cot available. All rooms have TVs, telephones and en suite bathrooms. Lift, lounge, guests' kitchen with dishwasher.

Prices s €68-€83; d €80-€120; t €100-€140; extra person fr €20; dinner fr €33 **On Site** ♟ **Nearby** ⛵ 6km ↝ 14km Water sports 6km ⌇ 6km ⋈ 14km **Notes** Pets admitted English spoken

---

LA FERTE-MACE

▦ ⏀ La Péleras

Christine VOLCLAIR

61600 LA FERTE MACE

☎ 02 33 37 28 23

email: auberge.lasource@orange.fr

web: http://perso.orange.fr/auberge.lasource/

Large Norman-style half-timbered house near Bagnoles de l'Orne, built by the owners, and furnished with antiques. There is a room with three singles, two rooms with a double and single, a double room and a room for four, all with private facilities and heating. Lounge; garden; terrace. Views extend over the lake and meadows to the little village of La Ferté-Macé.

Prices s fr €46; d fr €54; t fr €72; extra person fr €18; dinner fr €14 **On Site** ⛵ Water sports **Nearby** ♟ 0.5km Sea 0.1km ♟ 0.5km ↝ 2km Restaurant 2km ⌇ 2km Spa 5km 🏛 2km ⋈ 11km **Notes** No pets English spoken

---

LA FORET-AUVRAY

▦ ⏀ Beaux Rêves

Margaret et Chris GALLACHER

Le Bourg, 61210 LA FORET AUVRAY

☎ 02 33 66 48 25

A modern bungalow with fantastic views and close to magnificent walks. There is a TV lounge and a double room with bathroom. A cot is available and each room has access to the garden and its own garden furniture.

Prices s fr €35; d fr €45; t fr €60; extra person fr €15; dinner fr €15 **Nearby** ⛵ 7km ♟ 17km ♟ 3km ↝ 15km Restaurant 0.4km Water sports 10km ⌇ 8km Spa 40km ⚑ 15km 🏛 5km ⋈ 15km **Notes** No pets English spoken Open Easter to October.

LA VENTROUZE

⁂ ◯ **Manoir de la Vallière**

Alain DE GIOVANNI
61190 LA VENTROUZE

☎ 02 33 85 46 13 & 06 10 27 62 47 🖹 02 33 73 54 20
email: degiovanni.alain@wanadoo.fr

An 18th-century manor house in its own enclosed grounds with a small lake, on the edge of the Parc Naturel du Perche. Three double rooms, all with television, en suite shower room and WC. Dining room, living room with open fire and books, and conservatory.

Prices s €75-€90; d €90-€105; dinner fr €25 **Nearby** ⚓ 14km ⚘ 20km ✦ 7km ⚹ 15km Restaurant 8km Water sports 7km ⚴ 9km Spa 20km ✤ 15km ⚑ 10km ⚭ 15km **Notes** No pets English spoken

LE CERCUEIL

⁂ **Aprel**

Dominique BOULET
61500 LE CERCUEIL

☎ 02 33 26 01 19

An old school building, attractively restored, in a hamlet near the forest of Ecouves. On the ground floor is a triple room with a kitchenette; upstairs is another triple, plus a grade 2 room for four with a double bed and twin beds. All have private facilities, but those for the room which sleeps four guests are not en suite.

Prices s fr €20; d €40-€45; t fr €60; extra person fr €20; dinner €12 **Nearby** ⚓ 5km ✦ 7km ⚹ 20km Restaurant 10km Water sports 35km ⚴ 12km Spa 45km ✤ 12km ⚑ 2.5km ⚭ 12km **Notes** Pets admitted English spoken

LES CHAMPEAUX-EN-AUGE

⁂ **Les Fermes de Florence**

F PINSARD-HUSZAR
Les Fonciers, 61120 LES CHAMPEAUX EN AUGE

☎ 02 33 39 15 56 & 06 10 76 11 67
email: mail@lesfermesdeflorence.com
web: www.lesfermesdeflorence.com

Charming collection of farm buildings in the Pays d'Auge. Three bedrooms are decorated with taste. All rooms have king size beds, hi-fi, TV/DVD and courtesy tray.

Prices s €60-€80; d €65-€90; t €80-€105; dinner fr €19 **Nearby** ⚓ 0.8km ✦ 9km ⚹ 20km Restaurant 0.7km ⚴ 2km ✤ 9km ⚑ 9km ⚭ 20km **Notes** No pets English spoken

LONGNY-AU-PERCHE

⁂ ◯ **L'Orangerie**

Edith et Marc DESAILLY
9, Rue du Docteur Vivares, 61290 LONGNY AU PERCHE

☎ 02 33 25 11 78 🖹 02 33 73 67 19
email: desailly-fondeur@tele2.fr
web: http://lorangerie.free.fr

An old orangery with comfortable rooms in the colours of meadow flowers: two doubles and a room with double and single beds, all

with heating and private facilities. Enormous guest lounge with open fire, garden and meals if booked. Longny-au-Perche is in a region of forests, manor houses and horses, in the Regional Nature Park.

Prices s fr €40; d fr €50; t fr €65; extra person fr €15; dinner €10-€14 **On Site** ⚹ **Nearby** ⚓ 7km ⚘ 30km ✦ 0.5km ⚹ 0.5km Restaurant 0.8km Water sports 2km ⚴ 1km ⚑ 0.8km ⚭ 22km **Notes** No pets English spoken

MARCHEMAISONS

⁂ **Boisaubert**

Nicole MOHA-CAMUS
61170 MARCHEMAISONS

☎ 02 33 27 02 95 🖹 02 33 31 91 31

In separate outbuildings of the proprietor's house, two double rooms, one twin room and one triple room, each with shower room and wc are offered. Lounge with open fire, heating, garden with two ponds. Stables for horses possible.

Prices s fr €45; d fr €50; t fr €65 **Nearby** ⚓ 1km ⚘ 18km ✦ 3km ⚹ 18km Restaurant 3km Water sports 3km ⚴ 3km ⚑ 3km ⚭ 18km **Notes** Pets admitted English spoken

MONTCHEVREL

⁂ **La Chapelle**

Monique et Judith GRIGNAUX
61170 MONTCHEVREL

☎ 02 33 27 68 10
email: au.gres.de.judith@wanadoo.fr

A restored old vernacular farmhouse, commanding panoramic views. Comfort and calm are assured, and guests can relax in the lounge, with its corner kitchen, or in the garden. There is a suite of two rooms containing two doubles and a single bed, a room with a double and a single bed, and a third room with a double bed and a sofa-bed. All have private facilities. Within the grounds is a craft shop where pottery, jewellery and wood paintings are for sale; pottery lessons are also available.

Prices s fr €28; d fr €36; t fr €44; extra person fr €8 **Nearby** ⚓ 6km ⚘ 30km ✦ 2km ⚹ 17km Restaurant 7km Water sports 7km ⚴ 3.5km ✤ 17km ⚑ 7km ⚭ 20km **Notes** Pets admitted English spoken

MONTGAUDRY

⬛⬛⬛⬛ Le Tertre

Anne MORGAN

61360 MONTGAUDRY

☎ 02 33 25 59 98 📄 02 33 25 56 96

email: annemorgan@wanadoo.fr

web: www.french-country-retreat.com

This magnificent farmhouse, which enjoys a wonderful outlook, has been authentically restored by its owners. It has three bedrooms - two twins and a double. All have private bath or shower rooms (one has a spa bath); two have independent access, and one has a possible supplementary room. Lounge with TV, internal courtyard and garden. Courses in art, yoga, meditation, etc.

Prices s €50-€89; d €72-€130; t €119-€200; extra person fr €35 **Nearby** ⛱ 2km ∅ 6km ⊀ 6km Water sports 6km ⊕ 6km Spa 50km 🖫 6km ⋙ 35km **Notes** Pets admitted English spoken

MOULICENT

⬛⬛⬛⬛ Château de la Grande Noë

P et J DE LONGCAMP

61290 MOULICENT

☎ 02 33 73 63 30 & 06 87 65 88 47 📄 02 33 83 62 92

email: contact@chateaudegrandenoe.com

web: www.chateaudelagrandenoe.com

In the calm of the open countryside of Perche, guests are welcome in this family home (a château dating from the 15th century). There is a double room, a twin and a room for three, each with bathroom, wc and heating. Large park, table tennis, bikes, stables for horses, harness.

Prices s €80-€100; d €100-€120; extra person fr €20 **On Site** ⊛ **Nearby** ⛱ 12km ∅ 6km ⊀ 8km Restaurant 5km Water sports 15km ⊕ 5km 🖫 5km ⋙ 25km **Notes** No pets English spoken Open March to November.

MOUTIERS-AU-PERCHE

⬛⬛⬛⬛ ⦿ La Louveterie

C et P COSSU-DESCORDES

61110 MOUTIERS AU PERCHE

☎ 02 33 73 11 63 & 06 87 14 23 32 📄 02 33 73 05 16

email: domainedelalouveterie@wanadoo.fr

web: www.domainedelalouveterie.com

An authentically restored 17th-century farmhouse with swimming pool. Ground floor double (splits to twin), bathroom, WC. First floor two doubles (split to twins), bathroom/WC for each. Two duplex suites comprising ground floor dining room, bathroom, WC and upstairs double (splits to twin). Lounge with fireplace. TV available for bedrooms. Central heating. Garden, meadow and woodland, organic produce.

Prices s €85-€145; d €85-€145; extra person fr €25; dinner €35-€65 **On Site** Restaurant ⊛ Private ⊀ **Nearby** ⛱ 5km ∅ 7km ⊕ 7km 🖫 5km ⋙ 15km **Notes** No pets English spoken

NEUILLY-SUR-EURE

⬛⬛⬛ ⦿ Les Hautes Bruyères

Monique et André DI GIOVANNI

61290 NEUILLY SUR EURE

☎ 02 33 73 92 23 & 02 37 52 08 10 📄 02 37 52 09 91

This is a famous hunting estate in the Perche, and the décor of the house is reminiscent of big game hunting. There are two rooms for three (single beds) and two doubles (one with cot), all with shower and wc. Two extra beds available. Central heating, enormous lounge with open fire. Hunting available on the estate.

Prices s fr €47; d fr €47; t fr €56; dinner fr €22 **On Site** ∅ ⊛ **Nearby** ⛱ 1km ∅ 12km ⊀ 8km Restaurant 9km Water sports 1km ⊕ 1km 🖫 0.8km ⋙ 10km **Notes** Pets admitted English spoken

NEUVILLE-PRES-SEES

⬛⬛⬛⬛ Le Lion du Haut Montrond

David et Véronique SCHNEIDER

61500 NEUVILLE PRES SEES

☎ 02 33 35 41 58 & 06 80 41 55 26 📄 02 33 35 41 58

email: schneider.veronique@tiscali.fr

web: http://site.voila.fr/lelionduhautmontrond

This old, renovated house is in a hamlet a few kilometres from Sées and has three double rooms, and two rooms for four (one double, two single beds), each with shower, wc and heating. The proprietor owns a pair of Percherons and is happy to share his passion for working horses. Stables available.

Prices s fr €40; d fr €47; t fr €60; extra person fr €13 **On Site** ∅ Private ⊀ **Nearby** ⛱ 5km ∅ 8km Restaurant 8km Water sports 17km ⊕ 12km 🖫 10km ⋙ 5km **Notes** No pets English spoken

NONANT-LE-PIN

⬛⬛⬛⬛ ⦿ Le Plessis

Marie-Claire RUAULT

61240 NONANT LE PIN

☎ 02 33 35 59 02 & 06 10 97 12 97

A fascinating old property, once a stud farm for trotting horses, which has been lovingly restored by its owners. There are three double rooms, one downstairs and two upstairs, each with an additional single bed. Each bedroom has a private bath or shower room and WC. Lounge, with open fire; outside is a garden with a lake.

Prices s fr €35; d fr €40; t fr €50; extra person fr €9; dinner fr €15 **On Site** ∅ **Nearby** ⛱ 15km ⊀ 10km Water sports 32km ⊕ 1km 🖫 1km ⋙ 7km **Notes** No pets

PACE

🏶 Le Haut Montrayé

Monique LETOURNEL
61250 PACE
☎ 02 33 31 09 95 & 06 71 66 18 42
email: letournel.monique@aliceadsl.fr

A beautifully decorated house with attractive gardens close to Alençon. The separate guests' entrance leads to a living room where there is a microwave, then to three bedrooms, each with a double bed (which in one case can be unzipped to make singles). Extra folding beds are available, and each room has en suite facilities. The owner keeps ornamental chickens.

Prices s €40-€45; d €45-€50; extra person fr €10 **On Site** 🐾
Nearby ⛳ 5km ⌁ 10km 🎣 12km ⬥ 5km Restaurant 1km ⌂ 5km
Spa 40km 🏠 3km 🚂 11km **Notes** Pets admitted English spoken

PASSAIS-LA-CONCEPTION

🏶 ⒾⓄⒾ La Bigottière

Julie et Tony WARREN
61350 PASSAIS LA CONCEPTION
☎ 02 33 38 63 35 📄 02 33 38 63 35
email: anthony.warren@orange.fr
web: www.labigottiere.com

A restored character house in lovely countryside offering individually decorated comfortable bedrooms and a private lounge with TV, video and jukebox. First floor: one double and cot; one single and optional extra bed. Second floor: one twin, one double. Each with shower room/private WC. Enclosed garden, covered terrace. Horse boxes and pasture available. Pétanque, swing.

Prices s fr €40; d fr €48; extra person fr €10; dinner fr €18
Nearby ⛳ 1km ⌁ 15km 🎣 5km ⬥ 12km Restaurant 1km Water sports 15km ⌂ 8km Spa 15km 🏠 1km 🚂 25km **Notes** No pets
English spoken CC

ST-BOMER-LES-FORGES

🏶 Château de la Maigraire

Jean-Louis FISCHER
61700 ST BOMER LES FORGES
☎ 02 33 38 09 52 & 06 76 83 36 17
📄 02 33 38 09 52
email: la.maigraire@wanadoo.fr
web: http://chateaudelamaigraire.monsite.wanadoo.fr

An 1860s château surrounded by delightful parkland with lawns, trees and lake. Two suites on the first floor, each with a double and a single bed and a shower room with WC. A third double suite on the second floor with bathroom, separate toilet and private terrace. There are two lounges, central heating, a garage and seasonal harpsichord concerts.

Prices s fr €90; d €100-€120; t fr €140; extra person fr €20
On Site 🎣 **Nearby** ⛳ 1.5km ⌁ 17km 🎣 17km Restaurant 6km
Water sports 15km ⌂ 1km Spa 19km 🐾 7km 🏠 1.5km 🚂 17km
Notes No pets English spoken

🏶 La Roculière

Pierre et M-Madeleine ROUSSEL
61700 ST BOMER LES FORGES
☎ 02 33 37 60 60 📄 02 33 37 60 60

In the bocage between Domfront and Flers, the hosts welcome guests to two comfortable and cosy double rooms on their farm, both with private facilities. Cot available. Old bread oven available for guests' use. Botanical trail and charming countryside.

Prices s fr €40; d fr €45; t fr €55 **On Site** 🎣 **Nearby** ⛳ 3km
⬥ 10km Water sports 10km ⌂ 3km Spa 25km 🏠 10km 🚂 10km
Notes No pets English spoken

ST-DENIS-DE-VILLENETTE

🏶 ⒱ ⒾⓄⒾ La Prémoudière

Marie et Pascal BRUNET
61330 ST DENIS DE VILLENETTE
☎ 02 33 37 23 27 📄 02 33 37 23 27

Old restored house in the forests and bocage country, lounge with open fire and TV, and a garden with apple and pear trees. There are two double bedrooms, one with a kitchenette, a twin room with cot, a room for three and one for four. All have private facilities and heating. Guests can sample farm produce.

Prices s fr €32; d fr €40; t fr €47; extra person fr €10; dinner fr €15
Nearby ⛳ 15km ⌁ 10km Sea 0.1km 🎣 15km ⬥ 10km Restaurant 2km
Water sports 20km ⌂ 6km Spa 13km 🏠 5km 🚂 30km **Notes** Pets
admitted English spoken

TRUN

††† ⦿ La Villageoise

Nathalie MANOURY

66 rue de la République, 61160 TRUN

☎ 08 71 38 56 87 & 06 79 49 49 64   📄 02 33 39 13 07

email: lavillageoise@wanadoo.fr

web: www.lavillageoise.org

An old 17th-century posting inn, offering guests a chance to step back in time. There are three double rooms, and a suite for five with two double beds and a single. All have private bath or shower room and WC. For relaxation, there is a lounge with an open fire, a billiard room and an enclosed courtyard.

Prices s €55-€100; d €60-€100; t €80-€100; extra person fr €20; dinner fr €25   **On Site** ❀   **Nearby** ⚓ 10km ♟ 2km ⌇ 12km Restaurant 7km Water sports 12km ⊰ 0.5km Spa 40km ⌂ 0.1km ⋙ 12km **Notes** No pets English spoken

SEINE-MARITIME

ANCEAUMEVILLE

††† ⦿ Chambre d'hôtes

Roger et Ginette ALEXANDRE

95 route de Sierville, 76710 ANCEAUMEVILLE

☎ 02 35 32 50 22   📄 02 35 32 50 22

A Norman-style farmhouse surrounded by a garden, in the middle of the village. There are three guest rooms with their own entrance: two triples and a double and triple, all with own bath and wc. Sitting room, living room, TV. Meals during the week by arrangement. Restaurant 3km.

Prices s fr €37; d fr €45; t fr €60; extra person fr €15; dinner fr €20 **Nearby** ⚓ 6km ⌇ 6km ♟ 4km ⌇ 4km Restaurant 3km Water sports 4km ⊰ 4km ⌂ 4km ⋙ 4km   **Notes** No pets

††† La Cambriere

Laurent SEYEUX

346, Route de Dieppe, 76710 ANCEAUMEVILLE

☎ 02 35 61 26 64 & 06 61 47 68 11   📄 02 35 61 26 64

email: lacambriere@wanadoo.fr

web: http://perso.wanadoo.fr/lacambriere

This house is easily accessible from the Dieppe/Rouen road - ten minutes from Rouen and half an hour from the sea. There are two double rooms (one at grade 2), a family room for four with a double bed and two singles, and another family room with two doubles and one single. All have private facilities. Cot available.

Prices s fr €38; d fr €48; t fr €58; extra person fr €10 **Nearby** ⚓ 3km ⌇ 6km ♟ 4km ⌇ 4km Water sports 4km ⊰ 4km ⌂ 3km ⋙ 3km **Notes** Pets admitted English spoken

ANCOURTEVILLE-SUR-HERICOURT

††† Hameau Petites Cours

Huguette DUVAL

2, Les Petites Cours,

76560 ANCOURTEVILLE SUR HERICOURT

☎ 02 35 56 41 84 & 06 10 57 97 07   📄 02 35 56 41 84

email: lespetitescours@free.fr

web: http://lespetitescours.free.fr

A modern house in a rural setting, in an enclosed garden with plenty of flowers. Three double rooms are all upstairs, with private shower room and WC. A cot is available. Home-made items for breakfast, and outside is garden furniture and a barbecue.

Prices s fr €36; d fr €40; t fr €55; extra person fr €20 **Nearby** ⚓ 10km ⌇ 30km Sea 15km ♟ 10km ⌇ 7km Water sports 12km ⊰ 7km ⌂ 3km ⋙ 12km **Notes** Pets admitted

ANGERVILLE-BAILLEUL

††† ⦿ Ferme de l'Etang

Jacques et Gilberte MADIOT

76110 ANGERVILLE BAILLEUL

☎ 02 35 27 74 89   📄 02 35 27 74 89

Close to the sea, this farm has a fine half-timbered farmhouse with four guest rooms with their own entrance. There is a triple, two doubles and a five-bed family room, all with private facilities. Sitting room, large living room with traditional open fireplace. Baby equipment. Farm produce for sale and featuring in the meals (by arrangement).

Prices s fr €58; d fr €60; t fr €88; extra person fr €25; dinner €22-€28 **Nearby** ⚓ 10km ⌇ 20km ♟ 5km ⌇ 5km Restaurant 5km Water sports 25km ⊰ 1km ❀ 10km ⌂ 5km ⋙ 7km **Notes** No pets

ANGERVILLE-LA-MARTEL

††† Les Hates

Gilbert et Michèle LEDOULT

Les Hates No 229, Miquetot,

76540 ANGERVILLE LA MARTEL

☎ 02 35 29 80 82

A large house with extensive landscaped garden, in peaceful countryside. There is a double, and in a separate building, a double and twin with kitchenette. Extra beds available; all rooms have private facilities. Special rates for groups of four. Parking. Pétanque. 8km from Fécamp.

Prices s fr €41; d fr €45; t fr €65; extra person fr €15 **Nearby** ⚓ 9km ⌇ 25km ♟ 3km ⌇ 9km Restaurant 1km Water sports 12km ⊰ 2km Spa 10km ⌂ 3km ⋙ 10km **Notes** No pets

ARGUEIL

⊪ *Domaine de Clairval*

GARY et M GLORIEUX
76780 ARGUEIL ☎ 02 35 09 00 72 📄 02 35 90 17 66
email: clairval@wanadoo.fr
web: www.domaine-de-clairval.com

Five bedrooms in a restored 19th-century farmhouse with grounds. Ground floor breakfast room. First floor three grade 3 bedrooms, with double and sofa bed, plus a dining area on the landing. Second floor two grade 2 bedrooms, each with a double and twin single beds and WC. All have shower or bathroom with adjoining WC. Guests can use eight bicycles, two billiard/games rooms, table-tennis, pétanque, large reception hall, garden rooms and portico. Two person self-catering gîte. Restaurant 9 km.

Prices not confirmed for 2008 **Nearby** ⛷ 9km ⌇9km ✎ 9km ⚓ 9km Water sports 9km ⌇ 9km 🏛9km ⋈ 10km **Notes** Pets admitted English spoken

AUBERVILLE-LA-MANUEL

⊪ ⓘ **Au Repos Cauchois**

Daniel et Yvette LEONARD
rue de Yaume, 76450 AUBERVILLE LA MANUEL
☎ 02 35 57 24 17 & 06 33 01 73 53 📄 02 35 57 24 17
web: www.repos-cauchois.fr

In a quiet village on the coast, five guest rooms are on offer in this large brick-built house with a courtyard garden. There is a twin, a family room for four, three doubles (one grade 2) and a triple. All have private facilities. Sitting room with TV and open fireplace. Table football, pétanque, archery, mountain bikes. Meals by arrangement. Restaurant 2.5km.

Prices s fr €38; d fr €50; t fr €69; extra person fr €12; dinner fr €22
Nearby ⛷ 12km ⌇40km Sea 2.5km ✎ 2km ⚓ 8km Restaurant 2.5km Water sports 8km ⌇ Spa 45km 🏛8km ⋈ 12km **Notes** No pets

AVREMESNIL

⊪ ⓘ **Le Marronnier Rouge**

Philippe et Françoise LAURENT
rue Vauban, 76730 AVREMESNIL
☎ 02 35 04 90 83
email: lemarronnierrouge@wanadoo.fr
web: www.marronnier-rouge.com

The grounds of this large house are bordered by beech trees. Situated in the village centre and near the beaches. The ground floor has a hall and lounge/diner with fireplace. Upstairs bedrooms comprise two doubles and a room with double and single beds. All are decorated with individual themes and have spacious adjoining facilities. Evening meal by reservation using local produce; garden room. Restaurant 6km.

Prices s fr €60; d fr €65; t fr €80; extra person fr €15; dinner fr €25
Nearby ⛷ 12km ⌇12km ⚓ 15km Water sports 15km ⌇ 0.5km ⋈ 15km **Notes** No pets English spoken

BARDOUVILLE

⊪ *Le Val Sarah*

Jean et Micheline LEFEBVRE
Beaulieu, 76480 BARDOUVILLE
☎ 02 35 37 08 07 📄 02 35 37 11 33
email: levalsarah@wanadoo.fr
web: http://le-val-sarah.com

In an attractively landscaped setting close to the River Seine, this detached house has two doubles and a triple room, all with own shower and wc. Well-equipped kitchen (washing machine, dishwasher), sitting room, living room with open fireplace, TV. Enclosed garden, outdoor furniture. Children's games, tennis, table tennis, pétanque. Banqueting hall (150 guests, parking for 90 cars) for hire. Restaurant at La Bouille 6km.

Prices not confirmed for 2008 **Nearby** ⛷ 5km ⌇20km ✎ 0.5km ⚓ 10km 🏛6km ⋈ 25km **Notes** No pets

BEAUMONT-LE-HARENG

⊪ ⓘ **La Cour Cormont**

Rémy et Marie-Claude LEMONNIER
20 chemin de l'Eglise, 76850 BEAUMONT LE HARENG
☎ 02 35 33 31 74 📄 02 35 33 11 53
email: rmc.lemonnier@wanadoo.fr

This quiet and peaceful property is close to the forest of Eauwy and the Saint-Saëns golf course. In the house there are two triple rooms, with private entrance and kitchenette; in the loft of an 18th-century stable are two further rooms, for three and four people. All rooms have private showers/WCs. Lounge available - a room full of character.

Prices s fr €45; d fr €55; t fr €75; extra person fr €15; dinner fr €23
Nearby ⛷ 6km ⌇4km Sea 30km ✎ 6km ⚓ 15km Restaurant 4km ⌇ 4km Spa 25km 🏛6km ⋈ 27km **Notes** No pets English spoken

BEAUVAL-EN-CAUX

⊪ ⓘ **La Boidelière**

P et C DELIERS-BOIDIN
Le Puits de Beaumont, 76890 BEAUVAL EN CAUX
☎ 02 35 32 89 76 & 06 61 72 36 34
email: patrickdeliers@aol.com
web: http://laboideliere.site.voila.fr

A house dating from the late 19th century set in a beautiful garden with some quiet, private places. There are four bedrooms: a spacious

CONTINUED

BEAUVAL-EN-CAUX CONTINUED

double room with lounge area and terrace on the ground floor, while upstairs there is a double, a twin-bedded room, and a triple (double bed plus a single). All have private facilities; baby equipment available. Meals by arrangement.

Prices s fr €53; d €58-€65; t fr €83; extra person €15; dinner fr €25
Nearby ⛟ 9km ⚓ 25km ✎ 6km ↖ 4km Water sports 20km ◷ 4km ⌂ 4km ⋙ 7km **Notes** No pets English spoken

BEC-DE-MORTAGNE

⁂ ❧ *La Vallée*

J-Pierre et Arlette MOREL
1 rue de la Chênaie, 76110 BEC DE MORTAGNE
☎ 02 35 28 00 81
email: becdemortagne.morel@wanadoo.fr

Close to a river in the middle of the village, this half-timbered residence has a large attractive garden. There are two doubles and a triple room, all with own shower and wc (extra bed available). Garden furniture. Restaurant 2km.

Prices not confirmed for 2008 **Nearby** ⛟ 9km ⚓ 18km ✎ 6km ↖ 9km ◷ 9km ⌂ 9km ⋙ 12km **Notes** No pets Open Easter to 1 November.

BERTRIMONT

⁂ ❧ Le Colombier

Marie-Louise DUVAL
76890 BERTRIMONT
☎ 02 32 80 14 24 ▤ 02 32 80 14 24
email: duval_alain@club-internet.fr
web: http://le-colombier.net

This old cider farm has three guest rooms. There are two grade 4 suites, one in the main house and one in a converted dovecote. They each have a lounge area, and sleeping accommodation for three. In the main house is a grade 3 family room. All rooms and suites have private bath/shower rooms, and WCs.

Prices s €55-€90; d €60-€95; t €80-€115; extra person fr €20; dinner fr €24 **Nearby** ⛟ 12km ⚓ 30km ✎ 8km ↖ 8km Restaurant 6km Water sports 34km ◷ Spa 40km ⚘ 25km ⌂ 5km ⋙ 20km **Notes** No pets

BOUVILLE

⁂ ❧ La Chic'Cotiere

Jacques et Véronique CHICOT
1364 rue d'Ybourville, 76360 BOUVILLE
☎ 02 35 91 68 13 & 06 20 65 87 28 ▤ 02 35 91 90 08
email: la-chic-cotiere@wanadoo.fr

Five guest bedrooms in two separate buildings in a quiet, green spot. In one building are two first floor suites, each with a double room and a single; on the second floor is a two-room family suite for four. The other building has a ground floor double, and a triple room upstairs. Landscaped gardens, kitchen, lounge, wonderful breakfasts. Meals available Saturday evenings.

Prices s fr €46; d €56-€60; t fr €71; extra person fr €16; dinner fr €30 **Nearby** ⛟ 2km ⚓ 8km Sea 40km ✎ 3km ↖ 3km Restaurant 10km Water sports 8km ◷ 1km Spa 20km ⌂ 2km ⋙ 3km **Notes** No pets English spoken

BUTOT-VENESVILLE

⁂ Hameau de Vaudreville

Marc et Marie-France MOSER
1 sente du Gite, 76450 BUTOT VENESVILLE
☎ 02 35 97 52 86 & 06 22 07 23 69

Only 5km from Petites Dalles beach, this fine 17th-century house stands in an attractively landscaped park, and has a grade 3 triple with private entrance. A separate 19th-century building has two grade 2 doubles and a grade 3 twin with their own entrance and private facilities. Restaurants 6km.

Prices s fr €30; d €40-€45; t fr €55; extra person fr €15 **Nearby** ⛟ 8km ⚓ 30km Sea 5km ✎ 5km ↖ 8km Restaurant 6km Water sports 8km ◷ 2km Spa 19km ⌂ 4km ⋙ 19km **Notes** Pets admitted English spoken

CANEHAN

⁂ ❧ Les Terres du Thil

Marie-Claire BLANGEZ
Rue de la Laiterie, 76260 CANEHAN
☎ 02 35 86 72 56
email: lesterresduthil@wanadoo.fr
web: http://ledomainedesterresduthil.com

This establishment is situated in a peaceful countryside setting on the banks of the River Yères. There is a family suite for four or five with terrace, separate entrance through the garden, and four doubles, all

ith own facilities and lovely views. Meals by arrangement. Garden
urniture, barbecue, seating, parking, private fishing lake. Close to
eaches at Criel and Le Tréport and to the Eu Forest.

Prices s fr €45; d fr €50; t fr €66; extra person fr €16; dinner fr €25
On Site ⌂ Restaurant ❦ **Nearby** ⛷ 5km ♨ 25km ⊰ 10km Water
ports 12km ♒ 10km ⊞ 5km ₩ 10km **Notes** No pets English spoken

CANOUVILLE

₩ **Chambre d'hôtes**

ean et Monique DOURY
4 rue du Bas, 76450 CANOUVILLE
☎ 02 35 97 50 41

his spacious residence stands in landscaped gardens and has two
iple rooms, a family room for four, a double and a triple, all with
ivate facilities. Sitting room.

Prices s fr €42; d fr €52; t fr €62; extra person fr €10 **Nearby** ⛷ 5km
30km Sea 4km ♨ 4km ⊰ 4km Restaurant 4km ♒ 4km Spa 30km
5km ₩ 30km **Notes** No pets

CRASVILLE-LA-ROCQUEFORT

₩ ⦿ *Chambre d'hôtes*

rançois et Jana HENNETIER
ue de l'Eglise, 76740 CRASVILLE LA ROCQUEFORT
☎ 02 35 97 63 31
mail: francois.hennetier@wanadoo.fr

his large red-brick house, just below the church in a peaceful and
elightful village 11 kilometres from the small resort of Veules-les-
oses, is surrounded by an enclosed garden. It has three double
oms, each with private shower room and WC. Lounge with TV.
arden room, games and barbecue. Your hosts will be delighted to
rovide meals, by arrangement.

Prices not confirmed for 2008 **Nearby** ⛷ 8km ♨ 28km ♨ 12km
18km Water sports 21km ♒ 6km ⊞ 1km ₩ 16km **Notes** No pets

CRIQUEBEUF-EN-CAUX

₩ ⦿ **La Criqueboise**

hierry et Véronique BAUDRY
2 rue de l'Eglise, 76111 CRIQUEBEUF EN CAUX
☎ 02 35 28 70 15   🖷 02 35 28 70 15
mail: gite.baudry@wanadoo.fr

his spacious brick and flint home, standing in attractive tree-lined
ounds, has three double rooms, a family suite for four and a family
om for three, all with own facilities. Dining room, billiard, games and
' room. Meals provided. Restaurant 2km.

Prices s €38-€39; d €47-€51; t fr €69; extra person fr €17; dinner fr €19
earby ⛷ 7km ♨ 14km Sea 2km ♨ 2km ⊰ 5km Water sports 26km
staurant 2km ♒ 0.5km ❦ 2km ⊞ 2km ₩ 5km **Notes** No pets

DIEPPE

₩₩₩ **Villa Florida**

Danièle NOEL
24 chemin du Golf, 76200 DIEPPE
☎ 02 35 84 40 37   🖷 01 72 74 33 76
email: adn@lavillaflorida.com
web: www.charmance-dieppe.com

Close to the sea in the exclusive surroundings of Dieppe-Pourville golf
course, this is a fine example of contemporary domestic architecture,
with well-proportioned and sunny rooms. The guest rooms include
two twins and a triple (single bed on mezzanine) with own facilities
and a terrace with golf course views. Restaurant 500mtrs.

Prices s fr €66; d €73-€78; t €90-€110; extra person fr €15
On Site ♨ **Nearby** ⛷ 4km ♨ 7km ⊰ 1km ♒ 2km ⊞ 1km ₩ 2km
Notes No pets English spoken

DOUVREND

₩₩₩ ⦿ **Le Farival**

Tan et Martine DO PHAT-LATOUR
Bois du Farival, 76630 DOUVREND
☎ 02 35 84 58 98
email: lefarival@neuf.fr
web: www.lefarival.com

This 18th-century hunting lodge, in a forest clearing with a view
over the Eaulne valley, feels in a time warp. On the ground floor
are two double rooms; upstairs is a family room with four single
beds. All of the rooms have a private bathroom and WC. Extra
bed available. Lounge with books; sauna with power shower.
Meals by arrangement.

Prices s fr €72; d €82-€92; t fr €112; extra person fr €22; dinner
fr €33 **Nearby** ⛷ 7km ♨ 20km Sea 15km ♨ 5km ⊰ 10km
Restaurant 5km Water sports 5km Spa 15km ⊞ 5km ₩ 15km
Notes No pets English spoken CC

ECTOT-L'AUBER

₩₩₩ ⦿ *La Hêtraie*

J-Pierre et Bénédicte VIN
Le Village, 76760 ECTOT L'AUBER
☎ 02 35 96 84 14   🖷 02 35 96 81 32
email: bjp.vin@wanadoo.fr
web: www.lahetraie.com

Surrounded by beech trees, and complete with dovecote, barn and
cart-shed, this fine old 18th-century farmhouse has been converted
to house three charming and attractively decorated rooms, all with
own shower and wc. Kitchenette, barbecue, table tennis, bikes. Meals
by arrangement. Hosts are a good source of information on nearby
attractions. Restaurant 3km.

Prices not confirmed for 2008 **Nearby** ⛷ 5km ♨ 25km ♨ 6km
⊰ 10km Water sports 32km ♒ 3.5km ⊞ 3km ₩ 10km **Notes** No pets
English spoken

La Gourmandine

Claude and Edith welcome you to their lovely brick house, surrounded by a flower garden just 10 minutes from Rouen.

The Gite can accommodate up to 5 people.

The chambres d'hôtes are within the main house, on the first floor and all enjoy private facilities.

- WiFi available
- Possibility of organised weekends
- Near to golf course, pool, museum and trains
- Table d'hôte available by reservation

La Gourmandine
69 rue des Lilas
76710 Eslettes
Tel/Fax: 00 33 (2) 35 33 14 75
e-mail: contact@gourmandine76.com

ESLETTES

₩ ⁍◯⁍ La Gourmandine

Jean-Claude MARNE
69 rue des Lilas, 76710 ESLETTES
☎ 02 35 33 14 75 📄 02 35 33 14 75
email: contact@gourmandine76.com
web: www.gourmandine76.com

Surrounded by flowers, this large red-brick village house is just ten minutes from Rouen. It has two double rooms, one of them an attic room, and a two-room family suite for six. All have private shower rooms and WCs. Lounge, with TV and books. Baby equipment available, possible baby-sitting. Theme weekends arranged - golf, walking, etc.

Prices s fr €35; d fr €40; t fr €63; extra person fr €18; dinner fr €20 **On Site** Restaurant ♚ **Nearby** ♣ 3km ⅃ 5km 🏊 1.5km ⚲ 1.5km Water sports 1.5km ⚲ 1.5km 🏛 7km ₩ 1.3km **Notes** No pets
see advert on this page

ETAINHUS

₩ Le Clair Logis

Chantal et J-Claude LECLERC
321 route du Moignan, 76430 ETAINHUS
☎ 02 35 20 98 55 & 06 82 62 15 84
email: leclair-logis@orange.fr
web: http://perso.orange.fr/leclair-logis

This house stands in the peaceful countryside, 15 minutes from Honfleur. There are three themed bedrooms: a twin-bedded room, and two rooms with three single beds. All of the rooms have TV and telephone sockets, private bathrooms and WCs. Separate guests' entrance; kitchen, large lounge with TV, books and children's games. Attractive garden, with furniture and barbecue.

Prices s fr €34; d fr €46; t fr €63; extra person fr €14 **Nearby** ♣ 11km ⅃ 19km Sea 19km 🏊 8km ⚲ 6km Restaurant 6km Water sports 43km ☺ 6km 🏛 1km ₩ 12km **Notes** Pets admitted

ETALLEVILLE

₩ ⁍◯⁍ *La Pommeraie*

Elizabeth SHIRLEY
28 rue des Chênes, 76560 ETALLEVILLE
☎ 02 32 70 86 29
email: the.shirleys@tiscali.fr
web: www.la-pommeraie-normandie.com

A half-timbered farmhouse dating from1780. On the first floor is a double room with two extra folding beds available; in a separate building is a double room with kitchenette, and another double with a folding bed and TV. All have en suite facilities, and a cot is available Meals available by arrangement.

Prices not confirmed for 2008 **Nearby** ♣ 15km ⅃ 34km 🏊 15km ⚲ 15km Water sports 18km ☺ 4km 🏛 3km ₩ 15km **Notes** No pets English spoken Open February to November.

EU

₩ Manoir de Beaumont

Jean-Marie DEMARQUET
76260 EU
☎ 02 35 50 91 91 & 06 72 80 01 04
email: catherine@demarquet.eu
web: www.demarquet.com

Set in a peaceful park overlooking the valley, this Anglo-Norman manor house and its 18th-century hunting lodge offers guest rooms including a triple, a double and a family suite for five with kitchenette; all with TV and private facilities. TV in all rooms. On the edge of the Eu Forest.

Prices s fr €36; d €48-€56; t fr €65; extra person fr €12 **Nearby** ♣ 4km ⅃ 37km 🏊 7km ⚲ 5km Restaurant 2km ☺ 2km Spa 3km ♚ 5km 🏛 2km ₩ 3km **Notes** Pets admitted English spoken

FESQUES

▥ Villa Caltot

Dany LUCAS

5 route de la Vallée, 76270 FESQUES

☎ 02 35 94 51 90 & 02 35 93 23 02 ▤ 02 35 94 47 52

e-mail: dany.lucas2@wanadoo.fr

web: www.danylucas.fr

19th-century house in a quiet village half an hour from Dieppe. On the ground floor is a double room; upstairs is a triple with a lounge area, plus another double. All have private shower room and WC. Baby equipment; kitchen for guests. Garden with lots of flowers and garden furniture. Baby sitting can be arranged.

Prices s fr €41; d fr €48; t fr €60; extra person fr €12 **On Site** ☜
Nearby ☰ 10km ≛ 18km ↗ 3km ↘ 10km Restaurant 8km Water sports 25km ☐ 10km Spa 25km ☖ 10km ➤ 45km **Notes** No pets
see advert on this page

FLAMETS-FRETILS

▥ ♥ ⍉ La Dranvillaise

Claudie PETIT

Dranville, Route de la Chapelle, 76270 FLAMETS FRETILS

☎ 02 35 93 31 29 & 06 81 73 70 80 ▤ 02 35 93 31 29

e-mail: la-dranvillaise@orange.fr

This restored farmhouse in the Bray countryside offers a traditional Norman atmosphere. With their own entrance, the three rooms include a pink family suite (three beds) in a separate building with cot, a green room (double), and a yellow room (triple). All have private facilities. Sitting room. Restaurant 10km.

Prices s fr €30; d fr €46; t fr €48; extra person fr €15; dinner fr €16
Nearby ☰ 8km ≛ 25km Sea 35km ↗ 15km ↘ 10km Restaurant 10km Water sports 17km ☐ 10km Spa 12km ☖ 10km ➤ 12km **Notes** Pets admitted English spoken

GODERVILLE

▥ ⍉ ♿ *Ferme du Bocage*

Philippe BELLET

Hameau Le Bocage, 76110 GODERVILLE

☎ 02 35 27 73 19 ▤ 02 35 27 15 63

e-mail: pbellet@terre-net.fr

web: www.multimania.com/fermebellet

In a converted outbuilding, this quietly situated farmhouse has two ground floor double rooms, and three further rooms, one of them a family room for four, on the first floor. They all have private facilities, and the style of decoration gives a warm and modern feel. Large lounge/kitchen area. Breakfasts served in the owners' house. Terrace, garden furniture, meals by arrangement.

Prices not confirmed for 2008 **Nearby** ☰ 1km ≛ 15km ↗ 15km ↘ 1km Water sports 30km ☐ 1km ☖ 1km ➤ 5km **Notes** No pets

HOUDETOT

▥ ⍉ Chambre d'hôtes

Catherine BOCQUET

21 Grand Route, 76740 HOUDETOT

☎ 02 35 97 08 73 ▤ 02 35 57 19 21

email: info@chambresbocquet.info

web: www.chambresbocquet.info

This property is an old building with a substantial modern extension. There are three tastefully decorated upstairs rooms, two doubles and a triple. All the rooms have private shower and WC. Lounge area and a cot is available. Pre-booked evening meals served all year except July and August.

Prices s fr €39; d fr €45; t fr €59; dinner fr €20 **Nearby** ☰ 8km ≛ 25km ↗ 7km ↘ 12km Water sports 14km ☐ 7km ☖ 4km ➤ 12km **Notes** Pets admitted English spoken

▥ *La Ferme des Etocs*

Michel DELAVIGNE

76740 HOUDETOT

☎ 02 35 97 10 87 & 06 07 13 27 27

email: michel.delavigne@wanadoo.fr

web: www.ferme-des-etocs.com

A 19th-century house with four prettily decorated rooms. Lilac has a double bed and two singles; Green has a double bed and a single; Yellow has a double and twin beds; Blue has a double bed. All rooms

CONTINUED

NORMANDY

HOUDETOT *CONTINUED*

have a private shower and WC, but those for Yellow and Blue, which are grade 2 rooms, are not en suite. Enclosed garden with furniture; children's games.

Prices not confirmed for 2008 **Nearby** ⚓5km ♨25km ♪7km ✈12km Water sports 12km ⛵7km ⓘ3km ﷼25km **Notes** No pets English spoken

HUGLEVILLE-EN-CAUX

⚜ Le Château de Grosfy

Pascale-Marie LEVISTRE
61 rue du Calvaire, Hameau de Grosfy,
76570 HUGLEVILLE EN CAUX
☎ 02 35 92 63 60 ▤ 02 35 91 33 87
email: chateaudegrosfy@wanadoo.fr
web: www.chateaudegrosfy.com

This is a great place to relax. It is a peaceful château in wooded grounds, half-way between Rouen and Dieppe. There are two double rooms and a triple, with private bathrooms, plus a family suite of two double rooms with private bathroom and WC across the landing. Lounge area with TV, books, billiards; farm animals to delight the children!

Prices s €34-€44; d €40-€51; t €53-€63; extra person fr €12 **Nearby** ⚓6km ♨12km ♪4km ✈5km Restaurant 4km Water sports 30km ⛵5km ⓘ5km ﷼5km **Notes** Pets admitted English spoken CC

INGOUVILLE-SUR-MER

⚜ ✿ Chambre d'hôtes

Christian et Nathalie OUIN
49 Grande Rue, 76460 INGOUVILLE SUR MER
☎ 02 35 57 26 45 & 06 22 58 31 18 ▤ 02 35 57 26 45
email: Nathalieouin@aol.com
web: http://meretcampagne.free.fr

This farmhouse property is not far from the coast, so guests can enjoy sea and countryside. A separate entrance leads to the four bedrooms, all on the first floor: a double room; two triples with double and single beds; and a twin-bedded room. All have a TV, private bath or shower room and WC. Baby equipment available.

Prices s fr €40; d fr €46; t fr €60; extra person fr €15 **Nearby** ⚓10km ♨30km ♪13km ✈3km Water sports 10km ⛵3km ⓘ3km ﷼3km **Notes** No pets English spoken

ISNEAUVILLE

⚜ La Muette

Jacques et Danielle AUFFRET
1057 rue des Bosquets, 76230 ISNEAUVILLE
☎ 02 35 60 57 69 & 06 86 78 43 91 ▤ 02 35 61 56 64
email: jdftm.auffret@wanadoo.fr
web: www.charmance-lamuette.com

On the very edge of the forest, this charming, fully restored Norman-style house has four guest rooms in an adjacent 18th-century cider press building with separate entrance. There are two doubles, one with small adjacent room with single bed and two triples, one with single bed on mezzanine and all with TV point, own shower and wc. Ground floor sitting room with open fireplace.

Prices s €55-€78; d €63-€78; t fr €73; extra person fr €10 **Nearby** ⚓4km ♨4km ✈5km Restaurant 2km ⛵1.5km ⓘ1km ﷼8km **Notes** No pets English spoken Open 21 March to 19 December.

JUMIEGES

⚜ Le Relais de l'Abbaye

Patrick et Brigitte CHATEL
798 rue du Quesney, 76480 JUMIEGES
☎ 02 35 37 24 98 ▤ 02 35 37 24 98

In a quiet location on the edge of a wooded park 25km from Rouen, this Norman-style house has a garden with terrace and six mini-gîtes. There is a twin, two doubles and a triple, all with own wc and shower. Separate entrance. Plenty of brochures and other material about the area. Country inn and restaurant nearby.

Prices s fr €40; d fr €44; t fr €54 **Nearby** ⚓3km ♨3km ♪3km ✈15km Restaurant 1km ⛵3km Spa 15km ⓘ1km ﷼25km **Notes** Pets admitted

LA CHAPELLE-SUR-DUN

⚜ *Chalet du Bel Event*

Daniel et Virginie WESTHEAD
Chemin du Bel Event, 76740 LA CHAPELLE SUR DUN
☎ 06 11 10 00 80 & 02 35 57 08 44
email: info@chaletdubelevent.com
web: www.chaletdubelevent.com

In a parkland setting midway between coast and countryside, the chalet has a traditional 19th-century seaside character. A nearby brick building has four double rooms, all with own facilities. Sitting room, living room, piano, tennis. Restaurant 200mtrs.

Prices not confirmed for 2008 **Nearby** ♨15km ♪15km ♬3.5km ♜12km Water sports 25km ♒0.5km ⚶25km **Notes** Pets admitted English spoken

LA HALLOTIERE

♨ ⬭ & Le Clos de la Normandiere

Alain et Liliane JAVAUDIN

D57, Hameau de Normanville, 76780 LA HALLOTIERE

☎ 02 35 90 96 71 ▤ 02 35 09 06 85

email: contact@normandiere.info

web: www.normandiere.info

A house standing in wooded grounds with a lake and a river between Lyons-la-Forêt and Forges-les-Eaux. There are four double rooms and a triple (three single beds), all with private shower room and WC. Two of the rooms can be linked for family use. Meals are available by arrangement. Outside are garden furniture and a barbecue; fishing possible on site.

Prices s fr €55; d fr €60; t fr €80; extra person fr €20; dinner fr €25 **On Site** ♬ **Nearby** ♨7km ♪25km ♜13km Restaurant 13km Water sports 50km ♒1km Spa 13km ♒3km ⚶15km **Notes** No pets English spoken

LA MAILLERAYE-SUR-SEINE

♨ *La Renardière*

M-A et M LEFRANCOIS

Route de Brotonne, 76940 LA MAILLERAYE SUR SEINE

☎ 02 35 37 13 25 ▤ 02.35.37.13.25

email: m-lefrancois2@wanadoo.fr

web: http://perso.wanadoo.fr/domaine.de.la.renardiere

This half-timbered house stands among attractive gardens in a four hectare estate in the Normandy Seine Regional Park. There are two double rooms (can be twin), one with extra single, and a triple room in an annexe, with sitting area and kitchenette. All have private facilities; extra beds available. Sitting room with open fireplace.

Prices not confirmed for 2008 **On Site** Private ♜ **Nearby** ♨7km ♬7km ♬7km Water sports 7km ♒2km ♒1km ⚶20km **Notes** Pets admitted English spoken

♨ ⬭ *Parkshore*

Alain BRIERE et Eric MERZ

Le Bourg l'Abbé, Route de Pont Audemer, 76940 LA MAILLERAYE SUR SEINE

☎ 02 35 75 52 67 & 06 16 46 00 72 ▤ 02 35 75 52 67

email: Parkshore-normandie@wanadoo.fr

web: www.parkshore-normandie.com

A peacefully situated Anglo-Norman style house with landscaped grounds, near the national park with walking and riding opportunities. Lounge/diner on the ground floor. Upstairs one grade 2 double, one grade 3 double, a grade 3 family room with single and double. All with private shower rooms. Horse riding/trekking by arrangement. Evening meal by arrangement.

Prices not confirmed for 2008 **On Site** ♨ **Nearby** ♪7km ♜2km Water sports 7km ♒1km ♒1km ⚶20km **Notes** Pets admitted English spoken Open January to October.

LANDES-VIEILLES-ET-NEUVES

♨ Château des Landes

J et G SIMON-LEMETTRE

76390 LANDES VIEILLES ET NEUVES

☎ 02 35 94 03 79 ▤ 02 35 94 03 79

email: jgsimon@chateaudeslandes.com

web: www.chateaudeslandes.com

A 19th-century château just a step from the Eu Forest. The five spacious rooms include two double rooms, a four-bed suite and two triple rooms, all with own shower and wc. No charge for child's bed. Dining room, sitting room/library. Breakfast served on veranda.

Prices s €45-€49; d €49-€59; t fr €78 **Nearby** ♨12km ♪30km ♬14km ♜12km ♒12km ♒12km ⚶12km **Notes** No pets English spoken

LE TILLEUL

♨ Hameau de Bonneville

J-Pierre et Sylviane LACHEVRE

934 route du Havre, 76790 LE TILLEUL

☎ 02 35 29 81 61

This house is very close to Etretat, with its famous cliffs. It has three bedrooms, two doubles and a twin, all with private showers/WCs. It is possible to walk down to the beach, and to come back up in a horse-drawn carriage. Peaceful, restful garden, with barbecue. Enclosed parking.

Prices s fr €40; d €45-€48 **Nearby** ♨1.5km ♪3km Sea 3km ♬3km ♜20km Restaurant 0.2km Water sports 40km ♒3km Spa 5km ♒0.5km ⚶15km **Notes** No pets English spoken Open March to November.

LE TREPORT

♨ *Prieuré Sainte Croix*

Romain et Nicole CARTON

76470 LE TREPORT

☎ 02 35 86 14 77 ▤ 02 35 86 14 77

email: carton.nicole@wanadoo.fr

web: http://prieuresaintecroix.free.fr

This building of character on the old farm of the Eu Château has a suite (double and sofa bed in sitting room) with kitchenette and private garden, three double rooms and a twin, all with own facilities. Two of the rooms can be linked. Sitting room. Garden and outdoor furniture, courtyard parking. Restaurant 2km.

Prices not confirmed for 2008 **Nearby** ♨2km ♪30km ♬2km ♜3km ♒1km ♒1km ⚶2km **Notes** No pets English spoken

MANNEVILLE-ES-PLAINS

♿ Le Clos Saint Vincent

Sophie et Alain JANNOT
434 rue du Bois, 76460 MANNEVILLE ES PLAINS
☎ 02 35 97 93 27
email: sophie.jannot@voila.fr
web: www.le-clos-saint-vincent.com

Peace and quiet in a seaside village mid-way between Veules-les-Roses and Saint-Valéry-en-Caux. This converted stable building has four bedrooms: on the ground floor is a twin-bedded room, and a double; upstairs is a triple (double bed plus a single) and a family room with a double bed, three singles and a cot. All have TV, private bathroom and WC. Big garden with a pond.

Prices s fr €65; d fr €68; t fr €84; extra person fr €26 **Nearby** ⛵ 0.5km
⚓ 27km ⚲ 3km ↘ 3km Restaurant 0.5km Water sports 3km ☖ 3km
Spa 30km ♞ 3km ⛺ 3km ⛟ 25km **Notes** No pets English spoken

MARTAINVILLE-EPREVILLE

⑩ Sweet Home

J-Y et M-L AUCRETERRE
534 rue des Marronniers, Epreville,
76116 MARTAINVILLE EPREVILLE
☎ 02 35 23 76 05 & 06 85 31 92 03 📄 02 35 23 76 05
email: jean-yves.aucreterre@libertysurf.fr
web: http://jy.aucreterre.free.fr

An attractive, peaceful spot in the village of Epreville, 15 kilometres from Rouen. There are four double rooms, one downstairs and three on the first floor. All have private bath or shower room and WC. Lounge with an open fire; superb garden with a terrace, a small wood and a fish pond. Private parking, meals by arrangement.

Prices s €46-€86; d €50-€90; extra person fr €15; dinner fr €15
On Site ⚲ Water sports **Nearby** ⛵ 7km ⚓ 40km ↘ 15km
Restaurant 4km ☖ 3km ⛺ 3km ⛟ 15km **Notes** No pets English spoken

MAUQUENCHY

⑩ ♿ Le Clos du Quesnay

J-Francois et Sabine MORISSE
651 route de Rouen, Le Grand Quesnay,
76440 MAUQUENCHY
☎ 02 35 90 00 97 & 06 71 44 82 44
email: info@leclosduquesnay.fr
web: www.leclosduquesnay.fr

This former farm building with four hectares, garden and orchard, has been transformed to provide spacious individually decorated bedrooms. A double with separate entrance; a family suite with double and twin rooms, a room with double and single beds and a double room. All have adjoining bath or shower room and WC; telephone and kettle in each room. Microwave available, lounge with fireplace and TV. Restaurants 3 km.

Prices s fr €48; d fr €58; t fr €73; extra person fr €10; dinner fr €23
Nearby ⛵ 4km ⚓ 21km ⚲ 3km ↘ 3km Restaurant 3km Water sports 37km ☖ 4km ♞ 3km ⛺ 3km ⛟ 5km **Notes** No pets English spoken

MONTVILLE

Le Domaine du Mont Real

Hélène LEPINE
4 Promenade des Chevreuils, 76710 MONTVILLE
☎ 02 35 33 25 48 📄 02 35 33 28 94
email: lepine6@wanadoo.fr

This property is not far from Rouen and close to the start of a long-distance footpath. In an annexe to the owners' home are four bedrooms: a double, two triples (double bed and a single), and a room for four (double bed and two singles). All have private facilities. Games room with billiard table; enclosed garden with furniture.

Prices s fr €49; d fr €59; t fr €69; extra person fr €10 **Nearby** ⚓ 1km ⚓ 3km ✎ 1.5km ⚓ 1.5km Water sports 1.5km ⚓ 1.5km ⚓ 0.7km ⚓ 1.5km **Notes** No pets English spoken

NESLE-NORMANDEUSE

⚏ Chambre d'hôtes

Jacqueline DUJARDIN
7 route de Campneuseville,
76340 NESLE NORMANDEUSE
☎ 02 35 93 54 96

18th-century property, 3 km from the Eu Forest, offering rooms in an annexe including two doubles and two triples, all with TV, own bath and wc. Breakfast served in the house. Garden with loungers. Fishing lake. Restaurant at Blangy-sur-Bresle 4km.

Prices s €40-€50; d €48-€60; t fr €70; extra person fr €15 **Nearby** ⚓ 20km Sea 27km ✎ 3km ⚓ 23km Restaurant 4km ⚓ 4km ⚓ 4km ⚓ 4km **Notes** Pets admitted

NEUFCHATEL-EN-BRAY

⚏ 🐓 Le Val Boury

Xavier et Valérie LEFRANCOIS
76270 NEUFCHATEL EN BRAY
☎ 02 35 93 26 95 ⚏ 02 32 97 12 30
email: xavier.lefrancois@wanadoo.fr
web: www.cellier-val-boury.com

In a peaceful setting just a few steps from the town centre, this 17th-century storehouse stands at the start of a footpath leading along the valley. There are three doubles with own shower and wc and a suite with three double beds (extra bed available), cot, and sitting area. Garden with furniture, barbecue, play area. Baby-sitting. Gîte 500mtrs.

Prices s €40-€50; d €48-€60; t €60-€75; extra person fr €15 **Nearby** ⚓ 15km ⚓ 10km Sea 35km ✎ 10km ⚓ 0.5km Water sports 0.5km ⚓ 0.5km Spa 10km ⚓ 0.5km ⚓ 0.5km ⚓ 1km **Notes** No pets English spoken

NEVILLE

⚏ Nature et Lin

Gladys LENDORMY
9, Rue de la Bergerie, 76460 NEVILLE
☎ 02 35 57 07 66 & 06 13 72 47 80
⚏ 02 35 57 05 95
email: accueil@nature-lin.com
web: www.nature-lin.com

A converted farm building offering four bedrooms, attractively decorated and with many thoughtful little touches. There are two double rooms and two triples, one with a double bed and a single, the other with three single beds. All have private bath or shower room and WC. Heated indoor swimming pool.

Prices s fr €120; d €120-€140; t €165-€205; extra person fr €45 **On Site** Private ⚓ **Nearby** ⚓ 4km ⚓ 25km ✎ 4km Restaurant 4km Water sports 3km ⚓ 4km ⚓ 4km ⚓ 4km ⚓ 25km **Notes** No pets English spoken

OMONVILLE

⚏ Les Ecureuils

Jérôme et Nicole LEMARCHAND
542 rue Jacob Bontemps, 76730 OMONVILLE
☎ 02 35 83 21 69 ⚏ 02 35 83 21 69
web: http://perso.wanadoo.fr/fermelesecureuils

In a quiet and leafy setting between the château and the church, this working farm with exposed timbers and open fireplace. There are two doubles, a twin and a triple, all with own shower and wc. Children's bed and games. Kitchen available. Garden. Sea-fishing 6km. Restaurant 4km.

Prices s fr €36; d €45-€49; t €60-€64; extra person fr €15 **Nearby** ⚓ 8km ⚓ 8km ✎ 3km ⚓ 15km Restaurant 4km Water sports 15km ⚓ 8km Spa 15km ⚓ 3km ⚓ 5km **Notes** No pets

OUAINVILLE

⚏ L'Estable

Jean-Luc et Nicole THONNAT
57 impasse de l'Eglise, 76450 OUAINVILLE
☎ 02 35 97 73 49 & 06 85 71 69 22
email: nthonnat@aol.com
web: www.gite-estable.com

A large building separate from the house, which looks out onto a flowery garden with a pond. On the first floor are two double rooms with private facilities, plus a grade 2 two-room suite with twin beds and a single, which has a private but not en suite bathroom/WC. Lounge with piano, and an artist host who can tell you all about this coastline.

Prices s fr €55; d fr €60; t fr €90 **Nearby** ⚓ 4km ⚓ 35km ✎ 3km ⚓ 3km Restaurant 4km Water sports 3km ⚓ 3km ⚓ 3km ⚓ 3km ⚓ 17km **Notes** No pets English spoken Open April to September.

OUVILLE-LA-RIVIERE

⋔⋔⋔ ⓘⓞⓘ Le Manoir de Tessy

Pascal et Marie-Agnès FRITSCH

76860 OUVILLE LA RIVIERE

☎ 02 32 06 34 44 & 06 08 22 05 93 📄 02 32 90 05 31

email: famfritsch76@wanadoo.fr

web: www.lemanoirdetessy.com

Ten minutes from the sea, between Dieppe and St-Valéry-en-Caux, this 16th-century manor house has a beautiful setting. There are two double rooms, a triple (three single beds), and a family room for four with a double bed and two singles. All have private bath or shower room and WC. Pre-booked evening meals available.

Prices s €56-€70; d €60-€80; t €80-€90; extra person fr €20; dinner fr €19 **Nearby** ⓩ 4km ⓩ 10km ⓟ 3km ⓣ 15km Restaurant 4km Water sports 9km ⓢ 4km Spa 15km ⓑ 1km ⓦ 15km **Notes** No pets English spoken CC

PALUEL

⋔⋔⋔ *Ferme du Château*

Virginie PHILIPPE

560 route du Bout Fleuri, Bertheauville, 76450 PALUEL

☎ 02 35 57 22 83

email: info@domaine-bertheauville.com

web: www.domaine-bertheauville.com

Stay in style on this 13-hectare estate 3 km from the sea, with Renaissance style château and 18th-century brick-built residence. Free access to the heated pool at the château. Ground floor rooms include a breakfast room, dining area with fireplace and kitchen, and a twin bedroom with shower room and WC. First floor: one double, one king-size. Second floor: two bedrooms with twin beds which can convert to a double, each with room for an extra double. All have bathroom with shower and own WC, TV. Restaurant 500mtrs.

Prices not confirmed for 2008 **On Site** Private ⓣ **Nearby** ⓩ 7km ⓩ 40km ⓟ 6km Water sports 6km ⓢ 3km ⓑ 4km ⓦ 6km **Notes** Pets admitted English spoken

ROUEN

⋔⋔⋔ Chambre d'hôtes

Philippe AUNAY

45 rue aux Ours, 76000 ROUEN

☎ 02 35 70 99 68

Philippe Aunay has an unparalleled knowledge of Rouen, and this 15th and 16th-century house has been in his family since the 19th century and is furnished in Norman style. There is a double, a twin, and a family suite for three, all with private facilities. Two rooms have cooking facilities. Sitting room.

Prices s fr €40; d fr €60; extra person fr €30 **Nearby** ⓩ 8km ⓩ 4km ⓟ 15km ⓣ 1km Restaurant 0.1km ⓢ 1km ⓒ 0.2km ⓑ 0.1km ⓦ 1km **Notes** Pets admitted English spoken

SAINNEVILLE-SUR-SEINE

⋔⋔⋔ Ferme Drumare

Bruno et Christine DERREY

Route de Montivilliers - CD31,

76430 SAINNEVILLE SUR SEINE

☎ 02 35 20 59 29 & 06 07 70 01 01 📄 02 35 13 94 84

email: derrey.bruno@neuf.fr

Guests can enjoy peace and quiet on this farm with 16th-century family home. The three rooms with own entrance include a double, a triple, and a family room for four, all with private facilities and TV point. Kitchenette, baby equipment, garden furniture, barbecue, children's games. Country inn 7km. Close to Honfleur, Etretat and Le Havre.

Prices s fr €37; d fr €45; t fr €70; extra person fr €15 **Nearby** ⓩ 6km ⓩ 12km ⓣ 6km Restaurant 5km ⓢ 1km ⓑ 1km ⓦ 7km **Notes** No pets

SASSETOT-LE-MAUCONDUIT

⋔⋔⋔ Hameau De Criquemanville

Michel et Danièle SOUDRY

76540 SASSETOT LE MAUCONDUIT

☎ 02 35 27 45 64

A lovely Norman-style house dating from the 18th century with two double rooms, a triple, and a family room for four with balcony, all with own shower and wc. Kitchenette, sitting room with TV, garden furniture, garage. Special rates for groups of four. Restaurants at Sassetot-le-Mauconduit 2km and Cany-Barville 6km.

Prices s fr €37; d fr €45; t fr €55; extra person fr €16 **Nearby** ⓩ 2km ⓩ 10km Sea 2.5km ⓟ 6km ⓣ 6km Restaurant 3km ⓢ 2km Spa 9km ⓑ 2km ⓦ 10km **Notes** No pets

⋔⋔⋔ Les Bruyères

Claude et Rolande BOURCIER

76540 SASSETOT LE MAUCONDUIT

☎ 02 35 29 77 18 📄 02 35 29 77 18

email: chambresdhotes.lesbruyeres@wanadoo.fr

web: www.chambresdhotes-gites-lesbruyeres.eu

This bright and welcoming house is close to the sea, and the hosts pride themselves on their Québecois hospitality. It has one double room, two triples and a room for four, all with private showers/WCs, and each with décor in the style of a painter: Boudin, Dufy, Monet or Morisot. Lounge with books. Good access to footpaths.

Prices s fr €46; d fr €51; t fr €63; extra person fr €12 **Nearby** ⓩ 6km ⓩ 28km ⓟ 11km ⓣ 11km Water sports 13km ⓢ 1km ⓑ 1km ⓦ 15km **Notes** No pets English spoken Open February to December.

SAUSSEUZEMARE-EN-CAUX

🍴 ⦿ *La Mare du Montier*

Josette COISY

D72, 76110 SAUSSEUZEMARE EN CAUX

☎ 02 35 27 93 55

email: nicole.coisy@wanadoo.fr

web: http://perso.wanadoo.fr/nicole.coisy

Between Etretat and Fécamp, this 18th-century Norman-style house stands in peaceful countryside. There are three attractive doubles with their own entrance, all with own shower and wc. Spacious living room with open fireplace. Meals by arrangement; refined cuisine featuring produce from the garden. Half-board available.

Prices not confirmed for 2008 **Nearby** ⇄ 10km ⚓ 10km ✐ 10km
↘ 2km ♨ 2km ⛪ 3km ⋙ 8km **Notes** No pets

SENNEVILLE-SUR-FECAMP

🍴 Val de la Mer

André et Mireille LETHUILLIER

37 Val de la Mer, 76400 SENNEVILLE SUR FECAMP

☎ 02 35 28 41 93

web: www.val-de-la-mer.com

A fine example of a Norman-style home, offering a twin, double and a triple room with private facilities.

Prices s fr €45; d fr €59 **Nearby** ⇄ 3km ⚓ 18km Sea 1km ✐ 6km
↘ 15km Restaurant 1.5km ♨ 3.5km ⛪ 3.5km ⋙ 3.5km **Notes** No pets
Open 21 September to 19 August

SOMMERY

🍴 ❧ Ferme de Bray

Patrice et Liliane PERRIER

76440 SOMMERY

☎ 02 35 90 57 27

web: http://ferme.de.bray.free.fr

This large and splendid 16th and 17th-century brick residence is in an attractive park and has five rooms including a double, three triples, and a family room for four, all with own bath and wc (children's bed available). Sitting room. Countryside activities include farm tours (mill, press, dovecote, dairy) and fishing. 100-seat hall and kitchen for hire. Forges-les-Eaux 7km.

Prices s fr €38; d €40-€45; t fr €55; extra person fr €10 **On Site** ♨ ✐
Nearby ⇄ 7km Sea 40km ↘ 7km Restaurant 1km ♨ 2km Spa 40km
⛪ 2km ⋙ 3km **Notes** No pets English spoken

SOTTEVILLE-SUR-MER

🍴 ⦿ Le Bout du Haut

François et Denise LEFEBVRE

Rue du Bout du Haut, Cidex 15,

76740 SOTTEVILLE SUR MER

☎ 02 35 97 61 05 ▤ 02 35 97 61 05

A farming couple offer accommodation in a modern building in traditional style close to their old weavers' house, in peaceful

surroundings only 800mtrs from the sea. Two doubles and a triple, all with own shower and wc. Sitting and living room, TV, parking, attractive garden. Stabling for horses. Restaurant 800mtrs. Veules-les-Roses 2.5km, Dieppe 20km.

Prices s fr €45; d fr €45; t fr €60; extra person fr €15; dinner fr €19
Nearby ⇄ 3km ⚓ 15km ✐ 1km ↘ 9km Restaurant 0.8km ♨ 0.5km
Spa 18km ⛪ 0.5km ⋙ 10km **Notes** No pets English spoken

ST-AUBIN-LE-CAUF

🍴 La Châtellenie

Agnès/Veronique BOSSELIN

76510 ST AUBIN LE CAUF

☎ 02 35 85 88 69 ▤ 02 35 85 84 21

email: lachatellenie@wanadoo.fr

web: www.lachatellenie.com

This château stands in an extensive park with a river in a lovely valley. There are three doubles, a triple and a twin, all with own shower and wc. Sitting rooms, reception room. River and lake fishing, table tennis, pétanque, bike shed, garden furniture and arbour.

Prices s €65-€80; d €70-€85; extra person fr €25 **On Site** ✐
Water sports **Nearby** ⇄ 3km ⚓ 12km ↘ 4km Restaurant 3km
♨ 10km Spa 10km ⛪ 3km ⋙ 10km **Notes** No pets English
spoken Open Easter to 1 November. CC

ST-AUBIN-SUR-MER

🍴 Ramouville

Gisèle GENTY

Route de Quiberville, 76740 ST AUBIN SUR MER

☎ 02 35 83 47 05

email: gisele.genty@wanadoo.fr

web: www.fermettederamouville.com

Guests can expect a warm welcome and choose between a triple or double room with separate access, or a twin, triple or room for four in an annexe, all with private facilities. Sitting and kitchen area, TV, 18th-century bread oven, baby equipment. Stabling for horses. Upholstery lessons by arrangement.

Prices s €42-€45; d €50-€54; t fr €63; extra person fr €14
Nearby ⇄ 6km ⚓ 18km ✐ 1km ↘ 14km Restaurant 3km Water
sports 27km ♨ 3km ⛪ 3.5km ⋙ 18km **Notes** Pets admitted

ST-AUBIN-SUR-SCIE

▒▒▒ *Rouxmesnil-le-Haut*

Gérard et Viviane LULAGUE
Route de Paris - D915, 76550 ST AUBIN SUR SCIE
☎ 02 35 84 14 89 ▤ 02 35 84 14 89
email: g.v@lulague.com
web: www.lulague.com

Separate from the owners' house, this fine old brick and flint house dates from the 17th-century and has a family room for four, two triples and two doubles, all with own shower and wc. Sitting room, use of kitchen. Landscaped garden, climbing frame, table tennis. Handy for Dieppe, marina, and Varengeville-sur-Mer. Restaurant 500mtrs and country inn at Eawy 20km.

Prices not confirmed for 2008   **Nearby** ♨ 0.5km ♨ 3km ♪ 3km ☂ 1km ♨ 0.5km 🏛 0.5km 🚂 3km   **Notes** No pets English spoken

ST-EUSTACHE-LA-FORET

▒▒▒ ♿ **La Petite Rue**

Agnès SAILLARD
65 A La Petite Rue, 76210 ST EUSTACHE LA FORET
☎ 02 35 38 34 36 & 06 62 61 37 22 ▤ 02 35 38 33 67
email: etcometa@wanadoo.fr

This old lodge, close to the owners' house, has been restored to provide two double rooms, a triple with disabled access, and a twin, all with own shower and wc. Sitting room, well-equipped kitchen, TV. The landscaped garden has a pool with black swans. Garden furniture, barbecue. Nearby: Etretat, Fécamp, Notre-Dame-de-Gravenchon and Gruchet-le-Valasse Abbey. Leisure park 5 minutes. Swimming pool with wave machine 11km.

Prices s fr €38; d fr €55; t fr €68; extra person fr €15   **Nearby** ♨ 6km ♨ 22km ♪ 11km ☂ 11km Restaurant 4km ♨ 1km Spa 11km 🏛 4km 🚂 10km   **Notes** No pets English spoken

ST-GEORGES-SUR-FONTAINE

▒▒▒ *Le Bout d'Amont*

Laurent et Sylvie VALLERAN
3 rue du Bout d'Amont,
76690 ST GEORGES SUR FONTAINE
☎ 02 35 32 62 43 & 06 33 57 83 59
email: valleran.l.s@wanadoo.fr

Not far from Rouen, a brick-built converted outbuilding with three guest rooms: a double, a twin and a room for four (with double bed and singles). All the rooms have a private bathroom or shower and WC. On the ground floor is the breakfast room, lounge and kitchenette. Garden with pond and furniture.

Prices not confirmed for 2008   **Nearby** ♨ 1km ♨ 8km ♪ 10km ☂ 10km Water sports 30km ♨ 1km 🏛 3km 🚂 8km   **Notes** No pets

ST-JEAN-DU-CARDONNAY

▒▒▒ **La Ferme du Vivier**

Marie-Cécile LAMBERT
88 route de Duclair, 76150 ST JEAN DU CARDONNAY
☎ 02 35 33 80 42 ▤ 02 35 33 80 42
email: Lambert76150@yahoo.fr
web: http://membres.lycos.fr/lambert76150

A 17th-century Norman home on a farm providing a twin room and double (with separate and disabled access), a family room for four, a triple and another double, all with own facilities. Children's bed available. Sitting and living room, TV, kitchenette, washing-machine. Garden with furniture. Jumièges 15km.

Prices s fr €35; d fr €45; t fr €60; extra person fr €22   **Nearby** ♨ 5km ♨ 15km ♪ 15km ☂ 4km Restaurant 4km Water sports 15km ♨ 1km 🏛 4km 🚂 4km   **Notes** No pets

ST-JOUIN-BRUNEVAL

▒▒▒ **Manoir de Guetteville**

Serge et Fabienne PREVOST
Rue Legros, Hameau de Guetteville,
76280 ST JOUIN BRUNEVAL
☎ 02 35 30 79 94 & 06 17 25 56 17 ▤ 02 35 24 82 29
email: manoirdeguetteville@free.fr
web: www.manoir-de-guetteville.com

This peaceful 17th-century flint-built Guetteville manor house is surrounded by extensive gardens and shady fruit trees. The four rooms with separate entrance include three doubles and a triple, all with own shower and wc. Sitting area with TV and games. Fine walk to the coastal coombe at Bruneval.

Prices s fr €42; d fr €50; t fr €70; extra person fr €16   **Nearby** ♨ 3km ♨ 5km ☂ 15km Restaurant 3km ♨ 2km 🏛 2km 🚂 12km   **Notes** No pets English spoken CC

ST-PAER

▒▒▒ La Ville des Champs

J-Pierre et Michèle DUCHET
1036 Ville des Champs, 76480 ST PAER
☎ 02 35 37 28 68
email: jpmduchet@wanadoo.fr
web: www.gite-villedeschamps.com

A former farmhouse surrounded by prairies and orchards, in the Regional Park of Boucles de la Seine Normande. It has a double room, a twin and a room with a double and single, each with private facilities. Extra bed possible. Enjoy picnics and relax on the shady and flowery lawns. Nearby: the Seine Valley with its abbeys and bridges, Caux and Rouen. Parking. Closed part of July.

Prices s fr €37; d €45-€48; t fr €63; extra person €12-€15   **Nearby** ♨ 10km ♨ 12km ☂ 4km ☂ 9km Water sports 12km ♨ 5km 🏛 1km 🚂 9km   **Notes** No pets English spoken

ST-SAENS

⬤ *Le Jardin de Muriel*

Muriel et J-Jacques DUBOC

23 rue Paul Lesueur, 76680 ST SAENS

☎ 02 35 59 86 18 & 06 08 47 86 84

email: muriel7623@free.fr

web: http://muriel7623.free.fr

This beautiful 19th-century house is tucked away in a quiet spot above the attractive little town of St-Saens. Upstairs is a double room and a twin-bedded room; in a separate building is a family room with four single beds, a little kitchenette, terrace and garden furniture. All have private bath or shower room and WC.

Prices not confirmed for 2008 **On Site** 🏊 **Nearby** ⬤ 0.5km ♨ 1km 🎣 15km Water sports 30km ⛵ 0.5km ⚏ 7km **Notes** No pets English spoken

⬤ ♿ Le Logis d'Eawy

Françoise BENKOVSKY

4 rue du 31 Août 1944, 76680 ST SAENS

☎ 06 19 15 52 04 🖨 02 35 34 60 29

email: fbenkovsky@freesbee.fr

web: www.logisdeawy.com

a charming residence in a town in the Bray countryside, close to the Eawy Forest. There is a double/twin with separate entrance and disabled access, a double and a family suite for four, all with own shower and wc. Internal courtyard and garden. Wonderful walking area.

Prices s €48-€50; d €52-€72; extra person fr €15 **On Site** 🎣 **Nearby** ⬤ 0.5km ♨ 1km 🎣 15km Water sports 30km ⛵ 0.5km ⚏ 7km **Notes** No pets English spoken

ST-VAAST-DU-VAL

⬤ Manoir de Fumechon

J et D FLAHAUT-BAEHR

76890 ST VAAST DU VAL

☎ 06 71 79 90 08 & 06 85 52 18 30

🖨 02 35 84 89 11

email: fumechon@ifrance.com

web: www.ifrance.com/fumechon

An elegant 19th-century Anglo-Norman manor, surrounded by a park with mature trees. It provides five charming rooms with private facilities: two doubles, two twins, and a room with a double and single bed. Lounge with TV, video and fireplace. Breakfasts served on the terrace with reading chairs, and table tennis.

Prices s €75-€105; d €75-€105; t fr €105; extra person fr €20 **Nearby** ⬤ 9km ♨ 19km 🎣 7km Restaurant 2km Water sports 30km ⛵ 7km ⚏ 7km 🏛 2km ⚏ 7km **Notes** No pets

ST-VALERY-EN-CAUX

⬤ Hameau d'Ectot

Annie PORCHER

76460 ST VALERY EN CAUX

☎ 02 35 97 88 05

email: patrick.porcher6@wanadoo.fr

Set in a peaceful hamlet between coast and countryside on the approach to the resort of Saint-Valéry-en-Caux, this restored farm building has two doubles and a triple room, all with own shower and wc. Large ground floor sitting and breakfast room. Extensive garden with parking.

Prices s fr €42; d fr €50 **Nearby** ⬤ 3km ♨ 27km 🎣 20km 🏊 2km Restaurant 0.8km Water sports 15km ⛵ 2km 🏛 2km ⚏ 2km **Notes** No pets English spoken

STE-BEUVE-EN-RIVIERE

⬤ ⊙ Le Moulin de l'Epinay

I-L et D BIRTLES

16 chemin du Moulin, 76270 STE BEUVE EN RIVIERE

☎ 02 32 97 13 01 🖨 02 32 97 13 01

email: ilbaumoulin@hotmail.com

web: www.moulin-epinay.com

Parts of this old water mill date from the 18th century. On the first floor is a family room for up to five; a grade 2 twin-bedded room; and

CONTINUED

STE-BEUVE-EN-RIVIERE CONTINUED

a double room. On the second floor is another double with TV, kitchenette, cot and high chair. All rooms have private facilities, but those for the grade 2 room are not en suite. Lounge; meals by arrangement.

Prices s €40-€60; d €40-€65; t €67-€77; extra person fr €12; dinner fr €24 **On Site** ⚲ **Nearby** ⛵ 14km ⚑ 25km ⚓ 8km Water sports 30km ⚘ 8km ⚜ 8km ⌂ 8km ⚐ 15km **Notes** No pets English spoken

🏵 🍴 Les Louxettes

Arlette et André LOUCKX
2 chemin du Moulin, 76270 STE BEUVE EN RIVIERE
☎ 02 35 93 20 81 & 06 86 14 86 25

This former village inn is now a peaceful guesthouse with walking and fishing nearby. Four charming country-style bedrooms include two ground floor doubles, one with separate entrance. First floor double. Second floor triple (two double beds, one single). All rooms have own shower room/WC. Terrace with garden room. Gastronomic dinners.

Prices s fr €35; d €40-€55; t fr €65; extra person fr €15; dinner €13-€30 **On Site** ⚲ ⚜ **Nearby** ⛵ 8km ⚑ 25km Sea 35km ⚓ 9km Restaurant 10km Water sports 30km ⚘ 9km Spa 15km ⌂ 9km ⚐ 15km **Notes** No pets English spoken

THIERGEVILLE

🏵 🍴 ♿ Domaine de l'Orval

Sylvie HERICHER
Route du Bec de Mortagne, 76540 THIERGEVILLE
☎ 02 35 28 54 81
email: domainedelorval@wanadoo.fr
web: www.domainedelorval.com

A small hamlet near the sea is the setting for this restored house. It has four bedrooms. There are three ground floor doubles, all with an additional single bed or cot, and one with disabled access. Upstairs is a two-roomed family suite for five. All rooms have a private shower room and WC. Lounge with TV and stereo; garden furniture; meals by arrangement.

Prices s fr €45; d fr €55; extra person fr €15; dinner €14-€20 **Nearby** ⛵ 12km ⚑ 27km Sea 12km ⚲ 5km ⚓ 12km Restaurant 3km Water sports 18km ⚘ 3km ⌂ 3km ⚐ 12km **Notes** Pets admitted

TURRETOT

🏵 🌿 Les Quatre Brouettes

Claudine et Alain RAS
986 rue Hermeville, 76280 TURRETOT
☎ 02 35 20 23 73 📠 02 35 20 23 73
email: claudine.ras@wanadoo.fr
web: www.gite-lesquatrebrouettes.com

This traditional Norman-style house is 20 minutes from the Pont de Normandie. The rooms have individual names: 'Poppy' is a double with sofa-bed, sitting area/kitchenette and TV; 'Forget-Me-Not' is a triple; 'Camellia' (triple) and 'Periwinkle' (double with cot) share a sitting room and kitchenette. Garden, bike hire.

Prices not confirmed for 2008 **Nearby** ⛵ 8km ⚑ 10km ⚲ 7km ⚓ 4km ⚘ 1km ⌂ 1km ⚐ 4km **Notes** Pets admitted

VARENGEVILLE-SUR-MER

🏵 Les Grandes Masures

Catherine BOSREDON
Route de Vasterival, 76119 VARENGEVILLE SUR MER
☎ 02 32 90 04 37
email: remy.bosredon@wanadoo.fr
web: http://lesgrandesmasures.ifrance.com

A modern house in a quiet, pleasant area 1 km from the sea. Enclosed flower garden with garden room. Ground floor lounge and breakfast room. First floor three double bedrooms and one triple (single beds), all with separate shower room/WC.

Prices s fr €60; d fr €75; t fr €85; extra person fr €10 **Nearby** ⛵ 6km ⚑ 15km Sea 0.9km ⚲ 1km ⚓ 15km Restaurant 0.5km Water sports 1km ⚘ 6km Spa 10km ⌂ 1km ⚐ 10km **Notes** No pets

VIBEUF

🏵 La P'tite Ferme

Isabelle LEFEBVRE
Rue de la Mare des Champs, 76760 VIBEUF
☎ 02 35 96 82 81 📠 02 35 96 82 81
email: lefebvre.isabelle@hotmail.fr

A working farm with spacious bedrooms in a building close to the owners' home. Downstairs are two triples (double bed and a single) and kitchenette; upstairs there is a lounge area on the landing and a family room with a double bed and bunks. A cot is available. Each room has television, shower and WC.

Prices s fr €40; d fr €48; t fr €58; extra person fr €10 **Nearby** ⛵ 6km ⚑ 3km ⚲ 14km ⚓ 6km Restaurant 3km Water sports 26km ⌂ 3km ⚐ 6km **Notes** No pets

VILLERS-ECALLES

🏵 Les Florimanes

Marie-Claire LEREVERT
850 rue Gadeau de Kerville, 76360 VILLERS ECALLES
☎ 02 35 91 98 59 & 06 74 12 82 65
📠 02 35 91 98 59
email: florimanes@wanadoo.fr
web: www.florimanes.net

In quiet countryside only 15 minutes from Rouen, this 17th-century manor house stands in landscaped grounds. The three spacious rooms (non-smoking) include two triples and a double, all with own shower, wc and separate access. Sitting room, music room and library. Unfenced lake. The hostess is a watercolour painter and gives courses in framing and book-binding. Restaurant 3km. 30 minutes from Saint-Valéry-en-Caux.

Prices s €76-€81; d €80-€85; t fr €110 **Nearby** ⛵ 8km ⚑ 8km ⚲ 3km ⚓ 3km Restaurant 3km Water sports 10km ⚘ 1km ⌂ 3km ⚐ 3km **Notes** No pets English spoken

NORMANDY

SEINE-MARITIME

Seine

Risle

EURE
27

Bernay

N 15

N 13

D 810

N 138

Risle

Le Havre

Honfleur

CriquebSuf

Équemauville

Genneville

Les Authieux-
sur-Calonne

Bonneville-
la-Louvet

Le Pin

Moyaux

Firfol

Marolles

St-Martin-de-la-Lieve

St-Germain-
de-Livet

Prêtreville

Ste-Marguerite-des-Loges

Préaux-
St-Sébastien

Touques

D 979

N 26

Risle

Argentan

D 916

D 579

St-Désir-
de-Lisieux

Lisieux

Manerbe

Cambremer

St-Aubin-
Lébizay

St-Laurent-
du-Mont

Le Mesnil-Mauger

Le Mesnil-
Durand

Tortisambert

St-Étienne-
la-Thillaye

Pont-l'Évêque

Bourgeauville

Gonneville-
sur-Mer

Bretteville-
sur-Dives

St-Pierre-
sur-Dives

Berville-
l'Oudon

Dives

D 53

THE ENGLISH CHANNEL

Bavent

Le Home-
Varaville

Croissanville

Vieux-Fumé

St-Aignan-
de-Cramesnil

N 158

Ussy

D 511

606 D

Rapilly

Le Mesnil-Villement

D 909

CAEN

Maltot

Bretteville-
sur-Laize

Clécy-le-Vey

La Pommeraye

Pont-d'Ouilly

ORNE
61

D 924

Mondrainville

Noyers-Bocage

Parfouru-sur-Odon

Ome

D 562

Graye-sur-Mer

Courseulles-sur-Mer

St-Côme-
de-Fresne

Crépon

Sommervieu

Banville

Beny-sur-Mer

Reviers

Basly

Rosel

Secqueville-en-Bessin

Authie

N 13

D 7

D 982

Manvieux

Longues-
sur-Mer

Magny-en-Bessin

Vaux-sur-Aure

St-Martin-
des-Entrées

Bayeux

Lingèvres

Tilly-
sur-Seulles

Cahagnolles

Livry

Longvillers

St-Jean-le-Blanc

St-Charles-
de-Percy

Montchamp

Colleville-
sur-Mer

Mosles

Commes

Subles

Cahagnes

A 84

Vire

Vire

St-Pierre-
du-Mont

La Cambe

Formigny

Tour-en-Bessin

Vaucelles

Campigny

Le Molay-Littry

Grandcamp-
Maisy

Géfosse-
Fontenay

Mandeville-en-Bessin

Colombières

Vouilly

Bricqueville

Ruberc/

A 84

N 174

Courson

D 524

MANCHE
50

SAINT-LÔ

N 175

D 999

D 966

D 972

15 km

N

Le Havre

D 940

A 29

A 131

A 13

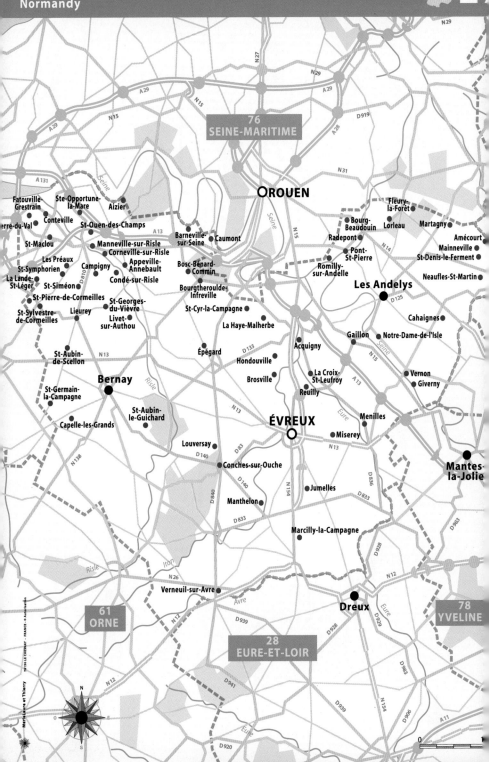

76 SEINE-MARITIME

○ROUEN

61 ORNE

28 EURE-ET-LOIR

78 YVELINE

Fatouville-Grestrain
Ste-Opportune-la-Mare
Aizier
Conteville
rre-du-Val
St-Ouen-des-Champs
St-Maclou
Manneville-sur-Risle
Corneville-sur-Risle
Barneville-sur-Seine
Caumont
Les Préaux
St-Symphorien
Campigny
Appeville-Annebault
Bosc-Bénard-Commin
La Lande-St-Léger
St-Siméon
Condé-sur-Risle
Bourgtheroulde-Infreville
St-Pierre-de-Cormeilles
St-Georges-du-Vièvre
St-Cyr-la-Campagne
St-Sylvestre-de-Cormeilles
Lieurey
Livet-sur-Authou
La Haye-Malherbe
St-Aubin-de-Scellon
Épégard
Hondouville
Bernay
Brosville
St-Germain-la-Campagne
St-Aubin-le-Guichard
Capelle-les-Grands
Louversay
Conches-sur-Ouche
Manthelon
Marcilly-la-Campagne
Verneuil-sur-Avre

Fleury-la-Forêt
Bourg-Beaudouin
Lorleau
Martagny
Radepont
Pont-St-Pierre
Amécourt
Mainneville
St-Denis-le-Ferment
Romilly-sur-Andelle
Neaufles-St-Martin
Les Andelys
Cahaignes
Gaillon
Notre-Dame-de-l'Isle
Acquigny
La Croix-St-Leufroy
Vernon
Reuilly
Giverny
Menilles
ÉVREUX ○
Miserey
Mantes-la-Jolie
Jumelles

Dreux

THE HAGUE PENINSULA

Fermanville
Gatteville-le Phare

Cherbourg
Tourlaville
Montfarville

La Glacerie

Benoitville
Tamerville
Videcosville

Les Pieux
Négreville
Valognes

Bricquebec
Lieusaint

THE ENGLISH CHANNEL

Fresville
St-Martin-de-Varreville

Barneville-Carteret
Rauville-la-Place
Ste-Mère-Église

Portbail
Angoville-au-Plain

Les Veys

Jersey
Montgardon
Bayeux

Graignes

14
CALVADOS

Vaudrimesnil

SAINT-LÔ

Blainville-sur-Mer
Coutances
Lamberville

Montchaton

Regnéville-sur-Mer
Orval

Chausey Island
Le Mesnil-Aubert

Tessy-sur-Vire

Lingreville

Longueville
Vire

La Beslière

61
ORNE

St-Michel-des-Loups

Genêts
Juvigny-le-Tertre

Saint-Malo
Avranches

Le Mont St-Michel
Le Val-St-Père

Céaux

Huisnes-sur-Mer
Ardevon
St-Cyr-du-Bailleul

Beauvoir
Servon

Juilley

Aucey-la-Plaine
Vergoncey
St-Aubin-de-Terregatte

La Croix-Avranchin

Vessey
St-James

35
ILLE-ET-VILAINE

Sélune

0   15 km

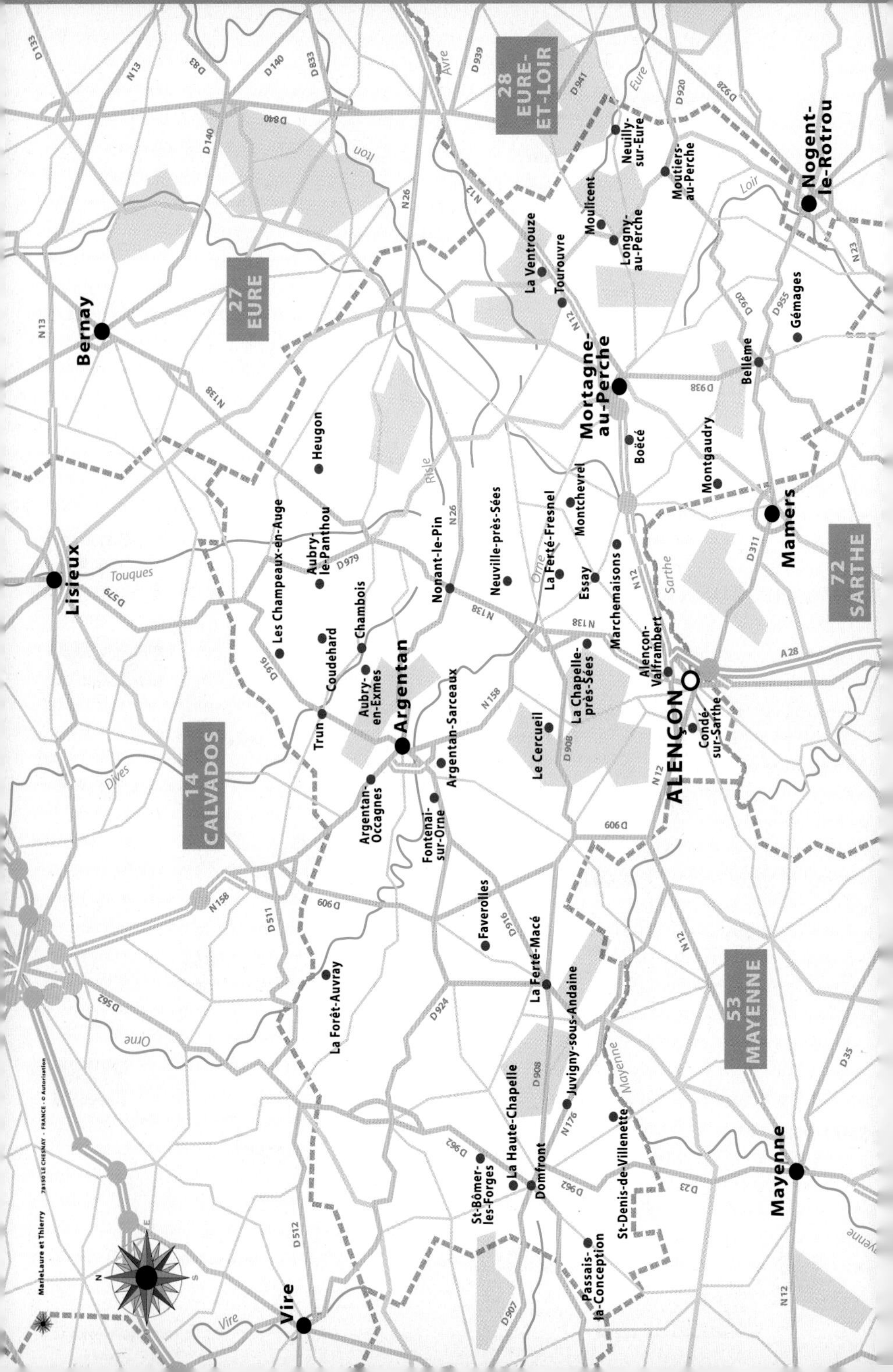

28 EURE-ET-LOIR

27 EURE

14 CALVADOS

72 SARTHE

53 MAYENNE

Nogent-le-Rotrou

Neuilly-sur-Eure

Moutiers-au-Perche

Moulicent

Longny-au-Perche

Tourouvre

La Ventrouze

Gémages

Bellême

Mortagne-au-Perche

Boëcé

Montgaudry

Mamers

Bernay

Heugon

Les Champeaux-en-Auge

Aubry-le-Panthou

Chambois

Coudehard

Aubry-en-Exmes

Trun

Nonant-le-Pin

Neuville-près-Sées

La Ferté-Fresnel

Montchevrel

Essay

Marchemaisons

Argentan

Argentan-Sarceaux

Le Cercueil

La Chapelle-près-Sées

Alençon-Valframbert

ALENÇON

Condé-sur-Sarthe

Argentan-Occagnes

Fontenai-sur-Orne

Lisieux

Faverolles

La Ferté-Macé

La Forêt-Auvray

Juvigny-sous-Andaine

Mayenne

St-Bômer-les-Forges

La Haute-Chapelle

Domfront

St-Denis-de-Villenette

Passais-la-Conception

Vire

Lisieux

Touques

Dives

Orne

Vire

Yonne

Moyenne

Sarthe

Eure

Loir

Risle

Iton

Mortelaure et Thierry

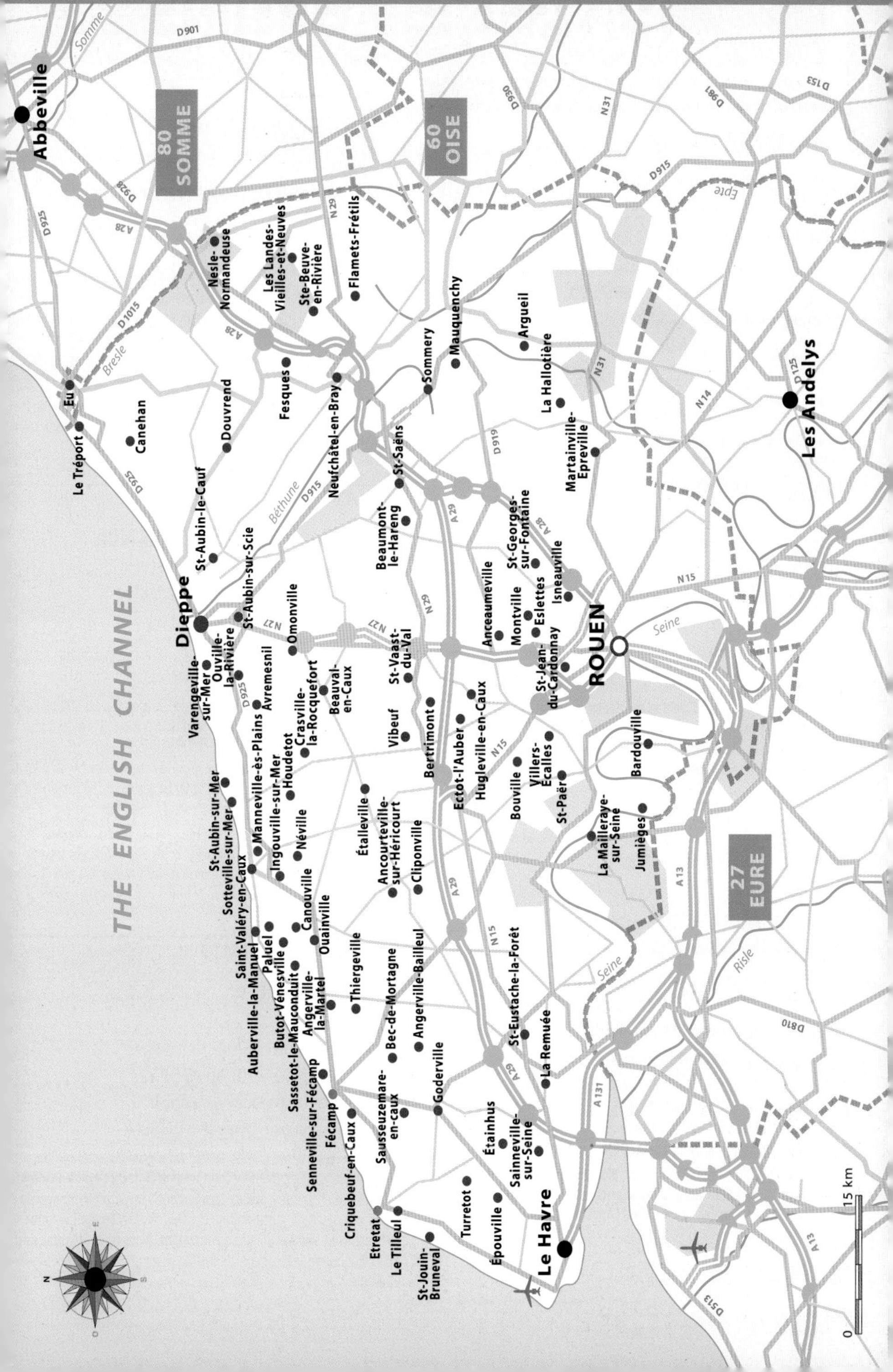

76

80 SOMME

60 OISE

27 EURE

Abbeville

Les Andelys

Le Tréport

Eu

Canehan

Douvrend

Fesques

Nesle-Normandeuse

Les Landes-Vieilles-et-Neuves

Ste-Beuve-en-Rivière

Flamets-Frétils

Mauquenchy

Sommery

Argueil

La Hallotière

Martainville-Epreville

Neufchâtel-en-Bray

St-Saëns

Beaumont-le-Hareng

Dieppe

St-Aubin-le-Cauf

St-Aubin-sur-Scie

Varengeville-sur-Mer

Ouville-la-Rivière

St-Aubin-sur-Mer

Omonville

Avremesnil

St-Vaast-du-Val

St-Georges-sur-Fontaine

Montville

Eslettes

Isneauville

Anceaumeville

ROUEN

St-Jean-du-Cardonnay

Crasville-la-Rocquefort

Beauval-en-Caux

Vibeuf

Bertrimont

Houdetot

Manneville-ès-Plains

Ingouville-sur-Mer

Néville

Canouville

Étalleville

Ancourteville-sur-Héricourt

Cliponville

Ectot-l'Auber

Hugleville-en-Caux

Villers-Écalles

Bouville

St-Paër

Bardouville

La Mailleraye-sur-Seine

Jumièges

St-Valéry-en-Caux

Sotteville-sur-Mer

Paluel

Butot-Vénesville

Auberville-la-Manuel

Sassetot-le-Mauconduit

Angerville-la-Martel

Ouainville

Thiergeville

Senneville-sur-Fécamp

Fécamp

Bec-de-Mortagne

Angerville-Bailleul

St-Eustache-la-Forêt

Criquebeuf-en-Caux

Saussuzemare-en-caux

Goderville

La Remuée

Étretat

Le Tilleul

Turretot

Épouville

St-Jouin-Bruneval

Étainhus

Sainneville-sur-Seine

Le Havre

THE ENGLISH CHANNEL

Seine

Béthune

Bresle

Epte

Risle

15 km

PAYS-DE-LA-LOIRE

LOIRE-ATLANTIQUE

ARTHON-EN-RETZ

⬚ & Chambre d'hôtes

Marie Claire MALARD
Route de Chauvé, 1 Rue Moulin de la Boizonnière,
44320 ARTHON EN RETZ
☎ 02 40 64 85 81 & 06 03 86 25 29 📄 02 40 64 85 81
email: malardpi@wanadoo.fr
web: www.gites-de-france-44.fr/moulin_boizonniere/

Close to the sea in peaceful countryside, the house has four en suite guest rooms, one accessible for the less mobile. Heating, breakfast room with kitchenette, separate entrance. The garden has children's games, BBQ and furniture. Private parking.

Prices s fr €32; d fr €37; t fr €42; extra person fr €5 **Nearby** ⛷ 9km
🏊 10km Sea 7km 🎣 7km ⬈ 10km Restaurant 1km Water sports 7km
🚲 1km 🏌 10km 🅿 0.4km ⭐ 10km **Notes** Pets admitted English spoken

ASSERAC

⬚ ⍥ La Baie des Dames

Christine JOSSO
Pen Bé, 44410 ASSERAC
☎ 02 40 01 72 45

Uninterrupted views of the sea are a feature at this house, which offers three rooms for two or three guests, each with TV, shower and wc. There is a library, lounge/games room, large enclosed garden with a terrace and garden furniture. Friendly atmosphere. Medieval city nearby.

Prices not confirmed for 2008 **On Site** Sea 🎣 Water sports
Nearby ⛷ 12km 🏊 20km ⬈ 20km 🚲 6km 🅿 6km ⭐ 20km
Notes No pets Open May to September.

⬚ Le Marquisat

Marie PHILIPPE-PAUVERT
15 Rue du Calvaire, 44410 ASSERAC
☎ 02 51 10 28 68 & 06 11 02 64 47
email: le.marquisat@caramail.com
web: http://le.marquisat.club.fr/

An early 18th-century manor house situated between the Parc de Brière and the salt marshes. Three en suite double rooms with shower and wc. Guests can use the main lounge with open fireplace, the attractive garden, furnished terrace, BBQ and parking.

Prices s fr €50; d €57-€63; t fr €73 **Nearby** ⛷ 8km 🏊 20km Sea 4.5km
🎣 12km Restaurant 4.5km 🚲 5km Spa 24km 🏌 0.1km 🅿 5km ⭐ 20km
Notes No pets English spoken Open April to October and reservations.

BASSE-GOULAINE

⬚ L'Orangerie du Parc

Bernard METRO
195 Rue du Grignon, 44115 BASSE GOULAINE
☎ 02 40 54 91 30 📄 02 40 54 91 30
email: lorangeduparc@voila.fr
web: www.gites-de-france-44.fr/lorangerie

Guests will enjoy the charming and refined setting of this gîte, in the orangerie of a lovely old residence. Ideal location to experience Nantes' traditional cuisine and there is a large dining room and a lounge for guests' use. The bedrooms are spacious and completely independent, all have private facilities.

Prices s €60-€65; d €72-€78; t €88-€91 **On Site** 🏌 **Nearby** ⛷ 4km
🏊 5km Sea 50km 🎣 1km ⬈ 2km Restaurant 0.1km Water sports 50km
🚲 1km 🅿 2km ⭐ 8km **Notes** No pets English spoken

BOUAYE

⬚ Château du Bois de La Nöe

Patrick et Valérie GUFFROY
8 Allée de la Roseraie, 44830 BOUAYE
☎ 02 51 11 10 94 & 06 33 52 71 45
email: pat.guffroy@wanadoo.fr
web: www.chateau-boisdelanoe.com/

A magnificent 17th-century property just 20 minutes from Nantes, with five spacious, elegantly decorated bedrooms. All are doubles, two with an additional single bed, and each room has a television, private shower room and WC. The grounds are spacious with a lake, swimming pool and tennis court. Plenty of garden furniture, and a games area for children.

Prices s €55-€65; d fr €75; t fr €85; extra person fr €10 **On Site** 🏌
Private ⬈ Private tennis court **Nearby** ⛷ 4km 🏊 15km Sea 30km
🎣 2km Water sports 30km 🅿 0.3km ⭐ 0.3km **Notes** No pets English spoken

CHATEAU-THEBAUD

⬚ La Pénissière

Gérard et Annick BOUSSEAU
44690 CHATEAU-THEBAUD
☎ 02 40 06 51 22 📄 02 40 06 51 22
email: hotes-bousseau@wanadoo.fr
web: www.domaine-penissiere-millaut.fr

Guests are warmly welcomed to this wine-growing estate in the heart of Muscadet, providing three tastefully decorated bedrooms, with antique furniture, private facilities and views of the vineyards. There is a separate guest entrance, a large warm reception room with exposed stonework and a mezzanine (with optional extra bed). Peaceful lounge area, fireplace and TV. Fishing on a private lake in 400mtrs.

Prices s fr €40; d fr €45; extra person fr €15 **Nearby** ⚓ 3km Sea 40km ⚓ 0.4km ⚓ 6km Restaurant 1.5km Water sports 0.4km ⚓ 3km ⚓ 2km ⚓ 18km **Notes** No pets

CHATEAUBRIANT

ⅢⅢ ⅠⓄⅠ Les Fougerays

Gilles SALMON

44110 CHATEAUBRIANT

☎ 02 28 04 07 56

email: salmongilles@orange.fr

web: www.chateaubriant-gite.com

The oldest parts of this château date back to the 15th century. It stands in four hectares of grounds, amongst ancient trees and in a French-style garden. The five elegantly decorated bedrooms are all doubles, and each has a private bath or shower room and WC. A peaceful spot, where relaxation comes naturally.

Prices s €77-€86; d €77-€86; dinner fr €23 **On Site** ⚓ **Nearby** ⚓ 7km ⚓ 15km ⚓ 1.5km Restaurant 1km ⚓ 1.5km ⚓ 2km ⚓ 1.5km **Notes** No pets English spoken

CHAUVE

ⅢⅠ La Caillerie

Colette LESUEUR

44320 CHAUVE

☎ 02 40 21 16 18 & 06 60 84 77 97

email: lesueurcolette@yahoo.fr

web: www.caillerie.com

A peaceful rural setting in the heart of the Pays de Retz, south of the Loire and 12km from Pornic and the Côte de Jade beaches. Four guest bedrooms are available for two to four people, all with private bathroom, TV and separate entrance. Large shady garden, private parking.

Prices d €52-€58; t fr €75; extra person fr €17 **Nearby** ⚓ 2.5km ⚓ 12km Sea 12km ⚓ 12km Restaurant 12km Water sports 12km ⚓ 3km ⚓ 12km ⚓ 3.5km ⚓ 12km **Notes** No pets English spoken Open April to September.

CHEMERE

ⅢⅠ Princé Neuf

Hubert HARDY

44680 CHEMERE

☎ 02 40 21 30 35 & 06 76 99 85 42 ⚓ 02 40 21 30 35

email: princeneuf@wanadoo.fr

A former hunting lodge dating from the 19th century, at the edge of the Princé Forest, close to Pornic. There are four first-floor en suite double bedrooms, heating and the estate has direct access to long forest walks and adjoining grounds.

Prices s fr €50; d fr €52; extra person fr €15 **On Site** Private tennis court **Nearby** ⚓ 10km Sea 15km Restaurant 4km Water sports 15km ⚓ 15km ⚓ 15km ⚓ 4km ⚓ 12km **Notes** No pets Open April to October.

FROSSAY

ⅢⅢ ⅠⓄⅠ Chambre d'hôtes

Rémy et Gabrielle LERAY

3 Rue Saint Front, 44320 FROSSAY

☎ 02 28 53 04 87 & 06 81 00 49 14

email: rgl.1328@wanadoo.fr

web: http://perso.wanadoo.fr/logis-de-saint-front/

In the town of Frossay, 20 kilometres from the sea, this property offers three first floor non-smoking bedrooms, with independent access. Each room sleeps up to three people and has an en suite shower room/WC. There is a lounge with kitchen area on the ground floor. Breakfast can be served on the terrace.

Prices d fr €52; t fr €65; dinner fr €15 **Nearby** ⚓ 10km ⚓ 20km Sea 18km ⚓ 2km ⚓ 18km Restaurant 1km Water sports 2km ⚓ 18km ⚓ 0.2km ⚓ 22km **Notes** No pets English spoken

ⅢⅢ Château de La Rousselière

Catherine SCHERER

44320 FROSSAY

☎ 02 40 39 79 59 ⚓ 02 40 39 77 78

email: info@larousseliere.com

web: www.larousseliere.com

An 18th-century château in beautiful grounds in the Pays de Retz, just 3km from the Canal de la Martinière. Three spacious en suite bedrooms with separate entrances are available. Lounge and dining room for guests, swimming pool, horses accepted. Forest, Pornic, St Brévin nearby.

Prices s fr €85; d fr €85; extra person fr €30 **On Site** Private ⚓ **Nearby** ⚓ 10km ⚓ 20km Sea 20km ⚓ 3km Restaurant 3km Water sports 3km ⚓ 1km ⚓ 20km ⚓ 1km ⚓ 25km **Notes** Pets admitted English spoken Open May to September. CC

GUEMENE-PENFAO

ⅢⅢ ⅠⓄⅠ ⚓ Callac

Chantal et Michel DEBARRE

44290 GUEMENE PENFAO

☎ 02 40 51 12 36 & 06 87 66 10 22

email: mic.debarre@wanadoo.fr

web: www.lesroseauxdecallac.com

Quietly situated in the heart of the Don Valley, this restored stone farmhouse has four comfortable double rooms. Breakfast is served in the rustic dining room; there is a lounge with a big fireplace and an attractive garden. Good walks in the area.

Prices s fr €40; d fr €49; t fr €62; extra person fr €12; dinner fr €17 **Nearby** ⚓ 4km ⚓ 40km Sea 50km ⚓ 1.5km ⚓ 2.5km Restaurant 2.5km Water sports 2.5km ⚓ 2.5km ⚓ 0.1km ⚓ 2.5km ⚓ 20km **Notes** No pets English spoken

HERBIGNAC

⊞ Chambre d'hôtes La Noe de Marlais

Henri et Josiane FRESNE

12 Rue Jean de Rieux, 44410 HERBIGNAC

☎ 02 40 91 40 83 & 06 88 50 35 24 ▤ 02 40 91 40 83

email: j.h.fresne@orange.fr

web: http://perso.orange.fr/lanoedemarlais

This converted longhouse is in a village within travelling distance of the coast around the Golfe de Morbihan. It has a double room with its own outside access, and two two-roomed family suites for four, all of them with private shower room and WC. Baby equipment available if needed. Off-road parking.

Prices s fr €40; d fr €51; t fr €69; extra person fr €16 **Nearby** ⚓ 6km ⚓ 13km Sea 12km ⚓ 1km ⚓ 13km Restaurant 5km Water sports 13km ⚓ 1.5km ⚓ 0.1km ⚓ 1.5km ⚓ 19km **Notes** Pets admitted English spoken

⊞ Château de Coëtcaret

Cécile DE LA MONNERAYE

44410 HERBIGNAC

☎ 02 40 91 41 20 & 06 98 40 20 74 ▤ 02 40 91 37 46

email: info@coetcaret.com

web: www.coetcaret.com

This small 19th-century château enjoys an exceptional setting on a large wooded estate between the ocean and the Parc Régional de Brière. There are three quiet, comfortable en suite bedrooms, one suitable for a family of three. Heating, table tennis, telephone, garden furniture, nature trail in the grounds, day trips arranged with help of hosts. Wi-fi available throughout.

Prices d €95-€100; extra person fr €28 **On Site** ⚓ **Nearby** ⚓ 12km Sea 14km ⚓ 2km ⚓ 12km Restaurant 1.5km Water sports 2km ⚓ 4km ⚓ 3km ⚓ 20km **Notes** No pets English spoken

JOUE-SUR-ERDRE

⊞ ♿ Les Ronderais

Marie-Béatrice CAROUR

44440 JOUE SUR ERDRE

☎ 02 28 24 80 98 ▤ 02 28 24 81 39

email: mbcarour@wanadoo.fr

web: www.lesronderais44.com

An old farmhouse, beautifully restored, in a truly rural spot close to a lake and about half an hour from Nantes. There are four spacious, comfortable en suite bedrooms, all with attractive views: a double and a triple on the ground, both with terraces, and a double and a triple upstairs; all have shower room and separate WC. Accommodation for horses (meadow or loose box). This is a non-smoking property.

Prices s fr €47; d fr €57; t fr €67; extra person fr €9 **On Site** Private ⚓ **Nearby** ⚓ 4km ⚓ 25km ⚓ 0.3km Restaurant 4km Water sports 4km ⚓ 6km ⚓ 4km ⚓ 10km ⚓ 40km **Notes** No pets English spoken Open April to 1 November.

LA CHAPELLE-SUR-ERDRE

⊞ La Gandonnière

Françoise GIRARD

44240 LA CHAPELLE SUR ERDRE

☎ 02 40 72 53 45

email: pierre.girard351@orange.fr

web: www.gites-de-france-44.fr

An 18th-century house with gardens and a lake, close to Nantes. There are three bedrooms, each with its own character: a twin-bedded room, a triple (double bed and single) and a family suite for four (double bed and singles). All have en suite facilities. Outside is a terrace and gardens with good views.

Prices d €79-€115; extra person fr €20 **Nearby** ⚓ 3km ⚓ 4km Sea 50km ⚓ 0.1km ⚓ 7km Restaurant 1.5km Water sports 0.1km ⚓ 1.5km ⚓ 1.5km ⚓ 12km **Notes** No pets Open May to September and reservations.

LA CHEVROLIERE

⊞ Chambre d'hôtes

Joseph et Danielle CHEVALIER

26 Thubert, 44118 LA CHEVROLIERE

☎ 02 40 31 31 26 & 06 89 99 19 80

Set in the country, this house offers four rooms with bathrooms and separate entrances, two with kitchenettes. Guest lounge, dining room with kitchen and TV. Terrace, lawn, garden furniture. Lake, restaurant, and leisure centre nearby, as well as Nantes and airport.

Prices s fr €36; d fr €45; t fr €61; extra person fr €16 **Nearby** ⚓ 4km Sea 35km ⚓ 10km ⚓ 10km Restaurant 3km Water sports 10km ⚓ 5km ⚓ 10km ⚓ 4km ⚓ 13km **Notes** No pets

LA LIMOUZINIERE

⊞ ▯◯▮ Chambre d'hôtes

Ghislaine PATRAULT

1 Rue Des Marronnier, La Touche Monnet,

44310 LA LIMOUZINIERE

☎ 02 40 05 52 83

email: lechironet@wanadoo.fr

web: www.le-chironet.com/

A property in a truly beautiful spot with three en suite bedrooms (tw doubles and a twin-bedded room) opening directly onto gardens wi mature lime trees and lots of flowers. The beds are top quality and t rooms are soundproofed. Extra bed if needed. A guests' living room available in another building in the grounds.

Prices s fr €52; d fr €54; t fr €68; extra person fr €14; dinner fr €24 **Nearby** ⚓ 1km ⚓ 30km Sea 20km ⚓ 5km ⚓ 5km Restaurant 3km Water sports 25km ⚓ 1km Spa 40km ⚓ 20km ⚓ 1km ⚓ 30km **Notes** No pets English spoken

LA PLAINE-SUR-MER

⊪ Chambre d'hôtes

Nicole FOUCHER

15 Rue de la Libération, 44770 LA PLAINE SUR MER

☎ 02 40 21 53 32   📄 02 40 21 53 32

web: www.gites-de-france-44.fr/chez_nicole

Three romantically-decorated first floor bedrooms at this property: a double with bathroom, another double with shower/WC, and a double of separable twin beds, also with shower/WC; extra folding beds are available if needed. Fridge and microwave; peaceful, shady enclosed garden. Off-road parking and under cover parking for bikes and motor bikes. October to May reservation only.

Prices s fr €48; d fr €50; t fr €53 **Nearby** ⛰ 6km ♨ 6km Sea 1.5km ✎ 1.5km ✗ 6km Restaurant 0.1km Water sports 3km ⌘ 0.3km ♜ 6km ⋈ 6km **Notes** No pets English spoken

LA TURBALLE

⊪ Les Belles Roches

Isabelle BRIAND

Cté Arturballe, 58 Rue de Bellevue, 44420 LA TURBALLE

☎ 02 40 22 10 72 & 06 73 45 76 43   📄 02 40 60 35 88

email: bellesroches@wanadoo.fr

web: www.lesbellesroches.com

In beautiful grounds with plenty of flowers, this is a house where peace and quiet can be guaranteed. There are three double rooms, a triple, and a family room for four, all with TV, private shower and WC. Indoor swimming pool, and a cooking area for guests with fridge-freezer and microwave.

Prices s fr €64-€74; d €64-€74; t fr €78; extra person fr €18 **On Site** Private ✗ **Nearby** ⛰ 5km ♨ 15km Sea 1km ✎ 1km Restaurant 1.2km Water sports 1km ⌘ 1km Spa 15km ♜ 1.2km ⋈ 1.2km ⋈ 15km **Notes** No pets English spoken CC

LE BIGNON

⊪ La Cour de l'Epinay

Martin et Caroline DURAND

44140 LE BIGNON

☎ 02 40 78 15 19 & 06 21 30 36 89   📄 02 40 78 15 19

In a relaxing riverside setting, this establishment offers five character rooms in the former outbuildings of a 19th-century château, each with a private washroom or bathroom. There is also a guest lounge. La Cour de l'Epinay is just 15 minutes from the centre of Nantes.

Prices s €41-€46; d €57-€62; extra person fr €7 **On Site** ✎ **Nearby** ⛰ 4km ♨ 20km Sea 40km ✗ 6km Restaurant 1km Water sports 10km ⌘ 3km ♜ 12km ♜ 3km ⋈ 12km **Notes** Pets admitted English spoken

LE LANDREAU

⊪ Le Relais de la Rinière

Françoise LEBARILLIER

44430 LE LANDREAU

☎ 02 40 06 41 44   📄 02 51 13 10 52

email: riniere@netcourrier.com

web: www.riniere.com

This charming house with large flower-filled gardens is in the heart of wine country and an ideal base for exploring the Loire. Three en suite bedrooms, picnics in the garden and children's games. Pony trekkers welcome.

Prices s fr €41; d fr €45; extra person fr €13 **On Site** ♞ **Nearby** ✎ 12km ✗ 6km Restaurant 3km Water sports 15km ⌘ 3km ♜ 3km ⋈ 25km **Notes** Pets admitted English spoken

LE TEMPLE-DE-BRETAGNE

⊪ ♿ Chambre d'hôtes

Marguerite DE SARIAC

52 Rue Georges Bonnet, La Mariaudais,

44360 LE TEMPLE DE BRETAGNE

☎ 02 40 57 09 38 & 06 30 59 98 64

email: mariaudais@free.fr

web: http://mariaudais.chez-alice.fr

Former stables have been renovated to offer four spacious triple bedrooms with showers and wcs. Dining room with TV and kitchen area for guests, separate entrance. Adjoining courtyard, orchard and vegetable garden.

Prices s fr €47; d fr €56; t €68-€72; extra person fr €15 **Nearby** ⛰ 5km ♨ 10km Sea 40km ✗ 10km Water sports 40km ⋈ 10km **Notes** No pets English spoken

LEGE

⊪ ⊙ ♿ La Mozardiere

Gérard et Christine DESBROSSES

Richebonne, 44650 LEGE

☎ 02 40 04 98 51   📄 02 40 26 31 61

email: christine@lamozardiere.com

web: www.lamozardiere.com

An 18th-century house in a peaceful spot quite close to the town. There are three bedrooms: a double on the ground floor, upstairs another double and a two-room family suite for up to five. All have

CONTINUED

LEGE *CONTINUED*

private bathroom and WC. Sitting room with open fireplace, and guests' kitchen area. No smoking; pre-booked meals some days.

Prices s fr €54; d fr €56; t fr €85; extra person fr €6; dinner fr €26 **Nearby** ⚓ 8km Sea 39km 🏊 1km ⌇ 1km Restaurant 0.6km Water sports 1km ⚘ 1km 🚲 1km ⚑ 22km **Notes** Pets admitted English spoken Open March to October.

MARSAC-SUR-DON

⋕⋕⋕ ⦿ La Mérais

Sylvie BRENON

44170 MARSAC SUR DON

☎ 02 40 79 50 78 & 06 64 47 16 98

email: daniel.brenon@wanadoo.fr

web: www.lamerais.com

This long-barn has been lovingly restored by the owners and offers two en suite rooms for two or three guests and a room with mezzanine for four, all with separate entrances. A large reception room has a kitchen and dining area, and there are terraces with garden furniture.

Prices s fr €42; d fr €55; t fr €65; extra person fr €10; dinner fr €25 **On Site** Restaurant ⚘ **Nearby** ⚓ 6km ⚘ 10km 🏊 1km ⌇ 5km Water sports 5km ⚘ 7km 🚲 1km **Notes** No pets English spoken

MESQUER

⋕⋕⋕ Clos de Botelo

Liliane LEDUC

249 Rue des Caps Horniers, Kercabellec, 44420 MESQUER

☎ 02 40 42 50 20 & 06 22 61 11 06 🖹 02 40 42 50 20

email: leduc.liliane@wanadoo.fr

web: www.leduc-liliane.fr/

A peaceful, character house with marsh views, furnished with antiques, a fireplace and a collection of paintings and works of art. Five rooms sleep four, three, or two people and each has private shower and WC. TV, terrace, orchard, lawns, parking.

Prices s fr €49; d fr €59; t fr €78 **Nearby** ⚓ 3km ⚘ 14km Sea 0.4km 🏊 0.4km ⌇ 8km Water sports 0.4km ⚘ 3km 🚲 1.3km ⚑ 14km **Notes** No pets

MISSILLAC

⋕⋕⋕ ⦿ Au Jardin d'Eau

Valérie BONDUELLE

La Saulzaie, 44780 MISSILLAC

☎ 02 51 76 89 82 & 06 75 63 81 53

email: valerie_bonduelle@yahoo.fr

web: www.gites-de-france-44.fr/au_jardin_d_eau/

In southern Brittany, in the Brière Park, this property offers four guest rooms, two of them family rooms. They all have a terrace, and a view over the lake. Fishing available; enclosed play area for children, kitchenette available. Meals by arrangement - house specialities are crêpes and galettes. Closed during February holidays.

Prices s fr €40; d fr €48; t fr €60; extra person fr €12; dinner fr €16 **On Site** 🏊 ⚘ **Nearby** ⚓ 8km ⚘ 5km Sea 25km ⌇ 8km Restaurant 4km Water sports 25km ⚘ 5km 🚲 4km ⚑ 8km **Notes** Pets admitted English spoken

MONNIERES

⋕⋕⋕ ⦿ Chambre d'hôtes

Jean Paul SAUVAGET

22 Rue de la Poste, 44690 MONNIERES

☎ 02 40 54 64 91

email: jpaul@topaze-monnieres.com

web: www.monnieres.com

An old farmhouse in the wine-growing village of Monnières. Three bedrooms sleep from three to five people, all with private bath or shower room and WC. The family room is grade 2. Plenty of walks, either beside the river or through the vineyards. Nantes and Clisson are easily accessible. Wine tasting on request.

Prices s fr €38; d fr €43; t fr €58; extra person fr €12; dinner fr €20 **Nearby** ⚓ 5km ⚘ 20km Sea 50km 🏊 0.3km ⌇ 5km Restaurant 5km Water sports 50km ⚘ 1km ⚘ 3km 🚲 5km ⚑ 2km **Notes** No pets English spoken CC

NORT-SUR-ERDRE

⋕⋕⋕ Le Patis Roux

M et J-P RAIMONDEAU

44390 NORT SUR ERDRE

☎ 02 40 85 01 02 & 06 63 28 85 14

email: jpraimondeau@wanadoo.fr

web: http://perso.wanadoo.fr/jpraimondeau/

In the peace and quiet of the countryside, this restored stone-built house has three double bedrooms. On the ground floor is a light and airy lounge area with open fire, books and a telescope. Upstairs is a mezzanine lounge area, and the three rooms, each with private facilities. Extra bed available. Garden, terrace, garden furniture, table tennis and barbecue.

Prices s fr €52; d fr €58; extra person fr €15 **On Site** Private ⌇ **Nearby** ⚓ 5km ⚘ 15km 🏊 3km Restaurant 5km ⚘ 5km ⚘ 5km 🚲 5km ⚑ 30km **Notes** No pets English spoken

NOZAY

⋕⋕⋕ Grand Jouan

Pierre et Monique MARZELIERE

44170 NOZAY

☎ 02 40 79 45 85 & 06 80 84 18 63 🖹 02 40 79 77 80

email: pierre.marzeliere@wanadoo.fr

web: http://grandjouan.online.fr/

This former agricultural school is situated between Nantes and Rennes. Four en suite bedrooms for two or three people. Guest TV lounge, games room and dining room. Shady grounds, horse boxes, lakes, mini-golf. Creperie and restaurants nearby.

Prices s fr €37; d fr €47; t fr €57-€60; extra person fr €12 **Nearby** ⚓ 10km 🏊 1km ⌇ 2km Restaurant 2km Water sports 1km ⚘ 2km 🚲 2km ⚑ 25km **Notes** Pets admitted

ORVAULT

⊪ ⌸ ⅃ Chambre d'hôtes d'Orvault

Thierry et Béatrice HARVEY
8 Chemin de la Provotière, 44700 ORVAULT
☎ 02 40 63 45 26 & 02 40 63 70 65 📱 02 40 63 45 26
email: harvey.bnb@wanadoo.fr
web: http://harveybnb.monsite.orange.fr

This house, in undulating grounds beside a lake, is just 15 minutes
from the centre of Nantes. The large comfortable rooms, one with
separate entrance, all have TVs and private bathrooms. One room has
disabled access. There is a lounge with open fire, and the dining room
opens directly on to the terrace. Attractive walks in the grounds.

Prices s fr €62; d fr €67; extra person fr €6 **On Site** ♟
Nearby ♣ 10km ♨ 5km Sea 50km ⚲ 2km Restaurant 1km Water
sports 10km ♒ 1km ⛪ 3km ⛵ 8km **Notes** Pets admitted English
spoken CC

PIRIAC-SUR-MER

⊪ Polohan

Sylvie GUILLARD
55 Route de Guérande, 44420 PIRIAC SUR MER
☎ 02 40 15 52 93
email: sylvie-guillard@wanadoo.fr

The three comfortable bedrooms at this property are in a converted
barn, just one kilometre from the town and the beaches: a ground
floor double with shower room, and the same configuration upstairs
together with a twin-bedded room with additional sofa bed and own
bathroom. Separate dining room for guests, with direct access to the
garden.

Prices s fr €45; d fr €55; t fr €65; extra person fr €10 **Nearby** ♣ 3.7km
♨ 22.5km Sea 1.2km ⚲ 1.3km ⚲ 2.2km Water sports 1.1km ♒ 1.5km
⛪ 0.8km ⛵ 18km **Notes** No pets English spoken Open February to
December.

⊪ Résidence Les Océans

MOREAU et R-A MALNOE
5 Rue de la Plage, 44420 PIRIAC SUR MER
☎ 02 40 23 26 10
email: lesbellenoes@wanadoo.fr

Tucked away among the twisting streets of the seaside village of
Piriac-sur-Mer, this house has four double rooms, each with a private
shower and separate WC. There is a patio for breakfast in the summer;
a little further away are the flower-filled streets, cliff-top walks, the
beach and Piriac's harbour.

Prices s fr €67; d fr €70 **Nearby** ♣ 5km ♨ 18km Sea 0.1km ⚲ 0.1km
♨ 3km Water sports 0.1km ♒ 1km ⛵ 18km **Notes** No pets English
spoken Open Easter to September.

PONT-ST-MARTIN

⊪⊪ Le Château du Plessis

Josiane BELORDE
44860 PONT SAINT MARTIN
☎ 02 40 26 81 72 📱 02 40 32 76 67
email: Josiane.Belorde@wanadoo.fr
web: http://belorde.leplessis.monsite.wanadoo.fr

In a peaceful setting, 11km south of Nantes and only 5km from
the airport (although not disturbed by its proximity), this château
is a historic monument dating from the 14th and 15th centuries.
It has three guest bedrooms, beautiful grounds and rose
gardens and exquisite cuisine and fine wine. Children's games.
Honeymoon package available, and special rates after two nights,
for children and for half board.

Prices s €90-€110; d €120-€175; t €225; extra person fr €40
Nearby ♣ 4km ♨ 15km Sea 30km ⚲ 1km ⚲ 7km Water
sports 10km ♒ 2km ⛪ 0.8km ⛵ 11km **Notes** No pets English
spoken

PORNIC

⊪ Chambre d'hôtes

Louis Marie BARREAU
18, La Tingère, 44210 PORNIC
☎ 02 40 21 78 29 & 06 11 80 09 18 📱 02 40 21 78 29
email: daveri44@wanadoo.fr
web: http://lesmandalas.fr

In a quiet spot close to the beaches, this house has four guest rooms,
all with double beds and one with an additional single. Each has a
private bath or shower room and its own external access. One upstairs
room has a private terrace. Baby equipment available; guests have use
of a kitchen. Outside is a pond, picnic area and parking space.

Prices d €59-€65; t fr €75; extra person fr €16; dinner fr €20
On Site Spa ♟ **Nearby** ♣ 5km ♨ 5km Sea 5km ⚲ 2km
⚲ 2km Restaurant 4km Water sports 5km ♒ 2km ⛪ 2km ⛵ 4km
Notes No pets English spoken

PORNIC *CONTINUED*

⚑ Cupidon

Françoise GAGNOT

Plage du Portmain, 44210 PORNIC

☎ 02 51 74 19 61 🖹 02 51 74 19 20

email: gagnot-catu@club-internet.fr

web: http://chambre-hote-pornic.com/

Cupidon is on Portmain Beach, just off a small country road in the heart of the Côte Sauvage. The prettily decorated rooms benefit from sea views. Large breakfasts are served on the terrace looking out to sea or in the lounge area by the fireplace. Guests can use a heated swimming pool, a terrace, parking, Coastal walks.

Prices s €54-€62; d fr €54; t fr €77 **On Site** Sea Water sports Private **Nearby** 5km 3km Restaurant 3km 3km 3km 3km 6km **Notes** No pets English spoken

⚑ Le Grand Large

Joël et Maud CHUNIAUD

1 la Basse Ficaudière, 44210 PORNIC

☎ 02 40 21 64 81 & 06 08 23 85 49

email: joel.chuniaud@club-internet.fr

web: www.pornic44.com

Very close to the pleasant seaside resort of Pornic, this is a newly-built house with three bedrooms which can sleep from two to four people. Each room has a television with DVD player, and access to a private terrace. Conservatory where breakfast is served and an outdoor swimming pool. Bikes available, and on-site parking.

Prices s €73-€84; d €73-€84; t €86-€96 **On Site** Private **Nearby** 3km 1.2km Sea 2km 2.5km Restaurant 2km Water sports 2.5km 3km 0.8km 2.5km **Notes** No pets English spoken Open March to November.

⚑ Le Jardin de Retz

M & J BLONDEAU-RAEDERSTOERFFER

1 Chemin des Mousseaux, 44210 PORNIC

☎ 02 40 82 02 29

Relax for a night, a weekend or longer break in the lush surroundings of a large botanical park and peaceful gardens. Three double guest bedrooms are available with independent access and private bathrooms. Private parking. Many leisure activities including sea-water therapy nearby.

Prices s €60-€65; d €70-€75 **On Site** Nearby 5km 0.5km Sea 0.1km 0.1km 1km Restaurant 0.1km Water sports 0.1km 5km Spa 1km 0.1km 0.5km **Notes** No pets

⚑ Le Reve Bleu

Jean Noël LEAUTE

10 Impasse Arc en Ciel, 44210 PORNIC

☎ 02 40 82 92 22 & 06 16 89 01 55 🖹 02 40 82 92 22

email: lerevebleu@orange.fr

web: http://lerevebleu.site.voila.fr

This is a large house right on the edge of Pornic, with a big garden, an open-air swimming pool, and a cheerful family atmosphere.

Accommodation comprises two double bedrooms, a suite for three, and a family room for five. They all have private bath or shower room and two of the rooms have their own outside access. Bikes available.

Prices s fr €42; d €54-€60; t fr €80; extra person fr €17 **On Site** Private **Nearby** 5km 5km Sea 2km 2km Restaurant 1.5km Water sports 4km 2km Spa 3km 1.5km 2.5km **Notes** Pets admitted English spoken

---

PORNICHET

⚑ Chambre d'hôtes

Catherine CARRE

97 Av de St Sébastien, 44380 PORNICHET

☎ 02 40 19 37 81 & 06 30 61 70 75 🖹 02 40 19 37 81

email: catherine.carremahe@free.fr

Three comfortable, tastefully decorated double rooms in a 'ville fleurie'; two of them have a shower room/WC and one a bathroom. In a small separate building is a guests' kitchenette and utility room, with fridge, electric hob and washing machine. Attractive terrace with garden furniture.

Prices s fr €50; d fr €55 **Nearby** 3km 3km Sea 1km 1km 2km Restaurant 1km Water sports 1km 0.8km 2km 1km 2km **Notes** No pets Open mid March to mid December.

PORT-ST-PERE

⚑ La Petite Pelletanche

Louis et Simone CHAUVET

44710 PORT SAINT PERE

☎ 02 40 31 52 44 🖹 02 40 31 52 44

A family house and separate accommodation at the centre of a farm, offering three guest bedrooms, each with shower and wc. Shared lounge with fireplace and kitchen area. Breakfast is served in your hosts' house, comprising Pays de Retz honey, jam, fruit juices, brioche or pastries and local bread. Garden furniture and barbecue, canoeing on the river and the Grand Lieu lake is 16km.

Prices s fr €38; d fr €42; t fr €53; extra person fr €11 **Nearby** 10km Sea 25km 0.3km 15km Water sports 7km 3km 6km **Notes** No pets

---

RIAILLE

⚑ La Meilleraie

J Paul et Madeleine HAREL

44440 RIAILLE

☎ 02 40 97 89 52 & 06 83 57 95 07 🖹 02 40 97 89 52

email: mjp.harel@free.fr

A character house near Meilleraye Abbey and Provostière Lake, ideal for fishing and walking and in an area covered with forests and ponds. Three en suite bedrooms with TV, lawn, garden furniture, BBQ, picnic area. Breakfast can be taken on the terrace or in the large reception room with fireplace. No smoking inside. Kitchen available.

Prices s fr €42; d fr €46; t fr €52 **Nearby** 1km 37km 0.5km 12km Restaurant 4km Water sports 9km 4.5km 20km 4km 25km **Notes** No pets Open May to September.

ROUGE

⅋ ⅋ La Touche

Hervé MOSER
44660 ROUGE
☎ 02 40 28 84 06 & 06 30 39 89 90
email: korrigans.moser@wanadoo.fr

Two kilometres outside the town, these old farm buildings have been sympathetically restored by the owners, using environmentally friendly materials. The setting is peaceful, and the five large rooms have each been decorated in an individual style. Two of the rooms offer disabled access.

Prices s fr €45; d fr €55; extra person fr €15 **Nearby** ⛳ 5km ♠ 10km ♦ 10km Restaurant 10km Water sports 25km ♨ 8km ⚷ 10km 🖭 2km ♨ 10km **Notes** No pets English spoken

SION-LES-MINES

⅋ ⏀ La Forgeraie

Bruno et Micheline BOURDEL
La Hunaudière, 44590 SION-LES-MINES
☎ 02 40 28 45 21 & 06 74 69 35 16 🖹 02 40 76 45 56
email: laforgeraie@yahoo.fr
web: www.laforgeraie.com

This converted blacksmiths' forge has three rooms, and can sleep up to nine guests. It stands among lakes and forests, in an area good for fishing and walking. Breakfast is served in a large room built entirely of local stone. Billiard table, piano and home cinema available; guests also have use of the excellent kitchen.

Prices s €51-€55; d €56-€60; t €66-€71; extra person fr €15; dinner fr €15 **On Site** ♠ **Nearby** ⛳ 10km ♦ 14km Restaurant 0.1km Water sports 30km ♨ 14km ⚷ 0.1km 🖭 5km ♨ 14km **Notes** No pets English spoken

SOUDAN

⅋ ⏀ La Boissière

Jacqueline NICOL
44110 SOUDAN
☎ 02 40 28 60 00 🖹 02 40 28 60 00
email: contact@lesmarchesdebretagne.com
web: www.lesmarchesdebretagne.com

This 17th-century long-barn is in a typical hamlet featuring local shale stone. Guest accommodation comprises a lounge with TV, fireplace and library and four bedrooms with private bathrooms, two with private terraces and two with mezzanines. Kitchenette, swimming pool, nature trail and astronomy evenings. A daily changing menu can be enjoyed in a warm and friendly atmosphere.

Prices s fr €40; d fr €55; t fr €68; extra person fr €10; dinner fr €17 **On Site** Private ⚷ **Nearby** ⛳ 14km ♦ 24km ♠ 9km Restaurant 6km Water sports 16km ♨ 6km ⚷ 13km 🖭 6km ♨ 13km **Notes** No pets English spoken

ST-JULIEN-DE-CONCELLES

⅋⅋⅋ La Gentilhommière du Bois Adam

Armelle GOBIN
96 Route de Beau Soleil,
44450 ST JULIEN DE CONCELLES
☎ 02 40 13 10 00 & 06 07 15 51 48 🖹 02 40 13 10 00
email: gentilhommiereduboisadam@wanadoo.fr
web: www.gentilhommiereduboisadam.fr

Tucked away in eight hectares of grounds, this small manor house overlooking wooded parkland offers peace, quiet and a happy atmosphere. Each of the four rooms is decorated to a theme, and all have their own facilities (one with WC accessed via a landing). Cot available. Picnics available by arrangement.

Prices s €62-€77; d €62-€77; t €87-€92; extra person fr €17 **On Site** ♠ **Nearby** ⛳ 9km ♦ 10km ⚷ 5.9km Restaurant 1.5km Water sports 10km ♨ 2.5km ⚷ 2.5km 🖭 2.5km ♨ 10km **Notes** Pets admitted English spoken

ST-MALO-DE-GUERSAC

⅋ ⏀ Chambre d'hôtes

Alain COLLARD
25 Errand, Ty Gween, 44550 SAINT MALO DE GUERSAC
☎ 02 40 91 15 04

A lovely old cottage on an island in the Brière marshes, with four spacious bedrooms with shower and wc: 'L'Ecossaise' (double), 'La Verte' (twin), 'La Bleue' (double and single) and 'La Rose' (double and single). Rustic dining room with fireplace; heating, parking, enclosed garden, separate entrance. Local attractions include a wildlife park 3km, walking routes, barge trips, cycling. Evening meals by arrangement.

Prices s fr €48; d fr €58; t fr €65; dinner fr €20 **Nearby** ⛳ 25km ♦ 25km Sea 14km ⚷ 1km Restaurant 7km Water sports 22km ♨ 2km ⚷ 20km 🖭 2km ♨ 14km **Notes** No pets English spoken Open April to September.

ST-MARS-DU-DESERT

⅋⅋⅋ Longrais

Dominique MORISSEAU
21 Du Village, 44850 SAINT MARS DU DESERT
☎ 02 40 77 48 25 & 06 80 62 95 63
email: longrais.accueil@wanadoo.fr
web: http://longrais.accueil-france.com

An 18th-century character property deep in the countryside, close to Nantes and Beaujoire. Relax in the enclosed landscaped gardens with furniture and parking and choose between three en suite bedrooms with antique furnishings (two for three people and a room for two). Satellite TV, guest kitchen, boat trips nearby on the River Erdre and the Loire. Restaurants 4km. Extra beds can be added. Reductions for long stays and low season.

Prices s €42-€50; d €48-€56; t €64-€68 **Nearby** ⛳ 4km ♦ 6km Sea 50km ♠ 8km ⚷ 6km Restaurant 4km Water sports 8km ♨ 4km Spa 50km ⚷ 6km 🖭 4km ♨ 17km **Notes** No pets English spoken

ST-PERE-EN-RETZ

♯♯♯ ⅠⓄⅠ L'Argoat

Louis CATACCHIO

Route de la Raterie, 44320 SAINT PERE EN RETZ

☎ 02 40 21 85 69

email: catacchio.louis@wanadoo.fr

web: www.largoat.com/

This is a spacious, very pleasant house in a woodland setting. All three bedrooms, individually decorated doubles and triples, are on the first floor. Each has a private shower and WC. There is a lounge area and a kitchenette with a fridge and microwave; baby equipment is also available. Meals by arrangement. Outdoors there is garden furniture.

Prices s fr €40; d fr €45; t fr €60; dinner fr €18   **Nearby** ⛷ 8km
🛶 10km Sea 8km 🏊 10km ⚓ 10km Water sports 8km 🚲 10km
🏛 1.5km ⇢ 10km   **Notes** No pets Open 16 December to 14 November.

STE-PAZANNE

♯♯♯ Chambre d'hôtes

Isabelle MANSAIS

24 La Boitellerie, 44680 SAINTE PAZANNE

☎ 02 40 02 62 56

email: maillet-mansais@club-internet.fr

A modern house in a small hamlet close to the 'Planète Sauvage' wildlife park and 20 minutes from Nantes. There are two double bedrooms and a triple, all with themed decorations and private shower room and WC. Children's games available. Good walks in the locality; fishing close by.

Prices s fr €40; d fr €45; t fr €55   **Nearby** ⛷ 20km 🛶 25km Sea 20km
🏊 0.8km ⚓ 15km Restaurant 2km Water sports 25km 🏊 10km
Spa 25km 🏛 3km ⇢ 4km   **Notes** No pets English spoken Open July to August, February holidays and weekends April to June.

STE-REINE-DE-BRETAGNE

♯♯♯ La Thorelle

Françoise et Michel PINTUREAU

27 Rue René Guy Cadou,

44160 SAINTE REINE DE BRETAGNE

☎ 02 40 01 03 50 & 06 03 52 33 02 🖨 02 40 01 03 50

email: pintureau@la-thorelle.com

web: www.charmance-bretagne.com

This early 20th-century house in spacious grounds has been completely renovated. Bedrooms, on the first floor, are bright, spacious and equipped with bathrooms. This is an ideal base for trips to the Brière Park, the Côte D'Amour, Guérande, La Roche Bernard and the Pays des 3 Rivières.

Prices not confirmed for 2008   **Nearby** ⛷ 10km 🛶 8km Sea 25km
🏊 2km ⚓ 8km Water sports 20km 🏊 2km 🏛 5km ⇢ 8km
Notes No pets English spoken

SUCE-SUR-ERDRE

♯♯♯ Chambre d'hôtes

Marie Claude COURANT

179 Rue de la Gamotrie, 44240 SUCE SUR ERDRE

☎ 02 40 77 99 61 & 06 19 41 90 70 🖨 02 40 77 99 61

email: courantbernard@wanadoo.fr

web: www.gites-de-france-44.fr/la_gamotrie/

This 19th-century building, at one time connected to the Château of la Gamotrie, stands beside the River Erdre. It has three bedrooms, all with private bathroom and WC. Breakfast is served in the splendid ground floor lounge, with its elaborate plaster cornices and mouldings. Guests' kitchen; covered swimming pool available from May to September. Garden furniture, barbecue, possible boat hire.

Prices not confirmed for 2008   **On Site** ⚓ Water sports Private ⚓
Nearby ⛷ 6km 🛶 12km 🏊 7km 🏛 5km ⇢ 20km   **Notes** No pets
English spoken

♯♯♯ Chambre d'hôtes

Patricia DEGREZ

2 Chemin de la Dolette, 44240 SUCE SUR ERDRE

☎ 02 40 77 96 25 & 06 82 66 19 25

email: gitplage.verte@free.fr

web: http://gitplage.verte.free.fr

Just a stone's throw from one of France's most beautiful rivers this property combines the modern and the traditional and offers two double rooms and a room for four. There is a ground-floor lounge with a private terrace and a kitchen shared by all three bedrooms. Proximity to the river provides the opportunity to take part in nautical activities.

Prices s fr €46; d fr €58; t fr €70; extra person fr €12   **Nearby** ⛷ 3km
🛶 5km Sea 70km 🏊 0.1km ⚓ 4km Restaurant 1km Water sports 0.1km
🏊 5km 🏛 1.5km ⇢ 16km   **Notes** No pets English spoken

♯♯♯ La Menade

Anne et Christian VINSOT

9 Chemin des Vignes, 44240 SUCE SUR ERDRE

☎ 02 40 77 39 70 & 06 61 54 32 40 🖨 02 40 77 32 44

email: cvinsot@wanadoo.fr

web: www.la-menade.com

This characterful house, with its beautiful peaceful setting and private river frontage to the Erdre, enables guests to relax completely. There are three bedrooms, one of them a suite, all facing the river and all with private bathroom/WC. Lounge/dining room, and separate guests' kitchen; swimming pool; boating on the river.

Prices s €69-€72; d €75-€78; t fr €96; extra person fr €18   **On Site** ⚓
Water sports Private ⚓   **Nearby** ⛷ 5km 🛶 5km 🏛 1km ⇢ 15km
Notes No pets English spoken

VALLET

🏴 Château d'Yseron

Olivier DE SAINT ALBIN

44330 VALLET

☎ 02 51 71 70 40 & 06 10 76 54 28

📠 02 51 71 70 11

email: ostalbin@wanadoo.fr

web: www.yseron.net

A beautiful period house, offering peace and comfort amongst the vines. There are three double rooms and a suite for four, all grade 4 except for one of the doubles which is grade 3. The wooded grounds has a lake where guests can fish. Wine tasting can be arranged.

Prices d €80-€130; extra person fr €15 **Nearby** ⛷ 2km ⌁ 20km ⌁ 0.1km ⌁ 3km ⌁ 3km ⌁ 3km ⌁ 10km **Notes** Pets admitted English spoken CC

VARADES

🏴 ᐃᐃ Le Grand Patis

Jacques ROY

44370 VARADES

☎ 02 40 83 42 28

This small renovated château is set in a large park. There are four guest bedrooms available for two, three and five people respectively, all with shower and wc. Lounge, parking.

Prices s fr €38; d fr €49; t fr €61; extra person fr €15; dinner fr €15 **Nearby** ⛷ 5km ⌁ 25km ⌁ 2km ⌁ 5km Restaurant 2km Water sports 40km ⌁ 2km ⌁ 2km ⌁ 2km ⌁ 3km **Notes** No pets English spoken

MAINE-ET-LOIRE

ANDARD

🏴 ᐃ La Pocherie

M-Madeleine BOUTREUX

Ferme Fruitière la Pocherie, 49800 ANDARD

☎ 02 41 76 72 25

This property, which is a market garden and fruit farm, has three very comfortable bedrooms. There is a ground floor double room; on the first floor is a triple, and a room for four which is accessed by an exterior staircase. Extra bed and cot available. All the rooms have private facilities. Library, board games, garden furniture.

Prices s fr €42; d fr €48; t fr €60; extra person fr €13 **Nearby** ⛷ 6km ⌁ 10km ⌁ 10km ⌁ 5km ⌁ 1km ⌁ 1km ⌁ 12km **Notes** No pets Open April to February.

🏴 ᐃ Les Champs

Catherine BOUTREUX

Rue des 4 Vents, 49800 ANDARD

☎ 02 41 76 49 02 & 06 24 74 23 25

email: contact@lelogisdeschamps.com

web: www.angers-charmance.com

In a beautifully quiet spot in the heart of the countryside, this 15th-century house has three bedrooms. There are two rooms which can be arranged as doubles or twins, one downstairs and one upstairs; the upstairs room has an additional single bed. Also upstairs is an ordinary double room. All have private facilities. Flower garden with furniture; generous breakfasts.

Prices s fr €50; d fr €52; extra person fr €15; dinner fr €20 **Nearby** ⛷ 5km ⌁ 20km ⌁ 5km ⌁ 10km Restaurant 5km ⌁ 2km ⌁ 6km ⌁ 1km ⌁ 14km **Notes** No pets English spoken

ANDREZE

🏴 ᐃ Château de la Morinière

Pascal et Muriel PRINGARBE

49600 ANDREZE

☎ 06 03 02 55 16

email: pringarbe.pascal@wanadoo.fr

web: www.chateau-de-la-moriniere.com

This 19th-century château has three guest bedrooms with themed decorations and antique furnishings, all on the second floor. The bathrooms are located in the towers of the château, each has a jacuzzi. Meals are available by arrangement, serving a creative style of cuisine based on ancient local varieties of fruit and vegetables.

Prices d €79-€85; extra person fr €20; dinner fr €30 **On Site** ⌁ **Nearby** ⛷ 0.2km ⌁ 10km Sea 50km ⌁ 3km Restaurant 2km ⌁ 0.5km ⌁ 0.8km ⌁ 12km **Notes** No pets English spoken

BOCE

ᴴᴴ ⁱ◎ⁱ Le Chant d'Oiseau

Jannick et J-Pierre GALLET

49150 BOCE

☎ 02 41 82 73 14 📄 02 41 82 73 14

email: jjp.gallet@orange.fr

web: www.gites-de-france-anjou.com

This restored house, close to the Chandelais Forest, has three bedrooms, in a separate building. There is a twin-bedded room; a split-level family room for four; and a triple room (double bed and a single) which is reached by an outside staircase. All have their own facilities. Lounge area with kitchenette. Garden with furniture and barbecue; bikes, table tennis.

Prices s fr €40; d fr €48; t fr €60; extra person fr €12; dinner fr €18
On Site Restaurant Spa ᴾ **Nearby** ⛵ 5km ᴶ 4km ᴾ 1.5km ᴿ 4km ᴾ 0.5km 🏠 4km 🚶 35km **Notes** Pets admitted

BRAIN-SUR-ALLONNES

ᴴᴴ ⁱ◎ⁱ La Michcatière

M ROTA et C GENTAUD

16, Rue de l'Eglise, 49650 BRAIN-SUR-ALLONNES

☎ 06 60 91 33 49

email: michcatiere@orange.fr

web: www.michcath.com

Tastefully furnished and restored, with many original features, this property is in a village in the heart of the Anjou region, not far from vineyards. Three double rooms and a two-roomed family suite for up to four; all have private bath or shower room, and baby equipment is available.

Prices s fr €70; d fr €77; t fr €95; extra person €15-€30; dinner fr €33
Nearby ⛵ 3km ᴶ 14km ᴾ 1.5km ᴿ 0.3km Restaurant 4km ᴾ 🚶 4km
Notes Pets admitted English spoken

BRIOLLAY

ᴴᴴ *Chambre d'hôtes*

Martine TREVET

3, Square de la Chansonnière, 49125 BRIOLLAY

☎ 02 41 37 91 98

email: christian.trevet@wanadoo.fr

web: www.haut-pressoir.com

On the outskirts of Angers and close to the Parc des Expositions, this property has three ground floor rooms - two doubles and a single.

Each room has a private terrace, and its own bath/shower room and WC. Large landscaped garden with swimming pool.

Prices not confirmed for 2008 **On Site** ᴾ Private ᴿ **Nearby** ⛵ 5km ᴶ 12km ᴾ 2km 🏠 2km **Notes** No pets English spoken

BROC

ᴴᴴ ⁱ◎ⁱ ⴺ Les Roberderies

Bruno et Jamila POUSSIN

49490 BROC

☎ 02 41 82 38 42 & 06 81 83 56 12

email: roberderies@aol.com

web: www.les-roberderies.com

In a quiet country setting between the valleys of the Loire and the Loir, this 18th-century house has three ground floor bedrooms. They can all be arranged as doubles or twins, and one of them has an additional single bed. All of the rooms have private facilities. Lounge with books and open fire. Wooded grounds with lake; meals available by arrangement.

Prices s fr €45; d fr €50; extra person fr €15; dinner fr €20 **On Site** ᴾ Private ᴿ **Nearby** ⛵ 2km ᴾ 2km Restaurant 7km ᴾ 8km 🏠 0.8km 🚶 38km **Notes** Pets admitted English spoken

CHALONNES-SUR-LOIRE

ᴴᴴ Le Logis des Mariniers

Annie DEMORE

35, quai Victor Hugo, 49290 CHALONNES-SUR-LOIRE

☎ 02 41 68 02 64 📄 02 41 68 02 64

email: annie.demore@wanadoo.fr

web: www.logisdesmariniers.com

Annie warmly offers three rooms in her historical home which dates in part back to the 15th century: two doubles and a three-person suite. Terrace and salon with views over the Loire.

Prices d €55-€70; t fr €70; extra person fr €15; dinner fr €20
On Site ᴾ **Nearby** ⛵ 0.1km ᴶ 20km ᴿ 0.5km Restaurant 0.2km ᴾ 0.1km 🏠 0.5km 🚶 1km **Notes** Pets admitted English spoken

CHARCE-SAINT-ELLIER

ᴴᴴ La Pichonnière

Jean-Claude COLIBET-MARTIN

49320 CHARCE-SAINT-ELLIER

☎ 02 41 91 29 37 📄 02 41 91 96 85

email: gite-brissac@wanadoo.fr

web: www.gite-brissac.com

This farmhouse has four bedrooms: on the ground floor is a double with lounge area and direct garden access; upstairs, with their own entrance, are two double rooms and a twin-bedded room. All of the rooms have their own showers and WCs, except that upstairs the twin bedded room shares a WC with one of the doubles.

Prices d €46-€58 **On Site** ᴾ **Nearby** ⛵ 3km ᴶ 6km ᴾ 3km ᴿ 3km Restaurant 3km ᴾ 3km 🏠 3km 🚶 20km **Notes** No pets English spoken

CHEMELLIER

⫴ ⏀ La Poirière

Eliette EDON

49320 CHEMELLIER

☎ 02 41 45 59 50

email: lapoirière@wanadoo.fr

web: www.hotes-en-anjou.com

This house, built in typical local style, provides a triple room, and two doubles, all with private facilities. Heating, lounge with fireplace, TV, games and billiard table. Bikes available, table tennis and porch. Table d'hôte meals on reservation.

Prices s fr €41; d fr €48; t fr €61; dinner fr €22 **On Site** 🐎
Nearby ✿ 4km ♨ 10km ♂ 1km ➤ 6km Restaurant 5km ♒ 2km
🏛 2km ᎊ 25km **Notes** No pets

⫴ Le Logis des Grainetiers

Chantal ARCHAUX

49320 CHEMELLIER

☎ 06 20 39 96 36

email: chantal.archaux@wanadoo.fr

web: www.logis-des-grainetiers.com

Three en suite rooms offered in a typical tuffeau house in the heart of the Aubance region, all spacious, comfortable and delightfully decorated. 'Romantique' and 'Clair de Lune' are double rooms with large lounge areas; 'Alizé' is a double with an adjoining suite ('Parfum d'Orient') of three single beds. Games room, outdoor leisure area.

Prices s fr €57; d fr €62; extra person fr €16 **Nearby** ✿ 8km ♨ 12km
♂ 1km ➤ 8km Restaurant 3km ♒ 2km Spa 28km 🎿 15km 🏛 0.5km
ᎊ 25km **Notes** Pets admitted English spoken

CHEMILLE

⫴ Clos du Marais

Hélène POIREAU

5, Chemin du Marais, 49120 CHEMILLE

☎ 02 41 30 08 04 & 06 62 00 12 77

email: poireauhelene@aol.com

web: www.closdumarais.com

This old farmhouse, in the Anjou wine-growing region, has five bright, spacious first floor bedrooms, all of them named after medicinal plants. Woody Nightshade, Peppermint, Camomile and Poppy are all doubles; Sage is a quadruple, with a double bed and a single. There is

a guests' entrance, and all rooms have en suite facilities. Guests' lounge. Beautiful surroundings; fishing lake.

Prices s fr €42; d fr €50; extra person €15-€18 **On Site** 🎣 🐎
Nearby ✿ 4km ➤ 1.5km ♒ 1.5km 🏛 1km ᎊ 1km **Notes** No pets
English spoken

CORNE

⫴ Chambre d'hôtes

Monique DESLANDES

47, Route du Point du Jour, 49630 CORNE

☎ 02 41 45 01 53

email: lalogecorne@aol.com

web: http://lalogecorne.free.fr

There are three bedrooms in this little farmhouse, two on the ground floor and one upstairs. One is a double room; another has twin beds; and the third is a triple, with a double bed and a single. All have shower rooms and WCs. Use of lounge and kitchen; garden; peaceful family atmosphere.

Prices s fr €41; d fr €46; t fr €62; extra person fr €15 **On Site** 🐎
Nearby ✿ 2km ♨ 25km ♂ 7km ➤ 10km Restaurant 2km 🏛 2km
ᎊ 15km **Notes** Pets admitted English spoken

⫴ Les Genêts

Michel et Nadeige BRIAND

63, route de Baune, 49630 CORNE

☎ 02 41 45 05 21

email: briand.michel@wanadoo.fr

web: www.loire-authion.com

Three very comfortable guest rooms in a 19th-century country house, on a peaceful one-hectare estate. 'Matisse' and 'Monet' are doubles, while 'Lurçat' is a twin room; each has a private shower room and wc. Extra bed available. Garden, terrace, outdoor furniture. Reduced prices for longer stays.

Prices s fr €40; d fr €49; extra person fr €12 **Nearby** ✿ 2km ♨ 15km
♂ 4km ➤ 15km Restaurant 2km ♒ 2km 🏛 1km ᎊ 15km
Notes No pets English spoken

DENEE

⫴ Manoir de la Noue

O et C DE CENIVAL

Domaine des Chesnaies, 49190 DENEE

☎ 02 41 78 79 80 & 06 82 37 73 50 📄 02 41 68 05 61

email: odecenival@wanadoo.fr

web: www.domainedeschesnaies.com

At the entrance to Angers, winegrowers have restored the outbuildings of a 16th-century walled house. Four spacious rooms open onto a romantic 19th-century listed garden: the Green and Yellow Room have twin beds, while the Raspberry Room and Blue Room have large double beds. Each has a private bathroom. Sample wines from the estate or home-made jam in the breakfast room, in front of the fireplace in the lounge, or in the garden.

Prices s fr €65; d fr €70; extra person fr €20 **Nearby** ✿ 5km ♨ 10km
♂ 1km ➤ 5km Restaurant 5km ♒ 0.5km 🎿 5km 🏛 1km ᎊ 18km
Notes No pets English spoken CC

DOUE-LA-FONTAINE

▓▓ |◯| & Le Chais de Taunay

Catherine PARMENTIER

15, rue d'Alger, 49700 DOUE-LA-FONTAINE

☎ 02 41 83 09 54

email: patcat.parmentier@wanadoo.fr

web: www.auchaisdetaunay.com

This old wine store, still with its extensive cellars, makes a very unusual setting for a chambre d'hôtes. Five bedrooms sleep from two to five people, all with private bath or shower room and separate WC. Four are non-smoking. Breakfast served in the dining room, out on the terrace or in guests' bedrooms.

Prices s fr €54; d fr €65; extra person €14–€19; dinner fr €20
On Site Restaurant **Nearby** ⚓ 8km ⚓ 18km ⚓ 15km ⚓ 2km ⚓ 1km
⚓ 20km **Notes** No pets English spoken

▓▓ |◯| Les Roses Roses

Françoise DOUET

34 rue de Soulanger, 49700 DOUE-LA-FONTAINE

☎ 02 41 59 21 43 & 06 98 80 91 98 📄 02 41 50 65 20

email: douet.f@wanadoo.fr

web: www.lesrosesroses.com

A house on an old wine-growing estate, next to the Jardin des Roses and close to Doué zoo. There are three rooms: the double Green Room and Le Pavillon, and the twin Pink Room, all with private facilities. Parking in courtyard.

Prices d fr €45; extra person fr €10; dinner fr €15 **On Site** ⚓
Nearby ⚓ 2km ⚓ 1km Restaurant 0.1km ⚓ 0.5km ⚓ 15km
Notes No pets English spoken

DRAIN

▓▓ |◯| Le Mésengeau

Brigitte et Gérard MIGON

49530 DRAIN

☎ 02 40 98 21 57 📄 02 40 98 28 62

email: le.mesengeau@wanadoo.fr

web: www.anjou-et-loire.com/mesangeau

This welcoming 19th-century manor house has lovely fireplaces, old beams and a six-hectare park with lake and chapel. The carefully-decorated bedrooms (four doubles and one twin) have a rustic charm, and each has its own facilities. Piano, billiards, bikes, table tennis, small driving range, outdoor furniture, summerhouse beside the lake. Table d'hôte meals by prior reservation only; restaurants nearby. Wine tasting in the village. Reduced rates after the third night.

Prices s €80–€100; d €90–€110; t fr €130; dinner fr €35
On Site ⚓ ⚓ **Nearby** ⚓ 8.5km ⚓ 15km ⚓ 8km Restaurant 8km
⚓ 8km ⚓ 4.5km ⚓ 12km **Notes** No pets English spoken

DURTAL

▓▓ |◯| Le Chaudron

M et Mme SZAPU

103 rue St-Pierre, 49430 DURTAL

☎ 02 41 76 39 09 & 02 41 76 04 77

email: szapu@wanadoo.fr

This is a beautiful 15th-century house, built in typical Anjou style. On the ground floor is a bedroom which can be arranged as a double or twin; upstairs is a double room, a twin-bedded room, and a suite with a double bed and three singles. All have private facilities, and there is a separate guests' entrance. Terrace with garden furniture.

Prices s fr €50; d fr €55; extra person fr €20; dinner fr €20
Nearby ⚓ 6km ⚓ 0.5km ⚓ 0.5km ⚓ 0.5km ⚓ 0.5km **Notes** No pet
English spoken Open April to October.

FAYE-D'ANJOU

⚑ Le Logis de la Brunetière

François BILLEROT
49380 FAYE-D'ANJOU
☎ 06 07 25 60 41
email: françois.billerot@wanadoo.fr
web: www.gite-logis-brunetiere.fr

Dating back to 1489, the Logis de la Brunetière has three double guest rooms: 'Aubance', 'Layon' and 'Lys', all with private bathroom and separate wc. Lounge room with kitchenette. Self-catering gîte on site. 500mtrs from the town centre.

Prices s fr €50; d €50-€60; extra person fr €20 **On Site** ✿
Nearby ⚲ 5km ⚱ 10km ✐ 4km Restaurant 4km ⌁ 0.5km ☖ 4km
⋙ 25km **Notes** No pets English spoken

FONTAINE-GUERIN

⚑ Moulin de Laveau

Charlotte CHARRIER
49250 FONTAINE-GUERIN
☎ 02 41 57 13 18 & 06 70 35 23 81
email: moulindelaveau@orange.fr
web: www.moulindelaveau.com

An old water mill set in eight hectares of grounds, in a wooded area. There are three bedrooms, two of them upstairs and one with a private terrace. All the rooms have views of the river, and each has a private bath or shower and WC. Footpath by the water, and animals and poultry on site - donkeys, chickens, etc.

Prices d €60-€70; extra person fr €15 **On Site** ✐ ✿
Nearby ⚲ 10km ⚱ 11km ✦ ⌁ 5km ☖ 5km ⋙ 30km **Notes** No pets English spoken

GREZ-NEUVILLE

⚑ ⦿ La Croix d'Etain

Auguste BAHUAUD
49220 GREZ-NEUVILLE
☎ 02 41 95 68 49 ▤ 02 41 18 02 72
email: croix.etain@anjou-et-loire.com
web: www.anjou-et-loire.com/croix

In the middle of a tree-lined park beside the Mayenne, this 18th-century mansion offers four stylish guest rooms - two doubles and two twins - each with private bathroom and wc. Lounge with TV, furnished terrace. Table d'hôte meals possible. Nearby: golf, marina, boat hire, museums and châteaux.

Prices s fr €60; d €65-€100; extra person fr €25; dinner fr €30
On Site ✐ **Nearby** ⚲ 2km ⚱ 10km ✦ 4km Restaurant 0.1km
⌁ 1km ☖ 4km ⋙ 20km **Notes** Pets admitted English spoken CC

⚑ ♿ Le Bois de Grez

M-L et J-G CESBRON
Route de Sceaux d'Anjou, 49220 GREZ-NEUVILLE
☎ 02 41 18 00 09 & & 06 22 38 14 56
▤ 02 41 18 00 09
email: cesbron.boisgrez@wanadoo.fr
web: www.boisdegrez.com

There are four spacious and bright rooms to welcome guests to this restored manor house, which dates back to the 15th century. Two of the rooms are doubles, one with room for a folding bed; another has twin beds, and the fourth has a double bed and a single. All the rooms have private facilities.

Prices s fr €65; d €70-€80; t fr €98; extra person fr €18 **On Site** ✐
✿ **Nearby** ⚲ 3km ⚱ 15km ✦ 4km Restaurant 3km ⌁ 0.5km
☖ 4km ⋙ 20km **Notes** No pets English spoken

INGRANDES-SUR-LOIRE

⚑ Chambre d'hôtes

Thérèse DOUGE
10 Place de l'Eglise, 49123 INGRANDES-SUR-LOIRE
☎ 02 41 39 21 83 ▤ 02 41 39 21 83
email: douge.resa@wanadoo.fr
web: www.chambre-hote-ingrandes.com

In the heart of the village, on the edge of the Loire, this property has three guest rooms. On the ground floor, with a separate entrance, is
CONTINUED

INGRANDES-SUR-LOIRE CONTINUED

one double room; upstairs are two more doubles. Each room has its own bath or shower room and WC. Breakfast served outside on the terrace.

Prices s fr €41; d €46-€52; extra person fr €15 **On Site**
Nearby ⚑ 9km ⚑ 17km Restaurant 0.2km ⚑ 0.2km ⚑ 0.1km ⚑ 0.1km
Notes No pets

JARZE

⚑ Le Point du Jour

Vincent et Véronique PAPIAU

49140 JARZE

☎ 02 41 95 46 04 📄 02 41 95 46 04

email: veronique.papiau@wanadoo.fr

web: http://perso.wanadoo.fr/veronique.papiau

Organic farmers who rear cattle welcome you to 'Le Point du Jour'. There is separate access to the three comfortable guest rooms, each decorated in period style: 'Saumon' has a double and single bed; 'A Rayures' is a double and 'Verte' is a twin room. Each has private facilities; extra bed and cot available. Kitchenette, barbecue, outdoor furniture. Reduced rates after three nights.

Prices s fr €35; d fr €45; t fr €60; extra person fr €15 **Nearby** ⚑ 12km
⚑ 10km ⚑ 10km ⚑ 10km ⚑ 30km ⚑ 0.7km ⚑ 30km **Notes** No pets
English spoken

LA BREILLE-LES-PINS

⚑ ⚑ Relais des Lys

François et Viviane SAUVAGEOT

49390 LA BREILLE-LES-PINS

☎ 02 41 52 74 72 📄 02 41 59 63 29

email: relaisdeslys@aol.com

This old posting inn is in a little town tucked away in the forest. It has three bedrooms: a double, a triple (double bed and a single), and a twin-bedded room which links to another similar room to provide accommodation for four. Each room has a TV, shower and WC. Lounge with open fire, billiard room, swimming pool.

Prices d fr €65; extra person fr €10; dinner fr €25 **On Site** Private ⚑
Nearby ⚑ 5km ⚑ 3km ⚑ 5km ⚑ 5km ⚑ 18km **Notes** No pets
English spoken

LA POSSONNIERE

⚑ ⚑ La Rousselière

François et Jacqueline DE BERU

49170 LA POSSONNIERE

☎ 02 41 39 13 21 & 06 60 67 60 69 📄 02 41 39 12 23

email: larousseliere@unimedia.fr

web: www.anjou-et-loire.com/rousseliere

Jacqueline welcomes you to her 18th-century family home and five spacious guest rooms with views of the park. There are three rooms with private bathrooms and windows over the garden. Mini-bar, TV, heating, lounge, billiard table, dining room with fireplace, veranda. Four-hectare park, walled courtyard, swimming pool, porch, table tennis, pétanque, parking, garden furniture. 17th-century chapel. Table d'hôte meals on reservation. Seventh night free.

Prices d €55-€80; t €55-€100; extra person fr €20; dinner fr €29
On Site Private ⚑ **Nearby** ⚑ 5km ⚑ 20km ⚑ 0.5km Restaurant 1.5km
⚑ 5km ⚑ 4km ⚑ 2km ⚑ 4km **Notes** No pets English spoken

LA RENAUDIERE

⚑ ⚑ La Foye Moreau

Annie DUGAST

49450 LA RENAUDIERE

☎ 02 41 30 85 20 📄 02 41 30 85 20

email: anniedugast@yahoo.fr

web: www.lafoymoreau.com

This grange provides a relaxing stop-over in the fragrant countryside and is set on a farm. The personalised rooms include La Paysanne and La Cholestaise (doubles), L'Espagnole (twin) and La Zen (double with two children's beds). Each has independent facilities and TV. Lounge with kitchenette, washing machine and cable TV available to guests.

Prices s fr €43; d fr €50; extra person fr €18; dinner fr €18
Nearby ⚑ 10km ⚑ 1km ⚑ 10km Restaurant 10km ⚑ 2.5km ⚑ 2.5km
Notes No pets English spoken

LE LION-D'ANGERS

⚑ Les Travaillères

J-L et J LECOURBE-VIVIER

49220 LE LION-D'ANGERS

☎ 02 41 61 33 56 & 06 77 86 24 33

email: jeanlouislecourbe@orange.fr

web: www.lestravailleres.com

This renovated farmhouse is in a peaceful countryside setting, 20 minutes from Angers. There are three double rooms, one with adjoining twin room, all with private facilities and access. Heating, lounge with fireplace, library, board games. Shady, relaxing garden with furniture, courtyard, terrace for picnics, barbecue.

Prices s fr €34; d fr €41; t fr €55; extra person fr €16 **Nearby** ⚑ 5km
⚑ 15km ⚑ 2km ⚑ 5km Restaurant 5km ⚑ 2km ⚑ 5km ⚑ 5km
⚑ 25km **Notes** Pets admitted English spoken

LE LONGERON

♯♯♯ **La Grande Fribaudière**

Monique et René PINEAU
49710 LE LONGERON
☎ 02 41 55 46 03 & 06 60 20 45 74
email: rm.pineau@wanadoo.fr

A quietly situated comfortable place, close to the river Sèvre, one of the tributaries of the Loire. Three en suite bedrooms: 'L'Angevine' with a double bed; 'La Vendéenne' with a double bed and a single; and 'La Clissonnaise' with three single beds. The whole site is non-smoking.

Prices s fr €40; d fr €50; t €60-€65; extra person €10-€15　**On Site** ⌇
Nearby ⛷ 6km ♨ 12km ⟲ 7km Restaurant 3km ♒ 2km ⌂ 2km
⚓ 12km　**Notes** No pets English spoken

♯♯♯ **La Promenade**

Marc et Monique VIGNERON
5, Rue d'Anjou, 49710 LE LONGERON
☎ 02 41 64 37 13 🖨 02 41 64 37 13
email: lapromenade.lelongeron@wanadoo.fr
web: www.lapromenade-France.com

A prominent house, in a large garden with lots of flowers, right in the centre of the village. The River Sèvre is close by. There is a double-bedded room, and a suite which can sleep up to five. Both the rooms have en suite shower room and WC. The whole site is non-smoking.

Prices s fr €54; d fr €59; dinner fr €20　**Nearby** ⛷ 10km ♨ 20km
♒ 0.5km ⟲ 8km ♒ 1km ♒ 15km ⌂ 0.1km ⚓ 18km　**Notes** No pets
English spoken

LE MAY-SUR-EVRE

♯♯♯ *Le Petit Cazeau*

Mme DAVOUST
49122 LE MAY-SUR-EVRE
☎ 02 41 63 16 88 🖨 02 41 63 16 88
email: lepetitcazeau@aol.com
web: www.lepetitcazeau.fr.st

Twenty minutes from Puy-du-Fou, this old farmhouse offers three themed guest rooms, each with private shower room and wc: 'l'Africaine' is a double room with exotic décor, 'la Romantique' is also a double, while twin-bedded 'la Provençale' has a sunny colour scheme. Flower-filled garden with furniture, heating.

Prices not confirmed for 2008　**Nearby** ⛷ 10km ♨ 3km ♒ 1km ⟲ 7km
♒ 3km ⌂ 3km ⚓ 7km　**Notes** No pets English spoken

LE PUY-NOTRE-DAME

♯♯♯ ◯ **L'Amandier**

Séverine et Olivier BRUNEAU
20, Rue de la Mairie, 49260 LE PUY-NOTRE-DAME
☎ 02 41 67 59 77 & 06 62 91 42 27
email: seve.lamandier@orange.fr
web: www.lamandieranjou.monsite.orange.fr

This welcoming house is in the heart of a delightful village in the wine-growing area. It has two double rooms, and a family suite for four. All rooms have en suite bath or shower rooms and WCs. Cot available. Lounge with billiard table, and a garden with terrace where meals can be served in the summer. Meals by arrangement.

Prices s fr €37; d fr €46; t fr €57; extra person fr €13; dinner fr €16
On Site Restaurant ♒　**Nearby** ⛷ 4km ♨ 20km ♒ 3km ⟲ 5km
♒ 25km ⚓ 25km　**Notes** No pets

LE VIEIL-BAUGE

♯♯♯ ☙ **La Guitoisière**

Chantal REVEAU
49150 LE VIEIL-BAUGE
☎ 02 41 89 25 59 🖨 02 41 89 06 04

Three guest rooms in an annexe building of a 13th-century farm: 'Echigné' and 'Montivert' are doubles, and 'Sensé' is a twin room. Each has its own shower room and wc. Heating, lounge with fireplace, library, dining room. Large landscaped garden with terrace, furniture and children's games. Farm produce available.

Prices s fr €40; d fr €45; extra person fr €15　**Nearby** ⛷ 12km ♨ 6km
♒ 4km ⟲ 5km Restaurant 5km ♒ 5km ⌂ 5km ⚓ 35km　**Notes** Pets admitted

♯♯♯ ◯ ♿ **Les Bouchets**

Géraldine et Michel BIGNON
49150 LE VIEIL-BAUGE
☎ 02 41 82 34 48 & 06 71 60 66 05
email: bignonm@wanadoo.fr
web: www.lesbouchets.com

This is a quiet place, ideal for charging your batteries. On the ground floor is a twin-bedded room; upstairs is a room with a double bed and a cot, and another room with a double bed and two singles. All of the rooms have private bath/shower rooms and WCs. Meals are available, using produce from the garden.

Prices s fr €45; d fr €50; t fr €70; extra person fr €15; dinner fr €25
On Site Restaurant ♒　**Nearby** ⛷ 5km ♨ 2km ⟲ 5km ♒ 4km
⌂ 4km　**Notes** No pets English spoken

LES CERQUEUX-DE-MAULEVRIER

ⅲ ⅰⓄⅰ La Hayère

Anne-Marie CHUPIN

49360 LES CERQUEUX-DE-MAULEVRIER

☎ 02 41 55 91 42   📄 02 41 55 91 42

email: gchupin@wanadoo.fr

web: www.lahayere.com

There are three first floor non-smoking bedrooms in this restored farmhouse, which is half an hour from Puy-du-Fou and ten minutes from the Parc Oriental Maulévrier. They are all double-bedded rooms, and they all have private bath/shower rooms and WCs. There is a lounge with open fire, and meals are available by arrangement.

Prices s fr €40; d fr €48; t fr €63; extra person fr €15; dinner fr €20 **Nearby** ⚓ 7km ⚴ 20km ⚘ 15km ⚹ 20km Restaurant 8km ⚘ ⚹ 20km ⋙ 20km **Notes** No pets   English spoken

LES ROSIERS-SUR-LOIRE

ⅲⅲ ⅰⓄⅰ Domaine de l'Oie Rouge

Christiane BATEL

8, Rue Nationale, 49350 LES ROSIERS-SUR-LOIRE

☎ 02 41 53 65 65   📄 02 41 53 65 66

email: c.batel@wanadoo.fr

web: www.domaine-oie-rouge.com

A magnificent 19th-century residence on the banks of the Loire, between Angers and Saumur. An outbuilding offers personalised rooms: a cosy double with views over the park (Romance), a twin decorated in homage to Rode (Iris), a vast 1930s-style room with views over the Loire (Camélia) and 'Santal' with momentos of journeys abroad. All have private facilities. Tree and flower-lined park to relax in after a day exploring tourist attractions and walks.

Prices s €63-€83; d €70-€90; t €88-€99; extra person fr €15; dinner fr €25   **On Site** ⚘   **Nearby** ⚓ 2km ⚴ 10km ⚹ 1km Restaurant 0.2km ⚘ 1km ⋙ 1km   **Notes** No pets   English spoken   CC

LONGUE

ⅲⅲ La Rigauderie

Yolande et Daniel LAURIOUX

18, Rue de la Rigauderie, 49160 LONGUE

☎ 02 41 67 73 86 & 06 07 66 18 50

📄 02 41 53 07 31

email: larigauderie@hotmail.fr

web: www.larigauderie-anjou.com

Between Saumur and Angers and about nine kilometres from the Loire, this 19th-century house has two double rooms and a family suite which can sleep up to four. All have private shower room and WC. Outside are two hectares of grounds surrounded by watercourses.

Prices s fr €70; d fr €75; t fr €93; extra person fr €18   **On Site** ⚘ Private ⚹   **Nearby** ⚓ 3km ⚴ 20km Restaurant 0.1km ⚘ 1km ⚹ 17km ⚐ 0.1km ⋙ 17km   **Notes** No pets   English spoken

MARTIGNE-BRIAND

ⅲⅲ Domaine de l'Etang

Gilles TENAILLON

49540 MARTIGNE-BRIAND

☎ 02 41 59 92 31   📄 02 41 59 92 30

email: domaine.etang@ifrance.com

web: www.domaine-etang.com

These guest rooms are on the first floor of an annexe building, set in a two-hectare park including private tennis court, table football, outdoor furniture and winter garden. The Blue Room and Red Room each offer a double and a single bed, the Green Room twin beds and the Yellow Room a double. Each has private facilities and heating. High chair available. Lounge room.

Prices s fr €55; d fr €60; t fr €75; extra person fr €15   **On Site** ⚘ Private ⚹   Private tennis court   **Nearby** ⚓ 5km Restaurant 3km ⚹ 3km ⚐ 3km ⋙ 35km   **Notes** Pets admitted   English spoken   CC

MAZE

ⅲⅲ Chambre d'hôtes

Nathalie GUERIN

78, Rue Grollay, 49630 MAZE

☎ 06 13 11 39 42   📄 02 41 74 97 90

email: maeno@free.fr

web: www.maeno-yn.com

This house in beautiful countryside has the feeling of a family home about it. Four large bedrooms, two of them family-sized suites, all have private bath or shower room and WC. Living room with a kitchenette. Plenty of good walks and other activities close by.

Prices s fr €50; d fr €53; extra person fr €20   **Nearby** ⚓ 2km ⚴ 17km ⚘ 2km ⚹ 7km ⚘ 2km ⚐ 3km ⋙ 22km   **Notes** No pets

ⵜⵜⵜ Rive Gauche

Joël et Sheena ANDROMAQUE
Le Gué de Mazé, Route de St-Mathurin, 49630 MAZE
☎ 02 41 66 67 93
email: andromaque@rivegauche-maze.com
web: www.rivegauche-maze.com

Beside the Authion River, mid way between Angers and Saumur, this conversion of a 19th-century barn has three beautiful bedrooms. They are all double-bedded, one with an additional single bed, and all of them with private shower room and WC. Outside are extensive wooded grounds bordered by water.

Prices s €47-€50; d €52-€55; extra person fr €15 **On Site** 🏊 🎾
Nearby ⛳5km 🎣 5km ⊕5km 🏛1km 🚲6km **Notes** No pets English spoken

MONTJEAN-SUR-LOIRE

ⵜⵜⵜ Les Cèdres

Nina et Serge MILLERIOUX
7 Rue du Prieuré, 49570 MONTJEAN-SUR-LOIRE
☎ 02 41 39 39 25 & 06 62 17 39 25
email: lescedres@les-cedres.net
web: www.les-cedres.net

family home in a pretty village beside the Loire. The individual double guest rooms have private bathrooms and include the 'Mozart', 'Bartok' and 'Mahler'. Breakfast is served in the dining room; large garden with furniture. Marked walking routes, boat trips. In summer: exhibition of giant sculptures in the village, hemp festival.

Prices s €49-€60; d €55-€65; extra person fr €17 **On Site** Private 🎣
Nearby ⛳3km 🎣20km 🏊 0.3km Restaurant 0.3km 🍷0.3km 🏛0.1km
🚲3km **Notes** No pets English spoken

MONTREUIL-BELLAY

ⵜⵜⵜ Chambre d'hôtes

Jacques et Monique GUEZENEC
Demeure les Petits Augustins, 49260 MONTREUIL-BELLAY
☎ 02 41 52 33 88 📠 02 41 52 33 88
email: lespetitsaugustins@yahoo.fr
web: www.les-petits-augustins.com

This peaceful 17th-century home has two double rooms with additional singles bed, and a room with a double and twin beds, each with private facilities and heating. Guest lounge. Village 500mtrs.

Prices s fr €50; d fr €58; t fr €70; extra person fr €10 **Nearby** ⛳ 6km
🎣15km 🏊 0.2km 🎣 0.2km Restaurant 0.1km ⊕0.5km 🏛0.5km
🚲0.3km **Notes** Pets admitted English spoken Open April to October.
CC

ⵜⵜⵜ 🍽 ♿ Les Murets

Liliane MERCIER
115 rue de la Société, 49260 MONTREUIL-BELLAY
☎ 02 41 50 84 85 📠 02 41 50 84 85
email: les-murets-de-treze@wanadoo.fr
web: www.murets.com

This old stone-built farmhouse, in a beautifully quiet setting, has five bedrooms. Downstairs there are two double rooms and a twin-bedded room; upstairs are two more doubles. All of the rooms have their own facilities, with shower rooms downstairs and bathrooms upstairs. Outside there is a garden and swimming pool - and in the stones of the walls surrounding them you can see ammonites. Evening meal by reservation only.

Prices s fr €50; d fr €59; extra person €15-€17; dinner fr €22
On Site 🎣 🎾 Private **Nearby** ⛳15km 🎣8km Restaurant 3km
🏊8km 🏛5km 🚲18km **Notes** No pets English spoken CC

MONTREUIL-JUIGNE

ⵜⵜⵜ Le Plateau

Jean-Louis HUEZ
Rue Espéranto, 49460 MONTREUIL-JUIGNE
☎ 02 41 42 32 35

Set in grounds with a terrace and outdoor furniture, this large family house offers four guest rooms, each with independent access and private facilities: 'Jacques' has a double and a single bed, 'Bernard' is a twin room, 'Geneviève' is a double and 'Antoinette' has three single beds. Mezzanine floor for breakfast and TV, lounge. Restaurant 2km.

Prices s fr €35; d fr €47; extra person fr €17 **On Site** 🎣
Nearby ⛳3km 🎣 2km Restaurant 1km 🏊1.5km 🏛1.5km 🚲9km
Notes Pets admitted

MONTREUIL-SUR-LOIR

‖‖ ✉ Château de Montreuil

Jacques et Marie BAILLIOU
Montreuil-sur-Loir, 49140 SEICHES-SUR-LOIR
☎ 02 41 76 21 03 & 06 66 68 90 29
email: chateau.montreuil@anjou-et-loire.com
web: www.anjou-et-loire.com/chateau

This château has panoramic views of the Loir Valley and the Forest of Boudre. There are two double guest rooms, one twin room, and one room with a double and a single bed; each room has private facilities. Dining room and lounge. Terrace overhanging the Loir, garden and large wooded park alongside the river. Village 200mtrs. Canoeing on site. Five golf courses within a 30km radius.

Prices s fr €75; d fr €85; t fr €130; extra person €15-€30; dinner fr €30 **On Site** ✿ **Nearby** ✿ 7km ⚓ 20km ↗ 5km Restaurant 5km ⚓ 5km ⛵ 5km ⚓ 20km **Notes** No pets English spoken Open 15 March to 15 November.

MOULIHERNE

‖‖ ✉ Le Cèdre de Monnaie

Marguerite DELVAL
49390 MOULIHERNE
☎ 02 41 67 09 27 & 06 08 97 48 34
email: lecedredemonnaie@tiscali.fr
web: www.cedredemonnaie.com

In the heart of the Monnaie Forest, this splendid 17th-century farmhouse offers the warmest of welcomes. Three guest rooms (one double and two triple) with private facilities and a vast lounge with fireplace, beams and half-timbering. Private terrace opening onto the park with its majestic cedar tree.

Prices s fr €45; d fr €55; t fr €70; dinner fr €19 **On Site** ⚓ **Nearby** ✿ 5km ✿ 4km Restaurant 4km ⛵ 10km ⚓ 4km ⚓ 15km **Notes** No pets English spoken

MOZE-SUR-LOUET

‖‖ Les Roches

Philippe CATROUILLET
49610 MOZE-SUR-LOUET
☎ 02 41 78 84 29
email: catrouillet.philippe@wanadoo.fr
web: www.accueil-anjou.com

This restored 18th-century house, with exposed stone and beams, is situated overhanging a river in a vineyard, in a peaceful hamlet at the entrance to Angers. The Green Room and the White Room are spacious rooms with queen-size bed and single bed, each with private facilities. In a converted outbuilding, there is a kitchenette and lounge area, with twin beds, shower room and wc on a mezzanine level. Outdoor furniture.

Prices s €45-€47; d €52-€62; extra person €15-€17 **On Site** ✿ ✿ **Nearby** ✿ 5km ⚓ 10km Restaurant 3km ⛵ 2km ⚓ 2km ⚓ 12km **Notes** No pets English spoken

MURS-ERIGNE

‖‖ ✉ Le Jau

Françoise TERRIERE
49610 MURS-ERIGNE
☎ 02 41 57 70 13 & 06 83 26 38 80
email: le.jau@anjou-et-loire
web: www.anjou-et-loire.com/jau

Amidst châteaux and vineyards, this attractive and welcoming house is in a verdant setting. There are three quiet, comfortable guest rooms with views over the park, each with private bathroom and wc. TV in two bedrooms. Large, welcoming kitchen, lounge with fireplace and TV, terrace, outdoor furniture, barbecue. Evening meals by reservation. Bathing 500mtrs. Special weekend rates.

Prices not confirmed for 2008 **Nearby** ✿ 0.5km ↗ 8km ⚓ 8km **Notes** No pets

NEUILLE

‖‖‖ Château le Goupillon

Monique CALOT
Neuillé, 49680 VIVY
☎ 02 41 52 51 89 ▤ 02 41 52 51 89
email: chateau-de-goupillon@wanadoo.fr
web: www.chateau-de-goupillon.com

Comfortable, quiet château in a lush four-hectare park with three bedrooms individually decorated with antique furnishings. The rooms have private facilities and include two doubles with extra single bed (one with adjoining twin room) and a room with four-poster bed. Beamed lounge with fireplace, heating, outdoor furniture. A timeless place, ideal for discovering the Saumur vineyards and visiting the châteaux of the Loire.

Prices d €75-€110; extra person fr €20 **Nearby** ✿ 6km ⚓ 10km ✿ 1.5km ↗ 7km Restaurant 3km ⛵ 10km ⚓ 1.5km ⚓ 10km **Notes** Pets admitted

NOYANT

⦀ Galmer

Guy COURAULT

49490 NOYANT

☎ 02 41 89 50 17　▤ 02 41 89 50 17

email: gmacouralt@yahoo.fr

Between Anjou and Touraine, set in peaceful countryside, this property offers a double room in the proprietor's house and a twin room with queen-size bed in an annexe, all with private facilities. Cot available, heating, kitchen, lounge.

Prices s fr €32; d €40-€42; extra person fr €10　**On Site** ⚑
Nearby ⛵ 15km ⚓ 18km ✎ 5km ⟋ 15km ⚓ 3km ⚑ 3km ⛵ 35km
Notes No pets　English spoken

NYOISEAU

⦀ ⦿ Les Hauts-de-Brèges

Stéphanie PELLIER

49500 NYOISEAU

☎ 02 41 61 39 07

email: b.pellier@wanadoo.fr

web: www.hauts-de-breges.com

Extensive wooded grounds surround this house, which has tremendous character. There are three double rooms, each with a private shower room and WC. Baby equipment is available. There is a lounge for guests' use, a games room, and bikes can be borrowed. Meals by arrangement. Closed Xmas & New Year.

Prices s fr €37; d fr €41; extra person fr €10; dinner fr €15　**On Site** ✎
⚑　**Nearby** ⛵ 1km ⟋ 3km Restaurant 0.3km ⚓ ⚑ 1km ⛵ 4km
Notes Pets admitted　English spoken

PONTIGNE

⦀ ✿ ⦿ Les Hautes Roches

M-Ange et Yannick SALLE

49150 PONTIGNE

☎ 02 41 89 19 63　▤ 02 41 89 19 63

email: gaec.deshautesroches@wanadoo.fr

With views of the Couasnon Valley and the Forest of Chandelais, this organic farm has two twin rooms and two doubles (one with child's bed), each with private facilities. Lounge with kitchenette, heating. Table d'hôte meals by reservation. Pétanque, table tennis, large courtyard, garden furniture, swings, barbecue. Walks nearby, fishing in the lake on the farm. Donkey rides for children. Château of King René V and the Vraie Croix nearby.

Prices s fr €40; d fr €48; dinner fr €17　**Nearby** ⛵ 6km ⚓ 4km
✎ 3km ⟋ 3km Restaurant 1.5km ⚓ 3km ⚑ 3km ⚑ 3km ⛵ 35km
Notes No pets

RABLAY-SUR-LAYON

⦀ La Girardière

Eliette PHELIX

49750 RABLAY-SUR-LAYON

☎ 02 41 78 65 51 & 06 21 11 46 94

In the peace of the Anjou countryside, amid the Layon vineyards, choose between three comfortable en suite rooms, one of which has kitchenette. Swim in the pool and visit the châteaux of the Loire, Angers' famous Apocalypse Tapestry or the Puy-du-Fou. Taste the famous Layon wines at one of several vineyards. Bikes may be borrowed. Parking. Reduced rates for longer stays.

Prices s fr €40; d fr €45; extra person fr €15　**On Site** ⚑
Nearby ⛵ 15km ⚓ 15km ✎ 1km Restaurant 3km ⚑ 1km ⛵ 26km
Notes No pets

SAUMUR

⦀ Ile du Saule

Mme KEMPCZYNSKI

49400 SAUMUR

☎ 02 41 51 38 71

web: www.iledusaule.com

In a green and pleasant setting, these three guest rooms include a double, a twin and a double room with adjoining twin room. All have private facilities and heating. Parking. Garden with outdoor furniture.

Prices s fr €38; d fr €45; t fr €61; extra person fr €18　**On Site** ⚓
Nearby ⛵ 5km ✎ 5km ⟋ 5km ⚓ 5km ✿ 0.8km ⚑ 0.8km ⛵ 1.5km
Notes No pets　English spoken

SAVENNIERES

⦀ ✿ Lorcival

Evelyne MARCHESI

Place du Mail No 3, 49170 SAVENNIERES

☎ 06 76 60 88 30

email: evelyne.marchesi@wanadoo.fr

This village has an 11th-century church and is surrounded by vineyards. The chambre d'hotes has three bedrooms in a building facing the owner's home. There are two double rooms, one downstairs and one upstairs; also upstairs is a triple room with a double bed and a single. All the bedrooms have private bath or shower rooms and WCs.

Prices not confirmed for 2008　**Nearby** ⛵ 2km ✎ 3km ⟋ 3km ⚓ 3km
Notes Pets admitted

SEICHES-SUR-LOIR

⦀ ⦿ ♿ Domaine de Bré

Brigitte DONON

49140 SEICHES-SUR-LOIR

☎ 02 41 76 18 61

email: dononbre@aol.com

web: www.domainedebre.fr

Dating from 1850, this attractive house is at the heart of a 400-hectare forest. A calm, relaxing spot, the grounds are crossed by a canalised

CONTINUED

SEICHES-SUR-LOIR *CONTINUED*

river. There are three very comfortable, individual guest rooms with private bathrooms and activities include walking, mountain-biking, fishing, canoeing and swimming on site. Many places of tourist, cultural and gastronomic interest nearby. Reservations are necessary out of season.

Prices s fr €60; d fr €77.50; extra person fr €20; dinner fr €23
On Site 🏊 🍽 **Nearby** ⛷ 8km ⌖ 18km Restaurant 7km 🏊 5km
Spa 25km 🏛 7km ⋙ 25km **Notes** No pets English spoken

SERMAISE

⌘ 🍽 Le Chalet

Guillemette et Pierre GRELIER
49140 SERMAISE
☎ 02 41 82 29 71 🗎 02 41 82 14 98
email: lechalet49@wanadoo.fr
web: www.lechaletchambresdhotes.com

The main building here is an old farmhouse dating back to the 19th century, but the three individually decorated guest rooms are all in a converted outbuilding. All the rooms are spacious; two are doubles and the third is a family room for four. All have a private bath/shower room and WC, and each also has its own lounge area.

Prices s fr €45; d fr €55; extra person fr €15; dinner fr €18 **On Site** 🍽
Private 🎣 **Nearby** ⛷ 15km ⌖ 10km 🚲 8km Restaurant 10km 🏊 4km
🏛 4km ⋙ 30km **Notes** No pets English spoken

ST-AUBIN-DU-PAVOIL

⌘ 🍽 Saint Aubin du Pavoil

Michel et M-Alice DE VITTON
La Grange du Plessis, Place de l'Eglise, 49500 SEGRE
☎ 06 07 97 77 37
email: domainevitton@wanadoo.fr
web: www.le-plessis.com

Three kilometres from a charming village, an historic 17th-century presbytery and authentic former barn offer a friendly welcome. There are three twin rooms (one with sofa) and a double, all with TV, phone and private facilities. Wooded park, access to the river, boat available. Bike hire on site. Wi-fi available for guests.

Prices s fr €51; d fr €64; extra person fr €18; dinner fr €25 **On Site** 🚲
🚲 🍽 **Nearby** ⛷ 3km 🎣 3km Restaurant 3km 🏊 3km 🏛 3km ⋙ 3km
Notes No pets English spoken CC

ST-CLEMENT-DE-LA-PLACE

⌘ 🍽 Chambre d'hôtes

Isabelle et Bruno BROCHARD
10, Rue de l'Abattoir, 49370 ST-CLEMENT-DE-LA-PLACE
☎ 02 41 77 31 63 & 06 73 46 11 69
email: saga.isa.bru@club-internet.fr
web: www.dormircheznous.free.fr

A little 16th-century house, adjacent to the owners' home in the centre of a small town, is the setting for this chambre d'hôtes. There are three double bedrooms, two downstairs and one upstairs. All of the

rooms have private facilities. Garden, above-ground swimming pool, table tennis. Meals and entertainment on some evenings.

Prices s fr €35; d €39-€42; extra person fr €12; dinner fr €11
On Site Private 🎣 **Nearby** ⛷ 5km 🎣 15km 🚲 5km Restaurant 5km
🏊 0.5km 🍽 17km 🏛 5km ⋙ 17km **Notes** Pets admitted English spoken

ST-GERMAIN-DES-PRES

⌘ Villa Loire

Isabelle SAINT-BRIS
La Grande Boire, 49170 ST-GERMAIN-DES-PRES
☎ 02 41 39 96 44 🗎 02 41 39 96 44
email: isasaintbris@aol.com
web: www.villa-loire.com

Right beside the banks of the Loire, this house enjoys a beautiful location. There are extensive grounds, and a heated indoor pool. The three bedrooms are all doubles, each with private shower room and WC. Picnic area in the grounds and picnics available to order, with local wine and food specialities.

Prices s fr €70; d fr €80 **On Site** 🚲 Private 🎣 **Nearby** ⛷ 5km
Restaurant 5km 🏊 5km 🍽 5km 🏛 5km ⋙ 30km **Notes** No pets
English spoken

THORIGNE-D'ANJOU

⌘ 🍽 Le Rideau Miné

Dany FABRY
49220 THORIGNE-D'ANJOU
☎ 02 41 76 88 40
email: rideau49@yahoo.fr
web: www.lerideaumine.com

Three comfortable bedrooms - spacious, bright, facing south-west and with beautiful river views - are available at this 17th-century property. There are two double rooms, and a triple with three single beds. All the rooms have private facilities. Fishing is available, and the property is very close to a famous stud farm.

Prices s fr €49; d fr €58; t fr €76; extra person fr €18; dinner fr €22
On Site 🚲 **Nearby** ⛷ 1km 🎣 2km 🏊 2km 🏛 2km **Notes** No pets
English spoken

THOUARCE

⌘ Le Clos des 3 Rois

Liliane et Marc DUSEAUX
13 rue du Bellay, 49380 THOUARCE
☎ 02 41 66 34 04 & 06 99 91 95 20
email: infos@closdes3rois.fr
web: www.closdes3rois.fr

In the heart of the Layon region, this property has five excellent bedrooms, one of them a family room, in the restored outbuildings of a 19th-century house. Everything has been arranged for guests' comfort, with superb quality bed-linen, air-conditioning, heated swimming pool and a billiard room. The entire site is non-smoking.

Prices s €64-€74; d €64-€74; extra person fr €16 **On Site** 🚲 Private 🎣
Nearby ⛷ 5km 🎣 20km Restaurant 0.1km 🏊 🍽 6km 🏛 0km ⋙ 30km
Notes No pets English spoken CC

VARENNES-SUR-LOIRE

⌖ Les Marronniers

France BODINEAU

Gaure, 49730 VARENNES-SUR-LOIRE

☎ 02 41 38 10 13

web: www.loireabracio-marronniers.com

This 19th-century house with panoramic views of the Loire offers five en suite guest rooms: two doubles, a room with a double and two singles, a triple and a room with a double and single bed. Landscaped garden. Peace and relaxation assured.

Prices s fr €42; d fr €47; t fr €62; extra person fr €16 **Nearby** ⚓ 8km ⚓ 7km ⚓ 0.1km ⚓ 8km Restaurant 3km ⚓ 10km ⚓ 10km ⚓ 1.5km ⚓ 10km **Notes** Pets admitted

---

VAUCHRETIEN

⌖ Le Moulin de Clabeau

François et Nelly DAVIAU

49320 VAUCHRETIEN

☎ 02 41 91 22 09

email: moulin-clabeau@gite-brissac.com

web: www.gite-brissac.com

In a verdant setting alongside the Aubance, close to Brissac Quincé, this old water mill offers three guest rooms. 'Agathe' is a family room with a double and twin beds, while 'Jeanne' and 'Valentine' both have queen-size beds. Each room has a private bathroom. Lounge area with kitchenette.

Prices s fr €56; d fr €60; t fr €85 **On Site** ⚓ **Nearby** ⚓ 7km ⚓ 6km ⚓ 3km Restaurant 2km ⚓ 3km Spa 15km ⚓ 3km ⚓ 15km **Notes** No pets

---

VAUDELNAY

⌖ ◯ La Pinsonnière

P et O PETITOUT-SCHWIRTZ

25 Rue du Château, 49260 VAUDELNAY

☎ 02 41 59 12 95 ▤ 02 41 59 12 95

email: pascale@la-pinsonniere.fr

web: www.la-pinsonniere.fr

A wonderful 17th-century property standing above 15th-century cellars which have seen use as troglodyte homes, a chalk quarry, temporary prison and more recently as a cellar for maturing wine! There are four large non-smoking bedrooms, with themed decorations, all with private bath or shower room and WC; one room sleeping up to five people includes a magical converted pigeon loft ideal for children up to ten years old. Meals available (pre-booking required).

Prices s €59-€70; d €63-€74; extra person fr €17; dinner fr €30 **On Site** ⚓ Private ⚓ **Nearby** ⚓ 3km ⚓ 15km ⚓ 3km Restaurant 2km ⚓ 2km ⚓ 2km ⚓ 20km **Notes** Pets admitted English spoken CC

⌖ Les Loges de Vignes

Bruno ALBERT

205 Rue du Château d'Oiré, 49260 VAUDELNAY

☎ 02 41 52 21 78 & 06 62 58 21 78 ▤ 02 41 38 85 83

email: vieuxpressoir@wanadoo.fr

This totally restored property is in the heart of a working vineyard. On the ground floor it has one double bedroom; upstairs is a two-roomed suite for four, plus two more double rooms. All have private bath/shower room and WC. Outside is an awning with a barbecue and garden furniture.

Prices s fr €49; d fr €55; extra person fr €15 **Nearby** ⚓ 10km ⚓ 15km ⚓ 6km ⚓ 10km Restaurant 10km ⚓ 3km ⚓ 7km ⚓ 25km **Notes** No pets CC

MAYENNE

BAZOUGERS

⌖ ◯ Domaine de la Houzardière

Marguerite MOENNER

53170 BAZOUGERS

☎ 02 43 02 37 16

email: marguerite@houzardiere.com

web: www.houzardiere.com

Old stables, which are part of a larger complex of farm buildings, have been converted to provide five attractive guest rooms, all individually decorated and furnished with antiques. All have private bath or shower room and WC; there is a kitchenette available, and outside there is garden furniture, table tennis, swimming pool and a barbecue.

Prices s €39-€45; d €48-€50; extra person fr €15; dinner fr €18 **On Site** Private ⚓ **Nearby** ⚓ 30km ⚓ 0.5km Restaurant 8km Water sports 6km ⚓ 0.5km ⚓ 8km ⚓ 16km **Notes** No pets English spoken Open March to December.

CHATEAU-GONTIER

⌖ ◯ La Coudre

Valérie BRUNET

53200 CHATEAU GONTIER

☎ 02 43 70 36 03

email: herbrun2@aol.com

web: www.lacoudre53.fr

An old farmhouse which has been beautifully restored. There are three double-bedded rooms, two with an extra single bed and all with

CONTINUED

CHATEAU-GONTIER CONTINUED

television, private shower room and WC. Guests' kitchenette; meals available by arrangement. Pleasant gardens.

Prices s fr €46; d fr €51; t fr €66; dinner fr €18   **On Site** ⚓
Nearby ⛵ 15km ♨ 20km Restaurant 3km Water sports 5km 🍴 2km
🚶 30km   **Notes** No pets English spoken

▦ ⧉ Le Chêne Vert

Caroline HERON
53200 CHATEAU GONTIER
☎ 02 43 07 90 48 & 06 81 84 48 66
email: caroline.heron@wanadoo.fr
web: www.chenevert-chateaugontier.com

In peaceful countryside just 1.5km from the village, the château is in wooded grounds with its own chapel. Breakfast is served in the period dining room or under the arbour. There are five large, themed bedrooms (Roses, Queen Elizabeth, Tropical, Oriental and Safari), two of which are family rooms. They all have private shower or bath rooms.

Prices s fr €55; d fr €65; extra person fr €20; dinner fr €23
Nearby ⛵ 1.5km ♨ 35km ✿ 1.5km ↖ 1.5km Restaurant 1.5km
Water sports 25km ♨ 1.5km Spa 1.5km ⛳ 1.5km 🍴 1.5km 🚶 25km
Notes Pets admitted CC

COUESMES-VAUCE

▦ ❦ *Froulay*

Hubert et Thérèse GARNIER
53300 COUESMES VAUCE
☎ 02 43 04 94 17 & 06 75 91 44 17
email: hubertgarnier@wanadoo.fr
web: http://perso.wanadoo.fr/hubert.garnier/

This ancient house is on a farm overlooking the valley of the Varenne. It has three delightful decorated and spacious bedrooms, one of them a grade 2 room. All have separate access, and private showers and WCs. There is a guests' lounge with kitchenette. Fishing, cycling, table tennis and canoeing are available, and there is a leisure centre close by.

Prices not confirmed for 2008   **Nearby** ♨ 30km ✿ 0.1km ↖ 7km
Water sports 10km 🍴 5km 🚶 50km   **Notes** No pets English spoken

COURBEVEILLE

▦ La Rênerie

Michel et Nicole BOUVIER
53230 COURBEVEILLE
☎ 02 43 64 17 64 & 06 80 00 85 09

A peaceful house just ten minutes from the historical art town of Laval, on the edge of the Pays de Craon. Your hosts invite you for an evening stroll round their garden surrounded by the perfume of roses, under the watchful eye of their swans and ducks. The three comfortable rooms are all individually decorated.

Prices s fr €48; d €58-€68; extra person fr €20   **On Site** ⛳
Nearby ♨ 15km ✿ 2km Restaurant 5km Water sports 15km ♨ 0.8km
🍴 5km 🚶 15km   **Notes** No pets English spoken

CRAON

▦ ⧉ La Demeure de l'Ile

Chantal BRETAUDEAU
16 Rue du Vieux Pont, 53400 CRAON
☎ 02 43 06 37 07 & 06 74 64 72 72
🖷 02 43 06 72 90
email: bretaudeau@wanadoo.fr
web: www.demeuredelile.com

Right beside the Oudon River, this former 18th-century washhouse has been magnificently restored to provide three delightful guest bedrooms, all elegantly decorated and furnished. All the rooms are doubles, two have a bathroom and the third has shower/WC. Breakfast is served in the bright and cheerful dining room; outside are extensive grounds with a swimming pool.

Prices s fr €85; d fr €95; extra person fr €25; dinner fr €27
On Site ✿ Restaurant ⛳ Private ↖   **Nearby** ♨ 4km ♨ 25km
Water sports 5km 🚶 30km   **Notes** No pets English spoken

ERNEE

▦ ❦ La Gasselinais

Florent et Catherine GENDRON
53500 ERNEE
☎ 02 43 05 70 80
email: gendron53@yahoo.fr
web: www.bienvenuealaferme.net

Expect a warm welcome at this restored farmhouse in the Ernée Valley. Discover life on the farm, with animals and organic produce, including apple juice, jam and milk, to taste. The three guest rooms have private facilities and one has a kitchenette and mezzanine floor for a family. Lounge with fireplace and kitchenette. Reduced rates from the third night.

Prices s fr €32; d fr €40; t fr €52; extra person fr €13   **On Site** ✿
Nearby ♨ 7km ♨ 25km ↖ 2km Restaurant 3km Water sports 23km
♨ 3km 🍴 2km 🚶 30km   **Notes** No pets English spoken

ERNEE-MEGAUDAIS

▦ ⧉ La Rouaudière

Thérèse et Maurice TRIHAN
53500 ERNEE-MEGAUDAIS
☎ 02 43 05 13 57
email: therese-trihan@wanadoo.fr
web: www.chambresdhotes-auxportesdelabretagne.com

This family house is on a smallholding and includes a relaxing garden with furniture and terrace, full of perennial plants, rose bushes and shrubs. The three guest rooms each sleep 2-3 people and benefit from a lounge, separate entrance and private facilities. Lounge with fireplace. Supplement payable for pets. Choice of restaurants nearby, one of which is fine dining and only five minutes away.

Prices s €38-€42; d €48-€56; extra person €12-€20; dinner fr €20
Nearby ♨ 30km ✿ 10km ↖ 5km Restaurant 0.5km Water sports 18km
♨ 5km ⛳ 5km 🍴 5km 🚶 35km   **Notes** Pets admitted English spoken

GREZ-EN-BOUERE

⫼ ⎢○⎥ **Château de Chanay**

Béatrice SIMONET BLAISEL
53290 GREZ EN BOUERE
☎ 02 43 70 98 81   📄 02 43 70 98 81
email: info@chateau-de-chanay.com
web: www.chateau-de-chanay.com

This beautiful historic house has three bedrooms, all now restored and featuring antique furniture. Two have double beds and the third has twin beds; all have en suite bathroom and separate WC. Elegant living room, and outside are grounds of five hectares.

Prices s €70-€100; d €80-€110; dinner fr €27   **On Site** 🌳
Nearby ⛷ 10km ⚓ 20km 🏊 7km ➹ 12km Restaurant 10km Water sports 10km 🛶 10km 🏛 3km ⛰ 30km   **Notes** Pets admitted English spoken

LA CROPTE

⫼ ⎢○⎥ **Hys**

Isabelle FREYSSENGE
53170 LA CROPTE
☎ 02 43 64 24 14
email: hys@free.fr
web: http://hys.free.fr

Expect a peaceful stay at this 17th-century mill surrounded by wooded parkland. Drop off to sleep to the gentle murmur of the millrace in one of the four cosy, tastefully decorated rooms - each with private facilities. Make use of the lounge, the garden furniture or reserve an evening meal.

Prices s €45-€55; d €50-€60; t €65-€80; dinner fr €20   **On Site** 🌳
Nearby ⛷ 10km ⚓ 17km ➹ 3km Restaurant 5km Water sports 2km 🏊 5km 🏛 5km ⛰ 20km   **Notes** Pets admitted English spoken

LASSAY-LES-CHATEAUX

⫼ ⎢○⎥ **Le Nouveau Gue**

Florence RICHEFEU
2 Rue des Tilleuls, Niort la Fontaine,
53110 LASSAY LES CHATEAUX
☎ 02 43 00 16 97
email: richefeu@wanadoo.fr

This is an old presbytery, dating back to the 18th and 19th centuries. It has three guest rooms: two upstairs in the owners' house, and a family suite in a converted outbuilding, with its own entrance. All have private bath or shower room and WC. Meals are available, by arrangement.

Prices s fr €40; d fr €45; extra person fr €20; dinner fr €20
Nearby ⚓ 18km 🏊 3km ➹ 3.5km Restaurant 3km Water sports 12km 🛶 3km Spa 18km 🌳 18km 🏛 3.5km ⛰ 40km   **Notes** No pets English spoken

MEZANGERS

⫼ **Le Cruchet**

Leopold NAY
53600 MEZANGERS
☎ 02 43 90 65 55 & 06 70 01 25 75
email: bandb.lecruchet@wanadoo.fr
web: www.lecruchet.com

This country house dates back to the 15th and 16th centuries. It has three guest bedrooms. On the ground floor is a double room, and upstairs is a room for four. In an adjacent building is a studio for four people. The rooms have private facilities and their own entrances. Kitchenette, garden furniture.

Prices s fr €35; d €40-€45; extra person fr €15   **Nearby** ⚓ 36km 🏊 1km ➹ 5km Restaurant 1km Water sports 1km 🏛 0.5km ⛰ 5km
Notes No pets English spoken

MONTSURS

⫼ ⎢○⎥ **Le Logis Deritel**

Bernard VALLEE
13 Av de la Libération, 53150 MONTSURS
☎ 02 43 37 33 01 & 06 89 76 77 86   📄 02 43 37 33 01
email: deritel@wanadoo.fr
web: http://chambre-hote-mayenne.com/gite-mayenne.html

This superb 19th-century house offers a warm welcome and three guest rooms, each with private facilities. The 'royal' room is particularly appealing and excellent breakfasts are served.

Prices s fr €35; d fr €45; extra person fr €16; dinner fr €18
Nearby ⛷ 4km ⚓ 20km 🏊 0.5km ➹ 10km Water sports 20km ⛰ 10km   **Notes** Pets admitted

OLIVET

⫼ *La Chaussée*

Nathalie MORAND
26 route de Saint Ouen, 53410 OLIVET
☎ 02 43 90 79 78 & 06 85 75 35 00
email: chambresdhotes.53olivet@wanadoo.fr
web: www.lachausseedolivet53.com

This characterful house with large country garden is in a charming village set around a 25-hectare lake. Art deco and 'art de vivre' combine to offer comfort and warmth, perfect for a romantic break

CONTINUED

OLIVET CONTINUED

with forest walks. Three themed rooms take you back in time. One room sleeps four, two further double rooms. Gastronomic restaurant with lake view nearby.

Prices not confirmed for 2008 **Nearby** ⌖ 5km 🌳 0.2km ↖ 14km Water sports 30km 🏛 1km ⚘ 14km **Notes** No pets English spoken

---

RUILLE-FROID-FONDS

⊞ ℃ **Chambre d'hôtes**

Christophe DAVENEL

Ville Prouvée, 53170 RUILLE FROID FONDS

☎ 02 43 07 71 62 & 06 89 81 50 13 📠 02 43 07 71 62

email: christ.davenel@wanadoo.fr

web: http://perso.orange.fr/villeprouve/bb

This 17th-century character house offers large, comfortable guest rooms with rustic furnishings: four-poster beds, hexagonal floor tiling, tufa stone fireplaces and half-timbering. There are two double rooms, one three-person room, and one four-person room, each with private bathroom and wc. Lounge, garden, stretch of water. Table d'hôte meals featuring farm produce.

Prices s fr €33; d fr €43; t fr €53; extra person fr €10; dinner fr €13 **On Site** 🌳 **Nearby** ⌖ 25km ↖ 9km Restaurant 1km Water sports 9km ⊰ 9km Spa 9km 🎾 12km 🏛 10km ⚘ 25km **Notes** Pets admitted English spoken

---

ST-BRICE

⊞ ℃ **Au Manoir des Forges**

Vincent et Sabine COLOMBANI

53290 ST BRICE

☎ 02 43 70 84 40 📠 02 43 70 84 14

email: contact@manoirdesforges.fr

web: www.manoirdesforges.fr

After a day of sightseeing, or sporting activities in the nearby village, come back to the sauna in the authentic setting of the 'Manoir des Forges'. In the main house are two large, comfortable rooms with private bathrooms and an en suite room in the annexe. Meals are served on the terrace in summer. Foodlit tennis court.

Prices d €85-€130; extra person fr €25; dinner fr €28 **On Site** Private ↖ Private tennis court **Nearby** ⌖ 6km ⌖ 8km 🌳 4km Restaurant 6km Water sports 8km 🏛 6km ⚘ 6km **Notes** No pets English spoken Open March to October.

⊞ ℃ **La Manchetiere**

Michael BARRETT

53290 ST BRICE

☎ 02 43 70 86 58 & 06 77 55 00 39

email: mike.barrett@wanadoo.fr

The house stands between Laval and Sablé, in an area rich in history. There are three spacious and elegant rooms, each with a private bath or shower room and WC. The grounds are extensive and close to the Forest of Bellebranche with its superb views across the countryside.

Prices not confirmed for 2008 **Nearby** ⌖ 10km 🌳 10km ↖ 10km Water sports 10km 🏛 1km ⚘ 10km **Notes** No pets English spoken

---

ST-GERMAIN-LE-FOUILLOUX

⊞ 🦋 *Fleurs des Champs* ⚘

Therese GEHANNIN

L'Hommeau, 53240 ST GERMAIN LE FOUILLOUX

☎ 02 43 01 18 41 📠 02 43 37 68 11

email: fleurs.des.champs@online.fr

web: http://fleurs.des.champs.online.fr

Guests can expect a quiet, restful stay at this farm in the middle of the Mayennais, 10km from Laval. Each of the renovated guest rooms has been individually decorated on the theme of wildflowers; there are two doubles with balcony and a room for four people, all with TV and private bathroom. Copious breakfasts are served in the bright lounge, or outside.

Prices not confirmed for 2008 **Nearby** ⌖ 10km 🌳 4km ↖ 10km Water sports 10km 🏛 3km ⚘ 10km **Notes** No pets

---

SARTHE

ANCINNES

⊞ **La Basse Cour**

Phil et Jude GRAHAM

3 Rue de l'Oisellerie, 72610 ANCINNES

☎ 02 33 82 01 19

email: gdf@normandie-chambres.co.uk

web: www.normandie-chambres.co.uk

Guest bedrooms are in the charming converted stables of an 18th-century house set in wooded and flower-filled gardens with a private lake. The lovely setting on the edge of the village affords forest views and proximity to shops, restaurant and bar. Guest lounge and library. Two bedrooms (one twin) with shower room, and one bedroom with bathroom (shower over bath), private WC. Exposed beams, tumble drier, guest lounge, garden rooms, two terraces, sheltered arbour, pétanque, skittles.

Prices s fr €45; d €50-€52; extra person fr €15 **On Site** 🎾 **Nearby** ⌖ 6km 🌳 1km ↖ 12.5km Restaurant 0.2km ⊰ 0.5km 🏛 0.2km ⚘ 8km **Notes** No pets English spoken

---

ASNIERES-SUR-VEGRE

⊞ ℃ ♿ **La Tuffière**

Mauricette et Yves DAVID

72430 ASNIERES-SUR-VEGRE

☎ 02 43 95 12 16 📠 02 43 92 43 05

email: tuffiere@yahoo.fr

web: www.tuffiere.com

Situated on the banks of the River Vègre, this house offers two guest rooms with a double and single bed and one room with a double and two singles, all en suite with heating. Fishing and boating on site. Table d'hôte meals.

Prices s fr €33; d €40-€44; t €51-€55; extra person fr €11; dinner fr €18 **On Site** 🌳 **Nearby** ⌖ 8km ⌖ 12km ↖ 12km Restaurant 6km ⊰ 5km 🎾 12km 🏛 4km ⚘ 12km **Notes** No pets Open March to December.

BEAUMONT-SUR-DEME

⊞ *Le Petit Hêtre*

Laurence LARIVIERE

72340 BEAUMONT-SUR-DEME

☎ 02 43 79 13 83 📄 06 16 30 18 94

email: lepetithetre@wanadoo.fr

A 19th-century farmhouse, very attractively restored to provide three bedrooms, each with independent access and a small living area. Two of the rooms have double beds, the third has twin beds, and they all have tea/coffee making facilities, private shower room and WC. The garden provides some secluded spots for sunbathing or picnics.

Prices not confirmed for 2008   **On Site** ☜   **Nearby** ⇕ 3km 🖋 2.5km ⟲ 3km ⟲ 3km 🏛 3km   **Notes** Pets admitted

BRULON

⊞⊞ Château de l'Enclos

Annie-C et J-Claude GUILLOU

2 Av de la Libération, 72350 BRULON

☎ 02 43 92 17 85

email: jean-claude.guillou5@wanadoo.fr

web: www.chateau-enclos.com

This elegant 19th-century château is in a beautiful village, close to long-distance footpaths, rivers and forests, and well-placed for mountain-biking. The Abbey of Solesmes is close by - well-known for its Gregorian chants and Malicorne pottery. It stands in its own enclosed grounds of three hectares. Enclosed parking.

Prices d fr €90; extra person fr €65   **On Site** 🖋   **Nearby** ⇕ 2km ⟲ 5km ☜ 2km   **Notes** No pets English spoken

see advert on this page

CHAMPFLEUR

⊞ ⏀ La Garencière

Christine et Denis LANGLAIS

72610 CHAMPFLEUR

☎ 02 33 31 75 84

email: denis.langlais@wanadoo.fr

web: http://monsite.orange.fr/garenciere/

This typical 19th-century farm enjoys a rural setting and provides five en suite guest rooms, sleeping two, three or four people. Lounge with TV, heating, table d'hôte (farm/regional specialities), covered swimming pool. Closed Xmas.

Prices s fr €47; d fr €56; extra person fr €16; dinner fr €22   **On Site** Private 🜄   **Nearby** ⇕ 10km ⌕ 7km 🖋 4km Restaurant 7km ⟲ 1km 🏛 1km ⛵ 11km   **Notes** No pets English spoken

CHANGE

⊞ Chambre d'hôtes

Daniel et Annick DUVAL

17 Route de la Californie, 72560 CHANGE

☎ 02 43 40 46 99 📄 02 43 40 46 99

email: duval.annick2@wanadoo.fr

web: http://24heures.free.fr

Close to Le Mans and with a relaxing atmosphere, this wooded property includes a swimming pool and is ideal for business trips and sports. Rooms available include a large room with a lounge area, satellite TV, double bed and single and two family rooms with two double beds; all have private facilities.

Prices s €35-€48; d €45-€60; t €60-€75   **On Site** Private 🜄   **Nearby** ⇕ 3km ⟲ 3km 🏛 1km ⛵ 8km   **Notes** No pets English spoken

CHANTENAY-VILLEDIEU

▦ ı◯ı �& *Chauvet*

Marylise VOVARD
72430 CHANTENAY-VILLEDIEU
☎ 02 43 95 77 57
email: marylise.vovard@wanadoo.fr
web: http://perso.wanadoo.fr/chauvet.hotes

The owners of this farmhouse will gladly show guests around their farm where they breed pigs and poultry. They offer three double en suite rooms, a living room, lounge with TV, cot/baby requirements, heating, garden furniture. Evening meals with the family (by arrangement). Mini-golf (2km).

Prices not confirmed for 2008 **Nearby** ᇂ 17km ℘ 2km ⚲ 2km ⌁ 2km ♔ 9km ⌂ 2km ⋙ 17km **Notes** No pets English spoken

CHEMIRE-LE-GAUDIN

▦ ı◯ı *Théval*

Anne-Marie FORNELL
72210 CHEMIRE-LE-GAUDIN
☎ 02 43 88 14 92
email: atheval@aol.com

Guests can enjoy a comfortable stay and friendly welcome, in a peaceful setting beside the River Sarthe. They offer four elegant, comfortable and spacious rooms accommodating two or three guests, all en suite. Enjoy sumptuous table d'hôte meals beneath 100-year-old plane trees or a game of boules. Nearby: boating, fishing and exploring the islands of the River Sarthe.

Prices not confirmed for 2008 **Nearby** ᇂ 5km ℘ 0.1km ⚲ 5km ⌁ 5km ♔ 0.1km ⌂ 2km ⋙ 5km **Notes** No pets English spoken

CLERMONT-CREANS

▦ **Le Château d'Oyre**

Karoline et Camille CONSTANTIN
Rue Galliéni, 72200 CLERMONT-CREANS
☎ 02 43 48 00 48 & 02 43 45 12 12
email: contact@moulindesquatresaisons.com
web: www.chateau-doyre.com

This property is a 15th-century château surrounded by French-style gardens and parkland. There are six double bedrooms, all with private shower room and WC. During the summer months a heated swimming pool can be used. A magnificent setting, with peace and quiet almost guaranteed. Jacuzzi available.

Prices s €45-€80; d fr €90 **On Site** Private ⚲ **Nearby** ᇂ 3km ⌥ 15km ℘ 2km Restaurant 4km ⌁ 2km ♔ 5km ⌂ 1km ⋙ 30km **Notes** Pets admitted English spoken

CORMES

▦ *La Ferté Bernard*

Odette et Désiré CHERRIER
Manoir de Planchette, 72400 CORMES
☎ 06 80 33 97 61
email: manoir.de.planchette@wanadoo.fr

A lovingly restored 13th-century manor, which is situated in quiet, rural surroundings. En suite rooms include a double and two rooms with two beds, with lounge, open fireplace, central heating, heated towel rail and TV. Large garden, children's games, walks, fishing lake.

Prices not confirmed for 2008 **On Site** ℘ ♔ **Nearby** ᇂ 4km ⚲ 4km ⌁ 3km ⌂ 3km ⋙ 7km **Notes** Pets admitted

COULAINES

▦ **Le Monet**

Lucette BORDEAU
72190 COULAINES
☎ 02 43 82 25 50

This detached property is close to the owners' home and offers four en suite double rooms. The house enjoys a rural location and is situated in wooded grounds. Facilities include central heating, living room, lounge, kitchen area, parking, covered terrace, picnic area. Restaurant, golf and racing circuit nearby.

Prices s fr €40; d fr €50 **Nearby** ᇂ 10km ⌥ 3km ℘ 3km ⚲ 1km Restaurant 3km ⌁ 1km ⌂ 3km ⋙ 3km **Notes** No pets Open April to December.

DISSAY-SOUS-COURCILLON

▦ **Le Moulin du Prieuré**

M-Claire BRETONNEAU
3 Rue de la Gare, 72500 DISSAY-SOUS-COURCILLON
☎ 02 43 44 59 79 ▤ 02 43 46 29 90
email: moulinduprieure@wanadoo.fr
web: www.moulinduprieure.fr

This 18th-century water mill is situated in the heart of the village and offers rooms for three, and a family room; all en suite with children's facilities. Breakfast is served in the mill and other facilities include an enclosed garden, parking, French/English books, packed lunch.

Prices not confirmed for 2008 **On Site** ℘ **Nearby** ᇂ 2.5km ⚲ ⌁ ⋙ 5km **Notes** Pets admitted English spoken CC

GUECELARD

⋕⋕ ⊚⋅ Château de Mondan

Catherine BABAULT
Route de la Suze, 72230 GUECELARD
☎ 02 43 87 92 16 ▤ 02 43 77 13 85
email: chateau.mondan@wanadoo.fr
web: www.chateaumondan.com

Relax in a peaceful, lush setting on the banks of the River Sarthe, either in the château, which offers four double rooms, or in the adjoining farmhouse, which has two grade 2 family rooms for three and four guests. All rooms are en suite. Golf driving range, two tennis courts, river walks, fishing, table d'hôte meals on request. Reduced rates, depending on number of nights. Closed 15 days in November.

Prices s fr €57; d fr €64; extra person fr €15; dinner fr €20
On Site Private ↖ Private tennis court **Nearby** ⛷ 5km Restaurant 1km
♨ 12km 🖫 1km ⋙ 15km **Notes** Pets admitted English spoken

JUILLE

⋕⋕ *Manoir de St Pierre*

Luc et Martine TRASSARD
15 Rue des Hauts-de-Sarthe, 72170 JUILLE
☎ 02 43 33 56 25 & 06 84 19 67 12
email: martine.trassard@wanadoo.fr
web: www.manoir-st-pierre.com

This property stands on the Hauts de Sarthe, half way between Le Mans and Alençon, close to the hills known as the Alpes Mancelles. It has four bedrooms, to accommodate a total of eight guests. All of the rooms have a private bathroom and WC. Breakfast is served in the dining room, and there is a guests' lounge.

Prices not confirmed for 2008 **On Site** ⌔ **Nearby** ⛷ 10km ↖ 1km
♨ 1km 🖫 1km **Notes** No pets

LE GRAND-LUCE

⋕⋕ ⊚⋅ ঙ **La Roiserie**

Martine et Gilbert ORY
72150 LE GRAND LUCE
☎ 02 43 85 81 54
email: roiserie@orange.fr

A 16th-century house with swimming pool, terrace and open views across the valley. A separate entrance leads to the bedrooms: two doubles on the ground floor, one with disabled access, and a family room for four upstairs. All have private shower room and WC. Meals are available by arrangement. Good walks close by.

Prices s fr €50; d fr €60; extra person fr €15; dinner fr €20 **On Site** ⌔
Private ↖ **Nearby** ⛷ 5km ⤓ 8km ⌔ 3km Restaurant 1km ♨ 1km
🖫 1km ⋙ 25km **Notes** No pets English spoken

LUCEAU

⋕⋕ ⊚⋅ Le Moulin Calme

M et Mme COMBRIES
Gascheau, 72500 LUCEAU
☎ 02 43 46 39 75 ▤ 02 43 46 49 96
email: moulincalme@wanadoo.fr
web: www.lemoulincalme.com

An old watermill in a peaceful green and grassy spot just outside the village. There are five bedrooms, all with private shower room and WC, with a mix of double beds and twin beds; two rooms make a family suite for four people. Outside are two lakes with boats and plenty of fish. Pre-booked meals can be served outdoors in the summer.

Prices s fr €47; d fr €57; t fr €82; extra person fr €25; dinner fr €20
On Site ⌔ ⛲ Private ↖ **Nearby** ⛷ 5km ⤓ 5km 🖫 3km ⋙ 6km
Notes Pets admitted English spoken

⋕⋕ ⊚⋅ Les Chataigniers

Muriel BRIDEAULT
72500 LUCEAU
☎ 02 43 46 69 28
email: muriel.brideault@wanadoo.fr

Between Tours and Le Mans, this house has three spacious individually decorated double rooms, each with private bathroom, hairdryer and separate WC. There is a games room, a fitness room and a sitting room with books to read; in the garden is a barbecue. Breakfast, with home-made jams from the fruit trees in the orchard, can be served outside in the summer.

Prices s €45-€60; d €55-€70; extra person €18-€25; dinner fr €18
Nearby ⛷ 5km ⌔ 1km ↖ 1km Restaurant 0.1km ♨ 1km 🖫 0.2km
⋙ 2km **Notes** No pets

MAYET

⋕⋕ Chambre d'hôtes

Patricia et Michel DELAHAYE
11 Place de Gaulle, 72360 MAYET
☎ 02 43 79 37 22 & 06 89 54 17 56
email: patricia.delahaye@wanadoo.fr

Well-placed for visiting the Loire châteaux, this property has one bedroom in the owners' home and three rooms in a separate building, all with private facilities. A room adjacent to the bedroom in
CONTINUED

MAYET CONTINUED

the main house can be used to provide family accommodation, but this second room does not have its own facilities.

Prices s fr €46; d fr €53; t fr €69; extra person fr €16 **On Site** ℰ
Private ⌇ **Nearby** ⚓ 2km ॒ 1km **Notes** No pets English spoken

MOITRON-SUR-SARTHE

⊪⊪ ⦿ Les Quatre Saisons

M et Mme RICORDEAU

Le Bourg, 72170 MOITRON-SUR-SARTHE

☎ 02 43 34 43 89 & 06 86 96 65 15

email: contact@lesquatresaisons.fr

web: www.lesquatresaisons.fr

On the edge of the Alpes Mancelles, in a green and tranquil country setting, this restored 19th-century house has four bedrooms. All of the guest accommodation is upstairs: two double rooms and two triples, each with a private shower room and WC.

Prices s fr €38; d fr €48; extra person fr €18; dinner fr €18
Nearby ⚓ 15km ॒ 20km ℰ 1km ⌇ 5km Restaurant 5km ॒ 5km
℀ 5km ॒ 5km **Notes** No pets English spoken

MONCE-EN-BELIN

⊪⊪ ⦿ Le Petit Pont

Bernard BROU

72230 MONCE-EN-BELIN

☎ 02 43 42 03 32 ॒ 02 43 42 97 95

This working cattle farm offers one grade 3 double guest room and four grade 2 double rooms, all en suite and located in the owners' house. There is a living room, lounge with TV, garage, garden, parking, stabling facilities. Restaurant nearby.

Prices s fr €50; d fr €60; extra person fr €15; dinner €18–€25
Nearby ⚓ 1km ॒ 5km ℰ 0.5km ⌇ 0.2km Restaurant 1.5km ॒ 0.4km
॒ 4km **Notes** No pets English spoken

MONHOUDOU

⊪⊪⊪ ⦿ Château de Monhoudou

Michel DE MONHOUDOU

72260 MONHOUDOU

☎ 02 43 97 40 05 ॒ 02 43 33 11 58

email: monhoudou@aol.com

web: www.monhoudou.com

This 18th-century château, set in fifty acres of English-style parkland, offers five double en suite guest rooms. Two lounges and a library are also available, as are horses, bicycles, tandems and candlelit table d'hôte meals by arrangement.

Prices d €100–€160; extra person fr €20; dinner €42–€69
On Site Spa Private ⌇ **Nearby** ⚓ 6km ॒ 15km Restaurant 2km
॒ 3km ℀ 0.1km ॒ 3km ॒ 40km **Notes** Pets admitted English
spoken CC

NOTRE-DAME-DU-PE

⊪⊪ ⦿ ⚅ La Reboursière

Gilles CHAPPUY

72300 NOTRE-DAME-DU-PE

☎ 02 43 92 92 41 ॒ 02 43 92 92 41

email: gilles.chappuy@wanadoo.fr

web: www.lareboursiere.fr.st

This quiet, comfortable house between Angers and Le Mans, has a beautiful setting with valley views. It has three bedrooms, one on the ground floor. Each room has an en suite shower room and WC. Guests' lounge with open fire and TV, central heating. Meals by arrangement; heated swimming pool in season. Wi-fi available. Hot-air balloon flights can be arranged.

Prices s fr €55; d fr €65; t fr €85; dinner fr €23 **On Site** Private ⌇
Nearby ⚓ 6km ॒ 12km ℰ 8km Restaurant 1km ॒ 6km ℀ 5km
॒ 5km ॒ 8km **Notes** No pets English spoken

OISSEAU-LE-PETIT

⊪⊪ *Chambre d'hôtes*

Jean PERCHERON

17 Rue de la Fontaine, 72610 OISSEAU-LE-PETIT

☎ 02 33 26 80 09 ॒ 02 33 26 82 62

email: jean-percheron@wanadoo.fr

web: www.ferme-de-la-fontaine.com

A friendly atmosphere and generous breakfasts in a setting of flowers, meadows, greenery and old stone. The accommodation comprises four double en suite rooms, all with a spare bed, and one with a TV. Other facilities include TV lounge and covered swimming pool from March to mid November.

Prices not confirmed for 2008 **On Site** ⚓ Private ⌇ **Nearby** ℰ 10km
॒ 10km ॒ 10km ॒ 10km **Notes** Pets admitted

ROUEZ-EN-CHAMPAGNE

⊪⊪ ⦿ L'Abbaye de Champagne

72140 ROUEZ-EN-CHAMPAGNE

☎ 02 43 20 15 74 ॒ 02 43 20 74 61

email: contact@abbayedechampagne.com

web: www.abbayedechampagne.com/

Eighteenth-century guest rooms available in this 12th-century abbey, all en suite with heating. Art courses on request. Gîte, two fishing lakes, hunting, pedalos.

Prices s €50–€70; d €55–€75; extra person fr €21; dinner fr €18
Nearby ⚓ 10km ॒ 30km ℰ 0.1km ⌇ 6km Restaurant 6km ॒ 4km
℀ 8km ॒ 4km ॒ 6km **Notes** No pets English spoken

SOLESMES

▦ ⦿ Le Fresne

M-Armelle et Pascal LELIEVRE
72300 SOLESMES
☎ 02 43 95 92 55 🗎 02 43 95 92 55
email: le.fresne@wanadoo.fr
web: www.lefresne.com

Expect a warm welcome at this home near Solesmes in the Sarthe
valley. The self-contained accommodation is located in a building
adjoining the owners' house and comprises a twin and two rooms
with a double and two single beds (one with mezzanine); all are en
suite with heating. Pets accepted for a charge. Table d'hôte meals on
request. Reduced rates from four nights.

Prices s fr €42; d fr €49; t fr €57; extra person fr €15; dinner fr €20
On Site Private ⚓ **Nearby** ⛴ 5km 🏊 0.2km ⚘ 3km ⛵ 6km 🚣 3km
🚶 7km **Notes** Pets admitted English spoken

SOUILLE

▦ ⦿ *Chantelouve*

Isabelle et Patrick RICHET
72380 SOUILLE
☎ 02 43 27 88 67
email: richet.chantelouve@wanadoo.fr

Just 12 kilometres north of Le Mans, this restored longhouse offers
three double bedrooms, each with a private shower room and WC.
The grounds extend to one hectare, and walking and fishing are
available on site. Meals can be served by prior arrangement.

Prices not confirmed for 2008 **On Site** 🏊 **Nearby** ⛴ 10km ⚓ 10km
🚣 3km 🚣 1km **Notes** No pets

SOULIGNE-FLACE

▦ ⦿ La Bertellière

Lily et Bruno PORTEHAULT
72210 SOULIGNE-FLACE
☎ 02 43 88 13 12
email: la.bertelliere@wanadoo.fr
web: www.labertelliere.net

The hosts of this restored farmhouse, which stands in extensive
grounds 15 kilometres from Le Mans, promise a calm, cheery
atmosphere. There are three guest rooms with separate access, en
suite bathrooms and WCs. The guests' lounge area is on a mezzanine
floor, with a beautiful view of the garden.

Prices s fr €38; d fr €44; extra person fr €12; dinner fr €18
On Site Restaurant **Nearby** ⛴ 4km 🏊 2km ⚓ 10km ⚘ 8km 🚣 3km
🚶 10km **Notes** Pets admitted

ST-JEAN-D'ASSE

▦ ⦿ Domaine des Sablons

Jérôme et Patricia COSNET
72380 ST-JEAN-D'ASSE
☎ 02 43 27 80 97 & 06 84 81 86 85 🗎 02 43 27 86 60
email: chambredhotes.lesabon@wanadoo.fr
web: www.chambresdhotesleslablon.com

This charming old riverside farmhouse has five bedrooms. One is a
family suite for five, with a private terrace at first floor level; another is
a two roomed family suite for four; the rest are doubles. All have a
private bathroom/WC, television and DVD player. Meals by
arrangement. Horses, bikes, boats and fishing all available, as well as
table tennis and badminton.

Prices s fr €51; d fr €60; extra person fr €16; dinner €8-€20 **On Site** ⛴
⚘ ⛵ **Nearby** Restaurant 3km ⚘ 7km 🚣 4km **Notes** Pets admitted
English spoken

ST-LEONARD-DES-BOIS

▦ Le Moulin de l'Inthe

Claude ROLLINI
72590 ST-LEONARD-DES-BOIS
☎ 02 43 33 79 22 🗎 02 43 33 79 22
web: www.moulindelinthe.fr

On the banks of the River Sarthe and in the heart of the Alpes
Mancelles, the Moulin de l'Inthe offers three double rooms, a triple
and a room for four, all en suite. Facilities include guest lounges with
TV, fishing and helipad.

Prices s fr €44; d €60-€70; t fr €83; extra person fr €19 **On Site** 🏊
Nearby ⛴ 0.2km ⚓ 12km Restaurant 0.4km ⚘ 0.4km ⛵ 0.4km
🚣 0.4km 🚶 18km **Notes** Pets admitted English spoken

THOIRE-SUR-DINAN

⚶ ⏅ **Le Saut du Loup**

Claudine et Jacques CISSE
72500 THOIRE-SUR-DINAN

☎ 02 43 79 12 36

web: www.lesautduloup62.com

A dairy farm bordering Bercé Forest (5500 hectares) in the Loir Valley providing a double room, a triple and two adjoining rooms with four single beds; all en suite with TV point and heating. There are books, a billiard room, fridge, TV, terrace with garden furniture, boules area, large garden. Public footpaths and mountain biking nearby. Table d'hôte meals by arrangement.

Prices s fr €41; d fr €48; t fr €64; extra person fr €17; dinner fr €17 **Nearby** ⛷ 5km 🏊 3km ⤚ 9km Restaurant 3km ⛵ 3km ⚑ 3km 🛆 3km ⚓ 9km **Notes** No pets

YVRE-L'EVEQUE

⚶⚶ ⏅ **Château des Arches**

Chantal et Michel METAIS
72530 YVRE L'EVEQUE

☎ 02 43 89 49 92 & 06 22 98 17 10

🖺 02 43 89 49 92

email: michel.metais@neuf.fr

web: www.chateaudesarches.org

This property can be found about five minutes from Le Mans, between parkland and forest with a river close by. The bright and spacious bedrooms are all upstairs - three doubles, a triple and a room for four. All have private bathroom and WC, and a cot and high chair are available. Stabling for horses.

Prices s €60-€90; d €70-€100; extra person fr €20; dinner fr €25 **On Site** ⤙ **Nearby** ⛷ 5km 🏊 4km ⤚ 4km Restaurant 2km 🛆 4km 🏛 1km ⚓ 7km **Notes** No pets English spoken

⚶⚶ **Les Turets**

Elizabeth et Jean-Paul GUITTET
72530 YVRE-L'EVEQUE

☎ 02 43 27 25 15 & 06 85 10 74 66

email: elisajousse@aol.com

Near to Le Mans and close to a small river, this is a late 19th-century house with four guest rooms. Two have double beds, and the other two have a total of five single beds and a child's bed. All have TV

and private shower room and WC. Living room with open fire; also available is stabling for two horses.

Prices d €70-€80; extra person fr €20 **On Site** ⤙ **Nearby** ⛷ 1km 🏊 5km ⤚ 4km Restaurant 5km 🛆 2km ⚓ 8km **Notes** No pets English spoken Open April to October, other times by reservation.

YVRE-LE-POLIN

⚶⚶ ⏅ *La Noirie*

M LARDY
72330 YVRE-LE-POLIN

☎ 02 43 42 48 96 & 02 43 42 02 17 🖺 02 43 47 08 36

email: info@lanoirie.com

web: www.lanoirie.com

In the heart of a forest estate with tree lined park, 20km from Le Mans, this chambre d'hôtes offers three rooms and two suites for three to four - sleeping a total of 13. Each room has a TV and possible internet access. There is a lounge with TV and library, a swimming pool, tennis and mountain biking on site. Restaurant 4km. Reductions from the second night.

Prices not confirmed for 2008 **On Site** ⛵ Private ⤚ **Nearby** ⛷ 5km ⤙ 15km 🏛 4km ⚓ 4km **Notes** No pets

AIZENAY

⚶⚶ **Sainte Marie**

Chantal CORBIERE
85190 AIZENAY

☎ 02 51 94 83 87 🖺 02 51 94 83 87

email: lafermesaintemarie@wanadoo.fr

Deep in the countryside, surrounded by seven hectares of land, the outbuildings of this 19th-century farm were adapted to create three guest rooms. A separate entrance leads to the bedrooms - a double, and two rooms for three, all with private showers and WCs. Guests' lounge with kitchen area. Three ponds, with private fishing available.

Prices s €38-€40; d €40-€42; t €50 **On Site** ⛵ **Nearby** Sea 25km ⤙ 0.2km ⤚ 4km 🏊 4km 🏛 4km ⚓ 15km **Notes** No pets English spoken

ANGLES

⚶⚶ 🍂 *Moricq*

Roger et Chantal GUIET
4 Route du Port, 85750 ANGLES

☎ 02 51 97 56 20

email: roger.guiet@wanadoo.fr

A working farm with four bedrooms, including two doubles and a triple - in a converted outbuilding. The fourth bedroom, a double is situated upstairs in another old building. All of the rooms have private showers and WCs, and TV sockets. Lounge with kitchen area. Terrace with garden furniture, covered play area.

Prices not confirmed for 2008 **On Site** ⤙ **Nearby** ⛷ 2km Sea 8km ⤚ 8km 🏊 1km 🏛 1km ⚓ 25km **Notes** Pets admitted

BENET

▦ Le Petit Paradis

Marie-Noëlle HOUCHE
La Meugne, 85490 BENET
☎ 02 51 00 99 10 & 06 64 32 26 64 🗎 02 51 00 99 10
email: accueil@le-petit-paradis.com
web: www.le-petit-paradis.com

A warm, unaffected welcome is promised at this restored barn in the marshlands. There are three triple rooms, with separate access, lounge and use of kitchen. There is another triple room, with small lounge area in a separate building. All rooms have private shower/WC and private terrace. Barbecue, mountain bikes, boat, table tennis and heated pool.

Prices s fr €45; d fr €55; t fr €67; extra person fr €12 **On Site** ✿ Private ⚲ **Nearby** ⛅ 4km ⌖ 1km Restaurant 4km ⌇ 4km ⛱ 5km ₩ 15km **Notes** No pets English spoken Open April to October.

CHAILLE-LES-MARAIS

▦ Côté Marais

Eric BESNIER
38 Rue du 11 novembre, 85450 CHAILLE LES MARAIS
☎ 02 51 27 07 66
email: contact@cote-marais.com
web: www.cote-marais.com

Half an hour from la Rochelle, this property is in the kind of village where time seems to have stood still. The guest accommodation is in the converted outbuildings of a 19th-century house, and the four double bedrooms, one with an extra single bed. Each has a private bath/shower room and WC. Parking.

Prices d €80-€95; t €100-€115; extra person fr €20 **On Site** Private ⚲ **Nearby** ⛅ 10km ⌇ 20km Sea 25km ⌖ 1km Restaurant 3km ⌇ 1km ✿ 10km ⛱ 0.1km ₩ 15km **Notes** No pets English spoken Open February to November.

CHAMBRETAUD

▦ ⵏⵣ Puycrotier

Laurent et Aurore BARON
85500 CHAMBRETAUD
☎ 02 51 91 50 08 🗎 02 51 91 50 08
email: chambresdhotes.baronaurorelaurent@wanadoo.fr
web: http://perso.wanadoo.fr/baron-chambresdhotes/

This farmhouse offers three bedrooms: a double, and two triples. The guest rooms have a separate entrance, and all have a private bath or shower room and WC. Lounge, with kitchenette area. Gardens, with garden room. Meals available by arrangement, except Sunday evenings. Guests are welcome to walk around the farm.

Prices s fr €37; d fr €47; t fr €62; dinner fr €16 **Nearby** ⛅ 15km ⌖ 7km ⚲ 4km ⌇ 6km ⛱ 2km ₩ 23km **Notes** No pets English spoken

CHATEAUNEUF

▦ ⵏⵣ ⵏⵣ Les Boulinières

Bernard et Martine BOCQUIER
85710 CHATEAUNEUF
☎ 02 51 49 30 81 & 06 87 98 75 18

Guest rooms provided in this renovated and refurbished farmhouse include one with two doubles and a single, one with double and single, and three doubles, all with private facilities. Living room, garden, games area, parking. Nearby: fishing, working windmill, riding, Marais Discovery Centre.

Prices d fr €43; t €52-€77; extra person fr €10; dinner fr €15 **Nearby** ⛅ 5km Sea 15km ⌖ 0.2km ⚲ 10km ⌇ 0.2km ⛱ 0.2km ₩ 10km **Notes** No pets

CHAUCHE

▦ ⵏⵣ L'Epiardière

Nathalie HERBRETEAU
85140 CHAUCHE
☎ 02 51 41 88 50 & 06 64 29 66 85 🗎 02 51 41 88 50
email: herbreteaun@wanadoo.fr

A working farm provides the setting for this chambre d'hôtes. The house dates from 1888; restored within the last few years it now has three bedrooms: on the ground floor a triple and a family room for four (double bed and two singles); upstairs is another triple. All have private shower and WC, and there is a private terrace with furniture. The day room has a kitchen area for guests' use.

Prices not confirmed for 2008 **Nearby** ⛅ 3km ⌖ 0.5km ⚲ 10km ⌇ 1km ⛱ 1km ₩ 15km **Notes** No pets

CHAVAGNES-EN-PAILLERS

⊪ La Déderie

Marie GAUVIN

No 18 La Déderie, 85250 CHAVAGNES EN PAILLERS

☎ 02 51 42 22 59

email: marie@gauvins.com

web: www.dederie.com

This renovated 18th-century manor house offers four guest rooms: a double, two other doubles with single beds and one with two doubles, all with private facilities. Living room with TV, walled garden, garage, parking. Restaurant, shops, châteaux nearby.

Prices s €42-€52; d €51-€61; extra person €18-€23 **On Site** ⌀ ⁂ **Nearby** ⌇ 5km Restaurant 0.3km 🏠 0.5km ₩ 12km **Notes** No pets

CHAVAGNES-LES-REDOUX

⊪ Les Guerinieres

Gérard et Anne-Marie CAILLAUD

14 Rue de la Muleterie, 85390 CHAVAGNES LES REDOUX

☎ 02 51 92 41 77

email: g.caillaud@libertysurf.fr

A restored 19th-century farmhouse built in the local style, that offers three upstairs guest bedrooms. There is a double room, a triple and a room for four, all with private shower room and WC. A small play space is provided for children, and in the day room is a kitchenette with buffet.

Prices not confirmed for 2008 **Nearby** ⌇ 10km ⌀ 3km ⌇ 10km ⌇ 0.8km 🏠 10km ₩ 12km **Notes** No pets

DOIX

⊪ Logis de Chalusseau

Marie-Thérèse BAUDRY

111 Rue de Chalusseau, 85200 DOIX

☎ 02 51 51 81 12 📄 02 51 51 81 12

email: chaluss@wanadoo.fr

Close to the Marais fen lands, the 17th-century Logis de Chalusseau offers three guest rooms, all full of character with original features: a double, a double with single and a suite with its own entrance, with double and twin beds, all with private facilities. Guests' own living room, salon and kitchen, outdoor seating area.

Prices not confirmed for 2008 **Nearby** ⌇ 9km Sea 40km ⌀ 6km ⌇ 9km ⌇ 6km 🏠 1km ₩ 9km **Notes** No pets Open April to 15 November.

FEOLE-LA-REORTHE

⊪ Chambre d'hôtes

Geneviève ROUAULT

36 Rue Georges Clémenceau, 85210 FEOLE LA REORTHE

☎ 02 51 27 83 33 📄 08 72 13 26 83

email: genevieverlt@free.fr

This 15th-century coaching house offers four individually styled double guest rooms with shower and wc. There is a kitchen and large living room with monumental chimney and TV, and parking is available in the enclosed courtyard. Walking tours with the proprietor can be organised.

Prices not confirmed for 2008 **Nearby** ⌇ 14km Sea 40km ⌀ 3km ⌇ 4km ⌇ 2km 🏠 4km ₩ 10km **Notes** Pets admitted

GROSBREUIL

⊪ Les Barbières

André et Bernadette PASCREAU

85440 GROSBREUIL

☎ 02 51 22 66 48 & 06 74 56 43 57

email: lesbarbieres@wanadoo.fr

Less than ten minutes from Sables d'Olonne, this barn has been converted to provide three double bedrooms: two downstairs, one upstairs, all three with private bath or shower room and WC. Outside is a large terrace with a pergola, and a swimming pool. Fridge and microwave available, also crockery and everything necessary for on-site picnics.

Prices not confirmed for 2008 **On Site** Private ⌇ **Nearby** ⌇ 1.5km Sea 10km ⌀ 7km ⌇ 6km 🏠 6km ₩ 10km **Notes** Pets admitted

LA BOISSIERE-DES-LANDES

⊪ Le Logis de la Lande

J-Marie et M-Claude STIMPFLING

85430 LA BOISSIERE DES LANDES

☎ 02 28 15 52 49 & 06 07 13 35 49

email: lelogisdelalande@wanadoo.fr

This guest house dates in part to the Wars of the Vendée. Rooms available include two family suites each sleeping four in two rooms, and two double rooms, each with private facilities and TV points. Guests may use the lounge with TV and video, the kitchen, garden furniture, parking facilities. There is also a private lake for fishing and a rural gîte.

Prices not confirmed for 2008 **On Site** ⌀ **Nearby** ⌇ 2km Sea 15km ⌇ 5km ⌇ 5km 🏠 5km ₩ 15km **Notes** Pets admitted

LA CHAPELLE-ACHARD

⊪ Le Plessis Jousselin

D et M CHIFFOLEAU

85150 LA CHAPELLE ACHARD

☎ 02 51 05 91 08 & 06 08 66 64 07

email: maite.chiffoleau@cerfrance.fr

In the heart of the countryside, near the sea, this newly renovated farmhouse has four double guest rooms with their own entrance and private shower rooms and wc. Cot and folding bed available. Communal living room with equipped kitchen area, TV, washing machine, terrace with outdoor seating.

Prices s fr €35; d fr €40 **On Site** ⁂ **Nearby** ⌇ 8km ⌇ 10km Sea 12km ⌀ 1km ⌇ 15km Restaurant 2km ⌇ 2km 🏠 2km ₩ 2km **Notes** No pets

LA FAUTE-SUR-MER

⏸ ❯◯❮ L'Estérel

André et Madeleine HERVE
12 Bis Rue des Oeillets, 85460 LA FAUTE SUR MER
☎ 02 51 97 02 14 ▤ 02 51 97 02 14
email: herve.esterel@wanadoo.fr

Surrounded by a shady, walled flower-filled garden, this guest house offers four rooms, each with double and single beds, their own entrances, shower rooms and wc, as well as individual terraces and outdoor seating areas. Kitchenettes, TV, washing machine available. Fine sandy beaches only 8km. Home-made baking and jam for breakfast. Evening meals offer local seafood.

Prices d €54-€60; dinner fr €21 **Nearby** ⛷ 10km ⌁ 40km Sea 0.3km ⌀ 0.4km ⤳ 5km Restaurant 0.3km ⌑ 0.3km ⛳ 0.3km ⓘ 0.3km ⋙ 20km **Notes** No pets Open April to November.

LE BOUPERE

⏸ Manoir de la Baussonnière

Pierre et Yvette SOULARD
85510 LE BOUPERE
☎ 02 51 91 91 48

In the Vendée Forest, this 16th-century manor house has five refurbished guest rooms: four doubles and a room with double and single, all with private shower and wc. Guests have use of small kitchen and living room with TV. Pleasant gardens with outdoor seating areas. Private parking. Restaurant 2km.

Prices s fr €45; d fr €52; extra person fr €15 **Nearby** ⛷ 3km ⌀ 2km ⤳ 3km Restaurant 2km ⌑ 2km ⛳ 3km ⓘ 3km ⋙ 3km **Notes** No pets Open Easter to 15 September.

LE CHATEAU-D'OLONNE

⏸ La Châtaigneraie

Didier et Martine BOULINEAU
85180 LE CHATEAU D'OLONNE
☎ 02 51 96 47 52

Enjoy the calm of the countryside at this farmhouse, close to the Sables d'Olonne. Three guest rooms above the main house with their own entrance: one with double and twin beds, one double and a double with large single, all with private bathroom. Folding bed and cot available. Communal living room with kitchen area, well-kept terrace with tables and chairs.

Prices s fr €35; d fr €46; t fr €58 **Nearby** ⛷ 3km ⌁ 6km Sea 6km ⌀ 15km ⤳ 7km Restaurant 6km ⌑ 3km ⛳ 6km ⓘ 3km ⋙ 7km **Notes** No pets English spoken Open February to 15 November.

⏸ ❯◯❮ Les Landes de Beauséjour

Josette HEITZ
48 rue des Parcs, 85180 LE CHATEAU D'OLONNE
☎ 02 51 21 36 84
email: leslandes.beausejour@wanadoo.fr

This modern house stands in its own wooded grounds five kilometres from Sables-d'Olonne. It has four guest rooms - two triples and two singles, with separate access. Each room has a private shower and WC. Lounge and guests' kitchen available. Swimming pool, barbecue, garden room, table tennis and badminton. Parking. Baby sitting available (chargeable).

Prices s €50-€55; d €58-€75; t €65-€75 **On Site** Private ⤳ **Nearby** ⛷ 8km Sea 5km ⌀ 5km ⌑ 2km ⓘ 2km ⋙ 7km **Notes** No pets English spoken

LE FENOUILLER

⏸ ♿ Chambre d'hôtes

Annie BARDU
142 Les Herbens, Route de St Révérend,
85800 LE FENOUILLER
☎ 02 28 10 27 06 & 06 87 45 37 56 ▤ 02 28 10 27 06
email: lesherbens85@orange.fr
web: www.lesherbens.com

In its own enclosed grounds, this property has four guest rooms with their own independent entrance. There is a double room, two triples, and a family room for four. All the rooms have a private bath or shower room and WC. There is a day room with a fridge and microwave; outside there is garden furniture and a swimming pool.

Prices s fr €50; d fr €67; t fr €83; extra person fr €16 **On Site** ⌁ ⛳ Private ⤳ **Nearby** ⛷ 2km Sea 5km ⌀ 2km Restaurant 5km ⌑ 2km ⓘ 2.5km ⋙ 5km **Notes** No pets

LE POIRE-SUR-VELLUIRE

⏸ Chambre d'hôtes

Paulette CHAMPENOIS
20 Rue de Lattre de Tassigny,
85770 LE POIRE SUR VELLUIRE
☎ 02 51 52 32 82 ▤ 02 51 52 32 82
email: champenois.paule@wanadoo.fr

Set in its own grounds, this 19th-century house is full of character. There are three individually decorated bedrooms; one large triple with a shower room, WC and fridge; one double room with a child's bed, shower room and WC. Upstairs in the owners' house is another large triple room with a mezzanine, bathroom and WC. There's a communal sitting room and dining room, and a swimming pool which is open from June to September.

Prices not confirmed for 2008 **On Site** Private ⤳ **Nearby** ⛷ 15km Sea 40km ⌀ 0.8km ⌑ 1km ⓘ 1km ⋙ 12km **Notes** No pets English spoken Open 15 March to October.

LES EPESSES

▥ Le Petit Bignon

Brigitte BRIDONNEAU
85590 LES EPESSES
☎ 02 51 57 45 57

This old, converted barn has three guest rooms with their own entrance. There are two doubles and one room with double and single, each with private shower room, wc, TV, terrace and outdoor seating area. Use of living room.

Prices s fr €60; d €60-€75; t fr €90 **Nearby** ☼ 10km 🏊 4km ⚲ 4km Restaurant 10km 🏊 4km 🏛 10km � 25km **Notes** No pets English spoken

LES HERBIERS

▥ L'Abri des Alouettes

Marie-Jeanne PINEAU
La Cossonnière, 85500 LES HERBIERS
☎ 02 51 67 11 42 📄 02 51 66 90 27

The owners of L'Abri des Alouettes welcome guests to their organic farm. There are four guest rooms in the modern farmhouse with individual entrances, private facilities and kitchen area: two with double and single beds, and two twins. Use of owner's living room with TV, library and telephone, open-air games, arranged visits around farm. Reduced rates for stays over three nights.

Prices s fr €42; d fr €48; t fr €58 **Nearby** ☼ 16km 🏊 3km ⚲ 3km Restaurant 1.5km 🏊 3km 🏛 3km � 25km **Notes** No pets Open May to September.

▥ La Jonchere

Laëtitia VERONNEAU
94 Rue du Château d'eau, 85500 LES HERBIERS
☎ 02 51 63 90 87
email: ch.veronneau@wanadoo.fr
web: www.lajonchere-chambresdhotes.com

This restored property, offers three guest bedrooms. On the ground floor is a room with a double bed and a single, with its own entrance. Upstairs are two double rooms. All have a private shower room/WC, and baby equipment is available. There is a day room with fridge and microwave.

Prices d fr €46; t fr €56 **On Site** Private ⚲ **Nearby** ☼ 5km ♨ 30km ⚲ 7km 🏊 5km 🎣 5km 🏛 5km � 35km **Notes** No pets

▥ La Petite Fételière

Pierrick et Marie-Luce THOMAS
85500 LES HERBIERS
☎ 02 51 66 92 43
email: pierrick.thomas4@wanadoo.fr

Four bedrooms are offered at this restored property. On the ground floor is a double room and a family room for four; upstairs is a twin-bedded room and a room with three single beds. All rooms have a private bath/shower room and WC, and also a TV socket. Day room with fridge and microwave; grounds with garden furniture.

Prices not confirmed for 2008 **Nearby** ☼ 4km ⚲ 7km ⚲ 4km 🏊 4km 🏛 4km � 25km **Notes** No pets English spoken Open May to September.

▥ La Petite Ganachère

Valérie VRIGNAUD
85500 LES HERBIERS
☎ 02 51 66 85 72 & 06 75 89 88 53 📄 02 51 66 85 72
email: laganachere@wanadoo.fr
web: http://laganachere.monsite.orange.fr/

This old farmhouse has three double bedrooms, with independent access. One of the rooms is on the ground floor; one is upstairs; and the third is in an annexe. They all have private bath or shower rooms and WCs, and there is a TV socket in each room. In the annexe is a lounge with TV, books, and a small kitchen area. Attractive garden, with furniture.

Prices s fr €38; d fr €48; extra person fr €15 **Nearby** ☼ 5km ⚲ 6km ⚲ 4km Restaurant 2km 🏊 5km 🏛 4km � 25km **Notes** No pets

LES LANDES-GENUSSON

▥ Le Colombier

Michel et Huguette BAILLY
38 Rue du Général de Gaulle,
85130 LES LANDES GENUSSON
☎ 02 51 61 60 06 & 06 80 81 81 31
email: michel_bailly@libertysurf.fr

This property stands in grounds of one hectare, on the edge of a small town. It has four big, comfortable bedrooms. On the ground floor is a double, and a room for three; upstairs is another double, and a family room for five. All have private facilities, but those for the family room are not en suite. Home-made breakfast items; attractive gardens with furniture.

Prices not confirmed for 2008 **Nearby** ☼ 6km ⚲ 0.5km ⚲ 12km 🏊 0.5km 🏛 0.5km � 6km **Notes** No pets English spoken

MAILLEZAIS

▥ Le Censif

Gabriel ROBIN
85420 MAILLEZAIS
☎ 02 51 00 71 50 📄 02 51 00 71 50

Discover the beauty and peace of the Marais-Poitevin in this authentic 17th-century farmhouse, surrounded by meadows and a working farm. Three very comfortable guest rooms are furnished with antiques: one double and two doubles with single, one with mezzanine. All have private facilities and independent access. Folding bed available. Communal living room with TV, kitchen and washing area, garden and terrace.

Prices s fr €35; d fr €40; t fr €50 **On Site** ⚲ **Nearby** ☼ 5km Sea 45km ⚲ 5km 🏊 2km 🏛 2km � 25km **Notes** No pets

648

MARTINET

||| |◎| Chambre d'hôtes Montmarin

Vincent et Joëlle HERBRETEAU

85150 MARTINET

☎ 02 51 34 62 88 🗎 02 51 34 62 88

Situated in a leafy spot near the sea, this working farm offers four guest rooms in a renovated 19th-century farmhouse: two doubles, a double with single and a room with two doubles, all with private shower and wc. Guests' living room with kitchen and washing area available. Dinner on reservation (except Fridays). Pond, outdoor seating area, parking.

Prices s fr €35; d fr €40; t fr €50; dinner fr €14 **On Site** ✐
Nearby ₫ 15km ↓ 10km Sea 20km ↗ 10km Restaurant 5km ⊕ 4km
🎿 5km 🖭 4km ⋙ 5km **Notes** Open May to September.

MOUILLERON-EN-PAREDS

|||| ⅙ La Boisnière

J-R et N PAUL et GUILMIN

85390 MOUILLERON-EN-PAREDS

☎ 02 51 51 36 39

email: laboisniere@wanadoo.fr

A late 18th-century restored farmhouse. A separate guests' entrance leads to a triple room on the ground floor (double bed and a single), and to three doubles upstairs. All have private shower room and WC. Extensive grounds with garden furniture and panoramic views; swimming pool available during the summer months.

Prices s fr €60; d €70-€90; t fr €110 **On Site** Private ↗
Nearby ₫ 3km ✐ 1km ⊕ 1km 🎿 20km 🖭 1km ⋙ 15km
Notes No pets

MOUZEUIL-ST-MARTIN

||| La Vérronnerie

Jocelyne DIBOT

85370 MOUZEUIL ST MARTIN

☎ 02 51 28 71 98 & 06 23 38 42 57

email: dibot.jocelyne@terre-net.fr

Enjoy the peace of the country in this house surrounded by an arable farm. Three guest rooms: one double, one with double and twin beds, and one with double and single, all with private facilities and independent access. Guests' living room with TV and kitchen area, garden with seating area. Animals accepted on reservation.

Prices not confirmed for 2008 **Nearby** ₫ 10km Sea 30km ✐ 5km
↗ 10km ⊕ 2km 🖭 2km ⋙ 15km **Notes** Pets admitted

NIEUL-LE-DOLENT

|||| ❤ Les Sorinières

Patrick et Françoise BOURON

85430 NIEUL LE DOLENT

☎ 02 51 07 91 58 & 06 85 20 88 73 🗎 02 51 07 94 78

email: bouronp2@wanadoo.fr

web: ww.camping-lessorinieres.com

Only 15 minutes from the Sables d'Olonne, this distinctive 1920s farmhouse offers a relaxed and simple atmosphere. It has four guest rooms: one with two doubles, one double with single and two doubles, all with private shower and wc. Use of reception room, sitting room with TV and kitchen. Camping and holiday cottages also on site. Private pool open June to September. Restaurant 15km.

Prices s fr €35; d fr €45; t fr €57; extra person fr €12 **On Site** Private ↗
Nearby ₫ 5km ↓ 12km Sea 20km ✐ 3km Restaurant 15km ⊕ 2km
🎿 17km 🖭 2km ⋙ 17km **Notes** No pets English spoken

NIEUL-SUR-L'AUTISE

|||| Le Rosier Sauvage

Christine CHASTAIN-POUPIN

1 Rue de l'Abbaye, 85240 NIEUL SUR L'AUTISE

☎ 02 51 52 49 39

email: rosier.sauvage1@tiscali.fr

At the entrance to the Marais-Poitevin, opposite the Royal Abbey, this delightful 18th-century townhouse has four comfortable and charmingly decorated guest rooms: two doubles and two with double and single, all with private facilities. Guest sitting room with library, TV and fireplace. Garden with table and chairs. Breakfast in a superbly renovated former stable. Restaurants nearby.

Prices not confirmed for 2008 **Nearby** ₫ 11km ✐ 15km ↗ 11km ⊕
⋙ 25km **Notes** No pets English spoken Open April to September.

POUZAUGES

|||| La Rémondière

Magalie BOTTON

85700 POUZAUGES

☎ 02 51 91 36 22 & 06 33 23 41 54 🗎 02 51 91 36 22

email: emmanuel.botton@wanadoo.fr

In the heart of Vendée farmland, this property has three bedrooms in a converted farm building adjacent to the owners' home. Each room

CONTINUED

POUZAUGES CONTINUED

has its own entrance, TV, shower and WC, and can sleep three people. Lounge with kitchen area; garden furniture.

Prices not confirmed for 2008 **Nearby** ⚓ 5km 🏊 0.6km ⚡ 4km 🚶 5km 🏠 5km 🚲 7km **Notes** No pets English spoken CC

REAUMUR

🏵 Le Prieuré

François GARRET

2 Rue du Prieuré, 85700 REAUMUR

☎ 02 51 63 36 41 & 06 82 06 64 92

email: sci.le.prieure@wanadoo.fr

A former priory dating from the 18th century standing in landscaped parkland. There is a double bedroom on the ground floor, with another double and a family room for four upstairs. Outside is a swimming pool and garden furniture; fishing is available in a private lake 500 metres away. Use of billiard room and tennis court.

Prices d fr €55; t fr €100; extra person fr €10 **On Site** Private ⚡ Private tennis court **Nearby** ⚓ 7km 🏊 0.5km Restaurant 7km 🏠 4km 🚲 20km **Notes** No pets English spoken

ST-CHRISTOPHE-DU-LIGNERON

🏵 L'Hubertière

Gérard et Michelle LOIZEAU

85670 ST CHRISTOPHE DU LIGNERON

☎ 02 51 35 06 41 & 06 81 73 13 07 📠 02 51 49 87 43

email: michelle.loizeau@terre-net.fr

Only 20 minutes from the ocean and in the heart of the Vendée, this friendly 18th-century home is on a working farm. There are two rooms with double and single, one with two doubles and a single in the main farmhouse, and a double with kitchen located in a converted stable, all en suite. TV available.

Prices s fr €40; d fr €45; t fr €75 **On Site** 🏊 **Nearby** ⚓ 7km Sea 20km ⚡ 7km 🚶 7km 🏠 7km 🚲 15km **Notes** No pets Open 15 March to 15 November.

🏵 La Marière

G TAVET et M-C MEUNIER

85670 ST CHRISTOPHE DU LIGNERON

☎ 02 51 35 28 67

This old farmhouse has been renovated to create the owner's home plus four upstairs guest rooms: three doubles and a triple. Each has private shower room with wc. Guests have use of the living room with TV and garden with outdoor furniture.

Prices s fr €38; d fr €42; t fr €48 **Nearby** ⚓ 4km ⚡ 12km Sea 20km 🏊 4km ⚡ 6km Restaurant 5km 🚶 4km 🏠 4km 🚲 12km **Notes** Pets admitted English spoken

🏵 La Vergne Neuve

Marylène BOURMAUD

85670 ST CHRISTOPHE DU LIGNERON

☎ 02 51 93 32 52 & 06 87 91 51 22 📠 02 51 93 17 08

email: mylene@la-vergne-neuve.com

Dating from 1880, this farmhouse is close to the sea and surrounded by peaceful countryside. The four guest rooms have been carefully restored, leaving the original walls and beams exposed and are furnished with antiques. All rooms have double and single beds, private shower room and wc. Folding bed available. Use of guest living room/kitchen, outdoor seating, fish pond.

Prices not confirmed for 2008 **On Site** 🏊 **Nearby** ⚓ 1km Sea 18km ⚡ 5km 🏊 4km 🏠 4km 🚲 10km **Notes** No pets

ST-CYR-EN-TALMONDAIS

🏵 🍽 L'Ardiller

Marie-France FAUCONNIER

8 Rue de la Saunerie, 85540 ST CYR EN TALMONDAIS

☎ 06 78 07 44 62 & 02 51 97 47 22 📠 02 51 97 47 22

email: thfauconnier@wanadoo.fr

The three bedrooms at this property - two doubles and a triple - are in adapted farm buildings. Each room has its own entrance, shower and WC. Cot available; lounge. Garden with furniture; owners' farm 300 metres away. Meals by arrangement, except Saturdays from July to September.

Prices s fr €37; d fr €42; t fr €54; dinner fr €15 **Nearby** ⚓ 15km ⚡ 15km Sea 15km 🏊 3km ⚡ 13km Restaurant 0.5km 🏊 0.4km Spa 36km 🍷 15km 🏠 7km 🚲 13km **Notes** No pets

🏵 🍽 La Maison Neuve

Gérard et Marie-Renée MASSON

85540 ST CYR EN TALMONDAIS

☎ 02 51 30 80 13 📠 02 51 30 89 37

email: massong@85.cernet.fr

Located in a protected area on the borders of the Marrais fen lands, this farmhouse has four guest rooms: a double with single and own entrance, a double and two more with double and single. All rooms have private shower, wc and TV. Use of reception room with TV, meadow, children's games.

Prices s fr €37; d fr €42; t fr €54; dinner fr €15 **Nearby** Sea 12km ⚡ 3km ⚡ 16km Restaurant 2km 🏊 2.5km 🍷 15km 🏠 2.5km 🚲 16km **Notes** No pets

ST-GERMAIN-L'AIGUILLER

🏵 🌾 🍽 La Berthomerie

Marcel et Suzanne BRIFFAUD

85390 ST GERMAIN L'AIGUILLER

☎ 02 51 00 32 66 📠 02 51 00 38 24

email: m.briffaud@85.cernet.fr

In the peace and quiet of the countryside, this working farm has four double/twin bedrooms in a separate building, close to the owners' house. Each room has a private shower and WC. Guests' lounge with kitchen area. Garden with garden room. Parking. Possible fishing in nearby lake. Meals by reservation. Good for walking and mountain biking.

Prices s fr €40; d fr €45; extra person fr €12; dinner fr €16   **On Site** ✐
Nearby ⚓ 5km ⚒ 15km Restaurant 1km ⚐ 0.8km ⛳ 40km 🏛 1km
🚣 50km   **Notes** No pets

ST-JEAN-DE-MONTS

⫘ La Bourrine

Isabelle BERNARD

184 Av d'Orouet, 85160 ST JEAN DE MONTS

☎ 02 51 59 55 31

This traditional renovated house, situated between St Jean de Monts and St Gilles Croix de Vie, has three guest rooms, all with antique furniture and views over the Marais. One room with double and single beds and disabled access, a double and twin; all with shower and wc. Walled garden with outdoor seating, parking. Restaurants nearby.

Prices s fr €47; d fr €47; t fr €61   **Nearby** ⚓ 4km Sea 3km ✐ 3km
⚒ 8km Restaurant 1km ⚐ 11km 🏛 1km 🚣 8km   **Notes** No pets Open 24 March to 24 September.

ST-JULIEN-DES-LANDES

⫘ ⫤ Les Suries

Alain et Monique GROSSIN

85150 ST JULIEN DES LANDES

☎ 02 51 46 64 02 & 06 86 67 35 20   📄 02 51 46 64 02

email: monique-et-alain.grossin@wanadoo.fr

Only a few minutes from the ocean, this farmhouse enjoys a beautiful wooded location. It provides three recently decorated rooms: a double, one with double and single and one with two doubles located in a converted barn. All have private shower room, wc and TV. Dinner by reservation. Holiday cottage and fishing pond also on site.

Prices s fr €34; d €44-€49; t fr €54; extra person fr €10; dinner fr
€17   **On Site** ✐ Private ⚒   **Nearby** ⚓ 2km ⚊ 20km Sea 15km
Restaurant 5km ⚐ 2km Spa 23km ⛳ 5km 🏛 2km 🚣 5km   **Notes** Pets admitted

---

ST-MATHURIN

⫘⫘ Château de la Millière

Claude et Danielle HUNEAULT

85150 ST MATHURIN

☎ 02 51 22 73 29   📄 02 51 22 73 29

email: chateaudelamilliere@club-internet.fr

web: www.chateau-la-milliere.com

This elegant 19th-century building houses four double rooms and a suite of two double rooms, all with private bathroom and wc. Guests are welcome to use library, billiard room, TV, telephone and swimming pool. Terrace with outdoor seating, fishing pond, barbecue, table tennis on site. Restaurants nearby.

Prices s fr €92; d fr €100; t fr €115   **On Site** ✐ Private ⚒
Nearby ⚓ 8km ⚊ 3km Sea 10km Restaurant 1km ⚐ 1km ⛳ 1km
🏛 1km 🚣 10km   **Notes** No pets English spoken Open May to September.

ST-MICHEL-EN-L'HERM

⫘ Basse Brenée

Michel et M-Noëlle ARDOUIN

85580 ST MICHEL EN L'HERM

☎ 02 51 30 24 09   📄 02 51 30 24 09

email: michel.ardouin@free.fr

web: www.visite-vendee.com

A warm welcome is assured at this 18th-century Marais farmhouse, set in a tranquil, rural setting. There is a double room, a room with two doubles and a single, and a completely separate double room with kitchen and sofa, all with private facilities. Use of sitting room with equipped kitchen area, games room. Camping on site.

Prices d fr €40; t fr €50; extra person fr €10   **Nearby** ⚓ 7km Sea 9km
✐ 2km ⚒ 15km ⚐ 3km ⛳ 3km 🏛 3km 🚣 15km   **Notes** Pets admitted

---

ST-MICHEL-LE-CLOUCQ

⫘ *Bel Air*

J-Christian et M-Jo BOURDIN

78 Rue de la Mairie, 85200 ST MICHEL LE CLOUCQ

☎ 02 51 69 24 24 & 06 33 50 03 65

email: info@gite-bourdin.com

Located in a small market town between the Marais-Poitevin and the great forest of Mervent, this 1850 renovated farmhouse is still full of character. It offers two double rooms and a double with single bed, all with private shower room and wc. Use of shared living room, outdoor seating area. Holiday cottage also on site. Reductions for longer stays.

Prices not confirmed for 2008   **Nearby** ⚓ 5km ✐ 3km ⚒ 5km ⚐ 1km
🏛 5km 🚣 30km   **Notes** No pets

ST-PAUL-EN-PAREDS

⫘ *La Gelletière*

Charly MERLET

85500 ST PAUL EN PAREDS

☎ 02 51 92 00 43 & 06 16 34 28 90   📄 02 51 92 00 43

email: contact@lagelletiere.com

This former barn on a working farm has been converted to include the owner's home, a holiday cottage and five en suite guestrooms: a double and four doubles with extra single, all with their own entrance.

CONTINUED

ST-PAUL-EN-PAREDS CONTINUED

Use of shared living room with kitchen area, private pool (open June to October), and leafy picnic area beside the river. Restaurant 3km.
Prices not confirmed for 2008 **On Site** Private **Nearby** 8km
2km 8km 30km **Notes** No pets Open May to September.

ST-PIERRE-LE-VIEUX

La Ferme des Ecluseaux

Chrystèle PEPIN
36 Les Bas 85420, 85420 ST PIERRE LE VIEUX
☎ 02 51 00 76 14 📄 02 51 00 76 14
email: chrystele.pepin85@orange.fr
web: www.lafermedesecluseaux.com

Find peace and relaxation on this organic farm, in the heart of the Marais-Poitevin fen lands. There are three double rooms, two with extra single, all with independent entrance, shower room and wc. Use of living room with kitchen area. Home-made breakfast with produce from farm. Camping and boat trips on site. Restaurants 3km.
Prices s fr €28; d fr €40; t fr €53; extra person fr €13 **On Site**
Nearby 10km Sea 50km 10km Restaurant 3km 3km 3km
3km 20km **Notes** No pets English spoken

STE-CECILE

La Grande Métairie

Serge et Nelly BOUDEAU
85110 STE CECILE
☎ 02 51 40 25 36 & 06 18 06 26 73
email: serge.boudeau@wanadoo.fr
web: www.alagrandemetairie.com

Four guest rooms in part of a barn close to the owners' home on a working farm 500 metres from the village. There are two separately accessed ground floor rooms for three people, and two upstairs doubles with access through the lounge. All rooms have private showers/WCs. Lounge with TV, garden room.
Prices s fr €37; d fr €41; t fr €55 **On Site** Private **Nearby** 10km
30km 0.2km Restaurant 2km 0.5km 10km 0.5km 10km
Notes Pets admitted Open May to September.

Logis de l'Aublonnière

Anne COUTANSAIS
85110 STE CECILE
☎ 02 51 40 26 43 & 06 62 10 90 09
email: logisaublonniere@wanadoo.fr
web: www.aublonniere.com

The three spacious guest rooms occupy the first floor of the main part of this 17th-century building. They are accessed by a stone staircase. There is a double room, and two rooms for three, one of which has a cot. There is a lounge on the ground floor, and a garden with garden room. On-site parking.
Prices d €72-€89; t fr €99 **On Site** **Nearby** 3km 15km
Sea 50km 0.2km 10km Restaurant 2km 10km 1km 20km
Notes No pets English spoken

TALMONT-ST-HILAIRE

La Pinière

Bertrand CARAYOL
85440 TALMONT ST HILAIRE
☎ 02 51 22 25 66 & 06 70 30 55 16

This renovated farmhouse is surrounded by an organic farm in a beautiful wooded valley. It houses four double en suite guest rooms, two with extra singles and all with their own entrance. Use of a shared sitting room with fireplace. Holiday cottage available on site.
Prices s fr €35; d fr €44; t fr €58 **Nearby** 5km 3km Sea 3km
1km 12km Restaurant 2km 0.8km Spa 12km 3km 1.5km
12km **Notes** Pets admitted

VAIRE

Chambre d'hôtes

Pascal et Marie HEILIGENSTEIN
1 Allée de la Noë, 85150 VAIRE
☎ 02 51 33 78 47 & 06 85 22 21 35
email: heiligenstein.pascal@tiscali.fr

Marie, Pascal and their daughters welcome you to their house, just 10 minutes from the sea. Four bedrooms with independent access, TV, and private facilities. Two double rooms with shower room/WC; one double room with bathroom/WC. Upstairs there's a triple room with bathroom and private lounge. There's also a communal sitting room with TV. Table d'hotes available on reservation.
Prices not confirmed for 2008 **Nearby** 3km Sea 6km 0.5km
12km 12km 1km 12km **Notes** Pets admitted

VENANSAULT

La Guérinière

Bernadette SELIN
85190 VENANSAULT
☎ 02 51 07 32 20 📄 02 51 07 32 20
email: selinb85@hotmail.com

This old traditional house is peacefully situated on a working farm, and offers three first floor guest rooms. There are two doubles and a room for three. Each has an en suite shower room and WC. There is a lounge, with board games and a small kitchen area. Garden; terrace and garden room. Parking.
Prices s fr €32; d fr €40; t fr €48 **Nearby** 12km 20km Sea 25km
5km 12km Restaurant 3km 5km 10km 5km 12km
Notes No pets English spoken

49 MAINE-ET-LOIRE

56 MORBIHAN

85 VENDÉE

ATLANTIC OCEAN

Noirmoutier Island

Sèvres Nantaise

Boulogne

Loire

Canal

Vilaine

Canal

Segré

Cholet

Varades

Ancenis

Riaillé

Joué-sur-Erdre

Châteaubriant

Rougé

Sion-les-Mines

Soudan

Nort-sur-Erdre

St-Mars-du-Désert

St-Julien-de-Concelles

Le Landreau

Vallet

Monnières

Basse-Goulaine

Château-Thébaud

Le Bignon

Marsac-sur-Don

Nozay

Sucé-sur-Erdre

La Chapelle-sur-Erdre

Orvault

NANTES

Pont-Saint-Martin

La Chevrolière

La Limouzinière

Legé

Guémené-Penfao

Bouaye

Port-St-Père

Ste-Pazanne

Chéméré

Arthon-en-Retz

Le Temple de Bretagne

Frossay

Chauvé

Redon

Missillac

Ste-Reine-de-Bretagne

St-Malo-de-Guersac

St-Père-en-Retz

Pornic

La Plaine-sur-Mer

Herbignac

Assérac

Saint-Nazaire

Pornichet

Mesquer

La Turballe

15 km

0

N

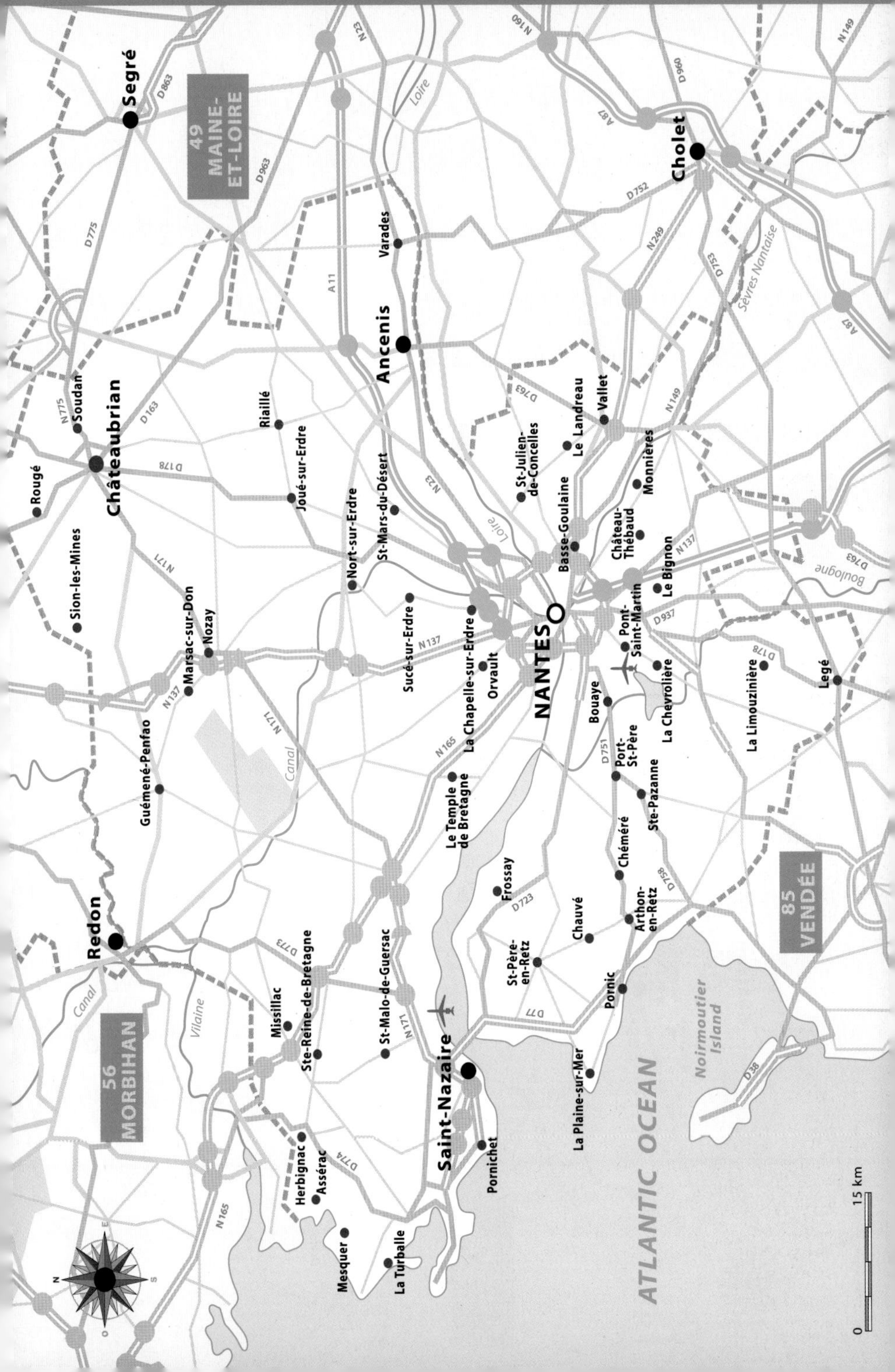

MAINE-ET-LOIRE

Pays-de-la-Loire

49

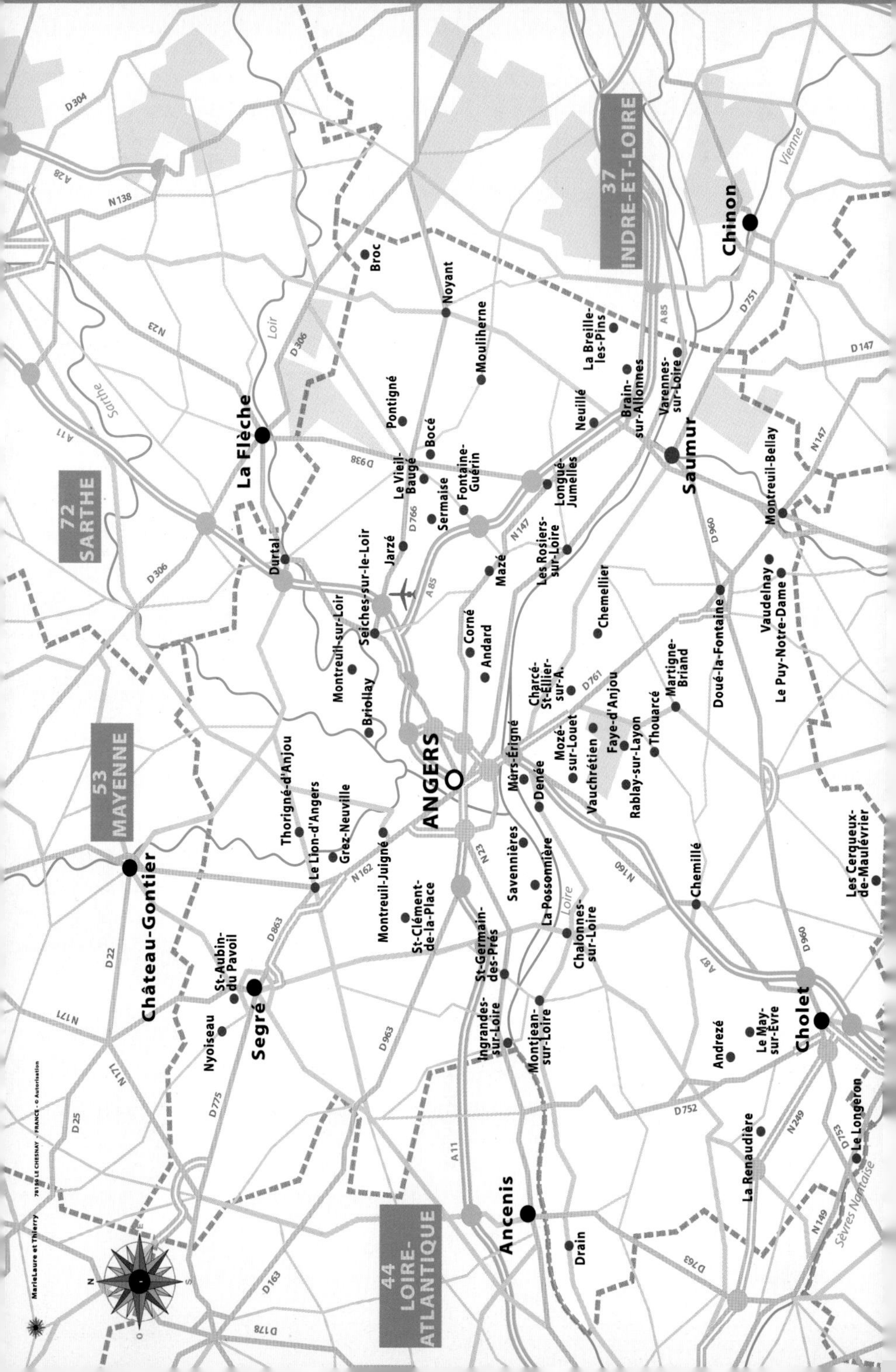

D304
A28
N138
N23
Loir
D306
Sarthe
A11
La Flèche
72 SARTHE
D306
Durtal
53 MAYENNE
Château-Gontier
D22
N171
N171
D25
D775
Nyoiseau
St-Aubin-du Pavoil
Segré
D863
N162
Le Lion-d'Angers
Thorigné-d'Anjou
Grez-Neuville
Montreuil-Juigné
St-Clément-de-la-Place
D963
D163
D178
44 LOIRE-ATLANTIQUE
Ancenis
A11
Drain
Ingrandes-sur-Loire
St-Germain-des-Prés
Montjean-sur-Loire
Chalonnes-sur-Loire
La Possonnière
Savennières
N23
Loire
ANGERS
Mûrs-Érigné
Denée
Briollay
Montreuil-sur-Loir
Seiches-sur-le-Loir
Jarzé
D766
Le Vieil-Baugé
Pontigné
Boçé
D938
Sermaise
Fontaine-Guérin
Broc
Noyant
Mouliherne
Corné
Andard
A85
Mazé
N147
Les Rosiers-sur-Loire
Longué-Jumelles
Neuillé
Brain-sur-Allonnes
La Breille-les-Pins
Varennes-sur-Loire
37 INDRE-ET-LOIRE
A85
Chinon
Vienne
D751
D147
Saumur
N147
Montreuil-Bellay
D960
Vaudelnay
Le Puy-Notre-Dame
Doué-la-Fontaine
Chemellier
Charcé-St-Ellier-sur-A.
D761
Faye-d'Anjou
Mozé-sur-Louet
Vauchrétien
Rablay-sur-Layon
Thouarcé
Martigné-Briand
N160
Chemillé
A87
D960
Les Cerqueux-de-Maulévrier
Cholet
Le May-sur-Èvre
Andrezé
D752
La Renaudière
N249
D753
Le Longeron
Sèvres Nantaise
N149
D763
MarieLaure et Thierry 78150 LE CHESNAY - FRANCE - © Autorisation

D 908
D 916
N 158
N 138
Orne
D 908
N 176
D 909
61 ORNE
N 12
D 938
N 12
Mayenne
N 138
N 12
ALENÇON
Sarthe
Mortagne-au-Perche
Champfleur
D 311
Loir
St-Léonard-des-Bois
Ancinnes
D 920
Mamers
D 955
53 MAYENNE
Oisseau-le-Petit
Nogent le-Rotro
Monhoudou
N 23
D 35
Moitron-sur-Sarthe
Juillé
Huisne
A 11
Cormes
Rouez-en-Champagne
D 304
A 28
N 138
D 301
A 81
N 157
Coulaines
N 23
Yvré-l'Évêque
LE MANS
Souligné-Flacé
Changé
Brûlon
N 157
Chantenay-Villedieu
Chemiré-le-Gaudin
D 304
Asnières-sur-Vègre
A 11
Guécélard
A 28
Solesmes
Sarthe
Moncé-en-Belin
Le Grand-Lucé
N 23
N 138
41 LOIR-ET-CHER
D 306
Yvré-le-Pôlin
Lavenay
Notre-Dame-du-Pé
Thoiré-sur-Dinan
Clermont-Créans
Mayet
Luceau
Beaumont-sur-Dême
La Flèche
Loir
Dissay-sous-Courcillon
D 306
D 938
49 MAINE-ET-LOIRE
D 766
N 138
37 INDRE-ET-LOIRE
D 766
N 147
A 85
D 959
A 10
N
O
E
S
A 28

0   15

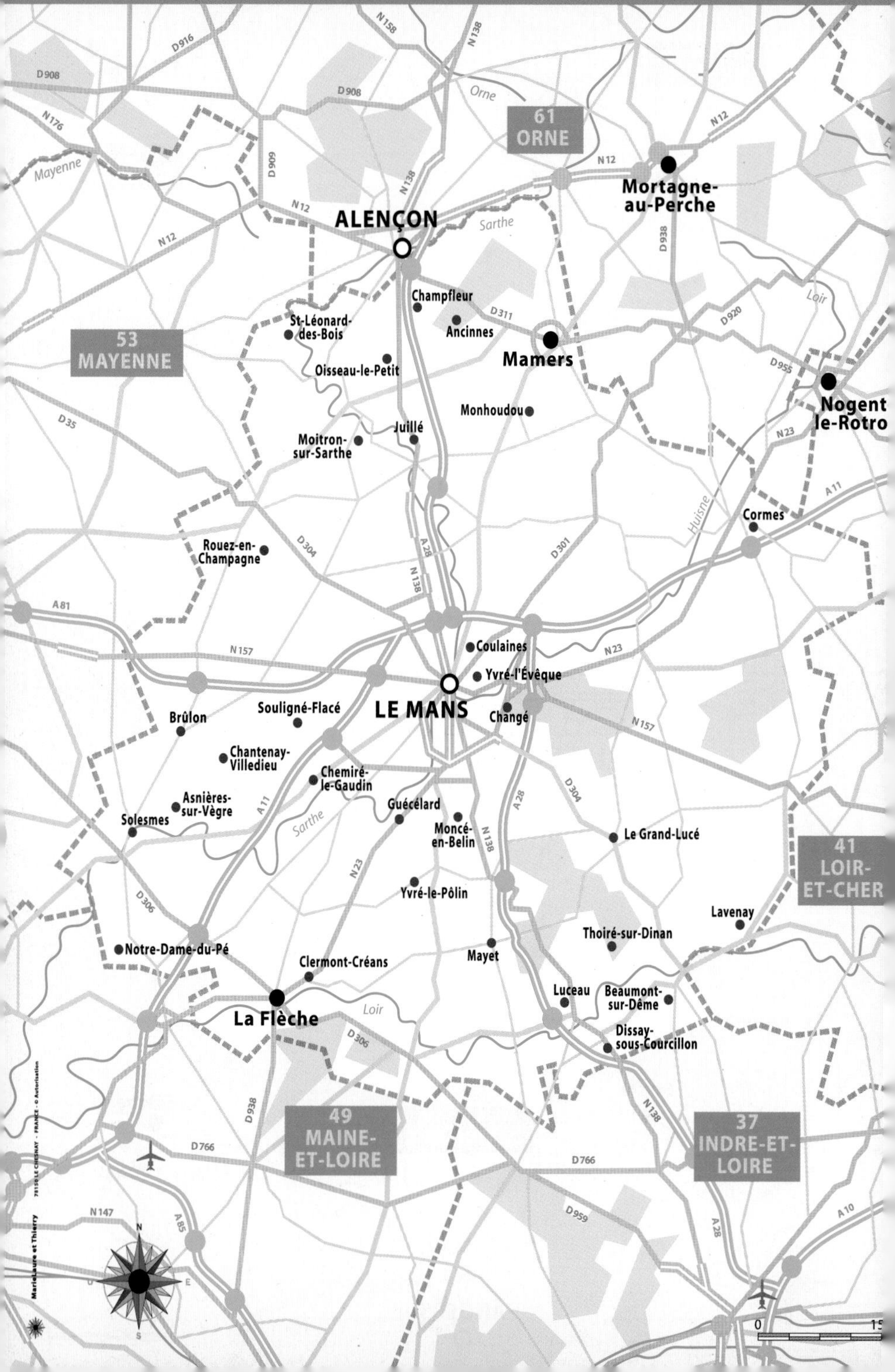

VENDÉE

Pays-de-la-Loire

85

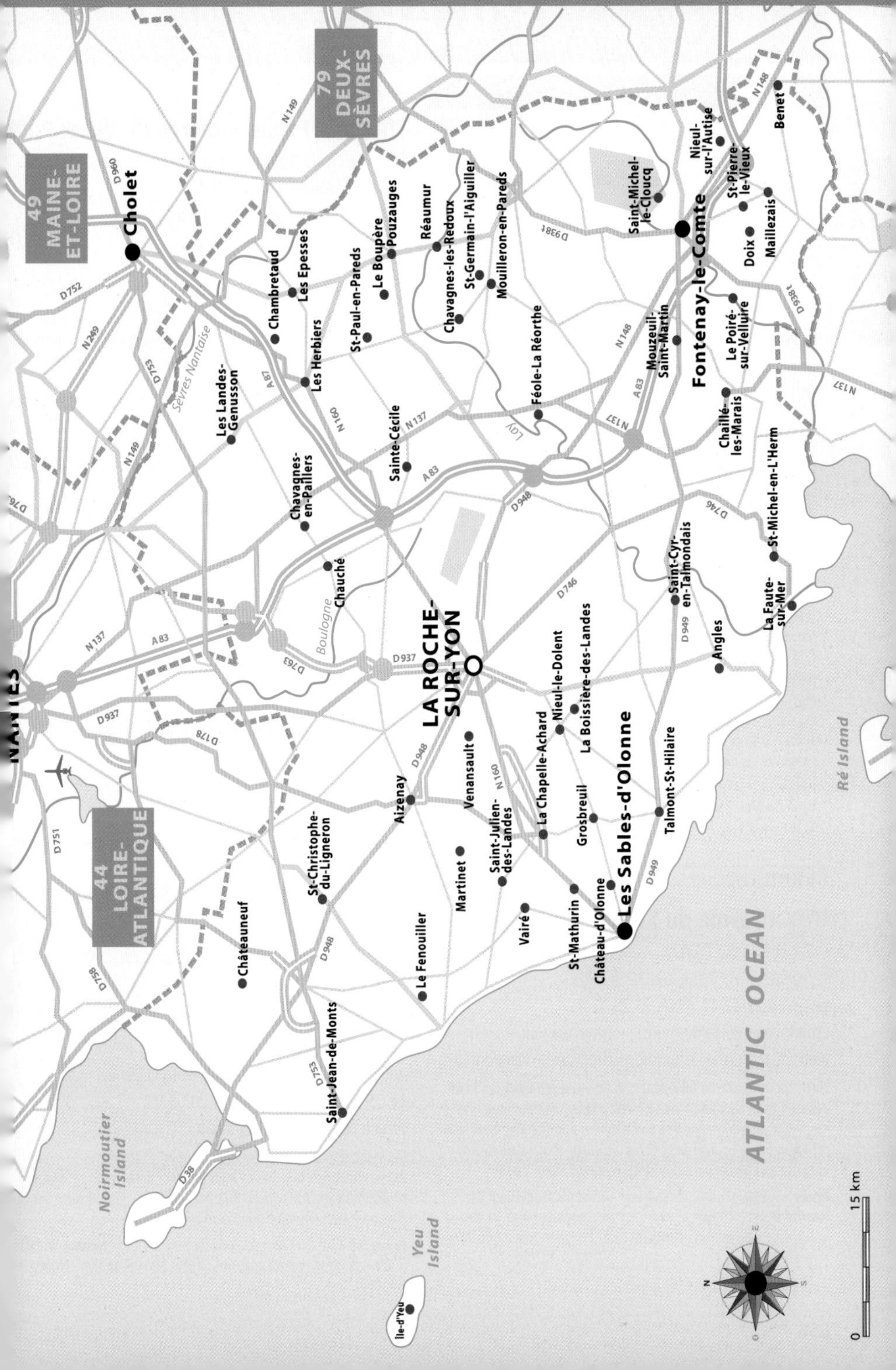

49 MAINE-ET-LOIRE
79 DEUX-SÈVRES
44 LOIRE-ATLANTIQUE
Cholet
Chambretaud
Les Epesses
Le Boupère
Pouzauges
Réaumur
St-Paul-en-Pareds
Les Herbiers
Chavagnes-les-Redoux
St-Germain-l'Aiguiller
Mouilleron-en-Pareds
Saint-Michel-le-Cloucq
Nieul-sur-l'Autise
St-Pierre-le-Vieux
Benet
Maillezais
Doix
Fontenay-le-Comte
Mouzeuil-Saint-Martin
Le Poiré-sur-Velluire
Féole-La Réorthe
Les Landes-Genusson
Sainte-Cécile
Chavagnes-en-Paillers
Chauché
Chaillé-les-Marais
St-Michel-en-L'Herm
Saint-Cyr-en-Talmondais
La Faute-sur-Mer
LA ROCHE-SUR-YON
Angles
Nieul-le-Dolent
La Boissière-des-Landes
La Chapelle-Achard
Venansault
Aizenay
Les Sables-d'Olonne
Talmont-St-Hilaire
Grosbreuil
Saint-Julien-des-Landes
Martinet
St-Christophe-du-Ligneron
Château-d'Olonne
St-Mathurin
Vairé
Le Fenouiller
Châteauneuf
Saint-Jean-de-Monts
Ile-d'Yeu
NANTES
Sèvres Nantaise
Boulogne
Lay
A87
A83
N137
N149
N148
N160
D960
D752
N249
D753
D938
D948
D746
D949
D937
D763
D178
D751
D758
D38
Noirmoutier Island
Yeu Island
Ré Island
ATLANTIC OCEAN
0
15 km

PICARDY

AISNE

AMBLENY

▦ ⏹ **Le Domaine de Montaigu**

Philippe DE REYER

16 rue de Montaigu, Hameau du Soulier,
02290 AMBLENY

☎ 03 23 74 06 62 📄 03 23 74 06 62
email: info@domainedemontaigu.com
web: www.multimania.com/domainemontaigu

Between Soissons and Compiègne, this lovely old vineyard house is in a peaceful haven, surrounded by extensive woodlands and parkland with a swimming pool, shady terrace and parking. The estate provides five stylish guest rooms with antique furnishings: Du Barry, Pompadour, Marie Antoinette, Colette and Georges V. There is a large lounge and dining room with open fire, and meals are available by reservation.

Prices s fr €65; d fr €75-€100; t fr €100; extra person fr €25; dinner fr €25 **On Site** Private ⚡ **Nearby** ⛳ 3km ♨ 35km ✎ 2km ♨ 8km 🏛 1km ⛵ 10km **Notes** No pets English spoken

BERRIEUX

▦ ⏹ **Ferme du Jardin Monsieur**

Gilles et Isabelle PAYEN

12 rue de la Fontaine, 02820 BERRIEUX

☎ 03 23 22 42 41 📄 03 23 22 42 41
email: payengil.jardinmonsieur@wanadoo.fr
web: http://ferme_jardinmonsieur.monsite.wanadoo.fr

Three spacious, comfortable rooms in an old stable block on a farm, between Laon and Reims with a forest nearby. Two doubles, one room with an extra single bed and a family room for five, each with private facilities. Lounge with television, dining room, garden with furniture and barbecue and enclosed courtyard with parking.

Prices s fr €38; d fr €43; t fr €58; extra person fr €15; dinner fr €18 **Nearby** ⚡ 1km ♨ 15km ✎ 4km ⚡ 10km Restaurant 4km ♨ 4km ⚡ 20km 🏛 4km ⛵ 4km **Notes** No pets English spoken Open February to 10 December.

BONY

▦ ⏹ & **Ferme Auberge du Vieux Puits**

Philippe GYSELINCK

5 rue de l'Abbaye, 02420 BONY

☎ 03 23 66 22 33 📄 03 23 66 25 27
email: pgyselin@terre-net.fr
web: www.isasite.net/ferme-du-vieux-puits

Four spacious and comfortable rooms above a farm hotel, all with private facilities, hairdryers, telephone and satellite television. Two rooms with a double and a single bed, one twin and one double room. Lounge and kitchenette for guest use with independent access. Other facilities include a heated swimming pool, garden furniture, a terrace, mountain bikes, table tennis, volley ball and basketball court.

Prices s fr €37; d fr €54; t fr €70; extra person fr €16; dinner €19-€23 **On Site** Restaurant ⚡ Private ⚡ **Nearby** ⚡ 6km ♨ 17km ✎ 5km 🏛 2km ⛵ 15km **Notes** Pets admitted English spoken Open 3 January to 23 December. CC

see advert on opposite page

BRAYE-EN-LAONNOIS

▦ ⏹ **Chambre d'hôtes**

David KACZMAREK

2 rue de l'Eglise, 02000 BRAYE-EN-LAONNOIS

☎ 03 23 25 68 55
email: kaczmarekda@wanadoo.fr
web: http://perso.wanadoo.fr/david.kaczmarek/

In a peaceful location surrounded by greenery, this establishment offers four spacious rooms on an old farm, each with private facilities. Two double rooms, one room for three people and one room for four; child's bed available on request. The facilities include a large communal lounge with fireplace, a cooker, enclosed parking, private courtyard and garden and generous breakfasts.

Prices d fr €46; t fr €69; extra person fr €23; dinner fr €20 **Nearby** ⚡ 10km ♨ 6km ✎ 6km ⚡ 6km Restaurant 8km ♨ 6km Spa 6km 🏛 10km ⛵ 20km **Notes** No pets

BURELLES

▦ & **Relais des Eglises**

Georges LOUVET

4 route de la Fontaine, 02140 BURELLES

☎ 03 23 90 03 03 📄 03 23 90 03 03
email: relaisdeseglises@free.fr

Set in the middle of the village, in the heart of Thiérache, there are three rooms with two double beds and two single beds each with private facilities (additional child's bed available). Guests have use of day room with television. Inn 200m away.

Prices s fr €32; d fr €43; t fr €60; extra person fr €20 **Nearby** ⚡ 25km ✎ 7km ⚡ 20km Restaurant 0.2km ♨ 6km 🏛 5km ⛵ 5km **Notes** Pets admitted

BUSSIARES

▥ La Grange du Moulin

Chantal BLOT

5 rue du Moulin, 02810 BUSSIARES

☎ 03 23 70 92 60

email: lagrangedumoulin@hotmail.fr

This is a pretty renovated country house where the ancient mill barn has been turned into four guest rooms: a double, two triples and a family room that can sleep five; all have shower room and WC. Kitchen, conservatory and BBQ at guests' disposal. Meals by arrangement. Close to Champagne tourist route.

Prices s fr €40; d fr €55; t fr €65; extra person fr €10 **Nearby** ⚓ 16km ⚑ 13km ◈ 0.5km ↖ 13km Restaurant 4km ⚲ ⚑ 13km ⋙ 13km **Notes** Pets admitted Open February to 15 December.

CESSIERES

▥ ⓘ La Forestière

Jacqueline et Jean DRU

7 ruelle Buet, 02320 CESSIERES

☎ 03 23 24 19 07 ▤ 03 23 24 19 07

email: jjdru@wanadoo.fr

A stone-built house in a forest clearing ten kilometres from Laon. A double bedroom is on the ground floor, and a family suite upstairs has its own separate entrance and living area. A veranda leads into the garden, where there is secure car parking and cycle storage.

Prices s fr €42; d fr €50; dinner fr €20 **Nearby** ⚓ 10km ⚑ 20km ◈ 3km ↖ 5km ⚲ 5km ⋙ 10km **Notes** No pets

CHAOURSE

▥ ⓘ Chambre d'hôtes

Jean BRUCELLE

6, rue du château, 02340 CHAOURSE

☎ 03 23 21 30 87 ▤ 03 23 21 20 78

Two triple rooms and two doubles, all on the first floor with independent access, shower room and WC, make up the accommodation in this house in a small village. Kitchenette available; enclosed courtyard with secure parking. Evening meals by reservation. Close to the Thiérache circuit of fortified churches.

Prices s fr €30; d fr €42; t fr €52; dinner fr €16 **Nearby** ⚑ 35km ◈ 15km ↖ 20km ⚲ 1km ⚑ 1km ⋙ 35km **Notes** No pets

CHARLY-SUR-MARNE

▥ Le Havre des Blanches Vignes

J-M et C CHARPENTIER

11 route de Paris, 02310 CHARLY-SUR-MARNE

☎ 03 23 82 10 72 ▤ 03 23 82 31 80

email: jean-marc@champagne-charpentier.com

web: http://champagne-charpentier.com

Your hosts at this property, set in a village in the heart of the Marne valley, are the eighth generation of a dedicated wine-growing family. There are four beautifully decorated bedrooms: two doubles, a king-size double, and a twin, all with en suite facilities. Mezzanine lounge area with TV and board games; extensive enclosed grounds. Closed 15 days in September.

Prices s €60-€65; d €65-€70; extra person fr €15 **On Site** ◈ **Nearby** ⚓ 3km ◈ 15km ↖ 15km Restaurant 0.5km ⚲ 0.5km ⋙ 2km **Notes** No pets English spoken CC

CHERET

⊪ ⚬⃝ Le Clos Cheret

Monique SIMONNOT

18 rue Principale, 02860 CHERET

☎ 03 23 24 80 64

email: leclos.cheret@club-internet.fr

web: www.leploscheret.com

An 18th-century winery surrounded by a large park. Two grade 2 rooms with a double and twin beds, sharing a shower room and wc. One room for three to five people and one twin, both en suite (cot available). Day room, lounge, library, parking, table tennis. Family table d'hôte by prior arrangement with wine included - except for Sunday evenings.

Prices s fr €40; d €45-€50; extra person fr €20; dinner fr €20
On Site ✎ **Nearby** ⛄ 7km ♨ 7km ⚲ 8km Restaurant 0.5km ⚲ 8km
🏠 2km ♨ 7km **Notes** No pets English spoken Open 15 March to 15 October.

CHIGNY

⊪ ⚬⃝ Chambre d'hôtes

M PIETTE

6 et 7 place des Maronniers, 02120 CHIGNY

☎ 03 23 60 22 04

An 18th-century brick and flint house, right on the village square. There is a double room and a room for three, both with private bath or shower room and WC. Three more rooms (grade 2) together make a family unit for up to six people, with a shared bathroom and WC. Garden, on-site parking.

Prices s fr €32; d fr €44; t fr €56; extra person €15; dinner fr €16
Nearby ⛄ 2km ♨ 15km ✎ 0.5km ⚲ 12km Restaurant 3km ⚲ 12km
🏠 2km ♨ 30km **Notes** Pets admitted

CONNIGIS

⊪ ⚬⃝ Ferme du Château

Pierre LECLERE

1 rue du Launay, 02330 CONNIGIS

☎ 03 23 71 90 51 📠 03 23 71 48 57

Expect a friendly winegrower's welcome at this ancient château's farm, on the Champagne tourist route. Five spacious rooms with private facilities: two doubles, two for three people and one double with a lounge is in a tower. Table d'hôte meals by reservation; billiard room; large wooded park; bicycles to hire; footpaths; fishing; local produce for sale. Heating supplement payable in winter.

Prices s €40-€45; d €48-€60; extra person fr €25; dinner fr €17
Nearby ⛄ 2km ♨ 12km ✎ 2km ⚲ 12km Restaurant 3km ⚲ 3km
🐎 12km 🏠 4km ♨ 12km **Notes** No pets

COUCY-LE-CHATEAU-AUFFRIQUE

⊪ Chambre d'hôtes

Michèle LEFEVRE-TRANCHART

3 rue Traversière,

02380 COUCY-LE-CHATEAU-AUFFRIQUE

☎ 03 23 52 76 64 & 06 61 70 13 25 📠 03 23 52 69 79

email: michele.tranchart@wanadoo.fr

This house is based on the 13th-century ramparts of a medieval village in the massive forest of Saint-Gobain. There are five rooms: on the first floor is a room for four people with shower and WC, and two doubles with shower/WC. On the second floor are another two doubles, both with shower/WC. Historical monuments on the doorstep; fishing in the local lake; good walking country.

Prices s fr €35; d fr €42; t €50-€70; extra person fr €10 **On Site** ✎
Nearby ⛄ 4km ♨ 30km ⚲ 13km Restaurant 0.1km ♨ 10km
Notes Pets admitted

CUIRY-HOUSSE

⊪ ⚬⃝ Chambre d'hôtes

Maryse et Jean-Louis MASSUE

6 rue de Soissons, 02220 CUIRY-HOUSSE

☎ 03 23 55 01 06 📠 03 23 55 01 06

email: jlmassue@wanadoo.fr

web: puitsetgirafe.fr

This huge, completely renovated house built in 1874 is set in a tranquil, pastoral environment and offers four rooms with private facilities and television (three doubles and one family). Large communal room, covered garage, terrace, summer kitchen, large park and bicycles; evening table d'hôte meals by reservation. 25 km from the Paris-Strasbourg, Calais-Lyon-Paris-Lille motorways and one hour from Disneyland Paris.

Prices d €53-€68; extra person fr €15; dinner fr €19 **Nearby** ⛄ 10km
♨ 20km ✎ 8km ⚲ 16km Restaurant 7km ⚲ 8km 🏠 6km ♨ 16km
Notes No pets

DANIZY

⊪ ⚬⃝ Domaine le Parc

Anne et Jos BERGMAN

02800 DANIZY

☎ 03 23 56 55 23 📠 03 23 56 55 23

email: contact@domaineleparc.fr

web: www.domaineleparc.fr

An 18th-century house with lots of character, perched on a hill with views of the Oise. There are five luxurious bedrooms on the first and second floors. Each has a king-size bed, lounge area, TV and private bathroom/WC. Three have views across the valley; the other two overlook the extensive wooded grounds. Not suitable for small children, for safety reasons. Meals by arrangement.

Prices s €60-€70; d €65-€85; extra person fr €25; dinner fr €35
Nearby ⛄ 15km ♨ 30km ✎ 8km ⚲ 25km Restaurant 0.5km
⚲ 25km 🏠 1km ♨ 1km **Notes** No pets English spoken

EPARCY

⚞ ⦿ Villa des Tilleuls

Nathalie FOURDRIGNIER POINTIER
7 route de Landouzy, 02500 EPARCY
☎ 03 23 98 46 17

A typical village in the heart of the Thiérarche, between Paris and
Brussels. Five rooms in a large mansion set in peaceful, wooded
parkland that stretches to the banks of the River Thon, where you
can fish. There are five double rooms, three sharing a wc. An extra
bed and child's bed is available. Set price table d'hôte meals by
reservation.

Prices s €27-€30; d €38-€42; extra person fr €12; dinner fr €15
On Site ⌀ **Nearby** ⛷ 5km ⤚ 5km Restaurant 5km ⦿ 5km ⛛ 5km
⬚ 5km ⋈ 5km **Notes** No pets

FERE-EN-TARDENOIS

⚞ Clairbois

François CHAUVIN
7 Résidence Clairbois, 02130 FERE-EN-TARDENOIS
☎ 03 23 82 21 72 ▤ 03 23 82 62 84
email: residence.clairbois@free.fr
web: www.clairbois.fr.fm

This beautifully situated property is just off the Champagne trail near
the Château de Fere-en-Tardenois. There is a large lake on site with
boating and a tennis court for guests' use. The three rooms (one
double, one twin and one family) all have private bathrooms. There is
a lounge and meals are available if reserved.

Prices s fr €55; d €65; t fr €80; extra person fr €25; dinner fr €18
On Site ⌀ **Nearby** ⛷ 3km ⚓ 20km ⤚ 1km Restaurant 1.7km ⦿
2km ⋈ 2km **Notes** No pets English spoken

LA CHAPELLE-MONTHODON

⚞ ⦿ Chambre d'hôtes

Christian DOUARD
7 Hameau de Chezy, 02330 LA CHAPELLE-MONTHODON
☎ 03 23 82 47 66 ▤ 03 23 82 72 96
email: christian.douard2@wanadoo.fr

Peaceful surroundings with a countryside view. Four double rooms
and one family room, all with private facilities and separate access.
Facilities include a charming lounge for guests' use, a games room, a
television, mountain bike hire and parking. Champagne tasting, golf
and archery nearby.

Prices s fr €45; d fr €50; t €61-€75; extra person fr €15; dinner fr
€15 **Nearby** ⛷ 5km ⚓ 5km ⤚ 5km Restaurant 5km ⦿ 5km ⬚ 5km
⋈ 5km **Notes** No pets English spoken Open March to 15 December.

MONDREPUIS

⚞ ⦿ L'Arbre Vert

Pascal DIVRY
70 route de Fourmies, 02500 MONDREPUIS
☎ 03 23 58 14 25

In the heart of the Thiérache, close to the tourist route for fortified
churches and near Belgium. This 19th-century house in typical local
style with five well-appointed rooms includes a room for three, a
family room and three doubles, all with private facilities. Guests' have
use of a lounge, a dining room, an enclosed courtyard, parking and
a garage.

Prices s fr €35; d fr €48; t fr €61; extra person fr €13; dinner fr €16
Nearby ⛷ 9km ⚓ 4km ⤚ 4km Restaurant 3km ⦿ 5km Spa 10km
⬚ 4km ⋈ 4km **Notes** No pets English spoken

MONS-EN-LAONNOIS

⚞ Chambre d'hôtes

Françoise WOILLEZ
2 rue Saint Martin, 02000 MONS-EN-LAONNOIS
☎ 03 23 24 44 52 & 03 23 62 36 41 ▤ 03 23 24 44 52
email: gitemons@aol.com
web: www.gitenfrance.com

There are three charming rooms, two doubles and a twin, each with
shower and WC, in this old winery. Enjoy the calm of its protected
environment in the middle of a 50-acre wood, lakes full of fish, and
views to a notable church. Living and dining rooms are panelled, and
there's a huge open fire for homely breakfasts and relaxing evenings.
Ideal for golfing break.

Prices s €50-€55; d €60-€65; extra person fr €15 **On Site** ⌀
Restaurant **Nearby** ⛷ 4km ⚓ 15km ⤚ ⦿ 0.8km ⬚ 0.1km ⋈ 7km
Notes No pets English spoken Open 15 March to 15 November, other
times by reservation.

MONTAIGU

⊞ ⭘ Chambre d'hôtes

Daniel et Josette IMMERY

22 rue des Charretiers, 02820 MONTAIGU

☎ 03 23 22 77 61 & 06 32 66 65 46 ▤ 03 23 22 62 18

Owned by asparagus growers, this modern, spacious house provides four guest rooms, as well as a day room with open fire and TV, large terrace and flower garden. Private parking is available and meals can be booked. Set on the edge of the village, near Saint-Erme, Laon and Reims with its champagne cellars. Two attached gîtes are also available, ideal for couples or families.

Prices s fr €35; d fr €40; t fr €60; dinner fr €20 **Nearby** ⛲ 7km
⚓ 20km ⚘ 0.8km ⭑ 8km Restaurant 2km ⊕ 1km ⊞ 2km ⋙ 2km
Notes No pets Open July to March.

NOUVION-ET-CATILLON

⊞ ⭘ Ferme de la Commanderie

José-Marie CARETTE

Catillon-de-Temple, 02270 NOUVION-ET-CATILLON

☎ 03 23 56 51 28 & 06 82 33 22 64 ▤ 03 23 56 50 14

email: carette.jm@wanadoo.fr

Just two hours from Calais, high on a hill, this house enjoys some exceptional views. It has four bedrooms - two doubles, a triple (double bed plus a single), and another triple with three single beds, one of them child size. All have private shower room/WC. Lounge with kitchenette, meals by arrangement. Open grounds with trees and flowers, garden furniture.

Prices s fr €31; d €42-€45; t €57-€60; extra person fr €15; dinner fr €15 **On Site** ⚘ **Nearby** ⭑ 10km ⚓ 20km ⊕ 2km ⊞ 4km ⋙ 14km
Notes Pets admitted

ORIGNY-EN-THIERACHE

⊞ ⭘ Chambre d'hôtes

Jacques TUPIGNY

9 bis rue de la Maladrerie, 02550 ORIGNY-EN-THIERACHE

☎ 03 23 98 13 47 ▤ 03 23 65 83 74

This interesting house can offer two twin rooms, three double rooms, and a double suite (where the salon can sleep another two people if required). All rooms are decorated in pastel shades, and have private facilities and satellite TV. Independent access, enclosed courtyard with parking, conservatory. Terrace with pond, country views. Two stables for guest horses. Breakfast features home-made breads and brioches cooked in a wood-fired oven.

Prices s fr €33; d €42-€49; t €52-€59; extra person fr €10; dinner fr €17
On Site ⚘ **Nearby** ⛲ 6km ⚓ 20km ⭑ 10km Restaurant 6km ⊕ 6km
⊞ 0.1km ⋙ 0.1km **Notes** No pets English spoken

RESSONS-LE-LONG

⊞ Ferme de la Montagne

Patrick et Solange FERTE

02290 RESSONS-LE-LONG

☎ 03 23 74 23 71 ▤ 03 23 74 24 82

email: lafermedelamontagne@free.fr

web: http://lafermedelamontagne.free.fr

This 14th-century mountain farm, originally belonging to the royal abbey of Notre-Dame de Soissons, overlooks the valley of the Aisne. It has five spacious bedrooms, sleeping two or three people, all with private facilities, and one of them on the ground floor. The large garden also has a tennis court.

Prices s fr €45; d fr €50; t fr €66; extra person fr €12 **Nearby** ⛲ 4km
⚓ 25km ⭑ 10km ⊕ ⚘ 3km ⊞ 4km ⋙ 15km **Notes** No pets English spoken Open March to December.

SEPTMONTS

⊞ ⭒ ⭘ La Carrière l'Evêque

Antoine et Sophie HUBERT

02200 SEPTMONTS

☎ 03 23 74 91 06 & 06 82 09 42 43

email: ahubert@carriereleveque.com

web: www.carriereleveque.com

A listed 12th century former residence of the Bishops of Soisson, the house has lovely views of the Vallée de la Crise. On the first floor, with its own entrance, are three spacious bedrooms with private facilities. Table d'hôte available.

Prices d €55-€65; extra person fr €20; dinner fr €20 **On Site** ⚘
Nearby ⛲ 1km ⚓ 30km ⚘ 25km ⭑ 5km Restaurant 1km ⊕ 1km
⊞ 5km ⋙ 6km **Notes** No pets English spoken

SOUPIR

⊞ ⭘ Sous Les Jardins

Claudine et Gérard LECLERE

2 rue des Bourbleux, 02160 SOUPIR

☎ 03 23 74 10 94

A country-style house of brick and stone which stands in the centre of the village. There is a family suite with two double-bedded rooms, one with an additional single bed; and a room for three with a double bed and a single. All have private facilities and TV, and baby equipment is available. Meals by arrangement. Courtyard with garden furniture.

Prices s fr €30; d fr €46; t fr €56; extra person fr €10; dinner fr €15
Nearby ⛲ 6km ⚓ 4km ⚘ 3km ⭑ 25km Restaurant 5km ⊕ 5km
⚘ 5km ⊞ 4km ⋙ 25km **Notes** Pets admitted

ST-MICHEL

||| Le Petit Château

Martine et Thierry GUILLAUME
8 rue Jean Charton,
02830 SAINT-MICHEL-EN-THIERACHE
☎ 03 23 58 45 56

A lovely 19th-century squire's house which sits in a peaceful wooded garden with flowers and the river running through. With own access, the two doubles and two triples all have bathroom and WC. Additional bed can be provided. Kitchenette, TV, library, conservatory, BBQ, table tennis, parking. Military and glass museums plus water park nearby. Belgium 10 kilometres.

Prices s fr €32; d fr €43; t fr €56; extra person fr €15   **On Site**
Nearby ⚓ 5km ♨ 12km ⚲ 4km Restaurant 0.2km ♒ 0.5km 🏛 0.5km
🚶 4km   **Notes** No pets

STE-CROIX

||| 🍽 La Besace

Jean LECAT
1 rue Haute, 02820 SAINTE-CROIX
☎ 03 23 22 48 74   📠 03 23 22 48 74
email: la.besace@wanadoo.fr
web: www.la-besace.fr

A small, ancient village farmhouse with stabling on site. Three double rooms, one twin room and one room with a double bed and bunks, all with private facilities. Other facilities include a lounge, television, fireplace, garden, playground, table tennis, volley ball and parking. Table d'hôte meals available. There is a river, a restaurant and the Vauclair Forest 3 km away.

Prices s fr €38; d fr €45; t fr €62; extra person fr €16; dinner fr €17
Nearby ⚓ 1km ♨ 6km ⚲ 18km 🏛 2km 🚶 15km   **Notes** Pets admitted
Open Easter to September.

VIELS-MAISONS

||| 🍽 Les Clos

Anna et Bertrand NEZEYS
4 rue des Barres, 02540 VIELS-MAISONS
☎ 03 23 82 74 53 & 06 32 36 16 30
email: bertrand.nezeys@wanadoo.fr

A large 17th-century house 40 kilometres from Disneyland Paris and 5 kilometres from Reims. Four double rooms, with two extra single beds available, all have private shower and WC. Large living area, and meals are available by arrangement. On site parking.

Prices s fr €40; d fr €50; t fr €60; extra person fr €10; dinner fr
€15   **Nearby** ⚓ 3km ♨ 20km ⚲ 10km ⚲ 18km ♒ 🚶 10km
Notes No pets   English spoken   Open April to November.

VREGNY

|||| 🍽 Les Terrasses de la Vallee

Odile et Hervé COLLIGNON
9 rue de l'Église, 02880 VREGNY
☎ 03 23 53 27 40 & 06 14 48 11 95
email: ohcollignon@wanadoo.fr
web: www.lesterrassesdoh.fr

A beautiful art deco house with a lot of history, in a green setting in the Aisne valley. There are four rooms, all upstairs with en suite facilities: three are double-bedded, and a room for four has a double bed and two singles. Meals are available by arrangement; the dining room opens onto a shady terrace.

Prices s fr €75; d €80-€100; t €100-€125; extra person fr €25;
dinner fr €40   **Nearby** ⚓ 10km ♨ 12km ♒ 6km ⚲ 10km
Restaurant 10km ♒ 12km 🏛 10km 🚶 10km   **Notes** No pets
English spoken

OISE

ANSAUVILLERS

||| 🍽 Chambre d'hôtes

F MILLECAMPS
2 place de la Mairie, 60120 ANSAUVILLERS
☎ 03 44 77 05 89 & 06 82 49 63 03

A late 19th-century house with three guest bedrooms. They are all doubles, one downstairs and two on the first floor. All have private bath or shower room and WC. An extra bed and a baby's cot are available. Table tennis, table football, sauna and piano. Garden with private parking; meals by arrangement.

Prices s fr €44; d €52-€65; extra person fr €10; dinner fr €22
Nearby ⚓ 12km ♨ 35km ♒ 10km ⚲ 20km Restaurant 4km ♒ 10km
🏛 7km 🚶 5km   **Notes** Pets admitted

AUGER-SAINT-VINCENT

||| 🐾 🍽 Chambre d'hôtes

Françoise MOMMELE
8 rue Raguet, 60800 AUGER SAINT VINCENT
☎ 03 44 59 03 61 & 06 17 68 44 20   📠 03 44 59 28 68
email: lafermeduraguet@orange.fr

There are three large guest rooms in the first-floor extension of this house, sleeping two to four people with a mix of double and single beds, each with en suite shower and WC. Table tennis, garden and swimming pool. Sale of farm produce on site.

Prices s fr €40; d fr €49; t fr €58; dinner fr €16   **On Site**
Nearby ⚓ 7km ♨ 8km ♒ 5km ⚲ Restaurant 7km ♒ 7km 🏛 4km
🚶 7km   **Notes** Pets admitted   CC

PICARDY

BARON

⚜️ Domaine de Cyclone

Denise PETITOT

2 rue de la Gonesse, 60305 BARON

☎ 03 44 54 26 10 & 06 08 98 05 50 📄 03 44 54 26 10

email: domainedecyclone@wanadoo.fr

web: http://chambres-hotes.org

On the edge of a regional nature park, this 17th-century mansion set in wooded parklands has five rooms, of which one is family-sized for three people, three are doubles, and one has three single beds. Breakfast is taken in a room with open fire, and a living room can be used. Riding school on site.

Prices s fr €70; d €80–€90; t fr €100; extra person €15–€40 **On Site** ♿ 🖉 ☺ **Nearby** ↨5km ↝ 10km Restaurant 3km ⌂1km 🏠0.1km ⋒1km **Notes** No pets English spoken

BELLOY

⚜️ 🍽️ Chambre d'hôtes

Bernard TOMAS

7 rue de Méry la Bataille, 60490 BELLOY

☎ 06 14 20 52 43 & 03 44 85 49 12 📄 03 44 85 49 11

email: bernard.tomas@wanadoo.fr

In a building adjacent to this old farmhouse are three rooms comprising a double on the ground floor with en suite shower and WC, and upstairs a triple and a double, both with en suite shower/WC. Also on the ground floor is a shared living room with TV. Large garden, children's games, table tennis, enclosed parking. Meals by arrangement.

Prices s fr €35; d fr €49; t fr €62; extra person fr €10; dinner fr €18 **Nearby** ♿2km ↨15km 🖉10km ↝ 20km Restaurant 6km 🏠6km ⋒20km **Notes** No pets English spoken

BERNEUIL-SUR-AISNE

⚜️ Le Manoir de Rochefort

Estelle ABADIE

Rochefort, 60350 BERNEUIL SUR AISNE

☎ 03 44 85 81 78 & 06 87 08 90 63 📄 03 44 85 81 78

email: rochefort1@orange.fr

Guest rooms at the 17th-century Manoir du Rochefort are located in the old chapel. There are four double rooms situated on the ground floor, each with en suite facilities. Its location is a focal point in the village of Berneuil-sur-Aisne.

Prices s fr €75; d fr €85; extra person fr €35 **On Site** ☺ **Nearby** ♿8km ↨12km 🖉1km ↝ 4km Restaurant 3km ⌂4km 🏠3km ⋒16km **Notes** No pets .English spoken

BONNEUIL-LES-EAUX

⚜️ 🍽️ Chambre d'hôtes

Catherine et James DAIX

16 rue de la Ville, 60120 BONNEUIL LES EAUX

☎ 03 44 80 56 07

email: catherine.daix@wanadoo.fr

web: www.hote-floralie.com

17th-century stone-built house. The four first-floor guest rooms with private access comprise two doubles and two twins, each with shower room and WC. Guests can relax among the flowers and fruit trees in the garden. Meals by reservation. Enclosed parking. Reductions for longer stays.

Prices s fr €36; d fr €46; t fr €55; extra person fr €12; dinner fr €18 **Nearby** ♿3km ↨25km 🖉15km ↝ 6km Restaurant 6km ⌂5km 🏠0.5km ⋒16km **Notes** No pets English spoken

ESPAUBOURG

⚜️ 🍽️ ♿ Le Clos des Avettes

Claude et Anne-Marie TIREL

26 rue des Clos, 60650 ESPAUBOURG

☎ 03 44 81 57 50 📄 03 44 81 97 57

email: tirelam@aol.com

web: www.ifrance.com/avettes

Two double rooms both with an additional sofa bed, and a single room, all with en suite bath or shower and private WC can be found on the first floor of the hosts' house. A family room may also be available. Secure parking, with large garden and terrace. Meals by arrangement.

Prices s fr €46; d fr €56; t fr €76; dinner fr €22 **Nearby** ♿4km ↨4km 🖉13km ↝ 15km Restaurant 15km ⌂15km 🏠18km ⋒15km **Notes** No pets English spoken

FAY-LES-ETANGS

⚜️ 🍽️ Le Clos

Philippe VERMEIRE

3 rue du Chêne Noir, 60240 FAY LES ETANGS

☎ 03 44 49 92 38 & 06 87 01 85 61 📄 03 44 49 92 38

email: philippe.vermeire@wanadoo.fr

web: http://leclosdefay.com

Four well-equipped rooms in an annexe with private entrance. There is private parking and guests have use of the garden, with furniture. Evening meals available if booked. There are two bedrooms on each floor with private shower rooms - a double, a twin and two singles which could take an extra bed.

Prices s fr €46; d fr €56; t fr €68; dinner fr €25 **Nearby** ♿0.4km ↨5km 🖉2km ↝ 5km Restaurant 5km ⌂2km 🏠2km ⋒5km **Notes** Pets admitted English spoken

FLAVACOURT

☷ *Ferme de la Folie*

Pascal VANHESTE

60590 FLAVACOURT

☎ 03 44 84 80 28 & 06 18 52 49 46 📄 03 44 84 80 28

With three guest rooms, this renovated farmhouse building has a double room with additional single bed located on the ground floor, and two double rooms on the first floor. All rooms have en suite shower rooms, and a guest lounge is provided with self-catering facilities available on request.

Prices not confirmed for 2008 **Nearby** ⚓ 10km ⚓ 13km ⚓ 5km
⚓ 13km ⚓ 2km 🏠 6km ⚓ 6km **Notes** No pets

FROISSY

☷ ❤ ⚬ ⚬ **Chambre d'hôtes**

Francine et Xavier HAMOT

3 rue du Château, 60480 FROISSY

☎ 03 44 80 71 43 & 06 11 41 18 64 📄 03 44 80 35 28

email: francinehamot@aol.com

web: www.francineetxavier.free.fr/

Five rooms in an 18th-century farm set in wooded parkland with lounge and bookable evening meals. A fully accessible ground floor room with a double and a single bed. On the first floor are a twin room, a family room, a triple room and a double with single bed. All have either bath or shower rooms.

Prices s fr €40; d fr €48; t fr €56; extra person fr €10; dinner fr €16
Nearby ⚓ 12km ⚓ 35km ⚓ 8km ⚓ 10km Restaurant 0.5km ⚓ 0.5km
⚓ 20km 🏠 0.4km ⚓ 20km **Notes** No pets English spoken

MACHEMONT

☷ *Château de Roberville*

Philippe GUEGAN

rue de Cavan, 60150 MACHEMONT

☎ 03 44 76 28 96

email: contact@roberville.com

web: www.chateauderoberville.com

A 19th-century building in a half-hectare park. On the first floor, it offers two rooms that have double beds and a family room with a double and two single rooms. On the second floor there are two rooms with a double bed and two singles. All rooms have private facilities.

Prices not confirmed for 2008 **On Site** ⚓ **Nearby** ⚓ 3km ⚓ 2km
⚓ 13km 🏠 3km ⚓ 2km **Notes** No pets English spoken Open April to September.

MELLO

☷ **Chambre d'hôtes**

Christelle GOFFAUX

1 Grande Rue, 60660 MELLO

☎ 03 44 26 17 17 & 06 24 76 30 43 📄 03 44 26 17 17

email: goffaux.christelle@wanadoo.fr

Three bedrooms here are all upstairs in the owners' home. There is a family room for four (two double beds) and two rooms for three (double bed and a single in each). All the rooms have television and private facilities; a cot is available, as well as fridge, microwave, and off-road parking.

Prices not confirmed for 2008 **On Site** ⚓ ⚓ **Nearby** ⚓ 15km ⚓ 6km
⚓ **Notes** Pets admitted

MONTEPILLOY

☷ **Chambre d'hôtes**

Virginie BLOT

13 rue des Bordes, 60810 MONTEPILLOY

☎ 03 44 54 23 80 📄 03 44 63 10 60

email: virginie.blot@free.fr

web: http://virginie.blot.free.fr

In a picturesque village, four rooms with independent access on a farm: three upstairs doubles in an extension to the owners' houses, and the fourth in an annexe accommodates three on two levels. All have private shower room/wc. Breakfast room with open fire. Enclosed parking in courtyard.

Prices s fr €45; d fr €55; t fr €65 **Nearby** ⚓ 8km ⚓ 8km ⚓ 8km
⚓ 10km Restaurant 5km ⚓ 5km 🏠 8km ⚓ 15km **Notes** No pets
English spoken

MONTREUIL-SUR-BRECHE

⚜ ❦ ◎ ⅄ Chambre d'hôtes

Annie FREMAUX

154 rue de Clermont, 60480 MONTREUIL SUR BRECHE

☎ 03 44 80 44 85 📄 03 44 80 08 52

email: info@lafermedes3bouleaux.com

web: www.lafermedes3bouleaux.com

A 19th-century timbered barn, recently restored to its original condition, housing guest rooms: two doubles (one with disabled access and the other with additional fold-down bed) and two twin rooms, all en suite with television. A lounge, barbecue and self-catering facilities are available to guests. The proprietor offers good food made from local produce by reservation. Reductions are available for extended stays.

Prices s fr €33; d fr €40; t fr €52; extra person fr €12; dinner fr €15
On Site ♪ **Nearby** ⚓ 3km ♪ 40km ➹ 10km Restaurant 10km ♨ 2km Spa 15km ♣ 0.2km 🏛 0.5km ⋙ 15km **Notes** No pets English spoken

NOYERS-SAINT-MARTIN

⚜ ◎ La Treille

Marie-Dominique GARCIA

292 rue des Marronniers, 60480 NOYERS-SAINT-MARTIN

☎ 03 44 15 57 42 & 06 72 98 57 97

email: la.treille@free.fr

web: http://la.treille.free.fr

Three rooms in a building separate from the owners' home, each with its own private access. There is a split-level double-bedded room, another double-bedded room, and a room for three; all have private shower and WC. Sitting room; meals available by arrangement. The enclosed garden has space for parking.

Prices s fr €40; d fr €47; t fr €57; dinner fr €18 **On Site** ♣
Nearby ⚓ 14km ♪ 35km ➹ 5km ➶ 15km Restaurant 10km ♨
⋙ 15km **Notes** No pets English spoken

ORROUY

⚜ ❦ ◎ Ferme de la Chaînée

Germaine et Daniel GAGE

60 rue de la Forêt, 60129 ORROUY

☎ 03 44 88 60 41 📄 03 44 88 92 09

email: sca.gage@wanadoo.fr

This property offers five double rooms. One room has disabled access and another an additional single bed. All rooms have en suite facilities. A vegetarian menu is available on request. Drinks not included.

Prices s fr €45; d fr €53; t fr €60; extra person fr €17; dinner fr €18
Nearby ⚓ 6km ♪ 10km ➹ 12km ➶ 10km ♨ 7km 🏛 7km ⋙ 3km
Notes No pets English spoken CC

see advert on opposite page

PIERREFONDS

⚜ Donjon House

David et Hanna BOURNE

10/12 rue Notre Dame, 60350 PIERREFONDS

☎ 03 44 42 37 59 & 06 26 37 70 73

email: donjon.house@free.fr

web: http://donjonhouse.blogspot.com

In the grounds of the château of Pierrefonds. At garden level and overlooking the château is a double with shower room. On the first floor is a family room with double and single beds and shower room. On the second floor is a large room with double bed and a divan bed with bathroom.

Prices s €60-€75; d €75-€100; t €120-€140; extra person fr
€25 **On Site** ⚓ **Nearby** ♪ 13km ➶ 17km ♨ 1km 🏛 16km
Notes No pets English spoken

⚜ L'Ermitage

Elisabeth DANDOY

74 rue de l'Impératrice Eugéni, 60350 PIERREFONDS

☎ 03 44 42 85 64

email: elizabeth.dandoy@wanadoo.fr

web: www.oisermitage.com

A house on the edge of the forest with four upstairs bedrooms: three have double beds and the fourth has twin beds; each has a private bath or shower room and WC, and a private terrace. There is a sitting room, also upstairs, and a living room with open fire on the ground floor. Accommodation for horses available.

Prices s €50-€60; d €60-€80; extra person fr €15 **On Site** ⚓ ♣
Nearby ♪ 12km ➹ 2km ➶ 5km Restaurant 3km ♨ 12km 🏛 1.5km
⋙ 12km **Notes** No pets English spoken

PLAILLY

▦ ♿ Chambre d'hôtes

Hervé et Céline PERREAU

19 rue du Docteur Laporte, 60128 PLAILLY

☎ 03 44 54 72 77 & 06 60 07 15 43 ▤ 03 44 54 72 77

email: perreau.celine@wanadoo.fr

web: www.lachasseroyale.typspod.com

Situated in its own grounds, this charming 19th-century house has three well-furnished double rooms, one with an additional single bed. In addition there are two communicating rooms, one double and one twin. The panelled dining room has an open fire, and the proprietors offer a warm welcome. Local attractions include the Parc Asterix.

Prices s €48-€58; d €58-€68; t €68-€78; extra person fr €16
On Site Restaurant **Nearby** ⚓ 5km ♨ 3km ♪ 5km ⚲ 3km ⚓ 1km
⚓ 5km ⚓ 5km **Notes** No pets English spoken

RAVENEL

▦ ⍾ Le Temps d'un Reve

P et A DERDERIAN

57 rue du Château, 60130 RAVENEL

☎ 03 44 19 05 01 & 06 61 16 83 79

email: derderian.patrick@wanadoo.fr

web: http://anneetpatrick.fr.nr

Four bedrooms in a 19th-century house, with furniture from the period. Three of the rooms are doubles, and the fourth is a two-roomed family suite for four with two double beds. All have private bath or shower room and WC. There is a living room with an open fire, and outside is a garden with space to park. Owners will meet guests at railway station.

Prices s fr €60; d fr €100; t fr €140; extra person fr €40; dinner €20-30 **Nearby** ⚓ 5km ♨ 30km ♪ 5km ⚲ ⚓ 0.5km ⚓ 5km ⚓ 5km
Notes No pets English spoken

REILLY

▦ Château de Reilly

David et Hilary GAUTHIER

60240 REILLY

☎ 03 44 49 03 05 & 06 15 22 29 54 ▤ 03 44 49 23 39

email: reilly@terre-net.fr

web: www.chateaudereilly.fr

In the heart of a medieval village, which has been awarded the title 'village que j'aime', the proprietors welcome you to the elegant sophistication of their 19th-century castle. Set in grounds of twelve hectares, there are three double bedrooms, and one suite with both double and twin beds, all en suite. There is a television lounge and hunting can be arranged for guests. Animals are welcome for a charge. Closed Xmas.

Prices s €65-€75; d €75-€85; t fr €115; extra person fr €18 **On Site** ♪
⚲ **Nearby** ⚓ 5km ♨ 4km ⚲ 4km Restaurant 4km ⚓ 3km ⚓ 3km
Notes Pets admitted English spoken CC

SAVIGNIES

🐾 ❤ ⭑ ⭑ Ferme du Colombier

J-C et A LETURQUE

14 rue du Four Jean Legros, 60650 SAVIGNIES

☎ 03 44 82 18 49 📠 03 44 82 53 70

email: ferme.colombier@wanadoo.fr

web: www.fermecolombier.org

This chambre d'hôtes offers four guest rooms housed in a converted farm building. There are two double rooms, one with child's bed, and two rooms sleeping three, each with a double and a single bed. All rooms are en suite, and additional children's beds are available on request. Food and drink is included, and reductions are available for extended stays.

Prices s fr €36; d fr €45; t fr €59; extra person fr €14; dinner €17-€22 **Nearby** ⛵ 5km ♨ 7km ♞ 6km ↘ 0.5km Restaurant 0.1km ♨ 0.5km ♞ 8km ⛺ 8km ➳ 9km **Notes** Pets admitted English spoken

ST-FELIX

⭑ ⭑ Villa les Iris

Jacqueline MARIANI

100 rue de Heilles, 60370 ST-FELIX

☎ 03 44 07 00 24 & 06 13 93 65 28 📠 03 44 07 00 24

email: jackprin@orange.fr

web: http://perso.orange.fr/chambres.dhotes/sommaire.htm

Five well-equipped rooms in the owner's 1930s Art Deco villa, set in wooded parkland. On the first floor are a double room and a room with a double and a single bed, both with balconies. On the second floor are two double rooms and a twin room. Each room is en suite, with television. Highchair and cot are available.

Prices s fr €50; d fr €65; t fr €75; extra person fr €15; dinner fr €18 **On Site** ♞ **Nearby** ⛵ 2km ↘ 10km ♞ 4km ➳ 4km **Notes** No pets English spoken CC

ST-PAUL

⭑ ⭑ Les Passereaux

Jacques et Annie BESMOND

23 rue de l'Abbaye, 60650 ST-PAUL

☎ 03 44 82 24 99 📠 03 44 82 14 91

email: lespassereaux@wanadoo.fr

web: http://perso.orange.fr/les-passereaux

This property has three guest rooms in a building separate from the owners' home. On the ground floor is a double-bedded room; upstairs there are two more doubles, with an extra single bed available if needed. All the rooms have private shower room and WC. Outside is a garden with a terrace, also parking space.

Prices s fr €39; d fr €49; extra person fr €13 **On Site** ♞ **Nearby** ⛵ 4km ♨ 6km ↘ 5km Restaurant 2km ♨ ♞ 6km ⛺ 3km ➳ 5km **Notes** No pets English spoken

THIBIVILLERS

⭑ ⭑ Le Puits d'Angle

Stéphane BEAUVIVRE

2 rue des Tilleuls, 60240 THIBIVILLERS

☎ 03 44 84 31 10 & 06 20 78 84 52

email: resa@lepuitsdangle.com

web: www.lepuitsdangle.com

Five guestrooms, with independent access, are available in this establishment, offering both rustic simplicity and luxury. Three rooms are on the first-floor of a barn, two doubles and a twin. Within the main residence are a further two rooms on the ground floor, both doubles. All rooms have private facilities, TV and wi-fi. Breakfast is served in front of the open hearth and meals are available with reservation. Turkish bath for guest use.

Prices s fr €66; d fr €76; extra person fr €20; dinner fr €25 **Nearby** ⛵ 8km ♨ 5km ♞ 8km ↘ Restaurant 8km ♨ 2km ⛺ 8km ⛺ 5km ➳ 5km **Notes** No pets English spoken

SOMME

ABBEVILLE

⭑ ⭑ *Fermette des Pres de Mautrort*

Brigitte & Joël DELAHAYE

10 Impasse de la Croix, 80100 ABBEVILLE

☎ 03 22 24 57 62 & 06 68 56 57 62 📠 03 22 24 57 62

email: brigitte.delahaye2@wanadoo.fr

web: http://perso.wanadoo.fr/lespresdemautort/

A former farmhouse in a hamlet about three kilometres from Abbeville. There are three double rooms, each with twin beds. One is in the owner's house on the ground floor, with en suite shower/WC. The other two each have independent access in a separate building: one on the ground floor has a bathroom with whirlpool bath, and kitchenette; the other is an attic room with shower/WC, kitchenette and air conditioning. Pleasant garden with covered swimming pool.

Prices not confirmed for 2008 **Nearby** ⛵ 3km ♨ 8km Sea 18km ♞ 3km ↘ ♨ 3km ⛺ 3km ➳ 3km **Notes** No pets

AILLY-SUR-NOYE

⭑ ⭑ *Les Ecuries du Val de Noye*

Grégoire BLONDEL

Passage du Hamel, Berny-sur-Noye,

80250 AILLY-SUR-NOYE

☎ 03 22 42 10 10 & 06 84 60 04 78

email: contact@ecuriesduvaldenoye.com

web: www.ecuriesduvaldenoye.com

An equestrian property in a village 15 minutes south of Amiens. On the first floor are four bedrooms, two doubles and two with three single beds. All have private shower room and WC. Meals by arrangement. Riding is available, and there is accommodation for horses.

Prices not confirmed for 2008 **On Site** ⛵ ♞ **Nearby** ↘ 10km ⛺ 3km ➳ 3km **Notes** Pets admitted

BAYONVILLERS

ⅲ ✣ La Ferme du Vent des Moissons

I & J-F DESSAINT

6 rue de Lamotte, 80170 BAYONVILLERS

☎ 03 22 85 85 84 & 06 68 71 14 15 🖹 03 22 85 85 84

email: la-ferme-du-vent-des-moissons@wanadoo.fr

web: www.leventdesmoissons.com

This village in the Somme valley is on the 'Circuit de Souvenir'. There are three bedrooms in a building separate from the owners' home. Two of the rooms are doubles, the third is a family room for four on two levels. All three have private shower and WC, and there is a shared living area with kitchenette.

Prices s fr €39; d €45-€48; t €58-€62 **Nearby** 🎣 3km ⚓ 8km Restaurant 2km 🏠 12km ⋙ 12km **Notes** No pets English spoken

BEHEN

ⅲⅲ ⅩⅠ Château de Béhen

Famille CUVELIER

8 rue du château, 80870 BEHEN

☎ 03 22 31 58 30 & 06 08 98 05 74

🖹 03 22 31 58 39

email: norbert-andre@cuvelier.com

web: www.chateau-de-behen.com

In the Vimeu Vert region, the Château de Béhen dates back to the 18th and 19th centuries. Set within a five-hectare park, this family home offers four bedrooms and two suites with TV, telephone, bathroom and wc. There is a sitting room and hall, and meals are available on request. Table tennis, horse riding and mountain biking are available and horses can be stabled. The GR125 walking route borders the property.

Prices s €95-€133; d €105-€143; t €150-€169; extra person fr €26; dinner fr €38 **On Site** ⚐ **Nearby** ⚓ 12km Sea 20km 🎣 8km ⚓ 10km 🏊 10km 🏠 10km ⋙ 10km **Notes** No pets English spoken CC

ⅲ ⅩⅠ Château des Alleux

⸱-F DE FONTANGES

⸱0870 BEHEN

☎ 03 22 31 64 88 🖹 03 22 31 64 88

⸱mail: chateaudesalleux@wanadoo.fr

⸱ the green Vimeu region, this 17th and 18th-century château is set ⸱ a large park. There is a family suite for four, a studio with a double ⸱ed and kitchen area in a separate building, and the château houses ⸱ double room. Cot and babysitting possible. Table d'hôte meals by ⸱servation; restaurant 12km. Bikes and pony rides. Reductions from ⸱e second night.

⸱rices s fr €45; d €55-€65; t fr €85; extra person fr €15; dinner fr ⸱20 **Nearby** ⚓ 8km 🎣 12km Sea 25km ⚓ 12km 🏠 12km ⋙ 12km **⸱otes** No pets English spoken CC

BELLOY-SUR-SOMME

ⅲ A la Closerie

Maryse et Hubert FLANDRE

29 rue Ch. de Gaulle, 80310 BELLOY-SUR-SOMME

☎ 03 22 51 41 05

email: contact@alacloserie.com

web: www.alacloserie.com

On the edge of the village in the main street, this traditional Picardy house offers three first floor bedrooms - one double room and two family rooms, all of which have private bath or shower room and WC. Garden with barbecue, and secure storage for motor bikes; fishing possible close by.

Prices s fr €48; d fr €57; t fr €73; extra person fr €16 **On Site** ⚓ 🎣 ⛳ **Nearby** Sea 40km ⚓ 20km Restaurant 3km 🏊 3km 🏠 0.5km ⋙ 16km **Notes** No pets English spoken

BERNAY-EN-PONTHIEU

ⅲ ✣ *La Bucaille*

Julie CHUFFART

121 rue de Bellevue, 80120 BERNAY-EN-PONTHIEU

☎ 03 22 29 92 55 & 06 86 81 89 31 🖹 03 22 29 44 68

email: julie.chuffart@ferme-bellevue.fr

web: www.ferme-bellevue.fr

In the vicinity of La Bucaille, this smallholding offers four double rooms and two mezzanine beds in a brick and white stone building, close to the owners' house. Rooms have private facilities and a lounge with kitchenette is available. Terrace with garden furniture and barbecue. A gîte can also be hired on a self-catering basis.

Prices not confirmed for 2008 **Nearby** ⚓ 5km 🎣 6km Sea 15km ⚓ 10km ⚓ 21km 🏊 5km 🏠 5km ⋙ 5km **Notes** Pets admitted English spoken CC

BLANGY-TRONVILLE

ⅲ Chambre d'hôtes

Patricia CORBIERE

9 rue Edouard Ruelle, 80440 BLANGY-TRONVILLE

☎ 03 22 47 50 64 & 06 29 35 07 12

email: corbiere.pat@wanadoo.fr

web: http://perso.orange.fr/patricia.corbiere/

Not far from the 'Circuit de Souvenir', this property has four bedrooms in converted farm buildings. Two of the rooms are doubles, two are triples (double bed and a single), and all have private shower and WC. Enclosed garden with parking space; breakfast served in the conservatory.

Prices s fr €50; d fr €65; t fr €80 **On Site** 🎣 **Nearby** ⚓ 4km 🎣 13km ⚓ 8km Restaurant 5km 🏊 7km 🏠 5km ⋙ 5km **Notes** No pets English spoken

BUIGNY-SAINT-MACLOU

⊪ Chambre d'hôtes

Sylvie & Gérard LEMOINE
6 rue du Haut, 80132 BUIGNY-ST-MACLOU
☎ 03 22 31 15 49 & 06 80 68 19 34 📄 03 22 31 15 49
email: lemoine11@wanadoo.fr
web: www.syl-ge-chambres-hotes.levillage.org

5km from the A16 exit (Abbeville Nord), this village house is opposite the church. It provides two double rooms and a room with a double and single, each with private facilities. Breakfast room, guests' lounge, courtyard, and garden. Tennis in the village.
Prices s fr €46; d fr €52; t fr €68; dinner fr €20 **Nearby** ⛷ 8km ☨ 3km Sea 13km ♂ 5km ⚲ 6km Restaurant 4km ⚓ 🏛 2km ⋙ 6km
Notes Pets admitted English spoken

BUSSY-LES-POIX

⊪ ❧ Chambre d'hôtes

Francis GUERIN
1 rue de l'Eglise, 80290 BUSSY-LES-POIX
☎ 03 22 90 06 73
email: guerin.francis@free.fr
web: http://bussy.guerin.free.fr

In a village setting, this property has three rooms on the first floor of an old farmhouse. There are two triple rooms (double and single beds) and another triple (twin beds and a child's bed). All of the rooms have a private bath or shower room and WC. Guests' lounge; garden with garden furniture.
Prices s fr €45; d fr €54; t fr €62; extra person fr €8 **Nearby** ♂ 6km ⚲ 6km Restaurant 6km ⚓ 6km 🏛 6km ⋙ 6km **Notes** Pets admitted English spoken

CAOURS

⊪ ❧ La Rivièrette

Marc & Hélène DE LAMARLIERE
2 rue de la Ferme, 80132 CAOURS
☎ 03 22 24 77 49 & 06 07 80 22 59 📄 03 22 24 76 97
email: helene-marc@voila.fr
web: www.de-lamarlierem.com

Opposite the owners' home, this renovated building offers five guest rooms with access straight into the garden running down to a river. There are four double bedrooms with an extra single bed in three, and one twin with a single; each has private facilities. Lounge with kitchen area; pets permitted for a charge. Facilities include mountain bikes, stabling, croquet, table tennis, basketball, a trampoline and an indoor swimming pool. Restaurants and tennis courts in the village.
Prices s fr €45; d fr €59; t fr €80; extra person fr €20 **On Site** 🏊 Private ⚲ **Nearby** ⛷ 4km ☨ 8km Sea 25km ♂ 4km Restaurant 0.5km ⚓ 1km 🏛 4km ⋙ 7km **Notes** Pets admitted English spoken

⊪ *Le Scardon et La Drucat*

M FLANDRIN
8 rue des Près, 80132 CAOURS
☎ 03 22 23 28 73 & 06 75 48 00 86
email: claudine.flandrin@wanadoo.fr

About 20 kilometres from the Baie de la Somme, this impressive 19th century brick-built house has been fully restored by its owners. There are four bedrooms, two with double beds and two with twin beds. All have private shower and WC, and there is a kitchenette for guest use. The extensive grounds have garden furniture, and good walks are available close by.
Prices not confirmed for 2008 **On Site** ♂ **Nearby** ⛷ 4km ☨ 12km Sea 20km ⚓ 1km 🏛 4km ⋙ 4km **Notes** Pets admitted Open Easter to 1 November. CC

CARREPUIS

⊪ Le Manoir Roses de Picardie

France MATHIEU
16 Grande Rue, 80700 CARREPUIS
☎ 03 22 87 84 84 📄 03 22 87 83 83
email: francemathieu@gmail.com

This manor house is situated within a lovely two and a half hectare park. There are three doubles, one part of a suite with a lounge area with sofa-bed, and one room with two double beds, all with private facilities. Breakfast is served in the owners' house. Boules pitch, children's play area, garden furniture, barbecue, garage, pony trekking, fencing lessons, table d'hôte meals by prior arrangement.

Prices s fr €50; d fr €55; t fr €70; extra person fr €15   **Nearby** ✖ 5km ↧30km ℘2km ↗1km Restaurant 2km ⌕2km ⇶13km   **Notes** Pets admitted English spoken

---

CAYEUX-SUR-MER

⌗ ⊙ *Les Années Folles*

Hélène DEBEAURAIN
270 Av Parmentier, Brighton-les-Pins,
80410 CAYEUX-SUR-MER
☎ 03 22 26 30 71 ▤ 03 22 26 32 35
email: helene.debeaurain@lesanneesfolles.com
web: http://lesanneesfolles.com

This is a big 1930s house, complete with lift! On the first floor is a double bedroom, linking through to a single; and a two-roomed suite for four with two double beds. There are two further similar suites on the second floor and two studio rooms in an annexe. All rooms have private facilities. Large grounds, terrace, garden furniture.

Prices not confirmed for 2008   **Nearby** ✖ 2km ↧15km Sea 0.3km ℘2km ↗14km ⌕2km ⓐ2km ⇶15km   **Notes** Pets admitted English spoken Open February to December.

⌗ Les Portes du Hable

Miguel BEAUDELIN
Route des Canadiens, 80410 CAYEUX-SUR-MER
☎ 03 22 26 58 74 & 06 73 40 29 43 ▤ 03 22 26 58 74
email: lesportes.duhable@wanadoo.fr
web: www.lesportesduhable.com

Three bedrooms, and a first-floor suite with private access, are available in this house just a stone's throw from Cayeux-sur-Mer. Two rooms are family size with small double and bunk beds in the living area, shower room and WC; the third room is a small double with shower/WC. The suite comprises two small double rooms, salon, shower and WC. Play area for children, two garages for closed parking. Pets by arrangement.

Prices s fr €56; d €63-€77; t €79-€111   **On Site** ⓔ   **Nearby** ✖ 1km ↧20km Sea 2km ℘3km ↗12km Restaurant 1km ⌕3km ⓐ2km ⇶15km   **Notes** Pets admitted

---

CITERNES

⌗ Château de Yonville

Philippe DES FORTS
rue de Yonville, 80490 CITERNES
☎ 03 22 28 61 16 ▤ 03 22 28 61 16
email: des.forts-philippe@wanadoo.fr
web: www.chateaudeyonville.com/

Situated in the hamlet of Yonville in the middle of a fifteen-hectare park, this property offers three guest rooms - two double bedrooms and one twin - each with private facilities and an extra bed on request. A kitchenette, lounge area and conservatory are available for guests' use. Reductions for extended stays.

Prices s fr €60; d fr €60; extra person fr €15   **Nearby** ✖ 5km ↧19km Sea 35km ℘12km ↗19km Restaurant 5km ⌕ ⓔ19km ⓐ5km ⇶15km   **Notes** No pets English spoken

---

COCQUEREL

⌗ La Grange

Maurice CREPIN
2 rue de Francières, 80510 COCQUEREL
☎ 03 22 31 82 00 ▤ 03 22 31 82 00
email: crepin.maurice@wanadoo.fr
web: http//:perso.orange.fr/lagrange.cocquerel

Located in the Somme Valley, on the outskirts of a village near d'Ailly-le-Haut-Clocher. Four guest rooms, each with private facilities, are available in a brick farm building near the owners' house. There is one twin and three double rooms, one with an extra single and one with kitchen area. The plant-lined courtyard has garden furniture and parking and pets are admitted by prior arrangement.

Prices s fr €34; d fr €44; t fr €50   **Nearby** ✖ 10km Sea 35km ℘2km ↗10km Restaurant 7km ⌕4km ⓔ4km ⓐ4km ⇶8km   **Notes** Pets admitted English spoken

---

COURCELLES-AU-BOIS

⌗ L'Amartinierre

Christine & Pierre PECOURT
1 rue de Mailly, 80560 COURCELLES-AU-BOIS
☎ 03 22 76 48 09 & 06 08 65 90 20 ▤ 03 22 76 48 09
email: lamartinierre@club-internet.fr
web: http://membres.lycos.fr/lamartinierre/

In a brick-built building facing the hosts' house are three rooms, all with shower and WC. On the ground floor, a family-size room with two small doubles; upstairs, a small double and a twin. Breakfast room with kitchenette. Bikes can be hired; garage parking. Visit to deer farm next door can be arranged.

Prices s fr €35; d fr €45; t fr €53; extra person fr €7   **Nearby** ✖ 7km ℘10km ↗15km Restaurant 13km ⓐ5km ⇶13km   **Notes** Pets admitted English spoken

---

CURLU

⌗ ▼ ⊙ ⟐ Le Pré Fleuri

Christiane et Gérard PLAQUET
11 rue de Maurepas, 80360 CURLU
☎ 03 22 84 16 16 & 06 77 18 80 54 ▤ 03 22 83 14 67
email: leprefleuri@yahoo.fr
web: www.leprefleuri.com

Situated in the Haute-Somme Valley, six rooms available include two double rooms, two twins and two rooms sleeping three and four, all with private facilities. There is a lounge for guests' use, table d'hôte meals on request, a private pond for carp fishing and bikes for hire. TGV station 17 km (pick up possible).

Prices s fr €40; d fr €50; t fr €65; dinner fr €22   **Nearby** ✖ 4km ↧10km ℘2km ↗10km Restaurant 0.2km ⌕10km ⓔ14km ⓐ0.3km ⇶10km   **Notes** No pets English spoken

DOMVAST

☰ ℺ *Le Bien Venant*

Marie & Christian PETIT
4 route de St Riquier, 80150 DOMVAST
☎ 03 22 31 09 62 & 06 79 40 29 12
email: marie-pierre@lebien-venant.com
web: www.lebien-venant.com

This 19th-century farmhouse stands in seven hectares of grounds. In a separate building, it has five rooms, all of them with a split level layout, sleeping from two to four people. All rooms have a private bath or shower room and WC. There is a guests' lounge area in a former stable; breakfast is served here, in the hosts' house, or on the terrace.

Prices not confirmed for 2008 **Nearby** ☘ 5km ↧ 12km Sea 25km ⬮ 10km ↰ 12km ☐ 1km 🏠 7km ⚒ 12km **Notes** No pets English spoken

DOULLENS

☰ ℺ **Chambre d'hôtes**

Françoise DE MUYT
Route d'Albert - D938, Hameau de Freschevillers, 80600 DOULLENS
☎ 03 22 77 15 56 & 06 64 95 67 22 ᠍ 03 22 77 15 56

This property is in the hamlet of Freschevillers, two kilometres from Doullens. It has three first floor bedrooms, all in the owners' house, but with independent access. Two of the rooms are doubles; the third has a double bed and a single. All have private shower room/WC and a TV socket. Guests' lounge, kitchenette, garden furniture.

Prices s fr €35; d €45-€52; t fr €60; extra person fr €20; dinner fr €18 **On Site** ⬮ **Nearby** ☘ 6km ↧ 30km ↰ 3km Restaurant 3km ☐ 3km 🎿 3km 🏠 3km ⚒ 30km **Notes** No pets

DRUCAT

☰ **La Houssaye**

Hélène D'AMECOURT
183 rue du Levant, 80132 DRUCAT
☎ 03 22 31 27 44 & 06 84 62 02 24 ᠍ 03 22 24 82 17
email: h.damecourt@wanadoo.fr
web: www.lahoussaye.com

In a village six kilometres from Abbeville, this house is surrounded by two hectares of wooded grounds. On the first floor is a twin-bedded room; on the second floor is a double-bedded room, and a room which can be arranged with a double bed or twins. Possibility of additional linked rooms. All of the rooms have a private bathroom and WC.

Prices s fr €60; d fr €76; t fr €130 **Nearby** Sea 17km ⬮ 13km ↰ 6km 🏠 6km ⚒ 6km **Notes** No pets English spoken Open March to 15 December.

DURY

☰ **Chambre d'hôtes**

Maryse et Alain SAGUEZ
2 rue Grimaux, 80480 DURY
☎ 03 22 95 29 52 ᠍ 03 22 95 29 52
email: alain.saguez@wanadoo.fr
web: http://perso.wanadoo.fr/am.saguez

Four bedrooms are available at this property: one twin, one double, one room with double and single and a suite with an adjoining double and twin, all with private facilities. A cot is also available. There is a lounge with TV, a living room, parking available and an excellent restaurant in the village. Outings in a horse-drawn carriage are available.

Prices s fr €55; d €70-€78 **On Site** ☘ **Nearby** ↧ 3km ⬮ 5km ↰ 5km Restaurant 0.1km ☐ 5km 🏠 0.1km ⚒ 6km **Notes** No pets English spoken

ESTREBOEUF

☰ **Ch'vrais Paradis**

Marie-Christine HOUART
15 route de Gamaches, 80230 ESTREBOEUF
☎ 03 22 26 80 61 & or 06 08 98 06 29
email: jacques.houart@wanadoo.fr
web: http://perso.wanadoo.fr/jacques.houart/

In a village near La Baie de Somme, four rooms are offered in the owners' house - three doubles and one with a double and single bed all en suite (extra bed on request). Facilities include a lounge/sitting room, flower-filled garden with furniture and stream for fishing, parking, bikes and barbecue. Restaurants in nearby Saint-Valery.

Prices s fr €44; d fr €50; t fr €65; extra person fr €20 **On Site** ⬮ **Nearby** ☘ 15km ↧ 20km Sea 17km ↰ 11km Restaurant 4km ☐ 4km 🏠 3km ⚒ 7km **Notes** No pets English spoken

FAVIERES

⁂ Chambre d'hôtes

Yvette DELAUNAY

773 rue de Romaine, 80120 FAVIERES

☎ 03 22 27 21 07 & 06 19 30 70 11 🖹 03 22 27 21 07

email: f.feron@wanadoo.fr

web: www.lesgarennes.com

This accommodation is in a newly built wing next to the main house and comprises three doubles and one twin, each with private facilities. There is a guests' lounge, parking, bike shed, barbecue and good quality restaurant in the village. Small pets may be allowed. Holiday tax is payable.

Prices not confirmed for 2008 **Nearby** ⚑ 4km ⚑ 6km Sea 4km ∥ 4km ⚑ 10km ⚐ 4km 🏠 4km 🚶 4km **Notes** Pets admitted

⁂ La Vieille Forge

C et F QUENNEHEN

930 rue des Forges, 80120 FAVIERES

☎ 03 22 27 75 58

email: lavieilleforge@wanadoo.fr

web: http://lavieilleforge.free.fr

Three rooms converted from an old forge alongside the owners' house: a ground-floor triple (double bed and single), and two doubles upstairs, all with shower room/wc. Further rooms available in another building. Breakfast room in the forge shared with the hosts; living room and kitchenette.

Prices not confirmed for 2008 **Nearby** ⚑ 4km ⚑ 15km Sea 4km ∥ 4km ⚑ 15km ⚐ 4km 🏠 4km 🚶 4km **Notes** Pets admitted

FAY

⁂ ❦ ⚏ Chambre d'hôtes

Bruno ETEVE

2 Grande Rue, 80200 FAY

☎ 03 22 85 20 53 🖹 03 22 85 91 94

This post-war house is situated on a smallholding and has a twin room and two doubles with private facilities. A cot is available and meals can be provided on request. The lounge has a library area and TV, or guests can relax in the garden. Private parking; restaurant 12 km and the Museum of the Great War at Péronne is nearby.

Prices not confirmed for 2008 **Nearby** ∥ 5km ⚑ 12km 🏠 12km 🚶 2km **Notes** No pets English spoken

FOREST-MONTIERS

⁂ Ferme de la Mottelette

Yves MANIER

80120 FOREST-MONTIERS

☎ 03 22 28 32 33 🖹 03 22 28 34 97

email: contact@la-mottelette.com

web: www.la-mottelette.com

This farmhouse is in an isolated position, near Rue. A separate entrance leads to the first floor, where there is a double room, and a

room with two double beds. These rooms both have TV and en suite facilities. There are also two grade 2 doubles, with en suite showers, but with WCs accessed via a corridor. Extra bed; kitchenette available for evening use.

Prices s €45-€50; d €50-€55; t fr €68 **On Site** ⚏ **Nearby** ⚑ 3km ⚑ 4km Sea 10km ∥ 2km ⚑ 8km Restaurant 3km ⚐ 2km 🏠 3km 🚶 3km **Notes** Pets admitted English spoken

⁂ ⚏ La Tour Blanche

Famille LEGRU

10 rue de la Ville, 80120 FOREST-MONTIERS

☎ 03 22 23 69 13 & 06 88 61 31 62

email: info@latourblanche.net

web: www.latourblanche.net

An 18th-century manor house set in parkland near the A16. There are four individually decorated double bedrooms on the first floor each with a private bathroom. Open fires and wood panelling are features of the rooms. Generous breakfasts are served in the dining room, and there's a lounge with games table. Children's play area, horse boxes and pony riding lessons. Pets welcome (by arrangement). Meals by arrangement.

Prices s fr €80; d fr €90; t fr €115; extra person fr €25; dinner fr €46 **On Site** ⚏ **Nearby** ⚑ 3km ⚑ 8km Sea 10km ∥ 5km ⚑ 18km Restaurant 3km ⚐ 5km 🏠 3km 🚶 6km **Notes** Pets admitted English spoken

FRANSART

⁂ Chambre d'hôtes

A & H DE BOUTEVILLE

1 rue Neuve, 80700 FRANSART

☎ 03 22 87 40 37 & 06 23 72 61 95

email: chateaudefransart@free.fr

web: http://chateaudefransart.free.fr

CONTINUED

FRANSART CONTINUED

This old family house was rebuilt after the 1914-18 war, and stands in three hectares of wooded grounds with 75 species of trees. There are three first-floor rooms: one with twin beds, and two rooms each with a double bed and a single. They all have a private bath or shower room and WC. Cot and child's bed available. Lounge, garden furniture, bikes.

Prices s fr €50; d fr €60; t fr €75; extra person fr €15; dinner fr €25
On Site ℘ **Nearby** ♿ 7km Restaurant 8km ♨ 8km 🏛 8km 🚣 12km
Notes No pets Open February to October.

FRESNES-MAZANCOURT

⠿ ⍥ *Chambre d'hôtes*

Martine WARLOP
1 rue Génermont, 80320 FRESNES-MAZANCOURT
☎ 03 22 85 49 49 📄 03 22 85 49 49
email: martine.warlop@wanadoo.fr
web: www.maison-warlop.com

This architect-designed house stands in a village and offers five bedrooms: one family room with a double bed and two singles, two bedrooms sleeping two and a further double has a communicating door with a twin room, all with private facilities. Large guest lounge and meals and cookery classes can be provided. The TGV station and autoroute are 6 km.

Prices not confirmed for 2008 **Nearby** ℘ 10km ⚲ 10km 🏛 10km
🚣 7km **Notes** No pets English spoken

FRISE

⠿ *Chambre d'hôtes*

Bernard DECROIX
24 rue Blaise Cendrars, 80340 FRISE
☎ 03 22 84 46 76 & 06 86 08 40 90 📄 03 22 84 46 76
email: bedecroix@wanadoo.fr
web: www.maison-decroix.com

Four guest rooms have been converted in a building opposite the hosts' house. On the ground floor with direct access to the terrace is a double with additional hidden bed, shower room and WC; on the first floor are a double and a triple, and a large room for four with kitchenette and sitting room; all have shower/WC. Reception room with kitchenette on ground floor. Pets by arrangement. Fishing in village.

Prices not confirmed for 2008 **On Site** ℘ **Nearby** ⚲ 10km 🏛 9km
🚣 10km **Notes** Pets admitted English spoken Open March to October.

⠿ 🐾 ⍥ *La Ferme de l'Ecluse*

Anik LEPINE
1 rue Mony, 80340 FRISE
☎ 03 22 84 59 70 & 06 16 36 25 87 📄 03 22 83 17 56
email: anik7@wanadoo.fr
web: http://lafermedelecluse.com

Situated on a smallholding in the Haute Somme Valley; this property is ideal for fishing, with ponds reserved for guest fishing nearby. The three en suite guest rooms (doubles, one with extra single) have a terrace and views over the ponds. The lounge has a TV and library, an open fireplace and an eating area. Meals can be supplied on request.

Prices not confirmed for 2008 **On Site** ℘ **Nearby** ⚲ 10km 🏛 7km
🚣 20km **Notes** No pets English spoken

GAPENNES

⠿ *La Nicoulette*

Solange NICOLLE
7 rue de St Riquier, 80150 GAPENNES
☎ 03 22 28 92 77 & 06 07 32 86 75
email: nicoulette@wanadoo.fr
web: http://monsite.wanadoo.fr/nicoulette

This property has five individually decorated rooms. In the owners' house is a room which can be arranged with twin beds or a double. In a separate building are four doubles, one of which also has twin beds on a mezzanine. All rooms have a private shower and WC. Breakfast room available for guests' use; terrace and large enclosed garden.

Prices d fr €78; t fr €90; extra person fr €15 **Nearby** ♿ 0.1km ⚲ 20km
Sea 25km ℘ 13km ⚲ 13km Restaurant 5km ♨ 5km 🏛 13km 🚣 13km
Notes Pets admitted English spoken Open March to October.

HATTENCOURT

⠿ *La Fontaine aux Iris*

J-J & M GONTHIER
7 rue de Fresnoy, 80700 HATTENCOURT
☎ 03 22 87 33 58 & 06 78 94 84 73
email: gonthierjj@wanadoo.fr
web: http://monsite.orange.fr/fontaine-aux-iris

There are three bedrooms at this property, in a separate building from the owners' home. Two of the rooms are doubles, with access from the living room; the third is a split-level room. All have bath or shower room and WC, and baby equipment is available. Garden with furniture and parking space.

Prices s €45-€50; d €50-€55; t €70-€80; extra person €15-€20
Nearby ♿ 6km ⚲ 40km ℘ 20km ⚲ 9km Restaurant 6km ♨ 6km
🏛 6km 🚣 12km **Notes** No pets English spoken

HEBECOURT

⠿ *Ferme du Bois*

N & P GLORIEUX-MALVOISIN
13 rue de la Vallée, 80680 HEBECOURT
☎ 03 22 42 73 62 & 06 88 79 42 60
email: earl.glorieux@wanadoo.fr
web: www.isasite.net/ferme-du-bois

This is a working farm on the edge of a village ten kilometres south of Amiens. In a converted outbuilding are four bedrooms: two doubles, one with disabled access, another double room which also has a folding bed, and a room for four with a double bed and two singles. All have private shower/WC. Covered parking, stabling for horses.

Prices s fr €55; d fr €60; extra person fr €18 **Nearby** ♿ 4km ⚲ 5km
℘ 4km ⚲ 10km Restaurant 0.5km ♨ 10km 🏛 10km 🚣 10km
Notes No pets

JUMEL

♿ Ferme Saint-Nicolas

M. COTEL
80250 JUMEL
☎ 03 22 42 74 85 & 06 22 37 26 67 ▤ 03 22 42 07 17
email: brigittecotel@wanadoo.fr
web: www.gite-leshirondelles.com

Four guest bedrooms with independent access are available at the entrance to Saint-Nicolas farm, a former monastery. Ground floor double with shower room and WC. Upstairs three doubles, all with fixed showers and separate WC. Large enclosed garden, garden rooms. Secure or garage parking on request. Games room. Pets by arrangement.

Prices s fr €42; d fr €55; t fr €65 **Nearby** ⚓ 5km ⚓ 15km ⚓ 6km
⚓ 17km ⚓ 5km ⚓ 5km ⚓ 5km **Notes** Pets admitted English spoken

L'ETOILE

Chambre d'hôtes

Janine et Laurent MERCHAT
10 rue Saint-Martin, 80830 L'ETOILE
☎ 03 22 51 02 84 ▤ 03 22 51 02 84

This renovated Picardy home in the Somme Valley offers two double rooms, one with bunk beds, and a room with one double bed and one single, all with private facilities. There is a TV, patio area, parking in an enclosed courtyard and 1.3 hectares of parkland surrounding with a pond and tennis court. Table d'hôte meals available by prior arrangement.

Prices not confirmed for 2008 **On Site** ⚓ **Nearby** Sea 40km
⚓ 25km ⚓ 5km ⚓ 5km **Notes** Pets admitted English spoken

LA CHAUSSEE-TIRANCOURT

Chambre d'hôtes

François CARRENCOTTE
rue à l'Avoine, 80310 LA CHAUSSEE-TIRANCOURT
☎ 03 22 51 44 37 & 06 81 96 37 59 ▤ 03 22 51 44 37
email: francois.carrencote@wanadoo.fr

Three double rooms in a former presbytery, near the owner's home. Each has private facilities and access to the garden with furniture. Guests may use the lounge and breakfast rooms and enjoy fishing in the nearby Chaussée ponds.

Prices s fr €40; d fr €49; dinner fr €20 **On Site** ⚓ **Nearby** ⚓ 1km
⚓ 25km Sea 40km ⚓ 15km Restaurant 1km ⚓ 15km ⚓ 1km ⚓ 1km
Notes Pets admitted English spoken

LA FALOISE

⚓ ♿ Couleur et Jardin

M C SERRAZ
22 rue de l'Eglise, 80250 LA FALOISE
☎ 03 22 41 41 88 & 06 86 86 86 80 ▤ 03 22 41 41 88
email: contact@couleuretjardin.com
web: www.couleuretjardin.com

In a small quiet village south of Amiens, this house has five rooms with themed decorations and painted furniture. On the ground floor is a twin-bedded room with disabled access; upstairs there is a further twin-bedded room, a double, and two triples (double and single beds). All have private facilities. Lounge, dining room, garden and parking.

Prices s fr €55; d fr €65; t fr €80; dinner fr €20 **On Site** ⚓
Nearby ⚓ 5km ⚓ 20km ⚓ 8km Restaurant 8km ⚓ 3km ⚓ 8km
⚓ 8km **Notes** Pets admitted English spoken

LAMOTTE-BULEUX

⚓ Domaine d'Isis et de Robinson

J et V TROLET-THERASSE
798 rue de Canchy, 80150 LAMOTTE-BULEUX
☎ 03 22 20 47 63 & 06 20 81 42 65 ▤ 03 22 20 47 63
email: isisetrobinson@wanadoo.fr
web: www.isis-et-robinson.com

An equestrian property on the edge of a village. There are three bedrooms, all on the first floor of the owners' house, each with twin beds and a double. All have private shower room and WC. Breakfast can be served in the lounge or outside on the terrace. There is accommodation for horses, and riding is available with a qualified instructor.

Prices s fr €46; d fr €56; t fr €70; extra person fr €15; dinner fr €20 **On Site** ⚓ **Nearby** ⚓ 10km Sea 16km ⚓ 7km ⚓ 11km Restaurant 3km ⚓ 5km ⚓ 10km ⚓ 3km ⚓ 10km **Notes** No pets
English spoken

LE CROTOY

✷✷✷ **La Maison Bleue en Baie**

Rosana CESSAC

12 rue de la Croix, 80550 LE CROTOY

☎ 03 22 27 73 86 📄 03 22 27 73 86

email: la.maison.bleue@baie-de-somme.fr

web: www.baie-de-somme.fr

A large house which is about 100 years old, right in the centre of Le Crotoy, not far from the harbour and the attractive beach. Three bedrooms, all upstairs, are brightly and individually decorated. Sitting room with TV and books. Outside is a flowery patio where breakfast can be served in good weather. Bike hire available.

Prices s €52-€82; d €75-€98; extra person fr €15 **On Site** ⚓ Sea 🏖 **Nearby** ⚘ 20km ⚓ 🚶 7km **Notes** No pets English spoken

✷✷✷ *La Villa Marine*

Isabelle DEWASTE

14-16 rue du Phare, 80550 LE CROTOY

☎ 03 22 27 84 56 & 06 88 46 75 68 📄 03 22 27 84 56

email: villamarine@wanadoo.fr

web: www.villamarine.com

In the heart of Le Crotoy, 100m from the sea, this 1930s villa has been totally renovated to provide comfortable guest accommodation: two double bedrooms, one room with a double and a single and a suite with one double bed and lounge. All rooms have private facilities and a cot is available. Lounge for guests, mountain bikes for hire and restaurant nearby.

Prices not confirmed for 2008 **On Site** ⚓ Sea 🏖 **Nearby** ⚘ 10km 🏖 20km ⚓ 🚶 8km **Notes** No pets English spoken

✷✷✷ *Les Abris Côtiers*

Pierrick LUKOWSKI

7 rue des Roulettes, 80550 LE CROTOY

☎ 03 22 27 09 45 & 06 07 58 77 13

email: contact@abris-cotiers.com

web: www.abris-cotiers.com

Only a stone's throw from the beach, next to the sports centre, this 1930s house has been renovated to provide four guest rooms with shower and WC: a double on the ground floor, two doubles and a twin on the first floor, one of which has a balcony. Living room, furnished terrace and garden. Pets by arrangement.

Prices not confirmed for 2008 **On Site** ⚓ Sea 🏖 **Nearby** ⚘ 15km 🏖 15km ⚓ 🚶 8km **Notes** Pets admitted

MACHY

✷✷✷ *Chambre d'hôtes*

M PETIT

141 route Départementale 938, 80150 MACHY

☎ 03 22 29 98 92

email: petitbrigitte@free.fr

web: http://petitbrigitte.free.fr

This 18th-century house, which stands on the edge of the village, has three bedrooms. On the ground floor is a double-bedded room, and a suite with two double beds. Upstairs is a room with three single beds. All rooms have a private shower room and WC. Extra bed available. Lounge available for guests' use. Enclosed garden with flowers and furniture. Stabling.

Prices not confirmed for 2008 **Nearby** Sea 14km 🏖 2km ⚓ 14km 🏖 6km 🚶 7km **Notes** Pets admitted English spoken

MAILLY-MAILLET

✷✷✷ 🍽 **Les Bieffes**

Paulette PECOURT

27 rue Pierre Lefebvre, 80560 MAILLY-MAILLET

☎ 03 22 76 21 44 📄 03 22 76 21 44

On the outskirts of a village bordering the D919 for Amiens and Arras this large house was used as a hospital during World War I. It now offers two twin rooms and a triple, with possible child's bed, a lounge TV room and garden with furniture. Small animals allowed. Some English spoken.

Prices s fr €33; d fr €44; t fr €55; extra person fr €15; dinner fr €24 **Nearby** 🏖 4km ⚓ 12km 🏖 13km 🚶 13km **Notes** Pets admitted

MONCHY-LAGACHE

✷✷✷ 🍽 **Le Château**

Jean-Luc DEQUIN

2 rue du 8 mai 1945, 80200 MONCHY-LAGACHE

☎ 03 22 85 08 49 & 06 88 99 92 55 📄 03 22 85 28 23

email: info@chateau-monchy.com

web: www.chateau-monchy.com

Opposite the 12th century church in the village, this château was buil in 1928 and is set in an enclosed park. There are three double rooms a single room with a child's room adjacent and a room with a double and two single beds. Each has private facilities. Dining room, lounge with fireplace, reading and kitchen areas, parking, table d'hôte meals by reservation. Fixed price activity weekends. Animals accepted by arrangement.

Prices s fr €50; d fr €60; t fr €85; dinner fr €22 **On Site** 🍽
Nearby ⚑ 3km ⚓ 30km ✎ 1km ⚲ 10km Restaurant 12km 🎣 1km
🏊 12km ⚐ 20km **Notes** Pets admitted English spoken Open to 15 January to 15 December.

NAOURS

🍴 🐓 🍳 Au Logis de l'Oie

Stéphanie et Gérard SOIRANT

10 rue du Cul de Sac, 80260 NAOURS

☎ 03 22 93 72 62 & 06 67 02 67 81 📄 03 22 93 08 85

email: gaecduplouy@wanadoo.fr

web: http://monsite.wanadoo.fr/aulogisdeloie/

An annexe of this restored Picardy farmhouse houses two double rooms, a twin and a family room with two double beds, a single and a mezzanine. Each has private facilities. There is a kitchen area, lounge with TV and books, and breakfasts are served in the living room. Mini-golf and restaurant in the village. Table d'hôte meals by reservation. Animals admitted by arrangement.

Prices s fr €35; d fr €45; t fr €65; extra person fr €10; dinner fr €18
On Site ⚑ **Nearby** ⚓ 0.5km ✎ 5km ⚲ 15km Restaurant 10km 🎣 4km ⚐ 18km **Notes** Pets admitted English spoken

NOYELLES-SUR-MER

🍴 🐓 🍳 Chambres a La Ferme

M CREPIN

rue Violette Szabo, 80860 NOYELLES-SUR-MER

☎ 03 22 23 40 96 & 06 10 56 43 95 📄 03 22 23 49 89

email: chambresalaferme@wanadoo.fr

web: www.chambresalaferme.com

A converted stable block is the setting for these four bedrooms, three doubles and a family room for four (double bed plus singles). All the rooms have private shower and WC. Breakfast is served in the living room which has a microwave for guest use. Fridge space also available.

Prices s fr €45; d fr €55; t fr €65; extra person fr €10 **Nearby** ⚑ 6km
⚓ 6km Sea 8km ✎ 1km ⚲ 13km Restaurant 6km 🎣 6km 🏊 4km
⚐ 0.3km **Notes** Pets admitted English spoken

🍴 La Criste Marine

M. DE LA SERRE

9 rue du Général de Gaulle, 80860 NOYELLES-SUR-MER

☎ 03 22 23 61 25 & 06 76 57 31 52

email: lacristemarine@hotmail.com

web: www.lacristemarine.com

Rooms are offered in the building at the entrance to this property near a village. They include two rooms with a double and a single bed, a double room and a twin room. Breakfast is taken in the owner's home. Parking on site.

Prices s €50-€60; d €55-€65 **Nearby** ⚑ 6km ⚓ 6km Sea 5km ✎ 5km
⚲ 13km 🎣 6km 🏊 6km ⚐ 1km **Notes** No pets English spoken Open March to November.

OCHANCOURT

🍴 Chambre d'hôtes

Jacques HUGOT

38 rue de Paris, 80210 OCHANCOURT

☎ 03 22 30 24 98

email: mf.hugot@wanadoo.fr

web: www.hugotine.fr.fm

Just 10 km from the Baie de Somme, this house offers a double bedroom, twin room and a double bedroom with a communicating door to a twin room, all with private facilities and entrances. There is a terrace with garden furniture, garage, enclosed garden and a barbecue.

Prices s fr €45; d fr €52; t fr €70; extra person fr €17 **Nearby** ⚑ 6km
⚓ 20km Sea 10km ✎ 15km ⚲ 5km Restaurant 5km 🎣 5km 🏊 4km
⚐ 20km **Notes** No pets

🍴 🐓 ♿ Ferme du Bois d'Hantecourt

E WYNANDS

13 rue de Paris, 80210 OCHANCOURT

☎ 03 22 30 25 53 & 06 84 83 20 13 📄 03 22 20 43 67

email: ewynands@momont.com

Four bedrooms with private access are available in this renovated Picardy farmhouse: two double bedrooms, one twin and one triple, all en suite. A barbecue and garden furniture is available for guests' use. Private parking is available.

Prices s fr €40; d fr €50; t fr €65; extra person fr €15 **Nearby** ⚑ 6km
⚓ 15km Sea 8km ✎ 12km ⚲ 6km Restaurant 6km 🎣 8km 🏊 3km
⚐ 3km **Notes** Pets admitted English spoken

PICARDY

OMIECOURT

⊞ Château d'Omiécourt

Dominique DE THEZY

Route de Chaulnes, 80320 OMIECOURT

☎ 03 22 83 01 75 🖹 03 22 83 09 56

email: thezy@terre-net.fr

web: www.chateau-omiecourt.com

Situated in a village with views over a 16-hectare park, this château offers two double bedrooms and one twin (en suite) and a two-bedroom suite comprising a double and twin room share a wc. There is a dining room where evening meals are available on request; a garden with furniture, children's games (table tennis, table football, board games) and parking. Golf driving range on site.

Prices s €65-€80; d €80-€95; t €100-€120; extra person €20-€25
On Site 🏊 **Nearby** ⛵15km ♨30km 🎣10km ⚓ Restaurant 13km
🏛3km ⛽6km **Notes** No pets English spoken CC

PORT-LE-GRAND

⊞ Bois de Bonance

Jacques et Myriam MAILLARD

80132 PORT-LE-GRAND

☎ 03 22 24 11 97 & 06 07 66 90 03 🖹 03 22 31 72 01

email: maillard.chambrehote@bonance.com

web: www.bonance.com

This fine 19th-century brick house, with a family swimming pool, is situated in the middle of a beautiful landscaped garden. There is a twin room, two suites with two twin rooms, a double and two twin bedrooms. Some rooms have private facilities and a cot is available.

Prices s fr €65; d fr €78; extra person fr €23 **On Site** 🏊
Nearby ⛵4km ♨4km Sea 10km 🎣5km ⚓ Restaurant 9km ♨
🏛8km ⛽9km **Notes** Pets admitted English spoken Open March to October. CC

QUEND

⊞ 🌿 🍽 *Ferme de la Motte*

Famille BOUTIN

38 route de Froise, Monchaux, 80120 QUEND

☎ 03 22 27 76 71 🖹 03 22 23 67 09

email: fermelamotte@aol.com

web: http://fermedelamotte.net

Just two kilometres from the beach at Quend, there are four rooms on this 18th-century Picardy farm in a building close to your hosts' house. On the ground floor are two triples with access to the courtyard and terrace, one with bathroom/WC, the other with shower/WC. Upstairs is a triple room on two levels, and another triple, both with shower/WC. Breakfast served in the farmhouse. Cot, horse-boxes; cycles for hire. Reductions for longer stays.

Prices not confirmed for 2008 **Nearby** ⛵5km ♨2km Sea 2km 🎣2km
⚓2km ♨2km 🏛2km ⛽8km **Notes** Pets admitted English spoken CC

RUE

⊞ 🌿 La Mare aux Iris

M. PETIT

262 Becquerel, 80120 RUE

☎ 03 22 25 03 98 🖹 03 22 25 03 98

email: la.mare.aux.iris@orange.fr

web: http://lamareauxiris.monsite.wanadoo.fr

A 19th-century Colomages farmhouse, surrounded by grounds of 1.2 hectares with flower filled garden and furniture, terrace and parking. Rooms available include two doubles and two doubles with singles, each with private facilities. Living room with lounge corner with fireplace. Near Somme Bay; the Marqenterre bird sanctuary, brick and shingle dovecote. Two Henson horses live on site.

Prices d €54-€62; t €70-€75; extra person fr €15 **Nearby** ⛵1km
♨12km Sea 5km 🎣2km ⚓10km Restaurant 1km ♨2km 🏛1km
⛽2km **Notes** No pets English spoken

⊞ 🍽 Le Thurel

Claudine et Patrick VAN BREE

80120 RUE

☎ 03 22 25 04 44 & 06 16 75 44 98 🖹 03 22 25 79 69

email: lethurel.relais@libertysurf.fr

web: www.lethurel.com

This small 19th-century manor house is surrounded by a 2.5 hectare park. There are three double en suite rooms and a family suite, with a double and twin room sharing a bathroom. The lounge has an open fireplace; there is a dining room, pond for private fishing, mountain bike hire, parking area and kennels and stables available.

Prices d €84-€95; t fr €135; extra person fr €27; dinner fr €29
On Site 🏊 **Nearby** ⛵7km ♨10km Sea 12km 🎣3km ⚓10km
Restaurant 2km ♨2km 🏛2km ⛽1.5km **Notes** No pets English spoken CC

SAIGNEVILLE

♯♯♯ Le Presbytere

Corinne et Franck SOUCHON
3 rue de la Falise, 80230 SAIGNEVILLE
☎ 03 22 60 98 34 & 06 85 59 89 55 📄 03 22 60 98 34
email: souchon.franck@akeonet.com
web: http://lepresbytere.akeonet.com/

A former presbytery, fully restored and within enclosed gardens, in a quiet village seven kilometres from St-Valéry-sur-Somme. There are four bedrooms - two double-bedded rooms, a twin-bedded room, and a family room for four with a double bed and two singles. Breakfast is served in the bright and attractive living room.

Prices d fr €58; t fr €75; extra person fr €10   **Nearby** ⚌ 20km ⚲ 6km
Sea 8km ⚓ 2km ⚒ 8km Restaurant 8km ⚑ 8km 🏢 3km ⋙ 8km
Notes Pets admitted   English spoken

SAINS-EN-AMIENOIS

♯♯♯ Les Bruyères

Nathalie VAGNIEZ
Ferme de Mamont, 80680 SAINS-EN-AMIENOIS
☎ 03 22 09 51 05 & 06 81 66 14 28
email: contact@chambre-hotes-bruyeres.com
web: www.chambre-hotes-bruyeres.com

Three guest bedrooms are available in a former farmhouse next to the owners' house, in enormous grounds including 120 hectares of woodland and 200 hectares of grassland. Ground floor double bed splits into two singles, bathroom and WC. Double with shower room and WC. Upstairs double (or two singles) under the eaves with shower room and WC. Extra beds available. Breakfast in the lounge/diner with fireplace or outside. Long distance path within the grounds, mountain bike hire, BBQ, garden room. Horses welcome, looseboxes for grazing.

Prices d €60-€75; extra person fr €20   **On Site** ⚌
Nearby ⚲ 12km ⚓ 5km ⚒ 12km Restaurant 3km ⚑ 12km 🏢 9km
⋙ 12km   **Notes** No pets   English spoken

SAVEUSE

♯♯♯ ♥ Les Kintrabell

FAMILLE DUFOUR
3 rue de l'Eglise, 80470 SAVEUSE
☎ 03 22 54 17 37 & 06 22 03 75 39 📄 03 22 54 17 37
email: contact@leskintrabell.com
web: www.leskintrabell.com

This village property has four bedrooms in a converted farm building close to the owners' home. There are three double rooms, one downstairs and two upstairs. There is also a family suite for four on two levels, with lounge and kitchenette, which can be used as a self-catering gîte. All have private facilities. Courtyard, terrace, garden furniture and barbecue. Farm visits.

Prices s fr €51; d fr €62; extra person fr €20   **On Site** ⚌
Nearby ⚲ 3km ⚓ 3km ⚒ 5km Restaurant 5km ⚑ Spa 5km 🏢 5km
⋙ 5km   **Notes** No pets   English spoken   CC

ST-BLIMONT

♯♯♯ ♿ Ebalet

Gilles THIEBAULT
12 Hameau Ebalet, 80960 SAINT-BLIMONT
☎ 03 22 30 61 41 & 06 82 22 87 24
email: gthiebault@wanadoo.fr

In a rural hamlet, this property offers five rooms in a wing of the owners' house with independent access, one of which is suitable for guests with disabilities. These include four double rooms and one with double and a single bed. There is a breakfast room, garden with furniture and private parking.

Prices s fr €43; d fr €50; t fr €65   **Nearby** ⚌ 5km ⚲ 20km
Sea 8km ⚓ 10km ⚒ 5km Restaurant 5km ⚑ 5km 🏢 5km ⋙ 15km
Notes No pets   Open February to December.

♯♯♯ 🍽 Le Château des Lumieres

F et Fabrice VOGEL GUILBERT
29 rue du Moulin, Offeu, 80960 SAINT-BLIMONT
☎ 03 22 60 68 20 & 06 64 54 33 04 📄 03 22 60 68 20
email: lechateaudeslumieres@free.fr
web: http://lechateaudeslumieres.free.fr

A large 19th-century 'maison bourgeoise', with five upstairs bedrooms. Two are doubles, one has twin beds, and the other two are family rooms for four (double bed and two singles in each). All have private bath or shower room/WC, and cots are available if needed. Living room, internet access, garden with furniture, parking space.

Prices s fr €60; d fr €60; t fr €70; dinner fr €22   **Nearby** ⚌ 4km
⚲ 17km Sea 9km ⚓ 10km ⚒ 4km Restaurant 7km ⚑ 9km ♞ 9km
🏢 2km ⋙ 8km   **Notes** Pets admitted   English spoken

PICARDY

ST-GERMAIN-SUR-BRESLE

ⅲ ⁖◎⁖ Le Moulin

Jean-Philippe PETIT
80430 SAINT-GERMAIN-SUR-BRESLE
☎ 02 35 94 23 78 🗎 02 35 94 23 78
email: moulinstgermain@aol.com
web: http://pageperso.aol.fr/moulinstgermain/
moulinstgermain.html

In a detached building at the entrance to a large estate with a
working windmill there are three guest bedrooms, two with their
own access. There is a twin-bedded room, a double room accessed
from the breakfast room, and a double with possible folding bed for
two children. All rooms have private facilities. Terrace with garden
furniture.

Prices s fr €45; d fr €60; t fr €80; dinner fr €25 **On Site** ✐
Nearby ⛷30km ♨40km Sea 35km ↘25km Restaurant 8km ♒1km
🎿8km 🏠8km ⋙8km **Notes** No pets English spoken

ST-RIQUIER

ⅲ ❦ ◎⁖ Le Relais du Beffroi

Patou DECAYEUX
7 Place du Beffroi, 80135 ST-RIQUIER
☎ 03 22 28 93 08 & 06 63 20 48 10 🗎 03 22 28 93 10
email: nadinedecayeux7@orange.fr
web: www.aurelaisdubeffroi.com

Full of character, this 18th-century house on a farm has five
individually styled rooms with private facilities, separate access and TV:
four doubles (one with canopy) and a family room with a double and
two single beds. Dinners and breakfasts are served in the dining room
with the hosts in front of a fireplace. Terrace, courtyard with parking.

Prices not confirmed for 2008 **Nearby** ⛷10km ♨6km Sea 27km
✐5km ↘8km ♒ ⋙8km **Notes** Pets admitted English spoken

ST-VALERY-SUR-SOMME

ⅲ La Gribane

Michèle & J-Pierre DOUCHET
297 quai Jeanne d'Arc, 80230 ST-VALERY-SUR-SOMME
☎ 03 22 60 97 55
web: www.cote-picarde-bresle.com/pages/48

Situated on a quayside opposite the Baie de Somme, accommodation
includes two suites sleeping four and two doubles (one with
fireplace), all with lounges and private facilities. Breakfast features
home-made specialities and is served in the owners' house or on the
terrace. There is a kitchen and dining room available for guests' use
and parking. Holiday tax not included; reduced rates for groups.

Prices s fr €68; d €78-€98; extra person fr €25 **On Site** Sea ✐ 🎿
Nearby ⛷15km ♨15km ↘10km Restaurant 0.1km ♒ 🏠0.3km
⋙6km **Notes** No pets English spoken Open February to November.

VARENNES

ⅲ La Maison Bleu

Jackie et Mimi PILLON
7 rue Warin, 80560 VARENNES
☎ 03 22 76 42 85 & 06 83 44 55 73
email: jackie.pillon@orange.fr

This village is not far from the town of Albert and the 'Circuit de
Souvenir', which links the region's battle sites and war cemeteries.
There are three bedrooms comprising two doubles and a room with
twin beds which can be linked. All have private shower room and WC.
There is a kitchen available for guests and reductions for longer stays.
Outside, guests have use of a tennis court and barbecue.

Prices s fr €40; d fr €50; extra person €15 **On Site** 🎿
Nearby ⛷15km ♨25km ✐15km ↘10km Restaurant 2km ♒ 🏠2km
⋙10km **Notes** Pets admitted English spoken

VAUCHELLES-LES-QUESNOY

ⅲ *Chambre d'hôtes*

Joanna CREPELLE
121 place de l'Eglise, 80132 VAUCHELLES-LES-QUESNOY
☎ 03 22 24 18 17 🗎 03 22 24 18 17
email: joanna_crepelle@yahoo.fr
web: http://perso.wanadoo.fr/crepelle-chambres

This house, in the centre of the village, has three bedrooms. On the
ground floor is a double room; upstairs is another double, which links
through to a single; there is also a grade 2 suite of two rooms with a
double bed and three singles. All rooms have private bath or shower
room and WC. Use of lounge, TV, garden with barbecue.

Prices not confirmed for 2008 **Nearby** Sea 15km ✐3km ↘3km
⋙3km **Notes** No pets

VECQUEMONT

ⅲ Chambre d'hôtes

Florence & Guillaume HEBDA
5 allée des Aubépines, 80800 VECQUEMONT
☎ 03 22 48 29 54
email: guillaume.hebda@orange.fr

You will be warmly received by Florence and Guillaume in their
modern Picardy house, where three individually decorated rooms are
accessed privately by a separate hallway. There are two doubles and
a twin, all with shower and WC. Breakfast room with kitchenette and
sitting area shared with hosts. Calm atmosphere, garden with terrace
and summerhouse. Tennis lessons; boules park close by.

Prices s fr €45; d fr €55; extra person fr €15 **Nearby** ⛷10km
♨10km ✐1km ↘7km Restaurant 7km ♒ 🎿10km 🏠7km ⋙2km
Notes Pets admitted English spoken

VILLERS-SUR-AUTHIE

⏛ La Bretagnère

Josette GAUDUIN

16 rue de Bretagne, 80120 VILLERS-SUR-AUTHIE

☎ 03 22 27 77 25 & 06 62 78 73 09 ◷ 03 22 27 77 25

email: contact@labretagnere.com

web: www.labretagnere.com

Not far from the Baie de la Somme and the attractive former fishing village of Rue, this property has four double bedrooms on the first floor of the owners' home. There is a separate entrance to the rooms, all of which have private bath or shower room and WC. The Marquenterre bird sanctuary is close by.

Prices s €50-€55; d €60-€65; t €70-€77; extra person €10-€12
Nearby ⛵ 10km ⚓ 4km Sea 12km ⚐ 3km ⚒ 10km Restaurant 4km
⚐ 11km ⚑ 4km ⚑ 4km **Notes** No pets

VIRONCHAUX

⏛ ✌ Ferme de Mezoutre

Patricia POUPART

80150 VIRONCHAUX

☎ 03 22 23 52 33 & 06 22 10 40 85 ◷ 03 22 23 58 17

email: ppoupart@wanadoo.fr

web: www.cerpicardie.fr/mezoutre

This Picardy farmhouse, a brick and stone building, once belonged to the Abbaye de Valloires (6km). There are four double en suite bedrooms, two with private access to the garden. The lounge/breakfast room has a kitchenette, and there is a large enclosed courtyard with a duck pond, terrace and garden.

Prices s fr €48; d fr €55 **On Site** Restaurant ⚒ **Nearby** ⛵ 10km
⚓ 9km Sea 21km ⚐ 4km ⚒ 2km ⚑ 7km ⚑ 14km **Notes** Pets admitted English spoken

Péronne

AMIENS

Somme
N29

A29

80
SOMME

Bonneuil-les-Eaux

Montdidier

Noyon

Oise

Froissy
Ansauvillers
Noyers-St-Martin
Belloy
Montreuil-sur-Brèche
Machemont

BEAUVAIS
Compiègne
Berneuil-sur-Aisne
Savignies
Aisne
Espaubourg
St-Paul

Clermont
Flavacourt
St-Félix
Pierrefonds
Thibivillers
Orrouy
Reilly
Fay-les-
Étangs
Mello
02
AISNE

N324
Auger-Saint-Vincent
Montépilloy
Baron
N2

Plailly

PONTOISE
95
VAL-D'OISE

Montmorency
78
YVELINES
Meaux
Argenteuil
Saint-Germain-
en-Laye
NANTERRE
BOBIGNY
93
Le Raincy
77
SEINE-
ET-
MARNE
PARIS
75
Boulogne-
Billancourt
Nogent-
sur-Marne
VERSAILLES
92
L'Haÿ-
les-Roses
CRÉTEIL
Antony
94
Palaiseau

0   15 km

SOMME
Picardy

80

Scarpe
Douai
59 NORD
Cambrai
Escaut
N45
N43
A2
N 44
Saint-Quentin
D 1
D 932
Monchy-Lagache
A 26
D 930
Noyon
Oise
Lens
ARRAS
Canal du Nord
D 917
Péronne
Fresnes-Mazancourt
Omiécourt
Carrépuis
D 935
N 17
Scarpe
A 26
A 1
Curlu
Frise
Fay
Bayonvillers
Hattencourt
Fransart
D 937
A 1
Somme
N 29
PAS-DE-CALAIS
62
N 25
N 39
Courcelles-au-Bois
Mailly-Maillet
Varennes
Vecquemont
Blangy-Tronville
A 29
D 934
D 935
Montdidier
Sains-en-Amiénois
Ailly-sur-Noye
La Faloise
D 916
Scarpe
Doullens
Canche
D 941
N 25
D 925
Naours
AMIENS
Dury
Jumel
Hébécourt
60 OISE
A 16
N 1
Authie
D 928
D 925
A 16
Gapennes
St-Riquier
Belloy-sur-Somme
La Chaussée-Tirancourt
Saveuse
Bussy-les-Poix
Domvast
Vauchelles-les-Quesnoy
Cocquerel
L'Étoile
D 901
D 990
N 1
Vironchaux
Machy
Lamotte-Buleux
Drucat
Caours
Abbeville
Béhen
Citernes
St-Germain-sur-Bresle
D 925
Villers-sur-Authie
Quend (Monchaux)
Rue
Bernay-en-Ponthieu
Forest-Montiers
Favières
Le Crotoy
Buigny-St-Maclou
Port-le-Grand
Noyelles-sur-Mer
Saigneville
Ochancourt
D 928
A 28
Cayeux-sur-Mer
St-Valery-sur-Somme
Estréboeuf
Saint-Blimont
Ault
Somme
D 925
Bresle
D 1015
76 SEINE-MARITIME
A 28
N 29
Béthune
D 925
D 919

Marie-Laure et Thierry
74130 LE CÉRSMY · 7W100.LE CÉRSMY · FRANCE · © Assistance

POITOU-CHARENTES

CHARENTE

ANAIS

⏚ *La Clavière*

Christelle MASSONNET

16560 ANAIS

☎ 05 45 90 67 23

email: la.claviere@free.fr

web: http://la.claviere.free.fr

This property, which stands in a small hamlet, makes an ideal location for a holiday in Charente. There are three double rooms, all with private shower rooms and WCs, and an extra bed is available. Lounge with books; washing machine; wooded grounds. Meeting room (80 square metres) available for hire.

Prices not confirmed for 2008 **Nearby** ⚓ 10km ⚓ 13km ⚓ 6km ⚓ 9km Restaurant 5km ⚓ 1km ⚓ 9km ⚓ 13km **Notes** No pets English spoken

ARS

⏚ *Chambre d'hôtes*

Yvon GROSSIN

2, rue de l'Eglise, 16130 ARS

☎ 06 76 29 04 80

email: ppatricia.pineau@wanadoo.fr

web: www.lefiefdeschevaliers.com

A typical Charentaise house with a large garden and swimming pool, right in the middle of the village of Ars. It offers three bedrooms - a double, a twin-bedded room and a room for three, all equipped with private bath or shower room and WC. Living/dining room, and use of a washing machine.

Prices not confirmed for 2008 **On Site** Private ⚓ **Nearby** ⚓ 8km ⚓ 10km ⚓ 1km ⚓ 0.5km ⚓ 1km ⚓ 10km **Notes** Pets admitted English spoken

BAIGNES

⏚ ⚏ *Haras du Fief de Montauzier*

Isabelle WILLIOT

16360 BAIGNES

☎ 05 45 78 37 65

email: haras.du.fief@infonie.fr

web: http://haras.du.fief.chez.tiscali.fr

This typical Charente house is bordered by vines, set in a four hectare park with equestrian centre, in countryside known for its Roman art, pine trees and Cognac. It offers two rooms for three people and two for two, with separate facilities. Guests have use of a lounge, dining room, fireplace, TV and washer-drier. Children's meals available.

Prices not confirmed for 2008 **On Site** ⚓ ⚓ **Nearby** ⚓ 1km Restaurant 1km ⚓ 1km ⚓ 1km ⚓ 18km **Notes** Pets admitted English spoken

CHADURIE

⏚ ⚏ *Les Vergers du Faure*

M et Mme STRALLA

16250 CHADURIE

☎ 05 45 24 80 06 ▤ 05 45 24 80 06

email: serge.stralla@wanadoo.fr

Undulating vineyard country with many Romanesque churches makes a fine setting for this late 19th-century property. There are three double rooms with private bath/shower room; a further two doubles suitable for family use share a shower room and WC. Cot available, and garden with shared swimming pool.

Prices not confirmed for 2008 **On Site** ⚓ Private ⚓ **Nearby** ⚓ 13km ⚓ 22km Restaurant 1km ⚓ 3km ⚓ 10km ⚓ 10km **Notes** No pets English spoken CC

CHAMPNIERS

⏚ ⚏ La Templerie

Claudine et Jean RICHON

Denat, 16430 CHAMPNIERS

☎ 05 45 68 73 89 & 05 45 68 49 00 ▤ 05 45 68 91 18

email: richon.jean@wanadoo.fr

Situated on a wine-making enterprise in the heart of a Charentais village, this chambre d'hôtes has three rooms sleeping three and one room sleeping two, all en suite. In addition, a family suite offers a double and a twin room. There is a dining room with an open fire and a lounge, plus a library, a games room and TV. The large wooded garden has a swimming pool and wine tasting is available.

Prices s fr €36; d €45-€47; t €57-€60; extra person €12-€13 **On Site** Private ⚓ **Nearby** ⚓ 10km ⚓ 8km ⚓ 3.4km Restaurant 1.5km ⚓ 3km ⚓ 3km ⚓ 8km **Notes** No pets English spoken CC

CHASSORS

⏚ Logis de Guîtres

Corinne AUBRIET

16200 CHASSORS

☎ 05 45 83 21 57 & 06 74 90 69 22 ▤ 05 45 83 18 29

email: aubriet@aubriet.com

web: www.logisdeguitres.com

Not far from Cognac this 18th- and 19th-century property has four delightful bedrooms. Three are doubles, and there is a family suite with two bedrooms and lounge which can sleep five or six people. All the rooms have private bath or shower room and WC. There is a lounge/dining room with open fire and books.

Prices s €60-€65; d €60-€65; t €100-€130 **Nearby** ⚓ 5km ⚓ 7km ⚓ 3km ⚓ 3km Restaurant 2km ⚓ 1km ⚓ 2km ⚓ 2km ⚓ 15km **Notes** No pets English spoken

CHENON

⌗⌗⌗ ⭗ **Les Cajets**

Pierre NADAUD

16460 CHENON

☎ 05 45 93 94 24 📄 05 45 69 25 80

email: pierjonadaud@tele2.fr

web: www.lescajets.com

Not far from Charente, this tastefully restored farmhouse offers three en suite rooms (two doubles and a family suite made up of two rooms, each sleeping two). Guests can make use of the lounge/diner with TV and an open fire. The garden has seating and a small boat with which you can explore the Charente.

Prices s fr €42; d fr €46; t fr €77; extra person fr €8; dinner fr €16
On Site ✎ **Nearby** ⛷ 1km ⚊ 12km Restaurant 4km ⚊ 3km ⛵ 4km
⚊ 12km **Notes** No pets English spoken

CONFOLENS

⌗⌗⌗ *Chambre d'hôtes*

D VALEYRE et N LORIETTE

9 rue du Pont de l'Ecuyer, 16500 CONFOLENS

☎ 05 45 85 32 06

Five guest rooms can be found in this stylish house in a park in the centre of town. All rooms are double, and a child's bed and TV is available. Guests have use of a lounge, library and swimming pool.

Prices not confirmed for 2008 **Nearby** ⛷ 2km ⚊ 20km ✎ 2km ⚊ 2km Restaurant 0.3km ⚊ ⛵ 1km ⚊ 17km **Notes** No pets

DIRAC

⌗⌗⌗ ⭗ **Le Thie**

Nazirah TRANCHET

16410 DIRAC

☎ 05 45 61 03 59 & 06 20 51 36 68

email: lethie@wanadoo.fr

web: http://perso.wanadoo.fr/gite.du.thie

An arable farm not far from Angoulême - a good base for exploring the Charente region. There are two double rooms on the ground floor, and a two-roomed family suite for four upstairs. All have private bath or shower room and WC. The garden has a Jacuzzi and swimming pool, which are shared with the hosts and residents of three 'gîtes ruraux'.

Prices s fr €50; d fr €55; t fr €65; extra person fr €15; dinner fr €15
On Site Private ⚊ **Nearby** ⛷ 5km ⚊ 7km ✎ 8km Restaurant 3km ⚊ 5km ⛵ 2km ⚊ 8km **Notes** Pets admitted English spoken

ECURAS

⌗⌗⌗ ⭗ **L'Etanchon**

Erna CLAESSENS

16220 ECURAS

☎ 05 45 70 38 61 & 06 81 33 90 89

email: info@letanchon.com

web: www.letanchon.com

An old house built in the local style offering five guest bedrooms, double-bedded or twin-bedded, and all with private bath or shower room and WC. The house stands in three hectares of grounds, with a lake which is good for boating, fishing or bathing. Sitting room with satellite.

Prices s fr €45; d fr €50; t fr €65; extra person fr €10; dinner fr €20
Nearby ⛷ 16km ⚊ 3km ✎ 6km ⚊ 6km Restaurant 3km ⚊ 1km ⛵ 6km ⚊ 20km **Notes** No pets English spoken

GARAT

⌗⌗⌗ **Au Chai**

Didier BALARESQUE

16410 GARAT

☎ 06 85 12 72 28

email: balaresquedidier@aol.com

Ten minutes from Angoulême, this property enjoys panoramic views across the surrounding countryside. The bedrooms are large and modern. On the ground floor there are two doubles; upstairs is a vast room for four people, with two double beds. All rooms have private facilities. Dining room with open fire, lounge. Guests have use of the kitchen. Private terrace for each room.

Prices s €45-€55; d €55-€65; t fr €70; extra person fr €10 **On Site** ✎
Nearby ⛷ 6km ⚊ 8km ⚊ 15km Restaurant 1km ⚊ 1km Spa 10km ⛵ 6km ⚊ 10km **Notes** No pets

LACHAISE-SUR-LE-NE

⌗⌗⌗ ⭗ ♿ **Domaine de Pladuc**

Nicole PROVOT

16300 LACHAISE-SUR-LE-NE

☎ 05 45 78 21 80 & 06 15 41 04 41

email: info@domainedepladuc.com

web: http://domainedepladuc.com

This is a restored Charentais property, close to a stream. On the ground floor is a twin-bedded room; upstairs are two doubles, and a family suite with two bedrooms which can sleep up to five (double bed and three singles). All have private bath or shower room and WC. Vast lounge with open fire and books. Swimming pool.

Prices s fr €60; d €80-€90; t €95-€105; extra person fr €15; dinner fr €25 **On Site** 🌳 Private ⚲ **Nearby** ⚑ 4km ⚓ 20km ℘ 5km Restaurant 5km ⚲ 5km Spa 20km 🏠 9km ⚙ 15km **Notes** No pets English spoken

LESIGNAC-DURAND

⚑ ❦ Château de la Redortière

Marie-Paule MICHAUD

16310 LESIGNAC-DURAND

☎ 05 45 65 07 62 📄 05 45 65 31 79

email: vandervelden@tiscali.fr

Situated in grounds of seventeen hectares, this 19th-century castle has three double rooms, and two family suites sleeping three or four people. The rooms all have private bathroom facilities. The castle overlooks the lake of Mas Chaban.

Prices s fr €42; d €50-€62; t fr €62; extra person fr €18; dinner €17-€23 **On Site** ❦ **Nearby** ℘ 10km ⚓ 10km ⚲ 8km ⚲ 3km 🏠 3km ⚙ 12km **Notes** Pets admitted English spoken

LIGNIERES-SONNEVILLE

⚑ ❦ Les Collinauds

Roland MATIGNON

16130 LIGNIERES-SONNEVILLE

☎ 05 45 80 51 23 📄 05 45 80 51 23

email: matignon.les-collinauds@wanadoo.fr

web: www.les-collinauds-charente.com

Furnished in period style, this 19th-century Charentais hostelry offers four en suite guest rooms: two double rooms, one sleeping three, and one sleeping four. A dining room, reading room with TV, video and games, plus a small kitchen with a dining area are available. For leisure there is bike hire, horse-drawn carriage rides, local tennis courts and a distillery, which dates from the 1870s.

Prices s fr €40; d fr €48; t fr €55; extra person fr €5 **On Site** Private ⚲ **Nearby** ⚑ 10km ⚓ 20km ℘ 1.5km Restaurant 2km ⚲ 1.5km 🏠 1.5km ⚙ 12km **Notes** Pets admitted English spoken

LINARS

⚑ ⦿ Château de Moulède

Dominique CATON

16730 LINARS

☎ 05 45 96 02 94

email: brian.caton@wanadoo.fr

web: http://chateaudemoulede.com

A small château on a one hectare property, set in a green, quiet wine-growing region. Four rooms are available, sleeping two in double or twin beds, each with private facilities. There is also a lounge, dining room, library, TV, garden with terrace, bikes and golf equipment.

Prices s fr €62; d fr €70; t fr €85; dinner fr €22 **On Site** 🌳 **Nearby** ⚑ 10km ⚓ 9km ℘ 3km ⚲ 6km Restaurant 0.8km ⚲ 1km 🏠 2.6km ⚙ 10km **Notes** No pets English spoken

LOUZAC-ST-ANDRE

⚑ Demeure du Chapître

Lucette JOUSSAUME

16100 LOUZAC-SAINT-ANDRE

☎ 05 45 82 90 34 📄 05 45 82 45 74

email: demeureduchapitre@wanadoo.fr

web: http://perso.wanadoo.fr/demeureduchapitre

Close to Cognac, this chambre d'hôtes has three guest rooms in a renovated stable: two doubles and a family suite of two rooms sleeping two. Child's bed available. There is a large lounge/dining room, with TV and a second lounge with an open fire and a kitchen. The garden has seating and a variety of games; parking.

Prices s fr €47; d fr €54; t fr €80; extra person fr €16 **Nearby** ⚑ 2km ⚓ 12km ℘ 3km ⚲ 6km Restaurant 6km ⚲ 0.5km Spa 30km 🌳 5km 🏠 0.5km ⚙ 6km **Notes** Pets admitted English spoken CC

MAGNAC-SUR-TOUVRE

⚑ Le Clos-Saint-Georges

Nadine JACQUEMIN

rue de Bel Air, 16600 MAGNAC-SUR-TOUVRE

☎ 05 45 68 54 33 📄 05 45 68 54 33

email: nadjacq@voila.fr

web: http://clos-st-georges.site.voila.fr

On the Dordogne side of Angoulême, this house has a swimming pool and panoramic views over the forest and countryside. There are three double bedrooms, all with private bath or shower room and WC. Lounge and dining room with open fire; billiard table. Garden with private parking; two cycles available.

Prices not confirmed for 2008 **On Site** Private ⚲ **Nearby** ⚑ 5km ⚓ 8km ℘ 3km Restaurant 9km ⚲ 3km 🏠 3km ⚙ 10km **Notes** No pets English spoken

MANSLE

⚑ La Fontaine des Arts

Marie-France PAGANO

13 rue du Temple, 16230 MANSLE

☎ 05 45 69 13 56 & 06 12 52 39 86 📄 05 45 69 48 66

email: mfpagano@wanadoo.fr

web: www.la-fontaine-des-arts.com

Three comfortably furnished and spacious rooms: 'Fanny' (double en suite), 'Cottage' and 'Manon' (sleeping three with en suite spa bath). Guests can use the lounge/TV room, with video and library and games, and a kitchen area with washing machine and dryer. Outdoors, there is a swimming pool, fishing, ping-pong and enclosed garden with a portico and a fountain.

Prices s €52-€59; d €62-€69; t €86-€93; extra person fr €21 **On Site** ℘ Private ⚲ **Nearby** ⚑ 5km ⚓ 25km Restaurant 0.5km ⚲ 1km ⚙ 15km **Notes** No pets English spoken

MERIGNAC

♯♯♯ ⏹ L'en Haut des Vignes

Josiane MEMETEAU
Villars, 16200 MERIGNAC
☎ 05 45 92 41 12 & 06 30 11 14 90
email: memeteau.family@wanadoo.fr
web: www.lenhautdesvignes.com

Set in a Charente village dating back nine hundred years, this early 19th-century house is in the heart of a Cognac vineyard between Angoulême and Cognac. It provides a double room, a king-size and a room with four single beds, each with private facilities. Lounge/dining room, fireplace, library, TV, washer-dryer, terrace and garden at guests' disposal.

Prices s fr €50; d fr €57; t fr €73; extra person fr €16; dinner fr €19
On Site Restaurant Private ⚹ **Nearby** ⛷ 6km ↟20km ⚓ 5km ⚄ 2km ⛲2km ⋙20km **Notes** No pets English spoken

MESNAC

♯♯♯ ♈ ⏹ Château du Mesnac

C et C CHURLAUD MOINARDEAU
Place de l'Eglise, 16370 MESNAC
☎ 05 45 83 26 61 ▤ 05 45 83 17 70
email: contact@dduveron.fr
web: www.dduveron.fr

In the heart of the Cognac vineyards, on the banks of the River Antenne, this 18th-century castle has one family and two double rooms, all with private facilities. Dining room and lounge, with TV; large country garden with swimming pool. Sample the gourmet food served at the local inn, and try local cognacs and wines on offer. Parking available.

Prices s €60-€70; d €60-€90; t fr €85; extra person fr €18; dinner fr €25
On Site ⚓ Private ⚹ **Nearby** ⛷ 4km ↟12km Restaurant 3km ⚄ 4km ⛲4km ⋙12km **Notes** No pets English spoken Open November to September.

MOULIDARS

♯♯♯ ♈ Malvieille

Jean-Bernard MAURIN
Le Prunier, 16290 MOULIDARS
☎ 05 45 96 40 38 ▤ 05 45 90 09 85
email: chleprunier@aol.com
web: www.giteleprunier.com

Stay at a wine grower's home on the road between Angoulême and Jarnac, 4km from the River Charente. Two doubles and a room for three, each with shower or bath and wc. Living room, dining room with open fire, and kitchenette for use by guests. Garden; parking in grounds of house.

Prices not confirmed for 2008 **Nearby** ⚹ 15km ↟20km ⚓ 4km ⚹ 10km ⚄ 3km ⛲3km ⋙10km **Notes** No pets English spoken

MOUTHIERS-SUR-BOEME

♯♯♯ Le Moulin du Duc

Danièlle ALLAIN
16440 MOUTHIERS-SUR-BOEME
☎ 05 45 67 81 57
email: allain.danielle@wanadoo.fr
web: www.moulinduduc.com

The river Boëme runs through this green valley and turns the wheel of the 17th-century Moulin du Duc. The guest accommodation is upstairs: two double rooms and a family suite for four, all with private shower room and WC. The dining room sits above the mill machinery. Outside is a fishing lake and a garden bordered by the river.

Prices not confirmed for 2008 **On Site** ⚓ **Nearby** ⚹ 15km ↟15km ⚹ 9km Restaurant 1km ⚄ 3km ⛲3km ⋙14km **Notes** No pets

PERIGNAC

♯♯♯ ⏹ Château de Lerse

François LAFARGUE
16250 PERIGNAC
☎ 05 45 60 32 81 & 06 08 51 08 65 ▤ 05 45 62 30 98
email: fl.lafargue@wanadoo.fr
web: www.chateaudelerse.com

Lerse is in southern Charente, far from hustle and bustle, in an area rich with Roman heritage and not far from the vineyards of Bordeaux and Cognac. The little fortified castle dates from 13th century and has three large and beautiful rooms, two triples and a double, all with bathroom and WC. Sitting room, dining room, historic fireplace, library, TV. Huge grounds. Reductions for longer stays.

Prices s €80-€100; d €90-€110; t €100-€120; extra person fr €10; dinner fr €30 **Nearby** ⚹ 5km ↟25km ⚓ 5km ⚹ 7km ⚄ 5km ⛲6km ⋙30km **Notes** Pets admitted English spoken Open May to September.

REPARSAC

🏵 *Domaine de la Vennerie*

Jean-Marie BRIDIER
16200 REPARSAC
☎ 05 45 80 97 00 📄 05 45 81 02 59
email: info@domainedelavennerie.com
web: www.domainedelavennerie.com

These four guest rooms are located in a Charentais home, on a wine-making enterprise. There is one double room and one room sleeping three, both en suite, and a family suite with private bathroom facilities. There is a lounge with an open fire, and a kitchen with TV. Visits can be arranged to the wine storeroom and the distillery. Fishing is available on a private lake.

Prices not confirmed for 2008 **Nearby** ⛷ 8km ♨ 8km ✎ 0.7km ⊀ 7km Restaurant 8km ⊰ 3km 🏛 7km ⋙ 7km **Notes** Pets admitted English spoken

---

SALLES-DE-VILLEFAGNAN

🏵 **La Cochere**

John et Kathy ANDERSON
16700 SALLES-DE-VILLEFAGNAN
☎ 05 45 30 34 60
email: la.cochere@wanadoo.fr
web: http://lacochere.com

In the heart of a small village in the Charente Valley, this restored farmhouse has two double rooms and one family room which comprises one double and one single bed. The rooms are en suite and there is a lounge/dining room and a library. The garden boasts a terrace and swimming pool.

Prices s fr €45; d fr €55; t fr €65 **On Site** Private ⊀ **Nearby** ⛷ 9km ✎ 8km Restaurant 7km ⊰ 5km 🏛 10km ⋙ 10km **Notes** No pets English spoken

SEGONZAC

🏵 🍽 *Chambre d'hôtes*

Thérésa KYNE
58, rue Gaston Briand, 16130 SEGONZAC
☎ 05 45 35 18 97
email: kynetcanada@yahoo.com
web: www.chezthomasfrance.com

This restored farmhouse and its adjacent distillery are in the heart of the Cognac region. There are four double rooms, each with a private bath or shower room and WC. Dining room and sitting room, with meals available by arrangement. Outside is a garden, and the area is good walking country.

Prices not confirmed for 2008 **Nearby** ⛷ 2km ♨ 11km ✎ 4km ⊀ 9km ⊰ 0.5km 🏛 0.5km ⋙ 9km **Notes** Pets admitted English spoken

ST-ADJUTORY

🏵 🍽 **Château du Mesnieux**

Sandrine GRACIA
16310 ST-ADJUTORY
☎ 05 45 70 40 18 & 06 08 05 27 46
email: contact@chateaudumesnieux.com
web: www.chateaudumesnieux.com

A château with towers dating back to the 15th and 16th centuries, which combines a feeling for the past with comfortable surroundings and tasteful decoration. There are two double bedrooms and two triples, each with a private bath or shower room and WC. Cot available. There is a guests' lounge with billiard table, and the garden has a lake for private fishing.

Prices s €70-€85; d €80-€95; t €100-€115; dinner fr €25 **On Site** ✎ **Nearby** ⛷ 3km ♨ 12km ⊀ 9km Restaurant 1km ⊰ 10km 🏛 10km ⋙ 10km **Notes** No pets English spoken

---

ST-CLAUD

🏵 **Manoir La Betoulle**

Penelope HITCHINGS
16450 ST-CLAUD
☎ 05 45 30 23 10
email: ph@manoir-la-betoulle.com
web: www.manoir-la-betoulle.com

A 20th-century manor house standing in 35 hectares of natural parkland. There are four spacious guest bedrooms, three doubles

CONTINUED

POITOU-CHARENTES

ST-CLAUD *CONTINUED*

and a twin-bedded room, all with private bathroom and WC. Lounge, dining room, swimming pool and tennis court. Very large garden.

Prices s fr €50; d €60–€70 **On Site** ✤ Private ✦ Private tennis court **Nearby** ⚓ 24km ⚲ 18km Restaurant 1.5km 🏛 1km �* 9km **Notes** No pets English spoken

ST-GENIS-D'HIERSAC

🍴 Les Negres de Soie

Françoise et Pascal BAUDOT

Grosbot, 16570 ST-GENIS-D'HIERSAC

☎ 05 45 21 07 20 📠 05 45 21 92 02

This renovated 18th-century farmhouse is located at the centre of a hamlet overlooking the Charente Valley. Five double rooms are available, and guests may use the lounge and dining room with its open fire. There is also a garden with a terrace, a swimming pool and an exhibition of paintings. Canoeing 5 km away; internet access available.

Prices s fr €46; d €52–€54 **On Site** ✤ Private ✦ **Nearby** ⚓ 5km ⚲ 25km ⚲ 3km Restaurant 1km 🏊 1km 🏛 1.5km 🚶 15km **Notes** No pets English spoken

ST-PREUIL

🍴 ⊙ Le Relais de Saint Preuil

Christine MONTEMBAULT

Chez Rivière, 16130 ST-PREUIL

☎ 05 45 80 80 08 📠 05 45 80 80 09

email: contact@relais-de-saint-preuil.com

web: www.relais-de-saint-preuil.com

In the heart of the Grande Champagne region, this beautifully restored old posting inn has five double bedrooms, with independent access. Two extra beds are available. All rooms have stereo, DVD player, telephone with free internet access, and a safe. Lounge/dining area with kitchen; extensive grounds with woods, tennis courts and a heated swimming pool (shared with three gîtes).

Prices s €80–€130; d €95–€145; t fr €160; extra person fr €20; dinner €28–€35 **On Site** ✤ Private ✦ Private tennis court **Nearby** ⚓ 3km ⚓ 12km ⚲ 11km Restaurant 7km Spa 40km 🏛 5km 🚶 14km **Notes** No pets English spoken Open 18 March to 16 February. CC

VARS

🍴 Logis du Portal

Liliane BERTHOMME

16330 VARS

☎ 05 45 20 38 19

email: logis-du-portal@netcourrier.com

web: www.logis-du-portal.com

Located on the banks of the Charente, this 17th-century residence has one single and two double rooms, each furnished in keeping with the property. There is a lounge/dining room with a kitchen area, and an open fire. The typically French garden has a swimming pool and parking is available.

Prices not confirmed for 2008 **On Site** ⚲ Private ✦ **Nearby** ⚓ 15km ⚓ 16km 🏊 3km 🏛 1km 🚶 16km **Notes** No pets

VERRIERES

🍴 La Chambre

Henri et Monique GEFFARD

16130 VERRIERES

☎ 05 45 83 02 74 📠 05 45 83 01 82

email: cognac.geffard@tiscali.fr

Five guest rooms are available, located on a wine-making farm in the heart of the Cognac vineyards. There are two doubles, two triples, and one room sleeping five; all are en suite (child's bed available). There is a lounge with television, and a kitchen area for guests. Local produce is available and includes pineau, cognac and local wines for sampling.

Prices not confirmed for 2008 **Nearby** ⚓ 8km ⚲ 18km ⚲ 2km ✦ 4km Restaurant 5km 🏊 4km 🏛 7km 🚶 15km **Notes** No pets English spoken

VERTEUIL-SUR-CHARENTE

🍴 ⊙ Le Couvent des Cordeliers

Alain BARBOU

8, rue du Docteur Deux Després,

16510 VERTEUIL-SUR-CHARENTE

☎ 05 45 31 01 19 📠 05 45 31 01 19

email: barbou@lecouventdescordeliers.com

web: www.lecouventdescordeliers.com

A former convent on the banks of the Charente, between Poitiers and Angoulême, at the heart of the historic village of Verteuil. One family suite for four (one double and a twin), bathroom and two WCs and a double with bathroom and WC. On the second floor are two more doubles and a twin, all with bathroom and WC.

Prices s fr €85; d fr €95; t fr €115; extra person fr €45; dinner fr €28 **On Site** ⚲ Restaurant ✤ Private ✦ **Nearby** ⚓ 8km ⚓ 40km 🏊 🏛 0.2km 🚶 5km **Notes** No pets English spoken Open February to December. CC

VILLEFAGNAN

🍴 ⊙ Le Logis des Tours

Chantal DUVIVIER

16240 VILLEFAGNAN

☎ 05 45 31 74 25

email: chantal.duvivier.fancy@wanadoo.fr

In a leafy setting, the 'Logis des Tours' gets its name from the two 15th-century towers, which stand guard over the entrance. It has two double rooms, one triple and a family suite comprising two rooms, capable of sleeping five. All rooms are en suite, and there is a lounge with a library, an open fire and satellite TV. In the grounds are old trees, and a terrace. Parking is available.

Prices not confirmed for 2008 **On Site** Private ✦ **Nearby** ⚓ 0.5km ⚓ 40km ⚲ 1km 🏊 1km 🚶 9km **Notes** No pets English spoken

CHARENTE-MARITIME

AIGREFEUILLE

⚲ Chambre d'hôtes

C et C JARROSSAY

13, Rue de la Rivière, 17290 AIGREFEUILLE

☎ 05 46 35 97 84 📠 05 46 01 98 04

Situated in a market town close to La Rochelle and Rochefort, this establishment offers three well-furnished rooms: two doubles and a twin, all en suite. The twin room has the option of an extra fold-away bed. A guest lounge is available, with TV and a library. The large, enclosed garden has seating and ping-pong, and bicycles are available. Private parking.

Prices s fr €46; d fr €54; t fr €69; extra person fr €15 **Nearby** ⚓ 8km ⚲ 15km ⚐ 2km ⚹ 1km Restaurant 3km ⚄ 1km ⛪ 0.5km ⛵ 20km **Notes** No pets English spoken Open April to October.

ANAIS

⚲ ⟨◯⟩ ⚅ *Le Clos d'Autrefois*

Danielle FISCHER

L'Impeau, 17540 ANAIS

☎ 05 46 00 48 38 & 06 08 09 07 95

email: leclosdautrefois@wanadoo.fr

There are five comfortable personalised rooms, all with shower and WC, on this superbly restored farm in the quiet of the countryside: a twin room suitable for disabled people, two double rooms, a room with three single beds, and a family room with mezzanine, having a double and two single beds. Salon, library, tea-room; cot available. Swimming pool, parking, boules park, bicycles, table tennis. Meals by reservation.

Prices not confirmed for 2008 **On Site** Private ⚹ **Nearby** ⚓ 6km ⚲ 25km ⚐ 6km ⚄ 6km ⛪ 6km ⛵ 16km **Notes** No pets English spoken

ARCHINGEAY

⚲ ⟨◯⟩ ⚅ Chambre d'hôtes

M-T et J-P JACQUES

16 Rue des Sablières, 17380 ARCHINGEAY

☎ 05 46 97 85 70 & 06 73 39 79 70 📠 05 46 97 61 89

email: jpmt.jacques@wanadoo.fr

web: www.gite-prop.com/17/5114

Not far from St Savinien, Rochefort and Saintes, this chambre d'hôtes has three very comfortable en suite rooms: two doubles and one suite for three (one double, one single and a fold-away bed if required). A lounge with an open fire is available to guests and there is a flower garden and terrace. Dinner is available by prior arrangement.

Prices s fr €49; d €52-€58; t fr €75; extra person fr €17; dinner fr €22 **On Site** ⚹ **Nearby** ⚓ 5km ⚲ 7km ⚐ 3km ⚹ 3km ⚄ 3km ⛪ 3km ⛵ 7km **Notes** No pets English spoken

ARTHENAC

⚲ ⟨◯⟩ ⟨◯⟩ *La Barde Fagnouse*

D et N CHAINIER

17520 ARTHENAC

☎ 05 46 49 12 85 📠 05 46 49 18 91

email: vignoblechainier@free.fr

Situated in the heart of the Cognac region on a vineyard which also produces Pineau (tastings available), this property offers three very comfortable first floor rooms. There are two doubles, and a family suite with a double and a twin-bedded room. All rooms have private bath or shower room and WC. Lounge with books, and an attractive garden.

Prices not confirmed for 2008 **Nearby** ⚓ 10km ⚲ 25km ⚐ 8km ⚹ 5km ⚄ 5km ⛪ 5km ⛵ 15km **Notes** No pets English spoken

BERNAY-ST-MARTIN

⚲ ⟨◯⟩ *Breuilles*

Catherine LANDRE

5, Rue de l'Ecole, 17330 BERNAY SAINT MARTIN

☎ 05 46 33 88 21 & 06 86 55 32 53

email: landreca@wanadoo.fr

Set in a quiet hamlet, this former farmhouse has two annexes housing three rooms (two twins and a family suite with two single beds and a double on the mezzanine), all with private facilities. Guests have access to the lounge, with open fire and library, as well as the garden and games. Dinner can be arranged except Sunday and Monday.

Prices not confirmed for 2008 **Nearby** ⚓ 10km ⚲ 10km ⚐ 6km ⚹ 10km ⚄ 2km ⛪ 2km ⛵ 10km **Notes** No pets English spoken Open 15 April to 15 October.

CHAILLEVETTE

⚲ Logis de Chatressac

G et J-C BOITTIN

13, Place de Chatressac, 17890 CHAILLEVETTE

☎ 05 46 47 96 60 & 06 15 88 60 02

email: jcboittin@wanadoo.fr

web: http://logisdechatressac.pagesperso_orange.fr

Close to a small oyster harbour, this 19th-century Charentais house offers five pleasant first-floor rooms: three doubles and two triples, all with shower and WC. Kitchenette, dining room with open fire, lounge, library, TV. Table tennis, bicycles, parking. Zoo, beaches, and one of France's prettiest villages, Mornac-sur-Seudre, nearby.

Prices s fr €47; d fr €53; t fr €68; extra person fr €12 **On Site** ⚹ **Nearby** ⚓ 5km ⚲ 10km Sea 8km ⚐ 0.5km ⚹ 15km Restaurant 0.5km ⚄ 0.5km Spa 15km ⛪ 0.1km ⛵ 15km **Notes** No pets English spoken

CHATELAILLON-PLAGE

▒▒▒ **Chambre d'hôtes**

Marie-Armelle SUZANNE

37, Bld Georges Clemenceau,

17340 CHATELAILLON-PLAGE

☎ 05 46 56 17 64 & 06 76 09 51 29

email: ma.suzanne@wanadoo.fr

web: www.gite-prop.com/17/2617

Close to La Rochelle and Rochefort, this modern property has three guest rooms in a recently built maisonette. All are en suite doubles and a child's bed is also available. Guests may make use of the veranda, sitting room and kitchen area, and the garden with swimming pool, barbecue and private parking. Nearby, Chatelaillon has a beach ideal for swimming.

Prices s €45-€52; d €53-€60; t fr €68; extra person fr €15
On Site Private ⚲ **Nearby** ⚑ 10km ⚓ 10km ⚘ 1km ⚒ 0.5km ⚑ 1km ⚒ 1km **Notes** No pets

---

CHERAC

▒▒▒ **Chez Piché**

M et J-C CHARBONNEAU

17610 CHERAC

☎ 05 46 96 30 84 & 06 30 18 17 25 ▤ 05 46 96 30 84

email: fermedechezpiche@orange.fr

web: www.gite-prop.com/17/7204

In the Charente Valley, on an agricultural and wine-growing smallholding, this chambre d'hôtes has three very comfortable double rooms, one with an extra single bed. Guests may use the lounge with TV, and the garden, which has seating and children's games. Visits to the wine storehouse on site can be arranged, and the chambre d'hôtes is ideal for visits to the regions of Charente, Pineau and Cognac.

Prices s fr €41; d fr €46; t fr €60; extra person fr €10 **Nearby** ⚑ 5km ⚓ 15km ⚘ 0.4km ⚲ 10km Restaurant 3km ⚒ 2km Spa 5km ⚑ 2km ⚒ 12km **Notes** No pets English spoken

▒▒▒ ⊚ **La Pantoufle**

Djahidé PAKSOY

5, Impasse des Dimiers, 17610 CHERAC

☎ 05 46 95 37 10

email: lapantoufle@free.fr

web: http://lapantoufle.free.fr

Three first-floor rooms furnished for complete comfort can be found in this house between Saintes and Cognac in the Charente valley. Accommodation comprises two double rooms with shower/WC, and a triple with bathroom/WC. Dining room, living room, TV and library, table tennis and bicycles at guests' disposal. Enclosed garden and conservatory.

Prices s fr €45; d fr €50; extra person fr €15; dinner fr €20 **Nearby** ⚑ 5km ⚓ 15km ⚘ 0.4km ⚲ 10km ⚒ 0.2km ⚑ 0.2km ⚒ 12km **Notes** No pets English spoken

CLION-SUR-SEUGNE

▒▒▒ ⊚ ⚹ **Chez Drillaud**

Claire et Patrick ESPINOSA

8, Chemin des Millauds, 17240 CLION-SUR-SEUGNE

☎ 05 46 70 38 97 & 06 81 13 23 84

email: delatoquealane@wanadoo.fr

web: www.delatoquealane.com

Three spacious and comfortable guest rooms in this Charentaise longhouse, one of them with access for disabled guests. Two of the rooms are doubles, the third is a triple, and they all have air-conditioning, private shower room and WC. Living room with piano, and garden with parking space. Meals available (pre-booking required).

Prices not confirmed for 2008 **Nearby** ⚑ 7km ⚓ 35km ⚘ 3km ⚲ 5km ⚒ 3km ⚑ 5km ⚒ 5km **Notes** Pets admitted English spoken CC

COURCON

▒▒▒ **Le Puits Sainte Claire**

Christiane DRAPPEAU

17 Grande Rue, 17170 COURCON

☎ 06 08 91 74 72 ▤ 05 46 01 62 93

email: contact@weekend-17.com

web: www.17-chambres-hotes.com

This beautifully restored 19th-century house has four luxurious guest bedrooms, three doubles and a two-roomed family suite with a double bed and two singles. All of the rooms are on the first floor, and all have private bath or shower rooms and WCs. Lounge with books, TV, billiard room. Enclosed garden; covered heated swimming pool available from April to October.

Prices s €62-€77; d €70-€92; t fr €110; extra person fr €10 **On Site** Private ⚲ **Nearby** ⚑ 1km ⚓ 30km ⚘ 4km Restaurant 2km ⚒ 1km ⚑ 0.2km ⚒ 15km **Notes** No pets

---

DOMPIERRE-SUR-MER

▒▒▒ **Logis Saint Leonard**

Marie-Paule SCHWARTZ

6 Rue des Chaumes, L'Abbaye,

17139 DOMPIERRE-SUR-MER

☎ 05 46 35 14 65 & 06 78 03 41 13 ▤ 05 46 35 14 65

email: logis-st-leonard@wanadoo.fr

A tastefully restored property, which looks out on wooded parkland. There are three bedrooms: a double room, a twin-bedded room, and a two-roomed family suite (two double beds). All have private bath or shower room and WC. Lounge with open fire and books, billiard room, swimming pool.

Prices s fr €65; d fr €70; t fr €102; extra person €15-€34 **On Site** ⚘ Private ⚲ **Nearby** ⚑ 4km ⚓ 8km Restaurant 6km ⚒ 1km Spa 6km ⚑ 1km ⚒ 6km **Notes** Pets admitted English spoken

ECHILLAIS

▦ ⑩ **Les Hibiscus**

Danièle COURAUD

5, Rue du Champ Simon, 17620 ECHILLAIS

☎ 05 46 83 11 60

This chambre d'hôtes has four comfortable en suite rooms situated in an annexe next to the proprietors' home: three double rooms, one with an additional single bed, and one twin. Guests may use the lounge and library, TV and garden, and dinner is available by reservation. Local attractions include the Charente River, the Bridge of Nartrou, L'Ile d'Oleron, La Rochelle and Royan.

Prices s fr €42; d fr €44; t fr €56; dinner fr €18   **Nearby** ♨ 2km ♨ 40km ♠ 1km ✈ 7km Restaurant 0.5km ⌂ 1km ♟ 1km ⌂ 5km ⋙ 7km   **Notes** No pets Open Easter to 1 November.

JARNAC-CHAMPAGNE

▦ ⑩ *La Feuillarde des Tonneaux*

SARL LASSALLE ET FILS

14, rue des Tonneaux, Domaine des Tonneaux, 17520 JARNAC-CHAMPAGNE

☎ 05 46 49 50 99 & 05 46 49 57 19

🖹 05 46 49 57 33

email: info@domainedestonneaux.com

web: www.domainedestonneaux.com

This typical Charentais house has two double rooms, one en suite and one with a separate bathroom, and an en suite twin room. All rooms have a fridge and guests have use of a sitting room, TV, the internet and a library. In the garden are children's games and petanque and there are visits to the distillery and wine storeroom on site. Local produce and dinner (by reservation) are available.

Prices not confirmed for 2008   **Nearby** ♨ 12km ♨ 25km ♠ 8km ✈ 10km ⌂ 1km ♟ 1km ⋙ 14km   **Notes** No pets English spoken Open March to October. CC

LA GRIPPERIE-ST-SYMPHORIEN

▦ **La Contadine**

Heidi ZELUS

Le Grand Breneau,

17620 LA GRIPPERIE-SAINT-SYMPHORIEN

☎ 05 46 82 03 34 & 06 17 70 76 64   🖹 05 46 82 03 34

email: lacontadine@wanadoo.fr

web: www.lacontadine.com

This building is a magnificent 18th-century farmhouse which has been restored and enlarged over the years. The guest accommodation is in a converted barn, and consists of two double bedrooms, a twin-bedded room and a triple room (double bed and a single). All have private shower room and WC. Gardens with parking space; much to see in the area.

Prices s fr €60-€62; d fr €68-€70; t fr €85; extra person fr €18   **On Site** ❀ **Nearby** ♨ 10km ♨ 20km ♠ 5km ✈ 8km ⌂ 8km ♟ 7km ⋙ 25km   **Notes** No pets English spoken

▦ ⑩ **Les Grandes Maisons**

V et J-M VAILLANT-MARESCAUX

10, Les Champs de la Croix, 17620 LA GRIPPERIE-SAINT-SYMPHORIEN

☎ 05 46 82 60 95 & 06 81 60 14 88   🖹 05 46 82 60 95

email: info@grandesmaisons.fr

web: www.grandesmaisons.fr

An old mansion house, tucked away quietly and discreetly in its walled grounds. There are three welcoming and comfortable guest bedrooms, all individually decorated and with private facilities. On the ground floor is a double; upstairs is a triple (double bed plus a single), and a two-roomed family suite for four (double bed plus twins). Lounge; meals by arrangement (except Wednesdays). Closed most of January.

Prices s €62-€75; d €66-€75; t €85-€94; extra person fr €18; dinner fr €25   **Nearby** ♨ 10km ♨ 25km ♠ 5km ✈ 8km ⌂ 8km ♟ 8km ⋙ 20km   **Notes** No pets English spoken

LE CHATEAU D'OLERON

▦ ♿ **La Cabane**

Vanessa PARENT

62, Route du Viaduc, Ors, 17480 LE CHATEAU D'OLERON

☎ 05 46 47 48 01 & 06 77 75 25 55   🖹 05 46 47 48 01

email: vanessa@alacabane.fr

web: www.alacabane.fr

There are four comfortable, individually-decorated bedrooms at this property. On the ground floor is a double room with disabled access; upstairs are two more doubles and a family suite for four, with a double room and a twin-bedded room. All have private facilities. There are two lounges, with open fire and books; outside is a garden with a terrace and enclosed parking. In an annexe at the bottom of the garden is a sauna and fitness area available for guests use on request.

Prices s fr €56; d fr €62; t €86-€104; extra person fr €15   **On Site** Spa **Nearby** ♨ 3km ♨ 8km ♠ 1km Restaurant 0.6km ⌂ 4km ♟ 4km ⋙ 35km   **Notes** No pets English spoken

LES ESSARDS

▦ **Le Pinier**

Francine JAMIN

10, Le Pinier, 17250 LES ESSARDS

☎ 05 46 93 91 43   🖹 05 46 93 93 64

This chambre d'hôtes offers four comfortable and well-furnished en suite rooms: three doubles located in a renovated stable, and a suite of two rooms (one double and one twin) housed in the main building. A guest lounge is available, as are a games room, kitchen area, washing machine, phone point and internet access. There is also a garden.

Prices s fr €40; d fr €50; t fr €62; extra person fr €12   **Nearby** ♨ 7km ♨ 2km ♠ 10km ✈ Restaurant 5km ⌂ 3km ♟ 10km ♟ 3km ⋙ 10km **Notes** No pets English spoken Open July to September & weekends May to June

POITOU-CHARENTES

LORIGNAC

⁂ Chez Poupot

Claude et Jacky PALISSIER

55, Rue de Chez Poupot, 17240 LORIGNAC

☎ 05 46 49 96 95 & 06 19 52 17 89 📄 05 46 49 96 95

This superb mansion, built in the local style, has three very comfortable bedrooms. There is a room for three; a family suite for four with a double room and a single; and a room with two doubles. All rooms have private bath or shower room and WC. Lounge with books, kitchenette, garden, parking.

Prices s fr €40; d fr €55; t €62–€70; extra person €10–€16
Nearby ⚓ 12km ⚑ 40km ✐ 5km ☇ 12km ☲ 3km 🏠 1km ₩ 20km
Notes No pets

LUCHAT

⁂ ◎ ♿ La Métairie

Martine TRENTESAUX

17, Rue de la Métairie, 17600 LUCHAT

☎ 05 46 92 07 73 & 06 83 58 25 55

web: http://lametairie2luchat.chez-alice.fr

This old renovated Charentais house, next to the proprietors' home, offers three comfortable and individually furnished rooms, a twin and two triples, each with en suite facilities. A lounge with open fire is available, along with TV room and library. The garden is charming and there is parking for guests. Saintes or Royan are not far off. Dinner is available by reservation.

Prices s fr €38; d fr €45; t €58–€60; dinner fr €18 **Nearby** ⚓ 4km
⚑ 12km ✐ 8km ☇ 10km ☲ 4km ♨ 10km 🏠 5km ₩ 10km
Notes No pets English spoken Open April to November.

MARANS

⁂ ◎ La Manoire

Claude BARRERIE

Le Marais Sauvage, 17230 MARANS

☎ 05 46 01 17 04 📄 05 46 01 17 04

email: cb.la-manoire@wanadoo.fr

web: www.marcireau.fr/marans/manoire

In a corner of the Marais Poitevin region, this chambre d'hôtes offers four individual rooms, 'The Exotic', a double, 'The Rose' a twin, 'The Rustic' with both double and single beds, and 'The Forget-me-not', with twin beds. There is a guest lounge with open fire and TV, a covered area for parking and dinner is available by reservation (Monday, Wednesday, Friday and Sunday only).

Prices not confirmed for 2008 **On Site** ✐ **Nearby** ⚓ 6km ⚑ 20km
☇ 6km ☲ 6km 🏠 2.5km ₩ 30km **Notes** No pets Open April to September.

MARENNES

⁂ Logis du Canal

Maryse BOUSSEREAU

5 Rue des Martyrs, Route de la Cayenne, 17320 MARENNES

☎ 05 46 85 67 88 & 06 18 29 34 13

email: logisducanal@wanadoo.fr

web: www.logisducanal.com

A property dating back to 1900, looking onto the Cayenne canal. On the first floor of the house are two double rooms and a twin-bedded room; on the ground floor of an annexe are two triple rooms (double beds plus singles). All have private facilities. Lounge with TV. Pleasant garden with swimming pool.

Prices s fr €57; d fr €62; t fr €83 **On Site** Private ☇ **Nearby** ⚓ 5km
⚑ 25km ☲ 3km Restaurant 0.4km ♨ 2km 🏠 1km ₩ 20km
Notes No pets English spoken

MESCHERS-SUR-GIRONDE

⁂ ◎ Chambre d'hôtes

Mauricette et Pierre REDEUILH

202, Route de Royan, 17132 MESCHERS-SUR-GIRONDE

☎ 05 46 02 72 72 📄 05 46 02 72 72

email: redeuilh.p@wanadoo.fr

This modern chambre d'hôtes has a large flower garden, terrace, veranda and parking. There are four en suite rooms: a double, two rooms with two double beds sharing a balcony, and a single. Guests are welcome to make use of the lounge, sitting room, TV and library. There are beaches and creeks in the area and the harbour at Meschers and local caves are worth a visit. Dinner is available by reservation.

Prices s fr €40; d fr €48; dinner fr €18 **Nearby** ⚓ 3km ⚑ 15km
✐ 2.5km ☇ 10km Restaurant 1.5km ☲ 0.8km ♨ 3km 🏠 3km ₩ 10km
Notes No pets

MIRAMBEAU

⁂ ◎ Haut Brochon

Monique et Michel MARTIN

17150 MIRAMBEAU

☎ 05 46 86 10 16 & 06 10 76 12 70 📄 05 46 86 10 16

email: martindavy@wanadoo.fr

web: www.haut-brochon.com

In this small hamlet there are four comfortable first-floor rooms on an ancient Charentais farm. Three of the rooms are doubles, while the fourth is a family suite of two rooms, one being a double and the other a twin; all have shower room and WC. Shared living room, TV, library. Garden with parking. Meals by reservation. Not far from Bordeaux vineyards and the Gironde estuary.

Prices s €49–€54; d €52–€60; t fr €68; extra person fr €16; dinner fr €20
Nearby ⚓ 3km ⚑ 50km Sea 45km ✐ 10km ☇ 4km Restaurant 4km
☲ 4km 🏠 4km ₩ 18km **Notes** No pets English spoken

⊯ La Bertonnière

Anne et Christian TARDY

17150 MIRAMBEAU

☎ 05 46 49 60 91 & 06 32 11 03 14　📄 05 46 49 83 31

email: labertonniere@aol.com

web: www.labertonniere.com

This late 19th-century property has three bedrooms in an old mill, one of them a split-level suite, and a further room in the owners' home which can sleep up to four people. The style of them all is a delightful mix of ancient and modern. Ornithologists will delight in the herons, wrens, kingfishers and chaffinches, but other possibilities here include fishing, mountain-biking and walking.

Prices s €45-€55; d €60-€70; t €70-€90; extra person fr €10　**On Site** Private ⭢　**Nearby** ⭐ 3km ⚓ 50km ⌫ 5km ⌂ 1km 🏠 1km 🚶 13km　**Notes** No pets English spoken Open April to October.

MONTENDRE

⊯ Les Chambres du Jardin

Valérie CAILLET

4, Rue des jardins, 17130 MONTENDRE

☎ 05 46 86 11 50　📄 05 46 86 11 50

email: valerie.verduzier@caramail.com

web: www.hotes-du-jardin.com

Cosy bedrooms available in a superb 19th-century house: two doubles and a twin with private facilities. Living room, lounge, TV, library, sauna, tree-lined garden with furniture and parking available. Unrestricted views over the Cité des Pines from rooms and the garden. Lake with watersports and fishing. Jonzac with aquatic park 20km.

Prices s fr €60; d fr €60; extra person fr €25　**On Site** 🏠　**Nearby** ⭐ 1km ⚓ 1km ⌫ 2km ⭢ 2km Restaurant 0.1km 🚶 2km 🏠 0.1km 🚶 0.3km　**Notes** Pets admitted English spoken

MONTLIEU-LA-GARDE

⊯ ✈ Les Galards

Pascal MENANTEAU

17210 MONTLIEU-LA-GARDE

☎ 05 46 04 53 62 & 06 15 42 95 25　📄 05 46 04 32 33

email: menanteau.pascal@free.fr

web: www.lesgalards.com

Situated on a working farm, each of the four rooms of this property is decorated in an individual style. On the ground floor are a double and single; upstairs are another double and single. All rooms have private bath or shower room and WC. Lounge with books, garden, fishing lake with pedalos, parking.

Prices s €46-€50; d €54-€59; extra person fr €20　**On Site** ⌫ 🏠　**Nearby** ⭐ 8km ⚓ 10km ⭢ Restaurant 1km 🚶 2km Spa 25km 🏠 1km 🚶 10km　**Notes** Pets admitted English spoken

MONTPELLIER-DE-MEDILLAN

⊯ 🍽 *Chambre d'hôtes*

Claude et Marie-Jeanne HUBIN

17, Rue de la Sauveté,

17260 MONTPELLIER DE MEDILLAN

☎ 05 46 90 92 70

email: hubin.c-mj@wanadoo.fr

web: www.lasauvete.com

In a quiet hamlet, this chambre d'hôtes offers three comfortable rooms, two double and one triple, all en suite. The rooms are located in an annexe, have separate access and look onto the garden. A lounge and dining room with open fire is available to guests; dinner is available by arrangement. Between the estuaries of the Gironde and the Charente, this is the home of oyster farming.

Prices not confirmed for 2008　**Nearby** ⭐ 15km ⚓ 25km ⌫ 0.5km ⭢ 5km 🚶 8km 🏠 3km 🚶 22km　**Notes** No pets English spoken Open Easter to 1 November.

NERE

⊯ ✈ 🍽 Le Chiron

Jacqueline GUIBERTEAU

17510 NERE

☎ 05 46 33 01 33 & 06 72 68 29 92

Three comfortable first-floor rooms are available in this house, where Jacqueline and Christian will share their enthusiasm for and appreciation of regional gastronomy and their rich cultural environment. All the rooms are doubles with shower and WC. Baby bed available; living rooms and conservatory; private parking; garden with small lake. Meals by arrangement.

Prices s €38-€40; d €43-€45; extra person fr €15; dinner fr €16　**Nearby** ⭐ 6km ⚓ 40km ⌫ 5km ⭢ 7km Restaurant 5km 🚶 5km 🏠 7km 🏠 5km 🚶 25km　**Notes** No pets English spoken

NIEULLE-SUR-SEUDRE

⊯ 🍽 ♿ Le Logis de Port Paradis

M et M MEBAUVE

12, Rue du Port Paradis, 17600 NIEULLE-SUR-SEUDRE

☎ 05 46 85 37 38 & 06 09 71 64 84

email: logis.portparadis@wanadoo.fr

web: www.portparadis.com

A beautifully restored Charentais house which has five very comfortable guest rooms, with independent access. Three of the rooms are doubles; the other two are two-roomed family suites for four, each with double bed and twin beds. All have private bath or shower room and WC. Lounge; attractive wooded gardens with swimming pool. Meals by arrangement (not Sundays or Thursdays).

Prices s fr €66; d €70-€90; t €95-€105; extra person fr €15; dinner fr €28　**On Site** 🏠 Private ⭢　**Nearby** ⭐ 7km ⚓ 20km ⌫ 4km Restaurant 3km 🚶 1km 🏠 0.5km 🚶 15km　**Notes** No pets English spoken

PISANY

⋕⋕⋕ La Chabotiere

M LE PENVEN-BOUCHER

42, Rue Julie d'Angennes, 17600 PISANY

☎ 05 46 94 80 31 & 06 77 48 28 33

email: monique.le-penven-boucher@orange.fr

Extensive wooded grounds provide the setting for this chambre d'hôtes, with its three individually styled bedrooms. All are double rooms, on the first floor, with en suite facilities. There is a lounge with books and open fire, a large terrace and private parking. Not far from the coast at Royan, and many other places to visit within easy reach.

Prices s fr €50; d fr €55 **Nearby** ⛵ 2km ⚓ 15km ⚙ 3km ⚲ 7km Restaurant 1km ⚘ 1km 🏠 1km ⚑ 15km **Notes** No pets English spoken Open Easter to 1 November.

PUYRAVAULT

⋕⋕⋕ ⬡ ⬡ Le Clos de la Garenne

Brigitte et Patrick FRANCOIS

9, Rue de la Garenne, 17700 PUYRAVAULT

☎ 05 46 35 47 71 ▤ 05 46 35 47 91

email: info@closdelagarenne.com

web: www.closdelagarenne.com

This 17th-century property is set in a four-hectare park with children's games, animals, table tennis and volleyball on site, and tennis courts nearby. The 'Linden' and 'Belle Epoch' rooms form a family suite which can sleep four to six, the 'Aunisienne' can sleep three and in an annexe, the 'Cottage' is a family suite sleeping five. All rooms have private facilities and there is a TV, billiards, a kitchen area and reading room. Baby facilities available.

Prices s fr €60; d fr €67; t €87-€105; extra person fr €20; dinner fr €25 **On Site** Restaurant ⚘ **Nearby** ⛵ 2km ⚓ 20km Sea 25km ⚙ 5km ⚲ 5km ⚘ 0.2km 🏠 5km ⚑ 5km **Notes** No pets English spoken CC

RETAUD

⋕⋕⋕ L'Orée du Bois

M-P CHAUVIN et F BOSSUYT

15, Route de Chez Touzeau, 17460 RETAUD

☎ 05 46 74 13 55 & 06 75 82 51 10

email: marie.pierre@club-internet.fr

web: www.retaud.com

The rooms here, in an annexe to the owners' home, are decorated in a theme set by the elements: 'Terre', 'Air', 'Feu', 'Eau'. Two of them are double rooms, one has twin beds, and the fourth has three singles. Each has independent ground floor access, and a private bath or shower room. Kitchenette; pleasant gardens and parking space.

Prices s fr €43; d fr €50; t fr €65 **Nearby** ⛵ 2km ⚓ 15km ⚙ 15km ⚲ 3km ⚘ 1km 🏠 3km ⚑ 12km **Notes** No pets English spoken

SAINTES

⋕⋕⋕ *Le Bois des Faux*

Nicole et Daniel BOULET

23, Rue du Champverdier, 17100 SAINTES

☎ 05 46 92 25 77 & 06 72 07 80 89 ▤ 05 46 90 00 91

email: leboisdesfaux17@wanadoo.fr

web: http://leboisdesfaux17.free.fr

In the heart of the countryside, this house overlooks the Charente and offers three guest rooms: the 'Wood,' the 'Cascade,' and the 'River' rooms, all double and en suite. There is a lounge with an open fire, a day room, TV and a library available to guests. Outside in the shaded garden are a terrace and a swimming pool and access to the River Charente.

Prices not confirmed for 2008 **On Site** ⚙ Private ⚲ **Nearby** ⛵ 3km ⚓ 10km ⚘ 2.5km 🏠 5km ⚑ 5km **Notes** No pets English spoken

⋕⋕⋕ *Le Haras du Grand Gaterat*

Rosine PONS

1, Route de Marennes, 17100 SAINTES

☎ 05 46 97 89 23 & 06 87 10 23 05 ▤ 05 46 97 89 23

email: bonsaipons@aol.com

web: www.gite-prop.com/17/7227

A superb late 18th-century property, with three very comfortable rooms upstairs in a part of the owners' home. The rooms sleep from two to four people; one of them is a suite, and each has a private bath or shower room and WC. The hosts cultivate bonsai trees and keep horses. The area is rich in history, with much to see.

Prices not confirmed for 2008 **Nearby** ⛵ 2km ⚓ 8km ⚙ 5km ⚲ 5km ⚘ 4km 🏠 6km ⚑ 6km **Notes** Pets admitted

SONNAC

⋕⋕⋕ Le Goulet

Frédérique THILL-TOUSSAINT

Le Clos du Plantis, 17160 MATHA

☎ 05 46 25 07 91 & 06 81 99 07 98

email: auplantis@wanadoo.fr

web: www.auplantis.com

This beautifully restored farmhouse, situated in a leafy hamlet, has three spacious and comfortable en suite rooms with private terraces: two double rooms, one with an additional single bed, and a family room made up of a twin and double room. Lounge and library, as well as a large garden bordering the river with a swimming pool. Cognac, Jarnac and Saintes are close by.

Prices s fr €45; d €52-€58; t fr €76; extra person fr €18 **On Site** Private ⚲ **Nearby** ⛵ 1.5km ⚓ 19km ⚙ 0.5km ⚘ 1km 🏠 0.5km ⚑ 19km **Notes** No pets English spoken

ST-BRIS-DES-BOIS

♯♯♯ Le logis de l'Astrée

Sophie BOUTINET-MANGEART
17770 SAINT-BRIS-DES-BOIS
☎ 05 46 93 44 07 & 06 09 62 47 65
email: smangeart@terre-net.fr
web: www.logis-astree.fr

Situated between woods and vineyards, this 17th-century property enjoys a delightfully peaceful location - although it has easy access to Cognac and Saintes. The four attractive rooms - two doubles and two triples - are on the ground and first floors; all have private bath or shower room and WC. Lounge with books.

Prices s €86-€98; d €96-€106; t fr €123; extra person fr €23
On Site Private ↖ **Nearby** ⛵ 6km ♨ 10km ⚡ 0.5km Restaurant 0.7km
♨ 1km ⛪ 0.2km ₩ 12km **Notes** Pets admitted English spoken

ST-CESAIRE

♯♯♯ ⚐ La Bujolière

Béatrice et Bernard MOULIN
5, Chez Lorain, 17770 SAINT-CESAIRE
☎ 05 46 93 08 56
email: bujoliere@wanadoo.fr
web: www.bujoliere.com

An old Charentais farmhouse which has been beautifully restored, this property has three spacious and comfortable bedrooms, all with air-conditioning and private facilities. On the ground floor is a double room, with space for an extra bed; upstairs are two more doubles, one with an additional folding single bed. Lounge with fire and books; garden with parking space. Meals by arrangement.

Prices s fr €50; d fr €55; t fr €70; extra person fr €15; dinner fr €22
Nearby ⛵ 6km ♨ 8km Sea 45km ⚡ 1km ↖ 1km Restaurant 0.8km
Spa 45km ♨ 1km ⛪ 2km ₩ 12km **Notes** No pets English spoken

ST-GEORGES-DES-COTEAUX

♯♯♯ *Chambre d'hôtes*

Anne et Dominique TROUVE
5, rue de l'Eglise, 17810 SAINT-GEORGES-DES-COTEAUX
☎ 05 46 92 96 66 ▤ 05 46 92 96 66
email: adtrouve@yahoo.fr

This 18th-century house close to Charente and Saintes offers guests a choice of accommodation: 'Moulinsart' is a three-bedded room; 'Pearl Buck' and 'Picardie' are doubles and 'Agatha Christie' has a double and single bed. Guests may use the lounge, a mezzanine sitting room, a library, a kitchen area, TV, French billiards, and garden with barbecue, sand pit, ping-pong, a portico and parking.

Prices not confirmed for 2008 **Nearby** ⛵ 3km ♨ 6km ⚡ 6km ↖ 6km
♨ 0.5km ⛪ 0.5km ₩ 6km **Notes** No pets English spoken Open April to 15 November.

ST-OUEN-D'AUNIS

♯♯♯ Les Palmiers

Evelyne et Rémy CARIOU
2, Rue du Beurre, 17230 SAINT-OUEN-D'AUNIS
☎ 05 46 68 99 52
email: evelyne.cariou@wanadoo.fr
web: http://perso.orange.fr/chambres.lespalmiers/

A 19th-century Charentaise house in a village about ten minutes from la Rochelle. Four bedrooms comprise a room for three (double bed and a single, with screen between) upstairs in the owners' house, and three double rooms in a separate building. All have private facilities. Fridge, microwave; garden furniture and a swimming pool.

Prices s fr €57; d fr €63; t €87-€112; extra person fr €15
On Site Private ↖ **Nearby** ⛵ 4km ♨ 12km ⚡ 2km Restaurant 1km
♨ 4km ⛪ 3km ₩ 15km **Notes** No pets English spoken

ST-PIERRE-D'OLERON

♯♯♯ ⚑ *Le Clos - La Menounière*

Micheline et J-Pierre DENIEAU
20 Rue de la Légère, 17310 SAINT-PIERRE-D'OLERON
☎ 05 46 47 14 34 ▤ 05 46 36 03 15
email: denieau.jean-pierre@wanadoo.fr
web: http://perso.wanadoo.fr/denieau-gites

En suite rooms in an annexe on a wine-making enterprise: one twin and four doubles, two of which have an additional single bed on a mezzanine. A foldaway bed can also be provided. There is a lounge with TV, a kitchen area available by arrangement, a garden with seating, portico, children's games and table tennis. The Ile d'Oleron, Continiere, oyster beds and marshlands are nearby.

Prices not confirmed for 2008 **On Site** Private ↖ **Nearby** ⛵ 4km
♨ 8km ⚡ 0.5km ♨ 0.5km ⛪ 3km ₩ 40km **Notes** Pets admitted English spoken

ST-PORCHAIRE

♯♯♯ *Chambre d'hôtes*

Jeanine TIRACCI
16 Rue du Cadran Bleu, 17250 SAINT-PORCHAIRE
☎ 05 46 95 55 05 & 06 83 19 98 28
email: perthuiserie@wanadoo.fr
web: http://perthuiserie.free.fr

Close to Saintes, famous for its Roman remains and art work, this superbly restored house has three big and very comfortable bedrooms - two doubles and a two-roomed suite with three single beds. All rooms have private bathrooms and WCs. Lounge with books; swimming pool and table tennis.

Prices d €70-€76; t fr €95; extra person fr €20 **On Site** Private ↖
Nearby ⛵ 8km ♨ 1.5km Sea 35km ⚡ 2km Restaurant 0.2km
♨ 0.5km Spa 35km ♨ 8km ⛪ 0.5km ₩ 8km **Notes** Pets admitted English spoken

ST-ROMAIN-DE-BENET

♨ Les Violettes de Malleville

Marie-Madeleine DOUAY
3, Rue Malleville, 17600 SAINT-ROMAIN-DE-BENET
☎ 05 46 96 92 05 & 06 30 70 17 24
email: mm48douay@yahoo.fr
web: http://perso.club-internet.fr/boogie/malleville/

Not far from the coast at Royan, and within easy reach of many other interesting sites, this rural property has four spacious and comfortable guest rooms. Two of the rooms are doubles (one on the ground floor); the others are triples. All have private bath or shower rooms and WCs. Lounge with books and an open fire, garden and parking space.

Prices s fr €44; d fr €50; t fr €60 **Nearby** ⚓ 2km ⌇ 25km ⌀ 7km
⚲ 6km ⌇ 2km ⌖ 6km ⋈ 6km **Notes** No pets English spoken

ST-SAVINIEN

♨ ⓘ Forgette

Jeannine et Gilbert LOIZEAU
17350 SAINT-SAVINIEN
☎ 05 46 90 21 20 & 06 08 32 20 29 ▤ 05 46 90 21 20
email: gloizeau@wanadoo.fr
web: www.chambre-hotes-valleedelacharente.com

Adjacent to the proprietors' home, these en suite guest rooms include two doubles (one with additional single bed) and a family suite made up of two rooms, one double and one three-bedded. A guest lounge and small kitchen area are available and there is a garden with a seating area. Bicycles can be hired, and dinner is available with advanced booking. A nearby leisure centre offers tennis, swimming, small boats and pedalos. Closed Xmas week.

Prices s fr €42; d fr €45; t fr €60-€75; dinner fr €15 **On Site** ⌀
Nearby ⚓ 3km ⌇ 20km ⚲ 2km ⌇ 2km ⌖ 2km ⋈ 2km
Notes No pets

ST-SORNIN

♨ ⓘ La Caussoliere

Alan GATES
10, rue du Petit Moulin, 17600 SAINT-SORNIN
☎ 05 46 85 44 62 ▤ 05 46 85 44 62
email: reservations@caussoliere.com
web: www.caussoliere.com

These four individually decorated rooms all offer a high level of comfort. One double is in the main house; a further two doubles (one with an extra bed) and a twin are in a restored barn. They all have private bath or shower room and WC. Lounge with books, large garden, bikes; meals by arrangement. Jacuzzi and spa available for guests use.

Prices s €67-€72; d €68-€88; t fr €82; extra person fr €15; dinner fr €24
On Site ♨ Private ⚲ **Nearby** ⚓ 1km ⌇ 20km ⌀ 1km Restaurant 5km
⌇ 0.2km ⌖ 6km ⋈ 10km **Notes** No pets English spoken Open 16 March to 14 November.

ST-SULPICE-DE-ROYAN

♨ La Closerie

Ebba et Brian LEWY
3, Rue des Morlons, 17200 SAINT SULPICE DE ROYAN
☎ 05 46 22 68 40 ▤ 05 46 22 68 40
email: brian.lewy@wanadoo.fr
web: www.la-closerie-france.com

A separate guests' entrance leads to four first floor rooms which have all been individually decorated. Three of the rooms are doubles, and the third has twin beds. All have private bath or shower room and WC. Guests' lounge, billiard table, TV and stereo. Attractive gardens with garden furniture and swimming pool.

Prices s €55-€60; d €60-€65; extra person fr €18 **On Site** Spa
Private ⚲ **Nearby** ⚓ 10km ⌇ 10km ⌀ 5km Restaurant 0.3km ⌇ 0.5km
⌖ 8km ⌇ 0.5km ⋈ 6km **Notes** No pets English spoken

ST-THOMAS-DE-CONAC

♨ ⓘ Les Caves

J et D DEGORCE-NOBLE
17150 SAINT-THOMAS-DE-CONAC
☎ 05 46 04 00 80 & 06 21 80 45 69
email: john.domi.lescaves@wanadoo.fr

This is an attractive house, built in the local style. All the guest accommodation is on the first floor. There is a three-roomed family suite for five (double bed, twin beds, and a single), a triple room (double bed plus single), and a double room. All have private facilities. Lounge with fire and books, extensive grounds, meals by arrangement.

Prices s fr €42; d fr €50; t fr €66; extra person fr €16; dinner fr €18
Nearby ⚓ 0.3km ⌇ 45km ⌀ 5km ⚲ 10km ⌇ 0.3km ⌖ 0.3km
⋈ 23km **Notes** No pets English spoken

ST-XANDRE

♨ Trente Vents

A et M AUTRUSSEAU
1, Rue de la Grâce par Hasard, 17138 SAINT-XANDRE
☎ 05 46 37 22 10

In a remote location, this chambre d'hôtes offers a twin room, a double with an additional single bed on a mezzanine, and a family suite with a double and single bed, all en suite. Lounge with mezzanine and sitting room with reading area, TV, fridge and microwave are all available. Outside, the enclosed garden has a lawn, a terrace, a barbecue, children's games and a portico.

Prices s fr €40; d €48-€50; t fr €65; extra person fr €15 **Nearby** ⚓ 5km
⌇ 5km ⌀ 8km ⚲ 8km Restaurant 8km ⌇ 1km ⌖ 8km ⌇ 1km ⋈ 8km
Notes No pets

STE-SOULLE

⊞ *Usseau*

Monique et Pierre GILBERT

3 Bis, route de Nantes, 17220 SAINTE-SOULLE

☎ 05 46 37 50 32 🖹 05 46 37 26 11

email: p-gilbert@wanadoo.fr

web: www.gite-prop.com/17/2618

The guest rooms at this chambre d'hôtes are in a restored barn and include a twin and two doubles, all en suite with a foldaway bed or cot available. There is a lounge reserved for guests, a TV, telephone and parking. A shaded garden offers a swimming pool, ping-pong and children's games. There are local tennis courts. La Rochelle and Ile de Re are nearby.

Prices not confirmed for 2008 **On Site** Private ⊀ **Nearby** ⛵ 2km ⚓ 10km ✐ 2km ◑ 0.5km 🏬 2km ⋙ 10km **Notes** No pets English spoken

THAIRE

⊞ **Chambre d'hôtes**

Brigitte FONTENAY-MANIEN

2, rue de Dirac, 17290 THAIRE

☎ 05 46 56 24 21

Three en suite double rooms are offered in this typical 18th-century house in the region of Charente. There is a lounge, a kitchen area and a games room available to guests and an English-style garden, with furniture and children's games, surrounds the house. There is a good restaurant only 100mtrs away and parking. La Rochelle, Iles de Re and Aix, Fouras and Rochefort are all within travelling distance.

Prices s €46-€49; d €50-€53; t fr €73 **Nearby** ⛵ 8km ⚓ 30km ✐ 7km ⋟ 7km Restaurant 7km ◑ 0.2km ◐ 0.2km 🏬 0.2km ⋙ 7km **Notes** No pets English spoken Open April to September.

TRIZAY

⊞ **Le Chizé**

Fabienne et Pascal PASQUIER

17250 TRIZAY

☎ 05 46 82 09 56 & 06 13 39 29 95 🖹 05 46 82 09 56

email: lechize@wanadoo.fr

web: www.chambre-hote-trizay.com

Guests can enjoy peaceful surroundings at this restored farmhouse. There are three very comfortable upstairs bedrooms, all with a double bed and a single, and all with en suite bathroom/WC. The guest rooms have an independent entrance. On the ground floor is a lounge/dining room with fireplace, TV and books. Use of kitchen.

Prices s fr €47; d fr €53; t fr €68; extra person fr €15 **On Site** ◐ **Nearby** ⛵ 5km ⚓ 30km Sea 20km ✐ 0.8km ⋟ 13km Restaurant 1km ◑ 2km Spa 25km 🏬 1km ⋙ 13km **Notes** No pets

VENERAND

⊞ *Au Point du Jour*

Danielle et J-Pierre GALAND

2, Chemin du Vallon, 17100 VENERAND

☎ 05 46 97 79 65 & 06 98 06 27 19

email: j.p.galand@wanadoo.fr

web: www.aupointdujour.net

A separate guests' entrance leads to three spacious guest rooms in the owners' house. On the ground floor is a family room (double bed and two singles); upstairs are two double rooms. All have private shower room and WC. Lounge with books and open fire. Open, wooded grounds, off-road parking.

Prices not confirmed for 2008 **Nearby** ⛵ 5km ⚓ 5km ✐ 7km ⋟ 7km ◑ 7km 🏬 8km ⋙ 8km **Notes** No pets English spoken Open Easter to 1 November.

VERINES

⊞ **Les Passeroses**

Quitterie et Serge AUBINEAU

6, Chemin de l'Ardillon, 17540 VERINES

☎ 05 46 37 32 98 & 06 76 95 64 36 🖹 05 46 37 06 44

email: contact@lespasseroses.com

web: www.lespasseroses.com

A twin room and two doubles with private facilities and modern décor, available in this renovated village. Living room/lounge with TV reserved for guests, kitchen corner, garden with swimming pool and parking. Close to La Rochelle, famous for its towers, aquarium and seafood restaurants. Discover le Marais Poitevin by boat or by bike.

Prices s fr €48; d fr €55 **On Site** Private ⊀ **Nearby** ⛵ 7km ⚓ 20km ✐ 4km Restaurant 5km ◑ 1km ◐ 12km 🏬 0.4km ⋙ 20km **Notes** No pets

DEUX-SÈVRES

AIRVAULT

⊞ 🍴 **Le Vieux Château**

Isabelle et Eric VILAIN

6 rue de Brelucan, 79600 AIRVAULT

☎ 05 49 64 25 78 & 06 09 61 85 38

email: levieuxchateau@free.fr

web: www.levieuxchateau-airvault.com

CONTINUED

POITOU-CHARENTES

AIRVAULT   CONTINUED

Close by the old château, this is a house with four guest bedrooms. On the ground floor there is a double room and a twin-bedded room; upstairs is another double, and a family suite for four. All have private facilities. Above-ground swimming pool, and meals available if pre-booked. Futuroscope is about 50 kilometres away.

Prices s €54-€66; d €59-€71; t fr €96; extra person fr €12; dinner fr €21 **On Site** Private ⚲ Restaurant ☂ **Nearby** ⚐ 9km ⚓ 26km ⚓ 0.8km ♨ ⋒ 25km **Notes** Pets admitted English spoken

ARCAIS

⫼ Chambre d'hôtes

E CHOLLET-PLAT
10 rue de l'Ouche, 79210 ARCAIS
☎ 05 49 35 42 59
email: chambres.dhotes@wanadoo.fr
web: www.chambre-dhote.com

This charming house is situated in a village near the port, with a garden running down to the water where boats and canoes are available; boat trips and bike rental on site. The main house has three stylish bedrooms for two to five people, doubles or singles, with TV and private facilities, whilst the annexe has one bedroom with disabled access. Cooking facilities; heated indoor swimming pool and solarium. Parking.

Prices s fr €45; d fr €50; extra person €12-€20 **On Site** ⚓ Restaurant Private ⚲ **Nearby** ⚐ 4km ⚓ 15km Sea 45km ♨ 0.3km ⚑ 0.1km ⋒ 20km **Notes** Pets admitted English spoken

⫼ ⚇ Les Bourdettes

Jean-Claude PEAN
14 chemin de la Foulée, 79210 ARCAIS
☎ 05 49 35 88 95
email: jc.pean@wanadoo.fr
web: http://jcpean.9online.fr

On the edge of Sèvre Niortaise in the Marais Poitevin area, three rooms in a typically traditional house: two doubles and one suite with a double and two twins, all with private facilities. There is a sitting room with TV and fireplace, large covered terrace with views, enclosed garden and parking. Walks and cycle paths on site.

Prices s fr €46; d fr €46-€50; extra person fr €19; dinner fr €16 **On Site** ⚑ **Nearby** ⚐ 3km ⚓ 27km ⚲ 1km Restaurant 0.5km ♨ 2.5km ⚑ 1.5km ⋒ 25km **Notes** No pets English spoken Open April to September.

CHENAY

⫼ ⚇ Chambre d'hôtes

Jean et Madeleine NAU
Place de la Mairie, 79120 CHENAY
☎ 05 49 07 31 28

Three rooms in the owners' house including a double room, a family room with one double bed and two singles, and one double room with a cot, each with private facilities. A terrace overlooks the garden and there is garage parking.

Prices s fr €31; d fr €32; extra person fr €9; dinner fr €12 **Nearby** ⚐ 10km ⚓ 2km ⚲ 7km ♨ 7km ⚑ 3km ⋒ 20km **Notes** Pets admitted

⫼ ⚇ Les Chenets

J-Yves & Micheline NAU
1 Rue des Ecoles, 79120 CHENAY
☎ 05 49 07 32 90
email: chenets_nau@yahoo.fr
web: www.chenets.fr/index4.htm

This is a traditional house opening on to a heated swimming pool and enclosed wooded garden. Three first-floor double rooms with shower and WC. Table tennis, bicycles; numerous walk routes near by. Micheline and Jean-Yves offer a friendly welcome, and encourage you to discover traditional cooking around a lively and convivial table.

Prices s fr €40; d fr €40; extra person fr €13; dinner fr €15 **On Site** Private ⚲ **Nearby** ⚐ 8km ⚓ 15km ⚑ 4km Restaurant 0.1km ♨ 8km ⚑ 8km ⋒ 22km **Notes** No pets English spoken

CHERVEUX

⫼ ⚇ Château de Cherveux

François et M.Thérèse REDIEN
2, place de l'Eglise, 79410 CHERVEUX
☎ 05 49 75 06 55 ▤ 05 49 75 06 55
email: redien@aol.com
web: www.chateau-de-cherveux.com

In the 15th century this was a Scottish fortress; today it is a farmhouse with superb architecture! It has three guest rooms, two of them over the old guardroom. There is a large room with a double bed and a single; a double-bedded room; and a two-roomed suite in the château for up to six people. Generous breakfasts; other meals by arrangement.

Prices s €45-€50; d €50-€60; t fr €75; extra person fr €20; dinner fr €20 **On Site** ⚑ **Nearby** ⚐ 0.5km ⚓ 20km ⚲ 11km Restaurant 3km ♨ 3km ☂ 3km ⚑ 0.2km ⋒ 15km **Notes** No pets English spoken

COULON

⫼ La Rigole

Sergine FABIEN
180 route des Bords de Sèvre, 79510 COULON
☎ 05 49 35 97 90

In the heart of the Marais-Poitevin region, this beautiful traditional house sits on the edge of the river and has four guest bedrooms: one room for three with a double and single bed, and three rooms with two doubles and two singles have private facilities, there is a sitting area and garden. Local excursions possible.

Prices s fr €42; d fr €45; t fr €50 **On Site** ⚑ **Nearby** ⚐ 15km ⚓ 12km ⚲ 7km Restaurant 0.8km ♨ 2km ⋒ 12km **Notes** No pets English spoken

♦♦♦ *Rigole du Grand Coin*

Antoine et Sabrina BERTRAND
79510 COULON
☎ 05 49 24 45 32
email: contact@relaisdelaveniseverte.com
web: www.relaisdelaveniseverte.com

Three huge first-floor rooms overlook the river in Antoine and Sabrina's old marshland farm two kilometres from Coulon. There is a light and airy triple, with large balcony; a twin room with small balcony; and another triple. All rooms have private shower room and WC. Two gîtes also available; swimming pool and outdoor games.

Prices not confirmed for 2008　**On Site** ✐　**Nearby** ☘ 6km　⚓ 2km
🏠 2km　🚴 14km　**Notes** No pets　English spoken

FRONTENAY-ROHAN-ROHAN

♦♦♦ Faugerit

Frédéric BERTHOME
Chemin du Marais, 79270 FRONTENAY ROHAN ROHAN
☎ 05 49 77 55 51 & 06 23 53 95 85
email: logis-de-faugerit@wanadoo.fr
web: http://perso.wanadoo.fr/logisdefaugerit/index.htm

This 15th century property has been recently restored and enjoys a verdant, flowery setting 2km from town. It has three double rooms and two rooms with a double and single bed, each with private facilities. Cot and high chair available. Private lounge; breakfasts served in the large dining room. Walks on site, Marais Poitevin (bikes, boats) 12km, Niort 12km.

Prices s fr €48; d fr €57; t fr €73; extra person fr €18　**Nearby** ✐ 0.5km
⚓ 12km　⚓ 3km　🏠 2.5km　🚴 14km　**Notes** No pets

GERMOND-ROUVRE

♦♦♦ ⚑ Breilbon

Didier et Josette BLANCHARD
40 Chemin de la Minée, 79220 GERMOND-ROUVRE
☎ 05 49 04 05 01 & 06 87 41 06 60
email: josette.didier@breilbon.com
web: www.breilbon.com

Three guest rooms in this beautifully restored property in a small village between Parthenay and Niort. There are two double rooms and a double with a single bed, all with private facilities. There is a sitting room with TV, open fireplace and card-phone. Child's bed, cot and high chair available. Table tennis, walks and enclosed garden.

Prices s fr €33; d €43-€47; t €55-€59; extra person fr €12; dinner fr €15　**Nearby** ☘ 6km　⚓ 10km　✐ 2km　⚓ 15km　Restaurant 2km　⚓ 2km
⚓ 20km　🏠 8km　🚴 15km　**Notes** Pets admitted　English spoken

LA MOTHE-SAINT-HERAY

♦♦♦ ⚑ Mouillage Vert

Uschi et J-Pierre ANCOT
79800 LA MOTHE SAINT HERAY
☎ 05 49 04 86 18
email: lemouillagevert@hotmail.com
web: www.lemouillagevert.com

A restored farmhouse set on a hillside among mature trees, ten kilometres from the historic village of Saint-Maixent-l'Ecole. There are three double rooms, one with an extra single bed, and all have private bath or shower room/WC. Meals available by arrangement.

Prices s fr €40; d fr €45; t fr €55; dinner fr €18　**Nearby** ☘ 15km
⚓ 25km　⚓ 2km　⚓ 10km　Restaurant 2km　⚓ 2km　⚓ 2km　🏠 2km
🚴 10km　**Notes** No pets　English spoken

LE BEUGNON

♦♦♦ ⚑ La Croisée des Chemins

Viviane BABIN
Chicheville, 79130 LE BEUGNON
☎ 05 49 69 15 65
email: babin.viviane@wanadoo.fr

Exposed stone and beams combine with modern design on the outside, and sympathetic, quality interior decor. Great view of the valley. Two street-level double bedrooms, well lit, with private shower room and WC. Upstairs a spacious pastel-decorated double with shower room/WC; two quality doubles with private shower room/WCs. Evening meal with local produce by arrangement.

Prices s fr €55; d fr €60; t fr €70; extra person fr €10; dinner fr €25　**Nearby** ☘ 20km　✐ 8km　⚓ 5km　⚓ 5km　🏠 5km　🚴 35km
Notes No pets　English spoken

LE VANNEAU-IRLEAU

♦♦♦ ⚓ Le Paradis

Philippe et Chantal ROUYER
29 Sainte Sabine, 79270 LE VANNEAU-IRLEAU
☎ 05 49 35 33 95
email: cp.rouyer@wanadoo.fr
web: www.gite-le-paradis.com

This traditional house sits in 5 hectares in the heart of Marais-Poitevin. Rooms include two doubles, one triple, one room for four and one for five with extra beds if required. Each room has a shower and wash basin. The kitchen is available for guests, as well as a large covered terrace ideal for breakfast. On site there is a private lake with fishing. Landing stage and boating activities.

Prices s fr €45; d €50-€58; t fr €65; extra person fr €15　**On Site** ✐
Nearby ☘ 5km　⚓ 20km　Sea 45km　⚓ 4km　Restaurant 2km　⚓ 2km
Spa 18km　⚓ 2km　🏠 2km　🚴 18km　**Notes** No pets　English spoken

LOUIN

⊞ Ô Trois Oliviers

Jocelyne et Michel PERICHON
route d'Amailloux, 79600 LOUIN
☎ 05 49 63 33 79 ▤ 05 49 64 58 25
email: michelperichon@aol.com
web: www.ripere-gites.com

This old farmhouse has a double room downstairs, and two rooms for three (one a grade 2 room) upstairs. In a separate building is another room for three, with a lounge area and kitchenette. All of the rooms have a private shower room and WC, but those for the grade 2 room are not en suite.

Prices s €41-€51; d €45-€55; t fr €66 **Nearby** ⛷ 5km ⚓ 30km ♂ 4km ⟋ 10km Restaurant 5km ⚓ 4km ⚘ 9km ⛪ 5km ⚠ 15km **Notes** Pets admitted

MARIGNY

⊞ Le Grand Mauduit

Francine GARNAUD
Le Vieux Fournil, 79360 MARIGNY
☎ 05 49 09 72 20 ▤ 05 49 09 72 20

A 15th-century house on the edge of the Chizé Forest, situated in a 5 hectare botanical park, full of wild flowers. There are two doubles, a room with double bed and convertible twin beds, and a single room with child's bed, all with private facilities. The patio is ablaze with flowers and there is a sitting room with fireplace and a cooking area for guests. Walking route GR 36 on site.

Prices d €60-€65; extra person €18-€20 **Nearby** ⛷ 12km ♂ 25km ⟋ 20km Restaurant 5km ⚓ 0.8km ⛪ 5km ⚠ 3km **Notes** Pets admitted Open April to 1 November.

NIORT

⊞ La Magnolière

Alain et Catherine MARCHADIER
16, Impasse de l'Abbaye, 79000 NIORT
☎ 05 49 35 36 06 ▤ 05 49 79 14 28
email: a.marchadier@lamagnoliere.fr
web: www.lamagnoliere.com

Peacefully situated on the edge of Marais Poitevin, this large residential property dominates Sèvre Niortaise. There are two double rooms and four singles, all with stylish furniture, TV, computer points, and spacious bathroom or shower room. Breakfast is served in the dining room or in the garden; there is a large sitting room, library, a swimming pool and exhibitions of contemporary paintings.

Prices s fr €76; d fr €80 **On Site** ♂ Private ⟋ **Nearby** ⛷ 7km Restaurant 0.8km ⚓ 1km ⛪ 4km ⛪ 4km ⚠ 5km **Notes** No pets English spoken

SAUZE-VAUSSAIS

⊞ ♥ La Ferme de Puy d'Anché

Didier RAGOT
79190 SAUZE-VAUSSAIS
☎ 05 49 07 90 69 ▤ 05 49 07 72 09
email: contact@ferme-puyanche.fr
web: www.ferme-puyanche.fr

Six bedrooms full of character in a restored old building situated close to the owners' farm. One double room on the ground floor and five on the first floor with four single beds as well. Shower room, wc, and TV points in each room.

Prices s fr €46; d €51-€55; t €70-€75; extra person fr €15 **Nearby** ⛷ 5km ♂ 2km ⟋ 0.3km Restaurant 0.1km ⚓ 0.3km ⛪ 1km ⚠ 12km **Notes** Pets admitted English spoken CC

SOUVIGNE

⊞ ⌘ Bois Bourdet

Louise et Leslie NICHOLSON
79800 SOUVIGNE
☎ 05 49 76 35 39
email: info@boisbourdet.com

This is a sensitively-restored 18th-century farmhouse, five kilometres from Saint-Maixent-l'Ecole. Two bedrooms are in the main house - a grade 2 double, and a family suite for up to four people; another double-bedded room is in the former bakehouse. All have private bath or shower room and WC. Living room, kitchen and heated swimming pool.

Prices s fr €50; d €60-€70; t fr €80; extra person fr €20; dinner fr €30 **On Site** ♂ Private ⟋ **Nearby** ⛷ 6km ♂ 15km ♂ 5km Restaurant 5km ⚓ 5km Spa 40km ⛪ 5km ⚠ 5km **Notes** No pets English spoken

ST-HILAIRE-LA-PALUD

⊞ ⌘ ♿ La Rivière

Monique Stoesslé
25 rue du Marais Sauvage,
79210 SAINT HILAIRE LA PALUD
☎ 05 49 26 07 32 ▤ 05 49 26 14 11
email: accueil@marais-sauvage.fr
web: www.marais-sauvage.fr

This is a quiet spot in the heart of the Marais Sauvage. The five very comfortable bedrooms are in converted barns - three doubles, a twin-bedded room, and a family room for four. All have television, internet access, private shower and WC. Pleasant garden with a terrace; a good area for walking and cycling.

Prices s fr €52; d fr €57; t fr €72; extra person fr €15; dinner fr €20 **On Site** Restaurant ♂ **Nearby** ⛷ 4km ♂ 0.8km ⟋ 9km ⚓ 3km ⛪ 2km ⚠ 9km **Notes** No pets

⊞ Les Lavandières

J-Claude et Catherine DESBAS
8, rue des Lavandières, 79210 SAINT HILAIRE LA PALUD
☎ 05 49 35 31 20 & 06 80 21 19 26　▤ 05 49 35 31 20
email: les.lavandieres@wanadoo.fr
web: www.marais-poitevin.com/heberg-ch/les-lavandieres/

The hosts here have converted the stables of their large house in a marshlands village to offer three stylishly-decorated double first-floor rooms with shower and WC. A large reception room with open fire opens on to a covered terrace and the unsupervised swimming pool. Gourmet breakfasts served buffet-style. Walks and bike routes; cycle hire and boat rides one kilometre.

Prices s fr €50; d fr €55; extra person fr €15　**On Site** Restaurant
Private ⚲　**Nearby** ⚑ 2.5km ⚓ 25km ⚐ 0.5km ⚓ 0.5km Spa 40km
⚑ 4km ⚑ 0.1km ⚑ 9km　**Notes** No pets

⊞ Logis de la Venise Verte

Monique PROUST
12, place de l'Eglise, 79210 SAINT HILAIRE LA PALUD
☎ 05 49 35 52 40 & 06 50 34 91 00
web: www.logisveniseverte.com

This converted barn has four double rooms upstairs, and a separate family suite, with a double bed and bunks, downstairs. All of the rooms have a private shower room and WC. There are enclosed wooded grounds, with Jacuzzi and a circular swimming pool.

Prices s fr €46; d fr €52; t €65-€79; extra person fr €13
On Site Private ⚲　**Nearby** ⚑ 2.5km ⚓ 25km ⚐ 3km Restaurant 4km
⚑ 1km ⚑ 23km　**Notes** No pets

ST-VINCENT-LA-CHATRE

⊞ ❦ Chambre d'hôtes

Béatrice BOUTIN
Le Bourg, 79500 SAINT VINCENT LA CHATRE
☎ 05 49 29 94 25　▤ 05 49 29 94 25
email: vieuxfour@mellecom.fr
web: www.mellecom.fr/fastvincent

Situated in the heart of the village, 10km from Melle, this stunning farm property has a small enclosed garden. One family bedroom has a double and two twin beds, and there are two twin rooms, all with private facilities. Ferme-auberge on site. Silver mines 10km.

Prices s fr €35; d fr €50; t fr €67　**Nearby** ⚑ 5km ⚓ 30km ⚐ 8km ⚲
Restaurant 0.1km ⚓ 0.3km ⚑ 10km ⚑ 25km　**Notes** No pets CC

TAIZE

⊞ La Closeraie

Frédérique HAMEURY
24 rue du Thouet-Maranzais, 79100 TAIZE
☎ 05 49 68 02 76
email: lacloseraie.duval@free.fr

Standing in its own grounds, this mansion has three first floor bedrooms. There is a two-roomed family suite for four (double bed and singles), a double room with a child's bed, and another double room with separate access via an outside staircase. All have private bath or shower room and WC.

Prices s fr €46; d fr €50; extra person fr €16　**On Site** ⚐ ⚓
Nearby ⚑ 5km ⚓ 30km ⚲ 7km Restaurant 2km ⚓ 7km ⚑ 5km
⚑ 3km　**Notes** No pets English spoken

VALLANS

⊞ ⃝⃝ Le Logis d'Antan

A RAGOUILLIAUX-DI BATTISTA
140 rue St Louis, 79270 VALLANS
☎ 05 49 04 86 75　▤ 05 49 32 85 05
email: info@logisdantan.com
web: www.logisdantan.eu

Only 10km from the Marais-Poitevin, this establishment offers a variety of rooms with private facilities. There are two doubles, a room with three singles, two bedrooms with a private entrance, each with two doubles and two twins, a sofa and TV, and a two-bedroom suite at the bottom of the park. Living room; library with TV; fridge; meals by reservation. Closed Xmas.

Prices s fr €65; d fr €65; extra person fr €16; dinner fr €25　**On Site** ⚓
Nearby ⚑ 15km ⚐ 1km ⚲ Restaurant 10km ⚓ 1km ⚑ 0.5km
⚑ 17km　**Notes** Pets admitted English spoken

VAUSSEROUX

⊞ ❦ La Ferme de la Roseraie

Ludivine BETIS
79420 VAUSSEROUX
☎ 05 49 70 05 54　▤ 05 49 70 05 54
email: lafermedelaroseraie@wanadoo.fr

A beautifully restored Gatinaise farm situated in beautiful wooded countryside with an 11-hectare park. There are two rooms with two double and two single beds, a double with sofa bed and TV and a

CONTINUED

VAUSSEROUX   CONTINUED

room in a separate building with a double and sofa bed; all with private facilities. Sitting room, kitchenette, table tennis.

Prices s fr €40; d fr €46; t fr €53; extra person fr €10; dinner €17-€35 **Nearby** ♿ 16km ⚓ 9km ➹ 16km ♨ 4km 🏛 1km ⛴ 19km **Notes** No pets English spoken

VERNOUX-EN-GATINE

▥ 🍴 *La Rémondière*

Jean-Louis MAURY

79240 VERNOUX EN GATINE

☎ 05 49 95 85 90 📠 05 49 95 96 07

email: remondiereweb@aol.com

This wonderful old bake house, surrounded by apple trees, is in the heart of the Gatinaise countryside. There are four rooms: a family room with two double beds and three double rooms on the same floor, two rooms with two double beds and one room with twin beds. It is possible to sleep extra people on a mezzanine and rooms have private facilities. A kitchenette allows for self-catering.

Prices not confirmed for 2008 **Nearby** ♿ 7km ⚓ 0.3km ➹ 9km ♨ 2km 🏛 9km ⛴ 45km **Notes** Pets admitted

VILLIERS-EN-PLAINE

▥ *La Dan de Champbertrand*

Francky BLANC

Le Prieuré de la Dan, 79160 VILLIERS EN PLAINE

☎ 05 49 25 63 55 & 06 71 86 89 83

email: blanc.francky@wanadoo.fr

web: www.leprieuredeladent.com

Part of this priory dates back to the 13th century. One bedroom has separate access via an internal courtyard (double with shower/WC). Two communicating family rooms have a double and two singles, shower room and WC. A further double has shower room and WC. Another two communicating family rooms offer two doubles and a single with shower room and WC. Swimming pool shared with two self-catering cottages. Breakfast is served in a large dining room or under an arbour.

Prices not confirmed for 2008 **Nearby** ♿ 5km ⚓ 1km ➹ 3km ♨ 5km ⛴ 18km **Notes** No pets English spoken

---

VIENNE

ARCHIGNY

▥ *Logis de la Talbardière*

Jacques LONHIENNE

86210 ARCHIGNY

☎ 05 49 85 32 52 📠 05 49 85 32 52

email: jacques.lonhienne@wanadoo.fr

web: www.la.talbardiere.archigny.net

Tranquillity is guaranteed in this 17th-century residence and its outbuildings. It has three rooms: two doubles, with beds which can act

as doubles or twins, and a triple room. Extra beds and cots if needed. Guests' lounge. Discounts for longer stays. Roche-Posay 15km: spa.

Prices not confirmed for 2008 **Nearby** ♿ 18km ⚓ 15km ➹ 6km ➹ 17km ♨ 6km 🏛 6km ⛴ 20km **Notes** No pets English spoken Open April to September.

ASLONNES

▥ *Le Port Laverre*

Mme CHOLET

86340 ASLONNES

☎ 05 49 61 08 38 📠 05 49 11 94 20

email: info@moulinlaverre.com

web: www.moulinlaverre.com

A former mill and tastefully restored outbuildings, in an exceptional setting at the gateway to Poitiers. A comfortable stay is assured in the three double rooms and two twins, each with air-conditioning and private facilities. Living room with TV, books and magazines. Lovely swimming pool on the banks of the river (young children must be supervised). Fitness room, garden furniture and parking available..

Prices s fr €65; d fr €80 **On Site** ⚓ 🏊 Private ➹ **Nearby** ♿ 10km ⚓ 25km Restaurant 1.5km ♨ 4km 🏛 4km ⛴ 14km **Notes** No pets English spoken

AVANTON

▥ *Martigny*

Annie ARRONDEAU

39 Route de Chasseneuil, 86170 AVANTON

☎ 05 49 51 04 57 & 06 07 24 75 30 📠 05 49 51 04 57

email: annie.arrondeau@libertysurf.fr

web: www.lafermeduchateau.fr

A restored Poitou farmhouse in the grounds of the Château de Martigny. There are three guest rooms, all with private facilities: two doubles, one with cot and the other with an extra single, and a grade 2 family room with a mezzanine which has one double and two singles. Kitchenette, sitting room; library; swimming pool. Delicious breakfasts can be enjoyed on the terrace overlooking the enclosed garden.

Prices not confirmed for 2008 **On Site** Private ➹ **Nearby** ♿ 10km ⚓ 12km ⚓ 3km ♨ 3km 🏛 3km ⛴ 2km **Notes** No pets English spoken Open 15 February to 15 November.

BENASSAY

▥ *Manoir Saint Hilaire*

Louis et Bernadette BOURBON

8 Route de la Gatine, 86470 BENASSAY

☎ 05 49 42 98 42 📠 05 49 42 98 42

email: manoirsthilaire@wanadoo.fr

The rooms here are all on the ground floor, in a converted outbuilding of the Manoir St Hilaire: a twin-bedded room, a double-bedded room and a room for three with a double bed and a single, all with private facilities. This is a good area for walking, with excellent way-marked footpaths close by.

Prices not confirmed for 2008 **Nearby** ↓6km 🏌 12km ⬙ 7km
🏊 12km 🎣 7km 🚲 26km **Notes** No pets

BEUXES

▦ Moulin Pallu

Danielle LECOMTE
86120 BEUXES
☎ 05 49 98 70 55

Close to the Châteaux of the Loire, a 19th-century family home with a
wonderful rustic feel. The property has three double guest rooms with
private facilities, two with an extra single bed and a cot if needed. Near
Richelieu, Fontevraud Abbey.

Prices s fr €36; d fr €42; t fr €50 **Nearby** ⬙ 12km ↓18km 🏌 3km
⬙ 12km Restaurant 0.8km 🏊 8km 🎣 1km 🚲 12km **Notes** Pets
admitted

BONNEUIL-MATOURS

▦ *Les Pierres Blanches*

Dominique GALLAIS-PRADAL
86210 BONNEUIL-MATOURS
☎ 05 49 85 24 75

Situated between forest and Vienne, a large house in a wonderful
wooded park which boasts over 200 rose bushes. Three double rooms
include a grade 2 and one with an extra single bed and have private
facilities. There is a private terrace overlooking the park, a sitting room
with an open fireplace and magazines, a private swimming pool. Fresh
sandwiches can be ordered. Parking.

Prices not confirmed for 2008 **On Site** 🏌 Private ⬙ **Nearby** ⬙ 10km
🏊 10km 🎣 1km 🚲 20km **Notes** Pets admitted English spoken

BOURNAND

▦ ⫶⊙⫶ *La Dorelle*

Jacqueline et Joseph THOMAS
4 La Dorelle, 86120 BOURNAND
☎ 05 49 98 72 23
email: ladorelle@voila.fr
web: www.ladorelle.com

In a calm hamlet close to Fontevraud Abbey and Roiffé golf course;
four guest rooms in a beautifully restored stone farmhouse, separate
from the owners' home. There are three doubles and a twin, each
with private facilities, a sitting room with open fireplace, magazines
and books as well as a kitchenette for self-catering. A terrace overlooks
the garden, with barbecue and garden furniture. Extra beds are
available on request.

Prices not confirmed for 2008 **Nearby** ↓10km 🏌 3km ⬙ 10km
🏊 2km 🎣 5km 🚲 30km **Notes** No pets English spoken

CELLE-L'EVESCAULT

▦ ⫶⊙⫶ Château de la Livraie

Lysiane MORIN
86600 CELLE-L'EVESCAULT
☎ 05 49 43 52 59
web: www.chateaulalivraie.com

This fabulous renovated château has a peaceful setting in a densely
wooded park, complete with a small river and farm animals. The three
double rooms are comfortable and have antique furniture; two have
extra beds and all have private facilities. There is also a family suite
consisting of two rooms, one double and one twin. Lounge with TV,
table tennis and other games. A guest menu is available on request.

Prices s fr €41; d fr €47; t fr €59; dinner fr €16 **On Site** 🏌 ⬙
Nearby ⬙ 15km ↓30km ⬙ 6km Restaurant 6km 🏊 3km 🎣 3km
🚲 6km **Notes** No pets English spoken

CHAMPNIERS

▦ ⫶⊙⫶ La Theophiliere

J-L et G FAZILLEAU
86400 CHAMPNIERS
☎ 05 49 87 19 04 📠 05 49 87 19 04
email: jlgfazilleau@cegetel.net
web: http://chambres-hotes-poitou-charente.ifrance.com

This traditional stone house is situated near St Nicolas de Civray,
famous for its Roman churches. There is a grade 3 room with a
double and two singles, a grade 2 twin room (both with private
facilities) and a grade 2 double room with a shower room on the
landing. Extra beds available. Sitting room with books, table tennis and
a piano; veranda overlooking a pretty garden. Parking.

Prices s €44-€48; d €48-€60; t fr €72; dinner fr €20 **On Site** Private ⬙
Nearby ⬙ 14km ↓30km 🏌 9km 🏊 2.5km 🎣 8km 🚲 14km
Notes Pets admitted English spoken

CHARRAIS

▦ ⫶⊙⫶ Chambre d'hôtes

Claudine COLLAS
35 Rue Des Ecoles, 86170 CHARRAIS
☎ 05 49 54 50 31 & 06 87 80 37 98 📠 05 49 54 50 31
email: collas.claudine@wanadoo.fr

An old farmhouse 14 kilometres from Futuroscope, with four
attractively decorated bedrooms. There is a two-roomed family suite
for four (double bed and two singles) with lounge and kitchenette,
and a triple double (double plus single). These rooms have private
facilities. There are also two grade 2 doubles, which share a shower
room and WC. Courtyard with furniture. Meals by arrangement.

Prices s €38-€39; d €40-€47; t €60-€62; extra person fr €15; dinner
fr €18 **Nearby** ⬙ 25km ↓20km 🏌 10km ⬙ 3km Restaurant 3km
🏊 3km Spa 25km 🎣 3km 🚲 20km **Notes** No pets

ⅢⅢ Charrajou

J-Y et M MARTINET

16 Rue des Ormeaux, 86170 CHARRAIS

☎ 05 49 51 14 62 🖹 05 49 51 14 62

web: www.chambrehote.net

A traditional stone Poitevin house situated in the heart of the Haut Poiteau wine region; the house has four guest bedrooms with separate access. There are two rooms with a double and a single, one room with three singles and one double, all with private facilities. Guests' lounge and kitchenette and large enclosed courtyard with parking.

Prices s fr €34; d fr €41; t fr €53 **Nearby** ⛳ 15km ⛷ 25km 🏊 25km ⌇ 2km Restaurant 2km 🍽 2km 🏛 2km 🚍 20km **Notes** No pets

CHAUVIGNY

ⅢⅢ *La Rivière aux Chirets*

Catherine FILIPPI

86300 CHAUVIGNY

☎ 05 49 56 41 70 & 06 82 23 58 59

email: filippi.catherine@wanadoo.fr

web: www.riviereauxchirets.com

Just two steps from the pretty medieval city of Chauvigny, this 17th-century residence is in calm countryside and features two fortified towers, a courtyard and garden with furniture and parking. The guest rooms are elegantly decorated, with private facilities, and include a twin room, a large double and a room with a double and single bed. Guests can relax in the living room and read a book or magazine.

Prices not confirmed for 2008 **On Site** 🏊 **Nearby** ⛳ 18km ⛷ 18km ⌇ 1km 🍽 1km 🏛 1km 🚍 23km **Notes** Pets admitted

ⅢⅢ La Veaudepierre

Jacques et Claude DE GIAFFERRI

8 rue du Berry, 86300 CHAUVIGNY

☎ 05 49 46 30 81 & 05 49 41 41 76 🖹 05 49 47 64 12

email: laveaudepierre@club-internet.fr

web: http://perso.club-internet.fr/laveaudepierre

A stunning 18th-century residence close to Chauvigny, with exceptional views of the châteaux. The accommodation comprises one single, and three doubles (one grade 2 and another with an adjoining single room). Extra beds are available on request. Sitting room. Parking on site and garden offering shade and excellent views.

Prices s €40-€45; d €50-€55; t €60-€70 **On Site** 🏊 **Nearby** ⛳ 21km ⛷ 18km ⌇ 1km 🍽 🚍 23km **Notes** No pets English spoken Open Easter to 1 November and school holidays.

CHENECHE

ⅢⅢ Château de Labarom

Eric LE GALLAIS

86380 CHENECHE

☎ 05 49 51 24 22 & 06 83 57 68 14 🖹 05 49 51 47 38

email: chateau.de.labarom@wanadoo.fr

A 16th and 18th-century château nestled in a park with a swimming pool. There is a twin room and two family suites, the first with a double bed and room with two singles, and the second with two twin rooms. All rooms have private facilities and there is a sitting room full of books for guests' use.

Prices s €59-€67; d €67-€75; t fr €93 **On Site** Private ⌇ **Nearby** ⛳ 16km ⛷ 18km 🏊 5km 🍽 2km 🏛 4km 🚍 22km **Notes** No pets English spoken Open April to 15 November.

COULOMBIERS

ⅢⅢ La Verrerie

Lucien et Isabelle PROVOST

86600 COULOMBIERS

☎ 05 49 43 71 69 🖹 05 49 43 71 69

web: http://laverrerie.free.fr

Futuroscope and the historic town of Poitiers are both within easy reach of this property. There are two family suites for up to four people: one on the first floor (grade 2), and another in a converted outbuilding which has a microwave and fridge. Both have private facilities. Generous breakfasts; enclosed gardens with furniture and picnic area; good cycling country.

Prices s fr €30; d €37-€39; extra person fr €15 **On Site** 🍽 **Nearby** ⛳ 2km ⛷ 25km 🏊 5km ⌇ 10km Restaurant 3km 🍽 3km 🏛 6km 🚍 18km **Notes** Pets admitted English spoken

COULONGES

ⅢⅢ 🍽 ♿ Domaine de la Porte

Joc et Judith HAUSERER

Les Herolles, 86290 COULONGES

☎ 05 49 48 33 81 & 05 49 48 98 58 🖹 05 49 48 98 58

email: info@domainedelaporte.com

web: www.domainedelaporte.com

An attractive property on the southern edge of the Brenne natural park, with its exceptional flora and fauna. There are five spacious rooms, tastefully decorated and comfortably furnished. Beds can be arranged as doubles or twins; one can be a family room, and one has disabled access. All have private facilities. Courtyard with garden furniture, grounds, swimming pool, table tennis. Meals by arrangement.

Prices s fr €67; d fr €90; t fr €100; extra person fr €25; dinner fr €30 **On Site** 🍴 Restaurant 🎾 Private ⚡ **Nearby** ⛵ 8km 🏊 5km 🏛 5km 🚶 30km **Notes** No pets English spoken

---

DANGE-SAINT-ROMAIN

🏨 🍴 Château de Piolant

Beatrice et Franck CHICOT

86220 DANGE-SAINT-ROMAIN

☎ 05 49 93 68 11 & 06 81 05 07 24 📄 05 49 93 58 05

email: franckchicot@wanadoo.fr

web: www.chateau-piolant.com

This château, the oldest part of which dates from the 11th century, has been some famous visitors - including Louis XIII and Honoré de Balzac. Now it has three first floor guest rooms - two doubles and a triple, all with private facilities. Lounge and sitting room. Extensive wooded grounds, where some of the trees are hundreds of years old; helipad. Meals by arrangement.

Prices s €55-€60; d €62-€135; t fr €85; dinner fr €23 **Nearby** ⚡ 25km 🏊 25km 🍴 8km ⚡ 3km Restaurant 4km 🏊 3km 🏛 4km 🚶 12km **Notes** No pets English spoken

---

🏨 🍴 ♿ La Grenouillère

Annie et Noel BRAGUIER

7 Rue de la Grenouillere, 86220 DANGE-SAINT-ROMAIN

☎ 05 49 86 48 68 📄 05 49 86 46 56

email: lagrenouillere86@aliceadsl.fr

19th-century farmhouse in a glorious wooded park with a river running through it. Rooms include a triple, two doubles and a further

---

double and triple in an annexe, all with private facilities. There is a sitting room with open fireplace, an enclosed courtyard, a conservatory, table tennis and other outdoor games available. Guest menu available by prior arrangement, except Sunday evening.

Prices s €33-€37; d €43-€49; t €54-€63; dinner fr €21 **On Site** 🍴 **Nearby** ⚡ 3km ⚡ 25km ⚡ 1.5km Restaurant 1km 🏊 1km 🏛 1km 🚶 1.2km **Notes** No pets English spoken

---

L'ISLE JOURDAIN

🏨 Les Chardes

Dany LABONNE

6 Rue de Chardes, 86150 L'ISLE JOURDAIN

☎ 05 49 91 80 99

email: info@les-chardes.com

web: www.les-chardes.com

A large 19th-century house in two hectares of grounds, overlooking the river. Three double bedrooms are all upstairs, one with an additional single bed. Each has a private shower room and WC. The garden has furniture and a barbecue; bungee jumping and water skiing close by.

Prices not confirmed for 2008 **On Site** 🍴 **Nearby** ⚡ 0.1km ⚡ 0.3km 🏊 0.1km 🏛 1km 🚶 19km **Notes** Pets admitted English spoken

---

LATILLE

🏨 🍴 La Colinière

J-M et C FERJOUX

86190 LATILLE

☎ 05 49 51 99 58 📄 05 49 51 99 58

email: jferjoux@wanadoo.fr

Fully restored, typical local house on a peaceful sheep farm. A grade 2 double attic room, a large, fully-accessible room with a double and two single beds, a double room, twin room and a family suite with double room and bunk bed room - all with private bathroom facilities. Guest lounge and terrace, kitchenette and bookable evening meals all available.

Prices not confirmed for 2008 **Nearby** ⚡ 10km ⚡ 10km 🍴 8km ⚡ 12km 🏊 5km 🏛 5km 🚶 30km **Notes** No pets

---

🏨 🍴 ♿ Relais Sainte Catherine

Alain et Martine DANE

12 Place Robert Gerbier, 86190 LATILLE

☎ 05 49 54 81 63 & 06 15 15 79 65

email: alain.dane@club-internet.fr

web: www.latille.org/relais-latille.html

This house stands in the heart of the village. It has three spacious bedrooms: two doubles (one with disabled access), and a two-roomed family suite for four (double bed and two singles). All have private bath or shower room and WC. Outside is a garden and off-road parking, and meals are available by arrangement.

Prices s fr €35; d fr €47; t fr €60; dinner fr €16 **On Site** 🍴 🎾 **Nearby** ⚡ 15km ⚡ 15km ⚡ 1km Restaurant 5km 🏊 0.5km 🚶 25km **Notes** No pets English spoken

POITOU-CHARENTES

MONTMORILLON

♦♦♦ Les Chambres de la Loge

Daniel et Nathalie CAPILLON
La Loge Monteil, 86500 MONTMORILLON
☎ 05 49 91 33 11 & 06 06 56 06 07
email: daniel.capillon@wanadoo.fr
web: http://chambresdelaloge.free.fr

Country calm in an old, restored house in a hamlet just outside a small town full of art and history. One double room, one room with a double and a single bed, and a grade 2 double room with kitchenette. They all have private facilities. A large, flowered garden and covered parking.

Prices s fr €37; d fr €47; t fr €62; extra person fr €15 **Nearby** ♨ 4km ⚬ 2km ✦ 4km Restaurant 3km 🏊 5km Spa 20km 🎿 20km 🏛 2km ₩ 3km **Notes** No pets English spoken

NEUVILLE-DE-POITOU

♦♦♦ ⦿ ⅚ La Galerne

Yvette PAVY
22 Chemin de Couture, 86170 NEUVILLE-DE-POITOU
☎ 05 49 51 14 07 📄 05 49 54 47 82
email: lagalerne@tiscali.fr
web: www.lagalerne.eu

In a park full of trees and flowers, this friendly contemporary house has five double guest rooms, two with extra beds and each with separate access and private facilities. Extra beds on request. There is a terrace looking out onto the park, garden furniture and a swimming pool.

Prices s fr €36; d fr €46; t fr €58; extra person fr €19; dinner fr €18 **On Site** Private ✦ **Nearby** ⛵ 16km ⚬ 16km 🏊 1km 🏛 1km ₩ 10km **Notes** No pets

♦♦♦ ⦿ La Roseraie

Michael et Heather LAVENDER
78 Rue Aramnd Caillard, 86170 NEUVILLE-DE-POITOU
☎ 05 49 54 16 72 📄 05 49 51 69 04
email: info@laroseraiefrance.fr
web: www.laroseraiefrance.fr

This beautiful property, standing in its own grounds, has five bedrooms. On the ground floor is a double; on the first floor are two more doubles; on the second floor are two family suites, one for four guests, the other for five. All have private facilities. TV and internet access available. Garden furniture, swimming pool, table tennis, meals by arrangement.

Prices s €58-€62; d €58-€68; t €98-€110; extra person €10-€15; dinner fr €23 **On Site** Restaurant Private ✦ **Nearby** ⚬ 9km 🏊 2km 🏛 1km ₩ 15km **Notes** No pets English spoken

ROMAGNE

♦♦♦ La Roseraie

Sidney LEE
86700 ROMAGNE
☎ 05 49 97 05 73
email: sidney.lee@wanadoo.fr
web: http://larosevacances.com

A peaceful, traditional old farm, fully restored to preserve the old beams, chimneys and tiles. Surrounded by a large garden with private parking. Two ground floor, double rooms with shower rooms. A family suite on the first floor with two rooms containing two double and two single beds, bathroom. Swimming pool.

Prices s fr €50; d fr €60; t fr €75 **On Site** Private ✦ **Nearby** ♨ 10km ⚬ 4km Restaurant 2km 🏊 2km 🏛 2km ₩ 40km **Notes** No pets English spoken

SAMMARCOLLES

♦♦♦ ⦿ Chambre d'hôtes

Benoit SAINT-MARD
18 Rue du Stade, 86200 SAMMARCOLLES
☎ 05 49 22 76 48
email: saint-mard@caramail.com
web: http://tenuedufougeray.free.fr

A lovely town house right in the heart of Sammarcolles. The three spacious rooms each have their own shower room and toilet: a double, two rooms with double and single beds each. Living room with library, large garden with furniture, flower beds, pool and parking. Evening meals are available if reserved.

Prices not confirmed for 2008 **On Site** Private ✦ **Nearby** ♨ 16km ⛵ 15km ⚬ 8km 🏊 1km 🏛 6km ₩ 20km **Notes** Pets admitted English spoken

SILLARS

𝔚 *La Cour de Villeneuve*

Philippe BALANCA-DUCHET

4 Route de la Barre, 86320 SILLARS

☎ 05 49 48 72 25

email: contact@pictavie.net

web: www.pictavie.net

An attractive, peaceful farm built by a ship-owner from Boulogne in 1842, ideal starting point for exploring the region. It surrounds a large courtyard with chapel and bread oven. Three double rooms, one twin and one triple all with private facilities. A lounge, terrace, garden and parking.

Prices not confirmed for 2008　**Nearby** ⛷12km ♨30km ℰ 3km
✦ 9km ⅃ 9km ≗ 3km ⋯ 3km　**Notes** Pets admitted　English spoken
Open April to October.

ST-SAVIN

𝔚 ❦ *Siouvres*

Jacky et Charline BARBARIN

86310 SAINT-SAVIN

☎ 05 49 48 10 19 & 06 08 76 18 32　📄 05 49 48 46 89

email: charline@lafermeapicole.com

web: www.lafermeapicole.com

A late 18th-century Poitevine farmhouse in a tranquil spot. Two double rooms, one with an extra double and kitchenette with private wash facilities for each room. Extra beds on request. There is a barbecue, children's toys and table tennis and bee-keeping on site.

Prices not confirmed for 2008　**Nearby** ⛷4km ♨35km ℰ 2km ✦ 2km
⅃ 2km ≗ 2km ⋯ 20km　**Notes** Pets admitted　Open 15 March to 15 October.

USSEAU

𝔚𝔚 ⓘ **Château de la Motte**

J-M et M-A BARDIN

86230 USSEAU

☎ 05 49 85 88 25　📄 05 49 85 88 25

email: chateau.delamotte@wanadoo.fr

web: www.chateau-de-la-motte.net

This 15th-century château, surrounded by ancient lime trees, offers a large suite with its own open fireplace, two rooms with double and single beds and a single room. Each room has private facilities. The grounds have a swimming pool and badminton court. Guests can enjoy local produce served in the dining room. Music, parlour games and books are provided in the elegant sitting room; there is also a library.

Prices d €75-€120; t €110-€130; dinner fr €28　**On Site** Private ✦
Nearby ⛷4km ♨20km ℰ 5km ⅃ 7km ≗ 8km ⋯ 8km
Notes No pets　English spoken　Open April to 15 November.

VARENNES

𝔚 **Manoir de Vilaines**

Philippe SIMONNET

86110 VARENNES

☎ 05 49 60 73 93 & 06 30 62 68 43　📄 05 49 60 73 93

web: manoirdevilaines@orange.fr

In the wine region of Haut-Poitou, this characterful house has a family suite with sitting room, a single and double bed; a room with one double and a single, and another family suite with two double rooms and a sitting room. All the rooms have private facilities; extra beds can be arranged. Large living room, garden furniture and landscaped grounds.

Prices s €37-€38; d €45-€46; t fr €59; extra person fr €15
Nearby ⛷20km ♨20km ℰ 1km ✦ 8km　Restaurant 1km ⅃ 4km
≗ 4km ⋯ 25km　**Notes** No pets　English spoken　Open February to 5 November.

VELLECHES

𝔚𝔚 ❦ ⓘ *La Blonnerie*

Marie-France MASSONNET

86230 VELLECHES

☎ 05 49 86 41 72　📄 05 49 93 68 17

email: marie_massonnet@yahoo.fr

In beautifully wooded surroundings close to the Châteaux of the Loire, this farm has three rooms: a suite with a double and two pull out beds; a double room with two extra pull-out beds and sofa-bed, and a room with single and double bed. Rooms have private facilities, sitting areas and TVs. Guests' lounge with games; terrace with wonderful views; lake in the grounds where guests can fish and a botanical park. Hunting in season. Inn on site.

Prices not confirmed for 2008　**On Site** ℰ　**Nearby** ⛷15km ♨35km
✦ 7km ⅃ 7km ≗ 7km ⋯ 13km　**Notes** No pets

VENDEUVRE-DU-POITOU

𝔚𝔚 ⓘ *Domaine de la Fuie*

Micheline CHAUZAMY

Bataille, 86380 VENDEUVRE-DU-POITOU

☎ 05 49 51 34 95　📄 05 49 54 08 81

email: jchauzamy@wanadoo.fr

web: www.lafuie.com

This 17th-century stately home is set in wonderful wooded grounds with lots of interesting flowers. The property offers a grade 2 double, three rooms with a double and a single (one grade 2) and a further grade 2 room with two double beds and a single. All the rooms have private facilities. Garden with a covered swimming pool, boules, table tennis and private parking.

Prices not confirmed for 2008　**On Site** Private ✦　**Nearby** ⛷10km
♨15km ℰ 3km ⅃ 3km ≗ 4km ⋯ 17km　**Notes** No pets

VOUNEUIL-SOUS-BIARD

⚏ Le Grand Mazais

Jean-Pierre CARCEL

86580 VOUNEUIL-SOUS-BIARD

☎ 05 49 53 40 31 📄 05 49 43 69 94

This beautiful late 17th-century master's house stands in one and a half hectares of grounds at the gateway of Poitiers. There are three double rooms and a family suite consisting of two rooms each with one double and two singles. Rooms have private facilities. There is a sitting room and swimming pool.

Prices s fr €70; d €80-€85; t fr €95 **On Site** Restaurant Private ⚡ **Nearby** ⚓ 2km ⛷ 6km ♟ 1km ⌣ 3km 🏛 2km ⋙ 5km **Notes** No pets English spoken

VOUNEUIL-SUR-VIENNE

⚏ La Pocterie

Martine POUSSARD

86210 VOUNEUIL-SUR-VIENNE

☎ 05 49 85 11 96

Close to a nature reserve, this pretty house is full of charm. There is a grade 3 room with one double and one single, a grade 2 double room and a large grade 3 room with one double and a sofa bed, all with private facilities. A terrace overlooks the large garden, which is full of flowers. There is a swimming pool and a leisure centre nearby.

Prices s fr €40; d fr €50; t fr €62 **On Site** Private ⚡ **Nearby** ⚓ 4km ⛷ 11km ♟ 1km Restaurant 3km ⌣ 3km Spa 18km 🏛 2km ⋙ 13km **Notes** No pets English spoken

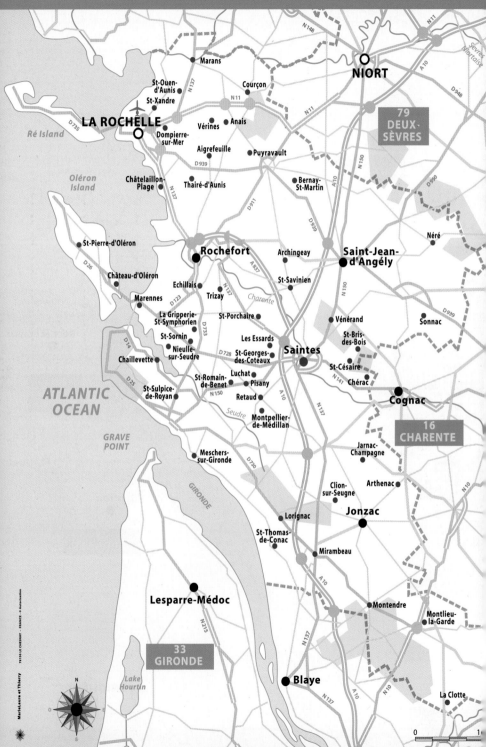

NIORT

79 DEUX-SÈVRES

Marans

St-Ouen-d'Aunis

St-Xandre

Courçon

LA ROCHELLE

Ré Island

Vérines Anais

Dompierre-sur-Mer

Aigrefeuille

Puyravault

Oléron Island

Châtelaillon-Plage

Thairé-d'Aunis

Bernay-St-Martin

Néré

St-Pierre-d'Oléron

Rochefort

Archingeay

Saint-Jean-d'Angély

Château-d'Oléron

Echillais

St-Savinien

Charente

Sonnac

Trizay

Marennes

La Gripperie-St-Symphorien

St-Porchaire

Vénérand

St-Bris-des-Bois

St-Sornin

Les Essards

Saintes

Nieulle-sur-Seudre

St-Georges-des-Coteaux

St-Césaire

Chaillevette

St-Romain-de-Benet

Luchat

Chérac

St-Sulpice-de-Royan

Pisany

Retaud

Cognac

ATLANTIC OCEAN

Seudre

Montpellier-de-Médillan

16 CHARENTE

GRAVE POINT

Jarnac-Champagne

Meschers-sur-Gironde

Clion-sur-Seugne

Arthenac

GIRONDE

Lorignac

Jonzac

St-Thomas-de-Conac

Mirambeau

Montendre

Lesparre-Médoc

Montlieu-la-Garde

33 GIRONDE

Lake Hourtin

N

Blaye

La Clotte

S

0   1

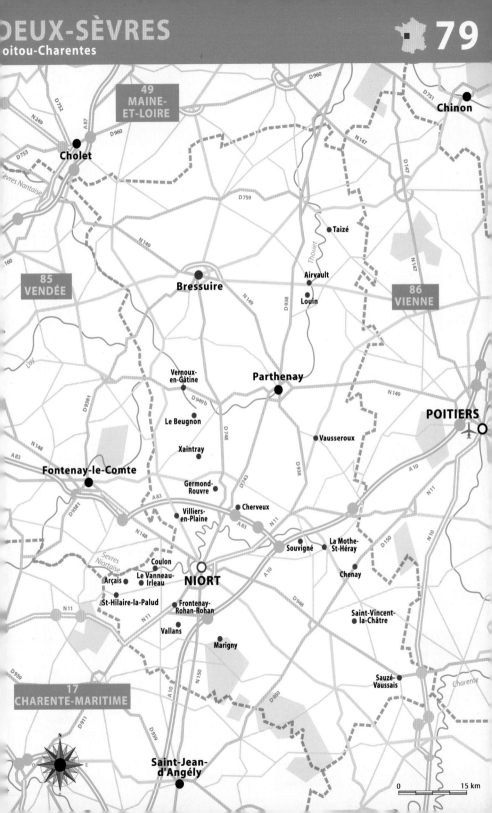

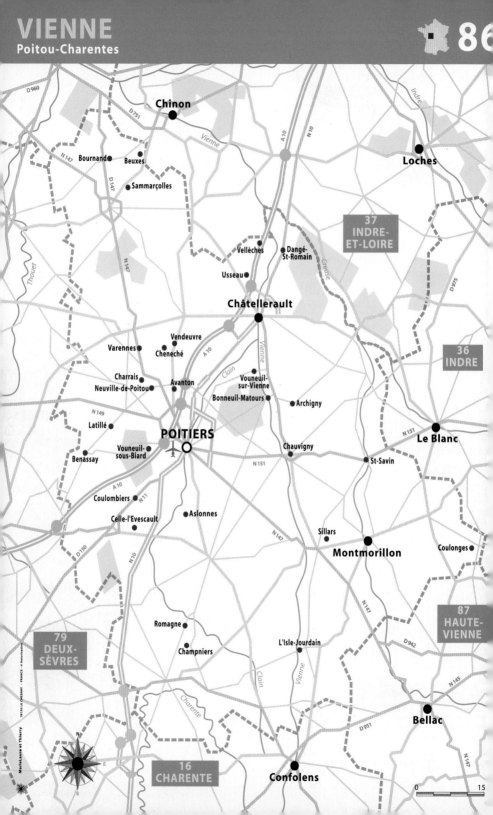

D 960

Chinon

D 751

Vienne

A 10

N 10

Indre

Loches

N 147

Bournand

Beuxes

D 147

Sammarçolles

Thouet

N 147

Vellèches

Dangé-St-Romain

Usseau

Creuse

37
INDRE-ET-LOIRE

D 975

Châtellerault

Vendeuvre

Varennes

Cheneché

A 10

Vienne

Clain

36
INDRE

Charrais

Neuville-de-Poitou

Avanton

Vouneuil-sur-Vienne

Bonneuil-Matours

Archigny

N 149

Latillé

POITIERS

Benassay

Vouneuil-sous-Biard

Chauvigny

N 151

Le Blanc

St-Savin

A 10

Coulombiers

N 11

Celle-l'Evescault

Aslonnes

N 147

Sillars

Montmorillon

Coulonges

D 150

N 10

87
HAUTE-VIENNE

Romagne

L'Isle-Jourdain

D 942

N 145

79
DEUX-SÈVRES

Champniers

Clain

Vienne

N 147

Charente

D 951

Bellac

N
E
S

16
CHARENTE

Confolens

0   15

MarieLaure et Thierry

PROVENCE-ALPES-CÔTE-D'AZUR

ALPES-DE-HAUTE-PROVENCE

AIGLUN

▦ ◌ **Le Vieil Aiglun**

Charles et Annick SPETH
04510 AIGLUN
☎ 04 92 34 67 00 ▤ 04 92 34 74 92
email: info@vieil-aiglun.com
web: www.vieil-aiglun.com/

Stone built house with views over the Bléone Valley and the 16th-century village. The five charming rooms offer a range of accommodation and there is a lounge, library and television. Neighbouring the owner's house and a self-catering cottage guests have use of the pool and quiet garden.

Prices s €60-€75; d €80-€95; t €100-€120; dinner fr €26
On Site Private ⸚ **Nearby** ⸚ 13km ⸚ 8km ⸚ 12km Restaurant 12km
⸚ 12km Spa 13km ⸚ 8km ⸚ 11km **Notes** No pets English spoken
Open 31 March to November. CC

BARCELONNETTE

▦ **Le Bosquet**

Claudine VILLAIN
2 Av Watton de Ferry, 04400 BARCELONNETTE
☎ 04 92 81 41 28 & 06 31 68 24 73 ▤ 04 92 81 41 28
email: lebosquet1@wanadoo.fr

This renovated property is in bustling Barcelonnette. It offers a double room, two with a double and a single bed, and one with a double and bunk beds, all with private facilities. Large lounge with fireplace. Swimming pool, forest walks, Mercantour National Park, paragliding, lake at Jausiers, skiing at Pra-Loup, and watersports on the Ubaye all nearby.

Prices d fr €52; t fr €65; extra person fr €15 **Nearby** ⸚ 1.5km ⸚ 1.5km
⸚ 0.5km ⸚ 0.8km Restaurant 0.2km ⸚ 12km ⸚ 0.4km ⸚ 0.2km
Notes Pets admitted English spoken Open February to 1 November.

CASTELLANE

▦ ◌ **Mas du Verdon**

Mélanie JACOBS
Quartier d'Angles, 04120 CASTELLANE
☎ 04 92 83 73 20 ▤ 04 92 83 73 20
email: info@masduverdon.com

This 18th-century house is in open countryside to the north of the Gorges de Verdon, just below the town of Castellane with its famous rock. There are five very comfortable en suite double rooms, some with space for an extra bed if needed. Several terraces outside, with wonderful valley views. Excellent walking country - the GR4 long-distance path passes close by.

Prices d €50-€65; extra person fr €15; dinner fr €16 **Nearby** ⸚ 1km
Notes No pets English spoken Open April to 15 October.

CERESTE

▦ ◌ **La Maison d'Emma**

Emmanuelle LIEBERT
Place Saint-Michel, 04280 CERESTE
☎ 04 92 74 19 21 & 06 15 17 27 61
email: e.liebert@wanadoo.fr

An 18th-century house in the centre of Cereste, an authentic Provençal village between Apt and Manosque. There are two double rooms and a twin-bedded room, all with private bathroom and lavatory. Outside is an enclosed garden, and the surrounding countryside is good for riding and walking. Meals are available by arrangement - Provençal cooking with local ingredients.

Prices s fr €60; d fr €65; dinner fr €25 **Nearby** ⸚ 2km ⸚ 15km
Sea 10km ⸚ 20km ⸚ 0.5km Restaurant 0.5km ⸚ 0.5km ⸚ 0.1km
Notes No pets English spoken

CHATEAUNEUF-VAL-SAINT-DONAT

▦ ◌ **Mas Saint-Joseph**

Olivier et Hélène LENOIR
04200 CHATEAUNEUF-VAL-SAINT-DONAT
☎ 04 92 62 47 54
email: lenoir.st.jo@wanadoo.fr
web: www.provenceweb.fr/04/st-joseph/

At the foot of the forested Lure Mountain, this 18th-century former farm is set in four hectares of land. There is a double room, a family room with double and two singles, a triple and a room sleeping four, all with private facilities. Table d'hôtes meals are served on the terrace, or in the converted wooden barn. Lounge, library, swimming pool, table-tennis, rambling and mountain biking - maps available.

Prices s fr €45; d fr €50; t fr €67; extra person fr €17; dinner fr €18
Nearby ⸚ 6km ⸚ 12km **Notes** Pets admitted English spoken Open April to November.

COLMARS-LES-ALPES

♥ ○ Les Transhumances

J-P et M-T BARBAROUX

Les Espiniers, 04370 COLMARS-LES-ALPES

☎ 04 92 83 44 39 ▤ 04 92 83 44 39

email: lestranshumances@wanadoo.fr

web: www.lestranshumances.fr/

A restored farmhouse in the peace and quiet of the countryside, with a wonderful view of Colmars-les-Alpes, an ancient village which was fortified by Vauban, the 17th-century military engineer. It has three rooms: two triples (double bed plus a single), and a room for five with a double bed, bunks and a single bed. All rooms have private facilities.

Prices s fr €55; d fr €70; t fr €78; dinner fr €20 **Nearby** ⌀ 1km ≈ 8km ⓘ 1km **Notes** No pets English spoken

CRUIS

○ Le Mas de Foulara

Richard et Odile HARTZ

04230 CRUIS

☎ 04 92 77 07 96

email: foulara@free.fr

web: http://foulara.free.fr/

Surrounded by hills and lavender fields, this 17th-century farmhouse is situated on an Arab stud farm at the foot of the Lure Mountain, close to hiking trail GR6. There are five bedrooms with private bathrooms, and a lounge with fireplace. Outdoor attractions include covered terraces, shaded park and a pond. Central heating.

Prices s fr €42; d fr €52; t fr €62; dinner fr €21 **Nearby** ⌀ 15km ♨ 40km ⟋ 5km Restaurant 2km ⌂ 5km Spa 40km ⓘ 2km ⋘ 20km **Notes** No pets English spoken Open April to 15 November.

DAUPHIN

Le Moulin des Encontres

M-C ROCHON-BOUFFIER

04300 DAUPHIN

☎ 04 92 79 53 84 ▤ 04 92 79 53 84

email: infos@moulindesencontres.com

web: www.moulindesencontres.com/

This restored mill in the heart of Luberon is set in tranquil surroundings. It offers three rooms: Elzéard for two to four people, the double Agathe, and Marthe et Anthonin is suitable for four. Rooms have bathroom and wc, a kitchen area, terrace and private entrance. Cycle track, lavender tours, Lure Mountain, Gorges of Verdon and the Regional Nature Park nearby.

Prices d €50-€60; t fr €75; extra person fr €15 **Nearby** ⌀ 2km ♨ 18km ⟋ 15km Restaurant 2km ⌂ 2km Spa 8km ⓘ 4km ⋘ 15km **Notes** No pets English spoken

DIGNE-LES-BAINS

♥ Les Oliviers

Jean-Pierre FRISON

1 Route des Fonts, Gaubert, 04000 DIGNE-LES-BAINS

☎ 04 92 31 36 04 ▤ 04 92 31 36 04

Situated in the geological reserve of Haute-Provence, this farmhouse is set in a peaceful and rural environment. Accommodation consists of four double rooms with either a bath or a shower and a wc. There is also a large lounge and terrace available for guests' use. Rural gîtes and camping available on site.

Prices s fr €37; d fr €42 **On Site** ♨ **Nearby** ⌂ 6km ⟋ 3km ⌲ 4km Restaurant 0.8km ⌂ 5km Spa 5km ⓘ 6km ⋘ 5km **Notes** No pets Open April to 1 November.

ENCHASTRAYES

○ Le Villard

Marc et Lyliane VAN ZURK

04400 ENCHASTRAYES

☎ 04 92 81 33 75

email: info@champ-rond.com

web: http://champ-rond.com/

In the heart of the Ubaye Valley, this mountain wood chalet offers two double rooms with balconies and one family room (double bed and one single), all with private facilities. Lounge with library and open fire available for guests' use. Evening meals can be ordered in advance. Local attractions include walks, alpine skiing, cross-country skiing, watersports, fishing, bike tours and hang-gliding.

Prices s fr €45-€46; d fr €48-€55; dinner fr €18 **Nearby** ⌂ 7km ♨ 7km ⟋ 4km ⌲ 4km Restaurant 4km ≈ 6km ⌂ 4km ⓘ 4km **Notes** No pets Open January to September.

FORCALQUIER

Bergerie la Beaudine

Marie-Louise PAGLIANO

Route de Banon, 04300 FORCALQUIER

☎ 04 92 75 01 52 & 04 92 75 36 86

email: malou.pagliano@wanadoo.fr

web: http://perso.wanadoo.fr/bergerielabeaudine/

Beautiful panoramic views from this old shepherd's house add to the peace and quiet of the shaded grounds. On the ground floor are three double rooms, each with independent access; on the first floor is a room for four, (double bed and two singles) and a triple (double and single beds); all rooms have private shower and WC. Dining and living rooms, TV and cot on request.

Prices s fr €49; d fr €59; extra person fr €19 **On Site** Spa Private ⌲ **Nearby** ⌂ 1.5km ♨ 20km ⟋ 5km Restaurant 0.2km ⌂ 1.5km ⓘ 0.8km ⋘ 8km **Notes** No pets English spoken

GREOUX-LES-BAINS

♦♦♦ Domaine de Pigette

Danielle et Christophe GORSE
04800 GREOUX-LES-BAINS
☎ 04 92 74 35 52 ▤ 04 92 74 35 52
email: chambres.dhotes.pigette@wanadoo.fr
web: http://perso.wanadoo.fr/pigette.chambredhote/
cariboost1/index.html

Meadows and market gardens surround this property, which has four air-conditioned bedrooms, two doubles and two triples, all on the second floor. All have private facilities. Cot available. Lounge with TV, and dining room with kitchen for guests' use. Terrace, garden furniture, barbecue and swimming pool. An international centre for gliding and canoeing is nearby at Vinon-sur-Verdon.

Prices s fr €45; d €50-€55; extra person fr €15 **On Site** Private ⚡
Nearby ⚡ 1km ⚓ 20km Restaurant 2km Water sports 3km ⚐ 2km
Spa 2km ⌂ 3km ⇶ 15km **Notes** No pets English spoken

JAUSIERS

♦♦♦ La Mexicaine

Cécile FONTAINE
Les Clos du Gueniers, 04850 JAUSIERS
☎ 04 92 84 69 63 ▤ 04 92 84 69 63
email: lamexicaine@wanadoo.fr
web: www.lamexicaine.com

With a furnished garden, barbecue and two gîtes, this house is built in the typical Mexican style of the region. Rooms include La Sinagote (a double/twin), La Romantique and La Montagnarde (doubles), and a family room with a double bed and two singles; all with private facilities. There is a dining room, lounge with fire, TV, hi-fi and library. Close to the Resteford Pass (highest road in Europe), Jausier Lake and the Mercantour National Park.

Prices s fr €45; d €52-€65; t fr €68; extra person fr €16
Nearby ⚡ 10km ⚓ 0.3km ⚡ 8km Restaurant 0.3km ⚐ 12km ⚐ 0.3km
⌂ 0.5km **Notes** No pets English spoken Open April to September.

LE CASTELLET

♦♦♦ Chambre d'hôtes

M et P CIRAVEGNA
Quartier Combe Croix, 04700 LE CASTELLET
☎ 04 92 79 60 97 ▤ 04 92 79 62 77
email: combe.croix@wanadoo.fr
web: www.combe-croix.com/

An independent chambre d'hôtes at the foot of the Valensole Plateau. Double bedrooms with an extra single bed, with shower room and wc. Private access. Terrace, solarium, swimming pool. Small room with stove, fridge, barbecue, crockery and washing machine. Garden furniture and boules are available for guest use. Situated in a green valley, Le Castellet is a quiet village with a restaurant and a fishing lake.

Prices s €40-€42; d €48-€50; t €58-€60; extra person fr €16
On Site Private ⚡ **Nearby** ⚡ 15km ⚓ 20km ⚐ 0.5km Restaurant 0.3km
⚐ 6km Spa 25km ⌂ 5km ⇶ 8km **Notes** Pets admitted

LES MEES

♦♦♦ ⊗ Campagne du Barri

Olga MANCIN
Quartier de la Croix, 04190 LES MEES
☎ 04 92 34 36 93 ▤ 04 92 34 39 06
email: olga.mancin@wanadoo.fr
web: www.guideweb.com/provence/bb/campagne-barri/

Set in the Val de Durance in two hectares of plush green fields, close to Digne-les-Bains, this rural gîte forms part of an 18th-century house which has retained its original charm with period furnishings. There are two family rooms (one with adjoining single), three doubles (one in a separate chalet) and a split-level apartment for four, all with private facilities. Meals feature home-grown vegetables.

Prices not confirmed for 2008 **Nearby** ⚓ 2km ⌂ 1km **Notes** Pets admitted English spoken CC

♦♦♦ ⊗ L'Oustaou

Jean-Marie et Josiane GALY
Les Bourelles, 04190 LES MEES
☎ 04 92 34 39 57
email: galy.lesmees@free.fr
web: http://oustaou.lesmees.free.fr/

A modern house with an expanse of shady garden and three bedrooms in a separate wing of the owners' home. The rooms are all doubles, and each has a private bath or shower room and WC. Guests have use of the owners' swimming pool, and the local area is excellent for walking and mountain-biking. Meals are by arrangement.

Prices d €52-€62; extra person fr €5; dinner fr €18 **Nearby** ⚡ 1km
⚓ 15km ⚓ 0.3km ⚡ Restaurant 1km ⚐ 0.3km ⌂ 1.4km ⇶ 10km
Notes No pets English spoken

♦♦♦ ⊗ La Bastide Blanche

Marie-Hélène MILLET
Dabisse, 04190 LES MEES
☎ 04 92 34 33 25 ▤ 04 92 34 33 25
email: milletmh@wanadoo.fr
web: http://perso.wanadoo.fr/lestroisgrains/

This house is in the valley of the Durance. On the ground floor it has one room for up to five people, with a kitchenette, and another room for up to four. Upstairs is a further room, also for up to four people. All rooms have private showers and WCs. Shady garden, private parking, swimming pool, meals by arrangement.

Prices not confirmed for 2008 **Nearby** ⚓ 10km Water sports 20km
⌂ 5km **Notes** Pets admitted English spoken

LES OMERGUES

▦ ◯ Le Moulin de la Viorne

D COLONNA-BOUTTERIN
04200 LES OMERGUES
☎ 04 92 62 01 65 🗐 04 92 62 06 03
email: moulindelaviorne@free.fr
web: www.guideweb.com/provence/bb/viorne/

Set in the countryside of the Jabron Valley, close to the River Drôme, this restored 17th-century mill offers a double, a twin and a family room (with one double bed and a single), all with private bathrooms. Central heating, billiard room, lounge with library, swimming pool, grounds, covered furnished terrace, parking and meals upon request. Display of paintings open to guests.

Prices s fr €57; d €59-€70; extra person fr €25   **On Site** ♪
Nearby ♨ 2km ⚲ Restaurant 1km ⌂ 8km 🏠 8km ⚑ 30km
Notes No pets English spoken Open Easter to 1 November.

MANE

▦ ◯ Le Jardin des Glycines

Myriam VIGNEAUX
Rue da la Bourgade, 04300 MANE
☎ 04 92 75 13 98
email: vigneauxroland@orange.fr
web: http://lejardindesglycines.free.fr/

A village squire's house, with parking opposite and a flowery garden. Period furniture and decorated ceilings. Ground floor dining room, living room with TV and a billiards room at guests' disposal. Two triple rooms, both with double bed and a single; and a double room, all with private shower/WC. Meals feature Provençal specialities.

Prices s fr €50; d fr €55; t fr €65; extra person fr €10; dinner fr €22
Nearby ♨ 3km ⚓ 21km ♪ 10km ⚲ 3km Restaurant 0.5km ⌂ 3km
Spa 8km ⚑ 18km   **Notes** No pets English spoken

MANOSQUE

▦ ♥ ◯ La Bastide des Collines

Francis et Christine CHAIX
Chemin de Valveranne, 04100 MANOSQUE
☎ 04 92 87 87 67 🗐 04 92 87 59 56
email: christine.chaix2@wanadoo.fr
web: http://monsite.wanadoo.fr/labastidedescollines/

This property has three independently accessed first floor rooms, each for up to three people and all with private showers/WCs. On the ground floor is a lounge in the Provençal style, with a large open fireplace, TV, books, children's games, etc. Central heating, private terrace, garden furniture. Parking; meals by arrangement. Walks among the olive groves and hills.

Prices s fr €36; d fr €45; t fr €55; dinner fr €14   **Nearby** ♨ 2km
⚓ 8km ♪ 1km Restaurant 0.8km ⌂ 5km Spa 25km 🏠 1km ⚑ 5km
Notes No pets English spoken

MEOLANS-REVEL

▦ Les Méans

Frédéric et Elisabeth MILLET
04340 MEOLANS-REVEL
☎ 04 92 81 03 91 🗐 04 92 81 03 91
email: elisabeth@les-means.com
web: www.les-means.com/

A restored 16th-century farm set in a mountain hamlet offering four double rooms, two with balconies, and a suite with balcony, all with private facilities. Lounge with TV, library and open fire. Fridge and washing machine on request. Garden with a working baker's oven. Rafting, fishing, mountain tours and climbing nearby.

Prices s fr €50; d €50-€70; t €80-€95; extra person fr €20   **On Site** Spa
Nearby ♨ 9km ⚓ 9km ♪ 9km ⚲ 9km Restaurant 0.1km ⌂ 20km
Water sports 0.5km ⌂ 9km 🏠 10km   **Notes** Pets admitted English
spoken Open May to 15 November.

MONTLAUX

▦ ◯ Grand-Champ

Philippe PATRIER
04230 MONTLAUX
☎ 04 92 77 01 10
email: ppatrier@aol.com
web: http://membres.lycos.fr/grandcham/

Flanked by the Lure Mountain, this large building is set in four hectares in the heart of the countryside, scented by thyme and lavender. There are five rooms with private facilities, three leading onto a covered terrace. A lounge, dining room with fireplace and library are available. Outdoor facilities include a swimming pool, toboggan run, table tennis and bowls. Mountain bikes available for hire. Camping area.

Prices s fr €40; d fr €50; t fr €60; extra person fr €10; dinner fr €17
On Site Private ⚲   **Nearby** ♨ 5km ⚓ 40km Restaurant 2km ⌂ 14km
⌂ 3km 🏠 2km ⚑ 16km   **Notes** No pets English spoken

MOUSTIERS-SAINTE-MARIE

♨ Le Mas du Loup

Edith ORIONE
04360 MOUSTIERS-SAINTE-MARIE
☎ 04 92 74 65 61
email: masduloup7@hotmail.fr

This property, in the Parc Naturel Régional du Verdon, is in one of the most beautiful villages of France. The Gorges de Verdon and the Lac de Sainte-Croix are both nearby. The house stands in its own grounds at the bottom of the village. There are five ground floor double rooms, each with private terrace, shower room and WC.

Prices s €60-€70; d €65-€75; extra person fr €20 **Nearby** ♿ 8km ⚡ 5km Restaurant 0.5km Water sports 2km 🏊 1km 🛍 1km **Notes** Pets admitted English spoken Open end of March to November.

♨ ⏹ Monastère de Ségries

Christian et Florence ALLEGRE
04360 MOUSTIERS-SAINTE-MARIE
☎ 04 92 74 64 32
email: c.allegre@free.fr

This renovated 19th-century former monastery enjoys a calm and privileged setting close to the Valensole Plateau. There are five spacious bedrooms all with private facilities. Table d'hôte meals, which are in the local style, can be booked in advance. Nearby attractions include the Verdon Regional Nature Park and Moustiers, a listed town famous for its earthenware.

Prices s fr €42; d fr €55; extra person fr €12; dinner fr €18 **Nearby** ♿ 4km ⚡ 40km ⚡ 15km Restaurant 6km Water sports 10km 🏊 6km Spa 45km 🛍 6km 🚴 45km **Notes** No pets Open April to 20 October.

NIOZELLES

♨ ⏹ Le Relais d'Elle

Jacques et Catherine PENSA
Route de la Brillainne, 04300 NIOZELLES
☎ 04 92 75 06 87 🖹 04 92 75 06 87
email: relais.d.elle@wanadoo.fr
web: http://relaisdelle.com/

Between Luberon and the Lure Mountain this restored former farmhouse offers five spacious bedrooms decorated in Provençal style, sleeping 13 in a mix of double beds and five singles. All have private facilities. Central heating, lounge, library and meals on request. Close to the Roman pathway, Via Domitia, numerous walks, mountain biking and horse riding.

Prices s fr €48; d €58-€65; t €70-€80; extra person fr €15; dinner fr €22 **Nearby** ♿ 6km ⚡ 20km ⚡ 1km 🔨 Restaurant 0.8km 🏊 6km Spa 6km 🛍 4km 🚴 5km **Notes** Pets admitted English spoken

NOYERS-SUR-JABRON

♨ ⏹ Le Jas de la Caroline

Françoise MAGENTIE
Chenebotte, 04200 NOYERS-SUR-JABRON
☎ 04 92 62 03 48 🖹 04 92 62 03 48
email: lacaroline@free.fr
web: http://lacaroline.free.fr

An idyllic country retreat in a beautifully converted old sheepfold. Each of the three rooms has a private balcony and home produced breakfasts are served on the terrace. The en suite rooms are well equipped and charmingly decorated with partly vaulted ceilings and private lounge.

Prices s fr €50; d €60-€77; t fr €99; dinner fr €25 **Nearby** ♿ 10km ⚡ 0.5km 🔨 10km Restaurant 10km 🏊 10km 🛍 10km 🚴 10km **Notes** No pets English spoken Open March to November.

PEIPIN

♨ Les Nialles

Eric et Agnès PUT
3 Rue de Piolard, 04200 PEIPIN
☎ 04 92 62 47 62 & 06 81 56 62 71
email: agnes64@free.fr

An 18th-century farmhouse, superbly renovated, on the edge of the village. There are two double rooms and two rooms for four people, one of which has a terrace; all have private shower room and WC. Beamed dining room with open fire and TV. Mountain bike track.

Prices d fr €65 **Nearby** ♿ 0.2km ⚡ 45km ⚡ 3km 🔨 Restaurant 9km 🏊 8km 🛍 0.2km 🚴 8km **Notes** No pets English spoken

PIERRERUE

♨ ⏹ Le Mas du Galoubet

C CUEREL et C BUSI
Quartier Julien, 04300 PIERRERUE
☎ 04 92 75 31 70
email: info@mas-du-galoubet.com
web: www.mas-du-galoubet.com/

This is a restored 19th-century house in a shady parkland setting in a quiet village. On the ground floor are a double room and a twin. On the first floor are a further three rooms: a double, a twin, and a suite for up to four. All rooms have private shower/WC. Guests' lounge, meals by arrangement: local cuisine.

Prices s fr €41; d fr €55; t fr €69; extra person fr €14; dinner fr €19 **Nearby** ♿ 5km ⚡ 25km ⚡ 8km 🔨 Restaurant 5km 🏊 5km 🛍 4.5km 🚴 7km **Notes** No pets English spoken Open 15 March to 1 November. CC

PIERREVERT

�#### Chambre d'hôtes

J-P et F SUPPLISSON
Ecuriel Bleu, Quartier Parrin, 7 Av René Bigand,
04860 PIERREVERT
☎ 04 92 72 88 93

Pine trees surround this big old Provençal house in the Lubéron, with its easy access to lakes for bathing and fishing. It has three spacious and comfortable guest bedrooms, all of them with private bathrooms. There is a shady terrace which offers plenty of space for rest and relaxation. Good walking country.

Prices s fr €38; d fr €50; extra person fr €20 **Nearby** ♨5km ♟ 3km ⚲ Restaurant 0.8km ☕0.8km 🏛1km ⛷5km **Notes** No pets English spoken

REVEST-DU-BION

⍟ ⌯⌾⍟ Le Petit Labouret

Yves VIALES
04150 REVEST-DU-BION
☎ 04 92 72 30 92 & 06 81 85 53 04
email: yves.viales@laposte.net
web: www.petit-labouret.com/

Between Mont Ventoux and the Lure Mountain, this renovated farmhouse has two double rooms, a room with two double beds and a room sleeping seven, all with private facilities and entrances and three with mezzanine floors. Lounge with fireplace, laundry with fridge-freezer, washing machine and tumble-dryer. Children's menu. Open grounds with woodland, lavender fields, and garden furniture. Country walks, horse riding and mountain biking nearby.

Prices s €46-€56; d €50-€62; t €65-€76; extra person fr €15; dinner fr €21 **On Site** Restaurant Private ⚲ **Nearby** 🏛2.5km ⛷50km **Notes** Pets admitted

ROUGON

⍟ La Bastide du Rocher

Serge et Annie QUESNOY
04120 ROUGON
☎ 04 92 83 73 58 & 06 81 51 31 04

This house is slightly outside the village, perched nearly 1000 metres up, between Castellane and Moustiers-Ste-Marie. It has three double rooms (extra bed available) with private entrances, each with a private shower room/WC. Breakfast served on the terrace with a wonderful view of the Gorges of Verdon and the vultures! Good area for walking, climbing and fishing.

Prices not confirmed for 2008 **Nearby** ♟ 6km Water sports 12km 🏛13km **Notes** Pets admitted English spoken Open March to November.

SEYNE-LES-ALPES

⍟ *Le Grand-Puy*

Guillaume et Isabelle HUTIN
04140 SEYNE-LES-ALPES
☎ 04 92 35 11 11 & 06 83 27 40 02
email: info@gitederocheclose.fr
web: www.gitederocheclose.fr/

This large detached house is only 100mtrs from the ski station, so there's plenty of storage space for skis and equipment. In summer you can ramble with a donkey to carry your bags, and the owners run courses on personal fitness. Four bedrooms sleep two to four people, all with private shower/WC. Shady garden with furniture.

Prices not confirmed for 2008 **On Site** ⚲ **Nearby** Water sports 20km 🏛5km **Notes** Pets admitted English spoken

SIMIANE-LA-ROTONDE

⍟ Les Granges de Saint-Pierre

Josiane TAMBURINI
04150 SIMIANE-LA-ROTONDE
☎ 04 92 75 93 81 📄 04 92 75 93 81

Set in the Luberon Regional Nature Park, these renovated 14th-century barns offer three bedrooms with private bathrooms. Kitchen, lounge, garage, laundry, TV, central heating, covered terrace, swimming pool and shaded park. In nearby Simiane-la-Rotonde, there are exhibitions, a music festival and local handicrafts. Close to several hiking trails. Reservations needed in winter.

Prices s fr €54; d fr €64; extra person fr €16 **On Site** Private ⚲ **Nearby** ♨15km ♨40km Restaurant 0.1km ☕9km Spa 20km 🏛0.2km **Notes** Pets admitted English spoken

ST-ETIENNE-LES-ORGUES

⍟ ⌯⌾⍟ *Chambre d'hôtes*

Sylvie MATHIEU
Rue de la Paix, 04230 ST-ETIENNE-LES-ORGUES
☎ 04 92 73 18 75 & 04 92 73 17 56 📄 04 92 73 17 71
email: sylvie.mathieu@wanadoo.fr
web: www.fourbanal.com/

This renovated stone built house is situated in a quiet lane in the village. It has one room for up to three people with a lounge and private terrace and two further doubles, all with private shower/WC. Large lounge with open fireplace and kitchenette. Good centre for exploring the area on foot, mountain bike or horseback.

Prices not confirmed for 2008 **Nearby** 🏛0.1km **Notes** No pets English spoken

ST-GENIEZ

⏸ ⏸ Domaine des Rayes

Bruno et Micheline MASURE
04200 ST-GENIEZ
☎ 04 92 61 22 76 ▤ 04 92 61 06 44
email: les.rayes@wanadoo.fr
web: www.lesrayes.fr

Deep in the countryside this renovated former sheepfold has four doubles and a family room sleeping four, all with private facilities and terraces with garden furniture. At the heart of the Geological Reserve of Haute-Provence, this chambre d'hôtes has views over the Durance valley and towards the Chapel of Dromon and is close to Sisteron with its lake, citadel, and Rock of Beaume. Rate reduction after two nights.
Prices s €72-€79; d €72-€79; t €105-€110; extra person €20; dinner fr €19 **Nearby** ♨ 2km ⊁ 18km ▦ 18km **Notes** No pets English spoken CC

ST-LAURENT-DU-VERDON

⏸ ⏸ La Colombiere

Paul et Véronique TEISSEIRE
04500 ST-LAURENT-DU-VERDON
☎ 04 92 74 06 32
email: colombiere.chateau@wanadoo.fr

This old farmhouse dates back to the 17th century, and has been beautifully restored. There are three ground floor bedrooms each with separate guests' entrance and own terrace, for two or three people; upstairs is another triple with balcony. All are non-smoking and have private shower room/WC. The hosts are guides to the area, and organise visits on foot or horseback. Lake close by, with boating and water sports available.
Prices d €70-€76; t fr €90; dinner fr €25 **On Site** ♨ **Nearby** ♨ 2km spa 20km ♂ 1km ⊁ 15km Restaurant 5km Water sports 1.5km ⊞ 5km ▦ 40km **Notes** Pets admitted English spoken Open February to December.

ST-MARTIN-DE-BROMES

⏸ Les Chaberts

André et Joelle LE METER
04800 ST-MARTIN-DE-BROMES
☎ 04 92 78 16 41
email: campagne.chaberts@free.fr
web: http://perso.wanadoo.fr/campagne-chaberts/

Fields of lavender, almond and olive trees surround this renovated farmhouse. On the mezzanine level is a reception hall with kitchenette; also two of the three bedrooms. The third bedroom is downstairs, with its own kitchenette and terrace. Cot available. Garden with table tennis; possibility of pottery courses; easy access to the GR4 long-distance path.
Prices not confirmed for 2008 **Nearby** Water sports 12km ⊞ 9km **Notes** No pets Open 31 March to 5 November.

ST-MICHEL-L'OBSERVATOIRE

⏸ ⏸ Le Farnet

Pascal et Cathy DEPOISSON
04870 ST-MICHEL-L'OBSERVATOIRE
☎ 04 92 76 65 52 ▤ 04 92 76 65 97
email: le-farnet@wanadoo.fr
web: www.lefarnet.com/

This renovated stone country house in the large Farnet Estate is surrounded by two hectares of woodland and offers five bedrooms, all with private bathroom, wc and entrance. Central heating and baby equipment on request. Swimming pool, furnished terrace, table-tennis, table football, bikes for hire and pétanque. Meals served every evening except Thursday and Sunday. Close to the Luberon Regional Nature Park and the Provençal Colorado.
Prices s fr €48; d fr €52; t fr €66; extra person fr €11; dinner €11-€17.50 **On Site** Private ♨ **Nearby** ♨ 20km ♂ 30km Restaurant 5km ☘ 5km Spa 25km ⊞ 5km ▦ 25km **Notes** Pets admitted English spoken Open 19 April to 5 October.

UVERNET-FOURS

⏸ ⏸ Le Rozet

Guy GARCIN
Route du Col d'Allos, 04400 UVERNET-FOURS
☎ 04 92 81 10 64 & 06 32 61 61 82
email: lerozet@club-internet.fr
web: www.guideweb.com/provence/bb/rozet/

Ancient restored beamed farmhouse and sheep barn, with five rooms - Ancolie, Neptune, Tajine, Amandine and Archipel, offering accommodation for two to five people and each with heating and private facilities. There is a lounge, library, sauna, fridge for use of guests, and meals (including Creole) are available. Set in peaceful countryside with a magnificent view over the summits of the Chapeau de Gendarme, the Pain au Sucre and the Vallon Bachelard.
Prices s fr €43; d fr €55; extra person fr €15; dinner fr €19 **Nearby** ♨ 6km ♂ 10km ⊁ 6km Restaurant 6km ☘ 5km Water sports 6km ⊞ 6km **Notes** No pets English spoken

VENTEROL

⏸ ✿ ⏸ La Meridienne

Sonia BOYER
Le Blanchet, 04130 VENTEROL
☎ 04 92 54 18 51 ▤ 04 92 54 11 31
email: sonia.boyer@lameridienne.com
web: www.lameridienne.com/

This renovated 18th-century farmhouse looks over the Durance Valley. Five bedrooms all with private bathroom and wc, three with a mezzanine floor. Lounge and library. The farm produces fruits and poultry, and is surrounded by two hectares of shaded parkland with 200 kilometres of forest tracks. 10% reduction for two people for one week and for children.
Prices not confirmed for 2008 **Nearby** ♂ 5km ⊞ 8km **Notes** No pets English spoken

VILLENEUVE

♦♦♦ ⏐◎⏐ La Maurissime

Nicole MOUCHOT

Chemin des Oliviers, 04180 VILLENEUVE

☎ 04 92 78 47 61 ▤ 04 92 78 47 61

Gourmet cuisine and a refined interior are promised at this beautiful residence surrounded by pine forest. Accommodation includes two doubles, a room for three and one for four, all with private facilities and terrace. Lounge with fireplace and TV, meeting room, large terrace with views over Oraison. Nearby attractions include Manosque, the Luberon Regional National Park, the Valensole Plateau, the Salagon and Ganagobie priories.

Prices s fr €45; d fr €60; t fr €70; dinner fr €20 **Nearby** ↧ 39km ✐ 5km ⚲ 6km ⛪ 1km **Notes** Pets admitted English spoken

ALPES-MARITIMES

ANDON

♦♦♦ ⏐◎⏐ Domaine de la Bécassière

Maurice BRUNE

Thorenc, 06750 ANDON

☎ 04 93 60 00 92 & 06 80 41 17 14

email: flo@floiazzetta.com

web: www.saintpaulweb.com/becassiere

This well-appointed house, in the heart of the countryside, has two bedrooms and a suite. On the ground floor is a double-bedded room; on the first floor is another double room, and a two-roomed suite with a double-bedded room plus a lounge with a bed settee. All rooms have private showers and WCs. Meals by arrangement.

Prices d fr €80; extra person fr €15; dinner fr €25 **On Site** ✾ **Nearby** ⚓ 15km ↧ 10km ✐ 0.5km ⚲ 20km Restaurant 0.5km ⚱ 12km ⛱ 0.5km ⛪ 0.5km ⋙ 50km **Notes** No pets English spoken

♦♦♦ ⏐◎⏐ Le Château

Germaine DAMIANI

Canaux, 06750 ANDON

☎ 04 93 09 13 01 & 06 09 55 49 98 ▤ 04 93 09 13 01

This split-level house in a small hamlet has three guest bedrooms. On the second floor are two triples; on the third floor is a room for four. All have private showers/WCs. On the ground and upper ground floors, both with garden access, are two large lounges (one with TV), games room and library. Central heating. Meals by arrangement.

Prices s fr €42; d fr €52; t fr €68; extra person fr €10; dinner fr €20 **Nearby** ⚓ 20km ↧ 10km ✐ 5km ⚱ 15km ⛱ 9km ⛪ 9km ⋙ 50km **Notes** No pets

BERRE-LES-ALPES

♦♦♦ Chambre d'hôtes Les Lys

Francois NOBILE

288 Chemin de Meingarde, 06390 BERRE-LES-ALPES

☎ 04 93 91 81 09 & 06 03 22 39 34 ▤ 04 93 91 83 04

email: chambres-hotes-les-lys@wanadoo.fr

web: www.chambresdhotes.les-lys.com

A peaceful chambre d'hôtes annexed from the owner's home situated between the sea and mountains; an ideal base for walking and mountain biking. Three double rooms have private facilities (extra be available on request). Lounge with open fire, TV and hi-fi; terrace with furniture and barbecue leading out to large enclosed grounds. Parking Medieval villages and numerous restaurants nearby.

Prices s fr €41; d fr €50; extra person fr €13 **Nearby** ⚓ 3km Sea 20km ✐ 5km ⚲ 5km Restaurant 1km ⚱ 30km ⛱ 1km ⛪ 2km ⋙ 4km **Notes** Pets admitted English spoken

CABRIS

♦♦♦ Chambre d'hôtes

Jocelyne FARAUT

14 Rue de L'Agaphon, 06530 CABRIS

☎ 04 93 60 52 36 & 06 03 44 16 84 ▤ 04 93 60 52 36

web: www.cabris-chambres-hotes.com

In the heart of Cabris, this chambre d'hôtes can be found amongst th picturesque houses that surround the ruins of the 10th-century castle in the Provençal village. Five guest rooms: on the ground-floor there is a double, while the first floor has a double room and two twins (one with balcony), all with showers and wcs. On the second floor is a double with bathroom and wc. The dining room has a panoramic view of Lake Saint-Cassien.

Prices d €50-€60; extra person fr €16 **Nearby** ⚓ 6km ↧ 3km Sea 22km ✐ 12km ⚲ 3km Restaurant 0.3km ⚱ 35km ⛱ 0.5km Spa 5km ⋙ 5km **Notes** Pets admitted English spoken Open April to September.

♦♦♦ Le Mas du Naoc

J et S MAINGRET

580 Chemin du Migranie, 06530 CABRIS

☎ 04 93 60 63 13

email: info@lemasdunaoc.com

web: www.lemasdunaoc.com

An 18th-century authentic mas providing five guest rooms: four doubles and a single each with private facilities. There is a communa dining room, a private terrace, a large park with swimming pool and spring and parking. Gourmet breakfasts are served in the garden, which enjoys panoramic views over Cannes Bay.

Prices d €120-€155 **On Site** Private ⚲ **Nearby** ⚓ 6km ↧ 1km Sea 22km ✐ 12km Restaurant 1km ⚱ 35km ⛱ 1km Spa 10km ⛪ 1.5km ⋙ 5km **Notes** No pets English spoken

CARROS

⬛⬛⬛⬛ Le Mas des Selves

Danielle RITUIT

427 Route des Plans, 06510 CARROS

☎ 04 93 29 10 27 & 06 15 19 10 78

email: aumasdesselves@aol.com

web: www.auxselves.com/accueil.htm

A beautiful property in modern Provençal style, with mountain views. There are three guest suites. The first has a double bedroom, twin beds in the lounge, and a terrace. The other two, in a separate building, each have a double room with a double bed-settee in the lounge. All have TV and private facilities. Attractive gardens with terraces and swimming pool.

Prices d €100-€130; extra person fr €25 **On Site** Private ⚲
Nearby ⛷20km ♨5km Sea 15km ✎4km Restaurant 0.1km
⚓45km ♒3km Spa 15km ♒15km ♨0.5km ⛟15km
Notes No pets English spoken

CAUSSOLS

⬛⬛⬛ ◯ Le Mas des Chardons

et P DORGE

64, Chemin des Chardons, 06460 CAUSSOLS

☎ 04 93 09 29 93 � 04 93 09 80 55

email: pierre.dorge1@wanadoo.fr

web: http://perso.wanadoo.fr/dorge

This country house has five guest rooms: two doubles, two triples and a room for four (twin beds plus bunks). Each room has private shower/WC. Lounge with TV and fireplace; cot available. Enclosed grounds with terrace, garden furniture and mini-tennis. Caving and astronomy on site, or explore this area around Bar-sur-Loup on foot, bike or horseback. Walking routes close by.

Prices s fr €45; d fr €52; t fr €69; dinner fr €21 **Nearby** ⛷1km
15km Sea 41km ✎12km ⚲10km Restaurant 0.5km ⚓33km ♨9km
41km **Notes** No pets

CHATEAUNEUF

⬛⬛⬛⬛ Bastide la Rouveirado

Carole COPPEL

22 Chemin des Colles, 06740 CHATEAUNEUF

☎ 04 93 77 78 49 & 06 11 48 27 66

email: info@larouveirado.com

web: www.larouveirado.com

Standing among ancient olive trees in a protected area, this house has five colonial-style guest rooms. There are two twin-bedded rooms; two rooms each with a double bed and a single; and a room with two small double beds. All rooms have a private shower or bathroom and WC. Guests' lounge; extensive grounds with swimming pool.

Prices d €110-€120; extra person fr €15 **On Site** Private ⚲
Nearby ⛷2km ♨0.5km Sea 15km ✎20km Restaurant 3km
⚓45km ♒1km ♨1km ⛟15km **Notes** Pets admitted English spoken Open February to December.

CHATEAUNEUF-VILLEVIEILLE

⬛⬛⬛ ◯ La Parare

S et K VAN VOLEN

GITES DE FRANCE DES ALPES-MARITIMES

☎ 04 93 79 22 62 & 06 89 79 20 93

� 04 93 79 46 99

email: karin@laparare.com

web: www.laparare.com

This house, peacefully situated among the olive trees on the edge of a village, has three double bedrooms. Two are on the second floor and one on the third. Each room has a lounge area and a private bathroom and WC. Extra bed available. Terrace with garden furniture, small swimming pool. Meals by arrangement.

Prices d €95-€110; extra person fr €25; dinner fr €29
On Site Private ⚲ **Nearby** ⛷6km Sea 22km ✎6km ⚓43km
♨0.5km ⛟22km **Notes** No pets English spoken

COARAZE

⬛⬛⬛ ◯ L'Alivu

Michele CESARI

816 Route des Baisses, 06390 COARAZE

☎ 04 93 80 86 68 & 06 25 19 86 24

email: reception@alivu.com

web: www.alivu.com

This is a peaceful place standing in its own grounds, with olive trees and open views over the valley. Four double bedrooms are on the ground floor, all with television, en suite shower room and WC; two have independent entrance. Large living room, swimming pool, table tennis, mountain bikes. Outdoor cooking area with barbecue.

Prices d fr €100; dinner fr €29 **On Site** Private ⚲ **Nearby** ⛷30km
Sea 32km ✎1km Restaurant 3km ⚓33km ♒10km Spa 10km ♨4km
⛟32km **Notes** Pets admitted English spoken

CONTES

⬛⬛⬛⬛ Les Cypres

C DJORDJIAN

GITES DE FRANCE DES ALPES-MARITIMES

☎ 04 93 62 58 77 & 06 03 88 14 71 � 04 93 96 02 50

email: info@lescypres.fr

web: www.lescypres.fr

A 1920s house with three ground floor double bedrooms, each with private shower and WC. Cot and a child's bed available. The garden has plenty of flowers, a pergola and a terrace. Not far from the town of Contes, with its good range of shops; Nice and the Alpes d'Azur are within travelling distance.

Prices d €68 €75 **On Site** ♒ **Nearby** ✎12km ♨20km Sea 18km
✎1km ⚲0.2km Restaurant 0.2km ⚓37km ♒0.2km ♨0.2km ⛟5km
Notes No pets English spoken

EZE

▦ La Bastide aux Camélias

F et S MATHIEU

23 C Route de L'Adret, 06360 EZE

☎ 04 93 41 13 68 & 06 22 33 15 45

📄 04 93 41 13 68

email: sylviane.mathieu@libertysurf.fr

web: www.bastideauxcamelias.com

La Bastide is set in a medieval village with panoramic views over the park, near all the attractions of the Riviera. It offers three rooms: 'Lilas' (twin), 'Jasmin' (double) and 'Carambole' (double with possible extra bed). Each room has a private bathroom and TV-video. Guests have use of the lounge, veranda, library, Jacuzzi, swimming pool, parking and enclosed grounds with garden furniture.

Prices not confirmed for 2008 **On Site** Private ⚡ **Nearby** ⚡ 3km Sea 8km ⚡ 8km 🏛 2km ⚡ 8km **Notes** No pets English spoken

GATTIERES

▦ Les Sources

Paule HEYBERGER

103 Impasse du Barry, 06510 GATTIERES

☎ 04 93 72 53 09 & 06 18 73 09 71

email: pauleheyberger@wanadoo.fr

web: www.aux-sources.com

Four first floor bedrooms in a Provençal style house. One is a double, the others have twin beds. All have private bathroom and WC; two have private garden areas, one has a balcony, and one has a terrace. Each room has a split-level layout, with space for an extra bed. Lounge, weights room, swimming pool. Wooded grounds.

Prices d €90-€95; extra person fr €20 **On Site** Private ⚡ **Nearby** ⚡ 13km Sea 11km ⚡ 6km Restaurant 0.3km 🏛 0.3km ⚡ 15km **Notes** No pets English spoken

GOLFE-JUAN VALLAURIS

▦ Le Mas Samarcande

Mireille DIOT

138 Grand Bld de Super Cannes,

06220 GOLFE-JUAN VALLAURIS

☎ 04 93 63 97 73 📄 04 93 63 97 73

email: mireille.diot@wanadoo.fr

web: www.mas-samarcande.com

Situated in Vallauris, a town famous for its art and pottery, this chambre d'hôtes has a view over the Baie des Anges and offers high levels of comfort in the peace of the hills. There are five guest rooms, two of which are adjoining, Manosque 1 (double) and 2 (twin). Lérins and Samarcande are also double rooms. Porquerolles contains one double bed and one small child's bed. All rooms have a bathroom, wc, TV and air conditioning. The lounge opens onto a large panoramic terrace, a garden and parking.

Prices d €120-€130; extra person €20-€30 **On Site** ⚡ Private tennis court **Nearby** ⚡ 5km Sea 3km ⚡ 3km ⚡ Restaurant 1km 🏛 0.7km ⚡ 3km **Notes** No pets English spoken Open February to 15 November.

GREOLIERES

▦ ⍟ Chambre d'hôtes

P DELGRANGE

440 Route de Gentelly, 06620 GREOLIERES

☎ 04 93 59 91 12 & 06 14 12 01 84

email: delgrange.pierre@wanadoo.fr

Three en suite double rooms here, with beautiful views of the village of Gréolières. Two of the rooms have a split-level layout, with room for an extra single bed if needed. Meals available if pre-booked; hang gliding school on site, and off-road parking.

Prices s fr €40; d fr €60; extra person fr €18; dinner fr €20 **Nearby** ⚡ 8km ⚡ 17km Sea 27km ⚡ 3km Restaurant 0.2km ⚡ 15km ⚡ 0.2km Spa 30km 🏛 0.4km ⚡ 27km **Notes** Pets admitted English spoken Open January to November.

LA COLLE-SUR-LOUP

▦ Bastide Saint-Donat

Alphonse ROSSO

Parc Saint-Donat, 06480 LA COLLE-SUR-LOUP

☎ 04 93 32 93 41 📄 04 93 32 80 61

web: www.bastide-saint-donat.com

This renovated riverside country house has three suites (double and single bed, one with lounge, another with private terrace) and two twin rooms, all with private facilities. Lounge with open fire and television, separate television room, telephone, terrace and parking. Close to the Gorges du Loup and the Côte d'Azur.

Prices s fr €40; d €65-€95; extra person fr €16 **On Site** ⚡ ⚡ Restaurant ⚡ **Nearby** ⚡ 10km Sea 7km ⚡ 40km ⚡ 🏛 2km ⚡ 7km **Notes** Pets admitted English spoken

▦ Un Ange Passe

B et M DELOUPY

419 Av Jean Leonardi, 06480 LA COLLE-SUR-LOUP

☎ 04 93 32 60 39 📄 04 93 82 45 29

email: contact@unangepasse.fr

web: www.unangepasse.fr

A beautiful Provençal style house with a family suite and four double bedrooms. The suite has two intercommunicating rooms, one with a double bed, the other with two singles. Two of the double-bedded rooms also have lounge areas, with additional folding beds. All rooms have private shower, WC, TV, fridge, cafetière and air-conditioning. Wooded garden, swimming pool.

PROVENCE-ALPES-CÔTE-D'AZUR

Prices s fr €80; d €80-€130; extra person fr €25   **On Site** ☺ Private ↘
Nearby ⚓ 0.4km ⌇8km Sea 7km 𝒫 1.5km Restaurant 1km ⚓40km
⚒ 1.5km Spa 6km 🖭1km ⋙7km   **Notes** Pets admitted English spoken

⁂ Villa Cédria

Rob Heuvers et Willem Zoon
Chemin de Vaulongue, 06480 LA COLLE-SUR-LOUP
☎ 04 93 32 15 99 & 06 31 57 20 60
email: info@villacedria.com
web: www.villacedria.com

The owners of this house welcome guests to three double rooms
('Jaune', 'Terra-Cotta' and 'Ivoire') each comfortably furnished with
private facilities, TV, heating and minibar. There is a lounge, shared
dining room, garden and terrace with furniture, swimming pool and
boules.

Prices d €85-€135   **On Site** Restaurant ☺ Private ↘
Nearby ⚓ 20km ⌇10km Sea 12km 𝒫 3km ⚓40km ⚒ 2km
⋙10km   **Notes** No pets English spoken

LA CROIX-SUR-ROUDOULE

⁂ ⏏ *Le Tilleul*

Marc et Odile VIGNAL
Leouve, 06260 LA CROIX-SUR-ROUDOULE
☎ 04 93 05 15 63 & 06 22 56 86 34   📄 04 93 05 09 94
email: chambreshotestilleul@wanadoo.fr
web: http://perso.wanadoo.fr/chambreshotestilleul

A property with five bedrooms, all on the first floor. There are two
double rooms and two twin-bedded rooms, plus a family room for
four with double and twin beds. All rooms have private showers and
WCs. On the same floor is a small guests' lounge, and there is another
lounge on the ground floor. Garden, terrace and a swimming pool.

Prices not confirmed for 2008   **On Site** 𝒫 Private ↘   **Nearby** ⚓ 29km
⌇8km ⋙8km   **Notes** Pets admitted English spoken

LA GAUDE

⁂ ⏏ L'Orangeraie

B LALLEMAND
6 Chemin du Maoupas, 06610 LA GAUDE
☎ 04 92 12 13 69 & 06 13 71 24 31   📄 04 92 12 17 44
email: lorangeraie@gmail.com
web: www.orangeraie.fr

This is a farm producing olives, citrus fruit, avocados, vegetables
and poultry. The four air-conditioned bedrooms are in a separate
building from the owners' home. Each room has twin beds which
can be linked to form a double. All have private facilities, including
power showers, also safes for valuables. Leisure room with TV, table
tennis and table football. Swimming pool, mountain bikes. Meals by
arrangement.

Prices s fr €85; d €85-€95; extra person fr €25; dinner fr €24
On Site Private ↘   **Nearby** ⚓ 2.5km ⌇10km Sea 6km 𝒫 0.5km
Restaurant 7km ⚓48km ⚒ 5km 🖭1km ⋙6km   **Notes** Pets admitted
English spoken CC

⁂ ⏏ *Le Clos des Lucioles*

C et R PARMENTIER-BRAUGE
87 Chemin de L'Adret, 06610 LA GAUDE
☎ 04 92 11 01 79   📄 04 92 11 01 79
email: cath.brauge@laposte.net
web: http://chambrehotes.site.voila.fr

This property has three ground floor bedrooms - three doubles,
one of which also has a lounge area with a bed-settee. Two of
the rooms have their own separate entrances, with a terrace; all
rooms have TVs and private facilities. Lounge with books, terrace
bordered by trees, semi-sunken swimming pool, bikes. Meals by
arrangement.

Prices not confirmed for 2008   **On Site** Private ↘   **Nearby** ⚓ 10km
Sea 10km 𝒫 5km ⚓48km 🖭1km ⋙12km   **Notes** Pets admitted
English spoken

LE ROURET

⁂ Le Grand Mas

C et V COMTE
1 Chemin Miejou Souro, 06650 LE ROURET
☎ 04 93 77 29 73 & 06 11 13 06 93   📄 04 93 77 29 73
email: christophe.cc.comte@wanadoo.fr
web: www.legrandmas-lerouret.com

An 18th-century stone-built house in its own grounds close to the
village of Le Rouret. On the ground floor is a double room with a
canopied bed; upstairs are two triples, each with a double bed and a
single. All rooms have en suite facilities and a safe for valuables. Sun-
room, living room with kitchenette, and a boules pitch.

Prices d €85-€105; t €100-€110; extra person fr €10   **Nearby** ⚓ 1km
⌇10km Sea 13km 𝒫 4km ↘ Restaurant 0.5km ⚓49km ⚒ 1km
Spa 5km 🖭1km ⋙5km   **Notes** No pets English spoken

⁂ ⏏ ⛔ Villa Rose de Mai

Rose-Marie FONTAINE
20 Chemin des Bourges, 06650 LE ROURET
☎ 04 93 77 33 09
email: gerard.fontaine19@wanadoo.fr
web: http://rmgfontaine.free.fr

A beautiful Provençal country house, with two double bedrooms and
one suite. Each has an en suite bathroom or shower and WC, and a
large private terrace; one room also has its own entrance. Sitting room

CONTINUED

LE ROURET *CONTINUED*

with TV, books, and outside are beautiful grounds with mature olive trees. Meals by arrangement; parking on site.

Prices d €65-€90; extra person fr €15; dinner fr €26 **Nearby** ⚑ 1km ♨ 2km Sea 13km ♻ 4km ↘ 10km Restaurant 1km ⚓ 49km ♋ 2km 🏛 1km ⋙ 15km **Notes** No pets English spoken CC

NICE

▦ ⟡ **La Lézardière**

Rudolph PAAUW

87 Boulevard de l'Observatoire, 06300 NICE

☎ 04 93 56 22 86 & 06 75 97 33 91

🖹 04 93 56 22 86

email: rpaauw@free.fr

web: www.villa-la-lezardiere.com

This lovely Provencal house has a sea view and provides a double room and four suites: Rosina (double with sauna and lounge area); Ellen (twin with lounge area); Bleue (double); and Orientale (twin with sitting room). Each has private facilities, and the suites feature mini-bars, satellite TV, safe and private terrace with furniture. Communal enclosed grounds with swimming pool, Jacuzzi, parking, table tennis, barbecue and outdoor kitchen. Table d'hôte meals available.

Prices d €110-€160; extra person fr €25; dinner fr €39 **On Site** ♨ Private ↘ **Nearby** ⚑ 3km Sea 5km ♻ 5km Restaurant 2.5km ♋ 🏛 2km ⋙ 3km **Notes** No pets English spoken CC

▦ **Le Castel Enchanté**

J et M FERRARY

61 Route Saint-Pierre de Feric, 06000 NICE

☎ 04 93 97 02 08 🖹 04 93 97 13 70

email: contact@castel-enchante.com

web: www.castel-enchante.com

A lovely relaxing Italian-style house dating from the turn of the last century, set on the hills of Nice. Spacious and comfortable rooms comprise a family room with two singles and a double, 'Rose d'été' (twin) and 'Capucine' (double), each with private facilities and TV. Terrace; large park with swimming pool.

Prices s fr €100; d fr €110; t fr €150 **On Site** Private ↘ **Nearby** ⚑ 6km Sea 2km ♻ 3km 🏛 1km ⋙ 2km **Notes** No pets English spoken Open April to 14 November.

PEONE-VALBERG

▦ ⟡ **Le Chant du Mele**

Patricia GUICHARD

GITES DE FRANCE DES ALPES-MARITIMES

☎ 04 93 02 57 88 & 06 81 98 53 90 🖹 04 93 02 57 88

email: contact@chambres-hotes-valberg.com

web: www.chambres-hotes-valberg.com

A mountain chalet with five upstairs bedrooms. Two are doubles, and the other three are family rooms. Each has a private shower and WC. Downstairs is a living room with open fire, and outside is a terrace, parking space, and a garage for motor bikes. Mountains and the Mediterranean coast are both within reach.

Prices d fr €78; t fr €113; extra person €17-€23; dinner fr €23 **Nearby** ⚑ 1km ♨ 2km ♻ 5km ↘ 2km Restaurant 1km ⚓ 1km ♋ 1km 🐾 1km 🏛 1km ⋙ 31km **Notes** Pets admitted CC

PIERREFEU

▦ ⟡ **La Maïoun aux Oliviers**

F AIMAR et J CIRILLO

GITES DE FRANCE DES ALPES-MARITIMES

☎ 04 97 02 12 81 & 06 07 38 24 91 🖹 04 97 02 12 81

email: contact@maioun-aux-oliviers.com

web: www.maioun-aux-oliviers.com

This pretty Provençal house in a restful country setting offers three themed bedrooms. On the ground floor is a triple, with private shower/WC; upstairs are two doubles, with private bath/shower and WC across the corridor. Lounge with TV, video and stereo; garden with terrace and garden furniture. Parking. Meals by arrangement.

Prices d €85-€95; t €85-€95; extra person fr €20; dinner fr €25 **On Site** Spa Private ↘ **Nearby** ⚑ 30km ♨ 30km Sea 45km ♻ 6km Restaurant 10km ♋ 30km 🏛 10km ⋙ 40km **Notes** Pets admitted English spoken

SOSPEL

▦ **Villa Amiel**

Patrick LE COUSTUMER

Ave Martyres de la Resistance, 06380 SOSPEL

☎ 04 93 04 12 69 & 06 83 42 65 61 🖹 04 93 04 12 69

email: plc@villaamiel.com

web: www.villaamiel.com

This house, set in an English-style garden, has three guest rooms, all with two double beds. All rooms have private bath or shower room and WC, also TV, mini-bar and courtesy tray. One room has a terrace with garden furniture; another has two balconies. Lounge with open fireplace and satellite TV. Parking. Generous and varied breakfasts, other meals by arrangement.

Prices s €59-€68.50; d €70.50-€77.50; t fr €99; extra person fr €22 **On Site** ♻ ♨ **Nearby** ⚑ 1km Sea 18km Restaurant 0.8km ⚓ 24km ♋ 0.8km 🏛 0.8km ⋙ 0.8km **Notes** No pets English spoken

TOURRETTES-SUR-LOUP

▦ ⟡ **La Demeure de Jeanne**

Y COHEN-DICHTEL

907 Route de Vence, 06140 TOURRETTES-SUR-LOUP

☎ 04 93 59 37 24 & 06 66 76 53 32 🖹 04 93 24 39 95

email: yolande6@libertysurf.fr

web: www.demeuredejeanne.com

A beautiful Provençal chambre d'hôtes with a sea view, close to the Esterel Mountains. There are two double rooms with lounge areas, one with private terrace, a twin room and a suite with double bed and lounge. All rooms have private facilities, TV and video, and guests can borrow films from a video library. Garden and swimming pool.

Prices s €100-€150; d €100-€150; extra person fr €35; dinner fr €45 **On Site** Private ↘ **Nearby** ⚑ 10km ♨ 15km Sea 12km ♻ 3km Restaurant 0.3km ⚓ 40km ♋ 0.4km ↘ 5km 🏛 0.9km ⋙ 12km **Notes** No pets English spoken Open March to 15 October.

⠿ La Rocheliere

G et M-N PICOT

260 Rte de la Chapelle, 06140 TOURRETTES-SUR-LOUP

☎ 04 93 58 81 38 & 06 20 54 72 96 ▤ 04 93 58 81 38

email: contact@la-rocheliere-tourrettes.com

web: www.la-rocheliere-tourrettes.com

A house with lots of character, set in the countryside within reach of the town of Vence. Four bedrooms are all doubles and twins, with air-conditioning, private shower room and WC. Each also has its own terrace, with a sea view. Parking, mountain bikes, boules pitch and swimming pool are all on site.

Prices d €100-€120; extra person fr €5   **On Site** Private ⤜
Nearby ⚲ 8km ⚲ 5km Sea 12km ⌀ 3km Restaurant 0.5km ⚓ 40km
⚲ 3km ⚲ 4km ⚏ 15km   **Notes** No pets English spoken Open March to October.

⠿ ⏣ *Le Mas de Tourettes*

Christian DAUPHINOT

13 Chemin des Gours, 06140 TOURRETTES-SUR-LOUP

☎ 04 93 32 16 42 & 06 24 48 57 31 ▤ 04 92 11 06 95

email: info@masdetourrettes.com

web: www.masdetourrettes.com

A house built in the local style, with two bedrooms and one suite. Each has a TV, en suite shower and WC, mini-bar and a private terrace. Outside is a large swimming pool and a pétanque pitch. Meals can be served on the patio near the pool.

Prices not confirmed for 2008   **On Site** Private ⤜   **Nearby** ⚲ 8km
Sea 14km ⌀ 3km ⚓ 40km ⚲ 1.6km ⚏ 15km   **Notes** No pets English spoken

⠿ Le Mas des Cigales

David PRIEUR-GELIS

1673 Route des Quenieres,

06140 TOURRETTES-SUR-LOUP

☎ 04 93 59 25 73 & 06 63 64 48 95

▤ 04 93 59 25 73

email: lemasdescigales@free.fr

web: www.lemasdescigales.com

A medieval village, renowned for its violet-growing, is the setting for this house, which has distant sea views. There are five bedrooms - some double-bedded, some with twin beds - two of which can be linked. All rooms have TVs and private bath or shower rooms and WCs. Generous breakfasts; internet access. Tennis, swimming pool with terraces, outdoor Jacuzzi.

Prices d €77-€105; extra person fr €25; dinner fr €25   **On Site** Spa
⚲ Private ⤜ Private tennis court   **Nearby** ⚲ 12km ⚲ 12km
Sea 14km ⌀ 7km Restaurant 1.6km ⚓ 40km ⚲ 1.6km ⚏ 15km
Notes No pets English spoken CC

⠿ Le Cheneau

A et C RINGENBACH

205 Route D'Antibes, 06560 VALBONNE

☎ 04 93 12 13 94 & 06 68 15 82 64 ▤ 04 93 12 13 94

email: ringbach@club-internet.fr

This completely non-smoking property stands in extensive level grounds. It has three guest bedrooms, one double and two with twin beds which can be linked. All the rooms have en suite bathrooms/WCs. There is a lounge area with TV and kitchen for guests' use. Outside is a covered seating area, and a big terrace with garden furniture. Parking on site.

Prices s €60-€80; d €65-€85; extra person fr €20   **Nearby** ⚲ 2km
⚲ 0.9km Sea 13km ⌀ 3km Restaurant 0.2km ⚓ 40km ⚲ 5km ⚲ 10km
⚲ 0.2km ⚏ 10km   **Notes** No pets English spoken

VENCE

⠿ La Bastide aux Oliviers

Claude OLLIVIER

1260 Chemin de la Sine, 06140 VENCE

☎ 04 93 24 20 33 & 06 16 09 85 73

▤ 04 93 58 55 78

email: frenchclaude@wanadoo.fr

web: www.bastideauxoliviers.com

Two kilometres from St-Paul-de-Vence, La Bastide aux Oliviers is a beautiful stone building situated in a one-hectare park with a magnificent view of the Plaine du Loup. Four double bedrooms, one of which is a suite with a private lounge, decorated in the Provençal style with a bathroom, TV and terrace or solarium. Swimming pool, tennis, terrace, parking, table d'hôtes meals. Mountain bikes, table tennis, table football, darts and pétanque available.

Prices d €100-€175; extra person €25-€35   **On Site** Private ⤜
Private tennis court   **Nearby** ⚲ 8km ⚲ 15km Sea 14km ⌀ 5km
Restaurant 2km ⚓ 40km ⚲ 3km ⚏ 13km   **Notes** Pets admitted
English spoken

⠿ La Colline de Vence

F et K BRONCHARD

808 Chemin des Salles, 06140 VENCE

☎ 04 93 24 03 66 ▤ 04 93 24 03 66

email: contact@colline-vence.com

web: www.colline-vence.com

Close to St-Paul-de-Vence, this authentic 200-year-old farm has three individually decorated rooms: Amandiers, Orangers (with fireplace) and Mimosas, all with panoramic views of the countryside and sea, king-size bed, private facilities, satellite TV and mini-bar. Extra bed available. Heating, terrace, private gardens and parking. Near country pathways and numerous leisure facilities and attractions. Low season discounts.

Prices d €90-€135; extra person fr €25   **On Site** Private ⤜
Nearby ⚲ 8km Sea 12km ⌀ 4km Restaurant 1.5km ⚓ 40km
⚲ 2km ⚲ 2km ⚏ 12km   **Notes** No pets English spoken

VILLARS-SUR-VAR

Le Château

M et V TAPIA
06710 VILLARS-SUR-VAR
☎ 04 93 05 70 10 & 06 61 92 90 06
📠 04 93 05 78 86
email: chateau-d-esperon@wanadoo.fr
web: www.chateau-d-esperon.com

A beautifully-appointed stone-built house overlooking the village. On the second floor it has two double-bedded rooms and two twin-bedded rooms. All the rooms have TVs, private bathrooms with spa baths and WCs; three of them also have lounge areas with convertible bed-settees. Guests' lounge, table tennis and table football, swimming pool. Generous breakfasts.

Prices d €100-€160; t €135-€180; extra person fr €25
On Site Private **Nearby** 30km 0.5km 30km 2km
Notes No pets English spoken Open February to mid October. CC

BOUCHES-DU-RHÔNE

AIX-EN-PROVENCE

Campagne Jeanne

Martine ALEXANDRIAN
670 Chemin des Loups, 13290 AIX-EN-PROVENCE
☎ 04 42 60 83 10 📠 04 42 20 16 35
email: martine@campagne-jeanne.com
web: www.campagne-jeanne.com

Set in the countryside around Aix, this house offers four pretty bedrooms decorated in the traditional colours of Provence. Three double rooms, one twin room and bathroom. Cot available. Private terrace with furniture. In the winter, guests are invited to share the lounge's open fire with their hosts. 4km from the town centre. Car park. Closed Xmas.

Prices s fr €55; d fr €60 **Nearby** 3km Sea 30km Restaurant 4km 3km 2km 10km **Notes** No pets English spoken

ARLES

Mas Sainte Cécile

Corinne et Michel MEGIAS
13200 ARLES
☎ 04 90 97 08 92 & 06 25 03 46 12 📠 04 90 97 08 92
email: michel.megias@wanadoo.fr
web: www.domainesaintececile.com

A former 17th-century monastery in the heart of the Camargue provides a striking setting for this chambre d'hôtes. On the ground floor is a double room and two suites, all with TV/DVD. Upstairs is a further double room (plus dressing room) with a canopied bed. All rooms have private facilities. Cot and extra beds available; meals by arrangement.

Prices s €65-€85; d €80-€105; extra person fr €18 **Nearby** 15km 25km Sea 30km Restaurant 5km 10km 15km 15km 12km **Notes** No pets English spoken

ARLES MOULES

Mas du Petit Grava

Ike ILOPUTAIFE
Quartier St Hippolyte, 13280 ARLES MOULES
☎ 04 90 98 35 66 📠 04 90 98 35 66
email: ekeneme2@aol.com
web: www.masdupetitgrava.net

Standing among gardens and orchards, this 18th-century property has four bedrooms, all beautifully restored and decorated. Upstairs are two doubles; downstairs are a double and a twin. All have private bath/shower and WC. Extra bed available. Use of lounge, with books. Terrace, garden furniture, table tennis, cycles, swimming pool. Enclosed parking. Evening meal by arrangement.

Prices s €90-€115; d €100-€120; dinner fr €29 **On Site** Restaurant **Nearby** 1km 10km Sea 20km 1km 4km 3km 4km
Notes No pets English spoken Open 15 March to October

AURONS-EN-PROVENCE

Château du Petit Sonnailler

Dominique BRULAT
13121 AURONS-EN-PROVENCE
☎ 04 90 59 34 47 📠 04 90 59 32 30
email: jc.brulat@club-internet.fr
web: www.petit-sonnailler.com

A pretty house situated on a site of archaeological interest, with a château dating from the 12th century and a vineyard. Set in 80 hectares, it offers three double rooms (one with single, extra beds available) and private facilities. Private terrace and garden with furniture, mini bar, microwave. Covered car park.

Prices s €55-€64 **Nearby** 5km 5km Sea 30km 15km 1km Restaurant 1km 9km 7km 9km **Notes** Pets admitted English spoken

Le Castelas

Monique BRAUGE
Vallon des Eoures, 13121 AURONS-EN-PROVENCE
☎ 04 90 55 60 12 & 06 83 25 86 76 📠 04 90 55 60 12
email: lecastelas@aol.com
web: www.le-castelas.com

The pretty house is situated in a village that dates from the 10th century. One twin, one double and one triple room, all with bathroo

and separate access, furnished with antiques. Situated in closed grounds with car park, a private terrace with furniture and a large veranda with panoramic views where breakfast can be taken.

Prices d €75-€95; extra person fr €25; dinner fr €25 **Nearby** ✿ 5km ⚐ 9km Sea 35km ↖ 0.1km Restaurant 5km ⚑ 5km ♔ 0.1km ☖ 8km ⋙ 8km **Notes** No pets English spoken

BARBENTANE

▦ Le Mazet de la Dame

Isabelle et Albert SILVESTRE
Draille Du Mas de le Dame, 13570 BARBENTANE
☎ 04 90 90 91 73 ▤ 04 90 90 91 73
email: ladame@free.fr
web: www.la-dame.com

In a wonderfully peaceful forest setting, standing in seven hectares of grounds, this property has a beautiful double bedroom, decorated in a Tuscan style, with a baby's cot, TV and en suite facilities. There are also two suites for two or three people with private facilities. Terrace with garden furniture.

Prices s fr €95; d fr €110; extra person fr €15 **On Site** ♔ **Nearby** ✿ 3km ⚐ 6km ℓ 6km ↖ 18km Restaurant 3km ⚑ 4km ☖ 3km ⋙ 11km **Notes** Pets admitted

CABRIES

▦ ⦿ La Bastide de la Cluée

J-M VINCENT et C PERRIER
Route de la Césarde, 13480 CABRIES
☎ 04 42 22 59 00 & 06 13 90 26 50 ▤ 04 42 22 59 00
email: bastide.cluee@wanadoo.fr
web: www.gite-prop.com/13/200311

This peaceful 19th-century house set in shady grounds offers four attractive guest rooms: two double rooms and a room with double bed and single bed on a mezzanine; and one suite with double bed and two bunk beds, small lounge and private entrance. Rooms have private facilities. A lounge with fireplace, living room with TV, dining room, kitchen, pool house, and swimming pool.

Prices s fr €64; d €75-€78; t fr €115; extra person fr €20; dinner fr €25 **On Site** Private ↖ **Nearby** ✿ 6km ⚐ 2km Sea 20km Restaurant 4km ⚑ 2km Spa 15km ☖ 2km ⋙ 5km **Notes** No pets English spoken

CASSIS

▦ *Chambre d'hôtes*

Valérie NEDERVEEN SIMANDOUX
22, Impasse des Brayes, 13260 CASSIS
☎ 06 67 10 88 71
email: nederveen@voila.fr

This property stands above Cassis, not far from the sea, with views across the hills. It has two double rooms and a two-roomed family suite for four (double bed and twins). All rooms have private facilities. Lounge for guests' use, with open fire. Swimming pool, table tennis, boules, and terrace with garden furniture. Good access to footpaths.

Prices not confirmed for 2008 **Nearby** ✿ 1.5km ⚐ 25km Sea 1.2km ↖ ⚑ 2km ♔ 0.5km ⋙ 4km **Notes** No pets English spoken

CAZAN VERNEGUES

▦ ⅋ Chambre d'hôtes

Evelyne et Régis LEBRE
Route de Charleval D22, Commanderie des Taillades,
13116 CAZAN VERNEGUES
☎ 04 90 59 76 75 & 06 12 28 63 08 ▤ 04 90 59 76 75
email: regis.lebre@wanadoo.fr
web: www.lacommanderie.net

This 200-year-old farmhouse stands peacefully in 250 hectares of grounds. On the ground floor is a double which is suitable for the less mobile guest; upstairs are four double-bedded rooms, two of which also have an additional single bed. All have en suite showers/WCs. Terrace with garden furniture.

Prices s fr €60; d fr €70; t fr €88; extra person fr €18 **Nearby** ✿ 4km ⚐ 5km ↖ 5km Restaurant 5km ⚑ 5km ☖ 5km ⋙ 18km **Notes** No pets

CEYRESTE

▦ Les Sorbieres des Oiseleurs

S et J-J CENTINO
Chemin des Lavandes, 13600 CEYRESTE
☎ 04 42 83 71 55 & 06 08 06 85 25
email: jjcentino@wanadoo.fr
web: www.lamusarde.com

A stone-built 19th-century country house with three guest rooms. There is a double room, which can also have a cot or child's bed; a triple room (double bed plus single on mezzanine); and a further double in a separate, small building. All have TV, private facilities and individual terraces. Use of fridge. Extensive wooded grounds. Secure off-road parking.

Prices s fr €60; d fr €70; t fr €90; extra person fr €20 **Nearby** ✿ 5km ⚐ 15km Sea 4km ℓ 4km ↖ 6km Restaurant 1.5km ⚑ 2km Spa 5km ♔ 4km ☖ 1.5km ⋙ 2km **Notes** No pets English spoken Open April to 1 October.

CHARLEVAL

▦ ⦿ Mas du Câprier

G GALLI et L ATAROFF
Chemin des Termes, Les Royères, 13350 CHARLEVAL
☎ 04 42 28 49 29 & 06 10 24 74 87 ▤ 04 42 28 49 29
email: lecaprier@wanadoo.fr
web: http://lecaprier.monsite.wanadoo.fr

This old Provençal farmhouse, with its views towards the Lubéron Hills has three attractive and tasteful bedrooms, all on the first floor. There are two double rooms and a twin-bedded room, all with private bath/ shower rooms and WCs. Extensive grounds with terrace and garden furniture. Good walking country. Provençal cuisine served.

Prices s fr €70; d fr €70; extra person fr €15; dinner fr €25 **Nearby** ✿ 4km ⚐ 4km ℓ 3km ↖ 3km Restaurant 1.5km ⚑ 3km Spa 30km ☖ 1.5km ⋙ 30km **Notes** Pets admitted

CHATEAURENARD

☷ Chambre d'hôtes

Jacqueline SARRAZIN

1001 Chemin du Mas Raton, 13160 CHATEAURENARD

☎ 04 90 94 00 33 & 06 20 80 40 64 📄 04 90 94 00 33

web: www.avignonetprovence.com

This large house close to Avignon offers three guest rooms with a separate entrance. One double room with private bathroom facilities opposite, and a further two rooms with bathroom. Private terrace with furniture, well-kept garden, swimming pool, table tennis, boules and car park.

Prices s fr €58; d fr €68 **On Site** Private ⚲ **Nearby** ⛵ 3km
⚓ 10km ⚐ 25km Restaurant 3km ⚑ 5km ⚐ 5km 🏠 5km ⚒ 8km
Notes No pets

☷ *Le Mas di Lioun*

Chantal et Gilbert GERVASONI

688, Chemin du Pont de Bois, 13160 CHATEAURENARD

☎ 04 90 94 27 66 & 06 17 27 98 95 📄 04 90 94 27 66

email: gervasoni.gilbert@wanadoo.fr

web: www.mas-di-lioun.com

Guests can expect a warm welcome at this 19th-century country house, set in extensive wooded grounds near les Alpilles. Rooms available are spacious, comfortable and carefully decorated and include a suite for three, a triple with terrace and a double room, each with private facilities and TV if required. Guests can sit out on the large flowery terrace.

Prices not confirmed for 2008 **Nearby** ⛵ 4km ⚓ 17km ⚲ 2km ⚑ 3km
🏠 2km ⚒ 6km **Notes** No pets English spoken

☷ *Li Tres Pichot*

Daniel BLACHON

621 B Chemin du Bigonnet, La Crau de Chateaurenard, 13160 CHATEAURENARD

☎ 04 90 94 07 44 & 06 13 41 16 44 📄 04 90 94 07 44

email: contact@litrespichot.com

web: http://li.tres.pichot.free.fr

This beautiful country house, in deepest Provence, has three magnificent ground floor air-conditioned rooms which have all been tastefully and sensitively decorated. Two are doubles; the third is a triple with access for disabled guests. All have private shower rooms/WCs, and a cot is available. Large dining room with lounge area. Garden room, shady terrace, parking.

Prices not confirmed for 2008 **Nearby** ⛵ 3km ⚓ 15km ⚲ 5km ⚑ 3km
🏠 3km ⚒ 10km **Notes** No pets English spoken

☷ Mas des Cactus

Françoise et Patrick BASNEL

3501 Chemin Roumieux, 13160 CHATEAURENARD

☎ 04 90 90 14 65 & 06 22 45 30 25 📄 04 90 90 14 65

email: patrick.basnel@neuf.fr

web: www.masdescactus.com

Charming guest rooms in a house set in two hectares of grounds and surrounded by farmland. One twin and one double room, both with shower room and wc. Lounge with library and TV, covered swimming pool and car park. Pleasant, shady garden.

Prices s fr €50; d fr €55 **Nearby** ⛵ 2km ⚓ 6km ⚐ 5km ⚲
Restaurant 2km ⚑ 2km ⚐ 3km 🏠 2km ⚒ 10km **Notes** No pets
English spoken

EYGALIERES

☷ Chambre d'hôtes du Contras

Danielle et Maurice PERNIX

Quartier du Contras, 13810 EYGALIERES

☎ 04 90 95 04 89 & 06 19 01 28 77 📄 04 90 95 04 89

A peaceful small farm, with beautiful views towards the Alpilles, is the setting for these five rooms. There are three doubles on the first floor, reached by an outside staircase, and two twin-bedded rooms downstairs, again with their own entrance. Cot and extra bed available. All have private shower rooms/WCs. Guests' lounge areas; also fridge, freezer and microwave.

Prices s €40-€45; d €50-€55; t €65-€70 **Nearby** ⛵ 1km ⚓ 15km
Sea 40km ⚐ 4km ⚲ 10km Restaurant 3km ⚑ 4km ⚐ 10km 🏠 3km
⚒ 8km **Notes** No pets Open 16 March to 14 October.

EYRAGUES

☷ L'Oustau de Mistral

Christiane et Marc MISTRAL

377 route de Chateaurenard, 13630 EYRAGUES

☎ 04 90 92 80 60 & 06 89 33 55 19 📄 04 90 24 97 34

email: c.mistral@wanadoo.fr

web: http://perso.wanadoo.fr/mas.mistral

A very pretty chambre d'hôtes in a 19th-century mas of provençal colours, set in large enclosed grounds featuring mature plane trees. There is a double suite, a room with two double beds, a room with a double and single, and a double, all with private facilities and air conditioning. Corner lounge, terrace with garden furniture and parking available.

Prices s €85-€120; d €85-€120; t €105-€140; extra person fr €20
On Site Private ⚲ **Nearby** ⛷ 5km ♨ 15km ⌘ 40km Restaurant 0.8km
⚓ 1km Spa 1km ☆ 5km ▣ 1km ⋙ 12km **Notes** No pets English
spoken

FUVEAU

⊪ |◎| *Chambre d'hôtes*

Francette et Daniel DUBOIS

39 chemin des Pradels, Quartier des Longs Cols,
13710 FUVEAU

☎ 04 42 68 15 88 & 06 76 03 68 12 ▤ 04 42 68 15 88
email: mas-papillons@cegetel.net
web: http://mas-papillons.perso.cegetel.net

Set on nine hectares of land, this house offers four attractive rooms
with great views, each with lounge area. Two double rooms, one twin
room and one suite consisting of a double room and single room,
with bath/shower. Cot available. Library, terrace with furniture, covered
swimming pool and car park. Walks and bike riding.

Prices not confirmed for 2008 **Nearby** ⛷ 5km ♨ 3km Sea 40km ⚲
♨ 3km ▣ 2km ⋙ 10km **Notes** No pets English spoken

GRANS

⊪ **Chambre d'hôtes Mon-Moulin**

Marie-Jehanne MARTINI

12 Rue des Moulins, 13450 GRANS

☎ 04 90 55 86 46 & 06 27 46 49 55 ▤ 04 90 55 86 46
email: monmoulin@aol.com
web: www.mon-moulin-en-provence.net

This 17th-century former mill, set in the heart of a historic village,
offers two triple rooms and a double with separate facilities looking
onto the garden. Rooms have direct access to the swimming pool and
solarium. Shady garden and communal patio. Large room with TV,
library, fridge and microwave.

Prices s fr €60; d fr €65; extra person fr €20 **On Site** Private ⚲
Nearby ⛷ 1km ♨ 10km Sea 40km ⌘ 0.1km ♨ 1km Spa 30km
▣ 0.1km ⋙ 4km **Notes** No pets English spoken Open April to
1 November.

⊪ **Domaine du Bois Vert**

V et J-P RICHARD

Quartier Montauban, 13450 GRANS

☎ 04 90 55 82 98 ▤ 04 90 55 82 98
email: leboisvert@hotmail.com
web: www.domaineduboisvert.com

Two triple rooms, and one double with private facilities available in
this pretty Provençal farmhouse situated in grounds on the river's
edge. Private terrace, garden furniture and independent guest
entrance. Lounge with fireplace, TV and library, fridge. Table tennis,
tennis and other games. Sculpture and literature courses offered in
the village.

Prices s fr €65; d €70-€77; t fr €95 **Nearby** ⛷ 2km ♨ 9km
Sea 25km ⚲ Restaurant 1.5km ♨ 0.5km ☆ 5km ▣ 1.5km ⋙ 6km
Notes No pets English spoken Open 20 March to 15 December.

GRAVESON

⊪ **La Demeure Toscane**

Chantal et J-François LEMAIRE

5, Place de l'Église, 13690 GRAVESON

☎ 04 90 95 89 79 & 06 71 50 28 75 ▤ 04 90 95 89 79
email: chantal.lemaire@9online.fr
web: www.lademeuretoscane.fr.st

Three beautiful rooms, warmly decorated, in a house in the heart of
the village. Two of the rooms are doubles, the third is a triple, and
they all have private bath or shower room and WC. Outside is a neat
garden, with a terrace and space for parking.

Prices s €80-€100; d €90-€110; t fr €130; extra person fr
€25 **On Site** Spa **Nearby** ⛷ 2km ♨ 10km ⌘ 10km ⚲ 10km
Restaurant 1km ♨ 1km ☆ 1km ▣ 1km ⋙ 15km **Notes** No pets

⊪ ♿ **Le Mas du Jujubier**

Christine et Michel PIN

2975, Route des Palunettes, 13690 GRAVESON

☎ 04 32 61 90 95 & 06 64 75 89 42 ▤ 04 32 61 90 95
email: michel.pin@wanadoo.fr
web: www.lemasdujujubier.com

A terrace shaded by a 100-year-old plane tree is one of the attractions
here. There are four individually decorated rooms: a ground floor
room with a double and a child's bed, suitable for guests with limited
mobility; upstairs are three doubles, one of them a small suite. All
have private facilities. There is also a sauna, spa bath, and billiards.

Prices s fr €65; d €85-€100; extra person fr €15 **On Site** Private ⚲
Nearby ⛷ 4km ♨ 6km ♨ 4km ▣ 2km ⋙ 8km **Notes** No pets English
spoken Open 25 March to 2 November.

JOUQUES

⊪ ♥ |◎| *Campagne le Catalan*

Magalie et Philippe MARY

13490 JOUQUES

☎ 04 42 67 69 43 & 06 14 13 20 05 ▤ 04 42 67 69 43
email: philippe.mary@libertysurf.fr
web: www.le-catalan.com

Peace and quiet guaranteed in this renovated stone house, set in 40
hectares. It offers guest rooms decorated in traditional local colours:
two doubles, a triple and a family room with double bed and twin
beds, all with private facilities. Terrace with furniture, boules, volleyball
and car park.

Prices not confirmed for 2008 **Nearby** ⛷ 5km ♨ 30km ⚲ ♨ 3km
▣ 3km ⋙ 10km **Notes** No pets English spoken

LAMBESC

♦♦♦ *Campagne la Mignarde*

Cathy et Adrien LEBRE

Chemin des Cairades, 13410 LAMBESC

☎ 04 42 92 72 27 & 06 21 09 64 52 📄 04 42 92 72 27

email: adrien.lebre@wanadoo.fr

web: www.lamignarde.com

A beautiful house shaded by plane trees, in the countryside between Aix and Salon-de-Provence. There are two double rooms and a family room with two double beds. Each has private bathroom and WC, and an extra bed is available. There are two shady terraces with garden furniture, and a well-equipped outdoor kitchen area.

Prices not confirmed for 2008 **Nearby** ⛷12km ♨10km Sea 40km ⤳2km ⌘2km 🏛2km ➰18km **Notes** No pets

LE PARADOU

♦♦♦ L'Espélido

Mireille JOLY

Route des Tours de Castillon, 13520 LE PARADOU

☎ 04 90 54 38 55 & 06 88 10 03 03

email: lespelido@wanadoo.fr

web: www.lespelido.fr

In the Baux de Provence Valley, this attractive old-fashioned house benefits from a large, shady garden. Three double rooms and a family room with private terrace all have private facilities. Telephone available. Reservations necessary in the winter. Close to Les Baux, St Rémy, Avignon, Arles, the Camargue, and Lubéron.

Prices s fr €65; d fr €65; t fr €85 **On Site** ♨ **Nearby** ⛷2km ⌘2km Sea 40km ♙5km ⤳ Restaurant 0.2km ⌘0.5km 🏛0.5km ➰15km **Notes** No pets English spoken

MAILLANE

♦♦♦ 🍴 *Le Mas de la Christine*

Caroline et Christian CRESTIN

Chemin du Mas des Gantes, 13910 MAILLANE

☎ 04 90 95 79 49 & 06 61 77 86 73 📄 04 32 60 16 77

email: crestincaro@aol.com

web: www.masdelachristine.com

This restored house has a beautiful view towards the Alpilles Hills. There are five splendid air-conditioned bedrooms: two doubles downstairs, and a twin-bedded room and two triples upstairs. All the rooms have private bath/shower rooms and WCs. Lounge with open fire. Terrace with garden furniture, summer kitchen and enclosed swimming pool.

Prices not confirmed for 2008 **Nearby** ⛷6km ♨6km ⤳3.5km 🏛3.5km ➰15km **Notes** No pets English spoken

RAPHELE-LES-ARLES

♦♦♦ 🐓 🍴 *Domaine du Grand Barbegal*

Julie ROUX

13280 RAPHELE-LES-ARLES

☎ 04 90 54 63 69 & 06 82 93 49 80 📄 04 90 54 89 85

email: ferme.auberge.barbegal@wanadoo.fr

web: www.barbegal.fr

These beautiful rooms in a restored 18th-century farmhouse are on a working sheep and mixed farm in the Baux Valley. There are three double rooms and two rooms for four (double bed plus two singles on a mezzanine). All have private bath or shower room and WC. Dining room with open fireplace, fridge. Terrace with garden room, parking.

Prices not confirmed for 2008 **Nearby** ⛷4km ♨9km Sea 40km ⤳6km ⌘6km 🏛6km ➰10km **Notes** No pets

ROGNES

♦♦♦ Le Grand Saint Paul

Joy et Michel GAYVALLET

13840 ROGNES

☎ 04 42 50 31 93

email: joy@le-grand-st-paul.com

web: www.le-grand-st-paul.com

A 12th-century house with views of the countryside and four colourful and warmly decorated bedrooms. On the first floor are two twin-bedded rooms, and a triple. On the second floor is a double room with lounge area and space for a child's bed on a mezzanine. All have private facilities. Outside, several terraces provide quiet and private sitting areas.

Prices s fr €55; d fr €65; t fr €80; extra person fr €20 **Nearby** ⛷10km ♨15km Sea 40km ⤳ Restaurant 2.5km ⌘1.5km 🏛3km ➰18km **Notes** No pets English spoken

♦♦♦ Le Moulin du Rossignol

B et J-M PARANQUE-LUNA

13840 ROGNES

☎ 04 42 50 16 29

email: lerossignol@free.fr

web: www.moulindurossignol.com

This 18th-century former mill provides three pretty guest rooms: a double, a twin and a double with single bed, each with private bathroom. Guests can relax in the lounge, and enjoy gourmet breakfasts in summer on the communal shaded terrace, with garden furniture and situated by a stream. Parking is available.

Prices s fr €63; d fr €68; t fr €83 **Nearby** ⛷4km ♨20km Sea 45km ⤳ Restaurant 0.5km ⌘4km 🏛0.5km ➰20km **Notes** No pets English spoken

SALON-DE-PROVENCE

⁂ **Le Mas des Vergers**

Veith et Sophie IVANSCHITZ

Chemin de Chaillol, 13300 SALON-DE-PROVENCE

☎ 04 90 59 64 81 & 06 73 26 39 56

📄 04 90 59 64 81

email: lemasdesvergers@aol.com

web: http://lemasdesvergers.free.fr

Beautiful rooms are offered in this early 18th-century sheep farm, surrounded by orchards in a lovely open setting. They include a room with three single beds, a twin room and two doubles, all with bath or shower, wc and TV. Terrace with patio furniture, table tennis, well maintained garden with swimming pool open in the summer, parking.

Prices s fr €55; d fr €69; t fr €79 **Nearby** ⚓ 10km ⚓ 12km Sea 35km ⚓ 12km ⚓ Restaurant 4km ⚓ 1km ⚓ 4km ⚓ 4km ⚓ 4km

Notes No pets English spoken

ST-CHAMAS

⁂ ⑩ ♿ **L'Escapade**

J-B MARECHAL et S VALERIAN

Route de Cornillon, 13250 ST-CHAMAS

☎ 04 90 50 73 30 & 06 71 40 61 54 📄 04 90 50 76 10

email: lescapadeii@wanadoo.fr

web: www.lescapadeprovence.com

This country guest house is ideal for families, and is set in large grounds complete with swimming pool, communal terrace with garden furniture and parking. There are four guest rooms: a triple with disabled access and three rooms upstairs for two, three and four, each with private facilities. TV also available to guests.

Prices s €55-€70; d €65-€80; t €75-€90; extra person fr €10; dinner fr €18 **Nearby** ⚓ 2km ⚓ 5km Sea 20km ⚓ 0.8km ⚓ Restaurant 3km ⚓ 3km ⚓ 3km ⚓ 3km ⚓ 2km **Notes** Pets admitted English spoken

ST-ETIENNE-DU-GRES

||| Mas de Ravert

Muriel et Vincent BERARD

24342 Chemin de la Theze, 13103 ST-ETIENNE-DU-GRES

☎ 04 90 49 18 11 & 06 84 14 30 45 📄 04 90 49 09 92

email: masderavert@wanadoo.fr

web: http://perso.wanadoo.fr/masderavert/

This stone-built 18th-century farmhouse has four spacious and beautifully-decorated bedrooms. On the ground floor is a two-roomed family suite for four, with double bed and twins; upstairs are two doubles and a twin. Each has a private bath/shower and WC. Air conditioning. Large lounge/dining room with exposed beams and stonework; billiards, table-tennis, garden furniture and parking.

Prices d €60-€105; t fr €120; extra person fr €15 **Nearby** ⛷ 8km
⛷ 8km ⌁ 0.8km 🎣 0.8km ⋙ 25km **Notes** No pets English spoken

ST-MARC-JAUMEGARDE

||| *Chambre d'hôtes*

J-C et M FOURNIER

Chemin de l'Ermitage, 13100 ST-MARC-JAUMEGARDE

☎ 04 42 24 96 40 & 06 85 71 36 40 📄 04 42 24 96 23

email: laferme-chambreshotes@wanadoo.fr

web: www.gite-prop.com/13/260405

A pretty house, in enclosed wooded grounds not far from Aix-en-Provence. There is a double room, a triple, and a family suite with two double beds. Each has a private entrance, bath or shower room and WC. Living room with open fireplace; outside is a pleasant shady terrace.

Prices not confirmed for 2008 **Nearby** ⛷ 4km ⛷ 10km Sea 45km
⌁ 4km ⌁ 3km 🎣 5km ⋙ 22km **Notes** No pets English spoken Open 28-5 August.

ST-REMY-DE-PROVENCE

||| ♿ Mas Clair de Lune

Myriam FEIGE

Plateau de la Crau, BP 90, 13533 ST-REMY-DE-PROVENCE

☎ 04 90 92 02 63 & 06 89 43 65 43 📄 04 90 92 02 63

web: www.mas-clairdelune.com

One twin, one triple and one single room, all with shower and wc facilities, are available in this detached house set in wooded grounds with panoramic views of the Alpilles. Each room has a private terrace and separate entrance. Lounge with TV and fireplace. Table tennis, swimming pool, boules and car park. Peace and quiet guaranteed.

Prices s fr €53; d fr €63; t fr €79 **On Site** 🏊 **Nearby** ⛷ 6km ⛷ 9km
🏌 10km ⌁ Restaurant 2km 🎣 2km 🎣 2km ⋙ 19km **Notes** Pets admitted English spoken

||| 🍴 ♿ Mas des Figues

A-M et P MICHELOT DUDOUIT

Vieux Chemin d'Arles, 13210 ST-REMY-DE-PROVENCE

☎ 04 32 60 00 98 & 04 75 41 55 96 📄 04 32 60 00 95

email: info@masdesfigues.com

web: www.masdesfigues.com

This characterful farmhouse has five guest bedrooms: on the ground floor, three doubles, each with a private terrace; on the first floor a further double and a two-roomed family suite for four. All have TV, air-conditioning, hairdryer and mini-bar.

Prices s €100-€130; d €120-€205; dinner fr €35 **Nearby** ⛷ 4km
⌁ 10km ⌁ 4km 🎣 4km ⋙ 20km **Notes** Pets admitted English spoken Open 22 March to 4 November & on request only from 5 November to 21 March CC

see advert on page 733

TARASCON

||| *Chambre d'hôtes*

Yvette et Yves JUMEAU

7 Rue du Progrés, 13150 TARASCON

☎ 04 90 43 52 52 & 06 08 09 28 99

📄 04 90 43 52 52

email: y.jumeau@wanadoo.fr

web: www.chambres-tarascon.com

An old town house, part dating back to the 17th century, in a quiet street close to a small park. There are two double rooms, one with a living area; a triple room (double bed plus a single); and a suite for two. All have private facilities and some antique furnishings. Lounge with books; large courtyard with garden furniture and fountain.

Prices s €85-€120; d €89-€120; t fr €129 **On Site** Restaurant 🍴
Nearby ⛷ 15km ⛷ 15km 🏌 20km ⌁ 0.8km ⌁ 1km 🎣 0.1km
⋙ 0.2km **Notes** No pets

VENTABREN

||| La Villa Rosalie

Agnès SCHEPMANS EBBINGHAUS

260 Chemin de la Bertranne, 13122 VENTABREN

☎ 04 42 28 94 20 & 06 77 24 44 10

email: agnes.schepmans@gmx.net

A newly built house, just below the village of Ventabren and 12 kilometres from Aix-en-Provence. There are four double rooms, each with private shower room and WC, internet access and safe for valuables. One room has a private terrace. Swimming pool, two terraces with garden furniture and plenty of flowers.

Prices s €80-€100; d €100-€120 **On Site** 🏊 Private ⌁
Nearby ⛷ 2km ⌁ 5km Sea 35km 🏌 10km Restaurant 2km 🎣 2km
🎣 2km ⋙ 15km **Notes** No pets English spoken

HAUTES-ALPES

ARVIEUX

⁞⁞⁞ La Girandole

Noël et Isabelle MOREL

Brunissard, 05350 ARVIEUX

☎ 04 92 46 84 12 & 06 12 41 09 47 ▤ 04 92 46 86 59

email: lagirandole@tiscali.fr

web: www.lagirandole.info

The owner and his family welcome you to their guest house which comprises their accommodation, two gîtes, and four double rooms and a suite for four with bathrooms and wc, plus a television lounge. There is a living room with open fireplace, kitchen for guest use, library, music area, children's games room and sauna. Outside: terrace, garden, enclosed grounds, summer swimming pool, balneotherapy bath.

Prices s fr €75; d fr €75; t fr €100; extra person fr €30
On Site Private ⚲ **Nearby** ⚑ 1km ⌖ 3km Restaurant 0.5km ⚓ 0.5km ⊕ 0.5km ⚑ 1km ⌂ 1km ⇢ 25km **Notes** No pets English spoken

ASPRES-SUR-BUECH

⁞⁞⁞⁞ *Le Château*

Albane JACQUART

La Grande Rue, 05140 ASPRES SUR BUECH

☎ 04 92 58 74 78

email: albane@chateaudaspres.com

web: www.chateaudaspres.com

A 15th-century house in the heart of the village with a swimming pool. Breakfasts are served either in the dining room with a coat of arms over the fireplace, or on the terrace. Two well-furnished suites can accommodate four people and contain a comfy corner with television. There is also a double room with a terrace.

Prices not confirmed for 2008 **Nearby** ⚑ 1.5km ⌖ 1.5km ⚓ 30km ⊕ ⌂ 0.1km ⇢ 0.5km **Notes** No pets English spoken

BARATIER

⁞⁞ ⁞◯⁞ La Fernande

Gisella et Pierre BELLOT

Champ Rambaud, 05200 BARATIER

☎ 04 92 43 81 13 & 04 79 00 21 57 ▤ 04 92 43 81 13

email: lpbellot.lafernande@wanadoo.fr

web: www.lafernande.com

This peaceful 17th-century farmhouse with its three spacious guest rooms, stands high above the village, with a wonderful view. The rooms, doubles and twins, all have private bath or shower rooms and WCs, and each room has a balcony or terrace. Baby equipment available. Large vaulted living room, with dining and lounge areas. Meals by arrangement: local and farm produce.

Prices d fr €68; extra person €14-€23; dinner fr €22 **Nearby** ⚑ 10km ⚓ 40km ⌖ 2km Restaurant 1km ⚓ 13km ⊕ 1km Spa 1km ⚑ 2km ⌂ 1km ⇢ 4km **Notes** No pets English spoken Open May to November.

BARCILLONNETTE

⁞⁞⁞ ⁞◯⁞ La Ferme du Lau

Hugues PHAM-PHU

05110 BARCILLONNETTE

☎ 04 92 54 26 27

email: sgphph@gmail.com

web: http://perso.wanadoo.fr/f.jp.cola

An old farmhouse, beautifully restored, with three bedrooms which sleep from two to four people. All have private shower and WC. Sitting room with open fire, internet, books and TV. Beamed dining room and shady terrace. Attractive garden with children's games and a shed for bikes. Evening meals and mid-day snacks are available with 24 hours notice, served inside or out.

Prices s fr €40; d €42-€45; t €61-€64; extra person €15-€16; dinner fr €15 **Nearby** ⚑ 6km ⚓ 40km ⌖ 6km ⚓ 15km Restaurant 6km ⚓ 35km ⊕ 15km ⌂ 8km ⇢ 23km **Notes** No pets English spoken

BENEVENT ET CHARBILLAC

⁞⁞⁞ ⁞◯⁞ Le Cairn

Brigitte GOURDOU

Charbillac, 05500 BENEVENT ET CHARBILLAC

☎ 04 92 50 54 87

email: gite.le.cairn@wanadoo.fr

web: http://perso.orange.fr/chambres.dhotes.le.cairn/

This village house has a vaulted ground floor, containing dining room and sitting area with fire. It offers four guest rooms each with shower room and wc, cooking over a wood fire, heating and enclosed grounds with garden furniture. Several mountain bike routes on the doorstep.

Prices s fr €38; d fr €44; extra person fr €22; dinner fr €14 **Nearby** ⚑ 7km ⚓ 6km ⌖ 4km ⚲ 3km Restaurant 3km ⚓ 11km ⊕ 5km Spa 20km ⌂ 5km ⇢ 20km **Notes** No pets English spoken

BUISSARD

⁞⁞⁞ ⁞◯⁞ Les Chemins Verts

Nathalie DUBOIS

05500 BUISSARD

☎ 04 92 50 57 57

email: lescheminsverts@free.fr

web: www.lescheminsverts.com

On this 18th-century renovated farm, as well as the owners' apartment, there are a country gîte, and four rooms for guests, each

CONTINUED

BUISSARD *CONTINUED*

with shower room and wc. On the ground floor: large dining room/lounge with open fire, TV, wc. First floor: two rooms for two and four people; and in the mansard: two rooms for two and three people. Central heating, garden, parking.

Prices s fr €40; d fr €46; t fr €55; extra person fr €10; dinner fr €14 **Nearby** ⚓ 3km ⚲ 10km ℰ 3km ⚐ 3km Restaurant 2km ⚶ 6km ⚱ 3km Spa 20km ⚑ 3km ⚓ 20km **Notes** No pets English spoken

CHABOTTES

⚏ ☙ ⦿ La Chabottine

Catherine et Alain DUSSERRE
Les Fangeas, 05260 CHABOTTES
☎ 04 92 50 72 29

Near the Park des Ecrins, on their working farm, Catherine and Alain offer you five guest rooms in a converted farm building. The ground floor contains a dining room, sitting area with fireplace and TV. The first floor has two three-bedded rooms opening on to a terrace. The mansard second floor has three double rooms. Each room has shower room and wc. Central heating. Garden furniture, garden and parking. Meals out of season if booked.

Prices s fr €36; d fr €45; t fr €55; dinner fr €14 **Nearby** ⚓ 3km ⚲ 8km ℰ 6km ⚐ 10km Restaurant 2km ⚶ 5km ⚱ 2km Spa 20km ⚑ 2km ⚓ 20km **Notes** No pets English spoken

CHAMPCELLA

⚏ ⦿ Le Chalet des Faures

J-Pierre et Christine ZOELLIN
05310 CHAMPCELLA
☎ 04 92 20 92 74 ▤ 04 92 20 92 74
email: zoellinjeanpierre@wanadoo.fr
web: www.chaletdesfaures.com

A traditional house set in the tranquillity of the National Park. All three rooms are en suite with king-size beds and one has a balcony. Guests have use of a large, vaulted lounge, games room, library, terrace and garden. A variety of local dishes are served at evening meals.

Prices s fr €70; d fr €70; t fr €80; extra person fr €10; dinner fr €23 **Nearby** ⚓ 11km ℰ 5km ⚶ 20km ⚱ 11km ⚑ 11km ⚓ 11km **Notes** Pets admitted English spoken

GAP-ROMETTE

⚏ La Belle Étoile

Ginette PAUCHON
Le Forest du Serre, La Montagne, 05000 GAP ROMETTE
☎ 04 92 52 37 71 & 06 23 87 49 73 ▤ 04 92 52 37 71
web: www.alabelletoile.com

This large detached chalet situated on a cattle farm enjoys panoramic views. There are five guest rooms, for two to four people, each one with a shower room/WC, TV, mezzanine and direct access to a terrace and small private sitting area. Cot available. Large lounge with open fireplace and picture windows opening on to the surrounding massifs. Parking.

Prices s fr €41; d fr €51; t fr €66; extra person fr €15 **Nearby** ⚓ 8km ⚲ 0.5km Sea 0.2km ℰ 5km ⚐ 7km Restaurant 4km ⚶ 6km ⚱ 7km Spa 7km ⚑ 7km ⚓ 7km **Notes** No pets

LA PIARRE

⚏ ⦿ ♿ Le Chanelou

Dominique et Bernard GIRAUD
GITES DE FRANCE - Service Réservation
☎ 04 92 67 08 35
email: contact@lechanelou.com
web: www.lechanelou.com

This renovated farmhouse overlooks the village of La Piarre. Dominique and Bernard offer four en suite guest rooms (in the style of the region) for two to four people. Swimming pool and terrace for guests' use. Meals feature regional cuisine and are served in a large vaulted dining room. Relaxing area exclusively for guests. Garage for bicycles and motor bikes.

Prices s €30-€33; d fr €55; dinner fr €18 **On Site** Private ⚐ **Nearby** ⚓ 15km ℰ 0.3km Restaurant 8km ⚶ 40km ⚱ 10km ⚑ 10km ⚓ 8km **Notes** Pets admitted Open April to October.

LA SALLE-LES-ALPES

⚏ ⦿ Le Grand Area

André et Ornella ARNAUD
2, Rue de la Teinture, 05240 LA SALLE-LES-ALPES
☎ 04 92 24 74 78
email: contact@grand-area.com
web: www.grand-area.com

18th-century former farm in an old village of La Salle-les-Alpes. It has five rooms for two to four people, each with private facilities and two with mezzanine. Dining rooms, lounge with fireplace in old stable, TV and kitchen corner with local information for guests. Sauna, terrace and grounds.

Prices s €58-€63; d €86-€92; extra person fr €25; dinner fr €20 **Nearby** ⚓ 1km ⚲ 15km ℰ 0.6km ⚐ 5km Restaurant 0.1km ⚶ 0.8km ⚱ 0.8km ⚑ 0.5km ⚓ 6km **Notes** No pets

LARAGNE-MONTEGLIN

⚏ ⦿ La Désirade

Antonia MANFREDI
Quartier Les Combes, Route du Poet, 05300 LARAGNE MONTEGLIN
☎ 04 92 65 09 00 ▤ 04 92 65 09 00
email: antoniamanfredi@hotmail.com
web: www.ladesirade05.com

A big Provençal-style house with three double bedrooms, each with themed decorations. All the rooms have private bath/shower room and WC. There is a large lounge, and breakfast is served on the shad terrace by the swimming pool. Meals are available by arrangement; choices can include Italian dishes.

Prices s fr €50; d fr €70; extra person fr €25; dinner fr €20 **On Site** Private ⚐ **Nearby** ⚓ 3km ℰ 1km Restaurant 2km ⚶ 45km ⚱ 1km ⚑ 2km ⚓ 2km **Notes** Pets admitted

LE NOYER

♦♦♦ ⓘⓞ La Griotte

Josiane et J-Claude ZEVACO
Hameau le Villard, 05500 LE NOYER
☎ 06 07 48 84 69
email: jczevaco@la-griotte.com
web: www.la-griotte.com

In this old 18th-century farmhouse, in the hamlet of Villard and near to the Ecrins National Park, there are five guest rooms. Each one sleeps two or three people, and has a private bath or shower room and WC. A large downstairs room with an arched ceiling has dining and lounge areas. Grounds, private parking. Good walking country.

Prices s fr €40; d fr €50; t fr €60; extra person fr €15; dinner fr €16 **Nearby** ⛷ 15km ♨ 12km ✎ 1km ⚲ 8km Restaurant 8km ⚐ 17km ⚓ 10km Spa 23km 🚲 8km ⛵ 23km **Notes** No pets

NEVACHE

♦♦♦ ⓘⓞ Histoire de Montagne

Fabienne et J-Pascal ADOLPHE
Plampinet, 05100 NEVACHE
☎ 04 92 21 23 05 & 06 07 29 21 23 📄 04 92 21 23 05
email: histoiredemontagne@plampinetenclaree.com
web: www.plampinetenclaree.com/page.php?page=56

Well-placed for walking and cross-country skiing, this is an 18th-century house with three bedrooms. There is a double room with balcony, a room for three (double bed and a single), and a large split-level room for up to four. All have private bathroom, WC and wonderful views. Meals are available by arrangement, with dishes from the local area.

Prices s fr €52; d fr €62; t fr €76; extra person fr €18; dinner fr €18 **Nearby** ⛷ 10km ♨ 20km ✎ 0.1km ⚲ 14km Restaurant 0.1km ⚐ 5km ⚓ 4km Spa 14km 🚲 4km ⛵ 15km **Notes** No pets English spoken

POLIGNY

♦♦♦ ⓘⓞ Le Filet d'Eau

Philippe et Dominick SUARD
Villeneuve, 05500 POLIGNY
☎ 04 92 49 07 13 📄 04 92 49 07 13
email: fildo@orange.fr
web: www.gdf05.com/fildo/

A large garden surrounds this old farmhouse with its vaulted ceilings, built in 1840. There is independent access to the four bedrooms, decorated in country style. The facilities include private bathrooms and central heating. Breakfasts are served in a large room on the ground floor with a rest area and television. Imaginative meals are on offer in the evenings.

Prices s fr €50; d €50-€55; t €55-€58; extra person fr €15; dinner fr €18 **Nearby** ⛷ 7km ♨ 10km ✎ 5km ⚲ 20km Restaurant 5km ⚐ 7km ⚓ 5km Spa 20km 🚲 5km ⛵ 20km **Notes** No pets

PRUNIERES

♦♦♦ ♿ Les Carlines

Louis VELAY
Les Vignes Larignier, 05230 PRUNIERES
☎ 04 92 50 63 27
web: www.gites.net/car6327

In a park with its own lake, the house looks out on the Lac de Serre-Ponçon and the Alps. Veranda, lounge, sitting room with kitchen for use of guests. At the garden level: three bedrooms with shower rooms/wcs. On the second floor: two rooms with shower/wc. All rooms have TV, fridge and air conditioning. Skiing and fishing. Picnic area, table tennis, barbecue, boules. Washing machine available.

Prices s €40-€45; d €45-€60; extra person €15-€18 **Nearby** ⛷ 3km ♨ 20km ✎ 1.5km Restaurant 0.8km ⚐ 12km ⚓ 5km 🚲 5km ⛵ 5km **Notes** Pets admitted

RISOUL

♦♦♦ ⓘⓞ La Maison de Joséphine

Philippe MAUREL
L'Eglise, 05600 RISOUL
☎ 04 92 45 28 01
email: maisonjosephine@yahoo.fr
web: www.maisonjosephine.com

Opposite Pelvoux in Risoul village, a traditional house with five guest rooms, each with shower room or bathroom and wc. Vaulted dining room, sitting area, library, games room and sauna for guests. Nearby swimming pool and children's area. Large terrace and managed grounds. Organic vegetarian meals.

Prices d €57-€62; t €66-€75; dinner €16-€18 **Nearby** ⛷ 5km ✎ 5km Restaurant 0.2km ⚐ 10km ⚓ 2.5km Spa 45km 🚲 2.5km ⛵ 5km **Notes** Pets admitted English spoken

♦♦♦ ⓘⓞ La Source

Cathy et Walter LUISELLI
Chauvet, 05600 RISOUL
☎ 04 92 45 37 48
email: lasourcerisoul@wanadoo.fr
web: www.gitelasource.com

An historic farm set in landscaped grounds with a view of the Durance Valley and Ecrins Massif. Traditional family meals using home-grown produce are served in the vaulted dining room. The four double and one single rooms have either a private bath or shower room - two have balconies. There is a free shuttle service to the station in winter.

Prices s €42-€49; d €60-€70; extra person fr €18; dinner €12-€20 **Nearby** ⛷ 5km ♨ 30km ✎ 5km ⚲ 3km Restaurant 3km ⚐ 15km ⚓ 5km Spa 35km 🚲 5km ⛵ 5km **Notes** No pets

ROSANS

††† ❤ ⋈ & La Conviviance

T DE SAINT-JEAN
05150 ROSANS
☎ 04 92 66 65 42
email: contact@laconviviance.com
web: www.laconviviance.com

The Saint-Jean family (market gardeners and cattle breeders) invite you to their completely restored traditional farmhouse. One family room for four, two doubles (with extra bed if required). Each room has private shower and wc. Living room and sitting room for guests (open fire, television, books). Shared dining room. Cooking based on the produce of the farm. Terrace, grounds, parking.

Prices s fr €42; d fr €50; t fr €62; extra person fr €20; dinner fr €21
On Site ⋒ **Nearby** ⛷ 1.5km Restaurant 1km ⌁ 1.5km 🏛 1.5km
🚤 23km **Notes** Pets admitted English spoken

SIGOTTIER

††† Le Moulin du Paroy

Pierrette AULONNE
Route de Sigottier, 05700 SIGOTTIER
☎ 04 92 67 13 95 & 04 42 05 31 44

A renovated old mill of considerable character on a 9ha estate. There are two double rooms and a large room with a double bed, two singles and a terrace in an annexe with its own access. Each has private facilities. Large living room, with kitchen area for guests. Summer kitchen, terrace, trout river.

Prices s fr €53; d fr €60; t fr €68; extra person fr €8 **On Site** ⋒
Nearby ⛷ 13km ↗ 2km Restaurant 0.8km ⌁ 35km ⌁ 2km Spa 0.8km
🏛 1.2km 🚤 1.5km **Notes** No pets Open June to September.

ST-ANDRE-DE-ROSANS

††† ⋈ Ferme de la Condamine

Hélène et Roland TAELMAN
05150 ST-ANDRE DE ROSANS
☎ 04 92 66 60 06 ▤ 04 92 66 60 06
email: contact@fermedelacondamine.com
web: www.fermedelacondamine.com

In a calm setting of 24 hectares, this typically renovated 18th-century farmhouse overlooks superb countryside of wooded hills bordered by L'Eygues. Three spacious rooms are offered, with independent access, private terraces and facilities and heating. Lounge corner, fridge, living room, TV corner in the former grange. Table d'hôte meals.

Prices s fr €48; d fr €55; t fr €68; dinner fr €18 **Nearby** ⛷ 6km ⋒ 1km
Restaurant 1.5km ⌁ 6km 🏛 5km 🚤 15km **Notes** No pets English spoken Open June to September. CC

ST-CHAFFREY

††† ⋈ Les Chambres du Soleil

Christophe MACOUIN
7 Rue des Aillauds, 05330 ST-CHAFFREY
☎ 04 92 24 02 18 & 06 86 91 42 78
email: mail@chambres-soleil.com
web: www.chambres-soleil.com

This 18th-century house has been restored using traditional materials and with full regard to environmental issues. Four bedrooms sleep from two to four people, all with television, internet access, private bath or shower room and WC. Meals available, with regional dishes. Excellent base for winter sports and a wide range of outdoor pursuits.

Prices d €70-€95; t €90-€105; extra person fr €20; dinner fr €20
Nearby ⛷ 3km ⌁ 15km ⋒ 0.1km ↗ 1km Restaurant 0.5km ⌁ 1km
⌁ 1km Spa 0.5km 🏛 0.1km 🚤 2km **Notes** Pets admitted English spoken

††† ⋈ Les Marmottes

Karin et Denis LUCAS
22, Rue du Centre, Chantemerle, 05330 ST-CHAFFREY
☎ 04 92 24 11 17
email: lucas.marmottes@wanadoo.fr
web: www.gite-serre-chevalier.fr

This old property near the Serre Chevalier ski runs has been extensively restored and your hosts are delighted to welcome you to their four guest rooms, all with private entrance, TV and en suite facilities. There is a guest lounge with open fire, and a balcony with a beautiful view over the valley. Meals by arrangement. Parking 20 metres.

Prices s €57-€95; d €76-€127; extra person €27-€45; dinner fr €22
On Site Restaurant ❦ **Nearby** ⛷ 3km ⋒ 0.1km ↗ 0.1km
⌁ 0.3km 🏛 0.5km 🚤 5km **Notes** No pets English spoken CC

ST-CLEMENT-SUR-DURANCE

††† ⋈ La Grange de Mon Père

Alain et Jeannine GERARD
Les Traverses, 05600 ST-CLEMENT-SUR-DURANCE
☎ 04 92 45 37 80 ▤ 04 92 45 37 80
email: lagrangedemonpere@free.fr
web: http://lagrangedemonpere.free.fr

Local specialities are served in a large vaulted room in this renovated old farm in the Parc National des Ecrins. There are five rooms available, two can sleep four people, and each has a private bathroom. Guest have use of a lounge and the garden. There is storage for cars, bicycles and skis.

Prices s €43-€48; d €50-€60; t €65-€75; extra person fr €15; dinner fr €18 **Nearby** ⛷ 2.5km ⋒ 1.5km ↗ 3km Restaurant 3km ⌁ 16km
⌁ 6km Spa 45km 🏛 5km 🚤 6km **Notes** No pets

ST-CREPIN

||| |◎| Les Eymards

Michèle et Francis BREUZA

05600 ST-CREPIN

☎ 04 92 45 01 36 & 06 25 33 71 52

web: www.geocities.com/lebalconstcrepin

A typical house with character, in the Eymards hamlets enjoying unrestricted views over the mountains and valleys of Durance. Three rooms for two to three people each with private facilities are available. Kitchen, dining room and lounge with fireplace and TV, balcony, enclosed garden. Parking nearby. Table d'hôte meals available.

Prices s fr €55; d fr €65; t fr €75; extra person fr €20; dinner fr €20 **Nearby** ⚓ 6km ⛷ 30km ↖ 5km Restaurant 3km ⚘ 25km ⚲ 2.5km Spa 25km 🏛 4km ⋙ 7km **Notes** No pets English spoken

ST-JACQUES-EN-VALGAUDEMAR

||| ❤ |◎| ♿ Les Clarines

J-Pierre BARBAN

Entrepierres, 05800 ST-JACQUES-EN-VALGAUDEMAR

☎ 04 92 55 20 31 📠 04 92 55 20 31

email: info@auberge-clarines.com

web: www.auberge-clarines.com

A farmhouse inn, with four double rooms and a country gîte. Some rooms are on the mansard level and one is in a separate annexe; each has private facilities and heating. Sitting room, TV, shady grounds with mountain. Many walks in the National Park des Ecrins.

Prices s fr €40; d €48-€50; t €65-€69; dinner €15.50-€16.50 **On Site** Spa **Nearby** ⚓ 7km ⛷ 11km ↖ 3km ↖ 3km Restaurant 3km ⚘ 15km ⚲ 3km 🏛 2.5km ⋙ 25km **Notes** No pets

ST-JEAN-ST-NICOLAS

||| |◎| L'Abondance

Fréderic et Delphine DEGRIL

Ruisseau Lacour, 05260 ST-JEAN-ST-NICOLAS

☎ 04 92 55 98 73 & 06 60 74 23 12 📠 04 92 55 98 73

email: info@labondance.com

web: www.labondance.com

Delphine and Fréderic, farmers and ski instructors, are happy to welcome you to their historic farmhouse, which has been renovated using original materials. Four very spacious bedrooms for two to four people, three of which have a mezzanine. Each has shower/WC, TV, and private sitting area. Meals are served in the ground floor dining room, which opens on to the terrace and garden.

Prices s fr €40; d fr €57; t fr €70; extra person fr €16; dinner fr €6 **On Site** Spa **Nearby** ⚓ 0.3km ⛷ 15km ↖ 0.3km ↖ 15km Restaurant 1km ⚘ 3.5km ⚲ 0.4km 🏛 0.6km ⋙ 24km **Notes** No pets English spoken

ST-LEGER-LES-MELEZES

||| |◎| La Coustille

Bettina et Guy MECHIN

05260 ST-LEGER-LES-MELEZES

☎ 04 92 50 76 74

email: info@lacoustille.fr

web: www.lacoustille.fr

Four of the five bedrooms at this house have direct access to the garden, where there are children's games, a swimming pool and a boules pitch. The en suite rooms sleep from two to four people, and there is a sauna and Jacuzzi. Meals include local specialities. The house is well placed for a whole range of winter sports activities.

Prices s fr €45; d fr €55; t €55-€70; extra person fr €15; dinner fr €15 **On Site** Spa Private ↖ **Nearby** ⚓ 0.5km ⛷ 10km ⚘ 4km Restaurant 0.5km ⚘ 0.5km ⚲ 0.9km ⋙ 25km **Notes** No pets English spoken

VILLAR-D'ARENE

||| La Roche Méane

Xavier et Sylviane CRET

rue de Fonton, 05480 VILLAR D'ARENE

☎ 04 76 79 91 43 & 06 88 60 46 11 📠 04 76 79 91 43

email: rochemeane@wanadoo.fr

web: www.rochemeane.com

A renovated farm with attractively laid out grounds is the setting for these five guest rooms. They sleep from two to four people, and they have independent access and private shower rooms/WCs. Dining room in an old barn; lounge area with stove, TV, books. Small kitchen area available for guests' use. Your host is a mountain guide.

Prices s €48-€51; d €61-€66; t €83-€92; extra person €23-€29 **Nearby** ⚓ 25km ⚘ 0.5km Restaurant 0.5km ⚘ 3km ⚲ 2km ⚘ 0.5km 🏛 0.1km ⋙ 35km **Notes** No pets English spoken

VAR

AUPS

||| Terre de Vigne

Danielle MARTINEZ

272 Route de Moissac D9, 83630 AUPS

☎ 04 98 10 29 36 & 06 62 06 24 60

email: chambres@terre-de-vigne.com

web: www.terre-de-vigne.com

Enclosed grounds with vines and olive trees surround this property. The three double rooms are all on the ground floor, each with private shower and WC, mini-bar, TV, safe, hairdryer, electric shutters. In the garden are terraces with furniture, a swimming pool and parking space.

Prices s fr €89; d fr €99 **On Site** Private ↖ **Nearby** ⚓ 8km ⛷ 30km ⚲ 0.5km 🏛 0.5km ⋙ 30km **Notes** No pets English spoken

BAGNOLS-EN-FORET

♦♦♦ ⍟ Villa Arcadie

Sylvie SITEAUD

Chemin Saint Denis, 83600 BAGNOLS-EN-FORET

☎ 04 94 40 68 36 & 06 61 83 07 04 📄 04 94 40 68 36

email: siteaud@orange.fr

web: http://monsite.wanadoo.fr/villaarcadie

This large Provençal-style villa, surrounded by greenery, has five bedrooms: three doubles, and two with twin beds. All rooms have private terraces, as well as their own shower rooms and WCs. There is a separate guests' entrance, giving access to the swimming pool and grounds. Fitness room; boules area. Meals available by arrangement.

Prices s fr €70; d fr €85; extra person fr €15; dinner fr €25 **On Site** ⍟ Private ⚲ **Nearby** ⚐ 4km ⚑ 10km Sea 18km ⚘ 10km Restaurant 4km ⚲ 4km 🏛 4km 🚗 22km **Notes** No pets English spoken

BARGEME

♦♦♦ ⍟ *Les Roses Trémières*

Annie NOEL

83840 BARGEME

☎ 04 94 84 20 86 & 06 19 36 36 11

email: rosesdebargeme@free.fr

web: www.rosesdebargeme.fr

In a medieval site - the highest in the Var - this house overlooks pretty, perfumed countryside and is near the Gorges of Verdon. Five individually styled rooms with private shower and wc, decorated in Provençal style.

Prices not confirmed for 2008 **Nearby** ⚐ 4km ⚑ 5km ⚲ 4km ⚲ 4km 🏛 4km 🚗 40km **Notes** No pets English spoken Open April to November.

♦♦♦ ⍟ St Pierre

C et B MARCELIN GABRIEL

83840 BARGEME

☎ 04 94 84 21 55 📄 04 94 84 21 04

email: marcelin.berte@wanadoo.fr

web: www.fermesaintpierre.net

This working farm stands at the foot of the hills, looking out over vast expanses of meadows and forest. It has four double bedrooms, one on the first floor and three on the second. They all have private bath or shower rooms and WCs. Extra bed available; meals available by arrangement.

Prices s fr €55; d €65-€75; t €89-€94; extra person fr €16; dinner fr €25 **On Site** ⚐ ⍟ **Nearby** ⚑ 3km ⚘ 1km ⚲ 3km Restaurant 2km ⚲ 5km 🏛 3km 🚗 50km **Notes** Pets admitted English spoken

BAUDUEN

♦♦♦ ⍟ Domaine de Majastre

Philippe et Rosy DE SANTIS

83630 BAUDUEN

☎ 04 94 70 05 12 📄 04 94 84 01 88

web: www.domaine-de-majastre.com

Le Domaine de Majastre is a 400 hectare truffle-growing estate which belonged to the last king of France. The guest rooms include four double rooms, a triple and a room for four, all with bath or shower and wc. Swimming pool.

Prices d €61-€71; extra person fr €10; dinner fr €61 **On Site** Private ⚲ **Nearby** Restaurant 5km ⚲ 5km 🏛 5km 🚗 30km **Notes** Pets admitted

BESSE-SUR-ISSOLE

♦♦♦ L'Oustaou

Fanny SALIGNAC

83890 BESSE-SUR-ISSOLE

☎ 04 94 86 14 85 & 06 70 16 39 90

email: oustaou.besse@cegetel.net

web: http://oustaou.besse.free.fr

In a quiet setting, one and a half kilometres from the village, this Provençal house has three guest rooms, two doubles and a twin, all with private shower rooms/WCs, TVs and independent access. Outside there is a terrace and a garden room.

Prices s fr €48; d fr €56; extra person fr €15 **Nearby** ⚐ 1km ⚑ 10km Sea 40km ⚘ 1km ⚲ 15km ⚲ 1km 🏛 1.5km 🚗 6km **Notes** Pets admitted English spoken

BRAS

♦♦♦ ⍟ *Les Restanques*

Christine IMBERT

Ancien Chemin de Barjols, 83149 BRAS

☎ 04 94 69 96 13 & 06 85 02 86 77 📄 04 94 69 96 13

email: christine.imbert@freesbee.fr

web: www.provenceweb.fr/83/lesrestanques

In green countryside among olives and oaks, on the Ste Baume. One suite with double bed, sitting room, and separate access, a twin room and a double room, all with private facilities. Swimming pool and barbecue. Meals available (regional dishes and family specialities).

Prices not confirmed for 2008 **On Site** Private ⚲ **Nearby** ⚐ 15km ⚑ 15km ⚲ 3km 🏛 0.7km **Notes** No pets

CALLAS

⊞ Les Clèdes

B et E BONNAIRE
Route de Grasse D 562, 83830 CALLAS
☎ 04 94 39 99 84 & 06 08 70 08 44   🗎 04 94 39 99 84
email: fret01@wanadoo.fr
web: www.callas-provence.com

This large Provençal villa enjoys a calm setting among pine trees, in a shady enclosed garden with terrace, parking and boules. It provides rooms with king-size beds, personalised decor, private facilities and access and fridges. 10km from Draguignan, between the sea and the Verdon caves.

Prices not confirmed for 2008   **On Site** Private ⚲   **Nearby** ⛵ 5km
⚲ 4km 🏛 4km ⋙ 25km   **Notes** No pets Open April to October.

CALLIAN

⊞ Domaine de Sainte Annette

Nathalie MUNOZ-RUIZ
83440 CALLIAN
☎ 04 94 76 59 59 & 06 86 49 26 26   🗎 04 94 76 59 39
email: melarab@wanadoo.fr
web: www.sainteannette.com

Just below the ancient village of Callian, this is a stud farm for pure-bred Arab horses. The house dates from the 18th century and has a twin-bedded room and two doubles, all upstairs with private facilities. Cot available also Jacuzzi and fitness room. Outside is a swimming pool, a sheltered sitting-out area, a fitness room and a summer house.

Prices d €95-€105   **On Site** ⚲ Private ⚲   **Nearby** ⛵ 8km
⚲ 2.5km ⚲ 4km Restaurant 2km ⚲ 2km Spa 5km 🏛 2km ⋙ 25km
Notes No pets English spoken Open 15 February to 15 January.

COLLOBRIERES

⊞ ❧ ⫶◯⫶ La Bastide de la Cabrière

Loïc DE SALENEUVE
83610 COLLOBRIERES
☎ 04 94 48 04 31   🗎 04 94 48 09 90
email: loic.de.saleneuve@wanadoo.fr
web: www.saleneuve.com

A renovated house set in peace and quiet in the heart of the Maures, in an oasis of greenery. Four double rooms and one triple, all with separate entrance, shower or bath and wc. Enclosed swimming pool, garden furniture, sitting room.

Prices d €92-€105; t fr €130; dinner fr €35   **On Site** ⛵
Nearby ⚲ 25km ⚲ 6km 🏛 6km ⋙ 50km   **Notes** No pets English spoken

COTIGNAC

⊞ ⫶◯⫶ Campagne Saint Martin

Sonia et Laurence ALLEGRE
83570 COTIGNAC
☎ 04 94 04 66 50 & 06 80 84 69 20   🗎 04 94 04 74 21
email: sonia.allegre@club-internet.fr
web: www.campagne-st-martin.com

The buildings of an old silkworm farm, dating back to the 19th century. There are four double rooms, and a family room for four with two double beds. Each has a private shower room and WC. The setting is very pleasant: beautiful views, terrace with furniture where guests can relax, footpaths close by. Meals by arrangement.

Prices d fr €55; t fr €80; extra person fr €20; dinner fr €17
Nearby ⛵ 2km ⚲ 20km ⚲ 8km ⚲ 6km Restaurant 3km ⚲ 3km
⚲ 3km 🏛 3km ⋙ 45km   **Notes** No pets English spoken

⊞ ❧ ⫶◯⫶ Domaine de Nestuby

Nathalie ROUBAUD
4540 Route de Montfort, 83570 COTIGNAC
☎ 04 94 04 60 02 & 06 86 16 27 93   🗎 04 94 04 79 22
email: nestuby@wanadoo.fr
web: www.sejour-en-provence.com/nestu01.htm

This beautiful restored 19th-century house is set in the middle of a 45 hectare wine-growing estate. A typical Provençal establishment with beautiful local furniture and sunny fabrics, offering four rooms: a double, a twin, one sleeping three and the other sleeping four, with private facilities. Reading room with television and hi-fi system, garden with furniture, swimming pool, children's games.

Prices s fr €65; d €75-€80; t €93-€98; extra person fr €18; dinner fr €27
On Site Restaurant ⚲ Private ⚲   **Nearby** ⛵ 10km ⚲ 20km ⚲ 5km
🏛 5km ⋙ 30km   **Notes** Pets admitted English spoken Open March to 15 November.

DRAGUIGNAN

⊞ ⫶◯⫶ Bastide des Micocouliers

Marie Dolores HEBERT
1653 Route de Grasse, 83300 DRAGUIGNAN
☎ 04 94 85 39 09 & 06 07 18 81 39   🗎 04 94 50 96 88
email: mariehebert2@wanadoo.fr
web: www.bastide-des-micocouliers.com

A beautiful country house above Draguignan, with five comfortable guest bedrooms. Four of the rooms are doubles; the fifth is a suite for three people with a double bed and a single. All have private bathroom, WC and TV. There is a swimming pool, and meals are available, by arrangement.

Prices d €85-€110; t fr €115; dinner fr €20   **On Site** Private ⚲
Nearby ⛵ 3km ⚲ 15km ⚲ 3km ⚲ 2km 🏛 3km ⋙ 10km
Notes No pets English spoken

EVENOS

ᵚᵚᵚ ᶦⓄᶦ **Le Mas du Cimai**

Frederic CERDAN

2473 Route d'Evenos, 83330 EVENOS

☎ 04 94 25 28 41 & 06 68 13 42 75

email: cerdanfrederic@hotmail.com

web: http://masducimai.com

Old restored wine-growing farm, in an outstanding location. Two ground floor rooms opening onto a shady terrace with outdoor furniture. View over the Falaises and the Restanques. Scrambling routes only 800mtrs away.

Prices s €56-€58; d €58-€62; t €78-€82; extra person fr €20; dinner fr €22 **On Site** Private ⚲ **Nearby** ⛵ 4km ⚓ 15km Sea 14km ⚐ 14km Restaurant 5km ⚲ 12km ⚘ 8km ⚑ 2.5km ⚘⚘ 12km **Notes** No pets

FAYENCE

ᵚᵚᵚ ᶦⓄᶦ **Chez Tonton Nini**

Pierre GUYOT

Quartier Jaumillot, 83440 FAYENCE

☎ 04 94 76 10 77 & 06 81 79 82 99

email: tontonnini@free.fr

web: www.tontonnini.info

Three double rooms in a villa in the heart of the country with access to waymarked tracks for rambling or mountain biking. Swimming pool, parking, terrace, garden furniture, table tennis, pétanque pitch. A fully equipped kitchen is available as well as a leisure room.

Prices s fr €48; d fr €60; extra person fr €22; dinner fr €22 **Nearby** ⛵ 10km ⚓ 5km ⚲ 4km Restaurant 4km ⚲ 4km ⚑ 4km ⚘⚘ 30km **Notes** Pets admitted English spoken

ᵚᵚᵚ ᶦⓄᶦ *l'Albatros*

Jacques VIROLLE

1434 Ancienne rte Draguignan, Quartier Baudisse, 83440 FAYENCE

☎ 04 94 47 65 58 & 06 81 54 69 54 ▤ 04 94 47 65 58

email: jv.lalbatros@wanadoo.fr

web: www.lalbatros83.com

Set in the heart of the woodlands, Nathalie and Jacques welcome you to their contemporary and original house, built from red cedar. Swimming pool, Jacuzzi, table tennis, boules. Ideal for golfers. Augusta has a double and a single bed, shower/wc; St Andrews and Sperone are both doubles with shower/wc. Air-conditioning, TV, DVD player.

Prices not confirmed for 2008 **On Site** Private ⚲ **Nearby** ⛵ 10km ⚓ 10km ⚲ 3km ⚑ 3km ⚘⚘ 30km **Notes** No pets

FREJUS

ᵚᵚᵚ ♥ ᶦⓄᶦ *Les Vergers de Montourey*

Christophe ARTAUD

Quartier Montourey, 83600 FREJUS

☎ 04 94 40 85 76 & 06 23 21 06 85

email: arttotof@wanadoo.fr

web: http://perso.wanadoo.fr/vergers.montourey

An 18th-century building on a fruit farm, offering four double rooms and two suites sleeping three or four, all with shower, wc, and television. Sitting room with open fireplace, terrace, barbecue and children's games. Baby equipment available.

Prices not confirmed for 2008 **Nearby** ⛵ 6km ⚓ 5km ⚲ 6km ⚲ 6km ⚑ 6km ⚘⚘ 6km **Notes** No pets English spoken Open April to 1 November.

GINASSERVIS

ᵚᵚᵚ ᶦⓄᶦ **La Rougonne**

Jean Marie PERRIER

83560 GINASSERVIS

☎ 04 94 80 11 31 & 06 82 57 18 69 ▤ 04 94 77 24 28

email: larougonne@club-internet.fr

web: www.larougonne.com

A 14th-century house on a hillside with three suites with private facilities and television; two rooms sleeping three, and one double room. Antique furniture, friendly hosts, billiards, library, open fires and sitting rooms.

Prices s €74-€82; d €77-€85; t €95-€102; extra person fr €17; dinner fr €24 **On Site** Private ⚲ **Nearby** ⛵ 10km ⚓ 35km ⚲ 9km Restaurant 3km ⚲ 3.5km ⚘ 9km ⚑ 3km ⚘⚘ 30km **Notes** No pets English spoken Open 10 January to 20 December.

GRIMAUD

ᵚᵚᵚ *Bastide de l'Avelan*

Patricia HERMANGE

Quartier Robert, 83310 GRIMAUD

☎ 04 94 43 25 79

email: bastide.avelan@wanadoo.fr

web: www.bastideavelan.com

Two minutes from the sea, surrounded by vineyards and shaded by enormous pine trees, the Bastide de l'Avelan is an ideal place to rest and relax. There is a double room, a twin-bedded room and two family rooms - one for three, the other for four; all have private facilities. Garden with swimming pool and shaded parking.

Prices not confirmed for 2008 **On Site** Private ⚲ **Nearby** ⛵ 1.5km ⚓ 3km ⚲ 1.5km ⚑ 2km ⚘⚘ 35km **Notes** No pets English spoken

⚏ & Domaine du Prignon

Paul et Christelle BERTOLOTTO

83310 GRIMAUD

☎ 04 94 43 34 84 & 06 81 67 30 93

web: http://laprignon.free.fr/

Only ten minutes from the sea, guests rooms in this twelve hectare vineyard have great character, separate entrances and private terraces. There is a double and two twin rooms, each with shower and wc. Outdoor furniture and deckchairs in the shade of the oak trees, refrigerator, lounge, library. Baby equipment available.

Prices d fr €69; extra person fr €15 **Nearby** ⚓ 3km ⚑ 8km Sea 7km ⚐ 0.5km ⚒ 10km Restaurant 4km ⚒ 7km ⚒ 6km ⚒ 4km ⚒ 35km
Notes Pets admitted English spoken

LA CADIERE-D'AZUR

⚏ Château St Come

Joel POUTET

Chemin de St Come, 83740 LA CADIERE-D'AZUR

☎ 04 94 90 07 71 & 06 20 30 37 98

📄 04 94 90 07 53

email: contact@chateaudestcome.com

web: www.chateaudestcome.com

A pretty 16th-century former coaching inn which has been traditionally renovated and decorated, and is set in the heart of a Bandolais vineyard, 3km from the beach. The rooms are decorated in colours of Provence and include Olivier, Lavande and Mimosa (twins) and Raisin and Calanque (doubles); each has private facilities. Guests have use of a swimming pool with summer kitchen and garden furniture, and gourmet breakfasts feature home-grown fruits.

Prices d €90-€140; extra person fr €20; dinner fr €25
On Site Private ⚒ **Nearby** ⚓ 2km ⚑ 6km Sea 3km ⚐ 3km Restaurant 2km ⚒ 2km Spa 4km ⚒ 2km ⚒ 2km ⚒ 2km
Notes No pets English spoken

LA MOLE

⚏ Domaine de Ventabren

Emmanuel DE BIZEMONT

Route des Guiols, 83310 LA MOLE

☎ 04 94 49 51 21 📄 04 94 49 57 89

email: debizemont.descombris@wanadoo.fr

web: www.le-domaine-de-ventabren.com

Built in typical Provençal style, this house stands in two acres of wooded grounds, with a fine swimming pool sheltered on three sides by the house. Five bedrooms, four doubles and one with twin beds, all have private bath or shower room/WC. Sunny patio, boules pitch, table tennis table and lots of garden furniture.

Prices not confirmed for 2008 **On Site** Private ⚒ **Nearby** ⚓ 5km ⚑ 10km ⚒ 8km ⚒ 3km ⚒ 35km **Notes** Pets admitted

---

LA MOTTE

⚏ Mas du Péré

Catherine et Gerard HUT

280 Chemin du Péré, 83920 LA MOTTE

☎ 04 94 84 33 52 & 06 13 22 09 45 📄 04 94 84 33 52

email: le.mas.du.pere@club-internet.fr

web: www.lemasdupere.com

Set in large verdant grounds, this stone mas is close to a small, typical village and provides four guest rooms: Le Jade and Topaze (double and single beds), Pierre de Lune (twin) and Opale (double with private lounge). Each has private facilities, access and terraces. There is also a living room with fireplace and a communal summer kitchen.

Prices s fr €74; d €74-€105; t €95-€125; extra person fr €18
On Site ⚐ Restaurant ⚒ Private ⚒ **Nearby** ⚓ 5km ⚑ 3km ⚒ 0.7km ⚒ 0.7km ⚒ 5km **Notes** No pets English spoken

---

LA ROQUE-ESCLAPON

⚏ ⚘ ◉ Ferme de Séjour Rebuffel

Jean-Guy REBUFFEL

Quartier Riphle, 83840 LA ROQUE-ESCLAPON

☎ 04 94 76 80 75 📄 04 94 76 80 75

email: isabelle.rebuffel@worldonline.fr

web: www.rebuffel.com

This working farm is 1000mtrs above sea level, a short distance from Verdon and its lakes and 18 kilometres from the Verdon gorges. It has four rooms, each of them with en suite shower room and WC. Library, garden room, games. Meals by arrangement.

Prices not confirmed for 2008 **Nearby** ⚓ 8km ⚑ 7km ⚒ 1km ⚒ 1km ⚒ 1km ⚒ 40km **Notes** Pets admitted English spoken

---

LA ROQUEBRUSSANNE

⚏ ◉ La Madrigale

Samuel RIAND

1 Chemin des 9 Fonts, 83136 LA ROQUEBRUSSANNE

☎ 04 94 86 89 27 & 06 98 07 59 09

email: lamadrigale@wanadoo.fr

web: http://perso.wanadoo.fr/lamadrigale/

A former winegrower's home in the heart of the village on the edge of the Sainte-Baume mountain range and the shores of the Issole. It provides three rooms overlooking the tree-lined garden, each with private facilities. There is a reading room, a TV room, a terrace, a swimming pool and table d'hôte meals are available by reservation.

Prices not confirmed for 2008 **Nearby** ⚓ 6km ⚑ 20km ⚒ 6km ⚒ 2km ⚒ 0.1km ⚒ 33km **Notes** Pets admitted English spoken

LE BEAUSSET

ⵜ *La Gîthomière*

Monique FAUVET

1253 Chemin de la Baro Nuecho, 83330 LE BEAUSSET

☎ 04 94 98 62 97 & 06 13 27 94 94

email: contact@githomiere-var.com

web: www.githomiere-var.com

Welcome to Le Vallon, a haven of peace in the hills, with its swimming pool, flower garden and trees. Three charming guest rooms with shower rooms and wc are offered, one with a private terrace. Laundry. Summer kitchen.

Prices not confirmed for 2008   **On Site** Private ⵜ   **Nearby** ⵜ 2km
⚲ 12km ⚲ 2km ⛫ 2km ⵜ 11km   **Notes** Pets admitted   English spoken

ⵜ **Le Cigalon**

Jacques et Marie-L PESENTI

Quartier Souviou, 83330 LE BEAUSSET

☎ 04 94 90 46 05 & 06 82 47 56 33

email: lecigalon@neuf.fr

web: http://lecigalon.site.voila.fr

This 19th-century house has an exceptional setting, with distant views of the sea. On the ground floor is a twin-bedded room; upstairs there are two doubles. All the rooms have private bathrooms and WCs. Landscaped grounds full of flowers, conservatory, garden furniture.

Prices d fr €70   **Nearby** ⵜ 5km ⚲ 15km ⵜ 20km ⚲ 5km ⛫ 5km
ⵜ 15km   **Notes** No pets   English spoken

ⵜ *Les Cancades*

Charlotte et Marceau ZERBIB

Ch. Fontaine 5 Sous No 1195, 83330 LE BEAUSSET

☎ 04 94 98 76 93 🗎 04 94 90 24 63

email: charlotte.zerbib@wanadoo.fr

web: www.les-cancades.com

Four guest rooms in the owners' house, in enclosed green grounds and remarkable quiet: three twins and a double with private facilities. Thoroughly equipped outside kitchen, garden furniture, park. One ground floor twin room with shower and wc and separate garden. Circuit du Castellet race track nearby.

Prices not confirmed for 2008   **On Site** Private ⵜ   **Nearby** ⵜ 0.5km
ⵜ 6km ⚲ 4km ⛫ 1km ⵜ 17km   **Notes** No pets

LE CASTELLET

ⵜ ⵏⵓ⍾ **Le Mas des Oliviers**

Alain TOKATLIAN

12 Chemin des Puechs, 83330 LE CASTELLET

☎ 04 94 32 71 80 & 06 62 35 09 16 🗎 04 94 32 65 38

email: le.mas.des.olivers@wanadoo.fr

Just 200 metres from the medieval village of Castellet, this peaceful property with its panoramic view across the bay of La Ciotat has five rooms, four doubles and a single, decorated in Provençal style. All have private bathrooms, private terraces, air-conditioning, TVs and hairdryers; three have an open view. Wooded grounds, swimming pool, terrace, barbecue, guests' kitchen, boules area.

Prices s fr €78; d fr €85; extra person fr €30   **On Site** Private ⵜ
Nearby ⵜ 3km ⚲ 10km Sea 7km ⵜ 7km Restaurant 0.8km ⚲ 1km
Spa 7km ⵜ 4km ⛫ 3km ⵜ 5km   **Notes** Pets admitted   English spoken

LE LUC-EN-PROVENCE

ⵜ ⵏⵓⵏ **Bastide de la Mourignette**

Claudette VILAREM

2915 Route de Toulon, 83340 LE LUC-EN-PROVENCE

☎ 04 94 60 94 06 & 06 08 26 61 05 🗎 04 94 60 94 06

email: claudette@vilarem.com

web: www.vilarem.com

This house, dating from 1900, stands at the foot of the hills, surrounded by vines, looking out over the Plain of Maures. It has three spacious double bedrooms, all on the ground floor and all with private shower rooms and WCs. Lounge, terrace, extensive grounds with swimming pool. Meals are available, by arrangement.

Prices s fr €55; d fr €60; extra person fr €20   **On Site** Private ⵜ
Nearby ⵜ 2km ⚲ 10km ⚲ 3km ⛫ 1km ⵜ 5km   **Notes** Pets admitted
English spoken   Open 15 March to 15 November.

LE MUY

ⵜ **Les Palmiers**

Yvette MERDJOYAN

1890, Route de la Motte, 83490 LE MUY

☎ 04 94 45 34 67 & 06 11 41 90 50

email: palmiers.yvm@free.fr

web: www.les-palmiers.fr

A newly-built house in large enclosed grounds on the outskirts of the village. Two double rooms and a twin-bedded room, all with fridge, private bath or shower room and WC. Sitting room with satellite TV, covered terrace with garden furniture, and swimming pool.

Prices s fr €75; d fr €75   **On Site** Private ⵜ   **Nearby** ⵜ 6km ⚲ 3km
Sea 18km ⵜ 6km Restaurant 1km ⚲ 4km Spa 20km ⛫ 2km ⵜ 15km
Notes No pets   English spoken

LE THORONET

⊪ ⫯◎⫯ La Gourgue de Blanc

Georges GEOFFROY

Bastide Saint Bernard, 83340 LE THORONET

☎ 04 94 73 83 39 & 06 33 08 69 83   ▤ 04 94 73 83 39

email: bastide.saint.bernard@wanadoo.fr

web: www.bastide-saint-bernard.com

This is a very comfortable modern Provençal house, in a beautiful situation. It has five guest bedrooms, spacious, attractively decorated, and all with TVs, private shower rooms and WCs. Lounge with open fire, swimming pool. Meals are available, including traditional dishes made with local ingredients.

Prices d fr €73   **Nearby** ⛵ 9km ⚓ 11km ⛳ 1km 🏛 10km ➤ 15km

Notes No pets English spoken

LES ARCS-SUR-ARGENS

⊪ ⫯◎⫯ Lou Nieu

Valter et Martine TOGNELLI

919 Rte Croisières, Quartier les Plaines,

83460 LES ARCS-SUR-ARGENS

☎ 04 94 85 28 15 & 06 14 30 71 66

email: martine.tognelli@wanadoo.fr

web: www.lou-nieu.com

Expect a warm welcome at this beautiful house in the quiet of the country. Enclosed grounds, terraces, swimming pool, garden furniture, deckchairs, books, boules. The three rooms each have their own entrance, shower, wc, television; 'Tournesol' and 'Papaye' are double rooms and 'Almande' sleeps three. Meals available.

Prices s fr €50; d fr €60; t fr €72; extra person fr €12; dinner fr €18

Nearby ⛵ 2km ⚓ 8km ⛳ 5km 🏛 2km ➤ 4km   **Notes** No pets English spoken

LES MAYONS

⊪ ❦ ⫯◎⫯ *Domaine de la Fouquette*

Michèle et Yves AQUADRO

83340 LES MAYONS

☎ 04 94 60 00 69   ▤ 04 94 60 02 91

email: domaine.fouquette@wanadoo.fr

web: www.domaine.de.la.fouquette.com

This welcoming vineyard and farm has panoramic views over the Plain of Maures. Three upstairs guest rooms, two twins and one sleeping three, each with shower and wc. Meals available. Television in the sitting room. Baby equipment available.

Prices not confirmed for 2008   **Nearby** ⛵ 10km ➤ 10km ⛳ 2km 🏛 5km ➤ 25km   **Notes** Pets admitted Open March to October.

LORGUES

⊪ Villa de Lorgues

Claude CAIS

7 Rue de la Bourgade, 83510 LORGUES

☎ 06 61 47 67 02   ▤ 04 93 99 33 03

email: cais.claudie@wanadoo.fr

web: www.villadelorgues.com

Right in the heart of the village, this large house sits in a pleasant flowery garden with shady places to sit. Three double bedrooms all have en suite bathrooms; two have satellite TV. Large sitting room with TV, books to read, and internet.

Prices s €75-€95; d €100-€140; t €140-€170   **On Site** Restaurant

🏖 **Nearby** ⛵ 2km ⚓ 20km ➤ 10km ➤ ⛳ 3km 🏛 1km ➤ 15km

Notes No pets English spoken

MONTAUROUX

⊪ Amboise

Sandie DOCHERTY

Chemin des Esclapieres, 83440 MONTAUROUX

☎ 04 94 76 46 55 & 06 18 58 40 00   ▤ 04 94 76 46 55

email: info@amboise-bnb.com

web: www.amboise-bnb.com

This house is in a quiet, restful spot close to a lake. It offers three air-conditioned bedrooms, two doubles and one with twin beds, all with private shower room and WC. Outside is a large garden with swimming pool, shady terrace, boules pitch and a summer kitchen for guests.

Prices s fr €50; d fr €65; t fr €84; extra person fr €19   **On Site** Private ➤

Nearby ⛵ 5km ⛳ 1km Sea 25km ➤ 1km Restaurant 1km ⛳ 5km Spa 7km 🏛 1km ➤ 25km   **Notes** Pets admitted English spoken

⊪ Villa Thocha

Dominique STRIBICK

Bd de Tournon, 83440 MONTAUROUX

☎ 04 94 67 62 73 & 06 72 04 59 20   ▤ 04 94 67 78 74

email: villa-thocha@wanadoo.fr

web: http://monsite.orange.fr/chambres-hote-thocha

A contemporary house in a quiet forest clearing above the village, surrounded by landscaped gardens. There are three double bedrooms, each with independent access, private shower room and WC. Terraces, garden furniture, games area. An ideal spot for a walking holiday, or just relaxing.

Prices s fr €52; d fr €57; extra person fr €15   **Nearby** ⛵ 15km ⚓ 12km Sea 30km ➤ 4km ➤ 12km Restaurant 3km ⛳ 3km 🏖 4km 🏛 2km ➤ 30km   **Notes** No pets English spoken

MONTMEYAN

⚑ Au Jardin de Mon Père

Louis et Dany FONTICELLI

2 Route de Régusse, 83670 MONTMEYAN

☎ 04 94 80 72 84 & 06 64 52 69 52 📄 04 94 80 72 84

email: fonti.l@wanadoo.fr

web: www.aujardindemonpere.com

This beautiful house is at the foot of the village and has a terrace and small garden with a magnificent view over the Préalpes. There are five rooms with shower and wc, parking and the Musée de la Préhistoire at Quinson.

Prices s fr €44; d fr €51; extra person fr €15 **Nearby** ⚓ 20km ⚘ 40km ⚑ 7km ⚘ 7km ⚓ 0.2km ⚑ 0.2km **Notes** No pets Open April to October.

PIERREFEU-DU-VAR

⚑ Le Clos de Lette

Alain CASAL

83390 PIERREFEU-DU-VAR

☎ 04 94 48 21 71 & 06 84 30 22 26 📄 04 94 48 21 71

email: clos.de.lette@club-internet.fr

web: www.closdelette.com

In open country between the Massif des Maures and the vineyards of the Provence coast, winegrowers from the oldest families in the region welcome you to their peaceful home. Two twin-bedded rooms and two double rooms, with private bath and wc and separate entrances are offered, with wonderful views and a cooking area for guests.

Prices s fr €59; d fr €63; extra person fr €19 **Nearby** ⚓ 6km ⚘ 25km ⚘ 15km ⚓ 0.5km ⚑ 2km ⚑ 6km **Notes** Pets admitted English spoken

---

PLAN-DE-LA-TOUR

⚑ ⦿ La Bergerie

Gilles CARANTA

Le Clos de San Peire, 83120 PLAN-DE-LA-TOUR

☎ 04 94 43 74 74 📄 04 94 43 74 74

email: labergeriecaranta@wanadoo.fr

web: www.la-bergerie-caranta.com

An old restored sheep farm with three guest rooms (two doubles and a twin, all en suite) and two gîtes. Communal gardens, private terrace, garden furniture, leisure area, swimming pool. Meals if required.

Prices d €75-€85; extra person fr €18; dinner fr €30 **On Site** Private ⚘ **Nearby** ⚓ 2km ⚘ 10km ⚓ 1km ⚑ 2km ⚑ 35km **Notes** No pets English spoken

---

PONTEVES

⚑ ⚘ Domaine de Saint-Ferréol

A et G DE JERPHANION

83670 PONTEVES

☎ 04 94 77 10 42 📄 04 94 77 19 04

email: saint-ferreol@wanadoo.fr

web: http://domaine-de-saint-ferreol.fr

This 100 hectare 18th-century farm and vineyard is set in the hillside. The rooms are located in a restored wing of the farm and are filled with antique country furniture and lovely Provençal fabrics. They include one double room, one sleeping three, and a suite for four, each with private facilities. Communal kitchenette.

Prices not confirmed for 2008 **On Site** Private ⚘ **Nearby** ⚓ 12km ⚘ 30km ⚓ 3km ⚑ 3km **Notes** No pets English spoken Open March to 15 November.

⚑ ⦿ La Sauvabelle

Sylvie POILLY

Quartier Rognette, 83670 PONTEVES

☎ 04 94 77 31 52

email: ppoilly@club-internet.fr

web: http://perso.club-internet.fr/ppoilly

In a tranquil and verdant setting, this property provides four guest rooms as well as a rural gîte. Each room is for two or three guests and has private facilities. There is parking, a communal swimming pool, living room with TV and telephone, and table d'hôte meals are available by reservation.

Prices not confirmed for 2008 **On Site** Private ⚘ **Nearby** ⚓ 6km ⚘ 40km ⚓ 8km ⚑ 5km ⚑ 45km **Notes** No pets English spoken

---

PUGET-VILLE

⚑ ⦿ Le Mas des Oliviers

Guy LEROY

Chemin des Grands Pres, 83390 PUGET-VILLE

☎ 04 94 48 30 89 & 06 16 82 60 32 📄 04 94 48 30 89

email: guy.leroy18@orange.fr

web: www.masdesoliviers.sup.fr

This property enjoys a typically provincial setting amongst vines and olive trees in three hectares of calm. There is a swimming pool, garden furniture, summer kitchen and horses on site, and the sea is just 25 minutes away. The three twin rooms are full of character and have their own facilities. Table d'hôte meals available by reservation.

Prices s fr €58; d fr €68; extra person fr €18; dinner fr €24 **On Site** ⚓ ⚘ Private ⚘ **Nearby** ⚘ 25km Sea 27km ⚑ 20km Restaurant 6km ⚓ 2km ⚑ 2km ⚑ 30km **Notes** No pets English spoken

RAMATUELLE

⁙ Leï Souco

Nathalie GIRAUD
Plaine de Camarat, 83350 RAMATUELLE
☎ 04 94 79 80 22 & 06 10 09 73 76 📄 04 94 79 88 27
web: www.leisouco.com

Four kilometres from Ramatuelle, near the beaches, Leï Souco is a beautiful Provençal house in 10 hectares of vines, olives, mimosas, eucalyptus and blackberries. The spacious rooms have Provençal furnishings and include four rooms and one suite, all with private terrace and facilities. Sample the local rosé with the friendly proprietors. Safe deposit box, fridge, private tennis, pétanque ground. Nearby restaurants.

Prices not confirmed for 2008 **Nearby** ⚑ 2km ⌀ 18km ⤍ 7km ⌂ 1km ⊶ 40km **Notes** Pets admitted English spoken Open Easter to 15 October.

RIANS

⁙ ⊙ & La Margottière

Anne DURAND
Chemin du Passet, 83560 RIANS
☎ 06 12 86 94 91
web: www.lamargottiere.fr

La Margottière stands on a hill looking towards Rians, a typical Provençal village. There are four ground floor double rooms, all with private shower and WC, mini-fridge, hot drink making facilities, and private entrance. Extra children's beds available. Meals served if pre-cooked. This is good walking country, and footpaths pass close by.

Prices s fr €65; d fr €75; extra person fr €15; dinner fr €20 **Nearby** ⚑ 1km ⌀ 30km ⤍ 1km Restaurant 0.3km ⊷ 1km ⌂ 0.3km ⊶ 40km **Notes** Pets admitted English spoken

ROCBARON

⁙ ⊙ La Maison de Rocbaron

Jeanne et Guy FISCHBACH
Rue Saint Sauveur, 83136 ROCBARON
☎ 04 94 04 24 03 & 06 87 31 77 61
email: maison.de.rocbaron@wanadoo.fr
web: www.maisonderocbaron.com

This converted 19th-century farm building stands in the middle of a typical Provençal village. The enclosed shady garden has a terrace, swimming pool, and parking space. Five bedrooms are all doubles with en suite facilities. Internet access available, sitting room with books; meals available if pre-booked.

Prices s fr €78; d €78-€108; t €103-€133; extra person €10-€25; dinner fr €32 **On Site** Private ⤍ **Nearby** ⚑ 5km ⌀ 20km Sea 35km Restaurant 3km ⊷ 1.5km Spa 30km ⌂ 2km ⊶ 10km **Notes** No pets English spoken

SALERNES

⁙ ⊙ & Chambre d'hôtes

Marie Claire BOISARD
1133 Route de Sillans, 83690 SALERNES
☎ 04 94 70 75 20 & 06 14 75 35 60 📄 04 94 70 75 20
email: aumasdesoliviers@aol.com
web: www.masdesoliviers-salernes.com

Set in shady grounds, there are two triple rooms and two doubles, two with separate access and all with fridge and private facilities. Satellite television room, reading room, billiard room. Meals if booked. Terrace, table tennis, swimming pool.

Prices s fr €53; d fr €61; t fr €78; extra person fr €16; dinner fr €24 **On Site** Private ⤍ **Nearby** ⚑ 2km ⌀ 25km ⌗ 1km Restaurant 1km ⊷ 1km ⵣ 1km ⌂ 1km ⊶ 35km **Notes** Pets admitted English spoken

⁙ ♥ ⊙ La Bastide Rose

Karel et Caroline HENNY
Haut Gaudran BP 24, 83690 SALERNES
☎ 04 94 70 63 30 & 06 19 48 41 40 📄 04 94 70 77 34
email: labastiderose@wanadoo.fr
web: www.bastide-rose.com

The Dutch proprietor extends a warm welcome at this pretty pink farmhouse amidst vines and fruit trees. There are three very comfortable suites: one with double bed and two singles on a half-floor with a balcony, and two with lounge/kitchenette and four single beds, two on a mezzanine. All have private facilities; terrace, garden, outdoor furniture, swimming pool. Baby equipment and holiday gîte available.

Prices not confirmed for 2008 **Nearby** ⚑ 3km ⌀ 35km ⤍ 3km ⊷ 3km ⌂ 3km ⊶ 35km **Notes** No pets English spoken Open Easter to 15 October.

SANARY-SUR-MER

⁙ Villa Lou Gardian

Bruno CASTELLANO
646 Route de Bandol, 83110 SANARY-SUR-MER
☎ 04 94 88 05 73 & 06 60 88 05 73 📄 04 94 88 24 13
email: annie-bruno.castellano@wanadoo.fr
web: www.lou-gardian.com

Between Sanary and Bandol, 400m from the beach, a vast 19th-century town house in a garden surrounded by palms and hundred-year-old cypresses. The four beautifully decorated rooms include three twins and a double, all with private facilities. Swimming pool, tennis, air-conditioning, library.

Prices s fr €71; d fr €82; extra person fr €37 **On Site** Private ⤍ Private ⊷ **Nearby** ⚑ 4km ⌀ 8km ⌂ 0.4km ⊶ 3.4km **Notes** No pets English spoken

SIX-FOURS-LES-PLAGES

⁂ La Griottière

Michel BERTRAND

1029 Av John Kennedy, 83140 SIX-FOURS-LES-PLAGES

☎ 04 94 25 92 12 & 06 74 28 24 48 📄 04 94 25 92 12

web: www.lagriottiere.com

Your hosts will be delighted to welcome you to this beautiful house on the edge of the village. It has three air-conditioned double rooms, all with televisions and private showers/WCs. One of them also has a balcony and covered terrace. Microwave, fridge, freezer. Enclosed wooded grounds, terrace (for breakfast in the summer), garden room, parking and cycle storage.

Prices s €45-€60; d €55-€60; extra person fr €15 **Nearby** ⚓ 5km
🏊 1km ⚲ 1.5km Restaurant 1km ⛴ 0.4km Spa 6km ⛵ 3km 🏛 0.5km
🚃 3km **Notes** Pets admitted

ST-MAXIMIN

⁂ L'Oree du Bois

Claudette DUBOIS

380 Chemin du Claret, 83470 ST-MAXIMIN

☎ 04 94 59 83 75 & 06 11 57 64 01 📄 04 94 59 83 75

email: claudette.loreedubois@cegetel.net

web: www.loree-du-bois.net

A country house three kilometres from the town, with three double bedrooms. One is on the ground floor; upstairs is another double, and a twin-bedded room. Possible space for a child's bed. All rooms have private shower and WC. Lounge with TV; air-conditioning. Swimming pool.

Prices not confirmed for 2008 **On Site** Private ⚲ **Nearby** ⚓ 2km
⚲ 15km ⛴ 2km 🏛 3km 🚃 30km **Notes** No pets English spoken

ST-RAPHAEL

⁂ 🏠 La Bergerie de Vaulongue

Elisabeth GAILLARD-LENOIR

1520 Boulevard Jacques Baudino, 83700 ST-RAPHAEL

☎ 04 94 53 66 65 & 06 09 33 16 44 📄 04 94 53 66 65

email: bergerie-vaulongue@orange.fr

web: www.bergerie-vaulongue.com

A 19th-century converted farm building which feels as if it is in the countryside, although it is actually on the outskirts of St-Raphaël. The three spacious, air-conditioned double rooms, all with private shower and WC, are decorated in warm Provençal colours. Outside is a courtyard with sitting and parking space, and Fréjus and St-Tropez are within travelling distance. Meals available by arrangement.

Prices s fr €57; d fr €68; dinner fr €25 **Nearby** ⚓ 5km ⚲ 1km ⚲ 5km
Restaurant 0.2km ⛴ 1km ⛵ 0.5km 🏛 0.5km 🚃 5km **Notes** No pets
English spoken

ST-ZACHARIE

⁂ Le Coup de Vent

Lionel FOURNIER

25 Rue Bringier Monnier, 83640 ST-ZACHARIE

☎ 04 42 72 99 92 & 06 61 00 49 52 📄 04 42 72 99 92

email: trivenel01@aol.com

web: www.lecoupdevent.com

A 17th-century former convent building in a village in the heart of Provence that has been sensitively restored. There are three double bedrooms, all on the second floor, all with TV, private bathroom and WC. Landscaped gardens, terrace, swimming pool. Good area for walking.

Prices not confirmed for 2008 **On Site** Private ⚲ **Nearby** ⚓ 2km
⚲ 10km ⛴ 1.5km 🏛 0.1km 🚃 33km **Notes** No pets

TAVERNES

⁂ Villa des Hermes

Bernard VILLEGIER

Chemin des Clots, 83670 TAVERNES

☎ 04 94 72 35 80 & 06 11 15 38 62

email: Bernard.Villegier@wanadoo.fr

This Provençal house is set in a field of olive trees, with lovely views over the village of Tavernes, renowned for its countryside and olive oil. It offers three double rooms with private facilities and access, a swimming pool, heating and two mountain bikes for guest use. 15km from prehistoric museum at Quinson/Verdon and 60km from Aix-en-Provence.

Prices s fr €40; d fr €55; extra person fr €15 **On Site** Private ⚲
Nearby ⚓ 4km ⚲ 30km ⛴ 1km 🏛 1km **Notes** No pets English spoken
Open April to 15 October.

TOURVES

⁂ Chambre d'hôtes

Pascal DAUGE

Chemin des Rabassieres, 83170 TOURVES

☎ 04 94 59 27 43 & 06 24 04 05 91 📄 04 94 59 27 43

email: ladryade83@orange.fr

web: www.ladryade.com

In a quiet rural spot on the edge of a forest, this is an attractive modern house with more than one hectare of grounds and terraces with garden furniture and plenty of sitting space. The bedrooms are a on the ground floor, three doubles and one with twin beds, each with a private shower room and WC.

Prices not confirmed for 2008 **Nearby** ⚓ 6km ⚲ 15km ⚲ 6km ⛴ 2km
🏛 1km 🚃 45km **Notes** No pets

⊞ ⌾ L'Espérel

Francois DESAUW

Route de Bras, 83170 TOURVES

☎ 04 94 69 32 96 & 06 75 25 89 40

email: contact@esperel.com

web: www.esperel.com

On the edge of a village below the Massif de la Ste Baume, this property is in a beautiful situation and ideally placed for exploring the many local places of interest. The large landscaped gardens face south with wonderful open views. The five bedrooms (three doubles and two twins) have their own entrance and private facilities. Swimming pool and boules pitch, solarium and other leisure facilities; hospitality is excellent and meals can be booked.

Prices s €50-€65; d €60-€70; t €80-€90; extra person fr €20; dinner fr €20 **On Site** Private ↖ **Nearby** ⚓10km ♨10km ♐3km Restaurant 1km ⚐1km ⚑1km **Notes** No pets English spoken

see advert on this page

TRANS-EN-PROVENCE

⊞ St-Amour

Marie-Camille WAHL

986 Route de La Motte, 83720 TRANS-EN-PROVENCE

☎ 04 94 70 88 92 & 06 81 33 43 80 🖺 04 94 70 88 92

email: wahl@domainedesaintamour.com

web: www.domainedesaintamour.com

A splendid 18th-century house in the peaceful solitude of a two hectare park. Ornamental lake, river, waterfall, swans, summer kitchen, barbecue, terrace, car shelter, swimming pool. Three rooms with terrace and separate entrance. Two double rooms, each with sitting area, shower, wc and television and one 'boat' for two people, with bathroom, wc, television and well-equipped kitchenette. Baby facilities.

Prices d €77-€81; extra person fr €19 **On Site** Private ↖ **Nearby** ⚓2km ♨5km Sea 20km ♐0.5km Restaurant 0.9km ♐3km ⚐1km ⚑6km **Notes** Pets admitted English spoken

---

TRIGANCE

⊞ ⌾ Le Priolat des Anges

Frank et Nadine DUPARANT

83840 TRIGANCE

☎ 04 94 85 67 07 & 06 07 68 08 06

email: lepriolatdesanges@wanadoo.fr

This 19th-century Provençal house in landscaped grounds close to the Gorges of Verdon has three bedrooms: a double, a split level room with a double bed and three singles, and another split level room with two doubles. All have private showers/WCs. The area offers an exceptional variety of flora and fauna, and many tourist sites. Meals by arrangement.

Prices s fr €55; d fr €65; extra person fr €25; dinner fr €25 **Nearby** ⚓45km ♨30km ♐4km ↖18km Restaurant 3km ♐2km ⚑18km ⚐2km **Notes** Pets admitted Open 22 March to 13 November.

VINON-SUR-VERDON

⊞ ⌾ La Clape

Thierry GILLET

735 Chemin de la Clape, 83560 VINON-SUR-VERDON

☎ 04 92 78 86 78 & 06 65 16 18 34

email: t.v.gillet@wanadoo.fr

web: http://perso.wanadoo.fr/la_clape_vinonsurverdon

One of the oldest farms in Vinon, situated on the borders of Verdon in the countryside in large grounds. Your hosts extend a warm, friendly welcome and offer five very comfortable rooms in an annexe to their home with private access. These include four doubles, two with extra single beds, and a suite with a lounge area with sofa. There is also a living room, with fireplace, to relax in. Sailing, gliding and kayaking nearby.

Prices s fr €43; d fr €50; t fr €65; extra person fr €12; dinner fr €19 **Nearby** ⚓2km ♨10km ↖10km Restaurant 1.5km ♐2km ⚐2km ⚑10km **Notes** Pets admitted English spoken Open March to 15 October.

VINS-SUR-CARAMY

⦀ Château de Vins

Jean BONNET
83170 VINS-SUR-CARAMY
☎ 04 94 72 50 40 📄 04 94 72 50 88
email: contact@chateaudevins.com
web: www.chateaudevins.com

A 16th-century château with courtyard, loggias, terraces and medieval bridge. Five guest rooms are offered: the 'Campra' suite (two rooms, double and single bed, kitchen area), the 'Couperin' suite for three, and three double rooms 'Fauré', 'Debussy' and 'Berlioz'. Rooms have private facilities.

Prices s fr €60; d fr €78 **Nearby** ⛷ 10km ⚓ 10km ⛳ 0.2km ⚲ 7km Restaurant 4km ⛵ 6km 🏛 0.1km **Notes** Pets admitted English spoken Open April to October.

VAUCLUSE

ALTHEN-LES-PALUDS

⦀ ⦿ Le Clos de la Cousin

Alain BONTON
426 Chemin de Toutblanc, 84210 ALTHEN-LES-PALUDS
☎ 04 90 62 13 88 📄 04 90 62 13 88
email: clos-cousin@wanadoo.fr

Set in verdant countryside, this old farmhouse is typical of the Comtadine region. There is independent access to the accommodation, comprising two rooms and a suite of two bedrooms, all with private facilities. Lounge, TV in the library, fridge, heating, fireplace, terraces with garden furniture and car park. Meals if booked in advance.

Prices s fr €57; d fr €60; t €72-€84; extra person fr €19; dinner fr €25 **Nearby** ⛷ 4km ⚓ 8km ⛳ 2km ⚲ 8km Restaurant 1km ⛵ 45km ⚑ 3km 🏛 0.8km ⚑ 13km **Notes** Pets admitted English spoken Open 15 March to 15 November.

⦀ Le Mas de la Grave

Danielle BUCHERON
181 Route de la Grave, 84210 ALTHEN-LES-PALUDS
☎ 04 90 62 17 53
email: masdelagrave@wanadoo.fr
web: www.masdelagrave.com

This is a restored 19th-century house, in enclosed grounds which open on to an orchard. It has three guest rooms, all with private bath or shower room and WC. Central heating. Lounge with library. Swimming pool, terrace with arbour, garden room and enclosed parking.

Prices s fr €66; d €70-€75 **On Site** Private ⚲ **Nearby** ⛷ 6km ⚓ 10km ⛳ 7km Restaurant 2km ⛵ 30km ⚑ 1km Spa 15km 🏛 1km ⚑ 15km **Notes** No pets English spoken Open December to October.

⦀ Mas de Claire Fontaine

Monique UVERGOELS
198 Chemin des Platanes, 84210 ALTHEN-LES-PALUDS
☎ 04 90 12 02 23 & 06 10 64 32 42
email: monique.uvergoels@wanadoo.fr
web: www.masdeclairefontaine.com

19th-century mas in enclosed grounds in the orchards of Comtat Venaissin. Rooms include three rooms with private bathrooms and heating, a communal lounge, terrace with bower and parking.

Prices s €75-€80; d €75-€80; t €110-€130; extra person fr €285 **On Site** Private ⚲ **Nearby** ⛷ 3km ⚓ 8km ⛳ 1.5km Restaurant 2km ⛵ 40km ⚑ 1km Spa 9km ⛵ 2.5km 🏛 1km ⚑ 17km **Notes** No pets English spoken

---

ANSOUIS

⦀ ⦿ Mas du Grand Lubéron

Gilles RAFER
La Parine, 84240 ANSOUIS
☎ 04 90 09 97 92 & 06 84 76 34 29
web: www.lemasdulub.com

An old house amongst the vineyards just below the village, with a wonderful view of the Lubéron. Five bedrooms are available: two doubles, a twin-bedded room, and two triples (one with three single beds, the other with double bed and single); all have a private shower room and WC. Open grounds, with swimming pool, terrace and parking space. Meals by arrangement.

Prices s fr €60; d fr €70; t fr €90; extra person fr €10; dinner fr €25 **On Site** Private ⚲ **Nearby** ⛷ 5km ⚓ 25km ⛳ 8km Restaurant 0.2km ⚑ 8km Spa 25km 🏛 1km ⚑ 25km **Notes** Pets admitted English spoken Open March to December.

ⅲ ⅰ○ⅰ Un Patio en Luberon

M CUCHE et J-M LEBOSQ

Rue du Grand Four, 84240 ANSOUIS

☎ 04 90 09 94 25 & 06 81 11 64 37

email: patio-en-luberon@wanadoo.fr

web: www.unpatioenluberon.com

This stone-built former royal inn dating back to the 16th century has been fully restored. Situated at the heart of the medieval village at the foot of the château. Open flowery patio, arcades, fountain, view over the Luberon. One first floor bedroom with private shower room/WC. Two second floor bedrooms with private shower room/WCs. Electric heating, shared lounge, dining room with TV and working fireplace. Three parking spaces, one 20mtrs away.

Prices s fr €45-€60; d €55-€70; dinner fr €20 **Nearby** ⛷ 5km ⚓ 45km ⚲ 5km ⚲ 8km Restaurant 0.1km ⚲ 10km ⚲ 8km ⚲ 0.1km ⚲ 40km **Notes** No pets English spoken Open 15 March to December.

APT

ⅲ Les Mylanettes

B HEUZARD LA COUTURE

Par la Rue des Bassins, 84400 APT

☎ 04 90 74 67 15 📠 04 90 74 67 15

email: hlc.jean@wanadoo.fr

Our spacious bedrooms in this fine house in a quiet area on the edge of the town, with panoramic views. Each of the bedrooms has a private bathroom and wc, with possibility of an extra bed. There is also a large living room with fireplace, TV, loggia and terrace. The town centre is within walking distance.

Prices s fr €48; d fr €60; t fr €70; extra person fr €15 **Nearby** ⛷ 5km ⚲ 20km ⚲ 4km Restaurant 0.5km ⚲ 4km ⚲ 0.6km ⚲ 0.5km ⚲ 50km **Notes** Pets admitted English spoken

AUBIGNAN

ⅲ ⅰ○ⅰ Mas d'Aubignan

Lionel ARAKELIAN

Route de Beaumes, Av Anselme Mathieu,

84810 AUBIGNAN

☎ 04 90 62 77 25 📠 04 90 62 68 01

email: mas.daubignan@wanadoo.fr

web: www.masdaubignan-vaucluse.com

A village house with terraces with a shady bower and enclosed garden. It offers three rooms with TV, private facilities and heating, as well as a communal lounge and courtyard with parking. Table d'hôte meals are available by arrangement.

Prices s €65-€110; d €70-€115; extra person fr €15; dinner fr €25 **On Site** Spa **Nearby** ⛷ 1km ⚓ 27km ⚲ 1km ⚲ 3km Restaurant 0.2km ⚲ 30km ⚲ 1km ⚲ 4km ⚲ 0.2km ⚲ 25km **Notes** No pets English spoken

AUREL

ⅲ ⅰ○ⅰ Pierre de Lune

Marie-José VINCENT

84390 AUREL

☎ 04 90 64 13 58

email: pierrelune@wanadoo.fr

web: www.guideweb.com

This is a modern house in a beautiful situation with a view of the village and the mountains. It has three bedrooms in an annexe, all with private bath or shower room and WC. Electric heating. There is a lounge with TV. In the open grounds are two terraces and shady parking. Meals by arrangement. Pets admitted by arrangement.

Prices s fr €78; d fr €78; extra person fr €17; dinner fr €27 **On Site** Private **Nearby** ⛷ 5km ⚲ 10km Restaurant 2km ⚲ 20km ⚲ 4km Spa 5km ⚲ 4km ⚲ 4km **Notes** Pets admitted English spoken Open 15 March to 15 November.

AVIGNON-MONTFAVET

ⅲ Chambre d'hôtes

Jean-Michel MOUZAC

1044 Chemin de Sourdaine, Montfavet,

84140 AVIGNON-MONTFAVET

☎ 04 90 89 77 81 📠 04 90 89 77 81

email: clos.st.pierre@libertysurf.fr

web: www.clos-st-pierre.fr.st

The green belt just south of Avignon is the location for this mas with swimming pool and enclosed grounds. The two bedrooms are accessible by a communal lounge reserved for guests and have private facilities, TVs and one has a kitchen. Heating and open fire, terrace, gardens and car park.

Prices s €50-€75; d €60-€90; t fr €105 **On Site** Private **Nearby** ⛷ 8km ⚓ 6km ⚲ 3km ⚲ 2km ⚲ 2.5km ⚲ 6km **Notes** No pets English spoken

AVIGNON/ILE-DE-LA-BARTHELASSE

ⅲ La Bastide des Papes

Laurence ROUBY

Des Poiriers, Ile de la Barthelasse,

84000 AVIGNON/ILE-DE-LA-BARTHELASSE

☎ 04 90 86 09 42 📠 04 90 82 38 30

email: bastidedespapes@free.fr

web: www.bastidedespapes.fr

This renovated country house, formerly home to the family of Pope Innocent VI, is set in the orchards of the Ile de Barthelasse. There is a private swimming pool on the four-hectare estate, and five bedrooms with TVs and private facilities. Heating and shared living room with fireplace. Library, TV and kitchen at the guests' disposal. Meals provided certain evenings.

Prices s €85-€114; d €90-€120; t €110-€140; extra person fr €20 **On Site** Private **Nearby** ⛷ 1km ⚓ 15km ⚲ 0.5km ⚲ 1km ⚲ 6km ⚲ 6km **Notes** No pets English spoken

AVIGNON/
ILE-DE-LA-BARTHELASSE CONTINUED

▦ ▯◯ï Le Mas de L'Ile

J SERGE et P DEMORISSI

1261 Chemin des Canotiers, Ile de la Barthelesse,
84000 AVIGNON/ILE-DE-LA-BARTHELASSE

☎ 04 90 85 68 65 & 06 87 84 93 29

email: info@masdelile.com

web: www.masdelile.com

A stone-built house in the countryside with three double bedrooms
and a family room for four. All the rooms are air-conditioned, with
private bathroom and WC. Sitting room with TV, and meals are
available by arrangement. The spacious grounds face south, with a
large terrace area.

Prices s €50-€80; d €50-€95; t €50-€115; extra person fr €20;
dinner fr €23 **On Site** Private ⚲ **Nearby** ⚑ 3km ⚓ 8km
⚑ 0.5km Restaurant 1km ⚓ 40km ⚓ 3km ⚑ 4km ⚑ 2km ⚑ 8km
Notes No pets

BEAUMES-DE-VENISE

▦ ▯◯ï Le Clos Saint Saourde

G et J THUILLIER

Route de St Véran, 84190 BEAUMES-DE-VENISE

☎ 04 90 37 35 20 & 06 99 41 44 19

email: contact@leclossaintsaourde.com

web: www.leclossaintsaourde.com

An 18th-century house with stylish and original decorations, in the
heart of the vineyards where Muscat wine is produced. Two
double bedded rooms, and two triples with a double bed and a
single in each, each having private bath or shower room/WC.
Outside is a salt-water swimming pool, and a wonderful view.
Meals by arrangement. A non-smoking property.

Prices d €120-€190; extra person fr €40; dinner fr €35
On Site Private ⚲ **Nearby** ⚑ 3km ⚓ 15km ⚓ 3km
Restaurant 2km ⚓ 25km ⚓ 2km ⚑ 4km ⚑ 2km ⚑ 18km
Notes No pets English spoken

BEDOIN

▦ Les Colombets

B et G BERARD

Chambre d'Hôtes de Curnier, 84410 BEDOIN

☎ 04 90 65 65 79 & 06 21 72 09 65

There are three ground floor bedrooms in an annexe to this old
farmhouse at the foot of Mont Ventoux, near to the GR3 long-distance
footpath. All of the rooms have TVs, and private shower rooms/WCs.
Lounge area with books; guests' kitchen, terrace, open grounds.

Prices s fr €45; d fr €54; t fr €64; extra person fr €15 **Nearby** ⚑ 3km
⚓ 30km ⚑ 10km ⚲ 3km Restaurant 2.5km ⚓ 15km ⚓ 3km Spa 30km
⚑ 2.5km ⚑ 30km **Notes** No pets

BOLLENE

▦ ♿ Au Cor de Chasse

Jean-Luc TAUPIN

159 Route de la Palud, 84500 BOLLENE

☎ 04 32 80 21 13 & 06 98 41 80 73 ▤ 04 32 80 21 13

email: au-cor-de-chasse@orange.fr

This property is the western part of a restored farmhouse with an
enclosed courtyard for the private use of guests. The three guest
rooms are in an annexe which adjoins the owners' house. They are
all on the ground floor with TVs and en suite shower rooms and WCs.
Electric heating. Terrace.

Prices s fr €40; d fr €52; extra person fr €16 **Nearby** ⚑ 7km ⚓ 10km
⚑ 1km ⚲ Restaurant 4km ⚓ 4km ⚑ 4km ⚑ 5km **Notes** Pets
admitted

▦ *Mas Lou Geneste*

P et T FERNANDEZ

Route de Suze, 84500 BOLLENE

☎ 04 90 40 01 07 ▤ 04 90 40 01 07

email: infos@lougeneste.com

web: www.lougeneste.com

A 19th-century Provençal property in large grounds with a swimming
pool, and south-facing terrace. One ground floor bedroom with
private terrace, one first floor bedroom, both with private bathroom
and WC. One first floor family room with two bathrooms and two
WCs. One bedroom sleeping four with shower room and private WC.
Electric heating. Kitchen shared between two bedrooms on request.
Shared lounge with fireplace. Parking.

Prices not confirmed for 2008 **On Site** Private ⚲ **Nearby** ⚑ 7km
⚓ 20km ⚑ 0.3km ⚓ 50km ⚓ 3km ⚑ 4km ⚑ 20km **Notes** No pets
English spoken

BONNIEUX

⅋⅋⅋ ⅋○⅋ Le Clos du Buis

M. MAURIN

Rue Victor Hugo, 84480 BONNIEUX

☎ 04 90 75 88 48 & 06 08 63 64 76   📠 04 90 75 88 57

email: le-clos-du-buis@wanadoo.fr

web: www.leclosdubuis.com

A beautifully restored village house with swimming pool and large enclosed garden with trees offering wonderful panoramic views of Mont-Ventoux and the Lubéron countryside. There are six rooms with private facilities, one of which is a family suite. Gas central heating, shared living room with library and TV, open fire, veranda, and enclosed parking. Meals if required. Wi-fi available.

Prices s €84-€120; d €84-€120; extra person fr €15; dinner fr €25 **On Site** Private ⅋ **Nearby** ⅋ 3km ⅋ 18km ⅋ 15km Restaurant 0km ⅋ 0.1km ⅋ 0.1km ⅋ 45km **Notes** No pets English spoken

⅋⅋⅋ ⅋○⅋ Les Terrasses du Lubéron

Sabine KEUKENBRING

Quartier les Bruillères, 84480 BONNIEUX

☎ 04 90 75 87 40

email: info@terrasses-luberon.com

web: www.terrasses-luberon.com

This property has three ground floor bedrooms in an annexe to the owners' home, all with a private bath or shower rooms and WCs. Each room has a private terrace with views towards Mont Ventoux. Swimming pool, enclosed parking. Low season reductions.

Prices s €60-€85; d €70-€95; extra person fr €20; dinner fr €25 **On Site** Private ⅋ **Nearby** ⅋ 0.8km ⅋ 15km ⅋ 10km Restaurant 0.5km ⅋ 0.8km ⅋ 0.5km ⅋ 0.5km ⅋ 40km **Notes** No pets English spoken Open 15 January to 15 December.

BUISSON

⅋⅋⅋ L'École Buissonnière

M et J ALEX-PARSONS

Les Prés - D75, 84110 BUISSON / VAISON LA ROMAINE

☎ 04 90 28 95 19

email: ecole.buissonniere@wanadoo.fr

web: www.buissonniere-provence.com

An attractive house, pleasantly restored on the edge of a quiet country lane with an enclosed courtyard, open garden and offering three bedrooms. Upstairs there is one room with shower and private wc, one with bathroom and wc, and a third with mezzanine, shower, wc, and private balcony. Central and underfloor heating. Shared living room with open fireplace, library, TV, telephone and car park.

Prices s €45-€48; d €55-€63; t €70-€78; extra person €16-€19 **Nearby** ⅋ 4km ⅋ 25km ⅋ 0.5km ⅋ 7km Restaurant 1km ⅋ 45km ⅋ 1.5km ⅋ 1km ⅋ 45km **Notes** Pets admitted English spoken Open Easter to 1 November.

⅋⅋⅋ ⅋○⅋ Mas de Grateloup

R PEILLOT et P DAVIET

84110 BUISSON

☎ 04 90 28 17 95 & 06 73 23 41 78

email: masgrateloup@wanadoo.fr

web: www.masgrateloup.com

Authentic Provençal farm dating back to the 18th century with a swimming pool. Terraces, two hectares of grounds with pine forest, hundred-year-old trees and lovely views. Two ground floor suites with separate entrance, one with terrace; private bathrooms and WCs. Two first floor bedrooms with separate entrance, private shower rooms and WCs. One first floor suite with separate entrance, bathroom, WC and private terrace. Electric heating. Lounge with TV, reading corner. Boules. Parking.

Prices s €50-€60; d €65-€75; t €80-€100; extra person €15-€20; dinner €15-€27 **On Site** Private ⅋ **Nearby** ⅋ 2km ⅋ 20km ⅋ 2km Restaurant 2km ⅋ 40km ⅋ 2km ⅋ 10km ⅋ 2km ⅋ 50km **Notes** Pets admitted English spoken

CABRIERES-D'AVIGNON

⅋⅋⅋ ⅋ Chambre d'hôtes Le Jardinage

André BRIEULLE

Clos de Roque, 84220 CABRIERES-D'AVIGNON

☎ 04 90 76 87 92   📠 04 90 76 87 46

email: closderoque@free.fr

web: http://closderoque.free.fr

This is the south-eastern part of a 19th-century house, with an enclosed courtyard, swimming pool and summer dining room. There are three first floor rooms with private showers and WCs, and a second floor room, also with private facilities, which has air-conditioning. Central heating, lounge with TV, terrace and parking. Pets admitted by arrangement.

Prices d €80-€100; extra person fr €15 **On Site** Private ⅋ **Nearby** ⅋ 10km ⅋ 12km ⅋ 10km Restaurant 1km ⅋ 12km Spa 5km ⅋ 1km ⅋ 1km ⅋ 30km **Notes** Pets admitted English spoken

⅋⅋⅋ La Magnanerie

Magali FRANTZ

84220 CABRIERES-D'AVIGNON

☎ 04 90 76 89 65   📠 04 90 76 82 35

email: magali.frantz@wanadoo.fr

Beautiful 18th-century mas, with swimming pool, patio and enclosed courtyard surrounded by vines. Three rooms with private facilities, one with private terrace. Central heating, shared living room, lounge, dining room and open fireplace. TV, telephone, terrace, and car park.

Prices d €65-€105 **On Site** Private ⅋ **Nearby** ⅋ 10km ⅋ 10km ⅋ 10km Restaurant 0.5km ⅋ 12km ⅋ 1km ⅋ 12km **Notes** No pets English spoken Open Easter to October.

CADENET

‖‖ ⏐◌⏐ Domaine du Colimaçon

E et D VELON

Chemin Desportis, 84160 CADENET

☎ 04 90 08 55 06

email: domaineducolimacon@wanadoo.fr

web: www.luberon-lourmarin.com

This is an authentic Provençal house one kilometre from the edge of the village, in a calm and serene setting. There are five guest rooms, three of them family rooms and one a suite, all with private facilities. From the vast terrace, the view is superb. Landscaped gardens bordering parkland. Parking. Meals available three evenings a week.

Prices s €67-€83; d €67-€83; t €83-€99; extra person fr €16; dinner fr €23 **On Site** ☀ Private ⌇ **Nearby** ⛵ 0.5km ↥15km ⚘ 2km Restaurant 1km ◔ 1km ⛪ 1km ⋙ 12km **Notes** No pets English spoken

‖‖ ⏐◌⏐ *La Bastide des Vérunes*

Sylviane et Lucien ROMAN

Route de Pertuis, 84160 CADENET

☎ 04 90 08 31 54 & 06 16 55 10 64 ⏐ 04 90 08 31 54

email: sylviane.roman@orange.fr

web: www.bastidedesverunes.com

A 12th-century house with a beautiful stone facade, standing in 10 hectares of grounds. There are four spacious first floor rooms - two doubles, a twin-bedded room and a triple, all with private shower room and WC; one has a small terrace. Living room with an open fireplace; outside are orchards and a terrace.

Prices not confirmed for 2008 **Nearby** ⛵ 0.5km ↥30km ⚘ 5km ⌇ 10km ◔ 2km ⛪ 1.5km ⋙ 35km **Notes** Pets admitted English spoken

‖‖ ⏐◌⏐ La Tuilière

C et D BORGARINO

84160 CADENET

☎ 04 90 68 24 45 ⏐ 04 90 68 24 45

email: clo@latuiliere.com

web: www.latuiliere.com

Large 18th-century farmhouse with gardens and swimming pool, on a private estate of 12 hectares of vines and woods just 700 metres from the village. There are five rooms with private facilities, heating and separate exterior access. Terraces and car park. Meals if required. Low season tariff.

Prices d €69-€85; t €86-€101; extra person fr €16; dinner fr €22 **On Site** Private ⌇ **Nearby** ⛵ 2km ↥20km ⚘ 2km Restaurant 0.7km ◔ 1km ☀ 6km ⛪ 1km **Notes** No pets English spoken CC

CAIRANNE

‖‖ ⏐◌⏐ Le Vieux Platane

Mirjam PHILIPPI

Les Sablières, 84290 CAIRANNE

☎ 04 90 30 77 04 ⏐ 04 90 30 78 15

email: mphilippi@levieuxplatane.fr

web: www.levieuxplatane.fr

An ancient mill standing in open country, in 1 hectare of unfenced grounds featuring a swimming pool, terrace and parking. The rooms have private facilities and heating and include two family suites (each two rooms). There is a communal living room and dining room where table d'hôte meals are served three evenings a week by arrangement. Apéritif, wine and coffee are included.

Prices s fr €64; d €80-€95; t €110-€125; dinner fr €30 **On Site** ☀ Private ⌇ **Nearby** ⛵ 0.1km ↥15km ⚘ 0.3km Restaurant 0.8km ⛵ 40km ◔ 1.5km ⛪ 0.8km ⋙ 15km **Notes** No pets English spoken

CAROMB

‖‖‖ Chambre d'hôtes

Françoise VAZQUEZ

24, Rue des Petites Aires, 84330 CAROMB

☎ 04 90 12 78 38 & 06 75 55 00 22

email: francoisevazquez@aol.com

At the heart of the village of Caromb, this lovely building has a large enclosed courtyard, terrace and ornamental pond. Lounge with library, TV and fireplace. First floor: two doubles with own shower room, WC and small lounge. Courtyard annexe suite with ground floor lounge, kitchenette, shower room and WC. First floor double bedroom (reached via loft ladder). Parking 200mtrs.

Prices s €70-€100; d €80-€110 **On Site** Private ⌇ **Nearby** ⛵ 7km ↥22km ⚘ 2km ⌇ 20km ◔ 1km ⋙ 25km **Notes** No pets Open May to July.

CARPENTRAS

‖‖‖ Bastide Sainte Agnès

Maryse et Michel PINBOUEN

Chemin de la Fourtrouse, 84200 CARPENTRAS

☎ 04 90 60 03 01 ⏐ 04 90 60 02 53

email: pinbouenmichel@aol.com

web: www.sainte-agnes.com

Numerous restaurants are within easy reach of this old, pleasantly restored mas with swimming pool. There is a suite of two bedrooms with living room, equipped kitchen, TV, telephone, terrace, garden and private barbecue, and five further bedrooms with private facilities. Lounge with TV, library, living room, dining room, fireplace and terrace. Beautiful enclosed garden, boules area and car park. Excellent breakfasts for those with a sweet tooth. Picnics and barbecues possible.

Prices s €72-€82; d €76-€120; t €105-€140; extra person fr €30 **On Site** Private ⌇ **Nearby** ⏚ 9km ⌇15km ✍ 6km Restaurant 3km ⛵25km ⌇2km ⌂2.5km ⋙20km **Notes** No pets English spoken CC

CAUMONT-SUR-DURANCE

▦ ⍾ *Chambre d'hôtes*

Patricia GROSJEAN

3 Rue du Posterlon, 84510 CAUMONT-SUR-DURANCE
☎ 04 90 22 21 20 & 06 60 83 93 71 📄 04 90 33 77 49

From its position just above the village, this house has a beautiful view of the Lubéron. There are two double bedrooms, two triples and a family room for four, all with TV, private bathroom and WC. The garden is enclosed, and there is a swimming pool. The breakfasts are generous with home-made items, and other meals are available by arrangement.

Prices not confirmed for 2008 **On Site** Private ⌇ **Nearby** ⏚ 2km ⌇6km ✍ 3km ⌇0.3km ⌂0.2km ⋙15km **Notes** No pets

▦ La Bastide des Amouriers

B et M DURAND-PROIA

117 Chemin de St Estève,
84510 CAUMONT-SUR-DURANCE
☎ 04 90 03 39 31 & 04 90 01 28 67
email: labastide@lesamouriers.com
web: www.lesamouriers.com

This is a 19th-century house which has been very pleasantly restored. It offers four spacious guest rooms on the first floor with private showers and WCs. Lounge with books. Central heating. Large unfenced garden with terrace. Parking. Possible courses in painting on wood, out of season.

Prices s fr €50; d fr €65; t fr €80; extra person fr €20 **Nearby** ⏚ 4km ⌇4km ✍ 2km ⌇ Restaurant 9km ⛵40km ⌇2km ❀5km ⌂2km ⋙18km **Notes** No pets English spoken

CAVAILLON

▦ ⍾ Le Mas des Amandiers

Chantal LORBER

1539 Chemin des Puits Neufs, 84300 CAVAILLON
☎ 04 90 06 29 60 📄 04 90 06 29 60
email: bb@mas-des-amandiers.com
web: www.mas-des-amandiers.com

A superb 18th-century property, the almond grove has a pool protected by a wall, pool-house, closed parking. One ground floor bedroom and two first floor bedrooms, all with private bathroom/WC. Electric heating. Breakfasts are served on the shady terrace amongst flowers or in the dining room. Evening meals offered Tuesday, Thursday and Saturday. Painting lessons available.

Prices s €70-€80; d €75-€85; extra person fr €20; dinner fr €27 **On Site** Private ⌇ **Nearby** ⏚ 10km ⌇15km ✍ 15km Restaurant 4km ⛵3km Spa 4km ⌂3km ⋙4km **Notes** No pets English spoken Open March to December.

▦ ⍾ Le Mas du Platane

Noël et Danièle MAUREL

22 Qu. des Trente Mouttes, 84300 CAVAILLON
☎ 04 90 78 29 99 📄 04 90 78 35 17
email: noel.maurel@wanadoo.fr
web: http://lemasduplatane.free.fr

Two suites and one bedroom are offered in this restored mas, set among fields in the countryside. Rooms have private facilities and benefit from heating, a shared living room with fireplace, library, TV and telephone. Terrace and car park; meals by reservation.

Prices s fr €75; d fr €85; t fr €105; extra person fr €15 **On Site** Private ⌇ **Nearby** ⏚ 3km ⌇8km ✍ 4km ⌇2km ⌂1km ⋙4km **Notes** No pets English spoken

CHEVAL-BLANC

▦ ⍾ La Malleposte

Colette et Thierry HAMEL

5760 B Route de Pertuis, 84460 CHEVAL-BLANC
☎ 04 90 72 89 26 📄 04 90 72 88 38
email: info@malle-poste.com
web: www.malle-poste.com

Old 18th-century coaching house on the banks of the Carpentras canal in a small Lubéron park with swimming pool and extensive wooded grounds. There are five bedrooms with TVs and private facilities, heating, dining room, sitting room with library and lounge with a fireplace. There is also a billiard room, terrace, boules area and table tennis.

Prices s fr €84; d €90-€110; t fr €110; extra person fr €20; dinner fr €26 **On Site** Private ⌇ **Nearby** ⏚ 0.5km ⌇10km ✍ 7km Restaurant 7km ⛵6km ⌂6km ⋙12km **Notes** No pets English spoken Open 15 March to 15 November. CC

CRESTET

▦ ⍾ *Les Romarins*

Marc UGHETTO

Chemin des Ramières, 84110 CRESTET
☎ 04 90 36 39 03 & 06 63 18 13 74 📄 04 90 36 39 03
email: ughettom@club-internet.fr
web: http://les.romarins.free.fr

This property consists of a small group of buildings in a peaceful position below Mont Ventoux and the medieval village of Crestet. It offers two double rooms, a twin-bedded room, and two family rooms for up to five people. Each has private facilities, fridge, microwave and a terrace. Guests' utility area with washing machine, dishwasher; large grounds with parking space.

Prices not confirmed for 2008 **On Site** Private ⌇ **Nearby** ⏚ 5km ✍ 5km ⌇0.5km ⌂3km **Notes** Pets admitted

CRILLON-LE-BRAVE

⊪ ⏃ Domaine la Condamine

Marie-Josée EYDOUX
84410 CRILLON-LE-BRAVE
☎ 06 77 98 21 29 & 04 90 62 47 28   04 90 62 47 28
email: domlacondamine@hotmail.com
web: www.lacondamine.info

This large mas is set in hills at the foot of the Mont-Ventoux, on a wine producing estate. There are four rooms and a suite of two bedrooms with kitchenette and living room; all have private facilities. Heating, lounge with reading material and TV, summer kitchen, barbecue and arbour. Terrace, car park and gardens with swimming pool. Meals by arrangement.

Prices s fr €62; d fr €64; t fr €120; dinner fr €27   **On Site** Private ⏃
Nearby ⚲ 4km ⚑ 30km ⚘ 5km Restaurant 1km ⚓ 15km ⚴ 1km
Spa 30km ⚘ 4km ⚑ 4km ⚌ 30km   **Notes** No pets English spoken

⊪ ⏃ Moulin d'Antelon

M-Luce et Valérie RICQUART
Route de Bédoin, 84410 CRILLON-LE-BRAVE
☎ 04 90 62 44 89   04 90 62 44 89
email: moulin-dantelon@wanadoo.fr
web: www.moulin-dantelon.com

An old wheat mill, this large 1820 farmhouse overlooks a park, with large swimming pool and stream. It has five bedrooms, three in an annexe and all with private facilities. Central heating and parking facilities. Pets allowed except July and August. Meals by reservation.

Prices s €59-€62; d €66-€68; t €95-€105; extra person fr €25; dinner fr €24   **On Site** Private ⏃   **Nearby** ⚑ 3.5km ⚑ 30km Restaurant 0.1km ⚴ 3.5km ⚑ 2km ⚌ 40km   **Notes** English spoken CC

ENTRAIGUES-SUR-LA-SORGUE

⊪ ⏃ Le Moulin de Souchière

Anca BOURDON
279 Route de Saint Albergaty,
84320 ENTRAIGUES-SUR-LA-SORGUE
☎ 04 90 48 00 20   04 90 31 71 95
email: souchieres@wanadoo.fr
web: www.lemoulindesouchieres.com

Old 19th-century mill set in wooded grounds with a swimming pool, bordered by two streams with a view of Mont-Ventoux. There are five rooms with private facilities, heating, shared lounge with fireplace and TV. Library, telephone, terrace, covered shelter and car park.

Prices s €76-€98; d €76-€93; t €76-€138; dinner €13-€29   **On Site** ⚘
Private ⏃   **Nearby** ⚲ 3km ⚑ 7km Restaurant 2km ⚓ 37km ⚴ 3km
Spa 15km ⚑ 2km ⚌ 15km   **Notes** No pets English spoken Open
2 April to 17 November.

⊪ ⏃ Villa Liberty

J et A-M VANHOORNE
744 Chemin du Rialet,
84320 ENTRAIGUES-SUR-LA-SORGUE
☎ 04 90 22 24 83 & 06 14 11 53 76
email: info@villa-liberty.com
web: www.villa-liberty.com

A Provençal house with swimming pool and spa bath. Four twin-bedded rooms and a family room with a double bed and two singles, all having private facilities - bath or shower room and WC. The property is among vineyards, and the grounds extend to two hectares, with trees. Prices include breakfast and dinner.

Prices s €90-€140; d €130-€190; extra person fr €35; dinner fr €25
On Site Private ⏃   **Nearby** ⚲ 5km ⚑ 6km ⚘ 0.3km Restaurant 5km
⚴ 5km Spa 12km ⚑ 4km ⚌ 12km   **Notes** No pets English spoken CC

ENTRECHAUX

⊪ ⏃ L'Escleriade

Mady ALEXANDRE
Route de Saint Marcellin, 84340 ENTRECHAUX
☎ 04 90 46 01 32 & 04 90 46 03 71   04 90 46 03 71
email: lescleriade@wanadoo.fr
web: www.escleriade.com

This rural property is in an exceptional setting with a swimming pool, shaded park and picnic area on the banks of the river. There are four bedrooms and a suite with telephone, TV, private facilities and some have a terrace. Heating, shared living room, library and fridge. Outside is a boules ground, enclosed garden and secure car park.

Prices s €98-€160; d €98-€160; t €118-€160; extra person fr €20;
dinner fr €25   **On Site** ⚘ Private ⏃   **Nearby** ⚲ 1.5km ⚑ 20km
Restaurant 6km ⚓ 25km ⚴ 1.5km ⚘ 6km ⚑ 2km ⚌ 30km
Notes No pets English spoken CC

⁝⁝⁝ La Bastide des Gramuses

Christiane REYNAUD

84340 ENTRECHAUX

☎ 04 90 46 01 08 🖹 04 90 46 01 08

email: contact@lesgramuses.com

web: www.lesgramuses.com

A beautifully restored 17th-century farmhouse with swimming pool and a panoramic view. There are three first floor bedrooms, two doubles and a twin, each with a private bath or shower room, WC, internet access and small fridge. Outside is a terrace, courtyard, parking space and a summer cooking area with barbecue.

Prices s fr €90; d fr €100; extra person fr €30　**On Site** Private ⚡ **Nearby** ⚓ 3km ⚡ 30km ✐ 3km　Restaurant 1.5km ⚓ 25km ☕ 1km ⚡ 7km 🏛 1.5km ⚓ 35km　**Notes** No pets English spoken

---

GORDES

⁝⁝⁝ ♿ La Badelle

Michèle CORTASSE

84220 GORDES

☎ 04 90 72 33 19 & 06 07 98 58 80 🖹 04 90 72 48 74

email: badelle@club-internet.fr

web: www.la-badelle.com

A pleasant new construction with terrace and awning, next to an old farm with open grounds of one hectare including a swimming pool. It offers five bedrooms with private facilities, heating, summer dining room, open kitchen and well-designed veranda at guests' disposal. Car park.

Prices s €79-€90; d €84-€111; t €116-€127; extra person fr €16　**On Site** ⚡ Private ⚡ **Nearby** ⚓ 7km ⚡ 15km ✐ 15km Restaurant 4km ☕ 7km Spa 6km 🏛 4km ⚓ 45km　**Notes** No pets English spoken

⁝⁝⁝ ♥ Les Martins

Martial PEYRON

84220 GORDES

☎ 04 90 72 24 15

email: lesdemoiselles@wanadoo.fr

Among the vines, just outside a hamlet, this charming farm has four bedrooms, each with private shower and wc. Heating, shared living room, enclosed garden and terraces, capturing the sun or shade. Reduction of 10% after ten nights.

Prices not confirmed for 2008　**Nearby** ⚓ 3km ⚡ 10km ✐ 10km ⚡ 5km ☕ 5km 🏛 2km ⚓ 15km　**Notes** No pets　Open 15 February to 15 November.

⁝⁝⁝ Mas de Belle Combe

Micheline et Alain BIDAULT

Les Rapières, 84220 GORDES

☎ 04 32 50 22 52 & 06 27 06 81 40

email: masdebellecombe@aol.com

web: www.masdebellecombe.com

An impressive property on a south-facing hill just outside the village. There are four double bedrooms, and a suite with a double bedroom and separate living area. All have television, private terrace, en suite bath/shower room and WC. The landscaped grounds have olive trees, oaks, lavender bushes, a swimming pool with pool house - and some wonderful views.

Prices s €90-€150; d €90-€150; t €115-€185; extra person €25-€30; dinner fr €35　**On Site** Private ⚡ **Nearby** ⚓ 5km ⚡ 15km ✐ 20km Restaurant 1km ☕ 45km ⚡ 5km Spa 5km 🏛 0.5km ⚓ 35km　**Notes** No pets English spoken Open 31 March to October.

⁝⁝⁝ Mas de la Beaume

Miguel et Wendy WILLEMS

84220 GORDES

☎ 04 90 72 02 96 🖹 04 90 72 06 89

email: la.beaume@wanadoo.fr

web: www.labeaume.com

This old mas at the entrance of a village enjoys a very fine view of a château, church and Lubéron countryside. There are three bedrooms and two suites, all with private facilities and terraces. Central heating, shared living room, car park and large enclosed garden.

Prices d €115-€175; extra person fr €35　**On Site** Private ⚡ **Nearby** ⚓ 10km ⚡ 20km Restaurant 0.8km ⚡ 2km Spa 0.8km 🏛 0.8km ⚓ 25km　**Notes** No pets English spoken

⁝⁝⁝ Mas des Oliviers

Isabelle DONAT

Près de Saint Pantaléon, Les Coucourdons, 84220 GORDES

☎ 04 90 72 43 90 & 06 77 70 90 92 🖹 04 90 72 43 90

email: mas-des-oliviers@club-internet.fr

web: www.masdesoliviers.fr

A new stone-built farmhouse and swimming pool in olive groves with a panoramic view of the Lubéron, Bonnieux and the Ochres de Roussillon. It provides five bedrooms, each with private facilities and terrace. Heating, dining room, veranda, terrace, barbecue and summer kitchen at guests' disposal in the pool house. Car park, boules area and table tennis.

Prices s €65-€72; d €74-€105; extra person fr €16　**On Site** Private ⚡ **Nearby** ⚓ 6km ⚡ 16km Sea 0.1km ✐ 15km Restaurant 4km ⚡ 7km 🏛 5km ⚓ 16km　**Notes** No pets English spoken

GORDES   CONTINUED

⁂ Mas des Poncets

Anne-Marie JOYEUX

Chemin de Fontcaudette, 84220 GORDES

☎ 04 90 72 26 58 & 06 62 33 56 64

email: masdesponcets@wanadoo.fr

web: http://perso.wanadoo.fr/masdesponcets

A beautiful stone-built house with swimming pool and a wonderful view across the Lubéron. There are two double rooms and a twin-bedded room with independent outside access. Each has a shower room and WC, fridge and a private terrace. Baby equipment available if needed. Enclosed garden with terrace.

Prices s fr €75; d fr €75; extra person fr €25   **On Site** Private ↖
Nearby ⛷ 12km ♨ 10km ⚓ 12km Restaurant 3km ♒ 5km Spa 4km
🏛 3.5km ⛵ 30km   **Notes** No pets English spoken

⁂ Mas des Étoiles

A et F FOREST-LEPOUTRE

Hameau des Imberts, Quartier Dragonne, 84220 GORDES

☎ 04 90 05 85 53 📠 04 90 05 85 53

email: francois@etoiles-luberon.com

web: www.chambre-hote-gordes.com

A beautiful stone-built house in quiet countryside with a swimming pool and views across vineyards and the Lubéron. There are four double bedrooms and a twin-bedded room, all with private bath or shower room and WC. Outside is a large enclosed garden with terrace and parking space.

Prices d €115-€170; extra person €20-€30   **On Site** Private ↖
Nearby ⛷ 6km ♨ 10km Sea 0.1km ⚓ 8km Restaurant 0.1km
♒ 3km Spa 0.5km 🏛 4km ⛵ 8km   **Notes** No pets English spoken
Open April to October. CC

GOULT

⁂ ۞ *La Borie*

D et A PAUWELS

Chemin de la Verrière, 84220 GOULT

☎ 04 90 72 35 84 📠 04 90 72 44 46

email: alfred.pauwels@wanadoo.fr

web: www.la-borie.com

A very fine 17th-century bastide with beautiful landscaped gardens which has been pleasantly restored to provide four bedrooms in an annexe, three with fridge and TV, and all with private facilities. Heating, shared living room with fireplace and library, swimming pool and tennis court. A well-placed awning for meals, which are available Mondays, Wednesdays and Fridays.

Prices not confirmed for 2008   **On Site** Private ↖   **Nearby** ⛷ 8km
♨ 25km ⚓ 20km ♒ 1km ⛵ 40km   **Notes** No pets

⁂ ۞ ۞ Mas Marican

Maryline et Claude CHABAUD

84220 GOULT

☎ 04 90 72 28 09 📠 04 90 72 28 09

Come and discover this restored 18th-century country mas, which is situated on a working farm and benefits from tranquillity and fine views. There are five bedrooms with private facilities, heating, shared living room, terrace, interior courtyard and car park. No meals provided on Sundays and public holidays.

Prices s fr €39; d fr €50; t fr €66; dinner fr €20   **On Site** ۞
Nearby ♨ 20km ⚓ 15km ↖ 15km Restaurant 3km ♒ 3km 🏛 2km
⛵ 40km   **Notes** No pets English spoken Open 15 February to 15 November.

GRAMBOIS

⁂ Le Jas de Monsieur

Monique MAZEL

84240 GRAMBOIS

☎ 04 90 77 92 08 & 06 72 79 32 51

email: lejasdemonsieur@orange.fr

web: lejasdemonsieur.com

Large 18th-century country residence set in 130 hectares in a charming spot in the heart of the South Lubéron national park. Choose between three bedrooms with bathroom and private wc. There is central heating, a terrace, and the park, with private footpaths at the guests' disposal.

Prices d €65-€80   **Nearby** ⛷ 5km ♨ 11km ⚓ 12km ↖
Restaurant 2.9km ♒ 5km Spa 30km ۞ 11km 🏛 3km ⛵ 11km
Notes No pets English spoken

GRILLON

⁂ ۞ Au Vieux Chêne

Yvette HILAIRE

Ancienne Route de Valréas, 84600 GRILLON

☎ 04 90 35 24 47 📠 04 90 35 24 47

Lavender fields are the setting for this property, which offers four bedrooms with private facilities, accessed from a covered terrace. Heating, lounge-living room and kitchen. Breakfasts are served in the living room or on the terrace; meals available by reservation.

Prices s fr €45; d fr €48; extra person fr €15   **Nearby** ⛷ 4km ♨ 10km
⚓ 3km ↖ 4km Restaurant 4km ♒ 1km 🏛 1km ⛵ 35km   **Notes** Pets
admitted Open 5 February to 15 November.

ⅢⅢ ⅠⓄⅠ Les Buis d'Augusta

Geneviève SPIERS

Av du Comtat, 84600 GRILLON

☎ 04 90 35 29 18 & 06 09 89 86 78

🗎 04 90 37 41 86

email: gdspiers@club-internet.fr

web: www.buisdaugusta.com

Set in a large shady park, this beautiful house has authentic charm and six spacious and well-decorated bedrooms, two of which are two bedroomed suites and one is a mezzanine. All have TV, private facilities, hairdryer and bathrobes. There is heating, a lounge with fireplace and magazines, courtyard, terraces, sauna, table-tennis, bicycles, saltwater swimming pool and phone.

Prices s €80-€100; d €85-€100; t €120-€135; extra person fr €30; dinner fr €35 **On Site** Private ⚲ **Nearby** ⚓ 4km ⚑ 8km ⚏ 1km Restaurant 3km ⚇ 1km 🏛 0.2km ⮔ 35km **Notes** Pets admitted English spoken

---

ISLE-SUR-LA-SORGUE

ⅢⅢ ⅠⓄⅠ Domaine de la Fontaine

I et D SUNDHEIMER

920 Chemin du Bosquet, 84800 ISLE-SUR-LA-SORGUE

☎ 04 90 38 01 44 🗎 04 90 38 53 42

email: contact@domainedelafontaine.com

web: www.domainedelafontaine.com

A restored 19th-century mas set in large open grounds with swimming pool, offers three rooms and two suites, one with private terrace, another with small lounge and all with private facilities. Heating, lounge, dining room, telephone and TV on demand. Terrace with shade and car park. Meals provided three times a week.

Prices d €94-€105; t €130-€152; extra person fr €25; dinner fr €28 **On Site** Private ⚲ **Nearby** ⚓ 2km ⚑ 3km ⚏ 2km Restaurant 0.8km ⚇ 2km ⚎ 2km 🏛 2km ⮔ 2km **Notes** No pets English spoken

ⅢⅢ Le Mas des Busclats

C et F DELEPLANQUE

1356 Route de Saumanes, 84800 ISLE-SUR-LA-SORGUE

☎ 04 90 38 67 61 & 06 77 95 54 65 🗎 04 90 38 67 61

email: deleplanque@busclats.net

web: www.busclats.net

An 18th-century property, former sheepfold, with exposed stonework and swimming pool. Close to a small road. Two first floor bedrooms with shower room or bathroom and private WCs. Two air-conditioned second floor rooms with shower room or bathroom and private WCs. Electric heating. Dining room with TV. Open grounds. Parking.

Prices s fr €70; d fr €80; extra person fr €15 **On Site** Private ⚲ **Nearby** ⚓ 0.5km ⚑ 1km ⚏ 1.5km Restaurant 3km ⚇ 3km Spa 30km 🏛 3km ⮔ 5km **Notes** No pets English spoken

ⅢⅢ Le Mas des Hirondelles

Sylvie et Thierry BURRIN

Chemin de la Cornette, 84800 ISLE-SUR-LA-SORGUE

☎ 04 90 20 21 97 & 06 22 58 63 30 🗎 04 90 20 26 38

email: thierry.burrin@tiscali.fr

web: www.mas-hirondelles.com

These rooms are in an annexe on the south-west side of the 19th-century main house. There is one room on the ground floor, and two (one of them a family suite) on the first floor. They all have private shower rooms and WCs. Electric heating. Lounge with TV. Terrace, swimming pool and pool house. Enclosed parking.

Prices s €70-€75; d €75-€85; extra person €20-€25 **On Site** Private ⚲ **Nearby** ⚓ 0.5km ⚑ 0.5km ⚏ 1km Restaurant 0.5km ⚇ 4km Spa 6km 🏛 2km ⮔ 30km **Notes** Pets admitted English spoken

ⅢⅢ ⅠⓄⅠ Mas les Fontanelles

Jacques KONINGS

114 Route de lagnes, 84800 ISLE-SUR-LA-SORGUE

☎ 04 90 20 72 59 🗎 04 90 20 72 59

email: lesfontanelles@wanadoo.fr

web: www.lesfontanelles.com

This is the eastern part of a house overlooking the fields beneath the cliffs of Vaucluse. The bedrooms are non-smoking: one on the ground floor and two large rooms, with lounges, on the first floor. They all have fridges, TVs and private facilities. Electric heating. Lounge with open fire, books and TV. Enclosed courtyard, shady terraces, enclosed parking. Meals by arrangement.

Prices s fr €95; dinner fr €30 **On Site** Private ⚲ **Nearby** ⚓ 2km ⚑ 4km ⚏ 2km ⚇ 3km 🏛 3km ⮔ 30km **Notes** No pets English spoken

---

LA BASTIDE-DES-JOURDANS

ⅢⅢ *Les Magnans*

Jérome ROBERT

Rue du Barri, 84240 LA BASTIDE-DES-JOURDANS

☎ 04 90 77 87 59 & 04 90 07 35 78 🗎 04 90 77 87 38

email: lesmagnans@hotmail.fr

web: www.les-magnans84.com

An 18th-century house in enclosed grounds with swimming pool, two terraces and a boules pitch. There is a double room, a twin-bedded room, a triple room (double bed and a single) and a room for four (two double beds). All have private bath or shower room and WC.

Prices not confirmed for 2008 **On Site** Private ⚲ **Nearby** ⚓ 5km ⚑ 5km ⚇ 0.1km 🏛 0.1km **Notes** No pets English spoken

LA MOTTE-D'AIGUES

▥ La Clef des Champs

G et L DROMENQ

Rte de la Tour, Ch. du Claux, 84240 LA MOTTE-D'AIGUES

☎ 04 90 77 69 80 ▤ 04 90 77 69 80

email: laurent.dromenq@wanadoo.fr

web: www.hotesdeschamps.com

This stone mas with swimming pool is situated 800mtrs from the Bonde Lake. Set in vineyards, there are two bedrooms and a family room (two bedrooms and kitchen) with TV, bathroom, wc, separate access and private terrace. Heating, shared room with fireplace and library.

Prices s €69-€75; d €75-€90; t €98-€130; extra person fr €20
On Site Private ⚲ **Nearby** ⚑ 3km ⚑ 30km ⚹ 1km Restaurant 1km
⚑ 3km ⚑ 3km ⚑ 10km **Notes** No pets

LACOSTE

▥ Bonne Terre

Roland LAMY

84710 LACOSTE

☎ 04 90 75 85 53 ▤ 04 90 75 85 53

email: roland.lamy@luberon-lacoste.com

web: www.luberon-lacoste.com

Personalised double rooms in a character house near a village, with panoramic views and situated in a site of exceptional natural beauty. Very tranquil, shaded park, and swimming pool. Five comfortable rooms with private facilities. Heating, terraces, telephone and car park. Dogs accepted.

Prices s €85-€100; d €90-€110; t €110-€130 **On Site** Private ⚲
Nearby ⚑ 2km ⚑ 25km ⚹ 40km Restaurant 0.1km ⚑ 4km ⚑ 17km
Notes Pets admitted English spoken Open February to November.

▥ Le Clos des Lavandes

Marie-José BORDIER

84480 LACOSTE

☎ 04 90 75 62 67

email: leclosdeslavandes@wanadoo.fr

web: http://perso.wanadoo.fr/leclosdeslavandes

This typical Provençal house has a lot of character. It stands among holm oaks, in its own enclosed grounds, facing the Lubéron. Its four bedrooms are all on the ground floor, with a separate entrance. All are attractively decorated, and they have private bathrooms/WCs. Terrace with garden furniture. Generous breakfasts include home-made produce.

Prices s €67-€72; d €70-€75 **Nearby** ⚑ 15km ⚑ 30km ⚹ 10km
⚲ 15km Restaurant 0.5km ⚑ 5km Spa 5km ⚑ 1km ⚑ 25km
Notes No pets English spoken Open 2 March to 4 November.

LAGARDE-PAREOL

▥ ⦿ Domaine les Serres

L KRIJGER et T BEAUMONT

84290 LAGARDE-PAREOL

☎ 04 90 30 76 10 & 06 07 49 39 23
▤ 04 90 30 74 31

email: domaine-les-serres@wanadoo.fr

web: www.domaine-les-serres.com

Five spacious bedrooms are located in this large stone mas, in a wooded park of one hectare with swimming pool and numerous terraces and gardens. Four of these are family rooms sleeping four, and all have private facilities. Heating, shared living room with fireplace, library, TV, video, telephone, car park. Meals three times a week.

Prices d €149-€169; dinner fr €29 **On Site** Private ⚲
Nearby ⚑ 6km ⚑ 8km ⚹ 10km ⚑ 30km ⚑ 2km ⚑ 3km ⚑ 10km
Notes No pets English spoken Open 15 January to 15 December.

LAGNES

▥ La Pastorale

Elisabeth NEGREL

Rte de Fontaine de Vaucluse, 84800 LAGNES

☎ 04 90 20 25 18

email: lapastorale84@free.fr

web: www.la-pastorale.net

A restored stone farmhouse in the country providing two single and two double rooms with private facilities. In addition there is heating, shared living room, dining room, and summer kitchen reserved for guests. Locked garage, terrace and open grounds providing shade.

Prices s fr €73; d fr €78; t fr €97; extra person fr €19 **Nearby** ⚑ 0.2km
⚑ 1.5km ⚹ 1km ⚲ 1km Restaurant 2km ⚑ 35km ⚑ 1km Spa 0.5km
⚑ 1km ⚑ 25km **Notes** Pets admitted English spoken

⚞ ⦿ Le Mas du Grand Jonquier

Ina FICHTEL

84800 LAGNES

☎ 04 90 20 90 13 🖹 04 90 20 91 18

email: masgrandjonquier@wanadoo.fr

web: www.grandjonquier.com

Two hectares of lawns, cherry and plum trees is the setting for this very fine 18th-century restored mas with private swimming pool. There are five double en suite bedrooms with TV, telephone and mini-bar, and a further double room has facilities on the landing. Heating, lounge with fireplace, living room, dining room, terrace and car park. Individual gourmet meals by reservation and generous breakfasts.

Prices s fr €90; d fr €93; t fr €102; extra person fr €16; dinner fr €29 **On Site** Private ⭢ **Nearby** ⭐3km ⭐5km ⭐ 5km Restaurant 8km ⭐4km Spa 6km ⭐3km ⭐8km **Notes** Pets admitted English spoken

LAURIS

⚞ Bastide du Piecaud

C SCHLUMBERGER-CHAZELLE

Chemin de L'Escudier, 84360 LAURIS

☎ 04 90 08 32 27 & 06 82 86 10 30 🖹 04 90 08 32 27

email: carolechazelle@free.fr

web: www.bastide-du-piecaud.com

This is a 17th-century house, with an internal courtyard and an external courtyard overlooking the surrounding hills. All of the guest accommodation is on the first floor: four rooms, and a suite for up to six people, all of them with private bath or shower room and WC. Central heating. Library/TV room; terrace, unfenced grounds. Parking.

Prices s €70-€90; d €70-€90; extra person fr €30 **On Site** Private ⭢ **Nearby** ⭐3km ⭐14km ⭐ 3km Restaurant 3km ⭐2km ⭐2km ⭐45km **Notes** No pets English spoken

⚞ La Maison des Sources

Martine COLLART-STICHELBAUT

Chemin des Fraysses, 84360 LAURIS

☎ 04 90 08 22 19 & 06 08 33 06 40 🖹 04 90 08 22 19

email: contact@maison-des-sources.com

web: www.maison-des-sources.com

This pleasantly restored mas in the country has a beautiful view of the Durance Valley, terraces and a private garden of three hectares. There are four bedrooms with private facilities, one ideal for four people. Central heating, shared living room, lounge, dining room, TV, library and fireplace. Telephone, table tennis and car park. Pets accepted with prior agreement.

Prices s €75-€79; d fr €89; t €108-€108; extra person fr €20 **Nearby** ⭐1.5km ⭐15km ⭐ 2km ⭢ 4km ⭐1km ⭐1km ⭐20km **Notes** Pets admitted

LE BARROUX

⚞ ⦿ L'Aube Safran

Marie et François PILLET

Chemin du Patifiage, 84330 LE BARROUX

☎ 04 90 62 66 91 & 06 12 17 96 94

🖹 04 90 62 66 91

email: contact@aube-safran.com

web: www.aube-safran.com

This is a modern house on a saffron-growing estate, in the middle of a pine forest. It has four non-smoking first floor guest rooms, all with private bath or shower room and WC. Lounge with TV, books and open fireplace. Central heating. Swimming pool with waves and "beach", Jacuzzi, pool house. Meals by arrangement, including dishes with saffron.

Prices s €80-€100; d €115-€135; extra person fr €25; dinner fr €39 **On Site** Private ⭢ **Nearby** ⭐12km ⭐20km ⭐ 8km ⭐31km ⭐0.4km Spa 8km ⭐5km ⭐40km **Notes** No pets English spoken Open 15 March to 15 November. CC

⚞ ⦿ La Ferme des Bélugues

Catherine PINCET

Chemin de Choudeirolles, 84330 LE BARROUX

☎ 04 90 65 15 16

email: lesbelugues@wanadoo.fr

web: www.lafermedesbelugues.com

This stately 18th-century farmhouse in the wooded foothills of Mont-Ventoux has a swimming pool (open 15 May to 30 Sep), and landscaped gardens opening onto two hectares with terraces. Four bedrooms in an annexe with private WC and shower or bathrooms. One suite (bedroom and lounge) with TV, shower room and private WC. Central heating, shared lounge (library). Kitchen area. Parking, games, cycles available. Discount after 3 consecutive nights. Walking routes from the farm. Organic breakfast.

Prices s fr €65; d fr €75-€100; t €90-€100; extra person fr €20; dinner fr €19 **On Site** Private ⭢ **Nearby** ⭐15km ⭐40km ⭐ 2km Restaurant 4km ⭐20km ⭐4km ⭐4km ⭐4km ⭐40km **Notes** Pets admitted English spoken Open September to June.

⚞ ⦿ Mas de la Lause

Corine et Christophe LONJON

Ch. Geysset - Rte de Suzette, 84330 LE BARROUX

☎ 04 90 62 33 33 & 06 33 53 18 66

email: info@provence-gites.com

web: www.provence-gites.com

A beautiful 19th-century house standing in two acres of grounds with cherry trees, apricot trees, olive trees and a wonderful view of the château. There is a double room, three twin-bedded rooms and a split-level family room for four with a kitchenette. The garden has a shady terrace and boules pitch, and meals are available by arrangement.

Prices s fr €56; d fr €64; t fr €89; extra person fr €25; dinner fr €20 **On Site** Private ⭢ **Nearby** ⭐7km ⭐20km ⭐ 5km Restaurant 0.8km ⭐25km ⭐0.5km ⭐1km ⭐20km **Notes** Pets admitted English spoken Open April to October. CC

LE THOR

⊞ *Domaine des Coudelières*

N MARCHAL et A BUSTILLO
560 Chemin des Coudelières, 84250 LE THOR
☎ 04 90 02 12 72 & 06 62 53 54 62 ▤ 04 90 02 32 69
email: domcoudelieres@free.fr
web: www.domainedescoudelieres.com

Charming, attractively restored 19th-century mas amidst three hectares of cypress trees, laurels, lavender, and apple orchards. There are four rooms, of which one is a family room, and a suite with a Provençal theme, all with private facilities. Central heating, lounge with fireplace and TV, reading material, car park, boules area, table tennis. Enclosed pool and summer house shared with a self-catering gîte and shaded terrace with old trees. Meals by reservation.

Prices not confirmed for 2008 **On Site** Private ⊰ **Nearby** ⇌ 5km
⌕ 10km ⌀ 1km ⇋ 40km ⊰ 1km ⊞ 1.5km ⋙ 1.5km **Notes** No pets English spoken Open April to 15 October. CC

⊞ iOi **La Garance**

Chantal et Régis SANGLIER
4010 Route de Saint Saturnin, 84250 LE THOR
☎ 04 90 33 72 78 & 06 07 56 06 23 ▤ 04 90 33 72 78
email: contact@garance-provence.com
web: www.garance-provence.com

A 17th-century country farm with 1.3 hectares including swimming pool (open 15 Apr to 30 Sep). View of the Château de Thouzon. Five large bedrooms (one ground floor) with private shower rooms/WCs. Solar heating. Lounge with fireplace, library, large dining room with fireplace, south-facing terrace, parking.

Prices s €90-€110; d €95-€120; t fr €145; extra person fr €25; dinner fr €28 **On Site** Restaurant ♔ Private ⊰ **Nearby** ⇌ 5km ⌕ 6km ⌀ 4km ⇋ 40km ⊰ 4km ⊞ 4km ⋙ 4km **Notes** No pets English spoken

⊞ iOi **Mas de la Martelière**

Patrick LAGET
888 Ch. du Réal de Montclard, 84250 LE THOR
☎ 04 90 02 37 90 ▤ 04 90 02 38 70
email: la-marteliere@wanadoo.fr
web: www.la-marteliere.com

This beautiful 19th-century house has been totally restored in a delightfully subtle Provençal style. In an annexe it offers one ground floor room, with four further rooms on the first and second floors, all with private shower rooms and WCs. Electric heating. Lounge with fireplace, books and TV. Swimming pool, shady terrace and enclosed parking. Meals available every day.

Prices s €64-€84; d €69-€89; extra person fr €30; dinner fr €28 **On Site** Private ⊰ **Nearby** ⇌ 5km ⌕ 15km ⌀ 3km Restaurant 3km ⊰ 3km ♔ 3km ⊞ 3km ⋙ 22km **Notes** No pets English spoken

LOURMARIN

⊞ *La Lombarde*

Eva LEBRE
BP32, 84160 LOURMARIN
☎ 04 90 08 40 60 ▤ 04 90 08 40 64
email: la.lombarde@wanadoo.fr
web: www.lalombarde.fr

Four bedrooms with exterior access have been incorporated into this 17th-century mas, situated in six hectares of wooded park with swimming pool. The bedrooms have a hall, fridge, TV, shower, wc and private terrace. Central heating, shared courtyard, dining room, reception room/lounge, kitchen. Bicycles, table tennis, pétanque, volley-ball, barbecue area.

Prices not confirmed for 2008 **On Site** Private ⊰ **Nearby** ⇌ 2km ⌕ 15km ⌀ 1km ⊰ 2km ⊞ 0.5km **Notes** No pets English spoken Open March to 10 November.

MALAUCENE

⊞ **Le Château Crémessières**

M et E DALLAPORTA-BONNEL
84340 MALAUCENE
☎ 04 90 65 11 13
email: e.dalla@provenceservices.com

In the village of Malaucène, this very attractive property is set in meadows and wooded grounds of two hectares. There are two rooms, one suite of two rooms with terrace, kitchen and TV and a further suite with terrace, kitchen, living room, TV and private fireplace. All have private facilities, use of fridge and heating. Shady terrace; car park; garden furniture; garage; picnics. Breakfasts served on the terrace; numerous restaurants close by.

Prices d €78-€88 **Nearby** ⇌ 3km ⌕ 35km ⌀ 3km ⊰ 9km Restaurant 0.1km ⇋ 10km ⊰ 1km ♔ 0.2km ⊞ 0.2km ⋙ 40km **Notes** Pets admitted English spoken Open June to 30 August.

MENERBES

⊞ **Les Peirelles**

D ANDREIS et M PILLODS
84560 MENERBES
☎ 04 90 72 23 42 ▤ 04 90 72 23 56
email: les-peirelles@worldonline.fr
web: www.lespeirelles.com

This property, separate from the owners' house, is set in a large park of one hectare with terraces and a swimming pool. There are three double bedrooms and two rooms for four people, with terraces and private facilities. Heating, use of shared room with kitchen, fridge, and microwave. Library, telephone, terrace, car park, locked garage for bicycles.

Prices s €85-€95; d €95-€109; extra person fr €20   **On Site** Private ↖ **Nearby** ♿ 10km ⚓ 15km Restaurant 2km ⌘ 2km Spa 10km 🏠 2km ⩫ 15km **Notes** No pets English spoken Open Feburary to December. CC

MODENE

� Villa Noria

Philippe MONTI

84330 MODENE

☎ 04 90 62 50 66

email: post@villa-noria.com

web: www.villa-noria.com

This house stands in wooded grounds at the entrance to the village, at the foot of Mont Ventoux. It has four bedrooms and one suite, all air-conditioned and all with private bath or shower rooms and WCs. Lounge with books, veranda, terrace and enclosed parking and swimming pool. Meals available by arrangement.

Prices d €50-€150; t €90-€180; dinner fr €35   **On Site** ℘ **Nearby** ♿ 10km ⚓ 30km Restaurant 3km ⛵ 18km ⌘ 3km ♞ 7km 🏠 3km ⩫ 10km **Notes** No pets English spoken

MONIEUX

⫿ ✦ ❍l Le Viguier

M. GIARDINI

Gaec le Viguier, 84390 MONIEUX

☎ 04 90 64 04 83 ▤ 04 90 64 11 39

email: le.viguier@wanadoo.fr

web: www.leviguier.com

This farm, between Mont-Ventoux and the Luberon, is in the heart of the lavender country, close to the Nesque gorges. The five bedrooms are on the ground floor of a separate building - all with en suite showers and WCs. Guests' lounge with open fireplace and TV, terrace, parking; mountain bikes available. Fishing lake nearby, courses available: truffles, walking, local foods.

Prices s fr €45; d fr €55; t fr €70; extra person fr €15; dinner fr €20 **Nearby** ♿ 5km ⚓ 25km ℘ 0.2km ↖ 7km Restaurant 2km ⛵ 25km ⌘ 7km 🏠 2km **Notes** Pets admitted English spoken

MONTEUX

⫿⫿⫿ L'Estiou

Sylvie et Yves GUEGUEN

2362 Route de Bédarrides, 84170 MONTEUX

☎ 04 90 66 91 83 & 06 19 89 15 23

email: lestiou@wanadoo.fr

web: www.lestiou.com

This is a restored farmhouse with three first floor rooms, one of them a family suite. They all have private bath or shower room and WC; central heating. Guests' lounge/dining room with open fireplace, books and TV. Swimming pool, and terrace with awning. Open garden, parking.

Prices s €60-€73; d €65-€78; t €70-€120; extra person fr €15; dinner fr €23   **On Site** ⛲ Private ↖ **Nearby** ♿ 5km ⚓ 12km ℘ 3km Restaurant 3km ⌘ 3km 🏠 3km ⩫ 20km **Notes** No pets English spoken

⫿⫿ ❍l La Capelo

Jo et Roger NALLET

1860 Chemin des deux Saules, 84170 MONTEUX

☎ 04 90 61 02 38 & 06 24 45 06 07

email: lacapelo@wanadoo.fr

This is an 18th-century house in enclosed wooded grounds. It has four first floor rooms, all with en suite shower rooms and WCs. Central heating. Spacious guests' lounge with TV and books. Swimming pool and large shady terrace. Parking. Meals available two days a week.

Prices s €70-€85; d €85-€100; dinner fr €27   **On Site** Private ↖ **Nearby** ♿ 5km ⚓ 12km ℘ 5km Restaurant 4km ⛵ 40km ⌘ 3km ⛲ 30km 🏠 4km ⩫ 20km **Notes** No pets English spoken Open 15 March to 15 December.

⫿⫿⫿ ❍l *Le Mas des Fleurs d'Hilaire*

Christèle et Olivier TORCK

709 Chemin de la Firmine, 84170 MONTEUX

☎ 04 90 66 91 82

email: fleurs-d-hilaire@wanadoo.fr

web: www.les-fleurs-d-hilaire.com

An 18th-century house with four hectares of pasture and enclosed swimming pool, views over Ventoux. Two ground floor bedrooms and three first floor bedrooms, all with private shower rooms and WCs. Gas heating. Shared lounge with TV and library. North-facing terrace. Parking. Low season tariff available.

Prices not confirmed for 2008   **On Site** Private ↖ **Nearby** ♿ 3km ⚓ 15km ⌘ 3km 🏠 3km ⩫ 25km **Notes** No pets English spoken

MORMOIRON

▦ ⌖ Lou Mas de Carboussan

Jean-Pierre ESCOFFIER
500 Chemin de Carboussan, 84570 MORMOIRON
☎ 04 90 61 93 02 & 06 11 21 71 64 ▤ 04 90 61 93 03
email: loumasdecarboussan@tiscali.fr
web: http://loumasdecarboussan.chez.tiscali.fr

A detached villa on the side of a hill, set in an orchard of cherry and olive trees. It provides five rooms with private facilities, three with terraces. Central heating, shared room with fireplace and kitchen available. Terrace, grounds, car park.

Prices s €44-€49; d €52-€57; t €69-€74; extra person fr €16
Nearby ⛵ 5km ⛳ 25km 🏊 2km ⌖ 5km Restaurant 0.6km ⛴ 20km
🏊 1km ⛺ 4km 🏛 0.5km ⛽ 40km **Notes** Pets admitted

MURS

▦ ⌖ Rocquejeanne

Chantal TAVERNE
84220 MURS
☎ 04 90 72 63 96
email: richard.taverne@rocquejeanne.com
web: www.rocquejeanne.com

Stone-built house in hills and orchards with a swimming pool and lovely view over the Monts de Vaucluse and Luberon. It offers four rooms with private facilities and heating, communal room, terrace, open grounds of six hectares and parking.

Prices s fr €70; d fr €75; extra person fr €20; dinner fr €25
On Site Private ⌖ **Nearby** ⛵ 10km ⛳ 28km 🏊 25km Restaurant 5km
🏊 6km 🏛 3km ⛽ 30km **Notes** Pets admitted English spoken Open March to November.

ORANGE

▦ ⌖ La Bastide des Princes

Annie et Pierre PAUMEL
Chemin de Bigonnet, 84860 CADEROUSSE/ORANGE
☎ 04 90 51 04 59 & 06 84 62 41 90 ▤ 04 90 51 04 59
email: info@bastidedesprinces.com
web: www.bastide-princes.com

A beautiful 17th-century Provençal house in landscaped grounds with a swimming pool. There are five spacious non-smoking rooms, three doubles and two with twin beds, each with a living area, private bath or shower room and WC. Sitting room, dining room and kitchenette. Outside is a large south-facing terrace and parking space. Chef will give cookery lessons.

Prices s €95-€120; d €105-€130; t €130-€155; extra person fr €25; dinner fr €45 **On Site** Private ⌖ **Nearby** ⛵ 2km ⛳ 10km 🏊 4km Restaurant 4km 🏊 3km ⛺ 4km 🏛 4km ⛽ 5km **Notes** No pets English spoken Open April to 15 November. (open wknds only Winter) CC

▦ ⌖ Le Mas Julien

Valère CARLIN
704 Rhemin de St Jean, 84100 ORANGE
☎ 04 90 34 99 49 & 06 62 47 99 43
email: valere.carlin@libertysurf.fr
web: www.mas-julien.com

This small stone-built 17th-century farmhouse stands in large wooded grounds. It has three first floor rooms, all with private bath or shower rooms and WCs. Lounge with open fire, books and TV. Terrace with awning. Swimming pool, boules, badminton, volleyball, weights room. Meals available three days a week. Wi-fi available and two rooms are air-conditioned.

Prices s fr €80; d fr €95; t fr €125; dinner fr €28 **On Site** ⛺ Private ⌖
Nearby ⛵ 1km ⛳ 25km 🏊 3km Restaurant 1km 🏊 5km 🏛 5km
⛽ 5km **Notes** Pets admitted English spoken

▦ Villa Aurenjo

Chantal FERAUD
121 Rue François Chambovet, BP 136, 84104 ORANGE
☎ 04 90 11 10 00 & 06 62 67 03 30
email: villa-aurenjo@wanadoo.fr
web: www.villa-aurenjo.com

In the heart of the historic town of Orange, this 18th-century mansion has been totally restored. It has one bedroom on the ground floor, and four on the first floor, two of them with a private terrace. All rooms have TV, telephone, private bath/shower room and WC. Lounge with books and TV. Swimming pool, tennis court and sauna.

Prices not confirmed for 2008 **On Site** Private ⌖ **Nearby** ⛵ 5km
⛳ 5km 🏊 🏛 0.2km ⛽ 2km **Notes** Pets admitted English spoken

PERNES-LES-FONTAINES

▦ ⌖ Domaine de la Nesquière

Isabelle DE MAINTENANT
5419 Route D'Althen, 84210 PERNES-LES-FONTAINES
☎ 04 90 62 00 16 ▤ 04 90 62 02 10
email: lanesquiere@wanadoo.fr
web: www.lanesquiere.com

A beautiful 18th-century farm property. There are four rooms, attractively decorated with some period furniture. All are upstairs: two doubles, and two family suites for up to four guests. All have private bath or shower room/WC, TV, fridge and tea-making equipment. One of the doubles has a small kitchenette. Lounge, laundry room, meals by arrangement. Garden, terraces, swimming pool.

Prices s €75-€92; d €83-€99; t €105-€115; extra person fr €15; dinner fr €32 **On Site** Private ⌖ **Nearby** ⛵ 5km ⛳ 15km 🏊 0.5km
Restaurant 5km ⛴ 35km 🏊 6km ⛺ 5km 🏛 5km ⛽ 20km **Notes** Pets admitted English spoken Open 16 January to 14 December. CC

see advert on opposite page

♨ ⱺ Le Mas Pichony

L et L DESBORDES
1454 Rte de St Didier (Rd28),
84210 PERNES-LES-FONTAINES
☎ 04 90 61 56 11 & 06 99 16 98 58 ▤ 04 90 40 35 02
email: laurent.desbordes@wanadoo.fr
web: www.maspichony.com

An independent 17th-century mas of much character in a beautiful setting in vineyards with swimming pool, shaded terrace and open grounds. Five bedrooms with private facilities, central heating, shared living room with fireplace, library, TV and telephone. Cot available. Car park, local produce, evening meals if booked in advance.

Prices s fr €76; d €82-€170; t fr €102; extra person fr €20; dinner fr €28 **On Site** Private ⚓ **Nearby** ⛵ 2km ⚓ 15km ⚐ 8km Restaurant 0.5km ⚓ 25km ⚓ 1.2km ⚑ 2km ⚐ 0.5km ⚓ 16km **Notes** No pets English spoken Open March to 30 October.

♨ Moulin de la Baume

Christine REYNARD
182 Route d'Avignon, 84210 PERNES-LES-FONTAINES
☎ 04 90 66 58 36 & 06 80 26 83 50 ▤ 04 90 61 69 42
email: contact@moulindelabaume.com
web: www.moulindelabaume.com

A pleasantly restored mill just outside a village, in open grounds with a swimming pool. Five bedrooms all have private facilities and TV, and one has a living room. Central heating, shared living room, terrace and car park.

Prices d €95-€120; extra person fr €20 **On Site** Private ⚓
Nearby ⛵ 2km ⚓ 10km ⚐ 4km ⚓ 25km ⚓ 1km ⚐ 1km ⚓ 15km
Notes No pets English spoken

♨ St-Barthelemy

Jacqueline MANGEARD
Chemin de la Roque,
84210 PERNES-LES-FONTAINES
☎ 04 90 66 47 79
email: mangeard.jacqueline@wanadoo.fr
web: www.ville-pernes-les-fontaines.fr/st-barthelemy

Fully restored 18th-century Provençal farmhouse in the country with swimming pool and tennis court. Five rooms with private facilities and central heating, shared lounge, dining room, fridge and terrace. Next to a shaded, enclosed park. Car park; phone booth, free bicycle, table tennis and badminton.

Prices s fr €60; d fr €70; t fr €90; extra person fr €20 **On Site** ⚐ ⚑
Private ⚓ **Nearby** ⛵ 5km ⚓ 10km Restaurant 0.5km ⚓ ⚐ 1.5km
⚓ 5km **Notes** No pets English spoken

PROVENCE-ALPES-CÔTE-D'AZUR

PUYMERAS

⊞ Domaine le Puy du Maupas

Christian SAUVAYRE

Route de Nyons, 84110 PUYMERAS

☎ 04 90 46 47 43   📄 04 90 46 48 51

email: sauvayre@puy-du-maupas.com

web: www.puy-du-maupas.com

A large, country house adjacent to a wine-tasting cellar. It offers three double bedrooms and two triples (double bed and a single in each). They all have private bath or shower room and WC. Sitting room with open fire, use of fridge, sink for washing picnic plates, etc. Terrace and parking space. This is a non-smoking property.

Prices s fr €50; d fr €55; t fr €70   **On Site** Private ↖   **Nearby** ♨ 8km
♨ 35km 🎣 5km Restaurant 3km ♨ 3km ♨ 5km 🏛 2km ➡ 35km
Notes No pets Open 15 March to 15 October. CC

⊞ ♥ |◯| L'Oustau des Oliviers

Marie-Françoise ROUSTAN

Quartier des Eyssarettes, 84110 PUYMERAS

☎ 04 90 46 45 89

email: marie-francoise.2@wanadoo.fr

web: www.guideweb.com/provence/bb/
oustau-des-oliviers

Situated amidst hills in the middle of a wine-producing enterprise, this house provides four bedrooms with private facilities. There is a living room, fridge, microwave, lounge, dining-room, and library inside and outside, a swimming pool, terrace, garden furniture, barbecue, ornamental pond, boules area and table tennis. Hiking trails and bike hire nearby; meals available if booked, except on Tuesday and Saturdays. Theme weeks.

Prices not confirmed for 2008   **Nearby** ♨ 7km ♨ 25km 🎣 15km ↖
♨ 35km ♨ 2km 🏛 5km ➡ 30km   **Notes** Pets admitted Open April to 15 October.

ROBION

⊞ ♥ |◯| Domaine de Canfier

Michel et Catherine CHARVET

84440 ROBION

☎ 04 90 76 51 54

email: info@domainedecanfier.fr

web: www.domainedecanfier.fr

This countryside farm has plenty of character and offers four rooms, all with private facilities and benefiting from central heating, a communal room, lounge, dining room, fireplace, library, piano and TV. There is also a telephone, terrace, enclosed garden, swimming pool and car park. Meals for residents three or four times a week.

Prices s €62-€94; d €73-€94; t €103-€113; extra person fr €23
On Site Private ↖   **Nearby** ♨ 5km ♨ 15km 🎣 0.3km Restaurant 1km
♨ 35km ♨ 1km 🏛 1km ➡ 5km   **Notes** No pets English spoken

⊞ |◯| Le Domaine d'Anthyllis

Liliane BOURQUIN

Le Plan de Robion, 84440 ROBION

☎ 04 32 52 91 30 & 06 08 32 42 72   📄 04 32 52 91 30

email: domaine@anthyllis.com

web: www.anthyllis.com

The separate western part of this house has one first floor room and one suite, with access by exterior stairs. There is another room on the ground floor of the owners' part of the house. All rooms have en suite bath or shower rooms and WCs. Central heating. Open grounds, shady terrace, swimming pool and parking. Meals by arrangement.

Prices not confirmed for 2008   **On Site** Private ↖   **Nearby** ♨ 3km
♨ 10km 🎣 10km ♨ 2km 🏛 3km ➡ 30km   **Notes** No pets English spoken

⊞ Mas la Pomarede

N et J-N POMAREDE

Chemin de la Fourmillère, 84440 ROBION

☎ 04 90 20 21 81   📄 04 90 20 37 99

email: contact@maslapomarede.com

web: www.maslapomarede.com

This 17th-century farmhouse stands in large wooded grounds. It has two rooms and two suites. All of them have private facilities, although those for one of the suites are not fully self-contained but are accessed via a landing. Lounge with books, terrace and swimming pool.

Prices s €100-€135; d €100-€135; t €141-€161; extra person fr €26   **On Site** ♨ Private ↖   **Nearby** ♨ 10km ♨ 10km 🎣 5km
Restaurant 3km ♨ 3km 🏛 3km ➡ 4km   **Notes** Pets admitted English spoken CC

ROUSSILLON

⊞ La Bastide des Ocres

Monique GOURICHON

Le Bois de la Cour, 84220 ROUSSILLON

☎ 04 90 05 64 50 & 06 19 35 26 81

email: bastidedesocres@orange.fr

web: www.bastidedesocres.com

A newly built house that offers four rooms in an annexe with private facilities, small terraces and heating. Communal room with library, information, board games and kitchen corner with fridge and microwave. Enclosed grounds with parking and swimming pool.

Prices d €62-€83; t €94-€100   **On Site** Private ↖   **Nearby** ♨ 4km
♨ 25km Restaurant 1km ♨ 0.2km Spa 10km ♨ 1km 🏛 1km ➡ 50km
Notes No pets English spoken

∰ Le Clos des Cigales

B et P LHERBEIL

Route de Goult, 84220 ROUSSILLON

☎ 04 90 05 73 72 & 06 62 15 81 88 ▤ 04 90 05 73 72

email: philippe.Lherbeil@wanadoo.fr

web: www.leclosdescigales.com

This property has five ground floor bedrooms in a newly built annexe in an enclosed pine grove. All of the rooms have private terraces and shower rooms/WCs. South-facing terrace, outdoor summer room provides a lounge area for guests. Swimming pool.

Prices s €65-€115; d €70-€115; t €115-€130; extra person fr €15
On Site Private ⚲ **Nearby** ⚓ 0.2km ⚑ 20km ⚐ 10km Restaurant 1km ⚓ 50km ⚑ 1.5km Spa 1km ⚑ 1.8km ⚑ 20km **Notes** No pets English spoken

RUSTREL

∰ La Forge

D BERGER-CECCALDI

Notre Dame des Anges, 84400 RUSTREL

☎ 04 90 04 92 22 ▤ 04 88 10 05 76

email: info@laforge.com.fr

web: www.laforge.com.fr

This large 19th-century building is situated on the edge of the Colorado Provençal Forest. Accommodation consists of three bedrooms in an annexe with terraced lawn and a suite, all with private facilities. Central heating, shared living room, fireplace, TV, telephone and barbecue. Garage and car park. Meals if reserved.

Prices d €91-€99; t fr €154; extra person fr €5 **On Site** ⚽ Private ⚲
Nearby ⚓ 10km ⚑ 35km ⚐ 7km Restaurant 0.2km ⚓ 7km ⚑ 2km
Notes No pets English spoken Open March to 20 November.

SAIGNON

∰ La Pyramide

C et P BOURDIN

Rue du Jas, 84400 SAIGNON

☎ 04 90 04 70 00 ▤ 04 90 04 78 87

email: lapyramide2@wanadoo.fr

An attractive house with shared swimming pool, patio, and enclosed landscaped garden on the outskirts of a village. It offers four rooms with private facilities, central heating, a shared living room and car park.

Prices s €55-€75; d €59-€90; t €90-€105; extra person fr €15
On Site Private ⚲ **Nearby** ⚓ 1km ⚑ 12km ⚐ 4km Restaurant 0.1km ⚑ 2km Spa 18km **Notes** No pets English spoken Open 16 January to 4 December.

SARRIANS/VACQUEYRAS

∰ ⏏ Le Mas de la Fontaine

M-Jeanne et Jacky LEROY

Gr. Roques, Rte de Vacqueyras,

84260 SARRIANS/VACQUEYRAS

☎ 04 90 12 36 63 & 06 70 80 06 55 ▤ 04 90 12 36 76

email: lemasdelafontaine@wanadoo.fr

web: www.lemasdelafontaine.com

This typical restored mas, at the foot of the Dentelles de Montmirail on the Route du Vin, is in a tranquil setting of three hectares of trees, with ornamental garden and private swimming pool. There are four bedrooms and a suite, each with private facilities. Heating, dining room, bar area, reading room, TV and phone, shaded terrace and car park. Evening meals if booked.

Prices s fr €67; d €72-€90; t €97-€110; extra person fr €20; dinner fr €25
On Site Private ⚲ **Nearby** ⚓ 5km ⚑ 15km ⚐ 7km ⚓ 30km ⚑ 7km ⚑ 2km ⚑ 30km **Notes** No pets English spoken

SAULT

∰ ⏏ *Les Bourguets*

Claudine et Stéphane JAMET

84390 SAULT

☎ 04 90 64 11 90 & 06 09 95 04 69 ▤ 04 90 64 10 92

email: bastidedesbourguets@hotmail.com

web: www.bastidedesbourguets.com

This mid 19th-century house has been fully restored. It stands peacefully in the countryside amid fields of lavender, with a wonderful view. It has four upstairs bedrooms, all with private showers/WCs. Lounge with open fire, TV and books. Meals by arrangement, three days a week.

Prices not confirmed for 2008 **On Site** Private ⚲ **Nearby** ⚓ 10km ⚑ 45km ⚐ 1km ⚑ 3km ⚑ 3km **Notes** Pets admitted Open February to November.

∰ Piedmoure

M-J et J-P BONNARD

Route de Saint Christol, 84390 SAULT

☎ 04 90 64 09 22 ▤ 04 90 64 17 19

email: piedmoure@aol.com

A large 17th-century mas, set in woods and lavender fields overlooking the Croc Valley. It offers four bedrooms on the first floor with private facilities, heating, shared living room, TV, terrace and enclosed garden.

Prices s fr €77; d fr €80 **Nearby** ⚓ 10km ⚑ 20km ⚐ 10km ⚲ 3km Restaurant 3km ⚓ 25km ⚑ 3km ⚑ 2.5km **Notes** No pets English spoken Open Easter to October.

ST-DIDIER

Le Mas des Abricotiers

Christine DUBUC
193 Chemin des Terres Mortes, 84210 ST-DIDIER
☎ 04 90 66 19 16 & 06 83 19 11 26
email: abricotier@bleu-provence.com
web: www.bleu-provence.com

A restored mas at the entrance to a village, set in lovely large grounds planted with apricot trees and enjoying views over Mont Ventoux and Dentelles de Montmirail. There are three rooms, one with mezzanine, with private bathrooms and heating. Dining room with TV, summer kitchen, parking, enclosed courtyard and swimming pool. Table d'hôte meals available twice a week.

Prices s €63-€98; d €63-€98; t €93-€123 **On Site** Private **Nearby** 2km 10km Restaurant 0.8km 30km 1km 0.8km 33km **Notes** No pets English spoken Open 30 March to October. CC

ST-PIERRE-DE-VASSOLS/BEDOIN

Les Conils

C DE CHABASSOL
Route de Bédoin, 84330 ST-PIERRE-DE-VASSOLS/BEDOIN
☎ 04 90 12 79 49 & 06 83 40 44 55 04 90 12 79 49
email: lesconils@yahoo.fr
web: http://les.conils.free.fr

This 12th-century house on the side of a hill commands a superb view. It has two bedrooms and one suite with bunk beds, all with private bath or shower rooms and WCs. Central heating. Lounge with open fireplace and TV. Two terraces and private parking. Swimming pool 75 metres away, available for guests' use.

Prices s €56-€66; d €60-€70; t fr €95; extra person fr €25; dinner fr €25 **On Site** Private **Nearby** 3km 30km 5km Restaurant 4km 25km 3km Spa 25km 3km 25km **Notes** No pets English spoken

ST-SATURNIN-LES-AVIGNON

Domaine des Gendalis

Edith BACULARD
200 Chemin des Gendalis,
84450 ST-SATURNIN-LES-AVIGNON
☎ 04 90 22 07 54 & 06 03 78 35 04 04 90 22 05 78
email: lesgendalis@free.fr
web: www.domaine-des-gendalis.com

Accommodation is housed in a large property with large enclosed wooded garden and swimming pool. There are five bedrooms on the ground floor with separate access, shower and private wc. Heating and air conditioning; shared living room with fireplace and terrace.

Prices s €73-€78; d €76-€80; t €98-€102; extra person fr €22 **On Site** Private **Nearby** 7km 5km 4km 1km 10km 1km 10km **Notes** No pets English spoken

Le Mas de l'Amandier

Nadine et Philippe AUGIER
102 Impasse des Centenaires,
84450 ST-SATURNIN-LES-AVIGNON
☎ 04 90 22 02 77 04 90 22 02 77
email: info@lemasdelamandier.com
web: www.lemasdelamandier.com

Village house in a large enclosed courtyard with swimming pool and summer house. The four bedrooms are in an annexe and have private facilities and terrace. Central heating and air conditioning. Dining room with fireplace, library and TV, enclosed garden, car park, evening meals available if booked.

Prices s €75-€85; d €80-€90; t €110-€120; extra person fr €25 **On Site** Private **Nearby** 8km 5km 0.5km Restaurant 0.1km 0.5km 0.2km 0.5km **Notes** No pets English spoken CC

UCHAUX

La Cabanole

Leen et Patrick DEBLAERE
Beauchamp, 84100 UCHAUX
☎ 04 90 30 07 28 04 90 30 08 75
email: deblaere.cabanole@wanadoo.fr
web: www.lacabanole.com

Castle farmhouse with swimming pool, set in vineyards and olive groves in an area of cultural and tourist interest. There are five bedrooms, two of which are for four people, with private facilities. Heating, shared reception room with fireplace, dining room, library, TV and telephone. Enclosed grounds, terrace, car park.

Prices s €68-€113; d €75-€120; t fr €130; dinner fr €28 **On Site** Private **Nearby** 1km 12km Restaurant 2km 4km 12km 4km 12km **Notes** No pets English spoken Open 15 March to 15 November. CC

Les Convenants

Sarah et Ian BANNER
84100 UCHAUX
☎ 04 90 40 65 64 04 90 40 65 64
email: sarahbanner@wanadoo.fr
web: www.lesconvenents.com

This is an 18th-century house, standing amongst the vines. There are two rooms on the ground floor; one family suite in an adjacent annexe, and two rooms for four on the first floor. All rooms have

private bath/shower rooms and WCs. Lounge with open fire, books and TV. Swimming pool, open garden, meals served twice a week.

Prices s €85-€90; d €95-€100; extra person fr €20 **On Site** Private ⚡
Nearby ⛵ 6km ♨ 10km ♿ 10km Restaurant 3km ♨ 5km 🏛 5km
🚶 10km **Notes** No pets English spoken Open 15 March to
15 November.

VAISON-LA-ROMAINE

⚜ Chambre d'hôtes

Anne et Laurent VIAU

1 Av J. Mazen, 84110 VAISON-LA-ROMAINE

☎ 04 90 35 63 04

email: anne.viau@vaisonchambres.info

web: www.vaisonchambres.info

A 19th-century farmhouse with vines in the garden, close to the centre of the village. There are three double rooms, a twin-bedded room and a family room for four - all with air conditioning and en suite facilities. The gardens are enclosed, and there is a large terrace. Closed Xmas.

Prices s €55-€60; d €60-€65; t €110-€120; extra person fr €10
Nearby ⛵ 4km ♨ 15km ♿ 3km ⚡ 0.3km Restaurant 0.2km 🥾 40km
♨ 0.4km Spa 30km 🏛 0.5km 🚶 25km **Notes** No pets English spoken

⚜ ⚐ Jade en Provence

Pierre ANTOINE

Av André Coudray, 84110 VAISON-LA-ROMAINE

☎ 04 90 28 81 60 & 06 09 98 23 46 🖃 04 90 28 81 60

email: contact@jade-en-provence.com

web: www.jade-en-provence.com

Five guest bedrooms quietly located in an annexe to the owner's home. Each room has a private bath or shower room and WC. Lounge with an open fire and TV, and outside there is a terrace and parking space. Meals are available, by arrangement, three days a week.

Prices s €60-€65; d €75-€85; t fr €16; dinner fr €30 **On Site** Private ⚡
Nearby ⛵ 3km ♨ 15km ♿ 35km ♨ 0.3km 🏛 0.5km 🚶 25km
Notes No pets English spoken

⚜ L'Évêché

Aude VERDIER

Rue de L'Évêché, Cité Médiévale,

84110 VAISON-LA-ROMAINE

☎ 04 90 36 13 46 & 06 03 03 21 42 🖃 04 90 36 32 43

email: eveche@aol.com

web: http://eveche.free.fr

This 18th-century restored house of character lies in the medieval town of Vaison-la-Romaine. There are four rooms with private facilities and telephone, heating, shared living room and lounge with fireplace. Terrace with superb view of the town where you can find a swimming pool and tennis court. Mountain bikes available.

Prices s €70-€105; d €78-€130; t €110-€150 **On Site** ⚑
Nearby ⛵ 5km ♨ 25km ♿ 0.1km ⚡ 0.5km Restaurant 0.2km ♨ 0.5km
🏛 0.2km 🚶 20km **Notes** Pets admitted English spoken

⚜ La Calade

C HAGGAI et R TERRISSE

Saint Romain en Viennois, 84110 VAISON-LA-ROMAINE

☎ 04 90 46 51 79 🖃 04 90 46 51 82

email: bb@la-calade-vaison.com

web: www.la-calade-vaison.com

Forming part of the ramparts encircling this small fortified village in northern Vaucluse, this quiet and charming chambre d'hôtes has a courtyard where breakfasts can be enjoyed, and a rooftop terrace affording wonderful views. Montmirail and Mont Ventoux are within easy reach, via the intervening vineyards and olive groves. Vaison-la-Romaine is only 3km away; a renowned tourist attraction with historic, artistic and cultural appeal.

Prices s fr €70; d fr €80 **Nearby** ⛵ 5km ♨ 30km ♿ 2km ⚡ 3km
Restaurant 0.5km 🥾 25km ♨ 3km Spa 40km 🏛 2.5km 🚶 40km
Notes No pets English spoken Open 10 April to 15 October.

VALREAS

⚜ ⚐ *Domaine les Grands Devers*

Paul-Henri BOUCHARD

84600 VALREAS

☎ 04 90 35 15 98 & 06 15 58 42 19 🖃 04 90 37 49 56

email: phbouchard@grandsdevers.com

web: www.grandsdevers.com

A house with four guest bedrooms on a 69 hectare estate - vines, truffles and woodland. The rooms are on the first floor, all with private shower and WC. Lounge and dining room with open fire; terrace and parking. Meals available on alternate days. During the truffle season the hosts can arrange for guests to participate in the truffle gathering.

Prices not confirmed for 2008 **Nearby** ⛵ 10km ♨ 25km ♿ 6km
⚡ 6km ♨ 6km 🏛 6km **Notes** Pets admitted English spoken

⚜ Le Mas de Manon

M DE DIEULEVEULT et C XIBERRAS

Ancienne Route de Grillon, 84600 VALREAS

☎ 06 09 44 92 22

email: masdemanon@aliceadsl.fr

web: www.masdemanon.com

This fully restored Provençal house in a rural setting offers one double room, one twin room and two triple rooms, all warmly decorated with shower and wc. Lounge with fireplace and satellite TV. Cot available. Barbecue, car park and covered terrace with furniture.

Prices s fr €65; d fr €75; t fr €95; extra person fr €20 **Nearby** ⛵ 3km
♨ 30km ♿ 2km ⚡ Restaurant 2km ♨ 2km Spa 30km 🎾 2km 🏛 2km
🚶 30km **Notes** No pets English spoken

VAUGINES

₩₩ *L'Eléphant de Vaugines*

Thierry CHOME
les Trailles, 84160 VAUGINES
☎ 04 90 77 15 85 📄 04 90 77 14 13
email: elephant@vaugines.com
web: www.vaugines.com

This modern house stands on a hillside with several wooded terraces and a beautiful view over the Durance Valley. On the ground floor are three bedrooms and a two-roomed suite; there is a further bedroom upstairs. All are air-conditioned, and they all have private bath or shower rooms and WCs. The suite also has its own kitchenette. Lounge with open fire, TV and books. Table tennis, pétanque.

Prices not confirmed for 2008 **On Site** Private ⊀ **Nearby** ⇔10km ♨35km ♨2km 🏠1km ⋙40km **Notes** No pets English spoken

₩₩ ᷑ **Les Grandes Garrigues**

Evelyne et Christian ARNOUX
Route de Cadenet, 84160 VAUGINES
☎ 04 90 77 10 71 & 06 13 61 47 90
email: carnoux@aol.com
web: www.lesgrandesgarrigues.com

Old Provençal mas in the country with panoramic views of the Lubéron, St-Victoire and the Alpilles. Five bedrooms (one with a lounge) that have independent entrances, TV, shower, wc and private terrace. Animals admitted by prior arrangement. Boules area, walking trails, summer kitchen for fine weather, swimming pool. Pets admitted by arrangement.

Prices s €75-€100; d €75-€105; t €90-€120; extra person fr €15 **On Site** Private ⊀ **Nearby** ⇔3km ♨15km ♠5km Restaurant 2km ♨3km ♨3km 🏠3km ⋙35km **Notes** Pets admitted English spoken

VEDENE

₩₩₩ **La Banastière**

Jeanie et Fréderic BUSSOT
Ch. de la Banastière, Rte du, 84270 VEDENE
☎ 04 90 01 35 25 & 06 10 80 66 52
📄 04 90 01 35 25
email: contact@labanastiere.com
web: www.labanastiere.com

Beautifully restored 18th-century Provençal house showcasing traditional methods and materials in Italian and Tuscan style. Swimming pool, wooded grounds, south-facing terrace. Heating/ air-conditioning. Three ground floor and two first floor bedrooms, all with satellite TV, internet, bathroom and private WC. Dining room/library with TV and internet. Covered shelter. Low season rates available. Gym on site.

Prices d €165-€185; extra person fr €30 **On Site** ♨ Private ⊀ **Nearby** ⇔0.3km ♨0.3km Restaurant 0.3km ♨2km 🏠2km ⋙10km **Notes** Pets admitted English spoken Open April to 1 November.

₩₩ ᷑◯᷑ **Le Pavillon Vert**

Anya MERAN
Chemin de la Banastière, 84270 VEDENE
☎ 04 90 31 13 83 & 06 11 49 49 19 📄 04 90 31 13 83
email: merananya@hotmail.com
web: www.lepavillonvert.com

Five kilometres from Avignon, in a grassy setting among ancient oak trees, this old farm building has been authentically restored in the country style. It has four guest rooms with a separate entrance. Each one has TV, heating/air conditioning, bath, shower, WC, and internet access on request. Terrace, swimming pool. Meals available three days a week (local specialities).

Prices s €65-€78; extra person fr €20; dinner fr €23 **On Site** Private ⊀ **Nearby** ⇔0.3km ♨0.5km ♨2km 🏠2km ⋙10km **Notes** No pets English spoken

VELLERON

₩₩ ᷑◯᷑ ᷑ **Villa Velleron**

Claudia et Christian HICKL
Rue Roquette, 84740 VELLERON
☎ 04 90 20 12 31 📄 04 90 20 10 34
email: info@villavelleron.com
web: www.villavelleron.com

This old olive oil mill has been converted into a village house with enclosed courtyard, terraced garden and swimming pool. On the first floor there are four bedrooms with bathroom and wc, and two rooms are in an annexe, of which one has a mezzanine, open fireplace, and private terrace. Heating, lounge, dining room, fireplace, library, TV and telephone. Car park.

Prices s €90-€115; d €95-€120; t €18; extra person fr €25; dinner fr €28 **On Site** ♨ Private ⊀ **Nearby** ⇔1km ♨8km ♠1km Restaurant 1km ♨30km ♨1km 🏠0.3km ⋙7km **Notes** No pets English spoken Open Easter to 1 November.

VENASQUE

₩₩ **Chambre d'hôtes**

Régis BOREL
Quartier du Camp-Long, 84210 VENASQUE
☎ 04 90 66 03 56 & 06 03 16 44 36
email: camplong84@aol.com
web: http://members.aol.com/camplong84

Restored farm in the hills near woods, with swimming pool, open shaded garden with barbecue and car park. Four bedrooms with private facilities; central heating lounge with video, hi-fi and TV; shared living room; fridge; microwave and grill. Hiking trails and footpaths.

Prices s €45-€48; d €52-€58 **On Site** Private ⊀ **Nearby** ⇔4km ♨10km ♠12km Restaurant 3km ♨30km ♨3km 🏠3km ⋙30km **Notes** No pets Open March to October.

⫼ ⫶◎⫶ La Maison aux Volets Bleus

Martine MARET
84210 VENASQUE
☎ 04 90 66 03 04 & 06 80 34 53 84   ▤ 04 90 66 16 14
email: voletbleu@aol.com
web: www.maison-volets-bleus.com

A Provençal house of character with exceptional panoramic views, set in a village. Four bedrooms with bathroom and wc; central heating; reception room; living room; lounge and working fireplace. Floral garden, terrace and tennis court. Hiking on the premises. Dinner served some evenings per week at discretion of hostess (individual tables).

Prices d €75-€92; t fr €125; extra person fr €20; dinner fr €26   **On Site** ☜   **Nearby** ⛷ 3km ♨ 15km ⚑ 6km ⚓ 10km Restaurant 0.1km ⚓ 0.5km ⇶ 30km   **Notes** Pets admitted English spoken Open March to 5 November.

⫼ ⫶◎⫶ Le Mas des Pierres Blanches

Alain et Laurence LUBIATO
Chemin de la Peirière, 84210 VENASQUE
☎ 04 90 66 60 71 & 06 17 98 43 83
email: pierresblanches84@wanadoo.fr

This white stone house has its guest accommodation in a separate annexe. There are four bedrooms, each one with en suite shower room and WC, and a private terrace. Solar heating. Meals available, by arrangement.

Prices d €60-€65; t €75-€80; dinner fr €22   **On Site** Private ⚓ **Nearby** ⛷ 2km ♨ 20km ⚑ 30km Restaurant 0.5km ⚓ 0.3km ⇶ 0.5km ⇶ 30km   **Notes** No pets Open Easter to 1 November.

⫼ Maison Provençale

Gérard et Jany RUEL
Grand rue, 84210 VENASQUE
☎ 04 90 66 02 84   ▤ 04 90 66 61 32
email: maisonprovencale@freesurf.fr
web: www.maisonprovencale.freesurf.fr

This Provençal house is situated opposite the village post office. Five bedrooms are offered with private facilities, one with kitchenette. Central heating, living room, TV and kitchen; cooking possible. Terrace with flowers and panoramic view, enclosed garden and car park.

Prices s fr €42; d fr €50; t fr €60   **Nearby** ⛷ 5km ♨ 7km ⚑ 10km ⚓ 10km Restaurant 0.2km ⚓ 0.7km ⇶ 0.1km ⇶ 30km   **Notes** Pets admitted English spoken

VIOLES

⫼ La Farigoule

Y et M-L FAVRAT-OGAY
Le Plan de Dieu, 84150 VIOLES
☎ 04 90 70 91 78   ▤ 04 90 70 91 78
email: yvette.favrat@bluewin.ch
web: www.la-farigoule.com

This 18th-century house stands amongst vines, with a large enclosed courtyard and summer kitchen for guests' use. There are five bedrooms - one on the first floor and four on the second. They all have private showers and WCs, and one of them has its own kitchen. Guests' room with open fire and books; lounge with TV; use of fridge. Terrace.

Prices s €35-€55; d €45-€55; t €60-€65   **On Site** Restaurant ☜ **Nearby** ⛷ 8km ♨ 10km ⚑ 3km ⚓ 5km ⇶ 1.5km ⇶ 10km   **Notes** Pets admitted English spoken Open Easter to 1 November.

VISAN

⊞ ❦ ⊙ Château Vert

Christian et Josiane TORTEL
84820 VISAN
☎ 04 90 41 91 21　▤ 04 90 41 94 63
email: contact@hebergement-chateau-vert.com
web: www.hebergement-chateau-vert.com

This Knights Templar farm has been converted into five guest rooms overlooking a terrace, olive groves and swimming pool, all with private facilities. There is also an 18th-century château in the wooded park. Shared living room with working fireplace, terrace, library and TV at guests' disposal.

Prices s fr €55; d fr €70; extra person fr €20; dinner fr €23
On Site Private ⊰　**Nearby** ≰ 9km ↥ 20km ⌔ 6km ⊋ 6km 🏠 6km
🚶 35km　**Notes** No pets

⊞ ⊙ Le Mas des Sources

Martine BARNOUIN
Quartier Lacoste, 84820 VISAN
☎ 04 90 41 95 90 & 06 98 10 13 00　▤ 04 90 41 95 90
email: contact@mas-des-sources.com
web: www.mas-des-sources.com

Restored mas set in grounds of one hectare with vines and woods, in an 'enclave des papes'. Guests have the choice of three rooms and a family suite with private facilities and heating. There are communal rooms with a working fireplace, library and TV and a swimming pool. Possible theme stays, such as olive picking, wine harvesting, and truffle hunting.

Prices s €65-€100; d €75-€100; t €93-€130; extra person fr €23; dinner fr €25　**On Site** Private ⊰　**Nearby** ≰ 2km ↥ 15km ⌔ 4km Restaurant 0.8km ⊋ 0.8km ⚑ 5km 🏠 0.8km 🚶 35km　**Notes** Pets admitted　English spoken

VITROLLES-EN-LUBERON

⊞ ⊙ Le Tombareau

Pierre BRUZZO
84240 VITROLLES-EN-LUBERON
☎ 04 90 77 84 26 & 06 75 47 38 67
email: le.tombareau@club-internet.fr
web: www.tombareau-luberon.com

A charming, old renovated sheepfold in a rural setting, in three hectares of grounds with a swimming pool, shady terraces and horses. Two quiet bedrooms and one spacious suite, each with private facilities. Shared living room with piano, games, TV, library, fridge and solarium. Central heating and open fire. Car park. Pitch and putt on site.

Prices d €80-€100; extra person fr €25; dinner fr €30　**On Site** ⚑ Private ⊰　**Nearby** ≰ 12km ↥ 10km ⌔ 20km Restaurant 5km ⊋ 7km 🏠 7km 🚶 20km　**Notes** Pets admitted　English spoken

38 ISÈRE

05 HAUTES-ALPES

26 DRÔME

GAP

Lake Serre-Ponçon

Jausiers

Barcelonnette

Venterol

Méolans-Revel

Enchastrayes

Uvernet-Fours

Seyne-les-Alpes

Saint-Geniez

Colmars-les-Alpes

Noyers-sur-Jabron

Les Omergues

Peipin

DIGNE-LES-BAINS

Châteauneuf-Val-St-Donat

Aiglun

vest-du-Bion

St-Étienne-les-Orgues

Cruis

Montlaux

Les Mées

miane-la-Rotonde

Pierrerue

Le Castellet

Forcalquier

Mane

Niozelles

St-Michel-l'Observatoire

Dauphin

Villeneuve

Castellane

Céreste

Manosque

Moustiers-Sainte-Marie

Rougon

Pierrevert

St-Martin-de-Brômes

Lake Ste Croix

Gréoux-les-Bains

St-Laurent-du-Verdon

Verdon

83 VAR

N

Draguignan

0   15 km

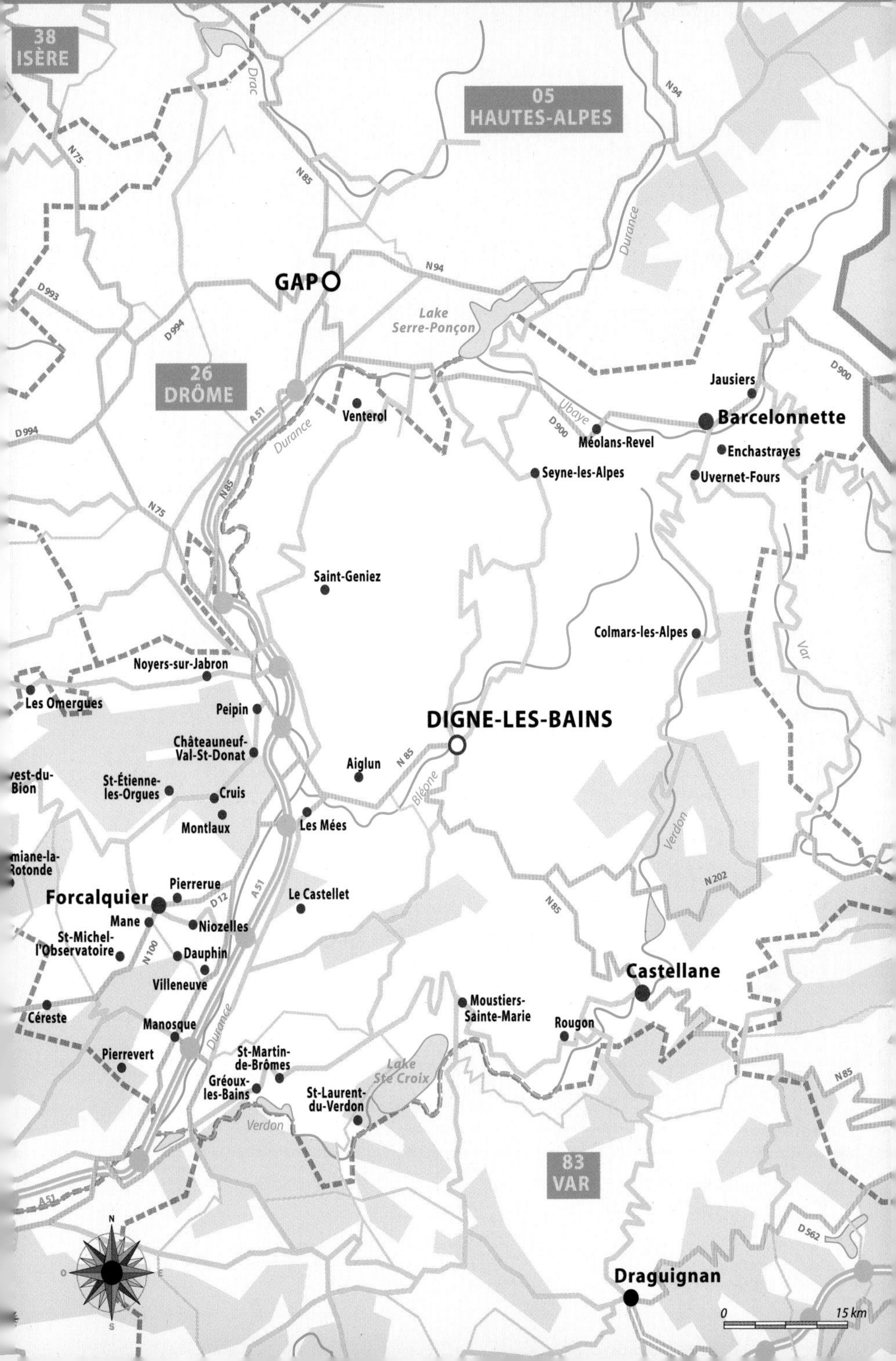

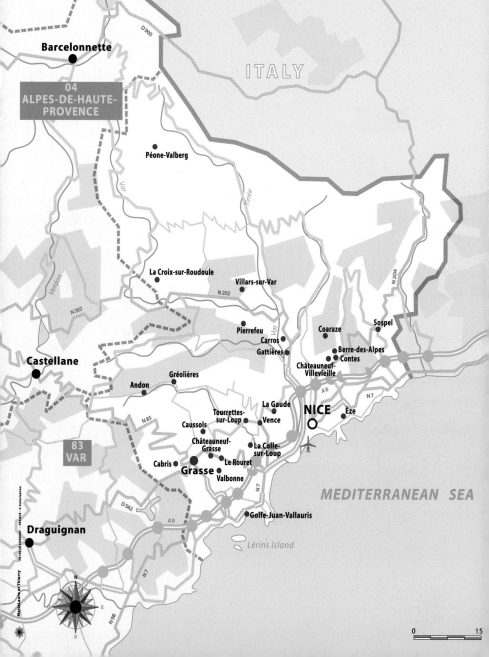

ITALY

04
ALPES-DE-HAUTE-
PROVENCE

Barcelonnette

Péone-Valberg

La Croix-sur-Roudoule

Villars-sur-Var

Castellane

Pierrefeu

Coaraze

Sospel

Carros

Gattières

Berre-des-Alpes

Contes

Châteauneuf-
Villevieille

Gréolières

Andon

La Gaude

NICE

Èze

Tourrettes-
sur-Loup

Vence

Caussols

Châteauneuf-
Grasse

La Colle-
sur-Loup

Le Rouret

Cabris

Grasse

Valbonne

Golfe-Juan-Vallauris

MEDITERRANEAN SEA

Lérins Island

Draguignan

83
VAR

M4 MARCHAND et Thierry

N

E

S

W

0   15

 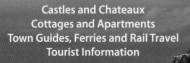

Notes

Please send this form to:
Editor, AA Bed & Breakfast France,
Lifestyle Guides,
The Automobile Association,
Fanum House,
Basingstoke RG21 4EA

Readers' Report Form

fax: 01256 491647
e-mail: lifestyleguides@theAA.com

Please use this form to recommend any establishment you have been to, whether it is in the guide or not currently listed. Feedback from readers helps us to keep our guide accurate and up to date. Please note, however, that if you have a complaint to make during a visit, we strongly recommend that you discuss the matter with the establishment management there and then so that they have a chance to put things right before your visit is spoilt. The AA does not undertake to arbitrate between you and the establishments management, or to obtain compensation or engage in correspondence.

Date:

Your name (block capitals)

Your address (block capitals)

....
....
....
....
....

e-mail address: ....

Comments (Please include the address of the establishment) ....
....
....
....
....
....
....
....
....
....

(please attach a separate sheet if necessary)

Please tick here if you DO NOT wish to receive details of AA offers or products

Bed & Breakfast France 2008

Have you bought this Guide before?   Yes   No

What other accommodation, restaurant, pub or food guides have you bought recently?
....
....

Why did you buy this guide? (circle all that apply)
holiday   short break   business travel
special occassion   Other...
....

How often do you stay in B&Bs? (circle one choice)
more than once a month   once a month   once in 2-3 months
once in six months   once a year   less than once a year

Please answer these questions to help us make improvements to the guide:

Which of these factors are most important when choosing a B&B?
price   location   previous experience
recommendation   Other...
....

Do you use the location maps in this guide?   Yes   No

Which elements of the guide do you find the most useful when choosing
somewhere to stay?
description   photo   advertisement

Do you have any suggestions to improve the guide? ....
....
....
....
....
....
....

Thank you for returning this form

Please send this form to:
Editor, AA Bed & Breakfast France,
Lifestyle Guides,
The Automobile Association,
Fanum House,
Basingstoke RG21 4EA

fax: 01256 491647
e-mail: lifestyleguides@theAA.com

Readers' Report Form

Please use this form to recommend any establishment you have been to, whether it is in the guide or not currently listed. Feedback from readers helps us to keep our guide accurate and up to date. Please note, however, that if you have a complaint to make during a visit, we strongly recommend that you discuss the matter with the establishment management there and then so that they have a chance to put things right before your visit is spoilt. The AA does not undertake to arbitrate between you and the establishments management, or to obtain compensation or engage in correspondence.

Date:

Your name (block capitals)

Your address (block capitals)

....

....

....

....

....

....

e-mail address:...

Comments (Please include the address of the establishment) ....

....

....

....

....

....

....

....

....

....

....

(please attach a separate sheet if necessary)

Please tick here if you DO NOT wish to receive details of AA offers or products

PTO

Bed & Breakfast France 2008

Have you bought this Guide before?   Yes   No

What other accommodation, restaurant, pub or food guides have you bought recently?

....

....

Why did you buy this guide? (circle all that apply)

holiday   short break   business travel

special occassion   Other...

....

How often do you stay in B&Bs? (circle one choice)

more than once a month   once a month   once in 2-3 months

once in six months   once a year   less than once a year

Please answer these questions to help us make improvements to the guide:

Which of these factors are most important when choosing a B&B?

price   location   previous experience

recommendation   Other...

....

Do you use the location maps in this guide?   Yes   No

Which elements of the guide do you find the most useful when choosing somewhere to stay?

description   photo   advertisement

Do you have any suggestions to improve the guide? ....

....

....

....

....

....

Thank you for returning this form